Current Biography Yearbook 2006

EDITOR
Clifford Thompson

SENIOR EDITORS
Miriam Helbok
Mari Rich

PRODUCTION EDITOR
Nathan E. Steffens

ASSOCIATE EDITOR
Andrew I. Cavin

ASSISTANT EDITORS
Jennifer Curry
Albert Rolls

CONTRIBUTING EDITOR
Kieran Dugan

STAFF WRITERS
Matt Broadus
In-Young Chang
Ronald Eniclerico
Kaitlen J. Exum
Dan Firrincili
David J. Kim
Nicholas W. Malinowski
Christopher Mari
Bertha Muteba
David Ramm

CONTRIBUTING WRITERS
Peter G. Herman
Cullen F. Thomas
Selma Yampolsky

EDITORIAL ASSISTANT
Carolyn Ellis

THE H. W. WILSON COMPANY
NEW YORK   DUBLIN

SIXTY-SEVENTH ANNUAL CUMULATION—2006

PRINTED IN THE UNITED STATES OF AMERICA

International Standard Serial No. (0084-9499)

International Standard Book No. – 10: 0-8242-1074-3

International Standard Book No. – 13: 978-0-8242-1074-8

Library of Congress Catalog Card No. (40-27432)

Table of Contents

PREFACE

The aim of *Current Biography Yearbook 2006*, like that of the preceding volumes in this series of annual dictionaries of contemporary biography, now in its seventh decade of publication, is to provide reference librarians, students, and researchers with objective, accurate, and well-documented biographical articles about living leaders in all fields of human accomplishment. Whenever feasible, obituary notices appear for persons whose biographies have been published in *Current Biography*.

Current Biography Yearbook 2006 carries on the policy of including new and updated biographical profiles that supersede earlier articles. Profiles have been made as accurate and objective as possible through careful researching of newspapers, magazines, the World Wide Web, authoritative reference books, and news releases of both government and private agencies. Immediately after they are published in the 11 monthly issues, articles are submitted to biographees to give them an opportunity to suggest additions and corrections in time for publication of the *Current Biography Yearbook*. To take account of major changes in the careers of biographees, articles are revised before they are included in the yearbook.

Classification by Profession–2006 and *2001–2006 Index* are at the end of this volume. *Current Biography Cumulated Index 1940–2005* cumulates and supersedes all previous indexes.

For their assistance in preparing *Current Biography Yearbook 2006*, I thank the staff of *Current Biography* and other members of The H. W. Wilson Company's General Reference Department, and also the staffs of the company's Computer and Manufacturing departments.

Current Biography welcomes comments and suggestions. Please send your comments to: The Editor, *Current Biography*, The H. W. Wilson Company, 950 University Ave., Bronx, NY 10452; fax: 718-590-4566; E-mail: cthompson@hwwilson.com.

Clifford Thompson

List of Biographical Sketches

Current Biography Yearbook 2006

Courtesy of Jeff Roberto, Friendster

Abrams, Jonathan

1970(?)– Founder of Socializr; founder and former chairman of Friendster

Address: Socializr Inc., 600 Fourth St., Suite 240, San Francisco, CA 94107

When Jonathan Abrams founded the on-line social network Friendster, in 2002, he envisioned it as a safer alternative to existing dating sites, one in which members would register, free of charge and by invitation only, to meet people through friends rather than total strangers. In designing the site, Abrams had in mind the concept of six degrees of separation (the theory that anyone on Earth can be linked to any other person anywhere in the world through a chain of acquaintances that has no more than five intermediaries); he aimed to give users access to the personal profiles of their friends, friends of friends, the friends of those people, and so on, thus making it possible for them to try to establish new personal or business relationships. By early 2003 Friendster's membership was growing at a weekly rate of 20 percent; by the following July

the number of registered users had reached one million. But in October of the same year, the demand for Friendster began to decline, partly because of server troubles and lack of innovation but mostly because of increasing competition from rival social-networking sites. In 2004 Abrams stepped down as Friendster's CEO while retaining the title of company chairman. Under its current CEO, Taek Kwon, Friendster has attempted to attract more customers by offering an array of multimedia features and an accessory that enables members to create their own on-line "radio stations" from a wide-ranging catalog of songs. Before launching Friendster, Abrams had started and later sold another company, called HotLinks; earlier, he worked in senior engineering roles at Bell-Northern Research, Nortel Networks, Netscape, and Bitfone. In 2003 Abrams was named *Entertainment Weekly*'s "breakout star," while *Time* listed Friendster as one of the "coolest inventions" of the year. In 2004 *Technology Review* named Abrams one of the world's top young innovators. Also that year he was listed among *Advertising Age* magazine's entertainment marketers of the year and nominated in the software-designer category for the Wired Rave Awards. Abrams has since left Friendster. In late 2006 he founded the social-networking Web site Socializr.

Jonathan Abrams was born in about 1970 in Toronto, in the province of Ontario, Canada, and raised in Thornhill, just north of Toronto. He told an interviewer for the Conference Guru Web site that his interest in computers and business began during his childhood. He attended McMaster University, in Hamilton, Ontario, where he majored in computer science. During summer breaks he worked in Ottawa, Canada's capital, as an intern for Bell-Northern Research, a telecommunications-equipment manufacturer. He earned a B.S. degree with honors from McMaster in 1995. After his graduation Bell-Northern hired him to write telecommunications software. Later, after Bell-Northern became Nortel Networks Corp., he worked on Internet software at the company's computing-technology laboratory. "After six months, I decided I wanted to move to where the action was, I wanted to move to where all the Internet stuff was being created. I was more interested in the Internet stuff than the telecom stuff," he told Kate Heartfield for the *Ottawa Citizen* (July 31, 2003). In 1996—at the height of the boom in Internet technology stocks—Abrams left Canada to accept a job as a senior software engineer at the Netscape Communications Corp. in Mountain View, California, in the heart of so-called Silicon Valley. "I wanted to be where I considered then to be the center of the universe," he told Todd Inoue for *Metroactive Features* (October 9, 2003, on-line). His responsibilities at Netscape involved managing the company's Web browsers and working on projects to promote open standards for Internet protocols. In 1998, after less than two years with Netscape, he lost his job—apparently for economic reasons, not poor performance.

In 1999 Abrams launched a business of his own—HotLinks Network, an on-line bookmark and Web directory service that enabled users to share their preferred Web sites with others. "We're trying to recapture the original idea behind the Internet—to bring people together in a spirit of discovery," he told Jayson Matthews for siliconvalley.internet.com (November 6, 2000). He funded the $2 million venture primarily with capital from an affiliate of CMGI, an investor in technology companies, and staffed it with former co-workers of his from Nortel. Along with many other Internet start-ups, his business (based in Mountain View) suffered during the dot-com downturn (the so-called dot-com bubble "officially" burst in 2000), and he was forced to reduce his payroll. "My greatest challenge was trying to run my first company in hyper-competitive 1999 with very limited business experience," Abrams told the Conference Guru interviewer, after admitting, "In many ways, I ended up in over my head." "Naturally, I made many mistakes, and while HotLinks was not a complete failure, it was a real disappointment for me to have had to lay off valued members of our team, and not provide a better outcome for the people who built the company with me." In 2001 Abrams sold HotLinks. Later that year he was hired to head the engineering group of Bitfone Corp., in Palo Alto, California, a fledgling wireless software company. Within nine months he found himself unemployed again, following Bitfone's merger with Digital Transit. He soon joined Ryze.com, a networking community, founded by Adrian Scott, whose members were categorized according to interests, location, and current and past employers.

At around that time Abrams broke up with his girlfriend of two years, and he began to explore the possibility of meeting single females through on-line dating sites. "But when I checked out these sites, I found that they were kind of anonymous and random and creepy, and I didn't find it very appealing," as he recalled to Robert Siegel for the National Public Radio (NPR) news magazine *All Things Considered* (July 10, 2003). "The other thing was that I noticed in real life, my friends preferred to meet people through their friends. So I kind of looked at those two things and thought it would be cool if there was a Web site where you could meet people through your friends online."

Inspired by the positive response he received from friends regarding his idea for an invitation-only on-line social network, Abrams left Ryze.com and, working from his apartment in Silicon Valley, created the software needed to launch the project. He decided against approaching venture capitalists for start-up funds; as he told Kate Heartfield, such investors "push you to spend a lot of money right away and in this economy, that didn't seem wise. I thought it would be more impressive to raise a small amount of money and go further with it." He raised $400,000 from friends and other investors, including Mark Pincus and Reid Hoffman, the founders of the networking sites Tribe and LinkedIn, respectively, whose combined investment was $310,000, as reported by Victoria Murphy in *Forbes* magazine (December 8, 2003). In August 2002, rather than actively promoting the service, Abrams tested Friendster by having 20 of his friends use it, in the hope that those people would invite 20 of their friends to join the site and the network would thus grow through word of mouth. "It was really like that old shampoo commercial where you tell two friends and then they tell two friends and so on," he told T. L. Stanley for *Advertising Age* (March 1, 2004). By the end of the year, although the site was still private, membership was growing at the rate of 4 percent to 7 percent daily, forcing Abrams to switch from a friend's server to a commercial server in January 2003.

In March 2003 Abrams offered a free trial version of Friendster to the public. Within three months the number of members registered to the site was increasing by about 20 percent every week, reaching a peak of 1.75 million in October 2003. The company's main sources of revenue initially were advertisements at the site and the sale of Friendster merchandise (T-shirts, hats, and mugs). Although Abrams had ruled out asking registered users to pay a subscription fee for basic service, in August 2003 he instituted an $8 per month charge for premium features, among them a chat room and a mechanism through which E-mail or instant messages could be sent to potential new friends outside the Friendster network. (By comparison, such on-line services as Match.com and Yahoo! Personals charged $20 to $25 monthly subscription fees.) In October 2003 Abrams agreed to accept venture-capital investments from Kleiner Perkins Caulfield & Byers and Benchmark Capital that totaled $13 million and reportedly raised the value of Friendster to an estimated $53 million, according to Ann Grimes in the *Wall Street Journal*. Abrams also received total investments of over $1 million from Tim Koogle, who was then CEO of Yahoo! and a member of the Friendster board of directors; Peter Thiel, the former chief executive of PayPal; and Ram Shriram, the former vice president of business development of Amazon.com and a former member of the executive team at Netscape Communications. Abrams used the money to expand the company's staff from 12 to 30 employees and to purchase additional servers, routers, and other machines to speed the network's processing time. The extra equipment had become vital with the surge in traffic, which had caused slowdowns. Contributing to that increase in usage was the registration at Friendster.com of imposters (commonly known as Fakesters), people posing as fictitious characters (the cartoon character Homer Simpson, for example) or as well-known personages (the actor Kevin Bacon was a popular choice).

In October 2003 Friendster switched the site's architecture from Java to the open-source Web server Apache (which costs nothing and allows users to modify software to fit their particular needs) and to the programming language PHP, thus enabling the company to add more features. That month only 1.75 million of its seven million registered users visited Friendster.com. In a conversation with Natalie Hanman for the London *Guardian* (April 28, 2005), Clay Shirky, a specialist on Internet technologies who teaches at New York University, attributed the decline in usage to a lack of technological innovation. In an attempt to make Friendster not merely a social networking site but also a for-profit company, Abrams agreed to relinquish his chief-executive role; he was replaced by Tim Koogle in March 2004. Koogle served as interim CEO until June 2004, when Scott Sassa, a former NBC head of entertainment, assumed the position. Sassa intended to generate most of Friendster's revenue through advertising on the site. "Friendster's mass appeal, viral growth and stickiness will make it one of the brands that will redefine the media landscape," he stated in a press release, as quoted by Elizabeth Millard on the CRM Web site. Besides posting horoscopes and news headlines at the site, Sassa made promotional tie-in agreements with DreamWorks and Sony Pictures, according to which Friendster would post profiles of fictional characters from their movies. In March 2005 Sassa offered members of Friendster, for a fee, the opportunity to create and update their own blogs. Beginning in April 2005 Friendster members could visit blogs created by more than 30 members of the Fox television series *Stacked* to promote the show.

While Friendster was attempting to appeal to a mass audience, similar social networking sites were having greater success targeting niche audiences. MySpace.com, for example, a social network (launched in October 2004) connected with the Los Angeles music scene, attracted 24.3 million unique visitors (visitors counted only once) in October 2005, according to ComScore Networks (on-line), while ComScore Media Metrix, a division of ComScore Networks, reported that Facebook.com (founded in February 2004), which is popular among college students, attracted 9.5 million unique visitors in October 2005. According to ComScore Media Metrix, that same month Friendster drew only 1.4 million unique visitors. Another of Friendster's competitors, Orkut, was launched by Google in January 2004—three months after Abrams turned down Google's

reported $30 million offer to purchase Friendster, according to Matt Marshall, writing for the *San Jose Mercury News* (October 3, 2003).

In May 2005 Friendster announced (without making its financial records public) that it expected its annual sales to total $10 million. The next month Sassa resigned. He was succeeded by Taek Kwon, formerly the executive vice president of product and technology for Citysearch.com, who believed that the solution to Friendster's problems lay in enhancing the site. In October 2005 Friendster launched a redesigned site that offered new features including extra photo storage space, free blogs, photo slideshows, classifieds, movie and music reviews, and, thanks to a so-called distribution partnership with Grouper Networks, new file-sharing capabilities. In March 2006, in partnership with Pandora and its Music Genome Project, Friendster offered its members the capability of creating playlists containing their favorite music. Earlier, Stefanie Olsen had reported for CNET News.com (November 14, 2005) that Friendster had hired Montgomery & Co., an investment bank in Santa Monica, California, to find a buyer for the company. (A spokesperson for Friendster declined comment while a spokesperson from Montgomery & Co. neither confirmed nor denied the report.)

Gary Rivlin, writing for the *New York Times* (October 15, 2006), gave an account of Friendster's sinking fortunes, describing the site as "the iconic case of failure" and noting that it was receiving less than 2 percent of the number of domestic visitors to Myspace each month. Abrams is no longer associated with Friendster. In the fall of 2006, he founded Socializr, an on-line network that offers information about parties and other social events.

Abrams is a member of the advisory board of the Silicon Valley Association of Startup Entrepreneurs. As far as is known publicly, he has never married.

—B.M.

Suggested Reading: *Advertising Age* S p8 Mar. 1, 2004; *Fortune* p30 June 28, 2004; Friendster.com; *Los Angeles Times* C p1 May 26, 2005; *New York Times* III p1 Oct. 15, 2006; *Newsday* B p3 Oct. 16, 2003; *Ottawa Citizen* F p2 July 31, 2003; *San Francisco Weekly* Aug. 13, 2003; Socializr.com

---

Alito, Samuel

(ah-LEE-toe)

Apr. 1, 1950– U.S. Supreme Court justice

Address: Supreme Court of the United States, Washington, DC 20543

"When I became a judge, I stopped being a practicing attorney. And that was a big change in role," Samuel Alito said on January 9, 2006, in his open-

Mark Wilson/Getty Images

Samuel Alito

ing statements to the Senate Judiciary Committee during the confirmation hearings for his nomination to the U.S. Supreme Court. "The role of a practicing attorney is to achieve a desirable result for the client in the particular case at hand. But a judge can't think that way. A judge can't have any agenda, a judge can't have any preferred outcome in any particular case and a judge certainly doesn't have a client. The judge's only obligation—and it's a solemn obligation—is to the rule of law. And what that means is that in every single case, the judge has to do what the law requires." He added, "There is nothing that is more important for our republic than the rule of law. No person in this country, no matter how high or powerful, is above the law, and no person in this country is beneath the law. Fifteen years ago, when I was sworn in as a judge of the court of appeals, I took an oath. I put my hand on the Bible and I swore that I would administer justice without respect to persons, that I would do equal right to the poor and to the rich, and that I would carry out my duties under the Constitution and the laws of the United States. And that is what I have tried to do to the very best of my ability for the past 15 years. And if I am confirmed, I pledge to you that is what I would do on the Supreme Court." In contrast to the case of John G. Roberts—the nominee for chief justice who received wide support in the Senate and coasted through his confirmation hearings in September 2005—Alito's nomination gave Democratic senators pause, as they considered his long, conservative-leaning record as a U.S. attorney, a member of the Justice Department in the administration of President Ronald Reagan, and, for over 15 years beginning in 1990, a jurist on the Third Circuit Court of Appeals.

Nonetheless, after answering more than 700 questions from Democrats and Republicans of the Judiciary Committee over the course of four days, Alito was confirmed on January 31, 2006 as the 110th justice of the Supreme Court.

The older of two children, Samuel Anthony Alito Jr. was born on April 1, 1950 in Trenton, New Jersey, to Samuel Anthony Alito Sr. and Rose (Fradusco) Alito. Alito's father, whose family had emigrated from Italy during his childhood, worked as a high-school teacher before attending law school and, later, rising to the position of executive director of New Jersey's bill-drafting Office of Legislative Services. Alito's mother was a schoolteacher and an elementary-school principal. "Both she and my father instilled in my sister and me a deep love of learning," Alito said at his hearings. His sister, Rosemary, has worked as a television reporter and is now an employment defense lawyer in the Newark, New Jersey, office of Kirkpatrick & Lockhart Nicholson Graham.

Alito was raised in the Mercerville section of Hamilton Township, New Jersey, a Trenton suburb that emerged during the years following World War II and was home to blue- and white-collar European immigrants. "It was a warm . . . unpretentious, down-to-earth community," Alito said about Mercerville in his opening statements at his confirmation hearings. He attended public schools. At Steinert High School he was active in the debate team, the band, the track team, and the student council, among several other groups, and was a member of the honor society. Alito was known in high school for his humble, quiet demeanor as well as his remarkable intellectual abilities. As a public speaker and debater, Alito "wasn't an in-your-face confrontational person," Victor R. McDonald, a classmate of Alito's, told Neil A. Lewis and Scott Shane for the *New York Times* (November 1, 2005). He simply gave a "well-reasoned, solid argument." After graduating as class valedictorian, Alito decided to stay close to his neighborhood, traveling only 12 miles to attend Princeton University.

During his sophomore year of college, which coincided with the most intense phase of the Vietnam War, Alito was assigned a low number in the military draft lottery, which meant that his chances of being drafted and placed on active duty were relatively high. He enrolled in the army's Reserve Officers' Training Corps (ROTC) program on the Princeton campus to become an officer rather than an enlisted man. As an increasing number of universities underwent the upheaval of student protests against the war, the Princeton administration was pressured to phase out the ROTC program, which ended in 1970, to Alito's disappointment. During that time, "I saw some very smart people and very privileged people behaving irresponsibly," Alito said in his opening statements at his confirmation hearings. "And I couldn't help making a contrast between some of the worst of what I saw on the campus and the good sense and the decency of the people back in my own community." Two years later the university reinstated the ROTC program. Alito completed his ROTC training in 1972 and was commissioned as a second lieutenant in the Signal Corps of the Army Reserve. He served active duty for three years and inactive duty until 1980, when he was honorably discharged with the rank of captain. While at Princeton Alito also actively participated in political discussions, leading a student conference in 1971 called "The Boundaries of Privacy in American Society." Although Alito held conservative beliefs stemming from his Roman Catholic upbringing, his political views were more moderate. The conference supported the legalization of homosexual acts, an end to hiring discrimination against homosexuals, and restraints on domestic intelligence gathering. During the conference Alito plainly stated his beliefs, saying, "No private sexual act between consenting adults should be forbidden." Despite such progressive positions on privacy rights, Alito's interest in constitutional law was triggered by his disagreements with the Supreme Court's decisions under the more liberal chief justice Earl Warren, specifically those concerning criminal procedure and reapportionment, a ruling on which had created the "one person, one vote" standard. (In the 1960s the Warren court heard reapportionment cases in *Baker v. Carr* and *Reynolds v. Sims*. Until then the Supreme Court had refused to hear cases of malapportioned districts, on the grounds that states should decide those matters. But the Warren court judged that state legislators probably would not reapportion district lines fairly, because doing so might leave them without constituents in newly created districts. The claims of malapportionment and unconstitutionality stemmed from situations in places such as California, where legislators representing rural and suburban areas outnumbered those in cities such as Los Angeles, which had only one representative. The Warren court ruled that state legislatures could not favor rural and suburban areas and held that all local and state legislative bodies must be elected from roughly equal-size districts—hence the "one person, one vote" standard.) Alito graduated from Princeton in 1972 with an A.B. degree in history and political science. His ambition was evident in the 1972 Princeton yearbook, which noted his intention "eventually to warm a seat on the Supreme Court."

Alito's disagreements with the Warren court's rulings motivated his decision to attend Yale University Law School, in New Haven, Connecticut, where he was in the graduating class behind that of another future Supreme Court justice, Clarence Thomas. Alito, who served as editor of the *Yale Law Journal*, was known among his peers as an articulate and sharp-witted student. "At Yale, he wasn't someone who spoke frequently in class," Peter Goldberger, a liberal law-school classmate of Alito's, told Lewis and Shane, "but when he did it was something you wished you had said." Goldberger, who later argued dozens of criminal appeals before Alito, noted, "It's the same way on the

bench. He's always asking the right question." In law school Alito's reserved and thoughtful disposition revealed little about his political beliefs. He built a reputation as a careful thinker, preferring a literal and traditionalist approach to jurisprudence over a "spirit of the law" approach. Upon receiving his juris doctorate, in 1975, Alito clerked briefly for a Trenton law firm and then for the moderate-conservative appellate judge Leonard I. Garth of the Third Circuit. Alito found in Garth a mentor whose logical methods suited his own conservative principles. "I had the good fortune to begin my legal career as a law clerk for a judge who really epitomized open-mindedness and fairness," Alito said during his confirmation hearings. "He read the record in detail in every single case that came before me; he insisted on scrupulously following precedents, both the precedents of the Supreme Court and the decisions of his own court, the 3rd Circuit. He taught all of his law clerks that every case has to be decided on an individual basis."

In 1977 Alito became an assistant U.S. attorney for New Jersey. Four years later he moved to Washington, D.C., to serve as the assistant to Solicitor General Rex E. Lee in the Justice Department of the newly instated Reagan administration. During his tenure under Lee, Alito argued 12 cases before the Supreme Court. On January 16, 1984 he presented arguments on behalf of the Federal Communications Commission (FCC) before the Supreme Court in *FCC v. League of Women Voters of California*. At issue was statute 399 under the Public Broadcasting Act of 1967, which established the nonprofit Corporation for Public Broadcasting (CPB) to "disburse federal funds to noncommercial television and radio stations in support of station operations and educational programming," according to the case text, available on-line. Section 399 of the act expressly forbids any noncommercial educational station that receives federal funds from CPB to "engage in editorializing." The appellees in the case were representatives of the League of Women Voters, part of Pacifica Foundation, a nonprofit corporation that received CPB funding and sought to engage in editorializing by challenging the constitutionality of Section 399—which they called a violation of the First Amendment. Alito argued that Congress may "exercise broad power to regulate broadcast speech because the medium of broadcasting is subject to the 'special characteristic' of spectrum scarcity—a characteristic not shared by other media—which calls for more exacting regulation." In writing the Supreme Court's majority opinion, Justice William J. Brennan declared, referring to Alito's argument, "This power, in the Government's view, includes authority to restrict the ability of all broadcasters, both commercial and noncommercial, to editorialize. . . . The Government concludes by urging that 399 is an appropriate and essential means of furthering 'important' governmental interests, . . . which leaves open the possibility that a wide variety of views on matters of public importance can be expressed through the medium of noncommercial educational broadcasting." The Supreme Court upheld the district court's judgment in favor of the appellees, holding that although Congress has the power to regulate the broadcast medium, "since broadcasters are engaged in a vital and independent form of communicative activity," Congress must not limit the First Amendment rights of free speech.

In 1985 Alito applied for a position in the White House's Office of Legal Counsel—that of deputy assistant to Attorney General Edwin Meese III. Meese was the object of much criticism for his involvement in the Iran-Contra affair, in which money from the sale of arms to Iran was illegally diverted to the anti-Communist Contra rebels of Nicaragua. Meese's alleged role as an adviser to the president in the exchange of HAWK missiles, the discrepancy between his and the president's testimonies, and his ideological disputes with liberal Supreme Court justices including John Paul Stevens made Meese a controversial figure. As attorney general Meese criticized the liberal-leaning Supreme Court for what he viewed as its unwillingness to adhere to the original intent of the Constitution. Moreover, Meese, who was responsible for recommending potential judicial nominees to the president, reportedly applied a "litmus test" to candidates for federal judgeship to determine their commitment to the conservative legal views of the Reagan administration, particularly with regard to *Roe v. Wade*, the landmark Supreme Court decision legalizing abortion. In his job application, Alito wrote a brief essay describing his political and legal views, which were closely aligned with those of Meese and other conservatives of the Reagan administration. Alito wrote, in part, "I am and always have been a conservative and an adherent to the same philosophical views that I believe are central to this Administration. . . . In the field of law, I disagree strenuously with the usurpation by the [Warren] judiciary of decisionmaking authority that should be exercised by the branches of government responsible to the electorate. The Administration has already made major strides toward reversing this trend through its judicial appointments, litigation, and public debate, and it is my hope that even greater advances can be achieved during the second term, especially with Attorney General Meese's leadership at the Department of Justice." Concerning his work under the solicitor general, Alito wrote, "I am particularly proud of my contributions in recent cases in which the government has argued in the Supreme Court that racial and ethnic quotas should not be allowed and that the Constitution does not protect a right to an abortion." Alito landed the position, and although his job application had emphasized his conservative views, Mark Levy—a Democrat who worked with Alito in the Meese Justice Department—told Lewis and Shane, "Nobody tagged Sam as a fire-breathing conservative. He had friends across every divide." Nevertheless, in both his capacity as the assistant to the solicitor general and his new role as deputy assistant attorney general, Alito helped to "advance legal positions in which I personally believe very strongly," as he wrote in his 1985 job application.

Alito left the Justice Department in 1987 and returned to New Jersey as a newly appointed U.S. attorney. Heading a 67-lawyer office, Alito focused his efforts on prosecuting cases involving organized crime, child pornography, environmental crimes, drug trafficking, violations of civil rights, and a planned terrorist attack by a member of the Japanese Red Army. On February 20, 1990 President George H. W. Bush nominated Alito to the Third U.S. Circuit Court of Appeals. The Senate confirmed him by a unanimous vote on April 27, 1990, and Alito took his place on the same bench as his former mentor, Appellate Judge Garth. (Michael Chertoff, currently the U.S. secretary of Homeland Security, succeeded Alito as U.S. attorney for the District of New Jersey.) During his tenure on the Court of Appeals, in which each case is heard by a panel of judges, Alito ruled on more than 1,000 cases, cementing his reputation as a traditionalist jurist who consistently gave fair rulings without regard to his own political ideology. Apparent in many of his rulings is a deeply held respect for the legal doctrine *stare decisis*—a Latin term that translates roughly as "to stand by things decided"—which recognizes past court decisions as precedents for future rulings. "There is nobody that I believe would give my case a more fair and balanced treatment," a more liberal former appellate judge, Timothy Lewis, who served with Alito, told Donna Cassata for the Associated Press (October 31, 2005). "He's open-minded, he's fair and he's balanced."

Despite Alito's reputation as a fair and scholarly jurist without an ideological agenda, as an appellate judge he compiled a record of decisions that came down more often on the conservative side, although rulings favorable to liberals were scattered throughout. Representative of his decisions where those in *ACLU v. Schundler* and *Abdul-Aziz v. City of Newark*, in which Alito ruled in favor of allowing religiously affiliated representations—such as holiday displays—to appear in the secular sphere. Also, his dissenting opinion in *Doe v. Groody* was that the police officers who strip-searched a mother and her 10-year-old daughter during an authorized search of a residence should have been protected from prosecution even though the official search warrant made no mention of searching occupants of the home. Alito's claim that the police officers did not violate the constitutional rights of the mother and daughter attracted a great deal of criticism, with detractors nicknaming him "Strip-Search Sammy." Alito also dissented in *United States v. Rybar*, citing the Supreme Court decision in *United States v. Lopez* (1995) as precedent and arguing that Congress had violated the Commerce Clause of the Constitution by establishing a federal law banning citizens from owning submachine guns. (The precedent in *United States v. Lopez* concerned the conviction of a Texas high-school student who was found guilty in a lower court of violating the Gun Free School Zones Act of 1990 by bringing a concealed firearm to school. The Fifth Circuit Court of Appeals had agreed with the student's argument that the Commerce Clause restricted Congress from legislating over public schools and had overturned the student's conviction. The Supreme Court also agreed and affirmed the decision.)

In the sphere of immigration cases, according to Stephen Henderson and Howard Mintz for Knight Ridder Newspapers (December 1, 2005), Alito's judicial record is "especially congenial to social conservatives"; even in instances when he sided with noncitizens fighting deportation, Alito typically remanded cases back to lower courts for further review, calling the noncitizens' legal victories into question. In *Gui Cun Liu v. Ashcroft* (2004) and *Xiu Ling Zhang v. Gonzales* (2005), for example, he vacated and remanded orders by the Board of Immigration Appeal (BIA) to deny asylum to married Chinese immigrants who were being forced by the Chinese government to undergo abortion or sterilization. In *Cai Luan Chen v. Ashcroft* (2004), he affirmed the deportation of a Chinese man who had sought asylum based on a 1996 decision by the BIA, which held that the "*spouse* of a person who was forced to undergo an abortion or sterilization is deemed . . . to have suffered past persecution." Alito noted that the 19-year-old Chen had intended to marry his pregnant fiancée but was prevented from doing so by a Chinese law stipulating that men must be at least 25 years of age to marry. Alito nonetheless reasoned that because Chen was not actually married to his fiancée he could not claim the rights and privileges covered by the BIA decision. In denying asylum to Chen and affirming his deportation, Alito wrote, "As we understand it, [Chen] uses marital status as a rough way of identifying a class of persons whose opportunities for reproduction and child-rearing were seriously impaired or who suffered serious emotional injury as the result of the performance of a forced abortion or sterilization on another person. Of course, this use of marital status as a proxy is undoubtedly both over- and under-inclusive to some extent, but neither over- nor under-inclusiveness is alone sufficient to render the use of a metric like marital status irrational." Perhaps the most controversial of Alito's rulings on the Third Circuit Court was his dissent in *Planned Parenthood v. Casey* (1991), concerning the constitutionality of a section of the Pennsylvania Abortion Control Act of 1982, which required married women to notify their husbands before undergoing abortions. The Third Circuit ruled that requiring spousal notification was unconstitutional, and the Supreme Court upheld the decision the following year. In his dissent Alito wrote, "I do not believe that Section 3209 has been shown to impose an undue burden. . . . The plaintiffs failed to show even roughly how many of the women in this small group would actually be adversely affected by Section 3209." While serving on the Third Circuit Court, Alito also taught courses on constitutional law, terrorism, and civil liberties at Seton Hall University School of Law, in South Orange, New Jersey. In 1995 Alito was presented with the school's Saint Thomas More Medal, "in recognition of his outstanding contributions to the field of law."

On July 1, 2005 Associate Justice Sandra Day O'Connor announced her intended retirement from the Supreme Court. President George W. Bush promptly nominated U.S. Appeals Court Judge John G. Roberts to fill the vacated spot on the high court. But with the death of Chief Justice William H. Rehnquist, President Bush recommended Roberts for Rehnquist's position instead. To replace O'Connor, Bush nominated Harriet Miers, his White House counsel, who soon withdrew her nomination amid fierce protests from both Republicans and Democrats regarding her relative unfamiliarity with constitutional law. On October 13, 2005 Bush nominated Alito to fill the seat being vacated by O'Connor. Republicans expressed approval of Alito's judicial record. Unlike Roberts, who sailed through his nomination hearings, Alito faced opposition from Democrats who, among other concerns, questioned whether he would remain committed to *stare decisis* if *Roe v. Wade* were to be reexamined by the Supreme Court. Democrats also voiced reservations about the conservatism expressed in past memos written by Alito and in the essay for his 1985 job application. Both Republicans and Democrats were aware that Alito's confirmation could signal an ideological shift in the Supreme Court, as he would replace the politically moderate O'Connor—who had cast the "swing" vote in key cases—and might well become part of a four-justice conservative bloc led by Chief Justice Roberts. (According to the February 1, 2006 edition of the *New York Times*, Justice Anthony M. Kennedy would then become "the court's new fulcrum.") On January 9, 2006 Alito appeared before the bipartisan Senate Judiciary Committee. "Good judges develop certain habits of mind," he said in his opening statements to the committee. "One of those habits of mind is the habit of delaying reaching conclusions until everything has been considered. Good judges are always open to the possibility of changing their minds based on the next brief that they read, or the next argument that's made by an attorney who's appearing before them, or a comment that is made by a colleague during the conference on the case when the judges privately discuss the case."

The committee's Democrats brought up Alito's membership in the organization Concerned Alumni for Princeton (CAP), which Alito cited in his 1985 job application but had not disclosed to the Judiciary Committee. Formed in October 1972, just as the university began incorporating affirmative action in its admission policy, CAP was committed to increasing alumni involvement in the university and to controlling "the University's anti-traditionalist leftist urges," as a former CAP member and New Jersey Superior Court judge, Andrew Napolitano, told Chanakya Sethi for the *Daily Princetonian* (November 18, 2005, on-line). Jerome Karabel's book *The Chosen*, a historical account of admissions at Harvard, Yale, and Princeton universities, included a passage in the CAP publication *Prospect* written in 1973 by CAP co-founder Shelby Cullom Davis, a member of Princeton's class of 1930. Davis wrote, as quoted by Sethi, "May I recall, and with some nostalgia, my father's 50th reunion, a body of men, relatively homogenous in interests and backgrounds, who had known and liked each other over the years during which they had contributed much in spirit and substance to the greatness of Princeton. I cannot envisage a similar happening in the future with an undergraduate student population of approximately 40% women and minorities, such as the Administration has proposed." Few students or members of CAP publicly recalled Alito's involvement with CAP, which disbanded in the early 1980s, and Alito distanced himself from the organization, saying that he did not inform the Judiciary Committee of his association with CAP because he could not recall ever being a part of the group.

In response to questions from Senator Richard J. Durbin of Illinois about his opinion regarding *Roe v. Wade*, Alito said, "It is a precedent that has now been on the books for several decades. It has been challenged. It has been reaffirmed. But it is an issue that is involved in litigation now at all levels. There is an abortion case before the Supreme Court this term. There are abortion cases in the lower courts. I've sat on three of them on the Court of Appeals for the 3rd Circuit. I'm sure there are others in other courts of appeals or working their way toward the courts of appeals right now. So it's an issue that is involved in a considerable amount of litigation that is going on." Some observers felt that such responses were evasive and masked Alito's intention of acting on his ideology if confirmed for the Supreme Court seat.

Shifting their questioning to matters concerning international affairs, Democrats pressed Alito for his views on the theory of the unitary executive. That theory, embraced by members of the George W. Bush administration, holds that the president has the power—and in some cases the obligation—to act without restraint by the legislative or judicial branches of government. Citing a memo Alito wrote during his tenure in the Reagan administration about expanding presidential powers, as well as a speech he gave before the Federalist Society in 2000, Democrats questioned Alito's meaning in the statement, "The president has not just some executive powers, but the executive power—the whole thing," which he made in the 2000 speech. Many feared that Alito's assessment of the unitary executive theory would lead him to favor giving President Bush the power to overstep constitutional boundaries. However, in response to Senator Dianne Feinstein's questions on the matter during the fourth day of the hearings, Alito stated, "The president, like everybody else, is bound by statutes that are enacted by Congress, unless the statutes are unconstitutional, because the Constitution takes precedence over a statute. But in general, of course, the president and everybody else is bound by statute. There is no question about that whatsoever."

Despite the issues that arose during the hearings, Alito's confirmation appeared likely. In a last-ditch effort to oppose it, Democrats led by Massachusetts senators John Kerry and Edward M. Kennedy attempted to galvanize their peers to support a filibuster. The attempt failed, however, and Alito's nomination was sent to the Senate floor for a vote. On January 31, 2006 the Senate voted 58–42 to confirm Alito as the Supreme Court's 110th justice. After being sworn in Alito said in a speech, according to the FDCH Regulatory Intelligence Database (February 1, 2006), "The many letters that I've received over the past three months have reminded me how much the people of the United States revere our Constitution and our form of government, and how much they look to the Supreme Court of the United States to protect our form of government and our freedoms. That is an awesome responsibility. . . . And so I simply pledge that I will do everything in my power to live up to the trust that has been placed in me." Hours later Alito broke with his conservative colleagues on the bench, Chief Justice Roberts and Justices Antonin Scalia and Clarence Thomas, ruling with the court's majority to grant a stay of execution to Missouri death-row inmate Michael Taylor, who had appealed his sentence based on the argument that lethal injection represents cruel and unusual punishment. During the remainder of the 2005–06 term, he ruled more or less conservatively.

Samuel Alito lives in West Caldwell, New Jersey, with his wife, Martha-Ann Bomgardner Alito, a former law librarian. The couple have a daughter, Laura, and a son, Philip.

—I.C.

Suggested Reading: Biography Resource Center (on-line) 2005; *Chicago Tribune* p1+ Nov. 1, 2005; *Congressional Quarterly* Jan. 9, 2006; Federal News Service Dec. 2, 2005, Jan. 12, 2006; FDCH Regulatory Intelligence Database Feb. 1, 2006; Findlaw Web site; Knight Ridder Newspapers (on-line) Dec. 1, 2005; *New Jersey Law Journal* (on-line) Nov. 2, 2005; *New York Times* p1+ Nov. 1, 2005, p19 Jan. 13, 2006, p1+ Jan. 31, 2006; Oyez Web site; *Washington Post* p1+ Jan. 10, 2006

Stephen Shugerman/Getty Images

Apple, Fiona

Sep. 13, 1977– Singer; songwriter

Address: c/o Sony BMG Music Entertainment,
550 Madison Ave., New York, NY 10022

When she made her first album, *Tidal*, in 1996, the singer/songwriter Fiona Apple was still in her teens and had never performed before a paying audience. Hailed as "the girl with the voice of Billie Holiday, the lyrics of Joni Mitchell and the looks of Kate Moss," as Emma Forrest reported in the London *Independent* (April 25, 1997, on-line), Apple went on to receive a great deal of attention, not only because of the almost universal critical praise that *Tidal* earned; she also raised eyebrows with the controversial video she made for the single "Criminal" and the angry, profane speech with which she accepted a prize at the 1997 MTV Music Video Awards ceremony. Meanwhile, *Tidal*, which represented her "jazz-tinged, brittle brand of artfully anguished pop," as Stephen Dalton wrote for the Glasgow, Scotland, *Sunday Herald* (February 6, 2000), sold more than a million copies within a year of its release—its total sales have topped three million to date—and won the 1998 Grammy Award for best female rock vocal performance. The 90-word title of Apple's second album, which begins *When the Pawn Hits*, was widely mocked, but the recording, released in 1999, earned mostly positive reviews and achieved platinum status (that is, a million copies were sold). Apple earned negative publicity again in 2000, when, apparently distraught and furious, she prematurely ended a concert in New York City because of trouble with the sound system. Rumors

that Sony/Epic was dissatisfied with her third album and was delaying its release spurred some among her many loyal fans to launch the Free Fiona Web site and to demonstrate publicly in her behalf; in addition, bootleg copies of some of the album's songs—most of which were later re-recorded with a different producer—were posted on the Internet. Called *Extraordinary Machine* (2005), the recording has largely solidified Apple's reputation as a highly distinctive and intensely emotional artist.

Fiona Apple Maggart was born on September 13, 1977 in New York City to Diane McAfee and Brandon Maggart, who met during rehearsals for the musical *Applause* in the early 1970s. (Maggart co-starred in the production; McAfee was replaced before the opening.) "Apple," the surname Sony used on the singer's first recording contract, was the maiden name of one of her ancestors. Apple's mother had a brief career as a singer and dancer; her father has appeared in films and on television as well as on the stage and is still a working actor. Apple's parents, who never married, separated when their daughter was four; her mother later married another man. Her older sister, Maude Maggart (originally named Amber), is an award-winning cabaret singer who has recorded three albums. On their father's side Fiona and Maude have two older half-sisters (a third was killed in a car crash) and two older half-brothers, one of whom, Garett Maggart, is a television actor.

Apple grew up on the Upper West Side of Manhattan. A loner, she was ridiculed as ugly by her classmates, who nicknamed her "Dog," partly because of her unruly hair. On more than a few occasions, sometimes for weeks at a stretch, she would pretend to be sick and play hooky. When she was in fifth grade, a teacher overheard her telling another pupil that she was going to kill herself and her sister. Although, by her own account, she never intended to carry out those acts, the teacher arranged for her to have a psychiatric evaluation, and she later had psychotherapy. Apple has maintained that during her adolescence, psychological counseling was of little benefit to her, because she was an unwilling patient and the sessions served mostly to convince her that there was something seriously wrong with her, further lowering her already low self-esteem. Earlier, when she was about eight, Apple had started taking piano lessons. In her first year of study, she performed an original composition at a recital. Within a few years she had begun writing lyrics as well as music, and composing became her primary emotional outlet.

One afternoon when Apple was 12, a stranger followed her home from school and raped her inside her apartment building. (The man was never caught.) In an attempt to alleviate her anguish, someone gave her a book by the poet and memoirist Maya Angelou, who was raped at age eight by her mother's boyfriend. "I slept with it under my pillow every night . . . ," Apple told Emma Forrest. "Angelou is so honest about her weakness and about times in her life when she has been humiliated. On the back [of the book] is her photo. You could see in everything about her—her posture, her smile—that she is so proud of herself. It gave me hope. If we had the same feelings of weakness, we could also have the same feelings of pride." After she became well-known, Apple began speaking publicly about the assault, whose aftereffects included nightmares and an eating disorder. Her song "Sullen Girl," from her first album, is about her painful experience.

Apple attended an "alternative" New York City high school until she was 16, when she quit and went to Los Angeles, California, to live with her father, as she had during summers. She completed most of her high-school requirements within a few months by means of a correspondence course but never earned a diploma. During that period she recorded three songs for a demo tape. She gave a copy of the tape to a friend in New York who babysat the children of a music-industry publicist, Kathryn Schenker. Schenker, in turn, gave the tape to the producer and manager Andy Slater, who arranged to meet Apple (in the company of her father) soon afterward. "I was not entirely convinced that this person sitting in front of me—who was clearly 17—had written those words," Slater, who is now the president and CEO of Capitol Records, told Dimitri Ehrlich for the *New York Times* (January 5, 1997). Slater became Apple's manager and producer and secured for her a contract with Sony Music.

Apple wrote all the songs for *Tidal*, her debut album, and played piano on many of its tracks. Released in July 1996, it was certified gold (half a million copies sold) the following December and platinum in July 1997. In the opinion of Emma Forrest, *Tidal* is "a 21st-century blues record. . . . [It] deserves its plaudits and not just . . . because the writing is so mature. . . . In her eloquence, [Apple] has made people realise that these are not 'grown up' feelings and experiences but human ones that teenagers also have a right to." Her lyrics struck Elysa Gardner, writing for the *Los Angeles Times* (November 3, 1996), as "stark, candid, eerily precocious accounts of romantic obsession and frustration," while her smoky alto drew comparisons to the voices of such singers as Nina Simone and Carole King. The videos of two tracks, "Shadow Boxer" and "Criminal," got heavy coverage on MTV; the latter, in which an exceedingly skinny Apple crawled on the floor wearing skimpy underwear, aroused complaints from feminists and others, mainly because they felt it served to glamorize unhealthy thinness. The shame that Apple later felt with regard to the video, which she described to Jeff Giles for *Newsweek* (November 8, 1999, online), and the feeling that she "deserved recognition but that the recognition I was getting was for the wrong reasons," as she told Chris Heath for *Rolling Stone* (January 22, 1998, online), triggered the remarks that she made at the MTV Music Video Awards ceremony held on September 4, 1997, in New York City. In accepting the prize for best new artist, for "Sleep to Dream," she said in part, "This world is bulls—t, and you shouldn't model your life about what you think that we think is cool, and what we're wearing, and what we're saying and everything." Quoting Maya Angelou, she added, "Go with yourself." When Tracey Pepper, writing for *Interview* (November 1997, on-line), asked her about the speech, she said, "I think I did a wonderful thing. I have absolutely no regrets."

Apple, who when *Tidal* reached stores had never performed live in front of anyone other than her family and friends, toured extensively to promote the record. For a while she opened for Chris Isaak. After attending a concert by her at the Rave/Eagles Club in Milwaukee, Wisconsin, Dave Tianen, writing for the *Milwaukee Journal Sentinel* (March 29, 1997, on-line), described Apple as "Eartha Kitt in the body of a mall rat." "Seldom have voice and physicality seemed more incongruent than in the person of singer, pianist, songwriter, temptress and sprite Fiona Apple," he continued. "The voice is deep and seasoned. It ought to belong to a 35-year-old woman who knows something about life, love, disappointment, sex and the commonplace flaws of men. Instead it belongs to . . . Apple, a slender, diminutive 19-year-old . . . who has to be one of the more intriguing child/women ever to cross the musical stage." Speaking to a *Billboard* (June 15, 1996) reporter after she performed in Paris, France, before an audience of about 800, Apple said, "When you really get down to it, the whole reason for doing this is that I have a certain psychological need to get in front of people and be understood. I spent a lot of my life being misunderstood, and it made for a lot of pain, and performing is a way of standing up and making yourself understood."

After reading a magazine article about herself that she viewed as unflattering, Apple wrote a poem in response: "When the pawn hits the conflicts he thinks like a king / What he knows throws the blows when he goes to the fight / And he'll win the whole thing 'fore he enters the ring / There's no body to batter when your mind is your might / So when you go solo, you hold your own hand / And remember that depth is the greatest of heights / And if you know where you stand, then you know where to land / And if you fall it won't matter, cuz you'll know that you're right." The poem became the title of her second album (which holds the record for longest album title), released in 1999. "I knew I didn't want to make [the poem] into a song, but I needed to write something for myself to remind me that everybody who was making fun of me wasn't right," Apple told the music writer Gary Graff, as quoted by Amy Reiter in *Salon* (November 19, 1999, on-line). "I needed to remind myself that I have not done anything to hurt anybody. It's saying . . . do not think that you're wrong because people are saying that to you." In an assessment of *When the Pawn . . .* for *Time* (November 8, 1999), Christopher John Farley wrote, "Like shards from a shattered mirror, Fiona Apple's new album . . .

glitters with reflective surfaces and sharp edges. The singer-songwriter's debut . . . was a work of ingenue ingenuity, delicately designed, bright with innocence, laden with the prospect of future accomplishment. This follow-up CD is a promise kept: the 22-year-old's new compositions, angry but articulate, veering between gentle balladry and art-pop, don't need the crutch of precociousness to establish their worth. These are songs that stand on their own."

During a concert at the Roseland Ballroom in New York City in February 2000, equipment problems prevented Apple from hearing her own singing clearly. Forty minutes into the concert, having by turns wept, shouted at the engineers, paced agitatedly, and screamed at journalists, she stalked off the stage and never returned. Later, she posted an apology on a fans' Web site and performed a make-up concert at the same venue. Karen Valby, writing for *Entertainment Weekly* (September 30, 2005), reported that Apple told the audience at the latter event, "You said you wanted me to be self-confessional. I thought you said selfish and unprofessional."

In 2001, following her breakup with her boyfriend of three years, the director Paul Thomas Anderson, Apple entered a long reclusive phase. "I didn't have an appetite for music in any way," she told Valby. Then, in mid-2002, Jon Brion, who had produced her albums, persuaded her to begin writing again, and the two ensconced themselves in the Paramour Mansion recording studio, in Los Angeles. Within a few months rumors began to spread that Apple had finished the album but that Sony, the parent company of her record label, Epic, had shelved it on the grounds that it contained no potential hit singles. In June 2004 two cuts from the recording sessions were leaked onto the Internet; the following March, a radio disk jockey in Seattle, Washington, aired a bootleg copy of the whole, unreleased album. Meanwhile, a few of Apple's fans had established a Web site called FreeFiona.com, posting demands that Sony release her album, and many others deluged Andrew Lack, who was then the chairman and CEO of Sony BMG Music Entertainment, with letters of complaint containing images of apples. In addition, in early 2005 several dozen fans staged a protest outside Sony's offices in New York City.

One day during that time, while on a visit to her mother's apartment, Apple and her sister looked at the Free Fiona Web site for the first time. "First I started laughing, saying, 'This is hilarious, people are protesting and I'm sitting on my ass watching reruns of *Columbo*,'" Apple recalled to Valby. "I'm not on the phone with my lawyers trying to get my album released, I'm applying to Green Chimneys!'"—an organization that serves children with emotional, behavioral, and learning problems. "And then I started crying because I really felt touched. It's an incredible feeling to feel like all these people who you don't know care about you. And it was bigger than me, it was about what was going on in the music industry and anybody deciding what's sellable. And then I started feeling guilty, because it wasn't the truth. The album hadn't really been shelved. . . . I quit because I felt that what was going to happen was what they thought was already happening." In June 2005 Apple returned to the studio, this time with Mike Elizondo as her producer, and *Extraordinary Machine* was released in October of that year. In a review for *Entertainment Weekly* (October 7, 2005), David Browne wrote that the original, bootlegged copy "had its moments. . . . But the album was clearly canned for a reason: It was a distracting mess. . . . The new, largely re-recorded *Extraordinary Machine* lives up to its name." Jill Kipnis wrote for *Billboard* (October 8, 2005), "The album has that signature Apple sound: sultry singing and smart lyrics combined with interesting arrangements and intriguing chord progressions. However, it also has a new element of musical spareness—evident in the title track—and a funkier feel in a number of the songs." In the *New York Times* (December 25, 2005), Jon Pareles, the paper's pop-music critic, ranked *Extraordinary Machine* number one on his list of the year's best albums; Ben Williams, in *New York* (December 26, 2005, on-line), placed it second; and it also appeared on the "year's best albums" lists of *Time Out New York*, the *New York Post*, *Details*, and the *Los Angeles Times*, among other publications.

The making of *Extraordinary Machine* and other recent experiences, Apple wrote for her Web site, as posted in early October 2006, "all just proves that you can grow up and be a happier person and make good things. You don't have to suffer . . . all the time." Apple is a vegan, meaning that she eats neither meat nor such animal products as eggs and milk. In 1997 she recorded a message for the organization People for the Ethical Treatment of Animals (PETA) in which she urged Americans to forgo eating turkey on Thanksgiving Day. She lives in California.

—C.M.

Suggested Reading: *Billboard* p18+ June 15, 1996, p11+ Nov. 2, 1996, p47+ Oct. 8, 2005; *Entertainment Weekly* p14 Mar. 17, 2000, p18+ Feb. 11, 2005, p28+ Sep. 30, 2005; Fiona Apple Official Web site; *Interview* p130+ Nov. 1997; *Los Angeles Times* Calendar p3 Nov. 3, 1996; *Newsweek* p94+ Nov. 8, 1999, p55 Apr. 4, 2005; Rock on the Net (on-line); *Rolling Stone* p124 Nov. 13, 1997, p30+ Jan. 22, 1998; *Spin* p84+ Nov. 1997

Selected Recordings: *Tidal*, 1996; *When the Pawn Hits . . .* , 1999; *Extraordinary Machine*, 2005

Courtesy of Universal Press Syndicate

Auth, Tony

May 7, 1942– Editorial cartoonist

Address: Philadelphia Inquirer, *P.O. Box 8263, Philadelphia, PA 19101*

The editorial cartoonist Tony Auth "draws like an angel and persuades like the devil, seducing us to his point of view with intelligence, insight and consummate artistry." That assessment, posted on the Herb Block Foundation Web site, came from Harry Katz, one of the judges who named Auth the winner of the 2005 Herblock Prize for editorial cartooning—an award named for Herbert L. Block (1909–2001), one of the 20th century's most prominent artists cum political commentators. Auth's renowned colleague Matt Davies, another of the judges for the prize, praised Auth's cartoons for "not only point[ing] out the flaws, ironies and injustices in the [political] system and its leaders, but simultaneously offer[ing] a playful sense of hope." In a statement widely quoted on the Internet, another celebrated writer and illustrator, Jules Feiffer, once said of Auth, "His perspective is that of a bemused and often angry comic historian. Irony, never a favorite form with Americans, is his meat and potatoes. He is not smug, and though he can be mean, he is never mean-spirited. Auth is a moralist and an optimist." Referring to the American comedian Bob Hope and U.S. president Ronald Reagan, Feiffer added that Auth "insists, even in this day and age, that hope is more than the name of a right-wing comedian or the shtick of a reactionary president."

Auth began his professional life working for six years as a medical illustrator before joining the staff of the *Philadelphia Inquirer,* in 1971. Since then he has produced five cartoons per week for that newspaper—a total of more than 8,000—among them one that earned him a Pulitzer Prize, in 1976. Auth has cited as his primary motivator the outrage that he often feels when he reads or hears news accounts about local, national, and international issues or events. He told Kenneth Turan for the *Washington Post* (November 2, 1977), "You have to be capable of reading something and saying, 'I don't believe that,' and then translate that into a drawing. Those are the most satisfying cartoons." Much of Auth's work has stirred controversy and drawn criticism, at times from those on opposite sides of the same issue. "Our job is not to amuse our readers," Auth said in his acceptance speech at the 2005 Herblock Prize awards ceremony. "Our mission is to stir them, inform and inflame them. Our task is to continually hold up our government and our leaders to clear-eyed analysis, unaffected by professional spin-meisters and agenda-pushers." "The ideal is to make people see something in a new light, to say 'Oh, yeah, that's right,'" he said to Kenneth Turan. "What we call information is really a glut of some facts, some public relations, some nonsense, some propaganda. I try and cut through it, illustrate what's really going on. The criticism of a cartoonist simplifying an issue is a criticism I hear from people who think I haven't simplified it correctly. Otherwise they say, 'Wow, you really cut through all the crap and got right to the point!'" At the time of the first Gulf War, in which the U.S. and a coalition of other Western countries attacked Iraq (then under the control of the despot Saddam Hussein) in response to Iraq's invasion of its neighbor Kuwait, Auth told Paul Dean for the *Los Angeles Times* (February 17, 1991), "I have no problem in painting Saddam Hussein as an absolute, maniacal tyrant, and then the next day being critical of us spending money on a war when our cities are going to hell. If people see a conflict in that, my response is: 'I'm not a propagandist. I just look for the truth wherever I find it.'"

Auth was born William Anthony Auth Jr. on May 7, 1942 in Akron, Ohio, to William Anthony Auth and Julia Kathleen Auth. He grew up in Southern California. For 18 months, beginning when he was five years old, he was bedridden with rheumatic fever. (The drugs now used to treat that illness were not available in the late 1940s.) To keep him occupied during his illness, his mother gave him crayons, pencils, and paper and encouraged him to learn to draw. "You might enjoy it. It's magical," she told him, as he recalled in his Herblock Prize acceptance speech. He especially enjoyed drawing pictures of his favorite comic-book characters and scenes inspired by the radio programs to which he listened while in bed. By the age of 12, Auth knew that he wanted to pursue a career as an artist. In an article he wrote for the magazine

Editor & Publisher (October 30, 1999), he credited a book by Herbert L. Block (known professionally as Herblock) with helping to steer him toward his life's work: "I read the text, studied the cartoons, and began to comprehend how opinions on what humankind was up to might be expressed with drawings. This was drawing with a purpose! I was hooked."

In 1961 Auth enrolled at the University of California at Los Angeles (UCLA), where he occasionally drew cartoons about student activities and sports events for the school's newspaper, the *Daily Bruin*. He studied art and zoology and earned a B.A. degree in biological illustration in 1965. After his graduation he found a job as a medical illustrator at Rancho Los Amigos, a teaching hospital (now a national rehabilitation center) that is an arm of the medical school of the University of Southern California. He told Kenneth Turan that he regarded himself as "apolitical" then but that knowing he might be drafted to serve in the Vietnam War any day, he learned what he could regarding the conflict. "I got gradually convinced that the war was stupid, obscene, wrong," he recalled to Turan. At around that time he began drawing political cartoons for *Open City*, a small weekly magazine founded by alumni of the *Daily Bruin*. After creating a political cartoon each week for one year, Auth showed his work to Paul Conrad, a cartoonist with the *Los Angeles Times*. Conrad advised Auth to take on a heavier workload, to prepare himself for the rigors of a cartoonist's job at any major newspaper. Auth then began producing several cartoons each week for the *Daily Bruin*. In time, according to the *New York Times* (May 4, 1976), his cartoons (for which he earned no pay) were syndicated in three dozen other school or alternative newspapers. At first they offered commentary on the Vietnam War, but, as Auth told a *Daily Bruin* interviewer, "one thing leads to another, so pretty soon there's the civil rights movement and the women's movement and pretty soon it was not a problem to do three cartoons a week, which convinced me that I really wanted to do this."

After putting together a portfolio with a substantial number of cartoons, Auth began looking for work at large-circulation newspapers. "The fact that I had done these drawings for the *Bruin* meant that if [potential employers] were interested, I had hundreds of cartoons to show them," he said in an interview for the *Daily Bruin* Web site. "If I'm doing three a week, after five years I could pull out 100 cartoons that were damn good, so it was incredibly invaluable." In 1971 the *Philadelphia Inquirer* hired Auth as an editorial cartoonist; he was one of the first opponents of the Vietnam War to land such a position with a major newspaper.

In 1974 Auth received the Thomas Nast Award from the Overseas Press Club for best cartoons on international affairs. (He won that award again in 1975, 1985, and 1991.) In 1975 he won the Sigma Delta Chi Award from the National Society of Professional Journalists, for a cartoon depicting Mus-lims and Christians killing each other in the names of their respective religions during a civil war in Lebanon. The next year he received the Pulitzer Prize for editorial cartooning, for a drawing (published on July 22, 1975 in the *Philadelphia Inquirer*) labeled "O beautiful for spacious skies, for amber waves of grain," which depicted Leonid Brezhnev, the chairman of the Communist Party of the Soviet Union, singing "America the Beautiful" while standing in a wheat field in the U.S. The cartoon referred to the Soviet Union's 1975 purchase from the U.S. of four times as much grain as it had bought the previous year, to prevent famine after a particularly poor harvest. In 2002 the Thomas Nast Foundation of Landau, Germany (named for a famous 19th-century American political cartoonist who was a native of Germany) selected Auth as the winner of that year's Thomas Nast Prize.

The first collection of Auth's work, *Behind the Lines*, was published in 1977. "The cartoons, though mainline political satire, are more funny than cynical, unlike much contemporary work," Patricia Goodfellow wrote in a review for *Library Journal* (December 1, 1977). Auth's second book, *Lost in Space: The Reagan Years*, with a foreword by Jules Feiffer, came out in 1988. Ten of his cartoons that he judged to be among his best appear in the collection *The Gang of Eight* (1988), along with work (self-chosen by each contributor) by his fellow cartoonists Feiffer, Paul Conrad, Jeff Mac-Nelly, Doug Marlette, Mike Peters, Paul Szep, and Don Wright; that book contains an introduction by the broadcast journalist Tom Brokaw. Auth's drawings appear in the *Gurl Engagement 2000 Calendar* (1999). He has illustrated seven children's books written by others: *That Game from Outer Space: The First Strange Thing that Happened to Oscar Noodleman* (1983), by Stephen Manes; *Mean Murgatroyd and the Ten Cats*, by Nathan Zimelman (1984); *Kids' Talk* (1993), by Linda K. Harris (1993); *Tree of Here* (1993) and *Sky of Now* (1994), both by Chaim Potok; *A Christmas Quartet* (2000), by Chris Satullo, the editorial-page editor of the *Philadelphia Inquirer*; and *My Curious Uncle Dudley* (2004), by Barry Yourgrau. Auth both wrote and illustrated *Sleeping Babies* (1989), a Big Golden Book, in which, according to a card-catalog description quoted on Amazon.com, "a human mother explains to her child who does not want to go to sleep that baby animals everywhere are fast asleep."

The Library of Congress owns six of Auth's original drawings, each of which is described in the library's Print and Photographs Online Catalog (PPOC). The first, from 1973, shows, according to PPOC, "a boy, wearing a dunce hat decorated with stars and stripes and having a sling shot in his back pocket, repeatedly writing on a blackboard 'I should not have gone into Vietnam.'" Auth drew the second, captioned "Pope John Paul II promoting man" (1979), during a visit by that pope to the U.S. during which the pontiff reaffirmed the Catholic Church's opposition to the ordination of women into the priesthood; the drawing shows John Paul II "wearing his ceremonial robes, raising the male sex symbol over his head," in the words of PPOC. The third (2000) shows Herb Block painting portraits of presidents Bill Clinton, Ronald Reagan, and Richard Nixon and the Republican U.S. senator Joseph McCarthy, who in the 1950s became notorious for exploiting Americans' fear of communism and accusing various public figures in government and the arts of being members of the Communist Party. In that cartoon all the subjects are nude; as the PPOC described the scene, "Clinton and McCarthy are bashful of their nudity, whereas Reagan and Nixon strike poses of a song and dance man and a muscleman, respectively. Seemingly ignoring his models, Herblock paints them as he sees them. Just visible on the far left is a portrait of [President] Franklin Delano Roosevelt." Auth created the fourth Library of Congress–owned cartoon, "Another victim of Bin Laden's terror," a month after the September 11, 2001 terrorist attacks on the World Trade Center, in New York City. The "victim" is Islam, as depicted by an minaret from which two fireballs explode, in an image reminiscent of the billowing smoke emerging from the burning twin towers after the terrorists flew airplanes into them. The fifth drawing (November 2001) shows President George W. Bush's first attorney general, John Ashcroft, standing at an altar, his arm upraised and a large knife in his hand; lying on the altar is the body of a woman, labeled "The rule of law"; the cartoon is captioned, "In the war on terror, sometimes sacrifice is necessary." The sixth drawing (December 2001) depicts Ashcroft as "a mullah seated on a rug, wearing a turban with [an] American flag design, and reading new rules to be imposed in the wake of the September 11th terrorist attacks," as the PPOC described it. Ashcroft is saying, "Music, kite-flying and women will be tolerated. Questions and dissent are forbidden."

Some of Auth's most controversial cartoons have focused on the conflict between Israel and its Arab neighbors, in particular Palestinians in refugee camps in the Gaza Strip and elsewhere; indeed, Auth has found himself attacked by supporters of each side. Some Jewish groups have condemned cartoons of his as anti-Semitic; a writer for *Jewish Exponent* (August 8, 2002), for example, accused Auth of making "inane cracks at Israel's expense," and Jonathan S. Tobin wrote for the *Jerusalem Post* (August 17, 2003) that Auth had a "long history of Israel-bashing images." Tobin labeled as an "atrocity" a drawing that commented on the security fence that Israel was erecting along some of its borders, with the stated aim of keeping terrorists out of Israel: the cartoon portrayed the wall in the shape of a Jewish star, with Palestinians inside the "walls" in poses of fear and suffering, each huddled in isolation from the others. "Tony Auth took our symbol of our people and turned it into a slur and a distortion and instead of a symbol of freedom, which it is, he was turning it into a symbol of imprisonment, which it is not," Steve Feldman,

the executive director of the Greater Philadelphia district of the Zionist Organization of America, told Andrea Schleider for the Jewish newspaper the *Forward* (August 15, 2003). Auth rejected demands from such groups that he apologize. "No one who's familiar with the body of my work can cling to this fantasy that I am an antisemite," he told Schleider. "The Star of David is the symbol of the Israeli state. The cartoon clearly says that the State of Israel is building a fence in such a way that it separates Palestinians and is an obstacle to peace. That's all it says. A drawing like that one I did is not done with glee; it's done with sadness." Palestinian sympathizers have criticized Auth as well. Palestine Media Watch, for example, a group devoted to promoting the Palestinian point of view in American broadcast and print journalism, complained on their Web site, "The striking fact that 80% of Mr. Auth's cartoons blame Arafat and the Palestinians either exclusively (57%) or partially (23%) for the violence in the Palestinian-Israeli conflict, vs. 20% that directly blame [the Israeli prime minister, Ariel] Sharon and the Israelis, places Mr. Auth squarely within the camp that puts the primary blame for the crisis on the Palestinians."

Among Auth's recent cartoons for the *Inquirer*, published in December 2005, is one that shows Vice President Richard B. Cheney—who had recently asserted that the CIA should be excluded from a proposed federal ban on cruel, inhuman, and degrading treatment of prisoners—yelling to a figure labeled "The English Language," whom he is stretching on a medieval torture rack, "Repeat after me! Mock executions are *not* torture! Sexual humiliation is *not* torture! Near drowning is *not* torture!" A third drawing shows President Bush, holding a report titled "Secret Spying on Americans," being visited by the ghost of Richard Nixon, who tells him, "You are not a crook."

Auth lives in Philadelphia with his wife, the former Eliza Drake, a professional artist. The couple have two daughters, Katie and Emily.

—R.E.

Suggested Reading: *Editor & Publisher* p43 Oct. 30, 1999; *Forward* p7 Aug. 15, 2003; Herb Block Foundation Web site; *Los Angeles Times* E p1 Feb. 17, 1991; *UCLA Daily Bruin* (on-line) Feb. 1, 1974; uclick.com; *Washington Post* B p1 Nov. 2, 1977

Courtesy of Sara Lee

Barnes, Brenda

Nov. 11, 1953– Business executive

Address: Sara Lee Corp., 3 First National Plaza, Chicago, IL 60602

Brenda Barnes is the president and chief executive officer (CEO) of the Sara Lee Corp., a worldwide manufacturer and marketer of foods and beverages, household products, and apparel. Since she took the reins of the company, in 2005, Barnes has faced the difficult task of reinvigorating the sluggish sales of Sara Lee's older products in the food business, an industry whose annual sale increases are typically in the single-digit percentages, while competing for market share with items named for grocery retailers, which provide a lower-priced alternative to traditional brand-name foods. Barnes began her career at PepsiCo, where she held a number of high-ranking positions and was the heir apparent to the CEO. She stunned observers in the business world in 1997, when, after 22 years at the company, she resigned her post as head of Pepsi-Cola's North American division to spend more time with her family. Seven years later she joined Sara Lee, where, as CEO, she has overseen the company's ambitious efforts to streamline its diversified businesses, with sales of its subsidiaries totaling $8.2 billion. She has also centralized Sara Lee's operations, concentrating more of its North American businesses in the Chicago, Illinois, area. "I am a marketing person by discipline. I'm also an operating person by discipline," she told Delroy Alexander for the *Chicago Tribune* (February 11, 2005), "and I think the transformation of those two [is] what is embedded in this transformation of Sara

Lee." In 2005 *Forbes* magazine ranked Barnes eighth on its list of the world's most powerful women, one step ahead of the talk-show legend Oprah Winfrey, and the *Wall Street Journal* named her one of its 50 Women to Watch.

The third of seven daughters, Barnes was born Brenda Czajka on November 11, 1953 in Chicago and grew up in nearby River Grove. Barnes has credited her mother, a homemaker, and her father, a factory worker, with being very influential figures in her life, telling Alexander that her parents gave her "a strong work ethic." Barnes attended East Leyden High School in Franklin Park, Illinois, where she was a member of the cheerleading squad and a frequent participant—and finalist—in the school's spelling bees. Following graduation, Barnes, whom her fellow students voted most likely to succeed, enrolled at Augustana College, a liberal-arts and science institution in Rock Island, Illinois. According to John Gogonas, Barnes's childhood neighbor and fellow student at Augustana, she maintained a single-minded focus on her studies. "She didn't join a sorority, didn't do cheerleading. She didn't get into that part of college," he told John Schmeltzer for the *Chicago Tribune* (October 28, 2005). In 1975, after graduating from Augustana with a degree in business and economics, Barnes worked for a year as a waitress and a postal clerk before becoming a business manager at Wilson Sporting Goods, which was then a subsidiary of PepsiCo Inc. Barnes was undeterred by the company's policy against hiring women in its team-sports division due to their perceived lack of knowledge regarding such items as baseball gloves and footballs. "I knew there were certain people who were uncomfortable dealing with me as a woman . . . but I went about doing my job. I probably wasn't terribly sensitive to those things," she told Shelley Donald Coolidge for the *Christian Science Monitor* (October 8, 1997). Barnes was promoted to head of sales at the company. Meanwhile, she completed night classes at Loyola University, in Chicago, where she received her master's degree in business administration in 1978.

In 1981 Barnes joined Frito-Lay, another Pepsi-Co subsidiary, serving as a brand manager before becoming vice president in charge of marketing for the Lay's, Ruffles, and O'Grady's brands of potato chips. She moved in 1984 to the company's beverage division, Pepsi-Cola. After being named the group vice president of marketing at Pepsi USA, she relocated to the company's headquarters, in Purchase, New York. In 1988 she made the decision to switch from marketing to sales and was appointed vice president of on-premise sales for the eastern region, based in Somers, New York. Two promotions at the senior-vice-president level followed, in the national sales department, in 1989, and in corporate operations, in 1991.

In January 1992 Barnes accepted the position of president of Pepsi-Cola South, succeeding Ron Tidmore. With that appointment Barnes reached a milestone in her career, becoming the highest-ranking female executive at the Pepsi-Cola division of PepsiCo. As president Barnes was in charge of Pepsi-Cola's manufacturing, sales, and distribution operations for the southern region, which covered 13 states. Her responsibilities also involved the operation of over 50 production and warehouse facilities. In 1993 Barnes was named chief operating officer for PepsiCo South. At the time PepsiCo was undergoing a reorganization, switching from 24 separate domestic areas of operation to one national business unit, consisting of 16 nationwide business and 100 separate market units in charge of front-line sales and marketing. That move, for which Barnes was one of the key planners, was meant to "put decision-making as close to the customer as possible," as she explained to Katherine Hauck for *Prepared Foods* (August 1993). Barnes led the company's market units for the southern and western regions, which also involved managing the operations of company-owned and franchise-business units. (Franchise business units are authorized to sell or distribute a company's goods or services in a particular region.) Barnes's regions were largely responsible for the company's 22 percent increase in first-quarter profits during fiscal year 1993. In 1994 Barnes was promoted to chief operating officer (COO) of the North American arm of Pepsi-Cola, also based in Somers; in April 1996 she became the president and chief executive officer of Pepsi-Cola, which was then a $3 billion business. Up until that time, the company had sold its beverages to licensed bottling companies, which then sold and distributed the products in designated regions of North America; as CEO Barnes oversaw the acquiring of bottling operations, resulting in a tripling of sales. Pepsi-Cola recorded operating profits of $1.43 billion and sales of $7.73 billion in 1996. Discussing her successful management of the Pepsi-Cola division, Barnes told Katherine Hauck, "I just had someone tell me they thought I was tough, but that I always treated them with dignity and respect. I set the bar high, but make sure people have what they need to jump over it."

In September 1997 Barnes shocked the business world when she resigned from her $2 million-per-year position as president and chief executive officer of Pepsi-Cola North America, after 22 years with PepsiCo. Although it had been widely speculated in the media that Barnes would succeed the chairman and CEO of PepsiCo, Roger A. Enrico, following his retirement in 2001, she cited a desire to devote more time to her husband, Randall C. Barnes, a retired PepsiCo executive, and their three young children. (As quoted by Delroy Alexander, Barnes told a TV talk-show host that she didn't want to miss "another of my kids' birthdays.") "I hope people can look at my decision not as 'women can't do it' but 'for 22 years Brenda gave her all and did a lot of great things.' I don't think there's any man who doesn't have the same struggle. . . . You have to make your choices. Maybe I burned [the candle] at both ends for too long," she told Nikhil Deogun for the *Wall Street Journal*, as

quoted in the Fort Lauderdale, Florida, *Sun-Sentinel* (September 25, 1997). Barnes did not completely disappear from the business world: from November 1999 to March 2000, she served as the interim president and chief operating officer of the Starwood Hotels and Resorts in White Plains, New York, whose luxury-hotel chains include the Sheraton, the Westin, the Luxury Collection, St. Regis, W, and Four Points by Sheraton. In 2002 she also became an adjunct professor at Northwestern University's Kellogg Graduate School of Management, in Evanston, Illinois, and at North Central College, in Naperville, Illinois.

In July 2004 Barnes accepted an offer from the Chicago-based Sara Lee Corp. to become the company's president and chief operating officer, replacing then-chairman and chief executive officer C. Steven McMillan, who had not hired a president and COO since he had vacated those posts in 2000. With her oldest child preparing for college and her two younger children in the eighth and 10th grades, respectively, Barnes felt ready to return to the corporate business world, following a seven-year hiatus. "Being away from the day-to-day was very helpful. I feel recharged," she told Michael Arndt for *Business Week Online* (May 17, 2004). Barnes was placed in charge of global marketing and sales and was expected to call upon her consumer-brand experience at PepsiCo to help implement Sara Lee's new brand-segmentation strategy. (That long-term strategy involved investing marketing, research and development, and management resources in the company's projected consumer brands while limiting the investment in its low-growth brands.) She was viewed in the media as the eventual successor to McMillan, who had overseen an unsuccessful four-year plan to restructure the company by consolidating acquisitions and streamlining the company's decentralized business operations.

The Sara Lee Corp. was established in 1935, when Charles Lubin acquired a small chain of local bakeries that he named Community Bake Shops. The first product Lubin launched was a line of cheesecakes, named after his eight-year-old daughter, Sara Lee; the company later introduced an all-butter pecan coffee cake and its signature all-butter pound cake. Lubin's manufacturing process involved freezing the baked products after they were removed from the oven to ensure freshness. In 1949 the business changed its name to Kitchens of Sara Lee, and six years later Consolidated Foods Corp. acquired the company. By 1985 Consolidated Foods Corp. had officially changed its name to the Sara Lee Corp., and Kitchens of Sara Lee was renamed the Sara Lee Bakery. Today, the Sara Lee Corp. manufactures and markets food, beverage, branded apparel, and household products.

Under McMillan Sara Lee had downsized its portfolio of 200 diverse brands, which ranged from Wonderbra and Kiwi shoe polish to Endust furniture polish, Ball Park hot dogs, and Chock Full O'Nuts Coffee, by selling off its unrelated product lines—including its Coach leather-goods business, Champion athletic wear, and the PYA/Monarch food-service unit—and investing the savings in the marketing of its core businesses: food and beverages, underwear/intimate apparel, and household products. (Sara Lee had only one billion-dollar product line, its Hanes line of underwear and socks.) McMillan's strategy to jumpstart the company's profits also involved the acquisition of the Brazilian coffee company Uniao and the Argentine underwear firm Sol y Oro and the purchase of a minority stake in the U.S.-based Johnsonville Sausage Co.—brands or product lines that were not only closer to Sara Lee's core businesses but appeared to have the potential for higher-than-average growth. However, his $2.6 billion acquisition of Earthgrains, America's second-largest fresh-bread manufacturer, in 2002, drew criticism from investors, who accused him of overpayment, and managed a return of less than $100 million in operating profits in 2003. Between 1998 and 2001 the price of the company's stock also plummeted, to $22.50 per share, a decrease of nearly 30 percent. During the same period sales grew by only 1.7 percent, to $17.7 billion, and operating earnings increased by only 5.6 percent, to $1.2 billion, according to Julie Forster, writing for *Business Week* (September 10, 2001, on-line). The Sara Lee Corp. also experienced a drop in sales in its apparel division, including Hanes, Playtex, and Wonderbra, as a result of competition from low-cost imports and high cotton prices; sales from its hosiery business, which accounted for 60 percent of the domestic market, dropped from $1 billion to $500 million between 2000 and 2004.

Following five years of substandard sales and growth-investment returns, Barnes was named to succeed McMillan in the position of CEO in February 2005. McMillan remained in the role of chairman until October of that year. In a company press release (February 10, 2005) posted on the Sara Lee Corp.'s Web site, Barnes said, "Today, Sara Lee is embarking on an aggressive, strategic plan that will transform the entire enterprise into a tightly focused food, beverage and household products company. We are taking bold actions that will enable Sara Lee to compete more successfully in today's dynamic marketplace and thereby generate consistent, long-term topline growth and bottom-line profitability for our shareholders." As part of her five-year plan, Barnes restructured the organization into three lines of business: North American retail, which targets bakery, packaged-meat, and coffee businesses on the continent; North American Foodservice, encompassing restaurants and other food-service businesses; and Sara Lee International, which focuses on brands outside North America. Barnes hired former employees of PepsiCo and H.J. Heinz to fill key roles in Sara Lee's executive ranks, including George Chappelle, who joined the company as chief information officer. She also moved the company's North American headquarters from downtown Chicago to Downers

Grove, a Chicago suburb, concentrating its domestic businesses there. "By bringing our North American businesses together in the Chicago area, we will provide a natural catalyst for sharing best practices and pursuing growth opportunities across the businesses, as well as provide great opportunities for career growth and development for our employees," Barnes added, according to the press release.

In February 2005 Barnes announced the company's intention to convert its remaining apparel business, Sara Lee Branded Apparel/Americas Asia, into an independent, publicly traded company; that process was completed in September 2006. In October 2005 Sara Lee's $300 million U.S. Retail Coffee business, including Chock Full O'Nuts, Hills Bros., and Chase & Sanborn, was sold to the Italian-based company Segafredo Zanetti Group, pending regulatory approval. The following month the company sold its European apparel business to Sun Capital Partners for $117 million, and it completed the sale of its European nuts and snacks businesses in France (Benenuts) and Belgium and the Netherlands (Duyvis) to PepsiCo for a reported $152 million in 2006. The Sara Lee Corp. also completed the sale of its $450 million direct-selling business in Latin America and Asia (encompassing cosmetics, skin-care products, fragrances, toiletries, and clothing) to the Tupperware Corp. in December 2005. While Barnes's plans include divesting Sara Lee of its $1.1 billion European meats business, she has decided to retain control over Senseo, a maker of coffee machines.

In fiscal year 2005 the Sara Lee Corp. reported revenues of $19.3 billion, an increase of only 1 percent from the previous year, and a net income of $719 million, a decrease of 43.5 percent from 2004. The company experienced a fourth-quarter net loss of $148 million, which was the result of an increase in commodity costs, millions of dollars in reorganization expenses, and a 5.2 percent decrease in sales revenue, for a total of $4.75 billion. The apparel division and the baked-goods division reported declines in revenue of 8 percent and 9.2 percent, respectively. Sara Lee showed no great financial improvement during the first quarter of fiscal year 2006; the company's net sales declined by 2 percent, to $4.4 billion, compared with $4.3 billion during the first quarter of 2005, whereas the company's goal had been $4.64 billion. While Sara Lee also experienced a 3 percent increase in the sales of its North American retail meats and sales increases of 4 percent and 3 percent, respectively, in its international beverage and bakery division, those boosts were accompanied by a decrease in sales in the North American retail bakery, household and body care, and branded-apparel lines. Despite the company's poor showing, Barnes remained optimistic. "While we exceeded our forecasted earnings per share target, we still are not satisfied with our business performance. However, our ongoing transformation initiatives are building the momentum needed to drive improvement," Barnes said, as quoted in the company's November 3, 2005 press release.

In January 2006 the company announced its acquisition of Butter-Krust Baking, a fresh baked-goods business, for nearly $72 million. In February 2006 Sara Lee announced that its Soft & Smooth whole-grain bread, which was launched in the U.S. in July 2005, held a 5.7 percent share of the combined packaged bread, buns, rolls, bagels, and English muffins category, as quoted in the company's second-quarter 2006 press release (February 2, 2006). Sara Lee also made its largest launch yet in the "air-care" business in February 2006, with the introduction of the air-freshener brand Ambi Pur 3volution, which emits a different scent every 45 minutes.

Barnes has been a member of the board of directors at the Sara Lee Corp. since she joined the company in 2004. She is currently on the board of directors of the New York Times Co., LucasFilm Ltd.,

Staples Inc., and the Grocery Manufacturers Association. Barnes is also a member of the board of trustees of Augustana College and a member of the steering committee of the Kellogg Center for Executive Women at Northwestern University. She has previously served as an advisory board member for the comedienne Rosie O'Donnell's All for Kids Foundation and as a corporate director with Avon Products Inc., PepsiAmericas Inc., and Sears, Roebuck and Co. Barnes lives in Naperville, Illinois, with her husband, Randall C. Barnes, and their children.

—B.M.

Suggested Reading: *Chicago Tribune* C p1 Feb. 11, 2005; *Christian Science Monitor* p1 Oct. 8, 1997; *Directors and Boards* p49 June 22, 1998; *Prepared Foods* p35 Aug. 1993; Sara Lee Corp. Web site

---

Courtesy of Creators Syndicate

Bartlett, Bruce

Oct. 11, 1951– Economist; syndicated columnist

Address: 439 Seneca Rd., Great Falls, VA 22066-1113

The economist, writer, and syndicated columnist Bruce Bartlett has "emerged as the most articulate spokesman for the view" that President George W. Bush has "betrayed conservatism," according to David Brooks, a columnist for the *New York Times* (October 23, 2005). Shortly before Brooks wrote

that piece, the National Center for Policy Analysis, where Bartlett had worked for a decade, fired him, after its president read a draft of his most recent book, *Impostor: How George W. Bush Bankrupted America and Betrayed the Reagan Legacy.* The dismissal prompted Brooks to declare that Bartlett "is a man of immense intellectual integrity. In an era when many commentators write whatever will affirm the prejudices of their own team, [he] follows his conscience and has paid a price."

A self-described libertarian Republican, Bartlett was an early advocate of supply-side economics, a term coined in 1975. His work has often been cited in congressional debate, mostly by Republican legislators but occasionally by Democrats, among them the two-term senator Paul Simon of Illinois. Bartlett, who began his career as a congressional legislative aide and later directed the Joint Economic Committee of Congress during the administration of President Ronald Reagan, has helped shape some of the most important and contentious tax-reform proposals introduced by Republican lawmakers in the past two decades. No longer working directly in government, Bartlett has continued to influence federal policy making through his weekly syndicated column. "Bartlett has long been one of Washington's most searching, thoughtful, and uncompromisingly candid economic analysts," E. J. Dionne Jr., a columnist for the *Washington Post*, is quoted as saying on the Doubleday Web site. "That's a view shared not only by those who agree with him, but also by people like me, who differ with him about 80 percent of the time."

Bruce Reeves Bartlett was born on October 11, 1951 in Ann Arbor, Michigan, to Frank and Marjorie Bartlett. Bartlett was a teenager in 1965, when the U.S. began air strikes targeting guerrilla forces in North Vietnam, and he initially supported the use of military force to prevent the spread of Communism in Asia. As the U.S.-led war progressed, however, he gradually came to believe that Vietnam in the 1960s "was the wrong place and the wrong time to confront the Communist menace," according to an article he wrote for the *National Review* (February 19, 2003). Nevertheless, as an undergraduate at Rutgers University, in New Brunswick, New Jersey, where he majored in history, Bartlett joined the Reserve Officers' Training Corps (ROTC). After he earned a B.A. degree, in 1973, he was commissioned as a second lieutenant in the U.S. Air Force. He did not serve in Vietnam, however; he told *Current Biography* that, with the war in its waning stages, the air force allowed him to withdraw from its ranks before his commitment had ended.

While at Rutgers Bartlett idolized Milton Friedman, one of the most prominent and respected advocates of free-market economics, a school of thought that posits that the allocation of resources should be determined only by supply and demand. Friedman, a Rutgers graduate who won the Nobel Prize in Economics in 1976, "was one of the few economists I could cite in class in support of free market policies who wasn't automatically dismissed as irrelevant," Bartlett wrote in an article published on the Web site of the National Center for Policy Analysis (July 31, 2002). "I learned far more economics from his books than the justly forgotten texts I was forced to study." As a graduate student at Georgetown University, in Washington, D.C., Bartlett mingled with and was influenced by such revisionist historians as Jules Davids, a professor of diplomatic history at Georgetown's School of Foreign Service, and Percy Greaves, who served as the chief of minority staff for the 1945–46 Joint Congressional Investigation of the Pearl Harbor Attack. "Percy introduced me to a wide range of people who were absolutely convinced that [President Franklin D. Roosevelt] had not only known about the Pearl Harbor attack in advance, but had done everything in his power to instigate it," Bartlett wrote for a column published in the *National Review* (February 19, 2003, on-line). "This argument was highly persuasive to me at the time and I eventually wrote a master's thesis on the topic at Georgetown University." The thrust of that thesis served as the foundation for Bartlett's book *Coverup: The Politics of Pearl Harbor, 1941-1946* (1979).

In 1976, after he graduated from Georgetown with an M.A. degree in American history, Bartlett took a job as a legislative assistant in the office of Republican congressman Ron Paul of Texas. The following year he published the pamphlet *The Keynesian Revolution Revisited* and became a special assistant to Republican congressman Jack Kemp of New York State. While in that position Bartlett drafted the Kemp-Roth tax bill (also named for Republican senator William Roth Jr. of Delaware), which proposed cutting federal tax rates across the board, with the rate for those in the lowest income bracket reduced from 14 to 10 percent

and for those in the highest bracket from 70 to 50 percent; the purpose of the proposed cuts was to offset the effects of inflation, as a result of which taxes accounted for a greater proportion of people's income than the tax laws passed in the early 1960s had originally intended. The Kemp-Roth tax bill was introduced in 1977 (apparently, it never came to a vote) and later served as the basis for the Economic Recovery Tax Act of 1981, which was signed by President Ronald Reagan.

In 1981, prior to the final vote on that legislation, Bartlett published *Reaganomics: Supply-Side Economics in Action*, which, according to M. S. Forbes Jr., writing for *Forbes* (July 20, 1981), presented "the history and thinking behind [the Reagan administration's] economics" in "a well researched, straightforward manner." The supply-siders were concerned with how the marginal tax rate—the amount of tax paid on each additional dollar of income—was influencing productivity. For example, if an individual earned $27,050 during the 2001 tax year, he would fall into the first tier of the graduated-tax system, in which income is taxed at a rate of 15 percent. He would thus owe approximately $4,000 in taxes. But if the taxpayer earned only one dollar more, so that his income fell in the next tier, his tax rate would climb to 27.5 percent, and he would owe more than $7,000 in taxes. Consequently, according to such supply-siders as Bartlett, if individuals know that working overtime, investing in businesses, or starting businesses on the side will push them into higher tax brackets, they will be less likely to engage in such activities; the net effect on the economy would be a reduction in the efficient use of resources and a retardation of output. According to their theory, the government could collect greater tax revenues by reducing taxes and, consequently, the marginal tax rate, because taxpayers would have a greater incentive to earn more money and, in addition, would be less inclined to cheat on their income-tax returns.

In an assessment of Bartlett's book for *Management Review* (September 1981), Marc E. Miller wrote that *Reaganomics* "often rings with that suspiciously utopian optimism peculiar to many new economic philosophies." Nicholas von Hoffman, writing for the *New York Review of Books* (June 25, 1981), thought that "within limits" there was much to be said in favor of Bartlett's arguments: "All other things being equal, going ahead with the Reagan/Kemp-Roth bill is a prudent risk. It may give the stimulative burst that's claimed for it." But, Von Hoffman argued, Bartlett had failed to take into account the cost of Reagan's plans for expanding the defense budget: "Neither the president nor [this] book is able to answer or even articulate the central dilemma of the administration's kind of conservatism—reconciling laissez-faire with a state of perpetual [military] mobilization." *Reaganomics* was selected as one of the best business books of 1981 by the *Wall Street Journal* and *Library Journal*.

Earlier, in 1978, Bartlett had left Kemp's office to become the economic adviser to a Republican member of the New York State Assembly, Perry B. Duryea, who was running for the governorship of New York. After Duryea lost to the Democratic incumbent, Hugh Carey, Bartlett returned to Washington, D.C., to join the staff of Roger Jepsen of Iowa, a Republican who had been elected to the U.S. Senate. He first served as Jepsen's legislative assistant for tax and economic policy and then, in 1980, was promoted to legislative director. From 1981 to 1983 he held the post of deputy director, and from 1983 to 1984 executive director, of the Joint Economic Committee of Congress, a counterpart to the president's Council of Economic Advisers. During that period, in 1982, he organized the first congressional hearing on the flat tax. His book *The Supply Side Solution*, a collection of essays co-edited by Timothy P. Roth, and his pamphlet *The Federal Debt: On-Budget, Off-Budget, and Contingent Liabilities: A Staff Study*, were both published in 1983.

In 1984–85 Bartlett was a vice president at the consulting firm Polyconomics Inc., and from 1985 to 1987 he was a senior fellow at the Heritage Foundation, a think tank whose mission, according to its Web site, is "to formulate and promote conservative public policies." In 1987, at the invitation of Gary Bauer, Reagan's chief domestic policy adviser, he joined the staff of the Office of Policy Development (an arm of the White House) as a senior analyst. When the Reagan administration ended, in early 1989, he took a job as a deputy assistant secretary for economic policy in the U.S. Treasury Department, where he stayed until Bill Clinton became president. In 1993 he served as a visiting fellow at the Cato Institute, a libertarian foundation, and starting later that year, into 1994, he was a senior fellow at the Alexis de Tocqueville Institution, which is devoted to the spread of democracy.

In 1990 Bartlett's political columns began appearing weekly on the editorial pages of the *Washington Times*. In 1997 Bartlett signed on with the Creators Syndicate, which also distributes the work of such well-known political columnists as Molly Ivins and Robert Novak. Currently, his column appears in the *Washington Times*, *Investor's Business Daily*, the *Indianapolis Star*, and the *New York Sun*, and it is posted on the *National Review* and *Townhall* Web sites.

In 1995 Bartlett accepted a position as a senior fellow at the National Center for Policy Analysis (NCPA), a conservative think tank with offices in Washington, D.C., and Dallas, Texas. The goal of the NCPA, according to its Web site, is to "develop and promote private alternatives to government regulation and control, solving problems by relying on the strength of the competitive, entrepreneurial private sector." For the NCPA Bartlett conducted research in economic policy and made frequent appearances on network and cable news shows. In 1996 the campaign team working for the election of the Republican presidential nominee,

Senator Robert Dole of Kansas, approached Bartlett for advice, hoping, as the *Economist* (June 1, 1996) put it, that by "jazzing up" his tax platform, Dole could make a dent in President Bill Clinton's lead in the polls. Bartlett recommended a 15 percent across-the-board cut in federal taxes, noting that in 1995 the total collected (as a share of the gross domestic product (GDP), had been 31.3 percent—the highest since the tax began to be collected, in 1913. Some observers were surprised when Dole integrated this plan into his platform, because, as Matthew Rees wrote for the *Weekly Standard* (February 15, 1999), there had been "a longstanding distrust between the Republican party and the noisy squad of supply-side economists, writers, and activists." Indeed, before Dole signed on to Bartlett's plan, the senator had joked, according to Rees, "The good news is that a bus of supply-siders went off a cliff. The bad news is that three seats were empty."

In the mid-1990s congressional leaders began considering a sweeping overhaul of the U.S. tax code, but within a few years, with many Americans enjoying growing prosperity, interest in tax cuts had waned; polls conducted in the late 1990s by various news agencies indicated that American voters placed a lower priority on tax cuts and tax reform than they had in previous years. Nevertheless, when the Republican governor of Texas George W. Bush campaigned for the presidency in 2000, he made tax cuts a central issue. Since proposed tax cuts had failed to win the presidency for Dole, Bartlett suggested that the Republican Party take a cue from private industry and learn how to better market tax reform to the electorate. GOP decision makers "need to ask themselves, 'What is wrong with this product?'" Bartlett said to Robert Dodge for the *Dallas (Texas) Morning News* (December 13, 1999). "In corporate America, they respond when they see demand declining. . . . People who support tax cuts need to stop using the old rhetoric and arguments." Bartlett's analysis drew criticism from some fellow conservatives: "No politician ever lost an election for promising to cut taxes," Stephen Moore, a policy analyst at the Cato Institute, told Dodge. "Republicans cannot as a party abandon the anti-tax message of their party, and they would be foolish to do so." In response, Bartlett told Dodge, "I'm not saying we should not push tax cuts. I am saying we should do a better job."

As president, Bush signed major tax-cutting legislation in 2001 and 2003. But by the time Bush ran for reelection, in 2004, Bartlett and other fiscal conservatives in the Republican Party had grown vocal in their discontent with the administration's economic policies. While in the last year of the Clinton presidency, the federal government had a budget surplus and the federal debt had decreased, under Bush the federal deficit reached a record-breaking $412 billion in 2004, and forecasts released by the nonpartisan Congressional Budget Office predicted that it would climb to

$427 billion in fiscal 2005. According to the *Philadelphia Inquirer* (March 28, 2004), Bartlett said that the president was almost "Nixonian" in his "willingness to subordinate everything to a reelection effort, including abrogation of one's own principles." Though Bartlett continued to advocate cuts in domestic discretionary spending (particularly in entitlement programs), he also predicted that—regardless of whether Bush won reelection or was defeated by the Democratic nominee, Senator John Kerry—tax hikes were inevitable. Several months after Bush's reelection, Bartlett told Bob Edwards for the National Public Radio program *Morning Edition* (March 5, 2005), "When the time for a fiscal readjustment comes, it will be absolutely necessary to both cut spending and to raise taxes. It's simply unrealistic to think that you can reduce the deficits of the magnitude we have to deal with just by cutting spending." Bartlett also made it clear that while he was predicting tax increases, he was not advocating them: "I figure that to be forewarned is to be forearmed," he told Edwards. "And if you know that a tax increase is coming, perhaps we can think about how to do that in a way that is the least damaging to our economy as possible and so that we don't just rush in with bad tax ideas that would be harmful to economic growth."

Earlier, in November 2004, in conjunction with the Ripon Society, Bartlett proposed that the federal government introduce a value-added tax. Used in many European nations, a value-added tax is applied at each stage of a product's manufacture; the cost of collecting it is largely borne by businesses rather than the government. Bartlett believes that such a tax would be the most effective means of cutting the deficit. Discussing Bartlett's proposal in the *New York Times* (December 5, 2005), Eduardo Porter wrote, "Reversing his previous stance that low taxes would force lawmakers onto a spending diet, he now says that adding a steadily increasing value-added tax is the best way to deal with what he now sees as an inevitable rise in federal spending, to as much as 30 percent of the gross domestic product, to cover expanding entitlements for baby boomers."

Bartlett was, however, less concerned with the increasing federal deficit than with the new entitlement programs created by the Bush administration, particularly the introduction of drug benefits for Medicare recipients. "From my own point of view, the drug bill was the line in the sand," he told Ryan Lizza for the *New Republic* (October 31, 2005). "That's the point I decided to write a book and say this guy [Bush] isn't one of us." In 2004 Bartlett reduced his workload at the NCPA in order to complete his most recent book, which the organization's administrators reportedly thought would focus on economic policy and taxation. In October 2005, shortly after Bartlett presented a draft of the book, *Impostor: How George W. Bush Bankrupted America and Betrayed the Reagan Legacy* (2006), to the organization's president, John C. Goodman, he was fired. A statement issued by the NCPA, according to Richard W. Stevenson in the *International Herald Tribune* (October 19, 2005), indicated that the organization had fired Bartlett because it did not want to be associated with a work that was "an evaluation of the motivations and competencies of politicians rather than an analysis of public policy."

Bartlett told Elisabeth Bumiller for the *New York Times* (February 13, 2006) that both Goodman and his wife, Jeanette Goodman, the NCPA's vice president, had told him that his criticisms of Bush administration officials and policies had jeopardized their ability to raise money for the NCPA from Republican donors. In an example of such criticism, Ron Suskind, writing for the *New York Times Magazine* (October 17, 2004), had quoted Bartlett as saying, "Just in the past few months, I think a light has gone off for people who've spent time up close to Bush: that this instinct he's always talking about is this sort of weird, Messianic idea of what he thinks God has told him to do. This is why George W. Bush is so clear-eyed about Al Qaeda and the Islamic fundamentalist enemy. He believes you have to kill them all. They can't be persuaded, that they're extremists, driven by a dark vision. He understands them, because he's just like them. . . . This is why he dispenses with people who confront him with inconvenient facts. He truly believes he's on a mission from God. Absolute faith like that overwhelms a need for analysis. . . . But you can't run the world on faith."

According to E. J. Dionne Jr., *Impostor* "is a perfect reflection of [Bartlett's] gifts: he cares far more about being honest and consistent than about following anyone's party line." A reviewer for *Publishers Weekly* (January 2, 2006) wrote, "Liberal commentators gripe so frequently about the current administration that it's become easy to tune them out, but when Bartlett, a former member of the Reagan White House, says George W. Bush has betrayed the conservative movement, his conservative credentials command attention."

Bartlett is a frequent commentator on CNN (on TV) and NPR (on radio), and he frequently contributes articles to such high-profile periodicals as the *Wall Street Journal*, the *New York Times*, the *Los Angeles Times*, and *USA Today*, among others. He also serves as a contributing editor of *Libertarian Review*. He lives in Great Falls, Virginia, a suburb of Washington, D.C.

—J.C.

Suggested Reading: *International Herald Tribune* p7 Oct. 19, 2005; *National Review* (on-line) July 15, 2002; *New York Review of Books* p24 June 25, 1981; *New York Times* VI p 4 Oct. 7, 2004

Selected Books: *Coverup: The Politics of Pearl Harbor, 1941–1946*, 1979; *Reaganomics: Supply-Side Economics in Action*, 1981; *Impostor: How George W. Bush Bankrupted America and Betrayed the Reagan Legacy*, 2006; as editor—

The Supply Side Solution (with Timothy P. Roth), 1983

Courtesy of the California Institute of Technology

Barton, Jacqueline K.

May 7, 1952– Chemist

Address: Dept. of Chemistry, M/C 12772, California Institute of Technology, 1200 E. California Blvd., Pasadena, CA 91125-7200

"Lovely . . . with beautiful shape and symmetry." That is how the chemist Jacqueline K. Barton described DNA (deoxyribonucleic acid) nearly 20 years ago, during an interview for *Fortune* (October 13, 1986). A half-dozen years before, Barton had started to conduct experiments with DNA, the molecule that is basic to nearly all forms of life, orchestrates the activities of living cells, contains the genetic instructions for growth, development, and reproduction, and is so long that it might be considered "the biological equivalent of a colossal run-on sentence," as the *Fortune* reporter put it. Unlike most DNA researchers, Barton is neither a biologist nor a biochemist; rather, she is a specialist in bioinorganic chemistry, the study of inorganic compounds or ions (those that do not contain carbon–hydrogen bonds) in living organisms. In her research, she has treated the DNA molecule "as if it were an inorganic crystal, such as a piece of a rock or a semiconductor in a cell phone," thus introducing "a radically different way to think about DNA," as K. C. Cole wrote for the *Los Angeles Times* (December 29, 1997). By her early 30s Barton had already made discoveries deemed so important that,

in 1985, she became the first woman to win the National Science Foundation's Alan T. Waterman Award, the federal government's highest honor for scientists 35 years old or younger. Those discoveries were products of her pioneering creation and use of chemical "tools," made with metallic compounds, to recognize and modify specific sites on the DNA molecule. Then and in the years since, she has illuminated aspects of DNA's structure and some of the ways in which the molecule functions, including its conducting of electricity (which previously most scientists in her field had dismissed as impossible) and abilities to maintain and repair itself. According to her profile on the Web site of the California Institute of Technology (Caltech), Barton's work "provides a completely new approach to the study of DNA structure and dynamics and may be critical to understanding the chemical consequences of radical damage to DNA within the cell"; as the National Science Foundation noted on its Web site, her findings have "important implications for drug design and for the theory of gene expression." "Perhaps because I'm a woman and now getting some attention I'm a role model," Barton told Steven Waldman for the States News Service (May 15, 1985) after receiving the Waterman Award. "That sort of thing makes me a little uncomfortable." However, she added, "young women need to see that women are doing science and doing it well." Barton taught and worked at Columbia University, in New York City, from 1983 until 1989, when she joined the faculty of Caltech, in Pasadena. There, she holds the title of Arthur and Marian Hanisch Memorial Professor of Chemistry. Barton has published as author or co-author more than 250 scientific papers and book chapters. Her many honors include seven awards from the American Chemical Society, election to the American Academy of Arts and Sciences and the National Academy of Sciences, and a 1991 MacArthur Foundation Fellowship, popularly known as the "genius" grant.

Jacqueline K. Barton was born on May 7, 1952 in New York City. She attended a private high school, the Riverdale Girls School (now part of the co-educational Riverdale Country School), in the Bronx, at a time when, as she told Natalie Angier for the *New York Times* (March 2, 2004), "young girls didn't take chemistry"; indeed, her school did not offer a course in that subject. She enrolled in a chemistry class for the first time as a student at Barnard College (which was associated with and later became a division of Columbia University), in New York City, which she entered in 1970. Barnard was then a women's school, and as an undergraduate Barton "learned that there wasn't anything strange about a woman going into science," as she told Steven Waldman. She majored in chemistry and graduated with an A.B. degree summa cum laude in 1974.

Barton next began graduate studies in physical chemistry at Columbia; it was only then that she noticed the prevalence of males in her field. But increasing numbers of women were becoming scientists, and she encountered little discrimination; in her experience, she told Waldman, scientists' work "generally speaks for itself." She was a National Science Foundation predoctoral fellow from 1975 to 1978. Barton chose as her Ph.D. adviser the bioinorganic chemist Stephen J. Lippard, after he aroused her curiosity about a substance in which he himself had grown interested—a compound of platinum called cis-diamminedichloroplatinum, or cis-platinum, which had proven to be highly effective in treating certain types of cancers. Barton struck Lippard as "clearly a very bright student, quite strong mathematically. Pure algebra, quantum mechanics—she was really good at that," as he told Will Hively for *Discover* (October 1994, online). Lippard suggested that she try to determine the structure of platinum blue, the compound formed by cis-platinum and uracil (the latter of which is very similar to thymine, one of the basic components of DNA)—"no easy task," as Hively wrote: "First she had to produce a crystal large enough to study; then she had to figure out the location of atoms in the crystal by analyzing the patterns produced by X-rays shot through the crystal." In what Lippard described to Hively as "a major breakthrough," Barton succeeded. The platinum-blue molecule, she determined, contained on its periphery several exposed platinum atoms that could potentially bond with other atoms— including those in components of DNA. Depending on the location, their bonding with the DNA molecule might hinder the further reproduction of cancer cells. Thus, as Hively wrote, "Barton's discovery opened up a whole new field of anticancer compounds." "Crystalline Platinum Blue: Its Molecular Structure, Chemical Reactivity, and Possible Relevance to the Mode of Action of Antitumor Platinum Drugs," by Barton and Lippard, was published in the *Annals of the New York Academy of Sciences* in 1978. Barton earned a Ph.D. in inorganic chemistry in 1979. During the next year, supported by postdoctoral fellowships, she worked with the biophysicist and biochemist Robert G. Shulman at Bell Laboratories and then, in 1980, at Yale University, in New Haven, Connecticut. From 1980 to 1982 she taught chemistry at Hunter College, a division of the City University of New York. She joined the faculty of Columbia in 1983 and remained there for the next six years, during the last three with the title professor of chemistry.

When Gary Taubes, writing for *Science Watch* (January/February 1997), asked Barton how she would describe the "overriding theme" of her research, she responded, "My interest is in using chemistry to ask molecular questions about biological systems—to explore on a chemical level the relationship of structure to function." The goal of Barton's work since the 1980s has been to gain a better understanding of DNA, a nucleic acid whose structure was discovered in 1953 to be a double helix. In humans, DNA is present in 23 pairs of chromosomes (each parent having provided one set of 23) located within the nucleus of almost every cell. (Among the few exceptions are mature red blood cells, which do not have nuclei, and reproductive cells, or gametes—sperm and eggs—each of which has only one set of 23, not two.) Each chromosome contains one DNA molecule. Infinitesimally narrow but about six feet long, the molecule is extremely tightly coiled; if stretched to its full length, it would resemble a ladder that has been twisted along its midline millions of times. Each side of the ladder (also referred to as a strand or a backbone) looks like a necklace strung with millions of linked beads, with each bead composed of a phosphate molecule bonded to a sugar molecule (the sugar being deoxyribose). The rungs, or steps, of the ladder are all of equal length, and the outer ends of each rung are connected to one of the sugar–phosphate "beads" that lie along each strand. The ladder has two types of rungs, with each type made up of a pair of molecules called bases; there are four bases, each of which is a different arrangement of carbon, hydrogen, oxygen, and nitrogen atoms. One type of rung, the A–T pair, consists of the base adenine (A) weakly linked by two hydrogen bonds to the base thymine (T); the other type, the C–G pair, consists of the base cytosine (C) weakly linked by three hydrogen bonds to the base guanine (G). In normal DNA, A connects only to T, and C connects only to G. Thus, one side of the ladder is the complement of the other: if a sequence of nine bases on one side of the ladder is CCTAGTTGG, the corresponding sequence of nine bases on the other side of the ladder must be GGATCAACC. The chemical "direction" of one side of the ladder is the opposite of the other's; the two strands are said to be "antiparallel," and each plays a different role in the cell. Among the findings of the federal government's ongoing Human Genome Project is that the number of base pairs (the "rungs") in a DNA molecule ranges from nearly 47 million in chromosome 21 to more than 245 million in chromosome one. A base plus its connected sugar and phosphate molecules is called a nucleotide. A gene is a connected series of nucleotides; every human's approximately 20,000–30,000 genes (the precise number has not yet been determined) range in length from fewer than 1,000 nucleotides to several million; the average number is about 3,000. Genes are described in terms of codons, each codon being a sequence of three of the four bases (TTT, TCC, CTA, CTG, etc.); the total number of codons is 64 (the four bases combined three at a time; $4^3 = 64$). Every codon contains information connected with the creation of one of 20 standard amino acids (aspargine, histidine, leucine, tryptophan, etc.), the components of proteins, from which muscle, nerves, blood vessels, bone, and everything else in the body is made. (Since there are only 20, each amino acid is associated with more than one codon.) Each gene is located in a specific position on a particular chromosome. Only about 2 percent of the nucleotide sequences of human DNA are genes; the functions of the rest—known variously as junk DNA or noncoding DNA—are only beginning to be elucidated. Although the media and scientists, too, refer to "the" human genome, "a" human genome would be more accurate, because no two individuals have precisely the same DNA; according to the Web site genome.gov, a comparison of the DNA of individuals will show variations of one nucleotide per 1,000 nucleotides, on average. (It is those variations that enable forensic scientists to identify criminals from blood or other body tissues.)

In 1979 scientists discovered that in some DNA molecules, dubbed Z-DNA, portions of the ladder "twist jaggedly to the left rather than spiraling smoothly to the right," as Julie Ann Miller wrote for *Science News* (April 20, 1985). At the same time researchers were trying to recognize patterns in the nucleotide sequences and to demarcate the beginnings and ends of individual genes. Barton approached that problem from the standpoint of inorganic chemistry; as she told the *Fortune* reporter, "At some level one gene must be chemically distinguishable from another." "Chemistry lets you look at a biological problem in a nice simple way," she added. To assess such chemical distinctions, she created compounds using atoms of transition metals, whose two outermost shells of electrons are similar and which easily form chemical bonds; among the transition metals, she chose rhodium, ruthenium, and others among the so-called platinum metals. She then custom-made mirror-image pairs of compounds (called complexes), octahedrons that had an atom of the metal at their cores. She likened the shapes to a pair of mirror-image propellers; one propeller of each pair had a left-handed form, and the other a right-handed form. When she exposed both normal DNA (called B-DNA) and Z-DNA to the complexes, she discovered that only the right-handed propellers could slip between nucleotides in B-DNA, while the left-handed propellers behaved similarly with Z-DNA. Moreover, she could pinpoint the precise locations of such activity, because the metallic complexes—her "little probes," as she called them—emitted light when they found comfortable lodgings. "Take rhuthenium," she explained to the *Fortune* reporter. "When it luminesces, it really shines. It's like day-glo. And it actually luminesces even more intensely when it is bound to DNA. When something happens, you know because the probe changes color." "That's part of the fascination," she added. By that method Barton saw that the complexes had bonded with the DNA molecules near the ends of genes—"sites where the Z-DNA is likely to exert gene control," as Julie Ann Miller wrote. Barton told the *Fortune* reporter, "We now have a little probe that is uniquely suited to detecting structural variations local to a site on the DNA strand." One potential benefit of such chemical tools lies in the treatment of disease. "Say you make an anti-HIV drug and you want to get it to bind to a certain spot on the DNA to stop cell division, for example," Barton told Cole. "So you take your drug, you attach a light switch. Then when it snuggles up in the DNA, when it's safe, it lights up. It's a good tracer. And it's nonradioactive." In one measure of Barton's influence, by the end of 1996 Barton's paper "Metals and DNA: Molecular Left-Handed Complements," in *Science* (Vol. 233, 1986), had been cited nearly 250 times in journal articles by other scientists.

In 1985 the National Science Foundation recognized the immense value of Barton's work by naming her the winner of that year's Waterman Award. Barton used the prize money ($100,000 each year for three years) to pay for new lab equipment and a larger staff. In the fall of 1989, she left Columbia and accepted a professorship at the California Institute of Technology. In 1991 she won a $250,000 MacArthur Foundation Fellowship. Two years later she was elected to the board of directors of the Dow Chemical Co., one of the world's leading manufacturers of chemicals. "For chemists and chemical engineers in industry and academia, it is important . . . that we find ways to enhance the public understanding of issues involving chemistry," she said, as quoted in PR Newswire (January 14, 1993).

Immeasurably aiding Barton in her work (and making possible the Human Genome Project) was the invention in the early 1980s by Leroy E. Hood (who was then at Caltech) of the DNA-sequencing machine, which can rapidly manufacture large quantities of synthetic DNA according to programmed instructions. About the size and shape of a microwave oven, the automated DNA synthesizer strings together fragments of genes to manufacture DNA whose base-pair sequences, unlike those in naturally occurring strands, are known precisely. With large quantities of such DNA at her disposal, Barton conducted research into the electrical conductivity of DNA and the ways in which the strand repaired itself. The latter was addressed in the abstract "Oxidative Thymine Dimer Repair in the DNA Helix," written by Barton and her colleagues Peter J. Dandliker and R. Erik Holmlin and published in the journal *Science* (March 7, 1997). Thymine dimers result from the linking of two thymine bases, an abnormality that can be caused by overexposure to ultraviolet light (a component of sunlight). That linkage leads to mutations when DNA replicates itself, which in turn may lead to the uncontrolled cell growth that characterizes cancer. In the experiment described in *Science*, a synthetic rhodium compound of Barton's design was bonded to one or the other end of a DNA strand that contained a thymine dimer some distance from its ends. In the presence of normal visible light, the abstract explained, the compound "catalyzed" the "long-range repair," which was "mediated by the DNA helix": that is, the rhodium compound, though at some distance from the thymine dimers, stimulated the DNA strand to repair itself and thus return to its normal state. "What I think is exciting is that we can use the DNA to carry out chemistry at a distance," Barton said, according to City News Service (March 6, 1997). "What we're really doing is transferring information along the helix."

Overexposure to ultraviolet light or gamma rays causes the displacement or loss of electrons (a process known as oxidation) at bonding sites on DNA molecules. The displaced electrons, Barton discovered, could then travel to the spot on the DNA most susceptible to damage. (That was found to be the spot where multiple guanine bases were adjacent to one another—"GG" and "GGG" sites.) Damaged GG sites, and the mutations they spawned, had already been believed to play an important role in cancer. "If researchers can locate vulnerable sites and understand how harm is done, they can then look for ways to protect DNA from damage," Jim Thomas wrote for *New Scientist* (February 7, 1998). The discovery of electron travel along the DNA strand is among the highlights of Barton's career. "I probably didn't realize what a crazy idea this was to some scientists," she told K.C. Cole. She also told Cole, "When you rattle the foundations [of science], people get nervous. But at a place like Caltech, it's OK to go out on a limb. It's OK to have an idea proved wrong. I'm supposed to be pushing the boundaries."

In 2001 Barton founded her own company, GeneOhm Sciences, to develop nucleic-acid–based tests "to detect and identify infectious agents and genetic variations" much more rapidly than is possible with other methods and thus enable physicians to begin treatment far sooner, according to the firm's Web site. Based in San Diego, California, GeneOhm acquired a Canadian company, Infectio Diagnostic, in 2004, and was itself purchased by BD (Becton, Dickinson and Co.) in early 2006. To date GeneOhm has developed a nucleic-acid–based test for a type of streptococcus bacteria and another for detecting the presence of a virulent antibiotic-resistant bacterium that has often caused outbreaks of the infection in hospitals. The latter test is 96 percent accurate and takes two hours, rather than the two to four days necessary with other tests. Barton currently serves as a GeneOhm board member. She also continues to lead a research group at Caltech. In May 2006 she received the prestigious Gibbs Medal, presented annually by the American Chemical Society. (Only one other woman has earned that award: the Nobel Prize–winning chemist and physicist Marie Curie, in 1921.)

—M.B.

Suggested Reading: Barton Group Web site; *Chemical & Engineering News* p256 Apr. 22, 1985; *Chemical Heritage* p6+ Fall 2002; *Discover* p130+ Oct. 1994; *Los Angeles Times* A p1+ Dec. 29, 1997; *New Scientist* Feb. 7, 1998; *New York Times* F p1+ Mar. 2, 2004; *Science Watch* (online) Jan./Feb. 1997

Beehler, Bruce

Oct. 11, 1951– Ornithologist; conservationist

Address: Conservation International, 1919 M St., Suite 600, Washington, DC 20026

In February 2006 the international news media reported excitedly on an expedition to the Foja Mountains, in the South Pacific island of New Guinea. The expedition's scientists were co-led by the ornithologist and conservation biologist Bruce Beehler of the Washington, D.C.–based Conservation International (CI), a nonprofit organization dedicated to the preservation of biodiverse ecosystems around the world; Beehler and his colleagues discovered what Ellen Nakashima, writing for the *Washington Post* (February 8, 2006), called "a lost world of rare plants, giant flowers and bizarre animals," including previously undocumented species of frogs and butterflies, possibly the largest rhododendron on record, and, of particular significance for Beehler, a species of bird perhaps never before seen by Westerners. As Shawn Donnan and Taufan Hidayat wrote for the *Financial Times* (February 11, 2006), in characterizing the region that Beehler explored as "lost," many journalists failed to note that the area had been studied in the late 1970s and early 1980s by the Pulitzer Prize–winning evolutionary biologist Jared Dia-

Courtesy of Conservation International

mond; Donnan and Hidayat's article also pointed out that some conservation groups have exaggerated the newness of their undertakings in their appeals to donors. (Beehler himself, as paraphrased by Donnan and Hidayat, admitted that conservation work "can be as much about publicity as it is about national parks.") But Beehler's findings, even if inflated by the news media, are of genuine significance. "This is the sort of expedition you heard about in the 1920s," the Princeton University ecologist David Wilcove told Linell Smith for the *Baltimore Sun* (April 10, 2006). "To launch an expedition where you find new species of birds, butterflies and frogs as well as very rare mammals! There are very few places left on Earth where you can do that sort of thing." In addition, Beehler's team witnessed the spectacular mating rituals of two bird species previously believed "lost" to science—the golden-fronted bowerbird and Berlepsch's six-wired bird of paradise. "I know the [George W.] Bush administration is talking about going back to the moon and going to Mars," Beehler said to Nakashima. "But there are plenty of new things to look for right here, in our rain forests, in our oceans. There are whole worlds that are unknown to us."

As vice president of the Melanesia Program at CI, Beehler travels extensively, advocating conservation to various governments and private foundations. He also establishes contact with indigenous populations, some of which are sufficiently endangered themselves to be a focus of CI's conservation efforts. One of CI's programs, for example, trains members of tribes to serve as archivists of their people's heritage. "The indigenous forest people are actually more at risk than the wildlife because their uniqueness does not come from their genetics, it's their knowledge, their culture," Beehler told Linell Smith. "And that can disappear, essentially in an instant. If the transmission fails one generation, it's gone forever and cannot be recaptured." Beehler relied on such ancestral knowledge in the Foja Mountains, as local Kwerba and Papasena tribe members who accompanied his team identified flora and fauna mentioned in family legends. Beehler aims to improve the relationships between such tribes and research organizations, in the hope that both can work together to conserve the world's increasingly scarce biodiverse areas, such as the Foja Mountains. Michael Hanlon and Richard Shears wrote for the London *Daily Mail* (February 8, 2006), "The sad fact is that were it not for the efforts of scientists such as Bruce Beehler, the first people into these remote, beautiful clearings could well come armed with chainsaws, rifles and bulldozers, rather than cameras, laptops and notebooks."

Bruce McPherson Beehler was born on October 11, 1951 in Baltimore, Maryland, the son of William Henry Beehler and Cary (Baxter) Beehler, both of whom worked in sales. As a boy, Beehler has said, he developed an interest in wildlife while spending summers in the Adirondack Mountains of northern New York, as well as picnicking around Baltimore. Beehler was a member of a junior-naturalist program held during the 1960s and 1970s at the Museum of the Birds of Maryland at

Cylburn Mansion, in northwest Baltimore, which displayed stuffed birds representing 350 species indigenous to the state. He recalled to Michael Ollove for the *Baltimore Sun* (March 30, 2004) that he was entranced by the museum's stuffed pileated woodpecker, the largest of all North American woodpeckers, a year before he spotted one in the wild. (All but a few ornithologists believe that the ivory-billed woodpecker, which was bigger, is extinct.) "It was an epiphany to see the real thing," Beehler told Ollove. Just as momentous for the future ornithologist was his sighting, at age eight, of a red-bellied woodpecker at Lake Roland, in Baltimore County, while he was on a family picnic. "At the time, I didn't know what the hell it was," he told Linell Smith. "I just knew it was the most beautiful thing."

Beehler attended high school at the private Gilman School, in Baltimore, where he briefly pursued interests besides bird-watching. ("I went through a butterfly phase and a girls phase," he told Smith.) He then enrolled at Williams College, in western Massachusetts, where, he told Smith, "I assumed I would major in biology, but I found out there weren't any birds in it. . . . It was all about DNA and premed stuff, meant to scare away and weed out undesirables. So I quickly said, 'This is too unpleasant . . . and where are the birds?'" He majored in American civilization—the subject that "football players major in, because it allows you to do anything," he said. In 1974 he won a William Bradford Turner Award for his senior honors thesis, "Birdlife of the Adirondack Park."

After graduating, in 1974, Beehler traveled to New Guinea—the first of 40 trips he has made to the island—on a Thomas J. Watson Fellowship for foreign study. There, he studied birds of paradise, a family of birds known for their elaborate and beautiful plumage. Beehler then attended Princeton University, in New Jersey, earning an M.A. degree in 1978 and a Ph.D. in 1983, both in biology. He worked at the Smithsonian Institution, in Washington, D.C., from 1981 to 1984 as scientific assistant to the secretary; from 1984 to 1988 he was the assistant to the secretary emeritus. Beehler served as a zoologist at the National Museum of Natural History from 1989 to 1991, before taking successive positions as associate research zoologist at Wildlife Conservation International, an arm of the New York Zoological Society (1991–93), and senior ecologist at Conservation International (1993–95). Starting in 1995 Beehler worked for three years at the State Department's Bureau of Oceans and International Environmental and Scientific Affairs (OES). Since 2003 he has served as vice president of CI's operations in Melanesia, a group of islands in the southwest Pacific. He has published several books that focus on birds of New Guinea, as well as *Ornithology of the Indian Subcontinent, 1872-1992: An Annotated Bibliography* (with Charles G. Burg and S. Dillon Ripley, 1994). Beehler also co-authored the 600-page field guide *The Birds of Paradise* (1998), with Clifford B. Frith, and has written for, among other publications, *American Naturalist*, *Science*, and *Scientific American*. For one day each spring, as billions of warblers and other songbirds that spend winters in Latin America and the Caribbean return to their North American breeding grounds, Beehler leads a warbler "hunt" in rural, wooded western Maryland. He and a small group of fellow watchers travel by bicycle, car, and foot, trying from dawn to dusk to record as many sightings of species as possible.

Prior to the expedition in the Foja Mountains, Beehler's work garnered the attention of the media in a few isolated instances. In 1988 he and a fellow researcher at the Smithsonian, Mercedes Foster, published an article in *American Naturalist* (February 1988) examining the mating behavior—known as "lekking"—practiced by a wide variety of animals, including birds, frogs, bats, and dragonflies. Lekking occurs when the males in a species gather in a group, or lek (a term thought to derive from a Swedish word meaning "play"), from which the females can select mates. After the females are impregnated, they depart and later raise their offspring alone. Disputing earlier theories, Beehler and Foster argued that males, not females, had the more significant role in the lekking process. In their report they offered the "hotshot theory," according to which competition among males narrows the female's choice prior to her arrival. As an example, Beehler and Foster pointed to a study of the lekking behavior of the lesser bird of paradise; it was found that a single male bird of paradise that emerged as dominant in the lek performed 24 of 25 successful copulations, each with a different female. While that outcome was previously attributed to the females' choice, Foster and Beehler contended that, since male birds of paradise were all similar in looks and behavior (at least to the human eye), the dominant male candidate had likely been determined by male competition within the lek before the females even arrived. Under the hotshot model, less successful males grouped around the dominant male, both for the access to females the grouping gave them and for safety in numbers in the face of predators. The hotshot, or dominant male, perhaps benefited from the presence of other males because a crowd of males attracted more females than might the hotshot male alone. The *American Naturalist* article was cited often in discussions of lekking, a topic that was much debated.

Beehler was the subject of news reports again in 1992, when a member of his team on a trip to New Guinea, a student at the University of Chicago Medical Center named Jack Dumbacher, inadvertently discovered the first known poisonous bird: a hooded pitohui (pronounced "PIT-a-hooey"), an orange and black songbird, roughly the size of a blue jay, that was common in the area and had been previously identified but had not been known to be poisonous. Dumbacher became aware of the bird's toxin as he and volunteer researchers literally licked wounds they had suffered while netting and releasing various jungle birds. Dumbacher thought that the numbness and tingling he felt on his tongue had been caused by a plant, until he began to suspect the pitohui; after licking the bird's feathers, he felt the effect again immediately. The chemist John Daly of the National Institutes of Health, in Bethesda, Maryland, identified the chemical as homobatrachotoxin, a neurotoxin, or nerve agent. The chemical was known to be fatal to small animals, disabling their nervous systems, and was found in greatest quantities in the bird's skin and feathers. Beehler told Robert Cooke for *Newsday* (October 30, 1992) that the discovery was significant because "there are 9,000 or 10,000 species of known birds, and to date there hadn't been any bird discovered that uses a toxin to protect itself."

Beehler had been trying for more than 20 years to organize the trip to the Foja Mountains, an undertaking that involved, among other tasks, putting together a competent team and raising money from donors including the National Geographic Society. Finally, in November and December 2005, a team of 13 scientists from Conservation International and the Indonesian Institute of Sciences, and co-led by Beehler and Stephen Richards of the South Australia Museum in Adelaide, went on a month-long expedition to New Guinea, two weeks of which were spent on the upper slopes of the Foja Mountains. The area, located in the easternmost and least explored province of western New Guinea, is considered one of the most biodiverse on Earth. Beehler's team could reach the region, which stretches over 700,000 acres, only by helicopter. After they arrived they discovered more than 20 new species of frogs (among 60 they identified), four new butterflies (among 150, including the giant bird wing, whose wingspan of up to seven inches makes it the world's largest butterfly), and a variety of plant species that the team's botanists pronounced to be unlike any they had seen before. "What was amazing was the lack of wariness of all the animals," Beehler said about the expedition, as quoted by Terry Kirby in the London *Independent* (February 7, 2006). "In the wild, all species tend to be shy of humans, but that is learned behaviour because they have encountered mankind. In Foja they did not appear to mind our presence at all." During the trip Beehler's team saw a golden-mantled tree kangaroo, a species that scientists had never seen before on the island and that is "considered the most beautiful but also the rarest of the jungle-dwelling marsupials," according to Kirby. Many of the hundreds of animal and plant species in the mountainous terrain were specific to small areas. "It is as close to the Garden of Eden as you're going to find on Earth," Beehler said, as quoted by Kirby. "We found dozens, if not hundreds, of new species in what is probably the most pristine ecosystem in the whole Asia-Pacific region. There were so many new things it was almost overwhelming. And we have only scratched the surface of what is there."

For its size, New Guinea has the greatest number of bird species in the world. Within minutes of landing on the island, one of Beehler's team members spotted a bird later determined to be the first new species discovered in New Guinea since 1939: a wattled smoky honeyeater. As Beehler explained to Alex Chadwick for National Public Radio's program *Day to Day* (February 7, 2006), honeyeaters are, for Australia and New Guinea, "sort of like the common sparrow group of birds"—that is, as common in those countries as sparrows are in the U.S. Prior to Beehler's expedition, Jared Diamond had explored the area in two trips in 1979 and 1981, during which he had studied birds exclusively. On his later trip Diamond discovered that the golden-fronted bowerbird lived in the Foja Mountains. The bowerbird, believed to be the most highly evolved of all bird species, had been identified from traded skins since 1825, but its place of origin had previously been unknown. Diamond's discovery, as Beehler explained to Ira Flatow for the National Public Radio program *Talk of the Nation* (February 10, 2006), was "announced to the world with great excitement . . . and it really got us motivated. Now, in the . . . years between his announcement, which was actually in 1981, I believe, and our trip, not a single western party of any sort, no scientists, no poachers, no loggers, nobody has actually gone into that mountain range." Beehler's team became the first to photograph the bowerbird as it performed its elaborate mating ritual, in which the male builds a large structure of twigs, ornamented with insects and other objects, to attract females. Other birds the team encountered included the Victoria crowned pigeon, the world's largest pigeon (which is the "size of a small turkey," Beehler told Alex Chadwick), and, perhaps most notably, Berlepsch's six-wired bird of paradise. Like the golden-fronted bowerbird, Berlepsch's six-wired bird of paradise had previously been identified—in the late 19th century, by the German ornithologist Hans von Berlepsch—but was thought to be "'lost' to science, previously identified from the feathers of dead birds," as Kirby reported. "It was very exciting," Beehler said, as quoted by Kirby, "when two [six-wired birds of paradise], a male and a female, which no one has seen alive before . . . came into the camp and the male displayed its plumage to the female in full view of the scientists." Beehler described the bird to Chadwick as "about the size of a robin, a bit chunky. . . . Then it's got these six wires sticking out of the back of its head, two sets of three, one on each side. So it does a dance on the ground and it actually shoots these feathers forward in front of its head like antennae and waves them at the female to get her worked up."

Beehler told Ellen Nakashima that he had wanted to go to the Foja Mountains since his days as a graduate student. "Naturalists love to go to places that haven't been visited before," he said. "And this was one of the last, perhaps the very last." The team's findings were to be submitted to scientific journals to be evaluated by other authorities, who could say for sure whether the honeyeater the team found was of a previously undiscovered species. Beehler planned to name the bird after his wife, Carol, a graphic designer whom he married in 1982, and with whom he has three children: Grace, Andrew, and Cary.

—M.B.

Suggested Reading: *Baltimore Sun* C p1 Apr. 10, 2006; (London) *Daily Mail* p22 Feb. 8, 2006; (London) *Financial Times* p5 Feb. 11, 2006; *Newsday* p4 Oct. 30, 1992; *Washington Post* A p1 Feb. 8, 2006

Selected Books: *Birds of New Guinea*, 1986; *Ornithology of the Indian Subcontinent, 1872-1992: An Annotated Bibliography* (with Charles G. Burg and S. Dillon Ripley), 1994; *The Birds of Paradise: Paradisaeidae* (with Clifford B. Frith), 1998

Courtesy of the Discovery Institute

Behe, Michael J.

(BEE-hee)

Jan. 18, 1952– Biochemist; "intelligent design" theorist; author

Address: Lehigh University, Dept. of Biological Sciences, Iacocca Hall, Rm. D-221, 111 Research Dr., Bethlehem, PA 18015

In 1859 the British naturalist Charles Darwin published *The Origin of Species*—more precisely, *On *the Origin of Species by Means of Natural Selection, or the Preservation of Favoured Races in the Struggle for Life*—which presents the theory that all plants and animals on Earth evolved from other life forms through a series of genetic modifications, in a process that favors those individuals that best adapt to their environments. Darwin's theory (and a similar theory proposed at virtually the same time by another British naturalist, Alfred Russel Wallace) was radically different from the then-prevailing school of thought among scientists in the Western world, which held that the planet and everything on it had been created by God in six days—an idea that came to be known as creationism—and that each life form was created separately and is distinct and unchanging. Many proponents of creationism maintain that dinosaur bones and other fossils are not evidence of evolutionary processes but rather were placed on Earth by God to test humans' faith in a supreme being. In the century and a half since the introduction of Darwin's and Wallace's revolutionary theories—which, in Darwin's case, were accompanied by a huge number of examples from nature—vast quantities of additional evidence gathered by other researchers have bolstered the idea that all living species have a common ancestry. Such evidence notwithstanding, through the years many Westerners have rejected the theory of evolution because it contradicts their religious beliefs—specifically, the teachings of the Bible, which, in the Book of Genesis, attributes the creation of the heavens and Earth, and everything in and on them, to God.

Although the 1993 edition of the *Columbia Encyclopedia* asserts that "in its basic outline Darwinism is now universally accepted by scientists," in recent years a small number of scientists have joined those among their religious brethren who question the validity of the theory of evolution, either in whole or, more commonly, in part. Prominent among those questioners is Michael J. Behe, a professor of biochemistry at Lehigh University, in Pennsylvania. Behe contends that while there is much of value in Darwin's theory of evolution, it fails to explain how life originated and how complex cellular systems came to be. Such phenomena, he believes, can be explained only by the intervention of an "intelligent designer"—most likely, God. According to Behe, the extreme complexity of cells and of many biochemical systems precludes the possibility that they came into existence in the absence of an intelligent designer. As Jim Holt explained in the *New York Times Book Review* (April 14, 2002, on-line), Behe argued (in Holt's words) in his book *Darwin's Black Box*, "If you peer inside a cell, . . . you see wonderfully intricate little machines, made out of proteins, that carry on the functions necessary for life. They are so precisely engineered that they exhibit what [Behe] calls 'irreducible complexity': alter or remove a single part and the whole thing would grind to a halt. How could such cellular machinery have evolved in piecemeal fashion through a series of adaptations, as Darwinism holds?"

Behe is a senior fellow at the Seattle, Washington–based Discovery Institute, which seeks to promote conservative Christian values in American institutions and is a principal mover behind the theory of intelligent design. As a spokesperson for that theory, Behe has often responded to scientists who have attacked intelligent design as simply creationism in a different guise and as fundamentally unscientific because it is not testable. He has also found himself at the center of a political maelstrom in the United States, where—much to the consternation of the scientific community—many local school boards are advocating or demanding that teachers present the theory of intelligent design along with, and as an alternative to, the theory of evolution.

In October 2005 Behe testified in a landmark federal-court case that addressed the constitutionality of the Dover, Pennsylvania, school board's requirement that teachers of ninth-grade biology read a statement in their classes describing intelligent design as "an explanation of the origin of life that differs from Darwin's view" and suggesting that students can learn more about intelligent design from a book in the schools' libraries called *Of Pandas and People*. During the trial Behe told a reporter for the Associated Press (October 16, 2005), "The fact that most biology texts act more as cheerleaders for Darwin's theory rather than trying to develop the critical faculties of their students shows the need, I think, for such statements." In his testimony, according to the Allentown, Pennsylvania, *Morning Call* (December 22, 2005, on-line), Behe acknowledged that belief in intelligent design is inseparable from a belief in God. "Prof. Behe's assertion constitutes substantial evidence that in his view . . . [intelligent design] is a religious and not a scientific proposition," Judge John E. Jones III wrote, in ruling that the Dover school board was in effect advocating "a particular version of Christianity" and therefore had acted unconstitutionally. In his 139-page ruling, Judge Jones also wrote, as quoted by Laurie Goodstein in the *New York Times* (December 21, 2005, on-line), "To be sure, Darwin's theory of evolution is imperfect. However, the fact that a scientific theory cannot yet render an explanation on every point should not be used as a pretext to thrust an untestable alternative hypothesis grounded in religion into the science classroom or to misrepresent well-established scientific propositions." "I'm very disappointed [by that ruling]," Behe told Alice Chasan, who interviewed him for beliefnet.com (2005), "because not only did [Judge Jones] say that the school board was motivated by religious feelings, but he said that intelligent design itself is religious. And I simply disagree with that." The argument for intelligent design, he agreed, is "falsifiable," but, he maintained, "it has not been falsified."

One of seven children in a middle-class family, Michael J. Behe was born on January 18, 1952 in Altoona, Pennsylvania. His father worked for the Household Finance Corp.; his mother was a homemaker. His family was Roman Catholic, and he attended Catholic parochial schools. As a youngster he developed an abiding interest in science, particularly chemistry. He grew up believing that God served as the guiding hand in the evolution of life on Earth. "In the seventh, eighth grades, I recall nuns teaching that God can make life any way he wants," Behe recalled to Josh Getlin for the *Los Angeles Times* (November 5, 2005, on-line). "If he wanted to create life by the outplaying of natural laws, well, who were we to tell him otherwise? Here was Darwin's theory, and it looks like God set up the world to begin producing life. I remember thinking, 'That's cool.'"

Behe received a B.S. degree in chemistry from Drexel University, in Philadelphia, Pennsylvania, in 1974. He then got a job as a chemist with the U.S. Department of Agriculture. In 1978 he was named a National Research Service predoctoral fellow at the University of Pennsylvania, also in Philadelphia. Later that year he earned a Ph.D. in biochemistry from the University of Pennsylvania. From November 1978 to September 1982 he worked at the National Institutes of Health as a Jane Coffin Childs Fund postdoctoral fellow.

Behe began his academic career in the fall of 1982, as an assistant professor of chemistry at Queens College, a division of the City University of New York. In 1985, having married and wanting to raise a family in an environment that he and his wife thought would be less stressful than New York City's, he moved with his wife to Pennsylvania, where he assumed the position of associate professor of chemistry at Lehigh University, in Bethlehem. In 1995 he became an associate professor of biological sciences at Lehigh, and in 1997, a full professor in the same field.

Since 1978 Behe has written or co-authored three dozen articles published in refereed biochemical journals, on such subjects as sickle hemoglobin gelation, an oligopurine sequence bias in eukaryotic viruses, and the structure of nucleosomal DNA at high salt concentration. Meanwhile, in the late 1980s, Behe had read *Evolution: A Theory in Crisis*, by the geneticist Michael Denton, which argues that there are unaddressed problems in the theory of Darwinian evolution—most significantly, its failure to explain how life began or how complex cellular systems evolved. "I became angry because here I was a professor of science at a leading university and had never heard these criticisms, let alone how to answer them . . . ," Behe recalled in an interview with Mario Seiglie for the *Good News* (May/June 2005, on-line), a publication of the United Methodist Church. "I had been led to believe in the Darwinian theory, not because the evidence was compelling, but because that's what I was expected to believe. After reading Denton's book, I decided to go to the science library and look at the science journals to see who had explained the complicated cellular systems by a Darwinian process. I was astounded to find there were no published papers, or none to speak of, that even *tried*

to explain how a step-by-step process could produce such complexity. At that point I figured a new idea was needed and so I started to think more about alternatives."

According to Behe, molecular biologists have discovered systems that are far too complex at the molecular level to be the result of random, unguided mutations. As Bob Harvey noted in the *Ottawa Citizen* (July 26, 1998), which he serves as religion editor, "Darwin himself admitted 'my theory would absolutely break down' if anyone could demonstrate the existence of a complex organism that could not possibly have been formed by numerous, successive small modifications." Edward B. Davis, a professor of the history of science at Messiah College, wrote for the *Christian Century* (July 15–22, 1998), "Darwin worried that the origin of complex organs such as the eye would be difficult to explain in terms of the gradual, stepwise evolutionary process outlined by his theory. The best he could do was to speculate that the complex eye might have developed from simple light-sensitive cells that could give a competitive advantage to an organism that possessed them. But the molecular biology of vision, as Behe notes, was a 'black box' to Darwin. Darwin and his contemporaries took the simplicity of cells for granted, treating them as black boxes that needed no further explanation. Now that we know how complex even the simplest cells are, Behe argues, we can no longer ignore the question of how they originated, nor can we deny the lack of progress in answering that question within a Darwinian paradigm." Behe came to believe that cells and other complex biological systems must have been designed by an intelligent entity. Further, he came to believe that Darwin's theory is fundamentally flawed, because it cannot explain the origin of life itself, while belief in the existence of an intelligent designer enables one to explain how life came to be. To better explain the existence of complex cellular systems, Behe developed the concept of irreducible complexity, according to which complicated biological systems cannot be the result of evolution, because they can function only if all of their component parts are in place simultaneously. To illustrate that idea, Behe has often used the example of a mousetrap, which, as he has pointed out, requires all of its parts in order to work.

Since 1996 Behe has described his ideas about intelligent design and irreducible complexity in articles and book reviews for professional journals (among them *Biology and Philosophy*, *Philosophy of Science*, and *Rhetoric & Public Affairs*), publications connected with religious groups (among them *First Things*, *Ethics and Medics*, *National Catholic Bioethics Quarterly*, *Touchstone*, and *Philosophia Christi*), and such widely circulated periodicals as *National Review*, the *New York Times*, and *Natural History*. He has also advanced his theories in his books, *Darwin's Black Box* (1996) and *Science and Evidence for Design in the Universe*; the latter book, comprising papers presented at a conference sponsored by the Wethersfield Institute, in New York City, on September 25, 1999, was edited by Behe and two other leading proponents of intelligent design, William A. Dembski and Stephen C. Meyer, and includes writing by Behe. In addition, Behe has made videos: *Intelligent Design: From the Big Bang to Irreducible Complexity* (which consists of an interview with him), *Unlocking the Mystery of Life, Irreducible Complexity: The Biochemical Challenge to Darwinian Theory*, and *Where Does the Evidence Lead?*, the last of which was made for students in seventh grade and above. (The videos and books are sold by the Access Research Network, which disseminates materials about intelligent design and asks buyers to send suggested "donations" for its products.)

Reactions to *Darwin's Black Box* ranged from enthusiastic to disparaging. The magazine *Christianity Today* named *Darwin's Black Box* its 1996 Book of the Year, and both the politically and socially right-wing *National Review* and the magazine *World* (which according to its Web site reports news "from a Christian perspective") named it one of the 100 best nonfiction books of the 20th century. Eric D. Albright, a Duke University librarian who specializes in biomedical literature, wrote in a review of *Darwin's Black Box* for *Library Journal* (July 1996), "The importance of this controversial work is in the questions it raises about the primacy of evolution as the sole creator of life." Scientists, by contrast, with very few exceptions, dismissed *Darwin's Black Box* as an example of faulty reasoning. They insisted that since there is no way to subject the theory of intelligent design to reproducible, empirical testing, and no one has provided any tangible evidence of its validity, it cannot be considered a scientific theory. In a review for *American Scientist* (September/October 1997), Robert Dorit, a professor of biology at Smith College, noted that the argument for intelligent design is an old one (the 18th-century British theologian William Paley, for example, argued that just as the existence of a complex article like a watch implies its creation by a watchmaker, the existence of the infinitely more complex Earth and its inhabitants implies their creation by a supreme being), and that Behe has merely formulated it differently. "Adorned this time around with the language of molecular biology, spiced up with charges of a conspiracy of scientists, masquerading as an appeal for truth and not for theology, it is nonetheless the same old thing," Dorit wrote. "There cannot be design without a designer. Although I do not doubt the sincerity of the author, nor scoff at his unease with a world apparently lacking purpose, the case for intelligent design put forth in *Darwin's Black Box* is built on some deep misunderstandings about evolution, molecular organization and, ultimately, about the nature of scientific inquiry. Because of these misperceptions, not a blow is landed on the central, radical claim of Darwinian thinking: Biological order and design emerge from the workings of the evolutionary process and not from the hand of a designer."

Andrew Pomiankowski, writing for *New Scientist* (September 14, 1996), had similar concerns: "Behe is good at exposing the paucity of evolutionary thought in the field of biochemistry. But in *Darwin's Black Box*, he reveals that he is also part of the problem, falling back on the old, limp idea of 'design'. He takes irreducible complexity as a statement of fact, rather than an admission of ignorance, claiming that the 'purposeful arrangement' of biochemical parts must be the result of an intelligent designer. So what we have here is just the latest, and no doubt not the last, attempt to put God back into nature. But it is an old blind alley. To understand molecular design, we need a biochemical account of evolution. . . . You can read [the book] to tell you what is wrong with biochemistry. Behe is also very good at making biochemistry easy to understand. But don't be fooled by his claim that molecular systems are irreducibly complex, or that a supernatural designer is needed." In a review of *Darwin's Black Box* for *Reason* (July 1997), a magazine that, according to its Web site, "provides a refreshing alternative to right-wing and left-wing opinion magazines by making a principled case for liberty and individual choice in all areas of human activity," its science correspondent Ronald Bailey referred to the Austrian economist Friedrich A. Hayek (1899–1992), writing, "Hayek long ago recognized the phenomenon of 'spontaneous order' and describes how it arose in markets, families, and other social institutions. Now, ingenious computer models are confirming Hayek's insights. It is increasingly obvious that social systems, from commerce to language, evolve and adapt without the need for top-down planning and organization. Order in markets is generated through processes analogous to Darwinian natural selection in biology. In other words, we can indeed have apparent design without a designer; the world is demonstrably brimming with just such phenomena."

As his prominence as a spokesperson for intelligent design has increased, Behe has found himself more and more isolated among his peers, who believe that his ideas amount to little more than a way to reinsert God into science classes. Some time ago he stopped trying to secure academic grants for his work, and since 1997 he has published in peer-reviewed scientific journals only three articles related to his biochemical research. In August 2005 the Department of Biological Sciences at Lehigh University posted on its Web site a statement disassociating itself with his views. It reads: "The faculty in the Department of Biological Sciences is committed to the highest standards of scientific integrity and academic function. This commitment carries with it unwavering support for academic freedom and the free exchange of ideas. It also demands the utmost respect for the scientific method, integrity in the conduct of research, and recognition that the validity of any scientific model comes only as a result of rational hypothesis testing, sound experimentation, and findings that can be replicated by others. The department faculty, then, are unequivocal in their support of evolutionary theory, which has its roots in the seminal work of Charles Darwin and has been supported by findings accumulated over 140 years. The sole dissenter from this position, Prof. Michael Behe, is a well-known proponent of 'intelligent design.' While we respect Prof. Behe's right to express his views, they are his alone and are in no way endorsed by the department. It is our collective position that intelligent design has no basis in science, has not been tested experimentally, and should not be regarded as scientific." In late 2005 Behe's Web page on the Lehigh Web site contained the following "official disclaimer": "My ideas about irreducible complexity and intelligent design are entirely my own. They certainly are not in any sense endorsed by either Lehigh University in general or the Department of Biological Sciences in particular. In fact, most of my colleagues in the Department strongly disagree with them."

When asked by a reporter for *Time* (August 15, 2005) if it is possible to believe in both God and evolution, Behe replied: "I'm still not against Darwinian evolution on theological grounds. I'm against it on scientific grounds. I think God could have made life using apparently random mutation and natural selection. But my reading of the scientific evidence is that he did not do it that way, that there was a more active guiding. I think that we are all descended from some single cell in the distant past but that that cell and later parts of life were intentionally produced as the result of intelligent activity. As a Christian, I say that intelligence is very likely to be God. Several Christian positions are theologically consistent with the theory of mutation and selection. Some people believe that God is guiding the process from moment to moment. Others think he set up the universe from the Big Bang to unfold like a computer program. Others take scientific positions that are indistinguishable from those atheist materialists might take but say that their nonscientific intuitions or philosophical considerations or the existence of the mind lead them to deduce that there is a God. I used to be part of that last group. I just think now that the science is not nearly as strong as they think."

Well more than 100 times since 1996, at seminars, symposia, or other gatherings, mainly at colleges and universities, Behe has given speeches with such titles as "Chance or Purpose?—The Argument for Intelligent Design in Biology," "Evidence of Design in Biochemistry," and "Science Stumbles on Design." His courses at Lehigh University in recent years have included "Popular Arguments on Evolution" and "Controversies in Biology" as well as ones devoted to principles of protein structure, elements of biochemistry, and physical biochemistry. From 1995 to 1997 he served as a member of the molecular-biochemistry review panel of the National Science Foundation's Division of Molecular and Cellular Biosciences. Between 2000 and 2003 he served as an expert analyst for *ChemTracts—Biochemistry and Molecular Biology*.

Behe and his wife, Celeste, live and homeschool their five sons and four daughters in Bethlehem, Pennsylvania.

—C.M.

Suggested Reading: *American Scientist* p474+ Sep./Oct. 1997; *Boston Globe* A p16 Aug. 14, 2005; *Christian Century* p678+ July 15–22, 1998; *Christianity Today* p26+ Nov. 15, 1999; Lehigh University Web site; *New Scientist* p44+ Sep. 14, 1996; *Ottawa Citizen* A p1+ July 26, 1998; *Reason* p22+ July 1997; *Time* p26+ Aug. 15, 2005

Selected Books: *Darwin's Black Box*, 1996; *Science and Evidence for Design in the Universe*, 2000

Courtesy of MIT

Belcher, Angela

June 21, 1967– Materials scientist; nanotechnologist; educator

Address: MIT Biomolecular Materials Group 16-244, 77 Mass Ave., Cambridge, MA 02139

Angela Belcher has won international renown as a scientist who thinks small. She began to focus on the infinitesimal as an undergraduate, when she realized that she "really liked molecules," as she said in an undated interview for the Texas Workforce Commission (TWC) Web site. Belcher is a world leader in nanotechnology, a science—named in 1974—in which the primary unit of measurement is the nanometer: one billionth of a meter, or about 10 times the radius of a hydrogen atom or approximately 1/100,000th the width of a human hair. Every four or five years, Belcher has said, she likes to learn a "completely new field"; as a nanotechnologist, or, more specifically, a bionanotechnologist, she has drawn upon her knowledge of many disciplines, among them organic and inorganic chemistry, organic-inorganic interfaces, biochemistry, molecular biology, materials chemistry, biomaterials, biomolecular materials, genetic engineering, and electrical engineering. She and others in her field have noted that nature is Earth's most accomplished nanotechnologist, and in her research she has studied "how nature makes materials," as she put it at a symposium called "Nanoscience—Where Physics, Chemistry and Biology Collide," sponsored by the Australian Academy of Science, as quoted at science.org.au (May 2, 2003). "We like to apply the ideas that nature has already used to make materials" so as to make other materials, ones "that we like to say nature hasn't had the opportunity to work with yet," as she said at that symposium. In another description of her approach, she told Elizabeth Corcoran for Forbes (July 23, 2001) that she and her research team are "working out the rules of biology" in a realm absent from the natural world. "The kinds of things that nature does that we like to do are basically self assembly, molecular scale recognition, nanoscale regularity and self correction," she said at the nanoscience symposium. "One of our goals is to have biological molecules that can actually grow and assemble electronic materials . . . on the nanoscale and also act like enzymes and self correct. So as they start to grow the materials, if there is a mistake they would be able to correct themselves." Building on what she discovered as a doctoral candidate about the processes by which abalones use proteins and minerals to form their shells, Belcher invented techniques for coaxing viruses harmless to humans to create crystalline films and minuscule inorganic wires and battery anodes that are far smaller than those currently in use. Moreover, she created them without using the tremendous heat and toxic chemicals required by traditional manufacturing processes, such as photolithography, the means by which semiconductor devices are currently fabricated. Belcher's discoveries and inventions may lead to the creation of new generations of unprecedentedly small circuit boards and solar cells and lighter, more durable construction materials.

Belcher worked at the University of Texas at Austin from 1999 until 2002, when she joined the faculty of the Massachusetts Institute of Technology (MIT), in Cambridge. Since 2005 she has held the title of Germehausen Professor of Materials Science and Engineering and Biological Engineering at MIT. Her many honors include a Presidential Early Career Award for Science and Engineering (2000), a Harvard University Wilson Prize in Chemistry (2001), a World Technology Award (2002), and a MacArthur Foundation Fellowship

(2004), the last of which is popularly known as the "genius" grant. In a conversation with Candace Stuart for Small Times Magazine (September 24, 2004, on-line), one of Belcher's mentors, Evelyn L. Hu, a professor of electrical and computer engineering at the University of California at Santa Barbara, said of her, "Angie has a special view of a way to change the world by thinking across disciplines and boundaries that is truly extraordinary. She has continuously looked into the future. She's very much in the excitement of the present but [has] always looked at the broader aspect."

A native of San Antonio, Texas, Angela M. Belcher was born on June 21, 1967. Readily available sources contain no information about her family and virtually none about her early years. In an undated interview for the TWC Web site, she said that as a 12-year-old she planned to become a physician, and as a high-school student, she read medical books and accompanied doctors on their rounds at a hospital associated with Rice University, in Houston. She attended Santa Barbara City College (SBCC), in California, from 1986 to 1988, supported in part by a William Olivarius Scholarship in Biology; while at the school she also won the SBCC President's Scholarship Award and the Outstanding Student Award in the Biological Sciences. She later transferred to the College of Creative Studies at the University of California at Santa Barbara (UCSB), which encouraged students to design their own curricula. "We could add or drop classes up to the week before finals, so that we could sign up for what we thought sounded interesting and after a few weeks pick what really was," she recalled in June 2003, in a commencement address presented at the College of Creative Studies and posted on the school's Web site. She concentrated in molecular biology and earned a B.A. degree in creative studies with highest honors from UCSB in 1991. During her undergraduate years she had served as an intern (1988) in gravitational and space biology at the Kennedy Space Center, a division of the National Aeronautics and Space Administration (NASA) in Florida; as a student researcher (1988–89) at the Center for the Study of Evolution and the Origin of Life and at the Plant Biochemistry Laboratory, both at the University of California at Los Angeles (UCLA), in the latter of which she studied metabolic pathways of a plant hormone called gibberellic acid; and as a student researcher (1989–91) at UCSB's Plant Molecular Biology Laboratory, where she investigated activity at the molecular level early in the formation of alfalfa root nodules. During the summers of 1989 and 1990, as a UCSB field researcher, she studied the foraging behavior of wild honey bees on Santa Cruz Island.

In pursuing a graduate degree in chemistry, also at UCSB, Belcher studied the processes involved in the formation of a natural biocomposite material—specifically, the shell of the abalone, a kind of mollusk. (Composites are materials whose constituent parts act together but retain their identities; the parts are physically distinguishable and do not dissolve or otherwise completely blend with one another. A biocomposite material contains organic as well as inorganic components and can grow without outside intervention. In addition to seashells, examples of biocomposites include bone, teeth, and ivory.) According to malacologists (experts on mollusks), at one time abalones had no shells; many millions of years ago, their internal proteins began to use calcium in seawater to produce shells composed of protein (2 percent) and calcium carbonate (98 percent). By means of chemical bonding, the proteins, working on the nanoscale at intervals of a millionth of a meter (called a micron), create hexagonal crystal-like tiles with carbonate particles; as more are created, the tiles become stacked, and the stacks form brick-like walls. A layer of protein "glue" binds each tile with the ones above and below it but does not bind the edges of horizontally adjoining tiles. The resulting walls are harder than synthetic ceramics and 3,000 times stronger than calcium carbonate. "The hardness and luster [of the shell] is a function of the very, very uniform structure of calcium carbonate, deposited a molecule at a time" under the control of the proteins. "That's also what makes pearls," Belcher—who as a graduate student herself created pearls, albeit flat ones—told Spence Reiss for *Technology Review* (February 1, 2005). As in such other natural materials as spider silk and horses' hooves, the organic and inorganic molecules in abalone shells are arranged in a highly durable configuration. "If you look at how nature makes these materials, it makes them just fine," Belcher told Cindy Tumiel for the *San Antonio (Texas) Express-News* (June 8, 2000). "We want to be able to use that same exacting assembly on materials that nature hasn't evolved to have these kinds of interactions."

Belcher won a Parson's Fellowship in Materials Research (1994–95), a Distinguished Research Presentation Award at PacificChem 1995, a conference organized by the American Chemical Society, and an Outstanding Chemistry Graduate Student Award from the American Institute of Chemists (1996). She earned a Ph.D. from UCSB in 1997. For the next two years, she worked as a postdoctoral fellow there. In 1999 she received young-investigator awards from the U.S. Army and the chemical company Du Pont. That same year she joined the faculty of the Department of Chemistry and Biochemistry at the University of Texas at Austin. She was given her own laboratory and became the director of a group of about 18 researchers.

In the June 8, 2000 issue of *Nature*, in an article entitled "Selection of Peptides with Semiconductor Binding Specificity for Directed Nanocrystal Assembly," Belcher, Evelyn Hu, and three of their colleagues announced that they had successfully bonded viruses to five inorganic materials commonly used in semiconductors, including gallium arsenide, indium phosphide, and silicon. Viruses are so small that they can be seen only with elec-

tron microscopes, not ordinary microscopes (in which specimens are illuminated by light). Unlike a typical cell or a single-celled organism, such as a bacterium—which, within its outer wall, has a nucleus surrounded by cytoplasm containing various small components, and which can reproduce on its own—a virus consists only of genetic material (one or another of the two kinds of nucleic acid) enclosed in a protein wall; it can reproduce only when it is inside a suitable living cell. Belcher used viruses known as bacteriophages, which are harmless to mammals and reproduce rapidly in bacteria; each bacteriophage was about 6.6 nanometers wide and 880 nanometers long. Belcher bred in bacteria and then genetically manipulated roughly a billion individual viruses, each identical except for the protein molecules (called peptide amines) at one end. She next covered them with semiconductor particles—gallium arsenide was one of the first to be tried—and then sifted out the relatively few virus molecules whose proteins successfully bonded with the semiconductor molecules. She made millions of additional copies of those viruses (by providing them with bacterial hosts) and then reexposed that batch to uncontaminated semiconductor material "under more chemically stringent conditions," as she explained in her nanoscience lecture. "We go through this process about seven times," she said in the same talk. "We think of it as a Darwinian kind of process: we are looking for the ones that survive under the conditions that we are interested in. . . . In my group we can evolve interaction for materials in about one week." She thus isolated viruses whose peptide tips "recognized" molecules of a specific semiconductor but did not bond with nearly identical molecules of the same semiconductor (that is, isomers, which have the same atomic formulas but differ in the molecular arrangement of their atoms) or with different semiconductors. In the following months Belcher engineered proteins on viruses that bonded with more than 20 different inorganic materials. In 2000 Belcher received a Presidential Early Career Award for Science and Engineering (which came with a $500,000 research grant) from President Bill Clinton for her work. Soon afterward Clinton officially launched the National Nanotechnology Initiative.

Belcher's next goal, as she described it in her nanoscience talk, was "to grow and assemble a material." At the fall 2001 meeting of the Materials Research Society, and later in *Science* (May 3, 2002), she announced that she and her colleagues had accomplished that feat—a significant step toward the realization of marketable bioelectronics. Using a process similar to the one described in the 2000 *Nature* article, the scientists combined a genetically engineered bacteriophage with zinc sulfide. In *Science* they described the resulting product as a "highly ordered composite material": a liquid crystal film that was "ordered at the nanoscale and at the micrometer scale into [approximately] 72-micrometer domains, which were continuous over a centimeter length scale"—that is, big enough to be grasped with tweezers. The proteins at the tips of the viruses were weakly magnetic, enabling Belcher and her graduate student Seung-Wuk Lee to create different structural patterns in the film by means of a magnetic field. "In one such film, . . . the viruses lined up in successive rows, like rows of pencils all with zinc selenide erasers at one end," Robert F. Service wrote for *Science* (December 21, 2001). "Other films have viruses lining up in either a zigzag pattern or all facing the same direction but not organized into orderly rows." After noting that polymer-based liquid crystal mixtures without living ingredients had already been integrated into laptop computer screens, Service wrote, "Although the viral liquid crystals aren't likely to displace their polymer counterparts anytime soon, they point the way forward in one of the hottest areas of materials science." The film was also durable: after seven months the viruses were still intact, which suggested that the film could be used for storage purposes—to preserve genetically altered DNA, for example, or as an alternative to refrigerating vaccines shipped overseas. "We're looking at these materials to grow and arrange electronic, magnetic and optical materials for devices, displays and sensors," Belcher told Kimberly Patch for *Technology Research News* (May 15, 2002).

In the fall of 2002, Belcher shifted her research to the NanoMechanical Technology Laboratory at MIT, where she joined the faculties of two departments as the John Chipman Associate Professor of Materials Science and Engineering and Bioengineering. Most of the postdoctoral students who had worked with her at the University of Texas accompanied her. The aim of her next undertaking was to tailor viruses to function as battery anodes—a first step toward the creation of small, malleable, and efficient viral-based batteries. With funding provided by the Army Research Office Institute of Collaborative Biotechnologies, Belcher and her team of researchers first altered the proteins of a bacteriophage so that the virus collected molecules of cobalt-oxide and gold when dipped in a solution; the virus then assembled the molecules into a single-layer nanowire that functioned as a battery anode. Belcher's team then demonstrated the virus's battery power, using a traditional lithium cathode to complete the circuit. Her research goals include creating a lithium cathode using similar means. Once the creation of an entire battery circuit based on viruses is complete, Belcher hopes to market the product commercially. "These batteries are like Saran wrap," she told R. Colin Johnson for *Electronic Engineering Times* (April 17, 2006). "They are thin, flexible and can be bent into any shape, making them good for lightweight conformable applications." She also told Johnson, "Potentially, when we grow a lithium layer on the other side of the polyelectrolyte for the other cathode, we could use this material to make batteries as thin as 100 [nanometers]." Belcher has predicted that such a battery will store two or three

times more energy for its size than standard batteries and will lead to the advent of portable battery-powered devices far thinner and smaller than existing ones.

In 2002 Belcher and Evelyn L. Hu co-founded Semzyme Inc., which was renamed Cambrios Technologies in 2004. Funded by several venture-capitalist groups and based in Cambridge, the company aims to develop commercial uses for Belcher's innovative techniques. The first product to be offered to the public, a transparent material that conducts electricity and can make TV screens clearer, is scheduled to go on sale in 2007.

Belcher lives near Cambridge with several dogs. She is a vegetarian, and her dogs, Rebecca Skloot reported in *Popular Science* (November 2002, online), "eat only homemade organic foods." In 2004, according to Ascribe Newswire (September 28, 2004), after she learned that she had won a $500,000 MacArthur Foundation grant, Belcher told a reporter that the money would serve as "a catalyst for exploring new ideas in my lab and, equally important, let me contribute more to my community through science outreach to kids." "Sometimes I can't sleep because I have so many ideas," Belcher told the TWC interviewer, to whom she revealed that, by choice, she was working at least 80 hours a week. In her 2003 commencement address at UCSB, Belcher said, "I have the career I have always dreamed of. . . . My advice is to follow your passion. Find that idea or topic that you're so excited about, that you wake up in the middle of the night and wish it was morning so that you can try it out. Or that when you e-mail a colleague in the middle of the night to bounce an idea off of them, they e-mail you right back, because they're also up, passionately pursuing an idea."

—M.B.

Suggested Reading: *Electronic Engineering Times* p38 Apr. 17, 2006; *Forbes* p96 July 23, 2001; (London) *Guardian* p11 May 9, 2002; MIT, Department of Materials Science and Engineering Web site; *San Jose Mercury News* C p1+ June 14, 2006; *Science* p2462+ Dec. 21, 2001; science.org.au; *Small Times* (on-line) Sep. 29, 2004; *U.S. News & World Report* p46 Jan. 12, 2004

Bell, James A.

1949– Chief financial officer of the Boeing Co.

Address: Boeing Co., 100 N. Riverside Plaza, Chicago, IL 60606-2609

James A. Bell was named the interim chief financial officer (CFO) of the Boeing Co. in November 2003, following the embarrassing and damaging news that his predecessor as CFO had violated fed-

James A. Bell

Scott Olson/Getty Images

eral conflict-of-interest statutes while negotiating a multibillion-dollar deal with a Pentagon official who soon afterward secured a highly paid job at Boeing. That scandal had prompted the resignation of the then–chief executive officer (CEO), who was replaced by Harry C. Stonecipher. Then, in March 2005, 14 months after Boeing's board of directors had officially installed Bell as CFO, he was tapped to serve also as the interim CEO, in the wake of another scandal, one that led to Stonecipher's dismissal. Bell remained in the top post until June 2005, when Boeing's board chose W. James Mc-Nerney as CEO. By all accounts, Bell's probity and sound judgment went far toward restoring Boeing's reputation during that difficult period. Trained in accounting, Bell began his career in 1972, in an entry-level position at Rockwell International, which specialized in manufacturing products for the space and defense industries. He steadily ascended the corporate ladder, assuming such positions as senior internal auditor, manager of accounting, and manager of general and cost accounting. Boeing, the largest aircraft manufacturer and second-largest military contractor in the world, acquired Rockwell in 1996, and soon afterward Bell was promoted to a vice presidency. Currently, he holds the title of executive vice president of finance as well as CFO of Boeing, which employs more than 153,000 people in nearly 70 countries and has customers in an additional 75 nations.

James A. Bell was born in 1949 in Los Angeles, California, the youngest of the four children of Mamie Bell, who worked as a Los Angeles County government clerk, and her husband, a mail carrier. (Readily available sources do not reveal his name.) As a youngster living in a low-income neighbor-

hood of South Los Angeles, where few people completed high school, Bell had modest career aspirations. "When I was growing up, I didn't know what a CEO or CFO was," he told Peter Pae for the *Los Angeles Times* (March 14, 2005). "I thought people who worked at the post office were those we could look up to. They were the ones making the honest living, and that was something I thought I could do." Bell's outlook changed when, in the summer of 1965, riots broke out in Watts, an overwhelmingly African-American section of South Los Angeles. "They had National Guards with rifles at each end of the block," he told Pae. "It opened my eyes and took me out of my cocoon." The riots occurred just before Bell entered his senior year of high school, and he became determined to attend college to ensure a better future for himself. After graduating from high school, he enrolled at California State University at Los Angeles (Cal State LA). He majored in accounting, because he believed it was a practical vocation. Bell received a partial scholarship that helped finance his first year at college. To earn enough to pay his tuition afterward, he took on odd jobs around the city, among them cleaning offices and assisting with the X-raying of patients in the emergency room at the University of Southern California Medical Center.

Bell completed his bachelor's degree in accounting in 1972. That year Rockwell International held job interviews on the Cal State LA campus to recruit prospective graduates. Although Bell missed the interviews, the company—having implemented an affirmative-action program—offered him a job as an entry-level accountant at its Atomic International Group in Canoga Park, California. Over the next 24 years, Bell steadily climbed the corporate ranks at Rockwell, becoming director of accounting in 1984 and business manager six years later for the unit developing the electrical system for the International Space Station. When the Boeing Corp. acquired Rockwell, in 1996, Bell was retained. He was subsequently promoted to vice president of contracts and pricing for Boeing's space and communications business in Seal Beach, California. He developed a close relationship with Department of Defense staff members while working on military space programs and export issues. Known among Defense Department officials as an honest businessman with intimate knowledge of the aeronautical industry, he helped to expand the government–Boeing partnership. In 2000 he relocated to Boeing's corporate headquarters in Chicago, Illinois, after his promotion to the dual positions of corporate controller and senior vice president of finance.

Founded in 1916, Boeing quickly emerged as the premier aircraft manufacturer in the aeronautical industry. The company launched its first commercial aircraft, the Boeing 314 Clipper, in the mid-1930s and branched into the military sector during World War II, producing the B-17 and B-29 bombers. During the 1960s Boeing extended its business to include space-related work; in the 1980s it drew much business from the space shuttle and International Space Station projects. Meanwhile, the company continued to improve its signature commercial aircraft, which evolved from the Boeing 727 to the present-day 777. The firm suffered heavily from stock losses after the September 11, 2001 terrorist attacks, in part because the four hijacked planes were manufactured by Boeing but mostly because the drastic decrease in air travel after the attacks severely hurt Boeing's commercial-airline customers. On a promising note, hundreds of advance orders for the much-anticipated Boeing 787 (also known as the 7E7 Dreamliner), which is scheduled for delivery in 2008 and is one of several new aircraft currently in Boeing's pipeline, have helped to increase the confidence of investors in the company.

Investor confidence was badly shaken in November 2003, when Boeing was rocked by a scandal involving its chief financial officer, Michael M. Sears, and Darleen Druyun, who had joined Boeing the previous January to assist the head of the company's Missile Defense Systems unit. Druyun had approached Sears about getting a job at Boeing while she was employed at the Pentagon as a senior air-force acquisitions official and was negotiating with Boeing the terms of a $23 billion contract for the air force's lease or purchase of Boeing air-refueling tankers. When her activities became known, both Sears and Druyun were fired; they were later convicted of violating federal conflict-of-interest laws and sentenced to brief prison terms. As a result of those employees' misconduct (and that of two other employees in another case, involving copies of thousands of pages of confidential documents from the files of Boeing's rival Lockheed Martin that illegally came into Boeing's possession), in 2006 Boeing was ordered to pay the federal government a total of $610 million—reportedly the largest financial penalty ever imposed on a military contractor, according to Leslie Wayne, writing for the *New York Times* (May 16, 2006, on-line). (The Pentagon contract involving the air-refueling tankers had been canceled earlier.) Meanwhile, simultaneously with the dismissals of Druyun and Sears, Boeing's board of directors named Bell interim CFO. The board formally elected him to the post in January 2004. "Boeing chose Bell to provide a sense of continuity, some stability. He's a trusted insider," Chris Mecray, a senior aerospace analyst at Deutsche Bank, told Lisa Troshinsky for *Aerospace Daily* (January 7, 2004). "He is someone who has proven himself over the years in finance. He is a known quantity, has excelled in the organization, is viewed as highly competent and easy to interact with." Earlier, in November 2003, following the ousters of Sears and Druyun, Boeing's then-chairman and CEO, Philip M. Condit, had resigned and had been replaced by Harry C. Stonecipher as president and CEO and Lewis E. Platt as non-executive chairman.

As CFO, Bell was primarily responsible for the financial management of Boeing, including its reporting and accounting in accordance with accepted corporate practices and federal law, in areas including taxes, dividends, and annual reports. In addition, he was responsible for Boeing's Shared Services Group, a $6.8 billion business unit with 16,000 employees who provide cost-effective services connected with all the company's activities, ranging from hiring and training to corporate travel, health and environmental affairs, and disaster preparedness. Bell's reputation as a skilled manager and affable leader began to spread throughout Boeing, particularly after he accepted the board's request to take on further responsibilities as interim chief executive officer and president. That occurred on March 7, 2005, after the resignation of Harry Stonecipher, following the discovery that he had been having an extramarital affair with a female executive at Boeing. (In an effort to restore Boeing's tarnished reputation following the Sears-Druyun scandal, Stonecipher had made attendance at half-day ethics sessions mandatory for all of the company's employees and had required all of them to sign "code of conduct" forms as assurances that they would "avoid doing anything that would embarrass the company," as Peter Pae reported for the *Los Angeles Times* [March 8, 2005, on-line].) Bell's swift ascent to the top leadership position surprised many, including Bell himself. "Fifteen months ago, I was a back-room corporate controller," he said in a speech at a conference supported by Smith Barney, according to Leslie Wayne for the *New York Times* (March 10, 2005). "And you know they don't let corporate controllers out in public. Now, today, I'm standing in front of you as chief executive officer, president and chief financial officer of Boeing." Boeing's board announced that it would search for a permanent replacement for Stonecipher both within and outside the company.

On May 2, 2005, after some two years of unsuccessful discussions, Boeing and Lockheed Martin announced that they had agreed to merge their rocket-launch businesses in a 50–50 venture called United Launch Alliance—a coup for Bell, who had entered talks about the matter only days before. (As of early June 2006, the companies were still waiting for the Federal Trade Commission's approval of the merger.) On another front, at Boeing's Global Diversity Summit in 2005, Bell spoke candidly to employees on the importance of diversity in maintaining the company's competitive advantage and assuring business success. "Clearly, the company's ability to address diversity at some level played a significant role in me standing before you today as the CFO of a Fortune 30 corporation," he said, as quoted by Edith G. Orenstein on the Financial Executives International Web site. Bell's performance as interim CEO was widely praised among aerospace-industry insiders. Although he had stated his intention to remain CEO only temporarily, many investors, analysts, and Boeing employees believed that his position should have been made permanent. Boeing's board of directors, however, believed that Bell's background was not broad enough for such an expanded role and that the company would fare best if he devoted himself to its financial well-being. In June 2005 the board appointed W. James McNerney, then the CEO of 3M and earlier a General Electric executive, as the new president, chairman, and CEO of Boeing.

Bell is a member of the board of directors of the Dow Chemical Co., the Joffrey Ballet, the Chicago Urban League, World Business Chicago, the Chicago Economic Club, and New Leaders for New Schools. He lives in Chicago with his wife, Mary Bell.

—I.C.

Suggested Reading: *Aerospace Daily* p2 Jan. 7, 2004; Boeing Co. Web site; *Business Week* p46 June 13, 2005; Financial Executives International Web site; *Los Angeles Times* C p1 Mar. 14, 2005; *New York Times* C p8 Mar. 10, 2005; *Who's Who Among African Americans*, 2006

Courtesy of the Biomimicry Institute

Benyus, Janine M.

June 17, 1958– Environmentalist; naturalist; science writer

Address: Biomimicry Guild, 2813 Caribou Ln., Stevensville, MT 59870

"We humans are at a turning point in our evolution," the environmentalist, naturalist, and science writer Janine Benyus declared on the Biomimicry

Web site. "Though we began as a small population in a very large world, we have expanded in number and territory until we are now bursting the seams of that world. There are too many of us, and our habits are unsustainable." Benyus has suggested that the best source of tactics and techniques to meet the enormous environmental challenges facing humans is nature. She has become one of the leading proponents of what she has dubbed biomimicry, an emerging scientific discipline that, as she wrote for the Web site biomimicry.net, "studies nature's best ideas and then imitates these designs and processes to solve human problems." In her book *Biomimicry: Innovation Inspired by Nature* (1997), she wrote, "Biomimicry is a new way of viewing and valuing nature. It introduces an era based not on what we can extract from the natural world, but on what we can learn from it." "If you have a design problem," Benyus told Anne Underwood for *Newsweek* (October 10, 2005), "nature's probably solved it already. After all, it's had 3.8 billion years to come up with solutions." (Scientists believe that life on Earth originated about 3.8 billion years ago; Homo sapiens, the species to which humans belong, appeared about 150,000 years ago.) "The core idea is that nature, imaginative by necessity, has already solved many of the problems we are grappling with," she explained on biomimicry.net. "Animals, plants, and microbes are the consummate engineers. They have found what works, what is appropriate, and most important, what *lasts* here on Earth. . . . After 3.8 billion years of research and development, failures are fossils, and what surrounds us is the secret to survival."

Benyus told Michelle Cole for the *Oregonian* (April 18, 2001), "I think biomimicry is actually an ancient art. For 99.9 percent of the time we were on the Earth, we were hunters and gatherers, and our survival depended upon us noticing the fine details of our world. Alaskan hunters to this day will crawl on their stomachs up to a hole in the ice, exactly the same motion of a polar bear. But in our last 100 years, we've pulled away from any dependence on nature to the extent that we honestly believe we're not of nature. And that's what keeps us from hearing all these great ideas." "Practicing ethical biomimicry will require a change of heart," she wrote for the Biomimicry Web site. "We will have to climb down from our pedestal and begin to see ourselves as simply a species among species, as one vote in a parliament of 30 million." Benyus directs the Biomimicry Guild, which she co-founded in 1998 to research ways in which scientists can emulate nature. She has lectured widely on the idea of tackling specific problems from a biomimetic perspective and has collaborated toward that end with General Electric, Levi's, and Nike, among other corporations, as well as the National Aeronautics and Space Administration (NASA). "We humans are imitating the best and brightest organisms in our habitat," Benyus wrote for biomimicry.net. "We are learning, for instance, how to harness energy like a leaf, grow food like a prairie, build ceramics like an abalone, self-medicate like a chimp, compute like a cell, and run a business like a hickory forest. The conscious emulation of life's genius is a survival strategy for the human race, a path to a sustainable future. The more our world looks and functions like the natural world, the more likely we are to endure on this home that is ours, but not ours alone."

Janine M. Benyus was born on June 17, 1958 and grew up near the Pine Barrens, a large wilderness area in southern New Jersey. According to an article by Penny Borda on the Web site Interiors and Sources, Benyus was a "self-proclaimed 'nature nerd.'" In an interview with Masao Yokota, the president of the Boston Research Center (BRC) for the 21st Century, as posted on the BRC's Web site (Spring 2004), Benyus described herself as a "dreamy" child. "I was just in my own world for a very long time," she said, in part to explain why she did not speak until age three. Every weekend Benyus's father would take his children "into forests, into as much nature as we could possibly get to," as Benyus told Yokota. As a 10-year-old Janine felt devastated when a meadow near her house was destroyed in preparation for the construction of new homes. To escape ever-expanding suburban sprawl, her father moved his family repeatedly, so that they could live in places that Benyus described to Yokota as "rural, rural suburbia," even though his commute to and from his job grew correspondingly longer. "He was a parent who said [of the natural world], 'Look at how amazing this is!,'" as Benyus recalled to Yokota. Her mother, Benyus said, was "a very warm person and had great *joie de vivre*"; she, too, loved the outdoors, but because of ill health, she rarely left the house. Her parents were also "incredible storytellers," and the family would often sit at the dining-room table "telling stories for hours and hours." Storytelling, as she told Yokota, thus "comes naturally" to her.

Benyus attended an unusual Catholic high school, in which the teachers—nuns belonging to the Sisters of St. Joseph, whose mission includes working toward social and economic justice, and some Jesuit priests as well—were not dogmatic, as she recalled to Yokota; they encouraged the students "to ask the big questions, the life questions, the great questions." After high school she attended a branch of Rutgers, the state university of New Jersey, where she majored in both natural-resource management (or forestry, according to some sources) and English literature. She earned a bachelor's degree summa cum laude in about 1980. She began her career, as she told *Current Biography*, by "translating science-speak" for laboratory researchers. For some years she also worked as a nature-tour guide, acquiring an encyclopedic knowledge and understanding of ecology and the relationships of species within specific habitats. She shared some of what she knew in her first three books, all of which were published in 1989: *Northwoods Wildlife: A Watcher's Guide to Habitats*,

which describes ecosystems in Michigan, Minnesota, and Wisconsin, *Field Guide to Wildlife Habitats of the Eastern United States*, and *Field Guide to Wildlife Habitats of the Western United States*.

Benyus's next book was *Beastly Behaviors: A Zoo Lover's Companion: What Makes Whales Whistle, Cranes Dance, Pandas Turn Somersaults, and Crocodiles Roar: A Watcher's Guide to How Animals Act and Why* (1992). "Animals have their own customs and their own language, their own body language, their own rituals and ceremonies," Benyus told Robert Siegel for the National Public Radio program *All Things Considered* (March 15, 1993). "And, you know, we wouldn't think of going to Tibet without reading a travel guide first. . . . I think of [*Beastly Behaviors*] as the guide that gives you insights about the animal world before you travel there." In a review for *Library Journal* (September 1, 1992, on-line), Edell Marie Peters wrote, "This is one of the best books published on animal behavior for the general reader. The author . . . brings a positive, upbeat attitude to the topic of zoos, their future, and the animal collections they maintain. Benyus's unique format provides a logical approach to the subject of animal behavior that the reader can apply to observations in zoos or in the wild." Audrey C. Foote, writing for *Smithsonian* (February 1993, on-line), declared, "This book should be in the bookcase or backpack of every nonprofessional zoophile, amateur ethologist, armchair naturalist, creature watcher or even just fond relative of young zoo fans."

Meanwhile, Benyus had been formulating the ideas that would contribute to the foundations of biomimicry. She was among a small number of individuals who, as she put it to Michelle Lalonde for the Montreal *Gazette* (October 15, 2000), "were squirreled away working in agriculture, energy, medicine, even architecture, in a lot of different fields where people were looking to nature, but they did not call themselves biomimics or even talk to each other." Fearful that humans were depleting Earth of its natural resources and polluting the land, air, and water so quickly that the planet was in danger of becoming unlivable, she began asking herself, as she recalled to Lalonde, "How do we live sustainably on Earth without destroying it?" "That is the same question I realized had been answered in all kinds of ways by the 30 [million] to 100 million species we live with," she explained. "Nature builds soil, trades goods, flies through the air, lights up the night, lassoes the sun's energy, learns to circumnavigate the globe, lives at the bottom of the ocean and the top of the mountains, does chemistry, makes miracle materials that are stronger and better than ours—all of this without mortgaging the future." Benyus has identified nine laws of the "circle of life," which, as quoted by Penny Bonda in the on-line magazine *ISdesigNET* (Spring 2001), are as follows: "Nature runs on sunlight," "fits form to function," "recycles everything," "rewards cooperation," "banks on diversity," "demands local expertise," "curbs excesses from within," and "taps the power of limits."

Benyus expanded on her ideas in her 1997 book, *Biomimicry: Innovation Inspired by Nature. Biomimicry* details some of the ways in which science has copied nature. The invention of Velcro, for example, was inspired by the outer structure of burrs—seed casings whose surfaces are covered with barbs. The book also brings readers into the laboratories of people who are striving to discover the secrets to some of nature's imitation-worthy designs. For example, most of the paints and inks used to color manmade products pollute the environment after those products are discarded. Such pollution could be avoided by developing materials that mimic the designs of peacock feathers, say, or butterfly wings: the colors of the feathers are actually illusions created by the scattering of light off melanin rods and thin layers of keratin, while the colors of butterfly wings are illusions created by means of iridescent, overlapping scales atop translucent membranes. In other examples of natural designs that are superior to anything yet manufactured by humans, certain species of mussels afix themselves to underwater surfaces with extremely powerful adhesives that, unlike manmade glues, can set underwater without chemical primers, initiators, or catalysts; the silk that orb-weaver spiders produce without heat in their bodies, using materials gleaned from the insects they catch, is far stronger than the strongest steel wire currently available; the mechanisms by which hibernating bears retain urine for months without succumbing to uremic poisoning might hold the key to prolonging the lives of people whose kidneys have failed; the natural sonar of bats and the means by which migrating birds find their way may offer clues to improving mechanisms for navigation.

Biomimicry received positive reviews and was noted for the ingenuity of its suggested solutions to longstanding problems. A reviewer for *Scientific American* (June 1997) wrote that Benyus "ably brings together many disparate tracks of biomimetic work in a wide-ranging overview of this emerging and still speculative field," while Sharon Oddie Brown wrote for the *Vancouver Sun* (February 7, 1998) that Benyus "writes like an angel from the moment of her opening sentence." According to Penny Bonda, "It is safe to say that . . . *Biomimicry* . . . has done more to teach an extremely diverse readership the mysteries of the natural world than any classroom possibly could."

Benyus has acknowledged that the science of biomimicry is far from having all the answers required for sustainable growth in the immediate future. In a compilation of extracts from speeches she has given at conferences organized by the Collective Heritage Institute (also known as Bioneers), as posted on the *Resurgence* magazine Web site (May/June 2005), Benyus noted, "A lot of the research in biomimicry is years and years from fruition, but it is a path, an approach. It requires us to

visit wild places and keep asking, How does nature teach? How does nature learn? How does nature heal? How does nature communicate? Quieting human cleverness is the first step in biomimicry. Next comes listening, then trying to echo what we hear. . . . Until we create products that, in their manufacturing, use, disposal, and marketing, are part of an economy that mimics a living system rather than a machine, we haven't reached the full extent of biomimicry."

Benyus lives in Stevensville, in the Bitterroot Valley of Montana. In 2005 she was the subject of a two-part installment of David Suzuki's television program *The Nature of Things*, which aired in Canada. She is creating a database of biological literature for the Internet search engine Google. She teaches interpretive writing at the University of Montana.

—R.E.

Suggested Reading: *American Forests* p24 Autumn 1998; Biomimicry Web site; *Esquire* p107 Dec. 2003; *ISdesigNET* (on-line) Spring 2001; *Montreal Gazette* A p1+ Oct. 15, 2000; *Oregonian* C p12+ Apr. 18, 2001; *Vancouver Sun* G p9 Feb. 7, 1998

Selected Books: *Northwoods Wildlife: A Watcher's Guide to Habitats*, 1989; *Field Guide to Wildlife Habitats of the Eastern United States*, 1989; *Field Guide to Wildlife Habitats of the Western United States*, 1989; *A Zoo Lover's Companion: What Makes Whales Whistle, Cranes Dance, Pandas Turn Somersaults, and Crocodiles Roar: A Watcher's Guide to How Animals Act and Why*, 1992; *Biomimicry: Innovation Inspired by Nature*, 1997

Bernanke, Ben S.

(ber-NANK-ee)

Dec. 13, 1953– Chairman of the Federal Reserve; economist

Address: Federal Reserve Board, 20th St. and Constitution Ave., N.W., Washington, DC 20551

Ben S. Bernanke, the 14th chairman of the board of governors of the Federal Reserve, has been "lauded by colleagues and others as a low-key, self-made, independent, extremely smart fellow who surprisingly made it to the top anyway," as David Streitfeld and James F. Peltz wrote for the *Los Angeles Times* (October 25, 2005). Bernanke's appointment as what has been described variously as the world's most influential economics policy maker, top banker, and second-most-powerful man after the U.S. president "is the closest you can come to pure meritocracy," as Adam Posen, a senior fellow at the Institute for International Economics, com-

Ben S. Bernanke

mented to Streitfeld and Peltz. Bernanke, who was nominated for his new position by President George W. Bush on October 24, 2005 and sworn into office on February 1, 2006, succeeds Alan Greenspan, who served as chairman of the Federal Reserve—also known as the Federal Reserve System or the Fed—for 18 and a half years (four and a half terms), beginning during the administration of President Ronald Reagan and ending with his retirement, on January 31, 2006. Unlike Greenspan, who prior to becoming Fed chairman worked mostly in business, as the head of an economic consulting firm, Bernanke has spent most of his professional life as a teacher of economics, first at the Graduate School of Business at Stanford University and then at Princeton University. He served as a member of the Fed's board of governors from August 5, 2002 until June 21, 2005, when he was named chairman of the president's Council of Economic Advisers. With few exceptions, Democratic and Republican lawmakers alike appeared satisfied with the appointment of Bernanke to chair the Fed. Though a registered Republican, throughout his career he has appeared to be nonpartisan in his approach to economic problems; as Frederick Mishkin, an economist with the Columbia Business School, who, like Posen, has co-written a book with Bernanke, commented to Streitfeld and Peltz, "It's not Republican economics or Democratic economics, it's just good economics."

Bernanke is a specialist in monetary economics and in macroeconomics (the analysis of the economy as a whole, by means of information about unemployment, inflation, the total amount of goods and services produced, interest rates, and price levels, among other things). He is known to be a pro-

ponent of proactive inflation targeting (a monetary policy that emphasizes the importance of maintaining a particular, low, stable rate of consumer price inflation—ideally, according to Bernanke, between 1 percent and 2 percent—and adjusting interest rates to achieve that goal); Greenspan opposed targeting a specific percentage. Bernanke has also advocated making the Fed's activities much more transparent than they were under Greenspan. As he said at his confirmation hearings, held by the U.S. Senate Committee on Banking, Housing and Urban Affairs, as reported in the *Washington Post* (November 15, 2005, on-line), "A more transparent policy process increases democratic accountability, promotes constructive dialogue between policymakers and informed outsiders, reduces uncertainty in financial markets, and helps to anchor the public's expectation of long-run inflation, which . . . promotes economic growth and stability." In contrast to Greenspan, who was notorious for the opaqueness, tortuousness, and enigmatic nature of his utterances, Bernanke is known for the clarity of his speech and writings. At his Senate hearings, according to the *Washington Post* transcript, Bernanke assured his questioners that "with respect to monetary policy, I will make continuity with the policies and policy strategies of the Greenspan Fed a top priority." But many observers have warned that the relatively benign economic climate that prevailed as Greenspan's tenure drew to a close might soon change for the worse, forcing Bernanke to shift the Fed's policies in a different direction. As Ben White wrote for the *Washington Post* (November 15, 2005, on-line), "Bernanke will take over the Fed at a moment of rising economic unease. The U.S. trade and budget deficits are soaring. The once-blistering housing market may be cooling. Rumors continue to rumble through Wall Street of dangerously overextended hedge funds ripe for collapse. The next Fed chairman could face significant challenges . . . within months of taking office." "There's no denying that a collapse in stock prices today would pose serious macroeconomic challenges for the United States," Bernanke wrote in a piece called "A Crash Course for Central Bankers" for *Foreign Policy* (September/October 2000, on-line). "Consumer spending would slow, and the U.S. economy would become less of a magnet for foreign investors. Economic growth, which in any case has recently been at unsustainable levels, would decline somewhat. History proves, however, that a smart central bank can protect the economy and the financial sector from the nastier side effects of a stock market collapse." In a talk entitled "The Transition from Academic to Policymaker" that he gave at the annual meeting of the American Economic Association on January 7, 2005, as posted on the Federal Reserve Web site, Bernanke said, "For me, knowing that I am using my skills to further the commonweal and the national interest is an important compensation for the personal sacrifices that a policy position can entail," and he advised both veteran and fledgling economists "to serve in a policymaking capacity, be it as a principal or as a supporting staff member," because, he declared, "You will feel good about it, and you will learn a lot."

The first of three children, Ben Shalom Bernanke was born in Augusta, Georgia, on December 13, 1953 to Philip Bernanke, a pharmacist, and Edna (Friedman) Bernanke, a homemaker and occasional substitute teacher. He has a sister, Sharon, and a brother, Seth, who is a lawyer. For many years his maternal grandfather lived with the family. When Ben was a few months old, his parents settled in Dillon, in rural, northeastern South Carolina, where Philip Bernanke worked in a pharmacy founded earlier by his father. The Bernankes were among a half-dozen Jewish families in the town—too few to support a full-time rabbi at their synagogue; to officiate at services on important Jewish holy days, the families would hire rabbinical students from New York (who would board with the Bernankes), and as an adolescent and teenager, Ben would help the visitors. Earlier, at age three, as his mother recalled to Ben White, he became adept at adding and subtracting numbers of pennies. He learned to read as a kindergartener and skipped second grade. In 1965, as a 12-year-old sixth-grader, he competed in the South Carolina state spelling bee; after being eliminated because he had supposedly made a mistake, he returned to the stage and proved that he had spelled his last word correctly, then went on to win the contest. At that year's national spelling bee, he misspelled "edelweiss," the name of a mountain flower made famous at the time by the blockbuster movie *The Sound of Music*, which he had not seen. During his high-school years, Bernanke played saxophone with the student band, helped out in his father's store, and enjoyed playing backyard basketball with his friends. Inspired by the integration of Dillon's schools, according to Ben White, he "drafted a novel about top white and black football players coming together to form a team at a new high school." Bernanke also learned to speed-read on his own and taught himself calculus, a subject not offered at his school. His score of 1590 out of a possible 1600 on the 1971 Scholastic Aptitude Test (SAT) was the highest attained by any student in South Carolina that year.

After graduating from high school as valedictorian of his class, Bernanke enrolled at Harvard University, in Cambridge, Massachusetts, where he majored in economics. During at least one summer recess (sources differ as to whether it was before or after he entered college), he worked as a waiter at South of the Border, a busy tourist stop on Route I-95; during another, he worked as a manual laborer at a construction site. For his senior honors thesis, he wrote a 102-page paper entitled "An Integrated Model for Energy Policy"; it earned him the prestigious Allyn A. Young Prize, for best undergraduate honors thesis in economics. He also won the John H. Williams Prize, awarded to the outstanding Harvard senior majoring in economics. Bernanke graduated from college summa cum laude, with a B.A. degree, in 1975. Also in 1975 he won a National Science Foundation graduate research fellowship and was elected to the national honor society Phi Beta Kappa. Four years later he received a Ph.D. in economics from the Massachusetts Institute of Technology, in Cambridge; his doctoral dissertation focused on factors leading to the Great Depression of the 1930s. In a highly original paper that brought him much favorable attention—"Nonmonetary Effects of the Financial Crisis in the Propagation of the Great Depression," published in the *American Economic Review* (June 1983)—he presented the argument that ill-considered responses of the Federal Reserve Board, which clung to what he has termed "gold-standard orthodoxy," "helped convert the severe but not unprecedented downturn of 1929–30 into a protracted depression," in his words. In a remark quoted by Greg Ip in the *Wall Street Journal* (December 7, 2005), Bernanke—a self-described "Great Depression buff"—once said, "If you want to understand geology, study earthquakes. If you want to understand economics, study the biggest calamity to hit the U.S. and world economies."

For six years beginning in 1979, Bernanke taught economics at the Graduate School of Business of Stanford University, in California, as an assistant professor for four years and then as an associate professor. In California he and his wife (they married in 1978) "were hesitant to buy a house since I was certain that prices could never stay as high as they were at that time," as he recalled in a speech given at Stanford in 2005, as quoted by Streitfeld and Peltz. "Since then I've developed a view that central bankers should not try to determine fundamental values of assets," he added, alluding to the fact that, as his audience well knew, housing prices had skyrocketed in subsequent years.

In 1985 Bernanke joined the faculty of Princeton University, in New Jersey, as a professor of economic and public affairs; he held a joint appointment in the Department of Economics and the Woodrow Wilson School of Public and International Affairs. In 1994 he was named the Class of 1926 Professor of Economics and Public Affairs, and in 1996, the Howard Harrison and Gabrielle Snyder Beck Professor of Economics and Public Affairs. He chaired the Department of Economics for three years, beginning in mid-1996, and was appointed chairman for another three-year term in mid-2000. As head of the department, Bernanke avoided displays of egoism; referring to his colleagues, he told a reporter for the campus newspaper, the *Daily Princetonian*, as quoted in the *International Herald Tribune* (October 26, 2005) by Louis Uchitelle and Eduardo Porter, "We're all the same rank. I'm just the one sitting in the chair."

While at Princeton Bernanke wrote or co-wrote chapters for books and dozens of articles for such periodicals as the *Journal of Monetary Economics*, the *Journal of Econometrics*, the *Quarterly Journal of Economics*, the *Journal of Political Economy*, and the *Journal of Money, Credit, and Banking* as well as the *American Economic Review*. In addition, he edited the book *Readings and Cases in Macroeconomics* (1987) and published the textbook *Macroeconomics* (1992), co-written by the economist Andrew B. Abel, a fellow graduate student of his at MIT, who teaches at the Wharton School of the University of Pennsylvania; the fifth edition of that book was published in 2005. Bernanke was a Hoover Institution National Fellow in 1982–83, an Alfred P. Sloan Research Fellow in 1983–84, and a Guggenheim Fellow in 1999. As a visiting professor of economics, he taught at MIT in the fall of 1983 and during 1989–90 and at New York University in the fall of 1993. For varying lengths of time, he served on the U.S. Census Advisory Board and as director of the Monetary Economics Program of the National Bureau of Economic Research (NBER); co-edited the journal *Economics Letters*, the *Journal of Business*, and the NBER's *Macroeconomics Annuals*; and for one year directed Princeton's Bendheim Center for Finance. In the only political position he held until 2002, he was a member of the board of education of Montgomery Township, in New Jersey, where he and his family lived and his children attended school, for two terms—what he described at the 2005 annual meeting of the American Economic Association, as quoted on the Fed's Web site, as "six grueling years during which my fellow board members and I were trashed alternately by angry parents and angry taxpayers." As a member of that board, he told Matthew Benjamin for *U.S. News & World Report* (December 29, 2003), "I learned something, I think, about public service, about working with other people, and dealing with sometimes emotional or otherwise highly charged issues." Linda Romano, who was president of the board when Bernanke served, told David Streitfeld and James F. Peltz that Bernanke "wasn't in your face, he didn't push things on you or say, 'I know what I'm talking about, listen to me.' But you knew he was right."

On May 8, 2002 President George W. Bush nominated Bernanke to fill the remaining three years in the term of a departing member of the Federal Reserve Board. (The board consists of seven members, each of whom may serve only one, 14-year term. The U.S. president chooses from among those seven members the board's chairman and vice chairman, who—if approved by the U.S. Senate—serve for four years in those posts and who, if they are not reappointed to those positions, may remain on the board for the remainder of their 14-year terms.) Among other responsibilities, the Fed sets monetary policy and controls the nation's money supply, strives to keep the dollar sound, regulates and supervises banks, protects consumers in their financial dealings by means of the creation and enforcement of appropriate regulations, and promotes overall financial stability. The U.S.

Senate confirmed Bernanke on July 31, 2002, and five days later he was sworn into office. In *USA Today* (October 25, 2005), Sue Kirchhoff wrote that during the next 35 months, "Bernanke became one of the most influential members of the Fed," in part because he gave several "groundbreaking speeches." Prominent among them was his talk "Deflation: Making Sure 'It' Doesn't Happen Here," given at the National Economics Club on November 21, 2002, in which he discussed ways in which the Fed could prevent the sort of downward spiral in prices that has afflicted Japan, to the great detriment of its economy. In another speech, "Trade and Jobs," given at the Fuqua School of Business of Duke University on March 30, 2004, Bernanke declared that although economists agree almost universally that "free trade among nations promotes economic prosperity," the problems of workers displaced directly or indirectly as a result of free trade must be addressed; he concluded by stating that "helping displaced workers is good policy for at least three reasons. First, reducing the burdens borne by displaced workers is the right and fair thing to do. Second, helping workers who have lost jobs find new productive work is good for the economy as well as for the affected workers and their families. Finally, if workers are less fearful of change, less pressure will be exerted on politicians to erect trade barriers or to take other actions that would reduce the flexibility and dynamism of the U.S. economy. In the long run, avoiding economic isolationism and maintaining economic dynamism will pay big dividends for everybody." In another important speech, "The Global Saving Glut and the U.S. Current Account Deficit," presented to the Virginia Association of Economics on March 10, 2005, Bernanke argued that a major cause of the U.S. trade deficit is the "significant increase in the global supply of saving," in his words.

With only a month or so remaining before Bernanke completed his truncated term as a Fed governor, President Bush named him chairman of the three-member Council of Economic Advisers; the Senate approved his nomination unanimously, in a voice vote, and he was sworn in on June 21, 2005. Four months later, on October 24, the president chose him to fill the chairmanship of the Federal Reserve upon the retirement on January 31, 2006 of Alan Greenspan. (Because his first stint with the Fed did not constitute a full term, he was also eligible to begin, concurrently, a regular, 14-year term—during which, at the discretion of whoever is president, he may be reappointed as chairman.) Unlike his predecessors, Greenspan had become an icon in the business and financial world—many referred to him as the Maestro—because during his tenure inflation had dropped to desirable levels, and on the whole, the country had enjoyed great prosperity. He had also become one of the most admired public figures in the U.S. and a celebrity, with popular magazines reporting on his romances. Although Bernanke was renowned in academic circles for his "incredible knowledge of monetary theory and history," as Alan S. Blinder, a Princeton economist who served as a Fed vice chairman under Greenspan, put it, he was virtually unknown among laypeople and little known among elected or other government officials. Despite—or perhaps because of—his obscurity, Bush's choice of Bernanke was met with bipartisan support. (According to various observers, Bush ruled out candidates from his inner circle of political loyalists because he wanted to avoid the sort of controversy that had erupted after his ultimately unsuccessful nomination of Harriet Miers, his White House counsel and longtime friend, for a seat on the Supreme Court.) Moreover, according to the *New York Times* (October 26, 2005, on-line), "Bernanke had what many outsiders wanted: a world-class reputation among economists; credibility on Wall Street; a confidence and an air of political independence that seemed free from hints of cronyism." Bernanke encountered no tough questioning during his one-day confirmation hearings in November 2005. On February 1, 2006 he officially became the new chairman of the Federal Reserve.

In the early months of his tenure, Bernanke continued the policy, pursued by the Fed under his predecessor, of gradually increasing interest rates as a means of avoiding inflation. In August 2006 he suspended that approach, in the belief that a modest economic slowdown at that point would be sufficient to keep inflation in check. Bernanke hoped to maintain a core rate of inflation of between 1 and 2 percent. He has also spoken about the importance of addressing the problems of people whose jobs are lost because of outsourcing or who are hurt in other ways because of the unprecedentedly rapid pace of globalization. "The challenge for policy makers," Bernanke said in his keynote speech at the annual retreat for Fed employees in 2006, as quoted by Edmund L. Andrews in the *New York Times* (August 26, 2006), "is to ensure that the benefits of global economic integration are sufficiently widely shared—for example, by helping displaced workers get the necessary training to take advantage of new opportunities—[and] that a consensus for welfare-enhancing change can be obtained."

According to Streitfeld and Peltz, Bernanke has compared the difficulties of applying economic theory to real-life problems to "learning how to repair a car while it is still running." In a speech called "The Logic of Monetary Policy," presented to the National Economists Club on December 2, 2004, as transcribed on the Fed's Web site, Bernanke joked, "If making monetary policy is like driving a car, then the car is one that has an unreliable speedometer, a foggy windshield, and a tendency to respond unpredictably and with a delay to the accelerator or the brake." "Bernanke's lack of pretension and sense of whimsy are among his most striking characteristics, according to many of his friends and colleagues," Nell Henderson and Paul Blustein reported in the *Washington Post* (October 25, 2005, on-line). Once, after President Bush

kiddingly reproached him for wearing tan socks with a dark suit and dark shoes to a meeting at the White House, Bernanke distributed tan socks to Vice President Richard B. Cheney and other administration officials, all of whom wore them the next day to another White House meeting. In a news release posted on the Web site of Princeton University (from which Bernanke took a public-service leave in 2002 and from which he resigned in 2005) after his nomination as Fed chairman, many of his former colleagues expressed their high regard for him, mentioning such qualities as his "incredible knowledge of monetary theory and history," his "honesty and integrity," his "excellent judgment," and his being "fair minded, politically astute, level headed and not ideological" as well as a "wonderful administrator" and a "great educator." Bernanke is a longtime fan of the Boston Red Sox and, more recently, of the Washington Nationals; as a lover of statistics and mathematical analyses and formulas, he admires the work of the baseball statistician Bill James.

Bernanke and his wife, the former Anna Friedmann, who has taught Spanish on the middle-school level, have two children, Joel and Alyssa. The couple live in Washington, D.C.

—I.C.

Suggested Reading: *BusinessWeek* p36+ Nov. 7, 2005; Federal Reserve Web site; *Forward* (on-line) Nov. 18, 2005; *Institutional Investor* 2003; *Los Angeles Times* (on-line) A p1+ Oct. 25, 2005; *Marquis Who's Who* (on-line); *New York Times* A p1+, C p1+ Oct. 25, 2005, A p1+ Oct. 26, 2005; *U.S. News & World Report* p59+ Nov. 7, 2005; *USA Today* (on-line) A p1+ Oct. 25, 2005; *Washington Post* (on-line) D p1+ Oct. 25, 2005, D p1+ Nov. 25, 2005

Selected Books: *Macroeconomics* (with Andrew B. Abel), 2000; *Principles of Economics* (with Robert H. Frank), 2001; *Inflation Targeting: Lessons from the International Experience* (with others), 2001; *Principles of Macroeconomics* (with Robert H. Frank), 2003; *Essays on the Great Depression*, 2004

Bettis, Jerome

Feb. 16, 1972– Former football player; sports commentator

Address: Jerome Bettis Bus Stops Here Foundation, P.O. Box 211089, Detroit, MI 48221

On February 5, 2006, standing on a podium at Ford Field, in his native Detroit, Michigan, speaking before a television audience exceeding 45 million homes in the United States alone, the football player Jerome Bettis—known to fans as "the Bus"—

Jerome Bettis
Paul Hawthorne/Getty Images

announced his retirement. "I played this game to win a championship," he said. "And I'm a champion. I think the Bus's last stop is here in Detroit." He made his announcement shortly after his team, the Pittsburgh Steelers, defeated the Seattle Seahawks by a score of 21–10 in Super Bowl XL, bringing him the rare experience of winning a National Football League (NFL) championship in his final game as a professional. The 13-year veteran's statistics in Super Bowl XL—43 rushing yards on 14 attempts—reveal little about his role as a mentor for, and inspiration to, the Steelers' star players during their championship run. Throughout his career Bettis, an oversized but surprisingly agile runner, pulverized opponents and thrilled NFL fans, "barrel[ing] his way up and down football fields across the country, leaving bruised, battered and frustrated defenders strewn all over the landscape," as Steve Springer wrote for the *Los Angeles Times* (January 4, 1997). Bettis ranks fourth of all time in rushing attempts (3,479) and fifth in the accumulation of rushing yards (13,662), both records attesting to his durability and to the frequency with which he was called upon to "move the chains," or gain enough yardage for a new set of downs. In his 10 seasons playing for the Steelers, Bettis "became the heart and soul of one of the most prosperous franchises in the NFL," according to Curt Sylvester, writing for SuperBowl.com (February 5, 2006). His aggressive inside-running style (or his running in plays designed to move the ball between defenders on the opposing team's line of scrimmage) epitomized the Steelers' offensive philosophy under Bill Cowher, the Steelers' head coach since 1992. Cowher said to Michael Silver for *Sports Illustrated* (February 6, 2006) that Bettis "exemplifies what

I think a football team should be—he brings a toughness, an identity, and, of course, he is the consummate pro." Bettis first received national attention in the early 1990s, at the University of Notre Dame, where in three seasons as a fullback he led the school's celebrated team to a victory over the University of Florida in the 1992 Sugar Bowl and over Texas A&M University in the 1993 Cotton Bowl. Following the 1993 NFL season, his first as a professional, he was named the Offensive Rookie of the Year, in acknowledgement of his 1,429 rushing yards, the second-highest total among all runners that season. Bettis began his professional career with the Los Angeles Rams, who relocated to St. Louis beginning in the 1995 NFL season, Bettis's last year with the franchise.

Bettis is known for his friendliness—toward his teammates and coaches, the media, NFL fans, and, indeed, almost anyone with whom he comes into contact. "He's always signing autographs, and I think he enjoys it more than the fans do," Lee Flowers, a former teammate, said to reporters for *People* (January 21, 2002). "People could take lessons from him on how to be the perfect athlete." In 1996 Bettis founded the Jerome Bettis Bus Stops Here Foundation, aimed at supporting "underprivileged children in America's inner cities," according to its Web site, through a variety of services and programs. Bettis is also a spokesperson for asthma awareness. When asked why football fans in Pittsburgh had developed such affection for him, Bettis said to Jarrett Bell for *USA Today* (December 30, 1997), "It's a blue-collar town and I'm a blue-collar player. I'm not a flashy guy. I think the fans identify with a back who is going to pound for 4 yards, then get up and pound for 4 more yards. And you know they identify with 'The Bus,' that big, bad, bruising kind of thing that carries people." In September 2006 Bettis debuted on NBC as a broadcast commentator for Sunday-night football games.

The youngest of three children, Jerome Abram Bettis was born on February 16, 1972 in Detroit, Michigan, to Johnnie and Gladys (Bougart) Bettis. He and his older siblings, Kimberly and John III, were raised in Detroit's west side in what is currently one of the city's most violent and poverty-stricken neighborhoods. His father, now retired, worked for the city as an electrical inspector (he later became the chief inspector); his mother held a series of jobs, including bank teller, during Bettis's growing-up years. Bettis's parents were watchful disciplinarians who scheduled a variety of activities to shield their children from the rougher elements of their neighborhood. The close-knit family often bowled together, an activity Jerome Bettis particularly enjoyed. Bettis has often mentioned his parents' positive influence on him. "What I am all stems from parenting and a loving environment," he said to Bernie Miklasz for the *St. Louis Post-Dispatch* (December 18, 1994).

By all accounts Bettis was a well-behaved, attentive, and bright boy. (He has also been described as having been a nerd: in his youth he wore oversized glasses and, mimicking his father, carried a brief-case to elementary school.) He attended public school until the fourth grade. After learning that he was misbehaving in class, his mother, knowing that such behavior was atypical for Bettis, "checked it out," as she recalled to Ron Cook for the *Pittsburgh Post-Gazette* (February 3, 2006). It turned out that her son "would get his work done and start fooling with his friends. There was no challenge for him there." The boy's parents trans-ferred him to the private Detroit Urban Lutheran School, which he attended without incident through the eighth grade. He played flag football on a field behind the school, which has since been re-named Jerome Bettis Field. His first encounter with organized football was in his freshman year of high school. Initially, his mother was deter-mined that her son continue to attend local private schools (which apparently offered no football pro-grams). But Leroy Bougart, Jerome's uncle and a high-school football coach, noticed in Bettis an agility that was uncommon for a boy of his large size; he convinced Bettis's mother that his chances of attaining a college scholarship would increase significantly with the proper football training. Bet-tis thus attended Henry Ford High School, a public school. It was after collapsing during football prac-tice at Henry Ford that Bettis discovered he had asthma. "I passed out," Bettis said to the reporters for *People*. "But my parents said, 'Don't let this change your plans. If you want to play football, you can.'" (Beginning when he was in high school, his parents attended every one of Bettis's games, save for two NFL preseason contests played on foreign soil.) While he enjoyed playing football at Henry Ford, he was often picked on by other students. His decision to leave the school after one year was made easier once Joe Hoskins, the football coach there, was fired.

Bettis transferred to MacKenzie High, also a public school, where, weighing more than 230 pounds by that time, he became a standout football player. (He also played on the basketball team.) Bob Dozier, then the football coach at MacKenzie, made Bettis an offensive lineman during his first year with the team. In his junior and senior years, Bettis played linebacker, a defensive position, and—albeit reluctantly—fullback, as part of the running offense. Dozier recalled in a conversation with Ron Cook, "Do you believe I had to con him into running the ball? He liked defense. He liked hitting people. But once he had some success and started scoring those touchdowns, it was like, 'Man, coach, I like this.'" In one particularly suc-cessful season, Bettis rushed for 1,355 yards and scored 14 touchdowns. The *Detroit Free Press* named Bettis the top football player in the state of Michigan in his senior year. That year he also earned distinction as Michigan's Gatorade Circle of Champions Player of the Year. In addition, *USA Today* and the *Sporting News* named him among the top 100 high-school seniors in the country. Be-cause of his combination of size and quickness,

many major universities courted Bettis, but most were interested in making him play linebacker, rather than fullback. Bettis said to Keith Dunna-vant for *Sport* (October 1992), "They couldn't un-derstand why anyone would actually want to play fullback when he could play linebacker. That's be-cause so many of those schools looked at the full-back position as just another blocker lined up in the backfield. But I knew I could be more."

Lou Holtz, the head coach at the University of Notre Dame from 1986 to 1996, persuaded Bettis to enroll at the school simply by offering him a chance to play in the Fighting Irish's backfield. Bettis accepted the offer, joining a team that al-ready featured the running backs Ricky Waters and Reggie Brooks, both future professionals. As a freshman Bettis served as backup for the starting fullback Rodney Culver; on the 15 carries Bettis was given that year, he gained 115 yards. In his sophomore season he took over the duties as start-ing fullback, and with an average of 5.8 yards each carry, he rushed for 972 yards. He also proved to be a capable blocker, opening up avenues for his teammates when they carried the ball. He shared team most-valuable-player (MVP) honors with the quarterback Rick Mirer and set a new Notre Dame single-season record by scoring 20 touchdowns, or 120 points, at that time the most by a player in one season in school history. Bettis ended his stellar sophomore year by gaining 150 rushing yards and three touchdowns and earning MVP honors at the 1992 Sugar Bowl, in Notre Dame's 39–28 victory against the University of Florida Gators. He had emerged as "the kind of go-to fullback unseen in college football since Texas' Earl Campbell rum-bled his way to the Heisman trophy in '77," Keith Dunnavant wrote, referring to the Houston Oilers' Hall of Fame fullback. In Bettis's junior season an ankle injury slowed him down; he nevertheless managed to gain 825 rushing yards and score 12 touchdowns. In three seasons at Notre Dame, Bettis rushed for 1,912 yards, scored 33 career touch-downs, and made 32 catches for an additional 429 yards. He finished his college career by scoring three touchdowns in the Fighting Irish's 28–3 vic-tory against the Texas A&M University Aggies in the 1993 Cotton Bowl.

Bettis decided to forgo his senior year at Notre Dame to turn pro. In 1993 he was picked 10th in the NFL draft by the Los Angeles Rams, who signed him to a five-year, $4.6 million contract. Chuck Knox, the Rams' head coach, who favored a formi-dable running attack, named Bettis the Rams' fea-tured ball carrier six weeks into the season. Despite suffering a shoulder injury early in the year, he needed very little time to emerge as a star, rushing for 1,429 yards and scoring seven touchdowns. His average of 4.9 yards per carry that season ranks as the best of his career. He finished 57 yards shy of the mark set by Emmitt Smith of the Dallas Cow-boys for the most rushing yards in the NFL that sea-son. Bettis was named the NFL's Offensive Rookie of the Year and was selected to play in the prestigious Pro-Bowl Game in Hawaii. Showing gratitude to the Rams' offensive line for having blocked for him all season, Bettis reportedly purchased a 45-inch color television set for each player.

The 1994 season was a frustrating one on the field for Bettis, who averaged only 3.2 yards per carry. With opponents committing as many as eight defenders to the line of scrimmage, he found little room to maneuver. The poundings he took repeatedly on the field began to exact a toll on the young running back. "On Monday mornings, I get up by sections," Bettis said to Bernie Miklasz. "The whole process takes about an hour. When I wake up it takes me 15 minutes just to turn my body over to get ready to rise. Then it'll take me another 15 minutes to flex one leg and get it ready. Then 15 minutes to shake the other leg loose. Then when the legs are set, it takes another 15 minutes to get the rest of my body set. I take a deep breath, and then I jump out of bed." He added, "I want to succeed at all costs. If it's at the expense of me getting hurt, I'll make that deal. I'm trying to help the team win and I'll do what it takes." For the season he compiled 1,025 rushing yards and made a career-high 31 receptions, good for 293 receiving yards, also a career high. Despite the noticeable drop in his rushing production, Bettis was again selected to play in the Pro Bowl Game.

Rich Brooks, who in January 1995 led the University of Oregon to the Rose Bowl, was named the Rams' head coach in the following month, replacing Knox. For two weeks beginning in late July of that year, citing frustration with his contract, Bettis refused to report to the Rams' preseason training camp. He incurred over $56,000 in fines, which were reportedly given to local charities. Bettis has called the season that followed his most frustrating as a professional. "I took a beating," he said to Steve Springer. "They said I was a malcontent, that I was lazy and that I was overweight. A lot of things that were said were untrue." That year the team moved from Los Angeles to St. Louis, Missouri. The already fractured relationship between Bettis and Brooks took a turn for the worse. Bettis's production fell significantly, and it was rumored throughout the season that he would be traded. (He also endured injuries to his groin and ankle that year.) Bettis gained only 637 yards on 183 carries, both career lows except for his final season with Pittsburgh. After the Rams selected the running back Lawrence Phillips from the University of Nebraska with the sixth pick in the 1996 NFL draft, on April 20, 1996, Bettis was traded, along with a third-round pick, to the Pittsburgh Steelers, in exchange for the Steelers' second-round pick and a fourth-round pick the following year. Bettis later said to Michael Silver for *Sports Illustrated* (October 7, 1996), "I'll never forgive the Rams for the way they treated me, especially [vice president of football operations] Steve Ortmayer and [coach] Rich Brooks. They had to justify getting rid of me when they knew I could still play, so they labeled me as a bad apple."

The Steelers, then known as a perennial presence in the NFL play-offs, were coached by the gruff Bill Cowher, himself a Pittsburgh native. The team featured an aggressive, blitzing defense and a relentless running attack. Entering the 1996 season, the Steelers were months removed from their 27–17 defeat by the Dallas Cowboys in Super Bowl XXX. In Pittsburgh Bettis worked hard to live down the reputation for being a malcontent that his uneasy final season with the Rams had brought him. His first two years on his new team were outstanding, as he rushed for 1,431 and 1,665 yards, respectively, achieving the third-highest total in the NFL in each of those seasons; he played in the Pro Bowl both years. Named the NFL's 1996 Comeback Player of the Year, Bettis quickly emerged as a fan favorite.

Bettis suffered an asthma attack in a regular season contest in 1997, the first time since his teen years that he had had such an attack, according to what Bettis told the reporters for *People*. He was carried off the field on a stretcher and has said that the experience was frightening. As a result of the incident, he began monitoring his condition daily. When he felt particularly short of breath during a game, he would ask to be replaced; he also kept an inhaler on hand at all times.

The Steelers qualified for the play-offs in both the 1996–97 and 1997–98 seasons, coming out on top in the American Football Conference (AFC) Central Division. In the opening round of the 1996–97 play-offs, the Steelers faced the Indianapolis Colts, in Pittsburgh. Bettis scored two rushing touchdowns and ran for 102 yards, helping the Steelers to a 42–14 victory. The following week, in the divisional round, the Steelers lost to the New England Patriots, 28–3; Bettis was slowed in the game after aggravating an injury to his groin and gained only 43 yards. He was again mostly thwarted, rushing for 67 yards, in a rematch between the Steelers and Patriots in the divisional round of the 1997–98 play-offs, which the Steelers entered with a first-round bye. Emerging with a 7–6 victory, Pittsburgh was just one game away from the Super Bowl. In the AFC Championship Game, against the Denver Broncos—the eventual Super Bowl champions—on January 11, 1998, Bettis scored a touchdown and gained 105 yards. The Steelers' 24–21 loss marked the second time in six seasons that they had hosted but failed to win the AFC Conference Championship game.

Bettis continued to be the focal point of the Steelers' offense in each of the next three seasons. Eclipsing the 1,000-rushing-yards mark each year, he gained, respectively, 1,185, 1,091, and 1,341 yards. Assessing Bettis for the *People* reporters, Tom Jackson, a former player and an analyst for the sports television and radio network ESPN, observed: "Yes, he can be a bus, but he can also be a Porsche. He has a rare combination of power and very quick feet." Despite Bettis' consistency, the Steelers compiled a mediocre overall record of 22–26 in that three-year span, failing each season to make the play-offs.

With a record of 13–3, the Steelers finished the 2001 regular season atop the AFC central division. Contributing to the team's revitalization, Hines Ward and Plaxico Burress, drafted in 1998 and 2000, respectively, emerged as reliable targets for the Steelers' versatile quarterback Kordell Stewart. Defensively, meanwhile, during the regular season the team allowed 207 points, the third-lowest total in the NFL. Bettis rushed for a league-high 1,072 yards, an average of 4.8 yards per carry, through the first 11 games of the regular season. He was on pace to have his finest statistical season since his rookie year when, on December 2, in a game against the Minnesota Vikings, he was tackled awkwardly, landing out of bounds and injuring his hip. That caused his groin injury to resurface, and he was sidelined for the final five weeks of the regular season. Although Bettis vowed to return to the roster in good condition for the play-offs, he reacted adversely to pain medication and was removed from the lineup prior to the Steelers' play-off contest against their divisional rivals the Baltimore Ravens. Pittsburgh won the game, 27–10. While Bettis kept his promise to play the following week against the Patriots in the AFC Championship Game, he was ineffective. The eventual Super Bowl Champions, the Patriots, defeated the Steelers by a score of 24–17, limiting Bettis to eight rushing yards on nine attempts. Bettis was selected for the Pro Bowl but declined to play due to his injuries.

In 2002 Bettis rushed for 666 yards and nine touchdowns; he missed several weeks of action toward the middle of the season due to a left-knee injury. His 187 carries were the second-fewest of his career, topping only his final season with the Rams, in 1995. Bettis was limited to four carries, for a combined four yards, in the Steelers' two play-off games following the regular season. The Steelers were stopped short of reaching the AFC Championship Game on January 11, 2003, losing 34–31 to the Tennessee Titans in a seesaw-like game.

In the 2003 preseason Bettis was demoted from the Steelers' starting ranks, replaced by a smaller runner, Amos Zereoue. He regained his starter's role, however, midway through the season, and finished the year with 811 rushing yards and seven rushing touchdowns, both team highs. The Steelers finished that season with a 6–10 record and failed to qualify for the play-offs for only the fourth time in Cowher's 12 years as head coach. The team's comparatively poor record afforded them the 11th overall selection in the 2004 NFL Draft, in which they picked the quarterback Ben Roethlisberger from Miami University, in Ohio. In 2004 Bettis was named to his sixth and final Pro Bowl, after emerging during the season as a reliable short-yardage and goal-line-situation runner. His 13 touchdowns that season, for instance, amounted to a career high. At season's end the Steelers owned a franchise-best 15–1 record, thanks in part to the efforts of Roethlisberger, who appeared ma-

ture beyond his years. Bettis explained in a conversation with Teresa Varley for Steelers.com some of the reasons that his relationship with the Steelers had profited both parties. "The majority of my career, we've been a run-dominated football team. . . . Defenses knew that we were going to run the football, and we found a way to do it. I understood how to work myself around the football field, around eight-man fronts. I would know there wasn't going to be a hole, there was only going to be a crack, and I needed to use my leverage to get three or four yards—it wasn't about breaking long runs. I understand the dynamics that go along with coming in in the second half and getting those tough yards, because that's what I've been able to do my whole career." Having earned an opening-round play-off bye, the Steelers edged out the New York Jets in the divisional round of the play-offs by a 20–17 score; Bettis gained 101 yards on the ground and scored a touchdown in the contest. The Patriots, the Steelers' opponents the following weekend, in the AFC Championship Game, intercepted three Roethlisberger passes, en route to a 41–27 win.

In the first 12 games of the 2005 regular season, the Steelers' record stood at 7–5. An injury to Roethlisberger, in particular, seemed to hamper the team, whose defense was one of the league's most formidable. On December 11, 2005, in snowy conditions, the Steelers defeated the Chicago Bears in Pittsburgh on the strength of Bettis's 101 yards rushing and two touchdowns, thus snapping a three-game losing streak and bringing their record to 8–5. Pittsburgh won its last three regular-season games, finishing with an 11–5 record. The team thus qualified for the play-offs as the AFC's lowest, or sixth, seeded team. Facing their divisional rivals the Cincinnati Bengals on the road, in the first round of the play-offs, the Steelers emerged victorious by a score of 31–17. Bettis rushed for 52 yards on 10 carries and scored a touchdown. In the much-anticipated, second-round match-up between Pittsburgh and the heavily favored Indianapolis Colts, on January 15, 2006, the Steelers held in check the Colts' vaunted offense, led by quarterback Peyton Manning, en route to an exciting and unlikely 21–18 victory. Roethlisberger threw a pair of touchdown passes against the Denver Broncos to lead the Steelers to a 34–17 win the following week, giving the Steelers their third consecutive road play-off victory. Bettis pitched in against Denver by scoring a touchdown and gaining 39 rushing yards. Pittsburgh advanced to take on the Seattle Seahawks in Super Bowl XL, in Detroit.

Bettis's homecoming in Detroit was treated by the media as one of the more compelling stories associated with Super Bowl XL. Thanks in part to Cowher's ingenuity in calling plays, the Steelers emerged victorious in the game, 21–10. Early in the fourth quarter, on a play that was intended to deceive the opposition, Pittsburgh receiver Antwaan Randle El—after appearing as though he would run the ball—completed a 43-yard touchdown pass to the receiver Ward (who was later voted the game's most valuable player), extending Pittsburgh's lead from 14–10 to 21–10 and effectively deciding the game. Bettis gained only 43 yards on 14 carries in the game but helped secure, with a block, the Steelers' first touchdown, a one-yard scamper by Roethlisberger. "Bettis wasn't the same back who punished defenders in the NFL for 13 years, but he didn't need to be on this team," Tim Dahlberg wrote for the Associated Press (February 6, 2006, on-line). "His role wasn't so much to run as it was to lead." Hines said after the game, as quoted by Dahlberg, that the Steelers' play "was all for Jerome. We were going to fight for him." After the game Bettis announced his retirement, during an on-field ceremony in which the Vince Lombardi Trophy was presented to the Steelers. (The Super Bowl victory was the fifth in the Steelers' history.)

Later that month Bettis announced that he would be joining NBC Sports as an analyst for the television series *Football Night in America*, which premiered in September 2006, airing immediately before the network's Sunday-evening coverage of NFL games. Bettis explained to a reporter for the Associated Press, in an article appearing on MSN-BC.com (February 20, 2006, on-line), that he intended to be frank in his analysis of players' performance. "The nature of the business is to call it as you see it," he said. "If you look at my track record in Pittsburgh, I've always told the truth. Honesty is the best policy. If a guy is not playing well, he knows it. I'm just telling the truth. As long as I call it like I see it I'll be fine." Bettis made his debut as an NBC commentator on September 7, 2006, at a contest between the Steelers and the Miami Dolphins. Before the game started, a yellow school bus drove onto the field with a large sign reading "The Bus." Bettis emerged from the vehicle and then crossed the field to the Steelers' benches, where he greeted many of his former teammates with hugs. Prior to his debut as a broadcaster, Bettis was an occasional guest on television talk shows, among them *The Tonight Show with Jay Leno* and *Last Call with Carson Daily*. He appeared as himself in a 2006 episode of the sitcom *The Office*.

In 1997 Bettis founded the Bus Stops Here Foundation, which focuses on improving the lives of underprivileged children. He was named the Walter Payton NFL Man of the Year in early February 2002, in acknowledgement of his many community service endeavors and his excellence on the gridiron.

Bettis and his fiancée, Trameka Boykin, married on July 8, 2006, in Jamaica. They have a baby daughter, Jada. According to Ron Cook, Bettis has homes in or near Pittsburgh; Atlanta, Georgia; and the South Beach section of Miami, Florida. During his NFL career the five-foot 11-inch, 250-pound Bettis spent several off-seasons training with Bob Kersee, a former U.S. Olympic track coach, to improve his quickness. He also prepared meticulously for opponents, watching films of opposing teams

to gain a competitive edge. He has remained an avid bowler, with an average above 200, and claims to have bowled perfect 300 scores on more than one occasion. "If you bowl with Jerome, you bowl until he wins," his mother told the *People* reporters. "He'll bowl 10, 12 games if he has to." Bettis himself told the reporters, "I can't just compete for fun because when I lose, I get mad."

—D.F.

Suggested Reading: *Los Angeles Times* C p8 Jan. 4, 1997; *Pittsburgh Post-Gazette* E p1 Feb. 3, 2006; Pro Football Reference Web site; *St. Louis Post-Dispatch* F p1 Dec. 18, 1994; *Sport* p 58+ Oct. 1992

Black Eyed Peas

Musical group

apl.de.ap
(apple-dee-ap)
Nov. 20, 1974– Rapper; break-dancer

Fergie
Mar. 27, 1975– Singer

Taboo Nawasha
July 14, 1975– Rapper; break-dancer

will.i.am
Mar. 15, 1975– Rapper; break-dancer

Address: A&M Records, 2220 Colorado Ave., Santa Monica, CA 90404

"I want to present a universal ethnic, cultural, positive, unification-type vibe," will.i.am, a founding member and the de facto leader of the musical group Black Eyed Peas, told Karen R. Good for *Vibe* (May 1998). Black Eyed Peas came into being in 1995, when will.i.am teamed up with two other rappers and break-dancers, apl.de.ap and Taboo Nawasha, and began performing in clubs in Los Angeles, California. Then, as now, rap music was associated with profane language and violent imagery, references to gang activity, drug use, prostitution, and promiscuity, hostility toward civil authorities, the derogation of women, and the glorification of hypermasculinity and a "bling-bling" lifestyle, involving ostentatious displays of expensive possessions—jewelry, clothing, and cars. While Black Eyed Peas emerged from the same hiphop culture that produced gangsta rap, as it became known, the group has distinguished itself as a "progressive hip-hop band," by offering, for the most part, affirmative, optimistic messages that will "bring people together" so that "love will spread," as Taboo told Ramsay Adams for Fox-News.com (August 17, 2003). "We're not gangsters

. . . ," apl.de.ap told Peta Hellard for the Perth, Australia, *Sunday Times* (January 25, 2004). "We're just a bunch of good friends that does music and enjoys playing in front of people and we just like to have a good time, be aware of what's going on in our surroundings and always have a positive outlook."

Black Eyed Peas' first two albums, *Behind the Front* and *Bridging the Gap*, earned critical praise but generated only modest interest among consumers. The band's fortunes changed dramatically for the better after their shift toward a more pop-oriented sound and the addition to the band in late 2002 of the vocalist Fergie. Their third release, *Elephunk*, was a huge crossover success. One song on that album, "Where Is the Love?," reached the top spot on two *Billboard* charts and remained at number one for six weeks on singles charts in the United Kingdom and Australia and nine weeks in Ireland; another song, "Let's Get It Started," won the Grammy Award for best rap performance by a duo or group in 2005. Jack Johnson, Sting, James Brown, and other guest artists contributed to the Peas' most recent album, *Monkey Business* (2005), which contains the Grammy-winning track "Don't Phunk with My Heart" and the controversial hit single "My Humps," which capitalized on Fergie's evolution into a sex symbol and by early 2006 had sold two million copies. *Monkey Business* moved the group solidly into prevailing musical currents and led to complaints that the Peas had abandoned their hip-hop roots for pop stardom. "We've always had it in us to be a mainstream band," will.i.am told Alexia Loundras for the London *Independent* (February 27, 2004). The Black Eyed Peas' charity, the Peapod Foundation, which was launched in early 2006 and is affiliated with the Entertainment Industry Foundation, aims to raise money to help poor children in the U.S. and overseas.

The members of the Black Eyed Peas were born within eight months of one another. Will.i.am was born William James Adams on March 15, 1975. He was raised by a single mother in a housing project in South Central Los Angeles, the scene of frequent gang fights between the Crips and the Bloods. From an early age will.i.am displayed a flamboyant fashion sense as well as a talent for music and break dancing. In 1989 an uncle of his introduced him to apl.de.ap, and the teenagers became friends. Born Allan Pineda Lindo on November 20, 1974 in a Philippine barrio, apl.de.ap is the son of a Filipino woman and an African-American serviceman, who left apl's mother before his birth. He spent his early years with six siblings, speaking Tagalog, the main Philippine language, and Kapampangan, a provincial language. With features and skin color distinctly different from those of others where he lived, he was often attacked physically and verbally by other youngsters. In 1989, through a program in which Americans sponsored children in Third World countries, Joe Hudgens, a lawyer, and his wife adopted Allan, and he moved to the Hudgens's predominantly black and Hispanic Los Angeles neighborhood. "I would get chased from junior high school to my house every day," he told Benjamin Pimentel for the *San Francisco Chronicle* (August 8, 2005). "All these kids are like, 'Where you from?' And I was like, 'From Philippines.'"

Apl and will.i.am shared a passion for break dancing, and the pair spent much of their time honing their dance skills. While in high school they formed the break-dancing duo Tribal Nation. After his graduation from Palisades High School, in 1993, will.i.am attended the Fashion Institute of Design & Merchandising (which has four campuses in California) for less than one semester, dropping out to pursue a music career with apl.de.ap. Earlier, in 1991, the two had formed a music duo called Atban Klann and had begun performing at venues in Southern California. Their work impressed the rapper and producer Eazy-E, who signed them to a contract with his company, Ruthless Records, in 1992. The label's roster consisted mainly of gangsta-rap acts, and after Eazy-E died, in 1995, Ruthless promptly dropped Atban Klann, despite their having completed the recording of an album.

Not long afterward will.i.am and apl.de.ap invited the break-dancer Taboo Nawasha to join them. Taboo was born Jaime Luis Gomez on July 14, 1975 to a Mexican father and a Native American mother and grew up in the predominantly Hispanic Rosemead area of Los Angeles. He told Christina L. Esparza for the *Whittier (California) Daily News* (August 10, 2005) that young people in his neighborhood often ridiculed him for being a Latino who "danced black." "I never felt like a normal kid," he told David Watkins for the *South China Morning Post* (March 21, 2004), a Hong Kong newspaper. "I always felt outcast because I was the only Mexican in my peer group. My neighborhood was Mexican, but my friends were black. People would be, like, 'What are you doing being down with the blacks? You're Mexican. Why you dancing like that?'" In 1993 Taboo graduated with honors from Rosemead High School. Afterward he held odd jobs while break dancing with the Devine Tribal Brothers. Adopting the name Black Eyed Peas—"a name that we felt was soulful, like our music," as Taboo told Ramsay Adams—Taboo, will.i.am, and apl.de.ap got bookings in Los Angeles clubs. They combined acrobatic break dancing with clever raps, and, unlike most rap artists, who relied on DJs for their background music, they used a live band in every performance. In 1997 the Black Eyed Peas signed a deal with Interscope Records.

Almost immediately the group began working on their debut album, along with an eight-member band and Kim Hill, a specialist in Christian-themed music, who provided backup vocals. Released after hip-hop had become linked with gangsta rap, *Behind the Front* (1998) offered a blend of genres including Latin, jazz, R&B, funk, and rock. Though faulted by some as occasionally sounding tepid, "Fallin' Up," "Joints and Jams," "Clap Your

Black Eyed Peas (left to right): Taboo Nawasha, apl.de.ap, will.i.am, Fergie

Hands," "The Way You Make Me Feel," "Karma," "Love Won't Wait," "Positivity," and others among the album's tracks were applauded by music critics as welcome reminders of the freestyle rap of such artists as Run-DMC, the Fugees, and the Roots. Konrad Zeno Foster, for example, writing for the British periodical *Journal* (September 4, 1998), called the Black Eyed Peas "a breath of fresh air in the current smog of trite predictability which has polluted hip-hop over the last couple of years." "There's so much crazy stuff going on, like shootings here and there," apl.de.ap told Tamara Conniff for the Entertainment News Wire (June 23, 1999). "I think kids need to hear more of a positive outlook on life—either making a fun song or [putting] a positive message into it. That's mainly our approach." "The challenge was how to make feel-good albums with substance, but not come off like we were preaching," will.i.am told Lorraine Ali for *Newsweek* (May 16, 2005).

The Black Eyed Peas toured extensively to promote *Behind the Front*, but the album sold fewer than 200,000 copies. The band took a break from their travels to work on their next album, which was co-produced by the Fugees' Wyclef Jean. Released in 2000, *Bridging the Gap* included the single "Request Line," with vocals by Macy Gray, which reached number 31 on the *Billboard* Top 100 chart. Nevertheless, sales of *Behind the Front* totaled only about 280,000 copies. "I think it's because [the Peas] were neither fish nor fowl," Ron Fair, the president of Interscope's A&M Records division, told Michael Endelman for *Entertainment Weekly* (May 27, 2005). "They weren't the main urban type of music, but there wasn't really a pop element, either, so they would sell a couple hundred thousand and just sort of stop."

After the release of *Bridging the Gap*, Kim Hill left the group. For the next two years, personal troubles beset the Peas. Taboo and apl.de.ap battled drug addictions, the latter also grappling with the suicide of a younger brother. Will.i.am became seriously depressed after separating from his long-standing girlfriend and discovering from his mother the identity of his biological father, whose name is the same as his. Fearing that Interscope would drop them if they remained unproductive, and strongly advised by Fair to adopt a style closer to pop, the group began working on their next album. The September 11, 2001 terrorist attacks pushed them to think even more deeply about the music they were making. "I remember, we sat, the three of us, and it was like: This is it. This could be our last record—so let's go out with a bang!" will.i.am told Alexia Loundras. Taboo explained, "If this was going to be our last chance, we wanted to make an album that described who we were. We thought: Let's write songs about our relationships, the world, our anxieties—let's make the most of this."

In late 2002 the Peas recruited the vocalist Fergie, who was born Stacy Ferguson on March 27, 1975 in Hacienda Heights, a section of Los Angeles. At the age of eight, Fergie landed a steady role on the television variety show *Kids Incorporated*. In the 1980s and 1990s, she appeared on TV in shows including *Married with Children* (1994), and she provided the voice of Sally Brown in two made-for-TV *Peanuts* movies. She graduated from Glen A. Wilson High School, in Hacienda Heights, in 1993 and continued acting until four years later, when she formed the pop vocal trio Wild Orchid. The group's eponymous debut album produced several *Billboard* Top 10 hits, but the trio's next albums, *Oxygen* (1998) and *Fire* (2001), did not fare well. In 2001 Fergie left Wild Orchid, and after conquering an addiction to drugs, she began to record a solo album, with will.i.am as producer. The two suspended work on it after Fergie joined the Black Eyed Peas. The presence of a white singer on stage generated "some flak," as Fahiym Ratcliffe, the editor in chief of the hip-hop magazine the *Source*, told Elizabeth Blair for the National Public Radio program *Morning Edition* (July 1, 2005). Apl.de.ap told Blair, "You know, the whole discourse involving black music and white artists is still an ongoing thing. It's been going on since Elvis, and Fergie's just—you know, it's a microcosm of that issue." Fergie told the same interviewer, "I was going, 'OK, do these people know who I am? Do they know what I've been through?' No, they don't. And I've had to prove myself show by show."

"Where Is the Love?," a song on which the three original Peas members collaborated, was lacking a melodic hook until, one day in 2002, the group sought help from Justin Timberlake, formerly of the pop band 'N Sync. "Where Is the Love?" was the first single released from the Peas' third album, *Elephunk* (2003), and, with a hook provided by Timberlake, it became the first of the group's songs to reach the top spot on a *Billboard* chart. (It made the Top 10 on a total of five charts, and the Top 20 on two more.) Some Black Eyed Peas fans complained that by collaborating with Timberlake, the group had sold its soul, giving up its trademark underground sound for the sake of money. But will.i.am insisted that the message of "Where Is the Love?" was more important to the Peas than the kind of audience it attracted. "It's like if you have a vaccine for ignorance, you don't send it on some unknown courier," will.i.am told Chris Salmon for *Time Out* (September 24, 2003). Also on *Elephunk* was "The apl Song," which apl.de.ap had written, partly in Tagalog, as a tribute to his deceased younger brother, and "Anxiety," in which Taboo expressed his concerns about raising his son, Joshua (born in 1993), as a single father. Another single from *Elephunk*, released in 2004, was "Let's Get It Started," which on the album had different lyrics and was called "Let's Get Retarded" ("retarded" referring not to a mental handicap but to letting go of inhibitions on the dance floor). In 2005 *Elephunk* earned a Grammy Award nomination as record of the year, and "Let's Get It Started" won the Grammy for best rap performance by a duo or group. As of mid-2006 *Elephunk*'s sales had topped nine million copies worldwide.

Monkey Business (2005), the Black Eyed Peas' most recent album—which, like its predecessor, was released on Interscope's A&M label—offered dance-hall beats created with a melding of jazz, funk, pop, and hip-hop. The lyrics of one track, "Bebot," are entirely in Tagalog. *Monkey Business* debuted among the Top 10 on the *Billboard* 200 chart and, as of early 2006, had sold more than six million copies. The disk (along with Coldplay's

X&Y) won the 2006 Juno Award (a Canadian prize analogous to the Grammy Award) as international album of the year. Among its admirers was Jim Abbot, who wrote for the *Orlando (Florida) Sentinel* (June 3, 2005), "*Monkey Business* is a kaleidoscopic groove-fest that manages to be fairly ambitious without forgetting the fun." Detractors included Kalefa Sanneh, who wrote for the *New York Times* (June 6, 2005, on-line), "*Monkey Business* is a collection of Day-Glo dance tracks that struggle mightily to be eclectic and fun. . . . Some listeners might be tempted to write off the Black Eyed Peas as a hip-hop act that's too cheerful, too silly, too frothy to take seriously. But by the end of this rather heavy-handed album . . . you may discover, with a sigh, that the opposite is true. This group isn't nearly frothy enough." Headlining the 2006 Honda Civic Tour, the Black Eyed Peas traveled to three dozen cities in the U.S. to promote *Monkey Business*. They were also scheduled to perform in China and South Africa, among other places.

In addition to their work as a group, the members of the Black Eyed Peas have engaged in individual pursuits. Will.i.am produced Sergio Mendes's album *Timeless* (2006) and Fergie's solo album, *The Dutchess* (2006), and he has served as a producer for Busta Rhymes, John Legend, Nas, Ricky Martin, and other musicians as well as for the Peas. He has also made two solo albums—*Lost Change* (2001) and *Must Be 21* (2003)—and contributed to albums made by Mendes, Erykah Badu, and Carlos Santana. In early 2006 he closed a deal with Interscope to launch his own record label, and he introduced a line of expensive street apparel called i.am Clothing. In the fall of that year, will.i.am and the singer Michael Jackson announced that they would be working together on new material for Jackson's next album, scheduled to be released in 2007 on the Bahrain-based label Two Seas Records. Apl.de.ap and Taboo are also reportedly working on solo albums, to be called "Half and Half" and "Spanglish," respectively. In 2005 Taboo helped to launch a program at the Rosemead Community Center to teach children break dancing, martial arts, and in-house music production. "Every time I do a show, I hear people yelling 'Rosemead, Rosemead,'" he told a reporter for the *San Gabriel Valley Tribune*, as quoted on eurweb.com (August 11, 2005). "I was never loved in Rosemead. I was an outcast with Rosemead, but now, wow, people look at me and they say 'He did it, why can't I?'"

—I.C.

Suggested Reading: Black Eyed Peas Web site; *Entertainment Weekly* p44 May 27, 2005; *Journal* p16 Oct. 23, 1998; *Newsweek* p66 May 16, 2005; *South China Morning Post* p4 Mar. 21, 2004; *Vibe* p60 May 1998

Selected Recordings: *Behind the Front*, 1998; *Bridging the Gap*, 2000; *Elephunk*, 2003; *Monkey Business*, 2005

Blake, James

Dec. 28, 1979– Tennis player

Address: c/o USTA, 500 Mamaroneck Ave., Harrison, NY 10528

Since his debut on the professional tennis circuit, in 1999, James Blake has been touted—along with Andy Roddick, Robby Ginepri, and Taylor Dent—as being among the successors of such American male tennis greats as Pete Sampras and Andre Agassi. Despite an 8–3 record in Davis Cup play, and eight Association of Tennis Professionals singles titles, Blake, a former top-ranked college tennis player, has failed to dominate other big-name players in the Grand Slam tournament, suffering early-round losses in the United States Open to Lleyton Hewitt in 2001 and 2002 and to Roger Federer in 2003. But in 2005, following his father's death from cancer and a neck injury that threatened his tennis career, Blake earned his biggest win at a Grand Slam event with his defeat of Rafael Nadal, the second seed, to advance to the round of 16 at the United States Open. Blake built on that success during the 2006 season, again reaching the quarterfinals of the U.S. Open and having, by all accounts, his strongest overall season yet: that year he won five singles titles and achieved his highest world ranking (five) to date. The highest-ranked African-American male tennis player, Blake is aware of his status as a role model. "You know that [young people] are going to go out and pick up a racket and try to be like their favorite player," he told Patrick Hruby for the *Washington Times* (August 12, 2002), "[Being a role model] just comes with the territory. That's our job. I take it seriously."

James Riley Blake was born on December 28, 1979 in Yonkers, New York, to Thomas and Betty Blake. His father, an African-American, was a salesman for the global technology company 3M; his mother, a British-born white woman, worked as a part-time receptionist at the Tennis Club in Trumbull, Connecticut. (The two have frequently been described in the press as "avid tennis players.") Blake grew up with his older brother, Thomas Jr.; he also has two older half-brothers, Christopher and Howard, on his mother's side and a half-sister on his father's side. Blake's mother has recalled that even as a toddler, her son displayed superior hand-eye coordination. During visits to the neighborhood park, as Betty Blake recalled to Tommy Hine for the *Hartford (Connecticut) Courant* (October 12, 2001), "the older kids would give James a [tennis] ball, and he'd throw it on the roof. All the kids would stand around and watch. . . .When James got tired of throwing balls on the roof, he'd get in his stroller and we'd go home." Blake's passion for tennis began at the Harlem Tennis Center, which was housed in the 369th Regiment Armory, where Thomas and Betty Blake helped to organize minority youth leagues and oth-

er programs; there, James and Thomas Jr. would spend their free time attending clinics at the Junior Tennis Program. "We really didn't think about them becoming professionals," Thomas Blake Sr. told an interviewer for *Black Enterprise* (September 1998). "We didn't take them to the courts with the intention of grooming them to be the next Arthur Ashes or anything like that. It was just something we enjoyed and we hoped it would be something we could enjoy for the rest of our lives." Tennis, however, quickly became more than just a recreational activity for James Blake, who was inspired by the tennis legend Arthur Ashe, his father's role model, after hearing him speak at one of these clinics. "Arthur Ashe was someone I learned more and more about as I grew up. . . . I appreciate everything he did. He made it possible to overshadow a great tennis career by being a good person, a humanitarian and a social activist," he told Selena Roberts for the *New York Times* (August 18, 2002). (Ashe had the distinction of being the first African-American tennis player to compete for the Davis Cup and to win the U.S. Open.) Blake's competitive nature and sheer force of will helped to compensate for his relatively small stature. Dante Brown, the executive director of the Harlem Junior Tennis Program, said to Erica Hurtt in an on-line interview posted at the Ivy League Sports Web site, "James always had to fight to stay with Thomas. He was smaller and younger than Thomas and every time you would think he's just not there yet, he would prove you wrong." While Blake's parents were supportive of their son's tennis lessons, they continually stressed the importance of education. Blake and his brother were allowed to remain in the program only if they maintained grades of C or better.

When Blake was six years old, his family moved from Yonkers to Fairfield, Connecticut, where they became members of the Tennis Club of Trumbull, an indoor facility. Blake and his brother received instruction from Ed Pagano, the owner of the tennis club, who was impressed with Blake's strength and leaping ability as well as his stroke and returns. Pagano found teaching Blake to be a challenge. As he told Hine, "He [Blake] was a perfectionist, but he was so impatient. He wanted to do everything his older brother could, even though Thomas was 3 years older. If I changed Thomas from a two-handed backhand to a one-hander, James wanted to hit it one-handed, too. That was James. After six years of coaching him, I got older and he got stronger. I couldn't keep up with him." Blake quickly developed a reputation at the tennis club for his volatility. "I was a brat. I used to whine and cry and yell and scream and throw my racket," Blake admitted to an interviewer for *People* (July 29, 2002). When Blake was 12 years old, Pagano assigned him to work with Brian Barker, the head of the junior program at the Trumbull tennis club. (Some sources have reported that Blake was 10 at the time.) Barker quickly grew impatient with Blake's demands that Barker hit the ball to him

David Hancock/AFP/Getty Images

James Blake

harder, and he limited their practice time on the court to five minutes; he spent the remaining 25 minutes of the lesson talking with Blake on the bench.

Blake gained his first tournament experience during that time, playing in a 12-and-under match at a tennis club in New England. After he had tried out for the tournament twice and failed both times to make the draw, Betty Blake persuaded the tournament director to include her son. The director responded by placing him in the strongest section of the draw, which apparently fueled Blake's competitiveness; he narrowly defeated New England's top 12-and-under tennis player on his way to winning the entire tournament.

Although Blake fared well in the 12-and-under tournaments, he lost a number of matches in the 14-and-under and 16-and-under tennis tournaments, as a result of his small size. When Blake was 13 years old, he was diagnosed with severe scoliosis, a curvature of the spine, and decided against corrective surgery, which would have ended his tennis career. Instead, he wore a back brace for 18 hours each day until he was 18 years old, removing it only to play tennis. The brace made Blake the constant target of classmates' jokes. "I know having to wear that brace made him tougher because of the abuse he took from other kids," Barker told Chip Brown for the *Dallas Morning News* (April 3, 2002). "He's used to having to grind through things."

Blake attended Fairfield Warde High School, in Fairfield, where he was a member of the tennis team. When he was 15 he tried unsuccessfully to qualify for the nationals. On the positive side, he began to learn to control his temper. "After I worked with [Barker], I realized . . . I would be so much better if I just relax a little and realize there are so many more matches in my career and that every match isn't the end of the world, every practice isn't the end of the world. And that I really don't know everything," he told Joe Burris for the *Boston Globe* (May 28, 1999). In 1996 Blake won the United States Tennis Association's (USTA) National Boys' 16 Indoor Singles Championship. At 18 Blake, whose growth spurt during his last two years of high school had added nine inches to his five-foot-three frame, won 49 straight matches to become the USTA's top-ranked player in the 18-and-under category. He also claimed the USTA's national 18-and-under clay-court title and succeeded in reaching the final, as the number-two seed, of the U.S. National 18-and-under division in Kalamazoo, Michigan, where he was defeated by Fort Lauderdale's Rudy Rake in four sets: 6–0, 4–6, 6–4, 6–4. Blake graduated from Fairfield High School with a meet record of 80 wins and three losses over his four years as a member of the school's tennis team.

Blake, like Thomas Jr., was admitted to Harvard University, in Cambridge, Massachusetts. During his freshman year Blake joined Harvard's tennis team, on which his brother was the top-ranked singles player. Blake was asked to fill his brother's spot on the team temporarily, following a hamstring injury that left Thomas Jr. sidelined in 1998. In January 1999 Blake claimed his first title in a professional tournament, the singles title at the USTA Futures of Seminole County tournament in Altamonte Springs, Florida, which he won with a straight-set victory (6-2, 6-2) over Irakli Labadze. In February 1999 Blake won the ITA Rolex Indoor

Championships, and with his win at the Intercollegiate Tennis Association (ITA) All-America Championships, he became the first player from an Ivy League school to earn that honor. His loss to Jeff Morrison of Florida in the National Collegiate Athletic Association (NCAA) singles final kept Blake from reaching his goal of becoming the first African-American tennis player since Arthur Ashe to win an NCAA singles championship and the first men's player since Sargis Sargsian to win three ITA Grand Slam events. At the end of his sophomore year at Harvard, Blake was ranked as the top men's Division I tennis player in the nation. Blake left Harvard University and turned pro in June 1999. (His brother had done so after graduating from Harvard in 1998 with an economics degree.) Blake continued to compete in Futures events, which are part of the USTA's professional circuit. (The circuit consists of two events: Futures events, in which players earn points by reaching the round of 16, and Challenger events, in which players who have qualified for the top-level tournaments in the Association of Tennis Professionals [ATP, which governs men's professional tennis] and World Tennis Association [WTA] earn higher ranking points and even earn a ranking point with a loss. Futures events award $10,000 or $15,000 in total prize money, while Challenger events award a minimum of $25,000 and a maximum of $75,000 in total prize money.)

In June 1999 Blake claimed another singles title at the ITF Futures event in Montreal, Canada, with a three-set victory (4–6, 6–2, 7–6) over Paul Hanley. After reaching the semifinals of the Binghamton Challenger event, Blake claimed back-to-back wins at the USTA Futures events in Clearwater, Florida, and Grenelefe, Florida. In 1999 Blake also competed, with Thomas Jr., in the doubles category, winning the doubles title at the Winnetka Challenger and reaching the semifinals at the ITF Futures event in Toronto and Montreal, in Canada; the brothers also reached the quarterfinals at the USTA Futures event in Altamonte Springs. The 1999 U.S. Davis Cup team selected Blake as a practice partner for its Davis Cup Centennial Celebration against Australia, held in in Boston, Massachusetts.

In 2000 Blake competed mainly in the Challenger events on the USTA's professional circuit. He lost six straight matches at the start of the year. Blake earned his first title on the Challenger circuit with his defeat of Michel Kratochvil in the final of the Houston Challenger in Houston, Texas, where he was also the runner-up (with Kevin Kim) in doubles competition. Blake also recorded a three-set victory over Cecil Mamiit to win his second singles title at the Rancho Mirage Challenger tournament. That same year he began to compete with various doubles partners; he reached the finals with Mamiit at the Waikoloa Challenger event, in Hawaii, and with Mitty Arnold at the Futures event in Tampa, Florida. Blake also reached the doubles semifinals with Kevin Kim and Mark Merklein, at

Challenger tournaments in Las Vegas, Nevada, and Austin, Texas, respectively. At the end of the year, Blake was ranked 212th in the world; although his ranking was an improvement over his 1999 ITA rank of 262, it was still nowhere near the ATP tour's main draw range. "When I first started out, I didn't know what to do," he told Hruby. "I felt like I could serve and volley, stay back and run and play defensive, chip and charge. I could do a whole lot of different things but never decided on one."

In 2001 Blake began competing on the ATP tour, the USTA's pro circuit, and built on his previous year's success with his runner-up showing in the men's final of the Waikoloa Challenger, where he lost to fellow American Andy Roddick in three sets (1–6, 6–3, 6–1). The results were similar in his loss to Labadze at the finals of the Birmingham Challenger, a clay-court event. That year, for the first time, Blake reached the semifinals of an ATP event, in Newport, Rhode Island, before losing a four-set match to Martin Lee (6–4, 1–6, 7–6). He defeated Marcelos Rios, the former men's top tennis player, to advance to the semifinals of Tokyo's Japan Open, and made it to the third round of the Tennis Masters in Cincinnati, Ohio, past Arnaud Clement, the 10th seed, before a third-round loss to the Australian Patrick Rafter. Blake made his debut as a Davis Cup player that year, winning both of his singles matches in the world group play-off tie against India.

Blake's biggest match in 2001 was his first career Grand Slam appearance, at the U.S. Open. Blake made it to the second round of the U.S. Open, leading the Australian Lleyton Hewitt 2–1 after three sets before suffering dehydration and losing in five sets (6–4, 3–6, 2–6, 6–3, 6–0) to Hewitt, who would go on to capture the U.S. Open title that year. The match was controversial, due to remarks Hewitt made after two foot faults were called against him. (A foot fault occurs when a player places his foot or feet outside the service zone while serving.) Addressing an umpire, Hewitt indicated Blake and Marion Johnson, an African-American linesman, saying, "Look at him . . . look at him, and tell me what the similarity is"—a comment widely interpreted to mean that Johnson had favored Blake because of race, in Hewitt's view. Blake said about Hewitt's comment, as quoted by the Westchester County *Journal News* (September 1, 2001), "In the heat of battle, you say things, but I didn't necessarily appreciate it." After a locker-room tête-à-tête with Hewitt, who denied that his remarks were racially motivated, Blake told Adam Rubin for the New York *Daily News* (September 2, 2001), "I try to give people the benefit of the doubt. People have said maybe I'm naive or maybe I give people the benefit of the doubt too much. But I'd much rather be that and try to have a positive outlook on things." Blake ended the 2001 season with a first-place win against Gabriel Trifu at the Knoxville Challenger and a second-place showing against Vince Spadea at the Houston Challenger. With his 21–7 record in Challenger tournaments, Blake broke the top 100 for the first time.

In 2002 Blake recorded another milestone, beating both Andre Agassi and Paradorn Srichaphan in the semifinals and finals, respectively, to win his first ATP title, becoming the fourth African-American to win an ATP title and the first African-American to win an ATP event in Washington, D.C., since Arthur Ashe in 1973. With fellow American Todd Martin as his partner, Blake also won his first ATP title in the doubles category. Blake's Grand Slam performance results were even more impressive that year than in 2001; he managed to get past the first round of all four Grand Slam tournaments. He not only made it to the second round of the Australian Open, before losing to Stefan Koubek in five sets—he also reached the second round of the French Open before suffering a four-set loss to Sebastien Grosjean. He posted his best Grand Slam result with an appearance in the third round at the 2002 U.S. Open, where he lost to Hewitt in a five-set match for the second consecutive year. Blake reached the second round at Wimbledon, losing to Richard Krajicek of the Netherlands in a five-set match (6–3, 6–4, 3–6, 4–6, 11–9). In his second year on the U.S. Davis Cup team, Blake recorded a 5–1 record and was undefeated in doubles matches (3–0), helping the U.S. team reach the semifinals. In January 2002 he won the singles title at the Waikoloa Challenger and was runner-up to Roddick at an ATP tournament in Memphis, Tennessee, and runner-up to Taylor Dent in Newport. He also lost to Roddick during the quarterfinals of tournaments in Houston, Texas, and San Jose, California. Blake teamed up with his brother for doubles competition, reaching the quarterfinals at the Tokyo Outdoor and the semifinals at Newport. He recorded better results at the Waikoloa Challenger, where he was runner-up with his partner, Justin Gimelstob, and at Basle, where he and Roddick reached the semifinals. At the end of the 2002 season, Blake was ranked 28th in the world with 36 match wins, a career high; he had records of 22–12 on hard courts, 7–7 on clay, 5–3 on grass, 2–2 on carpet.

In the following year Blake topped his career-best Grand Slam showing at the 2002 U.S. Open by making it to the fourth round of the Australian Open (before losing to Rainer Schuettler). He followed up the Australian Open with his third appearance on the U.S. Davis Cup team and a 1–1 draw, which contributed to a first-round tie with Croatia. In February Blake advanced to the semifinals in San Jose with a victory over Agassi and reached consecutive quarterfinals in Scottsdale, Arizona, and Indian Wells, California, losing to Mariano Zabaleta and Gustavo Kuerten, respectively. He was the runner-up to Srichaphan at a tournament in Long Island, New York. In Grand Slam competition Blake reached the second rounds of the French Open and Wimbledon, and for the second straight year, he made it as far as the third round of the U.S. Open, where he defeated Zabaleta and Sargsian before losing to the top-ranked men's player, Roger Federer. He won his

second career doubles title with Mark Merklein in Scottsdale and reached the semifinals with Gimelstob in Memphis. Also for the second straight year, Blake finished the season ranked in the top 40 (37), with a career-best record of 24 wins and 14 losses on hard courts, a 5–7 record on clay, and 2–3 record on carpet; his indoor circuit record was 1–4.

In 2004 Blake made his second straight fourth-round appearance at the Australian Open, losing in four sets to Marat Safin (7–6, 6–3, 6–7, 6–3), who would go on to win the tournament. He recorded back-to-back quarterfinal victories in matches in Scottsdale and Indian Wells and also advanced to the quarterfinals in Houston before losing to Andrei Pavel. Blake won three doubles titles: two with Mardy Fish (in San Jose and Houston) and one with Merklein (in Munich, Germany). Blake's 2004 season was also plagued by injury and illness. In the spring he collided headfirst into the metal net post after chasing a drop shot during a practice session with Robby Ginepri, following the Italian Open in Rome. He suffered a broken vertebra in his neck and narrowly escaped paralysis. As he told Oprah Winfrey on the October 21, 2005 installment of the *Oprah Winfrey Show*: "Luckily, as soon as I kind of went airborne, just, I guess, out of instinct my head turned a little bit and I hit my neck instead of hitting right on top of my head. And the doctors said the force I was going at, if I had hit on top of my head, I probably wouldn't be walking anymore." Blake was sidelined for two months and was forced to miss the French Open and Wimbledon. While the injury kept Blake off the professional tennis circuit, it gave him the opportunity to spend time with his father, who had been diagnosed with stomach cancer in June 2003. "The best thing that could have happened to me was breaking my neck. I came home from Europe, and that was the last six weeks of my dad's life. I'm so thankful, in all seriousness. I'm thankful I got hurt," he told Charles Bricker for the *Lexington (Kentucky) Herald Leader* (December 23, 2004).

Within days of his father's death, on July 3, 2004, Blake suffered another setback in his recovery. He developed a case of shingles, a viral infection that caused a rash covering most of his head and temporarily numbed the left side of his face. Antibiotics prescribed by a doctor blurred his vision and affected his hearing. Still, in July, Blake, who was ranked 210, was back on the ATP Tour circuit, where he played in five matches and suffered three losses. He continued to experience blurry vision playing against Spadea during a tournament in Delray Beach, Florida, in September. After the second-round defeat, he left the tour and went home, where doctors predicted that his recovery would take a year.

In 2005 Blake played for the United States team at the Hopman Cup tournament, which he followed up with a four-set loss to Hewitt in the second round of the Australian Open and a straight-set loss to Bob and Mike Bryan in the quarterfinals with his doubles partner, Mardy Fish. He qualified for Wimbledon as a wild-card entry and suffered a first-round loss; he posted better results at the Legg Mason Classic, in Washington, D.C., advancing to the finals before losing to Roddick. Blake's first tournament win since his neck injury came in August, at the 2005 Pilot Pen tournament, which took place in New Haven, Connecticut. With his upset win against second-seeded Rafael Nadal at the U.S. Open, a tournament in which Blake was an unseeded wild-card entry, Blake reached the round of 16 for the first time, going head-to-head with Agassi in an epic five-set loss that lasted almost three hours. That match is widely considered one of the greatest ever in the history of the U.S. Open and was even nominated for a 2006 ESPY Award. In October 2005 Blake defeated Srichaphan to win the Stockholm Open, his first European title and his first ATP event since his loss to Agassi. The victory also marked Blake's 20th win in his last 23 matches in ATP events.

Blake captured his fourth career title in January 2006, when he defeated Igor Andreev of Russia in three sets (6–3, 2–6, 7–6) to win the Medibank International in Sydney, Australia. (In his two previous appearances at this event, Blake had suffered first-round losses.) The victory marked Blake's 24th win in his last 30 matches on the ATP tour, dating back to his 2005 victory at the Legg Mason Classic. The win also made Blake the ninth American and the first African-American since Arthur Ashe in 1970 to win the event. At the 2006 Australian Open tournament, Blake suffered a third-round loss against Tommy Robredo of Spain (3–6, 4–6, 4–6). Despite that defeat Blake's world ranking improved, and he cracked the top 20 for the first time. In March 2006, at the Tennis Channel Open in Las Vegas, Blake finally overcame Hewitt (7–5, 2–6, 6–3) en route to his fifth ATP Tour title. Also in March Blake upset second-ranked Rafael Nadal in the semifinals of the Pacific Life Open, a Tennis Masters Series event held in Indian Wells, California, before falling to Roger Federer in the final round (7–5, 6–3, 6–0). Simply by reaching the final, Blake boosted his ranking to nine, making him the first African-American male to reach the top 10 since Ashe. At the 2006 French Open, Blake outlasted his American counterparts but lost in the third round to the home favorite, Gael Monfils, in five sets. In the semifinals at the Stella Artois Championships in London, England, Blake defeated Roddick for the first time in his career, before losing to Hewitt in the final (6–4, 6–4). At Wimbledon Blake advanced to the third round, where he fell to Max Mirnyi in five sets. (That loss brought Blake's career record in five-set matches to a disappointing 0–9.) Blake rebounded in his next tournament, the RCA Championships, in Indianapolis, Indiana, defeating Roddick (4–6, 6–4, 7–6) in the final. With that victory, his fifth title in 11 months, Blake improved his world ATP ranking to five. At the U.S. Open in New York City, Blake matched his success from 2005, advancing to the quarterfinals, where he was defeated by the eventual champion,

Roger Federer (7–6, 6–0, 6–7, 6–4). Next, Blake made his first appearance at the Thailand Open, in Bangkok, where he won his seventh singles title, defeating Ivan Ljubicic in the final (6–3, 6–1). He then defended his Stockholm Open title and defeated Jarkko Nieminen in the final (6–4, 6–2). In the first 10 months of 2006, Blake compiled a 55–22 record in singles play and an 8–9 record in doubles matches and had earned $1,165,865 in prize money; his career earnings amount to nearly $3.5 million. He is currently ninth in the world in ATP rankings. His five ATP titles in 2006 placed him in a tie, with Nadal, for second place; the first-place Federer had nine titles.

Blake has kept up his connection to the Harlem Tennis Center, where he teaches tennis clinics along with his older brother, Thomas. He raised money for a girls' inner-city basketball team in New Haven by shaving his trademark dreadlocks and selling them for $2,300 at auction; he also donated $10,000 to Shriners Hospital, the Springfield, Missouri-based facility where he received treatment for his facial condition. Blake signed with IMG Models in 2002; he has been featured in *People* as the magazine's Sexiest Man Alive (2002) and appeared in a 10-page pictorial in *GQ Magazine* (2003). Blake lives in Fairfield, not far from his childhood home.

—B.M.

Suggested Reading: *Boston Globe* E p1 May 28, 1999; *Los Angeles Times* D p1 Mar. 10, 2005; *New York Times* D p7 Jan. 17, 2005, p18 Aug. 28, 2005; *Hartford (Connecticut) Courant* C p1 Oct. 12, 2001; USTA.com

---

Boehner, John

(BAY-ner)

Nov. 17, 1949– U.S. representative from Ohio (Republican)

Address: 1011 Longworth House Office Bldg., Washington, DC 20515

On February 2, 2006 John A. Boehner, a U.S. representative from Ohio, was elected House majority leader by his Republican colleagues. Boehner succeeded Roy Blunt of Missouri, a temporary replacement for Congressman Tom DeLay of Texas, who had resigned the post in September 2005 after being indicted in his home state on charges of illegal campaign financing. As majority leader, Boehner has faced, among other challenges, that of addressing mounting public concern over the influence of Washington, D.C.'s powerful and deep-pocketed lobbyist community—commonly referred to as K Street—on policy making and other activities by members of the U.S. House and Senate. Having assumed the post of majority leader in

Alex Wong/Getty Images

John Boehner

a congressional-election year, Boehner was also charged with trying to maintain the GOP's majority in the House, where Republicans held a 232–202 edge over Democrats. His efforts fell short, as Democrats regained control of the House in the balloting of November 7, 2006.

Boehner is known among members of Congress as a serious, pro-business lawmaker and as one of the few senior Republicans who can work well with Democrats. Early in his career as the representative from Ohio's traditionally conservative Eighth District, which began in 1991, he was identified as a close ally of Congressman Newt Gingrich of Georgia, who was Speaker of the House from 1995 until 1999. Prominent in rallying support for Gingrich's so-called Contract with America, he advanced quickly in the House hierarchy; in January 1994 he became that body's fourth-ranking Republican, after his election as chairman of the Republican Conference. He lost that position in 1998. In January 2001 Boehner became the chair of the House Committee on Education and the Workforce. According to various observers, his greatest achievement to date as a legislator came in 2002, when he helped shepherd through Congress President George W. Bush's No Child Left Behind Act, the goal of which is to ensure that all schoolchildren become proficient in math and reading (to the extent expected of them in each grade) by 2014.

Among the oldest of the 12 children of Earl Henry Boehner and Mary Ann (Hall) Boehner, John Andrew Boehner was born on November 17, 1949 in Cincinnati, Ohio. His father owned a local tavern. Boehner was raised in Cincinnati in the Roman Catholic faith. He attended Archbishop Moeller High School, an all-male Catholic school, where he

was a linebacker and long snapper on the football team. Despite a back injury that forced him to wear a brace on the gridiron, he was "a leader from day one" and "played with intensity," as his coach, Gerry Faust (later the head football coach at Notre Dame University), told Jonathan Riskind for the *Columbus (Ohio) Dispatch* (December 14, 1995). Faust told Mei-Ling Hopgood for the *Dayton (Ohio) Daily News* (May 13, 2001) that Boehner "had a great desire to win, and was concerned about the team first before himself."

After he graduated from high school, in 1968, Boehner began taking night classes at Xavier University, a Jesuit institution in Cincinnati. To pay for his tuition, he held various day jobs. In 1969 he enlisted in the U.S. Navy, because, as he told Weston Kosova for the *New Republic* (February 20, 1995), the U.S. was at war in Vietnam, and, although he "didn't know enough about the intricacies of why we were there, . . . I wanted us to win. The people with the long hair who were protesting against the war I thought were un-American." Within a few weeks of his joining the military, his back problem flared up, and he was discharged. He then reenrolled at Xavier, earning a bachelor's degree in business in 1977. (He is the only college graduate among his siblings.) For several years during his time as an undergraduate, he worked for Merrell Dow Pharmaceuticals as a management trainee. In 1976 he was hired by Nucite Sales, which represented manufacturers of plastics and packaging materials. After a series of promotions, Boehner was named president of the company; he later became a part owner. He left Nucite in 1990. According to the *Cincinnati Post* (June 16, 2005), Nucite accounts for most of Boehner's current assets. Specifically, in 2005 his interests in the Nucite Sales Pension Plan Trust and the Nucite Sales Profit Sharing Trust totaled between $1 million and $2 million.

Earlier, in 1978, "when I paid more in taxes than I had earned gross in 1976," as he told Kosova, Boehner switched his allegiance from the Democratic Party to the GOP. "I was frustrated with government," he explained to Riskind, "and I realized it wasn't going to change until real people from the real world decided to take a more active interest in politics." At that time Boehner, who had married in 1973 and had become a father, was serving as the president of a homeowners' association. His appetite for elective office grew when he attended meetings of the local school board and of the Union (now West Chester) Township board of trustees. He successfully ran for election as a township trustee and served from 1982 to 1984.

In 1984 Boehner was elected to the Ohio state House as a representative from West Chester. During his third term, in 1990, he made a bid for the seat in the U.S. House held by Donald E. "Buz" Lukens, a Republican, who was seeking reelection despite having been found guilty of a misdemeanor after having sex with a minor. Others opposing Lukens in the Republican primary included Thomas N. Kindness, a former six-term House member. In his advertisements Boehner cast himself as a responsible business owner while characterizing Kindness, the front runner, as a dishonest lobbyist. In the primary election Boehner, who reportedly spent five times as much as Kindness on the campaign, won by more than 17 percentage points. In the general election, which pitted him against Gregory V. Jolivette, a former Hamilton, Ohio, mayor, Boehner earned 61 percent of the 163,000 votes cast. He has since easily won reelection to the House, with 71 percent of the vote in 1992 (against the Democrat Fred Sennett), 70 percent in 1996 (against Jeffrey Kitchen), 71 percent in 1998 (against John Griffin), 71 percent in 2000 (against John Parks), 72 percent in 2002 (against Jeff Hardenbrook), and 69 percent in 2004 (against Hardenbrook). He ran unopposed in 1994.

In the 102d Congress (January 1991–January 1993), which coincided with the last two years of the administration of President George Herbert Walker Bush, a Republican, Boehner joined other freshman Republicans to form the so-called Gang of Seven. The group's self-proclaimed mission was to root out congressional corruption. Toward that end, they denounced the behavior of members of Congress who—without penalties of any kind— had overdrawn their accounts in a bank maintained by the House (by more than $500,000, in the case of one congressman). The scandal (sometimes referred to as "Rubbergate") involved more than 300 representatives and revealed extensive flaws in the rules governing the House bank. In October 1991, amid mounting public pressure, the House bank was closed.

In what became known as the Republican Revolution of 1994, Republicans gained 54 seats in the House in that year's elections, giving the GOP its first majority in that body since the 83d Congress (1953–55). Representative Newt Gingrich was named Speaker of the House. Boehner, who had become one of Gingrich's's most trusted freshman lieutenants, was elected chairman of the Republican Conference by Republican congressmen in late 1994 and thus became the fourth-ranking member of the House Republican leadership. The conference (consisting of all Republican congressmen) meets weekly to discuss party policies and legislative issues. As conference chairman Boehner had frequent contact with rank-and-file party members and the media. Early in the 104th Congress, at Gingrich's behest, Boehner worked diligently to champion among lawmakers and members of the media the Contract with America, which had been written a few weeks before the November 1994 election, with much of it taken verbatim from President Ronald Reagan's 1985 State of the Union Address. The contract (referred to by some of its opponents as the Contract *on* America) was presented as the Republicans' promise to the American people to pass, within 100 days of Congress's opening day in 1995, legislation aimed at shrinking the federal government, lowering taxes, limiting the role of the

United Nations in U.S. foreign policy, and reforming welfare, among other provisions. A tireless spokesman for the contract, Boehner became "easily the most-quoted member of the House GOP leadership," according to *Politics in America 1998*, and he helped Gingrich to maintain control over the GOP's message and strategies. As reported in *Time* (January 23, 2006) and other sources, Boehner held weekly meetings with a dozen of the business community's most influential lobbyists. In the waning months of the 104th Congress, he was roundly criticized when he distributed campaign donations from tobacco lobbyists to Republican congressmen on the House floor.

In late 1995 and early 1996, when budget negotiations between then–President Bill Clinton and the Republican-controlled Congress stalled and partial government shutdowns ensued, Boehner's popularity among his Republican colleagues endured a blow—even though he had been following orders from Gingrich—largely because of the disgust and dismay expressed by laypeople, many of whom blamed congressional Republicans for the impasse. *Politics in America 2000* reported that in the wake of the budget turmoil, Gingrich relieved Boehner of his duties as the party's principal spokesperson, but he restored Boehner to that position later in 1996, to help rally support for GOP-sponsored legislation involving education, taxes, and the restructuring of the Internal Revenue Service.

In late 1996 Boehner's Republican colleagues reelected him GOP conference chair. At that time Gingrich was steeped in controversy, stemming from his having accepted a $4.5 million advance to write a book. In late December 1996, while vacationing in Florida, Boehner participated in a conference call, made on his cellular phone, in which Gingrich and other high-ranking house Republicans also took part, on the subject of the House Ethics Committee's investigation of Gingrich's advance. Unbeknownst to the callers, two registered Florida Democrats, John and Alice Martin, intercepted and taped the call; they then gave the tape to Congressman Jim McDermott of Washington State, the ranking Democrat on the House Ethics Committee, and to several news outlets, among them the *New York Times*. In late April 1997 the Martins were fined $500 each after pleading guilty to federal charges that they had intercepted a cellular phone conversation. For his part, Boehner called upon Attorney General Janet Reno to investigate the matter further; he also filed a civil suit, on March 9, 1998, seeking punitive damages against McDermott. Eight years later the suit, which is the first ever to be brought by one sitting congressman against another, had neither come to trial nor been settled out of court.

A few days after the November 1998 elections, in which Republicans lost five seats in the House (thus decreasing the party's majority to six seats), Gingrich announced that he would not seek reelection as Speaker and would leave Congress altogether the following January, despite his election to an 11th term. Boehner soon felt the effects of Gingrich's resignation: he was unseated as Republican Conference chairman by J. C. Watts of Oklahoma in a vote that some interpreted as signaling a call for change by House Republicans. "I'm sure it was an unpleasant experience to lose the leadership election in 1998," Rob Andrews, a Democratic congressman from New Jersey, told Mei-Ling Hopgood. "But losers never get over the loss; they just throw in the towel." Referring to Boehner, Andrew added, "Winners refocus their energies and figure out how to pursue goals on another path." Congressman Michael G. Oxley, an Ohio Republican, expressed a similar view. "It was a bitter pill," he said to Jessica Wehrman for the *Dayton Daily News* (January 15, 2006). "A lot of members would have folded tent, attended to their own districts and maybe retired. It's rare to take that kind of defeat and turn it into a positive direction." "I think at the time I didn't take my loss personally," Boehner told Wehrman. "I kept my chin up, went to work, went back to my committee assignments and devoted my efforts to being a legislator, you know, the reason I really came to Congress."

In January 2001 Boehner's Republican colleagues selected him to chair the House Committee on Education and the Workforce. In that capacity he helped push through Congress the No Child Left Behind Law, which President George W. Bush signed on January 8, 2002. "This is [the] biggest challenge I've had since I've been in Congress," Boehner said to Mei-Ling Hopgood. "Because I'm a new chairman. Because we've got a new president and this is his number one issue and because some of my colleagues on both sides of the aisle might have seen this as an opportunity to undermine me." By means of yearly tests, the No Child Left Behind Law makes public schools accountable for the performances in math and reading of students in the third through eighth grades and enables children in failing public schools to transfer to more successful public or charter institutions. Education officials in many states complained that the law interfered with their own school-accountability systems and that the federal government had not given the states enough money to fulfill the law's requirements. Some of those states (among them Michigan, Vermont, Texas, and Connecticut) have sued the federal government on those grounds, as has the National Education Association (NEA) and NEA affiliates in a dozen states.

In June 2005 Boehner and two other congressmen introduced legislation to reform pension laws in the U.S. The move came a few weeks after a federal court approved United Airlines' decision to terminate its employee pension plans, as a way of avoiding bankruptcy—which forced the federal Pension Benefit Guaranty Corp. (an institution that was already deep in debt) to assume billions of dollars' worth of United's pension obligations. According to information on the Web site of the House Education and Workforce Committee, the measure introduced by the congressmen was designed to strengthen workers' retirement security and protect taxpayers by "fixing outdated worker pension laws." At the end of 2005, the House and the Senate approved conflicting versions of the legislation (the Senate but not the House bill extended certain tax cuts). In the summer of 2006, after months of negotiations, Senate Majority Leader Bill Frist removed the conflicting clauses; the resulting legislation was signed into law by President Bush that August.

On January 8, 2006 Boehner announced his intention to seek the position of House majority leader, the second-ranking position within the House leadership. Two of his colleagues also sought the post. One was Missouri congressman Roy Blunt, who was serving as the majority leader as a temporary replacement for Congressman Tom DeLay of Texas, who had resigned as majority leader in September 2005 after being indicted on charges of illegal campaign financing. The other candidate was John Shadegg of Arizona. Each of the three vigorously solicited the support of their Republican colleagues, all of whom were under a cloud in the wake of revelations of activities by Republicans that were unquestionably unlawful or highly improper. In November 2005, for example, Representative Randy Cunningham, a Republican from San Diego, California, had resigned from Congress after admitting that he had taken more than $2.4 million in bribes. On another front, several Republican legislators had become implicated in illegal ventures undertaken by the Republican lobbyist Jack Abramoff, who in early January had agreed to a plea bargain after being charged with mail fraud, conspiracy, tax evasion, and fraudulent dealings with politicians, and who seemed ready to accuse some members of Congress of corrupt practices. Commenting on the contest for House majority leader, Carl Hulse wrote for the *New York Times* (January 30, 2006, on-line), "In light of the Abramoff scandal, [Cunningham's] admission of bribery, and inquiries into the conduct of other lawmakers and former aides, an internal fight that would typically turn on legislative skills, fundraising power and political savvy has centered on whether the contenders can help dispel an impression that Republicans are too cozy with special interests." After a secret-ballot vote in which Blunt received 110 votes, seven short of the required 117 needed to win, Shadegg dropped out of the race. Republican House members then elected Boehner majority leader by a vote of 122 to 109.

A week after his election, Boehner told Chris Wallace, host of the Fox News Channel program *Fox News Sunday* (February 6, 2006, on-line), that he preferred to reform the lobbying industry by insisting on greater transparency rather than on instituting various prohibitions. "I believe that disclosure of the relationship between those who lobby us, whether they be paid lobbyists here in Washington, those from agencies, or others—disclosure of those relationships—and let the American people take a look at how this relationship works," he said. "Sunlight's the best disinfectant. I think it will help." Boehner also talked to Wallace about legislative earmarking, a tactic through which members of Congress insert into major budget bills provisions allocating federal funds for particular projects requested by their constituents—projects that may be peripheral or entirely unconnected to purposes of the bills and that completely escape congressional or any other scrutiny as to their necessity or value. In 2005, for example, a federal highway bill contained appropriations for more than 6,000 local projects. The bill called for $223 million to be spent on the construction of a bridge "nearly as long as the Golden Gate and higher than the Brooklyn Bridge," as Nick Jans wrote for *USA Today* (May 17, 2005, on-line), to connect the town of Ketchikan, in Alaska, whose population is less than 9,000, with a tiny airport on a neighboring island; in addition, a total of $498 million would go toward similar projects in the same state. The "ultimate beneficiaries" of that money, according to Jans, included private companies and Don Young, Alaska's sole congressman, who—thanks in large measure to such successful earmarking—virtually ensured his reelection. "I've never called for an outright ban on earmarks," Boehner told Wallace. "I've never asked for one in the 15 years that I've been in Congress. I told my constituents in 1990 that if they thought my job was to go to Washington and rob the federal treasury on their behalf, they're voting for the wrong guy. . . . But I don't think I want to hold all my colleagues to the same standard. There's an appropriate place for some of these earmarks, but we need less numbers of earmarks and more transparency and more accountability. Members' names ought to be associated with them. . . . And members ought to have a chance to see these before they become law."

Boehner's months as majority leader coincided with growing difficulties for the Republican Party. Uncertainty among Americans about the course of the war in Iraq and publicity surrounding the Abramoff and other scandals involving Republicans weakened Republicans' standings in polls and threatened to cost them control of Congress in the November 2006 elections. In one highly embarrassing incident, the Republican congressman Mark Foley of Florida resigned after the public learned that he had engaged in sexually explicit Internet conversations with underage congressional pages. After the Speaker of the House, Dennis Hastert, came under fire for allegedly attempting to cover up the scandal, Boehner said, as quoted by the *Dayton (Ohio) Daily News* (October 4, 2006), that he was "99 percent sure" that he had told Hastert before Foley's resignation about the latter's inappropriate and possibly illegal behavior. "I think I did what I should have done," Boehner told Malia Rulon, a reporter for the Gannett News Service (October 6, 2006). "Hindsight is 20-20. I didn't know the content of the instant messages. No one knew. If I had known, we would have thrown him out."

Despite his party's troubles, most of Boehner's colleagues professed to be satisfied with his work as majority leader. He acquired a reputation for being inclusive in discussions within the party. "Based on both style and performance, Boehner has secured his position in the next Congress," Republican representative Patrick McHenry of North Carolina told Susan Davis for *Roll Call* (September 28, 2006). Another Republican congressman, Tom Feeney of Florida, told Davis, "John inherited the environment we've got today, he didn't cause it. If things go poorly, he'll get none of the blame, and if things go well, he'll get a great deal of credit." In the elections of November 7, 2006, Democrats gained a majority of seats in the House, ending Boehner's tenure as majority leader as of early 2007. (Boehner himself defeated his challenger, the Democrat Morton Meier, with 64 percent of the vote.) Boehner was expected to retain a leadership position among House Republicans, however, particularly given reports that Hastert would likely step down as party leader.

Boehner sparked controversy when, several days after the fifth anniversary of the September 11 terrorist attacks on the United States, he responded to criticism of interrogation methods sanctioned by the Bush administration by saying, as quoted by Patrick O'Connor in the *Hill* (September 13, 2006), "I listen to my Democrat[ic] friends, and I wonder if they are more interested in protecting the terrorists than protecting the American people." The chairman of the Democratic Congressional Campaign Committee, Rahm Emanuel, countered by saying, according to O'Connor, "I wonder if John Boehner is more interested in protecting his majority than protecting the American people. . . . Instead of coming up with new ways to scare Americans into voting Republican, George Bush and John Boehner ought to be doing what needs to be done to secure our country."

Throughout his career in Washington, Boehner has been a diligent fund-raiser for the Republican Party. According to the nonpartisan group Center for Responsive Politics, during the 2004 campaign season, Boehner's political action committee (PAC), the Freedom Project, which he founded in 1995 and currently serves as chairman, raised some $1.5 million for Republican coffers—far more than most other Republican PACs. He has also maintained close ties with powerful lobbies. According to the independent news Web site alternet.org, "Boehner got $32,500 in campaign contributions from Abramoff and his clients, more than DeLay hauled in." *USA Today* (January 25, 2006) reported that since 2000 Boehner "has taken $157,000 worth of 'fact-finding' trips, many to resorts and European capitals, paid for by special interests and non-profit groups—the 9th highest ranking in Congress." Boehner has also reportedly forged a close relationship with Sallie Mae, the nation's largest student-loan provider, which severed its links with the federal government during a seven-year period that ended in 2004. In 2003–04, according to Federal Election Commission records, as Stephen Burd reported for the *Chronicle of Higher Eduction* (January 13, 2006, on-line), while Boehner was helping to draft legislation to reauthorize the Higher Education Act, part of which governs federal student-aid mechanisms, Sallie Mae contributed more than $100,000 to Boehner's PAC. (On February 6, 2006 President Bush proposed a $2.77 trillion federal budget for the fiscal year 2007, which began on October 1, 2006, that called for increases in interest payments for some federal student loans.) After Sheryl Gay Stohlberg, writing for the *New York Times* (February 3, 2006, on-line), characterized Boehner as "cozy with lobbyists," she quoted Congressman Michael G. Oxley as saying to her, "He is, and he doesn't make any bones about it. He's not a phony like some of my colleagues. He has an up-front relationship with these guys. He's a very pro-business, pro-free enterprise kind of guy, and he makes no apologies for it."

After he became majority leader, Boehner's fund-raising efforts came under closer scrutiny. According to an article in the *Cleveland Scene* (June 21, 2006), Boehner received $32,500 in campaign contributions from Jack Abramoff. An editorial in the *New York Times* (July 20, 2006) declared that Boehner's "fund-raising pace with powerful special-interest groups . . . already is challenging the achievements of his predecessor, Tom DeLay." "Mr. DeLay made the symbiosis of lobbyist and lawmaker an unabashed money machine that scandalized Congress," the editorial continued. "Mr. Boehner took over with vows to reform Congress. But he's busier beating Mr. DeLay's game at extracting contributions from power [sic] lobbyists and their corporate clients. He's averaged $10,000 a day since February, according to an article in The Times by Mike McIntire, with banks, health insurers and drug, oil and cigarette corporations among the biggest donors. As for golf junkets and other 'educational' freebies, Mr. DeLay scored 18 trips financed by private interests since 2000; Mr. Boehner has racked up 39 in that time. . . . It's all too clear that nothing serious can come of the vows of Mr. Boehner and other Congressional leaders to rein in ethical lapses so long as members remain addicted to lobbyist-generated campaign money."

Boehner is "easygoing and well liked, with a perpetual tan, a low golf handicap and an ever-present Barclay cigarette between his fingers," Stohlberg wrote. According to *Time* (January 23, 2006) and various other sources, he enjoys late-night carousing with colleagues and friends. Boehner told Wallace, "I'm an ordinary guy with a big job. And while I take my work very serious, I don't take myself very serious. And I don't allow my staff to call me Congressman or Mr. Leader. They call me John, or most of them just refer to me as hey, Boehner." "I'm just open," he added. "You know, what you see is what you get. I've got a very good relationship with the media, with my colleagues, frankly, the people downtown, and my constituents, be-

cause this is the way I am." Boehner and his wife, the former Deborah Gunlack, live in West Chester, Ohio, and have two daughters, Lindsay and Tricia.

—D.F.

Suggested Reading: *Columbus (Ohio) Dispatch* D p8 Dec. 14, 1995; *CQ Weekly* p336+ Feb. 6, 2006; *Dayton (Ohio) Daily News* A p1 May 13, 2001; johnboehner.house.gov; *New Republic* p22+ Feb. 20, 1995; *New York Times* (on-line) Feb. 3, 2006; *Politics in America*, 1993, 1999

Alex Wong/Getty Images

Bolten, Joshua

Aug. 16, 1954– White House chief of staff

Address: The White House, 1600 Pennsylvania Ave. N.W., Washington, DC 20500

On March 28, 2006 Joshua Bolten was appointed as chief of staff to President George W. Bush. The position entails many duties, including managing the president's schedule, deciding which policy recommendations the president should address, and generally overseeing activity in the West Wing of the White House, the main office of the executive branch of government. Bolten's predecessor, Andrew H. Card Jr., had been the longest-serving chief of staff in half a century; prior to his departure, many political observers had seen personnel changes in the White House as being overdue, as most of Bush's staff, including Card, had been on board since the president took office, in early 2001. Bolten's appointment came at a time when the president's approval ratings were at record lows and his administration's relations with Republicans on Capitol Hill were deteriorating. Previous presidents had restructured their staffs in response to low approval ratings—notably Ronald Reagan, who in 1987 hired a large number of new staff members to fill key positions, including a U.S. senator from Tennessee, Howard Baker, as chief of staff. Bush, his supporters believed, might benefit from a similar overhaul. But while the top presidential aide Karl Rove and others predicted that Bolten's appointment would help the troubled administration regain its footing, with Rove telling Peter Baker for the *Washington Post* (March 29, 2006) that Bolten would "challenge [aides] to think outside the box," many—including some prominent Republicans—doubted that Bolten, himself a member of Bush's team from its inception, could supply the new perspective the White House needed. Democrats argued that the appointment would do little to alter the administration's course.

Bolten served as director of policy for Bush's 2000 presidential run, helping to shape many of the positions that the candidate articulated on the campaign trail. As deputy White House chief of staff, from 2001 to 2003, he worked to put such policies—including those concerning health care and education reform—into practice. Beginning in 2003 he served as director of the Office of Management and Budget (OMB). Regarding his relatively low public profile prior to his appointment as chief of staff, he said, as quoted by Baker, "It's best that you keep yourself out of the equation, and in that way make sure that others have confidence that you're not running your own agenda—you're just running the president's agenda, which was my objective. Still is." Bolten has been described as hardworking and as demanding but likable. Assistant Secretary of State Kristen Silverberg, who worked with Bolten during Bush's first term, described him as being both "very funny" and passionate about developing innovative policies. "If you had to pick one person who was the architect of all the big first-term domestic policy initiatives," it would be Bolten, she told Baker. No one who knew Bolten, it seemed, was surprised by his rise to prominence. "I can only think of one person who could rival Andy Card in terms of being as cool-tempered, and that would be Josh," Jerry Cox, a classmate of Bolten's at Princeton University, told Angela Cai for the *Daily Princetonian*, as printed in University Wire (March 29, 2006). Such testimonials revealed precisely why many believed that Bolten would not bring anything new to the table: in important ways, they felt, Bolten was much like his predecessor. "What is not clear is how much change Bolten will feel is needed to convince a wary Congress and the public that the administration is turning a new page," Deb Reichmann wrote for the Associated Press Online (April 2, 2006).

Joshua Brewster Bolten was born on August 16, 1954 in Washington, D.C. His father was a covert CIA operative. (As a child Bolten reportedly had to tell friends that his father worked at the Pentagon rather than the CIA.) He attended public schools before enrolling at St. Albans, a prestigious, all-boys prep school in Washington (which was also attended by the former vice president and 2000 Democratic presidential nominee, Al Gore). Bolten then attended Princeton University, in New Jersey, where he served as class president and president of the Ivy Club, the university's storied dining and social club. One of his college friends, Peter Segall, told Cai that Bolten "was very well-liked, less perceived as a politico and more thought of as somebody who has the class' interest at heart, a doer rather than a talker." Segall added that Bolten "got things done quietly, by building relationships and quiet persuasion." In 1976 Bolten received a B.A. degree with distinction from the university's Woodrow Wilson School of Public and International Affairs. He then attended law school at Stanford University, in California, where he served as editor of the *Stanford Law Review* and earned a J.D. degree in 1980.

Bolten's brother Randall said about Joshua, as quoted by Cai, "I don't know if he always had specific aspirations to work in the government, but policy has always fascinated him." Upon graduating from law school, Bolten worked as a clerk for U.S. District Judge Thelton Henderson in San Francisco, California, before serving in the legal office of the State Department and as executive assistant to the director of the Kissinger Commission on Central America. (The National Bipartisan Commission on Central America, led by former secretary of state Henry Kissinger, was a panel established in 1983, made up of 12 members from both major political parties, who studied Central America with the goal of developing long-term policy for the region. The commission unanimously agreed that Soviet- and Cuban-backed insurgencies posed a threat to the region's security. In early 1984 they released their findings and recommended an $8.4 billion U.S. economic aid program and "significantly increased" military assistance for the region, with assistance contingent on observance of human rights and support for democratic processes in local governments.) Bolten was international trade counsel to the Senate Finance Committee from 1985 to 1989. In the latter year he joined the administration of President George H. W. Bush, in which he served for four years—three as general counsel for the U.S. trade representative, and one as deputy assistant to the president for legislative affairs.

After the first President Bush left office, in early 1993, Bolten taught international trade at Yale University Law School for a semester before taking a high-paying position in private industry, as executive director of legal and governmental affairs at the London, England, office of the investment firm Goldman Sachs. (Jon Corzine, a future Democratic governor of New Jersey, was then the company's chairman.) After five years with Goldman Sachs, Bolten turned down an offer to serve as Corzine's aide there and instead joined the presidential campaign of Texas governor George W. Bush, for which he served as policy director from March 1999 to November 2000. "I fell in love with the governor and the whole operation, the whole spirit of the operation," Bolten said in a 2005 interview with the cable channel C-SPAN, as Peter Baker reported. According to Cai, Bolten said that when he was introduced to Bush, during Christmas of 1998, "I found him to be sharp and energetic and charismatic and with a tremendous philosophical compass. . . . Then a bunch of his friends came over for dinner, and he took us all to a [University of Texas] basketball game. So I knew he was my kind of guy." Bolten introduced Bush to several advisers who would become senior Bush administration officials—including Condoleezza Rice, who was to serve as national security adviser before becoming secretary of state, and future deputy defense secretary Paul Wolfowitz.

After Bush won the 2000 presidential election, Bolten became deputy White House chief of staff. In that capacity he played a significant role in the implementation of the No Child Left Behind Act, aimed at improving public schools through methods that include standardizing tests and allowing parents the choice of moving their children out of underperforming schools. Bolten also led the push for a $15 billion plan to battle AIDS worldwide. He was responsible for coordinating the administration's policy initiatives in such diverse areas as antiterrorism and health care, drafting legislation, for example, on the proposed Patients' Bill of Rights. During Bush's first term Bolten demonstrated the loyalty to the president that would later lead many to question his potential to bring change to the administration as chief of staff. "Bolten operates with two guiding principles: absolute loyalty to the boss and absolutely no attention to himself," Richard S. Dunham wrote for *BusinessWeek Online* (December 3, 2001). After the terrorist attacks of September 11, 2001, Bush appointed Bolten chairman of the Domestic Consequences Principals Committee, a body created to ensure that policy responses to terrorist acts were developed swiftly. In 2003 the president named Bolten director of the Office of Management and Budget. In that position Bolten created budget policies for U.S. military operations in Iraq and Afghanistan, for Medicare, and for the government's response to the flooding and devastation caused by Hurricane Katrina in 2005. He managed the budget at an especially difficult time—Medicare and military expenses, in particular, contributed to the largest national deficits in U.S. history. (Bolten, like Bush, is known as a proponent of tax cuts, another factor in the growth of the deficit.)

On March 28, 2006, in announcing Bolten's appointment as chief of staff, Bush described him as "a man with broad experience," "a creative policy thinker," and "a man of candor and humor and directness, who is comfortable with responsibility and knows how to lead." Bolten thanked the president and the departing chief of staff, Andrew Card,

saying, "You've set a clear course to protect our people at home, to promote freedom abroad and to expand our prosperity. I'm anxious to get to work." Peter Baker wrote, "Bolten will take over a political operation gone astray—mired in an overseas war, stalled in its domestic agenda, sagging in the polls and alienated from congressional Republican allies." Indeed, the Bush administration has come under fire for what critics see as its insularity and flawed judgment. As of mid-May 2006, the president's approval rating had sunk to 29 percent, owing to factors including the slow federal response to Hurricane Katrina; Bush's nomination of Harriet Miers for a seat on the Supreme Court (she stepped aside after being widely criticized as unqualified); the thwarted plan to turn over some U.S. port operations to Dubai Ports World, a company based in the United Arab Emirates; and the U.S.-led war in Iraq, launched in 2003 ostensibly to rid that nation of so-called weapons of mass destruction, which never materialized. Since Bolten assumed his new post, he has been involved in the hiring of a number of new administration officials, with Henry Paulson becoming treasury secretary, Tony Snow joining the White House as press secretary, and Michael Hayden stepping in as director of the CIA—changes aimed at reinvigorating the administration. Also, in an effort to improve Republicans' chances of victory in the 2006 mid-term elections, Bolten relieved Bush's chief political adviser, Karl Rove, of managing day-to-day policies and assigned him instead to focus on the party's politics and overall message. In examining Bolten's performance as chief of staff thus far, Sheryl Gay Stolberg, writing for the *New York Times* (June 19, 2006), identified the Republicans' retention of control of Congress as Bolten's "real challenge" and quoted a conservative advocacy group leader, Grover Norquist, as saying, "If he does that, everyone will be extremely pleased. If he doesn't, then it doesn't really matter what other decisions he makes." In the elections of November 7, 2006, Democrats regained control of the House of Representatives and the Senate.

Though much has been written about Bolten's shunning of the spotlight, some of his more unusual personal traits have been well publicized since his appointment as chief of staff. Peter Baker wrote that Bolten "shows up at policy meetings with a giant calculator to add up the cost of anyone's ambitious ideas. And when someone strays off course, he throws a yellow penalty flag onto the conference table like a football referee." Bolten owns several motorcycles, one of which he keeps at the Bush ranch, in Crawford, Texas. In a 2005 interview with Brian Lamb for C-SPAN, according to Cai, Bolten said that he finds motorcycle riding to be "a form of relaxation and diversion that's beautiful and exhilarating." (His preferred model is the 2003 anniversary edition Harley-Davidson Fat Boy.) Bolten also plays the electric guitar. The new chief of staff, who, as his brother Randall told Cai, has "always been a very good guitarist," plays in a rock group called Deficit Attention Disorder (a name inspired in part by the budget troubles Bolten faced as OMB director). Only the second Jewish presidential chief of staff in U.S. history (the first was Kenneth M. Duberstein, chief of staff for President Reagan), Bolten has reportedly been nicknamed "Bad Mitzvah" by Karl Rove, and President Bush calls him "Yosh." Bolten is single.

—M.B.

Suggested Reading: *Financial Times* p17 Mar. 30, 2006; *New York Times* A p15 June 19, 2006; *Slate.com* Mar. 28, 2006; University Wire Mar. 29, 2006; *Washington Post* A p4 Mar. 29, 2006

Mark Wilson/Getty Images

Bolton, John R.

Nov. 20, 1948– U.S. ambassador to the United Nations

Address: United Nations, 79 United Nations Plaza, 11th Fl., New York, NY 10017

When President George W. Bush nominated John R. Bolton to the position of American ambassador to the U.N., on March 7, 2005, most political observers predicted that Bolton's controversial attitudes toward the U.N. would provoke heated exchanges during the hearings of the U.S. Senate's Foreign Relations Committee but that eventually Bolton would receive Senate confirmation. The hearings turned out to be even more bitter than predicted. While Bolton's admirers hailed him as a dedicated and clear-headed reformer, unafraid to challenge a U.N. bureaucracy that is corrupt, prof-

ligate, and reflexively hostile to the U.S.—the country that provides the organization with its single largest annual financial contribution—detractors called him a rude, reckless ideologue, an enemy rather than a reformer of the U.N., and a neoconservative determined to throw over decades' worth of international agreements in a short-sighted display of American power. Former employees and co-workers of his came forward to accuse Bolton of being vindictive and throwing temper tantrums, while his most recent supervisor, former secretary of state Colin L. Powell, reportedly conducted a behind-the-scenes campaign against the confirmation of Bolton, who had been only a few rungs lower than Powell on the Department of State ladder. With the controversy threatening to delay Bolton's appointment indefinitely, or possibly derail it, President Bush gave Bolton the position on August 1, 2005, during a congressional recess, as the Constitution entitles him to do. If the Senate does not approve his appointment on or before January 3, 2007, his post will become vacant again.

The debate about Bolton's personality and ideology notwithstanding, almost everyone agreed that President Bush's confidence about his qualifications and work ethic was well founded. During the past four decades, Bolton has served all but one Republican administration, distinguishing himself as an unusually intelligent, direct, and hardworking political appointee. The product of a blue-collar neighborhood, he helped to argue a landmark case before the U.S. Supreme Court not long after he earned a law degree from Yale University. In the last 25 years, he has held many positions associated with foreign relations, most recently that of undersecretary of state for arms control and international security, the fourth-most-powerful position in the State Department. Many foreign-policy commentators have said that Bolton is not really a neoconservative, as he has often been labeled, but rather a "realist" or an "aggressive nationalist," since he lacks the enthusiasm for spreading democracy abroad that is said to be a hallmark of neoconservatives. He does share with them, however, a firm belief that the U.S. must embrace a strong, proactive approach to self-defense and a refusal to shrink from military engagement. "I'm pro-American," Bolton told Caroline Daniel for the London *Financial Times* (December 19, 2002). "That means defending American interests as vigorously as possible and seeing yourself as an advocate for the US rather than as a guardian of the world itself." Bolton's

John Robert Bolton was born in Baltimore, Maryland, on November 20, 1948, the first of Edward Jackson Bolton and Virginia (Godfrey) Bolton's two children. His father was a professional firefighter who had been wounded in Normandy, on June 6, 1944 (D-Day), at the start of the Allied invasion of France during World War II. Some have attributed John Bolton's intense work ethic to his family's lack of social connections or wealth and to his childhood surroundings, a working-class neighborhood called Yale Heights. Beginning in seventh grade Bolton boarded during the week at a private, all-male military academy, the McDonogh School, in Owings Mills, a Baltimore suburb, which he attended on a scholarship. At the McDonogh School (which dropped its military curriculum and became co-educational in the decade after Bolton's graduation), he was conspicuous for his outstanding academic performance and his clear commitment to conservative principles. In 1964 he led a student group in support of the ultimately unsuccessful Republican presidential candidate, Barry Goldwater, and in 1966, the year he graduated, he wrote for the school newspaper (which he helped to edit) an essay strongly defending the U.S. military presence in Vietnam.

In the fall of 1966, Bolton enrolled at Yale University, in New Haven, Connecticut, where he majored in political science. He was a member of the Yale Young Republicans all through his undergraduate years and in at least one year served as the editor in chief of the *Yale Conservative*. By all accounts he and his fellow conservatives felt relatively isolated and powerless on the Yale campus, where left-wing political voices were then in the majority, but he expressed confidence that the Republican Party would someday dominate American politics. As he said in an often-quoted part of the speech he gave at his graduation ceremony, in 1970, "The conservative underground is alive and well here. If we do not make our influence felt, rest assured we will in the real world." Bolton earned a bachelor's degree summa cum laude and was elected to membership in the national honor society Phi Beta Kappa. He then entered Yale's law school, where, for one year, he held the prestigious position of editor of the *Yale Law Journal*. Around that time he began a six-year-long stint in the National Guard, which, as he later acknowledged, he joined in order to avoid being drafted to fight in Vietnam, despite his steadfast support for the war. "I confess I had no desire to die in a Southeast Asian rice paddy," he wrote for a book commemorating the 25th reunion of Yale's class of 1970, according to Ross Goldberg and Sam Kahn in the *Yale Daily News* (April 28, 2005, on-line). "I considered the war in Vietnam already lost."

On May 6, 1972 Bolton married his first wife, Christina. That same year he began an internship in the office of the U.S. vice president, Spiro Agnew (who served under President Richard Nixon until the following year). After he earned a J.D. degree, in 1974, he became as an associate with the firm Covington & Burling in Washington, D.C. Bolton entered the national political sphere a year later, acting as one of the lawyers for the plaintiffs in a case known as *Buckley vs. Valeo*, which addressed the constitutional validity of limits on campaign spending. The lead plaintiff in the case was Senator James L. Buckley of New York; its lead defendant was Francis R. Valeo, a member of the newly formed Federal Elections Commission.

When the Supreme Court unanimously ruled in favor of the plaintiffs, in January 1976, and established the far-reaching precedent that campaign spending was a form of free speech, Bolton became a recognized expert on the legalities of American elections.

In 1976 Bolton lent his legal expertise to Ronald Reagan, a former governor of California, in Reagan's unsuccessful bid for the Republican presidential nomination. Reagan won the nomination four years later, and after his election Bolton was immediately named to the president-elect's transition team. A few months later, in March 1981, he was sworn in as general counsel for the United States Agency for International Development (USAID). Later that year he was promoted to USAID assistant administrator, in which job he helped to develop American foreign-assistance policies. The loyalty and dedication Bolton showed to Reagan throughout his term at USAID prompted colleagues to give him a bronzed hand grenade with an inscription calling him "the truest Reaganaut."

Bolton's tenure at USAID ended in 1983, when he returned to Covington & Burling, this time as a partner. At around the same time, he began to work for the Republican National Committee (RNC). In 1984 he played a central role in the RNC's efforts to construct a broadly popular and unified platform for that year's national convention. After Reagan's reelection to the presidency, Bolton again left Covington & Burling and became an assistant attorney general for legislative affairs under Attorney General Edwin Meese. Bolton's work at the Department of Justice ranged from an unsuccessful pursuit of a means for indicting the Palestinian leader Yasir Arafat (who was thought to have been involved in the murders of two American diplomats in the Sudan in 1973) to a failed attempt to block the payment of reparations to Japanese Americans whom the U.S. government had forcibly held in internment camps during World War II. Bolton was also involved in 1986 and 1987 in the response of the Department of Justice to congressional investigations into the Iran-Contra affair. (The term refers to an illicit program of the Reagan administration in which money gained from arms sold to Iran was used to fund insurgents fighting the Communist Sandinista government of Nicaragua, as part of the U.S. government's larger Cold War strategy to prevent the spread of communism in Central America.) Bolton opposed, on constitutional grounds, congressional appointment of an independent counsel to investigate that or any other possible presidential misdeeds. In 1986 Bolton's work on behalf of Republican electoral candidates came under fire when an organization that he and Brice Clagett, a Covington & Burling lawyer, had helped form was fined $10,000 for evading campaign-finance laws. Called Jefferson Marketing, the firm aided a political action committee called the Congressional Club, which was associated with U.S. senator Jesse Helms, a North Carolina Republican.

In 1988, while still an assistant attorney general, Bolton became the head of the Justice Department's civil-law division. Bolton's job changed in May 1989, under President George Herbert Walker Bush, when he was named the assistant secretary of state for international organizations under Secretary of State James Baker III. Bolton had first worked with Baker in 1978, when Baker made an unsuccessful bid for attorney general of the state of Texas; their association reportedly helped make possible a number of Bolton's career moves. At the Department of State, Bolton chaired an interagency task force on Afghanistan, where a series of internal military conflicts had led to widespread suffering among the populace. He also offered stern criticisms of the management and politics of the United Nations Educational, Scientific and Cultural Organization (UNESCO), from which the United States had withdrawn in 1984, partially as a result of Bolton's lobbying, and which still was not functioning to Bolton's satisfaction. In 1991 he successfully led a joint U.S. and Israeli effort to repeal United Nations General Assembly Resolution 3379, a motion dating from 1975 that equated Zionism (a political movement and ideology that led to the creation of Israel as a homeland for Jews, in 1948) with racism; 111 nations voted for repeal and only 25 voted against. In 1992 Bolton urged the U.N. to act to stop what was to become a massive human rights crisis in the states that formerly made up Yugoslavia. On August 13, 1992, at an unusual two-day-long meeting of the U.N. commission on human rights, Bolton—in a comment widely quoted afterward—described the U.S. as "appalled at the unspeakable, immoral savagery being unleashed" in Bosnia and neighboring regions.

In 1993, after Bill Clinton succeeded George H. W. Bush in the White House, Bolton became a partner in the law firm Lerner, Reed, Bolton & McManus, where he remained until 1999. From 1994 to 1996 he served as an adjunct professor at the George Mason University School of Law, and in 1995 and 1996 he was the president of the National Policy Forum in Washington, D.C. In 1997 he became the senior vice president of the American Enterprise Institute for Public Policy Research (AEI), a conservative think tank with which he had been associated at least since 1977; according to its Web site, the AEI is committed to "preserving and strengthening the foundations of freedom—limited government, private enterprise, vital cultural and political institutions, and a strong foreign policy and national defense—through scholarly research, open debate, and publications." At AEI Bolton published and spoke widely on national and international issues, often returning to themes that had long dominated his thinking—problems with campaign-finance reform, for example, or the dangers of a simplistically multilateral approach to U.S. foreign policy—while also applying his ideology to specific issues that emerged at the time, such as plans for an international criminal court or the importance of independence for Taiwan, an island off

mainland China that was once a territory of China and whose claims to administrative autonomy China does not recognize. Concurrently, in 1999 Bolton became a senior fellow at another conservative think tank, the Manhattan Institute.

Bolton's knowledge of election laws and his loyalty to both former president Bush and former secretary of state Baker brought him into the thick of the dispute that erupted in Florida after the November 2000 presidential election. That election, in which Governor George W. Bush of Texas (running on the Republican ticket with Richard B. Cheney, a former government official) opposed Vice President Al Gore (running on the Democratic ticket with Senator Joseph I. Lieberman of Connecticut), failed to produce a clear victor. While attending a vote-counting session in the Leon County Library in northern Florida, Bolton told the assembled officials and workers, according to *Newsweek* (December 18, 2000): "I'm with the Bush-Cheney team, and I'm here to stop the vote." (The count was stopped on December 12, 2000 by order of the U.S. Supreme Court, which effectively made Bush the winner.) Cheney was later reported to have said at an AEI event that he was sometimes asked what job Bolton should have in the new administration. "My answer is, anything he wants," Cheney said, according to Carla Ann Robbins in the *Wall Street Journal* (July 19, 2002).

On February 21, 2001 Bush nominated Bolton for the post of undersecretary of state for arms control and international security. Bolton's frequently expressed disapproval of many arms-control agreements immediately made him the object of sharp criticism. "It's like putting the wolf in the hen's house," Don Kraus, a former executive director of the Campaign for U.N. Reform and currently the executive vice president of the left-wing group Citizens for Global Solutions, told Bill Nichols for *USA Today* (March 29, 2001). "This is a guy who, as best I can tell, has never seen a multilateral agreement that he liked." Bolton's supporters were equally vehement. "John Bolton is the kind of man with whom I would want to stand at Armageddon, for what the Bible describes as the final battle between good and evil in this world," Jesse Helms was widely quoted as telling the Senate Foreign Relations Committee (which he then chaired) on March 29, 2001, when it met to discuss Bolton's nomination. "John is a patriot. He is a brilliant thinker and writer. And, most importantly, he is a man with the courage of his convictions. John says what he means and means what he says." Although Bolton received more nays in the full Senate than any other person nominated by President George W. Bush up to that date, he was confirmed as an undersecretary of state. He was sworn in on May 11, 2001.

During the next two years, Bolton was influential in the Bush administration's decision to withdraw from both a 1972 Anti-Ballistic Missile Treaty between the U.S. and what was then the Soviet Union and a Clinton-era treaty, never ratified by

Congress, that established the International Criminal Court. With the expressed goal of creating more effective and realistic foreign-relations policies, Bolton also demanded radical changes to an agreement to limit the international sale of small arms and to a 1972 biological-weapons agreement—changes so extreme that they prevented further negotiations because the gulf between the U.S. position and the position of most other negotiating states was too wide to be bridged. While critics have cited those actions as proof that Bolton takes a dangerously unilateral approach to national security, Bolton and his supporters have argued that the above-cited agreements and various others are either unenforceable or threaten the national sovereignty of the U.S. Moreover, while at the Department of State, Bolton and others worked out dozens of bilateral agreements, including one with Russia that even Bolton's critics acknowledge has led to reduced stockpiles of nuclear weapons. A number of those agreements exempted Americans from prosecution in the International Criminal Court. Other agreements have emerged from the Proliferation Security Initiative (PSI), which allows signatories to intercept ships thought to be carrying weapons of mass destruction or the components that might allow countries to build them. Bolton told Rich Lowry for the *Wall Street Journal* (December 18, 2001), "We'll undertake obligations only when it's in our interest. But if we sign a treaty, we'll abide by it."

Meanwhile, reports had surfaced of tensions between Bolton and Secretary of State Colin L. Powell and of efforts by Powell and others among Bolton's superiors to tone down his uncompromising rhetoric. When President Bush, two months after his second inauguration, nominated Bolton to serve as the American ambassador to the U.N., Bolton's inability or unwillingness to maintain the calm, measured speaking style associated with diplomats again came under severe criticism. Democrats and other critics of Bolton claimed that such a fierce critic of the U.N. could not function effectively as a U.N. ambassador. Among other pieces of evidence, they noted that in 1994, at an event called the Global Structures Convocation, Bolton had told the audience, "There is no United Nations. There is an international community that occasionally can be led by the only real power left in the world, and that's the United States, when it suits our interest, and when we can get others to go along, and I think it would be a real mistake to count on the United Nations as if it's some disembodied entity out there that can function on its own." Speaking metaphorically of the United Nations' bureaucracy, Bolton added, "If the U.N. secretariat building in New York lost 10 stories, it wouldn't make a bit of difference." What seemed to dismay less-partisan senators more than such decade-old remarks were repeated accusations from former subordinates of his that Bolton often lost his temper and acted vindictively. On August 1, 2005, after a five-month-long debate within the Senate Foreign Relations Committee that failed to end in a vote, President Bush used his constitutional power to make temporary appointments during Congress's annual recess to install Bolton at the U.N. until January 3, 2007.

Bolton arrived in New York in August 2005, weeks before a U.N. summit meeting on global security, nuclear disarmament, and nonproliferation. Bolton had an integral part in shaping the final edition of the 35-page document that the summit produced; notably, he deleted passages that referred to disarmament, because he believed that the language empowered the U.N. to regulate the defense strategy of the U.S. Douglas Roche, writing for the *Catholic New Times* (October 9, 2005), described Bolton's actions as "bullying" but also as helpful in reinforcing "the dominance of the U.S. in international relations." Since January 2006 Bolton has worked to negotiate a plan to reform the U.N. The plan, no parts of which had been adopted as of late October 2006, falls short of the ideal, as he told members of Congress, but has still won his support. He has actively resisted attempts by countries less powerful than the U.S. to expand the U.N. Security Council, a body composed of 15 of the organization's 191 member nations. Bolton has remained stubborn in his goals and ideology, and his conduct has been alternately described as fiercely patriotic or obstinately unilateral. As an example of his negotiating ability, his supporters have pointed to his orchestration of a unanimous vote in the Security Council in October 2006 on a U.S. resolution that imposes limited sanctions on North Korea; others see his lack of success in the General Assembly, a more difficult arena for establishing a consensus, as evidence of his inability to build coalitions and of his commitment to a unilateral, uncompromising approach to diplomacy. His failed efforts at U.N. management reform and his handling of the matter of the U.N. Human Rights Council—the U.S. was one of only four nations to vote against the establishment of the council, and it later refused to nominate a candidate for membership on the council—are widely cited as examples of Bolton's ineffectiveness.

Among Bolton's strongest supporters is U.S. senator Norm Coleman, a Republican from Minnesota. "What John offers is what the U.S. needs at the U.N. today," Coleman told Warren Hoge for the *New York Times* (July 23, 2006). "John is the right kind of change agent in a universe that is resistant to change. In order to get reform done, you're going to have to push, you have to be assertive." Bolton's critics include Edward C. Luck, the director of the Center on International Organization of the School of International and Public Affairs at Columbia University, who said to Hoge, "I actually agree with Bolton on what has to be done at the U.N., but his confrontational tactics have been very dysfunctional for the U.S. purpose. . . . [I]f you take unilateral action the way Bolton has, you're isolated, and if you're isolated, you can't achieve much." More generally, Bolton has made it clear that the

Bush administration will pursue international multilateral diplomacy by means other than the United Nations if the organization fails to adopt adequate reforms. "We look at [the U.N.] in a kind of cost-benefit way," he said, according to Beth Gardiner, a reporter for the Associated Press (October 15, 2005). "If it's not solving problems, what do we do to fix it? And if we can't fix it, where else can we look to have those problems solved?"

Bolton and his first wife divorced in 1984. In 1986 Bolton married Gretchen Louise Brainerd, with whom he has one daughter, Jennifer.

—D.R.

Suggested Reading: *Bulletin of the Atomic Scientists* p24+ July/Aug. 2005; *Legal Times* p7 Nov. 23, 1987; *Los Angeles Times* A p1 May 1, 2005; *New Republic* (on-line) Mar. 29, 2004; *New York Times* p1+ May 1, 2005, p1+ July 23, 2006; *USA Today* A p10; *Wall Street Journal* A p14 Sep. 17, 2005; *Yale Daily News* (on-line) Apr. 28, 2005

Star Black

Bosselaar, Laure-Anne

(BOSS-uh-lahr, LORE-an)

Nov. 17, 1943– Poet; educator

Address: 122 Washington Pl., New York, NY 10014

"Poetry for me is passion, solace, joy . . . ," the poet Laure-Anne Bosselaar told Suzanne Frischkorn for the *Samsära Quarterly* (Vol. 2, Issue 2,

2000–01, on-line). "The poet's job is to reach out, grab, and give back the truth." Bosselaar, in the opinion of Barbara Hoffert, as expressed in *Library Journal* (April 1, 1998), "writes wonderfully evocative poems, pinpointing with exquisite accuracy 'the worlds in this world' even as she airs personal and spiritual concerns." Strongly autobiographical, Bosselaar's work "embodies the concept that poetry springs from moments of intense emotion recalled at leisure," as Lynn Flewelling wrote for the *Bangor (Maine) Daily News* (May 10, 1997). Within the past 20 years, Bosselaar has published three volumes of her poetry: *Artemis*, which came out in Belgium, her native land; *The Hour Between Dog and Wolf*; and *Small Gods of Grief*. Some of her poems have appeared in *Ploughshares*, the *Harvard Review*, the *Georgia Review*, the *Washington Post*, and *Agni*, a literary magazine published at Boston University, among other periodicals, and her poetry has been included in many anthologies. She has edited three collections of poems by others—*Outsiders: Poems about Rebels, Exiles and Renegades* (1999), *Urban Nature: Poems About Wildlife in the City* (2000), and *Never Before: Poems About First Experiences* (2005)—and with her husband, Kurt Brown, she co-edited the anthology *Night Out: Poems about Hotels, Motels, Restaurants, and Bars* (1997). Also with Brown, she translated from Dutch into English the poems in *The Plural of Happiness: Selected Poems by Herman de Coninck* (2006). Bosselaar teaches a graduate course in poetry at Sarah Lawrence College, in Bronxville, New York, and has led many poetry workshops. She has also given many public readings of her poems. At one of them, Flewelling reported, Bosselaar "read a few well-chosen poems that rocked a roomful of experienced poets and poetry-phobic prose artists such as myself back on our emotional heels."

An only child, Laure-Anne Bosselaar was born on November 17, 1943 in Belgium. Her parents maintained a home in the Belgian port of Antwerp. In her poem "The Worlds in This World," she wrote that while one of her grandfathers was imprisoned by the Germans during World War I, he "sewed perfect, eighteen-buttoned / booties for his wife with the skin of a dead / dog found in a trench." During World War II her father sympathized with the Nazis. Bosselaar's "deepest shame," she told Suzanne Frischkorn, was "being the daughter of anti-Semites"; her knowledge of her father's wartime activities "haunted" her, as Lynn Flewelling wrote. Her father in effect benefited from the war, becoming wealthy as a merchant of steel and iron after its conclusion, during the massive rebuilding effort in Europe. Her father's manner and behavior at home further alienated her from him. In her poem "The Cellar" (*Massachusetts Review*, Spring 1995), in which she recalled being sent to her family's basement on an errand, she wrote, "From up there, comes father's call, weary / irked, the same every time, with the same pitch and / threat after the last consonant in my name. / Deaf with terror, I grab the potatoes or his gin, / run out, slam the door, slap the hasp, / holding my offering to father as far as I can / from my body, throw it on the kitchen formica / in the escape to my room . . . " In her poem "Seven Fragments on Hearing a Hammer Pounding," from *Small Gods of Grief*, she recalled her parents' laughter when remarks they had made about Jews led her, at age five, to ask out of ignorance what sort of animals Jews were. In the same poem she wrote about a visit to her father's office as a seven-year-old; when her father discovered that she had used his pen, he slapped her face and struck her chest with his knee.

For much of her childhood, Bosselaar lived in misery in a Roman Catholic convent in Bruges, Belgium. She was "more often punished than praised," as she wrote in her poem "English Flavors," and had "no access to radio, television, or movies," as she recalled to Frischkorn. "We were only allowed to read books given to us, most of which were telling religious stories. I had to make up the outside world because I didn't see it. So I would tell myself stories. I would see the Atlantic Ocean in a mud puddle for example. . . . I would make up people's lives just by looking at them, to the point of imagining the color of their towels, how they ate and where, in the kitchen or in the living room?" In her poem "The Rat Trinity," published in *Ploughshares* (Fall 2001), Bosselaar wrote of seeing a rat waiting "with the same tenacity I had / as a child, hungry to grow strong / enough to escape the nunnery / without being caught. . . . There were times, when / beatings seared my skin with hues / of oil on the river Scheldt, and I / squeezed my thumbs / in my fists through dormitory / nights, there were times I prayed / to the Rat Trinity. To show me the way / out of the convent." In another poem, "The Pallor of Survival," she wrote of the experience of a childhood friend: "I'd seen / what the nuns did to her when she confessed / she masturbated: bending her over, pulling down / her panties to ram the longest part of an ivory crucifix / into her, hissing: HE is the Only One Who Can Come / Inside You—No One Else—You Hear?" In her conversation with Flewelling, Bosselaar alluded to being the victim of a rape as a young adult.

Bosselaar attended the Conservatoire Royal de Bruxelles, in Belgium, a school that specializes in music, theater, and "the art of the word," according to its Web site. She earned a First Prize in Elocution and a B.A. degree in French literature in 1962. She remained in Brussels to enroll at what is now called the Institut National Supérieur des Arts et Spectacles et des Techniques de Diffusion, which offers courses in many aspects of the entertainment industry; there, in 1964, she earned another B.A., in theater arts. During the next decade she devoted herself to homemaking and motherhood. She entered the workforce in 1974, taking voice-over and other jobs in theater, television, and radio in Belgium and neighboring Luxembourg. She next taught literature and poetry courses at the Interna-

tional School of Brussels, a day school for students up to age 18. She left that job in 1986, the year that her first volume of poetry, *Artemis*, was published. The poems in *Artemis* are in French, one of the four languages in which she is fluent. Bosselaar told Frischkorn that her knowledge of idioms in French, Dutch, and Flemish that don't exist in English is helpful to her as a poet writing in English; since "a cliché in one language isn't a cliché in another," knowing them helps her to meet "the challenge of finding an exact way of describing an image, emotion, or sensory detail," which is of prime importance to her.

In 1987 the now-divorced Bosselaar settled in the United States. From 1989 until 1991 she co-directed the Aspen Writer's Conference, in Colorado. When it was founded, by the poet Kurt Brown, in the mid-1970s, it served as a retreat for poets. By the time Bosselaar had joined the staff, it was catering to a range of prose writers as well. (Currently called Aspen Summer Words, it now welcomes readers as well as writers.) In 1992 Bosselaar and Brown married. At around that time Bosselaar entered the graduate writing program at Warren Wilson College, in Asheville, North Carolina. A so-called low-residency program, it requires a master's-degree candidate to complete four half-year semesters, during each of which the student spends 10 days on campus. Before graduation, according to the school's Web site, each student "must complete an analytical paper on some topic of literature, contemporary letters or craft; read 50-80 books; teach a class to fellow students; give a public reading of his or her work; and prepare a manuscript of fiction or poetry." Bosselaar earned an M.F.A. degree from the college in 1994.

Bosselaar's first collection of poems in English, *The Hour Between Dog and Wolf*, was published in 1997 by BOA Editions, a nonprofit publishing company, located in Rochester, New York, that is devoted to encouraging the writing, reading, and teaching of poetry. The book contains an introduction by the Pulitzer Prize–winning, Yugoslavian-born poet Charles Simic and poems whose subjects include both Bosselaar's childhood experiences and aspects of her adult life. Its first poem, "The Worlds in This World," opens with lines by the poet Stephen Dobyns—"This is the world to love. There is no other"—and begins, "Doors were left open in heaven again: / drafts wheeze, clouds wrap their ripped pages / around roofs and trees. . . . / all this in one American street. / Elsewhere, somewhere, a tide / recedes, incense is lit, an infant / sucks from a nipple, a grenade / shrieks, a man buys his first cane. / Think of it: the worlds in this world." In the year 1916, the poem continues, "thousands and thousands of Jews / from the Holocaust were already—were / still—busy living their lives; / while gnawed by self-doubt, [the German poet Rainer Maria] Rilke couldn't / write a line for weeks in Vienna's Victorgasse, / and fishermen drowned off Finnish coasts, / and lovers kissed for the very first time, / while in Kashmir an old woman fell asleep, / her cheek on her good husband's belly." The poem's last stanza, after mentioning a speck of dust that has landed on the poet's desk, reads, "Say now, at this instant: / one thornless rose opens in a blue jar above / that speck, but you—reading this—know / nothing of how it came to flower here, and I / nothing of who bred it, or where, nothing / of my son and daughter's fate, of what grows / in your garden or behind the walls of your chest: / is it longing? Fear? Will it matter?" The poem ends with the words, "Listen to that wind, listen to it ranting / *The doors of heaven never close, / that's the Curse, that's the Miracle.*" In a review of the book for *Ploughshares* (Fall 1997, on-line), the poet Wyn Cooper wrote that the poems set in Belgium "do more than address life there—they evoke it in every color, smell, texture, and taste." Another poet, Andrea Hollander Budy, writing for the *Arkansas Democrat-Gazette* (April 26, 1998), found "the foreignness of Bosselaar's perspective [to be] especially enlightening, whether she is describing her Flemish neighbors in postwar Belgium, or when she turns her focus onto things American." A third poet, Marilyn Krysl, in an assessment for the *Iowa Review* (Summer/Fall 1998), remarked on the coexistence of Bosselaar's attention to "the smallest detail" and capacity to "encompass the whole" and noted her ability to articulate in her poems "a child's rich chiaroscuro of emotion," her "gift for humor, whimsy, [and] irony," her "preoccupation with the sensuous and sensual," and the "ardor with which Bosselaar embraces her material." *The Hour Between Dog and Wolf* was a finalist for the Nicholas Roerich Prize and the Walt Whitman Award, among other honors.

In her conversation with Frischkorn, Bosselaar described in detail her creative process: "I work exclusively when an image strikes me; that for me, is the beginning of a poem. An image is like opening the door to a poem. Often I'll start by describing things around me to get into the imaginative space of a poem, and later I'll discard those descriptions because I don't need them anymore. . . . Once an image has triggered my imagination and/or a memory I will then introduce characters, dialogue or lyric based on the image. What I also do is listen to the sounds of the first line, and use that as guide for the rest of the poem. The sound of the first line, for me, sonorously tells me the emotion of the poem." She also said, "Nine times out of ten I will start a poem *in answer* to a poem I have just read. When I was writing *The Hour Between Dog and Wolf*, it was as if I was in constant dialogue with a novelist I have never met: Ron Hanson who wrote the extraordinary novel *Mariette In Ecstasy*." (That novel is set in a convent). An extremely slow writer, by her own account, Bosselaar typically rewrites every poem 20 to 30 times and discards 85 percent of her work. She has named Brigitte Pegeen Kelly, Louis Aragon, and the Flemish poet Herman de Coninck as "masters" whose poems she has studied in depth.

Bosselaar told Frischkorn that many of the poems in *Small Gods of Grief* (2001) were inspired by writings of the poet Jane Kenyon. That collection earned for Bosselaar the 2001 Isabella Gardner Prize for Poetry, which BOA Editions (the book's publisher) gives every other year to a poet in mid-career for work of "exceptional merit." The title of the book comes from one section of the seven-part poem "Seven Fragments on Hearing a Hammer Pounding," in which news accounts about the increasing influence of right-wing politicians in some countries spark Bosselaar's fears that her father's "tongue" is still alive. "O Gods of Grief, grant me this," she wrote: "some tongues will die, some tongues must." In an evaluation of the book for the *Crab Orchard Review* (on-line), Debra Kang Dean wrote, "*Small Gods of Grief* is marked by [Bosselaar's] irrepressible spirit and essentially redemptive imagination." A reviewer for *Poetry* (July 2003) wrote, "As good poems ought, Bosselaar's best suggest more than they say, but they do so with refreshing clarity. . . . With admirable economy, Bosselaar makes a near-epigram out of material lesser poets would belabor." In an assessment for the *Harvard Review* (Spring 2002), Andrea Hollander Budy wrote, "Bosselaar's concision is equaled by her ability to choose exactly the right details—a vital attribute in a genre so dependent upon the relative power of an image." Noting that she did not want to "neglect the book's pulse and heart," Budy added, "Good lyric poems allow us to empathize with their author; the best rouse our own emotional centers. Bosselaar's poems do both."

Bosselaar's poem "English Flavors" won First Prize in the 1996 National Poetry Contest. Bosselaar has taught at the University of Southern Maine as well as at Sarah Lawrence College and has been a writer in residence at Hamilton College and the Vermont Studio Center. Another collection of her poems, to be called *New Hunger*, is due to be published in 2007.

A "small, serene woman with a wonderfully gentle accent," according to Flewelling, Bosselaar has what she described to Frischkorn as "a maniacal curiosity—I'm so curious that I could stay in a hotel lobby all day and never be bored." She lives in New York City with her husband, Kurt Brown. She told Frischkorn that she and Brown are "each other's first readers. When I show a poem to Kurt 90 percent of the time he'll read it and say, 'So?' 'And?' and 75 percent of the time he's right. When he shows me work I will often say, 'This is great but . . .' and he will energetically defend the part that I doubt, then hours later come back and say, 'You were right again, damn it!'" "We're very, very supportive of each other. The only time we literally had a fight was one day in the car. The radio commented on something so fascinating that I said 'I'm going to write a poem about that,' and he had the guts to say 'I thought about it first!'" She told Frischkorn that she adopted the habit of writing from 4:30 to 10:30 a.m. when she was raising her son and daughter and, for a number of years, the child of a friend. Her son is a physician; her daughter works as a food stylist in Hollywood. Bosselaar is a passionate cook and gardener.

—R.E.

Suggested Reading: *Bangor (Maine) Daily News* May 10, 1997; Laure-Anne Bosselaar's Web site; *New York Times Book Review* p14 July 6, 1997, p32 Nov. 4, 2001; *Samsāra Quarterly* (on-line) Vol. 2, Issue 2, 2000–01

Selected Books: *The Hour Between Dog and Wolf*, 1997; *Small Gods of Grief*, 2001; as editor—*Night Out: Poems About Hotels, Motels, Restaurants, and Bars* (with Kurt Brown), 1997; *Outsiders: Poems About Rebels, Exiles, and Renegades*, 1999; *Urban Nature: Poems About Wildlife in the City*, 2000; *Never Before: Poems About First Experiences*, 2005

Frederick M. Brown/Getty Images

Bourdain, Anthony

June 25, 1956– Chef; writer; television host

Address: c/o Bloomsbury USA, 175 Fifth Ave., Suite 300, New York, NY 10010

"What Jean Genet was to the prison, what Tom Waits is to the lowlife bar, Anthony Bourdain is to the restaurant kitchen: a charmingly roguish guide to a tough, grimy underworld with its own peculiar rules and rituals," Adam Shatz wrote for the *New York Times* (May 13, 2001). A graduate of the Culinary Institute of America, Bourdain conquered a years'-long addiction to illegal drugs to gain respect as a chef in some of New York's most exclusive restaurants. With his best-selling book *Kitchen Confidential: Adventures in the Culinary Underbelly* (2000)—a brutally honest memoir and a "half-humorous, half-frightening expose of the restaurant industry," in the words of Bill Gibron, writing for popmatters.com (August 1, 2005), Bourdain became a celebrity. On the strength of the enormous popularity of *Kitchen Confidential*, which has been translated into 15 languages, he launched another career, as the host of a short-lived television show for the Food Network, *A Cook's Tour: Global Adventures in Extreme Cuisines*; the prize-winning book he wrote to accompany the program became another best-seller. Well-known for his profane wit, he has appeared since mid-2005 in a series for the Travel Channel called *No Reservations*, in which, according to Virginia Heffernan in the *New York Times* (July 25, 2005, on-line), he "indulges wanderlust and regular lust. Or rather," she added, "it's not clear whether he'll get into sex and drugs, the mainstays of . . . *Kitchen Confidential.* . . . But he's not saying no to anything here, and one of his many principles about food is that 'it does lead to sex, and it should.'" Bourdain published another nonfiction book, *The Nasty Bits: Collected Varietal Cuts, Usable Trim, Scraps, and Bones*, in 2006. Bourdain's books also include three novels—*Bone in the Throat, Gone Bamboo,* and *The Bobby Gold Stories*—and a book based on items on the menu of the Brasserie Les Halles, a New York City restaurant with which Bourdain has been associated since 1998: *Anthony Bourdain's Les Halles Cookbook: Strategies, Recipes, and Techniques of Classic Bistro Cooking.*

The first of the two sons of Pierre Bourdain, a Columbia Records executive who died in the late 1980s, and Gladys Bourdain, a *New York Times* editor, Anthony Bourdain was born on June 25, 1956 in New York City. He grew up with his brother, Christopher (who is now a currency analyst), in Leonia, New Jersey. By his own account, he was a precocious child: as a preschooler, for example, he told Deborah Ross for the London *Independent* (June 11, 2001), he found a copy of Rudolf Flesch's book *Why Johnny Can't Read* (1955) in his parents' bedroom and proceeded to teach himself to read "way beyond what should have been my level." He has traced his love of food to a summer holiday in 1966, when he traveled with his family to France (his father's birthplace) to stay with relatives. In Paris some of what he had most enjoyed eating in New Jersey—hamburgers and peanut butter and jelly sandwiches—could not be found, so he was forced to taste other foods. Eating his first oyster, he recalled to Deirdre Donahue for *USA Today* (November 29, 2001, on-line), affected him "viscerally, instinctively, spiritually—even in some small . . . way, sexually—and there was no turning back. . . . My life as a cook, and as a chef, had begun. Food had power. It could inspire, astonish, shock, excite, delight and *impress*. It had the power to please me . . . and others."

During his teens in New Jersey, Bourdain has said, he often felt angry—though he has maintained that he cannot remember why—and he developed a drug habit, which became the focus of many fights he had with his parents. Nevertheless, in his high school, the Dwight-Englewood School, in Englewood, New Jersey, he performed well enough to gain admission to Vassar College, an elite institution in Poughkeepsie, New York, that had opened its doors to men in 1969 (after more than 100 years as a women's college). He chose Vassar in order to be with his high-school girlfriend, Nancy Putkoski, who later became his wife.

Bourdain has claimed that at Vassar, which he entered in 1973, he did not attend any classes but wrote papers for other students so as to earn money to buy drugs. In the summer of 1974, he got a job as a dishwasher in a restaurant in Provincetown, on Cape Cod, Massachusetts. There, for the first time, he told Andrew Billen for the London *Times* (July 12, 2005), he felt respect for others—the people with whom he worked in the kitchen—and tried to gain their respect, though up until then he had never felt any for himself. After he completed his sophomore year at Vassar, he transferred to the Culinary Institute of America, in Hyde Park, New York, one of the most prestigious cooking schools in the U.S. After his graduation, in 1978, he began working in the kitchen of the Rainbow Room, a glamorous restaurant in Rockefeller Center, in Manhattan, where he stayed for 18 months. During the next half-dozen years, Bourdain made his way up the hierarchy in New York's culinary world at a variety of restaurants, among them Chuck Howard's, Nicki & Kelly, and Gianni's. Then, in the mid-1980s, he again became a heavy user of drugs and alternately worked briefly in a series of restaurants or did not work at all. His stint as a short-order cook led him to hate such food as French toast or fried eggs, "because, to me, it smells of failure and defeat," as he told Ross. In time he developed an addiction to heroin and found himself with neither a job nor a home. In 1988 he entered a methadone program, "which got me off the street overnight," as he told Deborah Ross, "but three times a week I had to queue up with other hideous junkies"—in his view, an unbearable indignity. He thus tried to go cold turkey, suffering through withdrawals and substituting cocaine for heroin in the process. Eventually he succeeded in ending his drug habit and began to rebuild his career, first as a chef at the Supper Club, then at Vince and Linda Ghilarducci's Italian Affair, where he stayed for two years and one year, respectively. In 1996 he worked for a few months at Coco Pazzo Teatro before handing in his resignation.

While he was reestablishing himself in New York restaurants, Bourdain was also trying his hand at writing. During the mid-1980s, to pass the time, he had written notes for a novel. While the story was expanding, and after he had conquered his heroin habit, he had taken a creative-writing course at Columbia University, in New York. The book was still unfinished when, in 1992, Gordon Howard, his Vassar roommate, urged him to complete it; indeed, Howard paid Bourdain's expenses for a 10-day vacation in Cozumel, Mexico, on the condition that Bourdain would do so. In 1993, within about six months of his return from Mexico, Bourdain had honored his pledge. Howard brought the novel to Random House, in New York City, which published it in 1995 with the title *Bone in the Throat*. Inspired in part by transcripts of the trial of the mobster John Gotti and by Bourdain's experiences as a restaurant worker, the book is a satiric thriller told from the perspective of Tommy Pagano, a chef at the Dreadnought Grill, a restaurant in the Little Italy section of Manhattan that is the cover for an FBI-financed sting operation. FBI officers hope that Tommy will help them to capture Sally Wig, an uncle of his, whom Tommy has witnessed committing a murder. Tommy, who hates everything associated with the mob, remains loyal to his uncle until faced with a crisis. Marilyn Stasio, who reviews crime and mystery fiction for the *New York Times Book Review* (August 6, 1995), described *Bone in the Throat* as a "prodigiously self-assured" and "deliciously depraved" first novel whose author's "comic vision goes beyond original."

When *Bone* was arriving in bookstores, Bourdain was busy creating the menu for the Italian Affair restaurant. He was also spending four hours a day working on his next novel, *Gone Bamboo* (1997), another satiric thriller involving mobsters, this time set on the Caribbean island of St. Martin. Bourdain's novels reportedly sold poorly, and journalists generally showed as much interest in his work as a chef as they did in his career as a novelist. The year *Gone Bamboo* was published, according to various sources, Bourdain became the chef at Sullivan's, in the Ed Sullivan Theater (from which David Letterman broadcasts his TV program, *The Late Show with David Letterman*). The following year Bourdain became the executive chef at Brasserie Les Halles, a New York restaurant specializing in French food; he currently holds the title "chef at large" there.

A major turning point for Bourdain came after he submitted a piece called "Don't Eat Before Reading This" to the *New Yorker* magazine. Although the *New Yorker* rarely accepts unsolicited manuscripts, the magazine published Bourdain's brief article in its April 19, 1999 issue. "Don't Eat Before Reading This," as Howard Seftel wrote for the *Phoenix (Arizona) New Times* (June 10, 1999), "exposed restaurant practices that chefs and restaurant owners would prefer the public didn't know"; for example, in it Bourdain warned diners to avoid ordering fish on Mondays, when it would be four days old, and revealed that when a customer orders a steak well-done, the chef chooses from among the worst cuts of meat. Only hours after the April 19 issue reached newsstands, Bourdain was offered a book deal. *Kitchen Confidential: Adventures in the Culinary Underbelly* was published in 2000. Going beyond simply telling readers unsavory details about restaurant kitchens, Bourdain took the opportunity to describe his alcohol and drug abuse, casual sexual encounters, and experiences in food preparation. Among those who expressed mixed feelings about the book was Sarah Billingsley, who wrote for the Pittsburgh, Pennsylvania, *Post-Gazette* (September 24, 2000) that the "richly described preparations and food references alone are enough to keep a reader entertained" but complained that "the chef's ego throbs on every page, even when Bourdain is self-deprecating. He is an unreliable and somewhat bitter narrator, with the limited writing skills of a college freshman who's been granted the 'literary' quarter to use profanity." More often, however, reviewers lavished *Kitchen Confidential* with praise. "In a style partaking of Hunter S. Thompson, Iggy Pop and a little Jonathan Swift," Thomas McNamee wrote for the *New York Times* (June 4, 2000), "Bourdain gleefully rips through the scenery to reveal private backstage horrors little dreamed of by the trusting public. He calls paying customers 'weekend rubes' and describes himself in an earlier, less enlightened incarnation as 'a shiftless, untrustworthy coke-sniffer, sneak thief and corner-cutting hack.' Thankfully, in his new life he has retained his brutal honesty."

Kitchen Confidential became a best-seller; by 2001, according to Deirdre Donahue, it had sold more than 700,000 copies and had been translated into 15 languages. Meanwhile, Bourdain had became a celebrity. He immediately signed contracts for two more nonfiction books. The first, *Typhoid Mary: An Urban Historical* (2001), tells the story of Mary Mallon, a cook whom the New York City Department of Health, in 1906, determined was spreading typhoid fever and who became famous as the first healthy carrier of the disease in the U.S. Despite the Health Department's insistence that she was spreading typhoid through her unwitting contamination of the food she prepared, she refused to stop cooking, even after she secured her release from a government-imposed quarantine by promising never to cook again. For Bourdain the "central question" regarding Mary was, as quoted by Adam Shatz, "Why did she go on cooking when she had every reason to believe she was spreading a possibly fatal disease?" Drawing on his own experiences, Bourdain suggested that Mary was simply a proud cook who wanted to work under any circumstances, even if she was sick or in pain. In an assessment for *Newsday* (April 15, 2001), Peg Tyre described Bourdain's retelling of the story as "competent" but felt that "his emphatic and sometimes coarse style . . . sometimes detracts from the story."

The second nonfiction book that Bourdain wrote to fulfill the terms of his contract was *A Cook's Tour: In Search of the Perfect Meal* (2001), which reached various best-seller lists. It was published as a companion to Bourdain's TV series, *A Cook's Tour,* which aired for 22 weeks on the Food Network in 2001; among other glimpses of Bourdain overseas, installments showed him in Vietnam eating a still-beating cobra heart immediately after it had been cut out of the snake and consuming sheep's testicles in Morocco. *A Cook's Tour* earned the Guild of Food Writers Award for Food Book of the Year in 2002 and was shortlisted for the 2002 Thomas Cook Travel Book Award. It also impressed critics. "Bourdain swaggers where the rest of us fear to tread," Karen Stabiner wrote for the *Los Angeles Times* (December 23, 2001). "Having scorched his way through the New York restaurant scene, he turns his attention in *A Cook's Tour* to the rest of the world. This time around, Bourdain is off in search of the perfect meal. Not your idea of a perfect meal, which might revolve around such civilized thrills as a beautiful wine or a bottomless bowl of caviar. His idea . . . reads more like a catered screening of *Apocalypse Now*." The book convinced some critics that Bourdain was, above anything else, a food writer. As Kathryn Hughes wrote for the London *Daily Telegraph* (December 29, 2001), "Take away the food, and Bourdain begins to sound like just one more middle-aged writer sent on assignment by a glossy American men's magazine to various hearts of darkness. But keep him close to the steam, the blood and the guts of everyday eating and he remains untouchable."

Bourdain's next book was the novel *The Bobby Gold Stories* (2003), about a mob-connected ex-convict who works in restaurants and clubs. In a review for the *Palm Beach (Florida) Post* (December 14, 2003), Scott Eyman wrote that *The Bobby Gold Stories* "isn't great, but it is good. It's all text and no subtext, which is why it's fun to read, but also why it doesn't hang in your head afterward." Jack Batten, a critic for the *Toronto (Canada) Star* (October 5, 2003), felt that the "tales of restaurant life behind the scenes radiate exotic authenticity" but complained, "Bourdain's touch is less convincing when he deals with the Mafia thugs who bring the violence to his books."

The Bobby Gold Stories was followed by *Anthony Bourdain's Les Halles Cookbook: Strategies, Recipes, and Techniques of Classic Bistro Cooking* (2004), which a number of laypeople posting their opinions on Amazon.com applauded. According to one reader, the book offers "great recipes with the clearest explanations I've seen anywhere," with everything written in Bourdain's "trademark prose"—which another Amazon.com contributor described as "brash, rude, [and] honest."

A sitcom called *Kitchen Confidential*, which was inspired by Bourdain's 2000 book, debuted on the Fox network in September 2005. It starred Bradley Cooper as a chef named Jack Bourdain, who is determined to rebuild his career after being mired in drug addiction and experiencing homelessness. The series was cancelled after 13 installments. In July 2005 Bourdain began appearing in the weekly series *Anthony Bourdain: No Reservations*; in that show, which airs on the Travel Channel, he introduces viewers to cuisine in different parts of the world. In his review of *No Reservations* for popmatters.com, Bill Gibron wrote, "Tony Bourdain is angry—and he's not afraid to share it with the world. He hates processed and pre-packaged foods. He loathes TV chefs who reduce classic cuisine to a series of easy to follow steps and perky soundbites. He argues for the purity of ingredients and the classicism of cultural culinary expression. But mostly he is mad at us, for allowing our taste buds to be tainted by fast food and microwaved mediocrity." Gibron continued, "When Bourdain turns off the anger and enjoys the food, he's fabulous. His obvious love of whatever he is eating, bordering on the orgasmic in some instances, is complemented by a complete knowledge of why the food has this effect."

Bourdain's fourth nonfiction book, *The Nasty Bits: Collected Varietal Cuts, Usable Trim, Scraps, and Bones* (2006), contains essays about food, leisure, and travel that originally appeared in such publications as the *New Yorker*, *Rolling Stone*, and *Gourmet* and that, in some cases, Bourdain updated for the collection. Various pieces make clear the writer's disdain for celebrity chefs and media food personalities and his intolerance for veganism in the U.S. Bruce Handy, in a review of *The Nasty Bits* for the *New York Times* (May 28, 2006), called it "a mix of the inspired, slightly less inspired . . . and the occasionally random or perfunctory" and concluded that overall Bourdain is a "vivid and witty writer" whose "greatest gift is his ability to convey his passion for professional cooking." After characterizing Bourdain as "the bad boy of the culinary world" and a knock-off of the cult hero and writer Hunter S. Thompson, Mia Stainsby, a *Vancouver Sun* (June 17, 2006) critic, described *The Nasty Bits* as "an entertaining, gritty, witty, nasty read."

In July 2006, while Bourdain was filming an installment of *No Reservations* in Beirut, Lebanon, violence erupted there between members of Hezbollah, an Islamic terrorist paramilitary group, and the Israeli Defense Forces (IDF). After only two days there, Bourdain left, along with other American evacuees. "We were there because of the food, of course; I'm in love with mezze [a selection of appetizers], huge, groaning tables everywhere filled with these little, delicious treats," he told a reporter for the London *Independent* (September 30, 2006). "The worst thing was that we had so little time to enjoy all this stuff." After declaring that his survey of Beirut restaurants was "the great unfinished business of my life," he said, "As soon as I can, I will go back and do that show."

Bourdain has an apartment in Manhattan but does not occupy it often. "I live in hotels much of the time," he told Billen. By early 2006 he and his wife had separated; according to several sources, they have since divorced.

—A.R.

Suggested Reading: (London) *Independent* p34 Sep. 30, 2006; (London) *Sunday Times* p3 Oct. 24, 2004; (London) *Times* p6 July 12, 2005; *Los Angeles Times* R p3 Dec. 23, 2001; *New York Times* C p1+ Sep. 10, 1997, IX p3 May 21, 2000, (on-line) July 25, 2005; *New Zealand Listener* (on-line) Nov. 8–14, 2003; *Newsday* May 31, 2000 B p15; popmatters.com Aug. 1, 2005; *USA Today* (on-line) Nov. 29, 2001; Bourdain, Anthony. *Kitchen Confidential: Adventures in the Culinary Underbelly*, 2000

Selected Books: fiction—*Bone in the Throat*, 1995; *Gone Bamboo*, 1997; *The Bobby Gold Stories*, 2003; nonfiction—*Kitchen Confidential: Adventures in the Culinary Underbelly*, 2000; *A Cook's Tour: In Search of the Perfect Meal*, 2001; *Anthony Bourdain's Les Halles Cookbook*, 2004; *The Nasty Bits: Collected Varietal Cuts, Usable Trim, Scraps, and Bones*, 2006

Paul J. Richards/AFP/Getty Images

Brazile, Donna

(brah-ZIL)

Dec. 15, 1959– Political consultant

Address: Brazile and Associates, LLC, 1001 G St., N.W., Suite 1001, Washington, DC 20001

When Donna Brazile was chosen to manage Vice President Al Gore's 2000 campaign for the presidency, she became the first African-American woman ever to run a major presidential candidacy. Brazile had begun her career in politics in the

1970s, as a teenager in Louisiana, working on the campaign of the state's attorney general; in the following decade she played important roles in the presidential bids of the Democratic luminaries Jesse Jackson, Richard A. Gephardt, and Michael S. Dukakis, winning admirers, and sometimes drawing censure, with her blunt style. The Democratic strategist Bill Carrick told Joyce Jones for *Black Enterprise* (April 2000) about Brazile, "She's a great organizer. She's a great manager of people. And she understands politics. She has a total inability to engage the ritual nonsense that defines many of the relationships between the news media and political operatives. She just cuts to the chase and tells the truth the way she sees things." In response to the outcome of the 2000 election, in which Gore won the popular vote but lost the electoral vote—and the presidency—to George W. Bush amid charges of vote suppression in Florida, Brazile helped to establish the Voting Rights Institute, dedicated to informing citizens about their rights. She is also the founder of Brazile and Associates, a grassroots-advocacy group, and contributes commentary to the CNN television program *Inside Politics*. Her memoir, *Cooking with Grease: Stirring the Pots in American Politics*, appeared in 2004.

The third of nine children, Donna Brazile was born on December 15, 1959 in New Orleans, Louisiana, and raised in Kenner, Louisiana, in a home located a block from the Mississippi River. Her father, Lionel Brazile, worked mostly as a janitor, and her mother, Jean Brazile, was a domestic worker. Brazile, who grew up in a segregated region, wrote in *Cooking with Grease*: "In Kenner, where you lived in relation to the railroad tracks was your destiny. My family didn't just live on the proverbial 'other side of the tracks.' No, we lived behind *two* sets of tracks. The middle-class Blacks lived between the main highway . . . and the working poor, like my family, lived behind the double railroad tracks. So in a way, if you really do the math correctly, we lived behind *three* sets of tracks pushed up against the banks of the Mississippi River." As a child Brazile helped to provide for her family financially by tending gardens, selling worms to fishermen along the river, and recycling bottles and cans. Brazile cited her grandmother, Frances Brazile, as the greatest influence on her decision to pursue a career in politics. Growing up, Brazile would rise by 5:30 a.m. to read the morning newspaper to her grandmother, who, as she told Melinda Henneberger for the *New York Times* (October 11, 1999), "gave me a thirst for knowledge." When Brazile was nine she heard a candidate for police chief make a campaign promise to pave the local roads, improve the schools, and build a neighborhood playground; she joined the campaign as a junior volunteer and traveled door-to-door, distributing literature. "I organized all the kids and told them that if he won, we'd get a playground. Which we did. So that was my first job in politics," she told Henneberger.

Brazile attended segregated public schools in Kenner until 1971, when the public schools in Jefferson Parish became integrated. She was then taken by bus about four miles from her home to attend seventh grade at T. H. Harris Junior High School, located in Metairie, a working-class, predominantly white suburb—many of whose residents opposed the decision to integrate. Brazile and the other African-American students were pelted every day with eggs and tomatoes and regularly subjected to racial epithets from their white classmates and their parents. Also, after they disembarked from the bus, they were forced to stand in an open area surrounded by a tall fence, while the white students were allowed to remain in the shaded area, away from the rain and sun. "After a couple of days of this I was fighting mad," Brazile wrote in her memoir. "I was a self-proclaimed militant. Although I was very eager to learn more about White people and to attend their schools, I was ready to start a revolution of some sort. I started to write poetry and essays about busing." Brazile launched a counterassault, hurling rocks, tomatoes, and eggs over the fence at the white students. Afterward the school principal began permitting Brazile and the other black students to stand in the shade and also encouraged them to interact with the white students. As she became more aware of the civil rights movement, Brazile continued to protest the conditions at the school, refusing, for example, to stand and recite the Pledge of Allegiance.

After two years Brazile left T. H. Harris High School and joined two of her sisters at Grace King High School, a racially integrated all-girls' school, located two miles from Kenner. There, her grades improved, and she also became active with the Soul Sisters Club, a group for politically active African-American students founded by her sister Cheryl. In 1975, following Cheryl's graduation, Brazile took on more of a leadership role with the club, working on campaigns for the Louisiana governor's race and the attorney general's race. In 1976 she worked as an organizer, taking part in a mock election between that year's Democratic presidential nominee, Jimmy Carter, and the Republican incumbent, Gerald Ford. She also worked on the campaign of Billy Guste, Louisiana's attorney general, helping to register Democratic voters. The experience of registering new voters for the Democratic Party was a turning point for Brazile, who began to identify with the party, which she felt represented the poor. That same year, for the first time, Brazile heard Barbara Jordan, the African-American U.S. representative from Texas who gave the keynote address at the Democratic National Convention. As Brazile recalled in *Cooking with Grease*, "I had never heard anyone so passionate and articulate, and she immediately symbolized everything I wanted to do and be politically. . . . I loved it when she said that we Black people may not have been written in the Constitution, but by a series of amendments we had finally got there.

She was not only eloquent, she told her story—she told *our* story." As a result, Brazile became inspired to pursue politics as a career, with the goal of gaining experience in Louisiana politics in order to manage a presidential campaign.

Having decided during her senior year of high school to study law in order to enter politics, Brazile enrolled at the predominantly white Louisiana State University (LSU), in Baton Rouge, on a partial athletic scholarship—once she realized that she would not be able to afford her first choice, the historically black Howard University, in Washington, D.C. "Everybody who wanted to be anybody in Louisiana state politics attended LSU undergraduate, graduate or law school. I was no exception," she wrote. With her previous experience in voter registration and protest organization, Brazile was an active member of LSU's student government, raising the level of representation of African-American students. She served as the university's statewide representative for external affairs and as its contact on the regional board of the U.S. Student Association (USSA), eventually becoming a board member. Brazile felt encouraged by the progress being made by African-Americans, who were now campaigning and holding political office nationwide.

Brazile changed her major from political science to psychology at the end of her second year of college; in the interest of supporting her family, she planned to work in human resources before attending graduate or law school at Harvard University. However, a job offer as a lobbyist with the National Student Education Fund (NSEF), coupled with the Republican Ronald Reagan's election to the presidency in 1980—which some attributed to low voter turnout—convinced Brazile that she had both the ability and the obligation to participate in national politics. After graduating from LSU in 1981, with a degree in psychology, Brazile traveled to Washington, D.C., to help organize the student committee lobbying Congress to make Martin Luther King Jr.'s birthday a holiday, in honor of the civil rights leader's achievements. (President Reagan signed the measure into law in January 1986.) Meanwhile, to gain experience as a lobbyist, Brazile accepted an internship on Capitol Hill working with the U.S. congressman Gillis Long of Louisiana. Her efforts as part of the Martin Luther King Jr. Holiday Committee brought her to the attention of the widow of the civil rights leader, Coretta Scott King. Coretta King asked Brazile to be the youth coordinator for the 20th anniversary commemoration of the historic 1963 March on Washington, at which Martin Luther King had given one of his most famous speeches. Some questioned Coretta Scott King's decision. "I thought Coretta had lost her mind. Why would you recommend somebody just out of college to do that?" Eleanor Holmes Norton, the congressional delegate from Washington, D.C., told Karin Miller for the Associated Press (May 23, 2000). "It had to do with raw talent."

In 1984 Brazile was chosen as the southern field director for the Reverend Jesse Jackson's campaign for the Democratic presidential nomination, which she regarded as a watershed event in her career. She had been inspired to join his campaign after hearing him speak at the 1983 March on Washington. As she told Robin Givhan for the *Washington Post* (November 16, 1999), "I will go to my grave remembering that run in 1984. It was not a campaign, it was a movement. . . . Jesse Jackson gave me my soul for this." In 1987 Brazile served as the campaign manager for Mary Landrieu's successful run for state treasurer of Louisiana. (Landrieu remained in that position until 1996.) During the Democratic primaries of 1988, Brazile served as the deputy campaign manager and national field director for House minority leader and Missouri U.S. representative Richard Gephardt, gaining notice within the Democratic Party for her expertise in political organizing and voter registration, which helped Gephardt win the Iowa caucuses. (Gephardt later bowed out of the race.) For the general election in 1988, she worked on the campaign of her party's nominee, Massachusetts governor Michael Dukakis, as deputy field director. Brazile was outspoken about her exclusion from the inner circle of the Dukakis campaign team and about the campaign's lack of focus on black voters. "I had been promised that despite my title I would be a major player in the campaign. And I had ended up flying all over the country with Dukakis just so he could avoid having an all-White campaign," she wrote in her memoir.

During a bus ride from New Haven, Connecticut, to New York with members of the press, Brazile accused the vice president and GOP nominee, George Herbert Walker Bush, of running a racist campaign. She focused on the campaign's television ad suggesting that Dukakis was soft on crime; the ad featured Willie Horton, a black prison inmate in a Massachusetts furlough program, who had escaped and committed rape during a weekend furlough. Brazile also alluded to reports that Bush was having an extramarital affair with a woman named Jennifer Fitzgerald, a claim that was unsubstantiated. As a result of the controversial remarks, Dukakis fired Brazile, who quickly earned a reputation as a loose cannon. The episode was an emotional blow to Brazile, who told Henneberger, "I thought I'd failed my mother. I've tried never to bring dishonor to my family and that was hard." Following the incident, Brazile, a devout Roman Catholic, volunteered at—and lived in—a homeless shelter in Washington, D.C., for nine months, as what she called her penance.

In 1990 Brazile returned to the political arena as a campaign manager for Eleanor Holmes Norton, who succeeded Walter Fauntroy to become Washington, D.C.'s delegate to Congress. (Fauntroy had stepped down to run—unsuccessfully, as it turned out—for mayor of Washington, D.C.) Following the successful campaign, Holmes offered Brazile a position as the chief of staff and press secretary in her administration, which Brazile accepted. "[Brazile] has the ability to look at a problem, see what everybody else misses, bring it all together and get it done," Norton told Jones. Discussing her work in national politics, Brazile told Robin Givhan, "I had to decide if I'd be a bitch or a whore. I chose bitch. I'd have to be strong, tough, abrasive. But I also knew I could be fair."

Beginning in 1991 Brazile served as an adviser for Bill Clinton's campaign for the 1992 Democratic presidential nomination, motivated, in large part, by her friendship with then–U.S. senator Al Gore, who would become Clinton's running mate in 1992. Brazile was encouraged by the attention Clinton paid to domestic issues, including the economy, as opposed to foreign policy. At the time President George H. W. Bush's approval ratings were high, following the U.S. victory in the Gulf War, and the Democratic Party was thought to have little chance of winning the White House. But as Brazile has recalled, African-American voters—most of them Democrats—turned out in record numbers due to the civil rights–minded campaign team that Clinton had assembled. Clinton became the first Democrat elected to the White House since 1976. Brazile wrote in her memoir about Clinton's victory over Bush in the general election: "I was so full of excitement. After years of weeping, joy had arrived. A Democrat was finally elected. I wrote in my diary, after the losses of the eighties, the Democrats got it right." Brazile assisted Clinton's presidential transition team while remaining in her position as Norton's chief of staff. In 1994 she worked with the Democratic National Committee to try to boost the party's chances of success in that year's congressional elections; she challenged the Democrats' decision to cut funding for voter-contact programs, rides to the polls, and other outreach efforts aimed at the African-American community. In the fall balloting the Republican Party took control of Congress for the first time in four decades.

In 1995 Brazile worked with the Nation of Islam leader Louis Farrakhan to organize the Million Man March, in Washington, D.C., which focused on African-American men's uniting and taking responsibility for their lives. While she was eager to manage a presidential campaign herself, Brazile took a leave of absence from Norton's office to work as a state director in Washington, D.C., for the Clinton-Gore 1996 reelection campaign, against Robert Dole. The campaign's focus on Clinton's success in turning around the economy proved successful. Brazile praised the racially diverse group Clinton chose for his Cabinet, which included Alexis Herman as his secretary of labor, Rodney Slater as his secretary of transportation, and Togo D. West Jr. as the secretary of veterans' affairs. "To his credit, Bill Clinton surrounded himself with African Americans, and we were always strategizing. After all, we had made both of his victories possible in terms of the large Black voter turnout. So when it came to putting our needs on the table, we had no second thoughts about it," Brazile noted

in her memoir. In 1998 Brazile designed the Voter/Campaign Assessment Program for the Democratic National Committee as a way to increase voter turnout among minorities in key congressional districts. The black voter turnout in 1994 was almost as low as 34 percent on the national level and only around 20 percent in some minority districts. According to Brazile, the turnout had increased 5 percent from the 1994 congressional campaigns. In recognition of Brazile's efforts to organize and mobilize Democratic constituencies, she was appointed to the Democratic National Committee (DNC) as an at-large member from the District of Columbia. In the lead-up to the 1998 congressional elections, she was asked to serve on the Rules and Bylaws Committee. Following the murder of Matthew Shepard, a gay Wyoming college student who was attacked because of his sexual orientation, Brazile joined the board of the Millennium March, a gay-rights demonstration, in Washington, D.C.

In 1999 Brazile resigned her post with Norton and fulfilled her dream when she was named campaign manager and national political director for Gore's presidential campaign, becoming the first African-American woman to manage a major presidential run. (The appointment was viewed by many as a tool to attract African-American and female voters.) "Gore wanted me to help him build a lean, mean aggressive fighting machine," she recounted in her memoir. Looking to distance Gore from President Clinton, Brazile relocated Gore's campaign headquarters from K Street in Washington, D.C., to downtown Nashville, in Gore's home state of Tennessee. Brazile also reworked Gore's campaign to make him more accessible to the voting public. In discussing her strategy, Brazile told Givhan, "I try to get [Gore's team] to know that you can say things with 5-cent words or 15-cent words and still reach people. When Gore talks about education and revolutionary changes, what does that mean? I say, 'Break that on down, brother, tell me how that will relate to my kids.'"

Brazile also worked to transform Gore's image in the media—that of a stiff and detached politician—through a series of debates against Senator Bill Bradley, his main opponent in the Democratic primaries. Gore labeled himself an underdog and called Bradley a quitter, for his decision to leave the Senate after the Republican takeover of Congress. He also criticized Bradley's plan for universal health care, which favored abolishing Medicaid and providing low-income families with subsidies to buy private insurance, as overly ambitious. "Brazile has re-energised Al Gore, turned him from a wimp into a fighter. No matter who faces Gore in November . . . they had better have a plan to deal with the Brazile factor," Kellyanne Fitzpatrick, a conservative pollster, told Roger Franklin for the *New Zealand Herald* (March 4, 2000). Perhaps because of Bradley's turn-the-other-cheek response to Gore's attacks, he failed to win state primaries in California, New York, Ohio, Vermont, Connecticut, Rhode Island, Massachusetts, Georgia, Maryland, Maine, and Missouri—his native state—and withdrew from the race in March 2000. (In July 2000 he endorsed Gore for president.)

In the general election, in which he faced the Republican George W. Bush, Gore won the popular vote but appeared to lose the electoral vote. As Gore prepared to concede the election to Bush, Brazile questioned the results, amid widespread reports of voter intimidation among Florida's African-American population; she persuaded Gore not to concede. After the U.S. Supreme Court's decision to stop the vote recount in Florida, Bush was awarded Florida's 25 electoral votes, which decided the election in his favor. In response to the irregularities of the 2000 election, Brazile persuaded the Democratic National Committee to create the Voting Rights Institute, an organization formed to educate poor and minority voters, many of whom were reportedly prevented from exercising their voting rights in 2000; Brazile also served as chairperson. Referring to the 2006 elections in an interview with Juan Williams for National Public Radio (March 23, 2006), she again stressed the importance of educating minority voters: "If you look at the 36 gubernatorial races, the 33 senatorial races, African American voters will make the difference in terms of who control[s] those state houses, as well as who controls the United States Senate." She also said, "It's important that the [Democratic] party understands and reach out and invest early in these communities and not ignore the black vote until three years before the [next presidential] election."

Earlier, in 2002, Brazile was the media consultant and grassroots organizer for Landrieu's winning reelection bid for senator from Louisiana. In 2004 she was a candidate to replace Terry McAuliffe, the departing chairman of the Democratic National Committee, but later removed her name from consideration. According to Jill Zuckman, writing for the *Chicago Tribune* (October 18, 2006), after the November 7, 2006 elections, Brazile plans to "talk politics" in a meeting with Senator Barack Obama of Illinois, who has not ruled out a run for the Democratic nomination for president in 2008.

Brazile has appeared on the CNN cable-television network as a commentator for the program *Inside Politics*. She also contributes commentaries to the National Public Radio series *Political Corner* and the on-line publication *Roll Call*, which covers activities on Capitol Hill. In 2005 she enlisted CNN's help to locate her family in New Orleans in the wake of Hurricane Katrina, which caused flooding that destroyed large sections of the city. Following Brazile's public appeal on CNN—and her offer of a $500 reward—the U.S. Fish and Wildlife Service succeeded in finding one of her sisters, who had resided in an assisted-living shelter in Louisiana before the flood. A Red Cross volunteer rescued her father after five days; after six days, another of Brazile's sisters was also rescued.

Brazile is the founder of Brazile and Associates, a consulting firm, and helped establish the National Political Congress of Black Women, which she serves as first executive director. She is also an adjunct professor of political science at the Academy of Leadership of the University of Maryland at College Park. As a senior fellow at the Institute of Politics at Harvard University's John F. Kennedy School of Government, she led a weekly study group focusing on the 2000 presidential campaign. In addition, Brazile has hosted and produced a weekly radio talk show heard in Washington, D.C., and Baltimore, Maryland. Among the honors she has received are the Congressional Black Caucus Youth Award, the National Women's Student Leadership Award, the Outstanding Young Achievers Award from *Ebony* magazine, and recognition from *Mirabella* magazine as one of the "Top 25 Smartest Women in America."

—B.M.

Suggested Reading: *Baltimore Sun* E p1 June 15, 2004; *Essence* p216 Aug. 2004; *Los Angeles Times* A p1 Jan. 10, 2000; *New York Times* A p10 Oct. 11, 1999; *New York Times Magazine* p54+ Oct. 1, 2006; *Washington Post* C p1 Nov. 16, 1999

Selected Books: *Cooking with Grease: Stirring the Pots in American Politics*, 2004

Brooks, Geraldine

1955– Writer

Address: c/o Viking Penguin, 375 Hudson St., New York, NY 10014

In both fiction and nonfiction, Geraldine Brooks has made her way into the lives of others, in a manner deemed by reviewers to be graceful and evocative. Her *Nine Parts of Desire: The Hidden World of Islamic Women* (1995) gave Westerners a nuanced picture of life behind the veil that has been thrust upon, or voluntarily assumed by, many Islamic women. For *Foreign Correspondence: A Pen Pal's Journey from Down Under to All Over* (1998), she reconnected with the pen pals who, during her youth, had helped her to escape—via her imagination—from what she saw as the provincialism of life in her native Australia. Brooks's first historical novel, *Year of Wonders: A Novel of the Plague* (2001), portrayed villagers of plague-ridden 17th-century England who sacrificed themselves for the common good, and her 2005 work, *March*, imagines the American Civil War from the point of view of the father in Louisa May Alcott's classic 1867 novel, *Little Women*. *March* earned Brooks, a former foreign correspondent for the *Wall Street Journal*, the Pulitzer Prize for Fiction.

Courtesy of Penguin Books

Geraldine Brooks

Geraldine Brooks was born in 1955 and grew up in the suburbs of Sydney, Australia. Her mother, an Australian, was a former radio announcer. Her father was an American singer and songwriter born with the surname Cutter. Several sources have referred to his "scandalous romantic past." When his agent advised him to begin life anew with a clean slate, by changing his name, he looked out of a window, saw a sign for Brooks Brothers, and adopted the name "Brooks" as his own. He was touring with a band in Australia when he met his fourth wife, who became the mother of Geraldine Brooks and her sister. In Australia he became a proofreader for a newspaper, and when Geraldine, at age eight, visited him in his office, she decided instantly to become a reporter when she grew up. "Something clicked inside me—I never doubted from that moment what I wanted to be," she told Murray Waldren for the *Weekend Australian* (March 19, 2005). That decision, as she mused to Marie Arana for the *Washington Post* (December 9, 2001, on-line), was "very much at odds with my excruciating shyness."

Brooks's childhood was an uneventful one. She was often ill and missed a lot of school. To gratify vicariously her longing for faraway places and exotic adventures, she maintained a correspondence with faraway pen pals. Her yearning for other locales, she suggested in a piece she wrote for the *Washington Post Book World* (December 9, 2001), was influenced by the books that were available to her, which were almost exclusively by and about English people. "My mind lived in a cold, Anglican place while my body lived in a hot Roman Catholic one," she wrote. "The real world of my 1960s Sydney childhood—the sweaty, salt-tanged

summer days when the smell of distant bush fires mingled with the car exhaust of suburban Sydney—was not set down between any hard covers, at least none that made it to my bedtime-story hour. . . . Because I did not read of my own world, it took me a very long time to learn how much I loved it."

After earning a B.A. degree in government from the University of Sydney, Brooks made her way to the U.S., attending the Columbia University School of Journalism, in New York City, which had awarded her a Greg Shackleton Australian News Correspondents Memorial Scholarship. In 1983 she was hired by the *Wall Street Journal*, which soon sent her to Cairo, Egypt, to cover the Middle East. During the years that followed, she filed reports for the newspaper about tumultuous events in Somalia, Eritrea, and Bosnia and about the Persian Gulf War of 1991. In 1994, while in Nigeria investigating the links between that country's military dictatorship and the Shell Oil Co., Brooks was jailed. As Murray Waldren reported, Brooks—who was by then married to the American-born writer Tony Horwitz—thought at the time, "If I get out of this alive, I want to have a child." After three days the Nigerian government deported her. She returned to the home she shared with her husband in Waterford, a town of 250 people in Virginia. In the following year the couple's son was born, and Brooks settled into a life of raising her child and writing books.

Brooks published her first book, *Nine Parts of Desire: The Hidden World of Islamic Women*, in 1995. The title comes from a saying attributed to Ali, the son-in-law of the prophet Muhammad and the founder of the Shiite sect of Islam, that "God created sexual desire in 10 parts; then he gave nine parts to women and one to men." While serving as a Middle East correspondent for the *Wall Street Journal*, Brooks had occasionally adopted Muslim-style veiling in order to gain access to and acceptance by the women she encountered, so that she could learn about the way women live in the Muslim societies of the Middle East and North Africa. She spoke to female soldiers, belly dancers, housewives, and professors whose ideologies ranged from feminism to radical orthodoxy. Remaining largely objective, Brooks nevertheless criticized Islamic women for not being sufficiently effective in struggling against "honor" killings (or the murders of women accused of having extramarital sex) and female circumcision—practices that are not prescribed by Islamic law but are encouraged by local custom and the clergy in many areas. At the same time, Brooks was careful in *Nine Parts of Desire* not to paint a one-sided picture of even the most extreme religious fundamentalists. She reported learning, for example, that the Ayatollah Khomeini, the radical Islamic cleric who became the leader of Iran, had been a jocular grandfather, allowing his grandchildren to play hide-and-seek under his robes, and that he had given his own infant children nightly feedings to relieve their mother. Brooks gave careful attention to the possibilities for change, with regard to attitudes about women, in Iranian society. She also wrote in *Nine Parts of Desire*, however, as quoted in the London *Guardian* (March 11, 1995), that until "Islam's articulate spokeswomen . . . target their misguided co-religionists with the fervour they expend on outside critics, the grave mistake of conflating Islam with clitoridectomy and honour killings will continue. And so will the practices themselves, at the cost of so many Muslim women's health and happiness." In a review of *Nine Parts of Desire* for the *Guardian* (March 14, 1995), William Taylor noted, "Although the book is clearly written by a journalist on the hoof, Brooks happily manages to avoid it becoming a series of international snapshots by her passionate exploration of its central question. 'Is it possible to reclaim the positive messages in the Koran and Islamic history, and devise some kind of Muslim feminism?'"

Brooks's second book, *Foreign Correspondence: A Pen Pal's Journey from Down Under to All Over*, appeared in 1998. She had gotten the idea for that volume when, during a visit to her dying father in Sydney, she found a pile of old letters that she had received from her pen pals in childhood. She decided to try to contact the writers of the letters to find out how they had fared in the intervening years. Among Brooks's former correspondents were Nell Campbell, who had grown up in another part of Sydney and gone on to become famous as an actress and owner of a New York nightclub; an American girl, Joanie, from New Jersey, who had shared Brooks's interest in the science-fiction TV series *Star Trek*—and had died of anorexia nervosa just before Brooks arrived at Columbia University; Brooks's French pen pal, Janine, who at 40 was still living in the small village where she was born and had three children and an apparently satisfying life; and an Israeli Jew, with the surname Cohen, who was embittered by the militarism that he felt had shaped his life. Valerie Sayers, writing for the *New York Times Book Review* (January 4, 1998), termed *Foreign Correspondence* "a layered portrayal of [Brooks's] own development" that is "full of a generous interest in the life beyond the self" and written "with grace and good humor. Her decision to seek out her childhood pen pals . . . is as straightforward and affecting as her writing." Brooks won the Kibble Award for Women Writers in 1998 for *Foreign Correspondence*, which the judges found to contain "subtle pleasures and insights."

For her first novel, which is based on historical fact, Brooks focused on the year 1666 in Derbyshire, England. There, the people of a village called Eyam decided to quarantine themselves to try to avoid further spread of the plague. Approximately four-fifths of the population of the village died. *Year of Wonders* (2001) is told from the viewpoint of a survivor, Anna Frith, a young shepherdess who helps the village parson in his effort to persuade the others to accept their fate and is, in turn,

helped and educated by the rector's wife. Brooks wrote for the *New York Times* (July 2, 2001) of how she came to defy the novelist Henry James's dictum, which he included in a letter to his fellow author Sarah Orne Jewett, that the "historical novel is . . . condemned. You may multiply the little facts that can be got from pictures and documents, relics and prints, as much as you like—the real thing is almost impossible to do." (By "the real thing," James apparently meant successful representations of the consciousness of premodern people.) Brooks noted that she had heard "similar opinions . . . when I worked as a journalist covering the Middle East and Africa. 'They don't think like us,' white Africans would say of their black neighbors, or Israelis of Arabs, or upper-class Palestinians about their desperately poor refugee-camp brethren. . . . 'They don't value life as we do.'" Brooks, she wrote, "knew they were wrong. A woman keening for a dead child sounds exactly as raw in an earth-floored hovel as it does in a silk-carpeted drawing room." She added, "The past may be another country. But the only passport required is empathy."

"In her first essay into historical fiction, Geraldine Brooks approaches the situation not as a novelist, but as a war correspondent whose experience of reporting from Gaza, Somalia and Bosnia is keenly felt on every page of this chilling, forensically detailed dispatch from the frontline of the 17th century," Alfred Hickling wrote for the *Guardian* (July 14, 2001). He concluded, "More than a mountain of corpses, more than a sensual evocation of the Sapphic bond between two women, more than a pulse-quickening tale of misplaced sadomasochistic zeal, *Year of Wonders* is a staggering fictional debut that matches journalistic accumulation of detail to natural narrative flair. Brooks has been posted to some of the most hellish combat zones of the modern world; but her most harrowing assignment has been the interior world of her historical imagination." By contrast, the critic and novelist John Vernon, writing for the *New York Times Book Review* (August 26, 2001, on-line), placed *Year of Wonders* in the "flourishing branch of historical fiction in Europe and America" that "has tended toward the lurid and the gothic." Another trend that Brooks's novel followed, in Vernon's estimation, was that of servant/narrators who "tend to be proud souls with democratic sympathies trapped in the wrong class and century. Brooks's Anna, at 18, not only reads English and has a smattering of Latin, she is smarter, sexier and more selfless, sensitive and independent than anyone else in her narrative. And from the opening paragraph, she tells her story with a descriptive tenderness that sounds suspiciously contemporary." The reviewer for the *Economist* (September 6, 2001, on-line) disagreed with that assessment, writing, "Anna's is a marvelous story. Through the rituals of childbirth, illness and death, she fights the villagers' fear and fanaticism, sorcery and witch hunts, and at the end of the novel is utterly redeemed by her courage."

The inspiration for *March*, Brooks's 2005 novel of the U.S. Civil War, was slow in coming. While her husband, Tony Horwitz, was writing *Confederates in the Attic*, a book about those who reenact Civil War battles, Brooks was "forever being dragged around Civil War sites," as she recalled to Murray Waldren. "And I was very ungracious about it too—it was either Gettysburg on the Fourth of July, which is as hot as Hades, or some desolate field in mid-winter with the winds howling through corn stubble, or some rare event"—such as the interment of Stonewall Jackson's horse. She added, "I mean, who really wants to give up their weekend for that, just you and 50 Daughters of the Confederacy in crinolines?" She had a change of heart after learning more about the very town where she and her husband were living. Waterford, she discovered, had been established by Quakers and other pacifists who were abolitionists. "They'd faced an agonising test of conscience over this—and some decided that slavery was a worse evil than war and they became among the few Virginians to fight on the Union side." The title character of *March* (who is largely absent from the narrative of *Little Women*) observes the horrors of the Civil War in his role as a chaplain for the Union Army. Reviewing *March* for the *Los Angeles Times* (March 6, 2005), Heller McAlpin called it "a beautifully wrought story about how war dashes ideals, unhinges moral certainties and drives a wedge of bitter experience and unspeakable memories between husband and wife," and Beth Kephart, writing for the *Chicago Tribune* (March 6, 2005), found the novel to be "a very great book" that "breathes new life into the historical fiction genre." In 2006 *March* won Brooks the Pulitzer Prize for Fiction.

Murray Waldren described the diminutive Geraldine Brooks as "someone who barely qualifies for the term petite when she is wearing heels. And high ones at that." Brooks and Tony Horwitz met as students at Columbia University; Horwitz, too, is a winner of the Pulitzer Prize, which he received for national reporting in 1995. In addition to Waterford, Brooks and Horwitz have shared homes in Sydney, London, and Cairo. The couple's son, Nathaniel, was named for the character Natty Bumppo in James Fenimore Cooper's novel *The Last of the Mohicans*.

—S.Y.

Suggested Reading: *Economist* (on-line) Sep. 14, 2001; (London) *Guardian* T p12 Mar. 11, 1995, T p6 Mar. 14, 1995; *New York Times* E p1 July 2, 2001; *New York Times Book Review* p14 Jan. 8, 1995, Jan. 4, 1998, (on-line) Aug. 26, 2001; *Washington Post Book World* p6 Dec. 9, 2001; *Women's Review of Books* p15 Apr. 1995

Selected Books: nonfiction—*Nine Parts of Desire: The Hidden World of Islamic Women*, 1995; *Foreign Correspondence: A Pen Pal's Journey from Down Under to All Over*, 1998; fiction—*Year of Wonders: A Novel of the Plague*, 2001; *March*, 2005

Courtesy of the Lavin Agency

Buckingham, Marcus

Jan. 11, 1966– Management consultant; lecturer; writer

Address: Marcus Buckingham Co., 3651 Peachtree Pkwy., Suite 330, Suwanee, GA 30024

"The real tragedy of life is not that each of us doesn't have enough strengths, it's that we fail to use the ones we have," the management consultant and business writer Marcus Buckingham declared in his book *Now, Discover Your Strengths*, co-authored by Donald O. Clifton. A native of Great Britain, Buckingham gained his expertise as a researcher and consultant for the Gallup Organization in the United States, with which he worked for the first 17 years of his career. His professional goal, as he and Clifton wrote, is to "start a revolution, the strengths revolution." The guiding tenets of the revolution, in their words, are that "each person's talents are enduring and unique" and "each person's greatest room for growth is in the areas of his or her greatest strength." "At the heart of the revolution," they explained, "is a simple decree": to gain success, an organization—that is, a company, a nonprofit group, or any other formally organized segment of society—"must not only accommodate the fact that each employee is different, it must capitalize on these differences. It must watch for clues to each employee's natural talents and then position and develop each employee so that his or her talents are transformed into bona fide strengths. By changing the way it selects, measures, develops, and channels the careers of its people, this revolutionary organization must build its entire enterprise around the strengths of each person. And as it does, this revolutionary organization will be positioned to dramatically outperform its peers." When one examines employee-performance appraisals, Buckingham told Tim Geary for the Amtrak Acela magazine *Arrive* (March/April 2006), "at least 40 percent of the time, managers discuss weaknesses, not strengths. That's about as fun and useful as going to a bad dentist. The whole self-help schtick has it that you can be anything you want to be if you just work at it. My argument has always been that, well, you can't! As you grow you don't become someone else. You become more who you are, which is why you have to focus on the strongest patterns in your life." Buckingham, who is on the roster of several speakers' bureaus, formed his own business, the Marcus Buckingham Co. Inc., in 2005. Greatly in demand as a lecturer, he earns tens of thousands of dollars for each of his lectures, and his three books—the other two are *First, Break All the Rules: What the World's Greatest Managers Do Differently*, written with Curt Coffman, and *The One Thing You Need to Know . . . About Great Managing, Great Leading, and Sustained Individual Success*—have sold a total of more than two million copies. He is a member of the U.S. secretary of state's Advisory Committee on Leadership and Management.

Marcus Buckingham was born on January 11, 1966 in England, where he grew up with one sister and one brother. His parents are divorced. Both his paternal grandfather and his father made their careers in the field of human resources. During Buckingham's childhood his severe, ever-present stammer led his peers to call him "BAAAAHkingham"; he escaped more-hurtful ridicule because of his athletic prowess, particularly in field hockey and cricket. Nevertheless, as he recalled to Del Jones for *USA Today* (March 4, 2005), "the stammer was the last thing I thought about when I went to sleep and the first thing when I woke up. [But] if you can hit the winning run, you can get away with a lot of imperfections." Buckingham attended the Edge Grove School, in Radlett, Hertfordshire, not far from London, which catered to both day and boarding students. One day when he was 13 years old, the headmaster selected him to speak in front of the whole student body at an assembly. When Buckingham rehearsed his speech in private, his stammer prevented him from uttering more than a few sentences in 20 minutes. But when he faced the 300 or so children and teachers in his audience, he completed the speech in four minutes, without stammering. He thus discovered, to his amazement, that when he addressed large gatherings, "my vocal cords could separate, my breath could come out," as he explained to Jones. Thereafter, he avoided stammering by imagining himself to be in the presence of a crowd whenever and wherever he spoke, whether it was in class, the schoolyard, a friend's house, or anywhere else.

After he completed secondary school, Buckingham enrolled at Cambridge University, in England. He earned a master's degree in social and political science there in 1987. Earlier, in 1984, he had spent the summer in the American Midwest, as an intern with the Gallup Organization. Founded by George Gallup in the mid-1930s, that company pioneered what is known as survey research, a method of studying human nature and behavior by means of carefully worded questionnaires. While Gallup is best known for its opinion polls, such surveys constitute only a small fraction of the company's business; its many other services include aiding personnel administrators by "conducting structured psychological interviews to identify the talents of individuals who 'fit' a designated position or role in an organization," according to the Gallup Web site. In 1988, some months after Buckingham graduated from Cambridge, he joined the Gallup Organization as a senior researcher and settled in the U.S.

Buckingham spent the next 15 years with Gallup, studying the relationship between workplace performance and bottom-line results for such corporate clients as Toyota and Wells Fargo. In 1994, having been promoted to management consultant, he was assigned to handle the Walt Disney account in Orlando, Florida, the site of Disneyland. His mission was to formulate a strategy for determining who among the people seeking jobs at Disneyland would prove to be the most productive workers. Prior to his arrival, Disney had used what Todd Mansfield, a Disney executive at that time, described to Del Jones as the "Ken and Barbie" approach, in which the company hired workers who "looked good in a theme park rather than people who had talent for it." After much research Buckingham concluded that, as a rule, the most effective workforces are composed of people who, temperamentally, are particularly well suited for their jobs. Jobs that some people might consider mind-numbing—housekeeper, doorman, or nanny, for example—others might regard as interesting and challenging. What was crucial was not the natures of the jobs themselves but the extent to which those filling the jobs felt "engaged" with their tasks—felt themselves to be "in the zone," as Buckingham put it. Employees who were "in the zone" would become so immersed in their work that they would lose track of time and forget their domestic troubles, but they would not be so busy that they would feel stressed. One Gallup survey found that 60 percent of workers felt engaged in their work less than once a week.

Intrigued by his findings, Buckingham teamed up with Curt Coffman—a fellow Gallup management consultant—and launched a huge study whose aim was to determine the extent to which workers' attitudes toward their jobs affected companies' performance. First, Buckingham and Coffman identified 12 main characteristics of a healthy work environment. Employees in such environments would answer "yes" to all or most of 12 questions (which the researchers labeled Q12), among them, "At work, do I have the opportunity to do what I do best every day?" "Does my supervisor, or someone at work, seem to care about me as a person?" "At work, do my opinions seem to count?" "Does the mission/purpose of my company make me feel that my work is important?" (None of the 12 questions mentioned salary, benefits, or pensions.) Then, by means of complex analyses of corporate data and more than 25 years' worth of Gallup written surveys and interviews of more than 80,000 managers and a million employees in some 400 companies, Buckingham and Coffman correlated the answers to Q12 with business results. They found that the most "engaging" workplaces—those whose Q12 scores ranked in the top 25 percent, in terms of affirmative answers—were 50 percent more likely to have lower turnover rates, 56 percent more likely to have greater customer loyalty, 38 percent more likely to have higher productivity, and 27 percent more likely to report higher profits than average. Buckingham and Coffman also found that three of the most widely held assumptions of managers were false: the beliefs, as Buckingham told Joel Schettler for *Training* (November 2001), that everyone who excels at a particular job does it the same way, that everything can be learned, and that eliminating employees' weaknesses will lead to their success.

The keys to corporate success, according to Buckingham and Coffman, are hiring people with desirable talents (that is, people with inborn qualities related to thought, feeling, and behavior), and not necessarily those with the most knowledge (learned information) or skills (learned behavior); focusing on those people's strengths; placing or keeping them in positions for which they are best fitted (rather than automatically promoting them from time to time to positions for which they may not be suited); and defining the right outcome for each person rather than telling them the right ways of fulfilling their responsibilities—in other words, viewing and treating people as individuals. "The major challenge for CEOs over the next 20 years will be the effective deployment of human assets," Buckingham told Polly LaBarre for *Fast Company* (August 2001). "But that's not about 'organizational development' or 'workplace design.' It's about psychology. It's about getting one more individual to be more productive, more focused, more fulfilled than he was yesterday." Buckingham and Coffman described their study and findings and offered recommendations for better management in *First, Break All the Rules: What the World's Greatest Managers Do Differently* (1999). The book quickly caught the attention of businesspeople; it became a *New York Times* best-seller and remained among the five best-selling business books for months.

Buckingham wrote his next book, *Now, Discover Your Strengths* (2001), with Donald O. Clifton, a former chairman of the Gallup Organization, who has been called the "father of strengths-based psychology." A unique numerical identification code (useable only once) inside each copy of the book enabled the reader to log onto the Gallup Web site to answer a 180-question personality test called the "StrengthsFinder," which was based on psychological surveys of close to two million workers in several dozen countries. The answers, according to Buckingham and Clifton, reveal the reader's five dominant "strength themes" out of a possible 34, those being a mix of abilities (for example, analytical, deliberative), values (fairness), and preferences (intellection, discipline). The book then offers suggestions for individuals and managers regarding the best ways to capitalize on particular strengths for personal development and success at work. "*First, Break All the Rules* blew away a lot of competing management theories, but it left a big question. How do you figure out someone's natural talents? The new book addresses that," Marta Salij wrote for the *Detroit Free Press* (January 31, 2001, on-line). "In the same clear language that made the first book a joy to read, Buckingham and Clifton distinguish between what can be changed and what can't. . . . What the book doesn't offer is a simple correlation between talent and profession. . . . Buckingham and Clifton warn that such a connection is impossible. 'Our research interviews indicate that thousands of people with very different theme combinations nonetheless play the same role equally well,' they write. They succeed by crafting their roles to fit their *strengths*." As of March 27, 2006, *Now, Discover Your Strengths* was number three on Amazon.com's list of its 10 best-selling business books, according to David Weinberger in *Advertising Age* (April 3, 2006, on-line).

Buckingham's third book, *The One Thing You Need to Know . . . About Great Managing, Great Leading, and Sustained Individual Success*, was published in early 2005, at around the time that Buckingham left Gallup. The book grew out of his interest in "the vividness of what excellence on the front line really looks like," as he told Bill Breen for *Fast Company* (March 2005). "By studying one person deeply, you might learn as much if not more than studying 10,000 broadly." "I identified one or two elite players, one or two people who, in their chosen roles and fields, had measurably, consistently, and dramatically outperformed their peers," Buckingham explained to Richard M. Vosburgh for *Human Resource Planning* (June 1, 2005). "Having identified them, I spent time with them in search of—not theoretical patterns, but specific actions—their day-to-day practice. My question: What were these special people actually doing that made them so very good at their role? . . . What intrigued me most about each of these people's endeavors were the practical, seemingly banal details of their actions and their choices." A great manager, he told Vosburgh, "shows two main talents: First, a natural coaching instinct . . . the ability to see and to derive satisfaction from seeing small increments of growth in someone else. Second, a quality I call individualization: namely, the ability to see fine shadings of uniqueness among the different people he/she manages." Great managers, he said, "are like catalysts, speeding up the reaction between the individual's talents and the company's goals." The main talents of a great leader, by contrast, are "optimism and ego. Optimism is the unflinching belief that things can and will get better," while a strong ego leads the optimist to believe that he or she is the one who can rally people to create that better future. In a review of *The One Thing You Need to Know* for *Personnel Today* (December 13, 2005, on-line), Bobby Chatterjee wrote, "You will instantly wonder why it requires 289 pages for the author to tell you one thing, but stick with it—it's well worth it. . . . This is a thoroughly enjoyable and very useful book."

Buckingham maintains offices in Beverly Hills, California, and near Atlanta, Georgia. His wife, Jane (Rinzler) Buckingham, is a professional trend spotter and the founder of the market-research firm Youth Intelligence, which publishes the thrice-yearly *Cassandra Report* and maintains the daily Web site TrendCentral. Jane Buckingham has written three books: *Teens Speak Out, The Modern Girl's Guide to Life,* and *The Modern Girl's Guide to Motherhood.* The Buckinghams live with their son, Jackson, and daughter, Lilia, in Beverly Hills.
—I.C.

Suggested Reading: *Across the Board* (on-line) May/June 2001; *Arrive* p21+ Mar./Apr. 2006; *Association Management* (on-line) p50+ Dec. 2001; *Fast Company* p88+ Aug. 2001; *Human Resource Planning* (on-line) p27+ June 1, 2005; Leading Authorities Speakers Bureau Web site; Marcus Buckingham Web site; *USA Today* B p1 Mar. 4, 2005

Selected Books: *First, Break All the Rules: What the World's Greatest Managers Do Differently* (with Curt Coffman), 1999; *Now, Discover Your Strengths* (with Donald O. Clifton), 2001; *The One Thing You Need to Know . . . About Great Managing, Great Leading, and Sustained Individual Success,* 2005

Burrows, James

Dec. 30, 1940– Television director; producer

Address: c/o Broder, Webb, Chervin, Silbermann Agency, 9242 Beverly Blvd., Suite 200, Beverly Hills, CA 90210

"My mind is never a blank," the sitcom director James Burrows told Bill Carter for the *New York Times* (May 14, 1995). "If something isn't funny, I'll try nine ways to make it funny. I won't just quit on it. I'll change the straight line to get more ideas, or find a funny position for the actors." The "sorcerer behind the sitcoms," as the *Times* headlined Carter's article, Burrows has helped to create and served as resident director of several of the most popular series ever to air on American television (and, through syndication, in many countries overseas): *Taxi, Cheers, Frasier, Friends,* and *Will & Grace.* He has also directed the pilots for and, in many cases, episodes of *Night Court, Dharma & Greg, NewsRadio, Veronica's Closet, 3rd Rock from the Sun, Caroline in the City, Wings,* and about 40 other television sitcoms, almost all of which went on to appear on prime-time lineups. "Millions of TV viewers owe him trillions of laughs," Sid Smith wrote for the *Chicago Tribune* (April 26, 1998). The shows Burrows has midwifed and nurtured are distinguished by their highly distinctive, quirky, flawed yet sympathetic characters, whose predicaments, yearnings, joys, and sorrows are portrayed with compassion and understanding as well as humor. Although many episodes of his shows have dealt with sensitive social issues, he has asserted that he and his collaborators refuse to

Stephen Shugerman/Getty Images

proselytize and aim only to entertain and make people laugh. "He's not like anybody else," Harriet Harris, who had a recurring role on *Frasier* and whom Burrows directed in a theatrical production in 1998, told Sid Smith. "With Jim, the jokes always come out of character. I've worked with a lot of fancy theater directors in my time, and, the truth is, most people just can't do that." Burrows is also known for his ability to turn his casts into close-knit ensembles, giving viewers "the sense that these actors have been with each other for a long time," as he explained to Bill Carter. "And I do it by creating a lot of stuff that's not necessarily on the page."

A keen observer of human nature, Burrows studied direction at the Yale School of Drama, but his education in the dramatic arts began long before, at home: his father was Abe Burrows, a successful playwright, director, producer, and occasional performer, whose friends included world-famous literary figures and people of renown in theater and film. "I look at it as if my father was a tailor, and I grew up in a tailor shop," James Burrows told Sid Smith. "The more I drifted into it, I realized I knew a lot more about making a suit than I thought." Burrows worked in theater for years before landing a job with MTM Enterprises, where he made his debut in television as the director of an episode of *The Mary Tyler Moore Show* in 1974. "When I was growing up I never thought I'd be as good as my father," he told Rick Marin for *Newsweek* (September 11, 1995). "I'm now coming to terms with the fact that maybe in my field I'm as successful as he was in his." According to Steve Johnson, writing for the *Chicago Tribune* (March 3, 2002), Burrows's achievements are a major reason why "the top shows have elevated the director from supporting player to co-star." A producer and executive producer as well as a director, Burrows has earned four awards for direction from the Directors Guild of America, nine Emmy Awards (five for direction and four for co-production), and an American Comedy Award for Lifetime Achievement, in 1996. In 2006 he received a Career Tribute Award at the United States Comedy Arts Festival in Aspen, Colorado, sponsored by HBO.

The second of two children, James Edward Burrows was born in Los Angeles, California, on December 30, 1940 to Abe Burrows and Ruth (Levinson) Burrows. He was raised in the New York City borough of Manhattan with his sister, Laurie Burrows Grad, a food writer who has hosted a television cooking show and currently edits the food and travel Web site Epicurus.com. Burrows's parents divorced in 1948; two years later his father married Carin Smith Kinzel. During Burrows's early years his father became celebrated among performers and writers for his extraordinary talents as a comic and satirist. Abe Burrows gained recognition among the public as a writer, from 1941 to 1945, for the radio show *Duffy's Tavern*; as the writer and star of his own radio programs, *The Abe Burrows Show* (1946–47) and *Breakfast with Burrows* (1949); and his appearances on *We Take Your Word* (broadcast on radio and TV in 1950), in which he displayed his erudition as well as his gift for extemporaneous comedy. His reputation grew exponentially with the success of the theatrical musical comedy *Guys and Dolls* (1950), which he co-authored. His many credits as a writer and/or director for Broadway and Hollywood also include *How to Succeed in Business without Really Trying, Cactus Flower, Can-Can, Silk Stockings, Breakfast*

at Tiffany's, and *The Solid Gold Cadillac.* His skill as a script doctor was legendary: the plea "Get me Abe Burrows!," according to various Web sites, remains a shorthand way of indicating that a script needs fixing.

As a youngster James Burrows was a member of the Metropolitan Opera Children's Chorus. He attended the High School of Music and Art (now known as the Fiorello H. LaGuardia High School of Music & Art and Performing Arts). After his graduation, in 1958, Burrows entered Oberlin College, in Oberlin, Ohio, where he majored in government and politics. "I had no desire to go into show business! New York was my father's town, and I was just Abe's kid," he told Caitlin Kelly for *Variety* (January 24, 2005). He earned a B.A. degree in 1962. Partly to avoid the military draft, he next enrolled at the Yale School of Drama, in New Haven, Connecticut. There, he learned directing from Nikos Psacharopoulos, who was a playwright as well as an instructor and whom Burrows described to Kelly as "inspirational." He earned an M.F.A. degree in 1965.

Later that year Burrows held a series of entry-level theater jobs. For a short while he worked as a dialogue coach for *O.K. Crackerby!,* a TV sitcom created by his father and Cleveland Amory that starred Burl Ives and ran for less than four months. In 1966 he served as the assistant stage manager for a musical adaptation of *Breakfast at Tiffany's,* starring Mary Tyler Moore, which his father directed and which closed after four preview performances. He next stage managed another show directed by his father—a touring production of *Cactus Flower.* In 1968, again under his father's direction, he stage managed *Forty Carats,* which starred Julie Harris and ran on Broadway for nearly two years. Watching and working closely with his father proved to be enormously valuable to Burrows. "In subsequent years, a lot of his gift and a lot of his skills seemed to come out of me at the strangest times," he told Terry Gross, who interviewed him for the National Public Radio program *Fresh Air* (March 9, 2006). "It's not that I learned them as much as . . . they were like osmosis. I absorbed them." During rehearsals, like his father, Burrows pays more attention to dialogue than to actors' movements or facial expressions, and he often paces. He also laughs heartily at every joke, in part to encourage his cast.

In late 1970 Burrows directed an original play, *The Castro Complex,* starring Raul Julia. Mounted on Broadway, it closed after 14 performances. For several years after that, Burrows stage managed or directed such shows as *The Odd Couple, Guys and Dolls,* and *The Last of the Red Hot Lovers* for dinner theaters and summer stock. One night, while he was watching *The Mary Tyler Moore Show* on TV, it occurred to him that his job and that of the director of that sitcom were similar, in that he had about eight days to prepare for each debut, while the director had a week in which to polish an episode that filled 20 minutes of air time. Burrows wrote a letter to Moore and her then-husband,

Grant Tinker, and secured an internship at their company, MTM Enterprises. In addition to *The Mary Tyler Moore Show*, which had premiered in 1970, MTM had launched *The Bob Newhart Show*, in 1972, and *Rhoda*, in 1974. For about two months Burrows observed the management, direction, and production of those programs. He paid particular attention to the camera work, which at first seemed "daunting," as he recalled to Terry Gross. In the memoir *Tinker in Television* (1994), Tinker recalled that when Bob Newhart complained that Burrows's presence was making him nervous, Tinker had Jay Sandrich take Burrows under his wing. Sandrich, who directed 119 episodes of the *Mary Tyler Moore Show*, became his mentor and close friend. Sandrich told Kelly that he immediately recognized that Burrows "was a very talented young man with a great sense of humor. We'd talk about how and why I did things. He really got it." In 1974, in his maiden effort on TV, Burrows directed an episode of *The Mary Tyler Moore Show* called "Neighbors." During the next few years, he directed episodes of such MTM programs as *The Bob Crane Show*, *The Bob Newhart Show*, *Rhoda*, *Phyllis*, and *Paul Sand in Friends and Lovers*, and he directed the pilot of *Lou Grant*.

In 1977 James L. Brooks, a creator and executive producer of *The Mary Tyler Moore Show*, and three others left MTM to create their own sitcom, and they hired Burrows as principal director. Called *Taxi*, the show was set in the dispatcher's office of a New York City cab company. All the cabdrivers—except the one played by Judd Hirsch, who accepted his lot in life—worked part-time and dreamed of success in other areas (one character, for example, was an actor, another a boxer), but every attempt they made to improve their circumstances ended in failure. In addition to Hirsch, the cast included Danny DeVito, Tony Danza, Marilu Henner, Christopher Lloyd, Andy Kaufman, J. Alan Thomas, Jeff Conaway, and Carol Kane. Burrows directed 76 of the 114 episodes, all of which were shot with four cameras operating simultaneously. He told Terry Gross that *Taxi*, which ran from 1978 until 1983, was "probably the most difficult show I ever did because the cast was so divergent, the writing was so outrageous, the set was so gigantic, and it was the first really big show where I was in charge from the beginning." *Taxi* won 20 Emmy Awards, and Burrows himself won two, for direction, in 1980 and 1981.

In 1982 Burrows co-founded a production company with Glen Charles and Les Charles, brothers who had worked as writers and producers for both *The Mary Tyler Moore Show* and *Taxi*. "I never learned more about writing than I did from those two guys," Burrows told Sid Smith. The first project of Charles Bros./Burrows Productions (later called Charles-Burrows-Charles) was *Cheers*, named for the fictional neighborhood bar in Boston, Massachusetts, that served as the setting for every show. (It resembled both the real Bull & Finch Pub in Boston and the fictional Duffy's Tavern from the radio show for which Abe Burrows wrote.) As at any bar, the main activity at Cheers (besides drinking) was conversation—indeed, as Burrows told Bill Carter, it seemed to him that that the Charleses' scripts "brought radio back to television"—with discussions among the characters about a great variety of mundane, frivolous, ridiculous, weighty, or sensitive subjects. The main characters were Sam Malone (played by Ted Danson), the libidinous, chauvinistic bartender and bar owner, a recovered alcoholic and onetime baseball player; Woody (Woody Harrelson), the childlike assistant bartender (a similar though much older character was played for three seasons, until his death, by Nicholas Colasanto); Carla (Rhea Perlman), a wisecracking waitress and harried mother of six; Diane (Shelley Long), a pretentiously intellectual graduate student who becomes a waitress—and, later, Sam's girlfriend—after being jilted by her fiancé in the first episode; and such steady customers as Norm (George Wendt), a frequently unemployed accountant, Norm's best friend, Cliff (John Ratzenberger), a postman and know-it-all, and Frasier (Kelsey Grammer), a pompous psychiatrist. Shortly before the series' 11th and last season, Bill Carter wrote in an assessment for the *New York Times* (May 9, 1993) entitled "Why *Cheers* Proved So Intoxicating," "The characters' very flaws are, in part, what makes them so irresistible."

For weeks after *Cheers* premiered, on September 30, 1982, it had very poor ratings; it avoided cancellation because of its fine critical reception and because NBC "had nothing to put on in its place," as Burrows told Kelly. Burrows nevertheless felt confident that the show was "something special," as he told Ed Will. *Cheers*'s viewership grew greatly during the 1984–85 season, when it aired after the already popular *The Cosby Show* and *Family Ties* and before *Night Court* and *Hill Street Blues*. In every season starting in its fourth, its Nielsen rankings placed it among the top-five TV shows; in its ninth season, 1990–91, it ranked first. Burrows directed about 235 of its 273 episodes and won Emmys as director in 1983 and 1991 and as coproducer in 1983, 1984, and 1990. The show itself won an Emmy as outstanding comedy series four times. When the last episode aired, on August 19, 1993, *Cheers* was being syndicated in three dozen countries, and revenues from syndication had topped half a billion dollars. In his 1993 *New York Times* appraisal, Carter reported that the *Cheers* cast described Burrows as "indispensable, the person most responsible for the show's longevity. . . . His leadership behind the scenes, they say, was equally essential to its success."

Burrows earned another Emmy, in 1994, for the direction of *Frasier*, a critically acclaimed and popular *Cheers* spin-off, in which Kelsey Grammer reprised his role as a psychiatrist, this time one who hosts a call-in radio show. *Frasier*, which debuted in September 1993 and ended its run in May 2004, also starred John Mahoney as Frasier's widowed father, Martin; Jane Leeves as Martin's health-care worker, Daphne; and David Hyde Pierce as Frasier's brother, Niles, also a psychiatrist. In *The 'Radio Times' Guide to Television Comedy* (2003), Mark Lewisohn described *Frasier* as a "comedy masterpiece," not least because it was "adult and sophisticated: the scripts were literate, the plots tight and the one-liners extremely funny and incisive." Burrows directed most of the first season's episodes and then, during the following three seasons, another 17.

Burrows's next project was *Friends*, the pilot for which aired in 1994. "I like to do shows with very strong writing," Burrows told Bill Carter in 1995. "When they sent me *Friends*, the writing just leaped off the page." The sitcom depicted six attractive 20-somethings (30-somethings by the end of the show's run) who relied on one another for emotional support. Roommates or neighbors living in the Greenwich Village section of New York, the three men and three women often hung out in a neighborhood coffee shop. In their conversations and approaches toward life, they displayed qualities associated with Generation X: "dissatisfaction with middle-class jobs and values, sexual angst in the age of AIDS, the disintegration of the nuclear family, and—most tellingly—fear of commitment to either love or career," as Joe Chidley wrote for *Maclean's* (October 2, 1995, on-line). As Jess Cagle and Dan Snierson wrote for *Entertainment Weekly* (December 29, 1995–January 5, 1996, on-line), however, *Friends* was "the first successful Hollywood offering in which Generation Xers aren't depicted as nihilistic, self-doubting pop culturaholics, as they are in films like *Clerks*, *Reality Bites*, and *Slacker*. . . . Our Friends are working and learning and growing. . . . We get the feeling that these Friends are going to be okay." In its first season *Friends* joined the ranks of the top 10 shows on television then, and its stars—Jennifer Aniston, Courteney Cox, Lisa Kudrow, Matt LeBlanc, Matthew Perry, and David Schwimmer—became celebrities. Burrows, who directed 16 episodes during the show's 11 seasons, earned an Emmy Award for his work in 1995.

To elicit good performances from actors, Burrows told Tom Walter for the *Chicago Tribune* (September 18, 1995), "you just try to make them feel they're part of the creative process." He and the actors "try to create things on the stage the writers haven't seen," he explained. He also said, "The best thing for an actor is to try it his way. The way they do it may not work but it may inspire me to try something else."

Most recently Burrows directed the sitcom *Will & Grace*, which ran from September 1998 until May 2006. The show was about a lawyer who is gay (played by Eric McCormack) and an interior designer who is heterosexual (Debra Messing); best friends, the two live in Manhattan, usually as roommates. Will's friend Jack (Sean Hayes), who appeared regularly, is also homosexual, but unlike Will, he displays stereotypically gay mannerisms. "Jack can be incredibly outrageous because Will is

not . . . ," Burrows told Terry Gross. "I think if Will wasn't on the show we would get letters from the gay community about how Jack's portrayed . . . but because of Will, it allows us to do that." "By the simple trick of sophisticated writing and great acting, [*Will & Grace*] creates an idealized reality within which sexual identity is no more or less interesting than a person's natural hair color," Tom Maurstad wrote for the *Dallas Morning News* (February 22, 2000, on-line). "It's something that can be fun to talk about, but, really, what difference does it make?" From 2001 to 2005 *Will & Grace* ranked second in popularity, after *Friends*, among viewers 18 through 49 years of age. It earned more than 80 Emmy nominations and won 12. As executive producer, Burrows shared one of them, in 2000, in the category of outstanding comedy series.

In 1982 Burrows directed the feature film *Partners*, written by Francis Veber (the scriptwriter for the 1978 motion picture *La Cage aux Folles*). The movie fared badly both critically and commercially. "I'm so sour on movies," Burrows told Bill Carter in 1995. "I don't like the two years you have to spend on them. I like the instant gratification, the eight-days-and-out of [a sitcom]. You know when you shoot in front of an audience if it's good." "If I found the right play," he added, "I would surely do theater." That opportunity came along in 1998, when Burrows directed a revival of the 1939 comedy *The Man Who Came to Dinner*, by George S. Kaufman and Moss Hart, presented at the Steppenwolf Theatre, in Chicago. "This is a joyous production . . . ," Richard Christiansen wrote for the *Chicago Tribune* (April 28, 1998). "Oh, what fun it is to see [the cast] all having such a good time—and giving us a wonderful night in the theater while they're at it." Christiansen also reported that "of the dozens of bits of business" that Burrows had "craftily invented," only three or four failed to produce laughs.

"For a guru of the funnybone, Burrows is a serious fellow," Sid Smith wrote. From his first marriage, which ended in divorce in the mid-1990s, Burrows has three daughters. (His production company is called Three Sisters Entertainment.) He has one stepdaughter from his second marriage, in 1997. He lives in Beverly Hills, California, and owns a large collection of modern art.

—M.B.

Suggested Reading: *Chicago Tribune* Tempo p5 Sep. 18, 1995, Arts & Entertainment p1+ Apr. 26, 1998, Tempo p2 Mar. 10, 2000; *Entertainment Weekly* p30+ Mar. 26, 2004; *Fresh Air* (transcript) Mar. 9, 2006; *GQ* p238+ May 1988; *New York Times* II p1+ May 14, 1995, E p1+ Sep. 29, 2005; *Newsweek* (on-line) Sep. 11, 1995; *Variety* (on-line) Jan. 24, 2005

Selected Television Shows: as director of pilot and/or further episodes during the years listed— *Fay*, 1975; *Phyllis*, 1975; *Mary Tyler Moore*, 1974–76; *Busting Loose*, 1977; *The Bob Newhart*

Show, 1975–77; Laverne and Shirley , 1976–77; Szysznyk, 1977; The Betty White Show, 1977; Lou Grant, 1977; Rhoda, 1977–78; Husbands, Wives & Lovers, 1978; Free Country, 1978; A New Kind of Family, 1979; The Associates, 1979; Good Time Harry, 1980; Best of the West, 1981; Taxi, 1978–82; Night Court, 1984; Valerie, 1986; All Is Forgiven, 1986; The Tortellis, 1987; Dear John, 1988; Disneyland, 1990; The Marshall Chronicles, 1990; Wings, 1990; The Fanelli Boys, 1990; Flying Blind, 1992; Cheers, 1982–93; Cafe Americain, 1993; The Boys Are Back, 1994; The Preston Episodes, 1995; Partners, 1995; Hudson Street, 1995; Caroline in the City, 1995; Newsradio, 1996; 3rd Rock from the Sun, 1996; Pearl, 1996; Men Behaving Badly, 1996; Chicago

Sons, 1997; Frasier, 1993–97; Fired Up, 1997; George & Leo, 1997; Dharma & Greg, 1997; Veronica's Closet, 1997; Union Square, 1997; Friends, 1994–98; Conrad Bloom, 1998; Jesse, 1998; The Secret Lives of Men, 1998; Ladies Man, 1998; Stark Raving Mad, 1999; Madigan Men, 2000; Cursed, 2000; Good Morning, Miami, 2002; Bram and Alice, 2002; Two and a Half Men, 2003; The Stones, 2004; Four Kings, 2006; Courting Alex, 2006; Teachers, 2006; Will & Grace, 1998–2006; The Class, 2006

Selected Films: Partners, 1982

Selected Plays: The Castro Complex, 1970; The Man Who Came to Dinner, 1998

Carone, Nicolas

(Ka-ROHN or Ka-ROHN-ay)

June 4, 1917– Artist

Address: 463 West St., Apt. B937, New York, NY 10014

The artist Nicolas Carone has synthesized a breadth of influences—some as remote as Michelangelo or Leonardo da Vinci, others as intimate as his friends and fellow painters Jackson Pollock and Roberto Matta—to create a body of work that has at times during his decades-long career swerved close to recognizable styles but has never settled comfortably into them. The winner of the prestigious Prix de Rome when he was only 23, Carone went on to participate in New York City's legendary 1951 Ninth Street Exhibition, which perhaps more than any other single show created a canon for mid-century American art and artists, as well as in such important international exhibitions as the 1956 Venice Biennale; the 1955 and 1958 Carnegie International; and the 1958 World's Fair, in Brussels, Belgium. In the mid-1980s, after more than 20 years of teaching at a variety of prominent art schools, Carone started his own school, the International School of Art (now called the International School of Painting, Drawing, and Sculpture). Located for most of its existence in Montecastello di Vibio, a tiny, ancient town on a hilltop in the Italian region of Umbria, the school is not far from the home where Carone, a first-generation American, has spent many of his summers for roughly the last 30 years. "You see," Carone told the curator and art historian Paul Cummings in a 1968 oral-history interview for the Smithsonian Institution's Archives of American Art (on-line), "living and working with the Italians, there's something about their aesthetic that sort of seeps in, you know. For instance, the Italians speak about tone. They don't paint pure color. It's a tonal idea. But that tonal idea also

has a metaphysical meaning. It has a time sense. It's like pushing; it's pushing forward in time."

The second of six children of Italian immigrants, Nicolas Carone was born on June 4, 1917 in the New York City neighborhood known as Little Italy. (His surname is pronounced Ka-ROHN-ay or the more Americanized Ka-ROHN.) His father was from Altamura, near the southeastern Italian port city of Bari, and his mother hailed from the village of San Costantino Albanese, in Basilicata. A traditional Italian family in many ways, the Carones were a large, closely knit group. His father was a dock worker for most of Carone's youth, and his mother worked in the home, making dinners for not only the immediate family but also for a group of artists, writers, and musicians who regularly visited the house in Hoboken, New Jersey, to which the family moved when Carone was about five.

Shortly before they moved, Carone began to do his first drawings from life, sketching horses in chalk on the cobblestones of the street in front of their home. His formal art education began in about 1928, when he traveled from Hoboken to Manhattan after school, to take night classes at the rigidly academic Leonardo da Vinci Art School. A few years later Carone persuaded his mother to let him leave A. J. Demarest High School to take full-time art classes. "I felt that I really wanted to be an artist," he told Cummings, "and why waste all this time at public schools when I could get an education in the meantime in a practical sense." (Carone is arguably the second-most-famous person ever to drop out of Demarest High School; the singer Frank Sinatra, then an acquaintance of Carone's, occupies the top spot.)

For the next few years, Carone studied at two venerable New York art schools, the Art Students League and the National Academy of Design (now the National Academy Museum and School of Fine Art). The National Academy was the home of his most important teacher during the 1930s, Leon Kroll, who "was more liberal and modern," as Carone told Cummings. "He had a very broad point of

Courtesy of David Ramm

Nicolas Carone

view." In 1939 Kroll was awarded a commission to create a set of three massive murals—the central one 31 feet high and 57 feet long—for the Worcester Memorial Auditorium in Worcester, Massachusetts. The mural filled a special hall dedicated to it with images expressive of New Deal–era political and social ideals; the central panel, for example, depicted Americans from a wide array of ethnic and racial backgrounds assembling around the country's flag. Carone served as Kroll's first assistant for almost three years, working on the mural from eight in the morning until six in the evening. He was responsible for transferring Kroll's drawings to the Belgian-linen canvas and roughly applying paint to parts of the landscape and the clothing on the figures in preparation for Kroll. It was "a good experience," Carone told Cummings, adding: "And actual work . . . a big surface."

In April 1941, the month before the Worcester murals were unveiled to the public, Carone participated in a show at the National Academy of Design, and in August of that year he won the highly prestigious Prix de Rome for painting, an annual award offered to emerging or mid-career artists by the American Academy in Rome. (The American award and similar awards offered by other countries are inspired by the prize the French government has sponsored since 1666.) Though the primary benefit of the award was normally free access to the facilities of the American Academy in Rome, World War II was already underway in Europe by the time Carone won, making the usual arrangement impractical. Instead, Carone was given $1,500, which he set aside so that he could travel to Italy once the war was over. "I was looking forward to that practically all my life," he told Cummings.

Carone enlisted in the U.S. Air Force not long after American involvement in the war began, late in 1941. He was assigned to the First Fighter Command, which initially stationed him in New York City before moving him to Long Island's Mitchel Field Air Force Base. Creating military maps and providing radar scopes by day, Carone spent the time he was allowed off the base hitchhiking into Manhattan, where he got to know members of the New York art scene, including the influential dealer of surrealist artwork Alexandre (sometimes spelled Alexander) Iolas and some of the artists associated with Iolas's gallery. At the same time, he continued his art education under the German expatriate painter Hans Hoffman, who directed a one-person art academy, the Hans Hoffman School of Fine Arts. Located most of the year in New York's Greenwich Village but relocating in the summer to Provincetown, Massachusetts, Hoffman's school had a revolutionary effect on both Carone and the New York art world in general. Among Hoffman's students were such important American painters as Joan Mitchell, Helen Frankenthaler, Lee Krasner, and Larry Rivers; the famed critic Clement Greenberg was also strongly influenced by Hoffman. Carone turned to Hoffman after growing "very dissatisfied with what I was doing before because I was looking for something more real," as he said to Cummings. By "something more real" Carone did not, in this case, mean paintings that offered a more convincing illusion of depth or of physical objects but work that captured what he called "the underlying abstract structure that I knew was in art."

Under Hoffman's tutelage, Carone's art went from figurative and largely realistic work, whose style approached the Impressionist-influenced manner of his former teacher Kroll, to increasingly abstract art, culminating in what he described to Cummings as "a very pure plastic approach to the work," one reminiscent of the highly simplified grids and flat colors of the Dutch painter Piet Mondrian. "And I think if you arrived at that . . . you were just ready to leave [Hoffman], that's all, because he couldn't take you anywhere else," Carone explained to Cummings. Hoffman's teaching and the work produced by students in the class nonetheless left a strong mark on Carone, affecting the way he painted and drew, shaping his own approach to teaching, and giving him a deeply informed and unusual perspective on the direction in which art would go as the 1950s and 1960s neared. "I think that the most advanced—and you can quote me now, boy—the most advanced art [of the time] was done in Hoffman's class," he told Cummings. Carone added, "I really think that Hoffman was probably the greatest teacher in the world. I really do."

Carone left the army in 1945, following the end of World War II, and in 1947, after about two years of working in a studio in New York, he moved to Italy, along with his first wife and young son. Using the money from his Prix de Rome and the G.I. Bill (a program that provided funds for education, housing, and other needs to returning veterans), he established a studio off a courtyard in the center of Rome. ("The rent was, oh, ten dollars a month," he told Cummings.) He began painting what he described to Cummings as "very abstract expressionist work." Carone and his wife lived on the via Margutta, an area famous as a home to Roman artists and the setting for a 1963 Italian film of the same name. He soon became familiar with important Italian artists from the postwar period, including the sculptor Pericle Fazzini and the painters Afro Basaldella, Giuseppe Capogrossi, and Alberto Burri, as well as the Chilean painter Roberto Matta, who would become a close friend of Carone's and a key influence on his work. Carone was also an acquaintance of the famed Italian painters Giorgio Morandi, Gino Severini, and Lucio Fontana. Rome was the site of Carone's first one-man show, as well as a base for explorations throughout Italy and into France. "It was really the most wonderful time of my life," Carone told Cummings. After about three and a half years in Italy, during which Carone had been awarded a Fulbright grant from the U.S. Department of State and had shown his work alongside Matta's at Rome's Museum of Modern Art, his marriage came to an end, and he returned to New York.

In 1951 Carone and a number of other artists who would eventually come to be called abstract expressionists held a show in a small space at 60 East Ninth Street, in Manhattan. Now referred to as the Ninth Street Exhibition (or Ninth Street Show), it has come to be considered by American art histo-

rians as one of the most important exhibitions of American art of the previous century, highlighting a distinctively American approach to painting and bringing together a group of artists who for the next decade or so commanded worldwide attention. In 1953 Carone began working with Eleanor Ward, an acquaintance of the dealer Iolas. Ward was opening a new gallery, located in an old carriage house (later destroyed) in Midtown Manhattan. Called the Stable Gallery, it became one of the most daring galleries in New York, giving such artists as Joseph Cornell, Robert Rauschenberg, and Cy Twombly—all of whom Carone recruited—much-needed exposure early in their careers; Andy Warhol and Alex Katz later became affiliated with the gallery.

Among the Stable's most important contributions to American art history was its hosting of the New York Artists Annuals that, between 1953 and 1957, helped give added cohesion to the New York painting scene. Carone participated in each of the annuals; a group of artists juried the shows, rather than Ward or Carone alone, thus eliminating any conflict of interest. Shortly before he began working with Ward, Carone had gotten married again, this time to Adele Bishop, a Juilliard-trained singer who would later be "instrumental in reviving the popularity of decorative stencils in the United States," according to her obituary in the *New York Times* (February 6, 1996). Bishop took up the practice of stenciling after she and Carone joined Pollock, Willem de Kooning, and others in moving out of Manhattan and onto Long Island, at that time a rural and more affordable place to live.

Over the years between the 1951 Ninth Street Show and his appearance in a show of abstract expressionists at the Solomon R. Guggenheim Museum in New York, in 1962, Carone enjoyed a strong period of sustained public exposure for his work. In addition to his appearances in the Stable annuals, Carone appeared in the 1955 and 1958 exhibitions of international paintings at the Carnegie Institute (now the Carnegie Museum of Art), in Pittsburgh; in the 1956 Venice Biennale; in the 1958 World's Fair, in Brussels; and in a show of abstract expressionists at the Walker Art Center, in Minneapolis, Minnesota. Along with those appearances in important group exhibitions, Carone's work was seen on its own in at least seven solo shows during the same period. The first was in Chicago's Allan Frumkin Gallery, in 1952. In April 1956, having apparently stopped working at Stable, Carone had his first one-person show there; a second one followed, in November 1957. The paintings Carone showed that year, as the critic Dore Ashton wrote for the *New York Times* (November 5, 1957), "present in abstract terms a chilly, wild, imaginary landscape filled with glacial abutments receiving the thrusts of dark currents. There are associations of underground streams and sudden draughts and quaking terrains." As Ashton's comments suggest, Carone's paintings during the 1950s and early 1960s were often completely abstract and muted in color, just a few shades of gray keeping them from being black-and-white works. (They could also be entirely black and white, as proven by Carone's participation in a December 1956 Stable show of work in that mode.) Carone's canvases during that period were often very large, and one criticism occasionally made of his work at the time was that the smaller canvases seemed more successful than the large ones. Ashton wrote in a *New York Times* article (November 13, 1959) about Carone's first solo show at New York's Staempfli Gallery, for example, that Carone's smaller works "show the artist in unguarded, natural moments when his innate love of detail is honored."

In 1956, meanwhile, Carone had participated in a show in Washington, D.C., titled New Approaches to the Figure in Contemporary Painting. Peppered throughout critical commentary on his work during that period are remarks about the sudden emergence of figures in otherwise abstract spaces. Writing about Carone's third solo show at Staempfli, in 1961 (the second had come in 1960), Brian O'Doherty opined in the *New York Times* (November 9, 1961), "Sometimes Mr. Carone introduces the figure to ignore it, and paint as it were, against it, so that it is immured in paint like a skiagram." (A skiagram is a photograph made with X-rays or gamma rays.)

In about 1960, with his second marriage coming to an end, Carone returned to Manhattan. By 1965 he had rented a studio and living space on the Upper East Side (in the same building in which the painter Mark Rothko lived) and begun the teaching career that would sustain him into the late 1990s. He took visiting-instructor positions at such universities as Yale, in New Haven, Connecticut; Columbia, in New York City; Brandeis, in Waltham, Massachusetts; and Cornell, in Ithaca, New York. In addition Carone taught for about six years at New York City's Cooper Union, and in 1964 he began a quarter-century association with the New York Studio School, where he was, according to Jennifer Sachs Samet in the *New York Sun* (February 17, 2005), "hugely influential."

By the end of the 1960s, Carone had returned to Italy, living on and off in Rome, particularly during the summers. In the 1970s he bought a remote piece of property in Umbria and, with it, an abandoned and at first uninhabitable stone house dating from the 16th century. Bit by bit, often camping there with his sons, who pitched in as well, Carone rebuilt the house and in the process increased his attachment to the country, growing frustrated that every fall he had to return to the U.S. in order to teach. In the mid-1980s a former student of Carone's offered to help him with the administrative work necessary to start his own school, and the International School for Art came into being, with a second business partner joining after a few years. The school's first home was in a still-functioning monastery in the hilltop town of Todi; it soon moved to the tiny village of Montecastello di Vibio. During the school's four- to six-week-long sessions, students worked much of the day in their studios or in classes—drawing, painting, or sculpting from models, still-life arrangements, or the green and brown hills around the town—while the night brought a communal dinner and visiting lecturers. Most Fridays there were excursions to Italian cities to view the artwork that had given the country such a prominent place in European art history. Though the school was an apparent success, the relationship between Carone and his business partners soured at the end of the 1990s, spurring Carone to bring a legal case against them in the Italian court system. (The case remains unresolved.)

Between 1962 and about 1999 Carone's work had been shown in public only intermittently, though he continued to sell it privately. In 1978 and 1993, however, Carone had solo shows in Florida, exhibiting exclusively a type of painting that he had been doing for decades: portraits, often of people in simple clothes, with firm gazes and wide noses—subjects that were not glamorous but suggested deep sensuality. In addition to those paintings, whose figures were not based on actual models, Carone was carving heads out of stones he found outside his home in Italy. Mysterious yet evocative like the paintings, following the contours and geologic makeup of the stones themselves, the heads have become important examples of Carone's work in sculpting, an art he had taken up in the mid-1960s at the suggestion of a friend.

The beginning of the 21st century brought a renewed interest in Carone and his work. In addition to his appearance in a variety of group exhibitions, in 2003 Carone had a solo show at the Butler Institute of American Art, in Youngstown, Ohio, that focused on his works on paper, especially gouaches, paintings made with a rich type of watercolor more closely resembling oil-based paints. Many of those works featured hunched male nudes in dreamlike atmospheres, their compositions reminiscent of Michelangelo's *Last Judgment*, a monumental fresco in the Sistine Chapel in Rome. A more wide-ranging exhibit of Carone's works on paper opened in October 2005 at the Lohin Geduld Gallery, in New York City. The exhibition brought emphatically positive reviews from the city's critics. "Mr. Carone's mixture of de Kooning-, Old Master-, and Greco-Roman-inspired works made up of nearly abstract figures [is] rich and absorbing—a rhythmic tumble of classicism, eroticism, and ambiguity," Lance Esplund wrote for the *New York Sun* (November 17, 2005). "Looking at his works, most of which, though fresh and alive, feel as if, half-baked, they had fallen straight out of mid-century, I could not help but think that here is an artist who is not anxious about what 'must-see' exhibition is currently showing. Here is an artist focused on his work who, moving picture to picture, line by line, is taking his own sweet time." With shows of his heads and other sculptures being planned for the near future, a reevaluation of Carone's work seems inevitable.

Now unmarried, Carone lives and works in Italy, New York City, and New York State's Hudson Valley, where he has a working space near the homes of his twin sons—Christian, a photographer, and Claude, a painter. David, a son by his first marriage, lives in Indiana.

—D.R.

Suggested Reading: *New York Observer* p1 Nov. 28, 2005; *New York Sun* p1 Nov. 17, 2005; *New York Times* p17 May 6, 1941, p37 Nov. 5, 1957, p58 Nov. 13, 1959, p31 Nov. 9, 1961; Smithsonian Institution's Archives of American Art (on-line)

Courtesy of Peter Smith

Carson, Anne

June 21, 1950– Poet; essayist

Address: c/o Knopf Publishing/Author Mail, 1745 Broadway, New York, NY 10019

Over the past decade Anne Carson has taken her place at the forefront of American poetry. In the *Village Voice* (May 19, 1998), Karen Volkman referred to Carson as "unclassifiable," due in part to the blurring of genres that takes place in many of her works, some of them blending poetry and prose, others story and essay. While Carson has been reluctant to discuss with interviewers more than the bare facts of her life, the sadder elements of that life—her father's dementia, the disappearance of her brother, the painful dissolution of her marriage—have often found their way into her work, which did not stop Gail Wronsky from writing in the *Antioch Review* (Spring 1997), echoing others, "Carson's poems are also sometimes wickedly funny." Carson, a university professor and scholar of classical literature, has often infused her poetry with references to mythology and the great works of antiquity, along with images from modern life; perhaps the most celebrated aspects of her work, in fact, are its eclectic nature and the connections made between things that are, on the surface, wildly unrelated. In her profile of Carson for the *New York Times Magazine* (March 26, 2000), Melanie Rehak reported, "When I try to get her to nail down her main themes as a writer, she's baffled: 'I have no idea. Whatever I bump into, I do. It's an act of impulse.'"

Carson's works include the essay volumes *Eros the Bittersweet* (1986) and *Economy of the Unlost: Reading Simonides of Keos with Paul Celan* (1999), the poetry volumes *Plainwater* (1995), *Glass, Irony and God* (1995), *Autobiography of Red: A Novel in Verse* (1998), and *Decreation* (2005), and translations of ancient works by the Greek masters Sophocles and Sappho. The winner of a number of prestigious awards, Carson was the recipient of a $500,000 MacArthur Fellowship, commonly referred to as the "genius" grant, in 2000.

Anne Carson was born June 21, 1950 in Canada and grew up in various towns in northern Ontario. Her father was a bank manager; her mother was a homemaker. Carson's early life was made difficult by her father's long struggle with Alzheimer's disease. Her older brother, Michael, who was addicted to drugs, dropped out of contact with the family in about 1970 and was in touch with Carson again only after their mother's death, in 1997. He died in 2000. Writing for the *New York Times* (March 27, 2004, on-line), Dinitia Smith reported that Carson's childhood was "redeemed" when, in her last year of high school, her Latin teacher introduced her to classical literature, giving her informal lessons in Greek and reading the works of Sappho with her. "She really changed my life," Carson told Smith about the teacher.

Carson pursued her interest in classical literature at the University of Toronto, in Ontario, where she earned a B.A. degree in 1974, an M.A. in 1975, and a Ph.D. in 1981. She was also awarded a diploma in classics by the University of St. Andrews in Scotland, in 1976. Carson began her academic career at the University of Calgary, Alberta, Canada, in 1979 and then taught at Princeton University, in New Jersey, from 1980 to 1987. She then went on to McGill University, in Montreal, teaching classics in the history department and directing graduate studies while devoting alternate semesters to visiting professorships at various universities in the United States. She has taught at the University of Michigan in Ann Arbor; the University of California, Berkeley; Emory University, in Atlanta, Georgia; and the California College of Arts and Crafts, in Oakland.

In 1986 Princeton University Press published Carson's *Eros the Bittersweet: An Essay*, which grew out of her doctoral dissertation. (Dalkey Archive reissued the book as a trade paperback in 1998.) The volume consists of 34 essays about the human expression of love and desire, with emphasis on how "the Greeks displayed *eros* in poetic discourse," according to John Peter Anton, writing for *Choice* (December 1986). Carson, he wrote, "combines critical insight, poetic sensibility, and intimate knowledge of classical literature" to "illustrate the multifaceted nature of *eros* and also provide a point of departure for expansive explorations into the depths of erotic myth and motive." Stephen Burt, in his article on Carson for *Publishers Weekly* (April 3, 2000), called *Eros the Bittersweet* "a startling, lucid argument about love, lust and jealousy in Greek poetry."

What Carson has described as a "changeful" occurrence in her career took place when she was living at the 92nd St. Y, in New York City, known as a venue for authors' readings, for a year in 1986 and 1987. As she told Stephen Burt, a friend of hers, a scholar, suggested that she contact Ben Sonnenberg, the founding publisher of the literary journal *Grand Street*, "since he was a man of letters and I was a person of letters." Carson took her friend's advice, with the result that Sonnenberg published her series of prose pieces, "Kinds of Water," which Carson described to Burt as "something in between a story and an essay" that traces the route of the Catholic pilgrimage to Santiago de Compostela, in Spain. Carson described Sonnenberg's response to her work as playing a crucial part in her development as a writer: "It's very important to have someone you trust tell you your writing is good," she told Burt, adding that Sonnenberg's acceptance of her writing "made me validate that way of writing, because up until that time . . . I thought I had to make things be either an academic thesis or else fiction, and I couldn't write fiction." A *New York Times Book Review* (November 20, 1988) critic called "Kinds of Water" an example of "a kind of inspired lunacy." Annie Dillard included an essay from "Kinds of Water" in *The Best American Essays 1988*.

In Carson's volume *Short Talks* (1992), prose works are intermingled with poems, each piece titled a "Short Talk" on a different subject, examples being "Short Talk on Hopes" and "Short Talk on Ovid." The pieces concern transformations, sometimes subtle, sometimes surreal, as in the transformation of the actress Brigitte Bardot into the mythological figure Circe in "Short Talk on Brigitte Bardot." Alexander M. Forbes wrote for *Canadian Literature* (Spring 1995), "If *Short Talks* transforms its subjects, it also transforms the prose paragraphs which comprise it. In Carson's hands the prose paragraph sometimes becomes a prose poem ('Short Talk on Autism') and sometimes an essay ('Short Talk on the Rules of Perspective'). . . . The stories that are told usually prove . . . to be 'parables and paradoxes'. . . . At every level, the *Short Talks* record unexpected transformations."

Carson's 1995 volume *Plainwater* includes "Kinds of Water" and *Short Talks* as well as "The Life of Towns" and "Canicula di Anna," a long poem based on the work of the 16th-century Italian painter Perugino. The book's overriding image is, as the title suggests, water. "The theme of water that floods each part lends credence to one's notion of seldom having a metaphysical floor to stand on, the aberrations of grammar, syntax, punctuation, and linear movement floating one weightless," Richard Holinger wrote for the *Midwest Quarterly* (Winter 1997). Holinger found the most successful part of the book to be "The Anthropology of Water," which consists of three essays. "At the outset of the third essay," he wrote, "Carson explains that her brother ran into 'bad luck' in high school, and then disappeared while trying to reach Asia. What follows is an anthology of lovely dreamlike prose poems about a man's daily swim in a beautiful lily lake. He is perfectly at home, as are we, thanks to Carson's sure, exquisite language." Brian Evenson, writing for the *Review of Contemporary Fiction* (Fall 1995), found Carson's "short essays on father's madness" to be "superb" and wrote that "at her best, Carson's imagination is so vivid and the links she makes so unexpected that her images are revelatory, skirting the very edge of madness. At her worst, which is seldom, a pretentiousness can creep into her style." He concluded that, like the poet Ezra Pound, Carson uses "erudition without obscurity, and knows how far her readers are willing to go with her."

Carson's *Glass, Irony and God*, also published in 1995, consists of five long poems and an essay, "The Gender of Sound." In *Publishers Weekly* (September 25, 1995), a reviewer wrote, "Fusing confession, narrative and classicism, Carson's poetry witnesses the collision of heart and mind with breathtaking vitality." Writing for the *New York Times Book Review* (May 14, 2000), Calvin Bedient judged the poem "The Glass Essay" from *Glass, Irony and God* to be (along with "The Anthropology of Water") one of Carson's strongest works, calling it "stunningly unsparing."

Autobiography of Red: A Novel in Verse, Carson's 1998 volume, is a modern retelling of the Greek myth of Geryon, a red monster with wings who, along with his red cattle, is killed by Herakles as one of the hero's 12 labors. Carson's Red is first a schoolboy, then an adolescent, and finally a mature artist with a passion for photography and volcanos. Years after he falls in love with—and is abandoned by—Herakles, the two meet again, when Herakles has a new lover. "The resulting love triangle erupts like a volcano," Anne Szumigalski wrote for *Quill & Quire* (July 1998). "*Autobiography of Red* is a strange bildungsroman, a portrait of the artist as red winged creature," Karen Volkman wrote. "With her unnerving gift for portraying inner turmoil and terror, Carson records the tremors of this fugitive sensibility, tracing Geryon's life through his childhood molestation, tortured romance with Herakles, obsession with photography, and impulsive pilgrimage to the extreme reaches of the Andes and the volcano Icchantikas, culminating in a delirious act of self-assertion as his dormant wings test themselves at last." *Autobiography of Red* was nominated for the National Book Critics Circle Award in Poetry in 1998.

In 1999 Carson and her students created the libretto for an opera, *The Mirror of Simple Souls*, based on the life of Marguerite Porete, a medieval French mystic who was burned at the stake for heresy. The original production, at the University of Michigan, required seven rooms—or installations—that corresponded to the seven parts of the opera. In the same year Carson published *Economy of the Unlost: Reading Simonides of Keos with Paul Celan*, comprising her Martin Classical Lectures, given at Oberlin College, in Ohio. The volume is a critical comparison of the writings of Simonides, who lived in the fifth century B.C.E. in Greece, with those of Paul Celan (1920-70), a Romanian Jew who lived in Paris and wrote in German.

Men in the Off Hours, Carson's 2000 offering, is another volume of poems and poetic essays. "Most verse collections are a miscellany of pieces written over a number of years, without much connection, and of uneven consistency," Phoebe Pettingell wrote in the *New Leader* (March/April 2000). "Carson's latest compilation should be read as a whole, for images and concepts accumulate meaning throughout the work, like a rolling snowball. A peruser might wonder why such diverse forms belong together, yet upon closer reading the work's coherence becomes luminous." In "Father's Old Blue Cardigan," from *Men in the Off Hours*, Carson addressed her father's decline into Alzheimer's disease: "His laws were a secret. / But I remember the moment at which I knew / he was going mad inside his laws. / He was standing at the turn of the driveway when I arrived. / He had on the blue cardigan with the buttons done up all the way to the top. / Not only because it was a hot July afternoon / but the look on his face — as a small child who has been dressed by some aunt early in the morning / for a long trip / on cold trains and windy platforms / will sit very straight at the edge of his seat / while the shadows like long fingers / over the haystacks that sweep past / keep shocking him / because he is riding backwards." *Men in the Off Hours* also contains an elegy for Carson's mother, "Appendix to Ordinary Time." Another section of the volume, entitled "TV Men," had its origins in the work Carson did for a 1995 public-television documentary on Nobel Prize winners. Since most of the laureates were scientists, "I was supposed to attack science from the view of a humanist in these little 30-second sound bites. It was just ridiculous," Carson told Melanie Rehak. "They referred to my function as 'putting the poetry in.'" She told Burt for the *Publishers Weekly* profile that her work on the documentary was "one of the worst experiences of my life." Calvin Bedient wrote in his assessment of *Men in the Off Hours* for the *New York Times Book Review*, "There's a good reason

that Carson's reputation has soared to a level equal to that of the half-dozen most admired contemporary American poets. She's tremendously gifted and, without lowering standards, often writes in a middle range between philosophy and lyricism, where many can find her. At the same time, she has great intellectual and emotional knowledge, a vast habitat, to every bit of which she brings powerful perception and a freshness as startling as a loud knock at the door."

In her 2001 volume, *The Beauty of the Husband: A Fictional Essay in 29 Tangos*, Carson returned to the autobiographical mode that had informed *Plainwater* and *Glass, Irony and God*. *The Beauty of the Husband* tells the story of a couple's courtship, marriage, and painful parting. "The plot emerges through Carson's meditative, elusive fragments, mysteriously isolated couplets, excerpts from versified conversations and letters, interior monologues and (as Carson's readers have come to expect) digressions on matters of classical scholarship," the *Publishers Weekly* (December 18, 2000) reviewer wrote. Over the next couple of years, Carson brought out her translations of work by Greek masters. Her edition of *Electra*, by the dramatist Sophocles, appeared in 2001, followed by *If Not, Winter: Fragments of Sappho*, her translation of the poet's work, in 2002. Her translation of Euripides's *Hecuba* had a staged reading in 2004 at the 92nd Street Y. *Decreation: Poetry, Essays, Opera* appeared in 2005. The volume is representative of the eclectic nature of Carson's work. The *Publishers Weekly* (August 15, 2005) reviewer wrote that in "13 intricately related, supple and confident works in verse and prose," Carson "takes on the meaning and function of sleep; the art and attitudes of Samuel Beckett; the last days of an elderly mother; guns; a solar eclipse; 'Longing, a Documentary'; the films of Michelangelo Antonioni; and the vexing, paradoxical projects of women mystics, among them Simone Weil and the medieval heretic Marguerite Porete." The *Publishers Weekly* reviewer concluded that for "all its variety . . . the strongest work in this strong collection may be the short, spiky, individual poems."

Carson received the prestigious Lannan Literary Award for Poetry in 1996. In the following year she was awarded the Pushcart Prize for Poetry, and she was the recipient of a Guggenheim Fellowship in 1998. In 2000 the John D. and Catherine T. MacArthur Foundation presented Carson with one of its coveted "genius" fellowships—a no-strings-attached cash award of $500,000, given both to recognize past accomplishments and to assist with future creative endeavors. One measure of the popularity of the poet's work is that it was mentioned on the television series *The L Word*, one of whose characters said that Carson's books "practically changed my life."

Dinitia Smith described Carson as "tall, lanky and shy"; Melanie Rehak noted, "She can seem reserved to the point of diffidence, but she's also prone to extravagant gestures like wearing green, purple and blue iridescent nail polish on alternating fingers." Carson's eight-year marriage to a man she described to Smith as "an entrepreneur" ended in 1980. Smith wrote in 2004 that Carson "lives by herself most of the time" and quoted the poet as saying, "Loneliness is not an important form of suffering. It's undeniable, but it's just not significant."

—S.Y.

Suggested Reading: *Antioch Review* p247 Spring 1997; *Choice* p637 Dec. 1986; *New York Times* E p13 Feb. 14, 2001; *New York Times Magazine* p36+ Mar. 26, 2000; *Ploughshares* p229+ Winter 1997; *Publishers Weekly* p77 May 29, 1995, p70 Feb. 7, 2000, p56+ Apr. 3, 2000, p73 Dec. 18, 2000; *Village Voice* p152+ May 19, 1998

Selected Books: essays—*Eros the Bittersweet*, 1986; *Economy of the Unlost: Reading Simonides of Keos with Paul Celan*, 1999; poetry—*Plainwater: Essays and Poetry*, 1995; *Glass, Irony and God*, 1995; *Autobiography of Red: A Novel in Verse*, 1998; *Men in the Off Hours*, 2000; *The Beauty of the Husband: A Fictional Essay in 29 Tangos*, 2001; as translator—*Sophocles's Electra*, 2001; *If Not, Winter: Fragments of Sappho*, 2002

Joe Raedle/Getty Images

Casey, George W. Jr.

July 22, 1948– U.S. Army general; commander of multinational forces in Iraq

Address: The Pentagon, Washington, DC 20310

When General George W. Casey Jr. assumed command of the multinational military force in Iraq, in July 2004, a year after the U.S.-led invasion of that country, he took on an extremely daunting task: supporting Iraq's fledgling democratic movement in the face of an insurgency fueled by remnants of the former Baathist regime, Shia militants, and foreign fighters with links to the Al Qaeda terrorist network—at a time when the American public's support for the war was waning. Since that time Casey has helped to oversee three successful and largely secure Iraqi elections, presided over the construction of schools and hospitals, and contin-

ued to improve Iraq's infrastructure, including its electrical power distribution and oil industry. While he has had to contend with a rebellion that seems resistant to suppression by traditional military means, and has had difficulty in preparing the Iraqi army and police force to take over security duties once coalition forces leave the country, Casey insists that the American public, watching daily television reports of violence in Iraq, is not seeing the progress being made there. "The media, especially the TV media, give you visual snapshots of what's happening," Casey explained in an interview with Larry Getlen for the *University of Denver Magazine* (Spring 2005, on-line). "They don't capture the overall, they don't capture trends, and they don't capture long-term change. What happens in these missions . . . is that you make progress in little steps. In the course of a week, you might not see much progress. In the course of a month, more is visible, and over the course of two months even more is visible. Then you get ready to leave, and you turn around and look backwards and you don't recognize the place. That's difficult to capture daily in a media snapshot."

George William Casey Jr., whose family hailed from Scitiuate, Massachusetts, was born on July 22, 1948 in Sendai, Japan, where his father—George W. Casey Sr., a career army officer—was then stationed with U.S. occupational forces following World War II. A self-described "army brat," Casey traveled the world through much of his childhood, living in cities and towns all over the United States and Europe, depending on where the elder Casey was stationed. After graduating from Boston College High School, Casey, who had little interest in pursuing a military career, applied to the United States Military Academy at West Point to satisfy his father; he later enrolled, however, at Georgetown University, in Washington, D.C. Still, in order to please his father, he joined the Reserve Officers Training Corps (ROTC) at Georgetown and planned to serve in the army for two years.

In July 1970, shortly after receiving his bachelor's degree in international studies from Georgetown, Casey learned that his father, then a major general, had been killed in a helicopter crash in

Vietnam. George Casey Sr. and six members of his staff had flown from Phuoc Vinh to Cam Ranh Bay to visit soldiers who had been wounded in combat; two days later their helicopter was found on a hillside. All aboard had been killed. His father's death reshaped Casey's thinking about a career in the army. "If he'd stayed alive, I probably would have gotten out," he told Larry Getlen. "I didn't necessarily want to stay in something my father was doing. I think his death had a kind of opposite effect." He added, referring to life in the military, "You get conditioned to it. I really enjoyed it—the challenges and the people. It was already in my blood, and I just didn't know it. Once I got in, I didn't want to stop."

That same year, after being commissioned a second lieutenant, Casey began his career in the United States Army. Over the next decade he moved up the ranks, serving in both field commands and staff positions. In 1978 he returned to school, this time at the University of Denver, where he again studied international relations. He received a master's degree in May 1980 and then continued his military education at the Armed Forces Staff College, in Norfolk, Virginia, completing his studies there in January 1981. Meanwhile, on September 6, 1980, he was commissioned as a major. Casey's first overseas assignment after his commission was to serve as a military observer for the U.S. Defense Department's Military Observer Group, working with the United Nations Truce Supervision Organization in Jerusalem. His time in the Middle East included a stint in Cairo, Egypt.

From February 1982 to July 1987 Casey was attached to the 4th Infantry Division (Mechanized), operating out of Fort Carson, Colorado. On August 1, 1985 he received his promotion to lieutenant colonel and served as commander of the 1st Battalion, 10th Infantry, 4th Infantry Division (Mechanized). Next, in August 1987, he moved to Washington, D.C., to continue his training, having earned the United States Army Senior Service College Fellowship for the Atlantic Council; he pursued his studies there until July of the following year. His next notable assignment came in December 1989, when he became the special assistant to Army Chief of Staff General Carl E. Vuono, a position he held until June 1991, shortly after he had received his promotion to colonel. Between August 1991 and March 1995, Casey was attached to the 1st Calvary Division operating out of Fort Hood, Texas, serving first as its chief of staff and later as commander of its 3rd Brigade. His next assignment was in Europe, as the assistant chief of staff of operations for V Corps; in October 1995 he was appointed chief of staff of V Corps. On July 1, 1996 he was promoted again, this time to brigadier general. From August 1996 to August 1997 he was the assistant division commander for the 1st Armored Division of the U.S. Army Europe and the 7th Army, Germany. During that time he served in a peacekeeping mission in Bosnia and Herzegovina.

In 1999, following his promotion to major general, Casey became commanding general of the 1st Armored Division of the United States Army Europe and the 7th Army, Germany. He remained in that position until July 2001, when he became commander of the Joint Warfighting Center and director of Joint Training, J-7, of the United States Joint Forces Command, operating out of Suffolk, Virginia. On October 31, 2001 he was promoted to lieutenant general and assumed the directorship of Strategic Plans and Policy, J-5, for the United States Joint Chiefs of Staff, in Washington, D.C. Now at the center of American military power, he displayed considerable management skill, and in January 2003 he became the director of the Joint Staff for the Joint Chiefs of Staff. On December 1, 2003, roughly two months after becoming vice chief of staff of the army, he became a four-star general.

Despite his elevated position in the military hierarchy at the Pentagon, Casey remained a relatively obscure figure. His primary duties involved training and providing supplies for military forces in Afghanistan, where the U.S. had engaged the Taliban regime in the wake of the 2001 terrorist attacks on New York City and Washington, D.C., and Iraq, where the U.S. had led an invasion to rid that country of weapons of mass destruction (which were not found). Then, in May 2004, he was charged with leading the investigation into the mistreatment by U.S. troops of prisoners in both Iraq and Afghanistan. Over the course of 16 months, the U.S. Army conducted some 30 investigations that included 10 suspicious deaths and 10 cases of abuse, as well as two deaths that had already been judged to be criminal homicides. Casey's investigation team took particular interest in the Abu Ghraib prison scandal in Iraq, where photographic evidence revealed that Iraqi prisoners and captured foreign fighters had been subjected to abuse, intimidation, and torture by American soldiers. While Lieutenant General Ricardo S. Sanchez, then the commander of forces in Iraq, was not indicted as a result of the investigations, he was sharply criticized for allowing the abuses, which he claimed not to have learned about until January 2004—some months after the abuses began. Compounding Sanchez's troubles was the fact that the Iraqi insurgency had flared up in southern Iraqi towns including Falluja.

Casey again found himself at the center of the media spotlight in July 2004, when he was tapped to take over command of the multinational force in Iraq, comprising 140,000 American troops and 25,000 soldiers from other nations. Pentagon officials claimed at the time that Sanchez's replacement by Casey had nothing to do with the former commander's performance but had come about because Sanchez, as a three-star general, would have needed Senate approval to achieve a higher rank and might have faced a drawn-out confirmation process. (The change of command was part of a plan to put a higher-ranking officer in charge in

Iraq; Casey, as a four-star general, did not need a promotion to fill the post and was able to sail through his confirmation process.) Described by Eric Schmitt for the *New York Times* (July 5, 2004) as a "forceful but low-key officer who is highly respected by Defense Secretary Donald H. Rumsfeld and Gen. Richard B. Myers, the chairman of the Joint Chiefs of Staff," Casey, while not an obvious candidate for the post, was refreshingly free of controversy, among other points in his favor. Commenting on the relative absence of press coverage of the confirmation process, U.S. senator Hillary Clinton of New York said, as quoted by Bryan Bender for the *Boston Globe* (June 25, 2004), "I think the fact that the press is not here and breathing down the general's neck is a good sign for the future."

When Casey assumed command of the multinational force, he faced a formidable task. Since the U.S. and its allies toppled Saddam Hussein's Baathist regime, in 2003, a small but very determined insurgency has subjected coalition troops, coalition-trained Iraqi forces, and civilians to guerrilla warfare. By the end of October 2006, deaths of U.S. troops alone had topped 2,800. In addition to fighting insurgents, the coalition has had to provide security for Iraq's leaders since sovereignty was handed over to an interim government in June 2004. The Iraqi government has held three elections—the first, in January 2005, for a Transitional National Assembly; the second, in October 2005, to vote on an Iraqi constitution, and the third, in December 2005, to elect the permanent, 275-member Iraqi National Assembly. Although all three elections brought very large voter turnouts and were relatively peaceful, many observers have expressed concern that the continuing violence in Iraq could derail the still-evolving democratic process and plunge the nation into a full-blown civil war.

After taking command, Casey worked closely with John D. Negroponte, then the U.S. ambassador to Iraq. (In April 2005 Negroponte left his post to become the first U.S. director of national intelligence; he was replaced by Zalmay Khalilzad, the U.S. ambassador to Afghanistan from 2003 to 2005.) Many praised the partnership of Casey and Negroponte, finding it an improvement over the difficult and often uncoordinated relationship between Sanchez and L. Paul Bremer, the head of the Coalition Provisional Authority, which governed Iraq between the fall of Saddam Hussein's regime and the establishment of the transitional government. Casey and Negroponte met on an almost daily basis and coordinated militarily and diplomatically with both Iyad Allawi, Iraq's first interim prime minister, and Ibrahim al-Jaafari, who served as prime minister from April 2005 to May 2006. Bradley Graham, a staff writer for the *Washington Post* (November 30, 2004), observed: "Although both men have attempted to keep somewhat low public profiles in the interest of letting the spotlight fall on the interim Iraqi government, Casey and Negroponte exercise exceptional authority in Iraq and remain essentially the midwives of the democratic system struggling to be born here."

Throughout 2005 Casey's command focused on two objectives: quelling the insurgency and training Iraqi martial and police forces to take over security detail for the country. Both goals, as of early November 2006, have proven elusive. In January 2005 it was reported that Casey wanted to add hundreds of American military advisers to Iraqi units, in the hopes of getting those units to the point of preparedness. The next month U.S. forces launched a new offensive against insurgents in Ramadi, Falluja's twin city, which they hoped to prevent from becoming a safe haven for the guerrilla fighters. That offensive was part of a plan, implemented by Casey in the summer of 2004, to keep guerrillas from maintaining control in a number of cities. "Between August and November [2004], the strategy drove Shiite rebels out of the holy city of Najaf, forced a standdown by the same group in Baghdad's Sadr City district, and ended Sunni insurgents' stranglehold on Falluja, a major post for attacks," John F. Burns reported in the *New York Times* (February 21, 2005). "The Falluja offensive ended with much of the city reduced to rubble, and insurgent groups still capable, weeks later, of mounting attacks from isolated pockets of resistance."

In August 2005 Casey and Pentagon officials, including General John P. Abizaid, head of the military's Central Command, suggested to reporters that the number of U.S. troops in Iraq might decrease by 20,000 to 30,000 by the following spring, if the political process remained on track and the Iraqi forces were in a position to take over day-to-day security issues. Though they denied that that prediction indicated the beginning of a phased withdrawal of American forces, Casey, Khalilzad, and Iraqi officials began meeting around that time to discuss plans to expedite the transition from coalition to Iraqi forces. Still, Casey admitted before Congress in September 2005 that only one Iraqi battalion was at Level 1 readiness—meaning that it could operate without supervision or support from coalition forces. U.S. senators and congressmen on both sides of the aisle criticized what they saw as a lack of progress in training Iraqi forces. Casey, defending the coalition's efforts, noted in his testimony that three dozen army and police battalions were at Level 2, meaning that they could lead combat patrols with support from the coalition. "Over the past 18 months, we have built enough Iraqi capacity where we can begin talking seriously about transitioning this counterinsurgency mission to them," Casey remarked, as quoted by Josh White and Bradley Graham in the *Washington Post* (September 30, 2005). In order to help expedite the training of Iraqi troops, Casey ordered the formation of a new school for officers at the military base in Taji, north of Baghdad. As reported by Eric Schmitt for the *Washington Post* (November 2, 2005), the school "is seen as a clearinghouse where field commanders can pass on the latest tactics and situations in the country. Among the topics will be patrol methods, techniques to find and destroy roadside bombs, and education on the various insurgent factions. And in the long term, it is hoped that the format can be passed on to the new Iraqi army and security forces."

Throughout the latter half of 2006, the U.S.-led coalition hoped to give more responsiblity to Iraq's security forces, but an increase in insurgent attacks prevented such a transfer of power. Although some 300,000 Iraqi troops and police officers have been trained by the coalition, many Iraqi army units are plagued with desertions, and some Iraqi police officers have been accused of being either corrupt or loyal to illegal sectarian militias. In a joint news conference held with Ambassador Khalilzad on October 24, 2006, Casey said, as quoted by Aamer Madhani and Stephen J. Hedges in the *Chicago Tribune* (October 25, 2006), "We are about 75 percent of the way through a three-step process in building [Iraqi security] forces. And it's going to take another 12 to 18 months or so until I believe the Iraqi security forces are completely capable of taking over responsibility for their own security—still, probably, with some level of support from us." Although in June 2006 Casey had outlined a plan for a gradual reduction in the number of U.S. troops in Iraq, from 14 combat brigades to eight or nine by December 2007, at the October 24 news conference he said that he may ask for additional troops to enforce security if conditions on the ground warrant such an increase. At that time there were 144,000 American troops in Iraq, many of whom were serving extended tours of duty.

George W. Casey Jr. is married to the former Sheila Lynch, the chief financial officer of the *Hill*, a newspaper that reports on the U.S. Congress. The couple have two grown sons, Sean and Ryan, and five grandchildren. In interviews Casey has admitted that being away from his family has become progressively more difficult during his career, but he believes that the mission in Iraq is worth the sacrifice. "Success in this mission is extremely important to the long-term security of the U.S.," he told Larry Getlen. "I firmly believe that a successful democracy can bring positive change to the region. And it's only by winning the battle of ideas—the battle of moderation over extremism, the battle of moderate Islam over extreme Islam—that we can win the war on terror. So we have to be successful."
—C.M.

Suggested Reading: *Baltimore Sun* A p4 June 16, 2004; *Boston Globe* A p3 June 25, 2004; BBC News (on-line) Oct. 25, 2005; MultiNational Force-Iraq (on-line); *New York Times* A p1 May 5, 2004, A p1 May 25, 2004, IV p5 June 27, 2004, A p5 July 5, 2004, A p1 Jan. 4, 2005, A p10 Feb. 21, 2005, I p1 Aug. 7, 2005, A p11 Nov. 2, 2005; *Newsweek* p20 July 4, 2005; *University of Denver Magazine* (on-line) Spring 2005; *Washington Post* A p27 June 25, 2004, A p12 Nov. 30, 2004, A p20 Mar. 18, 2005, A p12 Sep. 30, 2005, A p10 Oct. 3, 2005

Chase, Alison Becker

Jan. 3, 1946– Choreographer; former artistic director, Pilobolus Dance Theater

Address: P.O. Box 3135, Black Bear Rd., Brooksville, ME 04617

"I don't think there's a choreographer going—none of them will admit it, of course—who hasn't been affected by the reach that Pilobolus has taken into what is possible in the shapes and forms of the human body," Charles L. Reinhart, the president and onetime co-director of the American Dance Festival, told Lesley Stahl for the television newsweekly *60 Minutes* (February 15, 2004). Pilobolus—formally, the Pilobolus Dance Theatre—germinated in an introductory class in modern dance taught in 1971 at Dartmouth College by the choreographer and dancer Alison Becker Chase, widely considered the "mother" of the troupe. Chase, at 24, was not much older than the seniors among her students when the class first met. "I realized that I couldn't teach them as I would teach dancers," she told Lisa Traiger for the *Washington Post* (December 6, 2002), "so I started teaching them improvisation and choreography instead." Several of the students began to experiment with "body-linked" acrobatics that blurred the lines separating modern dance, gymnastics, pantomime, and slapstick; accomplished athletes, they developed routines centered on an array of visually striking formations, displaying what one student—Moses Pendleton—dubbed "collective muscle," as he recalled to Alan M. Kriegsman for the *Washington Post* (April 13, 1977). In 1973 Chase joined her former students as choreographer and dancer and, with another addition to the group, Martha Clarke, enhanced Pilobolus's aggressively physical routines with touches of femininity. Pilobolus became hugely popular on college campuses and other venues in the U.S. and overseas, and in 1977 the troupe made their critically acclaimed debut on Broadway. The company, then comprising Chase, Clarke, Pendleton, and three others, struck the dance critic Anna Kisselgoff, writing for the *New York Times* (November 25, 1977), as "American free enterprise's best advertisement. Investing in a little ingenuity, they have come up with something different and fresh. Yes, it is dance if the definition of dance is stretched. Certainly, it is an experiment in a new movement vocabulary and in an appeal

Mac Herrling, courtesy of Island Heritage Trust

Alison Becker Chase (left) working with dancers during a 2006 summer program at the Island Heritage Trust's Settlement Granite Quarry, in Maine

to the senses. That appeal, incidentally, cuts across all ages and all audiences. . . . Pilobolus is a Mad Hatter's tea party: Children of the 60's and 70's, they have created their own wonderland. The marvelous part is that all of us enjoy ourselves at the party."

Individually or with others, Chase choreographed more than 40 major works for Pilobolus and performed in many of them before she was ousted from the company in 2005 by the board of directors—an action almost universally regarded as unconscionable among those in the world of dance. As the artistic or co-artistic director of the troupe, she won a Guggenheim Fellowship in 1980 and the Connecticut Governor's Award in 1997. Pilobolus, meanwhile, earned the Scotsman Award for performances at the Edinburgh Festival, in 1973; the Berlin Critic's Circle Prize, in 1975; the New England Theatre Conference Prize, in 1977; a Brandeis University Creative Arts Award, in 1978; the Connecticut Commission on the Arts Award for Excellence, in 1979; a 1997 Primetime Emmy Award for outstanding achievement in cultural programming, for a televised performance at the Kennedy Center's 25th anniversary celebration, held in 1996; and the Samuel H. Scripps American Dance Festival Award for lifetime achievement in choreography, in 2000. In 2005 Chase received a commission (funded with a grant from the National Endowment for the Arts) to choreograph a piece for Professional Flair/Dancing Wheels, a company that includes disabled performers. In 2006 she directed the first of two proposed summer workshops at the Island Heritage Trust's Settlement Granite Quarry, a preserve in Oceanville, Maine.

The goal of the project is the development of a performance work that will include dance, puppetry, percussion, and the operation of quarrying machines.

Alison Becker Chase was born on January 3, 1946 in Eolia, Missouri, just north of St. Louis, where she grew up. She attended the Mary Institute and St. Louis Country Day School, in Ladue, a St. Louis suburb. In 1964, after she completed her secondary education, she enrolled at Washington University, in St. Louis, where she studied philosophy and history; she also took a class in modern dance taught by Annalise Mertz, who established the school's first degree program in dance. Chase earned a B.A. degree in 1969. She next entered the graduate school of dance at the University of California at Los Angeles. She earned a master's degree in 1970, and that same year she was hired as the choreographer-in-residence and as an assistant professor of dance at Dartmouth College, in Hanover, New Hampshire. According to Paul Ben-Itzak, writing for the *Dance Insider* (June 20, 2006, online), her resumé includes training with the modern dancers and choreographers Merce Cunningham and Murray Louis and with the European-born ballerina Mia Slavenska.

Dartmouth, which was then a men's college, required all students to take at least one class in art, music, or dance. Chase's introductory modern-dance class attracted athletes with no prior training in dance. Instead of teaching classical technique, Chase encouraged experimentation and improvisation—in particular, a form of contact improvisation in which "partners and small groups give and take their weight by leaning, carrying, and lifting one another in unscripted, gamelike fashion," as Lisa Traiger wrote. Chase watched her students transform simple exercises into idiosyncratic, interdependent acrobatics that were more reminiscent of artful gymnastic maneuvering than of modern ballet. "They had a sports vocabulary," Chase told Jennifer Dunning for the *New York Times* (July 18, 1996). "They brought in terrifically fresh choreography. . . . They were fresh and off the wall and radical because they didn't know. They didn't come with all the baggage." She told Tim Matson, the author of *Pilobolus* (1978), "I tried to see that from the beginning they choreographed and performed and got used to performing and to bringing in pieces of choreography every day, the way a writer gets used to writing every day."

After Chase encouraged them to organize their improvisations into repeatable arrangements, three students—Jonathan Wolken, Moses Pendleton, and Steve Johnson—came up with what John Skow described for *Time* (November 20, 1978) as an "acrobatic slapstick, abstract-expressionist mime, [a] muscular, head-over-heels tableau vivant," a dance that offered explosions of flailing arms and legs and other movements, all intermingling to form seamless formations of torsos, limbs, and heads. Wolken named the 11-minute dance for a species of fungus, *Pilobolus*, which, in releasing its spores, "explodes with unearthly energy," as Pendleton explained to Anna Kisselgoff for the *New York Times* (March 5, 1976). The students "took shape as one rather than as individuals . . . [resembling] a gigantic ball that would re-shape and re-group," Chase said to Jennifer MacAdam for the *St. Louis Post-Dispatch* (January 19, 1992). "I was struck by the exchange of weight between them, the counter-balances and leverages."

In 1971 Wolken, Pendleton, and Johnson performed *Pilobolus*, to music by Jon Appleton, as the opening act for the progressive-rock musician Frank Zappa at Smith College, in Northampton, Massachusetts. The audience's highly enthusiastic response to the work led Chase to select *Pilobolus* to represent Dartmouth in a 12-college dance festival held later that year at New York University (NYU). When Murray Louis saw the dancers perform at NYU, "I was knocked off my socks," as he recalled to Paul Ben-Itzak for *Dance Magazine* (June 1996, on-line), and afterward he invited the men to dance at the space in New York City in which he and the choreographer Alwin Nikolais rehearsed their own companies. The troupe's informal New York debut took place on December 29, 1971 at the Louis-Nikolais Dance Theater Lab, with Pendleton (then using the given name Robb) and Wolken, both of whom had graduated from Dartmouth by then, joined by two undergraduates, Robby Barnett and Lee Harris. (Steve Johnson had entered medical school.) "The group displayed amazing physical fearlessness, humor, inventiveness and unselfconsciousness . . . ," Anna Kisselgoff wrote in a *New York Times* (December 31, 1971) review that brought them to the attention of the dance world. "That they can do so much with so little is astounding." In 1972 Pendleton, Wolken, Barnett, and Harris named their quartet the Pilobolus Dance Company. The following year Pilobolus performed at the American Dance Festival, an influential showcase for modern dance, at the invitation of Charles Reinhart, its president. "Out of their innocence," as Reinhart recalled to Lesley Stahl, "they created a new artistic direction based on what they knew, which was athletics, science and bodies." In 1973 Chase left Dartmouth, and she and Martha Clarke, a classically trained ballerina who had been a member of Anna Sokolow's modern-dance troupe, joined Pilobolus to form a sextet. "[The] male relationship began to go stale. We needed the input of female energy and sexual tension," Pendleton told Hubert Saal for *Newsweek* (December 5, 1977). Chase and Clarke softened Pilobolus's edgy, super-physical antics, layering the acrobatics with elements of eroticism, intrigue, romance, gentleness, and delicacy, and bringing "a theatrical element to the company," as Chase noted to Jennifer MacAdam.

Among Pilobolus's early dances was the vaudeville-inspired *Walklyndon* (1971), which demonstrated the artfulness and tremendous skill of the performers' bumps, clumps, romps, kicks, and leaps. In *Ciona* (1974) the dancers bent and leapfrogged in one fluid motion, resulting in the "unlikely blend of primitive physicality and sophisticated humor, practiced with an innate seriousness that [is] cloaked in playful irony," as Dunning wrote in 1996. With *Monkshood's Farewell* (1974) the group "began to organize the material with a dramatic logic," Pendleton recalled, as quoted in Robert Coe's book *Dance in America* (1984). In *Untitled* (1975) two Victorian women evade a pair of eager suitors, until, after they "grow" to a height of nine feet, their billowing skirts reveal the hairy legs of the two nude men who hold them aloft. Later, the men are "expelled" in a surreal depiction of birth and become the women's beaus. *Untitled* struck Saal as "a comic, Freudian, dreamlike excursion into personal relationships." *Day Two* (1980), set to music by the Talking Heads and Brian Eno, which purportedly depicts the second day of creation as described in the Bible, mirrors the release and freedom the dancers felt when, after a frustrating workday, they cavorted during a thunderstorm; it ends with the dancers sliding vigorously across the stage through puddles of water. For some time the Pilobolus dancers refined their routines while living and working together, first at a farm in Vermont and then in Washington Depot, Connecticut, in what Jennifer Dunning described in the *New York Times* (December 20, 1981) as "an extension of close, communal college living that set the pattern of their dance." By early March 1976, when they performed to sold-out audiences at the Brooklyn Academy of Music, in New York City, they had abandoned their cooperative living arrangements.

Early on in the troupe's development, the fashion designer Pierre Cardin became a Pilobolus fan; he provided financial assistance to the group for three years in the 1970s, and he helped fund their tours of Europe and South America as well as their Broadway debut, at the St. James Theatre in 1977. At that time Pilobolus still consisted of two women and four men (with Michael Tracy having replaced Harris). In one of the two programs prepared for their premiere, Chase and Pendleton performed *Shizen* (which they had choreographed together), accompanied by music for Japanese bamboo flute by Riley Lee. A "knowing but beautiful love duet," *Shizen* showed Pilobolus "at its most sophisticated," as Anna Kisselgoff wrote for the *New York Times* (November 25, 1977). In another duet of their creation, *Alraune*, Chase and Pendleton "play[ed] upon the theme of two equals one . . . with some striking geomorphic forms," in Kisselgoff's words. The critic also wrote, "Steps have no meaning for Pilobolus but motion does, and 'motion studies' would not be a misnomer for the ever-changing flow of linked body shapes that the troupe molds and remolds into space with such skill and sophistication. There is a kinetic and visual impact to these designs that other dance does not have."

In 1979 Clarke left Pilobolus. The next year Chase and Pendleton, while remaining with Pilobolus, launched an offshoot dance group called Momix, which provides "entertainment with beautiful bodies doing amazing things" and "performs dance for people who don't like dance," as Pendleton said to Susan English for the *Spokane (Washington) Spokesman Review* (April 5, 2001, online). At the 1980 Winter Olympic Games, held in Lake Placid, New York, Pilobolus performed *The Empty Suitor*, a series of seemingly unconnected gags that Kisselgoff, in a *New York Times* (March 23, 1980) review of a Pilobolus concert at the McCarter Theatre Center, in Princeton, New Jersey, described as "very funny." In the same review Kisselgoff praised Chase's performance in her solo piece *A Miniature*, in which Chase danced on a dark stage, holding two flashlights that provided the only light. "The solo was a detailed self-analysis, a tour de force because of its combination of subjectivity and objectivity," Kisselgoff wrote. "Objective because it described a woman looking at herself, a view dependent upon what the flashlight revealed. . . . Subjective because character was illuminated as much as body parts. Fears, fantasies and yearnings were implied in the silhouettes and do-it-yourself spotlighting by the performer."

In the 1980s Pilobolus added to its staple of dancers a pickup pool of 50 others. "I find that it's through the dancers' bodies and minds and souls that this stuff is birthed," Chase told Laura Bleiberg for the *Orange County (California) Register* (December 3, 2000). Also during that decade, as Jack Anderson pointed out in the *New York Times* (July 22, 1992), the group "increasingly tried to invest its

gymnastic technique with dramatic significance." The two-character *Cedar Island*, (1990), choreographed by Chase, Duffy Wrede, and Nina Winthrop, is an example of that trend. A meditative work that explored family relationships, it was danced by Chase and a 10-year-old boy at its premiere, at the Joyce Theater in New York. According to Jack Anderson in the *New York Times* (December 28, 1990), it was "notable for its sweetness and delicacy," and its choreography, "though always tender, avoided cheap sentimentality." In another example, in 1992 Chase and her Pilobolus colleagues created *Sweet Purgatory*, a melancholy dance set to Dmitri Shostakovich's Chamber Symphony. In 1996, to mark Pilobolus's 25th anniversary, the company's four artistic co-directors—Chase, Tracy, Barnett, and Wolken—choreographed *Aeros*, a fantasy about a space traveler who finds love on a distant planet.

By the late 1990s creative tensions had begun to mount among the artistic co-directors. Chase began to work exclusively with Michael Tracy, while Robby Barnett collaborated with Jonathan Wolken on most new works. With her family, Chase moved to Brooksville, Maine, and focused her energies on her own projects, while occasionally teaming up with a few others. "I found that I was able to listen in a different way to what was being generated," she said to Gia Kourlas for the *New York Times* (June 23, 2002). "I've always needed a little time or distance. Instead of having someone buzz in my ear, saying, 'Well, gee, I think this is the wrong direction,' you just sit and listen and feel. It made a huge world of difference, and I found that I really enjoyed it." She also acknowledged that Pilobolus was "born and raised on collaboration, and I think that it will always be a part of our process. . . . You might have to change it to keep it invigorated, but I think that we will always be collaborative souls." In *Ben's Admonition* (2002), a dance loosely based on an event involving Benjamin Franklin and the Continental Congress, Chase and the Pilobolus members Ras Mikey C and Matt Kent experimented with "upper torso hydraulics . . . that whole illusion of float," as she described it to Lisa Traiger, by having Ras Mikey C and Kent hang upside-down in midair and then twist and turn acrobatically. Gia Kourlas, in reviewing *Ben's Admonition* for *Dance Magazine* (November 1, 2002), described the dancers as seeming "at once urban and otherworldly. Clearly, Chase's ability to conquer both qualities is a credit to her choreographic sophistication and understanding of theater." Chase joined with the composer Edward Bilous and the documentary filmmaker Mirra Bank to create *Lucid Dreams* (2005), which explored new ways of perceiving dance movement through music and video.

A $50,000 deficit led Pilobolus's board of directors, in 2004, to establish a new position, that of executive director, with responsibility for restructuring the troupe's management and business practices, and they hired the theater director Itamar Kubovy to fill it. Kubovy's bottom-line, corporate-minded agenda alarmed Chase. "He began dismantling the fabric that was the artistic soul of Pilobolus. As this autocratic regime was being established, I realized this was stifling me creatively," she told Daniel J. Wakin for the *New York Times* (July 24, 2006). Chase particularly objected to Kubovy's insistence that Pilobolus retain copyrights to already produced work, including her own. For his part Kubovy argued to Frank Rizzo for the CT-Now Web site (August 6, 2006), "[Pilobolus] began as a collective in every great sense of the word. We paid salaries to the artistic directors. . . . You make work, and that work is owned by the company." In October 2005, after several weeks of contentious negotiations, Chase was ousted from the Pilobolus board and given a few weeks to sign over her creative rights to the company. When she refused, she was fired. Chase told Paul Ben-Itzak for *Dance Insider* in 2006 that Kubovy and the three remaining board members maintained that their stance mirrored that of the Martha Graham Dance Center, which, in a so-called work-for-hire case, sued successfully in federal court in 2002 for ownership of all of Graham's choreography. In the introductory paragraphs of the *Dance Insider* article, Ben-Itzak wrote, "This is the story of the day a dance company fired its mother and lost its soul. This is the story of the day an artistic enterprise founded on collaboration . . . acted like a corporation. . . . This is the story of a dance company which shows every intention of performing the work of a fired choreographer/director against her objections and without her supervision of the work, which the company apparently insists it owns."

In an appreciation of Chase for the *Dance Insider* (June 20, 2006, on-line), Rebecca Stenn, who danced with Pilobolus Too, a Pilobolus offshoot, for six years after a seven-year stint with Momix and now heads her own dance company, described Chase as "sweet, funny, and incredibly demanding in the best possible way. . . . From Alison I learned stamina and grace. . . . I think it is her sense of humor, and her enthusiasm that gave her the fortitude to achieve all that she has over the years. She is a creative force, a whirlwind . . . , irreverent and loving." Chase taught theater studies at the Yale School of Drama, in New Haven, Connecticut, from 1991 to 1997, and she has given classes in improvisation for YARD (Youth at Risk Dancing), a program affiliated with the Cleveland School of the Arts. She lives in Brooksville, Maine, with her husband, Eric Chase, an architect, who occasionally designed scenery for Pilobolus productions. The couple have three children.

—D.J.K.

Suggested Reading: CTNow Web site; *Los Angeles Times* p84 Sep. 29, 1996; *New York Times* A p27 Dec. 20, 1981; *New York Times* p2 June 23, 2002; *St. Louis Dispatch* C p3 Jan. 19, 1992; *Newsweek* p89 Dec. 5, 1977; *Time* Nov. 20, 1978; *Washington Post* T p29 Dec. 6, 2002;

Stephen Jaffe/Getty

Clarke, Richard

1951– Writer; commentator; former U.S. government official

Address: c/o Bruce Nichols, Free Press, Simon & Schuster, 1230 Ave. of the Americas, New York, NY 10020

"Your government failed you. Those entrusted with protecting you failed you. And I failed you. We tried hard, but that doesn't matter, because we failed." Those words were uttered on March 24, 2004 by Richard Clarke, the counterterrorism czar under President Bill Clinton and a high-ranking official in the administrations of Presidents Ronald Reagan, George H. W. Bush, and George W. Bush; he was testifying before the panel investigating inadequacies in U.S. antiterrorism efforts prior to the attacks of September 11, 2001. Clarke retained the position of counterterrorism adviser when, in January 2001, George W. Bush succeeded Clinton, and he was a member of Bush's National Security Council (NSC) when the 2001 attacks occurred. In October of that year, he became President Bush's special adviser for cyberspace security, a post he held until his retirement from government service, in February 2003. Days before his 2004 testimony, Clarke appeared on the CBS news magazine *60 Minutes* and charged the Bush administration with having grossly underestimated the threat posed by the terrorist organization Al Qaeda and its leader, Osama bin Laden. Clarke claimed that in the days after Bush took office, and intermittently throughout Bush's first eight months in the White House, he and Central Intelligence Agency (CIA) director George Tenet had requested a meeting with the president and his Cabinet members to discuss Al Qaeda and bin Laden, but that their attempts to call attention to the imminent threat were ignored. Clarke's book *Against All Enemies: Inside America's War on Terror*, published in 2004, is a scathing criticism of Bush's handling of intelligence prior to September 11, 2001, and charges further that Bush encouraged Clarke and other top advisers to find a connection between the September 11 attacks and Iraq as a justification for military engagement in that country, which the U.S. and its allies invaded in 2003. Asked by the *60 Minutes* interviewer, Lesley Stahl, whether an official in the White House owed the president loyalty, Clarke responded by saying, "Yes. . . . Up to a point. When the president starts doing things that risk American lives, then loyalty to him has to be put aside. I think the way he has responded to al Qaeda, both before 9/11 by doing nothing, and by what he's done after 9/11 has made us less safe. Absolutely."

A reporter for *BBC News* (March 22, 2004, online) called Clarke, who has long been known for his nonpartisanship, "a man whose expertise cut across party boundaries and a voice few presidents could afford to ignore." His career in government began in 1973, in the U.S. Department of Defense; he later moved to the U.S. State Department and then to the National Security Council, where he was appointed in 1992 as special assistant for global affairs by President George H. W. Bush's national security adviser, Brent Scowcroft. In 2005 Clarke published his first novel, *The Scorpion's Gate*, a story—set in the near future—in which the House of Saud falls to radical Islamists. Clarke is currently employed by ABC News as an expert on national security and terrorism and can be seen regularly on the programs *Good Morning America* and *ABC World News Tonight*.

The son of a factory worker and his wife, a nurse, Richard Alan Clarke was born in Dorchester, Massachusetts (some sources say Pennsylvania) in 1951. According to the CNN program *Wolf Blitzer Reports* (March 25, 2004, on-line), Clarke was raised primarily in Pennsylvania. At age 12 he won a scholarship to attend Boston Latin School, in Massachusetts, a prestigious private school founded in 1635, whose distinguished former pupils include Benjamin Franklin and Samuel Adams. He next attended the University of Pennsylvania, graduating in 1972. By that time he had decided to pursue a career in national security. Clarke embraced the anti–Vietnam War movement that was then in full swing. "I wanted to get involved in national security . . . as a career to make sure that Vietnam did not happen again," he told Andrew Buncombe for the London *Independent* (June 14, 2004). Clarke later attended the Massachusetts Institute of Technology (MIT), in Cambridge, receiving a master's degree in political science in 1978.

Clarke began his career in government, meanwhile, in 1973, as a weapons and European-securities analyst for the Defense Department, in the administration of President Richard M. Nixon. Then–Secretary of Defense James R. Schlesinger was reshaping U.S. foreign policy in light of the curtailment of U.S. military involvement in Vietnam. Clarke's post, which he held until 1977, primarily involved limiting the proliferation of nuclear weapons in Europe and elsewhere. From 1977 to 1979 Clarke worked in the private sector, as a senior analyst for the independent defense-strategy consulting firm Pacific Sierra Research.

In 1979 the Soviet Union invaded Afghanistan, leading many officials in Washington, D.C., to fear that the Soviets would carry out similar actions in other countries in the Middle East. That year Clarke was hired by the U.S. State Department and assigned to the Bureau of Politico-Military Affairs. During that period his extensive research into political conditions in the Middle East and the Persian Gulf made him a recognized expert on those regions.

In 1985, at age 34, Clarke was named assistant secretary of state for intelligence under George P. Shultz, President Ronald Reagan's secretary of state. A year later Clarke received negative publicity when he and others at the State Department devised a plan, later abandoned, to disrupt the Libyan leader Muammar Qaddafi's harboring of terrorist groups. The plan included flying airplanes over Libya's capital city, Tripoli, to generate sonic booms, and sending unmanned rafts onto Libya's beaches—all to mimic military action. "It seemed to me at the time that booms were better than bombs," Clarke told Pat Milton for the Associated Press (October 10, 1998). In 1989 Clarke was appointed assistant secretary for political-military affairs, a position in which he remained in the State Department, in the incoming administration of President George H. W. Bush.

At the time of the 1991 Persian Gulf War, which followed the invasion of Kuwait by Iraq, Clarke accompanied then–Defense Secretary Richard B. Cheney on a mission to Saudi Arabia, to ask the heads of the country for permission to station U.S. troops there for the impending military action against the forces of Iraq's leader, Saddam Hussein. In 1992 Clarke was relieved of his duties at the State Department after failing to inform the U.S. Congress of the illicit transfer of U.S. military technology, believed to be related to air defense, from Israel to China and other countries. Regarding Clarke's dismissal, Sherman Funk, a former high-ranking official in the State Department, told Michael Dobbs for the *Washington Post* (April 2, 2000) about Clarke, "He is very intelligent and quick on his feet, but in this one case he was dead wrong." Clarke said, as paraphrased by the *Washington Post* (April 2, 2000), that he had "run afoul of an anti-Israel lobby that had seized on misleading intelligence," and he defended his actions in the incident involving Israel, telling Dobbs, "I was not about to lie against a good ally like Israel for somebody else's political agenda." Soon afterward Brent Scowcroft hired Clarke as the president's special assistant for global affairs; Clarke remained an NSC member for more than a decade, until February 2003, serving in the administrations of both Clinton and George W. Bush.

U.S. efforts to combat terrorism were stimulated on February 26, 1993, when a bomb was detonated in the underground garage of the World Trade Center, in New York City. Six people were killed and more than a thousand injured by the blast. (Ramzi Yousef, the mastermind of the bombing and a member of the Al Qaeda terrorist organization, was sentenced in January 1998 to 240 years in prison.) That event and others, including a gas attack on the subway in Tokyo, Japan, in March 1995, signaled to Clarke that terrorists would attempt further strikes on U.S. soil. He grew increasingly concerned with the threat posed by terrorists, especially the Al Qaeda network, and became outspoken in government circles about the danger facing the U.S.

By the time of the 1993 World Trade Center bombing, Bill Clinton had succeeded George H. W. Bush in the White House. An avid reader of books on global terrorism, Clinton shared with Clarke the view that terrorists posed a major threat to the U.S. Over the course of Clinton's two terms as president, several incidents traced to Al Qaeda took place overseas, pointing further to the possibility of future acts of terrorism within the U.S. borders. Under Clinton, Clarke played an integral role in the ultimately unsuccessful 1993 manhunt for the Somalian warlord Mohamed Farah Aideed, and he helped determine the U.S. response to the August 7, 1998 bombings of the U.S. embassies in the East African countries of Kenya and Tanzania. (On August 20 of that year, U.S. warships in the Red Sea launched a missile strike against terrorist targets in Afghanistan and the Sudan, specifically the Al-Shifa pharmaceutical factory, in Khartoum, where administration officials believed chemical weapons were being produced for Osama bin Laden, the mastermind of the embassy bombings. Many Muslims denounced the military response, named Operation Infinite Reach, at the time; investigations later showed that the Al-Shifa factory was not producing weapons for bin Laden. Fears about airline safety increased in July 1996, after TWA Flight 800 exploded off the coast of New York State, killing the 230 passengers and crew. The White House and U.S. law enforcement officials investigated the explosion as a possible terrorist act. (No connection to terrorism was found.) Clarke, displaying an unusual knowledge of the budgetary process, helped to push for a $1.1 billion plan to enhance airport security.

In May 1998 Clinton signed Presidential Directive 62, which established the post of national coordinator for security infrastructure protection and counterterrorism. Clinton asked Clarke to take the position, in which he would be responsible for coordinating federal agencies to defend against possible chemical or biological attacks and organizing counterterrorism efforts. Clarke thus became the

nation's first special assistant to the president on terrorism, or counterterrorism czar. According to Dobbs, powerful players within the Pentagon, the FBI, and other corners of the government became concerned that the new position would encourage Clarke to intrude on their turf. As counterterrorism czar Clarke was widely credited with thwarting Al Qaeda's efforts to unleash several coordinated attacks in the U.S. on New Year's Eve in 1999. After learning in December 1999 through "chatter" picked up by the CIA of the possibility of an attack on the Los Angeles International Airport, President Clinton ordered his Cabinet members to hold daily meetings on terrorism. Clarke ordered the FBI to be put on high alert, dispatched counterterrorism teams to Europe and elsewhere, and instructed the State Department to issue an ultimatum to the leadership in Afghanistan to keep bin Laden under surveillance. On December 14 a suspect driving a vehicle full of explosives was arrested at the U.S.-Canadian border. The arrest was believed to have prevented an attack on the Los Angeles airport. Also under Clarke's watch as counterterrorism czar, spending on counter-terrorism initiatives rose from approximately $5.7 billion in 1995 to $11.1 billion in 2000.

In January 2001 George W. Bush became the 43d president of the United States, succeeding Clinton. Prior to September 11, 2001, Clarke told Michael Dobbs, regarding the possibility that biological or chemical weapons could be obtained by terrorists, "The notion that this is an analytical problem and one can quantify the threat is naïve. This is not the Cold War." Noting that Clarke's job during the Cold War had been that of "calculating the relative strength" of the U.S. and the Soviet Union, Dobbs quoted Clarke as saying, "You can't do that with these [new] kind of threats. We don't know how many bio labs there are out there, how many tons of chemical agents. Frankly, it will only take one." He also said, "They will come after our weakness, our Achilles heal, which is largely here in the United States." Referring to the threat posed by bin Laden, Clarke told Dobbs, "It's not enough to be in a cat-and-mouse game, warning about his plots. If we keep that up, we will someday fail. We need to seriously think about doing more. Our goal should be to so erode his network of organizations that they no longer pose a serious threat."

In the wake of the 2001 terrorist attacks, which killed 3,000 people, destroyed the World Trade Center, and severely damaged the Pentagon, just outside Washington, D.C., Clarke remained inside the Situation Room in the West Wing of the White House, helping to manage the government's response. Clarke was appointed as President Bush's special adviser for cyberspace security, a newly created position, in early October 2001; concurrently, he served as chairman of the president's Critical Infrastructure Protection Board. In the latter capacity, Clarke was "the federal official most directly responsible for protecting not just IT [information technology] systems and electronic networks such as telecommunications infrastructure," according to John Rendleman, writing for *Information Week* (December 24, 2001), "but all essential utility systems, including energy, water, and transportation." In that role Clarke warned of a possible "digital Pearl Harbor," or a terrorist attack on the nation's information-technology infrastructure, which he believed would cripple hospitals, airports, utility centers, and other places where essential public services are performed. "Our enemies know our technology as well as we do, and our enemies will use our technology against us," Clarke told Rendleman. "Our enemies will find the fissures and the seams in our high-tech economy." He added, "We need to insist that the next generation of hardware and software systems have security built into their basic architecture. As long as we're a superpower, there will be people who will come after us." Clarke urged telephone companies to give rescue personnel first priority over their wireless networks during emergencies, and called for the creation of a separate and more secure Internet for government employees and officials. He resigned the position in February 2003.

On March 21, 2004, several months before that year's presidential election, Clarke appeared on the CBS news magazine *60 Minutes* to discuss the events of September 11, 2001 and the Bush administration's response to the attacks. "Frankly, I find it outrageous that the president is running for reelection on the grounds that he's done such great things about terrorism. He ignored it. He ignored terrorism for months, when maybe we could have done something to stop 9/11. Maybe. We'll never know," he told Lesley Stahl. Clarke later added, "I think he's done a terrible job on the war against terrorism." The Bush administration made counter-accusations, claiming that Clarke's team had put forth no plan for addressing the threat. Vice President Richard Cheney told the radio talk-show host Rush Limbaugh in a nationally syndicated interview, "Well, [Clarke] wasn't in the loop, frankly, on a lot of this stuff. As I say, he was head of counterterrorism for several years there in the '90s, and I didn't notice that they had any great success dealing with the terrorist threat." In addition, Bush administration officials portrayed Clarke's accusation against Bush as politically motivated, citing connections Clarke had with high-ranking members of Democratic senator John Kerry's presidential campaign. Paul Krugman, meanwhile, writing for the *New York Times* (March 30, 2004) called the Bush administration's statements about Clarke "a campaign of character assassination."

In the *60 Minutes* interview Clarke suggested that as early as the day after the attacks, Defense Secretary Donald Rumsfeld began recommending that the U.S. strike Iraq, despite the fact that bin Laden and Al Qaeda were known to be based in Afghanistan. Describing the day's activities, Clarke told Stahl, "The president dragged me into a room with a couple of other people, shut the door, and said, 'I want you to find whether Iraq did this.' Now he never said, 'Make it up.' But the entire conversation left me in absolutely no doubt that George Bush wanted me to come back with a report that said Iraq did this." According to several sources, Clarke had written a memo on January 24, 2001 to Bush's then–national security adviser, Condoleezza Rice, urgently requesting a Cabinet-level meeting to brief the president about the serious threat Al Qaeda posed. As late as June 2001, no Cabinet-level officials had met with Clarke to be briefed about bin Laden and Al Qaeda. Clarke told Stahl: "There's a lot of blame to go around, and I probably deserve some blame, too. . . . I blame the entire Bush leadership for continuing to work on Cold War issues. . . . It was as though [officials in the administration, some of whom had worked in the first Bush White House] were preserved in amber from when they left office eight years earlier. They came back. They wanted to work on the same issues right away: Iraq, Star Wars. Not new issues, the new threats that had developed over the preceding eight years."

Clarke also generated headlines by criticizing the Bush administration for its insistence on taking military action in Iraq, a move he believes to have strengthened the cause of Al Qaeda and the network of radical Islamic organizations around the world. "Osama bin Laden had been saying for years," Clarke told Stahl, "'America wants to invade an Arab country and occupy it, an oil-rich Arab country'. . . . This is part of his propaganda." Clarke added: "So what did we do after 9/11? We invade an oil-rich [country] and occupy an oil-rich Arab country which was doing nothing to threaten us. In other words, we stepped right into bin Laden's propaganda. And the result of that is that al Qaeda and organizations like it, offshoots of it, second-generation al Qaeda have been greatly strengthened."

On March 24, 2004, days after his interview with Stahl aired, Clarke testified before the panel investigating inadequacies in U.S. antiterrorism efforts prior to the attacks of September 11, 2001, telling those present, "The reason I am strident in my criticism of the president of the United States is because . . . by invading Iraq, the president of the United States has greatly undermined the war on terrorism." Some families of the victims of the September 11 attacks were supportive of Clarke, while others reportedly felt that his actions were self-aggrandizing. Clarke's book *Against All Enemies: Inside America's War on Terror* (2004), which contends that the Bush administration failed to address the threat of Al Qaeda prior to the terrorist attacks and turned its attention to Saddam Hussein quickly afterward, became a best-seller. Reviews of *Against All Enemies* were mixed, with some speculating that the decision to publish the book during an election year was politically motivated. Writing for *Time* (March 25, 2004), Romesh Ratnesar cited passages that seemed to him to "reveal the polemical, partisan mean-spiritedness that lies at the heart of Clarke's book, and to an even greater degree, his television appearances flacking it. That's a shame, since many of his contentions—about the years of political and intelligence missteps that led to 9/11, the failure of two Administrations to destroy al-Qaeda and the potentially disastrous consequences of the U.S. invasion of Iraq—deserve a wide and serious airing." Robin Cook had a more favorable view, writing for the London *New Statesman* (May 3, 2004): "[Clarke] has done more than any other US voter in the past four years to embarrass George Bush. His book is a revealing and intelligent record of a quarter-century spent in the national security corridors in and around the White House. He is commendably honest about the failures along the way."

In 2005 Clarke turned his attention to fiction, publishing the novel *The Scorpion's Gate*. The book depicts a near future in which Muslim fundamentalists revolt against Saudi royalty to take control of Saudi Arabia, renamed the Republic of Islamyah. The resulting struggle between the U.S. and China for oil leads to the brink of world war. "Though [the novelists] Graham Greene and John le Carré are under no threat from Clarke, he does demonstrate a flair for action fiction," Gary Hart wrote for the *Washington Post Book World* (October 23, 2005), in a review of *The Scorpion's Gate*. Hart added that Clarke's "handling of personal relations" is "less successful" and that his "dialogue also needs work," but concluded, "If Clarke does nothing else but cause some readers to question our ludicrous reliance on unstable oil supplies, wonder whether we have even begun to understand Islamic culture, begin to demand a more subtle and layered approach to the Middle East, doubt our ability to export democracy at the point of a bayonet, or gain maturity in foreign affairs, he will have done a service." Discussing whether he intended *The Scorpion's Gate* as a prediction of the future, Clarke said to a reporter for *ABC News* (October 24, 2005, on-line), "The book intends to raise these issues, but I'm not giving odds that these things will happen. As a matter of policy, for example, our country advocates democracy in the Middle East. That could lead to the overthrow of the Royal House in Saudi Arabia. If that country did become a republic, it's not clear that the good guys would be in charge. So while I'm not predicting the fall of the House of Saud, I am raising questions that would emerge if that were to happen."

After leaving government service, Clarke joined ABC News in April 2004 as an on-air analyst of issues related to national security. He is featured regularly on *Good Morning America* and *World News Tonight*. In addition, Clarke is the chairman of Good Harbor Consulting, based in Virginia, which, according to its Web site, "provides strategic advice and counsel for a broad range of clients—including Fortune 500 companies, industry associations, systems integrators, and innovative technology start-ups—in the fast developing areas of homeland security, cyber security, critical infrastructure protection and counterterrorism."

Clarke is a lecturer at Harvard University's Kennedy School of Government. His pastimes include playing racquetball. He is single.

—D.F.

Suggested Reading: Associated Press Oct. 10, 1998; *BBC News* (on-line) Mar. 22, 2004; *CBS News* (on-line) Mar. 21, 2004; *Information Week* p36 Dec. 24, 2001; (London) *Independent* p29 June 14, 2004; *Slate* (on-line) Mar. 23, 2004; *Time* (on-line) Mar. 25, 2004; *Washington Post* (on-line) Apr. 2, 2000

Selected Books: nonfiction–*Against All Enemies: Inside America's War on Terror*, 2004; fiction–*The Scorpion's Gate*, 2005

Kevin Winter/Getty Images

Clarkson, Kelly

Apr. 24, 1982– Singer; songwriter

Address: c/o RCA Records, 1540 Broadway, New York, NY 10036

In 2002 Kelly Clarkson became familiar to pop-music fans, millions of whom voted her the winner on *American Idol* in the first season of that immensely popular singing-competition TV program. Given the unusual nature of her rise to stardom, some critics dismissed her as being less an artist than a creation of the media. But with her rock-tinged brand of pop, her country-girl persona, and a "belting, soulful style" that "brings to mind such towers of singing prowess as Etta James and Ethel Merman," as Andrew Marton wrote for the *Houston Chronicle* (September 9, 2002), Clarkson has continued to win the approval of fans, who have purchased millions of copies of her albums, *Thankful* and *Breakaway*, and of the singles "A Moment Like This," "Breakaway," "Since U Been Gone," "Behind These Hazel Eyes," and "Because of You." The music industry has been equally taken with Clarkson, the winner of two Grammy Awards in 2006.

The youngest of three children, Kelly Brianne Clarkson was born on April 24, 1982 in Burleson, Texas, a town of 28,000 located outside Fort Worth. When Clarkson was six years old, her mother, Jeanne, separated from her biological father, Steve Clarkson, after 17 years of marriage; while Clarkson's brother, Jason, lived with his father, and her sister, Alyssa, resided with an aunt, Clarkson was raised by her mother, an elementary-school teacher, and her stepfather, Jimmy Taylor, a contractor. From a very early age, Kelly Clarkson demonstrated a passion for performing, staging productions of musicals, including *Beauty and the Beast* and *The Little Mermaid*, in the living room of her home. For a time she wanted to become a marine biologist—an aspiration that ended when she saw the movie *Jaws*. Her interest in a musical career was sparked in 1995, while she was attending Pauline Hughes Middle School. The school's choir teacher, hearing Clarkson singing in the hallway, suggested that she join the choir. Clarkson took that advice and discovered that she had an impressive vocal range. "I didn't even know what a range was," she told Lisa Chant for the Melbourne, Australia, *Sunday Herald Sun* (July 31, 2005). As a member of the choir, Clarkson received training in different musical styles, including classical and opera.

Clarkson also sang in the chorus at Burleson High School. "Already then, Kelly could do any and all musical styles. She could sing the classical literature but didn't sound like a rhythm-and-blues singer trying to sing classical," her chorus teacher, Philip Glenn, told Andrew Marton. She landed starring roles in school productions of such musicals as *Seven Brides for Seven Brothers* and *Brigadoon*. During that time Clarkson also began writing songs and poems. At 15 she was offered a contract by a record label, but she turned it down, deciding to complete her high-school education. She felt, however, that singing would be a part of her future. "Singing gave me confidence," she told Barry Koltnow for the *Orange County (California) Register* (June 18, 2003). "Friends at school were nervous because they didn't know what they wanted to do with the rest of their lives, but I had a peaceful feeling inside because I knew. I knew that I would make a living at this since a seventh-grade assembly, when I was about to go out and sing a Mariah Carey song in front of the whole town. Other singers were throwing up out of fear but I wasn't afraid at all. Singing just seemed a natural thing."

Following her graduation from high school, in 2000, Clarkson decided not to pursue a college education. "Kelly is the type of person who always wanted to get to the very meat of things. College is just not made for kids like that, who know exactly what they want for their career," her mother, Jeanne Taylor, told Marton. Instead Clarkson remained in Burleson for a year and held a series of low-paying jobs, as a waitress in a comedy club and as a worker at a pharmacy, a zoo, and a movie theater, in order to finance a demo tape of her original compositions, which she planned to send to record labels. In 2001 Clarkson headed with a friend to Los Angeles, California, in an attempt to break into the recording industry. While mailing out audition tapes, Clarkson sought opportunities to perform in front of live audiences. Her first professional job was as an extra on the ABC television series *Sabrina the Teenage Witch*. Clarkson also began working with Gerry Goffin, a renowned songwriter who had collaborated with the singer Carole King, among others. Then she had a run of bad luck: first, Goffin contracted a serious illness, and then Clarkson's apartment was destroyed in a fire. Her roommate's decision to leave Hollywood led Clarkson to return to Burleson, where she worked part-time, distributing promotional samples of Red Bull, an energy drink. Despite the setbacks, she did not abandon her hopes for a singing career.

In 2002 Clarkson's best friend, Jessica, suggested that Clarkson attend auditions that were being held in Dallas, Texas, for a new "reality" TV series, a singing-competition program called *American Idol: The Search for a Superstar*. Auditioning along with 1,000 other candidates, Clarkson impressed the show's judges, Paula Abdul, Simon Cowell, and Randy Jackson. After several callbacks she was one of 119 contestants invited to Los Angeles, where she competed successfully for a spot as one of the top 30 finalists, who would appear on the show.

American Idol, which premiered in June 2002, was based on a live weekly British television program in which contestants performed songs, in a variety of musical styles; each performance was followed by critiques—often frank to the point of cruelty—from the three judges. Each week television viewers were given the opportunity to vote by telephone for their favorite performers. In the American version of the show, which quickly became a hit, Clarkson won over audiences with her renditions of soulful ballads written or made famous by Mariah Carey ("Without You"), Celine Dion ("I Surrender"), and Aretha Franklin ("[You Make Me Feel Like] A Natural Woman"). It was Clarkson's version of another Aretha Franklin tune—"Respect"—that garnered her a position among the show's top 10 contestants. On the following September 4, 2002, Clarkson reached the finale, competing against Justin Guarini of Doylestown, Pennsylvania. Each performed two songs written for the show, "Before Your Love" and "A Moment Like This." For the third and final round of performances, each of the two finalists was allowed to choose a tune he or she had previously performed during the season. Clarkson sang "Respect" and Guarini selected "Get Here," a ballad made famous by Oleta Adams. Following their final performances, more than 15.5 million television viewers called in, and Clarkson was crowned the winner of *American Idol*, receiving 58 percent of the votes. At the close of the show, she tearfully sang "A Moment Like This."

As part of the publicity tour, Clarkson reunited with the other 29 *American Idol* top finalists at the MGM-Grand Hotel in Las Vegas, Nevada, for a television special that aired on the FOX network on September 23, 2002. The next month she embarked on a 30-city national tour that featured the top 10 performers from *American Idol*. Clarkson's video for "A Moment Like This" premiered on the cable channel MTV's "Total Request Live" countdown in October 2002, and she was a featured performer on four tracks of the *American Idol* compilation CD, *American Idol Great Moments*, released in the same month. Most significantly during that time, Clarkson signed a $1 million recording contract with RCA; her first single, "A Moment Like This," was released on September 17, 2002. The single sold an impressive 236,000 copies in its first week of release in the U.S. and also set a record on *Billboard*'s Hot 100 chart when it jumped from number 52 to number one within one week in December 2002. The song occupied the top of the charts in Canada for five weeks.

In January 2003 Clarkson was nominated for an American Music Award in the category of favorite pop/rock artist, along with the post-grunge band Puddle of Mudd and the R&B singer Ashanti (who won the award). On April 15 of that year, Clarkson released her debut album, *Thankful*, which was produced by the legendary Clive Davis. Clarkson co-wrote four of the album's 12 tracks, which also included "A Moment Like This." While Clarkson's album received generally favorable reviews, she drew criticism for what some critics perceived as a lack of personality, reflected in her attempt to cover a wide range of musical genres. Joanna Hensley wrote for the Lafayette, Indiana, *Journal and Courier* (May 9, 2003), "Clarkson is sweet and has tons of talent, unlike some big-selling artists out there. Her voice is also strong, sexy and mature, which is pretty amazing considering she's never had a professional voice lesson. But her versatility is also the album's major downfall. One minute she sounds like Christina Aguilera; the next moment she sounds like Sheryl Crow or Faith Hill. And while it's great to pander to several genres, it's also hard to find a niche with fans when you're obviously trying to sound like every other star." In its first week of release, Clarkson's album debuted at number one on the *Billboard* 200 chart in the U.S. and on the Canadian album chart, driven by a second single, "Miss Independent." That rock-influenced song was co-written and nearly recorded by Christina Aguilera, who left the song un-

finished when she decided not to include it on her own album; Clarkson collaborated with Rhett Lawrence, the co-writer and co-producer of the track, to finish writing the lyrics.

June 2003 saw the premiere of the film *From Justin to Kelly*, in which Clarkson starred with the *American Idol* runner-up, Justin Guarini. A musical in the tradition of the lightweight 1960s beach-themed movies starring Frankie Avalon and Annette Funicello, *From Justin to Kelly* found Clarkson portraying a girl from Texas who, on spring break in Florida, falls in love with a young man from Pennsylvania (played by Guarini). In September of that year, Clarkson appeared on the NBC television series *American Dreams*, set during the 1960s; she portrayed the singer Brenda Lee and performed Lee's classic song "Sweet Nothin's." Shortly afterward *Thankful* received both gold and platinum certification (indicating sales of 500,000 and one million copies, respectively) from the Recording Industry Association of America (RIAA).

In January 2004 Clarkson took part in the *World Idol* competition in London, England, which pitted her against the winners of *American Idol*–like programs from countries around the world, including Australia (*Australian Idol*), Belgium (*Idool*), Britain (*Pop Idol*), Canada (*Canadian Idol*), Poland (*Idol, Poland*) and South Africa (*Idols, South Africa*). Clarkson, who performed "(You Make Me Feel Like) A Natural Woman" at the competition, was the early favorite to win; she ultimately placed second behind the Norwegian "idol," Kurt Nilsen, and was criticized for being a poor sport after she abruptly left the set of *World Idol* following her loss. In the next month Clarkson was nominated for a Grammy Award for best female pop vocal performance for "Miss Independent"; she faced competition from Christina Aguilera ("Beautiful"), Sarah McLachlan ("Fallen"), Dido ("White Flag"), and Avril Lavigne ("I'm with You"), with the award going to Aguilera. Also in February 2004 Clarkson co-headlined a 30-city tour with Clay Aiken, the runner-up to the winner, Ruben Studdard, in the second season of *American Idol*. In August Clarkson had her biggest U.S. hit since her debut single, with the release of the song "Breakaway," which was featured on the soundtrack of the movie *The Princess Diaries 2: Royal Engagement* (2004). The song reached the number-six position in the United States on the *Billboard* Hot 100 chart and the number-one spot on its adult-contemporary chart.

For her sophomore album, also entitled *Breakaway* (2004), Clarkson received songwriting credit on six of the album's tracks. Critics contrasted *Breakaway* favorably with *Thankful*, praising its harder, rock-and-roll-influenced sound, which drew comparisons to the Canadian singer and songwriter Avril Lavigne—who co-wrote the title song on Clarkson's album. In reviewing *Breakaway*, Natalie Nichols wrote for the *Los Angeles Times* (December 15, 2004): "This time, the Texas-born chanteuse digs deeper emotionally, and the songs . . . generally fit better with her upbeat, down-to-earth personality. Perhaps the greatest asset of *Breakaway*—whose title track plays like Clarkson's anthem, about a small-town girl going for it—is that she sounds more like herself, which allows her to move beyond the typical." *Breakaway* spawned several more hit singles: "Since U Been Gone," "Behind These Hazel Eyes," and "Because of You." The album had sold five million copies by January 2006. In February Clarkson defeated the music veterans Mariah Carey, Sheryl Crow, Bonnie Raitt, and Gwen Stefani to capture the Grammy Award for best pop vocal female performance. She won a second Grammy during the ceremony, in the best-pop-album category. Afterward Clarkson traveled to Turin, Italy, where she performed at the 2006 Winter Olympics. She then began a 24-city North American summer tour.

Discussing her third album, which is scheduled for release in 2007, Clarkson told an interviewer for the MTV Web site, "Some of the stuff on the new album is very singer/songwriter, because I love people like Patty Griffin and Ryan Adams. And then there is other stuff that's real intense rock stuff, more rock than *Breakaway*. It's going to be a cool album." She introduced several songs while touring during the summer of 2006. In addition to her Grammy Awards, Clarkson won an ASCAP Pop Music Award (2004) for the song "Miss Independent," an American Music Award (2005) in the category of favorite adult contemporary artist, and two MTV Video Music Awards in 2005 in the categories of best female video and best pop video, for the single "Since U Been Gone." She also received 12 *Billboard* awards in 2005. In 2006 she was nominated for American Music Awards in the categories of pop/rock favorite female artist and adult contemporary favorite artist. In February 2006 Clarkson bought a home in Mansfield, Texas.

—B.M.

Suggested Reading: *Dallas Observer* June 19, 2003; *Houston Chronicle* p3 Sep. 9, 2002; *Los Angeles Times* E p2 Feb. 10, 2006; (Melbourne, Australia) *Sunday Herald Sun* E p6 July 31, 2005; *Time* (on-line) Feb. 13, 2006

Selected Recordings: *Thankful*, 2003; *Breakaway*, 2004

Cohen, Sasha

Oct. 26, 1984– Figure skater

Address: c/o www.sashacohen.com, 132 Waterford Park Dr., Greer, SC 29650

Sasha Cohen came to widespread attention with her silver medal–winning performance at the 2000 U.S. Figure Skating Championships, exhibiting impressive athleticism—along with the flexibility of a ballet dancer and the dramatic ability of a seasoned actress. "Sasha is elegance personified," John Nicks, Cohen's coach, told Mark Emmons for the *Orange County (California) Register* (February 12, 2000). "She is naturally unable to get into an ugly position. She looks fragile, but that's deceptive, she's a very tough young lady." Until recently, while many observers had long believed that Cohen had the potential to be the country's top female skater, her performances during major competitions were inconsistent, and she accumulated a string of second-place wins, often trailing the nine-time U.S. champion and five-time world champion, Michelle Kwan. "A beautiful body, beautiful smile, angelic face—[Cohen] has the most beautiful lines I've seen in skating," Peggy Fleming, a 1968 Olympic gold medalist and now a popular skating commentator, told Frank Litsky for the *New York Times* (September 26, 2003). "They are pure and look natural, not taught. She has incredible extension. The technique is there. But mentally, control has been her problem. She is awesome in practices. Then, when she gets out, she just loses focus. She's got to overcome that. She just has to be able to do

Matthew Stockman/Getty Images

it under pressure." On January 14, 2005 Cohen, proving that she could excel under incredible pressure, won the U.S. championship, finishing the competition with 199.18 points—more than 28 points ahead of the second-place skater, Kimmie Meissner. (Kwan did not take part in the competition because of an injury.) By dint of her performance at the U.S. championships, Cohen represented the U.S. at the 2006 Winter Olympics, in Turin, Italy, where she earned the silver medal.

Alexandra Pauline Cohen was born on October 26, 1984 in Westwood, California. (Sasha is a common Slavic nickname for those named Alexander or Alexandra.) Her mother, Galina, a former ballet dancer, is a native of Odessa, Ukraine, who immigrated to the United States in the early 1970s. (Cohen's maternal grandfather was part of a children's gymnastics troupe that once performed for the Soviet dictator Joseph Stalin.) Her father, Roger, is an attorney and international-business consultant. Her younger sister, Natasha, is an aspiring pianist. At the age of five, Cohen began studying gymnastics, just as Galina had done during her own childhood in Odessa. By the time Cohen was six years old, she was attending two-and-a-half-hour gymnastics classes four times a week.

Cohen was first exposed to figure skating as a seven-year-old. "I was in gymnastics with a close friend of mine, and she also skated. So she took me to the rink with her, and I loved it," Cohen told *USA Today* (September 30, 2003, on-line). "My mom said you have to pick one, so I chose figure skating." Cohen started taking the weekly group lessons offered at her local rink. Although she was initially behind other serious skaters her own age, most of whom had started studying at four or five, within three years she had added two double jumps—a double salchow and a double toe loop—to her repertoire. When she was 10 Cohen and her family moved from the coastal village of Westwood to the city of Laguna Niguel, located in South Orange County. She attended the now-defunct Ice Chalet ice rink in Costa Mesa, where she caught the attention of Nicks, a Hall of Fame coach whose previous pupils included Tai Babilonia and Randy Gardner, a pair who had won five U.S. Figure Skating Championships. "I could see immediately that she was somebody very special," Nicks told Amy Shipley for the *Washington Post* (February 5, 2002). "She was skating two times as fast as everyone else, and she had no fear at all. Also, at her age, she had a great elegance—a natural elegance that can't be taught." By the time she was 11 her arsenal of jumps included all of the double jumps, except for the double axel, which she learned, along with the triple toe loop, when she was 12 years old.

In 1996 Cohen, training under Nicks, qualified for her first major competition, the U.S. Southwest Pacific Regional; still needing to catch up to skaters her own age, she recorded a fourth-place finish in the juvenile-girls' division. In 1997, after a second-place showing in the intermediate-ladies' division at the U.S. Southwest Pacific Regional, Cohen came in fourth at the Pacific Coast Sectional (also in the intermediate-ladies' division) and fifth at the intermediate level of that year's Junior Olympics. "That's when I started getting very serious and began realizing what I was going to have to sacrifice in order to be a good skater," she told Mark Emmons for the *Orange County Register* (February 9, 2000). To accommodate her weekly training sched-

ule, which included several hours of practice time at the rink, ballet lessons, and Pilates classes, Cohen enrolled in the Futures High School, a private school in Mission Viejo that provides flexible, individual instruction.

In 1998 Cohen's two second-place finishes—in the novice divisions of the Southwest Pacific Regional and the Pacific Coast Sectional—qualified her for the State Farm U.S. Figure Skating Championships. (To advance to the U.S. Championships, skaters must first place in the top four at the regional level and must then post a top-four finish at the Pacific Coast Sectional, the Eastern Sectional, or the Midwestern Sectional Championships.) That year Cohen finished sixth in the final standings. The following year she took first place at both the Southwest Pacific Regional and the Pacific Coast Sectional and qualified for the 1999 U.S. Figure Skating Championships in the junior division. Cohen led the field of 11 junior female skaters after the short program and finished second in the free skate—and the overall competition—to Sara Wheat. She made additional good showings in 1999, with first-place wins at the Gardena Winter Trophy and the Junior Grand Prix (held in Stockholm, Sweden) and a second-place finish (as a member of Team USA) at the Keri Lotion Figure Skating Classic, a competition pitting a U.S. team against a Russian team.

After coming in first at the 2000 Pacific Coast Sectional, Cohen—despite having missed training time for the event because of an injury to her right heel—delivered what is widely considered to be her breakthrough performance, at the 2000 U.S. Figure Skating Championships, held in Cleveland, Ohio. That marked her first appearance at the nationals at the ladies' senior level, where she was part of a group of promising female skaters that included her training partner, Naomi Nari Nam; Sarah Hughes, a fourth-place winner at the 1999 nationals; and Wheat. They were pitted against Michelle Kwan, who already had a string of U.S. and world championships to her credit.

Cohen's short program, set to classical music by Antonio Vivaldi and Tomas Albinoni, demonstrated a level of athleticism and artistry that was surprising in a skater of her youth. Her performance earned Cohen solid technical and presentation marks from the judges and a standing ovation from the audience. Her strong scores put Cohen in first place, ahead of Hughes and Kwan—who found herself in third place after falling during a triple toe loop. Calling Cohen "wonderfully lyrical and impossibly flexible," Jere Longman wrote for the *New York Times* (February 12, 2000), "She wore a white costume, which can engulf a skater on an ice surface, but Sasha Cohen hardly disappeared tonight." Cohen, however, fell during her long program, and Kwan, by capturing high scores for her own long program, which accounts for two-thirds of a skater's final score, claimed the overall competition and her fourth national title. The 2000 U.S. Figure Skating Championships marked the first of several competitions in which Cohen would come in second, behind Kwan.

Age restrictions prevented Cohen from automatically competing at the 2000 World Championships, in Nice, France. (She could qualify for the competition only by first winning a medal at the World Junior Championships.) Although Cohen was the heavy favorite to win a medal at that year's World Junior Championships, she came in sixth, well behind her American teammates Jennifer Kirk and Deanna Stellato, who finished in first and second place, respectively, thus making her ineligible to attend the senior championships. "I was looking at that competition like, 'Oh, this is going to be easy, I just won a silver at nationals,'" Cohen told Philip Hersh for the *Chicago Tribune* (January 9, 2001). "I guess that was a little much. I learned I have to go to a competition to skate my best. Not to do well here so I can make it there." Cohen finished the rest of the 2000 season with similarly disappointing results, taking fifth place in the Nations Cup, fourth place in the Cup of Russia, and fifth place in the Sparkassen Cup on Ice.

In 2001 Cohen suffered an injury, variously reported as a stress fracture in the vertebrae of her lower back or an inflammation in her back joint. The result of excessive jumping during practice, the injury forced her to withdraw from the 2001 nationals and kept her sidelined from competition for nine months, during which she underwent physical therapy and made changes in her training regimen and diet. "I had to keep in mind what my goals were and the steps to get there. I took every day one at a time and looked to where my dreams were," Cohen told Carin Davis for the *Jewish Journal of Greater Los Angeles* (January 25, 2002, on-line). Cohen was determined to regain her place among her fellow skaters and rebuild her reputation with the judges. She decided to try to become the first female skater to land a quadruple salchow in competition—a jump she had successfully landed in practice. (During quadruple salchows, which were then being performed regularly only in men's competitions, skaters launch themselves from the back inside edge of one blade, revolve in the air four times, and land on the back outside edge of the other blade; a figure-skating blade is only three to four millimeters thick.)

Cohen returned to competitive skating in the fall of 2001, when she took part in the Goodwill Games, held in Brisbane, Australia, where she finished in fourth place. She followed up her appearance at the Goodwill Games with a gold-medal win at the Finlandia Trophy competition in Helsinki, Finland, and a bronze-medal finish at the Trophée Lalique, in Paris, France—her first showing in a senior Grand Prix skating event. (Grand Prix events are sanctioned by the International Skating Union, or ISU.) She also placed fourth at the Masters of Figure Skating event, second at the Hershey's Kisses Challenge team competition, and fifth at the Smart Ones Skate America contest. After failed attempts to land the quadruple salchow at three competitions (the Finlandia Trophy, the Masters of Figure Skating, and Skate America), Cohen and Nicks feverishly debated the wisdom of attempting the difficult move. As Nicks told Rachel Blount for the *Minneapolis-St. Paul Star Tribune* (February 6, 2002), "She is a very ambitious young lady. It's a gamble, and I'm a conservative Englishman. I don't like to gamble. But I always get outvoted. She will do it. It's just a question of when and where."

There was intense media speculation regarding whether or not Cohen would perform the quadruple salchow at the 2002 nationals, in Los Angeles, California, and she ultimately announced that in order to increase her chances to qualify for the Olympic team she would not try to execute the risky jump. Cohen finished the nationals in second place—once again behind Kwan—earning her a berth, alongside Kwan and Hughes, at the 2002 Olympics, to be held in Salt Lake City, Utah.

In preparation for the Olympics, Cohen and Nicks decided against including the quadruple jump in her routine, instead opting for a series of triple jumps, including a triple lutz–triple toe loop combination. The two disagreed about the music Cohen had chosen, selections from Georges Bizet's opera *Carmen.* Although Nicks argued that the choice lacked originality, as both Katarina Witt and Debi Thomas had skated to the same music at previous Olympic Games, Cohen, much like the character Carmen herself, was insistent. "It's music that I've always loved, and I feel the character's personality is similar to mine," Cohen told Davis. On the first day of the Olympics, Cohen was seated next to President George W. Bush at the opening ceremonies, and much to the amusement of reporters, she handed him her cell phone so that he could chat with her mother.

In an article for the *New York Times* (February 21, 2002) describing Cohen's performance during the short program, Selena Roberts wrote, "In her moment Tuesday night, she was at ease from the first note of her short program to the last. With her graceful spirals, Cohen skated lines into the ice with the elegant touch of a calligrapher. Accelerating into each jump, she approached her triples with a daredevil's confidence She had it all: beauty, style, athletics—and gall. Suddenly, the same judges who have been [blasted] for scoring skaters on reputation accepted the coltish 17-year-old Cohen into the elite." During her long program, however, Cohen fell during a combination jump; she finished in fourth place, out of medal contention. (With her long-program win, Sarah Hughes took home the gold medal, upsetting Russia's Irina Slutskaya and Kwan, who finished second and third, respectively.)

Following her disappointing finish at the 2002 Olympics, Cohen abruptly left California—and Nicks—to train with the legendary Russian skating coach Tatiana Tarasova in Simsbury, Connecticut. (Tarasova had coached seven Olympic gold medalists, including the male skater Alexei Yagudin, who took home a gold medal in 2002.) Under Tarasova, Cohen claimed the top spot at several 2002 competitions, including Skate Canada, Trophée Lalique, the Sears Figure Skating Open, and the Crest Whitestrips International Figure Skating Challenge. Her wins at Skate Canada and Trophée Lalique, along with her silver medal from the 2002 Cup of Russia, made her eligible for her first ISU Grand Prix Final, at which she had a triumphant first-place finish.

Cohen's winning streak continued in 2003. The Campbell's Classic, held in New York City that year, marked the first time that Cohen defeated Kwan. She followed up her season-opening win at the Campbell's Classic with her first Skate America gold, as well as first-place wins at Skate Canada and Trophée Lalique. Although she placed fourth overall at the 2003 World Championships, Cohen successfully completed her first triple lutz–triple toe loop combination during the competition. Cohen fell three times during the ABC Winter Challenge, but still earned a bronze, and three times at the Grand Prix Final, at which she still earned a silver. In all, Cohen earned seven perfect marks of 6.0 during 2003.

In early 2004 Cohen left Tarasova to train with Robin Wagner, Sarah Hughes's former coach. (Hughes had left competitive skating to attend Yale University, where she is a member of the class of 2007.) Under Wagner's tutelage Cohen won silver medals at both the 2004 nationals and the World Championships, as well as a gold at the 2004 Marshalls World Skating Challenge with a flawless free skate. She managed only third-place finishes at the 2004 Marshalls World Cup and the Campbell's Classic, however, and within six months, her relationship with Wagner was strained. "She is a magnificent skater with magnificent artistic qualities, but why not push yourself? Why not do a new spiral sequence, a triple-triple [jump] combination, something challenging musically? You can do those things only if you are willing to accept mental and physical discomfort on a daily basis," Wagner told Hersh for the *Chicago Tribune* (January 12, 2005). "It is very difficult for Sasha to get out of her comfort zone. . . . Talent, greatness and potential sometimes causes an athlete to become complacent. Sasha was becoming complacent. If you're not number one, you can't go into a holding pattern,"

In December 2004, weeks before the 2005 U.S. Figure Skating Championships, Cohen returned to California, where she reunited with Nicks, who came out of retirement to coach her. "The main thing was that I just realized nothing was really right, nothing was really in place in my life, and that's when I knew I had tried to stick it out for so long [on the East Coast] and that it wasn't working," Cohen told Reid for the *Orange County Register* (January 10, 2005). "As soon as I thought about it, as soon as the idea came in my head to go back to California, I thought, 'Yeah, this is right. Let's pack.' And there was never a second thought."

Cohen felt that a new ISU judging system recently put in place by U.S. Figure Skating, the sport's national governing body, would work to her advantage. Under the new system skaters accumulate points based on program difficulty and successful execution of various elements; it replaces a system in which skaters were judged on a maximum scale of 6.0. In her first competition under the new scoring system, Cohen came in second to Slutskaya at the World Championships. She also earned a silver at the Marshalls U.S. Figure Skating Challenge, behind Kwan, who also topped her at that year's nationals. Kwan, however, withdrew from the 2006 nationals, held in January, because of an injury, and there was rampant speculation in the press that her absence made it likely that Cohen would earn the championship and secure a spot on the Olympic team. (Only the first-place finisher in each event is guaranteed a spot on the team. The other team members are chosen by a committee.)

On January 14, 2006, after skating a four-minute program set to the musical theme from the 1968 film version of *Romeo and Juliet*, by the composer Nino Rota, Cohen was named U.S. champion, thereby ensuring a spot on the team traveling to Turin, Italy, in February for the Winter Games. She received a long ovation from the crowd after the program, and a reporter for the Associated Press (January 15, 2006, on-line) wrote of the performance, "She doesn't skate so much as float, and her expression told of all the pain and heartache that Juliet felt. When she spins, she looks like that ballerina in the music box." Kimmie Meissner, the second-place winner, was also named to the Olympic team. In a widely debated move, the selection committee granted Kwan a medical waiver: if her injury healed sufficiently she could compete in the Olympics. She eventually withdrew, however, and was replaced on the team by Emily Hughes, winner of the bronze medal at the U.S. championships and the sister of Sarah Hughes.

At the 2006 Winter Olympics, Cohen got off to a promising start. Drawing the last performance slot, after the other 28 competitors, she ranked in first place, 0.03 points ahead of Russia's Irina Slutskaya, when all of the short programs were completed. Her performance during the four-minute free skate, which is weighted more heavily than the short program, was imperfect, a result perhaps foreshadowed by a spill in her warmup routine. "I was probably, not nervous, but a little apprehensive knowing I missed the [triple] lutz and [triple] flip in the warmup," Cohen explained after the event, as reported by John P. Lopez in the *Houston Chronicle* (February 24, 2006) and by journalists in many other publications. "You know, when you go out there and you have all the people watching and you know what you want to do and you know your practices are not exactly right, it's kind of hard to feel like you're getting churros at Disneyland." Cohen fell on her opening combination, a triple lutz, double toe loop, double loop; on her second combination she nearly repeated the misstep, but managed to stay upright by bracing her hand against the ice. She regained her composure and skated flawlessly throughout the remainder of her program, which included five more triple jumps. Cohen's program was considered one of the more difficult, and because the figure-skating scoring system rewards aggressiveness and ambition, deductions for the flaws in her performance were not as heavy as they might have been otherwise. Indeed, her scores were good enough to earn her a silver medal. Japan's Shizuka Arakawa, who performed a similarly demanding program without falling, won the gold medal.

In Cohen's first event following the Olympics, the World Championships, held in Calgary, Alberta, Canada, she repeated her exquisite performance in the Olympics short program, building a 3.62-point lead. She was again undone by her long program, in which she fell once and botched the landings of several jumps; she finishing third overall. "It is frustrating and disappointing," Cohen said afterward to Helene Elliot for the *Los Angeles Times* (March 26, 2006), "but I know I gave it my best effort and I kind of have to be happy with that part. . . . I still haven't found that automatic robot to pump out perfect performances. That's something I'm still searching for." Some observers suggested at the time that the World Championships would be Cohen's final competition; speculation increased when Cohen passed up the 2006 International Skating Union Grand Prix of Figure Skating Series, which began in October.

Cohen plans to divide her time between skating and acting before she begins serious preparations for the 2010 Olympics. She was cast as the equestrian diva Fiona Hughes in Michael Damian's film *Moondance Alexander*, and she has a cameo role in a movie starring Will Ferrell; both pictures were to be released in 2007. On the small screen, Cohen has appeared as herself on episodes of NBC's *Las Vegas*, CBS's *CSI: New York*, and Bravo's *Project Runway*. She has helped to create many of her own skating costumes and has expressed a desire to study fashion design. Regarding her future, she told Ramona Shelburne for the *Los Angeles Daily News* (August 12, 2006), "I want to just play it by the moment and see what's out there for me."

Cohen currently lives in Orange County, California, where she recently purchased a home located a block from the beach. She chronicled her skating career in her memoir, *Fire on Ice: Autobiography of a Champion Figure Skater*, which was published in 2005. She has signed a modeling contract with the prestigious Wilhelmina Agency and has appeared in several magazines, including *Seventeen*, *Vogue*, and *Teen People*. Cohen is also active in several charitable ventures, among them Covenant House; the Connecticut Children's Medical Center; Soldiers' Angels; and Girls Inc.

—B.M.

Suggested Reading: Associated Press (on-line) Jan. 15, 2006; *Chicago Tribune* N p1 Jan. 9, 2001, C p2 Jan. 12, 2005; *Jewish Journal of Greater Los Angeles* (on-line) Jan. 25, 2002; *Minneapolis-St. Paul Star Tribune* Feb. 6, 2002; *New York Times* D p1 Feb. 12, 2000, D p1 Feb. 21, 2002; D p4 Sep. 26, 2003; *Orange County (California) Register* Sports Feb. 9, 2000, Feb. 12, 2000, Jan. 6, 2002, Jan. 10, 2005; *USA Today* (on-line) Sep. 30, 2003; *Washington Post* D p1 Feb. 5, 2002, D p1 Jan. 15, 2005

Selected Books: *Fire on Ice: Autobiography of a Champion Figure Skater*, 2005

Kevin Winter/Getty Images

Colbert, Stephen

(kohl-BEAR)

May 13, 1964– Comic actor

Address: Comedy Central, 513 W. 54th St., New York, NY 10019

Stephen Colbert came to national attention as one of the correspondents on the fake news program *The Daily Show*, which airs on the cable network Comedy Central. More or less regularly for eight years, beginning in 1997, the year after *The Daily Show*'s debut, Colbert played a self-important reporter who exhibited, to a comical degree, the self-important speech, attitudes, and mannerisms of legitimate news correspondents. "Since Bill Murray's departure for the movies, no one has done fatuous like Colbert does fatuous: the serious-reporter-guy ability to cock a brow with bogus knowing, his way of tilting his head to indicate sincerity worthy of an Airedale," David Remnick wrote for the *New Yorker* (July 25, 2005). In the fall of 2005, Comedy Central added to its schedule, immediately after *The Daily Show*, *The Colbert Report* (pronounced with a French accent: kohl-BEAR ray-PORE), a half-hour program that parodies *The O'Reilly Factor* and other right-wing talk shows. *The Colbert Report* has been a critical and commercial success—drawing 1.2 million viewers per night in late 2005, more than double the network's rating for the 11:30 time slot the previous year—and it has further elevated Colbert's status among the premier political and media satirists of the day.

Stephen Tyrone Colbert was born to James W. Colbert Jr. and Lorna Tuck Colbert, both of Irish-Catholic ancestry, on May 13, 1964 in Charleston, South Carolina. He was the youngest of eight brothers (the others were James III, William, Edward, Thomas, John, Peter, and Paul) and three sisters (Mary, Margo, and Elizabeth). His family was "very devout but joyful," as he told Gavin Edwards for *Rolling Stone* (November 3, 2005, on-line). His father, a physician specializing in immunology, was the vice president for academic affairs at the Medical University of South Carolina; his mother was a homemaker. Colbert grew up on James Island, which encompasses sections of Charleston. During his earliest years members of his family pronounced their surname in the English way, with a hard *T* at the end, but, as he told Bryce Donovan for the Charleston, South Carolina, *Post and Courier* (April 29, 2006), his father "always wanted to be Col-BEAR" and told his children that they could use whichever pronunciation they preferred. "So we made a choice, and it's about half and half. The girls for the most part are like, 'Get over it, you're Colbert,' but I was so young when this choice was given to us, I think that if somebody woke me up in the middle of the night and slapped me across the face I'd still say Stephen Col-BEAR." As a boy Colbert enjoyed listening to comedy albums by George Carlin, Bill Cosby, and Dean Martin. To eradicate his southern accent, he imitated the "deep, rich, buttery, confident tones" of John Chancellor, Frank Reynolds, and other newscasters, as he recalled to Jacques Steinberg for the *New York Times* (May 4, 2005). In 1974, when he was 10, his father and his brothers Peter and Paul were killed, along with dozens of others, in a plane crash in Charlotte, North Carolina, caused by pilot error. "Nothing made any sense after my father and brothers died. I kind of just shut off," Colbert told Donovan. After his father's death his mother moved the family to downtown Charleston, where young Stephen had difficulty in adjusting. "I was not from downtown, I did not know the kids there," Colbert told Donovan. "I love Charleston, I love the Lowcountry, but it's very insular. Or peninsular. I just wasn't accepted by the kids."

As a way to escape his unhappiness, Colbert began reading books of fantasy and science fiction—he read the Lord of the Rings trilogy many times—and playing the fantasy game Dungeons and Dragons. In a conversation with Nathan Rabin for the *Onion A.V. Club* (January 25, 2006), he asked rhetorically, "Who really wants to be themselves when they're teenagers? [In Dungeons and Dragons] you get to be heroic and have adventures. And it's an incredibly fun game. They have arcane rules and complex societies and they're open-ended and limitless, kind of like life. For somebody who eventually became an actor, it was interesting to have done that for so many years, because acting is role-playing." Colbert began to show a comedic streak in his teens, as a student at the private Porter-Gaud School, in Charleston. He told Donovan, "That's when people said, 'Oh, Colbert's funny.' Then a year later, I was voted wittiest at my high school. And that's when I thought maybe I should be a comedian."

An indifferent student, Colbert earned poor grades at Porter-Gaud. After he graduated, in 1982, he spent two years at the all-male Hampden-Sydney College, in Hampden-Sydney, Virginia, a school that he has described as "an inorganic rock of ultra-conservatism," according to Robin Finn in the *New York Times* (August 27, 2004). He then transferred to Northwestern University, in Chicago, Illinois, where he majored in theater. Colbert told Nathan Rabin, "My mom kind of led me toward acting. She wanted to be an actress when she was younger." During his college years Colbert studied improvisation with Del Close, considered one of the pioneers of improvisational theater. A co-founder of the San Francisco-based 1960s comedy troupe the Committee, a performer with and director of the Second City, a Chicago comedy troupe, and an acting coach with the TV series *Saturday Night Live* during its early years, Close had previously taught the comedians John Belushi, Bill Murray, John Candy, and Gilda Radner, among others. In 1984 Close joined Charna Halpern to run ImprovOlympic, an acting school and performance space (now known as the iO Theater). "At the time, it was a competitive, freeform, one-act, long-form improvisation," Colbert recalled to Rabin. "And they were looking for colleges to do competitions at their theater. . . . A friend of mine said, 'We should go down and check this out.' . . . And I went and saw it once and was stunned by how much I wanted to go do it. We formed a team—we would go down on Tuesday nights and perform for audiences at the cabaret." At 22, some years after breaking away from the Catholic Church, Colbert began attending services again. He told Gavin Edwards, "That whole relativistic thing of 'Any path to God is a good one'—I thought, 'Well, if that's the case, I should stick with this one because I've got a head start.'"

Colbert graduated from Northwestern in 1986. With the help of a friend who worked as the box-office manager for the Second City, he got a job with the troupe, manning the phones and selling souvenirs. He also took classes there (they were free to employees). "I wanted to do something other than try to go get an acting job . . . ," he told Rabin. "I was so afraid of not being hired. And I found out that I really liked the people who worked there, that they were really trying hard to do something new and interesting." Colbert has said that at that time he did not know about Second City's storied past—its alumni included many performers who appeared on *Saturday Night Live*, some of whom became film stars—and "hadn't intended to end up there," as he told Rabin. "I meant to be a serious actor with a beard who wore a lot of black and wanted to share his misery with you." Colbert said, though, that his experiences at the Second City provided him with "a great education about what I was able to do and what audiences enjoyed, and the limits of self-indulgence, and the need to please and how you balance those." In his first acting job on the Second City's main stage, Colbert understudied for Steve Carell (who would become a *Daily Show* correspondent and, later, star of the TV comedy *The Office* and several films). While at Second City, Colbert met Amy Sedaris and Paul Dinello, both of whom appeared in skits with him. With Sedaris and Dinello, Colbert wrote installments of Comedy Central's first original sketch-comedy series, *Exit 57*. The show survived for two seasons, in 1995 and 1996, during which 12 episodes aired, and earned several CableACE Award nominations.

Also in the mid-1990s, after moving to New York, Colbert served as a writer for and performer on the *Dana Carvey Show*, which the Fox network canceled after eight episodes; worked for a few weeks as a field correspondent for the ABC weekly news show *Good Morning America*; and co-created and provided the voice of Ace in the *Saturday Night Live* cartoon called *Gary and Ace: The Ambiguously Gay Duo*. He was often unemployed, and because by that time he had married and become a father, he tried to do "everything and anything" that he could to earn money, as he recalled to Donovan. His luck changed after his agent arranged an audition for him with *The Daily Show*, then under development. "I really didn't want to do [it] because I hated *Good Morning America*, and I figured it was going to be the same type thing," he told Donovan. Colbert joined *The Daily Show* in 1997, when Craig Kilborn was its host.

After six months as a regular on the *The Daily Show*, Colbert decreased his appearances to fewer than once a week, on average, instead devoting most of his time to writing scripts, in collaboration with Sedaris and Dinello, for the Comedy Central series *Strangers with Candy*, which aired in 1999–2000. Presented as a parody of inspirational after-school specials, the show starred Sedaris as Jerri Blank, who returns to high school after spending years in jail. The same-titled, 2006 film, co-written by Colbert (cast as a science teacher), Dinello (who directed and played an art teacher), and Sedaris (in the leading role), earned mixed reviews.

Colbert told Rabin that when Jon Stewart replaced Kilborn on *The Daily Show*, in January 1999, the program "turned from local news, summer kicker stories, celebrity jokes, to something with more of a political point of view. Jon has a political point of view. He wanted us to have a political point of view, and for the most part, I found that I had a stronger one than I had imagined." Recurring segments in which Colbert appeared included "Even Stevphen," in which he and Steve Carell debated each other; "This Week in God," which satirized religion (as well as atheism, which Colbert defined as "the religion devoted to the worship of one's own smug sense of superiority"); and "The Jobbing of America," a cynical depiction of political campaigning. During Colbert's association with *The Daily Show*, the program won four Emmy Awards and two Peabody Awards for writing.

Airing Monday through Thursday immediately after *The Daily Show*, *The Colbert Report* began its run on October 17, 2005. Colbert told Rabin that the show "is a direct extension of the work [Stewart and the writers] did on *The Daily Show*, and it plays very much the same game as my character, who is a well-intentioned, poorly informed, high-status idiot." According to Marc Peyser, writing for *Newsweek* (February 13, 2006), "Both shows dissect the idiocy and hypocrisy of politicians and the media, and both do it with eyebrows cocked clear to the top of their heads." But whereas on *The Daily Show* Stewart plays himself while delivering fake headlines, on *The Colbert Report* its host remains in character throughout, presenting the news with an ill-informed, highly conservative slant. In an effort to mimic such right-wing pundits as Bill O'Reilly and Sean Hannity, as Colbert told Nathan Rabin, "we just try everything we can to pump up my status on the show. There are no televisions behind me, like the way [the *NBC Nightly News* anchor] Brian Williams has, or even [Stewart]. At certain angles, there are monitors behind Jon that have the world going on, which implies that that's where the news is, and that's where the information is, and the person in front of it is the conduit through which this information is given to you. But on my set, I said, 'I don't want anything behind me, because I am the sun. It all comes from me. I'm not channeling anything. *I am* the source.'" In his interview with David Remnick, Colbert, referring to the Fox News commentator Greta Van Susteren, the talk-show host and interviewer Larry King, and the broadcast journalist Aaron Brown (who was dropped from CNN in late 2005), as well as O'Reilly and Hannity, described his approach as "like O'Reilly segueing into Hannity, Hannity into Greta, Larry King into Aaron Brown."

"Truthiness," a satirical Colbert locution that is not in any American dictionary (it appears, as an archaic term with a different definition, in the *Oxford English Dictionary*), has become popular among his admirers since he introduced it, in a recurring segment called "The WØRD," on his debut show. Colbert told Rabin that "truthiness" refers to an attitude prevalent among government representatives and conservative members of the media. "I don't know whether it's a new thing, but it's certainly a current thing, in that it doesn't seem to matter what the facts are. It used to be, everyone was entitled to their own opinion, but not their own facts. But that's not the case anymore. . . . Truthiness is 'What I say is right, and [nothing] anyone else says could possibly be true.' It's not only *that* I feel it to be true, but that *I* feel it to be true. There's not only an emotional quality, but there's a selfish quality."

In 2006 the White House Correspondents Association chose Colbert to be the main entertainer at the group's annual dinner, held on August 29 that year. Appearing in character, as a strong Bush supporter, Colbert delivered a mock tribute to the president, who was seated just a few feet away from the podium. Commenting on a recent comparison of a shake-up among White House staffers to a rearrangement of deck chairs on the *Titanic*, and referring to the explosion that destroyed a German zeppelin in 1937, Colbert said, "This administration is soaring, not sinking. If anything, they are rearranging the deck chairs on the *Hindenburg*." Regarding the president's well-known reluctance to change his mind or deviate from any of his chosen courses of action, Colbert said, "When the president decides something on Monday, he still believes it on Wednesday—no matter what happened Tuesday." He also urged Bush not to worry about his low approval ratings: "We know that polls are just a collection of statistics that reflect what people are thinking in 'reality.' And reality has a well-known liberal bias." Colbert did not spare the journalists in his audience, either. "Over the last five years you people were so good—over tax cuts,WMD [weapons of mass destruction] intelligence, the effect of global warming," he said. "We Americans didn't want to know, and you had the courtesy not to try to find out. Those were good times, as far as we knew. But, listen, let's review the rules. Here's how it works: the president makes decisions. He's the Decider. The press secretary announces those decisions, and you people of the press type those decisions down. Make, announce, type. Just put 'em through a spell check and go home. Get to know your family again. Make love to your wife. Write that novel you got kicking around in your head. You know, the one about the intrepid Washington reporter with the courage to stand up to the administration. You know—fiction!" Reactions to Colbert's monologue ranged from condemnation to unequivocal approval.

"Off-camera," Gavin Edwards wrote, "Colbert carries himself with the same upright posture and serious demeanor that he employs on camera, only he's incredibly sane and literate." "He's like a living wall of encyclopedias that like to drink beer," Paul Dinello told Edwards. With Dinello and Sedaris, Colbert wrote the book *Wigfield: The Can-Do Town That Just May Not* (2003), a satire cum social commentary. Colbert met his wife, the former Eve-

lyn McGee, an actress and homemaker, in Charleston in 1990. The couple live in suburban New Jersey with their three children—Madeline, Peter, and John, the oldest of whom was born in 1995. Colbert teaches Sunday school at his church. His home contains his huge collection of Lord of the Rings dolls.

—M.B.

Suggested Reading: *60 Minutes* transcript (on-line) Aug. 13, 2006; (Charleston, South Carolina) *Post and Courier* F p1+ Apr. 29, 2006; *New York Times* B p2 Aug. 27, 2004, A p20 May 3, 2006, (on-line) May 4, 2005, Oct. 12, 2005, Oct. 25, 2005; *New York Times Magazine* (on-line) Sep. 25, 2005; *New Yorker* (on-line) July 25, 2005; *Newsweek* (on-line) Feb. 13, 2006; *Rolling Stone* (on-line) Nov. 3, 2005; *Salon* (on-line) Feb. 13, 2006; *Washington Post* (on-line) Jan. 10, 2005

Selected Television Shows: *Exit 57*, 1995–96; *Saturday Night Live*, 1996; *The Daily Show*, 1997–2005; *Strangers with Candy*, 1999–2000; *The Colbert Report*, 2005–

Selected Films: *Snow Days*, 1999; *Nobody Knows Anything*, 2003; *Bewitched*, 2005; *Strangers with Candy*, 2006

Selected Books: *Wigfield* (with Amy Sedaris and Paul Dinello), 2003

Cooper, Anderson

June 3, 1967– Broadcast journalist

Address: CNN, One Time Warner Center, New York, NY 10019

"I didn't go to anchor school or work in a local station," the journalist Anderson Cooper of the cable channel CNN told Jonathan Van Meter for *New York* (September 19, 2005, on-line), "so I never really learned the patter and the emphasis, the one-word-in-the-sentence kind of cadences. The best thing I can do is just be myself and not pretend to be this hard-bitten reporter. I feel like I'm making it up as I go along. I'm not the best TelePrompTer reader and I say *um* too much and I stumble and I stutter a lot." Despite that lack of polish, or because of his perceived genuineness, Cooper, the host of *Anderson Cooper 360*, has carved a niche for himself in the world of broadcast news. On September 1, 2005, with his interview of U.S. senator Mary Landrieu of Louisiana, Cooper made news himself—confronting Landrieu about the federal government's response to Hurricane Katrina, one of the worse natural disasters ever to occur in the United States. According to a CNN transcript of the interview, Cooper said to Landrieu, referring to the

Peter Kramer/Getty Images

Anderson Cooper

flooding that left much of New Orleans, Louisiana, and neighboring areas underwater, "For the last four days, I've been seeing dead bodies in the streets. . . . I got to tell you, there are a lot of people here who are upset, and very angry, and very frustrated. . . . And when they hear politicians . . . thanking one another . . . it kind of cuts them the wrong way. . . . Do you get the anger that is out here?" In an industry ostensibly concerned with objectivity, Cooper's impassioned style of reporting in the aftermath of the hurricane struck a chord with viewers. In explaining Cooper's appeal, Van Meter wrote, "He didn't calm us down; he made us feel even more unsettled. He became a proxy, both for the victims of Katrina and for his viewers, building a bridge between the two. He reacted the way any of us might have—raging against government officials when help didn't come fast enough, and weeping when it all got to be too much. But it wasn't just his raw emotion that set him apart. . . . It was his honest humanity. . . . He connected to those in the hurricane's path, and to the people watching at home. He removed the filter."

Cooper began his career with Channel One, working his way up from fact checker to chief international correspondent, a position in which he covered war-torn regions including Somalia, Rwanda, and Bosnia. In 1995 he became the youngest correspondent at ABC, where he served as a weekend reporter and co-anchor of *World News Now*. His decision to become the host of *The Mole*, a so-called reality series, was widely criticized by industry observers, who predicted that the move would mean the end of his journalism career. In 2001 Cooper defied those predictions when he

joined the news staff at CNN, serving as the weekend anchor before becoming a prime-time anchor in March 2003 and the host of *Anderson Cooper 360* the following September. Since he joined CNN, Cooper has reported on major breaking news stories, including the Asian tsunami of 2004, the Iraqi elections, and the funeral of Pope John Paul II in Vatican City.

Anderson Hays Cooper was born on June 3, 1967 in New York City, the younger of the two children of Wyatt Emory Cooper and Gloria Morgan Vanderbilt. His father, a writer, had come from a poor farming family in Mississippi; his mother is a renowned, New York–born socialite and fashion designer whose paternal great-grandfather, the shipping and railroad tycoon Cornelius Vanderbilt, had amassed a fortune estimated at $100 million at the time of his death. Cooper was raised with his older brother, Carter, on the Upper East Side of Manhattan. "Certainly, growing up, there was a nice apartment and nice things in the apartment, but for me, one of the greatest privileges of my background was realizing that what a lot of people think they want will not ultimately make them happier. If money is the goal, you will end up as desperately unhappy as everyone else. Learning that frees you up," he told Brad Goldfarb for *Interview* (October 1, 2004). "Neither of my parents believed in joining clubs or being involved in anything that reeked of elitism or exclusiveness. Growing up, 'elitist' was the worst thing you could say about someone," he added. Beginning when he was six or seven years old, Cooper showed a great fondness for television, usually watching programs from the time he got home from school until his bedtime (with breaks for dinner and homework). His television schedule comprised the cartoon *Magilla Gorilla*, followed by the 4:30 movie on Channel 7, the local ABC affiliate, and then the news. Growing up, Cooper admired the television news anchors more than he did the actors and writers who were frequent guests at his parents' home. "Some of my earliest memories are of watching Eric Sevareid and Walter Cronkite on the *CBS Evening News*. I don't know what it is. I was always fascinated with history, particularly military history," he told Mike McDaniel for the *Houston Chronicle* (September 5, 2003).

In January 1978, when Cooper was 10 years old, his father died of a heart attack. "The world seemed a very scary place," Cooper said about that time, in a conversation with George Rush and Joanna Rush Molloy for the New York *Daily News* (May 2, 2006). At the age of 11, Cooper, who was determined to be as financially independent as possible, began working as a model for the well-known, New York–based Ford Models agency. As a teenager he spent his summer vacations waiting tables at Mortimer's, a now-defunct restaurant in New York City. Meanwhile, he attended the Dalton School, an arts-oriented, coeducational private high school in Manhattan, which his parents had believed would provide him with a strong educational foundation. For a few months during his senior year, having become restless with his regimented high-school life, Cooper went on a survival trip through Africa. Gloria Vanderbilt told Van Meter about her son, "I knew it was in his nature to take risks, live on the edge. He got malaria and was in a hospital in Kenya, and he never told me about this until he came home safe." Cooper documented his experience for his teachers as a final paper.

After graduating from the Dalton School, in 1985, Cooper attended Yale University, in New Haven, Connecticut. He studied political science and international relations with the aim of becoming a diplomat and perhaps a member of the Foreign Service. He devoted his extracurricular hours to the university's crew team; after failing to make the team as a rower, he found another place, at the front of the boat, as a coxswain, and committed himself to maintaining the 125-pound race-weight requirement. (The coxswain is responsible for steering the boat and directing the speed and rhythm of the rowers.) "It was sort of absurd. I was probably normally 145 or 150 regularly, so it was a little extreme looking back on it. It's probably why I went grey early. I think I've always been sort of intense or obsessive. . . . I wanted to stick with the sport. I don't know if that was a very good idea, but it was a great experience," he told Hillary August in an interview for the *Yale Daily News* (September 29, 2005, on-line).

In the summer of 1988, before the start of Cooper's senior year, his older brother, Carter, who was being treated for emotional problems, committed suicide by leaping from a window in the family's 14th-floor New York City penthouse apartment. The suicide was witnessed by Cooper's mother, who told reporters that Carter's allergy medication may have triggered a psychotic episode. In the wake of the tragedy, Cooper wanted to remain at home to take care of his mother, but at her urging he returned to Yale for his senior year and earned a bachelor's degree in political science and international relations in 1989. As he recalled in an October 2003 piece for CNN (excerpted from an article published in the September 2003 issue of *Details*) that discussed his brother's suicide, his last year of college was "a blur," during which he spent most of his time "trying to figure out what had happened . . . I worried that whatever impulse drove my brother might be lurking out there, somewhere, waiting for me." After graduation Cooper took a yearlong break from school and career pursuits, working on his family's house on Long Island. He then decided that he wanted to work in television news. "I was feeling obviously an amount of pain over the loss, [and] I wanted to be in an environment where emotion and pain and suffering was something that was acceptable to talk about. Some people would join a support group. I was drawn to a combat zone," he explained to Verne Gay for *Newsday* (October 12, 2003).

When Cooper failed to get an entry-level position at the ABC Television Network, he accepted a job as a fact-checker at Channel One News, which was broadcast directly to 12,000 middle-school and high-school classrooms across the country. He remained with Channel One for six months before leaving the United States to study Vietnamese at the University of Hanoi. On his way there Cooper gained illegal entry into Burma; armed with a home-video camera and a counterfeit press pass, he documented the ongoing conflict between the Burmese government and pro-democracy students, sending the stories to Channel One News. "I figured if I put myself in situations where there weren't many Americans around and I shot little stories, then I could sell them to Channel One. I wanted to make it impossible for them to not put me on air," he told David S. Hirschman in an interview posted on the Media Bistro Web site (May 11, 2004). Continuing on to Vietnam, Cooper studied for six months, surviving on $2 per day and eating mostly chicken noodle soup. He continued to shoot freelance stories for Channel One from Cambodia, Thailand, and Vietnam, which he edited upon his return to the United States. When his reports failed to net him a job offer from Channel One News, Cooper traveled to Africa in August 1992 and filed stories from the war-torn regions of Somalia, Mozambique, and Uganda. "I sort of had all these questions of loss and survival. I kind of wanted to go where those issues were very much in the forefront of people's minds," he told Jill Vejnoska for the *Atlanta Journal-Constitution* (November 23, 2003). He explained to Goldfarb, "From watching news growing up, I kind of knew how stories were put together, but because I was shooting by myself, I was forced to do it in a different way. . . . As a result, my stories were much more of a personal journey." As a freelance reporter Cooper did not have access to hotel-room and transportation accommodations that were available to network-news reporters; forced to fend for himself, he slept on the roofs of houses while covering the famine in Somalia and used his press pass to hitch rides.

In 1993 Cooper's hard work paid off when Channel One News hired him as its chief international correspondent. Over the next two years, while he continued to report from war zones including the Balkans and Rwanda, he began attracting the attention of the major news organizations. In 1995 Cooper joined the staff of ABC News, becoming, at 27, the network's youngest correspondent. He also served as a reporter for ABC's weekend-news segments and as co-anchor of its overnight program, *World News Now*, which was mostly unscripted and included offbeat first-person stories, such as a piece on riding public transportation at 3 a.m. In 1998 Cooper became a contributor to ABC's news magazine *20/20* and its spin-off, *20/20 Downtown*. Cooper came to be dissatisfied with the type of stories he was covering at the network, telling Goldfarb, "I wasn't doing the kinds of pieces that really spoke to me." He was also unhappy with his grueling schedule, which, during his last year at ABC, consisted of anchoring *World News Now* from 3 a.m. until 5 a.m., returning to his apartment after leaving the studio at 8 a.m., and getting only four hours of sleep before heading back to the studio to work on *20/20*.

In 2000 Cooper turned down ABC's offer to renew his contract, instead signing with USA Networks to host and produce a weekly, one-hour, single-topic documentary program, which was given the working title "Anderson Cooper News Project." Six months later, following the cancellation of the documentary series due to creative differences, Cooper accepted an offer from ABC Entertainment to host *The Mole*, a new entry in the burgeoning reality-television genre that was designed to compete with CBS's *Survivor*. *The Mole* focused on 10 contestants, five men and five women, who engaged in mental and physical challenges as one of them, the "mole," whose identity was unknown to the others, attempted to sabotage the rest of the group. Each week the competitors answered questions about the mole, and the least knowledgeable contestant was eliminated; the contestant who was eventually able to figure out the mole's identity was awarded the prize money. According to Nielsen data, *The Mole*, which debuted on January 9, 2001, averaged 12.6 million viewers each week, becoming the network's top-ranked entertainment program among 18-to-34-year-olds; the two-part finale ranked as the number-one program among adults aged 18 to 49 in its time period, prompting the network's decision, in February 2001, to film a second season of the series, with Cooper returning as host. However, *The Mole II: The Next Betrayal*, which debuted on September 28, 2001, was pulled from the network's prime-time schedule after three installments, after it drew an average of only 5.6 million viewers. The network broadcast the full season of the show (13 episodes) in May 2002. Cooper's decision to host the show drew criticism from broadcast-journalism insiders who believed that he had damaged his chances of returning to the television-news industry.

Nonetheless, after hosting two seasons of *The Mole*, Cooper returned to television news, his interest having been rekindled by the September 11, 2001 terrorist attacks on the World Trade Center and the Pentagon. Cooper learned about the attacks while riding in a cab in New York. He rushed back to his downtown apartment to get his camera but instead ended up watching television coverage of the event, after he discovered that he had no videotape or working batteries. Cooper, who was still under contract at ABC, tried without success to cover the subsequent war in Afghanistan for the network. In January 2002, after his contract had expired, Cooper signed with CNN (Cable Network News), where he served as co-anchor, alongside Paula Zahn, of the network's New York–based program, *American Morning with Paula Zahn*. (When *The Mole* returned to ABC's prime-time lineup in 2003, Ahmad Rashad had replaced Cooper as the

host.) The hiring of Cooper was part of the plan by Jamie Kellner, the former head of CNN News Group, to compete with the Fox News Channel in the ratings. In June 2002, when Cooper returned from covering the war in Afghanistan for CNN, he filled in for one week as a substitute host on the program *NewsNight with Aaron Brown*. "I loved working that show. It was a better format for me. The week I was there, they let me play with stuff and morph things around, and the audience responded because I was just being real, being myself, because I had nothing to lose," he told Van Meter.

In the fall of 2002, Cooper was selected as the network's weekend prime-time anchor, and the following year found him anchoring the first hour of *Live from the Headlines*, a two-hour program that also featured Paula Zahn. In September 2003 CNN gave Cooper the opportunity to host his own, one-hour show, *Anderson Cooper 360*, which functioned as the 7 p.m. lead-in to *Paula Zahn Now*. In explaining the program's name, Cooper told McDaniel, "It's 360 degrees in terms of the scope of what we're talking about, whether it's foreign policy, political events or pop culture things." During the first 30 minutes of the show, Cooper covers the day's major stories, which are followed by regular segments on media obsessions ("Overkill"), hot topics in current magazines ("Fresh Print"), and upcoming movies and entertainment events ("Weekender"). In December 2003 executives at CNN reported that *Anderson Cooper 360* had recorded a 15 percent increase among viewers aged 18 to 49, who are highly coveted by advertisers. In September of that year, *Details* published Cooper's article about his search for the reasons behind his brother's suicide. "It's something I've been writing in my own head for 15 years. There's something about suicide . . . no one really talks about it in polite company. But I had all these questions about why he did this and why it happened. It stays with you," he told Eric Deggans for the *St. Petersburg Times* (September 8, 2003).

As part of his duties for *Anderson Cooper 360*, Cooper also covered breaking news stories. In January 2005 he traveled to Sri Lanka to report on the damage caused by the tsunami. That year he also covered the elections held in Iraq, the funeral of Pope John Paul II, the royal wedding of Prince Charles and Camilla Parker-Bowles, and the damage caused in Pensacola, Florida, by Hurricane Dennis. It was his emotional coverage of another hurricane—Katrina—in September 2005 that garnered the most attention. Cooper was almost reduced to tears on the air on two occasions; at one point he became so choked up that he stopped the camera during his report about homes lost in the flooding that resulted from the hurricane. "I have been tearing up on this story more than any story I've worked on. I can't really explain why that is. . . . It's hard not to be moved. The fact that it is in the United States, for me, added a layer and dimension to the story," he explained to Elizabeth

Jensen for the *New York Times* (September 12, 2005). The cameras also recorded such candid moments as Cooper's playing with stray dogs that were stranded following the hurricane. His frustration and anger at government officials' recovery efforts—widely condemned as slow and ineffective—were evident during a heated interview with Senator Mary L. Landrieu of Louisiana, in which he criticized her as she thanked officials of the Federal Emergency Management Agency (FEMA) for their work. During the first week of the hurricane coverage, *Anderson Cooper 360* had a nearly 400 percent increase in viewers, according to *New York*. During the same month Cooper was enlisted by Jonathan Klein, president of CNN's U.S. operations, to serve as co-anchor with Aaron Brown on CNN's *NewsNight*, which was expanded from one to two hours.

In October 2005, following Cooper's coverage of Hurricane Katrina, *Anderson Cooper 360* averaged 811,000 viewers, a 36 percent increase over the same period from the previous year. In November 2005 Klein revamped the network's schedule, canceling *NewsNight* and replacing it with *Anderson Cooper 360*, which was expanded to two hours and moved to the 10 p.m. Eastern Standard Time slot previously occupied by *NewsNight*.

Cooper's memoir, *Dispatches from the Edge*, was published in May 2006. Excerpts from the book appeared in the June 2006 issue of *Vanity Fair*, whose cover showed an image of Cooper taken by the photographer Annie Leibovitz. Also in June Cooper landed the first exclusive U.S. interview with the movie actress Angelina Jolie after she gave birth to her daughter in Namibia. Their conversation aired on *Anderson Cooper 360* in mid-June, in connection with World Refugee Day; according to the *Chicago Tribune* (June 28, 2006), the interview, in which Jolie discussed motherhood and her humanitarian work as a United Nations goodwill ambassador, attracted 1.33 million viewers, more than twice the usual number for the broadcast. During the first week of October 2006, Cooper reported from the Democratic Republic of the Congo, which has been wracked by ethnic conflict and civil war. Earlier in 2006 CBS announced that Cooper had been named as a contributor to its long-running newsmagazine program, *60 Minutes*. His stories were to begin airing before the end of the year.

Since 2003 Cooper has also been the host of CNN's *New Year's Eve with Anderson Cooper*, which is broadcast live from Times Square in New York City, the site of the famous ball drop. He serves as a contributing editor for *Details* and has received several awards, including a National Headliners Award for his tsunami coverage, the Chicago International Film Festival's Silver Plaque for his report on the Bosnian civil war, a Bronze Telly for his coverage of the famine in Somalia, a Bronze Award from the National Educational Film and Video Festival for a story on Islam, and the GLAAD (Gay & Lesbian Alliance Against Defama-

tion) Media Award for Outstanding TV Journalism for his *20/20 Downtown* profile on a gay high-school athlete, Corey Johnson. In 2004 Cooper was named sexiest male newscaster in a *Playgirl* online poll, and *People* magazine featured him in its "Sexiest Man Alive" issue in 2005. Cooper's sexual orientation has become the subject of speculation by the media, with some having theorized that he is gay—a rumor that Cooper has refused to address. "You know, I understand why people might be interested. But I just don't talk about my personal life. It's a decision I made a long time ago, before I ever even knew anyone would be interested in my personal life. The whole thing about being a reporter is that you're supposed to be an observer and to be able to adapt with any group you're in, and I don't want to do anything that threatens that," he told Van Meter. Cooper lives in a loft in midtown Manhattan with Molly, his Welsh springer spaniel.
—B.M.

Suggested Reading: *Atlanta Journal-Constitution* MS p1 Nov. 23, 2003; *Boston Globe* B p5 Sep. 8, 2003; *Interview* p122+ Oct. 1, 2004; *New York* (on-line) Sep. 19, 2005

Selected Television Shows: *20/20*, 1998-2000; *The Mole*, 2001; *The Mole: The Next Betrayal*, 2001–02; *Live from the Headlines*, 2003; *Anderson Cooper 360*, 2003–

Selected Books: *Dispatches from the Edge*, 2006

Corbijn, Anton

(kor-BIN)

May 20, 1955– Photographer; music-video director

Address: Anton Corbijn Ltd., 10 Poplar Mews, London W12 7JS, England

"Smooth and sexy is boring," the photographer Anton Corbijn told Degen Pener for *Entertainment Weekly* (August 9, 1996). "My pictures are either not properly lit or not properly balanced, but there's much more life in imperfection." Corbijn has set himself apart from other photographers with his uncanny ability to counter the popular images of his celebrity subjects and reveal the humanity audiences rarely see or imagine in their favorite performers. Once a shy and reclusive teenager from a Dutch family that favored Calvinist asceticism over the material excesses of the secular world, Corbijn found that photography allowed him to enter a life surrounded by the music he loved and the people he idolized. Now a celebrity in his own right, Corbijn is known for his skill at helping popular icons to shed their public images and bare their true selves to the camera lens, which

Andrew H. Walker/Getty Images

Anton Corbijn

has made him a sought-after commodity in both the music and acting industries. "His photographs are a 50-50 mix of his own personal vision and style as well as bringing out emotion and feeling in the people he's photographing," Jodi Peckman, the photo editor of the music magazine *Rolling Stone*, told Howard Rombough for the *Creative Review* (September 2, 1996). "A lot of times, photographers' photos are all about them, all about what they do and you don't really get a sense of the artist, but Anton always seems to find one little quirky thing about somebody."

The eldest of four children, Anton Corbijn Jr. was born on May 20, 1955 in Strijen, a small village on the island of Hoeksche Waard, in the Netherlands. His mother was a nurse, and his father was a Protestant minister who emphasized "humility, honesty, and hard work," as Rombough wrote. Throughout his formative years Corbijn looked out on the island's church spires and stark skyline, which for him symbolized the unforgiving austerity of the local culture, and he hoped for a more colorful future. As a bashful and rather quiet teenager with a love of punk music, he fantasized about a life on the road playing in a band—though he was acutely aware of his musical shortcomings. When a local band called Solution held a live concert, Corbijn, then about 18 years old, took his father's camera to snap pictures of the group; it seemed that he had found his niche in the music scene. "It was just because I loved music so much," he told Paul Freeman for the Albany, New York, *Times Union* (April 10, 1994). "[Using the camera] gave me an excuse to go to the front of the stage. I managed to get these photos of a local band published. That got me hooked."

Over the next two years, Corbijn regularly sent his photographs to *Oor*, a music magazine that he believed was the best in Holland. Despite his local success with the pictures of Solution, the editors of *Oor* declined to publish any of his submissions. After graduating from high school, Corbijn studied at the School of Photography, in the Hague. The creative inflexibility of the program proved too restricting for him, and he dropped out after a year and a half. "It was horrendous, almost put me off photography. It was very technique-based. I've always tried to steer far from that. I felt that any introduction of technique into my photography would inhibit the character or the atmosphere I was seeking. I was afraid that, if I focused on technique, I would lose my momentum," he told Freeman. After leaving photography school he worked for several months as an assistant to Gijsbert Hanekroot, an Amsterdam-based photographer known for his pictures of musicians. All the while the determined Corbijn continued to submit his photographs to *Oor*. In 1975 the magazine finally published a Corbijn original, and he soon became their chief photographer. The job, which he had dreamed of for years, turned out to be incredibly demanding. He spent four years darting from one concert to the next, snapping pictures of anyone who might be of interest to the publication's readers. "It taught me to take pictures very quickly," Corbijn told Andrew Harrison for *Photo District News* (April 2005). "You had limited time so you were very inventive with your immediate surroundings. I can still take pictures very quickly." One of his best-known photos from that era is of Elvis Costello, taken in a tiny Amsterdam hotel room. To get the shot, which shows Costello sprawled across the single bed with his guitar, Corbijn, who stands six feet five inches, had to crouch in a cramped closet.

In 1979 Corbijn purchased the Joy Division album *Unknown Pleasures* and instantly became an ardent fan of the group. He left the Netherlands that year and moved to London, England, to be closer to the band and to the burgeoning punk scene there. "Within two weeks of arriving I was photographing the band on spec in an Underground tunnel. I remember I was very shy and formal and tried to shake hands with them, but they refused," Corbijn told Joanna Pitman for the London *Times* (February 14, 2005). His regular photo sessions with Joy Division soon led to a job as the main photographer for the *New Musical Express*, a British music magazine similar to *Rolling Stone*. Corbijn's stern upbringing was evidenced by the simplicity and undeniable forcefulness of his photographs, qualities that distinguished them from many others exhibited at the time. "I guess [the landscape] has an influence on the way I photograph," Corbijn told Rombough. "I'm looking at the person behind the surface as it were. Also in my visual style . . . you can see an emphasis on the surroundings." With his photos being published regularly in one of the U.K.'s most popular magazines,

Corbijn gained worldwide recognition for his signature dark-toned, black-and-white photographs, which had been inspired by photojournalism. "[Newspaper photos] were very dramatic and it was sort of a social comment. Holland was quite interested in the whole social-political kind of photojournalism," Corbijn explained to Richard Harrington for the *Washington Post* (October 9, 1996). One of his most iconic photojournalistic images is a shot of the jazz legend Miles Davis, taken in a Montreal hotel room in 1985. Davis's fingers are splayed across his face, and a careful viewer will see Corbijn's image darkly reflected in the musician's eyes.

Working in a profession in which his peers often need an entourage to help carry their supplies and set up ideal lighting arrangements, Corbijn is known for using little more than a Hasselblad camera, a few lenses, and film. He prefers to work with natural conditions. "I'm not sure if it's laziness on my part, but I find it so tedious to have to set up a shoot with lights. It's really not my element," he told Harrington. "I much prefer to be dumped somewhere, in any situation, and just make it work than carry lights with me and make everything look the same. It's also the reason I don't do studio photography very much—you have your same environment all the time and I don't find that interesting."

Corbijn himself has said that his long career consists of four distinct periods, beginning with what he has called his *NME* (*New Musical Express*) years. The second phase of Corbijn's career had its genesis in 1982, when he met the members of the Irish band U2 at a photo shoot for *NME* in New Orleans, Louisiana. Corbijn began documenting the band's rise to stardom. "He gave U2 a visual strength we didn't have at that point," Bono, the lead singer, once said, as quoted by Harrington. Perhaps the image with which both the band and Corbijn are most closely identified is the album cover for U2's *The Joshua Tree* (1987), which features a bleak panoramic view of Death Valley, with the band members, looking serious, off to one side. "Instinctively, he got us. He saw the possibilities," Bono told Sean O'Hagen for the London *Observer* (February 6, 2005). "The general look at the time was effete and homoerotic, but we were Irish; we couldn't be that. We looked like we'd just got off the boat. Because we had. In truth, I think Anton found a masculinity in us that was very out of step with the time, but that has stood the test of time." Corbijn's connection with U2 opened up a number of opportunities, making it easier for him to gain access to major stars. He thus calls the second phase of his career his Star Trak period, and in 1996 he published a compilation—called *Star Trak*—of photographs he took of such celebrities as Luciano Pavarotti, Johnny Depp, Jodie Foster, and Frank Sinatra. "There's the challenge with really famous people to do a picture that is very ordinary, because that's not how people see them usually," Corbijn told Chris Willman for the *Los Angeles*

Times (November 18, 1993). Thus, for example, the anguished Pavarotti of Corbijn's photo is a very different character from the ebullient bon vivant so many fans assume the singer to be. In a review of the volume for the London *Guardian Weekly* (September 15, 1996), Rombough wrote, "He doesn't make people look beautiful. Some pictures are unflattering and that's the point. They bring out the human side of his subjects, hinting at complex lives full of torment, reflection or even giddiness."

Corbijn's second stage culminated in the photographer's exploring new mediums; in 1983, for example, he directed a music video for the German band Propaganda, and his reputation as an innovative maker of music videos grew considerably in the U.S. after the 1986 release of Depeche Mode's "Question of Time" video. (Although he had dismissed Depeche Mode when they first met, in 1980, as a group of musical lightweights, he agreed to the project because he wanted to direct a video in the U.S.) Corbijn's nontraditional and visually stimulating music videos are markedly different from those of other artists because he acts as both director and cameraman, recording with a hand-held video camera. He has continued to work with Depeche Mode, acting as the band's exclusive music-video director and photographer. Corbijn has now directed more than 70 music videos, 20 of them for Depeche Mode. In 1993 Corbijn's video "Heart-Shaped Box," which he filmed for the band Nirvana, received an MTV Music Video Award for best alternative video and another for best art direction. (He has since been nominated for numerous awards from MTV.) That same year Corbijn also produced a 13-minute documentary piece entitled *Some YoYo Stuff*, profiling Don Van Vliet, a rock innovator also known as Captain Beefheart. Other legendary musicians he has filmed include Joni Mitchell and Johnny Cash. Despite his success in the music-video industry, Corbijn has said that he will not abandon photography. He told Freeman, "Now I have enough offers that I could go on making videos for the rest of my life. But photography is still my first love, so I keep much of my time for that. I don't believe that making videos is a better profession or a higher art form than photography."

Corbijn became disillusioned with the uniformity of photographic styles in magazines during the early 1990s. It seemed that the images he was known for—black-and-white photos revealing the deeply authentic personality of a celebrity—had become the norm, as magazine editors began to do more in-depth pieces on their subjects. "People gave away all their secrets in their images. You saw how the subject lived, everything about them. There was a lack of mystery," Corbijn told Harrison. In an attempt to differentiate his work once more, Corbijn entered what he considers his third phase, using blue and brown duotones and staging what looked like paparazzi pictures of his subjects. (Corbijn, however, has always been careful to distance himself from the label of rock photographer because of its implied connection to the paparazzi.) In 1999 Corbijn published *Still Lives*, a compilation of those ironic and satirical photos.

Corbijn's humor has been more blatantly displayed during his fourth phase, with *a. somebody, strijen, holland*, a somewhat autobiographical series of photographs. Returning to his isolated childhood neighborhood in Strijen, Corbijn dressed up as various dead musicians, including Frank Zappa, John Lennon, and Jimi Hendrix, and took portraits of himself walking through the streets and alleys of his hometown. "There was nothing there. To me, everything outside the island looked mysterious and exciting," he told Pitman. "So I set the photos there. I wanted something to happen there. I thought it would be funny to photograph Jimi Hendrix visiting my tiny village."

Throughout his four distinctive phases, a constant in Corbijn's work has been his close relationship with U2, which he has maintained for more than two decades. The trajectory of Corbijn's career paralleled, in some ways, that of the band, with his photos on the early albums *The Joshua Tree* and *Achtung Baby* (1991) helping to launch the group into the higher echelons of rock stardom, as he himself was becoming known as one of the world's premier photographers. In 2005 Corbijn published *U2 & I: The Photographs 1982–2004*, a book chronicling his years traveling the world with the band. "Each time they went anywhere, they said, 'Can you come?' Each time I thought it would probably be the last time they'd use me," Corbijn told Pitman. "But I don't know anyone else who's photographed a band for over 20 years. You see in these photographs their ageing, the change in their attitudes to being photographed, and also my development as a photographer. I taught myself, and I think over the years I've moved from being intuitive to being more conceptual. I never want to be predictable in my work." The compilation, more than 400 pages long, follows the group from the time they were four young Irishmen coming into their own as viable musicians to the current era, in which they are a legendary rock band championing awareness of problems in Africa. "[Corbijn] is the eye that has defined the band's look in publicity shots and on album and magazine covers," Orli Low wrote in a review for the *Los Angeles Times* (December 4, 2005). "These photographs make you pine for the days when an album cover had a feel to it, was a canvas."

Corbijn's celebrated photos have been compiled in more than a dozen books and published in numerous magazines, including *Rolling Stone, Vogue, W, Entertainment Weekly, Details*, and *Icon*. He was nominated for a Grammy Award for his 1993 Depeche Mode video, "Devotional." He is currently working on a feature-length film about Ian Curtis, the former Joy Division singer who committed suicide at age 23, in 1980, shortly after Corbijn began photographing the band. The film, titled *Control*, is scheduled to premiere in 2007. Corbijn also recently finished assembling a vast annotated collection of his work in photography and film for an installment of the *Director's Label DVD* series.

Corbijn, whose work has been the subject of several museum retrospectives throughout the world, has at times wrestled with the issue of the legitimacy of his oeuvre. "I've been asked many times if I felt I was cheating in that my pictures are all of famous people," he told Kristine McKenna for the *Los Angeles Times* (June 29, 1997). "That's undeniably a central element of my work, and early in my career I constantly asked myself, 'Why am I successful? Is it the photograph or the person I'm photographing?' I finally concluded it's a mixture of the two."

— I.C.

Suggested Reading: (Albany, New York) *Times Union* H p6 Apr. 10, 1994; *Billboard* p36 Dec. 18, 1993; *Creative Review* p65+ Sep. 2, 1996; *Entertainment Weekly* p47+ Feb. 18, 1994, p34+ Aug. 9, 1996; (London) *Guardian* Weekly p27 Sep. 15, 1996; (London) *Observer* p14 Feb. 6, 2005; (London) *Times* p16 Feb. 14, 2005; *Los Angeles Times* F p1 Nov. 18, 1993, Calendar p56 June 29, 1997, R p13 Dec. 4, 2005; *Photo District News* p62 Mar. 1997, p30+ Apr. 2005; *Washington Post* C p7 Oct. 9, 1996

Selected Books: *Famouz*, 1989; *Allegro*, 1991; *Star Trak*, 1996; *33 Still Lives*, 1999; *Werk*, 2000; *a. somebody, strijen, holland*, 2002; *U2 & I: The Photographs 1982–2004*, 2005

Corzine, Jon

Jan. 1, 1947– Governor of New Jersey (Democrat); former businessman

Address: New Jersey Office of the Governor, P.O. Box 001, Trenton, NJ 08625

Among the prominent figures in government for whom politics is a second career, Jon Corzine is unusual, for his combination of great personal wealth and far-left-of-center views. Once the chief executive officer (CEO) of the Wall Street investment-banking firm Goldman Sachs, Corzine entered politics in 2000, after being ousted from that company's top position. He proceeded to win a U.S. Senate seat in New Jersey, in a campaign that set new national records for spending. As a senator Corzine championed the liberal ideas he had embraced in his campaign, supporting such causes as abortion rights and affirmative action, and he defied the expectations of critics by attaining a position of influence among his colleagues. Five years after his election to the Senate, he entered New Jersey's gubernatorial election, narrowly defeating the Republican Doug Forrester.

William Thomas Cain/Getty Images

Jon Corzine

James Traub described Corzine for the *New York Times* (February 13, 2000) as having "the balding pate, rimless spectacles, mild gaze and fuzzy beard of an English professor in a small private college. He is a good listener, a slow ruminator, a modest man who takes up less space than any zillionaire you've ever met." Indeed, it is universally observed of Corzine that he embodies none of the stereotypes attached to those in positions as powerful as those he has held. His popularity within Goldman Sachs has become near-legendary. "It's hard to find people, within Goldman or outside it, who have anything bad to say about Corzine. In an often nasty business, he seems to symbolize the qualities investment bankers would like the world to think they have, even when they don't," Brett D. Fromson wrote for the *Washington Post* (November 6, 1994). Mark O. Winkleman, a partner at Goldman Sachs, told Fromson, "Jon's values are terrific. Pure. It is always very clear to others what his values are. . . . There is no deviousness, no hidden agenda, no politicking. That is easy to recognize and therefore trust."

Jon Stevens Corzine was born on January 1, 1947 in Willie's Station, a town of roughly 50 people in Illinois. His father, Roy Allen Corzine, was a wheat farmer who also sold insurance; his mother, Nancy June (Hedrick) Corzine, was an elementary-school teacher. Both his parents were Republicans. Brett D. Fromson noted that Corzine "was no prodigy as a kid. He wasn't the smartest pupil, the most talented athlete, the most popular guy, according to those who knew him when." Still, he showed determination as an athlete, at nearby Taylorville High School. Discussing Corzine's tryouts for the basketball team, one of his former English teachers told Fromson, "He was not really athletic. But Jon determined that he was going to make the team and he did. It was pure guts that got him through."

Corzine enrolled, along with his high-school sweetheart and future wife, Joanne Dougherty (whom he had known since kindergarten), at the University of Illinois. There, he was president of his fraternity, Phi Delta Theta, as well as a walk-on guard for the basketball team. Corzine attended college during the period of campus protests over the Vietnam War; he held a more moderate political outlook than many of his peers. "I had a growing distaste for our involvement [in the war]," he told Fromson, "but I wasn't prepared to renounce my citizenship. I like to work within the system for change." Corzine graduated Phi Beta Kappa, with a B.A. degree in economics and political science, in 1969. To avoid being drafted into the army, he joined the U.S. Marine Corps Reserves, serving from 1969 to 1975 and rising to the rank of sergeant in his infantry unit.

In 1971 Corzine took a job as an analyst at Continental Illinois National Bank, meanwhile earning his M.B.A. degree through night classes at the University of Chicago. It was during that time that he decided to become a bond trader. People in that profession "seemed to be having a lot of fun," he told Fromson. In 1975 Corzine joined the bond department at Goldman Sachs, located in Lower Manhattan, in New York City, and later he took up residence in Summit, New Jersey. Founded in 1869 and considered to be among the most prestigious firms on Wall Street, Goldman Sachs provides financial services for a wide variety of institutional and individual clients. With more than 30,000 employees and offices in more than 20 countries, the company is also a leading dealer of U.S. government bonds to large corporations and investment funds. (The bonds have a fixed rate of interest and serve as investments in, or loans to, the U.S. government, with the agreement that each loan will be repaid on a certain date—the maturation date.)

At the beginning of his career at Goldman Sachs, Corzine had a relatively low position. Then, in 1976, the top five government-bond traders at Goldman quit, enabling Corzine to take a more prominent role in his department. He soon became known for making substantial investments for Goldman Sachs that were inspired by those the company's clients were making—thereby both contributing to, and profiting from, investor trends. Corzine was made a partner at Goldman Sachs in 1980. In 1986 he orchestrated a risky trade that enhanced his reputation greatly within the company. That year the U.S. Treasury had replaced its traditional, 30-year bond with a 10-year bond that had a lower yield, or rate of interest. While most Wall Street investors, including Goldman, bought the new bond, the price of the old bond rose dramatically, due to Japanese investors' preference for its higher yield. Frightened, many on Wall Street cut their losses and left the market for those particular bonds. While Goldman faced losses for having invested in the new bond, Corzine predicted that since the new and old bonds were actually quite similar, investments in the two would eventually balance out, and he chose to hold onto, and trade, the new bonds. His actions saved the company many millions of dollars. "It was a very painful exercise. Took about four months and half a lifetime," he told Fromson. "But I've been blessed with an ability to compartmentalize the stresses and strains of a position." Corzine was named a member of the company's managing board later that year.

In September 1994 Goldman's departing chief executive, Stephen Friedman, recommended Corzine—who by then was co-head of the company's bond business and its de facto chief financial officer—to take over as CEO. That year the market had dropped, and the company, like many other Wall Street firms, experienced net losses, in Goldman's case $41 million in its fourth quarter. Of the company's partners, who then numbered 160, 38 retired—taking with them much of Goldman's capital. For most of the time Corzine had worked at Goldman, Robert Rubin and Stephen Friedman had been its co–chief executives; Rubin left in 1993 to serve as President Bill Clinton's economic adviser, while Friedman continued to run the firm as both chairman and vice chairman, with support from a six-member management committee. In the fall of 1994, amid the pressures of the company's dwindling earnings, Friedman, too, retired. "We got hit with a double whammy, with the chairman walking out and the partners having their first experience at losing capital," a former partner at the company told Harry Hurt III for *U.S. News & World Report* (July 20, 1998).

As Friedman's successor in the CEO position, Corzine took over a company that many observers described as being in a state of disarray, although he denied it. "I wouldn't be jumping into a mess, willingly or unwillingly," he told Anthony Ramirez for the *New York Times* (September 14, 1994). Along with the newly appointed chief operating officer, Henry M. Paulson (who would later become Goldman's CEO and, in 2006, the U.S. secretary of the treasury), Corzine helped the firm regain its footing by strengthening relationships with clients, limiting risks, tightening the firm's management structure, cutting Goldman's annual spending by 25 percent, and laying off 12 percent of the company's nonpartner work force (1,500 workers in all). He also organized committees that included both operations staff and partners, to involve employees in tracking the company's progress. Corzine's measures paid off: between the time he became CEO and the end of 1995, the company had earned pretax profits of nearly $1.4 billion. Nonetheless, the departure of many of Goldman's partners had made apparent its need for a larger, more permanent store of capital, which the company could attain by selling its shares to the public. In 1996 Corzine proposed that Goldman Sachs go

public, an idea that most of the firm's employees opposed. "You want to do initial public offerings in periods of strength, and a lot of people still didn't feel secure about the firm," Corzine told Hurt. "I think we in leadership felt more secure about it."

In the next two years, the firm steadily prospered. By the first half of 1998, it had earned another $7.6 billion in pretax profits and was "on track to hit Corzine's five-year, $10 billion target by the end of September—16 months ahead of schedule," as Hurt wrote. At that year's annual meeting, Goldman's partners voted 60–40 in favor of an initial public offering (IPO), and Corzine announced the decision in June. Goldman planned to sell 10 to 15 percent of its stock—roughly $30 billion worth of shares—in what would be the largest single initial sale of shares in U.S. history. But then a market decline shook the entire financial industry, diminishing the value of most publicly traded companies by half. The value of Goldman's stock fell from $30 billion to an estimated $16 billion in late September, and the IPO was withdrawn. Corzine found himself in an unenviable position: after leading the push for the IPO, support for which had been less than unanimous, he could now be held accountable, fairly or not, for its collapse.

Henry Paulson, who represented the company's investment-banking sector, had opposed the IPO, voting "yes" only in return for Corzine's granting him a co-CEO position, which he assumed in May 1998. Corzine, who represented the trading sector, saw his position worsened by the company's trading losses that year, which approached $1 billion. In January 1999 the firm announced that he would step down as CEO, with Paulson staying on as sole chief executive. Two other investment bankers, John Thornton and John Thain, were elected co–chief operating officers. While the company presented the decision as a simple restructuring associated with its forthcoming IPO, it was generally regarded as the result of a power struggle in which Corzine had lost. Corzine was to remain at the firm long enough to oversee the company's public offering, which finally came about in May 1999. His ouster was reported to be emotionally devastating for Corzine, despite his leaving Goldman Sachs with a personal net worth of between $300 million and $400 million.

Following those developments, Corzine's "plans for life after Goldman all involved making yet more money," James Traub wrote. "And then sheer accident intruded into what had been a very orderly life." In February 1999 U.S. senator Frank Lautenberg of New Jersey, a Democrat, announced that he would retire in 2000. Another Democrat, Jim Florio, a former New Jersey governor, immediately declared his candidacy for the seat to be vacated. While governor in the early 1990s, Florio had instituted record-high tax increases, which had damaged his reputation among voters. Hoping to prevent a Florio victory in the Democratic primary (in the belief that Florio would then lose to the Republican candidate for senator—the state's governor, Christine Todd Whitman—in the general election), party leaders courted Corzine as a possible candidate—in large part because he could finance his own campaign. After consulting with Robert Rubin and others about running for the Senate, Corzine formed an exploratory committee in June 1999. He began collecting endorsements from various state Democratic officials who would serve as campaign advisers, including the other New Jersey U.S. senator, Robert G. Torricelli, as well as Lautenberg himself. In a move that shocked Republicans, Governor Whitman, who was ahead of both Florio and Corzine in the polls, dropped out of the Senate race in September, figuring that she could not raise the funds needed to compete with Corzine.

A few weeks before Whitman's announcement, Corzine had formally declared his candidacy, at a ceremony held in front of his home in Summit. There, he outlined his liberal platform, which included opposition to the death penalty and support of universal health care as well as universal access to four-year colleges for students with a "B" average in high school. In addition, he was a strong advocate of abortion rights and of affirmative action, for women as well as minorities. Corzine's campaign, especially in the early stages of the race, was widely criticized as amateurish. Critics saw it as embarrassingly clear that his wealth was the only factor allowing him to be taken seriously as a candidate. "Corzine's Midwest liberalism . . . can be distilled to two words: 'universal' everything," George Will wrote for the Chicago Sun-Times (December 11, 1999). David Plotz wrote for Slate (June 3, 2000, on-line), "If [Corzine] has a clue how he's going to pay for any of his universals, he isn't sharing it. Most businessmen in politics pride themselves on their sharp edges. Corzine is all fuzzy: He has a fuzzy beard. He wears fuzzy sweater-vests. He has fuzzy ideas." Corzine's lack of political credentials was epitomized by the fact that he had not voted in a primary for 10 years. But Traub wrote that Corzine, in spite of his perceived shortcomings, "has precisely the gift you wouldn't expect from a Wall Street baron, which is the common touch. After [a] speech, he squeezed biceps and draped an arm over shoulders; he grinned and guffawed and gave every impression of having a swell time."

The primary campaign was filled with increasingly negative exchanges between the two Democratic candidates. Florio accused Corzine of planning to use Wall Street tactics to lead a "hostile takeover" of the Senate, while Corzine abandoned his pledge not to attack the former governor on the subject of his much-loathed tax hikes. Corzine also came under fire for refusing to reveal his tax returns from his years at Goldman Sachs and for his connection to some of the more questionable business dealings conducted at Goldman. Andrew Jacobs reported for the New York Times (June 7, 2000) that in the late stages of the race, Florio's supporters sent brochures to black voters accusing Corzine of brokering a business deal in the African nation of Sudan that "led to the enslavement of people in that country's civil war." In the primary, held in early June, Corzine took 58 percent of the vote. By that time his spending had reached $35 million, while Florio had spent $2 million.

In the general election Corzine faced U.S. representative Bob Franks, who had little name recognition even after winning the Republican primary, mainly because the Democratic primary had commanded most of the press's attention. Franks attacked Corzine on many of the same points that Florio had emphasized, questioning his refusal to give details of his finances and criticizing as unrealistic his plans for universal federal programs. (Corzine said that he was prevented from releasing his tax records by a legal agreement with Goldman Sachs, and he continued to defend his proposed programs.) Franks put Corzine on the defensive, criticizing his decision to wait until after the election to reveal the names of those who had received millions from his private foundation—and citing that refusal as evidence that Corzine was buying community support. While some polls indicated that Corzine's campaign spending was troubling to voters, Franks was unable to capitalize on that concern. As David M. Halbfinger wrote for the New York Times (October 15, 2000), "While Mr. Corzine is running attack ads and more positive commercials extolling his own ambitious proposals, Mr. Franks is telling voters only why they should not elect Mr. Corzine. He has yet to broadcast a commercial that gives them a reason to elect him." On Election Day Corzine won 50 percent of the vote, and Franks 47 percent. Though Corzine lost in most of New Jersey's counties, he prevailed on the strength of the votes in heavily populated urban communities with minority voters. Corzine outspent Franks 10 to one; the total cost of his campaign topped $60 million, the most of any Senate candidate in U.S. history.

As a senator Corzine played a more integral role in national policy than many had expected. Corzine's Wall Street experience came in handy as the Democrats, reacting to scandals involving the companies Enron and WorldCom, passed legislation meant to crack down on corporate corruption. While two of Corzine's seniors in Congress—Democratic senator Paul S. Sarbanes of Maryland and Republican representative Michael G. Oxley of Ohio—received most of the credit for the corporate-reform legislation known as the Sarbanes-Oxley Act, Corzine was its chief architect. (The act imposed stricter rules governing companies' financial disclosures and required that all publicly traded companies, beginning in 2006, submit to the Securities and Exchange Commission annual reports on the effectiveness of their internal-accounting controls.) Corzine also encouraged Democrats to project stronger images and to "speak like Democrats," as Raymond Hernandez reported in the New York Times (March 16, 2003)—that is, to embrace the party's core values without fear of alienating moderate voters. He opposed many of President George W. Bush's policies, including his tax cuts, which Corzine argued would benefit mainly the country's wealthiest taxpayers, and criticized what he viewed as the inadequacy of the Bush administration's funding for health care. Corzine voted against granting the president the power to wage war in Iraq—which put Corzine in the minority even among Democrats. He was active on numerous Senate committees, including the Intelligence, Budget, Energy, and Natural Resources Committees.

In August 2004 New Jersey Democrats again called on Corzine to run for office, this time to replace Governor James E. McGreevey, the Democrat who resigned after revealing that he had had an extramarital homosexual affair with a former aide. Richard Codey, who served as acting governor for the final 14 months of McGreevey's term and expressed interest in running for governor in 2005, ultimately announced that he would not seek the office. That cleared the way for Corzine, who won the Democratic primary in June 2005. In the general election Corzine faced Doug Forrester, a former mayor of West Windsor, New Jersey, who had run unsuccessfully for the U.S. Senate in 2002. The two candidates' debates centered on their respective proposals to decrease property taxes in the state, which were (and, as of November 2006, remained) the highest per capita in the country, and on how to clean up corruption in New Jersey politics. Forrester's main criticism of his opponent was that Corzine himself, as head of the state Democratic Party's fund-raising efforts, embodied insider politics and corruption. It was revealed in August 2005 that Corzine had given a union leader, Carla Katz, $470,000 for a mortgage payment in 2002, while the two were involved romantically. Forrester, along with members of Katz's union, Communications Workers of America Local 1034, accused Corzine of having a conflict of interest that might influence his decisions on policies affecting union pay. Two lawyers filed a complaint with the Senate Ethics Committee over Corzine's actions. Corzine claimed that the money he gave Katz was not an investment but a loan and thus did not need to be recorded on the annual disclosure form every Senate member is required to file. He added that he and Katz were dating at the time he made the payment, and that he forgave the loan after they ended their relationship. Corzine's former wife, Joanne, claimed that his affair with Katz had contributed to the dissolution of their marriage; the two had separated in 2002 and were divorced in 2003. In early November 2005 she criticized Corzine in newspaper interviews, saying that he had failed his family and would likely fail New Jersey as governor, and the Forrester campaign quickly produced a television ad based on her comments. A few days later, despite those events, Corzine defeated Forrester in the general election with 53.9 percent of the vote, while Forrester captured 43.2

percent. Corzine got nearly all of the state's black votes and received more female votes than Forrester by over 20 percentage points. In December 2005 Corzine appointed the Democratic representative Robert Menendez to serve the remainder of his term in the U.S. Senate.

One of Corzine's first actions as governor was to sign an executive order aimed at strengthening ethics guidelines in state politics, which included a code of conduct for the governor. Republicans charged that he broke those guidelines himself when, in March 2006, he lent $5,000 in bail money to a lobbyist and former campaign aide, Karen Golding, who was accused of stalking, and trying to break into the car of, the chairman of the state Democratic Party, Joseph Cryan. Republicans said that the loan represented another conflict of interest, since Golding was a lobbyist for Prudential Financial, which was managing a $1.3 billion deferred-compensation fund for state employees.

In March Corzine passed legislation to improve funding for the state's roads and bridges. That month he also introduced a plan for a series of budget cuts to deal with the state's deficit, which was over $4 billion. The plan included an increased sales tax as well as an extension of the tax on services provided by tattoo parlors, limousine companies, and health spas, among other businesses. It also included $169 million in cuts to higher education in the state as well as a proposed monthly tax to be paid by private hospitals for each of their beds. In addition, the plan included freezes (at the previous year's levels) on financing for poorer school districts. In July 2006 Corzine signed a law creating a Cabinet-level Department of Child and Family Services for the state.

Meanwhile, in the summer of 2006, the New Jersey government temporarily shut down after legislators failed to agree on a budget plan. The crisis began when Democrats who controlled the state Assembly rejected a proposal by Corzine to increase the sales tax, thereby missing a July 1 deadline for passing a new budget. With no authority to spend money, the government was forced to suspend nonessential services, including the state lottery and operations of Atlantic City casinos. The shutdown lasted for a week, during which 45,000 state employees were kept from work. It ended when Corzine signed a $30 billion budget plan that included a sales-tax increase from 6 to 7 percent. Half of the new money raised was to be used to reduce property taxes.

In September 2006 Corzine proposed measures to lower New Jersey's property taxes, including the decreasing of benefits for new state employees and the leasing of portions of the New Jersey Turnpike for corporate advertising. "Everything must be on the table," he told a joint session of the state legislature, as quoted by Anthony Birritteri in *New Jersey Business* (September 2006). "The sacred cows, third rails and 800-pound gorillas; all the issues that government for too long has been unwilling to address." Corzine announced that if the legislature could not agree upon a tax-relief plan before January 1, 2007, he would convene a citizens' convention to produce one; whatever they came up with would be placed on the ballot in November 2007 for voter approval.

Corzine's hobbies include playing basketball and tennis as well as jogging. He and his ex-wife have three grown children: Jennifer, Joshua, and Jeffrey.

—M.B.

Suggested Reading: *New York Times* I p33 Apr. 9, 2000, XIV p1 Nov. 3, 2002, XIV p1 Nov. 13, 2005; *New York Times Magazine* p48+ Feb. 13, 2000; *Slate* (on-line) June 3, 2000; *U.S. News & World Report* p39 July 20, 1998; *Washington Post* H p1 Nov. 6, 1994, E p1 Oct. 7, 1999

Getty Images

Cowher, Bill

(kar)

May 8, 1957– Football coach

Address: Pittsburgh Steelers, 3400 S. Water St., Pittsburgh, PA 15203-2349

On February 5, 2006 Bill Cowher, currently the longest-serving coach in the National Football League (NFL), led the Pittsburgh Steelers to a 21–10 victory over the Seattle Seahawks in Super Bowl XL, in Detroit, Michigan. That championship win, Cowher's first, broke the Steelers' years-long pattern of success in the regular season followed by heartbreaking losses in the play-offs. Cowher be-

came the Steelers' head coach in 1992, after playing for five seasons with the Cleveland Browns and serving variously as a special-teams coach, secondary coach, and defensive coordinator for the Browns and the Kansas City Chiefs. As coach of the Steelers, he led his team to the play-offs in each of his first six seasons, becoming one of only two coaches to achieve that feat. The Steelers under Cowher are known for their strong running attack and a blitzing defense. An ESPN television analyst, Paul Maguire, said to Jeff Ryan for *Sport* (November 1998) about Cowher, "There aren't many head coaches who are better. When players leave, it doesn't make much difference because the Steelers stick with the same basic offense and defense. They beat you with execution." Cowher, known throughout the world of football for his high-decibel, "in-your-face" exchanges with players and NFL officials alike, explained to Gerry Dulac for the *Sporting News* (August 3, 1992) that as a coach he emphasizes "mak[ing] the game simple, you've got to make the game fun. That's the thing any coach tries to do—create a winning atmosphere, yet one that stresses the team element of it."

One of the three sons of Laird and Dorothy Cowher, William Laird Cowher was born on May 8, 1957 in Pittsburgh, Pennsylvania, and raised in the suburb of Crafton. Beginning when the Cowher sons were very young, their father instilled in them a belief in the importance of hard work, determination, and courage. "My father said three things to us: Don't quit anything you start, work harder than the other person, and don't be intimidated by anything or anybody," Bill Cowher said to Jeff Ryan. Laird Cowher owned season tickets to the Steelers' home games when Bill was a boy, and both enjoyed following the fortunes of the Steelers and the Pittsburgh Pirates baseball team. While growing up Cowher and his brothers attended football camps. At Carlynton High School Cowher was a linebacker on the football team and also played basketball and ran track. His most memorable achievements were on the gridiron, where he achieved all-state honors. In an interview with Tim Crothers for *Sports Illustrated* (January 9, 1995), Tom Donahoe, the coach of a team that played against Cowher's, recalled that Cowher's ferocity was evident even in high school. "His face was so intense that our players were scared to death of him," Donahoe said. "He even had some of my coaches intimidated." (During Cowher's tenure with the Steelers, Donahoe has served as the franchise's director of football operations.)

Though Cowher hoped to attend college in Pennsylvania, two of the state's major football programs—those at Penn State University and the University of Pennsylvania—showed little interest in him. Recruited by Lou Holtz, Cowher enrolled at North Carolina State University, where he received a full scholarship to play football. He started at linebacker for three seasons, making significant contributions on the field and emerging as a team leader. He led the team in tackles in both his junior and senior seasons, and as a senior he was selected as captain and named most valuable player. Cowher also received the 1978 Cary Brewbaker Award, given by the school's coaching staff to the team's best linebacker. He graduated with a B.A. degree in education in 1979. That year he gained some coaching experience as a graduate assistant.

Cowher was not selected by an NFL team in the 1979 draft. He later signed a free-agent rookie contract with the Philadelphia Eagles and played three preseason games at linebacker for the team but was released before the start of the regular season. The following year Cowher signed a contract with the Cleveland Browns, earning a roster spot after training camp. He appeared mostly as a special-teams player for the Browns in 1980, starting two games at inside linebacker as well. In the third preseason game of the 1981 season, Cowher sustained an injury to his knee that sidelined him for the rest of the year. In 1982 he returned to the field as the Brown' special-teams captain, also seeing action at the outside linebacker position. Before the start of the 1983 NFL season, the Browns traded Cowher to the Eagles in exchange for a ninth-round draft pick. He appeared in all 16 Eagles games that year, and his fellow players voted him most valuable special-teams player. In 1984 Cowher injured his knee a second time, which limited his contribution to four games that season and effectively ended his playing career.

In 1985, eager to return to football, Cowher—then 28—took a job coaching special teams, under his former coach, Marty Schottenheimer of the Browns. At the time Cowher was the league's second-youngest assistant coach. He held that position, with some success, until 1987, when he was promoted to the team's secondary (or defensive backfield) coach. The Browns' defense made 23 interceptions, the third-highest total in the NFL, in 1987. In 1989 Schottenheimer became the head coach of the Kansas City Chiefs, and Cowher followed him there, serving for three seasons as the team's defensive coordinator; in those years the Chiefs were rated statistically among the best defensive units in the American Football Conference (AFC). During his time with Kansas City, Cowher emerged as a viable candidate to serve as head coach elsewhere in the NFL. Schottenheimer said to Timothy W. Smith for the New York Times (January 26, 1996) about Cowher, "When he was here [in Kansas City] he was able to implement a defensive system that plays to the style of our people. . . . He's a creative guy, a flexible guy. There was very little doubt in my mind that he'd be successful." For his part, Cowher—who once admitted to Gerald Eskenazi for the New York Times (January 15, 1995) that he "was never a really gifted athlete"— told Erik Brady for USA Today (August 31, 2004) that less-than-stellar players "sometimes make good coaches. Those are the guys who do the little things. I wasn't a guy who was going to get by on athletic ability."

On January 21, 1992, at age 34, Cowher became the head coach of the Pittsburgh Steelers. In the second half of the 1970s, the Steelers had enjoyed one of the most successful periods of any team in NFL history, but beginning in the early 1980s, following the retirement of several key players, they saw their success diminish. In his first season as head coach, Cowher turned the Steelers around. He was named NFL coach of the year by the Associated Press and the Sporting News after the 1992 season, in which he directed the Steelers to an 11–5 record and to its first central-division crown since 1984. Cowher emphasized both a rushing attack and an attacking defense, features that have become the Steelers' signatures. The third-year running back Barry Foster finished the season with 1,690 yards rushing, the highest total in the AFC that year. On defense the Steelers ranked first in the NFL in takeaways (or forced turnovers), with 22 interceptions and 21 fumble recoveries. In Pittsburgh on January 9, 1993, following an opening-round bye, the Steelers were defeated in the divisional round of the play-offs by the Buffalo Bills, winners of the AFC wild card, by a score of 24–3. (Foster rushed for a respectable 104 yards, but the Steelers committed four turnovers, enabling the Bills quarterback Frank Reich to pass for two touchdowns.)

The Steelers' 1993 and 1994 seasons provided a similar story line: after strong play in the regular season, the team stumbled in the play-offs. Pittsburgh's record after the 1993 regular season was 9–7, which earned the Steelers an AFC wild-card berth and a road play-off game against the Kansas City Chiefs, winners of the AFC Western Division. The Steelers' 17–7 halftime lead against Kansas City was erased in the game's final minutes, when the Chiefs quarterback Joe Montana completed a touchdown pass to the receiver Tim Barnett, tying the score. Kansas City's kicker Nick Lowrey managed a 32-yard field goal in sudden-death overtime and ended the game, 27–24. In 1994, en route to their second Central Division championship in three seasons under Cowher, the Steelers won 12 games, the highest total in the AFC that season. The team's 2,180 rushing yards in 1994 were the most in the NFL; Foster and the rookie running back Bam Morris each rushed for more than 800 yards, pacing a Steelers offense that also relied upon well-timed contributions from the quarterback Neil O'Donnell in the passing game. On January 7, 1995 Cowher recorded his first play-off victory, a 29–9 win against the Cleveland Browns. In the AFC Championship Game, in Pittsburgh, contested eight days later, the favored Steelers lost to the San Diego Chargers by a score of 17–13. San Diego's ability to thwart the Steelers' ground attack was the main cause of the upset, in the opinion of sportswriters.

As the Steelers' performance won respect among fans and football experts, Cowher developed a reputation as a great motivator of players. He also became known for dramatic encounters with both players and NFL officials. "When Bill Cowher wants to make a point," Paul Needell wrote for the New York *Daily News* (January 28, 1996), "his eyes lock into yours. His nose duels yours. His prominent chin grows a few inches. And his breath bounces off your face." Cowher himself said to Needell, "I'm not as intense as you think I am. I think there's a difference between being intense and having a great passion for the game. I love the game of football. . . . I'm just kind of an emotional guy." He added, "I think the people that try to hide how they feel and try to keep things inside 'em, well, I think that eats at you more than just letting it show. This is healthier."

Achieving an 11–5 record in the 1995 regular season, which earned the Steelers their third AFC Central Division championship under Cowher, the team entered the play-offs as the AFC's highest-scoring team—averaging slightly more than 25 points per game in the regular season—and boasting one of the league's most multitalented offenses. Kordell Stewart, for example, was nicknamed "Slash" by Cowher for his ability to play quarterback, receiver, and kick returnee, among other positions. Adding a new dimension to Pittsburgh's offense, Cowher designed unconventional plays that utilized Stewart's speed, elusiveness, and versatility. A first-round bye in the AFC play-offs, followed by a 40–21 victory in the divisional round against the Buffalo Bills and a 20–16 win against the Indianapolis Colts in the AFC Championship Game, netted the Steelers their fifth Super Bowl appearance and their first under Cowher. At age 38 Cowher became the youngest person up until then to lead his team to the Super Bowl.

On January 28, 1996 the Steelers squared off against the Dallas Cowboys in Super Bowl XXX, held in Tempe, Arizona. Winners of two of the previous three Super Bowl contests, the Cowboys were overwhelming favorites. In the hard-fought contest, the Steelers gained more yardage than the Cowboys, but Super Bowl XXX was decided by mistakes, with the Steelers, baited by the Cowboys, making the greater number. Pittsburgh's quarterback Neil O'Donnell threw three interceptions, two into the hands of the game's most valuable player, Larry Brown, leading directly to Dallas touchdowns. The Cowboys won their third Super Bowl in four seasons, by a score of 27–17. Despite the loss, Cowher was praised by many. Dave Goldberg wrote for the Associated Press (January 29, 1996), "Cowher enhanced his standing as the game's best young coach by outmaneuvering the more talented Cowboys and almost winning." Super Bowl XXX was "fun, and exciting, because Cowher's team wouldn't fold up and crawl into a hole when the Cowboys put on the heat," Timothy W. Smith observed for the *New York Times* (January 29, 1996). "Cowher had the guts to call some risky plays, and it gave the game a jolt of electricity and uncertainty almost to the end." (Cowher himself said to Jeff Ryan on another occasion, "Our players understand we're going to take chances and play to win, not to avoid losing.")

In both the 1996 and 1997 seasons, Pittsburgh won the AFC Central Division title, then suffered disappointing play-off losses—to the New England Patriots and Denver Broncos, respectively. Particularly frustrating for Cowher and the team was the 24–21 loss to the Broncos, on January 11, 1998, which marked the second time in six seasons that the Steelers hosted the AFC Conference Championship Game but lost to their opponents. Cowher nonetheless shared a distinction with the Hall of Fame coach Paul Brown, becoming the only other NFL coach to lead his team to the postseason in each of his first six seasons. Following the 1997 NFL season, the Steelers made key personnel changes, and concerns about the future direction of the team proved to be well founded. The Steelers failed to qualify for the play-offs in 1998, 1999, and 2000, posting a combined record of 23–26 over that span.

The Steelers returned to form in 2001, finishing the regular season atop the AFC Central Division with a 13–3 record. Cowher, meanwhile, won admiration for his ability to adjust his game plan according to his players' strengths. Pittsburgh ran for 2,774 combined yards, the most in the league that year, and the team's passing attack was also formidable. On defense during the regular season, the Steelers allowed 207 points, the third-lowest total in the NFL. Again earning an opening-round bye, Pittsburgh advanced to the AFC Championship Game by defeating the Baltimore Ravens, 27–10, in the divisional round of the play-offs, on January 20, 2002. A week later they lost to the New England Patriots, the eventual Super Bowl champions, 24–17. Two touchdowns by Patriots special teams gave New England a lead sufficient to stave off the Steelers' second-half resurgence. A crestfallen Cowher told reporters after the game, as quoted by Alan Robinson for the Associated Press (January 28, 2002), "It's hard to put into words the disappointment that exists. . . . The further you go, the greater the disappointment and the harder the hurt."

Pittsburgh's 2002 regular season began inauspiciously, with consecutive losses to the Patriots and Oakland Raiders. To rejuvenate his team, early in the season Cowher replaced Stewart, who was struggling at quarterback, with the journeyman pass-thrower Tommy Maddox. The Steelers responded positively, finishing the regular season with a record of 10–5–1. (The Steelers played the Atlanta Falcons to a 34–34 tie on November 10.) The 2002 season brought the team its seventh Central Division crown under Cowher. In the opening round of the play-offs, Pittsburgh edged out the Cleveland Browns, 36–33, thanks to the efforts of Maddox, who threw three touchdowns. In the following round the Steelers lost to the Tennessee Titans in Nashville in overtime, 34–31. The loss dropped Cowher's play-off record to 7–8 (0–3 in road contests).

In 2003 the Steelers finished with a 6–10 record and failed to qualify for the play-offs for only the fourth time in Cowher's 12 seasons as head coach. The team's poor record afforded them the 11th overall selection in the 2004 NFL Draft, which they used to select the quarterback Ben Roethlisberger from Miami University, in Ohio. On September 19, 2004, in a game against the Baltimore Ravens in Baltimore, Maddox suffered an injury to his elbow, and Roethlisberger replaced him—throwing two touchdown passes. Pittsburgh went on to win its remaining 14 games in the regular season, on the way to an NFL-best 15–1 record. In a vote taken among NFL head coaches, Cowher was named the *Sporting News* coach of the year. Having earned an opening-round play-off bye, the Steelers outplayed the New York Jets, 20–17, in the divisional round to advance to play the New England Patriots in the AFC Championship Game, Cowher's fifth since 1992. The poise that Roethlisberger had displayed earlier seemed to vanish: New England's defense intercepted three Roethlisberger passes, en route to a 41–27 win. After the game Cowher acknowledged Roethlisberger's mistakes but stood up for his young quarterback, telling Tom Pedulla for *USA Today* (January 24, 2005), "The kid will learn. He's going to be a good quarterback, he really will. It's a tough learning experience."

For the first 12 games of the 2005 regular season, the Steelers' record stood at 7–5. An injury to Roethlisberger, in particular, seemed to hamper the team, whose defense remained one of the league's most formidable. On December 11, 2005, in snowy conditions, the Steelers defeated the Chicago Bears, 21–9, in Pittsburgh on the strength of their rushing attack, breaking a three-game losing streak and bringing their record to 8–5. Pittsburgh won its last three regular-season games, finishing with an 11–5 record and qualifying for the play-offs as the AFC's sixth- and lowest-seeded team. Facing their divisional rivals, the Cincinnati Bengals, on the road in the first round of the play-offs, the Steelers emerged victorious, by a score of 31–17. In the much-anticipated second-round match-up between Pittsburgh and the heavily favored Indianapolis Colts, on January 15, 2006, the Steelers held in check the Colts' vaunted offense, led by quarterback Peyton Manning, en route to an exciting and unlikely 21–18 victory. The Steelers' third consecutive road play-off game, against the Denver Broncos the following week, was also a success: Roethlisberger tossed a pair of touchdown passes to lead the Steelers to a 34–17 win. The Steelers thus advanced to take on the Seattle Seahawks in Super Bowl XL, in Detroit, Michigan, on February 5. Early in the game's fourth quarter, on a play intended to deceive the opposition, the Pittsburgh receiver Antwaan Randle El appeared as though he would run the ball—then completed a 43-yard touchdown pass to Hines Ward, the game's most valuable player. The score extended Pittsburgh's lead from 13–10 to 21–10—the final score of the game that brought Cowher his first Super Bowl victory. After the game, in a conversation with Rick Reilly for *Sports Illustrated* (February 13, 2006), Cowher described his attitude toward the championship game: "To be honest, all those championship-game losses hurt me so bad, I stopped thinking about titles. I just refused to think about a championship. I learned to think about the game and nothing else. Nothing about what it meant. I just always prepared myself for the worst. I never let myself think about what it'd be like to win a Super Bowl. I didn't want to be hurt again."

Cowher is said to be unassuming, quiet, even self-deprecating when he is not coaching. He eschews the publicity some NFL coaches seem to crave, often turning down requests for interviews. He does not project the image of a workaholic; for example, by his own account, he rarely stays up late reviewing tapes of games. Instead, Cowher tries to strike a balance between his family and football. Rick Reilly wrote that Cowher has "the nose of a nearsighted boxer, rock-pile teeth and a mustache stolen from the Village People." During the week of the Super Bowl, Reilly added, Cowher dressed in "flood-ready khakis, logoless tennis shoes and what looked like a $40 watch."

Cowher met his wife, the former Kaye Young, when both were students at North Carolina State University. Kaye Cowher once enjoyed celebrity in the New York area when she and her twin sister, Faye, played basketball for the New York Stars of the now-defunct Women's Professional Basketball League. Bill and Kaye Cowher live in Pittsburgh and have three daughters: Meagan, Lauren, and Lindsay. Kaye is currently a basketball coach in the Pittsburgh area and has coached each of her daughters in the sport. Discussing her husband's public persona, Kaye Cowher told Erik Brady, "That's not the father and husband we see at home. One woman stopped me at a grocery store and said, 'How can you live with that man?' They think he yells and screams at home. He saves that for football."

—D.F.

Suggested Reading: *New York Times* VIII p2 Jan. 15, 1995; Pittsburgh Steelers Web Site; *Sport* p44+ Nov. 1998; *Sports Illustrated* p52+ Jan. 9, 1995, p96 Feb. 13, 2006

Davis-Kimball, Jeannine

Nov. 23, 1929– Archaeologist

Address: 577 San Clemente St., Ventura, CA 93001-3649

The archaeologist Jeannine Davis-Kimball is best known for providing the most concrete evidence to date that the myth of the Amazons, the female warriors described in ancient Greek texts, may have some basis in fact. Through her excavation of buri-

Courtesy of Jeannine Davis-Kimball

Jeannine Davis-Kimball

al mounds left by nomadic tribes that roamed the steppes of central Asia more than 2,500 years ago, she has uncovered the remains of women that not only bear the marks of battle but were also buried with weapons of war, including armor, daggers, and long swords—evidence that suggests that these women fought in battle alongside men. As that was an uncommon occurrence in the ancient world, Davis-Kimball and others now believe that these women, while not Amazons themselves, inspired the Greek myth, which still resonates in modern culture.

In an interview with Jacqueline Fitzgerald for the *Chicago Tribune* (August 4, 2004), Davis-Kimball attempted to explain the enduring appeal of the myth: "The Greeks began using the idea of the Amazons, and [the] Greek hero fighting the Amazon [to convey] that it was better to be a good wife and stay home so you don't end up dead like the Amazons. That was actually what some of the Greek orators talked about. In our culture, women are supposed to, in general, be sort of docile and to follow the lead of men. . . . When you have a culture that's entirely women, that's entirely independent and in fact dominant, and can go out and fight the men, that creates some sort of tension and probably that's the reason [the interest] has continued so long." Davis-Kimball is the author, with Mona Behan, of *Warrior Women: An Archaeologist's Search for History's Hidden Heroines* (2002).

The daughter of Elmer Jacob Davis and Cora (Kimball) Davis, Jeannine Davis-Kimball was born on November 23, 1929 in Driggs, Idaho. As a child she enjoyed reading "adventure books, particularly about women, such as a nurse in Alaska and stories of other cultures and ethnic groups," she told

an interviewer for the Time Warner Bookmark Web site. It was not until relatively late in life, however, that Davis-Kimball discovered her passion for archaeology. Before that she worked as a nurse in Idaho, a cattle rancher in South America, an administrator of a convalescent hospital in Southern California, and an English-language teacher in Bolivia and Spain, where she also completed a degree in Hispanic studies at the University of Madrid. During that time she also raised six children—Teresa, Mary Patrice, Stephen, John Eric, Christopher, and Leslie Ann—with her husband, Wayne Elbert Hargett, whom she divorced in 1980.

Davis-Kimball returned to school in her 40s, receiving her bachelor's degree in art history from California State University at Northridge in 1978. From 1976 to 1980 she also served as a curatorial assistant at the Los Angeles County Museum of Art, cataloging artifacts from the ancient Near East. "I became very curious about the collection's two hundred bronze plaques and animal statuettes from Eurasia, a legacy of the steppe nomads," she wrote in *Warrior Women*. "Although these artifacts were between two and three thousand years old, the casting was impeccable. . . . The detailed depictions of flying deer with massive antlers twined over their backs or a tiger savagely attacking a horse enthralled yet perplexed me. I felt they held some special significance to their owners that I couldn't quite reach." She grew increasingly fascinated as she read about the Eurasian steppes, a region of grassy plains that stretches some 6,000 miles, from the mouth of the Danube River, in Romania, to the Altai Mountains, in China.

After earning her master's degree from Goddard College, in Plainfield, Vermont, in 1980, Davis-Kimball enrolled in the doctoral program in Near Eastern studies at the University of California at Berkeley. In 1985 she assisted her doctoral adviser in an excavation at Tel Dor, an archaeological site located 15 miles south of Haifa, Israel. "I loved the freedom of working outdoors, and digging for artifacts that might reveal some tiny clue to the mystery of an ancient world fired my imagination and lent purpose to every task," she wrote in *Warrior Women*. "I hoped that archaeology would shed light on the original sources and meanings of the variety of motifs that most intrigued me as an art historian. . . . I realized that the answers to the questions I found most pressing lay not in museums and research libraries, but out in the field." In 1989 Davis-Kimball earned her doctorate and founded the American Eurasian Research Institute (AERI)—along with its subsidiaries, the Center for the Study of Eurasian Nomads (CSEN) and the Zinat Press—and she continues to serve as its executive director.

Davis-Kimball first travelled to Eurasia in 1985. Accompanied by Warren B. Matthew, an engineer whom she would marry two years later, she visited central Asia, specifically Samarkand and Bukhara in Uzbekistan, two cities that had been major stops along the Silk Road, an ancient trade route that linked China to the Roman Empire. On the visit they were constantly accompanied by a government-appointed guide, who made sure that they visited only officially sanctioned tourist spots. In 1986, when the Soviet leader Mikhail Gorbachev introduced *glasnost*, a policy of open discussion of political and social issues, the couple returned to Uzbekistan, hoping to see more. Nevertheless, the populace still feared the consequences of engaging in conversation with outsiders. "Frustrated by our inability to penetrate the tourist facade, we returned home and I vowed never to return to the USSR unless I first established connections with Soviet scholars who could grant me access to the information and sites needed for meaningful research," Davis-Kimball wrote in *Warrior Women*. That opportunity presented itself when an exhibition of Kazakh (or Kazak) art, "Nomads of Eurasia," was shown in Southern California in 1989, and she was able to establish relationships with the curators. She began collaborating with archaeologists in the Soviet Union, becoming the first American woman to contribute to excavations in Kazakhstan. Following the collapse of the Soviet Union, in 1991, she was granted more freedom to conduct digs with Russian archaeologists at Pokrovka, a collective farm located near the Russia-Kazakhstan border.

In an article published on the Time Warner Bookmark Web site, Davis-Kimball described her expeditions: "To understand the nomadic world on both ends of the great steppe lands, one summer I led excavations in Moldova and another summer in Mongolia. In 1991, I traveled with UNESCO's 'Dialogue of the Silk Road' expeditions in [Kazakhstan], but it was during the extensive journey with the same group through Mongolia in 1993 that I learned about Kazaks nomadizing in valleys guarded by the glistening glaciers high in the Altai Mountains. It was 1996 before I could break from my excavations to journey to those truly remote mountainous valleys. During that summer, I drank salt-milk tea in Kazak yurts [while] listening to their stories and songs, and often was a spectator at festivities that featured horse races, wrestling and singing competitions."

The majority of Davis-Kimball's digs involved kurgans, ancient Indo-European burial mounds; those that Davis-Kimball excavated were typically 60 feet across and as high as seven feet above the ground. The oldest of these mound-like graves, which were built by the nomadic peoples who lived in the region thousands of years ago, are pits dug typically four to six feet deep and surrounded by a low wall; other graves were later dug beside the pits and reveal niches where the dead were placed. A tribe would bury its dead in the same kurgan over a period of centuries, thereby allowing archaeologists a means to compare how people lived during different eras.

The kurgans offered a wealth of artifacts, as the dead were usually buried with the accoutrements of their occupations in life. In the 1950s Soviet ar-

chaeologists discovered that many of the women's graves contained weapons, including long swords, daggers, and bronze arrowheads—a finding that was given very little consideration at the time. As Davis-Kimball and her team further excavated those kurgans along the Russian-Kazakhstan border, they discovered that the society who buried those dead seemed to have little interest in defined gender roles. They found not only warrior men, but warrior women dressed in full battle armor, men entombed with children, women buried with seeds and baskets, priestesses, and even warrior-priestesses. Just as their weapons, made with smaller handgrips, indicated that these women were capable of fighting, their remains, often riddled with battlefield scars, proved that they had indeed fought. "[These women] seem to have controlled much of the wealth, performed rituals for their families and clan, rode horseback, and possibly hunted saiga, a steppe antelope, and other small game," Davis-Kimball told David Perlman for the *San Francisco Chronicle* (January 28, 1997).

The discoveries made by Davis-Kimball's expeditions led many scholars to suggest that the existence of such women warriors lent credence to the myth of the Amazons, a legendary band of female soldiers known for their skills as archers and horseback riders, who were later described by the Greek historian Herodotus. In his writings Herodotus chronicled a trip he made in 450 B.C. to the Scythian lands north of the Black Sea, where he first heard stories of armed horsewomen who could not marry until they had killed an enemy in battle. Tall, blond, and fierce, the female warriors Davis-Kimball uncovered roamed the southern Russian steppes and had a linguistic connection to the Scythian peoples. Those nomads were known by Herodotus as the Sarmatae or Sauromatae and are referred to as the Sauro-Sarmatians by modern ethnographers. Their culture existed roughly between the seventh century B.C. and second century A.D., and their habits, most notably the leadership roles in their society, were remarked upon by later writers, who often called them the "woman-ruled Sarmatae."

Though Davis-Kimball has dismissed the idea that these ancient women were Herodotus's mythical Amazons, she acknowledges that their existence indicates a kernel of truth in the legend, despite the fact that they lived so far from the Black Sea, where myth had placed them. "It's clear that either through firsthand or secondhand reports, the Greeks knew of women warriors and they elaborated on the stories," she told Peter N. Spotts for the *Christian Science Monitor* (January 28, 1997). Like the Amazons of myth, the Sauro-Sarmatian women took to their saddles with bows and arrows to defend their territory, families, animals, and pastures whenever they were threatened. There is no evidence, however, that they, like the Amazons, killed their male offspring or burned off their breasts in order, as some experts maintain, to more effectively shoot their arrows. In 2003, working with the German forensic anthropologist Joachim Burger, Davis-Kimball established a direct genetic link between one of the warrior women that she had excavated and a nomadic girl living in present-day Mongolia whose hair was blond—a color unusual among Mongolians.

Davis-Kimball has served as editor of the *Guides to the California Indian Library Collections* (1993), as the technical editor of *Catalogue Raisonne of Alaska Commercial Company Collection, Pheobe Apperson Hearst Museum of Anthropology* (1995), as co-author (with Leonid T. Yablonsky) of *Kurgans on the Left Bank of the Ilek: Excavations at Pokrovka, 1990–1992* (1995), as co-editor (with Vladimir A. Bashilov and Yablonsky) of *Nomads of the Eurasian Steppes in the Early Iron Age* (1995), and as editor (with Eileen M. Murphy, Ludmila Koryakova, and Yablonsky) of *Kurgans, Ritual Sites, and Settlements: Eurasian Bronze and Iron Age* (2000). She has also contributed to professional journals and provided research for or otherwise contributed to numerous television documentaries. Most recently she wrote (with Mona Behan) of her archaeological work in the Russian steppes in her 2002 book, *Warrior Women*. In a review for the *Edmonton Journal* (July 14, 2002), Dana McNairn wrote, "*Warrior Women* is best taken as a readable history wrapped around a travelogue, rather than serious scholarship. There is only haphazard regard for chronology or geography or the context of Davis-Kimball's finds. Not all of her claims are backed by academe because, understandably, the research doesn't exist yet. But it's fun to speculate that the remains found in the Russian kurgans might be the mythical Amazons. While it may well never be confirmed, I say let's keep the battle-axes sharp, just in case."

Davis-Kimball has said in interviews that she has no plans to undertake any more excavations, though she remains committed to the American Eurasian Research Institute. She also continues to contribute to the Web site of the Center for the Study of Eurasian Nomads, which she has maintained since the earliest days of the Internet's public use. She enjoys spending her leisure time with her large extended family.

—C.M.

Suggested Reading: *Chicago Tribune* C p2 Aug. 4, 2004, with photo; *Christian Science Monitor* p15 Jan. 28, 1997; *Edmonton Journal* D p12 July 14, 2002; *Los Angeles Times* II p3 Nov. 15, 2001; *New Scientist* p1717 Feb. 8, 1997; *San Francisco Chronicle* A p1 Jan. 28, 1997, with photo; *Secrets of the Dead* Web site

Selected Books: *Kurgans on the Left Bank of the Ilek: Excavations at Pokrovka, 1990–1992* (with Leonid T. Yablonsky), 1995; *Warrior Women: An Archaeologist's Search for History's Hidden Heroines* (with Mona Behan), 2002

Davis, Shani

Aug. 13, 1982– Speed skater

Address: Team Shani Davis, 815 Dempster St., Evanston, IL 60201

On February 18, 2006, in Turin, Italy, the speed skater Shani Davis—who holds the world records in the men's long-track 1,000- and 1,500-meter distances—became the first black person in the history of the Winter Olympics to capture an individual gold medal, crossing the finish line in the 1,000-meter event with a time of one minute, 8.89 seconds. While such a watershed accomplishment usually brings an athlete universal applause, Davis, who also won a silver medal in the 1,500-meter race, received as much criticism as praise at the Winter Games: a week before the 1,000-meter event, Davis publicly stated that he would not participate with his teammates in the new team-pursuit competition, a decision that was thought to decrease the U.S. team's chances for a medal in that event and that some criticized as unpatriotic. The U.S. men's Olympic long-track coach, Tom Cushman, and other high-ranking U.S. Speedskating officials expressed the view that those who had judged Davis negatively for his decision had done him an "injustice." As quoted by Philip Hersh for the *Chicago Tribune* (March 8, 2006, on-line), Cushman explained Davis's desire to focus on the 1,000- and 1,500-meter distances and said, "I would have done the same thing. His reasons were completely legitimate. I have nothing but respect for Shani." For Davis the attainment of a gold medal at the Winter Games represented the fulfillment of a lifelong dream. "One of the hardest things for me, being an African-American, is being in the sport of speedskating," Davis said to reporters after winning the gold medal, as quoted by Jay Mariotti in the *Chicago Sun-Times* (February 19, 2006). "As you know, African-Americans enter sports like track and field and basketball. I chose a different route. But I wake up every morning and love what I'm doing, regardless of color. To be able to achieve a dream is wonderful, whether I'm white, black, Hispanic or whatever."

The only child of Reginald Shuck and Cherie Davis, Shani Davis was born on August 13, 1982 in Chicago, Illinois. His first name is the creation of his father, who combined the Swahili words for "light" and "weight." Shani was raised by his mother in the tough, predominantly low-income area of Hyde Park, on Chicago's South Side. His parents divorced when he was a boy. When Davis was two years old, his mother introduced him to

Carlo Allegri/Getty

Shani Davis holding his Olympic medals

roller skating, seeing it as an activity they could enjoy together and as a way to shield him from the rougher elements of their neighborhood. Even at a very young age, Davis was able to perform aerial tricks and other advanced maneuvers, wearing traditional "quad" roller skates. (Quad roller-skating is different from inline skating, which became immensely popular in the U.S. in the early 1990s and involves skates with four or five wheels arranged in a single line.) Although he was eager to become a better skater, in time Davis grew bored with trick skating, preferring to skate circles around the rink at increasing rates of speed. Davis's official Web site reports that beginning when he was about three, he would "dart around the roller rink so fast that many times the skate guards would chase him just to ask him to slow down."

When Davis was around six years old, his mother was advised by her then-employer, Fred Benjamin, an attorney and member of the U.S. Speedskating board of directors, to enroll her son at the Evanston Speedskating Club, in Evanston, Illinois, directly north of Chicago. Mother and son began spending a lot of time at the rink in Evanston, as Davis honed his speed-skating abilities under the tutelage of Sanders Hicks, the founder and president of the club, among others. When Shani was a little older and had shown himself to be particularly adept at the sport, Cherie Davis took him jogging nearly every morning before school, to help him develop cardiovascular strength and endurance and also to nurture his competitive spirit.

Those living in his neighborhood, meanwhile, criticized Davis's dedication to a sport typically practiced by whites. Their view was that a black person as physically gifted as Davis should pursue a career in football or basketball, and that success in those sports would bring greater fame and fortune than he could enjoy as a speed skater. His neighbors' comments were "pretty derogatory stuff, especially at that young of an age," Davis said to Paul Newberry for the Associated Press (December 23, 2005). "But what I was doing was so different. Now, when I see some of those same people, they truly respect what I do. A lot of them say they're sorry for what they said. I don't hold it against them. They just didn't know anything about it."

By the time he was eight years old, Davis was winning regional speed-skating competitions in his age group. He began to feel that competing in the Olympics in the future was an attainable goal. In 1992 Davis and his mother moved to Rogers Park, a Chicago suburb, to be closer to the training facility in Evanston. Davis began to compete at the national level in 1994, finishing second in that year's competition for 10- and 11-year-olds and winning the championship for his age group in 1995.

Davis entered the prestigious U.S. Olympics developmental program in Lake Placid, New York, at age 16. "It was hard," Davis said to Tina Akouris for the *Chicago Sun-Times* (December 3, 2001), referring to the adjustment of being away from home for the first time, "but I knew it would be for a greater reason and I tried to look at the overall picture. I saw greater plans for myself and it was one of the many stepping-stones." In Lake Placid, Davis, who was accustomed to training with a diverse group of athletes in the Chicago area, was for the first time part of a predominantly white group of skaters. "That was the biggest culture shock of my life, going to Lake Placid," he said to Marty Motzko for nbcolympics.com. He trained there for a year before returning to the Chicago area to finish his junior year of high school. After spending the first part of his senior year in the Chicago area, Davis left for Marquette, Michigan, to continue his training as a speed skater. While there he graduated from Marquette Senior High School, where in 2000 he was a state champion in track in the 1,600- and 3,200-meter relay competitions. At age 17 Davis made history by becoming the first U.S. skater to earn a place on both the short- and long-track teams for the Junior World Team. He accomplished that feat again in 2001 and 2002.

In September 2001 Davis traveled to Canada to train with that country's national team in preparation for the Olympic trials. As Davis told Tina Akouris, the two months of intense workouts there helped him to become a faster skater. At the trials, held in Kearns, Utah, in late December 2001, Davis entered the last 1,000-meter short-track event. He needed a first-place finish to have a chance at coming in sixth in the overall points standings, which would make him the first African-American to qualify for a U.S. Olympic speed-skating team. Though his chances of winning were considered slim, due to the presence of the speed skater Apolo Anton Ohno, a rising star on the short track, who was competing in the same race, Davis finished in first place. Days afterward the skater Tommy O'Hare alleged that Ohno and another skater, Rusty Smith, had deliberately stayed behind Davis and had kept another competitor from passing them so that Davis—Ohno's friend—could make it to the Olympics. O'Hare's complaint was brought before the U.S. Olympic Committee, putting Davis in jeopardy of being thrown off the speed-skating team. The arbitrator of the case, James R. Holbrook, ruled that the race had been run and officiated fairly, and Davis was cleared to skate in the 2002 Olympics, held in Salt Lake City, Utah. An alternate on the team, he did not, in the end, participate in any short-track events. "I didn't even consider myself an Olympian. One day I was a hero, the next day I was a cheater," he said to Greg Couch for the *Chicago Sun-Times* (February 8, 2006, on-line), adding, "My name was run through the mud."

Before the Olympics were over, Davis went to Italy, where he helped the U.S. take first place in the 1,500-meter relay at the World Junior Long-Track Championship. Later that year, at the Junior Country match, also in Italy, Davis took home top honors in the 1,500-meter long-track race, with a time of one minute, 51.50 seconds. At the U.S. National Long-Track Speed-Skating Championships, held in Kearns, Utah, at the end of December 2002, Davis took first place in the 10,000-meter race, posting a time of 13 minutes, 53.39 seconds. Two thousand three marked the first year that he competed on the regular men's circuit. He found himself competing against more-seasoned athletes, and his results revealed his relative inexperience. For example, he finished 16th at the World All-Around Championships, held in Göteburg, Sweden, in early February.

In 2004 Davis became the first male U.S. skater to make both the long-track and short-track World Teams. He also won the 1,500-meter race at the World Single Distance Championships and took second place overall at the World Overall Championships. Davis began 2005 by breaking two world records in Salt Lake City at the North America & Oceania Regional Qualifier, the qualifying meet for the long-track World All-Around Championships. In the 1,500-meter long-track event, he set a record time of one minute, 43.33 seconds, .62 seconds faster than the previous mark, held by the U.S. speed skater Derek Parra. With 149.359 total points in that event, he also set a new mark for overall points by a skater. Davis won the 2005 long-track World All-Around Championships, in Moscow, Russia, in early February 2005. In November of that year, at the Fall World Cup event, Davis set a new world record in the 1,000-meter event, achieving a time of one minute, 7.03 seconds.

In early 2005, when Davis refused to remove from his uniform during competition the logo of the Netherlands-based bank DSB, with which he had recently signed an endorsement contract, U.S. Speedskating officials reacted by reducing his monetary compensation for travel and other expenses. (U.S. Speedskating has its own sponsors and claimed to have an agreement with its athletes that they wear the logos of those sponsors exclusively.) During that time it was widely reported that Davis had referred to U.S. Speedskating as "the enemy," further irritating members of the sport's governing body. (Several of Davis's teammates have engaged in similar disputes with U.S. Speedskating.) According to the *Denver Post* (December 12, 2005), Davis filed a grievance against U.S. Speedskating, which is to be settled by an arbitrator.

In December 2005 Davis fell just short of qualifying for both the short- and long-track U.S. Olympic teams; he would have been the first ever to do so. He was nevertheless regarded as a medal favorite on entering the 2006 Winter Olympics, in Turin, Italy. So, too, was his teammate and rival Chad Hedrick, who had stated publicly prior to the Turin Games that he was capable of winning multiple gold medals. Davis finished seventh in his first event, the 5,000-meter race, in which Hedrick took gold. Davis then announced that he would skip the team-pursuit event in order to concentrate on his signature individual event, the 1,000-meter race. Davis's decision became one of the most talked-about stories among U.S. observers of the 2006 Winter Olympics, and it rankled many, including Hedrick, who felt that Davis had compromised the U.S. team's chances of winning a medal in the team event. In the remaining days of the Games, the two engaged in a well-publicized war of words. In the team pursuit the U.S. was eliminated in the quarterfinals by Italy. Days later, Davis became the first black athlete in Winter Olympics history to win a gold medal in an individual competition, when he posted a time of one minute, 8.89 seconds in the 1,000-meter event. Davis also took home the silver medal in the 1,500-meter race. In his conversation with Jay Mariotti, Davis defended his actions: "When I was a kid, I'd say, 'Someday, I want to win the 1,000 meters at the Olympics.' To have the opportunity to chase that dream, then have the team pursuit, is a conflict of interest. All my life, I've been concentrating on individual events. If [U.S. Speedskating] could have let me know in advance . . . If things were more organized and I would have been notified earlier, maybe I could have done what's best for myself and the sport."

Davis's decision, regarded as selfish and even unpatriotic by some, set off a furious debate among speed-skating enthusiasts and sportswriters. Harvey Araton, writing for the New York Times (February 19, 2006), commended the skater. "In other settings, we salute premier athletes who approach their work with a single-minded purpose," Araton wrote. "Derek Jeter comes to mind. Tiger Woods. Hideki Matsui says he wants to win a World Series so much that he won't play for Japan in the World Baseball Classic. . . . Davis won the race that always suited him best, the one he predicted he would win when he was just a kid talking, playing, dreaming. He made it come true. He deserves credit, admiration, not scorn."

Other controversy surrounding Davis involved his mother, Cherie, who served until recently as his manager and agent and whom critics accused of tarnishing her son's image through her combativeness. She is known, for example, for sending scathing E-mail messages and other correspondence to speed-skating officials, journalists, and Shani's teammates, accusing them of racism and of failing to support her son. Some also felt that Cherie Davis exerted an undue influence on the skater, and she drew criticism for chastising Shani at the Olympic trials held in December 2005. As revealed by a Dutch television documentary that aired during the Winter Games, she told Shani after he failed to qualify for the short-track squad, "Somebody's going to see what a loser you are." "Shani should've been the feel-good story of the Turin Olympics . . . ," Rick Reilly argued in Sports Illustrated (March 6, 2006). "Instead, he came off as icier than Admiral Byrd's axe. And almost everybody blames his mom for it." Davis, for his part, has defended his mother. In a conversation with Carl Quintanilla for CNBC.com (February 27, 2006), Davis said that he owes his mother "everything," adding, "When I was tired and didn't want to get up, I would think about how hard my mom worked to get to where I'm at. And if she could do it, then why am I not doing the same thing that she would do?"

Immediately following the Olympics, competing in Heerenveen, Netherlands, Davis won the overall World Cup championship in the 1,000-meter long-track competition, posting a time of one minute, 8.91 seconds. At the International Skating Union World All-Around Speed-Skating Championships held in Calgary, Alberta, on March 18 and 19, 2006, Davis broke the men's 1,500-meter world record, finishing in one minute, 42.68 seconds—one 10th of a second faster than the previous record, set by Hedrick. In addition, Davis, who had grabbed first place in the 500-meter race held a day earlier, secured the event's overall men's title. "To me, this is bigger than the Olympics," Davis said, as quoted by a reporter for the Associated Press (March 20, 2006). "This medal is prestigious. Not only do you have to skate 500 meters, but you have to skate 10,000, you have to skate a 1,500 and a 5,000, and you only have two days to do it."

Shani Davis is six feet two inches tall and weighs approximately 185 pounds. Observers have noted that his tall frame is particularly suited to long-track speed-skating events. Davis has expressed a desire to be a positive role model for young people and has said that he would like to see speed skating become more popular among youth, especially in inner-city areas. "I want to be a breath of fresh air," he said to John Crumpacker for the U.S. Olympic Team Web site. "I want to show kids it's OK to break away from that bubble [of such conventional sports as football and basketball] and do something different." According to Time (January 23, 2006), Davis enjoys a considerable following in Europe, where speed skating is more popular than in the U.S.

Davis, who maintains a busy training schedule, lives in Calgary, in the province of Alberta, Canada. Interested in science, he has said that he would like to become a teacher when his speed-skating career is over. In his spare time he enjoys playing video games, listening to rap music, and practicing tae kwon do. He is currently working toward his undergraduate degree at Northern Michigan University, in Marquette.

—D.F.

Suggested Reading: Chicago Sun-Times p80 Dec. 3, 2001, A p119 Feb. 19, 2006; nbcolympics.com; New York Times I p1+ Feb. 19, 2006; shanidavis.org

Dawdy, Shannon Lee

July 19, 1967– Archaeologist; anthropologist; historian

Address: Dept. of Anthropology, Haskell 202, University of Chicago, 1126 E. 59th St., Chicago, IL 60637

"Although I am an archaeologist who deals in artifacts, old buildings, and musty documents, in recent days I have realized more than ever that what I love about New Orleans is intangible and immaterial," the anthropologist, historian, and archaeolo-

Shannon Lee Dawdy

Courtesy of Dan Dry

history," Dawdy told John Schwartz for the *New York Times* (January 3, 2006). "If anyone is going to stick it out, out of a sense of history, out of a sense of tradition, it is New Orleans."

The older of two children, Shannon Lee Dawdy was born on July 19, 1967 in Santa Rosa, California, to James H. Dawdy, a small-business owner, and Arletta Dawdy, a social worker. She told *Current Biography*, "From a very young age, I would often [say] that I would be a Ph.D. when I grew up, though I had no idea what that meant or in what field." Her father, who had an interest in the sciences, hoped that she would become an astronomer, and her mother loved writing historical novels; Dawdy has theorized that her parents' combined interests influenced her own decision to become an archaeologist. At Reed College, in Portland, Oregon, she majored in anthropology while maintaining her interest in archaeology, an interest that was further fueled—though not in a traditional way—by one of her instructors. "Gail Kelly, [a] professor of anthropology at Reed College, was a frightening dragon lady of a mentor, but she scared me into stretching my known limits, a habit that has stuck and served me well," Dawdy told *Current Biography*. "She abhorred archaeology, thinking of it as a knuckle-headed kind of anthropology, but that has just challenged me more, to make it a thinking-person's anthropology." After earning her bachelor's degree in anthropology, in 1988, Dawdy took time off from her studies and traveled to Spain to teach English. She returned to the U.S. in 1989 and worked for the next three years as a docent for the Fine Arts Museums of San Francisco.

In 1992 Dawdy enrolled in the master's program in anthropology at the College of William and Mary in Virginia, where she received her first formal training in archaeology. During the last few months of her master's program, she began working as a contract archaeologist in New Orleans. After completing her degree, in May 1994, Dawdy moved to New Orleans with her husband, Dan Mc-Naughton, a jazz musician. "My research soon became rooted in local history, where it has remained to this day," she told *Current Biography*.

Immersing herself in the history and culture of the city, in 1995 Dawdy helped found a pilot program called the Greater New Orleans Archaeology Program at the University of New Orleans. The main purpose of the program, which called for consultations with city planners, was to preserve historical artifacts through "excavation, oral history and hands-on work," as John Schwartz wrote. As a research associate and director of the program, Dawdy oversaw excavations for 10 different projects while also becoming heavily involved with public-outreach work in the area. Despite the difficulty of finding a building in New Orleans—much less a historical artifact—that remains untouched by the area's volatile weather or by the fires that plagued the city's past, two digs undertaken during Dawdy's tenure with the Greater New Orleans Archaeology Program resulted in important discover-

gist Shannon Lee Dawdy wrote in a column for the Web site About.com in 2006. "It has always been the people. That cultural heritage is hard to describe. People in New Orleans are wonderfully expressive, improvisational, irreverent, impetuous, and eccentric. They live their lives with all five senses. And they often eschew the commercial and the crass for community and tradition." Specializing in topics including race and ethnicity, the formation of Creole societies, and sexuality and tourism in post-colonial New Orleans, Dawdy was the founding director of the Greater New Orleans Archaeology Program at the University of New Orleans and has spent nearly 12 years at the helm of some of the most productive archaeological projects in the New Orleans, Louisiana, area. Much evidence of New Orleans's historical past has been erased by a constant barrage of storms during the annual hurricane season. Dawdy has been more successful than many archaeologists at rendering a detailed picture of New Orleans society—from its Native American ancestry to the influx of French immigrants to the formation of the ethnically mixed Creole culture. Now an assistant professor at the University of Chicago, in Illinois, Dawdy still maintains strong ties to New Orleans in the wake of Hurricane Katrina, which devastated much of the city in 2005. Working with the Federal Emergency Management Agency (FEMA), Dawdy has used her archaeological expertise to safeguard what remains of the city's past and current culture during the rebuilding efforts, thereby helping to preserve the social integrity of New Orleans and helping natives to reconnect with their hometown. "The thing about New Orleans that gives me hope is [that its residents] are so tied to family, place, ies. With a team of 135 local volunteers, Dawdy excavated the site of the historical Madame John's Legacy, a colonial-era house—one of the few remaining pieces of French colonial architecture and culture left in the city. (The house took on the name Madame John's Legacy in the late 1800s, after the short story "Tite Poulette," by George Washington Cable, who used it as the setting for his tale.) During the excavation, Dawdy was able to identify such items as shards of pottery as having been in use during the slave era. Paraphrasing Dawdy, Jason Bullock wrote for the New Orleans *Times-Picayune* (August 2, 1997), "In addition to the two-story main house, Madame John's Legacy includes separate buildings for the kitchen and an apparent garconniere, or bachelor's quarters, which was added in the 1820s. The garconniere also may have been used to house slaves." Dawdy explained to Bullock, "The boys would live outside the house so they wouldn't disturb their mother with their sexual exploits." Many of the dig's most significant findings came from a trash pit underneath the site that dated back to 1788, the same year a fire destroyed much of the city's French Quarter. "The volume of stuff we're finding is more striking than any particularly spectacular artifact," Dawdy told Bullock. Items in the trash pit suggested much about the diet and living conditions in the 1800s of New Orleans inhabitants, who included people of Latin, French, and Spanish heritage. For example, the discovery of a goat horn suggested that people of the era and region may have had "a broad diet," in Bullock's words. Dawdy said to the reporter, "There's the old stereotype that Cajuns will eat anything. But it's not really a cliche. It's a cultural characteristic of the French." The team also found remnants of pottery that Dawdy thought was perhaps a gift exchanged between the Native Americans and European settlers during peace settlements during the mid-18th century.

The second notable dig to take place during Dawdy's three-year stint with the Greater New Orleans Archaeology Program occurred at the old Maginnis Cotton Mill in the city's Warehouse District, which dates back to the slavery era. Dawdy and her team found evidence that the structure was built in the fashion of a French West Indies–style plantation constructed in 1765, a discovery that shed light on the ethnic mix of the city and its French-Creole ancestry. French residents of the house on the mill property included Francois Duplessis as well as the Fouchers, the Delord-Sarpys, and the du Plantiers, among other families; such details, about a city where scarcely more than a few documents describing daily life in the 19th century are available, have helped to paint a fuller picture of the lives of the Europeans and Creoles who once made up the Big Easy, as New Orleans is nicknamed.

In 1999 Dawdy left New Orleans to work as a graduate student/instructor in the Anthropology and History Departments at the University of Michigan in Ann Arbor. In addition to teaching undergraduate courses in archaeology and history, Dawdy worked toward a second master's degree—in history—which she received in April 2000. Dedicated to earning the Ph.D. she dreamed of as a child, Dawdy completed work on a double doctorate, in anthropology and history, from the University of Michigan in December 2003. Her dissertation, entitled "La Ville Sauvage: 'Enlightened' Colonialism and Creole Improvisation in New Orleans, 1699-1769," focused on French colonial times in New Orleans and was based in part on findings from the numerous digs she organized in the city. In 2004 Dawdy won a coveted assistant professorship in anthropology and social sciences at the University of Chicago. Meanwhile, she maintained her ties to New Orleans, accepting a visiting-scholar position that same year at the University of New Orleans. She made frequent trips there to work on digs and delve ever deeper into the city's literally buried past.

When the Historic New Orleans Collection acquired property located on Conti Street, directors of the collection commissioned Dawdy to oversee an archaeological dig there, scheduled to take place before the one-story parking garage on the property was slated to be demolished, in February 2005. With less than a year to work, Dawdy chose seven sites for full-scale excavations—each three feet square and four feet deep. At one site, about two and a half feet below the surface, Dawdy and her team of researchers found a large number of liquor bottles and a collection of rouge pots, a combination suggesting that the team had discovered the site of the early-19th-century Rising Sun Hotel, which was destroyed by a fire in 1822. Dawdy's discovery earned her considerable recognition and attracted the attention of people outside the archaeological and historical fields. Many wondered if there was a connection between Dawdy's findings and the classic love ballad "The House of the Rising Sun," a song of unknown origin. (Georgia Turner first recorded it in 1937.) The song centers on "a whorehouse in the heart of the [French] quarter," according to David Usborne, writing for the London *Independent* (March 21, 2005). Although local historians had long assumed that the Rising Sun Hotel was nothing more than an ordinary inn, the vast number of liquor bottles and rouge pots made the site look "impressively like a bordello," Dawdy told Bruce Eggler for the *Times-Picayune* (March 6, 2005). "Can you prove archaeologically is this a brothel? I can't prove it with a yes or no answer," she told Schwartz. In search of more evidence, Dawdy sifted through the city's meager historical records and newspaper clippings and found a January 1821 advertisement for the hotel in the *Louisiana Gazette*, which pointed further to the possibility of a connection between the Rising Sun Hotel and the similarly named song. In the ad the hotel's new owners stated, as quoted by Eggler, that they would "maintain the character of giving the best entertainment, which this house has enjoyed for twenty years past. . . . Gentlemen may here rely upon finding attentive Servants. The bar will be supplied with genuine good Liquors; and at the Table, the fare will be of the best the market or the season will afford." Although the ad does not explicitly mark the hotel as a brothel, researchers and historians agree that it has risqué undertones. "The archaeology is suggestive at this point," Dawdy told David Usborne. "I'm certainly excited just for the possibility. But I don't want to add to the mythology of New Orleans unnecessarily until I know more. Everything needs a caveat for now."

On August 29, 2005 Hurricane Katrina ravaged the Gulf Coast with 160-mile-per-hour winds and unremitting rain. The resulting floods left much of New Orleans in ruins: hundreds of people died or went missing, homes and other buildings were destroyed, and entire neighborhoods sat under as much as 15 feet of water. Dawdy, who had completed her research at Conti Street, had returned to Chicago just three weeks before the storm hit the city. "It is heart-wrenching to watch a place that you love, and people you love but don't know, suffering like that," she told Current Biography. Soon after the floodwaters receded, Dawdy went back to New Orleans, working with the Federal Emergency Management Agency as a liaison with the state's historic preservation office, in order to preserve any remaining historical and cultural artifacts during the city's rebuilding process. "It's a way that archaeology can contribute back to the living," she told Schwartz, "which it doesn't often get to do."

One of Dawdy's main projects related to that effort centers on Holt Cemetery, described by Schwartz as "a final resting place for the city's poor." Unusual makeshift headstones, rather than traditional custom-made headstones, mark the graves. The teddy bears, ice chests, plastic jack-o'-lanterns, chairs, and occasional liquor bottles strewn throughout the graveyard all suggest that mourners regularly visit the graves. "Holt cemetery is a place where New Orleanians, mainly poor and African American, bury and remember their dead with artistic tenderness. . . . The colorful contrast with the more typical white-washed tombs in other New Orleans cemeteries is dramatic," Dawdy told Current Biography. The cemetery is an example of "the amazing improvisational impulse of New Orleans," Dawdy told Schwartz. Every year on All Souls' Day, the cemetery would be filled with people coming to pay their respects and replace worn grave decorations. But since Hurricane Katrina, few people have visited. "The saddest thing to me now was how few people we see. I realize we're having enough trouble taking care of the living," she told Schwartz, but the interruption of such customs in New Orleans, which normally places importance on its ties to the dead, "drove home how far out of whack things are." Dawdy has proposed that the cemetery be treated in the same manner as archaeologists would treat an ancient site where objects have surfaced because of erosion. "While in the face of this, archaeology may seem like a trivial pursuit to many, what I have come to realize is that

for New Orleanians to move forward with hope and vision, they need not only to preserve, but to comprehend, the past," she told Current Biography. "That is where I have found a new value and motivation for my work."

Dawdy is currently writing a book that "addresses the role of New Orleans in the popular imagination, both historically and through recent Katrina-related events," as she told Current Biography. Among other honors, she has received a National Endowment for the Humanities Scholarly Editions grant, the Distinguished Dissertation Award (twice) from the University of Michigan, and the Rackham Fellowship, also from the University of Michigan. She lives in Chicago with her husband and their five-year-old son.

—I.C.

Suggested Reading: About.com (online) 2006, with photo; (London) *Independent* p25 Mar. 21, 2005; *Los Angeles Times* A p1 Mar. 20, 2005; (New Orleans) *Times-Picayune* B p1 Aug. 2, 1997, B p1 Mar. 23, 1998, Metro p1 Mar. 6, 2005; *New York Times* (on-line) Jan. 3, 2006

Selected Books: as editor–*Creolization: Thematic Issue of Historical Archaeology*, 2000; *Dialogues in Cuban Archaeology* (with Antonio Curet and Gabino La Rosa), 2005

---

de Waal, Frans

(duh WAHL, frahnz)

Oct. 29, 1948– Primatologist; ethologist

Address: Yerkes National Primate Center, 954 N. Gatewood Rd., Atlanta, GA 30329

Frans de Waal is "one of the subtlest, most knowledgeable and most cheerful students of great ape behaviour," according to the biologist Alison Jolly, writing for the *London Review of Books* (September 20, 2001). For more than 20 years, de Waal has championed a view of primates (animals including monkeys, apes, lemurs, and humans) that stresses how similarly members of this group behave, whether they are the capuchin monkeys associated with organ grinders in times past or actual Capuchin monks. De Waal is not only a primatologist but also an ethologist, someone who studies animal behavior and its biological basis. He rose to international prominence while in his early 30s, with the publication of his book *Chimpanzee Politics: Power and Sex among Apes* (1982), which helped give scientific substance to shifting scholarly ideas about animal (and human) behavior. Openly ascribing such supposedly human-specific traits as feelings of affection and rational intentions to animals—a descriptive method known as anthropomorphism, which is viewed with suspi-

Courtesy of Emory University

Frans de Waal

despises the 'Bambification' of animals. The chimpanzees he watches have been known to kill each other. They have castrated their rivals. But chimpanzees also hug and kiss in reassurance and friendship. After fights, they are likely to make up with extra shows of affection. They need each other, and they seem to know it." That intergroup dependency also gives rise to specific group identities. In *The Ape and the Sushi Master: Cultural Reflections of a Primatologist* (2001), as well as a book that he co-edited with the oceanographer Peter L. Tyack, *Animal Social Complexity: Intelligence, Culture, and Individualized Societies* (2003), de Waal and others have not hesitated to refer to those group identities as cultures, despite the somewhat controversial question of whether animals can be said to have something as distinctly human as culture. Since his years at the Arnhem zoo, de Waal has photographed his primate subjects, and many of his photos appear in his books. In 2003 he published more than 120 pictures of primates in his book *My Family Album: Thirty Years of Primate Photography*.

The acclaim accorded de Waal's popular writing—including a 1989 *Los Angeles Times* Book Prize for *Peacemaking among Primates*—has been echoed in responses to the more than 100 articles in scientific journals that de Waal has written or co-written in English, Dutch, and German. He currently holds four professional positions, including dual appointments as a research professor of psychobiology at the Yerkes National Primate Research Center at Emory University, in Atlanta, Georgia, and as the founding director of the Yerkes's Living Links Center, where researchers study the evolution of human behavior. He is also the C. H. Chandler Professor of Primate Behavior in the psychology department at Emory and an affiliate scientist with the Wisconsin National Primate Research Center at the University of Wisconsin in Madison, where he worked after he came to the U.S. in 1981. De Waal has been inducted into the Royal Netherlands Academy of Arts and Sciences and its American counterpart, the National Academy of Sciences. De Waal's success as both a popular writer and a serious scientist impresses many of his peers. "I marvel at how he can do both of these things at the same time," the ecologist William McGrew told Regina Nuzzo. "Frans can make statements that can be understood by the average person, but he can back it with carefully designed studies and data. He has a such a high standing with his fellow scientists because he does hard work in order to get good data and form his opinions."

Born on October 29, 1948 in the city of 's-Hertogenbosch (more commonly known as Den Bosch), about 50 miles south of Amsterdam, Holland, Frans B. M. de Waal was the fourth of six boys born to Jo A. de Waal, a bank director, and Francis (van Dongen) de Waal. (De Waal told *Current Biography*, "My official name is Franciscus Bernardus Maria de Waal, but no one uses those

cion by many scientists—de Waal described in *Chimpanzee Politics* a set of behaviors that he and others meticulously recorded over thousands of hours at the largest colony of chimpanzees in the world, at the Burgers' Zoo in the Dutch city of Arnhem. His experiences there continue to inform his work. "All the issues that I'm at the moment still working on I basically saw in front of me in that colony of chimps," de Waal told Regina Nuzzo for the *Proceedings of the National Academy of Sciences* (August 9, 2005). The chimps that de Waal observed so closely acted in surprisingly human ways, fighting and helping each other with equal intensity, eagerly forming and defending coalitions that contributed to a hierarchy, which promoted group stability. The unusual mix of rich storytelling and clearheaded scientific exposition in *Chimpanzee Politics* made it a critical success, praised even in business magazines and in a statement by a former Speaker of the U.S. House of Representatives, Newt Gingrich, who recommended the book to incoming members of Congress in 1994.

To some degree in that book but particularly in such later ones as *Peacemaking among Primates* (1989), *Good Natured: The Origins of Right and Wrong in Humans and Other Animals* (1996), *Our Inner Ape: A Leading Primatologist Explains Why We Are Who We Are* (2005), and *Primates and Philosophers: How Mortality Evolved* (2006), de Waal emphasized the reconciliatory and not merely self-interested inclinations that primates demonstrate; an important part of de Waal's *Bonobo: The Forgotten Ape* (1997) examines the sexual methods of peacekeeping by humans' closest relative. Still, as Alison Jolly noted, "De Waal is not mawkish. He names.") De Waal's maternal grandfather owned a pet store, the genetic source (de Waal has jokingly claimed) of his marked interest in animals. From a young age de Waal enjoyed scooping up creatures—fish, salamanders, and little eels, for example—with a net in ditches outside Waalwijk, the town where he was raised. He brought some of them home and kept them in buckets in his family's backyard, creating a hybrid of zoo and laboratory, where he bred mice and stickleback fish. He also kept jackdaws, smaller, grayer relatives of the crow, which he described as "still my favorite bird" in an autobiographical sketch he wrote for the Web site for *Our Inner Ape.* In 1966 de Waal began studying biology at the University of Nijmegen (now Radboud University Nijmegen). "Most of the animals I saw smelled of formaldehyde," he wrote in his sketch, "and had no behavior left in them." While conducting cognition tests on two male chimpanzees in Nijmegen's Psychology Department, he became convinced that what interested him most were living animals. In 1970 de Waal received a *kandidaats* degree, a rough equivalent of the British or American bachelor's degree. Rather than staying at Nijmegen to pursue a *doctoraal* (typically, a two-year degree, similar to a British or American master's, completed at the same university as the *kandidaats*), de Waal transferred to the University of Groningen and began to study ethology, both by observing a colony of jackdaws and investigating how the behavior of rats was affected by brain stimulation. "It was the heyday of Dutch ethology," de Waal wrote in his autobiographical essay, "and I took full advantage." De Waal earned his *doctoraal* from Groningen in 1973, by which time he had taken up the study of primates at the University of Utrecht under professor Jan van Hooff. In 1975, after about three years in Utrecht, studying aggression among a largely arboreal primate known as the long-tailed macaque—the subject of his doctoral dissertation—de Waal went to Arnhem to write his thesis and to observe chimpanzees at the Burgers' Zoo, which van Hooff's brother directed.

When de Waal began his work at the zoo, which opened in 1971, the chimpanzee colony numbered roughly 25 chimpanzees, ranging from newborns to adults of about 40 years of age. Using a stool near the animals' one-hectare (2.47-acre) island as his observation post, de Waal spent about 6,000 hours watching and recording his subjects's activities, sometimes using binoculars. Though carefully designed, the environment in which the chimps lived could not, of course, duplicate the wild, and in *Chimpanzee Politics* de Waal wrote that one key difference involved the procurement of food. Captive chimpanzees, freed from having to worry about finding food, put more of their energy into their social lives. Though those circumstances served de Waal's purpose well, it also meant that to make any claims about chimpanzees in general, he had to compare his findings with information available from field observations. As de Waal later explained in *Peacemaking among Primates*, "Ethologists base their conclusions on observable behavior, following rigorous methods of data collection. For a certain action to be classified as 'aggressive,' for instance, the action has to include several specific behavior patterns that previous analyses have shown to be associated with chasing and biting. Subjective determination of the meaning of the action is thus eliminated. I have consistently followed these procedures: for every anecdote in [*Chimpanzee Politics*] hundreds of records have been entered into our computer."

In 1979, having published a number of papers about the chimps in scientific journals, de Waal began writing, in longhand and in Dutch, what would eventually be published in 1982 as *Chimpanzee Politics* (by his own account, his most frequently cited book). Originally conceived as a somewhat formal scientific text with a popular bent, the book takes an openly anthropomorphic and anecdotal approach, with the personalities of many members of the Arnhem zoo's chimp colony described in page-long sketches, along with portrait-like photos that accentuate their individuality. In the introduction to the revised edition (1998), de Waal wrote that the book "demonstrates something we had already suspected on the grounds of the close connection between apes and humans: that the social organization of chimpanzees is almost too human to be true." Instead of detailing spontaneous outbursts among a rigidly hierarchical and largely aggressive group of animals, *Chimpanzee Politics* reveals the premeditation and social back-and-forth that allow dominance within the colony to pass from one group member to another, while the chimps' society remains stable—a process so intricate and so dependent on cultivating support from key individuals that de Waal calls their behavior Machiavellian (after the Italian writer Niccolò Machiavelli [1469–1527], whose most famous work, *The Prince*, prescribes methods for acquiring and maintaining power).

Although his dissertation adviser, van Hooff, recommended that he steer clear of descriptions or conclusions that might upset other scholars, and although he had been trained to avoid assigning humanlike feelings—let alone subtle political intentions—to animals, de Waal wrote in the preface to a revised edition of *Chimpanzee Politics*, "I didn't mind following my intuitions and convictions, however controversial these might be," in part because he saw himself as "a beginning scientist, in my early thirties, without much to lose." His instincts proved to be sound: *Chimpanzee Politics* was widely lauded by the popular press, and most scientists greeted de Waal's analyses with interest rather than shock or outrage. In the London *Times Literary Supplement* (October 15, 1982), R. A. Hinde praised de Waal's "careful observation" and wrote that his book "achieves the dual goal which eludes so many writers about animal behavior—it will both fascinate the nonspecialist and be seen as an important contribution to science." Businesspeople, too, expressed enthusiasm for the book, discovering in it a clear prescription for building support within a group and prospering thereby. In a 1985 article from *Success!* magazine reprinted in the *Chicago Tribune* (March 10, 1985), Duncan Maxwell Anderson wrote that de Waal's first book "has been hailed by numerous biologists as the most important book on animal behavior in the last 50 years."

In 1981 de Waal came to the U.S. for what was supposed to be a yearlong research appointment at the Wisconsin National Primate Research Center at the University of Wisconsin in Madison. Less than a month after his arrival, he agreed to stay for the long term. In Wisconsin de Waal shifted his focus to reciprocal social behavior and the then-unknown study of peace and reconciliation among primates. Over the next 10 years, he pursued those avenues of study through different approaches. In his longest project (1981–91), he investigated modes of dominance among a group of macaques that lived in Madison's Henry Vilas Zoo. (Later, until 2001, de Waal studied rhesus monkeys—also called rhesus macaques—and stump-tailed macaques at other zoos as well as research centers in Wisconsin and Georgia.) Another project began in 1983 at the San Diego Zoo, in California, where de Waal made detailed observations of bonobos. Many of his subsequent books and articles offer research findings and photos connected with that project. The foundations of de Waal's current research into feelings of empathy and various forms of selfless behavior began with a brief stint at the Yerkes National Primate Research Center in 1986.

In addition to writing or co-authoring dozens of articles for scientific journals in the years following the publication of *Chimpanzee Politics*, de Waal wrote another book: *Peacemaking among Primates* (1989). In it he reviewed the evidence of reconciliatory behavior in chimpanzees, bonobos, stump-tailed macaques, rhesus monkeys, and humans. Though most of the book is about nonhuman animals, de Waal wrote in the prologue that his "main purpose here is to correct biology's bleak orientation on the human condition." "In a decade in which peace has become the single most important public issue, it is essential to introduce the accumulated evidence that, for humans, making peace is as natural as making war," he declared. Widely reviewed and widely praised, *Peacemaking among Primates* won the 1989 *Los Angeles Times* Book Prize for science and technology. "De Waal demonstrates that science can be like poetry: Once a truth is stated, our vision shifts and we cannot imagine how we did not see it before," Betty-ann Kevles wrote for that newspaper's book-review section (November 5, 1989).

In 1991 de Waal accepted a full-time teaching position in the Psychology Department at Emory University. He became a full professor in 1993 and was named to an endowed professorship in 1996. Also in 1991 he accepted a research professorship—a university-affiliated position, of the sort he had held at Wisconsin, that does not necessarily involve teaching—with the Yerkes National Primate Research Center, the nation's oldest and largest primate center, with some 3,400 individuals representing seven primate species. By teaching, as he told Regina Nuzzo, he would leave a "legacy" in the form of students whose future work will be inspired to some degree by his own. At the primate center, by contrast, he could devote himself full-time to the chimpanzees at the center's field station in Lawrenceville, Georgia. "There's lots of good stuff you can do in monkey work," de Waal told Nuzzo, "but if you're interested in questions of higher cognition and human evolution, then apes have a great advantage." During that period de Waal began to perform more experiments than he had previously, studying what he termed cultural transmission among the chimpanzees and a number of similarly complex behaviors among a group of more than 30 brown capuchin monkeys in a laboratory established especially for de Waal.

De Waal's third book for a popular audience, *Good Natured: The Origins of Right and Wrong in Humans and Other Animals* (1996), examines primate behaviors that seem to indicate that animals can recognize distinctions between just and unjust acts. Drawing on his own research and the work of others, especially that of the biologist Robert Trivers, who developed the concept of reciprocal altruism—the idea that animals will assist each other in the expectation that they will be repaid in the future—de Waal examined evidence that animals, like humans, can experience such feelings as sympathy and empathy. "Mr. de Waal wisely avoids drawing social or political conclusions from his work," the linguist Derek Bickerton wrote for the *New York Times Book Review* (March 24, 1996). "However, politicians, social scientists and moral philosophers alike will ignore his insights at their peril. Anyone who cares about humans or their future will profit from this excellent book, which sheds at least as much light on our own lives as it does on those of other creatures."

The following year de Waal and the renowned wildlife photographer Frans Lanting published *Bonobo: The Forgotten Ape*, about a rare and endangered species. De Waal has said that that book represents a way of confronting what he sees as a particularly American prudishness, because a discussion of peacemaking and other social-stabilization skills among bonobos necessarily involves a discussion of their sexual behavior. With frequent, brief sexual encounters many times a day among bonobos of both sexes and virtually all ages, the animals use sexuality, according to de Waal, to soothe one another and keep the group functioning well. Furthermore, the fact that bonobos—which, genetically, are humans' closest relatives—have pacific natures casts doubts on descriptions of human evolution that have emphasized our similarities to more aggressive primates. De Waal's essays brought him commendations in the popular press, though some specialists considered the book a flawed introduction to the bonobo as a whole.

In *The Ape and the Sushi Master* (2001), de Waal offered a far-ranging discussion of culture as it manifests itself among both humans and other animals, especially primates, and even among dogs and tigers. To de Waal culture is essentially learned behavior—or, as he wrote in the book's prologue, "the nongenetic spreading of habits and information." He added: "The rest is nothing but embellishment." The book received highly positive reviews on both sides of the Atlantic, though a minority took issue with de Waal's broad definition of culture. Among the latter was Kenan Malik, who in the London *Sunday Telegraph* (June 24, 2001) wrote that humans "constantly innovate, transforming ourselves, individually and collectively, in the process," whereas what de Waal considers chimpanzee culture, for example, has stayed virtually the same for its entire existence.

In 2003 de Waal selected more than 120 photographs from the estimated 50,000 he had taken over the past three decades to create *My Family Album*, a coffee-table book in which full-page reproductions of photos appear opposite brief notes about each image. In *Natural History* (December 2003), Laurence A. Marschall wrote that de Waal's "tight focus on faces, made possible because his subjects knew him so well, conveys a genuine sense of intimacy." De Waal, Marschall concluded, "obviously has a great love for the apes and monkeys he's known, and his pictures and anecdotes invite the reader to feel, rightly, that primates are members of our own extended family." De Waal's book *Our Inner Ape* (2005) argues for a revised picture of human nature based on the behavioral and biological similarities between humans and the two species most closely related to us—the bonobo and the chimpanzee. With characteristics of the peace-loving bonobos and the far more aggressive and status-minded chimps, humans are "bipolar apes," de Waal claimed. Spiced with anecdotes and supported by decades of careful study, *Our Inner Ape* won over many critics, even ones who disagreed with details of his arguments.

De Waal's most recent book, *Primates and Philosophers: How Morality Evolved* (2006), is based on the Tanner Lectures, which he delivered at the Center for Human Values at Princeton University in 2004. In that volume de Waal suggested that humans share with our evolutionary predecessors such traits as fairness, reciprocal altruism, and morality, and that those characteristics have developed through natural selection. While the idea that altruism is a product of evolution is not new, de Waal's thesis is distinguished by the empirical evidence that backs his arguments.

In 1980 de Waal married Catherine C. Marin. He and his wife live in Stone Mountain, Georgia. De Waal's leisure activities include playing the piano, baking, and taking care of his cats. He also raises freshwater fish in a 120-gallon tank in his study.
—D.R.

Suggested Reading: Living Links Center Web site; *London Review of Books* (on-line) Sep. 20, 2001; *Our Inner Ape* Web site; *Paula Gordon Show* Web site, 1997; *Proceedings of the National Academy of Sciences* p11137+ Aug. 9, 2005

Selected Books: *Chimpanzee Politics: Power and Sex among Apes*, 1982; *Peacemaking among Primates*, 1989; *Good Natured: The Origins of Right and Wrong in Humans and Other Animals*, 1996; *Bonobo: The Forgotten Ape* (with Frans Lanting), 1997; *The Ape and the Sushi Master: Cultural Reflections of a Primatologist*, 2001; *My Family Album: Thirty Years of Primate Photography*, 2003; *Our Inner Ape: A Leading Primatologist Explains Why We Are Who We Are*, 2005; *Primates and Philosophers: How Morality Evolved*, 2006; as editor—*Tree of Origin: What Primate Behavior Can Tell Us about Human Social Evolution*, 2002; as coeditor—*Coalitions and Alliances in Humans and Other Animals* (with Alexander H. Harcourt), 1992; *Natural Conflict Resolution* (with Filippo Aureli), 2000; *Animal Social Complexity: Intelligence, Culture, and Individualized Societies* (Peter L. Tyack), 2003

Dionne, E. J. Jr.

Apr. 23, 1952– Journalist; author

Address: Washington Post, 1150 15th St., N.W., Washington, DC 20071

The op-ed columnist and political commentator E. J. Dionne Jr. has been hailed as one of the most thoughtful and articulate analysts currently covering national politics. A former domestic and foreign correspondent for the *New York Times*, Dionne has written a syndicated column for the *Washington Post* since 1993 and has aired his views regularly on CNN, National Public Radio, and NBC's *Meet the Press*. He has also written three well-received books on Washington, D.C., politics and co-edited a number of others. In a review of Dionne's 2004 title, *Stand Up Fight Back: Republican Toughs, Democratic Wimps, and the Politics of Revenge*, David Greenberg wrote for the *Washington Post* (July 18, 2004), "Painstakingly fair-minded, his writings radiate an earnest resolve to ponder complex problems and reach reasoned judgments." Critics have praised Dionne for the intellectualism that informs his writing and for his willingness to take into account both liberal and conservative views. In the magazine *America* (February 17, 1996), George W. Hunt described Dionne as "arguably the finest political commentator in our nation. Other columnists are more famous—often to the same degree that they are more partisan, opinionated or simply outrageous—but he repre-

Alex Wong/Getty

E. J. Dionne Jr.

sents that bright handful who are not only judicious, fair-minded and gifted with a sense of American history but who compose their reflections in intelligent, lucid prose." In his columns and books, Dionne discusses in their complexity political issues that are often simplified in the media and illuminates the role that government plays in the lives of citizens. While exhibiting a belief in progressive ideals (he favors the word "progressive" over "liberal," which he feels has acquired negative connotations), he dissects and criticizes the actions of Republicans and Democrats alike. In an interview with Harry Kreisler, published on the Web site of the Institute of International Studies at the University of California at Berkeley (March 8, 2001), Dionne described his politics as "a combination of . . . Catholic tradition, a sort of . . . social democratic tradition, and then a practical moderate tradition. . . . Sometimes I say my heart's on the left and my head's more in the center. But my heart is still on that side."

Dionne's views—liberal while stressing the importance of family and community—were clearly influenced by his upbringing. He told Kreisler that debating political issues (along with attending church) was a staple of his household: "My dad had a wonderful idea, which I hope to stick to. He thought it was a good thing for kids to argue with their parents. . . . He would usually take a position well to the right of his own, and I would often take a position to the left of my own, and we would go at it." Those arguments, Dionne said, led to his belief that "you can disagree with someone and love them all the same; that argument, itself, is not a bad thing."

Eugene J. Dionne Jr. was born on April 23, 1952 in Boston, Massachusetts, and grew up in Fall River, about 50 miles south of Boston. His father was a dentist, his mother a teacher and librarian. Dionne told Harry Kreisler that Fall River was an unusually political town. "A friend of mine," he noted, "once said that there were three kinds of people in Fall River: people running for office, people getting ready to run for office, and people recovering from running for office." Dionne described his father as having been "a compassionate conservative before compassion and conservatism was cool. He was also very independent minded, so he was against the Vietnam War before I was, which is very much the reverse of what happened with a lot of people at that time."

In 1969 Dionne enrolled at Harvard University, in Cambridge, Massachusetts, not far from his hometown. He found that his exposure in Fall River to people of all economic classes gave him a perspective on the socioeconomic aspects of the antiwar movement that some of his college peers lacked. He told Kreisler, "I used to bring down lots of my friends to work on various political campaigns in Fall River. That was a time when there were a lot of people who were Marxist or claiming to be Marxist, and I always told them it was about time they actually met the working class that they talk about so much." At Harvard Dionne's interest in political debate was further fueled, in particular by a course called Capitalism and Socialism, taught jointly by professors who argued passionately with each other: Michael Walzer, whom Dionne described to Kreisler as a "great democratic socialist and political philosopher" who "very much shaped my view," and Robert Nozick, "the libertarian political philosopher." Dionne also gained experience in practical aspects of political journalism, such as using computers and polling. He graduated from Harvard summa cum laude with a B.A. degree in social studies in 1973. He later attended Oxford University, in England, as a Rhodes Scholar, earning a Ph.D. in sociology in 1982. His first job was to prepare polls for the *New York Times* and CBS. From 1975 to 1989 Dionne worked as a reporter for the *Times*, covering national and global politics and corresponding from such locales as Rome, Italy; Paris, France; and Beirut, Lebanon. He also lived in Albany, New York, for two years, reporting on state politics. In 1990 he joined the *Washington Post*, where he continued to cover national politics.

Dionne's first book, *Why Americans Hate Politics: The Death of the Democratic Process*, was published in 1991. In the book Dionne summarized American political thought from the 1960s onward and examined what he believed to be a growing indifference among the American public toward a political system that was increasingly irrelevant to their lives. Politicians, Dionne claimed, had become too absorbed in arguing ideological points with their opponents, leading those outside politics to lose interest. Dionne told Kreisler, "The core argument of the book is that politics in America was cast as a series of false choices. That we argued, say, about whether feminism was a good thing, or the family was a good thing. In fact, most Americans think equality between men and women is a good thing, and that the family is a good thing, and that the false choice perspective wasn't a very constructive or helpful way to talk about the problem." Dionne suggested that the most relevant ideas across the political spectrum (for example, conservatives' stance on "family values" and liberals' concern for racial equality) should be combined and put to more practical use. Norman J. Ornstein wrote for the *New York Times Book Review* (May 19, 1991) that the book is "knowledgeable and sympathetic to all viewpoints while comprehending and communicating intricate personality, policy and doctrinal disputes. Mr. Dionne writes with the sprightly facility of a good journalist, while displaying the intellectual depth of the Ph.D. historian he is." *Why Americans Hate Politics* was a 1991 National Book Award finalist and won the *Los Angeles Times* book prize in the current-interest category.

Dionne served as a guest scholar at the Woodrow Wilson International Center, a nonpartisan center for political dialogue in Washington, D.C., in 1994 and 1995. Earlier, in 1993, he had begun writing an op-ed column for the *Post*, which became syndicated in 1996 and is now featured in more than 90 newspapers in the U.S. and abroad. Dionne's next book, *They Only Look Dead: Why Progressives Will Dominate the Next Political Era*, was published in 1996. That volume predicted that the politics of limited government and free-market capitalism endorsed by House Speaker Newt Gingrich and the Republican-led 104th Congress would be countered increasingly from the left by a revival of progressivism and an emphasis on government activism—the latter of which, Dionne argued, was not synonymous with a loss of personal freedoms. Reviewers pointed out that Dionne used the term "progressive" both because of the negative connotations of the word "liberal" and because the viewpoints he believed would, or should, become more prevalent were closely aligned with those of such American progressives of the past as Presidents Theodore Roosevelt and Woodrow Wilson. Those leaders believed that a strong, active central government was capable of promoting political awareness and virtuosity among citizens. *They Only Look Dead* contended that the majority of Americans belonged to the "Anxious Middle," a class of citizens increasingly concerned about their place in an ever more technologically oriented, globally competitive world. Such voters, Dionne suggested, elected the politicians, Republican or Democratic, whom they saw as most capable of addressing those concerns. In a review of *They Only Look Dead*, James Fallows wrote for *Washington Monthly* (May 1996), "Dionne does not pretend that he has solved the problem of reconceiving government's role. But he has given us much to think about."

Stand Up Fight Back: Republican Toughs, Democratic Wimps, and the Politics of Revenge (2004), Dionne's third book, examines the ways in which the Democratic and Republican Parties present themselves in the media. The book attributes the Republicans' continued electoral success in recent years—which belied the fact that the public did not necessarily favor their policies—to the Democrats' own failure to show themselves as representing a clear set of values in opposition to those of the GOP. On a number of issues, including the vote recount in Florida after the 2000 presidential election, the 2003 U.S.-led invasion of Iraq, and the tax cuts instituted by President George W. Bush, Democrats failed to take a firm stand, according to the book. Dionne argued that Democrats had internalized Republicans' charges that they were "soft" (a label dating back to the Cold War, when Democrats were deemed "soft on communism") and that, in trying to avoid appearing soft, they came across as indecisive and divided. Fearful of alienating moderate voters, Dionne contended, the Democrats were often vague in expressing their beliefs, in contrast to Republicans, whose consistently savvy media manipulation helped them to project clear messages. Dionne wrote, according to the *Austin-American (Texas) Statesman* (July 25, 2004), that the Democratic Party, which "once galvanized a nation by declaring that there is nothing to fear but fear itself became afraid—afraid of being too liberal, of being weak on defense, of being culturally permissive, of being seen as apologizing for big government." Dionne was praised for his balanced analysis of the state of the Democratic Party. An uncredited article in *Kirkus Reviews* (April 15, 2004) called *Stand Up Fight Back* "balm for those who long to see a revivified—and not-quite-so-spiteful—opposition and a return to Kennedy era liberalism."

Dionne has been a senior fellow in the Governance Studies Program at the Brookings Institution, in Washington, D.C., since 1996. The aim of the program, according to the institution's Web site, is to analyze "the means or mechanisms by which Americans and citizens in other democracies govern themselves." In 2001 Dionne helped found the Pew Forum on Religion and Public Life, which gathers information through polls and provides government officials, journalists, and others with reports on topics pertaining to religion and public policy. The forum also serves as a "town hall," according to its Web site, "provid[ing] a neutral venue through its various issue roundtables and briefings for discussions of important issues where religion and domestic and international politics intersect." Since 2003 Dionne has held a tenured position as professor of foundations of American democracy and culture at Georgetown University, in Washington, D.C. In addition to the books he has written, he has served as co-editor of volumes including *What's God Got to Do with the American Experiment?* (with John Dilulio Jr., 2000), *Bush V. Gore* (with William Kristol, 2000),

Sacred Places, Civic Purposes: Should Government Help Faith-Based Charity? (with Ming Hsu Chen, 2001), and *One Electorate Under God: A Dialogue on Religion and American Politics* (2004). In 1997 he was named one of the 25 most influential Washington journalists by the *National Journal* and as being among the capital city's top 50 journalists by *Washingtonian* magazine. Dionne lives in Washington, D.C., with his wife, Mary, and their three children, James, Julia and Margot.

— M.B.

Suggested Reading: *America* (on-line) Feb. 17, 1996; Brookings Institution Web site; Institute of International Studies, University of California at Berkeley, Conversations with History Web site; *Time* (on-line) Mar. 11, 1996

Selected Books: *Why Americans Hate Politics: The Death of the Democratic Process,* 1991; *They Only Look Dead: Why Progressives Will Dominate the Next Political Era,* 1996; *Stand Up Fight Back: Republican Toughs, Democratic Wimps, and the Politics of Revenge,* 2004

Dobbs, Lou

Sep. 24, 1945– Broadcast journalist; author

Address: CNN, One Time Warner Center, New York, NY 10019

"Night after night, Lou Dobbs slides into his anchor chair, turns to the camera and becomes the sober and steady face of CNN . . . ," Rachel L. Swarns wrote for the *New York Times* (February 15, 2006) about the longtime host of CNN's series *Moneyline* and, since 2003, of the show *Lou Dobbs Tonight.* "He has more than three decades of experience . . . and a voice that rumbles with authority. And for most of his program, he looks and feels like a traditional, nothing-but-the-news television host. Then the topic turns to illegal immigration, and the sober newsman starts breathing fire." Television's "first economic populist," as Ellsworth Quarrels characterized him in *Across the Board* (May/June 2005), Dobbs vehemently opposes the increasingly common practice among U.S. corporations—as well as in government at the city, state, and federal levels—of outsourcing jobs to other nations. He has condemned that practice, along with tolerance of illegal immigration in both the public and private sectors, as a betrayal of middle-class Americans. "The power of big business over our national life has never been greater," he wrote in the second of his three books, *Exporting America: Why Corporate Greed Is Shipping American Jobs Overseas.* "Never have there been fewer business leaders willing to commit to the national interest over selfish interest, to the good of the country over that of

the companies they head." A self-described moderate Republican, Dobbs "is not content merely to lay out every new permutation in these stories," as Robert Wilson, the editor of the *American Scholar,* wrote for the Winter 2006 issue of that publication; "each night he blusters and gets red in the face, making it clear that he does not attribute the deficiencies he reports to incompetence or corruption. No, every instance is prima facie evidence of treason. His passion . . . seems to me unique in public life, both for its sincerity and its single-mindedness."

Except for the years (1999–2001) when he served as the chief executive officer and chairman of a start-up company called Space.com, Dobbs has appeared on CNN since 1980 (the year the cable station came into existence), reporting on business events, issues, and trends and their implications nationally and internationally. Since 2003 he has reported on a wider range of happenings. "Lou Dobbs basically did an astounding thing," Roger Ailes, the chief executive and chairman of the Fox News Channel, said to Richard Katz for *Variety* (June 14–20, 1999). "He went into a general news franchise . . . and with pure tenacity and force of will and vision, created himself as a leading business news anchor in the industry." Dobbs's first position at CNN was chief economics correspondent; he has also held such titles there as vice president and managing editor of business news, senior vice president, and executive vice president. Currently, he is the anchor and managing editor of *Lou Dobbs Tonight.* From 1995 to 1999 he served as the president and executive vice president, respectively, of the now-defunct CNNfn and CNNfn.com. He has anchored the syndicated radio program *The Lou Dobbs Financial Report* since 2001, and he has written columns for *Money* magazine (2001–04) and *U.S. News & World Report* (2002–05).

Every month since 2003 Dobbs has published the *Lou Dobbs Money Letter,* which offers investment advice and includes in every issue an interview with the CEO of a featured company. For the annual price of $199, subscribers also receive a "weekly hotline update" and access to an exclusive Web site. As Zachary Roth pointed out in *CJR Daily* (June 17, 2004, on-line) and as James K. Glassman noted for *Capitalism Magazine* (March 4, 2004, on-line), in articles whose titles both included the words "Two Faces of Lou Dobbs," Dobbs has often recommended investments in companies that he has included on a list of hundreds of firms that are "either sending American jobs overseas, or choosing to employ cheap overseas labor, instead of American workers." When Roth asked him about the "contradiction in fingering outsourcers with one hand, while recommending the same companies as investment opportunities with the other," Dobbs responded, "You seem to be suggesting that one cannot criticize corporate America without calling for its destruction. Or because one believes a company to be well-managed that it's beyond criticism. . . . Surely, you don't believe that

Evan Agostini/Getty Images

Lou Dobbs

your readers or my viewers are incapable of abhorring a business practice, and at the same time acknowledging the success of a corporation." When Bill Moyers, interviewing Dobbs for alternet.org (August 21, 2004), referred to Roth's article and then asked Dobbs about his seemingly contradictory stances, Dobbs said, "I've never suggested [to] anyone they make an investment judgment based on whether a company outsources or does not outsource. I suggest people make investment decisions based on the value of the company, the importance, the relevance, the success of its products. And the commitment of its management . . . to being a better corporate citizen." Among Dobbs's honors are the Man of the Year Award from the Organization for the Rights of American Workers and an Emmy Award for his single-item newscast "Exporting America" (both in 2004) and a Lifetime Achievement Emmy for business and financial reporting (2005).

Louis Dobbs was born on September 24, 1945 in Childress, a rural community in the Texas panhandle, where his parents, Frank and May Dobbs, owned farm-supply and propane-gas businesses. His family moved to Rupert, Idaho, when he was about eight years old. "I feel very fortunate for growing up in southern Idaho," he told Dan Fields for the Idaho *Times-News* (April 16, 2001). "There's that code of the West. I've always prized individualism." He told Joyce Saenz Harris for the *Dallas Morning News* (January 3, 1999) that his family was poor, "but I didn't know it for the most part because nearly everyone in a farming community was [poor]. Some people might have a newer car or an older pickup, but that was just about the difference." He told the same reporter that his fa-

ther always advised him to "say what you mean, and mean what you say," and both his parents emphasized that nothing is impossible, "as long as I worked in school." During his youth Dobbs worked on farms, sometimes with migrant workers. He also hunted, skied, and went fishing and whitewater rafting, and he enjoyed stargazing as well. When he was a teenager, he and a few of his friends "took out a semi-truck and started contract-hauling hay for a nickel a bale," as he recalled to Saenz Harris. "What we hadn't calculated was that, all summer long, those bales kept getting heavier. Actually, it took an embarrassingly long time to figure out that those bales had started out at about 80 pounds, and by the end of the summer were 120." "That was my first experience in watching numbers a little more closely than I had before," he added.

At Minidoka County High School, in Rupert, Dobbs excelled in science, mathematics, English, and history and was a member of the football team. In his senior year he was elected student-body president. One of his teachers, Elizabeth Toolson, "took me under her wing and taught me how to debate and how to organize my thinking," he told Saenz Harris. Toolson helped Dobbs fill out an application to Harvard University, in Cambridge, Massachusetts, a school about which Dobbs had only the vaguest knowledge. He gained admission, with a scholarship, and entered the freshman class in 1963. "I had a terrific experience there—but boy, the culture shock was extraordinary," he told Saenz Harris. He considered majoring in political science until he attended a debate between Paul Samuelson and Milton Friedman, each of whom later won the Nobel Prize in Economics. Friedman, an advocate of laissez-faire capitalism, "instantly became one of my heroes," Dobbs said to Saenz Harris. He added, "There's no question about the drudgery of it"—that is, economics as a discipline—"the dreariness of much of it. But the fact is, economics—I believed then and I believe now—is absolutely essential to an understanding of our society and our political system." At Harvard Dobbs joined the Marine Corps Reserves after injuring a knee while playing with the campus football team. Dobbs earned a bachelor's degree at Harvard in 1967.

After his graduation Dobbs, "committed to what I saw as some idea of serving the community," as he put it to Saenz Harris, got jobs in the private and public sectors helping unemployed people gain skills. He soon grew disenchanted with that work; his next position, too, at a bank near Los Angeles, California, failed to engage his interest. Noting that a few of his friends seemed happy as reporters, he tried to get work with KABC-TV in Los Angeles but was told that he first had to have relevant experience. Within weeks he had secured a job as a news reporter with KBLU, a radio station in Yuma, Arizona. "Suddenly, I was getting up at 4 o'clock in the morning and going around to the police department, the Yuma County sheriff's office, the fire department . . . and I loved it," he recalled to Saenz Harris. He later worked for KING-TV, in Seattle, Washington, as a reporter and weekend news anchor, and for the *Los Angeles Times* as a copy reader.

In June 1980, when Ted Turner launched CNN as a 24-hour, live-news television network, Dobbs came on board as the chief economics correspondent and the anchor of *Moneyline*. (Some sources identify him as a "founding member" of CNN.) On *Moneyline*, which aired every weeknight, Dobbs and prominent guests discussed national and international business issues and news in the context of other current events and public policy. In 1970, when about 10 million shares were traded daily on the New York Stock Exchange (NYSE), viewers interested in more than the minute or two of business news offered on TV news broadcasts had no source other than the Friday-night public-television program *Wall Street Week*, anchored by Louis Rukeyser. By late 1981, as John J. O'Connor noted in the *New York Times* (November 1, 1981, online), the number of shares traded on the NYSE had increased fivefold, and growing numbers of working people in addition to investment specialists and the wealthy were seeking up-to-the-minute information on the stock market and other aspects of the economy. *Moneyline* thus had a ready-made audience. In terms of revenue from advertising dollars, it became CNN's most profitable program; because its viewership was relatively small (fewer than half a million individuals at most), for many years it reportedly earned more money per viewer than any other program on TV. Dobbs won the George Foster Peabody Award for his coverage of the stock-market crash of October 19, 1987, when—for reasons never determined—the Dow Jones Industrial average fell nearly 23 percentage points in one day (the second-largest percentage drop in stock-market history, after one that occurred in 1914). In 1988 *Moneyline* earned a CablACE Award for "extended news coverage." Two years later Dobbs received the *Business Journalism Review*'s Luminary Award for his "visionary work, which changed the landscape of business journalism in the 1980s." *Moneyline* was expanded from a half-hour to an hour in 1998. Earlier, and concurrently, in late 1995 Dobbs was named president of CNNfn and executive vice president of CNNfn.com when they debuted. According to Jon Lafayette in *Electronic Media* (June 14, 1999, on-line), Ted Turner agreed to set up CNNfn and its associated Web site "to keep Mr. Dobbs from jumping to business news rival CNBC." Aired on the CNN International channel, CNNfn provided business news every weekday from 7:00 a.m. to 7:00 p.m. (and, subsequently, for another two hours).

In June 1999 Dobbs left CNN to assume the post of chief executive officer and chairman of the company Space.com, which, along with its associated Web site, was launched in July of that year. Media observers linked Dobbs's headline-making departure from CNN to his increasingly strained rela-

tions with Richard N. "Rick" Kaplan, who had become president of the network in 1997. Dobbs, however, told Lafayette that his differences with Kaplan and others at CNN were "irrelevant to my career decision." He also said, "I wanted a new challenge." Dobbs has said that his interest in space and space travel stems in part from his belief in the existence of extraterrestrial intelligence. Cofounded by Dobbs and Rich Zahradnik (a former CNNfn vice president), Space.com was financed by the venture-capital firm SpaceVest, NBC (through its parent company, General Electric), and Venrock, an investment arm of the Rockefeller family, among others. According to a CNN biography of Dobbs, it was "the first multimedia company dedicated to space and space-related content." Its advertiser-supported Web site, as Gillian Flynn wrote for *Entertainment Weekly* (August 13, 1999), was "designed as a repository of news and entertainment about the cosmos." The bursting of the so-called dot.com bubble in 2000 left the company near collapse. An infusion of cash from new investors later revived it, but by that time Dobbs remained only as a minority shareholder and member of the board; in early April 2001 he had signed a five-year contract with CNN worth a total of between $15 million and $25 million. The network's executives "made me a terrific offer," he told Dan Fields. "It was one, frankly, that I couldn't refuse." He told a reporter for the New York *Daily News* (April 11, 2001, on-line) that the timing of CNN's offer was perfect, in part because Rick Kaplan was no longer with CNN and Dobbs liked the network's new management team. In his book *Space: The Next Business Frontier* (2001), which he co-wrote with H. P. Newquist, Dobbs touted the potentials of "S-commerce," or entrepreneurship that takes advantage of opportunities connected with outer space.

Describing *Lou Dobbs Moneyline*, as his program was rechristened, Dobbs told Dan Trigoboff for *Broadcasting & Cable* (May 13, 2002), "The broadcast has always been about the political economy. We've always had a broader context [than pure business news]. I cannot think of any part of this news environment—education, war . . .—that does not influence or is not influenced by economics and our standard of living. This is business news for know-it-alls. This broadcast is aimed at the highest common denominator." In 2003 *Lou Dobbs Moneyline* was renamed *Lou Dobbs Tonight*. That year, with the introduction on his program of a regular segment called "Exporting America," Dobbs became a point man on cable television on the issue of international free trade, the expansion of which, by means of the North American Free Trade Agreement and other pacts, has gravely worsened the United States' trade deficit, in his opinion. "I think every American should be offended by anyone . . . who would suggest there are only two choices in trade policy, protectionism or free trade," Lou Dobbs told a reporter for the Associated Press (April 9, 2004, on-line). "There are a host of choices between those polar extremes. The policy I favor is balanced trade, which is the policy pursued by all of our principal trading partners." Dobbs is similarly critical of outsourcing, or "the shipment of American jobs to cheap foreign labor markets," in his words, which he charges has taken away an enormous number of jobs previously filled by middle-class Americans. "For the first time in the country's history," Dobbs said to Steve Cocheo for *ABA Banking Journal* (May 2004), "we are shipping jobs overseas to provide products and services for export *back* into this country. That's never happened on the scale on which it now appears to be happening. And never before have businesses tried to either rationalize or camouflage what they are doing by saying it's a question of competitiveness and productivity and efficiency when what they really mean is that it is a question of labor price." "The ultimate message in outsourcing is this: America be damned," Dobbs said to Michael McCarthy for *USA Today* (February 23, 2005). "It's all about the lowest cost. . . . The pain that's being exacted on our middle class from so many quarters is intolerable." Dobbs has also taken a hard-line stance against the presence of illegal immigrants in the U.S. He presented arguments in support of his positions on outsourcing and illegal immigrants in his books *Exporting America: Why Corporate Greed Is Shipping American Jobs Overseas* (2004) and *War on the Middle Class: How the Government, Big Business, and Special Interest Groups Are Waging War on the American Dream and How to Fight Back* (2006).

In his *CJR Daily* article, in which he took Dobbs to task for the seeming contradiction between his anti-outsourcing stance and some of the recommendations in the *Lou Dobbs Money Letter*, Zachary Roth wrote, "[Dobbs] makes a distinction, he said, between bad practices and those who practice them. . . . But Dobbs's newsletter doesn't just 'acknowledge' successful corporations. He goes further, painting his featured companies as good corporate citizens—and encourages readers to invest in them partly on that basis—without mentioning that they conduct business practices that, by his own admission, he 'detests.' Most of Dobbs's CNN viewers don't have access to the information in . . . his investment guide. So the larger public sees only one Lou Dobbs: the outspoken anti-outsourcing crusader. The other Lou Dobbs is available only for . . . [a] fee. And that's the Lou Dobbs who doesn't appear to be putting his money where his mouth is."

Writing for *In These Times* (April 4, 2006, online) Susan Douglas, a professor of communications at the University of Michigan, recalled that she "used to watch Dobbs for what are called surveillance purposes; how do right-leaning, pro-business types report and spin the news?" "Now," she continued, "I try not to miss Dobbs, in part because he seems to be deliberately crafting a new kind of anchor persona—that of the outraged everyday American, the one who is indeed 'mad as hell and not gonna take it anymore.' He expresses his incredulity over [President George W. Bush's] pronouncements and policies in his give-and-take with CNN reporters, addresses the audience directly with sarcastic rhetorical questions and has abandoned the more neutral, objectivity-adhering stylings of news anchors. He has also been walking an interesting political line, conservative about some issues, especially American immigration policy, populist about others, including corporate giveaways and the privileging of business interests over national security." By contrast, Peter Tirschwell, writing for the *Journal of Commerce* (April 10, 2006), called Dobbs "a modern-day Charles Lindbergh, a new face of isolationism," and for the *San Francisco Chronicle* (May 9, 2005, on-line), Tim Goodman wrote, "Dobbs is running amok inciting the nation about undocumented immigrants while CNN chooses to do nothing about his fearmongering."

Dobbs's current wife, the former Debi Segura, is a one-time CNN sportscaster. The couple live on a 300-acre horse farm in Sussex County, New Jersey; Dobbs also raises horses on two farms in Texas. The Dobbses' twin daughters, Hillary and Heather, who entered college in 2006, are prize-winning equestrians. From his first marriage Dobbs has two adult sons, Chance and Jason, and one granddaughter. His recreational activities include playing golf.

—D.F.

Suggested Reading: *ABA Banking Journal* p32+ May 2004; *Across the Board* p57+ May/June 2005; CNN.com; *Broadcasting & Cable* p95 June 14, 1999, p41 Aug. 20, 2001, p30 May 13, 2002; *Dallas Morning News* E p1+ Jan. 3, 1999; emmyonline.org; *In These Times* (on-line) Apr. 4, 2006; *New York Times* (on-line) Feb. 15, 2006; *SmartMoney* p69+ June 1997; *USA Today* B p3 Feb. 23, 2005

Selected Books: *Space: The Next Business Frontier* (with H. P. Newquist), 2001; *Exporting America: Why Corporate Greed Is Shipping American Jobs Overseas*, 2004; *War on the Middle Class: How the Government, Big Business, and Special Interest Groups Are Waging War on the American Dream and How to Fight Back*, 2006

Tony Avelear/AFP/Getty Images

Donovan, Landon

Mar. 4, 1982– Soccer player

Address: Los Angeles Galaxy, 18400 Avalon Blvd., Suite 200, Carson, CA 90746

The soccer player Landon Donovan "has the whole package," a writer for JockBio.com wrote in 2004. "He is quick on his feet and fast in the open field. He has a strong and accurate right leg, and is lethal with his left one, too. He combines these qualities with a scorer's instinct, which means there is no real ceiling on his potential." Donovan was not yet 20 when he established himself as one of the most prominent soccer players in the U.S. Playing with the American national team in international competition at all levels, he won admirers among fans and professionals in both Europe and the U.S. At the age of 17, he became the youngest American to sign a professional contract with a team (the German Bayer Leverkusen) in a top-level European soccer league. At 19, on loan from Leverkusen, he played a major role in transforming one of the worst teams in Major League Soccer (MLS), the Earthquakes, into league champions. "Landon is a very special, special player. He's high-caliber, high-quality, and high-octane," Ray Hudson, the coach of the Miami Fusion in 2001, observed at the end of the Earthquakes' championship season, as Dave Brousseau reported for the Fort Lauderdale, Florida, *Sun Sentinel* (October 10, 2001). "He's the sort of player this country has always yearned for." In both 2002 and 2003 Donovan was named the Honda U.S. Player of the Year, one of his sports' highest honors, and in 2003 and 2004 he was named U.S. Male Soccer Player of the Year by the

U.S. Soccer Federation (USSF). In 2004, for the Web site of the U.S. National Soccer Players Association, Earnie Stewart, the USSF's U.S. Soccer Player of the Year in 2001, said about Donovan, who was then 19, "He's a great player already. He has speed; he's great on the ball; he can dribble opponents. Because he's a young kid, he likes to take on people all of the time." According to a biography of Donovan on the same site, he "is lightning quick on the ball and possesses a lethal touch in front of goal. His vision and skill make him one of the most highly touted players ever to come out of the U.S. youth programs." Donovan has taken on the role of ambassador for soccer in the U.S.; he tirelessly promotes the sport, spending as much time as possible signing autographs and posing for photos with fans. Since 2005 Donovan has been a member of the Los Angeles Galaxy. He was the team's highest scorer during the 2005 season, helping it win the MLS Cup Final.

In 2006 Donovan made a lackluster showing in the World Cup, in Germany, failing to score a goal in three consecutive matches. The U.S. team endured humiliating defeats to the Czech Republic and Ghana (and drew one tie with Italy) and did not advance past the first round. In an interview with Steven Goff for the *Washington Post* (August 26, 2006), Donovan described the criticism he endured as "a little eye-opening." "The human psyche is [conditioned] to find blame somewhere," he said, "and I realize that a lot of times when the team does well, I get credit I shouldn't get, and . . . when it goes bad, I get criticism I don't deserve. A lot of the criticism after the World Cup was fair, too. I know I didn't play well." He finished the 2006 season with the Los Angeles Galaxy with a record of 12 goals and seven assists, while the team plummeted from a first-place finish in 2005 to last place.

Landon Timothy Donovan was born on March 4, 1982 in Ontario, California, and grew up in Redlands, California, a small city that lies 75 miles west of Los Angeles. His mother, Donna Kenney Cash, is a special-education teacher; his father, Tim Donovan, is an employee of a pharmaceutical company who played hockey semi-professionally in Canada when he was young and harbored hopes of joining the National Hockey League. Donovan's parents divorced when he was two; thereafter, he lived with his mother, his older brother, Joshua, and his twin sister, Tristan, with whom he is very close. His father later remarried, moved to Nebraska, and lost contact with his children until Landon entered adolescence and began making a name for himself with the U.S under-16 and under-17 soccer teams. (From his father's second marriage, Landon has two older step-siblings.) Donovan had been playing soccer almost from the moment he could walk. Learning the basics from his brother, who also loved the sport, at age five Donovan begged his mother to allow him to join a league. She agreed, and he found himself competing with six- and seven-year-olds. The other children's added years failed to give them an advantage: during Donovan's first game he scored seven goals. The boy immediately became obsessed with soccer. "He wore soccer clothes to . . . school every day," his sister told Joe Hamelin for the Riverside, California, *Press Enterprise* (June 2, 2002). "He walked around with a soccer ball. All day long. Our . . . babysitter, Connie, who was like our second mom from age 2 to 10, gave him a stuffed soccer ball the size of a regular soccer ball. He slept with that." As a youngster Donovan took violin lessons.

By the time he reached high school, Donovan was receiving expert training from Clint Greenwood, a former player in the Welsh Soccer League and the coach of the Rancho Cucamonga, California, club—called Cal Heat—for which Donovan played. Greenwood, Donovan told Ridge Mahoney for *Soccer Magazine*, as posted on greenwoodsoccer.com, "was always focused on a lot of ball contact. His theory was absolutely perfect: As a kid you need to touch the ball as much as you can. You should always be with the ball." He also said of Greenwood, as quoted on ussoccerplayers.com, "Clint taught me almost every technical skill I have." During his freshman year at Redlands High School, Donovan became a soccer star and was named the Most Valuable Player (MVP) of the area league. The soccer program at Redlands High was weak, however, so the following year he transferred to East Valley High, also in Redlands, to take advantage of its superior coaching. But he spent less time playing for the school than for the U.S. national teams. In the 10 games in which he participated at East Valley High, he scored 16 goals. On the international stage he was also a standout, scoring his first goal in his debut with the U.S. Under-17 team, in a game in which Mexico earned a 2–1 victory. The following year Donovan played increasingly for U.S. national teams. He was instrumental in bringing its Under-16 squad to victory in the Christchurch Cup in New Zealand, a tournament in which he scored 11 goals and was named best player of the tournament by the Fédération Internationale de Football Association (FIFA), the international governing body of soccer. At the season's end he was also named an All-American by the National Soccer Coaches Association of America.

At the age of 16, Donovan was attracting the attention of European teams, especially Bayer Leverkusen, one of the top teams in the Bundesliga, a German league. Officials from Bayer Leverkusen were particularly impressed by his scoring of two goals during the U.S. Under-17 team's 4–3 victory over Argentina at the beginning of 1999. (Donovan told ussoccerplayers.com that John Ellinger, the head coach of the Under-17 team, "turned me into a professional.") By the end of March 1999, Donovan had been offered a $400,000, four-year contract with Bayer Leverkusen. (He had also become the youngest person to play with the U.S. national Under 23 team.) His mother, who wanted him to attend college, urged him to turn the contract down,

but his father encouraged him: "Landon had a chance to do exactly what I had hoped to do," his father told Marc Spiegler for *Sports Illustrated* (April 17, 2000), "but I didn't have the ability or the talent." Donovan, who for several years had dreamed of playing in a European league, eagerly accepted the Germans' offer. But after he joined Bayer Leverkusen, he discovered that the style of play favored in the German league was more physical than what he was used to, and he was relegated to Leverkusen's reserve team in Germany's fourth division, where the level of play was not the best. He also felt lonely, and by the end of 2000, he was reportedly seeking to be loaned to the MLS. (MLS, America's professional soccer league, consists of 12 teams; its season runs from April 1 to the beginning of October and is followed by a postseason competition that culminates with the MLS Cup Final on November 12.) Indeed, negotiations toward that end were taking place behind the scenes, and in March 2001 Leverkusen and the MLS agreed to lend him to an MLS team for two years. (At the end of the 2002 season, the deal was extended for another two years.) Earlier, in 1999, Donovan had participated in the Pan American Games as a member of the U.S. Under-23 team, which won a bronze medal; he started in four games and played in all six. Also in 1999 he was named a parade High School All-American. In 2000 he played in four games at the Summer Olympics, and the USSF named him U.S. Soccer Youth Male Athlete of the Year.

In April 2001 Donovan began playing for the San Jose, California, Earthquakes, which had ended the previous season as one of the worst teams in the league. Donovan flourished on his new team, becoming one of its biggest stars and one of the MLS's best players. On June 2 and July 16 he was named to the Team of the Week, a fantasy squad formed weekly by the magazine *Soccer America* to celebrate players' performances during the previous week. Donovan also won a place on the Western Division's All-Star team, capturing 26,151 votes from fans, more than any other midfielder. He was named MVP after he scored a record-breaking four goals during the All-Star match, which pitted Eastern Division players against their Western Division counterparts. By the end of the regular season, he had scored seven goals and registered 10 assists for the Earthquakes. The accomplishment made him the team's second-leading scorer and helped the Earthquakes reach the playoffs. In the ensuing six matches, Donovan scored five goals, one of which occurred during the cup final, a 2–1 Earthquake victory over the Los Angeles Galaxy. Meanwhile, Donovan was also performing well on the international level. In June he had joined the Under-20 national team and played in the Under-20 World Cup; while the U.S. won only one match, Donovan worked noticeably hard to strengthen the weaknesses in the U.S.'s game plan. In October 2001 he joined the senior national team in its must-win World Cup qualifier against Jamaica. Providing "just the spark the Americans needed after three sluggish losses," as Glenn P. Graham put it in the *Baltimore (Maryland) Sun* (October 8, 2001), Donovan drew the penalty that gave the U.S. its second goal, leading to a 2–1 victory and qualification for the World Cup for the fourth straight year.

In 2002 Donovan scored seven goals and made 20 assists during regular-season play. The team again made it into the play-offs but lost to the Columbus Crew in the opening round, despite Donovan's one goal and one assist. Donovan's greatest successes in 2002 were achieved on the international stage, where he was the only player to start in every game the U.S. played. At the beginning of the season, he was a key member of the squad that won the Gold Cup Championship: he scored that tournament's first goal, in the U.S.'s 2–1 victory over South Korea. For his efforts during that game, he was named Man of the Match, an honor he won again during the U.S.'s shootout victory over Canada in the tournament's semifinals. He was also valuable in the U.S.'s surprising World Cup run to the quarterfinals in Korea/Japan (both countries hosted the competition). He scored two goals during the World Cup tournament. Fútbol de Primera, a Mexican football organization working to promote international soccer in the U.S., honored him for his performance in international play by naming him the Honda Player of the Year. He was the youngest player ever to receive that honor.

In 2003 Donovan scored 12 goals and made six assists for the Earthquakes during the regular season and four goals and two assists during the play-offs. Five of his regular-season goals came in two consecutive games in late September, when he registered a hat trick against the Kansas City Wizards and two goals against FC Dallas. He thus became the 15th player in the history of the MLS to score five goals in two games. Two of his postseason goals came in the MLS Cup Final, in which the Earthquakes took the championship for the second time in three years, beating the Chicago Fire 4–2. Donovan was subsequently named the MLS Cup MVP. His achievements earned him a number of other honors throughout the season, including being named player of the month in both April and September, player of the week in the third week of September, the Los Gatos Brewing Co. Earthquakes' player of the month for September, and the Earthquakes' MVP for the year. He was also named U.S. Soccer Male Athlete of the year. In international competition Donovan led the U.S. team in scoring: his seven goals included four made during the 5–0 win over Cuba in the Gold Cup on July 19. He also registered five assists during the season. Those accomplishments earned him his second Honda U.S. Player of the Year award, making him the first player to be so honored in consecutive years.

During the Earthquakes' regular 2004 season, Donovan scored only six goals and registered 10 assists. The team reached the MLS Cup semifinal,

where it fell to the Kansas City Wizards, 3–2. In international play Donovan performed better, scoring fives goals in 14 games and earning the title Man of the Match four times. He was again named Honda U.S. Player of the Year. In November 2004, as many observers had expected, Donovan announced that he would return to Germany and play with Leverkusen, and he did so in January 2005. "They have assured me that it is not prison I'm going back to," he said, according to Jonathan Nierman, writing for MLSnet.com (November 23, 2004). "I don't expect to go in and just play. You can't just go and be given anything, you have to earn it and I expect to do that, but it's nice to know that they are backing you and supporting you."

Donovan's stay in Germany proved to be short-lived. In January 2005 he made two appearances as a substitute in the closing minutes of two games. He later substituted in four more games and started in two. Dissatisfied with the amount of time he spent on the field, he expressed his desire to play with the Los Angeles Galaxy. That team soon worked out a deal with Leverkusen and bought out Donovan's contract. Donovan returned to the U.S. and began playing with the Los Angeles Galaxy at the beginning of April. "My decision to return to the MLS is one that I have made with thoughtful consideration," Donovan said, as quoted by Agence France Presse (March 31, 2005). "If we as Americans can't contribute to our league, it's a bit of a disservice in growing soccer here in the US." During the regular season with the Galaxy, Donovan registered 10 assists and was the highest-scoring player on the team, with 12 goals in 22 games. In the opinion of George Dohrmann, writing for *Sports Illustrated* (November 2, 2005, online), Donovan pushed the Galaxy "farther into the playoffs than they deserved." Indeed, he led the Galaxy into the finals, which it won in overtime, beating the New England Revolution 1–0. In the qualifying round of the World Cup, he scored six goals in 12 games, helping to assure the U.S. a place in the 2006 tournament.

In June 2006 the U.S. national team, ranked fifth in the world by FIFA, competed in the World Cup, held in Germany. "Americans' success will depend heavily on Donovan, who scored twice in 2002 and was the most influential U.S. player during the recent qualifying campaign," a *Washington Post* (December 10, 2005) writer predicted. Yet from the get-go, Donovan and his teammates performed in a pedestrian manner; in their first match, with the Czech Republic, they were defeated, 3–0. One observer, Jeff Carlisle, wrote for ESPN (June 12, 2006, on-line), "Four years after a sparkling World Cup debut, it appears that Donovan's game hasn't progressed enough to have an impact at the highest level." Though the U.S. bounced back in their second match, which ended in a 1–1 draw against the heavily favored Italy (which went on to win the World Cup), their hope of advancing to the second round ended with their third match, a 2–1 loss to Ghana. As the team's bright young star, Donovan took the brunt of the media criticism aimed at the team. He told Steven Goff, "I should've been more aggressive. I just felt like half the time I was out there I was just going through the motions. What's the point of being there? That's really disappointing for me because I thought I was smarter and I thought I would realize that more. I didn't until it was over, and that's frustrating because you can't go back."

In the summer of 2006, Donovan resumed his professional play with the Los Angeles Galaxy, which had gone from being the MLS Cup champion, in 2005, to occupying the bottom spot in the Western Conference standings. Donovan tried his best to salvage the season, scoring three goals in one two-game stretch in July. The Galaxy failed to qualify for the postseason; Donovan finished the year with an admirable record of 12 goals and seven assists. "I'm not on this Earth to go be in Europe and become the best soccer player in the world," he told Goff. "My life is about being happy. I want to enjoy it, and I think I can balance all of that and still be a good soccer player."

The five-foot eight-inch Donovan weighs about 150 pounds. He has appeared in ads for Gatorade, Pepsi-Cola, and Verb, a program developed by the Centers for Disease Control and Prevention, a division of the U.S. Department of Health and Human Services, that encourages youngsters to engage in physical activities. According to ussoccerplayers.com, Donovan's leisure activities include playing video games and golf.

—A.R.

Suggested Reading: Agence France Presse Mar. 31, 2005; *Baltimore Sun* D p6 Oct. 8, 2001; (Fort Lauderdale, Florida) *Sun-Sentinel* C p1+ Oct. 10, 2001; jockbio.com; *MetroActive* (on-line) July 7, 2002; MLSnet.com Nov. 23, 2004; (Riverside, California) *Press Enterprise* C p1 June 2, 2002; *Sports Illustrated* R p27 Apr. 17, 2000, R p16 Nov. 27, 2000, (on-line) Nov. 2, 2005; ussoccerplayers.com; *Washington Post* E p9 Dec. 10, 2005

Douglas, Dave

Mar. 24, 1963– Composer; trumpeter

Address: Greenleaf Music, P.O. Box 4773649, Chicago, IL 60647; c/o Sooya Arts, PO Box 87, Tappan, NY 10983-0087

The trumpeter, composer, and bandleader Dave Douglas has been one of the most critically acclaimed jazz musicians of the last decade. Douglas first received recognition in the mid-1990s, for his skillful playing and for the diversity of elements his records incorporated. Genres as disparate as Balkans music, classical, and electronica all found their way into his repertoire, though Douglas seldom played in any one style for very long. "Douglas' stylistic range is broad, yet unaffected," as a profile on the All Music Guide (on-line) noted. "His music is not a pastiche, but rather, a personal aesthetic that reflects a wide variety of interests." "In the hands of a curatorial genius such as Douglas," Joseph Hooper wrote for the *Los Angeles Times* (September 3, 2000), "the jazz past is a different country, as ripe for exploration as the Balkans but, from the point of view of the general audience, much more accessible." Indeed, Douglas's accessibility has made him something of a jazz ambassador to listeners who know little about the music—to the dismay of some purists, who consider his reputation to be inflated. For example, while Phil Johnson wrote for the London *Independent* (April 7, 2000) that "heard live, [Douglas] can sound every bit as in the tradition as Wynton Marsalis, blowing expressionist raspberries of Louis Armstrong-like phrases," comparisons to such leg-

Courtesy of Jimmy Katz

ends as Armstrong are seen as unfounded by critics including Stanley Crouch, who argued that the championing of Douglas—a white musician—by white jazz critics suggests a desire to distance the music from its history as a black art form.

In the midst of such controversy, Douglas has continued to release several albums per year; his more than 20 albums of original music include *Parallel Worlds* (1994), *Soul on Soul* (2000), *Freak In* (2003), and *Keystone* (2005). Hooper wrote, "That

Dave Douglas, a shortish, balding and uncharismatic guy, should have become downtown jazz's ambassador to the rest of the world might not have been predicted. There are, however, reasons: a blazing musical intelligence, the work habits of a Puritan and, not to be underestimated, a diversified portfolio." Douglas's portfolio consists of many simultaneous projects with different groups, each with its own musical aesthetic and instrumental makeup. The Tiny Bell Trio, for example, played a combination of jazz and Balkans music, while the Dave Douglas Sextet had a more traditional jazz sound; its three albums, which consist mostly of Douglas's original tunes, are tributes to under-appreciated jazz musicians and composers. Charms of the Night Sky centered on the work of the accordion player Guy Klucevsek, while the group Parallel Worlds combined contemporary classical and improvised music, recording new arrangements of works by Igor Stravinsky, Thelonious Monk, and Duke Ellington, among others. In all, Douglas is said to have worked with 10 groups, not including his extensive recordings as a sideman. Discussing the diversity of his musical output, he told Tom Cardy for the Wellington, New Zealand, *Dominion Post* (October 31, 2002), "I like playing with a lot of different people. I don't like doing the same thing over and over. That's why each record I make is a new challenge to make. I like playing with my friends and I have a lot of friends." In the judgment of Fred Kaplan, writing for the *New York Times* (March 23, 2003), "What makes Mr. Douglas a pivotal figure of modern (or postmodern) music, as opposed to a mere emblem, is not so much that he leads 10 bands. It's that he imbues them all with a sound expansive enough to encompass their disparate dynamics and timbres, yet distinctive enough to bear a clear, consistent signature."

The youngest of the four children of Damon Douglas Jr., an executive at IBM, and Emily Douglas, a schoolteacher and landscape designer, Dave Douglas was born on March 24, 1963 in Montclair, New Jersey, and grew up in the New York metropolitan area. From an early age, Douglas was an avid music fan, listening to his older siblings' pop and rock albums as well as his father's jazz records. He told Cardy, "When I was very little I was listening to [Stevie Wonder's] records daily with my eyes closed. I found this a way of getting into music in a really organic, interior kind of way." He still cites Wonder as one of the top three influences on his work, along with Igor Stravinsky and the jazz saxophonist John Coltrane. Taught privately, Douglas learned to play the piano at age five, the trombone at age seven, and the trumpet at age nine. He practiced trumpet using the Music Minus One record series, which he said allowed him, in effect, to improvise with bands in his own home. (The Music Minus One recordings feature performances with one instrument absent, allowing the listener to supply the missing part.)

Douglas attended the New Hampshire prep school Phillips Exeter, where, he has said, he made up his mind to become a musician. He learned jazz and classical harmony while in high school. As part of a foreign-exchange program, he traveled to Spain, where he played live with professional musicians for the first time. From 1981 to 1982 he attended the Berklee School of Music, in Boston, Massachusetts, and from 1982 to 1983, he was enrolled at the New England Conservatory, also in Boston. At the conservatory Douglas learned the Carmine Caruso method, which greatly influenced his technique on the trumpet. The method involves controlling the muscle movements of the player, allowing him or her more freedom and fluidity when performing. Douglas then studied under the saxophonist Caruso himself, at New York University (NYU), where he enrolled in 1984. While completing an undergraduate music degree at the Gallatin School for Independent Study at NYU, he played in various jazz and experimental funk bands and also performed on street corners in Times Square, in Manhattan.

Upon graduating, Douglas toured internationally with a series of musical acts that included the saxophonist Tim Berne, the avant-garde rock ensemble Dr. Nerve, and, most notably, the group led by the famed jazz pianist Horace Silver. Silver, a veteran performer of hard bop, a jazz style that had by then become conventional, did not readily appreciate the young trumpeter's brash approach to ensemble playing. Douglas told Lloyd Sachs for the *Chicago Sun-Times* (September 15, 1996), "I was 23 and still thought I was single-handedly changing modern American music. I was trying to play modern while [Silver] wanted something more literal. It wasn't the smoothest ride, but ultimately, learning that language was very important to me." Douglas also toured with the saxophonist Vincent Herring and the experimental clarinetist Don Byron during that period. The trumpeter received offers to record albums of his own, but, as he has recalled, at the time he could not find a proper platform for his ambitious, eclectic vision. He told Cardy, "It had been presented to me 'Well, you can make this album. We'll record you playing [jazz] standards.' . . . That was not what I was interested in."

In 1993 Douglas played alongside the violinist Mark Feldman on *Don Byron Plays the Music of Mickey Katz*, a Don Byron album of Katz's klezmer music. Douglas and Feldman parlayed that collaboration into a group project of their own, with the cellist Erik Friedlander. Alternately calling themselves Parallel Worlds and the Dave Douglas String Group, they released three albums: *Parallel Worlds* (1994), *Five* (1996), and *Convergence* (1998). The recordings reflected the range of Douglas's influences—from classical to jazz—and placed an emphasis on stringed instruments. Glenn Astarita, in *All About Jazz* magazine (April 1, 1999), wrote, "*Parallel Worlds* and *Five* were landmark recordings for Douglas' chamber-like excursions with his lead trumpet, string arrangements, pounding back-beats and keen sense of swing which comprised a sound that added a new and refreshing dimension to modern jazz."

After hearing *Parallel Worlds*, the saxophonist and composer John Zorn invited Douglas to join the group Masada, whose sound was inspired by traditional Hebrew music and the free-jazz style pioneered by Ornette Coleman. Masada performed selections from an extensive songbook of Zorn's original compositions. Douglas recorded and toured intermittently with them over the next decade, and Masada's performances were touted for the rapport that developed between the two lead horn players. "Douglas would burnish his musical reputation as the resident WASP in Zorn's Jewish folk-tinged Masada quartet," Hooper wrote, "finding a mentor of sorts in the industrious and prolific Zorn."

In 1994 the Tiny Bell Trio, consisting of Douglas, Brad Shepik on guitar, and Jim Black on drums, released their eponymous debut album. The group took its name from the Bell Café in New York City, where they had held a weekly gig in 1991. The Tiny Bell Trio was inspired by Serbian, Macedonian, and Bulgarian music, though its influences were not exclusively Balkan. Lloyd Sachs cited the group as being among a wave of new artists who took inspiration from Eastern European song structures, writing for the *Chicago Sun-Times* (November 11, 1997): "What is so appealing about this movement is how happily it serves the improvisational bent of jazz. Drawing no lines between Hungarian folk melodies, the quirky bop of neglected genius Herbie Nichols and show tunes, Douglas and company attain a bracing wholeness out of the sum of its disparate parts." Following its debut, the Tiny Bell Trio released three more albums: *Constellations* (1995), *Live in Europe* (1996), and *Songs for Wandering Souls* (1999).

With his sextet (Chris Speed, clarinet and tenor saxophone; Joshua Roseman, trombone; Uri Caine, piano; James Genus, bass; and Joey Baron, drums), Douglas recorded new songs that reinterpreted works by musicians, some of them relatively obscure, who had inspired him. The 1994 effort *In Our Lifetime* was a tribute to the trumpeter and composer Booker Little. That album was followed by *Stargazer* (1997), made up of music "by and for" the saxophonist and composer Wayne Shorter, and a tribute to the pianist and composer Mary Lou Williams, *Soul on Soul* (2000). Douglas said that those albums were attempts to play more conventional, "straight-ahead" jazz without reverting to clichés, as he felt that many of his contemporaries had done in that era of classic-jazz revivalism. "I spent years and years practicing straight-ahead jazz, but it never seemed distinctive enough," he told Hooper. "It was like, 'This could be Joe Blow down on the corner, what am I really trying to get at here?'"

Soul on Soul was Douglas's first release on RCA, the major record company with which he signed. (Before that, Douglas had released music on various independent labels, including Soul Note, Hat Art, and Arabesque.) Under the contract Douglas was to release four albums over two years, each with a different group. Subsequent albums he recorded for RCA included Charms of the Night Sky's *A Thousand Evenings* (2000) and the Dave Douglas Septet's *Freak In* (2003). In addition to the leeway the label allowed him with regard to his groups, RCA gave Douglas full creative control over his material, a contractual clause that is highly coveted by major-label recording artists.

Beginning in the late 1990s, Douglas's albums had featured an increased emphasis on electronic instrumentation. In 1997 his eight-piece group Sanctuary had released its self-titled debut. Sanctuary was notable for its use of a sampler, an electronic device that loops segments of other records. On *Witness* (2001), Douglas unveiled an even larger (10-piece) and more electronics-friendly lineup. Along with a spoken-word contribution from the singer and songwriter Tom Waits, *Witness* featured Ikue Mori playing percussion generated entirely on a laptop computer, as well as further use of samplers. *Freak In* represented Douglas's furthest venture into electronic territory. The album was composed on computer, and its synthetic textures and beats led some critics to dub the new Douglas sound "jazztronica."

Douglas received his first Grammy Award nomination, in the category of best jazz instrumental album, individual or group, for his quintet album *The Infinite* (2002). Douglas cited the legendary trumpeter Miles Davis as a major influence on the record—both in its sound and in its inclusion of unlikely pop covers, such as versions of Rufus Wainwright's "Poses" and Mary J. Blige's "Crazy Games." (Davis had revived that practice in jazz, covering Cindy Lauper and Michael Jackson songs in the 1980s.) Explaining his choice of covers, Douglas told Aaron Cohen for the *Chicago Tribune* (May 3, 2002): "I was listening to all these pop records and feeling that there are these incredible pop musicians again with compositions and melodies and all those good things that we love. It was a natural step for me to want to cover these tunes. It just felt like it was speaking to the tradition that I come out of, which is American jazz music." Prior to his Grammy nomination for *The Infinite*, Douglas had won numerous Trumpet Player of the Year awards from *Down Beat* magazine (2000–04) as well as that magazine's Composer of the Year (2001–02) and Jazz Artist of the Year (2000) honors. Other awards Douglas received included the Jazz Journalists Association's Trumpet Player of the Year award (1998–99, 2001–04) and the Musician of the Year award from the Italian Jazz Critics Society in 2001.

As Douglas gained more recognition, he was able to participate in increasingly unusual and innovative projects. In 2003 he was commissioned to compose a score for Sound of the Dolomites, a jazz festival that combined mountain hiking and music and took place on a mountaintop in the Italian Alps. He told John Kelman for *All About Jazz* (April 2, 2004, on-line), "The weirdest and most wonderful gig I've ever done in my life was taking a funicular up to about ten thousand feet, and then hiking about three hours from there with all our instruments, and then getting to the top, this mountainous, rocky crag. There were a thousand people, who'd hiked up to see this, and we played all this music." He undertook another unconventional project in 2005, when the National Endowment for the Arts offered Douglas a grant to compose soundtracks to silent films of his choice. He picked movies directed by and starring Roscoe "Fatty" Arbuckle (with whom he shared a birthday). Arbuckle was a pioneering comic and filmmaker of the silent-film era who was falsely accused of a rape and murder at a San Francisco party. Though he was exonerated and given an apology by the courts, Arbuckle's film career was ruined by the negative attention the case generated. Douglas's soundtrack project was called *Keystone*, after the film company for which Arbuckle worked. The music, in keeping with Douglas's penchant for experimentation, featured scratching by the turntablist DJ Olive as well as Wurlitzer keyboard and saxophone. The *Keystone* CD was packaged with a DVD of Arbuckle's films *Fatty and Mabel Adrift* and *Just Another Murder*, complete with the Douglas band's accompaniment. Peter Hum wrote for the *Ottawa Citizen* (November 6, 2005), "If the Arbuckle connection is too much of a stretch, music lovers can enjoy *Keystone* thoroughly on its own, especially if they're in the mood for substantial but trippy jam jazz." *Keystone* was the first release on Douglas's own label, Greenleaf Records, which he launched in 2005. The following year he released the album *Meaning and Mystery* on Greenleaf, as well as *Rue de Seine*—duets with the French pianist Martial Solal—on Sunnyside Records. In a review of *Meaning and Mystery*, in which Douglas plays as a member of his quintet, Mark Keresman wrote for *Cleveland Scene* (June 14, 2006), "While stylistically hard bop, it has unexpected twists and turns aplenty. . . . Douglas' nine compositions range from the pensive, suitelike 'Invocation' to the slyly impassioned, blues-saturated 'Elks Club,' evoking Charles Mingus at his peak." Greenleafmusic.com stated that the company aimed to advance Douglas's "vision of an American Music moving forward in all directions." In 2006 *Keystone* earned the trumpeter his second Grammy nomination, for best contemporary jazz album.

Douglas lives in Croton-on-Hudson, New York, with his wife, Suzannah Painter Kincannon, and her son, Drummond Dominguez-Kincannon. From a previous relationship the musician has a daughter, Mia Douglas, who attends college in Atlanta, Georgia.

—M.B.

Suggested Reading: *LA Weekly* p118 Oct. 14, 2005; Greenleaf Music Web site; *Los Angeles Times* Calender p6 Sep. 3, 2000; *New York Times* II p27 Mar. 23, 2003

Selected Recordings: with the Dave Douglas Quintet—*The Infinite*, 2002; *Strange Liberation*, 2004; *Meaning and Mystery*, 2006; with the Dave Douglas Septet—*Freak In*, 2003; with the Dave Douglas Sextet—*In Our Lifetime*, 1994; *Stargazer*, 1997; *Soul on Soul—Celebrating Mary Lou Williams*, 2000; with Charms of the Night Sky—*Charms of the Night Sky*, 1998; *A Thousand Evenings*, 2000; with Martial Solal—*Rue de Seine*, 2006; with Parallel Worlds—*Parallel Worlds*, 1994; *Five*, 1996; *Convergence*, 1998; with Sanctuary—*Sanctuary*, 1997; with the Tiny Bell Trio—*Tiny Bell Trio*, 1994; *Constellations*, 1995; *Live in Europe*, 1996; *Songs for Wandering Souls*, 1999; with Witness—*Witness*, 2001

Duany, Andrés and Plater-Zyberk, Elizabeth

Duany, Andrés
(doo-AH-nee, ahn-DRAYZ)
Sep. 7, 1949– Architect; town planner

Plater-Zyberk, Elizabeth
Dec. 20, 1950– Architect; town planner

Address: 1023 S.W. 25th Ave., Miami, FL 33135

Over the last 25 years, Elizabeth Plater-Zyberk and Andrés Duany have led a revolution in town planning and urban design that has begun to reshape the suburbs and cities of North America. University-trained architects, Duany and Plater-Zyberk, who are married, worked for six years with a cutting-edge firm in Miami, Florida, before setting out on their own to design traditional houses, large buildings, and wholly new towns and neighborhoods. The firm they founded and still lead, Duany Plater-Zyberk & Co. (DPZ), draws on pre–World War II models of town planning and architectural design to create or reconfigure sites with the goal of building so-called mixed-use communities, in which stores and homes are juxtaposed, and people do not have to depend on cars to get from place to place. DPZ's regional plans, urban-revitalization projects, and design codes for more than 250 new towns generally forgo the usual methods of zoning real estate. Instead of rigidly separating areas by use, as most codes and designs do—keeping offices and retail stores apart from residences, requiring that each single-family house be built on a large parcel of land, and rarely if ever laying sidewalks outside the city center—Plater-Zyberk, Duany, and their staff use a process called a charette ("a creative process akin to visual brainstorming that is

Courtesy of Duany Plater-Zyberk & Co.

Andrés Duany (left) and Elizabeth Plater-Zyberk

used by design professionals to develop solutions to a design problem within a limited timeframe," according to englishrules.com) to help them plan neighborhoods in which houses are built very close together along tree-lined sidewalks; back alleys lead cars to garages behind the houses; and stores, schools, and churches are all a few minutes' walk from one another.

Most often called New Urbanism and sometimes referred to as neotraditional design or traditional neighborhood development, the movement that Plater-Zyberk and Duany initiated in the U.S. had by 2004 inspired the creation of more than 600 new communities in North America and at least 14 large-scale planning initiatives in American metropolitan areas, according to Robert Steuteville, writing in the *New Urban News* (July 8, 2004, on-line). Duany and Plater-Zyberk's work has won them acclaim from their professional peers, dozens of awards to their or their firm's credit, and teaching appointments at some of America's most prestigious schools of architecture. Among all their work, the first of Plater-Zyberk and Duany's New Urbanist towns, the resort village of Seaside, Florida, has been singled out for the highest praise, with both *Progressive Architecture* and *Time* calling it one of the most remarkable architectural or design achievements of the 1980s. Kurt Andersen later summed up the value of Seaside and DPZ's work in another issue of *Time* (May 20, 1991), writing: "It seems incredible, that such a simple, even obvious premise—that America's 18th and 19th century towns remain marvelous models for creating new suburbs—had been neglected for half a century. Yet until Duany and Plater-Zyberk came along, even envisioning a practical alternative to dreary

cookie-cutter suburbs had become almost impossible."

The first of three children, Andrés Duany was born on September 7, 1949 in New York City and grew up in his parents' native Cuba, in the Vista Alegre neighborhood of the town of Santiago. Duany's grandfather had planned Vista Alegre early in the 20th century; the site was so large that Duany's father was still working to finish the development during the 1950s. In 1960, the year after the Communist leader Fidel Castro assumed control of Cuba, the Duanys left the country and moved to Sands Point, Long Island, where they lived for three years before settling in Barcelona, Spain. At that time Spain was ruled by the Fascist dictator Generalissimo Francisco Franco; in an interview with Karl Zinsmeister and Eli Lehrer for the *American Enterprise* (October–November 2002), Duany credited Franco for the virtual absence of crime in Spain and thus for the freedom of movement he enjoyed as a child in Barcelona. "I don't think I would be as confirmed in the pleasures and assets of cities if I hadn't been wandering around Barcelona as a kid," he told Zinsmeister and Lehrer.

The parents of Elizabeth Plater-Zyberk, Josaphat and Maria (Meysztowicz) Plater-Zyberk, also fled communism, immigrating to the U.S. from Poland in the late 1940s. They, too, were involved in building and design, her father as an architect and her mother as a landscape designer. Born on December 20, 1950 in Paoli, Pennsylvania (or Bryn Mawr, according to some sources), Plater-Zyberk was the youngest of four children. A precocious designer, she drew plans for the interior of a house when she was eight. Plater-Zyberk and Duany met at Princeton University, in Princeton, New Jersey (where Duany's father had also studied); both earned bachelor's degrees in architecture and urban planning. They grew close as graduate students in architecture at Yale University, in New Haven, Connecticut, where Duany had enrolled after a year of study at the École des Beaux Arts, in Paris, France.

After each of them had earned a master's degree from Yale, in 1974, Duany and Plater-Zyberk moved to Miami, Florida. They married in 1976. The following year they joined three other architects to form Arquitectonica, now one of the most famous architecture firms in the U.S. Almost immediately the new firm began changing the skyline of Miami with striking modernist designs. Arquitectonica's most famous work during Duany and Plater-Zyberk's six years with the firm was a sleek glass building in Miami known as the Atlantis apartments. Its blue-glass exterior, which is interrupted near the roof by a high, wide, window-like opening in which a tree grows, figured prominently in the credits for the 1980s television series *Miami Vice*. The building won an award from the magazine *Progressive Architecture* in 1980. In 1979 Plater-Zyberk began teaching at the School of Architecture of the University of Miami. The next year she and Duany left Arquitectonica to form Duany Plater-Zyberk & Co. Duany has said that the move was prompted by a lecture on traditional urbanism given by Léon Krier, a Luxembourg-born architect and planner; as Duany told Zinsmeister and Lehrer, "Krier introduced me to the idea of looking at people first, and to the power of physical design to change the social life of a community." A time of "real agony and crisis" followed the lecture, Duany said, during which "I realized I couldn't go on designing these fashionable tall buildings, which were fascinating visually, but didn't produce any healthy urban effect."

DPZ's earliest work did not stray far from commonly encountered styles of architecture and planning, and most were for sites in the Miami area. Their first housing development, built in the early 1980s in Boca Raton, Florida, was named Charleston Place, because its look was inspired by houses in Charleston, South Carolina. Charleston Place features the closely spaced houses and comfortable porches that became characteristic of DPZ's designs, but does not offer the corner stores and other small-town elements DPZ later embraced. It also represents the only time that Plater-Zyberk and Duany designed all the houses in one of their planned communities. They have since decided that the uniformity of the houses' exteriors, as Duany told Chuck Twardy for the *Orlando (Florida) Sentinel* (July 11, 1991), detracted from the community's visual appeal. Ever since then Duany and Plater-Zyberk have eschewed designing homes in favor of writing the building codes that govern everything from the dimensions of every part of edifices to the distances between sidewalks and front porches. As Duany told Twardy, "Who-

ever controls the codes controls the city and ultimately the society."

The first DPZ community built largely according to New Urbanist principles was the 80-acre resort town of Seaside, located along a white sand beach in Walton County, Florida. Planning for the community had begun in 1978, when Plater-Zyberk and Duany joined Seaside's developer, Robert Davis, on information- and impression-gathering trips through small towns in Florida and other places in the South. The design developed slowly, with aspects of it being evaluated by Plater-Zyberk's students at the University of Miami. In 1981 the building code that Duany and Plater-Zyberk wrote was approved. It called for a town square in the center of the development, not far from the beach, with retail stores in close proximity to a Greek Revival–style post office and a conference center that would double as Seaside's administrative headquarters. So as to keep a tight rein on vehicular traffic and encourage people to walk, the streets are relatively narrow and the sidewalks meet at 90-degree angles, to discourage drivers from making fast turns of the sort that curved corners allow. (Slower-moving cars, New Urbanists contend, generate more easily walkable residential areas.) To control the pace of development, the individual lots were sold at the rate of roughly 20 a year, and architects and builders of individual homes or civic offices had to adhere to Plater-Zyberk and Duany's guidelines, with many specifications varying according to the locations of the lots. For the town's widest street, Seaside's codes called for three-story homes fronted by verandas, while on streets closer to the beach, houses had to be a greater distance from the sidewalk, so as to avoid obstructing ocean views. Traditional grass lawns were forbidden; the code permitted only native plants, such as scrub oak and scrub pine, which require less maintenance than typical lawn grasses.

Seaside, which currently contains 430 private residences, has demonstrated the strengths of New Urbanist principles. It has been an impressive financial success, as is evident from the dramatic increase in the value of its lots: though relatively small (on average, about 5,000 square feet), its lots currently sell for 20 to almost 200 times the original prices of equivalent lots. In 2001, according to Beth Dunlop in the *New York Times* (December 9, 2001), inland lots in Seaside, which had sold initially for around $15,000, were selling for at least $300,000 each, while the cost of beachfront lots had exceeded $1 million apiece. Aesthetically, too, Seaside is a success, judging by the prominence of the architects who have designed homes there despite the strictures of the building code, among them Robert Stern, Stuart Cohen, Deborah Berke, and Léon Krier. Krier helped design the town's central tower, and architects including Aldo Rossi and Steven Holl have contributed designs for public buildings. DPZ's plans for Seaside have won architecture and urban-planning awards since 1983 and have continued to receive professional and public approbation regularly since then. In addition, Seaside has become a touchstone for New Urbanist approaches to design. As the project description for Seaside on DPZ's Web site explains, the town exemplifies the "underlying principles" of New Urbanism: "The built environment must be diverse in use and population; it must be scaled for the pedestrian yet capable of accommodating the automobile and mass transit; and it must have a well defined public realm supported by an architecture that reflects the ecology and culture of the region."

Also in the 1980s Plater-Zyberk and Duany designed traditionally styled homes, such as the Clary House in Sanibel, Florida, and commercial spaces, such as the Galen Medical Building, in Boca Raton. In 1987 they began one of their most famous urban-renewal projects: the revitalization of the downtown of the city of Stuart, Florida, which had been largely abandoned by businesses and residents alike. After interviewing laypeople and city officials, Plater-Zyberk and Duany and their staff presented a plan that called for a more pedestrian-friendly downtown and the preservation of a historic courthouse. The presentation was met with such enthusiasm that by the end of the following day, the town council had voted it into law. DPZ's work in Stuart has been repeatedly credited with revitalizing the town, with both businesses and home dwellers moving into the downtown area and with the consequent boosting of the city's tax revenues.

In 1988 Duany and Plater-Zyberk started work on another of their most frequently praised commissions. Named the Kentlands, the project was initiated by the developer Joe Alfandre, who had purchased a 352-acre Gaithersburg, Maryland, farm for a reported $40 million in 1987. In June 1988 Plater-Zyberk, Duany, and Alfandre held an intensive charette in Gaithersburg. Over the course of six days, DPZ and the developer worked on the plans along with builders, local government officials, engineers, and consultants on matters ranging from architecture to traffic. The result of that intensive process was a plan for a 1.2 million-square-foot retail center and 1,600 residential units, some of them to be constructed within the development's 900,000 square feet of office space. The 19th-century farmhouses at the heart of the property were to be retained, and an elementary school and a firehouse were to be built. The construction of Kentlands began in 1989; by mid-1992 roughly 750 residential lots had been sold. Eight years later, after a second charette in which DPZ and members of the local community participated, Kentlands had 3,000 residents, and by the end of 2005, almost 1,800 residences had been built.

In the early 1990s, just as New Urbanism was gaining momentum, the tentative success of Kentlands, along with continuing acclaim for Seaside, brought Duany and Plater-Zyberk an increasing number of commissions for the designing of new communities or rehabilitating of established communities. In its January 1, 1990 issue, writers for *Time* called Seaside possibly "the most astounding design achievement of its era and, one might hope, the most influential," and the following year architects surveyed by *Progressive Architecture* (October 1991) selected the Seaside plan as one of the 10 best designs of the past decade. In 1991 the first of several book-length studies of DPZ's work appeared. Titled *Towns and Town-Making Principles* and edited by Alex Krieger with William Lennertz, the book presents selections from 13 of DPZ's plans and discussions of their work and its implications by Krieger, Krier, and others. *Seaside: Making a Town in America* (1992), edited by David Mohney and Keller Easterling, offers a similarly detailed look at their work, this time focusing on their most famous creation.

By early 1991 DPZ had completed commissions for more than 30 plans for new communities or urban and suburban transformations. The number had grown to 120 by the middle of 2000 and to more than 250 by the end of 2005. Among the most important was an ambitious plan to revitalize downtown Los Angeles. The planning began in 1990, when DPZ joined another firm in addressing the problems of urban sprawl, among them increased traffic and accompanying air pollution. A similar project by DPZ to revitalize an established urban locale developed from a 1992 charette in a historic neighborhood of Cleveland, Ohio, called Central. In that case, 21 vacant acres became the site of 60 single-family homes for moderate-income citizens, the idea being in part that this one site might become a model for future developments in the area. That same year, in the Toronto suburb of Markham, Duany and Plater-Zyberk began participating in a two-year series of charettes to help guide the development of more than 4,000 acres in a rapidly growing part of Canada. In 1993 the burgeoning interest in newly created small towns and controlled development resulted in the formation of the Congress for the New Urbanism, which Plater-Zyberk and Duany helped found, along with other architects or planners Peter Calthorpe, Elizabeth Moule, Stefanos Polyzoides, and Dan Solomon. The organization's rapid growth and the ever-widening influence of its philosophy—as evidenced by the decision of the U.S. Department of Housing and Urban Development to revitalize some public-housing developments in adherence to New Urbanist ideas—prompted the architecture critic Herbert Muschamp to praise the Congress for the New Urbanism in the *New York Times* (June 2, 1996) as "the most important phenomenon to emerge in American architecture in the post–Cold War era."

In 1995, after 16 years of teaching and administrative work at the University of Miami, Plater-Zyberk was named dean of the university's school of architecture, a position she still holds. In around 1997 Duany and his brother Douglas began a more than four-year process of developing a comprehensive revision of zoning rules. The first and most far-reaching product of their work was a tool called the Transect, in which a spectrum of urban and rural uses are designated for a landscape, with each point along the spectrum assigned a different set of design principles depending on the density of its human population. The second product of the brothers' work was a set of building rules that in a sense served as an application of the principles of the Transect. Called SmartCode, those rules consist of a set of highly detailed but flexible regulations for construction along New Urbanist lines.

For the last five years, Duany and Plater-Zyberk have been active as writers as well as planners. In 2000 the couple collaborated with Jeff Speck (at that time the head of DPZ's town planning unit and since 2003 the director of design for the National Endowment for the Arts) to publish what is now often called the Bible of New Urbanism, *Suburban Nation: The Rise of Sprawl and the Decline of the American Dream*. Written for a popular audience, the book argues that American cities and their suburbs should be rebuilt so that they serve the needs of people rather than cars. The authors' clear, informative, and often cuttingly humorous presentation received widespread praise, though critics sometimes took issue with their conclusions. Three years later Duany and Plater-Zyberk joined with another architect and planner, Robert Alminana, to publish *The New Civic Art: Elements of Town Planning*, a densely illustrated guide to planning aimed largely at professionals and students of the field. Their latest book, which Duany and Plater-Zyberk wrote with Speck, is *Smart Growth: New Urbanism in American Communities* (2005).

After Hurricane Katrina devastated coastal towns in Louisiana, Mississippi, and Alabama at the end of August 2005, Duany and other planners and architects offered their services for free or for greatly reduced rates. Building on his experience in planning for the reconstruction of Florida City after it was destroyed by Hurricane Andrew, in 1992, Duany initially focused his efforts on rebuilding southern Mississippi towns affected by the disaster, meeting with Mississippi's governor and the mayors of towns affected by the disaster prior to holding a series of charettes. "The architectural heritage of Mississippi is fabulous, . . . really, really marvelous," Duany told Haya El Nasser for *USA Today* (October 13, 2005). "However, what they have been building the last 30 years is the standard, tawdry strip developments. The government's vision is to start again and do it right." In 2006 Duany hosted charettes and community meetings to help local planners in St. Bernard Parrish and the Gentilly neighborhood of New Orleans, Louisiana. At least two DPZ projects have been planned for areas in and around New Orleans.

Duany and Plater-Zyberk live in Coral Gables, Florida.

— D.R.

Suggested Reading: *American Enterprise* p14 Oct./Nov. 2002; Duany Plater-Zyberk & Co. Web site; *Florida Trend* p32 July 1992; *New York Times* E p1+ May 24, 2006; *People* p72 Mar. 28, 1990; *Tampa Tribune* p8 Jan. 31, 2000; *Time* p52 May 20, 1991

Selected Books: *Suburban Nation: The Rise of Sprawl and the Decline of the American Dream* (with Jeff Speck), 2000; *The New Civic Art: Elements of Town Planning* (with Robert Alminana), 2003; *Smart Growth: New Urbanism in American Communities* (with Jeff Speck), 2005

Kevin Winter/Getty Images

Duff, Hilary

Sep. 28, 1987– Actress; singer; clothing designer

Address: c/o PMK Public Relations, 650 Fifth Ave., 33d Fl., New York, NY 10019

While some "tween" actresses—or those whose films appeal to viewers between childhood and teenagerhood—are desperately shedding their wholesome images in favor of edgier personae, Hilary Duff has maintained the aura of youthful innocence that is the hallmark of her career, making her, in the words of *Vanity Fair* (April 2003), "The Tween Queen." Duff first earned the adoration of the "tween" crowd when she played the title character in the hit Disney Channel sitcom *Lizzie McGuire*, a junior-high-school girl whose life was a constant mix of comedy and misadventure. Although the show, which aired from 2001 to 2003, targeted viewers from ages eight to 14, Duff's charm and the show's universal themes appealed to audiences of all ages, making it the most successful teen sitcom on the Disney Channel. "There's a level of sophistication that's brought to the show so it can be viewed with a parent," the program's co-executive producer Stan Rogow told Fred Shuster for the *Daily News of Los Angeles* (February 7, 2002). "The experiences are rather universal. Just because you're now an adult doesn't mean at some point you weren't 12 or 14." On the strength of her work on *Lizzie McGuire*, Duff has made forays into the worlds of pop music, fashion, and the big screen—releasing three albums, designing a line of clothing, and appearing in films including *Cheaper by the Dozen* and its sequel and *The Lizzie McGuire Movie*. Duff told Taylor Hanson for *ASAP* (February 1, 2004), "I want to do it all! I don't want to choose."

The second of two daughters, Hilary Ann Duff was born on September 28, 1987 in Houston, Texas, to Bob and Susan Duff. Hilary and her sister, Haylie, were exposed to show business at an early age, touring as children with a ballet company. In 1993 Hilary made her professional debut, with the Columbus Ballet Met touring company's production of *The Nutcracker*. Soon afterward Haylie Duff pursued a career in acting. Duff followed her sister to acting classes, unenthusiastically at first. Then, at age six, she auditioned successfully for a regional cable-service commercial, and the experience led her to take acting more seriously. Bob and Susan Duff adapted their lifestyles to accommodate their children's career ambitions. For years, with their mother managing their careers and home-schooling them, the sisters made regular treks to Los Angeles, California, for auditions for movies and TV pilots. Their father, meanwhile, stayed in Houston to manage a chain of convenience stores.

Duff appeared at age 10 in the TV miniseries *True Women* (1997) as an uncredited extra. Her first starring role came when she portrayed the red-caped witch Wendy in *Casper Meets Wendy* (1998), based on the animated cartoon *Casper the Friendly Ghost*. Duff was chosen from among hundreds to portray Wendy, who tries, with Casper's help, to escape the evil designs of the warlock Desmond Spellman (played by George Hamilton). Of the four finalists interviewed, Duff had the least experience, but the actress Shelley Duvall, who starred in the movie alongside Duff, saw special potential in the young actress—as did the film's producers. Duvall told Nancy Churnin for the *Dallas Morning News* (October 27, 1998), "[Duff] is the best Wendy and so bright and talented. I've worked with a lot of kids and done a lot of children's programming, and I think she's got it in store to be a big star in the firmament." In 1999 Duff had a role in the made-for-television movie *The Soul Collector*; for her work in that film, she was named the best young supporting actress in a TV movie or pilot by a group known as the Young Artist Awards.

Duff's career received a major boost in 2001, when she gained worldwide exposure for her work on the television series *Lizzie McGuire*. Duff starred as the 13-year-old Lizzie, a normal if accident-prone junior-high-school student, frequently embarrassed by her unhip parents and tormented by her younger brother, Matt. The show followed the experiences of Lizzie and her two best friends, Gordo, an aspiring filmmaker, and Miranda, a musician. An animated version of Lizzie, representing the character's inner self, appeared occasionally to voice the teenager's thoughts. "It's a series that really speaks to 'tween girls who really identify with Hilary," the series' co-executive producer Susan Jansen told Fred Shuster for the *Daily News of Los Angeles* (February 7, 2002). "The idea that here's this charismatic girl who doesn't really fit in speaks to kids. It connects on an emotional level to kids in a way they find entertaining and helpful." Duff beat out thousands of actors to land the role. "Each time we saw Hilary, she was more interesting to watch," Stan Rogow said to Shuster. "So, while the auditioning process can be painful, part of what's revealed is who you're not getting bored with. Slowly, you began not to be able to take your eyes off Hilary. It became, 'That's the girl.'" During its 65-episode run, which ended in 2003, *Lizzie McGuire* became Disney's top-rated sitcom ever.

As Disney's fast-rising star, Duff was given the leading role in the Disney television movie *Cadet Kelly* (2002), in which she played 14-year-old Kelly Collins, a spirited New York City girl who finds herself enrolled in a military academy after her divorced mother (played by Linda Kash) marries the new commandant of the school (Gary Cole). Kelly struggles to find her place amidst the school's atmosphere of strict discipline, enforced with zeal by Cadet Captain Jennifer Stone (Christy Carlson Romano). She faces an additional challenge when a victory at the drill-team championships depends on her ability to rise to the occasion. So that the on-screen military drills would be as authentic as possible, Duff underwent weeks of intensive training in the U.S. and Toronto, Canada, before filming began. "It was great fun, and I can arm wrestle with the best now . . . ," she told Alicia Clott for *Girls' Life* (April 2002). "It was really challenging because I had to learn all the rifle drills and had a lot of stunts. I loved it, and loved working with the producing team and director."

Duff's career on the silver screen took off in 2003, with her role in the action comedy *Agent Cody Banks*, which starred the teen screen idol Frankie Muniz as a school-age covert CIA operative. In the film Duff played Natalie Connors, the object of Cody's affection. Comparing Connors with the character Lizzie McGuire, Duff told Larry Ratliff for the *San Antonio Express News* (March 12, 2003), "Lizzie McGuire is a kind of like shy-and-trying-to-find-her-way-through-life kind of girl. Natalie's really popular. She has everything going for her. She's really independent." That same year Duff took on a small role in the movie

Cheaper by the Dozen as the fashion-crazed, angst-ridden teenage daughter—one of 12 children—of the character played by Steve Martin. She also revisited her wholesome television character, starring in *The Lizzie McGuire Movie* (2003), which picked up where the series had ended. That popular film follows McGuire to Rome, where she is mistaken for Isabella, a member of a famous pop duo. McGuire is forced to pose as Isabella and simultaneously falls for the other half of the duo, Paolo. McGuire goes through a process of self-discovery while exploring the depths of her friendships with Gordo and two of her other friends, Ethan and Kate. Duff received $1 million for the role.

Duff began her music career with *Santa Claus Lane*, a Christmas album, in 2002. She next sang on the *Lizzie McGuire* soundtrack, following that project up with songs on the *Agent Cody Banks* soundtrack, each of which achieved platinum status, or sales of at least one million copies. Having built a solid fan base through her work on the screen and through film songs, Duff released "So Yesterday," her debut single, in 2003. Her subsequent pop album, *Metamorphosis*, which appeared the same year, sold more than two million albums in the U.S. alone, as it capitalized on the "average girl" persona she had made popular on *Lizzie McGuire*. "There's a whole bunch of people who look like pop stars, and then there's Duff, who looks like a 16-year-old girl, if with more make-up and more expensive clothes, but looking like part of her audience, and they love that," Joe Levy, the music editor of *Rolling Stone*, told Steve Hochman for the *Los Angeles Times* (January 26, 2004). "They loved it on *Lizzie McGuire*, and now she's doing it on stage." Still, the album also marked a change for the maturing Duff, who hoped to separate herself from her quirky Disney character. "I think a lot of people knew me as characters that I've played on TV or in movies," she told Seamus O'Regan for *Canada AM* (October 13, 2003), "and I wanted them to get to know more about Hilary. So, we decided to call [the album] *Metamorphosis*." She followed up *Metamorphosis* the next year with a second, self-entitled album, which featured a more aggressive rock edge.

Duff's early films and albums were undeniable hits at the box office and on billboard charts, but critics had little praise for the rising star. In a review of *The Lizzie McGuire Movie*, Liz Braun wrote for the *Toronto Sun* (May 2, 2003), "There's no plot. . . . The film is a series of bad sight gags, overacting, music videos, heinous pop and shopping, and all of it meant to be tied together by the cuteness of Hilary Duff. It is fabulously stupid." Allison Stewart wrote in a review of Duff's *Metamorphosis* album for the *Chicago Tribune* (October 12, 2003), "Even after the release of several hit singles, a 'Lizzie McGuire' soundtrack and a 2002 Christmas album, it's impossible to tell whether 16-year-old Disney Channel phenom Hilary Duff can actually sing, and at this point, it seems almost impo-

lite to ask." The music critic Malcolm Mayhew wrote for the *Fort Worth Star-Telegram* (September 6, 2003) that Duff "sings the songs [on *Metamorphosis*] with so little conviction and sentiment, you know that someone just handed her a sheet of paper and said, 'Sing this line.' In other words, this isn't all that different from her day gig: She's still acting." Such comments notwithstanding, every critic conceded that Duff's loyal fan following would make her projects resoundingly successful.

In 2004 Duff starred in the movie *Cinderella Story*, a contemporary retelling of the fairy tale, which grossed more than $50 million in American theaters. The actress played Sam Montgomery, a high-school senior who works at a diner once run by her deceased father. Sam strives relentlessly to maintain a near-perfect grade-point average, so that she can attend Princeton University and escape life with her stepsisters and stepmother. Between scrubbing floors at the diner and playing maid to her demanding family, Sam finds herself in a romance with the popular Austin Ames (Chad Michael Murray). Duff next combined her musical and acting talents to star in *Raise Your Voice* (2004), in which she played an eager-to-please high-school student, Terri Fletcher, from Flagstaff, Arizona, who sings in the school choir. After a harrowing personal tragedy, Terri hopes to attend an exclusive summer music program at the prestigious Los Angeles Conservatory, but her conservative and overprotective father (David Keith) disapproves of his daughter's spending the summer in California without her parents. Her sympathetic mother (Rita Wilson) concocts a secret plan with her aunt (Rebecca De Mornay), who lives in California, so that Terri can attend the music program and experience life in a big city.

In 2005 Duff starred as Holly Hamilton in *The Perfect Man*, opposite Heather Locklear and Chris Noth. Holly's mother (Locklear), a divorcée, gravitates toward ill-advised romantic relationships, then moves to a new city for a fresh start after each dramatic breakup. To distract her mother from those relationships, Holly conjures up a mythical perfect man; the well-intended deception nearly prevents a romance between her mother and a man to whom she is well-suited. "I really liked the idea of playing Holly because there's absolutely nothing of me in her," Duff told the *Chicago Tribune* (June 17, 2005). "When I first read it, I just thought, I don't even relate to this girl. I don't have a family like that or a mother like that, and I don't have those problems, so I could just have fun playing a completely different person." The movie had only modest success in theaters and drew harsh reviews from critics. One of the most scathing was by Stephen Hunter, who wrote for the *Washington Post* (June 17, 2005), "Not to be too rough on one so young, but it's hard to see a single thing about the pleasant but eminently forgettable Duff that makes her so essential to today's Hollywood." In response to such criticism, Duff told Lola Ogunnaike for the *New York Times* (October 13, 2004), "The 50-year-old person that's writing the review is not who is meant to see my movie. I don't care what they think of the movie. They're 50. They're not the demographic."

Discussing her wholesome persona, which stands in sharp contrast to the sexy and rebellious images many Hollywood actresses her age try to project, Duff told Brad Barnes for the *Columbus Ledger-Enquirer* (July 31, 2005), "I hear 'goody good' all the time. I'd rather be called that than be called anything else. . . . I think I'm a pretty positive role model, and someone who isn't too scandalous and stays out of the focus of that kind of thing—the partying and stuff like that. I don't want girls to think . . . that it's normal for people to live like that, 'cause it's not, you know?" In response to criticism of Duff's image, her mother said to Ogunnaike that the actress's detractors "hate on goodness. They want controversy, but there is no controversy. My kids don't drink, they don't do drugs, they aren't promiscuous. Sometimes I feel like I should apologize because they haven't stolen a car or gotten arrested." Many parents reportedly see Duff as a good role model for their children, in that she appears unfazed by the pressure on many female performers to be rail-thin. (Duff's sister told *People* [August 2, 2004], "We have a mom in our house who buys Krispy Kremes.")

Duff recently ventured into the fashion world, becoming the chief executive officer of her own fashion-and-lifestyle company, called Stuff by Hilary Duff. She has also taken on the title of chief designer for a clothing line for female tweens, available in K-Mart stores nationwide. Duff has closed a deal with Elizabeth Arden to produce a perfume, which is scheduled to go on the market in the fall of 2006, and intends to have her clothing label available in 20 countries by 2008.

In August 2005 Duff released a greatest-hits album entitled *Most Wanted*, which includes three new tracks written in collaboration with her sister, Haylie, and her boyfriend, Joel Madden, the lead singer of Good Charlotte. Later that year she was seen in *Cheaper by the Dozen 2*. In 2006 she co-starred with Haylie in the comedy *Material Girls*. Other upcoming films starring Hilary Duff are *Outward Blonde* and *Foodfight!*

—I.C.

Suggested Reading: *Dallas Morning News* C p1 Oct. 27, 1998; *Los Angeles Times* E p1 Jan. 26, 2004; *New York Times* E p1 Oct. 13, 2004; *San Antonio Express-News* G p1 Mar. 12, 2003; *Seventeen* p118+ June 2005

Selected Films: *Casper Meets Wendy*, 1998; *Agent Cody Banks*, 2003; *Cheaper By the Dozen*, 2003; *The Lizzie McGuire Movie*, 2003; *Raise Your Voice*, 2004; *The Perfect Man*, 2005; *Cheaper by the Dozen 2*, 2005; *Material Girls*, 2006

Selected Television Shows: *Lizzie McGuire*, 2001-03

Selected Recordings: *Metamorphosis*, 2003; *Hilary Duff*, 2004; *Most Wanted*, 2005

Duke, Annie

Sep. 13, 1965– Professional poker player

Address: c/o Hudson Street Press, 375 Hudson St., New York, NY 10014

In 1992, after spending five years in graduate school and nearly completing her Ph.D. degree in psycholinguistics, Annie Duke left academia—to become a professional poker player. Today, in an arena almost completely dominated by men, Duke is regarded as one of the world's best poker players and has benefited from the card game's explosion in popularity in the United States. In September 2004 she took home $2 million by winning the inaugural World Series of Poker Tournament of Champions, dispatching her brother, Howard Lederer, along the way. On the strength of the game's newfound appeal and her unofficial status as its best female competitor, Duke has branched into other areas, developing the program *Annie Duke Takes on the World* for the Game Show cable-TV network and publishing a memoir, *Annie Duke: How I Raised, Folded, Bluffed, Flirted, Cursed, and Won Millions at the World Series of Poker*, which she co-authored with David Diamond, in 2005. Duke—who has sometimes won, and occasionally lost, staggering monetary sums in the course of a day—explained to Tamar Alexia Fleishman, for an interview appearing on the Web site Bankrate.com, that successful professional poker players view money in an unconventional manner. "Poker players have an interesting disconnect about the value of money," she said. "You have to look at the chips on the table, even if it's $100,000, like tools, like a hammer. You can't look at it like money."

The second of three children, Duke was born Annie Lederer on September 13, 1965 in Concord, New Hampshire. Her father, Richard Lederer, a recognized linguist and scholar of the English language, is the author of *The Miracle of Language*, *The Play of Words*, and *Anguished English*, among other books. He served for more than two decades as chairman of the English Department at St. Paul's Preparatory School, a private, co-educational institution in Concord, on whose campus Annie Duke and her siblings were raised. Duke's mother was also a teacher. Her older brother, Howard Lederer, is a two-time bracelet winner, or top-prize winner,

Ethan Miller/Getty Images

Annie Duke

in the World Series of Poker and has also won two World Poker Tour championships. (His peers gave him the nickname "Professor" for his impassivity during competition.) Katy Lederer, Duke's younger sister, is a poet and former magazine editor and the author of *Poker Face: A Girlhood Among Gamblers* (2003). In her own memoir Duke revealed that she had a difficult relationship with her mother, who was an alcoholic. Duke and her siblings, while close-knit, were highly competitive with one another. The family frequently played cards together. (Duke has recalled that poker was not one of the games she often played growing up.) "I was encouraged to be supercompetitive as a child," she said to Michelle Stanistreet for the *Sunday Express* (September 4, 2005), a British newspaper. "It was all about winning and that hasn't changed."

According to her Web site, at St. Paul's Duke "struggled to fit in as a liberal product of two teachers in a sea of conservatism and privilege." That difficulty notwithstanding, she excelled in her classes and went on to enroll at Columbia University, in New York City, receiving bachelor's degrees in both English and psychology in 1987. During her years at Columbia, she went with her brother, Howard, who briefly attended the school before pursuing poker full-time, to local, underground poker and chess games and tournaments. While she did not participate then in the sometimes high-stakes games in which her brother was building a reputation as a gifted player, she was attracted to the atmosphere of competitiveness.

Duke's original intention was to become a professor, following in the footsteps of her parents. After graduating from Columbia she enrolled at the University of Pennsylvania, in Philadelphia, re-

ceiving a National Science Foundation scholarship. For the next several years, she pursued an advanced degree in psycholinguistics, doing research specifically in the area of "bootstrapping," the theory that children learn language by mentally assigning words they have learned to grammatical categories. According to persons close to her then, she was an exceptional Ph.D. candidate and took her work seriously; her CV was filled with honors and published papers. In 1991, in an example of the impulsiveness for which she is known, she proposed marriage to Ben Duke, a fellow student at the University of Pennsylvania—with whom she had not been romantically involved. After getting married the two moved to Billings, Montana, where Duke continued working toward her degree. The couple lived in "romantic poverty," as Duke's Web site put it, getting by with money that Ben Duke received from his family's trust fund. Then, in 1992, when she was very close to obtaining her Ph.D. degree, she quit academics. She has since recalled that the thought of having to defend her thesis made her physically ill. (Indeed, she reportedly landed in the hospital for two weeks after an interview for a position at New York University.) Also influencing her decision was her desire for competition and winnings. Ginia Bellafante wrote for the *New York Times* (January 19, 2006) that that desire had its origins at St. Paul's Prep School, where Duke and her siblings "felt like outcasts in the world of the exceedingly well-born" and craved money because of "the intimate distance" from which they viewed it. "In order to be a successful scholar—which I was—you have to have exceptional critical thinking skills. And you have that same set of skills playing poker. So much of what I did academically had to do with statistical analysis, and that comes in very handy playing poker at this level," Duke said to Mark Kram for the *Philadelphia Daily News* (May 20, 2004).

Using $2,400 sent to her by her brother, who was by then a successful professional poker player based in Las Vegas, Nevada, and employing the tips he passed on to her, Duke began winning money in card rooms in Montana. She has credited her brother with giving her insight into the finer points of poker strategy. "Almost everything I know about poker is a direct result of him," Duke told Melinda Murphy for CBS News (June 4, 2003, on-line). She said to Jamie Berger for *Columbia Magazine* (Spring 2002), "We talked a little about the game, and he told me to read [poker expert] David Sklansky's books for a foundation. I did the reading and started winning regularly almost right away." (Sklansky has authored or co-authored 13 books on gambling theory and poker and is widely considered a foremost expert on those subjects.)

The game of poker "rewards wit, skill, nerve, bravado, deception, patience, discipline and luck, elements embraced as quintessentially American," according to Mark Sauer, writing for the *San Diego Union-Tribune* (August 22, 2004). Poker may be played in hundreds of variations. Tournament play, the type of play predominantly featured on television today, gained popularity in American casinos in the 1970s. In the game Texas Hold 'em (or simply Hold 'em), which is played in the main event of the World Series of Poker and is the centerpiece of poker's surge in popularity, players receive two cards dealt face down, which are called "hole cards." After a round of betting, the dealer turns over three "community cards" (so-called because the players share those cards)—the stage of the game called "the flop." Another round of betting ensues, followed by the dealing of a fourth community card, or "turn card"; the turning of the fifth and final community card, or "the river," is preceded and followed by a round of betting. The winner is the player who holds the best five cards—using any combination of community and hole cards.

In the spring of 1994, Duke went to Las Vegas to enter, for the first time, the World Series of Poker tournament. She finished 13th, after eliminating her brother from competition. According to her Web site, Duke won $70,000 in her first month of competition in Las Vegas. She and her husband then moved there so that she could play poker professionally. For the next several years she built a reputation as a savvy competitor, entering and faring well in private cash games, at such Las Vegas casinos as the Bellagio and the Mirage. In May 2000 Duke placed 10th in the World Series championship event, earning $52,000. (At the time she was eight months pregnant with her third child.) In 2001 she suffered a losing streak, which cost her $250,000. She moved in the following year to Portland, Oregon, to be near the main offices of UltimateBet.com, an on-line poker site for which she serves as a consultant. At that time, seeking exposure, she abandoned cash games in favor of televised tournaments.

The year 2004 was Duke's most successful as a tournament player thus far. In early May she defeated 234 players in winning the $2,000 buy-in World Series of Poker Omaha Hi/Lo Split tournament; the victory brought Duke her first World Series bracelet and made her the all-time money winner among women at the World Series, raising her earnings above $500,000. In August she won $2 million in the No-Limit Texas Hold 'em Tournament of Champions, established by Harrah's Entertainment and ESPN (which televised the event). The invitation-only event included Howard Lederer and nine of the game's other marquee players, all of whom were male.

Since ESPN's broadcast of the World Series of Poker in 2003, which was won by a former accountant, Chris Moneymaker, several television networks, taking advantage of the game's appeal, have aired programs devoted to poker. The programs have received high ratings. The poker boom has likewise spawned an increase of activity on poker Web sites, in some instances tripling business on those sites. Some have cited as a defining moment in the national appeal of poker the decision in 2002

by Steven Lipscomb, a documentary filmmaker and the founder and CEO of the World Poker Tour, to place a camera (about the size of a lipstick tube) beneath the poker table during the Travel Network's coverage of the World Poker Tour, so that viewers could see the cards that players were holding. ESPN used that feature during its broadcast of the 2003 World Series and also borrowed graphics that Lipscomb had used on the Travel Network that explained the odds each player faced in a given hand based on the player's hole cards. Writing for *Entertainment Weekly* (October 15, 2004), Daniel Fierman and Michelle Kung observed that the camera angle enabled viewers "to know when [players] were bluffing, when they had set a trap, or when they were headed for certain, multimillion-dollar disaster on live television." "Before all the (TV) coverage came along, I spent most of my poker career having to explain to people what I do for a living," Duke said to Mark Sauer. "Now everyone thinks what I do is really cool." She added, "When you think about the lipstick camera, the popularity of poker becomes obvious. If you have no access to the players' hole cards, then watching poker becomes like watching paint dry."

Duke has advised poker neophytes and more experienced players alike to make decisions during games in part by observing their opponents' facial expressions, body posture, and betting strategies. Also, she said to Michelle Stanistreet that poker "is an extremely mathematical game" and that "the combination of math and controlled aggression, with a little psychology thrown in, makes you a great poker player." Duke told Jamie Berger, "I approach it [poker] completely as a business. I do no other gambling. I don't let my emotions get in the way of how I play."

Duke has said that being a woman sometimes gives her a psychological advantage over her male opponents. "I think women are better readers in general . . . ," she said to Melinda Murphy. "I think men find women hard to read and women don't find men hard to read." In a conversation with Stephen McDowell for the London *Financial Times* (June 25, 2005), she explained her theory that male poker players, in their interactions with female players, largely fit into two categories: the flirtatious and the chauvinistic. "You can really profit off the chauvinists," she said. "They go off and play . . . to get away from their old lady and sit around bitching about them. So when the old lady pitches up at the table they quickly get bent out of shape. They tend to play worse than they would against a man. And that is to my advantage." Male players in the other category, she said, "are the guys who are thinking with the wrong parts of their bodies, who want to take you to the cocktail lounge. I am quite happy to flirt right back and then walk away." She also said to Michelle Stanistreet, "Unfortunately, there's a lot of stigma attached to gambling for women and people see poker as gambling, rather than a skill. Women are considered the keepers of the [hearth], people look at them and think they're gambling away their grocery dollars." Although the organizers of women-only poker tournaments have urged her to participate in them, Duke has declined to do so. "I don't play in them for two reasons," she said in her interview with Tamar Alexia Fleishman. "First, the money"—which amounts to substantially less than in other poker competition. "The other is I consider the [open] tournaments an equalizer, with age, sex, background. The ladies' tournaments, it's segregation. It's a bad message to send, to say that women can only win in the ladies' tournaments. I mean, it's not the NFL, where men have more strength."

Duke has parlayed her celebrity into numerous product endorsements and other opportunities. For the Game Show Network, she developed the program *Annie Duke Takes on the World*, in which four amateur players compete for the opportunity to face her, one-on-one, in Texas Hold 'em. The show premiered in May 2006. She has also produced a series of instructional DVDs, among them *Annie Duke's Advanced Texas Hold 'Em Secrets—How to Beat the Big Boys* (2005) and three discs in the *Masters of Poker* series: *Annie Duke's Conquering Online Poker* (2005); *Annie Duke's Beginner's Guide to Texas Hold 'Em* (2005), and *Annie Duke's Girl's Guide to Texas Hold 'Em* (2005).

Duke continues to serve as a consultant for the Web site UltimateBet.com, and she has personally tutored such celebrities as the actor Ben Affleck. In addition, she worked with her brother on the design and promotion of a video game featuring herself as a virtual character. Duke's life story was the basis for *All In*, a sitcom that was developed in 2005 for NBC and that was to star Janeane Garofalo; the show did not appear in the network's fall lineup. Since 2005 Duke has made endorsements for the ESPN Poker Club, a line of poker-related products, including chips, tables, and other accessories. She also recently formed her own film production company, Ten Dime Productions ("ten dime" is gambling slang for $10,000), and is writing the screenplay for a horror film. Duke has said that she has received criticism from fellow professional players for maintaining such a high profile and for cashing in, so to speak, on her celebrity. "I had another player once criticize me for being a media whore," Duke recalled to Fierman and Kung. "My response was 'And that's bad because . . .?' You only have so many opportunities that come your way in life. I'm going to take my window the moment I have it. Because in a couple of years it may not be there." In late 2005 Hudson Street Press published *Annie Duke: How I Raised, Folded, Bluffed, Flirted, Cursed and Won Millions at the World Series of Poker*, a memoir, which Duke co-wrote with David Diamond. Ginia Bellafante described the book as "rarely burdened by self-effacement." The book also profiles some of her fellow poker professionals, including Johnny Chan and Phil Hellmuth.

Duke often wears jeans and a T-shirt when playing poker, in order to be comfortable—which, she feels, helps her to win games. She is "chatty and vivacious, with a brush of brown bangs and an enthusiasm that can sometimes rattle her opponents," Matt Surman wrote for the *Los Angeles Times* (March 27, 2002). Jamie Berger wrote that Duke "tends toward polarities: humility and cockiness, sassy charm and in-your-face competitiveness, raise or fold. . . . Both her humility and her pride seem completely genuine." Duke lives in Hollywood Hills, California. She divorced Ben Duke in 2004 and is currently living with Joe Reitman, an actor and producer. Her four children, Maud, Leo, Lucy, and Nell, range in age from 11 to four years old. Duke also owns two homes in Montana that she "will never sell" because, as she explained to Fleishman, she purchased them with the winnings from her first World Series of Poker competition, in 1994. "They have huge sentimental value," she said. Regarding her poker-playing abilities, Duke said to Anna Dubrovsky for the *Miami Herald* (June 26, 2005), "There are times when I lack confidence in my decisions, and there are times when I falter. I'm getting much better at it. What makes poker such a great game is you never master it."

—D.F.

Suggested Reading: AnnieDuke.com; *Columbia Magazine* (on-line) Spring 2002; *Entertainment Weekly* p41+ Oct. 15, 2004; *New York Times* F p1 Jan 19, 2006; *San Diego Union-Tribune* E p1 Aug. 22, 2004; Duke, Annie. *Annie Duke: How I Raised, Folded, Bluffed, Flirted, Cursed, and Won Millions at the World Series of Poker*, 2005

Selected Books: Duke, Annie. *Annie Duke: How I Raised, Folded, Bluffed, Flirted, Cursed, and Won Millions at the World Series of Poker*, 2005

Selected Television Shows: *Annie Duke Takes on the World*, 2006–

Selected DVDs: *Annie Duke's Advanced Texas Hold 'Em Secrets—How to Beat the Big Boys*, 2005; *Masters of Poker: Annie Duke's Conquering Online Poker*, 2005; *Masters of Poker: Annie Duke's Beginner's Guide to Texas Hold 'Em*, 2005; *Masters of Poker: Annie Duke's Girl's Guide to Texas Hold 'Em*, 2005

Courtesy of Senator Richard Durbin

Durbin, Richard J.

*Nov. 21, 1944– U.S. senator from Illinois
(Democrat)*

*Address: 332 Dirksen Senate Office Bldg.,
Washington, DC 20510*

The United States senator Richard J. Durbin of Illinois, now in his second term, has earned a reputation as a hard-working liberal legislator whose knowledge of parliamentary rules and procedures has proven to be an asset to the Democratic Party. In 2004 he was appointed assistant minority leader, also known as the minority whip, making him the second-highest-ranking Democrat in the Senate. Known as an eloquent speaker, he has become one of his party's leading spokesmen. "Durbin has the knack for matching his rhetoric to the occasion: catchy when the subject is broad political themes, detailed when the subject is the nuts and bolts of legislation," a profile in *Congressional Quarterly's Politics in America: 2004* (2003) noted. "He can shift gears between details and the big picture in a way that few members of Congress can. Somehow, he stops short of sounding like a robot—but it is also clear that it is virtually impossible to knock him off message."

Durbin's career in politics stretches back to the 1960s, when he interned for then-Senator Paul Douglas, a revered Illinois Democrat. He later set up a law practice and provided counsel for Paul Simon, a lieutenant governor of Illinois who went on to serve for 22 years in Congress. In 1982 Durbin was elected to the U.S. House of Representatives, defeating the 11-term Republican incumbent in an upset. He served seven consecutive terms; during

that time he distinguished himself as a major opponent of the tobacco industry, leading the successful effort in the late 1980s to ban smoking on most domestic airline flights. For his efforts he received a Lifetime Achievement Award from the American Lung Association. In 1996, when Simon retired from the Senate, Durbin campaigned successfully for his seat, becoming the 47th senator from Illinois. He was promptly appointed to the powerful Senate Appropriations Committee, becoming the first Illinois senator to serve on the committee in more than 25 years. (The committee oversees all legislation regarding federal discretionary spending.) Durbin, a strong supporter of Bill Clinton during Clinton's presidency, has been deeply critical of the administration of President George W. Bush. He voted against congressional authorization of the U.S. invasion of Iraq and has repeatedly attacked the administration's handling of the war. He also voted against Bush's $1.35 trillion tax cut and against several of his appointments, including those of Supreme Court justices John G. Roberts and Samuel Alito. Durbin, however, prefers to emphasize his positive efforts, such as modernizing the federal food-safety system, advancing gun-safety legislation, and helping farmers by promoting ethanol and securing the deductibility of health-insurance costs for the self-employed. "As they say downstate, any jackass can kick down a barn door but it takes a carpenter to build one, and I want to be a builder," Durbin has said, as quoted in a profile for the Associated Press Candidate Biographies (November 16, 2004). "I don't want them to say, Well, he made a career of some of the greatest 'no' votes in the history of the Senate. I want them to say he left behind a legacy that may improve the lives of people."

The youngest of three brothers, Richard Joseph Durbin was born on November 21, 1944 in East St. Louis, Illinois. His father, William Durbin, was a night watchman, and his mother, Ann (Kutkin) Durbin, a Lithuanian immigrant, was a switchboard operator; both worked for the New York Central Railroad Co. When Durbin was 14 years old, his father, a heavy smoker, died from lung cancer. "It was one of the defining moments of my life," Durbin wrote in an article for the *Chicago Sun-Times* (October 16, 1996). "My two older brothers had left home by then and mom and I had to pull together and move forward." Durbin briefly attended St. Louis University, then transferred to Georgetown University, in Washington, D.C., after receiving a government student loan. As an undergrad he interned for Senator Paul Douglas. After graduating from college, in 1966, with a bachelor's degree in foreign service and economics, Durbin volunteered for Douglas's reelection campaign that year. (Douglas lost to the Republican Charles Percy.) He then returned to Georgetown University, receiving a law degree in 1969. Durbin moved to Springfield, Illinois, where he set up a law practice and worked as legal counsel to Paul Simon, then lieutenant governor, from 1969 to 1973. Durbin also provided legal counsel for the Illinois State Senate Judiciary Committee. From 1969 to 1982 he worked as the parliamentarian for the Illinois Senate, a position that involves advising Senate leaders on procedures and rules. In 1976 Durbin ran unsuccessfully for a seat in the Illinois State Senate; two years later he lost his bid for lieutenant governor of Illinois on a ticket with Michael J. Bakalis.

In 1982 Durbin challenged Republican incumbent Paul Findley for a seat in the U.S. House of Representatives., representing the 20th Congressional District of Illinois. Although Findley's popularity was initially daunting, redistricting had added Democratic constituents to his district; in addition, Findley was critical of U.S. support for Israel and had met with the Palestinian leader Yasir Arafat, angering Jewish groups; Durbin subsequently drew large campaign contributions from pro-Israel organizations. Durbin won the election with a margin of only 1,410 votes, or 50.3 percent of the ballots cast, becoming the first Democrat to represent the district in four decades. He quickly became a key player in the House. After serving a term on the Agriculture Committee, he was appointed, in 1985, to a seat on the House Appropriations Committee. "An expert on the rules, an amiable in-house politician and a student of 'new ideas' for the Democratic Party, Durbin is one of the more versatile members to arrive in Congress in recent years," *Politics in America* (1985) noted.

In July 1987 Durbin proposed pioneering legislation to ban cigarette smoking on all domestic air flights. The bill drew intense opposition from cigarette companies and lawmakers from tobacco-producing states. "It is absolutely an infringement on individual rights to prohibit smoking on airplanes," Representative James Quillen of Tennessee told the Associated Press, as quoted by the *Chicago Tribune* (July 14, 1987). Durbin countered, "The rights of smokers to smoke end where their smoking affects the health and safety of others." Though Durbin's initial bill was defeated by the House Appropriations Committee, it was amended to ban smoking on domestic flights of less than two hours; the new bill passed by a vote of 198–193. Approved by the Senate and signed into law by President Ronald Reagan, it went into effect on April 23, 1988. Two years later Durbin was able to extend the ban to include all domestic flights of six hours or less. "My work has earned me a prominent place on the tobacco lobby's hit list . . . ," he wrote in his article for the *Chicago Sun-Times*, "and I wear that badge with honor."

Durbin made national headlines in 1989 for his tongue-in-cheek response to calls for a constitutional amendment to ban the burning of the American flag. As his colleagues debated the amendment, Durbin made a speech on the House floor in which he denounced the recent shift from wooden baseball bats to aluminum bats, calling it "the desecration of a great American symbol," according to the Associated Press (July 27, 1989). "Are we willing to hear the crack of a bat replaced by the dinky

ping? Are we ready to see the Louisville Slugger replaced by the aluminum ping dinger? Is nothing sacred?" Durbin's sarcasm received more press than he had expected. "The response to that was amazing," he told Peter Ellertsen for *Illinois Issues* (April 1991), as reprinted on the Northern Illinois University Library Web site. "I still have people whom I meet for the first time, and they'll say, 'Oh, you're the guy who gave the speech about the baseball bat.'"

Durbin was challenged in the 1990 congressional elections by Paul Jurgens, a Republican who took issue with Durbin's support of tightened gun-control regulations. "I took a lot of heat for voting for the Brady Bill [which required a five-day waiting period for hand-gun purchases] and the assault weapons ban," Durbin told Rick Pearson for the *Chicago Tribune* (March 8, 1996). "Some of the more extreme people in my district shot up my campaign signs with shotguns, made threatening phone calls to my home and family. It was a pretty nasty time." Jurgens challenged Durbin to a target-shooting contest, which Durbin declined. Durbin easily won reelection with 66 percent of the vote.

That same year Durbin voiced hesitation about President George H. W. Bush's plans to go to war with Iraq in response to that country's invasion of Kuwait. When President Bush asserted that he did not need approval from Congress to lead the nation to war, Durbin co-authored a resolution stating that Congress alone had the power to approve a declaration of war. "There are a lot of guys [in Congress] who wonder why anybody would want to take this on," Durbin told Steve Daley for the *Chicago Tribune* (January 13, 1991), referring to his efforts to question the decision to go to war. "We were having this debate everywhere but Congress. I tried to tell my colleagues that the Constitution didn't allow a debate on war powers. It required it." A bill sponsored by Durbin, requiring congressional approval before military action could be initiated against Iraq, passed by a vote of 302–131. (Congress subsequently voted to authorize the war.)

Throughout his final two terms in the House, Durbin was a staunch supporter of Democratic president Bill Clinton, voting in favor of several Clinton-led initiatives, including increasing taxes and ending a ban preventing homosexuals from serving in the military. In the November 1994 elections Durbin won a seventh term, surviving the widespread defeat of the Democratic Party that year. Shortly thereafter Senator Paul Simon announced that he was retiring and would not seek reelection in 1996. While many prominent Illinois Democrats sought Simon's seat, Simon endorsed Durbin as his successor, telling Thomas Hardy for the *Chicago Tribune* (June 13, 1995) that Durbin was "a person of unquestioned integrity, of great ability and of uncommon courage."

In the election Durbin faced the Republican Al Salvi, a conservative who characterized Durbin as "a big taxin', big spendin', pay grabbin', liberal congressman," according to Scott Fornek and Dave

MicKinney in the *Chicago Sun-Times* (September 19, 1996). "This is going to be a confrontational campaign," Durbin said, as quoted in a profile for the Associated Press Candidate Biographies (1996). "I will not stand back and be [Salvi's] punching bag." In his article for the *Chicago Sun-Times*, Durbin defended his record, writing, "Paul Simon and I joined forces to pass a law which stops convicted felons from purchasing handguns. We beat the National Rifle Association and now they are pouring more money into this race to elect Al Salvi than any other Senate race in America." Durbin also rejected assertions that he was too liberal, noting his support of President Clinton's controversial welfare-reform bill. "Though many of my fellow Democrats opposed welfare reform," Durbin wrote, "I voted for it. The measure is not perfect but the current welfare system is clearly failing both taxpayers and recipients. This plan rewards creative state and local efforts to put welfare recipients to work and includes basic protections for children." On Election Day Durbin captured 55.8 percent of the vote.

Durbin stood out among the 15 incoming senators, according to the Associated Press Candidate Biographies (November 16, 2004), with observers and colleagues describing him as "articulate," "likeable," and "easygoing but unintimidated." During his first term he pursued many of the same causes he had championed in the House. Granted a coveted spot on the Appropriations Committee, he was able to push for the elimination of government subsidies for tobacco farmers, telling Dave Williams for the Jacksonville *Florida Times-Union* (April 25, 1997), "There is absolutely no justification for taxpayers subsidizing the production and marketing of a product that causes so much death, disease and suffering." The following year he supported legislation that would raise taxes on tobacco. Over the next several years, Durbin fell solidly behind President Clinton, voting against Republican efforts to impeach the president on charges of perjury in connection with his extramarital affair.

After Republican president George W. Bush took office, in January 2001, Durbin went on the defensive. That year he voted against confirming Bush's candidate for attorney general, John Ashcroft, and against the Bush administration's $1.35 trillion tax cut, although he voted in favor of the USA Patriot Act, which expanded the government's power to investigate suspected terrorists. The following year he voted against oil drilling in the Arctic National Wildlife Refuge and supported the creation of an independent commission to investigate intelligence failures leading up to the terrorist attacks of September 11, 2001. In 2002, as the administration prepared to invade Iraq in the event that Saddam Hussein failed to comply with U.N. resolutions, Durbin was one of 23 senators who voted against giving President Bush the authority to use military force against the country.

Meanwhile, in late 2001 Durbin became embroiled in a bitter dispute with his fellow Illinois senator, the Republican Peter Fitzgerald, over a plan to expand Chicago's O'Hare Airport. The expansion, which was proposed by Chicago's mayor, Richard Daley, was intended to alleviate excessive air traffic at O'Hare, one of the most overcrowded airports in the U.S., by adding several new runways. Local governments and community groups staunchly opposed the project, citing the extra noise, pollution, and traffic that would result. Fitzgerald and others endorsed an alternate plan to build a new airport in Chicago's impoverished South Side, asserting that the project would create needed jobs in the area. In December 2001 Durbin inserted a $6.6 billion provision for the O'Hare expansion into a defense appropriations bill, but Fitzgerald filibustered the bill, catching Durbin off-guard and dealing him a significant political blow. "I never believed for a moment we would face a filibuster over this," Durbin told Renee Trappe for the *Chicago Daily Herald* (December 8, 2001). "I was told there would be an up or down vote and I was prepared to accept the outcome." The debate over the O'Hare expansion lasted throughout 2002, with Fitzgerald insisting that the city had underreported the costs and the amount of land that would be appropriated for the expansion. For a time Durbin's failure to secure legislation threatened to be a political liability. Although Durbin did not succeed in getting the legislation passed, in November 2002 he was easily reelected to the Senate over the Republican Jim Durkin, receiving more than 60 percent of the vote. (The city has since moved forward with the expansion, although some aspects of it remain in dispute. In November 2005 a federal judge dismissed a lawsuit filed on behalf of the opponents; Transportation Secretary Norman Mineta subsequently pledged $337 million in federal discretionary funds toward the expansion. According to an Associated Press article that appeared in *USA Today* [April 3, 2006], work began on the expansion in April, 2006.)

In his second term Durbin voted in favor of an $87 billion funding bill for military operations in Iraq and Afghanistan; voted to reduce U.S. dependence on foreign oil; and voted against a bill that would prevent civil lawsuits against gun manufacturers. Durbin also voted against banning partial-birth abortions; a Roman Catholic, Durbin was once opposed to abortion, but over the years he has grown more supportive of the practice as an option, especially in cases involving rape, incest, or the endangerment of the mother's health. In 2004 Durbin's nemesis, Peter Fitzgerald, opted not to run for a second term in the Senate (a move some analysts attributed to his unpopular opposition to the O'Hare expansion). Durbin backed Barack Obama, an Illinois state senator and rising star within the Democratic Party, who went on to win the vacant U.S. Senate seat.

In November 2004 Senate Minority Leader Tom Daschle lost his reelection bid to the Republican John Thune; the Democrats named Harry Reid of Nevada to replace him as minority leader and chose Durbin to be the assistant minority leader. "Durbin's reputation as a fierce partisan who is comfortable in front of a camera is seen as a counterbalance to the more soft-spoken Reid, who is known as a skillful behind-the-scenes negotiator," Dori Meinert wrote for the Copley News Service (November 16, 2004). Republicans gained four seats in the Senate in the 2004 elections, and Democrats found themselves in a weakened position. In 2005 Durbin voted against President Bush's nomination of Condoleezza Rice for secretary of state and Alberto Gonzales for attorney general, and he later voted against Bush's Supreme Court nominees John G. Roberts and Samuel Alito. Durbin also emerged as one of the Senate's most vocal critics of the war in Iraq. Though U.S. forces had ousted the Iraqi dictator Saddam Hussein in a matter of months, the occupation faced a growing insurgency from militant groups who rejected the American military presence. "We've seen a litany of serious miscalculations from Pentagon leaders, stretching back to the earliest stages of this war when [Secretary of Defense Donald Rumsfeld] ignored warnings from top military experts that success in Iraq would require far more troops and that our troops were likely to be met with strong resistance, not parades and flowers," Durbin said in a radio address, as quoted by FDCH Political Transcripts (December 18, 2004).

In mid-2005 Durbin voiced concerns about the U.S. detention center at Guantánamo Bay, Cuba, where people deemed "enemy combatants" have been detained without trial since they were captured during U.S. military operations after the 2001 terrorist attacks. "Most of those captured in Afghanistan and Iraq are people who have never raised arms against us, but they've been taken prisoner far from the battlefield," Durbin said on the Senate floor, as quoted by the Agence France-Presse (June 15, 2005). Durbin provoked a controversy when, on June 16, 2005, he read from a report alleging instances of prisoner abuse and torture, saying, as quoted on National Public Radio's *Morning Edition* (June 17, 2005), "If I read this to you and I did not tell you that it was an FBI agent describing what Americans have done to prisoners in their control, you would most certainly believe this must have been done by the Nazis or Soviets in their gulags or some mad regime, Pol Pot or others, that had no concern for human beings. Sadly, that is not the case. This was the action of Americans in the treatment of their prisoners." Durbin faced many attacks from politicians and commentators who called it inappropriate to liken the actions of U.S. forces to the regimes of Adolf Hitler, Josef Stalin, and Pol Pot, each of whom was responsible for millions of deaths. Republican senators John Warner of Virginia and Mitch McConnell of Kentucky admonished Durbin on the Senate floor, and White House press secretary Scott Mc-Clellan said that Durbin's remarks were, as quoted by *Morning Edition*, "simply reprehensible." Paul Begala, a Democratic strategist, told Mark Leibovich for the *Washington Post* (June 22, 2005) that such comments "will always be misconstrued and turned around, and that's why you should never compare anything to Nazis or Hitler. It's as basic a rule as there is in politics." On June 22 Durbin apologized in front of the Senate, saying, as quoted by the *Frontrunner* (June 22, 2005), "Some may believe that my remarks crossed the line. To them, I extend my heart felt apologies."

By 2006 Durbin had become one of the prominent figures of the Democratic Party, frequently called upon to explain the Democrats' views of major issues to media outlets. In May 2006 Durbin supported the Senate's immigration-reform bill, which called for stronger border security, a guest-worker program, and a process to allow illegal immigrants already in the U.S. to earn citizenship—although he supported an amendment that would have eliminated the program to grant temporary guest-worker visas. "I'm worried about the impact on American workers," he told Chris Wallace for the television program *Fox News Sunday* (May 28, 2006). "We tried to put a sunset [ending date] on it so that in five years we take a look. I don't want to lose American jobs as a result of this. But unfortunately, we didn't prevail." In June the Senate passed a bill increasing standards of safety in mines, which was a slightly altered version of a bill proposed by Durbin after recent disasters in West Virginia and Kentucky, where 18 miners were killed. In the summer of 2006, the Senate voted on amending the Constitution to ban the burning of the American flag. Durbin proposed an alternative law that would have made it illegal only to desecrate a flag on federal property, but the proposal was defeated. He later voted against the flag-burning amendment, which was defeated by one vote. In September 2006 Durbin voted against the Military Commissions Act, which allowed President Bush to interpret whether interrogation techniques authorized under his presidency constitute torture, as barred by the Geneva Conventions. The bill passed in both the Senate and the House, and President Bush signed it into law on October 17, 2006.

In addition to the Senate Appropriations Committee, Durbin has served on the Judiciary Committee, the Rules and Administration Committee, and the Select Intelligence Committee. He is a founding member of the Senate Global AIDS Caucus. In 1999 he was named Legislator of the Year by the American Public Health Association, and in 2001 he received the American Medical Association's Dr. Nathan Davis Award for outstanding government service.

Durbin lives in Springfield, Illinois, with his wife, Loretta Schaefer Durbin. They have three grown children—one son and two daughters—and one grandchild.

—R.E.

Suggested Reading: *Chicago Tribune* p1 Mar. 8, 1996, C p14 Apr. 22, 2001; *CQ Weekly* p68+ Jan. 5, 2002; *Crain's Chicago Business* p10 Oct. 21, 2002; *Nation* p11+ Feb. 14 2005; *New York Times* A p20 Jan. 27, 2006; *Washington Monthly* p12+ July/Aug. 2005

Courtesy of Suzette Haden Elgin

Elgin, Suzette Haden

Nov. 18, 1936– Linguist; writer; educator; artist

Address: Ozark Center for Language Studies, P.O. Box 1137, Huntsville, AR 72740-1137

"The power of language—to change attitudes, to persuade, to comfort, to teach, to create whole worlds, to heal (and to hurt), to forge and maintain relationships, and much more—has always seemed to me to be the most interesting thing that exists in this universe," Suzette Haden Elgin told Jenna Glatzer for the Absolute Writer Web site. Elgin is a specialist in linguistics and applied psycholinguistics—in particular, the psychological processes involved in language and the relationships among language, thinking, and culture; she is an outspoken feminist (especially with regard to the use and abuse of language) and an educator as well. Among her more than 30 books are 11 science-fiction novels; the self-help series that began with the guide *The Gentle Art of Verbal Self-Defense* (1980); and the reference works *What Is Linguistics?* (1973), *A Primer of Transformational Grammar for Rank Beginners* (1975), and *The Science Fiction Poetry Handbook* (2005). She has also written poetry and a dozen science-fiction novellas

or short stories. In 1986, in a talk at the feminist science-fiction convention known as WisCon, held annually at the University of Wisconsin since 1977, Elgin said that if one assumes (as she does) that language plays a huge role in structuring people's perceptions of reality, it follows that "language is one of the most powerful instruments for social change in existence. And it follows from that that the more effective the language is, the more profound the social change will be." Moreover, as she has said on various occasions, she believes that science fiction "is our best tool for testing such changes before they are implemented in the real world; therefore the conjunction of [science fiction and linguistics] is desirable and should be useful." One of relatively few female science-fiction writers, Elgin has written three series in that genre: the Communipaths quartet, whose hero is Coyote Jones, an agent for the Tri-Galactic Intelligence Service; the Ozark trilogy, about a dozen families who leave a sullied Earth and settle on the planet Ozark, where their society operates by means of a magical system based on generative transformational grammar (a term connected with theories of the linguist Noam Chomsky); and the Native Tongue trilogy—already a classic among aficionados of feminist literature—in which a group of female linguists in 22d-century America create a new language, Láadan, which, unlike English or other existing languages, enables women to express their thoughts, feelings, and perceptions accurately. Elgin devised a grammar system for Láadan and created a vocabulary for it containing thousands of words. *A First Dictionary and Grammar of Láadan* was published by the Society for the Furtherance and Study of Fantasy and Science Fiction in 1985.

According to the article about her in *Twentieth-Century Science-Fiction Writers* (1991), Elgin has said that in her science-fiction works, she focuses on "problems of communication as they are now and as they are likely to develop in the future." Many of her nonfiction books, such as *You Can't Say That to Me!: Stopping the Pain of Verbal Abuse—An 8-Step Program* (1995), deal with similar problems in the here and now and offer laypersons practical suggestions for handling them. In 1981 Elgin founded the Ozark Center for Language Studies, a business that she operates out of her home in Arkansas and that is "dedicated to the two goals of reducing violence in the U.S. and getting information about linguistics out to the public," as she put it on her personal page on the Web site of the Science Fiction & Fantasy Writers of America (sfwa.org). Her center issued the bimonthly newsletter *The Lonesome Node* from 1981 to 2000, when it switched from print to three separate E-mailed newsletters: *The Linguistics & Science Fiction Newsletter*, *The Verbal Self-Defense Newsletter*, and *The Religious Language Newsletter*. (The mission of the last-named publication, which is posted on the site forlovingkindness.org, is to analyze and disseminate "information about the *ef-*

fects of religious language (in particular, religious language in English)." Elgin also maintains a blog, ozarque.livejournal. In her book *The Grandmother Principles* (1998), she offered advice about the responsibilities and joys of grandmotherhood. Elgin is also an artist. Examples of her artwork are posted on sfwa.org.

Elgin was born Patricia Anne Wilkins in Louisiana, Missouri, on November 18, 1936 and grew up in Jefferson City, the state capital, on the Ozark Plateau (also known as the Ozark Mountains). Her mother, Hazel (Lewis) Wilkins, was a teacher; her father, Gaylord Lloyd Wilkins, was a lawyer, as was one of her grandfathers and four of her uncles. From an early age, she told Linda Hicks for the *Arkansas Democrat-Gazette* (June 29, 1997), she was exposed to "very stimulating conversation" and intellectual arguments. She loved words and learned to read when she was a toddler, while sitting on her grandfather's lap and "'helping' him do the daily crossword puzzle in the newspaper," as she recalled to Glatzer. She also told Glatzer, "I can't remember ever not wanting, and needing, to write, once I'd learned to make my letters." When her homework in second grade called for her to make up sentences using the day's spelling words, she would write a story incorporating all of them. As a youngster she spent much of her free time at the local library. By the time she was eight, local newspapers had published some of her poems. Throughout elementary, junior-high, and high school, she earned superior grades. By choice, she studied Latin, French, German, Russian, and Italian. "I did this for just one reason," she told Linda Hicks. "I was very weary of the myth of the ignorant hillbilly."

After she graduated from high school, in 1954, Elgin enrolled at the University of Chicago, in Illinois. Her distinctive speech, marked by a strong Ozark twang, made her a "laughingstock" among her fellow students, as she recalled to Hicks. "Everyone would burst out laughing. They bought me a year's worth of *New Yorker* magazines to help educate me." During her first year she earned an Academy of American Poets Award. That same year she married Peter Haden, a foreign-exchange student from Switzerland. During the next half-dozen years, while her husband completed his schooling and became an air-force officer, Elgin worked as a secretary and a translator and also gave birth to two daughters, Patricia and Rebecca, and a son, Michael. According to her entry in *Contemporary Authors* (New Revision Series, Volume 83, 2000), in 1958 she won a Eugene Saxon Memorial Trust Fellowship in poetry from *Harper's* magazine. In about 1963 her husband died, at age 29. The next year she married again; she became the stepmother of the child of her second husband, George Elgin, a sales manager, and with him she had another son, Benjamin. She also returned to school, this time attending Chico State College (since renamed California State University at Chico), where she earned a B.A. degree in 1967. She

next entered the University of California at San Diego in pursuit of a graduate degree in linguistics. To help pay her tuition, she wrote several science-fiction novels, taught classes in French, music theory and guitar, and linguistics, and entertained in coffeehouses, playing the guitar and singing. Despite her hectic schedule and what she has described as the efforts of several professors to discourage her, she earned an M.A. degree in 1970 and a Ph.D. in 1973. For the latter, she wrote two dissertations, one on the English language and the other on the Navajo language. (She has also studied the Hopi and Kumeyaay Amerindian languages.) Earlier, in 1972, she had joined the faculty of San Diego State University, where she taught linguistics. A textbook, titled "The Joy of English," which she wrote at the behest of a publisher, was judged by the company's peer reviewers to be unmarketable. "I then used it in my own courses . . . and it was pirated far and wide," she wrote for the *Linguistics and Science Fiction Bulletin* (April 1996). In 1980 health problems forced her to retire.

Elgin's first book was the science-fiction novel *The Communipaths* (1970). It is set in the distant future in the Three Galaxies, which are connected by a telepathic communication system that makes possible transmission of messages through unimaginably large distances. A "rogue telepath" sparks a series of vibrations that threaten to destroy a peaceful planet, and Tri-Galactic Agent Coyote Jones is recruited to capture the scoundrel. *Furthest* (1971), the second book in the Coyote Jones series, is named for a far-off planet whose seemingly perfect averageness invites officials' suspicions. Coyote Jones's investigations lead him to a "psychic concubine," or "mindwife," who no longer accepts her societal role. In the next book, *At the Seventh Level* (1972), Jones must find whoever is planning to murder a woman whose high status as a poet is offset by her lack of status due to her gender. In the fourth book, *Star-Anchored, Star-Angered* (1979), Jones discovers that the charismatic female messiah whose activities threaten the economic stability of the planet Freeway is not a fraud, and he embraces her beliefs.

In Elgin's next series, the Ozark Trilogy— *Twelve Fair Kingdoms*, *The Grand Jubilee*, and *And Then There'll Be Fireworks* (all published in 1981), the writer drew upon her knowledge of American Ozark culture in creating characters who establish a semi-utopian society with minimal government and little technology on the planet Ozark. The trilogy, as she wrote for sfwa.org, referring to the disciple who betrayed Jesus and three principal young female characters in the books, is "a story with a different sort of Judas in it, where the relationship isn't 'good versus evil' but the mutual interactions of good (whose agent is Silverweb of McDaniels) and evil (agent, Troublesome of Brightwater) and the balanced middle (headed up by Responsible of Brightwater)." In *Yonder Comes the Other End of Time* (1986), in which the TriGalactic Federation discovers the planet Ozark, Elgin blended elements of both the Communipaths and the Ozark novels.

Elgin set the Native Tongue trilogy in the United States in the 22d century. The 19th Amendment to the Constitution has been repealed, thus depriving women of the right to vote. A new amendment deprives women of other civil rights, bans them from public life, and reduces their status to that of property; they are valued solely for their breeding capabilities and their superior linguistic skills, with the most expert linguists serving as translators of other worlds' languages. As part of an underground rebellion against men, the experts, who live in isolated compounds, begin forming their own language, Láadan. (The accent indicates a syllable with a high tone.) Elgin chronicled the spread of Láadan and the growing success of the women's revolution in the next two books of the Native Tongue trilogy, *The Judas Rose* (1987) and *Earthsong* (1994). Elgin has said that she hoped that people reading the series would regard it as a warning about events that might actually come to pass.

Relying on the vocabulary currently available in English, Elgin has written more than a dozen books on what she has called "the gentle art of verbal self-defense" (GAVSD), the term she used as the title of her first book on that subject, published in 1980. "There are two goals in verbal self-defense," she wrote in an article posted on the Alternative Dispute Resolution Resources Web site (adrr.com): "To establish and maintain a language environment around you, by your own behavior and by the power of your presence, in which verbal violence almost never happens, [and] to be able to deal with verbal violence—on those rare occasions when it really cannot be avoided—efficiently, and effectively, with no loss of face on either side." The first principle of verbal self-defense, she explained, is to "know that you are under attack." The second, third, and fourth principles are, respectively, "Know what kind of attack you are facing" (which requires asking oneself such questions as "Why is the attack happening? What would be the reason behind it?" and "What is the attacker trying to accomplish?"), "Know how to make the defense fit the attack," and "Know how to follow through." Among Elgin's dozen other books on GAVSD are *The Gentle Art of Verbal Self-Defense for Business Success* (1989); *The Gentle Art of Verbal Self-Defense for Parents and Teenagers* (1990); *The Gentle Art of Written Self-Defense* (1993); *The Gentle Art of Communicating with Kids* (1996); *How to Turn the Other Cheek and Still Survive in Today's World* (1997); and *The Gentle Art of Verbal Self-Defense at Work* (2000). In *Peacetalk 101* (2003), Elgin presented in the form of a parable 12 rules for conversing amicably and preventing verbal abuse.

Elgin founded the Science Fiction Poetry Association in 1978; a few of her poems have appeared in the organization's journal, *Star*Line*. With John Grinder, she wrote *Guide to Transformational Grammar: History, Theory, Practice* (1973). Among her other books are the English textbook *Pouring*

Down Words (1975) and *The Language Imperative: The Power of Language to Enrich Your Life and Expand Your Mind* (2000). Elgin wrote the last-named book, as she explained for sfwa.org, because she believes that "learning a language is different from learning a sport or learning to play a musical instrument or learning physics. Learning a language is the *only* kind of learning that brings with it a new way of perceiving the world—what's often called a new 'worldview.'"

Elgin lives with her husband in a partly underground house in Huntsville, Arkansas. The couple have a dozen grandchildren, some of whom have accompanied Elgin to some of the many science-fiction conferences that she has attended regularly. At such conferences she has often displayed her artwork—fiber-art pictures (almost entirely crocheted), ink-and-pencil drawings, small crocheted and embroidered figures that she calls Ozarques, and painted gourds, made with fruits harvested from her own garden.

—K.J.E.

Suggested Reading: *Arkansas Democrat-Gazette* p10 June 29, 1997; *Houston Chronicle* p9 Nov. 8, 1998; ozarque.livejournal.com; sfwa.org/members/elgin; Women Writers Web site; *Women's Studies* p175+ Vol. 14, 1987

Selected Books: fiction—*The Communipaths*, 1970; *Furthest*, 1971; *At the Seventh Level*, 1972; *Star-Anchored, Star-Angered*, 1979; *Twelve Fair Kingdoms*, 1981; *The Grand Jubilee*, 1981; *And Then There'll Be Fireworks*, 1981; *Native Tongue*, 1984; *The Judas Rose*, 1987; *Earthsong*, 1994; nonfiction—*The Gentle Art of Verbal Self-Defense*, 1980; *More on the Gentle Art of Verbal Self-Defense*, 1983; *The Last Word on the Gentle Art of Verbal Self-Defense*, 1987; *Success with the Gentle Art of Verbal Self-Defense*, 1989; *Staying Well with the Gentle Art of Verbal Self-Defense*, 1990; *The Gentle Art of Verbal Self-Defense for Parents and Teenagers*, 1990; *The Gentle Art of Written Self-Defense*, 1993; *Genderspeak: Men, Women and the Gentle Art of Verbal Self-Defense*, 1993; *BusinessSpeak: Using the Gentle Art of Verbal Persuasion to Get What You Want at Work*, 1995; *You Can't Say That to Me!: Stopping the Pain of Verbal Abuse: An 8-Step Program*, 1995; *The Gentle Art of Communicating with Kids*, 1996; *How to Disagree without Being Disagreeable: Getting Your Point Across with the Gentle Art of Verbal Self-Defense*, 1997; *Try to Feel It My Way: New Help for Touch Dominant People and Those Who Care About Them*, 1997; *How to Turn the Other Cheek and Still Survive in Today's World*, 1997; *The Grandmother Principles*, 1998; *Language in Emergency Medicine: A Verbal Self-Defense Handbook*, 1999; *Peacetalk 101*, 2003

Courtesy of Mary Cross

Fagles, Robert

Sep. 11, 1933– Translator; educator; poet

Address: c/o Penguin Classics Publicity, 375 Hudson St., New York, NY 10014

For many of those who have no knowledge of ancient Greek, Robert Fagles is the voice of some of the most important literature written in that language. While teaching English and comparative literature at Princeton University, in New Jersey, beginning in 1962, Fagles made a name for himself outside the academy by translating plays by Aeschylus and Sophocles and the epics of Homer. He distinguished himself from other 20th-century translators by rendering such works in an idiom that simultaneously captures the essence of the originals and clarifies elements that would otherwise be obscure to contemporary readers. He thus seems to have come uncommonly close to accomplishing what he called in his introduction to The Oresteia "a translator's best hope," which, as he went on to note, was that of the 17th-century British poet and playwright John Dryden: the hope that "his author will speak the living language of the day. And not in a way that caters to its limits, one might add, but that gives its life and fibre something of a stretching in the process." With over two million copies of his translations in print, Fagles may justly be ranked with the primary popularizers of classical Greek literature.

Robert Fagles was born in Philadelphia, Pennsylvania, on September 11, 1933 to Vera (Voynow) Fagles, an architect, and Charles Fagles, a lawyer, the latter of whom died when he was 14. He was raised in Bala Cynwyd, Pennsylvania, where he at-

tended Bala Grammar School, Bala Cynwyd Junior High School, and Lower Merion Senior High School. After graduating from high school, Fagles entered Amherst College, in Massachusetts, where he majored in English and earned a bachelor's degree in 1955. It was at Amherst that he fell in love with Greek literature. Reading Homer's *Iliad* and *Odyssey* in translation, he was inspired to take up the study of ancient Greek so that he could read the poems in their original language. His focus, though, remained English; as a graduate student at Yale University, in New Haven, Connecticut, he enrolled in the school's English program and studied Greek in his free time. After receiving his Ph.D. in English, in 1959, he taught the subject at Yale for three years. Then, in 1962, he became an assistant professor of English at Princeton University, where he remained for the next 40 years, becoming an associate professor of English and comparative literature in 1965 and a full professor in 1970.

Fagles's first translations to be published were the poems of Bacchylides, a Greek lyric poet who lived in the fifth and sixth centuries B.C. and whose poems were rediscovered in 1896. *Complete Poems/Bacchylides* (1961) introduced Fagles as a translator who was capable of conveying the words of an ancient Greek poet in a way that made them relevant to English-speaking readers. "[Fagles] has produced a work which is at once a faithful translation of Bacchylides in the fullest sense and something which stands and lives in its own right as a work of art," the British classical scholar Maurice Bowra wrote in the foreword to the 1998 reprinting of the book. Earlier, in assessments of the first edition, the Harvard University classicist Emily Vermeule wrote for the *American Journal of Philology,* according to the Yale University Press Web site, "Fagles has created . . . a musical and craftsmanly series of verses. As a translator, Fagles has the merits of . . . keeping the lilting rhythms of Bacchylides alive in one's ear . . . and unearthing metaphors behind faded Greek words, of splitting the strings of compound adjectives into pungent clauses which lose nothing in color but make coordinated English." After that success Fagles took up more traditional scholarly pursuits, editing *Homer: A Collection of Critical Essays* (1962) with George Steiner and working on an edition of the 18th-century poet Alexander Pope's translations of the *Iliad* and *Odyssey,* which was published in 1967.

Fagles's next major work was his translation of the Greek dramatist Aeschylus's trilogy *The Oresteia,* made up of *Agamemnon, The Libation Bearers,* and *The Eumenides.* He chose to make those works seem somewhat dated in their use of language, an approach that Robert Dyer, in the *Yale Review* (Summer 1976), deemed to be appropriate. "The energy of the translator's celebration rings through in the rich strength of the translation," Dyer wrote. "If it seems sometimes Shakespearian and unmodern we must remember that Aeschylus seemed that way in antiquity, perhaps already in his own lifetime. If the techniques of celebration employed by Aeschylus and his translator seem mannered to a modern audience, as I suspect this translation may, we should not criticize adversely, for in the ritual mannerism is Aeschylus's personal manner. The strength of the translation and introduction lies, however, less in the established unity than in brilliant and provocative analyses and renderings of the ambiguities and complexities of the text." The classics educator Bernard Knox, who assessed Fagles's work for the *New York Review of Books* (February 5, 1976), thought the translation's power lay in its ability to make Aeschylus's world more comprehensible to the reader. "But the question . . . is this: what is the difference between this *Oresteia* and that of Richmond Lattimore, a version which, greatly (and justly) admired, has been the authorized version for the postwar years?" Knox asked. "The first impression that emerges from a comparison of individual passages is that Fagles is more solicitous of the needs of the Greekless reader. . . . The over-all result of this bias . . . is not only greater immediate intelligibility but also . . . English verse which is 'actable.'" Nominated for a National Book Award, the Fagles translation of *The Oresteia* became the standard text in the last years of the 20th century and prompted the British writer Francis Spufford to declare in the London *Guardian* (April 12, 1994), "Aeschylus is now lucid because of Robert Fagles."

During the 1970s Fagles was also working on his own poems; in 1978 he published a book of his original poetry, *I Vincent: Poems from the Pictures of Van Gogh*. He described the poems, according to Lynn Emanuel in *Library Journal* (October 15, 1978), as "'very free translations' of Van Gogh's paintings and letters." Each poem takes as its subject a painting and attempts to express in language its visual effects. Among those who praised the book was a critic for the *Virginia Quarterly Review* (Autumn 1979), who wrote that Fagles had "produced a work of insight and artistic virtuosity. His knowledge of Van Gogh's life and work appears profound; more importantly, Professor Fagles reveals a deep imaginative sympathy with the painter. His poems do not use Van Gogh's works merely as an occasion but try to enrich our understanding of the paintings. What surprises is that, without loss of poetic integrity and without sounding 'academic,' they splendidly succeed." Others, however, were not favorably impressed. A reviewer for *Choice* (September 1979), for example, wrote, "The black-and-white, diminished reproductions cannot convey the color and texture of the paintings, and the poems are often derivative of the paintings and/or amateurish. . . . A poem about a painting must transcend the painting and illuminate the life beyond the work of art. Fagles consistently fails in this regard." Fagles never published another book of his own poems. His verses occasionally appear in literary journals, however.

Fagles's translations of three of Sophocles's plays, *Antigone, Oedipus the King,* and *Oedipus at Colonus,* were published together under the title *The Three Theban Plays* (1982). Those translations were less well received than Fagles's Aeschylus translations. Indeed, the value of the book, according to some reviewers, derived not so much from the translations of the plays as from the introductions and explanatory notes provided by Bernard Knox, a classical scholar with whom Fagles had studied at Yale. In terms of their relationship, Knox is, as Fagles told Chris Hedges for the *New York Times* (April 13, 2004), "very much the professor, and I am still the student . . . I stand in awe of him. I cherish our friendship." Hugh Lloyd-Jones, an Oxford University professor of Greek, writing for the *New York Review of Books* (October 7, 1982), expressed the view that Fagles's translations were "the least inadequate versions of the three plays in modern times" but that Knox's commentaries might provide contemporary readers with the needed "assistance in understanding a work coming from a culture and religion remote from those of [their] own time, and no other translation of Sophocles now available is anything like so well equipped in this respect." M. D. Northrup was more positive, writing for *Library Journal* (August 1982), "Fagles is a skillful translator of Greek drama, a fact amply demonstrated by his 1976 translation of Aeschylus' *Oresteia.* The translations under review further confirm his competence." Northrup also wrote, "It is the happy combination of Fagles' translations and Knox's supplementary material that makes the present work compare quite favorably with other English treatments of the same plays."

Throughout the 1980s Fagles devoted much of his energy to a translation of Homer's *Iliad*; his version was published, with an introduction by Knox, in 1990. That work brought him greater success than any of his previous ones, winning him the 1991 Harold Morton Landon Translation Award from the Academy of American Poets, an award from the Translation Center of Columbia University, and the New Jersey Humanities Book Award. Reviewers voiced their admiration for Fagles's ability to render an ancient text in modern terms without losing sight of the original's spirit. "Fagles . . . offers a verse translation that explains what readers need to know, in clear, vigorous language that still retains a sense of the sweep and the sonority of the original," Mary Lefkowitz, who taught classical studies at Wellesley College, wrote for the *Washington Post* (September 16, 1990). Oliver Taplin, a professor of classical languages at Oxford University, wrote for the *New York Times* (October 7, 1990) that Fagles's translation "has real pace, it presses onward, leading the reader forward with an irresistible flow. [Fagles] achieves this, among other ways, by going for relatively short words that accumulate rhythm in long, lightly punctuated sequences." Taplin had some reservations, though: "My chief unease is, perhaps, over the patchy use of archaism and odd phraseology in the attempt, I presume, to get over the point that the language of Homer was not a natural spoken language, far from it. But when Agamemnon says to the prophet Calchas near the beginning: 'Now, again, you divine god's will for the armies,/ bruit it out, as fact, why the deadly Archer/ multiplies our pains,' the verb 'divine' is too peculiar." Despite the qualms of a few critics, Fagles's *Iliad* proved to be an overwhelming success for a work of that kind. As Paul Gray reported for *Time* (October 28, 1996), as of mid-1996 it had sold 22,000 hardcover copies and 140,000 paperback copies (and was in its eighth printing in the paperback edition). In addition, sales of an abridged audio cassette of the book, read by Derek Jacobi, had exceeded 35,000 copies.

Like eminent translators of Homer before him, Fagles also translated Homer's other great epic, the *Odyssey*. Published in 1996 with an introduction by Knox, it earned Fagles the Academy Award in Literature from the American Academy of Arts and Letters and the PEN/Ralph Manheim Medal for Translation. It also found favor with reviewers. Ian Thomson, for example, wrote for the London *Guardian* (June 19, 1997) that the translation "triumphantly restores the poem to its Hellenic toughness. The *Odyssey* unfolds in a real world of rawhide sandals, brine-soaked mariners and bronze shinguards. As Ezra Pound said, Homer had an 'ear for the sea-surge,' and Fagles captures it superbly in images of dripping oarblades and pitchers of shining wine." The translation was a commercial success and brought Fagles more publicity than he had ever enjoyed before; for instance, he was interviewed on the nationally televised PBS weeknight show *The NewsHour with Jim Lehrer*. Fagles's *Odyssey* also began to replace earlier ones as the standard modern translation. As Peter Green wrote for the *New Republic* (February 24, 1997), "In comparing Robert Fagles' translation to those of his predecessors, the first thing we should stress, and by far the most important, is that this is an *Odyssey* consciously crafted for performance. The wheel has indeed come full circle. Just as it was for centuries an article of faith that Homer wrote his poems, so, virtually since the Renaissance, all translations, even the best, have been composed to be read. But Fagles' Homer is accompanied by an audiotape version, and this is not an electronic gimmick, it is an integral part of this translation's purpose: to recreate, for those who have ears to hear, the ambience and the impact of the rhapsode's magic, his voice, like that of Odysseus, 'holding them spellbound down the shadowed halls.' Its spoken force is what gives Fagles' version its unique quality. We are caught, like Coleridge's wedding-guest, by this other ancient mariner: we cannot choose but hear."

Fagles completed his most recent project, a translation of the *Aeneid*, by the Roman poet Virgil, in 2006. He had to return to his study of Latin to accomplish the task, which he had worked on since 1997 for four or five hours a day at home. Fagles's version is distinguished stylistically from other recent translations of the *Aeneid* by the absence of meter, which, according to a favorable review in *Publishers Weekly* (September 18, 2006), allowed Fagles to "stay literal when he wishes, and grow eloquent when he wants." (In Allen Mandelbaum's 1972 translation, the English is in blank verse, which has meter but not rhyme.) Fagles has expressed the hope that his latest work will be as widely read as his previous ones. "The *Aeneid* is a cautionary tale," he told Chris Hedges. "It is one we need to read today. It speaks of the terrible price of victory in war, for Virgil knew that victory is finally impossible, that it always lies out of reach. He saw the unforeseen aftermath, the way war could all go wrong whether from poor planning or because of the gods on high. He knew the sheer accumulation of death, the destruction, the pain we inflict when we use force to create empire." *Publishers Weekly* agreed with the timeliness of Fagles's edition, which joined more than a dozen translations currently for sale, suggesting, "Aeneas' story might prompt new reflection now, when Americans are already thinking about international conflict and the unexpected costs of war." Fagles's publisher, Viking Penguin, issued a 60,000-copy first printing of the book. Its preface contains a discussion by Bernard Knox of Virgil's place in history.

When Fagles retired, in 2002, he held the title Arthur W. Marks '19 Professor of Comparative Literature at Princeton. He lives in the town of Princeton with his wife, Lynne (identified in some sources as Marilyn), an English teacher who for years spent much time as a literacy volunteer in New Jersey prisons. The couple, who married in 1956, have two daughters.

—A.R.

Suggested Reading: *Choice* p831 Sep. 1979; (London) *Guardian* p10 Apr. 12, 1994; *New Republic* p30+ Feb. 24, 1997; *New York Review of Books* p11 Feb. 5, 1976; *New York Times* VII p1 Oct. 7, 1990, Apr. 13, 2004; *Paris Review* p142+ Summer 1999; *Time* p90+ Oct. 28, 1996; *Virginia Quarterly Review* p147 Autumn 1979; *Washington Post* X p5 Sep. 16, 1990; *Yale Review* p600 Summer 1976

Selected Books: translations—*Complete Poems/Bacchylides*, 1961; *The Oresteia*, 1976; *The Three Theban Plays*, 1982; *The Iliad*, 1990; *The Odyssey*, 1996; *The Aeneid*, 2006

Robert Mora/Getty Images

Falco, Edie

July 5, 1963– Actress

Address: c/o ICM, 8942 Wilshire Blvd., Beverly Hills, CA 90211

"All I ever wanted to do was act. And pay my bills," the actress Edie Falco told Robin Finn for the *New York Times* (April 24, 2001). The order in which she listed those desires is perhaps telling; a look at her 15-year career in television, film, and theater makes it clear that Falco has long placed artistic integrity ahead of financial reward. It was not until she landed the part of Carmela Soprano on the highly successful HBO cable-TV series *The Sopranos*, which debuted in 1999, that Falco could claim both. A seasoned New York theater actress whose work included parts in Off-Broadway plays and television police dramas, Falco spent over a dozen years working day jobs to support herself before finding success with *The Sopranos*, whose seventh and final season is scheduled to begin in 2007. (Frequently mentioned in interviews is that immediately prior to the show's debut, Falco—who was in her mid-30s—could not afford cable television.) By the start of the show's second season, in 2000, she had become the first actress ever to win all of television's major awards: an Emmy, for outstanding lead actress in a dramatic series; a Golden Globe, for best performance by an actress in a dramatic television series; and a Screen Actors Guild (SAG) Award, for outstanding performance by a female actor in a drama.

Falco's role on the show, as the put-upon wife of the fictional New Jersey Mafia boss Tony Soprano (played by James Gandolfini), has been ac-

claimed for its subtlety and lack of pretense. Mark Morris commented in the London *Observer* (September 24, 2000), "Falco is effortless in the role, utterly real: despairing, loyal, tough, able to hold her own at unexpected moments. The Mafia wife who flirts with the priest, who makes the cannelloni, who seems so ordinary and decent and yet is an expert at stashing the cash when the Feds come calling. The fact that she's not flashy or obvious but you still notice her is what makes her performance special." Falco's theater work has also been commended. Her notable stage appearances have included a 2001 run of the *Vagina Monologues* at London's Ambassador Theater, as well as a performance of that show in New York as part of the events of V-Day, which sought to raise awareness about violence toward women. She also starred in the 2002 revival of Terence McNally's 1987 play *Frankie and Johnny in the Clair de Lune*, which broke four box-office records at New York's Belasco Theater and was the most successful Broadway show of its season. In 2004 she played a suicidal daughter in Marsha Norman's *'night, Mother*, at the Royale Theater on Broadway. Describing that performance, Jesse Green wrote for the *New York Times* (November 7, 2004) "Critics and colleagues reach for words like 'transparency' and 'vulnerability' to describe her work because the work itself is almost invisible. Her characters come across directly, without the semaphore of actorly style."

Edith Falco was born in Brooklyn, New York, on July 5, 1963, the second of four children. When she was four, her family relocated to Long Island, where the actress spent the remainder of her childhood, moving among neighboring towns. Green, paraphrasing Falco, described the actress's family as "nutty and bohemian"; both of her parents were involved in the arts—Edie's father, Frank Falco, as a graphic artist and jazz drummer, and her mother, Judith Anderson, as an amateur actress. Her parents divorced when she was 14. Falco told Bruce Fretts for *Entertainment Weekly* (January 15, 1999), "I grew up as a tomboy. I was always barefoot, running races with the guys on the block, climbing trees, and beating kids up." As a young girl she performed plays in a wooden theater her mother constructed in their backyard. She also accompanied her mother to community theater performances, which inspired Falco to take a more serious interest in drama. She joined Northport High School's theater and choral groups, and she also auditioned (unsuccessfully) for a part in the Broadway production of *Dreamgirls*.

In 1982 Falco enrolled at the State University of New York (SUNY) at Purchase, studying drama at the school's Conservatory of Theatre Arts and Film. The conservatory's reputation for producing famous actors had led its alumni to be nicknamed "The Purchase Mafia." Falco found the environment intimidating and was unhappy with the parts she received. "I spent four years with blacked-out teeth and a Cockney accent. It broke my heart," she told Michael A. Lipton and Ken Baker for *People*

(March 13, 2000). She was often cast in the parts of aging women, overlooked for starring roles because she lacked the conventional looks of a lead actress. "I had problems with my weight, being heavy, and some people were not very nice about that. I spent a lot of time crying. . . . At that point it had been drilled into me that the pretty, confident girls would get the work," she told Green. After a professor warned her that she "would never work in television or film because of the way I talk—I have a slight sibilance," Falco took speech therapy and, upon graduating, in 1986, set out to be a professional actress in New York City.

Over the next five years, Falco acted in Off-Broadway plays and got small parts in soap operas, working as a waitress to earn additional income. She also appeared in independent films by SUNY Purchase graduates, such as Hal Hartley's *The Unbelievable Truth* (1989), in which she had her first professional film role; Hartley's *Trust* (1990); and Nick Gomez's *Laws of Gravity* (1992). In addition to waitressing, Falco trained as both a legal proofreader and a graphic artist. She also worked for a company that hired her out as an entertainer at parties and other functions. She told Morris, "I had to dress up as Betsy Ross once, sit on the centrepiece of a table while people ate their dinner. Guys got drunk and started looking under my skirt, it was a . . . nightmare. Other times, we had to dress up in outfits and pull people on to the dancefloor. At weddings, I'm the one in the chair praying that no one comes near me. And there I was, having to put on Cookie Monster with this giant head." During that period Falco struggled with substance addiction and experienced anxiety attacks. She told Jeff Giles for *Newsweek* (September 16, 2002), "You go to college and you go off and do plays and then when the dust clears, you are left alone in your crazy apartment at 4 in the afternoon with no job, no prospects and a waitressing shift to go to. And real, heavy-duty darkness can set in." One day Falco walked off her job at a hardware store and boarded a train to Long Island, where she rested at her mother's home. Asked if her mother advised her at that point to give up acting, Falco told Giles, "No, she just talked me through it. Anxiety attacks have been in my family for years. We are sort of a high-strung bunch."

In the early 1990s, after overcoming her addiction through a variety of methods, Falco was cast in more visible, recurring television roles: as an attorney on *Law and Order* and as a police officer's wife on *Homicide: Life on the Street*. She also landed small parts in feature-length films, including Woody Allen's *Bullets Over Broadway* (1994); *Cop Land* (1997), starring Sylvester Stallone; and the Howard Stern vehicle *Private Parts* (1997). As she had during college, Falco often felt typecast—either as "The Diane Keaton type, sort of fumbling around" or as the no-nonsense "district attorney type," as she told Kamau High for the *Financial Times* (October 30, 2004). But as a writer for *Celebrity Biographies* (2005) noted, she approached even those limited parts with ingenuity, bringing "increased dimensionality to the stereotypical hardened woman." For two years beginning in 1997, she played one such part—that of a corrections officer—on the HBO series *Oz*.

It was her work on *Oz* (a show created by Tom Fontana, who had previously directed Falco in *Homicide: Life on the Street*) that caught the attention of *The Sopranos*' creator, David Chase, who asked Falco to audition for the part of Carmela. Chase said to Lipton and Baker about the role, "Without a real strong, shrewd wife like Carmela, what you'd have is just another conventional Mob show with a bunch of wiseguys sitting around b.s.-ing and smoking in bars." Once she got the part, Falco initially doubted her ability to portray her character adequately. Falco, who had no children when *The Sopranos* began filming, told Jane Pauley on NBC's program *Dateline* (January 18, 2002, on-line), "When I was first cast in the part, . . . my biggest fear was being able to pull off being the mother of two teenagers." Her fear subsided, though, as she spent more time on the set. "Something very organic happens when you're around two young kids, and you're behaving as their mother, something bigger than me starts to take place, and I start to think, 'I think I could do this.' Not only could I, but I think I'd like to," she said to Pauley. (Indeed, in 2004 Falco adopted a son, whom she named Anderson—her mother's maiden name.) Discussing her preparation for playing Carmela, Falco told Pauley, "I get on the set, truly it is a Pavlovian experience. There's the house, there's Tony, me and my kids and there's my fingernails and my jewelry and the hair and the outfit. And I am suddenly a different person."

Falco had to adjust to a newfound celebrity she had not expected. Of her sudden fame, she told Robin Finn, "I'm very happy for it, but it also makes you kind of quizzical about the world; you know, they see you on a television show and suddenly you're more worthy than you were five years ago, which is malarkey, frankly." In 2003 Falco was diagnosed with breast cancer. She continued to work on *The Sopranos* while receiving treatment; to protect her privacy, she kept her condition concealed from the media until her treatment was completed.

Falco's heightened profile also created new expectations on the part of celebrity watchers. At the 1999 Emmy Awards ceremony, at which she won the honor for outstanding lead actress in a dramatic series, Falco was also named "worst dressed" by *E! Television*'s fashion critics Joan and Melissa Rivers. "I grew up a tomboy," Falco said to Morris. "Here I was, thrust into this world where I feel so out of place. I'm trying to do my best, to show up for these things. The truth is that it goes against my nature." She also told Morris, "It felt like the popular girl at junior high had put gum on my back."

Falco reportedly feels fulfilled by her work. "I'm the happiest person I know," she told Green. Asked what she plans to do after *The Sopranos* concludes, Falco told Pauley, "Some place or other, I will be acting after this is done, because it is what I love to do. It is the only time I really feel sure that I know why I am alive. . . . It doesn't matter if . . . I remain in the public eye or, you know, the level at which, you know, I'll be recognized . . . nobody can stop me from doing it." In the past half-dozen years, Falco has been featured in a number of mainstream films. In 1999 she played a supporting role in the Sydney Pollack drama *Random Hearts* (1999), starring Harrison Ford. In 2002, in a role written specifically for her, she appeared as the divorcée and motel manager Marly Temple in John Sayles's *Sunshine State* (2002). She has a role in the film *Freedomland*, starring Samuel Jackson, which opened in theaters in February 2006.

—M.B.

Suggested Reading: *New York Times* B p2 Apr. 24, 2001, II p1 Nov. 7, 2004; *New York Times Magazine* p28+ July 7, 2002; *Newsweek* p52+ Sep. 16, 2002; *Observer* Life Pages p12 Sep. 24, 2000; *TV Guide* p32+ May 19–25, 2001

Selected Films: *The Unbelievable Truth*, 1989; *Trust*, 1990; *Laws of Gravity*, 1992; *Bullets Over Broadway*, 1994; *Cost of Living*, 1997; *Cop Land*, 1997; *Private Parts*, 1997; *Random Hearts*, 1999; *Sunshine State*, 2002; *The Great New Wonderful*, 2005

Selected Television Shows: *Oz*, 1997–99; *The Sopranos*, 1999–

Selected Plays: *Side Man*, 1999; *The Vagina Monologues*, 2001; *Frankie and Johnny in the Clair de Lune*, 2002; *'night, Mother*, 2004

Mark Wilson/Getty Images

Fitzgerald, Patrick J.

1960– Federal prosecutor; U.S. Attorney, Northern District of Illinois

Address: U.S. Attorney's Office, 219 S. Dearborn St., Fifth Fl., Chicago, IL 60604

On July 6, 2005 Judith Miller, then a reporter for the *New York Times*, was sent to prison for her refusal to testify about a confidential source before a federal grand jury in a widely publicized case. The special prosecutor in that case, United States attorney Patrick J. Fitzgerald, explained his decision to

imprison a journalist by saying, according to Julie Hirschfeld Davis in the *Baltimore Sun* (July 19, 2005), "At a certain point we have to yield to law because if we don't, we're lost." Fitzgerald's words and deeds that day epitomized his approach to his position as a federal prosecutor. In his primary post he heads one of the nation's largest and most important federal-attorney's offices, and in his temporary post he serves as a special prosecutor for a case involving the leak of a CIA (Central Intelligence Agency) operative's name to members of the press—the case with which Miller was involved. In both capacities, Fitzgerald has combined a high-minded belief in the laws of the land as society's fundamental ordering principles with a willingness to use any legal means at his disposal to have lawbreakers punished, even if doing so means riding roughshod over such conventions as the shaky legal protections traditionally granted journalists or the guidelines for prosecuting terrorists. By all accounts sincere, gifted, modest, and so hardworking that for 14 years he lived in an apartment without ever bothering to have the gas turned on, Fitzgerald has a long history of successfully and relentlessly pursuing convictions for crimes ranging from drug trafficking to seditious conspiracy. His work has earned him virtually universal acclaim from other law-enforcement officials. Having begun as an assistant U.S. attorney in 1988 and worked almost constantly on some of America's most important terrorism cases since 1993, Fitzgerald has been credited with honing the legal techniques necessary to prosecute terrorism successfully. He is regarded as a foremost expert on the terrorist organization Al Qaeda and its head, the wealthy Saudi Arabian exile Osama bin Laden. "He is a one-man encyclopedia on al Qaeda because he has this absolutely scary photographic memory," his close friend and former colleague, U.S. deputy attorney general James Comey, told

Chitra Ragavan and Eric Ferkenhoff for *U.S. News & World Report* (July 4, 2005). "He is a one-man dot connector, which is very valuable." Even Fitzgerald's recent entry into the typically polarized activity of investigating the administration of a sitting president, which Fitzgerald is doing in connection with the CIA leak case, has not tarnished his reputation as a politically independent prosecutor. His treatment of Miller, however, and to a much lesser degree his approach to prosecuting other cases, has brought harsh criticism of his methods, particularly from members of the media, who argue that his willingness to jail Miller for maintaining the confidentiality of her source might make it harder for journalists to gather the sort of information necessary for maintaining a truly free press. Still, even those critical of Fitzgerald have generally questioned only his means, not his ends. "He's a real prosecutor," an assistant U.S. attorney under Fitzgerald told Matt O'Connor for the *Chicago Tribune* (July 1, 2002). "He's not here for advancement to a powerhouse law firm for a gazillion dollars. That's not his agenda. He's got one agenda: doing the job the best possible way."

One of four children, Patrick J. Fitzgerald was born in 1960 in the Flatbush area of Brooklyn, a borough of New York City. His parents had both immigrated to the U.S. from County Clare, Ireland. His mother, Tillie, came when she was young, while his father, also named Patrick, arrived at age 31. In New York his father worked as a doorman at a building in Manhattan's well-to-do Upper East Side; he is said never to have taken a vacation and always to have arrived early for his shift. Fitzgerald has credited his work ethic and his attitude toward justice to his parents. "They were very hardworking, straight, decent people," he told Peter Slevin for the *Washington Post* (February 2, 2005). "The values we grew up with were straight-ahead. We didn't grow up in a household where people were anything but direct." Fitzgerald added: "I'm hoping that if you're a straight shooter in the world, that's not that remarkable."

An excellent student at Our Lady Help of Christians, a private Catholic primary school in Brooklyn, Fitzgerald was admitted to Regis High School, a highly prestigious Jesuit academy in New York City that is free of charge to the select few who are admitted. At Regis he studied Latin and other required subjects and served on the debate team. After his graduation he majored in economics and mathematics at Amherst College, in Massachusetts. There his tuition was paid in part by his earnings from a job as a janitor during his high-school years and by summer stints in college as a doorman for a building not far from the one where his father was employed. He graduated from Amherst in 1982 with a B.A. degree and as a member of the prestigious national honor society Phi Beta Kappa. Instead of seeking a job in the financial industry, which his undergraduate courses had prepared him for—as he told Kristen Scharnberg for the *Chicago Tribune Magazine* (February 27, 2005), the idea of "sitting around predicting turns in the stock market" seemed unappealing—he enrolled at Harvard Law School, in Cambridge, Massachusetts. In a Boston courtroom during his final year at Harvard, he accidentally bumped into a man later described to him as "the head of the New England mob." The episode inspired him to become a government prosecutor, according to Scharnberg. Nevertheless, for three years after he earned a J.D. degree from Harvard, in 1985, he worked in private practice, as a litigation associate at the New York City law firm of Christy & Viener (now a part of the international law firm Salans).

Fitzgerald's career as a public prosecutor began in 1988, when he became an assistant U.S. attorney for the Southern District of New York, one of the most prominent of the nation's 93 federal district-attorney offices. Fitzgerald's first high-profile case came to trial in 1991, when he helped to prosecute a New York drug lord named George Rivera, who in his late teens and early 20s had amassed $15 million from heroin dealing and was believed to have been responsible for six murders. Known as "Boy George," Rivera was sentenced to life in prison for tax evasion and narcotics conspiracy; the jury was deadlocked as to whether he was guilty of the 12 other charges brought against him. Succeeding in getting a long sentence meted out for relatively minor charges became a leitmotif in Fitzgerald's career, as did (though to a lesser degree) prosecuting cases that ended in hung juries.

Fitzgerald's next widely publicized case involved two important Mafia figures, the brothers John and Joseph Gambino, who had been charged with crimes related to drug smuggling and murder. The four-month trial was closely followed by the media. The jury deliberated for 10 days but could not reach a verdict, leading the judge to declare a mistrial and forcing the U.S. attorney's office to try the case again. Fitzgerald was devastated, and when he and his new partner, Richard Zabel, began pretrial hearings for the second trial, he showed little interest in what was happening, going so far as to write Zabel a note in court that—instead of offering some procedural advice or a reminder about a small but important detail—merely asked, "Is there beer back in the fridge?" It was the "lowest point in his career," Scharnberg wrote. The Gambinos did not have a second trial; in January 1994 the brothers pleaded guilty to a variety of charges, among them drug trafficking—a startling admission. "The defendants had maintained at the last trial that they were against drugs and that, if there is a Mafia, it's against drugs," a United Press International reporter quoted Fitzgerald as saying (January 7, 1994). "We argued that that's a myth."

After a six-week vacation in Australia and New Zealand—which marked the first time in almost two years that he had left his office for more than a few hours—Fitzgerald returned to the New York district and was soon assigned to his first terrorism case. The defendants were Omar Abdel Rahman, a blind Muslim religious leader in exile from his native Egypt, and nine of his associates. Rahman had come to the attention of U.S. authorities because other associates of his had been involved in the 1993 bombing of the World Trade Center, which had killed six people and injured about 1,000 others. The 10 people Fitzgerald and his partners prosecuted in the new case were tried under a seldom-cited law (dating from 1861) that made it illegal to plan to commit a crime against the United States, regardless of whether the crime was even attempted. That risky prosecutorial technique had only occasionally been successful in the recent past, but for Fitzgerald and his colleagues the gambit worked. On October 1, 1995, after an eight-month trial in which more than 200 witnesses testified and a summation by Fitzgerald that continued for three days, all 10 defendants were convicted. Rahman and one other defendant later received life sentences, while prison terms for the remaining eight men ranged from 25 to 57 years. Later in 1995, in recognition of his work on the case, Fitzgerald was named co-chief of his district's organized-crime and terrorism unit, and in July 1996 Fitzgerald and two other prosecutors involved in the case received the U.S. attorney general's highest honor, the award for exceptional service.

Over the next few years, Fitzgerald continued to prosecute terrorists, tax evaders, and other suspected lawbreakers. During that time he began a criminal investigation of Osama bin Laden, seeking clues in Africa, Asia, and the Middle East for bin Laden's whereabouts and operations. On August 7, 1998, while Fitzgerald was on vacation, working on his apartment to make it more habitable, bombs exploded almost simultaneously in front of the American embassies in Kenya and Tanzania, killing 257 people, most of them local civilians. Fitzgerald was immediately dispatched to Africa to begin an investigation that would take up most of his working life for the better part of the next three years. In the end he brought charges against bin Laden and 22 other people for the bombings, but he was able to locate and try only four.

As the trial got under way, at the beginning of 2001, a Republican U.S. senator from Illinois, Peter Fitzgerald (who is not related to Patrick Fitzgerald), began looking for a new head of the Northern District federal attorney's office in his state. (U.S. senators are granted the opportunity to propose candidates by tradition rather than law, as it is nominally the attorney general who appoints an attorney to the position. The president then nominates the candidate and the Senate votes to confirm.) The Northern District of Illinois is one of the nation's largest, most visible, and most influential U.S. attorneys' offices. It employs 300 lawyers, roughly half of them assistant U.S. attorneys, and covers an area of 18 counties, whose total population is about nine million. The top job in the Northern District has traditionally gone to an attorney from Chicago, where the office is based, or from elsewhere in that part of the state. But since 1998

the Northern District office had been investigating and prosecuting dozens of local and state officials for corruption, among them Illinois's then-governor, George Ryan, and Peter Fitzgerald feared that appointing a local attorney might cause the investigation to lose momentum—or at least give it the appearance of doing so. Turning to the then-director of the FBI, Louis Freeh, and then to several other knowledgeable people, Peter Fitzgerald asked each in turn, according to Peter Slevin, "Who's the best assistant U.S. attorney you know of in the country?" Everyone reportedly responded, "Patrick Fitzgerald." After meeting Patrick Fitzgerald, the senator decided to recommend him for the position. One potential problem was that Patrick Fitzgerald is a confirmed political independent (he has never registered to vote as a member of a national party and has been universally described as having no aspirations to elective office), and as a Republican, Peter Fitzgerald was expected to choose a member of his party. But on May 13, 2001, as the trial of the men held responsible for the embassy bombings was nearing its end, Peter Fitzgerald's recommendation was announced to the press. While most welcomed the choice, it surprised some Chicago-area lawyers; others were put off by the implication of corruption in Chicago, however mild, that followed from Peter Fitzgerald's emphasis on the New York attorney's independence. A few weeks later, on May 29, the four men on trial for the embassy bombings were convicted. They were later given life sentences. (Fitzgerald had sought the death penalty for the two convicted of planting the bombs.)

On September 1, 2001, after a visit to relatives in Ireland, Fitzgerald started working in Chicago, even though the U.S. Senate had not yet confirmed his appointment. Ten days later 19 terrorists commandeered four airplanes in the northeastern part of the U.S. They flew two of the planes into the twin towers of the World Trade Center, in New York City, and one into the Pentagon; one crashed in a field in Pennsylvania. Nearly 3,000 people died in the attacks. The massive damage and loss of life were precisely what Rahman and his associates had been convicted of planning, and, as Fitzgerald told Mike Robinson for the Associated Press (November 13, 2001), while watching the towers fall on television, he immediately thought of bin Laden. Federal officials soon contacted Fitzgerald, mining him for information about Al Qaeda and its leaders and for some time keeping his location secret. "He knows more about the bin Laden network than anyone else in the world, and [federal officials] need him now," an unnamed prosecutor told Jerry Markon and Laurie P. Cohen for the *Wall Street Journal* (September 21, 2001). On October 23 the U.S. Senate voted unanimously to approve his appointment to the Northern District. By late November Fitzgerald had returned to his Chicago office. (Currently, he still maintains close ties to various federal investigations of terrorists, especially as the head of a subcommittee on terrorism that is an arm of the U.S. attorney general's advisory committee.)

For most of the next two years, Fitzgerald's work was largely restricted to overseeing cases involving corruption, drug sales, gang activities, fraud, and white-collar crime cases. During that time any lingering resentment over his outsider status faded from view. Office morale was reported to have improved, and other federal law officials said that his work was helping to motivate their staffs as well as his own. Among other actions, he set in place new rules governing how his office can negotiate plea agreements with defendants.

During the first third of 2002, according to O'Connor, Fitzgerald's office brought 229 indictments against a total of 457 felony defendants—55 and 137 more, respectively, than for the same period the year before. The first of the indictments to attract national attention was against Enaam Arnaout, the executive director of an Islamic charitable organization known in the U.S. as the Benevolence International Foundation (BIF). Though the government acknowledged that Arnaout's organization operated in part as a charity, when he was arrested in May 2002 it alleged that BIF directed a portion of its funds toward the support of terrorists and that Arnaout had direct ties to Al Qaeda. In addition to accusing him of providing material support to terrorists, the government indicted Arnaout for fraudulently obtaining funds for his charity (technically, the charge was racketeering) and for perjury. Arnaout denied any connection to Al Qaeda, but on the eve of the trial, he pleaded guilty to one count of racketeering and promised to provide the government with information. The judge in the case emphasized that no connections with Al Qaeda had been proven, and to many the plea to the lesser charge and the relatively light sentence (11 years in prison) that Arnaout received were evidence that Fitzgerald's case had been weak from the beginning. An independent government commission (the National Commission on Terrorist Attacks upon the United States) charged with investigating the events of September 11, 2001 later concluded that the methods used to prosecute BIF and another Islamic charity that had been charged around the same time raised "substantial civil liberty concerns" and that the two investigations "revealed little compelling evidence that either of these charities actually provided financial support to al Qaeda—at least after al Qaeda was designated a foreign terrorist organization in 1999." According to Kirsten Scharnberg, Fitzgerald nonetheless remains pleased with the results of his investigation.

In December 2003 the continuing federal investigation into corruption among Illinois state-government officials, named Operation Safe Roads after the trucking-license scandal that inspired the original inquiry, led to the conviction of former Illinois governor George Ryan on charges of racketeering conspiracy, false statements, and tax and mail fraud. Fitzgerald had alleged in the indictment that Ryan had obtained $167,000 by illegal means during his time in office and had funneled to a friend over $300,000 worth of gifts, services, and loans. Ryan, who could have received a maximum penalty of 95 years in prison, was sentenced to six-and-a-half years behind bars (which nevertheless, as some observers pointed out, could amount to a life sentence for the septuagenarian. who suffers from diabetes and Crohn's disease). According to reporters for the Web site Bloomburg.com (September 6, 2006), Fitzgerald called the sentence "appropriate."

Less than a month after he indicted Ryan, Fitzgerald was named by James Comey, his former colleague in New York and currently the assistant U.S. attorney general, to lead a grand jury investigation into the revealing of the name of a covert CIA agent to the syndicated newspaper columnist and cable-television commentator Robert Novak. The CIA agent, whom Novak identified by her maiden name, Valerie Plame, was the wife of a former U.S. ambassador, Joseph Wilson, who, in an op-ed piece published in the *New York Times*, had criticized the intelligence used to justify the invasion of Iraq in March 2003 by a coalition of forces led by the U.S. The leak of the agent's name was said to have come from members of the administration of President George W. Bush in retribution for Wilson's making his criticisms public. Fitzgerald's political independence was one of the qualities that stood most strongly in his favor as the potential prosecutor of what became known as the Plame case. "He is an absolutely apolitical career prosecutor," Comey said in his formal announcement, according to Charlie Savage in the *Boston Globe* (December 31, 2003). "He is a man with extensive experience in national security and intelligence matters, extensive experience conducting sensitive investigations, and in particular in conducting investigations of alleged government misconduct."

As the Plame case proceeded, the media watched Fitzgerald closely, but very little information about his activities was revealed. From early on, speculation as to the identity of the leaker focused on senior officials in the Bush White House, in particular Karl Rove, President Bush's senior adviser and current deputy chief of staff, and I. Lewis "Scooter" Libby, who was then serving as the chief of staff of Vice President Richard B. Cheney. Fitzgerald was permitted to interview President Bush and Vice President Cheney together for an hour, though not under oath, and many other senior officials spoke to him as well. Almost from the beginning, Fitzgerald stirred controversy because of his expressed determination to force journalists connected with the case to testify, even if in doing so they would have to reveal the names of sources who had given them information in strict confidence. Though it has been upheld in certain circumstances by Supreme Court rulings, the confidentiality of journalistic sources is not protected explicitly by legislation. Journalists have long insisted that such confidentiality is essential to their work, and for the most part prosecutors have recognized it as a proper privilege of the press.

Most journalists connected with the case have either acknowledged testifying for the grand jury or refused to comment to other members of the press about their involvement in the investigation. One influential reporter, the *New York Times* journalist Judith Miller, vocally and repeatedly refused to tell Fitzgerald about her involvement with the case, despite Libby's having signed a formal letter releasing her from the confidentiality agreement after Fitzgerald began working on the case; Libby's signature was viewed by Miller as having been coerced. Her determination to protect her source brought the somewhat controversial Miller admiration from members of the media even before Fitzgerald succeeded in putting her in jail for contempt of court, on July 6, 2005. The columnist William Safire, for example, wrote for the *New York Times* (September 29, 2004), "This principled journalist is risking her freedom and defending us all by fighting the subversive subpoena" brought against her by Fitzgerald, whom Safire described as a "runaway Chicago prosecutor." Editorial writers around the country concurred with Safire's argument that the pursuit of Miller constituted a threat to the freedom of the press. Miller spent 85 days in jail, gaining her release only after she agreed to testify, having received a second letter from Libby. In an appearance on the Cable News Network show *Lou Dobbs Tonight*, Miller said after her release, according to a transcript on the Web site for the magazine *Editor and Publisher* (October 4, 2005), that if Fitzgerald succeeds in bringing "serious" indictments "then I might have to say that perhaps his zealousness with respect to his mission was justified. . . . But if he doesn't have anything, I will wonder about why I had to spend 85 days in jail, and why I may be the only one to spend time in jail." (Miller and the *New York Times* ended their association on November 9, 2005.)

On October 28, 2005, three days before the grand jury was scheduled to be dismissed, Fitzgerald announced at a press conference in Washington, D.C., that he was bringing five charges against Libby, who insisted that he was innocent but offered his resignation at virtually the same time that Fitzgerald made his announcement. (One charge against Libby was for obstruction of justice, two were for perjury, and two were for making false statements to FBI agents who interviewed him in the case.) During his 66-minute session with the press, Fitzgerald fielded questions from reporters but pointedly refused to provide more information than his indictment mentioned. "My job is to investigate whether a crime was committed, can be proved and should be charged," Fitzgerald said, according to Richard B. Schmitt in the *Los Angeles Times* (October 30, 2005). "I'm not going to comment . . . beyond that. It's not my jurisdiction, not my job, not my judgment." Less than a month later, on November 17, Fitzgerald announced an eight-point indictment for fraud against another high-profile figure, the financier Conrad Black, in a matter not connected to the Plame case. The following day Fitzgerald said that he planned to convene another grand jury to look into the Plame case, which had taken an unexpected turn only a few days before, when the *Washington Post* reporter Bob Woodward revealed that he had been told Valerie Wilson's name by a White House official before Libby had allegedly leaked it to a number of other reporters, including Miller. Fitzgerald's investigation ended in 2006, and as of late October 2006—to the frustration of many observers—the prosecutor had not charged anyone with the crime he set out to investigate, the leaking of Plame's identity. Neither Rove nor Richard Armitage, who later admitted to being a source of the CIA leak, were indicted. Thus Libby, whose trial was to begin in early 2007, remained the only person to be prosecuted in the case.

In the *National Law Journal* (December 19, 2005, on-line), which named him 2005 Lawyer of the Year, Leigh Jones described Fitzgerald as "famously shy." Never married, he has been unable to sustain an intimate relationship, according to friends of his, because of his long work hours.

—D.R.

Suggested Reading: *American Lawyer* (on-line) May 2003; *Boston Globe* (on-line) July 19, 2005; *Chicago Tribune* C p10 Feb. 27, 2005; *Irish America* p78 May 31, 2004; *U.S. News & World Report* p23 July 4, 2005; *Washington Post* C p1 Feb. 2, 2005

Flagg, Fannie

Sep. 21, 1941– Novelist

Address: c/o Random House Trade Group, 299 Park Ave., Eighth Fl., New York NY 10171

Fannie Flagg has had a variety of successful careers. In addition to acting in more than a dozen stage and silver-screen productions from the mid-1960s to the early 1990s, Flagg wrote original material for, and appeared on, such television shows as *Candid Camera*, the *Tonight Show with Johnny Carson*, and the *New Dick Van Dyke Show*. She also became known to many as a celebrity guest on such TV game shows as *Liars' Club*, *Password*, *Match Game*, and *Hollywood Squares*. The career path Flagg has found most gratifying, by her own account, is her current one—as a novelist. In 1981 she impressed critics and won over readers with her debut novel, *Coming Attractions* (reissued in 1992 as *Daisy Fay and the Miracle Man*), a fictionalized account of Flagg's early years. *Fried Green Tomatoes at the Whistle Stop Café* (1987), her immensely popular second novel—a multigenerational tale set in Alabama—confirmed her standing as a talented storyteller; with Carol Sobieski, Flagg later adapted the book for the 1991 film *Fried*

Suze Lanier, courtesy of Random House

Fannie Flagg

Green Tomatoes, which starred Jessica Tandy, Kathy Bates, and Mary-Louise Parker and won an Academy Award nomination for best screenplay. Flagg has since authored the commercially successful novels *Welcome to the World, Baby Girl!* (1998), *Standing in the Rainbow* (2002), *A Redbird Christmas* (2004), and *Can't Wait to Get to Heaven* (2006). Flagg said to Susan Salter Reynolds for *Publishers Weekly* (September 21, 1998) that as a writer she has a particular interest in people who live "quiet lives, nurses and firemen and those people who never get recognized. They don't really have a voice. In the South, we hear about the very poor or the very wealthy. There aren't many people writing for middle-class America."

The writer and former comic actress was born Patricia Neal on September 21, 1941 (1944, according to one source) in Birmingham, Alabama, the only child of William H. Neal and Marion Leona (LeGore) Neal. Raised in the relatively populous Birmingham area, Flagg said to Ellen Kanner for *BookPage* (August 2002, on-line) that she would have preferred growing up with many brothers and sisters in a tranquil town like those portrayed in her novels. "I write about families because it's what I longed for. I'm trying to rewrite my childhood," she said. The experience of Daisy Fay Harper, the adolescent protagonist of *Coming Attractions*, specifically the character's relationship with her feckless father, is based in part on the author's childhood. Flagg's father is reported to have been a heavy drinker; after returning in 1944 from Europe, where he served in World War II, he took on a number of jobs, including one as a projectionist at a local movie house, and tried various get-rich-quick schemes. Flagg told Vernon Scott for United

Press International (June 26, 1981) that as a girl she spent a lot of time watching movies at the Birmingham theaters where both her father and grandfather worked. That experience kindled her interest in acting and performing. As a fifth-grader in a Catholic school, she wrote a play entitled "The Whoopee Girls." "Thanks to all the B pictures I saw, my idea of sophistication was drinking martinis," she said to Scott. "So in my play the two leading characters, both young Alabaman women who had moved to New York, drank 32 martinis in three acts." She added, "The nuns were scandalized and expelled me. They called my parents in for a conference and I was reinstated after my father told Sister Mary Jude, 'My daughter always had a dry wit.'" Asked by Bronwyn Miller for Bookreporter.com (December 17, 2004, on-line) about the presence of "strong, irrepressible women" in many of her books, Flagg said that she has created such characters "because both my grandmother and mother, and most of the women I know, are strong." In a biographical sketch appearing on the *Reader's Digest* Web site, Flagg was quoted as likening her writing success to "a one-legged person becoming a tap dancer." She was referring, at least in part, to her having suffered from dyslexia. Her fifth-grade play notwithstanding, she explained to Reynolds, "I always wanted to write but acting came so much more easily. I didn't pursue writing because I always assumed and was told that if you can't spell you can't be a writer. I'd get Cs and Ds in creative writing. It was so embarrassing."

During her early teenage years, Flagg joined a local theater group. She also entered a series of Miss Alabama contests in the hope of winning a scholarship to attend college. She explained to Jill Lai for United Press International (October 23, 1987), "At that time the only way women could get scholarships was literally through the beauty pageants. People forget about that. I had girlfriends who went to Yale and all over through beauty pageants [scholarships]." She often performed original comedy material during the talent portion of the beauty contests. In the last Miss Alabama contest she entered, she placed among the winners and received a scholarship to attend the Pittsburgh Playhouse, the performing-arts arm of Point Park University, in Pittsburgh, Pennsylvania. Flagg attended the school for one year, encountering problems there due to her dyslexia. She also struggled to learn the complicated dance routines for which the school was known. "I . . . was told that I was a nice little girl, but I should just go home and get married and forget acting, because my southern accent was too bad," she said for the *Reader's Digest* Web site. She had also been told that since she shared her birth name with a famous film and stage actress, she should change it if she intended to pursue a career in entertainment. She said to Kenneth R. Clark for United Press International (August 28, 1981) that she chose the name Fannie Flagg because it "was the funniest one I could think of. It still is."

Flagg left Pittsburgh and returned to Birmingham, where she worked in 1964 and 1965 at WBRC, a local ABC television affiliate, co-hosting, producing, and writing much of the material for the *Morning Show*, a 90-minute local news and variety program. "There was nobody famous in Birmingham," she said to Reynolds, "so we'd interview men who worked in the zoo and women from the garden club." (She recalled to Kanner that during one particularly slow news cycle she interviewed the cameraperson's mother several times.) In 1966, at the Town and Gown Theatre in Birmingham, she appeared in a production of *Cat on a Hot Tin Roof.*

Flagg next moved to New York City, where she wrote comedy material for a troupe performing at Upstairs at the Downstairs, in Manhattan. When one cast member was sick, Flagg filled in and drew laughs from the crowd, which led to other performances. Her work at Upstairs at the Downstairs led to an association with Allen Funt, the creator and host of the television show *Candid Camera*. An early example of what later came to be known as reality TV, *Candid Camera* showed real people placed in bizarre or frustrating situations while, unbeknownst to them, television cameras captured their reactions. In the late 1960s Flagg was a writer for the show and, later, had an on-camera role.

During that particularly busy period of her career, Flagg also made regular appearances as a comedian on the *Tonight Show with Johnny Carson*, writing her own material. Flagg was noted for performing, on that program and others, a dead-on imitation of Lady Bird Johnson, the wife of President Lyndon Johnson. The popularity of such impressions led Flagg to make a number of comedy albums with RCA Victor in the late 1960s. Flagg made her feature-film debut alongside Jack Nicholson in *Five Easy Pieces* (1970). Later in the decade she appeared in the movies *Stay Hungry* (1976), *Grease* (1978), and *Rabbit Test* (1978). From 1971 to 1973 she appeared as the sister of Dick Preston, played by Dick Van Dyke, on the *New Dick Van Dyke Show*, on CBS. In 1981 she played Cassie Bowman on the NBC sitcom *Harper Valley P.T.A.*; in addition, Flagg guest-starred on the ABC television series *The Love Boat* in 1979 and 1983. Perhaps her best-remembered contributions to television during the 1970s were her appearances as a panelist on the popular game shows *Match Game*, *Liars' Club*, *Password*, and *Hollywood Squares*. Also throughout that period Flagg was active on the stage. She appeared in the Broadway productions of *Patio/Porch*, in which she played the lead, in 1977; *Come Back to the Five and Dime, Jimmy Dean, Jimmy Dean*, in 1979; and the Tony Award–winning musical *The Best Little Whorehouse in Texas*, in which she also had the lead role, in 1980. Flagg told the editor Sam Vaughan, her interviewer for the Web site of the book publisher Random House, that she "got sidetracked for many years as an actor. It took me many years to realize that acting and performing did not make me as happy as

it did other performers. I always felt that something was missing from my life. Much later, I realized that although I was doing quite well, I was in the wrong profession."

When Flagg was in her late 30s, she attended a writers' conference, where she entered a short-story contest whose theme was childhood. "I bought a child's notebook and wrote a story from the eyes of a 7-year-old girl," she recalled to Nadine Brozan for the *New York Times* (November 17, 1994). "I made all my spelling mistakes and said, 'Oh, they will think I'm diabolically clever.'" The story won first prize. Barnaby Conrad, the conference's founder, introduced Flagg to a book editor, who encouraged her to expand her story into a novel. Her initial reaction, as she said to Nadine Brozan, was to "burst into tears" and explain that because of her dyslexia she could not possibly write a novel. The editor then "took my hand and said the most wonderful thing I've ever heard," she said to Brozan. "He said, 'Oh, honey, what do you think editors are for?'" Flagg also said to Reynolds, "To have gone from being a girl who could not spell her name to an author with her own books on a library shelf is the most rewarding thing that has ever happened to me." (Flagg, who had long adored the work of the Pulitzer Prize–winning writer Eudora Welty, a Mississippi native, met her idol in the mid-1970s at a Santa Barbara, California, writers' conference at which Welty was a guest speaker; the two became close friends.)

In 1981 William Morrow & Co. published Flagg's first novel, *Coming Attractions* (later republished as *Daisy Fay and the Miracle Man*) to mostly favorable reviews. Set in Mississippi, the semi-autobiographical book is told in the form of a diary kept by Daisy Fay Harper from April 1952, when the protagonist is 11, until she is 17. The story recounts Daisy's coming of age, culminating with her being crowned Miss Mississippi, and includes several humorous passages involving her father, who tries, for example, to start a mail-order taxidermy business. *Coming Attractions* spent 10 weeks on the *New York Times* fiction best-seller list. Buoyed by the success of her first book, Flagg gave up acting and decided to pursue writing full-time. She spent five years researching her next book, part of which would be set during the Great Depression. Random House purchased the book, which was published in 1987 as *Fried Green Tomatoes at the Whistle Stop Café* and spent 36 weeks on the *New York Times* best-seller list.

The novel's multi-generational story alternates between 1980s Birmingham and Depression-era Whistle Stop, Alabama. In it Cleo Threadgoode, an elderly woman residing in a nursing home, recounts to Evelyn Couch, a middle-aged woman visiting her mother there, the story of Idgie, Cleo's sister-in-law, and Idgie's companion, Ruth. Idgie and Ruth become proprietors of the Whistle Stop Café. The novel was a critical favorite. "Beneath the jokes (which are wonderful) lurk anger, tragedy, a murder mystery and a deceptively casual collage of what life was like in an Alabaman hamlet in the middle-half of the [20th] century," Charles Champlin wrote for the *Los Angeles Times* (November 19, 1987). "What it was like to be white, what it was like to be black."

The 1991 film *Fried Green Tomatoes*, adapted by Flagg and Carol Sobieski and directed by Jon Avnet, was nominated for two Academy Awards, including the Oscar for best adapted screenplay. Flagg and Sobieski's screenplay also won a Scripters Award. (Idgie and Ruth's relationship in the book is a romantic one, which is obscured in the movie.) Flagg recalled to Reynolds, "I went down to Alabama to watch them filming. I visited the set on a Sunday, when no one was around. I walked into the café they had created and it was the strangest thing. Like being a painter and walking into your own painting." (The café is based on a real-life restaurant, the Irondale Café in Irondale, Alabama, run by Flagg's aunt.) The end of the novel contains recipes for the southern dishes described in the book; in 1993 Flagg published *Fannie Flagg's Original Whistle Stop Café Cookbook*.

Flagg's next novel was *Welcome to the World, Baby Girl!* (1998). The book is set in the mid-1970s and focuses on Dena Nordstrom, who has a successful career in New York City as a television anchorperson. She begins to feel wistful about Elmwood Springs, Missouri, the midwestern town where she was raised, and returns there. Robert Plunket, reviewing the novel for the *New York Times Book Review* (November 1, 1998), found it to be "too long" but "enjoyable," adding that it "has a very ingratiating cast and the unusual quality of getting better as it goes along."

Elmwood Springs is featured prominently in *Standing in the Rainbow* (2002), Flagg's fourth novel, whose events take place from the late 1940s to the 1960s. The book received mixed reviews. Ellen Feldman, writing for the *New York Times Book Review* (August 11, 2002), complained, "Sometimes there is so much going on that the novel threatens to spin out of control. One of the charms of *Fried Green Tomatoes at the Whistle Stop Café* was watching the narrative threads come together, but the disparate pieces of *Standing in the Rainbow* never quite coalesce. Incidents accumulate, but the action does not build because everything carries the same weight." Ron Charles, on the other hand, wrote for the *Christian Science Monitor* (August 8, 2002), "Beneath the sentimentality, there's a real celebration of life here, an affirmation that success and happiness are the results of simple kindness, gratitude, and courage." Describing her reasons for writing *Standing in the Rainbow*, Flagg explained to Kanner, "The world is getting so crazy, I needed to remind myself and others that most of these people still exist. We shouldn't let go of that wonderful heritage we have—middle class America is the heroic class. . . . They don't get written about much, and they never got much credit or appreciation. They're laughed at or thought of as sort of sappy."

For *A Redbird Christmas*, published in 2004, Flagg returned to the setting of Alabama—specifically, the fictional town of Lost River. The book concerns Oswald T. Campbell, who returns to the town to spend what he believes will be his final Christmas, after receiving a grim diagnosis from his doctor in Chicago. A reviewer for *Publishers Weekly* (September 27, 2004) wrote that Flagg "makes this down-home story about good neighbors and the power of love sparkle with wit and humor." With Jon Avnet, Flagg adapted *A Redbird Christmas* into the screenplay for a full-length film Avnet is slated to direct. Flagg's most recent novel is *Can't Wait to Get to Heaven* (2006). The story's events are set in motion when Elner Shimfissle, who is in her 80s, falls from a ladder while trying to pick fruit and ends up in the hospital in Elmwood Springs. The accident is an occasion for her neighbors and relatives to reflect on the ways she has affected their lives. Flagg "has a well-deserved reputation for humanity and hilarity, and her latest yarn is no exception . . . ," Jay Strafford wrote for the *Richmond (Virginia) Times Dispatch* (July 30, 2006). "*Can't Wait to Get to Heaven* is another warm, wise and witty novel from an accomplished writer whose insights into people never fail to remind us of those we know—and of ourselves."

Flagg's fiction has often been criticized for being sentimental and trite. When Ellen Kanner asked about the novelist's reaction to the *Christian Science Monitor* review of *Welcome to the World, Baby Girl!*, which described Flagg as "the most shamelessly sentimental writer in America," Flagg said: "I thought, isn't that fabulous? And my friends said, 'No, Fannie, that's not good.' But it is. The easiest thing in the world is to be smart-alecky and cynical and snide and jaded. It's hard to keep your heart open."

Flagg told Bronwyn Miller that she does not know how a book will develop before she begins writing it. "I usually have some vague idea of the beginning and the end when I start a book, but I have no idea what will come in the middle or how I will get to the end," she said. "I am always surprised at what happens in between." In a conversation with Jeff Guinn for the *Fort Worth (Texas) Star-Telegram* (September 26, 2002), Flagg said, "I think every book is like a child that grows up into its own little person." The author has said that in her novels, the setting is usually the main character.

Fannie Flagg lives in Santa Barbara, California. According to Teresa K. Weaver, writing for the *Atlanta Journal-Constitution* (October 4, 1998), Flagg's home is "a 1913 frame house with a porch, nestled amid all the modern, Spanish-style haciendas in Santa Barbara." "It could be an Alabama house," Flagg said to Susan Salter Reynolds. "I came to Santa Barbara to visit in 1975, . . . and I've been there ever since." She received an honorary doctorate from Franklin Pierce College, in Rindge, New Hampshire; her novel *Fried Green Tomatoes at the Whistle Stop Café* is part of the freshman curriculum there. Flagg said to Jill Lai, "Nothing has pleased me more than to write. I think it's because I'm curious about people, I'm fascinated with people. It's a legitimate way to sit around and talk to people. You can say, 'Oh yes, it's for a project.'"

—D.F.

Suggested Reading: *BookPage* (on-line) Aug. 2002; Bookreporter.com (on-line) Dec. 17, 2004; *Publishers Weekly* p30+ Sep. 21, 1998; United Press International June 29, 1981

Selected Books: *Coming Attractions* (reissued in 1992 as *Daily Fay and the Miracle Man*), 1981; *Fried Green Tomatoes at the Whistle Stop Cafe*, 1987; *Welcome to the World, Baby Girl!*, 1998; *Standing in the Rainbow*, 2002; *A Redbird*

Christmas, 2004; *Can't Wait to Get to Heaven*, 2006

Selected Television Shows: *Candid Camera*, 1966–67; *The New Dick Van Dyke Show*, 1971-73; *Harper Valley P.T.A.*, 1981-82

Selected Films: as actor—*Five Easy Pieces*, 1970; *Some of My Best Friends Are*, 1971; *Rabbit Test*, 1978; *Grease*, 1978; *Crazy In Alabama*, 1999; as screenwriter—*Fried Green Tomatoes*, 1991

Selected Theatrical Productions: *Cat on a Hot Tin Roof*, 1966; *Patio/Porch*, 1977; *Come Back to the Five and Dime, Jimmy Dean, Jimmy Dean*, 1979; *The Best Little Whorehouse in Texas*, 1980

Matthew Stockman/Getty

Flowers, Vonetta

Oct. 29, 1973– Bobsledder

Address: P.O. Box 360226, Hoover, AL 35236

At the sound of the bell, 500 tiny spikes of a specially made pair of Adidas shoes dug into the slippery ice of a 13,000-meter track. A 28-year-old former track-and-field star pushed the 450-pound, two-person bobsled for a crucial five seconds, then jumped in behind the driver and raced down the icy track at 80 to 90 miles per hour, shifting her weight to help guide the sled along the curves, against the impact of up to 4 G-forces. Crossing the finish line in 48.95 seconds, the former track star

dropped a metal-claw brake to bring the massive sled to a halt. On the scoreboard, the number one flashed next to the names Bakken and Flowers. Vonetta Flowers, the college track-and-field athlete from the University of Alabama, and the driver, Jill Bakken, thus became gold-medal winners in the first-ever women's bobsled competition at the Winter Olympics, in Salt Lake City, Utah, in 2002. Flowers also became the first person of African descent ever to win a gold medal at the Winter Games. The winner of 35 Southeastern Conference track-and-field titles and a seven-time All-American, Flowers had spent years trying to make the Olympic team for the Summer Games. After failed attempts at the Olympic trials in 1996 and 2000, she responded to a flyer aimed at recruiting track athletes for the U.S. bobsledding team. Though she did not expect to succeed, she tried out and, two months later, found herself training with the former Olympic luger Bonny Warner and traveling around the world to compete as a member of the U.S. bobsled team in international tournaments. Flowers's success at the 2002 Winter Olympics helped associate black athletes with winter sports in the public consciousness, and she inspired people around the world with her story of perseverance, which is rooted in her Christian faith. "To me, it still doesn't quite feel real in a lot of ways," Flowers told Fran Blinebury for the *Houston Chronicle* (February 20, 2006) about her 2002 triumph. "I mean, I grew up in Alabama, where it never snows. Then to be not only the first African-American, but the first black athlete from any nation [to win a gold medal], I just feel blessed and honored and a little odd. It doesn't feel real to be the first. You look in the history books and think of . . . older people who have passed on. You don't ever think of yourself as part of history. But I'm delighted that years from now, my grandkids will be able to open up those books and read about me." Flowers went on the compete in the 2006 Winter Games, in Turin, Italy.

Flowers was born Vonetta Jeffery on October 29, 1973 in Birmingham, Alabama, to Jimmie Jeffery, a maintenance director for a truckline, and Bobbie Jeffery, a hotel maid. In 1982, when Flowers was eight years old, Coach DeWitt Thomas of the Marvel City Striders track team showed up at Jonesboro Elementary School looking to recruit its fastest boys and girls. Students of all ages lined up in the school's parking lot and raced to the finish line. When the fastest time was recorded alongside the name V. Jeffery, Thomas assumed that the V stood for Victor, Vincent, or another boy's name; he was surprised to find that it was Vonetta Jeffery who had beaten boys and girls alike for first place. From that day, Flowers competed successfully in track-and-field events, hoping to qualify one day for the Summer Olympics. She attended P. D. Jackson Olin High School, where she joined the track, volleyball, and basketball teams. In her senior year alone, Flowers won four events at the Alabama State Championships in track and field and was offered athletic scholarships by several schools. When she enrolled at the University of Alabama at Birmingham (UAB), she became the first in her family to attend college. While a freshman there, she met her future husband, Johnny Flowers, a minister's son who was also a member of the track team. Encouraged by him, Flowers became intensely involved in the church and was "born again." She began looking to her faith for the strength to continue working toward her goal of competing in the Olympics. While at UAB Flowers won the gold medal in the long jump at the 1994 Olympic Festival, earned a total of 35 Southeastern Conference titles in the 100-meter and 200-meter races, the long jump, and the triple jump, and set six individual university track records. In 1997, as the university's only seven-time National Collegiate Athletic Association (NCAA) All-American, Flowers graduated with a bachelor's degree in physical education.

During her senior year at UAB, Flowers traveled to Atlanta, Georgia, to compete in the 100-meter dash and the long jump at the Olympic trials for the 1996 Summer Games. Failing to earn a spot on the U.S. team, she spent the next four years focusing her efforts on the event in which she was strongest: the long jump. But in 2000, five months before that year's trials for the Summer Games, Flowers was forced to undergo surgery on her ankle—her fifth operation in eight years. Afterward, though she continued to prepare for the Olympic trials, Flowers began to feel dejected, as she grappled with the likelihood that her dream of competing in the Summer Olympics would never be realized.

Two days after Flowers's unsuccessful attempt to make the U.S. track-and-field team, her husband picked up a flyer left at the hotel by the former Olympic luge athlete Bonny Warner and calling on track athletes to try out for the U.S. bobsled team. The couple, half-jokingly at first, began to consider doing so. Flowers agreed to accompany her husband to tryouts for the men's bobsled team; when

he pulled his hamstring at the trials, Johnny Flowers suggested, again half-jokingly, that his wife take up the challenge. Neither Flowers nor her husband knew anything about bobsledding beyond what they had seen in *Cool Runnings* (1993)—the Disney movie about the Jamaican bobsled team—but she nevertheless gave it a try. "It felt like I was put in a trash can and thrown down a hill," Flowers told Bill Ward for the *Tampa (Florida) Tribune* (February 10, 2005), describing her first experience in the sport. "No one tells you at first about the G-forces. I thought it was going to be this fun little ride down a hill." (One G is the force of gravity, which is related to weight. At four Gs a bobsledder would experience pressure equal to four times her weight.) As it turned out, Flowers was an ideal candidate for Warner's two-person bobsled team, in that her running ability and strength enabled her to give the sled the quick and powerful push so crucial in the first five seconds of a race. Within two months of trying out, Flowers was preparing to compete in tournaments around the world as a member of the U.S. bobsled team. "People in Alabama laughed when we told them," Johnny Flowers recalled to *Jet* (March 11, 2002). Indeed, many of Flowers's family members and friends found it odd that a black woman who grew up experiencing Birmingham's humid summers, and who had never seen snow as a child, would pursue a form of competition held mainly among whites, in frigid temperatures. Such attitudes notwithstanding, Flowers soon became recognized as the best brake woman in the U.S. "Since I was [a] 9-year-old, I wanted to be like [the Olympic heptathlete] Jackie Joyner-Kersee, and I tried but it just wasn't for me," Flowers told Ward. "God just had a different plan for me." By the end of her first year in her new sport, Flowers and Warner were ranked second among female bobsledding teams in the U.S. and third in the world.

With their rapid rise in the sport, the duo of Flowers and Warner came to set their sights set on winning a medal at the 2002 Winter Olympics in Salt Lake City. In late December 2001, two months before the start of the Games, Flowers became embroiled in a highly publicized drama when Warner suddenly dropped Flowers from her team in favor of Gea Johnson, a former NCAA heptathlon champion whose four-year suspension from track for using anabolic steroids had just ended. Deeply disappointed, fearing that her dream of competing in the Olympics would be dashed once again, Flowers nonetheless continued to train as if she would be competing. "Faith pulled me through. I still had a goal and I was going to keep trying. It was as though [God] was telling me, 'Your day is coming,'" Flowers said, as quoted by Laurie Stroud for a biographical piece published on Flowers's Web site. "[Johnny] would repeatedly tell me, 'God has put you in this sport for a reason.'" She soon received an offer to push the sled for Jill Bakken, and the pair went into the 2002 Olympics as a team. "I began to realize maybe God does have me in this sport for a reason. Every time a door would close another would open. I really began to develop a peace about it," Flowers said, as quoted by Stroud. The teammate-swapping continued as Jean Racine dropped her own longtime sled partner to lure Johnson away from Warner. Going into the Olympics, Racine and Johnson were the American favorites among U.S. bobsledders to win a medal, and little media attention was given initially to the Flowers-Bakken team. Then, two days before the bobsledding competition at the Winter Olympics, Johnson injured her left hamstring in a practice run. Racine immediately petitioned the bobsled-federation officials to have Flowers replace Johnson as her brake woman. The United States Olympic Committee intervened and gave Johnson the option of having Bethany Hart as her stand-in for Racine's team. Johnson declined the offer and competed with a strained hamstring.

On February 19, 2002 Flowers and Bakken took to the icy track at the inaugural women's bobsledding event at the Winter Olympics. Having had little time to train together amid the chaos of the preceding weeks, and having had, between them, a concussion, a bulging disk, and seven operations (on their knees, hips, and ankles), the two women faced steep odds. The team of Johnson and Racine had ended up in fifth place in the actual Olympic competition, after Johnson injured her hamstring in their second run. Flowers and Bakken entered the race with confidence and finished their first run in 48.81 seconds, to take the lead. Their second run was slightly slower, ending in 48.95 seconds, for a combined time of 1:37.76, .30 seconds better than the top German team of Sandra Prokoff and Ulrike Holzner. More importantly, the time was good enough to capture the gold medal. "I knew we had a good run," Flowers told Bob Ryan for the *Boston Globe* (February 20, 2002). "We had a good start, and it was a good, clean run. I kept looking for a clock, then I saw the '1,' and I think my heart dropped." Flowers and Bakken's gold medal was the first in bobsledding for the U.S. in 46 years and the first ever for a person of African descent at the Winter Olympics. Flowers said to Jay Mariotti for the *Chicago Sun-Times* (February 20, 2002), "Hopefully, it will encourage other African-American girls and boys to give the winter sports a try because we don't see too many of them out here." She added, on the subject of the various betrayals that marked the competition, "Jill and I tried to stay out of the soap opera. We just tried to stay focused and win a medal. A lot of people saw us as the other team, so we got to come in and prove a lot of people wrong." U.S. Olympic athletes and the press corps voted to give Flowers and Bakken the 2002 U.S. Olympic Spirit Award, for exemplifying the spirit of the Olympic Games through their sportsmanship.

Having fulfilled her Olympic dream, albeit in the Winter Games, Flowers decided to retire from bobsledding and return to Alabama. A week after winning the gold medal in Salt Lake City, she discovered that she was pregnant with twins. During the next several months, Flowers relaxed at her home in Hoover, Alabama, working on her autobiography, *Running On Ice: The Overcoming Faith of Vonetta Flowers* (2005), written with W. Terry Whalin. On August 30, 2002, only six months into her pregnancy, Flowers gave birth to twin sons, Jaden Michael and Jorden Maddox. Despite being born prematurely, the twins appeared to be healthy, though Jorden showed some signs of hearing problems. Just five weeks after giving birth, and seven months into her retirement, Flowers began training to compete in the 2006 Winter Games, in Turin, Italy. Flowers teamed up with Racine—the controversial figure in the 2002 Olympic bobsledding competition—since Jill Bakken had retired from the sport. Finishing third in the 2003-04 World Championships, the new partnership showed promise. In preparation for the 2006 Winter Games, Flowers's husband quit his job as a manager at Blue Cross Blue Shield to act as the full-time physical trainer for both his wife and Racine, whose surname was now Prahm, following her recent marriage. Though it is not common for U.S. Olympic athletes to travel with their families while competing, both of Flowers's sons accompanied their mother in her daily training routines as well as in international tournaments. "Vonetta needs [her] family here," Bill Tavares, one of the U.S. women's bobsled coaches, told Karen Rosen for the *Atlanta Journal-Constitution* (January 8, 2006). "I think it'd be more of a distraction if she didn't have them here because she'd be worried about them all the time." Prahm told Rosen that Flowers never allowed her attention to her children to interfere with her training, saying, "If I can tell she's got some little bags under her eyes, I know she's had a rough night, but she never complains. She's just thankful to have the kids and have them here."

In 2005 Flowers's family life and athletic career converged in an unexpected way. Flowers's son Jorden, it turned out, had been born with a rare auditory condition that left him deaf. After years of research and consultations with several doctors, Vonetta and Johnny Flowers were referred to Vittorio Colletti, the only surgeon in the world who performs the auditory brainstem implants (ABI) operation—which restores hearing after a year of therapy—on children. The Flowers family considered it providential that Jorden could receive the ABI surgery only in Verona, Italy, where Colletti was based, while his mother raced at a World Cup competition in Cortina d'Ampezzo, only two hours away, the day before his scheduled operation. In the following year Flowers told Jemele Hill for the *Orlando Sentinel* (February 26, 2006), "We feel like this is all part of God's plan—for me to come into the sport of bobsledding, have a race in Italy last year to meet [the doctor] and the Olympics are in Italy this year." The operation appeared to be successful, though Colletti said it would be months before he could measure Jorden's hearing ability accurately. Encouraged by the news, Flowers entered the 2006 Winter Olympics unfazed by the fact that she and Prahm had finished only fifth in the 2005–06 World Cup standings and were riding in the USA-2 sled (USA-1 is reserved for the team considered to be gold-medal favorites, a status determined by runs at the World Cup competition and the Olympic trials.) Prahm and Flowers had a rough first run, grazing the wall on a particularly difficult section of the track and finishing far down in the standings. They finished their second run in 57.81 seconds, which put them out of the running for a medal. Their third run was gold-medal worthy, but Prahm grazed the wall on their fourth. The Flowers-Prahm team finished in sixth place, with a combined time of 3:51.78. Flowers nonetheless was so exuberant as she crossed the finish line that onlookers and reporters were confused. "It feels like I won," Flowers told Hill. "I did win because in this country, my son had surgery and he lived through it. This place is very special to me."

In addition to her 2002 Olympic gold medal, Flowers is the recipient of numerous awards, including the Dodge National Athletic Olympian Award (2003), the U.S. Olympic Committee Team of the Year Award (2003), and the Rainbow/PUSH Coalition's Wilma Rudolph Athlete of the Year Award (2002). In 2002 she was named one of the "50 Most Inspiring African-Americans" by *Essence* magazine and one of *People* magazine's "50 Most Beautiful People." According to her Web site, Flowers is now training to become a bobsled driver. She currently resides in Hoover, Alabama, with her husband and sons.

—I.C.

Suggested Reading: *Atlanta Journal-Constitution* A p1 Jan. 8, 2006; *Chicago Sun-Times* p135 Feb. 20, 2002; *Chicago Tribune* p4 Jan. 29, 2006; *Orlando Sentinel* C p17 Feb. 26, 2006; Vonetta Flowers Web site

Selected Books: *Running on Ice: The Overcoming Faith of Vonetta Flowers* (with W. Terry Whalin), 2005

Franco, Julio

Aug. 23, 1958– Baseball player

Address: New York Mets, Shea Stadium, 123-01 Roosevelt Ave., Flushing, NY 11368

In 2005 the Dominican-born Julio Franco, currently a first baseman for the New York Mets, became the oldest regularly appearing position player in the history of Major League Baseball (MLB). In 2006 he became the oldest player ever to participate in an MLB postseason game, according to the Elias Sports Bureau. Franco holds many oldest-player records—the oldest to hit a grand slam, to hit a home run, and to play 100 games in a season, among others—and he threatens, with every at-bat, to add to records that will likely stand long after his playing days are over. Franco has said that he will not retire until he is 50 years old, joking to Hal Habib for the *Palm Beach (Florida) Post* (March 28, 2006), "One day I'm going to collect a paycheck, my pension and Social Security in the same year." (MLB players can start receiving their pensions at age 45—one measure of the improbability of Franco's longevity.) Franco's distinction as a ballplayer is not limited to his age. After 28-plus seasons as a pro, which have seen him play for the Cleveland Indians, the Texas Rangers, the Atlanta Braves, and teams in Japan, Mexico, and South Korea, Franco has maintained a career batting average of just under .300. He has also compiled more than 4,100 hits, 2,566 of them in the major leagues, and he leads all Dominican-born players in MLB history in seasons and games played, at-bats, hits, and bases on balls. He is also in better physical condition

Victor Baldizon/Getty Images

than some players half his age. The Braves' general manager, John Schuerholz, told Tim Povtak for the *Orlando (Florida) Sentinel* (February 29, 2004), "Julio's amazing. . . . He's the oldest guy in the game, but he's probably the best conditioned, strongest guy in the game."

One of four brothers, Julio Cesar Robles Franco was born on August 23, 1958 in San Pedro de Macoris, in the Dominican Republic. A city of 80,000 people, San Pedro de Macoris is known as a producer of sugar cane—and as the birthplace of many

Major League Baseball players, including George Bell, Tony Fernandez, Rafael Ramirez, Juan Samuel, Sammy Sosa, and the current stars Luis Castillo, Alfonso Soriano, and Robinson Cano. Franco grew up playing different versions of baseball in the streets and fields of his hometown with Samuel, Ramirez, and Fernandez, among others. "We played stickball; we played street ball . . . ," Samuel recalled to Joe Gergen for the *Sporting News* (July 3, 1989). "We used to grab nine guys and go out and play. Everybody got to pitch, to catch, to hit, to play third base." Joe McIlvaine, a former MLB scout in Latin America, described the Dominican Republic to Gergen: "As in a lot of Latin America, much of the country is poor. Five percent of the people control the wealth. There is no middle class. Baseball is an escape. Everywhere you go, you see kids throwing balls against a wall, hitting rocks with a stick. All the good athletes play baseball." Though some MLB teams have sports academies in the Dominican Republic, in his teens Franco played baseball for the team sponsored by the sugar-cane processing facility in the nearby town of Consuelo, where he and his father worked. "I dusted the floors, worked the machines, moved the sugar from one place to the other, but I also played baseball for the factory. That's one reason to play amateur baseball, so you can get a job with the factory," Franco told Steve Wulf for *Sports Illustrated* (February 9, 1987). Many men saw professional baseball as the only way to escape from the poverty of their communities, and often amateur baseball players would forge their birth certificates to make themselves appear younger and thus more enticing to MLB teams. Franco himself did that, signing with the Philadelphia Phillies in 1978 with the aid of a fake birth certificate, according to which he was 16 years old. In fact, Franco was nearly 20, and a graduate of Devine Providence High School, when he moved to the United States.

Franco started off in the minors, playing in Butte, Montana, for the Phillies' affiliate in the Pioneer League. That was in some ways the toughest year of his professional career: he was unused to the cold and without any warm clothing, and he could not talk to his teammates, because none of them spoke Spanish and he was struggling to learn English. Those difficulties aside, Franco, who was then a tall, skinny shortstop, breezed through the Phillies' minor-league system, finishing every season with a batting average above .300. He made his major-league debut on April 23, 1982 and played in 16 games for the Phillies that year. Franco spent the rest of the season with the Phillies' Class AAA affiliate in Oklahoma City, Oklahoma, where he amassed 21 home runs, 66 runs batted in (RBIs), and 33 stolen bases and came to be considered an elite prospect.

At the conclusion of the 1982 season, Franco was traded, along with four other players, to the Cleveland Indians for Von Hayes, a highly regarded outfielder. Franco began the 1983 season as the starter at shortstop for the Indians. Prior to the season Milton Richman, writing for United Press International (March 31, 1983), declared: "[Franco] is all you could possibly ask for at shortstop. He has a strong arm, good speed and fine range." In his rookie season Franco played in 149 games and led the team in hits with 153. His other totals of a .273 batting average, eight home runs, 80 runs batted in, and 32 stolen bases were so impressive that he was voted runner-up for the American League Rookie of the Year Award. Franco's only apparent deficiency was his defense, as he led the team in errors, with 28. Errors plagued the young star throughout his tenure with the Indians; because of his exceptional athleticism, coaches attributed that shortcoming to carelessness rather than lack of ability. The former Indians manager Pat Corrales told John Leptich for the *Chicago Tribune* (May 5, 1985), "[Franco] could be a great defensive player. It's all up to him. He has the capabilities of making an outstanding play on one ball, then booting the next. For some reason, he loses concentration in the field." After the 1987 season the team moved Franco to second base, a position that is considered less demanding defensively. Meanwhile, he continued to blossom as a hitter, consistently leading the team in hits, and raised his batting average in each of his first five seasons with Cleveland. Franco has one of the most recognizable batting stances in all of baseball: using one of the heaviest bats in the majors (36 ounces), keeping his torso twisted and elbows raised, he bats from the left side of the plate, with the barrel of the bat parallel to the ground, pointing toward the pitcher.

Though Franco was making a name for himself on the field as one of the most promising young players in the league, he was also attracting attention in undesirable ways. He sometimes carried a gun to the stadium, was followed by an ever-growing entourage, and was late to team functions, sometimes skipping meetings altogether. He was married and divorced twice during that time and spent his money recklessly. "I was going to discotheques, drinking and staying out late. I didn't think I'd live to be 30," Franco told Terry Pluto for the *Akron (Ohio) Beacon Journal* (February 25, 1996) about his early career. Though he received fines for his misconduct, his teammates were willing to overlook what they saw as youthful indiscretions, until they carried over onto the baseball diamond. One Saturday in 1987 Franco did not show up for a game in New York against the Yankees. The night before he had hit a game-winning home run against the Yankee ace Ron Guidry. "The next day was my brother's birthday," Franco told Pluto. "After the game, we began to celebrate. . . . We went to bed about four in the morning. I didn't get up until noon. The game was at 1 p.m. I could have rushed over and made it. But I told my brother, 'I'll spend today with you. I'm leading the league in hitting, what are they going to do to me?' I really didn't care about the team." Franco rejoined the team the following day, but he had lost the respect of his teammates. After the 1988 season, in which he played second base almost exclusively, Franco, who had received the Silver Slugger award for the best offensive player at his position, was traded to the Texas Rangers.

The trade was controversial, as sportswriters and fans of both teams were conflicted about Franco's value. Some thought that Cleveland was making a mistake in trading away a hitter who in the last five years had totaled 898 hits, good for fifth-best in the major leagues over that span. Others thought that Texas was taking too large a risk on a player who many felt was inconsistent on the field and a headache for management away from it. Regardless of his reputation for being fiercely independent and a malcontent, the Rangers were glad to add Franco's talent to its roster. Tom Grieve, the general manager of the Rangers at the time, told Phil Rogers for the *Sporting News* (May 15, 1989), "[Franco] will be a good player for us. . . . If there is something to his reputation, it's the job of the manager to handle it. That was not a concern for us." As it happened, the trade was a turning point for Franco, who clearly benefited from a change of scenery. In his first season for Texas, Franco batted .316 while hitting 13 home runs and contributing 92 runs batted in, both career highs. He also took his defensive assignments more seriously, committing a career-low 13 errors, and showed additional patience at the plate, earning 66 bases on balls, also a career high. For his efforts Franco earned his first trip to the All-Star Game and a second Silver Slugger award. Franco admitted that playing for a winning team, after losing so much while with Cleveland, contributed to his new focus. "In a situation where you're winning consistently . . . you try to bear down," Franco told Chuck Melvin for the Associated Press (July 14, 1989). Franco spent five years with the Texas Rangers, winning the Silver Slugger award three more times, and led the American League with a .341 batting average in 1991. He went to the All-Star Game in 1989, 1990, and 1991, an acknowledgement from fans and managers that he was one of the best players in the major leagues.

While Franco was enjoying his best seasons up to that time, he was also trying to erase his image as a troublemaker by taking on the role of clubhouse leader. He was especially conscientious about reaching out to the team's two young, Spanish-speaking, Caribbean stars, Ruben Sierra and Rafael Palmeiro. "[Franco's] been a great influence," the Rangers' manager, Bobby Valentine, told Ken Picking for *USA Today* (April 25, 1989). Franco acknowledged that he was a changed man, dedicated to the game and to maintaining his health. He told Phil Rogers for the *Sporting News* (July 31, 1989), "I learned that God gives you talent, but you still have to be on time and do what the manager says. You can't let your ego control you. Spanish ball players have reputations for egos that go too far. . . . Julio is not going to break rules in Texas." Franco helped Palmeiro and Sierra to develop extensive exercise routines to maximize their potential, and the three hitters became known collectively as the "Artilleria Pesada," or heavy artillery, and as the most productive three-hitter combination in the major leagues. In addition to providing stability for the young players on the team, Franco was settling down in his private life. In 1991 he remarried, and partly at the urging of his brother Jose, he became a dedicated born-again Christian. (Franco nonetheless remained something of a cutup, once bringing a pet tiger to batting practice.)

The 1992 season was the first in which Franco had to deal with physical adversity. In part because of the zeal with which he had pursued his weight-lifting regimen, his knees started to give out. After playing in only 35 games, Franco had knee surgery and was unable to compete for the rest of the year. The following season was the last remaining on his contract with Texas, and Franco felt that the end of his career might be coming. "With all the injuries I have had in the last two years, I play every game like I want to win this game because it could be my last," he told Gerry Fraley for the *Dallas (Texas) Morning News* (August 22, 1993) at the time. Though the team listed his age at 32, Franco was actually 35, an age at which many ballplayers enter or near retirement. Playing exclusively at the designated-hitter position to preserve his knees from the rigors of defense, Franco batted .289 with 14 home runs and 84 runs batted in during the 1993 season. Texas, which did not make it to the play-offs that year, allowed Franco to become a free agent in order to open up a roster position for a younger player. "What I want to do is get out as a winner," Franco told Fraley, and with that goal in mind, after the 1993 season the 11-year veteran signed a contract with the defending division champion Chicago White Sox. Franco had his finest season yet with the White Sox, batting .319 while hitting 20 home runs and contributing 98 RBIs in just 112 games during the 1994 season. The White Sox were in first place when the season was abruptly ended by a labor dispute. Franco was bitter about that development, since the strike had likely cost him his first opportunity to appear in the play-offs.

Frustrated with Major League Baseball and worried that the following season, 1995, would also be canceled, Franco signed a contract with the Chiba Lotte Marines of Japan, a team managed by his former manager in Texas, Bobby Valentine. Valentine was impressed by the way that Franco attempted to adapt to Japanese culture. "Some guys learn a few words," Valentine told George Vecsey for the *New York Times* (April 15, 2002). "Julio was speaking in sentences. He knew the right endings to verbs. He knew the right times to speak politely to elders. He ate the food. He was truly a delight. And he can still play." Playing first base for his new team, Franco won the Japanese equivalent of the Gold Glove, given to the best defensive player at his position. He was successful at bat as well, hitting .306, and the team ended the season in second place, their highest finish in a decade. Despite the success of the team, Valentine was fired after the season. In protest, Franco ignored the second year of his two-year contract and returned to the United States to play for the Cleveland Indians. He was grateful that the Indians were giving him another chance. "It makes me feel good that I [changed] and that the Indians recognized that and brought me back," Franco told Paul Hoynes for the *Cleveland Plain Dealer* (February 21, 1996). "I think they [the Indians] realized that maybe I can prevent some of the young players on this team from making the same mistakes I did."

Franco had a good year in Cleveland in 1996, playing first base and designated hitter and appearing in the play-offs for the first time in his career. (He performed poorly, contributing only two hits in 15 at-bats. Cleveland lost the best-of-five series to Baltimore, three games to one.) During the following season, however, he struggled with injuries and was released by the Indians, finishing the season with the Milwaukee Brewers. After the 1997 season concerns about his age, health, and ability to play in every game kept MLB teams from showing an interest in Franco. He spent the following four years playing in foreign countries, while believing that he still had the ability to contribute to an MLB team. During the 1998 season he was in Japan, for a second stint with the Chiba Lotte Marines, and achieved a .290 average. In 1999 he earned a tryout with the Tampa Bay Devil Rays of the MLB, but ended up spending the season with their affiliate in the Mexican League, which he led in batting with a .423 average. In 2000 he returned to Asia to play for a South Korean team, the Samsung Lions; he was considered the biggest baseball star ever to play in Korea, which had only had a baseball league for 18 seasons. Franco returned to the Mexican League for the 2001 season and hit .437, then was picked up by the Atlanta Braves for the end of the MLB season. Atlanta reached the play-offs that year; Franco appeared in 25 games, with a batting average of .300. He has played in the major leagues ever since.

The Braves, a National League team, did not use the designated-hitter position, and Franco, for the first time, was not playing in every game. He did well enough in his 2001 return to be asked to sign another one-year contract with Atlanta for the following season. The Braves hoped that Franco could serve as a part-time player and tutor for their young first baseman, Adam LaRoche. Franco was happy to be playing baseball in the United States again and embraced his new role, telling T. R. Sullivan for the *Fort Worth (Texas) Star-Telegram* (July 20, 2003), "I know if I played regularly I'd put up good numbers, but that's not the situation here. It's not about me, it's about the ballclub. It's about winning and I'm happy to be part of it." Franco maintained his position on the Atlanta roster through 2005, appearing in postseason play each season he spent with the team and hitting .309 in his final year.

Prior to the 2006 season, the New York Mets signed the 47-year-old Franco to a two-year contract worth $2.2 million. Many were surprised by the length of the deal, unusual for a backup player of any age. But the Mets' general manager, Omar Minaya, coveted the veteran for a variety of reasons: he desired the clutch hitting that Franco could provide off the bench; he wanted to establish a winning environment, and Franco had by then gained play-off experience; and the Mets had two young stars, David Wright and Jose Reyes, who Minaya hoped could learn from Franco "how to play the game," as he told Mike Fitzpatrick for the Associated Press (December 10, 2005, on-line).

The Mets performed very well in 2006, compiling a 97–65 record to win the National League East Division title by the resounding margin of 12 games. In his final game of the regular season, Franco hit a home run and plated a career-high five RBIs. The Mets advanced to the postseason but failed to reach the World Series, losing four games to the St. Louis Cardinals in the play-offs. Franco, who had achieved a batting average of .273 and 26 runs batted in during the regular season, did not make an impact in the postseason, earning no hits in two at-bats. Mark Bowman, writing for the Web site MLB.com (October 6, 2006), expressed the opinion that the Mets' contractual obligation to Franco over two seasons "will be money well spent."

Franco has said that he would like to manage a team when he retires as a player. That he speaks Spanish, English, Japanese, and a little Korean should prove useful in a sport that continues to inspire interest around the globe. Franco became a citizen of the United States in 1991 and currently resides in Lighthouse Point, Florida, with his wife, Rosa, and son, Joshua Cesar. Joe Lapointe wrote for the *New York Times* (May 23, 2005) that "the Franco of today" is "6 feet 1 inch and 210 pounds, muscles sculptured like those of a bodybuilder, head shaven, speaking often of God and the greatness of baseball and of the United States, his adopted nation." Franco told Mike Fitzpatrick, "I don't work out and train . . . like this because I play baseball, I do this because I've got one life to live. When I stop playing baseball, I'm going to continue to do this. I think everyone should take care of their body. It's your best investment." Franco's hobbies include boxing and playing basketball

—N.W.M.

Suggested Reading: Associated Press July 14, 1989; *Atlanta Journal-Constitution* G p1 Aug. 22, 2003, D p1 Mar. 5, 2004; *Chicago Tribune* C p4 May 5, 1985; *New York Times* D p3 Apr. 15, 2002, D p5 May 23, 2005; *Sporting News* p12 May 15, 1989, p6 July 3, 1989, p40 July 24, 1989, p10 July 31, 1989; *Sports Illustrated* p88 Aug. 13, 1984, p132 Feb. 9, 1987

William Thomas Cain/Getty

Friedlander, Lee

July 14, 1934– Photographer

Address: c/o Janet Borden Inc., 560 Broadway, New York, NY 10012

"Every time you turn around, it sometimes seems, the versatile and prolific Lee Friedlander is having a show . . . or a book of his photographs is coming out, or he is being given an award or is otherwise making news," Margarett Loke wrote for the *New York Times* (May 4, 2001, on-line). Discussing Friedlander's 50-year career as a photographer, Andy Grundberg wrote for the *Washington Post* (June 21, 2005), "There is no single subject or genre that defines Friedlander. . . . He embraces the world with an idiosyncratic style that confounds, amuses and occasionally instructs, [making him] a kind of latter-day, lens-based Walt Whitman. What he has to teach us is a democratic way of seeing." Friedlander has forged what an Associated Press (March 8, 2005) writer called a "new documentary paradigm," one in which "stylistic innovations and freedom from established formal practices [have] influenced the work of subsequent generations of photographers." His broad array of subjects has included shop windows, cityscapes, outdoor monuments, desert scenes, flowers, trees, fruits, office and factory workers, musicians, nudes, his family, and himself, and he shoots primarily in black and white. The most recent of his more than 20 books, *Apples and Oranges* (2005), was published in conjunction with an exhibit of his pictures in a San Francisco gallery. After seeing that show, which opened when Friedlander was 72, Kenneth Baker wrote for the *San Francisco Chroni-*

cle (December 10, 2005), "Without overt trickery or politics, Friedlander exposes to us the constructed nature of every photographic fact. Each presentation of his work confirms afresh his standing as one of the great American artists of his day." A 50-year retrospective of Friedlander's work was mounted at the Museum of Modern Art, in New York City, in 2005; in October 2006 the show, which included some 500 photographs, opened at the Galerie Nationale du Jeu de Paume, a museum of contemporary art, in Paris, France.

Lee Norman Friedlander was born on July 14, 1934 in Aberdeen, Washington. Arthur Ollman reported in his book *The Model Wife* (1999), as quoted on tfaoi.com, that Friedlander's mother died when he was seven; afterward, "his father felt unable to raise him and sent him to live with a farmer about 110 miles south of Seattle, where he grew up." Friedlander began taking pictures at the age of 14. He soon built a darkroom, in which he developed his photographs and became fascinated with the gradual appearance of images on blank sheets of paper. "I got involved in the process. I still am," he told Douglas Davis for *Newsweek* (July 24, 1978). "You put a piece of paper in some water [actually, a special chemical] and an image comes out—it's magic." After completing high school Friedlander enrolled at the Art Center School in Los Angeles, California, and began studying under the photographer Edward B. Kaminski. "I used to skip classes to go to his class. . . . He was a very interesting character, and he talked interestingly. He sort of encouraged a certain kind of experimentation," Friedlander has recalled, as Steve Appleford reported for the *Los Angeles Times* (April 25, 1993). After two years at the art school, Friedlander left, but he continued studying with Kaminski; he even lived for about a year in Kaminski's studio, where he was treated like a family member.

In 1956 (some sources say 1955), heeding advice from Kaminski, Friedlander moved to New York and launched his career as a freelance photographer. He supported himself with assignments for such magazines as *Esquire*, *Holiday*, and *Sports Illustrated* and through portraits (usually for use on album covers) of jazz musicians, among them John Coltrane, Charlie Parker, Big Joe Turner, Duke Ellington, Miles Davis, and Ornette Coleman. Some of those portraits have become iconic images of the era's jazz greats, and many of them were published in 1998 in Friedlander's book *American Musicians* or in 2000 in *Lee Friedlander: Jazz Portraits*. Friedlander's experiences as a peripheral member of the jazz world inspired his own art and "made me understand things that were possible," as he recalled to Appleford. "I think everybody finds it some way. When I first heard Charlie Parker, Coleman Hawkins or Louis Armstrong even, I realized things that normally weren't heard were being heard there, and it made the world seem like an oyster that was available for anybody." Living in New York and working as a freelancer had other benefits for Friedlander. He became acquainted with so-called art photographers, among them Robert Frank, Richard Avedon, Garry Winogrand, and Diane Arbus.

In the early 1960s Friedlander began to establish himself as an art photographer in his own right, becoming known for his images of urban landscapes. Writing for the *Albuquerque (New Mexico) Journal* (July 25, 2003), Tom Collins described him as "a direct photographic descendant in a line of documentors of the 'social landscape'—what the actual physical environment tells us about the culture and politics of a society—that began with Parisian Eugene Atget and developed in its own particularly American, 'on-the-road' vernacular from Walker Evans to Robert Frank." Friedlander was awarded a Guggenheim Fellowship in 1960 and another in 1962. In 1963 his work appeared in his first solo exhibition, Little Screens, at the George Eastman House, in Rochester, New York. The show was devoted to photos of televisions in American hotel rooms. "The slightly sinister Cyclopian glow from the television heightens the forlorn, anonymous aspect of the hotel room and, by inference, of the American experience," Collins wrote. "Also, the flavorless homogeneity of American culture is portrayed as we see the same leotard-clad exercise lady on a television in Nashville '63 and in Atlanta '62, in rooms that are morbidly alike." The images were published in the book *Little Screens* (2001).

Coining a now-common phrase, Friedman said during the 1960s that he was seeking to photograph the "American social landscape," as Abigail Forester reported for the *Chicago Tribune* (October 27, 1989). In 1967 the Museum of Modern Art (MoMA) in New York mounted an exhibition, called New Documents, containing works by Friedlander, Arbus, and Winogrand. Although each of the three photographers was forging a new documentary style that was distinct from that of the others, all of them had departed "from the traditionally committed statement of the Thirties and Forties . . . in favor of observing, understanding and 'leaving alone' that which exists," as John Gruen wrote for the New York *World Journal Tribune* (February 26, 1967). With regard to some of Friedlander's New Documents images, Linda Yablonsky wrote for the Bergen County, New Jersey, *Record* (July 1, 2005) that Friedlander's "best documentary pictures give us eyes in back of our heads. A 1962 image shows a portly man and a young boy standing in a Newark diner window that reflects the parade they are watching and the stores across the street. A 1963 picture of a parking meter, a telephone and a car blends inside and outside with equal dexterity, as does a whiz-bang 1969 image of a New Orleans street. Taken from a car, it employs both the window and a side mirror to offer a nearly 360-degree view of the scene." The New Documents exhibit brought Friedlander, Arbus, and Winogrand to the attention of a wider audience but did not lead to immediate sales of their pictures. Friedlander has referred to the exhibit, as Sam Whiting reported for the *San Francisco Chronicle* (September 25, 1996),

as "the phantom show—the show that nobody saw but everybody talks about." "You would have thought we would have gotten a lot of inquiries about the pictures," Friedlander told Abigail Forester. "But only one person inquired—a guard at the museum who wanted to buy a picture from each of us. We got together and decided, 'Well, $25 sounds about right.'"

The 1967 MoMA exhibition solidified Friedlander's reputation as a photographer of cityscapes, particularly those containing storefronts, but he has never limited himself to one or only a few subjects. Nevertheless, as Malcolm Jones wrote for *Newsweek* (June 6, 2005), "the combination of intention, point of view and subject matter is so distinctive that you could pick one of his photographs out of a lineup every time, though the variety of his work still manages to stun." During the 1960s that variety encompassed unvarnished pictures of himself, such as *Self-portrait, Philadelphia* (1965), which shows the photographer dressed only in boxer shorts and slumped in a hotel-room chair. Friedlander also experimented with capturing his shadow, "using its clumsy presence to add humor and shape to a picture," as Appleford wrote. "One photograph from 1966 has that same shadow heavy against the back of a woman waiting to cross a New York street, her blond hair and fur-collared coat virtually eclipsed." "Photographers are always struggling to keep their shadow out," Friedlander has explained, according to Appleford. "And I always thought it was a funny creature, so I let him in for awhile."

In the 1970s Friedlander began photographing monuments in parks, on town squares, and in other settings. His monuments project was the first that he undertook with a specific theme in mind; it produced 1,000 photos, 200 of which were published under the title *The American Monument* (1976). The book inspired praise from Leslie Katz, as posted on Amazon's Web site: "This photographer . . . understands and brings us human civilization, embattled but intact in the various wilds of American enterprise, whether downtown, in suburbia, or on the roof." The ultimate subject of the photographs, Fred Schruers wrote for the *Los Angeles Times* (December 6, 1992), "is time itself. Time mocks our pretense when he shows us the small bust of Kennedy on a drab street in Nashua, N.H.; and it can roar like a Beethoven symphony in the snowy silence around the Spirit of the American Doughboy statue in St. Albans, Vt." While he was working on the monuments project, and afterward, Friedlander also focused on the natural world, taking "unconventionally beautiful" photos of flowers and trees, as Andy Grundberg wrote in his *Washington Post* article; those images appear in Friedlander's books *Photographs of Flowers* (1975) and *Flowers and Trees* (1981).

In 1978 the Hudson River Museum, in Yonkers, New York, mounted the first of many retrospectives of Friedlander's work, and at about the same time, he accepted his first commission, when the

Akron Art Museum, in Ohio, hired him to photograph industrial areas in that state. The commission led to the publication of *Factory Valleys* and to an accompanying exhibition in 1982. The photographs represent, as Andy Grundberg wrote for the *New York Times* (December 26, 1982), "both a summation and an extension of Mr. Friedlander's immense talents. In his views of drab manufacturing cities are echoes of his early syncopated street photographs, but also of his more recent, more elegiac depictions of flowers and trees. Yet the real surprise comes with his portraits of workers at their jobs, which show man and machine in an equilibrium that conceals none of the boredom of mass production." In a similar project, in 1985, Friedlander spent months photographing office workers. Those pictures were published, along with some of the factory photos, in *Art Work* (2002). Such images, Jacob Stockinger wrote for the *Wisconsin State Journal* (January 2, 2003), might make one "pause and ask again: Is this what I want to do? How much time and identity do I want to invest in my job? Is my job where I—and others—will find the meaning and measure of my life?"

In 1989 Friedlander included a number of nudes in his exhibition Like a One-Eyed Cat at the Seattle Art Museum; the show, which included photos taken from 1956 to 1987 (photos that appear in a book with the same title, with text by Rod Slemmons), subsequently traveled to nine other U.S. museums. The images struck Andy Grundberg, writing for the *New York Times* (March 12, 1989), as "conventional, despite their uncommon poses and unvarnished skin tones. One wonders if the bite has gone out of Mr. Friedlander's wit, or if he means them to be as lyrical as his landscapes." Friedlander's book *Nudes* was published in 1991, the year that Like a One-Eyed Cat came to MoMA. In a review of the MoMA show, Charles Hagen wrote for the *New York Times* (August 4, 1991), "These are not particularly erotic images. Even when the women are lolling about on their beds or sofas, there's an almost analytical, detached quality to the pictures. The models are doing a job, and Mr. Friedlander is, too. This down-to-earth quality is heightened by the inclusion of everyday objects—cheap bedspreads, ashtrays and so on—that furnish the women's rooms." Unlike the Seattle show, the one at MoMA included photographs that Friedlander had taken of Madonna in the late 1970s, before she became a pop singer, and had been published in *Playboy* in September 1985.

Friedlander's *Letters from the People* (1993) is a collection of images of handwritten words, graffiti, and signs, which were also exhibited at MoMA in 1994. At around that time, as the photographer told Richard Williams for the London *Independent* (August 15, 1993), he began "trying to learn how to do landscapes. In the western part of America—the Rockies, the deserts. Places that have an intensity." The results appeared in the show The Desert Seen and in a book with the same title in 1996. When viewing The Desert Seen, according to Jacob Stock-

inger, writing for the Madison, Wisconsin, *Capital Times* (November 20, 1996), "you leave behind that traditional, even stereotypical, notion of the desert. Images as idiosyncratic as these are not likely to reappear in calendars stocked by gift shops in Arizona and New Mexico or as backdrops in TV and Hollywood westerns. The scene that is seen—hence the punningly postmodern title—is unique and unsettling. . . . What's seen is a scene, not scenery." Other critics were equally impressed. To Francine Prose, writing for *Newsday* (December 1, 1996), "These black-and-white pictures reveal a passionate concern for—and curiosity about—the unpopulated natural world. With sharply focused, detailed precision, [Friedlander] captures the riotous profusion of thorns and branches, cactus and trees, the chaotic swirl and richness of plant life in this supremely inhospitable climate. These striking pictures are hard to focus on for very long; they're so dizzying in their complexity that one's eyes begin to hurt."

In 1995 the George Gund Foundation commissioned Friedlander to take pictures of workers in Cleveland, Ohio, to accompany its annual report. Of the 3,000 photographs that he took, 49 accompanied the report, and in 1997 the selected pictures were exhibited at the Cleveland Museum of Art. Steven Litt, who reviewed the show for the Cleveland *Plain Dealer* (December 19, 1997), found the images stylistically repetitious, but they impressed him nonetheless. "The photographs are in many ways an old-fashioned hymn to labor," Litt wrote. "Friedlander often focuses on people who operate machines in settings where a moment's inattention would result in serious injury. It's a nitty-gritty world far from the downtown skyscrapers where lawyers, bankers and accountants work. In Friedlander's show, nobody sits in front of a computer screen. His workers are on their feet, embroiled in sweaty, physical tasks requiring skill and mental focus."

Starting in the late 1950s, Friedlander began taking pictures of Maria DiPaoli, whom he married in 1958; he also captured on film many images of his children (Erik, born in 1960, and Anna, born in 1962) as they grew up. A few photos of Maria, spanning four decades, appear in Arthur Ollman's *The Model Wife*, which also includes pictures of the wives of eight other photographers. Friedlander, Mike Daniel wrote in a review of the book for the *Pittsburgh Post-Gazette* (December 14, 1999), "has used his neutral, documentary style to capture Maria . . . , but in a different way than the detached portraiture for which he is better known. His Maria pictures are still spur-of-the-moment and loosely staged. But they are full of warmth, reverence and admiration for his wife." Quoting Ollman, Daniel wrote, "'He's showing her with such love, such regard, such affection,' that the viewer might, in the more recent photos of Maria, miss her signs of age." Other portraits of Friedlander's family members, along with self-portraits, have been displayed publicly in the 2000s. In 2001, for example, in an exhibit called Face to Face, he presented "images of himself partially obscured by grasses (in Tuscany) and by bare, winter branches (in New York and Santa Fe). Others contrast his somewhat aged face with those of his infant grandchildren. The impressions range from discomfort to joy," as Paul Weideman wrote for the Santa Fe New Mexican (October 19, 2001). Friedlander's book Kitaj (2002) contains photos of the artist R. B. Kitaj, one of his longtime friends.

Another recent book, Stems (2003), offers still lifes from the mid-1990s that Friedlander shot while he was recovering from knee surgery. The subjects were the stems of flowers standing in water-filled glass vases. "Not only would the stems fall into wild array," Friedlander wrote in the book, as quoted by Mitch Alland on photo.net (September 12, 2003); "the vases produced with them a kind of optical splendor. . . . Helter-skelter light refractions and optical exaggerations, as well as compound reflections, happened naturally." Jacob Stockinger, writing for the Wisconsin State Journal (November 6, 2003), found the book to be "memorable and original." "It may not be to your taste—especially if you crave colorful, greeting card cheerfulness—but you are unlikely to forget these images any time soon," he continued. "These photos force you to look differently at the same old world." Similarly, Friedlander's images in Sticks & Stones: Architectural America (2004), a book that accompanied an exhibition of the same name, violate "all the pieties of architectural photography," as Nicholas Howe wrote for the New Republic (April 25, 2005). "[Friedlander] does not render buildings placeless by isolating them from their surroundings; he does not use the proper equipment to prevent distortion; and he clutters the view with signs, shadows, fences, trees, utility poles. Everything that a photographer for a glossy architectural magazine would consider amateurish becomes triumphant art in Friedlander's new book." Friedlander's book Family (2004) contains photos of his wife, dating back more than four decades, and of his children and grandchildren.

Among other honors, Friedlander has earned five National Endowment of the Arts Fellowships (1972, 1977, 1978, 1979, and 1980), a Friends of Photography Peer Award (1980), the Edward MacDowell Medal for lifetime achievement in the arts, and a MacArthur Foundation Award (1990). In late 2000 MoMA announced that it had acquired 1,000 of Friedlander's photos—"the museum photography department's biggest purchase ever of works by a living artist," as Margarett Loke reported—and the National Gallery of Art, in Washington, D.C., bought 459 of his prints, in each case for the museum's permanent collection. Friedlander has not tried digital photography. "I've got nothing against it, but I'm not a computer person," he told Paul Weideman for the Santa Fe New Mexican (October 19, 2001). "When it gets to the point where all my friends aren't talking about these things crashing all the time and I know I can walk into a room and say, 'Make me two 11 x 14s,' maybe I'll do it. But I'm quite happy with the process I have now." Friedlander and his wife live in New York State.

—A.R.

Suggested Reading: Albuquerque Journal p6 July 25, 2003; Chicago Tribune p53 Oct. 27, 1989; (London) Independent p31 Aug. 15, 1993; Los Angeles Times p2 Dec. 6, 1992; New York (online) June 5, 2005; New York Times II p27 Dec. 26, 1982, C p12 Aug. 18, 1986, II p25 Aug. 4, 1991; New Republic p35 Apr. 25, 2005; Newsweek p77 July 24, 1978; San Francisco Chronicle E p1 Sep. 25, 1996

Selected Books: The American Monument, 1976; Flowers and Trees, 1981; Factory Valleys, 1982; Nudes, 1991; Letters From the People, 1993; The Desert Seen, 1996; Little Screens, 2001; Art Work, 2002; Lee Friedlander: Kitaj, 2002; Stems, 2003; Lee Friedlander: Family, 2004; Sticks & Stones: Architectural America, 2004; Apples and Olives, 2005; Lee Friedlander: Self Portrait, 2006

Fu, Ping

1958– Software developer; president and CEO of Raindrop Geomagic

Address: Raindrop Geomagic, P.O. Box 12219, Research Triangle Park, NC 27709

In 2005 Ping Fu was named entrepreneur of the year by the editors of the magazine Inc. for her work in Digital Shape Sampling and Processing (DSSP) technology. At the helm of Raindrop Geomagic, the company she founded in 1996, Fu has developed computer programs that allow designers and engineers to digitally scan an object with optical beams and then use the scan to generate a precise three-dimensional model. The first product manufactured using DSSP was a doll based on the character Pikachu from the cartoon series Pokemon. Today, the technology Fu pioneered is used by thousands of clients, including the National Aeronautics and Space Administration (NASA), which employed DSSP in 2005 to evaluate the damaged tiles on the space shuttle Discovery while the craft was in orbit, and the National Association for Stock Car Auto Racing (NASCAR), for which DSSP provides an efficient method of inspecting engine parts. Additionally, DSSP has many applications in the medical industry, including the development of artificial hearts, hearing aids, prosthetic joints, and dental braces. Recently, Raindrop Geomagic software was used to make a massive laser scan of the Statue of Liberty, so that the monument could be repaired or replaced in the event of a terrorist attack.

Courtesy of Raindrop Geomagic

Ping Fu

Ping Fu was born in Nanjing, China, in 1958. Her father was an aerospace engineer and professor, and her mother was the chief financial officer of a large company. When Fu was just 11 days old, her mother, intent on her own career, sent her to be raised by an aunt and uncle (a successful entrepreneur) in Shanghai. Fu became devoted to the couple, whom she remembers as loving, responsible surrogate parents. "[My uncle] taught me so much about integrity and trust of others," Fu told Becky Suzik for *Business Leader* (January 2005, online). "His constant reinforcement of integrity, honesty, trust, and efficiency had a huge influence on how I conduct myself." When she was seven years old, Fu and her sister, Hong, who was then three, were removed from the care of their aunt and uncle by members of the Red Guard, a youth militia organized by Mao Zedong to purge the People's Republic of China of bourgeois influences. The two children were taken from Shanghai to Nanjing just as Mao's Cultural Revolution, a program aimed at instilling proletarian values in the country's educated elite, was getting underway. After their biological parents were sent to forced-labor camps in the countryside, the girls were placed in a dormitory under the control of the often brutal Red Guard.

During the Cultural Revolution Fu witnessed a series of violent events. She once watched members of the Red Guard tie a teacher to four horses—with one limb attached to each horse. They then startled the horses, which galloped away in different directions, killing the teacher. Fu witnessed another teacher being dropped headfirst down a dry well. Her sister was once scalded with boiling water by a guard as punishment for playing too noisily. In another instance Hong was thrown into a river to drown, and Fu, then 10 years old, leapt in to pull her out of the water. When the two crawled from the river, they were beaten, and Fu was raped.

Shortly after Hong's near-drowning, the girls' mother was released from the camp and returned to Nanjing. (Their father remained imprisoned.) Instead of offering her daughters the joyous reunion they had envisioned, their mother emerged from her ordeal embittered and unable to cope with daily life. "She whipped me and slapped me, she took my flesh between her fingers and pinched me," Fu told John Brant for *Inc.* (December 2005). "Intellectually, I understood. I understood my mother was not herself, that her own misery was such that she had to lash out at me. I knew that in my head, but in my heart it was something different. I could forgive my mother for sending me away when I was a baby—she had a career, she never wanted to be a mother—but I could not forgive her for what happened when she came back from the camp."

In 1976, upon Mao's death, the Cultural Revolution ended and schools began reopening. Fu, then 18, had not attended classes for over a decade. She was accepted into a literature program at Suzhou University, from which she graduated with a bachelor's degree in 1980. (She had originally hoped to study business or engineering; some sources state that Fu was forced into her field of study by the Communist Party.) As a student Fu took an interest in journalism, and at the urging of a teacher, she embarked on an investigation into the reported killings of newborn girls in some of China's rural provinces. The practice had presumably become common because of the government's policy of limiting each family to one child and the culture's entrenched preference for male offspring. In the course of her investigation, which lasted two years, Ping witnessed several such killings herself. Her findings were published in the largest newspaper in Shanghai in January 1981 and shortly after that in the national *People's Daily*. When the story was picked up by the international media, a public outcry arose, and the United Nations was forced to impose sanctions on China. Embarrassed by the attention, the Chinese government decided to punish Fu. In February 1981 she was put in solitary confinement in Nanjing Prison. For three days she was kept in a cell with no heat, light, or toilet facilities. When she emerged, she thought she would be executed; instead, she was brought before a government official, who informed her that she was to be deported. The official told her, according to Brant, "You must never say a word about your involvement in this project. You are forbidden to engage in any political activity. You will never return to China, but your family remains here. If in any way you disobey these instructions, your family will suffer the consequences. Have I made myself clear, Comrade?" Fu was put on a flight from Shanghai to San Francisco, California, and told, for reasons she did not understand, that she was to make her way to Albuquerque and enroll at the University of New Mexico to study English.

Fu's first days in the U.S. were filled with confusion. She arrived in San Francisco with too little money for airfare to Albuquerque—Communist officials had given her only $80 in traveler's checks, and the ticket cost $85. She was able to secure a ride with a Vietnamese man she met at the airport, who spoke some Chinese. Instead of taking Fu to the university, however, the man took her to a suburban house, then disappeared, locking her inside with his three children for three days. A neighbor eventually overheard Fu's cries for help from within the house and called the police, who helped Fu get to the university.

Once there Fu worked at various restaurant and housecleaning jobs to help pay her tuition and gained a reputation as a diligent, disciplined employee and student. Fu had begun studying comparative literature, but realizing the relative lack of opportunities for students in that field, she switched her focus to computer science. She had been casually told by a professor, as Brant wrote, "The best way for [Asian students] to learn about America . . . was to enter a university as an undergraduate: Live in a dorm, eat greasy pizza in the dining hall, play foosball in the student union." Taking the advice seriously, she left her master's program in New Mexico and transferred to the University of California, San Diego, as an undergraduate.

In California Fu met Len Sherman, the owner of a start-up software company, who hired her to write computer codes part-time. In 1986, after finishing her bachelor's degree in computer sciences, she turned down a 5 percent share in Sherman's already lucrative company and moved to Illinois, to work at Bell Labs and study at the University of Illinois, home to the National Center for Supercomputing Applications (NCSA). According to its Web site, the NCSA, which opened in 1986, "has contributed significantly to the birth and growth of the worldwide cyberinfrastructure for science and engineering, operating some of the world's most powerful supercomputers and developing the software infrastructure needed to efficiently use these systems. . . . Today the center is recognized as an international leader in deploying robust high-performance computing resources and in working with research communities to develop new computing and software technologies."

Fu worked for four years at Bell Labs while beginning to study for her Ph.D., then moved on to the NCSA while completing her doctoral work. There she proved a talented designer of computer-visualization applications, a field that Brant described as "opening an exciting new playground between science and art." At the NCSA she designed the software used for the acclaimed special effects for the film *Terminator 2: Judgment Day* (1991), in which the cyborg villain melts into a puddle of liquid metal before assuming a new shape.

After earning her doctorate Fu accepted a full-time staff position at the NCSA, where she supervised a talented student named Marc Andreeson. Andreeson developed the Mosaic software browser, a user-friendly application that allowed text and images to be displayed on the same Web page and introduced the now-common system of hyperlinking. Andreeson, eager to profit from his work, soon left the NCSA and developed the Netscape search engine, which was built on the system he had created in Illinois. The NCSA responded by suing him, claiming that it owned the rights to the work done in its laboratories, and ultimately came away with $3 million, a small fraction of what Andreeson eventually earned. Andreeson's success in some ways inspired Fu, who strove to create something equally beneficial to society. (She has told journalists, however, that she cares little for the kind of financial gain Andreeson has enjoyed.)

At the University of Illinois, Fu had met Herbert Edelsbrunner, an Austrian computer-science professor and expert in computational geometry and algorithms, and in 1991 the couple married. Soon after the wedding, a friend asked Fu about the possibility of digitally computing negative or empty spaces as well as objects and shapes. She turned her attention to the issue and discovered that her husband had already developed algorithms that could be applied to the task. By 1996 she had developed Alpha Shapes, a program that allowed users to create three-dimensional prototypes of objects. Such clients as Boeing and General Motors immediately began licensing the software from the NCSA for use in their design and manufacturing processes.

DSSP technology involves aiming a laser scanner at an object. The scanner's beams strike the object's surface, creating what is known as a point cloud (or shadow image) of the object, which is displayed on a computer screen. Brant explained, "Point clouds form a decisive step in the DSSP process . . . and distinguish the technology from its cousin, computer-aided design and manufacturing, or CAD/CAM. In CAD/CAM, the designer creates the product, employing the software as a digitally enhanced pencil and drawing board. In DSSP, by contrast, the designer does not create. The image on the screen originates from the product itself, not the hand, brain, and eye of a human." Next, the software connects each point in the cloud to two neighboring points, thereby creating a multitude of triangles. The triangles are then interconnected, forming a more detailed digital draft of the object. The next phase involves the creation of nonuniform rational B splines, known as NURBS, a mathematical model useful for representing curved surfaces. Once the software generates the NURBS—within roughly three minutes—the digital model exhibits a realistic surface; the models are said to be size-accurate to within three-thousandths of a millimeter and can be used in various ways. Some manufacturers, for example, virtually redesign the model and then compare it with the original before making changes to their product; others age the computer image to help predict how their product will perform after years of use.

In 1997 Fu left the NCSA to start her own company, Raindrop Geomagic, along with Edelsbrunner. After borrowing $500,000 from her sister, who had moved to the U.S. and married a successful Arizona businessman, Fu began pitching her ideas to venture capitalists, who provided another $1.5 million. Fu, aware that she was a more skilled computer scientist than business manager, hired an experienced CEO and moved the fledgling company to Research Triangle Park (RTP), North Carolina, a center for high-tech commerce located near Raleigh, Durham, and Chapel Hill. RTP was closer than Illinois to the major coastal centers for new technology, and Fu realized that it would be easier to lure talented employees to North Carolina than to the Midwest. RTP is also close to Duke University, where Edelsbrunner had been hired as a professor. (In addition to his academic duties, he serves on Geomagic's board of directors and still provides the algorithms needed to develop new products.)

Fu proved especially good at attracting new investors, and by 1999 Geomagic had more than $6 million in additional capital. Still, due in part to her CEO's lack of experience with small start-up companies (rather than large technology firms), the first two years were difficult ones, and sales of Fu's innovative DSSP programs were slow. By the end of 2000, the company had lost most of its capital, and, as it was often phrased in the media, the high-tech "bubble" seemed to have "burst." Fu chose to take more extensive control of Geomagic. She told Brant, "All of my instincts kicked in. . . . In a crisis mode, you lose all self-doubt—at least I do. I couldn't afford the luxury of doubt. I had too many people depending on me. I knew I had to make Geomagic's story so compelling that no potential customer could possibly turn me down." After Fu had stepped into the CEO position and handed the company's salespeople pink slips, mortgaging her home to pay their severance packages, Geomagic's fortunes improved considerably, and by 2002 the firm had begun to make a profit. One of Fu's first major sales was to Align Technology, a dental firm, which used her software to make custom implants and crowns. Dental companies still make up a large portion of Fu's client base, as do manufacturers of individually fitted hearing aids. Brant wrote, "Ping likes to imagine that each of us will soon be in possession of a DSSP model of our feet, and when we need new shoes, we'll transmit that model to a manufacturer, which will make shoes that fit like no off-the-shelf shoes can." Meanwhile, Geomagic technology is now a standard tool in a number of other arenas: turbine companies, for example, are using it to manufacture and inspect new blades; toy companies use it to design molds for increasingly elaborate playthings; and archaeologists are creating virtual museums made up of digitized images of their finds. As the scanning and processing hardware necessary for DSSP becomes less expensive and the software more sophisticated, Fu's list of clients continues to grow. Although she does not release exact details of her company's earnings, a November 2005 press release, as posted on the Geomagic Web site, states, "During the last five years, Geomagic revenues have grown by 2,105 percent. In the 2004 fiscal year, net income rose by 615 percent, the number of Geomagic employees doubled, and the company became international, establishing fully owned subsidiaries throughout Europe and Asia."

Ping Fu became a U.S. citizen in 1993. In addition to her work at Raindrop Geomagic, she is an adjunct professor at Duke University and a frequent lecturer at international conferences. She and Edelsbrunner have one daughter, XiXi.

—M.B.

Suggested Reading: *All Things Considered* (on-line) Apr. 5, 2006; *Business Leader* (on-line) Jan. 2005; *Inc.* Dec. 2005; Raindrop Geomagic Web site; (Raleigh, North Carolina) *Metro Magazine* (on-line) Jan. 2006; (Raleigh, North Carolina) *News and Observer* D p1+ Apr. 7, 1999; *U.S. News & World Report* p48 Feb. 5, 1996

Gaines, Donna

Mar. 21, 1951– Sociologist; writer

Address: 350 E. 52d St., #8A, New York, NY 10022

"I'm a writer that loves sociology. Sociology opened my eyes and my heart; it explains the world to me, everyday," the sociologist, journalist, and author Donna Gaines told Johanna Ebner for *Footnotes* (April 2004), an American Sociological Association publication. Gaines is an authority on the behavior and emotional lives of teenagers—in particular, suburban teenagers and their feelings of alienation and hopelessness, suicidal impulses, and survival tactics, including their identification with rock, punk-rock, and heavy-metal music and musicians. Her first book, *Teenage Wasteland: Suburbia's Dead End Kids* (1991), is an ethnographic study of teenagers (born during the decade starting in the mid- to late 1960s and called generation X or the baby-bust generation) living in Bergenfield, New Jersey, where in 1987 four teens ended their lives after signing a suicide pact. Described by Gil Asakawa for the Denver, Colorado, *Rocky Mountain News* (March 14, 2003) as a "landmark empathetic look at adolescent anomie," *Teenage Wasteland* is widely considered a classic in sociology, and it has appeared on the reading lists of college courses nationwide. Gaines's second book is *A Misfit's Manifesto: The Spiritual Journey of a Rock & Roll Heart* (2003). In an interview with Benjamin Frymer for *InterActions: UCLA Journal of*

Donna Gaines

Education and Information Studies (Volume 2, Issue 1, 2006), Gaines described that book as a "sociological memoir"; Frymer characterized it as "an exploration of relationships between identity formation, popular culture, addiction, and spirituality." As a social worker for a decade beginning in 1976, Gaines specialized in substance-abuse counseling, suicide prevention, community organizing, advocating for children and parents, and "streetwork," as she has called it, using a term common overseas but not in the U.S. She herself, as she revealed in *Teenage Wasteland* and explained in greater detail in *A Misfit's Manifesto*, had felt burdened by negative feelings about herself during her teens and had spent much of her time on the streets or by herself in her room, listening to rock-and-roll music; she had also drunk to excess and become a drug abuser. In 1986, with the first of many articles written for the *Village Voice*, she "ventured into journalism," as she recalled on her Web site, because she saw it "as a means to an end: making social theory more accessible, and reaching more people on critical issues like youth suicide, class, and the redemptive power of subculture (i.e. music)." Gaines has also written for *Rolling Stone*, *Spin*, *Long Island Monthly*, and *Newsday*, on subjects including tattoos, pornography, spirituality, and intergenerational love as well as music and young people in American society. She was a visiting professor in the Department of Sociology of Barnard College (a division of Columbia University), in New York City, from 1996 to 1999, and in the fall of 2002, she taught graduate students at the New School, also in New York.

Gaines was born Donna Denmark on March 21, 1951 in the New York City borough of Brooklyn. Her mother, Betty Bradley, had been a successful big-band singer before her first marriage (which ended in divorce); among other jobs, she had worked with the bandleader Bob Chester and performed with the comedian Milton Berle in the famous New York nightclub the Latin Quarter. Gaines's father, Herbert Denmark (Bradley's second husband), managed his family's kosher-catering enterprise; he died of Hodgkin's disease less than a month after his daughter's birth. For Gaines, as she wrote in *A Misfit's Manifesto*, "Herbie . . . [was] an icon, a mythic figure I knew only as the great love of Mom's life." In 1954 her mother remarried; her new husband, Arthur Gaines, an Oldsmobile dealer, legally adopted Donna. In her memoir Gaines described her first stepfather as well-meaning but passive and remote. For years he suffered from worsening heart disease, and when she was in ninth grade, he died. The next year (1966) her mother married again; her fourth husband worked in his family's liquor store. Gaines has always referred to her second stepfather only as D.O.M., for "Dirty Old Man," a name inspired by the song with that title by the rock group the Fugs, and one she chose because D.O.M. used to tease her about her use of garish makeup and provocative dress. In her memoir she described D.O.M. as "a functional parent" and as "protective; he didn't want me to be vulnerable. He also didn't want to push the dad thing too hard. But he was in full parental mode, looking out for his daughter." Her mother's parental style, by contrast, she wrote, "was an incongruent mix of devouring need and free-spirited permissiveness. . . . Fiercely possessive and overindulgent, neglecting me and spoiling me at the same time, Betty was a pal, more like a sister than a mother." For half a dozen years, until Gaines was about 10, a live-in maid was her primary caregiver.

Gaines grew up in the Rockaway Beach section of the New York City borough of Queens. Until ninth grade she attended a Jewish day school. For the next three years, except for one term at a private school in Brooklyn, she was enrolled at Far Rockaway High School. As a child and adolescent, she felt isolated and ashamed of being overweight. "In those days if you were fat or queer or if you were adopted, forget about it. If your parents were divorced or drunks, if you were an only child or interracial, you were a weirdo. Shamed, you suffered silent and alone," she wrote in her memoir. For solace, she listened to doo-wop and then rock-and-roll music in her room. Later, she also sniffed glue, drank alcohol, and took illegal drugs. Referring to Arthur Gaines and her mother, respectively, she told Susan Brenna for *Newsday* (May 29, 1991), "If one of your parents is dying and the other one is preoccupied with taking care of him, and you're the rowdy teenager, the best thing you can do is disappear. Think about it—how many women get to be free on the street when they're 14? And I'm enormously independent because of it." She considers herself fortunate, too, because in the latter half of the 1960s, as she wrote, "Youth was exploding": "Thanks to drug culture and flower power, misfits like me had other choices. People would respect me for my street smarts, for my accumulated knowledge of toxicology and pharmacology. . . . I was free, lost in the crowd."

After Gaines graduated from high school, she spent three months at Rider College (now Rider University), in Lawrenceville, New Jersey, before dropping out. At 18 she was arrested on a narcotics charge while at a party (though she herself had not been using drugs that night); the next day she was released into the custody of her stepfather, and later the charges were dropped. The following September she enrolled at Chamberlain Junior College, in Boston, Massachusetts, where she remained for only two months. Soon after she left school, her mother was diagnosed with breast cancer and underwent a double mastectomy. Her stepfather sold the liquor store and devoted himself to his wife's care. (Gaines's mother lived for another 18 years.) After failing at a series of unskilled jobs, Gaines made up her mind to "show D.O.M. I could be something more. . . . I had to grow up, prove to [my parents], to the neighbors, . . . to the world and to myself that I was not . . . a pathetic loser."

At 19 Gaines entered Kingsborough Community College, in Brooklyn, with the intention of studying sociology. "I was born with a sociological imagination," she told Johanna Ebner. "It's the way my brain was wired. I looked at groups and social norms and began to reflect on them." In her memoir she described Kingsborough as "a benevolent parent, indulgent and generous, nurturing in every possible way—emotionally, financially, spiritually, and mentally." "It was . . . my first positive experience of self in the legitimate world," she wrote. "Here I encountered adults in authority who treated me like I knew something, like I had something to offer. I read all the books, then asked for more. I spoke up in class. . . . I took every sociology course I could. . . . Tricks of the trade, tools of craft, sociological concepts clarified so many things. My career as a teenage misfit and an outcast was dignified through the study of *deviance*. My identity as a 'problem child,' an 'underachiever,' was vindicated by *labeling theory*. My early forays to [parts of Far Rockaway] were *ethnographies*, *community studies*, albeit exploratory. . . . I had felt like a vapor for most of my life, and even this was explained. In fact, vast bodies of knowledge addressed it. It was called *alienation*. The idea that human interactions were governed by norms, and that we paid a price for violating them, clarified childhood experiences. . . . It was my introduction to formal sociology that made me feel ironically grateful for a ruptured childhood. Exposure to four extended family groups"—those of her biological parents and of her two stepfathers—"hand-fed me social class and cultural process as lived experience." She also wrote, "As I began to understand myself as a member of a race, a sex, a class, a generation, as a creator and consumer of culture, I saw that my personal experiences were both political and sociological. I understood from my professors that no matter how hip or smart I thought I was, social roles, rules, norms, mores, and rituals bound me too. As sociological thought began to formalize my life into a coherent and manageable package, things started making sense. . . . In passing sociology on to me, my professors handed me the keys to my own freedom."

Readily available sources do not mention whether Gaines earned an associate's degree. She next entered Harpur College, a division of the State University of New York (SUNY) at Binghamton, where she majored in sociology and received a B.A. degree in 1974. During her last year at SUNY Binghamton, she worked on campus as an assistant director of the High Hopes Counseling Center. In 1977 she earned a master's degree in social work (MSW) from Adelphi University, in Garden City, New York, where, in 1976–77, she held a Levenstein Fellowship in Research. Earlier, in 1976, she had launched a decade-long career as a social-work consultant; she specialized in child-abuse prevention, special adoptions, social-program evaluation, and street work with youths. Meanwhile, at the age of 31, she had entered the graduate program in sociology at SUNY Stony Brook, on Long Island. There, she was strongly influenced by the eminent sociologist Lewis Coser, who, in one seminar that he led, as she wrote in her memoir, "mesmerized us with stories of our forefathers, our heroes, the masters of sociological thought. . . . It felt like a tribal campfire, a ceremonial rite of passage." His course in classical sociological theory "changed my life. From cosmetology to cosmology, the sociology of knowledge slowly lifted me up from the gutters of positivism." (Positivism is a school of thought, introduced by the "father of sociology," the 19th-century French philosopher August Comte, according to which the only true, reliable knowledge is scientific knowledge.) Gaines continued, "Once, pointing from his office window out to the snowy walkways and trees of Eastern Long Island, Professor Coser referred to data as 'anything out there.' After that, anything seemed possible."

For the better part of two decades starting in 1978, Gaines was romantically involved with a man she called Nick, a member of a rock group. She also forged close friendships with the rock-and-roll singer and guitarist Johnny Thunders and members of the punk-rock group the Ramones—in particular, Joey Ramone (born Jeffrey Ross Hyman). By her own account, as a graduate student she maintained two separate lives, even two separate personas: one, that of a workaholic driven by a fierce determination to excel in school; the other, that of "Tessa," as Nick and others called her, a person who wore punk-style dress, drank to excess during club crawls and on other occasions, took an array of illegal and prescription drugs, and gorged on sugary foods. (In the late 1990s she conquered her addictions to drugs and sugar and swallowed her last alcoholic drink.)

Gaines completed an M.A. degree at SUNY Stony Brook in 1984 and remained at the school to work on her doctoral dissertation. A suggestion from a SUNY employee that she study what she loved led her to consider writing about popular culture—an idea that she had previously rejected, fearing both that she had to keep the nonacademic part of her life private and completely separate from her academic pursuits, and that, as she wrote in her memoir, "academic discourse has the power to render anything banal and dull—including sex, drugs, and rock & roll." In 1985 she founded, and chaired briefly, the cultural section of the American Sociological Association, which has grown into one of that organization's largest special-interest sections. Shortly afterward, thanks to the journalist Ellen Willis, whom Gaines has described as "rock's first feminist critic" and whom she met through Willis's partner, the sociologist Stanley Aronowitz (both of whom she has cited as mentors), the Village Voice hired her as a freelance writer. The Voice published her first article, about the punk-rock and "new-wave" radio station WLIR-FM, on September 23, 1986.

In mid-1987 the Voice assigned Gaines to investigate the planned, simultaneous suicide by carbon-monoxide poisoning of four Bergenfield, New Jersey, teenagers, which had occurred in March of that year. She approached friends of the four and soon gained their trust; the breakthrough moment came, as she recalled to Susan Brenna, when the teenagers noticed a button on her lapel that read "Ace of Spades," the title of a song by the British heavy-metal band Motörhead. Gaines—who dressed in black leather, had visible tattoos, sometimes dyed her hair purple, carried a knife in one of her boots, used profanity, often stayed out all night in clubs, and shared the teenagers' taste in music—spent much time during the next two years on suburban streets, in New Jersey and elsewhere, in an attempt to understand not only the motives behind the quadruple suicide but the reasons for the pervasive hopelessness that she had detected among the teens she befriended. Some of the young people had already attempted suicide, and a few were likely to try again, she believed. She described her findings in the Village Voice, in "Teenage Wasteland—Bergenfield's Dead End Kids" (July 14, 1987). (The title is from the chorus of the Who's "Baba O'Riley," which has been called "the definitive rock anthem.") Gaines's doctoral dissertation, similarly titled and written under the guidance of Lewis Coser, grew out of that article; she completed it in 1990 and earned her Ph.D. the same year. Her dissertation, in turn, with some modifications, was published in 1991 as her book Teenage Wasteland: Suburbia's Dead End Kids. The book appeared in paperback in 1992; in a "scholarly edition," with an afterword, under the imprint of the Chicago University Press, in 1998; and in an Italian version in 2001.

Most of the Bergenfield teenagers whom Gaines got to know were from unstable, lower-middle-class (or "upper poor") families. They were unlikely to attend college but, rather, with industrial and manufacturing jobs growing increasingly scarce, would accept or had already started working at low-wage jobs with little or no potential for advancement. Moreover, they blamed themselves for their circumstances and felt "like they're losers," as Gaines put it when talking to Susan Brenna. Desperate to grasp at some hope, they turned to what Gaines called "white suburban soul music": heavy metal. According to Susan Brenna, "Kids see in their metal heroes people who broke out of their grungy suburban traps, and they dream of having a glorious moment of their own before life grinds them down."

The culture and behavior of the teenagers whom Gaines wrote about in Teenage Wasteland served as examples of theories presented by the pioneering French sociologist Émile Durkheim (1858–1917) in his book Suicide and other writings. As Gaines wrote in her memoir, "In my investigation, I had discovered that most rare of Durkheimian types, the fatalistic suicide. I could explain [what led to the four Bergenfield suicides] using theories of alienation and anomie. I was adamant that sociology, not psychology, could and should explain teenage suicide. That suicide was a social, cultural, and historical phenomenon—not an exclusively medical, psychiatric one." (Later, as she told Benjamin Frymer, she realized that she had "underestimated the impact of alcohol and addiction" and had erroneously "dismissed concepts like low self-esteem, spiritual dis-ease.") In his review of Teenage Wasteland for Billboard (May 9, 1992), Chris Morris praised "this compassionate book" for being "one of the only works of its kind to view teenage America from the teenager's perspective." In the St. Petersburg (Florida) Times (May 12, 1991), Ann G. Sjoerdsma described Teenage Wasteland as "an alienating, disturbing book about alienated, disturbed kids. Not bad kids, really, just lost, forgotten, cast-off kids, kids of the 1980s for whom the American dream no longer exists, kids who seek refuge from abusive parents, apathetic teachers and a hypocritical society in heavy-metal music, Satanism, sex, drugs, alcohol and hanging out at the 7-Eleven. Kids who think daily about suicide." "It is Ms. Gaines's provocative thesis that in postindustrial America these working-class children are denied the real or metaphorical mobility that could liberate them from their limited lives," Samuel G. Freedman wrote for the New York Times Book Review (June 16, 1991). "The wanderlust and social experiments of the 1960's, which the author credits with rescuing her from desperation, were no longer options once the guns-and-butter economy that undergirded them slid into recession. The boom of the 1980's saw a decline in meaningful and remunerative work for high school graduates, leaving little besides fast-food and gas station jobs. Drug abuse, alcoholism and even suicide, Ms.

Gaines argues, are the symptoms of a larger cultural and economic disease."

In around 2000, when she began to write *A Misfit's Manifesto*, as she told Liza Featherstone for *Newsday* (March 9, 2003), Gaines felt as if she was "just exploding with rage, and I couldn't figure out where it was coming from. . . . So I saw all manner of healers—Native American healers, Buddhist healers, Christian healers, 12-step therapists—to try to figure out where this anger came from and who I was, because I was split off. I was, as an adult, this attractive, successful, strong woman, but somewhere, dragging behind me, was this bottled-up misery and sorrow." In *A Misfit's Manifesto* she wrote, "For a long time, rage and fear were my survival tools. I took abuse and I dished it out. . . . I viewed the world as a hateful, unloving place where people were out to demolish me." In time, she came to believe that "God works in us, and we work in God," that people are "not alone" but are in "God's world." "As God reopened my heart, my capacity for joy, my ability to love myself and to feel part of the world were restored," she wrote. In a review for *Elle* of *A Misfit's Manifesto*, as quoted on Gaines's Web site, a critic wrote, "If, like me, you're drawn to confessions of love for loud guitars, Pepperidge Farm's finest and the Man upstairs, this is your sort of tell-all. If you have a

low tolerance for astrology or fits of self-congratulation, then this isn't—but you'll miss out on a slyly poignant one-woman social history of postwar America."

Gaines has presented many talks and served on panel discussions on dozens of occasions at universities and other places in the U.S. and abroad. She lives in Manhattan. Her recreational activities include target shooting, body surfing, hiking, and studying metaphysics. She practices and is a master healer and teacher of Usui Reiki, which the Web site usuireiki.org defines as a "system of natural healing for body, mind and spirit."

—K.J.E.

Suggested Reading: *Billboard* p75 May 9, 1992; (Denver, Colorado) *Rocky Mountain News* D p29 Mar. 14, 2003; Donna Gaines Web site; *Footnotes* (on-line) Apr. 2004; *New York Times Book Review* p20 June 16, 1991; *Newsday* II p46 May 29, 1991, D p31 Mar. 9, 2003; *St. Petersburg (Florida) Times* D p6 May 12, 1991; Gaines, Donna. *A Misfit's Manifesto: The Spiritual Journey of a Rock & Roll Heart*, 2003

Selected Books: *Teenage Wasteland: Suburbia's Dead End Kids*, 1991; *A Misfit's Manifesto: The Spiritual Journey of a Rock & Roll Heart*, 2003

Galbraith, James K.

Jan. 29, 1952– Economist

Address: c/o Levy Economics Institute, Bard College, P.O. Box 5000, Annandale-on-Hudson, NY 12504-5000; c/o Palgrave Macmillan, Houndmills, Basingstoke, Hampshire RG21 6XS, England

"What is modern economics about?" James K. Galbraith asked in "How the Economists Got It Wrong," an article he wrote for the *American Prospect* (February 14, 2000, on-line). "It seems to be, mainly, about *itself*: The AEA [American Economic Association] meets to celebrate the importance of its members, their presence in high public positions, their influence in foreign lands, and the winning of the Nobel Prize." In that article, Galbraith, an economist who is noted for his iconoclastic streak, expressed his dissatisfaction with a recent meeting of the AEA, in which "radicals and Keynesians," he wrote, had been effectively relegated to the sidelines. "What was therefore most conspicuously missing from this meeting of America's premier social science organization, was any actual discussion of economic ideas. But what am I thinking? Of course they don't want to discuss ideas. Would you, with the record of this professorate?"

Courtesy of the University of Texas

James K. Galbraith is the son of John Kenneth Galbraith, who was widely regarded as one of the most important economists of the 20th century. (The elder Galbraith died in 2006, at the age of 97.) "The most important thing about my dad's influence is a critical perspective," Galbraith told Kenneth N. Gilpin for the *New York Times* (April 2, 1989). "My father is both a leading economist and a leading critic of economists. I can't escape from that perspective, nor do I want to." Like his father, Galbraith is considered a Keynesian economist, a student of the school of economics propounded by John Maynard Keynes in the 1920s and 1930s. Keynes was a stern critic of the laissez-faire economic policies of the day, arguing instead that governments needed to spend significant amounts of money on public-works programs to help reduce unemployment rates and fight poverty during slow economic times. That idea, according to an article by the economist Robert Reich for *Time* (March 29, 1999), "probably saved capitalism from itself." Reich explained that Keynes saw deficit spending by the government as a necessity "because the private sector won't invest enough. As their markets become saturated, businesses reduce their investments, setting in motion a dangerous cycle: less investment, fewer jobs, less consumption and even less reason for business to invest." John Kenneth Galbraith, a Democrat who served in the presidential administrations of Franklin D. Roosevelt and John F. Kennedy, championed public spending on infrastructure and criticized prevailing opinions about consumerism and corporate power in a series of successful, if controvesial, books, including *The Affluent Society* (1958) and *The New Industrial State* (1967). James K. Galbraith, commonly known as Jamie, has followed in his father's footsteps; as Robert Reno wrote for the *Austin American-Statesman* (February 9, 2000), "One of the most provocative and eloquent voices in 21st-century economics is coming from the son of one of the most provocative and eloquent economists of the 20th century." Because the bylines of both father and son have appeared (separately) in many periodicals, their identities have at times been confused, with articles written by James K. Galbraith mistakenly attributed to John Kenneth Galbraith. "It is true that I share my father's middle name Kenneth, although I have made a practice for the sake of those who may be easily confused to use only the initial," Galbraith told Renee Montagne for National Public Radio's *Morning Edition* (July 29, 2002). Dimitri Papadimitriou, an economist and colleague of James Galbraith, told Bill Day for the *San Antonio Express-News* (November 25, 2001), "He cannot avoid the reputation by association, but he stands on his own merit. Genes have something to do with it, clearly. He's a very articulate speaker and very clear in his writing, and that follows the tradition of John Kenneth Galbraith. But Ken Galbraith was not a theoretician. His son Jamie combines theory and practice."

The younger Galbraith has written many books and articles on economics and speaks frequently on various television programs about the state of the economy. He has argued vociferously, and unfashionably, against the ideas that the best way to fight inflation is to raise interest rates, that higher

minimum wages will lead to unemployment, and that rising pay inequality is acceptable and due to technological change. According to Galbraith, the economy is a "managed beast" that the government has forgotten to manage, as he told Gene Marlowe for the *Richmond (Virginia) Times Dispatch* (August 22, 1998). Over the years he has grown increasingly and primarily concerned about the issue of economic inequality, which he examined in his book *Created Unequal: The Crisis in American Pay* (1998). As he told Anne Morris for the *Austin American-Statesman* (September 7, 1998), "I started out with a substantially more detached view than I have now. I came to a realization that this issue—inequality—really connected to questions of economic policy, to monetary policy, interest rates, to the great issue of unemployment, to growth, to the minimum wage. These are questions I had been working on all my professional life . . . questions I feel passionate about. A society that becomes too badly split really isn't a single society any more. One group is concerned to protect the wealth that they have; the other feels that the political system doesn't have much to offer them."

James Kenneth Galbraith was born on January 29, 1952 in Boston, Massachusetts, to the author Catherine Atwater and John Kenneth Galbraith, who was at that time an economics professor at Harvard University. He has two brothers, John Alan and Peter W. Galbraith. (Another brother, Douglas, died at a young age from leukemia.) From 1961 until 1963 John Kenneth Galbraith, who had been deputy administrator in the Office of Price Administration under President Roosevelt, served as John F. Kennedy's ambassador to India, bringing his family to live there with him. Then nine years old, James was struck by the massive gap in India between rich and poor and later credited the experience with sparking his interest in economic inequality. Beginning in 1969 he studied French and art history at the University of California at Berkeley, where he took part in marches to protest the Vietnam War. "My father and I never had that characteristic conflict of our generation over Vietnam," he told Morris. "We were on the same side." He later transferred to Harvard University; in 1974 he graduated magna cum laude with a degree in economics. He then spent a year in England, studying economics as a Marshall Scholar at King's College, part of Cambridge University, before returning to the United States, where he received a Ph.D. in economics from Yale University, in New Haven, Connecticut, in 1981. While working toward his degree, Galbraith served on the staff of the Banking and Financial Services Committee of the U.S. Congress. From 1981 to 1982 he was the executive director of the Joint Economic Committee of Congress, an advisory panel that includes members of the House of Representatives and the Senate as well as public citizens. In 1985 Galbraith became a professor at the Lyndon B. Johnson School of Public Affairs at the University of Texas at Austin, where he has taught courses in economics as well as public policy and government. (During the 2006 fall term, he was on a leave of absence.) He directed the school's Ph.D. program in public policy from 1995 to 1997.

Galbraith's scholarly output has been prodigious, much like his father's. He has written two major books, *Balancing Acts: Technology, Finance, and the American Future* (1989) and *Created Unequal*. He has co-authored two textbooks, *The Economic Problem* (1990), written with Robert L. Heilbroner, and *Macroeconomics* (1994), written with William Darity Jr.; he is also the co-editor (with Maureen Berner) of *Inequality and Industrial Change: A Global View* (2001), which features articles from several graduate students of the Lyndon B. Johnson School. In addition, he has penned an enormous number of articles for such periodicals as *Salon*, the *American Prospect*, and the *Nation*, as well as served as an occasional commentator for the National Public Radio program *Marketplace*. He writes the column "Econoclast" for *Mother Jones*. As Galbraith explained to Morris, "Long ago my father . . . realized that writing had become a bad habit he couldn't break. I've caught the habit, I'm afraid."

In his first book, *Balancing Acts*, Galbraith offered several ideas for policies to help the U.S. achieve a competitive advantage in the global economy. He attacked the reigning conservative anti-inflation policies as well as the liberal "industrial policy" ideas that aimed at preserving existing factory jobs. Regarding the latter, according to Hobart Rowen in the *Washington Post* (April 23, 1989), he "shrewdly observes that 'industrial policy arose to meet an explicitly political need, to fill a vacuum in the political agenda, specifically, of congressional Democrats.'" Galbraith made the suggestion, unpopular with liberals, that the older consumer-jobs sectors should be allowed to shrink. The U.S., moreover, ought to focus on producing high-end capital goods, placing it in competition with such industrially advanced countries as Japan and Germany, rather than consumer goods, which are better left to newly industrialized nations. By investing in research and development in high-tech industries, he reasoned, the U.S. could tap into its burgeoning "knowledge" sector, enabling it to build the equipment that other nations would need to run their factories.

One of Galbraith's core arguments in *Balancing Acts* was that policy makers needed to overcome the fear of inflation. In his view, the Federal Reserve Board, which manages the monetary supply by raising and lowering interest rates, had erred in fighting inflation with high interest rates and a stable dollar; that combination had hurt America's competitiveness abroad during the early 1980s. He argued that the nation would be better served through low interest rates and dollar devaluation—which would mean, however, an increased tolerance for modest inflation. "Indeed, in Mr. Galbaith's hands, inflation in proper doses is an economic benefit, not a drawback," Louis Uchitelle observed in a review for the *New York Times* (April 2, 1989). "If most Americans think otherwise, that's because they deal with inflation as an emotional issue, a 'public evil,' a phenomenon that somehow threatens constitutional order and 'inspires public citizens to oppose it with an energy and perseverance devoted to few other tasks.'" In addition to claiming that we should place less power in the hands of the Federal Reserve, Galbraith maintained that the president could manage inflation expectations by synchronizing all major wage negotiations in the private sector and issuing an annual inflation estimate that would be used to make cost-of-living adjustments for the year ahead.

"The hardest thing to explain to Americans these days is the behavior of their economy," Uchitelle wrote. "The major concepts of mainstream economics are turning out to be inadequate, and only slowly are new explanations emerging. One of the better efforts comes from James K. Galbraith in *Balancing Acts*. Mr. Galbraith's contrarian, sometimes fanciful theories may not be an improvement over the prevailing concepts, which say such things as: inflation is almost always destructive; efforts to direct the economy never work; and investment requires prior savings to pay for it. But in a period of so much economic malaise, contrarian ideas can be very helpful in sorting out solutions—particularly when the ideas are as insightful as Mr. Galbraith's." Bill Barnhart wrote for the *Chicago Tribune* (April 9, 1989), "To some, Jamie Galbraith, as he is known, comes off as a John Kenneth Galbraith in sheep's clothing. He's more successful than other recent liberal economic gurus in adopting the lingo and logic of conservative peers. Yet his formula unabashedly requires new and bigger involvement of the federal government in economic planning and decision-making." Although reviewers generally praised the book, most correctly surmised that Galbraith's policy proposals would have little effect on the administration of then-President George H. W. Bush. As Barnhart observed, "It's . . . hard to imagine how any of Galbraith's ideas will attract a significant constituency. Certainly the Bush ('read my lips') administration is unlikely to make the kind of public investment Galbraith seeks. Democrats, on the other hand, again are trying to redefine their party but probably won't stray too far from populist appeals to protectionism and full employment."

In Galbraith's more recent major work, *Created Unequal*, he argued that growing economic inequality—the gap between rich and poor—has reached a crisis point. In the years following World War II, he explained, the country enjoyed a progressive income tax, Social Security, a minimum wage, and strong trade unions, all of which placed it on the path toward becoming a prosperous, functioning middle-class society. In the 1970s, however, the picture started to worsen for many, as real wages (which take inflation into account) began slipping. The income gap grew and the wealthy gained in political power. "What we had under the

Nixon administration was . . . an unwillingness to use the tools that had been used before—willingness to tolerate more instability, much higher rates of unemployment," Galbraith told Anne Morris. "It's just at that point you get the beginnings in the rise of inequality."

Inequality, Galbraith asserted, as quoted by Michael Lind in the *Washington Monthly* (November 1998), "is the cause of our dreadful political condition. It is the cause of the bitter and unending struggle over the Transfer State, of the ugly battles over welfare, affirmative action, health care, social security, and the even uglier preoccupation in some circles with the alleged relationship of race, intelligence, and earning." "Transfer State" is the term Galbraith uses to describe the redistribution of wealth in society. Welfare, he notes, comprises only a small fraction of the total; Social Security and Medicare account for the bulk of transfer payments. In addition to redistribution through taxation, Galbraith's conception includes transfers to the wealthy in the form of interest payments. As inequality grows and society becomes polarized, however, the wealthy classes have aggressively sought tax cuts and reductions in welfare and entitlement programs. Galbraith bemoans the fact that liberals have largely acquiesced to conservative attempts to move the country away from the goal of an equitable pattern of income distribution. "There is a common ground on the unchallengeable authority of markets that now stretches, with differences only of degree, from the radical right to the mainstream liberal," he wrote, as quoted by Sam Pizzigati for *Working USA* (January/February 1999). "The poor are voiceless, the middle class marginalized; in the new theology of economic governance, only dollars vote, and only the rich have them."

Galbraith also makes the case that this growing income gap is not the result of technological change, as many economists have been eager to claim. Those economists rationalize inequality by saying that the market is simply adapting to new technology in the habitual way: those with high-tech skills benefit, while those without are left behind. Inequality, in that view, is ultimately a good thing, in that it encourages workers to gain new skills. Galbraith, however, roundly dismisses that idea. "I think there is a tendency for each generation to exaggerate the novelty of what's happening at that particular moment," he told Morris in 1998. "I'm 46 now. When I was growing up, there was the Jet Age, the Atomic Age—a number of other exciting ages. When my father . . . was growing up, there was the Automobile Age. Every generation has its own. Technological change is not new in America. It's been the characteristic signature of the American economy for 150 years." Rather than technology, he maintains, inequality is the result of political decisions—in particular, the failure of the federal government to pursue full employment and the use of high interest rates to fight inflation. Liberal economists, meanwhile, have mistakenly focused on education as the solution. "The notion that education can cure the inequality problem remains a staple of economics teaching," Galbraith wrote in the *American Prospect* article. "It also remains the central policy approach to inequality of 'third way' politicians in the United States and Europe, including President [Bill] Clinton. Once again, conventional policy thought lingers on, even after the research fad has faded out."

Galbraith, in *Created Unequal* and his other writings, reserves his most strident criticism for the monetary policies of the Federal Reserve Board, which continues to make fighting inflation its priority. As he told Aaron Zitner for the *Boston Globe* (June 25, 1999), "The notion that we live in a world in which inflation is an ever-present threat—that you always have to be standing in a door with a crowbar to clobber it on the head—is contrary to fact." He attacks the conventional theory that there exists a natural rate of unemployment, known as NAIRU (nonaccelerating inflation rate of unemployment). According to the theory, when unemployment falls below a certain figure, about 5 or 6 percent, then businesses, competing to find workers, will have to raise wages. Increased wages will lead to increased prices, and therefore inflation. The economy of the 1990s, however, appeared to prove that theory wrong. "The number, it turns out, has no basis in serious study; it was first made up by Robert J. Gordon as an illustration for his textbook [*Macroeconomics*, 1978]," Galbraith wrote in the *American Prospect* article. "Since that time, unemployment has been continuously below 6 percent, without rising inflation." Inflation fears, however, have continued to guide the Federal Reserve Board's decisions. In 2004 Galbraith criticized the board's chairman, Alan Greenspan (who retired in February 2006), for initiating a new series of interest-rate hikes. "The Fed is driving blind," he wrote for the *Washington Monthly* (September 2004), adding that "higher interest rates will mean more pressure on debt-ridden households, slower consumer spending growth, and stagnant or falling stock prices—as anyone can see."

Galbraith has been a consistent advocate of raising the minimum wage. A major misunderstanding among economists, he has written, is that a high minimum wage makes it more difficult for American companies to compete in the global market and as a result leads to higher unemployment. He told Morris, "Most of the goods we trade in world markets are produced by people who earn a good deal more than minimum wage. What the minimum wage affects is the wages of the large number of Americans who work largely in the service sector. People who work in day-care centers. . . . Really, should a company be paying its chief executive officer a hundred or two hundred times what it pays its least well-paid worker? Inside individual companies you get a small-scale replication of what's going on in society as a whole."

As the director of the University of Texas Inequality Project (UTIP), Galbraith has worked recently to make the lessening of inequality an economic priority. A small research group, UTIP seeks to measure and explain wage inequality, not just in the U.S. but globally. As Galbraith told Bill Day, "In the three areas that have the highest levels of inequality in the world, you see the seat of the drug problem in Latin America, the seat of a public health collapse in Central Africa and the seat of failed states, terrorism and war in the Middle East. I can't help but think that these problems are related."

Galbraith has been a critic of the administration of President George W. Bush; on several occasions he has called for a repeal of the tax cuts that critics say disproportionately favor the wealthy. Much like his father, he advocates government spending on such public goods as libraries, parks, and mass transit. Unlike most economists and policy makers, he is not concerned about balancing the budget. "Full employment, sustainable development, and national security are proper goals for policy," he wrote in the *American Prospect* (May 2000). "Deficit reduction, as such, is not. Public debt to enrich the wealthy is one thing. Debt to rebuild the country is something else again. If we have to go that route, we should do it and not look back."

Galbraith is the chairman of the economists' committee of the Campaign for a Fair Minimum Wage and chairman of the board of Economists for Peace and Security (EPS), formerly known as Economists Allied for Arms Reduction. EPS is a group that seeks to raise awareness of the fiscal costs of war while suggesting peaceful alternatives to armed conflict. Galbraith is also a senior scholar at the Levy Economics Institute of Bard College.

Galbraith has been married to Ying Tang, his second wife, since 1993. Ying Tang is a social-science research associate at the Ray Marshall Center for the Study of Human Resources at the Lyndon B. Johnson School of Public Affairs. The couple have a daughter, Eve. Galbraith also has a son, Douglas, and a daughter, Margaret, from his previous marriage, to Lucy Ferguson, an architect.

—R.E.

Suggested Reading: *American Prospect* (on-line) Feb. 14, 2000; *Austin American-Statesman* E p1 Sep. 7, 1998; *Journal of Post Keynesian Economics* p347+ Spring 2002; *San Antonio Express-News* K p1 Nov. 25, 2001; *Texas Monthly* p56+ Dec. 1998; *Washington Monthly* p39+ Nov. 1998; *Working USA* p89+ Jan./Feb. 1999

Selected Books: *Balancing Acts: Technology, Finance, and the American Future*, 1989; *Created Unequal: The Crisis in American Pay*, 1998; as co-author—*The Economic Problem* (with Robert L. Heilbroner), 1990; *Macroeconomics* (with William Darity Jr.), 1994; as co-editor—*Inequality and Industrial Change: A Global View* (with Maureen Berner), 2001

Jed Jacobsohn/Getty Images

Glavine, Tom

(GLAH-vin)

Mar. 25, 1966– Baseball player

Address: New York Mets, Shea Stadium, 123-01 Roosevelt Ave., Flushing, NY 11368-1699

Tom Glavine, a 20-year veteran of Major League Baseball (MLB) and currently a member of the New York Mets, has proven to be one of the sport's most durable pitchers. In the last two seasons, following a slump, the southpaw has strengthened his performance by throwing "inside" with both his change-up and his fastball, and he has enhanced his control with a quickening of his pitching motion; the result, in particular since the 2005 All-Star Break, has been a return to form that has brought him closer to an illustrious benchmark for starting pitchers—300 career victories. (Only 22 men have won 300 or more big-league games, a fraternity that includes baseball's most renowned hurlers.) Glavine spent the first 16 years of his career with the Atlanta Braves, the Mets' chief rival in the National League Eastern Division. While with the Braves he won the National League Cy Young Award in 1991 and 1998 and was elected to the All-Star Game eight times. He was selected as an All-Star representing the Mets in 2004 and 2006. Among the active leaders in career wins, innings pitched, games started, complete games, shutouts, batters faced, and strikeouts, Glavine ranks as one of the best pitchers of his generation.

In a conversation with Scott Freeman for *Atlanta Magazine* (April 2001), Leo Mazzone, the Braves' pitching coach from 1990 until 2003, offered the following assessment of Glavine: "Steady, consistent, stubborn, on the edge, never giving in. He has tremendous arm action and change of speed, and that makes him deceptive. Hitters know he's going to throw down and away, and they still can't do anything about it." Echoing a commonly held sentiment, Mazzone also praised Glavine's ability to alter his game plan while on the mound, according to the effectiveness of certain pitches in particular situations. "He does it in different fashions," Mazzone told Steve Marantz for the *Sporting News* (May 1, 1995). "I've seen him throw 79 pitches in a 9-inning game. I've seen him do it with change of speed. Whatever is working for him on a particular night, he'll use. He's the type of pitcher who wins when he doesn't have his best stuff. I've seen him throw a shutout striking out one, and I've seen him throw a shutout striking out 10." Glavine is a crafty rather than overpowering pitcher, baiting his opponents into ineffectual swings instead of facing them down with blazing fastballs. Leigh Montville, writing for *Sports Illustrated* (July 13, 1992), noted, "He goes about his business with precision, not angst. He deceives. He fools. One pitch sets up another pitch, and another, and another. His dominant pitch, for goodness' sake, is the changeup."

One of four children, Thomas Michael Glavine was born on March 25, 1966 in Concord, Massachusetts, and raised in a blue-collar, middle-class household in Billerica, in the greater Boston area. He has one sister, Debbie, and two brothers, Fred and Mike. (On September 14, 2003, at the age of 30, Mike Glavine made his major-league debut with the New York Mets, after an extensive minor-league career.) Tom's father, Fred, was a construction worker in Billerica, where he later started his own company, Fred Glavine Construction. Tom's mother, Mildred, was a school secretary. Fred Glavine encouraged Tom's interest in sports but did not pressure him to excel, merely wanting his son to enjoy himself. Tom Glavine played baseball, street hockey, and football with the other children in his neighborhood. He told an interviewer for *Sports Illustrated for Kids* (December 1992) that he "dreamed" of becoming a professional athlete, "but I knew that millions of kids had the same dream."

Glavine played baseball and hockey at Billerica Memorial High School, concentrating on one sport per season and becoming a standout in both. He was so proficient at hockey, in which he played center, that National Hockey League (NHL) scouts sometimes attended his games. One scout, who ranked Glavine 56th out of some 240 prospective NHL players, noted in a written report the teenager's "good skating ability," "long stride with good balance," and "good acceleration," and found Glavine to be "an excellent scorer, smart around net . . . tough and durable," a player who "[would] not be intimidated," and an "excellent competitor," as quoted by Montville. At the end of his senior year, Glavine was named the Boston area's high-school hockey player of the year, an award that was presented to him at the Boston Garden, the former home of the Boston Celtics basketball team and the Boston Bruins hockey team. He also earned the *Boston Globe*'s All-Scholastic and All Player of the Year honors for his efforts on the ice. (Playing hockey in high school, Glavine competed against such future NHL stars as Kevin Stevens, Tom Barrasso, and Brian Leetch, each of whom lived in the greater Boston area.)

On the baseball diamond, meanwhile, Glavine played multiple positions, including pitcher and center fielder. The most memorable achievement of his high-school baseball career came in his senior year, in the 1984 Massachusetts state championship game, against Brockton High School. He started the game on the pitcher's mound, throwing for nine innings in which he surrendered only one run, and had been moved to center field, with the score tied 1–1, when the game went into extra innings. In the 11th inning, from the outfield, he threw out an opponent attempting to score. In the 13th inning, with his team at bat, he led off with a single, and later that inning he scored the championship-clinching run.

On June 9, 1984 the Los Angeles Kings hockey team drafted Glavine with the 69th overall pick in the fourth round. (He was selected ahead of such players as Brett Hull and Luc Robitaille, who both went on to stardom in the NHL.) He was also offered a scholarship to play hockey at the University of Massachusetts at Lowell. In the summer of 1984, when the Atlanta Braves baseball team selected Glavine in the second round of the amateur draft, he was faced with having to pick a career path. He chose baseball, signing with the Braves. Glavine said to John McMurray for *Baseball Digest* (October 1, 2005), "You just go through the plusses and minuses of both sports. I think that two things that weighed heavily with me in both sports were the health factor and the ability to play baseball probably longer than hockey."

Just a few weeks after the Braves signed him, Glavine headed to Bradenton, Florida, to play in the minor leagues. In the 32 innings he pitched, he struck out 34 batters, triggering his promotion, in 1985, to the Braves' South Atlantic League team in Sumter, South Carolina. He spent the 1986 season in Greenville, South Carolina, with the Braves' double-A affiliate, and began the 1987 campaign playing triple-A ball in Richmond, Virginia, in the International League. On August 14, 1987 he was promoted to the big leagues and joined the Braves.

From the 1984 season through the 1990 season, the Braves finished no higher than third place in the National League Western Division. They became the laughingstock of the National League, and their home attendance figures slumped mightily. Glavine attained his first victory in Atlanta on August 22, 1989, in a game against the Pittsburgh Pirates. In the 50.1 innings he pitched that year, he won two games, lost four, and compiled a 5.54 ERA. In 1988, his first full season in the big leagues, Glavine won seven games, lost 17, and had a 4.56 ERA.

One day in spring training in 1989, while standing in the outfield during batting practice, Glavine picked up a ball that had rolled toward him and, without intending to, hurled it back toward the infield with his middle and index fingers placed along the baseball's seams and the tip of his index finger and resting atop his thumbnail. Experimenting with the new grip in subsequent games, Glavine found that he could use it to reduce the velocity of his pitches while maintaining his normal arm speed—thereby coaxing hitters to swing prematurely. "Throwing that way just seemed natural to me," Glavine said to Leigh Montville, adding, "If I hadn't found that pitch, picked up the ball that way . . . I don't know. Maybe I would have found some other pitch. I don't know. I'm just glad I found it." The changeup pitch he developed (often called a circle-changeup) became Glavine's most reliable "out pitch," or pitch meant to secure a strikeout; he continues to throw it as many as 50 times in a game. He employed his new changeup with great frequency and success during the 1989 season. Of the 22 games in which he was the pitcher of record, he won 14, and recorded a 3.68 ERA. In 1990, taking a step backward, he won 10 and lost 12, compiling a 4.28 ERA.

For both Glavine and the Braves, 1991 was the start of over a decade of highly successful seasons. Midway through the preceding season, on June 22, 1990, Bobby Cox had replaced Russ Nixon as the team's manager. Cox named Leo Mazzone as the Braves' pitching coach. Together, Cox, Mazzone, and John Schuerholz, hired as the team's general manager after the 1990 season, formed baseball's soundest and most successful brain trust. From 1991 through 2005 (except for the strike-shortened 1994 season), the Braves won an unprecedented 14 straight division titles. The strongest element of the team was its rotation of mostly young starting pitchers, including Glavine, who benefited from Mazzone's counsel. From 1992 through 2002, for example, the Braves had the lowest or second-lowest ERA in the major leagues. The team also took home six of the eight National League Cy Young Awards (presented to pitchers) given from 1991 to 1998.

The Braves won 94 games in 1991 to take the National League Western Division title, advancing to the play-offs for the first time since 1982. They defeated the Pirates, four games to three, in the National League Championship Series (NLCS). In that series Glavine was saddled with two losses, despite pitching to a 3.21 earned-run average and surrendering less than one hit per inning pitched. In the World Series the Braves lost in seven games to the Minnesota Twins. In two starts in the World Series, Glavine pitched to a slightly higher ERA (4.05) but picked up a victory in the Braves' 14–5 victory in Game Five.

Never the ace of the Braves' pitching staff, Glavine was nonetheless regarded as a model of consistency and durability. From 1991 to 1993, for example, he posted three consecutive 20-win sea-sons, leading the National League in victories in each of those years. In 1991, in recognition of his 20–11 record, 2.55 ERA, and nine complete games, the Baseball Writers Association of America named Glavine the Cy Young Award winner in the National League. The following year he became the first National League pitcher to start consecutive All-Star Games since Robin Roberts of the Philadelphia Phillies—who had accomplished the feat in 1954 and 1955. The Braves advanced to the World Series for a second straight season, winning a rematch against the Pirates in the 1992 NLCS, four games to three. Glavine rebounded from a Game Six start that lasted just one inning—one in which he surrendered eight runs—to toss a complete game in Game One of the 1992 World Series, a four-hitter against the Toronto Blue Jays, which the Braves won, 3–1. His performance in Game Four was equally strong: in notching his second complete game of the series, he allowed six hits, four walks, and two runs. The Braves, however, lost that game, 2–1, and went on to lose the series, four games to two. In the 1993 NLCS the Braves were thwarted by the Phillies from qualifying for their third consecutive World Series.

Between the 1993 and 1994 seasons, when the National League was expanded to include a third division, the National League Central, the Atlanta Braves were moved from the National League West to the National League East. Baseball's realignment also included a restructuring of the play-offs, which would double the number of teams invited to the play-offs from two to four—the three division winners and a wildcard team. In 1994 Atlanta's hope of reaching the National League championship for the fourth consecutive time was dashed by the players' strike, which arose over plans to impose a salary cap on the MLB athletes. Glavine posted 13 wins, the fifth-highest total in the league, and an earned-run average of 3.97, his highest since the 1990 season, during the abbreviated 1994 season. Ironically, Glavine attributed those relatively modest figures to the strengthening of his left arm, which added roughly five miles per hour to his fastball and caused him to lose some control of his pitches. Glavine, who had become the players' union representative for the Braves in 1991, emerged as a target of many fans' ire because of his visible role in the strike and negotiations. The players' strike ended on April 1, 1995, and games resumed on April 25.

Atlanta finished that season with a record of 90 wins and 54 losses. In the first round of the National League play-offs, beginning on October 3, 1995, the Braves faced the Colorado Rockies, the league's wild-card finisher. Taking the ball in Game Two, Glavine hurled five scoreless innings before surrendering a three-run homer to the Rockies' outfielder Larry Walker, with one out in the sixth inning—a blow that tied that game at three. (The Braves went on to win the game, 7–4.) After winning the series against the Rockies three games to one, the Braves swept the Cincinnati Reds in four games for the National League championship. In Game One of the pennant series, on October 10, 1995, Glavine pitched seven strong innings, striking out five opposing batters; the Braves won in 11 innings, 2–1. In the World Series, against the Cleveland Indians, Glavine won the first two games. (In Game Two he surrendered a second-inning two-run home run to the Indians' first baseman Eddie Murray before recording a 4–3 victory.) With Glavine resting, Cleveland took Game Three, Atlanta Game Four, and Cleveland Game Five. In Game Six, on October 28, 1995, Glavine took the mound at Atlanta's Fulton County Stadium to give what still stands as his most dazzling performance in a pressurized situation. He allowed only one hit over eight innings, striking out eight batters, and pitched the Braves to a 1–0 victory—and their first World Series championship since 1957. Glavine was named the series' most valuable player.

The Braves advanced to the World Series again in 1996 and 1999, both times losing to the New York Yankees. In his 16 years in Atlanta, Glavine started 32 postseason games, racking up 12 wins and 15 losses and a 3.58 earned-run average. In World Series play during those years, in eight games started, he won four, lost three, and recorded three complete games. In 1998 Glavine took home his second Cy Young Award. That season he posted a career-best 2.47 ERA, 20 wins, and six losses.

On December 5, 2002, after contract negotiations with the Braves failed to work out to his satisfaction, Glavine signed a four-year, $42.5 million deal with the New York Mets. Sportswriters believed that in signing Glavine the Mets had obtained a veteran leader who would bolster their pitching rotation. The Mets had reached the World Series in 2000 (in which they were defeated in five games by the New York Yankees), then finished in third place in their division in 2001 and compiled a disappointing 75–86 record under Bobby Valentine the following season. Art Howe replaced Valentine after that year. Acknowledging the team's recent decline, Jack Curry wrote for the *New York Times* (January 24, 2003), "[Glavine] walks, talks and acts like a leader, something the Mets desperately need."

Glavine's career with the Mets began inauspiciously. On the cold and windy afternoon of March 31, 2003, in New York's Shea Stadium, he surrendered eight hits, four walks, and five runs in a game against the Chicago Cubs, in less than four innings pitched. (Speaking to reporters after the game, Glavine said that he had had trouble gripping the ball in the way needed to throw his changeup in the 39-degree weather.) The season as a whole was substandard for Glavine: he posted a 9–14 record (his first losing record since 1990) and a 4.52 earned-run average, which was uncharacteristically high. Also, in pitching only 183.1 innings, he ended a streak of seven seasons with at least 200 innings pitched. The Mets sank even lower in the standings, finishing with a 66–95 record (the second-worst in the NL in 2003), 34.5 games behind the division-champion Braves.

In the first half of the 2004 season, Glavine seemed poised to bounce back, pitching to a 2.66 earned-run average and a 7–7 record. He was selected to play in the 2004 All-Star Game, held in Houston, Texas, in July. In early August his record stood at 8–10, with a 2.92 ERA. Then, on August 10, an SUV (sport utility vehicle) slammed into the taxi transporting Glavine from LaGuardia Airport to Shea Stadium. Glavine lost two front teeth. (He underwent extensive surgery, mostly after the season.) He returned to the field later that month but pitched poorly for a time, saddling himself with a 5.71 ERA. In his first two seasons with the Mets, he collected only 20 wins against 28 losses—while watching his former team, the Braves, win the Eastern Division championship both years. (They did so again in 2005.) Meanwhile, the Mets' 71–91 record in 2004 represented the team's third consecutive losing season.

At the time of the 2005 All-Star Break, Glavine's record stood at 6–7 with a 4.94 earned-run average—numbers that fell short of the pitcher's past performance and did not meet the Mets' standards. Glavine's pitching increasingly drew boos from the Mets fans gathered at Shea Stadium. Because of his reluctance to pitch inside, which he had never done with consistent success, the hitters facing him were free to ignore that area of the strike zone and look instead for pitches over the outer area of the plate. To address the problem, Glavine worked with Rick Peterson, the Mets' pitching coach, and expanded his repertoire to include more pitches designed to cross the inner area of home plate. Also, he sought to unsettle hitters by occasionally throwing a curveball, a pitch he had consciously avoided since his days in Atlanta. Beginning after the All-Star Break, he won seven of the 13 games for which he was the pitcher of record and pitched to a 2.22 ERA. His final statistics for the season—a 13–13 record with a 3.53 ERA and two complete games, one shutout, and 211 innings pitched—belied his value to the Mets in the latter part of the year. Glavine has admitted that in his first two and a half seasons in New York, stubbornness played a part in his unwillingness to change his style. "My natural reaction was, 'I was successful for 17 years this way. . . . Surely, when I fix my mechanics I'll be all right,'" he said to Paul White for *USA Today* (June 29, 2006). Guided by first-year manager Willie Randolph, who stressed to his players the importance of mastering baseball's fundamentals and encouraged aggressive base-running, the Mets finished 2005 with an 83–79 record, registering their first winning season since 2001.

In 2006 the Mets won the National League East Division Championship for the first time since 1988, finishing the regular season with a record of 97 wins and 65 losses. Glavine had begun the season by picking up where he left off the previous year, keeping hitters off-balance by throwing his fastball inside with greater frequency and by using a faster pitching motion. In July he was selected to play in his 10th All-Star Game. Glavine's sterling first half of the 2006 season refueled interest in his pursuit of 300 career victories. He finished the regular season with a record of 15 wins and seven losses and an ERA of 3.82. In the second game of the divisional series against the Los Angeles Dodgers, Glavine pitched six scoreless innings, leading the Mets to a 4–1 victory; the Mets shut the Dodgers out, three games to zero, to win the series. Facing the St. Louis Cardinals in Game One of the National League Championships, Glavine pitched seven scoreless innings en route to a Mets victory. In Game Five of the series, he gave up a fourth-inning home run to the Cardinals' Albert Pujols, leading to a 4–2 defeat for the Mets, who ultimately lost the series, four games to three. By the close of the 2006 season, Glavine had 290 career wins, and he stood an excellent chance of reaching the 300 mark in 2007. If he accomplishes that feat, he may be one of the last starting pitchers to do so for the foreseeable future—in part because of the introduction in the 1970s of five-man pitching rotations, which decrease the number of starts per pitcher. (Another factor is the rise of specialized bullpens, which lead to the departure of starters earlier in games.)

"I know I am very stubborn in terms of my pitching, and that's part of what's made me successful," Glavine told John McMurray. "But I think away from the field, I would characterize myself as pretty quiet and very unassuming." Glavine is six feet one inch tall and weighs roughly 190 pounds. He and his wife, Christine, have two sons, Peyton Thomas and Mason Riley; Glavine also has a daughter, Amber Nicole, from his first marriage, which ended in divorce, and a stepson, Jonathan, from his current marriage. The pitcher and his family divide their time between homes in Greenwich, Connecticut, and Alpharetta, Georgia. Glavine is an avid golfer; his Georgia home sits on a golf course. He also enjoys listening to music by James Taylor. Among the most articulate players in baseball, Glavine said recently that he may pursue a career in broadcasting when his pitching days end.

—D.F.

Suggested Reading: *Baseball Digest* (on-line) Oct. 2005; Baseball Reference Web site; New York Mets Web site; *New York Times* D p1 Jan. 24, 2003; *Sporting News* (on-line) May 1, 1995; *Sports Illustrated* p42+ July 13, 1992

Grossman, Edith

Mar. 22, 1936– Translator

Address: c/o Knopf Publicity, 1745 Broadway, New York, NY 10019

"Fidelity is surely our highest aim, but a translation is not made with tracing paper. It is an act of critical interpretation," the translator Edith Grossman said during a tribute to the Nobel laureate in literature Gabriel García Márquez (November 5, 2003) hosted by the literary and human rights organization PEN, as quoted on the Modern World Web site. "Let me insist on the obvious: Languages trail immense, individual histories behind them and no two languages, with all their accretion of tradition and culture, ever dovetail perfectly. . . . Fidelity is our noble purpose, but it does not have much, if anything, to do with what is called literal meaning. A translation can be faithful to tone and intention, to meaning. It can rarely be faithful to words or syntax, for these are peculiar to specific languages and are not transferable." In a profession that has been largely unrecognized, Grossman has emerged as a celebrity of sorts. Her ability to interpret and convey in English the meanings and flavors of works originally written in Spanish has been highly praised by admirers of such literary figures as Mario Vargas Llosa, Ariel Dorfman, Julián Ríos, Julio Ortega, Alvaro Mutis, and, most prominently among contemporary Spanish-language authors, Gabriel García Márquez, five of whose books she

Courtesy of HarperCollins

has translated. Grossman, who taught at colleges from 1970 to 1990, has translated more than 30 books. They include works by lesser-known writers—among them the Cuban-born Eliseo Alberto, Marcelo Birmajer of Argentina, and Mayra Montero of Puerto Rico—that she has helped to promote. Grossman's translation of the 17th-century masterpiece *Don Quixote*, by Miguel de Cervantes, published in 2003, was hailed as a "major literary achievement," as the preeminent Mexican writer Carlos Fuentes put it in the *New York Times Book Review* (November 2, 2003, on-line). In a review for *Publishers Weekly* (November 10, 2003), Jeff Zaleski described Grossman's translation as "an honest, robust and freshly revelatory *Quixote* for our times."

"I think I have an ear for language because I was able to speak all the ones I studied: Spanish, Italian, and French," Grossman told Caleb Bach for *Americas* (November 1, 2004). Grossman was born Edith Marian Dorph on March 22, 1936 in Philadelphia, Pennsylvania, one of several daughters of Jewish immigrants from Eastern Europe. Her father, Alexander Dorph, was a shoe salesman and small-business owner; her mother, Sally Stern Dorph, was a homemaker. Grossman was not a stellar student and, by her own account, did not like school, but while attending the Philadelphia High School for Girls, she became keenly interested in Spanish. "My high school Spanish teacher reached me. I said whatever this woman is doing I want to do," she told Caleb Bach. She won a scholarship to the University of Pennsylvania, where she steeped herself in the works of great Spanish authors. As an undergraduate she translated poems by Juan Ramón Jiménez, a Spanish poet who won the Nobel Prize in literature in 1956; the translations, her first, were published in the university's literary magazine. After earning an A.B. degree in Spanish, with distinction, in 1957, she remained at the school to pursue a master's degree. Concurrently, she taught Spanish literature as a "hardnosed and strict" teacher's assistant, as she described herself to Max Gross for the *Forward* (January 23, 2004, on-line). "I was failing half the class [when] the professor said to me, 'You know 'D' is a very bad grade; you don't have to fail everybody.'" In 1959, after she received a master's degree, Grossman moved to the West Coast, where she began studying toward a doctorate at the University of California at Berkeley. (She did not complete the requirements for a Ph.D. at that school.) In 1961 she won a Woodrow Wilson fellowship, and a year or two later, she studied Spanish literature in Spain on a Fulbright grant. She abandoned her plan to write her dissertation on a literary figure from the Spanish Baroque period or on medieval Spanish poetry after she read works by the Chilean poet Pablo Neruda and the Peruvian poet Cesar Vallejo. "I said no, I'm going to Latin America, the twentieth century, something is going on there," she told Bach. Her dissertation examined the work of Nicanor Parra, a Chilean poet who was also a professor of physics and mathematics. She earned her Ph.D. in Latin American literature at New York University (NYU), in New York City, in 1972. Over the next two decades, Grossman wrote literary criticism and taught Spanish literature at Hunter College, a division of the City University of New York; Dominican College, in Orangeburg, New York; and NYU.

In the early 1970s Ronald Christ, the editor of the literary journal *Review*, asked Grossman to translate a story by Argentine writer Macedonio Fernández. Although she had little experience in translating prose from Spanish to English and had doubts about her ability to do a satisfactory job, she nevertheless agreed. She discovered that the work suited her, in part because she enjoyed working at home. She also found that because many Spanish writers use vivid imagery and rhythmically flowing language, translating prose was not very different from translating poetry. Translation was not practical as a full-time job, though, because she was paid only 50 cents a line. Thus, she continued to teach while also translating poems, short stories, and excerpts of longer pieces for the *Review*.

In 1977, for the first time, Grossman translated a full-length novel: *Drums for Rancas*, by the Peruvian writer Manuel Scorza. By the late 1980s Grossman's reputation as a gifted and careful translator had grown significantly. One day during that period, she received an invitation to submit a 20-page sample for consideration for the job of translating *Love in the Time of Cholera*, by the Colombian writer Gabriel García Márquez. (The previous translator of García Marquez's work into English, Gregory Rabassa, was unable to work on *Love in the Time of Cholera*.) Grossman won the assignment. She modeled her translation after the style of the American novelist William Faulkner, who favored long, complex sentences (and who is García Márquez's favorite English-language writer). She told Lewis Beale for the *Los Angeles Times* (November 30, 2003), "I didn't use any contractions in the narration, and I used Latinate words, polysyllabic words, instead of German monosyllables. Any time I could, I chose a longer word rather than a shorter word, as if Hemingway had never lived"—a reference to the short, simple sentences that characterize the writing of Ernest Hemingway. The English translation of *Love in the Time of Cholera* was published, to much critical acclaim, in 1988. Although reviewers rarely mention translators, the novelist Thomas Pynchon praised Grossman in his assessment of the book for the *New York Times* (April 10, 1988), writing that she had been attentive to the "many nuances of the author's voice to which she is sensitively, imaginatively attuned." He also wrote that Grossman "catches admirably and without apparent labor the swing and translucency of [García Márquez's] writing, its slang and its classicism, the lyrical stretches and those end-of-sentence zingers he likes to hit us with. It is a faithful and beautiful piece of work." In 1990, thanks to the success of the English translation of *Love in the Time of Cholera*, Grossman left academia to devote herself full-time to the craft of translating the works of celebrated Spanish and Latin American writers.

Grossman later translated García Márquez's novels *The General in His Labyrinth* (1990), *Strange Pilgrims* (1994), *Of Love and Other Demons* (1995), *News of a Kidnapping* (1998), and

Memories of My Melancholy Whores (2005), as well as the first volume of his memoirs, *Living to Tell a Tale* (2004). "You are my voice in English," García Marquez once told her, according to Jay Tolson in *U.S. News & World Report* (January 26, 2004). Grossman told Bach, "I feel as if I know him better than anyone else in the world because I have spent so much time with his language and his books. But in truth we are not really close." Grossman and García Márquez meet for lunch or coffee during the writer's occasional trips to New York, but Grossman has never visited him in his native land.

In about 2002 David Halpern, an editor at HarperCollins, asked Grossman to translate one of the earliest and most famous novels in the Spanish language—*Don Quixote*, by Miguel de Cervantes. "I remember telling her that she couldn't really feel like she'd completed her life as a translator in Spanish until she'd done *Don Quixote*, and it seemed to me she was the only person to do it," Halpern told Tanya Barrientos for the *Philadelphia Inquirer* (December 9, 2003). Halpern's proposal "astounded" Grossman, as she recalled to Bach. "I said, you know I only do contemporary authors. But of course I said okay because what translator would not want to try? Besides, great books need to be translated periodically." "*Don Quixote* is a great monument of world literature, a pillar of the Western literary tradition, and it's at the center of the Spanish-language literary tradition, so the responsibility and challenge of translating it into another language was just enormous," she confessed to Adriana Lopez for *Publishers Weekly* (November 10, 2003). "Up until the present, I had translated only living authors, which meant that, when I was stymied, there was someone I could call. Certainly I couldn't channel Cervantes. So it was a leap into an abyss." Working from a 940-page edition of *Don Quixote*, Grossman devoted seven days a week for nearly two years to her translation. In a note that appears in the book, Grossman explained, "Shortly before I began work, while I was wrestling with the question of what kind of voice would be most appropriate for the translation of a book written some four hundred years ago, I mentioned my fears to Julian Rios, the Spanish novelist. His reply was simple and profound and immensely liberating. He told me not to be afraid; Cervantes, he said, was our most modern writer, and what I had to do was to translate him the way I translated everyone else—that is, the contemporary authors whose works I have brought over into English. Julian's characterization was a revelation; it desacralized the project and allowed me, finally, to confront the text in Spanish and find the voice in English." She realized that "Cervantes' language wasn't quaint when he was writing. He wasn't archaic," as she told Barrientos. "He was pushing the envelope of Spanish. He was writing a very creative, very original book." For those reasons, Grossman endeavored to write the English text with a contemporary flair that would enable English speakers to read

Cervantes's work with the same ease as Spaniards had in the 17th century; at the same time, she tried never to distort either the culture as Cervantes presented it or the connotations associated with his words and phrases. A big hurdle for Grossman was the translation of the opening sentence of *Don Quixote*, which is "the most famous sentence in Spanish," as she told Tom Devaney for *Penn Arts & Sciences Magazine* (Spring 2004, on-line): "*En un lugar de la Mancha, de cuyo nombre no quiero acordarme, no ha mucho tiempo que vivía un hidalgo de los de lanza en astillero, adarga antigua, rocín flaco y galgo corredor.*" "I translated it, 'Somewhere in la Mancha, in a place whose name I do not care to remember, a gentleman lived not long ago, one of those who has a lance and ancient shield on a shelf and keeps a skinny nag and a greyhound for racing.' What I really wanted was to get that drive—the momentum. And after I was pretty satisfied with my opening sentence, I said, OK, I can do this now," she told Devaney.

The renowned and notoriously harsh literary critic Harold Bloom wrote in his introduction to Grossman's translation, "Though there have been many valuable English translations of *Don Quixote*, I would commend Edith Grossman's version for the extraordinarily high quality of her prose. The Knight [Don Quixote himself] and Sancho [his companion] are so eloquently rendered by Grossman that the vitality of their characterization is more clearly conveyed than ever before. . . . Reading her amazing mode of finding equivalents in English for Cervantes's darkening vision is an entrance into a further understanding of why this great book contains within itself all the novels that have followed in its sublime wake." In his review for *Publishers Weekly*, Jeff Zaleski wrote, "Her translation is admirably readable and consistent while managing to retain the vigor, sly humor and colloquial playfulness of the Spanish." Carlos Fuentes, in his assessment for the *New York Times Book Review*, wrote, "This *Don Quixote* can be read with the same ease as the latest Philip Roth [novel] and with much greater facility than any [novel by the 19th-century writer Nathaniel] Hawthorne. Yet there is not a single moment in which, in forthright English, we are not reading a 17th-century novel. This is truly masterly: the contemporaneous and the original co-exist. . . . To make the classic contemporary: this is the achievement."

Grossman is what she calls "a secondary author," one who considers not only texts but also subtexts and shades of meanings so as to produce translations that are as faithful as possible to the originals. She aims to make it possible for English-language readers to enjoy the same experiences that readers of the original Spanish might have. "To recreate significance for a new set of readers, translators must make the effort to enter the mind of the first author through the gateway of the text— to see the world through another person's eyes and translate the linguistic perception of that world into another language," she said during the PEN tribute to García Márquez in 2003. "The better the original writing, the more exciting and challenging the process is."

In Grossman's six-room apartment on the Upper West Side of Manhattan, there are 15 bookcases filled with both classic and contemporary books. Every morning the 69-year-old Grossman goes for a walk; then, back home, she sips a cup of coffee while reading the newspaper and tackling the daily crossword puzzle. After that she remains at her computer for six to 10 hours, working to the accompaniment of radio broadcasts of jazz. She is aided in her translations by six Spanish-language dictionaries and the suggestions and advice of a slew of United Nations translators, Latino friends, and native speakers of various regional Spanish dialects. Usually, she waits until she has completed a translation before showing it to the author of the original book. She rarely travels and has never visited South America. "I never want to leave New York," she told Tanya Barrientos. "I love my neighborhood. I love my apartment. I suppose it's a failing on my part."

The poet and translator Alastair Reid told Jay Tolson that Grossman "remains infinitely curious about the mysterious alchemy of translation." Tom Devaney described her as having a "deep voice and smoky gray hair." Her marriage to Norman Gross-man ended in divorce. She has one son, Matthew Grossman, and a stepson, Kory Grossman, both of whom are musicians. In 2005 she won the University of Pennsylvania's Distinguished Alumni Award.

—I.C.

Suggested Reading: *Americas* p24+ Nov. 1, 2004; *Forward* (on-line) Jan. 23, 2004; *Los Angeles Times* Nov. 30, 2003; *Miami Herald* Entertainment News Apr. 5, 2001; Modern Word Web Site Nov. 5, 2003; *New York Times Book Review* (on-line) p15 Nov. 2, 2003; *Penn Arts & Sciences Magazine* (on-line) Spring 2004; *Philadelphia Inquirer* D p1+ Dec. 9, 2003

Selected Books: as translator–*Drums for Rancas*, 1977; *Last Waltz in Santiago: And Other Poems of Exile and Disappearance*, 1988; *Love in the Time of Cholera*, 1988; *The General in His Labyrinth*, 1990; *Strange Pilgrims: Twelve Stories*, 1994; *Of Love and Other Demons*, 1995; *Death in the Andes*, 1996; *In the Palm of Darkness*, 1997; *The Messenger: A Novel*, 2000; *Caracol Beach: A Novel*, 2001; *The Red of His Shadow: A Novel*, 2001; *The Feast of the Goat*, 2003; *Don Quixote*, 2003; *Living to Tell a Tale*, 2004

Guerrero, Vladimir

Feb. 9, 1976– Baseball player

Address: Los Angeles Angels of Anaheim, 2000 Gene Autry Way, Anaheim, CA 92806

In 1997 the baseball player Vladimir Guerrero was 21 years old and coming off a rookie season in which he had played in only 90 games and endured injuries to his back, left and right quadriceps, left foot and hand, and right hamstring—when Tom Verducci, writing for *Sports Illustrated* (September 1, 1997), declared his potential to be "Griffey-like." Verducci was referring to Ken Griffey Jr., then one of baseball's most feared sluggers (and the son of a former major leaguer of the same name), and the judgment proved to be accurate: each season since then, Guerrero has posted statistics equaling or surpassing a .300 batting average, 30 home runs, and 100 RBIs (runs batted in), becoming one of the most consistent hitters in baseball. Guerrero received the American League (AL) Most Valuable Player Award in 2004, the year he led the Los Angeles Angels of Anaheim to the AL Western Division crown and posted a career high in runs scored, with 124. In his eight seasons prior to joining the Angels, as a member of the beleaguered Montreal Expos, Guerrero was frequently touted as baseball's unsung hero.

A veteran of 10-plus big-league seasons, Guerrero is known for his uncanny plate coverage—that is, his ability to connect solidly with pitches thrown above or below the strike zone and on the inside or outside corners. (Legend has it that on more than one occasion in the minor leagues, Guerrero got extra-base hits on pitches that bounced in front of the plate.) His aggressiveness at the plate, while unrivaled among his peers, belies his modesty away from it and has never led to an unusually high number of strikeouts, a testament to his natural ability as a hitter. "Since I was a little boy, I've been swinging at everything I see that comes near home plate," Guerrero said to Mark Saxon for *Sports Illustrated for Kids* (August 2005). "It doesn't really matter whether they're giving me pitches to hit or not, because I spread the [strike] zone myself." Guerrero, an outfielder, also boasts one of baseball's most accurate and powerful throwing arms. "I believe God reached out with a finger and touched him and said, 'You are a baseball player,'" Rondell White, a former teammate of Guerrero's, said to Tom Verducci for *Sports Illustrated* (May 1, 2000). "He's blessed. God gave him everything to be a baseball player. He's the best in the game—by far." Guerrero "plays baseball with a purity of purpose and talent rarely seen in a game that increasingly rivals the Academy Awards for overproduction," Verducci wrote. Teammates and sportswriters alike also laud the outfielder for what they perceive as his humility. John Lackey, one of

Vladimir Guerrero

Guerrero's teammates on the Angels, said to Esmeralda Santiago for *Sports Illustrated* (August 30, 2004), "He's a superstar who doesn't act like one."

The fourth of the five children (he also has four half-siblings) of Damian Guerrero and Altagracia Alvino, Vladimir Guerrero was born on February 9, 1976 in Nizao Bani, on the southwest coast of the Dominican Republic. His father, a cab driver, worked long hours but earned only a modest salary. (One source indicates that Guerrero's father was a farmer.) His mother earned a small income by running a food stand near the town center, selling such popular Caribbean dishes as fried pork, fried plantains, and rice and beans. The close-knit family lived in a one-story dwelling built by Guerrero's father in the village of Don Gregorio, near Nizao Bani; his parents later added two floors to the home, which they maintained until after Guerrero signed with the Angels. (The family currently lives near the town where Guerrero was raised, in a "sprawling house . . . in a valley surrounded by mountains," as reported by Esmeralda Santiago.) When Vladimir was 12 years old, his mother traveled to Venezuela, working as a maid for a well-to-do family there and for years seldom seeing her own family.

Growing up, Guerrero and his brothers were avid fans of the meringue group Los Kenton, and Guerrero reportedly aspired to be a singer and dancer before considering a career in baseball. Still, he was an excellent baseball player from a very early age. On the dusty ball fields and the streets of Nizao Bani, using a stick as a bat and "lemons wrapped in rags for balls," according to Santiago, Guerrero played the sport with his friends. (The infielder Devi Cruz, currently a ma-

jor-league free agent, was a childhood friend of Guerrero's.) "Whenever the kids got together to play," his mother said to Santiago, "they always chose him for their team because he could hit." Guerrero dropped out of school before his 16th birthday, taking a job selling fish at a local market and, later, rounding up cattle. "The bulls were stubborn," he recalled to Santiago, "and I had to pull them until they did what they were supposed to." Guerrero has credited that work with strengthening his arms.

One of the outfielder's earliest baseball instructors, Victor Franco, recalled to Luciana Chavez for the *Sporting News* (February 15, 2001) that Guerrero was not fond of vigorous physical training in his youth. "He just wanted to play," Franco said. That did not go unnoticed by professional scouts, who, despite Guerrero's developing batting prowess and strong throwing arm, considered him to be overweight; his lack of foot speed, in particular, was a concern. In the 1992–93 off-season Guerrero tried out unsuccessfully for both the Los Angeles Dodgers and the Texas Rangers, at those teams' training facilities in the Dominican Republic. (Guerrero's brothers Wilton and Elieser had made it into the Dodgers' camp by that time.) The early rejection did not discourage Guerrero, who said to Tom Verducci, "I knew I would be signed." He added in a conversation with Luciana Chavez for the *Sporting News* (February 19, 2001), "I'm not mad [at the Rangers or Dodgers]. They didn't like me when they saw me. The Expos said they'd give me a chance, so I said, 'Let's go. I only want to play. That's it.'"

At his tryout with the Expos, Guerrero, then 17 years old, pulled a muscle in his groin while running to first base, after hitting a ground ball weakly in his only turn at bat. Earlier that day, however, Guerrero had displayed his major-league-caliber arm strength in the outfield. Fred Ferreira, then a scout and later the director of international scouting for the Expos, was impressed with Guerrero's throwing ability and physique (particularly his broad shoulders) and by the fact that the young man was noticeably upset after the injury, which indicated that he took the game seriously. The Expos signed Guerrero to a $2,000 free-agent contract on February 24, 1993. He made his professional debut later that year in the Dominican Summer League, playing in 34 games. He hit safely in 35 of his 105 at bats, recording a .333 batting average.

In 1994 Guerrero hit .424 with 12 home runs and 35 RBIs in the Dominican Summer League, triggering his promotion to the Expos' rookie Gulf Coast team in Florida. There, he kept up his extraordinary batting statistics, finishing in a tie for third place in extra-base hits (21); at the conclusion of the season, he was named the Gulf Coast League's Most Valuable Player. In 1995 *Baseball America* named Guerrero as the Expos' best prospect and as the second-best prospect in the South Atlantic League, where Guerrero, by then playing for Albany, Georgia, recorded a .333 batting average, the best among the league's players that season. Guerrero started the 1996 season playing single-A ball in West Palm Beach, Florida, where he launched five home runs, batting .363 with 18 RBIs. His continued success enabled him to move quickly to a double-A team in Harrisburg, Pennsylvania, where, at age 20, he became the youngest player in Eastern League history to win a batting title. Guerrero was named the *Sporting News* minor-league player of the year, Eastern League MVP, and rookie of the year; *Baseball America*, meanwhile, selected him as double-A player of the year.

On September 19, 1996 Guerrero was called up to the majors. He made his debut with the Expos on the road, in a game against the Atlanta Braves, reaching base safely with a single in five at bats. After the Major League Baseball (MLB) season, to keep in shape for the Expos, Guerrero played in the Dominican Winter League, where he batted .258. In 1997, Guerrero's rookie season with the Expos, his mother relocated to the apartment complex in downtown Montreal, Canada, where he lived. In keeping with a tradition she had started in Los Angeles, California, when Guerrero's older brother Wilton broke into the big leagues, she helped Vladimir acclimate himself to the big city, cooking for him and other major-league players who had come from the Dominican Republic, including visiting players from other teams. Altagracia Alvino has thus become a maternal figure to many of the sport's Dominican stars, such as Miguel Tejada of the Baltimore Orioles and Manny Ramirez of the Boston Red Sox. In July 1998 Wilton was traded to the Expos, joining Vladimir; the two were team-

mates until Wilton signed a free-agent contract with the Cincinnati Reds, in 2001. Wilton played for the St. Louis cardinals in 2006.

Heralded in 1997 upon his arrival at the Expos' spring-training facilities in Jupiter, Florida, Guerrero did not disappoint. He compiled a .358 batting average with four doubles, four home runs, and 11 RBIs and was named the best rookie of spring training by the Montreal chapter of the Baseball Writers' Association of America. In the Expos' final spring-training game, he drove a foul ball into his left foot, breaking a bone, thus starting the season on the disabled list (DL). The only rookie named to the Expos' big-league roster, he appeared in 90 games over the course of the season, missing time due to injuries to his left foot, right hamstring, left hand, left and right quadriceps, and back. Those setbacks notwithstanding, Guerrero batted .302, with 35 extra-base hits and 40 RBIs—solid numbers, most sportswriters agreed, that would have increased with more playing time. Tom Verducci, for example, observed in 1997, "If the Expos' Guerrero can get a break from injuries, he could be one of the game's big guns."

During the 1998 season Guerrero became just that. At age 22 he was the youngest player in Expos' history to equal or surpass in a single season 30 home runs, 200 hits, and 100 RBIs. He also set a franchise record for home runs (38), extra-base hits (82), and total bases (367), finishing third in the National League in that category. On September 1, 1998 the Expos signed Guerrero to a five-year contract valued at $28 million, the largest sum the team had ever committed to a single player and a sign of their hope that Guerrero would help them reach the play-offs. Nonetheless, the Expos won only 65 games that year, losing 97, and went on to lose 90-plus games in each of the next three seasons.

Continuing his stellar play in 1999, Guerrero slugged 42 home runs and 131 RBIs, becoming the first Expos player to record at least 30 home runs and 100 RBIs in consecutive seasons. From July 27 to August 16, he hit safely in 31 consecutive games, baseball's longest hitting streak of the 1990s. In July he represented the Expos at the All-Star Game, in Boston, Massachusetts. Two thousand was another successful year for the Expos outfielder, if not his team. He established new club records in seven offensive categories, including batting average (.345), home runs (44), total bases (379), and slugging percentage (.664). In addition, he joined Ted Williams, Joe DiMaggio, and Jimmy Fox as the only players in baseball history to record at least 30 home runs, 100 RBIs, and a batting average of .300 in three consecutive seasons before age 25. (The St. Louis Cardinals first baseman Albert Pujols has since accomplished that feat.) In July, in Atlanta, Georgia, Guerrero made his first All-Star Game start, replacing the injured San Francisco Giants outfielder Barry Bonds. Guerrero played in his third consecutive All-Star Game in 2001 and set career highs that year in doubles, with 45. He became the first Expos player to attain at least 30 stolen bases and 30 home runs in one season, recording 37 and 34, respectively, in those categories. During spring training in 2002, he was named the team captain, and over that season he maintained his standing as one of the league's best all-around talents. His 206 hits in 2002 set an Expos franchise record. In addition, Guerrero played in his fourth All-Star Game and recorded a fifth consecutive season of at least 30 home runs, 100 RBIs, and a .300 batting average. (He joined Hall of Famers Babe Ruth, Lou Gehrig, and Jimmie Fox, along with his contemporary Frank Thomas, currently of the Oakland Athletics, as the only players to have done so.)

By that time the notion of Guerrero as his sport's most underappreciated and enigmatic hero had spread throughout the world of baseball, helped by several factors. Considered a shy person, Guerrero, who has trouble speaking English, turned down requests for interviews. His resulting air of mystery was increased by what sportswriters called the "anonymity" of playing for the struggling Montreal Expos in the late 1990s and early 2000s. Indeed, average attendance for Expos' home games sank below 10,000 in the 2001 season, and the team's games were hardly ever broadcast nationally. Still, Guerrero revealed in a conversation with Paul Gutierrez for the *Los Angeles Times* (September 15, 1999) that he found the level of recognition he commanded in Montreal to be enjoyable. "The experience has been good for me because this is still the major leagues and it's a good job to go to work to every day," he said in Spanish. "I've felt really welcomed in Montreal. The people salute me and welcome me when I'm just walking down the street."

February 2002 brought the news that Major League Baseball's owners had purchased the Expos from the team's principal owner, Jeffrey Loria, for $120 million. MLB intended to eliminate the Expos, along with the Minnesota Twins, from baseball, but a collective bargaining agreement reached at that time between MLB and the players' association prohibited such actions through the 2006 season. Rumors that the franchise would relocate were widespread; in 2003 the Expos played 22 of their home games in San Juan, Puerto Rico (a location MLB was testing as a possible future site for a big-league team). That season was Guerrero's eighth and last with the Expos. He played in 112 games, missing significant time during the months of May, June, and July because of a herniated disk, which caused him back pain but did not require surgery. Making limited plate appearances, he compiled a .330 batting average along with 25 home runs for the year. In September 2004 MLB officially announced that beginning in 2005 the Expos would be relocated to Washington, D.C., and be renamed the Nationals.

Meanwhile, many teams had expressed a desire to sign Guerrero, who became a free agent after the 2003 season. The only uncertainty about the out-

fielder had to do with his back, which was a potential cause of disability. In January 2004 the Anaheim Angels (currently known as the Los Angeles Angels of Anaheim) signed Guerrero to a five-year, $70 million contract. The Angels, winners of the 2002 World Series, had failed to make the play-offs in 2003, but the acquisition of Guerrero, along with the free-agent pitcher Bartolo Colon (formerly of the Cleveland Indians), served as an indication to Angels fans that the team's ownership was serious about returning to the Fall Classic. In 2004 Guerrero had his finest season to date, tying or posting career highs in hits (206) and runs scored (124). He was named to his fifth All-Star Game at midseason. The Angels and their divisional rivals, the Oakland Athletics, engaged in a tight race to the regular-season finish line, separated in the standings by the slimmest of margins through much of late September and early October. Guerrero emerged as the American League's best player in the season's waning days, posting over the final seven games, according to Mark Saxon, a .536 batting average, with six home runs, 11 RBIs, and 10 runs scored. The Angels finished one game clear of the Athletics in the final standings to win their first divisional title since 1986. In November Guerrero was named the AL's Most Valuable Player, receiving 21 of the possible 28 first-place votes cast. "Not many players can do what he did at that point of the season with the pressure and the pitchers he faced," Mike Scioscia, the Angels' manager, said to Mike Scarr for MLB.com (November 16, 2004). "It was fun to watch." In the divisional round of the play-offs, the Angels were dispatched in three games by the eventual World Series champions, the Boston Red Sox. In Game Three of the series in Fenway Park, in Boston, Guerrero clubbed the first postseason home run of his career—a grand slam off reliever Mike Timlin in the seventh inning that tied the score, 6–6.

Although he finished only third in the MVP race in 2005, Guerrero posted excellent statistics that season, finishing third in the AL in batting average with .317. Despite missing several games in late May due to a partially separated left shoulder, Guerrero recorded 32 home runs and 108 RBIs. During the season he joined 12 others in major-league history by swatting his 300th career home run before reaching his 30th birthday. The Angels won 95 games in 2005 and finished seven games ahead of the Oakland Athletics in the AL Western Division, then entered the American League Divisional Series as underdogs against the New York Yankees. Guerrero scored five runs in the five-game series and batted .333, helping Anaheim earn a three-games-to-two victory. Facing the eventual World Series champions, the Chicago White Sox, in the American League Championship Series, the Angels outfielder was held in check by Chicago's formidable pitching staff, which limited him to only one hit in 20 at bats. The White Sox took the best-of-seven series in five games, advancing to the World Series to face the Houston Astros. The Angels failed to return to the play-offs in 2006, finishing in second place in the AL Western division, behind the Athletics. Guerrero, for his part, finished the season with a batting average of .329, scoring 33 home runs and 116 RBIs. He also played in his sixth All-Star Game, scoring his first All-Star home run in the second inning of a 3–2 victory for the American League.

Vladimir Guerrero stands six feet three inches tall and weighs about 225 pounds. He is unmarried but has reportedly fathered four children, each of whom has a different mother. In the off-season he returns to the Dominican Republic to live with his family. He also has a home in the Anaheim area, where he lives during the baseball season; Guerrero pays for the members of his large extended family (his mother is said to be one of 21 siblings) to visit California and stay with him at his home. "My nieces and nephews are my children," he said to Esmeralda Santiago. "I don't distinguish between my kids and those of my sisters or brothers. I love them all as if they were my own and treat them all as if I were their father." Guerrero appeared on the cover of *989 Sports' MLB 200*6 video game. He also appeared in Pepsi commercials in 2005, with Alex

Rodriguez of the New York Yankees. Guerrero has been known to listen to meringue music and play video games in the locker room prior to the start of games. In his native Dominican Republic, a national holiday was established to commemorate his winning the 2004 American League MVP award. To provide job opportunities for those near his hometown in the Dominican Republic, Guerrero has opened a factory, a propane distributorship, a supermarket, a women's clothing store, and livestock and vegetable farms.

Discussing Guerrero with Luciana Chavez, the San Diego Padres' manager, Bruce Bochy, said, "He's kind of a throwback. You know, no batting gloves. It's good old hardball with him. You're talking about an unbelievably talented kid. There's nothing he can't do."

—D.F.

Suggested Reading: Baseball Reference Web site; Los Angeles Angels of Anaheim Web site; *Sporting News* p46+ Feb. 19, 2001; *Sports Illustrated* p42+ May 1, 2000, p74+ Aug. 30, 2004

Guillen, Ozzie

(GEE-yen)

Jan. 20, 1964– Manager of the Chicago White Sox

Address: Chicago White Sox, U.S. Cellular Field, 333 West 35th St., Chicago, IL 60616

"Managers don't win games—players do," Ozzie Guillen, the manager of the Chicago White Sox baseball team, told Josh Elliott for *Sports Illustrated* (June 14, 2004). "So what's a good manager? Someone other people want to play for. A good manager is Bobby Cox [of the Atlanta Braves], is Joe Torre [New York Yankees], is Tony La Russa [St. Louis Cardinals]. They're so good, people forget they played the game. So that's what I want: To be so good, they forget I ever played." That sentiment notwithstanding, many recall Guillen's days as a player with the White Sox and other major-league teams from 1985 to 2000, in particular his steady defense, leadership qualities, sharp understanding of baseball strategy, and enthusiasm for the sport. In 1985 he was named the American League's rookie of the year, in acknowledgement of his solid play at shortstop and keen batter's eye. In 2005, after he became the first Venezuelan-born manager in Major League Baseball (MLB) history, Guillen achieved a number of other firsts as well: he led the White Sox to their first American League pennant since 1959 and their first World Series victory since 1917, and he became the first Latino manager, and the first person born outside the United

Tim Boyle/Getty

States, to lead a big-league baseball team to a world championship. Guillen was named the 2005 American League manager of the year.

Guillen is an advocate of "small ball"—the art of using base steals, bunts, singles, and other "small" moves, as opposed to extra-base hits, as means of accumulating runs. One assessment of Guillen's approach to the game was offered by Ken Williams, the White Sox's general manager, who told Michael Farber for *Sports Illustrated* (May 16, 2005), "If he has a style, it's, Do whatever the hell you have to do to win on a given day." Guillen is known in baseball circles for his candor, which has occasionally led to disagreements between him and his players, among others. Michael Farber remarked that Guillen "was born without a mute button. . . . grabbing listeners' attention with observations and Ozzie-isms that are wry and sometimes ribald." Members of the sports press find the White Sox skipper's colorful and forthright manner to be refreshing. Tom Verducci, writing for *Sports Illustrated* (October 3, 2005), declared, "Caffeine has nothing on Ozzie Guillen," whom he described as "a fast-talking, expletive-spewing, insult-chucking, ego-bruising, gut-churning, headline-making natural stimulant."

The oldest of five children, Oswaldo José Guillen Barrios was born on January 20, 1964 in Ocumare del Tuy, in northern Venezuela, about 25 miles south of Caracas, the country's capital. Ocumare del Tuy is located in the central region of the Miranda State, one of Venezuela's 23 states, which, with more than 2,300,000 people, is the second-most-populous in the country. Guillen's mother, Violeta, worked as a high-school principal in Ocumare del Tuy before transferring to a school in Los Teques, a suburb of Caracas, moving there with her family when Guillen was about 10 years old. Guillen's father, Oswaldo Sr., was the manager of a General Electric plant. Guillen's parents divorced around the time that he relocated with his mother to Los Teques. While attending high school Guillen struggled to make passing marks, and when his teachers approached his mother, the school's principal, about his poor grades, she ordered them not to give her son any special treatment. "Ooh, my mother, she tough," Guillen told Richard Hoffer for *Sports Illustrated* (April 6, 1992). "She tells the teachers, 'Flunk him.'" They took her advice, and Guillen flunked out of high school.

Growing up, Guillen played *pelota de goma*—a variant of baseball in which participants strike a rubber ball with their fists and field with their bare hands. An all-around athlete as a boy, Guillen also played volleyball in his grammar-school years for Venezuela's national youth team. Later, while playing a traditional form of baseball in Los Teques, where he "was just hanging around, trying to survive," as Guillen told Mike Dodd for *USA Today* (October 21, 2005), he was discovered by Ernesto Aparicio, the uncle of the baseball Hall of Fame member Luis Aparicio, a former shortstop for the Chicago White Sox and other major-league teams. In Los Teques Ernesto Aparicio had built a reputation as a knowledgeable baseball coach, due in part to his having tutored his nephew in Venezuela for a time before Luis played in the United States. Ernesto Aparicio took Guillen under his wing as well. "First thing I ever remember doing was taking grounders," Guillen told Richard Hoffer. He added, referring to Venezuelan athletes,

"We are built to be shortstops—small, with quick hands, always wanting to take ground balls. When scouts come to Caracas, they naturally ask to see infielders." Venezuela's history of producing talented shortstops began with Chico Carrasquel, who made his MLB debut with the Chicago White Sox on April 18, 1950. In his youth Guillen was a particular admirer of the Venezuelan player Dave Concepcion, whose prominence as a shortstop with the Cincinnati Reds, beginning in the 1970s, coincided with Guillen's teenage years. (In homage to Concepcion, Guillen wore the uniform number 13 when he joined the White Sox and copied Concepcion's style of wearing his uniform pants so long that they reached his shoes.) "All of the great Venezuelan shortstops—Carrasqual, Aparicio, Dave Concepcion—use the same style as I do in fielding practice," Guillen explained to Jim Kaplan for *Sports Illustrated* (September 2, 1985). "They take a small glove and try to catch everything one-handed. That makes your hand strong."

At 16 Guillen joined a winter-league baseball team coached by Aparicio in Venezuela. On December 17, 1980, five weeks before his 17th birthday, Guillen signed a contract as an undrafted free agent with the San Diego Padres. Guillen, who spoke little English when he arrived in the U.S., played four seasons with the Padres' minor-league affiliates. On December 6, 1984 the Padres traded him to the White Sox along with his fellow infielder Luis Salazar and the pitchers Tim Lollar and Bill Long, in exchange for the pitchers LaMarr Hoyt, Todd Simmons, and Kevin Kristan.

In 1985, as a 21-year-old rookie, Guillen played in 134 games for the White Sox, scoring 71 runs, a career high, and recording nine triples, the fifth-highest total in the American League that season. By September 1985 Guillen was considered the favorite to win the American League's Rookie of the Year Award, which he was given at the season's conclusion. (The *Sporting News* also named Guillen its rookie of the year for 1985.) Most impressive to many baseball veterans were Guillen's defensive abilities, strong instincts for the game, and eagerness to learn from his coaches. Guillen set a record in 1985, committing only 12 errors, at the time the fewest by a shortstop in White Sox history. Referring to Guillen's defensive and leadership skills alone, Tony La Russa, then the manager of the White Sox, said to Kaplan, "He could be hitting zero and still be helping us." Roland Hemond, the White Sox general manager, who had acquired Guillen from the Padres, told Kaplan, "Ozzie reminds me of [the Hall of Fame member] Red Schoendienst when he came over to Milwaukee and solidified the defense in 1957. We'd say, 'What a great fielder, what instinct, what knowledge of the hitters.' But Red was 34; Ozzie's 21."

In 1988 Guillen set a White Sox franchise record for shortstops, with 588 assists in a single season. Also that year he was selected to appear in his first All-Star Game; he went on to play as an All Star in 1990 and 1991. Though his offensive numbers would pale in comparison with those of the preeminent MLB shortstops of today—for example, Derek Jeter and Alex Rodriguez of the New York Yankees and Miguel Tejada of the Baltimore Orioles—Guillen had a reputation around the league as a patient and dangerous hitter. He consistently placed in the top 10 in the American League for most at-bats per strikeout, ranking first in the American League in that category in 1996 and 1997. His signature qualities on the diamond, however, were his defensive ability and his fiery personality. Richard Hoffer noted, "He is best known for extending the defensive legacy of Venezuelan shortstops. . . . He flops all over the field, not necessarily with the elegance of his mentors but with the same wonderful effect." In 1990 Guillen received his first and only American League Gold Glove award for his work at shortstop. Throughout the world of baseball, and particularly with his teammates, Guillen earned a reputation for being a leader and speaking his mind. "He's the type of guy who's going to say what nobody else is going to say," Robin Ventura, one of his teammates, told Alan Solomon for the *Chicago Tribune* (April 7, 1991). "If something has to be said, he's going to say it—and not even worry about it. That's good. Every team needs that. It just has to be the right person to do it, and he has the right personality to be able to do it." Referring to Guillen's talkativeness on the field, Ventura told Richard Hoffer, "He's nonstop, never shuts up. Not one unspoken thought. He's talking about something he saw on TV, about the batter, about how some event here might translate in Venezuela. He's talking to me, he's talking to umps, he's talking to fans, he's talking to base runners. I've seen it so bad out there that the third base coach is beside himself trying to get the runner's attention."

Guillen's 13th and final season with the White Sox ended on October 31, 1997, when he was granted free agency. Among White Sox shortstops he ranked first of all time in fielding percentage, with .974, and ranked second behind Luis Aparicio in five categories, with 1,724 games played, 7,900 total fielding chances, 2,735 putouts, 4,962 assists, and 1,027 double plays. "I know the White Sox, through their history, have had many outstanding shortstops. Some of them may have been as good as Ozzie, but I doubt any were better. Not better all-around," the Hall-of-Famer Carlton Fisk, a former teammate of Guillen's, told Jerome Holtzman for the *Chicago Tribune* (August 25, 1990). "Some might have stolen more bases and had more speed, but as far as reading the hitters and making the plays, Ozzie could be the best."

Guillen's final three seasons as a player found him with three different teams: the Baltimore Orioles, the Atlanta Braves, and the Tampa Bay Devil Rays. On May 6, 1998, having already signed with the Orioles before the season, he was acquired by the Braves, joining the perennial play-off qualifiers midway through the season. He appeared in the play-offs for Atlanta in 1998 and 1999, helping the Braves reach the 1999 World Series, where they lost to the Yankees. (Guillen had appeared in the 1993 play-offs for the White Sox, garnering six hits and scoring four runs in the best-of-seven series against the Toronto Blue Jays, who went on to win the 1993 World Series.) Guillen finished his career with 1,764 hits, 773 runs scored, 275 doubles, 69 triples, 169 stolen bases, and a lifetime .264 batting average.

Aspiring to a new career as a manager, Guillen sought the counsel of Bobby Cox, the Braves' skipper, who is widely thought to be one of the best managers in baseball. (Cox has been named National League Manager of the Year four times, in 1985, 1991, 2004, and 2005.) "When I played for him, I said, 'If you don't mind, I want to learn from you. Can I ask you questions during the game, why are you doing this?'" Guillen said to Mike Dodd. "He explained it to me." In 2001 Guillen took a job with the Montreal Expos under the team's manager, Jeff Torberg; Guillen had played for Torberg from 1989 until 1991, while both were with the White Sox. On June 4, 2001 Guillen was named the Expos' third-base coach. The following season landed Guillen in Miami, home of the Florida Marlins, where he served as third-base coach under manager Jack McKeon. In 2003, Guillen's second year with the team, the Marlins won the World Series, defeating the Yankees four games to two.

On November 3, 2003 Guillen was named the 37th manager in the White Sox's history, taking over for Jerry Manual, who had served in the position for the previous five seasons and had led the team to one play-off berth, in 2000. Responsible for Guillen's hiring was Ken Williams, the White Sox general manager and a former teammate of Guillen's on the White Sox. At the press conference introducing Guillen as the team's manager, Williams cited "the passion, the commitment, the energy, the game knowledge, the aggressive attitude" of Guillen, as quoted by Nancy Armour for the Associated Press (November 4, 2003): "He bleeds White Sox baseball. There is no doubt in my mind that he is going to provide something here we desperately need. A jolt, if you will." Guillen's promise to the media and White Sox fans, as quoted by Armour, was, "Every player who wears this uniform is going to play the game right. If they don't play the game right, they're not going to play for me." He added, "We're going to have fun. But fun is winning."

Prior to 2005 the White Sox had won two world championships—in 1911 and 1917—and had appeared in the World Series only three other times, in 1901, 1919, and 1959. The franchise was best known to some for the "Black Sox" scandal of 1919, the year that members of the team accepted money from gamblers in exchange for intentionally losing the World Series to the Cincinnati Reds. (The Reds went on to beat the White Sox—who were the heavy favorites—fives games to three in the best-of-nine-game series.) The betting conspiracy led to the banning from baseball of eight White Sox players, including the legendary outfielder

"Shoeless" Joe Jackson. The White Sox bore the stigma of the scandal for several decades. In the nine seasons that preceded Guillen's hiring, the White Sox had qualified for the play-offs once, in 2000, but were quickly dispatched by the Seattle Mariners in the first round.

Sports Illustrated reported that over the course of Guillen's first 25 games as manager, in 2004, attendance for White Sox home games increased by more than 4,000 tickets per game. Guillen set about remaking the White Sox in his own likeness, preferring scrappy overachievers to established stars. So that his players understood that they were under his constant scrutiny, Guillen frequently criticized them in front of the media. "I don't want them to be excuse players," Guillen explained to Mike Dodd. "If you fail, you fail. Come on. As soon as you make any excuse, you're not a winner." With an 83–79 record the team finished the 2004 season in second place in the American League (AL) Central Division, nine games out of first place, a slight decline from the 86–76 record Manual had posted a season before.

At Guillen's urging Williams made several changes to the White Sox roster prior to the 2005 season. With the hope of minimizing the team's reliance on home runs and extra-base hits, Carlos Lee was traded to the Milwaukee Brewers for the outfielder Scott Podsednik, who in 2004 was noted for stealing 70 bases, the most in the National League. Saving money on the Lee-for-Podsednik trade, Williams added the catcher A.J. Pierzynski to help stabilize the team's core of talented but mostly young starting pitchers. The team's pitching staff featured the left-hander Mark Buehrle and the right-handers Freddy Garcia, José Contreras, Jon Garland, and the veteran Orlando "El Duqué" Hernandez, whom Guillen favored for his experience and versatility. During the off-season the White Sox also jettisoned the talented but injury-prone outfielder Magglio Ordoñez, who signed with the Detroit Tigers—and with whom Guillen had traded jabs through the press in 2004.

By the middle of May 2005, with a win-loss ratio of 24–7, the White Sox were owners of the best record in professional baseball. On August 1, 2005 the team held a 15-game lead over the Cleveland Indians in the AL Central Division. After a ferocious charge by Cleveland, however, the White Sox entered the final series of the regular season with their lead trimmed to less than two games. The White Sox's precipitous decline rankled Guillen, whom Tom Verducci quoted as saying, "Many times I'm sick—physically sick. I'm that upset" after a loss. The White Sox swept the Indians in three games in Cleveland to finish the regular season six games ahead of their divisional rivals, with a record of 99–63, the best in the American League. The designated hitter and first baseman Paul Konerko, who hit 40 home runs and drove in 100 runners, was the team's most consistent offensive player in the regular season. Meanwhile, the free-agent hires Jermaine Dye and Tadahito Iguchi pro-

vided the batting lineup with stability, behind lead-off hitter Podsednik.

The White Sox, considered underdogs, opened the play-offs as hosts to the Boston Red Sox, winners of the 2004 World Series. Predictions that the Red Sox's dynamic lineup would overpower the White Sox's relatively unseasoned pitching staff proved inaccurate, and after scoring five times in the first inning of the series, the White Sox won the first game in Chicago by a score of 14–2 and the second by 5–4. The highlight of the best-of-five series came in the bottom of the sixth inning of Game Three, played in Fenway Park in Boston, Massachusetts. The Red Sox had the bases loaded with no outs, with the White Sox leading, 4–3, Guillen called on the pitcher Orlando Hernandez to relieve the starter, Freddy Garcia. Hernandez drew the next three batters into harmless outs and finished the inning with a strikeout of the centerfielder Johnny Damon. The White Sox went on to win the game by a score of 5–3.

In the American League Championship Series, the White Sox faced the Los Angeles Angels of Anaheim, winners of the Western Division play-offs. After losing the first game in Chicago, the White Sox took the second, aided by a controversial call that came with two outs in the bottom of the ninth inning; the call enabled Pierzynski to reach base when the Angels thought that he had struck out and that the inning was over. Game Two also featured the first of four consecutive complete games tossed by White Sox pitchers. (Buehrle, Garland, Garcia, and Contreras, respectively, were the winners of Games Two, Three, Four, and Five.) In Anaheim the White Sox were helped by a pair of first-inning home runs by Konerko—in Games Three and Four, respectively—and took the best-of-seven series in five games. (Konerko was named the series' most valuable player.)

The 2005 World Series pitted the White Sox against the Houston Astros, the winners of the National League's wild-card berth. Whereas the White Sox had not won a championship in 88 years, the Astros, who had joined MLB as an expansion team in 1962, had never before reached the World Series. Both teams featured dominant starting pitching staffs, with the Astros' led by the trio of Roy Oswald, Roger Clemens, and Andy Pettitte. The White Sox's Jermaine Dye, later named World Series MVP, opened the scoring in Game One, played in Chicago, with a solo home run against Clemens. The White Sox won, 7–6. Game Two, in Chicago, was thought by many to be the most memorable game of the World Series. The contest was a taut, seesaw affair, featuring a seventh-inning grand slam by Konerko that gave the White Sox a seemingly insurmountable 6–4 lead. A two-run, ninth-inning rally by the Astros tied the score, but Podsednik managed a walk-off home run against the reliever Brad Lidge with one out in the bottom of the inning, winning the game for the White Sox. "You follow the team year round, that's the way we play all year," Guillen said in the postgame press conference, as quoted by MLB.com (October 24, 2005). "We keep fighting, making big pitch. When somebody fail, somebody pick them up." The White Sox went on to win the next two games, played in Houston, Texas, to capture their first championship since 1917. In his postgame press conference, as quoted by MLB.com (October 27, 2005), Guillen acknowledged the patience of the White Sox fans, who had waited so long for a World Series victory: "The fans in Chicago . . . are still there for us, and rooting for us for I don't know how many years, 80 or whatever it is, good thing we did it." In 2006 the White Sox were unable to repeat their successes of the previous season, failing to reach the play-offs. They finished the regular season with a record of 90 wins and 72 losses, thereby placing third in the American League Central division.

Guillen frequently contributes a column to the Venezuelan newspaper El Universal, based in Caracas. He has also appeared on television movies and soap operas in his native country. In addition, Guillen heads the Ozzie Guillen Foundation, founded in 1997 to raise funds for young people suffering from AIDS and cancer. In the winter of 1999, Guillen donated $200,000 to families in Venezuela who were affected by a mudslide. He received the Dr. Martin Luther King Jr. Excellence in Leadership Award in January 2005.

Guillen is married to the former Ibis Cardenas and has three children: Oswaldo Jr., Oney, and Ozney. Oswaldo Jr. works for the White Sox as a liaison and interpreter for Spanish-speaking players. Guillen, known for dreading Midwest winters, divides his time between homes in Miami, Florida, and Caracas. He practices the religion of Santería (also called Lukumí), which fuses Catholic and traditional Yoruba beliefs and sometimes involves the sacrificing of animals. (The Yoruba are the largest ethnic group in Nigeria.) In his spare time Guillen enjoys golfing. He is working to attain dual citizenship in the United States and Venezuela.

—D.F.

Suggested Reading: Baseball Reference Web site; Chicago White Sox Web site; New York Times A p1+ Oct. 22, 2005; Sports Illustrated p 42+ Sep. 2, 1985, p 92+ Apr. 6, 1992, p 95+ Jun. 14, 2004; USA Today A p1+ Oct. 21, 2005

Gupta, Sanjay

Oct. 23, 1969– CNN medical correspondent; neurosurgeon

Address: Dept. of Neurological Surgery, Grady Memorial Hospital, Faculty Office Bldg. #339, 80 Jesse Hill Dr. S.E., Atlanta, GA 30303

As a senior medical correspondent for CNN, Sanjay Gupta has provided audiences with insightful looks at the implications of a potential avian-flu outbreak and the problems facing doctors in war-torn areas of Iraq, among many other such issues. Concurrently a practicing neurosurgeon, he is affiliated with Emory University Hospital and Grady Memorial Hospital, well-regarded institutions in Atlanta, Georgia. "We all know smart doctors, but they're not compassionate and empathetic," Daniel L. Barrow, the chairman of the Emory Neurological Surgery Department, told Jill Vejnoska for the Atlanta Journal-Constitution (September 30, 2004). "[Gupta] possesses all those qualities that make a physician truly outstanding. And frankly, those are the necessary qualities to make a good reporter." At times his dual career as television correspondent and working neurosurgeon have converged on the air, attracting criticism from those who contend that Gupta cannot act both as an objective journalist and as a doctor when reporting news pieces. He shrugs off such criticism, insisting that "putting a press badge on does not bar you from humanity," as he stated in a speech he gave at the University of Texas–Pan American on March 21, 2006, posted on the school's Web site.

Carlo Allegri/Getty Images

Sanjay Gupta was born in Dearborn, Michigan, on October 23, 1969 to Subhash and Damyanti Gupta, first-generation Indian immigrants who worked as engineers at the Ford Motor Co. (Damyanti Gupta was the first female engineer hired by the automotive giant.) Raised, along with his younger brother, in Livonia and Novi, cities in the Detroit metropolitan area, Gupta excelled academically and was valedictorian of his graduating class at Novi High School. After completing high school, Gupta, then 17 years old, enrolled in an accelerated program at the University of Michigan, earning both his undergraduate and medical degrees in six years. As a medical student Gupta frequently contributed to the university newspaper, investigating and writing articles on health-care policies and issues. After earning his M.D. degree, in 1993, he stayed on at the University of Michigan Medical Center as a neurosurgery resident.

In 1997 Gupta was selected to participate in the prestigious White House Fellows Program. The fellowship, which is awarded to approximately 15 young people annually, provides qualified candidates in various fields with the opportunity to put their specialized knowledge to political use. (Past fellows who have gone on to high-profile careers include Wesley K. Clark, a retired four-star general in the U.S. Army and former NATO supreme allied commander; Marsha Evans, a former head of the American Red Cross; and Colin L. Powell, a former U.S. secretary of state.) Keenly interested in health-care policy, Gupta served his year-long fellowship as a special adviser and speechwriter for then–First Lady Hillary Rodham Clinton. During that time he became well-versed in media communication, learning that complicated medical jargon must be refashioned in understandable terms for the general public. Gupta told Pradeep Shankar for *Silicon India* (June 2, 2003, on-line), "People get medical information from different mediums—magazine, radio, television. . . . It is important for doctors to be involved in that process so that the medical information [the public is] getting can be credible."

After completing the fellowship, Gupta began working as a neurosurgeon at the University of Tennessee's Semmes-Murphy clinic, in Memphis. Although Gupta had returned to practicing medicine full-time, his experience in Washington had only increased his attraction to a media career. He consulted several contacts he had made during the fellowship, and in the summer of 2001, he landed a position as a medical correspondent for CNN. Gupta initially assumed that he would work mostly behind the scenes at the network, offering medical advice to the on-air talent. After the terrorist attacks of September 11, 2001, however, Gupta found himself in front of the camera, interviewing burn victims about their excruciating ordeals in several nationally televised pieces. In the weeks following September 11, Gupta also reported on the anthrax scare, in which letters containing the potentially deadly bacteria were anonymously mailed to newsrooms and the offices of U.S. senators, and he was called on to speculate about the health of Osama bin Laden, the terrorist mastermind who was known to suffer from kidney disease. When coverage of the attacks waned, Gupta worked on such general-interest stories as the likelihood of being exposed to dangerous germs while hospitalized and the effectiveness of Melanotan, a drug said to curb the appetite, increase the libido, and tan the skin. (Melanotan was dubbed the "Barbie drug" by several headline writers.)

In 2003, as U.S. military forces drove into Iraq to depose the dictator Saddam Hussein, American and Iraqi casualties steadily rose. While other reporters devoted much of their coverage to the ongoing political turmoil and military strategizing, Gupta provided a look at the experiences of medical units entrenched within the war's fiercest battle zones. At the outset of the war, Gupta filed reports from Camp Iwo Jima, in Kuwait. He explained to viewers that medical stations had become more sophisticated since the Persian Gulf War, in 1991, when battle locations changed frequently and were often far from where medical personnel were stationed. In response to such situations, according to Gupta, the military adopted mobile operating rooms called "forward resuscitative surgical suites" to deliver care to soldiers at the front lines. The operating tents—which can be reached only by passing through series of zippered layers, to maintain sterility—were designed to be set up or broken down within one hour. As tensions began to escalate in Iraq, Gupta traveled with the U.S. Navy's forward resuscitative surgical unit, called the Devil Docs, a play on the nickname Devil Dogs, which refers to U.S. Marines. Gupta gave exclusive live coverage on CNN of the first surgery performed during the war from a makeshift operating room in the middle of the Iraqi desert. The doctors are "obviously much more in harm's way than they were ever before, because they are so close to the front line," he told Julie Hinds for the *Detroit Free Press* (April 4, 2003). "They are right here with the troops, taking care of the injured essentially right as they are injured. It's a totally different concept, different from Vietnam or Korea, but it appears to be working."

Though Gupta was reporting in extremely dangerous circumstances, with death being an ever-present possibility even for journalists, he told Hinds, "We don't want to be the story, we want to tell the story. And that's what we're out here doing." When U.S. Marines opened fire on a taxi that had ignored a checkpoint south of Baghdad, however, Gupta, the only neurosurgeon present, undeniably became a participant in the story, operating on a two-year-old Iraqi boy who had been in the car and consequently suffered severe head trauma. "If the child weren't operated on immediately it would certainly die. I had to remove the blood clot as well as the fluid that were causing pressure on the child's brain," Gupta told Shankar. Because the medical unit was not equipped to handle complicated neurosurgical procedures, Gupta sterilized a drill that had been used to put up the medical tent, then used it to open the boy's skull in order to treat the injuries. (The toddler succumbed to his other injuries hours later.) "I didn't intend to work as a doctor while [in Iraq], but there was no neurosurgeon in the field," Gupta told a writer for *Emory Magazine* (Spring 2004). "So they started saying, 'If someone gets shot in the head, we'll just call Sanjay.' Then it happened—five times." Among the other patients he treated were two Iraqi combatants and two coalition-force members.

CNN applauded Gupta's efforts, and the Devil Docs made him an honorary member of their unit. At least one media analyst began criticizing Gupta's actions, however, contending that he had blurred the lines of objectivity by performing surgery in Iraq. Bob Steele, an expert on journalistic ethics at the Poynter Institute for Media Studies, wrote in a column for the institute's Web site (April 4, 2003), "How does Gupta the reporter and Gupta the doctor reconcile his competing roles and competing obligations? Does the Hippocratic oath [of medical] duty always trump the journalistic responsibility to gather information and report stories?" Steele told Suzanne C. Ryan for the *Boston Globe* (April 4, 2003), "I'm hoping and trusting that [Gupta] and CNN set some thresholds. I think it's problematic if this is a role that he's going to be playing on any kind of frequent basis. I don't think he should be reporting on it if he's also a participant. He can't bring appropriate journalistic independence and detachment to a story." Surprised by such criticism and unapologetic about his actions, Gupta told Vejnoska, "I had a very clear moral compass out there. You never stop being a doctor, and you never stop being a human being."

In 2004 Gupta traveled to the 15th International AIDS Conference, held in Bangkok, Thailand, to report on the epidemic plaguing many countries throughout the world. Later that year he returned to South Asia, this time to Sri Lanka, to cover the devastating effects of the tsunami that destroyed coastal communities there and in Indonesia, India, and Thailand, claiming the lives of more than 155,000 people. In order to show viewers the scope of the destruction, Gupta filmed reports from ravaged villages, where displaced victims scavenged through the wreckage for signs of family members and friends. Gupta's in-depth news pieces addressed topics ranging from the health hazards posed by decomposing corpses to the difficulties of meeting basic needs for subsistence. He contributed in large part to CNN's overall coverage of the tsunami, which was awarded the prestigious Alfred I. duPont Award for excellence in broadcast journalism. Touched by his experiences in Sri Lanka, Gupta donates all proceeds he receives from speaking engagements to an organization that offers aid to orphaned children there.

In 2005 Gupta reported from similar circumstances in flooded areas of New Orleans, Louisiana, after Hurricane Katrina tore through the Gulf Coast region, causing one of the worst natural disasters in American history. Reporting from Charity Hospital, a large facility that lost all running water and electricity and was unable to be evacuated for several days, he told CNN (September 2, 2005, on-line), "It's gruesome. I guess that is the best word for it. If you think about a hospital, for example, the morgue is in the basement, and the base-ment is completely flooded. So you can just imagine the scene down there. But [now] when patients die in the hospital, there is no place to put them, so they're in the stairwells. It is one of the most unbelievable situations I've seen as a doctor, certainly as a journalist as well."

Gupta's compelling and timely reporting of such devastating events made him a popular contributor on CNN. Today he makes regular appearances on the weekday program *American Morning* and hosts his own half-hour weekend show, *House Call with Dr. Sanjay Gupta.* (In 2002 he also began co-hosting *AccentHealth*, a patient-education program produced by CNN and shown in hospital waiting rooms.) He has hosted numerous prime-time health-related specials, including *New You Resolution, Life Beyond Limits,* and *The First Patient: Health and the Presidency.* (For *Life Beyond Limits,* which focused on such people as fire eaters, deep-sea divers, mountain climbers, and Arctic swimmers, Gupta himself ate fire.) In addition to his on-air reporting, Gupta writes a weekly health column for *Time.* In early 2006 he toured university campuses all across the country to educate students about the growing obesity problem in the U.S.

Despite his journalistic accomplishments, Gupta considers his medical career of primary importance. "Being a doctor is my greatest passion and brings me the most satisfaction," he told *Emory Magazine.* "I've spent half my life training to be a neurosurgeon." He serves as the associate chief of neurosurgery at Grady Memorial Hospital, where he still performs operations regularly. Additionally, as an assistant professor of neurological surgery, he teaches at the Emory University School of Medicine. "I always tell my residents, 'It's OK to have butterflies [in your stomach]. Just make sure they're flying in formation,'" he quipped to Vejnoska.

Gupta has published articles in medical journals on brain tumors and spinal-cord abnormalities, and most recently he wrote articles on the subject of percutaneous (passing through the skin) placement of pedicle screws—a fairly new procedure in spinal surgery—for the *Journal of Neurosurgery* and *Neurosurgical Focus.* Gupta is the recipient of numerous awards, including the National Headliner Award from the Press Club of Atlantic City for his television special *The First Patient,* the Humanitarian Award from the National Press Photographers Association, and the GOLD Award from the National Health Care Communicators. In 2003 he was called one of the sexiest men alive by *People* magazine and deemed a "pop culture icon" by *USA Today.* In 2004 the Atlanta Press Club named him Journalist of the Year.

Gupta splits his time between New York City and his home in Atlanta, which he shares with his wife, the attorney Rebecca Olson Gupta, and their daughter.

—I.C.

Suggested Reading: *Atlanta Journal-Constitution* E p1 Sep. 30, 2004; *Boston Globe* A p24 Apr. 4, 2003; CNN (on-line) Sep. 2, 2005; *Detroit Free Press* H p1 Apr. 4, 2003; *Emory Magazine* Spring 2004; *Philadelphia Daily News* p10 Mar. 28, 2003; Poynter Institute for Media Studies Web site; *Silicon India* (on-line) June 2, 2003; University of Texas–Pan American Web site

Selected Television Shows: *House Call with Dr. Sanjay Gupta*, 2004–

Mandel Ngan/Getty Images

Hadley, Stephen

Feb. 13, 1947– U.S. national security adviser

Address: National Security Council, Executive Office Bldg., 17th St. and Pennsylvania Ave., N.W., Washington, DC 20001

In January 2005 Stephen Hadley was appointed assistant to the president for national security affairs, a position commonly referred to as national security adviser. In that role, which has been filled in recent decades by such political luminaries as Colin Powell, Henry Kissinger, Brent Scowcroft, and McGeorge Bundy, Hadley is responsible for reviewing information, such as that in intelligence reports, and deciding which foreign-policy issues are deserving of the president's attention; he also accompanies the commander in chief on visits with other world leaders. Hadley, a veteran foreign-policy and defense specialist, served in the administrations of presidents Richard M. Nixon, Gerald R. Ford, Ronald Reagan, and George H. W. Bush. Dur-

ing the first term of President George W. Bush, as deputy national security adviser under Condoleezza Rice, his immediate predecessor as national security adviser, Hadley was one of the architects of U.S. policy in Iraq. He earned particular notoriety for his role in a controversy surrounding the claim that Iraq had tried to purchase uranium from the African country of Niger for the purpose of building nuclear weapons, a claim that was used to justify the 2003 U.S. invasion of Iraq. Hadley took responsibility for the inclusion of that claim in Bush's State of the Union address in 2003, by which time the intelligence supporting it had already been discovered to be faulty. Many saw Hadley as the "fall guy" in that controversy, or the one to accept the blame for the administration's missteps.

Hadley is generally characterized as low-key, deferential to the president, and respectful of the established processes by which policies are created. "With his oversize tortoise-shell glasses and lawyerly manner, Stephen Hadley . . . seems to be studying for the role of Clark Kent, not Superman," David Ignatius wrote for the *Washington Post* (February 11, 2005), also describing Hadley as "meticulous, well-organized," and "self-effacing." "In a town populated by people nursing grandiose views of their own importance and scheming for greater glory, Hadley still thinks of himself as a staff man," Peter Baker wrote for the January 29, 2006 edition of the same newspaper. "He sits at the pinnacle of power, but articulates no sweeping personal vision of the world and has made a point of staying in the shadows." In interviews Hadley has tended to reinforce such characterizations. "There is a lot of attention to what does . . . Condi Rice think, what does [Secretary of Defense Donald] Rumsfeld think, or what does the national security adviser think," he said to Sabrina Eaton for the *Cleveland Plain Dealer* (April 24, 2005). "What really matters is what the president of the United States thinks. The president is the architect of American foreign policy, and our job is to support him in his role."

Stephen Hadley was born on February 13, 1947 in Toledo, Ohio, the second of three children of Robert Hadley, an electrical engineer, and Suzanne Hadley, a homemaker. He grew up outside Cleveland, Ohio, and became interested in politics after reading Allen Drury's novel *Advise and Consent*, a thriller centering on the Senate confirmation of a nominee for secretary of state. At Brush High School in Lyndhurst, Ohio, Hadley was elected student-body president; he graduated in 1965 as valedictorian of his class. "He always seemed a little older than he was, but he wasn't stuffy or anything," Hadley's schoolmate Keith Kerr told Eaton. "He was pretty much a straight arrow, very bright and focused." Hadley attended Cornell University, in Ithaca, New York, where he served on the Scheduling Coordination and Activities Review Board (SCARB), a body overseeing various campus activities. SCARB dealt with occurrences related to many of the social issues of that time—the politically turbulent 1960s. According to Eaton, "Hadley fought a local prosecutor's efforts to censor a student publication, helped negotiate a peaceful conclusion when armed black students took over a campus building and refused to sanction events where draft cards were burned." After graduating, in 1969, Hadley attended Yale University Law School, in New Haven, Connecticut, where he met and befriended the future First Lady and Democratic U.S. senator Hillary Rodham Clinton, one of the few women then enrolled in the program. Arthur C. Kaminski, a lawyer and a classmate of Hadley's from both Yale and Cornell, recalled to Eaton that he once asked Hadley if he thought that Clinton "was the smartest woman in the class, and he looked at me and said, 'I thought she was the smartest of all of us.'" That comment, Kaminski said, was "quintessential Hadley. He is the most open-minded guy in the world. Even though his politics are much different from Hillary's, he recognizes her intelligence. A lot of people in D.C. have no use for people who aren't on their side, and that isn't him at all." (According to Eaton, Hadley "remains cordial" with Clinton, "although they don't talk much anymore.")

After graduating from Yale, in 1972, Hadley served a tour of duty in the U.S. Navy. Concurrently, he worked as an analyst for the comptroller of the secretary of defense from 1972 to 1974, during the Richard Nixon administration. Hadley next became a junior staff member of the National Security Council's Office of Program Analysis, under President Gerald R. Ford. He was hired by Brent Scowcroft, who was national security adviser under Ford and, later, George H. W. Bush. Scowcroft told David Ignatius that Hadley is "just one of the nicest human beings I ever met. He's incredibly smart, works just all the time, is meticulous almost to a fault." Indeed, according to Baker, in his first government posts Hadley was "a serious young man who remained late to pore through endless cables." Baker quoted one of Hadley's former colleagues as saying, "Steve was one of the guys who would read all the time. It was the '70's, and we would say, 'Come on, Steve, it's time to party.' But he would stay and read."

In 1977, when the Democrat Jimmy Carter assumed the presidency, Hadley joined the Washington law firm Shea & Gardner, specializing in commercial litigation and public-policy work. The firm was "known around Washington as a haven for intellectually elite, highly skilled craftsmen who had quietly earned a solid reputation for top-quality work," Laura A. Kiernan wrote for the *Washington Post* (September 1, 1980). (Shea & Gardner merged with the Boston law firm Goodwin Proctor LLP in 2004, adopting that firm's name.) Hadley would continue to work off and on for the firm until 2001, by which time he had become a partner. He returned to government service in 1986 as counsel to the Tower Commission, appointed by President Ronald Reagan to investigate the Iran-Contra affair, in which White House officials stood accused of il-

legally funneling money from the sale of arms to Iran to anti-Communist rebels in Nicaragua. That experience, Baker wrote, "cemented" Hadley's view that the National Security Council, whose members were implicated in the scandal, "should serve only as staff, never as an operational agency." From 1989 to 1993, the years of George H. W. Bush's presidency, Hadley served as assistant secretary for international security policy in the Defense Department. He was chosen for the job by Richard B. Cheney, then the defense secretary and later vice president under George W. Bush. During the two-term presidency of Bill Clinton, Hadley returned to corporate practice, both as a principal in the Scowcroft Group Inc., an international consulting firm headed by Brent Scowcroft, and as a partner at Shea & Gardner.

Hadley served as a senior foreign- and defense-policy adviser for George W. Bush's 2000 campaign for president. During Bush's first term, Hadley was an assistant to the president and deputy national security adviser. In 2003 he became involved in the controversy surrounding the claim—made in Bush's State of the Union address—that Iraq's leader, Saddam Hussein, had tried to purchase uranium in Africa for the purpose of making weapons of mass destruction. That claim, used to help justify the U.S. invasion of Iraq, was based in part on documents later shown to have been forged. In July it was revealed that Hadley and others had known about the faulty nature of the intelligence prior to drafting Bush's speech: after the CIA had warned the previous fall that the reports were unsubstantiated, references to the uranium purchases had been removed from a speech Bush gave in Cincinnati, Ohio, in October 2002. In his January 2003 State of the Union address, however, Bush declared, "The British government has learned that Saddam Hussein recently sought significant quantities of uranium from Africa." The statement would be cited frequently by critics of the war in Iraq. Hadley took responsibility for the statement's inclusion in the speech, saying that although he had seen the memos countering the false claim in October 2002, he and other White House officials had forgotten about them when the State of the Union address was being written. "I should have recalled at the time of the State of the Union speech that there was controversy associated with the uranium issue," Hadley said in a widely quoted statement later in 2003. According to Baker, Hadley offered to resign in the wake of the controversy, but Bush refused to accept his resignation.

In January 2005 Hadley was appointed as head of the National Security Council, or national security adviser, when Condoleezza Rice replaced Colin Powell as secretary of state. In that position, working 14-hour days, six days per week, Hadley has maintained a more agreeable relationship with Rice than previous national security advisers have had with secretaries of state; often, individuals holding those respective posts have competed for dominance in matters of foreign policy. "My approach is going to be more offstage," Hadley said, as quoted by Baker. "Condi has established herself as an articulator of the president's policies. . . . It's very important that she carry that out and there not be competing voices or any sense of possible competition. And as long as we're both in these two jobs, there won't be." (Rice was one of the more prominent advocates of the invasion of Iraq and has continued to support the U.S. occupation of that country.) Because of his record of having supported the more outspoken Rice in her policy decisions when he served as her deputy, many predicted that Hadley's appointment to her old office signaled no significant changes in the administration's direction.

In 2005 Hadley was called on to represent the Bush administration in several highly publicized episodes related to the war in Iraq. That summer, Cindy Sheehan, the angry mother of a soldier killed in Iraq, camped out near the president's Texas ranch to protest the war. Hadley was sent to talk with her in a "futile bid to halt the public relations fiasco," as Eaton wrote for the *Cleveland Plain Dealer* (December 18, 2005). Then, in November, as the White House faced increasing criticism from Congress over the war, Hadley publicly defended the administration's actions. After several government investigations concluded that the U.S. had been wrong in its assessments of Iraq's chemical, biological, and nuclear-weapons programs before the war, Democrats accused the administration of having deliberately exaggerated the contents of intelligence reports in order to proceed with the war. In a press briefing, Hadley accused such critics of hypocrisy, since many of them had voted in favor of using force against Iraq. In a briefing, as quoted by Baker for the *Washington Post* (November 11, 2005), Hadley dismissed "the notion that somehow the administration manipulated prewar intelligence" and said that the decisions made about the threat posed by Iraq "represented the collective view of the intelligence community," which "was shared by Republicans and Democrats alike."

In May 2006 Hadley defended the controversial policy of intercepting, without warrants, E-mail messages and telephone calls to and from the United States that were thought to involve terrorists or their affiliates. The program, which Bush instituted following the September 11, 2001 attacks, was overseen by the National Security Agency (NSA), which also built a database of the domestic calling records of millions of people, obtained from the telephone companies AT&T, BellSouth, and Verizon. Many lawmakers and others criticized such surveillance as illegal. After *USA Today* had reported news of the database, Hadley appeared on the CBS program *Face the Nation* to verify the story and assert the program's legality. As quoted by Josh Meyer in the *Los Angeles Times* (May 15, 2006), he said that the *USA Today* article "does not claim that the government was listening to domestic phone calls. It does not claim that names were passed, that addresses were passed, that content

was passed. It's really about calling records . . . who was called when, and how long did they talk?" Hadley also said appropriate members of Congress had been briefed on the program and that the surveillance had "prevented attacks and saved lives." Lawmakers who responded critically to Hadley's comments included Representative Jane Harman, the top Democrat on the House Intelligence Committee, who had been briefed on the program but said, as quoted by Meyer, "This is a lawless White House, out of control with respect to programs like this."

In an interview with Wolf Blitzer for the CNN program *The Situation Room* (June 14, 2006), Hadley acknowledged reports about North Korea's development of nuclear weapons, a topic that would come to the world's attention on July 4, 2006, when the country launched one long-range and five medium-range ballistic missiles into the Sea of Japan, breaking a seven-year self-imposed moratorium on nuclear tests that it had affirmed as recently as 2005. The long-range missile, known as the Taepo Dong-2, was thought to have a range of roughly 9,300 miles, sufficient to carry a warhead to the U.S. "They have basically defied the international community," Hadley said, as quoted by Stephen J. Hedges, writing for the *Chicago Tribune* (July 5, 2006). "It's hard to get a sense of what they think could be achieved by this." In the wake of reports about North Korea's nuclear test in October 2006, Hadley and Condoleezza Rice met with a senior Chinese diplomat, Tang Jiaxuan, to discuss steps for dealing with the threat to peace in Asia and elsewhere.

In her April 2005 article, Sabrina Eaton described Hadley as a "movie buff who relaxes on Friday nights by watching videos and eating pizza" with his family. He is also said to enjoy listening to opera and classical music. He lives in Washington, D.C., with his wife, a Justice Department attorney, and their teenage daughters.

—M.B.

Suggested Reading: *Chicago Tribune* C p1 July 5, 2006; *Cleveland Plain Dealer* Sunday Magazine p9 Apr. 24, 2005, p12 Dec. 18, 2005; *Washington Post* A p25 Feb. 11, 2005, A p4 Jan. 29, 2006

Haggis, Paul

Mar. 10, 1953– Screenwriter; director

Address: c/o Larry Becsey, Becsey-Wisdom-Kalajian, 9200 Sunset Blvd., Suite 820, Los Angeles, CA 90069

Paul Haggis's career amounts to one of the longest overnight success stories in American film history: after more than 20 years as a television writer, producer, and director—whose most recognized cre-

Chad Buchanan/Getty Images

Paul Haggis

ation is the oft-maligned crime drama *Walker, Texas Ranger*—Haggis decided in 2000 to turn his back on his lucrative television career to write and direct serious dramatic films. His first feature-film release, *Million Dollar Baby* (2004), for which he had penned the screenplay, nearly swept the top honors at the 77th Annual Academy Awards, winning the statuettes for best actress, supporting actor, director, and picture. The following year he won the Academy Award for best original screenplay for his directorial debut, *Crash* (2005), which also beat the odds-on favorite in the best-picture category. Andrew Pulver wrote for the London *Guardian* (March 7, 2006), referring to filmmakers and screenwriters real and fictional: "The Lubitsch touch. The Barton Fink feeling. The Haggis . . . halo? A new Hollywoodism may have to be coined. Because it's now clear that whatever that secret thing is that the Academy of Motion Picture Arts & Sciences wants, Paul Haggis has it in spades. . . . Haggis has won, for himself and his collaborators, a staggering total of seven Oscars with his first two films. He's clearly got something. The question is, can you bottle it and sell it on eBay?"

Paul Edward Haggis was born on March 10, 1953 in London, Ontario, Canada. He gained an interest in the performing arts as a youth; his parents, Edward H. Haggis, a road-construction–company executive, and the former Mary Yvonne Metcalf, were the owners of the Gallery Theatre in London, Ontario, where Paul Haggis learned the principles of stage production and playwriting—which he would later apply to great advantage as a television and film producer and writer. (Haggis's two sisters also went on to pursue careers in the entertainment

industry: Kathy is a television producer and writer, and JoAnne works as a film editor.) While a student at the H. B. Beal Secondary School, he began writing plays and developed an eclectic taste in films, enjoying mysteries directed by Alfred Hitchcock as well as the work of the avant-garde auteur Jean-Luc Godard. Inspired by Michelangelo Antonioni's thriller *Blowup* (1966), the tale of a fashion photographer who becomes entangled in a mystery after snapping a photo of a couple in a park, Haggis moved to London, England, as a young man to pursue a career in fashion photography. He failed to break into that highly competitive field, and after a year he returned, penniless, to Canada. He worked briefly as a theater photographer before enrolling in a cinematography program at Fanshawe College, in London, Ontario. During that time he also performed in stage shows with his sister Kathy at the Gallery Theatre.

In the mid-1970s Haggis reluctantly joined his father's construction business. "But [my father] knew I had a different dream," he told Jim Bawden for the *Toronto Star* (April 12, 1986). "Finally one day he just blurted out, 'Son, you're really not that good at doing this!' And he was right. My heart wasn't in it at all." With his father's financial assistance, Haggis moved to Los Angeles, California, and for his first couple of years there, supported himself by working as a furniture mover, a writer of cartoon dialogue, and an on-spec screenwriter, writing for films that either were never made or for which he received no credit. During the late 1970s and throughout the 1980s, Haggis wrote for a number of the most popular shows on network television, including *The Love Boat* and *Who's the Boss?*, and he worked as a story editor for the sitcoms *Diff'rent Strokes* and *One Day at a Time*. At the beginning of the 1984 fall television season, he was hired as a writer for the NBC sitcom *The Facts of Life*, later serving as a producer for that show. At the start of the 1987 season, he was at another network, ABC, serving as a writer for and the supervising producer of the television drama *thirtysomething*, a position he held until 1988. For the 1987–88 season, he received two Emmy Awards (one as producer, the other as a writer), a Humanitas Prize, and the Golden Globe Award in the television-drama category.

Over the next few years, Haggis wrote for the hit TV drama *L.A. Law* while also creating and producing shows of his own, including such short-lived programs as *You Take the Kids* (1990), *City* (1990), and *Michael Hayes* (1997). Along with some misfires, he helped develop four noteworthy programs. Beginning in 1994 he produced, wrote, and directed *Due South*, a comedy series of his own creation that poked fun at American stereotypes about Canadians; in a classic odd-couple scenario, a virtuous, polite Mountie moves to Chicago and is assigned a rough-around-the-edges American street cop for a partner. Though the show was a hit with audiences in Canada, where it aired on CTV, American audiences, who could see the show on

CBS, were less enthusiastic; the American network canceled the show after one season. It continued to air in Canada until 1996, but without the co-production money from CBS, Haggis had to take a pay cut and assume the title of creative consultant. In 1995 Haggis won four Gemini Awards from the Academy of Canadian Cinema and Television for *Due South*, and the following year he received three more awards from the academy, including the Chrysler's Canada's Choice Award.

Haggis then served as the executive producer of *EZ Streets* (1996–97), another program that he had created and for which he received a Television Critics Association Award for best program of the year. Critics raved about that gritty crime drama, and Elaine Showalter, writing for *People* (October 28, 1996), described Haggis as the "new TV genius on the block," declaring the show an instant classic. "The most innovative show of the season, *EZ Streets* has plenty of action and some scenes of shocking violence," Showalter wrote, "but Haggis's vision is brilliant TV-noir (think *Chinatown* or *The Usual Suspects*), complete with murky urban settings, a haunting score, suave sociopaths and even a slumming femme fatale." Despite its popularity with the press, the show lasted for only one season.

Haggis's next project, *Family Law*, which featured the small-screen luminaries Dixie Carter and Tony Danza, fared miserably with critics and was canceled after three seasons due to low ratings. His most enduring television creation of all was *Walker, Texas Ranger* (1993–2001), a crime drama starring the martial-arts expert Chuck Norris that was critically panned but proved to be extremely popular, much to Haggis's later embarrassment. In an interview with a reporter for *Entertainment Weekly* (May 20, 2005), Haggis explained that his jump into serious filmmaking was due in part to his dislike of that series: "I had to do something to erase that. I wanted to find something that scared me. I had written too many things that didn't ask questions about who I am."

In 2000, burned out from his TV work, Haggis turned to writing for feature films. (In 1993 he had written and directed *Red Hot*, a direct-to-video release about rock music in the Soviet Union of the 1950s, but that movie had garnered little attention.) He had recently secured the film rights—paying the fee by mortgaging his home—to *Rope Burns: Stories from the Corner* (2000), a collection of tales written by F. X. Toole, the pen name of Jerry Boyd, a former boxing manager. Haggis shaped two of the stories into a screenplay titled *Million Dollar Baby*. Adapting the stories was difficult, as they were not obviously movie material, and securing funding for the film and attracting big-name actors to the project proved to be even more arduous. Eventually, Haggis managed to sign on the Academy Award–winning actors Morgan Freeman and Hilary Swank, but he still needed a leading man. After much effort he attracted the interest of the legendary actor and director Clint Eastwood, who

was not only eager to star in the film but wanted to direct it as well—which Haggis had planned to do himself. Wanting to get his screenplay produced, Haggis agreed to let Eastwood helm the film, which debuted in 2004.

In the film Maggie Fitzgerald (played by Swank) is an impoverished 31-year-old waitress who dreams of success as a boxer. She recruits the hardened boxing trainer Frankie Dunn (played by Eastwood) to coach her and manage her career. Though he has no interest in training her at first, Frankie is persuaded to do so by his old friend, Eddie "Scrap-Iron" Dupris (played by Freeman), who recognizes Maggie's potential to become a champion. The film was roundly praised by critics. In a representative review, A. O. Scott wrote for the *New York Times* (December 15, 2004, on-line) that the film was "the best movie released by a major Hollywood studio this year, and not because it is the grandest, the most ambitious or even the most original. On the contrary: it is a quiet, intimately scaled three-person drama directed in a patient, easygoing style, without any of the displays of allusive cleverness or formal gimmickry that so often masquerade as important filmmaking these days." Haggis won the University of Southern California Scripter Award and was nominated for the Academy Award for best adapted screenplay in 2005. Though Haggis lost to Alexander Payne and Jim Taylor, who won with their screenplay for *Sideways, Million Dollar Baby* garnered four of the most prestigious statuettes, winning not only the best-picture award but also a best-director award for Eastwood, a best-actress award for Swank, and a best-supporting-actor award for Freeman.

Despite the critical acclaim that Haggis received for his script, he came under fire—from advocates for the disabled and such conservative commentators as Michael Medved and Rush Limbaugh—for the ending of *Million Dollar Baby*, in which Maggie requests assistance in committing suicide after suffering a spinal-cord injury that has left her paralyzed. "This movie is a corny, melodramatic assault on people with disabilities," Stephen Drake wrote for the Web site of the activist group Not Dead Yet, which picketed the film in Chicago, according to Sharon Waxman in the *New York Times* (January 31, 2005). "It plays out killing as a romantic fantasy and gives emotional life to the 'better dead than disabled' mindset lurking in the heart of the typical (read: nondisabled) audience member." Haggis and Eastwood, however, were unapologetic. "People trying to politicize these difficult decisions—decisions that people have to make every day, decisions that I have had to make in my own life—is just insensitive," Haggis told Katherine Monk for the *Edmonton Journal* (May 7, 2005). "For someone to judge someone else's morality based on these decisions is just the height of arrogance."

At about the same time that Eastwood was filming *Million Dollar Baby*, Haggis was at work directing *Crash* (2005), a film that dealt with an equally controversial issue—race relations. Four years earlier Haggis and Bobby Moresco had written the screenplay, which, like the script of *Million Dollar Baby*, had initially garnered very little interest in Hollywood. The film's overlapping story lines about race, class, and crime in modern-day Los Angeles were based on Haggis's own experience as the victim of a carjacking in the early 1990s. The controversial nature of the story scared away most producers. Eventually, Haggis's production partner, Mark R. Harris, secured funding, and Haggis began filming in 2003 with an all-star cast that included Don Cheadle, Sandra Bullock, Matt Dillon, Brendan Fraser, Thandie Newton, and Ryan Phillippe. In the middle of filming, Haggis suffered a heart attack and returned to work two weeks later. "The doctor said, 'I'm sorry, but I can't let you go back. It's too much stress,'" Haggis recalled to Coeli Carr in an interview for *Time* (April 3, 2006). "I said, 'I totally understand. So how much stress do you think it'll be for me to be sitting at home while, say, another director finishes my film?' We had a nurse on the set."

Unlike *Million Dollar Baby*, *Crash* received mixed reviews. In the *Los Angeles Times* (May 6, 2005, on-line), Carina Chocano described it as "a grim, histrionic experiment." She complained, "What really makes you want to screw up your eyes, clap your hands over your ears and belt out a show tune, though, is the nagging feeling that Haggis . . . seems to have experienced some misplaced guilt over his lingering low opinion of the gentlemen who took his car, followed by anger at the guilt, more guilt at the anger, and so on. I'm only guessing, of course, but upon meditating on the lives of his assailants—what were they like in their free time, when they *weren't* sticking guns in people's faces?—the director has written them a funny valentine. They are reborn in his imagination as a couple of charming, clever, philosophical, socially committed young car thieves who, when not busy jacking SUVs, enjoy ice hockey, Merle Haggard and liberating smuggled Asian sweatshop workers into the free market wonderland of downtown L.A." On the other hand, David Denby, in his review for the *New Yorker* (May 2, 2005, on-line), cheered: "*Crash* is hyper-articulate and often breathtakingly intelligent and always brazenly alive. . . . In the first twenty minutes or so, the racial comments are so blunt and the dialogue so incisive that you may want to shield yourself from the daggers flying across the screen by getting up and leaving. That would be a mistake. *Crash* stretches the boundaries: after the cantankerous early scenes, it pulls us into the multiple stories it has to tell and becomes intensely moving."

Though critics were at odds over the film's merits, *Crash* was nominated for six Academy Awards, including best picture. Few observers felt that *Crash* had much of a chance at winning the best-picture award in 2006; the director Ang Lee's *Brokeback Mountain* (2005), a film about the forbidden love between two homosexual cowboys,

seemed to have generated most of the season's buzz and was considered the favorite. When the winner was announced, on March 5, 2006, at the 78th Annual Academy Awards, an audible gasp went through the crowd: *Crash* had upset *Brokeback Mountain* to win the academy's top award. (Lee had won the best-director statuette only minutes before, and typically the two prizes are won by the same film.) When Haggis was asked by David Carr for the *New York Times* (March 7, 2006) why he thought the academy honored him, he responded: "I am the wrong guy to ask because I never even thought the picture would get made. . . . To the extent that it connected with people, I think it was time to address the fear and intolerance that we all live with." Haggis also received the Academy Award for best original screenplay and a Golden Globe nomination for best original screenplay.

Three motion pictures for which Haggis co-wrote the screenplays were released in 2006: *The Last Kiss*, a remake of the Italian director Gabriele Muccino's *L'Ultimo Bacio* (2001); *Flags of Our Fathers*, directed by Clint Eastwood, which depicts the Battle of Iwo Jima in World War II, and *Casino Royale*, the latest installment in the James Bond spy series. He also wrote the screenplay for *In the Valley of Elah*, which is scheduled to premiere in 2007; the story is based on an account for *Playboy* by Mark Boal of the disappearance of an American soldier after he returned to the U.S. from the war in Iraq. Haggis is also writing and directing *Honeymoon with Harry*, which is due to be released in 2008.

A co-founder of Artists for Peace and Justice, Haggis has received numerous awards for his commitment to humanitarian and environmental causes, including the Valentine Davies Award from the Writers Guild of America, West, for "contributions to the entertainment industry and the community-at-large [that] have brought dignity and honor to writers everywhere," according to the organization's Web site. He serves on the boards of directors of the Hollywood Education and Literacy Project, the Environmental Media Association, and the Earth Communications Office. He also serves on the advisory board of the Center for the Advancement of Nonviolence and is a member of the President's Council of the Defenders of Wildlife.

Paul Haggis's first marriage, to Diane Christine Gettas (sometimes printed as "Gattas"), lasted from 1977 to 1994 and produced three daughters. He has been married to the actress Deborah Rennard since 1997; they couple live in Santa Monica, California, and have one son.

—C.M.

Suggested Reading: All Movie Guide Web site; *Chicago Sun-Times* (on-line) Jan. 7, 2005; *Entertainment Weekly* p38+ May 20, 2005; Internet Movie Database Web site; *Los Angeles Times* (on-line) May 6, 2005; *New York Times* (on-line) Dec. 15, 2004; *New Yorker* (on-line) May 2, 2005

Selected Films: as screenwriter—*Million Dollar Baby*, 2004; *The Last Kiss*, 2006; *Flags of Our Fathers*, 2006; *Casino Royale*, 2006; as screenwriter and director—*Crash*, 2005

Selected Television Shows: *The Facts of Life*, 1984–1986; *thirtysomething*, 1987–88; *Walker, Texas Ranger*, 1993; *Due South*, 1994–96; *EZ Streets*, 1996; *Family Law*, 1999–2002

Scott Gries/Getty Images

Hammer, Bonnie

1951(?)– Cable-television executive

Address: Sci-Fi Channel, c/o Vivendi Universal, 100 Universal City Plaza, Universal City, CA 91608

"Why is Sci Fi so hot?" Kevin D. Thompson wrote for the *Palm Beach (Florida) Post* (July 12, 2001). He was referring to the USA Network's Sci-Fi Channel, the science-fiction-oriented cable station launched in 1992. Answering his own question, Thompson wrote, "Two words: Bonnie Hammer." After taking charge of the Sci-Fi Channel's programming, in 1998, Hammer quickly revamped its lineup to include fewer old, syndicated shows and more original programs, including miniseries produced by the film luminary Steven Spielberg and a multi-part program based on Frank Herbert's novel *Dune*. The result, as Thompson wrote, is that the Sci-Fi Channel went "from being an industry joke to one of cable TV's hottest networks." In 2004 Hammer became president of USA Network—whose programs include the highly regarded series

Monk—while maintaining her title as president of the Sc-Fi Channel.

Hammer began her career in the 1970s, as a producer for public television, and went on to oversee the creation of award-winning cable-TV documentaries on subjects including racism and child abuse. She moved in the late 1980s to the USA Network, where, in a highly unusual shift, she subsequently found herself in charge of revitalizing the network's wrestling programs. Her success in drawing viewers to the sport, about which she previously knew very little, brought her the opportunity to achieve similar results in the area of science fiction. "In my view," Hammer told James Hibberd for *Television Week* (June 27, 2005), "in terms of production value, USA and Sci Fi can go toe to toe with HBO or any network broadcast any day."

Bonnie Hammer was born around 1951 into an upper-middle-class family in Brooklyn, New York, and raised in the New York borough of Queens. Her mother was a homemaker; her father, an immigrant from Russia, was a former teacher at the Cooper Union for the Advancement of Science and Art, in New York City's East Village, and the owner of a now-defunct, Brooklyn-based company that manufactured pens and pencils. Hammer has credited her father with instilling in her, when she was very young, a determination to succeed. As she told James Hibberd, "There was no sexism, no 'Your brother can do this, but you can only do that.' Everything was on an equal playing field." When Hammer was a child, her parents enrolled her in piano and voice lessons as well as drama classes, and they took her to a Broadway show every month. Hammer also developed an interest in photography during her youth. She attended Boston University, in Massachusetts, where she studied communications and received a B.A. degree in 1972. She then entered the university's graduate program, earning her master's degree in media and new technology in 1974.

After graduate school Hammer embarked on a career as a photojournalist, landing assignments with such renowned publications as *Time* magazine, the *Boston Herald*, and the *Los Angeles Times*. In 1974, while working as a freelance photographer for *Infinity Factory*, a half-hour children's TV series airing on the Public Broadcasting System (PBS), Hammer was offered her first full-time television job, as a production assistant for the show, which was based in the Boston area. The position (which required Hammer to clean up after a sheepdog, among other duties) provided her with the opportunity to observe firsthand how a television program was filmed, and the experience sparked her desire to work in the industry. Following that assignment Hammer worked at the PBS television affiliate WGBH, where she gained even more experience, serving as a producer for *Infinity Factory*, the home-remodeling series *This Old House*, and the critically acclaimed children's program *Zoom*. During that time she also worked on *Good Day*, a morning program broadcast by the

ABC affiliate WCVB-TV in Boston. "I went from the public broadcasting arena where the kind of attitude was 'We don't care who watches as long as it's quality,' to the ABC affiliate, which was 'We don't care about the quality necessarily, as long as people watch.' So it was a great education on two really opposing points of view," she recalled to Hibberd.

After seven years in Boston, Hammer relocated to Los Angeles, California, having been appointed director of development at Dave Bell Associates. There, she worked on the programming side of television, creating reality-based shows and also taking on the role of executive producer for the talk show *Alive and Well*. In 1987 Hammer accepted a position in New York City as a programming executive with the cable network Lifetime Television for Women. She was creator and executive producer of the network's Signature Series, comprising documentaries that tackled the weighty subjects of child abuse (*Child Abuse: Innocence on Trial*), women living with AIDS (*AIDS: Dying for Love*), children in gangs (*Gangs: Not My Kid*), and post-partum depression (*Post-Partum: Beyond the Blues*). Despite her having had no marketing budget to promote the series, *Gangs: Not My Kid* (1988) garnered Hammer several awards, including the Cine Golden Eagle, the National Association for Youth's Mentor Award, and the Lillian Gish Award from the organization Women in Film.

In 1989 Hammer became vice president of original programming at USA Network, where she created the pioneering Erase the Hate documentary series, focusing on issues of racism, sexism, and homophobia. Hammer received a National Emmy Governor's Award for her work on that project. Next, in 1992, she was entrusted by then–USA Network president Rod Perth with overseeing production for the network's wrestling franchise, then known as the World Wrestling Federation (WWF). Hammer, who had not previously watched the sport, initially viewed the new assignment as a demotion and seriously considered resigning from USA Network. "I went home and said to my husband, 'This is where my career has come to?' But I took it with a sense of humor and ended up having the most fun I've had in television," Hammer told Paula Bernstein for *Daily Variety* (November 14, 2001). She watched a televised wrestling match for the first time only two weeks before meeting with Vince McMahon, the chairman and promoter of the wrestling franchise. Hammer took on the formidable challenge of increasing the viewership of the franchise, which consistently drew television ratings of 3.0 in the early 1990s. (A single ratings point represents one percent of viewing households.) Hammer faced heavy competition from Ted Turner, who in 1988 had acquired the promotion company National Wrestling Alliance, renaming it World Championship Wrestling (WCW). Hammer was also forced to contend with the declining popularity of the professional wrestling superstars Hulk Hogan and "Macho Man" Randy Savage, among other WWF personalities.

In January 1993 the WWF premiered the groundbreaking series *Monday Night RAW*. In 1994 the content of the new program was overshadowed by allegations of illegal steroid use among wrestlers and by a sexual harassment suit filed by WWF employees. Although McMahon was acquitted of distributing steroids, the trial tarnished the image of the World Wrestling Federation and took a financial toll on the already struggling franchise. As a result, Turner's World Championship Wrestling organization was able to lure away the WWF's roster of established wrestlers, including Hogan, Savage, Lex Luger, and Scott Hall. In 1995 Hammer moved up the ranks from vice president of current programs to vice president of original productions and current programming for the USA Network. By 1996 the WCW's wrestling show, *Monday Nitro*, had surpassed its head-to-head competition, *Monday Night RAW*, in the television ratings for 88 consecutive weeks, helped, in large part, by the story lines the WCW attached to its wrestlers and by the resurgence of former superstar Hogan, who became the face of the new wrestling franchise. McMahon responded by integrating sex and soap-opera-style story lines into the WWF wrestling show, improving the production values of the match coverage, and developing new talent, particularly "Stone Cold" Steve Austin, in order to appeal to the show's target audience of males aged 12 to 34. The overhaul was successful in reversing the one-and-a-half-year dominance by the World Championship Wrestling. In March 1999 *Monday Night RAW* drew 4.7 million viewing households, and between April and August of 1998, the show ranked ahead of WCW's *Monday Nitro* in the ratings for nine out of 11 weeks. The show regularly ranked among the 10 highest-rated weekly programs in basic cable. Hammer credited McMahon with the turnaround, telling Cindy Kranz for the *Cincinnati Enquirer* (March 12, 1999), "[The WWF's] story lines have become far more fun and interesting and unpredictable. They've developed their stable of characters as bigger than life. They've created an attitude with humor and edginess." McMahon, for his part, gave a great deal of the credit to Hammer. "When she first got the account," he told Kate Aurthur for the *New York Times* (December 4, 2005), "she said, 'Well, Vince, where are the relationship stories?' The what? 'And this story arc needs to be longer.' The what? 'The story arc, Vince.' She defines things for us that open our eyes."

Hammer, who reviewed the content of the wrestling telecasts before they aired, also responded to criticism from parents and child-development experts regarding the increased sex, violence, and profanity in televised professional wrestling. "If you really take a look, the show has no more violence [or] aggressiveness than any prime-time series you have on the air," she told Ann Oldenburg for *USA Today* (August 6, 1998). "Any of the cop shows—look at *NYPD Blue*—they're far more violent. Yeah, there's some sexual innuendo. It's fun though; it's humor. Am I going to have my 4-year-old watch it? No. But my husband grew up watching it, and he wound up in Harvard Divinity School." Hammer was equally successful with the August 1998 debut of another hour-long prime-time wrestling show, *WWF Sunday Night Heat*, which recorded a better-than-expected rating of 4.2. (In September 2000 MTV acquired the broadcast rights to WWF programming, renaming the wrestling show *WWE Heat* after the WWF became World Wrestling Entertainment, or WWE; that change followed a legal dispute with the World Wildlife Fund, over the use of the WWF initials. The National Network [TNN], the network that became Spike TV in August 2003, acquired the WWE's programming rights from MTV in April 2003.) Hammer said to James Hibberd about her experience with the wrestling programs, "I learned a lot about managing, about having to deal with people who had a vision of what they wanted and yet trying to get them to understand your own vision of what you needed for television."

In recognition of Hammer's success in revitalizing the USA Network's wrestling shows, in 1998 she was promoted to senior vice president for programming for Sci-Fi Channel, a USA subsidiary, and for USA Original Productions. The Sci-Fi Channel, launched in 1992, initially offered very little original programming; its schedule featured many old movies and TV shows and only two "home-grown" series per year. Not coincidentally, in Hammer's view, the channel struggled for several years. "We can't exist on acquired shows alone," she told Kevin D. Thompson. "There is no identity connected to taking shows off network or syndication and calling them your own. You can get ratings, you can get visibility that way, but it doesn't help define you." She thus oversaw the creation of new shows for the channel. As Hammer told Diane Werts for the *Milwaukee Journal Sentinel* (April 6, 2000), another of her responsibilities was to make the cable channel more "fun and light and approachable, as opposed to the darker, more Gothic image"—examples of the latter being the old television series *Twilight Zone, The Outer Limits, Ray Bradbury Theater Presents, Swamp Thing, Night Gallery*, and *Mystery Science Theater 3000*. In an effort to make science fiction more accessible to a mainstream television audience, Hammer increased the network's programming budget by 30 percent, resulting in the creation of a greater total of original prime-time programs in the Sci-Fi Channel's lineup, more than other network channels were running. Those original programs included *Farscape*, a space comedy featuring human and Muppet-inspired characters, and *Crossing Over with John Edward*, an unconventional talk show hosted by a medium who claims to communicate with both living and deceased guests. *Farscape* became recognized as the network's first true breakout series. In November 1999 Hammer was named by Barry Diller, then the chairman and CEO of USA Networks, and Steven Chao, then the network's president, to the newly created position of executive vice president and general manager at the Sci-Fi Channel, where she was placed in charge of marketing, advertising sales, and licensing in addition to programming. (Both the Sci-Fi Channel and USA Network are currently owned by NBC Universal.) Her attempt to promote the network as a brand also included the creation of television spots with the tagline, "I Am SCI FI."

In 2000, following a 50 percent growth in the Sci-Fi Channel's television audience, Hammer increased the network's original programming budget by an additional 85 percent. In June 2000 she debuted *The Invisible Man*, a weekly series about a criminal recruited by the federal government for experiments in human invisibility. In December of that year, Hammer doubled the network's previous viewership record with a six-hour miniseries based on Frank Herbert's novel *Dune*; the promotional campaign included video billboards, movie trailers, and Internet advertising. In another effort to develop shows outside the weekly-drama genre, she expanded the *Crossing Over* franchise to include a series, set in the studio, that focused on psychic readings of audience members.

In April 2001 Hammer was promoted to president of the Sci-Fi Channel. Along with her continued focus on heavily promoted miniseries, she actively recruited Hollywood talent to help develop some of the network's programs. The most prominent example was *Steven Spielberg Presents TAKEN*, an ambitious, 20-hour miniseries that aired in December 2002. During that program's 10-night broadcast, the Sci-Fi Channel ranked as the top basic-cable network on television, with an average of five million viewers. The series brought the Sci-Fi Channel its first Golden Globe Award nomination and its first Emmy Award, for best miniseries. By the end of 2002, the Sci-Fi Channel had become the fastest-growing basic-cable prime-time network. The network also had the most-watched cable miniseries in 2003—*Battlestar Galactica*, based on the 1970s television series.

In May 2004 Hammer returned to the USA Network, when she was named president of the cable channel. She retained the title of president of the Sci-Fi Channel. As USA Network president Hammer is primarily responsible for creating a distinct brand image for a lineup of seemingly unrelated programs, including *Monk*, the Emmy Award–winning show starring Tony Shalhoub as a detective who suffers from obsessive-compulsive disorder; the television adaptation of Stephen King's novel *Dead Zone*; the music-competition show *Nashville Star*; and reruns of *Law and Order* spin-offs (*Law and Order: Criminal Intent* and *Law and Order: Special Victims Unit*). In July 2005 Hammer launched a rebranding campaign at the USA Network, using the tagline "Characters Welcome" as a promotional tool for the full range of programs in the network's lineup. Meanwhile, she also continued her focus on new programming, as evidenced by the March 2005 launch of *Kojak*, a remake of the

1970s police drama starring Telly Savalas. (The show, which starred Ving Rhames in the title role of the bald detective, lasted only one season and originally aired on the network as a two-hour television movie.) In October 2005 Hammer brought World Wrestling Entertainment back to the USA Network under the name *WWE Monday Night RAW*.

In 2006 the Sci-Fi Channel began carrying the series Extreme Championship Wrestling and launched several new shows, among them *Eureka*, a drama about a seemingly ordinary town inhabited by scientific geniuses assembled by the government to conduct top-secret research in various fields, and *Psych*, a comedy about an amateur detective who fools the police into believing that he is a psychic. In May the Sci-Fi Channel purchased 11 episodes of *Dresden Files*, about a private eye who is also a wizard. Based on novels by Jim Butcher, *Dresden Files* is scheduled to premiere in January 2007 with a two-hour episode. The actor Nicolas Cage serves as the series' executive producer. Hammer's plans include the development of *Caprica*, a prequel to *Battlestar Galactica*, one of the channel's highest-rated original series and the winner of a George Foster Peabody Award in 2006.

Hammer has received *Hollywood Reporter*'s Top 100 Women in Hollywood Award for four consecutive years and the New York Women in Film's Muse Award for Outstanding Vision and Achievement. She is a member of the board of directors of the National Association of Television Program Executives (NATPE) and the CableACE awards as well as a member of the board of advisers of MPH Connective, a firm that offers media solutions for educational and other projects. She also serves on the Museum of Radio and Television's "Celebration of Women's Achievements in Television and Radio" steering committee and is a mentor for the nonprofit organization Women in Film & Television. Hammer is married to Dale Heusner and has two children, Jesse and Kimae. She lives in Westport, Connecticut, and enjoys photography as a hobby.

—B.M.

Suggested Reading: *Broadcasting & Cable* p49 June 19, 2000; *Daily Variety* A p12 Nov. 14, 2001; *New York Times* p26 Dec. 4, 2005; *Television Week* p18 June 27, 2005

Hammons, David

July 24, 1943– Artist

Address: c/o Jack Tilton Gallery, 8 E. 76th St., New York, NY 10021

"The art audience is the worst audience in the world," the artist David Hammons declared in 1986, according to Kenneth Baker, writing for the *San Francisco Chronicle* (March 27, 1994). "It's overly educated, it's conservative, it's out to criticize, not to understand, and it never has any fun. . . . So I refuse to deal with that audience, and I'll play with the street audience. That audience is much more human, and their opinion is from the heart." Though much of Hammons's work has indeed "played to," or been inspired by, urban street life—as is particularly evident in his assemblages compiled from the debris he has gathered from New York City's streets—his work has also been lauded by critics, shown in some of the world's most prestigious museums, and incorporated into the canon of American art. Still, Hammons prefers to keep the art world at arm's length, occasionally skewering its pomposity in his work—as with a performance piece he called *Blizaard Ball Sale* (1983), in which he stood on a snowy street corner in Manhattan and sold snowballs, presenting a critique of the idea of art as commodity. "Hammons's continuing reworking of the relationship between materials, images, and their meanings focuses on two primary targets—the pretence and commercialism of 'high' art and its ex-

Courtesy of Tribes Gallery

clusionary milieu, and the misguided, even limiting objectives and values of sectors of the black middle class . . . ," Coco Fusco wrote in *The Bodies That Were Not Ours: And Other Writings* (2002). "Other works take swipes at short-sighted materialist values in American life. Indeed, part of Hammons's way of tempering his own success has been to play the role of sly jester, pointing to the hypocrisies and contradictions implicit in whatever context he finds himself." Hammons's reputation as an art-world maverick is such that when the nonprofit Harlem gallery Triple Candie put on an "unauthorized retrospective" of his work in 2006—hanging photocopied images of Hammons's work, after they failed to secure his cooperation in obtaining the originals—many observers wondered whether he, in fact, was behind the show.

David Hammons was born on July 24, 1943 in Springfield, Illinois, the youngest of 10 children—three girls and seven boys—raised by a single mother. "I still don't know how we got by," he told Peter Schjeldahl for the *New Yorker* (December 23, 2002). Hammons, who was placed in vocational classes, excelled at drawing from an early age. In 1962 (some sources say 1963), he moved to Los Angeles, California, where he was exposed to and inspired by the work of such avant-garde artists as Bruce Nauman and Chris Burden. Hammons studied commercial art at the Los Angeles Trade Technical College from 1964 to 1965 and attended the Chouinard Art Institute (now California Institute of the Arts) from 1966 to 1968. He then transferred to the Otis College of Art and Design, also in Los Angeles, which he attended from 1968 to 1972.

During the height of the civil rights movement, Hammons developed a technique known as "body printing," in which he coated himself in margarine from head to toe and then pressed his body against an illustration board. After carefully rising from the board, he used a strainer to sift powdered paint over the entire board, with the margarine-coated sections creating a more intense color. Those pieces, as typified by the ghostly, bound figure in *Injustice Case* (1970), frequently incorporated the American flag and served as commentary on inequality in the U.S. In 1973 Hammons began working on his "Spade" series, in which he incorporated the image of the spade—which was a derogatory term for African-Americans—into his mixed-media work and body prints. "I was trying to figure out why black people were called spades, as opposed to clubs," Hammons said, as quoted by Ruth Mayer in *Artificial Africas: Colonial Images in the Times of Globalization* (2002). "Because I remember being called a spade once and I didn't know what it meant; nigger I knew but spade I still don't. So I just took the shape and started painting it. . . . Then I started getting shovels (spades); I got all of these shovels and made masks out of them. It was just like a chain reaction. . . . I was running my car over these spades and then photographing them. I was hanging them from trees."

In the early 1970s Hammons became restless in Los Angeles—"tired of being the best of a second-rate city," as he told Amei Wallach for the *Los Angeles Times* (August 18, 1991). Additionally, Hammons, who was by then married and the father of two young boys, felt that family life was an impediment to his art. "As an artist, you have to keep reinventing yourself," he told Peter Schjeldahl. "In a marriage, you have to be consistent. It's difficult."

In 1974 Hammons moved to New York City, leaving his family behind. "He wanted to be his own person, not be answerable to anyone, live his own experiences without conforming to anyone," his ex-wife, Roberta Hammons, told Wallach. "He has to live it as well as produce it, and he feels most comfortable immersing himself totally."

In New York City Hammons began to immerse himself in the avant-garde art world, and like the urban-centered artists of the Italian *arte povera* movement that had influenced him, he drew inspiration from street life. Working with the detritus—empty wine bottles, greasy paper, shopping bags, gnawed bones from barbecue ribs, and bottle caps—that he collected from African-American neighborhoods throughout the city, he constructed such assemblages as *Greasy Bags with Barbecue Bones* (1975) and *Lady with Bones* (1983), which were shown in New York galleries and both evoked and challenged stereotypes about African-Americans through the cultural tokens associated with them. "Old dirty bags, grease, bones, hair . . . it's about us, it's about me . . . it isn't negative . . . we should look at these images and see how positive they are, how strong, how powerful . . . ," Hammons explained, as quoted by Sharon F. Patton in the book *African-American Art* (1998). "There's nothing negative about our images, it all depends on who is seeing it and we've been depending on someone else's sight. . . . We need to look again and decide." Though Hammons believed that the full meaning of such works might elude white audiences, critics praised his assemblages. "David Hammons's gifts are many and wondrous," Michael Kimmelman wrote for the *New York Times* (December 28, 1990). "He can take a piece of wire and a few cigarettes and turn them into a chandelier. He can transform a bunch of brown-paper shopping bags, some grease, a few clumps of hair from the floor of a barber shop, bits of broken records and some half-eaten spareribs into something as elegant and ornate as a Japanese kimono. Or into what resembles a folding fan. Or, in the case of *Bag Lady in Flight*, into what seems a tongue-in-cheek reference to [Marcel] Duchamp's *Nude Descending a Staircase*. He is a master of metamorphosis and rejuvenation."

Duchamp, the famous French artist who invented the ready-made (an everyday object selected and designated as art), was an important influence on Hammons's work, but the Harlem-based artist's work emerged from his own cultural milieu. Shortly after arriving in New York, Hammons saw an African sculpture that incorporated human hair and was inspired to use the same material in his own work, sweeping up the clippings from the floors of local barber shops and using them to create tapestries, sculptures, and such Plexiglas mixed-media works as the Dreadlock series (1976). He also pasted the hair on top of stones and returned them to the very same barber shops from which they had come for a trim. According to Sharon F. Patton, Hammons sees hair as "the essential sign of blackness," and he has continued to work with it throughout his career. *Hair Relaxer*, a 2001 installation that illustrated Hammons's penchant for wordplay, featured a pile of clippings spread out, as if relaxing, on a chaise longue, serving as a commentary on the pressure for African-Americans to use chemical products in order to give their hair a more European appearance.

In 1983 he first exhibited one of his most indelible pieces, *Higher Goals*, on 125th Street in Harlem. *Higher Goals* featured basketball hoops held 20 to 30 feet above the ground by telephone poles, which were decorated with bottle caps patterned after Islamic and African designs. "It's an antibasketball sculpture," he told Merrell Noden for *Sports Illustrated* (December 24, 1990). "Basketball has become a problem in the black community because kids aren't getting an education. They're pawns in someone else's game. That's why it's called *Higher Goals*. It means you should have higher goals in life than basketball." Hammons has continued to create representations that reflect on the impact of basketball on the African-American community. *High Falutin* (1990), a heavily adorned basketball hoop, and *Money Tree* (1992), a sepia photograph of a hoop attached to a tree, comment on the importance of money in the sport.

Jazz is another motif in Hammons's work. In a 1989 exhibition at Exit Art, in the Soho section of Manhattan, Hammons explored "the many train references in the music and artifacts of black culture," according to Michael Kimmelman, writing for the *New York Times* (May 19, 1998). A model train snaked through the gallery, burrowing through a mountain of coal, while the music of the jazz legend John Coltrane played. "Next to where Mr. Hammons has glued into an elegant circle several dozen empty green Night Train Express wine bottles, the song 'Drinkin' That Wine' plays on a tape deck," Kimmelman wrote, describing the exhibit. "Bottles of Thunderbird wine, in this punning context, recall the jazz great Charlie (Bird) Parker. And so on. It is, all in all, an amusing idea that arguably has its dark underpinnings. The drug and alcohol problems of Parker and Coltrane are inevitably echoed in the liquor bottles and in the train tracks, a play on the idea of needle marks on an addict's arm."

That same year Hammons gained national attention with the controversy that arose over his piece *How Ya Like Me Now?* For an outdoor installation series that ran in conjunction with the show The Blues Aesthetic: Black Culture and Modernism, which was curated by the Washington Project for the Arts (WPA), Hammons had painted a 14-by-16-foot portrait of the African-American leader Jesse Jackson, portraying him as a white man with blond hair, blue eyes, and the words "How Ya Like Me Now?" written across his chest. The WPA planned to place the portrait for public exhibition in a parking lot in Washington, D.C. However, as the piece, which was painted on tin, was being erected, it was noticed by a group of African-American passersby who took offense, thinking that the piece was disrespectful to the political activist. One person took a sledgehammer to the portrait, knocking down and damaging, but not destroying, most of it. Rick Powell, the curator of the series, told Elizabeth Kastor for the *Washington Post* (November 30, 1989) that the protesters should have taken the time to analyze the piece; the picture, he argued, asks "a simple yet profound question to viewers: Are our likes, dislikes and expectations of people based on their race?" When Jackson himself saw the portrait, he was not offended but said that he understood why the crowd had become upset. "Sometimes art provokes," he told the *New York Times* (December 4, 1989). "Sometimes it angers, which is a measure of its success. Sometimes it inspires creativity. Maybe the sledgehammers should have been on display, too." Hammons took Jackson's advice, remounting the piece elsewhere and surrounding it with sledgehammers.

In addition to addressing racial tensions, Hammons continued to lampoon the consumerism of the art world: at the 1990 Venice Biennale, he displayed *Bag Lady*, a copy of the ancient Greek sculpture Venus de Milo draped with fake Louis Vuitton bags. Back at home, Hammons again found his work raising controversy. P.S.1 Contemporary Art Center, in Queens, New York, an affiliate of the Museum of Modern Art, hosted a retrospective of Hammons's work in 1991 and ran one of his pieces—an American flag with red, white, and blue replaced by green, red, and black (the colors of the African National Congress)—up the flag pole. Displayed at the time of the U.S.-led 1991 Persian Gulf War, the flag drew complaints from local residents who felt it was unpatriotic. Some anonymous residents called in threats to the museum, but the flag remained. According to *Newsday* (February 1, 1991), both Hammons and the museum, represented by managing director Tony Vasconcellos, insisted that the flag "is a positive statement and not intended as a symbol of protest or negativity toward current events in the gulf." To quell the complaints, a conventional American flag was flown outside the art center as well.

Hammons told Peter Schjeldahl that he prefers to exhibit his work in European museums, and he had not mounted a solo show in New York City for 10 years before the Ace Gallery presented the installation *Concerto in Black and Blue*, beginning in the fall of 2002. Inspired by a visit Hammons paid to the Zen Gardens in Kyoto, Japan, the installation consisted of a room that was kept in total darkness, requiring visitors to find their way through the room with flashlights that emitted tiny blue rays of light. "This room is full of light," Hammons explained to one of the gallery's visitors, as quoted by Herb Boyd in the *New York Amsterdam News* (December 11, 2002). "There is a lot of light here, just as the space is full of visibility. It is the absence of something that makes it present." Upon exiting the exhibit, another visitor asked the artist, according to Boyd, "Was there something I was supposed to see?" Hammons responded only by saying, "You saw what you saw." Kenneth Baker, writing for the *San Francisco Chronicle* (February 9, 2003), suggested a connection between Hammons's installation and the work of the composer John Cage, who, in one of his most famous pieces of music, had a pianist simply sit in silence, forcing the audience to listen to the noises around them. *Concerto in Black and Blue* worked similarly; the audience expects to see something, and upon seeing nothing is forced to focus upon itself and the details of its environment. "You meet yourself," Hammons told Boyd of the exhibit. "Of course, *Concerto in Black and Blue* is also Mr. Hammons's latest nose thumbed at the art world, and an especially elegant one," Roberta Smith wrote for the *New York Times* (November 22, 2002). "It mocks the taste for festival art, specifically expensive digital light pieces (those of Tatsuo Miyajima, for example) with a down-home, handmade version. It mocks, as well, the New York art world's expectations of Mr. Hammons's return after more than a decade of self-imposed invisibility. And unlike those snowballs, this new piece requires you to be there to get any inkling of its sly combination of politics, beauty and visual perception." In the last several years, Hammons has shown his work mainly in Europe.

Hammons is the recipient of numerous honors, including a Guggenheim Fellowship, a MacArthur Fellowship, and a Prix de Rome. Since 1989, when Hammons served as a fellow at the American Academy in Rome, he has divided his time between Rome and New York City. "I decided a long time ago that the less I do the more of an artist I am," Hammons told Peter Schjeldahl. "Most of the time, I hang out on the street. I walk."

—R.E.

Suggested Reading: *Los Angeles Times* p3 Aug. 18, 1991; *New York Times* C p33 May 19, 1989, C p24 Dec. 28, 1990; *New Yorker* p156+ Dec. 23, 2002; *San Francisco Chronicle* p37 Mar. 27, 1994, p9 Feb. 9, 2003

Hancock, Trenton Doyle

May 1, 1974– Artist; graphic novelist

Address: c/o Dunn and Brown Contemporary, 5020 Tracy St., Dallas, TX 75205

Trenton Doyle Hancock, one of the best-known artists of his generation, has built his reputation by combining images and narratives to form what could be described as fine-art comic books, ones inhabited by characters named Loid, Painter, Torpedo Boy, the Mounds, and the Vegans. Janet Kutner, commenting for the *Dallas Morning News* (July 4, 1998) on some of Hancock's earliest works, has commended his putting "a fresh spin on 'bad art,'" a paradoxical phrase used to describe sophisticated, well-crafted artworks that seem crude to the untrained eye. "Done on scraps of used canvas or paper glued together piecemeal," Kutner went on to explain, "his mixed-media paintings are full of cartoony characters and childish scribbles, to which he has applied off-the-street materials such as plastic bottle caps and fake fur. But [his] loose narratives . . . are tightly bound compositions reflecting an uncanny sense of line and color." Hancock has since been included in two Whitney Biennials, one in 2000 and another in 2002, as well as in the 2003 Istanbul Biennial, in Turkey, and the 2003 Lyon Biennial, in France. In 2003 he was featured on the PBS series *Art: 21*, which introduced viewers to representative contemporary artists. Hancock has continued to maintain the "cartoony" quality of his art, integrating his characters into a mythological-style narrative. Referring to the British poet and artist William Blake (1757–1827), Lynn Herbert, a senior curator at the Contemporary

Courtesy of Trenton Doyle Hancock and the James Cohan Gallery, New York

Arts Museum in Houston, Texas, observed, as quoted by Jeanne Claire van Ryzin in the *Austin (Texas) American-Statesman* (February 7, 2002), "Trenton is in some ways like a William Blake of our time. In one package you have a gifted artist, a captivating storyteller—someone brave enough to develop his own singular style."

When the interviewer for *Art: 21* mentioned that Hancock has said that the story of the Mounds "comes to [him] in flashes," the artist responded, "I like to refer to it as visions. But when you break it down, you can actually break down a vision into a series of questions. Like after I realized what Mounds were, I had a lot of questions for myself. So where do they come from? How tall are they? Do they eat? Like just all of these types of things. In asking a question you can then have an epiphany because it'll open up the floodgate to twenty new questions. And from there you just keep going and it snowballs. And to me that's what the vision is all about. It's taking notice of things that are around you and then questioning them. And out of those questions will come answers but hopefully a lot more questions. And from there you can just keep your vision growing."

Trenton Doyle Hancock was born on May 1, 1974 in Oklahoma City, Oklahoma. He was raised in Paris, Texas, by his mother, who taught fifth grade, and his stepfather, a Baptist minister, in "a very, very religious family," as he described it to Dan Tranberg for the Cleveland, Ohio, *Plain Dealer* (December 19, 2003); the members of his immediate and extended families attended church at least twice a week. "That's just how I grew up and it was a sense of community," Hancock told the *Art: 21* interviewer. "The church was filled with beautiful stories and great music and it was a very visceral type of experience." An aunt of his introduced him to drawing when he was two, and he immediately became enamored of that activity. "I drew through church when I was little," he told van Ryzin. "It kept me quiet." At school he spent much of his time drawing, but, as he told Kutner, "all my teachers, from kindergarten up, were very supportive. They realized what art meant to me." As a child he also loved comic books and video games, and he dreamed of becoming a comic-book artist. As a fourth-grader he created Torpedo Boy, whom he described on *Art: 21* as "a super hero: he can fly, he can lift things." Torpedo Boy became "a lot more flawed" after his creator reached adulthood, as Hancock told the PBS interviewer, and his uniform, once white, became pink and yellow—"one of the most obnoxious color combinations I could think of. . . . It's very loud and that's kind of what Torpedo Boy is all about. His ego is his force field. That's just how he takes on the world." In high school Hancock drew comics for the student newspaper. He earned an A.A.S. degree from Paris Junior College, in Texas, in 1994, and continued his undergraduate education at Texas A&M University at Commerce. A class in painting that he attended led him to alter his artistic aspirations. "I wanted to bring my first love"—comic books—"back into what I had learned about the Modernists and merge my new experiences with these stories into the physicality of paint," he told Dorothy Shinn for the *Akron (Ohio) Beacon Journal* (December 21, 2003). He graduated from Texas A&M with a bachelor of fine arts degree in 1997.

Hancock made his debut in the art world in 1997, with a solo exhibition, held at a Texas A&M gallery, called Autobiodegradable (which he had put together for his undergraduate honors thesis).

He literally slept through the opening while sitting in a high chair, having forced himself to stay awake for the two or three days preceding the event and then taken over-the-counter sleeping pills an hour before it started. "At least two interpretations of this performance/stunt suggest themselves," Charles Dee Mitchell wrote for *Art in America* (November 1998). "One is that Hancock was lightheartedly forestalling the 'Where do you get your ideas?' questions that his chaotic paintings inevitably prompt, by showing the artist immersed in his unconscious. Or, since this was the qualifying exhibition for his BFA, he could have been presenting himself as a poor overworked artist, so exhausted from cranking out work for his degree that he could not enjoy his own triumph." In 1998, during his first commercial show, called Off Colored—the double entendre of the title simultaneously referring to his race and to the bathroom humor he had incorporated in the works on display—Hancock again slept during the opening while perched on a thronelike chair. In a variation on his previous year's performance, the ringing of an alarm clock would awaken him every half hour, and when his eyes opened, the gallery director would feed him Jell-O—red Jell-O the first time, then yellow, blue, and finally green—while an assistant released similarly colored balloons from under Hancock's tentlike costume. (Hancock has since turned other openings into performance pieces. At one, he hid in a back room while a man who looked very much like him greeted the guests.)

Off Colored, which contained about 20 autobiographical works, was held at the prestigious Gerald Peters Gallery in Dallas, Texas. The themes of the show, according to Mike Daniel in the *Dallas Morning News* (May 29, 1998), included "black masculinity in contemporary life and what [Hancock] sees as an abstraction of emotion: language. The interplay between these two forces could prompt discussions on both how we function as a society and how Mr. Hancock interprets society." Michael G. Auping, the chief curator of the Modern Art Museum of Fort Worth, Texas, told Michael Ennis for *Texas Monthly* (February 2000) that Hancock's themes "are not overtly about racism. They're about Trenton finding his way through life's various social and political complexities as a black male. He's sort of a black Woody Allen, with drawing as his medium." The works in Off Colored introduced to the public such Hancock characters as Torpedo Boy and Coon Bear, some of whom have since been integrated into a larger pictorial narrative. Hancock had already started thinking about this narrative. As he told van Ryzin, "At first I was concerned with getting the whole story into one painting. Then I decided to break it up into chapters. There's still so much about the story I haven't even begun to work out yet."

Also in 1998 Hancock entered the master of fine arts program at the Tyler School of Art, in Philadelphia, Pennsylvania, widely considered one of the best art programs in the country. In 1999 he was awarded a $15,000 Joan Mitchell Foundation artist grant. By the following year, as he was finishing work on his master's degree, Hancock had already established himself among the country's prominent artists, as evidenced by his inclusion in the 2000 Whitney Biennial (held at the Whitney Museum of American Art, in New York City), arguably the nation's most important show of contemporary art. One art dealer thought that that honor was premature in Hancock's case, telling Christina Rees for the *Dallas Observer* (February 10, 2000), "Trenton will be great when he figures out what he wants to do. There's enough in his work to suggest that one day he'll arrive. But if the Biennial was going to include one wildcard young Texan, you have to wonder if Trenton deserved that spot." Most critics who voiced their opinions publicly agreed with that view. Mary Sherman, in the *Boston Herald* (April 9, 2000), described Hancock's contributions as "sophomoric excesses," while Raphael Rubinstein, in *Art in America* (July 1, 2000), derided them as "crushingly derivative." By contrast, Michael Auping, who was one of the curators of that year's Biennial, described what he viewed as Hancock's "sophisticated, sometimes grotesquely self-deprecating autobiographical drawings, such as *Ambijest*, 1998" to be "representative of a new global outlook filtered through personal experience," as Michael Ennis reported.

In 2000 Hancock's work appeared in a solo exhibit called Wow Thats Me at Dunn and Brown Contemporary, a Dallas gallery. The title, purposely incorrectly punctuated, was also that of a painting in the show, which Kutner described in the *Dallas Morning News* (August 5, 2000) as "an entangled web of intestinal shapes struggling to escape, like snakes trapped in a morass, or feelings inside a person. The prevalent color, aside from black, white and gray, is bubble-gum pink, an evocation of flesh." The color pink, which became increasingly prominent in Hancock's work thereafter, signified "intolerance," as Janet Kutner opined in the *Dallas Morning News* (November 18, 2001). The exhibit—in particular, the disappearance of Coon Bear from his paintings—indicated a lessening of Hancock's overt concern with being a black man in America. "People told me I was a black painter," he later explained during a lecture at the Jones Center in Austin, Texas, in 2002, according to van Ryzin. "But I got bored with the dead-end quality of identity politics. The issues just ran in circles, and they weren't as universal as I wanted them to be." In Wow Thats Me, Hancock dealt instead with such issues as alienation, oppression, and otherness—all of which spurred critics to continue to discuss racism when commenting on his work. He also incorporated into his images the Mounds, each a blobbish character that seemed to Kutner to serve as "a surrogate figure with no arms and no legs, battered in some instances—the quintessential suggestion of 'me against the world,'" as she wrote in her 2001 *Dallas Morning News* article. Also present for the first time in Hancock's paint-

ings in public display were the Vegans, creatures who Hancock has described as living underground and as being in conflict with the Mounds.

In 2001 Hancock made his New York City gallery debut, at the James Cohan Gallery. The show, like his previous ones, contained semi-autobiographical drawings and collages, this time telling the story of Legend, a "bulging tree-human mutant who in these works is set upon by vegan gremlins, despite the efforts of the action heroes Torpedo Boy, Painter and Loid," as Roberta Smith explained in the *New York Times* (July 13, 2001). Smith then wrote, "This wouldn't be too interesting if Mr. Hancock's obsessive language didn't also give voice to some of the inner demons that many artists contend with. 'You Deserve Less' rants the roiling surface of the work titled *Painter and Loid Struggle for Soul Control*. Even more important is the voracious, carpet-chewing physicality of his collage technique, which evokes quilting, lace-making and outsider art and, like a lot of more or less two-dimensional art today, seems to push the layered, often collaged images of 1980's painting to new extremes." The exhibit convinced Mario Naves, writing for the *New York Observer* (July 30, 2001), that Hancock is "an artist with a real feel for collage, for the choppy contour created by a pair of scissors and the electricity that is sparked when materials, textures and spaces are juxtaposed just so. He even makes a case for shag carpeting as a viable means of artistic expression. Yet Mr. Hancock's work is never as outrageous or gutsy as it prides itself on being. It's kid's stuff writ with a grubby expertise. If Mr. Hancock wants to build on his gift, he's got to put more effort into getting out of his own head—or at least out of the back pages of old art magazines."

In his interview for *Art: 21*, Hancock said that his mother "is Painter and she is Loid wrapped up into one. She is the smiling face of Painter. She is the color that you get from Painter, but at the same time she could be stern. When she put her foot down, when she spoke her word, you had to listen and if you didn't she made . . . sure that you listened the next time. So she was also Loid. So in a way the mother and father energy in my universe are both my mother."

Hancock's first solo show at a museum, also held in 2001, was The Life and Death of #1, at the Contemporary Arts Museum in Houston, Texas. That exhibition presented the story of Mound #1. As Patricia C. Johnson described it for the *Houston Chronicle* (September 15, 2001), "This primeval, benign creature is a heap of black and white stripes pockmarked by large areas of bubble-gum pink. Usually the stripes are defined by furry fabrics or heavily textured paint and the pink spots slick and soft-looking, like exposed skin or viscera. Mound has a globular head with lidless eyes on extended stems and a round, lipless mouth." The annihilation of Mound #1 was depicted with "an explosion of canvas and paint," in Johnson's words, in the painting *Torpedo Boy Tries His Darnedest to Stop an Oozing Moundmeat*.

Hancock was represented a second time in a Whitney Biennial in 2002. Jerry Saltz, in an admiring review for the *Village Voice* (March 19, 2002), wrote that Hancock, "whose complex narrative canvases looked promising in the last Biennial, delivers on that promise here." Referring to the show's chief curator, Lawrence Rinder (the Whitney's curator of contemporary art), Alice Thorson wrote for the *Kansas City Star* (March 24, 2002), "An almost Calvinist distrust of pleasure pervades Rinder's choices of paintings and sculpture, which are by and large either concept-driven or doggedly representative of non-mainstream approaches," and she cited as an example of the latter Hancock's "hallucinatory collages created from pieces of painted canvas."

In 2003 Hancock was included in the prestigious Istanbul Biennial and the Lyon Biennial. He also had a number of one-man shows in the U.S., among them It Came from the Studio Floor, in the Museum of Contemporary Art in Miami, Florida, and For a Floor of Flora, in the James Cohan Gallery. In the latter exhibition, Hancock presented Homerbuctas, a creature resembling the cartoon character Homer Simpson, who "has a knack for turning impulsion into compulsion," as Hancock wrote on the gallery's wall, according to Karen Rosenberg in the *Village Voice* (March 25, 2003). Rosenberg then noted, "This unfortunate trait leads the ape to indulge an unholy affection for flower beds, siring hundreds of Mounds and ultimately estranging his wife and children." Ken Johnson, writing for the *New York Times* (March 28, 2003) and referring to two giants of 20th-century art and a well-known contemporary artist, saw Homerbuctas as a manifestation of the artist as the "self-gratifying wildman (think Picasso, Pollock and Matthew Barney). He represents a struggle not only within Mr. Hancock himself but within modern art in general: how to reconcile artmaking's self-gratifying pleasures with expectations that arts have social value."

Hancock's exhibition Moments in Mound History began toward the end of 2003 and ran until April 2004 in Cleveland, Ohio. The work on display struck a reviewer for the *Cleveland Scene* (December 17, 2003) as "an excuse to explore various cultural and elemental aspects of Hancock's life, using wallpaper, watercolors, drawings, etchings, and paintings." Describing the exhibit in more detail, Dan Tranberg wrote, "Loosely painted words scrawled across the normally stark white walls wrap around the gallery entrance, describing Hancock's wacky, invented characters, the 'mounds' and the 'vegans.' Inside the gallery, the words continue, casually winding around the space as if an angry child decided to spontaneously compose a story on his bedroom walls. Hancock's more traditionally composed work, some of which is neatly framed, hangs in the same space, creating an intentionally chaotic vibe. Beautifully executed etchings, densely organized mixed-media collages and colorful drawings are hung in discreet groupings.

One wall is covered with brightly patterned wallpaper of Hancock's own creation."

Hancock's next major exhibit, St. Sesom and the Cult of Color, opened in 2005 at the Dunn and Brown Contemporary in Dallas. "Hancock has hit the mark with this multimedia installation," a critic wrote for the *Dallas Observer* (October 6, 2005), "bringing together his talents as graphic artist, conceptualist, painter and, above all else, visionary storyteller." In that exhibition Hancock related the story of the Vegans, telling how St. Sesom, the Vegans' leader, guides his followers from their underground home to the world's surface. "Simply stated," Janet Kutner wrote for the *Dallas Morning Observer* (October 13, 2005), "Sesom, whose name spelled backward is Moses, heeds a call not from a burning bush but from a dream in which he discovers color, a liberating force he wants to share with his flock. Together they embark on a search for a more vibrant existence, an adventure that pits them once more against the Mounds." Charissa N. Terranova, writing for the *Dallas Observer* (October 13, 2005), regarded the show as "a celebration of carefully modulated mess and cleanly delineated lines [that] tells us that craft is back in vogue. Hancock is a young raconteur, and the story he tells goes something like this: In a peculiarly un-PC turn of thought, Hancock has dreamed up a world where Vegans live underground in stoic monochromy. Life for these would-be do-gooders is literally colorless until St. Sesom's prophecy. . . . The tale that unfolds along the walls and in the space of the gallery reveals the Vegans' discovery and production of color by way of Miracle Machines. *Sesom's Mission* and *Sesom's Dream*, mixed-media works on canvas, offer postmodern pastiche disciplined by the tightness of narrative storytelling."

The character Sesom was featured in an exhibit of Hancock's work titled In the Blestian Room, mounted at the James Cohan Gallery in 2006. Near the entrance of the gallery, a pail of Pepto-Bismol dangled from a sculptured arm—a touch that Grace Glueck described, in her review of the show for the *New York Times* (April 7, 2006), as "a fitting accompaniment to a funky but somewhat indigestible extravaganza." The exhibition also included a piece that filled an entire wall with handwritten satirical biblical references and paintings of Sesom leading the Vegans against the Mounds and saluting, in Glueck's words, "the power of color." Also in 2006 Hancock was one of 33 artists featured in an exhibit, called Reverence, at the Hudson Valley Center for Contemporary Art, which celebrated contemporary religious art. Benjamin Ganocchio, who critiqued the show for the *New York Times* (June 11, 2006), found that rather than trying to compete with traditional motifs of religious art, the artists—among them Hermann Nitsch, Damien Hirst, and Shirin Neshat in addition to Hancock—opted "for a display of artworks that trade less in conventional ideas of religious faith than in a wider feeling of profound awe, respect and devotion." "The curators call it reverence," Ganocchio continued, "but essentially this is an exhibition about belief." Hancock's piece, an entire wall filled with text describing his experiences as a Baptist in the South, was one of two pieces (the other was a photograph of Neshat at a mosque) that overtly conveyed the artist's religious affiliation.

In May 2006 Hancock published a graphic novel, *Me a Mound*, which depicts adventures of the Mounds and the Vegans. The book, which offers personal-identity explorations, biblical allusions, references to food and sex, and scatological humor, contains inserts and trading cards. In the opinion of Lisa Gray, who reviewed *Me a Mound* for the *Houston Chronicle* (May 14, 2006), the combination of personal reflections and "poop jokes" was somewhat dissonant. Referring to a comment made by a curator of Fort Worth's Modern Art Museum, who had described Hancock's previous installation there as "seriously weird," Gray wrote that *Me a Mound* "is both serious 'and' weird."

Hancock was awarded a $30,000 grant from the Penny McCall Foundation in 2004. In 2002 he was the Core Fellow at the Museum of Fine Arts in Houston, the city in which he lives.

—A.R.

Suggested Reading: *Art in America* p138 Nov. 1998, p114 June 1, 2003; *Austin American-Statesman* XL p25 Feb. 7, 2002; (Cleveland, Ohio) *Plain Dealer* p54 Dec. 19, 2003; *Dallas Morning News Guide* p52 May 29, 1998, C p8 July 4, 1998, C p5 Aug 5, 2000, C p1 Nov. 18, 2001; *Houston Chronicle* p9 Sep. 15, 2001, p14 Sep. 7, 2003; *New York Observer* p12 July 30, 2001; *New York Times* E p31 July 13, 2001; PBS Web site; *Texas Monthly* p131 Feb. 2000

Selected Exhibitions: Autobiodegradable, 1997; Off Colored, 1998; Wow Thats Me, 2000; It Came from the Studio Floor, 2003; Moments in Mound History, 2003; For a Floor of Flora, 2003; St. Sesom and the Cult of Color, 2005; In the Blestian Room, 2006

Selected Books: *Me a Mound*, 2006

Hastings, Reed

Oct. 8, 1960– President and CEO of Netflix Inc.

Address: Netflix, 970 University Ave., Los Gatos, CA 95032

In the mid-1990s Reed Hastings neglected to return a rented videotape of the film *Apollo 13* (1995) for weeks. The hefty late fee he had to pay worried him, because, as he told John Petkovic for the Cleveland *Plain Dealer* (March 8, 2004), "I didn't want to tell my wife I had blown $40 on a video." "It was my fault in some sense . . . ," Hastings told Damien Cave for *Salon* (June 6, 2002, on-line). "But I realized immediately that it was a poor customer experience. It was also suboptimal for the companies—the retailers and vendors." Hours later, while Hastings was at a local gym, a simple idea came to him: instead of paying to rent each video and keeping track of due dates, customers could subscribe to a watch-all-you-want video service, just as he could work out at his gym whenever he wanted for a monthly fee.

A computer programmer and entrepreneur, Hastings had the business and technical skills to launch an Internet-based movie-rental business. The first company he started, Pure Software, had grown into one of the 50 largest software companies in the U.S. within a few years of its founding, in 1991. After he sold Pure Atria, as his firm was renamed, to a competitor for $525 million (or $750 million, according to some sources), Hastings also had the resources and time to develop virtually any business. Netflix, the company Hastings and

Justin Sullivan/Getty Images

his partner formed after his epiphany in the gym, opened for business in 1998, and during its first year, when Netflix customers had to pay for each movie separately and late fees were charged, it earned $5 million in revenues. Five years later, its revenues had reached more than 100 times that amount. On October 19, 2005, in a conference call to a journalist and financial analysts, Netflix's chief financial officer, Barry McCarthy, predicted that the company would record at least

$940 million in revenues for fiscal year 2006, almost all of it earned from Netflix's patented subscription service. That service, which became available in 2000, allows subscribers to rent—from among some 65,000 titles—an unlimited number of DVDs each month for a single fee (though at any one time customers may keep no more more than a set, maximum number). "Consumers enjoy and are willing to pay for an unlimited model because it gives them freedom," Hastings told Damien Cave. "Some months they watch a lot of DVDs; some months they don't. But regardless, they have the freedom to decide for themselves. It's the same reason why people get the unlimited mileage when they rent a car—they don't want to feel nickel-and-dimed." The phenomenal growth that Netflix has experienced is to some extent attributable to Hastings's luck. Even industry insiders have expressed amazement at how quickly and enthusiastically Americans have adopted the DVD as their preferred medium for watching movies at home. But Netflix's success is particularly noteworthy because the company has had to fight off attempts to win over its customers by the largest company in its field, Blockbuster, and the largest company in the world, Wal-Mart.

In addition to serving as Netflix's president, chief executive officer, and chairman of its board, Hastings devoted much of his time, between 1997 and 2005, and more than $5 million of his own money to reform for California's public schools. A champion of the charter-school movement and president of the state's board of education for most of his four-year term as a member, Hastings also took the helm of the Technology Network (TechNet), a bipartisan educational-reform organization, for six months during its formative years. "I don't know anybody [else] who does all this stuff," the Stanford University education and business professor Michael W. Kirst told Caroline Hendrie for *Education Week* (February 25, 2003). "I've never seen anything like it, and I've been around a long time. [Hastings is] very interesting and unique." In April 2005 the editors of *Time* named Hastings one of the 100 most influential people in the world.

Wilmot Reed Hastings Jr. was born on October 8, 1960 in the Boston, Massachusetts, area. His father, a lawyer, held various governmental positions before serving, during President Richard Nixon's first term, as general counsel in what was then called the U.S. Department of Health, Education, and Welfare. The elder Hastings later returned to private practice in Boston. Reed Hastings finished his secondary education at the Buckingham, Browne, & Nichols School in Cambridge, Massachusetts, before enrolling at Bowdoin College, in Brunswick, Maine, where he studied math. In 1981, at the end of his sophomore year, he won Bowdoin's Smyth Prize, for having the highest math grades during his first two years of college. In 1983 the school's Mathematics Department awarded him its Hammond Prize, given to an outstanding graduating senior. Hastings was accorded highest

honors for his senior project, on Riemann surfaces, which are a way to represent complex functions. After graduating cum laude from Bowdoin, with a B.A. degree in 1983, Hastings spent two years teaching high-school mathematics as a Peace Corps volunteer in the African nation of Swaziland. In 1988 Hastings earned a master's degree in computer science from Stanford University, in California, where he had specialized in the study of artificial intelligence as a member of the university's now-defunct Adaptive Intelligent Systems Project. Before he founded his own company, Hastings is said to have worked for a number of others: the once cutting-edge software company Symbolics Inc. (now no longer in business in its original form); the Palo Alto, California, research offices of the international oilfield technology corporation Schlumberger; the now-defunct software company Coherent Thought; and the networking company Adaptive.

While at Adaptive Hastings met Audrey MacLean, one of the company's co-founders. By then he wanted to start his own software company, and, as he had with other potential investors, he explained to MacLean that his plan was to invent a way to help other programmers speed their products to market by enabling them to identify programming errors called bugs. The process, termed debugging, is one of the most tedious and time-consuming parts of programming, but it is also essential, since bugs can frustrate and even infuriate the people who buy the software (its so-called end-users). Impressed by Hastings's idea, MacLean provided seed money for what Hastings named Pure Software Inc. Hastings readied the company's first product, a program called Purify, in a matter of months; it debuted in January 1992. The key difference between Hastings's program and those of most of his competitors was that Purify ran alongside the program it was debugging, detecting errors that could be found only when the program under development was carrying out the many highly technical and unpredictable tasks performed by all but the most rudimentary of programs. (Competing programs, by contrast, tested the software under development without its running—a much less meaningful measure of how it would work for end-users.)

By most measures Pure was a resounding success. Revenues doubled every year for the first five years, and by 1994 the company became profitable. In February 1995 Hastings announced that Pure was opening subsidiaries in Japan and in several European countries. The following month he acquired a competing maker of programming tools, Qualtrak Corp. On August 2, 1995 Pure began to trade publicly on the Nasdaq stock exchange, in New York, beginning the day at $17 per share and ending at $29.75. Hastings and his early investors became richer by millions of dollars, on paper at least, the moment trading began. Reported to have earned $2.3 million in cash and 10s of millions' worth of stock from Pure's initial public offering

(IPO), Hastings celebrated on the day of the sale by buying an $80,000 car, and not long afterward he left the small house in the woods he had been living in and moved into a house on the beach in Santa Cruz, according to Julie Schmit in *USA Today* (December 26, 1995). "It's like—boom!—you are rich," Hastings told Schmit. Hastings stayed on at Pure, continuing as its president and chief executive officer, after the company merged with its competitor Atria Software, in June 1996. Less than a year later, the combined company, Pure Atria, was acquired by Rational Software in a stock trade worth well over half a billion dollars, with Hastings's share reportedly valued at over $35 million. This time Hastings cashed out, abandoning Pure Atria and, for a brief time, entrepreneurship.

Hastings next entered a master's degree program in education policy at Stanford. His pursuit of the degree, which he never completed, was driven, he has often said, by his frustration at being unable to find qualified employees to staff Pure. While at Stanford Hastings set out to learn how California's educational system, among the most poorly funded in the country, could be reshaped so that it would produce the graduates that the state's technology-driven economy needed. "More and more it's becoming that you have to think for a living," Hastings told Timm Herdt for the *Ventura County (California) Star* (October 17, 1999). "I can't change that, but what I can do is try to help more people get the kind of education that prepares them for that." Like many others interested in education, Reed believed that one way to bring change to American public education was through licensing new or newly reorganized schools that, in exchange for public funding and greater degrees of accountability, are freed from certain government-imposed restrictions and thus able to try a greater variety of approaches to teaching. Called charter schools because the states in which they are located have given them charters or contracts specifying the conditions under which they can operate, these types of schools serve students better, their proponents argue, because they allow local schools to respond to local needs, and they typically involve parents in curriculum development and other aspects of school life to a greater extent than do larger public schools with established and often legally mandated curricula.

At first, in late 1997, Hastings tried to advocate for charter schools by appealing directly to legislators, but they turned him away almost immediately. "I still have scars from that experience," he told Dan Moran for the *Los Angeles Times* (April 16, 1998). Hastings then paired with Don Shalvey, at that time the superintendent of the San Carlos, California, school district, to fashion a ballot measure that would have radically increased the number of schools chartered in California. Called the Charter Public Schools Act of 1998, the act was developed in close consultation with a legal and political team Hastings hired with his own money and was intended to appear on ballots on Election Day in November 1998. Then, in May 1998, California's Republican governor, Pete Wilson, signed a law that enacted many of the reforms sought by Hastings and Shalvey. Beginning in 1999 Hastings and other school-reform supporters introduced a different ballot initiative, that one making it easier for school districts to sell bonds to pay for new public-school facilities; the measure passed in 2000. By then a Democrat, Gray Davis, had been elected California's governor; he appointed Hastings (who had contributed heavily to Davis's election campaign) to the state's 11-member board of education. By March 2001 Hastings had been named president of the board; he retained that position after Davis was voted out of office, in 2003, in a special election won by Arnold Schwarzenegger, a Republican. In early 2005, when Hastings's appointment came up for renewal, Democratic as well as Republican state senators, angered at Hastings's support for the costly bond initiative and for certain types of bilingual education, scuttled his nomination for a second term.

Meanwhile, Hastings had been developing his idea for the mail-order movie-rental business that became Netflix. The biggest problem was that the cost of mailing a videotape to and from a customer could amount to as much as $8, a prohibitively high price. Before long, that roadblock vanished: Hastings learned that the electronics industry would soon offer an alternative to videotape—the DVD (digital versatile disc, or digital video disc), a more highly compressed version of the compact disc. Like CDs, DVDs are roughly 4.7 inches wide and less than one-20th of an inch thick, and they can be mailed as easily and cheaply as a letter, a fact Hastings verified by buying a batch of CDs and sending them to himself through the mail. "I waited for two days—and they all arrived in perfect condition," Hastings told Aline van Duyn for the *Financial Times* (October 4, 2005). "All the pieces started to fall into place after that."

In 1997 Hastings co-founded Netflix with Marc Randolph (formerly, an executive with Integrity QA, a company that Pure Atria had bought earlier that year), who served for about a year as the company's president and chief executive officer; the two were helped by what would ultimately total more than $100 million in outside investments. A press release announcing Netflix's startup was disseminated in April 1998. From the start Netflix offered virtually every movie available on DVD, including obscure experimental films and documentaries and excluding only pornography; unlike any other mainstream rental businesses, the company also featured videos emanating from India's thriving movie industry. Initially Netflix hewed to the traditional rental line: each DVD cost $4, and there were additional charges for delivery and discounts for renting multiple movies simultaneously. Renters were allowed to keep their movies for only seven days, and a late fee applied; customers could also use Netflix to buy DVDs. By the end of the first year and a half, the business was taking in about half a million dollars a month in gross income, but its potential for further growth seemed exhausted. Disappointed, Hastings and his partners decided that to reap a profit, they would have to take bold steps—specifically, introducing movie-rental subscriptions, a service never before tried. "What gave us the courage to switch was the necessity to switch," Hastings told Megan Lindow for the *Silicon Valley/San Jose Business Journal* (November 23, 2001). In mid-1999 Netflix dropped due dates for its films and eliminated late fees, and in December it introduced a flat-rate service that allowed customers to rent four movies a month for $15.95. The changes brought immediate success. Rentals surged 300 percent, and the company began mailing more than 400,000 DVDs a month. Then, in February 2000, Netflix began to offer its unlimited rental program, whereby for $19.95 per month, subscribers could watch as many movies as they wanted (but have at one time only four DVDs). In addition, shipping charges were eliminated. A year later the company had more than 500,000 subscribers, making it by far the leading Internet-based rental company in the world and the fourth-largest film rental service in the U.S. By February 2003 more than one million customers subscribed to Netflix; as of late 2006, the number was 5.7 million.

Earlier, on May 23, 2002, Netflix went public. By the end of its first day of trading, the value of its stock had increased by 12 percent, despite the fact that it had yet to turn a profit on paper. The price of its stock has since risen and fallen several times. One reason for the stock's volatility was business analysts' fear that the company would never reach a broad market because it required consumers to choose movies days in advance of receiving them. To speed the receipt of selections to a day or two, Netflix increased the number of its distribution centers: as of late October 2006, there were 41 of them around the country. Also, analysts and investors have worried that a more established company—Blockbuster or the on-line retail giant Amazon.com, for example—would crush their comparatively tiny rival Netflix; persistent rumors of takeovers have also long threatened Hastings's company, since no one person has a controlling interest in it. (Hastings's share in the company when it went public was 14.9 percent.) For years Blockbuster dismissed mail-order rental as a minor, niche business. Then, in 2002, Blockbuster began to test-market a subscription-like service that cost more than Netflix's and relied on customers' bringing videos to and from their stores, and by the end of 2003, both Blockbuster and the superstore retailer Wal-Mart were offering DVD rentals by mail. Despite such competition, Hastings remained unperturbed, telling Stacey Grenrock-Woods for *Esquire* (December 2003), "There are a hundred details that we've got right that they haven't yet." Among those details were Netflix's admired Cinematch program, which analyzes customers' movie ratings to determine and suggest other films that they might enjoy, and the complex logistics programs that run the company's distribution chain. With its easily recognizable red envelopes, Netflix also had a clear brand identity. In May 2005 Wal-Mart gave up trying to compete with Netflix and recommended that its subscribers join the smaller company; in exchange, Netflix agreed to refer its customers to the Wal-Mart Web site; and while as of February 2006 Blockbuster was continuing to rent films to Internet subscribers, it had suffered stiff losses because of a price war with Netflix and was in the process of closing many of its stores. (In November 2005 Blockbuster announced that its financial troubles might force it to file for bankruptcy.)

In the long run, Hastings has predicted, Netflix will take a leading role in what he and many others have long argued is the next step in home movie watching: video-on-demand, whereby movies or other media products are downloaded via the Internet. He also hopes that Netflix will become a way for less mainstream movies to reach wider audiences. With that goal in mind, he gave postproduction financial support to the documentary *Born into Brothels*, which he had seen on his yearly trip to the Sundance Film Festival, in Utah, and which won the festival's audience award in 2004. The following year the film went on to win the Academy Award for best documentary. Armed with an exclusive distribution deal in exchange for the company's funding, Netflix enjoyed what Hastings described to Julie Schlosser for *Fortune* (June 13, 2005) as the first "exclusive on an Oscar-winning film in the history of retailing."

Hastings lives in Santa Cruz with his wife, Patty Quillin, whom he married in the early 1990s, and their two young children. He and Quillin donated $1 million to Aspire Public Schools, which, according to its Web site, is "a not-for-profit organization that builds and operates high quality public charter schools to prepare urban students for college." The schools have no admission requirements and charge no tuition.

—D.R.

Suggested Reading: *Education Week* p14+ Feb. 26, 2003; *Financial Times* p15 Oct. 4, 2005; *Inc.* p118+ Dec. 2005; *Los Angeles Times* A p1+ Apr. 16, 1998; Netflix Web site; *New York Times* G p1+ Feb. 22, 2005; *New Yorker* p26 Aug. 28, 2006; *Stanford Magazine* (on-line) Jan./Feb. 2006; *USA Today* A p1 Dec. 26, 1995; *Ventura County (California) Star* A p1 Oct. 17, 1999

Mark Wilson/Getty Images

Hayden, Michael V.

Mar. 17, 1945– Director of the Central Intelligence Agency

Address: Central Intelligence Agency, Office of Public Affairs, Washington, DC 20505

When Michael V. Hayden became director of the Central Intelligence Agency (CIA), in late May 2006, he took on what Michael Vickers, a Pentagon consultant and former CIA official, described to reporters for the *Washington Post* (May 7, 2006, online) as "the most important job in the U.S. government when it comes to fighting the global war on terrorism." He also assumed responsibility for restoring the reputation of an agency whose place in the U.S. intelligence community had become uncertain, in part due to the creation in 2005 of the Office of the Director of National Intelligence, which was charged with overseeing all national intelligence activity. Hayden brought a wealth of experience to his new post. A former intelligence officer in the U.S. Air Force, in which he attained the rank of general, Hayden served as the director of the National Security Agency (NSA) from 1999 to 2005 and as the CIA's deputy director in 2005 and 2006. In those positions he earned a reputation as a low-key but strong and thoughtful leader. The retired vice admiral Thomas Wilson, a former head of the Defense Intelligence Agency and a longtime friend of Hayden's, said to Greg Miller for the *Los Angeles Times* (May 7, 2006) that with Hayden at the helm of the CIA, "I would expect to see a real strong effort to bring the agency more fully engaged with the rest of the intelligence community. Always, one of the issues with the CIA was its unwill-

ingness to share information and sources. I would think [Hayden] would try to further the progress that has been made [in sharing information]." Hayden is "exceedingly smart, he's very hardworking, he has great integrity, and he knows the intelligence business," Brent Scowcroft, a former government official and air force general, said to Scott Shane for the *New York Times* (May 18, 2006). "That's a combination that's really needed right now at C.I.A."

Michael Vincent Hayden was born on March 17, 1945 in Pittsburgh, Pennsylvania, into a large extended Irish-Catholic family, and raised on Pittsburgh's working-class North Side. His father, Harry Hayden, was a welder for a company that produced electrical transformers; his mother, Sadie, was a homemaker. Hayden has one brother, Harry III, and one sister, Debbie. As a boy Hayden was an exceptional student; his father has recalled returning home from work after midnight, or leaving the house before dawn, and finding Hayden alone in his room, studying. Hayden also played quarterback for the football team at St. Peter's parochial school. Dan Rooney, the son of Art Rooney, who founded the Pittsburgh Steelers professional football team in 1933, was Hayden's football coach. (Dan Rooney is currently the owner and chairman of the Steelers.) "He wasn't the biggest or the strongest kid on the team, but he was the smartest," Rooney recalled to Scott Shane. "He exuded confidence, and the other kids gathered confidence from him." Hayden's family and the Rooneys were well acquainted as parishioners at the same local church, and as a teenager Hayden took a job as a ballboy for the Steelers.

After graduating near the top of his class at North Catholic High School, Hayden enrolled at Duquesne University, a private Catholic institution in Pittsburgh. (While in college he worked as an intern in the Steelers' offices.) He earned a B.A. degree in history in 1967, the year he joined Duquesne's Air Force Reserve Officers' Training Corps (ROTC) program; he later graduated with distinction from the ROTC. In 1969 Hayden received a master's degree in modern American history from Duquesne; he wrote his master's thesis on the effects of the Marshall Plan on post–World War II Europe. During that period he supported himself and his wife, Jeanine Carrier, whom he had married shortly after completing his undergraduate studies, by driving a cab, teaching, coaching football at St. Peter's, and also moonlighting as a bellhop at the private Duquesne Club.

Also in 1969 Hayden went on active duty with the air force. He was promoted to the rank of first lieutenant on June 7, 1970 and to captain on December 7, 1971. Meanwhile, from January 1970 until January 1972, he was stationed at the headquarters of the Strategic Air Command at the Offutt Air Force Base, in Nebraska, where he was an analyst and briefer. From 1972 to May 1975, he was assigned to Anderson Air Force Base, in Guam, where he was the chief of the Current Intelligence

Division. In the summer of 1975, Hayden completed coursework at the air force's Academic Instructor School, located on the Maxwell Air Force Base, in Montgomery, Alabama. He would go on to complete assignments at Squadron Officer School at the Maxwell Air Force Base, in 1976; at Air Command and Staff College, also in Montgomery, in 1978; at Defense Intelligence School at Anacostia Naval Annex, in Washington, D.C., in 1980; at the Armed Forces Staff College in Norfolk, Virginia, in 1983; and at Air War College at the Maxwell Air Force Base, also in 1983. After completing instructor school, Hayden served until 1979 as an academic instructor and commandant of cadets at the St. Michael's College ROTC program, in Winooski, Vermont. He was promoted to the rank of major on June 1, 1980.

That same month Hayden was assigned the post of chief of intelligence in the 51st Tactical Fighter Wing, at Osan Air Force Base, in South Korea. There, he earned a reputation among the officers assigned to his command as an affable leader, more of "a mentor than a commanding officer," as Vernon Loeb reported for the *Washington Post* (July 29, 2001). Gene Tighe, an intelligence officer under Hayden's command, said to Loeb, "[Hayden] wanted us to see the temples, the rice paddies, go shopping in Hong Kong. He took a vested interest in making you feel important." After spending more than a year, from January 1983 until July 1984, at Air Attache Training School, in Washington, D.C., where he learned to speak Bulgarian, Hayden moved to the U.S. Embassy in Sofia, in the Republic of Bulgaria. In one of his many assignments there, according to the *Washington Post* (May 7, 2006, on-line), Hayden traveled by train across the countryside disguised as a working-class native in order to eavesdrop on the conversations of Bulgarian soldiers. He was promoted to the rank of lieutenant colonel on February 1, 1985.

When he returned to the U.S., in July 1986, Hayden was without assignment until recruited by Charles Link, then a colonel, for a position at the air force's headquarters, at the Pentagon, in Washington, D.C. For the next three years, Hayden served as a politico-military affairs officer in the strategy division of the air force. His deft handling of his responsibilities there won him the approval of General Charles Boyd, then the air force's director of plans, who observed in Hayden an "ability to think conceptually and put his thoughts down on paper," as Vernon Loeb phrased it. Boyd said to Loeb, "[Hayden's] got the soul of a historian. . . . He thinks things are explainable on the basis of how things have been. It's a scholarly bent, combined with an exceptional sensitivity to human behavior." Boyd later recommended Hayden for a position on the National Security Council, under Brent Scowcroft, President George H. W. Bush's national security adviser. Hayden worked for two years as the director for defense policy and arms control on the National Security Council (alongside the current U.S. secretary of state, Condoleezza Rice); part of his responsibility in that position was to write the national security adviser's annual strategic policy document. He was promoted to colonel in 1990. From July 1991 to May 1993, Hayden was the chief of staff for the secretary of the air force at the Pentagon. He was again promoted, this time to the rank of brigadier general, on September 1, 1993.

In May of that year Hayden had moved to Stuttgart, Germany, to the headquarters of the U.S. European Command, as the head of intelligence directorate. That period coincided with conflict in the former Yugoslavia and saw the Bosnian Serbs' violent campaign of "ethnic cleansing" against Bosnian Muslims, with the support of neighboring Serbia. On June 2, 1995 Hayden learned that an American F-16 fighter aircraft, piloted by air-force captain Scott O'Grady, had been shot down over Bosnia, as the craft was patrolling a no-fly zone. O'Grady ejected from the craft, evaded capture, and was later rescued by a Marine unit. The incident had a profound effect on Hayden's view of the role of military intelligence. Hayden had previously recommended that the U.S. take seriously the warnings by Rathko Mladic, a general in the Serbian army, that NATO aircraft must avoid Serb airspace. O'Grady's being shot down demonstrated for Hayden that the traditional role of the intelligence community—to provide support for the military—needed to be rethought, that intelligence "was becoming so essential to make use of and counter sophisticated weaponry that it had become as much of a weapon in its own right as any bomb or missile," in Loeb's words. "It was a kind of redefinition of self, as a professional," Hayden said to Loeb about the O'Grady episode. "It's not about intelligence successes or failures; it's just successes or failures."

Hayden was next appointed as the special assistant to the commander at the Air Intelligence Agency, at Kelly Air Force Base, in Texas. In January 1996 he assumed the duties of commander of the agency and, simultaneously, became the director of the Joint Command and Control Warfare Center. In the former position, as the head of the air force's so-called "cyberwar department," he was responsible for planning the air force's strikes against enemies' computer systems. He was promoted to the rank of major general on October 1, 1996. His next assignment took him to the Yongsan Army Garrison, in South Korea, as deputy chief of staff of U.N. Command and U.S. Forces Korea, from September 1997 until March 1999. According to Loeb, the move signaled that Hayden "had crossed the divide between the bookish world of intelligence into the front-line world of operations."

In 1999 the U.S. House Permanent Select Committee on Intelligence reported that the National Security Agency was in need of a new leader and desperately short on capital. George Tenet, then the director of the CIA, offered the job to Hayden, who became the NSA director in March of that year. Created by President Harry Truman in 1952, the NSA specializes in signals intelligence (or SIGINT), encoding secret U.S. communications and decoding those of other nations; for decades prior to the Internet age, the NSA was the undisputed leader in such activities worldwide. With the end of the Cold War, the shift in focus from monitoring the activities of the Soviet Union to combating such enemies as terrorist groups, and sweeping changes in technology, the NSA found itself struggling to maintain its dominance. In addition, following revelations in the mid-1970s that the NSA had engaged in domestic spying—on individuals ranging from the civil rights leader Martin Luther King Jr. to the singer Joan Baez—many called the agency a threat to the privacy of American citizens and questioned its very purpose.

As NSA director Hayden was credited with fostering the pooling of information between the NSA and the CIA, and he took steps to counter the agency's reputation for being hermetic. He invited journalists and others on tours of the agency's facilities and reportedly brought reporters to his home. Hayden was praised in government circles for bringing the NSA up to date in terms of its surveillance technology. Not all of the reports about Hayden's performance were positive, however. He invested $1.2 billion in a program called Trailblazer, which was meant to streamline the NSA's capacity for sorting through the millions of messages it intercepts each day; the program was reported to be largely ineffective. Also, NSA officers cited frequent malfunctions and system crashes in the agency's computers. "Hayden had a lot of great ideas," Matthew M. Aid, a former NSA analyst, said to Scott Shane. "But when he left N.S.A. . . . none of his modernization programs had been completed, and the agency's fiscal management was still broken." Damaging to the reputation of the intelligence community as a whole was the failure to prevent the September 11, 2001 terrorist attacks.

As the director of the NSA, Hayden was perhaps best known for presiding over a controversial domestic-wiretapping program. A front-page *New York Times* article, among other reports, publicized the program in early December 2005, revealing that the NSA, beginning in the months after the September 11, 2001 terrorist attacks, had been—without warrants—wiretapping the international communications of people in the U.S. who were suspected of having ties to terrorism. Republican and Democratic lawmakers called in early 2006 for a congressional inquiry into the NSA's practice of domestic wiretapping. On January 23, 2006, addressing the National Press Club, Hayden defended the NSA's use of the controversial program, saying, as quoted by the Web site globalsecurity.org: "The 9/11 commission [which investigated intelligence failures prior to the 2001 attacks] criticized our ability to link things happening in the United States with things that were happening elsewhere. In that light, there are no communications more important to the safety of this country than those

affiliated with [the terrorist network] al Qaeda with one end in the United States. The president's authorization allows us to track this kind of call more comprehensively and more efficiently. . . . The intrusion into privacy is . . . limited: only international calls and only those we have a reasonable basis to believe involve al Qaeda or one of its affiliates." He added, "The purpose of all this is not to collect reams of intelligence, but to detect and prevent attacks. The intelligence community has neither the time, the resources nor the legal authority to read communications that aren't likely to protect us, and NSA has no interest in doing so. . . . The program has . . . been reviewed by the Department of Justice for compliance with the president's authorization. Oversight also includes an aggressive training program to ensure that all activities are consistent with the letter and the intent of the authorization and with the preservation of civil liberties."

Meanwhile, on December 17, 2004 President George W. Bush had signed into law the Intelligence Reform and Terrorism Prevention Act, which the U.S. Senate had approved by a vote of 89–2. Many of the provisions of the legislation had been recommended by the bipartisan National Commission on Terrorist Attacks Upon the United States (often called the 9/11 commission), which released a report on July 22, 2004 that identified the major intelligence failures leading up to the events of September 11, 2001. The Intelligence Reform and Terrorism Prevention Act called for the overhaul of the U.S. intelligence community, including the establishment of an Office of the Director of National Intelligence, which would oversee all intelligence operations. In May 2005 Hayden was nominated by President Bush to be second in command to John D. Negroponte, the new director of national intelligence. Hayden's new duties included overseeing the budgets of the various intelligence organizations.

On May 5, 2006 Porter Goss resigned his post as director of the CIA. Goss's appointment, in September 2004, had been disquieting to many in Washington, as he had shown fierce partisanship with regard to important national issues during his tenure as a Republican congressman from Florida. Under Goss the CIA had come to focus on rigorous intelligence analysis rather than hands-on intelligence gathering. Morale among its employees had sunk to all-time lows, according to several reports. The establishment of the Office of the Director of National Intelligence had put Goss at loggerheads with Negroponte; the two disagreed about the direction of the CIA. On May 8, 2006 President Bush nominated Hayden to succeed Goss as CIA director. In light of his role in the controversial domestic-wiretapping program, the American Civil Liberties Union (ACLU) objected to his nomination. As quoted by *BBC News* (May 8, 2006, on-line), Anthony Romero, the executive director of the ACLU, said, "Hayden's approval of warrantless surveillance on Americans raises serious questions about whether the CIA would be further unleashed on the American public." Others wondered if putting Hayden atop the civilian CIA would concentrate too much power in the hands of the military.

In his testimony before the Senate Select Intelligence Committee on May 18, 2006, Hayden elaborated on the NSA domestic-wiretapping program, noting that the program had proved helpful in tracking those suspected of links to Al Qaeda; he did not comment specifically, however, on any of the program's accomplishments. He also shed light on the origin of the domestic-wiretapping program, explaining that he had proposed the program in the days after September 11, 2001, following his meeting with then–CIA director George Tenet. Hayden disputed the notion that President Bush, Vice President Richard B. Cheney, or other administration officials had put pressure on the NSA to ramp up spying on Americans. When pressed by senators to assess the constitutionality of the program, Hayden argued that in a time of war Article II of the Constitution expands the president's authority to conduct domestic surveillance. He also stated that the NSA's lawyers had assured him of the program's legality and that no lawmaker had called for significant changes to the program during the several classified briefings NSA had given before the program was made public. Hayden said that if confirmed as CIA director, he would work to "reaffirm CIA's proud culture of risk-taking and excellence" and ensure that the agency is "field-centric, not headquarters centric," while also maintaining its strong record on intelligence analysis. He also stressed the importance of the CIA's "fitting in seamlessly with an integrated American intelligence community." As quoted by reporters for the *Washington Post* (May 19, 2006), Hayden said: "It's time to move past what seems to me to be an endless picking apart of the archaeology of every past intelligence success or failure. CIA officers . . . deserve recognition of their efforts, and they also deserve not to have every action analyzed, second-guessed and criticized on the front pages of the morning paper." He added, "While the bulk of the agency's work must, in order to be effective, remain secret, fighting this long war on the terrorists who seek to do us harm requires that the American people and you, their elected representatives, know that the CIA is protecting them effectively and in a way consistent with the core values of our nation." On May 23, 2006 the Senate Intelligence Committee voted 12–3 to send Hayden's nomination to the full Senate, which confirmed the nomination on May 26 by a vote of 78–15. He was sworn in as the CIA director on May 30. In mid-June 2006 Hayden announced the hiring of Stephen R. Kappes, who had left the CIA in November 2004, as the agency's deputy director. Hayden and others hoped that Kappes would help boost morale at the CIA and help "stem the outflow of trained clandestine officers," as Walter Pincus wrote for the *Washington Post* (June 19, 2006, on-line).

Hayden's wife, the former Jeanine Carrier, is active in the National Military Family Association. The couple have three adult children—Margaret, Michael, and Liam—and live in Fort Meade, Maryland. Hayden has been described as unassuming and cerebral. "He's not the flashy, fiery kind of guy," Charles Link said to Scott Shane for the *New York Times* (February 18, 2005). "His strength is the power of his intellect and his ability to articulate ideas." Hayden is known to be an avid fan of the Pittsburgh Steelers and often attends the team's home games. He also enjoys cross-country skiing and reading and attending Shakespeare plays. Hayden attained the rank of lieutenant general on May 1, 1999 and, on April 21, 2005, the rank of general. His military decorations include the Defense Distinguished Service Medal; the Defense Superior Service Medal with Oak Leaf Cluster; the Legion of Merit; the Bronze Star Medal; the Meritorious Service Medal with Two Oak Leaf Clusters; the Air Force Commendation Medal; and the Air Force Achievement Medal.

—D.F.

Suggested Reading: Central Intelligence Agency Web site; *Los Angeles Times* A p4 May 7, 2006; *New York Times* A p16 Feb. 18, 2005, I p1+ May 7, 2006, A p22 May 18, 2006; *Pittsburgh Post-Gazette* A p8 Mar. 12, 1999; *Washington Post* W p8+ June 29, 2001, (on-line) May 7, 2006

Hayes, Edward

Nov. 2, 1947– Lawyer

Address: c/o Random House Publicity Dept., 1745 Broadway, 18th Fl., New York, NY 10019

"Criminal law is the only profession in which the better you get, the worse the class of people you represent," the attorney Edward Hayes told David Margolick for the *New York Times* (February 5, 1988). It follows from that statement that Hayes, who currently represents a police officer who was found guilty of carrying out assassinations for the Mob while on duty, has gotten quite good as a defender of criminals. Hayes began his career with a four-year stint as an assistant district attorney in the Bronx in the 1970s, and he has maintained a private law practice in New York City ever since. He has advised or represented such well-known figures as the singer, actor, and record producer Sean "P. Diddy" Combs, the architect Daniel Libeskind, the fashion editor Anna Wintour, the publicist Elizabeth S. "Lizzie" Grubman, and the actor Robert De Niro, "as well as lots of guys with names like Pistol Pete and Little Georgie," as Charles McGrath wrote for the *New York Times Book Review* (February 19, 2006), in an assessment of Hayes's memoir, *Mouthpiece: A Life In—and Sometimes*

Courtesy of Doubleday Broadway Publishing Group

Edward Hayes

Just Outside—the Law. For nearly a decade beginning in 1987, Hayes was ensnared in a high-profile case involving the estate of the Pop artist Andy Warhol; since March 2005 he has been in the news as the attorney defending Stephen Caracappa, a retired detective whom, on April 6, 2006, a jury found guilty of serving as an assassin for the Mafia while working for the New York City Police Department. Writing for *Newsday* (February 14, 2006), Dennis Duggan described Hayes as "the go-to criminal-defense lawyer of the moment . . . and, at 57, sitting pretty much where every lawyer who has scrambled for a buck in crummy courtrooms would like to be." Noted for his colorful persona, Hayes is "serious but fun-loving, hard-boiled but sentimental, the type who hides his book-learning under layers of profanity, who talks tough but is moved to tears at the mention of his mother," according to Margolick. David Friedman, also writing for *Newsday* (December 20, 1999), characterized Hayes as "a dandy who's as at home on Southern Boulevard" (a somewhat shabby section of the Bronx) "as on Savile Row" (the upscale section of London, England, where Hayes buys his custom-made clothing). Hayes counts among his friends Governor George Pataki of New York State, the current (and also a former) New York City police commissioner, Raymond W. Kelly, and the writer Tom Wolfe, who dedicated his novel *The Bonfire of the Vanities* to Hayes. In his assessment of *Mouthpiece* for the *New York Times Book Review*, Charles McGrath wrote, "Every now and then another, possibly more authentic Hayes makes an appearance in the book, one who has troubles with intimacy, suffers from depression, crying jags and rage attacks, and has been in therapy for 30 years. But whenever

that fellow turns up, Hayes quickly ushers him off the page. It's not so much that he's embarrassed as that his self-transformation is so complete he barely recognizes this other guy."

One of the three children of Edward Hayes and Jean (Sowden) Hayes, Edward W. Hayes was born on November 2, 1947 and grew up in a working-class household in the Jackson Heights section of the New York City borough of Queens. His father's job involved both the manufacture of submarine parts and the servicing of submarines; his mother worked at various times as a librarian, salesperson, and package wrapper. He has one sister, Barbara; his brother, Steven Hayes, is an entertainment lawyer. His father was an alcoholic; often, he was physically abusive to both young Eddie and his mother. Once, the elder Hayes ordered his wife to bring his son home from school so that he could thrash him. "The most important thing I learned in the world is that I could take a beating," Edward Hayes recalled in his book. He told Joyce Wadler for the *New York Times* (March 6, 2002), "When you learn at 11 or 12 that even if somebody beats you bad, you will eventually get up, it makes you smart."

Hayes attended the University of Virginia, where he was active in school politics. He graduated in 1969, with a B.A. degree, and then enrolled at the Columbia University School of Law, in New York City. "I was a terrible law student, near the bottom of my class," he told Anthony DeStefano for *Newsday* (March 6, 2006). Of more importance to Hayes than schoolwork were adventures in Manhattan; in his book, he wrote that he frequented late-night clubs in Times Square and supported himself by working at an Irish saloon patronized by prostitutes. "What I liked about New York at the time was that you could go out and something was always going to happen, something you couldn't begin to predict," he wrote. Upon earning a J.D. degree, in 1972, Hayes took a job in the Bronx district attorney's office, where he remained for four years. He was admitted to the state bar in 1973. At the time the Bronx was notoriously crime-ridden, and working in its district attorney's office appealed to him, because he had opportunities to prosecute an unusually high number of courtroom cases. By all accounts, that period was a formative one for Hayes; he "befriended the shrewdest and toughest of the homicide detectives and came to relish what he calls the 'action, intensity and the constant revelation of what was most ragged and raw about human life,'" as McGrath reported. "The two main things he learned in the Bronx . . . ," McGrath also wrote, "are that 'most of the time, law is about power,' and is less concerned with justice than with money, and that 'everything works the same way as the crime business'—meaning that there is always a way around the rules."

When Hayes entered private practice in Manhattan, in 1976, he "spen[t] the first two weeks . . . reading [detective stories by] Raymond Chandler in an empty office at 225 Broadway," according to

David Margolick. Eventually, he benefited from acquaintanceships he had made in nightclubs. He attracted clients with his street smarts, which "appealed equally to lowlifes and to Park Avenue types," as McGrath put it. He also began associating with celebrities, among them the actor Robert De Niro and the writer Tom Wolfe, the latter of whom he met in 1978 at the summer house of a mutual friend, the painter Richard Merkin. Margolick wrote that the two men admired each other's fashion sense. "There is no stratum of life that Eddie can't walk right into," Wolfe told Margolick. When Wolfe was doing research in preparation for writing his novel *The Bonfire of the Vanities* (1987), Hayes and a friend of his, a city detective, gave Wolfe a tour of parts of the Bronx and showed him some of the workings of the New York legal system. Wolfe based one of *Bonfire*'s key characters, the Yale Law School graduate Tommy Killiam, on Hayes, to whom the book was dedicated.

On February 22, 1987, within a few hours of the death of Andy Warhol, Warhol's close friend and business manager, Fred Hughes, who was also the executor of Warhol's will, hired Hayes to manage the artist's estate. Warhol's will stipulated that a foundation was to be formed in his name, for the purpose of encouraging the visual arts; projected sales of Warhol's artwork and his vast collections of knickknacks and other items would generate the money for the foundation, and Hayes would receive 2 percent of whatever such sales brought. Hayes, who at first knew next to nothing about art or the art market, worked full-time on the Warhol estate; for long periods he virtually lived in the Warhol studio in Manhattan, where, as Margolick wrote, he "[ran] the cottage industry of litigation that invariably emerges when the rich and famous die." Hayes secured Warhol's estate, probated his will, sold the late artist's assets, and filed negligence charges against New York Hospital, where Warhol had died following routine gallbladder surgery. He also began taking legal action against profiteers who, without authorization, had produced merchandise featuring copies of Warhol's famous depictions of Marilyn Monroe, Campbell's soup cans, and other images and were attempting to sell it. Hayes believed that at auctions, Warhol's estate would bring as much as $600 million, but the administrators of the newly formed Warhol foundation placed the probable total at closer to $100 million. Hayes, who had been paid a substantial retainer, believed that the administrators had underestimated the estate's worth out of laziness and because they did not want to pay him what he felt he would be owed. For complicated reasons, according to McGrath, Hughes and the Warhol foundation "decided that the assets were actually more valuable to them if they were worth less, and charged Hayes with incompetence and money-grubbing." Ultimately, Hayes was forced to file for bankruptcy after a judge ruled that he owed the foundation money, rather than the other way around. The case ended when Hayes paid the foundation a $700,000 settlement.

For some time after that, Hayes took whatever cases he could get, including very ill-paying ones emanating from Bronx family court; eventually, he succeeded in getting more-remunerative divorce cases. In recovering from bankruptcy he was helped by his connections to Si Newhouse, the owner of the Condé Nast Co., and Newhouses's chief financial officer (CFO), both of whom banked with Chase. After Hayes did a favor for the CFO's brother, Chase decided not to foreclose on Hayes's home. During that period Hayes also became a volunteer commentator for Court TV. Then, in 2000, thanks to the intervention of the channel's president, Henry Schleiff, he became a paid daytime co-anchor on the show *Both Sides*, along with Rikki Klieman. The program was later canceled.

In 2005 and early 2006, Hayes worked alongside his longtime friend Bruce Cutler (an attorney famous for his defense of the Mob boss John Gotti in the 1980s) to defend Stephen Caracappa (Hayes's client) and Louis Eppolito (Cutler's client), two former New York City police detectives accused of secretly working for the Luchese crime family. In what was called the worst scandal in the police department's history, the two men allegedly carried out eight killings for the Luchese underboss Anthony ("Gaspipe") Casso. During some of the early court hearings, Hayes argued that Caracappa was innocent and claimed that his indictment reflected the overzealous drive of the federal government to punish members of the Mob. Alan Feuer wrote for the *New York Times* (April 22, 2005), "It is highly unlikely that there exist in New York City two trial lawyers who get more publicity than Mr. Hayes and Mr. Cutler. Both speak off the cuff, if not always to the point." As an example, Feuer wrote of Hayes's pretrial comments to the press: "After chastising Mr. Cutler for monopolizing the microphones—a gentle joke—Mr. Hayes made a statement that managed to mix together references to a well-known Mafia killer, Representative Tom DeLay and Genghis Khan." After Eppolito and Caracappa were found guilty, on April 6, 2006, a tearful Hayes said to reporters, "I try as hard as I can. You're not doing your job in these cases if you're not doing your best," as quoted by Alan Feuer in the *New York Times* (April 7, 2006). Shortly after the trial Eppolito and Caracappa sought to have their convictions overturned, on the grounds that their respective lawyers had defended them inadequately. In June 2006 Judge Jack Weinstein, who had presided over the case, dismissed those allegations against Hayes and Cutler and described their work during the trail as "highly professional," according to Anthony M. Destefano in *Newsday* (June 28, 2006). Less than a week later, however, Weinstein overturned key racketeering charges against the two officers, because the trial had not taken place within five years of the crimes for which they had been convicted, as federal criminal law requires. After the ruling was announced, Anthony M. Destefano, writing for *Newsday* (July 1, 2006), quoted Hayes as declaring, "We won the case! We won the case!" U.S. attorneys have appealed Judge Weinstein's decision. Meanwhile, a new trial has been ordered for the former officers on more-recent drug-trafficking charges.

Also in early April 2006, Hayes was in the news as one of the attorneys hired by Jared Paul Stern, a *New York Post* gossip writer who was accused of trying to extort money from the billionaire Ronald W. Burkle, in exchange for refraining from including negative comments about Burkle in the *Post*.

Hayes's book, *Mouthpiece: A Life In—And Sometimes Just Outside—The Law* (2006), was written with Susan Lehman, a journalist, editor, and former criminal-defense lawyer. *Mouthpiece*, which is dedicated to Tom Wolfe, who wrote its introduction, describes Hayes's early years and career and offers revelations about some of his past clients. "There is a certain amount of profanity and a certain amount of self-promotion (you would never mistake Hayes for a shy fellow), but there's no denying that he has plenty of charisma," David Pitt wrote of an advance copy of *Mouthpiece* for *Booklist* (December 1, 2005, on-line). "Hayes has made his bones as a go-to guy—as Wolfe calls him in the book's introduction—and at its center, his book is the story of a man who believes so passionately in a person's right to representation that he will put his own reputation on the line for even the most unsavory of clients." A critic for *Kirkus Reviews* (November 1, 2005) described the book as a "tough-guy memoir" that "reveals what drives an archetypal New York lawyer" and as "a brag book about criminals, contacts and cordovans." "It's

also a primer on the machinery that makes Manhattan go . . . ," the critic wrote. "[Hayes's] practice clearly depended on three things: connections, connections and connections—and, maybe, availability."

Hayes was married in 1984 to Susan Gilder, a former model and actress. The couple have two children, Avery and John. Hayes told Joyce Wadler that in one of his first cases as a lawyer in private practice, he defended a gangster called "Pistol Pete" Spriggs who was tried on charges of having had a submachine gun, two kilograms of cocaine, and $30,000 in his possession when investigators, in pursuit of another man, happened to come upon him. Thanks to Hayes's representation, Spriggs was acquitted, and in payment he gave Hayes some of his jewelry. Hayes got cash for it and used the money to buy clothes and shoes on Savile Row. According to Hayes's Court TV profile on the Internet and his book, the lawyer is in the International Best Dressed Hall of Fame.

—M.B.

Suggested Reading: *New York* (on-line) May 23, 2005; *New York Times Book Review* p15 Feb 19, 2006; *Newsday* II p92 Dec. 20, 1990; Hayes, Edward. *Mouthpiece: A Life In—and Sometimes Just Outside—the Law* (with Susan Lehman), 2006

Selected Books: *Mouthpiece: A Life In—and Sometimes Just Outside—The Law* (with Susan Lehman), 2006

Haysbert, Dennis

June 2, 1955– Actor

Address: c/o Paradigm Talent Agency, 10100 Santa Monica Blvd., 25th Fl., Los Angeles, CA 90067

"I don't like stereotypical characters," the actor Dennis Haysbert told Mike Duffy for the *Detroit Free Press* (June 26, 2002). "I always want to be challenged. I always want to have something that's out of the ordinary and something that people can look at and say, 'Oh, that's interesting.'" Haysbert has become best known for his role as David Palmer, the fictional first African-American president, on the Fox network's action series *24,* in which he appeared from 2001 to 2005. He also impressed critics and moviegoers with his performance as Raymond Deagan, a gentle, educated black gardener in segregated 1950s America, in the 2002 film *Far from Heaven*, and he is known by millions for his commanding, trust-inspiring presence in television ads for the insurance company Allstate. Haysbert played guest roles in TV sitcoms and dra-

mas in the late 1970s and 1980s before making his film debut, in 1989, as a voodoo-practicing baseball player in the comedy *Major League*. The six-foot four-inch actor went on to win supporting roles in such high-profile films as *Heat, Waiting to Exhale, Insomnia*, and *Absolute Power*, bringing to those parts authority and a voice described by Jenelle Riley for *Back Stage West* (June 25, 2002) as "a low bass that would make [the actor] James Earl Jones tremble." Haysbert has lent that voice to characters in the Dreamworks film *Sinbad: Legend of the Seven Seas* as well as other animated projects. Noting the variety of roles the actor has played, Duffy wrote, "In an era when television networks are being criticized for a lack of racial and ethnic diversity, Haysbert is a one-man wrecking crew of stereotypes."

The eighth of the nine children (two girls and seven boys) of Gladys Haysbert, a homemaker, and Charles Haysbert Sr., a sheriff's deputy at the San Francisco Airport, Dennis Haysbert was born on June 2, 1955 in San Mateo, California, near San Francisco. Haysbert was born with a hole in his heart, a life-threatening condition that corrected itself during his grade-school years. Even after his heart condition improved, his mother told him that

François Durand/Getty Images

Dennis Haysbert

peared on many other television series, including *Buck Rogers in the 25th Century*, *The Incredible Hulk*, *Laverne and Shirley*, and *The White Shadow*. His first film appearance was in the 1989 comedy *Major League*, as Pedro Cerrano, a Latin American outfielder who practices voodoo in the locker room. (Haysbert also appeared in the film's sequels, released in 1994 and 1998, respectively.) He had his first starring role in *Love Field*, a film made in 1990 but not released until two years later. In a role originally offered to Denzel Washington, Haysbert played Paul Cater, a black man who travels across the country with his daughter in the early 1960s and enters into a love affair with a white woman, played by Michelle Pfeiffer. With its delayed release and lack of publicity, *Love Field* did little to raise Haysbert's profile, although both actors won critical praise and Pfeiffer earned an Academy Award nomination for best actress. Later in the 1990s Haysbert played supporting roles in such hit films as *Waiting to Exhale*, *Heat*, *Insomnia*, and *Absolute Power*. "His turn as a shady Secret Service man [in *Absolute Power*] is a testament to his status as one of Hollywood's top character actors," Kyle Smith and Lynda Wright wrote for *People* (March 17, 1997)..

Haysbert received greater exposure with the success of the TV show *24*, which premiered in 2001. In it he played U.S. senator and presidential candidate David Palmer, who, in the show's first season, is the target of an assassination plot on the day of California's presidential primary; Palmer is guarded by Special Agent Jack Bauer, played by the show's star, Kiefer Sutherland. *24* used an innovative, "real-time" format, consisting of 24 episodes per season, each depicting a single hour of the same day. *24* was critically acclaimed and received 10 Emmy Award nominations after its first season. The show did not find popular success, however, until its second season, in which Palmer took office as the first African-American president. Haysbert liked the complexity of the character, whom he modeled on former secretary of state Colin Powell and former presidents Jimmy Carter and Bill Clinton. He told Peter Brunette for the *Boston Globe* (November 10, 2002), "[Palmer is] a great politician with a dark secret, who really cares about people. He's not a black president, just a president who happens to be black." During the show's second season, Palmer had to contend with a nuclear bomb threat in Los Angeles, the possibility of biological warfare, and potential global war. Brunette wrote, "In dealing with [those issues], he brings a dignity and sense of self-possession to the role that its real-life occupants have not always achieved. Beneath it all, he still manages to suggest the soft core of a vulnerable, caring human being."

he could not play sports until he was older and stronger. She encouraged him to cultivate interests other than sports, which led him to drama. "I used to watch and was fascinated with movies and television shows," he said to a writer for *Ebony* (June 1993). "It wasn't until I was finishing up junior high school that the interest really peaked." "Dennis was a born actor," his brother Al told Jason Lynch for *People* (March 31, 2003). "When we would play cowboys and Indians, you saw the actor in him. He was dramatic." As it turned out, Haysbert also excelled as an athlete in high school and was offered sports scholarships by several colleges, but he was much more interested in theater. "With acting there was a calling and I said, 'I got to do this.' It was about emotional fulfillment," he told the *Ebony* reporter. Still, after graduating from high school, he lacked direction for a time, dropping out of one college (some sources say two) and pursuing acting only tentatively, until an encounter with his oldest brother, Charles, strengthened his resolve. Charles, who was dying of bone cancer at 34, advised Dennis to pursue his passion, telling him from his deathbed, "Tomorrow is not promised." Weeks later Haysbert moved to Los Angeles, California, and auditioned successfully for enrollment at the American Academy of Dramatic Arts in Pasadena. He graduated in 1977. During that time he also spent a season studying and acting at the American Conservatory Theater in San Francisco.

Haysbert next found small roles in local stage productions and television shows. His first TV role was on the CBS series *Lou Grant*, in an Emmy Award–winning episode that also guest-starred the Reverend Jesse Jackson. In subsequent years he ap-

During his tenure on *24*, Haysbert won his most prominent film role to date, that of Raymond Deagan, a gardener, in Todd Haynes's *Far from Heaven* (2002). Deagan is working for an upper-middle-class white family in Hartford, Connecticut, in the late 1950s. The family's homemaker, Cathy, played by Julianne Moore, discovers that her husband, Frank (Dennis Quaid), is having a homosexual affair. Distraught and unable to turn to her gossiping neighbors for support, she begins a friendship with the well-educated, cultured Raymond, a character also confined by the era's mores. "Most black people didn't fit into that '50s Tupperware *Leave it to Beaver/Father Knows Best*/Donna Reed world because we weren't invited," Haysbert told Riley. "What I like to think of with Raymond is that he invited himself." In a review of *Far from Heaven* for the *New York Times* (November 8, 2002, on-line), A. O. Scott called Haysbert's performance "powerful," adding, "On the surface, Raymond is all reticence, decency and good manners—liberal Hollywood's dream of the noble, upwardly mobile Negro. But Mr. Haysbert and Mr. Haynes conspire to subvert this stereotype. . . . They pay homage to [Douglas] Sirk's grandest, most radical picture, *Imitation of Life* (1959), in which Juanita Moore took the cinema archetype of the selfless black servant and turned her into a human being."

In 2003 Haysbert lent his voice to Kale, the title character's first mate, in the animated film *Sinbad: Legend of the Seven Seas.* The co-director of the film, Patrick Gilmore, told Terry Lawson for the *Detroit Free Press* (July 2, 2003) that Kale's becoming the "little voice that challenges Sinbad to do the right thing" reflected Haysbert's influence: "When we first started working on the story, Kale was sort of a yes man. He did whatever Sinbad needed." Eventually, though, "Dennis gave so much spirit, confidence and nobility to the character that Kale's role was actually expanded. There were whole scenes written for Kale based on what Dennis brought to the part." Haysbert has also supplied the voices of characters in animated TV series including *Static Shock, Justice League, Superman,* and *The New Batman Adventures.*

As *24* continued its run, Haysbert expressed a desire to appear in more action roles. Referring to the series of films starring Harrison Ford as a CIA agent turned president, Haysbert told Lynch, "I like where Palmer is going now, but I would love to see him become more action-oriented, like in *Air Force One.*" He added jokingly, "I'm a frustrated action hero." Instead, in a move unpopular with fans—many of whom had suggested that Haysbert himself run for political office—Haysbert's character was written out of *24* during its third season. (On the show, Palmer chose not to serve a second term.) Though he would have preferred to remain on *24*, Haysbert was now able to pursue roles in more action-packed films and series. Beginning in March 2006 he appeared on the CBS show *The Unit,* about a Special Forces unit in the U.S. military, playing the no-nonsense team leader Jonas Blane. The series disappointed most critics. "The jargon-heavy lines in *The Unit* drip with self-importance and drag the series dangerously close to self-satire . . . ," Mark Dawidziak wrote for the *Cleveland Plain Dealer* (March 7, 2006). "When this misfire is on target, it's mostly because Hays-

bert is so much fun to watch, sizing up a mission-impossible situation and taking command." (The show has not been canceled, however, and is now in its second season.) Meanwhile, in 2005 Haysbert returned to *24* for the final six episodes of the show's fourth season, in which Palmer filled in for his successor in the Oval Office, John Keeler (played by Geoffrey Pierson), after Keeler was critically injured in a plane crash. Haysbert's return was short-lived: Palmer was assassinated in the first episode of the next season. The actor was not happy with that decision, telling Andy Smith for the *Providence Journal* (March 5, 2006), "There's not one person I see on the street who says 'I'm glad they killed that character.'"

Haysbert could still be seen during *24*'s commercials breaks, in ads for the Allstate insurance company. Introduced in 2004, the spots feature the actor speaking in his resonant voice about the advantages of Allstate policies. Haysbert, who became an Allstate policyholder when he began doing the commercials, told Theresa Howard for *USA Today* (August 16, 2004), "I like the fact that [in the ads] I'm an advocate, not a pitchman. I'm like a third person experiencing what the company has to offer, but I'm not necessarily connected to the company." For over a decade prior to his work for Allstate, Haysbert had avoided acting in commercials, feeling that most were "not very dignified," as he told Howard.

In recent years Haysbert has taken on more action-oriented parts, appearing in the film *Jarhead* (2005), about the 1991 Gulf war, and in the 2005 ABC miniseries *Empire,* about ancient Rome. Upcoming projects include an appearance in the film *Breach* and the role of the South African activist and statesman Nelson Mandela in the forthcoming *Goodbye Bafana.* Haysbert is a spokesperson for the National Leadership Commission on AIDS, as well as the Western Center for Law and Poverty. In his spare time, he enjoys playing sports, reading, and cooking. Haysbert has been divorced twice and has two children, Charles and Katherine, from his second marriage. According to Jason Lynch, Haysbert lives in a Tudor-style home in San Marino, California.

—M.B.

Suggested Reading: *Back Stage West* June 25, 2003; *Detroit Free Press* July 26, 2002; *People* p77 Mar 17, 1997, p77 Mar. 31 2003

Selected Films: *Love Field,* 1992; *Absolute Power,* 1997; *Far From Heaven,* 2002, *Sinbad: Legend of the Seven Seas,* 2003

Selected Television Shows: *24,* 2001–05; *The Unit,* 2006–

Courtesy of Peter Carni, Banff Centre, Alberta, Canada

Hersch, Fred

Oct. 21, 1955– Jazz pianist; composer

Address: c/o Robert Rund, Arts Consultant, 109 Armellino Court, Hightstown, NJ 08520; 548 Broadway, Apt. 5J, New York, NY 10012

"Fred Hersch is a pristine technician with a poet's soul—a pair of qualities that combine to especially dazzling effect in a jazz pianist," the music critic Joan Anderman wrote for the *Boston Globe* (October 15, 1998, on-line). "He investigates the shape of rhythm and the mathematics of motion as graciously as he coaxes the layers of feeling from a bittersweet melody." Another of Hersch's admirers, Fernando Gonzalez, a jazz critic and producer who is the curator of jazz programming at the Miami Performing Arts Center, in Florida, described the pianist in the *Miami Herald* (February 5, 1999) as "a brilliant technician, a thoughtful, elegant improviser and an artist with a curious ear" and also as "a musician's musician." Expressing similar enthusiasm, the freelance jazz writer Ed Hazell wrote for *Jazziz* (on-line), in a review of Hersch's 2002 three-CD release, "There are plenty of jazz pianists who boast a beautiful tone and an encyclopedic knowledge of the great American Songbook, and pianist Fred Hersch certainly ranks among them. But there is much more to Hersch than lyrical command. As his . . . *Songs Without Words* demonstrates, Hersch is a risk taker who can swing hard and play with emotional immediacy. Few jazz pianists have ever struck as beguiling a balance between technique, feeling, insight, and imagination. . . . Hersch's engagement with each of these songs is so complete that he evokes the sort of secret meanings words cannot."

Hersch, who began performing in public nearly three decades ago, is a composer, arranger, and producer as well as a pianist. He has collaborated with many masters of jazz, among them the saxophonists Stan Getz, Lee Konitz, and Billy Harper, the bassists Charlie Haden and Drew Gress, the drummers Billy Hart and Ed Blackwell, the harmonica player Toots Thielemans, the guitarist Bill Frisell, and the vocalists Diana Krall and Jane Monheit. He has also worked with many lesser-known jazz specialists, including the saxophonist Jerry Bergonzi, the bassist Matt Kendrick, the soprano saxophonist Jane Ira Bloom, the clarinetist Michael Moore, the percussionist Gerry Hemingway, the vibraphonist Jon Metzger, and the vocalists Janis Siegel, Jay Clayton, and Norma Winstone. As the founder of a trio that bears his name (and has had a changing roster of members), he has concertized and recorded since 1986. In total, Hersch has made three dozen albums as leader or co-leader, many of which contain his own compositions, and dozens more recordings as a sideman. His most recent albums are *Leaves of Grass* (2005), with music that he wrote to accompany poems by Walt Whitman, played by an instrumental octet and sung by Kurt Elling and Kate McGarry, and *In Amsterdam: Live at the Bimhuis* (2006), recorded at a solo concert in the Netherlands.

Fred Hersch was born in Cincinnati, Ohio, on October 21, 1955. In his interview with *Current Biography*, he recalled how his interest in music developed: "There was a baby grand piano in the house and I just went to it naturally around the age of four. I picked up themes from [TV] cartoon shows by ear and started class [piano] lessons at five, private lessons at six. Since I always improvised as well as played classical music, the best thing my parents did for me was, starting in third grade, [was to provide me with] private theory, composition and musicianship lessons. So by the time I was out of elementary school, I had studied what most freshmen and sophomores did at a conservatory. This gave me a great and life-long understanding of the building blocks of Western music and made it much easier to transition later in life to jazz and composition." As a youngster he became interested in styles of music in addition to classical, starting with the popular songs he found in his grandmother's collections of Broadway original-cast albums and sheet music. After he completed high school, he enrolled at the New England Conservatory of Music, in Boston, Massachusetts, from which he graduated with honors in 1977. When asked by *Current Biography* how he decided to pursue a career as a jazz pianist, Hersch explained: "I stumbled into it. . . . I always improvised, and jazz is the great common language for improvising with others. I enjoyed the social milieu of the jazz scene in Cincinnati, and the older musicians were very supportive of me (youngsters playing jazz were much more of a novelty in 1973). It seems to be the perfect medium for my particular set of skills."

In about 1978 Hersch moved to New York City, where he hoped to earn a living as a professional musician. Like many others before him, he tried to make a name for himself by working in jazz clubs. He told *Current Biography*, "After I had been in New York for a year . . . I got a week playing duo with the late, great bassist Sam Jones at a now-defunct and legendary club, Bradley's. It was where all the great jazz pianists and bassists played, and I was the first young player to get a week there. Sam subsequently became a mentor to me, and through him I met and started working with flugelhornist Art Farmer and tenor sax legend Joe Henderson, among others. This connection to him and them was the beginning of my apprenticeship phase which lasted through my twenties." "I did a lot of sideman gigs with the greats . . . ," he told Tim Blangger for the Allentown, Pennsylvania, *Morning Call* (November 6, 2004). "I was lucky. I arrived at a time when it was possible to play for the people who created this music." Much of his work was far less glamorous and fulfilling, though. "I spent all of my 20s playing basically in dumps," he told Blangger. "I played the Catskills. In restaurants. I played with singers who don't merit the word singer." Meanwhile, starting in 1980, he taught at the New England Conservatory and, in New York City, at the New School for Social Research (now known simply as the New School).

By early 1983, when he was 27, Hersch had "built a steadily growing reputation as a jazz pianist in a variety of situations," as the jazz critic John S. Wilson wrote for the *New York Times* in a review of a concert Hersch had given with the bassist Ratso Harris at a Greenwich Village club. "Mr. Hersch's approach is full-bodied and flowing," Wilson continued. "But it has a lighter touch, a more varied development and a more open exposure with melody than most of his colleagues who work in much the same basic style. Mr. Hersch is a romantic. He is openly involved in what he is playing and projects this involvement with body English and facial expressions that subtly underline the sense of his music. His lines often become gently billowing waves of sound, and he rises and falls, tenses and relaxes along with them."

"I have countless influences," Hersch told *Current Biography*: "jazz musicians (those I have played with and many I have heard on recordings), classical composers and performers, music of Brazil and Africa, but J[ohann] S[ebastian] Bach has been the biggest influence for sure. Much of what I write and play involved four musical voices, and Bach wrote the book on that." Ever an experimenter, Hersch has often blended jazz with classical music in arrangements and original pieces. For a 1989 concert, to cite one example, he arranged works by such classical composers as Mozart, Ravel, Scriabin, and Debussy for the Concordia Orchestra, conducted by Marin Alsop, who had founded the group in 1984 to help break through barriers between traditional classical music and contemporary musical genres. What Hersch referred to as "classical" works that he has composed for solo piano include "24 Variations on a Bach Chorale," a 25-minute piece based on the chorale from Bach's *St. Matthew's Passion*; "Three Character Studies," which include a nocturne for the left hand, a "perpetual-motion Spinning Song," and "a study in thirds and sixths in the style of a chorinho, a Brazilian tango that's a cousin of ragtime," as he put it on his Web site; and "Saloon Songs," which were inspired, in his words, by his "mental images of Lower Manhattan in the early part of the 20th century. All three pieces use dance forms that were popular at that time—the slow drag, the waltz, and ragtime." On a commission from the Doris Duke Foundation, he wrote a score, called *Out Someplace: Blues for Matthew Shepard*, for the Bill T. Jones/Arnie Dane Dance Company; the work premiered at the Kennedy Center, in Washington, D.C., in 1999. The subtitle refers to a young gay man who was tied to a fence post, brutally beaten, and left to die in freezing temperatures in Wyoming in 1998. Hersch has explained that the eight movements of the score "loosely illustrate different meanings of the phrase 'out someplace': social, geographic, gay identity, zaniness, etc." Hersch has performed with such classical musicians as the opera singers Renée Fleming and Dawn Upshaw, the pianist Jeffrey Kahane, and the violinist Nadja Salerno-Sonnenberg, and also as a soloist with symphony orchestras, including the Pittsburgh Symphony, the Toronto Sinfonietta, the BBC Radio Orchestra, and the Sinfonietta Caracas of Venezuela.

The first album that Hersch recorded as a leader was *Horizons* (1984), which featured his trio, with Marc Johnson on bass and Joey Baron on drums. That was followed by, among other disks, *Sarabande* (1986), with Baron and Charlie Haden; *E.T.C.* (1988), with the bassist Steve LaSpina and the drummer Jeff Hirshfield; *Heartsongs* (1989), with the bassist Michael Formanek and Hirshfield; *Evanessence: A Tribute to Bill Evans* (1990), with Toots Thielemans and the vibraphonist Gary Burton; *Dancing in the Dark* (1992), with Drew Gress and the drummer Tom Rainey, and *I Never Told You: Fred Hersch Plays Johnny Mandel* (1994), both of which were Grammy Award nominees; *Red Square Blue: Jazz Impressions of Russian Composers* (1993), with Hirshfield, Thielemans, Steve LaSpina, the saxophonist and clarinetist Phil Woods, the flutist James Newton, and the cellist Erik Friedlander; *Passion Flower: Fred Hersch Plays Billy Strayhorn* (1995); *Fred Hersch Plays Rodgers and Hammerstein* (1996); *Thelonious: Fred Hersch Plays Monk* (1997); and *The Fred Hersch Trio: Live at the Village Vanguard,* (2003), with Gress and the drummer Nasheet Waits, the last of which, Hersch told *Current Biography*, is one of the two recordings of his of which he feels most proud. (The other is the boxed set *Songs Without Words*, with one disk containing original pieces by Hersch, a second offering works by such composers as Thelonious Monk, Duke Ellington, Dizzy

Gillespie, and Wayne Shorter, and a third devoted to songs by Cole Porter.)

Richard Cook, writing for the *New Statesman* (November 6, 1998), expressed the view that Hersch's single-composer compilations—those devoted to Johnny Mandel, Billy Strayhorn, and Rodgers and Hammerstein—were "astoundingly good," and he described the last-named as "a flawless effort." Cook continued, "He picks tunes that jazz players have seldom looked at—'A Cock-Eyed Optimist,' 'Getting to Know You'—and he muses his way through each piece, rarely letting the melody drift from sight. The choruses of each tune seem to unfold as he walks through them, but the voicings and harmonies turn them into arias." *The Fred Hersch Trio: Live at the Village Vanguard*, too, inspired rave reviews. Mark Miller, writing for the Toronto *Globe and Mail* (February 13, 2003, on-line), described the trio as one that "swings easily from the robust to the romantic . . . without every losing its collective sense of balance. Hersch has always been an expansive improviser," he continued, "and it's his imagination that once again animates this performance. . . . There's usually an all-for-one, one-for-all quality to the very best piano trios, and so there is here."

In 1986 Hersch discovered that he was infected with the AIDS virus, but it was not until 1993 that he revealed publicly that he was a gay man living with HIV. "I knew I was gay when I came to New York in the early '80s," he told Kenny Fries for the *Advocate* (April 1, 2003). "I wondered what people would think. I didn't talk about it." Many legendary jazz musicians have also been notorious womanizers; Charlie Parker and Duke Ellington, for example, were well-known for such behavior. Although there have been gay jazz musicians throughout the genre's history, notable among them Ellington's frequent writing partner Billy Strayhorn, few if any had been openly homosexual. As Hersch told Don Heckman for the *Los Angeles Times* (July 4, 1994), "At that time, I knew no other gay jazz musicians, so I led a kind of dual existence—gay friends on one side, musician friends on the other, but never the same. And the funny thing is that the feeling of isolation I experienced in the jazz community [as a gay man] wasn't really that unfamiliar to me, because that's how gay people often feel throughout their lives." By the mid-1980s he had begun coming out to his fellow musicians because "it was starting to mess with my creativity," as he explained to Tom Masland for *Newsweek* (June 20, 1994). "I stopped worrying about what people think." As of late 2005 Hersch had developed no symptoms of AIDS. In interviews Hersch has admitted that he has felt somewhat "up against the clock" since he learned about his infection with HIV, and in some years he drove himself harder than he might have otherwise to accomplish his goals as an artist.

Hersch has worked with the organizations Classical Action: Performing Arts Against AIDS and Broadway Cares/Equity Fights AIDS to raise money for AIDS education and research. As an AIDS fund-raiser, he produced and (along with 12 other musicians) performed on the record *Last Night When We Were Young: The Ballad Album* (1994). According to Celeste Sunderland in *All About Jazz* (February 27, 2003, on-line), that album and two others of his—*Fred Hersch and Friends* and *The Richard Rodgers Centennial Jazz Piano Album*—have raised more than $250,000 for AIDS-related causes. His most recent AIDS-related effort was *Two Hands/Ten Voices* (2003), in which he accompanied jazz, cabaret, and Broadway vocalists in renditions of songs by George Gershwin, Carole King, and others.

On February 28, 2006 Hersch began a one-week engagement at the Village Vanguard, in New York City, thus becoming the first pianist in the 70-year history of that jazz club to play solo for a weeklong gig. In his assessment of one of those performances for the *New York Times* (March 2, 2006), Ben Ratliff wrote, "Mr. Hersch turned songs into double exposures, or triple exposures if you want: melody, harmony and rhythm. That's a visual metaphor, not a musical one, but he has earned it. Mr. Hersch . . . has evolved his solo playing over the years into something special. It plays games with the listener's brain, and can make music seem to spill over into the other senses." Rafliff ended his review by describing Hersch's rendering of Joni Mitchell's song "My Old Man": "Here was a good example of the rapturous Fred Hersch and the meticulous one together: bringing out the richness in the song, he also kept isolating micro-phrases and building logical superstructures on them. He made an incontrovertible argument on behalf of the song, but also on behalf of his own process."

Four years ago, at age 47, Hersch told Celeste Sunderland that his career "keeps branching out and getting richer and more interesting. I still feel like I'm getting better as a player. I feel like I'm just now getting to a point where I'm playing at my potential. Put aside the bull_ _ _ _ and get to the music. I have a lot more confidence now. I'm blossoming right now." When *Current Biography* asked Hersch what advice he might have for an aspiring jazz musician, he responded, "Be a great (not good) musician; be prepared to pay dues; don't focus too early on marketing yourself, focus on what you have to say as an artist; really learn to play your instrument; really study the whole history of jazz music and other genres; don't be afraid to be different as a person and as a musician; don't be afraid to make mistakes, that's how you learn; and stay humble and open to whatever comes your way."

For over 20 years, Hersch told *Current Biography*, he has studied piano with Sophia Rosoff. "She really taught me about sound and continues to help me with the physicality of playing the piano," he said. Hersch lives in New York City.

—C.M.

Suggested Reading: *Advocate* p50 Apr. 1, 2003; (Allentown, Pennsylvania) *Morning Call* D p1 Nov. 6, 2004; allmusicguide.com; *Boston Globe* D p15 Mar. 16, 2001; fredhersch.com; *Los Angeles Times* F p1 July 4, 1994; *New Statesman* p40+ Nov. 6, 1998; *New York Times* I p19 Mar. 26, 1983, C p22 Oct. 29, 1989, E p6 Dec. 9, 2004; *Newsweek* p61 June 20, 1994; *Ottawa Citizen* D p15 June 23, 2004

Selected Recordings: *Horizons*, 1984; *Sarabande*, 1986; *E.T.C.*, 1988; *Heartsongs*, 1989; *Evanessence: A Tribute to Bill Evans*, 1990;

Forward Motion, 1991; *Red Square Blue*, 1992; *Dancing in the Dark*, 1992; *Live at Maybeck Recital Hall*, 1993; *Fred Hersch Trio Plays*, 1994; *I Never Told You*, 1994; *Point in Time*, 1995; *Passion Flower: Fred Hersch Plays Billy Strayhorn*, 1995; *Beautiful Love*, 1995; *Fred Hersch Plays Rodgers & Hammerstein*, 1996; *Thelonious*, 1997; *The Duo Album*, 1997; *Thirteen Ways*, 1997; *Songs We Know*, 1998; *Let Yourself Go: Live at Jordan Hall*, 1999; *Focus*, 2000; *The Fred Hersch Trio: Live at the Village Vanguard*, 2003; *Songs and Lullabies*, 2003; *Fred Hersch Trio + 2*, 2004

Alexander Hassenstein, Bongarts/Getty Images

Holdsclaw, Chamique

(shuh-MEE-kwah)

Aug. 9, 1977– Basketball player

Address: Los Angeles Sparks, 1111 S. Figueroa St., Los Angeles, CA 90015

The six-foot two-inch basketball player Chamique Holdsclaw is widely regarded as the "female Michael Jordan." A forward who developed her scoring and rebounding skills on the outdoor courts of a housing project in the New York City borough of Queens, Holdsclaw led the Christ the King Regional High School women's basketball team to four consecutive championships while the team compiled a 106–4 record. As an undergraduate she helped the University of Tennessee's Lady Volunteers gain three straight championships while she

became the all-time leading scorer and rebounder among men and women in the school's history, with a total of 3,025 points and 1,295 rebounds. She also became only the fifth women's basketball player in the history of the National Collegiate Athletic Association (NCAA) to score at least 3,000 points. In 1999 Holdsclaw was the only college player chosen in the first round of the Women's National Basketball Association (WNBA) draft. That year, as a player with the Washington Mystics, she started 31 of 32 games, scoring an average of 16.9 points per game and earning the league's Rookie of the Year Award. With the Mystics, Holdsclaw did not experience the same success that she had enjoyed as a Lady Vol. In the 2000 WNBA Eastern Conference play-offs, the team failed to make it past the first round, and in their second postseason appearance, in the 2002 WNBA Eastern Conference Finals, the team was again defeated. In 2004 Holdsclaw took a leave of absence because of depression. After requesting that she be traded, she returned to the WNBA in 2005 as a player with the Los Angeles Sparks. Holdsclaw finished the 2005 regular season ranked third in the league in scoring, with an average of 17.0 points per game. She announced that the following season would be her last in professional basketball. She ended the 2006 season with a career average of 17.7 points, 8.3 rebounds, and 2.6 assists per game.

Chamique Shaunta Holdsclaw was born on August 9, 1977 to William Johnson and Bonita Holdsclaw in the Flushing section of Queens, New York. Her father, an auto mechanic, and her mother, who held a civil-service job in data entry, never married but lived together during her early years. When she was five the family, which included her younger brother, Davon, moved to Jamaica, in another part of Queens. Holdsclaw's childhood memories include both fond recollections of barbecues and picnics and troubled ones stemming from her parents' arguments. "The fighting . . . always came after the drinking," as she recalled in her book, *Chamique: On Family, Focus and Basketball*, written with Jennifer Frey. "My mom drank the most, though I think my dad had a problem too. I just remember hearing them scream at each other at night." Holdsclaw and her brother spent much time on weekends and school holidays and during the summer in a public housing project in Astoria, Queens, at the home of their maternal grandmother, June Holdsclaw. A medical-records clerk at a local hospital, their grandmother, and her mother as well, had played basketball as youngsters themselves. During the children's visits to Astoria their mother's brother, Thurman, who then played basketball as a Manhattan private-school student, introduced Holdsclaw to basketball on the large court at Astoria Houses. Although she was not a naturally gifted athlete, she became passionate about the sport. "When I played, it was like everything was okay. Basketball became my shield, a way to protect myself from what was going on in my life," she explained in her book. Indoors, she would practice shooting for hours, using a pair of rolled-up socks and a hoop made with bent clothes hangers. As a youngster Holdsclaw often looked out for her brother. As she wrote in her book, "My parents weren't ready to raise kids. . . . They had their own lives to figure out, their own demons to fight. So Davon and I, we became our own little family. I was the mom, he was the kid . . . he looked to me to bring him dinner, to watch over him, to take care of him, no matter what."

When Holdsclaw was 11 her parents separated, and she and her brother moved in with their maternal grandmother, who provided them with much-needed stability. "My grandmother was older and wiser. She put a lot of restrictions on me. I kind of liked it," Holdsclaw told Maria M. Cornelius for the *Knoxville News-Sentinel* (August 30, 1998). She later became her grandmother's permanent ward. (Her brother returned to their mother's home after two years.) By her own account, Holdsclaw soon became troubled and depressed. "I talked back to my grandmother," she recalled in her book. "I got into more and more fights. . . . I started to reject things that had always been important to me or had made me happy. Once a good student who'd liked school, I stopped caring about my classes." At the local intermediate school in Astoria where she had enrolled, she began to play hooky; once, she skipped school for three days in succession, traveling into Manhattan to play pickup basketball. Rather than repeat sixth grade, as her school's administrators deemed necessary, she gained admission to a small private school, Queens Lutheran School, in Astoria; her grandmother paid the tuition. At Queens Lutheran Holdsclaw began playing organized basketball, on the boys' team, wearing the number 23 on her jersey. (The number refers to Psalm 23, in the Old Testament of the Bible, which, her grandmother advised her, as Holdsclaw told Milton Kent for *TV Guide* [March 13, 1999], "would carry me through whatever happens in life.") Under the close supervision of her teachers, Holdsclaw's grades improved; the stricter rules that her grandmother set (with regard to fixed mealtimes and nighttime curfews, for example) strengthened her psychologically.

Holdsclaw spent her Saturdays at the local Boys and Girls Club, and she was required to attend Sunday church services as a condition for playing basketball. At age 12 she joined the local Police Athletic League (PAL) boys' basketball team, coached by Tyrone Green. She developed her outside shot, fadeaway, and crossover dribble by competing against older neighborhood boys in one-on-one or three-on-three pickup games in which she was usually the only female player; on some days she would remain on the court for as many as eight hours, sometimes until darkness fell. "The boys never liked when I beat them, so we had to keep playing," she told Kelly Whiteside for *Newsday* (March 14, 1999). "They would try to beat me again." Before long she was being chosen ahead of other boys for their pickup teams.

At age 13, as a student at Queens Lutheran School, Holdsclaw and her teammates on the school's girls' basketball team won the Eighth Grade Championship title. Eager for Holdsclaw's talents to develop, in July 1991 Tyrone Green invited to a PAL practice session Vincent Cannizzaro, the coach of Christ the King Regional High School in Middle Village, New York (considered one of the top girls' secondary-school basketball programs in the nation). Holdsclaw's first play, in which—in one fluid motion—she made a quick move against a defender to receive the ball and elevated herself above her opponents to score a basket, so impressed Cannizzaro that he soon recruited her for Christ the King High School.

Holdsclaw made the varsity team, the Royals, in her freshman year at Christ the King (becoming only the fourth girl to accomplish that feat in the school's history), but she went virtually unnoticed, primarily because the team's five starters were all excellent, veteran players, all of whom received Division I college scholarships at the end of the school year. "A lot of times I didn't want to go in the game," Holdsclaw told Michael Dobie for *Newsday* (November 6, 1994). "I didn't want to play in front of a bunch of people. I was hiding at the end of the bench." During her first season Holdsclaw averaged six points per game in limited playing time. Her first start came during her freshman year, in the Catholic High School Athletic Association (CHSAA) Class A State Championship game against St. Peter's in Staten Island, which the Royals won , 58–43. After a 71–42 victory against August Martin High School in the state Federation Class A girls' basketball semifinal, the Royals captured their third straight Class A state Federation Championship, following a 63–43 win against Hopewell Junction John Jay High School. Speaking of the victory against St. Peter's, Cannizzaro told Dobie, "That was the first game she was asked to step up and do something and she did. From then on, the level of play she's been at is phenomenal."

During Holdsclaw's sophomore year, Cannizzaro, whose experienced starting players had all graduated, relied increasingly on Holdsclaw's offensive skills. "She can score inside, she can score up on the perimeter, she can shoot three-pointers as well as any of the guards," he told Dobie for *Newsday* (December 6, 1992). "Her leaping ability is phenomenal, she's almost dunking the ball. Her explosiveness off the floor will be heart stopping. She's the type of player who not only can dominate a game but can create a lot of outstanding moments during the game. She can add a dimension of entertainment to the game." Christ the King was undefeated (26–0) in 1992–93 and captured their second consecutive New York State championship later that season, against Shenendehowa High School, in Clifton Park, New York, thereby earning *USA Today*'s top national ranking; with 22 points and 20 rebounds in the championship game, Holdsclaw recorded a double-double and was named the tournament's top female player. She was similarly outstanding in her junior and senior years, leading her team to two additional state championships in 1994 and 1995. During her senior year she averaged 25 points per game. Over her four-year high-school career, she scored 2,118 points, while the Christ the King team set a remarkable win–loss record of 106–4. As the top female high-school player in the U.S., she was recruited by the University of Virginia, Penn State, the University of Connecticut, and the University of Tennessee. She chose the last-named, in part because her grandmother believed that Pat Summitt, the head coach of Tennessee's Lady Volunteers (familiarly known as the Lady Vols), would prove to be a strong positive influence on her.

Holdsclaw graduated from Christ the King in 1995 and made an apparently seamless transition to college basketball. She became the only freshman in the history of the University of Tennessee Lady Volunteers to start every game. Mickie DeMoss, who was then a Lady Vols' assistant coach, told Wendy Smith for the *Tennessean* (May 3, 1999), "Our first game when she was a freshman, she nailed some jumpers with people right in her face. I kept saying surely this is going to wear off pretty soon, this freshman thing. Then she did it the whole year. She was able to score against big time defenders when she was a freshman. She'd have seniors guarding her. It didn't matter. They couldn't stop her." In her first three games Holdsclaw averaged almost 13 points per game; her 19 points in a November 1995 exhibition against the 1995–96 USA Women's National Team was equally impressive, leading observers to compare her to the Women's Basketball Hall of Famer Cheryl Miller. On March 4, 1996, in the Southeastern Conference (SEC) title game against the University of Alabama, Holdsclaw—the Lady Vols' leading scorer during the early part of the 1995–96 season—suffered a partial tear of the medial collateral ligament in her right knee, forcing her to miss the final games of the regular season. On March 16, following nonsurgical rehabilitation, which included wearing a protective brace, Holdsclaw returned to the lineup for the first round of the NCAA tournament, against Radford University, a winning effort

in which she recorded 14 points and eight rebounds. Tennessee reached the tournament's Final Four, where they faced the University of Connecticut Huskies (whose 59–53 win during the regular season game on January 6, 1996 had ended the Lady Vols' home-game winning streak at 69); Holdsclaw scored 13 points as the team beat the Huskies, 88–83, in an overtime victory that advanced the Lady Vols to the NCAA championship game, against Georgia. In that contest, Holdsclaw's 16 points and 14 rebounds were part of a successful, balanced offensive attack by the Lady Vols lineup: all five starting players reached double figures in scoring and vaulted the team past Georgia, with an 83–65 victory. In addition to being part of the 1996 NCAA championship-winning team in her freshman year, Holdsclaw was the team's leading scorer (an average of 16.2 points per game) and rebounder (an average of 9.1 per game). She became the first Lady Volunteer rookie to be selected as a Kodak All-American and was named SEC Freshman of the Year; she was also voted to the All-American team by the Associated Press, the U.S. Basketball Writers Association, and United Press International.

During the 1996–97 season, when Holdsclaw was a sophomore, the Lady Vols won only six of their first 16 games. Before the start of the season, the team had lost its back-court leader and point guard Michele Marciniak, who had graduated, and struggled to overcome the successive absences of two injured point guards, the sophomore Kellie Jolly and the junior Laurie Milligan. That season's team achieved the distinction of being Tennessee's first female team to lose to both the University of Arkansas and the University of Florida. "We were setting so many bad records, we were wondering if anything positive would come out of the season," Holdsclaw said to Kelli Anderson for *Sports Illustrated Online* (April 7, 1997). Holdsclaw carried the bulk of Tennessee's offense, with an average of 20.6 points per game and 9.4 rebounds per game. She also got career high marks in assists (eight), in a game against Mississippi State University; in steals (seven), in a game against the University of Wisconsin at Green Bay; and in blocked shots (four), against the University of Memphis. At a team meeting held in January 1997, Holdsclaw, frustrated by the Lady Vols' sixth loss of the season (which marked the first time since the 1989–90 season that they experienced a six-game losing streak), demanded more effort from her teammates. "I think as a basketball team, you need five players on the floor who are committed to doing the same thing. If you have one individual standing out and the other four not making a contribution, everyone is not giving what they can . . . ," she told Lorraine Kee for the *St. Louis Post-Dispatch* (March 20, 1997). "I'll joke with them but when it comes to basketball, I try to be serious about it. And they knew they weren't getting the job done." Perhaps inspired by her words, and demonstrating the benefits of additional workouts, the Lady Volunteers won 13 of the next 17 games; nevertheless, for the first time since 1986, the team dropped out of the top 10. Tennessee still managed to advance to the Final Four, thanks to a 91–81 win over Connecticut. They followed up with a semifinal victory (80–66) against Notre Dame. With her 24 points and seven rebounds, Holdsclaw led the Lady Volunteers past Old Dominion in the final game for their second straight NCAA title. (The only other team to earn the title two years in a row was the University of Southern California, in 1983 and 1984; later, the University of Connecticut did so as well, in 2002 and 2003.) Holdsclaw received the NCAA Women's Final Four Most Outstanding Player Award, having led in points (803), assists (114), turnovers (139), blocks (35), and steals (93) during her sophomore year.

In the summer of 1997, Holdsclaw was selected as a member of the USA World Championship Qualifying Team and went on a 13-game pre-competition tour, during which the American team suffered only one loss, capturing a silver medal and a berth to compete in the 1998 World Championships. Holdsclaw missed part of the pre–World Championship tour due to school-related obligations; in four of the six games in which she participated, she was a starting player. The only college player, she led the team in both scoring (an average of 13.1 points per game) and rebounding (an average of 6.5 per game). In the summer of 1998, she joined the U.S. women's team at the World Championships, during which she averaged 10.9 points per game and 5.4 rebounds per game and ranked third in scoring and rebounding averages. The team defeated Russia in the finals, 71–65, and won the gold medal. While playing in the World Championships, Holdsclaw had difficulty adjusting to the more physical style of play that prevailed in international competition, and afterward she began a weight-training program, adding muscle to her slender build. The regimen increased her agility and helped her to improve her passing skills.

Earlier, prior to the start of the 1997–98 college basketball season, Holdsclaw, rather than leaving school to join the WNBA or the American Basketball League (ABL), returned to the University of Tennessee for her third year. "I don't think females should be allowed to decide to go pro. The leagues need mature young ladies who have their degrees," she told Kelli Anderson. As a junior Holdsclaw teamed up with two freshmen players, Tamika Catchings and Semeka Randall (the trio became known as the "Three Meeks") to lead the Lady Vols to a 39–0 record. The team dominated that year's SEC Tournament, achieving a 92–54 victory against the Lady Rebels of the University of Mississippi. In the NCAA championship game, against Louisiana Tech, Holdsclaw's 18 points, seven rebounds, and five assists, which were all scored before intermission, propelled Tennessee to a 22-point lead and a third consecutive national title. She completed her junior year with her highest season points-per-game average (23.5) and as the team leader in rebounds (an average of 8.4 points per game).

In Holdsclaw's senior year she was considered by many to be the best female player in the U.S., and the Lady Vols were the overwhelming favorites to capture a fourth national title. The team advanced into the Final Eight before being defeated by Duke University in the NCAA regional finals, in March 1999; during that game, Holdsclaw landed only two of 18 shots before fouling out and leaving the court in tears. After she graduated from college, where she had majored in political science, in 1999, the Washington Mystics signed Holdsclaw as the number-one overall pick in the WNBA draft. The WNBA immediately recruited her for an 11-city summer tour as an ambassador for the league, which was just three years old. The WNBA's president, Val Ackerman, likened Holdsclaw's appeal to that of Michael Jordan, telling *Sports Illustrated Online* (May 5, 1999), "There are players in sports who transcend the consciousness and it seems she has the potential to perhaps bring herself into that category, that very special class of athlete."

The year 1999 saw Holdsclaw's first season with the Mystics. (Unlike the NBA's season, the WNBA's runs only from May until September within one calendar year). That year she averaged 16.9 points, 7.9 rebounds, and 2.4 assists per game and provided a powerful offensive complement to the guard Nikki McCray (the team leader in scoring, with an average of 17.5 points per game). Although, with a record of 12 wins and 20 losses, the Mystics performed better than they had in 1998, when they won only three of their 30 games, they failed to make the play-offs. Holdsclaw, though, was named the 1999 WNBA Rookie of the Year and earned more votes (31,002) than any other player when she was chosen for the inaugural WNBA All-Star Game. In that meet (won by the West, 79–61) she served as starting forward for the East.

With the addition of the starting point guard Andrea Nagy and the forward Vicki Bullett, the Mystics' prospects seemed to be brighter when the 2000 season opened. Holdsclaw's offense improved, from 16.9 points per game in her 1999, rookie season to 17.5 points per game in 2000, despite two stress fractures in her right foot, which were discovered in March 2000, and an undesired weight gain of 20 pounds. Rumors of conflict between Holdsclaw and the Washington Mystics' head coach, Nancy Darsch, began to spread after Holdsclaw was benched in July 2000, following a loss to the Sacramento Monarchs. Holdsclaw publicly criticized Darsch, telling Rick Freeman for the *Washington Post* (July 15, 2000), "I think we'll win basketball games with [Darsch], but I don't think we'll ever be a great team." Darsch resigned several weeks later and was replaced as interim head coach by the team's assistant general manager, Darrell Walker, a former Knicks player. Under Walker the team made it to the postseason for the first time, with a 14–18 record; they then suffered a first-round defeat by the New York Liberty. In 2001 the

Australian Olympic coach Tom Maher was hired to replace Walker.

In the summer of 2000, Holdsclaw traveled to Sydney, Australia, where she won a gold medal as a member of the U.S. women's Olympic basketball team. Also during the off-season, thanks to a conditioning program, she lost 20 pounds and developed more muscle. Although her rebounding numbers had improved, from an average of 7.5 rebounds during 2000 to 8.8 during 2001, her points-per-game average dropped, to 16.8 points from 17.5. Holdsclaw and her teammate McCray carried on a public feud with each other in the media . The Mystics finished the 2001 season with a record of 10–22, leaving them in a tie for eighth (and last) place in the Eastern Conference. Maher resigned and was replaced by assistant coach Marianne Stanley, and Pat Summitt was hired as a consultant. McCray was traded to the Indiana Fever for forward Angie Braziel and draft picks. Holdsclaw's position changed from small forward to power forward, and she changed her jersey number from 23 to 1.

The death of her grandmother before the start of the 2002 WNBA season forced Holdsclaw to miss two games. She later missed 12 more games, because of an ankle injury. Nevertheless, the Mystics ended the regular season with their best record ever (17–15). In the Eastern Conference Finals, the Mystics defeated the Charlotte Sting in two games before losing to the New York Liberty. Holdsclaw was the regular season's league leader in scoring (19.9 points per game, on average) and rebounding (11.5 per game, on average); she also made her fourth straight All-Star Game appearance. During the 2003 off-season, Holdsclaw played with a team belonging to the Women's Korea Basketball League. During the 2003 season she averaged 20.5 points and 10.9 rebounds per game; she missed the final six games due to an injury to her right ring finger. Despite her efforts the Mystics finished last in the Eastern Conference, with nine wins and 25 losses.

Holdsclaw turned down an invitation to train with Team USA for the 2004 Olympics. In July of that year, with 10 games left in the regular season, she took a leave of absence from the Mystics, citing "undisclosed medical reasons." In the fall she revealed that she had been battling severe depression, triggered by her grandmother's death, and was under the care of a psychiatrist; she was also considering retirement from the WNBA. In an effort to regain her enthusiasm for the game, she played overseas for Ros Casares, a team based in Valencia, Spain; she performed well, averaging 18.8 points per game. Her team reached the second round of the Euroleague play-offs before being defeated by the Russian team VBM-SGAU. When she returned to the U.S., Holdsclaw asked the Washington Mystics to trade her. On March 21, 2005 the Mystics announced that she would be traded to the Los Angeles Sparks, in exchange for Delisha Milton-Jones and a first-round pick. As a member of

the Sparks, she has been surrounded by three established All-Stars (the center Lisa Leslie and the guards Nikki Teasley and Mwadi Mabika) and has not been expected to carry the offense. Under the Sparks' first-year coach, Henry Bibby, in the 33 games of the 2005 season, she averaged 17 points, 6.75 rebounds, and 3.2 assists per game. The Sparks reached the 2005 WNBA Western Conference Finals, where they were defeated by the Sacramento Monarchs.

Holdsclaw missed the first two weeks of the 2006 season, instead spending time with her father and stepfather after learning that both had been diagnosed with cancer. In September, in the Western Conference Finals, the Sacramento Monarchs again defeated the Sparks, 72–58. Holdsclaw finished the season with an average of 15 points, 6.1 rebounds, and 2.2 assists per game. Earlier, in June, she had announced that that season would be her last in the WNBA. "I've been doing this since I was 18 years old," she explained to Melody Gutierrez for the *Sacramento (California) Bee* (June 23, 2006). "I'm a creative person. I look forward to what else life has to hold."

Holdsclaw lives near Venice Beach, California.
—B.M.

Suggested Reading: *Knoxville News-Sentinel* E p1 Aug. 30, 1998; *Sports Illustrated for Kids* p73 Sept. 2005; *Sports Illustrated* p87 May 30, 2005; *Washington Post* D p1 Aug. 12, 2002; *Washington Times* A p1 June 27, 1999

Selected Books: *Chamique: On Family, Focus, and Basketball*, 2000

Hollander, Robert B.

July 31, 1933– Translator; literary scholar

Address: Dept. of French and Italian, Princeton University, 303 E. Pyne, Princeton, NJ 08544-0001

"Reading Dante is like listening to Bach. You just can't understand how a human being could produce that," Robert B. Hollander, an internationally renowned Dante scholar, colloquially known as a *dantista*, remarked to Marianne Eismann for the *Princeton Alumni Weekly* (September 13, 2000). While neither he nor anyone else can fully account for the extraordinary creativity that sets the composer Johann Sebastian Bach, the 13th–14th-century Italian poet Dante Alighieri, and other geniuses apart from the rest of humanity, Hollander arguably knows as much about the writings and life of Dante—and the commentaries of others on Dante's writings and life—as anyone in the world. Hollander is a professor emeritus at Princeton University, where he taught famously popular courses

Denise Applewhite, courtesy of Princeton University
Robert B. Hollander

the Hollanders is probably the most finely accomplished and may well prove the most enduring." In an evaluation of their *Purgatorio* for the *National Review* (April 21, 2003, on-line), the former Dartmouth University English professor Jeffrey Hart described the Hollanders' work as "one of the most exciting literary and scholarly projects of our time" and as "the definitive translation." He also praised Robert Hollander's "copious notes" as "both invaluable and civilized" and added, "With regard to Dante scholarship, I do not hesitate to apply to the Hollanders what Dante said of Aristotle in the *Inferno*: They are 'the master[s] of those who know.'"

Robert Hollander is also a specialist in the works of the Italian author and poet Giovanni Boccaccio (1313–75), whose best-known work is the *Decameron*. Hollander's writings include more than 70 journal articles and books; among the latter, in addition to his *Inferno* and *Purgatorio* translations, are *The Art of the Story: An Introduction* (1968), co-written by Sidney E. Lind; *Allegory in Dante's Commedia* (1969); *Boccaccio's Two Venuses* (1977); *Studies in Dante* (1980); *Dante's Epistle to Cangrande* (1994); *Boccaccio's Dante and the Shaping Force of Satire* (1997); and *Dante: A Life in Works* (2001). Hollander was the originator of and prime mover in the launching of an ambitious project in which huge amounts of material related to Dante were gathered into two databases and made available on the Internet for use in teaching and research. He began the project in 1982, when he was a visiting professor at Dartmouth College, in New Hampshire. He remains the director of the Dartmouth Dante Project (DDP); the database, which bears the same name, became available in 1988 (http://dante.dartmouth.edu). Since 1997 he has also directed the Princeton Dante Project (PDP); the PDP, as that database is known, became operational in 1999 (www.princeton.edu/dante). The material in the PDP includes texts of *The Divine Comedy* in Italian and English; a voice recording of the poem in Italian, read by the Harvard professor Lino Pertile, and samples of the not-yet-completed English-language recording, read by the Hollanders; centuries' worth of interpretive notes and other commentaries, selected from the more than 50,000 articles and books that have been written about Dante and his writings; "lectures," as Hollander called them, reproduced from the introduction to the Hollanders' *Inferno*, on such subjects as Dante's life, Dante's use of allegory, his "appropriation" of the Roman poet Virgil's epic poem the *Aeneid*, and the problem for the contemporary reader of "find[ing] a moral point of view from which to consider the actions portrayed in the poem," in Hollander's words; minor works by Dante; illustrations by the French artist Gustave Doré (1832–83) and the Italian artist Amos Nattini (1892–1985), whose depictions of scenes in *The Divine Comedy* are among those most widely admired; and links to other Dante Web sites, including the DDP. The DDP and the PDP are continually being expanded. The PDP, Hollander told Jennifer

in medieval Italian literature for more than four decades. He gained celebrity in literary circles outside academia in 2000, with the appearance of his translation into contemporary English of Dante's *Inferno*, the first part of the immortal, three-part, 14,233-line poem *Commedia*, which Dante wrote in vernacular Italian and which in the 1550s became known as *La Commedia Divina—The Divine Comedy*. Hollander produced his translation, and that of the *Purgatorio* (2003), the second part of *The Divine Comedy*, in collaboration with his wife, Jean Hollander. The Hollanders' renditions of the *Inferno* and the *Purgatorio*, which were preceded by dozens of others during the past six centuries or so, earned universal praise. In an assessment of the Hollanders' *Inferno* for the *Los Angeles Times Book Review* (April 29, 2001), the distinguished literary scholar and longtime Yale University professor R. W. B. Lewis wrote about Dante's work first and then about the Hollanders': "The answer to the question 'Why attempt another Englishing of all or any part of the *Comedy*?' must be the same as that to the question 'Why does anyone want to climb Mt. Everest?' Because it's there. The *Divine Comedy* is there, overwhelmingly there. It is rich in poetry and drama, and far-reaching in its visionary enactment of human behavior. . . . In a culture like ours, which thrives on the contradictory, the incomplete, the absurd, *The Divine Comedy* is the place to go to, when you want to find yourself." After mentioning various 20th-century translations by others—John D. Sinclair (whose work was published in 1939), Charles Singleton (1970), Allen Mandelbaum (1980), Mark Musa (1984), Robert Pinsky (1994), and Robert Durling (1996)—Lewis wrote, "Among the new versions of *Inferno*, that of

Maloney for the *Daily Princetonian* (September 29, 1999), is "one of the most powerful instruments we've ever had for the study of a literary work." Hollander founded, in 1995, and edited, until 2004, the *Electronic Bulletin of the Dante Society of America*, which publishes short articles on Dante-related subjects. His many honors include a Guggenheim Fellowship (1970), two National Endowment for the Humanities Senior Fellowships (1974 and 1982), and the Gold Medal of the City of Florence, Italy, for his contribution to Dante studies. In 1997 the city of Certaldo, Italy, Boccaccio's birthplace, made him an honorary citizen.

Robert B. Hollander Jr. was born on July 31, 1933 in New York City to Robert B. Hollander Sr., a stockbroker, and Laurene (McGookey) Hollander. After graduating from high school, Hollander attended Princeton University, in Princeton, New Jersey, where he received an A.B. degree in 1955. For the next two years, Hollander taught Latin and English at the Collegiate School, a private boys' school in New York City. He began teaching literature at Columbia University, also in New York, in 1958, while pursuing a doctoral degree at the same university. At that time Hollander had little appreciation for Dante and included works by him in his syllabus only because the university's core curriculum required him to do so. Then 25, he read Dante "seriously," as he put it on the PDP site, for the first time while preparing his lectures for what is known at Columbia as the "Great Books" course. "I didn't like [Dante's *Divine Comedy*] very much," he told Lynne Weil for the *New York Times* (April 8, 2001). "I kept saying, 'This is the greatest work of the Middle Ages?'" But while reading an article on Dante, Hollander suddenly understood the importance and relevance of the Italian writer's work. "I came to myself several hours later, holding the periodical in my hand," he told Weil. "I can remember that my first thought was, 'So that's how it works.' And I walked out of the library having decided that I was going to be a Dante scholar." He earned a Ph.D. from Columbia in 1962 and that year joined the Princeton faculty as a lecturer on European literature in the Department of Romance Languages. He was named a full professor of European literature, comparative literature, and Romance languages and literatures in 1974. Earlier, in 1964, he had married the former Jean Haberman, a poet, college teacher of literature, and translator. Jean Hollander has published two prize-winning books of poetry and translations from German into English of two books: *Woman Without a Shadow: Die Frau Ohne Schatten*, by Hugo von Hofmannsthal (the libretto of an opera by Richard Strauss), and *I Am My Own Wife: The True Story of Charlotte von Mahlsdorf*, the memoir (originally titled *Ich Bin Meine Eigene Frau*) of a controversial transvestite and museum founder. (Van Mahlsdorf was the subject of a Tony Award– and Pulitzer Prize–winning play by Doug Wright.)

Robert Hollander's first scholarly article, "Dante's Use of *Aeneid* I in *Inferno* I and II," was published in the journal *Comparative Literature* in 1968. The second, "Dante's Use of the Fiftieth Psalm (A Note on *Purgatorio* XXX, 84)," appeared in *Dante Studies* in 1973. Others among his many articles on Dante are "Dante's Poetics" (*Sewanee Review*, 1977); "Dante on Horseback? (*Inferno* XII, 93-126)" (*Italica*, 1984); "Dante's Pagan Past: Notes on *Inferno* XIV and XVIII" (*Stanford Italian Review*, 1985); and "Dante's Harmonious Homosexuals (*Inferno* 16.7–90)" (*Electronic Bulletin of the Dante Society of America* [*EBDSA*], June 27, 1996). Both *Dante Studies* and *EBDSA* are published by the Dante Society of America. Hollander served as president of the society from 1976 to 1985. In the 1980s and early 1990s, he was the editor in chief of Lectura Dantis Americana, a three-volume series.

In "Dante: A Party of One," which appeared in *First Things* (April 1999, on-line), Hollander wrote, "Rarely has a writer left a more indelible mark—and under less favoring circumstances—than Dante. . . . His major work is considered one of the crowning achievements of human expression. It lives even today, nearly seven hundred years after its making, as one of the two or three greatest poems ever written." The *Commedia* was most likely written between 1306 and 1321, the year Dante died; because of his political activities and refusal to bend to authority, Dante was then in permanent, sorrowful exile from Florence, his native city, from which he had been banished in 1302, the year he turned 37. In the poem Dante himself is the unnamed protagonist. The poem begins on an evening in 1300, when "midway in the journey of our life / I came to myself in a dark wood, for the straight way was lost." "The wood indicates not sin itself, but human life lived in the condition of sin," as Hollander wrote in his introduction to his translation of *The Inferno*; "the straight way" refers to the path that leads one to God. Summoned by the spirit of Beatrice, who is based on a young woman (possibly fictitious) whom Dante loved spiritually and who dwells in Paradise, the shade of the Roman poet Virgil appears and invites Dante to tour the underworld with him. With Virgil guiding him, first in Hell and then in Purgatory (as a pre-Christian, Virgil cannot enter Paradise), Dante meets many individuals from ancient times as well as his own, many of whom give him their accounts of their lives. Beatrice guides him through the nine heavenly spheres into Paradise, where Dante's week-long journey ends. In addition to views of the next world and visions of a pure Christian way of life, the poem offers a spiritual autobiography, portraits of people with whom readers could easily identify, and presentations in various forms of much of the knowledge available in Dante's day; as Hollander wrote, it "tackled everything: theology, religion, philosophy, politics, the sciences of heaven (astronomy/astrology) and of earth (biology, geology), and, perhaps most of all, the study of human behavior." Quite unusually, Dante wrote the poem not in Latin but in vernacular Italian (which differs from modern Italian far less than Shakespearean English differs from modern English) and in a rhyme scheme of his own invention: 10- or 11-syllable lines grouped in threes, in each of which the middle line rhymes with the first and third lines of the next three. The poem "began to be talked about, known from parts that seem to have circulated before the whole, even before it was finished . . . ," as Hollander wrote. "By the time [Dante] had completed it, . . . people were eagerly awaiting the publication of *Paradiso* [hundreds of hand-written copies were circulated, the invention of the printing press being more than a century in the future]. And within months of his death (or even before) commentaries upon it began to be produced. It was, in short, an instant 'great book.'"

In "A New Translation of Dante," published in the *Literary Review* (Fall 2000, on-line), Hollander recalled that a chance event led him and his wife to devote themselves to the "demanding task" of producing another translation of *The Divine Comedy*. One afternoon in early 1997, Jean Hollander happened to look over her husband's shoulder while he was preparing John Sinclair's translation of the *Commedia* for the Princeton Dante Project, and after reading some of it, she declared it to be "un sayable." "It was awful, not poetic . . . and it really read very badly," as she explained to Lynne Weil. "So my husband challenged me. He said, 'Well, can you do any better?' And I said, 'Well, let me see.'" Robert Hollander judged the small section that his wife reworded to be truer to the meaning of Dante's Italian, and thus began their collaboration. During the year that they worked on the *Inferno*, they consulted earlier translations, particularly those of Sinclair and Charles Singleton, as well as a draft that Robert Hollander and Patrick Creagh had struggled with for four years in the 1980s before they abandoned it in frustration when it was about 80 percent completed. "The project's intricacies highlighted a natural tension between [Robert's] scholarly instincts and [Jean's] poet's ear," Weil wrote, noting that the Hollanders often disagreed "over distinctions as fine to the untrained eye as whether sinners are hurled 'down' or 'below.'" In his "Note on the Translation" in *The Inferno*, Robert Hollander wrote, "This is not Dante, but an approximation of what he might authorize had he been looking over our shoulders, listening to our at times ferocious arguments. We could go on improving this effort as long as we live. . . . Every translation begins and ends in failure. To the degree that we have been able to preserve some of the beauty and power of the original, we have failed the less."

The enthusiasm with which critics greeted the Hollanders' *Inferno* and *Purgatorio* suggests that the degree to which they "failed" is not significant. In a representative assessment of *The Inferno*, a reviewer for *Publishers Weekly* (January 1, 2001)

wrote that the Hollanders' translation, "remarkably, is by no means redundant and will for many be the definitive edition for the foreseeable future. . . . While there will be debate about the relative poetic merit of this new translation in comparison to the accomplishments of Mandelbaum, Pinsky, . . . and others, the Hollanders' lines will satisfy both the poetry lover and scholar; they are at once literary, accessible and possessed of the seeming transparence that often characterizes great translations." In an article for the *Literary Review* (Summer 2003), the poet Rita Signorelli-Pappas wrote that the Hollanders had "rendered both the supple lyricism and the rich imagery of the *Purgatorio* with an admirably informed expertise, preserving the stately economy of Dante's Italian throughout." The scheduled publication date of the Hollanders' translation of *Paradiso*, the third section of *The Divine Comedy*, is April 2007.

Kimberley A. Strassel, in an op-ed piece for the *Wall Street Journal* (June 8, 2001, on-line), described Robert Hollander as "handsome and dapper . . . with a neatly trimmed mustache over a mischievous smile." "To his former students," she wrote, "Prof. Hollander's most enduring quality is his enthusiasm for anything Dante, and for anyone—no matter how unscholarly—who is willing to learn about the poet. He has convinced his alumni that they can all be scholars of the classics and that learning need not stop at graduation." Every year Hollander organizes a "Dante reunion" for former students of his; in 2001 the event took place in Italy and included a 14-hour recitation in English or Italian of the entire *Divine Comedy*, with all the participants taking turns as readers. "People are often 'afraid' of Dante," Hollander said during an on-line chat posted on *Wordsmith* (January 17, 2001). "They have heard so much about him; he seems imposing. Here's what I advise my first-time students to do. Sit down after supper with the entire poem and just read it through as though it were a novel. I have done this myself, and it is a wonderful experience." Hollander published a book of poetry, *Walking on Dante*, in 1974 and has occasionally written poems since then. He is fluent in French as well as Italian and has a working knowledge of several other languages.

Hollander has served on the boards of the National Council on Humanities, the National Humanities Center, and the New Jersey Committee for the Humanities, among others. He and his wife live in Hopewell, New Jersey. The couple have two adult children: Cornelia Vanness Hollander and Robert B. Hollander III.

—I.C.

Suggested Reading: *Christian Science Monitor* p21 Mar. 29, 1985; *Los Angeles Times* p12 Apr. 29, 2001; *New York Times* XIV NJ p3 Apr. 8, 2001; *Princeton Alumni Weekly* Sep. 13, 2000; Princeton University Web site; *Wordsmith* (on-line) Jan. 17, 2001

Selected Books: *Allegory in Dante's Commedia*, 1969; *Walking on Dante*, 1974; *Boccaccio's Two Venuses*, 1977; *Studies in Dante*, 1980; *Boccaccio's Last Fiction: Il Corbaccio*, 1988; *Boccaccio's Dante and the Shaping Force of Satire*, 1997; *Dante: A Life in Works*, 2001; with Jean Hollander—*Inferno*, 2000; *Purgatorio*, 2003; *Paradiso*, 2006

Courtesy of Hunt Alternatives Fund

Hunt, Swanee

May 1, 1950– Former ambassador; philanthropist; organization official; public-policy educator; writer

Address: John F. Kennedy School of Government, 79 John F. Kennedy St., Rm. T110A, Cambridge, MA 02138-5801

As a daughter of the legendary Texas billionaire oilman H. L. Hunt, Swanee Hunt was born to a life of wealth and privilege. To an extent that is rare even among the charitable of those similarly favored, Hunt has used her affluence and position in society to better the lives of others in the United States and overseas. A co-owner of the Hunt Oil Co., she was trained in psychological and pastoral counseling and in her 20s devoted herself to church-related jobs and activities. During her long residency in Denver, Colorado, she contributed—both as a member of various public-sector groups and as the founder of the Hunt Alternatives Fund—to community efforts to improve public education, make available more affordable housing, and provide more and better mental-health services.

Through the fund, which she continues to serve as president, she has also strived to alleviate poverty and promote programs that assist women and children in other places as well. For four years in the 1990s, she held the post of U.S. ambassador to Austria; in that capacity she helped victims of the violence that was then engulfing the Balkan region and worked with women in post-Communist Eastern Europe who were eager to help create democracies in their native lands. Her experiences in Europe helped to shape her current work: since 1997 she has been the director of the Women and Public Policy Program and the chair of the Initiative for Inclusive Security, which are dedicated to promoting women's roles in shaping public policy and helping to build and sustain peace within and among nations. A writer and photographer as well, Hunt is the author of the book *This Was Not Our War* (2004), for which she conducted interviews with female survivors of the 1990s Balkans violence. Her memoir, *Half-Life of a Zealot*, was published by Duke University Press in late 2006.

One of the 15 children and the youngest daughter of H. L. (Haroldson Lafayette) Hunt, an oil tycoon once reputed to be the richest man in the world, Swanee Grace Hunt was born on May 1, 1950 in Dallas, Texas. Her father, whose formal education stopped after the third grade, worked his way up from odd jobs—shepherd, short-order cook, lumberjack—to become the owner of some of the richest oil fields in the United States; reportedly, he won some of his holdings through his skills at poker. Her mother, née Ruth Ray, was working as a Hunt Oil Co. secretary when she met H. L. Hunt, who was already married (bigamously) to two other women. When Swanee was born—out of wedlock, like her older brother, Ray, and two older sisters, June and Helen—her father was 60; her parents married when Swanee was seven. According to Nancy Bartosek, writing for the Texas Christian University publication *TCU Magazine* (Winter 2005, on-line), Swanee was "raised in a strict Southern Baptist home by a compassionate mother and a politically arch-conservative father." "Home life was pretty tough; there were a lot of strains," Swanee Hunt told a reporter for *On the Issues* (Spring 1997). "I had an extraordinarily strange upbringing. My father was a very eccentric man, very involved with a lot of right-wing causes. And being a Hunt in Dallas was isolating, like being a Rockefeller on the East Coast or part of the royal family in London."

From an early age Hunt displayed a determination to work hard and do well. She received a B.A. degree in philosophy from Texas Christian University, in Fort Worth, in 1972. In 1976 she earned an M.A. degree in counseling and psychology from Ball State University, in Muncie, Indiana, as a participant in an extension program held in Rhein-Main, Germany. During her four years in Germany, she learned to speak German, a skill that she later put to good use as ambassador to Austria. She earned a second master's degree, in religion, from the Iliff School of Theology (a graduate school of the United Methodist Church), in Denver, Colorado, in 1977 (some sources say 1980); at the Fort Logan Mental Health Center, in Denver, she studied clinical pastoral education. In 1986 she earned a doctorate in theology, with a specialty in ethics and pastoral care and counseling, from the Iliff School.

During the early part of her career, Hunt divided her time between her duties as a minister (serving at one time in the Capital Heights Presbyterian Church in Denver) and her responsibilities as a co-owner of the Hunt Oil Co. In the early 1980s she also established several foundations, among them the Karis Community, a therapeutic residence for people with persistent mental illness, and, in 1981, the Hunt Alternatives Fund, which she directed with her sister Helen Hunt (not the same-named actress). The Hunt Alternative Fund, which now operates out of Cambridge, Massachusetts, provides funding for programs aimed at combating poverty and racial discrimination in the inner cities of Denver, Dallas, New York City, and other urban areas; it also supports women's programs, particularly the Colorado Women's Foundation. (Since its founding, according to its Web site, the fund has contributed, through grants and operating programs, some $50 million to further its goals.) From 1983 to 1987 she served as the vice chair of the Denver Community Mental Health Commission. From 1989 to 1990 she assisted Colorado's Government Policy Academy on Families and Children at Risk, and from 1989 to 1992 she served on the Colorado Governor's Council on Housing and the Homeless. Speaking of her civic work, Hunt told Sharon Silvas for Colorado Women's News (January 31, 1990), "I've been on lots of boards of lots of organizations, although I've been sparing in my board involvement unless there is a critical reason for me to be on it. I don't join just for the sake of having my name on the board list."

During the 1992 race for the U.S. presidency, Hunt threw her support behind the Democratic candidate, Governor Bill Clinton of Arkansas. (According to various reports, Hunt donated more than $200,000 of her own money to Clinton's campaign.) As is not uncommon among generous donors to successful presidential candidates, in September 1993 President Clinton nominated Hunt for the post of U.S. ambassador to Austria. She was confirmed by the U.S. Senate by voice vote two months later. As the ambassador to Austria until 1997, Hunt oversaw a staff of 500 people. "To reach an otherwise elusive audience," as Carla Koehl and Marc Peyser put it in Newsweek (April 24, 1995), she wrote about the U.S. and American values in a weekly column published in the right-wing Austrian newspaper Neue Kronenzeitung and spoke about the U.S. and other topics in addresses broadcast over Austrian radio. During her ambassadorship she stressed the importance of the role of women in Eastern European societies following the collapse of the Soviet Union. To foster the

fledgling democracies in the region, she established the Vienna Women's Initiative. In an article for Foreign Affairs (July/August 1997), she wrote: "In this brave new world, the voices of women are vital to healthy social and political discourse. The dramatically low status of women in post-communist Europe is an issue that goes beyond the well-being of women per se to the fostering of economic development and democracy. American interests require that we help the region's women carve out their rightful place in the mainstream of society." She also became indirectly involved with the then-ongoing ethnic wars in the Balkans, having become concerned about the welfare of the approximately 70,000 people from that region who had taken refuge in Austria to escape the fighting. As ambassador she supported relief initiatives in the region, including an effort to restock the National Library in Sarajevo, in what had been Yugoslavia and is now Bosnia and Herzogovina. Also as ambassador she arranged the shipment of musical instruments to devastated Bosnian schools and organized an effort to plant trees in parks that had been destroyed. In addition, she helped to relocate temporarily to Vienna, Austria, the U.S. mission to Sarajevo. Hunt recalled to Rose Marie Berger for Sojourners (November 2004): "For over a year, the U.S. mission to Bosnia was actually in our embassy in Vienna. As a result, I was meeting the political figures [involved in the ethnic conflicts] and hosting negotiations."

After leaving the State Department, Hunt accepted a position at the John F. Kennedy School of Government at Harvard University, in Cambridge, Massachusetts. Since 1997 Hunt has been the director of the Women and Public Policy Program (WAPPP) at Harvard. In that position she has tried to involve women in working toward peace in the wake of conflicts around the world. In an interview with Thane Peterson for Concerning Women (online), she recalled, "I brought, ultimately, women from 25 different conflicts to Harvard for a week or two, listening to them exchange their strategies. . . . What we found is that there were some extraordinary strengths among these women that would be very useful in trying to avert or stop violent conflicts. The women were bridging the divide. They tended to not see the person on the other side as the demon. They would often talk about how, 'We're all mothers, and as mothers we understand each other.' One of the sayings was, 'As mothers, we all cry the same tears.'" WAPPP focuses on research and education that helps to advance and support women's voices in the public arena. According to its Web site, its projects have entailed educating African women about AIDS, developing a worldwide database regarding the trafficking of women and children, and examining the roles of women in elected governments, particularly in terms of how their gender roles affect their political decisions. Hunt is an adjunct lecturer in public policy at the Kennedy School. She has taught a course called "Inclusive Security," which, according to its description on the Kennedy School Web site, "examines the work of women-led, peace-building initiatives around the world."

Hunt organized the Initiative for Inclusive Security (originally called Women Waging Peace) in 1999, as an activity of the Hunt Alternatives Fund. The initiative seeks to help women worldwide get involved in peace processes and reconstruction efforts following civil wars and other fighting. A worldwide program, it includes among its members female government and military officials, lawyers, journalists, teachers, scholars, religious leaders, and heads of organizations and businesses.

As a means of promoting her humanitarian efforts, Hunt has contributed hundreds of articles to such journals and periodicals as *Foreign Affairs*, *Foreign Policy*, the *International Herald Tribune*, the *Chicago Tribune*, the *Boston Globe*, the *Denver Post*, the *Dallas Morning News*, and the *Rocky Mountain News*, and she writes a column for the Scripps Howard News Service. Recent columns of hers have discussed the paucity of females or people of color on the U.S. Supreme Court (as she pointed out, of the 110 justices who have served on the court since 1789, 106 have been white men); the importance of cultural activities in communities ("Thriving cultural institutions bring sizable financial and spiritual returns: they build neighborhood identities, lift local economies, boost student achievement and bridge social divides," she wrote); the benefits of nuclear energy as an alternative to petroleum-based fuels and the importance of finding ways to make nuclear plants secure from terrorists and ways to safely store spent nuclear fuel; and the injustice of the nation's continuing denial to homosexuals of more than 1,000 federal benefits available to heterosexuals.

Hunt's book, *This Was Not Our War: Bosnian Women Reclaiming the Peace* (2004), grew out of her seven years' worth of interviews with 26 women who had been caught up in the ethnic fighting in the former Yugoslavia. A reviewer of the book for *Publishers Weekly* (December 4, 2004) wrote: "Hunt juxtaposes private moments with public meetings and differences of opinion with common convictions. Women speak wrenchingly and courageously about the fight to save their homes and protect their children; the decision to stay or flee; the attempt to preserve their own bodies and souls; and the ongoing challenge to rebuild their lives and society. . . . Despite differences of opinion on most other issues, Hunt's ethnically and religiously diverse interviewees all agree that political greed rather than obstinate ethnic hatred fueled the conflict. . . . Hunt succeeds in capturing, organizing and analyzing the complexities inherent in conversations with 26 very different people during and after an abhorrent war. 'Life goes on, and life wins,' says Mediha Filipovic, the only female member of parliament in the first Bosnian national assembly and Bosnia's current ambassador to Sweden. Readers will be inspired by her courage, and that of the others here, in saying so." In the *London*

Review of Books (March 3, 2005), Gabriele Annan, by contrast, complained that at times Hunt sounded "irritatingly upbeat. There wasn't much for her to do in Vienna, so she took up Bosnia in a big way, and especially Bosnian women. This is a feminist work, and the 'our' in the title means 'us Bosnian women.' . . . Most of those Hunt interviewed were professional women. . . . All of them spoke in favour of peace among the different races, and most of them thought that women would have handled the situations that led to war better than men could or did. Well, they would think that: that was the sort of women they were. But there must be quite a lot of Serb women who carried on hating the Croats, and vice versa. Hunt sees herself as a sort of missionary. . . . No one could deny that her mission for peace in Bosnia was a good cause. But people don't always like being preached at." Accompanying the text of *This Was Not Our War* are photos taken by Hunt of devastated sites in Bosnia. Others of Hunt's photos have been exhibited in one-woman showings of her work.

Hunt has earned many honors for her charitable and humanitarian work, among them the National Mental Health Association Award (1985), the Martin Luther King Humanitarian Award from the University of Colorado (1992), the Mile High Award from the United Way (1993), the American Heritage Award from the Anti-Defamation League (1995), three decorations from the Austrian government (1997), and awards from the International Women's Forum (1989) and the Institute for International Education (1998). While she was serving as ambassador, the Together for Peace Foundation, in Rome, named her Woman of Peace.

Hunt's first, 15-year marriage, to Mark Meeks, a pastor and social worker, ended in divorce in about 1984, when her daughter, Lillian Hunt-Meeks, was two years old. In an article that they co-wrote for *Good Housekeeping* (November 1996), Lillian described the pain and enormous difficulties she had suffered as a manic-depressive before a successful combination of drugs was prescribed for her, after she entered her teens, and Hunt revealed her anguish and travails as the mother of a child with that disorder. In 1986 Hunt married the orchestra conductor Charles Ansbacher, who led the Colorado Springs Symphony Orchestra from 1970 to 1989. Ansbacher is the founder and conductor of the Boston Landmarks Orchestra and currently the principal guest conductor of the Sarajevo Philharmonic and the Ala-Too Symphony Orchestra (based in the Kirgiz Republic). Hunt and Ansbacher have a son, Ted, and live in Cambridge, Massachusetts. Hunt is the stepmother of Ansbacher's son, Henry, from his previous marriage. *The Witness Cantata*, a musical composition that Hunt wrote to memorialize the victims of war, was recently performed at the Arlington Street Church in Boston, Massachusetts, with Ansbacher conducting.

—C.M.

Suggested Reading: *BusinessWeek* p58 Jan. 29, 1990; *Christian Century* p6 Oct. 9, 2002; *Colorado Business* p58 Feb.1994; *Colorado Woman New*s p7 Jan. 31, 1990; Harvard University, John F. Kennedy School of Government Web site; Initiative for Inclusive Security Web site; *London Review of Books* p27+ Mar. 3, 2005; *On the Issues* p32 Spring 1997; *Newsweek* p4 Apr. 24, 1995; *Soujourners* p39+ Nov. 2004; Women and Public Policy Program Web site; Burst, Ardis. *The Three Families of H. L. Hunt*, 1988; Hunt, Swanee. *Half-Life of a Zealot*, 2006

Selected Books: *This Was Not Our War: Bosnian Women Reclaiming the Peace*, 2004; *Half-Life of a Zealot*, 2006

Courtesy of Jonathan Ive

Ive, Jonathan

Feb. 1967– Vice president of industrial design at Apple Computer

Address: Apple Computer Inc., 1 Infinite Loop, Cupertino, CA 95014

"Products have a significance way beyond traditional views of function," Jonathan Ive, the head of Apple Computer's design team, told an interviewer for the Design Museum of London, England, in 2005. Although neither Ive's name nor his face are widely recognized in the United States, his fingerprints, metaphorically speaking, mark products that have become icons of modern design—most prominently, the iMac desktop computer and the

iPod digital music player. By early 1999, according to Matt Richtel, writing for the "Home Design" section of the *New York Times Magazine* (April 11, 1999, on-line), Ive, who was then 32, had become "perhaps the most influential designer in the computer world." "Ive's visions have transformed his company and are forcing the industry to transform, too," Richtel added. Trained in industrial design, the British-born Ive began creating designs for commercial products in 1989, when, with three partners, he co-founded the innovative London-based design-consultancy firm Tangerine. His unconventional approach to design became known to Apple a year or two later, when, as a Tangerine consultant, he worked on a notebook prototype for Apple. He joined Apple in 1992, during a period when the company's serious financial troubles, along with other factors, had eclipsed its reputation for creativity and novelty. The company's slide toward bankruptcy—and Ive's mounting professional frustration—ended in 1997, when Apple's co-founder Steve Jobs regained the reins of power. The "Versace of computers" and the "Armani of Apple," as he has been called (the references are to two of the most famous names in contemporary fashion design), Ive inaugurated a new era in consumer-oriented technology by artfully integrating colors, materials, and forms to create products that are not only functional but visually and tactilely appealing and satisfying to people's sensibilities in other ways as well. "My view is that surfaces and materials and finishes and product architecture are about telling a bigger story," he told Josh Quittner for *Time* (January 14, 2002). Ive's honors include the 2002 and 2003 Designer of the Year Prizes from the Design Museum of London and the 2005 President's Award for Outstanding Contribution to the Industry from the British educational organization Design and Art Direction. He ranked number one among British culture's top 50 movers and shakers in a poll conducted by the British Broadcasting Corp. (BBC) in 2004, and *BusinessWeek* included him on its list of 25 masters of innovation in 2006. In 2005 he was named a Commander of the Most Excellent Order of the British Empire (CBE).

Jonathan Ive was born in February 1967 in Chingford, in the borough of Waltham Forest, in Greater London, England. His father, Michael Ive, a silversmith, became a teacher and, later, evaluated design and technology courses in British schools as an inspector for the country's Office for Standards in Education. Clive Grinyer, the director of design at Britain's quasi-governmental Design Council, who was a classmate of Jonathan Ive's and co-founded Tangerine with him, told Nick Webster for the British newspaper the *Mirror* (June 5, 2003) that Ive's patience, passion for design, and various other qualities are evidence of his father's influence on him. Ive's interest in the structure of electronic gadgets and other objects was aroused during his childhood. "As a kid, I remember taking apart whatever I could get my hands on," he told an interviewer for the Design Museum of London, as posted on its Web site. "Later, this developed into more of an interest in how they were made, how they worked, their form and material." By his early teens, he told the same interviewer, "I was pretty certain that I wanted to draw and make stuff." The subjects of his designs and drawings included furniture, jewelry, cars, and boats.

In 1985, after he completed his secondary education, Ive attended a few classes at Central St. Martins College of Art and Design, in London, before transferring to Newcastle Polytechnic (now called Northumbria University), in northeastern England, where he studied industrial design. During his college years he "figured out some basic stuff—that form and color defines your perception of the nature of an object, whether or not it is intended to," as he told the Design Museum interviewer. "I learnt the fundamentals of how you make things and I started to understand the historical and cultural context of an object's design." Clive Grinyer told Webster that for the final project required of seniors, Ive built 100 models as part of a "system of hearing aids for teachers and deaf pupils"—an accomplishment that became legendary among Polytechnic students, who would typically build five or six models for the final-year design showcase. "You realized he was totally dedicated to his art," Grinyer said. As an undergraduate Ive earned two design awards, in 1988 and 1989, from the Royal Society for the Encouragement of the Arts, Manufactures, and Commerce (usually referred to as the Royal Society of Arts, or RSA). He graduated from Newcastle Polytechnic with a B.A. degree in 1989.

That same year Ive teamed up with Grinyer, Marty Darbyshire, and Peter Phillips to form Tangerine, in London. The men "planned to design products that met genuine consumer needs and delivered demonstrable difference," according to the Tangerine Web site, in the belief that "product design aligned to their clients' overall business objects could make a tangible contribution to business." While designing products including washbasins, hair combs, televisions, and power tools, Ive told the Design Museum interviewer, "I worked out what I was good at and what I was bad at. . . . I was really only interested in design. I was neither interested [in] nor good at building a business." According to Grinyer, in his designs Ive developed a knack for accommodating the sometimes quirky habits of consumers. In designing a pen for the design consultants Roberts Weaver Group, for example, he "built in what he called a 'fiddle factor' because he knew that was what people like to do" with pens, as Grinyer told Webster. "That's a trait of his. He looks for something people will latch on to." In an interview with Peter Burrows for *BusinessWeek* (September 25, 2006), Grinyer, who was then a Roberts Weaver employee, said that the additions to the pen made it "something you always wanted to play with." "We began to call it 'having Jony-ness,' an extra something that would tap into

the product's underlying emotion." For another client, Grinyer recalled to Webster, Ive constructed "a bizarre telephone with a receiver you held [next to] your waist. It was off-the-wall but it showed he thought about things in a different way." Although the design pleased Ive, the telephone, which resembled a microphone, proved to be hard to use, as he discovered when he tested it. "People were so obviously uncomfortable using it," he recalled to Sheryl Garratt for the London *Times* (December 3, 2005). "They were self-conscious and felt stupid, because it was such an odd thing." From that experience, Garratt wrote, Ive gained a better appreciation of the importance of enabling consumers to "connect" with a new device and "relate it to products [they have] used before."

One of Tangerine's clients was Apple Computer, which was seeking new looks for its portable computers. Unveiled in 1984, Apple's Macintosh (or Mac, as it is universally known) was the first personal computer to be equipped with both a graphical user interface and a mouse; rather than having to learn a complex command language, users could manipulate text and images by means of an easy-to-learn point-and-click system. By his own account, Ive already knew a lot about Apple's beginnings and corporate structure and philosophy, having researched the company after happening upon a Mac while he was in college. "The more I learnt about this cheeky almost rebellious company the more it appealed to me, as it unapologetically pointed to an alternative in a complacent and creatively bankrupt industry," he told the Design Museum interviewer. As an undergraduate, Ive told that reporter, he had wanted to use computers in his design courses but had had a "real problem" with them and had become certain that he was "technically inept." "I remember being astounded at just how much better [the Mac] was than anything else I had tried to use. I was struck by the care taken with the whole user experience. I had a sense of connection via the object with the designers." Ive's mock-ups of portable computers greatly impressed Apple representatives, and after an international search for a director of design, Apple recruited him for the position. By that point, despite the assortment of clients and projects that had come his way at Tangerine, Ive had grown frustrated by what he felt were the creative limitations imposed on him as a member of an independent consulting firm. "Working externally"—that is, as someone not on the staff of any company in the market for a new design—"made it difficult to have a profound impact on product plans and to truly innovate," he explained to the Design Museum interviewer. "By the time you had accepted a commission so many of the critical decisions had already been made. Increasingly, I had also come to believe that to do something fundamentally new requires dramatic change from many parts of an organization." Eager for the chance to fulfill his ambitions with a company that he admired, in 1992 Ive left Tangerine to join Apple, and he and his wife (he had married several years before) settled in California, near Apple's headquarters, in Cupertino.

When Ive arrived at Apple, morale among the staff was low and the company was in trouble financially and technologically, largely because of competition from IBM and, especially, Microsoft and partly because of management problems that had sprung up following the forced departure of Apple's visionary co-founder Steven Jobs in 1985. The company "seemed to have lost what had once been a very clear sense of identity and purpose," Ive told the Design Museum interviewer. "Apple had started trying to compete to an agenda set by an industry that had never shared its goals. While as a designer I was certainly closer to where the decisions were being made, . . . I was only marginally more effective or influential than I had been as a consultant." One of his projects, the Newton MessagePad, a pen-based personal organizer, failed commercially because of its "bloated price tag," as Rob Walker put it in the *New York Times Magazine* (November 30, 2003), early problems with handwriting recognition, and bulkiness (it was too big to fit into average-size pockets). As "sanity exercises," Jennifer Tanaka wrote for *Newsweek* (May 18, 1998, on-line), Ive and some of his colleagues made "gorgeous but doomed prototypes on the side." Named head of Apple's design team in 1996, Ive was "at wit's end," as he told Tanaka, and he was contemplating leaving Apple and returning to England when, in July 1997—three months after Apple reported a quarterly loss of $708 million—the company announced that Steve Jobs would take on an expanded role, as interim CEO. (Apple had rehired Jobs as an adviser in 1995, when Apple had purchased Jobs's company NeXT and Apple's share of the personal-computer market had dropped to less than 6 percent.) "Suddenly, the reason we came to Apple was back at Apple," Ive told Tanaka. Within weeks, as John Markoff wrote for the *New York Times* (August 1, 1997), employees had thrown off the "malaise" that had gripped Apple. In 1998, the year Jobs was officially named CEO, he promoted Ive to senior vice president of industrial design, in charge of overseeing Ive's handpicked, elite team who were now encouraged to push the boundaries of creativity. "[Our] effectiveness as a design team is so dependent on someone like Steve. He has rendered us effective and valuable to the company," Ive told Chris Ward for the London *Times* (May 20, 1998). Jobs, Ive told Tanaka, understands the "emotional side" of objects.

The first of Jobs's assignments for Ive was to design an attractive, compact, all-in-one desktop computer—the iMac, as it became known, with the "i" standing for "Internet." As he had in the past, Ive approached his task by studying everyday objects. After deciding to use translucent plastic for the computer's shell, "we needed to understand the science of how you control color production over millions of units, to make the first and the last look the same, [which led us to] the sweet candy

industry," as he explained to Ward. "Because so many sweets are translucent they also have this problem of how to make the first the same as the last." Ive and his team also drew inspiration from the TV series *The Jetsons* (1962–63), an animated family sitcom set in a utopian, futuristic U.S. "Early on," Ive told Garratt, "we talked about designing a computer for the Jetsons," one that would also offer contemporary consumers "a comforting portrayal of the future that's nostalgic," as he described it to Tanaka. The first iMacs, which went on sale in August 1998, looked distinctly different from other desktop computers: the screen was backed by what looked like a truncated egg, one covered in a translucent shell colored "Bondi blue" (said to resemble the color of the water at Bondi Beach, in Australia, a site popular with surfers; the shade, Apple believed, would now be associated with Internet surfing). Before long, consumers could choose from a dozen additional colors, among them grape, lime, tangerine, and sage. "The back of our computer looks better than the front of anyone else's," Apple advertisements boasted, while also emphasizing how much easier the device was to install than other brands. The iMac became the fastest-selling personal computer in history, with two million purchased within the first year. "Most computer makers don't realize how afraid many people are of computers," Ive told Kristi Essick for IDG News Service (September 18, 1998). "The idea that the iMac comes in one box, has clear plastic that catches the light and shows its changing nature and has a shape that 'looks like it just arrived' all contribute to [its] overall approachability and appeal." The iMac's handle also added to its allure, according to Ive; as he explained to the Design Museum interviewer, "While [the handle's] primary function is obviously associated with making the product easy to move, a compelling part of its function is the immediate connection it makes with the user by unambiguously referencing the hand. . . . Seeing an object with a handle, you instantly understand aspects of its physical nature—I can touch it, move it, it's not too precious." By mid-1999 Apple's finances had improved dramatically: most of its debt had been paid off, and the value of its stock, which had plummeted earlier in the 1990s, had increased by about 450 percent.

Ive and his team next designed a cigarette-box–sized, 6.5-ounce digital music player dubbed the iPod, which could store 1,250 songs and allowed users to create their own playlists. An example of elegant minimalism, the first-generation iPod had neither latches nor battery covers and was completely sealed. On its pearly façade the iPod displayed a monochrome screen, four navigational buttons (Menu, Play/Pause, Forward, Back), and a mechanical scroll wheel, and it came with tiny earphones, called earbuds, on a white cord. Speaking of the iPod's initial blueprints, Ive told Marcus Fairs for *Icon Magazine* (August 2003) that he and his colleagues adopted "a very honest approach and an exploration of materials and surface treatment . . . to get to a point where the solution seems inevitable: you know, you think 'of course it's that way, why would it be any other way?'" When it debuted, in November 2001, the iPod earned high praise for its design as well as its capabilities. "The kind of insidious revolutionary quality of the iPod is that it's so elegant and logical, it becomes part of your life so quickly that you can't remember what it was like beforehand," the recording artist Moby told Rob Walker. Ive later modified the iPod's exterior, designing a slimmer, rounder encasement that contained "touch sensitive," glow-in-the-dark buttons. By the end of 2003, Rob Walker reported, Apple had estimated that iPods constituted nearly one-third of MP3 players sold, and that the company's share of industry-wide revenues was more than half; in addition, Apple was selling more iPods than any other product. Twelve months later, according to Michel Marriott in the *New York Times* (December 16, 2004, on-line), an estimated nine out of 10 high-capacity portable music players sold in the U.S. were iPods. According to Nate Mook in *BetaNews* (January 20, 2006, on-line), in the fourth quarter of 2005, iPods were selling at the rate of 100 per minute. By October 2006, Jim Dalrymple reported in *Playlist* (October 23, 2006, online), more than 67 million iPods had been purchased, and it had become a widely embraced pop-culture icon. In preliminary figures released for the fourth quarter of its fiscal year 2006, which ended on September 30, 2006, Apple announced that it had shipped nearly 8.7 million iPods during that three-month period—35 percent more than had been shipped during the same quarter in 2005. Ive's iPod designs also include the iPod mini, the iPod shuffle, the iPod nano, and the iPod video, as well as such accessories as a leather case, a remote control, and in-ear headphones.

Ive was also the lead designer for such products as Apple's small, mobile notebooks—the iBook, which went on sale in 1999, the PowerBook G4 (2001), which came with a titanium or an aluminum body, and the 17-inch PowerBook (2003), the slimmest and lightest computer of its size to that date. (In mid-2005, at its annual Worldwide Developer Conference, Apple announced a new partnership with the world's largest computer chipmaker, the Intel Corp., with the goal of having faster, more-efficient processors in Apple's portable and desktop computers. Beginning in 2006 both the Ive-inspired 15-inch and 17-inch PowerBooks were newly minted as MacBook Pros, while the iBook, updated in May 2006, was renamed as the Mac-Book.) Ive also headed the design team for the PowerMac G4 (1999), PowerMac G4 Cube (2000), and revisions to the iMac desktop computer—the iMac G4 (2002), which had a "floating" flat screen, and the iMac G5 (2004), with a flat-panel display and a revolutionary all-in-one enclosure. In addition, he spearheaded designs for the landmark, high-end professional desktop computer Power-Mac G5 (2003) and, in 2005, the Mac mini, Apple's smallest desktop computer, housed in a two-inch-tall cuboid case.

In September 2006 Apple introduced new iPod nanos and iPod shuffles. (The iPod Video underwent minor software changes.) Originally launched in September 2005 as a replacement for the iPod mini, the iPod nano had turned out to be a rare Apple mistake—a "customer relations disaster," as Sheryl Garratt put it—because the screens of a few owners (less than one-tenth of 1 percent, according to Apple) "reportedly scratched easily." While the number of complaints was tiny, there was much media coverage of the problem, owing to Apple's prominence. With the second-generation iPod nano, Ive and his team reverted to the sleek, anodized-aluminum enclosure of the iPod mini, offering the nano in a range of colors—blue, green, silver, pink, and black. Then, in October 2006, Apple introduced a red iPod nano, as a licensee of the Product Red brand, introduced by Bono, the lead singer of the rock band U2, and Robert Sargent "Bobby" Shriver 3d, co-founders of the organization Debt, AIDS, Trade in Africa (known by its acronym, DATA). Portions of the profits from sales of Product Red items will be contributed to the Global Fund to Fight AIDS, Tuberculosis and Malaria. Also in September 2006 Apple announced that the following month it would begin shipping the second-generation iPod shuffle; about a quarter of the length of a typical computer mouse, it comes with a belt clip and weighs only 1.6 ounces.

In interviews Ive has always emphasized that his creations result from a collaborative approach; indeed, he has referred to his colleagues as "a heavenly design team." When the Design Museum interviewer asked Ive, "What is it that distinguishes the products that your team develops?," Ive answered, "Perhaps the decisive factor is fanatical care beyond the obvious stuff: the obsessive attention to details that are often overlooked, like cables and power adaptors." Some of his designs are in the permanent collections of the Museum of Modern Art in New York City and the National Museum of Modern Art at the Centre Georges Pompidou, in Paris, France. In 2002 both *Esquire* and *Details* magazines included him in their choices of the "best and brightest" of the year. In the British magazine *Creative Review*'s "peer poll" in 2003, Ive was named the person most admired in the creative industries. Also in 2003 the RSA named Ive Royal Designer for Industry, and the British Interactive Media Association named him New Media Hero. In 2000 he earned an honorary Ph.D. from Northumbria University.

In *Wired News* (June 25, 2003, on-line), Leander Kahney described Ive as a "quiet-spoken, somewhat shy man. . . . He is accessible and friendly, almost egoless." Ive lives on the outskirts of San Francisco, California, with his wife, Heather, and their twin toddler sons.

—D.J.K.

Suggested Reading: *BusinessWeek* p26+ Sep. 25, 2006; *Icon Magazine* (on-line) July/Aug. 2003; London Design Museum Web Site; (London) *Mirror* p6 June 5, 2003; (London) *Observer* p19 Dec. 21, 2003; (London) *Sunday Times* p24+ Feb. 29, 2004; (London) *Times* p41+ Dec. 3, 2005; *New York Times* F p1+ Feb. 5, 1998; *New York Times Home Design Magazine* p48+ Apr. 11, 1999; *New York Times Magazine* p78+ Nov. 30, 2003; *Newsweek* p48 May 18, 1998; *Time* p63+ Sep. 19, 2005

Carlo Allegri/Getty

Jarecki, Eugene

Oct. 5, 1969– Filmmaker

Address: Keppler Speakers, 4350 N. Fairfax Dr., Suite 700, Arlington, VA 22203

In the motion picture *Why We Fight*, the filmmaker Eugene Jarecki examined a phenomenon that had troubled him for some time: what seemed to him and many others to be the United States' obsession with unending preparations for warfare. In trying to explain that fixation, Jarecki was drawn to the nationally broadcast address in which, on January 17, 1961, a few days before the end of his second term in the White House, President Dwight D. Eisenhower bid farewell to the American people. The commander of Allied forces in Europe during World War II, a five-star general, and a moderate Republican, Eisenhower warned in his address of the dangers of what he termed the military-industrial complex—the increasingly close, mutually beneficial connections among people of influ-

ence in the armed forces, the weapons industry, and the U.S. Department of Defense and certain other government agencies—which took root during World War II and grew tremendously afterward. "The potential for the disastrous rise of misplaced power exists and will persist," Eisenhower cautioned. During the course of his speech, parts of which Jarecki interspersed among other footage in *Why We Fight*, the president also said, "Down the long lane of the history yet to be written America knows that this world of ours, ever growing smaller, must avoid becoming a community of dreadful fear and hate, and be, instead, a proud confederation of mutual trust and respect. . . . Together we must learn how to compose differences, not with arms, but with intellect and decent purpose. Because this need is so sharp and apparent I confess I lay down my official responsibilities in this field with a definite sense of disappointment. As one who has witnessed the horror and the lingering sadness of war—as one who knows that another war could utterly destroy this civilization which has been so slowly and painfully built over thousands of years—I wish I could say tonight that a lasting peace is in sight." Since Eisenhower uttered those words, members of the U.S. military have fought in the Vietnam War, the 1991 Gulf War, the wars in Afghanistan and Iraq that the U.S. launched in 2001 and 2003, respectively, and nine other large and small armed conflicts around the world. As described by Noy Thrupkaew in the liberal publication the *American Prospect* (February 2006), "*Why We Fight* digs into the incestuous relationships between corporate, military, and governmental interests, tracing back 50 years of wartime history in an attempt to demonstrate how decisions about military engagement are increasingly motivated by 'profit rather than public good,' as . . . Jarecki asserted in a phone interview." *Why We Fight* won the American Documentary Grand Jury Prize at the 2005 Sundance Film Festival. With the hope of sparking a national discussion on the current powerful military-industrial influence in American politics, Jarecki founded the Eisenhower Project, an "academic public policy group" dedicated to "studying the forces that shape American foreign policy," according to the *Why We Fight* Web site; as executive director of the organization, he works with students at universities who are interested in the same subject. "I definitely have an agenda," Jarecki told Laura Metzger for the British Broadcasting Corp. (BBC) World Web site (January 25, 2005). "It's an agenda toward a very free and open discussion about issues that will make or break the future for all of us. And that is no small challenge, because we live in a time when there is almost an embrace of ignorance in America." Jarecki's earlier films include the fictional *Season of the Lifterbees* and *The Opponent* and the documentaries *Quest of the Carib Canoe* and *The Trials of Henry Kissinger*, the last of which won the 2002 Amnesty International Award and has been released in more than 30 countries worldwide.

Eugene Jarecki was born on October 5, 1969 in Rye, New York, the youngest of the three sons of Henry G. Jarecki and Gloria Jarecki. According to the Web site islandsun.com, he also has a younger sister, Lianna. Jarecki's parents are Jewish; both of them fled despotic, oppressive governments early in their lives—his father, that of Nazi Germany, and his mother the Soviet Union. His parents' backgrounds contributed to their development of progressive, goal-oriented outlooks. Jarecki's father practiced clinical psychiatry for a year before becoming "a legendary figure in the world of metals trading," as futuresindustry.org described him; later, he turned to investment banking. Currently, he manages his own highly successful firm, the Falconwood Corp., and also teaches psychiatry at the Yale School of Medicine. Jarecki's mother is the president of Guana Island Corp., a business his parents began in the mid-1970s after purchasing the island of Guana in the British Virgin Islands. Committed to protecting the island's ecological integrity, the Jareckis established a wildlife preserve there, as well as a small, technologically modest resort. Henry Jarecki donated the funds to build the four-classroom Gloria Jarecki School as part of the Cambodia Rural School Project; the school opened in 2004. Jarecki's brothers, Tom and Andrew, with their father, co-founded Moviefone, a movie information and ticket service. Andrew is the director of the critically acclaimed documentary *Capturing the Friedmans* (2003).

After graduating from high school, Eugene Jarecki entered Princeton University, in New Jersey. He majored in English, with an emphasis on stage directing and political drama, and earned a bachelor's degree in 1991. He then enrolled in the Film Intensive Program at New York University, where he made the short feature *Season of the Lifterbees*, a fairy tale in which a boy leaves his forest home to attend his first day at school. When the work was accepted for the 1993 Sundance Film Festival, he became, at 21, the youngest entrant in that event that year. *Season of the Lifterbees* won the Student Academy Award and the Time Warner Grand Prize at the Aspen Film Festival. Seven years went by before the appearance of Jarecki's next film: the 50-minute documentary *Quest of the Carib Canoe*. That movie shows Jacob Frederick, a Carib Indian artist and activist, as he travels with other members of his community from the island of Dominica in the British West Indies to South America in a hand-built canoe—a voyage of 1,000 miles—with the aim of honoring their people's ancestral heritage. The film officially premiered on BBC television before being distributed to more than 15 countries, but it received little media attention.

After years of near anonymity, in 2000 Jarecki began establishing himself in the film industry with his first dramatic feature, *The Opponent*. Set in Port Chester, New York, the movie centers on Patty Sullivan, played by Erika Eleniak, known for her performances on the TV series *Baywatch*. Sullivan enrolls in boxing classes as a means of defending herself against a physically abusive boyfriend. As her obvious boxing talent becomes apparent, she starts working with a professional trainer, who helps her rise in the female boxing circuit and realize that she need not remain with her boyfriend. Jarecki wrote and directed the low-budget film, drawing inspiration from his childhood friendship with the heavyweight boxing champion Mike Tyson. The two met through Jarecki's uncle, who was Tyson's doctor, and Jarecki came to view his relationship with Tyson as "eye-opening and inspiring and ultimately disheartening," as he told Chris Hansen for the Westchester County, New York, *Journal News* (April 6, 2001). According to Jarecki, boxers often feel a "paradox of rage," and with *The Opponent* he attempted to illuminate and explore it. "The very rage that gets you into boxing will undo you if you don't arrive at a mechanism for its control," he told Hansen. The movie was released in 2000 to disappointing reviews. The film critic Robert Koehler wrote for *Variety* (November 9, 2000), "While Jarecki avoids an easy triumph-over-adversity ending as he tells the story of an abused woman who finds that there's more to boxing than self-defense, pat characters and episodes tend to flatten what could have been a multidimensional drama that, after fest bouts, should find a home base in cable." Despite such criticism, the film won the award for best narrative feature at the Westchester Film Festival in March 2001.

Following the release of *The Opponent*, Jarecki directed minor television projects for the National Geographic channel, *60 Minutes*, and HBO International. He was also asked by the BBC to produce and direct a documentary exploring the role in foreign-policy actions of Henry Kissinger, who had served as the U.S. secretary of state during the administrations of Presidents Richard Nixon and Gerald R. Ford, and the merit of the war-crime accusations that had been leveled against him for decades by political watchdogs and reporters. Jarecki's indecision about taking on the project ended when, in May 2001, Kissinger refused to testify in the case against the former Chilean dictator Augusto Pinochet, who was standing trial for torturing Spanish citizens. Jarecki agreed to direct the film, which was written by Alex Gibney and was based on Christopher Hitchens's book *The Trial of Henry Kissinger*, a scathingly critical view of its subject's record as the head of the State Department. Jarecki entitled his film *The Trials of Henry Kissinger*. Adding the letter "s" to "trial," he told Terry Armour for the *Chicago Tribune* (December 19, 2002), "seems like a little different but it actually means a lot. By pluralizing the title we meant very much to pluralize the voices being heard from in the film, a chorus of his friends and detractors." Unlike such filmmakers as Michael Moore, who were producing fiercely polemic political documentaries attacking President George W. Bush, his administration, and its policies, Jarecki, by his own account, went out of his way to give voice to both supporters and detractors of Kissinger and tried to avoid a partisan slant or condemnatory tone. "One of our goals in making this film was to make very clear to people that this is not a personal attack. The fact that we focused on Dr. Kissinger is a way to bring people's attention to the public policies and the cruelties of those policies that he's come to represent for millions of people from around the world," Jarecki told Armour. "But by focusing on that, we certainly did not want to create the impression [such that] people would leave the theater and say, 'Well, if we just took care of Dr. Kissinger's guilt or innocence—if we were to bring him to justice—the world would be safe for democracy.' It's a look at U.S. policy through the prism of Dr. Kissinger's experience and the prism of his conduct."

Jarecki designed *The Trials of Henry Kissinger* both as a forum for an open discussion on American foreign affairs and a scrupulous assessment of Kissinger's role in several events: the secret bombing of Cambodia in 1969; the death of the Chilean president-elect Salvador Allende in a political coup led by Pinochet in 1970; and the Indonesian invasion of East Timor in 1975, in which American-made weapons were used. Kissinger declined Jarecki's invitation to appear before the camera and state his side on those matters, and when the film opened, in 2002, he dismissed its charges as "frivolous," according to Sulaiman Beg in the *Journal News* (March 7, 2003). In March 2003, a few months after the picture's premiere, the U.S. invaded Iraq. "We want people to see the movie as a cautionary tale on current events. It's a vision of how a past administration, given carte blanche, broke laws and broke basic accepted notions of plain old human decency," Jarecki told Beg. In a review of the film for *Newsday* (September 25, 2002), John Anderson wrote, "What we have is a movie that informs, fascinates and leaves one with an ugly taste in the mouth. There's nothing intentionally sensationalistic about *The Trials of Henry Kissinger*, no overheated narration . . . and there are only timid juxtapositions of implicating footage. What we see in *Kissinger* is less devastating than what we hear, and what we hear is truly stranger than fiction. And much, much uglier than fiction ever dares to be." Others who reviewed *The Trials of Henry Kissinger* thought that Jarecki's attempts at neutrality had failed. Among those who nevertheless approved of its presentation was Deborah Hornblow, who wrote for the *Hartford (Connecticut) Courant* (October 19, 2002), "The film oversteps in its zealous attempt to pin all the deaths in Vietnam from 1969 to 1975 on Kissinger, who is charged with undercutting the Paris peace talks in 1969 that would have ended the war. But with strong evidence linking Kissinger to the assassination of [the Chilean army general Rene] Schneider [in 1970] . . . and documents to support Kissinger's role in the carpet-bombing of Cambodia, the filmmakers secure their conviction. The film's evident bias notwithstanding, *The Trials* amounts to a chilling echo of the events of our pres-ent time, one in which the United States' penchant for 'regime change' has become an isolating agenda. The current U.S. president seems a proponent of the doctrine practiced by Kissinger that says, as one British source put it, 'international law applies to everyone except the Americans.'"

After the release of the film, many viewers and reporters entertained the idea that Kissinger, who won the Nobel Peace Prize in 1973, should be made to stand trial for his alleged complicity in certain violent conflicts overseas. *The Trials of Henry Kissinger* also contributed to the public outcry that followed President George W. Bush's appointment in November 2002 of Kissinger to head a commission charged with investigating the ways in which the federal government had failed with regard to events leading up to the September 11, 2001 terrorist attacks. (The commission was formed only after many months of pressure exerted by many groups on the White House.) A month after his appointment, Kissinger resigned, ostensibly because the work of the consulting firm he had formed, and his ties to various organizations and public figures, might subject him to accusations of conflict of interest.

Jarecki's next documentary, *Why We Fight*, explores the reasons why the U.S. has fought so many wars. (*Why We Fight* has the same title as Frank Capra's 1940s propaganda film series, which expressed the conviction that the U.S. entered World War II because it was morally right to do so.) To provide a framework for the film, Jarecki used President Dwight D. Eisenhower's farewell address to the nation, on January 17, 1961, in which Eisenhower warned, "In the councils of government, we must guard against the acquisition of unwarranted influence, whether sought or unsought, by the military-industrial complex." "Eisenhower thought . . . this confluence of power, this unholy alliance between the defense industry and government . . . was a risk factor for the future, . . . he thought it would threaten democracy and the purity of our decision-making process about foreign policy and even domestic policy," Jarecki told Metzger. "I really wanted to visit, today, Eisenhower's prophecy. I wondered to what extent that warning has come to pass."

When Jarecki was making his film, in 2004, the U.S. defense budget had climbed to three-quarters of a trillion dollars (taking into account expenditures that appeared elsewhere in the budget, such as veterans' benefits and military-related homeland-security projects, or did not appear at all, such as the costs of the military operations in Afghanistan and Iraq), and constituted about 50 percent of the entire federal budget; moreover, the defense industry's profits were 25 percent greater than they had been the previous year. Curious about the reasons for such a rise in military expenditures, Jarecki questioned Republican and Democratic politicians and government officials in the Pentagon and Congress. Among others, he spoke with Arizona's Republican senator John McCain;

the Bush strategist Richard Perle; a Vietnam refugee and former bomb engineer; a retired New York City police officer whose son was killed in the September 11, 2001 attacks on the World Trade Center; and a retired army lieutenant colonel. Jarecki's objective for the film was to present the audience with a fair assessment of why the U.S. entered into wars—from Vietnam to the current war in Iraq—while reminding viewers of Eisenhower's warnings. "What I want most people to find in the film is that they find voices with whom they resonate and they find in the film voices with whom they might not agree but they can't simply disagree. It is meant to make people think twice," Jarecki told Peterson Gonzaga for VNU Entertainment News Wire (January 19, 2006). The film concludes that the U.S. fights because for various groups, wars and preparing for them is lucrative. "When war becomes that profitable, you're going to see more of it," a former CIA consultant, Chalmers Johnson, says in the movie. *Why We Fight* also warns that along with the growth in the armaments industry, some of the nation's traditional values are withering away. "The forces that are imperiling [our democracy] are the forces Eisenhower warned us about," Jarecki told Teresa Wiltz for the *Washington Post* (February 12, 2006). "It begins with his concern about the military-industrial complex and extends to other forces of corporatism in our society. Which is what he meant when he said, 'The power of money is ever-present and is gravely to be regarded.' They're not only trying to build a product; they're trying to keep it from being shut down. . . . And so we find the B-2 bomber has a piece of it made in every single U.S. state. Why? . . . Because everybody is getting a piece of the action." Released nationally in February 2006, *Why We Fight* won the 2005 Grand Jury Prize at the Sundance Film Festival. Owen Gleiberman wrote in a review of it for *Entertainment Weekly* (January 27, 2006), "*Why We Fight*'s analysis of the Iraq war as imperialist folly is the least original thing about it. Yet by the end of the movie, with its images of Saddam Hussein videogames, crowds being roused by the explosions at an air show, and a desolate recruit who joins the Army because he has nothing else to do, we're left with a vision of America grown accustomed, if not addictively numb, to the deadening spirit of war." Robert Koehler wrote for *Daily Variety* (January 27, 2005), "Combining the skills of journalist and poet, Eugene Jarecki joins the top ranks of non-fiction filmmakers with *Why We Fight*, a thoroughgoing and affecting film on the nature and causes of the American military-industrial complex."

Jarecki lives in Waitsfield, Vermont, with his wife, Claudia Becker, and their two young children. Becker served as a production assistant on *The Trials of Henry Kissinger*. She directed MountainTop, a human-rights film festival, held in January 2006 in Waitsfield at the Eclipse Theater, which she owns.

—I.C.

Suggested Reading: *BBC World* (on-line) Jan. 15, 2005; *Boston Globe* Jan. 29, 2006; *Chicago Tribune* Dec. 19, 2002; (Westchester County, New York) *Journal News* p2A Apr. 6, 2001, p2A Mar. 7, 2003; (Sarasota, Florida) *Herald-Tribune* G p1 Jan. 5, 2003; *Washington Post* N p3 Feb. 12, 2006

Selected Films: *Season of the Lifterbees*, 1993; *Quest of the Carib Canoe*, 2000; *The Opponent*, 2000; *The Trials of Henry Kissinger*, 2002; *Why We Fight*, 2005

Ethan Miller/Getty Images

Jefferts Schori, Katharine

Mar. 26, 1954– Presiding bishop of the Episcopal Church in the United States

Address: Episcopal Church Center, 815 Second Ave., New York, NY 10017

Katharine Jefferts Schori, who was installed as the presiding bishop of the Episcopal Church in the United States on November 4, 2006, has described her religious philosophy as "progressive," meaning a "willingness to use all of one's faculties to examine the faith rigorously and to advocate justice for everyone," as she defined the word during a conversation with John Przybys for the *Las Vegas (Nevada) Review-Journal* (June 11, 2006). On June 18, 2006, when Jefferts Schori's fellow bishops elected her to a nine-year term as the next presiding bishop and spiritual leader of the 2.4 million-member Episcopal Church in the United States, many Episcopalians felt increased fear of an impending schism, one that would separate the church from the worldwide, 77 million-member Anglican Communion, of which it is currently a part. The fear stemmed from fierce controversy among church members over the ordination of openly homosexual men, the blessing of same-sex marriages by priests, and Jefferts Schori's approval of both practices. Opponents of her positions on those issues have condemned her for voting in 2003 to confirm as bishop of New Hampshire the openly gay V. Gene Robinson. They have also decried her recent, widely quoted response to a question posed by a CNN interviewer as to whether being homosexual is a sin. "I don't believe so," Jefferts Schori said. "I believe that God creates us with different gifts. Each one of us comes into this world with a different collection of things that challenge us and things that give us joy and allow us to bless the world around us. Some people come into this world with affections ordered toward other people of the same gender, and some people come into this world with affections directed at people of the other gender." Jefferts Schori's remarks stirred one of her opponents, Les Kinsolving, a White House reporter, Anglican minister, and former Episcopalian priest, to write in his column for the on-line news service WorldNetDaily (June 24, 2006), "This astounding statement amounts to a contention that homosexuals are born that way—a claim that has been made, recurrently, by the Sodomy Lobby—with no such scientific evidence ever determined." Jefferts Schori has disputed such assertions: "For us to say in this day and age that homosexuality is sinful is to ignore evidence science has brought us," she declared to Christina Littlefield for the *Las Vegas Sun* (July 1, 2006, on-line). When the Episcopal gay activist Louie Crew asked Jefferts Schori for the *Witness* (April 18, 2006, on-line), a magazine produced by the Church Publishing Co., an arm of the Episcopal Church, "What do you most value about the Episcopal Church?," she said, "I value most its historic ability to live with diversity and to celebrate that diversity. We have gotten better in some areas over the years, like liturgical diversity. We are wrestling mightily at the moment with theological diversity. I love the Episcopal Church's ability not to define everything, to allow for a varied interpretation. Some see that as a mighty sin, but I see it as one of the gifts of the creator. To be created in the image of God doesn't mean just one thing."

Jefferts Schori, who has attended Episcopal churches since the age of nine, has served the church in official capacities only since 1994, when she was ordained as a deacon and then a priest, at age 40. In early 2001 she was elected bishop of the Episcopalian Diocese of Nevada, which consists of three dozen congregations (including one in Arizona) with a total of about 6,000 members. She remained in that post until she was installed as the head of the Episcopal Church in the United States, becoming the first woman to lead any branch of the worldwide Anglican Communion and the first woman in the U.S. to lead a major Protestant denomination. Earlier, for about a decade in the 1980s, Jefferts Schori had worked as an oceanographer. Discussing with Nancy Haught, a reporter for the Religion News Service (July 5, 2006), her transition from scientist to minister, she said, "In the Middle Ages, theology was called the queen of the sciences. What science means is a way of knowing, of seeking knowledge. The kind of science that I did as an oceanographer involved looking at the world in all its diversity and making sense out of that. The kind of knowing that I'm engaged in now involves meaning issues: Why are we here? What are human beings' roles in creation? How do we live together? I see them as complementary ways of looking at the world. When I'm feeling flip, I tell people that I'm still fishing."

The oldest of four children, Katharine Jefferts was born into a Roman Catholic family on March 26, 1954 in Pensacola, Florida. She has a sister, Ingrid, and two brothers, Steven and Erik. Her father, Keith B. Jefferts, was a navy pilot; after earning a doctorate in physics, he worked in the field of radio astronomy at Bell Laboratories with Arno Penzias and Robert Wilson, who won the Nobel Prize in Physics jointly in 1978. Keith Jefferts also revolutionized salmon management; while still at Bell Labs, he collaborated with a childhood fishing friend of his to develop a system for tracking salmon, and later, in the 1970s, he invented a magnetic, coded wire tag that could be implanted in juvenile salmon and detected in captured adult fish. A billion of the tags have since been sold for use with salmon and hundreds of other types of fish and other animals. Jefferts Schori's mother, Elaine Ryan (now deceased), was a microbiologist and virologist. She and Jefferts Schori's father divorced in 1981. Jefferts Schori began her formal education at a Catholic parochial school, where she was taught by nuns and performed well. "It was a very strict environment, and I remember we got numerical grades in things like diction and deportment," she said to John Przybys. "But, at the same time, it was a very gracious place." Occasionally the nuns would play kickball with the children, indicating to them, as Jefferts Schori told Christina Littlefield, that "joy is a central part of the Christian life." When she was in the fifth grade, the Jefferts family moved to New Jersey, where young Kate attended public school. Soon after the move her parents converted to Episcopalianism. Recalling the event to Przybys, she said, "As I've put it together since, I think it was their own frustration about [a] lack of change in the Roman tradition." She recalled to Neela Banerjee for the *New York Times* (June 21, 2006), "We went from a liturgy in Latin to one in English, from a large and anonymous church to a small and intimate one."

As a seven- or eight-year-old, Jefferts Schori knew that she wanted to make her career "in the ocean or in medicine," as she told Susan Skorupa for the *Reno (Nevada) Gazette-Journal* (February 27, 2001). After her high-school graduation, she enrolled at Stanford University, in California, and majored in biology. In science, she told John Przybys, she found "a sense of mystery and the presence of God in the natural order of creation." After she earned a B.S. degree, in 1974, she entered Oregon State University, in Corvallis, where she studied squid and octopuses and other marine invertebrates, and in particular their evolution. Her research, she told Alan Cooperman for the *Washington Post* (July 3, 2006, on-line), helped her to appreciate "the great wonder and variety of creation." She received a master's degree, in 1977, and a Ph.D., in 1983, both in oceanography. She then took a job with the National Marine Fisheries Service. Before long she began to feel frustrated in her work, not least because federal funding for oceanographic research was shrinking.

Earlier, when Jefferts Schori was about 22, a close friend of hers and his family were killed in a plane crash. In the wake of their deaths, she spent much time pondering fundamental spiritual questions. Also during that period Jefferts Schori took a graduate course in the philosophy of science, which further stirred her interest in the universe's great mysteries. "And that led me back to the church looking for answers," she said to John Przybys. She became a regular churchgoer, joining an Episcopal church in Seattle, Washington, and later the Episcopal Church of the Good Samaritan in Corvallis. In the mid-1980s several of the congregants suggested that she consider becoming a priest. "I was astounded. I laughed," she said to Przybys. "When I was growing up, little girls didn't think about things like that." After speaking to a priest at her Corvallis church about pursuing ordination, she concluded that she was not yet ready. For a while she taught religion at the college level. Then, at the time of the 1991 war in the Persian Gulf, she preached a sermon at the church, at the invitation of a clergyman, and found the experience rewarding. For a brief period afterward, she prayed with her pastor for spiritual guidance. Feeling more prepared to seek ordination, in the fall of 1991 she enrolled at the Church Divinity School of the Pacific, in Berkeley, California, one of the 11 seminaries of the Episcopal Church in the U.S. She earned a master of divinity degree in 1994 and that same year was ordained as both a deacon and a priest. "My sense of call was like looking at a series of doors closing and others opening, not like there were words on fire on the wall," she said to Neela Banerjee. "It was this dawning awareness that, 'Yes, it makes sense, that there is a coherence to the pieces I am experiencing.'"

The Episcopal Church in the United States (ECUSA), or the Episcopal Church (TEC), as it is known informally, currently has 108 dioceses within nine so-called provinces. Two provinces include churches outside the U.S. (with Haiti, the U.S. Virgin Islands, and the Convocation of American Churches in Europe included in one province and Taiwan in the other). One province includes overseas churches only (in Colombia, Ecuador, Honduras, Puerto Rico, the Dominican Republic, and Venezuela). All are under the jurisdiction of the presiding bishop (currently, Frank Tracy Griswold III). The General Convention, which meets every three years, serves as the ECUSA's governing and legislative body; it consists of the House of Deputies, with up to four laypersons and four clergy representatives from each diocese, and the House of Bishops, which includes retired as well as active bishops. Individual churches, or congregations, are categorized as cathedrals, parishes, missions, or chapels, with parishes being most common. Depending upon the congregation's category, its leader is called a dean, a priest (or rector), a chaplain, or a vicar; deacons rank below priests, and lay leaders are called wardens. The head of each diocese is a bishop; there are no archbishops. ECUSA descended from the Church of England, or Anglican Church (which came into being in the 16th century, when King Henry VIII, born a Roman Catholic, was excommunicated and broke completely with the Catholic Church after defying the pope by divorcing his first wife and remarrying). ECUSA became independent after the American Revolution but remains closely affiliated with the Anglican Communion. The archibishop of Canterbury heads the Church of England and the Anglican Communion only symbolically, but he is considered "first among equals" among the presiding bishops (also called primates). Like Roman Catholic churches, the churches in the Anglican Communion use the Old and New Testaments and part of the Bible known as the Apocrypha, incorporate the Nicene and Apostles' Creeds (statements of belief) in their services, celebrate communion and four other sacramental rites, and recognize saints. Unlike Catholic churches, they involve laypeople in decision-making, allow married and other uncelibate men as well as women to be ordained, use the Book of Common Prayer in services, and do not recognize the authority of the pope. A few U.S. dioceses do not permit the ordination of women. Around the world, 13 of the Anglican Communion's 38 constituencies have never ordained women, and the only countries to date that have installed female bishops are the U.S., Canada, and New Zealand.

After her ordination Jefferts Schori became the assistant rector at her church. Fluent in Spanish, she served as pastor to the Spanish-speakers in the congregation, whose numbers she was instrumental in increasing. In October 2000, at a state convention in Reno, Nevada, a majority of the clergy and laypeople present elected her bishop of the diocese of Nevada. (In the Anglican Church, bishops are appointed.) Jefferts Schori was consecrated bishop on February 24, 2001 and thus became the ninth woman in the ECUSA to hold that title. (The Episcopal priesthood was opened to women in 1977.) Jefferts Schori "has a good mind," V. James Jeffery, an Episcopal priest from Reno, told Susan Skorupa. "I think she can draw us all together and make us feel like we're one." David Funk, a member of the Episcopal bishopric search committee, told Skorupa, "I look for a new vision from her—another approach to church activities within the state as well as on a national level. I think it was the wish of the convention delegates for change and they liked her approach to change, her openness, honesty and vision of the future." A licensed pilot, Jefferts Schori has flown to visit congregations within the sparsely populated state, working to close divisions between rural and urban congregations and between churches in the northern and southern parts of Nevada. She has also made special efforts to reach out to Filipino, Hispanic, African-American, and Native American church members. "I think we've gone a long way toward bridging the chasms—toward building a greater sense of community in the different regions of the diocese," she said to Geralda Miller for the *Reno Gazette-Journal* (May 28, 2005). She also said to Miller, "We need to be starting new faith communities in rapidly growing parts of the diocese. . . . We're not just a white church, which is our reputation unfortunately." She told Skorupa that she wanted the church to serve as "an advocate for people who are exploited" by legal gambling in Nevada (a major source of revenue for the state) and, in some counties, legal prostitution. "The Gospel tells us to help the oppressed, the forgotten, the exploited," she said. According to Skorupa, "The motivating theme in her ministry has come from the prophet Isaiah—to feed the hungry, console the brokenhearted, bring sight to the blind and free the captives."

At the 2006 General Convention, the 188 attending bishops chose their next presiding bishop from a slate of one female and six male candidates. Jefferts Schori led on the first four ballots and won the election on the fifth, held on June 18, by a vote of 95 to 93. When Rowan Williams, the archbishop of Canterbury, spoke to her by phone the next day, "he was . . . a bit anxious," as Jefferts Schori told Stephen Bates for the London *Guardian* (June 24, 2006, on-line). "As well he might be," Bates wrote. "Jefferts Schori's unexpected election . . . was an indication that the Americans were not going to roll over and allow conservative forces elsewhere to dictate to them." The conservative forces to which he referred urged the archbishop not to invite Jefferts Schori to the next international gathering of Anglican bishops and primates, scheduled for 2008. At the last such meeting, known as the Lambeth conference, held in 1998, the participants issued a resolution, approved by a vote of 526 to 70, declaring that "homosexual practice" was "incompatible with Scripture." (Later, 182 bishops and primates apologized to lesbian and gay Anglicans in a public Pastoral Statement.) The resolution also stated that the church "cannot advise the legitimising or blessing of same sex unions nor ordaining those involved in same gender unions." At the same time, it left the door open to changes in the church's position, by requesting that "Primates and the [Anglican Communion Office] establish a

means of monitoring the work done on the subject of human sexuality in the Communion and to share statements and resources among us." Then, in 2004, following the turmoil provoked by the consecration of V. Gene Robinson as the bishop of New Hampshire, a commission appointed by the archbishop of Canterbury issued a document, known as the Windsor Report, which called for a moratorium on both the ordination of openly gay men and the blessing of same-sex unions.

Among many conservatives in the U.S., too, Jefferts Schori's election as presiding bishop triggered dismay and, in some cases, outrage. "The incoming presiding bishop has made her positions very clear—that she is committed to the new agenda, committed to same-sex blessings, committed to having same-sex partners in the leadership in the church—which means she is also *not* committed to the faith as delivered to the saints," Bishop Robert W. Duncan, head of the Pittsburgh diocese, said to Alan Cooperman. Jefferts Schori further angered many church members when, in her homily on June 21, 2006 at the last communion at the 75th General Convention, she referred to Jesus as a mother, saying, "Our mother Jesus gives birth to a new creation—and you and I are His children." In response to charges that she was "preaching heresy," in Bates's words, she told Bates that her choice of words "was very deliberate and conscious" and that medieval Christians had used the same imagery. "I was trying to say that the work of the cross was in some ways like giving birth to a new creation," she explained to Alan Cooperman. "That is straight-down-the-middle orthodox theology." She also said to Cooperman, "All language is metaphorical, and if we insist that particular words have only one meaning and the way we understand those words is the only possible interpretation, we have elevated that text into an idol." She added, "I'm encouraging people to look beyond their favorite understandings." The Pittsburgh diocese and a half-dozen others in the U.S. have announced that they will not recognize Jefferts Schori's authority and have asked the archbishop of Canterbury to assign a conservative primate from another nation as their leader, at least temporarily.

On November 4, 2006, at a ceremony held at the National Cathedral, in Washington, D.C., Jefferts Schori was installed as presiding bishop of the Episcopal Church. (Jerry Lamb, the retiring bishop of Northern California, will serve as bishop of Nevada until October 2007, when an election will determine Jefferts Schori's permanent successor.) In her first sermon in her new position, Jefferts Schori talked about the controversy surrounding her appointment, telling the assembled crowd, as quoted by Louis Sahagun in the *Los Angeles Times* (November 5, 2006), "If some in this church feel wounded by recent decisions, then our salvation, our health as a body, is at some hazard, and it becomes the duty of all of us to seek healing and wholeness. As long as children live exposed on the streets, while seniors go without food to pay for life-sustaining drugs, wherever people are sickened by industrial waste, the body suffers, and none of us can say we have finally come home."

Neela Banerjee described Jefferts Schori as "a tall, slender woman who speaks in a soft alto"; Stephen Bates characterized her as "a model of self-possession"; and Christina Littlefield wrote that she "emits an inner joy that is inspiring and soothing" and that "fellow clergy describe her as a tension diffuser, able to build bridges and push boundaries at the same time." John Kater, one of her divinity-school professors, told Jennifer Garza for the *Sacramento (California) Bee* (June 24, 2006), "She's always been an extremely good listener and very perceptive. . . . She's calm, but she is also very tough." In 1979 Jefferts Schori married Richard Miles Schori, a now-retired college teach-

er of theoretical mathematics. Their only child, a married daughter, Katharine Schori Harris, who was 24 in 2006, is a U.S. Air Force pilot. In her leisure time Jefferts Schori enjoys backpacking, rock climbing, and camping with her husband. She runs several miles a few times a week.

—D.F.

Suggested Reading: *Christian Century* p13 July 11, 2006; Episcopal Church Web site; *Las Vegas (Nevada) Review-Journal* K p1 June 11, 2006; *Las Vegas (Nevada) Sun* (on-line) July 1, 2006; (London) *Guardian* (on-line) June 24, 2006; *New York Times* A p10 June 21, 2006; *Reno (Nevada) Gazette-Journal* E p1+ Feb. 27, 2001; *Sacramento (California) Bee* K p1 June 24, 2006; *Time* p6 July 17, 2006; *Washington Post* (on-line) July 3, 2006

Courtesy of the Steven Style Group

Jones, Scott

Oct. 5, 1960– Inventor; technology entrepreneur

Address: Gazelle TechVentures, 11611 N. Meridian St., Suite 310, Carmel, IN 46032

Though few people outside the high-tech industry know his name, Scott Jones has the potential to reinvent everyday life in the 21st century, just as Thomas Alva Edison did in the 19th. He has already made a tremendous impact on people's daily interactions: more than a half-billion people worldwide use his patented voice-mail system every day. In addition, as the chairman of companies

including Gracenote Inc. and the founder of Escient Technologies, he has taken steps toward merging Internet technology with ordinary electronic devices and appliances, reinventing our idea of entertainment and accessibility; many of the innovations of his companies are integral to such products as Apple's iPod, a portable device for storing and playing music that is currently in the hands of more than 40 million consumers, and iTunes, which allows users to purchase and download music on-line, among other functions. "I have a strong desire to help change our world for the better," Jones remarked in an E-mail interview with *Current Biography*.

The brave new world Jones envisions—in which people can contact anyone in the world, or enjoy any mode of entertainment they desire, at the touch of a button—frightens some, who believe that too great a reliance on technology can be harmful. If the fulfillment of our needs and desires is too easy, too close to our fingertips, they maintain, then human individuality may begin to erode. Jones argues that technology is only what we make of it. "Technology can't make moral judgments; people can and do, sometimes not for the better," he said to *Current Biography*. "However, if correctly deployed, technology can help us further amplify what is most human about ourselves. Technology can save lives, significantly enhance the quality of life, and enrich the human experience. That is what motivates me."

Scott Alan Jones was born on October 5, 1960 in Louisville, Kentucky, to George and Barbara Jones. He was raised in Indiana, surrounded by a loving extended family. His interest in building and invention seems to have stemmed in part from his father, an engineer who, among other projects, had overseen the construction for St. John's Medical Center in Anderson, Indiana. Jones's childhood was a happy one, in part because his relatives encouraged his inquisitiveness. "I had a wonderful childhood," Jones remarked in his interview with *Current Biography*. "I always had 'projects' where I was inventing and discovering things, and it helped to have access to my father's woodworking and metalworking shop. I conducted experiments with chemistry sets and electronics, that sort of stuff. At a fairly young age, my uncle taught me how to solder (he was a horse trainer at Churchill Downs who used some of the first PC's to help him manage his horses). I was very close to my grandparents, too."

Unlike the stereotypical inventor locked in a basement and isolated from the rest of the world, Jones was very outgoing and involved with people as a youth. As he told *Current Biography*, "Many times, I went on daylong 'adventures' that took me biking/hiking much further from home than my parents ever knew. I spent a lot of time reading 'classics' and I devoured *Popular Science* and *Scientific American* magazines. I loved math and science and had a particularly motivating set of science/math teachers in public junior high and high school. I also engaged in many entrepreneurial activities in my neighborhood: door-to-door sales of seeds [and] holiday gifts, [and I] organized and sold tickets to carnivals and haunted houses, etc. I also played basketball in high school, which helped me acquire valuable team-building skills that have served me well in business."

One of Jones's childhood hobbies was to take apart electronic devices in order to see how they worked. His first contact with computers only deepened his desire to do so. "When I was 12 years old, I saw my first big computers at the local university while I was in Boy Scouts (my scoutmaster was a professor there) and I had the opportunity to program in BASIC during my teens," he recalled. "So, the interest was there at a very young age."

An excellent student, Jones acquired two years' worth of college credits during his time at North Central High School in Indianapolis. In the fall of 1978, he entered Indiana University (IU) with the intention of taking pre-med courses and ultimately becoming a doctor. Just one computer-science course, however, convinced him that his talents lay in engineering rather than medicine. Since Indiana University did not offer a degree in electrical engineering, he had to teach himself. The inventor told *Current Biography*: "I put an ad in *Byte* magazine for companies to send me their used electronics and computer 'leftovers'. . . and they did, but by the busload: I filled my basement with an electronics lab and taught myself a great deal about electronics and computers from the ground up. At IU, I was able to get a thorough grounding in chemistry, biology, math, physics, and computer science. This broad knowledge helped me to make various 'connections' in technologies in a Renaissance fashion."

While at IU, Jones worked at the university's speech-recognition laboratory, as a programmer, and at its neurochemistry laboratory, as a consultant. In the latter position he helped to develop cutting-edge technologies to monitor the electrochemical activities of the human brain. After graduating with honors in 1984, he served as a researcher for the Artificial Intelligence Laboratory at the Massachusetts Institute of Technology (MIT), in Cambridge. His position at the lab gave him access to advanced technology in robotics and the Internet—some years before those technologies were available to the general public.

In 1986 Jones left MIT to found his first company, Boston Technology Inc. (BT), with his friend Greg Carr. Jones's experience at the speech-recognition laboratory, as well as at MIT, convinced him that it was possible to build an electronic system that could record, store, edit, and play back human voices without the need for bulky answering machines and magnetic tape. "Starting in college, I developed an interest in having computers that were able to talk and hear—voice recognition stuff," he explained to *Current Biography*. "While working at IU, I discovered a way to store human voice on the computer's tiny hard drive (these were the very first personal computers and were not very powerful at all). At MIT's Artificial Intelligence Lab, I discovered more about computerizing voice. I learned more about voice recognition, but decided that one of the most important uses of the current technologies was the storage and distribution of digitally encoded voice. My patents relate to building massive storage networks that can handle the bandwidth requirements of voice. When we started the business (Boston Technology), I built a prototype of the first voice mail system on a first-generation IBM-PC. It was used to demonstrate the technology to investors in order to raise financial capital for my company. We then sold relatively small voice mail systems to small businesses. Meanwhile, I talked with patent attorneys about designs that I had to build very large, fully integrated voice mail systems. These systems were not commercially viable until the federally mandated break-up of [the communications network] AT&T ('Ma Bell') created a situation where the resulting Baby Bell companies could sell 'enhanced services' such as voice-mail."

While the Baby Bells—or the Regional Bell Operating Companies, as they are officially known—could offer voice-mail services to their customers, they were forbidden by law from manufacturing those systems themselves, as part of the effort to keep any telephone company from developing a monopoly. They therefore began looking for a company that had the technology to build an extensive, adaptable voice-mail system—in a very short period of time. Jones, as it happened, had already developed a design for such a system; he needed only a team in place to make it work. "I pulled together a team of a half-dozen engineers in Cambridge, Massachusetts, to help build the first fully distributed, massively parallel computational platform for voice messaging," he recalled. "In order to build it, we had to merge technologies from separate industries: PC's from the computer industry and digital switching from the telecommunications industry. The really difficult parts of the project had more to do with making the system ultra-reliable and 'foolproof' rather than simply making it work."

Jones clinched the deal with the Regional Bells by telling them that he could deliver an inexpensive system 20 times bigger and more reliable than anything on the market—in just three months. The Bells jumped at the chance to get such a system so quickly, as Jones's competitors had claimed that it would take 18 to 36 months to design and build something similar. At the time that the Bells entrusted Boston Technology with the project, BT's boss and principal architect was only 26 years old.

"It was intimidating, challenging and exciting all at the same time," Jones recalled to Current Biography. "We had good ideas and theories about how to build a massive voice-processing system, but nobody had ever done it before. We had to conduct many 'experiments' to determine what the various components were capable of doing. We had to merge together technologies that had not been combined before (PC's, local area networking, and switching technology). At times, we were not sure that we had all the 'right' pieces of technology to get the job done, but fortunately 'necessity was the mother of invention.' We found a way to meet our three-month deadline, but only by working around the clock—literally. For a month, I didn't even leave the office building. When I slept, it was under my desk using a sleeping bag that I kept in my office."

In 1988 Bell Atlantic became the first customer for Boston Technology's scalable voice-mail system (that is, a system that could be adjusted according to the size of the company), with Southwestern Bell and BellSouth quickly following suit. The voice-mail architecture Jones created can be found in many businesses and homes, as it is now the standard for telephone companies worldwide. As of 2001, more than 500 million people across the globe were using Jones's system; it remains the invention of which he is most proud. "It is very gratifying to know that this innovation has had a broad and pervasive impact on business and society," he remarked. "I believe that the 'time shifting' of voice communications has substantially changed our world at several levels. In addition to making life more manageable at a personal and business level in developed countries, it has had arguably even more impact in developing countries where voice mail provides a 'multiplier effect' for villages that have only one telephone among dozens of families and individuals, for example. And, for communities that have more cellular phone infrastructure than copper/fiber telecommunications infrastructure, voice messaging has allowed for a 'virtual answering machine' that further enhances and leverages newer communications technologies."

The scalable voice-mail system made Jones a multimillionaire, which allowed him the freedom to do some things he had always wanted to do. Beginning in 1992 he left the daily operations of Boston Technology to pursue other interests, which included learning to pilot a variety of aircraft; he has since flown everything from gliders and hot-air balloons to helicopters and jets and has expressed an interest in developing technologies for the aviation field. After a few years of traveling and enjoying time with his family, he decided to return to his roots in Indiana. Meanwhile, Boston Technology had merged with Comverse Technology Inc. to form a multibillion-dollar provider of products and services to telephone companies the world over.

When Jones returned to Indiana, in 1995, he began developing the ideas that led to the launch of Escient Technologies LLC, the high-tech company he co-founded in 1996 with Tom Doherty. Escient was established on the principle that as technology developed, the power of the Internet would merge with electronic appliances used in the home and office. The company's motto was, "We make technology behave." During his interview with Current Biography, Jones elaborated on the company's work, explaining that Escient was devoted to "building entertainment solutions for homes and businesses that make it easier for people to enjoy and manage their music, movies, video content, home videos, personal photos, web sites, etc. Today, homes typically have central heating and air conditioning powered by a furnace that distributes the heated or cooled air to all parts of the house." Escient, he said, sought to build "the technologies to make an 'entertainment furnace' possible, only instead of distributing air, these technologies will distribute entertainment content." In the years after its founding, Escient acquired more than a dozen businesses.

Jones remarked to Current Biography, "I believe there are ways to significantly enhance the impact that music has on our lives by making it much more accessible. This applies to music that one currently owns, as well as music that is yet undiscovered for a particular individual. I have found that music can substantially alter attitudes, motivation, and mood. While intangible, I think this has [a] broad, pervasive impact on the world." In 1998, having already licensed compact-disc database (CDDB) technology to use in a 200-CD changer, Escient acquired the CD-technology company ION, merging it and other companies into a firm christened Gracenote Inc., of which Jones is chairman. According to an on-line company profile, Gracenote "provides music recognition technologies that compare digital music files to a worldwide database of music information, enabling digital audio devices to identify the song or track you're listening to." The company states on its Web site, "Leading Gracenote-enabled brands include: media players such as Apple's iTunes, RealNetworks RealPlayer, AOL's Winamp, Napster's Napster 3.0, and CD/DVD PC applications from Roxio and Sonic Solutions."

In 2000 Jones and Gerry Dick co-founded Grow Indiana Media Ventures, a disseminator of business and technology news, of which Jones is chairman. He also chairs Gazelle TechVentures, a venture-capital firm established in the previous year, and is the founder of PowerFile Inc., "the world leader in DVD storage libraries," according to its Web site. Jones sold Escient Technologies to D&M Holdings, a Japanese electronics manufacturer, in May 2003. Inspired to participate in the 2005 DARPA Grand Challenge, a 175-mile race across the Mojave Desert by unmanned vehicles, Jones became the chairman and CEO of IndyRobotics, parent company of the Indy Robot Racing Team—which entered a vehicle in the race. The DARPA (Defense Advanced Research Project Agency) Grand Challenge is "the result of a mandate by Congress and the Department of Defense . . . that by 2015, one-third of operational ground vehicles of the armed forces must be unmanned," according to *Inside INdiana with Gerry Dick* (August 15, 2005, on-line). Jones served as co–team leader of the Indy Robot Racing Team.

Jones's home in Carmel, Indiana, has become something of a showroom for the technologies he has helped to develop. A 27,000-square-foot home on a 46-acre property, Jones's estate is at once old-fashioned and decidedly contemporary. Built in the 1930s, the house resembles a 19th-century English manor; after five years of renovation and extension, it is now a monument to modernity, one with which Jones is in continual contact via the Internet. From almost anywhere in the world, he can control the heat, lights, and music playing in any part of the house, and through a vast array of cameras and heat sensors in every room and on the grounds, he can keep track of servants or check in on his sons. The house also boasts a 20-seat movie theater, a 28-foot slide, a library of more than 1,600 books, and a 2,500-gallon aquarium.

Jones believes that such connectivity allows him to be more productive. When asked by *Current Biography* if he ever felt himself to be a prisoner of his own technology, he replied, "I have the freedom to connect. And, being human, there are times when I want (and really need) to disconnect. I love having the power and freedom to be connected, to accomplish my goals from anywhere and at anytime. I love having access to my best tools without the constraints of location or time. However, it is important for me to understand that I control the technology—it doesn't control me. This can be difficult for some people who either become addicted to the technology or feel pressure from others to utilize the technology when it invades their personal boundaries. To use these sorts of technologies effectively, people must understand their priorities in life and be able to effect those priorities through their conscious use of these powerful technologies."

When asked to imagine the life of an average American a generation in the future, Jones predicted: "Because of the work of companies like Escient, I believe that in 20 years (probably less) people around the world will have a much greater ability to access whatever content they desire 'on demand' at anytime and from anywhere. Just as the Internet has dramatically changed people's ability to access and search broad amounts of information, this increased ability to do so with entertainment content will dramatically enhance the way people 'do' education, training, business presentations, business communications, and home entertainment."

In September 2006 Jones and Brad Bostic, the chairman of Bostech Corp., announced the debut of ChaCha, a so-called social search engine that allows Internet users to interact with paid human researchers (called guides). After a user accesses ChaCha and types in a search term, he or she has the option of initiating a real-time, typed conversation with a ChaCha researcher. As of mid-October 2006, about 7,000 guides had signed on to ChaCha.

Jones sits on the boards of a variety of institutions, including the Art Technology Group, the Indianapolis Zoo, and the Children's Museum of Indianapolis. In 1994 he established a charitable organization in his name, which has made substantial contributions toward helping children reach their full academic potential while also exposing them to the benefits of technology. He has also served as chairman of the Indiana Technology Partnership, whose goal is to make Indiana the Midwest's center of the high-tech field in the 21st century.

Jones maintains a close relationship with his parents, who helped oversee the renovation of his estate, as well as with his sister, Susie. He has three sons, Benjamin, Andrew, and Daniel, who divide their time between their parents' homes.

—C.M.

Suggested Reading: *Business Wire* May 8, 2000; *Fortune* p140 Oct. 11, 1999; Indiana University Web site; *Indianapolis Monthly* p108+ Oct. 2001; *Indianapolis Star* C p1 Apr. 19, 2000; Scott A. Jones Web site

---

Karpinski, Janis

May 25, 1953– Former U.S. Army general; business consultant

Address: c/o Miramax Books, 99 Hudson St., Fifth Fl., New York, NY 10013

Janis Karpinski, a former brigadier general in the U.S. Army, became the first woman in the country's history to command troops in a war zone when she was put in charge of thousands of sol-

Spencer Platt/Getty Images

Janis Karpinski

diers in Iraq, following the 2003 U.S.-led invasion of that country. She also became the highest-ranking officer to be reprimanded in connection with American soldiers' abuse of prisoners at Iraq's Abu Ghraib detention facility, which came to light in the early months of 2004. In the midst of the scandal, which damaged the image of the U.S. military, Karpinski categorically denied responsibility for the abuses, claiming that she had been made a scapegoat by higher-ranking army and government officials. Karpinski is the author, with Steven Strasser, of the memoir *One Woman's Army: the Commanding General of Abu Ghraib Tells Her Story*, published in the fall of 2005.

The third of six children—and one of four daughters—of Nelson Arthur Beam, a Dutch-German chemical engineer, and his wife, Ruth (Sorenson) Beam, Karpinski was born Janis Leigh Beam on May 25, 1953 near Rahway, New Jersey. Her mother was an active member of the Republican Party at the local level; her father had served in Germany on the Allied side during World War II. Karpinski's family was close-knit, and her parents instilled conservative values and patriotism in their children. For example, on holidays her mother often displayed the family's American flag outside their home.

Karpinski decided at a very early age that she wanted to be a soldier. As a girl she preferred her brothers' GI Joe action figures to her own toys, and she is said to have paraded her Barbie dolls in military formation with the words "A-OK US Army" written on their backs. Karpinski's siblings have described their sister as having had a strong sense of adventure and wonder as a child, which she exhibited during their travels to the arcade-lined

boardwalks in towns on the New Jersey seashore and elsewhere. "She loved the wild rides at the boardwalk," Karpinski's sister Debby Russell told Libby Copeland for the *Washington Post* (May 10, 2004). "She was always the one that ran into the ocean and worried about whether it was cold [only] when she got there." According to several sources, her mother once had to stop Karpinski from leaping from her family's second-story window. (To Karpinski, as Copeland reported, "it didn't seem that far down.")

For fear of upsetting her parents, Karpinski did not embrace the antiwar sentiment that was widespread during her teenage years, when the Vietnam War was at its peak. While attending Rahway High School and, later, Kean College, in Union, New Jersey, she worked as a waitress in nearby Seaside Heights. There, she befriended and later fell in love with George Karpinski, who ran an amusement-park booth with his brother. The two later married, and after finishing college—Janis Karpinski graduated from Kean with a degree in English in 1975—they both became teachers.

Before long Karpinski found her duties as a substitute teacher to be dull. After discovering a magazine advertisement for the U.S. Army, she contacted an army recruiter. Karpinski explained to Helena de Bertodano for the London *Times* (August 13, 2004) that her decision to join the army grew in part from "a restlessness" to travel. Both she and her husband, who was then working as a biology teacher, joined the army and later decided to make careers of the military. After completing officer training, military police training, and airborne course work (or jump school), Karpinski was assigned to active duty. She was commissioned as a second lieutenant in 1977. Over the course of the next decade, she was stationed at U.S. military installations in a variety of locations, beginning with Fort Bragg, North Carolina, where she did intelligence work, and later including Fort McPherson, Georgia, and Mannheim, Germany, where she was an antiterrorism officer. In 1987 she was assigned to the army reserves and took on various positions related to military police work and intelligence gathering.

Beginning with the 1991 Persian Gulf War, Karpinski returned to active duty, serving as an operations and targeting officer with allied Special Forces in Riyadh, Saudi Arabia, in Operation Desert Shield (which involved the buildup of troops); she received a Bronze Star for her service during the conflict. (The 1991 Gulf War took place following Iraq's invasion of Kuwait; a coalition of forces led by the U.S. drove Iraqi troops from the country.) Continuing her active duty after the war, Karpinski was stationed in Abu Dhabi, United Arab Emirates (UAE), where she helped set up military training programs for women in the Gulf region and, through her post at the U.S. Embassy, advised the UAE government on ways to integrate women into the army. During the 1990s Karpinski served as commander of the 160th Military Police Battalion in Tallahassee, Florida; director of operations for the 641st Area Support Group in Saint Petersburg, Florida; and chief of staff for the Readiness Command in Fort Jackson, South Carolina.

At the outset of the American-led invasion of Iraq on March 20, 2003, Karpinski was stationed in Birmingham, Alabama, serving as chief of staff of the 81st Regional Support Command. The U.S. and its allies deposed Iraq's leader, Saddam Hussein, for failure to comply with the United Nations Security Council's Resolution 1441, regarding possession of so-called weapons of mass destruction. (No such weapons have been found during the U.S. occupation.) By May 2003 American soldiers had reached Iraq's capital city, Baghdad. Several days later the Security Council approved the installation of a U.S.-led administration in Iraq until a new government could be established. In June 2003 Karpinski was appointed brigadier general of the Army Reserve's 800th Military Police in Iraq. She thus became the only female commander in Iraq, and, according to several sources, the first woman in U.S. history to command troops in a war zone. She was put in charge of eight battalions and approximately 3,400 reservists, and was made responsible for the prison facilities in Iraq (as many as 17) that were controlled by allied forces—despite having no prior experience overseeing a prison facility. As reported in the press, those imprisoned included three major groups: civilians, security detainees (those suspected of crimes against the U.S.-led coalition), and top officials of Hussein's regime.

Earlier, in the fall of 2002, Hussein had emptied Iraq's detention facilities of their prisoners without explanation, leaving many of the facilities unguarded. Many of the prisons were ransacked and rendered useless. "Looters had a field day. They stole all the doors, the windows and in some locations, they took bricks out of the walls and the tile off the floor," Karpinski explained to Susan Taylor Martin for the *St. Petersburg (Florida) Times* (December 23, 2003). "The prisons were in absolute disrepair when we came into Iraq." Upon assuming control in Iraq, the U.S. coalition made repairs to many of the prison facilities. Karpinski told Martin that conditions were improved for the Iraqi prisoners and that great care was being taken to ensure that those prisoners were treated differently from those being held at Guantanamo Bay, Cuba. (The prison camp at Guantanamo Bay, where Iraqi and Afghan soldiers, among others, are detained, has also been the subject of controversy; since January 2004 reports of abuse and torture of prisoners there have prompted demands from United Nations officials to inspect the camp.)

In January 2004 a member of the U.S. military police alerted superiors to prisoner abuse on the part of U.S. soldiers at Abu Ghraib. (Under Hussein the Abu Ghraib prison, located 20 miles west of Baghdad, had a reputation as a site of gruesome torture and execution of political prisoners.) General Ricardo Sanchez, then the commander of the Combined Joint Task Force on the ground in Iraq, ordered an investigation into the allegations, which was carried out by Major General Antonio Taguba. On April 28, 2004 the CBS program *60 Minutes II* broadcast a story about Abu Ghraib, including in the telecast photographic documentation of the abuse and humiliation of Iraqi prisoners, which included being stripped naked and forced to engage in simulated sex acts. Seymour Hersh, writing for the *New Yorker* (May 10, 2004), reported that the investigation had uncovered several instances of "sadistic, blatant, and wanton criminal abuses" that occurred at the prison between October and December 2003. Taguba's report, which was completed in February 2004, concluded that the abuse was carried out by soldiers of the 372d Military Police Command, then under Karpinski, as well as by members of the U.S. intelligence community. In January 2004, before those events were publicized, Karpinski was formally admonished by General Sanchez; Karpinski and 16 others in the military were suspended with undisclosed reprimands and left Iraq. (Karpinski's suspension was explained at the time as part of a routine troop rotation.) On May 5, 2005, following allegations that she had misrepresented a shoplifting incident that occurred in October 2002 on a U.S. Air Force base, President George W. Bush approved the army's decision to demote Karpinski to the rank of colonel in the U.S. Army Reserve. (Karpinsky denied having shoplifted or having lied about the episode, in which, she said, a store guard mistakenly thought she had stolen an item.) She thus became the first general to be punished in connection with the abuse of detainees at U.S. military prisons, and as of March 2006, she remains the highest-ranking officer to be disciplined.

In the months that followed the scandal, Karpinski made appearances on many talk shows, including ABC's *Good Morning America* and the cable network MSNBC's *Hardball*. She asserted repeatedly that higher-ranking military officials, including Secretary of Defense Donald Rumsfeld, had made her a scapegoat for the incidents at Abu Ghraib, which had tarnished the reputation of the U.S. military and the Bush administration. She also insisted that she had had no knowledge of the prisoner abuse. In addition, she claimed that in September 2003, military intelligence personnel led by Major General Geoffrey Miller, previously the commandant at the military detention facility in Guantanamo Bay, had taken control of cell blocks 1-A and 1-B of the Abu Ghraib prison, where the torture and other abuse were believed to have been carried out. In an interview with Ted Koppel on the ABC News program *Nightline* (May 12, 2005,) Karpinski said: "Had I known, had I been made aware in any way, shape or form, I would have stopped it. I would have demanded an investigation. I would have screamed and yelled and protested. . . . And I believe that the people at headquarters knew that."

To the consternation of many in the military community, Karpinski, assisted by Steven Strasser, wrote a memoir about her part in the Abu Ghraib prison scandal. In October 2005 Miramax Books published *One Woman's Army: The Commanding General of Abu Ghraib Tells Her Story*, in which Karpinski claimed that the abuses of Iraqi prisoners were perpetrated by contract employees of the U.S. Army trained in Afghanistan and Guantanamo Bay. According to the book, the abuse could be tied to an order that came directly from Secretary Rumsfeld. Karpinski also maintained that her demotion amounted to political retribution for her outspokenness during the media firestorm that ensued after the reports of abuse were made public. In a review of the book for the *American Prospect* (March 2006), Karen J. Greenberg wrote that Karpinski "depict[s] the Army overall as a troubled institution in dire need of reform." She also wrote that Karpinski's account "suggest[s] that disarray, tolerance of abusive behavior toward detainees, and a willingness to disregard the law are all too frequent at every level and that the military, consequently, is poorly prepared to act consistently in the country's highest interests." In an assessment of the book for Salon.com (November 10, 2005), Jan Banbury wrote, "Karpinski makes a strong argument that she was made a scapegoat by George W. Bush, Donald Rumsfeld, her immediate bosses and military intelligence commanders. Frustratingly, Karpinski never steps up and takes responsibility, in any way, for what happened at Abu Ghraib. Yet, despite her lack of accountability or mea culpa, the book is an often shocking, guns-a-blazing indictment of the inept occupation of Iraq, and of the men who planned it and continue to run it today."

Echoing the arguments she made in *One Woman's Army*—that the abuse occurred after the period in which she was responsible for Abu Ghraib—Karpinski said to those gathered for a speech she made to the Commonwealth Club on April 8, 2005, as quoted on commonwealthclub.org: "I have never in my career tried to shirk my responsibilities, and I've not tried to avoid any responsibility at Abu Ghraib. . . . Hold me responsible for those things I could control. When my authority for Abu Ghraib was removed, I no longer had authority out there. I knew those soldiers, and I continued to visit Abu Ghraib, on [many] fewer occasions than I had when I was completely responsible for it."

Karpinski currently works as a consultant, offering a course designed to prepare individuals for the rigors of the business world, with emphasis on stressful situations. She explained to Susan Taylor Martin that the courses are "not a lot of fun . . . but are a true test of the toughness of an individual's mettle." Karpinski and her husband, George, make their home on the resort island of Hilton Head, South Carolina. George Karpinski, a lieutenant colonel in the U.S. Army, is currently stationed with the U.S. Embassy in the small Arab nation of Oman. The couple, who have no children, see each other as seldom as once a year; they stay in touch frequently through E-mail. Karpinski is a devout Presbyterian. On December 13, 2003, prior to the Abu Ghraib scandal, she wrote in an E-mail message to a priest she had befriended in Rahway, New Jersey, as quoted by the Newhouse News Service (May 6, 2004): "I find myself relying very heavily on my faith, and have managed so far because of it. There certainly have been, and no doubt will still be, many tests of one's faith and beliefs, in this setting. I cannot imagine trying to do any of what I do without God's constant help, inspiration, strength, and direction." Karpinski and her husband own an African gray parrot named Casey, who often travels with Karpinski. In her limited spare time, Karpinski enjoys reading and golfing. She and her husband play golf together near their home.

—D.F.

Suggested Reading: (London) *Times* II p4 Aug. 13, 2004; *New Yorker* p42+ May 10, 2004; Newhouse News Service May 7, 2004; *Newsweek* p32+ May 17, 2004; *Nightline* (on-line) May 12, 2005; *St. Petersburg (Florida) Times* A p1 Dec. 14, 2003; *Washington Post* C p1 May 10, 2004

Selected Books: *One Woman's Army: The Commanding General of Abu Ghraib Tells Her Story* (with Steven Strasser), 2005

Kavafian, Ani

(kah-VAHF-ee-an)

May 10, 1948– Violinist

Address: c/o Chamber Music Society of Lincoln Center, 70 Lincoln Center Plaza, New York, NY 10023-6582

"Sometimes one is lucky enough to catch a performer at the precise moment in his or her career when all technical problems have been resolved and youthful fervor is at its height. Such was the happy combination when violinist Ani Kavafian performed Bruch's Concerto No. 1 in G minor . . . ," Florence Fisher, a music critic for the *Sarasota (Florida) Herald-Tribune* (February 4, 1996), wrote about a performance Kavafian gave with the Florida West Coast Symphony, at the Van Wezel Performing Arts Hall, in 1996. "Her tone is best described as luminous, but 'rich,' 'round,' 'sweet' are other adjectives one might use. But they cannot convey the throat-catching effect that sound, combined with an instinctive musicality, produced in the listener." In a professional career that has spanned three decades and more than 2,000 performances around the globe, Kavafian has established herself as one of the premier violinists in the world. Her energetic, physical style, while criticized by some for being overly emotional, lends a

Ani Kavafian (right) performing with her sister, Ida Kavafian, in 2001

dramatic quality to her performances. Equally adept at performing as a soloist or as part of a chamber-music ensemble, Kavafian has appeared with almost all of the top orchestras in the United States, including the New York Philharmonic, the Philadelphia Orchestra, the Pittsburgh Symphony, the Minnesota Orchestra, the Los Angeles Chamber Orchestra, and the symphony orchestras of St. Louis, Delaware, San Francisco, Atlanta, Seattle, Minneapolis, Utah, and Rochester; among the elite venues in which she has given solo recitals are New York City's Carnegie Hall and Alice Tully Hall. Kavafian has made recordings not only of works by Bach, Beethoven, Brahms, and Mozart but of pieces by such 20th- and 21st-century composers as Aaron Copland and Ned Rorem, and a number of contemporary works have been composed specifically for her. She has performed at the White House on several occasions and has been featured on a number of PBS television music specials. She is the artistic director of the New Jersey chamber-music series Mostly Music.

The older of two daughters, Ani Kavafian was born on May 10, 1948 in Istanbul, Turkey, to Peruz and Yenovk Kavafian. Her father, whose parents were refugees of the 1915 Armenian Genocide, in which more than one million Armenians perished in Turkey, was born in Bulgaria and moved to Turkey as an adult. Kavafian's parents, both musicians, had met while performing with the Istanbul State Symphony Orchestra, her father as principal violist and her mother as a member of the first-violin section. Kavafian and her sister, Ida, who is also a professional violinist, were exposed to music at an early age, as their parents often invited friends to the house to play music. In 1956 the family moved to the United States, settling in a suburb of Detroit, Michigan. Kavafian, who had begun to study piano at the age of three, had always been intrigued by the violin. When she was nine years old, Kavafian's school offered her a scholarship for five free violin lessons if she agreed to perform the instrument at a school concert. She agreed and began studying violin with Ara Zerounian, while continuing her lessons on piano as well. "We didn't know this at the time," Kavafian explained to Lisa Boghosian Papas for *AGBU: Armenian General Benevolent Union* (November 30, 1999), "but Mr. 'Z' was the foremost violin teacher in the area." After her initial five lessons, Kavafian continued studying with Zerounian until she was 14. (After the death of Kavafian's father, Zerounian married her mother.) By that time Kavafian had displayed such extraordinary musical ability that Zerounian insisted that it was in his pupil's best interest to change instructors. She next studied with Mischa Mischakoff, a renowned violinist and concertmaster, who was extremely demanding of his students. At 16 Kavafian attended the National Music Camp at Interlochen, Michigan, where she earned first place in both the piano and violin competitions. Eventually her schedule required that she concentrate on only one instrument, and she decided to drop piano lessons. "There were many reasons why I picked violin," Kavafian told Papas. "Not the least of which is that my hands are tiny. As a pianist, having small hands was much more of a handicap. I also enjoyed playing in an orchestra and sitting first chair. The violin was just a more social instrument." In 1966, following her high-school graduation, Kavafian left Michigan to attend the Juilliard School of Music, in New York City.

In order to matriculate at Juilliard, Kavafian had to audition for the influential violinist and instructor Ivan Galamian. "When Mr. Galamian accepted me, I felt pretty confident about myself," Kavafian recalled to Papas. Then, at Galamian's request, Kavafian participated in an intensive violin summer camp prior to attending the school. At the camp she felt humbled by the abilities of Galamian's other students. "I was put on scales and arpeggios, while I witnessed other students give full concerts," she told Papas. "I mean we are talking about people like Pinchas Zukerman, Young Uck Kim and Kyung-Wha Chung. These are people who are famous now, but at that time they were [Galamian's] stars. After I heard them play, all I really wanted to do was pack up my violin and go right back to Detroit." Despite that blow to her confidence, she attended Juilliard, where she quickly overcame her insecurities and became one of Galamian's most promising pupils. While working under Galamian, Kavafian developed her skills as a soloist but was more interested in performing chamber music. When she said as much to Galamian, he was disappointed, because he wanted all of his students to be soloists. "But he told me something that I never forgot," Kavafian told Papas. "He said that if I could be the best chamber music player then he thought it was a great thing. He was so attuned to being the best that one could be." Perhaps the person who most influenced Kavafian during her time at Juilliard was Felix Galamir, who, as Kavafian told Papas, "taught me that the way to be is to have your own voice and to know something about the composers. If you play Tchaikovsky the same way you play Bach, then you are really not doing the composers justice. The two are completely separate personalities who lived 120 years apart from each other. The best way to play is to have a recognizable style that adheres to the composer's wishes." Kavafian began practicing up to eight hours per day, continually striving to improve. She was never reluctant to try different techniques in her efforts to become as accomplished a violinist as possible. While at Juilliard Kavafian played chamber music, served as concertmaster of the school orchestra, and made her debut at Carnegie Hall, in 1969.

After earning a master's degree with highest honors from Juilliard, in 1972, Kavafian began playing with the Chamber Music Society (CMS), in New York City. In the following year she was one of three musicians—selected from 400 applicants—to join Young Concert Artists (YCA), a nonprofit group that assists musicians with the transition from music school to professional life. YCA offered a platform for performances, which increased musicians' exposure, and organized classes that focused on the business side of musical careers. Kavafian toured extensively with YCA throughout the 1970s, making her European debut in Paris, France, in 1973. She won a number of prizes during that time, including, in 1976, the inaugural Avery Fisher Prize, which brought her the chance to appear with the New York Philharmonic Orchestra and six other orchestras. Another prize, in 1978, earned her a recital at Alice Tully Hall, where she caught the attention of—and was soon represented by—the respected manager Herbert Barrett. In 1980 she became an artist-member of CMS and began touring with the group in the United States and Canada. (Her sister, Ida, later joined CMS, and the two have often performed together.) While appearing with CMS throughout the 1980s and 1990s, Kavafian became a sought-after soloist and performed with most of the leading orchestras in the United States. She was also in high demand for summer festivals, including the Santa Fe Chamber Music Festival, Chamber Music Northwest, and Bridgehampton Chamber Music Festival. Her performance schedule came to encompass more than 90 concerts a year; meanwhile, in the 1980s, she had begun teaching at the Manhattan School of Music and the Mannes College of Music, both in New York. She worried initially that the busy schedule would compromise her performance, but soon found that she was able to maintain her performance standards, even if it meant practicing in hotel rooms instead of conventional rehearsal spaces. "Believe me, if I wasn't keeping up [my musical standards] I would have to do something about it," Kavafian explained to Martin Renzhofer for the Salt Lake (Utah) Tribune (March 22, 1998) at the time. "Right now, I'm taking advantage of the fact that it works for me. Right now, I turn very few things down."

During the 1990s, having immersed herself for years in the traditional canon of classical music, Kavafian began to focus on modern and contemporary works, performing pieces by such composers as Henri Lazaroff, Samuel Barber, and Erich Korngold. The work of those composers makes different demands on performers from those Kavafian had encountered in older music, and she relished the opportunity to perform pieces that made her think, listen, and play in new ways. "One feels freer," Kavafian explained to R. M. Campbell for the Seattle Post-Intelligencer (July 1, 1994) about performing newer works. "Playing contemporary music also gives you a break from the standard repertory. I've played a lot of Beethoven." In 1993, with the St. Paul Chamber Orchestra, Kavafian debuted Tod Machover's Forever and Ever, which had been written for her. For that piece she played the hyperviolin, an instrument developed by Machover, which resembles a traditional violin but has electronic devices inside it that amplify the sound and transmit to a computer information about the the motion of the violinist's wrist, the pressure on the strings, and other factors; the computer uses the information to provide musical accompaniment. (Machover's hope was that his instrument would expand the possibilities of what an individual musician could accomplish. His goal, he said, was not to subordinate the artist through technology, but to enhance human virtuosity.)

A decade earlier Kavafian had begun playing the 1736 Muir McKenzie Stradivarius violin, crafted by the famed stringed-instrument maker Antonio Stradivari in the northern Italian town of Cremona. (It is believed that following the creation of that violin, Stradivari made only two more before his death, in 1737.) Kavafian's violin was named after two of its previous owners, members of European nobility. Until 1982, when Kavafian acquired the instrument, it had never been used as a concert violin, as its previous owners had played only avocationally; as a result, the violin had minimal wear, despite its age. Kavafian had to secure a loan to purchase the violin; she has never publicly revealed how much she paid for the instrument, but some estimate its 1982 value at $250,000. (Its current estimated value is over $2 million.) In a conversation with Nancy Stetson for the Florida News–Press (February 25, 2000), Bruce Price, a violin dealer who specializes in rare instruments, explained the value of such unique instruments to musicians: "Can you imagine how it would be for a great singer to go out and pick their own voice? The match that you have in your mind to what sound you'd like to produce, and then to go out and find it is a very exhilarating experience and will generally inspire music making of an even higher level."

In 1997 Kavafian premiered another piece written for her: Michelle Ekizian's Red Harvest, Concerto for Violin and Orchestra. Ekizian, who, like Kavafian, is of Armenian heritage, described their collaboration as an homage to the women of the Armenian Genocide of 1915. In a review of a performance of the piece, at the Cathedral of St. John the Divine, in New York, a writer for the Armenian Reporter (October 25, 1997) found that the concerto featured "staggering virtuosity" from Kavafian and a "tremendous emotional range from deep lament to joyous renewal." "Being Armenian is an incredibly important part of me," Kavafian explained to Papas. "And I believe that our background has prepared us for a much richer existence than normal. Knowing that struggle that others had before us, and seeing how many successful Armenians there are in the world today, lends a richness that when combined with belief in oneself can only yield the positive."

Discussing her extensive touring schedule, Kavafian said to Renzhofer that performing with a variety of professional musicians "makes you a better-rounded musician. . . . One of the great things not being in a group, every experience is nearly always brand new." In recent years Kavafian has dedicated more time to teaching at universities such as Yale, in New Haven, Connecticut, and the State University of New York at Stony Brook, as well as at summer camps for younger musicians. She told one group of students, as reported by John Fleming for the St. Petersburg (Florida) Times (April 29, 2005), "There are fine violinists, and there are fine musicians. I'll go for the fine musician any day. Obviously there are violinists who can play incredibly well, but if they can move me as a musician, I'm the happiest." She also said, "The times that I have been most inspired at concerts are the times when the instrument has not come into play, that I've heard only the music coming out. I want the violin to stay out of the way and for people to learn to communicate musically." Kavafian often returns to the camps and festivals she attended as a young musician, to help aspiring professionals. "As a student, the [Sarasota Music Festival] was a phenomenal, eye-opening experience for me in every way," she explained to Charlie Husking for the Sarasota Herald-Tribune (June 2, 2006). "As a teacher here now," she continued, "I'm careful to do the same thing, to make sure the students get what they need. I don't expect to change every student's life, as [former instructor Joseph] Silverstein did for me. But I take this extremely seriously. And I want to be not just their teacher, but their colleague, their friend." Since the mid-1990s Kavafian has been the director, with the cellist Carter Brey, of Mostly Music, a chamber-music series based in New Jersey.

Kavafian has recently recorded music with the Chamber Music Society and, as a soloist, has collaborated with other musicians and contemporary composers. Her most recent compact-disc releases include a live recording with Kenneth Cooper of Bach's Six Sonatas for Violin and Fortepiano, in 2005, and Mozart Sonatas for Piano and Violin, with Jorge Federico Osorio, in 2006. Kavafian also recorded Machover's Forever and Ever on Hyperstring Trilogy in 2003. The Chamber Music Society frequently records live concerts for release on compact disc, most notably The Chamber Music of Claude Debussy—Complete, which was recorded between 1995 and 1999 in various venues throughout the United States and includes performances by Kavafian. The recording garnered the group a 2001 Grammy Award nomination.

Kavafian makes her home in Westchester County, New York. She lives with her husband, Bernard Mindich, a multimedia artist, and their son, Matthew. Her interests include gardening and cooking.

—N.W.M.

Suggested Reading: Christian Science Monitor p14 Oct. 13, 1993; New York Times C p22 Nov. 2, 1987; Newsweek p74 Feb. 24, 1986; San Jose Mercury News E p5 Aug. 3, 2004; Sarasota Herald-Tribune p23 June 2, 2006

Selected Recordings: Musica da camera italiana, 1998; Hyperstring Trilogy, 2003; J. S. Bach: Six Sonatas for Violin & Fortepiano, 2005

Karim Sahib/Getty Images

Khalilzad, Zalmay

(KAH-leel-ZAHD, ZAHL-may)

Mar. 22, 1951– U.S. ambassador to Iraq

Address: Embassy of the United States, APO AE 09316, Baghdad, Iraq

In the midst of rampant violence on the part of insurgents, which confines U.S. officials to a heavily guarded compound in the so-called Green Zone of Baghdad, Iraq, the U.S. ambassador to that country, Zalmay Khalilzad, is charged with the seemingly impossible task of ensuring stability and guiding Iraq to self-sufficiency in order to allow for the withdrawal of American troops. Khalilzad's exceptionally thorough knowledge of Middle Eastern affairs is perhaps the most important resource for the reconstruction of Iraq in the wake of the 2003 overthrow of its leader, Saddam Hussein, by U.S. and coalition forces. A strategic and scholarly thinker, Khalilzad has had an extensive career as an adviser for U.S. policies toward the Middle East, dating back to the Iran-Iraq and Afghan wars in the 1980s. A background figure in the administrations of the Republican presidents Ronald Reagan and George H. W. Bush, Khalilzad rose to prominence immediately following the terrorist attacks of September 11, 2001 and held a number of high-level government positions, in quick succession, in the George W. Bush administration: counselor to Secretary of Defense Donald Rumsfeld, special assistant to President Bush for the Middle East and Southwest Asia, special envoy to Afghanistan, and U.S. ambassador to Afghanistan. In the last-named position, Khalilzad gained the approval of Afghani

leaders in large part because he showed a genuine interest in seeing his native country reestablish itself as a democracy. His Muslim Pashtun heritage was an especially welcome commodity among officials of that nation who saw many U.S. diplomats as being detached from Middle Eastern culture. Much to the disappointment of the Afghani leadership, on April 5, 2005 President Bush nominated Khalilzad as ambassador to Iraq.

The mistakes of former U.S. officials in Iraq who did not understand Middle Eastern culture—Paul Bremer and John Negroponte—added to the chaos in post-Hussein Iraq; during their tenures the country moved closer to civil war, as political infighting among factions increased. To his current post, Khalilzad "brings a lot more to bear than his predecessors, who knew nothing about Iraq . . . ," Khalilzad's mentor and former colleague at Columbia University, Zbigniew Brzezinski, told Jon Lee Anderson for the *New Yorker* (December 19, 2005). "It was a gutsy decision to put himself in the line of fire. He is a broad-minded pragmatist and an insightful strategist. He has a unique advantage in a part of the world in which the United States has become massively engaged and does not have many people at the top equipped to deal with it. The top decision-makers today are ignorant and Manichaean." With Iraq divided along ethnic and religious lines, Khalilzad's main challenge is to help the nation's various groups to form a viable government while remaining sensitive to the interests of each faction. At the same time, he must keep in mind that the volatile political situation in the Middle East has far-reaching consequences for the international realm, which could include the continued fostering of terrorism. Although Khalilzad's work in Afghanistan and Iraq has been praised, several policy recommendations he made earlier in his career have been the targets of criticism, since past U.S. actions in the Middle East were brought to the public's attention by the 2001 terrorist attacks. Nevertheless, he is widely seen as one of the American officials best suited to handle the volatility of Middle Eastern politics in the post-9/11 world.

Zalmay Khalilzad was born on March 22, 1951 in the northern Afghan city of Mazar-i-Sharif. His father, a Sunni Muslim, worked as a civil servant for the government of King Zahir Shah in the local office of the Ministry of Finance. His mother, a Shiite Muslim and a homemaker, was the main caregiver for Khalilzad and his two brothers and three sisters. When Khalilzad completed eighth grade, his father moved the family to Kabul, the capital, where Khalilzad resumed his education at the elite English-speaking school Ghazi Lycee. He excelled academically and had become the top student in his class by his sophomore year of high school. As a result, he was given the chance to participate in a student-exchange program run by the American Friends Service Committee, a Quaker charitable organization. In 1966 Khalilzad left Kabul to spend a year living with an American family on their walnut ranch in Ceres, California, experiencing a life that was starkly different from his Muslim upbringing. The subservient maternal figure who often brought Khalilzad's father and brothers their slippers was absent from his surrogate family; instead, he witnessed a partnership between the husband and wife, in which both performed daily household chores. Khalilzad returned to Afghanistan in 1967 with a new perspective on life and, in particular, gender relations. He now believed that his mother, who had married at the age of 12 and was illiterate, might have become a great political figure had she been given the opportunity to pursue an education. "I had different values, greater interest in sports, a more pragmatic way of looking at things, and a broader horizon," Khalilzad told Jon Lee Anderson. "I had a sense of how backward Afghanistan was. And I became more interested in how Afghanistan needed to change."

Upon graduating from high school, Khalilzad enrolled at Kabul University. In what he described to Anderson as "a prank," he and his friends took tests for scholarships to study at the American University of Beirut, in Lebanon; to his surprise, he passed and was offered a scholarship. Khalilzad arrived at American University in 1970 and began studying political science and the history of the Middle East. There, he met his future wife, Cheryl Benard, an Austrian-born writer of feminist novels who was then conducting research on Arab nationalism for her dissertation. After earning both his bachelor's and master's degrees at American University, Khalilzad left Beirut in 1974, the year before civil war broke out in Lebanon. The following year he moved to the U.S. to pursue his doctorate at the University of Chicago, in Illinois, where he was a student of the military-strategy expert Albert Wohlstetter. (Wohlstetter is best known for his argument that the U.S. should gain global dominance by strategic development of nuclear weaponry, a view that had a profound influence on the neoconservative political movement). During one lecture, in which Wohlstetter talked about the "inevitability of war," Khalilzad caught his professor's attention by raising his hand and asking about the "inevitability of permanent peace." The remark earned Khalilzad an invitation to attend a small seminar Wohlstetter taught in his Chicago apartment; the other students included Paul Wolfowitz, a future deputy secretary of defense in the administration of President George W. Bush. Khalilzad thrived on the passionate, in-depth political discussion of the seminar and soon began writing papers on nuclear proliferation for Pan Heuristics, a think tank formed by Wohlstetter, which had contracts with the U.S. government. Khalilzad completed his dissertation on Iran's nuclear program and earned his Ph.D. degree in 1979. He accepted a position as an assistant professor of political science at Columbia University, in New York City.

In 1984 Khalilzad acquired U.S. citizenship and was also awarded a fellowship by the Council on Foreign Relations. At that time, during the dec-ades-long Cold War between the U.S. and the Soviet Union, U.S. officials feared a Soviet military victory in Afghanistan; Muslims there had banded together in a force called the mujahideen to drive the Soviets out of the country, which they had invaded in 1979. Though Khalilzad had intended to use his fellowship to work in the area of nuclear proliferation, President Reagan's secretary of state, George P. Shultz, saw Khalilzad's Afghani heritage as a potential asset for American interests in both the war between Iran and Iraq and the Afghan war. Khalilzad was thus named special adviser to the undersecretary for political affairs in the State Department in 1985, just as President Reagan authorized an increase in weaponry aid to the mujahideen. With the support of other conservative policymakers, Khalilzad argued fervently that in order to ensure an Afghan victory, the U.S. should provide the mujahideen with American heat-seeking stinger missiles, known to be among the most effective of antiaircraft weapons. The White House approved the recommendation, and in 1986 and 1987 approximately 900 stinger missiles were supplied to the Afghans. The invaluable American technology helped to bring about the Afghan victory and led to the Soviet withdrawal, in February 1989. Afterward the U.S. significantly decreased its financial and military support of Afghanistan. Even so, at the close of the war, the mujahideen were left with 200 unused stinger missiles and a large cache of other arms. In the years following the Soviet pullout, Afghanistan fell into a civil war that gave rise to the Muslim extremist government of the Taliban, who were helped to victory by the mujahideen's use of American-made weapons. After the attacks of September 11, 2001, it became well-known that the Taliban had allowed Osama bin Laden's terrorist organization, Al Qaeda, to establish its base in Afghanistan. Critics have pointed to Khalilzad's 1985 recommendation that the U.S. supply the mujahideen with stinger missiles as having provided the foundation of the brutal Taliban government and the springboard for Al Qaeda's effective terrorist attacks.

After the Soviet withdrawal from Afghanistan, Khalilzad's reputation as a strategic political thinker became well known in U.S. government circles. Still, most officials dismissed a policy paper he wrote in 1988, calling for a shift in focus from Iran—with which the U.S. had had an antagonistic relationship for the past decade—to Iraq. In the paper Khalilzad staunchly supported a regime change in the latter nation, suggesting that while Iran had become weaker as its war with Iraq progressed, Iraq under Saddam Hussein now presented a grave risk to stability in the Middle East. In 1989 General H. Norman Schwarzkopf, the head of the U.S. Army's Central Command, saw value in Khalilzad's paper and asked him to lend his expertise to a study assessing the threat posed by Hussein. The following year Hussein deployed troops to invade neighboring Kuwait, under the pretense that Kuwait was threatening Iraq's oil supplies.

Khalilzad's warnings began to gain credibility in the State Department, and in 1991 the U.S. launched the Gulf War to protect American and Kuwaiti interests against Iraq. Richard B. "Dick" Cheney, then the secretary of defense, invited Khalilzad to work for the Defense Department. Khalilzad, who at the time was an associate professor of international affairs at the University of California at San Diego, accepted the offer and helped mold the government's Middle East policies throughout the war. (Khalilzad was displeased with the war's outcome, in which Hussein was expelled from Kuwait but remained in power. "I thought, frankly, that we should have helped the Iraqis get rid of Saddam," he said to Anderson.) After the war he remained at the Defense Department as the assistant undersecretary for policy planning, assessing America's position as the only superpower in the post–Cold War era that followed the 1991 collapse of the Soviet Union. He produced a draft of the Defense Planning Guidance (DPG) of 1992, which argued that "bipolarity had ended, and the U.S. was now the world's single leading power, and that our goal in this new era was to preclude a return to a bipolar system, or a multipolar system," as Khalilzad told Anderson. The document called for using force, if necessary, to maintain America's global supremacy. Although the DPG was widely criticized after it was leaked to the press and was later rewritten in a less harsh tone, the original draft, according to Anderson, is "seen as the defining hard-line neoconservative doctrine that contemplated, among other things, preemptive warfare." In 1993 Khalilzad left the Department of Defense to join the RAND Corp., a political think tank. As the group's director of strategy, Khalilzad founded its Center for Middle Eastern Studies and continued working with the government, which relied on his expertise to carry out policy studies for the U.S. military.

In late 2000 Khalilzad returned to Washington, D.C., as the head of the Pentagon's transition team for the incoming administration of President George W. Bush. The following year he was appointed to the National Security Council. Still, he held relatively little influence in the White House until September 11, 2001. As it became clear in the days following the attacks that Osama bin Laden's Al Qaeda organization had been responsible for hijacking the airplanes flown into the World Trade Center towers, in New York, and the Pentagon building, White House staffers saw Khalilzad as a much-needed asset in its relations with Afghanistan, the home base of Al Qaeda. "It was momentous," Khalilzad told Anderson. "I realized that we were now going to get involved in a war and that Afghanistan was the likely theatre. At that moment, the post–Cold War era was being defined. Afghanistan was marginal to U.S. interests, and then became very central, overnight." Khalilzad's familiarity with Pashtun culture, his fluency in both national Afghan languages, Dari and Pashtu, and his prodemocracy stance with regard to Mid-

dle East politics made him the ideal "go-to" person for the White House as it prepared for an invasion to depose the Taliban regime and weed out terrorists. He quickly ascended the administration's ranks, becoming a counselor to Secretary of Defense Donald Rumsfeld and special assistant to the president on the Middle East and Southwest Asia. When U.S. forces entered Afghanistan, in October 2001, Khalilzad worked closely with leaders of the Northern Alliance, a coalition of various Afghan groups opposing the Taliban, and reported directly to Condoleezza Rice, then the national security adviser.

Leaders in the U.S. and other countries were impressed by Khalilzad's ability to represent U.S. interests effectively without appearing unsympathetic to those in the Middle East. "A good negotiator listens to the views that are expressed and tries to find a sentence—even a single word—that coincides with the opposite view, and uses that to create a common ground. [Khalilzad] can do that," a U.N. official, Lakhdar Brahimi, told Anderson. Brahimi also noted that Khalilzad has "a unique capacity to listen." After the Taliban fell from power, in November 2001, Khalilzad was named special envoy to Afghanistan and worked with the Northern Alliance and the U.N. to form the transitional Afghan government, with Hamid Karzai as the acting chairman. By 2003 Khalilzad had made such impressive progress toward the formation of Afghanistan's post-Taliban government that President Bush appointed him as the U.S. ambassador to Afghanistan. Dubbed "viceroy" by Afghanis, in 2004 Khalilzad helped bring about cooperation among opposing political factions, resulting in the historic democratic elections in which Karzai became Afghanistan's first president.

Relying on faulty intelligence, which indicated that Iraq held a large cache of weapons of mass destruction, the U.S. invaded Iraq in March 2003 to depose Saddam Hussein. In the months preceding the invasion, Khalilzad was also named the ambassador at large for free Iraqis—in addition to his diplomatic duties in Afghanistan—and met with pro-American Iraqi exiles to discuss a strategy for a transitional government. Although Khalilzad preferred a provisional government that put Iraqis in an advisory role to occupation forces, the leading Iraqi exiles staunchly opposed the idea and instead favored an interim government of Iraqi leaders. Khalilzad listened carefully to the group's thoughts and grievances and relayed their concerns to other U.S. government officials. A sharing of power in the interim government among leaders of the Kurdish, Sunni, and Shiite populations was thought to be the best means of avoiding resentment of U.S. forces and violence among opposing factions. Plans were made to accept the terms Khalilzad had negotiated at his meetings with Iraqi exiles before the invasion. But after President Bush named Paul Bremer as director of the Office for Reconstruction and Humanitarian Assistance in Iraq, the plans were ignored. After the fall of Saddam

Hussein's government, the U.N. placed Iraq under a U.S.-British trusteeship. "We were all angry when we found out," Adel Abdul Mahdi, the Shiite vice president of Iraq, told Anderson.

In the two years following the March 2003 invasion, Iraqi politics and security fell into disarray, as Bremer failed to communicate effectively with Iraqi factional leaders. His successor, John Negroponte, who was named ambassador to Iraq in June 2004, similarly failed to understand the intricacies of Arabic culture and politics, thus further alienating Iraqi leaders. A series of political missteps by American officials in Iraq contributed to a rise in violence by insurgents, bringing Iraqi factions closer to civil war. President Bush, recognizing Khalilzad's breadth of knowledge of Middle Eastern affairs and having seen his effectiveness in Afghanistan, looked to him to quell the divisive rhetoric among ethnic and religious groups in Iraq and also to secure a measure of governmental stability. On April 5, 2005 Bush nominated Khalilzad as ambassador to Iraq. President Karzai and several other Afghani officials pleaded with Washington to keep Khalilzad in Afghanistan, but the U.S. Congress quickly confirmed Bush's nomination, and Khalilzad moved to Baghdad.

Upon arriving in Iraq, in the summer of 2005, Khalilzad immediately attempted to break the political stalemate that was stalling an election on an Iraqi constitution. The Sunni population felt that their interests had been ignored after the group boycotted the January 2005 election for a constitutional assembly. Previous U.S. officials in Iraq had had little sympathy for the Sunni minority's position and had given their support to the Shiite religious parties, which won a majority in the January election. Khalilzad, however, saw that it was important to bring the Sunnis into the political fold and extended the constitutional deadline two weeks beyond the planned date of August 15, 2005 in order to broker a deal with Sunni leaders. He persuaded Tariq al-Hashemi, the leader of the Sunni-dominated Iraqi Islamic Party, to support the constitutional draft. The effects of his negotiating were still felt at the parliamentary election in December 2005, when many Sunnis voted..

The philosophical differences separating Khalilzad's approach to Iraqi politics from those of his predecessors account for much of the way the Iraqi government has evolved since March 2003. According to Peter Galbraith, an informal adviser to Kurdish leaders during political negotiations, Bremer and Negroponte failed to understand that Iraq could not become a unified nation. Deep political, religious, and ethnic divisions rendered such a notion impractical; Iraqi leaders put more faith in the possibility of Iraq's consisting of three separate states. "[Khalilzad] understood quickly that this constitution was more of a peace treaty than a nation-building exercise, and that what he had to produce was a road map to avoid a future civil war," Galbraith told Anderson. Khalilzad's familiarity with Middle Eastern social customs has put Iraqi

officials at ease, despite the fact that he does not speak Arabic fluently. Mahdi told Anderson, "Zalmay . . . understands the culture here and knows he can invite himself to come and see us. He'll drop in and say, 'Can we have a moment together?,' knowing that other people will come by, as is our custom, and that he will be there, and he will discuss things with them, be part of our discussions." The cordial personal relationships Khalilzad has painstakingly established with various political factions have noticeably diminished Iraqi politicians' bitterness toward the U.S. Though diplomatic progress has been made in Iraq since his arrival, Khalilzad still sees a need for Americans to make a redoubled effort to understand the complexities of Middle Eastern politics and culture so that its nations may advance further into the democratic realm. Addressing the violence that continues to plague Iraq—driven by the presence of Al Qaeda operatives as well as the Shiite campaign against Sunnis and Sunni guerrilla warfare against the new Iraqi government—Khalilzad has hinted that continued unrest could result in Iraq's being abandoned by the U.S. Iraqis "understand that the United States could not be counted on to support a kind of indefinite tribal warfare," he told Ned Parker for the London *Times* (May 31, 2006). On October 24, 2006, despite mounting violence in many parts of Iraq and shrinking support for the war among U.S. citizens, Khalilzad publicly expressed confidence about the situation in Iraq. In a joint interview with General George W. Casey Jr., the commander of American forces in Iraq, that aired on CNN, he declared, according to Frank Rich in the *New York Times* (October 29, 2006), "Success in Iraq is possible and can be achieved on a realistic timetable."

Khalilzad is the author of a number of books, including *The Government of God: Iran's Islamic Republic* (1984), written with his wife, Cheryl Benard; *Sources of Conflict in the 21st Century: Strategic Flashpoints and U.S. Strategy* (1998); and *Strategic Appraisal: United States Air and Space Power in the 21st Century* (2002), written with Jeremy Shapiro. He received the King Ghazi Ammanullah Medal, Afghanistan's highest honor, and, twice, the Defense Department medal for outstanding public service. He has published articles and studies in newspapers and political journals and in more than 200 books. His works have been translated into Arabic, Chinese, German, Japanese, and Turkish, among other languages.

Khalilzad divides his time between Baghdad and his home in Maryland. He and Cheryl Benard have two sons, Alexander and Max.

—I.C.

Suggested Reading: Biography Resource Center Online, 2003; *Chicago Tribune* C p9 Mar. 5, 2006; *Los Angeles Times* A p3 Dec. 18, 2001; *Modesto (California) Bee* A p1 Jan. 8, 2002,; *New York Times* B p8 Oct. 28, 2001; *New Yorker* p54+ Dec. 19, 2005; *Time* p38 Mar. 20, 2006; *Washington Post* A p41 Nov. 23, 2001

Selected Books: *The Government of God: Iran's Islamic Republic* (with Cheryl Benard), 1984; *Sources of Conflict in the 21st Century: Strategic Flashpoints and U.S. Strategy*, 1998; *Strategic Appraisal: The Changing Role of Information in Warfare*, 1999; *The Future of Turkish-Western Relations: Toward a Strategic Plan*, 2000; *The United States and Asia: Toward a New U.S. Strategy and Force Posture*, 2001; *Strategic Appraisal: United States Air and Space Power in the 21st Century* (with Jeremy Shapiro), 2002

Antonio Scorza/Getty Images

Kim, Jim Yong

Dec. 8, 1959– Physician; public-health-service officer; educator; co-founder of Partners in Health; social activist

Address: *François-Xavier Bagnoud Center for Health and Human Rights, Harvard School of Public Health, 651 Huntington Ave., Boston, MA 02115*

"I'm a physician and an anthropologist, but essentially I'm an activist," Jim Yong Kim told an interviewer for *KFLA Connectivity* (November 2004, on-line), the newsletter of the Kellogg Fellows Leadership Alliance. As a student in the mid-1980s, Kim co-founded the organization Partners in Health (PIH), to provide medical care to impoverished people in rural Haiti; currently, PIH addresses the medical needs of poor people in parts of seven countries. "The basic idea is that we believe very strongly that all people in the world deserve excellent health care, at a minimum," Kim told Stephen

Byrd for the *Muscatine (Iowa) Journal* (November 26, 2005, on-line). "And we believe that the world has more than enough resources to be able to provide it." A native of South Korea who earned M.D. and Ph.D. degrees at Harvard University, Kim is an authority on the treatment of tuberculosis (TB), multidrug-resistant TB (MDR-TB), and HIV, the virus that causes AIDS. In the nations served by PIH, he has demonstrated that, contrary to long-held assumptions in the medical community, attempts to treat, and contain the spread of, such infectious diseases as TB and AIDS among those on the lowest rungs of the economic ladder, even in Third World countries, can succeed. His tactics have ranged from the distribution of watches, to enable people to take medications at the proper time of day, to his successful campaign to obtain effective drugs at a small fraction of the prices usually charged by pharmaceutical companies for similar medications. As director of the HIV/AIDS program of the World Health Organization (WHO) from 2004 to 2006, Kim aimed to provide medications to three million HIV/AIDS victims in the developing world by the end of 2005. Although WHO failed to achieve that outcome, the consensus among professionals was that because the goal was so ambitious, AIDS medications reached far more people than they would have otherwise. In September 2006 Kim became the director of the François-Xavier Bagnoud Center for Health and Human Rights at the Harvard School of Public Health, with the title of Bagnoud Professor of Health and Human Rights. He is also a professor at the Harvard Medical School, chair of the school's Department of Social Medicine, and chief of the Division of Social Medicine and Health Inequalities at Brigham and Women's Hospital, in Boston, Massachusetts. Earlier, he co-directed Harvard's Program in Infectious Disease and Social Change and was a founding member of WHO's Working Group on DOTS-Plus (an acronym for Directly Observed Treatment, Short-course), a strategy for treating and stopping the spread of TB and drug-resistant TB. With three others, Kim co-edited *Dying for Growth: Global Inequity and the Health of the Poor* (2000). In 2003 Kim won a $500,000 MacArthur Fellowship, commonly referred to as the "genius" grant; the next year he was elected to the Institute of Medicine of the National Academy of Sciences. "To me, there is something fundamentally wrong about how a person—through no fault of his own—because of where he or she was born, can't go to school, can't have access to health care, and can't feed his children," Kim told the *KFLA Connectivity* interviewer. "I'm working toward a fairly universal concept of social justice." He added, "We all know that there are complexities, but I feel that we must insist—out of simple decency as human beings—on universal access to the most basic services."

One of three siblings, Jim Yong Kim was born on December 8, 1959 in Seoul, South Korea, to Nhak Hee Kim, a dentist, and his wife, Oaksook Chun Kim, an expert in neo-Confucianism who directed the Korea Program at the University of California at Los Angeles in the 1990s. He has a brother, Bill, a physician, and a sister, Heidi. When Kim was about five years old, his family immigrated to the U.S. After a couple of moves they chose to settle in Muscatine, in eastern Iowa, so that his mother could complete her doctorate at a nearby campus of the University of Iowa. Besides the Kims, the only Asian residents in Muscatine, according to Kim, were the owners of the town's Chinese restaurant. He told Steven Byrd that Muscatine's residents "have always been decent, friendly and warm. That fairness and decency have been a big part of my interest in working with the poor." Kim attended Muscatine High School, where he was a member of the basketball and football teams. As a teenager he attended lectures sponsored by the Muscatine-based, nonprofit Stanley Foundation, whose mission, according to its Web site, is to build support for "principled multilateralism in addressing international issues." Speeches made by such renowned figures as the Harvard Medical School psychologist and humanist Robert Coles and the liberal Christian clergyman and peace activist William Sloane Coffin "made me want to get out and see the world to pursue the values I had learned," as Kim told Byrd. He graduated from high school, as the class valedictorian, in 1978.

Kim began his undergraduate career at the University of Iowa. "At the urging of friends," as Byrd wrote, he transferred to Brown University, in Providence, Rhode Island. He received a B.A. degree at Brown in 1982 and then enrolled at Harvard Medical School and Harvard University, in Cambridge, Massachusetts, where he pursued both a medical degree and a doctoral degree in anthropology. He earned his M.D. degree in 1991 and completed his internship and residency at Brigham and Women's Hospital, Harvard's teaching hospital. He was awarded his Ph.D. in 1993.

At Harvard Kim had befriended Paul Farmer, who, like him, had been working toward earning degrees in both medicine and anthropology. In the early 1980s Kim, Farmer, and several others established Zanmi Lasante ("Partners in Health" in Creole, one of Haiti's two official languages), with the aim of bringing medical care to impoverished Haitians; the Boston-based Partners in Health, Zanmi Lasante's sister organization, came into being in 1987. (For a while Kim served as PIH's executive director; currently, he is a member of its board of trustees.) Early on, Farmer and Kim had no money to buy medical supplies for the sick people they hoped to treat; in desperation, they took a microscope and medications from the Harvard Medical School and Brigham and Women's Hospital. Soon afterward Thomas White, a Boston-area philanthropist, paid the hospital and the school for the missing supplies. With contributions from White (who through the years has donated millions of dollars to PIH), Kim and Farmer arranged for the construction of a medical facility, named Clinique Bon Sauveur, in Cange, a rural slum in one of Hai-

ti's poorest regions, where many people were suffering from AIDS and TB. The men set up a program in which they trained teams of community-health workers, who then monitored AIDS and TB patients every day to ensure that they were following the prescribed drug regimens. (Their approach mirrored that of DOTS, WHO's worldwide treatment regimen for TB patients, which called for regularly administered doses of mostly inexpensive but powerful antibiotics for six to eight months.) The health of many patients improved dramatically. In addition to Haiti, PIH currently supports community-based health networks in Guatemala, Mexico, Rwanda, Lesotho, Russia, and the Boston area.

In 1995 the Reverend John J. Roussin (known as Father Jack), a member of the Society of St. James in Boston and of the PIH team in Carabayllo, a shantytown on the outskirts of Lima, Peru, died at age 48 after contracting a drug-resistant form of TB. In investigating the source of Father Jack's illness, Kim and Farmer discovered that most of the PIH patients in Carabayllo were suffering from a type of TB that was resistant to all of the readily available drugs that were commonly used to treat TB. Earlier, WHO officials had ruled that it would be too costly to treat people in poor areas of developing countries who were suffering from MDR-TB. Determined to help those patients, Kim and Farmer "created a plan that flew in the face of the accepted ideas about treatment costs," as Tyler D. Johnson wrote for the Denver, Colorado, *Rocky Mountain News* (September 19, 2003). Their new treatment regimen required the daily administration for up to two years of as many as seven so-called second-line medications, which were weaker than the preferred, standard drugs used to combat the disease and produced unpleasant side effects. Residents of Carabayllo were trained to administer the complex drug therapies in patients' homes. The strategy had a high success rate: over 80 percent of those patients regained their health. (WHO has stressed that curing people infected with MDR-TB is important not only in terms of the well-being of those people, their families, and others in their communities, but also in terms of the well-being of people everywhere, because of the ease with which infectious diseases can spread in the 21st century's global society.)

As the founding chairperson of WHO's Green Light Committee for Access to Second-line Anti-Tuberculosis Drugs, Kim spent much time during the late 1990s striving to get reductions in the prices of second-line medications while ensuring that their quality was not compromised. As he and colleagues of his explained in their article "Responding to Market Failures in Tuberculosis Control" for *Science* (August 10, 2001), negotiations handled by Médecins Sans Frontières (Doctors without Borders) resulted in savings of nearly 94 percent on expenditures for the second-line drugs. Also during that period Kim helped write protocols for the treatment of persons with MDR-TB.

"To us, those with drug-resistant TB are among the most outcast, the most marginalized people in the world," Kim told John Donnelly for the *Boston Globe* (November 1, 1999). "We will always remain grounded in the experiences of the poor."

In 2003 Kim took a three-year leave of absence from Harvard to become a senior adviser to Lee Jong-wook, who was then the general director of WHO. In December 2003 WHO launched what was dubbed the "3 by 5" initiative, with the goal of delivering, by the end of 2005, antiretrovirals (anti-AIDS drugs) to three million people in the Third World who were infected with HIV. "No matter how many people get on treatment by 2005, we will show that we take seriously the loss of a life," Kim, who helped design the "3 by 5" project and became its head in 2004, told John Donnelly for the *Boston Globe* (December 1, 2003). According to the Web site of the Global Fund to Fight Aids, Tuberculosis, and Malaria, of the estimated 40 million people worldwide who are infected with HIV, about 95 percent live in Third World countries; HIV/AIDS "is the leading cause of death in Africa and the fourth-leading cause of death worldwide"; and in 2004 approximately 3.1 million people died of AIDS-related causes. Speaking of the "3 by 5" project, Eric Goemaere, the head of the South African program of Doctors without Borders, told a reporter for *Africa News* (January 20, 2006), "It's good to have an ambitious target. People are under pressure to move—and things are moving, and moving fast." Mostly because of insufficient funding, the "3 by 5" initiative fell more than one million people short of its goal. Kim was nevertheless encouraged by the results; according to the Brigham and Women's Hospital Web site, he explained, "At the time of 3x5's inception, there was really no clear target for HIV treatment that changed the way the world responded to the epidemic next week, next month, next year. Treatment goals can be very concrete, and we felt that naming a really concrete, difficult, and compelling target would get things moving, which it did. Now, the challenge is to bring the same momentum to prevention."

Kim is an adherent of "liberation theology," which maintains that organized religions should place much greater emphasis than they have in the past on trying to end poverty and fighting for social justice and human rights. "Paul [Farmer] and I are both Christians, but our commitments and work go well beyond our faith," he told Stephen Byrd. "We have worked very hard to break through what we feel are incorrect arguments about what can and can't be done in poor countries in terms of the delivery of health care."

Kim and his wife have a young son, Thomas, who was named in honor of Thomas White. Information about Kim appears in the book *Mountains Beyond Mountains: The Quest of Dr. Paul Farmer, a Man Who Would Cure the World* (2003).

—D.F.

Suggested Reading: Harvard School of Public Health Web site; kelloggfellows.org; *Muscatine Journal* Nov. 26, 2005 (on-line); Partners in Health Web site; *Satya* (on-line) Jan. 2001; *U.S. News & World Report* p60+ Oct. 31, 2005; World Health Organization Web site

Selected Books: as co-editor—*Dying for Growth: Global Inequity and the Health of the Poor*, 2000

Courtesy of *National Review*

King, Florence

Jan. 5, 1936– Writer

Address: P.O. Box 7113, Fredericksburg, VA 22404

The essayist, novelist, and former columnist Florence King embodies several contradictions. A political and social conservative, pronounced by Julia Watson in the *Washington Post* (March 13, 1992) to be "the Right's most crotchety sage," she is also a professed bisexual and the author of dozens of books of erotica, published under a number of pseudonyms; a trailblazer for female writers, she has often turned her satirical powers on the feminist movement; and she is a self-described "failed southern lady" and celebrated lampooner of American southern cultural mores who, as quoted by Alex Heard in the *Washington Post* (July 10, 1980), declared that she would live in a present-day Confederacy "without a moment's hesitation." Her early writing focused mainly on the South: *Southern Ladies and Gentleman* appeared in 1975, and she is perhaps best known for the comic energy and intelligence displayed in her partially embellished memoir *Confessions of a Failed Southern Lady* (1985). Her later books, including *Reflections in a Jaundiced Eye* (1989), *Lump It or Leave It* (1990), and *With Charity Toward None: A Fond Look at Misanthropy* (1992), broadened the scope of King's work. From 1991 to 2002 she penned "The Misanthrope's Corner," a weekly column that appeared in the conservative publication *National Review*. In an assessment of *Stet, Damnit! The Misanthrope's Corner, 1991-2002* (2003), an anthology of King's *National Review* columns, Colby Cosh wrote for the *American Spectator* (March 2004), "Anyone with even a hint of literary or comic sensibility who now attempts to parse Southern society has to acknowledge a debt to her books and journalism." Sam Staggs, writing for *Publishers Weekly* (June 22, 1990), described King as "an equal-opportunity provocateuse with a bad word for everybody, including a number of America's special-interest groups: women, feminists, gays and lesbians, ethnics; also children, 'Helpists' (King's term for do-gooders), even morning people."

The label that rests most easily on King is the one she has chosen herself: that of misanthrope. In the *Florence King Reader* (1996), King wrote, "Misanthropy is a realistic attitude toward human nature for Americans who do not necessarily hate everybody, but are tired of compulsory gregariousness, fevered friendliness, we-never-close compassion, goo-goo humanitarianism, sensitivity that never sleeps and politicians paralyzed by a hunger to be loved." Regarding her popularity, King told Alanna Nash for *Writer's Digest* (July 1990): "I say what I think, and that's so refreshing nowadays. So many writers are fence-straddling, state-of-the-art wimps. . . . And too, the novelty of a *woman* who rips the teats off sacred cows probably has something to do with it. We're supposed to be nurturing, and I come through as Medea."

Florence King was born in Washington, D.C., on January 5, 1936, the only child of Herbert Frederick King and the former Louise Ruding. Her mother's family traces its heritage in the state of Virginia to 1672. King's father, an English expatriate and the more intellectually inclined of her parents, was a trombone player in a traveling jazz band. King has described her mother, who left high school to earn a living as a telephone operator, as a tomboy. *Confessions of a Failed Southern Lady*, for example, revealed that Louise King "once hung a punching bag in the gazebo" and "could out-cuss a sailor," as Sam Staggs put it. Florence King noted for her April 22, 2002 column in *National Review* that her mother "never read a book in her life, including mine, but she had the sharpest brain I've ever encountered." King was raised in part by her maternal grandmother, who attempted to mold the irascible girl into a model of feminine southern charm. Her grandmother's harangues were to have a profound impact on King's sense of herself and of those around her. King wrote in *Reflections in a Jaundiced Eye*, for example, as quoted by Frank Gannon in the *New York Times* (April 9, 1989), "Living with Granny taught me that aging does not make women powerless objects of pity but colorful and entertaining individuals, and on occasion, fire-breathing dragons that wise people don't cross."

At school King excelled in French. She hoped to major in that subject at American University, in Washington, where she won an academic scholarship; to her dismay, she learned upon arriving on campus that the university did not offer a French major. "To lose French was to lose a certain girlhood innocence," she explained to Staggs. "I think that warped me greatly, far more than some experience such as a broken romance. Breaking up with someone never bothered me but losing French did, because that was my real life." She studied history instead, graduating from the school with a bachelor's degree in 1957. While at American she began to experiment sexually, having affairs with both men and women. She also joined a sorority, which revoked her membership when she professed to be a lesbian. After her graduation King made a brief attempt to become a marine, training at the Women Officer Candidate School in Quantico, Virginia, before dropping out.

King next attended graduate school at the University of Mississippi (known popularly as "Ole Miss"), in Oxford. While there she began writing "true confession" stories—for three to five cents per word—for such pulp magazines as *True Story*, *Modern Romances*, and *Uncensored Confessions*. According to one source, while in Oxford King fell in love with a young woman who was later killed in a car accident, a tragedy that led her to turn inward emotionally and focus more on her writing. King left graduate school short of the requirements for a master's degree and then, in the late 1950s, supported herself with a string of temporary jobs. In Suitland, Maryland, she taught history to 10th-graders, once getting into trouble for telling her students about Nell Gwynne, an English actress who in the 17th century became the mistress of King Charles II of England and bore him two sons. Also during that period King worked temporarily as a file clerk at the National Association of Realtors. Afterward she returned to writing true confessions anonymously for pulp magazines. In 1961 King began writing "sweet, virtuous" short stories for small-circulation religious magazines, as she later recalled for her column in *National Review* (September 30, 2002). Later, in a different vein, she used the pseudonym Ruding Upton King to write for adult publications including *Sir*, *Escapade*, *Dude*, and *Gent*—precursors to such magazines as *Playboy* and *Penthouse*.

In 1964 King left the Washington, D.C., area, heading to Raleigh, North Carolina. From 1964 to 1967 she worked as a feature-page writer for the newspaper *Raleigh News and Observer*. The experience enabled her to meet with and interview the opera performers who were passing through the city. In 1965 she received the North Carolina Press Woman Award for her reporting. From 1967 to 1968 she served as the assistant editor for *Uncensored Confessions* magazine. During the late 1960s King also churned out more than 35 erotic novels under several pseudonyms; she told Staggs that the experience taught her about creating plots and characters as well as "how to apply the seat of the pants to the seat of the chair, which was good discipline." (She added, "I don't approve of pornography, and I wish I hadn't written it. But it was nothing like porn as we know today; it was very soft. I couldn't write the stuff they sell now.") Discussing other influences on her work, she said, "I learned to write by reading Aristotle's *Poetics*, Horace's *Ars Poetica* and Boileu's *L'art poétique*. Read these books and you will never have to take a creative writing course, because it's all there."

In 1972, inspired by Mary Brinker Post's 1949 novel *Annie Jordan*, which she had enjoyed reading as a teenager, King moved to Seattle, Washington, the city in which the book is set. She remained in Seattle for the next decade, a period in which her writing career flourished, beginning with the publication, in 1975, of *Southern Ladies and Gentlemen*, the first book she wrote under her own name. The book, in part a comedic guide for northerners venturing south, was based largely on an article she had written for *Harper's*. An unsparing, "comic piece of regional sociology," in the words of Margo Jefferson, writing for *Newsweek* (June 30, 1975), *Southern Ladies and Gentleman* brought King notice as a distinctive observer of social behavior in the American South. The book takes issue with several customs associated in the South with manhood and, especially, womanhood. Assessments of *Southern Ladies and Gentleman* were mostly favorable, with reviewers pointing to King's alternately glib and caustic prose. Jefferson wrote, "King is an adept, clever Southern taleteller who assigns her gallery of everyday eccentrics tags like 'The Good Ole Boy' and 'Dear Old Thing' and knows how to set up scenes in which they play out their contradictions for us." Noting the author's "sprightly wit," Jefferson added, "At times her sallies are poorly and tastelessly aimed—as when she turns them on Southern homosexuals. She is best when letting situations speak for themselves as in her description of Northern reactions to Southerners." David Loftus, writing for the Web site allreaders.com, remarked on King's "sharp-tongued" and "witty" prose, observing: "From Debutantes, Dowagers, and Dear Old Things to all the different kinds of Good Old Boys, King explains their crazy motivations and behaviors. The fascination Southern women have for one another's plumbing, and the critical importance of wedding announcements are also dissected in this breezy and urbane set of essays."

King followed up her successful debut with *WASP, Where Is Thy Sting?* (1976), which grew out of an article she had written earlier for *Penthouse* entitled "Lay Me, I'm WASP." Next came *He, An Irreverent Look at the American Male* (1978), which Jerry Tallmer described for the *New York Post* (February 3, 1979) as "204 quite thoroughly salty pages [in which] Miss King gives a hilarious and detailed description of her own sexual growing-up in Washington, D.C., and at college, complete with wrestling matches, front seats, ironmaiden undergarments, flashlighting campus police, errant diaphragms, and young men's lies." Between *WASP, Where Is Thy Sting?* And *He*, King found time to write the romance novel *The Barbarian Princess* (1977) under the pseudonym Laura Buchanan.

The 1982 publication of King's next book, the novel *When Sisterhood Was in Flower*, one of the author's favorites of her own works, established her reputation as a satirist of the feminist movement. Set in the late 1960s and later, *When Sisterhood Was in Flower* tells the story of the aspiring writer Isobel Fairfax, who leaves her conservative family in the Deep South and moves to Boston, Massachusetts, where she encounters feminist activists—including the members of the Women's International Terrorist Conspiracy from Hell, or WITCH. A reviewer for *Resident Scholar*, quoted by the Web site allreaders.com, praised the book as "truly, unbelievably hysterical, and a marvelously caustic commentary on the Era of Love, feminism, and life."

In the opinion of many reviewers and fans, the memoir *Confessions of a Failed Southern Lady* (1985) remains the author's best work to date, and it increased her readership significantly. Clancy Sigal wrote for the London *Guardian* (August 29, 1985) about the book, "In form this is an autobiography. . . . In substance it is a gag strewn, very dirty *Pilgrim's Progress* of a young Upper South woman who, trapped in a divided sexual self in the 1950s, despised other women ('a pretty girl was supposed to be a melody, not a misanthrope') but finessed, rather than fought, her way out of a strangling Scarlett O'Hara stereotype." Carolyn See, reviewing the book for the *Los Angeles Times* (February 4, 1985), wrote that it "is so original, so odd, so wonderful, so bizarre and finally so heartwrenching that it can't easily be summed up. . . . This is a stunning book, a masterpiece, a book that should be read 50 times and then put carefully away in case you ever have cancer and care to try the Norman Cousins cure-by-laughter."

The irreverent King next offered *Reflections in a Jaundiced Eye* (1989), a collection of essays of social criticism. Many observers noted that King's tone in *Reflections* had become more harsh, a fact that the author attributed, with seeming seriousness, to her having passed through menopause. (She explained to Staggs, "*Reflections* was the first book I wrote post-menopause. By then, I was free at last; I became once more the way I was as a child, that is, more like my masculine mother, whereas during my menstruating years I was more like my father—quiet, gentle and thoughtful. I suppressed my true personality.") Among other American trends that King attacked in *Reflections* are "helpism," political correctness, and the tendency of many to seek expert problem solvers to improve their personal lives. In *Lump It or Leave It* (1990), King's second book of essays, she took aim at, among other targets, the system of democracy—which she referred to as "the crude leading the crud." (She told Staggs, "You must have an elitist republic before you can have excellence. Democracy is the rule of the mediocre. Americans call anything good elitist. . . . You can't have excellence and democracy.") *Lump It or Leave It* disclosed King's political leanings toward the Republican Party. Writing about the volume for the *Washington Post Book World* (July 10, 1990), Alex Heard noted that King had been praised for "say[ing] what others are afraid to"; Heard himself, however, criticized King's writing as unfunny and racially offensive, and he concluded his review by advising readers not to buy the book.

In many ways *With Charity Toward None: A Fond Look at Misanthropy* (1992) represented the height of the author's curmudgeonly tone. The book includes a detailed look at misanthropes of the past, among them the French novelist Gustave Flaubert, the French philosopher Jean-Jacques Rousseau, and G. Gordon Liddy, a former aide to U.S. president Richard Nixon. *With Charity Toward None* "puts [King] in the curmudgeonly tradition of such professional sourpusses as H. L. Mencken, W. C. Fields, and John Simon," in the words of Grace Glueck, writing for New York *Newsday* (March 8, 1992). "I say *tradition*, not company, because she has a long way to go to achieve their swordsmanship. But she's in there lunging. . . . When King is good, she is very, very good, but when she is bad, she is florid, as in her purple-prose assault on the 'feminization' of America."

In the 1980s King had reviewed books for *Newsday*. From 1991 to 2002 she contributed the column "Misanthrope's Corner" to the *National Review*. That period coincided with the presidential administration of Bill Clinton, whom King described, according to Colby Cosh, as "the Man on the Plane, the ubiquitous middle-aged businessman with *husband* written all over him who lives for out-of-town flings." King attacked what she viewed as the era's effeminacy and oversensitivity. For her May 28, 2001 column in the *National Review*, in response to numerous articles and books about overcoming stress, she wrote: "The American way of stress is comparable to Freud's 'beloved symptom,' his name for the cherished neurosis that a patient cultivates like the rarest of orchids and does not want to be cured of. Stress makes Americans feel busy, important, and in demand, and simultaneously deprived, ignored, and victimized. Stress makes them feel interesting and complex instead of boring and simple, and carries an assumption of sensitivity not unlike the Old World assumption that aristocrats were high-strung. In short, stress has become a status symbol." On September 30, 2002 the *National Review* published what King declared was to be her last column for that periodical. "As to why I'm leaving," she wrote, "the simplest reason has to do with those 'clicks' we hear in our heads: Ten years is enough. I've written this column for so long that you know everything I think about everything under the sun. . . . If I were to continue, it would just be overkill." Her announced retirement notwithstanding, in 2006 columns as well as book reviews by King appeared in the *National Review*. In 2003 an anthology of her *National Review* columns were collected in book form. (The book's title, *Stet, Damnit!*, refers to a proofreading mark signalling that a deletion or change made by an editor should be ignored.) The conservative magazine *American Spectator* has also carried articles by King.

King, who has never married, remarked to Jerry Tallmer that she does not "believe in living with men" because "it doesn't look right." She resides in Fredericksburg, Virginia. Her interests include turn-of-the-century popular songs, horseback riding, and collecting guns. She is an Episcopalian and a member of the history honor society Phi Alpha Theta. King has served on the *American Heritage Dictionary*'s usage panel since 1986.

Explaining to Sam Staggs the attitude one must develop to become a wit, a label she prefers to "humorist," King said: "You must have a dismal outlook on life and human nature. You have to be a misanthrope, a loner, an introvert—all the things Americans don't want to be and don't think people should be. Wit goes for the jugular; humor goes for the jocular." Jack Nichols wrote for the Gay Today Web Site (February 3, 1997), in a piece titled "Florence King: World's Funniest Bi-Sexual Republican," that King "is, actually, an astute student of human nature, amazingly aware of funny foibles and facetious faults. She draws stereotypes of various human classes not to be believed. In fact, it is hard to believe, almost, that she doesn't like her species since, obviously, she seems to have derived and given so much pleasure describing it."
—D.F.

Suggested Reading: *American Spectator* p57+ Mar. 2004; (London) *Guardian* Aug. 29, 1985; Mississippi Writers and Musicians Web site; *New York Post* p34 Feb. 3, 1979; *New York Times* VII p27 Feb. 10, 1985; *Newsweek* p66 June 30, 1975; *Publishers Weekly* p38+ June 22, 1990

Selected Books: *Southern Ladies and Gentlemen*, 1975; *WASP, Where Is Thy Sting?*, 1976; *He: An Irreverent Look at the American Male*, 1978; *When Sisterhood Was in Flower*, 1982; *Confessions of a Failed Southern Lady*, 1985; *Reflections in a Jaundiced Eye*, 1989; *Lump It or Leave It*, 1990; *With Charity Toward None: A Fond Look at Misanthropy*, 1992; under pseudonym Laura Buchanan—*The Barbarian Princess*, 1977; *Satan's Child: A Survivor Tells Her Story to Help Others*, 1994

Courtesy of Knopf Books

Klinkenborg, Verlyn

June 16, 1952– Writer

Address: New York Times, *229 W. 43d St., New York, NY 10036*

In the mid-1990s Verlyn Klinkenborg revived an old tradition at the *New York Times* by writing short pieces about the cycles, visible developments, and all-but-hidden meanings in nature, as he observed them from his farm in upstate New York. He became a member of the newspaper's editorial board in 1997, the year that his nature writings were made into a permanent feature of the *Times* and given the name "The Rural Life." In his position Klinkenborg helps to make decisions regarding the newspaper as a whole and writes editorials about issues affecting the nation. He is the author of the nonfiction books *Making Hay* (1986), *The Last Fine Time* (1991), and *The Rural Life* (2002) and the genre-straddling *Timothy, Or, Notes of an Abject Reptile* (2006).

The oldest of four children, Verlyn Klinkenborg was born on June 16, 1952 in Colorado and raised in a small town in Iowa. His paternal grandparents, who were farmers in Iowa, did not have enough land to divide among their sons, and Verlyn Klinkenborg's father, Ronald, became a public-school music teacher. Klinkenborg's mother, a nurse, became ill during his childhood; in the mid-1960s, when he was 14, the family moved to California for his mother's health. Klinkenborg attended high school in Sacramento and then enrolled at the University of California at Berkeley, ultimately graduating from Pomona College, in Claremont, California. He was 19 when his mother died of leu-

kemia. Her death led Klinkenborg to draw closer to his father. "My mother was our interpreter, and when she died we were left speechless," he wrote for *Harper's* (May 1992). "In the silent period that followed, I think we saw in my mother's death how much we stood to lose in each other. . . . Death makes individuals of us all. The individual it made for me was my father."

After spending a year in Europe, Klinkenborg entered graduate school at Princeton University, in Princeton, New Jersey, earning a Ph.D. degree in 18th-century English literature. As a graduate student in 1978, Klinkenborg worked at the Morgan Library, in New York City, as a curatorial assistant, cataloging British literary and historical manuscripts. (He later wrote about the experience for the *New York Times* [April 29, 2006].) After receiving his doctorate Klinkenborg taught creative writing and literature at Fordham University, in New York City; St. Olaf College, in Northfield, Minnesota; Bennington College, in Bennington, Vermont; and Harvard University, in Cambridge, Massachusetts. His first published works were a Morgan Library catalogue, which he wrote, and *Mrs. Piozzi to Mr. Conway* (1981), which he edited. (Hester Lynch Piozzi [1741–1821] was a friend of the English writer and lexicographer Samuel Johnson.)

Klinkenborg's book *Making Hay* was published in 1986. The volume is an account of Klinkenborg's visits to the farms of friends and relatives in Minnesota and Iowa, where the author participated in making hay. He had wanted to write the book because, although he had grown up around farmers, he had never understood the processes of such tasks as making hay—which, nevertheless, remained a part of his consciousness and evoked "all the epiphanies I have ever had," as he wrote, according to Christopher Lehmann-Haupt of the *New York Times* (December 8, 1986). "Whether the book means to or not, it evokes the ugliness of farm work as well as its beauty," Lehmann-Haupt noted, "but what is most admirable about *Making Hay* is that it memorializes a way of life we take for granted. Its language celebrates both the changes and permanence of modern farming, its earthiness and ethereality. 'Behind us the steers drooled and the pigs clanked their self-feeders and ran about in high heels while we looked at the afternoon past an old metal sign that marked the far end of the bottom feedlot to which the floods had risen last spring.' What activity there is in that sentence. Yet what it sneakily tells us is that people have stopped to daydream for a moment. There isn't much to dream about on these farms, but what there is Mr. Klinkenborg has caught." Assessing *Making Hay* for the *New York Times Book Review* (October 12, 1986), Sue Hubbell wrote, "Farmers, the author observes, do not rhapsodize. [Klinkenborg] does not either, but in writing in loving detail about one part of farming—making hay—Verlyn Klinkenborg gives the reader some understanding of why in these hard times those of us who do farm stay on the land and still farm."

In 1982 Klinkenborg had married Regina Wenzek. Wenzek's father, Eddie, had been a restaurateur and barkeep in a heavily Polish working-class community of Buffalo, New York, the locale that served as the setting for Klinkenborg's nonfiction volume *The Last Fine Time*, published in 1991. The narrative focuses largely on Eddie Wenzek, who in 1947—the eponymous "fine time"—took over his father's bar, an ethnic hangout, and tried to turn it into an upscale nightspot. The book portrays the life of the community over a period of decades and describes the experiences of European immigrants in the U.S. JoAnn Wypijewski complained in the *Nation* (April 1, 1991) that Klinkenborg had told Eddie's story and the stories of the other Buffalonians not in their own words but in those of "a creative-writing teacher from Harvard who seems oblivious to the delicate means by which people may choose to mediate their own life histories." Many other reviewers, however, were more positive. "*The Last Fine Time* is an evocative story, detailing the immigrant experience with precision . . . ," Stephen Amidon noted in the *Financial Times* (August 10, 1991). "This book's unique strength lies in the empathy Klinkenborg has for vanished people and events. . . . Klinkenborg concludes his account of the Wenzeks' compromised American dream with a chapter on Niagara Falls, waiting just downstream for city dwellers who take a wrong turn. It's a fitting reminder of a nation whose boundless hope has always been balanced by an equal potential for plummet." Klinkenborg won the Lila Wallace–Reader's Digest Writer's Award for *The Last Fine Time* in 1991. In the following year the volume won the American Book Award from the Before Columbus Foundation.

In 1995 Klinkenborg, who had contributed pieces on a freelance basis to the *New Yorker*, *Harper's*, *Esquire*, *Mother Jones*, and other magazines, and had owned and lived on farms in Massachusetts and upstate New York, began to write unsigned essays on nature for the editorial pages of the *New York Times*—reviving a tradition at the newspaper previously practiced by Hal Borland and Edward Hoagland. After two years, "when it became clear I could make editorials about things besides spring, winter and summer and fall," as he told James Norton for *flakmagazine* (December 11, 2002, on-line), Klinkenborg joined the *Times*'s editorial board. Also that year his nature essays began appearing with his byline in a regular column, called "The Rural Life." He collected many of those columns in a book of the same name, published in 2002. A writer for *Kirkus Reviews* (September 15, 2002) called the book "nonfiction storytelling at its highest: unflaggingly lovely, with scope, profundity, and power achieved through a mastery of the delicate." Klinkenborg said to James Norton, "The trick about writing ['The Rural Life'] for me, and the thing I try to pay close attention to, is that [the] world up there is very complicated. I don't believe that there's any kind of virtue in giving a false picture of the serenity or simplicity of the country. It's not simple, it's not serene—it's rewarding and engaging and as intellectually and ethically challenging as anything you can do in the city."

As a member of the *Times* editorial board, Klinkenborg is, as Ed Nawotka put it in *Publishers Weekly* (September 23, 2002), "one of a dozen people responsible for formulating the newspaper's national agenda." He also writes about "what I would call the national emotional issues," as he said to James Norton. In the wake of the 2001 terrorist attacks on the U.S., he wrote pieces about their effects on the public mind-set. "In the first few days after the attack, cultural prognosticators announced the death of irony and the end of cynicism," he wrote for the September 30, 2001 edition of the paper. "The sitcom would be reborn, regaining its rightful dominance over reality TV, whose fortunes would wane in the wake of a televised reality more overpowering than anyone had ever imagined. Disaster movies were over. Hollywood needed the dawn of a new Doris Day. . . . Behind all these cultural predictions lies the assumption that what we really need to do is avert our eyes from what we have already watched in horror, that we need, somehow, to prevent our innocence from being further impaired by the smoke and ash and death that rained down on this country that day. That is a false, not to say a vain, assumption. . . . What we need most is the work of artists who do not flinch. . . [Their] work, whatever form it takes, may not offer the consolation we feel we need now, but then it is not the job of artists to console us. Their job, however unseemly it may feel, will inevitably be to fracture this momentary mood, to lead us beyond what is merely safe and consoling."

Klinkenborg told James Norton that he believes "in the glory of nonfiction. . . . I don't believe in the hierarchy of genres that seems to prevail in the United States. Is the novel the higher calling, or is poetry the higher calling? Frankly I think nonfiction is equally great and equally profound—and often gloriously better." While he has maintained that he writes strictly nonfiction, his most recent book is narrated from the point of view of a tortoise—the real-life pet of the 18th-century British naturalist Gilbert White. Klinkenborg told Emily Chenoweth for an interview in *Publishers Weekly* (January 30, 2006) that in writing *Timothy, Or, Notes of an Abject Reptile* (2006), he was influenced by White's 1789 work *The Natural History and Antiquities of Selborne*, in which White described the tortoise that lived in his garden. Josh Kun noted in the *Los Angeles Times Book Review* (February 12, 2006) that the book "is Selborne [a town in England] through Timothy's eyes; this is White under observation by a tortoise. Which makes *Timothy* a work of both speculative naturalism and speculative biography. . . . Klinkenborg imbues Timothy with a profound sense of apartness, a lonely being at home in the space of a singular shell. It is the author's greatest triumph: He makes us believe we are reading not just the thoughts of a tortoise but those of a Turkish tortoise, uprooted from the craggy coast of the Mediterranean to spend cruel, solitary winters in a British garden." David Gessner, who assessed *Timothy* for the *New York Times Book Review* (May 7, 2006), was of the opinion that "writing from an animal's point of view . . . always risks coming off as just plain goofy." He added, "As our narrator (a misnamed female, it turns out) tells the 'true story' of her life, I found myself having a hard time suspending disbelief. But then slowly (as befits her kind) Timothy starts turning on the turtle charm."

Klinkenborg lives on a farm in the Hudson Valley of New York with his wife, Lindy Smith, a photographer. James Norton reported that Klinkenborg usually goes to his office at the *Times* three days a week and is "otherwise . . . typically upstate on the farm, looking after his livestock and watching the natural world." His introduction prefaces *Portraits: Photographs of Farm Animals* (1994), by

Danielle Weil, and he wrote the text for *Straight West: Portraits and Scenes from Ranch Life in the American West* (2000), with photographs by Lindy Smith, and *Gardenscapes* (2003), with photographs by Lynn Geesaman.

—S.Y.

Suggested Reading: *America* (on-line) Jan. 20, 2003; *Financial Times* X p1 Aug. 10, 1991; *Kirkus Reviews* p1367 Sep. 15, 2002; *Mother Jones* p48+ Feb. 2002; *Nation* p420+ Apr. 1, 1991; *New York Times* C p28 Dec. 8, 1986; *New York Times Book Review* p20 Oct. 12, 1986, p1 Jan. 20, 1991; *Washington Post* C p3 Jan. 3, 1991

Selected Books: *Making Hay*, 1986; *The Last Fine Time*, 1991; *The Rural Life*, 2002; *Timothy; Or, Notes of an Abject Reptile*, 2006; as editor—*Mrs. Piozzi to Mr. Conway*, 1981

Knoll, Andrew H.

Apr. 23, 1951– Paleontologist

Address: Harvard University Botanical Museum, 26 Oxford St., Cambridge, MA 02138

"There are times when I wake up and wish I could find something as sexy as a dinosaur," the paleontologist Andrew Knoll told an interviewer for CNN.com in 2001. "On the other hand, what I'm trying to find out is how the modern fabric of the world came to be and what was in place long before the dinosaurs existed." As a specialist in what is called the deep history of Earth, Knoll has spent his career collecting microscopic fossils from remote regions around the globe and drawing new conclusions about early climate conditions and the evolution of plant and animal species. Knoll is a leading authority on the Proterozoic period (2.5 billion to 544 million years ago), an ecologically unique time in Earth's history that immediately preceded the era known as the Cambrian period, during which there appeared the types of plant and animal life that exist today. Knoll told *Current Biography* that among his most important scientific contributions, made with the help of others, are the discovery and systematic interpretation of Proterozoic fossils and the discovery that the increase in oxygen levels in the atmosphere that occurred during the late Proterozoic period was concurrent with the appearance of plants and animals that required high levels of oxygen for their survival. In collaboration with scientists from China, Knoll has studied fossil embryos of animals from the Cambrian period. He has also applied his geological expertise to studying Martian sediment samples, as a member of the National Aeronautics and Space Administration (NASA) Mars Exploration Rovers

Science Team. Knoll has taught at Harvard University, in Cambridge, Massachusetts, since 1982. He has held the title of professor in the Department of Earth and Planetary Sciences there since 1985 and was named Fisher Professor of Natural History in 2000. He has served as the curator of the paleobotanical collections in Harvard's Botanical Museum since 1985 and as an associate dean in the Faculty of Arts and Sciences since 2000.

Andrew Herbert Knoll was born on April 23, 1951 in Wernersville, Pennsylvania. His father, Robert S. Knoll, was a banker; his mother, Anna A. (Meyer) Knoll, was an elementary-school teacher. He grew up near Reading, Pennsylvania. Knoll's first encounter with fossils came when, as a fourth-grader, he went with the junior-high class of his brother, John, on a field trip to the foothills of the Appalachian Mountains. The sight of a fossil in a rock that had been split open made a lasting impression on him. "From that first fossil I never stopped being fascinated by how the Earth records life's history," he told David S. F. Portree for the *Earth and Sky Radio Series* (June 2004, on-line). Although he remained interested in paleontology, Knoll entered Lehigh University, in Pennsylvania, as an engineering major. "Where and when I grew up," he told Portree, "there were only three professions. You could be a doctor, a lawyer or an engineer. I knew that I didn't want to be a doctor or a lawyer, so I went to an engineering school." After a year, however, Knoll "had an epiphany—that I could perhaps make a living by doing my hobby, which was paleontology." He spent the next three years pursuing a double major in biology and geology. While at Lehigh he sang with the glee club, whose director, Robert Cutler, as he told Portree, helped young people "grow up." "I learned my science from other people, but everything I learned about how to negotiate and appreciate the world,

Andrew H. Knoll at work in British Columbia, Canada

Courtesy of Andrew H. Knoll

I learned from Professor Cutler." Knoll graduated from Lehigh with a B.A. degree, with highest honors, in 1973.

Knoll told Portree that his decision to study fossilized specimens of Earth's earliest life forms was inspired by an introductory botany course he took as a Lehigh senior. While writing a term paper on the origin of chloroplasts (organelles in the cells of green plants where photosynthesis takes place), Knoll learned about the endosymbiotic theory of photosynthesis, a then-controversial view revived by the biologist Lynn Margolis, which holds that chloroplasts were originally freely roaming bacteria that were "captured and, in essence, made metabolic slaves," as Knoll put it in his interview with Portree. "The endosymbiotic theory really altered the way I thought about the history of the planet. I thought that this was one of the most powerful ideas of all time—I still think that." In the course of researching the term paper, Knoll also read about early fossils discovered by Elso Barghoorn of Harvard, among them fossilized algae from Lake Superior and fossils from South Africa. Those discoveries pushed back by billions of years, to more than 3.4 billion years ago, the estimates of when life had appeared on Earth. Knoll later worked with Barghoorn while a graduate student at Harvard, where Knoll earned an M.A. and a Ph.D. in geology in 1974 and 1977, respectively. He told Portree that Barghoorn, whom he regards as his primary professional mentor, "taught me it was all right to think broadly about the world and find the connections." After he completed graduate school, Knoll taught geology for five years at Oberlin College, in Ohio. In 1982 he joined the faculty of Harvard as an associate professor of biology.

Much of Knoll's fieldwork in the 1980s was conducted in the Arctic and was concerned with discerning patterns of diversity and evolutionary changes in early eukaryotic cells (those having a nucleus), both one-celled individuals and cells in multicelled creatures. While there had been previous paleontological studies of diversity among invertebrates through time, Knoll was the first to try to construct the diversity history of early eukaryotes or land plants. In 1983 he and the Swedish scientist Gonzalo Vidal, of Uppsala University, reported finding evidence of the earliest known mass extinction of species, gathered from fossilized algae at sites in Spitsbergen (an island in the Svalbard Archipelago, in the Arctic Ocean), Scandinavia, the Baltic region of northern Europe, and eastern Greenland. Knoll and Vidal suggested that as many as 70 percent of the single-celled algae species living in those areas disappeared about 650 million years ago, probably because of climate changes and widespread glaciation. Prior to Knoll and Vidal's report, the earliest known mass extinction was one that took place around 450 million years ago, when many shell-covered animals disappeared. (The most well-known extinction occurred roughly 65 million years ago, when dinosaurs and many other species died out, apparently after a meteor struck Earth.)

Knoll told Portree that his favorite research site is Spitsbergen, which he described as "shockingly foreign and beautiful. It's like having the Alps at sea level." In 1988 Knoll, his Harvard colleague Nicholas Butterfield, and Keene Sweet of the University of Iowa reported finding marine fossils at Spitsbergen that dated from a time when the region's climate was tropical. The 700-million-year-old fossils, which included both single-celled algae and the first known multicelled algae, were of "a much greater number of forms and greater complexity" than had previously been seen in specimens from that period. The collection included algae resembling those that currently carpet coral reefs in the Caribbean Sea. Some of the fossilized algae had been in the process of germinating when they were covered by clay. The clay "preserved them and sealed them off from bacteria that would have eaten them or compounds in the percolating water that would have caused chemical breakdown," Knoll told Delthia Ricks for United Press International (August 3, 1988). In addition to their discoveries of those fossils, Knoll told *Current Biography*, "perhaps the most important result from our Spitsbergen work was geochemical—we showed that the carbon isotopic composition of seawater shows remarkable variation in 550 [million]–800 million-year-old oceans, with major excursions reflecting ice ages."

In a 1994 paper Knoll suggested that rates of evolution and diversification among microscopic eukaryotes, especially algae, increased dramatically with the introduction of animals into marine ecosystems. The fossil record, he wrote, showed a rapid increase in the number of single-celled planktonic algae species and replacement of old with new species among algae occurring along with the arrival of early plant and animal forms immediately prior to the Cambrian explosion. He hypothesized that that increase among algae and animals might have resulted from the rise of oxygen levels in the atmosphere or another widespread ecological change.

In the 1990s Knoll turned his attention from the Arctic to China and parts of Russia below the Arctic Circle. He told *Current Biography*, "The Russian work was successful—most notable for collecting volcanic ash beds that provided the first good radiometric dates for the Cambrian explosion, but the Chinese work turned out to be special." The latter was the discovery in 1998 by Knoll and a team of researchers, including his Harvard student Shuhai Xiao, of a large number of well-preserved fossils in phosphatic rock in southern China. The fossils, about the size of grains of sand, were roughly 580 million to 600 million years old and provided evidence of the oldest known animals on record. They dated from a time when living creatures existed only in aqueous environments and before any had skeletons, shells, or limbs. The extensive collection included the oldest known remains of soft-bodied creatures known as bilaterians, which, unlike the jellyfish and sponges prevalent during that era, had left and right sides. Bilaterians include a wide range of present-day animals as well—"everything from worms to us," as Knoll told Malcolm Ritter for the Associated Press Online (February 4, 1998).

In 2001 Knoll and his Harvard colleague Richard K. Bambach, a paleontologist, argued for the removal of two of what had been considered the "Big Five" mass extinctions in the last 500 million years, as identified by the paleontologists John Sepkoski and David Raup in the early 1980s. Using the same fossils that Sepkoski and Raup had studied, Knoll and Bambach showed that two of the events labeled extinctions—those of the late Devonion period, 365 million years ago, and of the Triassic period, 200 million years ago—were not large, sudden, or unusual enough to be called extinctions. Both events fell within a series of occurrences of similar magnitude, and their levels of depletion did not stand out among those neighboring events enough to qualify them as "big." Furthermore, though both periods in question contained a noticeable decline in the diversity of species, the drop was due not to increased extinction rates (the rates before and after those events were similar) but to a decline in the production of original species. Knoll and Bambach's proposal that the events be labeled "mass depletions" drew little argument from others in their field.

Knoll's Martian investigations began in 1998, when NASA recruited researchers from American and European institutions to a network connected to its recently founded Astrobiology Institute, at the Ames Research Center in Mountain View, California. Eleven teams were formed to research the evolution of life on Earth and other planets. Knoll was the leader of the Harvard team, which focused on comparing geological records from Earth and Mars, with the aim of determining whether life might ever have existed on Mars. Knoll and Steven W. Squyres, a professor of astronomy at Cornell University, orchestrated the planning of missions on Mars of two small mobile geological rovers, called Opportunity and Spirit, equipped with technology for collecting, dusting off, and photographing rock samples, to analyze the planet's surface. "In some ways," Knoll told *Current Biography*, "[the Mars research] can be seen as an extension of my earlier work—looking at ancient sedimentary rocks to learn about conditions early in planetary history." Knolls's team had a breakthrough in 2004 when the Opportunity rover reached Meridiani Planum, a Martian plain containing the mineral hematite. On Earth, hematite is usually found only near water, and this, along with several other clear geological indicators, assured the team that water had once been present in some form. However, further investigation led Knoll to question the possibility of life on Mars. "Mars was probably pretty acidic in most places for most of its history. And, if that's true, then regardless of whether habitable environments ever existed, it's probably a long shot to think that life would have originated on Mars," he was quoted as saying in the *Belleville (Illinois) News-Democrat* (October 26, 2004).

For his contributions to the Mars project, Knoll earned NASA's Group Achievement Award in 2004 and 2005 and the National Air and Space Museum Trophy in 2006. He won a Guggenheim Foundation fellowship in 1987 and, that same year, won the Charles Schuchert Award from the

Paleontological Society, an international organization. In 1991 he was elected to the National Academy of Sciences—an honor that, for most scientists, as he told Sarah L. Park for the *Harvard Crimson* (August 17, 2001), "tells you you've arrived." In 2001 he received the Chang Ying-Chien Prize in Paleontology from the American Museum of Natural History. Knoll was named an honorary fellow of the European Union of Geosciences in 2003. He won the Phi Beta Kappa Book Award in Science in 2003 for *Life on a Young Planet: The First Three Billion Years of Evolution on Earth* (2003), which he wrote for a popular audience, and he was given a Paleontological Society Medal in 2005. He has received honorary doctoral degrees from Lehigh University and Uppsala University. His scientific papers (he has written or co-written more than 200) are among those most frequently cited by others working in the geosciences, according to the ISI Web of Science. With the British ecologist and environmental economist Norman Myers, he edited

the volume *Colloquium on the Future of Evolution* (2002).

Knoll and the former Marsha Craig, whom he married in 1974, have two children, Kirsten and Robert. For *Who's Who in America*, he listed his recreational interests as traveling, reading, cooking, and choral music. Marsha Knoll teaches a class in Japanese culture in a program called Harvard Neighbors.

—M.B.

Suggested Reading: *Earth & Sky Radio Series* (on-line) June 2004; ISI Highly Cited Researchers (on-line); *Nova* at pbs.org; *Time* p48+ Aug. 20, 2001; *Who's Who in America*

Selected Books: *Life on a Young Planet: The First Three Billion Years of Evolution on Earth*, 2003; as co-editor—*Colloquium on the Future of Evolution*, 2002

Sarah Shatz

Koh, Jennifer

Oct. 8, 1976– Violinist

Address: c/o Colbert Artists Management Inc., 111 West 57th St., New York, NY 10019

By her early teens the violinist Jennifer Koh was already considered one of the world's best young classical musicians by those who had seen her perform in national competitions, and her reputation has only grown since then. A native of Chicago, Il-

linois, Koh began studying violin at age three, performed with the Chicago Symphony Orchestra at 13, and has since played with a host of top orchestras around the world, including the Los Angeles Philharmonic, the Czech Philharmonic, the Cleveland Orchestra, and the KBS Symphony of Seoul, South Korea. She is known for the insight and appreciation she brings to her interpretations of both well-known and obscure compositions, and as many have observed, she conveys a passion for music that is rare, or at least rarely so freely demonstrated, even among her fellow musicians. "I love being on stage," Koh, then 14, told Shirley Barnes in a story about rising young stars for the *Chicago Tribune* (February 17, 1991). "People talk about stage fright, but I just enjoy being up there." In 2003, reviewing a performance Koh gave as a soloist with the Grant Park Orchestra, in Chicago, Ted Shen wrote for the *Chicago Tribune* (June 29, 2003), "Her playing is so fluent and assured that she can breeze through the toughest technical hurdles, and she's exciting to watch, a petite firebrand who revels in emotional display. Yet, she's also capable of the delicate touch and beguiling sweetness." Koh tours extensively, playing roughly 100 concerts a year, in which she is featured both with orchestras and in solo recitals. She has given recitals at such venues as Carnegie Hall, in New York; the Kennedy Center, in Washington, D.C.; the Marlboro Music Festival; and the Ravinia Festival. Koh has also recorded albums for several labels, on which she has explored parallels between pieces from widely different eras and showcased the work of lesser-known—though to her mind eminently worthy—composers. While her performance repertoire consists largely of classics by Beethoven, Mozart, Schubert, and other universally known names, Koh has, as Jeremy Eichler noted for the

New York Times (January 20, 2004), "distinguished herself as an adventurous musician with a flair for performing contemporary music"—including concertos by the New York downtown avant-gardist John Zorn and the West Coast–based composer Lou Harrison.

It was a piece by Harrison, the Indonesian-influenced *Concerto in Slendro*, that Koh played at the 2003 opening of Zankel Hall, a 644-seat facility located directly below Carnegie Hall. Several years earlier she had given her first performance at Carnegie Hall, playing Mozart's Concerto in A Major with the New York String Orchestra, conducted by Jaime Laredo. Her many other career highlights include a performance of Tan Dun's *Water Passion*, conducted by the composer at New York's South Street Seaport, and annual appearances at Italy's Spoleto Festival. Koh told Wynne Delacoma for the *Chicago Sun-Times* (June 26, 2005), "I knew from when I was very young that I wanted music in my life. But it was never very career-oriented for me; it was always musically oriented. Ultimately, that developed [into the desire] to become a great musician, a great artist." Still, she added, "I am in no way saying I'm a finished artist. I hope I'm not. That's an ongoing process."

Jennifer Koh was born on October 8, 1976, the only child of Gertrude Koh, a professor of library science, and John Koh, a small-business owner. Her parents had moved to the United States from Korea and settled in the Chicago area in the 1960s; Koh grew up in the suburb of Glen Ellyn. When she was three years old, her parents enrolled her in a program at nearby Wheaton College to learn music through the Suzuki method, which introduces very young children to instrumental study; she took up the violin, she has said, because the class for that instrument was the only one open at the time. At age eight she began studying under the renowned instructors Roland and Almita Vamos at the Music Center of the North Shore (now known as the Music Institute of Chicago). Each week the couple traveled from Minnesota, where they were professors, to teach gifted students in Chicago. Almita Vamos told Barnes in 1991, "Jennifer's one of the few young children I know who's totally happy playing the violin. She doesn't regret having to sacrifice [her time]." She said about Koh several years later, in a conversation with Elaine Guregian for the *Akron (Ohio) Beach Journal* (January 23, 1997), "She's not laid back at all. She likes a challenge. She can be a very sweet person and also temperamental. You can hear it when she plays." Koh made her concert debut at 11. At 12 she placed among the finalists at the Folkeston Menuhin International Competition, in Kent, England, and she earned top honors at the same contest two years later. She performed with the Chicago Symphony Orchestra at 13. Koh also participated in a number of other activities, including track, ice skating, and ballet, before her parents pressed her to choose between her two favorites—violin or competitive swimming. Koh reportedly did not waver in her choice, telling James D. Watts Jr. for the *Tulsa (Oklahoma) World* (January 12, 2001), "I grew to love music, and I reached the point where I could not imagine not playing and performing."

In 1991, when she was a freshman at Benet Academy, a high school in Lisle, Illinois, Koh won the prestigious National Concerto Competition, earning a prize of $5,000. In 1993 she won the $9,500 first prize in the Irving M. Klein International String Competition, held in San Francisco, California. The next year, at age 17, Koh tied for top violin prize and won all of the special prizes, including best performance of a Tchaikovsky work, at the International Tchaikovsky Competition in Moscow. (She had won the gold medal in the contest's Young Musicians category in 1992.) During the 1994–95 concert season, she won two top U.S. music prizes: the Concert Artists Guild Competition and an Avery Fisher Career Grant. "When it comes to violin competitions," Delacoma observed for the *Chicago Sun-Times* (June 30, 1994), "Glen Ellyn teenager Jennifer Koh is a regular Energizer bunny: She just keeps winning and winning and winning . . ."

Koh attended Oberlin College, in Ohio, where she received a bachelor's degree in English and a performance diploma in music from the Oberlin Conservatory in 1997. Though she continued to perform in contests during college, she devoted more time to her literature classes—an unusual route for a musician with the kind of credentials she had already established. "I think I surprised a lot of people when I decided to go for the English degree," she told Delacoma in 2005. "I needed that time to grow up, to open a lot of doors to different sources of knowledge. I was able to meet a lot of people who are passionate about things other than music. That was very important for me personally." After graduating Koh attended the Curtis Institute of Music, in Philadelphia, Pennsylvania, where she studied under the famous violinist Jaime Laredo, who would become a close friend and frequent professional collaborator. "I adore that lady," Laredo told Delacoma about Koh in 2005. "She was one of the greatest people to teach and work with. Most of the students I get at Curtis are 14 or 15. Being a little bit older, she was on a different level. She had such great interest in all facets of music. . . . You don't get many students like that. She was just like a sponge. Whatever she was doing, it was never enough. She always wanted more." At Curtis Koh was also instructed by another distinguished violinist, Felix Galimir, who earlier in the century had worked with such legendary composers as Anton Webern and Arnold Schoenberg. Koh greatly appreciated having a living connection to those past musical greats. "I've always been very intrigued by composers," she told Delacoma in 2005. "But having known Felix Galimir, I see an amazing kind of relationship between composers and performers. You're so close to the creative process."

Koh's career has been marked by several collaborative relationships with established artists who have inspired her. After she won the gold medal in the Young Musicians category at the Tchaikovsky Competition, the Russian composer Andrei Eshpai wrote a piece specifically for her—Violin Concerto no. 4, which she premiered in St. Petersburg, Russia, in 1996. Koh told Elaine Guregian, "It was really exciting to have [Eshpai] asking 'How exactly do you interpret this?' and to see this whole creative process work." Koh's performance of that piece was included with two others on the 1998 recording *Andrei Eshpai Edition, Volume Number 1*. As a result of that collaboration, she was asked to record music by the Finnish composer Uuno Klami (1900–61). The recording, *Whirls: Act 1*, appeared in 1997. Koh also developed a fruitful relationship with the Italian composer and librettist Gian Carlo Menotti, who in 1958 founded the Spoleto Festival, in Italy, at which Koh performs annually. Koh has vacationed with the elderly composer and his son, Francis, the festival's current director, at Menotti's castle in Scotland. In 2001 she made a live recording of Menotti's Violin Concerto with the Spoleto Festival Orchestra, conducted by Richard Hickox, as part of a 90th-birthday celebration for the composer. "I really feel this is one of the most beautiful violin concerti out there," Koh told Donald Rosenberg for the *Cleveland Plain Dealer* (August 22, 2003). "It's a shame it's not part of the standard repertoire. It was so special to have a chance not only to record it but to play it for Gian Carlo, who's been such a wonderful mentor and supporter."

Koh's first solo recording was *Solo Chaconnes* (2001), which included Bach's Chaconnes for Solo Violin along with works by the composers Richard Barth (Ciacona in B Minor, 1908) and Max Reger (Chaconne in G Minor, 1914). That year she also performed *Contes des Fées*, a violin concerto by John Zorn, at the Miller Theatre at Columbia University, in New York. In 2004 Koh's album *Violin Fantasies* was released on the Cedille recording label. The album contains four pieces, each by a different composer and from a different period, all of them "fantasies"—free-form, imaginative explorations—written for violin. Koh was accompanied by the pianist Reiko Uchida on works by Franz Schubert, Robert Schumann, Arnold Schoenberg, and Ornette Coleman. *Portraits*, Koh's recording of violin concertos by the composers Karol Szymanowski (1882–1937), Bohuslav Martinu (1890–1959), and Béla Bartók (1881–1945), was released in May 2006. Reviewing that recording, on which Koh accompanied the Grant Park Orchestra, conducted by Carlos Kalmar, Mark Swed wrote for the *Los Angeles Times* (July 23, 2006) that Koh "brings fresh rapture" to the music. Koh's album of the complete Schumann Sonatas for Violin and Piano, with accompaniment by Reiko Uchida, is scheduled to appear in 2007. Koh also performed with others on a 1997 recording of concertos by the Danish composer Carl Nielsen (1865–1931).

In addition to performing and recording, Koh has earned much praise for her involvement in music education. She serves on the board of directors of the National Foundation for the Advancement of the Arts, a scholarship program for high-school students. In 2001 she founded Jennifer Koh's Music Messenger program, for which she performs in classrooms around the world. The program, which she began as a way of addressing the lack of classical-music education in schools, was later expanded to include schools with music classes as well. Koh told Jacob Stockinger for the *Wisconsin State Journal* (March 11, 2004) that the program was "a mix of playing the violin and unpeeling all the layers of music—the difference between loud and soft passages, phrasing, the use of color, vibrato. It's becoming aware of music everywhere around us as a conversation. It connects music to everyday life." Koh schedules appearances at schools in cities she tours as a performer. She told Stockinger that the program is designed to reach those children whose parents do not ordinarily take them to classical-music concerts: "For me, it's a very idealistic thing about reaching other people in the community who aren't ticket holders and for children to realize there is another voice they can speak through. It's about giving kids a voice and a different form to express themselves in an artistic way." Koh also gives lectures and teaches master classes for students at the high-school and college levels.

For nearly a decade Koh has performed on a Stradivarius, a creation of the famed Italian stringed-instrument maker Antonio Stradivari (1644–1737). The violin, made in 1727 and known as the "Ex Grumiaux Ex General DePont," was lent to her by private sponsors—a couple who have chosen to remain anonymous. The violin has an impressive history: one of its several owners was the Belgian violinist Arthur Grumiaux (1921–86), who used it to record sonatas by Mozart and Bach. Koh's sponsors were reportedly moved to allow Koh to use the violin after witnessing one of her performances. Koh told Beth Ramirez de Arellano for the *Pensacola (Florida) News Journal* (March 2, 2005), "The moment I played it, I knew it was my soulmate."

—M.B.

Suggested Reading: *Akron (Ohio) Beacon Journal* F p13 Jan. 23, 1997; *Chicago Sun-Times* p1 June 26, 2005; *Chicago Tribune* p12 June 30, 1994, D p1 Feb. 17, 1991, C p8 June 29, 2003; jenniferkoh.com; *Tulsa (Oklahoma) World* Jan. 12, 2001

Selected Recordings: *Solo Chaconnes*, 2001; *Violin Fantasies*, 2004

Courtesy of the University of North Carolina

Krawcheck, Sallie

1965– Finance executive

Address: Citigroup Inc., 399 Park Ave., New York, NY 10043

Beginning in 2001, Citigroup Inc., one of the most profitable financial-services companies in the world, found itself at the center of an extensive conflict-of-interest scandal that tarnished several Wall Street firms, including Salomon Smith Barney, Citigroup's retail-brokerage and stock-research unit. The following October Sanford I. Weill, the founder and then-CEO of Citigroup, sought to restore credibility to Salomon Smith Barney by hiring as its chief executive a comparative novice who, as a stock analyst, had once given Citigroup a low rating. While decision makers at rival firms questioned that move, the person Weill chose, Sallie Krawcheck, had built a reputation for reliability and independence as an analyst and, later, as an executive at Sanford C. Bernstein, a small investment-research firm. In her two years as the CEO of Citigroup's research and brokerage arm, renamed Smith Barney, Krawcheck proved a capable leader, furthering her reputation for forthrightness while strengthening both the quality and transparency of Smith Barney's operations. In November 2004 Krawcheck was named Citigroup's chief financial officer; she also currently serves as the company's head of strategy. The following year *Forbes* magazine ranked Krawcheck seventh in its annual list of the "World's 100 Most Powerful Women."

The third of the four children born to Leonard Krawcheck, an attorney of Jewish descent, and his wife, Sallie Krawcheck was born in 1965 in Charleston, South Carolina. Each of her siblings became an attorney. While growing up, Krawcheck has recalled, she was teased and perceived as an outsider by children her age, and she felt awkward around them, in part because of her appearance. "I was so ugly. I had braces, glasses, and bad hair, and I was skinny," she said to David Rynecki for *Fortune* (June 9, 2003). "I wore corrective shoes because I had pigeon toes." Krawcheck has attributed her professional accomplishments in part to the social difficulties of her youth, which "created an abject fear of failure for which I am grateful now but that was awful as a kid," as she told Rynecki. Krawcheck attended Ashley Hall, an elite girls' school in Charleston, where her marks were routinely well above average. At home she and her siblings often engaged in spirited debates on a variety of topics at the family dinner table, discussions moderated by their father.

At age 14 Krawcheck transferred to the college-preparatory school Porter-Gaud, a coeducational institution in Charleston that has ties to the Episcopal Church and is known for its challenging academic curriculum. There, Krawcheck became much more popular and self-confident than she had been at Ashley Hall. She shed her braces and corrective shoes, replaced her glasses with contact lenses, and excelled on the school's track team, ranking among the state's best in the high-jump competition. In addition, she joined the cheerleading squad and was voted the school's homecoming queen. Meanwhile, she continued to perform well in her studies. She also became very interested in dating boys—so much so that Nancy Wise, a guidance counselor at the school, advised her to focus less on romance and more on schoolwork. "She was in danger of becoming terminally cute," Wise told Daniel Kadlec for *Time* (2002). Legend has it that Wise gave Krawcheck a picture of a princess standing over a slain dragon to stoke her career ambition.

Apparently heeding Wise's advice, Krawcheck won a prestigious Morehead scholarship to attend the University of North Carolina at Chapel Hill, where she majored in journalism and minored in political science. During her college years Krawcheck and some of her friends wrote and edited their own campus publication, *Omnibus*. The future executive's interest in finance was kindled by an internship she secured at an investment house; her father later recalled in an interview with John Engen for *US Banker* (October 1, 2003) that he "knew when she returned from that summer job that she would go into the financial world." "She just loved it," he told Engen. After graduating from college Phi Beta Kappa, in 1987, Krawcheck briefly pursued a career as a business reporter, working at *Fortune* magazine. She then enrolled at Columbia University, in New York City, where she earned an M.B.A. degree in 1992.

Krawcheck worked for a short time in investment banking, as a research analyst at Salomon Brothers and, later, as a corporate finance associate at Donaldson Lufkin & Jenrette. At the latter firm she met Gary Appel, who was employed there as a merchant banker. The two married in 1994, and soon afterward Krawcheck gave birth to their first child, Jonathan. The professional demands placed upon her in investment banking, coupled with her responsibilities as a new mother, led to a career change, and in 1994 she became a financial analyst, moving to Sanford C. Bernstein & Co., a small, independent research firm with no ties to banking clients. Founded in 1967, Bernstein provides its clients with a broad range of research on stocks and bonds, real estate and cash management, and mutual funds, to help advise them on investments.

At Sanford Bernstein Krawcheck began as an associate under the firm's insurance-industry analyst, but soon after her arrival she took on duties related to brokerage stocks. In her five years as a senior analyst at Sanford Bernstein, during which she became an analyst of financial-services companies, Krawcheck earned a reputation for honesty and even outspokenness. She also became known as a perfectionist and a skeptic. "I always took the attitude that I was being misled," she told David Rynecki for *Fortune* (June 10, 2002). "If I went into a meeting with a company and it turned out they were telling the truth, I was pleasantly surprised." For three years consecutively, from 1997 to 1999, *Institutional Investor* magazine's annual poll of mutual-fund and money managers ranked her as the top analyst among those covering financial-services firms, due largely to the reputation she had earned for providing dependable research. Concerning the importance of impartiality to a research company, Krawcheck explained to Caroline Merrill for the London *Times* (August 1, 2003), "I do not care if a negative stock recommendation leads to an analyst being cut off from information by the company [being analysed]. Getting too close to the company can sometimes be bad for analysts. . . . You may end up feeling some empathy for the company you are analysing."

In 1999 Krawcheck was named Sanford Bernstein's director of research. The promotion coincided with the height of the so-called dot-come craze in the business world, which led many institutional investors to seek quicker—and less meticulous— research and caused Sanford Bernstein's revenues to slide. So that the company would remain attractive to portfolio managers who were using its services, Krawcheck persuaded her superiors to ramp up spending on researching small companies, tripling it in some instances. "Our view was that the pendulum would swing back to valuing thorough, objective research," Krawcheck told Rynecki in 2002. Later, after the Internet "bubble" burst and the stock market declined, investors again came calling at Sanford Bernstein, drawn by its reputation for dependable investment research for long-term growth. In June 2001 Krawcheck was named chairman and CEO of the company, which had been acquired by Alliance Capital in 2000; in that position she oversaw the company's 400 employees and $295 million in revenues. Krawcheck adhered to many of the company's core practices, such as hiring analysts who were already knowledgeable about the fields they would be assigned to evaluate. She also deflected attention away from herself by highlighting the hard work of her analysts in her interviews with the business press. *Fortune* magazine ran her image on the cover of its June 10, 2002 issue, along with the words "In Search of the Last Honest Analyst."

Fortune's allusion to Krawcheck's integrity had to do with the highly publicized ethical scandals that had befallen such Wall Street financial firms as Salomon Smith Barney, a division of Citigroup, as well as Merrill Lynch, J.P. Morgan Chase, and others, beginning in 2001. After winning a case against Merrill Lynch that year, in which it was proved that the securities and investment firm had routinely and intentionally misled clients by publishing false or misleading stock recommendations for the benefit of Merrill Lynch or its investment partners, New York State's attorney general, Eliot Spitzer, expanded his investigation to include virtually all major Wall Street banking firms. Chief among Spitzer's investigations was that focusing on the Salomon Smith Barney stock analyst Jack Grubman, who had arranged to give certain companies a "buy" rating, a designation that amounted to a recommendation, with the understanding that those companies would conduct investment-banking business with Citigroup. In a 2003 settlement with securities regulators, Citigroup was slapped with approximately $400 million in penalties and saw its reputation suffer major damage.

Sanford Weill personally chose Krawcheck, in late October 2002, to head Smith Barney, the stock-research and brokerage division of Citigroup. (The name "Salomon" was dropped due to its historical association with investment banking.) Many observers noted the irony of Weill's hiring Krawcheck, who had been one of Citigroup's sharpest critics during her time at Sanford Bernstein. Krawcheck had been especially critical of Citigroup in 1997, when Weill's Traveler's Group acquired Salomon Smith Barney; working for Sanford Bernstein at the time, she expressed her concern by downgrading the company's stock. Reacting to her appointment, some observers questioned whether Krawcheck, a relative neophyte as a chief executive, could make the transition from heading the small firm of Sanford Bernstein to guiding the second-largest retail-brokerage firm in the U.S. "This is the kind of spectacular career leap that tends not to happen in real life," Rynecki wrote in 2003. "It's like telling the pitching coach of the Staten Island Yankees to catch the next bus to the Bronx to manage the New York Yankees, or maybe promoting a promising lieutenant, mid-battle, to commander of the Third Infantry." According to reports, Krawcheck was given a two-year, $29.7 million compensation package.

Weill gave Krawcheck complete autonomy in her post at Smith Barney. For her part, the new CEO began a reorganization of the research department of Smith Barney, which involved firing some analysts and consolidating the remaining group under the leadership of Bill Kennedy and Jon Joseph. "The public is like a jilted lover," Krawcheck explained to David Rynecki in 2003. "It's going to take some time to win them back. We've got to start by saying we're sorry." In other efforts to renew client faith in the company's stock research, Krawcheck changed the way in which the firm's analysts were paid, separating their compensation from the performance of Citigroup's investment bank. The new pay structure is believed to have remedied the problem of analysts' potentially inflating the ratings they gave to companies. Krawcheck also simplified the analysts' ratings model, replacing jargon with everyday terms such as "add," "hold," and "reduce." "She took the biggest thorn in our foot and removed it," a person identified as "one longtime advisor" told David A. Gaffen in an interview for the industry publication *Registered Rep.* (December 1, 2004, on-line). "Because of that, we now have the confidence back in the research department."

In November 2004 Krawcheck became Citigroup's chief financial officer, replacing Todd Thompson, who took over Krawcheck's duties as CEO of Smith Barney. Industry observers have speculated that the juggling of the two executives may have been aimed at preparing each for a higher position within Citigroup. In E-mail correspondence with *Registered Rep.*, Krawcheck described the decision as sensible: "In this role I'll be meeting more people across Citigroup and then actively engaging outside our organization with investors and the analyst community." She added, "Chuck [Prince, CEO of Citigroup] and Bob Willumstad [president and chief operating officer of Citigroup] are committed to giving managers a broad range of experiences—my background as an analyst and Todd's background, having previously run the private bank, really made this a natural swap."

Krawcheck possesses a "razor-sharp intuition," her friend and former colleague Lisa Shalett—currently the CEO of Sanford C. Bernstein—told Engen; she is also noted for her ability to motivate those working under her. Shalett said to Engen, "She's able to find the right hook for each person, and make every person feel like she's managing them individually." The business press and others have depicted Krawcheck as a charming and self-effacing leader. "I don't want this to be 'Look at me, look at me,'" she told Engen shortly after she was named CEO of Sanford Bernstein. "I think this is the greatest firm on Wall Street—that the analysts have the independence they have, the ability to make controversial calls." Despite being called one of the most powerful businesswomen in the world, Krawcheck claims not to think about her accomplishments in terms of gender. "I no more think about being a woman than I do about being a Southerner, being a bottled blonde or having brown eyes," she told Zach Hoskins for the University of North Carolina's alumni publication *Carolina Communication* (Summer 2003).

Krawcheck has endowed the Porter-Gaud school with a fund that provides students with full-tuition academic scholarships, based on need, each year. She serves as a member of the board of directors for Carnegie Hall and the University of North Carolina at Chapel Hill Foundations Inc. and of the board of overseers for Columbia Business School. In addition, Krawcheck is an advisory board member for Columbia University's Center for Excellence in Accounting and Security Analysis.

Krawcheck and her husband, Gary Appel, have two children, Jonathan and Katherine. From her husband's previous marriage, she has two stepchildren—Alex and Lizzie. Krawcheck has said that the challenges of helping to run a multibillion-dollar company and being a mother have been made easier by her husband, her mother, and two babysitters. She also explained to Hoskins that her children and her career are her two main areas of concern: "I don't get caught up in being good at too many things. Focus is the real issue, and so is forgiving yourself."

—D.F.

Suggested Reading: *Carolina Communicator* (on-line) Summer 2003; *Fortune* p 85 June 10, 2002, p68+ June 9, 2003; (London) *Times* p31 Aug. 1, 2003; *Money* p76+ Oct. 2001; *Registered Rep.* (on-line) Dec. 1, 2004; *US Banker* p22+ Oct. 1, 2003

Kristof, Nicholas D.

Apr. 27, 1959– Journalist; columnist

Address: New York Times*, 229 W. 43d St., New York, NY 10036*

Nicholas D. Kristof, who joined the *New York Times* in 1984 and became a columnist for the newspaper in 2001, has sometimes been chided by the left for being too conservative and by the right for being too liberal. That seeming contradiction is perhaps best explained if he is viewed as a pragmatist, one who urges governments and individuals to follow the best possible course rather than dream of the ideal. For example, he argued against the 2003 U.S.-led invasion of Iraq—but also argued, in the wake of the invasion and in the midst of the troubled U.S. occupation of that country, that immediate withdrawal would result in a catastrophe. Having pleaded for American agricultural aid to famine-plagued nations in Africa, he has also defended the system of overseas sweatshops, maintaining that they are vital to the strengthening of economies in developing nations.

Courtesy of the *New York Times*

Nicholas D. Kristof

Kristof, who has reported from six continents, regularly travels to foreign regions to talk to individuals—both ordinary citizens and government leaders—about their aspirations and ideas for a better life. His style combines folksy metaphors and locutions with hard statistics, as when he began a column about Niger in the *New York Times* (October 11, 2005) by writing, "Welcome to the most wretched country in the world"; revealed that in Niger, there is one doctor for every 33,000 people and that 160,000 children under the age of five die every year; and pinpointed what he saw as a critical American failure with regard to Africa: "our refusal to provide substantial agricultural assistance to increase African food production. Instead, we ship tons of food in emergency aid after people have already started dying. It's like a policy of scrimping on manhole covers because we're too busy rescuing people who fall into manholes." Kristof was among the first to apply the term "genocide" to the murder of hundreds of thousands of African villagers in Darfur, Sudan, by rebel militias. With graphic intensity, he recorded in the region acts of extreme brutality, including rape, torture, and murder, reports that earned him a Pulitzer Prize for commentary in 2006. With his wife, Sheryl WuDunn, Kristof has reported on matters of economics and human rights in China, South Korea, Japan, and other Asian nations, in dispatches that won the two journalists the first Pulitzer Prize ever given to a married couple. Kristof and WuDunn are the authors or editors of *China Wakes: the Struggle for the Soul of a Rising Power* (1994), *The Japanese Economy at the Millennium: Correspondents' Insightful Views* (1999), and *Thunder from the East: Portrait of a Rising Asia* (2000).

Nicholas D. Kristof was born to Jane (McWilliams) and Ladis K. D. Kristof on April 27, 1959 in Chicago, Illinois. His father was of Armenian origin. Kristof grew up on a cherry farm four miles north of Yamhill, Oregon, a rural town. In the area where he lived, "far more children studied welding than French . . .," he wrote in the *New York Times* (April 5, 2000). "In my sophomore year of high school, we boys judged ourselves largely on our ability to make straight welds in vocational agriculture class. School had generally been easy for me, so it was mortifying—but also painfully edifying—to discover that I was a terrible welder." He noted in the *New York Times* (June 10, 2001) that as teenagers he and his friends "would disappear into the [Cascade] mountains for up to 10 days at a time and emerge blistered, sunburned, tired and thrilled." At his small high school, as he wrote in the April 5, 2000 *Times* piece, he was "pressed into service as a distance runner, despite a lack of any ability, and running ultimately became an important part of my life." Kristof left the rugged atmosphere of his childhood for Harvard University, in Cambridge, Massachusetts, where he earned his B.A. degree in 1981, after only three years, and joined the prestigious Phi Beta Kappa society.

Kristof was the recipient of a Rhodes Scholarship that enabled him to study at Magdalen College of Oxford University, in England. There, he received a second B.A. degree as well as an M.A. degree in law, in 1983. He went on to earn a diploma in Arabic studies at the American University in Cairo, Egypt, in 1984. Afterward he worked in France, then backpacked through Africa and Asia, supporting himself through writing assignments; for one of them, for the *Washington Post* in 1982, he was given the byline "staff writer." He became a reporter for the *New York Times* in 1984, specializing in economic issues, and went to Los Angeles as a financial correspondent for the newspaper in 1985. In 1986 Kristof was named chief of the *New York Times* Hong Kong bureau; from 1987 to 1988 he studied Chinese at the Taipei Language Institute. There, he met Sheryl WuDunn, whose forebears had gone to the U.S. from Guangdong province. Kristof and WuDunn married in 1988, then went to Beijing, where Kristof headed the *New York Times* bureau. They arrived in time to cover the birth and subsequent suppression of the student-led Chinese democracy movement, culminating in the events of June 1989 in Tiananmen Square, in which attacks by army troops left thousands dead. Kristof and WuDunn were awarded the Pulitzer Prize for international reporting in 1990 for their dispatches. They also were recipients of the George Polk and Overseas Press Club awards for foreign reporting that year.

In China, where Kristof and WuDunn remained until 1993, what had "been an exhilarating land of pandas and peasants steeped in history" turned into "a blood-stained nation of repression," Kristof wrote, as quoted by J. D. Brown in the *Chicago Tribune* (January 1, 1995). During their stay, as Kristof and WuDunn related in *China Wakes: The Struggle for the Soul of a Rising Power* (1994), China underwent an additional transformation: while the authoritarian one-party system—with its disregard of human rights—still prevailed, the Chinese people were adjured to "get rich" by their leader, Deng Xiaoping, and China's economy began to grow at the fastest rate in the world. As Brown noted, Kristof and WuDunn, who wrote alternating chapters of the book, were undecided over whether to "portray China 'as the evil empire, a disintegrating dynasty, the last bastion of Communism' or 'as an awakening giant, one that is raising the living standards of its citizens more quickly than any other major country in the world.'" In the end, "by overlapping these two Chinas, Kristof and WuDunn expose the evils of a society that is rotting away while paying attention to its presumed replacement, a 'civil society' with room for limited democracy and increased human rights," Brown concluded. Ian Buruma wrote in the *New York Times Book Review* (September 18, 1994), "Mr. Kristof and Ms. WuDunn have raised the right questions about China. Yet they have written an unsatisfying book. This is partly a question of style. Like many journalistic books, this one. . . . should have been more tightly edited, and organized with more care. . . . When they concentrate on the serious argument that runs through the book, about the connection between politics and economic prosperity, . . . their conclusions are plausible."

Upon returning to New York in 1993, Kristof was named a senior writer for the *Times*, a position he held until 2000. He also served as chief of the newspaper's Tokyo bureau from 1995 to 1999. Kristof tended to express pessimism about the Japanese economy. In columns from 1998 and 1999, he cited Japan's overwhelming national debt, shrinking workforce, and over-large subsidies to failing industries among the problems that were prolonging Japan's economic crisis. Kristof and WuDunn edited *The Japanese Economy at the Millennium: Correspondents' Insightful Views* (1999). Kristof observed in the book that Japan, "instead of 'picking winners' . . . is now picking losers and subsidizing them on a huge scale."

Using the same method—writing alternate chapters—that they had used to produce *China Wakes*, Kristof and WuDunn wrote *Thunder from the East: Portrait of a Rising Asia* (2000). The volume covers almost all of the vast Asian continent from India and Pakistan to China, Cambodia, Indonesia, Singapore, Malaysia, and Thailand. Their approach was to examine individual lives, such as those of a child prostitute in Cambodia and a food-service entrepreneur in Thailand, in order to integrate personal experiences into an analysis of the state of an entire continent. Because the couple lived in Japan, where their children attended school, they became especially familiar with the Japanese educational system. "Kristof and WuDunn describe Asians in every imaginable circumstance," Walter Russell Mead noted in *Foreign Affairs* (December

2000), "from Japanese politicians revealed in private moments of frankness to Cambodian child prostitutes interviewed in front of their brothels; from bankrupt Thai ex-millionaires rebuilding their fortunes to Javanese peasants hacking 'sorcerers' to death with machetes. The authors have captured the kaleidoscopic realities of contemporary Asia as few others have and reproduced them sympathetically." Mead concluded by calling *Thunder from the East* a "remarkable book."

Upon Kristof's return to New York in 2000, he was appointed associate managing editor of the *New York Times*, with responsibility for the Sunday editions. That year he covered the presidential election campaign, particularly the candidacy of George W. Bush (about whom he wrote a chapter for a reference book, *The Presidents*). In November 2001 he became a regular columnist for the *Times*. In that position Kristof has addressed issues around the world from a humanitarian viewpoint. His columns have dealt with famine, female genital mutilation, human trafficking for purposes of slavery and prostitution, Third World sweatshops, massacres, the globalization movement, and economic turmoil in Asia, among other topics. He has often expressed outrage over cruelty to vulnerable women and children. In columns in January 2005, he revealed that he had purchased two female sex slaves in Cambodia and freed them. (One of them, he reported, later returned to the brothel.) Kristof opposed the 2003 invasion of Iraq, undertaken ostensibly to rid that nation of so-called weapons of mass destruction. As the American occupation has continued, and as Iraq has taken tentative steps toward democratic rule while Iraqi rebels continually mount lethal attacks on military personnel and civilians, Kristof has expressed a more nuanced position. In his column of November 13, 2005, he wrote, "So how do we get out of Iraq? . . . CUT OUR LOSSES—This has an obvious merit: Iraq may fall apart no matter what we do, and if we're going to give up and pull out we should do so now rather than wait until after we've spilled more blood. That said, immediate withdrawal strikes me as utterly immoral. A surgeon who botches an operation should not walk off and leave the patient on the table with a note: 'Oops. This didn't go as planned. Good luck, but I'm outta here.'" In his follow-up column, published on November 15, he wrote, "My vote is to set target dates for withdrawing our troops. I suggest that we announce that we intend to pull out at least half our troops by the end of 2006—and the very last soldier by the end of 2007. . . . I have to acknowledge that the big disadvantage of target dates is that they can encourage insurgents to think, 'We just need to hang on for one more year, and then Iraq will be ours for the taking.' That's a legitimate concern, but a tentative timetable does avoid the worse pitfalls of the other two approaches. And target dates and a renunciation of bases at least show some sensitivity to the resentment of our presence, while giving the Iraqi political system and Army more time to coalesce. . . . If we can make it clear that we're headed for the exits, that'll make it harder for the insurgents to portray themselves as nationalist heroes. . . . All the Iraq options are bad. But this is the least bad."

An ongoing concern for the welfare of disadvantaged mothers and children has motivated Kristof's constant calls for the Bush administration to pay attention to their needs. After Hurricane Katrina destroyed much of New Orleans, Louisiana—particularly its poor, largely African-American neighborhoods—in 2005, Kristof wrote in the *New York Times* (September 6, 2005), "The wretchedness coming across our television screens from Louisiana has illuminated the way children sometimes pay with their lives, even in America, for being born to poor families. It has also underscored the Bush administration's ongoing reluctance or ineptitude in helping the poorest Americans. The scenes in New Orleans reminded me of the suffering I saw after a similar storm killed 130,000 people in Bangladesh in 1991—except that Bangladesh's government showed more urgency in trying to save its most vulnerable citizens. . . . If it's shameful that we have bloated corpses on New Orleans streets, it's even more disgraceful that the infant mortality rate in America's capital is twice as high as in China's capital. That's right—the number of babies who died before their first birthdays amounted to 11.5 per thousand live births in 2002 in Washington, compared with 4.6 in Beijing."

Given his pleas on behalf of poor children in the U.S., some have been surprised by Kristof's support of sweatshop labor in other parts of the world. Kristof and WuDunn published an article in the *New York Times Magazine* (September 24, 2000), "Two Cheers for Sweatshops," adapted from *Thunder from the East*. Kristof and WuDunn wrote, "Sweatshops that seem brutal from the vantage point of an American sitting in his living room can appear tantalizing to a Thai laborer getting by on beetles. . . . The campaign against sweatshops risks harming the very people it is intended to help. For beneath the grime, sweatshops are a clear sign of the industrial revolution that is beginning to reshape Asia. This is not to praise sweatshops. Some managers are brutal. . . . Agitation for improved safety conditions can be helpful, just as it was in 19th-century Europe. But Asian workers would be aghast at the idea of American consumers boycotting certain toys or clothing in protest. The simplest way to help the poorest Asians would be to buy more from sweatshops, not less." The negative reaction provoked by the article did not stop Kristof from issuing a half-serious call, in a *Times* piece (June 25, 2002) he wrote after a visit to Pakistan, for "an international campaign to promote imports from sweatshops, perhaps with bold labels depicting an unrecognizable flag and the words 'Proudly Made in a Third World Sweatshop!'"

Kristof won a Pulitzer Prize for commentary in 2006 for his accounts of his six trips to Darfur, in the Sudan, in which he labeled the torture, rape, and murder of African villagers by Arab militias "genocide." Kristof's trips to Darfur "have taken him through desolate no-go areas menaced by land mines, bandits and trigger-happy fighters—areas the United Nations and humanitarian aid groups avoid," the *New York Times* (April 18, 2006) reported in announcing the award.

According to the profile of Nicholas Kristof on the *New York Times* Web site, the journalist has "traveled to well over 100 countries" and has "had unpleasant experiences with malaria, mobs, war and an African airplane crash." Kristof and Sheryl WuDunn live in New York. They have three children, Gregory, Geoffrey, and Caroline, who, as reported on the *Times* site, correct their father's Chinese and Japanese. The family enjoys backpacking together in Oregon.

—S.Y.

Suggested Reading: *Business Week* (on-line) Oct. 9, 2000; *Chicago Tribune* XIV p43 Sep. 11, 1994, IV p4 Jan. 1, 1995; *Dissent* p41+ Spring 2005; *Foreign Affairs* p156+ Dec. 2000; *Nation* p11 Mar. 1, 2004; *New York Newsday* p43 Sep. 11, 1994; *New York Times* B p8 Apr. 5, 2000, A p25 Mar. 26, 2002, A p15 Nov. 27, 2004, A p25 June 25, 2002, A p31 Apr. 25, 2003, A p19 Jan. 14, 2004, A p27 Sep. 6, 2005; *New York Times Magazine* p70 Sep. 24, 2000

Selected Books (with Sheryl WuDunn): *China Wakes: The Struggle for the Soul of a Rising Power*, 1994; *The Japanese Economy at the Millennium: Correspondents' Insightful Views*, 1999; *Thunder from the East: Portrait of a Rising Asia*, 2000

Labov, William

(la-BAHV)

Dec. 4, 1927– Sociolinguist

Address: Linguistics Laboratory, 3700 Market St., #300, Philadelphia, PA 19104

On February 6, 1984 Paul Prinzivalli, a native of Long Island, New York, and a cargo handler for Pan American Airlines at Los Angeles International Airport, was arrested for allegedly making bomb threats in repeated phone calls to Pan Am. According to police, the caller had a thick East Coast accent, and prosecutors asserted that the baggage handler's voice matched that on tape recordings of the caller. After spending more than nine months in jail, Prinzivalli was released—thanks, in large part, to the testimony of the renowned sociolinguist William Labov. After having spent two decades studying linguistic variation and change, Labov was able to make fine, quantifiable distinctions between the caller's New England accent and

Courtesy of the University of Pennsylvania

William Labov

that of the defendant. As Judge Gordon Ringer, who dismissed the case against Prinzivalli, told Robert Schwartz for the *Los Angeles Times* (July 8, 1985), it was "the 'ah's' and the 'oh's'," that convinced him of the baggage handler's innocence; Ringer noted that the caller sounded like the Massachusetts native Robert F. Kennedy when saying the words "nuclear bomb."

Labov is known as the father of sociolinguistics—the study of language as it affects and is affected by social relations—and in his long and prestigious career he has focused on advancing the study of linguistics from a theoretical abstraction to a quantified science, making it possible to determine with certainty whether linguistic analyses are "right or wrong." He is perhaps best known for documenting the differences between Standard English and so-called Black English, also known as Ebonics. Though derided by some who see Ebonics as simply "bad English," Labov has held, based on his extensive studies in the field, that Black English is actually a legitimate dialect with its own grammatical system and should therefore be treated as a foreign language in schools. Labov has helped educators in failing inner-city schools to develop new teaching methods for African-American students. Most recently, he published *The Atlas of North American English: Phonetics, Phonology and Sound Change* (2005), the first graphic and computer-interactive representation of all major dialects spoken in the continental U.S. and Canada. "William Labov is to American dialect what Lewis and Clark are to American geography," John Seabrook wrote for the *New Yorker* (November 14, 2005, on-line). "He's the pathfinder."

William Labov was born on December 4, 1927 in Rutherford, New Jersey. When he was 12 years old, his family moved to Fort Lee, New Jersey, across the Hudson River from New York City and, as Labov would discover later, within the area where the New York dialect was spoken. He has recalled watching the 1938 film version of the George Bernard Shaw play *Pygmalion* and his amazement during the scene in which the hero, Henry Higgins—who was modeled on the renowned English phonetician Henry Sweet—apparently wrote down every sound that the uneducated Eliza Doolittle uttered in her Cockney accent. Labov attended Harvard University, in Cambridge, Massachusetts, where he earned a bachelor's degree in English and another in philosophy in 1948. He had no specific career plans when he graduated but wanted to write. "I lost several jobs in rapid succession: writing blurbs for Alfred Knopf, writing boiler plate for *Drug Trade News*, writing down what people said for market surveys," he recalled in an autobiographical essay posted on his Web site (October 1, 1997).

In 1949 Labov got a job as an industrial chemist at the Union Ink Co., in Richfield, New Jersey. He enjoyed working and conversing with the firm's pressmen, mill hands, and truck drivers, learning from those interactions that "there were a lot of people in the world who [knew] what they were doing, but that salesmen earned most of the money," as he wrote in his essay. That realization and his growing interest in class dynamics later informed much of his work in linguistics. At Union Ink he also developed "a firm belief in the existence of the real world": "It often happens in work of this type that you coat a panel with an enamel and expose it southward to the sun," he wrote. "If you come back in six months and find the coating cracked and peeling, you know that you were wrong six months ago. You may not know why you were wrong, but you can be sure that some part of the real world has defeated your real effort to protect a metal surface."

Labov left Union Ink in 1961 and enrolled as a master's student in the linguistics program at Columbia University, in New York City. There, he was surprised to learn that his colleagues did not share the same regard for the "real world"; rather, he found that many linguists, having no objective, scientific way of gathering information, were making broad conclusions based on material that they simply thought up. "I thought that I could do better," Labov wrote in his essay. "I would make good capital of the resources I had gained in industry. I would develop an empirical linguistics, based on what people actually say, and tested by the experimental techniques of the laboratory." Although he did not realize it at the time, Labov found that he "was also bringing to linguistics two other resources that were missing in the university: the belief that working class people have a lot to say, and that there is such a thing as being right or being wrong."

For his graduate thesis Labov conducted research on Martha's Vineyard, a small island off Cape Cod, Massachusetts. After interviewing people of various backgrounds, Labov found that individuals had distinctive ways of pronouncing the "i" in such words as "right" and "ice." This tendency varied by occupation, locale within the island, age, and the speaker's ethnic background (the majority of the population were Yankee, Portuguese, or Gay Head Indian). Older Portuguese or Gay Head Indian residents did not share in the local phonetic variables (or sound changes), but the younger residents of the two groups did possess the sound changes in their speech once they began gaining more prominent positions within the community. Labov concluded that sound changes served as a "symbolic claim to local rights and privileges, and the more someone tried to exercise that claim, the stronger was the change," as he wrote in his autobiographical essay. Essentially, sound changes in language occur more quickly when once-excluded groups begin to share in the power of the community. That finding became the basis for nearly all of Labov's future work in the developing field of sociolinguistics. Much to his surprise, when Labov sent his master's thesis to the Linguistic Society of America, the connections he had made between social factors and linguistics were well received by his peers and caused revolutionary advances in the understanding of language. "I had imagined a long and bitter struggle for my ideas, where I would push the social conditioning of language against hopeless odds, and finally win belated recognition as my hair was turning gray," Labov wrote in his essay. "But my romantic imagination was cut short. They ate it up!"

In 1963 Labov received his master's degree in linguistics. He stayed on at Columbia to pursue his doctorate. Under the guidance of Uriel Weinreich, the head of Columbia's Linguistics Department, Labov wrote his dissertation on speech patterns in New York City. He conducted his research at three retail stores: the high-end Saks Fifth Avenue, the mid-priced Macy's, and the discount store S. Klein, each of which had very different clientele. He went to each store and would ask salespeople for directions to a department on the fourth floor. After each person responded, he would say, "Excuse me?," to force him or her to repeat the words more carefully. In *The Social Stratification of English in New York City* (1966), Labov wrote that speech patterns in the city demonstrated sharp class distinctions, a conclusion that is similar to the theory presented in his master's thesis. He found that the more affluent the store's clientele was, the more likely workers were to pronounce the "r" in the words "fourth floor." Employees at S. Klein would frequently drop the "r," thus pronouncing the words as "fawth flaw." Labov also noticed that New Yorkers seemed to have an attitude of "linguistic self-hatred." Dennis Preston, a sociolinguist at Michigan State University, told John Tierney for the *New York Times* (January 22,

1995) that most people associate the New York accent with "immigrants, criminals and rude, uneducated people." Perhaps for that reason the accent had never spread, remaining exclusively in New York City, parts of Long Island, and a narrow strip of New Jersey that includes Fort Lee.

Labov received his doctorate in linguistics in 1964. That same year he was appointed an assistant professor at Columbia. While there, from 1964 to 1970, Labov conducted a landmark research project supported by the city's office of education, with the aim of learning whether the dialect spoken by African-American children in Harlem was related to the failure of schools to effectively teach them to read. Working with colleagues of black and white ethnic backgrounds—Paul Cohen, Clarence Robins, and John Lewis—Labov studied the language spoken by people in south-central Harlem. The researchers concluded that although there were major differences in the speech patterns among racial groups, "the main cause of reading failure was the symbolic devaluation of African American Vernacular English that was part of the institutionalized racism of our society, and predicted educational failure for those who used it," as Labov wrote in his autobiographical essay. In an article entitled "The Logic of Non-Standard English," which was published in the series *Georgetown Monographs on Languages and Linguistics* in 1969, he defended the Black English vernacular as "perfectly adequate for logical thought and learning."

While conducting field research in Harlem and the Lower East Side neighborhoods of New York City, Labov and his colleague Joshua Waletzky were confronted with what Labov termed the "observer's paradox." If a field worker approaches native speakers to ask questions and record their responses, the native speakers, aware that their responses are being analyzed, will tend to "correct" typical speech patterns to conform more closely to Standard English. "Among the partial solutions to that paradox within the face-to-face interview, the elicitation of narratives of personal experience proved to be the most effective," Labov wrote for the *Journal of Narrative and Life History* (1997). "We were therefore driven to understand as much as we could about the structure of these narratives and how they were introduced into the every-day conversation that our interviews simulated." In 1967 Waletzky and Labov's seminal work in narrative studies, "Narrative Analysis: Oral Versions of Personal Experience," was published in *Essays on the Visual and Verbal Arts*, edited by June Helm. Labov continued to examine narrative analysis in later papers and such books as *Therapeutic Discourse: Psychotherapy as Conversation* (1977), which he co-authored with David Fanshel. He later abandoned such studies in favor of investigating language variation and change.

In 1971 Labov accepted a position as associate professor at the University of Pennsylvania, in Philadelphia. Working with his colleague Gillian

Sankoff, he developed the Linguistics Laboratory to allow University of Pennsylvania students to interact closely with the community and to study the inner workings of language scientifically.

In 1977 Labov's work in south-central Harlem had a significant impact on a heated national debate concerning Black English vernacular. The parents of 11 elementary-school children in Ann Arbor, Michigan, filed a suit against a public school, claiming that teachers did not provide their children with an equal education because the children spoke an African-American variant of Standard English and were not receiving the bilingual education that they needed. Labov testified on behalf of the parents at the 1979 trial, saying, "Teachers must approach teaching standard English with the recognition of the differences of black English," as quoted by Kathy Horak for the Associated Press (June 26, 1979). Based on his research and findings in Harlem, Labov considered Black English a valid dialect; he stated in his testimony that Standard English should be taught as a foreign language to students who speak Black English. He offered theories and arguments presented in his book *Language in the Inner City: Studies in the Black English Vernacular* (1972), in which he stated that the Black English vernacular, as with any other fully formed language, could be used as a basis for learning. In the book he derided the notion that children who speak the Black English vernacular are "unworthy of attention and useless for learning" and that the use of the dialect is "evidence of [the child's] mental inferiority." Labov has unequivocally held that such notions are false. In *Language in the Inner City*, he wrote, "That children should be the victims of this ignorance is intolerable," and thus educating teachers and others about Black English "is an important job for [linguists] to undertake." Labov's testimony, based on such arguments, led the judge to rule in favor of the parents, stating that the children's problems were mostly due to language differences and "an unconscious prejudice on the part of teachers," according to William Robbins in the *New York Times* (March 30, 1981). As a result of the decision, teachers in Ann Arbor were given afterschool training.

In the mid-1980s Labov's investigations led to the discovery that, contrary to popular belief, radio and television were not leveling influences in speech; in other words, widespread exposure to Standard English spoken on television and radio did not affect people's speech. More startling was that differences in American dialects were increasing rather than diminishing. "It's a warning flag. The great majority of urban blacks hear whites as radio or television figures, but don't engage whites in personal contact. It's that contact that makes the difference," Labov told Clarence Page for the *Chicago Tribune* (March 24, 1985). "It means an inner city child has more work to do in understanding his teachers in school. It's like he's hearing a foreign dialect. He's more likely to be discouraged and perform poorly." Labov has also noted that

since textbooks are written in Standard English dialect, children raised in inner cities who speak Black English often have trouble understanding what they are reading.

In light of that growing trend, Labov was concerned that a permanent black underclass would be established as neighborhoods became increasingly divided along racial lines. "I went to Battersea Park in London and I taped six kids—black and white. The English themselves had trouble telling which was which! You'd never have that trouble in America," Labov told Jim Quinn for the *Nation* (November 9, 1985). "Blacks born in England sound English. Blacks born in America sound black. Now part of the reason is that the black population in England is relatively small. But part of the reason is segregation. . . . And language—language is telling us what we already know. Inner-city blacks are remote from the centers of power, divorced from the community, so remote that they don't even make a claim to local rights and privileges. They know that for them making that claim doesn't work." As an example of the differences between Standard English and Black English, Labov cited the statement, "He come telling me this and that," which sounds similar to "He came telling me" in standard dialect. Someone speaking standard dialect would never say, "He come coming up to see me," but, according to Labov, a black person might, because "come" in that particular sentence means "He has the nerve to." According to Labov's research, the tendency toward racial segregation in residential communities inevitably meant that lower-income African-Americans who have little or no contact with whites are unlikely to use the Standard English dialect, while the speech of businesspeople, members of the military, and other relatively successful African-Americans, whose exposure to whites is greater, bears increasing resemblance to the standard dialect. "There is a close parallel between residential segregation and linguistic segregation, and between residential segregation and educational failure," Labov told Quinn. He has advocated integrating school systems so that blacks and whites are in constant contact, thus ending the isolation of inner-city blacks and their resulting linguistic segregation.

In December 1996 a national debate over Black English arose when the board of the Oakland Unified School District in California passed a resolution claiming that Ebonics is the primary language of African-American children and calling for the curriculum to accommodate that finding. Those who considered Ebonics "bad English" deplored the resolution, while Labov and other linguists defended the resolution as a major advance. On January 23, 1997, in connection with the controversy in Oakland, Labov testified before Congress about the role of Ebonics in public education. After presenting his arguments, he closed his statement by saying, as quoted by the Federal Document Clearing House Congressional Testimony, "At the heart of the controversy, there are two major points of view taken by educators. One view is that any recognition of a nonstandard language as a legitimate means of expression will only confuse children, and reinforce their tendency to use it instead of standard English. The other is that children learn most rapidly in their home language, and that they can benefit in both motivation and achievement by getting a head start in learning to read and write in this way. Both of these are honestly held and deserve a fair hearing. But until now, only the first has been tried in the American public school system. The essence of the Oakland school board resolution is that the second deserves a fair trial as well."

Starting in 1992, Labov and a team of researchers began collecting data for his most recent book, *The Atlas of North American English: Phonetics, Phonology and Sound Change* (2005). Using census data and local telephone books, Labov's team called residents of the most dominant ethnic groups in major cities to hear how they spoke. Labov chose to interview only residents who still lived in their birth cities, because they had the strongest ties to the local dialects and traditions. Covering nearly two thirds of the population of North America, the atlas is the first of its kind. It includes 139 color-coded maps, representing dialects spoken in the continental U.S. and Canada, as well as a CD-ROM with audio clips and accompanying data. The software allows the user to listen to pronunciations of the same words in different parts of the continnent. The atlas functions primarily as an educational tool. It can also help companies develop voice-recognition technology that can distinguish among North American accents.

Labov is the author or editor of many books, and he has been honored many times for his work in sociolinguistics. He was a Guggenheim Fellow in 1970 and in 1987. He received the Leonard Bloomfield Book Award of the Linguistic Society of America (which he served as president in 1979) for *Principles of Linguistic Change, Volume 1: Internal Factors* (1994). The third and last volume, *Principles of Linguistic Change: Synthesis*, is scheduled for publication in December 2006. Labov is a member of the National Academy of Sciences and the American Association for the Advancement of Science. He has earned honorary degrees from the Uppsala University, in Sweden, the University of York, in England, and the University of Edinburgh, in Scotland.

Labov lives in Philadelphia with his second wife, Gillian Sankoff, a professor of linguistics at the University of Pennsylvania and his sometime collaborator. The couple have two daughters. Labov has five children from his first marriage, to the sociologist Teresa Gnasso Labov, which ended in divorce.

—I.C.

Suggested Reading: *Nation* p479+ Nov. 9,1985; *New York Times* B p15 Mar. 30, 1981; *New Yorker* (on-line) Nov. 14, 2005; *U.S. News &*

World Report (on-line) Jan. 25, 1999; William Labov's Web site

Selected Books: *The Social Stratification of English in New York City*, 1966; *Sociolinguistic Patterns*, 1972; *Language in the Inner City: Studies in the Black English Vernacular*, 1972; *Therapeutic Discourse: Psychotherapy as Conversation* (with David Fanshel), 1977; *Principles of Linguistic Change, Volume 1: Internal Factors*, 1994; *Principles of Linguistic Change, Volume II: Social Factors*, 2001; *The Atlas of North American English: Phonetics, Phonology and Sound Change* (with Sharon Ash and Charles Boberg), 2005

Tom Pidgeon/Getty Images

Laimbeer, Bill

May 19, 1957– Basketball coach; former basketball player

Address: Detroit Shock, The Palace of Auburn Hills, 4 Championship Dr., Auburn Hills, MI 48326

Writing for the *Detroit News* (January 22, 2004), Jerry Green described Bill Laimbeer, a basketball coach and former center for the Detroit Pistons basketball team, as a "human quilt." "A patch of him is on local TV as an analyst on Pistons games," Green explained. "Another segment is on national TV, a studio talking head on ESPN, dissecting NBA [National Basketball Association] games. Still another section is his achievement in coaching, rescuing women's pro basketball in Detroit, the coach who built the Shock into WNBA [Women's National Basketball Association] champions." Before Laimbeer retired, in 1993, after almost 14 years as a player in the NBA, he had participated in four All-Star Games, helped the Detroit Pistons win NBA titles two years in a row, and become one of 19 players in NBA history to score career totals of more than 10,000 points and more than 10,000 successful rebounds. He had also been fined $92,171 for his conduct on the court, which had earned him a reputation for being the quintessential bad boy on a team of bad boys, and he was widely disliked by the members of other teams as well as those teams' fans, who regarded him as a dirty player. After a failed business venture, in 2002 Laimbeer returned to the Pistons as a TV news analyst; he also became a commentator for the cable sports channel ESPN. Later that year he became the coach of the Detroit Shock, a four-year-old team that was playing more poorly than any other in the WNBA. In just one year he turned the squad into the best performers in the league.

Born in Boston, Massachusetts, on May 19, 1957 to Mary Laimbeer and William Laimbeer Sr., a corporate executive, William Laimbeer Jr. grew up in Clarendon Hills, an upper-class suburb of Chicago, Illinois, with his two sisters, Susan and Lee-Ann. As a child he played basketball purely for fun, and he approached the sport in a similar spirit while on his high-school teams in Clarendon and then Palos Verdes Estates, in California, where his family moved during his junior year. Having impressed a college basketball recruiter, after he graduated from high school, he enrolled at the University of Notre Dame, in Indiana, on a basketball scholarship. He flunked out after his first year, apparently because of a lack of self-discipline. He then attended Owens Technical College, in Toledo, Ohio, for two semesters and improved his grades sufficiently to gain readmission to Notre Dame, in 1977. He again took a place on the school's basketball team and played for the next two years. Averaging 7.3 points and 6.0 rebounds per contest, Laimbeer served as a substitute and was rarely on the court for more than 20 minutes a game. Nevertheless he made an appearance in the Final Four of the National Collegiate Athletic Association (NCAA) basketball tournament in 1978 and in the tournament's regional finals in 1979.

Although he has claimed that he was not particularly interested in becoming a professional basketball player, Laimbeer made himself eligible for the NBA draft in 1979 and was drafted by the Cleveland Cavaliers in the third round. But the team's decision makers felt unsure about his fitness for the squad and waited until the middle of August to offer him a contract. By that time Laimbeer had signed with Pinti Inox of Brescia, a team in the Italian Basketball League. During the year he played in Italy, he averaged 21.1 points and 12.5 rebounds per game. When he returned to the United States, in 1980, he tried out for the United States Olympic team, which did not compete that year.

(The United States boycotted the Olympics, which were held in Moscow, in what was then the Soviet Union, to protest the Soviet invasion of Afghanistan.) Instead, Laimbeer played in the Southern California Summer Pro League. He then signed a contract with the Cavaliers, with whom he played in 1980–81 and until February 1982 of the next season, when he was traded to the Detroit Pistons.

It was while playing for the Pistons that Laimbeer came into his own. As a second-string player with the Cavaliers, he had been a mediocre participant and seemed satisfied with his status. "I've always felt that my time was my time," he explained to Anthony Cotton for *Sports Illustrated* (November 22, 1982), "whether I wanted to travel or fish or just lie around and do nothing. Basketball never entered into it." Being with the Pistons changed his attitude. "After I came here to Detroit last season and everyone showed such confidence in me," he told Cotton, "I felt I had to do something to repay them." The Pistons had made Laimbeer the first-string center, and he began working hard on and off the court. The team's coach, Scotty Robertson, was pleased with his performance and noted, as the *New York Times* (March 7, 1982) reported a little less than a month after Laimbeer joined the Pistons, "Getting Laimbeer just shows you how smart we were. We have been after him since last summer. We got him 15 minutes before the trading deadline ended and he's been just great. He went into tonight's game [against the Knicks] averaging 15.9 points and 14.6 rebounds. How much more can you ask?"

After the season ended Laimbeer practiced basketball during the summer, something he had not done since junior high school. The work paid off: during the 1982–83 and 1983–84 seasons, he averaged 12.1 points and 12.2 rebounds and 13.6 points and 17.3 rebounds per game, respectively, and was selected for those years' All-Star teams. He was also gaining a reputation for antagonizing his opponents, by using his elbows and bulk to interfere with them. Laimbeer justified his aggressiveness on the court by saying, as Peter Alfano reported for the *New York Times* (November 4, 1983), "This is a competitive business, and everyone is looking for an edge. Players will try to get away with as much as possible." During a game at the beginning of the 1983–84 season, the Milwaukee Bucks center Bob Lanier punched him in the face and broke his nose in response to an aggressive defensive move. He nevertheless rejected the charge that he was a "dirty player." "I'm probably in the Top 10 among players who can't jump," Laimbeer told Anthony Cotton for *Sports Illustrated* (February 27, 1984). "In order to play in this league I have to do things like lay in the lane and fight for position, but I'm not a dirty player."

Laimbeer's protests did little to suppress opponents' complaints, and over the years various confrontations confirmed the belief of many that he tended to cross the bounds of fair play. One such skirmish occurred during the second game of the postseason contest between the Pistons and the Boston Celtics in 1985, when Laimbeer knocked down Larry Bird, who was bleeding when he got off the floor; during the third game Laimbeer nearly came to blows with the Celtics' Ropert Parish, who complained afterward, as Harry Atkins reported for the Associated Press (May 4, 1985), that Laimbeer "took some cheap shots at me." When the Pistons and Celtics met again, in January 1986, Parish was ejected from the game for punching Laimbeer, who, despite being the victim, was portrayed by the media as the villain. The 1985–86 season had not yet ended when the renowned sportswriter Jack McCallum labeled him in *Sports Illustrated* (April 7, 1986) "one of the NBA's most disliked players." Even Isiah Thomas, Laimbeer's close friend on the Pistons, admitted, as McCallum reported, "If I didn't know Bill, I wouldn't like him, either." Such opinions notwithstanding, his performance placed Laimbeer among the best players in the NBA. He played in his third All-Star Game in 1986 and was the number-one rebounder in the league during the 1985–86 season.

Before the 1986–87 season had even begun, Laimbeer again sparked controversy, by knocking the Phoenix Suns' center Alvan Adams to the floor during an exhibition game. Midway through the season Bob Sakamoto wrote for the *Chicago Tribune* (February 2, 1987), "Laimbeer, whose reputation precedes him wherever he goes, might as well put a black hood over his head and snarl at everything in sight." Although Laimbeer was chosen for another All-Star Game, the press devoted more words to discussions of his reputation as a villain than to his successes on the court. Then, in the postseason, during Game Three of the NBA Eastern Conference Finals, Larry Bird got caught between Dennis Rodman, the Pistons' forward, and Laimbeer under the basket, and all three players fell to the floor. Certain that Laimbeer had knocked him down, Bird took a swing at him, and both players were ejected from the game. "Wanted" posters and T-shirts with images of Laimbeer's face began selling in large numbers in Boston. In Game Five of the series, Parish punched Laimbeer three times without being called for a foul. The Celtics, the series' winners, emerged with an untarnished reputation, while Laimbeer and the Pistons projected an air of indifference to what people thought. By December of the following season, the latter were "developing a reputation as the bad boys of the NBA," as Bob Sakamoto wrote for the *Chicago Tribune* (December 15, 1987).

"Bad boys" or not, the Pistons' fortunes improved in the 1987–88 season. They set a club record by winning 54 games, became the only team in NBA history to have attracted more than a million spectators, and beat the Celtics in the conference finals. "We learned how to win this year," Laimbeer said, as quoted by Bill Barnard for the Associated Press (July 19, 1988). "We learned what it takes when you get in the later rounds to win the big series." Seeming to foster their notoriety, they

began to refer to themselves as the "hit men." Laimbeer threw his first punch on the court, an action that led to his being suspended, thus ending his streak of 685 consecutive regular-season games—the longest in the league at the time and currently the fourth-longest in the NBA. The following year the Pistons win:loss ratio improved, to 63:19. They also won their first NBA title. Laimbeer, however, did not play as well as he had in previous years; according to Paul Attner in the *Sporting News* (June 26, 1989), he was viewed as "a symbol of sorts," one that showed that it was possible for a team to win an NBA title without a dominating center. The following season the Pistons won the title again, becoming the third team to repeat a championship win. Laimbeer's contributions to the team's 1990 NBA championship were his last notable achievements as an NBA player. In December 1993 he announced his retirement, observing, according to a United Press International (December 1, 1993) reporter, "You have to have total disregard for the well-being of your body and I no longer have that. I want to go out with my body intact so I can walk a golf course and take up skiing. But most important, I no longer have the desire to compete as a basketball player."

Laimbeer next entered the corporate world, as the founder, owner, and manager of a company (Laimbeer Packaging) that manufactured cardboard boxes. The company earned profits of about 10 percent in its first year but failed to perform well in the following years. It remained solvent until 2001, when it lost one of its biggest customers (reportedly DaimlerChrysler), and by October of that year, the company was losing $100,000 to $200,000 a month. Laimbeer began shutting down the operation a few months later, selling off assets in an attempt to pay debts and fighting a union over vacation pay that he owed his employees. He later admitted that he had mishandled matters at Laimbeer Packaging, in part because he could not accommodate himself to the vagaries of business. "In my old job," he told Tom Walsh for the *Detroit Free Press* (February 26, 2002), "I knew in the evening whether we won or lost and how to fix it." He also said, "'My philosophy is to be the best. It's been frustrating that I couldn't get to that point."

While in the process of closing his business, Laimbeer took on a part-time job as an analyst on the Pistons' local television station. In 2002, in addition to his appearances on the TV station, he went back to work for the Pistons full-time, as a special consultant to the Detroit Shock, a Pistons-owned team in the Women's National Basketball Association. His idea was to learn about sports management and become knowledgeable about financial aspects of the basketball business. Soon afterward he took on an additional job, as a broadcaster on the cable-TV station ESPN. A few months later, when it became apparent that the Shock would rank as the worst-performing franchise in the WNBA, he offered to become the team's coach, notwithstanding the fact that his coaching experience was limited to practice with his daughter's Amateur Athletic Union team, and despite the skepticism of Tom Wilson, the president of the group that owns the Pistons. "Are you sure you want to risk your reputation to protect a sinking ship?" Wilson asked him, according to Laura Bailey in *Crain's Detroit Business* (September 22, 2003). Without giving up his responsibilities on television, Laimbeer began coaching the 0–10 team on June 19, 2002, halfway through the season. After the Shock finished the season with a 9–23 record, Laimbeer promised Wilson that given one more year, he could turn the Shock into Eastern Conference champions and contenders in the WNBA finals. He fulfilled his promise: the Shock won the finals, beating the Los Angeles Sparks, the two-time defending champions, in three games. The WNBA named Laimbeer coach of the year in 2003. The Shock made it to the postseason in both 2004 and 2005 but were knocked out of contention each year in the Eastern Conference semi-finals— by the New York Liberty in 2004 and the Connecticut Sun in 2005.

In 2006 the Shock had another memorable season, achieving a record of 23 wins and 11 losses and finishing second in the Eastern Conference, behind the Connecticut Suns. In the play-offs the Shock bested the Indiana Fever and the Suns, losing just one game during the first two rounds, and earned a berth in the WNBA finals, where they faced the Sacramento Monarchs. The Monarchs, winners of the 2005 championship, led the series two games to one after the first three games of the best-of-five series. In the crucial fourth game, Laimbeer orchestrated a masterful defense, which held the Monarchs to just four points during the fourth quarter and led to a Shock victory (72–52). The next, decisive game, at the Joe Louis Arena in Detroit, was the first-ever Game Five in WNBA finals history. In front of a sold-out crowd of 19,671 fans, Detroit prevailed, 80–75, bringing the Shock and Laimbeer their second title in four years.

Laimbeer lives in Orchard Lake, a waterfront community outside Detroit, with his wife, Chris. The couple have a son, Eric, and a daughter, Kerriann. Laimbeer's favorite pastimes are fishing and golfing.

—A.R.

Suggested Reading: Associated Press May 29, 1987, July 19, 1988; *Chicago Sun Times* p107 Sep. 21, 2003; *Chicago Tribune* C p3 Dec. 15, 1987, C p10 Jan. 27, 1988; *Detroit Free Press* C p1+ Feb. 26, 2002, p2 Sep. 11, 2006; *Detroit News* D p4 Dec. 8, 2003, H p4 Jan 17, 2003, X p9 July 14, 2004; *New York Times* V p1 Feb. 13, 1983; *Sporting News* p9 June 26, 1989, p30 June 25, 1990; *Sports Illustrated* p71+ Nov. 22, 1982, p56 Feb. 27, 1984, p71+ Apr. 7, 1986; *USA Today* C p7 Dec. 2, 1994

Lawal, Kase L.

June 30, 1954– Chairman and CEO of CAMAC International

Address: CAMAC Holdings, 4669 Southwest Freeway, Suite 600, Houston, TX 77027

Kase L. Lawal is the chairman and CEO of CAMAC International, which *Black Enterprise* named company of the year in 2006. CAMAC and its affiliates "collectively represent the largest African-American owned energy services enterprise in the United States," according to the company's Web site. CAMAC was established in 1986 as a buyer and seller of agricultural products. Three years later Lawal changed its focus to exploring for oil and gas for other firms, and since 1999, when CAMAC acquired its first refinery, the company has reaped profits from sales of oil as well. In the first nine months of 2006, CAMAC moved, produced, or traded an average of 100,000 barrels of oil a day. "Sometimes people think I'm crazy because I can sink in $40 million looking for oil or gas," the Nigerian-born Lawal told Kevin Chappell for *Ebony* (January 2006). "But if you catch it, if you get it, if you are able to get the reserves [strike oil], it pays for all of the other times you were unsuccessful. It's an interesting business to be in." "The numbers game is not important to me," Lawal insisted to Chappell, on the subject of his running what is arguably the largest black-owned business in the United States. (Sources differ as to whether CAMAC or World Wide Technology occupies the top spot.) "Whether it's $1 billion today or $2 billion tomorrow, is neither here nor there. All I tried to do is to satisfy myself that I had done the best that I could do, and take advantages of opportunities that I had." Lawal considers part of his mission to be economic empowerment for blacks in the U.S. and citizens of his native Africa. "All kids can look at City Hall and say 'I can be mayor,'" Lee P. Brown, the former mayor of Houston, Texas, told Lauren Bayne Anderson for the *Houston Chronicle* (August 9, 2002). "But now, most are saying, 'I want to be Kase Lawal.' I look at the kids and say, 'Me too.'"

Kase Lukman Lawal was born on June 30, 1954 in Ibadan, Nigeria, a city of 2.2 million residents about 80 miles inland from the former capital, Lagos. He grew up in what he has described as a large, traditional, devoutly Muslim family. His father was a politician and his mother a textile trader. Inspired by the American civil rights movement of the 1960s, Lawal developed a desire to travel to the United States. He spent many hours at the United States Information Service, reading and gathering information about the struggles of African-

Kase L. Lawal

Courtesy of CAMAC

Americans. "I was fascinated by the plight of Blacks," he told Kevin Chappell. "America had a tremendous influence on young people all over the world during those days. We were very interested in knowing what was happening. And most young people wanted to come to America. I was just one of the fortunate ones." Lawal researched every possible means of attending college in the U.S., and in 1971 he gained admission to Fort Valley State University, a historically black institution in Fort Valley, Georgia, known for its strong biology and engineering departments. Despite their trepidation, his parents consented to his enrolling there. "I remember that morning," Lawal told Chappell about leaving Nigeria for the first time. "I can still see my mother at the airport crying. It was the first time a person in my family was leaving home and going overseas." Lawal studied chemistry at Fort Valley State while becoming involved in the ongoing southern freedom movement, which reminded him of Nigeria's struggle for independence. He later transferred to Texas Southern University, from which he graduated in 1975 with a bachelor's degree in chemical engineering.

Lawal next took a job with Shell Oil, as a chemical engineer at a refinery in Deer Park, Texas. He did not enjoy his work there and began to feel that his training had limited him. "Of course, I didn't want to be wearing the hard hat," Lawal said to Hughes and Robinson. "I decided I wanted to go for my business degree so I could wear suits." Shell Oil paid for his studies at Prairie View A&M University, in Prairie View, Texas, where he earned his M.B.A. degree in finance and marketing. Starting in 1977 Lawal worked as a research chemist at Dresser Industries, now Halliburton. In the follow-

ing decade he held executive positions in the oil and finance industries, including vice president at the Suncrest Investment Corp. and president of Baker Investments. In 1986, while at the latter company, Lawal learned of a business opportunity involving a group of entrepreneurs from Cameroon, a nation that borders Nigeria. The company would purchase tobacco from the United States and sell it to a Cameroonian cigarette manufacturer, which conducted business throughout the Middle East. Taking the name CAMAC (Cameroon-America Corp.), the company expanded to trade other agricultural commodities, such as rice and sugar. Soon after involving himself in CAMAC, Lawal purchased 80 percent of the company, with the rest being divided among his brothers and sisters. To Lawal CAMAC has always been a family business.

In 1989, when Lawal first tried to steer CAMAC into the oil business as an exploratory company, he found that the industry was highly competitive and that entering it required a large amount of capital. The search for oil involves drilling, which requires a permit; after participating unsuccessfully in nearly two dozen auctions (the process through which permits are awarded) in the U.S., Lawal decided to try his luck overseas. He caught a break later in 1989, when Rilwanu Lukman, the foreign minister of Nigeria and later the secretary general of OPEC (the Organization of the Petroleum Exporting Countries), approached him about taking advantage of his dual U.S.-Nigerian citizenship. The Nigerian government wanted its citizens to get involved in the lucrative oil industry off Nigeria's coast and estimated correctly that Lawal would be interested. Most of the people in the industry there were Nigerians, "but their bosses were the major oil company employees from the West," as Lawal explained to Chappell. "The government asked me to try to organize Nigerians in the U.S. who were working for the oil companies and would be interested in being technical partners with indigenous companies." Securing foreign drilling rights required intimate knowledge of local political and regulatory governance; Lawal, who was familiar with decision makers in Africa, was able to maneuver successfully through the process. Soon Lawal had reached agreements for joint ventures in Africa between CAMAC and some of the larger companies, such as the Houston-based Conoco, which provided financing while CAMAC located the drilling sites and acquired the necessary permits. "The best way for me to get into the industry was to know what the big boys wanted, the major oil companies, the big 10, the big 50," Lawal explained to Chappell. "Did they have an interest in West Africa? If they did, I would go to West Africa and look for what they wanted and [make] it available to them. I understood the political landscape and business environment in those countries in Africa. When you merge these two together, there was a good synergy that was very attractive to the major oil companies." CAMAC was the first independent oil company to secure a deep-water exploration permit in Nigeria and one of the first to make a successful exploration there. CAMAC's alliance with Conoco alone reportedly produced more than 20,000 barrels of oil per day, and soon CAMAC was growing in size and profits. Lawal has often given credit for much of his business success to one of his mentors, Reginald Lewis, the founder of the black-owned TLC Beatrice International, who taught him about navigating the American business world.

CAMAC's operations changed in 1999, when Lawal purchased the company's first oil refinery. That enabled CAMAC to offer "downstream" services, such as the trading and refining of products, along with its "upstream" services, including exploration and drilling. CAMAC's revenues increased dramatically between 1999, when it recorded $114.3 million, and 2001, when its earnings reached $979.5 million. In 2002 the company moved its Blue Island Refinery from Illinois to a new complex in Cape Providence, in the Republic of South Africa. Lawal came under criticism for the move, as some thought he was attempting to dodge environmental regulations in the United States in favor of less stringent standards in South Africa. Lawal vowed to maintain the same standards set by the U.S. and claimed that his decision reflected an effort to involve Africans in the process; the new facility employed more than 2,000 workers. "I want to encourage more blacks to get involved in the oil industry as entrepreneurs," Lawal explained to Alan Hughes for Black Enterprise (June 30, 2002). "Through CAMAC, I want to be one of the architects of black empowerment globally."

In 2003 the company split its operations. Lawal's firm remained a United States corporation, while his brothers and sisters controlled a separate incorporated offshore entity based in a tax haven—the Cayman Islands—in which Lawal did not hold any interest. In 2002 CAMAC earned the top spot on the Black Enterprise Industrial/Service 100 list, and the same publication listed CAMAC as the largest black-owned company in the United States. (In order to qualify as "black-owned," according to Black Enterprise, a business must be at least 51 percent black-owned and -operated and manufacture or own the products it sells.) CAMAC was ranked second on the Industrial/Services list in both 2004 and 2005. By 2006 CAMAC had affiliates in Colombia and England, as well as in Nigeria and South Africa.

Lawal's business success has led to his activities in other areas. In 1999 he was appointed by the city of Houston to serve as a commissioner on the Port of Houston Authority Board. Houston's seaport is the United States' largest receiver of foreign tonnage and the sixth-largest port in the world; as a commissioner Lawal organized the Port of Houston Authority International Corp., which provides management consulting and technical assistance to foreign ports. In 2002, while working with the Port of Houston Authority Board, Lawal helped establish its Small Business Development Program, which helps Houston-area small businesses ac-

quire contracts connected with the port. The program's goal was to award at least 35 percent of all eligible contracts to certified small businesses. Between 2002 and 2005, the first three years of the program, a total of $76.2 million in contracts was given to small businesses. "Our small business owners and employees are vital links in the port's supply chain. They are the leading employers in the Houston area and provide nearly half of all jobs in Texas," Lawal explained to PrimeZone Media Network (February 15, 2005). The Houston City Council member Ada Edwards told a writer for the same publication (August 24, 2005), "The Port of Houston Authority has benefited greatly from the leadership of Kase Lawal. Since his original appointment, Lawal has been instrumental in developing trade cooperatives and memorandum of friendship agreements with 20 global ports, including several in Africa and South America. These relationships strengthen Houston's status as a world-class port and bring vital import and export business to our port."

Also in 1999 Lawal was appointed by President Bill Clinton's administration to the U.S. Trade Advisory Committee on Africa; he was reappointed by George W. Bush's administration in 2001. As a committee member Lawal was responsible for helping to develop a U.S.-Africa trade policy. Lee P. Brown felt that Lawal's experience and international contacts made him a good fit for the job. "He's developed relationships not only in this country but in other parts of the world," Brown told Alan Hughes and Tennille M. Robinson for Black Enterprise (June 2006). "He's someone who can drive up to the president of Nigeria's gate, they look in the back to see who he is, and the gates open up like he's at home. We went with him to Namibia, and he calls the president and the prime minister and they all rearrange their schedules to meet with him." Lawal's position on the U.S. Trade Advisory Committee on Africa increased the visibility of his own U.S.-Africa business dealings; in 2003 Lawal was involved in a controversy involving CAMAC's purchase of oil from Nigeria through its South African affiliate, the South African Oil Co. The deal was publicly described as a "government-to-government" sale, until later disclosure proved that the oil was actually sold to CAMAC's Cayman Island entity rather than to the Republic of South Africa.

In 2005 Lawal acquired a controlling interest in Unity National Bank, making it the only black-owned federally chartered bank in Texas. Lawal intended to use the bank as an instrument of economic development for African-Americans. He served as Unity National Bank's vice chairman and developed its financial-services arm, which provides loans to African-American entrepreneurs and also offers insurance, asset management, investment advice, and securities brokerage. He explained to Hughes and Robinson that while he intended for oil and gas exploration, production, and trade to remain the foundation of CAMAC, financial services would become an important part of the company. "[Lawal] understands that in the African American community, the economic element is extremely important to everything we do. Politics is important, obviously, but so is economics," Lee Brown told Hughes and Robinson. "So if you have an institution such as a bank that can serve the community, that's a major contribution."

Lawal has suggested that a major challenge facing CAMAC involves human resources; he believes that there are far too few African-Americans interested in engineering, geological sciences, and petroleum economics and in careers within the energy sector. To address that issue Lawal established a $1 million endowment for the Kase and Eileen Lawal Center for International Business Development at Texas Southern University's Jesse H. Jones School of Business. He also established an endowment at the University of Houston for the study of petroleum engineering; the amount of the endowment in 2005 was $600,000. Among other philanthropic endeavors, Lawal co-chairs, with his wife, Eileen, Hope Lives Here, a $300 million UNICEF campaign against AIDS. Lawal also chairs several programs to support the arts and cultural ex-

changes between Africa and the West. Through its South African affiliate, CAMAC provided the first-ever curb-to-curb school-bus service for students in Johannesburg.

When he is not working, Lawal enjoys jogging, playing tennis, and spending time with his wife and their three children. He built a 21,000-square-foot home in Houston in 1998. Lawal considers the large prayer mosque, with a dome-shaped roof, to be the centerpiece of the house. He and his wife collect art from around the world, particularly Africa. Lawal would like to see his children take over the family business someday, but he is not pressuring them to do so. "I want them to do what they want to do," he told Chappell. "They can take over the business. But they will have to work for it. . . . It's not going to be easy."

—N.W.M.

Suggested Reading: *Black Enterprise* p127+ June 30, 2002, p128+ June 2006; *Ebony* p74+ Jan. 2006; *Houston Chronicle* p1+ Aug. 9, 2002; *PrimeZone Media Network* Feb. 15, 2005, Aug. 24, 2005

Ledger, Heath

Apr. 4, 1979– Actor

Address: c/o Creative Artists Agency, 9830 Wilshire Blvd., Beverly Hills, CA 90212-1825

"I don't really like to do the same thing twice," Heath Ledger explained to Rachel Abramowitz for the *Los Angeles Times* (November 20, 2005). "I like to do something I fear. I like to set up obstacles and defeat them." After attracting attention as a young hunk in the teen comedy *10 Things I Hate About You* (1999), the Australian actor resisted the attempts of Hollywood to capitalize on his youthful good looks by casting him in similar lighthearted fare; he passed up several scripts before taking a role in the grisly war drama *The Patriot* (2000), about the American Revolution. That high-profile film, and Ledger's subsequent leading role in *A Knight's Tale* (2001), propelled him into the spotlight; he appeared on the covers of glossy magazines and was named one of *People* magazine's 50 most beautiful people of the year (2001). Uncomfortable with the limelight and afraid of being typecast, Ledger sought out what seemed to be unusual or challenging films; he took a supporting role in *Monster's Ball* (2001) and starred in *The Four Feathers* (2002), *The Order* (2003), and *Ned Kelly* (2003). With the exception of *Monster's Ball*, most of his films flopped. In an interview with Andy Dougan for the Glasgow *Herald* (December 24, 2005), Ledger explained, "In a way I was spoon-fed a career. It was fully manufactured by a studio that

Jeff Haynes/AFPGetty Images

believed it could put me on their posters and turn me into a product. . . . I hadn't figured out properly how to act, and all of a sudden I was being thrown into these lead roles." In 2005 Ledger appeared in several films, including *Lords of Dogtown*, *The Brothers Grimm*, and *Casanova*—and though most of those fared little better than his previous films, Ledger again found himself the center of media attention, following his acclaimed performance in *Brokeback Mountain*, a drama about two cowboys who carry on a furtive homosexual relationship. Directed by Ang Lee and co-starring Jake Gyllenhaal, the film impressed critics and audiences alike, earning Ledger an Academy Award nomination for best actor. "I hope I will always be learning the craft," Ledger told Dougan, adding that until recently, "I felt that the choices were being made for me, so I feel this has been my time now to find the good stories and test myself. . . . It has been an interesting year, where I finally have a sense of accomplishment."

Heathcliff Andrew Ledger was born on April 4, 1979 to Sally Ledger, a French teacher, and Kim Ledger, an engineer. Named after the main characters of Emily Brontë's *Wuthering Heights*, Ledger and his older sister, Katherine, grew up in Perth, in Western Australia, where Ledger attended Guildford Grammar, a private boys' school. His parents divorced when their son was about 10 years old, and for the next few years he divided his time between them. (Both parents found new partners and each had another daughter.) At about the same time, at his sister's urging, Ledger joined a local theater company and appeared in a production of *Peter Pan*, which led to his being cast in children's television programs. Ledger appeared in the 1992 film *Clowning Around* and the 1993 TV series *Ship to Shore* before deciding to pursue acting as a profession. He had been involved in numerous sports and other activities: he was the state junior chess champion at age 10 and a junior go-kart racing champion, played hockey for the state team, and dabbled in cricket. However, when his hockey coach issued an ultimatum, forcing Ledger to choose between drama and hockey, he stuck with the former. "Heath is extremely dedicated and follows his passions," his father recalled to Maree Curtis for the Sydney *Sunday Telegraph* (June 11, 2000). "I picked him up late one night after a rehearsal. He was about 13, and we were lying on his bed looking at the stars [stuck] on his ceiling and he said, 'I'm going to have to get used to these late nights. I'm going to do really well in this industry. I love it.' I knew he meant it. If Heath said he was going to do something, we knew he would."

When he was 16 years old, Ledger drove across the Australian continent to Sydney, where he believed he would find more acting opportunities. He landed the role of a gay cyclist in the short-lived TV series *Sweat* (1996), found small parts in the films *Paws* and *Blackrock* (both 1997), and did a brief stint on the long-running soap opera *Home and Away* (1997). His largest role was that of Conor, a Celtic warrior, in the medieval fantasy TV series *Roar* (1997), but that project did not last long. "It was shot beautifully, and the script was half decent. But by the fifth episode the ratings weren't going well, and all of a sudden sea sprites in bikinis were popping up," Ledger explained to Jeff Giles and Suzanne Smalley for *Newsweek* (July 10, 2000). After the show was canceled, Ledger moved to Los Angeles, California. "I went over there with no expectations and all the confidence of youth," he told Curtis. "I never let anything faze me or anyone look down on me." His next film, *Two Hands* (1999), necessitated a brief return to Australia. Although the movie, in which he played an amiable but bumbling strip-club bouncer and aspiring gangster, received little exposure outside Australia, film-industry insiders took notice of his compelling performance when the movie was screened at the 1999 Sundance Film Festival. The Australian Film Institute (AFI) nominated Ledger for a best-actor award.

Ledger's first American film was *10 Things I Hate About You*, which Peter Ross described for Scotland's *Sunday Herald* (July 9, 2000) as "an above-par teen flick based on Shakespeare's *Taming of the Shrew*." A lightweight comedy, it won praise for its two leading actors, Ledger and Julia Stiles. In the *Atlanta (Georgia) Journal-Constitution* (October 14, 1999), Steve Murray called the pair "captivating," adding, "[Ledger is] equally comfortable playing a dangerous loner or doing a goofy song and dance to impress [Stiles's character]." Following the success of *10 Things I Hate About You*, Ledger was offered numerous similar roles in the teen-heartthrob vein, but he turned them all down in an effort to avoid getting pigeonholed.

Nearly a year passed before Ledger found a script that appealed to him. During that period he was so poor that he was forced to borrow money from his agent, and often he could not afford to eat. "I was literally living off ramen noodles and water, because I was sticking to my guns," he told Rupert Mellor for the London *Evening Standard* (July 25, 2001). "I'm happy without money, I never did have it, so that was no big deal. And it was fun saying no—because they really don't like to hear that word in Hollywood." Eventually he earned an audition for *The Patriot* (2000), starring Mel Gibson and directed by Roland Emmerich. He prepared two scenes to perform for the filmmakers but flubbed the audition. "Halfway through the second scene, I stood up and left," he told Giles and Smalley. "I said, 'I'm awfully sorry and I'm awfully embarrassed, but I'm wasting your time. I'm going to get up right now, and I'm going to walk out that door. Thanks for your time, but I'm giving you a bad reading. Catch you later.'" Yet Ledger made an impression, for when his agent requested a second audition, the filmmakers agreed. That time, Ledger excelled and was promptly cast as the son of the character played by Gibson. Although the movie garnered mixed reviews (many found it overlong and historically inaccurate), the young actor received raves. "[Ledger] comes of age as an actor, smouldering on screen as Gibson's eldest son Gabriel who goes off to war against the wishes of his anxious parent," Peter Ross wrote. "Shame, pride, rage, courage, pain—he emotes up a storm."

Ledger, who found himself dubbed "the next Russell Crowe" (the Australian star of the 2000 blockbuster *Gladiator*), was tapped to star in *A Knight's Tale*, playing the part of a squire who disguises himself as a nobleman in order to joust. "[The film] imagines that the medieval tournament sport of jousting was the World Wrestling Federation of its day, where superheroes and supervillains faced off in arenas surrounded by fanatical supporters and intense hype," Kirk Honeycutt observed for the *Hollywood Reporter* (April 19, 2001, on-line). Directed by Brian Helgeland, the film debuted at the number-two spot on the box-office charts and spent five weeks in the top-10 list. Critics largely panned the film, though some praised it as playful and spirited. Despite the film's being "more or less a cartoon" and "too long," Nicholas Barber wrote for the London *Independent on Sunday* (September 2, 2001), "it's terrific, innocent, old-fashioned entertainment." "Ledger has a strong masculine screen presence that allows him to dive bravely into a scene's emotions," Honeycutt opined. Ledger, however, was uncomfortable with his emerging stardom. "When I saw the poster for the movie [which features a portrait of a resolute-looking Ledger], I was pretty freaked," he told Rupert Mellor. "The film is an ensemble piece, and there's just my great, big mug. I'm just doing what I've always done—being an actor. Now I'm being made into a 'star', a product, and it's out of my control."

Unsurprisingly, given his feelings, Ledger was very interested when a supporting role in *Monster's Ball*, a drama starring Halle Berry and Billy Bob Thornton, became available. Ledger's part, that of the prison guard Sonny—the deeply troubled son of the character played by Thornton—was originally to be played by the actor Wes Bentley, who had appeared in *American Beauty* (1999); when Bentley had to pull out of the project, he reportedly asked Ledger, a friend, to take over for him so as to avoid delaying the production. That development proved to be serendipitous for Ledger, as the role displayed his talent as a serious actor capable of complexity. "A fable of absolution and redemption, *Monster's Ball* is a dauntingly ambitious work," Kevin Thomas wrote in a review for the *Los Angeles Times* (December 26, 2001). "Ledger expresses the torment of the conflicted Sonny perfectly; it was a smart move for an actor whose star is ascending so swiftly to commit to a supporting role in so venturesome a project as this."

Ledger's next part was in the much-anticipated 2002 film *The Four Feathers* (the fifth version of A. E. W. Mason's 1902 novel), in which he played a conflicted Victorian-era British soldier who resigns from the army as it prepares to do battle in the Sudan. The film, directed by Shekhar Kapur (who had earned high praise for his 1998 film *Elizabeth*), disappointed the critics. Although Ledger "broods prettily and holds your attention during the crowd scenes," the film as a whole "is still as moth-eaten as a Bengal tiger rug on the floor of a London men's

club," Ty Burr wrote for the *Boston Globe* (September 20, 2002). Ledger's subsequent films—*Ned Kelly*, in which he starred as a legendary Irish-Australian outlaw, and *The Order*, a religious thriller—were trounced by critics and generally ignored by moviegoers.

In 2005 Ledger appeared in *Lords of Dogtown*, a dramatization of the story of the Zephyr Team (also known as Z-Boys), a group of talented skateboarders living in and around Venice, California, in the 1970s. Directed by Catherine Hardwicke, the film was based on a script by Stacy Peralta, who had covered the same material in the noted documentary *Dogtown and Z-Boys*, which had premiered in 2001. In Hardwicke's telling, Ledger played Skip Engblom, a surf-shop owner who serves as an unlikely mentor to the pioneering teens. "Engblom is crass, excessive, decadent and a control freak. But he is fun," Regina Campbell wrote for the *Daily Yomiuri* (December 8, 2005), a Japanese newspaper. "Ledger dominates the screen in each of his scenes, and through his take on the well-meaning but rough-and-ready character, the audience comes to understand that Engblom may be tough, but he cares." "Played by Heath Ledger in what seems to be a demented tribute to Val Kilmer's performance in *The Doors*, Skip is always volatile, frequently drunk and consistently the most entertaining figure in this movie," A. O. Scott wrote for the *New York Times* (June 3, 2005). "Which is saying something, since *Lords of Dogtown*, from start to finish, is pretty much a blast."

In *The Brothers Grimm* (2005), Ledger starred alongside Matt Damon in a fictional portrayal of the German folktale writers Jacob and Wilhelm Grimm. Directed by Terry Gilliam, the film reimagines the brothers as a pair of con men who stage hauntings, then pretend to vanquish the otherworldly creatures—for a fee. Complications arise when the brothers are called upon to solve the disappearance of a village's children, leading them on a quest involving an enchanted forest and an evil queen. The big-budget film generally failed to impress. "Despite a few early sparks of promise," Manohla Dargis wrote for the *New York Times* (August 26, 2005) in a representative review, "*The Brothers Grimm* sputters and coughs along like an unoiled machine, grinding gears and nerves in equal measure." The lead actors, however, earned a degree of praise. "Damon and Ledger give game and wry performances," Michael Phillips wrote for the *Chicago Tribune* (August 26, 2005), "Ledger twitching his way through the twittier role with a touch of wit." Likewise, a review in the U.K. paper the *Express* (November 4, 2005) applauded the "real charm and energy in the performances of Matt Damon and Heath Ledger who both display a fine talent for comedy."

Brokeback Mountain was released in December 2005. The movie follows the difficult lives of two young ranch hands, Ennis Del Mar (Ledger) and Jack Twist (Gyllenhaal), who meet in Wyoming in

1963; looking for work, they are assigned to spend the summer together in an isolated mountain range, keeping watch over sheep. Del Mar is tight-lipped and emotionally reserved; Twist is talkative and outgoing. As the days go by they come to enjoy each other's company, until one night, huddling for warmth in a tent, they succumb to an unexpected mutual attraction and fall in love. When their jobs end abruptly, they are forced to move on with their lives; they marry women and become fathers, but they cannot forget about their time together. Four years later they meet again, and their passion is reignited, but Del Mar is haunted by an incident from his past that prevents him from accepting his relationship with Twist.

Based on a 1997 short story by E. Annie Proulx, *Brokeback Mountain* was a project that remained in limbo for years; the homosexual love story was deemed commercially risky, and the making of the film was repeatedly postponed until Ang Lee signed on to direct. Impressed by Ledger's performance in *Monster's Ball*, Lee offered him the part of Del Mar. "When I met [Ledger], the moment I saw him, that was it," Lee told Rachel Abramowitz. "He's the person that's the best to carry that western brooding mood—elegiac and fearful and violent, all the complexities, all the poetic qualities." But the actor was initially unsure about the project. "There was this kind of industry-manufactured fear and risk factor that was surrounding the script," Ledger told Steven Rea for Knight Ridder, as reprinted in the *Bradenton (Florida) Herald* (January 8, 2006). He had read Proulx's story and the screenplay adaptation, by Larry McMurtry and Diana Ossana, and found both deeply moving. "I truly had a lump in my throat, but . . . these manufactured fears started to bleed into my response to the script—'Oh, this is risky,' that sort of thing," he explained. "But then that just started to fade away and I thought . . . 'What exactly am I risking?' I didn't feel like I had a career to risk, and I'm a little ruthless about it anyway. If it went away based upon a creative choice I made, then it's not really an industry I want to be in."

The film solicited widespread praise from critics. "An achingly sad tale of two damaged souls whose intimate connection across many years cannot ever be resolved, this ostensible gay Western is marked by a heightened degree of sensitivity and tact, as well as an outstanding performance from Heath Ledger," Todd McCarthy wrote for *Variety* (September 3, 2005, on-line). "As Del Mar, Ledger emits the kind of loneliness that seeps into your bones like the dampness of a bad winter cold," Rachel Abramowitz wrote. "He's unvarnished, understated and stoic, fiercely determined to keep his longing and fury and grief pent up for the rest of his life." Proulx herself concurred, telling Howard Feinstein for the London *Guardian* (January 6, 2006): "Ledger erased the image I had when I wrote [the story]. He was so visceral. How did this actor get inside my head so well? He understood more about the character than I did." "Heath is very me-

ticulous," Lee explained to Feinstein. "I don't advise actors to come to the monitor to watch themselves, but he's the only exception I made. He gets better as he gets more self-conscious. He sets himself in a zone and believes in it and keeps refining it. Jake [Gyllenhaal] sets himself this way and that way, he tries everything, like [Robert] De Niro. Heath is not like that. He has a specific target within him."

Ledger was nominated for a Golden Globe Award for best actor, and the film won Golden Globes for best dramatic picture, best director, best screenplay, and best original song. The film led the Academy Awards with eight nominations, of which it won three, for best director, best adapted screenplay, and best score. (Ledger was also nominated for an Oscar for best actor; the award went to Philip Seymour Hoffman for his role in *Capote*.) The film performed well at the box office, though some religious groups urged a boycott due to the homosexual content. "I think people should see it before they make any judgment on it," Ledger told Des Partridge for the Queensland, Australia, *Courier Mail* (January 14, 2006). "It seems a shame they put so much energy into expressing their disgust and their negative views about it when it is a story about people who love each other." He continued, "They may not agree with the subject matter, but there are worse things in life than love. They should demonstrate about the amount of anger and violence [in films] perhaps."

Casanova, in which Ledger played the title character, was also released in late 2005. A comedic love story directed by Lasse Hallström, it garnered mostly derisory reviews, although Ledger was again singled out for praise. "I admit that the picture is handsomely designed in gold and pale blue, but none of the tumult and pomp have any dramatic, comic, or erotic effect whatsoever," David Denby commented in the *New Yorker* (January 9, 2006). "Yet there *is* humor in Heath Ledger's performance. After his powerful work in *Brokeback Mountain*, in which he plays a man all tied up inside himself, it was fun to see him leaping out of bedroom windows and prancing around, sword in hand. His Casanova is seductive yet reserved, and Ledger's extraordinary baritone voice, which registers clearly at the lowest volume, may be the best asset any actor has had in years." In the *Baltimore Sun* (January 6, 2006), Michael Sragow described the picture as "refreshingly uninhibited" and full of subplots "like sumptuous chutes and ladders that turn the canalworks of Venice into a romantic slip'n'slide." Sragow concluded, "Ledger has never been so charming."

In 2006 Ledger appeared with Abby Cornish and Geoffrey Rush in the Australian film *Candy*, directed by Neil Armfield, about a poet who falls in love with an artist and, at her insistence, introduces her to heroin, to which he has become addicted. "Heath has this incredible ability to maintain a sort of guileless charm, despite the fact [that] this character is ultimately selfish and makes so many mistakes," Armfield, who is among his nation's pre-eminent theater directors, told Clint Morris for webwombat.com in early 2006. "He just has this beautifully focused concentration." Ledger's upcoming projects include the film *I'm Not There*, scheduled for release in 2007, in which he will portray the singer/songwriter Bob Dylan, and the next *Batman* film, *The Dark Knight*, expected to premiere in 2008, in which he will appear in the role of the Joker.

Ledger found real-life romance on the set of *Brokeback Mountain* with Michelle Williams, who played his on-screen wife, Alma, and also has a role in *I'm Not There*. The two are engaged and in 2005 became the parents of a child, named Matilda Rose. The family live in a brownstone in the New York City borough of Brooklyn. "That's where Mi-chelle is happiest, and I think it's important that we rear our daughter . . . where the mother is happiest," Ledger told Partridge.

—K.J.E.

Suggested Reading: (Glasgow) *Herald* p14 Dec. 24, 2005; (London) *Guardian* p3 Jan. 6, 2006; *Los Angeles Times* E p1 Nov. 20, 2005; (Queensland, Australia) *Courier Mail* M p1 Jan. 14, 2006

Selected Films: *Two Hands*, 1999; *10 Things I Hate About You*, 1999; *The Patriot*, 2000; *A Knight's Tale*, 2001; *Monster's Ball*, 2001; *The Four Feathers*, 2002; *Ned Kelly*, 2003; *The Order*, 2003; *Lords of Dogtown*, 2005; *The Brothers Grimm*, 2005; *Brokeback Mountain*, 2005; *Casanova*, 2005; *Candy*, 2006

Vince Bucci/Getty Images

Lee, Debra L.

Aug. 8, 1954– Chairman, CEO, and president of Black Entertainment Television

Address: One BET Plaza, 1235 W St., N.E., Washington, DC 20018-1211

"I grew up with *Ebony* and Motown. BET has surpassed those brands to become the No. 1 brand in African-American media," Debra L. Lee told a reporter for *Women's Biz.US* (June 2005, on-line), shortly after she was named the chief executive officer (CEO) and president of BET Holdings Inc. Six months later, while retaining those two titles, Lee became its chairman as well, succeeding Robert L. Johnson, the founder of BET—Black Entertainment Television. Lee has been with BET since 1986, when the company was six years old; she joined the staff as its first corporate attorney, after working for over five years at a Washington, D.C., law firm. She organized BET's legal department and remained there for a decade, during which she was instrumental in helping BET to become the first firm owned and controlled by African-Americans to be listed on the New York Stock Exchange. (Two years later, in 1998, BET turned private again, when Johnson bought back all of its publicly traded stock.) Concurrently, from 1992 to 1996, Lee served as BET's corporate secretary and president of its publishing division. In the latter role she oversaw the publication of the magazines *YSB*, *Heart & Soul*, *Emerge*, and *BET Weekend* (the last two of which ceased operation in 2000) and several imprints of BET Books, which published romances for black women until its purchase by Harlequin Enterprises in late 2005. From 1996 to 2005 Lee held the titles of corporate president and chief operating officer (COO) of BET.

Owned by the media conglomerate Viacom since 2000, BET Holdings Inc. has diversified widely since its launch, with the introduction of the Internet portal BET.com; the digital networks BET Jazz, BET Gospel, and BET Hip Hop; BET Pictures, a film-making enterprise; BET Event Productions (which handles such aspects of events as management, selection of venues, and recruitment of talent); BET Home Entertainment, which aims to produce DVDs and videos; and BET Mobile, among other offshoots. In the quarter-century of its existence, the company has enjoyed huge increases in revenues, and its television audience has grown steadily. In 2005 alone, according to CTIA Wireless (2006, on-line), viewership grew by 17 percent. As of early 2006, according to Nielsen Media Research, BET reached 80 million homes in the U.S., Canada, and the Caribbean, and of its viewers, 78 percent were African-American and 18 percent were white. Its commercial success and popularity notwithstanding, BET has been the target of strong criticism. Keith Boykin, a writer who served as an assistant to President Bill Clinton in the mid-1990s, complained on his Web site on December 18, 2002 that under Johnson, BET aired "a steady stream of mindless, degrading music videos, comic shows and infomercials playing to the lowest common denominator in black 'entertainment.' He squandered an opportunity to help uplift a race of people as he amassed billions of dollars in new capital for his own personal fortune." More recently, Allen Johnson, the editorial page editor of the Greensboro, North Carolina, *News & Record* (August 14, 2005, on-line), complained, "The problem with Lee and Johnson is not what they've done with their remarkable success at BET. It's what they haven't done. The network has jettisoned all of its news and public affairs shows. The latest casualty was its nightly news report. Meanwhile, BET increasingly has catered to the lowest common denominator, accenting its popular staple of rap videos prominently featuring barely covered women's bottoms and less-than-uplifting themes. . . . Now Lee calls most of the shots. By most accounts, she's a brilliant woman. . . . Still, you've got to wonder. At the 2005 BET Awards Show, it was business as usual. Singer Beyonce gave actor [Terrence] Howard a lusty onstage lap dance." A half year later, when Lynette Clemetson interviewed Lee for the *New York Times* (January 10, 2006) and mentioned such complaints, Lee said, "We're not PBS, and we'll never be PBS."

The youngest of three children, Debra Louise Lee was born on August 8, 1954 in Fort Jackson, South Carolina. Her father, Richard M. Lee, was a U.S. Army major. Her mother, Delma L. Lee, was a nurse's aide; later, she got a job as a receptionist in the BET corporate office building where Debra worked in Washington, D.C. The family was living in Compton, California, a suburb of Los Angeles, when five days of massive riots occurred in the Watts section of Los Angeles in August 1965, following physical brutality against an African-American man by an officer in the city's then all-white police force. "I think that's when I realized race was a big issue, because we had to stay inside for two weeks," Lee said to a reporter for the *Washington Business Journal* (June 29, 2001). Not long afterward Lee and her family moved to the Benbow Park section of Greensboro, North Carolina. According to the *Washington Business Journal*, despite the prevalence of racial segregation in Greensboro and its environs then, racial hostility in the family's new, predominantly black neighborhood was uncommon, and Lee felt comfortable with her surroundings for the first time that she can remember. She became a hard-working and accomplished student. "For the first time in my life, teachers took a real interest in me and pushed me," she said to the *Washington Business Journal* reporter. "They knew my parents. It was a nurturing environment where you felt like you could do any-

thing." Her image of herself as an uncommonly reserved person notwithstanding, Lee was elected class president at Lincoln Junior High in Greensboro. Also during her middle-school years, she started a business to help parents plan parties for their children, and she was inducted into the National Junior Honor Society. At Dudley High School, also in Greensboro, Lee joined with a group of classmates protesting the desegregation of their school. She told the *Washington Business Journal* that they did so "because we were so proud of our school." In calling for continued segregation, she challenged her father, a member of the local National Association for the Advancement of Colored People (NAACP) chapter, which supported extensive desegregation in Greensboro. "I think that was the first time I stood up to him and said, 'That's wrong,'" Lee said to the *Washington Business Journal* reporter. Despite that difference of opinion, Lee also said that in adulthood, when she feels unusually challenged by a task, she has thought of the values passed on to her by her parents. "A lot of the things they both stood for, I hear in my head," she said. "They motivated me, and I think they both had a big influence."

At Brown University, in Providence, Rhode Island, Lee majored in political science, with a focus on politics in Communist China and other Asian nations. She received a B.A. degree in 1976; she also won the Eva A. Mooar Premium that year, for academic achievement and her contributions to Brown. She then entered Harvard University, in Cambridge, Massachusetts, where she studied both law and public policy. In 1980 she earned a J.D. degree from the Harvard Law School and a master's degree in public policy (MPP) from the John F. Kennedy School of Government. She had hoped to start her career as an employee of the federal government, in the field of public policy, but she did not want to be associated with the administration of President Ronald Reagan, a Republican, who was then in the White House; in any event, Reagan had imposed a hiring freeze in all federal agencies. Instead, she accepted a position as a law clerk for Barrington D. Parker Sr. of the U.S. District Court for the District of Columbia. In 1981 she was hired to practice corporate law with the firm of Steptoe and Johnson, also in Washington, D.C. Steptoe and Johnson handled the accounts for the cable network BET. In 1986 Robert L. Johnson hired her as BET's first corporate attorney, with the titles of vice president and general counsel. As such, she set up and directed BET's legal department.

BET made its cable-television debut on January 25, 1980, airing on the USA Network, which then reached some 3.8 million homes in 250 markets. For several years BET's transmissions were limited to a two-hour broadcast every Friday night beginning at 11:00 p.m. In 1982 BET's airtime increased to six hours daily, and it began broadcasting music videos that it received free of charge from record companies. On October 1, 1983, a week after Home Box Office (HBO), then a cable subsidiary of Time

Inc. (now Time Warner), agreed to become a minority equity partner of BET, BET expanded its daily offerings to fill 24 hours; it thus severed its ties with the USA Network and became a full-fledged network. (HBO officially became a minority partner in BET in 1984.) By early 1990, when the network celebrated its 10th anniversary, BET was reaching 30 million subscribers in 1,900 markets.

Early on, one of Lee's most important tasks at BET was the selection of a site in northeast Washington, D.C., for the company's corporate headquarters, which would also be the home of its broadcast studios; she oversaw the construction of the building as well in 1989. Later, Lee was instrumental in helping BET become a publicly offered company: on October 31, 1991 BET Holdings (established by Johnson to serve as the parent company of BET) became the first firm controlled by African-Americans to be listed on the New York Stock Exchange. "The fact that we had an offering price of $17 and that it went up to $28 or $29 that first day proved that BET was not just a successful black company but a successful American company," Lee told Rashaun Hall for *Billboard* (October 29, 2005), citing the day of the initial public offering (IPO) as her "proudest" moment as a television executive.

Over the course of the next decade, BET diversified, launching several new networks—BET on Jazz, BET Starz! (now Black Starz!), and BET Action Pay-Per View; in the process it changed its image, to some extent, from that of a mostly music-oriented network to one that included documentaries and other movies, talk shows, and issues-oriented shows. In 1989 the cable network introduced *Teen Summit*, the first talk show geared toward black teenagers. Other programs, such as *On Stage*, which featured performances of original plays, and *Screen Scene*, which focused on news about African-American celebrities, helped to place BET on the cutting edge of black entertainment and culture. Also in 1989 BET entered the publishing business, with the debut of the magazine *Emerge*, a news and general-interest magazine aimed at black readers; the magazine *YSB* (Young Sisters and Brothers) followed in 1991. The company also bought Arabesque Books, which publishes black-themed romance novels, and *Heart and Soul* magazine, possibly the first health-and-fitness magazine for black women in the U.S. Between 1992 and 1996 Lee served as both corporate secretary and president and publisher of the publications division. In 1996 she was named president and chief operating officer of BET Holdings.

On November 3, 2000 the media conglomerate Viacom bought BET Holdings for about $3 billion. The sale was deemed both "a testimony to the growing consumer power of blacks" and "the end of black control for one of the nation's most prominent minority-owned businesses," in the words of a reporter for the Associated Press Online (November 3, 2000). The transfer of ownership dismayed some members of the black community. Teresa

Wiltz, a black staff writer with the *Washington Post* (November 4, 2000), for example, complained that BET "was ours. . . . We might not have liked the content, we might have cringed at the comedians, [shaken] our heads at the rump-shaking hootchy mamas and the glorification of the playa lifestyle. But some of us had high expectations for the first black-owned network, our first black-owned network. We took it to task because its name was Black Entertainment Television. And we wanted it to represent. Expected it to. . . . Which is why, perhaps, at the news [that BET was sold to Viacom], there is among some African Americans a sense of loss. Fifty-two percent of members polled by BlackPlanet.com, for example, saw the acquisition as 'another Black company sells out.'"

In early June 2005 Lee was formally named Johnson's successor as BET's president and CEO. (Johnson remained a high-profile spokesperson until his retirement, in January 2006.) Comparing himself with Lee, Johnson told Lynette Clemetson, "I was an entrepreneur, a 'let me do it, get out of the way and I'll show you' type of person. She's more a step-to-the-background leader, more analytical, let's-sit-down-and-debate-the-issue." He also said, "She is far more adept at integrating everybody's interests and bringing people in to create a little bit of harmony." In July 2005 Lee hired Reginald Hudlin, a writer, director, and producer of films for the big screen and television, as BET's president of entertainment. In 2006 Hudlin, in turn, recruited Denys Cowan as senior vice president for animation, charged with developing animated series for BET's TV lineup and for the home-video market. On January 9, 2006, at the annual meeting of the Television Critics Association, Lee announced that BET would be adding three new original programs to its television lineup: two so-called reality programs—*Lil' Kim: Countdown to Lockdown* and *Season of the Tiger*—and a Sunday-morning half-hour talk show called *Meet the Faith*, which premiered on May 7, 2006 and features roundtable discussions with religious leaders on current trends in politics and society. The six-installment *Lil' Kim: Countdown to Lockdown* followed the rapper Lil' Kim for two weeks preceding her incarceration, for a year and a day, for perjuring herself before a grand jury. Its premiere was watched by more people than any other series debut in BET history. *Season of the Tiger*, which also premiered in 2006, follows five Grambling State University students who are involved in either the football or the marching-band programs on campus.

Earlier, in July 2005, BET had canceled its nightly newscast, replacing it with shorter news briefings airing throughout the day. That cancellation followed those of such news or issue-discussion shows as *Tonight with Tavis Smiley*, in 2001; *Lead Story* and *BET Tonight with Ed Gordon* in 2002; and *Teen Summit* in early 2003. In *Black Press USA.com* in 2002, Artelia C. Covington quoted Lee as having said when Viacom bought BET, "The acquisition will have no impact on the voice of BET. . . . We will continue to have an independent Black voice." Covington then wrote, "Obviously, that's not the case." Referring to a BET press release in which the company described the cancellation of *Lead Story*, *BET Tonight*, and *Teen Summit* as a "restructuring," the journalist George E. Curry, a longtime panelist on *Lead Story*, told Covington, "Regardless of how BET tries to spin it, the loss of these important programs represents a major setback for the Black community." Kevin Powell, a journalist and activist who has spoken out against the potentially harmful effects of reality television, told Clemetson, "There has been such a pandering to younger people [by BET]. I'm on the college circuit a hundred times a year, and people always ask me what is wrong with BET. We have to stop participating in the one-dimensional portrayal of ourselves. And BET as the premier television network for black people has to take the lead on that." For her part, when Rashaun Hall asked Lee, "How do you balance the day-to-day business of running a network with representing an entire community?," Lee answered, "We are a business, and our primary responsibility is to create returns for our shareholders. We really are a successful business and have to do all the things that you need to do to keep being successful." "We program to 18-to-34-year-olds, and music is an important part of what we do . . . ," she added. "We . . . make decisions based on what we think will work. And we know what works, because we get Nielson ratings every day. We're an entertainment network, and we try to put on the best programming that we can to appeal to the audience we serve."

Currently, a significant portion of BET's lineup is devoted to the broadcast of such programs as *The Wayans Brothers*, *The Jamie Foxx Show*, *In Living Color*, and *Girlfriends*, all of which aired earlier on other networks. The music-video countdown-show *106 & Park*, which airs every day except Sunday, has offered more than 1,100 installments since 2000 and is one of BET's most popular shows. The program *BET's Morning Inspiration with Brother Gerard*, hosted by Gerard Henry, airs daily for three hours beginning at 6:00 a.m.; according to the BET Web site, it "showcases top ministers in the African-American community" and "provides updates on gospel and religious events."

Lee's many honors include, in 2001, the Woman of the Year Award from Women in Cable and Telecommunications; in 2003, the Distinguished Vanguard Award for Leadership from the National Cable Television Association and the Positively Visionary Award from Cable Positive; and in 2005, the Madame C. J. Walker Award from *Ebony*. Lee sits on the boards of directors of Revlon Inc., the Eastman Kodak Co., Marriott International, and the Washington Gas & Light Co. In addition, she is a board member of the National Cable & Telecommunications Association; the Center for Communication; Girls Inc.; the Kennedy Center's Community

& Friends; the National Symphony Orchestra; National Women's Law Center; and the Alvin Ailey Dance Theater.

Lee's marriage, in 1985, to Randall Coleman ended in divorce. From that union she has a son, Quinn, and a daughter, Ava. Lee lives with her children in the Washington, D.C., area. Among her avocational activities are collecting glass art, reading, cycling, and playing tennis.

—D.F.

Suggested Reading: BET.com; *Billboard* p21 July 2, 2005, p30+ Oct. 29, 2005; *Black Enterprise* p68 Aug. 1997; *Broadcasting & Cable* p70 June 8, 1998; CTIA Wireless (on-line) Apr. 2006; *New York Times* E p1+ Jan. 10, 2006; *Washington Business Journal* p24 June 29, 2001; *Women's Biz.US* (on-line) June 2005

Courtesy of Union University

Leo, John

June 16, 1935– Columnist; author

Address: U.S. News & World Report, *450 W. 33d St., 11th Fl., New York, NY 10001*

"I'm a moralist," the columnist John Leo told Warren Bird during an interview for *Christianity Today* (October 7, 1996, on-line). "It's a dirty word these days, but I approach things in terms of right and wrong." Labeled "the first standard-bearer of the Politically Incorrect" by *Vanity Fair* (July 1994), Leo considers himself to be the "founder of the anti-sensitivity movement," as he told Elise O'Shaughnessy, his *Vanity Fair* interviewer; he has also characterized himself as a social conservative. Leo's career in journalism began in 1957, and except for three years in the early 1970s, he has worked as a reporter, editor, and/or columnist ever since. His employers have included a local New Jersey newspaper, two Roman Catholic periodicals, the *New York Times*, the *Village Voice*, *Time* magazine, and *U.S. News & World Report*, for the last of which he has written a column nearly every week since 1988. Called "On Society," his column has been syndicated to as many as 140 newspapers nationwide; in late 2005, about 80 papers published it. At that time the column was renamed "John Leo's Blog." As of mid-2006 it no longer appeared in the printed version of *U.S. News*. Instead, it was posted regularly only on the *U.S. News* Web site and uexpress.com, maintained by Universal Press Syndicate.

Leo believes that for too long, most Americans have thoughtlessly or approvingly complied with—or have failed to confront effectively and vigorously—what he has characterized as "a very broad and serious assault on traditional Western culture" that has led to nothing less than "a vast social disaster": "teen pregnancy, family breakup, teen suicide, street violence, murders by children, the burgeoning jail population, sexual disease, child sex abuse, drug use, gun incidents in school, and so forth," in his words, as quoted by O'Shaughnessy. "Every aspect of Western culture is under assault now . . . ," Leo declared to Warren Bird. "I think it's a very grave crisis." Elements of that crisis, in Leo's view, include the supplanting of communal standards and ties by personal, subjective standards and a "me-first" individualism; increasingly egregious corporate and individual greed; excessive consumerism; attempts to remove religion or references to religion from public life; insistence on political correctness (encompassing women's studies, gay rights, animal rights, bilingualism, and "censorship in the pursuit of tolerance," in his words) in language and elsewhere; affirmative action and diversification efforts in behalf of members of minorities and women; "extreme" forms of multiculturalism; what he terms "victimology," whereby homosexuals, the disabled, the elderly, and other groups claim that they have been victims of social neglect or abuse, with the goal of benefiting politically or in other ways and without regard for basic American conceptions of fairness; and the transfer of life-and-death decisions (in particular, those connected with abortion and euthanasia) from society to the individual. Leo said to Bird that "choice," as in "pro-choice," is "a consumerist, libertarian word that effectively keeps morality at bay." Leo has used his columns as a bully pulpit from which to convince readers that "this is not the way our culture has to go," as he said to Bird, and that many of the beliefs of the "elites," as he refers to people generally considered liberal or leftist, are variously shortsighted, senseless, willfully ignorant, perverse, and harmful. He told Bird, "My message is, 'Let's hang in

there, let's make our case, and maybe we can turn the culture around.'" "Although Leo's opinions are strong, and his allegiance is never in doubt, his prose is calm, well-reasoned and often witty," Douglas A. Sylva, who served as vice president of the Catholic Family and Human Rights Institute in the early 2000s, wrote for the *New York Times Book Review* (December 31, 2000), after reading Leo's most recent book, a collection of his columns titled *Incorrect Thoughts: Notes on Our Wayward Culture* (2000). To readers less or not at all sympathetic with his viewpoints, his words can also seem caustic, sarcastic, satirical, and mocking. "Not surprisingly," O'Shaughnessy wrote, "he is controversial, with detractors as vehement as his fans." Among those who have offered praise as well as criticism of his columns is Robert G. Hoyt, who reviewed Leo's book *Two Steps Ahead of the Thought Police* (1994) for *Commonweal* (November 18, 1994). Acknowledging disagreement with "from one- to two-sevenths" of Leo's opinions, Hoyt called the book "a sharper, and certainly funnier, work of social commentary than others you're likely to see" but also complained that Leo "sometimes gets a little mean"; worse, he wrote, Leo paid little attention to the economic and political causes of such "evils" as "poverty, racial discrimination, crime, drugs, broken homes, and child abuse," although, in Hoyt's view, "they are far more threatening to our future as a society than, say, the jejune deconstructionist babblings Leo recorded at a meeting of the Modern Language Association." Leo's book *How the Russians Invented Baseball and Other Essays of Enlightenment* (1989) is an earlier collection of his columns.

The eldest son of Maurice Matthew Leo, a designer of stainless-steel fixtures who was of Irish descent, and Maria (Trincellita) Leo, a schoolteacher of Italian descent, John P. Leo was born on June 16, 1935 in Hoboken, New Jersey. He has at least two brothers, one of whom, Peter Leo, is a journalist with the Pittsburgh *Post-Gazette*. Raised in the Roman Catholic faith, John Leo received a Jesuit education from grade school through high school. He attended St. Michael's College, a Catholic institution that is connected with the University of Toronto, in Canada. In 1957, upon earning a B.A. degree, Leo returned to New Jersey, where he was hired as a reporter for the Bergen County, New Jersey, *Record*. He left the *Record* after three years to edit the *Catholic Messenger*, a weekly published by the Roman Catholic Diocese of Davenport, Iowa. Writing for *Commonweal* (November 18, 1994), Robert G. Hoyt noted that the *Catholic Messenger* was "one of the country's best diocesan papers before [Leo] arrived" but "got more reader-friendly after he took over." In 1963 Leo moved to New York City to become the associate editor of *Commonweal*, "an independent journal of opinion edited and managed by lay Catholics," as its Web site describes it. "Liberal in temperament—opinionated and engaged, but tolerant in tone—the magazine's editorial strategy was (and continues to be) to reject sectarianism and to rely on reasoned discussion," according to its Web site. During Leo's four years with *Commonweal*, the civil rights movement in the United States and the widening Vietnam War were much in the news; the magazine supported both racial integration and resistance to the war, and the positions that Leo took were "probably as liberal as John gets," as Wilfrid Sheed, who served as a drama critic and book-review editor for *Commonweal* from 1964 to 1971, told Elise O'Shaughnessy.

Concurrently with part of his stint at *Commonweal*, Leo wrote a column called "Thinking It Over" for the *National Catholic Reporter* (*NCR*), an independent newsweekly founded in 1964 by Robert G. Hoyt. Leo seemed to be "a natural-born columnist," as Hoyt wrote for his 1994 *Commonweal* article. "He would dictate the column by phone. . . . It always fitted the allotted space exactly, was reasonable, readable, and witty, needed no editing, and was sometimes devastating, as the late Cardinals Spellman of New York and McIntyre of Los Angeles had reason to know. As for style: Some people think in sentences, some in paragraphs; Leo thinks in 750- to 1,000-word [chunks], each one a seamless entity. Besides which, somewhere in his brain there is a figure-of-speech machine that grinds out a steady product line of nicely turned metaphors, similes, and other tropes that divert the reader while conveying the intended message." At *NCR*, according to Hoyt, Leo "departed from his inborn moderate conservatism"; the views he offered in "Thinking It Over" "usually appeared to the left" of those in the column written by *NCR*'s "house conservative, Garry Wills." "Today" (that is, in 1994), Hoyt continued, "insofar as either of them can be labeled, Wills is the more liberal and Leo has gone back to his roots."

According to O'Shaughnessy, Leo was "segueing his way out of Catholicism" during the 1960s. She added that he had "blown the whistle on frauds, cover-ups, and piousness in the church, even taking up the cause of radical priest Daniel Berrigan [an outspoken opponent of the Vietnam War who was jailed for his illegal anti-war activities], and being banned in one diocese." In 1967 Leo left *Commonweal* and joined the staff of the *New York Times* as a reporter in the areas of sociology, psychology, and anthropology; on rare occasions he reported on religious matters as well. He had rejected the *Times*'s invitation to specialize in religion, because, as he told O'Shaughnessy, "I didn't want to be a professional Catholic the rest of my life." Bird reported that Leo "does not consider himself a Christian believer"; nevertheless, Leo told Bird that having grown up "in the Catholic tradition . . . my head is permanently shaped by it. I believe its social principles, and I defend religion against the assaults of a wrong-headed culture."

In 1969 Leo quit his job and stopped earning his living as a journalist. The following year he became an administrator at the New York City Department of Environmental Protection. He returned to writing in 1973, as a reporter for the *Village Voice*. In 1974 he launched the *Voice* column "Press Clips," which focuses on the print and broadcast media. That same year he took a new job, as an associate editor and writer for *Time*. His byline appeared mainly in the magazine's "Behavior" section, for which he wrote (sometimes using material gathered by other *Time* reporters) on such topics as problems common among single parents and their children (January 4, 1982); the tendency of "too many people [to] look upon themselves as helpless children" (May 27, 1985); and the growing skinhead movement in the U.S. (January 25, 1988). Others among his articles appeared in sections headed "Nation," "Sexes," "Medicine," "Ethics," "Living," and "Essay." For the last-named section, he wrote about a favorite subject of his—the silliness of journalese (February 6, 1984, March 18, 1985, and September 1, 1986). "Cunningly similar to English," Leo wrote for the *Columbia Journalism Review* (November/December 1994, on-line), "Journalese is the official language of American reporters and pundits, most of whom achieve fluency in this arcane tongue toward the end of their first full hour in any newsroom." Journalese is "prized for its incantatory powers," he noted in *Time* (March 18, 1985), and it relies on euphemisms and phrases that have become clichés: "Every cub reporter, for instance, knows that fires rage out of control . . . and key labor accords are hammered out by weary negotiators in marathon, round-the-clock bargaining sessions, thus narrowly averting threatened walkouts." In his essay "Journalese, or Why English Is the Second Language of the Fourth Estate," included in *How the Russians Invented Baseball* (and also in *Russell Baker's Book of American Humor*), he explained, "In general, adjectives in journalese are as misleading as olive sizes. . . . Thus the use of *soft-spoken* (mousy), *loyal* (dumb), *high-minded* (inept), *ageless* (old), *hardworking* (plodding), *irrepressible* (insanely giddy), and *pragmatic* (morally appalling, felonious). . . . A journalist may write: 'A private, deliberate man, Frobisher dislikes small talk, but can be charming when he wants to.' In translation, this means 'An antisocial and sullen plodder, Frobisher is outstandingly obnoxious and about as articulate as a cantaloupe.'" He also noted, "The hyphenated modifier is the meat and potatoes of journalese," citing such commonly seen written companions as "scandal-plagued," "debt-laden," "war-torn," "much-troubled," and "wide-ranging."

Occasionally, *Time* published one of Leo's "Ralph and Wanda" columns, in which a fictitious couple—the husband a conservative masculinist, the wife a liberal feminist—discuss social and political issues, thus enabling Leo to deal "quickly and lightly with a lot of ephemera," as he told John A. Meyers for *Time* (April 9, 1984). In the early dialogues, he admitted to Meyers, he would have "Ralph the triumphant curmudgeon teasing Wanda the trendy feminist. But Wanda has become a lot smarter. For one thing, the column worked better that way. Each of them could express sharper opinions and then get corrected or put down or yelled at by the other. . . . So now Wanda has acquired 60 to 70 additional IQ points, and the dialogue has become a moderately baroque version of a real debate." Many "Ralph and Wanda" columns appear in *How the Russians Invented Baseball*.

In 1988 Roger Rosenblatt, then the editor in chief of *U.S. News & World Report*, recruited Leo to write a column, called "On Society," for that magazine. Nearly every week for the next 17 years, Leo offered in his column his opinions about a broad array of social and political issues. A representative sample from recent years includes a column entitled "Insensitivity Is Now the Greatest Crime of All" (January 28, 2001), in which he wrote that several people nominated for Cabinet positions in the administration of President George W. Bush had been "indicted by a jury of Democratic politicians and columnists for sensitivity failures"—"a very effective tool of intimidation." "John Ashcroft, of course [who later became the U.S. attorney general], has been the main target," Leo wrote. "Though Ashcroft did not cover himself in glory by opposing Judge Ronnie White [an African-American and one of President Bill Clinton's unsuccessful nominees for the federal bench] and calling him 'pro-criminal,' there is zero evidence on the table of racist intent. . . . No matter. For two months now the Democrats have talked about nothing but race, so Ashcroft's opposition must have been racial. . . . Sen. Chuck Schumer, D-N.Y., knows how this game is played: 'I don't think he's a racist, but at certain instances, I don't think he has shown enough sensitivity . . . ' This, of course, allows the connection between the words 'Ashcroft' and 'racism' to linger in every mind, though the connection is piously denied. It also indicates a way for worried conservatives to clear themselves of the potentially career-killing charge of racial insensitivity: just abandon opposition to the alarming racial plans of the left (quotas, preferences, identity politics, hate crime laws). Nobody who favors quotas has ever been accused of racial insensitivity."

In his column "Pledge Furor More Evidence of Elites' Hostility to Religion" (June 30, 2002), Leo wrote in response to the ruling by the Ninth Circuit Court, a federal appeals court in California, that teacher-led recitation of the Pledge of Allegiance in public schools is an unconstitutional "endorsement of religion" because it includes the phrase "under God" (words added to the pledge by Congress in 1954). "By revealing so clearly the foam-at-the-mouth hostility to religion that grips our elites, the 9th Circuit's 'under God' decision is proving a Godsend . . . ," Leo wrote. "To religious conservatives, 'under God' is a crucial symbol, the last religious reference left in the schools since the separationist makeover of education. . . . The court ruling opens the door to a serious discussion of the aggressive ideological campaign against religion. As Christopher Lasch wrote in *The Revolt of the Elites*,

the elites' attitudes toward religion 'range from indifference to active hostility,' which is not much of a gamut. While using high-road rhetoric (safeguarding church-state separation allows all faiths to flourish, etc.) the elites have pursued low-road politics, relentlessly working to drive religion from the public square."

In "It's a Gamble to Trust Democrats to Run [a] War Against Terror" (October 24, 2004), Leo wrote that "a good many Americans don't trust the Democrats to run a war on terror." Supporters of John Kerry as the Democratic candidate for president in 2004, he wrote, "turned the Democratic National Convention into an improbable flag-waving, pro-military pageant. But this was marketing, not conviction." Referring to demonstrations by opponents of the war in Iraq, he wrote, "Ordinary Democrats raised almost no objection to the many hate-America themes at these marches. (Few liberals and almost no reporters mentioned that the rallies were organized by unreconstructed communist-front groups and Maoist fans of North Korean dictator Kim Jong Il.) . . . Maybe Andrew Sullivan [a former editor of the *New Republic* and current blogger] is right that electing John Kerry can bring the Democratic Party fully into the war on terror. But given the forces at work among Democrats, it's surely a gamble." Leo addressed the same theme in "The Left Still Doesn't Take Terrorism Seriously" (July 31, 2005): "The Bush administration has botched many things, but large numbers of Americans go along with the president because he displays what the left apparently cannot: moral clarity and seriousness about what must be done. When the ideas of the left come into view, the themes often include the closing of Guantanamo, attacks on the Patriot act, opposition to military recruitment on campuses, casual mockery of patriotism . . . and a failure to admit that defeating terrorism will require some trade-offs between security and civil liberties. Is this a serious program?"

In one of his most recent columns, "Stem Cell Morals," which appeared on "John Leo's Blog" (July 20, 2006), Leo wrote, "Are social and religious conservatives antiscience? Many are. But resistance to public funding of stem cell research is not an example of it. . . . The issue is one of moral judgment, as it is in abortion, infanticide, and euthanasia (though the claims that can be made on behalf of an infinitesimal embryo, though similar, are weaker). . . . The mainstream press would be lost without the semiofficial newsroom adjectives of 'placate' and 'appease' to explain why President Bush occasionally responds to the people who elected him. Those who allegedly are being placated and appeased fear that public funding of embryo killing is a gateway issue sure to lead to more morally obtuse decisions. Columnist and author Anna Quindlen, who favors [funding for stem-cell research], frankly thinks and hopes it will help increase support for abortion. It undoubtedly would. This is why many of us who cannot think of the killing of infinitesimal embryos as murder are still willing to be 'placated' and 'appeased' on this worrisome issue. At least it's worth keeping our tax money away from such stuff."

In the last column by Leo that appeared in the printed version of *U.S. News & World Report* (August 13, 2006), he wrote, "Now that I'm leaving, I should acknowledge that writing a column has to be one of the best jobs in the world. At a cost of only 750 words per week . . . you get to join what my friend and fellow columnist Richard Reeves calls 'the conversation.' He means the national dialogue, or whatever part of it you can shoulder your way into by being pertinent, witty, original, or whatever other trait induces people to read you. . . . I've tried to sound conversational, as if I were talking to a friend about a subject that interests us both. . . . The problem is that the tone may be conversational, but we are still talking about a one-way monologue. This is one reason why columnists seem to be losing out to Internet commentators. . . . Immediate feedback . . . allows real conversation that anyone can join, as well as a sense that all speakers are equal. The whole model of anointed commentators talking down to mostly passive readers has crumbled. If column-writing were a stock, I would sell now." He also announced that he planned to launch his own Web site in the near future, and he invited readers to write to him at johnleo2@optonline.com.

"Even people who don't like what John Leo writes like John Leo," James Brady wrote for *Crain's New York Business* (July 25, 1994), naming a bevy of well-known liberals who came to a party to celebrate the publication of Leo's second book. An avid baseball fan, Leo founded and presides over a softball team in Sag Harbor, on Long Island, New York, that plays weekly in the spring and summer. He lives in New York City and Long Island with his wife, Jacqueline (McCord) Leo, currently the editorial director of the *New York Times*'s women's magazines, and their daughter, Alexandra. Leo also has two daughters, Kristin and Karen, from his marriage in 1967 to Stephanie Wolf, which ended in divorce in the mid-1970s.

—I.C.

Suggested Reading: *Christianity Today* p62+ Oct. 7, 1996; *Commonweal* p38 Nov. 18, 1994; *Time* p3 Apr. 9, 1984, with photo; *Vanity Fair* p32+ July 1994

Selected Books: *How the Russians Invented Baseball*, 1989; *Two Steps Ahead of the Thought Police*, 1994; *Incorrect Thoughts: Notes on Our Wayward Culture*, 2000

Lethem, Jonathan

Feb. 19, 1964– Novelist; short-story writer; essayist

Address: c/o Random House, Inc., 1745 Broadway, New York, NY 10019

An author of short stories, essays, and six novels, Jonathan Lethem is known for his ability to develop unusual themes in unexpected genres and to blur the lines between "serious" and "popular" fiction. *Gun, With Occasional Music*, his first novel, was hailed for its unusual fusion of the detective story and science fiction. His second, *Amnesia Moon*, combines elements of a road novel with a postapocalyptic vision of the future. *As She Climbed Across the Table* focuses on a man losing the love of his life to an interdimensional anomaly. *Girl in Landscape* is a coming-of-age story set in a distant world ruled by creatures who are fascinated by anything human. *Motherless Brooklyn* takes readers inside the mind of a detective who suffers from Tourette's syndrome. Lethem's most recent novel, *The Fortress of Solitude*, which details events that begin in the 1970s in Brooklyn, New York, where Lethem spent his early years, was lauded as a sprawling bildungsroman. Reviewing *The Fortress of Solitude* for the *Nation* (October 27, 2003), Melanie Rehak wrote, "It has always been one of Lethem's gifts as a writer to make even his

Courtesy of Symphony Space

most futuristic, postapocalyptic universes and characters as humane and well observed as the city streets he chronicles in *The Fortress of Solitude*. If anyone can make you believe it's possible to fall in love with a void, or that a homeless man can fly and a prison break can be aided by powers of invisibility, it's him." In the *New York Review of Books* (April 7, 2005), David Leonard described Lethem as "a young writer as clever as they come and as crafty as they get, who skinwalked and shape-changed from Kurt Vonnegut into Saul Bellow before our starry eyes, whose Huckleberry Brooklyn novel brought municipal fiction back from the dead." Regarding the mixture of the realistic and the fantastic in much of his work, Lethem explained to Robert Birnbaum for the on-line newspaper the *Morning News* (January 7, 2004), "Life itself is made up of things that we experience as prosaic and things we experience as dreamlike, or disruptive, or metaphoric, or hallucinogenic. And so I've always wished to push some version of those distortions I sense pushing at the surface of every-day life into prominence in the work. Whether it's a fantastic element, one that created a resonance with science fiction, or fantasy, or magic realism, or a linguistic or metaphorical distortion, or a neurological distortion, or whether the distortion is archetypal, symbolic—say, the superhero plopping into the everyday realm—for me it's the same chase. I'm on the same trail."

In 2005 Lethem was one of the 25 individuals to receive a MacArthur Foundation fellowship, commonly referred to as the genius grant, which includes a no-strings-attached cash award of $500,000. A description of his work on the foundation's Web site cited his "keen powers of observation and description" and ability to draw readers "deeply within the physical and social worlds his characters inhabit, in the midst of the energetic dialogue and pop riffs that pulse throughout." The MacArthur Foundation site also stated that Lethem's "allusions to popular genres with his fiction" and his distortion of "boundaries across a broad spectrum of cultural creations" have extended "the frontier of American fiction." Lethem's oeuvre includes two collections of short stories, *The Wall of the Sky, The Wall of the Eye* and *Men and Cartoons*. He has edited an anthology of stories, *The Vintage Book of Amnesia* (2000), as well as the 2002 edition of *Da Capo Best Music Writing: The Year's Finest Writing on Rock, Pop, Jazz, Country*. Among other periodicals, his writings have appeared in the *New Yorker*, *Rolling Stone*, and *McSweeney's*. A collection of his essays, *The Disappointment Artist*, appeared in 2005. His most recent novel, *You Don't Love Me Yet*, about a Los Angeles rock band, was published in September 2006.

Jonathan Allen Lethem was born on February 19, 1964 in New York City and grew up in Brooklyn. He was raised with his two younger siblings—his brother, Blake, and his sister, Mara. Lethem's parents were political activists whose progressive ideology was shared by many of their neighbors. They welcomed foreign expatriates into their home for varying periods, and at times also provided bed and board for former students of Lethem's father, Richard Lethem, who had once taught in Kansas

City, Missouri. "Eventually we rented out rooms to people from Africa, England, Germany, some visiting New York on and off. And they became our friends," Richard Lethem said to Barbara Trachtenberg for *Words and Images* (February 2005, online). "So an international environment affected our kids' growing up. It was extremely diverse. There was always a lot of intellectual ferment going on. Judith [Jonathan's mother] was a talker who related to people intensely, and there was always over our dinner or breakfast table an intellectual give-and-take that was exciting, stimulating, politically and artistically." Lethem's mother died of cancer when he was a teenager. His father supported his family by means of various salaried jobs while he also pursued a career as an artist. As a teenager Jonathan intended to follow in his father's footsteps; he studied painting at the High School of Music and Art (now called the Fiorello H. LaGuardia High School of Music & Art and the Performing Arts), a prestigious New York City public school. As a student there he produced the *Literary Exchange*, a magazine featuring his writing and artwork along with work by others. On his subway rides to and from school, he read novels by authors who would later influence his own work—Thomas Pynchon, Kurt Vonnegut Jr., Philip K. Dick, and Jim Thompson, to name a few. Starting at the age of 15, he worked at a series of secondhand bookstores, where he read works by other authors who inspired him.

After high school Lethem enrolled at Bennington College, in Vermont. He stayed at the college for three semesters before dropping out, in 1984, to write a novel. The book, which took him three years to complete, has never been published. "It was just the X number of bad pages I had to write," he told Elizabeth Gaffney for *Publishers Weekly* (March 30, 1988). In the late 1980s Lethem moved to Berkeley, California, where he again got jobs in used-book stores and wrote whenever he had a spare moment. "If you asked me then, I would have said I'd be working at bookstores until I was 45," he told Gaffney. While in Berkeley Lethem was married briefly to Shelley Jackson, a graduate student.

After about a year in Berkeley, Lethem found a literary agent, Richard Parks. Parks later sold *Gun, With Occasional Music* to Harcourt Brace, which published it in 1994. Lethem's novel combines elements of the detective novels of Raymond Chandler with aspects of the science-fiction writings of Philip K. Dick. The story is set in the near future in Oakland, California, where children and animals speak and behave like adult human beings as a result of "evolution therapy." The experimental therapy proves to be disastrous: the "babyheads," as the children are called, become bitter, spending their days drinking and smoking in bars and speaking in a language unknown to adults. The animals, in turn, gain nearly human status as replacements for the lost generation of children. The main character is a detective named Conrad Metcalf. While trying to track down the killer of a physician's wife, Metcalf encounters shady characters, among them a kangaroo who puts him into a frozen state that lasts for six years. When he awakens, Metcalf scrambles to piece together the remaining clues to the murder in a society in which all memory has been outlawed.

Very luckily for Lethem, the *Newsweek* book critic Malcolm Jones discovered *Gun, With Occasional Music* in a pile of review copies of books awaiting his attention. "Novelists and moviemakers have fused sci-fi with detective stories for a long time . . . ," Jones wrote for *Newsweek* (April 18, 1994). "But nobody has ever done it this well. Lethem has conflated the two genres to fabricate a future that is frightening and funny and ultimately quite sad—a place where pleasure is had for the asking but happiness is hard to find. . . . *Gun, With Occasional Music* is a dazzling debut." Most other reviewers also praised the novel. A writer for *Booklist* (February 15, 1994), for example, described it as "a sparkling pastiche of Chandleresque detective fiction displaced to an almost comical postmodern landscape."

Amnesia Moon (1995), Lethem's second book, is a postapocalyptic road novel. The story's central character is Chaos, who learns that the devastated landscape that he inhabits is merely a subjective reality. In the company of a furry mutant, he sets out to explore his surroundings. The pair travel through a town whose populace was blinded when its air turned green; in another, people's social status is determined by a government test that measures luckiness. Chaos and the mutant later arrive in what may or may not be the actual San Francisco. Among the critics who praised Lethem's overt nods to Philip K. Dick was Gregory Feeley, who wrote for the *Washington Post Book World* (November 26, 1995), "By deploying Dick's quirky and numinous sensibility to tell a story that is Dickian but ultimately Lethem's own, Lethem creates a postmodern pastiche that speaks in its own voice—and is incidentally better written and more carefully structured than the revered Saint Phil's work usually managed to be."

Lethem's next book, *The Wall of the Sky, The Wall of the Eye,* (1996), was a collection of seven science-fiction tales, five of which had appeared previously in periodicals. In one story, "The Happy Man," the dead are resuscitated, but their souls must journey back and forth between Earth and hell. Another, "Vanilla Dunk," is about basketball players who take on the skills of former greats via computer. In "Light and the Sufferer," small feline creatures feed on crack cocaine, and in "The Hardened Criminals," malefactors are literally hardened and embedded in prison walls. Lethem's second short-story collection, *Men and Cartoons*, was published in 2004.

As She Climbed Across the Table (1997), Lethem's third novel, is loosely based on the writer's relationship with his first wife and is dedicated to her. In it Philip Engstrand, a professor of anthropology, loves a particle physicist, Alice Coombs. As the unexpected result of an experiment, one of Alice's colleagues, the Nobel Prize–winning Professor Soft, has opened a spatial anomaly, or void, that could be a portal to an alternate reality. The void gains a name—Lack—and a personality. Philip senses that Alice has fallen in love with Lack, because she spends most of her time in the chamber in which he/it exists; indeed, she eventually leaves Philip for Lack. A writer for *Kirkus Reviews* (January 15, 1997) remarked that "the intriguing, if gimmicky, premise sometimes feels a bit thin, like a Donald Barthelme story stretched to novel length. But Lethem's clear-eyed prose and believably strange people ultimately make for a moving tale of narcissism and need."

The title character of the novel *Girl in Landscape* (1998) is Pella, a 14-year-old. Lethem set Pella's coming-of-age story in a far-off world where she, her father, and her two younger brothers settle after the death of the girl's mother. Pella's father, a failed Brooklyn politician, cannot adjust to his new surroundings and deserts Pella and her brothers. The children have little problem finding food, which mysterious aliens called Archbuilders have provided. Pella becomes entangled with a ludicrously masculine character before discovering the truth about the seemingly benign virus that has infected both humans and aliens; she also uncovers the dirty secrets of some of her fellow settlers. A reviewer for *Booklist* (March 15, 1998) called *Girl in Landscape* "a cool, quirky, and oddly compelling . . . story that raises questions that linger long after the book is read." A *Kirkus Reviews* (February 1, 1998) critic concurred: "Lethem's people are fully as real as the locale seems unreal. . . . Pella, a sturdy girl-woman altogether equal to the tests she undergoes, is especially memorable. Wonderful stuff." By contrast, Gerald Jonas, a *New York Times Book Review* (May 24, 1998) science-fiction critic, lamented, "Pella's involvement with a macho character out of a John Wayne western seems strained, the product not of her own needs but of the author's determination to reinvent this backward-looking genre in a science fictional framework."

In his 1999 novel, *Motherless Brooklyn,* Lethem focused on a detective, Lionel Essrog, who, along with his three co-workers, endeavors to find the killer of their boss and mentor. The mind of Essrog, who is afflicted with Tourette's syndrome, serves as the alternate universe that is a hallmark of Lethem's earlier books. The novel represents a departure in Lethem's thinking about fiction. Prior to *Motherless Brooklyn*, Lethem told Robert Birnbaum, "I was very rigorous about being a fiction writer who always stuck to invention in creating my worlds. If my characters in my earlier novels went to a movie or listened to a record it would have to be a fictional one. I would have to make it up. Lionel Essrog in *Motherless Brooklyn* was very free in a way I had never been as a writer to stop the progress of the books and give a brief appreciation of *Mad* magazine or a certain song by Prince."

He also said, "To appreciate the real world very directly in the voice of the book—that was actually something that was a kind of breakthrough for me in *Motherless Brooklyn* and obviously necessary if I was going to write this panorama of pop culture and historical reality." In an assessment of the novel for the *New York Times Book Review* (October 17, 1999), Albert Mobilio wrote, "By littering the inductive process with babble, Lethem produces a Keatonesque detective who stumbles gracefully upon solutions rather than rooting them out. In *Motherless Brooklyn*, solving crime is beside the point. . . . Instead, this is a novel about the mysteries of consciousness, the dualism Essrog alludes to when he talks about his 'Tourette's brain' as if it were an entity apart from him." The *Library Journal* (July 1999) critic wrote, "Plot twists are marked by clever wordplay, fast-paced dialog, and nonstop irony. The novel pays amusing homage to, and plays with the conventions of, classic hard-boiled detective tales and movies while standing on its own as a convincing whole." *Motherless Brooklyn* earned a 2000 National Book Critics Circle Award and a *Salon* Book Award and was named Book of the Year by *Esquire*; it also catapulted Lethem to the forefront among his fiction-writing contemporaries. An adaptation of the story for the silver screen by the actor Edward Norton has not yet been scheduled for release.

Lethem's next book, *The Fortress of Solitude* (2003), is the most autobiographical and socially relevant of his novels. It centers on Dylan Edbus, the son of a discontented Jewish artist and his bohemian wife, and Mingus Rude, whose father, a black soul singer, gets addicted to drugs. The boys become best friends while growing up in the 1970s in the Boerum Hill section of Brooklyn, on a street where the Edbuses are the only white family. The childhoods of Dylan and Mingus are marked by broken relationships at home and are affected by changes in the neighborhood wrought by gentrification, the spread of crack-cocaine abuse, and the emergence of hip-hop music. An element of magical realism enters the story after a homeless man gives the 14-year-old Dylan a ring that endows its wearer with the power to fly. Using the ring, Dylan and Mingus together are transformed into a crime-fighting superhero named Aeroman. Later the ring's powers change, and its bearer can become invisible. As an adult Dylan writes the liner notes for a boxed set of recordings made by Mingus's father. Mingus has been sent to jail; when Dylan visits him there, the two reflect on their formative years.

The Fortress of Solitude struck Melanie Rehak, writing for the *Nation* (October 27, 2003), as "Lethem's valentine to the complicated, perilous and intermittently gorgeous hours of his childhood." "He writes as only the truly smitten can," she added. Peter Bradshaw, in *New Statesman* (January 19, 2004), wrote, "Everything about Mingus's and Dylan's lives in 1970s Brooklyn is realised in distinctively and thrillingly American prose: sinewy, vivid, tougher than leather." Max Watman, reviewing

the book for the *New Criterion* (November 2003), was less enthusiastic: "Lethem wants it both ways: he wants to write a big novel and still be quirky—and I think he should be able to. I do not think he's done it. He has foiled his ambition with low metaphors, and he has soiled his fun with ambition. He has evaded his characters, and rested on their interactions, their society."

The Disappointment Artist and Other Essays (2005) explores the relationship between so-called high art and popular culture. In his conversation with Robert Birnbaum, Lethem referred to its nine essays as "sleight-of-hand pieces." "I began by pointing outward at some cultural object and then kind of looped around into confession," he explained. "By the end of the sequence—which is how I think of it, a sequence of essays—it seemed to me I had written a backdoor memoir. Not a comprehensive one, more a series of glances, a series of entrees into memoir." In one essay Lethem wrote about his admiration for the John Ford Western *The Searchers*. In "13, 1977, 21" he discussed his obsession with the original *Star Wars* movie, which in 1977, as an adolescent, he saw 13 times. Critical assessments of the collection were generally mixed. Reviewing it for the *New York Review of Books* (April 7, 2005), David Leonard wrote, "Whole chapters are devoted to John Ford's westerns, Philip K. Dick's science fiction, *Star Wars*, John Cassavetes, and Stanley Kubrick. Page after page celebrates recording artists such as Chuck Berry, David Bowie, the Beatles, Elvis Costello, Brian Eno, Pink Floyd, and Cheap Trick, and such science fiction writers as Frank Herbert and Jules Verne. And when the loftier likes of Kafka, Borges, and Lem, or Faulkner, Beckett, and Joyce, or Cynthia Ozick, Grace Paley, and William Gass are mentioned at all, they will be fingered in brusque passing as 'professional Bartlebys' [a reference to the antihero of Herman Melville's story 'Bartleby the Scrivener']. It's not as if [Lethem has] never met them, they show up in his novels, wearing turtlenecks and trench coats; they hang in his closet. Yet not one is worthy here even of a paragraph." Marc Weingarten, writing for the *Los Angeles Times* (March 15, 2005), was more enthusiastic: "By connecting rich critical insight with moving emotional subtext, Jonathan Lethem has produced a disarming treatise on the essential connectivity between life and art," he wrote.

Lethem maintains residences in Brooklyn and Maine. His marriage in about 2000 to Julia Rosenberg, a Canadian who is the head of production and development for Serendipity Point Films, ended in divorce. He has described himself as a fervent baseball fan and follower of the New York Mets. By his own account, he finds listening to music helpful to the process of writing.

—C.M./D.F.

Suggested Reading: *Library Journal* p133 July 1999; (London) *Times Literary Supplement* p25+ Dec. 24–31, 2004; *Morning News* (on-line) Jan. 7,

2004, Oct. 19, 2005; *New York Times* E p2 Feb. 2, 1998; *Newsweek* Apr. 18, 1994; *Publishers Weekly* p50 Mar. 30, 1998; *Washington Post Book World* p11 Sep. 29, 1996, p15 Feb. 9, 1997; *Contemporary Authors*, vol. 150, 1996

Selected Books: fiction—*Gun, With Occasional Music*, 1994; *Amnesia Moon*, 1995; *The Wall of the Sky, The Wall of the Eye*, 1996; *As She Climbed Across the Table*, 1997; *Girl in Landscape*, 1998; *Motherless Brooklyn*, 1999; *The Fortress of Solitude*, 2003; *Men and Cartoons*, 2004; *You Don't Love Me Yet*, 2006; nonfiction—*The Disappointment Artist and Other Essays*, 2005; as editor—*The Vintage Book of Amnesia*, 2000; *Da Capo Best Music Writing: The Year's Finest Writing on Rock, Pop, Jazz, Country*, 2002

Courtesy of Random House Publishing Group

Lewis, Dorothy Otnow

July 23, 1937– Psychiatrist

Address: Yale University Child Study Center, 230 S. Frontage Rd., New Haven, CT 06520

"Most violent men I see would much rather be considered bad or evil than crazy," the psychiatrist Dorothy Otnow Lewis told Alison Bass for the *Boston Globe* (July 7, 1991). "So they really don't want to talk about the voices they hear or the times they have blacked out. And many of them, particularly the juveniles on death row, are still intent on protecting their families, even though their families hideously abused them." Lewis has won renown in part because of her ability to coax out of murderers—some of them among the most infamous serial killers in recent American history—accounts of their sometimes bizarre behavior and, in some cases, of the cruelty to which they have been subjected. Lewis's careful examination of those and other characteristics of people who became homicidal has earned her a reputation as an innovative and influential psychiatric researcher and as "a pioneer in the relationship between childhood abuse and brain damage and subsequent criminal violence," as the Georgetown University neuropsychiatrist James Merikangas described her to Bass. The University of Southern California law professor Elyn R. Saks told Laura Mansnerus for the *New York Times* (July 21, 2001) that Lewis "has revolutionized the way people think about criminal behavior."

Lewis has had a virtually lifelong curiosity about what makes some people commit appalling acts of violence while others go through life without so much as pounding a fist against a table. In her memoir *Guilty by Reason of Insanity: A Psychiatrist Probes the Minds of Killers* (1998), she recalled her childhood feelings of isolation and how they contributed to her identification with the underdog. Lewis has argued that murderers—even those who do not, or cannot, deny their crimes—should not pay for their actions with their lives, because what drove them to kill was a blend of childhood abuse, brain damage, and psychosis, among other causes, none of which by themselves would be likely to make a person violent but which may in combination create people whom Lewis herself has labeled "monsters." Though not by training a forensic psychiatrist (an expert in psychiatry with regard to law), she has become a sought-after witness for the defense at many trials and appeals, most famously for the serial killers Ted Bundy and Arthur Shawcross. Her appearances in court have sometimes made her the target of stinging criticism. As Richard Burr, formerly the head of the Death Penalty Project of the National Association for the Advancement of Colored People (NAACP), told Bass, "Testifying for serial killers is not a popular thing to do. But Dorothy is willing to put her reputation and honor on the line because she is trying to change the conditions today for children who might be Arthur Shawcross tomorrow." Some of her research, much of it in collaboration with the neurologist Jonathan Pincus and the psychologist Catherine Yeager, was cited in two Supreme Court decisions pertaining to the execution of juveniles. In a conversation with Malcolm Gladwell for the *New Yorker* (February 24, 1997), Lewis said, "I just don't believe people are born evil. . . . Forensic psychiatrists tend to buy into the notion of evil. I felt that that's no explanation. The deed itself is bizarre, grotesque. But it's not evil. To my mind, evil bespeaks conscious control over something. Serial murderers are not in that category. They are driven by forces beyond their control."

Lewis was born Dorothy Otnow in New York City on July 23, 1937, the second of two daughters. Her parents were middle-class Russian-Jewish immigrants; her mother, a committed Socialist, once dreamed of being a journalist but gave that ambition up when she met Lewis's father, who had worked his way up in the New York garment industry. Lewis has recalled that as a child in 1945, when she heard that the Nazi leader Adolf Hitler had killed himself, she regretted that his death would prevent people from understanding what had driven him to commit atrocities. Even then, as she wrote in her memoir, "I was convinced . . . that Hitler could not have been born that way. No one could be born that way. I still believe that." Raised on Manhattan's Upper West Side, Lewis received her education from preschool through high school at the Ethical Culture School (now the Ethical Culture Fieldston School), a private institution long associated with progressive labor and social movements. Lewis next attended Radcliffe College, then for women only, in Cambridge, Massachusetts (it is now a part of Harvard University). In 1957 she won the college's History and Literature Prize, and the next year its French Prize. She received a B.A. degree in French, magna cum laude, in 1959, and was elected to the honor society Phi Beta Kappa. Her interest in psychology, particularly the work of Sigmund Freud (1856–1939), led her to enroll at the Yale University Medical School, in New Haven, Connecticut. She earned an M.D. from Yale in 1963. In the same year she married Melvin Lewis, a London-born child psychiatrist, who worked at the Yale University Child Study Center from 1961 to 2002. She completed an internship at Yale–New Haven Hospital (1964–65) and then a residency in psychiatry at Yale (1965–67) before becoming a fellow in child psychiatry there (1968–69). She was named a clinical instructor of psychiatry in 1970, rising to clinical professor of psychiatry in 1979. (Her position carried no salary; the title itself was considered a form of compensation.) During those years she also maintained a small private practice and became the mother of a daughter, Gillian, and a son, Eric.

Part of Lewis's training had required her to spend one day a week studying the development of ordinary children at Yale's Child Study Center. "I had to observe normal children doing normal things," she told Bass, "and it bored me out of my mind." After she convinced her Yale supervisor that she could learn about the behavior of typical children by observing her own daughter, she shifted her focus to young people in New Haven's juvenile court. In 1971, with help from a government grant, she created a psychiatric clinic for the juvenile court and became its sole practitioner. One particularly difficult case led her to consult the neurologist who had tutored her for the neurological sections of the psychiatric certification exams: Jonathan Pincus, at that time a Yale faculty member (and currently the chief of neurology at the Veterans Affairs Medical Center in Washington, D.C.).

Pincus became Lewis's longtime collaborator, joining her in examining killers on death row and working with her to develop the idea that extreme violent behavior may be caused by a confluence of physiological and environmental factors.

Based on her work at the court clinic, Lewis wrote or co-wrote (sometimes with her husband) a steady stream of papers for psychiatric journals. In 1977 she won a grant from a Connecticut state agency to study violent juveniles whose cases were deemed serious enough to warrant their being tried as adults and possibly even be put to death. Lewis's research over the years had made her suspect that the health of violent delinquents was worse than that of their nonviolent counterparts, but Pincus, like most others at that time, doubted that the juveniles' behavior was evidence of anything other than antisocial attitudes, which were due to poor parenting and/or impoverished backgrounds. Even so, Pincus reluctantly agreed to conduct neurological exams of Lewis's subjects. What he found shocked him. "I've never seen anything like it before," he said, according to Lewis in *Guilty by Reason of Insanity*. "I've never seen so many neurologically impaired kids together in one place at one time."

In 1976 Lewis and the developmental psychologist David A. Balla published *Delinquency and Psychopathology*, which summarizes the results of a five-year study of children Lewis and Balla saw at the juvenile-court clinic in New Haven. Tentative in its conclusions and aimed at professionals, *Delinquency and Psychopathology* presents data suggesting that psychiatric problems were rife among delinquent juveniles and their parents and that those problems were often ignored by the courts and other state and local agencies.

In 1979, after her husband was diagnosed with a serious heart disease, Lewis successfully sought a full-time, paid professorship in psychiatry at New York University. A decade earlier, the university's medical school had assumed full responsibility for clinical services at Bellevue Hospital, the oldest public hospital in the country, and Lewis thus gained access to the patients in Bellevue's psychiatric wards. During the 1980s her research—particularly her findings connecting violent behaviors to earlier abuse, psychiatric problems, and head injuries or brain abnormalities—began to bring her greater attention. One of her 1983 journal articles led to her appearance on an installment of the *CBS Morning News*. A public defender in Florida who saw her on the show arranged for Lewis and Pincus to evaluate 10 killers on death row in Florida prisons. Later, in 1986, with the financial support of the international law firm Shearman & Sterling, Lewis launched a study of half of the juveniles on death rows throughout the U.S., in which she evaluated each prisoner's medical history and neurological condition and the results of psychological and intelligence tests. She cut her project short after screening 14 subjects (the number of juveniles on death row had risen from 33 to 37 during her study), having learned that the U.S. Supreme Court intended to consider, in *Thompson v. Oklahoma* in November 1987, whether executing people younger than 16 violated the Eighth Amendment of the Constitution, which prohibits cruel and unusual punishment. The plaintiff in the case, William Thompson—one of Lewis's death-row subjects—had at age 15 murdered his sister's ex-husband. Lewis presented evidence to the court demonstrating that Thompson and each of the other death-row teenagers she had studied had psychiatric problems, and that all had previously endured injuries to their heads. All but two of them had suffered grievous abuse at home; the same number had IQ scores lower than 90 (100 is considered normal); and nine had serious neurological problems, among the most significant of them being frontal-lobe dysfunction, which greatly affects an individual's ability to exercise judgment and control impulses. (Those findings were published in the May 1988 issue of the *American Journal of Psychiatry*.) Lewis's research was among the material the court cited when, in June 1988, it announced that the justices had ruled by a vote of 5–3 that states may not impose the death penalty on people who had committed capital crimes before turning 16. In 1990 Lewis enjoyed another success when her testimony at an appeal hearing in Louisiana for a convicted murderer named David Earl Wilson helped to persuade a district judge to overturn the man's death sentence.

Bracketing Lewis's efforts on behalf of Wilson were the cases in which she became involved with the serial killers Ted Bundy and Arthur Shawcross. Bundy had confessed to killing and raping dozens of women in the mid-1970s. Sentenced to death in 1979, he received two stays of execution; after the second, in 1988, he was evaluated by Lewis and Pincus. Over the next two years, Lewis interviewed him four or five times; she also spoke with members of his family. In January 1989, three days before Bundy's final execution date, Lewis talked with him again, at his request, for four and a half hours. In *Guilty by Reason of Insanity*, Lewis wrote that when she asked Bundy why he wanted to see her when there were so many other people clamoring to talk to him, Bundy said, "Because everyone else I've talked to these past days only wants to know what I did. You are the only one who wants to know why I did it."

In 1990 Lewis evaluated Arthur Shawcross at the request of his lawyers. In 1973, while in his 20s, in a plea bargain, Shawcross had been sentenced to 25 years in prison for killing an eight-year-old girl and a 10-year-old boy. He was incarcerated for only 15 years before being released. Afterward, within less than two years, he murdered 11 women in or near Rochester, New York, in what became known as the Genessee River killings. According to Lewis's account in *Guilty by Reason of Insanity*, her psychiatric analysis of Shawcross uncovered evidence of serious physical abuse when he was a child; she also learned from his medical

history that he had a series of head injuries and displayed symptoms of a seizure disorder. The neurological tests that Lewis asked Shawcross's lawyers to arrange were never conducted. During the killer's trial Lewis was the only expert witness who testified for the defense. During the three weeks that she spent on the witness stand, Lewis played videotapes of her interviews with Shawcross, emphasized the importance of the limited neurological information available to her, and argued that Shawcross's medical and family history provided clues to why he became a killer. The local media as well as the prosecutor pilloried Lewis, and the judge repeatedly chastised her for not answering questions with a simple yes or no. Perhaps the most painful charge against Lewis came from a fellow professional. Speaking of a videotape that showed Shawcross under hypnosis, acting out the abuse he said he had suffered when he was 10, a forensic psychiatrist working for the prosecution told the court, according to Lisa W. Foderaro in the *New York Times* (December 2, 1990), that Lewis's work was "not psychiatry," and that what Shawcross was doing was "a performance elicited by Dr. Lewis." In her memoir Lewis wrote that she had made a serious mistake by agreeing to testify after finding out that the tests necessary to evaluate Shawcross had not been conducted. The resulting experience, she later told Bass, "was horrible. But I felt I was the only voice for Shawcross. There was no one speaking out on his behalf."

A description of Lewis's ideas concerning the psychology of killers appeared in the *New Yorker* (February 24, 1997) in an article by Malcolm Gladwell. The article attracted the attention of a literary agent, Jonathan Lazear, and led to the publication in 1998 of *Guilty by Reason of Insanity*, which Lewis had started to write several years earlier. The book contains summaries of Lewis's research and attempts to convince readers of the urgent need to discover, through research, ways to prevent people from developing violent tendencies. *Guilty by Reason of Insanity* also offers a self-critical meditation on psychiatry and details aspects of Lewis's professional life, at times in a novelistic style.

Unbeknownst to Lewis, her book and Gladwell's 1997 article inspired the English playwright Bryony Lavery to write a drama about a woman whose daughter is missing, a female New York University psychiatrist who studies murderers, and a male killer. Called *Frozen*, Lavery's play received scant attention when it debuted, in 1998. Another mounting, in 2002 at London's Royal National Theatre, however, drew rave reviews, and that production came to a New York City theater in March 2004. Soon after it opened, friends of Lewis's urged her to see it, but she resisted. Then, at the request of the producers, who wanted her to talk to audiences after performances, she read a copy of the script. The parallels in it between her life and the psychiatrist's, and the similarities between long passages in the play and material in her book and Gladwell's article, were obvious. "The whole thing was right there," Lewis told Gladwell for the *New Yorker* (November 22, 2004). "I was sitting at home and reading the play, and I realized that it was I. I felt robbed and violated in some peculiar way. . . . I don't believe in the soul, but, if there was such a thing, it was as if someone had stolen my essence." Gladwell, too, felt outraged initially, but after he read the play, he changed his mind. He refused to help Lewis with the legal case that she said she intended to initiate, and in a 2004 *New Yorker* article, Gladwell concluded that Lavery—following a long tradition among writers, musicians, and artists—had used his words in the service of art. As of early April 2006, Lavery had not acknowledged her debt to Lewis; the legal case was reportedly on hold, and the two were said to be in the later stages of negotiations.

Meanwhile, in 2004, Lewis and a group of other researchers—among them Catherine Yeager, who had been collaborating with Lewis for over a decade—were preparing an article about 18 of the 26 men on death row in Texas who had been convicted of capital crimes committed before the culprits were 18. Lewis and her colleagues tested the 18 neurologically and psychologically and examined their educational and medical histories. Their research uncovered histories of harrowingly violent, often sexual abuse and mental illness, among other grave problems, and the failure of Texas courts to pay any attention to the subjects' mental health. Their discoveries were brought to the attention of the Supreme Court, which cited them in its decision in *Roper v. Simmons* (2005), which ruled the death penalty cruel and unusual punishment for crimes committed when the perpetrators were under 18.

Malcolm Gladwell described Lewis in 1997 as "petite" and as having "large, liquid brown eyes." In 2003, after commuting from her home in New Haven to her job in New York for more than 20 years, she left New York University to supervise psychiatric trainees at the Yale Child Study Center and treat clients in her private practice. In November 2005 Lewis told *Current Biography* that she was "working on some new, fascinating cases. Just when you think you've seen everything, you discover syndromes you had never heard of before. It's a humbling experience and I feel sorry for all those patients I saw earlier when I may have missed the diagnosis." Lewis's honors include the Blanche F. Ittleson Award for research in child psychiatry, from the American Psychiatric Association (1982) and the Wilfred C. Hulse Award for outstanding achievement in adolescent psychiatry, from the New York Council on Child and Adolescent Psychiatry (1988). She was listed among the best doctors in New York City by *New York* magazine in 1996 and in the books *The Best Doctors in America: Northeast Region, 2001–2003* and *America's Top Doctors* (2003). She lives with her husband in New Haven.

— D.R.

Suggested Reading: *Biography* p86+ Sep. 2000; *Boston Globe Magazine* p12 July 17, 1991; *New Yorker* (on-line) Feb. 24, 1997, p40+ Nov. 22, 2004; Lewis, Dorothy. *Guilty by Reason of Insanity: A Psychiatrist Probes the Minds of Killers*, 1998

Selected Books: *Delinquency and Psychopathology* (with David A. Balla), 1976; *Guilty by Reason of Insanity: A Psychiatrist Probes the Minds of Killers*, 1998; as editor— *Vulnerabilities to Delinquency*, 1981

Evan Agostini/Getty Images

Logan, Lara

Mar. 29, 1971– Print and broadcast journalist

Address: 60 Minutes, *524 W. 57th St., New York, NY 10019*

Having spent almost her entire adult life as a journalist—from the weekends in high school when she conducted the "death run" for a major metropolitan newspaper in her native South Africa to her months on the front lines of battle in Afghanistan and Iraq as a correspondent for television and radio stations in Great Britain and the U.S.—Lara Logan is baffled by press reports that describe her as a former model. "To me, it's strange," she told Stephen Battaglio for the New York *Daily News* (December 2, 2002). "I did some modeling when I was in college to earn extra money. I also worked in an ice cream parlor at 14. Does that make me a former ice cream parlor attendant?" After more than a decade of steady and often remarkable work in print, radio, and television, Logan came to sudden prominence in 2001, during her coverage of the U.S.-led war in Afghanistan. Having made her way to the front lines of the battle near the Afghan capital of Kabul, she provided the U.S. and U.K. with radio and television reports that carried an unusual degree of authority and immediacy. In 2002 Logan, the winner of four awards for her broadcast journalism, joined CBS News, where she became a regular correspondent for daily news broadcasts and for the widely admired, long-running news magazine *60 Minutes*. In February 2006 she was named the network's chief foreign correspondent.

Her professional accomplishments notwithstanding, comments about Logan's appearance have nonetheless become inseparable from descriptions of her meteoric rise through the ranks of television journalism, if only because of her colleagues' sometimes acrimonious comments about the privileges her looks supposedly give her. Returning to London after the defeat of Taliban forces in Kabul, Logan found herself the object of intense scrutiny, her name bandied about in a debate over whether female journalists were increasingly just "cute faces and cute bottoms and nothing else in between," as one prominent female news reporter put it. She was also dogged by press reports that she had dressed in skimpy clothes and flirted heavily with soldiers in attempts to pry information from them. While she has denied many of the specific claims against her in the press, she has repeatedly argued that all journalists do what is necessary for their stories. "There isn't a journalist alive who won't admit to you they use every advantage they have . . . ," she told Jacques Steinberg for the *New York Times* (November 23, 2005). "As a woman, I have lots of advantages [male reporters] don't have. I can be vulnerable. Usually you don't have to do anything. Men do it themselves. They feel like they want to protect you." Those issues aside, the quality of Logan's reporting and the fearlessness with which she has pursued stories have made her a star in her field. "I've never done anything other than to the best of my ability," Logan told Helena de Bertodano for the London *Sunday Telegraph* (June 2, 2002). "If I set about cleaning the bathroom I don't stop until it's spotless. I don't know how to do anything by halves."

Lara Logan was born on March 29, 1971 in the South African beach-resort city of Durban, sometimes called by its Zulu name, eThekwini. Her parents divorced when she was young, after the disclosure that her father, a retail businessman, had been having a long extramarital affair. Logan's mother went on to take a job as a sales representative for a glass company. During Logan's childhood South Africa was controlled by its white minority government; the system of racist policies known as apartheid sparked acts of rebellion on the part of the black majority and its supporters, which in turn led to brutal governmental repression. The intense struggle being waged within her own country led Logan, she has suggested, to a career in journalism. "I knew there were things happening in my country that weren't right, particularly in places a young white girl didn't go," she told Frazier Moore for the Associated Press (July 1, 2003). "I wanted to see them myself and make my own judgments." By all accounts an exceptional student, Logan began her journalism career when she was 17, before she left high school; a former editor at the first newspaper to employ her, the *Sunday Tribune* of Durban, told Steinberg that Logan had tried to work on the paper beginning at age 12. Among her regular assignments for the *Sunday Tribune* was to visit morgues, hospitals, and fire stations in search of reports of injuries and deaths as well as other stories. "She did everything a seasoned journalist would have done and more," the former editor told Steinberg. Upon graduating from high school, Logan moved to Paris, France, where she worked as a nanny and earned a diploma in French language, culture, and history from the country's century-old language school, the Alliance Française. After six months she realized that she was unsuited to work as a nanny. She told Steinberg, "I would be on my hands and knees, cleaning up urine from a spoiled little French brat. I realized then that my place was not in the home and never was going to be." She went next to Durban's *Daily News*, where she served as a reporter from 1990 to 1992. She attended Durban's University of Natal during that period as well, taking her degree in commerce in 1992.

Logan's first work in television began that same year. Moving from Durban to South Africa's financial hub, Johannesburg, Logan began working for Reuters Television, eventually earning the title senior producer. She covered the violence gripping her own country (according to recent U.N. statistics, South Africa has the highest rate of rapes per capita and the highest number of firearm-related murders overall of any country in the world) as well as the changes that made South Africa a more fully realized democracy, including its first post-apartheid elections, in 1994. She also began reporting on the military conflicts and other world crises that would become her primary subjects. She traveled to the nearby countries of Mozambique and Angola, both in the grip of civil war during the early and mid-1990s, and farther north to Malawi, where she covered the spread of AIDS, which is devastating many parts of sub-Saharan Africa.

Logan left South Africa in 1996 for London, England, where she worked as an editor for ABC News—her first of many assignments with American news companies. Over the next three years, still based in London, she held a variety of positions. She reported on environmental issues for the international satellite TV network Sky, a division of the News Corp., which owns the U.S. cable-news channel Fox, among scores of other media outlets. She then worked as a freelance correspondent for both Britain's Independent Television News (ITN) and the Cable News Network (CNN) in the U.S., covering current affairs in Britain and traveling throughout Europe, the Middle East, and Africa as well. She broadcast reports on such important stories as the simultaneous terrorist bombings on August 7, 1998, which killed hundreds of people in and near the U.S. embassies in Kenya and Tanzania, and the 1998–99 crisis in the former Yugoslavian province of Kosovo, which began as an outgrowth of an older civil war between Serbian nationals and ethnic Albanians and ended with a U.S.-backed bombing campaign. What she saw in Kosovo affected her so deeply that she left television work for a time to take a position with the International Medical Corps, serving primarily as a spokesperson. Meanwhile, she also wrote occasional articles for the London *Mirror*, the *Milwaukee Journal Sentinel*, and other newspapers.

In 2000 Logan began working as a correspondent for the British morning news program *GMTV*, by far that nation's most-watched "breakfast show." Covering both domestic and foreign news, Logan reported on such events as the floods in Mozambique in early 2000 that killed 700 people and left 500,000 homeless, and the ongoing conflict in Israel and the Palestinian territories, which flared up with particular intensity at the end of 2000, when the so-called second *intifada*, or uprising by Palestinians, began. (The first *intifada* lasted from approximately 1987 to 1993.) Logan's radio reports on the *intifada* won her a Gracie Allen Award for best news story from the organization American Women in Radio and Television. Logan also offered *GMTV* viewers an in-depth look at her home country, filming a five-part series on contemporary life in South Africa.

Logan's visibility within both Britain and the U.S. rose rapidly after the September 11, 2001 terrorist attacks on the U.S. She argued with her editors for the chance to cover the U.S.-led military campaign in Afghanistan, which was known to have provided a haven to the mastermind of the attacks, Osama bin Laden. Within a week of the attacks Logan was in Afghanistan, in close contact with soldiers connected to the Northern Alliance, a coalition of rebel groups united primarily by their opposition to the country's theocratic Taliban government. Logan's contacts with highly placed Northern Alliance leaders, particularly the top commander, General Babajan, put her closer than all but a handful of other reporters to the front lines, near the Afghan capital of Kabul. As a result her morning broadcasts to *GMTV* were unusually informative. Her work in Afghanistan also brought her to the attention of CBS, and she began filing dozens of radio reports a day, both for London's Capital Radio and for stations associated with the CBS Radio network. She also worked for the *CBS Evening News* and continued writing stories for newspapers as well.

Logan faced harsh conditions in Afghanistan. She ate very little during her first days there, gradually building up tolerance to the bacteria in the food. On one occasion a Taliban sniper fired at her. She slept in places that were filled with vermin—including bedbugs that sent her to the hospital, where her treatment went awry, leaving her unconscious for almost a full day. She told Rosa Prince for the *Mirror* (November 27, 2001) that a pair of Northern Alliance soldiers even plotted to rape her, offering her driver money if he would wait until after dark to take her away from an already unsafe area. In addition to those hardships, Logan had to adapt to cultural norms radically different from those of her background. Although the constant wind coated her with sand, she had to go for days at a time without a bath—and at least once she had to bathe in pajamas, to keep from offending the Afghanis around her, who expected women to cover themselves fully in accordance with the Taliban's strict interpretation of the Koran's calls for modesty on the part of women. For the same reason Logan had to cover her arms, legs, and hair. For a time she even donned a burqa, the full-body robe and veil worn in some cultures in keeping with Islamic traditions—a practice she found demeaning. "Without a face you become a non-person . . . ," she wrote for the London *Mirror* (November 15, 2001), adding: "I find it extremely difficult to accept the way women are treated in Afghanistan—even though I know I have no right to judge. But I believe the mandatory veil undermines every freedom I treasure as a western woman." On November 12, 2001, when Kabul fell to Northern Alliance forces, Logan was on the scene almost immediately. After choosing places from which to file her stories, she would remain in her car until the last moment, when she would run out and quickly film reports using the videophone she carried everywhere—a method she found necessary because of the attention she attracted as a Western woman in Western clothes and the resulting risk of physical abuse. "Sometimes it was so strange to look at [Afghanis'] faces," she told an interviewer for the *Scotsman* (May 25, 2002), "and think they had not seen a woman like me in public for seven years. It was depraved."

Logan emerged from Afghanistan as a major star on British television news. In 2002 she collected a second Gracie Award, for the best news story on radio, given in recognition of her work on CBS News Radio. She also got a taste of the less pleasant side of fame. Even before she returned home, a male television journalist, Julian Manyon, compared her in an article for the English magazine *Spectator* (November 3, 2001) to the World War I–era spy Mata Hari, who was known for learning secrets through seduction. Referring to General Babajan, who at that time controlled the airbase Bagram, near Kabul, Manyon wrote: "The general has the reputation of a bon viveur, and some of our jealous competitors have unkindly suggested that the unique access we have hitherto enjoyed to Bagram has less to do with my journalistic talents than with the considerable physical charms of my travelling companion, the delectable Lara Logan of *GMTV*, who exploits her God-given advantages with a skill that Mata Hari might envy. It is certainly true that whenever we appear the general's attention fixes on her with searchlight intensity, and a slow grin spreads across his face." Days later, in an interview for an article in the *Mirror* (November 6, 2001), Logan responded to Manyon's suggestions, saying, "If General Babajan smiles around me, perhaps it is because I offer him respect and attempt, at least, to talk to him in a non-demanding manner. It's an elementary part of making contacts and thereby getting the story." Manyon's comments coincided roughly with reports that Logan had worked as a model in her student days and with comments made by the famed television reporter Kate Adie, who claimed that news executives favored beautiful but incompetent female journalists over more serious and experienced women in the field. Television news stations, Adie said in widely reported comments, "want people with cute faces and cute bottoms and nothing else in between"; Logan was often mentioned in articles concerning Adie's remarks—though usually to suggest that such claims seemed hard to make against as accomplished a reporter as Logan. But Logan came under scrutiny most intensely when the *Sun* (May 22, 2002), an English tabloid, ran a front-page story titled "Put Those Bazookas Away, Lara," which claimed to detail complaints by U.S. and coalition soldiers about Logan's flirtatious behavior and provocative clothes. In the subsequent media storm, Logan denied the specific charges in the article. She has also acknowledged repeatedly that, to the degree that her attractiveness is an advantage, she is perfectly willing to put it to use— just as male reporters use their advantages. "Men play on the military thing," she told Emma Brockes for the *Guardian* (May 24, 2002), "they play on the macho thing, they play on the brotherhood thing. No one accuses them of using gender to their advantage. The fact is that sometimes being a woman can open doors for you, but more often than not it makes things more difficult. If I approach somebody as an attractive woman, especially an official, the first thing they think is: 'Oh, she thinks she can get anything she wants from me, because she's attractive, therefore I'm going to go out of my way to show her that she can't manipulate me.' That's even worse for me after the *Sun*'s coverage. People will go out of their way not to give me anything."

During that time Logan also received publicity for signing on as a regular correspondent for CBS News and its program *60 Minutes II*, the companion to the network's flagship magazine *60 Minutes*. "It's the most sought-after position in the world in my business, it's huge," Logan told Liz Jones for the London *Evening Standard* (May 31, 2002). "No one in America would challenge my credibility now [that] I have that job." While television networks on both sides of the Atlantic had wooed Logan, she chose CBS News after the longtime anchor and *60 Minutes II* correspondent Dan Rather made a personal appeal for her to join the network. Logan told Battaglio, "He said if reporting the news is the most important thing to you and the love of stories

around the world is what motivates you, then this is the place for you." At CBS Logan immediately began covering the tense international situations that, she has often said, motivate her as a journalist. Her reporting on the September 2002 assassination attempt on Afghanistan's then-interim president, Hamid Karzai, earned her a third Gracie Award for best news story—her first for television work.

In 2003 Logan was sent to Baghdad to cover the invasion of Iraq by U.S.-led forces. In mid-March of that year, she was among the last television reporters from the invading countries to leave Iraq's capital for safety in Jordan; she was also among the first to return, on April 4, 2003—the first, in fact, from a U.S. news network. Only a few days later, a shell landed in the hotel where Logan and other reporters were staying, killing three members of the press, including a cameraperson Logan had worked with at Reuters Television. Sending home reports about the incident "brings [the war] home to us," Logan told Walt Belcher for the *Tampa Tribune* (April 10, 2003), "because we're here on the ground. But this is happening to Iraqi families all across Baghdad." Logan's interest in the lives of Iraqis, and her refusal to become officially attached to a single military unit, as are most major U.S. journalists in Iraq, stemmed from her view of her mission in that country. "I think it's important to be here to tell the Iraqi side of the story in whatever way I could," Logan told Hal Boedeker for the *Orlando Sentinel* (April 13, 2003). "It's important that the American people get to understand the Iraqi people better. . . . If you only see the perspective from the American side, you won't understand why other people might feel differently. There's a widening gap between the West and the Muslims that's a danger to all of us." Logan did work as an "embedded" reporter (a journalist attached to one military unit) for later CBS reports, both in Iraq and Afghanistan. On one such occasion, in November 2003, while filming on the Afghan border near Pakistan, she came close to losing her life—when the Humvee in which she was riding ran over an antitank mine, sending the 5,200-pound vehicle hurtling eight feet forward and 12 feet in the air. Slightly injured, she went on to file a report on the story for CBS's *Early Show*. Logan's reporting from Iraq and Afghanistan contributed to her winning her fourth Gracie Award.

When *60 Minutes II* (for a time renamed *60 Minutes Wednesday*) was canceled, in mid-2005, Logan was reassigned to the original *60 Minutes*. Her first report for the program described the dangers faced by people traveling on the road to the airport in Baghdad. The ongoing conflict in Iraq and the related trial of its former leader, Saddam Hussein, have been primary subjects of her work since that time, despite the evident danger of her assignments. Logan pointed out to Gail Shister for the *Philadelphia Inquirer* (June 1, 2006) that as a television journalist she was particularly vulnerable. "Once the camera comes out, there's no secret about it," Logan said. "You can't blend in." At the end of May 2006 in Baghdad, two members of a CBS News crew were killed and another seriously injured when a car bomb exploded. Logan, who apparently was in South Africa at the time, was determined to return to Iraq. "I have a constant commitment to the story and to the people—my colleagues in the CBS bureau and my Iraqi colleagues," she told Shister. "I want to show my solidarity with them. . . . When you're invested in a place and in the people, every time you leave there, you feel like you're abandoning them." On February 2, 2006 Logan was named CBS's chief foreign correspondent. Since then she has reported on location about armed conflicts in Iraq, Afghanistan, Israel, and the Sudan.

Logan lives in London with her husband, Jason Siemon, an American, who until recently played professional basketball in the British Basketball League. The two married in December 1998, not long after they met. Logan has told interviewers that she hopes to have children someday and that she also would like to write a novel. She speaks three languages (English, Afrikaans, and French) fluently and knows some Portuguese.

—D.R.

Suggested Reading: Associated Press July 1, 2003; CBS News Web site; (London) *Sunday Telegraph* p3 June 2, 2002; *New York Times* E p1 Nov. 23, 2005

Magliozzi, Tom and Ray

Radio talk-show hosts; auto mechanics

Magliozzi, Tom
(molly-OTT-zee)
June 28, 1937–

Magliozzi, Ray
1949–

Address: P.O. Box 3500, Car Talk Plaza, Harvard Sq., Cambridge, MA 02238

To the more than four million listeners who tune in to hear them each weekend on National Public Radio (NPR), the colorful Bostonians Tom and Ray Magliozzi are better known as "Click and Clack, the Tappet Brothers," names inspired by the sounds of old automobiles. The Magliozzis host the immensely popular, nationally syndicated program *Car Talk*, which can be heard on close to 600 NPR stations worldwide. On their show the Magliozzis diagnose the various malfunctions of their audience's cars (sometimes after simply hearing a caller imitate the strange sounds his or her automobile is making), then give helpful tips for fixing the problems. The two are noted for their irreverence toward each other, their callers, and the automotive industry as well as their outspokenness about trends affecting U.S. drivers; for example, in 1999 the increase in the number of people who talk on mobile devices while driving goaded the *Car Talk* hosts into giving away bumper stickers that read, "Drive Now Talk Later." The hour-long *Car Talk* offers "advice about automobiles with a sassy aplomb reminiscent of the attitude evinced by the sisters Ann Landers and Abigail Van Buren," in the words of Stuart Elliot, writing for the *New York Times* (April 8, 1996). *Car Talk* began as a program on a local station in Boston, Massachusetts, in 1976 and was picked up by NPR nine years later; the Magliozzis' are now among the most recognizable voices on NPR's weekend programming. In October 2004 the brothers signed a contract with NPR and WBUR (the largest of three NPR affiliates in Boston) ensuring that *Car Talk* will be broadcast on public airwaves into 2009. The two write a twice-weekly column, also called "Car Talk," which is distributed by King Features Syndicate to some 330 newspapers nationwide as well as overseas. In 1992 the Magliozzis received a Peabody Award in recognition of their achievements. "They've become a great expression of American humor," Murray Horwitz, NPR's cultural programming director, said to Susan Diesenhouse for the *New York Times* (February 28, 1999). "And they really do know cars."

The oldest of three children, Thomas Louis Magliozzi (pronounced "molly-OTT-zee") was born to Louis and Elizabeth Magliozzi on June 28, 1937 in East Cambridge, Massachusetts, part of the greater Boston area. Tom, who grew up in a "gritty section" of the "erudite town" of Cambridge, in the words of Diesenhouse, has recalled his childhood environment fondly, writing for the *Car Talk* Web site, "This was the greatest neighborhood on the planet. Kids everywhere. Just hangin' out. Nothing much happened. Just good times." Diesenhouse reported that Tom and Raymond Magliozzi (born in 1949) became interested in cars during the 1950s, "when Tom did emergency repairs on his father's 1932 Chevy as Ray watched in awe." As a boy Tom attended the Gannett School (where his brother was later a student), the Wellington School, and the Cambridge High and Latin School, which is now known as the Cambridge Rindge and Latin School. After high school he enrolled at the Massachusetts Institute of Technology (MIT), in Cambridge, which he "hated," mostly because he "worked [his] butt off for four long years," he wrote for the *Car Talk* Web site. As a student he joined the U.S. Air Force Reserve Officers' Training Corps (ROTC) program. He graduated from MIT in 1958 with a degree in chemical engineering and economics.

Richard Howard

Tom (left) and Ray Magliozzi

Like his brother, Ray Magliozzi remembers a pleasant childhood, writing for the *Car Talk* Web site, "I had everything a kid could want: two square meals a day and a basket to sleep in and an imaginary dog." Tom and Ray have a sister, Lucille (younger than Tom and older than Ray), who works in music promotion and is unlike her siblings in that she is "likable, well mannered and successful," Ray said jokingly to Diesenhouse. Even as a boy Ray "loved to take things apart to see how they work," as he wrote for the *Car Talk* Web site. "That was my hobby." Growing up, Ray enjoyed watching Tom make repairs on the family's car and, later, his own cars, "which, as you might suspect," Ray wrote, "were complete junkboxes, veritable heaps of automobile refuse."

Ray Magliozzi also graduated from MIT, with a degree in science and humanities in 1972. Taking a year off from his studies during college, he joined Volunteers in Service to America (VISTA), traveling with the program to Texas, where "we did things like organize high school equivalency programs for adults, and some community organizing," he wrote. "It was pretty enlightening, all in all—basically we were radicals causing trouble." While in Norman, Oklahoma, with VISTA, Ray met a woman named Monique, whom he married shortly thereafter. After college Ray taught science at a junior high school in Bennington, Vermont, where he and Monique "froze our butts off," he recalled for the *Car Talk* Web site. "We couldn't wait to get out of there. Between the snow, the mud season, and the black flies, it was too much for us to handle."

Due to his involvement with the college ROTC program, after graduating from MIT Tom Magliozzi completed six months of military duty in Fort Dix, New Jersey. As a result of his outspokenness, he spent a great deal of his time there on kitchen patrol. (As he put it for the *Car Talk* Web site, "I was always in trouble because I couldn't shut up.") He next accepted a position with the lighting company Sylvania, working in its semiconductor division, in Woburn, Massachusetts. Approximately six months later he moved to the Foxboro Co. (which supplies instruments, systems, and services connected with industrial processes), located in Foxboro, Massachusetts, starting in the international division and later becoming the Far East administrator, a post that required him to travel to such places as Taiwan, Singapore, and the Philippines. While working at Foxboro Tom returned to school, receiving his M.B.A. degree, and began teaching part-time at universities near Cambridge. He was next promoted to the position of Foxboro's long-range planner.

After becoming frustrated with the long commute from Cambridge to Foxboro, which on one occasion involved an experience with a "tractor-trailer truck that almost did me in," Tom Magliozzi quit his job with the company and for about a year spent most of his time "hanging out in Harvard Square, drinking coffee," as he recalled. During that period he started a painting business, with the twofold intention of making a few extra dollars and meeting single women. To supplement his income he accepted a position as a teacher with the International Marketing Institute (IMI), which sent him to such places as Saudi Arabia and Kuala Lumpur, Malaysia, to train business managers.

Ray Magliozzi had become disenchanted with teaching in Vermont when he learned about Tom's idea for starting a do-it-yourself auto-repair shop, "where people could do their own work and we'd rent space and tools to them," as Ray wrote for the *Car Talk* Web site. The idea immediately appealed to Ray. Tom himself was initially reluctant to pursue it, for fear of compromising his cushy lifestyle. (Each brother has claimed that his own self-sacrifice, coupled with his brother's career dissatisfaction, allowed the do-it-yourself shop to get started.) In 1973 Tom and Ray Magliozzi opened Hacker's Haven—"hacker," at the time, being a popular term for one engaged in a particular pursuit without expert knowledge. The venture was unsuccessful at first, and Tom and Ray ended up performing the majority of the auto repairs themselves, for a fee of $2.50 an hour. By 1977, however, the business—renamed Good News Garage—had grown in popularity. Soon afterward it was converted into a full-service auto-repair station. (It is currently known as Ray's Garage.)

When the garage was in its infancy, Tom Magliozzi worked part-time at Technology Consulting Group, which was owned by a friend and located in Boston. He also began working toward his doctorate at Boston University, where he spent the next nine years "busting my cookies sitting at my computer day and night writing my dissertation," as he wrote for the *Car Talk* Web site. After receiving his Ph.D., Tom taught marketing and other subjects at Boston and Suffolk Universities for eight years before reaching what he called "a miraculous epiphany: Teaching sucks."

Meanwhile, in 1977 the Magliozzis and a handful of other mechanics were invited by Vic Wheatman, then the program director of Boston University's public radio station, WBUR-FM, to field listeners' questions during the broadcast of a call-in radio show focusing on auto repair. Tom Magliozzi, the only mechanic who showed up for the broadcast, was asked to return the following week for the airing of another, similar show. Upon doing so he learned that Wheatman had been fired, and he received a note instructing him to proceed with the broadcast. The following week Tom brought in Ray to help with the program, and the current format of *Car Talk* was born.

According to the *Car Talk* Web site, in the show's early stages, Tom and Ray Magliozzi "answered a lot of questions like, 'I'm stuck with my left arm in the transmission, how do I get it out?' and, 'I lost a three-eighths hex wrench taking off the cylinder head, but I can't bend down to pick it up because I have the timing chain in my right hand—could you send your brother over to help me?'" The Magliozzis were not paid by WBUR for their services during the first two years *Car Talk* aired locally, but later they were given a modest compensation. In the beginning the program aired for 90 minutes each week; by the summer of 1986, *Car Talk* was drawing an estimated 11,500 listeners and had become the third-most-popular show

on WBUR, behind two prominent NPR newscasts. With *Car Talk* established as a hit on local radio, NPR began searching for creative ways to expand its audience, and in January 1987 Susan Stamberg, then the host of the NPR program *Sunday Weekend Edition*, invited the Magliozzis to tape a regular segment for her show. In June 1987 *Newsweek* reported that *Car Talk* was attracting a listenership in the greater Boston area of between 15,000 and 20,000 listeners each week.

Car Talk began reaching most parts of the U.S. on October 31, 1987. By April 1988 the show could be found on 90 U.S. public-radio stations. Also in 1988 Tom and Ray appeared on the *Tonight Show with Johnny Carson*, with Jay Leno serving as the guest host. In the 1990s *Car Talk* continued to grow in popularity, serving, for example, as an inspiration for the short-lived 1995 NBC program *The George Wendt Show*, for which the Magliozzis were consultants. In November 1995 the *Boston Globe* reported that 370 NPR stations had picked up *Car Talk* and that the show was reaching two million listeners each week. In 1998 the brothers were inducted into the Radio Hall of Fame. The show currently attracts more than 4.5 million listeners weekly and can be heard on approximately 600 NPR stations, according to the *Washington Post* (May 4, 2005, on-line).

In 1989 (some sources say 1992), with the aim of achieving some autonomy from WBUR, the Magliozzis founded Dewey, Cheatham, and Howe (pronounced "do we cheat 'em, and how"), a production company with offices in Harvard Square, in Cambridge. The Magliozzis appointed Doug Berman to lead the new entity and were granted final say over, and ownership of, *Car Talk*'s editorial content. In 1989 the two began writing a twice-weekly newspaper column for King Features Syndicate that, like their radio show, includes automotive advice. The Magliozzis launched a Web site in 1996 that is visited by some 400,000 people each week. They have also written several books, including *Car Talk: with Click and Clack, the Tappet Brothers* (1991), *A Haircut in Horse Town . . . and Other Great Car Talk Puzzlers* (1999), and *In Our Humble Opinion: Car Talk's Click and Clack Rant and Rave* (2000).

The Magliozzis have often used their show as a forum for sounding off about trends among auto companies or U.S. drivers. In 2002 the Magliozzis attempted to stem the proliferation of gas-guzzling sport-utility vehicles (SUVs) in the U.S., teaming with Stonyfield Farm, an environmentally conscious yogurt company, to create the slogan "Live Larger, Drive Smaller." The slogan was to be placed on bumper stickers and the lids of Stonyfield Farm products, but NPR, whose initials were slated to appear alongside the slogan, prevented the stickers' distribution, citing reservations about advocating a potentially controversial position. "Everyone knows that S.U.V.s are big," Tom Magliozzi told Jane Mayer for the *New Yorker* (September 2, 2002), "they block everyone's view, they get five miles to the gallon, they roll over and kill people, and when you get hit by one the bumper comes right in your window and takes your head off."

A number of observers have tried to identify the source of *Car Talk*'s popularity. "The point of *Car Talk*, it turns out," according to Elizabeth Kolbert, writing for the *New York Times* (April 5, 1993), "is not to talk about cars, but to have fun: fun at the expense of people who make cars, people who buy them, people who ask for advice about them, and, above all, people who pretend to give out such advice over the radio." Kolbert added that the show's hosts speak in "a pure Bostonese that sounds a lot like a truck running over vowels." Susan Diesenhouse wrote, "[The Magliozzis] offer a weekly hour of general silliness sandwiched between car advice, automotive puzzlers and relentless irreverence (directed toward the callers as well as each other.)" David Hosley, a former station manager of KQED-FM, the NPR affiliate that airs *Car Talk* in San Francisco, California, told Laura Mansnerus for the *New York Times* (May 25, 1988), "The people who grew up in Boston and New York like it. My own sense of it is that it's East Coast humor. It's this intense, yammering humor. Part of its wonderfulness is its Italianness. I think Italians think it's an Italian thing, people who are Jewish think it's Jewish, people who are Greek think it's Greek: everybody sitting around the table talking at once."

Tom Magliozzi is responsible for organizing and writing the bulk of the content for the radio show's Web site. He also runs his own consulting business and still does odd jobs, such as painting. He has been married several times and has two daughters

and a son. Tom Magliozzi does not drive regularly; according to the show's Web site, the last car he owned was a 1952 MG TD. Ray Magliozzi is the shorter and stockier of the Magliozzi brothers. (Diesenhouse reported that Ray is "the teddy bear of the pair," while Tom is "a bit more of a grizzly.") Ray and his wife, Monique, have two grown children, Louis and Andrew. Ray continues to service cars at Ray's Garage, in Cambridge. In his spare time he enjoys gardening and woodworking. He is also a member of the National Car Care Council. The Magliozzis do not claim a high rate of success in helping their audience members; their popularity may simply result, as Bill Barol and Sue Hutchinson wrote for *Newsweek* (June 1, 1987), from the fact they "understand Americans' love-hate relationship with cars."

—D.F.

Suggested Reading: *Boston Globe* C p1 Jan. 12, 2005; *Car Talk* Web site; *New York Times* C p1 May 25, 1988, C p13 Apr. 5, 1993, II p43 Feb. 28, 1999; *Washington Post* (on-line) May 4, 2005

Selected Radio Shows: *Car Talk*, 1977–

Selected Books: *Car Talk: with Click and Clack, the Tappet Brothers* (with Terry Bisson), 1991; *A Haircut in Horse Town . . . and Other Great Car Talk Puzzlers* (with Doug Berman), 1999; *In Our Humble Opinion: Car Talk's Click and Clack Rant and Rave*, 2000

Marcus, George E.

Oct. 17, 1946– Anthropologist

Address: Anthropology Dept., University of California, Irvine, CA 92697–5100

During the course of his 30 years with the Anthropology Department at Rice University, George E. Marcus spearheaded what Piper Fogg and Eric Wills referred to in the *Chronicle of Higher Education* (August 5, 2005) as "a revolution within his discipline." Largely on the strength of his two volumes of critical essays—*Writing Culture: The Poetics and Politics of Ethnography* (1986), co-edited with James Clifford, and *Anthropology as Cultural Critique: An Experimental Moment in the Human Sciences* (1986), written with Michael M. J. Fischer—Marcus helped transform anthropology, the study of human beings and their cultures, from a field that focused primarily on studies of isolated communities into a comparative discourse on the nature of societies, placing an unprecedented emphasis on modern Western society. According to

Fogg and Wills, "Now, instead of studying just the local traditions of people who have lived in one place for hundreds of years, cultural anthropologists look at how communities evolve and cope with contemporary influences, such as financial markets and modern warfare." Marcus's most recent book is *Ocasião: The Marquis and the Anthropologist, a Collaboration* (2005). In mid-2005 Marcus joined the faculty of the University of California at Irvine as a Chancellor's Professor in the School of Social Sciences.

George E. Marcus was born on October 17, 1946, in Pittsburgh, Pennsylvania, to Samuel and Rose (Shriber) Marcus. He graduated magna cum laude from Yale University, in New Haven, Connecticut, in 1968, with bachelor's degrees in politics and economics. After studying for a year at Queens' College at the University of Cambridge, in England, he served briefly in the U.S. Army. He then enrolled in the anthropology doctoral program at Harvard University, in Cambridge, Massachusetts. There he followed what he described for *Anthropological Quarterly* (Summer 2005) as "the usual apprentice model" of anthropology, studying in-

Courtesy of the University of California, Irvine

George E. Marcus

own social, political and literary history" and were inclined "to study people with less power and status than themselves." In March 1979 he attended a seminar entitled "Anthropological Perspectives on Elites in Complex Societies" at the School of American Research in Santa Fe, New Mexico. Marcus edited a collection of essays that emanated from the seminar: *Elites, Ethnographic Issues* (1983), which included both discussions of theoretical issues and case studies from the U.S., Sicily, and India.

In 1984 Marcus returned to the School of American Research to participate in a seminar entitled "The Making of Ethnographic Texts." Many of the participants—most of whom were experienced ethnographers—shared Marcus's concerns; the result was a collection of essays, *Writing Culture: The Poetics and Politics of Ethnography*, which Marcus co-edited with James Clifford. According to a *Washington Post* (May 4, 1986) reviewer, "This volume sets out to answer the question [of] why ethnography is now suspect, more particularly why anthropologists seem to have lost their confidence in their ability to sum up other cultures with some claim to attaining objective truth. The answer formulated by anthropologists steeped in deconstructionism and post-modernist literature lies in acceptance of the reality that 'ethnographic truths are . . . inherently partial'—much, one supposes, like the rest of human knowledge." Credited by some with giving rise to postmodern anthropology, *Writing Culture* became "influential but incendiary" among anthropologists, as Stephen Phillips put it in the *Times Higher Education Supplement* (December 20, 2002), because many in the field believed that it "impugned anthropology's scientific efficacy with its thesis that ethnographies are narrative fictions." While *Writing Culture*—which has since been translated into Japanese, Italian, Chinese, Korean, and Croatian—was addressed to social scientists, H. Leedom Lefferts, writing for *Science Books & Films* (January/February 1987), noted that for lay audiences, "the volume presents a rare, considered introduction to the complexities of social scientific thinking about our own and other cultures."

Marcus cemented his reputation with the publication of *Anthropology as Cultural Critique* (1986), which he co-authored with Michael M. J. Fischer. In the introduction the authors explained that in a "time of reassessment of dominant ideas across the human sciences," their book was primarily concerned with what they described as "a crisis of representation," which "arises from uncertainty about adequate means of describing social reality." Noting the similarity between the attitude of superiority among colonial powers and the assumption of objectivity among ethnographers, the authors argued that anthropologists should be recast as cultural critics who seek to determine underlying assumptions in their own cultures. Marcus explained to Daniel Goleman for the *New York Times* (April 2, 1991) the value of this approach: "The

digenous peoples in Tonga, a nation comprising 150 islands in Polynesia. Marcus wrote that his fieldwork "was shaped categorically through basic concerns with kinship, ritual, politics, and religion by means of resident inquiry in local communities." From those studies he produced a string of often-cited publications throughout the 1970s and early 1980s, including his first book, *Nobility and the Chiefly Tradition in the Modern Kingdom of Tonga* (1980). When Marcus earned his doctorate, in 1976, he had already begun working as an associate professor at Rice University, in Houston, Texas. In 1980 he rose to the position of associate professor and became chair of the university's Anthropology Department. He was promoted to full professor in 1985.

At the time of Marcus's entry into the field, the discipline of cultural anthropology was largely concerned with studying the characteristics of small, isolated communities—"basic 'people and places' ethnographic research," as Marcus described it for *Anthropological Quarterly* (Summer 2005). That traditional approach was embodied by Margaret Mead's influential book *Coming of Age in Samoa* (1928), which "was meant to teach Americans about their own society through the study of another way of life," as Hymie Rubenstein wrote for *Anthropologica* (December 1995). Marcus, in his article for *Anthropological Quarterly*, noted that "the special task of social and cultural anthropology" then was "to describe and analyze forms of life that were, if not pre-modern, then nonmodern." Marcus also observed, according to a press release posted on the Web site of the University of California at Irvine, that anthropologists "typically frame their thoughts according to their idea is to use ethnographic methods to touch a nerve, to raise questions for the people studied themselves, so that the scientists, bankers, lawyers or whoever the subjects happen to be can't shrug it off as the work of someone who doesn't know their world."

In a blurb on the back cover of the book's first edition, the anthropologist David Schneider praised *Anthropology as Cultural Critique* as a "remarkable and very important book" that "considers the present state of anthropology, situating that state in its recent history and in relation to other social sciences—economics, politics, sociology, history—and, most importantly, to the major features of the social and intellectual scene—art, literature, literary criticism, cultural criticism, relativism, and the various states of *Zeitgeist* from the 1900s through today." According to Schneider, the book is "not merely . . . about anthropology but is in the widest sense about the major features of the intellectual climate of today." David Brent, then the editor in chief of the University of Chicago Press, which published *Anthropology as Cultural Critique*, told Goleman that the book "caused a sensation in the field" upon its initial publication and sold unusually well.

In 1992, after having conducted ethnographic research on two families in Galveston, Texas—the Kempners and the Moodys—Marcus published *Lives in Trust: The Fortunes of Dynastic Families in Late Twentieth-Century America*, an ethnographic account of wealthy American families; it also includes an essay on the Rockefeller family by the historian Peter Dobkin Hall. Eschewing the standard narrative of the triumphant magnate and his kin, Marcus and Hall attempted to "decenter" the discussion by examining the larger social implications of the institutions established by the families. "The imperative of perpetuating their fortunes, Marcus and Hall argue, led the patriarchs of the first and second generations to look for help outside the family itself," Michael McGerr wrote for *American Historical Review* (October 1994). "As a result, wealth typically became separated from family members through the creation of trusts and foundations managed by outsiders. The dynasty was not simply the family, but rather a whole apparatus of legal institutions and cultural images. In effect, the family took on a life apart from itself."

In 1998 Marcus published a collection of his essays, entitled *Ethnography through Thick and Thin*. In a review for the *American Anthropologist* (March 2000), Fred R. Myers wrote that the essays "provide an important and timely statement, both for anthropology as a discipline currently and as a comment on contemporary knowledge production." He continued, "Neither moralistic nor judgmental, Marcus builds his argument for the necessity and value of 'multi-site ethnography' and 'experimental writing,' not so much from a simple claim about what should and what shouldn't be, but rather from a consideration of what actual practitioners are doing and what these practices might

mean. . . . Marcus provides the strongest, most original reinvention of the field I have seen. . . . The ways in which he explores the values of ethnographic research and the changing conditions of knowledge production are both innovative and illuminating. It is difficult to imagine any syllabus for the field that will not include some of these essays in presenting the possibilities of a contemporary anthropology." Glenn Petersen wrote for *Library Journal* (February 1, 1999) that the essays "are mostly about the business of anthropology and as such are more pertinent to the realms of sociology and intellectual history than to traditional social and cultural anthropology," and thus would have little appeal for laypeople.

Marcus has edited and co-edited many volumes, among them *Rereading Cultural Anthropology* (1992), *The Traffic in Culture: Refiguring Art and Anthropology* (with Fred R. Myers, 1995), and *Critical Anthropology Now: Unexpected Contexts, Shifting Constituencies, and Changing Agendas* (1999). From 1994 to 2000 he also edited eight volumes for the series Late Editions: Cultural Studies for the End of the Century, published by the University of Chicago Press. That fin de siècle series addresses the challenges likely to face the field of cultural studies in the 21st century. Marie Gillespie described the series for the *Journal of the Royal Anthropological Institute* (December 1999) as "the product of an ongoing experiment in research and writing, with cultural and political activist intentions," that is "powered by a hyper-anxiety about the epistemological and political crisis that has shaken anthropology." Marcus has also written many articles for academic journals; in 1986 he founded *Cultural Anthropology*, the official journal of the Society for Cultural Anthropology. He served as one of its editors until 1991. His most recent book, *Ocasião: The Marquis and the Anthropologist, a Collaboration* (2005), offers letters and commentaries exchanged between Marcus and a member of the Portuguese nobility, Fernando Mascarenhas, Marques of Fronteira and Alorna.

In 2005, after spending a year as a visiting fellow at Stanford University's Center for Advanced Study in the Behavioral Sciences, Marcus announced that he was leaving Rice University, where he had headed the Anthropology Department for 25 years, to join the University of California at Irvine (U.C.-Irvine) as a Chancellor's Professor in the School of Social Sciences. "With my new colleagues," Marcus was quoted as saying in a press release posted on the latter school's Web site, "I'm hoping to continue contributing to the reinvention of my field's research approach, so that it will make the valuable interventions it always has, but in radically changing intellectual and social environments." In 2006 Marcus became a board member of U.C.-Irvine's newly created Center for Ethnography, which was created, according to its Web site, to "support innovative collaborative ethnographic research as well as research on the theoretical and methodological refunctioning of ethnography for contemporary cultural, social and technological transformations."

Marcus has been married to the historian Patricia Seed since 1984. The couple have a son and a daughter.

—R.E.

Suggested Reading: *Chronicle of Higher Education* p7 Aug. 5, 2005; *New York Times* C p1+ Feb. 20, 1990, C p1+ Apr. 2, 1991; *Journal of the Royal Anthropological Institute* p678 Dec. 1, 1999

Selected Books: *Nobility and the Chiefly Tradition in the Modern Kingdom of Tonga*, 1980; *Anthropology as Cultural Critique: An Experimental Moment in the Human Sciences* (with Michael M. J. Fischer), 1986; *Lives in Trust: The Fortunes of Dynastic Families in Late Twentieth-Century America* (with Peter Dobkin Hall), 1992; *Ethnography through Thick and Thin*, 1998; *Ocasião: The Marquis and the*

Anthropologist, a Collaboration (with Fernando Mascarenhas), 2005; as editor or co-editor— *Elites, Ethnographic Issues*, 1983; *Writing Culture: The Poetics and Politics of Ethnography* (with James Clifford), 1986; *Rereading Cultural Anthropology*, 1992; *Perilous States: Conversations on Culture, Politics, and Nation*, 1994; *Technoscientific Imaginaries: Conversations, Profiles, and Memoirs*, 1995; *The Traffic in Culture: Refiguring Art and Anthropology* (with Fred R. Myers), 1995; *Connected: Engagements with Media*, 1996; *Cultural Producers in Perilous States: Editing Events, Documenting Change*, 1997; *Corporate Futures: The Diffusion of the Culturally Sensitive Corporate Form*, 1998; *Critical Anthropology Now: Unexpected Contexts, Shifting Constituencies, and Changing Agendas*, 1999; *Paranoia within Reason: A Casebook on Conspiracy as Explanation*, 1999; *Para-Sites: A Casebook against Cynical Reason*, 2000; *Zeroing in on the Year 2000*, 2000

Martin, Jesse L.

Jan. 18, 1969– Actor

Address: c/o NBC Studios, 30 Rockefeller Plaza, New York, NY 10112

Each week since 1999, millions of viewers have watched Jesse L. Martin in his role as Detective Ed Green on the acclaimed NBC crime drama *Law & Order*. Prior to joining the cast of that show, Martin won attention in the mid- and late 1990s with his performance as Tom Collins in the hit Broadway musical *Rent* and his appearances as Greg Butters, the love interest of the title character in the popular television show *Ally McBeal*. Martin, who is six feet two inches tall with leading-man looks, told Nick Chiles for *Savoy* (November 2002) that he is "flattered" to be called a sex symbol, "and if that's the reason I keep working, I'm down with that, too. You gotta take that stuff with a grain of salt. . . . I'm not one of those actors who needs to be in the latest blockbuster film. As long as I have a job where I'm comfortable doing what I'm doing, I'm cool."

The third of five brothers, the actor was born Jesse Lamont Watkins (his family calls him Lamont) on January 18, 1969 in Rocky Mount, Virginia, a small town in the Blue Ridge Mountains. His mother, Virginia Price, was a college career counselor, and his father, Jesse Reed Watkins, was a truck driver. His parents divorced when he was very young, and his mother moved with the children to Buffalo, New York. Upon their mother's remarriage, the children took their stepfather's last name, Martin. In Buffalo Martin attended Public School 27, where he was afraid to speak in front of

Vince Bucci/Getty Images

his classmates. "I had a very thick accent and was a very shy kid. Everyone thought I was some kind of quiet hillbilly," he recalled to Cindy Pearlman for the *Chicago Sun-Times* (November 20, 2005). When he was in the fourth grade, his teacher suggested that he act in the school play, *The Golden Goose*. "Me being this sort of naive country boy, I knew it meant staying after school, and I knew that meant trouble; so I was scared to do it," he told Julie Hinds for the *San Jose (California) Mercury News* (June 4, 1999). Martin overcame his fears, as he recounted to Ken Tucker for *Entertainment Weekly* (November 12, 1999): "I was the pastor, which I associated with a brimstone-and-fire, Southern Baptist sort of preacher, so that's the way I played it. None of the white kids there had ever seen anything like that, and everyone was impressed, thought it was very funny. I got so much positive feedback, I knew I was on my way to being a performer."

Martin next attended the magnet school Campus West, at Buffalo State College, and he spent his high-school years at the Buffalo Academy for the Visual and Performing Arts. When Martin was 16 he and a friend drove to Brockport, New York, to audition for a summer production of *West Side Story*. Martin was cast in the show, to the exasperation of his mother. "When I told my mom, she freaked because she'd be the one to drive me back and forth all summer, and she worked and was in school and needed me at home to help out," Martin explained to Maria Pascucci for the *Buffalo News* (November 28, 2004). "But she did it anyway, and I'll love her forever for that." When Martin interned at the Shakespeare in the Park festival one summer, his friends were scornful of his activities. "My friends used to call me 'Shakespeare' and laugh at me for going to work all summer while they were playing football," Martin recalled to Maria Pascucci. "Don't get me wrong, I like football, but I knew what I was doing. . . . I took the abuse, but I would think, 'One day you'll see.'" After graduating from high school, in 1987, Martin was accepted at New York University, in New York City, where he studied drama. He worked multiple jobs to pay his tuition. He was ultimately unable to graduate, because his schoolwork took too much time away from his jobs—"and I couldn't afford not to work," he told Martha Frankel for *Cosmopolitan* (May 1, 2001). Upon leaving college Martin began auditioning for parts in plays, films, and television. To support himself he held a variety of jobs, which included washing dishes, waiting tables, bartending, peeling onions (his least favorite occupation), and working at the department store Macy's, where he sprayed female shoppers with perfume.

Martin's first acting jobs included bit parts in the Broadway productions of *Timon of Athens* (1993) and *The Government Inspector* (1994) and a single-episode role on the television show *New York Undercover* (1995). In 1996, though he initially told his agent that he did not want to appear in a musical, Martin took on a role in *Rent*, written by Jonathan Larson. A modernized version of Puccini's opera *La Bohème*, *Rent* told the story of a group of young artists and performers struggling with poverty, love, drug addiction, and AIDS while living in New York City's East Village. *Rent* was unusual in its frank depiction of homosexual relationships and the AIDS crisis. On the night of the final dress rehearsal for *Rent*, Larson died of an aortic aneurysm. As the cast member who had had the lengthiest relationship with Larson, Martin

was deeply saddened by the writer's unexpected death. "Jonathan trained me as a waiter at the Moondance diner down in SoHo," he told Patricia O'Haire for the New York *Daily News* (March 3, 1996). "He'd worked there 10 years, I lasted four days. He said the happiest day of his life was when he was able to quit that job." *Rent* won five Tony Awards, the New York Drama Critics Circle Award for best musical, six Drama Desk Awards, three Obie Awards, and the 1996 Pulitzer Prize for drama, among other honors. In the *New York Times* (February 14, 1996), Ben Brantley called Martin and his fellow cast members "performers of both wit and emotional conviction." Reviewing a performance in London, England, Matt Wolf enthused in *Variety* (May 18–24, 1998), "Playing Tom Collins, [the character] Angel's computer genius boyfriend, Jesse L. Martin impresses with a sincerity that never once becomes stolid: His reprise of the wrenching 'I'll Cover You' emerges tearfully from someplace within."

While appearing as an HIV-positive man in *Rent*, Martin also played an AIDS counselor in the TV drama *413 Hope St.*, which aired during the 1997–98 season on the Fox network. Later in 1998 Martin was cast as Quincy, a line cook in a bar and grill, in the movie *Restaurant*. His character "has a little problem getting out of a rut," Martin commented to Julie Hinds. "He realizes he's sort of stuck in this restaurant that has its good days and bad days, but it's never going to change." The film did not receive much exposure but earned respectable reviews. Meanwhile, Martin's performance in *Rent* led to his winning another role. David E. Kelley, the producer of the comedy series *Ally McBeal*, and his wife, the actress Michelle Pfeiffer, had seen the musical, and when Martin sent his audition tape to Kelley, Pfeiffer recognized the actor. Upon his wife's recommendation, Kelley cast Martin in *Ally McBeal* as Dr. Greg Butters, the boyfriend of the title character, a neurotic lawyer played by Calista Flockhart. In 1998 and 1999 Martin appeared in 11 episodes of the series. Martin was happy that, while he is African-American and Flockhart is white, that aspect of their characters' relationship was not treated on the show as a significant issue. "Everybody in the world can see that I'm black and that she's white, but it doesn't mean there's a problem there," Martin commented to Kevin D. Thompson for the *Palm Beach (Florida) Post* (September 22, 1999). Also in 1999 the actor appeared in an episode of *The X-Files* and in the made-for-television movie *Deep in My Heart*.

That year, in addition, Martin got the chance to fulfill a longstanding desire. He explained to Thompson, "If you talk to any New York actor, *Law & Order* is one of those shows you've either been on or want to be on." Martin had not been on NBC's long-running, critically acclaimed police and courtroom drama. Although he had once been offered a small, single-episode part as a car-radio thief, he had turned it down, preferring to hold out for a more substantial role. When, years later, he heard that the actor Benjamin Bratt was leaving the series, he jumped at the opportunity to replace Bratt. "I called my agent, got an interview with [the series' creator,] Dick Wolf, and basically begged him for the role, said I'd read with anyone, do anything," Martin recollected to Ken Tucker. Martin impressed Wolf, who cast him as Ed Green, a passionate, even hotheaded young detective. In his new role, Martin joined a distinguished cast that included Sam Waterston as Executive Assistant District Attorney Jack McCoy and Jerry Orbach as Green's partner, Detective Lennie Briscoe. Martin was nervous about becoming the newest member of an already established cast. "The first scene we were shooting, all I had to do was walk to a file cabinet, pull out a file and say a line," Martin recalled in an interview with Sharon Rainsbury for the Melbourne, Australia, *Sunday Herald Sun* (April 30, 2000). "But I was so nervous that when I went to grab the file my hand was shaking like crazy. I could never get the line out. It was so embarrassing." Soon, though, Martin developed a rapport with his fellow actors, particularly Orbach and S. Epatha Merkerson (who plays Lieutenant Anita Van Buren), both veteran stage performers themselves. "We sing here, literally non-stop," Martin told Sharon Rainsbury. "Epatha and Jerry know every song in the world. So someone will start a song and the next thing you know we are all in for three-part harmony—it's great." In December 2004 Orbach died of prostate cancer. Noting that Orbach had been an integral part of *Law & Order*, Martin told Lewis Beale for *Newsday* (November 23, 2005), "I honestly couldn't imagine [the show] going on. I knew it was going to, but I couldn't imagine why or how . . . Jerry made the show. I couldn't imagine anyone taking Jerry's place." Soon afterward the show's producers hired Dennis Farina to replace Orbach, a choice that met with Martin's approval. The actor told Lewis Beale, "Jerry would OK this. [Farina is] a class act all the way, fun to hang out with and we have a great rapport." (It was announced in the spring of 2006 that Farina was leaving the cast of *Law & Order*.)

Since he began his tenure on *Law & Order*, Martin has become a much-recognized presence on the streets of New York City, where the series is filmed. While he generally enjoys the attention (actual police officers often praise his performance), he has expressed bemusement over some aspects of his fame, telling Rainsbury, for example, that some people write to him with "ridiculous requests—can we get married, or we don't have to get married but I would love to have your child . . . I don't really know what to say to that."

In between filming episodes of *Law & Order*, Martin has worked on several other projects. In 2002 he appeared in the film *Burning House of Love*, and the following year he played another policeman, in the movie *Season of Youth*. Martin next did what Robert Bianco described in *USA Today* (November 26, 2004) as "a show-stopping musical hall turn as the Ghost of Christmas Present"

in a television version of Charles Dickens's *A Christmas Carol*. While Bianco praised the NBC special as a "cinematic cup of Christmas cheer," other critics were less favorably impressed. Writing for the *Boston Globe* (November 27, 2004), Matthew Gilbert dubbed the project "a cup of no-fat eggnog sipped to the accompaniment of jaunty, generic stage music."

Martin's next project—a film version of *Rent*—had taken nearly a decade to come to fruition. When the director, Chris Columbus, began work on the production, he invited nearly all of the original cast members to reprise their roles in the movie. "I would have been devastated if I [weren't] in the film," Martin confessed to Cindy Pearlman. (He needed to take a leave of absence from *Law & Order* for the duration of the filming. Explaining how his character's absence was handled on the show, Martin told Pearlman, "NBC was so great. They let me get shot . . . in the chest"—a plot development that allowed for a lengthy, off-screen recuperation period for Detective Green. While the movie *Rent* was a labor of love on the part of the cast members, critics were less affectionate toward it. In a representative review, Jorge Morales complained in the *Village Voice* (November 29, 2005) that the film "is not an update so much as a throwback. . . . Instead of bringing a universal love story to the living present, the film traps it in a frozen past like a prehistoric bug in amber, as removed from moviegoers' experience as a dusty diorama at the American Museum of Natural History." Morales, like many reviewers, expressed mixed feelings about the cast: "While I welcomed the familiar faces like old friends, it's been a long decade—part of me wanted to yell at the screen, 'You're pushing 40! Get a job!'" For his part, Martin disagreed. "I was too young to play the part when I played it on Broadway," he told Lewis Beale. "The initial idea for the role of [the character] Tom Collins was he was the oldest one in the bunch." Moreover, he firmly believed that the messages of *Rent* remained relevant, though some of the plot details were specific to the 1990s. "Let me just put it this way: Isn't it relevant to say in these times that love is still the most important thing in the world?" he asked Cindy Pearlman rhetorically. "Isn't it relevant to say that love is still the only thing most people are willing to die for and fight for—and love is the only thing in this world that's still free?"

Martin, who is single and lives in New York, continues to appear in *Law & Order* and, occasionally, its offshoots, *Law & Order: Special Victims Unit*, *Law & Order: Criminal Intent*, and *Law & Order: Trial by Jury*. He is one of only four actors who have played the same characters on all four shows. Martin is also involved with charitable work and sits on the board of trustees of the Jonathan Larson Performing Arts Foundation. He told Lewis Beale in 2005 that his dream was to portray the late soul singer Marvin Gaye, to whom, many have remarked, the actor bears a strong resemblance. "I think Marvin's music is beautiful and incredible, and I have such an affinity for it," he said. "I would do anything to be able to sing those words. And he was such a complex person; what a great character to play. There's so much there." Martin is reportedly preparing a one-man show about the singer. In addition, he was given the starring role in a biographical movie about Gaye, written and directed by the independent filmmaker Lauren Goodman. Tentatively titled "Sexual Healing" (the name of one of Gaye's best-selling singles), the picture is scheduled for release in 2007.

—K.J.E.

Suggested Reading: *Buffalo (New York) News* H p1 Nov. 28, 2000; *Entertainment Weekly* p33 Nov. 12, 1999; Internet Broadway Database;

(Melbourne, Australia) *Sunday Herald Sun* X p4 Apr. 30, 2000; *Palm Beach (Florida) Post* D p4 Sep. 22, 1999

Selected Films: *Restaurant*, 1998; *Burning House of Love*, 2002; *Rent*, 2005

Selected Television Shows: *413 Hope St.*, 1997; *Ally McBeal*, 1998-99; *The X-Files*, 1999; *Deep in My Heart*, 1999; *Law & Order*, 1999–; *A Christmas Carol*, 2004

Selected Plays: *Timon of Athens*, 1993; *The Government Inspector*, 1994; *Rent*, 1996–98

Peter Kramer/Getty Images

McCain, John S.

NOTE: An earlier article about John S. McCain appeared in *Current Biography* in 1989.

Aug. 29, 1936– U.S. senator from Arizona (Republican)

Address: 241 Russell Senate Office Bldg., Washington, DC 20510

In 1982, only one year after he settled in Arizona, John S. McCain rose from relative obscurity to win the first of two terms as a Republican member of the U.S. House of Representatives, and in 1986 he was elected to the Senate to succeed the retiring senator Barry M. Goldwater. McCain's popularity stemmed in large part from his heroism during the Vietnam War, for McCain holds the unenviable distinction of being the most severely injured pilot ever to withstand the rigors of a North Vietnamese prison camp. The strength of character that he displayed in surviving over five years as a prisoner of war, often tortured and most of the time in solitary confinement, and his ability to put the remnants of his life back together so quickly after that ordeal, won the admiration of Arizonans. Although proud of his service in Vietnam and grateful for the impetus it has given his political career, McCain prefers not to dwell on it. "I don't want to be the POW senator," he told Susan F. Rasky for the *New York Times* (August 9, 1988). "What I've tried to do is position myself so that if opportunities come along, I'm qualified and ready."

Now in his fourth term in the U.S. Senate, McCain sees his mission, according to the Web site for his 2004 reelection campaign, as being to "make government smaller and reduce federal spending, so American families have the freedom to chart their own course and small business can create new opportunities." Despite such traditionally Republican goals, he has ruffled the feathers of the more conservative elements in his party with his refusal to toe the line on a number of issues and with his insistence on pushing through campaign-finance reform. Indeed, McCain is, according to the *Economist* (June 18, 2005), "every American liberal's favourite Republican"—so much so that Senator John Kerry, the 2004 Democratic presidential nominee, courted McCain as a potential running mate. McCain, who lost to George W. Bush in his 2000 bid for the Republican presidential nomination, has remained noncommittal regarding his plans for the 2008 race. Many observers, however, view his recent triumph in passing anti-torture legislation, despite resistance from the White House, as an indication that he may have the cachet with moderates in both major parties to pull off a victory in the next presidential election.

John Sidney McCain 3d was born on August 29, 1936 in the Panama Canal Zone to John S. McCain Jr. and Roberta (Wright) McCain. He comes from a long line of military commanders dating back to Captain William Young, an ancestor who served on the staff of General George Washington during the American Revolution. His paternal grandfather, Admiral John S. McCain, was commander of all the aircraft carriers in the Pacific during World War II. His father, also an admiral, was commander in chief of all United States armed forces in the Pacific during the Vietnam War. The two were the first father and son in navy history to become full admirals. McCain has a sister, Jean (McCain) Flather, and a younger brother, Joseph Pinckney McCain.

McCain grew up at various naval bases in the United States and abroad with the assumption that he would follow in the family's military tradition. On graduating from Episcopal High School in Alexandria, Virginia, in 1954, he entered the United States Naval Academy at Annapolis. Although his grades as an electrical-engineering student there were satisfactory, he drew so many demerits for breaking curfew and other infractions that he graduated fifth from the bottom of the class of 1958. He was commissioned an ensign and, despite his low class standing, was granted his request for a training slot as a navy pilot.

During the Vietnam War, McCain flew carrier-based attack planes on dangerously low-altitude bombing runs against North Vietnamese positions. On July 29, 1967 he was sitting in the cockpit of his A-4 Skyhawk awaiting takeoff from the deck of the carrier *Forrestal* when his fuel tank was struck by an errant rocket from one of the other bombers. The resulting chain of explosions and fire killed 130 crewmen and disabled the ship. McCain, who somehow escaped without serious injury, promptly requested transfer to the carrier *Oriskany* while the *Forrestal* underwent repairs.

Less than three months later, on October 26, McCain, by then a lieutenant commander, took off from the *Oriskany* on his 23d air mission, his first against the North Vietnamese capital of Hanoi. Directly over the city, the aircraft's right wing was sheared off by a North Vietnamese surface-to-air missile, and McCain was forced to eject. He plunged into a lake, breaking both arms and his right leg. Fished out by Vietnamese onlookers, he was dragged ashore before an angry crowd of thousands that had by then gathered at the crash site. There, he was beaten and stabbed twice before being taken into custody. For five days he was denied medical attention, but when authorities learned that his father was a high-ranking naval officer, he was taken to a hospital and assigned a cellmate to nurse him back to health.

Five months later McCain, though weak, was able to get about on crutches. His cellmate was removed, and McCain spent the next three and a half years in solitary confinement. Meanwhile, the Vietnamese, who tried to exploit the status of Mc-Cain (whom they called the "crown prince") and his father for propaganda purposes, offered to release him ahead of the other prisoners in a grand ceremony meant to influence world opinion. When McCain refused to cooperate, he was severely beaten, an incident that he has described as the low point of his captivity. He was similarly mistreated for trying to communicate with other prisoners through an improvised wall-tapping code. Extremely malnourished, given just a single daily ration of noodles, some of which was eaten by his guards, he lost more than a third of his weight in prison. Throughout his confinement he was denied all mail and was permitted only once to write a brief postcard home.

In 1971 McCain was transferred from solitary confinement to a cell with 50 other prisoners, but though he was grateful for the company, conditions remained all but unbearable. Months later the men staged a riot, for which some of them, including McCain, were punished at a harsher facility outside Hanoi. The most difficult part of captivity, McCain has said, was not the physical abuse but the psychological strain and the uncertainty of his fate. Because he was deprived of news from the outside, he rode a roller coaster of emotions with each unfounded rumor of imminent release.

On March 17, 1973, two months after the cessation of hostilities, McCain and the other prisoners were turned over to U.S. authorities. When he underwent medical treatment at Clark Air Force Base in the Philippines and, later, in Jacksonville, Florida, it was obvious to observers that the years of captivity had taken their toll. Although he was only 36 years old, his hair had turned white. Once a robust 160 pounds, he then weighed about 100. Racked by arthritis and deformed joints, he could no longer bend his right knee, raise his right arm above a 45-degree angle, or elevate his left shoulder. Yet despite the permanent disabilities and the long years of torture and solitary confinement, McCain emerged from the war remarkably sound of mind. "Perhaps it has made me more sensitive to the underdog than I otherwise would have been," he said in an interview with Susan F. Rasky of the *New York Times* (August 9, 1988). "I know what it is like to be humiliated and degraded. But I don't think it made any change in my basic character." For his wartime service, he was awarded the Silver Star, the Legion of Merit, the Distinguished Flying Cross, and other decorations.

After spending four months in recuperation, McCain enrolled at the National War College in Washington, D.C., but he longed to fly again. Through sheer determination he passed the rigorous flight physical and returned to the skies for two years as commander of a training squadron. In 1977 he was promoted to captain and reassigned to the Department of the Navy's Office of Legislative Affairs, where he served as director of the Navy Senate Liaison Office. Over the next four years, he made extensive legislative contacts and struck up lasting friendships with such politically diverse senators as the Republicans John G. Tower of Texas and William S. Cohen of Maine and the Democrat Gary Hart of Colorado. By 1981 it had become obvious that his ultimate goal of commanding an aircraft carrier was now out of his reach. No longer able to pass the flight physical, he retired from the United States Navy.

Upon his discharge McCain accepted a job offer from his father-in-law, Jim Hensley, a beer distributor in Phoenix, Arizona. In 1982 a vacancy in Arizona's First Congressional District, a solidly Republican region comprising the greater Phoenix area, was created with the retirement of Congressman John J. Rhodes. Although McCain had been living in Arizona for less than a year, he entered the Republican primary against three seasoned contenders. Since early polls revealed that 97 percent of the people in the district had never heard of him, McCain devoted as many as 30 hours a week to knocking on some 16,000 doors in the Phoenix area. His opponents denounced him as a carpetbagger, a new resident unfamiliar with the state. Although that charge has been effective from time to time in states where many voters are life residents, it counts for considerably less in Arizona, which since World War II has attracted millions of Americans from out-of-state. Quickly silencing his critics, McCain pointed out that having been born into a navy family and having been a career naval officer himself, he never really had a home state. "The longest place I ever lived was Hanoi," he said, pointedly reminding voters of his war record. With fund-raising assistance from his friend Senator John Tower and the dedication of a hustling corps of volunteers, McCain topped the four-man field with a third of the vote and went on to defeat the Democrat William E. Hegarty by a two-to-one margin in the general election. In 1984 he ran for re-election unopposed in the primary and buried his Democratic opponent, Harry W. Braun 3d, taking 78 percent of the vote to Braun's 22 percent.

During his four years in the House, McCain consistently won high marks from conservative groups, earning a perfect 100 rating from the National Security Index of the American Security Council in 1984. He joined Newt Gingrich of Georgia and other young "new Right" Republicans in clashing with Thomas P. ("Tip") O'Neill, the Speaker of the House. On the House floor he voted in support of prayer in public schools, the 1985 Gramm-Rudman deficit-reduction package, the 1986 tax-reform act, continued tobacco subsidies, a resumption of certain handgun sales, and the continued use of the polygraph as a condition for employment under certain circumstances. He opposed the Equal Rights Amendment for women, increased funding to implement the Clean Air Act, trade protection for the textile and apparel industries, the 1983 domestic content bill restricting the use of foreign parts in American automobiles, and the 1986 Immigration Reform and Control Act. In foreign affairs, he opposed the 1983 nuclear-freeze resolution and approved funding for the research and development of the MX missile and the Strategic Defense Initiative, increased aid to El Salvador, and arms for the Contra rebels fighting in Nicaragua and the pro-Western guerrillas in Angola.

Although on those and most other issues, McCain fell in line with the Republican administration of President Ronald Reagan, he did not hesitate to oppose the administration on certain critical matters. In a major floor speech in 1983, for example, McCain called for the withdrawal of all United States Marines from Lebanon. In 1986 he joined the two-thirds majority in voting to override President Reagan's veto of sanctions against South Africa, whose black majority then suffered under a brutal system of racial segregation. Although he supported the Contra rebels, he urged the administration to abandon its effort to overthrow the Marxist-led Sandinista regime in Nicaragua and instead focus its resources on encouraging the democratic process there. In 1987 McCain exposed and thwarted an administration attempt to remove $28 million from an antipoverty food program to pay for a salary increase for Agriculture Department employees. He criticized the administration's handling of the Iran-Contra affair (in which officials had illegally diverted to the Contras money from the sale of arms to Iran), though he blamed both Congress and the White House for failing to work more closely on a coordinated foreign policy, and he empathized with his fellow Vietnam veteran Oliver North, a central figure in the scandal. "Some of these people like Ollie North," he explained to Michael Killian for the *Chicago Tribune* (July 29, 1987), "who saw their comrades and friends spill blood and die on the battlefields in a war that they believe the politicians wouldn't let them win—I think that leads to a mind-set which could rationalize deviating from the established rules and regulations."

Because of his own wartime experience, McCain was active in pressing the Hanoi government to provide more information about those American servicemen still reported as missing in action (or MIAs) from the Vietnam War era. While condemning the Vietnamese government for cynically using MIA information as a bargaining chip to win United States diplomatic recognition and aid in rebuilding the country, he privately urged the Reagan administration to restore low-level relations between the two nations. After his election to the Senate, in 1986, however, McCain became more outspoken in his criticism of the Reagan administration's approach to Vietnam, and in the early 1990s, while serving on the Senate Select Committee on POW/MIA Affairs, McCain worked closely with Democratic senator and fellow veteran John Kerry to investigate claims that Vietnam still detained American prisoners of war. After years of lobbying on McCain's part, the U.S. normalized relations with Vietnam on July 11, 1995.

In 1985 McCain accompanied the CBS news broadcaster Walter Cronkite to Vietnam for a special program marking the 10th anniversary of the fall of Saigon. While there, he warned authorities in Hanoi that resolution of the MIA issue was a precondition to resumption of diplomatic ties. He came away convinced that the dire state of the Vietnamese economy and the people's longstanding fear of the Chinese were prompting Hanoi to seek improved relations with the West. In one poignant episode, McCain and Cronkite returned to the Hanoi lake where the veteran had crashed 18 years earlier. To his surprise, the Vietnamese had erected a monument bearing the likeness of a kneeling American soldier with his arms held up in surrender and an inscription marking the spot where "the famous air pirate" John McCain was shot down. Recognizing him instantly, a gathering crowd began chanting his name as though he were a celebrity. Only in Hanoi, McCain joked, was he more famous than Walter Cronkite.

By 1986 McCain had become so popular among Arizona Republicans that he ran unopposed in the Senate primary for the seat long held by Barry Goldwater, who had announced plans to retire. Early polls gave McCain a comfortable lead over his Democratic opponent, Richard Kimball, but the race tightened somewhat after McCain upset the state's large elderly population with an offhand remark referring to the retirement community of Leisure World as "Seizure World." Moreover, McCain became unnerved by Kimball's charge that his votes on national-security matters were influenced by campaign contributions from the political action committees of defense-related industries. But McCain, outspending Kimball by three to one, recovered to win handily, by a margin of 60 percent to 40 percent. Senator McCain was assigned to the Senate Armed Services Committee and its subcommittees on manpower, projection forces, and readiness; the Senate Commerce, Science and Transportation Committee and its subcommittees on aviation, communications, and consumer affairs; and the Senate Select Committee on Indian Affairs.

McCain was a featured speaker at the Republican National Convention in New Orleans, Louisiana, in 1988, and was reportedly among those considered as a possible running mate with George Herbert Walker Bush. Although McCain was not enthusiastic about the eventual vice-presidential nominee, Senator Dan Quayle of Indiana, he defended Quayle's Vietnam War–era service in the National Guard. "I've spent the last ten years of my life trying to foster an atmosphere of reconciliation in this country and to get people to move beyond the hurts and the scars of that time," he told R. W. Apple Jr. of the *New York Times* (October 25, 1986). "Now we're threatened, because of the Quayle episode, with another round of finger-pointing, veiled accusations, biography-checking. . . . There's nothing to be gained by going back over that ground." McCain was a part of the Republican "truth squad" that kept a close critical watch on the eventual Democratic nominee, Michael S. Dukakis, early in the campaign. Meanwhile, he criticized his own party for not reaching out more effectively to African-Americans or to the poor.

In 1989 McCain was accused, along with four other senators, of trying to shield a campaign donor from a federal investigation into one of the largest-ever savings-and-loan scandals. Charles Keating, the owner of Lincoln Savings and Loan, was under investigation for illicit financial dealings, which had ruined his institution and cost taxpayers more than $3 billion in a federally funded bailout. McCain had received nine free trips to the Bahamas and $112,000 in campaign contributions from Keating, and shortly after the 1986 election, the senator attended two meetings with savings-and-loan regulators on behalf of the embroiled financier, who was later convicted and served jail time. Investigations and hearings into the scandal lasted for four years; the other senators involved—John Glenn, Donald W. Riegle Jr., Dennis DeConcini, and Alan Cranston—were all Democrats, and while McCain was the least culpable of what became known as the "Keating Five," the Democrats on the Senate Ethics Committee did not want to exonerate him unless their party members were cleared as well. Eventually the committee chastised McCain for displaying poor judgment but stopped short of actually accusing him of any wrongdoing. He was the only senator of the five to be absolved.

McCain has said that his embarrassment over that scandal was more trying than what he endured during his imprisonment in Hanoi. Connie Bruck, writing for the *New Yorker* (May 30, 2005), theorized that the savings-and-loan episode marked a turning point in McCain's career, in which he "learned how to use the press" and "developed an intense aversion to partisanship." "He believed that he had been held hostage by the Democrats, and that his own party had not demanded his release," she continued. "After that, he determined that he would take on fights over issues without regard to whether his opponents were Democrats or Republicans. And he decided that he would not merely apologize for his error in having sought to wield his influence on behalf of a generous contributor; he would also try to remake the system that encouraged such transgressions." McCain came to believe that private funding of political campaigns was having a deleterious effect on public life. He held a particular disdain for pork—legislation that yields rich benefits for campaign supporters and is usually attached to an unrelated bill shortly before the bill's passage—and in 1991 he began agitating for campaign-finance reform. After the 1994 congressional elections, in which Republicans took control of Congress for the first time in four decades, he joined forces with the Democrat Russell Feingold of Wisconsin to begin drafting a bill for campaign-finance reform. The bill that the two senators introduced in 1997, the Bipartisan Campaign Reform Act, more commonly known as the McCain-Feingold bill, was treated by their colleagues at first as something of a joke. "We were like the guys who introduced the bill to convert to the metric system," McCain told Michael Lewis for the *New York Times Magazine* (May 25, 1997). Most notably, the bill called for the elimination of "soft money," donations that are made to the national party ostensibly for general purposes but are later redirected to specific campaigns, and a ban on "issue ads," supposedly nonpartisan ads that actually advocate for or against a particular candidate.

In August 1999, apparently in preparation for his bid for the Republican presidential nomination—which he formally announced in the following month—the senator published his first book, *Faith of My Fathers*. Co-written with his longtime aide, Mark Salter, the book relates the senator's time in Vietnam to the wartime experiences of his father and grandfather. Writing for the *National Review* (September 27, 1999), Norman Geoffrey noted that McCain's book was clearly intended as a campaign tool, but asked rhetorically, "Does this mean that it is necessarily a bad book? A self-serving book? A suspect book? Actually, none of the above. It is, as they say, a good read, which even registered Democrats and just about anyone on the political spectrum right of Jane Fonda would find engaging, sometimes funny, and often profoundly moving." Assessing the book's usefulness for the senator's campaign, Evan Thomas wrote for *Newsweek* (September 13 1999), "The book amply demonstrates that McCain was a brave warrior and an honorable man. Whether it shows that McCain would make a good president is a more complicated question. . . . Many Americans would welcome a politician with the integrity to stand up to the hacks. As president, McCain would undoubtedly try to shake up the system, particularly campaign finance. But presidents, like senators, have to know when to compromise, and McCain has never been known as a dealmaker. . . . Still, McCain's character has withstood tests the average politician can only imagine." (*Faith of My Fathers* was later made into a television miniseries, which aired on Memorial Day in 2005 on the cable network A&E and received four Emmy Award nominations.)

Then–Texas governor George W. Bush was favored to win the Republican presidential nomination in 2000, but McCain—whose platform included responsible tax cuts, a plan to use the budget surplus to pay down the deficit, and campaign-finance reform—made a strong showing in the upper Midwest during the primaries. After McCain pulled off an upset victory in the New Hampshire primary, cutting significantly into Bush's lead in the polls, the governor's team reportedly began to worry that he could not win without introducing a negative tone into the campaign. Gathering in South Carolina for the primaries in February 2000, they "decided to take the gloves off," as Nancy Gibbs wrote for *Time* (February 14, 2000), quoting "a participant." Voters in South Carolina received E-mail messages and found fliers on their windshields—planted by unidentified sources—

alleging that McCain was the father of an illegitimate, racially mixed child. (McCain's wife, Cindy, had adopted a girl she met while on a relief mission in Bangladesh in 1991.) Other rumors circulated: McCain had slept with prostitutes and given his wife a venereal disease; the senator was a "Manchurian candidate," brainwashed during his detention in Hanoi to destroy the Republican Party; Cindy McCain was a drug addict (she did admit to pilfering prescription drugs from a relief agency for which she worked in 1994). Rumors were also spread through "push polling," a practice in which people posing as pollsters call voters in order to spread false, damning information. "What happened in South Carolina is as bad as you've been told and worse," the Republican senator Lindsey Graham of South Carolina told Connie Bruck. "Most of it was about campaign-finance reform and special-interest groups—they were going to kill him before he got any stronger. It was sheer rumor demagoguery."

Bush won the South Carolina primary by an 11-point margin, and McCain dropped out of the race shortly thereafter. Though he lost the nomination, McCain had gained nationwide exposure, and his candor earned him support from both registered Republicans and Democrats. According to Joshua Micah Marshall, writing for the *American Prospect* (December 18, 2000), McCain had "as solid a claim as any to credit" for the "Republicans' unexpectedly strong showing" in elections for the House of Representatives in 2000, having traveled to make appearances in support of 50 Republican congressional candidates: "Even a cursory look at this year's election map shows why McCain was a key factor. Republicans retained their majority in the House largely because of wins in a string of super-competitive races stretching the broad arc from Michigan down into Pennsylvania and up into Connecticut. . . . Each of these candidates ran on McCain-like agendas, each ran in parts of the country where McCain was particularly popular, each got generous campaign assistance from the senator (often with widely publicized joint appearances in the campaign's final days), and each pulled through by an exceedingly small margin."

After the election, McCain decided to use his newfound political leverage in order to advocate for positions that were not popular with the Republican leadership. With the Democratic senator Joseph Lieberman of Connecticut, he co-sponsored legislation to reduce the emission of greenhouse gases. He also voted against Bush's tax cuts, sponsored the Patients' Bill of Rights, called for the president to ease restrictions on embryonic stem-cell research, proposed legislation that would close a loophole in the law that allows people to purchase guns at gun shows without being subjected to background checks, refused to support a constitutional amendment banning gay marriage, and criticized the administration's handling of the postwar reconstruction in Iraq (though he had voted in support of the 2003 invasion). Nevertheless, he has consistently received high ratings for his legislative record from the American Conservative Union. "McCain really is a Republican," Anthony Cordesman, who worked for McCain in the late 1980s and early 1990s, told Connie Bruck, explaining why McCain appeals to many registered Democrats. "One of the difficulties you have with someone that active who starts out on the right and often ends up in the middle is that people assume—because of his pragmatic approach—that he agrees with them politically. But he does not."

Though his allegiance may have lain with the GOP, McCain continued to frustrate his own party with his determination to pursue campaign-finance reform. "On most issues, Republican legislators have presented a solid phalanx to give the Bush administration whatever it wants," Robert Kuttner wrote for the *American Prospect* (April 23, 2001). "The exception is campaign finance reform—and the chink in the Republican armor is Arizona Senator John McCain." In 2002, after years of stonewalling from the Republican leadership, McCain finally mustered enough support—mostly from Democrats—to pass the McCain-Feingold bill: the House voted 240–189 for the bill on February 14, and on March 20 the Senate approved the House's version of the bill by a vote of 60–40. President Bush signed the bill into law on March 27, 2002. Libertarians opposed the new regulations because, as they saw it, the restrictions limited not only private financing for campaigns but, in effect, free speech as well. The last attempt to reform campaign finance had been hobbled by just such an argument; the 1974 Supreme Court ruling in *Buckley v. Valeo* had virtually defined the right to contribute to campaigns as being part of free speech. After the bill's passage, Senate majority whip Mitch McConnell challenged its legality in court, and in December 2003 the Supreme Court ruled on *McConnell v. FEC*, allowing most of the bill's original provisions to stand.

In 2002 McCain also published his second book, *Worth the Fighting For: A Memoir*, another collaboration with Salter, in which the senator combined autobiographical sketches with musings on figures that he admires—including Ernest Hemingway, whose novel *For Whom the Bell Tolls* contains the passage that supplied the book's title. In her review for the *New York Times* (October 3, 2002), Janet Maslin wrote that though McCain had collaborated with an "auxiliary author," the book does not read as if he did, since it presents the "emphatic, familiar voice of a strongly outspoken public figure eager to announce his guiding ideals." Russell Baker, writing for the *New York Review of Books* (October 24, 2002), characterized the memoir as being less a political move than a book about self-discovery: "McCain has clearly advanced to a new stage of his career. Now he no longer feels compelled to be discreet about his discontent with conservative domination of his party. Personal dislikes and policy disagreements with party leaders are voiced in remarkably plain speech. . . . It is the work of someone who has found out, rather late in life, who he is and what he truly believes. Self-discovery seems to give him the nerve to speak with a candor rare among politicians. The result is a book packed with extraordinary indiscretions for a still-practicing politician." In one passage in the book, McCain, who was suffering from skin cancer at the time, admitted to wondering whether it was time for him to withdraw from public life, fueling speculation that he planned to retire. Nevertheless, McCain sought reelection to the Senate in 2004 and won with more than 76 percent of the vote.

Despite his uneasy relationship with the president, McCain supported Bush's reelection campaign, in 2004. In an election season that was considered to be particularly divisive, McCain's influence with moderate and undecided voters was highly valued by both parties; both Bush and Kerry used his image in their television ads. Kerry even asked McCain to join his ticket as the vice-presidential candidate; a CBS News poll released in June 2004 showed that while Kerry held a slight lead over Bush, a Kerry-McCain ticket would enjoy a lead of 14 percentage points over the Bush-Cheney ticket. Nonetheless, the senator remained loyal to his party, appearing at more than 20 events to stump for the president.

In *Why Courage Matters: The Way to a Braver Life* (2004), also co-written with Mark Salter, McCain suggested that "the definition of courage has been stretched thin in contemporary parlance, where it can be applied to acts as insignificant as cutting or not cutting one's hair," according to a reviewer for *Publishers Weekly* (February 9, 2004), who noted that with this slim meditation, the senator hoped "to return to the word's fundamental meaning not just of 'the capacity for action despite our fears' but self-sacrifice for the benefit of others as well as for oneself." McCain cited as an example of that quality the valor exhibited by American soldiers on the battlefield, and also related tales of the Navajo leaders Manuelito and Barboncito, the Jewish freedom fighter and writer Hannah Senesh, the Nobel Peace Prize recipient Aung San Suu Kyi, and the congressman John Lewis, who was involved in the civil rights movement. "These compelling life stories stand up against the best passages of McCain's previous works," the reviewer for *Publishers Weekly* wrote. "Alas, his writing becomes more vague and less interesting when he shifts to a more abstract discussion of the need for courage in the post–September 11 era. One of McCain's greatest strengths as a writer has been that he doesn't sound like just another politician, and while the drop-off in quality here isn't significant, it is noticeable."

McCain and Salter's most recent collaboration, *Character Is Destiny: Inspiring Stories Every Young Person Should Know and Every Adult Should Remember* (2005), discusses 34 notable individuals, including George Washington, Sojourner Truth, Queen Elizabeth I, and Mother Teresa, each representing a particular quality that McCain admires. E. J. Dionne Jr. described the book for the *Washing-*

ton Post (December 11, 2005, on-line) as "a series of morality tales pitched at America's youth," in which the primary moral is that "everything depends on the capacity of human beings to will themselves to transcend their egos."

In 2005 McCain proposed what would become known as the McCain amendment, which sought to bar any American—whether a civilian or a member of the military—from treating detainees in a cruel, inhumane, and degrading manner. The proposal came in the aftermath of reports of mistreatment of prisoners by U.S. troops in Iraq and elsewhere and the more recent revelation that the U.S. was running secret prisons in Europe and Asia, where CIA agents were authorized to practice torture. McCain's measure was backed overwhelmingly in both the House and the Senate, but the White House fought against the measure for months, despite increasing pressure both at home and abroad. Vice President Richard B. Cheney was the most vocal opponent of the measure, meeting with McCain to try to persuade him to accept an exemption for CIA operatives. Though McCain refused to make such concessions, the administration signed the bill on December 15, 2005, after the senator offered a provision that would allow those accused of torturing detainees to defend themselves against charges by arguing that a "reasonable person" could have thought that his or her actions were legal. (The White House later released a "signing statement" indicating that the executive branch would interpret the new law as it saw fit.) According to editors of the *Economist* (December 16, 2005), McCain's position as a potential presidential candidate in 2008 was strengthened by that victory: "Mr. McCain is often called a Republican Maverick who cannot win the conservative base necessary to get the Republican nomination. But the big majorities he won in Congress for his amendment show that Mr. Bush and his administration no longer have the lock on the party they once did."

In 2006 McCain became embroiled in two of the year's more noteworthy political issues—immigration reform and the limitations regarding the legal rights of detainees suspected of terrorism—both of which sparked fierce debates among members of the legislative and executive branches of government and complicated party loyalties. Regarding the first issue, McCain collaborated with the longtime Democratic senator Edward M. "Ted" Kennedy of Massachusetts to sponsor an immigration-reform bill. Among other provisions, the bill sought a temporary guest-worker program (enabling U.S. employers to hire illegal immigrants for restricted periods before such employees would risk deportation if they had not pursued proper steps toward obtaining citizenship); it also sought to grant illegal immigrants the right to apply for citizenship only after the U.S. Immigration and Naturalization Service had processed the applications previously filed by other foreigners. McCain characterized the immigration debate as representing

"a defining moment in the nation's history," as Carl Hulse and Rachel L. Swarns reported in the *New York Times* (March 31, 2006), and he asked rhetorically, "Are we going to continue our rich tradition of hundreds of years of welcoming new blood and new vitality to our nation? Or are we going to adopt a protectionist, isolationist attitude and policies that are in betrayal of the very fundamentals of this great nation of ours, a beacon of hope and liberty and freedom throughout the world?" The Senate, in a rare gesture of bipartisanship, passed the McCain-Kennedy bill by a 62 to 36 margin in late May 2006. The House passed a significantly different immigration-reform bill, and no attempt was made to hammer out a compromise between the two. The legislation of both arms of Congress was shelved until 2007.

Regarding foreign nationals and U.S. citizens imprisoned by the U.S. on suspicion of terrorism, McCain battled the Bush administration in its attempt to reinterpret the Geneva Conventions, four treaties that set international standards regarding the treatment of prisoners of war. "This issue is not about them [detainees]—this issue is about us," McCain declared, as quoted by Adam Nagourney in the *New York Times* (September 18, 2006). "The United States has always been better than our enemies. I'll tell you right now: one of the things in prison, in North Vietnam, that kept us strong was that we knew we were not like our enemies. That we came from a better nation, with better values, with better standards." Nevertheless, McCain, along with 52 other Republicans and 12 Democrats, voted for a bill that denies habeas corpus to foreigners considered "enemy combatants" rather than prisoners of war; thus, such detainees cannot legally challenge their detention, examine evidence against them, or—at trials conducted by military officers—seek to bar testimony against themselves on the grounds that it was obtained through coercion. McCain lauded the legislation, insisting that "the integrity and the letter and the spirit of the Geneva Conventions have been preserved," according to Kate Zernike in the *New York Times* (September 22, 2006). A similar bill passed in the House. President Bush signed the new law, known as the Military Commissions Act of 2006, on October 27 of that year.

Although, as of early November 2006, McCain had not formally announced that he planned to seek the presidency in 2008, he has taken steps indicating that he is seriously considering doing so. For example, he has conferred with many political consultants, fund-raisers, and others active in politics, some of whom—including the media consultant Mark McKinnon and the veteran GOP strategist Terry Nelson—had played important roles in the 2004 reelection campaign of President George W. Bush. In May 2006, in an effort to court the more conservative, evangelical base of the Republican Party, McCain delivered the commencement address at Liberty University, a Baptist college founded by the Reverend Jerry Falwell, whom Mc-

Cain had once denounced as an "agent of intolerance," as Adam Nagourney reported in the *New York Times* (April 9, 2006). In response to accusations that he has apparently altered his positions so as to retain the support of Republican moderates and lure centrist Democrats to his camp, McCain asserted, according to Nagourney, "I would argue that I have not changed any of my positions, and if I did really change my positions on issues, that I would lose what is probably one of the greatest attractions that people have for me, and that is as a person who stands up for what he believes in."

McCain stands five feet nine inches tall and is somewhat overweight. He was first diagnosed with skin cancer in 1993 and had two tumors removed in 2000, which left a scar on his neck, where skin was removed for a graft on his left temple; he currently visits his dermatologist every three months. The senator has been described as affable and unassuming, quick to laugh, and possessed of an irreverent sense of humor; he likes to do impressions of his fellow politicians. He also grows impatient easily and struggles to check his temper. In 1965 he

married his first wife, Carol, and adopted her two sons, Douglas and Andrew. The couple had a daughter, Sidney Ann, before their divorce, in 1980. Later in the same year McCain married Cindy Hensley, with whom he has four children, Meghan, Jack, Jimmy, and Bridget. The senator has four grandchildren.

—J.C.

Suggested Reading: *Economist* June 18, 2005; *Esquire* May 1998; *New York Times* A p12 Mar. 31, 2006, p33 Apr. 9, 2006, A p21 Sep. 18, 2006; *New Yorker* p58 May 30, 2005; *Time* p45 Nov. 17, 1986, p26 Feb. 14, 2000; *U.S. News & World Report* p42 Mar. 28, 1983, p33+ Mar. 11 1985; *Vanity Fair* p193 Nov. 2004

Selected Books: with Mark Salter—*Faith of My Fathers*, 1999; *Worth the Fighting For*, 2002; *Why Courage Matters: The Way to a Braver Life*, 2004; *Character Is Destiny: Inspiring Stories Every Young Person Should Know and Every Adult Should Remember*, 2005

McDonough, William

Feb. 21, 1951– Architect

Address: William McDonough + Partners, 700 E. Jefferson St., Charlottesville, VA 22902

In the late 1990s many corporate executives regarded the architect William McDonough's environmental philosophy with contempt. A pioneer of what has come to be known as the Green Building Movement, McDonough championed the "cradle-to-cradle" approach to architecture, according to which the raw materials for buildings and other objects are taken from, and harmless to, the immediate environment—and can return to that environment in the form of biodegradable matter. His hope to create the "next industrial revolution" was often dismissed by business leaders who argued that being environmentally conscious meant earning less profit. When McDonough told a manager at the automotive company Ford that he would like to put skylights in the roof of the company's River Rouge car plant, in Michigan, the manager retorted, as quoted by Brian Dumaine for *FSB* (December 2001/January 2002), "Do you know what we do with skylights at River Rouge? We tar them over." McDonough, far from being discouraged, drove the manager to a nearby plant owned by the office-furniture company Herman Miller, which he had designed in 1996. There, the bow-tied architect explained to the Ford manager the effectiveness of his "green" designs: the vertically placed skylights in the Herman Miller plant let in natural light and fresh air and never leaked, but more importantly, from a business standpoint, the design of the build-

Kevin Winter/Getty Images

ing helped increase productivity—so much so that the new, energy-efficient features paid for themselves. "This is not environmental philanthropy," William Ford Jr., the chief executive officer of Ford, stated in announcing McDonough's River Rouge plant project, according to Josey Ballenger for *Grid* (May 2001). "It is sound business, which . . . balances the business needs of auto manufacturing with ecological and social concerns. . . .

This new facility lays the groundwork for a model of 21st-century sustainable manufacturing."

McDonough's achievements in the area of what is called sustainable design have gained increasing attention in both corporate and ecological conservation circles. Working with Michael Braungart, a German chemist and conservationist, McDonough has designed environmentally sound buildings for several large companies and has also delved into product design, creating soles for Nike shoes, for example, that can be used to enrich soil when discarded, and designing a 99 percent biodegradable chair for Herman Miller. In 2002 McDonough and Braungart co-authored *Cradle to Cradle: Remaking the Way We Make Things*, a book explaining their approach to design. (The book itself is a manifestation of McDonough's values: the pages were made from plastic resins and inorganic fillers that are infinitely recyclable, and even the ink can be reused.) The winner of the Presidential Award for Sustainable Development in 1996, the Presidential Green Chemistry Challenge Award in 2003, and the National Design Award in 2004, McDonough was also named "Hero for the Planet" in 1999 by *Time* magazine, which credited the architect with a "unified philosophy that—in demonstrable and practical ways—is changing the design of the world."

William Andrews McDonough was born on February 21, 1951 in Tokyo, Japan, to James Edwin and Sara McDonough. His father's position as the Far East representative of the liquor company Seagram International required the family to move frequently within Asia. The McDonoughs settled in Hong Kong, China, at a time when water was available only every fourth day for four hours during the dry season and many people, as a result, suffered from dehydration and died of cholera, typhoid, typhus, yellow fever, or scarlet fever. McDonough was able to spend summers with his grandparents at Puget Sound, Washington, in a log cabin surrounded by Douglas firs and cedars. The tall trees and the clear springs with drinkable water contrasted sharply with the scarcity of land and natural resources McDonough had known in Hong Kong. Even while he was living amid such abundance, his grandparents taught him to respect his environment. When James McDonough became president of Seagram, the family returned to the U.S. William McDonough attended high school in Connecticut, "where there were 16-year-olds with Porsches," as he told Michael Bond during an interview for *New Scientist* (March 20, 2004). "All of a sudden I saw this profligate consumption. People would leave the showers running in the locker room. This was unbelievable to me. Even in Washington state with all the water in the world you never left the tap running. I went around turning off all the taps—they thought I was crazy."

McDonough enrolled at Dartmouth College, in Hanover, New Hampshire, where he obtained his bachelor's degree in art in 1973. During his college years he joined a team that was entering a contest, sponsored by King Hussein of Jordan, to produce a long-term plan for housing in the Jordan River valley, where significant numbers of Bedouins were settling. McDonough and the other members of the team proposed that Jordanians design housing based on ancient Bedouin principles, which suited the area's remoteness and arid environment. The Bedouins, nomadic tribes dwelling in the desert regions of Sinai, used available resources—which included mud and, most importantly, materials from goats—to build adobe huts that would protect them from the intense heat. For example, woven goat hair, when built into tents, draws the hot air up and out while also protecting against rain. McDonough and the others in the group also suggested that if the homes were built from mud, the local people could readily build and repair the homes themselves, since steel and other modern structural materials would not be needed. King Hussein selected the group's plan, and today the Jordan River valley is filled with adobe huts.

McDonough's experience with the Jordan River valley housing project played a part in the development of his architectural philosophy, which calls for using relatively inexpensive natural resources in ways that are environmentally sound and at the same time fulfill the needs of consumers. "In Jordan I was sitting in a Bedouin tent, and instead of saying, 'Oh, my God, I've gone back centuries to some primitive ways,' I saw it as one of the most elegant structures I've ever seen. You've got your factory—goats—following you around and eating what you can't eat and making hair out of that for you. At the same time it gives you meat, milk, and entertainment. And then rejuvenates the soil with its droppings—a full cycle," McDonough told Brian Dumaine for *FSB*. He wrote in *Cradle to Cradle*, "This ingenious design, locally relevant, culturally rich, and using simple materials, contrasted sharply with the typical modern designs I had seen in my own country, designs that rarely made such good use of local material and energy flows."

With that philosophy as a foundation for his future work, McDonough enrolled at Yale University's School of Architecture, in New Haven, Connecticut. In the course of working toward his master's degree, McDonough successfully designed and built the first solar-heated house in Ireland—an especially difficult task, given that Ireland receives a limited amount of sunshine. After completing his degree, in 1976, McDonough moved to New York City to apprentice at the firm Davis Brody & Associates, which was known for its socially responsible approach to designing urban housing.

In 1981 McDonough struck out on his own, establishing William McDonough Architects. Three years later his firm was selected to design the New York City headquarters of the Environmental Defense Fund (EDF), the project that brought McDonough into the architectural and ecological limelight. The greatest challenge McDonough faced with regard to the assignment was the EDF's insistence that the building contain no materials that were, or could become, toxic. "The executive director [of the EDF] told us that if anybody got sick from our building, he would sue," McDonough told Michael Bond. Focusing his efforts on avoiding "sick-building syndrome" (a term, according to the Environmental Protection Agency's Web site, used to describe cases in which buildings' occupants suffer "acute health and comfort effects that appear to be linked to time spent in a building, but no specific illness or cause can be identified"), the up-and-coming architect attempted to eliminate paints, wall coverings, carpets, and fixtures that might contain any volatile organic compounds or carcinogenic materials that could adversely affect the air quality in the building. Manufacturers of the materials offered McDonough little help in revealing what was in their products, merely citing vague federal safety warnings and saying that further information was proprietary. "We did the best we could," McDonough told Bond. "We used water-based paints and tacked down carpet instead of gluing it. For each person we provided a cubic metre per minute of fresh air, instead of a sixth of that, which is standard. We had the granite checked for radon. We tried to be less bad." (McDonough said to Bond that with regard to environmentally sound architecture, "being less bad" than other builders "is not the same as being good.") The building was completed in 1985 and has been credited with launching the Green Building Movement. (Among the many adherents of the movement are the Santa Monica–based architecture firm Pugh + Scarpa and the architect David Hertz. Pugh + Scarpa is credited with designing Colorado Court, the nation's first large residential complex that combines advanced sustainability with low-income housing. Hertz is known to capitalize on the versatility of natural surroundings to optimize the efficiency of his buildings.)

In 1991 McDonough met Michael Braungart, the founder of the Environmental Protection Encouragement Agency, an organization that specializes in environmental chemistry research. "He made me think, how can I make a beautiful building if it destroys the planet or makes people sick?" McDonough told Bond. McDonough and Braungart shared a deep conviction that products needed more sensible design in order to contribute to, rather than detract from, the soundness of the environment. In 1995 the two founded McDonough Braungart Design Chemistry (MBDC) to help large companies use the concept of sustainable design in their products and materials. Their clients have included Ford, Nike, and Herman Miller. In order to contribute to the health of the environment, reduce the impact of human activity on ecosystems, and help sustain those ecosystems over time, McDonough reconsidered his approach to architecture and developed a new philosophy, which he often explains by using an illustration of a triangle. The three points of the triangle, he says, represent economic returns, social good, and environmental benefits, respectively. Instead of making the common choice between "building green or building cheap," McDonough aims for the middle of the triangle, which satisfies all three concerns. Being "less bad" was, in McDonough's view, no longer acceptable. "To be less bad is to accept things as they are, to believe that poorly designed, dishonorable, destructive systems are the *best* humans can do. This is the ultimate failure of the 'be less bad' approach: a failure of the imagination. From our perspective, this is a depressing vision of our species' role in the world," McDonough wrote in *Cradle to Cradle*.

In the book McDonough and Braungart advanced the theory that the world has two types of metabolisms: biological and technical. In biological metabolism, biodegradable materials proceed through natural cycles, so that one organism's waste is another's sustenance. In technical metabolism, the man-made industrial system uses Earth's resources to design and manufacture products for consumption. McDonough and Braungart asserted that technical metabolism is a "cradle-to-grave" system that produces environmental hazards and excessive waste. Many products are packaged, for example, in containers that remain in landfills for over a century. The existing system of recycling does little, the authors maintained, to reduce the dependency on ever-growing landfills; it merely slows the depletion rate of Earth's resources. "It's not the person who throws away a Coke can that's the problem," Braungart told Leslie Close for the *Detroit News* (October 17, 1999). "It's the person who designs a Coke can that you can't throw away. All it is is light-weight packaging. Can't we develop polymers that we can throw away?" In order to remedy the problem of inherently destructive building materials, McDonough and Braungart proposed a "cradle-to-cradle" system, which would utilize "biological nutrients" (biodegradable materials) and "technical nutrients" (synthetic polymers) in an environmentally friendly and still profitable way. Such an approach would significantly reduce the amount of materials that go to landfills and also reduce costs of raw material. "Michael Braungart and I coined the term upcycling, meaning that the product could actually get better as it comes through the system. For example, some plastic bottles contain the residues of heavy-metal catalysts. We can remove those residues as the bottles come back to be upcycled," McDonough told Anne Underwood for *Newsweek*, in an interview that appears on the MSNBC Web site (May 16, 2005). By employing such methods and converting manufacturers from a "cradle-to-grave" system to a "cradle-to-cradle" system, McDonough hopes to create the "next industrial revolution."

MBDC has already worked with the textile company Designtex to develop fabrics using the Climatex Lifecycle system, the only 100 percent safely biodegradable fabric-manufacturing system in the world. The practice of sustainable design extends even to production at Rohner Textil, the Swiss mill that weaves Designtex's fabrics. MBDC helped the mill to isolate 16 nontoxic chemical dyes, out of 1,600, to use for textiles. According to Swiss government officials, the water leaving Rohner Textil is as clean and pure as the water going into the mill. No waste is created in the production process because all byproducts are designed to return safely to biological systems. Swiss farmers use the extra trimmings from the fabric as ground cover for crops; the material decomposes gradually and becomes food for worms and microorganisms.

Returning to architecture, McDonough began applying the principles of his "cradle-to-cradle" approach to his projects. In 1994 he relocated his architectural firm from New York City to Charlottesville, Virginia, where he began a five-year stint as the dean of the School of Architecture at the University of Virginia. While teaching courses at the university, McDonough continued working with his firm, which he renamed William McDonough + Partners. He created a research division of the firm, in which materials and processes are analyzed, engineering solutions are developed, and operational cost savings are projected. In 1996 McDonough designed an energy-efficient factory and showroom for Herman Miller that saved the company $35,000 a year on electrical costs and significantly reduced turnover and absenteeism among employees. The following year McDonough completed work on the corporate campus of the clothing company the Gap, in San Bruno, California. The native grasses and wildflowers planted on the roofs of the Gap campus serve as a thermal and acoustical insulator, so that employees are not disturbed by the constant air traffic from the nearby San Francisco Airport. All the wood used in the building and furniture was harvested from sustainable forests, and large atriums bring sunlight deep into the building. McDonough raised the floors to create a network of ducts and a ventilation system that pulls in cool breezes at night, eliminating the need for air conditioning. As a result of McDonough's creativity and ecological resourcefulness, the Gap campus became 30 percent more energy efficient than California law requires. McDonough's firm won an award from Pacific Gas & Electric for designing one of the most fuel-efficient buildings in the state. "We weren't trying to be efficient—we were trying to be effective," McDonough told Dumaine. "And we did this without minimizing the amount of daylight or fresh air in order to minimize the air conditioning. This is what traditional energy-efficient buildings try to do. But you end up living in the dark with bad air."

In 2000 Ford's CEO, William Ford Jr., hired McDonough as chief architect for the 10-year, $2 billion redesign of the River Rouge car factory, where the legendary Henry Ford had manufactured Model T's nearly a century earlier. Since its creation the plant, with its billowing smokestacks, has served as the quintessential symbol of the industrial revolution. Under the guidance of McDonough, the plant will, perhaps, take on a new reputation of ecological responsibility. The first phase of the project was completed in 2003: the entire one-million-square-foot assembly plant was refitted with a grass roof, to cut back on water-filtration costs as well as to meet federal regulations on pollution. "Most factories are designed today so that if you get a one-inch rainfall, it hits the roof and rushes down the gutters into big pipes and into the river as fast as possible," McDonough explained to Dumaine. "The runoff picks up all the particulates that may have dropped on the site—everything in the soil, the detritus, the harmful chemicals. Wouldn't it be interesting if we could make the water travel from the building to the river in three days rather than three minutes? Then you avoid flooding and the dangerous water. Then we said, 'What if we used the green roof of the Ford assembly plant to absorb water and make oxygen?' The water that does run off falls onto a porous paving in the parking lot, so the water is absorbed, and it's filtered through wetlands with native trees and habitat on the way back to the river." The grass roof and the new parking lot cost the company $13 million. Had Ford followed convention and built a chemical-treatment facility instead, the cost would have been $48 million, not including the ongoing expense of meeting governmental regulations. "Regulation is a sign of design failure," McDonough told Kermit Whitfield for *Automotive Design & Production* (January 2003). "If you bump into a regulation, clearly something is not optimized, because the state feels compelled to make you stop or slow down, or fill out paperwork or do something that is otherwise wasteful. We would rather see commerce act in a way that is totally unregulated because it didn't need to be regulated. Companies like what we do because we remove regulations from their worries." McDonough is mindful that business executives are wary of the costs of environmentally safe systems and products. "The fundamental thing to point out about our work is that what we do is hugely profitable for companies. If it isn't, we don't think they should do it," McDonough told Whitfield.

McDonough's most recent project appears to be his most ambitious one as well. With the ever-growing population in China, the China Housing Industry Association has the responsibility to build housing for 400 million people in the next 12 years. The association commissioned McDonough to help design seven new cities. "We are about to witness the largest migration in human history," McDonough told Brian Dumaine for *Fortune International* (May 16, 2005). "About 40% of China's population lives in cities. The government estimates that by 2050 nearly 70% of its people will live in cities and new towns. If China follows the Western model of development, it will end up degrading the environment. The numbers are just too big. . . . They're already running out of water, and their air is terrible. The government is very aware of this. . . . This will be the largest economic opportunity in human history if we get it right. The business opportunity is figuring out how to build cities and towns that don't suck resources out of the earth." McDonough has designed for those cities buildings that will be heated and cooled by solar panels, with rooftops doubling as farmland, so that farmers can live downstairs from where they work. With the help of newly designed toilets, the cities' waste systems will also generate fertilizer and methane gas for cooking. The bowl of each toilet, McDonough has said, is to be so smooth that nothing, including bacteria, sticks to it; as a result, water usage from flushing will be significantly reduced, because only a light mist will be needed to clear away waste. Nearby bamboo wetlands will purify the waste, and the bamboo can be harvested and used for wood.

In McDonough's view, the Ford project and the new housing communities in China represent the first steps toward a productive marriage between business growth and environmental awareness. "We won't get everything right the first time. Change requires experimentation. But no problem can be solved by the same consciousness that created it," McDonough told Underwood. "Our job is to dream—and to make those dreams happen."

In 2004 McDonough published *Something Lived, Something Dreamed: Urban Design and the American West*. Nearly three years in the making, the book consists of an essay written by McDonough concerning the relationships among the varying landscapes of cities in the American West. Following McDonough's green-design philosophy, the limited edition, fine-print book was made from aluminum and reclaimed sycamore trees, with no chemical additives. More than 50 people worked together to create 125 copies of the handcrafted book, which includes colorful images that visually express McDonough's ideas for a mutually beneficial coexistence of the natural world and urban design. Priced at $695, *Something Lived, Something Dreamed* was included in the American Institute for Graphic Arts' "50 Books/50 Covers" national tour in 2005, which showcases the best-produced books and covers.

McDonough lives in Charlottesville, Virginia, with his wife, Elizabeth Demetriades.

—I.C.

Suggested Reading: *Automotive Design & Production* p32+ Jan. 2003; *Fortune International* p60 May 16, 2005; *FSB* p44 Dec. 2001/Jan. 2002; *Grid* p60+ May 2001; *MSNBC* (on-line) May 16, 2005; *New Scientist* p46+ Mar. 20, 2004; *Newsmakers* 2003; *Time* p70 Feb. 22, 1999

Selected Books: *Cradle to Cradle: Remaking the Way We Make Things* (with Michael Braungart), 2002; *Something Lived, Something Dreamed: Urban Design and the American West*, 2004

Selected Works: Environmental Defense Fund National Headquarters, New York, New York, 1985; Herman Miller "GreenHouse" Factory and Offices, Holland, Michigan, 1995; Gap Campus, San Bruno, California, 1997; Oberlin College's Adam Joseph Lewis Center for Environmental Studies, Oberlin, Ohio, 2000; Ford River Rouge Center, Dearborn, Michigan, 2001–

Meat Loaf

Sep. 27, 1947(?)– Rock singer; actor

Address: c/o Virgin Records America, 150 Fifth Ave., New York, NY 10011

"You can't live your life trying to beat *Bat Out of Hell*," Meat Loaf told an interviewer for the VH1 Web site (May 16, 2002) about his 1977 album, one of the best-selling records of all time. "You can't live your life trying to duplicate it. I don't live my life because of it. *Bat Out of Hell* and three bucks will get me a grande cappuccino at Starbucks. That's how I look at my life. It still takes me three bucks to get the coffee. And I still gotta go get it." With an estimated 34 million copies shipped worldwide, at least 14 million of them in the U.S., *Bat Out of Hell* is a landmark in the history of rock. It introduced three Top 40 singles—"Two Out of Three Ain't Bad," "You Took the Words Right Out of My Mouth," and Meat Loaf's signature song, "Paradise by the Dashboard Light"—and turned Meat Loaf from a moderately successful theater and film actor, with a notable appearance in *The Rocky Horror Picture Show* (1975), into a sui generis rock star, famous for his operatic voice, life-threateningly physical live performances, and outsize girth. "There almost certainly will never be any pop singer describable as Loafesque," David Hiltbrand wrote for *People* (July 22, 1985). "When it comes to Tin Pan Alley rock delivered in the style of a Wagnerian stomp, Meat Loaf has the field to himself." Yet after the phenomenal success of *Bat Out of Hell*, the performer's U.S. career stumbled. He fell into alcohol and drug abuse and weathered a plague of lawsuits that pushed him out of the limelight in the U.S., even as he stayed popular in the United Kingdom and Europe, with such albums as *Dead Ringer* (1981), *Bad Attitude* (1984), and *Blind Before I Stop* (1986). The release of *Bat Out of Hell II: Back into Hell*, in 1993, unexpectedly propelled him to the top of the *Billboard* charts again, with the single "I'd Do Anything for Love (But I Won't Do That)" hitting number one in as many as 38 countries and netting Meat Loaf a 1994 Grammy Award for best male rock solo vocal performance. Subsequent studio albums— including *Welcome to the Neighborhood* (1995) and *Couldn't Have Said It Better* (2003)—never reached the heights of the first two installments of

Jo Hale/Getty Images

Meat Loaf

Bat Out of Hell, which collectively have sold more than 50 million copies. After resolving a trademark dispute with Jim Steinman, the songwriter behind the first two *Bat Out of Hell* albums, Meat Loaf completed *Bat Out of Hell III: The Monster Is Loose*, which was scheduled for release at the end of October 2006. "A *Bat Out of Hell* record goes past being Meat Loaf," he told John Dingwall for the Glasgow, Scotland, *Daily Record* (September 8, 2006). "It's about an event. It has my name on it but it is not about me."

Throughout his up-then-down-then-up-then-down-then-up-again career, Meat Loaf has toyed with journalists and fans by offering contradictory information about his history, even giving what he has come to claim is a false date of birth in his autobiography, *To Hell and Back* (1999), co-authored with David Dalton. Chris Campion, in the London *Daily Telegraph* (October 30, 2004), suggested that it seems "as if the big ham in [Meat Loaf] can't help acting up, improvising new riffs on his life that lend it the same kind of mythic dimension as his music. You sense that the confabulations serve to provide some distance between the man and the persona." Meat Loaf has, for example, offered more than half a dozen explanations for his nickname. By most accounts, the name was given to him in his early childhood by his father, but other stories have it coming from the mouths of bullies or from friends razzing him about a near-fatal stunt he performed as an adolescent. Leslie Aday, Meat Loaf's wife for more than 20 years, told Kimberly Goad for the *Dallas Morning News* (December 12, 1993) that she did not know exactly how he had been given the name, but added: "I think it is probably rather painful, the true story. Can you imagine being a prepubescent child weighing 200 pounds?"

In addition to his role in *The Rocky Horror Picture Show*, Meat Loaf has claimed more than 50 other film and television appearances, including important parts in the films *Roadie* (1980), *Crazy in Alabama* (1999), and *Fight Club* (1999), and he has described himself not as a singer who also acts but as an actor who sings. "I can't sing unless there's a character," he explained to Lynn Barber for the London *Observer* (December 7, 2003). "Because I don't sing. It's almost like being schizophrenic—I don't sing, the character sings. And if I'm not in touch with my characters on any given night—sort of like channeling—I can't sing." His voice, however, is remarkably strong and has been classified as a heldentenor (heroic tenor), a German classification used to describe a tenor whose voice has certain elements of a baritone and an unusual degree of fullness. Such a voice, Meat Loaf has sometimes lamented, can be a liability in rock. "I don't have a rock voice," he told Barber, "I have to force it." Meat Loaf is also set apart from many rock musicians by the element of self-parody he brings to his performances. "A lot of what I do onstage is blatantly funny; it's meant to be hilarious; it's meant to be melodramatic," he told Jim Sullivan for the *Boston Globe* (November 19, 1993). "But that's what makes me different from U2 or Pearl Jam. . . . And I'm sorry—everybody can make fun of me or Jim [Steinman], but I'll tell you, when we capture the heart of an audience, we get it lock, stock and barrel."

Meat Loaf was born Marvin Lee Aday in Dallas, Texas; his legal name is now Michael Lee Aday. Though he has given a consistent answer over the years regarding the month and day of his birth—September 27—Meat Loaf has offered various birth years, generally either 1947 or 1951. (Some sources, including the Library of Congress, give 1948.) The year cited in his autobiography is 1947, but more recently he has insisted on 1951, going so far, in 2003, to adduce his passport as proof. Several sources confirm that he graduated from high school in 1965, however, making 1947 (or possibly 1948) more likely.

Meat Loaf's father, Orvis Wesley Aday, was a salesman, a former police officer, and an alcoholic; his mother, Wilma Artie Hukel, was an English teacher who sang in a gospel choir. Because of the instability that Orvis's alcoholism brought to the household, Meat Loaf spent long periods at his grandmother's home, and his obesity—he has said he weighed 240 pounds in seventh grade—isolated him socially. At Dallas's Thomas Jefferson High School, he played football and acted and sang in school plays. After graduation Meat Loaf remained in Texas to attend Lubbock Christian College (now Lubbock Christian University), before transferring, at the beginning of 1966, to North Texas State University, in Denton (now the University of North Texas), where he studied accounting for one year. In 1967 his mother died of cancer, and Meat Loaf, unable to bear living with his sometimes violent father, moved to Los Angeles, California. His father died of emphysema a few years later, not long after the two of them were reunited.

During the late 1960s, living primarily in Los Angeles, Meat Loaf looked for work as an actor while also singing in a number of bands, including Meat Loaf Soul, Popcorn Blizzard, and Floating Circus. Those bands enjoyed some regional success, with Popcorn Blizzard even releasing a single, "Once Upon a Time," which sold about 5,000 copies, but Meat Loaf's most important break came when he landed two parts in a Los Angeles production of the Broadway musical *Hair* (1967). When that production ran its course, Meat Loaf took on the same material in Detroit, Michigan, and the publicity generated by those performances led to a recording contract with Rare Earth, a short-lived division of Motown Records. Performing songs created by Motown's production team, Meat Loaf and the singer Cheryl "Stoney" Murphy, a fellow cast member in *Hair*, recorded and released their only album together, *Stoney & Meatloaf*, in 1971. Their single "What You See Is What You Get" reached number 36 on the rhythm-and-blues charts and number 71 on the *Billboard* Top 100. Backed by a band called Jake Wade and the Soul Searchers, Meat Loaf and Murphy also toured in support of the album, sometimes opening for such famous performers as B. B. King, Bob Seger, and Alice Cooper. During that period Meat Loaf, somewhat in the shadow of Murphy, who had a better-trained voice, began to give the highly physical, almost acrobatic performances that now define his stage persona.

The duo with Murphy, however, did not last beyond that tour, and Meat Loaf moved to New York City to continue his acting career, having been invited to reprise his roles in *Hair* in its Broadway production. In 1973, looking for other work, he auditioned for a part in the musical *More than You Deserve*. Produced at Joseph Papp's Public Theater, the musical was co-written by Michael Weller and Jim Steinman, the latter of whom, a few years earlier, while still in college, had attracted Papp's attention by writing, scoring, and starring in his own musical, a sex-heavy science-fiction story called *The Dream Engine*. At the audition Meat Loaf came across as an "enormous, heroic monster; a grotesque, bloated creature, who stalked the stage like an animal but acted as if he were a prince," Steinman told Lynn Barber. After *More than You Deserve* ran its course, and after working as an understudy for the comic actor John Belushi on a Broadway production of the *National Lampoon Show*, Meat Loaf took Belushi's part in a touring version of the show, which also paired him with the singer Ellen Foley. During that period Meat Loaf and Steinman, with some help from Foley and others, began developing the material they later used for *Bat Out of Hell*, which they tried in vain to sell to record companies. In 1974 Meat Loaf took the parts of Eddie and Dr. Everett von Scott in the U.S. theater premiere of *The Rocky Horror Show* (1973), and he reprised the role of Eddie in the 1975 film version, in which he sang the song "Hot

Patootie," a fan favorite. Meat Loaf's last performance in a Broadway musical came in 1976, with *Rockabye Hamlet*, which ran for only a week.

Though Meat Loaf and Steinman's collaborations are now routinely called Wagnerian rock, record executives were initially befuddled by their work. Heavily influenced by musical theater, Steinman wrote operatic songs filled with plot-heavy lyrics about the desires, pains, and fantasies of teenage life. Meat Loaf's voice gave the songs a hyperbolic urgency that bordered on self-parody. Meat Loaf has often emphasized that another important collaborator on his most popular album was the producer and guitarist Todd Rundgren, who championed the project to record companies and nursed it through its final stages.

The album sold slowly at first, and the critical response was generally negative. In an interview with Tim Dowling for the London *Guardian* (May 5, 2003), Meat Loaf recalled one review that came out before the album was released: "*Melody Maker* . . . called us the worst rock and roll band in the history of rock and roll. But that did more for me than anything else in the world. That sold more records." *Bat Out of Hell* gained momentum thanks to Meat Loaf's relentless tour schedule and a 1978 musical performance on NBC's *Saturday Night Live*. Soon *Bat Out of Hell* was one of the top albums in the world, dominating the charts in the U.S., the U.K., and Australia, with more than 2.5 million copies shipped in its first year of release. It went on to spend a reported 474 weeks—a little more than nine years—on the British Top 100 charts, driven to some degree by its hit singles, which in the U.S. included "Paradise by the Dashboard Light," an eight-and-a-half-minute odyssey of teenage trial and seduction, which featured a cameo by the former New York Yankees announcer Phil Rizzuto.

The live concerts that Meat Loaf performed to promote *Bat Out of Hell* became legendary. Describing Meat Loaf as "the ultimate 'must see,'" Mark Kernis wrote for the *Washington Post* (April 14, 1978), "After seeing [Meat Loaf's] stage act, it's hard to believe that he'll make it to 30. 'No holds barred' is an understated way of putting it." At times Meat Loaf's stage antics got the better of him, and he ended up splitting his pants after doing running somersaults or needing to use an oxygen mask to help soothe his asthma. During a show in Ottawa, Canada, in 1978, Meat Loaf broke his leg after falling off the stage and performed subsequent shows for the tour in a wheelchair.

The unanticipated success of *Bat Out of Hell* strained Meat Loaf's relationship with Steinman, who believed that he was not receiving enough credit for his contributions to the album. Meat Loaf also struggled to adapt to his sudden celebrity. "As *Bat* got bigger," he recalled in *To Hell and Back*, "I got crazier. It was like some terrible curse where everything I'd ever wished for turned into a nightmare, and it was rapidly turning me into a maniac." During that period Meat Loaf struggled with severe depression and began to abuse alcohol and cocaine. "It was a crazy time," he explained to C. Johnston for the Melbourne, Australia, *Herald Sun* (January 31, 1991). "I didn't really want to be a star. You can't go anywhere, you've got everyone bugging you, you feel like you're under the microscope all the time." His self-destructive behavior culminated one night in a half-hearted suicide attempt, which he dismissed in his autobiography, writing: "I don't think people who are trying to kill themselves show the empty bottle of pills to their best friend right after they take them."

Meat Loaf's best friend, in this case, was Steinman, with whom he had reunited, in late 1978, to work on a follow-up to *Bat Out of Hell*. By that time Meat Loaf, still overwhelmed by success and exhausted from touring, had stopped singing—partially for psychosomatic reasons but also because he wanted to delay production of his second album. Under pressure from the record label to complete an album, Steinman told Meat Loaf, toward the end of 1979, that he was going ahead alone; the result was Steinman's only solo album, *Bad for Good* (1981). Meat Loaf's 1978 attempts to cut a second record had results of a nonmusical nature: At a recording studio in Woodstock, New York, Meat Loaf fell in love with one of the studio assistants, Leslie Edmonds, and before a week had passed he asked her to marry him. Edmonds already had a daughter, Pearl, and in 1981 the couple had their only child together, Amanda.

Unable to record any music, Meat Loaf continued to act, taking parts in such films as *Americathon* (1979) and *Scavenger Hunt* (1979) and starring in *Roadie* (1980). None of those fared well commercially, but they provided Meat Loaf with an income and a chance to perform and, along with his new family, gave his life a measure of stability. In 1981, working from material written by Steinman, Meat Loaf released *Dead Ringer*, which failed commercially in the U.S. but became a major success in the U.K., selling more than a million copies, thanks in large part to the single "Dead Ringer for Love," which featured supporting vocal work by Cher. By the time the album was released, Meat Loaf was being managed by the talent agents David Sonenberg and Alfred Dellentash. His short-lived relationship with them prompted a series of acrimonious lawsuits on both sides—lawsuits that eventually grew to include the record labels involved in Meat Loaf's work. He was forced to declare bankruptcy in 1983. Steinman had retained Sonenberg and Dellentash as managers, preventing Meat Loaf from working with his most important collaborator. After *Dead Ringer*, Meat Loaf recorded several albums that met with uneven sales and little critical approval: *Midnight at the Lost and Found* (1983), *Bad Attitude* (1984), and *Blind Before I Stop*.

By 1989 Meat Loaf had put the worst of his financial troubles and self-destructive habits behind him. His years of constant touring, playing at small venues in the U.S. and sometimes selling out major arenas in the U.K., had brought him enough attention that he was offered a recording contract by the Music Corporation of America (MCA). The following year he received $1 million to act as a spokesperson for the Slim Fast brand of diet shakes, which helped him lose at least 40 pounds in a matter of months. He also gained exposure with an appearance in the hit film *Wayne's World* (1992). Meanwhile, Meat Loaf had slowly repaired his relationship with Steinman, and they began discussions about working on another album. The result was *Bat Out of Hell II: Back into Hell*, which Steinman wrote and produced.

Appearing 16 years after the original, *Bat Out of Hell II* was replete with the imagery, themes, and Wagnerian rock sound of the original. The album divided critics, with most dismissing it but many finding its theatrics charming. "From the arrangements to the lengths of the tracks, everything on the album is overstated; even the album version of the hit single, 'I Would Do Anything for Love (But I Won't Do That),' is 12 minutes long," Stephen Thomas Erlewine wrote for the All Music Guide Web site. "Yet that's precisely the point of this album, and is also why it works so well. No other rock & roller besides Meat Loaf could pull off the humor and theatricality of *Back Into Hell* and make it seem real. In that sense, it's a worthy successor to the original." The album debuted at number three on the *Billboard* charts and within weeks had reached number one, representing one of the greatest comebacks in rock history. Meat Loaf's next effort, *Welcome to the Neighborhood*, provided him with a Top 10 hit, "I'd Lie for You (And That's the Truth)," and significant sales, but critics generally described the album as formulaic and comparatively humorless.

At the end of the 1990s, Meat Loaf toured less frequently and acted more often. He earned acting credits for various TV shows and several films, most notably *Spice World* (1997); *Black Dog* (1998), in which he had a starring role opposite Patrick Swayze; *Crazy in Alabama*; and *Fight Club*, in which he played Robert Paulson, a former steroid abuser and testicular-cancer survivor.

The material for Meat Loaf's next album, *Couldn't Have Said It Better*, was developed over more than three years, an unusually leisurely pace for him. Mötley Crüe's Nikki Sixx and his writing partner, James Michael, wrote about half of the album's songs, and on one track, "Man of Steel," Meat Loaf sang with his stepdaughter, Pearl Aday, who became a full-time backup singer in his band. Meat Loaf's tour to promote the album was derailed by his ill heath, which hit its lowest point in November 2003, when an undiagnosed heart problem caused him to collapse during a performance at London's Wembley Arena.

Following the 2003 tour Meat Loaf began working on *Bat Out of Hell III: The Monster Is Loose*. He originally offered Steinman the role of writer and producer for the album, but contract negotiations fell through. After Meat Loaf hired Desmond Child to produce the record, Steinman asserted that he had trademark rights to the phrase "Bat Out of Hell" in the U.S. (Meat Loaf has told interviewers that he controls them elsewhere in the world.) The dispute was resolved in a matter of months, with both parties retaining rights to use "Bat Out of Hell" in future projects. Steinman ultimately wrote half of the album's 14 tracks, though five were covers of songs that had been previously recorded, including "It's All Coming Back to Me Now," made famous by Celine Dion. *Bat Out of Hell III* was introduced to audiences on October 16, 2006 as the last section of a three-part concert at the Royal Albert Hall, in London. Titled "Meat Loaf: *Bat Out of Hell*, Acts I, II, and III," the show was scheduled to travel, in November, to New York City, where it was to be called "Bat on Broadway," marking an end to Meat Loaf's 30-year separation from the Broadway stage.

Divorced from Leslie Aday in 2001, Meat Loaf now lives in California. His stepdaughter, Pearl Aday, is a singer, and his daughter, Amanda Aday, is an actress.

—N.W.M.

Suggested Reading: *Boston Globe* p105 Nov. 19, 1993; *Calgary Herald* C p1 Dec. 5, 1993; *Dallas Morning News* E p1 Dec. 12, 1993; (London) *Guardian* Features p8 May 5, 2003; (London) *Observer* p16 Dec. 7, 2003; *Newsweek* p 97 Sep. 11, 1978

Selected Books: *To Hell and Back* (with David Dalton), 1999

Selected Recordings: *Bat Out of Hell*, 1977; *Dead Ringer*, 1981; *Midnight at the Lost and Found*, 1983; *Bad Attitude*, 1984; *Blind Before I Stop*, 1986; *Bat Out of Hell II: Back into Hell*, 1993; *Welcome to the Neighborhood*, 1995; *Couldn't Have Said It Better*, 2003; *Bat Out of Hell III: The Monster Is Loose*, 2006

Selected Films: *Rocky Horror Picture Show*, 1975; *Roadie*, 1980; *Wayne's World*, 1992; *Fight Club*, 1999; *Crazy in Alabama*, 1999

Meier, Deborah

Apr. 6, 1931– Educator; education reformer; writer

Address: Mission Hill School, 67 Alleghany St., Boston, MA 02120

"If we took into account half of what we know about how human beings learn, and what we ourselves need to learn, we wouldn't organize schools the way we do," the educator, educational theorist, educational reformer, and writer Deborah Meier asserted to Catherine Foster for the *Christian Science Monitor* (October 30, 1987). "We wouldn't assume that decisions can come from some distant place"—such as a state- or federal-government office—"telling a teacher and school what to do with kids, and that some completely mystical way that none of us understand—the modern standardized test—would be used to assess whether we're doing well." Moreover, she continued, "We wouldn't block schedules into 40-minute periods and assume that every 40 minutes kids can turn their minds off one thing and on to another thing. We wouldn't teach literature, history, and science as though they were all absolutely unrelated subjects, but would help students connect them." Meier began teaching as a substitute in the Chicago, Illinois, public-school system in 1961, while raising her own three children. "At first I thought teaching was unprestigious 'women's work,'" she told Foster. "I wanted to change the world: write the world's best novel, be a foreign correspondent. But then I got captivated by the children. It's still un-

Courtesy of Deborah Meier

prestigious, and it's still mainly women doing it. But I thought it was challenging, amazing work." Since the mid-1970s Meier has helped to found four so-called alternative public schools in the East Harlem neighborhood of New York City—three elementary schools and one high school—and an elementary school in Boston, Massachusetts, and she served as the principal of three of them. Those schools, which had no admission requirements, were distinguished in part by their small classes—

which enabled teachers to give each student far more attention than could teachers in neighboring schools—and the active involvement of teachers in the development of curricula and other aspects of school life. The schools became renowned as "laboratories," as Meier labeled them in an interview with Irene Sege for the *Boston Globe* (January 13, 1999), that showed "what can happen if school communities are allowed—nay, required—to use their resources, energies, ideas, and skills more freely." Meier is the author of more than 70 articles, which have appeared in publications ranging from the *Christian Science Monitor* and the *Boston Globe* to *Educational Horizons* and the *American School Board Journal*, and she has written, co-written, or edited five books. She has earned 14 honorary degrees, from schools including Harvard University and Teachers College of Columbia University. In 1987 Meier became the first person who works full-time in education to win a prestigious MacArthur Fellowship. "What I wanted was to create thoughtful citizens—people who believed they could live interesting lives and be productive and socially useful," she explained on the Public Broadcasting Service Web site. "So I tried to create a community of children and adults where the adults shared and respected the children's lives."

In an article for *Connection: New England's Journal of Higher Education & Economic Development* (Fall/Winter 1999, on-line), Meier, referring to Central Park East Secondary School, which she co-founded, wrote that years after students had graduated, they "were convinced that their survival over the many tough years that lay ahead depended upon the strong personal passions and relationships that the school had honored and nurtured. The school also had helped them weave a host of adults into a support network, aided by community service and school-to-work programs, as well as music classes, drama clubs and extended lab work. Many also noted that Central Park East was a school where families and teachers were partners and where students felt respected as individuals with different styles and concerns. Ongoing teacher-family ties helped make allies out of otherwise edgy rivals. Every family had at least one full-time staff member designated as its special ally for two years or more. Kids and their parents said they felt they had belonged to a powerful little community that stood for something. And its strength added to their own personal staying power. The students described the intervening years as difficult. But they attributed their perseverance to the kind of schooling we had offered. . . . Studies of other successful schools point to similar effects. They are not miracles. They are distinctly 'replicable' if we take them seriously."

In the same article Meier wrote, "At the same time, we must make sure that pressure to cover more and more material does not reduce opportunities for students and teachers to get to know each other well. Furthermore, as teachers have less say in what and how they teach, their knowledge of their students and their subject matter seems more and more superfluous. When teachers are seen as mere conduits of other people's expertise, the alienation between student and teacher grows apace. At Central Park East, we insisted that it was our job to model what it was like to be responsible citizens of our school. . . . If small schools are good for young people, maybe they're good for older ones too—even folks as old as us, their teachers. Shouldn't all educators join together to bring the advantages of a powerful school composed of powerful adults to all children regardless of where they start from? Shouldn't this be a common task for all educators ranging from kindergarten teachers to college professors?"

The daughter of Joseph Willen and Pearl (Larner) Willen, Meier was born Deborah Willen in New York City on April 6, 1931. She has an older brother, Paul Willen; as an adult, after her mother's death and her father's remarriage, she acquired two stepsiblings. She has named among her idols both her father, who, as executive vice president with the Federation of Jewish Philanthropies for 26 years, helped to secure $1 billion in donations for that organization, and her mother, who served for six years as president of the National Council of Jewish Women, contributed much time to the organization Women in Community Service, and co-founded the New York branches of the American Labor and Liberal Parties. "At a time when feminism was not fashionable, I learned from [my mother] that it was important and satisfying to be a mother and to try to make a difference in the world," Meier told Kathleen Teltsch for the *New York Times* (June 16, 1987). From the primary grades through high school, Meier attended the private Fieldston School, in the Riverdale section of the Bronx, which sought to instill in its students the values associated with Ethical Culture, "a humanistic religious and educational movement inspired by the ideal that the supreme aim of human life is working to create a more humane society," according to the Web site of the American Ethical Union. Classes were small, and the curriculum included discussions about ethics and emphasized hands-on learning (with instruction in the lower grades in such areas as woodworking and sewing) and first-hand experiences (including frequent field trips).

After she completed high school, Meier attended Antioch College, in Yellow Springs, Ohio, from 1949 to 1951. (Her Web site does not mention her earning a bachelor's degree.) She received an M.A. degree in history from the University of Chicago in 1955. While in graduate school she got married. Her formal education also includes courses taken at the City College of New York, the Bank Street College of Education, in New York City, and Temple University, in Philadelphia, Pennsylvania. In 1961, while living in Chicago, Meier decided to find part-time work, so as to have enough extra income to pay someone to clean her house once a week and also to have time both to be at home with her three young children (Roger, Nicholas, and Rebecca) and to serve as a volunteer in activities connected with the civil rights movement. She found what she was seeking in the Chicago public-school system, for which she became a substitute teacher. In 1963 she was hired as a half-time kindergarten teacher at her children's school. "It was never something that in the least bit interested me" before then, she told Irene Sege. "Outside of my own children I didn't find anybody else's children fascinating. I grew up in a climate in which teaching young children was considered [an occupation] for people who weren't too smart. But I found 5-year-olds absolutely staggeringly interesting. Seeing them day after day, I fell in love with the questions they raised that were so exciting." She began teaching Head Start prekindergarten classes and then classes in primary grades, and she continued to teach after moving with her family to Philadelphia and, later, in 1966, New York City. She developed a reputation for being an innovative educator and an iconoclast who openly voiced her disdain for overreliance on standardized testing and her belief in a personalized approach to teaching.

Meier was working with public-school teachers in a program at the City College of New York when, in 1974, Anthony J. Alvarado, who was then the superintendent of Community School District Four, in the East Harlem neighborhood of Manhattan, invited her to open a new elementary school where she could put her theories into practice. The test scores in District Four, on average, were lower than those in any other region of New York City, and the students, Alvarado thought, needed far more help than they were getting. Meier set up what became the Central Park East Elementary School, housed in a wing of the preexisting Public School 171. When the school opened, in 1974, the student body numbered 50, and all the children were black or Hispanic. Meier served as principal, and she hired teachers who expressed a desire to work with her in an innovative facility. The curricula that Meier and her staff developed together emphasized the quality of learning rather than the quantity of topics covered or test scores. Subjects were integrated rather than compartmentalized, and standardized testing was abandoned in favor of semi-personalized assessments. Meier and her staff made communication—among teachers, students, and parents—a top priority; indeed, parents were not only encouraged but required to become involved in their children's education. Students were not a carefully chosen educational elite but an assortment of area students, including those who had been struggling with their schoolwork. Central Park East quickly became a great success, in terms of students' academic performance and teachers' job satisfaction. "I look back at it and don't know how I did it," Meier told Irene Sege in 1999, referring to the fact that when she was establishing Central Park East, she was in the midst of a divorce, and her father had recently suffered a debilitating stroke. (Her mother had died in a car accident a few years earlier.) "I think the work was enormously stabilizing," she said to Sege. "Work has always been that for me. When I walked into that school I forgot everything else."

Within six years of its founding, the number of students at Central Park East had risen to 210. Moreover, about one-quarter of them were not members of minority groups but were white children, from outside East Harlem, whose parents had heard about the high quality of education offered at the school. There was not enough room in the school for all the children whose parents wanted them to be enrolled there, so, again supported by Alvarado, Meier opened a second school, called Central Park East II, in 1980. A third, River East Elementary School, opened a few years later.

In 1985 Meier helped to found the Central Park East Secondary School, and she became its principal. Class size was set at a maximum of 20. Students were strongly encouraged to participate in class discussions and, if they saw fit, to challenge what they heard from teachers as well as their peers. No longer confined to discrete 40-minute chunks of subject matter, most classes were two hours long and interwove topics—specifically, science and math, or social studies and the humanities. Students were required to perform community service for a minimum of three hours weekly, and interested students could undertake extracurricular career-oriented apprenticeships arranged through the school. Three times a week, for 45 to 60 minutes, juniors and seniors met with teacher/advisers; their advisers also maintained regular contact with the students' parents or guardians. Thus, as Meier has put it, adults and children became "part of the same culture." Instead of assessing progress by means of standardized tests, students were judged on the contents of portfolios submitted during their junior and senior years; examples of portfolio items, as listed on the Web site of the School Redesign Network, are reports entitled "The Effects of Alzheimer's Disease," "Education in South Africa and Cuba," and "A Comparison of the Effects of Hair Straighteners and Hair Removers on Skin and Hair." Seniors made presentations before a graduation committee, much as Ph.D. candidates defend their dissertations. "I'm for high standards. I'm not for standardization," Meier declared to Pat Wingert for Newsweek (June 12, 2000). "I'm not in favor of more multiple-choice tests, or important decisions being made using only one instrument—while ignoring the input of the teachers who know these kids. . . . There is no evidence that standardization produces more equality. This is a lazy and cheap way of trying to provide equity." According to a report on the Ford Foundation Web site, in the early 1990s only 5 percent of the students in Central Park East Secondary School, on average, dropped out before graduating, and 90 percent of those who earned their diplomas entered four-year colleges.

Between 1992 and 1996 Meier co-directed the Coalition Campus Project, which, as she wrote for her Web site, "successfully redesigned the reform" of two large, failing New York City high schools and led to the creation of a dozen new alternative schools. In late 1994 she resigned as principal of Central Park East Secondary School, after winning a two-year senior fellowship from the Annenberg Institute for School Reform, which is based at Brown University, in Providence, Rhode Island. As an Annenberg fellow she acted as a liaison between New York City public schools and the bureaucracy that oversaw them. While in that role she began to grow restless; after she realized that she missed her more intimate interactions with students, she decided to start another school, this time in the Boston area, where school-system officials had recently been soliciting proposals for innovative new schools. A little more than a year later, in September 1997, Meier, as principal, welcomed the first students to the Mission Hill School, located in the Roxbury district of Boston, which accommodated 180 students from kindergarten through eighth grade. Although the opening days of the school were plagued with difficulties (the furniture did not arrive on time, for example), and Meier suffered illnesses that resulted in her being hospitalized twice that winter, the first year at the Mission Hill School was more pleasant for her than what she had experienced in founding the schools in New York. One reason for that, as she told Irene Sege, was that her children were grown, and she no longer had to devote much of her energies to raising a family. Another reason, as she said to Sege, was that she knew "what to expect. I'm not thrown by the fact that it's not utopia immediately."

Meier's books are *The Power of Their Ideas: Lessons to America from a Small School in Harlem* (1995); *Will Standards Save Public Education?* (2000), which contains essays by the progressive school reformer Theodore Sizer, the conservative scholar Abigail Thernstrom, and the historian and standards-setter Gary Nash, as well as Meier; *Keeping School: Letters to Families from Principals of Two Small Schools* (2004), co-written by Theodore Sizer and Nancy Sizer; and *Many Children Left Behind: How the No Child Left Behind Act Is Damaging Our Children and Our Schools* (2004), which she edited with George Wood and which contains contributions, in addition to theirs, by Alfie Kohn, Linda Darling-Hammond, and Theodore Sizer. In an interview for the *Boston Globe* (September 26, 2004), when Katie Oliveri asked her why she believes that the No Child Left Behind Act (signed by President George W. Bush on January 8, 2002) "is actually leaving our children behind," Meier answered, "Because . . . it begins to create schools that place focus on students doing well on tests. . . . Children need to learn in school how to reason and how to communicate. . . . You can't test for mind and heart matters such as these. . . . It distorts intellectual life and ignores things kids need." She also said, "We need to be clear that it's

important to use our minds well and become educated people and not to just settle for high test scores and hard classes."

Currently, Meier is a senior scholar and adjunct professor at New York University's Steinhardt School of Education. She is on the editorial boards of *Dissent* magazine, the *Nation*, and the *Harvard Education Letter* and is a board member of the Mission Hill School, the Coalition of Essential Schools, the Educational Alliance, the Association of Union Democracy, Educators for Social Responsibility, the National Board of Professional Teaching Standards, and the National Academy of Education, among other groups. She is the director of the Forum for Democracy and is much in demand as a speaker.

Meier has a home in Hillsdale, New York, about two hours north of New York City, where she lives with her ex-husband, Fred Meier, whom she refers to now as her partner. She has four grandchildren.

—K.J.E.

Suggested Reading: *Boston Globe* F p1+ Jan. 13, 1999, A p15 Nov. 27, 2000, A p33 Sep. 26, 2004; *Christian Science Monitor* p19 Oct. 30, 1987; *Connection* (on-line) Fall/Winter 1999; Deborah Meier's Web site; Mission Hill School Web site; *New York Times* B p8 June 16, 1987; *Newsweek* p79+ June 12, 2000; pbs.org; *Teacher Magazine* (on-line) Aug./Sep. 2002; *University of Chicago Magazine* (on-line) Oct. 1995

Selected Books: *The Power of Their Ideas: Lessons to America from a Small School in Harlem*, 1995; *Will Standards Save Public Education?*, 2000; *Keeping School: Letters to Families from Principals of Two Small Schools* (with Theodore and Nancy Sizer), 2004; *Many Children Left Behind: How the No Child Left Behind Act Is Damaging Our Children and Our Schools* (with Alfie Kohn, Linda Darling-Hammond, Theodore Sizer, and George Wood), 2004

Miller, Judith

Jan. 2, 1948– Journalist

Address: c/o Jason Epstein, New York Review of Books, 1755 Broadway, Fifth Fl., New York, NY 10019

Since the September 11, 2001 terrorist attacks on New York City and Washington, D.C., the administration of President George W. Bush has advocated the establishment of democratic governments in the Middle East, contending that such governments would act as a stabilizing force in that region of the world and extend to its people the rights long taken for granted by Americans. Freedom of

Judith Miller

Win McNamee/Getty Images

Judith Miller was born on January 2, 1948 in New York City, to a Jewish father and an Irish-Catholic mother. Her father, Bill Miller, had emigrated with his parents from Pinsk, Russia, in 1905 and grown up in Brooklyn. He worked as a dancer and then, in 1929, opened his own club, the legendary Bill Miller's Riviera, located in Fort Lee, New Jersey, outside New York City. As an agent and producer (in addition to club owner), Miller booked such top entertainers as Frank Sinatra, Dean Martin, and Sophie Tucker at the Riviera. When the club closed, in 1953, Bill Miller moved with his family to Las Vegas, Nevada. While her father pursued his entertainment career there (he has been credited with pioneering the lounge act), Judith Miller settled in Los Angeles, California, where she graduated from Hollywood High School. She went on to attend Ohio State University and the University of Brussels, in Belgium, before earning her B.A. degree in economics in 1969 from Barnard College, in New York. In 1972 Miller received an M.A. degree in public affairs from the Woodrow Wilson School of Public and International Affairs at Princeton University, in Princeton, New Jersey. During her years there, Miller traveled to Jerusalem in 1971 to research a paper and became fascinated by the issues surrounding the territorial dispute between Israelis and Palestinians. In pursuit of her newfound interest, she spent the rest of the summer traveling through Egypt, Jordan, and Lebanon.

In the U.S., the next couple of years brought the Watergate affair, in which members of President Richard Nixon's administration engineered the 1972 burglary of the Democratic National Committee headquarters at the Watergate complex, in Washington, D.C. Amid the subsequent scandal, which led to the imprisonment of many administration officials and to the president's resignation, the public came to revere the *Washington Post* reporters Bob Woodward and Carl Bernstein, who broke the story and exposed corruption at the highest levels of government. Miller, too, saw journalism as a noble profession, thinking that "it was the way of doing something that was good, that was public-spirited, that exposing wrongdoing was a good thing to do," as she told Gabe Pressman for WNBC (June 19, 2005). Already knowledgeable about Middle East issues, Miller began a career in investigative journalism as a correspondent for the *Progressive* and for National Public Radio. Her work took her to regions of the world ruled by Muslim fundamentalists who were known to be unwelcoming to Westerners, particularly Western women; nonetheless, Miller's fearlessness and headstrong attitude allowed her to cultivate a network of sources with firsthand experience and knowledge of the topics she covered. In 1977 she was hired by the *New York Times* as a correspondent for the Washington bureau and assigned to cover the Middle East and nuclear-proliferation issues. As she rose through the ranks of the news organization, she continued to travel to the most volatile ar-

speech, among other priviliges, would be not a dream but a reality. Ironically, as Iraq—in the wake of the U.S.-led invasion—seeks to establish a democratic government, American journalists battle on the home front to protect a central constitutional tenet: freedom of the press. Since the identity of the former CIA operative Valerie Plame was revealed in the press, in July 2003, the establishment of a federal shield law, protecting reporters from having to reveal their sources, has been a subject of national debate. The former *New York Times* investigative journalist Judith Miller has been a major proponent of advancing such a measure in Congress. Over nearly three decades beginning in the 1970s, the Pulitzer Prize– and Emmy Award–winning reporter built an impressive career, filing stories on Middle East issues while ensuring the anonymity of her sources around the world. Her expertise in national security as well as her access to high-level government officials were matched by few other reporters and allowed her to climb the ranks of the prestigious *New York Times*. But on November 9, 2005, Miller resigned from the newspaper, after several years of controversy surrounding her reporting on the war in Iraq and her involvement in the federal investigation concerning the leak of Plame's status as an operative. (Her refusal to name sources during that investigation led to her imprisonment for 85 days in 2005.) In her resignation letter to the editors of the *Times*, Miller indicated that she intends to "continue speaking in support of a federal shield law" and to continue her long career as an investigative journalist by writing on national security—despite the controversies that plagued her last few years at the *Times*.

eas of the Middle East, constructing an extensive group of sources, both abroad and in Washington; her access to top officials in the White House was the envy of her journalistic colleagues. Miller was promoted to Cairo bureau chief in 1983, becoming the first woman ever to fill that position. Four years later she returned to the U.S. as the news editor and deputy chief of the Washington bureau, only to return to the Middle East in 1990, as a special correspondent during the Persian Gulf crisis. In 1996 Miller published the book *God Has Ninety-Nine Names: A Reporter's Journey Through a Militant Middle East.*

Miller's expertise in the issues of international security and terrorism became a much-sought-after commodity in the wake of the September 11, 2001 attacks against the U.S. (She even became a victim of terrorism herself when, on October 12, 2001, she was one of several journalists who received letters made to look as if they contained anthrax—a hoax perpetrated weeks after anthrax was sent anonymously through the mail, killing five people who came in contact with the lethal powder.) In 2002 Miller won an Emmy Award for a documentary based on the book *Germs: Biological Weapons and America's Secret War*, which she co-wrote with William Broad and Stephen Engelberg. In the same year she was one of a team of *New York Times* reporters who won the Pulitzer Prize for exploratory journalism for their coverage of the terrorist network Al Qaeda, and she was one of a *Times* group given the Dupont Award for a series of installments of the PBS program *Frontline.*

Few people ever questioned the validity of Miller's sources in Washington and the Middle East, or of the accuracy of her investigative reporting, until the United States invaded Iraq in 2003, deposing the country's leader, Saddam Hussein, who was said to have amassed weapons of mass destruction. In the months after the September 11 attacks, high-level officials of the George W. Bush administration had begun focusing their attention on Iraq; the government's case for invasion was based on the accounts of Iraqi defectors produced by the Iraqi National Congress (INC)—an umbrella group, headed by Ahmad Chalabi, that opposed Hussein's regime. The Pentagon's Defense Intelligence Agency was receptive to information from Chalabi's group of defectors, but the CIA, based on its past encounters with Chalabi, was critical and dismissive of his sources. Nonetheless, the Bush administration took Chalabi's accounts seriously. As a result, since Miller maintained sources in the top echelons of the White House, she wrote a series of articles based on the testimony of Chalabi's informants, which pointed to a large hidden cache of weapons of mass destruction in Iraq.

For the December 20, 2001 edition of the *New York Times*, Miller wrote an article detailing the experiences of an Iraqi defector, Adnan Ihsan Saeed al-Haideri, who claimed to have worked on renovation projects at sites where chemical and nuclear weapons were produced and stored. Miller wrote, "Mr. Saeed's account gives new clues about the types and possible locations of illegal laboratories, facilities and storage sites that American officials and international inspectors have long suspected Iraq of trying to hide." The following year Miller co-wrote a story about supposed evidence that Hussein was purchasing parts to build an atomic bomb. Citing another account by a defector, Miller and Michael R. Gordon reported for the September 8, 2002 edition of the paper, "In the last 14 months, Iraq has sought to buy thousands of specially designed aluminum tubes, which American officials believe were intended as components of centrifuges to enrich uranium. . . . The diameter, thickness and other technical specifications of the aluminum tubes had persuaded American intelligence experts that they were meant for Iraq's nuclear program, officials said." (The officials mentioned in the article were Miller's sources from within the White House.) Later, members of the Bush administration including Vice President Richard B. Cheney appeared on news programs, citing Miller's articles in their claims about the existence of an Iraqi weapons program. That sequence of events aroused skepticism—at the very least—among some journalists, including Bob Simon of CBS News, who told Charles Layton for the *American Journalism Review* (August/September 2003), "You leak a story to the *New York Times* and the *New York Times* prints it, and then you go on the Sunday shows quoting the *New York Times* and corroborating your own information. You've got to hand it to [the Bush administration]. That takes, as we say here in New York, chutzpah." By 2003 the Defense Intelligence Agency had discredited the information in both of the above-cited articles as well as several others.

It was Miller's April 21, 2003 article, however, that later drew the harshest criticism. Traveling with the Mobile Exploitation Team (MET) Alpha unit of the U.S. Army in Iraq as it searched for weapons of mass destruction, Miller wrote a piece about an Iraqi scientist who told MET Alpha that chemical- and biological-warfare agents had been destroyed just four days before President Bush issued his 48-hour warning to Hussein. (On March 17, 2003, after Hussein had refused to cooperate with the U.N. investigation of Iraq's weapons, Bush warned Hussein that if he did not leave Iraq within two days, the U.S. would commence military action against Iraq at a time of its own choosing.) The claim about the weapons was later found to be false, but what Miller's detractors condemned most strongly was that she had obtained the information from the government and not a firsthand source. (She was not allowed to speak with the scientist but merely saw him from a distance, "clad in nondescript clothes and a baseball cap," as she later described him.) The scientist also told MET Alpha that Iraq had worked with Al Qaeda. Miller wrote that U.S. officials viewed the scientist's account as "the most important discovery to date in the hunt for illegal weapons" and one that "supports the Bush administration's charges that Iraq continued to develop those weapons and lied to the United Nations about it." The story spread through news organizations all across the country and played a major role in Bush's post-invasion justification for having entered Iraq. When Ray Suarez asked Miller on the PBS program *The NewsHour with Jim Lehrer* if MET Alpha had found any proof of weapons of mass destruction in Iraq, Miller responded, "Well, I think they found something more than a smoking gun. What they've found is . . . a silver bullet in the form of a person, an Iraqi individual, a scientist, as we've called him, who really worked on programs, who knows them firsthand, and who has led MET Alpha people to some pretty startling conclusions," according to the *American Journalism Review* article. Skeptics, such as Jim Naureckas, editor of *Extra!*, a magazine published by the media watchdog group Fairness & Accuracy in Reporting, told the *Chicago Tribune* (May 27, 2004) that "the stories Judith Miller wrote were incredibly important in selling the idea that Iraq posed an immediate threat to the world."

On May 26, 2004 the *New York Times* published an editorial about the paper's failure to examine its sources sufficiently in its coverage of the events leading up to the war in Iraq. "The problematic articles varied in authorship and subject matter," the editorial read, "but many shared a common feature. They depended at least in part on information from a circle of Iraqi informants, defectors and exiles bent on 'regime change' in Iraq, people whose credibility has come under increasing public debate in recent weeks." Alluding to the controversy over Miller's articles, the editors wrote, "Complicating matters for journalists, the accounts of these exiles were often eagerly confirmed by United States officials convinced of the need to intervene in Iraq." An article by Douglas McCollum in the *Columbia Journalism Review* (July/August 2004) discussed a memo submitted to Congress in June 2002 by a member of the Iraqi National Congress; the memo described the Information Collection Program, designed by the INC to provide U.S. news organizations with fabricated information about Hussein's illicit weapons program and his ties to terrorist organizations, for the purpose of persuading the U.S. to effect regime change in Iraq. The memo contained a list of 108 news stories containing misinformation supplied by the Information Collection Program. While Miller was known to many as *the* journalist who had reported inaccurate information on Iraq, she was one of dozens of journalists listed in the memo. Miller eventually acknowledged the flaws in her reporting prior to the Iraq war, telling Don Van Natta Jr., Adam Liptak, and Clifford Levy for the *New York Times* (October 16, 2005), "WMD [weapons of mass destruction]—I got it totally wrong. The analysts, the experts and the journalists who covered them—we were all wrong. If your sources are wrong, you are wrong. I did the best job that I could."

In July 2003 Miller became the central figure of another controversy, this time involving the "outing" of the CIA operative Valerie Plame. In January 2003, during the State of the Union address, President Bush warned Americans, "The British government has learned that Saddam Hussein recently sought significant quantities of uranium from Africa"—referring to a substance used to build nuclear weapons. However, a former U.S. ambassador, Joseph C. Wilson IV, had already traveled to the African nation of Niger to investigate the issue and concluded that it was highly unlikely that Niger had sold uranium to Iraq. On July 6, 2003, the *New York Times* published an op-ed piece by Wilson revealing his findings in Niger, which contradicted the president's statements from earlier in the year. A week later, on July 14, 2003, Robert Novak revealed in his syndicated column that according to two senior administration officials, Wilson's wife, Valerie Plame, "a [CIA] agency operative on weapons of mass destruction," had suggested sending Wilson to Niger to investigate. Under the Intelligence Identities Protection Act, enacted in 1982, the intentional leak of a covert CIA agent's identity is a federal crime. Novak's column thus came under intense scrutiny, and U.S. attorney Patrick Fitzgerald was appointed as a special counsel to discover the source of the leak. Fitzgerald immediately subpoenaed Novak, Matthew Cooper of Time Inc., and Miller. Although only Novak had actually written an article revealing Plame's identity, the other two journalists were subpoenaed for discussions they had had with high-level officials concerning Plame's status as an operative. Initially both Cooper and Miller refused to testify before a federal grand jury and reveal their sources, but when Time Inc., Cooper's employer, complied and turned over his E-mail messages, Cooper decided to testify. According to Cooper's account, he spoke with President Bush's deputy chief of staff, Karl Rove, and Vice President Cheney's chief of staff, I. Lewis "Scooter" Libby, on successive days, asking them about the false information Bush had given in his State of the Union address concerning the Iraqi uranium purchase in Africa. Cooper asserted that Rove and Libby attempted to protect their bosses and contradicted the assertions in Wilson's op-ed piece. Both officials, Cooper recalled, said that Wilson's wife, not the CIA itself, had coordinated his trip to Niger—thus implicitly impugning the legitimacy of Wilson's trip and, some suspected, punishing Wilson by revealing his wife's identity. Fitzgerald's investigation, while focused on discovering the source of the leak, also aims to determine whether or not the White House intentionally leaked Plame's identity as revenge for Wilson's op-ed piece contradicting the administration's claims.

Miller, unlike Cooper, refused to testify. The *New York Times* had stood by Miller as soon as she was subpoenaed and immediately retained the acclaimed First Amendment lawyer Floyd Abrams to defend her. "She'd given her pledge of confidentiality," Arthur Sulzberger Jr., the newspaper's publisher, told Van Natta, Liptak, and Levy. "She was prepared to honor that. We were going to support her." On July 6, 2005 Miller was found in contempt of court and sentenced to prison until she testified before the grand jury. The newspaper's leadership never requested to see Miller's notes, nor did they press her to reveal her source. They left the major decisions of the case to Miller. Miller subsequently spent 85 days in jail, claiming that a waiver signed by Libby in 2004, freeing Miller to cooperate with investigators, had been coerced and that she could not honor it. While in prison, Miller became a public symbol of journalistic integrity for her refusal to betray her sources, despite the personal cost. Although she had never published an article that even alluded to Plame, Miller was the central figure in the CIA leak controversy because of her unwavering stance against revealing a source. Miller's lawyers contacted Libby to obtain another waiver, which he granted both verbally and in writing. Miller then agreed to testify, on the condition that Fitzgerald question her only about her conversations with Libby. Fitzgerald accepted the condition, and on September 29, 2005 Miller was released from jail.

The following day, Miller testified before the grand jury that at the time of her first meeting with Libby, on June 23, 2003, her assignment was to write an article on the failure of the U.S. government to find unconventional weapons in Iraq. Libby, however, had wanted to discuss a diplomat's 2002 fact-finding trip to Niger to determine whether Iraq had bought or was looking to buy uranium to build nuclear weapons. She stated that Libby defended Cheney, saying that the vice president knew nothing about Wilson or his findings. During their second meeting, two days later, according to Miller, Libby informed her that Wilson's wife worked for the CIA unit Winpac (weapons intelligence, nonproliferation, and arms control). In Miller's subpoenaed notebook, notations of "Valerie Flame" (apparently a misspelling of "Plame") and "Victoria Wilson," another misnomer, were found. When asked about those notations, Miller testified that she could not recall who had first mentioned Valerie Plame's name to her. Bound by the agreement made before Miller's release, Fitzgerald could not ask her where she might have first heard the name, if not from Libby. While some praised Miller for following her convictions, others began to question her motives for remaining silent. Some members of the media, recalling Miller's inaccurate reporting leading up to the Iraq war, expressed suspicions that Miller was attempting to cover up the extent of her relationship with the White House. For her part, Miller said in her interview with Gabe Pressman that her refusal to reveal her contacts was "not about me. It's not about the New York Times or Time or Matt Cooper. It's about the public's right to know. Do you want to hear from authorized government spokesmen, authorized corporate spokesmen alone, or do you want to hear

what's really going on inside an organization? We can't operate without confidential sources." Upon her release, mindful of the cause she had come to symbolize in the public perception, Miller said, as quoted by CNN.com (September 30, 2005), "I am hopeful that my very long stay in jail will serve to strengthen the bond between reporters and their sources. I hope that blanket waivers [which would allow reporters to discuss freely any conversations they had with signatories in connection with investigations] are a thing of the past. They do not count. They are not voluntary, and they should not be accepted by journalists. I am also hopeful that my time in jail will help pass a federal shield law"—to protect journalists from being prosecuted for refusing to reveal sources—"so that the public's right to know can be protected."

As Miller's critics have gained a stronger voice in the media, however, many feel that the potential for a federal shield law to be passed is extremely small with the controversial reporter as its leading spokesperson. "I wish it had been a clear-cut whistle-blower case. I wish it had been a reporter who came with less public baggage," Bill Keller, the Times's executive editor, told Van Natta et al, referring to the newspaper's decision to take a stand on the ambiguous issue of the Plame affair—and in support of Miller, whose conduct some had questioned. The article by Van Natta, Liptak, and Levy shed light on perceptions of Miller within the Times offices. The journalists referred to Miller as "an intrepid reporter whom editors found hard to control" and as "a divisive figure," and they quoted Keller as saying that he had removed Miller from coverage of Iraq and weapons issues, but that "she kept kind of drifting on her own back into the national security realm." Rather than receiving a hero's welcome from her colleagues at the New York Times upon her release from prison, Miller returned to a newsroom where there was an undercurrent of puzzlement and resentment regarding her action. Miller said to Van Natta, Liptak, and Levy, "You could see it in people's faces. I'm a reporter. People were confused and perplexed, and I realized then that The Times and I hadn't done a very good job of making people understand what has been accomplished." "Everyone admires our paper's willingness to stand behind us and our work," Todd S. Purdum, a Times reporter, said to Van Natta et al, "but most people I talk to have been troubled and puzzled by Judy's seeming ability to operate outside the conventional reportorial channels and managerial controls. Partly because of that, many people have worried about whether this was the proper fight to fight."

On November 9, 2005 Miller reached an agreement with the New York Times ending her career at the newspaper, which had spanned almost three decades. After two weeks of negotiations, lawyers for Miller and the paper negotiated a severance package. In her letter to the editor, published in the New York Times on November 10, 2005, Miller wrote that she had decided to leave the paper partly because of the criticisms from her colleagues concerning her actions in the Plame case. She went on to write, "But mainly I have chosen to resign because over the last few months, I have become the news, something a *New York Times* reporter never wants to be." Aware that she had become a controversial figure in the journalistic realm, Miller wrote, "Even before I went to jail, I had become a lightning rod for public fury over the intelligence failures that helped lead our country to war." Although the relationship between the *Times* and Miller had been fraught with tension for years, in the end many within the newspaper conceded Miller's legacy as an intrepid reporter during her 28-year career at the *New York Times*. Arthur Sulzberger Jr. said of Miller, "We are grateful to Judy for her significant personal sacrifice to defend an important journalistic principle," adding, "I respect her decision to retire from The *Times* and wish her well," as reported by Katharine Q. Seelye for the newspaper (November 10, 2005). Miller left the newspaper on amicable terms, assured that "the *Times* will continue the tradition of excellence that has made it indispensable to its readers, a standard for journalists, and a bulwark of democracy," as she wrote.

Judith Miller currently resides in New York with her husband, Jason Epstein, a publisher and writer.

—I.C.

Suggested Reading: *American Journalism Review* p30 Aug./Sep. 2003; *Columbia Journalism Review* p31 July/Aug. 2004; *New York Times* I p1 Oct. 16, 2005; *New Yorker* p48+ Nov. 7, 2005

Selected Books: *God Has Ninety-Nine Names: A Reporter's Journey Through a Militant Middle East*, 1996; *Germs: Biological Weapons and America's Secret War* (with William Broad and Stephen Engelberg), 2002

Courtesy of Kumiko Higo

Miller, Marcus

June 14, 1959– Jazz bassist, producer, and composer

Address: c/o Takamasa Honda, P.O. Box 49365, Los Angeles, CA 90049

At the age of two, Marcus Miller could be seen in New York City clubs, padding alongside his cousin, the jazz pianist Wynton Kelly, who was a member of Miles Davis's band during the late 1950s and early 1960s. Twenty years later, already a successful jazz bassist and session player, Miller made an indelible mark on the jazz scene after being invited to work with Davis on his Grammy Award–winning album *Tutu* (1986). Over the next two decades, Miller went on to produce, compose, arrange, and play on everything from jazz albums to movie soundtracks to commercial jingles. He has worked with such luminaries as Luther Vandross, Aretha Franklin, Frank Sinatra, Mariah Carey, and LL Cool J, and has played on more than 400 albums. Launching his solo career in 1983 with the album *Suddenly*, Miller has since released eight albums, which have made him a musical star in his own right. Named one of the 10 most influential bass players of the 1990s by *Bass Player* magazine, he has enjoyed continued success throughout his 30-year career, earning a reputation as the "Superman of Soul," thanks to his musical ingenuity—he pioneered a thumb-driven slap that is now commonplace among jazz bassists—and his virtuosic skills. Davis once described Miller, according to Rob Adams for the Glasgow *Herald* (July 25, 2002), as "so hip that he even walks in tempo."

Marcus Miller was born on June 14, 1959 in Brooklyn, New York, and raised in the Jamaica neighborhood of Queens. His father was a public-transportation supervisor for the city's Metropolitan Transit Authority, and his mother was a nurse. The elder of two boys, Miller came from a musically gifted family; his father played the pipe organ and served as the choir director at the family's church. "My father was always having rehearsals in the house," Miller told Rashod D. Ollison for the *Baltimore Sun* (May 8, 2003). "After church, my family would sing downstairs at the piano. My aunts would sing. Wynton would play, or my daddy would play, at the piano. So there was all this music around. I thought everybody's house was like mine." At eight years of age, Miller began his musical education with the recorder, and at age 10 he began playing the clarinet. In 1970 Miller saw the Jackson 5 perform, and inspired by their youthful ingenuity, he began putting together singing groups with other children in his neighborhood, which at the time was a hotbed of rising funk and jazz talents. By the age of 13, Miller was proficient on the clarinet, piano, and bass guitar, and had already begun composing music. In his early years as a musician, Miller was heavily influenced by his father. "When I was thirteen, fourteen, I would buy the sheet music to all the popular songs and want to play them," Miller wrote for his Web site. "My pops would show me shortcuts to playing the songs. He taught me how to just read guitar chord symbols and make up my own accompaniment instead of laboring to decipher the written accompaniment. . . . I didn't learn to read piano music that well, but I learned a lot about chord changes, voicings, and harmony."

Miller was admitted to a prestigious magnet school, the Fiorello H. LaGuardia High School of Music & Art and Performing Arts. There he received a formal education in the clarinet, but back on the streets of Jamaica, Queens, Miller was receiving a more funk-and-jazz-infused education on his bass guitar. "I have to say I learned at least as much in the street with my bass as I did in the schools with my clarinet," he wrote for his Web site. By the time Miller graduated from high school, at just 16 years of age, he was already working as a professional musician in the clubs around New York City, often playing with the flutist Bobbi Humphrey and the keyboardist Lonnie Liston Smith. In 1976 he enrolled in the City University of New York's Queens College, where he studied music theory and composition. That same year Miller made his recording debut as a bassist on the drummer Lenny White's album *Big City* (1977).

Miller's talent as a bassist got him noticed as a session player, and he was soon in high demand among R&B singers and jazz combos. But in 1977, just as his career was on the rise, his first two bass guitars were stolen within the same week. He lost the first when he was mugged, and the second was taken from his car. "I was devastated," Miller told James McBride for the *Washington Post* (October 11, 1987). "My mother didn't say a word. She went to the bank, withdrew some more money and got me another one. Twice in the same week. The second one she bought me is the one I still play today." Miller's parents encouraged their son in his endeavors and had an unflagging confidence in his abilities; although education was valued highly in his family, shuttling between classrooms and club gigs began to take a toll on Miller, and after four years of college, with his parents' blessing, he decided to drop out and work full-time as a bassist.

In the late 1970s, when Miller was launching a career as a full-time musician, most bassists in New York City could not read written music because many of them learned the instrument in the streets and not in schools. His ability to read written charts made Miller a desirable and a highly successful session player. Relying on his formal education in music, Miller began to style the charts that were given to him in sessions with his own unique flair. "I challenged myself by not only playing the notes correctly, but by trying to make it sound as if I'd been playing that particular part for years (instead of for just minutes)," Miller wrote for his Web site. "I tried to incorporate nuances into the parts that would make them sound really natural. . . . I really tried to make everything sound easy." He began receiving a steady stream of job offers and rarely felt the financial strains common to most young musicians. His musical dexterity was becoming well known among commercial jingle writers such as Leon Pendarvis, who had a reputation for writing very detailed parts for his jingles. "[Pendarvis] used to get a kick out of transcribing something he'd heard you play on a record and writing it out for you to play on his jingle! Imagine how I felt when I realized that this difficult part I was reading was actually nothing but one of my own licks!" Miller wrote for his Web site. Within a few years he was regularly being asked to play at sessions in his own style, without notated music, for commercial jingles or for major recording artists including Roberta Flack, Elton John, and Frank Sinatra.

In 1980, while playing at a recording date, Miller received a note that read, "Call Miles." At first the young session player thought the note was a joke, since the renowned jazz trumpeter Miles Davis had already retired. But Miller took a chance and called the number anyway. "Miles answered and told me to be at CBS recording studio in two hours. Two hours later I was recording with him, along with Bill Evans, Barry Finnerty, Al Foster, and Sammy Figueroa," Miller wrote for his Web site. "Those sessions eventually became part of the *The Man with the Horn* album." Coming out of retirement, Davis was in need of a bass player, and the saxophonist Bill Evans (not to be confused with the pianist Bill Evans, who had also worked with Davis), who had recognized the young bassist's talents in recording sessions and club gigs, recommended Miller to him. What Miller originally thought was a joke turned into a long-term collaboration with Davis, during the last phase of the jazz marvel's career. In 1981 the 22-year-old Miller went on the road with Davis, and the trumpeter's demanding and relentless work ethic profoundly influenced his own music. "[Miles] didn't settle for anything mediocre. And this helped me develop my style," Miller said, according to the official biography posted on his Web site. "I learned from him that you have to be honest about who you are and what you do. If you follow that, you won't have problems."

Meanwhile, Miller also began producing albums. His first major production, the saxophonist David Sanborn's *Voyeur* (1980), won a Grammy

Award for best R&B performance in 1981. The first of three albums that Miller produced for Miles Davis, *Tutu* (1986), won a Grammy for best jazz instrumental performance by a soloist, and critics praised the album as one of the most important jazz recordings of the 1980s. Incorporating traditional jazz elements with a more electronically driven sound, Miller worked closely with Davis, writing six of the eight tunes, playing most of the instruments, and creating the arrangements. In a review for the London *Times* (October 11, 1986), Richard Williams wrote, "What Davis does here is doodle his spindly muted-horn lines against sumptuously textured backing tracks whose high-gloss finish is a tribute to the skill of Marcus Miller." As a result of the album's success, Miller's prominence as a musician, producer, and composer grew enormously, leading to collaborations with R&B artists, among them Luther Vandross's "Power of Love," which won a Grammy Award for best R&B song in 1991.

Introduced to film scoring by the filmmaker Reginald Hudlin, in the late 1980s, Miller found that composing for movies required the songwriter to appreciate the visual and emotional nuances of the film. "Composing for films requires you to focus on moods and colors. You have to focus on moods and colors when composing a song too but, for movies, the mood and the color are the most important thing," Miller wrote for his Web site. "I think the movie scores have helped my other writing because I'm more tuned in to the emotional effect of my songs these days." Miller has composed scores for numerous films including *House Party* (1990), *Boomerang* (1992), and *Deliver Us from Eva* (2003).

Throughout his career, Miller has been prolific in a variety of genres; his innovative bass-slap sound and cool, easy instrumentation style have been much sought after in the music industry. And even while working on various projects with others, Miller still found time to launch a solo career. In 1983 he released his first solo album, *Suddenly*, which was followed by a self-titled album the following year. With both albums featuring a heavy R&B sound and not the jazz-fusion style that was characteristic of Miller's other work, the bassist later felt that his real personality did not come through in those recordings. "I kind of short changed myself," he told Kevin Le Gendre for *Jazzwise* (June 2001). "I really didn't have a strong musical identity and maybe needed to wait a little longer. I was heavily influenced by Luther [Vandross] and that R&B thing so my album reflected that. I needed to hold off a little because I wasn't really sure who I was. When I started again I had a much clearer sense of who I was and started to include a lot more jazz elements from my past."

In 1988 Miller began working as the music director for *Sunday Night*, an hour-long show that aired at midnight on NBC. The hosts, David Sanborn and the noted keyboard player Jools Holland—both legendary jazz musicians themselves—showcased live improvisational music ranging from popular music to funk and jazz. "For music-loving viewers, [*Sunday Night*] is a breath of fresh air," Bill Barol wrote for *Newsweek* (February 13, 1989). "It may be the hippest thing to happen to the tube since the [David] Letterman show." The casual, club feel of the show was popular even in its late-night time slot, and *Sunday Night* was syndicated to 45 stations weekly, with a viewership of two million television households. Nevertheless, the show was cancelled in 1990.

Eight years after his second solo album, a more experienced Miller returned to the studio to record a third, *The Sun Don't Lie* (1993). The album featured what Miller described as a "fusion" sound. "It's a word I avoided for 10 years, but that's the best one to describe it. It's been so long since fusion was around that people no longer have preconceived notions about it. I combine different elements . . . with jazz," he told Zan Stewart for the *Los Angeles Times* (September 17, 1994). Miller's album garnered much praise and was nominated for a Grammy Award for best contemporary jazz album. In 1994 Miller released *Tales*, which highlighted the avant-garde aspects of the bassists' rich, soulful style. Tracks on the album contained spoken-word introductions that were combined with R&B rhythms and jazz melodies that had hip-hop undertones. "I wanted *Tales* to put you in the mind that you were on the road with the musicians and having them telling you stories," Miller told Emenike Masi for the *Weekly Journal* (April 20, 1995). "Miles, Joe Sample, Bill Withers were always telling me stories about how things were and what they were going through. It made me listen and think about what I and younger musicians were going through and it's all the same: they all talked about 'you gotta play with feeling, soul and you gotta be real.'" In a review for the *Washington Post* (October 6, 1995), Geoffrey Himes wrote that *Tales* "boasts thought-out compositions that bring together disparate elements in unexpected and rewarding ways."

In 1998 Miller released a collection of concert recordings, *Live & More*, and he later issued two other well-received live albums: *The Ozell Tapes: The Official Bootleg* (2003) and *Dreyfus Night in Paris* (2004). But Miller earned the greatest critical acclaim for his 2001 studio album, *M²*. With its mix of Miller's original compositions and jazz standards by the saxophonist John Coltrane and the bassist Charles Mingus, the album earned Miller the number-one spot on *Billboard*'s contemporary jazz chart within weeks of its release. Reviewing the album for the *Philadelphia Tribune* (June 8, 2001), Kimberly C. Roberts wrote, "Miller's bold style virtually slaps you in the face, right from the opening notes of the first track. . . . *M²* is an artistically satisfying project by a musician's musician." *M²* won the Grammy Award for best contemporary jazz album in 2001.

Miller's most recent album, *Silver Rain* (2005), features eclectic collaborations that cross musical genres. Back in 1997 Miller had toured Europe as a member of the band Legends, an ensemble that included Eric Clapton on guitar, Steve Gadd on drums, Joe Sample on piano, Sanborn on saxophone, and Miller on bass. At the time, he and Clapton discussed teaming up to record one of Miller's compositions, which had been inspired by a Langston Hughes poem, "In Time of Silver Rain," but it took several years before they could find the time to record the song that would become the title track for Miller's latest album. "Marcus Miller demonstrates his enormous multiple talents on *Silver Rain* (Koch Records)," a reviewer wrote for *Ebony* (May 2005), "and adeptly demonstrates why he is considered one of the great all-around talents in the music business today. . . . Miller's emphat-ic bass guitar is front and center while engaging the listener's body and soul."

Miller currently lives in Los Angeles, California, with his wife and four children.

—I.C.

Suggested Reading: (Glasgow) *Herald* p19 July 25, 2002; Marcus Miller Web site; *Washington Afro-American* p6 Apr. 27, 2001; *Washington Post* F p1 Oct. 11, 1987

Selected Recordings: *Suddenly*, 1983; *Marcus Miller*, 1984; *The Sun Don't Lie*, 1993; *Tales*, 1994; *M²*, 2001; *The Ozell Tapes: The Official Bootleg*, 2003; *Silver Rain*, 2005

Tom Pidgeon/Getty Images

Moss, Randy

Feb. 13, 1977– Football player

Address: Oakland Raiders, 1220 Harbor Bay Pkwy., Alameda, CA 94502

In his seven seasons with the Minnesota Vikings, the wide receiver Randy Moss dazzled spectators and broke National Football League (NFL) records, while also engaging in highly publicized, controversial acts—ranging from mischief to criminal misdemeanors—both on and away from the field. Some have pointed to Moss as a symbol of the mollycoddling of athletes and of all that ails professional sports; others see him as a misunderstood figure whose negative publicity overshadows his essentially good nature and the charity work in which he has long been involved. Whatever one thinks of him, his on-field accomplishments are impressive: among other statistics, he has played in five Pro Bowls and holds the record for receptions and yardage for players in their first seven seasons. In 2005 Moss left Minnesota to play for the Oakland Raiders.

Randy Moss was born on February 13, 1977 in Rand, West Virginia. His father, Randy Pratt, did not spend much time with Moss; the boy was raised primarily by his mother, Maxine Moss, a nurse's aide. Moss grew up with his half-sister, Latisia, and an older half-brother, Eric, who himself went on to play for the Minnesota Vikings. Moss showed an early aptitude for sports, starting with Little League baseball. He continued to excel at that sport as a student at Dupont High School, in Belle, West Virginia, where he also competed successfully in track, winning the 100- and 200-meter state championships. In basketball he was twice named state player of the year. Meanwhile, as a football player, he took on a number of positions, including receiver, place-kicker, punter, kick returner, and free safety, and led his team to two state titles. As might be expected, Moss garnered a great deal of attention—too much, in the opinion of his mother, who told S. L. Price for *Sports Illustrated* (August 25, 1997), "I couldn't shield him enough. You couldn't turn on the TV or open the newspaper without seeing him there. We're talking about a high school sophomore getting interviewed, and I never thought that was needed. But the more I didn't want it, the more it would come."

Moss's first run-in with the law occurred when he was a senior at Dupont. The small, rural town of Belle was plagued by racial tensions; one day Moss's friend Rayeshawn Smith, finding his name and racial slurs carved into a desk at school, enlisted Moss's help in getting even with Ernest Roy Johnson, whom Smith believed to be the culprit. In the school hallway Moss reportedly punched Johnson until he fell to the floor, then kicked him while he was down. Johnson was hospitalized with a lacerated spleen, a concussion, blood around his kidneys, and fluid around his liver. Moss was charged with the felony of malicious wounding, but later pleaded guilty to two counts of battery (a misdemeanor) and was sentenced to 30 days in prison and a year's probation. At the hearing, Moss apologized before the county circuit judge and afterward shook Johnson's hand, apologizing once more to him and his mother. He was allowed to serve three days of his sentence immediately and defer the remainder until after his freshman year of college. (The University of Notre Dame, in Notre Dame, Indiana, which Moss had long dreamt of attending, had accepted his letter of intent.) At a banquet to accept a basketball award, Moss issued a public apology for the beating, for which he was given a standing ovation.

In the opinion of some, apologies were not sufficient. Moss was expelled from Dupont and forced to finish his high-school education at Cabell Alternative School. Then the University of Notre Dame rejected his application, informing him that he had filled it out incorrectly. In 1995 Moss was given a football scholarship to Florida State University (FSU), in Tallahassee, on the condition that he sit out his first year on the bench. In practices it soon became obvious that no one on the team could defend against Moss; he was able to score almost at will. But in April 1996 Moss ruined his chances at FSU when, on the day he was to begin serving the rest of his prison sentence, he smoked marijuana. After failing a prison drug test, Moss was placed in solitary confinement for a week and had 60 days added to his term. FSU revoked his scholarship. "I'm the dummy," Moss admitted to S. L. Price, adding that the consequences of his actions "hurt inside" but that "the only thing I couldn't do was cry, because I did it."

After getting out of jail, Moss was given a scholarship at Marshall University, in Huntington, West Virginia, whose Division I-AA football program was not of the same athletic stature as those of Notre Dame or FSU. Moss immediately helped to put Marshall on the college football map. Marshall went 15–0 during the 1996 season and won the division championship when Moss caught nine passes for 220 yards and scored four touchdowns to beat Montana, 49–29. Moss had 28 touchdowns that season, scoring the most ever for a freshman and beating Jerry Rice's Division I-AA record of 27.

But during the season Moss had gotten into more trouble. One day, shortly after breaking up with his girlfriend, Libby Offutt, he returned their daughter, Sydney, to Offutt's parents' house—driving his new girlfriend's car. The sight of the car sparked a violent argument between Moss and Offutt, and Offutt reportedly came away with abrasions around her neck and minor cuts and bruises on her arm. Though Moss claimed that he had merely been trying to defend himself, both were arrested on misdemeanor charges of domestic battery. The charges were later dropped, after Offutt and Moss agreed to counseling. Despite Moss's transgressions, many people maintained that the

criticism he received in the press was unwarranted. Moss's Little League baseball coach attested to his character, pointing out that Moss had volunteered to help children in a special-education class. Even Libby Offutt's father said that he liked Moss and felt that the incident involving his daughter had been blown out of proportion.

Afterward Moss managed to stay out of trouble for a time, and his athletic prowess once again began to overshadow questions about his character. In 1997, Moss's sophomore year, Marshall was promoted into Division I-A and became part of the Mid-American Conference (MAC). That year they won the MAC Championship. Moss caught 90 passes for the season for 1,647 yards and 25 touchdowns. With 53 touchdowns in two years, he more than doubled Marshall's previous career-touchdown record. He came in fourth place for the prestigious Heisman Trophy and was the only sophomore contender. In addition, he was a unanimous first-team All American and All-MAC selection and won the Fred Biletnikoff Award for best college receiver. *USA Today* rated him the premier college football receiver. Eric Kresser, a former Marshall quarterback who went on to play for the NFL, praised Moss in a conversation with Curry Kirkpatrick for *Sport* (October 1997): "The routes, the precision! Look at his reach! The discipline and focus. . . . I don't say this without knowing what's out there. Randy Moss is the best player in America."

For all the praise Moss had garnered at Marshall, NFL teams were hesitant to draft him because of his history. "You get a lot of attention at a young age, and it can really screw you up," Moss remarked to Mark Starr and Allison Samuels for *Newsweek* (May 29, 2000). "You get into things and you don't know how much they're going to haunt you down the road. It's so easy to get caught up in the moment, and one thing leads to another until you can't stop it. Then you deal with the consequences—and boy do you have to deal with them for a long time." Moss was the 21st pick in the 1998 NFL draft when Minnesota's head coach, Dennis Green, snatched him up. Had he been drafted sooner, he could have made an estimated $5 million or $6 million more than he made at Minnesota, where he was given a contract for $4.5 million over four years.

In Minnesota Moss joined his half-brother, Eric Moss, but the Pro-Bowl receiver Cris Carter quickly became his closest friend on the team. Carter's early years in the NFL had been plagued by controversial off-field behavior, so he felt that he could relate to and help Moss. In uncharacteristically laudatory comments, Moss shared his opinion of Carter with David Scott for *Sport* (August 1999): "He has all kinds of money, has his family, has appearances, he's busy, and he took time out of his schedule for me, to teach me how to be a pro, how to work out, how to look at the other side of things. . . . I'm thankful for that, and hopefully one day I can do that for somebody."

Moss had an astounding rookie season in Minnesota. During the preseason he made 14 receptions for 223 yards and four touchdowns, as the Vikings went 4–0. On August 15, 1998 Moss faced the Kansas City Chiefs, who possessed one of the best pass defenses in the league. The Chiefs' defenders tried to bait Moss by roughing him up and twisting his helmet, but Moss maintained his composure, responding only with solid play. He caught four passes, including one for a touchdown, and the Vikings went on to win the game, 34–0. In his first regular-season pro game ever, Moss caught two touchdown passes against the Tampa Bay Buccaneers, becoming the first Minnesota rookie to score two touchdowns in his first game. In the *Sporting News* (September 14, 1998), Chris Jenkins raved, "After Moss's brilliant preseason and thrilling two-touchdown debut against the Buccaneers, he has gone from being the football equivalent of Billy Zane's character [the snooty villain] in *Titanic* to possibly shifting the balance of power in the NFC Central."

On October 5, 1998 the undefeated Vikings played against their archrivals, the Green Bay Packers. In the previous three seasons, Green Bay had won in four of the two teams' six meetings, but Moss helped turn the tide. He made five catches for 190 yards, including two touchdowns for 52 and 44 yards, respectively, as the Vikings won the game, 37–24. On November 22, when they played Green Bay again, Moss hauled in eight catches for 153 yards and a 49-yard touchdown to help win the game and put the Vikings at 10–1 for the season.

The Vikings went on to win 15 games that season while losing only one. In the process they set the record for the most points ever in a season, with 556. Moss compiled impressive numbers: 69 catches for 1,313 yards and 17 touchdown receptions (the highest touchdown total in the league and the most ever for a rookie). Despite Moss's play-off contribution of 10 catches for 148 yards and two touchdowns, the Vikings lost the National Football Conference (NFC) championship game to the Atlanta Falcons, 30–27. Moss, though, was voted rookie of the year and went on to play in the Pro Bowl.

The following season was less successful for the Vikings, with their record falling to 10–6. In their third game, a loss against the Green Bay Packers, Moss was held to two catches for 13 yards. Some teams succeeded in neutralizing his performance by positioning a cornerback in front of him at the beginning of each play and covering him with a safety downfield. Critics noted that Moss appeared to be bored on the field and was prone to lapses in concentration. Showing shades of his former self, Moss was fined $10,000 by the league for verbally abusing a referee during a game against the Chicago Bears on November 14, 1999. Then, during the NFC Divisional Play-off game on January 16, 2000, which the Vikings lost to the St. Louis Rams, Moss squirted a referee with his Gatorade bottle after an

incomplete pass and was fined $40,000. In the end, however, Moss had a very good season. He caught more passes than he had the previous year, with 80, up from 69. He also had more yardage: his 1,413 yards receiving set a Vikings team record. Only his touchdown production decreased, to 11—still a highly respectable figure. Moss was again elected to the Pro Bowl, where he set reception and yardage records, with nine catches for 212 yards and one touchdown. That performance was enough to win him the most-valuable-player award of the 1999 Pro Bowl.

In 2000 Moss played basketball in the Southern California Summer Pro League. ("Moss . . . has never hidden his desire to play the sport professionally one day," Mike Freeman reported in the July 16, 2000 edition of the *New York Times*.) Returning to the gridiron, he racked up impressive numbers that year, making 77 receptions for 1,437 yards and 15 touchdowns, as the Vikings put together an 11–5 regular-season record and captured the NFC Central Division title. Minnesota's season was marred the following January by the team's devastating 41–0 loss to the New York Giants in the NFC title game—the second-worst defeat in Viking history as well as its worst-ever play-off loss and first play-off shutout. Moss made a comparatively modest two receptions for 18 yards in the game.

During the 2001 regular season, after Moss had inked an eight-year, $75 million contract with the Vikings and received an additional $18 million as a signing bonus, his number of receptions rose to 82, while his yards gained (1,233) and number of touchdowns (10) both fell; the Vikings, meanwhile, compiled a 5–11 record, their worst in 17 years. Off the field Moss publicly shed tears over the death of his teammate and friend Korey Stringer, who had succumbed to heatstroke during training camp. He also received a $15,000 fine from the Vikings, after heaping verbal abuse on the team's corporate sponsors during a bus ride to Philadelphia; he had become angry upon discovering that the individuals were occupying seats he felt should be reserved for players. Moss underwent anger-management counseling following that episode. He stirred up even more controversy in November of that year, when, asked by Sid Hartman for the Minneapolis *Star Tribune* (November 23, 2001) if he felt motivated on the field by Cris Carter, he replied: "I play when I want to play. Do I play up to my top performance, my ability every time? Maybe not. . . . When I make my mind up, I am going out there to tear somebody's head off. When I go out there and play football, man it's not anybody telling me to play or how I should play." The words "I play when I want to play" echoed throughout the sports media and brought condemnation of Moss from players, journalists, and even a Minnesota state senator.

The Vikings saw a number of changes at the end of the 2001 season: their coach, Dennis Green, was replaced by Mike Tice; Carter, whose relations with Moss had become strained, particularly after the team's 2000 play-off loss to the Giants, was not re-signed; and Moss appeared to take his role on the squad more seriously, displaying leadership among his teammates and spending the spring and summer of 2002 in the Vikings' off-season workout program rather than playing basketball. Off the field, however, he once again found himself in trouble with the authorities. In September 2002 he was arrested for assault with a dangerous weapon after bumping a Minneapolis, Minnesota, traffic-control agent with his car, knocking her to the ground. While the felony charge was dropped, Moss was charged with misdemeanors—careless driving, failure to obey a traffic officer, and possession of marijuana (found in his car at the time of the arrest). The Vikings responded to the traffic incident by fining Moss $50,000. Those troubles aside, Moss had a stellar year as a player, completing a career-high 106 receptions for seven touchdowns and 1,347 yards.

Moss's numbers the following year, 2003, were better still, as he grabbed 111 receptions for 1,632 yards and 17 touchdowns; the Vikings chalked up nine wins over seven losses, improving on their 6–10 record of the previous season. In 2004, as the team went 8–8, Moss was hampered by a hamstring injury but nonetheless pulled in 49 catches for 767 yards and 13 touchdowns. By the end of that season, Moss had caught 574 career passes for a total of 9,142 yards—the most by any player in his first seven seasons—and his 90 touchdown catches were eighth-best in NFL history. He had also played in five Pro Bowls, in 1998, 1999, 2000, 2002, and 2003, and in three of those years—1998, 2000, and 2003—he led the league in receiving touchdowns. On the other hand, while he managed to avoid trouble with the law in 2004, he nonetheless raised eyebrows. During the course of a Viking victory over the Green Bay Packers for the NFC wildcard spot, he pretended to moon the opposing team's fans (for which he was fined $10,000); he also left the field with time remaining in a game against the Washington Redskins (for which he later apologized).

By the end of the 2004 season, the Vikings appeared to have had their fill of Moss's antics, and Moss, for his part, yearned to play on a team that seemed to be Super Bowl–bound. In the winter of 2005, in exchange for the linebacker Napoleon Harris and two draft picks, the Vikings traded Moss to the Oakland Raiders. Moss called the move "a new start," as quoted by the New York Times (March 3, 2005); he added that Al Davis, the Raiders' owner, "told me he had some [Super Bowl] rings and now I need to get me one." In the preseason the Raiders got off to a shaky start, losing three of their four games; Moss himself, however, performed well. He also made five catches for 130 yards in the team's first regular-season game, against the New England Patriots (which the Raiders lost, 30–20). As reported by the New York Times (August 2, 2005), Moss seemed to anticipate his own future devilment with his new team, say-

ing during an interview at the Raiders' camp, "There's no telling what you're going to see. I love what I do. I love having fun. When it comes to big games, you never know what you're going to see out of me. As long as we win, I'm just having fun. If the antics come, then I'm here to apologize first before they even happen. I'm going to have fun, man, believe that." The fun he anticipated having in the 2005 season was limited early on by his injuries, which included back and rib problems. He finished the year with several strong showings, however. In a New Year's Eve match against the New York Giants, he caught seven passes for 116 yards and two touchdowns, pushing his season yardage total to over 1,000. In the previous game—the Raiders' Christmas Eve appearance in Denver, Moss's 124th career game—Moss reached the mark of 10,000 receiving yards; only three other players in NFL history have achieved that feat earlier in their careers. Moss had 60 catches for 1,005 yards and eight touchdowns during the season. As of early November 2006, he had made 26 receptions for 371 yards and three touchdowns, while Oakland had won two games and lost five.

The six-foot four-inch Randy Moss has "starkly angled cheeks," a "prominent chin," and "wide, deep-set eyes," as described by Karl Taro Greenfeld in Sports Illustrated (May 16, 2005). Greenfeld wrote about Moss's relatively modest house in Boca Raton, Florida, "This is one of four houses he owns, but this is the one he calls home." Moss's four children by Libby Offutt—Sydney, Thaddeus, Montigo, and Senali—live with their mother in Charlotte, North Carolina; Moss visits his children frequently during the NFL off-season and as much as possible during the season. "He's a great dad," Offutt told Greenfeld, "when he's around." Offutt said to Curt Brown for the Minneapolis Star Tribune (October 6, 2002) about Moss, "I've known him forever, and he's not what the media have made him out to be." Brown reported on Moss's extensive charity work in Minnesota, where he has been particularly active in support of children; Brown also noted that Moss usually requests that TV news crews not cover his philanthropic activities. Greenfeld wrote about Moss, "He is funny, quick to laugh and the sort of thoughtful talker who takes his time; his diction and argot—the 'yups,' the 'gollys,' and the 'baby dolls' he uses when addressing females—are those of a small-town boy from Rand, W.Va., who has grown into kingfish." In 2005 Moss's number 17 Raiders jersey was the top-selling NFL jersey, with over $10 million in retail sales (of which Moss received between $300,000 and $400,000).

—P.G.H./C.T.

Suggested Reading: New York Times VIII p7 July 16, 2000, D p1+ Mar. 3, 2005; Sport p58+ Oct. 1997, p50+ Aug. 1999; Sporting News p45+ Sep. 16, 1996, p12 Jan. 25, 1999; Sports Illustrated p130+ Aug. 25, 1997, p66+ Sep. 7, 1998, p54+ Jan. 18, 1999, 68+ Sep. 2, 2002, p36+ May 16, 2005; Washington Post p2 Aug. 2, 1995

Courtesy of Ballantine Books

Murray, Donald M.

Sep. 16, 1924– Columnist; journalist; novelist; textbook writer; educator

Address: c/o Boston Globe, 125 William T. Morrissey Blvd., Boston, MA 02125

"I write because I love writing," Donald M. Murray said in his keynote address to the National Writers' Workshop (NWW) in 1995, as posted on poynter.org. A self-described "cross-writer," he has "explor[ed] the possibilities of fiction and poetry, books and articles, columns and textbooks," as he said in the same talk. "Each genre illuminates the other." Murray was not yet 30 when, in 1954—six years after he had begun his professional life, as a copy boy for the *Boston Herald*—he won a Pulitzer Prize for editorials he had written for the same newspaper. Later in the 1950s and in the early 1960s, he contributed articles to magazines as a freelance writer. In a more recent foray into journalism, starting in the mid-1980s, he has written a weekly column for the *Boston Globe*; originally called "Over Sixty" and renamed "Now and Then," the column covers a wide range of subjects, all discussed from the point of view of a man whose memories date from the 1920s and who, as he said in his NWW address, "live[s] in a curious and delightful state of intense awareness and casual reflection." "My writing has made me a better reporter on my life," he added. "I pay attention to my living." Murray's published works also include a novel, two memoirs, poems, and many books on the art and craft of writing and on teaching would-be writers. For 23 years beginning in 1963, he taught writing at the University of New Hamp-

shire; during that time he introduced a course of study in journalism at the school and helped to set up a Ph.D. program in composition studies there. As a writing coach, he has taught journalists at the *Boston Globe* and the *Providence Journal*, among other newspapers. His credentials, achievements, and advanced age notwithstanding, when he spoke at the NWW, he regarded himself as "a young writer who is still trying to learn his craft." "I will return to my writing desk Monday and still try to learn the journalist's craft," he declared. "Then Tuesday through Sunday I will try to learn how to finish yet another book on writing, how to plan a new novel, how to write a great poem."

Donald Morison Murray was born to John W. Murray and the former Jean Edith Thomas Smith on September 16, 1924 in Boston, Massachusetts. An only child, he grew up in the Wollaston section of the nearby town of Quincy. His father, whose education ended with grade school, held various positions in department stores. Murray has described his childhood as very unhappy. Neither his father nor his mother ever hugged him, and they both beat him, his father with a leather strap and his mother with a wet hairbrush. He has few positive memories of elementary school, because he was bullied relentlessly by his peers, and, in addition, he "hated all but three teachers between kindergarten and graduate school," as he wrote in a column for the *Globe* (January 10, 2006). One of those three was his fourth-grade teacher, Miss Chapman, who announced that he would be the class editor. "My bones may creak, I may live on a diet of pills, I may forget names, but when I shuffle down to my computer I see Miss Chapman standing in the corner of the room, nodding [her] encouragement," he said in his NWW address. To escape from his childhood woes, he created an imaginary family, including siblings, who lived in the walls of his house; he also took comfort in writing and reading. In another *Globe* column (December 6, 2005), he wrote that his real family, who were of Scottish descent, never "attempted joy": "We didn't play, step over the line to pleasure, dance, drink, or frolic. We worked. . . . I was a child of the Great Depression, when we wore pencils down to the nub, resoled our shoes, turned the collars on our shirts, darned each sock even if the darns made walking painful, and ate everything on the plate—even slimy, overcooked spinach." In the same column he wrote, "My parents and my teachers got together and decided I was stupid. My response was to develop a private mantra: 'I'm stupid but I can come in early and stay late.' . . . It worked. Good work habits will beat talent every time." Murray's relationship with his father improved after he became an adult. Separated by many miles, the two communicated mainly through phone calls.

Murray attended North Quincy High School, where he had a less-than-stellar career; as he wrote for a *Globe* column (May 2, 2006), perhaps the most important thing he learned there was "how to fail": "It is essential to discover that the sky doesn't crack if you fail. . . . School wants only successes, but failure should be taught, encouraged, supported." He did not earn a diploma when he completed high school, in 1942, because, as he recalled in the same column, "the principal took away my A in art, [and] I was short a point." In 1943, during World War II, he became a paratrooper in the United States Army's Airborne Division. In Europe he experienced the loneliness, confusion, fear, and horrors of ground combat; once, while digging a foxhole, he came upon bones that were most likely those of soldiers who had died during World War I. After the war ended he served in the military police until 1946. His description in the *Globe* (May 22, 2001) of some of his wartime memories prompted a reader, Ann B. Gordon, to write in a letter to that newspaper (May 28, 2001), "Murray's column recalling his combat experiences during World War II was an act of heartbreaking courage. . . . He may always wonder whether or not he acted heroically during the war. But let him, and us, harbor no doubts about the depth and the character of the courage it took for him to tell us, in words simple and startling, how decent men saw, felt, and did indecent things in utterly indecent circumstances. He says his experience was common. His story reveals, however, that he is a very uncommon man."

Murray's marriage to Ellen Pinkham, in 1946, ended in divorce in 1948. Also in 1948 Murray earned a B.A. degree in English, cum laude, from the University of New Hampshire. The school invited him to remain there to teach, but he was determined to make writing his career. Soon after his graduation he took a job as a copyboy with the *Boston Herald*. He became a staff reporter in 1949 and began to write editorials for the same paper in 1951. That year he received the New England Award from the Associated Press for his editorials. In 1954 he won the Pulitzer Prize for editorial writing, after having entered into competition more than 100 samples from 1953, all pertaining to changes in U.S. military policy and national defense related to the progression of the Cold War. Around that time he was offered a position as an editor at the *Herald*, along with a larger salary and stock options, but he turned it down. In a column for the *Boston Globe* (January 10, 2006), he recalled that he responded to the offer by saying that although he knew he could do the work, "I want a job I don't know if I can do. Writing." "That decision was easy," he wrote. "I left the room, still a writer running after the meaning of my unexpected sentence." Earlier, between 1949 and 1951, he had taken courses in writing at Boston University. In 1953–54 Murray moonlighted as a journalism instructor at that school. In 1954 he moved with his family (he had remarried in 1951 and had become a father) to New York City and became a freelance contributing editor for *Time*. He grew unhappy with that job, and one day in 1956 he discussed with his wife the possibility of quitting. Unexpectedly, the next day he was relieved of his duties and

was told, "We're going to make you a TV producer." He had no interest in such work, however.

For the next seven years or so, Murray continued to support his family as a freelance writer, but with no official affiliation with any employer. His first book, which he wrote as Don Murray, was *Man Against Earth: The Story of Tunnels and Tunnel Builders* (1961). The next was a novel, *The Man Who Had Everything* (1964), in which Brad Hastings, a 36-year-old man with a successful career and happy home life, becomes a quadriplegic after a freak accident. In the course of the story, Brad, his wife, Bets, and his doctor, Irving, who is also a good friend of his, come to grips with his transformation from energetic professional man and contented husband and father to complete invalid. In a review for *Library Journal* (June 1, 1964), W. K. Beatty wrote, "Murray has written a beautifully moving and acutely understanding story. Each incident is pertinent and realistic." Haskel Frankel, reviewing the novel for *Book Week* (July 19, 1964), wrote, "Murray works so deeply within his characterizations, the reader is one with each of them. Brad, Bets and Irving are three people, never three characters. What they think and do to themselves and to each other is beyond judgment: there is no good and no evil, no hero or villain—just three decent people chained together by a situation as immovable and unchangeable as Brad's physical condition. Their reactions can hit with the shock of complete surprise, but each person is so thoroughly alive that the unexpected carries the clear ring of truth with it."

Murray's years as a freelance writer were difficult financially and psychologically. As Murray recalled for the *Boston Globe* (January 10, 2006), "The choices narrowed. I wanted to write high art but my children, wife, and I wanted to eat. I had to turn in drafts that I thought were inadequate. I had no Keogh [retirement] plan, no medical program." In 1963 Murray took a full-time job as a faculty member of the University of New Hampshire at Durham (UNH). Until the mid-1980s, when he became professor emeritus, he taught English composition. He also served as chairman of the Department of English for two years (1975–77). He won two UNH awards for his teaching and received an honorary doctoral degree from the university in 1990. One of his former students, the novelist, editor, and journalist Janice Harayda, wrote for her Web page that "a generation of students is grateful" to Murray. "He has been an inspiration to me—and countless other writers—for years." In 1981 he won the Yankee Quill Award, given by the New England Society of Newspaper Editors and the New England Chapter of the Society of Professional Journalists, for his significant positive influence on journalism in New England.

Readers' comments about Murray's textbook *Crafting a Life in Essay, Story, Poem* (1996) hint at some of his skills as an educator. Sue Weinstein, for example, wrote of the book, as posted on Amazon.com, "Murray's appeal to . . . a diverse audience begins with his development of an intimate relationship with the reader in the introduction, entitled 'Why I Write.' The reader can easily imagine having a cup of coffee with Murray while he shares the story of his birth as a writer and what motivates him to continue his writing life. But it's not just about him. . . . While encouraging us to overcome our fear of writing and to develop a writing discipline, Murray comes across as a combination fairy godmother and Olympic training coach. [In a] maternal tone [he] . . . provides comforting advice. Yet, like a coach, he also expects us to challenge ourselves, set goals, and stop making excuses for not writing. . . . Murray generously shares samples of his own early drafts with crossed-out lines, notes in the margins and detailed discussions of why he made the changes he made. Anyone who thinks that professional writers simply sit down, receive inspiration and then spontaneously produce masterpieces will learn a lesson from Murray about the energy and commitment involved in the craft of writing. Every step of the way, Murray displays rigorous honesty about himself as a writer, about the joys and struggles of the writer's life and about what it takes to please a reading audience."

Among Murray's other books on the art and craft of writing are *Writer Teaches Writing: A Practical Method of Teaching Composition* (1968), *Writing for Your Readers: Notes on the Writer's Craft from the Boston Globe* (1983), *Write to Learn* (1984), *Read to Write: A Writing Process Reader* (1986), *Expecting the Unexpected: Teaching Myself—and Others—to Read and Write* (1989), *Shoptalk: Learning to Write with Writers* (1990), *The Craft of Revision* (1991), *A Writer in the Newsroom: A Moving Narrative of a Life as a Reporter, Writer, Teacher and Above All, Student of the World* (1995), and *Writing to Deadline: The Journalist at Work* (2000). In an assessment of the last-named book, Carl Sessions Stepp, a professor of journalism at the University of Maryland, wrote for the *American Journalism Review* (June 2000): "*Writing to Deadline* is oddly mistitled. It is not mainly aimed at journalists crunching against the clock, though it can certainly help them. At heart, this book embraces writing with a capital W, the craft and soul and lifestyle of writers, the compulsions and idiosyncrasies and rituals that define them and their work. . . . The book teems with good advice on large and small issues. Murray specializes in introducing a topic with a nice conceptual insight, then following up with specific advice on technique." While some of Murray's books are out of print, others have been reissued several times. In 1993, for example, the third edition of *Read to Write* appeared, and in 2004 the fifth edition of *The Craft of Revision* and the eighth edition of *Write to Learn* were published.

Since shortly before his retirement from teaching at UNH, at age 62, Murray has written a weekly column for the *Boston Globe*. His column—called "Over Sixty" when it debuted and later renamed "Now and Then"—currently appears every Tuesday in the Living/Arts section of the newspaper. In most of the columns, he has written about himself, his family, and his past and present experiences, while also depicting the elderly in general as vigorous individuals who continue to make an impact on the lives of those around them. Pamela Hanson, in a letter to the *Globe* (February 15, 2001), wrote, "With all the celebration of youth in our culture, there are few role models for elegant aging. Murray is surely one of the most elegant of all." In recent columns he has described his daily schedule (November 8, 2005), his firsthand experiences of war and the futility of Hollywood's attempts to portray combat and soldiers' lives realistically (November 22, 2005), his struggles with feelings of guilt when he buys things for himself (December 6, 2005), his fears about his health since he suffered a heart attack and underwent triple bypass surgery in 1986 (May 16, 2006), and the "quiet moments of insight" that marked some of the turning points in his life (May 23, 2006).

In his columns Murray has frequently written about his second wife, the former Minnie Mae Emmerich, whom he married in 1951, and about their three daughters, Anne, Lee, and Hannah. He described his familial relationships in greater detail in his memoir *My Twice-Told Life* (2001), whose title refers to his habit not only of thinking (often repeatedly, sometimes daily) about what he has experienced but also writing about it (which inevitably leads to more reminiscence, not least because he always revises what he writes, sometimes more than a dozen times). *My Twice-Told Life* contains a brief account of the death of his daughter Lee at age 20, in 1977, and longer descriptions of the day-to-day difficulties and heartache connected with his wife's long, losing struggle with Parkinson's disease. (She died in early 2005.) In a review for the *New York Times* (July 23, 2002), John Langone called the book a "reflective, elegant" memoir "about coping with what life deals us and seizing control of it, about living in the moment, and, ultimately, accepting our lot." In an assessment for the *Fort Worth (Texas) Star-Telegram* (June 3, 2001), Catherine Newtown wrote, "The quest to assign meaning to life makes this personal account a page turner for people of all ages."

In his second memoir, *The Lively Shadow: Living with the Death of a Child* (2003), Murray wrote in detail about Lee and the illness (Reye's syndrome, which is fatal in 20 percent of cases) that struck her after she took an aspirin to break a high fever. After she was admitted to a hospital, Lee slipped into a coma. When her doctors told Murray and his wife that there was no chance of her recovery, they agreed to end life-support measures, and she died within a few days. Lee remains with Murray, he wrote, as a "lively shadow." In a critique for the "Forecast" section of *Publishers Weekly* (November 11, 2002), Sarah F. Gold wrote, "In this deeply felt, nicely written reminiscence, Murray . . . explains how he never truly recovered from the death of Lee. . . . Although [he] is initially shocked when a neighbor who has lost a son tells him 'It won't get any better,' he comes not only to agree with this prediction, but to be grateful for it. Murray writes that he now understands that he can accept Lee's death, not by forgetting, but only by continuing to live each day, loving his family and celebrating the commonplace occurrences of daily life in her memory." Bella English, a reviewer for the *Boston Globe* (June 19, 2003), wrote, "Murray is a generous and eloquent tour guide to a place that few of us want to go, but many of us ultimately will, be it with a cherished child or another loved one."

The magazines *Boston* and *Improper Bostonian* named Murray Boston's best columnist in 1991 and 1996, respectively. In 1997 the University of New Hampshire named its new journalism laboratory for him. In 2001 Murray received a New Hampshire Literary Award, from the New Hampshire Writers' Project, for lifetime achievement. *Writing on the Edge*, a journal (published at the University of California at Davis) that focuses on writing and the teaching of writing, established the Donald M. Murray Prize in 2003, to recognize the author of the best work on the subject of writing published during the previous year.

Murray has described himself as a lapsed Baptist. In addition to his two surviving daughters, he has three grandchildren. He meets friends at a local coffee shop every morning, often before sunup, and writes at least 500 words every day. In his leisure time he enjoys painting in watercolors, reading mystery novels (his favorite authors include Henning Mankell, Donna Leon, Peter Robinson, and Ed McBain), watching reruns of the TV series *Law and Order* and its spin-offs, and ruminating. He lives by himself in Durham and, by his own account, treasures his hours of solitude.

—C.M.

Suggested Reading: *Boston Globe* D p5 June 19, 2003, B p1 Feb. 9, 2005, C p17 Dec. 6, 2005, C p2 Dec. 27, 2005, C p3 Jan. 10, 2006; *Fort Worth (Texas) Star-Telegram* p6 June 3, 2001; *New York Times* F p8 July 23, 2002; Murray, Donald M. *My Twice-Told Life*, 2001, *The Lively Shadow: Living with the Death of a Child*, 2003; *Who's Who of Pulitzer Prize Winners*, 1999

Selected Books: fiction—*The Man Who Had Everything*, 1964; nonfiction—*Writer Teaches Writing: A Practical Method of Teaching Composition*, 1968; *Learning by Teaching: Selected Articles on Writing and Teaching*,1982; *Writing for Your Readers: Notes on the Writer's Craft from the Boston Globe*, 1983; *Write to Learn*, 1984; *Expecting the Unexpected: Teaching Myself—and Others—to Read and Write*, 1989; *Shoptalk: Learning to Write with Writers*, 1990; *The Craft of Revision*, 1991; *A Writer in the Newsroom: A Moving Narrative of a Life as a Reporter, Writer, Teacher and Above All, Student of the World*, 1995; *Crafting a Life in Essay, Story, Poem*, 1996; *My Twice-Told Life*, 2001; *The Lively Shadow: Living with the Death of a Child*, 2003

Musk, Elon

Nov. 7, 1971– Aerospace executive; Internet entrepreneur

Address: c/o Space Exploration Technologies, 1310 E. Grand Ave., El Segundo, CA 90245

By his early 30s the Internet entrepreneur Elon Musk was a multimillionaire: PayPal, a company he had created, which offers an on-line payment service used by millions, was purchased in 2002 for $1.5 billion. Afterward, rather than remain in that industry, Musk turned his ambitions in a different direction—toward space. In 2002 he founded Space Exploration Technologies, better known as SpaceX, with the goal of providing inexpensive spaceflight to governments and private companies. SpaceX's debut rocket, named Falcon after the Millennium Falcon spacecraft in the *Star Wars* films, was built as cheaply as possible, with simpler and more efficient parts than those used by such established aerospace companies as Boeing and Lockheed Martin. SpaceX is still in its formative period—its first launch, in March 2006, was unsuccessful; nevertheless, Musk has many customers lined up, including the U.S. Defense Department. "Their engine design is less than perfect, but it is good enough," Robert Sackheim, a NASA engineer who was an early consultant to Musk, told Leslie Wayne for the *New York Times* (February 5, 2006). "I think [Musk is] doing all the right things. This can be an incredibly important advance to the country."

Aside from the potential to profit in the space-launch industry, Musk's motivations for improving space travel include loftier goals relating to the future of the human race. "If we can be one of the companies that makes it possible for humans to become a multi-planetary species, that would be the Holy Grail," he told Josh Friedman for the *Los Angeles Times* (April 22, 2003). "It sounds a bit crazy but it's going to happen, and only if people build the means to do so. We're making progress toward a greater philosophical goal while building a sound business." Musk is not alone in his dream of improving humankind's access to space in the near future. Among others who have used Internet-fueled fortunes to support similar space ventures are Microsoft's co-founder Paul Allen, the software

Elon Musk

Courtesy of Elon Musk

programmer John Carmack, and the founder of Amazon.com, Jeff Bezos. Allen financed *SpaceShipOne*, the first private manned space flight to exceed an altitude of 100 kilometers (roughly 62 miles), for which its designer, Burt Rutan, won the $10 million Ansari X-Prize; Carmack, the creator of the video games *Doom* and *Quake*, fronts Armadillo Aerospace, the goal of which is to build a small personal spacecraft; and Bezos founded a secretive company called Blue Origin to build a manned spacecraft. "So far [such] efforts have either ended in failure or have been just ventures in 'space tourism' that brought test pilots to the fringe of space," Wayne wrote. Musk claims that SpaceX is different, because it has more technical talent and capital to compete with established players. Tom Mueller, the company's vice president of propulsion, who worked with the former aerospace giant TRW, told Friedman, "I had several other [employment] opportunities, but when Elon approached me I could see he was different. . . . The others all had a gimmick, like a helicopter blade or some miracle technology. Elon just wanted to take the best technology already out there, build a simple vehicle and use the right propellants." As Michael Griffin, an aerospace veteran and the president of the investment firm In-Q-Tel, told Friedman, "At some point the rocket industry needs a Henry Ford, and maybe Elon will be that guy."

Elon Musk was born on November 7, 1971 in Pretoria, South Africa. His father was a South African engineer; his mother was a Canadian-born fashion model and nutrition consultant. At age 12, according to Friedman, Musk made $500 selling the code for a video game he had created—along the lines of *Space Invaders*—to a gaming magazine.

He later invested the money in a pharmaceutical stock he had been following in the local newspaper. He sold the shares for "a few thousand" dollars, as he told Friedman. When Musk was 17 his parents divorced, and he moved to Canada, financing the trip with his own money. Musk left South Africa in part to avoid compulsory military service; he came to Canada because, as he told Friedman, "if you wanted to be close to the cutting edge, particularly in technology, you came to North America." He enrolled at Queen's University, in Kingston, Ontario. After two years (during which he interned at a Canadian bank), Musk transferred to the University of Pennsylvania, in Philadelphia, from which he earned bachelor's degrees in both physics and business. In 1995, at 23, he was accepted into the doctoral physics program at Stanford University, in California, and took on a summer internship doing high-energy physics research at Pinnacle Research Institute, in Los Gatos, California.

Before classes started at Stanford, however, Musk had made up his mind to drop out and pursue a business idea inspired by the Internet boom taking place in Southern California. "It was clear that the Internet was going to be big outside the academic world," he told Alice LaPlante for *Upside* (November 1998). He had an idea for software that would help media companies create Web sites tailored to local markets. Featuring classified ads, movie listings, event listings, and business directories, Zip2, as Musk's company came to be known, was born in mid-1995, with Musk's Palo Alto apartment as headquarters. His younger brother, Kimbal, joined Zip2 later that year, along with Greg Kouri—a former real-estate developer and a friend of Musk's mother. "Our beginnings were quite humble," Musk told Steve Lubove for *Forbes* (May 12, 2003); in those days, Musk has said, he showered at a local YMCA, and he told Lubove, referring to a fast-food restaurant, "Jack in the Box was a splurge." Though at first they had trouble finding financial support, the Zip2 team was aided by the success of the Web browser Netscape and the subsequent hype among investors surrounding the Internet. In early 1996 the venture-capital group Mohr Davidow gave Musk and his partners $3.6 million in exchange for majority control of the company. Zip2, under the group's leadership, brought in a more experienced manager, Richard Sorkin, to help run the company.

In September 1996 Zip2 launched its Web site. "[Musk] claimed no special knowledge of or insight into the future of the media," Mark Gimein wrote for the *Ottowa Citizen* (August 23, 1999), "aside from the simple and fairly obvious principle that a lot of what newspapers did . . . worked better online." Many newspaper companies needed help in putting their material on the Internet; Zip2 provided training to newspapers' marketing and sales teams and licensed its tools for Internet-technology development to the newspapers. Among the many newspapers that relied upon

Zip2 for their Web sites were the *New York Times*, the *Chicago Tribune*, and several belonging to Knight-Ridder and the Hearst Corp.

While outwardly successful, the company experienced internal difficulties, with Musk and Sorkin disagreeing over its future. Musk apparently was not satisfied with Zip2's background role; according to Gimein, "The sites [Zip2] created for the *New York Times* and other smaller newspapers bore the names of their sponsoring papers, with a little logo and the words, 'Powered by Zip2.' To users of its sites, Zip2's work was almost invisible." In 1998 a merger between Zip2 and CitySearch, a competitor offering similar services, was called off at the last minute at Musk's urging. Musk felt that CitySearch's chief executive, Charles Conn, would try to force him out of the position of executive vice president after the two companies merged. The failed deal cost both Musk and Sorkin their jobs. Derek Proudian, one of Mohr Davidow's venture capitalists, took over as acting CEO of Zip2, and in 1999 Compaq Computer bought the company for $307 million in cash, planning to combine it with its own search engine, AltaVista. The 28-year-old Musk's 7 percent share in the company brought him $22 million in cash.

Musk put $10 million of his fortune into his next undertaking, X.com, an Internet-based financial-services provider. After the success of Zip2, he was able to attract investor support quickly. Sequoia Capital, a leading venture firm, provided $25 million in start-up capital, and Bill Harris, a former CEO of Inuit (the makers of Quicken and TurboTax software), became president and CEO of the company. X.com went on-line in December 1999, initially offering a large number of financial services, including banking, investing options, and mortgages and loans via affiliated banks. Though X.com proved unsuccessful as a one-stop provider of finance services, one of the site's features—a program allowing users to E-mail money to one another—was popular with users of on-line auctions who needed a quick and secure way to send and receive payments. At the time, another company, Confinity, offered a similar service, called PayPal, that allowed wireless devices (such as PalmPilots) to move money between bank accounts. Musk bought that company, renamed his entire operation PayPal, and improved the money-transfer service by allowing users to make on-line payments using regular PCs. He drew in many new customers with a "viral marketing campaign," as he told Friedman, which included offering customers $10 for opening an account with PayPal, as well as $10 for referring a new user to the company. By October 2000 PayPal was operating more than three million accounts, with much of its success due to its popularity with users of eBay, a leading on-line auction service. In 2002 PayPal held what proved to be one of the year's few successful initial public offerings (IPOs) for technology stocks. Eight months later, in October 2002, eBay purchased PayPal for $1.5 billion, an 80 percent premium over the initial offering price. Musk, who was the company's largest individual shareholder, with an 11.7 percent stake, sold some of his shares but held onto the majority. With an estimated fortune of $165 million, he was included in *Fortune*'s list of the "40 Wealthiest People Under 40" in its September 2002 issue.

With his sizeable fortune, Musk was faced with a decision as to what to do next. According to Michelle Kessler, writing for *USA Today* (September 3, 2003), he asked a friend, "What is the most important thing that we can and should be doing?" He contemplated philanthropy but soon decided on space exploration, believing, as quoted by Mark Carreau in the *Houston Chronicle* (November 25, 2005), that "the extension of life to another planet is arguably one of the most important things in the whole history of Earth."

Musk initially planned to send a small life-supporting greenhouse to Mars to "gather scientific information and create excitement about space travel," as Wayne wrote. Although he could afford the estimated $20 million that the experimental system would cost, the high price of launching it into space using rocket technology presented a significant obstacle; the cost of launching commercial payloads, such as weather and telecommunication satellites, can range from about $20 million to $85 million. Musk began negotiating with a Russian firm offering a cheaper alternative, but he decided that the operation was too risky. Then it occurred to him that he should try to build his own rocket. He commissioned a study of the market and found that the prospects for business looked favorable: in 2005 governments and private companies paid a total of $4 billion for 55 launchings. Eighteen of those launchings—about $1 billion worth—were commercial. In addition, the two major U.S. companies in the rocket industry, Boeing and Lockheed Martin, had been undercut in recent years by lower-cost competitors from Russia, Ukraine, and France—but the prices were still high. As Musk told Lubove, "It was clear there was a need for a reliable, low-cost method of getting to space."

Musk moved to Southland, California, a center for the aerospace industry, and founded SpaceX in 2002. He bankrolled the company using $100 million of his own money, with hopes that venture capitalists who were reluctant to invest would back the project after successful launches. SpaceX currently employs about 150 people, including many engineers formerly with Boeing and TRW. It is located in "a gritty industrial zone," as Wayne described it, in a 25,000-square-foot warehouse in the town of El Segundo. Musk's Falcon rockets are manufactured there and field-tested in McGregor, Texas. SpaceX has established launch complexes at Vandenberg Air Force Base, in California, as well as on Kwajalein Atoll, in the Marshall Islands.

As SpaceX's CEO and chief technology officer, Musk has tried to hold costs down by focusing on efficient design and reusable parts. "SpaceX is optimizing for simplicity rather than performance, and that's what sets it apart from the others," Jeffrey Foust, an analyst at the aerospace consulting firm Futron, told Wayne. "When you have a limited number of things that could fail, you can increase a rocket's reliablity." SpaceX's debut rocket, the Falcon 1, is 68 feet long, weighs 60,000 pounds, and has kerosene and liquid-oxygen rockets. Although most rockets have several stages (individual sections that separate from the rocket after their engines have been used), Falcon 1 has only two, each with one engine. Accordingly, with only one stage-separation event, the chances for failure are kept to a minimum. The first-stage rocket is reusable; after separation, the first stage will descend by parachute to the ocean and be retrieved. "Throwing away multi-million-dollar rocket stages every flight," Musk told Wayne, "makes no more sense than chucking away a 747 after every flight." To further lower costs, SpaceX designs and builds its own engines rather than buying engines from suppliers. The Merlin, as the engine is called, "is much more analogous to a truck engine than a sports car engine, which is how all other [rocket] engines are designed," he told Wayne. "Instead of designing it to the bleeding edge of performance and drawing out every last ounce of thrust, we designed Merlin to be easy to build, easy to fix and robust. It can take a beating and still keep going."

SpaceX intends to attract customers with prices that are a fraction of those charged by other space-launch outlets. For a launch of the Falcon 1, which is designed to lift payloads of up to 1,256 pounds into low Earth orbit, SpaceX charges $6.7 million—the price includes, according to the SpaceX Web site, the launch range, third-party insurance, and standard payload integration costs. Falcon 1 is intended as a competitor of the Pegasus rocket, designed by Orbital Sciences, whose launch has a price of about $30 million. Other rockets in development are the Falcon 5 and the Falcon 9—the numbers correspond to the number of first-stage engines. Both rockets, like the Falcon 1, use two stages. The Falcon 5, which is priced at $18 million per flight and can take payloads of up to 9,000 pounds, will compete with Boeing's Delta II craft, which costs $85 million per flight. The Falcon 9, which will take payloads up to 20,000 pounds, is priced at $27 million per launch. As of early 2006 SpaceX had received $200 million worth of launching orders, many of them from the Defense Department, which has agreed to pay $100 million for the launching of military satellites through 2010. Among SpaceX's other clients are the government of Malaysia, the Swedish Space Corp., and the American venture group Bigelow Aerospace (which is seeking to develop habitable space structures—an orbiting hotel for space tourists, for example).

In August 2006 NASA announced that SpaceX was one of two companies (the other being Rocketplane Kistler) that would receive a total of about $500 million worth of contracts to build spacecraft to service the International Space Station. The work was scheduled to be accomplished between 2010 and 2014. SpaceX's share of the contract reportedly amounted to about $278 million.

SpaceX launched its first Falcon rocket on March 24, 2006, carrying as its payload the FalconSAT-2, a $380 million, 43-pound satellite designed by the Air Force Academy to study the ionosphere. The launch failed, due to a fuel fire in the engine. The rocket reached an altitude of about one mile before the engine shut off. Musk said that the fire resulted from "one little process error," as quoted by Michael A. Dornheim for *Aviation Week & Space Technology* (April 3, 2006), and was not caused by a serious design or manufacturing problem. "It is perhaps worth noting," Musk wrote for the SpaceX Web site, "that [other] launch companies that succeeded also took their lumps along the way. A friend of mine wrote to remind me that only 5 of the first 9 Pegasus launches succeeded; 3 of 5 for Ariane [designed by Arianespace]; 9 of 20 for Atlas [designed by Boeing]; 9 of 21 for Soyuz [designed by the Korolev Design Bureau, in Russia]; and 9 of 18 for Proton [designed by the Khrunichev State Research and Production Space Center in Moscow]." Musk added, "Having experienced firsthand how hard it is to reach orbit, I have a lot of respect for those that persevered to produce the vehicles that are mainstays of space launch today." A second attempt, dubbed Falcon 1.1, was to take place in November or December 2006.

Elon Musk has been described as tall, soft-spoken, and boyish-looking. "Although he speaks rapidly and dresses as casually as any Silicon Valley techie, he has the clean-cut appearance and impeccable manners of a Mormon missionary," LaPlante wrote. He owns a mansion in Bel Air, California, a McLaren F1 sports car, and a Dassault Falcon 900 business jet. He is married to Justine Wilson, a Canadian-born novelist.

—M.B.

Suggested Reading: *Forbes* p54 May 12, 2003; *Los Angeles Times* p1 Apr. 22, 2003; *New York Times* III p1 Feb. 5, 2006; *Ottowa Citizen* D p1 Aug. 23, 1999; *Wired News* (on-line) Apr. 22, 2003

Courtesy of Paul Nachtigall

Nachtigall, Paul E.

Jan. 21, 1946– Marine scientist

Address: Hawaii Institute of Marine Biology, P.O. Box 1346, Kaneohe, HI 96744

By March 26, 2003 six days had passed since U.S.-led coalition forces invaded Iraq for the stated purpose of locating so-called weapons of mass destruction, allegedly hidden by Iraq's leader, Saddam Hussein. Televised reports on the campaign showed armor units on the ground moving toward Baghdad, fighter jets bombing major Iraqi strongholds, and dolphins swimming in the port of Umm Qasr. An unusual military tool, the dolphins were part of the U.S. Navy's Special Clearance Team One from San Diego, California, working to locate lethal anti-ship mines scattered across the seafloor below southern Iraq. The dolphins will probably soon be out of a job they have held since the 1960s, however, as a result of over two decades of research by one of the leading experts on the sensory and perceptual processes of dolphins, Paul E. Nachtigall, director of the Marine Mammal Research Program. "Dolphin Biosonar: A Model for Biomimetic Sonars," written in collaboration with Whitlow Au, the program's chief scientist, provided the navy with a plan to build a sonar system to spot dangerous mines—a system that is based on the dolphins' echolocation abilities, or their use of sound waves to interpret their surroundings. While expanding the bounds of knowledge of the echolocation abilities of cetaceans—toothed whales, including sperm whales and dolphins—Nachtigall's work has served the health and environmental interests of those marine mammals as well. Although Nachtigall has encountered critics throughout his career who oppose his belief in confining marine animals for purposes of scientific research, his academic and philanthropic work have left little room for critics to doubt his intention to improve life for marine mammals.

Paul Eugene Nachtigall was born in San Jose, California, on January 21, 1946 to Elmer V. Nachtigall, a carpenter widely respected for his workmanship in showcase and fixture installation, and Melba Nachtigall. His parents were devout members of the Mennonite Brethren Church, and Paul and his three siblings, Judy, Dale, and Bruce, were raised in that conservative Protestant faith. After graduating from high school, Paul Nachtigall attended nearby San Jose State University, where he earned his B.A. degree with distinction in 1967, and his M.A. degree in 1970, both in experimental and comparative psychology—the latter being the study of animal behavior. Although Nachtigall began publishing his findings about various marine animals as early as 1969, it was not until the early 1970s that he began to focus his research on dolphins. While continuing his studies in experimental and comparative psychology, working toward his Ph.D. degree at the University of Hawaii, he began doing research at the Naval Undersea Center, in Kailua, Hawaii. In 1976 he completed his doctorate with the publication of his dissertation, "Food-Intake and Food-Rewarded Instrumental Performance in Dolphins as a Function of Feeding Schedule." Nachtigall worked at the Naval Undersea Center as a scientist until 1981, when the lab changed its name and he became the head of the Research Branch and Division at the Naval Ocean Systems Center, at Kaneohe Marine Corps Base in Windward Oahu, Hawaii. Nachtigall worked with two bottlenose dolphins, BJ and Boris, and a false killer whale (a species closely related to the bottlenose dolphin) named Kina. Collaborating with Whitlow Au, a fellow researcher at the Naval Ocean Systems Center research laboratory, Nachtigall dedicated much of those years to studying and publishing numerous articles on dolphins' echolocation abilities.

In 1993 the U.S. Base Realignment and Closure Commission decided to restructure operations at Kaneohe Marine Base and close the Naval Ocean Systems Center research lab. The navy offered Nachtigall and Au the opportunity to transfer to a similar lab in San Diego, but they declined the offer. Instead, the pair set up the University of Hawaii's Marine Mammal Research Program, with Nachtigall as director of the program and Au as chief scientist. They moved BJ, Boris, and Kina to pens on Coconut Island, and with the help of the Marine Corps, they set up operations in a building they constructed out of eight shipping containers. From their paltry beginnings in a roughly constructed office in Hawaii, Nachtigall and Au completed a great deal of significant work, attracting the attention of fellow marine scientists. For example, until the 1970s little was known about how marine mammals used echolocation, but through decades of research, Nachtigall and other researchers began to understand the uniquely evolved biological structure of cetaceans. They found that bodies such as those of dolphins, which do not include sharp angles, enhance the mammals' vocal range, thus intensifying sounds in their heads. They are therefore able to hear the echoes of their vocal clicks bounce off objects around them, forming acoustic pictures of their physical surroundings. "The animals are excellent signal processors. They know exactly what they are looking at with their clicks, and they can look precisely at one particular target. Even if it moves back and forth, they can stay locked onto it," Nachtigall told *Hawaii Business* (January 2004).

Nachtigall and Au collected millions of dollars in research grants over the next 10 years, which have gone toward supporting a full-time and part-time staff as well as feeding and otherwise caring for the scientists' research subjects, BJ, Boris, and Kina. "There is nobody that treats animals better than we do," Nachtigall told *Hawaii Business*. Nachtigall's background in experimental and comparative psychology and Au's knowledge of engineering, together with the expertise of their colleagues, made possible the discoveries detailed in such important publications as "Dolphin Biosonar: A Model for Biomimetic Sonars." In an interview with Discovery of Sound in the Sea (an Internet-based group devoted to educating people in the use of sight and sound among "all working or living in the ocean," according to its Web site), Au said that the study of dolphin echolocation is a multidisciplinary field, and that the key to its success is to "have a combination of several different kinds of people with different kinds of disciplines . . . if you can merge the disciplines together then you get the best results."

In addition to conducting research and teaching classes in the zoology and psychology departments at the University of Hawaii, as well as its School of Ocean Earth Sciences and Technology, Nachtigall has simultaneously held positions on a number of advisory boards. In 1992 he was selected as editor and publisher of *Aquatic Mammals*, a journal of the European Association for Aquatic Animals; he held that title until 2000, when he became an editorial board member and editor emeritus. In 1995 he was appointed research representative and vice chair of the Sanctuary Advisory Council of the Hawaiian Islands Humpback Whale National Marine Sanctuary, an organization committed to the protection of humpback whales and their habitat in the surrounding regions of Hawaii. In 1998 Nachtigall became the chair of the international Society for Marine Mammalogy's Scientific Program Committee. He was elected president of the 200-member organization in 2000.

Nachtigall has devoted his time not only to teaching and research in the area of marine mammals but to efforts to save creatures stranded along the Hawaiian shorelines. He has used his connec-tions within the marine-science field to bring together professionals of varying specialties for that purpose. Along with Bob Braun, a veterinarian specializing in marine mammals, and Marlee Breese, a research associate with the University of Hawaii Marine Mammal Research Program at Coconut Island, Nachtigall founded the Hawaiian Islands Stranding Response Group, which is currently made up of approximately 100 volunteers, including marine and ocean experts, veterinarians, and students. Because the government does not provide experts and specialists, members of the response group provide emergency treatment for the animals and arrange their transport, if necessary for medical care, to Nachtigall's facility at the Marine Corps Base in Kaneohe. "We come with experience as well as good hearts," Nachtigall told Eloise Aguiar for the *Honolulu Advertiser* (October 7, 2003). On August 19, 2003 the group responded when two melon-headed whales, weighing 285 and 260 pounds, respectively, were found beached at Hauula Beach Park. Originally, the whales were diagnosed with food poisoning and received around-the-clock care, which required the work of three volunteers per day. The older of the two whales, known as No. 2, died of congestive heart failure only five days after the rescue. Though volunteers had hoped that No. 1 would recover, since he had showed signs of improvement, he was euthanized one month after the death of No. 2; his condition had suddenly worsened, causing him pain and a loss of appetite, as Braun, president of the Hawaiian Islands Stranding Response Group, told Leila Fujimori for the *Honolulu Star-Bulletin* (September 17, 2003). A necropsy revealed that the whale was suffering from severe pancreatitis. "The unfortunate reality is there's a reason those two were on the beach," Marlee Breese, vice president of the response group, told Diana Leone for the *Honolulu Star-Bulletin* (August 20, 2003), suggesting that despite the group's efforts, more often than not the stranded animals die because they are beyond the point of rehabilitation. Many of the volunteers feel that although the work might seem futile, "as a human, you feel like you have to do something," as one of the volunteers, Becky Roten, told Eloise Aguiar.

On May 6, 2003 Nachtigall testified before the Congressional Committee on Resources during the hearing on a bill to amend the Endangered Species Act and the Marine Mammal Protection Act. During his testimony he stated, as quoted on the committee's Web site, "I am very concerned about both the ability to continue to conduct research, and the effects of sound on populations of marine mammals. It is my opinion that one cannot know about the effects of sound on animals without conducting well-planned and executed basic research. There appears to be a current trend among some marine mammal advocates to be very conservative when it comes to science. Some apparently advocate that no research involving sound should be done. I think it is unreasonable to do nothing. Basic research is essential to understand the animals and to assist in preservation of their populations." His statements alluded in part to a heated debate that had begun in 2001, in which some protested the construction of a dolphin exhibition facility at the proposed $20 million Maui Nui Park in North Kihei (which as of December 2005 had not been created). When the Maui County Council committee heard from a panel of speakers on either side of the issue, Nachtigall argued that observation of captive marine mammals plays a vital role in research and education in the area of marine conservation. Those who opposed the facility maintained that holding the dolphins in tanks was inhumane, even if it would help researchers learn more about the animals. "Imagine if studies of human behavior, cognition and physiology were based almost entirely on prisoners," Hannah Bernard, education director for the Maui Ocean Center aquarium, said to Timothy Hurley for the *Honolulu Advertiser* (September 21, 2001). In his testimony to the Committee on Resources, Nachtigall responded to such arguments, saying, "How will we know what the effects of sound are on marine mammals if in fact scientists are not allowed to study it. . . . Scientists do have an obligation to be concerned about the effects of their scientific investigation on the environment. I believe that this case identifies a critical need for basic research on the effects of [manmade] sound [from motorboats, for example] on whales." In November 2003 the Marine Mammal Commission, an independent agency of the U.S. government, established the Advisory Committee on Acoustic Impacts on Marine Mammals, appointing Nachtigall as a committee member.

It is possible that without extended research conducted on captive marine mammals, Nachtigall would not have been able to write his groundbreaking paper on dolphin biosonars, which, since its publication in 2000, has given way to technological advancements that benefit humans and dolphins alike. Those advances include the invention of biomimetic sonar, designed not only to improve the military's capability to clear away hazardous underwater mines, but to save dolphins the dangerous job of doing it themselves. The invention has borne fruit in the commercial sector as well. According to a January 2004 *Hawaii Business* article featuring Nachtigall and Au, software mimicking the noise-cancellation and signal-processing methods of sonar and cetaceans could conceivably be used in consumer products. Telecommunications companies could use the technology to make cell phones that have better noise-cancellation capabilities, to enable use of the phones in places where they do not currently function. Neptune Technologies, a firm based in Hawaii, has used Nachtigall's technology for a project to design an artificial dolphin for the U.S. Special Forces. The California-based firm DolphinSearch, founded in 1999 by a former University of Hawaii researcher and colleague of Nachtigall's, Herbert Roiblat, uses the same type of signal-processing sonar to search through large amounts of text for useful news items or legal documents.

Nachtigall continues his work at the Marine Mammal Research Program, which has offices on Coconut Island and at the Marine Corps Base in Kaneohe Bay. The University of Hawaii provides the program with the services of employees, volunteers, and students while the Office of Naval Research provides the funding and support facilities. The program's research goals are twofold: to improve mining and sonar techniques and to ensure the safety of marine mammals. "We do research on hearing primarily because we're concerned about the loud sounds in the ocean and its effects on the animals," Nachtigall told Jessica B. Davis for the U.S. Department of Defense Information (May 5, 2005). Because echolocation is fundamental in the daily lives of marine mammals such as whales and dolphins, loud noises from sonar use could potentially be harmful to their health. The navy has taken significant steps to minimize harm to marine mammals from sonar by suspending sonar operations when there is a risk to the animals. The research facility is also outfitted with a complete laboratory, surgery, and necropsy facility for beached or stranded mammals that are brought to the base by the Hawaiian Islands Stranding Response Group. In May 2005 the U.S. House of Representatives passed a bill providing $2.2 million to the University of Hawaii program to continue researching the effects of sound on whales and dolphins. The group hopes that the Senate will pass a similar measure. Nachtigall indicated to Timothy Hurley for the *Honolulu Advertiser* (May 22, 2005) that little is known concerning the effects of sound on cetaceans. In his testimony before the Committee on Resources, Nachtigall explained that there are audiograms (graphical representations of the softest sounds an individual can hear at different pitches) for only 10 or 11 of the 85 species of dolphins and whales. However, his program, working with Alexander Supin from the Russian Academy of Sciences, has constructed a method of measuring hearing in the cetaceans and plans on obtaining audiograms for more species.

Nachtigall has written, edited, or co-edited five books, among them *Sensory Systems of Aquatic Mammals* (1996) and *The Biology of the Harbour Porpoise* (1997). He is also the author of more than 75 peer-reviewed journal articles and chapters in reviewed books and has given more than 15 addresses at scientific meetings in the last three years alone. He is frequently invited to speak at scientific meetings and serves on numerous advisory boards. Nearly all of Nachtigall's work has had underlying aim of preserving the vitality of marine life as much as possible. He hopes to conduct future studies on vision and taste reception in cetaceans while also continuing his work in aiding stranded animals. Nachtigall and Au are research professors at the Hawaii Institute of Marine Biology.

For 38 years Nachtigall has been married to Cynthia Taylor Nachtigall, a pediatric medical social worker who works at the Tripler Army Medical Center with children diagnosed with cancer or other ailments. The couple have three children: Alysha and Emilie, who attend Mills College, and Nathan, who attends Windward Community College. Nachtigall "enjoys his friends, his garden, and raises bananas and avocados," as he wrote to *Current Biography*, adding that his "latest recreational venture" was a visit to Kolmården, Sweden, with three of his students, Michelle Yuen, Aran Mooney, and Kristen Taylor, "to measure the hearing of three polar bears" with his colleagues Alexander Supin and Mats Amundin. His "visit with Mats' wolves at the Kolmården Zoo," he wrote, "was a special treat."

—I.C.

Suggested Reading: *Hawaii Business* p22 Jan. 2004; Hawai'i Institute of Marine Biology Web site; Marine Mammal Commission Web site; U.S. Congress Web site

Chris Graythen/Getty Images

Nagin, C. Ray

June 11, 1956– Mayor of New Orleans (Democrat)

Address: New Orleans City Hall, Mayor's Office, 1300 Perdido St., Rm. 2E04, New Orleans, LA 70112

Images and stories of death and anguish filled television screens and newspapers throughout the world in the late summer of 2005, as New Orleans, Louisiana, was decimated by flooding in the aftermath of Hurricane Katrina, one of the worst natural disasters in the history of the United States. Thousands of people left homeless were herded into the Superdome, which came to look more like a disease- and war-ravaged Third World country than a sports complex. As some citizens looted stores for food, water, and other items, federal response teams were slow to provide aid to displaced residents. "We have small children and sick and elderly people dying every day. Small children being raped and killed. People running around with guns. I'm scared for my life, my wife and my 5-year-old daughter's life. We don't want to live here anymore . . . ," one New Orleans resident, Alan Gould, told CNN (September 2, 2005, on-line) over the telephone from the city's Convention Center. "We need the federal help . . . we just need to be out of here. They keep telling us the bus is coming, the bus is coming, and nobody showed up yet." Such frustration was conveyed not only by the hurricane's victims but by local government officials as well. New Orleans mayor C. Ray Nagin, known regionally prior to the disaster for his calm manner, projected a different image to the nation, as he tearfully demanded that federal authorities act immediately to help evacuate victims from devastated sections of the city. In an interview with Garland Robinette for a local radio station, WWL, which was broadcast nationally less than a week after Hurricane Katrina struck, Americans heard Mayor Nagin lashing out in sometimes profane language at President George W. Bush and Louisiana's governor, Kathleen Blanco: "This is ridiculous. I don't want to see anybody do anymore [expletive] press conferences. Put a moratorium on press conferences. Don't do another press conference until the resources are in this city. And then come down to this city and stand with us when there are military trucks and troops that we can't even count. . . . Let's do something, and let's fix the biggest [expletive] crisis in the history of this country."

Nagin had been a successful businessman when he was elected as New Orleans's mayor in 2002, with 59 percent of the vote. Taking the reins of a city plagued by violent crime, governmental nepotism, and poverty, he initially set about attempting to root out corruption and revive a dismal economy. But in the wake of Hurricane Katrina, with extremely limited resources and a divided constituency, Nagin has faced the more immediate and massive task of rebuilding what is left of the city known as the Big Easy.

Clarence Ray Nagin Jr. was born on June 11, 1956 in New Orleans. Raised with his two sisters, Wanda and Alana, in a low-income neighborhood of the city's Seventh Ward, Nagin came to appreciate the strong work ethic of his parents, who labored tirelessly to better the family's circumstances. While his mother ran a lunch counter at K-Mart, Nagin's father had two jobs: cutting fabric at a clothing factory by day and serving as a custodian at City Hall or working as a mechanic by night. The family eventually moved to the more affluent and predominantly white neighborhood of Algiers, where Nagin attended O. Perry Walker High School. Although his grades were less than stellar, Nagin received a baseball scholarship to Tuskegee University, a historically black school in Tuskegee, Alabama. The university, founded in 1881 by the famous black leader Booker T. Washington, gave Nagin a new perspective on his heritage. "That's when I realized how naive I was to the accomplishments of African-Americans," Nagin told Gordon Russell for the New Orleans *Times-Picayune* (May 5, 2002). "Because that school teaches black pride, not from a put-down-other-races perspective. It's more of an understanding of where you come from and what other African-Americans have done throughout history. . . . It made me feel like I could do just about anything. Like at the end of the day, if I had applied myself, I could do it." Nagin graduated from Tuskegee in 1978, earning his bachelor of science degree in accounting and becoming the second member of his family to receive a college degree.

After his graduation Nagin worked for General Motors in Detroit, Michigan, until 1981, when he moved to Dallas, Texas, to work at Associates Corp., a financial-services company. In 1985 he returned to his home state to become controller of Cox Communications, a cable-service provider. It was at Cox that Nagin established his reputation as a creative businessman. Soon after his arrival there, he was transferred to Cox New Orleans, the poorest-performing region in the company's network. He emphasized customer service, starting a cable-TV show that allowed customers to phone in their concerns to Nagin, who appeared on the program; he also revamped the cable system through a $500 million initiative. Nagin's innovations revitalized Cox New Orleans, making it one of the most profitable performers in the network. Continuing his education on a part-time basis, in 1994 he received his M.B.A. degree from Tulane University, in New Orleans, to prepare himself for additional responsibilities at Cox. By 2002 Nagin had been promoted to vice president and general manager of Cox New Orleans. He also applied his business ingenuity to the world of sports, bringing an East Coast Hockey League franchise to the city, where they became the New Orleans Brass, in 1998. With Nagin serving as one of the team's principal owners and as president of the franchise, the minor-league team won unexpected popularity in the city.

Nagin had never imagined himself as a politician, but after a conversation with his son, who saw few career opportunities in New Orleans, he considered pursuing a role in government, to help improve economic and employment conditions in the city. Nagin commissioned a poll of the public's opinions about those who were already campaigning for the 2002 mayoral election, and he found that much of the city, like him, was unimpressed by the contenders. "At that point, I kind of decided I was either going to be part of the problem or part of the solution, so I jumped in," he told *Contemporary Black Biography* (2004). The New Orleans native joined the 2002 mayoral race just two months before the Democratic primary. Largely self-funded, Nagin triumphed in the primary, to the surprise of many. In the general election he faced Police Chief Richard Pennington. Seen by voters as a no-nonsense man committed to bringing business to New Orleans and putting a stop to its long history of political corruption, Nagin easily beat Pennington to win the office. Afterward he spoke to well-wishers outside City Hall, saying, as quoted by Frank Donze in the *Times-Picayune* (March 3, 2002), "I'm going to need your help, a lot of help. I'm going to need your prayers. I'm going to need your support. And I'm going to need your patience. I don't have a Superman undershirt on underneath this coat. It didn't take us one year to get in this mess, and it's not going to take us one year to get out of it."

Nagin addressed the issue of corruption in a dramatic move in July 2002, sending police out in the early-morning heat to arrest dozens of suspected criminals in their homes. The sweep was aimed at low-level city officials who had taken bribes, brake-tag inspectors who accepted money in exchange for approving substandard vehicles, and illegally licensed cab drivers. Although few arrests resulted in convictions, many New Orleans residents welcomed the raid as a step toward a brighter future. "I think it sent a signal not only to ourselves but to the rest of the world that we were serious about cleaning the city up," Nagin told Juan Williams for the National Public Radio program *Morning Edition* (November 5, 2003). As mayor Nagin relied on his business sense, surrounding himself with business leaders instead of political insiders. Using that approach he eliminated a $25 million budget deficit, renegotiated public contracts to benefit the city, and streamlined bureaucracies, making government forms available on-line, for example.

Despite the many advances Nagin made in New Orleans, he found sharp critics among the city's black clergy, which accused him of failing to defend the economic, social, and political gains made by the city's black residents (who made up two-thirds of the city's population). To voice their concerns, they formed the Greater New Orleans Coalition of Ministers; the group accused Nagin of staying within a closed circle of associates and of ignoring the example of his predecessors by failing to reach out to the black community in a meaningful way. Unlike previous African-American New Orleans mayors, Nagin attended a small number of churches, rather than courting influential black preachers at as many churches as possible. Bishop Paul S. Morton Sr. of Greater St. Stephen Full Gospel Baptist Church, one of the most influential black preachers in Louisiana, even called Nagin "a white man in black skin" who had allowed New Orleans to slip into an "apartheid state."

In late August 2005 such conflicts were eclipsed by the most devastating natural disaster ever to hit New Orleans. Reports of a category-five hurricane heading straight for the Gulf Coast region caused some anxiety among New Orleans's approximately 460,000 residents, but 10 to 20 percent of them (as many as 92,000 people), having weathered a number of reportedly "severe" storms, did not heed the mayor's call to evacuate. Nagin reassured the thousands of people who remained in the city due to medical conditions or other causes that resources were available to meet their needs in the face of the hurricane; he directed them to the evacuation center set up at the Superdome as a refuge of last resort. "If you can't leave the city and you have to come to the Superdome, come with enough food, perishable items to last for three to five days. . . . No weapons, no alcohol, no drugs. . . . It's not going to be the best environment, but at least you will be safe," Nagin said at a press conference, as quoted by *CNN Breaking News* (August 28, 2005, online). The day before Hurricane Katrina struck, the federal government promised Nagin that 1,500 National Guard troops would be ready for deployment at a moment's notice, with another couple of thousand standing by.

Hurricane Katrina battered New Orleans on August 29, its 160-mile-per-hour winds uprooting trees, knocking down power lines, and strewing roadways with debris. The following day residents woke to find the city—already six feet below sea level—completely flooded. Entire neighborhoods were submerged under eight to 15 feet of water; levees had collapsed at three points, leaving New Orleans awash in floodwater, sewage, and corpses. Mayor Nagin, who had set up temporary operations on the 27th floor of a structurally damaged and powerless Hyatt Hotel, near the Superdome, remained upbeat at first—assuring people that 3,500 National Guard troops were on their way. Signs of doubt began to surface in the mayor's words, however, when he spoke with Charles Gibson for *Good Morning America* (August 31, 2005). "I am very concerned. I am, we are looking for help. There's supposedly 3,000 National Guard troops that are on their way. . . . Food is starting to become an issue. We have a shelter of last resort with about 15 or 20,000 people and it's almost unbearable in the Superdome. The Superdome's roof has been breached. There's holes in it. . . . Power is becoming an issue because the generators are failing at strategic locations because the water is rising." As the floodwaters began to rise and claim more lives, helicopters were dispatched to rescue victims from rooftops of homes and buildings, and the city's few rescue workers went to the aid of stranded residents. Despite those efforts, the confidence Nagin expressed before the hurricane vanished as time wore on. "I see the same thing I've been seeing for six or seven days now. I see destruction. I see despair. I see suffering. I see death," the mayor told Nic Robertson for CNN's *Late Edition with Wolf Blitzer* (September 4, 2005, on-line).

Desperate residents broke into the New Orleans Convention Center on August 30, seeking refuge from the growing chaos outside. Those who entered the Convention Center were ignored for two days before any relief came, at which point the facility was declared to have been made unsafe and unsanitary by the influx of people. A Federal Emergency Management Agency (FEMA) official, after seeing the devastation in the city firsthand from a helicopter, went to Nagin's center of operations at the Hyatt and immediately called Washington for help. According to a *Newsweek* (September 19, 2005) reporter, Evan Thomas, when the FEMA representative got in touch with senior officials in Washington, Nagin's staff heard him say repeatedly, "You don't understand, you don't understand"—an indication that those at the top level of the federal government did not grasp the scale of destruction Katrina had caused. (FEMA's director, Michael Brown, and the Homeland Security secretary, Michael Chertoff, both blamed for not acting quickly enough to help those in New Orleans, claimed not to have even known until September 1 that the Convention Center was being used as a shelter.) While some praised Mayor Nagin for his decision to remain in the city, others accused him of avoiding some of the sites of the worst suffering. At the Superdome—which Mayor Nagin, days earlier, had said would be a safe place for residents to weather the storm—squalid conditions gave rise to sharp criticism from flood victims including Donnieka Rhinehart, who told Susan Saulny for the *New York Times* (September 3, 2005), "We've been in here for five days, and [Nagin] still hasn't shown his face to us." Estimates indicate that as many as 60,000 people were gathered at the Superdome, living in hazardous conditions for nearly a week. By the time the centers were completely evacuated, four people had died at the Convention Center and six at the Superdome.

When the situation at the two evacuation centers became intolerable, city officials suggested that those who were able to do so make their way out of New Orleans to the Crescent City Connection Bridge, where buses were available to transport them to less-crowded evacuation centers. Mayor Nagin told FEMA to give water and supplies to the people as they made their way across, but instead of meeting relief workers, the evacuees encountered sheriffs from Gretna, Louisiana. The sheriffs forced the evacuees at gunpoint to turn back to their flooded city, fearing that the looting, murder, and rape rumored to have taken place within New Orleans would occur in other towns the evacuees were allowed to enter. (Such acts had occurred but were not as widespread as some sources reported.) "That says that people value their property, and were protecting property, over human life," an outraged Nagin told John Donvan for *Nightline* (September 4, 2005, on-line). "And look, I was not suggesting . . . to the people that they walk down in those neighborhoods. All I wanted them to do, and I suggested, walk on the interstate. . . . Those people were looking to escape, and [the Gretna sheriffs] cut off the last available exit route out of New Orleans."

In the absence of federal relief, the city's own rescue workers were overwhelmed by the burden of helping victims, leading Nagin to take a day to see to the needs of the rescuers. "I've got some fire-fighters and police officers that have been pretty much traumatized. And we've already had a cou-ple of suicides . . . ," he told Robertson. "They've been holding the city together for three or four days, almost by themselves, doing everything imaginable, and the toll is just too much for them. So I need to get them out." To add to the fray, accu-sations of racism were leveled at the government and the media. Nationally broadcast television news stories showed predominantly black masses of flood victims, convincing many that the victims' race accounted for the federal government's slow response; and many noted that black New Orleans residents searching for supplies were labeled in the media as "looters" while their white counter-parts were referred to as "starving victims." Mayor Nagin, however, viewed the issue in terms of class rather than race. (The majority of the lower-income neighborhoods with predominantly black popula-tions were located in the low-lying regions of the city and consequently had more severe damage than the wealthier French Quarter.)

While the National Guard troops began arriving in New Orleans toward the end of the week that Hurricane Katrina struck, two weeks passed before the promised number of them showed up. After nearly two weeks of repeatedly requesting troops and aid, a frustrated Mayor Nagin spoke to Garland Robinette for WWL Radio, saying, "I told [the pres-ident] that we had an incredible crisis here and that his flying over in Air Force One does not do it justice. And that I have been all around this city and I am very frustrated because we are not able to martial resources and we're outmanned in just about every respect." Critics accused President Bush, who was on vacation in Texas when the storm hit the Gulf Coast, of failing to comprehend the magnitude of the hurricane's destruction and of thus delaying the authorization of federal aid to the affected regions. Among the many critics was Mayor Nagin. "We authorized $8 billion to go to Iraq lickety-quick. After 9/11, we gave the presi-dent unprecedented powers lickety-quick, to take care of New York and other places. Now, you mean to tell me that a place where most of your oil is coming through, a place that is so unique—when you mention New Orleans anywhere around the world, everybody's eyes light up—you mean to tell me that a place where you probably have thou-sands of people that have died and thousands more that are dying every day that we can't figure out a way to authorize the resources we need? Come on, man." According to Evan Thomas, when Nagin fi-nally met with President Bush and Governor Kath-leen Blanco aboard Air Force One, on September 2, the sleep-deprived mayor demanded answers

and action from the president. He reportedly slammed his hand down on the table and told Bush, "We just need to cut through this and do what it takes to have a more-controlled command structure. If that means federalizing it, let's do it." A week later, however, there was still no agree-ment about federal oversight of the relief effort.

While Mayor Nagin spoke out pointedly against federal leaders' slow response to the crisis, many of his New Orleans constituents stood by him. But as the weeks wore on, Nagin himself became a tar-get of criticism, both regionally and nationally. De-tractors saw the mayor's decision to stay in the abandoned Hyatt hotel, rather than go to Baton Rouge, Louisiana, where there was a communica-tion system in place that might have allowed him to better coordinate the relief effort, as evidence of stubbornness. Supporters, such as Rodney Brax-ton, the city's chief legislative lobbyist, saw mat-ters differently. "It's exactly like this: The ship is full of water, but the captain is not leaving. Not without the crew. The crew are those poor people you see on TV in wheelchairs at the Superdome. That's his crew," Braxton told Saulny. On the na-tional level some accused Nagin of wildly exagger-ating the death toll, which he warned could reach 10,000; the final death toll was just over 1,000. Per-haps what hurt Nagin's reputation most among his constituency was his over-zealousness in bringing residents back to New Orleans before conditions were safe for human habitation. Nagin reopened the city just weeks after Hurricane Katrina hit, and residents who returned were forced to evacuate once again, when Hurricane Rita brought even more damage to the already suffering city. Some former residents resented what they felt were emp-ty promises made by Nagin in the course of the cri-sis. "Before Katrina, the man used to give us straight yes and no answers, and we liked that," John Washington, an owner of a small print shop in the Ninth Ward, told Tim Padgett and Kim Hum-phreys for *Time* (October 24, 2005). "But I guess you never really know the measure of a man until disaster strikes." In addition, Nagin and the New Orleans superintendent of police, P. Edwin Com-pass 3d, were criticized because of the failure of many law-enforcement officers to report for duty, the alleged looting by some of them, and the police department's failure to prevent disorder in the af-termath of the hurricane. (Compass resigned on September 28, 2005.)

"I was naive to think that higher levels of gov-ernment could come in and rescue me. I've had to really step up to the plate . . . ," Nagin told Arnold Hamilton and Colleen McCain Nelson for the *Dal-las Morning News* (October 6, 2005). "The things I used to think were very important, like air condi-tioning, showers, running water, I now know that they're not that critical. I've seen so much—such misery, death and despair. It makes my heart grow stronger for this city." Nagin maintains a vision of rebuilding a safer and more prosperous New Orle-ans. He said to John Donvan that New Orleans "has an incredible future. As you go around the city, you will see that some of the key assets of New Orleans are still intact. . . . some of the historic buildings are still intact. It's pretty amazing. So, we do have the fundamentals and the foundation to rebuild [the] city to a great city again." Toward that end, Nagin set up the Bring New Orleans Back Commission, consisting of 16 community and business leaders, to help him to develop a blueprint for the rebuilding of New Orleans. In an effort to meet the city's payroll, he announced the layoffs of 6,000 public employees in the recreation, economic-development, housing, finance, and law departments, effective October 2005. He also abandoned a plan to revive the city's economy by converting several of the city's largest downtown hotels to gambling casinos.

In the months following Katrina, independent investigators began blaming a faulty levee system for the submerging of 80 percent of the city under floodwater. At 15 feet in height, the levees, which were designed by the U.S. Army Corps of Engineers and built by contractors hired by the Corps, were reportedly built to withstand category-three–level storms. Although Katrina was a category-five hurricane, the findings confirmed that rising floodwaters never overtopped the levees. Rather, the brunt of the destruction came when the concrete walls of the levees gave way, after their unstable foundations were significantly weakened. On November 2, 2005 investigators accused contractors of the levee system of using "weak, poorly compacted soils in levee construction and deliberate skimping on steel pilings used to anchor floodwalls to the ground," Joby Warrick and Spencer S. Hsu reported for the *Washington Post* (November 3, 2005). Allegations of such criminal acts are currently under investigation by federal law-enforcement officials as well as the U.S. Army Corps of Engineers. The Corps has pledged to rebuild the levees back to category-three levels, but in order to give former New Orleans residents reassurance that they can return to a safe city, Nagin asked President Bush and Congress for funds to rebuild the levee system to withstand a category-five hurricane, which could cost upwards of $2.5 billion. On December 15, 2005 the Bush administration pledged to add $1.5 billion to the $1.6 billion that had already been promised for the project. Also in December, Governor Blanco announced the indefinite postponement of New Orleans's mayoral and City Council elections, which had been scheduled to take place on February 4, 2006.

In January 2006 a study conducted by Brown University raised concerns regarding the full impact of the hurricane on the future of New Orleans. The report concluded that of those who left New Orleans during the Katrina crisis, 80 percent of the minority population and half of the white population would not come back, if they were limited to neighborhoods undamaged by Katrina. At around the same time, Nagin unveiled the mayoral commission's proposal to give homeowners in the city's hardest-hit (and predominantly African-American) neighborhoods four months to rebuild their neighborhoods or convert the property into parks or marshland that would serve as extra flood defenses, a plan that brought much opposition from African-American business leaders and community activists in the city. Nagin remained a lightning rod for controversy, in part for remarks made at a Martin Luther King Day celebration in New Orleans. In his speech he referred to the hurricanes as indications that "God is mad at America" and also used the often divisive "chocolate city" metaphor to appeal to displaced African-American residents to return to New Orleans and restore its African-American majority, which is "the way God wants it to be," in Nagin's words. In an interview with CNN (January 18, 2006, on-line), Nagin explained that his "chocolate city" reference had been misinterpreted. "How do you make chocolate? You take dark chocolate, you mix it with white milk, and it becomes a delicious drink. That is the chocolate I am talking about. New Orleans was a chocolate city before Katrina. It is going to be a chocolate city after. How is that divisive? It is white and black working together, coming together and making something special."

In the 2006 New Orleans mayoral campaign, Nagin, whose reelection platform centered on a 100-day plan to rebuild New Orleans, faced 21 opponents (mostly white), including Lieutenant Governor Mitch Landrieu and Ron Forman, head of the Audubon Institute. He succeeded in capturing 38 percent of the vote in the primary; Landrieu and Forman came in second and third, with 29 percent and 19 percent of the vote, respectively. Less than two weeks before the runoff election, Nagin faced negative publicity from a recently published book, *The Great Deluge: Hurricane Katrina, New Orleans, and the Mississippi Gulf Coast*, by Douglas Brinkley, which presented Nagin as an ineffectual leader during the post–Hurricane Katrina crisis. Nagin nonetheless won 52 percent of the runoff vote to earn a second term as mayor. Asked for his response to those surprised by his reelection, Nagin said, according to Shaila Dewan, reporting for the *New York Times* (May 22, 2006), "They don't get the uniqueness of New Orleans, they don't really get what really happened during Katrina—all they saw was those awful images—and they really don't get Ray Nagin." He added, "Sometimes I don't get Ray Nagin, so it's all right."

Upon taking office on June 1, 2006, Nagin pledged to spend the first 100 days of his second term honing his rebuilding plan. He was criticized for failing to publish any details of the plan at the conclusion of the 100-day period and for his extensive travel outside New Orleans, as part of a national speaking tour, to seek funding for the rebuilding of the city. Nagin attracted negative publicity for a remark made during an interview in August for the CBS program *60 Minutes*, in which he responded to criticism of the pace of New Orleans redevelopment by finding fault with ongoing rebuilding efforts at New York City's Ground Zero: "You guys in New York can't get a hole in the ground fixed and it's five years later. So let's be fair." He later expressed regret for the statement, during a two-day visit to the World Trade Center site in September. In November 2006 Nagin unveiled his $405 million budget plan for 2007, which includes increased spending on crime prevention, parks, and youth programs.

In 1982 Nagin married Seletha Smith, whose parents lived across the street from his own mother and father in Louisiana. The couple have three children: Jeremy, Jarin, and Tianna.

—I.C.

Suggested Reading: CNN (on-line) Aug. 25, 2005, Sep. 4, 2005, Jan. 18, 2006; *New York Times* p1+ Apr. 24, 2006, p1+ May 22, 2006; *Newsweek* (on-line) Sep. 19, 2005; *Time* p34+ Oct. 24, 2005; *Contemporary Black Biography*, 2004

Courtesy of PepsiCo Inc.

Nooyi, Indra K.

Oct. 28, 1955– President and CEO of PepsiCo. Inc.

Address: PepsiCo, Inc., 700 Anderson Hill Rd., Purchase, NY 10577

On October 1, 2006 the 51-year-old Indra Nooyi succeeded Steve Reinemund as chief executive officer (CEO) of PepsiCo Inc., one of the world's largest food-and-beverage companies. In doing so she not only entered the rarefied group of female heads

of Fortune 500 companies (she is the 11th), but shattered the so-called glass ceiling for minority advancement, becoming the most prominent Indian-born executive in the United States and Pepsi-Co's first Indian-born CEO. Nooyi immigrated to the United States in 1978 to study business at Yale University's prestigious graduate school of management. She held high-level positions at the Boston Consulting Group, the Motorola Corp., and Asea Brown Boveri in the 1980s and early 1990s before beginning her tenure at the Purchase, New York–based PepsiCo, in 1994, as the company's senior vice president for corporate strategy and development. Among other successful moves there, in 1997 Nooyi persuaded then-CEO Roger Enrico to divest the company of its restaurant chains—Taco Bell, Kentucky Fried Chicken, and Pizza Hut—and refocus its mission on its core business, snack-and-beverage brands such as Frito-Lay corn chips and multiflavored soft drinks. Nooyi later became the chief architect behind PepsiCo's $3.3 billion purchase of the Seagram Co.'s Tropicana juices, in 1998, and its $13 billion acquisition of Quaker Oats, in 2001, key mergers that diversified the company's product portfolio in the United States and increased its presence overseas. In 2000 she became chief financial officer (CFO) of Pepsi-Co, and in the following year she took on the additional duties of president, teaming with the new CEO, Reinemund, to enlarge the company's global profile and work to surpass its archrival, the Coca-Cola Co. As a result of their partnership, PepsiCo has increased its profits by 24 percent since May 2001 and nearly doubled the value of it shares, from $37 in 1999 to $64 in 2006. Nooyi told a writer for the *Hindu* (January 2, 2001), "Much like GE [General Electric] was one of the most admired companies in the 20th century, we want people to look back and say PepsiCo [was] the defining corporation for the way they treated their employees, the way they created shareholder value and the way they thought about growth. We do want to set the standards for being the greatest corporation in the 21st century." Known for her singular style, Nooyi has enlivened PepsiCo's conservative corporate culture with her sense of humor and bicultural ethos, frequently wearing a flowing scarf and a sari (a traditional Indian dress) to PepsiCo functions and promoting a "be yourself" atmosphere among her colleagues. *Forbes* recently pronounced Nooyi to be the fourth most powerful woman in the world.

The second of three children, Indra Krishnamurthy Nooyi was born on October 28, 1955 in Chennai (formerly known as Madras), India's fourth-largest city, located in the southeastern state of Tamil Nadu. Her father was an employee at the State Bank of Hyderabad, her mother a homemaker. Her aunt Aruna Sairum is a renowned singer. Nooyi had a strict but supportive upbringing in a conservative Hindu family that valued religious faith, academic excellence, and a strong work ethic. Nooyi recalled, as quoted in an on-line transcript from the question-and-answer portion of a lecture she gave at the Tuck School of Business, at Dartmouth College (September 23, 2002), "My grandfather who was very tough on us said, 'The only thing that matters in life is grades.' As long as you got good grades you were okay. If you didn't get good grades you were not worth it. . . . The 30th day of every month you got a report card and my grandfather would stand at the door waiting for the report card. If you didn't get one of the first three ranks of the class, you might as well kill yourself on the way back from school because he was going to kill you. So those were your two choices, killed by own grandfather or jump in front of the bus. When you have that sort of goal to make all the time, you just work your tail off." Nooyi's mother often gave her and her older sister, Chandrika, speaking exercises that called for them to articulate their career aspirations in creative ways. The better speaker was rewarded with chocolate. "It didn't matter what they said, but it instilled in them a sense of pride and the urge to dream big and chase that dream. It made them achievers," one family friend told Nandini Lakshman for *Daily News & Analysis* (August 14, 2006, on-line).

In the early 1970s Nooyi enrolled at Madras Christian College (MCC), one of the oldest colleges in India, where she studied chemistry and physics and quickly impressed her teachers and peers with her intellectual drive and quick wit. V. J. Phillip, a former principal of the college, told Lakshman that Nooyi was "always a go-getter who had the capacity to rally around people and get them excited." As an example, Phillip recalled that when Nooyi's chemistry class was assigned a particularly difficult test paper, she led her fellow students in solving it—then "barged into the lecturer's room to show him why everybody had performed badly," as Lakshman reported. As a result, a retest was given. "When others shied away from a task, she would come forward to complete it. Indra is someone who grabbed all opportunities that came her way with both hands," Phillip told a writer for the *South Asian News* Web site (August 17, 2006). Nooyi participated in a host of extracurricular activities, serving as captain of the women's cricket team and playing guitar for the all-girls rock band Log Rythms.

After earning her bachelor's degree from MCC, in 1976, Nooyi enrolled at the prestigious Indian Institute of Management (IIM) in Calcutta, as one of only six women in the incoming class. Nicknamed "IK" by her IIM classmates, Nooyi drew their praises for her spunk and spontaneity. She earned her master's degree in business administration from IIM in 1978. She then worked briefly for Mettur Beardsell, a British textile company in India, before assuming the post of product manager at Johnson & Johnson, a global consumer-products company, in Bombay (now called Mumbai). As product manager Nooyi helped launch Stayfree, a brand of sanitary pads, by generating awareness among female consumers through an innovative marketing strategy. "It was a fascinating experience because you couldn't advertise personal protection in India so you had to go from school to school and college to college teaching people," Nooyi told Sarah Murray for the London *Financial Times* (January 26, 2004). "And it was very embarrassing to put out personal care items in retail stores. So even persuading retailers to carry it was difficult. But it was terrific and I learned a lot." During her tenure at Johnson & Johnson, Nooyi happened upon a magazine advertisement that featured Yale University's newly launched graduate school of management. She applied to the program "on a whim," as she said to Murray, and was accepted and offered financial aid. Nooyi then faced the task of persuading her family to let her pursue higher education in the United States. "It was unheard of for a good, conservative, south Indian Brahmin girl to do this. It would make her an absolutely unmarriageable commodity after that," Nooyi told Murray. But to her astonishment, her parents were already softened to the idea of her relocation, since their elder daughter, Chandrika, had left India to work for Citibank in Beirut, Lebanon.

Nooyi enrolled at Yale, in New Haven, Connecticut, in 1978 and covered her expenses by working odd jobs, often wearing a sari (a traditional Indian dress) out of necessity. "When you don't have a safety net, when you don't have money to buy clothes for interviews and you are going to a summer job in saris, all of a sudden life gives you a wakeup call and you realize that you have got to work extremely hard to make it happen in this country for you," Nooyi said to the students at the Tuck School of Business. At Yale, in addition to her traditional seminars in business-case study, Nooyi took mandatory courses in organizational behavior, which left an indelible impression on her. Discussing Yale's approach to teaching teambuilding, Nooyi explained to the Tuck students, "We went through two exercises. One was a desert survival and one was arctic survival. . . . What we had to do was pretend we were in a desert and were only given ten things. Everybody in the group had to prioritize because you were only allowed to pick up five things and decide whether to stay or to walk and then they would videotape you. The OB [organizational behavior] professors would sit outside this one-way room and watch the group dynamics. How you bring others along with you was one of the biggest lessons Yale taught me, both in the desert survival and arctic survival." Courses in communication were also a part of Yale's curriculum. "That was invaluable for someone who came from a culture where communication wasn't perhaps the most important aspect of business at least in my time," Nooyi told Sarah Murray. She added, "When I was growing up in India, we tended to draw conclusions too quickly and it was all in black and white. The thing I learned in my time at Yale was that shades of grey predominate. You need to think about an issue in its full glory and richness before you jump to a conclusion so I came an intelligent person and left an educated person."

Nooyi graduated from the Yale School of Management in 1980 with a master's degree in public and private management. She then joined the Boston Consulting Group (BCG), in Massachusetts, where she directed international corporate-strategy projects. In 1986 Nooyi went to work at the Motorola Corp., a mobile-communications company, where she was vice president and director of corporate strategy and planning. In the early 1990s she briefly held a senior-level post as vice president of corporate strategy and strategic marketing at Asea Brown Boveri Group (ABB), a Connecticut-based engineering firm. When Nooyi left ABB, in the mid-1990s, she declined a job offer from Jack Welch, the legendary CEO of General Electric, to join PepsiCo. Her decision was influenced by PepsiCo's then-CEO, Wayne Calloway, who said to her, as quoted by Nandini Lakshman, "Jack Welch [is] the best CEO I know, and GE is probably the finest company. But I have a need for someone like you, and I would make PepsiCo a special place for you." Nooyi became PepsiCo's senior vice president for corporate strategy and development in 1994. She helped to transform the company, which had seen lagging sales, from an ill-focused conglomerate to a company specializing once more in beverages and so-called convenience foods, such as Frito-Lay corn chips, which PepsiCo had owned since 1965. Nooyi particularly impressed CEO Roger Enrico, the successor to Wayne Calloway, with her ability to "look over the horizon," as he told Diane Brady for *BusinessWeek On-line* (August 14, 2006). In 1997 Nooyi initiated PepsiCo's spin-off of its fast-food restaurant chains, including Kentucky Fried Chicken, Taco Bell, and Pizza Hut, as Tricon Global Restaurants (now renamed Yum! Brands Inc.). Under Nooyi's influence PepsiCo similarly spun off its bottling operation, the Pepsi Bottling Group, which underwent an initial public offering (IPO) in March 1999.

Beginning in 1998 Nooyi served as the chief negotiator in a number of key PepsiCo acquisitions, which positioned the company atop the snack-and-beverage industry. For example, Nooyi aggressively pursued the Seagram Co.'s Tropicana juice line, recognizing the enormous potential of the Tropicana brand in the evolving consumer market that, as market researchers had forecast, favored fruit juices and functional drinks (that is, energy drinks for athletes) over carbonated beverages. Faced with skepticism from PepsiCo's executive board, Nooyi pressed forward and enlisted Enrico's support to execute the $3.3 billion acquisition. Regarding the transaction, Andrew Conway, a beverage analyst with Morgan Stanley Dean Witter, told Betsy McKay for the *Contra Costa Times* (December 10, 2000), "Indra is extraordinarily financially detailed. With Tropicana, she was willing to take a lower-return-on-asset business because she saw a way to improve it to get strong margin growth. Her ability to find value in an acquisition

is very high." The success of the Tropicana acquisition contributed to Nooyi's promotion to chief financial officer of PepsiCo in February 2000. Later that year Nooyi spearheaded PepsiCo's acquisition of the Quaker Oats Co. PepsiCo's bid was initially topped by Coca-Cola, whose board of directors then backed away from the deal; PepsiCo then made the purchase for less than Coca-Cola had offered. As Nooyi pointed out, the Quaker bid announced PepsiCo's further expansion into the snack-foods industry. "For any part of the day we will have a little snack for you," Nooyi quipped to Nanette Byrnes for *BusinessWeek* (January 29, 2001). In August 2001 PepsiCo sealed the $13.8 billion takeover deal, acquiring Quaker Oats's cereals and breakfast bars and its well-known sports drink, Gatorade; with that move PepsiCo increased its share of the noncarbonated beverage market from 18 percent to 33 percent, surpassing Coca-Cola's 22 percent share in the process. Talking with John Schmeltzer for the *Chicago Tribune* (August 15, 2006), Matt Riley, the beverage analyst for Morningstar Inc., a Chicago-based investment research firm, described the Quaker Oats deal as "a double win for PepsiCo and a double loss for Coke."

In the spring of 2001, meanwhile, Enrico had resigned from his post as CEO, naming Steve Reinemund as his successor. At Reinemund's invitation, Nooyi also moved up, becoming the company's president while retaining her position as CFO. According to Byrnes, Nooyi and Reinemund formed "what could be one of the most unusual management teams in Corporate America," with their distinctly different personalities and approaches to business—as Byrnes noted, Nooyi liked "to joke around" while Reinemund, a former Marine, was "all spit and polish." (Nonetheless, Reinemund moved Nooyi to tears by telling her, upon being named CEO, "I can't do it unless I have you with me," as quoted by Byrnes.) Gordon J. Davis, president of Lincoln Center for the Performing Arts, in New York City, told Byrnes about Nooyi, "She has a sort of guileless, unencumbered quality. She'll say something almost naïve, very personal and romantic in a sense, but totally truthful." Betsy McKay noted that Nooyi tried in a variety of ways to keep the office mood light. She was known to sing around her colleagues, for example, and "once kept a 'yes' man statuette on her desk at work; when touched, it made ingratiating utterances." The Reinemund-Nooyi partnership ushered in a new age for PepsiCo, as the two executives tried to integrate PepsiCo's Tropicana and Quaker brands through a profitable, seamless sales and marketing strategy. PepsiCo endured an awkward transitional phase with its new acquisitions. Combining its Tropicana and Gatorade sales forces, for example, resulted in miscommunication, botched promotions, and the resignation of a senior Gatorade executive during the final quarter of fiscal year 2001. But by the end of 2002, Nooyi had managed to fully integrate Quaker Oats's sales and distribution networks into PepsiCo's previously existing businesses, which resulted in a 7 percent increase in total sales and a boost in the company's annual revenue beyond its usual 6 percent growth. The Frito-Lay division also thrived, comprising 56 percent of the company's operating income, while the successful launches of the beverages Mountain Dew Code Red, Aquafina water, Lipton flavored iced tea, and Pepsi Blue gave the company an ongoing competitive edge over its rival soft-drink makers. In 2003 Nooyi helped implement an even broader marketing strategy, one that differentiated PepsiCo's products portfolio into three parts—"fun for you" products (Pepsi soft drinks and Lays potato chips), "better for you" products (Baked Lays and Rold Gold Pretzels), and "good for you" products (Tropicana juices and Quaker Oats)—which enabled the company to leverage its more nutritious offerings. The strategy earned plaudits for putting PepsiCo "closer to being a friend rather than a foe of the health community with moves like switching its chips from oils containing trans-fats to more heart-healthy versions," as Diane Brady noted for *Business Week* (October 20, 2003). PepsiCo's year-end profits climbed 13 percent, to $1.07 billion.

Along with its increasing profits, PepsiCo saw its share of controversy. In the fall of 2003, the Delhi, India–based Center for Science and Environment (CSE) issued reports mentioning the presence of pesticide residue in soft drinks sold by PepsiCo and Coca-Cola in India, one of the emerging overseas markets. The CSE's findings led in the short term to a 15 percent reduction in sales of soft drinks in India. According to Ratna Bhushan, writing for the *Hindu Business Line* (December 29, 2003), Pepsi and Coke brands were even "banned in [India's] Parliament." Nooyi, however, aggressively countered the CSE's claims, standing behind the safety of PepsiCo's products and remaining optimistic about PepsiCo's future in the country. "We are making cash profits from our Indian business. I am bullish on India and looking at the market as a long-term bet," Nooyi said, according to a writer for the *Economic Times of India* (March 30, 2005). By 2005 PepsiCo had restored its reputation in India, capturing 46.7 percent share of its soft-drink market. Meanwhile, Nooyi proposed a three-year investment of $300 million to $500 million toward product development for the Indian market.

In May 2005 Nooyi delivered the commencement address for Columbia University's graduate school of business. Her speech sparked controversy for its inclusion of a provocative analogy, which likened the world's major continents to the five fingers of a hand. According to a transcript of her speech, as quoted by *Business Week On-line* (May 20, 2005), Nooyi chose the middle finger to represent "North America, and, in particular, the United States." The middle finger "really stands out," she said, since it "anchors every function that the hand performs and is the key to all of the fingers working together efficiently and effectively. . . . However, if used inappropriately—just like the U.S. itself—

the middle finger can convey a negative message and get us in trouble." Her comments incited a wave of criticism from pundits and on-line bloggers, who saw them as an unpatriotic, thinly veiled swipe at U.S. foreign policy. Nooyi later apologized for her comments and issued a statement on PepsiCo's Web site, which read in part, as quoted by Brady, "I have come to realize that my words and examples about America unintentionally depicted our country negatively and hurt people."

In 2006 Nooyi succeeded Steve Reinemund, who announced his early retirement from the company, to become the fifth CEO in PepsiCo's 41-year history. With her appointment Nooyi also became the highest-ranking Indian-born executive in the United States and joined an exclusive group of 10 other women who currently preside over Fortune 500 companies. "Indra's record of transforming PepsiCo speaks for itself, and she has been an invaluable partner and ally throughout my time as CEO," Reinemund said in his statement, as quoted by Amy Joyce for the *Washington Post* (August 15, 2006). John Sicher, editor and publisher of trade magazine *Beverage Digest*, described Nooyi to Joyce as "not only an incredibly talented executive but a brilliant strategist. She is one of these executives who, in the chess game of business, moves ahead of other people." Nooyi assumed the post of chief executive officer of PepsiCo on October 1, 2006.

Asked by one of the Tuck students what lessons she had learned as a woman in the business world, Nooyi replied, "I will tell you one thing which some of you women may not like to hear, but accept it for whatever it is. The fact is that if you are a woman and especially a person of color woman, there are two strikes against you. Immigrant, person of color, and woman, three strikes against you. I can go on. If you want to reach the top of a company, . . . you have got to start off saying that you have got to work twice as hard as your counterparts. If you decide to get on a crusade and argue for equality and some kind of promotion, you could be on that crusade forever." In response to a different question, she said in part, "My parents taught me and my grandfather taught me . . . when you do a job you [have] to do it better than everybody else. You cannot let anybody down. . . . People who work with me . . . will tell you that if Indra is dying she will make sure the job gets done because I just don't know any other way to do the job."

Nooyi maintains close ties to Yale University, serving as a trustee of the Yale Corporation and as a member of the Yale President's Council on International Activities and the Yale School of Management Advisory Board. She is also a member of the Boards of Motorola, the International Rescue Committee, and Lincoln Center for the Performing Arts. In 2001 Nooyi received the Hunt Scanlon Human Capital Advantage Award for excellence in human capital management, given by the Connecticut-based Hunt Scanlon Advisors, an executive-recruitment firm. Recently, *Fortune* magazine ranked Nooyi 11th in its annual survey of the 100 most powerful women in business. Nooyi makes her residence in Greenwich, Connecticut, with her husband, Raj K. Nooyi, a management consultant, and their two daughters.

—D.J.K.

Suggested Reading: *Chicago Tribune* p1 Dec. 5, 2000; Dartmouth College Tuck School of Business Web site; (India) *Daily News and Analysis* (on-line) Aug. 14, 2006; (London) *Financial Times* p3 Jan. 26, 2004; *South Asian News* (on-line) Aug. 17, 2006; *Washington Post* D p1 Aug. 15, 2006

Matthew Stockman/Getty Images

Ohno, Apolo Anton

May 22, 1982– Speed skater

Address: c/o U.S. Speedskating, P.O. Box 450639, Westlake, OH 44145

A decade after short-track speed skating was introduced into the Winter Olympics, the 19-year-old Apolo Anton Ohno became the sport's most visible symbol, capturing the gold medal in the 1,500-meter race and the silver in the 1,000-meter event at the 2002 Games, in Salt Lake City, Utah; his exotic looks (accented by his "soul patch") and bad-boy reputation, meanwhile, made him a darling of the fans and one of the more compelling figures to emerge from that year's Olympics. Much of the attention on Ohno at the time centered on the unusual, and sometimes controversial, nature of his

wins: he took the silver medal by crawling across the finish line after he and several other skaters had crashed to the ice, and he received the gold after Kim Dong-Sung of South Korea was disqualified for blocking him. But his performances prior to the 2002 Olympics, and since that time, suggest that those victories were not flukes. Ohno, who had already been the U.S. overall short-track champion three times and the World Cup overall champion in 2001, went on to secure two more World Cup overall titles, in 2003 and 2005, and a total of seven U.S. championships. At the 2006 Winter Olympic Games, in Turin, Italy, any lingering doubts as to his abilities were dispelled, as Ohno won three medals for the U.S., including a gold in the men's 500-meter event.

Apolo Anton Ohno was born on May 22, 1982 in Seattle, Washington. His first name is the creation of his father, who put together the Greek words for "away" and "look out." Ohno's father, Yuki Ohno, emigrated from Japan at age 18 and later opened a hair salon, Yuki's Diffusions, in Seattle. Ohno's mother, Jerrie Lee, an American, left her husband and son when Ohno was a year old. He has never seen or spoken to her since then, and he has said that he does not have any interest in doing either. During his son's childhood Yuki Ohno had an active social life and often stayed out late. On the subject of raising a child alone, Yuki Ohno told S. L. Price for *Sports Illustrated* (February 4, 2002), "It was a mystery. I was incompetent. I didn't think I could pull this thing off." He said to Amy Shipley for the *Washington Post* (December 22, 2001, on-line), "At the beginning . . . I had no confidence. I thought, I'm the only male caring for a one-year-old baby, facing all the other mothers at day care. I was very depressed. But you just develop. You build up confidence." As a small boy Ohno spent time in day care or with his father at the hair salon. When he grew older his father had to take a second job at another salon and was unable to supervise Ohno much of the time. Seeing that his son needed structure beyond what he was able to provide, Yuki steered Apolo toward athletics, at which the boy excelled. Ohno took up in-line skating at Pattison's West Skating Center in Federal Way, Washington, and went on to win a national title as a preteen. As a swimmer Ohno became a state champion in his age group in the breaststroke. But in his early teenage years, he drifted into a crowd of older friends who drank, smoked, and committed such mischievous acts as blowing up toilets at school. Ohno has recalled that some of his friends belonged to street gangs and robbed houses and cars, used weapons, and spent time in jail. Ohno himself would sometimes stay out all night or even stay away from home for days at a time. Ohno said to Shipley, "The lifestyle I was living just wasn't healthy. It was overall just a bad lifestyle. I was rebelling against my dad."

Meanwhile, while watching television coverage of the 1994 Winter Olympic Games, in Lillehammer, Norway, Ohno and his father witnessed short-track speed skating for the first time. In that sport, which has been characterized as "roller derby on ice," the competitors—wearing skates with long blades—race around a small, oval surface at speeds of up to 35 miles per hour. They use quick, slicing moves to pass each other and lean so far into the turns that they appear to be nearly horizontal. Falls and collisions are common. Ohno commented about the sport to Sean McCollum, for an article that appeared on the Web site scholastic.com, "It's fast, lots of passing. And then a skater will lose an edge or get bumped and go down. It's real exciting, very dynamic." Yuki and Ohno were fascinated by short-track speed skating, and soon after watching the Olympics, Yuki bought his son his first pair of ice skates. Ohno joined the Tacoma Speedskating Club, and after just a year of skating and going to competitions, he participated in the Junior World Short Track Speedskating Championships in Milwaukee, Wisconsin, where he twice broke the national record for 12-year-olds in the 1,000-meter event. Pat Wentland, who would go on to become the U.S. national speed-skating team coach, saw Ohno's talent and invited him to join the U.S. Olympic Training Center residency program, in Lake Placid, New York. Wentland told Paul Newberry for an article that appeared on the *Sports Illustrated* Web site, "[Ohno] was so explosive and strong for his age. I knew this kid had talent. You could just see it." Although Ohno was still younger than the age required for the program (15), Wentland made sure that he was accepted. Ohno did not want to leave his friends in Seattle, but his father saw the program as a special opportunity and a way to give Ohno discipline and structure. When Yuki dropped him off for his flight to New York, Ohno waited until his father left the airport, then called a friend to pick him up and skipped the flight. The second time that he took his son to the airport, Yuki made sure that Ohno boarded the plane.

In the early days of his training at the speed-skating team's facilities in Lake Placid, Ohno lacked focus. He would stop to eat pizza during the team's five-mile runs, then jump back into the pack of runners when they came back past the fast-food restaurant. A change in Ohno's attitude came about as a result of a body-fat test that was done on all the skaters at the training center. Despite his natural skating ability, Ohno (who had picked up the nickname "Chunky" in Lake Placid) had the highest body-fat percentage of all the teammates, and as he recalled to Shipley, "I was mad about it. . . . It had an immediate effect." Wentland commented to Price that the body-fat test "got him. He came up to me and said, 'I don't want to be the fattest, I don't want to be the slowest, I want to be the best.' He totally changed. Every workout from then on, he had to win. Even now, at this level, if he decides one day that he's not feeling right, he won't skate well. But if he knows that he can win, I don't care if all the other skaters are having the best day of their lives, he'll beat them."

In 1997 Ohno won the U.S. men's national overall short-track speed-skating championship. He was just 14 years old; the second-place finisher was 32. The resulting high expectations began to take a mental toll on Ohno. He failed to reach the finals of the junior championships later in 1997, and at the Olympic trials for the upcoming Winter Games, in Nagano, Japan, in 1998, he came in last in a field of 16 skaters. That failure was difficult for Ohno to bear. Back in Seattle, Ohno spent a week at a cabin in the woods on the rugged coast of Washington, where he and Yuki had vacationed in the past. Without a telephone, a television, or the company of other people, Ohno was able to do some soul-searching. One day, while running in a driving rain, he developed a blister on his foot. Disgusted and frustrated, he sat on a rock and thought about whether he wanted to continue skating. He later recalled to Shipley, "I realized if I really desired to keep speedskating, I'd keep running. I got up and kept running." Speaking of that revelatory moment, he told Newberry, "It just came to me. [Skating] is something I was meant to do."

Ohno was World Junior Short Track champion in 1999, and in the 2000–01 season, he won 15 World Cup gold medals on his way to the overall World Cup title. He was also the U.S. overall national champion in 1999, 2001, and 2002. Susan Ellis, the coach of the elite U.S. short-track team, said to Paul Newberry, "[Ohno]'s got real good agility. He's strong. He's got endurance and power. He's got great race awareness. He's got the whole package." At the U.S. Olympic trials in December 2001, Ohno redeemed his 1998 failure by dominating the field, winning all but one of his races. In his last contest, a 1,000-meter race, Ohno took third place. His teammate Tommy O'Hare alleged that Ohno and the skater Rusty Smith had deliberately stayed behind another skater, Ohno's good friend Shani Davis, and had also blocked O'Hare from passing them, so that Davis could make it to the Olympics. Davis won the race and thus qualified for the Olympics, while O'Hare did not. (Davis became the first African-American to win a place on the U.S. Olympic Speedskating Team.) O'Hare's complaint was brought before the U.S. Olympic Committee, and so Ohno, despite being the pre-Olympic favorite in the short-track events and perhaps the U.S. athlete most likely to win multiple gold medals at the Winter Games, was in jeopardy of being thrown off the speed-skating team. The controversy surrounded Ohno in the weeks leading up to the Games in Salt Lake City. The arbitrator of the case, James R. Holbrook, ultimately ruled that the race had been fairly run and fairly officiated and that there was no conclusive evidence to the contrary. Ohno was cleared to skate in the Olympics.

Ohno's first short-track event at the Salt Lake City Games, in February 2002, was the 1,000-meter race. He skated well and was in the lead on the last lap of the final heat when several skaters in the tight pack around him went down in a heap and slid across the ice, bringing Ohno down with them. In the crash, Ohno suffered a gouge in his left thigh, probably caused by his own sharp skate, but he was alert enough to crawl across the finish line for a second-place finish and a silver medal. He thus became the first American to win an Olympic medal in short-track speed skating. In the 1,500-meter final, Ohno, skating with stitches in his thigh, crossed the finish line second, behind the South Korean Kim Dong-Sung, who had also come in first ahead of Ohno at the 2001 World Championships. Kim Dong-Sung, however, was disqualified by the Australian chief referee for cross-tracking—blocking another skater's forward progress by altering one's own path on the ice—and Ohno was awarded the gold medal. The South Korean Olympic team protested the decision and threatened to boycott the closing ceremonies of the Olympics, but the disqualification was upheld. Some felt that Ohno had been blocked illegally as he was about to pass Kim with one of his trademark bursts of acceleration, while others believed that Ohno, in raising his arms to avoid colliding with Kim, had exaggerated the gesture in an attempt to draw the referee's attention. In response to the episode involving Ohno—who had already received death threats via E-mail following his scramble across the line for the silver medal—South Koreans sent thousands of angry E-mail messages to the U.S. Olympic Committee, causing the organization's Internet server to crash. "Months later, at the soccer World Cup," Devin Gordon wrote for *Newsweek* (January 23, 2006), "a South Korean player scored on the United States and celebrated by miming a speed skater. By then, most Americans had forgotten about the incident; Koreans, evidently, had not." As quoted in an article that appeared on the Web site dailycamera.com, Ohno said, "I think [controversy] is just something I have to throw out of my mind. I just have to go into each race and push as hard as I can."

Ohno was disqualified in the semifinals of the next race, the 500 meters, for pushing the Japanese skater Satoru Terao. He later said that the ruling was fair and correct. In the final short-track event, the 5,000-meter team relay, Ohno's teammate Rusty Smith, who had been accused of colluding with Ohno at the U.S. Olympic trials, fell during his run, and the team finished fourth. Ohno told Ailene Voisin for the *Sacramento Bee* (February 24, 2002, on-line), "I got a silver medal and a gold medal and another two awesome performances, so this is definitely the highlight of my career."

Following his performance at the 2002 Olympic Games, Ohno found himself in the role of a celebrity—receiving an official public celebration in his hometown, attending exclusive Oscar parties, ringing the opening bell at the New York Stock Exchange, and appearing on the *Tonight* show. Later in the year, after "relaxing and eating . . . a lot," as he told *Sports Illustrated Women* (July/August 2002), he got back in shape to compete in late November and early December at World Cup events

in St Petersburg, Russia. (Each season World Cup meets are held in several different locations, with results from all races counted in the final World Cup rankings.) In St. Petersburg Ohno won a 1,500-meter short-track event, thanks in part to the disqualification of Li Jia Jun of China, who blocked skaters in the race's seventh lap. Ohno himself was disqualified in the 500-meter quarterfinals for blocking an opponent. Still, after winning the 3,000-meter competition, he captured the overall title at the St. Petersburg World Cup meet. Later in December 2002, at the World Cup meet in Bormio, Italy, he won the 1,500-meter event, was eliminated in the quarterfinals for the 500-meter race, won the 1,000 meters, and placed second in the 3,000. Ohno emerged as the 2002–03 overall World Cup champion. Also in 2003, for the third consecutive time, he became the U.S. short-track overall champion. (He missed one race in South Korea that year after receiving death threats.)

Ohno was U.S champion again in 2004, a year in which he also won four medals at the World Cup in Madison, Wisconsin. In 2005 he won his third short-track overall World Cup title, as well as the U.S. overall championship—his fifth consecutive U.S. title and seventh in all. In November of that year, in Bormio, he won the 1,500-meter and 3,000-meter races at the World Cup short-track meet, and in December, in Marquette, Michigan, he was victorious in seven of eight events at the trials for the 2006 Olympics. At the Winter Games, held in Turin, Italy, Ohno had a shaky start. He failed to qualify for the final of his first event—the 1,500-meter race—after he stumbled and finished last in a semifinal heat. He succeeded in winning the bronze medal in the 1,000-meter contest, finishing behind Ahn Hyun Soo and Lee Ho-suk of South Korea. (In a sign of renewed goodwill between South Korea and the U.S., the three men shared the top spot on the ceremonial pedestal.) In the 500-meter event, Ohno led from the start and captured the gold medal. Some observers complained that he had begun too early, but officials ruled in Ohno's favor. In the men's 5,000-meter relay, Ohno edged past the Italian skater Nicola Rodigari to secure a bronze medal for the U.S.—and the fifth Olympic medal of his career. (He thus tied the speedskater Eric Heiden's career record for most medals won by a U.S. male Olympian in Winter Games.) At the medals ceremony for the event, the U.S. and Korean teams embraced and posed for pictures together.

Ohno is five feet eight inches tall (five-seven, according to some sources) and weighs roughly 165 pounds. Lynn Zinser reported in the *New York Times* (June 21, 2005) that the Olympic training center in Colorado Springs, Colorado, has been the skater's "second home" since the late 1990s. Ohno enjoys R&B and rap music, break dancing, and playing badminton, and says that his father, Yuki, who stands trackside during Ohno's races, videotaping his son's performances and shouting encouragement to him, has been the greatest influence on his life. Concerning his father, Ohno told

Paul Newberry, "We're definitely closer than ever. That's something I'm really proud of. When I was younger, I never thought it would be like this." With Nancy Ann Richardson, Ohno penned his autobiography, *A Journey* (2002), for young readers; in a later edition, published the same year, the title was changed to *Apolo Anton Ohno: My Story*. Also available for youngsters are the books *All About Apolo*, by Joe Layden, and *Going for the Gold: Apolo Anton Ohno*, by Thomas Lang, both published in 2002.

—C.F.T.

Suggested Reading: *Baltimore Sun* D p1+ Feb. 26, 2006; *New York Times* D p7 June 21, 2005; *Sports Illustrated* p122+ Feb. 4, 2002, with photo; usspeedskating.org; *Washington Post* D p1 Dec. 22, 2001

Selected Books: *Apolo Anton Ohno: My Story* (with Nancy Richardson), 2002

Courtesy of the University of Chicago

Olopade, Olufunmilayo

(oh-loh-PAH-day, oh-loo-FOON-mih-lay-oh)

Apr. 29, 1957– Oncologist; geneticist

Address: University of Chicago Medical Center, #MC2115, 5841 S. Maryland Ave., Chicago, IL 60637

Assessing the groundbreaking research of the Nigerian-born geneticist and oncologist Olufunmilayo Olopade, James Madara, dean of the Pritzker School of Medicine at the University of Chicago, told a writer for the Healthy Life for All Foundation Web site, "Big thinking is what translates into big discovery. Dr. Olopade's thinking has been precisely on this scale: a world- and genome-wide view of connections between African descent and one of the most common cancers in women." Over the last two decades Olopade's ability to think in big and small ways as a researcher and physician—bridging intellectual zeal with patient advocacy, scientific inquiry with cultural empathy, medical ethics with social justice—has established her as a leading voice in the international medical community. In the 1990s Olopade launched a series of landmark, cross-cultural studies to identify the nature of gene mutations in breast cancer, particularly in the cases of women of African descent. With support from the National Institutes of Health and the Breast Cancer Research Foundation, Olopade compared the genetic profiles of several hundred women across Africa, North America, and Europe; her research revealed that women of African descent expressed different gene mutations than their Caucasian counterparts and stood at higher risk for more aggressive forms of breast cancer at younger ages. She also found that the gene mutations expressed in African women resisted the conventional therapies prescribed to patients of European descent. Motivated by the cultural and environmental facets of her research, in 1992 Olopade established the Cancer Risk Clinic at the University of Chicago Medical Center to translate her findings into effective clinical practice, addressing the cases of African women whose genetics made them particularly susceptible to disease. Currently, Olopade heads the Center for Clinical Cancer Genetics in the Department of Medicine at the University of Chicago.

In 2005 Olopade received a $500,000 John D. and Catherine T. MacArthur Foundation fellowship—often called the "genius grant"—for her pioneering research into the molecular genetics of breast cancer. The MacArthur award underscored the importance of Olopade's cross-continental, interdisciplinary approach to the prevention, detection, and treatment of breast cancer. It also served as an acknowledgement of Olopade's efforts to apply scientific inquiry to social activism. After receiving the award, Olopade told Charles Storch for the *Chicago Tribune* (September 20, 2005), "People in Africa have been understudied, and even African-Americans in this country have been understudied." She will, she added, "continue . . . advocating for the vulnerable."

The fifth of six children, Olopade was born Olufunmilayo Falusi on April 29, 1957 in Nigeria, in West Africa. (She is known to friends and colleagues as Funmi, pronounced FOON-me.) Details surrounding Olopade's formative years in Nigeria remain scant; it is known, however, that her early interest in medicine was sparked by her parents' concern over the dearth of trained physicians in their village. When she reached her late teens, Olopade enrolled in medical school at the University of Ibadan's College of Medicine, Nigeria's oldest and most prestigious institution of higher learning. As a student she showed exceptional promise, garnering departmental honors in pediatrics, surgery, and the clinical sciences. In 1980 Olopade received her M.D. degree and was awarded, among other distinctions, the University of Ibadan College of Medicine's Faculty Prize and the Nigerian Medical Association Award for excellence in medicine. After graduation Olopade participated in the National Youth Service Corps—a Nigerian government-sponsored mandatory program for university graduates—serving as a medical officer at the Nigerian Navy Hospital, in Lagos. After working for a year in that program, she relocated to the United States to serve an internship and residency in internal medicine at Cook County Hospital, in Chicago, Illinois. A year after her arrival, a military coup took place in Nigeria, leading to Olopade's decision to settle in the U.S. In 1986 she was promoted to chief resident at the hospital.

In 1987 Olopade accepted a postdoctoral fellowship in hematology and oncology at the University of Chicago. Under the advisement of Janet Rowley, Blum-Riese Distinguished Professor of Medicine, Olopade researched the molecular genetics of cancer, examining the specific link between genetic mutation and susceptibility to the disease. She completed her fellowship in 1991 and accepted a faculty appointment as assistant professor of hematology and oncology at the University of Chicago. At around the same time, Olopade combined her interests in cancer genetics, prediction, and prevention to establish the Cancer Risk Clinic, an affiliate of the University of Chicago Hospitals, which integrated cutting-edge scientific research with clinical care. In an interview for the Web site of the Breast Cancer Research Foundation, Olopade described the clinic's objectives as being to "coordinate preventive care and testing for healthy patients and their families who because of genetics or family history are at increased risk for cancer" and to focus "on quality-of-life issues for young breast cancer patients, including concerns related to pregnancy, fertility, and employment." The Cancer Risk Clinic's own Web site summed up its mission as three-fold—patient care, clinical research, and education (for medical students).

In the mid-1990s Olopade focused her scientific and clinical research on the area of breast cancer—the leading cause of death among American women ages 40 to 55—and its prevalence among young nonwhite women, particularly those of African descent. (A cousin of Olopade's had succumbed to the disease at age 32.) Her efforts were motivated in part by a widely celebrated breakthrough in the greater scientific community regarding the identification of *BRCA1*, a gene "believed to cause about half of all inherited cases of breast cancer," as reported by Thomas H. Maugh III for the *Los Angeles Times* (September 15, 1994). Originally pinpointed in 1990 by the geneticist Mary-Claire King of the University of California at Berkeley, *BRCA1* was found to be a tumor-suppressor gene that, when healthy, prevents the aberrant replication of cells; when dysfunctional it "can certainly cause cancers," as Jon Turney remarked for the London *Independent* (June 6, 1994). Citing a study published in the *Lancet*, a medical journal, Turney further noted, "A woman carrying the altered form of the gene has an 80 percent chance of contracting breast cancer before she reaches 70." He qualified that statement, however, by adding that "only around 5 per cent of all breast cancer cases are linked to mutations inherited from the patient's parents, and only around half of these are due to BRCA1. . . . Most cancer researchers think that the inheritance of a BRCA1 mutation represents one stage of a multi-step process which is seen in every case of breast cancer." That qualification aside, medical professionals received news of *BRCA1*'s discovery with great optimism. In 1995 *BRCA2*, a second gene linked to breast cancer susceptibility, was identified. The discovery of *BRCA1* confirmed prior studies that linked heredity to cancer susceptibility and strengthened the case for genetic testing as a viable detection measure. An early and passionate advocate of genetic testing, Olopade explained in the portion of the article she wrote for the *Chronicle of Higher Education* (July 3, 1998), "It is now widely accepted that cancer is a genetic disease, and that an accumulation of genetic defects can cause normal cells to become cancerous. . . . The most effective approach to preventing, diagnosing, and treating cancer is to identify individuals who are at risk. Genetic testing for cancer susceptibility can identify these individuals and provide unique opportunities to develop new strategies for early detection and prevention."

The *BRCA1* discovery introduced a host of ethical and socioeconomic questions and implications for clinical practice. With regard to genetic testing, which had become the preferred method for amassing statistics on breast-cancer susceptibility, for instance, why did the findings not reflect a more diverse sampling of patients? Olopade addressed that question in an editorial column for the *New England Journal of Medicine* (November 7, 1996): "At present, the only women at high risk who are not being tested are those who are economically disadvantaged or uninformed. The situation is clearly unfair. How should physicians responsibly address this latest challenge when there are no prospective, randomized clinical trials on which to base decisions?" In particular, Olopade cited the disparities between breast-cancer victims of African heritage and those of European ancestry, which she had observed in part through years of treating and observing patients at the Cancer Risk Clinic. While visiting Nigeria for a niece's wedding in 1997, Olopade spent time at a breast-cancer clinic and was struck by how young the patients there were, in comparison with white breast-cancer patients. From the well-documented research performed by the scientific community throughout the 1990s, Olopade noted that while African-American women experienced a lower incidence of breast cancer than Caucasian women, they had developed its more virulent forms at younger ages, contributing to higher mortality rates from the disease among black women. Determined to unravel the medical mystery presented by that finding, Olopade launched a cross-continental research project that sought to collect and analyze the genetic profiles of more than 100,000 breast-cancer patients under the age of 45 in the United States, Africa, and the Caribbean; with the resulting data she hoped to identify the environmental, social, and nutritional factors that increased a woman's susceptibility to breast cancer.

Olopade presented some of her findings in 2004 at a landmark conference she helped organize—the First International Workshop on New Trends in the Management of Breast and Cervical Cancers, held in Lagos. Drawing experts from the University of Chicago, the University of Ibadan, and the Medical Women's Association of Nigeria, the symposium addressed the issues of cancer awareness, detection, and prevention in African nations including Nigeria, whose breast-cancer patients' rate of surviving for five years stood at 10 percent. (By contrast, five-year survival rates for breast-cancer patients in the United States exceeded 85 percent.) As quoted in an on-line news release from the University of Chicago Hospitals (May 14, 2004), Olopade assessed the state of Nigeria's medical practices in stark terms: "Cancer awareness, even among physicians, and much more so among women at risk, needs an enormous boost in Nigeria. . . . We were trying to follow about 500 young Nigerian women who had been diagnosed with breast cancer, but in a very short time, without access to optimal treatment, almost all of them had either died or been lost to follow-up." Cancer, Olopade observed, remained a leading cause of death for Africans, despite the overshadowing urgency of the continent's AIDS pandemic.

In 2005, over a decade after the identification of *BRCA1*, Olopade and other researchers from the University of Chicago produced evidence that suggested unique gene expressions in the breast cancers of African women. Through an ongoing study funded by the Breast Cancer Research Foundation and the National Women's Cancer Research Alliance, Olopade compared cancer tissue from 378 women in Nigeria and Senegal with tissue samples from 930 women in Canada, deriving a number of significant conclusions in the process. Olopade determined that breast cancers in African women, for instance, originated from basal-like cells rather than the milk-secreting luminal cells of their white American and European counterparts (tumors caused by basal-like cells are more dangerous). She further observed that most African breast cancers lacked the estrogen receptors found in 80 percent of Caucasian breast cancers. Cancer tumors in African women, as a result, were largely unaffected by hormonal stimulus and neutralized the power of

such conventional, estrogen-blocking drugs as Tamoxifen. On the positive side, Olopade found that African cancers were less likely to express HER2 (or human epidermal growth factor receptor), a protein that when mutated stimulates aggressive cancer-cell growth; only 19 percent of Africans expressed that cell, compared with 23 percent of Caucasians. (Those statistics have implications for black American women, 40 percent of whom "have a lineage that can be traced back to historical Nigeria," as Lovell A. Jones, a researcher at the University of Texas, told Cynthia Daniels for the December 30, 2005 edition of *Newsday*.) As quoted in a University of Chicago Hospitals on-line news release (April 18, 2005), Olopade concluded that while breast cancer struck fewer women in Africa than in the Americas, it "hits earlier and harder." She hoped that her findings would initiate new testing measures for breast-cancer patients of varying ethnicities. "We need to reconsider how to screen for a disease that is less common but starts sooner and moves faster," she said. "Obviously, an annual mammogram beginning at 50 is not the best route to early detection in African women, who get the disease and die from it in their 40s, and it also needs to be adjusted in African Americans and high-risk women of all racial/ethnic groups."

Olopade continues to refine predictive models for cancer risk that incorporate patients' genetics, ancestry, and ethnicity. "Breast cancer isn't one single disease," she told Kimberly L. Allers for *Essence* (January 2006). "It affects women of different populations in different ways." For her pioneering research in the molecular genetics of breast cancer and for the development of genetic testing measures for women of African heritage, Olopade was awarded a MacArthur Foundation grant in September 2005. On its Web site, the MacArthur Foundation explained the selection of Olopade, stating, "In bridging continents with her innovative research and service models, Olopade is increasing the probability of improved outcomes for millions of women of African heritage at risk for cancer here and abroad." In April 2006 Olopade was awarded the inaugural Minorities in Cancer Research Jane Cook Wright Lectureship by the American Association for Cancer Research (AACR), in recognition of her contributions as a minority physician and scientist to cancer research. At the AACR annual meeting in Washington, D.C., Olopade delivered a lecture titled "Nature or Nurture in Breast Cancer Causation." According to Sola Ogundipe, writing for *Vanguard* (April 18, 2006), the lectureship honored Olopade's recent discovery of a so-called putative suppressor gene "that is involved in several other solid breast cancer tumors," a finding that "eventually led to the identification of the gene tagged p16INK4." In April 2006 Olopade traveled to China Medical University, in Shenyang, for a two-week visiting professorship, through which she presented her groundbreaking research on cancer genetics and women of color. Regarding her decision to lecture in China, Olopade told Bennie M.

Currie for *Crisis* (May/June 2006), "Our work on women of color has impact for other minority women, too. . . . Breast cancer is a disease that globally affects more than a million women."

Olopade is currently overseeing a trial run in West Africa for Capecitabine, a pill form of chemotherapy aimed at African women with advanced stages of breast cancer. With additional funding from the Breast Cancer Research Foundation, she is also examining the destructive interactions between Fanconi anemia–associated genes and *BRCA1*. (Fanconi, or Fanconi's, anemia is a rare genetic disease that is marked by congenital abnormalities and bone-marrow failure. Victims of the disorder have a significantly higher-than-average chance of getting cancer or other diseases.)

Olopade holds memberships in a number of professional organizations, including the American Association for Cancer Research, the American Association for the Advancement of Science, and the American College of Physicians. She continues to

lecture as professor of medicine and human genetics at the University of Chicago Medical Center, where she is now a full professor, and to direct the Cancer Risk Clinic at the University of Chicago Hospitals. Olopade also serves on the board of trustees of the Healthy Life for All Foundation, an advocacy group that promotes the advancement of medical technology in Nigeria.

Olufunmilayo Olopade is married to Christopher Olopade, an associate professor of medicine and director of clinical research at the University of Illinois at Chicago. The couple have three children and live in the Kenwood community, outside Chicago.

—D.J.K.

Suggested Reading: Breast Cancer Research Foundation Web site; *Los Angeles Times* A p1 Sep. 15, 1994; *New England Journal of Medicine* p1455 Nov. 7, 1996; *New York Times* A p16 June 7, 2006; University of Chicago Hospitals Web site

Courtesy of Oppenheim Architecture + Design

Oppenheim, Chad

Jan. 8, 1971– Architect

Address: 245 N.E. 27th St., #102, Miami, FL 33137

"Architecture ideally should interact with all the senses: sound, the rippling of water or rustling of bamboo; smell, fragrant flowers and vines as plantings; touch, the tactile quality of the materials; and even taste, an edible landscape of fruit trees and

banana palms," the strikingly innovative and much-in-demand architect Chad Oppenheim told the Miami, Florida, entrepreneur Michael Capponi (one of his business associates) for *Ocean Drive Magazine* (March 2004, on-line). Acknowledging the existence of more practical considerations, Oppenheim also said, "Of course, I have limitations as well. On any given day I have hundreds of millions of dollars of my clients' and investors' money at stake, people who trust us to do something that works. Architecture is, after all, a very complex three-dimensional puzzle in which the stakes are very high. We do try to find the perfect balance, an equilibrium between design and economics." Since 1999, when, while still in his 20s, he founded Oppenheim Architecture + Design, based in Miami, Oppenheim's name has become "synonymous with Miami's condominium boom," as Jennifer LeClaire wrote for *Architectural Record* (April 2006, on-line). According to the Miami *Sun-Post* (April 20, 2006, on-line), "In the next three years, over 10 million square feet of new skyline [designed by Oppenheim's firm] will come into being. . . . And—here's a switch—these towers look fairly pretty." The five-story, 16-unit Ilona condominium, the 17-story, 49-unit Sky condominium, and the 54-unit, 15-story Space 01 (all of which won awards from the Miami Chapter of the American Institute of Architects), the Clinique La Prairie Residences at Ten Museum Park, on Biscayne Boulevard, and Oppenheim's distinctive creations for more than a dozen other projects in Miami have garnered the praise of architects, real-estate developers, and buyers alike. Indeed, according to a description of him for WPS1 Art Radio (the Internet station of P.S. 1 Contemporary Art Center, an affiliate of the Museum of Modern Art in New York), he is "almost single-handedly bringing the Miami skyline . . . into the 21st century." "Unlike so many people who have spent a far longer time working and living here, Oppenheim 'gets' Miami," Michael Capponi wrote. "And he not only gets it, but he's also defining it in concrete and glass. He has even invented a new Miami lifestyle." "My inspiration is about beauty and a sort of happiness," Oppenheim told Cara Buckley for the *Miami (Florida) Herald* (January 14, 2002). "That's what architecture is. A vessel for living and enjoying life." Recently, Oppenheim has strived to create more environmentally friendly designs, ones that exemplify the precepts of the so-called Green Building Movement. He has also begun to accept more varied jobs, both within and outside Miami. Among them are the design for the renovation of a 13,000-foot industrial space for use by the Emmanuel Perrotin art gallery, in Miami.

Chad L. Oppenheim was born on January 8, 1971 and grew up in New Jersey with his sister, Meredith. Meredith Oppenheim is a principal in her brother's firm; a specialist in residential design for the elderly, she also works as a consultant for others. As a young child Chad Oppenheim spent much of his time playing with Matchbox cars, and he developed an appreciation beyond his years for automobile design. On paper he drew original car designs that featured sleek aerodynamic forms. His fascination shifted from cars to buildings in the late 1970s, when his parents decided to have a house built on land they had bought in Holmdel, New Jersey, near where they were then living. "Watching [the architect] listen to my parents and interpret their thoughts and wishes was a terrific experience," Oppenheim wrote in an autobiographical piece for the London *Financial Times* (February 4, 2006). "It opened up a whole new art form for me. I could move from elaborate dream cars to fantastic dream houses." His parents encouraged his interest in architecture; his mother, for example, bought him a calendar with photos of buildings by the architect Frank Lloyd Wright. Another influence, Oppenheim told Fabiola Santiago for the *Miami Herald* (July 30, 2006, on-line), was the 1980s TV show *Miami Vice*, which he used to watch with his father. "In the show there was interesting architecture, fast cars, beautiful women," he recalled to Santiago. While in high school, where he took art classes, he enrolled in architecture courses at the local community college. During summers he studied architecture at Cornell University, in Ithaca, New York. His teachers at Cornell "taught you to ask the right questions," as he told Cara Buckley. "How to create a space, make something better and more sensitive to its context." After he graduated from high school, Oppenheim entered the undergraduate architecture program at Cornell. As a college student he completed architecture internships in New Mexico and Israel; for one semester he studied in Rome, Italy. He earned a bachelor's degree in architecture in 1994 and stayed on at the school for a brief stint as a lecturer. (More recently he has taught architecture as

an adjunct professor at Florida International University and the New Jersey Institute of Technology.) Also in 1994 he won a fellowship that enabled him to study in Japan.

Although many prestigious architecture firms are based in New York City, in 1995 Oppenheim accepted a position in Miami, with the cutting-edge firm Arquitectonica. "Miami seemed more open to unique and original design than New York," he told Buckley. (He told Fabiola Santiago, "I came to Miami because of *Miami Vice*.") At Arquitectonica Oppenheim worked on more than 70 projects, for both domestic and overseas sites. After four years he left the firm to study industrial, product, and graphic design at the Graduate School of Design at Harvard University, in Cambridge, Massachusetts. He also worked on a few projects for private clients. He earned an architect's license in 1998.

In January 1999 Oppenheim founded his own firm, Oppenheim Architecture + Design. Working with a handful of employees (he now has three dozen), he landed contracts calling for the renovation of beachfront hotels in the Miami area. He soon began collaborating with "up-and-coming developers," as he told Sara Hart for *Architectural Record* (July 2005). "Many of them did not own the prime, oceanfront properties. They had infill parcels [vacant land within built-up areas] and residual pieces of land, which were blocks from the beaches. Our goal was to create a product that would draw buyers away from the waterfront. When these apartments started selling at higher prices than the waterfront condos, other developers started to pay attention to what we were doing." "Architecture in Miami must be open, clean, bold and minimal juxtaposed against Miami's incredible light, the colors of sea and sky, the brilliance of the gardens," Oppenheim told Michael Capponi. "It must be a sponge absorbing beauty."

In 2000 Oppenheim won an Award of Merit for an unbuilt design (that is, a design that has not yet become a reality) from the Miami Chapter of the American Institute of Architects (AIA). The winning design was that of the Ilona condominium, named for Ilona Mattli, a Swiss-born graphic designer who later became Oppenheim's wife. The five-story, concrete-and-stucco building, completed in 2002 (when it won an AIA Miami Merit Award), has 16 duplex units, each with a double-height living room, kitchen, bedroom, and bathroom on the first floor and a "master suite" on the second. A public space on the roof includes a swimming pool, cabanas, and plantings: dune grass, tropical shrubs, and palm trees. Bamboo, jasmine trees, and banana palms—the last "with fruit ready for picking and eating" when Beth Dunlop wrote about the condo for *Interior Design* (November 1, 2004, on-line)—stand in part of the entry-way, which also contains a triangular fountain and a "lozenge-shaped swing of perforated aluminum, the exterior painted in silver and the interior covered in apple-green marine-grade leather," in Dunlop's words. "The sound of water, the rustling of the leaves—a connection to nature is important," Oppenheim commented to Dunlop.

A 17-story condominium called Sky, in North Bay Village on Miami's Harbor Island, won for Oppenheim's firm an "unbuilt" award in 2001 from AIA Miami, which at the same time honored Oppenheim as Young Architect of the Year. Now completed, each of Sky's apartments is a duplex "loft" with a "flow-through" floor plan, meaning that no walls separate its first-floor living room, bedroom, and kitchen; the 18-foot outer walls of each unit are all glass and overlook downtown Miami, Miami Beach, and the ocean. The apartments of Sky, which has a rooftop pool and solarium, fetched the highest prices ever paid for inland condominium units. Oppenheim incorporated similar features in the 50-story condominium known informally as Ten Museum Park, located in downtown Miami and scheduled for completion in 2007. A joint project of Oppenheim's firm and Clinique La Prairie Lifestyle Developers, which is owned by Armin Mattli, Oppenheim's father-in-law, Ten Museum Park will house 200 residences along with such amenities as a wellness center, a restaurant, a lounge, and a spa complete with roof garden and several swimming pools. "When Ten Museum Park hit the supposedly saturated Miami market," Oppenheim and his sister wrote for *Multi-Housing News* (January 1, 2005, on-line), "it pre-sold for $150 per square foot more than similar product[s] in more ideal locations. Even at these high prices, the project sold out in 8 days." Sara Hart found much to praise in Ten Museum Park. "Oppenheim's brand of Modernism resists the invariability that often defines skyscrapers," she wrote. "After all, he's giving form to lifestyle, not maximizing square footage. Within the exoskeleton, his interlocking volumes create soaring spaces and frame dramatic views—a strategy that celebrates living up high."

Oppenheim's current projects include Ice2 ("Ice Squared"), a 56-story condominium with eight adjoining townhouses in Miami, which he designed in collaboration with the New York City–based architect Walter F. Chatham; on June 26, 2004, the first day that the Ice2 units went on sale, 42 percent of them were sold, at prices ranging from between $1.1 million and $1.7 million, or an average of $630 per square foot—"far exceeding prices at other leading projects in the area," as Oppenheim and his sister wrote for *Multi-Housing News*. That publication named Oppenheim among the top 100 multi-housing architects in 2004. In the same article the Oppenheims reported, "Also in the works is a 2.5 million-square-foot project designed in collaboration with the Pei Partnership slated for Downtown Miami. This project will take the concept of combining a luxury spa with cutting-edge architecture to the max: It will comprise 450 condominium units, a 400-key condominium hotel, 80,000 square feet of office space and a 150,000-square-foot multi-story spa/health club with roof-top gardens." Another project, the Cube condominium, is "structured in modules to allow residents to configure dwellings both vertically and laterally," as Jennifer LeClaire wrote.

In 2006 Oppenheim's buildings Three Midtown Miami and Montclair Lofts won AIA Miami Awards of Excellence (in the unbuilt and built categories, respectively). His current projects include Cor, a 25-story condominium in Miami's Design District, and Element, a 56-story waterfront highrise in downtown Miami. The announced $1.2 billion expansion and renovation of the Hard Rock Hotel, in Las Vegas, Nevada, which was to include the development of a 372-unit luxury highrise condominium, an 800-unit combination condo/hotel, and 32 poolside bungalows, all designed by Oppenheim, has been indefinitely postponed.

Oppenheim and his wife live on Sunset Island, near Miami Beach, in a house called Villa Allegra, which won an AIA Miami Award of Excellence in 2005. Representing a style that he has labeled "romantic minimalism," the house and its surrounding grounds provided the settings for some scenes in the 2006 film *Miami Vice*, directed and written by Michael Mann and based on the TV series.

—I.C.

Suggested Reading: *Architectural Record* p67+ July 2005, p46 Apr. 2006; *Interior Design* p52+ Nov. 2004; (London) *Financial Times* p12 Feb. 4, 2006; *Miami Herald* Jan. 14, 2002; *New York Times* F p1 Dec. 2, 2004; oppenoffice.com; *South Florida CEO* p26 Oct. 1, 2002

Selected Buildings (all in Miami, Florida): Ilona; Sky Residences; Space 01; Ten Museum Park; Three Midtown Miami; Ice; Ice2

Osteen, Joel

Mar. 5, 1963– Pastor; television minister; writer

Address: Joel Osteen Ministries, P.O. Box 4600, Houston, TX 77210

"Raise your level of expectancy," the Christian pastor Joel Osteen wrote in his best-selling 2004 book, *Your Best Life Now: 7 Steps to Living Your Full Potential.* "It's our faith that activates the power of God. Let's quit limiting Him with our small-minded thinking and start believing Him for bigger and better things. Remember, if you obey God and are willing to trust Him, you will have the best this life has to offer—and more!" Each Sunday more than 30,000 people flock to Lakewood Church, the largest church in the United States, at the Compaq Center, in Houston, Texas, to hear such encouraging and motivational messages from Osteen. Millions of others watch the services from their homes, on the television show *Joel Osteen*, which

Greg Schneider, courtesy of Time Warner Book Group

Joel Osteen

is seen in more than 150 countries and is "the world's most popular religious program," according to William Martin, writing for *Texas Monthly* (August 2005). Before 1999 few who knew Osteen would have believed that he could almost single-handedly quadruple the weekly attendance of Lakewood Church, founded by his father, John, in 1959. Unlike his parents and siblings, Osteen had often shied away from taking on prominent roles behind the pulpit during Sunday services, preferring instead to stay behind the cameras, directing the telecasts of the show that was then called *John Osteen* and that featured the older man's sermons. But in January 1999 John Osteen, who was then hospitalized, unexpectedly called his youngest son and asked him to preach in his stead that coming Sunday, saying, "Joel, you're my first choice." Insisting that he was not up to the task, Joel hung up the telephone and sat down to dinner. But minutes later a new attitude had come over him, and he called his father back, saying that he would fill in for him. Although he had been ordained by his father's church in 1983 and had been associated with Lakewood for 17 years, Joel Osteen had never preached to the congregation. "It was kind of a weird thing. I never wanted to preach, but I knew in my heart it was what I was supposed to do. I knew I was supposed to step up," Osteen recalled to Mark I. Pinsky for the *Orlando Sentinel* (November 27, 2004). Joel approached the stage that Sunday wearing a pair of his father's shoes to help alleviate his considerable anxiety. The sympathetic audience was drawn to Joel's sermon, as he told stories about his family. "I made them laugh. . . . The Lord just helped me get my message, and I could speak," he told Jennifer Mathieu for the

Houston Press (April 4, 2002). Less than a week after his son's first sermon, John Osteen died, at age 77, of a sudden heart attack. To everyone's surprise, on October 3, 1999 Joel assumed the position of senior pastor at Lakewood, and over the next six years, he turned the institution into the fastest-growing, largest, and most ethnically diverse "mega-church" in America.

One of six siblings, Joel Scott Osteen was born on March 5, 1963 in Houston to Dolores "Dodie" Osteen and John Osteen. The success enjoyed today by Lakewood Church is largely due to the efforts of John Osteen, the church's founder. The son of a cotton farmer, John—a high-school dropout—had a religious epiphany at age 18, as he was leaving a Fort Worth, Texas, nightclub. According to William Martin, John "had the feeling that God was tapping him on the shoulder." He went on to earn degrees from John Brown University and Northern Baptist Seminary, becoming an ordained Southern Baptist minister. He served as pastor of Central Baptist Church and, later, of Hibbarb Memorial Baptist, in Houston. In 1958, while at Hibbarb Memorial, John experienced the "baptism of the Holy Spirit," a spiritual experience often described by Pentecostal and charismatic Christians, who say that they receive "gifts of the Spirit" such as visions or the ability to speak in tongues. Instead of entering into contention with the Baptist church, which eschews such displays of the Holy Spirit, John left Hibbarb Memorial in 1959 and founded the nondenominational Lakewood Church in an abandoned feed store on Houston's northeast side. The church began with only 90 members. Establishing it in a predominantly black neighborhood, John Osteen envisioned a racially diverse church and welcomed local residents. As is common among Pentecostal pastors, John preached what is called Word of Faith sermons, saying in one sermon, as quoted by Martin, "It's God's will for you to live in prosperity instead of poverty. It's God's will for you to pay your bills and not be in debt. It's God's will for you to live in health and not in sickness all the days of your life." His core idea was that with enough faith, Christians could ask God for blessings and have their requests fulfilled. Calling Lakewood an "oasis of love in a troubled world," John Osteen spread his message to people from all walks of life, and the congregation quickly grew into the thousands.

In 1982, when he was only a freshman at Oral Roberts University, in Tulsa, Oklahoma, Joel Osteen had an idea for bringing his father's ministry to thousands more in the Houston area as well as to homes across America. After he discussed with his father the prospect of televising the Sunday services, the older man consented, on the condition that they never petition television viewers for money. Joel promptly agreed and dropped out of college (he finished one year) to begin producing and directing broadcasts of Lakewood's Sunday service, which aired at first on local Houston stations and was being seen nationally, via the Family

Channel, by the mid-1980s. "We don't have much drive-by visibility where we are," Osteen told Mathieu. "So TV was a big impact. That's when the church really began to grow." With the influx of people attending the weekly services, the church moved in 1987 to a newly built facility in Houston to accommodate Lakewood's 6,000 Sunday worshippers. That same year, Joel married Victoria Iloff, whom he had met when she sold him a watch battery in her family's jewelry store.

Lakewood churchgoers have become familiar with the Osteen family over the years, as members of the immediate and extended family have become deeply involved in the church, making it a family-run operation. Joel's older siblings Lisa and Paul speak regularly at the Wednesday-night services; Dodie Osteen and other family members serve as prayer partners. (Because membership at Lakewood Church is so large, individual prayer requests are sent to numerous church members, who pray for those requests, which Joel Osteen is unable to do. Those members, or prayer partners, also keep up contact with those who send the requests and encourage them in their "daily walk with the Lord." On Sundays there is a portion of the service during which prayer partners are stationed throughout the audience to pray briefly with individual congregants.) After Joel assumed the pastorship, his wife, Victoria, began delivering "a little encouraging piece" at each of the four Sunday services. As the Osteen family became recognizable evangelical figures, John Osteen was targeted along with a number of other well-known televangelists, among them Pat Robertson, who received anonymously mailed bombs. On January 30, 1990, while working in an office at an auxiliary building across the street from Lakewood Church, Lisa Comes Osteen opened a package sent from a small town in North Carolina and addressed to her father. When she did so, a pipe bomb exploded, shooting six- to eight-inch nails. Lisa was hospitalized for a week after undergoing surgery on her leg and abdomen. John Osteen told reporters, as quoted in the *Orlando Sentinel* (January 31, 1990), "The devil did his best, but his best was not enough. We are just going to go on doing the Lord's work." The culprit has never been found. "It was weird, because my dad was uncontroversial," Joel Osteen told Mathieu.

Joel himself has made it a point to avoid divisive topics in his ministry. In an interview with Paula Zahn for CNN (July 18, 2005, on-line), Osteen said, "I think everybody is called to different things. And I've never been—my dad's never been political, and I just—you know, that's just not me. I know my gifts are to encourage people, to inspire them, to motivate them . . . if you get into areas that you're not called to, you know, it just divides the very audience that I'm trying to reach." Osteen's desire to avoid divisiveness has, ironically, led some to criticize him. Calling his sermons "cotton-candy theology" or "prosperity gospel," detractors accuse Osteen of using God as a means of personal gain while evading critical issues of sin

and condemnation. Lynn Mitchell, director of religious studies at the University of Houston, said to John Leland for the *New York Times* (July 18, 2005), "The idea of suffering as a Christian virtue is not part of his worldview. Some call it Christianity Lite—you get all the benefits, but don't pay attention to the fact that Jesus called for suffering. He doesn't tackle many problems of the world." Although doctrinal theology may be absent from Osteen's sermons, his style of preaching has brought masses of people to Lakewood, not counting the millions of people who watch him from home. Nevertheless, critics such as Randall Balmer, a professor of religion at Barnard College, insist that Osteen's success actually has very little to do with religion. "Chances are, you're not going to draw huge crowds with a very dark and censorious message. Osteen is relentlessly sunny and positive. Self-help is very popular. It has a real appeal to the masses, and in some ways, it's kind of akin to the latest diet book: Somebody has a new formula and people kind of glom onto that," Balmer told Cathy Frye for the *San Antonio Express* (July 31, 2005).

Osteen, whose charming demeanor and ever-present smile have led some to dub him "The Smiling Preacher," has defended himself against such critics, telling William Martin, "People will probably laugh, but I don't feel like I am a prosperity preacher. I do believe, though, that God wants us to prosper. . . . I just don't think Christians should feel that they have to stay at the lower rung of the ladder. I also point out that prosperity is not just money. It's a healthy relationship with your wife, with your kids; it's a healthy body." Listening to the day-to-day problems of his congregants, Osteen feels that the "cotton-candy theology" many accuse him of representing is more appropriate for his followers than traditional doctrines. "If you want to reach the culture, you need to speak in their terms," he said to Martin. "When Jesus was here on this earth, he did such practical stuff. He taught using simple examples like the parable of the prodigal son; everybody can relate to that. I tell a lot of stories in my sermons. Most of what I preach is about simple things." On the subject of suffering, Osteen said to Martin, "I have a file in my mind called an 'I don't understand it' file. There are some things we are not going to understand, and we must say, like Job, 'Though he slay me, yet will I trust in him.' I think God will give us peace to go through anything. How do you tell somebody why their kid got killed in a car wreck? You just say, 'I can't understand it. I can't explain it to you.' You can't dwell on that. You just know that God is in control. It's a tough issue."

Although some who joined Lakewood during John Osteen's pastorship had doubts about Joel Osteen's ability to take over for his father, Lauro Cavazos, a longtime Lakewood member, told Bruce Nichols for the *Dallas Morning News* (November 29, 1999), "He's doing OK. He's improving. We were thinking that after John passed away, [the church] would struggle for a while. But evidently the Lord is giving us his support. New people are still coming." What sets Osteen apart from his father and other evangelical preachers is his self-help style of ministry, which dictates much of the content of his sermons. "Daddy would often just teach the Bible," Osteen told Martin. "I take a little different approach. I may give a whole sermon and give the scripture at the end. . . . I know doctrine is good. We need doctrine, but I think the average person is not looking for doctrine." Joel Osteen's warm, humble demeanor, coupled with his youthful looks, is apparently refreshing to many people, given that most other prominent figures in the world of evangelical Christianity are older men—another factor that may account for Osteen's popularity and the growth of his church's membership. But Osteen has occasionally experienced criticism from evangelical Christians. On June 20, 2005, for example, during an interview on CNN's *Larry King Live*, he angered many viewers when he told King, in response to questions about whether good deeds were sufficient to gain entrance into heaven or whether Jews or Muslims or others who don't believe in Jesus would be welcomed there, "I'm very careful about saying who would and wouldn't go to heaven." A few days later, after he received many E-mail messages and letters of complaint, Osteen posted, temporarily, a letter on his Web site in which he apologized for "leav[ing] any doubt" because of his words on King's show "as to what I believe and Whom I serve." "I believe with all my heart that it is only through Christ that we have hope in eternal life," he wrote, describing that belief as "the very thing in which I have decided my life."

Among the many legacies left by John Osteen, one of the most visible is the ethnic diversity of the congregation that continues to thrive under the care of Joel. Just as many Hispanics and blacks as whites sit in the stadium-style seats listening to Osteen's inspirational sermons at Lakewood. The church even provides a lunchtime service in Spanish every Sunday. Osteen's reach extends far beyond the doors of Lakewood, especially with the publication of his book, *Your Best Life Now: 7 Steps to Living Your Full Potential*, in October 2004. As of October 30, 2005 Osteen's 320-page book had been on the prestigious *New York Times* best-seller list for 52 weeks, and it has sold an estimated three million copies worldwide. *Your Best Life Now* is written in an upbeat tone and is aimed at helping readers live more prosperous lives. The "Smiling Preacher," who has no formal theological education, has thus joined the growing ranks of popular evangelical preachers who have written religious-themed motivational books. He wrote in *Your Best Life Now*, "God is saying get ready for more. Make room for increase. Enlarge your tents. He's saying expect more favor, more supernatural blessings. Don't become satisfied with where you are." Osteen asserted that Christians are entitled to lives of prosperity and can "expect preferential treatment, not because of *who* [they] are, but because of *whose* [they] are." He added, "We can expect people to want to help us because of who our Father is." With the success of his book and the 2005 publication of the supplementary guide *Your Best Life Now Journal*, Osteen has forgone his annual $200,000 salary from the church. "I never dreamed that I could be one of the biggest givers in our church, and now I can. . . . We are stewards of God's money," Osteen told Martin. In March 2006 Osteen signed a contract with the Free Press, a division of Simon & Schuster, for his next book. Unnamed sources told Ralph Blumenthal, who interviewed them for the *New York Times* (March 30, 2006), that the agreement calls for payments to Osteen of a modest advance and 50 percent (rather than the usual 15 percent) of the profits from sales, which are expected to reach more than $10 million.

In the hope of spreading his message even further, in September 2005 Osteen launched the multicity tour "An Evening with Joel Osteen." He preached to sold-out audiences at Madison Square Garden, in New York City, and was forced to add another night to his appearances there to meet demand. In Atlanta, Georgia, 4,000 people were turned away after the venue was filled to capacity. In July 2005 Lakewood took steps to ensure that no one would be turned away from the Sunday services: After a couple years of renovations whose costs topped $90 million, the church relocated to the Compaq Center, the former home of the National Basketball Association's Houston Rockets, to accommodate Lakewood's 30,000-member congregation. Absent from the newly remodeled church are the religious iconography, stained glass, and crosses that adorn most traditional churches. Instead, the former stadium is replete with state-of-the-art media equipment that includes Jumbotrons (used to show large images of a speaker); a café with wireless Internet access; 32 video-game kiosks; and even two waterfalls. "I just think we're in a society these days that we're so distracted or busy. . . . It's harder to hold people's attention," Osteen told Lois Romano for the *Washington Post* (January 30, 2005). "We try to package the whole service—I hate to use the word production or show." At an average Sunday service at Lakewood, congregants hear a 500-member choir, a band with a pop-inflected sound, and the familiar Texas twang of the renowned pastor. The service is televised every week on six cable networks and in 150 countries, making Joel Osteen an international household name. Based on his phenomenal success in the span of only six years, Osteen told William Martin that he is confident that "in twenty years we'll look up and realize that the Compaq Center isn't big enough to hold all the people."

Osteen was described as "a trim five nine" by Martin, who added, "He is not classically handsome, but his face is instantly appealing, both because of the lively energy in his intense blue eyes and a smile that never seems forced and is seldom missing." Joel and Victoria Osteen have two children, Jonathan and Alexandra.

—I.C.

Suggested Reading: *CNN Larry King Live* (on-line) July 3, 2005; *Houston Press* Apr. 4, 2002; *Texas Monthly* p106+ Aug. 2005

Selected Books: *Your Best Life Now: 7 Steps to Living Your Full Potential*, 2004

Joe Raedle/Getty Images

Pace, Peter

Nov. 5, 1945– U.S. Marine Corps general; chairman of the Joint Chiefs of Staff

Address: Office of the Chairman of the Joint Chiefs of Staff, U.S. Dept. of Defense, Pentagon, Rm. 2E873, Washington, DC 20318

On September 30, 2005 the four-star general Peter Pace of the U.S. Marine Corps was sworn in as the 16th chairman of the Joint Chiefs of Staff (the highest military rank in the nation after the president), becoming the first marine appointed to the post. Having served as the vice chairman from October 2001 to August 2005, Pace assumed the responsibilities of the top military position having already established ties with leading political officials, including President George W. Bush and Secretary of Defense Donald Rumsfeld. Although Pace has come under fire from some critics for his supposed acquiescence to the policies of those officials, the general has nevertheless earned a reputation as a strong yet quietly thoughtful leader whose main concern is for the men and women serving in the

armed forces. Pace, who has 39 years of military service, including combat experience in Vietnam and Somalia, will likely be judged in his role as chairman of the Joint Chiefs by the effectiveness of his military advice concerning the involvement of U.S. forces in the Middle East. Referring to the increasingly violent insurgency in Iraq, led by Abu Musab al-Zarqawi (a rebel leader with ties to Al Qaeda who was killed by U.S. forces in June 2006), Pace stated on June 29, 2005, while testifying before the Senate's Committee on Armed Services, "This is going to be a war on terrorism that's going to pit freedom loving men and women against those small cells supported by thieves and others who would want to take away the way we live. . . . This is going to be a long, tough fight for the nation globally to defend ourselves and our friends. But there's also absolutely no doubt that this country and our friends are very capable of doing it. It will not be easy. But . . . I look forward to having the opportunity to participate."

Peter Pace was born on November 5, 1945 in Brooklyn, New York, and raised in nearby Teaneck, New Jersey. He is the second of the four children (three sons and one daughter) of Doris Pace and her Italian-immigrant husband, John. During congressional hearings on immigration reform in 2006, Pace wept as he recalled the experiences of his father in the U.S, telling those present, as quoted by Glenn Frankel and Daniela Deane in the *Washington Post* (July 11, 2006), "There is no other country on the planet that affords that kind of opportunity to those who come here." As a teenager Pace exhibited leadership qualities as the vice president of his senior class at Teaneck High School, where he was also a member of both the soccer and track-and-field teams. Upon graduating from high school, Pace enrolled in the United States Naval Academy, in Annapolis, Maryland, with the intention of pursuing a career in the navy. However, just before earning his B.S. degree from the academy, in 1967, Pace decided to join the Marine Corps—a smaller branch of the armed forces—instead. After completing basic training at the Marine Corps Base Quantico, in Virginia, in 1968, Pace was commissioned as a second lieutenant. He was soon deployed to join U.S. troops in Vietnam, and just one week after arriving there, Pace was sent to replace a wounded platoon leader in the city of Hue. He was the third commander of the platoon in only three weeks; his predecessors had both been killed in battle. As the rifle platoon leader, Pace was forced to educate himself quickly in urban combat: during his basic training at Quantico, a snowstorm had shut down the base on the days designated to train new marines in urban combat, and Pace had spent the time watching World War II movies. The officers at Quantico had assured the young marines that they would still be prepared for the war in Vietnam, as much of the fighting took place in the country's jungles and rice paddies. Nonetheless, Pace found himself leading a platoon through Hue—the site of the worst street battles in the Vietnam War—dodging bullets from rooftop snipers and clearing enemy troops from alleys and abandoned homes. Five men in Pace's platoon were killed while carrying out their mission to retake the city's citadel from the North Vietnamese army. Staff Sergeant Willie Williams fell after stepping in front of Pace and taking bullet that would have killed the young officer. More than 35 years later, Pace still remembers the sacrifices of those men and keeps a picture of Marine Corps lance corporal Guido Farinaro—the first marine he lost to combat in Vietnam—on his desk at the Pentagon. "I remember Lance Corporal Charlie Hale, Lance Corporal Whitey [Travis], Corporal Mike [Witt], Staff Sergeant Williams, Lance Corporal Little Joe Arnold, Lance Corporal John Miller. I can . . . tell you where they died. I knew where they were from. If I was sitting here, not remembering the individuals who lost their lives under my command, not remembering Vietnam, I should not be chairman," Pace told Barbara Starr and other reporters for CNN (November 11, 2005, on-line). In the end, he was one of fewer than a dozen marines in a company of 160 men to come out of Hue uninjured. Before ending his tour of duty in Vietnam, he advanced to the rank of assistant operations officer.

In 1969 Pace returned to the U.S. as a first lieutenant and was assigned to the Marine Barracks, in Washington, D.C., where he served first as the security detachment commander at Camp David, then as a White House social aide, and finally as the platoon leader of the Special Ceremonial Platoon. Two years later Pace was promoted to the rank of captain. He attended the Infantry Officers' Advanced Course at Fort Benning, Georgia, in September 1971, and was assigned to the Security Element of the Marine Aircraft Group 15 in the First Marine Aircraft Wing, in Nam Phong, Thailand, the following year. Before leaving for Thailand, Pace received an MBA degree from George Washington University, in Washington, D.C. During his one-year tour in Southeast Asia, Pace served as the operations officer and then the executive officer, before again returning to Washington, D.C., in October 1973, for an assignment at the Headquarters Marine Corps as the assistant major's monitor. In 1976 he moved cross-country to serve as the operations officer of the Second Battalion of the Fifth Marines at Camp Pendleton, in California. He also served as the executive officer of the Third Battalion and eventually the staff secretary of the entire Fifth Marine Division, before being promoted to major in November 1977. In August 1979 Pace enrolled in the Marine Corps Command and Staff College at Quantico. Upon completing that program, the following year, he was assigned to a recruiting station in Buffalo, New York, as the commanding officer. Two years later he was promoted to the rank of lieutenant colonel.

Pace returned to Camp Pendleton in June 1983 to serve as commanding officer of the Second Battalion of the First Marines, until June 1985, when he was selected to attend the National War College, in Washington, D.C. There, Pace became well-versed in the international implications of military strategy in times of war and peace, preparing him for a career as a high-level marine officer. He graduated in 1986 and was assigned to the Combined/Joint Staff in Seoul, Korea, where he served as the chief of the ground forces branch until April 1987. Pace was then promoted to executive officer to the assistant chief of staff of the United Nations Command/Combined Forces Command of U.S. forces in Korea. In August 1988 Pace returned to the Marine Barracks in Washington, D.C., to serve as the commanding officer and was promoted to the rank of colonel two months later. After briefly serving as the chief of staff and assistant division commander of the Second Marine Division, at Camp Lejeune, in North Carolina, Pace advanced to the higher echelons of marine command as a brigadier general on April 6, 1992. He returned to the basic-training facilities at Quantico to serve as the president of the Marine Corps University and the commanding general of Marine Corps Schools at the Marine Corps Combat Development Command.

During his stint at Quantico, starting in December 1992, Pace was called upon to serve as the deputy commander of the marine forces in Somalia. At the time two insurgent forces were battling for political legitimacy after having ousted the government of President Siad Barre in January 1991. Besieged with constant civil war, many Somalis died of hunger as warlords prevented civilians from receiving food from U.N. relief workers. President Bill Clinton dispatched troops to Somalia to spearhead a U.N. peacekeeping effort. "We were told to circle the wagons and not get Americans hurt," Pace said, according to Evan Thomas, Karen Breslau, Rod Nordland, and Ron Moreau in *Newsweek* (September 11, 2002). After three months in the embattled African nation, Pace returned to the U.S. and attended the Program for Senior Executives in National and International Security at Harvard University, in Cambridge Massachusetts. In October of that same year, he was dispatched to Somalia once again, this time as the deputy commander of the Joint Task Force, overseeing the withdrawal of U.S. troops—a move that was spurred by the disastrous attempt to capture two warlords at the Battle of Mogadishu, in which two army helicopters were shot down and the bodies of the dead soldiers were paraded through the streets. According to David S. Cloud, writing for the *New York Times* (April 23, 2005), Pace was dissatisfied with the outcome of events in Somalia and stated years later that "expanding the American mission, from humanitarian aid to include disarming Somali militias, had been a mistake." Pace returned to the U.S. in March 1994 and was advanced to the rank of major general. He served in Japan for two years before returning to Washington, D.C., and being promoted to lieutenant general on August 5, 1996. From 1997 to 2000 he served as the commander of the Marine

Corp Forces, Atlantic/Europe/South. In September 2000 Pace became a four-star general and the commander in chief of the United States Southern Command, which is responsible for all U.S. military activities in South and Central America.

In October 2001 President George W. Bush appointed Pace vice chairman of the Joint Chiefs of Staff, under the chairmanship of General Richard B. Myers of the United States Air Force. Pace became the first marine to assume the vice chairmanship since its creation in 1986. (Previously, only air force or navy officers had filled the position.) As the White House planned a military response to the terrorist attacks of September 11, 2001, with Al Qaeda training camps in Afghanistan as key targets, Pace became integral to the development of the Pentagon's strategy in the so-called war on terror. He chaired the Joint Requirements Oversight Council and acted as vice chairman of the Defense Acquisition Board. In addition, he served as a member of the National Security Council Deputies Committee and the Nuclear Weapons Council, while also acting on behalf of the chairman of the Planning, Programming and Budgeting System. Through his many roles in the Pentagon, following the events of September 11, 2001 and well into the U.S.–led invasion of Iraq (which began in 2003), Pace crafted a reputation as a quiet-spoken but well-informed leader, commanding the respect of his officers and the civilian leaders from the Bush administration. "You name it, and I think he brings it," General Carl Mundy, a retired marine, told Douglas Jehl for the *New York Times* (April 9, 2003). "He is bright, he is sophisticated, he is persuasive, and he very obviously has tremendous rapport and recognized credentials with Mr. Rumsfeld and the administration." Known in the Pentagon as "Perfect Pete," Pace has made it a priority to refashion the language of military missions in order to assure that rookie soldiers understand the purpose of their work. During meetings with high-level military officials, Pace regularly refers to the fictional "Private Pace" to test whether missions have been explained in uncomplicated terms. Pace's constant concern for soldiers, grounded in his own days in battle, has earned him much respect among the rank and file. "It goes through your mind—your fellow Marines, your fellow soldiers are in combat and you feel like you should be too. That's the heart. The mind says you have a very important job in Washington and you got it for a reason and you are better applying all your experience and all your memory of what you did when you were younger to make sure that what bothered you doesn't bother these guys," Pace told Esther Schrader for the *Los Angeles Times* (February 23, 2003).

In April 2005 it was announced that President Bush intended to nominate Pace to replace Myers, whose term was to end later that year. Critics began speculating on how effective Pace would be if he were to serve under Secretary of Defense Donald Rumsfeld as the military's leading official. In the

lead-up to the war in Iraq, political opponents had seen Myers's and Pace's support for Rumsfeld's strategic and tactical plans as unquestioning acquiescence. Within the Pentagon it was well known that Rumsfeld regarded Pace as one of his leading men in the military's long-term strategy toward the Middle East, and many critics saw the rapport between the two men as further evidence that Pace was Rumsfeld's "yes man," according to senior officials who spoke with Schrader. The *New York Times* reporter David S. Cloud expressed the concerns of many political analysts and military officers, writing in an April 21, 2005 article, "If General Pace is confirmed by the Senate, former officers say, one of his main challenges will be dealing with the perception among military officers that he would not be willing to challenge Mr. Rumsfeld's priorities aggressively if . . . disagreements arose." Loren Thompson, a Pentagon analyst from the policy center Lexington Institute, told Cloud, "Donald Rumsfeld's main concept for the Pentagon is a tight ship organized along the lines of a large corporation. Pace fits in because he's a team player who does not argue in public and will execute Rumsfeld's wishes." Pace's support for Rumsfeld's strategy was evident during his nomination hearings before the Armed Services Committee. Responding to the concerns of Democratic and Republican senators over the number of troops needed in the Middle East, Pace reiterated Rumsfeld's strategy, stating, "There's . . . a balance that must be accommodated or understood that is the balance between having enough forces to provide sufficient security for the political governance to take place and having too much force that presents more targets, more what would be viewed as oppression. From my standpoint, sir, sitting where I sit and listening to what I've heard, doing the analysis I've done, talking to the leaders I've talked to, I am personally comfortable with the size force we have." Pace's military outlook coincided with that of the Bush administration: frustrated by the defensive stance the military took while he was stationed in Somalia, Pace welcomed the Bush administration's offense-oriented approach to the war on terror. "If people think you're going to sit there and you're afraid to attack, they're going to pick at you," he told the reporters for *Newsweek*. After September 2001, he added, "we were going to take the war to the enemy."

Despite the reservations of some, Pace was confirmed by the Senate as the 16th chairman of the Joint Chiefs of Staff and was sworn in on September 30, 2005. As chairman, Pace is the primary military adviser to the president, the secretary of defense, and the National Security Council. In his testimony to the Armed Services Committee during his nomination hearings, Pace stated that he would adhere to the same priorities that Myers had advanced during his two terms—winning the war on terror, improving joint warfare (or the coordination of efforts of separate branches of the military), and continuing the modernization of the nation's military—by focusing on goals that included executing comprehensive strategy to undermine and defeat extremists, strengthening military capability to prevent conflict, shaping and sizing the joint force to meet future challenges, and continuing to pursue quality-of-life initiatives. Though Pace shares the Bush administration's stance on military strategy, he publicly disagreed with Rumsfeld during a joint news conference, in November 2005, over a journalist's question about reports that Iraqi authorities were torturing prisoners. "It is the absolute responsibility of every U.S. service member, if they see inhumane treatment being conducted, to intervene, to stop it," Pace told the reporter, as quoted by Dana Milbank in the *Washington Post* (November 30, 2005). After Rumsfeld responded, "I don't think you mean they have an obligation to physically stop it; it's to report it," Pace remained unequivocal, replying, "If they are physically present when inhumane treatment is taking place, sir, they have an obligation to try to stop it." Pace's unshakable views on that matter quelled much of the criticism that he would serve mainly as Rumsfeld's strongman.

In April 2006, as insurgency violence was mounting in Iraq, bringing the country to the verge of civil war, six retired generals from the armed forces called for the resignation of the secretary of defense for what they saw as his mishandling of the war in Iraq and the overall war on terror. The generals accused Rumsfeld of ignoring advice from military leaders, who had argued that more troops were needed for the war in Iraq. A month before the invasion, General Eric Shinseki, the former chief of staff of the United States Army, told Congress that several hundred thousand troops would be needed to effectively oust the regime of Saddam Hussein, limit anticipated insurgency violence, and begin taking steps toward reconstruction. Rumsfeld, however, supported a smaller, more mobile force, a recommendation most military leaders viewed with much apprehension. The questioning of the civilian leader of the armed forces by former high-level military officials caused approval ratings for the Bush administration, which had been on the decline as the war in Iraq dragged on, to fall even further. A harsher blow for the White House was that several of the retired generals had firsthand experience commanding troops in Iraq—including Major General Charles H. Swannack Jr., who had commanded the Army's 82d Airborne Division in Iraq, in 2004—which gave significant weight to calls for Rumsfeld's resignation in the eyes of the American public, whose support for the war was dwindling.

Few politicians besides Bush defended Rumsfeld from the political firestorm that followed the calls for his resignation. However, in a press conference held at the Pentagon in mid-April 2006, Pace stood by Rumsfeld and staunchly expressed his confidence in the secretary of defense. "As far as Pete Pace is concerned, this country is exceptionally well-served by the man standing on my left," Pace said, referring to Rumsfeld, according to Scott Shane of the Minneapolis, Minnesota, *Star Tribune* (April 16, 2006). "Nobody—nobody—works harder than he does to take care of the PFCs and lance corporals and lieutenants and the captains. He does his homework. He works weekends; he works nights." Pace added in a separate press conference, as quoted by Peter Spiegel in the *Los Angeles Times* (April 12, 2006): "We had then, and have now, every opportunity to speak our minds, and if we do not, shame on us because the opportunity is there. The plan that was executed [in Iraq] was developed by military officers, presented by military officers, questioned by civilians as they should, revamped by military officers, and blessed by the senior military leadership." Although some critics viewed Pace's support for Rumsfeld as another instance of flattery and compliance, others understood that the general's comments were not necessarily tantamount to full-fledged support. "This is what the chairman of the joint chiefs is expected to do by tradition and law," Dennis Showalter, a military historian, told Shane. "If he had not spoken out, he would have been making a very strong statement." According to Showalter, apart from submitting his own resignation, Pace had little choice but to provide a public statement of support for the secretary of defense lest he add to the increasing political derision of the Bush administration.

In June 2006, in the wake of allegations that U.S. Marines had murdered 24 innocent Iraqi civilians in the town of Haditha in November 2005, Pace announced that special training in ethics would be required for American troops in Iraq, in part to "provide comfort to those looking to see if we are . . . a nation that stands on the values we hold dear," as he told Lolita C. Baldor for the Associated Press Online (June 4, 2006). Pace also pledged to conduct investigations into both the killings and alleged attempts to cover them up. In August 2006 Pace and General John Abizaid, the highest-ranking U.S. commander in the Middle East, acknowledged during a meeting of the Senate Armed Services Committee that increasing violence in Iraq between Sunni and Shiite Muslims might escalate into civil war, a possibility that most American officials had previously refused to recognize publicly. However, Pace also told the committee that he did not believe that such an outcome was probable. Several days later he vowed to redeploy American troops to four of the most violence-ridden areas of Baghdad, the Iraqi capital. To achieve a permanent resolution to the conflict, Pace told Jim Garamone for the American Forces Press Service (October 13, 2006, on-line), "the Shiite and Sunni leaders are going to have to love their kids more than they hate each other, so they can go about building their country."

Pace's military decorations include the Defense Distinguished Service Medal, with two oak-leaf clusters; the Defense Superior Service Medal; the Legion of Merit; the Bronze Star Medal, with Combat V distinction; the Defense Meritorious Service Medal; the Meritorious Service Medal, with one gold star; the Navy Commendation Medal, with Combat V distinction; the Navy Achievement Medal, with one gold star; and the Combat Action Ribbon.

Pace currently resides in Washington, D.C., with his wife, Lynne Ann (Holden) Pace. The couple have two children, Tiffany Marie, an accountant for the National Rifle Association, and Peter Jr., a first lieutenant in the Marine Corps.

—I.C.

Suggested Reading: *Christian Science Monitor* p16 Apr. 10, 2003; Department of Defense Web site; Federal News Service June 29, 2005; *Los Angeles Times* I p14 Feb. 23, 2003; *New York Times* B p10 Apr. 9, 2003, A p18 Apr. 21, 2005, A p10 Apr. 23, 2005; *Newsweek* p36+ Sep. 11, 2002; *Washington Post* A p18 Nov. 30, 2005

Lisa Blumenfeld/Getty Images

Palmer, Violet

Feb. 20, 1964– Referee with the National Basketball Association

Address: c/o National Basketball Association, Olympic Tower, 645 Fifth Ave., New York, NY 10022

Violet Palmer is currently the only female referee in the male-dominated National Basketball Association (NBA). She shattered the glass ceiling in professional basketball in 1997, when she became one of only two female referees in the NBA's history.

She began her career in the sport as a point guard at California State Polytechnic University, where she led the women's team to two consecutive National Collegiate Athletic Association (NCAA) Division II women's championships. Following her college career Palmer joined the officiating ranks of women's basketball, developing into one of the leading officials at the Division I level and officiating in five consecutive NCAA Final Four games. She subsequently spent three years in an NBA development program before becoming the first female official to referee an NBA game. The same year she also served as referee during the first season of the Women's National Basketball Association (WNBA). After an eight-season career in the NBA, during which she worked more than 400 regular-season games, she reached another milestone in April 2006, when she became the first female to officiate at an NBA play-off game.

Violet Palmer was born in Compton, in southern California, on February 20, 1964, the second-oldest of four children. Some sources indicate that her father, James, is a retired foreman for an airplane-parts company, while others say that he is a retired metalworker and furnace operator. Her mother, Gussie, was a homemaker during Palmer's youth. Palmer's family was close-knit and had a long tradition in sports, particularly basketball; her father played the game at the college level, her mother in high school. When she was five or six years old, Palmer began honing her skills at basketball, in games against her younger brother, Rod, in the family's backyard, where her father had installed a hoop. She also competed alongside her brother as a shortstop and pitcher in the boys' baseball league at Victory Park in Compton. The only girl on the team, "she was right there with us," as her brother told an interviewer for the Associated Press (October 30, 1997). "She was a lot better than some of the guys. She was very athletic."

At Compton High School Palmer shone as the starting point guard for the girls' basketball team and as a member of the track and softball teams. She caught the attention of Darlene May, then the head coach at California State Polytechnic University at Pomona (Cal Poly-Pomona), who recruited her to play for the women's basketball team. Palmer enrolled at the school on an athletic scholarship and played point guard for the Broncos at the NCAA Division II level. During her three years as captain, she led the team to two consecutive NCAA women's championships, in 1985 and 1986. As part of the requirement for her major, recreation administration, Palmer started officiating at basketball games. She had a role model in May, who, at the 1984 Summer Olympics, became the first female referee to oversee an Olympic women's basketball game. She began contemplating her career choices when she reached her senior year of college. "I knew I didn't want to play women's basketball overseas, which was the only choice at the time," she told Alan Eisenstock for an interview posted on Referee.com (October 31, 1997).

Palmer graduated from Cal Poly-Pomona in 1988. She spent a year as a graduate assistant and coached high-school basketball before deciding that it "just wasn't for me," as she told Paul Helms for the Cal Poly-Pomona publication *Panorama* (Spring 2006, on-line). She next accepted the position of recreation director at the Placentia Recreation Department, in northern Orange County, California. As part of her job, she performed referee duties. At the suggestion of a friend, she joined the Los Angeles branch of the California Basketball Officials Association (CBOA), and during her free time she started to oversee girls' high-school basketball games and men's recreational-league contests. After officiating at a semifinals match at a local high-school basketball tournament during her first year as a referee, Palmer was contacted by several junior colleges with offers to referee games. Following her performance in 1989 at the All-American Basketball Camp in Santa Clara, California, she was hired by the NCAA and scaled the ranks of women's college basketball competition, refereeing games in NCAA Divisions I, II, and III. A knee injury she sustained in a collision during a softball game in 1992 sidelined her for a year. The forced inactivity inspired in Palmer a renewed commitment to pursue a career as a referee. "Until my injury, I didn't realize how important officiating was to me. How much I really wanted to do it," she said to Eisenstock.

In the summer of 1993, Palmer attended a referee training camp in Minnesota operated by June Courteau, a former Division I women's referee and currently a referee official with the WNBA. Among the people in attendance were Marcy Weston, the now-retired NCAA coordinator of women's basketball officials, and fellow trainee Dee Kantner. Based on Palmer's solid performance at the camp, which included officiating at the championship game, she was scheduled to referee 50 NCAA Division I matches. In 1994 Carter Rankin, Palmer's supervisor at the NCAA Pacific 10 (Pac-10) conference, selected her as a referee for the NCAA women's basketball tournament, and she advanced in that capacity to the national semifinals games, also known as the Final Four. She did so again in 1995.

That May Palmer was a member of the officiating crew for the State Farm Hall of Fame Tipoff Classic. By that time she had come to be regarded as one of the best referees in women's college basketball, along with Kantner, then also a referee at the women's NCAA Division I level. The same year Palmer received a phone call from Aaron Wade, then the chief of staff of the Continental Basketball Association (CBA) officials, who offered her entry into the referee developmental program of the NBA, managed by Darell Garretson. Garretson was responsible for recommending staff additions to Rod Thorn, then the NBA's vice president of basketball operations. Palmer, who thought at first that Wade's proposal was a practical joke, had never entertained the thought of working in the NBA. "The NBA was never my goal because I thought it

was unattainable," she told Jill Lieber for *USA Today* (November 8, 2005). "I was a college referee. I was the No. 3 referee in the world for women's basketball. I had everything. The Final Four. Big TV games. All the limelight I wanted. But my personality is if you give me a challenge, I'm going to take it. In the back of my mind, I said, 'It doesn't cost me anything. I can just try it. If nothing happens, the training will be good.'"

In July 1995 Palmer attended two NBA-affiliated, professional-league camps, the Southern California Summer Pro League (SPL), in Long Beach, and the Rocky Mountain Review Summer League, in Salt Lake City, Utah. At the former, Palmer and Kantner were the only women present, and the players appeared suspicious of them, but "by the end of camp, I was just one of the guys," as Palmer recalled to Alan Eisenstock. During that time Palmer also officiated at a number of pro-am summer-league games, in which NBA players competed with amateurs. Talking with Valerie Lister for *USA Today* (October 29, 1997), she described the differences between overseeing women's college games and refereeing men's professional games: "One, the [NBA] players are extremely large, and also the play is a lot more above the rim. You find yourself having to really look above that rim a lot because you have to deal with them swatting the balls off the baskets, the slam dunks and all that type of stuff. That was a huge adjustment for me." Palmer quickly demonstrated that she could handle herself among NBA players. In one of her early camp games, as Amy Shipley reported for the *Washington Post* (September 23, 1997), a second-string player told Palmer that one of the calls she had made "wasn't an NBA call." She responded by telling him that he wasn't "an NBA player." As Shipley wrote, "The player fell silent as other players stifled laughter." "Nobody messed with me again," Palmer recalled to Shipley.

In the fall of 1995, Palmer officiated at her first exhibition game in the NBA. The following year she served as a referee, along with Kantner, during the 1996 NCAA women's finals in April and performed referee duties at her second consecutive State Farm Hall of Fame basketball tournament in May. Also in 1996 officials from the NCAA Big West Conference offered her the opportunity to officiate at men's basketball games during the upcoming season. The offer ultimately failed to materialize. "To make a long story short, they pretty much copped out. It wasn't a matter of ability. I think it was a matter of them not wanting to deal with the pressure [associated with hiring a female referee]," she told Mark Alesia for the *Chicago Daily Herald* (October 30, 1997). After attending NBA camp for her second consecutive summer, Palmer received an offer from Thorn to attend the NBA veterans' camp, an invitation-only training facility for the 58-person roster of NBA officials. After she was assigned to referee preseason games in Portland, Oregon, and Sacramento, California, Palmer saw a career in the NBA as a realistic possibility.

"A light bulb went off in my head. I said to myself 'you're gonna' do this. You're gonna show everybody that thought this was impossible that it is possible. I wasn't scared—I knew I could do it. I had been an athlete all my life and knew I just needed the training. But I was totally nervous. I couldn't believe it was happening, but that's a normal feeling," she told Christina Crews for the *Philadelphia Tribune* (June 19, 2001). Palmer's work during the two preseason games was part of a tryout to fill an available position on the theretofore all-male NBA referee officiating staff, following the retirement of Lee Jones. Among the other candidates being considered for the job were Kantner and four replacement referees who had worked during the previous season's lockout, including the former NBA and Cal State Fullerton player Leon Wood, who was selected for the available position in October 1996.

By January 1997 Palmer was in great demand as a lead official, managing a schedule that included games in the Pac-10 Conference and in the Western Athletic Conference (WAC) as well as her full-time job as a recreation director. Her referee duties that year included the NCAA women's championship game between Old Dominion University and Tennessee, which she refereed alongside Kantner, and her third consecutive State Farm Hall of Fame game. In August 1997 Palmer was selected as an official at the first WNBA championship game.

That September five officiating positions in the NBA became available, after members of the officiating crew were forced to resign, having pleaded guilty to falsifying their income-tax returns. There was intense media speculation regarding the possible hiring of Palmer and Kantner, following the league-wide distribution of a memo from the National Basketball Association league office during the summer, requesting that each NBA team reserve an available room to be used as a locker room for female officials. Rod Thorn ended the speculation on October 28, 1997, at the conclusion of the NBA exhibition season, when he selected both Palmer and Kantner to join the NBA officiating crew. Palmer thus became one of the first two women ever assigned to officiate at regular-season games in a major all-male professional sports league. On signing with the NBA, Palmer resigned from her job at the recreation department.

The hiring of Palmer and Kantner elicited differing reactions from NBA coaches and players, who had become familiar with both female referees during officiating appearances at NBA preseason and summer-league games. The Boston Celtics' head coach, Rick Pitino, told Mark Cofman for the *Boston Herald* (October 29, 1997), "There's no reason why women should not officiate men's basketball or men should not officiate women's basketball. It should be allowed if they're competent enough." Some prominent players in the league, however, were opposed to the appointments. Charles Barkley, then a forward for the Houston Rockets, remarked, "I don't think women should be in the army and I don't think they should be NBA refs," as reported by Amy Shipley for the *Washington Post* (October 30, 1997). Tim Hardaway, a guard for the Miami Heat, said, "[Women have] got their own game. Let them go over there and do their game."

As an incoming NBA referee, Palmer was assigned to work between 50 and 55 NBA games as well as games in the CBA, a standard schedule for rookie officials, while earning a reported annual salary of $80,000. Palmer made her official debut on October 31, 1997 at the Vancouver Grizzlies Stadium in Canada, in front of a crowd of more than 17,000 people, during a regular-season game between the Grizzlies and the Dallas Mavericks. In January 1998 Palmer officiated at a televised game between the Miami Heat and the Chicago Bulls at Miami Arena, becoming the first female official in the history of South Florida major-league sports to referee a basketball game.

Palmer's performance evaluation following the 1997–98 season included largely unfavorable feedback from the 58 coaches and general managers, whose input represented 40 percent of the evaluation. "She's just terrible. She's the worst thing I've seen in years. She's timid, and that's the worst thing you can be as a ref," an unidentified basketball executive told Mitch Lawrence for the New York *Daily News* (April 19, 1998), expressing an opinion held by others as well. However, league executives, who provided the remaining 60 percent of the overall evaluation, appeared determined to see Palmer succeed. "It would be bad publicity if the league fired her. That's the last thing they want," an unnamed general manager commented to Lawrence. In February 1999 Palmer returned for her second season in the NBA, which was delayed by a lockout—the result of a labor dispute between NBA owners and players. The lockout lasted 191 days, reducing the number of NBA preseason games from eight per team to two and the regular-season games from 82 to 50. Over the next four months, Palmer appeared as part of the three-person officiating crew in regular-season games between the Houston Rockets and the Golden State Warriors; between the Orlando Magic and the Detroit Pistons; and between the Los Angeles Lakers and the Vancouver Grizzlies (now known as the Memphis Grizzlies).

By the start of her fourth season in the NBA, Palmer had begun to gain acceptance from players and others. "I could kind of see the heads not turn anymore. I could see players come up to me and just talk. At first it was one of those arm's-distance kind of things. [They seemed to be thinking] 'She has this strength, she reminds me of my mother, but I'm not sure how to deal with her.' As time went on, it became, 'Wow, she's just cool. She's just as cool as the guys,'" she told Jill Lieber for *USA Today* (November 8, 2005). NBA players have also commented favorably on her officiating skills. Tim Duncan of the San Antonio Spurs remarked to Lieber that "once you're in the heat of battle, you don't notice her gender. Her strengths are she doesn't stick out. . . . She's a solid official." Duncan's teammate Robert Horry added, "She's good. At first a lot of guys challenged her on calls, like 'Come on,' but she stood up for herself. That says a lot about her. Guys respect her. . . . She doesn't back down from anybody." In July 2002, after the end of Palmer's fifth season, she became the sole female referee in the NBA, following Dee Kantner's dismissal from the league. Kantner had received poor mid- and postseason reviews from league officials, including 29 head coaches and general managers, reportedly earning her a last-place ranking among 59 officials, as reported by K. C. Johnson in the *Chicago Tribune* (July 16, 2002).

In the spring of 2004, Palmer became the first-ever female alternate referee for the NBA play-offs, during the first round of play; as such, she waited in the wings at five different games in case of an injury to one of the three officials on the court. "I'm almost there. I'm going to get there. I'm working my way, big time. It has nothing to do with gender. You've got to pay your dues. . . . When the opportunity knocks, you've got to be ready, and I'm ready," she told Lieber. In May 2006, during her ninth season with the NBA, Palmer fulfilled a long-time goal—and made history— when she officiated at the second game of the first-round play-off series between the Indiana Pacers and the New Jersey Nets, thus becoming the first woman to referee an NBA play-off game. Palmer's next goals include becoming the senior member of an officiating corps and serving as an official during an NBA finals game.

Palmer is a member of the board of directors of the National Association of Sports Officials (NASO). She is also the founder of the Violet Palmer Referee Camp, for men and women, which convenes annually, July 9–11. Every summer she volunteers her services at the City of Los Angeles Youth Referee Clinic, instructing girls between the ages of 15 and 18 in the art of officiating. Palmer lives in Los Angeles.

—B.M.

Suggested Reading: *Chicago Tribune* N p1 July 16, 2002; *Ebony* p172 Feb. 1998; *Essence* p60 Aug. 1998; *Jet* p59 May 15, 2006; *Newsweek* p38 Mar. 8, 2004; *Philadelphia Tribune* D p1 June 19, 2001; *USA Today* A p1 Nov. 8, 2005

Parker, Mary-Louise

Aug. 2, 1964– Actress

Address: c/o William Morris Agency, 151 El Camino Dr., Beverly Hills, CA 90212

"Mary-Louise Parker underplays more beautifully, and convincingly, than just about any other actress today. Set her on a marble bench surrounded by statues—just set her there—and after a while you'll think the statues are overacting and you'll want to ask them please to knock it off with all the voguing," Tom Gliatto wrote for *People* (August 15, 2005). Parker is famously focused on her craft, often continuing to hone her performance during the run of a play until her final curtain call. Mark Brokaw, who directed her in the play *How I Learned to Drive*, recalled to Sylviane Gold for the *New York Times* (July 13, 1997) a telephone call he received from the actress the day after the critics had given the play, and Parker's performance in particular, rave reviews: "I said, 'Congratulations,'" Brokaw recollected. "And she said, 'What do you mean?' I said, 'The press, Mary-Louise. It's incredible.' She said, 'Oh, great.' And then she said: 'Well, the reason I was calling is, you know in that second monologue I have? Do you think I'm missing something? Because it doesn't seem to be working the way it should.'"Aware of her reputation for single-mindedness, Parker told Benji Wilson for the London *Times* (October 8, 2005), "I think I've always gotten on people's nerves, but I'm just super-serious about the work." Her perfection-

Frazer Harrison/Getty Images

ism has helped to bring her a number of prestigious awards: a Tony Award for her work in the play *Proof*, Golden Globe Awards for her performances in the cable-television miniseries *Angels in America* and the cable comedy series *Weeds*, an Emmy Award for *Angels in America*, and an Emmy nomination for her recurring role on the NBC drama *The West Wing*, among other honors that have confirmed her status as one of today's most luminous stars of the stage and screen.

Parker is notoriously reluctant to discuss her personal life. "I'm not trying to be cryptic," she said in an interview with Devin Gordon for *Newsweek* (October 7, 2002). "There are just things I don't like to talk about. They might be simple things to someone else, but to me they're important. It would cost me more than anyone would gain by reading it." Parker was born on August 2, 1964 in Fort Jackson, South Carolina, to a Swedish mother and a father who was an army officer and, later, a city magistrate. Parker and her parents and siblings lived the typical peripatetic life of an army family, spending time in Tennessee, Texas, Thailand, Germany, and France, among other locations. As a child Parker was reportedly quiet and socially awkward. "My dad says I didn't say more than 10 words a week growing up," the actress told Sylviane Gold. Early on she developed a deep appreciation of the arts, which she credits to her father, who, as she told Joan E. Vadeboncoeur for the Syracuse, New York, *Post-Standard* (January 23, 1992), "had a great understanding and appreciation of art. My father loved literature and encouraged me to read." As she recalled in an interview with the director Joe Mantello for the *New York Times* (October 8, 2000), Parker discovered her affinity for the stage at the age of four, during her first performance—as a tap dancer: "Apparently, all the other little girls were crying. I just wanted more lipstick. I was ready to go. No fear." She later harbored dreams of becoming a ballerina before deciding that, although she had talent, she could not reach the height of that profession.

Parker attended high school in Arizona, then went to the North Carolina School of the Arts, in Winston-Salem. "It was the only acting school I knew, except Juilliard and I couldn't afford Juilliard," she explained to Joan E. Vadeboncoeur. Her decision to act was almost instinctive, she told Simon Fanshawe for the London *Sunday Times* (April 20, 2003). "I don't ever remember wanting to be an actress before I knew what it was. I was too shy at school to do it. I was terribly unsocial. Very solitary. I oftentimes felt a real inability to communicate as a child. It was excruciating. It was funny when I started acting, because it was just easy, natural. It is the one time I can fully communicate with the world, and I feel completely unselfconscious, honest and present in the world in a way that it is often difficult for me to feel in life. Before, I was this incredibly awkward, lonely, look-at-me-wrong-and-I'll-cry kind of girl. It transformed me, absolutely, socially."

The same day that she graduated, Parker left North Carolina for New York, intent upon making her career on the stage. To support herself she took a variety of jobs, which included selling shoes, waiting tables, working as a cashier in an Italian restaurant, and doing telephone sales. Also during that period, the mid- and late 1980s, she acted in regional theater, appearing in productions of *The*

Importance of Being Earnest in Hartford, Connecticut, *Up in Saratoga* in San Diego, California, and *The Miser*, in Syracuse, New York. In 1989 Parker landed a role in *The Art of Success* at the Manhattan Theatre Club. While she considered stage acting to be her true calling, Parker readily accepted film and television parts to pay her bills. She found a recurring role on the soap opera *Ryan's Hope* and had small parts in the television movie *Too Young the Hero* (1988) and the feature film *Signs of Life* (1989). She appeared in the AIDS-themed film drama *Longtime Companion* in 1990, and, under the auspices of the prestigious Circle Repertory Company, she starred in the plays *Prelude to a Kiss* (1990), which marked her Broadway debut, and *Four Dogs and a Bone* (1993). For her performance in *Prelude to a Kiss* as Rita, a bride who temporarily and accidentally switches bodies with an old man, Parker received Drama Desk Award and Tony Award nominations.

Despite her growing reputation as a lead actress in the theater, in films Parker was often relegated to supporting roles—when she was cast at all. (In the film version of *Prelude to a Kiss*, for example, the role of Rita went to Meg Ryan. Devin Gordon offered the theory that Parker is "too good an actress" for films. "She utterly vanishes in her roles; movie stars do not.") Parker's movie work in the 1990s included roles in *Grand Canyon* (1991); *Naked in New York* and *Mr. Wonderful* (both 1993); the made-for-television movies *A Place for Annie* and *Sugartime* (1994 and 1995, respectively); *The Portrait of a Lady* (1996); *The Maker* and *Murder in Mind* (both 1997); *Goodbye Lover* and the television movies *Legalese* and *Saint Maybe* (all 1998); and *The Five Senses*, *Let the Devil Wear Black*, and the television movie *The Simple Life of Noah Dearborn* (all 1999). Parker did receive special notice for some of her roles, most notably her portrayal of a southern belle turned café owner in *Fried Green Tomatoes* (1991), a trailer-park mother in *The Client* (1994), a playwright's neglected girlfriend in *Bullets Over Broadway* (1994), a deaf paraplegic in *Reckless* (1995), and an AIDS-stricken career woman in *Boys on the Side* (1995). "Honestly, as long as I like the writing, I'll do anything," she told Steve Hedgpeth for the Spokane, Washington, *Spokesman Review* (August 9, 2004). "I have no snob appeal."

Although good writing (and financial necessity) prompted Parker to work in a variety of media, she continued to prefer theater acting, which, in contrast to film and TV projects, is "never completely complete," as she explained to Sylviane Gold. "It can always be improved upon." In 1996 she starred in a Broadway revival of the play *Bus Stop*, reprising the role made famous by Marilyn Monroe in the 1956 film version. Parker's performance, and the production as a whole, drew largely positive notices from critics. David Patrick Stearns wrote for *USA Today* (February 26, 1996) that Parker "captures the fun and poignancy of the dizzy, drifting Cherie" and "makes the role of the randy, tone-deaf nightclub singer completely her own." She next appeared in Paula Vogel's Pulitzer Prize–winning *How I Learned to Drive* and garnered rave reviews for her performance in what William K. Gale described in the *Providence (Rhode Island) Journal-Bulletin* (March 27, 1997) as "a very funny, very loving piece about pedophilia, about an uncle and his niece caught in a dance neither can control." As the action in the play moves back and forth through time, Parker faced the daunting task of portraying her character at ages ranging from 11 to 35. "In a stunning performance, she skips from teenage temptress to girl filled with confusion and trepidation," Gale enthused. "Parker's great good looks don't change in this role; her acting simply takes her from a beauty to scared doe and back again in a microsecond." Mark Brokaw, who directed the production, was equally impressed with his leading actress: "She seemed to possess some sort of crystalline empathy—not just with the character but with the audience," he told Adam Green for *Vanity Fair* (October 2004). "It was as if she gave off light. I have never seen anything like it."

After a brief (but highly praised) stint playing a time-traveling prostitute in the Off-Broadway comedy *Communicating Doors* (1998), Parker won acclaim for her Broadway performance in David Auburn's Pulitzer Prize–winning play *Proof*. In it she played Catherine, the daughter of a brilliant mathematician who suffers from dementia. The eccentric Catherine has inherited some of her father's mathematical skills and worries that she may have inherited the dementia, too. In the *Boston Globe* (November 12, 2000), Patti Hartigan wrote that the actress's "exhilarating performance" was "matched by an impressive supporting cast and an intelligent script" and praised Parker's "aura of fierce vulnerability." Robert Trussell wrote for the *Kansas City Star* (July 8, 2001), "Parker employs no hyperbole, no mugging. Instead, she plays the part with a directness that makes the other competent actors on stage seem phony. It's a revelation and nothing short of inspiring." *Proof* swept the Tony Awards, earning six nominations and winning three awards, including a best-leading-actress statuette for Parker.

After playing Catherine in *Proof* from May 2000 through September 2001, Parker returned to films and television. She appeared in the TV movies *Cupid & Cate* (2000), *Master Spy: The Robert Hanssen Story* (2002), *Miracle Run* (2004), and *Vinegar Hill* (2005) and the feature films *Pipe Dream*, *The Quality of Mercy*, and *Red Dragon* (all 2002), *The Best Thief in the World* and *Saved!* (both 2004), and *Romance and Cigarettes* (2005). Through an unusual series of events, Parker also wound up with a recurring guest role on the TV political drama series *The West Wing*. The series' creator, Aaron Sorkin, wrote a part specifically for Parker after she left a message telling him of her admiration for the show. Parker played the fiercely intelligent, willful Amy Gardner, a political activist and the love interest of White House deputy chief of staff Josh Lyman

(played by Bradley Whitford). Although the initial plan was for Parker to appear in only one episode, she made an immediate impression on Sorkin and Whitford. Sorkin recalled to Devin Gordon that Whitford "came running up to me, saying, 'I love her! I love her! Can we keep her?' And I said, 'Well, OK, if you promise to walk her and feed her and everything.'" Sorkin promptly wrote Parker's character into more episodes, and the actress received a 2002 Emmy Award nomination for outstanding supporting actress in a drama series. Her work on the series was interrupted in 2003, when it became difficult to conceal her pregnancy, which did not fit the show's plot. (She made additional appearances on *The West Wing* in 2005.)

When Parker's agent and manager told her that the director Mike Nichols was casting an HBO miniseries based on *Angels in America*, Tony Kushner's award-winning drama about the AIDS crisis in the 1980s, she trained her sights on the character Harper Pitt. Based on her experiences with *Prelude to a Kiss* and *Proof* (the film version of which would star Gwyneth Paltrow), Parker assumed that she had little chance of being cast in the televised version of *Angels in America*; she nonetheless auditioned for Nichols, and to her considerable surprise, she landed the role she wanted: that of a sexually deprived, self-medicating, occasionally hallucinatory Mormon wife of a closeted gay man. "Playing Harper was one of the best experiences I've ever had. I wanted to keep doing it forever," she told Brad Goldfarb for *Interview* (December 1, 2003), and she said to Steve Hedgpeth, "I've never been that proud to be in anything, and probably never will again." Both Parker and the miniseries as a whole drew rave reviews from critics and viewers; the production and those involved with it also collected five 2004 Golden Globe Awards (including one for Parker for best actress in a supporting role in a series, miniseries, or television movie), and 11 Emmy Awards (among them the award for best supporting actress in a miniseries or movie, which went to Parker).

In 2004 Parker appeared in a Broadway revival of the play *Reckless*, in which she played the role of Rachel, a naïve housewife with a contract on her life (rather than Pooty, the wheelchair-bound deaf woman she had played in the 1995 film version). Most recently, she was cast in a leading role in *Weeds*, a sitcom on the Showtime cable network. Created by Jenji Kohan, *Weeds* tells the story of Nancy Botwin, a recently widowed mother who turns to dealing marijuana in order to support her family in the lifestyle to which they are accustomed. The darkly comedic suburban satire finished its first season to largely positive reviews and was renewed for a second season. Parker in particular came in for praise. John Leonard wrote about the show for *New York* (August 15, 2005), "Despite the jokes about . . . a stolen goat, a hungry mountain lion, sex online and in saunas, a nanny-cam in the teddy bear and marijuana in the sponge cake, *Weeds* moves steadily toward the daunting and ambiguous, where laughter in the dark is a gag reflex. In a drug-deal drive-by, Mary-Louise actually gets shot at, and the funny face she makes while trying to pretend it didn't happen, that it isn't even imaginable, broke all the hearts in my house." Parker's work on *Weeds* won her a Golden Globe Award for best performance by an actress in a television series, musical or comedy. She will next co-star with Brad Pitt in the film "The Assassination of Jesse James by the Coward Robert Ford," due for release in 2007.

From her seven-year relationship with the actor Billy Crudup, which ended in late 2003, Parker has a son, William Atticus, born on January 7, 2004. In her spare time she enjoys watercolor painting, knitting, and writing poetry.

—K.J.E.

Suggested Reading: Internet Movie Database; (London) *Sunday Times* p14 Apr. 20, 2003; *New York Times* p5 July 13, 1997, p1 Oct. 8, 2000; *Newsweek* p66 Oct. 7, 2002; *People* p73+ Aug. 21, 2006; (Syracuse, New York) *Post-Standard* Jan. 23, 1992

Selected Films: *Signs of Life*, 1989; *Longtime Companion*, 1990; *Grand Canyon*, 1991; *Fried Green Tomatoes*, 1991; *Naked in New York*, 1993; *Mr. Wonderful*, 1993; *The Client*, 1994; *Bullets Over Broadway*, 1994; *Reckless*, 1995; *Boys on the Side*, 1995; *The Portrait of a Lady*, 1996; *The Maker*, 1997; *Murder in Mind*, 1997; *Goodbye Lover*, 1998; *The Five Senses*, 1999; *Let the Devil Wear Black*, 1999; *Pipe Dream*, 2002; *The Quality of Mercy*, 2002; *Red Dragon*, 2002; *The Best Thief in the World*, 2004; *Saved!*, 2004; *Romance and Cigarettes*, 2005

Selected Television Shows and Films: *Too Young the Hero*, 1988; *A Place for Annie*, 1994; *Sugartime*, 1995; *Legalese*, 1998; *Saint Maybe*, 1998; *The Simple Life of Noah Dearborn*, 1999; *Cupid & Cate*, 2000; *The West Wing*, 2001-03, 2005; *Master Spy: The Robert Hanssen Story*, 2002; *Angels in America*, 2003; *Miracle Run*, 2004; *Vinegar Hill*, 2005; *Weeds*, 2005–

Selected Plays: *The Miser*, 1987; *The Art of Success*, 1989; *Prelude to a Kiss*, 1990; *Four Dogs and a Bone*, 1993; *Bus Stop*, 1996; *How I Learned to Drive*, 1997; *Communicating Doors*, 1998; *Proof*, 2000; *Reckless*, 2004

Pennington, Ty

Oct. 19, 1965– Television host; carpenter; designer

Address: c/o Lock and Key Productions, 1149 S. Gower St., Suite 10, Los Angeles, CA 90038

Ty Pennington first came to national attention in 2000 as the handsome handyman with a sense of humor and washboard abs on the Learning Channel series *Trading Spaces*. In December 2003 he began hosting his own reality program, *Extreme Makeover: Home Edition*. On that program Pennington and his team—which includes a slew of contractors, designers, and laborers—completely remodel or rebuild houses for such worthy beneficiaries as a family of orphans and a deaf couple with an autistic child. "It's tempting to dismiss [*Extreme Makeover: Home Edition*] as treacle—*Habitat for Humanity: The Series*—but with Pennington as megaphone-toting cheerleader the show has achieved a kind of delirious grandeur," Bryan Curtis wrote for *Slate* (March 9, 2005, on-line).

Ty Pennington was born on October 19, 1965 in Atlanta, Georgia. Some sources list his full name as Gary Tygert Pennington, others as Tygert Burton Pennington. (He has confirmed in various interviews that Ty is short for Tygert, which is also his father's name.) "I've always been building or breaking something," Pennington told Lori Lundquist for *Channel Guide Magazine* (on-line). "I

Carlo Allegri/Getty Images

should have been born wearing a helmet." His mother, Yvonne, is a psychologist. "I was like her guinea pig the entire [time] she was in college," Pennington told Lundquist. "I was a really hyperactive child back in the day when they didn't have meds for that. They just put you on Benadryl [an allergy medication], which made you drowsy, and hoped that would calm you down." (Pennington is currently a spokesperson for Adderall-XR, a prescription drug used to treat attention deficit/hyperactivity disorder, more commonly referred to as ADHD.) Pennington expended some of his extra energy playing soccer, surfing, and skateboarding.

Pennington, according to most sources, attended a variety of schools in Georgia, including Kennesaw State University, the Atlanta Art Institute, and the Atlanta College of Art. He funded his studies by working as a carpenter, a skill he had learned from his father. During one of Pennington's final semesters at school, a modeling scout noticed his muscular good looks. He began appearing in ads for J. Crew, Swatch, Land's End, Diet Coke, and Levi's, among other companies, as well as in a music video for the country song "I'm Gone," by Cyndi Thompson. Pennington was also involved in the 1995 film *Leaving Las Vegas*— behind the scenes as a set painter.

In 2000 Pennington was hired as a carpenter for the Learning Channel's reality show *Trading Spaces*, an Americanized version of the popular British series *Changing Rooms*. For each episode of the show, two pairs of friends or neighbors swapped houses for two days; working with a designer, a carpenter (either Pennington or the show's other on-air woodworker, Amy Wynn Pastor), and a budget of $1,000, each pair redecorated a room. The newly redecorated rooms were revealed to their owners, who were sometimes delighted and sometimes mortified, at the end of the episode. Pennington became an immediate favorite with viewers, both for his charismatic personality and his sex appeal, which was on frequent display because of his penchant for stripping off his shirt when he got too warm. Pennington became the subject of several on-line fan sites and received several thousand pieces of viewer mail a week. Some critics, however, questioned whether he and the many attractive imitators he spawned on similar shows were truly qualified workmen or were simply sex symbols in tool belts. "Gone are bearded, thoughtful men in plaid shirts [as exemplified by Bob Vila and Norm Abram of the long-running PBS series *This Old House*]. Now it's all about sexy nail-gun-wielding handyman hunks and, in the newest trend, hunkettes," Ann Oldenburg wrote for *USA Today* (October 15, 2004). "It's as if the pages of a bodice-ripping romance have come to life." Pennington, who was named one of the 50 Top Bachelors of 2002 by the editors of *People*, has expressed surprise at his status as a pinup; he told Elizabeth Rhodes for the *Miami Herald* (November 23, 2003), "I've always been the class clown. I guess I find it hard to believe that people look at me the other way." Pennington found occasional aspects of his new fame irritating: he disliked, for example, when fans lurked around his work sites and filched construction materials. "They actually steal . . . pieces of wood that I need—as souve-

nirs," he told Amber Nimrock for the *Chicago Tribune* (April 30, 2004). Additionally, he has said, according to Bryan Curtis, "If I hear the words 'hunky handyman' one more time, I will freak."

Initially Pennington, who had studied graphic design, painting, and sculpting while in school, contributed numerous project ideas to *Trading Spaces*. "There was a bunch of stuff I was doing at home that I wanted to put on the show," he recalled to Nina Metz for the *Chicago Tribune* (December 7, 2003). "But I realized I was giving my ideas away and I wasn't getting paid for it. . . . I didn't catch on to that game till three years into it, and I [thought], 'Oh, anything I put on the show [the producers] own. . . .' But there's tons of stuff nobody even knows that I know. They just think of me as the carpenter." Pennington, however, had also proven himself a savvy businessman and a creative designer; he had by that time renovated a downtown Atlanta warehouse into seven loft apartments (making a healthy return on his investment) and founded a company, Furniture Unlimited, which sold his own innovative designs. He was also a budding author. In 2003 Pennington published *Ty's Tricks: Home Repair Secrets Plus Cheap and Easy Projects to Transform Any Room*, a book that included a chapter titled "How I Built a Champagne House on a Beer Budget," detailing how he had remodeled his own Atlanta home for a mere $10,000 by fashioning light fixtures from toilet plungers and creating a sink out of a metal salad bowl, among other creative cost-cutting measures. The book also featured decorating advice, repair tips, and numerous photos—including one of Pennington in the shower. His nationwide book tour attracted thousands of fans, most of them female, and the book landed on the *New York Times* best-seller list.

Pennington appeared for four seasons on *Trading Spaces*. In December 2003 he became the host of his own show, *Extreme Makeover: Home Edition*, which premiered on the ABC network. During each episode of the new series, Pennington and his team remodel, expand, or even demolish and completely rebuild the homes of deserving individuals, who are sent on luxury vacations while the work is being done. "You could dismiss all this as a mere exercise in . . . tear-jerking do-goodism, and on one level it is: the families chosen have heartbreaking back stories, and the only element more common than children with disabilities are scenes in which grown men cry," Rob Walker wrote for the *New York Times* (December 4, 2005, on-line). "On the other hand, there is often a social component— these are American families who are stuck in tough neighborhoods, whose children die in Iraq, who have no health care, who are swindled by contractors or who are so close to the edge that a lost job is a financial catastrophe. Episodes last year featured a Hispanic family who lost a mother to a stray bullet and a young African-American man in South Central Los Angeles crippled in a mistaken gang hit. . . . These are, in other words, the American families who do not exist in the world of more traditional TV hits." Those subjects who are disabled sometimes require special or expensive equipment in their newly remodeled houses. In one episode, for example, the team added such high-tech aids as flashing-light smoke detectors and Braille wall labels for a family that included two deaf parents and a blind, autistic son. The 2004 season finale involved the complete rebuilding of a home for eight siblings whose parents had both recently died. "As astounding as the construction miracles are, the rebuilding of people's hopes and dreams are even more impressive," Bill Brioux wrote for the *Toronto Sun* (May 30, 2004).

One problem with the show's formula, however, which Anthony DeBarros pointed out in an article for *USA Today* (October 15, 2004), is that upon completion of the renovations, property taxes increase dramatically, with potentially devastating financial consequences for the recipients of *Extreme Makeover*'s largesse. David Goldberg, a producer of the show, explained to DeBarros, "We're very upfront with the families in telling them that there's a likelihood that the value of the house will increase, and therefore there will be a resulting property tax increase. . . . But we see that as a worthwhile tradeoff for receiving a new home, and I can't tell you how many letters I've received from families saying, 'You changed my life.'"

In 2004 Pennington signed a lucrative, multi-year deal with Sears, Roebuck and Co. to act as a spokesman and product developer. The retailer now carries numerous products, including bedding, dishes, flatware, glassware, bath accessories, lamps, and decorative pillows marketed under Pennington's name. A 2006 study conducted by the market research firm NPD Group found Pennington to be the celebrity with the greatest influence on consumers' purchasing decisions. "More than a third of people who knew of him said his endorsement would help sell them a product," Alex Mindlin reported for the *New York Times* (May 8, 2006).

When not hosting *Extreme Makeover: Home Edition*, designing products and appearing in ads for Sears, or creating new items for his Furniture Unlimited line, Pennington enjoys painting and sculpting. He also plays the guitar and sings in a duo called Thick and Vainy, whose CD is available on his official Web site, tythehandyguy.com. In a separate, solo musical project, Pennington told *People* (November 29, 2004), "I wear a [white leisure] suit full of Christmas lights and perform a combination of reggae, country and hip-hop." He also acts occasionally, taking a bit part as the legendary aviation pioneer Wilbur Wright in the children's film *The Adventures of Ociee Nash* (2003) and appearing in an episode of the Lifetime network series *Wild Card* in 2004. Additionally, he appeared on five installments of the television game show *Hollywood Squares* in 2003.

Pennington currently lives in Venice, California, where he has purchased a home for a reported $1.1 million. "When my 15 minutes of fame is over, I hope to retire to a little shop somewhere and just make paintings and sculptures," he told *People*.

—K.J.E.

Suggested Reading: *Channel Guide Magazine* (on-line); *Chicago Tribune* p1 Dec. 7, 2003, p20 Apr. 30, 2004; *Dallas Morning News* G p4 Nov. 14, 2003; *Miami Herald* HS p15 Nov. 23, 2003; *New York Times* (on-line) Dec. 4, 2005; *People* p113 Nov. 29, 2004; *Slate* (on-line) Mar. 9, 2005; *Time* p159 Dec. 20, 2004; *Toronto Sun* TV p2 May 30, 2004; tythehandyguy.com; *USA Today* E p10 Oct. 15, 2004

Selected Television Shows: *Trading Spaces*, 2000–04; *Extreme Makeover: Home Edition*, 2003–

Selected Books: *Ty's Tricks: Home Repair Secrets Plus Cheap and Easy Projects to Transform Any Room*, 2003

Selected Films: *The Adventures of Ociee Nash*, 2003

Pevear, Richard and Volokhonsky, Larissa

Translators

Pevear, Richard
Apr. 21, 1943–

Volokhonsky, Larissa
1946–

Address: c/o Vintage Publicity, 1745 Broadway, New York, NY 10019

Russian literature indisputably had its golden age during the 19th century, when such masters as Leo Tolstoy, Fyodor Dostoyevsky, and Anton Chekhov created their rich and vibrant characters. The theme of adultery in Tolstoy's *Anna Karenina*, the tragedy and comedy in Dostoyevsky's *The Brothers Karamazov*, and the exploration of the human condition in Chekhov's short stories were introduced to the English-speaking world in the early part of the 20th century by the British translator Constance Garnett. Few disputed Garnett's technical accuracy or the fidelity to literal meaning in her translations of Russian texts, and she was held for the better part of the 20th century to be the preeminent authority on Russian-to-English translations, even though she worked at such a feverish pace that much of the flavor of the original works was,

PEVEAR and VOLOKHONSKY

Courtesy of the American University of Paris

Richard Pevear

in the opinion of some, lost in translation. Nearly 90 years after Garnett had begun translating the great literary works of Russia, Richard Pevear, an American, and the Russian-born Larissa Volokhonsky teamed up to offer new English-language versions of those books, which have since been widely recognized as definitive, particularly in the cases of novels by Dostoyevsky and Tolstoy. Pevear and Volokhonsky, who have been married for 22 years, have surpassed Garnett in their ability to keep intact the cultural colorings and stylistic nuances of the Russian authors. "We're sort of an ideal bilingual translator," Volokhonsky told Lisa Simeone for the National Public Radio program *All Things Considered* (March 11, 2001). "We're also married to each other, so we live together. And when we translate, we live together with the author in a way, eat with him, and drink with him, and go for a walk with him. We can discuss it all the time."

Richard Pevear was born in Waltham, Massachusetts, on April 21, 1943, and Larissa Volokhonsky was born three years later in Leningrad (now St. Petersburg), Russia, then part of the Soviet Union. Little has been made public about Pevear's early life. Volokhonsky shared a literary sensibility with her brother Henri, a poet who was a rival of the renowned Russian poet Joseph Brodsky. While still living in Russia, Volokhonsky learned English and attended translation seminars. She eventually translated for publication a story by the celebrated American writer John Updike from a smuggled copy of the *New Yorker*. In 1973 Volokhonsky immigrated to the U.S. and soon translated "Introduction to Patristic Theology," by John Meyendorff, a Russian Orthodox priest and thinker. Pevear and Volokhonsky met in the early 1970s, when

Volokhonsky first visited the U.S. and read Pevear's article in the *Hudson Review* about the Soviet dissident author Andrei Sinyavsky. "Larissa had just helped Sinyavsky leave Russia," Pevear told Alex Abramovich for *Newsday* (August 1, 2004). "And she let me know that, while I'd said he was still in prison, he was actually in Paris. I was glad to know it." The two married in the early 1980s and made their home on the Upper West Side of Manhattan, in New York City. Pevear, who had earned a B.A. degree from Allegheny College, in Meadville, Pennsylvania, and an M.A. degree from the University of Virginia, made ends meet mainly by making custom furniture; he supplemented his income by cutting roses in commercial greenhouses, publishing verse in such literary journals as the *Hudson Review*, and translating works from French, Italian, and Spanish.

One day in the mid-1980s, Pevear began reading an English translation of *The Brothers Karamazov*. Volokhonsky, who had read the classic in Russian many times, saw the translation Pevear was reading and was aghast at its faithlessness toward the original. Pevear and Volokhonsky decided to combine their skills in their respective native tongues and experiment with their own English translation of *The Brothers Karamazov*. Focusing their efforts on three chapters, they hoped to produce a version of the narrative that did not mute the stylistic repetition, purposeful awkwardness, and melodrama that are of a piece with, and inseparable from, Dostoyevsky's unique voice. Volokhonsky began by writing a highly detailed, literal, interlinear translation of the original, complete with annotations concerning style, syntax, and diction. "I try to be very literal, sometimes even to the point of distorting the English sentences, so that Richard knows what is happening in the Russian text. I also sometimes indicate stylistic points—say, if an archaic word is used, or if there is some slang or a wrong word, especially in dialogue," Volokhonsky told Mikhail Ivanov in an interview for *Russian Life* (August 31, 2001). Pevear then used Volokhonsky's translations and notes to produce a more fluid English text. "There is also . . . a poetic quality for translating texts, because you are dealing with it not the way a novelist deals with big materials. . . . He has to compose the quality, he has to create characters, whereas the translator is concerned with the words with which it has already been done," Pevear told Ivanov. "[Translating] is much closer to mimicking the sounds of words . . . much closer to a kind of poetic writing than to novel writing." Throughout the process the two reached joint conclusions about how much flexibility Dostoyevsky would have approved in a translation. As the final step in the process, Pevear read the new English version aloud while Volokhonsky followed along in the original Russian. After completing the three chapters of the work, Pevear and Volokhonsky sent copies to a number of publishers, including Random House, Oxford University Press, Holt, Harcourt Brace, and Farrar, Straus & Giroux.

For decades Constance Garnett had been known as the leading English-language interpreter of Russian literature, having translated 70 volumes for commercial publication during her career. But a number of Russian writers, most famously Vladimir Nabokov, had criticized Garnett's efforts, complaining that her impressive productivity came at the cost of the books' literary integrity. As quoted by David Remnick in the *New Yorker* (November 7, 2005), Nabokov called Garnett's translation of *Anna Karenina* "a complete disaster." Joseph Brodsky once said, as quoted by Remnick, "The reason English-speaking readers can barely tell the difference between Tolstoy and Dostoyevsky is that they aren't reading the prose of either one. They're reading Constance Garnett." Pevear explained to Remnick that the American literary giant Ernest Hemingway "read Garnett's Dostoyevsky and . . . said it influenced him. But Hemingway was just as influenced by Constance Garnett as he was by Fyodor Dostoyevsky. Garnett breaks things into simple sentences, she Hemingwayizes Dostoyevsky, if you see what I mean." Nevertheless, Garnett still had major standing in the English-speaking world. After reading Pevear and Volokhonsky's translation of chapters from *The Brothers Karamazov*, an editor at Random House wrote the couple a note that read, as Pevear recalled to Remnick, "No, thanks. Garnett lives forever. Why do we need a new one?" Of all the publishers to whom Pevear and Volokhonsky sent their translation, only Jack Shoemaker of North Point Press (which is no longer in operation) called to make the couple an offer.

In 1988 the couple illegally moved to Paris, France, on tourist visas, with the notion that their $6,000 advance from the publisher and Pevear's $36,000 grant from the government-sponsored National Endowment for the Humanities would stretch further in France than in New York City. Working in their small Paris apartment, adhering to the process they had developed earlier, the couple sought to translate the "true" Dostoyevsky and not create their own version of his work. "Dostoyevsky's roughness, despite the rush and the pressure, was all deliberate. No matter what the deadline, if he didn't like what he had, he would throw it all out and start again. So this so-called clumsiness is seen in his drafts, the way he works on it. It's deliberate. His narrator is not him; it's always a bad provincial writer who has an unpolished quality but is deeply expressive. . . . He stumbles. It's all over the place . . . ," Pevear told Remnick. "Other translators smooth it out. We don't." In order to maintain the tone of the original work, the couple were careful not to use English words that, according to the *Oxford English Dictionary*, came into use after the publication of the novel—a standard they continue to use for all other projects as well. "These changes [from Garnett's version] seem small, but they are essential. They accumulate," Pevear told Remnick. "It's like a musical composition and a musician, an interpreta-

tion. If your fingers are too heavy or too light, the piece can be distorted." Volokhonsky added, "It can also be compared to restoring a painting. You can't overdo it, but you have to be true to the thing."

Pevear and Volokhonsky's translation of *The Brothers Karamazov* was published in February 1990 to modest sales but rave reviews. Donald Fanger wrote in an assessment for the *Washington Post* (November 11, 1990), "I suspect, and Pevear and Volokhonsky clearly do too, that individual words and phrases matter a great deal, producing a cumulative effect at least subliminally. For that reason, their scrupulous rendition can only be welcomed. In it, the movement of the novel becomes a little less febrile. Theirs is an adagio reading, distinctive and fresh, that returns to us a work we thought we knew, subtly altered and so made new again." Andrei Navrozov wrote for the *New York Times* (November 11, 1990), "Until the arrival of new translators like Mr. Pevear and Ms. Volokhonsky on the scene, readers of the English versions were in the position of Dostoyevsky's misled contemporaries of a century ago. By restricting the freedom of his genius within an interpretive straitjacket of what they think is good prose, their literary guides, rarely Russian by birth, had transgressed the . . . genuineness." Navrozov went on to write, "It is indeed astonishing that such a necessary effort—as has been made by Mr. Pevear and Ms. Volokhonsky—to correct (without quotation marks) an approach so obviously defective, and one that has brought about a misunderstanding so vast, should have been so late in coming. It is more astonishing still that any such effort should require justification in the first place, or that a grant from the National Endowment for the Humanities and a small press—rather than a major publishing house—should make it possible." In 1991 the Pevear-Volokhonsky translation of *The Brothers Karamazov* won the prestigious PEN/Book of the Month Club prize for translation.

After the success of *The Brothers Karamazov*, the couple began translating novels and short stories by other Russian writers, including Mikhail Bulgakov, Chekhov, and, most notably, Leo Tolstoy, employing the process that had worked so well with Dostoyevsky's novel. In the 1990s Pevear and Volokhonsky took on Tolstoy's *Anna Karenina*—the celebrated, tragic novel of 19th-century aristocratic Russia, in which the title character finds herself trapped in a loveless marriage and grapples with the guilt of her adulterous affair. Translating the novel proved to be a challenge for the couple, as Tolstoy's voice was difficult to capture. "Tolstoy's style is the least interesting thing about him, though it is very peculiar," Pevear told Remnick. "It seems like most, translators included, are insensible to the crudeness of Tolstoy's style, but Tolstoy liked to be crude, he was crude provocatively. *Anna Karenina* is interesting very often for how the prose is deliberately not smooth or fine. Nabokov apologizes for Tolstoy's bad writing. But

Tolstoy himself said the point is to get the thing said and then, if he wasn't sure he had said it, he would say it again and again." After a couple of years of extensive contact with editors at the publishing company Penguin, the translation was published in the United Kingdom in 2000 and in the U.S. the following year.

Pevear and Volokhonsky's interpretation of *Anna Karenina*, the first English version in 40 years, won the 2002 PEN/Book of the Month Club prize and was unanimously praised by critics. James McQuillen wrote for the *Oregonian* (February 25, 2001) that Pevear and Volokhonsky "combine a profound knowledge of the language with clear and vivid prose, and they bring Tolstoy, whom Vladimir Nabokov called 'the greatest Russian writer of prose fiction,' back to life." He added, "A literal English rendering of Russian would be unreadable, however illuminating to linguists: A scholar may want to explore the chasms of difference between original text and translation, but most of us just want a straight and steady bridge to get across. Pevear and Volokhonsky have given us one that is not just straight and steady, but beautifully engineered as well." Ironically, in light of that comment, Pevear wrote in an article for the *Times Higher Education Supplement* (December 15, 2000) that he and Volokhonsky "have no interest in putting *Anna Karenina* into contemporary 'reader-friendly' English. . . . Our only aim as translators has been to bring into English as much as possible of this 19th-century novel, meaning also its rhythms, tone and temperament."

Pevear and Volokhonsky's translation of Tolstoy's novel gained mass exposure on May 31, 2004, when the talk-show host Oprah Winfrey picked it for her book club, whose members number in the hundreds of thousands. At the time neither Pevear nor Volokhonsky knew who Winfrey was or comprehended how the development would affect their lives. (Pevear thought perhaps Winfrey was a country singer.) Executives at Penguin, however, grasped the significance of the event and decided to print an additional 800,000 copies of the translation in one month, in the hope of meeting the demand created by Winfrey. "I didn't understand what it could possibly mean. We're glad if we sell 20,000 copies of a book in a year," Volokhonsky told Edward Wyatt for the *New York Times* (June 7, 2004). Indeed, since its publication the Pevear-Volokhonsky translation of *Anna Karenina* had sold a respectable 60,000 copies over the course of three years. After Winfrey announced her choice of the book, sales instantly skyrocketed, and by the end of the day on May 31, the book held the number-one spot on Amazon.com, where just hours before it had ranked at number 26,206. When Remnick asked the couple what the "Oprah moment" meant for them, Pevear responded, "It means I have an accountant." In June 2006 the European University in St. Petersburg, Russia, honored Pevear and Volokhonsky with the first Efim Etkind Translation Prize, for

their translation of Dostoevsky's *The Idiot*. Pevear's solo translation of Alexandre Dumas's novel *The Three Musketeers* was published soon afterward.

Pevear and Volokhonsky are currently working on perhaps the most challenging translation of their 20-year collaboration: Tolstoy's epic novel *War and Peace*. At the end of 2005, Volokhonsky was about two-thirds of the way through her preliminary translation, and Pevear was approximately 600 pages into his. "There is a real challenge in *War and Peace*, a vast amount of historical detail," Pevear told Remnick. "The novel has five hundred historical figures and fictional figures, so we have to write commentaries for the historical ones, which are the vast majority. In the battle scenes, we have to come up with the words for particular kinds of guns and cannons, for military tactics. There is a huge hunting scene, so we have to find very particular words for the wolves, the foxes, the kinds of dogs. . . . Tolstoy knew all this as second nature." Publication of the translation is slated for the fall of 2007.

Since 1998 Pevear has been an adjunct professor of comparative literature at the American University of Paris. Pevear and Volokhonsky divide their time between their homes in Paris and Burgundy, in France. They have two children, both of whom are trilingual.

—I.C.

Suggested Reading: *New York Times* E p1 June 7, 2004; *New Yorker* p98+ Nov. 7, 2005; *Newsday* C p32 Aug. 1, 2004; *Russian Life* p40+ Aug. 31, 2001

Selected Translations: as a team—*The Brothers Karamazov*, 1990; *Crime and Punishment*, 1993; *Notes from the Underground*, 1994; *Demons*, 1995; *The Eternal Husband and Other Stories*, 1997; *The Collected Tales of Nikolai Gogol*, 1998; *Stories of Anton Chekhov*, 2000; *Anna Karenina*, 2001; *The Idiot*, 2002; *The Adolescent*, 2003; *Anton Chekhov: The Complete Short Novels*, 2004; *Dead Souls*, 2004; *The Double and the Gambler*, 2005; by Pevear alone—*The Three Musketeers*, 2006

Posen, Zac

Oct. 24, 1980– Fashion designer

Address: Outspoke, 1317 Laight St., New York, NY 10013

"I am trying to provide classics for the future, clothes that offer eternal, timeless femininity," the fashion designer Zac Posen told a reporter for *InStyle* (December 2003). "To make a woman look glamorous, you must pay obsessive attention to de-

Paul Hawthorne/Getty Images

Zac Posen

Cathy Horyn, writing for the *New York Times* (February 22, 2004), "Success in fashion is one part talent, one part luck and one part a tireless ability to hold a gaudy marquee over your head. Posen has all these qualities in excess." She added, "The most important thing that Posen has going for him is his talent."

The younger of the two children of Stephen Posen and Susan Posen, Zachary Posen was born on October 24, 1980 in New York City. His sister, Alexandra, who is about seven years his senior, is a fine artist, as is his father; the Guggenheim Museum and the Virginia Museum of Fine Art, among other places, have works by Stephen Posen in their permanent collections. Posen's mother worked as a corporate lawyer for more than two decades; she also founded a venture-capital firm that invested in businesses owned by women. Raised in the SoHo section of Manhattan, Zac Posen was regularly exposed to artists and designers and their creations virtually from birth. His fascination with fashion dates back nearly as far. As a preschooler he would dress dolls in clothes that he made from scraps of fabric that his father had left lying around the family loft, as well as from such unusual materials as seaweed, rock candy, and aluminum foil. He discovered that yarmulkes (stolen from the synagogue his family attended) were perfect for converting into miniature bell-shaped frocks. His enjoyment of such pursuits set him apart from his peers; indeed, "it was definitely something, when you're a boy, that you're ashamed of," as he told Michelle Tauber and Rebecca Paley for *People* (September 15, 2003). His parents always encouraged him to pursue his interests, cultivate his talents, and express his individuality. Similarly, the administrators and teachers at his school—the St. Ann's School, in the New York City borough of Brooklyn, which is renowned for its strong arts curriculum—tolerated his wearing eccentric outfits, in which such accessories as a 1920s nurse's cape, second-hand muffs, and even antlers were parts of the ensembles. "My entire life I've dressed in couture for the people," Posen remarked to Eva Friede for the Montreal, Canada, *Gazette* (February 26, 2002). His accomplishments in high school in the visual arts included creating a robe for the character Prospero for a student production of Shakespeare's play *The Tempest*. The robe, constructed from a huge piece of fabric, doubled as part of the set. According to an article in the news archive of *Vogue.com*, as a youngster he was afflicted with attention-deficit disorder. Although he is dyslexic, and thus had difficulty with reading and writing, he excelled in math.

While he was in high school, Posen took precollege summer courses in fashion at the Parsons School of Design, in Manhattan (an arm of the New School, a university). He also landed an internship at the Costume Institute of the Metropolitan Museum of Art, also in Manhattan, under the tutelage of its curator, Richard Martin, whose knowledge of art and fashion history and popular culture was

tail, love construction, and be obsessed with history, because by absorbing the knowledge and the rules of your predecessors, and adapting them to how modern women live, you can treat sophistication in a cool new way. The fun part is, the shopper doesn't need to know any of this. She just has to feel wonderful when she wears it." In the seven years since he started his first business, when he was 18, Posen has become one of the most recognized designers in fashion—a feat few ever accomplish in an industry that is notoriously competitive and even cutthroat. In 2002 Posen launched his own label, Outspoke, with his mother as chief executive officer and his sister as creative director. The few catwalk shows that he has so far produced attracted Hollywood celebrities as well as fashion's most influential critics. "The Zac Posen world is not just about the young starlet," he told Maureen Jenkins for the *Chicago Sun-Times* (April 21, 2005). "Beyond just taking clothing or expanding to designing furniture, it's really about expanding the world of taste and refining it." Famous for his bias-cut retro gowns, Posen has been nominated three times (2002, 2003, and 2004) for the Perry Ellis Award for Emerging Talent, and he was named among *Crain's New York Business* "40 under 40" in 2004. One of his creations is in the permanent collection of the Victoria and Albert Museum, in London, England. "I don't believe in one ideal beauty," he has said, as quoted by Tresanna Hassanally in the on-line magazine *Hilary* in late 2003. "You have to reinterpret what you do based on whether the body belongs to a real woman who is 5-foot-2 or a model who is 6-foot-1. In its present state, fashion is killing women's body image of themselves." According to the fashion reporter legendary. In addition, he interned at the company founded by the designer Nicole Miller and served as a design assistant with the clothing firm Tocca. He benefited as well from his social connections: one of his high-school classmates, for example, was Lola Schnabel, a daughter of the noted painter and sculptor Julian Schnabel, and he became friendly with both Lola and her younger sister, Stella. When he was 15 Posen received from the 12-year-old Stella his first commission—to design a dress that would make her look nude, to wear at an event that she would be attending with the actor Christopher Walken. Posen fashioned a form-fitting dress of velvet for her that was the color of her skin.

Posen graduated from high school in 1999. Accepted for admission to Brown University, in Providence, Rhode Island, he chose instead to enroll at the prestigious Central Saint Martins College of Art and Design, in London. He split his time between attending classes and making clothing of his own design for friends. In 2001 the supermodel Naomi Campbell noticed a Posen-designed dress worn by a guest at a party in Paris, France, hosted by the designer Azzedine Alaia. After learning the name of its designer, Campbell visited Posen in London and commissioned him to design and sew a dress for her. Posen, who has said he was both surprised and flattered by her praise, produced an intricate gown in which 36 separate pieces were stitched together. Campbell, he recalled to the *InStyle* reporter, told "everybody" about his work, and his name became mentioned with increasing frequency among elite circles of the fashion world. That same year he was selected along with 10 other students from Saint Martins to create an original design for an exhibition of Victorian undergarments at the Victoria and Albert Museum. According to Naomi West, writing for the *Fashion Telegraph* Web site (October 7, 2001), Posen's piece was "made from thin vertical strips of shiny brown leather fastened together with hundreds of hand-sewn hooks," which could be "unfastened anywhere to reveal the body beneath." Posen's design remained on display for nearly a year, and the museum acquired it for its permanent collection.

Although he was performing well academically, Posen left Saint Martins in 2001, after his sophomore year, partly for financial reasons and partly because he had been lured back to New York by the possibility of devoting himself full-time to his career. An opportunity had come his way from Mark Bagutta, the owner of the chic couture boutique Bagutta, in Manhattan, who had offered him space to work above his store, along with the promise to display Posen's designs on his shop floor. "Zac has something I haven't seen for a long time," Bagutta told Naomi West. "He makes dresses that bring out everything in a woman—they are very feminine, but not too sexy." Posen made his debut on the runway in October 2001, as one of 12 participants in the annual Fresh Faces in Fashion show, organized by Gen Art, a nonprofit group that supports up-and-comers in fashion, film, music, and the visual arts.

Posen funded his first solo show in large part with the prize money he had received upon winning the Award for Young Designers from the wine company Ecco Domani. The show was held in February 2002, during New York Fashion Week, at an abandoned synagogue; in the audience were the actresses Natalie Portman and Claire Danes, both of whom are among his clients; Julian Schnabel; and Anna Wintour and André Leon Talley, the editor and the editor at large, respectively, of *Vogue*. Cathy Horyn, the *New York Times* (February 14, 2002, on-line) fashion critic, had a mixed response to the show. Comparing the designer with Isaac Mizrahi, who had "made it perfectly clear what inspired him when he first hit the scene in the late 1980's," she wrote that Posen "could only express a kind of camp couture: trousers with one leg opened to the thigh, dramatic cowl necklines of the old Claude Montana genre, long Morticia dresses with witchy collars or sleeves. Here and there was clear evidence of talent—a deep red flannel skirt coyly wrapped around the hips with an embroidered turned-down waistband that was shown with a crisp man's pinstripe shirt. . . . The fact that the clothes were all over the place, with no clear line of thought, suggested that Mr. Posen couldn't sustain a design idea long enough either to see it through completely or to scrap it altogether." Two years later, when Horyn, writing for the *New York Times* (February 22, 2004), asked André Leon Talley for his impression of the 2002 event, Talley responded, "It was a swashbuckling student show. It was disjointed and messy." Horyn also reported, however, that Talley said that the show "not only anticipated the craze among young women for flirty dresses with a slight attic quality, but it also demonstrated, even in its messiness, that Posen is driven hardest by technique." Talley later told A. Scott Walton for the *Atlanta (Georgia) Journal-Constitution* (May 15, 2004) that Posen "gained notice immediately. People stood up and took notice because of his talent." Indeed, upscale New York retailers placed orders for his garments, which ranged in price from $400 to $3,000. "All the B's are really interested," Posen told Eva Friede, referring to Barneys, Bloomingdale's, Bergdorf Goodman, and Henri Bendel. "It's wild. There's some kind of war going on. They're all trying to charm me."

Also in 2002 Posen launched his own company, Outspoke, with his mother taking on the job of CEO and his sister that of creative director. "They're feminists who love their femininity, and their style and input surround me every day," Posen told *InStyle*. "My greatest inspiration is my mother," he told Kathryn Wexler for the *Miami (Florida) Herald* (April 7, 2004). "She's a very strong woman, and my sister as well." He also told Wexler that he felt it was extremely important to produce "clothing that was fun and represented strong femininity and intelligent femininity, which was something that I thought wasn't very present in what I was seeing in fashion. I designed for every different race, every body shape—important clothing that worked on very curvaceous women as well as very petite women because I didn't think there was clothing out there that was celebratory of women and their eccentricities." In 2002 he was named a finalist in the international design competition sponsored by Enkamania, a leading manufacturer of viscose.

In his next, highly anticipated catwalk show, Posen offered a fresh take on his original style by translating his retro look into daywear. According to *Biography Resource Center Online* (2003), a fashion critic for *Vogue* wrote, "Posen displayed a collection that included more daywear than normal, proving his label is no two-season wonder, as critics had whispered. . . . Zac Posen lived up to his reputation as the coolest new designer on the New York scene." The show featured collaborations with the noted shoe designer Manolo Blahnik and music by the Grammy Award–winning musician, producer, and fashion mogul Sean "P. Diddy" Combs. During that period Combs invested an undisclosed sum in Outspoke. Posen's partnership with Combs enabled him to expand his designs into menswear and ready-to-wear. "I see Zac as someone who shares the same drive and vision that I have," Combs told Eric Wilson and Julee Greenberg for *WWD* (April 21, 2004). "I also saw an opportunity for Sean John [Combs's fashion label] to make an impact with Zac Posen by giving him the tools and resources that he needed for his business to grow and mature. He has been able to establish a real profile as an American contemporary and evening designer. He dresses amazing women, the stores love him and clearly he is a force to be contended with in the designer ready-to-wear scene."

The fruits of the partnership were displayed in the runway show in which Posen's spring 2005 collection debuted. The Hollywood stars Demi Moore, Julianne Moore, and Liv Tyler were among the celebrities in front-row seats at the show. Posen's most commented-upon pieces included a black cocktail dress with horizontal slits, a white pantsuit with golden stripes running down the length of the legs, and a green pleated skirt paired with a navy polo. The collection impressed the critic Booth Moore, who wrote for the *Los Angeles Times* (September 14, 2004), "Posen has the talent to live up to the hype." He added, "Posen was a baby designer with a few celebutante clients a mere two years ago. But this season he has hit the big time."

For his fall 2005 collection, Posen again borrowed from earlier styles, this time from the 1960s and 1980s. Given the name "Perfectionist Rebel," the collection featured plainly styled clothing sewn with lightweight fabrics; some items had umbrella sleeves, with widely scalloped borders. One of the more highly praised pieces was a tuxedo jacket made of swakara, a fur derived from very young karakul lambs. Posen's spring 2006 collec-

tion displayed what observers considered to be a more aggressive approach. A long black mohair vest, for example, and leather straps on some garments were seemingly meant to appeal to the "power personalities" among the designer's typical clients. In a review for the *New York Times* (September 16, 2006) of one of Posen's shows, Cathy Horyn noted his evolution as a designer. Observing that he is a member of a generation that looks askance at "slick clothes," she praised him for his ability to make clothing "right but not too grown-up." "Zac Posen . . . may have finally earned his right to sit at the big people's table," she wrote.

Along with his sister, Posen has hosted benefits for the organization TeachersCount. His public appearances include, in 2004, a talk presented before students of the Harvard Business School and the Harvard Graduate School of Design and service as a panelist at a program called "Keeping Ahead of the Economic Crunch: Strategies and Success Stories," sponsored in part by the Manhattan Chamber of Commerce and the Manhattan International Development Corp.

Posen's sister wore a dress of her brother's design at her wedding, in 2004. According to Rebecca Paley in the *New York Times* (July 4, 2004, online), "Seventy-two hours before the wedding, the . . . dress, with its geranium-red bodice and six-foot train, was still in pieces. Twenty company employees were summoned to complete it in time." The train consisted of deep fuchsia poppies made of organza.

In the House and Home/Style section of the *New York Times* (September 15, 2005, on-line), Elaine Louie described the rental apartment that Posen shares with his boyfriend, Brian Callahan, an interior designer, in the West Village section of Manhattan. On display were a dozen pairs of antlers, "with and without heads," as she wrote. According to Louie, in his speech Posen "favors flights of verbal fancy over straightforward talk."

—I.C.

Suggested Reading: *Biography Resource Center Online* 2003; *Fashion Telegraph* (on-line) Oct. 7, 2001; *Harper's Bazaar* p376+ Mar. 2004; *InStyle* p152+ Dec. 2003; *Interview* p52+ May 2002; *Miami Herald* E p10 Apr. 7, 2004; *New York Times* p66 Feb. 22, 2004; *People* p153+ Sep. 15, 2003; *Vogue* p117+ May 2002; zacposen.com

Giuseppe Cacace/Getty Images

Prada, Miuccia

(PRAH-duh, MEW-chee-ah)

1949– Fashion designer

Address: 2 via Andrea Maffei, Milano 20135, Italy

Under the creative direction of Miuccia Prada, the small leather-goods company founded in 1913 by Prada's grandfather has blossomed into an international conglomerate, currently boasting more than 200 stores around the globe and ringing up billions of dollars each year from sales of its accessories and clothing lines. In certain circles the Prada name has become virtually synonymous with high fashion and understated elegance. "I have a kind of complex of this work being superficial and dumb," Prada told Michael Specter for the *New Yorker* (March 15, 2004). "It's my personal drama. Not the world's. Everyone who is smart says they hate fashion, that it's such a waste of time. I have asked many super-serious people, 'Then why is fashion so popular?' Nobody can answer that question. But *somebody* must be interested, because when I go to the stores the people are there. Thousands of them. So I have grown tired of apologizing for being in this profession." In 2005 the Prada family was listed in *Forbes* as one of the world's wealthiest, with an estimated worth of $3 billion, and the editors of *Time* named Miuccia one of the most influential people of the 20th century.

Miuccia Prada was born in Milan, Italy, in 1949. (Some sources state 1950.) In 1913 her paternal grandfather, Mario, founded Fratelli Prada (Prada Brothers), a maker of luxury leather goods located in Milan's renowned Galleria Vittorio Emanuele II shopping arcade. Within five years Mario had been appointed by the Italian royal family to fashion valises, trunks, and cases from leather and such exotic skins as walrus and alligator. When Mario died, he left his business not to his son, who had expressed no interest in making leather goods, but to his daughter-in-law, Luisa, Miuccia's mother. Despite Mario's long-held opinion that women belonged at home, rather than in the workplace, he recognized Luisa as his most worthy successor.

Miuccia and her two brothers were raised in an atmosphere that she described to Susannah Frankel for the London *Independent* (February 21, 2004) as "serious. It was a serious, Catholic family. My mother liked clothes but she liked correctness more." Luisa stringently dictated what sorts of outfits her daughter could wear, and Prada's childhood wardrobe consisted primarily of conservative blue or beige pleated skirts and sensible flat shoes. "I was always frustrated, because I had to dress so seriously," she told Specter. "I was a proper young girl and I was *dreaming* of pink shoes, red shoes, pink dresses. Anything with color. Exciting underwear. Everybody had this kind of dull underwear and wore boring striped dresses. I couldn't stand it."

As a teenager Prada joined the Communist Party. "I was young in the Sixties, when Italian society was first becoming obsessed with consumerism, but my big dreams were of justice, equality and moral regeneration," she told Frankel. "I was a Communist but being left wing was fashionable then. I was no different from thousands of middle-class kids." Despite this assertion, she did stand out in one way: "I'd always loved fashion. Yves Saint Laurent was my favourite," Prada told Alice Rawsthorn for the *Financial Times* (February 11–12, 1995). "I wore his things all the time in the 1970s—even to political protests. People looked at me strangely when I handed out pamphlets in my expensive clothes." Although Prada—who sported miniskirts, maxi coats, and vintage outfits long before those items caught on with her peers—found fashion entertaining, she did not initially consider a career in the industry. Instead, she studied political science at the University of Milan, graduating in 1970. In 1973 she earned a doctoral degree in political science from the same university. Prada also trained for several years to become a mime at the Piccolo Teatro, in Milan. Despite her singular sense of style, Prada was a shy young woman and found the art of pantomime, which allowed her to express herself without words, vastly appealing. "It was an excuse not to talk," she explained to Frankel. Prada stopped pursuing mime only at her parents' insistence.

When Luisa decided to retire in the mid-1970s, her daughter, who was by then deeply involved in the fight for women's rights, assumed control of the family business. "You know, I had to have a lot of courage to do fashion," Prada told Frankel, "because in theory it was the least feminist work possible—and at that time . . . that was very complicated for me. Of course, I liked it a lot but I also wanted to do something more useful."

Prada began by designing handbags, which were popular enough to spawn imitations. A leather-factory owner named Patrizio Bertelli, for one, produced what Prada deemed inferior knockoffs. When Bertelli and Prada met at a Milan trade fair, in 1978, she considered him brash, argumentative, stubborn, and arrogant. Nonetheless, both a romantic and a business relationship developed between them. They moved in together, and Prada awarded Bertelli the exclusive rights to manufacture her leather goods. She soon made him chief executive officer of the company. He is said to be one of the most temperamental and difficult figures in the business world. "[His] expressions of fury have been known to include throwing merchandise through office windows, smashing mirrors, or dramatically ripping up sketches submitted by his studio staff," John Davidson wrote for the *Scotsman* (May 28, 2005, on-line). "If you want to see some really frightened retail workers, just call into any Prada store the day they're anticipating a visit from their chief executive."

Bertelli continually advised Prada to expand her product line and heighten her ambitions. He suggested, for example, that she create a line of shoes in addition to her handbags. When Prada demurred Bertelli announced his intention to hire someone else to design the footwear; Prada, as she would do repeatedly in the future, accepted his challenge. "I am egotistical, so in the end he knows I will do the work," she told Specter. "If I could, I would make every single piece myself. Bertelli was right. I would have been bored only doing bags."

It was a handbag, however, that first brought Prada's name to widespread attention. In 1985 she introduced a simple black bag made from Pocone, a sturdy industrial nylon used by the Italian army for constructing parachutes, trimmed with leather and bearing a small, triangular metal tag with the Prada name. It had taken Prada more than three years to develop the proper technique for working with the nylon; her effort was rewarded, as women around the world purchased the expensive bag, which became ubiquitous in the pages of fashion magazines and on the streets. (The bag also spawned numerous inexpensive knockoffs.)

Bertelli and Prada were married in 1987, after living together for eight years. Their relationship, both at home and at the office, is famously tumultuous, and many media stories about them include mention of their stormy arguments. In 1989, at Bertelli's urging, Prada debuted a ready-to-wear collection of women's clothing, which received mixed reviews from the fashion critics. Prada explained to Annalisa Barbieri for the London *Independent* (July 7, 1996) that her colleagues had urged her to create clothing that was commercial because they were afraid that her original ideas would not sell. "I hated all the people around me and I told them it was the last time others would

push me to do what I didn't want to do," she said. Thereafter, Prada opted to follow her own instincts. "I have nobody in mind when I design, only what I like and what I think is right, and very often it happens that a lot of women think the same," she told Barbieri. "I can be insecure about many things but in my work I am 100 percent secure." Prada's subsequent collections, unlike her first, garnered significant praise. While her contemporaries were designing overtly sexual or impractical clothing, Prada focused on modern lines, conservative hemlines, classic tailoring, and quality details. Prada explained to Susannah Frankel, "For many years I've tried to work with an idea that you can be sexy without being obvious." Her clothes, often in shades of brown (Prada's favorite color) or other conservative hues, were lauded by fashion writers for suggesting a certain intellectuality.

In 1993, a year in which she won an award for her accessories from the Council of Fashion Designers of America, Prada introduced a whimsical, lower-priced line called Miu Miu (her nickname), aimed at younger women. Miu Miu allows the designer to incorporate vintage or bohemian influences and receives consistently good reviews. The same year Prada introduced a well-regarded line of menswear, and two years later she added a sportswear line. She introduced a fragrance for men in 2006. With each collection, Prada continued to challenge herself. "To work on what you like is too easy; it's not challenging. When I'm working with a colour or a shape that I have always hated, I'm always happy. It gives me space to be intrigued," Prada told Dominic Rushe for the London *Sunday Times Magazine* (March 27, 2005).

In 1999 Prada bought controlling stakes in the companies of the popular German designers Helmut Lang and Jil Sander; by early 2000, however, both designers, bristling at their interactions with Bertelli, left their namesake companies—Sander within only five months of the purchase. (Sander returned in 2003 but within a year had parted ways with the company again.) Such acquisitions resulted in Prada's amassing a reported debt of more than $500 million, which has since been reduced through a series of property deals and asset transfers. Despite such difficulties, in 2000 the company had sales totaling more than $1.4 billion and profits of more than $260 million. There is frequent speculation in the business press about a long-anticipated initial public offering (IPO); currently more than 60 percent of the company is held privately by Bertelli and Prada.

Prada and her husband are avid art collectors and reportedly own one of the most important contemporary-art collections in Italy, which includes pieces by Damien Hirst, Brice Marden, Andrea Zittel, Mark Rothko, and Frank Stella. In 1995 they founded the Fondazione Prada, which, since its creation, has hosted shows by such artists as Marc Quinn, Dan Flavin, and Anish Kapoor. Although some observers have speculated that Prada and

Bertelli founded their organization in order to gain publicity for their business, Prada told Specter, "I laugh when they talk about fashion as art. It's ridiculous. When I buy art, I want to keep it separate. You don't want people to think you are doing what you are doing because you want to make your company better."

Prada and Bertelli, an avid yachtsman who has competed in the America's Cup, live in the same Milan apartment in which Prada was raised. Of their much-discussed fractiousness, Bertelli told Dominic Rushe, "Of course, sometimes we don't agree, but our relationship is a very successful one. Think about it: we built a company together, we work together, we spend our holidays together. How many people would be happy to spend 24 hours a day for 25 years with their [spouses]?" The couple have two teenaged sons, Giulio and Lorenzo, who have not yet decided if they will enter the family business.

While it is customary for designers to walk triumphantly down the runway after a showing of their collections, Prada does not do so. She instead peeks from the wings and modestly waves. When asked by Colin McDowell about the gesture, during a public interview held at the British Museum and excerpted in *Vogue* (November 24, 2005, on-line), she explained, "Historically I tend to refuse any of the clichés of my job. Besides I'm not stupid—I don't want to compete with all the gorgeous models who have just appeared before me!"

Although Prada herself eschews the limelight, her creations are often the subject of intense media attention. When the actress Uma Thurman appeared at the 1995 Academy Awards wearing a lilac-colored Prada gown, for example, reporters barraged her with questions about the dress, and that development is credited with sparking the trend for red-carpet interviews in which reporters ask, "Who [which designer] are you wearing?" In 2005 Pope Benedict XVI was widely photographed wearing red Prada loafers, visible when he lifted the hem of his cassock. Prada and her company received much free publicity in 2006, when the film *The Devil Wears Prada* premiered. Based on Lauren Weisberger's 2004 novel of the same title, the movie focuses on a young midwestern woman who becomes an assistant to the editor of one of the world's top fashion magazines.

—K.J.E.

Suggested Reading: *Financial Times* II p4 Feb. 11–12, 1995; (London) *Independent* p17 July 7, 1996, p20+ Feb. 21, 2004; (London) *Sunday Times Magazine* p28 Mar. 27, 2005; (London) *Times* p24 Sep. 23, 2006; *New Yorker* p104 Mar. 15, 2004; *Scotsman* (on-line) May 28, 2005; *Vogue* (on-line) Nov. 24, 2005

Randall, Lisa

June 18, 1962– Theoretical physicist

Address: Harvard University, Jefferson 461, 17 Oxford St., Cambridge, MA 02138

"The cosmos could be larger, richer and more varied than anything we imagined," the physicist Lisa Randall wrote in her book, *Warped Passages: Unraveling the Mysteries of the Universe's Hidden Dimensions*. In an article written for the London *Daily Telegraph* (June 1, 2005), Randall explained, "My recent studies of extra dimensions of space, beyond the familiar 'up-down,' 'left-right' and 'forward-backward,' have made me more than usually convinced that they must really exist." "I really don't see any reason why these extra dimensions should not exist," she told Michael Brooks for *New Scientist* (June 18, 2005). "At the moment we see things over a very limited range of distance and energy. Every time we have looked beyond the boundaries of what we could see before, we have found new phenomena." Randall was a professor of physics at the Massachusetts Institute of Technology (MIT) when, in 1998, in collaboration with the particle physicist Raman Sundrum, who is now at Johns Hopkins University, she developed a theory to explain why gravity is by far the weakest of the four fundamental forces of nature. (The oth-

Courtesy of Lisa Randall

ers are the electromagnetic force, which acts on atomic particles carrying an electrical charge; the strong nuclear force, which holds atomic nuclei together; and the weak nuclear force, which is associated with particle emission and nuclear decay.) Gravity, Randall argued, seems weaker than the other forces because only a small portion of it is being exerted in the three-dimensional universe with which humans are familiar (in which time is considered a fourth, nonspatial dimension); the rest, she hypothesized, might be found in other dimensions—dimensions that, as she wrote for the *Daily Telegraph*, "might be tiny, far smaller than an atom, or they might be big, or even infinite in size." Furthermore, she theorized, those dimensions might exist beyond the boundaries of our universe, in other universes; that is, our universe may simply be what has been dubbed a brane and may be surrounded by other branes. Two 1999 papers in which Randall and Sundrum presented their unprecedented ideas are among the most frequently cited in the professional literature of physics, and many scientists who at first expressed skepticism about their theories have come to embrace them. Since 2001 Randall has expanded on her ideas along with the University of Washington particle physicst Andreas Karch, among others. In the widely acclaimed *Warped Passages*, Randall wrote, "Research into extra dimensions has also led to other remarkable concepts—ones that might fulfill a science fiction aficionado's fantasy—such as parallel universes, warped geometry, and three dimensional sinkholes. I'm afraid such ideas might sound more like the province of novelists and lunatics than the focus of real scientific inquiry. But outlandish as they might seem at the moment, they are genuine scientific scenarios that could arise in an extra-dimensional world." "I want to be clear that this is science and not just science fiction," Randall said to Jane Ganahl for the *San Francisco Chronicle* (September 1, 2005). "That even though these are still theoretical ideas, they are consequences of Einstein's theory of gravity." In a review of *Warped Passages* for the *Times Higher Education Supplement* (June 3, 2005), Lorna Kerry wrote, "Anyone accusing [Randall] of straying into fantasy would be brought up sharp by the detailed grounding in physics she provides. . . . Reading *Warped Passages* gives an insight into how people must have felt on discovering that the Earth was not flat." Randall, who has taught at Harvard University since 1999, hopes that an experiment slated to be conducted at the European Organization for Nuclear Research (CERN) in 2007 will offer evidence for the existence of additional dimensions.

Science, Randall told Sarah Baxter for the London *Sunday Times* (June 19, 2005), focuses as much on questions as it does answers, which is what "makes it fun." "Very often research is about finding the small glitch or inconsistency that is at the root of the really big issues," she said. According to Raman Sundrum, Randall has "a great nose" for identifying fruitful areas of investigation. He said to Dennis Overbye for the *New York Times* (November 1, 2005), "It's a mystery to those of us— hard to understand, almost to the point of amusement—how she does it without any clear sign of

what led her to that path. She gives no sign of why she thinks what she thinks." Similarly, Andrew Strominger, a professor of physics at Harvard, told Adrian J. Smith for the *Harvard Crimson* (January 6, 2006, on-line), "She is very intuitive. She often understands things in her own mind before she is able to formulate it mathematically." Randall told Michael Brooks that one reason she devoted so much time away from her research to write *Warped Passages* was that she "wanted to show why physicists think about things like extra dimensions, and how they might tie into 'real' observable phenomena." Another reason, she told Anna Fazackerley for the *Times Higher Education Supplement* (June 3, 2005), was that she "thought it was important . . . to get the message across that you don't have to look like a weirdo to do science."

The middle of the three daughters of a salesman for an engineering company and a schoolteacher, Lisa Randall was born on June 18, 1962 in the New York City borough of Queens. Her younger sister, Dana Randall, teaches math and computer science at the Georgia Institute of Technology. By her own account, Lisa Randall was drawn to mathematics at an early age; as she told Sarah Baxter, "I was looking for certainty. What I liked [about math] was that there were definite, nice, neat answers." Randall attended Stuyvesant High School, a New York City public school for academically gifted students, who are admitted on the basis of their performance on a competitive examination. While enrolled in her first physics class at Stuyvesant, as she recalled to an interviewer for *American Scientist* (September 28, 2005,on-line), she "began to think science could provide a better outlet for my interests, one that is more grounded in the physical world." Randall was the first female student to serve as the captain of Stuyvesant's math team. As a senior she tied for first place in the 1980 national Westinghouse Science Talent Search (now named for a different sponsor, Intel), with a project on complex numbers; the oldest and most prestigious precollege science competition in the U.S., recognition in the Science Talent Search is considered by many to be equivalent to a "junior Nobel Prize."

After her high-school graduation, Randall entered Harvard University, in Cambridge, Massachusetts. During her summer breaks she conducted research, in 1981, at the Smithsonian Astrophysical Observatory, which is affiliated with Harvard; in 1982, at the IBM facility at Poughkeepsie, New York, and then the Fermi National Accelerator Laboratory (FNAL), near Chicago, Illinois; and in 1983, at Bell Labs, in New Jersey. She earned a B.A. degree in physics from Harvard in 1983, after only three years. She remained at Harvard to pursue a Ph.D. in particle physics, a subject that had captured her imagination during her stint at FNAL. Her Ph.D. adviser was Howard Georgi, a strong supporter of women in science; her dissertation, entitled "Enhancing the Standard Model," about the theory of fundamental particles and how they interact, was based on collaborative work of Georgi and Sheldon Glashow, the latter of whom won the Nobel Prize in Physics in 1979. She was awarded a Ph.D. degree in 1987, by which time she had co-authored seven papers published in physics journals. Next, as a postdoctoral fellow, she worked at the University of California at Berkeley (1987–89), the Lawrence Berkeley Laboratory (1989–90), and Harvard (1990–91).

In 1991 Randall joined the faculty of MIT, in Cambridge, as an assistant professor of physics; four years later she was promoted to associate professor. Earlier, in 1992, she had won an Outstanding Junior Investigator Award from the Department of Energy; a Young Investigator Award from the National Science Foundation; and an Alfred P. Sloan Foundation Research Fellowship. While at MIT she wrote or co-wrote some 50 papers. She left that school in 1998 to teach at Princeton University, in New Jersey, where she became the first female professor of physics to earn tenure. In 2000 she returned to MIT; there, she held the distinction of being the school's first female theorist in particle physics.

Meanwhile, in 1998, Randall and Raman Sundrum, who was then a postdoctoral fellow at Boston University and whom Randall had worked with earlier, had begun to meet at an ice-cream parlor at the MIT student center to discuss some baffling problems regarding gravity. Sundrum, who is now a professor at Johns Hopkins University, "had already thought about branes and extra dimensions, and he was an obvious person to join forces with," Randall explained to Marguerite Holloway for *Scientific American* (October 2005, on-line). Describing the questions that she and Sundrum grappled with, Randall told John Crace for the London *Guardian* (June 21, 2005), "The Standard Model of particle physics describes forces and particles very well, but when you throw gravity into the equation, it all falls apart. You have to fudge the figures to make it work. We know how gravity works, but no one had properly answered the question of what determines its strength. Why is it so much weaker than standard theory would predict?" Gravity is by far the weakest of the four fundamental forces of nature—trillions of trillions of trillions of times weaker. "Gravity might not appear to be all that weak when you're hiking up a mountain, but bear in mind that the gravitational force of the entire Earth is acting on you," Randall wrote for the *Daily Telegraph*. "Think how feeble gravity must be for you to counter the force of the much larger Earth when you pick up a ball." In another common example of gravity's weakness, a magnet can hold a paper clip many times its size above the ground, even though Earth's gravity is pulling at it.

Randall and Sundrum theorized that gravity may be so weak because much of its force is being exerted in dimensions that humans are unable to perceive. While humans have traditionally thought of themselves as functioning spatially in three dimensions, Randall views dimensions as "the number of quantities you need to know to completely pin down a point in a space," as she put it in *Warped Passages*. Randall told Ira Flatow for the National Public Radio program *Talk of the Nation* (September 30, 2005), "One of the things that makes [the idea of additional dimensions] difficult to get across is that you can't picture it. We are not physiologically designed to picture more than three dimensions. It doesn't mean they're not there, but we certainly can't just picture them very simply. What we can do is we can try to extrapolate our ideas mathematically or in words, and we can find shortcuts for trying to picture things, the same way we try to picture three-dimensional worlds on two-dimensional pieces of paper." The idea that the universe is composed of more than three spatial dimensions is a crucial element of string theory, a central component of modern physics. String theory was developed as a way of reconciling classic, Newtonian physics, which explains the basic laws of motion, and quantum mechanics, which is concerned with the movement of atomic particles. According to Randall in the *Daily Telegraph*, string theory "doesn't naturally describe a world with three dimensions of space. It more naturally suggests a world with many more, perhaps nine or 10. A string theorist doesn't ask whether extra dimensions exist; instead, two critical questions that a string theorist asks are: where are they and why haven't we seen them?" String theorists had so far posited that the extra dimensions are undetectable by humans, theoretically as well as in actuality, because each is "rolled up" into a tiny bit of space far smaller than an atom.

"Many physicists are willing to overlook the lack of experimental evidence [for the validity of string theory] because they believe that string theory will eventually reconcile quantum mechanics, which governs atoms and all other particles, with general relativity, which describes how matter and gravity interact on the very largest scales," the science writer and editor Tim Folger noted in a review of *Warped Passages* for the *New York Times* (October 23, 2005). "Randall, though, argues that without any experimental feedback, string theorists may never reach their goal. She prefers a different strategy, called model building. Rather than seeking to create an all-encompassing theory, she develops models—mini-theories that target specific testable problems and that might then point the way to a more general theory." Adopting that approach, in 1999 Randall and Sundrum published a pair of papers, "Large Mass Hierarchy from a Small Extra Dimension" and "An Alternative to Compactification," in the journal *Physical Review Letters*, the first of which discusses the weakness of gravity in the known universe (the hierarchy problem, as it is labeled), and the second of which proposes that the existence of so-called branes would account for the existence of an infinitely large extra dimension. A brane (the word, coined by cosmologists, comes from "membrane," something that, on the cellular level, acts as a barrier), according to Randall in her book, is an "object in higher-dimensional space that can carry energy and confine particles and forces." Human beings exist on a "weak brane," while the brunt of gravity's force would be exerted on a stronger brane. "The world of branes is an exciting new landscape that has revolutionized our understanding of gravity, particle physics, and cosmology," Randall wrote in *Warped Passages*. "Branes might really exist in the cosmos, and there is no good reason that we couldn't be living on one." Randall told Gary Taubes for the Web site Special Topics that her work with Sundrum "went in the face of what everyone who has studied gravity has believed. We always thought if we have extra dimensions, we had to do what's called compactifying them, which is to say they curl up so that they can't be seen from our point of view. . . . It wasn't thought to be possible to have a theory with extra dimensions that wouldn't compactify and still have the physics reduce to four-dimensional physics here. So our theory, that you could have an infinite extra dimension that wasn't compactified, was a radical departure from conventional wisdom." As Anna Fazackerley wrote for the *Times Higher Education Supplement* (June 3, 2005), Randall's work with Sundrum "transformed the way that theoretical physicists think about the underlying structure of space." Randall wrote in *Warped Passages*, "Physicists have now returned to the idea that the three-dimensional world that surrounds us could be a three-dimensional slice of a higher-dimensional world."

Fundamental to Randall's theory about extra dimensions is the presumed existence of what are called Kaluza-Klein particles. As Randall wrote in *Warped Passages*, "KK [Kaluza-Klein] particles are the additional ingredients of an extra-dimensional universe. They are the four-dimensional imprint of the higher-dimensional world. . . . Just as Flatlanders [characters from Edwin A. Abbott's 1884 book *Flatland*], who see only two spatial dimensions, could observe only two-dimensional disks when a three-dimensional sphere passed through their world, we can see only particles that look like they travel in three spatial dimensions, even if those particles originated in higher-dimensional space. These new particles that originate in extra dimensions, but appear to us as extra particles in our four-dimensional spacetime, are Kaluza-Klein (KK) particles." According to a Fermi National Accelerator Laboratory Web site (www-cdf.fnal.gov) that discusses the search for extra dimensions by observing what is called missing energy, a Kaluza-Klein particle is a graviton—"the particle that mediates the force of gravity." If two atomic particles on the brane produce sufficiently high energy when they collide—specifically, in a collision in a high-energy particle accelerator—they will produce a graviton. "The graviton flies out of the brane . . . carrying away energy and momentum. . . . An observer on the brane witnessing the outcome of the collision would see the usual particles produced in such experiments, with a large imbalance of energy and momentum. Instead of detecting the Kaluza-Klein graviton directly, we observe its 'missing energy' signature." "The most exciting feature of any extra-dimensional theory that explains the weakness of gravity is that if it is correct, we will soon find out," Randall wrote in *Warped Passages*. An experiment designed to test the theory will be carried out in 2007 at CERN, on the border of France and Switzerland near Geneva, where the most powerful atom-smasher on Earth—what has been dubbed the Large Hadron Collider—is under construction. If the experiment turns out as Randall hopes it will, the collision of high-energy particles will produce evidence of additional dimensions. "If this is the way gravity works in high-energy physics, we'll know about it," Randall told Dennis Overbye.

Randall completed the writing of *Warped Passages* (2005) in three years. The 512-page book, whose title refers to the warping of the so-called space-time continuum, offers a history of modern theoretical physics along with a description of her own theories. Among the many enthusiastic reviews it earned was that of Brian Cox, who wrote for the *Times Higher Education Supplement* (September 16, 2005), "It is difficult stuff, but [Randall] makes it as simple as possible without diluting the content." In an assessment for *Library Journal* (September 1, 2005, on-line), Sara Rutter wrote, "To explain and illustrate the complex models and mathematical calculations used to develop groundbreaking new theories in physics, Randall employs stories, analogies, and drawings. In this way, she is like an extraordinarily smart and lively college professor working to engage her students in the excitement of discovery."

In 2005 Lawrence Summers, then the president of Harvard University, appointed Randall to a school task force whose mission was to recruit female science professors. Shortly before that happened Summers had ignited a fierce controversy on and off the Harvard campus by remarking in a speech that the significantly greater representation of men in the hard sciences might be attributed to inborn differences in ability between men and women. Randall disputed that idea, telling Michael Brooks, "There are lots of social factors that influence performance so it's impossible at this point to isolate innate differences in intelligence. You can only say something reliable about innate differences in scientific ability if the differences are so big they cannot be explained by social factors. And so far as we can tell, they are not." She told Matin Durrani for *Physics World* (May 2005, on-line) that women "just need a level playing field. There really are prejudices [against women], both inadvertent and deliberate, and if we get rid of those, we don't need any targets"—that is, minimum numbers of women on the faculty of any department of physics.

Many reporters have used words such as "glamorous" to describe Randall's looks. In her leisure time she enjoys skiing, rock climbing, and watching movies.

—R.E.

Suggested Reading: *Boston Globe* pE1 Sep. 4, 2005; (London) *Daily Telegraph* June 1, 2005; (London) *Guardian* p20 June 21, 2005; *New Scientist* p88 Dec. 18, 1999, p48 June 18, 2005

Selected Books: *Warped Passages: Unraveling the Mysteries of the Universe's Hidden Dimensions*, 2005

Evan Agostini/Getty Images

Reeves, Dianne

Oct. 23, 1956– Jazz singer

Address: c/o Blue Note Records, 150 Fifth Ave., Sixth Fl., New York, NY 10011

The late, celebrated jazz vocalist Joe Williams told a writer for *Down Beat* in 1997 about the singer Dianne Reeves, "I think Dianne's the legitimate extension of all the good things that have gone on before, from Ethel Waters to Ella Fitzgerald and Sarah [Vaughan] and Carmen [McCrae]. . . . She is earth mother, lover, she is the hurt child; she manages to get inside each one of those things." Though known primarily as a jazz vocalist, Reeves draws on a variety of influences, among them African, Brazilian, and Caribbean music and gospel, rhythm and blues, and pop. The albums of the four-time Grammy Award–winner include *In the*

Moment: Live in Concert (2000), *The Calling: Celebrating Sarah Vaughan* (2001), *A Little Moonlight* (2003), and the soundtrack to the film *Good Night, and Good Luck* (2005).

Dianne Reeves was born on October 23, 1956 in Detroit, Michigan, into a musical family. Her mother, Vada Swanson, a nurse, played the trumpet; her father sang tenor; her uncle Charles Burrell played the bass in the San Francisco and Colorado Symphony Orchestras; and one of her cousins is the keyboardist George Duke. Reeves was only two years old when her father died. Her mother then moved with Reeves and her sister, Sharon, to Denver, Colorado, to be close to the girls' grandmother, Denverada, and their aunt, Mary Beth Mitchell. Reeves found her female relatives to be a source of strength and inspiration. "They were all fighters, and I picked that up from them," she told John Pitcher for the *Rochester (New York) Democrat and Chronicle* (June 3, 2002). "But they were also rich in their collective spirituality and always found a way to celebrate and support the aspirations of their children."

As a youngster in the 1960s, Reeves was one of the first African-American students to participate in Denver's busing program, in which black children were required to commute to predominantly white schools in order to integrate the school system. "They were sending us off to neighborhoods that we didn't even know existed, and the authorities didn't do anything to prepare us for what we were in for," Reeves told Pitcher. At the school where she was sent, Hamilton Junior High, many parents of white students were hostile toward the young African-Americans. "It dawned on me that this was truly ignorance—ignorance in not wanting to understand one another," Reeves told an interviewer for the Europe Jazz Network Web site. Reeves participated in events, such as assemblies and sit-ins, designed to enlighten the adults in the community. A choir teacher who was sympathetic to the black children's predicament sought to diffuse the tension by helping to put on a show of songs and skits featuring all the eighth-grade students; the songs included "You've Got a Friend" and "He Ain't Heavy, He's My Brother"—"the kind of music that had a positive message," Reeves told Pitcher. She recalled to the interviewer for the Europe Jazz Network Web site, "Fortunately it all ended in a positive way. People started to look at themselves and be kind of ashamed of the way they acted." That experience led Reeves to realize, as she told Norman Provizer for the Denver *Rocky Mountain News* (April 7, 2001), "that music—art—can have a soothing impact, especially on young people. After that, I decided that I loved what the music made me feel, and I knew I wanted to sing."

When Reeves's uncle Charles Burrell learned that his niece had a strong singing voice, he promptly took an interest in cultivating her talents and broadening her musical horizons. As Reeves told John Pitcher, her uncle "started giving me every jazz record he could find. . . . I heard Ella Fitzgerald, Billie Holiday, Sarah Vaughan, and I became hooked on that kind of singing." At 17 Reeves got the opportunity to meet one of her idols when her cousin George Duke secured backstage access for her at a Cannonball Adderley tribute concert. While standing in the wings, Reeves struck up a conversation with a friendly woman who expressed an interest in the teen's career ambitions. "I told her I listened to Sarah Vaughan. I just talked and told her all about Sarah Vaughan," Reeves recalled in an interview with Adrian Chamberlain for the Victoria, British Columbia, *Times Colonist* (June 28, 2005). Several minutes later the woman was called onstage to perform and was introduced to the audience—as Sarah Vaughan. "I stood in the wings and listened to her. I just disappeared afterwards," Reeves admitted to Chamberlain. "I didn't know what to say."

While attending George Washington High School, Reeves was a member of a jazz band and sang at her own prom. When she performed with the school band at a convention of the National Association of Jazz Educators, in Chicago, Illinois, the famous trumpeter Clark Terry, impressed by the 16-year-old girl's voice, asked her to join his group. Soon Reeves found herself performing with Terry's bands, which featured the jazz luminaries Tommy Flanagan and Eddie "Lockjaw" Davis, among others. Meanwhile, after graduating from high school, she enrolled at the University of Colorado at Denver, leaving after a year. At the invitation of Philip Bailey, a member of the group Earth, Wind & Fire, who had heard about Reeves's talent through mutual friends, Reeves moved in 1976 to Los Angeles, California, to become the vocalist for another band that Bailey had formed. She quit the group a year later. "I really wanted to sing jazz," she explained to Norman Provizer, "and what they were doing wasn't really jazz-oriented. It was great music, but there was a really great jazz scene in Los Angeles at the time, and I wanted to be part of it." She performed with Caldera, a Latin-jazz group, in which she met the keyboardist Eduardo del Barrio, who was to become her frequent songwriting collaborator. From 1978 to 1980 she held a full-time gig with the pianist Billy Childs. "Billy gave me license to go anywhere musically," she said, as quoted by the Europe Jazz Network Web site. In 1981, when she heard that the pianist Sergio Mendes needed a singer, she gave an audition and before long was touring the world with Mendes and his band. Having acquired from Mendes an appreciation for Brazilian music, Reeves recorded her first album, *Welcome to My Love*, for the Palo Alto Jazz label, in 1982. Shortly thereafter she relocated to New York City in order to collaborate with the singer Harry Belafonte, whom she has credited with teaching her the importance of lyrics. While on the East Coast, Reeves continued performing live. In a review of one of her shows for *Newsday* (May 2, 1985), Wayne Robins praised Reeves's "awesome technical gifts: Pitch that you could set a tuning fork by is matched by enough lung power to raise

the roof at a Pentecostal church service." She also released a second album with Palo Alto, *For Every Heart* (1985), before returning to Los Angeles in the following year.

Reeve's 1987 album, the rhythm-and-blues-inflected *Dianne Reeves*, released on Capitol's Blue Note label, earned the singer widespread attention. The album included the R&B ballad "Better Days," a poignant melody about Reeves's grandmother, which became a hit; Reeves praised her grandmother to Norman Provizer as "a very strong and wise person who really kept the family close." She also told *Jet* magazine (December 26, 2005–January 2, 2006) that the song was "dedicated to grandmothers everywhere." *Dianne Reeves* was nominated for a Grammy Award. In 1989 she released *Never Too Far*, followed two years later by *I Remember*. In 1992 Reeves moved back to Denver to be closer to her family. Her return to her childhood home apparently had a positive influence on Reeves's music: in 1994 she released *Art and Survival*, which, she told Provizer in 2001, was "the most important record I've ever made." Reeves then proceeded to record albums at the rate of one a year, including the Grammy-nominated *Quiet After the Storm* (1995), *The Grand Encounter* (1996), and another Grammy nominee, *That Day* (1997). Two years later came still another Grammy nominee, *Bridges* (1999).

Given her history with the Grammy Awards, Reeves was pleased but not particularly hopeful when her album *In the Moment: Live in Concert* (2000) was nominated for the honor. She had planned to attend the awards ceremony, but a family emergency necessitated her presence in Denver, where she and her relatives watched the ceremony on television. While Reeves was watching the show, a friend from the East Coast (whose telecast was an hour ahead of Denver's) called with the news that Reeves had won the award for best jazz vocalist. Reeves was elated. "Everyone just started coming over. It was family, kids, cousins. Old friends were coming by, calling. Everybody was jumping around. It was really wonderful," she told Norman Provizer. Because Reeves could not be present at the live ceremony, her family and friends reenacted the event for her, even presenting Reeves with a photo of the Grammy Award and having her deliver an acceptance speech. Winning the Grammy was important to Reeves partly because, she told Provizer, it brought about "a healing experience. . . . There were people with whom I'd had misunderstandings and people with whom I'd fallen out of touch. They called. We talked and things were forgiven. You can say you're a Grammy winner, and maybe some things change. But most important, it brought people I really love together."

As a tribute to her longtime idol, Sarah Vaughan, Reeves recorded an album of classic Vaughan songs entitled *The Calling: Celebrating Sarah Vaughan* (2001). "When I was in high school, in the beginning of trying to find my own voice, dealing with my own raging hormones and angst—in the midst of all that, I heard her voice," Reeves recalled to Norman Provizer. "I heard her voice and a light came on. It opened a door to my understanding of my own voice and how I would use it." For her work on *The Calling*, Reeves won a second Grammy Award. She secured a third for *A Little Moonlight* (2003), which Nate Chinen described for the *New York Times* (February 7, 2006) as "an exquisitely focused standards album and her finest recorded work." Reeves became the first singer in any genre to win Grammy Awards for three consecutive releases. She next appeared as a 1950s TV-studio singer in *Good Night, and Good Luck*, a 2005 film about the broadcast journalist Edward R. Murrow, directed by George Clooney. Reeves also recorded the film's soundtrack. Both the movie and the album earned honors, which included a fourth Grammy Award for Reeves. "The powerful but mellow alto of Ms. Reeves wafts through the film, as ubiquitous and atmospheric as the smoke from Murrow's cigarettes," Nate Chinen wrote. Chinen described the soundtrack album, also called *Good Night, and Good Luck*, as "the leanest, most instantly gratifying album of [Reeves's] career." Also in 2005 she released *Christmas Time Is Here*, an album of what the *Sacramento (California) Observer* (November 9, 2005) called "stylish and sophisticated renditions of classics" delivered with a "strong, agile voice, rhythmic virtuosity and improvisational ease." Reeves's 2006 tour schedule included venues in the United Kingdom, the Netherlands, Norway, Spain, and Australia as well as the U.S.

Throughout her career Reeves has performed live as well as on recordings. In 2001 she appeared as part of the Jazz at Lincoln Center program in New York City. Writing about her performance, Ben Ratliff declared in the *New York Times* (February 20, 2001) that Reeves "sings the truest note in jazz. Ms. Reeves stays perfectly on pitch, and her notes, individually packaged like Valentine chocolates, have a perfect roundness." The following year she performed at the closing ceremony of the 2002 Winter Olympic Games, in Salt Lake City, Utah. She has since been awarded the Ella Fitzgerald Award at the Montreal International Jazz Festival, and in 2003 she received an honorary doctorate from the Berklee College of Music. Since 2002 she has held the position of creative chair for jazz with the Los Angeles Philharmonic Association. Reeves continues to make her home in Denver.

—K.J.E.

Suggested Reading: (Denver, Colorado) *Rocky Mountain News* E p1 Apr. 7, 2001; *New York Times* E p5 Feb. 20, 2001, E p1 Feb. 7, 2006; *Newsday* p35 May 2, 1985; *Rochester (New York) Democrat and Chronicle* C p1 June 3, 2002; (Victoria, British Columbia) *Times Colonist* D p5 June 28, 2005

Selected Recordings: *Welcome to My Love*, 1982; *For Every Heart*, 1985; *Dianne Reeves*, 1987; *Never Too Far*, 1989; *I Remember*, 1991; *Art and Survival*, 1994; *Quiet After the Storm*, 1995; *The Grand Encounter*, 1996; *Palo Alto Sessions, 1981–1985*, 1996; *That Day*, 1997; *Bridges*, 1999; *In the Moment: Live in Concert*, 2000; *The Calling: Celebrating Sarah Vaughan*, 2001; *The Best of Dianne Reeves*, 2002; *A Little Moonlight*, 2003; *Good Night, and Good Luck*, 2005; *Christmas Time Is Here*, 2005

Stephen Shugerman/Getty Images

Reichs, Kathy

(rikes)

1950– Forensic anthropologist; novelist; educator; television producer

Address: Dept. of Anthropology, University of North Carolina, Charlotte, NC 28213

When Jeanne Le Ber (1662–1714), who is known as "Montreal's Joan of Arc," was recommended for sainthood, in 1991, representatives from the Catholic archdiocese of Quebec asked the forensic anthropologist Kathy Reichs to help confirm that the remains interred in Le Ber's supposed grave actually belonged to the would-be saint. Accustomed to more gruesome cases, such as identifying the remains of victims of murder (through her work with law enforcement officials) or genocide (through her work with the U.N.), Reichs enjoyed comparing the details of Le Ber's life with the clues embedded in the skeletal remains exhumed by the

church. "When [Le Ber] was 18 she went into se-
clusion and stayed there until she died in her fifties," Reichs told Ann Treneman for the London
Independent (January 29, 1998). "She did two
things: praying and weaving tapestries. . . . When
you kneel a lot you hyper-flex your toes; we found
the right arthritic pattern and a flattened heel. She
also had lovely grooves in both her upper and lower incisors from year after year of pulling the thread
through her teeth. By also establishing the age and
sex, I had a positive identification." Using her skill
in reading human remains, Reichs has also helped
convict murderers, testified about the genocide in
Rwanda, and assisted in the recovery and identification of remains found in mass graves in Guatemala and in debris retrieved from the site of the
World Trade Center.

In 1997, to help offset the cost of her three children's college tuition, Reichs penned her first novel, *Déjà Dead*, which won an award from the Crime
Writers of Canada and became a *New York Times*
best-seller. Fans of *Déjà Dead* have since been
treated to eight other novels by Reichs, all of which
feature the character Dr. Temperance Brennan,
whose life and career resemble the author's in important ways. Brennan also serves as the central
character in the television drama *Bones*, which airs
on the Fox network. *Bones* is a recent addition to
a slew of television shows about forensic science;
Reichs has attributed the public's budding fascination with her field, and consequently the popularity of her novels, to the media spectacle surrounding O.J. Simpson's murder trial in the mid-1990s.
"We watched it wall-to-wall, morning until night
and we heard about DNA and blood-spatter patterns and pathology reports. People got curious
about it," she told Richard Ouzounian for the *Toronto Star* (October 23, 2004). "It may seem morbid, but I think there's a lot of fascination with
death. Most individuals don't have to become involved with the details of mortality on a day-to-day
basis, so they can afford to be terribly intrigued by
it."

One of four daughters, Kathleen Joan Reichs was
born in 1950 and raised in an Irish Catholic neighborhood in the suburbs of Chicago, Illinois. Her father worked as a manager in the food industry; her
mother played trumpet in the city's symphony orchestra. From an early age Reichs was interested in
becoming a scientist. "I had an ill-formed idea of
what it was, someone in a white coat in a lab
which, ironically, is what I am now," she told
Candida Crewe for the London *Times* (June 19,
1999). "I was never interested in dolls or playing
house. I was always collecting insects and snakes
and looking at them under my microscope. . . . I
set up a science lab in the cellar with shelves and
chemicals." She was also intrigued by archaeology
and enjoyed reading, as she recalled to Alden
Mudge for *BookPage* (September 1997, on-line): "I
was always reading books on places like Easter Island. I also had an interest in mysteries like Nancy
Drew and the Hardy Boys. I think that's the appeal

of forensic anthropology: it brings the science and
mystery together." As a nine-year-old, Reichs told
Ouzounian, she penned her first story, a whodunit
titled "The Mystery of the Old House."

Despite her early appetite for fiction, Reichs
avoided literature courses when she attended
American University, in Washington, D.C., as an
undergraduate. "I'd rather dissect a frog than ana-
lyse a poem," she told Iain Sharp for the *Sunday
Star-Times* (March 26, 2000), a New Zealand weekly. Reichs "bounced around, doing several majors," as she recalled to Crewe, before settling on
anthropology and earning a B.A. degree in that
field in 1971. She received her master's degree in
physical anthropology from Northwestern University, in Evanston, Illinois, the next year. While
completing a Ph.D. in physical anthropology at
Northwestern in 1975, Reichs worked, from 1974
to 1978, as an assistant professor at Northern Illinois University, in DeKalb. She also worked as an
instructor, from 1975 to 1978, at the Stateville Cor-
rectional Center in Joliet, Illinois.

When the police first asked her to examine a set
of human remains, Reichs had not been planning
on a career in forensic anthropology, thinking instead that she would study prehistoric Native
American burials. "I was especially interested in
North American peoples dating from 500 BC–500
AD: the disease patterning, what people ate and
died of, who was dying and when . . . ," she told
Crewe. "We went through a lot of skeletons. I suppose that it was because I was a bones person, the
police started coming to me with cases. This was
the mid-Seventies when the field was just beginning to crystallise. I could already tell the age, sex
and race of a skeleton, but forensic anthropology
goes beyond that—there's a lot of trauma analysis.
In archaeology you are dealing with broad groups,
not the specific identity of an individual. Working
for the police was so compelling because it was really going to have an impact. Archaeology is fascinating but, if you are wrong, no one is going to jail.
With forensic anthropology, I liked that relevance."

In 1981 Reichs accepted a job as assistant professor at Davidson College, in Davidson, North Carolina, and then, two years later, joined the Anthropology Department at the University of North Carolina
at Charlotte, where she has remained. In 1985 she
became a forensic-anthropology consultant for the
North Carolina Office of the Chief Medical Examiner and the Office of the Mecklenburg County
Medical Examiner (also in North Carolina). The
next year she received certification from the American Board of Forensic Anthropology; today, she is
one of about 65 certified forensic anthropologists
in the U.S. In 1988, as a visiting associate professor
at Concordia University, in Montreal, Canada,
Reichs began working as a forensic anthropologist
there as well, assuming the title *anthropologue
judiciare*, with the Laboratoire de Sciences Judi-
ciaires et de Médecine Légale in the province of
Quebec.

Reichs has said that when she started writing fiction, in the 1990s, she found her own voice when she switched from third-person to first-person narration. She modeled Temperance Brennan (or simply Tempe), the impassioned heroine of her first novel, *Déjà Dead* (1997), after herself. "What makes *Déjà Dead* unique is that I write about the things I actually do," Reichs told Alden Mudge. "Being in the autopsy room, autopsy procedure, skeletal analysis. I don't need to research that. That's what I do every single day." In her first adventure Brennan helps the Montreal police hunt a serial killer by decoding clues she finds on the mutilated cadavers of his victims. Like many other reviewers, Bill Bell, writing for the New York *Daily News* (September 28, 1997), compared Reichs to the popular mystery writer Patricia Cornwell, noting several similarities between Brennan and Cornwell's heroine, Kay Scarpetta. Reichs "puts a lot of personal stuff into the story, as Cornwell does in hers," Bell wrote, "but Brennan, a recovering alcoholic, is more emotionally involved with her work [and] as the medical shop talk and dead bodies pile up, Brennan is both outraged and numbed. It's hard not to like her." A critic for *Kirkus Reviews* (June 15, 1997) made a less favorable comparison: "Tempe is an appealing new heroine, and the forensic detail is gripping, but because Reichs . . . lacks the whiplash control of Patricia Cornwell at her best, the story seems overlong, overpeopled . . . and overwrought." Notwithstanding that assessment, the reviewer added: "Readers ravenous for ghoulish detail and hints of unfathomable evil, spruced up by the modishly effective Quebec setting, will gobble this first course greedily and expect better-balanced nutrition next time." As the reviewer predicted, many readers were delighted with Reichs's debut, which became a best-seller. The novel won the Arthur Ellis Award from the Crime Writers of Canada.

After the publication of her second novel, *Death du Jour* (1999), Reichs still found herself compared with Cornwell, with Wilda Williams writing for *Library Journal* (April 1, 1999) that Reichs's sophomore novel "offers an enjoyable read for Cornwell fans who want something new." Though Marilyn Stasio, in an assessment for the *New York Times Book Review* (June 13, 1999), wrote that Reichs stuffed "the story with so many characters that even the living ones seem half-dead," Patricia Craig argued in the *Times Literary Supplement* (June 25, 1999) that "Reichs's narrative approach is more engaging than Cornwell's, and her locations are richer in atmosphere." Craig acknowledged, however, that "there is something a bit excessive about the denouement of *Death du Jour*."

Reichs's next book, *Deadly Decisions* (2000), was also set in Montreal. In it Brennan is drawn into the world of fugitive motorcycle gangs, after she is forced to identify the remains of the targets of bomb-lobbing bikers. "Reichs . . . is regressing rather than improving," Anthony Wilson-Smith complained in a review for *Maclean's* (November 13, 2000). "Though the author speaks fluent French in real life and knows her way around Quebec, her cartoonish characters and dialogue seem to put the lie to that. Her cops run around saying things like 'sacré bleu'—an expression once popular in France that Quebec francophones never use—and there are frequent references to life in 'Quebec province,' which no one in Canada says in either official language. The plot line . . . offers potential, but to get from beginning to resolution, Reichs relies on visits from bumbling relatives, improbable coincidences and turncoat characters whose evil intent is telegraphed from their first appearance. . . . As whodunits go, Reichs's latest is deadly all right—but not in the way she intended."

In Reichs's *Fatal Voyage* (2001), Brennan travels to the site of an airline crash in the Great Smoky Mountains to help identify the victims. "With four crime thrillers to her name, Reichs . . . seems to have settled into a comfortable routine with forensic anthropologist Temperance Brennan, whose adventures grow more engrossing with each outing . . . ," a reviewer wrote for *Publishers Weekly* (May 21, 2001). "She capitalizes on the morbid yet captivating aspects of the forensic trenchwork, yet never lets it overwhelm her story. But it is Reichs's ongoing development of Tempe—a woman in her 50s with a mature understanding of human nature, and a self-deprecating sense of humor—that truly lifts the book above many of its peers."

Reichs's next novel, *Grave Secrets* (2002), was inspired by her work in Guatemala. "Reichs is living proof that following the 'write about what you know' edict can lead to a magnificent piece of fiction," Donna Lypchuk wrote for *Quill & Quire* (August 2002). On the other hand, Marilyn Stasio wrote for the *New York Times Book Review* (August 4, 2002), "Reichs is not what you would call a natural-born writer, so the emotional responses of her heroine . . . to the atrocities to which she bears witness can elicit more squeamishness than the actual bones and tissue she digs up. . . . But you can always trust Tempe to get through these rough literary patches and go back to work dissecting a shrunken head or unearthing pieces of a skeleton from the 'stew of human feces and microbial dung' of a septic tank."

In *Bare Bones* (2003) Reichs's heroine is on vacation, attempting to relax, but keeps getting summoned to investigate human remains that turn up unexpectedly. Like some of her earlier books, her next two books, *Monday Mourning* (2004) and *Cross Bones* (2005), are set in Montreal. In her most recent novel, *Break No Bones* (2006), Brennan is supervising the excavation of prehistoric Native American burial grounds just outside Charleston, South Carolina, when she unearths recent remains. While most reviewers predicted that the book would sell well due to the success of *Bones*, they disagreed about the quality of the book: Teresa L. Jacobsen, writing for *Library Journal* (July 1, 2006), complained that "the case itself is lackluster and the plot exceedingly predictable," but Sue

O'Brienin described the novel for *Booklist* (July 1, 2006) as "an engrossing entry in a widely read series."

In the fall of 2005, the Fox television network launched *Bones,* an hour-long drama series with Temperance Brennan as its main character. "I have always loved the idea of taking my character . . . from traditional literature to the small or big screen," Reichs, who serves as a producer for the show, wrote for her Web site. "I love writing novels, but there are more plot lines than I can work into a lifetime of books. My years of experience in the lab and at the crime scene have provided a storehouse of ideas that are intense, chilling, heartwarming, and powerful. Television will now provide the opportunity to share these stories through a brand new medium." Transplanted from Montreal to Washington, D.C., the television version of Brennan (played by Emily Deschanel) frequently clashes with a stubborn FBI agent, Seeley Booth (David Boreanaz), who prefers to solve crimes the old-fashioned way. In a nod to the fans of Reichs's novels, the television character Brennan also writes fiction—about a character named Kathy Reichs. While critics tended to find the premise of the series formulaic—comparing it to *CSI, The X-Files, House,* and *Hart to Hart,* among other shows—it was popular with audiences in its first season and was renewed for a second.

Earlier, in 1998, Reichs was called upon by the U.N. to give expert testimony before a special tribunal, held in the nation of Tanzania, regarding the 1994 genocide in the central African nation of Rwanda. She testified in a case that involved 27 mass graves found in and around a garage in Rwanda's capital city, Kigali. (In the spring of 1994, over a 100-day period, more than 800,000 people— mostly members of Rwanda's minority ethnic group the Tutsis—were slaughtered by members of the nation's majority ethnic group, the Hutus.) "It's important to get concrete evidence on the record so that years down the road someone can't say, 'This didn't take place,'" Reichs told Liz Hoggard for the London *Observer* (May 21, 2006). "There's a huge danger in human rights cases of accusing anyone, so that someone takes the blame for an atrocity. Our work has to be done to the same standard as a forensic criminal investigation here, which is hard, given the circumstances."

In May 2000 Reichs volunteered her services as a consultant with the Fundación de Antropología Forense de Guatemala (Guatemalan Forensic Anthropology Foundation, or FAFG), assisting with the exhumation and analysis of mass graves around Lake Atitlán in the highlands of southwestern Guatemala. An estimated 200,000 people, mostly indigenous Mayans, were killed during Guatemala's brutal civil war, which lasted for three decades, beginning in the early 1960s. In October 2001, as part of the federally coordinated Disaster Mortuary Operational Response Team (DMORT), Reichs traveled to New York City in the wake of the September 11, 2001 terrorist attacks. (DMORT, a component of the National Disaster Medical System [NDMS], comprises volunteer medical and forensic professionals and morticians; its members are called upon in situations of mass casualty. Following the attacks, for the first time in the organization's history, NDMS professionals from around the nation went into action at once, at the behest of then–U.S. secretary of health and human services Tommy G. Thompson.) Working mostly in the New York City borough of Richmond (Staten Island), Reichs and her colleagues helped local authorities sort through mountains of wreckage from the World Trade Center site in search of human remains.

Reichs edited *Hominid Origins: Inquiries Past and Present* (1983) and *Forensic Osteology: Advances in the Identification of Human Remains* (1986); she has also written many academic papers. From 1986 to 1993 she served on the American Board of Forensic Anthropology; she was its vice president from 1989 to 1993. As a member of the American Academy of Forensic Sciences, she chaired the physical anthropology section from 1995 to 1996, when she joined the organization's board of directors. In 1988 she was named to the Phi Beta Delta honor society. She has received many other honors as well.

Reichs has been married to the attorney Paul Reichs for more than 30 years. The couple have three adult children. Reichs has homes in Charlotte, North Carolina, and Montreal. She reveals little else about her private life for "security reasons," as she told Bob Minzesheimer for *USA Today* (August 28, 1997), noting, "I've testified against some less-than-stellar citizens." She admitted to Mudge that she shares some personality traits with Brennan. "Friends who have read the book [*Déjà Dead*] tell me that her dialogue sounds like me. She can be a bit of a smartass . . . a bit abrasive. But in terms of her personal life, it's fiction. And while I do go out to exhumations if we get a tip, I would never pursue the investigation in the way that she does. I stay in the lab." Reichs enjoys spending her free time on the beaches near her North Carolina home. She is also an avid tennis player.

—D.F.

Suggested Reading: *BookPage* (on-line) Sep. 1997; (Charlotte, North Carolina) *Observer* H p1 July 4, 2004; Kathy Reichs's Web site; (London) *Times* Features June 19, 1999; *Quill & Quire* p1+ Aug. 1997; *Weekend Australian* R p1 Aug. 10, 2002

Selected Books: *Déjà Dead,* 1997; *Death du Jour,* 1999; *Deadly Decisions,* 2000; *Grave Secrets,* 2002; *Bare Bones,* 2003; *Monday Mourning,* 2004; *Cross Bones,* 2005; *Break No Bones,* 2006; as editor—*Hominid Origins: Inquiries Past and Present,* 1983; *Forensic Osteology: Advances in the Identification of Human Remains,* 1986

Selected Television Shows: *Bones,* 2005–

Chip Somodevilla/Getty Images

Roberts, John G.

Jan. 27, 1955– Chief justice of the U.S. Supreme Court

Address: Supreme Court of the United States, Washington, DC 20543

Sitting in 2003 before the Senate Judiciary Committee, as part of the confirmation hearings for his third nomination to the United States Court of Appeals for the District of Columbia Circuit, John G. Roberts seemed to win over even Democratic senator Edward M. Kennedy with his answer to a question Kennedy put to him about Roberts's ability to set aside his personal or political views in favor of an open-minded application of legal precedents and the language of particular statutes. "My practice has not been ideological in any sense," Roberts said, as quoted in the official transcript of the hearings—referring to his more than 13 years of private advocacy, all of which were devoted principally to arguing before the United States Supreme Court and other federal courts. "My clients and their positions are liberal and conservative across the board." Roberts then alluded to a number of cases he had handled over the years, particularly emphasizing his work for a joint California-Nevada planning board in *Tahoe-Sierra Preservation Council, Inc. v. Tahoe Regional Planning Agency* (2002) and on behalf of the mining industry in a 2001 case in which he successfully argued that West Virginians who suffered property damage or ill health as a result of mining could not sue for damages. "I would urge you to look at cases on both sides," Roberts told Kennedy. "Look at the brief, look at the argument where I was arguing the pro environmental

position. Take a brief and an argument where I was arguing against environmental enforcement on behalf of a client. See if the professional skills applied, the zealous advocacy is any different in either of those cases. I would respectfully submit that you'll find that it was not. Now, that's not judging, I understand that, but it is the same skill, setting aside personal views, taking the precedents and applying them either as an advocate or as a judge."

Roberts faced similar questions in September 2005, during confirmation hearings before the committee for his nomination by President George W. Bush to the position of chief justice of the United States, more commonly referred to as chief justice of the Supreme Court. Unlike the other eight justices on the court (termed associate justices), the chief justice is vested by the Constitution with presiding over any impeachment trial of the president. In both of Roberts's Senate confirmation hearings, he generally avoided answering questions intended to draw out his personal views. Instead, he emphasized that, as he said in his opening remarks at the 2005 hearing, a "certain humility should characterize the judicial role." He added: "Judges and justices are servants of the law, not the other way around. Judges are like umpires. Umpires don't make the rules; they apply them. The role of an umpire and a judge is critical. They make sure everybody plays by the rules. But it is a limited role. Nobody ever went to a ball game to see the umpire." After both confirmation hearings Roberts went on to receive the approval of the committee by a wide margin (16–3 in 2003 and 13–5 in 2005); he received the approval of the Senate without any expressed dissent on May 8, 2003 and by a vote of 78–22 on September 29, 2005. Within hours of the 2005 vote, Roberts was sworn into office by the court's most senior associate justice, John Paul Stevens. (Roberts succeeded Chief Justice William H. Rehnquist, who died on September 3, 2005.) Following his swearing-in ceremony, Roberts noted with pleasure the relatively broad support he had received from the Senate. "I view the vote this morning as confirmation of what for me is a bedrock principle, that judging is different from politics," Roberts said, in widely reported comments. "And I appreciate the vote very, very much."

Born in Buffalo, New York, and raised in northwestern Indiana, Roberts spent his early life far from the seat of American governmental power, but virtually all of his adult life has been passed in influential legal posts in the nation's capital. Immediately after graduating from Harvard Law School, Roberts clerked for two of the 20th century's most famous jurists, Henry Friendly and William Rehnquist, and he served in two key legal posts under President Ronald Reagan before moving into private practice at the prestigious law firm of Hogan & Hartson. Between his years with Hogan & Hartson and his time working in the Justice Department's Office of the Solicitor General during the presidency of George H. W. Bush, Roberts argued 39 cases before the Supreme Court and won 25 of them, making him a member of "one of the legal world's most exclusive clubs: the small community of attorneys who specialize in guiding clients through the upper stratosphere of the federal judiciary," according to Dan Carney, writing for *Business Week* (October 9, 2000). Serious, by all accounts, about the responsibilities and limitations of the law, Roberts is also said to be quick-witted and so socially conservative that he decided against attending Stanford Law School after meeting a university representative who wore sandals. A registered Republican, Roberts is considered to be politically conservative as well, though both he and people who know him take pains to emphasize that he is not an ideologue. The law professor Cass Sunstein came to that conclusion when he surveyed Roberts's work as a jurist in an editorial for the *Wall Street Journal* (September 5, 2005). To Sunstein Roberts is a judicial minimalist—someone concerned with keeping the judiciary's role as limited as precedents will allow—rather than a judicial fundamentalist, someone who would overturn any number of Supreme Court decisions so as to restore the federal government to an earlier form, one more closely in keeping with what is thought to be the original scope of the Constitution. "In his two years on the federal bench," Sunstein wrote, Roberts "has shown none of the bravado and ambition that characterize the fundamentalists. His opinions are meticulous and circumspect. He avoids sweeping pronouncements and bold strokes, and instead pays close attention to the legal material at hand. He is undoubtedly conservative. But ideology has played only a modest role in his judicial work." Announcing Roberts's nomination to the Supreme Court on July 19, 2005, President Bush described Roberts in even broader and more glowing terms. "John Roberts has devoted his entire professional life to the cause of justice and is widely admired for his intellect, his sound judgment and his personal decency," Bush said, in widely quoted comments. "He has the qualities Americans expect in a judge: experience, wisdom, fairness and civility."

The only boy among John Glover Roberts and Rosemary (Podrasky) Roberts's four children, John Glover Roberts Jr. was born on January 27, 1955 in Buffalo, New York. His mother was a homemaker and his father an electrical engineer who had moved up through the ranks to become a plant manager with Bethlehem Steel. When Roberts was in elementary school, the company transferred his father to a plant in northwestern Indiana, near Chicago, Illinois, and for the rest of Roberts's youth, the family lived in the small, relatively affluent village of Long Beach. Roberts finished his education at Catholic schools not far from home, first at the Notre Dame elementary school and later at La Lumiere, then an all-boys' boarding school. Both institutions were extremely small, and La Lumiere required all students to play three sports so that no team lacked players. Roberts ran track but favored

wrestling and later football, playing fullback in his senior year and serving as a co-captain. As a student Roberts excelled at all things verbal; he studied Latin, acted in the drama group, and worked on the school newspaper all four years at La Lumiere, eventually becoming a co-editor.

In 1973 Roberts graduated from La Lumiere at the top of his class of 25 students and began studying at Harvard University, in Cambridge, Massachusetts, where he entered with sophomore status. A history major, Roberts was by all accounts a driven, sharp-witted, socially conservative, and essentially even-keeled student. Roberts shared a sophomore history prize called the William Scott Ferguson award with another student, and two years later he won the 1976 Bowdoin Prize for Undergraduates, given each year for an outstanding essay on any subject. He also submitted a senior honors thesis on the early 20th-century history of the British Liberal Party. A member of the prestigious honor society Phi Beta Kappa, Roberts graduated summa cum laude from Harvard in 1976 and entered the university's law school the same year. Between 1977 and 1979 Roberts worked on the *Harvard Law Review*, serving as its managing editor during his final year. He earned his juris doctorate in 1979. The stress of achieving the high honor of magna cum laude that accompanied his law degree took a toll, and Roberts—said by an undergraduate friend to have always kept medicine at hand to soothe his perennially upset stomach—ended up in the hospital after graduation, suffering from exhaustion.

Roberts's first position after Harvard was as a law clerk to a federal judge in New York on the second of the 12 regional courts (termed "circuits") of the courts of appeals. In the hierarchy of the federal judicial system, the courts of appeals stand between the almost 100 federal trial courts spread throughout the country and the Supreme Court in Washington, D.C., and because of its jurisdiction over New York City, the Second Circuit is considered one of the most important of them all. The judge Roberts clerked for, moreover, was Henry Friendly, who is considered possibly the greatest American appeals court judge of the previous century. Roberts's year-long appointment with Friendly, Evan Thomas and Stuart Taylor Jr. argued in *Newsweek* (August 1, 2005), left a lasting mark on his approach to the law. Friendly took an open-minded attitude toward each case, Roberts explained in his 2005 Supreme Court confirmation hearings, giving ample room in his written legal opinions to the evidence presented and to the legal precedents that informed his conclusions, even noting cases in which similar precedents could have been chosen and why he selected the ones he did. Thomas and Taylor described Roberts as having followed that approach in the 49 decisions he wrote more than 20 years later, when he served as a federal appeals court judge on the circuit court for Washington, D.C.

In 1980 Roberts finished his appointment with Friendly and moved on to an even more prestigious clerkship, this time with Supreme Court justice William H. Rehnquist. Appointed chief justice in 1986, Rehnquist was at the time of Roberts's clerkship one of the court's eight associate justices and was among its most politically conservative members, taking a consistent stand against the desegregation of public schools, for example, and dissenting from the majority opinion in the Supreme Court case that established the unconstitutionality of most laws restricting abortion, *Roe v. Wade* (1973). Over the following decades Roberts's early alliance with Rehnquist was used by both supporters and detractors as evidence of his clearly conservative values, but to some people who knew him at the time, Roberts's conservatism was less a product of his exposure to Rehnquist than of an already established attitude toward the law. John A. Siliciano, a clerk with the liberal Supreme Court justice Thurgood Marshall during Roberts's time under Rehnquist and currently the vice provost of the Cornell University Law School, told Adam Liptak and Todd S. Purdum for the *New York Times* (July 31, 2005), "John's conservatism was in fact a sign of intellectual courage, coming out of Harvard and being surrounded by law clerks from mainly liberal, East Coast, Ivy League institutions." Roberts's work as one of Rehnquist's three clerks revolved around administrative tasks and legal research, with much of his time given over to assessing the merits of the thousands of petitions sent to the court every year requesting that it hear a case.

In 1981, with Rehnquist's behind-the-scenes help, Roberts moved from the Supreme Court to the Justice Department for another roughly year-long position: as a special assistant to William French Smith, the attorney general during Reagan's first term. The following year Roberts moved even closer to the president, serving as an associate counsel to his chief counsel, Fred F. Fielding. Much of Roberts's work under Fielding was serious but routine—reading laws the president was asked to sign and speeches he planned to give, researching the legalities of proposed presidential decisions, and answering requests for the president's endorsement of some product or action or for his appearance at an event.

Given the nature of his position, however, some of Roberts's otherwise routine work had far-reaching implications, both for Reagan and eventually, in his bid to become a Supreme Court justice, for Roberts as well. In one 1985 memo Roberts argued that the U.S. should not be a party to the two 1977 protocols intended to update the Geneva Conventions, the 1949 international agreements governing wartime behavior. Roberts's "main objection," according to Jess Bravin and Jeanne Cummings, writing for the *Wall Street Journal* (August 16, 2005), was that the later protocols "would treat many terrorist organizations as if they were countries engaged in war, legitimizing their activities and offering them protections and courtesies that should not be extended to common criminals." (The U.S. has yet to ratify either of the 1977 protocols.) Another important memo involved a 1984 district court ruling that called on Washington State to adjust its pay scales for positions usually filled by women so as to compensate for the historical tendency to pay less for jobs associated with women. This approach, called "comparable worth," differed from the already widely embraced notion of "equal pay for equal work" in that it sought to bring into balance dissimilar jobs—to even out, for example, the pay of such male-dominated positions as construction worker with those of such female-dominated ones as nurse's aide. "It is difficult to exaggerate the perniciousness of 'comparable-worth' theory," Roberts wrote in a widely quoted memo from 1984. "It mandates nothing less than central planning of the economy by judges." The slogan of the theory's supporters, he added, "may as well be, 'From each according to his ability, to each according to her gender.'" Other memos Roberts wrote during that time which later became controversial included a number addressing racial discrimination and one attacking a 1984 Supreme Court decision that had ruled silent meditation or prayer in public schools unconstitutional. Assessing Roberts's views in these memos and work he did later for the executive branch, Stuart Taylor Jr. wrote for the *Legal Times* (September 26, 2005): "Roberts' interpretations of anti-discrimination laws . . . were sometimes too narrow, in my view. But his positions were both well-reasoned and consistent with his restrained view of judicial power."

Roberts left the White House in May 1986 to become an associate at Hogan & Hartson, one of Washington, D.C.'s oldest and largest legal firms; under two years later he was made a partner. Both during his first tenure at Hogan & Hartson and in the following decade, when he returned to the firm for a 10-year stint, Roberts's area of specialization was appellate law—in his case, crafting legal appeals to federal courts, particularly the Supreme Court, and also to some of the district circuit courts. As this was a private practice, Roberts's work with Hogan & Hartson lacked the partisan political flavor that had previously characterized his work. Even the clear and consistently expressed belief he had as a political appointee in the strength of privilege of the executive branch fell to the side. His most prominent case during his first tenure with the firm served as a check on federal prosecutors' powers to punish offenders; Roberts argued in *United States v. Halper* (1989) that Irwin Halper, at one time the manager of a medical laboratory in New York City, had already been punished once in criminal court with a sentence of two years in jail and a $5,000 fine for defrauding the federal Medicare program of $585 and thus could not be punished again in civil court, as he had been by being fined an additional $130,000. The Supreme Court voted unanimously in agreement with Roberts that prosecuting Halper a second time violated the double-jeopardy clause in the Fifth Amendment.

In October 1989 Roberts left Hogan & Hartson to return to the government's executive branch, becoming the principal deputy solicitor general to Solicitor General Kenneth Starr. Later famous for leading the Office of the Independent Counsel's investigations into people tied to President Bill Clinton and for laying the groundwork for Clinton's impeachment in the sex scandal involving the former White House intern Monica Lewinsky, Starr was appointed solicitor general by President George H. W. Bush and, like all solicitors general, was primarily charged with arguing on behalf of the federal government in cases before the Supreme Court. The principal deputy solicitor is distinguished from the five other deputy solicitors general by the power of becoming acting solicitor general in cases in which the solicitor general deems it inappropriate to be involved in the case directly; Roberts took on this duty at least four times in no fewer than 16 appearances before the court. The work of the solicitor general and his deputies can also extend beyond arguing cases before the Supreme Court, a point Roberts himself made in an editorial for the *Wall Street Journal* (May 5, 1993). While most of "what the government's chief litigator does before the court—defending federal statutes, programs and convictions—generally continues unchanged from one administration to the next," Roberts wrote, the solicitor general's office can also present courts with legal arguments—called briefs of amicus curiae or amicus briefs—to support cases that further a particular administration's political views, even if the U.S. government is not directly involved in the case and even if the case is not being heard (or not yet being heard) in the Supreme Court. The strength of such briefs can be considerable. (Roberts wrote that research suggests "the side, that] the government supports as amicus prevails about 75% of the time.") Taken altogether, Roberts's arguments during the slightly over three years he served as principal deputy solicitor general covered a wide range of topics, many of them hinging on technical questions, including what constituted the proper procedures for filing and distributing legal documents (*Irwin v. Department of Veterans Affairs*, 1990) and whether more than 1,000 specific, local decisions by the Bureau of Land Management could be challenged at once and by an organization that was not directly affected by those decisions (*Lujan v. National Wildlife Federation*, 1990); others involved similarly abstruse details about finance or tax laws (*Grogan v. Garner*, 1991), *Cottage Savings Association v. Commissioner of Internal Revenue*, 1991), and *United States v. Centennial Savings Bank*, 1991). Only a few touched on more sensitive areas, such as the government's ability to force the sale of land needed for public use (*National Railroad Passenger Corporation v. Boston & Maine Corporation*, 1992), prisoners' rights (*Hudson v. McMillian*, 1991, *Helling v. McKinney*, 1993, and *Withrow v. Williams*,

1993), the limits placed on the police in search-and-seizure activities (*Florida v. Jimeno*, 1991), affirmative action (*Metro Broadcasting, Inc. v. Federal Communications Commission*, 1990), and, the most divisive judicial issue of all, abortion (*Bray v. Alexandria Clinic*, 1993). It should be noted, though, that in the case of *Bray v. Alexandria Clinic* the questions put to the court were about protesting abortion rather than abortion per se. Similarly, another important case that Roberts participated in that involved abortion was not directly related to the freedoms granted by *Roe v. Wade*. Called *Rust v. Sullivan* (1991), the case questioned regulations laid out by Secretary of Health and Human Services Louis Sullivan that forbade the use of federal funds to support abortion, with "support" being defined to include telling women the names of clinics that perform abortions. While it was Starr who argued the case before the Supreme Court, Roberts co-authored the brief submitted on the government's behalf, and one sentence in that brief later became a lightning rod for pro-choice activism against Roberts's many nominations to the bench: "We continue to believe that Roe was wrongly decided and should be overruled." The court never responded to that part of the government's argument, though it decided by one vote (5–4) in favor of the government's overall position that Sullivan's regulations had not violated the First or Fifth Amendment.

In January 1992, while still working for the Office of the Solicitor General, Roberts was nominated to fill a position on the United States Court of Appeals for the District of Columbia Circuit formerly held by current Supreme Court justice Clarence Thomas. Like dozens of other judicial nominations put forward by the first Bush administration, however, Roberts's nomination lingered untouched throughout the rest of the year, the victim of the Democrats' desire to put off confirming nominees until after the 1992 presidential elections. When Bill Clinton won in November, Roberts's chances evaporated. In their article in *Newsweek*, Thomas and Taylor pointed to that development as Roberts's "lowest moment" and reported that "friends say he was crestfallen." Publicly, Roberts never missed a beat; his return to Hogan & Hartson to direct its appellate law practice was announced in January 1993, even before he had argued his last case before the court as principal deputy solicitor general.

Over his next 10 years at Hogan & Hartson, Roberts amassed both an impressive record of appearances before the Supreme Court and a small fortune, earning more than $1 million during the final year of his private practice. The range of cases he argued during that phase of his career covered everything from patent law (*TrafFix Devices, Inc. v. Marketing Displays, Inc.*, 2000) to state policies governing the behavior of sexual offenders (*Smith v. Doe*, 2003), with only one clear trend: Roberts tended to represent large, well-established groups—businesses, universities, industry-wide organizations, or state or local governments—rather than individuals, unions, or political groups of any stripe. One reason for that may have been his experience advocating for the federal government in the Solicitor General's Office; another may have been the extremely high fees of Hogan & Hartson, which in at least one instance ran to $500,000 to argue a single case before the Supreme Court, a charge that put his expertise far beyond the reach of most private individuals. In this phase of his private practice, Roberts showed a particularly strong tendency to represent the interests of manufacturers, especially mining corporations, in suits directly or indirectly related to workers' rights, a tendency that also put him on the losing side on a relatively high number of occasions. In *United Mineworkers of America v. Bagwell* (1994), Roberts argued on behalf of the state of Virginia's attempt to recover more than $64 million in fines from a miners' union; the attempt failed when the Supreme Court decided that the decision to award the fines had been reached unfairly. In 2000 Roberts argued in *Eastern Associated Coal Corp. v. United Mine Workers of America* that a mining company had the right to fire an employee who had twice tested positive for marijuana use, despite a private arbitration decision that reinstated the employee; the Supreme Court again decided against Roberts's clients. Roberts met the same fate in *Barnhart v. Peabody Coal Co.* (2003), when the Supreme Court sided against the coal company in a suit involving the Coal Industry Retiree Health Benefit Act of 1992, with much of the case hinging on the interpretation of a single word: "shall." A year earlier, however, Roberts enjoyed an important victory, one with far-reaching implications for the interpretation of the 1990 Americans with Disabilities Act (ADA), when the Supreme Court voted unanimously in support of Roberts's client, the car company Toyota, in its suit against a former employee, Ella Williams. Williams had been fired from Toyota after developing carpal tunnel syndrome and had claimed that the company acted negligently by not making the accommodations for her disability required by the ADA.

Roberts's success with *Toyota Motor Manufacturing v. Williams* was more characteristic of his record in private practice than his handful of losses against mining workers. Indeed, Roberts was extraordinarily successful in his appearances before the Supreme Court, winning 25 of the 39 cases he argued—a figure that combines his private practice with his time in the Solicitor General's Office and that made him, as Adam Liptak wrote for the *New York Times* (July 20, 2005), "one of the great Supreme Court advocates of his generation." Among the most important cases that Roberts won for Hogan & Hartson were two in which he represented the state of Alaska. The first case was *Alaska v. Native Village of Venetie Tribal Government* (1998), which revolved around whether the state or a village of Neets'aii Gwich'in people—one of Alaska's many Native American groups—had the right to

impose taxes on business conducted on its land. The Supreme Court decided that it was the state's right since the land occupied by the village of Venetie no longer qualified as "Indian country" after a 1971 federal law eliminated all but one of Alaska's Native American reservations. A second victory for the state of Alaska came five years later, with *Smith v. Doe* (2003), in which Roberts successfully argued that an act requiring sex offenders to register with the state could be applied to people who had been convicted of sexual offenses before the act became effective, in August 1994. But perhaps the most widely discussed case of Roberts's private-practice career was *NCAA v. Smith*, in 1999. Representing the National Collegiate Athletic Association, Roberts took the position that the NCAA was not subject to the gender equity requirements set forth in Title IX of the Education Amendments of 1972 because it did not directly receive the federal funding from which it admittedly benefited from by virtue of its intimate ties to American colleges and universities. The Supreme Court unanimously agreed.

In November 2000, while still at Hogan & Hartson, Roberts went to Florida to support the campaign of George W. Bush and Richard B. Cheney when that year's election results were in dispute. In 2001, when Bush became the first Republican president in eight years, he immediately nominated Roberts to fill an open position on the Washington, D.C., federal circuit court—the same position Bush's father had hoped Roberts would fill. Though buoyed by a letter from a bipartisan group of 150 lawyers offering Roberts unqualified praise, he was an object of particular opposition by groups seeking to ensure that *Roe v. Wade* remain in place, as Roberts's record on abortion did not suggest he supported it. For two years Roberts and 29 other nominees languished, not even offered the opportunity to air their views in hearings in front of the Senate Judiciary Committee. In 2003, however, Roberts received a third nomination, and this time, with a clear Republican majority in place in the Senate, Roberts was given the spot he had first been offered over a decade earlier.

Roberts's appointment began on June 2, 2003, and over the next two years, he heard scores of cases but wrote opinions on only 49, dissenting only three times from the other judges who heard the same cases. Out of all his work on the court, three cases in particular were frequently mentioned during his nomination hearings in 2005. The first came in 2003, when the court was asked in *Rancho Viejo, LLC v. Norton* to decide whether the Department of the Interior had the right under the Endangered Species Act to regulate development that might harm the arroyo southwestern toad, a species found only in California. When the standard three-judge panel found that the Department of the Interior did have that power, the circuit court was asked to consider the case en banc—that is, to consider it before the whole court, a move that would necessarily bring a wider array of opinions. On July 22, 2003 the court rejected the petition for an en banc hearing, and Roberts authored one of two dissents. He argued that hearing the case before the full court was justified by the misapplication of certain Supreme Court precedents by the smaller panel of judges; he also seemed to doubt that the federal government had the power to protect what he called "a hapless toad that, for reasons of its own, lives its entire life in California," and thus cannot be protected under the federal government's power to regulate interstate commerce. (The Supreme Court refused to hear the case in 2004.) The second case seized on by Roberts's critics centered on a 12-year-old girl who in October 2000 was caught eating a single french fry in a Washington, D.C., subway station. Because the city's laws did not allow for a minor to be simply fined for the offense, the child was handcuffed and searched and had her shoelaces removed before she was taken to a police station, where she was fingerprinted and held for nearly three hours prior to her release. In the opinion of the child's mother, the police's extreme response violated her daughter's constitutional rights, but to the district court that first heard the case, and to Roberts and the other members on the circuit court panel that reviewed it, the city's law might indeed have been a "bad idea" but did not violate the girl's rights. The final case, decided after Roberts's initial contact with Bush about the Supreme Court position but several days before his nomination, was called *Hamdan v. Rumsfeld* (2005) and concerned a man, Salim Ahmed Hamdan, who in 2001 was captured by Afghani military forces and accused of having been the driver for terrorist mastermind Osama bin Laden. The government tried Hamdan for his terrorist activities under a system of military tribunals, as he was what it termed an "enemy combatant"; Hamdan and his supporters, however, petitioned for a full jury trial in American courts. Roberts and the other two judges who heard the case refused to grant Hamdan his petition, and the continued detention ordered by the military trial was allowed to stand.

On July 19, 2005 Bush nominated Roberts to fill a spot that had just been vacated by the politically moderate associate justice Sandra Day O'Connor, who on July 1 had announced her decision to retire. Responses to Roberts's nomination from conservatives were swift and generally emphatic in their support, while liberal responses varied from cautious approval to forceful denunciations. To most political observers, though, Roberts's nomination seemed assured almost from the beginning—barring unexpected revelations about his past during his hearings in the Senate. Only one surprise emerged, and it came just before those hearings were set to begin: on September 3, 2005 Rehnquist died of thyroid cancer. Three days later Bush withdrew Roberts's first nomination and recommended him instead for Rehnquist's spot. The hearings before the Senate Judiciary Committee lasted from September 12 to 15, and in the views

of most observers, Roberts sailed through them, little troubled by the persistent questions from Democrats about his opinions, especially on abortion. As Democratic senator Charles Schumer told Roberts on the last day of the hearings: "Your knowledge of law and the way you present it is a tour de force. You may very well possess the most powerful intellect of any person to come before the Senate for this position." Two weeks later, before the full Senate, Schumer nonetheless joined 22 of his Democratic colleagues in voting against Roberts. The remaining 22 Democrats voted to support him, while all 55 Republican senators and the one independent did as well.

Before the start of the 2005–06 session, many observers expected to see more divisiveness among the members of the Roberts Supreme Court than had existed under Chief Justice Rehnquist, but, as Jeffery Rosen wrote for *Time* (July 10, 2006), "the Roberts court is, at least so far, less fractured than the court led for 19 years by William Rehnquist. Almost half its decisions this year had no dissents, compared with 38% in Rehnquist's final term, and the tally of 16 cases decided by a 5-to-4 vote is seven fewer than under Rehnquist. That is a tribute to the personality and leadership skills of Roberts, who has made issuing strong decisions and encouraging collegial debate top priorities." Rosen added that in a speech that Roberts gave during the graduation ceremony held in May at Georgetown University Law Center, he stated that he hoped that upcoming Supreme Court rulings would be decided unanimously or nearly so, so as to promote "clarity and guidance for lawyers and lower courts trying to figure out what Justices meant."

Roberts lives in Chevy Chase, Maryland, with his wife, Jane Marie Sullivan Roberts, a fellow attorney. They married in July 1996 and have two adopted children, Josephine (known as Josie), who was five at the time that Roberts's nomination was announced in 2005, and John (known as Jack), who was four.

—D.R.

Suggested Reading: Federal Judiciary Web site; FindLaw Web site; *Harvard Crimson* (on-line) July 19, 2005; *Indianapolis Star* (on-line) July 20, 2005; *New York Times* A p1 July 22, 2005; *Newsweek* Aug. 1, 2005, with photos; Oyez Project Web site; *Time* p26 July 10, 2006; *U.S. News & World Report* p32+ Oct. 2, 2006; U.S. Senate Judiciary Committee Web site; U.S. Supreme Court Web site; *USA Today* (on-line) July 20, 2005; *Weekly Standard* (on-line) Aug. 8, 2005

Peter Kramer/Getty Images

Roberts, Tony

Oct. 22, 1939– Actor

Address: c/o Innovative Artists, 1505 10th Ave., Santa Monica, CA 90401

"I never look down on work," the theater, film, and television actor Tony Roberts told Michael Riedel for the New York *Daily News* (April 21, 1996). Now in his late 60s, Roberts has seldom been without acting jobs since the age of 23, when he made his debut on Broadway in a short-lived drama. He earned two Tony Award nominations in the late 1960s and, as Brooke Allen wrote for the *City Journal* (Winter 1995, on-line), "assumed he would have a lifelong career on the New York stage." Not by choice, however, he has spent a considerable portion of his professional life in front of a camera. "What you want to be is a working actor," his father once told him, as he recalled to Riedel. "If you can be a star, that's fine. But your goal should be to get work." Among Roberts's dozens of credits are starring roles on Broadway, in the comedies *Barefoot in the Park*, *Arsenic and Old Lace*, and *The Tale of the Allergist's Wife*, and the musicals *Promises, Promises, Jerome Robbins' Broadway, Cabaret*, and *Victor/Victoria*, and Off-Broadway, in the drama *Endgame*. He has had co-starring parts in *Play It Again, Sam, Annie Hall*, and other Woody Allen films and in such motion pictures as *Serpico, Just Tell Me What You Want*, and *Switch*; he has also played leading and supporting roles in made-for-TV movies, among them *The Lindbergh Kidnapping Case, A Question of Honor*, and *The American Clock*. His work in regional theater includes performances at such venues as the Yale Repertory

Theatre, the Paper Mill Playhouse, the Berkshire Theatre Festival, and the Saratoga Performing Arts Festival. In addition, Roberts had regular roles on TV, in the short-lived sitcom *The Four Seasons*, which ran for half a year in 1984, three shorter-lived series—*Rosetti and Ryan* (1977), *The Lucie Arnaz Show* (1985), and *The Thorns* (1988)—and appeared on the soap opera *Edge of Night* in the 1960s. His resumé also includes work as a radio announcer, voiceover artist, and, early in his career, actor in advertisements. "My earliest ambition was to be an American Laurence Olivier, a great Shakespearean actor or at least 75 percent that and 25 percent Gene Kelly . . . ," he told Frederick M. Winship for United Press International (April 22, 1988). "I didn't particularly think of myself as a comic actor, but that's the way it's developed over the years." Roberts appeared most recently behind the footlights in a Broadway revival of *Barefoot in the Park*, which ran for 109 performances between February and May 2006. An actor's life, he told Simi Horwitz for *Back Stage* (March 24, 2005, on-line), is a series of "peaks and valleys." If an actor is in a valley, he has to believe a peak will be coming. It's the only way to avoid despair."

The son of Kenneth Roberts and Norma Roberts, David Anthony Roberts was born on October 22, 1939 in New York City and grew up there with his sister, Nancy. His father worked as an announcer for such radio programs as *The Shadow, Joyce Jordan: Girl Intern*, and *The Milton Berle Show* and for such TV series as *The Electric Company* and the soap operas *Love of Life* and *Secret Storm*. Still working at 96, Ken Roberts has also acted in many TV series and has had roles in dozens of films and made-for-TV movies. Actors including Zero Mostel and Jack Gilford were Roberts family friends, and one of Tony Roberts's cousins, Everett Sloane, was a film, television, and radio actor. Ken Roberts told Michael Riedel, "I first suspected that Tony would become an actor when he was 4. I remember one Saturday afternoon, Laurence Olivier was doing *Henry V* on the radio, and there was little Tony glued to the loudspeaker. I'd never seen a child so fascinated by the sound and the words coming from the radio; we couldn't drag him away. From then on, all he ever thought about or dreamt about was being an actor." Tony Roberts has traced his love of acting in part to the theatrical performance of *Around the World in 80 Days*, starring Orson Welles, that he saw in 1946. He told Hollie Saunders for the *Lancaster (Ohio) Eagle Gazette* (July 27, 2004), "I thought this was something I had to do. I was completely enchanted with theater." Watching his father and others at work in radio studios, speaking with different voices and accents, also influenced his choice of vocation. "It was fascinating to see grownups with scripts in their hands creating this fantastic adventure, and making the people listening at home think everything was really happening," he told Michael Riedel. "This was a very important connection for me to make."

Roberts attended New York City public schools, including P.S. 6, on East 81st Street, and what was then known as the High School of Music and Art (it is now the Fiorello H. LaGuardia School of Music & Art and Performing Arts). When he was about 11, he appeared in a production mounted at the 92nd Street Y. "Acting was what I did best when I was growing up, and it's what I got stroked for," he told Enid Nemy for the *New York Times* (July 26, 1985). On the advice of the legendary acting instructor Lee Strasberg, Roberts attended Northwestern University, in Evanston, Illinois, where he studied under the acclaimed and demanding drama teacher Alvina Krause. Krause "saw the theatre as the salvation of mankind, nothing less," Roberts told Michael Kuchwara for the Associated Press (August 11, 1985). "She believed in it the way a fanatic believes in the afterlife. You could change an audience's life. And if you didn't do that every performance, . . . you were missing the boat." Once, Krause told him, as he recalled to Michael Elkin for the *Jewish Exponent* (January 18, 1996), "One of the prime responsibilities of theater is to illuminate life, and it's wonderful to do it through laughter." Roberts majored in both speech and theater and earned a B.S. degree from Northwestern in 1961.

As Roberts recalled to Riedel, his father advised him when he was still in his teens "to be forceful about getting out there, creating your destiny, never resting on your laurels." Within months of his college graduation, Roberts (calling himself Anthony Roberts, as he was to do for several years) secured a part in a Broadway play, an adaptation for the stage of Mark Harris's novel *Something About a Soldier*. The production closed in January 1962 after a week's run. Later in 1962 he appeared with a national touring company in Neil Simon's *Come Blow Your Horn*. In 1963 he became the understudy for Robert Redford, a star of Neil Simon's comedy *Barefoot in the Park*, after the original understudy broke an ankle. When Redford left the cast of the show, which Mike Nichols directed, Roberts replaced him. Roberts earned $400 a week (equivalent to $2,440 in 2005) to portray the male lead, a stuffy, newly married lawyer, eight times a week for 17 months. In 1964 he appeared in Saul Bellow's *The Last Analysis*, which closed after 28 performances. For three years (1964–67) he played the character Lee Pollock on the television soap opera *Edge of Night*. He received excellent notices for his portrayal as Axel Magee, the bumbling son of an ambassador, in Woody Allen's comedy *Don't Drink the Water*, which opened on Broadway in November 1966. According to various critics, he came across as "both personable and comical," "likably fatuous," "disarming," and "the most charming bubblehead we have met on stage in some time."

Roberts received top billing in his next Broadway outing, *How Now, Dow Jones*, a musical comedy with a score by Elmer Bernstein, lyrics by Carolyn Leigh, and book by Max Shulman, directed by the venerable George Abbott. The role is one of very few that Roberts has originated in the legitimate theater. Although the show, which opened in late 1967 and closed in mid-1968, elicited mixed reviews, critics universally praised Roberts for his performance as Charley, "a young failure whose charming inabilities turn out to be just the thing to make him a success as a stock salesman," as a writer for *Newsweek* (December 18, 1967) described the character. "Mr. Roberts was applauded last year in *Don't Drink the Water*," Haskel Frankel wrote for the *National Observer* (December 11, 1967), "and now that he has added singing and dancing to his other boyish confusions, he has become an all-around, unstoppable star." Clive Barnes, in the *New York Times* (December 8, 1967), wrote, "Roberts, tousle-haired and with an aggressively untamed terrier face and eyebrows with independent suspension, is a bundle of talent." In 1968 Roberts received a Tony Award nomination, for best actor in a musical, for his work in *How Now, Dow Jones*. The next year he made his London stage debut, in a role originated in 1968 by Jerry Orbach on Broadway—that of Chuck Baxter, in the hit musical *Promises, Promises*, based on the movie *The Apartment*, with book by Neil Simon, score by Burt Bacharach, lyrics by Hal David, and choreography by Michael Bennett. For his efforts, he earned a London Critics Poll Award as best actor in a musical. In 1972 he succeeded Orbach in the same role in New York.

Earlier, in Woody Allen's stage comedy *Play It Again, Sam* (1969–70), Roberts depicted Dick Christie, who, with his wife, Linda (played by Diane Keaton), comes up with a series of miniskirted dates for the recently divorced, desperately insecure, monumentally inept protagonist, Allan Felix (Allen). David Merrick, a co-producer of the show, had recommended Roberts for the role, but Allen remained unimpressed after seeing Roberts in five auditions. Allen changed his mind after attending one of Roberts's performances in *Barefoot in the Park*, at Merrick's urging. As Roberts recalled to Jan Herman for the *Los Angeles Times* (October 31, 1997), Allen came backstage and said, "This is great. You're very good. I'll give you the part in my play. Why are you so bad at auditions?" Roberts told Herman that auditions are "every actor's nightmare, and with me they're worse." "I have to have rehearsals," he explained. "They're a collaboration that helps you come up with a performance. Going into a strange room with strange people who don't give you confidence, who are saying, 'Show me,' is entirely different. It's a tremendous burden." Roberts's work in *Play It Again, Sam* brought him a second Tony Award nomination, in 1969, for best featured actor in a play, as well as critical plaudits. Roberts reprised the role in Allen's well-received adaptation for the silver screen of *Play It Again, Sam* (1972). On Broadway in 1972 he appeared in the musical *Sugar*, based on the film *Some Like It Hot*, portraying Joe/Josephine, the character played by Tony Curtis in the movie; Robert Morse was cast as his sidekick, Jerry/Daphne.

Roberts had made his film debut in 1971, with the Walt Disney feature *The Million Dollar Duck*. While the film was a box-office success, Roberts found his role—which included barking at ducks while on his hands and knees—"properly humbling," as he told Michael Riedel. "When I first went to [Hollywood] . . . they were very impressed if someone could memorize more than a page of dialogue," he told Lawrence Van Gelder for the *New York Times* (October 20, 1989). "Somehow or other I was given the label New York actor because I was a fairly reliable study." "I'm very proud to be known as a New York actor . . . ," he added. "I probably have some kind of urbane street-smart wisdom that comes from the New York public school system, my greatest teacher." In 1973 Roberts had a supporting role in the film *Serpico*, directed by Sidney Lumet and starring Al Pacino in the title role, that of a police officer whose attempts to blow the whistle on police corruption turn him into a pariah. The next year Roberts appeared as Deputy Mayor LaSalle in *The Taking of Pelham One Two Three* and, on Broadway, as Geoffrey in the opening-night cast of Alan Ayckbourne's play *Absurd Person Singular*.

Roberts portrayed Rob, the longtime actor friend of the character Alvy Singer, in *Annie Hall* (1977), a semi-autobiographical movie that Allen directed, co-wrote (with Marshall Brickman), and starred in (as Alvy), along with Diane Keaton as the title character. Roberts's was among several "superb" performances that Frank Rich mentioned in his assessment of *Annie Hall* for the *New York Post* (April 21, 1977), one of many enthusiastic reviews of the film. Roberts was also cast in the Allen-written and -directed movies *Stardust Memories* (1980), as the confidant of the main character, a renowned but unhappy film director; *A Midsummer Night's Sex Comedy* (1982), as an egotistical, philandering physician; *Hannah and Her Sisters* (1986), as Norman, a former business partner of Mickey Sachs (Allen), the title character's ex-husband; and *Radio Days* (1987), as the "Silver Dollar" emcee. According to Charles Isherwood in the *New York Times* (February 25, 2005), Allen used Roberts in his films to "epitomize suave charm in contrast to his own hapless shlubbery." There was a major drawback to his association with Allen: as Roberts told Jan Herman, "I was always so vividly the guy Woody wrote, that everybody in the business, casting agents, for instance, would think of me that way. The persona I was for Woody is a hard thing to break out of." Roberts has not appeared in any of the two dozen movies Allen has made since *Radio Days*. "At some point I think I probably outlived my usefulness in his lexicon or repertoire of characters," Roberts told Herman. Nevertheless, his name is still often automatically linked with Allen's films.

Meanwhile, Roberts also worked on the New York stage, with parts in the musical *They're Playing Our Song* (1979), the comedies *Murder at the Howard Johnson's* (1979) and *Doubles* (1985), and a revival of another comedy, *Arsenic and Old Lace* (1986). In 1990 he starred in *Jerome Robbins' Broadway*, a revue, directed by Robbins, consisting of many of the legendary director and choreographer's best-known dances. Replacing Jason Alexander (who had won a Tony Award for his performance), Roberts sang and danced in seven roles, among them that of the narrator (a part that Alexander had written for the show); Pseudolus from *A Funny Thing Happened on the Way to the Forum*; and Tevye from *Fiddler on the Roof*. In addition to using "a lot of Velcro and false hair," as he told Larry King, who interviewed him for CNN (July 12, 1991), he changed his persona for each role by imagining people from his past or anything else that reminded him of the character. Taking a brief break from that job, he played an obnoxious advertising executive in Blake Edwards's film *Switch* (1991). Edwards directed him again in 1995, this time on Broadway, in Edwards's adaptation of his 1982 movie *Victor/Victoria*, which had starred Julie Andrews, Robert Preston, and James Garner. Roberts was cast as "Toddy" (the Preston role), a gay cabaret performer who helps Victoria (Andrews) get work by having her pose as a female impersonator named Victor. "The excellent cast is anchored by Tony Roberts, sweetly world-weary as a gay blade who's not the hot Toddy that he was," Jack Kroll wrote in a review for *Newsweek* (November 6, 1995, on-line).

In 1997 Roberts starred in a Los Angeles production of Stuart Flack's drama *Sidney Bechet Killed a Man*, as a successful heart surgeon and jazz lover who commits murder. "Roberts seems to have arrived at a late-breaking state of grace," Laurie Winer wrote for the *Los Angeles Times* (November 7, 1997). "The mellow fatuousness he embodied in early Woody Allen films has graduated into something layered and interesting: He has become a worldly citizen with a touch of melancholy, a man who possesses the hard-won ease to soar above earthly troubles while still respecting their power." From October 2000 to May 2002, in another leading role, Roberts played Ira Taub in Charles Busch's comedy *The Tale of the Allergist's Wife*, directed by Lynne Meadow. Charles Isherwood, in a critique for *Variety* (November 3, 2000, on-line), praised Roberts's "priceless underplaying."

In 2005 Roberts was offered what he described to Simi Horwitz as his first "heavyweight" role: that of the blind, wheelchair-bound Hamm in Samuel Beckett's drama *Endgame*. Charlotte Moore, who directed the production, which was mounted at the Irish Repertory Theatre in New York, told Horwitz, "There was something about [Roberts's] voice. Beckett says that his work is a matter of 'sounds made as fully as possible. They should be intoned, sonorous, or pompous at times.' Tony has that quality in spades. There is grandness in his voice. He also holds himself theatrically. And this play is about theatre. There are endless references to theatre—dialogues and asides." "The biggest acting challenge for me in *Endgame* is remembering all those lines," Roberts told Horwitz. He also told her, "There are so many contradictions [in *Endgame*] you're stymied. So you try to gravitate toward an intuitive connection with the material. My abusive relationship with my parents [in the play] is stimulated by my own feelings toward my father on occasion. I love you, but move over." *Endgame* also marked Roberts's first performance of a blind man. "I keep my eyes closed from the beginning to the end. Doing that immediately creates another reality," he told Horwitz. In an assessment for the *New York Times* (February 25, 2005, on-line) of Roberts's performance, Charles Isherwood wrote, "There is more than a smidgen of the ham in Hamm, and Mr. Roberts, with his sharp actorly instincts, proves surprisingly at ease in the strange wilds of Beckett's universe. His urbanity is naturally translated into imperiousness, as Hamm growls with exasperation at the grinding pointlessness of his exchanges with his three ungrateful dependents. . . . Mr. Roberts's polished tones lend richly funny colorations to Hamm's more high-minded monologues, the excursions into storytelling annotated with exclamations of satisfaction. . . . Mr. Roberts's Hamm is a man pompously orating his way into darkness, clinging fiercely to language in the face of the smudgy nothingness all around."

"An affable actor stunningly devoid of pretension," as Horwitz described him, Roberts lives in New York City. Recently, for three years, he served as first vice president of the Screen Actors Guild. In the early 1980s he started taking piano lessons. Roberts's marriage to Jenny Lyons, in 1969, ended in divorce in 1975. His only child, Nicole Roberts, is an actress.

—R.E.

Suggested Reading: *Back Stage* (on-line) Mar. 24, 2005; ibdb.com; imdb.com; *Lancaster (Ohio) Eagle Gazette* A p1+ July 27, 2004; *Los Angeles Times* F p1+ Oct. 31, 1997; (New York) *Daily News* Spotlight p28 Apr. 21, 1996; United Press International Apr. 22, 1988

Selected Plays: *Something About a Soldier*, 1962; *Barefoot in the Park*, 1963; *The Last Analysis*, 1964; *Don't Drink the Water*, 1966; *How Now, Dow Jones*, 1967; *Promises, Promises*, 1968; *Play It Again, Sam*, 1969; *Sugar*, 1972; *Absurd Person Singular*, 1974; *They're Playing Our Song*, 1979; *Murder at the Howard Johnson's*, 1979; *Doubles*, 1985; *Arsenic and Old Lace*, 1986; *Jerome Robbins' Broadway*, 1990; *The Seagull*, 1992; *The Sisters Rosenweig*, 1993; *Victor/Victoria*, 1995; *Cabaret*, 1998; *The Tale of the Allergist's Wife*, 2000; *Short Talks on the Universe*, 2002; *Endgame*, 2005; *Barefoot in the Park*, 2006

Selected Films: *The Million Dollar Duck*, 1971; *Star Spangled Girl*, 1971; *Play It Again, Sam*, 1972; *Serpico*, 1973; *The Taking of Pelham One Two Three*, 1974; *Le Sauvage*, 1975; *The Lindbergh Kidnapping Case*, 1976 (TV); *Annie*

Hall, 1977; *Rosetti and Ryan: Men Who Love Women*, 1977 (TV); *The Girls in the Office*, 1979 (TV); *If Things Were Different*, 1980 (TV); *Just Tell Me What You Want*, 1980; *Stardust Memories*, 1980; *A Question of Honor*, 1982 (TV); *A Midsummer Night's Sex Comedy*, 1982; *Packin' It In*, 1983 (TV); *Key Exchange*, 1985; *Hannah and Her Sisters*, 1986; *Seize the Day*, 1986; *Radio Days*, 1987; *A Different Affair*, 1987 (TV); *18 Again!*, 1988; *Fist Fighter*, 1989; *Popcorn*, 1991; *Switch*, 1991; *Our Sons*, 1991; *Not in My Family*, 1993 (TV); *The American Clock*, 1993 (TV); *A Perry Mason Mystery: The Case of the Jealous Jokester*, 1995 (TV); *Surprise!*, 1996; *Sounds from a Town I Love*, 2001; *My Best Friend's Wife*, 2001; *Twelve and Holding*, 2005; *A Get2Gether*, 2005; *Well Fed and Comfortable*, 2006

Selected Television Programs: *The Edge of Night*, 1964–67; *Rosetti and Ryan*, 1977; *The Four Seasons*, 1984; *The Lucie Arnaz Show*, 1985; *The Thorns*, 1988

Courtesy of Rudy Rojas

Rojas, Rudy

(ROW-hahs)

1959(?)– Founder and CEO of Native Threads

Address: Native Threads, P.O. Box 232386, Leucadia, CA 92023

On a fall night in 1989, while chanting in the intense heat and darkness of a sweat lodge on the

Viejas Indian Reservation, in Alpine, California, Rudy Rojas felt that his spirit self was speaking to him. Its message, he recalled to Gil Griffin for the *San Diego Union-Tribune* (July 25, 2002), was simple: "You're learning your culture—get involved with it." "It was gnarly," he said to Griffin (using a term that, among surfers, means "very powerful"). "Going into the spirit world? That's stuff you don't play with." Rojas, who belongs to the Tiwa (or Tigua) tribe and seems to embody equal parts spiritual Native American and laid-back California surfer, took the advice to heart. In 1990 he launched a line of clothing and accessories decorated with Native American–influenced graphics and bearing the label Native Threads. What began as a one-man enterprise in which Rojas traveled from one powwow to the next with a truck full of T-shirts has become a profitable business, complete with catalog and Web site (native-threads.com); its projected earnings for 2006 are $3 million. "I think one of the reasons people have responded the way they have is because the designs are contemporary, yet the messages are traditional," Rojas explained in an article for the *Native American Times* (November 15, 2001). "By having a constant reminder of the past, I believe it also helps bring to the surface the pride we carry inside of us."

Rudy Rojas, his parents' sixth child, was born in 1959 or 1960 on the Ysleta Del Sur Pueblo Reservation near El Paso, Texas. The reservation is home to Tiwa Indians, the only branch of the Pueblo that still exists in Texas. "In the late '50s and early '60s, life in our pueblo, like other reservations, was an endless struggle," Rojas told Paige Price and Dale Di Pietro for *Indian Country Today* (May 12, 1997). "It was yet another example of proud people caught straddling two worlds—trying to earn a living with very [few] opportunities, while at the same time trying to cope with the pressures to adapt to the ways of modern society." Rojas's father, a full-blooded Tiwa Indian, was a carpenter who struggled with alcoholism and substance abuse. Rojas's mother struggled, too, trying to deal with her husband's addictions while raising her large family. Determined to show her children that there was more to life than what the reservation offered, she sold the family's furniture when Rudy was a few years old and, with her young children in tow, moved without her husband to the barrio of East Los Angeles, California, where her sister was living. Though Rojas's family no longer had to contend with dirt floors and a lack of running water, life in Los Angeles presented its own challenges, among them gang violence, the activities of drug dealers and users, and burglaries and other criminal behavior. "My brothers and I had friends that overdosed on heroin, were stabbed in gang fights, and were sent to either juvenile hall or jail for a wide array of criminal offenses, from drug trafficking and car theft to armed robbery," Rojas wrote for his Web site, nativethreads.com. As a boy Rojas enjoyed reading and drawing. He often landed in trouble, however. To remove their little brother from their dangerous neighborhood for a few hours now and then, two of Rojas's older brothers, Arturo and Raul, began taking him along when they went to the beach to surf. "From the very first time I stood up on a surfboard and rode a wave, I was hooked," Rojas recalled to Price and Di Pietro. "The beach and the ocean were such a radical departure from the volatile day-to-day life on Isabel Avenue." Those outings ended after Raul went to Vietnam, to serve in the Vietnam War, and Arturo moved to Hawaii, upon completing high school. Left to fend for himself in the barrio, Rojas began to succumb to peer pressure, hanging out with a rough crowd of kids. Arturo, worried about Rudy's well-being and future prospects, sent Rojas money to buy an airplane ticket to Hawaii.

The summer Rojas spent in Hawaii, surfing and enjoying time with Arturo, "really straightened out my head," as he told Price and Di Pietro. "When I got back home, I felt different. There was a distance between me and the kids I had been hanging out with. Somehow I was able to focus more on school—especially my art classes." He made new friends, people who shared his passion for surfing and would go with him to the beach. "Surfing is so much more than riding waves," he told Price and Di Pietro. "To me, it's like meditation, prayer, mental therapy, nature, adrenaline, and physical conditioning all rolled into one. I need it for my sanity." Following the advice of one of his high-school teachers, Rojas applied successfully for a grant to attend California State University at Fresno. As an undergraduate he transferred to San Diego State University, also in California, because of its strong graphic-arts program and its proximity to the beach. At San Diego State Rojas majored in graphic communications. He left without graduating, in his senior year, after securing an internship with the Phillips Ramsey advertising agency. "Working as a production artist [at Phillips Ramsey] offered very limited creative freedom, but it did open my eyes to mass communications—advertising, marketing—and what powerful tools they are. It was a valuable lesson," Rojas told Price and Di Pietro. Eager to combine his knowledge of graphic design and communications with his passion for surfing, he left the agency to work as the advertising art director of a California surfing magazine. He next became the advertising manager and art director for Flojos, a beach footwear and clothing company. Toward the end of his employment at Flojos, Rojas began designing ethnic-inspired graphics for T-shirts and sandals. "Traditional Indian imagery began to flood my imagination and emerge in my work. I felt as though I was being guided, and I became increasingly drawn to that energy," he told Price and Di Pietro. "Those feelings, combined with a growing contempt for the commercial mentality and other b.s. that was dictating my work, inspired me to begin creating Native American imagery for my own T-shirts line. The name 'Native Threads' just came to me." While excited about his new project, Rojas felt conflicted and confused about his Native American ancestry. At about that time, he met a fellow surfer, Tim Flannery (then an infielder for the San Diego Padres baseball team), who talked to Rojas about his Cherokee heritage and introduced him to the Kumeyaay Indian spiritual leader Ron Christman. At Christman's invitation, Rojas visited the sweat lodge on the Viejas Indian Reservation. His experience there led him to return to his birthplace and reconnect with his father.

In 1990 Rojas launched Native Threads, funding the venture with his savings and loans from friends. After printing some T-shirts, he began traveling to reservations, showing his designs and trying to attract buyers. It was a lengthy, complicated process, as Tim Flannery recalled to Gil Griffin. "You can't just show up and start selling stuff at the powwow," Flannery explained; rather, Rojas "had to go to the elders and take them tobacco, before they agreed to talk to him. He had to do sweats and pray over the project with them. This stuff doesn't happen over e-mail, like in the mainstream corporate world." Initially, many tribal elders did not approve of Rojas's first T-shirt illustration—an image, which he called "sacred warrior," of a skull wearing a feathered headdress. "They thought it was showing elders who had passed on," Rojas said to Gil Griffin. "To me, it was saying, 'This is what happens when you can't recognize your spirit self.'" For a few years Rojas drove his truck to one powwow after another, selling T-shirts. His income from sales was barely enough to cover his personal expenses, order supplies of T-shirts, and keep his truck in good repair. "But more importantly, with each new pow wow, I felt I was planting seeds, hoping they would take root and perhaps drop new seeds that would help spread the awareness of what Native Threads had to offer," he told Price and Di Pietro. To supplement his meager earnings, Rojas took freelance graphic-design and art-direction jobs, working on such projects as brochures for the Indian Health Service, posters and advertisements for powwows and cultural events, and materials for the National Congress of American Indians. With time, most of the tribal elders came to support Rojas and his product line, and after several years and thousands of miles, Rojas had secured merchandising contracts with many Indian nations. He produced a Native Threads catalog and sent it to tribal offices, Indian health centers, universities with Native American studies departments, and individuals. The reaction, Rojas told Price and Di Pietro, overwhelmed him. "I started receiving letters, phone calls and faxes from all over the country. People were telling me that they had never seen a catalog and clothing line that touched them quite this way. And once they receive their shirts, sweatshirts and caps in the mail, people often respond with even more encouraging feedback. It has been very gratifying to get this response from such a diverse mix of Native people." On the strength of steadily increasing profits, Rojas

expanded his line to include baseball caps, accessories, sweat suits, and additional T-shirt designs, and he created a Web site. Native Americans, Rojas told Price and Di Pietro, "have grown tired of purchasing shirts and caps with corporate logos that are meaningless to the past and present realities of Indian life. Now they have a new alternative. I feel honored to have this chance to help fill that void."

Rojas has engaged in several charitable activities: he provides Native Threads uniforms to an amateur basketball team in Alaska; held a photo contest and sent the winner and the winner's wife and baby to the 2004 Gathering of Nations events; and sponsored a fundraising raffle at the 10th Annual First American Leadership Awards (FALA) banquet, also in 2004. In highly visible venues during the months preceding the 2004 U.S. presidential election, he urged his compatriots to vote. "Being people of the Earth, it's important we not become passive and assume things are going to be OK," he told Steve Schmidt for Copley News Service (September 27, 2004, on-line).

Rojas and his wife, Donna, married in about 1991. Donna Rojas works with her husband in the Native Threads warehouse in Carlsbad, California. The couple have one son, Hunter Ryan Rojas, who was seven years old in 2006 and who has modeled children's clothing for the Native Threads catalog. The family live in Leucadia, California.

—K.J.E.

Suggested Reading: *Indian Country Today* p8 May 12, 1997; *Native American Times* B p5 Nov. 15, 2001; nativethreads.com; *San Diego Union-Tribune* T p1+ July 25, 2002

Romney, Mitt

Mar. 12, 1947– Governor of Massachusetts (Republican)

Address: Governor's Office, State House Room 360, Boston, MA 02133

When the Republican Mitt Romney, a former investment banker and devout Mormon, defeated the Democrat Shannon O'Brien in the 2002 Massachusetts gubernatorial election to become the state's 70th governor, he achieved one of the more noteworthy political comebacks in recent memory. Nearly a decade earlier, the Harvard-educated Romney ventured on his first campaign, a bid to unseat the longtime Massachusetts U.S. senator Edward M. "Ted" Kennedy. Hoping that his reputation for reviving foundering businesses as CEO of Bain Capital, a venture-capital investment firm, would garner votes from the state's heavily Democratic and blue-collar constituencies, Romney presented himself as a fiscal wizard and critic of Massachusetts's liberal, big-government establish-

Alex Wong/Getty Images

Mitt Romney

ment. In an initially competitive race, Kennedy succeeded in portraying his novice opponent as an out-of-touch elitist and went on to a decisive victory. Romney resumed his duties at Bain Capital before taking on the project that would help pave the way for his political future: restoring the integrity and solvency of the Salt Lake Organizing Committee (SLOC)—which had been mired in scandal and debt—in time for Utah to host the 2002 Winter Olympic Games.

Sridhar Pappu, profiling Romney for the *Atlantic Monthly* (September 1, 2005), wrote, "How did a Mormon become governor of a state where Roman Catholics are by far the largest religious group? And how did a now avowed conservative rise to power in a place where . . . [President] George Bush is 'the Devil?' What, in short, is Mitt Romney's secret?" The answer seems to involve Romney's capacity for "turning around"—or restoring to financial health—institutions ranging from private companies to the SLOC to state bureaucracies. As governor Romney has not only eliminated Massachusetts's daunting budget deficit but helped the state to achieve a sizeable surplus. Romney said to Shawn Macomber for the *American Spectator* (March 2006), "I don't measure myself on a win/loss record. It's not like a baseball team where you're worried about any loss. Every time you win something I figure it's another step in helping people, and I take a great deal of satisfaction in every single victory." With his announcement that he would not seek a second term in 2006, Romney has increased speculation that he has set his sights on the White House. He has refused to reveal until January 2007 his decision about running for the presidency. Meanwhile, in

the media, more questions have arisen about his persona than about his competence. Neil Swidey, for example, mused in the *Boston Globe* (August 13, 2006), "Will [Romney] remember to breathe? Will he allow himself to go off script? Will he be able to get past that reputation for being so polished that he sometimes seems almost plastic?"

The youngest of the four children of George and Lenore Romney, Willard Mitt Romney was born on March 12, 1947 and grew up in Bloomfield Hills, Michigan, an exclusive suburb of Detroit. He was named in honor of two individuals—J. Willard Marriott, the founder of the famed Marriott Hotel chain and a close friend of the Romney family, and Mitt Romney, a cousin of his father's who played professional football with the Chicago Bears in the 1920s. In kindergarten Romney chose to go by "Mitt." The Romney family, who belonged to the Mormon Church, were immersed in business and high-level Republican politics. George Romney was the chairman of the American Motor Corp., based in Detroit, where he challenged the inefficient, gas-guzzling models of his competitors by introducing the Nash Rambler, the country's first compact car. He also served as president of the network of local Mormon churches. In 1962 he entered state politics and won the first of three successive terms as governor of Michigan. Lenore Romney, a former film and radio actress, ran unsuccessfully for one of Michigan's Senate seats in 1970. George Romney became known for his moderate conservatism and his civil rights advocacy. At the 1964 Republican National Convention, he walked out during the hard-line acceptance speech by the party's presidential nominee, Barry Goldwater, who famously declared, "Extremism in the defense of freedom is no vice, and . . . moderation in the pursuit of justice is no virtue." In the late 1960s Romney sought the GOP's presidential nomination and emerged as an early favorite. But his campaign derailed after remarks he made in 1967 on a local Detroit-area talk show, called *Lou Gordon's Hot Seat*, in which he explained his previous support for the war in Vietnam as the result of his having been "brainwashed" by U.S. military officials. The reaction to that statement was such that he dropped out of the race two weeks before the New Hampshire primary. Mitt Romney recalled to Shawn Macomber an early political lesson he learned from his father's failed presidential bid: "Be careful in the words you select, because he got hung with one word, the word 'brainwashing.'"

While a high-school student at the elite, all-boys' Cranbrook Academy, Mitt Romney joined his father's first gubernatorial campaign. Romney told Stephanie Ebbert for the *Boston Globe* (August 11, 2002) that his father "would ask my opinion in a way that would make me believe I was an important part of his decision-making. Now, most likely, he was just giving me a chance to learn and not hanging on my every word, but he was kind enough to let me become exposed to politics and to that part of his life."

After graduating from Cranbrook, in 1965, Romney enrolled at Stanford University in Palo Alto, California, where he immediately impressed his peers as a leader and gifted student. After his freshman year Romney spent two and a half years in France as a Mormon missionary, a traditional service commitment for members of the Church of Jesus Christ of Latter Day Saints (LDS), the official name of the church. In 1969 Romney returned to the U.S. and married his high-school sweetheart, Ann Davies, who had enrolled at Brigham Young University (BYU), in Provo, Utah. Romney transferred to BYU and majored in English, graduating in 1971 with a grade-point average of almost 4.0 and serving as class valedictorian. He next relocated to Boston, Massachusetts, where he enrolled in Harvard University's dual-degree graduate program in law and business. (Romney overlapped with another future politician, George W. Bush, in business school.)

In 1975 Romney graduated near the top of his class in both law and business and took his first job, at the Boston Consulting Group, a management-consulting firm. Three years later he moved to Bain & Co., which advises companies around the world. Romney had ascended to the position of vice president at Bain & Co. before its founder, William W. Bain Jr., tapped him in 1984 to spearhead a new spin-off venture-capital firm, Bain Capital Inc., which would invest in struggling companies, retool their business practices, and sell the reformed models for profit. Bain Capital also invested in viable startup ventures, counting among its early successes Staples Inc., an office-supply company; Babbages Inc., a software retailer; and the Sports Authority, a sporting-goods chain. Under Romney's leadership Bain Capital averaged an annual rate of return of over 50 percent, showcasing his talent as a "turnaround artist."

While Romney steered Bain Capital into increased prosperity throughout the 1980s, its parent company slowly unraveled. By 1990 Bain & Co., $150 million in debt and headed for nearly 1,000 employee layoffs, was on the brink of collapse. William Bain Jr. offered Romney the responsibility for a complete restructuring of the company. Romney agreed to the task, on the condition that he have absolute authority and that all 70 company partners give him their support. (For his part, Romney refused to accept compensation or equity stake for his new duties.) The partners agreed, and within three years, Bain & Co. had increased its business by 20 percent; the first quarter of 1994 was the best the company had ever seen.

Having guided Bain back to health, Romney, spurred by his wife, Ann, turned his thoughts toward politics. Ann Romney revealed to Ben Bradlee Jr. for the *Boston Globe* (August 7, 1994) the nature of her advice: "I said, 'Mitt . . . you can gripe and gripe and gripe all you want about how upset you are about the direction the country's going. But if you don't stand up and do something about it, then, you know, shut up and stop bother-

ing me.' . . . I really do think it came to the point where I said enough is enough." In 1994 Romney entered the Massachusetts senatorial race, challenging the incumbent, Ted Kennedy, in his bid for a sixth term. Heavily Democratic, Catholic, and a known bastion of liberalism, the Massachusetts constituency stood in stark contrast to Romney, a fiscal conservative, devout Mormon, and proponent of limited government. When asked why he chose to spend $3 million of his personal income in an attempt to unseat Kennedy, Romney told Pappu, "I felt very strongly that the social programs of the sixties and seventies, the liberal agenda—I'll call it the [President Lyndon B.] Johnson agenda—had hurt working families, had hurt the poor in many instances. And while the liberals had the best of intentions, I felt that the programs themselves had created a permanent underclass and had fostered poverty instead of eliminating it." Romney campaigned on a platform extolling the virtues of economic expansion. He outlined strategies to stimulate low-level investment and healthy economic risk-taking by granting tax breaks to entrepreneurs and small-business owners. One Romney initiative—a training tax credit—called for granting $5,000 credits to employers who hired welfare recipients. In another he proposed that publicly traded companies disclose the earnings of their female employees, to allow consumers to reward companies committed to gender equality and a more diversified labor force. "In my view, the best way to break the glass ceiling is to make sure we can see where it is . . . I am going to get a spotlight on it. I'm going to get out the hammer, and we're going to break it," Romney said at a campaign fund-raiser, as reported by Scott Lehigh for the *Boston Globe* (October 8, 1994). Romney's message attracted supporters across the political spectrum. Kennedy, whose brothers John and Robert were, respectively, the 35th president of the United States and a U.S. senator, was considered to be a formidable opponent; in previous races he had "devour[ed] one Republican sacrificial lamb after another," in Bradlee's words. But many, including Gerry Chervinsky, a pollster and the head of KRC Communications Research, viewed Romney as an attractive alternative to the aging, freewheeling Kennedy. "He's younger, he's well spoken, he's good looking, and he's in good shape. He has a pretty blond wife, and five kids. He doesn't smoke and he drinks milk. He's the perfect anti-Kennedy," Chervinsky said to Sara Rimer for the *New York Times* (October 25, 1994).

Romney and Kennedy entered the election season in a virtual deadlock at the polls. According to Pappu, the Kennedy camp, complacent during the early stages of the race, "awakened" after witnessing Romney's giant strides at the polls. Kennedy attacked Romney's lack of political experience and attempted to portray him as a cold and calculating profiteer, an "enemy of the blue-collar worker," as Charles Stein noted for the *Boston Globe* (October 9, 1994). Kennedy's attacks intensified in September 1994, when, according to Scott Lehigh and Sally Jacobs in the *Globe* (October 13, 1994), he accused Romney of having mistreated his employees in business dealings and having "put profits over people." Kennedy buttressed his claims by citing a case involving Ampad Corp., a paper company in which Bain Capital was a major investor. Ampad had acquired an Indiana-based factory owned by SCM Office Supplies Inc.; when news erupted over the takeover, which resulted in lower wages—and, in some cases, layoffs—for existing employees, a worker strike ensued. Disgruntled employees traveled to Massachusetts during the campaign to protest what they saw as Romney's disregard for blue-collar workers, creating a media frenzy. Though Romney was on leave from Bain Capital, he was seen by some as being responsible for what had happened; his public response to the accusations, slow and muddled, only fueled the criticism. Romney admitted to Sridhar Pappu, "I got caught up in all the 'Romney's a venture capitalist, he's laid off people.' Well, no, I didn't—it wasn't my factory." Nonetheless, public support for Romney began to wane.

As the November elections neared, and the tide clearly turned in Kennedy's favor, mudslinging from both camps increased. A controversy arose over Romney's Mormon faith, with Kennedy suggesting that Romney should be questioned about the church's pre-1978 policy of excluding African-Americans from its priesthood. On the subject of introducing religion into the political maelstrom, a Kennedy spokesman, Rick Gurgehian, said to Scott Lehigh and Frank Phillips for the *Boston Globe* (September 28, 1994): "This is not about religion. This is about racial prejudice, racial bigotry and bias toward people." A former bishop in the Mormon church (he served in that role in the early 1980s), Romney himself said at a press conference, as quoted by Lehigh and Phillips, "In my view the victory that John Kennedy [the first Catholic U.S. president] won was not for just 40 million Americans who were born Catholic, it was for all Americans of all faiths. And I am sad to say that Ted Kennedy is trying to take away his brother's victory." In the end, Kennedy withstood Romney's challenge, winning the election with 58 percent of the vote to Romney's 41 percent. Still, Romney's better-than-expected performance against a political legend made him a rising star in conservative circles.

Romney resumed his executive duties at Bain Capital in the mid-1990s, managing five equity funds, which, according to Steve Bailey and Steven Syre in the *Boston Globe* (December 19, 1997), "put [Bain's] compounded annual returns . . . at more than 100 percent." Then, in 1999, he received another job offer. The Salt Lake Organizing Committee, in the heavily Mormon state of Utah, host of the 2002 Winter Olympic Games, was scandalized by allegations that its members had bribed International Olympic Committee (IOC) officials during the bidding to host the event. The SLOC, facing a $379 million deficit, dwindling sponsorship, and multiple legal investigations, needed "a white knight who [was] universally loved" to restore its integrity, as the organization's chairman, Robert Garff, declared to John Powers for the *Boston Globe* (February 3, 2002). When the SLOC asked Romney to fill that role, he resisted. Since the fall of 1998, Romney had focused largely on his wife's struggle with multiple sclerosis. It was Ann Romney, however, who encouraged her husband to accept Garff's offer. After Mitt Romney formally accepted the post as head of SLOC, his wife told Powers, "He loves emergencies and catastrophes. He would never have considered doing it if it wasn't a big mess." David D'Alessandro, the chairman of the insurance firm John Hancock (which pulled its SLOC sponsorship when the scandal broke, then reinstated it), said to Powers, "I was surprised [Romney] took the job, because he didn't have to. I think he took it because he felt that the Mormons were in trouble. He never said that, but I think he saw the scandal as a stain on his religion."

Romney teamed with Fraser Bullock, a former colleague at Bain Capital, to treat the SLOC entanglements as a corporate-restructuring project. After examining the organization's finances, Romney slashed its administrative expense accounts, then lobbied the administration of President Bill Clinton for increased federal security for the Games. His actions inspired the trust of corporate sponsors, whose contributions exceeded those lavished on the 1996 Summer Olympics, in Atlanta, Georgia. The SLOC's turnaround under Romney boosted his popularity, and he was considered a potential front-runner for a host of 2002 political races. Many suspected that Romney's success in Utah would lead to his running for the Senate there. Romney, however, continued to set his sights on Massachusetts.

In the spring of 2002, all signs pointed to a Romney gubernatorial run. When Massachusetts's Republican interim governor, Jane M. Swift, the successor to Paul Cellucci (who had resigned in 2001 to accept a diplomatic post), withdrew her bid for a second term amid dismal poll numbers, Romney seized the opportunity. He entered the race in March, promising, as Joe Battenfeld and David R. Guarino reported for the *Boston Herald* (March 20, 2002), "better management" of the state's finances. Romney's campaign stumbled out of the gate, with reports about discrepancies in his income-tax filings and related disputes about his residency (for 1999 and 2000 Romney filed his returns as a Utah resident). Democrats tried to disqualify Romney from the race based on his three-year stint in Utah as SLOC chairman, since Massachusetts required a seven-year state residency for political candidates. That approach failed, however, when the state's Ballot Law Commission accepted Romney's explanation that he had merely signed returns prepared by his accountants and had not sought to change his residence.

In his campaign Romney tried to eschew party-line ideology, promoting ideas that incorporated both classically liberal and conservative values, including limitations to public-school teachers' tenure (granting principals of underperforming schools the power to remove up to 10 percent of the teachers they deemed ineffective), more expedient English-immersion programs for bilingual students, and increases in the minimum wage. On the polarizing issue of abortion, Romney said, according to Battenfeld and Guarino, "I'll say the same thing that I've said since 1994 and probably before. That is, on a personal basis, I do not favor abortion. However, as governor of the commonwealth, I will protect the right of a woman to choose under the laws of the country and the laws of the commonwealth." In the fall of 2002, Romney gained support in traditionally Democratic cities including Lowell, Salem, and Revere and defeated the Democratic candidate, Shannon O'Brien, a former state legislator, in the November election. Romney took 50 percent of the vote to O'Brien's 45 percent.

As governor-elect Romney vowed to first address the state's fiscal challenges, by bridging its $1 billion to $2 billion budget gap. "I believe that we will find a solution to balance our budget without having to raise taxes, and without hurting the essential services that we provide to our schools, to our elderly, to our people in need," he said, as reported by Rick Klein for the Boston Globe (November 7, 2002). Though Romney faced stark opposition from a largely Democratic state legislature, he was able to slash costs by eliminating excess government jobs and merging state agencies. In two years' time, Romney, true to his reputation as a "turnaround artist," achieved not only a balanced budget but a $700 million budget surplus as well as a $2.3 billion state "rainy-day" fund.

In 2004 Governor Romney stood at the forefront of the gay-marriage debate that swept the state and the nation. In an attempt to overturn the Massachusetts Supreme Court's November 18, 2003 ruling legalizing same-sex marriage, a position that was widely criticized by social conservatives as evidence of judicial activism, Romney introduced legislation that sought to define marriage in strictly heterosexual terms. In April 2004, lacking support from the Democrat-controlled legislature, Romney forced the issue by filing emergency legislation to halt pending same-sex weddings until Massachusetts citizens had the opportunity to examine and vote on Romney's original proposal. Regarding the emergency legislation, Romney said at a press conference, as reported by Tim Macolm for the Daily Free Press (April 6, 2004), a Boston University newspaper, that it "will allow me to protect the integrity of the constitutional process" and "preserve the right of the citizens to make this decision rather than having it made for them by the Court." In May the state legislature rejected Romney's legislation, in effect bringing the issue to a close in Massachusetts.

Romney worked to distance himself from his legislative debacle by channeling his efforts toward social-service reforms, among them a 2005 education-reform package inspired by One Laptop per Child, a nonprofit organization started by the Media Laboratory of the Massachusetts Institute of Technology (MIT). Romney's legislation aimed to equip every Massachusetts middle- and high-school student—nearly 500,000—with his or her own laptop computer. It also outlined a plan to recruit 1,000 new math and science teachers, through the formation of a selective Commonwealth Teaching Corps. Romney's proposals drew praise from legislators, educators, and community advocates alike. "Governor Romney's education reform plan addresses the single biggest challenge for our state's economy, which is supplying the pipeline of skilled workers that technology employers need for sustained future growth," in the words of Christopher R. Anderson, president of the Massachusetts High Technology Council, quoted by US States News (September 22, 2005). In early 2006 Governor Romney initiated more landmark legislation, specifically in the area of health-care reform, signing a bill that provided nearly all of the state's 515,000 uninsured citizens with coverage. Romney explained to Pam Belluck for the New York Times (April 5, 2006) that his plan showed that "we can get health insurance for all our citizens without raising taxes and without a government takeover. The old single-payer canard is gone." In other accomplishments during his term as Massachusetts governor, he vetoed a bill that would have ended funding for the state's successful charter-school program and championed zoning for multi-family housing, a measure that significantly lowered rents in Boston. On the negative side, his attempt to reinstate the death penalty was rejected by the Massachusetts House in November 2005, by a 99–53 vote.

In mid-2006 Romney initiated a state and federal inspection into the structural vulnerabilities of Boston's Central Artery/Tunnel Project—better known as the Big Dig—after a portion of the tunnel's concrete ceiling fell on a motorist, killing her instantly. The tunnel collapse forced the Massachusetts Turnpike Authority chairman, Matthew Amorello, to resign. After the Massachusetts legislature granted Romney full authority to control an investigation into possible additional structural defects in the tunnel, he sought the expertise of the Federal Highway Administration and the U.S. Department of Transportation in implementing adequate safety measures. Romney's response to the Big Dig calamity left some observers unsatisfied. The Boston Globe reporter Neil Swidey, for example, expressed the opinion that "the Big Dig crisis hints at an emotional deficit in the public Romney. It's a safe bet that either Bill Clinton, with his ability to speak from the heart, or George W. Bush, with his ability to speak from the gut, would have known that shaken citizens needed more from their chief executive in his first comments after the tragedy than a perfunctory apology to the family of the deceased and a lengthy exposition on how the courts would be used to settle an old political score."

Romney has continued to raise his public profile by addressing hot-button issues, such as the debate over stem-cell research. At an education conference held in Cambridge, Massachusetts, in 2006, for example, Romney referred to the process of embryo creation for scientific purposes as crossing "a very bright moral line. . . . It is Orwellian in its scope in that in laboratories you can have trays of new embryos being created," as Russell Nichols reported for the *Boston Globe* (September 1, 2006). In August 2006, apparently laying the foundation for a possible bid for the presidency in 2008, Romney organized steering committees and recruited political field operatives in Michigan and Iowa. David Yepsen, writing for the *Des Moines (Iowa) Register* (August 1, 2006), described Romney as the "best organized of any of the GOP presidential candidates in Iowa" and as being "well on his way toward winning the 2008 Iowa Republican caucuses."

With a political record of sound fiscal policy and visionary social reform, Romney has earned the admiration of his state's overwhelmingly liberal constituency, while his hard-line stance on abortion and gay marriage continues to attract the support of social conservatives—making him, as John H. Bunzel noted for the *Boston Globe* (February 19, 2006), a potential "dream candidate" for the Republican Party's conservative and moderate bases. However, as Bunzel's article also observed, one question continues to arise in connection with Romney's possible candidacy: Is America ready for a Mormon president? Perhaps more importantly, would members of his own party—specifically, its evangelical wing—support him? Michael Cromartie, the director of the Evangelical Studies Project at the Ethics and Public Policy Center, told Kathryn Jean Lopez for the *National Review* (December 20, 2005), "While many religious conservatives may have qualms with aspects of Mormon theology, they have even greater problems with religious bigotry and intolerance. Any candidate that chooses to attack his faith in a personal fashion will surely run the risk of a backlash." Romney himself explained to Pappu on the subject of his faith: "How Mormon am I? You know, the principles and values taught to me by faith are values I aspire to live by and are as American as motherhood and apple pie. My faith believes in family, believes in Jesus Christ. It believes in serving one's neighbor and one's community. It believes in military service. It believes in patriotism; it actually believes this nation had an inspired founding. It is in some respects a quintessentially American faith."

Pappu wrote about Governor Romney, "The guy just looks like a president—hardly a negligible consideration. . . . Standing over six feet, graying neatly at his temples, with a sharply cut jaw and the whitest teeth I've ever seen." His "appeal,"

Pappu added, "also comes from the natural ease and warmth that one feels in the vicinity of a man who unselfconsciously uses words like 'neat' and 'gosh' and 'wow,' as if everyone spoke that way." Others have reported on Romney's sense of humor. Raphael Lewis noted for the *Boston Globe* (March 21, 2005) that the governor once began a speech in Boston by saying, "It's great to be here in Iowa this morning," then feigned confusion and added, "Oops. Wrong speech. Sorry about that." Carrying on the philanthropic traditions of his late father, George Romney, Governor Romney sits on the boards of numerous charities, including the Points of Light Foundation and City Year. He was also recently appointed by President George W. Bush to serve on the Homeland Security Advisory Committee. Romney and his wife, Ann, have been married for 37 years and have five sons and nine grandchildren. They make their home in Belmont, Massachusetts.

—D.J.K.

Suggested Reading: *American Spectator* Mar. 2006; *Atlantic Monthly* p106+ Sep. 1, 2005; *Boston Business Journal* I p1 June 10, 1994; *Boston Globe* A p1 Aug. 7, 1994, A p1 Nov. 10, 1994, A p1 Aug. 11, 2002, p24 Aug. 13, 2006

Rounds, Michael

Oct. 24, 1954– Governor of South Dakota (Republican)

Address: Office of the Governor, 500 E. Capitol Ave., Pierre, SD 57501

Michael Rounds, the Republican governor of South Dakota, drew national attention in March 2006, when he signed into law a bill that made abortion in his state a felony except when the procedure is necessary to save the life of a pregnant woman. The most sweeping state abortion ban in over a decade, the legislation represented an attempt by South Dakota lawmakers to provoke the filing of a lawsuit that would wend its way through the justice system until it reached the Supreme Court. Governor Rounds and the lawmakers who voted for the bill expressed the hope that the majority of the justices on the Supreme Court would overturn the ruling in *Roe v. Wade* (1973), which legalized abortion in the U.S. "I've indicated I'm pro-life, and I do believe abortion is wrong and that we should do everything we can to save lives," Rounds said at a news conference on February 24, 2005, according to Monica Davey, writing for the *New York Times* (February 25, 2006). Although many antiabortion advocates had advised against a ban that made no exceptions for victims of rape or incest or cases in which a woman's pregnancy seriously jeopardized her health, Rounds signed the legislation, in part

Courtesy of the office of Governor Rounds

Michael Rounds

to show, as he said to Davey, a "united front among the pro-life groups" and partly because, as Monica Davey quoted him as saying, "Many people will never believe that this [approach to reducing the number of abortions in the U.S.] will not work unless it is tried." After the ban was signed into law, abortion rights groups succeeded in obtaining enough voters' signatures to take the issue before the public on Election Day. On November 7, 2006 voters overturned the ban.

Before he entered the public sector, in 1991, Rounds was a partner in a South Dakota insurance and real-estate agency. He served in the South Dakota state Senate for nearly a decade, for six of those years as majority leader, before running for governor in 2002. The surprise victor in the Republican gubernatorial primary, he won the general election with 57 percent of the vote. According to the state's Web site, since he became governor Rounds has balanced the state budget, reduced the state deficit from $28 million to $20 million without raising taxes, increased funding to public schools and universities, and "reorganized the South Dakota Department of Education to better embrace the concepts of 'No Child Left Behind'"—a reference to the 2001 federal law that aimed to improve the nation's primary and secondary schools by strengthening the standards of accountability maintained by the states (standardized-test scores, for example) and offering parents more flexibility in choosing which schools their children attend. Rounds was reelected by a comfortable margin in 2006.

The oldest of the 11 children of Don Rounds and the former Joyce Reinartz, Marion Michael Rounds was born on October 24, 1954 in Huron, South Dakota. Since as far back as he can remember, he has been called Michael or Mike, and he signs his name "M. Michael Rounds." According to Wikipedia.org, at various times his father's jobs included director of highway safety in South Dakota and executive director of the South Dakota Petroleum Council (in the latter position, he was a lobbyist); he also worked for the federal Rural Electrification Administration. Tim Rounds, one of Rounds's brothers, is a South Dakota state legislator. When Rounds was three the family moved to Pierre (pronounced "Peer"), the state capital (whose population in 2000 was less than 14,000), where he spent the rest of his childhood with his nine brothers and one sister. His father told Joe Kafka for the Associated Press (September 30, 2002) that the family often talked about politics at the dinner table. Rounds himself told Kafka, "From the time I was 4, I wanted to be a farmer or a flyer. I've always loved tractors and airplanes." Rounds began flying solo at age 16 and earned a pilot's license at 17. In high school he excelled at track and played baseball as well. Although friends of his have described him as a very poor pitcher, he showed enough talent as an undergraduate at South Dakota State University, in Brookings, to play for the school's baseball team. During his college years he interned at a state senator's office, an experience that led him to change his major from engineering to political science. According to Terry Woster of the Sioux Falls, South Dakota, *Argus Leader* (October 27, 2002), while in college he also ran his own bail-bondsman business. He earned a B.S. degree in 1977. In his first job after graduating, he worked for several months on a farm, planting wheat and tending cattle. He then entered the insurance business. In 1982 he was hired to sell insurance and real estate for a Pierre company owned by Karl Fischer. By 2002 Rounds had bought enough of the company's stock to become one of its owners. It is now called Fischer, Rounds & Associates Inc.

Earlier, in 1978, Rounds had worked on the successful reelection campaign of a South Dakota congressman, the Republican James Abdnor; two years later he again aided that politician, this time when Abdnor defeated the former Democratic presidential nominee George McGovern in a bid for a seat in the U.S. Senate. Rounds began his own political career in 1990, entering the race for state senator against the incumbent, Jacqueline Kelley, a Democrat; he won, with 52.5 percent of the votes. He was reelected four times, with 59.9 percent of the vote in 1992; 77.3 percent in 1994; 66 percent in 1996; and 74.9 percent in 1998. In the South Dakota Senate, which has 35 members, he represented District 24, which included Pierre and surrounding areas. (The state legislature also has a House of Representatives, with 70 members.) In 1994 his colleagues in the Senate elected him majority leader, a position he held for the remainder of his time in the legislature. As a senator Rounds displayed a "patient and inclusive style," according to the Biography

Resource Center (on-line). "His approach combined non-combativeness with delaying tactics. In short, voting on really big issues was often postponed until opposing factions had thoroughly argued them through." "I try to let everyone have a voice and to listen to what they say . . . ," Rounds said, as quoted on the Biography Resource Center's Web site. "If people know they've had a chance to be heard, they feel a lot better about the process." Rounds's achievements in the Senate, as listed on the state Web site, included helping to balance the budget, reducing property taxes, and authorizing and funding the largest four-lane highway-construction project since the Interstate Highway System was officially completed, in 1991. Since the South Dakota legislature meets only 35 days a year in even-numbered years and only 40 days annually in odd-numbered years, as a senator Rounds continued working at Fischer, Rounds & Associates.

In South Dakota a 1972 state law forbids the governor from serving more than two terms consecutively, and a law that took effect in 2000 forbids legislators from serving for more than four terms consecutively. For those reasons Rounds could not run for reelection in 2000, and the then-governor of the state, William "Bill" Janklow, could not run again in 2001. Rounds decided to seek the governorship. He entered the 2001 primary campaign as very much the underdog. His two principal opponents were Mark Barnett, the state attorney general for the past 11 years, who had run unopposed in 1998 and was considered the odds-on favorite to win the governorship, and Steve Kirby, a member of a prominent Sioux Falls family and a wealthy investor. Unlike Barnett and Kirby, Rounds had negligible name recognition among voters, despite his work as Senate majority leader; indeed, a pollster who questioned South Dakotans about their preferences in August 2001 did not even list him among the candidates. Moreover, according to estimated figures supplied by David Beiler in *Campaigns & Elections* (August 2002), Barnett spent almost eight times, and Kirby 11 times, as much as the amount that Rounds spent (about $250,000) during the primary campaign. Rounds saved money by having his campaign managed by two of his siblings (his sister, Michele Rounds Brich, and his brother Jamison, who was then a Roman Catholic seminarian and is now the director of the Governor's Office of Strategic Initiatives) rather than by outsiders; in addition, according to Beiler, "his only paid consultant was a fledgling ad agency in Pierre." Rounds also benefited significantly from voter dissatisfaction with Kirby's and Barnett's highly negative campaigns, in which, in widely disseminated attack ads, they incessantly questioned each other's integrity, honesty, and competency, all the while leaving Rounds unmentioned. By contrast, as Beiler wrote, Rounds "missed debates, talked to small knots of voters ad nauseum, criticized his opponents for their ideas only (rarely and mildly), and never seemed to offer major policy initiatives

or anything else that would generate press coverage." On Primary Day, in June 2002, Rounds was victorious, capturing 44 percent of the 110,079 votes cast—18 percent and 15 percent more than the totals for Kirby and Barnett, respectively. (In 2000 about 259,000 South Dakotans were registered as Republicans and 211,000 as Democrats.) "I don't want to burst Mike Rounds' bubble. He really thinks people voted for him because they like his ideas," the *Argus Leader* reporter David Kranz told Beiler. "But I have a very difficult time getting people who voted for Rounds to tell me what he stands for."

In the general election Rounds faced the Democrat James W. "Jim" Abbott, the president of the University of South Dakota. Rounds's popularity exceeded Abbott's throughout the campaign. According to Stateline.org, Rounds "shunned negative campaigning and earned a 'good guy' reputation, benefiting from a strong Republican base and support among conservative Democrats for his pro-life position." Joe Kafka reported that Rounds's campaign "focused almost entirely on bread-and-butter political issues, such as the economy, education and leadership abilities." On Election Day Rounds won the governorship with 57 percent of the vote. On January 7, 2003 he was sworn in as the 31st governor of South Dakota.

South Dakota, a midwestern state, had an estimated population of about 776,000 in 2005. The vast majority—88 percent—of the population are white; 8.3 percent are Native American, 1.4 percent Hispanic, 0.6 percent black, 0.6 percent Asian, and 1.3 percent of mixed race. Its economy is based largely on cattle and sheep ranching and the manufacture of livestock products. The Mount Rushmore National Memorial and the Crazy Horse Memorial attract many tourists to South Dakota. Problems that Rounds inherited as governor included a poorly funded educational system (the average salary for teachers in South Dakota is the lowest in the nation, and the amount of money spent per student in elementary and secondary schools is among the lowest) and decreasing populations in rural areas and small towns. According to the state Web site, Rounds has increased state aid for local public schools and for public universities. In response to problems caused by shrinking populations, he has promoted the so-called 2010 Initiative, a series of specific goals for economic growth and visitor spending in the state. By all accounts, as governor Rounds has displayed the same fondness for personal interactions with his constituents that had helped him to win the election. Early on, for example, he joined leaders of the state's Native Americans at a dinner at his home to discuss tourism and race relations.

In 2004 Rounds vetoed a bill banning abortions in South Dakota, on the grounds that it jeopardized the state's existing abortion restrictions. He said that a high court might overrule those restrictions while it awaited a decision on the ban. "The way the law is written, there's no provision to let those [established restrictions] stay in law while this law is tested," he was quoted as saying in the *Houston Chronicle* (March 10, 2004). He signed a new bill on March 6, 2006, thus instituting a ban on all abortions (except in cases in which continuing a pregnancy threatened a woman's life) starting on July 1 of that year. "In the history of the world, the true test of a civilization is how well people treat the most vulnerable and helpless in their society," Rounds said, as quoted by Monica Davey in the *New York Times* (March 7, 2006). "The sponsors and supporters of this bill believe that abortion is wrong because unborn children are the most vulnerable and most helpless persons in our society. I agree with them." Legislators knew that the bill would be challenged in court before the ban took effect, and they felt confident that the legal battle would end in the Supreme Court (since the side that lost at any point in the judicial process would appeal the latest decision), and that the court would decide that *Roe v. Wade* was unconstitutional. Such a decision appeared to have become more likely with the arrival on the court of two conservatives—Chief Justice John G. Roberts Jr., in September 2005, and Justice Samuel A. Alito Jr., in January 2006.

Rounds had initially felt uncertain about the timing of the passage of the bill, but he chose to sign it rather than alienate pro-lifers. He described the ban as a "direct frontal assault" on *Roe v. Wade*. "The reversal of a Supreme Court opinion is possible," Rounds maintained in a statement following the bill's passage, according to Monica Davey's March 7, 2006 *New York Times* article. "For example, in 1896, the United States Supreme Court ruled in the Plessy vs. Ferguson case that a state could require racial segregation in public facilities if the facilities offered to different races were equal. However, 58 years later, the Supreme Court reconsidered that opinion and reversed itself in Brown v. Board of Education."

Many within antiabortion circles, however, saw the bill as too extreme to be upheld by the Supreme Court. Such opponents, who now found themselves placed, "somewhat awkwardly, on the same side as abortion rights advocates," as Monica Davey wrote for the *New York Times* (February 22, 2006), had called instead for more-moderate abortion restrictions—for example, ones requiring spousal and parental notification of a desired abortion, measures more acceptable to the nation at large. As Morton M. Kondracke noted in *Roll Call* (March 16, 2006), "Polls overwhelmingly indicate that Americans favor retention of Roe, even if they also support limitations on abortion." Others critical of the bill noted that a Supreme Court vote in favor of a nearly complete ban on abortions was far from assured. As Kondracke wrote, "Both [Alito and Roberts] are conservatives, but both also told the Senate Judiciary Committee that they value precedent, which Roe definitely is after 33 years on the books." Furthermore, Kondracke wrote, the Supreme Court's approval of the bill would hurt the conservative Republican presidential hopeful John S. McCain, a U.S. senator from Arizona and a professed pro-lifer, who would need the votes of moderates to win in 2008. "McCain now wins in most 2008 matchups against Democrats, but this lead could evaporate if voters begin to consider him an opponent of Roe," Kondracke wrote.

"It's a sad day for the women of South Dakota," Cecile Richards, the president of Planned Parenthood of America, who ran the state's sole abortion clinic, in Sioux Falls, told Davey (March 7, 2006). "We had really hoped that the governor would weigh women's health as more important than politics," she added. The clinic performed about 800 operations a year, and women in the state often had to drive as far as 350 miles to be treated. Davey reported that clinicians spent much of the day after the bill's passage consoling women. Richards told Davey that her organization intended to challenge the law however they could, either by a statewide referendum or a federal lawsuit. "We're trying to evaluate the timing and options now, but we're committed to making sure this does not come into effect." Under state law, the effective date of the abortion bill would be delayed and the issue presented to the public on Election Day if the law's challengers were to collect the signatures of 16,728 registered voters (approximately 3.5 percent of the total number of those registered) before mid-June. They accomplished just that, and on November 7, 2006 voters overturned the abortion ban.

Recently, Rounds has come under attack for using state-owned planes for personal purposes, even though in most cases he reimbursed the government for the expenses incurred. According to an editorial in the *Argus Leader* (April 30, 2006, online), the reimbursements came from "an unregulated political slush fund known as the Governor's Club." The editorial also reported that the Federal Aviation Administration (FAA) is investigating Rounds's practice, and that in a similar case that occurred in Kansas, "such reimbursements violated federal regulations." In addition, Rounds has been criticized for what some regard as excessive secrecy regarding government-related issues and activities. In one instance, Rounds refused to divulge the names of business people who had attended the 2005 Governor's Invitational Pheasant Hunt, an event paid for with private funds but organized by the governor's Office of Economic Development. Rounds contended that making the names public (as had been done for previous hunts) would place South Dakota at a disadvantage, because, as he was quoted as saying in the *Aberdeen (South Dakota) American News* (April 24, 2006, on-line), it would "provide the economic development agencies of other states or cities with nothing less than a list of businesses which are willing to relocate or expand if given the proper business climate." In another case, the South Dakota state epidemiologist refused to answer questions posed by the *Argus Leader* about the outbreak of mumps in the state, because Rounds had ordered members of his cabinet and other government officials "not to comment without approval by the governor's lawyer," as an *Argus Leader* editorial (April 20, 2006, on-line) put it.

For much of 2006 Rounds was on the campaign trail, seeking a second term in the governor's mansion. He promised that if reelected, he would reintroduce bills (rejected by South Dakota lawmakers in 2006) to raise the state's minimum wage, which has remained at $5.15 an hour since 1997, and to offer incentive pay to teachers. In the general election he faced the Democrat Jack Billion, a former surgeon and former state legislator from Sioux Falls. Rounds was reelected easily.

"Soft-spoken with boyish good looks," according to Joe Kafka, Rounds married the former Jean Vedvei in 1978. The couple have four grown children: three sons—Chris, Brian, and John—and one daughter, Carrie. In his leisure time Rounds enjoys flying (he co-owns two airplanes), boating, camping, playing racquetball, and hunting.

—M.B.

Suggested Reading: Associated Press Sep. 30, 2002; *New York Times* A p14 Feb. 22, 2006, A p9 Feb. 26, 2006, A p2 Mar. 7, 2006

Courtesy of Edward M. Rubin

Rubin, Edward M.

Feb. 17, 1951– Geneticist

Address: JGI Production Genomics Facility, 2800 Mitchell Dr., Walnut Creek, CA 94598

James Watson, the famed scientist who co-discovered the double-helix structure of DNA, predicted that the international effort to map the human genome "will change mankind, like the printing press," according to a reporter for the BBC (June 26, 2000, on-line). Now that an international team of scientists has carefully transcribed the three billion base pairs that comprise the human genome—the "Book of Life," as scientists call it—geneticists such as Edward M. Rubin, the director of the U.S. Department of Energy's Joint Genome Institute and the genomics division at the Law-

rence Berkeley National Laboratory, are left with the daunting task of finding the meaning in the text.

Rubin is a pioneer in the study of DNA sequences that do not code for genes but rather play an important role in regulating gene expression. "I've been very interested in the part of the genome that does not code for proteins," he told *Current Biography*. "Some call this junk DNA, but clearly it's not all junk and some is functional. About 98 percent of the genome might be categorized as junk DNA and we really don't know how to read meaning in that part of the genome." Through the use of large-scale cross-species DNA sequence comparisons, he has indeed proven that there are "jewels of function amongst the junk," as he says. "The hotbed of medical research was the gene itself," Rubin told Sophia Kazmi for the *Contra Costa (California) Times* (October 17, 2003). "Now there is reason to look outside."

Known to associates and friends as Eddy, Edward M. Rubin was born in New York City on February 17, 1951. He and his older sister, Penny, were raised on the outskirts of the city. His father, Sol, was an accountant who also ran a small business, and his mother, Irene, was a homemaker. Even as a child Rubin took an interest in science, working on science projects and playing with his home chemistry set. He received a bachelor's degree in physics from the University of California (UC)–San Diego in 1974. After reading James Watson's *Molecular Biology of the Gene*, he was inspired to focus his studies on genetics. "[The book] made me appreciate for the first time how beautiful the machinery of life was with DNA, RNA and the building of proteins eventually leading to cells and organisms. Simple and elegant, in some ways like an erector set," Rubin told *Current Biography*. "Suddenly, in a flash, I realized that biological systems did not have infinite complexity, but were decipherable." In 1980 he earned an M.D. degree and a Ph.D. degree in biophysics from the University of Rochester School of Medicine, in New York State. He then served a clinical residency and a genetics fellowship at UC–San Francisco. Later, he worked as a research associate at the Howard Hughes Medical Institute, in Chevy Chase, Maryland.

In 1988 Rubin started working at the Lawrence Berkeley National Laboratory, an arm of the U.S. Department of Energy that is managed by the University of California. Two years after Rubin's arrival at the lab, the Energy Department and the National Institutes of Health launched the historic Human Genome Project, a collaborative effort by hundreds of researchers at colleges, universities, and laboratories throughout the world to catalog, or "sequence," all of the three billion chemical base pairs that make up human DNA. The project was completed ahead of schedule, in 2003—50 years to the month after James Watson and Francis Crick discovered the double helix shape of DNA; the Berkeley Lab had contributed significantly to the project, sequencing 11 percent of the human genome (more specifically, chromosomes 5, 16, and 19).

Rubin, who played a major role in the final phase of sequencing the human genome, has worked throughout his scientific career to develop computational and biological approaches to decipher the information encoded by the sequence of the genome. To that end, in 1992 he founded the Rubin Lab at the Berkeley National Laboratory. There, using transgenic mice—mice that have had DNA from another species, usually Homo sapiens, inserted into their own DNA—Rubin and his staff attempted to identify the genetic links to such common ailments as heart disease. "You can't look at heart disease in a test tube, so these transgenic animals have a very major impact," he told Marla Cone for the *Los Angeles Times* (May 9, 1993). "They contribute to our understanding of how things work in a setting fairly close to the way it works in people. It's really been a gold mine for researchers." In the May 1, 1997 issue of the journal *Nature Genetics*, Rubin and his research associates reported their discovery of a major genetic factor contributing to mental retardation in Down syndrome, which affects an estimated one million Americans and is the leading cause of mental retardation in the U.S. Most individuals afflicted with Down syndrome carry a complete extra copy of chromosome 21, which also results in problems with the immune and endocrine systems, as well as skeletal and tissue deformities, but because there are rare forms of the syndrome in which patients carry only a portion of chromosome 21 in triplicate, Rubin suspected that only a limited number of genes on the chromosome were responsible for mental retardation. To test his hypothesis Rubin's team inserted different adjacent segments of human chromosome 21 into mice and then tested their learning skills. The researchers found that inserting an additional copy of a particular gene, *DYRK*, affects the ways in which neural pathways are constructed and impairs learning ability. "Our strategy made no prior assumptions about individual genes, but rather, allowed the behavior of the mice to guide us to a crucial gene on chromosome

21," Rubin told a reporter for *Gene Therapy Weekly* (June 2, 1997). "This approach of using the whole animal is likely to become increasingly important as geneticists attempt to investigate the basis of other complex human conditions such as hypertension or schizophrenia."

Later in 1997 Rubin and Tim Townes of the University of Alabama–Birmingham reported in *Science* (October 31, 1997) that their labs had found a way to replicate sickle-cell anemia in mice. Every year thousands of human babies are born with sickle-cell anemia, a sometimes fatal disease in which a mutant form of hemoglobin distorts red blood cells into a sickle (crescent) shape, which makes it difficult or impossible for the cells to pass through small blood vessels. In time, without the normal flow of blood, such tissue becomes damaged. Victims of the disease suffer intense pain. Although scientists have known for more than 50 years which mutant gene causes the disorder, they have yet to develop a cure. Several scientists had attempted without success to introduce the mutant gene into mice in the 1980s and early 1990s, in the hope of being able to test a greater range of possible treatments than would be permitted on human subjects. Franklin Bunn of the Harvard Medical School, in Boston, Massachusetts, an authority on hemoglobin diseases, told Marcia Barinaga for the same issue of *Science* that Rubin and Towne's breakthrough was "a critically important advance" in the search for a treatment for sickle-cell anemia.

In 1998 Rubin was appointed head of the Genome Sciences Department at UC–Berkeley. The following year his research team reported in *Nature Genetics* (October 1, 1999) that by using a new technique, they had isolated two genes that increase an individual's odds of contracting asthma. Instead of relying on the usual "brute-force method" of comparing the DNA sequences of individuals afflicted with asthma with those from people who are not, the team examined sets of genes on chromosome 5 associated with allergic activity, inserting them into mouse DNA. Each mouse carried a different portion of the chromosome, allowing Rubin and his team to identify genes IL4 and IL13 as those responsible for asthma susceptibility by simply observing the outcomes in the mice.

Before scientists had set about sequencing the DNA of humans and animals, it was thought that genes—segments of DNA that build, or "code," proteins (the building blocks of life)—were the crucial elements of the genome. That raised a puzzling question, because 95 percent of the human genome consists of non-coding DNA, otherwise known as "junk" DNA. Some scientists hypothesized that those DNA "deserts," as these long stretches of junk DNA were called, had once served an evolutionary purpose but were now dormant. As scientists began sequencing the genomes of mice, rats, and humans, they discovered matching patterns in the DNA deserts of all three species. The idea emerged that if those segments had been preserved long after mice and rats diverged from the same evolutionary chain, and humans diverged from rodents, then those segments must present some evolutionary advantage. Scientists then discovered that some segments of noncoding DNA could be used to regulate the expression of particular genes. In *Science* (April 7, 2000) Rubin and his associates at the Berkeley Lab and UC–San Francisco reported that the technique Rubin's lab had been using to identify genetic links to disease could also be used to mine DNA deserts for regulatory DNA. "You could call this finding jewels in junk DNA," Rubin told a reporter for Ascribe Newswire (April 11, 2000). "By comparing human and mouse sequences we can identify those segments of the genome that contain information which instructs surrounding genes on when and where they are to be active. Identifying these regulatory sequences using classical biological approaches is labor intensive and difficult." In a subsequent issue of *Science* (October 18, 2001), Rubin and his team announced that by using that method they had discovered such a "jewel"—an apolipoprotein that plays an important role in regulating triglyceride levels in the blood. Triglycerides and cholesterol, the two major blood fats, pose important risk factors in the development of heart disease, the leading cause of death in the United States.

The next year the Rubin Lab, in conjunction with 27 other institutions in six countries, completed a project that sequenced the mouse genome and compared it with the human genome. Published in the journal *Nature*, the study revealed that mice share a genetic heritage with humans; depending on various measurements, the number of common genes might be as high as 99 percent of the genome and could be traced back 75 million years. The mouse was the second mammal to be decoded, and its genetic similarity to humans provided scientists with the opportunity to further investigate DNA deserts; the research team was surprised to discover that almost three times as much of the genome common to mice and men lay in DNA deserts as in genes. "Now instead of a landscape with no common points, we have a map that scientists can travel over," Rubin told Ian Hoffman for the *Oakland (California) Tribune* (December 5, 2005). "Now they have really vital highways into all kinds of biomedical research."

In January 2003 Rubin was appointed director of the U.S. Department of Energy's Joint Genome Institute and the genomics division at the Lawrence Berkeley National Laboratory. The Walnut Creek, California–based Joint Genome Institute (JGI) employs about 240 people and is managed by the Berkeley Lab in conjunction with two other UC-affiliated facilities: the Lawrence Livermore National Laboratory, near San Francisco, California, and the Los Alamos National Laboratory, in New Mexico. Rubin had been serving as the interim director since the spring of 2002 and was selected for the position after a nationwide search.

In the February 28, 2003 issue of *Science*, the JGI and the Berkeley Lab announced the development of what is known as phylogenetic shadowing, a new technique for deciphering the biological information encoded in the human genome. The technique enables scientists to make meaningful comparisons between the DNA of humans and monkeys, apes, or other primates. Previously, contrasting the human genome with those of chimpanzees or baboons had been difficult, because the sequences are so much alike—only 2 percent of the chimp sequence is different, and only 5 percent of the baboon's—and it is difficult to distinguish which segments encode functional elements. Instead of comparing the genetic sequence of one primate with that of the human genome, Rubin and his team compared segments from the genomes of several different primates and found enough small differences among species to compile a phylogenetic shadow. Using the shadow, Rubin and his team were able to identify DNA sequences that regulate the activation of a gene that is found only in primates and is an important indicator of an individual's risk of developing heart disease. "The ability to compare DNA sequences in the human genome [with] sequences in nonhuman primates will enable us in some ways to better understand ourselves than [will] the study of evolutionarily far-distant relatives such as the mouse or the rat," Rubin told a reporter for *Genomics & Genetics Weekly* (March 28, 2003). "This is important because as valuable as models like the mouse have been, there are many physical and biochemical attributes of humans that only other primates share."

Later that year, in *Science* (October 17, 2003), researchers at the Berkeley and JGI labs led by Rubin announced that the sequences in DNA deserts that regulate particular genes and the genes being regulated may be located surprisingly far from one another in the genome. "The distance from which these long-range enhancers can reach out across the genome to regulate a gene is a hundredfold greater than anyone thought," Rubin told a reporter for *Genomics & Genetics Weekly* (November 7, 2003). "Gene deserts may not be home to any genes but they can host DNA sequences that act as long-distance switches to activate far-away genes. This suggests that the idea that all gene deserts could be eliminated with no consequences to the organism is wrong." Rubin's team reached this conclusion after studying a human gene called DACHI, which is involved in the development of the brain, limbs, and sensory organs. Because DACHI resides between two large gene deserts, Rubin thought that regulatory elements for the DACHI gene might lie in the adjacent deserts. By comparing the human and mouse genomes, the researchers were able to identify seven long-range gene enhancers buried in the surrounding gene deserts. The discovery may prove useful in the treatment of diseases. "Regulatory elements that are very far away from a gene can cause serious problems," Rubin told the reporter for *Genomics & Genetics Weekly*. "You can think of these long-range enhancers like the root system of a tree. Previously we thought that roots only extended a short distance from the tree. Our new study suggests that some roots can extend far away from the tree's trunk and branches, [and that] cutting those distant roots can still do harm to the tree."

In a study published in *Nature* in October 2004, however, Rubin demonstrated that certain portions of the DNA desert could be deleted without any negative effects. Rubin's team deleted large segments of seemingly functionless stretches of mouse DNA, producing mice that exhibited no apparent abnormalities. The 1,234 non-coding sequences deleted from the mice were identical to sequences found in the human genome. "In these studies, we were looking particularly for sequences that might not be essential," Rubin told a reporter for the Wellcome Trust's Web site (October 20, 2004). "Nonetheless we were surprised, given the magnitude of the information being deleted from the genome, by the complete lack of impact noted. From our results, it would seem that some non-coding sequences may indeed have minimal if any function." In similar studies, parts of the genome of similar sizes had been deleted in mice, but because those sequences contained important genetic information, none of those mice survived. "If you're an architect and you want to see if a wall is weight bearing, you remove the wall and see if the ceiling caves in," he told Bryan Nelson for *Newsday* (October 21, 2004). "That's what we did and were expecting the roof to fall in, and it didn't." The discovery could also prove useful to scientists scouring the human genome for genes that cause or contribute to disease: Rubin's results could help them to eliminate large stretches of the three billion base-pair human genome that are likely irrelevant. "Looking for genes involved in human diseases is like looking for a needle in a haystack," he told Betsy Mason for the *Contra Costa Times* (October 21, 2004). "Here's a big part of that haystack where you don't have to look."

Rubin served as the lead researcher for a study in which his team demonstrated that the signatures of genes in terrestrial and aquatic environmental samples could be used to diagnose the health of environments. As described in *Science* (April 22, 2005), those DNA fingerprints, called Environmental Genomic Tags, or EGTS, serve as a DNA profile of a particular site and reflect the presence of levels of nutrients, pollutants, and other environmental features. For example, microbial creatures living in surface water rely heavily on light as a source of energy; consequently, samples taken from shallow seawater contain an abundance of genes involved in photosynthesis, the process by which sunlight is converted into energy. "EGT fingerprints may be able to offer fundamental insights into the factors impacting on various environments," Rubin said, as quoted in a JGI press release (April 21, 2005, online). "With EGTs we don't actually need a complete genome's worth of data to understand the

functions required of the organisms living in a particular setting. Rather, the genes present and their abundances in the EGT data reflect the demands of the setting and, accordingly, can tell us about what's happening in an environment without knowing the identities of the microbes living there." Instead of sequencing the genomes for all of the microbes in the environment—a daunting task, given the large number of different organisms present in nearly all environments—the EGT approach allows scientists, by means of an abbreviated sequencing technique, to form a useful metabolic picture of an environment. "Enivronmental systems are extremely complex, harboring numerous diverse species coexisting in a single locale," Rubin explained in the press release. "By focusing on the information encoded in the DNA fragments sequenced, independent of the organisms from which they derived, we were able to get around the problem of species diversity."

On June 2, 2005, in an on-line supplement to *Science*, Rubin and other Berkeley Lab researchers announced a breakthrough that could help resolve the controversy over the relationship between modern humans and Neanderthals (Homo neanderthalensis). Working with James Noonan of the Berkeley Lab and experts in ancient DNA in Austria and Germany, Rubin sequenced portions of nuclear DNA taken from two specimens of an extinct cave bear (Urus spelaeus) that died in Austria more than 40,000 years ago. Previously, scientists had been unable to reconstruct the genome of an extinct animal, because the nucleic acid that comprises DNA begins to degrade rapidly after death; moreover, such samples are easily contaminated with the DNA of the people who find it and the microbes that devoured the animal after it died. In rare instances, in which specimens had been unusually well preserved in permafrost or snow, scientists had succeeded in extracting nuclear DNA from their remains, but only from specimens less than 20,000 years old.

Many of the previously successful studies of ancient DNA had focused on mitochondrial DNA, which is more abundant and easier to extract than nuclear DNA. For example, the typical human cell contains 11,000 copies of mitochondrial DNA and only two copies of nuclear DNA. Mitochondrial DNA, however, is much less useful to scientists; it contains only DNA from the mother's side, and scientists need information from the father's DNA, too, to understand biological differences between species. "While mitochondria are great for learning about evolutionary relationships between species, to understand the functional differences between extinct and modern species we really need nuclear or genomic DNA," Rubin told David Gilbert for *US Fed News* (June 3, 2005).

Rubin and his team were able to reconstruct the cave bear genome using a tooth from one animal and bone from the other. They sequenced all of the DNA in the two samples, including the contamination. (It turned out that only 6 percent of the DNA sequenced from the sample contained the cave bear's DNA sequence; the other 94 percent came from various contaminants.) Aided by computers, the researchers compared the cave bear DNA with that of a dog—which diverged from bears around 50 million years ago but still share 92 percent of their genes with bears—so as to pinpoint what is identical to the cave-bear sequences in the lengthy sequences of human and microbial DNA. "We were looking for the proverbial needle in the haystack . . . ," Rubin told Lee Bowman for the Scripps Howard News Service (June 2, 2005). "Among the expected lion's share of contaminants we recovered reasonable amounts of 40,000-year-old cave bear DNA and useful information from it. We were lucky in that we had a very powerful magnet in the form of industrial strength computing to tease out the interesting data from a hodgepodge of different DNAs."

The sequence produced was only about 1/1,000th of 1 percent of the total bear DNA, but according to the team, it proved that given sufficient time and resources, the researchers could indeed sequence the genome of an entire extinct animal. "This is very much a proof in principle," Rubin told a staff writer for *New Scientist* (June 11, 2005). "We're not interested in cave bears—we're interested in Neanderthals." For the past century there has been a fierce debate surrounding the exact relation of modern humans to Neanderthals, hominids that lived in Europe and Asia during roughly the same period as cave bears. There is some evidence that Neanderthals, humans' closest prehistoric relatives, coexisted with early people. Though they possessed shorter, broader bodies than ours, their anatomy was so similar that in 1964 it was suggested that modern humans and Neanderthals actually represent subspecies: Homo sapiens sapiens and Homo sapiens neanderthalensis. This view held great currency in the 1970s and 1980s, but many anthropologists today have returned to the two-species hypothesis.

It will be more difficult but, the team believes, not impossible to distinguish Neanderthal DNA from human DNA that has contaminated a Neanderthal sample. On July 6, 2005 the Leipzig, Germany–based Max Planck Institute for Evolutionary Anthropology announced the launch of a joint project between German and U.S. scientists to reconstruct the Neanderthal genome. Rubin, who was also participating in the project, spoke of the effort to the German weekly *Die Zeit*, according to a reporter for the Associated Press Worldstream (July 6, 2005). "Firstly, we will learn a lot about the Neanderthals," he said. "Secondly, we will learn a lot about the uniqueness of human beings. And thirdly, it's simply cool." In July 2006 the Swedish-born anthropologist Svante Pääbo, who directs the Max Planck Institute for Evolutionary Anthropology, made public a two-year plan to complete the first part of the construction of the Neanderthal genome. According to a press release on the Max Planck Society Web site (July 20, 2006), Rubin,

Pääbo, and their collaborators "have already sequenced approximately one million base pairs of nuclear Neanderthal DNA from a 38,000-year-old Croatian fossil." In the next few years, the team intends to sequence the remainder of the three billion base pairs that composed the Neanderthal genome.

Rubin has served as co-chair of the Cold Springs Genome Sequencing and Biology Meeting and was scientific chair of the International Human Genome Organization. He lives in Berkeley with his wife, Joan Emery, a genetic counselor. They have two teenage children, Ben and Rachel. In his leisure time Rubin likes to surf in the nearby Pacific Ocean.

—J.C.

Suggested Reading: *Contra Costa Times* F p4 Oct. 21, 2004; *Genomics & Genetics Weekly* p21 Mar. 28, 2003, p54 Nov. 7, 2003; JGI Web site

Matthew Stockman/Getty Images

Santana, Johan

(YO-hahn)

Mar. 13, 1979– Baseball player

Address: Minnesota Twins, Hubert H. Humphrey Metrodome, 34 Kirby Puckett Pl., Minneapolis, MN 55415

The Minnesota Twins' starting pitcher Johan Santana is, in the estimation of the noted baseball journalist Jack Curry, writing for the *New York Times* (March 13, 2006, on-line), "one of the elite pitchers walking the earth." In 2004 Santana became the first Venezuelan-born player to receive the Cy Young Award, given to the best pitcher in each league of the majors. Few baseball players in recent memory have so dominated a single season as Santana did that year. Boasting three precise pitches—a 95-mile-per-hour fastball, a sweeping slider, and his signature, a deceptive changeup—the southpaw won 20 games in regular-season play and was, more than any other major-league pitcher, responsible for leading his team to the play-offs. He also led all American League (AL) pitchers in 2004 in earned-run average (ERA) and strikeouts and was named the *Sporting News*'s AL pitcher of the year. Santana had a similarly impressive season in 2005, again leading all AL hurlers in strikeouts. The New York Mets' ace right-handed pitcher Pedro Martinez, a three-time Cy Young Award winner, said to Albert Chen for *Sports Illustrated* (August 30, 2004), "[Santana] reminds me of myself when I was younger," adding, "His stuff is probably a little bit better than mine was at that age."

The fourth of five children, Johan Alexander Santana was born on March 13, 1979 in Tovar, a town of approximately 40,000 in western Venezuela. Tovar is located in Mérida, one of Venezuela's 23 states, which, with more than 710,000 people, is among the most populous in the country. Santana's father, Jesús, nicknamed "El Pulpo" (Spanish for "the octopus") for his ability to field ground balls, was a middle infielder on amateur teams during Johan's boyhood; he aspired, but failed, to make the pros in Venezuela. Jesús Santana worked a handful of jobs, ultimately becoming a repairman for Mérida's electric company. Johan was raised primarily by his mother, Hilda. His older brother, Franklin, was considered by Jesús to be a better professional baseball prospect than the slightly built Johan, who was the more serious student of the two. Their parents expected Johan to take up engineering.

Nevertheless, Santana, who grew up throwing right-handed because the only baseball gloves available to him were cast-offs from his father, was enamored of baseball from an early age. He and Franklin tagged along to their father's games, carrying his equipment. "I always wanted to be like [my father]," Santana said to S. L. Price for *Sports Illustrated* (May 23, 2005). At age 10 he played on his first team, at shortstop. In time Santana's coaches discovered that he was a left-handed thrower and made him an outfielder. Later, playing center field for a team called the Chiquilines, who frequently competed in events in other parts of Venezuela, Santana displayed a strong throwing arm and a knack for chasing down fly balls.

When Santana was 15 his play at center field in a national tournament in Guigue, Venezuela, caught the eye of Andres Reiner, a baseball scout who then worked for the Houston Astros. Reiner wanted to offer Santana the opportunity to join a baseball academy in Guacara, Venezuela, that he

ran in conjunction with the Astros. Because that period coincided with the professional baseball strike of 1994, which resulted in the cancellation of that season's World Series, the Astros initially expressed no interest in pursuing Santana as a prospect. In time, however, Reiner secured the funds needed to travel to Tovar. Santana, who at the time was working at his uncle's bakery and was about to graduate from Liceo Jose Nucete Sardi High School, where he also played soccer, did not at first receive his father's blessing to go north with Reiner. Jesús Santana wanted his son to pursue an education instead. "[My father] didn't get to be a baseball player, and right there I have the chance," Santana said to S. L. Price. "I was like, 'Dad, maybe you get this opportunity once in your life; you never know. If I fail, I'll go back to school. Let me take my chance.'"

Upon arriving at the academy, in January 1995, Santana was made a pitcher. While there he had to face prejudice on the part of his peers; in Venezuela people from Santana's home state are often called *gochos*, a derogatory term whose approximate English translation is "hillbillies" or "rednecks." While Venezuela had produced such professional baseball players as Luis Aparicio, Chico Carrasquel, and, later, Ozzie Guillen and Andres Galarraga, none were from the Andes region that Santana called home. Previously, those from that area had been known to become soccer players, cyclists, and bullfighters, but not baseball players. Santana, who today is celebrated as a national hero in Venezuela, has done much to alter that perception. "Every time they say 'Gocho' now, the people there feel better," he said to S. L. Price. "Because the others always thought those bad things, that gochos weren't smart. But it's not that way; gocho doesn't mean people live in cabins and they're shooting people. I'm going to make people proud of being from where I'm from. I'm going to make sure that everywhere I go my people will be represented the way they should be."

On July 2, 1995 Santana signed with the Astros as an amateur free agent, thus becoming the first Venezuelan from the Andes region to have signed with a U.S. team. By the following year he had performed well enough in his new role as a pitcher to earn a promotion to the organization's summer-league team, which played in the Dominican Republic. There, appearing primarily as a relief pitcher, he tossed 40 innings and held opposing batters to a low .178 batting average. He started the 1997 season in Kissimmee, Florida, with the Astros' Gulf Coast League affiliate. Over a span of 36 innings, however, he did not fare particularly well. On July 4, 1997 Santana made a start for the Auburn Doubledays of the New York–Penn League, but just days later he was transferred back to Kissimmee. He returned the following year to pitch for the Doubledays, winning seven games, which tied him for first place among the team's pitchers, and tossed 88 strikeouts in 87 innings. In 1999 he played in Michigan with the Astros' Class-A club of the Midwest League. Leading the team in strike-outs (150) and games started (26), by mid-season he had earned a spot in the Midwest League All-Star Game.

Despite the new pitches he had added to his repertoire, including a fastball that reached 95 miles per hour and an improving changeup, the Astros cut their ties with Santana on December 13, 1999. He thus entered that day's Rule V draft, in which the Florida Marlins chose him as the second overall pick, then traded him to the Minnesota Twins, in exchange for the pitcher Jared Camp and a monetary sum. Santana's chance of making the Twins' big-league roster was strengthened by the conventions of the Rule V baseball draft, which stipulate that a player so chosen must remain on the major-league roster of his new team for one season or be offered back to his original team. In the spring-training session before the 2000 Major League Baseball (MLB) season, Santana performed well enough to persuade Tom Kelly, the Twins' manager, to grant him a place in the big-league team's bullpen. Appearing in 30 games and starting in five, Santana finished the season with a 2–3 record and a 6.49 ERA. That inauspicious start aside, Santana's demeanor and guile on the mound had impressed the organization, which retained him for the start of the 2001 season. Midway through that year, however, he suffered a partial tear in the muscle in his left elbow, which sidelined him from mid-June until late September. In a limited role he registered a 1–0 record, with an ERA of 4.74. The Twins, with a talented but inexperienced roster, had a respectable 85–77 record at the end of the season.

Santana opened the 2002 season with the Twins' AAA affiliate in Edmonton, Canada, where in nine starts, due largely to the improvement of his changeup, he recorded 75 strikeouts in 48 and two-thirds innings. Santana credits Bobby Cuellar, Edmonton's pitching coach, with helping him sharpen his changeup. "He always had the pitch," Cuellar said to Mel Antonen for *USA Today* (July 27, 2004). "Johan had to learn to trust it. I told him, 'Don't be afraid to throw it at any time. Trust it, and it will do what it is supposed to do.' It's the hardest thing for a young pitcher to do." Santana's change-up, which is slower than his fastball by as much as 20 miles per hour, is delivered with the same arm speed—which tricks batters into swinging at it too early. Though he was still perfecting the pitch when he was recalled to the Twins' roster, in late May 2002, Santana subsequently employed it with great frequency and success. That season, splitting his time between relief pitching and serving as a starter, Santana reached a career high in innings pitched (108.3), struck out more batters (137) than he had in his entire career to that point, and recorded his lowest-ever ERA (2.99). The Twins, meanwhile, enjoyed one of their best seasons of recent memory; their 94–67 record earned them the AL Central Division crown. Playing against the Oakland Athletics in the first round of the play-offs, after falling behind two games to one, the team won the final two games of the best-of-five series. They were then dispatched in five games by the high-scoring Anaheim Angels in the American League Championship Series. Santana was not as effective in the play-offs as he would have liked, surrendering several runs in his six relief appearances.

Before the start of the 2003 season, while playing winter ball in Venezuela, Santana injured his hamstring. He hoped in spite of that that the Twins' coaching staff, on the strength of his pitching in the 2002 season, would name him as one of the team's starting pitchers. On March 13, 2003—Santana's 24th birthday—the Twins reached an agreement with the veteran southpaw Kenny Rogers to round out their starting staff; Santana, feeling betrayed, voiced his displeasure to Ron Gardenhire (the Twins' manager since 2002). Gardenhire, who told La Velle E. Neal III for the *Minneapolis Star Tribune* (March 15, 2003) that Santana would someday "get his chance to be a starter in this league," had Santana start the season as a reliever. The young left-hander did not disappoint. He allowed no runs in his first seven relief appearances, and by late June he had achieved a 2.41 ERA. Thrust into the role of starting pitcher in July, Santana employed his arsenal of pitches and quickly emerged as the team's ace. He was named the AL Pitcher of the Month for August; finished the year with a 12–3 record, which included a stretch of eight straight wins; and led the team with 169 strikeouts. "I figured he was trying to prove us wrong, and I figured once he got in the rotation and did well, it would come back and I'd hear it: 'I could've been doing this a long time ago,'" Gardenhire said to S. L. Price. "And I have heard that. You know what? I agree with him. Maybe we were stupid."

The Twins, considered underdogs, faced the mighty New York Yankees in the 2003 play-offs. Santana, the Twins' Game One starter, hurled four scoreless innings before succumbing to cramps in his hamstring, which forced his removal from the game. The Twins won, 3–1. With the Yankees leading by two games to one, Santana was given the ball again in Game Four, played in Minnesota. After retiring 10 of the first 11 batters he faced, Santana surrendered six runs in the fourth inning, before Gardenhire removed him; the Yankees went on to win the game, 8–1, and take the series. "I was doing what I was doing before, just trying to throw the ball for strikes," Santana explained after the game, quoted by Mark Sheldon for MLB.com (October 5, 2003). "They were able to hit the ball in the right spot. It's about adjustments. They made the right adjustments and hit the ball very well."

Gardenhire selected Santana as a starter for the 2004 season. He fared poorly early in the season, which some attributed to an off-season procedure to remove bone chips from his throwing arm. Beginning with his first start following the All-Star Break, in July, Santana had one of the most successful stretches of any pitcher in MLB history. He won all 13 of the remaining games in which he was the pitcher of record and was named the AL Pitcher of the Month for July, August, and September. During one especially remarkable period, Santana allowed four or fewer hits in 10 straight starts; he became the first pitcher to do so since 1961. Santana had proved to be the rare pitcher able to strike out a large number of batters while maintaining a low number of walks. S. L. Price observed, "In terms of power and control, only two pitchers in their 20s have ever had a season comparable with Santana's . . . year in 2004: Sandy Koufax in 1965 and Pedro Martinez in '99." During the 2004 season Santana posted a record of 20–6 with an earned-run average of 2.61, leading in both categories in the American League. He also led the American League in strikeouts (265), strikeouts per nine innings pitched (10.46), WHIP, or walks and hits per inning pitched, (0.92), batting-average allowed (.192), on-base percentage allowed (.249), and slugging-percentage allowed (.315). "Sandy Koufax, another left-hander, used to have numbers like that," Joe Torre, the Yankees manager, said to Jason Beck for MLB.com (October 4, 2004). "Those numbers don't exist anymore." Santana was named the AL Pitcher of the Year by the *Sporting News*. In addition, he was named by his peers the AL's Most Outstanding Pitcher and was the unanimous choice for the AL Cy Young Award, receiving all 28 first-place votes. (When that occurred, the people of Tovar swarmed into the streets surrounding Santana's family's home, mistakenly believing that he was inside and refused to address them. Santana, who was in Caracas, the country's capital, at the time, appeared on television to pacify the mob; the National Guard was also called in to restore calm.) He was given the Calvin R. Griffith Award as the Most Valuable Twins player and the Joseph W. Haynes Award as the team's Pitcher of the Year. "I used to be hyper, throw crazy and not think about what I wanted to do with each pitch. Now I have a better understanding of what it is to be a major league pitcher," Santana said to Albert Chen. Santana's father was filled with pride at his son's accomplishments. "I look at him, and I see me. Every time he played, I saw a part of me," Jesús Santana said in his conversation with S. L. Price. "A part of me that's better than me."

The Twins again opened the play-offs against the Yankees. Santana pitched well in New York in Game One (which the Twins won, 2–0), allowing no runs in seven innings and striking out five batters. In Game Four, with the Twins facing elimination, he took to the mound in Minnesota, working for the first time in his career on three days' rest—less than starting pitchers are accustomed to in contemporary times. Although he was effective over five innings, surrendering just one run, Gardenhire removed him from the game after the Twins scored three runs in the bottom of the fifth inning, acquiring a seemingly insurmountable 5–1 lead. The move proved to be premature, as the Yan-

kees scored five runs against the Twins' bullpen to win the extra-inning game by a score of 6–5 and take the series, three games to one.

In 2005 Santana did not win as many games or strike out as many opponents as he had the previous year, though the number of innings he pitched increased slightly. Nevertheless, he became the first Twins pitcher to lead both leagues in strikeouts (238) and topped the AL in strikeouts per nine innings pitched (9.25) and opponents' batting-average against (.198). Moreover, he ranked second in innings pitched, earned-run average, and shutouts. In 2005 the Twins finished 16 games behind the Chicago White Sox, the eventual winners of the World Series. Santana ended the season with a 16–7 record and an ERA of 2.87. "His stuff is absolutely amazing," Frank Viola, a former Twins pitcher and the winner of the 1988 AL Cy Young Award, said to S. L. Price. "If he's left alone and just goes out there, he will be the most dominant pitcher over the next five or six years. He's got a swagger now."

Santana started two games for Venezuela in the inaugural World Baseball Classic, played March 3–20, 2006 in locations including Tokyo, Japan; San Juan, Puerto Rico; and several cities on the U.S. mainland. Though he was saddled with two losses, he achieved a 2.16 ERA in the tournament. Venezuela advanced to the second round of play before being dispatched by the Dominican Republic. (Japan, the eventual winners, defeated Cuba in the final round by a score of 10–6.) In 2006 Santana led the American League in ERA (2.77), wins (19), and strikeouts (245), an accomplishment referred to as the Triple Crown in pitching; he was the first player to accomplish that feat since Randy Johnson in 2002, making him a favorite to win the 2006 Cy Young Award. That season the Twins won the AL Central Division and proceeded to the American League Division Series, facing the Oakland Athletics. Santana earned a defeat in Game One of the series after giving up a home run to Frank Thomas and a run-scoring double to Marco Scutaro; the Twins were swept in the series, three games to zero.

Johan Santana stands six feet tall and weighs about 205 pounds. He often wears a goatee. His teammates and coaches have described him as a jovial person with an uplifting presence. "This is a game, that's what I think," Santana said to S. L. Price. "I try to make people laugh. I see people on the team with a frown on their face, I think they'll go out and play with a frown." Unlike many of his pitching peers, who prepare for games by poring over notes and statistics on batters in the opposing lineups, Santana claims that while on the mound he observes subtle cues in hitters' postures that determine the speed and direction of his pitches. He also professes a love for video games, particularly those modeled on baseball; playing them on the nights before games, he has said, helps his pitching performance. "Believe it or not, sometimes I see things in video games that will come true," Santana explained to Price. "Particularly in the last year, they're coming up with some good games, so realistic—the stats are so accurate, and you can go from there. I'm sure a lot of players will agree with what I'm saying. Because it gives you ideas. I see the scouting reports, though I don't go by that, and in these video games you can see what the hitters have, how to approach them."

Santana participates in TwinsCare, a program that provides tickets for the team's home games to underprivileged youth in the Minnesota area. He has also been known to provide donations to families in Venezuela affected by floods. Santana is

building several new baseball and softball fields in Tovar; he is proud that his success has brought an influx of big-league scouts to Mérida, where the Twins have reportedly set up an outpost for scouting. He lives in Fort Meyers, Florida, with his wife, Yasmile, whom he has known since his childhood, and their two daughters, Jasmily and Jasmine.

—D.F.

Suggested Reading: Jockbio.com; Minnesota Twins Web site; *St. Paul Pioneer Press* A p1+ Jan. 28, 2005; *Sports Illustrated* p103+ Aug. 30, 2004, p42+ May 23, 2005

Courtesy of Buzzword

Scelsa, Vin

(SKEL-suh)

Dec. 12, 1947– Disc jockey; host of the radio program Idiot's Delight

Address: WFUV, Fordham University, Rose Hill Campus, Bronx, NY 10458

At a time when a handful of media conglomerates control the majority of radio stations in the U.S., and some stations have eliminated disc jockeys altogether in favor of computerized playlists and prerecorded announcements, Vin Scelsa's show *Idiot's Delight*, which currently airs in New York City on WFUV (90.7 FM), is an anomaly. In the 1960s Scelsa spearheaded the free-form radio movement, in which the DJ has complete—often idiosyncratic—control over program content, and

he continues to broadcast an eclectic mixture of jazz, folk, rock, and other styles, without targeting a specific marketing demographic. "The idea with free-form radio is there's lots of different kinds of music in the world and they all have relationships to each other, whether conscious or unconscious," Scelsa told Steve Inskeep for the National Public Radio show *Talk of the Nation* (September 6, 2001). "Why not take advantage of that fact? Why not create a new art out of this art that's already been created? Why not take these recordings and weave them together, from rock to jazz to pop to schmaltz to classical to lounge . . . weave all of this together in a very creative sort of soundtrack-like way that will take your very thinking and very listening listener on a kind of a journey?"

Scelsa is known not only for the wide variety of music he plays but also for the lengthy in-depth interviews he conducts with the guest artists who have appeared on his program, among them such legendary figures as John Lennon, Joey Ramone, Leonard Cohen, and Lou Reed. "I think of myself as a teacher with a missionary zeal, educating people to all kinds of new music," Scelsa told Lee R. Schreiber for the *New York Times* (March 13, 1994). "Though I try not to come in with all sorts of prepared, arcane knowledge."

Vincent Scelsa was born on December 12, 1947 in Bayonne, New Jersey, to S. Vincent and Antoinette Scelsa. (The family later moved to nearby Roselle Park.) Scelsa has credited his father, an accountant and amateur violinist, with instilling in him a love of music. "My father got very involved in my musical education," Scelsa told Claudia Perry for the *New Jersey Star-Ledger* (March 10, 2005). "He took me to a [clarinet] teacher in Jersey City. . . . My father would come and sit with us while I had my lesson. He wanted to learn more about music theory and things like that." Scelsa and his two sisters were frequent participants in the informal weekly gatherings their father arranged, at which guests played instruments or listened to old Italian songs on the radio.

Scelsa, who had attended Bayonne's Marist High School, enrolled at the now-defunct Upsala College, in East Orange, New Jersey, where he edited the campus literary review. Already interested in radio thanks to his father's influence, he began hosting a program called *The Closet* on the Upsala radio station, WFMU, in November 1967. Richard Neer, in his book *FM: The Rise and Fall of Rock Radio* (2001), explained how the program got its name: "From the thirties until the early fifties, *Fibber McGee and Molly* had been a popular radio sitcom. Often, the final punch line consisted of Fibber opening his overstuffed closet. Regular listeners knew that merely cracking the door would create a landslide of junk. . . . So at the end of the program when he finally opened the door after many false starts, the sound effects of junk tumbling from its shelves could be heard for several seconds." Neer continued, "Scelsa began his show by opening such a door, and when the noise of falling debris finally abated, he would calmly sort through the garbage. He'd find a new album by the Kinks—he'd have to play that later. An interview with a noted poet—he'd use that as well." *The Closet* became popular at Upsala and soon other students started hosting similar programs. Neer wrote, "Scelsa and his cohorts never thought about ratings or revenue as his commercial brethren were forced to: They were students having the time of their lives. Some of them actually lived at the station, and sex and drugs on the property were routinely accepted." Upsala's administration, however, was growing concerned about WFMU's overt leftist political leanings and began placing restrictions on the staff. Faced with new regulations, Scelsa left both the station and the college in 1969. After working briefly for his in-laws' jewelry business, Scelsa was again drawn into radio when Larry Yurdin, who worked for the radio station ABC-FM, convinced the station's head, Alan Shaw, that investing in a commercial free-form radio station would be worthwhile. Shaw agreed, and Scelsa was recruited as a part of the inaugural on-air staff of the newly minted WPLJ. According to Neer, "WPLJ was undoubtedly the most radical commercial radio New York had ever heard. Other than [disc jockey Dave Herman], the PLJ jocks did not have the deep professional radio voices one expected from syndication. Most sounded like the just barely above adolescents they were, and their musical taste was all over the map." Scelsa's show featured a mix of jazz, show tunes, and psychedelic rock music. Before long, however, WPLJ bowed to market pressures and adopted a more conventional Top 40 music format, and Scelsa left the station.

In 1973 Scelsa joined the staff at WNEW-FM, a well-respected station considered revolutionary during the 1960s and '70s for championing such artists as Bob Dylan and Bruce Springsteen before their music had broken into the mainstream. "WNEW was the hip place, where the hip people who were into music went," Pat St. John, a former DJ, told an interviewer for CNN (March 3, 2003, online). Neer wrote, "At various times in the last decades of the past millennium, the glamour profession might have been professional athlete, politi-

cian, actor, rock star, TV talk show host. But I'm convinced that at the beginning of the seventies, there was no greater glory than being a disc jockey at WNEW-FM." Though it would later narrow its focus to a rock-oriented format, in its formative years WNEW imposed few restrictions upon its on-air staff. Scelsa's show ran on weekends until 1979, when he joined forces with Tom Morrera, another DJ, to form the *Butch and the Brick Show*, which ran from 10 p.m. to 6 a.m. For the show Scelsa adopted an alter-ego known as Bayonne Butch. (Morrera's on-air name was a reference to a brick of hashish.)

One of Scelsa's most difficult moments on the air came on December 8, 1980, when the ex-Beatle and cultural icon John Lennon was shot by Mark David Chapman outside his apartment building in New York City; Scelsa had been in the middle of a show when he received the news, and many New Yorkers first heard of Lennon's death from that broadcast. "I am at a loss for words," Scelsa said at the time, as quoted on a recent edition of the television program *Dateline NBC* (November 18, 2005). "I think for the first time in my career on the radio I don't have anything to say." Scelsa, crying and shaking, then played the Beatles' song "Let it Be."

By the early 1980s WNEW had been purchased by the Infinity Broadcasting Corporation, and pressure was mounting for the station to switch to a format in which on-air talent picked their selections from a set list of records. Fearing that that move would compromise the artistic integrity of his show, Scelsa quit in 1982 and joined the staff of WNEW's chief competitor, WXRK (usually referred to as K-Rock), in 1985. (Sources do not indicate what he did in the interim.) Though K-Rock was dedicated to playing classic rock—as older, established rock music is often called—Scelsa was given a time slot on Sunday nights in which he could have free rein. His new show was christened *Idiot's Delight* and generated a cult following in the New York City area. Scelsa became known for punctuating his eclectic sets of music with in-depth discussions of film, literature, and theatre. "I view radio as very one-on-one," Scelsa told an interviewer for the Bergen County, New Jersey, *Record* (December 12, 1997). "There's me on the broadcasting side and there's one listener on the receiving end. And that one listener is alone somewhere: in a room, in a car. It's a community of these loners who are totally unconnected to each other, except for the common fact that they're listening to me."

In the mid-1990s K-Rock switched from classic rock to modern rock, and its management wanted Scelsa to change the direction of his program to better fit the new format; he refused and quit the station, telling David Hinckley for the New York *Daily News* (January 23, 1996), "They told me they wanted to talk about 'adjusting' my show to their new target audience, and that's something I won't do. I've never 'targeted' the show, period. It's for anyone with a mind and ears." Scelsa returned to

WNEW in 1996, where he broadcast *Idiot's Delight* on Sunday evenings (though the program's name was temporarily changed to *Vin Scelsa's Sunday Night* due to copyright issues). By that time Scelsa had become a celebrated figure in New York City broadcasting. In December 1997 a group of musicians that included Lou Reed, Joey Ramone, Ronnie Spector, Steven Van Zandt, and others gathered at the Bottom Line, a popular Manhattan nightclub, to celebrate Scelsa's 50th birthday and 30th anniversary on the radio. (From 1990 to 1995 Scelsa had hosted a series of shows at the club called "In Their Own Words: A Bunch Of Songwriters Sittin' Around Singin'.")

WNEW, meanwhile, under increasing pressure from Infinity Broadcasting and a constantly changing staff of executives, went through a series of rock-oriented formats before switching to an all-talk format in 1999 and unceremoniously firing almost its entire on-air staff, many of whom had been revered by New York audiences for decades. Scelsa, whose contract was not set to expire until 2001, remained at the station, though he spoke openly of his distress at the firing of his colleagues. "The difference between the '60s and the '90s is money," Scelsa told David Hinckley for the New York *Daily News* (November 17, 1998). "This kind of [free-form] radio started because you weren't risking anything. The economics of radio are into the stratosphere now. I understand that. I just don't like it." "The airwaves belong to a few big corporations," Scelsa told the Associated Press (June 14, 2000). "The notion that I grew up with in the '60s, that the airwaves belonged to the people and the owners held the license in public trust, has completely disappeared."

Scelsa's run on New York commercial radio ended at the close of 2000, when WNEW chose not to renew his contract. "Vin's standards are very high," WNEW's program director, Jeremy Coleman, told the *New York Times* (January 4, 2001). "His vision is pristine. Better not to continue with the show than to corrupt that." Scelsa was not unhappy to be done with the station; he was distressed by its new format, which consisted entirely of brash "shock jocks." Scelsa told the *New York Times* reporter, "In my heart it was beginning to make less and less sense to be [at WNEW]. The environment was so different from what I do."

Less than a month later it was announced that Scelsa would continue *Idiot's Delight* on Saturday nights, starting in February 2001, on Fordham University's member-supported public radio station, WFUV. (Fordham is a Jesuit-run institution whose main campus is in the New York City borough of the Bronx, from which the WUFV programs emanate.) Noting that he was returning in a sense to his roots at Upsala's WFMU, Scelsa told David Hinckley for the New York *Daily News* (January 18, 2001), "How ironic that all these years later I find salvation from the musical mediocrity of commercial radio in this marvelous offer from WFUV—the only broadcast station in New York playing a wide range of 'pop' music for thinking adults."

Scelsa also broadcasts an exclusive edition of *Idiot's Delight* on Sunday nights over Sirius Satellite radio, whose noncommercial format proved ideal for Scelsa's free-form show. He told Jim Beckerman for the Bergen County, New Jersey, *Record* (August 8, 2004), "I feel the way I felt in 1967, when we were doing free-form radio on WFMU. . . . I can now play art without having to censor it. I used to be faced with the idea of putting a bleep in a Lou Reed song, which seems sacrilegious to me, or not playing it at all, which also seems sacrilegious. With Sirius, I don't have that problem. That's a thrilling thing for someone who's been on the radio for 37 years." Scelsa was able to broadcast his Sirius show from his home studio in New Jersey; he told Robert Strauss for the *New York Times* (October 24, 2004), "Even the best studios I worked in, like WNEW in the 1970's, these stations have great libraries, but it is not my library. First, psychologically, [this] is my home. It is physically more comfortable than a radio studio. It is also necessary to have my tools, my recordings, my stuff to do the show. I have to know that I have the Chiffons CD and a complete collection of John Coltrane and every Bob Dylan album."

Vin Scelsa, who took a brief hiatus from *Idiot's Delight* in March 2006 to be treated for prostate cancer, currently lives in Essex County, New Jersey, with his wife, Freddie, and his daughter, Kate. In addition to his work in radio, from 1988 to 1992 Scelsa was the music editor and monthly columnist for the adult publication *Penthouse*, and he edited the music magazine *Grooves* from 1994 until 1996. He is affiliated with the Luna Stage, a professional theater company in Montclair, New Jersey. Besides serving as the company's musical director and sound designer, he has taken an occasional stage role, once starring in a production of Samuel Beckett's *Waiting for Godot*.

—R.E.

Suggested Reading: Associated Press June 14, 2000; (Bergen County, New Jersey) *Record* E p7 Jan. 23, 1996, E p1 Aug. 8, 2004; CNN (on-line) Mar. 3, 2003; *Dateline NBC* Nov. 18, 2005; (New Jersey) *Star-Ledger* (on-line) Mar. 10, 2005; (New York) *Daily News* p67 Jan. 23, 1996, p100 Nov. 17, 1998, p95 Jan. 18, 2001; *New York Times* IX p4 Mar. 13, 1994, XIII p1 Aug. 25, 1996, E p10 Jan. 4, 2001, XIV p1 Oct. 24, 2004; *Rolling Stone* Mar. 1, 2001; *Talk of the Nation* Sep. 6, 2001; *Washington Times* D p1 Aug. 6, 2004; Neer, Richard. *FM: The Rise and Fall of Rock Radio*, 2001

Evan Agostini/Getty Images

Schieffer, Bob

(SHEE-fer)

Feb. 25, 1937– Television journalist

Address: Face the Nation, *CBS News, 2020 M St., N.W., Washington, DC 20036*

The veteran journalist and CBS television news anchor Bob Schieffer is a "very rare individual in his business," Tom Brokaw, the longtime anchor of NBC's *Nightly News*, told Andrew Marton for the *Fort Worth (Texas) Star-Telegram* (February 2, 2003). The reason is that "as long as he has been in [journalism]"—nearly a half-century—"he still has many admirers [among his colleagues]. And he wouldn't get the accolades from that circle of admirers if he wasn't a rock-solid reporter in addition to being an engaging storyteller. The other thing you need to know about Bob is that in Washington's very competitive environment, he has always been a gentleman." Employed by CBS since 1969, when he was hired as a general-assignment reporter, Schieffer is among the few journalists who have covered news emanating from the Pentagon, Congress, the U.S. State Department, and the White House—considered the four major beats in the nation's capital. He has anchored *CBS Sunday Night News*, *CBS Saturday Evening News*, *CBS Morning News*, and, since March 2005, on an interim basis, *CBS Evening News*, the CBS network's flagship news program, which for 24 years had been the domain of Dan Rather and, for nearly two decades before that, was anchored by Walter Cronkite. Writing for *Journalism & Mass Communication Quarterly* (Spring 2004), Mark Feldstein, who teaches

media and public affairs at George Washington University, described Schieffer's reporting as "solid and without pretense, covering the basics with honesty and humor and occasional insight." Since 1991 Schieffer has hosted *Face the Nation*, a half-hour Sunday-morning interview show that has aired on CBS since 1954 and, in the main, features political figures from the U.S. and overseas. He has reported on every Democratic and Republican National Convention since 1972, and in 2004 he moderated the third televised debate between the U.S. presidential candidates—the incumbent, George W. Bush, and his Democratic challenger, Senator John Kerry of Massachusetts. Schieffer began his career as a radio reporter and spent several years with the *Fort Worth (Texas) Star-Telegram*. He has written or co-written three books. His honors include six Emmy Awards and, in 2002, being named Broadcaster of the Year by the National Press Association.

Bob Lloyd Schieffer was born on February 25, 1937 in Austin, Texas, to John Schieffer, who worked mostly in construction, and Gladys (Payne) Schieffer. He has two younger siblings. His brother, John Thomas "Tom" Schieffer, a friend and former business partner of President George W. Bush, was appointed U.S. ambassador to Japan in 2005, after four years as the ambassador to Australia. The Schieffer family moved often within Texas during Schieffer's early childhood before settling in Fort Worth, in 1943. One of Schieffer's most vivid memories is of the day in 1947 when the future president Lyndon B. Johnson, then a U.S. congressman from Texas running for a seat in the U.S. Senate, made a campaign stop at a Fort Worth vacant lot where the boy used to play baseball with his friends. "He gave a great speech, and before he left, he threw his hat into the crowd," Schieffer recalled to Christopher Keyes for *Texas Monthly* (December 2005). "From then on I would look in the paper every day to see where Lyndon Johnson was going to be. I guess that was the day I sort of fell in love with politics."

After his graduation from North Side High School, Schieffer remained in Fort Worth to enroll at Texas Christian University (TCU). Out of deference to his mother, who wanted him to become a doctor, he took pre-med courses. After two years he switched his major to journalism. He began writing for the campus newspaper, the *Daily Skiff*, and working part-time as a crime reporter at the local radio station, KXOL-AM. "I've always believed the police beat is the best training ground at any news organization, because no matter where a police reporter goes, no one wants him there," Schieffer told Mark Millage for the *Communicator* (April 2003), published by the Radio-Television News Directors Association & Foundation. "Generally, the police reporter is intruding in someone's life at the worst possible moment. I've always thought if you could conduct your business under those circumstances, then you could conduct it under most any circumstances." In 1959 Schieffer earned a B.A.

degree from TCU. In the same year he joined the U.S. Air Force, where he served as an information officer. Immediately after he completed his three-year stint, with the rank of captain, he returned to KXOL as a reporter. In September 1962 he was assigned to cover what proved to be a historic moment in the civil rights movement: the enrollment of the first African-American (James Meredith) at the University of Mississippi, an event that followed riots in which two bystanders were killed and 28 federal marshals injured by gunshots. "I had been in the Air Force, but I'd never heard a shot fired in anger," Schieffer told Millage. "When those snipers started shooting down into that crowd, we didn't know who they were shooting at. It was the most terrifying experience of my life."

Later that year Schieffer left his radio job to work as a police-beat reporter for the *Fort Worth Star-Telegram* during the night shift, which ended at 3:00 a.m. He was asleep at home in the early afternoon of November 22, 1963 when his brother phoned to tell him that President John F. Kennedy had been shot in Dallas, Texas. Schieffer rushed to the paper's newsroom, arriving just in time to answer a phone call from a woman who was seeking a ride to Dallas. "Lady, you know, the president has just been shot, and besides, we're not a taxi service," he told her, as he recalled in an interview for the PBS television show *NewsHour with Jim Lehrer* (November 20, 2003, on-line). The woman turned out to be Marguerite Oswald, the mother of Lee Harvey Oswald, the man who had just been arrested on charges of murdering the president. With another reporter driving, Schieffer accompanied Mrs. Oswald from her house to the Dallas police station to which her son had been brought. "She was making these outrageous statements," he told the *NewsHour* interviewer, "statements that were so outrageous that I didn't include some of them . . . in the story I wrote the next morning for the *Star-Telegram*. . . . And I learned a great lesson . . . that you have to be very careful about censoring yourself. I think probably had I put some of those quotes in the paper people might have had a better understanding of what kind of person she was . . . , and through that, might have had a better understanding of what kind of person Lee Harvey Oswald was." Schieffer noted on the *NewsHour* that people's reliance on television for news following the killing of President Kennedy (and the subsequent capture of Oswald, Oswald's murder in the police station by Jack Ruby, the ceremonies connected with Kennedy's lying-in-state and burial, and the transfer of power to the new president, Lyndon B. Johnson) led to TV's dominance over print media as the main source of news for most Americans.

Soon after President Kennedy's assassination, Schieffer left the police beat to cover what he considered more newsworthy events. In 1965 he persuaded his *Star-Telegram* editors to send him to Vietnam, where the war between North Vietnam and its allies, on one side, and South Vietnam and its allies—principally, the U.S.—on the other, "was really beginning to heat up," as Schieffer told a *Chicago Sun-Times* (February 9, 2003) interviewer. Assigned to interview soldiers from Texas, and Fort Worth in particular, Schieffer sought them out while traveling with armed convoys. After *Star-Telegram* readers learned about his activities, he received letters from many parents imploring him to find their sons in the war zone. During the five months he spent in Vietnam, he interviewed and wrote about 235 Texas soldiers for the *Star-Telegram*. "That was the most rewarding thing I ever did," he told Mark Millage. In *This Just In*, however, he criticized his reporting from Vietnam as "jingoistic."

Upon his return to Texas, Schieffer discovered that he had become a local notable during his absence, in part because of full-page ads that the *Star-Telegram* had printed about his work. His celebrity and reputation led executives at WBAP-TV (known as Channel 5) in Dallas/Fort Worth to recruit him for the job of evening news anchor. They won him over with the offer of a weekly salary of $135—$20 more per week than he was earning. "The odd thing about getting into television, coming from the newspaper, was I actually started out as the anchorman," he told Millage. "That's unheard of in this day and time." Despite the limited resources he had at his disposal, Schieffer gave the program an air of credibility. "Title cards would flash, 'Two Killed in Freeway Wreck,' and the music—a funeral dirge—would come on," he recalled to Millage. "I also did all the graphics. If we wanted a picture of somebody, I'd cut it out of a newsmagazine and paste it on a piece of red or blue cardboard." By that time Schieffer had begun what became a years-long attempt to be interviewed for a job at one of the three major television networks: ABC, NBC, and CBS, the last of which especially attracted him, because of his admiration for Walter Cronkite. In January 1969 Schieffer landed a position in the Washington, D.C., newsroom of Metromedia, which, he thought, was angling to become the fourth major network. The unlikelihood of that coming to pass soon became apparent to him. One day, in desperation, Schieffer went uninvited to the office of William J. "Bill" Small, then the chief of the CBS News Washington bureau, and the receptionist, mistaking him for the man who had an appointment but had not yet arrived, ushered him in. Small told Schieffer that he would not consider hiring him, because of his Texas twang. But but 10 days later, thanks to a taped news report Schieffer had sent, in which his accent was less noticeable, and a recommendation from James A. Byron, the WBAP-TV news director, Small changed his mind and hired Schieffer.

Schieffer joined *CBS News* in 1969 as a general-assignment reporter. In 1970 he was promoted to Pentagon correspondent. "The Pentagon was a great place to be, because it was like covering a town's courthouse or the police beat of Washington," he told Marton. "You could always find a story about the Army by talking to someone in the Air Force and vice-versa." He told Larry King on CNN's *Larry King Weekend* (February 16, 2003) that the Pentagon is "just a great place to learn a little about everything in Washington." Melvin R. Laird, who was the secretary of defense during most of Schieffer's time there, was trying to decentralize policy making within the Pentagon and also attempting to "de-Americanize" the Vietnam conflict and shift the brunt of the war effort to the South Vietnamese. "On so many of these issues, Bob Schieffer really persevered, getting under your skin, pushing hard," Laird told Marton. "Bob Schieffer was the most thorough in his questioning of any of the press. Even when Bob let you know he disagreed with you, that never once influenced his stories." During his last year (1973–74) as a Pentagon reporter, Schieffer also anchored *CBS Sunday Night News*.

In 1974, when Dan Rather left the post of principal White House correspondent for CBS and assumed those of correspondent and anchor for the nightly TV program *CBS Reports*, Schieffer succeeded him at the White House. Rather "was the most famous correspondent in America . . . ," Schieffer told Larry King. "He was just almost larger-than-life in those days. . . . It took me awhile to kind of escape Dan's shadow." Schieffer spent the next five years reporting on the presidencies of Gerald Ford and Jimmy Carter. In 1976, while he was still covering the White House, he was named the anchor of *CBS Saturday Evening News*. By that time he had spent three years shuttling weekly between Washington, D.C., and New York City. In 1979 he also began anchoring *CBS Morning News*, having been led to believe that doing so would increase his chances of replacing Walter Cronkite when Cronkite retired, in early 1980. The morning news program drew harsh critical reviews, and after 21 months Schieffer stepped down from the position. "When I left that show and came back to Washington, I felt like a complete failure, and I had never failed at anything before," he told Marton. Adding to his disappointment, he was passed up for Cronkite's position in favor of Dan Rather. "I was sort of a long shot," he admitted to Ellen Edwards for the *Washington Post* (January 4, 1994). "And I'm sure nobody thought I was going to get the job, but I sort of thought I might. . . . But once that happened I said to myself, this is going to be Dan's job and he's going to have it as long as I'm here and that's great and I'm not going to have my life come to the fact that I wasn't a success because there was one job in the world that I didn't get."

In 1982 Schieffer became both the State Department correspondent and the chief Washington correspondent for CBS. Seven years later he left the State Department to report on Congress. He greatly enjoyed the environment surrounding Congress and the absence of the sort of bureaucracy that elsewhere presented obstacles that he had to overcome in order to get interesting stories. "At the White House, everybody works for the same guy so

they're all on the same team," Schieffer told Millage. "At the Capitol, they're all independent contractors. I guess I'm like a cowboy. Cowboys just like horses. They like good horses, but they're also interested in bad horses. I'm the same way about politicians. I've always found them fascinating. Nothing compares to the fun of covering Congress." Schieffer's book *The Acting President*, written with Gary Paul Gates, was published in 1989. In it the writers argued that because of President Ronald Reagan's passivity and disengagement from both day-to-day White House business and policy making, his advisers gained unchecked powers, a situation that led to the Iran-Contra scandal and other schemes and misdeeds that were either criminal or of dubious legality.

In 1991 Schieffer replaced Lesley Stahl as the moderator of the Sunday-morning interview series *Face the Nation*. The show had lost viewers to NBC's *Meet the Press* and ABC's *This Week with David Brinkley* in recent years. Within months Schieffer turned it into a viable contender for the Sunday-morning news audience. "Sunday morning, to me, is the smartest time period on television," he told Millage. "We all feel like we're curators of something that is very special, because these programs are the last place people can really lay out the issues in a civil way." Schieffer's book *Face the Nation: My Favorite Stories from the First 50 Years of the Award-Winning News Broadcast* was published in 2004. It came with a DVD; a recorded version, narrated by Schieffer, is also available.

In 1996, after 20 years as the anchor of *CBS Saturday Evening News*, Schieffer left that job, while continuing to cover Washington news for CBS and host *Face the Nation*, as he still does. In 2003 Schieffer published his memoir, *This Just In: What I Couldn't Tell You on TV*. "What I try to show through [the book's] stories," he told Millage, "is that if you pick out something you like to do, and you learn to do it well, then you can be successful. That will follow. Don't just try to be successful. Find something you like to do. That ought to be a major factor when you decide how you want to spend your life." The book debuted at number three on the *New York Times* best-seller list and received mostly rave reviews. "Schieffer has written a candid, engaging, and humorous account of his career that every broadcast student should read," Mark Feldstein wrote for *Journalism & Mass Communication Quarterly*. "In fact, because Schieffer witnessed firsthand so many momentous stories of the past forty years, his memoir also provides students with a good overview of Washington politics and television news as they evolved together over the past generation."

On March 10, 2005 Schieffer assumed the much-coveted position of anchor of *CBS Evening News*, as a temporary replacement for Dan Rather, who had appeared on the show for the last time the night before. Rather had resigned in the wake of widespread criticism following a report on *60 Minutes* in which he had presented as evidence of

George W. Bush's unsatisfactory service in the U.S. National Guard in the early 1970s documents that he had insisted were authentic but had not been properly checked and were later described by various experts as probably forgeries. According to Gail Shister in the *Philadelphia Inquirer* (April 17, 2006, on-line), the *CBS Evening News* audience grew by some 220,000 viewers during Schieffer's first 13 months as anchor. Schieffer remained in that post until Katie Couric took over as permanent anchor, in early September 2006. He currently provides commentary several times a week on the *Evening News*, as Eric Sevareid did during Walter Cronkite's tenure and Bill Moyers did during Dan Rather's.

In addition to six Emmy Awards, Schieffer's honors include two Sigma Delta Chi Awards, from the Society of Professional Journalists; the 2003 Paul White Award, from the Radio-Television News Directors Association, for lifetime contribution to electronic journalism; in 2004, an International Radio and Television Society Foundation Award and the American News Women's Club Helen Thomas Award for Excellence in Journalism; and, in 2006, the Al Neuharth Award for Excellence, with which the University of South Dakota honors lifetime achievement in journalism. He was named Broadcaster of the Year by the National Press Foundation in 2002 and was inducted that year into the Broadcasting/Cable Hall of Fame. In 2005 Texas Christian University renamed its journalism school in his honor. Schieffer holds the rank of distinguished professor of broadcast journalism at the university and occasionally gives guest lectures there.

Dan Rather told Ellen Edwards that Schieffer may be the only person in network television "to never have backstabbed anyone else, and I do not exclude myself. He just does not do that." Some years ago Schieffer conquered his addiction to smoking and ended his reliance on daily alcohol consumption. He was treated for bladder cancer in 2003 and is now in remission. He and his wife, the former Patricia Penrose, who married in 1967, live in Washington, D.C. The couple have two married daughters, Susan and Sharon, and several grandchildren. Schieffer's recreational pursuits include drawing and painting.

—I.C.

Suggested Reading: *Baltimore Sun* Telegraph A p1+ Mar. 10, 2005; CBSNews.com; *Chicago Sun-Times* Show p1+ Feb. 9, 2003; *Communicator* (on-line) Apr. 2003; *Fort Worth (Texas) Star-Telegram* Life p1+ Feb. 2, 2003; *Television Week* p39+ Nov. 1, 2004; *Texas Monthly* p102+ Dec. 2005; *TV Guide* p12+ Nov. 8, 1986; *Washington Post* Style C p1+ Jan. 4, 1994; Schieffer, Bob. *This Just In: What I Couldn't Tell You on TV*, 2003

Selected Books: *The Acting President* (with Gary Paul Gates), 1989; *This Just In: What I Couldn't Tell You on TV*, 2003; *Face the Nation: My Favorite Stories from the First 50 Years of the Award-Winning News Broadcast*, 2004

Scott, H. Lee

Mar. 14, 1949– President and CEO of Wal-Mart

Address: Wal-Mart Stores Inc., 702 SW 8th St., Bentonville, AR 72716-6299

Writing for the September 12, 2004 edition of the London *Observer*, Paul Harris called H. Lee Scott "the most important man you have never heard of," then predicted, "That won't be true for much longer." That prediction has been borne out: his reputation for being folksy and unassuming aside, Scott—as the president and chief executive officer (CEO) of Wal-Mart—stands at the helm of the world's largest retail company and, over the past two years, its largest target for charges of worker exploitation, anti-labor activity, gender discrimination, and environmental recklessness. Scott began his career at Wal-Mart in 1979 and worked in a variety of capacities before succeeding David D. Glass, in 2000, as the company's chief executive. Under his watch Wal-Mart, which has nearly 6,500 stores and employs 1.8 million people worldwide,

has seen its revenues grow, exceeding $312 billion for 2005. Scott has also taken recent steps to improve Wal-Mart's reputation, donating millions of dollars to charity and disaster-relief efforts, seeking to make the company's operations more environmentally sound, and publicly urging managers to exercise fairness in their relations with employees.

The second of the three sons of a gas-station owner and an elementary-school music teacher, Harold Lee Scott Jr. was born on March 14, 1949 in Joplin, Missouri, and grew up in Baxter Springs, Kansas, near the Missouri border. Those who knew him in his youth have recalled his easygoing nature. He attended Baxter Springs High School, where he played clarinet in the school's orchestra, sang in the choir, and was a member of the football team. Jack Shewmaker, a member of Wal-Mart's board of directors and a former executive at the company, said to Christina Veiders for *Supermarket News* (July 21, 2003) that Scott's roots had served him well at Wal-Mart, which has been run by midwesterners since its founding, in 1962. "If you drew a triangle around where Sam Walton, David Glass, Lee Scott and I all grew up, it's a very

H. Lee Scott

Courtesy of Wal-Mart

small area. It made the group particularly compatible. We all had this intense need to learn—experience the unknown—and we weren't threatened [by] new developments or new ideas. Lee is an exponential force in that equation."

Scott earned a bachelor's degree in business administration from Pittsburg State University, in Pittsburg, Kansas, in 1971. He went on to complete executive-development programs at Penn State University and Columbia University, in New York City. To help pay his college tuition, he worked at McNally's, a tire-mold manufacturer; meanwhile, he and his wife, Linda, whom he had met in college, and their son, Eric, lived in a rented trailer in Pittsburg, Missouri. "Those hard times taught Scott the value of money," Paul Harris wrote. "I worked at McNally's from about 3:30pm to midnight, and studied between midnight and 2am," Scott recalled to Harris. "At the time, it didn't seem difficult, it just seemed cold because the heater in the trailer didn't work." After college his career began unpromisingly: he was turned down for a spot in the management-training program at Yellow Freight System, a Kansas-based trucking company. Later a friend intervened on his behalf, persuading the company's officials to hire him as a salesman. Scott rose through the company's ranks to earn a managerial position, for which he was stationed in Springdale, Arkansas.

In 1977, in his capacity as a manager at Yellow Freight System, Scott first crossed paths with David D. Glass, then Wal-Mart's head of distribution and finance. Scott had contacted Glass in an attempt to collect payment for a $7,000 bill, which Wal-Mart was disputing. Though Glass refused to pay it, he was impressed by Scott's skills as a nego-

tiator and offered him a position in one of Wal-Mart's new distribution centers—which Scott did not accept. Speaking to Wendy Zellner for *Business Week* (November 15, 1999), Scott recalled telling Glass: "I'm not the smartest guy that's ever been in your office, but I'm not going to leave the fastest-growing trucking company in America to go to work for a company that can't pay a $7,000 bill." Nonetheless, Scott joined Wal-Mart in 1979, becoming an assistant director in the transportation department. (In the interim, from 1978 to 1979, he worked for Queen City Warehouse, in Springfield, Missouri.)

Sam Walton, Wal-Mart's magnetic and cost-conscious founder, began his career in retailing in the 1940s, purchasing an outlet of the Ben Franklin five-and-dime chain in Newport, Arkansas, that proceeded to outperform others in the region. Walton's success was due in part to his novel and effective sales concepts, which included buying wholesale goods for the lowest prices available, which in turn enabled him to offer extremely low prices to his customers. Earning profits through a high volume of inexpensive goods became a cornerstone of his business strategy. A high premium on friendly, attentive service was another hallmark of Walton's early stores and remains a Wal-Mart trademark. In 1962 the first Wal-Mart store opened, in Rogers, Arkansas. Typically establishing outlets in small towns and rural areas, Walton developed Wal-Mart into a chain of massive, centrally located stores. He gradually introduced concepts that are now commonplace in the business world, such as profit sharing among managers, who were allowed to put a percentage of their wages toward subsidized Wal-Mart stock, a practice Walton instituted in 1971. Wal-Mart was incorporated in October 1969; it began trading stock as a publicly held company on October 1, 1972. David Glass, who succeeded Walton as CEO of Wal-Mart in 1988, guided the company through a period of unprecedented growth, highlighted by international expansion and innovation. During his tenure Wal-Mart developed the Wal-Mart Supercenter, a chain of "hypermarkets"—facilities that offer both grocery and traditional department-store goods—that on average occupy 200,000 square feet. Membership in Wal-Mart's Sam's Club stores (named for Sam Walton), a chain of warehouse clubs, also increased steadily under Glass. Today there are more than 570 Sam's Club stores and 3,900 Wal-Mart outlets in the U.S. Glass had encouraged Walton to invest heavily in information technology and to push manufacturers to adopt a universal barcode, which enabled Wal-Mart and other retail giants to track the goods consumers purchased in any given period. That information allows the company to predict seasonal sales activity. The world's largest retail chain, Wal-Mart has approximately 6,500 facilities worldwide, including stores in Brazil, China, Costa Rica, El Salvador, Germany, Guatemala, Honduras, Japan, Nicaragua, and South Korea, and its revenues for the fiscal year ending January 31, 2006 exceeded $312 billion. More than 176 million customers visit Wal-Mart stores each week. Wal-Mart is the largest private employer in the U.S. and employs some 1.8 million people worldwide. The company has prospered in part through what industry analysts call a "buyer-driven" global economy. Until about the mid-1980s, manufacturers produced goods for myriad retailers, while today they sell a sizeable percentage of their output to just a handful of mammoth retailers, including Wal-Mart. "The power of Wal-Mart is such, it's reversed a hundred-year history in which the manufacturer was powerful and the retailer was sort of the vassal," Nelson Lichtenstein, an economics professor at the University of California at Santa Barbara, said to Hedrick Smith, as quoted on the Web site of the PBS program *Frontline*. "It's changed that. . . . Now the retailer, the mass global retailer, is the center, the power, and the manufacturer becomes the serf, the vassal, the underling, who has to do the bidding of the retailer."

In his early years at Wal-Mart, Scott became known for his stern treatment of those beneath him. Reacting to the behavior of drivers who were consistently late in making deliveries, Scott wrote letters to all drivers, threatening to fire them in the event of unsatisfactory performance—an act the company's conscientious drivers found objectionable. Walton ordered Scott to address each driver's complaints individually, a development that is believed to have helped make Scott a better listener. "You couldn't be around Sam Walton and not fully understand the culture of the company," Joseph S. Hardin Jr., the CEO of Kinko's Inc. and a former executive at Wal-Mart, said to Wendy Zellner. "That's one of the things that has helped Lee so much."

Scott rose steadily through the ranks of Wal-Mart's distribution network, which is reputed to be one of the best-organized and most technologically sophisticated in the world. He served successively as director of transportation, vice president of transportation, vice president of distribution, and senior vice president of logistics. In 1993 he was promoted to executive vice president of logistics, a position he held until 1995. That year's announcement that Scott would take over as the head of Wal-Mart's merchandising unit surprised some, given his background in a different area; but with its stock price slumping and its sales slowing after years of the company's rapid growth, Wal-Mart needed, as Wendy Zellner put it, "a kick in the pants." Rising to the challenge of helping to rejuvenate the company, Scott slashed approximately $2 billion in inventory in two years' time and ramped up the company's price-rollback program, cutting prices to increase sales and revenue, among other measures that had positive results. "He asked the right questions, listened intently, and listened to a number of different opinions," John Lupo, a former Wal-Mart executive, said to Zellner; and Don S. Harris, an executive at the company, added, "He didn't come in with a preconceived notion of

exactly how to do it." Scott was named the president and chief executive of the Wal-Mart Stores Division in 1998. A year later he took on the duties of Wal-Mart's chief operating officer and vice chairman, and in 2000 he was named as Glass's successor.

Scott maintained a relatively low profile in his first few years as CEO while presiding over substantial sales growth, from 2001 to 2003. Matters changed in 2004, in part due to a class-action lawsuit accusing Wal-Mart of discrimination against as many as 1.6 million current and former female employees, with regard to promotions—a case that has been called the nation's largest sex-discrimination suit. In July 2005 two African-American truck drivers filed a race-discrimination suit against the company. Also in recent years, advocacy groups have excoriated Wal-Mart for its anti-union posture and labor standards, charging the company with having poor health-care benefits, paying low salaries that lead to wage depression throughout the industry, and illegally hiring undocumented aliens as workers. In December 2005 Wal-Mart was ordered by a California court to pay $172 million to more than 100,000 current and former employees for denying them meal breaks. In addition, there has been growing concern about the company's activities overseas. Wal-Mart has maintained its practice of purchasing wholesale goods as cheaply as possible and offering discounts to consumers, in part through pressuring U.S. manufacturers in several sectors to cut costs; the manufacturers, in turn, "outsource" jobs overseas, where labor is cheaper. Exasperating to many is Wal-Mart's presence in China, where an estimated 80 percent of its approximately 6,000 worldwide suppliers are based; many have charged that the company is exploiting foreign workers, lending tacit support to substandard human-rights practices in China, and taking jobs away from Americans.

In 2004 Scott oversaw Wal-Mart's purchase of some 100 newspaper advertisements in an attempt to counter the myriad criticisms the company faced. In the ads the company defended its wage and insurance policies and claimed that it had created jobs in many U.S. communities. Deemed a "charm offensive" by Nancy Gibbs, writing for *Time* (April 18, 2005), the gesture struck many as a hollow response to the allegations, which threatened to harm the company's bottom line. In January 2005, in an effort to set the record straight about the company's labor practices, offshore activities, and the general air of disapproval surrounding Wal-Mart domestically, Scott appeared on *Good Morning America*, and Fox News, and CNBC programs, saying that Wal-Mart treats its workers fairly and has helped small communities.

Wal-Mart has been charged, as Amanda Griscom Little wrote for the environmental news Web site *Grist* (April 12, 2006), with "exacerbating suburban sprawl, burning massive quantities of oil via its 10,000-mile supply chain, producing mountains of packaging waste, polluting waterways with runoff from its construction sites, and encouraging gratuitous consumption." In October 2005 Scott announced an ambitious plan to remake Wal-Mart into an environmentally friendly company. The plan included setting a timetable for having the company run completely on renewable energy. To that end Scott has implemented plans aimed at reducing Wal-Mart's greenhouse-gas emissions by 20 percent over the next decade, enhancing the fuel efficiency of its truck fleet, easing the solid waste its U.S. stores produce, and increasing its organic-food offerings to customers. (According to Marc Gunther in *Fortune* [August 7, 2006], Wal-Mart has become the "biggest seller of organic milk and the biggest buyer of organic cotton in the world.") The move surprised many observers. Scott has said that Wal-Mart's new environmentally friendly policies may have a positive impact on Wal-Mart's bottom line, which in turn will lead to lower costs for its customers. Discussing the reasons for his decisions, Scott said to Little, "I think two things happened. One . . . I had embraced this idea that the world's climate is changing and that man played a part in that, and that Wal-Mart can play a part in reducing man's impact. We recognized that Wal-Mart had such a footprint in this world, and that we had a corresponding part to play in sustainability. On a personal level, as you become a grandparent—I have a granddaughter—you just also become more thoughtful about what will the world look like that she inherits."

In the wake of Hurricane Katrina, which battered New Orleans, Louisiana, and surrounding areas in late August 2005—killing more than 1,000 people and leaving entire neighborhoods underwater—Wal-Mart was among the U.S. corporations that provided assistance to those affected in the region by the disaster. The company reportedly made $32 million in direct cash donations to aid relief efforts in the region. According to its Web site, Wal-Mart made an additional $245 million in cash donations to various charitable organizations in 2005. The company also appears to have considered substantive steps toward improving its reputation and its relations with employees. In October 2005 the company announced that it was setting up a $25 million private equity fund to support firms owned by minorities and women. In February 2006 Scott wrote a message to Wal-Mart managers that was posted on the company's internal Web site. As quoted by T. A. Frank in the *Washington Monthly* (April 1, 2006), the message read in part: "If you choose to do the wrong thing . . . if you choose to take a shortcut on payroll, if you choose to take a shortcut on a raise for someone, you hurt this company. And it's not unlikely in today's environment that your shortcut is going to end up on the front page of the newspaper."

In 2006, in what Jonathan Birchall, writing for the London *Financial Times* (April 25, 2006), described as "one of the most dramatic strategic shifts of recent US corporate history," Wal-Mart unveiled an additional series of initiatives aimed at counteracting its negative corporative image. "Wal-Mart is a company in transformation," Scott assured a group of journalists in Arkansas in April 2006, as quoted by Birchall. "[We are] a company that is out in front of the changes in the world around us." In one action, Wal-Mart changed the eligibility requirements for company-sponsored health insurance, extending benefits to part-time employees (and their children) who had logged one year of service (instead of two years, as in the past); in another, Wal-Mart increased the base wage for new hires by 6 percent at more than 1,200 stores nationwide. In addition, the company, in cooperation with the All-China Federation of Trade Unions, pledged to grant nearly 23,000 employees the right to unionize at the more than 60 Wal-Mart outlets in China.

Such moves notwithstanding, Wal-Mart experienced a rare decline in profits over the latter half of 2006, caused in part by the implementation of merchandising strategies that backfired. To compete with the more upscale offerings of such retail rivals as the Target Corp., for example, Wal-Mart began to add trendier, pricier fashion labels to its apparel collections, among them the Metro 7 line for women and the Exsto urban-clothing brand for men. Metro 7 sold well only initially at 600 stores and failed to generate interest at additional outlets. "We over expanded it. We had a pretty good idea. I think what happened is we didn't follow the strategy. We overloaded the fashion part. We need to remember who we are," Scott told Parija B. Kavilanz for *CNNMoney.com* (October 30, 2006). In mid-August 2006 Wal-Mart saw its stock value drop 1.6 percent, to below $45 a share, "its first quarterly decline in profits in over 10 years," as Joseph Weber and Michael Arndt wrote for *BusinessWeek* (August 16, 2006, on-line). The following October Wal-Mart failed to meet expected sales projections, reporting a 0.5 percent sales increase, well short of the anticipated 2 to 4 percent rise. Nevertheless, Scott has spoken optimistically about Wal-Mart's latest merchandising tactics, among them full-scale remodeling projects at nearly 300 stores. "We are confident that we will see good returns on the capital that we are investing," he told Weber and Arndt.

Scott has been said to have boyish charm and a self-effacing and low-key demeanor, attributes that belie a voracious drive to stimulate Wal-Mart's revenues. "He wields his power in subtle but unmistakable ways," Devin Leonard wrote for *Fortune* (August 9, 2004). The Wal-Mart CEO reportedly spends one day each week visiting a Wal-Mart store, where employees frequently address him as "Lee." He is married to the former Linda Gale Aldridge and has two sons: Eric Sean and Wyatt Parson. According to Paul Harris, "[Scott's] accent is still Midwestern and his speech is peppered with folksy turns of phrase." He owns homes in Arkansas and California. His hobbies include quail hunting, reading, golfing, and fly-fishing. Lee is on the board of directors of the United Negro College Fund. In 2004 and 2005 he was included on *Time* magazine's list of the 100 most influential people.

—D.F.

Suggested Reading: *BusinessWeek* p84+ Nov. 15, 1999; *CNNMoney* Web site; *Fortune* p42 Aug. 7, 2006; *Grist Magazine* (on-line) Apr. 12, 2006; (London) *Financial Times* p15 Apr. 25, 2006; (London) *Observer* p27 Sep. 12, 2004; pbs.org; Wal-Mart Web site; *Washington Monthly* (on-line) Apr. 1, 2006

Semel, Terry

(SEHM-uhl)

Feb. 24, 1943– Chairman and CEO of Yahoo!

Address: Yahoo! Inc., 701 First Ave., Sunnyvale, CA 94089

During a period of over two decades at Warner Bros., Terry Semel became known as one of the most powerful figures in Hollywood, ultimately serving as co-chairman and co-CEO with his close friend Robert Daly. As the duo turned Warner Bros. into one of the world's largest media and entertainment companies, they presided over a wide domain that included the company's lucrative film, television, music, and merchandise businesses. Their stable of hits included such movies as *Lethal Weapon* (1987), *Batman* (1989), and *The Matrix* (1999) and the television shows *Friends* (1994–2004) and *ER* (1994–present). Semel and Daly's departure from the company, in 1999, was called the end of an era. Despite Semel's success in the entertainment industry, many were surprised when, in early 2001, it was announced that he would become the new chairman and CEO of Yahoo!, a popular but struggling Internet company. Industry analysts and media pundits questioned his credentials, characterizing him as an "old media guy" and chiding him for being a luddite who did not even know how to use E-mail. Nevertheless, Jerry Yang, a co-founder of Yahoo!, believed that Semel had the expertise and vision that Yahoo! needed to survive the recent collapse of the dot-com market. "Everyone talks about what [Semel] did with movies and entertainment," Yang told Fred Vogelstein for *Fortune* (April 5, 2004), "but what he really did was pioneer how to take a piece of content and get it out there. He has a distribution mentality, which at the end of the day is what Yahoo! does on the Internet."

When Semel took over Yahoo!, it was the Internet's most-visited Web site, but it was in dire shape; the company was losing money fast, and its market value had dropped from a peak of $127 billion, just before the crash, to only $12.6 billion. Semel reduced the workforce, made several important acquisitions, focused the company on a few major areas, and strengthened its relationships with advertisers. The fixes worked: in 2001 the company had lost almost $100 million on $717 million in revenues; in 2005 it earned $1.2 billion on sales of $5.3 billion. Yahoo! currently has more than 400 million unique users per month and almost 250 million registered users, and the company boasts some of the most popular E-mail, instant-messaging, music, Web-search, and photo-sharing services. As Daly recalled to Richard Siklos for the *New York Times* (January 29, 2006), he had warned the skeptics that Semel was not to be underestimated: "I told them, 'You don't understand Terry Semel. He knows what they need, and that is to bring a sense of not only leadership but marketing and how to put things together.' At Yahoo!, he is the father."

Terence Steven Semel was born in the New York City borough of Brooklyn on February 24, 1943. His father, Benjamin, worked as a women's coat designer; his mother, Mildred, was an executive at a bus company. In 1964 Semel graduated from Long Island University, in Brooklyn, with a B.S. degree in accounting. Three years later he earned his M.B.A. degree from the City College of New York, having specialized in market research. From 1965 to 1966 he worked at an accounting firm, after which he joined Warner Bros. as a sales trainee, selling films to theaters. He demonstrated skills as a salesman and was later hired by CBS as a domestic sales manager and theatrical distributor; in 1972 he was promoted to president of the movie-marketing department. The following year Semel left CBS for Walt Disney's Buena Vista Entertainment, where he served as vice president and general sales manager. In 1975 Warner Bros. hired him as vice president and general sales manager, and a few years later he was named executive vice president and chief operating officer (COO) of the company.

During the 1970s Semel developed a close relationship with Daly, who became chairman and CEO of Warner Bros. in about 1980. For many years Semel and Daly were neighbors and carpooled to work almost daily. In 1982 Semel was promoted to president, while retaining his post as COO, and he and Daly formed a legendary business partnership, in which Semel was officially Daly's second-in-command, although eventually they governed the company as a team. "We never formally divide responsibilities in any definite way," Semel told Bernard Weinraub for the *New York Times* (March 31, 1994). "It's like a wonderful marriage. I say, 'I'll handle this movie thing,' and he'll say, 'I'll go to the meeting on the fifth network.'" Both reported to Steve Ross, the longtime CEO of Warner's parent company, Warner Communications. In 1994 Daly made their tight-knit relationship official by sharing his title, naming Semel co-chairman and co-CEO of Warner Bros. As Daly told Laura Landro for the *Wall Street Journal* (March 31, 1994), "We've always run the company as a partnership, and I

Terry Semel

thought Terry should get the recognition he deserves now, both on the inside of the company and on the outside."

Under the stewardship of Semel and Daly, Warner Bros. increased its annual revenues from about $1 billion in 1980 to about $11 billion by 1999. They helped the company navigate the 1989 merger of Warner Communications and Time Inc., creating Time Warner. In 1995 they established the WB Television Network, a station geared toward younger viewers, which launched the hit teen drama series *Buffy the Vampire Slayer* (1997–2003). In November 1995 Gerald M. Levin, who had replaced Ross as Time Warner's chairman in 1992, entrusted Semel and Daly with leading Warner Music Group, which is now one of the world's largest recording companies. Executives at rival studios have readily acknowledged Semel and Daly's clout: "They're extraordinary competitors," Jeffrey Katzenberg, the former chairman of Walt Disney Studios, told Bernard Weinraub. "They're risk takers. They've got taste. They consistently turn out eclectic, quality movies and they've done it now for a decade. Nobody else does it like them." The duo was responsible for such hit films as *Chariots of Fire* (1981), *Police Academy* (1984), *National Lampoon's European Vacation* (1985), *Unforgiven* (1992), and *Eyes Wide Shut* (1999); in television they produced such successful series as *Murphy Brown* (1988–98), *The Drew Carey Show* (1995–2004), and *Dawson's Creek* (1998–2003). They also helped make Warner a brand name, with the opening of a chain of Warner Bros. Studio retail outlets across the United States. Semel was named Pioneer of the Year by the Foundation of Motion Picture Pioneers in 1990, and he and Daly shared the

Producers Guild of America Milestone Award in 1998. During the late 1990s their success seemed to fade, as they produced some notable flops, including *The Postman* (1997), *The Avengers* (1998), and *Wild Wild West* (1999). Critics noted that they had built their empire on expensive production deals with aging stars, such as Mel Gibson and Kevin Costner, and that they had lost touch with younger audiences.

Nevertheless, when Daly and Semel both left Time Warner, in 1999, they made news headlines. "That resounding thud you heard when the two most powerful and senior moguls in the entertainment industry resigned last Wednesday night was the sound of a T-rex crashing to the pavement outside Rockefeller Center [the company's headquarters, in New York City]," Nikki Finke wrote for *New York* (July 26, 1999). To mark their retirement, the pair left their handprints in the celebrity sidewalk outside Hollywood's famous Mann's Chinese Theatre (now known as Grauman's Chinese Theatre). The reasons for their departure were never made clear. Some attributed it to clashes with studio vice chairman Ted Turner, whose company Turner Broadcasting had been acquired by Time Warner in 1996; others suggested that Levin and Turner had growing concerns about Daly and Semel's penchant for lavishing large sums on stars and blockbusters—as well as concerns about the size of Daly and Semel's salaries, estimated at $25 million each.

Semel reportedly received employment offers from almost all of the major Hollywood studios, but he had a new direction in mind: the Internet. He created an investment firm called Windsor Media and invested $2 million of his own money in

Digital Entertainment Network, a venture designed to provide on-line video; at that time, however, most computer users did not have the high-speed Internet connections necessary to make on-line video an option, and the company went bankrupt in 2000.

In May 2001 Semel accepted the position of chairman and CEO of the struggling Internet company Yahoo!. Founded in 1994 by Jerry Yang and David Filo, two students at Stanford University, Yahoo! had originated as a search engine but grown rapidly into the World Wide Web's most popular Internet portal (a Web site that organizes and displays information from the Web and offers users various specialized services). Yahoo!'s revenues had grown from about $70 million in 1997 to more than $1 billion in 2000, but the company had suffered greatly as a result of the stock market downturn of 2000–01, which had caused a precipitous decline in Web advertising, the company's primary source of revenue.

Semel had met Yang a few years earlier at a media conference; Yang was interested in Semel's work in media, and the two developed a friendship. When Yang and Filo decided it was time to find someone to replace Ted Koogle as Yahoo!'s CEO, Yang thought of Semel. Industry observers and Yahoo! insiders, however, initially had misgivings about the former Hollywood executive. "We think a more perfect fit in terms of background would have been someone from print, or advertising-driven media, with strong relationships among the advertising community," Henry Blodget, a former Merrill Lynch Internet analyst, told a reporter for BBC News (April 18, 2001, on-line). Semel also clashed with the casual dot-com culture at Yahoo!, which is headquartered in Sunnyvale, in Silicon Valley, a region of California known for its conglomeration of computer-related industries. He balked at Yahoo!'s cubicle-only policy, for example, in which everyone in the company, executives included, worked in cubicles of the same size. Semel instead set up his own, separate office next to the conference room, for privacy. He also kept to himself and did not chat with employees, as had his friendly and well-liked predecessor, Koogle (known to his employees as T.K.). "T.K. was just one of the guys," a former manager at Yahoo! told Ben Elgin for *BusinessWeek* (June 2, 2003). "When Semel talked to you, it felt like he was consciously making an effort to talk to employees."

Semel slowly earned his colleagues' respect, in part by showing a willingness to learn, not just about Yahoo!'s business operations, but about basic computing concepts. "Sometimes we'd just walk him over to the computer and show him what we were talking about," Jeff Mallett, Yahoo!'s former president, told Vogelstein. "Then he'd say, 'Let me repeat it back.' And we'd go over it again. He'd stay in that conference room for hours until he got it. I think he learned three years of information in six months." "I'm never going to be a technologist, but I have to be conversant," Semel explained to Siklos, adding that in that respect his new position was not so different from his jobs in the entertainment industry: "I was never an actor or a director or a singer—I had to understand the process well enough to help make decisions."

Some of Semel's first acts included laying off 12 percent of Yahoo!'s workforce and whittling the company's 44 businesses down to four: media and entertainment, communications, premium services, and search. "Terry's relentless focus on focus is probably the most important thing we as a team or as a company are doing," Yang told Siklos. Semel then created what was known as the product council, in which all new product ideas were subjected to vigorous review; the council enabled coordination and ensured that the heads of every division were aware of every upcoming project. He also began a series of major acquisitions, beginning in late 2001 with HotJobs, a leading recruitment Web site, for $436 million. Although Semel decided that advertising would remain Yahoo!'s main source of income, he sought out new sources of revenue, developing subscription-based premium services for such popular products as fantasy football, E-mail, and music. He also improved Yahoo!'s advertiser base, increasing the number of clients to the thousands. In addition, he established a partnership with SBC Communications to offer a co-branded broadband service, generating income from fees and securing Yahoo! a foothold in the high-speed Internet-service market. (SBC was later acquired by AT&T.)

Semel's changes were rewarded with increased revenues and growing investor confidence; Yahoo!'s stock-market price has tripled since he arrived, despite a considerable downturn in 2006. (In the early fall of 2006, segments of the company's advertising revenues fell, leading to a noticeable loss of confidence among investors.) "Semel has done nothing less than remake the culture of the quintessential Internet company," Ben Elgin wrote. "The new Yahoo is grounded by a host of Old Economy principles that Semel lugged up the coast from Los Angeles. The contrast with Yahoo's go-go days is stark. At Terry Semel's Yahoo, spontaneity is out. Order is in. New initiatives used to roll ahead following free-form brainstorming and a gut check. Now, they wind their way through a rugged gauntlet of tests and analysis. Only a few make the grade. It's a wrenching change. But Semel's self-effacing style, honed over years of navigating through the towering egos of Hollywood, helps soften the shock."

Semel also gradually refined the company's search capabilities. In 2002 Yahoo! replaced its directory listings, which had been compiled by editors, with search-engine results powered by Google, the leader in search technology. (Search engines use complex computer algorithms to search the Internet's ever-expanding store of information and display relevant results.) In 2004, after purchasing Inktomi (a designer of search technology) and Overture (a designer of software that links ads to searches and tracks the results, sometimes referred to as a pay-per-click business model), Yahoo! was able to create its own unique Internet search. Yahoo!'s proprietary search engine is currently the second-most-popular engine on the Web, although it has been losing ground to Google; as of July 2006 it had a market share of 24 percent, while Google's market share was 49 percent. Yahoo! has recently unveiled new forms of search technology, such as "social search" and Yahoo! Answers, which Semel has said may ultimately change the dynamics of the search business. Yahoo! has pioneered the area of social search, a method of searching that takes into account personal preferences and those of one's peer group, by tracking and analyzing searches and allowing users to "tag" useful results; the technology is based in part on del.icio.us, a Web site acquired by Yahoo! that enables users to store and share bookmarks of their favorite Web sites. Yahoo! Answers allows users to ask and answer questions, thereby replacing the mechanical feedback of a search query with an on-line community of human knowledge. The service had 60 million monthly users by November 2006. "We didn't get into search to do what everyone else is doing," Semel explained to Vogelstein. "We got into search to change the game."

One of the fastest-growing features of the Internet is user-generated content, an area that includes personal photos, videos, blogs, and product reviews, and Semel hopes to position Yahoo! as a leader in the field. In 2005 Yahoo! streamed four billion music videos; the company also acquired Flickr, a photo-sharing Web site that has surged in popularity over the past year, so much so that *Time* (May 8, 2006) included its two co-founders on its annual list of the world's 100 most-influential people. As of November 2006 Yahoo!'s photo-sharing Web site had 20 million monthly users. "The big change in technology is that we used to have someone else program everything for us," Semel said in a speech hosted by the San Francisco–based Jewish Community Federation, as quoted by Maureen Earl for the Jewish newspaper *J.* (February 17, 2006). "Someone else programmed television, so you watched what was on when it was on. Internet has turned the user into programmers—we want what we want, when we want, and we get it."

Yahoo! continues to face stiff competition—Google earns twice as much in advertising revenue and such companies as Microsoft and AOL are following Yahoo!'s lead in creating social-networking features and facilitating user-generated content. In 2005 Rupert Murdoch's media company News Corp. purchased MySpace, a wildly popular social-networking Web site, which has cut into Yahoo!'s audience. Then, in 2006, Google purchased YouTube—the largest site for user-uploaded videos—after negotiations between Yahoo! and YouTube broke down. "That lack of deal momentum exacerbated by the delay of Yahoo's search-advertising system . . . and decelerating revenue

growth have pounded Yahoo's stock, which is down 35%" from its value at the same time in 2005, Tim Arango and Adam Lashinsky wrote for *Fortune* (November 13, 2006). Semel, however, remains optimistic about Yahoo!'s potential for growth, given the considerable number of new markets opening up, among them advertising space on cell phones and social-networking sites. In October 2006 he told investors, according to Arango and Lashinsky, "With the landscape changing, I am very, very excited about the opportunities for Yahoo."

Yahoo! recently found itself mired in controversy, after media reports revealed that the company had provided information to the Chinese government that led to the imprisonment of two Chinese dissidents who had used the company's E-mail service. Google and Microsoft have gotten attention of a similar sort for cooperating with Chinese authorities, and executives at all three companies were called to testify before a congressional committee in early 2006. Semel has defended his company's actions, telling audiences at a technology convention that Yahoo! has no choice other than to comply with government authorities in countries where it operates; he has argued, moreover, that Yahoo!'s presence in China will foster openness in the long run: "The best gift we bring to the world is to expose them to information," he said, as quoted by John Shinal for *MarketWatch* (June 1, 2006). "What's the alternative, to walk away?"

In mid-2006 Yahoo! reduced Semel's salary to $1; in place of receiving a traditional salary, he will be granted stock options, thereby tying his income to the company's performance. Google and other technology companies have recently enacted similar pay cuts for executives. Semel earned $600,000 in salary in 2005 and has earned a reported $429 million over the last few years by selling stock options.

Semel lives with his family in the posh Bel Air section of Los Angeles; he commutes to Yahoo!'s headquarters, in Sunnyvale, three or four days a week, using a private corporate jet that he and Daly purchased from Warner Bros. when they resigned. He and his wife, the former Jane Bovingdon, have been married since 1977. They have three daughters, Courtenay, Lily, and Kate; Semel also has a son, Eric, from a previous marriage.

—K.J.E.

Suggested Reading: *BusinessWeek* p70 June 2, 2003; *Economist* Apr. 22, 2006; *Fortune* p220 Apr. 5, 2004, p33 Nov. 13, 2006; *New York Times* D p3 Mar. 31, 1994, III p1 Jan. 29, 2006

David Livingston/Getty Images

Silverman, Sarah

Dec. 2, 1970– Comedian

Address: Creative Artists Agency, 9830 Wilshire Blvd., Beverly Hills, CA 90212

Sarah Silverman has made a name for herself in comedy circles over the last 16 years by perfecting an act characterized by what her fellow comedian Michael McKean called "quiet depravity," as Dana Goodyear reported in the *New Yorker* (October 24, 2005). "No subject is taboo and she has jokes for seemingly every occasion, including 9/11 (among other things, she suggests that American Airlines adopt a new advertising slogan, 'First through the Towers') . . . ," Pam Grady wrote for Film-Stew.com (September 9, 2005). "She is a piece of work, Miss Sarah is, but just when it seems she has gone too far, she pushes even farther and just try in those moments not to laugh. It may not be the most comfortable laughter in the world—she has a way of exposing assumptions and stereotypes that is a lot like ripping off a band-aid—but she is funny." Silverman has flirted with mainstream fame over the years, making appearances on *Seinfeld*, *The Larry Sanders Show*, and other popular television programs, starring in such failed series as *Greg the Bunny* (2002) and *Pilot Season* (2004), and playing small- to medium-sized parts in a number of movies, including *There's Something About Mary* (1998), *Say It Isn't So* (2001), *The School of Rock* (2003), and *School for Scoundrels* (2006). Silverman was probably best known, however, for the controversy surrounding her use of a racial epithet in a joke that she told on *Late Night with Conan O'Brien*—at least until 2005, the year she earned

widespread attention for her part in the movie *The Aristocrats* and for *Sarah Silverman: Jesus Is Magic*, a film version of the stage show that she had been performing since 2001.

The youngest of four girls, Sarah Bennett Silverman was born on December 2, 1970 (1971, according to some sources) in Bedford, New Hampshire. She grew up there and in nearby Manchester, where she attended high school at the private Derryfield School. Her father, Donald Silverman, was a businessman who owned Junior Deb/Varsity Shops, a regional chain of clothing stores, and Crazy Sophie's, a discount clothing outlet. Her mother, Beth Ann Silverman, was a drama coach at a liberal-arts college in Manchester and established a theater company, the New Thalian Players, which took its name from the Greek Muse of comedy. Silverman's parents divorced when she was seven (some sources say six), but she remained close to both of them while growing up. Her interest in comedy dates back to her early childhood, when her father taught her to curse, amused by people's reactions to a vulgar toddler. "Here I was, this toddler saying a bunch of swears and getting this total attention, focus, and laughter," Silverman told Mark Shanahan for the *Boston Globe* (November 22, 2005). "From there, I guess I just sought out more of the same." Throughout her childhood Silverman pursued her interest in performing, winning the lead in a local production of *Annie* when she was 12. She continued performing even after she began, at the age of 13, to suffer from a deep depression—which lasted three years and recurred later in her life—playing the Jester in *Once Upon a Mattress* and Charity in *Sweet Charity* in high school. (Experiences that she has had as a result of her depression have since provided the wry comic with material. For example, in a November 3, 2005 interview with Vanessa Grigoriadis for *Rolling Stone*, she said that her parents, in an attempt to find a cure for her depression, took her to a psychiatrist, who prescribed Xanax and asked her to return the next week. In the intervening week, Silverman discovered when she arrived for her appointment, he had hanged himself. "I had to sit in the waiting room for an hour until my mom picked me up," Silverman told Grigoriadis. "The first thing I thought of was that he had braces. I was like, 'Wow, he didn't even wait to get his braces off.'") She also performed at a local Mexican restaurant called La Cantina, singing "Mammaries," a song she had written to the tune of "The Way We Were (Memories)," about her wishing that she had breasts, and at 17 she managed to land stand-up gigs in Boston, Massachusetts, where she stayed while attending summer school. After graduating from high school, she entered New York University, in New York City. More interested in comedy than in school, she spent much of her freshman year distributing flyers for comedy clubs in exchange for the chance to do five-minute comedy sets.

After her freshman year Silverman left college to pursue a career as a stand-up comic. "With her easygoing manner and unthreatening, child-woman good looks, she quickly became the naughty tomboy in an unshaven community that [talk-show host Conan] O'Brien describes as 'a cruddier version of expatriate 1920's modernist poets,'" according to Alexander Jacobs in the *New York Observer* (August 6, 2001). In 1993 she landed a job as a writer and performer on *Saturday Night Live*, which, in its more than 30 years on the air, has helped to launch the careers of such noted comedy stars as Bill Murray and Eddie Murphy. Silverman, however, had little success among the highly competitive group of writers and performers: only one of her skits made it past the development stage, reaching the show's Saturday rehearsals before getting cut. Her single, small triumph was her only appearance on the "Weekend Update" segment, the faux news program that has appeared regularly on the show since its first broadcast. Presenting a news report on her sister Susan's wedding, Silverman quipped, according to Goodyear: "It was a really neat wedding, too, you know, 'cause they took each other's last names and hyphenated it. So now my sister's name is Susan Silverman-Abramowitz. But they're thinking of shortening it to just 'Jews.'" When the season ended, in 1994, the show's producers sent her the news of her dismissal by fax. Bob Odenkirk, who wrote for *Saturday Night Live* for several years and later hired Silverman to play a variety of roles on his HBO sketch-comedy show, *Mr. Show with Bob and David*, told Goodyear, "I could see how it wouldn't work at *S.N.L.*, because she's got her own voice, she's very much Sarah Silverman all the time. She can play a character but she doesn't disappear into the character—she makes the character her. . . . She puts out stuff that she would appreciate and then you can like it or not—she doesn't give a [expletive]."

Silverman then returned to stand-up and began finding work on television and in the movies, appearing on *Mr. Show with Bob and David* from 1995 to 1997 and securing the part of Wendy Traston on *The Larry Sanders Show* in 1996. In 1997 she played the character Kramer's girlfriend in an episode of the sitcom *Seinfeld* and Susan Underman, the female lead, in *Who's the Caboose?*, a mock documentary spoofing the trials and tribulations of up-and-coming comedians. Over the following few years, she landed small parts in numerous movies, including *Overnight Delivery* (1998), *Bulworth* (1998), *There's Something About Mary* (1998), *The Bachelor* (1999), *The Way of the Gun* (2000), and *Screwed* (2000). She also appeared in the made-for-TV movies *Late Last Night* (1999) and *Smog* (1999).

A working comedian rather than a star, Silverman was carving out a niche for herself in the alternative-comedy scene and earning the respect of those in the entertainment industry. "She's what everyone says they want: 'Where's the really smart young women comics who are saying edgy stuff that's really intelligent?,'" Conan O'Brien told Alexander Jacobs. "And it's like: 'Uh, she's right here. Here she is!'" Such respect failed to earn her any major roles in 2001, though she played a number of small ones, landing parts in four movies—*Black Days*, *Say It Isn't So*, *Heartbreakers*, and *Evolution*. She gained a certain notoriety, however, from a set she performed on *Late Night with Conan O'Brien*, capturing the attention of the public with a joke about trying to get out of jury duty. "My friend is like, why don't you write something inappropriate on the form, like 'I hate chinks,'" Silverman said, according to Lynn Elber for the Associated Press (July 17, 2001). Continuing in her sweetly naive stage persona, she explained that she did not want people to think she was racist, so, "I just filled out the form and I wrote 'I love chinks'—and who doesn't?" A media storm followed: Guy Aoki, president of Media Action Network for Asian Americans, demanded that both NBC and Silverman apologize, and the debate over the joke was given national attention, getting discussed, for instance, on Barbara Walters's daytime talk show *The View*. Silverman, refusing to apologize, debated Aoki on Bill Maher's program *Politically Incorrect*, arguing that her joke was about racism but was not itself racist.

Later, in her act, Silverman joked about the controversy, saying, as Carina Chocano reported for the *Los Angeles Times* (November 11, 2005), "What kind of world do we live where a totally cute white girl can't say 'chink' on network television? As a member of the Jewish community . . . I'm totally concerned we're losing control of the media." The episode has not deterred Silverman from making similarly shocking jokes. "She's not just a critic of PC culture: She's a connoisseur," Sam Anderson wrote for the on-line magazine *Slate* (November 10, 2005). "She handles the complex algorithms of taboo—who's allowed to joke about what, to whom, using what terminology—with instant precision: 'Everybody blames the Jews for killing Christ, and then the Jews try to pass it off on the Romans. I'm one of the few people that believe it was the blacks.' (The joke exposes not the ancient perfidy of any particular race but the absurdity of blaming entire races for anything.)"

In 2002, in addition to making appearances in two movies—*Strippers Pole* and *Run Ronnie Run*—she returned to television with a full-time role as Alison Kaisor, a television executive who champions a children's show starring a rabbit puppet, on Fox's *Greg the Bunny*. As did *The Larry Sanders Show*, *Greg the Bunny* took a satirical look at the behind-the-scenes antics in a television studio, poking fun at "the legendary ego problems, rampant insecurities and high-camp high anxiety behind the scenes of your favorite network product," Carina Chocano wrote for the on-line magazine *Salon* (March 28, 2002). The show was canceled in May of that year. In June Silverman was working again, lending her voice to Comedy Central's *Crank Yankers*, a show that featured the voices of such noted comedians as Adam Carolla and Drew Carey, who are portrayed on-screen by puppets as they make prank phone calls. According to Richard B. Woodward, writing for the *New York Times* (August 4, 2002), the show was like "*Sesame Street* with Larry Flynt as host." Beginning in 2000, with a single-episode appearance on Matt Groening's *Futurama*, Silverman has also lent her voice to some of the most popular adult-oriented cartoons on television, including *Aqua Teen Hunger Force* (2004), *American Dad!* (2005), and *Tom Goes to the Mayor* (2005).

All along, Silverman continued to work on her stand-up act, telling Ed Condran for the Bergen County, New Jersey, *Record* (June 14, 2002), "That's my bread and butter. No matter what happens to me, I have that. I need something like that because God knows how short-lived some projects are. As long as I can be creative on a stage, I'm happy." She earned the moniker "hit-and-run comic" for her "quick, nasty barbs," as Gene Stout observed in the *Seattle Post-Intelligencer* (September 3, 2002). Silverman's one-woman show, *Jesus Is Magic*, was first staged near the end of 2001 and was praised by David C. Nichols in the *Los Angeles Times* (July 19, 2002) as being "savagely effective, as ruthlessly provocative as anything since the heyday of Lenny Bruce." The show, Nichols continued, is a "scabrously funny, Voltaire-level satire in stand-up guise, grounded by Silverman's central tenet: Mankind's only remaining means by which to conquer fear is ridicule. No taboo topic escapes her, from her interfaith relationship (supplying the show's title), through her gasp-inducing analogy concerning the way 9/11 has conjoined the mundane to the monumental, to the riotous finale, a rendition of 'You Are My Sunshine' that must be seen to be disbelieved."

Silverman's reputation for outrageousness continued to grow, which led David Thorpe, writing for the *Forward* (January 3, 2003, on-line), to wonder if mainstream audiences were ready for her: "Only a few punch lines into a recent gig opening for the indie-rock band Yo La Tengo at their Chanukah performances in New Jersey, Silverman remarked casually, 'I was raped by a doctor—which is a bittersweet experience for a Jewish girl.' Thanks to Silverman's sly timing and cocky attitude—not to mention her coltish beauty—the Yo La Tengo crowd erupted in guffaws of titillated disbelief. Silverman went on to tell equally jaw-dropping jokes about how Mexicans love to pass wind and how her half-black boyfriend was upset when she told him he would have made 'an expensive slave.' . . . Is Silverman a racist? Is she a self-hating Jew? These are the questions that she forces her audiences to ask themselves—along with the more troubling one: Should I be laughing at this?"

In 2003 Silverman appeared on HBO's *Real Time with Bill Maher* and *Howard Stern*, landed a part in *The School of Rock*, playing Patty, the girlfriend of Ned Schneebly (Mike White), and

brought *Jesus Is Magic* to New York for an extended engagement. The following year Silverman lent her voice to *Hair High*, a cartoon feature about a couple murdered on prom night who return the following year, and she opened the 2004–05 television season by reprising her role as the struggling actress Susan Underman from *Who's the Caboose?* in *Pilot Season*, a satire about Hollywood and the development of television series. "In Susan Underman, Sarah Silverman has finally found a role worthy of her deadpan stand-up persona," Dana Stevens wrote for *Slate* (September 8, 2004). "She's a very funny woman, but her combination of Parker Posey-like good looks and grating voice has condemned her to play the shrewish girlfriend in movies like *The School of Rock* and *There's Something About Mary*. In *Pilot Season*, Silverman spoofs this very typecasting. . . . Silverman's character is so deliciously bitchy she could carry the show on her own."

Pilot Season's run was not long; it was an original series produced by the cable network Trio, which folded at the end of 2005. Silverman turned to other projects, appearing in the film adaptation of the Tony Award–winning musical *Rent*, the romantic comedy *I Want Someone to Eat Cheese With*, and two of what Roger Moore, writing for the *Orlando Sentinel* (December 30, 2005), deemed the three dirtiest movies of 2005—*The Aristocrats* and *Sarah Silverman: Jesus Is Magic*, a film version of her one-woman show. (The other movie on Moore's list was Michael Winterbottom's *Nine Songs*.) *The Aristocrats* is a documentary film that was described by A. O. Scott for the *New York Times* (December 25, 2005) as a "scholarly inquiry into the world's filthiest joke," which shows "that filth knows no limits, and that exploring the far boundaries of taste and propriety demands fortitude, hard work and a commitment to craft." Silverman's contribution, which concluded with the assertion that Joe Franklin, the legendary 80-year-old talk-show host, had raped her, proved the most talked-about segment in the movie. Franklin was not pleased, telling Goodyear that he feared people would take the joke seriously: "The look on her [Silverman's] face is severe," he said. "The other guys in that movie, most of them had a happy, jolly look. What's the word? Spoofing, tongue-in-cheeking. But she was very, very harsh and very convincing." Later, in a television appearance, Silverman poked fun at reports that the older comic was considering litigation against her, declaring, according to Goodyear, "He doesn't have the balls to sue."

Sarah Silverman: Jesus Is Magic, which opened in seven theaters in Los Angeles, California, and New York—later spreading to others parts of the country—followed *The Aristocrats*, drawing mostly positive reviews. Allison Benedikt, for example, wrote for the *Chicago Tribune* (November 11, 2005), "Silverman throws her carefully crafted persona a proper, and hilarious, coming-out party in *Sarah Silverman: Jesus Is Magic*." David Edelstein, writing for *Slate* (November 11, 2005), called the film "a glorious piece of showmanship, easily the best stand-up film by a Jewish comedian (let's jettison comedienne, shall we?) I've ever seen. It's not a cultural milestone like *Richard Pryor Live in Concert*, but it has its own explosively twisted originality. It's a geyser of exhilarating tastelessness." Christy Lemire, writing for the Associated Press (November 9, 2005), admitted that "many of her jokes are breathtakingly funny in their wrongness," but complained that "after less than an hour the motif feels redundant, worn-out."

Jesus Is Magic has turned Silverman into a mainstream celebrity, a development she is not sure she is happy about. "I'm grateful, but by the time this is over—there was *The New Yorker* piece, *Rolling Stone* is coming out tomorrow—all of my jokes are now on paper," she told John Anderson for *Newsday* (November 13, 2005). "Plus, one reporter came to my show at the Improv and wrote this story, and these jokes I was doing are in their infancy. So much of what I do is about surprise. I mean, it's not a bad problem to have, but still."

In 2006 Silverman appeared in a small part in Todd Phillips's film *School for Scoundrels*, had a role in the video for Jenny Lewis's song "Rise Up with Fists," and appeared onstage at MTV's Music Video Awards. She was booked to perform with the comedians Brian Posehn and Zach Galifianakis during the Comedy Festival at Caesars Palace, in Las Vegas, Nevada, in November of that year. She is currently developing a show for HBO.

Silverman lives in Los Angeles. She is romantically involved with the talk-show host Jimmy Kimmel, who hosted the notoriously foul and riotous *Comedy Central Roast of Pamela Anderson* (2005), for which Silverman also performed, leading Manuel Mendoza of the *Dallas Morning News* (August 14, 2005) to declare, "No one is as brilliantly blue as Sarah Silverman." In her free time she likes to play poker, and she is a regular at a Saturday-night poker game attended by a number of other comedians. She has competed twice on the Bravo network's *Celebrity Poker Showdown.*

—A.R.

Suggested Reading: (Bergen County, New Jersey) *Record* p18 June 14, 2002; *Boston Globe* C p1 Nov. 22, 2005; *Chicago Tribune* C p2 Nov. 11, 2005; *Forward* (on-line) Jan. 3, 2003; *Los Angeles Times* E p6 Nov. 11, 2005; *New York Observer* p11 Aug. 6, 2001; *New York Times* II p27 Aug. 4, 2002; *New Yorker* p50 Oct. 24, 2005; *Newsday* C p3 Nov. 13, 2005;

Selected Television Shows: *Saturday Night Live*, 1993–94; *Mr. Show with Bob and David*, 1995–1997; *The Larry Sanders Show*, 1996–98; *Greg the Bunny*, 2002; *Crank Yankers*, 2002–04; *Pilot Season*, 2004; *Comedy Central Roast of Pamela Anderson*, 2005

Selected Films: *Who's the Caboose?*, 1997; *Bulworth*, 1998; *There's Something About Mary*, 1998; *The Bachelor*, 1999; *The Way of the Gun*, 2000; *Screwed*, 2000; *Black Days*, 2001; *Say It Isn't So*, 2001; *Heartbreakers*, 2001; *Evolution*, 2001; *Strippers Pole*, 2002; *Run Ronnie Run*, 2002; *The School of Rock*, 2003; *The Aristocrats*, 2005; *Sarah Silverman: Jesus Is Magic*, 2005; *Rent*, 2005; *School for Scoundrels*, 2006

Chris Jackson/Getty Images

Smith, Ali

Aug. 24, 1962– Writer

Address: c/o Pantheon Books, 212 E. 50th St., New York, NY 10022

The work of the Scottish writer Ali Smith is influenced by modernists of the early 20th century, particularly the Irish novelist and short-story writer James Joyce and the American poets Wallace Stevens and William Carlos Williams. In her fiction, Smith has continued the experimental tradition of those literary giants, defying readers' expectations through her use of form and through the kinetic nature of her narratives and viewpoints. In her books, the story collections *Free Love* (1995), *Other Stories and Other Stories* (1999), and *The Whole Story and Other Stories* (2003) and the novels *Like* (1997), *Hotel World* (2001), and *The Accidental* (2006), Smith has often written about lesbian love, but she resists the label "lesbian writer"—as she resists categories in general. Smith told Anna Burnside in an interview for Scotland's *Sunday Herald* (October 7, 2001), "We all live in boxes and if there's one thing I want to do it's push the edges of boxes and make them open." Brooke Allen, writing for the *Atlantic Monthly* (January 2002), called Smith "one of Britain's major talents."

Ali Smith was born on August 24, 1962 in Inverness, Scotland, to Donald Smith, an electrician who worked on hydroelectric projects, and Ann Smith, a bus conductor and switchboard operator. Her family was Catholic. The youngest of five children, Smith has told interviewers that her growing-up years were happy. "It's very safe to be the fifth child in a family," she said to Gillian Bowditch for the London *Sunday Times* (October 14, 2001). "The next brother was seven years older than me so I had the benefits of an only child as well as belonging to a big family." As a child Smith was an enthusiastic reader; by the time she was eight years old, she had read *Dubliners*, by James Joyce, *Animal Farm*, by George Orwell, and *Gulliver's Travels*, by Jonathan Swift. Despite the sense of security she enjoyed, Smith was "conscious that she was different long before she understood what that difference was," as Bowditch phrased it. Smith and another girl were "deeply in love" with each other, as the writer told Bowditch. "Growing up knowing most things are not about you, that you are excluded from most things, makes you feel different. There is nothing like feeling different to make you a writer. Any foreignness, any exile, any sense of the outside position is incredibly important."

Smith's parents, who had had to leave school at age 14, were determined that their children pursue university degrees. An an undergraduate Smith attended Aberdeen University, in Scotland, where she received an M.A. degree in 1984 and was awarded an M.Litt. degree the following year. During her college years Smith felt ambivalent about her sexual orientation. She dated men, which "was terrible and . . . fine," she said to Bowditch. "It was terrible because it was a mistake and it was fine because it was real. I don't think I'll ever live such a double life again." Upon leaving Aberdeen Smith went on to study for a doctorate in literature at Newnham College of Cambridge University, in England; her advisers, however, considered her proposed thesis topic, "Modernism and Joy in Irish and American Literature," to be too broad, and she left the program. By that time she had begun writing plays. Smith next taught English at Strathclyde University, in Scotland, an experience she reportedly found loathsome.

During that time Smith suffered what was diagnosed in 1992 as chronic fatigue syndrome. She went on sick leave and "had two months of not doing anything at all, lying on my back and being unable to move," as she told Bowditch. "It was absolutely terrifying. You just lie there waiting for things to change. Then you stop waiting for anything. You just close down." She added that her illness was "a phenomenally life changing, life stopping thing. . . . It was a visionary experience. You're faced with a different world and, if you are going to live, you have to renegotiate this world.

The illness was the catalyst for my next stage. It allowed me to write." After six months of sick leave, Smith left her teaching post and returned to Cambridge, where she lived with her partner, Sarah Wood. Smith received disability payments and consulted an expert on chronic fatigue syndrome. Meanwhile, she and Wood wrote a number of plays that had well-received stagings at the Edinburgh Fringe Festival. In 1994 Smith won the Macallan *Scotland on Sunday* short-story competition with "Text for the Day."

Smith's first book was a collection of short stories, *Free Love*, published in 1995. Many of the stories deal with lesbian love, and perhaps for that reason Smith struggled to get it published before Virago, a press that specializes in feminist books, took it on. Critical reception of *Free Love* was excellent. Kristina Woolnough wrote for *Scotland on Sunday* (June 18, 1995) that with "deceptively uncluttered language," Smith "homes in on the pinpoints of pain involved in the awakening of selfhood, first love . . . first sexual experiences . . . the flint of unshakeable memories in the whirl of the present, the transience of love. . . . The tension and interplay between what Smith is saying and how she says it is the most striking feature of her writing." For the *Sunday Times* (July 9, 1995) reviewer, most of the stories are about "the ways in which people come together, and are separated again." The stories, the reviewer found, are "brief, rather fragmented . . . , yet they are often memorable as well." *Free Love* won the Saltire First Book Award.

Smith's next book, the novel *Like* (1997), was also greeted enthusiastically. Its principal characters are Amy Shone, a scholar whose nervous breakdown has left her unable to read; her seven-year-old daughter, Kate, with whom Amy lives an itinerant life; and Amy's old friend, called Ash, who wants to be Amy's lover. The cause of Amy's breakdown is not fully revealed, but as Claire Messud wrote for *Newsday* (August 13, 1998), "Smith's novel is wise even in its obliqueness, in its masking of what cannot be known. . . . In often incandescent prose, with a quicksilver capacity to inhabit the psyches of her characters, Ali Smith has composed a lingering threnody of love." In the London *Guardian* (July 20, 1997), Christina Patterson gave *Like* qualified praise, writing that the stories of Amy and Ash "are beautifully written in precise, poetic prose that successfully evokes the love of like for like. But they do remain separate stories, echoing against each other with great subtlety, but not, finally, working as a novel."

With *Other Stories and Other Stories*, which appeared in 1999, Smith established a pattern she has followed since: alternating story collections with novels. The book contains stories about the Other, the narrator's lover, who is addressed as "you," and stories about other people; the latter include "Kasia's Mother's Mother's Story," in which a woman seems to be caught in a war zone, and "Blank Card," which depicts the effect of anonymously sent flowers on a pair of lovers. "On the surface, the tales appear disparate, but on deeper consideration, there are myriad connections," Denyse Lyon Presley wrote for the London *Independent* (April 4, 1999), noting also that "through pared down prose [Smith's] tales uncover some essence of truth without recourse to overt didacticism."

Smith's *Hotel World* (2001), a novel, follows five characters who inhabit a hotel and its periphery. One is the ghost of Sara, a 19-year-old chambermaid who as a result of a bet has died from a fall down a hotel dumbwaiter. Another is Sara's sister, who mourns her obsessively and takes to a life in the streets outside the hotel; there, the narrative also focuses on Else, a tubercular beggar. Inside the hotel are Lise, the desk clerk, who is having a nervous breakdown, and Penny, an ad copywriter who turns out blurbs for the hotel chain. "The one uniting factor that brings together these individual threads is not so much the hotel or [Sara's] death, as the haunting, dream-like note Smith has imbued into every line," Adam Vaughan wrote for the *Richmond Review* (on-line). The critical response to *Hotel World* was mainly positive. In the minority was Chauncey Mabe, who wrote for the Fort Lauderdale, Florida, *Sun-Sentinel* (January 30, 2002), "As if another example were needed to prove that literary modernism is utterly played out, along comes . . . Ali Smith with a novel chock full of the sort of dreary, self-conscious narrative trickery that was already threadbare by the middle of the last century." Most, however, agreed with Vicky Hutchings, who wrote for the *New Statesman* (May 21, 2001) that *Hotel World* is a "many-layered book" and that "Smith's writing is haunting and acute." In Great Britain *Hotel World* was placed on the short lists for the Booker Prize (now the Man Booker) and the Orange Prize.

In keeping with her pattern, Smith's next book was a collection, *The Whole Story and Other Stories*, which was published in 2003. The stories include one that begins, "I was on my way across King's Cross station concourse dodging the crowds and talking to you on my mobile when Death nearly walked into me," and another in which the narrator falls in love with a tree. The title of the collection is ironic, since, as Laura Baggaley noted for the London *Observer* (May 25, 2003), "Throughout, Smith shifts the narrative perspective so that 'I' becomes 'you,' making us question whether it is possible to grasp the complete story." Baggaley also observed, "Smith's prose captures moments in time like those sharp, seemingly insignificant memories which stick in the mind. Her protagonists share memories and we follow the workings of their minds, absorbing past and present, reflection and reminiscence. Reading this collection is like reading a brain in the process of thinking, flitting between subjects, every detail vivid." Writing for the *Miami Herald* (March 21, 2004), Connie Ogle called *The Whole Story and Other Stories* "wonderfully strange and exhilarating."

In Smith's most recent volume, the novel *The Accidental* (2006), a mysterious woman named Amber enters and changes the lives of the Smart family, whose members are Eve, an author with writer's block; her philandering husband, Michael, a college literature professor; the suicidal Magnus, Eve's teenage son from a previous marriage; and Astrid, her 12-year-old daughter. In an assessment of *The Accidental* for the *Threepenny Review* (Spring 2006, on-line), Sigrid Nunez declared, "Smith's writing is so fine, it is naturally the first thing one wants to praise. Her cleverness and exuberance, her unflagging verbal virtuosity, delight the reader page after page. But stylistic tour de force is hardly Smith's only concern, and though *The Accidental* is not a realistic novel, its characters are not only believable but brimming with life." *The Accidental* won the Whitbread Novel Award and was shortlisted for the Man Booker Prize and the Orange Prize.

A production of Smith's first full-length play, *The Seer*, was mounted in 2006 after a five-year delay. Susan Irvine, writing for the London *Sunday Telegraph* (June 4, 2006), described it as "a kind of metaphysical farce exploring the relation of truth to fiction. . . . In *The Seer* the invisible wall between art and life is permeable, allowing us to question what a real existence might be, with a humour at times so plain silly that the audience forgets itself and gets carried away across the fourth wall, too, in a moment that is both cheesy and strangely moving."

Melissa Denes wrote for the London *Guardian* (April 19, 2002, on-line) that Smith's "eyes are very blue, slightly slanted, and there is a point to her chin—an intelligent, slightly mischievous face." The writer is a liberal, as suggested by her desire, which she revealed to the *Scotsman* (June 7, 2001), to "lock [former British prime minister Margaret Thatcher] in a room and punch her—and I've got quite a good right hook." (Indeed, Gillian Bowditch reported that Smith's body is "muscular" if "compact.") Denes noted that Smith "strikes you as a generous person—in the space of an hour she will have recommended at least five writers," and she added that Smith, who reviews fiction for the *Guardian*, "doesn't like to take on anything she instinctively knows she won't like." Smith lives with her partner, Sarah Wood. With Wood and Kasia Boddy, she edited *Brilliant Careers: The Virago Book of Twentieth-Century Fiction* (2000). She also selected the stories for *Shorts3: The Macallan/Scotland on Sunday Short Story Collection* (2000).

—S.Y.

Suggested Reading: *Atlantic Monthly* p139+ Jan. 2002; *Boston Globe* G p3 Jan. 20, 2002; (London) *Guardian* p17 July 20, 1997, (on-line) Apr. 19, 2003; (London) *Observer* p16 May 25, 2003; (London) *Sunday Times* (on-line) July 9, 1999; *Miami Herald* M p6 Mar. 21, 2004; *Newsday* B p2 Aug. 13, 1998; *Publishers Weekly* p51 Mar. 1,

2004; *Review of Contemporary Fiction* p256 Summer 1998; *Scotland on Sunday* S p11 June 18, 1995; *Washington Post* C p4 Jan. 22, 2002

Selected Books: *Free Love*, 1995; *Like*, 1997; *Other Stories and Other Stories*, 1999; *Hotel World*, 2001; *The Whole Story and Other Stories*, 2003; *The Accidental*, 2006; as editor—*Brilliant Careers: The Virago Book of Twentieth-Century Fiction* (with K. Boddy and S. Wood), 2000; *Shorts3: The Macallan/Scotland on Sunday Short Story Collection*, 2000

Selected Plays: *The Seer*, 2006

Getty Images

Smith, Steve

May 12, 1979– Football player

Address: Carolina Panthers, 800 South Mint St., Charlotte, NC 28202

On September 9, 2001, in his first game as a professional football player, Steve Smith of the Carolina Panthers returned the opening kickoff for a 93-yard touchdown against the Minnesota Vikings. The five-foot nine-inch, 185-pound wide receiver has since earned the admiration of his peers in the National Football League (NFL) with a number of other, equally highlight-reel-worthy dashes, receptions, and leaps. Following the Panthers' 29–21 victory against the Chicago Bears in the divisional round of the 2005–06 play-offs, in which Smith caught two touchdown passes and established a franchise record with 218 receiving yards, the

Bears' All-Pro linebacker Brian Urlacher called Smith "the best offensive player in the league," according to Jerry Crowe in the *Los Angeles Times* (January 20, 2006). Among receivers Smith led or co-led the NFL in three important statistical categories in 2005: receptions (103), receiving yards (1,563), and touchdowns (12). At 27 years of age, he is generally regarded as one of the most versatile players in the game.

Early in his NFL career, Smith was often criticized by sportswriters for his fierce temper, an aspect of his nature that carried over from his days as a college player and earlier, when he grew up in various rough neighborhoods in South Central Los Angeles, in California. His teammate Ken Lucas told Nunyo Demasio for *Sports Illustrated* (January 23, 2006), "He plays with a chip on his shoulder, which helps him. He probably has the biggest heart in the game. . . . He doesn't care who's [covering him]. He's going to go up and get that ball." In a sport in which the average player stands above six feet and weighs approximately 245 pounds, Smith has acknowledged that he uses his relatively small stature to his advantage. "I'm real compact so guys think they can just jam me, push me back, out jump me, or out hustle me and that's completely the opposite of what's going to happen with me," he said to Michael Donnelly for NFLPlayers.com (February 16, 2006). Lee Jenkins wrote for the *New York Times* (January 19, 2006), "The National Football League has tons of receivers taller than Smith and some faster, but . . . no receiver is more relentless."

Stevonne L. Smith was born on May 12, 1979 in Lynwood, California. He was raised primarily by his mother, Florence Young, a drug counselor, and grew up with his brother, Raymond, currently an emergency technician in the Los Angeles area. Lee Jenkins reported that during the days when Smith went with his mother to work, "he looked at all the addicts and promised himself that he would never turn out like them." Florence Young said to Jenkins, "I prayed it would have some effect." Smith's father, also named Steve, had met his mother when both ran track in college; his uncle Martin played football for the University of Southern California, where he served as a backup to the legendary running back O. J. Simpson.

Speaking with Lee Jenkins, Smith's mother said that her son "has always been tenacious," a trait he displayed in his athletic endeavors while growing up. At University High School, in West Los Angeles, Smith was a standout hurdler on the track team. He was also a star on the football team, helping to lead the school to the city's 3A divisional semifinals in 1996. Smith excelled on both sides of the line of scrimmage, playing running back and wide receiver on offense and safety on defense. In his junior year he led the defense in tackles resulting in a loss of yards. As an upperclassman, Smith was named to the All-California Interstate Football and the All-Metro League teams. Marshall Jones, Smith's high-school coach, explained to Jerry

Crowe that at the time he considered it an "extremely long shot" that Smith would play in the NFL, "just because he was a little guy. I don't know if he weighed 150 pounds as a senior." (When Smith was a freshman, Jones added, "it was difficult fitting him into a helmet that didn't rattle around his head.") Smith struggled to make passing grades and decided not to take the college-entrance exam, or Scholastic Aptitude Test (SAT). "I just didn't have the drive," Smith said to Billy Witz for the *Daily News of Los Angeles* (January 31, 2004). Not sought after by many colleges, Smith enrolled at nearby Santa Monica College, where he played on the football team as a wide receiver and a kick returner. Meanwhile, he worked at a local Taco Bell fast-food restaurant, manning the cash register, sweeping the parking lot, and scrubbing floors. Recalling his job there, he told Jenkins, "I knew it wasn't what I wanted to do with my life, but I knew that I was going to need a lot of determination and a lot of persistence to do something else."

Robert Taylor, the head coach at Santa Monica, told Jenkins that Smith was a "really angry young man" during that time. Perhaps influenced by the violence of the neighborhoods in which he was raised, Smith engaged frequently in physical and verbal clashes with both his teammates and his coaches. In a conversation with Jerry Crowe, Eugene Sykes, a teammate of Smith's at Santa Monica, sought to explain Smith's violent behavior: "He was just so intense about the game. If a new receiver came to the school and he wasn't working hard, he'd get on him real quick. And a lot of people didn't know that was just his passion for the game. . . . That's how he ended up in a lot of fights." In Smith's first year at Santa Monica, when his temper had become a distraction to the team and overshadowed his stellar play, Taylor called Smith into his office and asked him, according to Jenkins, "Who are you angry at?" When Smith said, "I don't know," Taylor decided to suspend him "until he had an answer," in Jenkins's words. That decision seemed to have a humbling effect on Smith, who soon curbed his irascibility and devoted himself to becoming a team leader and a better student. On the field Smith teamed with Chad Johnson (currently of the Cincinnati Bengals of the NFL) to form one of the Los Angeles area's most imposing wide-receiver combinations. In his sophomore season he tallied 54 receptions, 847 receiving yards, and 13 touchdowns and was named to the Second Team All-Western State Conference South. In the 1998 South Bay Classic, Smith's final game with Santa Monica, he racked up close to 300 yards in kick returns, leading Santa Monica to a thrilling 71–67 victory against El Camino College.

Smith's quickness and play-making ability attracted Fred Graves, who was then the wide-receivers coach at the University of Utah and was also responsible for recruiting for the school in the Los Angeles area. "I met Steve one day at the Taco Bell," Graves told Jenkins. "I fell in love with him

right there." Smith enrolled at Utah in his junior year, earning an athletic scholarship. In his first year there, he caught 43 passes and gained 860 receiving yards, including eight touchdowns. He also ranked fifth nationally in yards gained per punt return, averaging 17.1 yards per kick. On November 22, 1999, in a game against Brigham Young University, Smith was tackled hard while returning a punt; he continued to play in that game despite a tingling sensation in his neck and shoulders—symptoms of what turned out to be a broken fourth cervical vertebra in his neck. (He also had a concussion.) He recovered from those injuries in time to return to the field the following year. He finished his two-year stay at Utah with an average of 20.6 yards per catch, a school record at the time. In addition, in both his junior and senior seasons, Smith performed well in All-Star Games and was named to the first team All-Mountain West Conference's squad as a wide receiver. His play drew the attention of pro scouts, who coveted him in part for his ability as a kick returner.

Smith was drafted by the Carolina Panthers in the third round of the 2001 NFL Draft, with the 74th overall selection. Although the Panthers—who had joined the NFL as an expansion franchise in 1995—qualified for the postseason in just their second year, they had compiled a mediocre overall regular-season record of 45–51 in their brief history. In Smith's rookie season the Panthers amassed an all-time franchise low with a league-worst one victory against 15 losses. Jeffri Chadiha, writing for *Sports Illustrated* (January 12, 2004), noted that in his first NFL year, Smith "ran sloppy routes and dropped too many passes." Smith made only 10 catches for 154 yards, with no touchdowns, as he was used sparingly on offense by the head coach, George Seifert. His play as a kick returner on special teams, however, was extremely impressive. Establishing several team records along the way, Smith gained 1,994 yards—the fourth-highest total in the NFL that season—thanks almost entirely to his efforts at returning kicks. He was the only rookie to be selected to play in the prestigious All-Pro Game in Hawaii at the season's conclusion. In addition, for his efforts on special teams, the Associated Press, *Sports Illustrated*, *Pro Football Weekly*, *Football Digest*, and the *Sporting News* each named him an All-Pro in 2001.

In the 2002 off-season John Fox replaced Seifert as the Panthers' head coach and began remaking the team's defense with young, versatile players. During the regular season the team improved its record to 7–9 and made significant strides in other areas—particularly in stopping opponents' rushing schemes. Smith's receiving in 2002 represented an improvement over his rookie year. He started in 13 games at the wide-receiver position and made 54 receptions, gained 872 receiving yards, and scored three receiving touchdowns for the season. As Chadiha reported, 2002 was the first NFL season in which Smith "showed a knack for making the difficult reception in a crowd and for gaining valuable yards after the catch." Meanwhile, Smith enjoyed another fine season as a kick returner. On December 8, 2002, in the course of contributing to a 52–31 victory against the Cincinnati Bengals, Smith made two punt returns (totaling 148 yards) for touchdowns and gained 144 receiving yards (including a receiving touchdown) in what was by far his best game as a professional up to that point.

Off the field, in late November 2002, Smith generated headlines by punching his then-teammate Anthony Bright during an argument. The altercation landed Bright in the hospital and Smith, briefly, in jail, where he was charged with misdemeanor assault. (The charges against Smith were dismissed in November 2003.) The team suspended Smith for one game and ordered him to attend anger-management classes.

The following year the Panthers won the National Football Conference (NFC) South division with a record of 11–5. The team's success was due in part to Smith, who had become a catalyst of the offense. He grabbed 88 receptions for 1,110 receiving yards and seven touchdowns—each a personal and team high. Returning punts, meanwhile, he gained 439 yards and another touchdown and recorded 309 kickoff return yards. At that time sportswriters began to note the positive effect that Smith's play had on the team. In an allusion to Fox's preference for calling for more running plays than passes, Chadiha wrote that Smith had become the Panthers' "big-play threat in a conservative, run-oriented offense." Smith attributed his success to his having matured as a professional. "I came into this league as a returner, and I wanted respect as a receiver," he said to Mark Whicker for the *Orange County (California) Register* (January 10, 2004). "I was trying to do things too quickly. I've learned to settle down and be patient, be more professional. You've got to have the same timing as everybody else." Despite the surge of positive feelings surrounding Smith's performance, in November 2003 he once again let his temper get the better of him, kicking the Houston Texans defensive lineman Jerry Deloach during a regular-season game and receiving a personal-foul penalty that effectively cost the Panthers a victory. Also during the 2003 season, Smith expressed his frustration with the Panthers' management for refusing to open negotiations on a new contract. Discussing those episodes, Smith told Chadiha, "I embarrassed myself, my family and the organization, and I learned I had to change. When you make mistakes that big, you're not going to repeat them because you simply can't afford to."

On the field Smith continued his stellar play in the 2003–04 play-offs, helping the Panthers reach the Super Bowl for the first time in the team's history. On January 3, 2004, in an NFC wild-card contest against the Dallas Cowboys, which the Panthers won by a score of 29–10, Smith recorded a team-high five receptions for 135 yards, including one for a touchdown. His performance in the following week's game against the strongly favored

St. Louis Rams was equally impressive. On the first play of the second sudden-death overtime period, Smith caught a short pass from the quarterback Jake Delhomme, then galloped 69 yards, past the Rams' secondary and into the end zone, winning the game for the Panthers. The following week the team defeated the Philadelphia Eagles, 14–3, to advance to Super Bowl XXVIII, where they faced the New England Patriots. In arguably the most exciting Super Bowl game of recent memory, Smith made four receptions for 80 yards and a touchdown. His performance on offense was not enough to hold off the efforts of the Patriots' quarterback Tom Brady, who in a high-scoring game set a Super Bowl record with 32 pass completions. Although the Panthers tied the score at 29–29 with slightly over a minute remaining in regulation play, the kicker Adam Vinatieri completed a 41-yard field goal with less than 10 seconds remaining, to lift the Patriots to a 32–29 victory—and to the team's second Super Bowl championship in three years.

In the off-season Smith signed a six-year contract extension with the Panthers valued at $27.5 million. Many observers expressed confidence that the Panthers could return to the Super Bowl, since most of the team's core remained intact. During the first week of the 2004 NFL season, however, Smith fractured his left fibula in a game against the Green Bay Packers. The injury forced him to miss the remainder of the season. Smith was one of several Panthers sidelined due to injury that year, and although the team finished the season by winning six of its final eight games, its 7–9 record was not strong enough to qualify for the play-offs. Smith spent most of his time away from the football field rehabilitating his leg in preparation for the 2005 NFL season. He also spent time with his wife and children. "It reminded me of when my time would be up in the NFL but at the same time it also reminded me of the financial opportunities the NFL has given me to be able to spend time with my family," Smith said to Michael Donnelly for NFL.com (February 16, 2006).

At the completion of the 2004 NFL season, in a move that was seen as a vote of confidence in Smith, the Panthers cut ties with the veteran wide receiver Muhsin Muhammad, who, with Smith, had formed the team's primary pass-catching duo. Smith became the focal point of the Panthers' offense in 2005 and emerged as one of the NFL's best players. Among all receivers that year, he led or co-led the NFL in receptions (103), receiving yards (1,563), and touchdowns (12). His team also enjoyed success in 2005, earning a play-off berth with an 11–5 record. It was Smith, however, who received most of the praise from football observers. "After 11 years of watching and covering the Carolina Panthers, I can tell you this with certainty: No Carolina player has ever been as valuable to his team as wide receiver Steve Smith has been to these Panthers," Scott Fowler declared in the *Charlotte Observer* (January 6, 2006). "On an offense that was otherwise mostly average, Smith made the

Panthers special." For the January 17, 2006 edition of that paper, Fowler wrote, "Steve Smith is cocky, irrepressible and constantly disrespected (in his own mind). He's also the most startling, exhilarating, eminently watchable player in the NFL. And, at this moment, the very best." Smith shared Comeback Player of the Year honors with the Patriots linebacker Tedy Bruschi and was selected as a starter at the wide-receiver position in the Pro Bowl. Earlier, during a regular-season game against the Dallas Cowboys, Smith was penalized and ejected after he made contact with an official. The sports agent Derrick Fox, who has been associated with Smith since the athlete's days at the University of Utah, said to Charles Robinson for Yahoo! Sports (January 19, 2006, on-line), "[Smith's] not your happy-go-lucky guy. He's got a hard shell. But when you break that hard shell, his heart is the size of Texas."

Smith's play did not falter in the NFL play-offs. After scoring two touchdowns (one rushing and one receiving) in the Panthers' 23–0 victory against the New York Giants in the wild-card round of the NFC play-offs, Smith turned in a second consecutive outstanding performance, gaining 218 receiving yards and again scoring two touchdowns, against one of the NFL's most formidable defensive units, that of the Chicago Bears, on January 15, 2006. (Smith's 218 receiving yards ranks fourth all-time in NFL play-off history.) "I'm just really utilizing my talents," Smith said after the game, playing down his performance, to a reporter for espn.com. "They throw me the ball, my job is to catch it. If I don't catch the ball, they will get somebody in here who will. I've got four people at home depending on me to do my job, so I can't come home with excuses." Against the Seattle Seahawks, in the NFC Championship Game, on January 22, 2006, the Panthers were frustrated by a defensive scheme designed almost entirely to hem in Smith: the Seahawks assigned as many as four defenders on each play to prevent Smith from catching the ball. (He recorded only five catches for 33 yards and no touchdowns.) In the second quarter Smith was able to return a punt 59 yards for a touchdown, but the Panthers were beaten 34–14 by the Seahawks, who advanced to Super Bowl XL. There, they were defeated, 21–10, by the Pittsburgh Steelers.

Smith suffered a thigh injury before the start of the 2006 NFL season and missed the first two games. The Panthers lost both of those contests. After Smith's return, in the third week of the season, the team won four games in a row and then lost one. Smith's receiving skills were on full display during those five games, particularly in the one against the Baltimore Ravens, in which he single-handedly outmaneuvered the Ravens' defense to net eight catches for 189 receiving yards (including one touchdown). As the mid-season mark approached, Smith had netted 39 receptions for 576 yards (and ranked third among the league leaders in receiving yards) and two receiving touchdowns; with four wins and three losses, the Panthers were in third place in the NFC South Division.

In 2004, after he signed his contract extension with the Panthers, Smith established a charitable trust in the name of his former Santa Monica College teammate Demetrius Posey, who was killed in a car accident in March 2003. The foundation was designed to provide recreational activities for underprivileged children in the Charlotte, North Carolina, area. Smith and his wife, Angie, have one daughter, Baylee, and two sons, Peyton and Boston. The sports media describes Smith as a fiercely devoted father and husband. He is known to have coached his son Peyton's soccer team, and he intends to become more involved in coaching youth sports when his NFL career ends. Smith, who has several tattoos, is known to perform wild dances in opposing teams' end zones after scoring touchdowns, an aspect of his play that exasperates tradition-minded fans of the sport.

—D.F.

Suggested Reading: Carolina Panthers Web Site; *Los Angeles Times* D p1 Jan. 20, 2006; *New York Times* D p1 Jan. 19, 2006; *Orange County (California) Register* Jan. 10, 2004; *Sports Illustrated* p68 Jan. 12, 2004

Smits, Jimmy

July 9, 1955– Actor

Address: c/o National Hispanic Foundation for the Arts, 1010 Wisconsin Ave., N.W., Suite 210, Washington, DC 20007

For two decades Jimmy Smits has been a familiar presence to television viewers, with his roles as Victor Sifuentes on *L.A. Law* from 1986 to 1991, Bobby Simone on *NYPD Blue* from 1994 to 1998, and, beginning in 2004, Congressman Matthew Santos—the (fictional) first Latino U.S. presidential nominee—on *The West Wing*. He has also broken ground for Hispanic actors with his portrayals of those admirable characters, who stand in contrast to the many negative screen images of Latinos. Smits began his career as an actor in Off-Broadway plays and soap operas before playing an attorney on *L.A. Law*, the role that brought him an Emmy Award. "As I become more successful," he told Gail Buchalter for the *Washington Post* (February 18, 1990), "I am aware that it affects other Latinos. It's imperative that I don't forget the homeboys and the old neighborhood. But I'm also an artist and an actor. The one thing I want to do with my career is be versatile—not limit myself."

Jimmy Smits was born on July 9, 1955 in the New York City borough of Brooklyn. His father, Cornelis Smits, who went on to become a manager for a silk-screening company, had come from Suriname, in South America; his mother, Emelina Smits, a nurse's aide, had come from Puerto Rico.

Frederick M. Brown/Getty

Jimmy Smits

While Smits was growing up, he was responsible for taking care of his two younger sisters while his parents worked. "I was never really young," Smits told Gail Buchalter. "I was raised to own up to my responsibilities." As their finances dictated, the family moved back and forth from Brooklyn to the Bronx and even lived in Puerto Rico for two and a half years, beginning when Smits was 10. At one point, when Smits was 13 and having a hard time adjusting to his family's recent relocation from Puerto Rico, he was caught shoplifting model-airplane parts. "My parents freaked" when the police notified them, Smits told Gail Buchalter. "It was very important to them not to be shamed around the neighborhood, and I had done just that. My father beat the hell out of me, my mother cried, and I felt awful. I never stole again." Smits also found more constructive ways to deal with the constant relocations. "One of the reasons I got into acting was, because we moved so much, I had no lasting friendships," he explained to Gail Buchalter. "I wasn't an outgoing kid, although I did have friends, but I also spent a lot of time alone and would act out different scenarios to keep myself amused."

As early as age six, Smits showed a fondness for doing impressions; he has recalled once banging his shoe on the kitchen table in imitation of the Soviet leader Nikita Krushchev. His early heroes were the actors Raul Julia and James Earl Jones. He acted in plays at George Gershwin Junior High School in Brooklyn, and, while at Thomas Jefferson High School, also in Brooklyn, he left the football team, on which he had been a linebacker, to join the drama club. That difficult decision led to his being ostracized at first by his former football

teammates; later, however, the team attended one of his first performances en masse, occupying the entire first and second rows of the auditorium and giving him a standing ovation. Upon finishing high school Smits attended Brooklyn College, earning a degree in 1980 and becoming the first member of his family to graduate from college. (When he switched his major from teaching to drama, his parents objected to what they considered an impractical career choice.) During those years he also performed public service, which ranged from cleaning streets to tutoring high-school dropouts, so that he could "stay involved with the community," as he told Buchalter.

Meanwhile, Smits faced crises and challenges in his personal life. When he was 18 his parents divorced, and at about the same time Smits learned that his girlfriend, Barbara, was pregnant. Smits moved in with her, and the two later married. Before divorcing amicably, in 1987, they had two children, Taina and Joaquin. During his senior year of college, Smits considered going to California after his graduation to try his luck as an actor in Hollywood. Instead, he enrolled at Cornell University, in Ithaca, New York, where he earned a master's degree in theater arts in 1982. Occasionally during that time he would "wonder if I had made the right choice," he recalled to Buchalter. "I would think, 'Maybe I should have gone to Hollywood. . . .' But I would have lost the grounding my education gave me, which is why I always tell kids to stay in school."

After completing his schooling, Smits returned to Brooklyn and began appearing in Off-Broadway plays while driving a cab to help support himself. During that time he also landed roles in soap operas. In 1984 he appeared in the pilot episode of the highly popular police drama *Miami Vice*; his character, the partner of the detective played by Don Johnson, was killed within the first 15 minutes of the show. In 1986 he played a policeman in the TV movie *Rockabye* and a drug dealer in the film *Running Scared*. He was also seen that year in an episode of *Spenser: For Hire*.

Following a disastrous audition in New York for the role of Victor Sifuentes on *L.A. Law*, Smits flew to Los Angeles, California, to audition again—this time successfully. The show, which debuted in 1986, followed the cases and personal lives of lawyers at a Los Angeles firm, where Smits's character, a Mexican-American, was a successful associate. "Back in the '30s and '40s, Latinos [in films] were the lady-killers, the suave lovers. Today, they're the crooks. And that's why the role of Victor Sifuentes is so appealing to me," Smits explained to Merrill Shindler for the *Chicago Tribune* (October 16, 1988). "I saw it as a chance to establish an intelligent, alternative image, someone who's neither a thug, nor a womanizer." In his portrayal of the passionate, dedicated Sifuentes, Smits soon became a favorite with both audiences and critics and earned an Emmy Award nomination for each of the six years he spent on the show. (He won the Emmy for Outstanding Supporting Actor in a Drama Series in 1990.) While starring on *L.A. Law*, he also appeared in the TV movies *The Highwayman* and *Stamp of a Killer* (both 1987) and *Glitz* (1988) and in the films *Hotshot* and *The Believers* (both 1987), *Old Gringo* (1989), *Vital Signs* (1990), and *Switch* and *Fires Within* (both 1991). Smits left *L.A. Law* in 1991 to pursue more film roles, returning to the series to make two guest appearances the following year.

After performing in the television movies *The Broken Cord* (1992) and *The Tommyknockers* (1993) and the film *Gross Misconduct* (1993), Smits found himself on another television series. When the actor David Caruso left the police drama *NYPD Blue* after the show's first season (1993–94), Smits took over as the Caruso character's replacement, Detective Bobby Simone. (A year earlier Smits had been offered the part of a detective named Flinn on the show; after he declined, the detective was renamed Kelly, and Caruso was cast in the role.) With a laid-back manner that contrasted with his predecessor's fiery personality, Simone replaced Kelly as the partner of Detective Andy Sipowicz (played by Dennis Franz). In an article for *USA Today* (November 15, 1994), Matt Roush wrote, "Jimmy Smits eases into *NYPD Blue* with an effortless, no-big-deal charisma, a low-key integrity that not only fills David Caruso's shoes but helps the entire show walk tall again." During the second season of *NYPD Blue*, Smits and the show's other actors won a Screen Actors Guild Award for outstanding performance by an ensemble cast. The Bobby Simone character "was the stable emotional center of [the show's] universe," David Milch, the co-creator and executive producer of *NYPD Blue*, told Peter M. Nichols for the *New York Times Television* section (November 22–28, 1998). "The essential decency of his nature allowed the audience to feel safe to explore the complexities and the woundings and scarrings of the other characters." While such traits made Bobby Simone a likable character, they also, Smits felt, made playing Bobby a somewhat unfulfilling exercise. "In some sense Jimmy felt it was a restriction, that it deprived his character of dimension," David Milch elaborated. "The healthy soul must be engaged with the world, whereas the wounded one can be interesting in its withdrawals. Jimmy felt the character lacked inwardness in that regard."

During his tenure on *NYPD Blue*, Smits also took on an assortment of other projects, including voice work on the TV series *Happily Ever After: Fairy Tales for Every Child* (1995) and *Mother Goose: A Rappin' and Rhymin' Special* (1997). He starred in the television movies *The Cisco Kid* (1994), *Solomon & Sheba* (1995), and *Marshal Law* (1996) and the films *My Family* and *The Last Word* (both 1995) and *Murder in Mind* and *Lesser Prophets* (both 1997). He earned particular praise for his performance in *My Family*, the story of several generations of a Mexican-American family living in East Los Angeles. "With a deft touch that lightens the story, and the charismatic presence this film has needed all along, Mr. Smits almost single-handedly makes *My Family* more engaging," Caryn James wrote for the *New York Times* (May 3, 1995). Smits, in her opinion, gave "a terrific, dominant performance." In 1998, after four years on *NYPD Blue*, Smits decided to move on. (On the show, his character died of a heart infection.) Caryn James wrote for the *Times* (November 24, 1998), "Though his level-headed approach offered Mr. Smits few opportunities for stormy acting, it is a huge and subtle accomplishment to have made Bobby so richly believable."

After leaving *NYPD Blue* Smits appeared in films including *The Million Dollar Hotel*, *Price of Glory*, and *Bless the Child* (all 2000) and *Angel* (2003). In 2002 he played the small but significant role of Senator Bail Organa, the adoptive father of Princess Leia, in the second *Star Wars* prequel, *Episode II: Attack of the Clones*. Although he told the Memphis, Tennessee, *Commercial Appeal* (April 14, 2005) that he had probably "spent more time in the wardrobe department than I did on the set" of *Attack of the Clones*, he found the experience sufficiently interesting to reprise his (now enlarged) role in *Episode III: Revenge of the Sith* in 2005. "It was fascinating to be there and watch the world [that George Lucas, the guiding force of the *Star Wars* series] has created over the past 30 years. . . . He'll start talking about it like it's real," Smits told the *Commercial Appeal*. Referring to the phenomenally successful *Star Wars* films, whose characters and story lines have taken on the status of myth for legions of fans, the actor told Sarah Rodman for the *Boston Herald* (April 6, 2005), "I'm just excited to be part of that lore."

Meanwhile, Smits had also returned to his first love, theater. He starred in a 2002 production of Shakespeare's *Twelfth Night*, in which he played the love-smitten Duke Orsino, for the yearly Shakespeare in the Park festival held in New York City's Central Park. While the overall production earned poor reviews, Smits was thought to have acquitted himself reasonably well. "His performance may not be memorable, but he conveys the core of the character very well and gets his laughs," Robert Feldberg wrote for the Bergen County, New Jersey, *Record* (July 22, 2002). "As the painfully smitten Orsino, Smits is a dashing figure . . . ," Charles Isherwood wrote for *Variety* (July 29–August 4, 2002). "With an equally handsome stage voice, Smits knows how to shape the verse and certainly savors the language, but the performance, perhaps like the character, is mostly style." In 2003 Smits starred in the Pulitzer Prize–winning play *Anna in the Tropics*, about a lector who reads Tolstoy's *Anna Karenina* to Depression-era cigar-factory workers in Florida and embarks upon an affair with one of the workers (played by Daphne Rubin-Vega). "Smits is sweetly seductive, matinee-idol handsome in a tropical white suit, a man who rides the passion of Leo Tolstoy's *Anna Karenina* to a different tragic ending," Christine Dolen wrote for the *Miami Herald* (November 17, 2003), and in the *New York Post* (November 17, 2003), Clive Barnes agreed that "the effortlessly accomplished" actor, "stylish, slightly remote, [and] haughty . . . is superb." Smits earned significantly better reviews during his next foray into the Shakespeare in the Park festival, which, in 2004, featured the actor as Benedick in *Much Ado About Nothing.* In the *Hartford (Connecticut) Courant* (July 15, 2004), Malcolm Johnson enthused that Smits "makes an amusingly divided Benedick, full of himself on the surface but less assured within." "Who knew he had perfect comic timing?" a pleasantly surprised Neil Genzlinger asked in a *New York Times* review (July 14, 2004). Genzlinger added that Smits "executes [physical comedy] with a crowd-pleasing fearlessness," yet manages to "show a great restraint, playing to the audience with subtlety rather than . . . lowest-common-denominator overkill."

In 2004 Smits joined the cast of another television series, the political drama *The West Wing.* At the conclusion of the 2004–05 season, his character, Congressman Matthew Santos, emerged from a deadlocked Democratic National Convention as his party's presidential nominee and the possible successor to the fictional Democratic president Josiah "Jed" Bartlet (played by Martin Sheen). In the 2005–06 season Santos ran in the general election against the wily, free-market Republican senator Arnold Vinick (Alan Alda). The two even faced off in November 2005 in a live episode that re-created the format of a presidential debate; minimally scripted, with plenty of room for improvisation, the debate episode was a hit among viewers and provoked disagreement over who had won—with one on-line source reporting that Santos had "edged out" Vinick and another finding that Alda had "waxed the floor" with Smits. The show's fictional voters were apparently of the former opinion, as Santos won a narrow victory over Vinick to become the first Latino president-elect. The debate and election did little to revive the diminished ratings of the long-running series, and in early 2006 NBC announced that *The West Wing* would go off the air at the end of the 2005-06 season. Asked by Holly Taylor for *Redbook* (March 2006) what it had meant to Smits "to play a politician who's also Latino and may well be the next president," Smits answered, "I got into acting because I've always believed that with any form of art, you have the ability to touch people in a profound way. And television can be a huge influence, especially for young people. The show gives them permission to aspire, you know? I run into young people all the time who are lawyers now and tell me the role I played on *L.A. Law* influenced their decision. That's a nice icing on the career cake."

"Ask anyone to describe Smits," Gail Buchalter wrote, "and most come up with the same simple word: nice." For many years the six-foot three-inch Jimmy Smits has lived with the actress Wanda De Jesus. In 1997 Smits co-founded the National His-

panic Foundation for the Arts, with the aim of helping Hispanics in creative endeavors. He narrated the documentary *Yo Soy Boricua, Pa' Que Tu Lo Sepas!* ("I'm Boricua, Just So You Know!"), which premiered on the Independent Film Channel in 2006. Directed by the actress Rosie Perez, the film is about the Puerto Rican–American experience. ("Boricua" connotes residents of Puerto Rico or descendants of native Puerto Ricans.)

—K.J.E.

Suggested Reading: *Chicago Tribune* p4+ Oct. 16, 1988; imdb.com; *New York Post* p41 Nov. 17, 2003; *New York Times* C p18 May 3, 1997, E p1 July 14, 2004; *New York Times Television* p4+ Nov. 22–28, 1998; *Variety* p29 July 29–Aug. 4, 2002; *Washington Post* p18+ Feb. 18, 1990

Selected Films: *Running Scared*, 1986; *Hotshot*, 1987; *The Believers*, 1987; *Old Gringo*, 1989; *Vital Signs*, 1990; *Switch*, 1991; *Fires Within*, 1991; *Gross Misconduct*, 1993; *My Family*, 1995; *The Last Word*, 1995; *Murder in Mind*, 1997; *Lesser Prophets*, 1997; *The Million Dollar Hotel*, 2000; *Price of Glory*, 2000; *Bless the Child*, 2000; *Star Wars: Episode II: Attack of the Clones*, 2002; *Angel*, 2003; *Star Wars: Episode III: Revenge of the Sith*, 2005

Selected Television Shows: *Miami Vice*, 1984; *L.A. Law*, 1986–91; *NYPD Blue*, 1994–98; *The West Wing*, 2004–06

Snow, Tony

June 1, 1955– Presidential press secretary; former television commentator

Address: The White House, 1600 Pennsylvania Ave. NW, 1st Floor, Washington, DC 20500

When Tony Snow succeeded Scott McClellan as White House press secretary in the administration of President George W. Bush, on April 26, 2006, he became the first professional journalist in three decades to assume the post. Prior to becoming press secretary, Snow, a former speechwriter for President George H. W. Bush, had built a distinguished career as a political columnist and radio and television news commentator. His syndicated columns for the *Detroit News* and *USA Today*, as well as his directorship of the *Washington Times* editorial page, established Snow as a voice for neoconservatism. But Snow's biggest splash in the national media had occurred in 1996, when the then relatively modest Fox News Network hired him as a commentator for its first weekend-news program, *Fox News Sunday*. During his seven-year tenure at Fox, Snow proved himself a congenial yet forceful ideologue, equally adept at praising and hammer-

Tony Snow

ing the politics of friend and foe. For Snow, no political party, including his own, was immune to criticism. As he explained to Chris Lamb for *Editor and Publisher Magazine* (September 7, 1996), his critiques were based on the fidelity of the party under discussion toward its own ideals: "I'm someone who believes that political parties should operate out of the passions and ideals of the people involved and not the sterile, finger-in-the-wind approach you get when you put a pollster in charge. . . . One of the big problems in American politics . . . is that people are far more afraid of being unpopular than being wrong. As a result, they're both."

Snow's early months as press secretary have garnered mostly praise. In his first televised briefing, he distinguished himself from his predecessor by assuming a comfortable affability, offering, in the words of Dana Milbank, writing for the *Washington Post* (May 17, 2006), "a sprightly blend of barbs, colloquialisms and one-liners," which made the 40-minute stand "entertaining." Snow's candor and self-deprecating style, as Julie Hirschfeld Davis wrote for the *Baltimore Sun* (July 25, 2006), have brought "fresh perspective to a press operation that was stuck in a rut of recycled responses and predictable dodges. . . . Snow's easy style is a marked departure from that of . . . McClellan, whose studied and stilted repetition of talking points often made him appear uneasy and defensive." In granting the press corps greater access to a reputedly hyper-secretive White House, Snow has striven to foster open and authentic exchange, sometimes telling reporters in response to questions about sensitive matters, "I just don't know the answer" or "That's just flat my fault," as Helen

Thomas observed for the *Houston Chronicle* (May 27, 2006). "He is a quick student and a showman, intense and glib," and is "slicker, smoother and more articulate than his . . . recent predecessors," Thomas wrote. The coming months will very likely prove to be more challenging for Snow, as some press corps members have admitted to cutting him some slack while he became accustomed to his position. "Tony's made some statements he regrets, and he gets a pass on some days because he's new," Martha Raddatz, ABC's White House correspondent, explained to Howard Kurtz for the *Washington Post* (October 12, 2006). "But I think that little honeymoon is over."

Robert Anthony Snow was born on June 1, 1955 in Berea, Kentucky, and spent his formative years in Cincinnati, Ohio. His father was a high-school teacher, his mother a nurse at an inner-city clinic. When Snow was in his late teens, Snow's mother died at age 38 from colon cancer. "The situation with his mother left him very attuned to mortality, how close we are to death," Ed Jones, an old friend of Snow's, told Howard Kurtz for the *Washington Post* (May 15, 2006). "That's why he's always been a grab-for-the-gusto kind of guy."

After graduating from Princeton High School, in nearby Sharonville, Ohio, Snow enrolled at Davidson College, in North Carolina. There, as a political philosophy major, he initially embraced leftist views. In a conversation with Kay McFadden for the *Charlotte Observer* (October 6, 1996), Snow recalled about his student days, "I was trying to plow through [the writings of Karl] Marx while fancying myself in favor of [re]distributing wealth. I was a cocky little kid from the Midwest, ready to shake up all these folks with deep Southern accents." A writer for *Davidson News & Events* (February 2004, on-line) reported about Snow's college years, "Tony wasn't satisfied with the status quo. He participated in late night rap sessions to debate and exchange philosophical ideas. . . . Tony took every opportunity to challenge other people's assumptions."

Snow studied under the Philosophy Department chair and libertarian thinker Lance Zell, who influenced his gradual shift toward conservatism. After graduating from Davidson, in 1977, Snow traveled to what was then the Soviet Union and was struck by the fatalism, as he saw it, of its Communist system. His stint as a teacher in Tanzania, Africa, confirmed for him that socialism had had a negative effect on African nations, and the experience contributed further to the change in his political views. Upon his return to the U.S., Snow worked in North Carolina as an advocate for the mentally disabled. He has said that during that period he learned a great deal in the South, a place "about which I had all kinds of prejudices," as he told McFadden. Southerners, he discovered, were not necessarily "slow," and he found that their "consensus-style politics often accomplished more than the contentious Northeast and Midwest," as McFadden put it. For the 1978–79 academic year, Snow enrolled in graduate courses at the University of Chicago, studying philosophy and economics; he did not earn a degree. He then took the first in a series of print-media jobs, as a writer for the *Greensboro Record*. Next he wrote editorials for the *Norfolk Virginian-Pilot* before becoming the youngest-ever editorial-page editor of the *Newport News Daily Press*, in Virginia. In 1984 Snow relocated to Detroit, Michigan, where he served for three years as deputy editor of the *Detroit News*.

In 1987 Snow accepted the position of editorial-page editor at a Washington, D.C., newspaper, the *Washington Times*. There, he quickly established himself as a reasoned conservative voice. The Democratic strategist Bob Beckel told Julia Malone for the *Atlanta Journal and Constitution* (May 11, 1991) that even then, Snow was "no doctrinaire conservative" but a conservative "with soul."

After four years at the *Washington Times*, Snow exchanged his role of political pundit for that of political insider. In 1991 President George H.W. Bush tapped Snow, then 35, for the post of chief White House speechwriter. Snow's former boss, Francis Coombs, the national editor of the *Washington Times*, described Snow to Malone as a clear thinker with the "gut instinct of a Midwesterner" and predicted that he would not "pound the table" and mount "in-your-face attacks" in his new post. Samuel Francis, a former *Times* colleague, also spoke glowingly of Snow, telling Malone that he would bring a "firmer philosophical edge" to the president's speeches. Indeed, it was generally agreed that Snow quickly brought a sparkle to President Bush's speeches. In May 1991 the president's graduation address at the University of Michigan highlighted the power of Snow's thoughtful rheto-

ric, which helped an otherwise predictable speech to take a turn for the memorable. As John E. Yang reported for the *Washington Post* (June 22, 1991), Bush waxed eloquent about the glory of American freedom before layering his remarks with an allusion to the debate over "political correctness" on college campuses. Bush declared, as quoted by Yang, that "what began as a crusade for civility has soured into a cause of conflict and even censorship. In their own Orwellian way, crusades that demand correct behavior crush diversity in the name of diversity." Snow's delicately woven allusion caused a stir. Landon Parvin, a former speechwriter for President Ronald Reagan, expressed to Yang his opinion that Bush's speech had "pushed a frontier" and added, "Tony Snow is just what was needed: someone who's not scared to serve up some ideas. . . . That's been lacking in the current White House." Snow himself said to Malone, "If there was an agenda to that speech, I guess it was 'Let us debate as reasonable people. Let us not assume that people who disagree with us are evil.'"

Snow's first priority upon becoming the president's chief speechwriter had been to have his staff work to grasp the nuances of Bush's personality and verbal predilections. Snow revealed to Jon Anderson for the *Chicago Tribune* (November 22, 1991), "The first thing George Bush said to me, when I came into the Oval Office, was, 'Well, you know, I'm not the world's greatest orator.'" Snow realized then, he said, that his job was to write for "a plain-spoken man with an innate sense of decency. You don't write florid passages or quote Thucydides. You talk like an American and quote [the country singer] Randy Travis." To achieve that end, Snow employed unorthodox methods. He hired Dana Carvey, who had performed impressions of Bush on the TV sketch-comedy show *Saturday Night Live*, to shed light on Bush's staccato syntax, while inviting novelists and playwrights to provide ideas for strengthening Bush's speeches. Snow's strategies mostly succeeded, as they lent depth and flourish to President Bush's speech at the University of Michigan and to his subsequent address at the Air Force Academy, where, as Yang reported, Bush uttered the much-quoted phrase "new world order" to refer to the post–Cold War era. Snow felt it important to keep in mind the context of a given speech and to remember that every presidential address is important. "It may seem like a terrible assignment, drafting remarks for greeting some high school basketball team. But it matters," he told Anderson. "It's a chance to say something interesting. You also know there are some people in each audience who will be seeing a president for the first, perhaps only, time. You owe it to those people to give them a memorable speech."

Snow's insistence on the politics of conviction, and his resistance to what is merely safe, have at times courted controversy. As Peter Wallsten and Joel Havemann noted for the *Los Angeles Times* (April 27, 2006), Snow drew ire from Democrats in the early 1990s for seeming to support those who championed aspects of the Louisiana gubernatorial campaign of the former Ku Klux Klansman David Duke. "You can't write off Duke's voters as racists," Snow told Dan Goodgame for *Time* (November 25, 1991). "Duke is talking about things people really care about: high taxes, crummy schools, crime-ridden streets, welfare dependency, equal opportunity. A lot of politicians aren't talking about these things."

After Bush lost his reelection bid, in 1992, Snow returned to journalism as a syndicated columnist for both the *Detroit Free Press* and *USA Today*. His columns appeared in 200 national papers. Snow also appeared as a guest host on radio and cable-news programs, including the *Rush Limbaugh Show*, National Public Radio's *Diane Rehm Show*, and CNN's *Crossfire*. In an interview with Barbara Matusow for the *Washingtonian* (February 1995), Diane Rehm noted, "Some of these conservatives get really nasty in their political opinions, but Tony is congenial. He says what he has to say but doesn't imply that the rest of the world is worthless."

In 1996 Snow became the host of his own broadcast-news program. Roger Ailes, the newly appointed president of Fox News, conceived *Fox News Sunday* as a vehicle for Snow's views, congeniality, and wit. "Frankly, Tony Snow is a star. He just pops through the screen. He's likable and he's got a sense of humor," Ailes told Howard Kurtz for the *Washington Post* (May 11, 1996). *Fox News Sunday* combined interviews, roundtable discussions, and commentary from pundits and was intended as a sprightly alternative to such established Sunday-morning news-discussion shows as *Meet the Press*. Snow saw the program as an opportunity to practice diplomacy. "You walk a fine like with a program like this. After all, I'm a practicing right-winger and everybody knows it. We have liberal guests on and the key for me is not to go in and club them . . . ," he mused to Michael Storey for the *Arkansas Democrat-Gazette* (September 1, 1996). "I get a lot of my conservative brethren angry at me because I sometimes don't leap in and argue or try to make it a polemical program." To distinguish itself from other shows, *Fox News Sunday* also integrated experimental features into its format. A segment called "Department of Corrections" poked fun at the malaprops of both liberal and conservative politicians, while the "Fox Movietone Newsreel" juxtaposed archival footage with coverage of current events. Snow said that *Fox News Sunday* incorporated fun and seriousness because politics itself involved both. "Politics is funny. It's love, sex, money, and death. Why not bring those elements to people? I try to draw the best from all along the spectrum and get crisp, active material—not that desiccated civics book stuff," he said to McFadden. *Fox News Sunday* received its share of criticism, with Frederic Biddle of the *Boston Globe* (April 29, 1996), for example, calling Snow a "helmet-haired traffic cop" and his

show a "free publicity meal" for the GOP faithful. Despite his detractors, Snow sustained a seven-year run on *Fox News Sunday* before it ended, in 2003. Snow later returned as host of a revised weekend-news program entitled *Weekend Live with Tony Snow*. Also in 2003 he branched out into radio, with *The Tony Snow Show*, a morning talk program on Fox News Radio.

Meanwhile, Snow had also resumed his duties as a syndicated columnist. His columns reflected his disenchantment with what he saw as the waning of conservatism in American economic policy. During the 2000 presidential campaign, for example, Snow published a series of commentaries for *Townhall* calling for a Republican return to classical conservatism. He labeled the Republican presidential nominee, George W. Bush—a son of the former president— a "classical dime-store Democrat" (August 25, 2000) and called for Republicans to "stop pandering incompetently and start making the limited-government case completely" (November 16, 2000). Snow was a staunch supporter of President George W. Bush's policies on global terrorism and of the U.S.-led war in Iraq, launched in the spring of 2003. In his column "Remembering the Real Enemy" for the *Jewish World Review* (May 13, 2004), Snow wrote, "We [must] return to the insights impressed upon us by the assaults of September 11, 2001. As President Bush reminded us back then . . . this is not a war over land or resources or old personal grievances. It is a battle of good and evil." At the start of George W. Bush's second term, Snow nonetheless grew critical of what he perceived as the president's cowardice in the face of his Democratic opponents. In his column "The Jury Is Still Out on Bush's Term" for *Townhall* (September 30, 2005, on-line), Snow wrote, "Begin with the wimp factor. No president has looked this impotent this long when it comes to defending presidential powers and prerogatives." Snow further argued, "The budget has grown nearly 50 percent on his watch, and [Bush] is vying to become the most free-spending president ever." In a November 11, 2005 column for *Townhall*, Snow also took exception to President Bush's "wavering conservatism" and his loss of swagger in his dealings with Democratic politicians such as Harry Reid and Nancy Pelosi, the result of which, in Snow's opinion, was that "the newly passive George Bush has become something of an embarrassment." Snow's criticism of the big-government tendencies of the Bush presidency continued in his *Townhall* column of March 17, 2006: "George W. Bush and his colleagues have become not merely the custodians of the largest government in the history of humankind, but also exponents of its vigorous expansion."

Snow seemed a curious choice, then, when President Bush appointed him as White House press secretary, the third of his presidency, on April 26, 2006. He became the first career journalist to be tapped for the role since the NBC correspondent Rob Nessen assumed the post under President Gerald R. Ford in 1974. As quoted in a White House on-line news release (April 26, 2006), President Bush introduced Snow by remarking, "Tony Snow understands the importance of the relationship between government and those whose job it is to cover the government." And of Snow's past criticisms of his administration, Bush said, "He's not afraid to express his own opinions. For those of you who have read his columns and listened to his radio show, he sometimes has disagreed with me. I asked him about those comments, and he said, 'You should have heard what I said about the other guy.'"

Media reactions to Snow's appointment were largely positive. Many, including Dee Dee Myers, who had been a press secretary in the administration of President Bill Clinton, believed that Snow would have credibility among journalists, having been one himself. Myers told Howard Kurtz of the *Washington Post* (April 26, 2006), "Tony has stature. He understands how the press works from both sides. He has a big personality, and that can be helpful." Peter Wallsten and Joel Havemann observed of Snow: "His voice is quiet and authoritative. Even critics conceded he has a talent for articulating policy issues and political philosophy." Others, like Julie Mason of the *Houston Chronicle*, believed that Snow's appointment was a slick attempt on Bush's part to appease the media with one of their own. Mason said, as quoted by Rebecca Dana for the *New York Observer* (May 1, 2006), "It's sort of the obvious elevation of style over substance. Not that he [Snow] doesn't have substance, but they do seem to be going with flash over someone who's a little wonkier."

For Snow, his acceptance of the appointment hinged on issues of health. Mason reported for the *Houston Chronicle* (April 27, 2006) that Snow had undergone a CAT scan, which confirmed that the colon cancer he had recently suffered had gone into remission. At a televised briefing, Snow's first as White House press secretary, Snow remarked candidly to the press corps, as quoted in a White House on-line news release (May 16, 2006): "It's going to sound stupid, and I'll be personal here. . . . Having gone through this [colon cancer] last year . . . was the best thing that ever happened to me. . . . It's one of these things where America—whatever we may say about a health care system, the technologies that were available to me that have me standing behind the podium today, where a doctor who said, you don't have to worry about getting cancer, just heartburn, talking to these people . . . that's a wonderful thing. And I feel every day is a blessing." Another factor in his decision was his desire to have a larger role than any previous spokesperson in the administration's policy discussions. Snow believed that greater insight into the making of the president's policies and strategies would increase his own effectiveness in articulating them. Snow explained to Byron York for the *National Review* (May 22, 2006), "The one thing I'm satisfied with is that I will have plenty of access and plenty of information so I can do my job right." Snow's openness has helped to alter the "make no mistake, admit no mistake" mentality of the White House, Terry Holt, a Republican communications consultant, told Julie Hirschfeld Davis.

By all accounts Snow has added personality to his role; indeed, Howard Kurtz wrote for the *Washington Post* (October 1, 2006), "There has never been a White House press secretary quite like Snow." Other White House correspondents agree that Snow seems to relish the daily repartee that is part of his job. "Sometimes it does feel like the Tony Snow Show," Richard Wolffe, *Newsweek*'s White House correspondent, said to Kurtz. "There are tactics he uses that are straight out of talk radio. The extent to which he personalizes things or comes back with a one-liner, it revs up the base. They love it when he takes us on." Snow himself believes that his years as host of *Fox News Sunday* prepared him well for his give-and-take relationship with the press corps; as he told Kurtz, "If you can't roll with the punches and give sensible answers, you're going to get killed." Bush administration officials describe Snow as a major asset. In an action unprecedented for a presidential press secretary, and one that provides evidence of both his party loyalty and his celebrity, he took part in fund-raising efforts for Republican candidates in the 2006 congressional elections.

Tony Snow lives in the Waynewood section of Northern Virginia with his wife, Jill Snow, and their three children. He plays flute, saxophone, and rhythm guitar for an oldies rock-cover band called Beats Workin.'

—D.J.K.

Suggested Reading: *Charlotte Observer* F p1 Oct. 6, 1996; *Editor & Publisher Magazine* p32 Sep. 7, 1996; *Los Angeles Times* A p8 Apr. 27, 2006; *Washington Post* A p8 Apr. 26, 2006, A p1+ June 22, 1991, C p1+ Oct. 12, 2006

Spelke, Elizabeth

(SPEL-kee)

May 28, 1949– Psychologist

Address: Dept. of Psychology, Harvard University, 1130 William James Hall, 33 Kirkland St., Cambridge, MA 02138

For three decades Elizabeth Spelke has been working to expand scientists' knowledge of which capacities humans are born with and how those capacities change with age. The simplicity of Spelke's experiments and the resulting clarity of her findings have illuminated infants' often surprising abilities and helped push away some older ideas about child development. Thanks to Spelke

Courtesy of Kirsten Condry

Elizabeth Spelke

and her collaborators, psychologists have come to realize that very young children are able to understand the world in ways that had once seemed possible only with formal education or later natural development. Whereas such important figures in the history of psychology as William James and Jean Piaget had judged infants incapable of making certain basic predictions about their environment—such as whether an object still exists after it is covered by a blanket—Spelke and her research partners have found strong evidence that infants as young as four months understand something about those types of phenomena. Named in *Time* magazine's August 20, 2001 issue among America's 18 best scientists, Spelke has also made significant contributions to research indicating that infants naturally develop a sense of numbers and numerical relationships ("numerosity," as it has been dubbed), and that, well before being taught arithmetic skills in school or elsewhere, children are able to perform basic addition and subtraction of very low numbers, as well as recognize differences between larger numbers that form simple ratios, such as 2:1. Spelke's research has also uncovered an intimate neurological connection between language and arithmetical calculation and provided support for the idea that language works hand in hand with innate mental categories and does not itself create those categories. As the American Psychological Society stated (as posted on its Web site) when it honored Spelke with its William James Fellow Award for lifetime intellectual achievements in 2000, "Spelke's work begins to answer perennial philosophical questions about the origins of human knowledge about space, objects, motion, unity, persistence, identity and number."

Spelke has come to believe that a set of innate "core knowledge systems," as she terms them, structures what we learn—a belief that makes her a nativist, as that word is used in discussions about the relative influences of nature and nurture on people's intelligence, personalities, and other characteristics. In an address to the American Psychological Association in August 2000, when she received that organization's award for distinguished scientific contributions, she defined core knowledge systems as "mechanisms for representing and reasoning about particular kinds of ecologically important entities and events—including inanimate, manipulable objects and their motions, persons and their actions, places in the continuous spatial layout and their Euclidean geometric relations, and numerosities and numerical relationships," as quoted in *American Psychologist* (November 2000). (Spelke was using "ecologically" in the sense of a person's response to all the elements in his or her environment, while "Euclidean" in that context denotes the familiar world of three dimensions.) Spelke has reported finding evidence for core knowledge systems in nonhuman primates, such as monkeys, as well as in humans, suggesting that such systems became part of the primate brain before humans appeared on Earth.

Spelke has taught at the University of Pennsylvania, in Philadelphia; Cornell University, in Ithaca, New York; and the Massachusetts Institute of Technology (MIT), in Cambridge, Massachusetts. Since 2001 she has held the title of professor at Harvard University, in Cambridge. In recent years she has spoken out publicly to urge Harvard to maintain an economic boycott of Israel, because of Israel's alleged abuse of Palestinians. She has also called on the university to refute claims that women are intellectually inferior to men—and that that supposed difference accounts for the fact that men greatly outnumber women in tenured professorships in mathematics and the so-called hard sciences. By her own account, part of what pushed Spelke to air her views in both cases was all the data produced by her own research, which support her nativist convictions. As she told David Dobbs for *Scientific American Mind* (October 2005), "We're getting evidence for an intricate and rich system of core knowledge that everyone shares and that gives us common ground." Describing Spelke as an "unabashed optimist," Dobbs quoted her as saying about that evidence, "In a world of so much conflict, I think that's something we badly need."

One of the three children of Ruth and Harold Spelke, Elizabeth Shilin Spelke was born on May 28, 1949 in New York City. She has two brothers. Her father was a writer and a filmmaker, and the family traveled often during Spelke's childhood. In 1967 she entered Radcliffe College (now part of Harvard University). She studied literature and history before changing her major to social relations, an offshoot of sociology. Her first opportunities to conduct experiments in psychology came in 1970, when she took a class with Jerome Kagan, a renowned developmental psychologist known for his work suggesting that individuals' temperaments can be traced to genes as well as environmental influences. According to Spelke's unsigned but plainly autobiographical sketch (written in the third person) in *American Psychologist* (November 2000), "Kagan taught Spelke that the deepest and most difficult questions can be asked in simple language and addressed by straightforward experiments." Spelke graduated from Radcliffe in 1971 with a B.A. degree and as a member of the honor society Phi Beta Kappa. After spending the 1972–73 academic year at Yale University, in New Haven, Connecticut, she began working toward a Ph.D. at Cornell University. She studied with the developmental psychologist Eleanor Jack Gibson, who specialized in infant perception, a field toward which Spelke gravitated early on in her career and one that remains of interest to her. Spelke's doctoral dissertation, which she completed in 1978, presented the results of her experiment on the ability of infants of about four months of age to relate what they hear to what they see. Spelke tested for that ability by observing the behavior of infants placed in front of two screens separated by a speaker that broadcast sounds synchronized with the images projected on one screen or the other. Spelke discovered that the babies, particularly at four months old or older, more often looked at the screen whose images were connected with the sounds—evidence that they could link the perceptual "modes" of sight and hearing.

Although Spelke did not originate the technique of determining what children intuit by observing what they prefer to look at—what is known as preferential looking—the Harvard psychologist and linguist Steven Pinker wrote, in an article for *Time* (August 20, 2001) in which he celebrated her achievements, that she "perfected" it. The technique "capitalizes on one thing babies are good at: getting bored," as Pinker put it: that is, if presented with two images, they prefer to look at the one that is more novel or unusual. In one experiment based on preferential looking, infants are placed in front of a screen that moves up and down. After they have watched the moving screen for a while, the infants barely glance at it. Researchers then have the screen hide a box that has been placed behind it or show what looks to be the screen passing magically through the box. If the infants spend less time looking at the plausible event (screen hiding box) than at the implausible one (screen passing through box), then one can conclude that they understand (at some level) how two solid objects can relate in the real world.

When Spelke and the psychologists Renée Baillargeon and Stanley Wasserman conducted precisely that experiment, using as subjects 21 babies between four months and just under six months of age, they discovered that the children apparently understood the concept of object permanence. The results of Baillargeon, Spelke, and Wasserman's experiment, published in 1985 in the technical

journal *Cognition*, supported an earlier experiment on preferential looking that Spelke had conducted with Philip Kellman, the results of which were published in *Cognitive Psychology* in 1983. The results of the two experiments indicated that the eminent Swiss psychologist Jean Piaget had erred when he suggested that children begin to grasp the concept of object permanence later in their development—a suggestion that scientists had assumed to be correct. More important, the findings of Spelke and her colleagues showed that Piaget had been wrong to assume that babies learned about object permanence as they moved around and tested object relations in their immediate environments. Instead, infants' ability to recognize how solid objects should relate seemed to result from inborn knowledge about the world that becomes manifest in normal development along with, rather than as a result of, sensory and motor skills. In other words, certain reasoning abilities come as naturally—and perhaps nearly as early—to humans as our abilities to move or perceive.

Long before Spelke had published those papers, she had made significant advances in her academic career. In 1977 she joined the Department of Psychology at the University of Pennsylvania as an assistant professor. In 1981 she earned tenure there and was promoted to associate professor. The following year she spent a sabbatical leave at the Center for Cognitive Science at MIT. The university's faculty included the world-renowned linguist Noam Chomsky and, at that time, Steven Pinker, both of whom were at the forefront of studies into humans' inborn abilities, particularly as revealed by and related to language. In her autobiographical sketch in *American Psychologist*, Spelke wrote that during that period she developed close working relationships with a number of people who have strongly influenced her research, and that "she began to see cognitive science as the interdisciplinary enterprise within which her kind of experimental and developmental psychology would grow."

In 1986 Spelke left the University of Pennsylvania and returned to Cornell, this time as a full professor. She stayed at Cornell for "10 happy years," as she recalled in her autobiographical sketch. During that time the primary aim of her research was to determine which qualities of objects (for example, shape or color) infants are able to distinguish. She also joined other psychologists in looking into how children, adults, and nonhuman primates orient themselves spatially, and she began to study infant numerosity. In a paper entitled "Origins of Knowledge" in *Psychological Review* (Volume 99, 1992), Spelke and three other researchers then at Cornell (Karen Breinlinger, Janet Macomber, and Kristen Jacobson) presented evidence that humans process and act on perceptual information by means of inborn mental categories. Spelke and her co-authors credited not only Chomsky with that hypothesis but also the philosophers René Descartes (1596–1650) and Immanuel Kant (1724–

1804). By far Spelke's most frequently cited paper, according to information on the reference database PsycINFO, "Origins of Knowledge" strongly challenged two rival theories (both of which still have adherents) about how children learn to understand their environments. One is related to Piaget's belief that sensory motor experience is the primary determining factor. The other, sometimes called "the theory theory," holds that children are born with very general dispositions toward ideas about the world but that they radically revise those ideas, or theories, as they experience their environments and new evidence presents itself. By contrast, Spelke and her collaborators maintained, "Cognition develops from its own foundations, rather than from a foundation of perception and action. Initial cognitive capacities give rise, moreover, to conceptions that are largely appropriate to the experience of children and (nonscientist) adults. Finally, initial conceptions form the core of many later conceptions; they are enriched and refined as knowledge grows, but they are rarely overturned." In a paper entitled "Science and Core Knowledge," published in the journal *Philosophy of Science* (Volume 63, Number 4, 1996), Spelke and her friend and later colleague Susan Carey tried to reconcile elements of the core-knowledge theory with the so-called theory theory.

Also in 1996 Spelke left Cornell to join the Department of Brain and Cognitive Sciences at MIT. During her five years at MIT, she continued to research object perception among infants and increasingly refined her ideas about how core knowledge systems might work. She also conducted studies on the perceptual clues people use to orient themselves in unfamiliar surroundings. Perhaps Spelke's most important contributions during that time related to the development of mathematical skills. In 1999 she and the French neuropsychologist Stanislaus Dehaene, along with three other researchers, drilled a group of adults who were fluent in both Russian and English on a set of exact sums and a set of approximate sums, using either Russian or English for each sum. Each subject was then tested on what he or she had learned. On the approximations, the subjects answered equally well in both English and Russian, regardless of which language had been used to teach a particular approximation. When asked for the answer to a particular exact sum, however, the subjects usually took a second longer, or sometimes slightly more than a second, to respond if they were questioned in the language that had not been used for that sum in the drill. That result constituted solid evidence that arithmetical skills and language skills are closely related. The experimenters then went one step further. Another set of bilingual subjects underwent similar training, but when tested, they also underwent brain-imaging scans, one for the approximations and a second for the exact sums. In the scans the researchers saw that when choosing between two approximations, the subjects used a part of the brain closely associated with, among

other things, the movements of the fingers, while choosing exact sums heightened the activity of parts of the brain associated with language. The clear neurological distinction between those two seemingly related skills suggested that each one might belong to a separate core knowledge system, while the close connection between approximations and physical movements—especially ones that might be related to the nearly universal arithmetical learning process of counting on one's fingers—surprised even the researchers. "I was amazed that the association could be so sharp," Dehaene told Nell Boyce for *New Scientist* (May 15, 1999).

In 2001 Spelke became a member of the Department of Psychology at Harvard University. There she has continued her investigations into the development of computational skills in children. Especially noteworthy among her discoveries is the finding, as reported by Spelke, the psychologist Hilary Barth, and two other researchers in the *Proceedings of the National Academy of Sciences* (September 2005), that even preschool-age children without any arithmetic training are able to perform rough calculations. An experiment, the results of which were published in *Nature* (July 22, 2004), addressed directly the question of whether perceptual categories precede language acquisition or vice versa. Working with the psychologist Susan Hespos, Spelke used an experiment in preferential looking to test whether a group of five-month-old babies, all of whom were to learn to speak English, distinguished objects that fit together loosely (for example, a block placed in a much wider container) from ones that fit tightly (that same block placed in a container outwardly identical to the other, except for its narrower mouth). Based on the infants' visual preferences, Spelke and Hespos concluded that the infants did make that distinction. She then tested English-speaking adults in the same way and found that they seemed oblivious to that distinction. Korean-speaking adults, on the other hand, noticed the difference—an effect, it would seem, of the fact that this distinction is reinforced in Korean speakers by their having a choice among verbs denoting that relation.

In addition to the attention her scientific work has brought her, Spelke has attracted widespread notice several times in the last few years because of her outspoken, controversial stands on some political and social issues. In 2002 she signed a petition asking Harvard to stop investing in companies that did business with or in Israel because of what she viewed as Israel's abuse of the human rights of Palestinians. "I was moved to take this action," Spelke told Scott Simon on the National Public Radio show *Morning Edition* (September 28, 2002), "because I believe that as an American, the best steps I can take to bring about a peace that is in the best interests of everyone in the Middle East and, in fact, all of us in the world, are to pressure my government and my university and the businesses in which it invests to pressure Israel to cease its occupation of this area." (Only 70 other members of the Harvard faculty signed the petition, while 439 signed a counterpetition.) According to Patrick Healy, writing for the *Boston Globe* (December 21, 2002), Spelke and other signatories received E-mail messages and letters labeling them anti-Semites and claiming that their stance lent support to terrorists. The president of Harvard at that time, Lawrence H. Summers, also raised the specter of anti-Semitism, saying in widely reported comments that the petition was "anti-Semitic in effect if not intent"—a charge that Spelke, born to Jewish parents and with strong familial ties to Israel, vehemently denied.

In 2005 Spelke and Summers again found themselves on opposite sides of an issue, this time concerning statements that Summers made in a speech to the National Bureau of Economic Research on January 14 of that year. According to a transcript made available later on Summers's Harvard Web site, Summers argued that differences in men's and women's "availability of aptitude at the high end" of science and engineering was "probably" one of the most important reasons for women's underrepresentation in those fields. His comments prompted an immediate and furious debate, to which Spelke initially contributed largely through her comments to journalists. In April 2005 Spelke participated in a public debate with Steven Pinker, one of Summers's most prominent defenders and the source of some of Summers's arguments in his talk. Spelke and Pinker's debate was wide-ranging and generally collegial, with both scientists emphasizing their support for a general nativist point of view. Spelke nonetheless strongly argued, according to a transcript of the debate on the science and culture Web site Edge.org (which preceded a scholarly review article Spelke published in December 2005 in *American Psychologist*), that "there are no differences in overall intrinsic aptitude for science and mathematics between women and men. Notice that I am not saying the genders are indistinguishable, that men and women are alike in every way, or even that men and women have identical cognitive profiles. I'm saying that when you add up all the things that men are good at, and all the things that women are good at, there is no overall advantage for men that would put them at the top of the fields of math and science." Earlier in 2005, when Edge.org asked Spelke and 119 other scientists what they believed but could not yet prove, Spelke had expressed similar views about the qualities humans share regardless of gender or culture. She wrote, in part, "I believe . . . that all people have the same fundamental concepts, values, concerns, and commitments, despite our diverse languages, religions, social practices, and expressed beliefs. If defenders and opponents of abortion, Israelis and Palestinians, or Cambridge intellectuals and Amazonian jungle dwellers were to get beyond their surface differences, each would discover that the common ground linking them to members of the other group equals that which binds their own group together."

Spelke's honors include the 1984 McCandless Young Scientist Research Award from the American Psychological Association and a Merit Award from the National Institutes of Health in 1993. She was elected to the American Academy of Arts and Sciences in 1997 and to the National Academy of Sciences in 1999 and was named a fellow of the American Association for the Advancement of Science in 2002. She received a Fulbright-Hays Senior Research Fellowship in 1983, a John Simon Guggenheim Memorial Fellowship in 1989, and a James McKeen Cattell Fellowship in 1992. She holds honorary degrees from Umeå University in Sweden and École Pratique des Hautes Études in Paris.

Spelke married Elliott M. Blass, a psychologist who teaches at the University of Massachusetts at Amherst, in 1988. The couple live near Harvard and have two children, Bridget and Joseph; Spelke also has two stepsons from her husband's first marriage. In her leisure time she enjoys traveling; she is particularly fond of France.

—D.R.

Suggested Reading: *American Psychologist* p1230+ Nov. 2000; Edge.org; *Scientific American Mind* p38+ Oct. 2005; *Time* p33 Aug. 20, 2001; wjh.harvard.edu

---

Squyres, Steven

Jan. 9, 1956– Planetary geologist; NASA scientist; educator

Address: 428 Space Sciences Bldg., Cornell University, Ithaca, NY 14853

"What really got me going on planetary exploration was the ability to take on a whole new world that [people] knew hardly anything about," Steven Squyres, a planetary researcher, geologist, and astronomy educator, told an interviewer for ABC News (January 9, 2006, on-line). Squyres is the director of the Mars Exploration Rover (MER) Mission, a project supported by the National Aeronautics and Space Administration (NASA), which has produced incontrovertible evidence that water existed on the Red Planet in the distant past—a discovery that the journal *Science* hailed as the Breakthrough of the Year in 2004. Working with a large team of scientists and engineers, Squyres designed and built two immensely complex instrument-laden robotic rovers—"twin robot geologists," as NASA calls them—named Spirit and Opportunity, which landed on Mars a few weeks apart in January 2006, after traveling for seven months and 303 million miles (in the case of Spirit) and 283 million miles (Opportunity) through space. Monitored and maneuvered from Mars Mission Control, in Pasadena, California, Spirit and Oppor-

Steven Squyres

Robyn Beck/Getty Images

tunity have relayed to Earth spectacular, crystal-clear images of parts of the martian surface as well as a treasure-trove of information regarding the geology and geological history of the planet. Although, as Squyres noted to John Schwartz for the *New York Times* (June 9, 2004), "there is no textbook that tells you how to explore a mountain range with a robot," the MER Mission rovers have done just that, even far exceeding expectations regarding their ambulatory and information-gathering capabilities, adaptability, and longevity. Squyres has acknowledged that the MER Mission, whose cost has totaled about $800 million, is not practical in the usual sense: as he told the ABC News interviewer, "It's not going to fill in the potholes. It's not going to put a roof over people's heads. What it does is it helps to address really fundamental questions of who we are, where we came from, by which I mean we can learn how life came about."

Squyres is the Goldwin Smith Professor of Astronomy at Cornell University, in Ithaca, New York, where he has taught for two decades. He is the author of *Roving Mars: Spirit, Opportunity, and the Exploration of the Red Planet* (2005), which provides "you-are-there thrills and chills . . . ," as Julie Mayeda wrote in a review of the book for the *San Francisco Chronicle* (August 7, 2005, on-line). In a critique for the *Chicago Tribune* (August 19, 2005, on-line), Jeremy Manier wrote, "The book's engine is the sense of curiosity and adventure that made Squyres devote his life to the ridiculously difficult enterprise of flinging delicate instruments and circuit boards to far-off worlds. . . . His message may not make great literature, but it's the inspiring plea of all great explorers: Here's how I did

it. Follow me." A 45-minute documentary film about the MER Mission, called *Roving Mars* and based in part on Squyres's book, premiered in IMAX theaters in 2006. "I'm a huge fan of sending robots to Mars, obviously—that's what I do for a living," Squyres told David Appell for *Scientific American* (September 27, 2004, on-line). "But even I believe that the best exploration, the most comprehensive, the most inspiring exploration is going to be conducted by humans." He also said, "I think people who point to the successes of these two rovers as evidence that you don't need to send humans to Mars are missing the point entirely. I view our rovers not as competitors to humans but as precursors."

Steven Weldon Squyres was born on January 9, 1956 in Woodbury, New Jersey, and grew up outside Camden, New Jersey, across the Delaware River from Philadelphia, Pennsylvania. His father was a chemical engineer with DuPont. Tim Squyres, his younger brother, is a Hollywood sound and picture editor; his credits include *Crouching Tiger, Hidden Dragon*, for which he earned an Academy Award nomination. As a child, as Steven Squyres wrote in *Roving Mars*, he loved studying maps and reading about 20th-century explorers, among them the oceanographers William Beebe and Otis Barton and the polar explorers Robert Falcon Scott and Roald Amundsen. He dreamed of making discoveries himself someday—of being the first person to set eyes on places on the ocean floor or even remote parts of Earth's surface. Young Steven's interest in rocks was kindled when, as an eight-year-old, he accompanied his family on a vacation to the Rocky Mountains. For Christmas one year he received a telescope, which with his father's help he used to trace the orbits of Jupiter's four largest moons. "I can't ever remember not wanting to be a scientist . . . ," he told the reporter for ABC News. "[I had] just a curiosity about how things work. That's really what science is, just trying to figure stuff out, and I like figuring stuff out." In his teens he became adept at rock climbing. He graduated from high school in 1974. By that time, as he wrote in *Roving Mars*, "reality [had] set in. There were no blank spots on the maps [of Earth] anymore," except for a few places on the sea floor.

Squyres pursued his interest in geology as a student at Cornell University. He was there when, in 1975, NASA launched the unmanned spacecraft *Viking 1* and *Viking 2*, both of which were headed for Mars. Each craft consisted of two parts, one designed to orbit Mars and transmit images of the planet to Earth, and the other designed to land on the martian surface and then move about, gathering and transmitting biological, chemical, physical, meteorological, seismological, and other information. The orbiters arrived at their destinations in mid-1976, the landers at theirs a few weeks later, and each continued to work for periods ranging from nearly two years (in the case of *Viking 2*'s orbiter) to more than six years (*Viking 1*'s lander). One member of the *Viking* team, Joseph F. Veverka,

taught a graduate-level course at Cornell that focused on Mars. As a junior Squyres signed up for
it, and Veverka—who had hesitated to include in
the class an undergraduate, especially one who
was not majoring in astronomy—soon came to rank
him among his best students. To get ideas for a research project required for the course, Squyres received permission to examine *Viking*-project images and other materials stored in the Astronomy
Department's warehouse-sized Mars Room. When
he emerged, four hours later, he recalled to the
ABC News interviewer, he knew "exactly what I
wanted to do with the rest of my life."

One reason why Squyres finds Mars so interesting is that in contrast to Earth, where nearly continual geological activity has destroyed evidence of
the beginnings of life, Mars has been geologically
quiescent, for the most part, so that the rocks on
half of its surface are more than four billion years
old—about as old as the planet itself. "So if life
arose on Mars," as Squyres explained to Don Hladiuk for the *StarSeeker* (September 2005, on-line), "a
big if, but if it did, the record of that event and how
it took place could actually still be preserved in
Martian rocks. It might be the place that we could
go to see how life originates." In *Roving Mars*
Squyres wrote, "Finding evidence that life arose
independently on another planet would be one of
the most profound discoveries that humans could
ever make. If you only know that a miracle has happened once, then it may be a rare, or even singular,
event. But if you can prove that it happened *twice
in the same solar system*—recognizing that there
may be countless solar systems out there—it means
that, while no less wondrous a miracle, it may be
a universal one. . . . And if we go [to Mars] and
find that the conditions were once warm, wet and
habitable, yet that somehow life *didn't* emerge,
then we have learned something profound about
the conditions that are required for life to develop."

Squyres earned a B.A. degree in geology in 1978
and a Ph.D. in 1981 in planetary science, both from
Cornell. Concurrently, from 1978 to 1981, he
served as an associate with a team that analyzed
images generated by *Voyager 1* and *Voyager 2*, unmanned spacecraft that were launched in 1977 to
convey data from flybys of Saturn and Venus.
(*Voyager 2* later transmitted information while
passing by Uranus and Neptune. Powered by plu-
tonium, both spacecraft are currently traveling in
the outer reaches of the solar system, and sometime
within the first quarter of the 21st century, they
will move into interstellar space, beyond the gravitational effects of the sun but not beyond the reach
of receivers on Earth.) For five years beginning in
1981, as a postdoctoral associate and research assistant, Squyres worked at Ames Research Center,
a NASA facility in Mountain View, California. Ex-
aminations of images of Europa, one of Jupiter's
four large moons (there are at least 59 smaller
ones), led him and another Ames researcher, David
Reynolds, to theorize that the existence of life on

Europa was remotely possible. Their theory, presented at a 1982 American Geophysical Union
meeting, was based on the presence of ephemeral
cracks that appear in the ice that covers Europa to
a depth of several miles; the cracks, Squyres and
Reynolds speculated, "could let through as much
sunlight as penetrates the perpetual ice of Antarctica," in the words of a reporter for the Associated
Press (December 14, 1982, on-line). Organisms that
live underneath Antarctica's ice "do quite well,"
Reynolds told that reporter.

In 1986 Squyres accepted an invitation to join
the Astronomy Department at Cornell. Eager to
participate in preparing a mission to Mars, he resolved to become an important contributor to such
a project, as an outside contractor. As he recalled
in *Roving Mars*, "At a minimum I was going to have
to learn how to build a scientific instrument that
could go into space." Since he had scientific kno-
whow but no engineering training, he recruited
others whose expertise would complement his, organizing a team whose proposal might someday
meet the requirements specified in one of NASA's
so-called Announcements of Opportunity (AOs).
An AO, in Squyres's words, "describes the spacecraft that NASA intends to fly . . . [and] in very
broad terms the science that the spacecraft is expected to do." In 1989 he and two collaborators
won a grant from NASA (worth $100,000 per year
for three years) to build the prototype of a camera
that would convey images of the surface of Mars
back to Earth. Their panoramic camera was completed in 1992, and that year NASA released the
AO for a similar camera, to be installed on Mars
landers for a project called the Mars Environmental Survey. In 1993 NASA rejected the model that
Squyres and his teammates had produced. A second, more ambitious proposal, submitted by
Squyres and his second team for a 1998 mission to
Mars, was also rejected. Then, in late 1995,
Squyres formed a new team, with the goal of producing a proposal for a mission to Mars as part of
NASA's Discovery program (which would support
acceptable plans for investigating any of the planets). "Under Discovery, a PI [principal investigator,
the person designated as the head of a research
project] could propose not just an instrument or a
payload, but an entire mission: payload, spacecraft, rocket, the whole shebang," Squyres explained in *Roving Mars*. In 1997 Squyres learned
yet again that his work, and that of his team, had
failed to win approval from NASA. That rejection
left him feeling both "drained and disheartened,"
as he wrote. "The main focus of my career for all
those years had been writing proposals to NASA,
all of them the best I could do, and all of them failures. It was time to now begin a fourth, but the fun
had gone out of it. The main thing driving me still
was fear: the fear that if we didn't try again, and if
we didn't win it this time, those years of work
would have been in vain." On November 2, 1997
Squyres learned that his fourth effort, a proposal
for sending an unmanned mission to Mars in 2001,

had met with success. His excitement diminished somewhat when, less than six months later, NASA pushed the mission back two years and decreased its budget. Then, following the extremely costly failures, in 1999, of two other Mars missions (with which Squyres was not associated), NASA decided that Squyres's team should send not one but two identical rovers to Mars as soon as that planet was at the point in its orbit when it was nearer to Earth than it had been for thousands of years and was in a good position relative to the sun. (The distance to both was crucial because the rovers were to be solar-powered.) That alignment was to occur in June 2003. Thus, 34 months remained in which to build and test models of the rovers and their payload and then the vehicles and instruments that were to be sent to Mars.

As Squyres made vividly clear in *Roving Mars*, completing that assignment (mostly at the NASA-supported Jet Propulsion Laboratory, a division of the California Institute of Technology, in Pasadena, California) involved not only repeated, frustrating failures in trials of many of the myriad parts of the instruments and vehicles, but also disagreements among members of the team, particularly between scientists, on one hand, and engineers on the other. As he explained in his book, "Scientists are seekers of truth. They're people who look at the world and wonder how it works. Scientists are people with hunches, and the good ones are people who know how to pursue those hunches to the correct conclusions, whatever they might be and however long it might take them. . . . Engineers, on the other hand, are creators. They are tinkerers and inventors. To an engineer, the goal is to build a machine that works. And even better is to build a machine that works right. The best engineers can look at a problem and not just find a design for a machine that can solve it. They can find the best design that can solve it. But engineering is a real-world pursuit, and in the real world you have to deal with realities like finite budgets and schedule deadlines. Engineers wrestle with these realities daily, often compromising their profound aesthetic sense of what makes a good design to arrive at one that is simply *good enough*—but that gets the job done on time and within budget. The problem when engineers and scientists have to work together is that 'good enough' is anathema to a scientist. There's no such thing as 'good enough' when what you're after is the truth. So on every space project, there is a tension: the idealistic, impractical scientists against the stubborn, practical engineers."

Arguments and tensions notwithstanding, the launches of the rovers, Spirit and Opportunity, took place on schedule, on June 10 and July 7, 2003, respectively. Spirit landed on Mars on January 3, 2004, and Opportunity set down on the opposite side of the Red Planet three weeks later. Each rover has six wheels and a robotic arm and is equipped with, among other devices, a high-resolution panoramic camera capable of recording and sending 360-degree, stereoscopic color im-

ages; magnets, for collecting magnetic particles of dust; a rock abrasion tool, for exposing the interiors of dusty or weathered rocks; a miniature thermal emission spectrometer, for determining the composition of rocks from a distance; a Mössbauer spectrometer, for identifying iron-bearing rocks and soils; and an alpha particle X-ray spectrometer, for identifying and measuring the concentrations of chemical elements in rocks and soils. Both spectrometers also analyze magnetic dust particles and airborne dust and rocks ground up by the rock abrasion tool. As a fact sheet mounted on jpl.nasa.gov explained, "Like a human field geologist, each Mars Exploration Rover has the capabilities to scout its surroundings for interesting rocks and soils, to move to those targets and to examine their composition and structure." According to marsrovers.nasa.gov, "Before landing, the goal for each rover was to drive up to 40 meters (about 131 feet) in a single day, for a total of up to one kilometer (about three-quarters of a mile)" during a three-month-long mission. But both rovers have traveled much farther per day and in total during the mission, which as of mid-October 2006 had continued for more than two and three-quarter years; indeed, on one day in 2004, Opportunity covered a distance of 140.9 meters (about 462 feet). When Don Hladiuk asked Squyres what he considered "the most important discovery made by the two rovers," he answered, "The most important discovery was the realization that at the Opportunity landing site there was once liquid water, not just beneath the ground, but water that came to the surface. Water that you could wade in, or swim in, or something. It was an environment that at some level would have been suitable for some kinds of life."

Squyres told David Brand for the *Cornell Chronicle* (August 19, 2004, on-line) that he will not direct NASA's Mars Science Laboratory, which is scheduled to launch in 2009. The MER Mission, he said, "has been an enormous amount of work. It has been a huge amount of time away from my family. I just cannot ask my wife and my daughters to make that kind of sacrifice again." Squyres and his wife, Mary, have two teenage daughters, Nicky and Katy, and live in Ithaca, New York. His honors include the 1987 Harold C. Urey Prize, from the Division for Planetary Sciences of the American Astronomical Society; the Space Science Award of the American Institute of Aeronautics and Astronautics and the Carl Sagan Award of the American Astronautical Society (the latter shared with his MER team), both in 2004; and a Rave Award from the publication *Wired* in 2005. Also in 2005 he was elected a Fellow of the American Academy of Arts and Sciences. Squyres carries a watch that keeps martian time, according to which a day (called a "sol") is 24 hours, 39 minutes, and 35 seconds long. His recreational interests include cycling and deep-sea diving.

—D.F.

Suggested Reading: ABC News (on-line) Jan. 9, 2006; *Cornell Chronicle* (on-line) Aug. 19, 2004; jpl.nasa.gov/missions; marsdaily.com; marsrovers.nasa.gov; pbs.org/wgbh/nova; *Science News* (on-line) Jan. 24, 2004; *Scientific American* (on-line) Sep. 27, 2004; solarviews.com; *StarSeeker* (on-line) Sep. 2005; Squyres, Steve. *Roving Mars: Spirit, Opportunity, and the Exploration of the Red Planet*, 2005

Selected Books: *Roving Mars: Spirit, Opportunity, and the Exploration of the Red Planet*, 2005

Bill Pugliano, Newsmakers/Getty Images

Stabenow, Debbie

(STAB-a-now)

Apr. 29, 1950– U.S. senator from Michigan (Democrat)

Address: 133 Hart Senate Office Bldg., Washington, DC 20510

Debbie Stabenow began her career in public service at age 25, winning election to a board of county commissioners in Ingham, Michigan. In 2000, after 30 years of service in county and state government and in the U.S. House of Representatives, Stabenow became Michigan's first female U.S. senator, narrowly defeating the one-term Republican incumbent, Spencer Abraham, in one of the country's most closely watched senate races. She has since gained a national reputation as a centrist Democrat, who embraces her party's traditional stances on many issues—supporting abortion rights, gun control, and funding for the arts—while backing Republicans' efforts to outlaw desecration of the flag and voting in favor of trying juveniles as adults in prosecuting violent crimes. Stabenow is perhaps best known for advocating the inclusion of prescription-drug coverage in Medicare, the federal program that serves nearly 40 million elderly and disabled Americans. She has also fought efforts by Senate Republicans and President George W. Bush to privatize Social Security, and she was the author of a bill that resulted in the first-ever federal ban on drilling for oil and gas in the Great Lakes. In the Senate she has served on the Agriculture, Nutrition and Forestry, Budget and Banking, Housing and Urban Affairs, and Special Aging Committees. Advancing quickly in the Senate, on November 16, 2004 she became the Senate Democrats' third-ranking member, having been elected by her colleagues as secretary of the Democratic caucus. In addition, the senator has been active in bolstering her party's ranks, serving as vice chair of the Democratic Senatorial Campaign Committee—charged with recruiting and fund-raising for prospective Senate Democrats—and chair of the Women's Senate Network, which encourages women, through financial support, to seek elective office. She told Eric Schmitt for the *New York Times* (November 13, 2000), "It is important that we have moms in the United States Senate, and daughters and sisters, as well as dads." The longtime Democratic U.S. senator Carl Levin of Michigan explained to Dee-Ann Durbin for the Associated Press (September 20, 2000) that Stabenow is "unusual in her innate ability to relate to people, and that's been there as long as I've known her." In a bid for a second term in the Senate, Stabenow ran against the Republican Mike Bouchard, a Michigan county sheriff, whom she defeated handily.

The oldest of three children, Deborah Ann Stabenow was born on April 29, 1950 to Robert Greer and Ann Greer in Gladwin, Michigan, and was later raised in the small town of Clare. Her father sold cars—Oldsmobiles and Cadillacs—and later became an insurance agent; her mother was a nurse. Stabenow's parents demonstrated little interest in politics. They nonetheless instilled in her a sense of responsibility toward others, setting an example by donating their time to their local church and hospital. Service was "a very strong value in our family, related to faith, but also civic responsibility," Stabenow, a devout Methodist, told Durbin. "Whenever we would complain about something, [our parents] would say, 'What are you going to do about it?'" When Stabenow was young, she and her parents and brothers, Lynn and Lee, formed a band, with Stabenow as the singer; they performed mostly for their own enjoyment or to entertain friends and other family members. "We still love to do that," Stabenow told reporters for *People* (November 5, 2001).

Stabenow's first foray into politics came during her junior year at Clare High School, when she was elected president of her class. (She had campaigned on a platform that called for improvements to the prom.) Her extra-curricular activities included playing the clarinet in the school band, serving as a cheerleader, and editing the yearbook. Stabenow's brother Lynn recalled to *People* that his sister was an excellent student who "came home with every book in her locker every night." While attending Michigan State University in East Lansing, Stabenow participated in protests against U.S. military involvement in the Vietnam War. To help finance her college education, she played folk songs in nearby coffeehouses. Also while a college student, Stabenow served as a volunteer in the campaign of the 1972 Democratic presidential nominee, George S. McGovern. "I began to see that government affected my life, whether I was paying attention or not," she told Durbin. (In the general election McGovern lost in a landslide to the incumbent president, Richard Nixon.) After she completed coursework in a multidisciplinary program, Stabenow received an undergraduate degree in 1972 from Michigan State University.

As an undergraduate the future politician had married Dennis Stabenow. In 1972 she helped him in his candidacy for a seat on the Ingham County Board of Commissioners. One of the more enjoyable assignments she undertook in that capacity was traveling door-to-door to greet her husband's prospective constituents. Noting her natural ability for such work, those close to Stabenow persuaded her to consider running for public office on her own in the future. After her husband failed to win election as a county commissioner, Stabenow returned to Michigan State to study social work, receiving a master's degree, magna cum laude, in 1975. Afterward she worked at area public schools as a counselor.

During that time Stabenow became incensed when a local county commissioner threatened to shut down the only nursing-home facility in Lansing that readily accepted recipients of Medicaid. "My mother's words came back to me," she told Durbin: "'What are you going to do about it?'" Absorbed by the issue, Stabenow took on a leadership role for a group protesting the planned closure. After the group succeeded in preventing the facility from being shut down, Stabenow decided to run for county commissioner. (According to Durbin, the nursing home is still open.)

In her 1975 run for a seat on the county board, Stabenow was pitted against the man who had defeated her husband earlier (and who referred to Stabenow as "that young broad"). The 25-year-old Stabenow stunned many when she won the election. Stabenow told Eric Schmitt, "I saw being involved in government as a vehicle to get things done in the community." She quickly began to use her influence to tackle issues she felt to be of concern to the people of her county. According to Durbin, during Stabenow's tenure on the board, the

county expanded its prison system, cleaned Lake Lansing, and streamlined its system of government. From 1977 to 1978 Stabenow served as the board's chair, becoming the youngest person and the first woman to do so.

In 1979 Stabenow was elected to Michigan's House of Representatives, from Lansing. Early in her career as a state legislator, she took on such issues as finance and taxation. In a move that surprised some colleagues, Stabenow chose to forgo an invitation from House leaders to sit with the body's six other female members on a women's rights committee, viewing the offer as patronizing. Turning her attention to issues affecting children, in 1982 Stabenow helped spearhead major reforms to Michigan law governing the collection of child support. Later, then-President Ronald Reagan used the law as a model for federal reforms. Stabenow became the first woman in Michigan to preside over the House. Her 12-year stay in the state House of Representatives ended in 1991, when she won election to the state Senate.

Over the next four years, Stabenow became a popular state senator, with a reputation as a hard worker and aggressive campaigner. Appealing to Michigan's families, she sponsored laws that stiffened penalties for drunk drivers. One of her more memorable acts as a state senator came in 1993, when she was a leading advocate of a bill to abolish Michigan's high property taxes, which were funding the state's public-school system. The bill became law in 1994, leading to wholesale changes to the state's apparatus for school finance; a sales tax was introduced to make up for the $6 billion in tax revenues that were to be lost.

Supporting a measure that was deemed conservative took a toll on Stabenow's popularity. In the wake of the bill's passing, she lost the backing of several influential unions, an occurrence that is believed to have cost her the Democratic Party's 1994 gubernatorial nomination for Michigan, which she lost to the Democratic Michigan congressman Howard Wolpe. Impressed by Stabenow, Wolpe picked her as his running mate, but the two were defeated by the incumbent governor, John Engler, and his running mate, Connie Binsfield. The loss ushered in the first—and to date, only—hiatus from public service in Stabenow's long career.

In 1996, in her bid to join the U.S. House of Representatives, Stabenow capitalized on her reputation as a hard worker on such issues as domestic violence, child-abuse prevention, and mental-health care to defeat the one-term Republican incumbent, Dick Chrysler, and claim the seat representing Michigan's Eighth District. Running as a moderate Democrat, Stabenow vowed to fight for the middle class, and some argued that her success in characterizing Chrysler as a disciple of then-House Speaker Newt Gingrich was helpful in securing her 10-point margin of victory. (For almost two decades prior to Chrysler's slight 1994 win, the Eighth District seat had been occupied by Democrats.) In the House Stabenow served on the Agriculture and Science Committees. Making a priority of applying technology to education, she co-sponsored legislation to provide tax incentives for businesses that donate computers and computer training to public schools. As a member of the Agriculture Committee, to help farmers within her own district, Stabenow supported funding for a Michigan State University study of a disease known as wheat scab, which had adversely affected crop growth.

Meanwhile, Stabenow also demonstrated a willingness to work with House Republican lawmakers. She voted for GOP-sponsored measures to restructure the nation's public-housing system and supported a Republican proposal to amend the Constitution to outlaw desecration of the U.S. flag. In addition, in July 1997 Stabenow supported the balanced-budget agreement settled on by congressional Republicans and then-President Bill Clinton; many liberal House Democrats opposed the agreement. Having successfully built a reputation as a "pragmatic problemsolver," according to Congressional Quarterly's Politics in America 2000: the 106th Congress, Stabenow easily won reelection in 1998, taking 57 percent of the vote against former Michigan representative Susan Grimes Munsell. Democratic representative Nancy Pelosi of California, currently the minority leader of the House, offered the following assessment of her colleague's demeanor to Dee-Ann Durbin: "Even though I've been in Congress much longer, I view her as a role model in the strong but gentle manner in which she wins the day for her issues. She knows her issues, she loves her constituents and she respects her colleagues."

Stabenow's hard-fought 2000 election-year battle against Michigan's first-term Republican incumbent senator, Spencer Abraham, attracted national attention. Abraham went into the contest with a financial advantage, having raised nearly $14 million. Early on, public-opinion polls suggested that Abraham would win handily; the incumbent built up double-digit leads in some parts of the state, largely through a blitz of aggressive television advertisements. Stabenow, however, mounted a successful counteroffensive. Among other stands, she championed prescription-drug benefits for the elderly; she sponsored a series of bus trips, collectively dubbed the Stabenow Express, that took seniors into Canada, where medications could be purchased at lower prices than in the U.S. She performed well in two debates with Abraham, eroding the incumbent's lead. According to Politics in America 2004, a large number of African-Americans and union members supported Stabenow, who was also the top recipient of donations from EMILY's list, a political action committee that backs abortion rights. On Election Day Stabenow won by slightly more than 67,000 votes of the 4.1 million cast. She thus became the first female U.S. senator elected from Michigan.

In the 107th Congress, which began in January 2001, as part of a push to include prescription-drug coverage in Medicare, Stabenow accepted the role of chairwoman of her party's prescription-drug task force. An outspoken opponent of powerful drug companies, she proposed limiting tax deductions for such businesses to the amount that they spend on developing new drugs. "We pay the pharmaceutical corporations at the prescription counter and through billions of dollars in taxpayer subsidies," she was quoted as saying in Politics in America 2004, "and they, in turn, spent more than twice as much on advertising and marketing techniques as they do on research and development. This is simply not acceptable." Thanks in part to Stabenow's efforts, Congress passed legislation allowing reimportation from Canada of U.S.-manufactured drugs and clearing the way for generic drugs—which are less expensive than brand-name medicines—to go on the market more easily. Also in the 107th Congress, turning her attention to protecting workers in Michigan's steel industry, Stabenow expressed her desire for a tariff on imported steel higher than the 30 percent imposed by President Bush.

Stabenow was appointed in late 2002 as vice chairperson of the Democratic Senatorial Campaign Committee, a group that works to get Democrats elected to the Senate through recruiting and fund-raising. In July 2004 she gave the opening speech at the Democratic National Convention in Boston, Massachusetts, rallying support for her party's 2004 presidential nominee, Senator John F. Kerry of Massachusetts. Heading into the general election, Republicans enjoyed a three-person majority in the Senate, with 51 seats to the Democrats' 48 and one seat occupied by an independent; the Democrats lost an additional four seats in the election. On November 16, 2004 Stabenow became the Senate's third-ranking Democrat, having been elected by her colleagues to the position of secretary of the Democratic caucus. "It puts me more in a role to be able to have influence, to have a stronger voice in setting policy," Stabenow said to Ruby L. Bailey for the Detroit Free Press (November 29, 2004). She also said that she planned to rally support for providing prescription-drug coverage for seniors. In the 108th Congress Stabenow once again took on drug companies, seeking to remove provisions from 2002 homeland-security legislation protecting vaccine makers from legal actions. Rankling some conservatives, in September 2005 Stabenow voted against the confirmation of John G. Roberts, President George W. Bush's nominee to replace William H. Rehnquist as chief justice of the U.S. Supreme Court. (Roberts was confirmed as the 17th chief justice of the U.S. on September 29, 2005, by a full Senate vote of 78–22.)

In 2006, with the goal of reducing the volume of trash exported from the Canadian province of Ontario (part of which borders Michigan), Stabenow and Michigan's other U.S. senator, the Democrat Carl Levin, introduced a bill that would require officials at the U.S.–Canadian border to inspect incoming municipal waste, with the haulers absorbing the inspection costs. "Until the [Bush] administration uses its authority to stop the trash completely, it should be the Canadian trash-haulers, not American taxpayers, footing the bill for these inspections," Stabenow said, as quoted by a writer for the Ontario *Welland Tribune* (July 14, 2006). In August 2006 Stabenow and Levin reached an agreement with the Ontario Ministry of the Environment that called for the gradual elimination of municipal waste shipped to Michigan sites, with the process complete by the year 2010. Also in mid-2006 Stabenow drew criticism from Republican campaign officials in Michigan who accused her of "straddling the fence" regarding a federal immigration-reform bill, as Donald Lambro reported in the *Washington Times* (June 5, 2006). One of four Senate Democrats to vote against the bill, Stabenow instead supported controversial amendments to it, one of which stated that "guest workers would not need an employer to attest forthcoming employment," as Lambro noted. To counter the perception of being soft on immigration reform, Stabenow, in an editorial published in the *Lansing State Journal* (May 31, 2006), reminded her constituency that she "do[es] not support amnesty. It is the wrong choice for our economy, rewards illegal behavior, and is unfair to people who have worked hard and come to our country legally." The Senate passed the bill, but the version passed in the House of Representatives was significantly different. Afterward leaders of both the House and the Senate decided to shelve the legislation until the next session of Congress.

In the weeks before the 2006 elections, Stabenow, seeking a second term in the Senate, continued to maintain a solid lead in opinion polls over her Republican challenger, Mike Bouchard. Nevertheless, with a substantial decline in Michigan's economy during the past year, she had to fend off charges of ineffective leadership and an overall lackluster record. "Only one state in America has lost jobs for three straight years and that's Michigan," Bouchard told Charles Hunt for the *Washington Times* (September 29, 2006). Stabenow was largely successful in blunting the force of her opponent's accusations, characterizing him as "someone who will support the failed Bush policies that have taken our jobs and threatened our middle-class way of life," according to Ken Thomas, a reporter for the Associated Press (August 9, 2006). On November 7, 2006 Stabenow easily defeated Bouchard, retaining her Senate seat in an election that saw Democrats regain control of the House and the Senate.

Debbie Stabenow—who "positively glows charisma," according to Marguerite Michaels, writing for *Time* (October 23, 2000)—has often distanced herself from the "liberal" label often attached to her party. *Politics in America 2000* quoted her as saying, "What I hear from people back home is, 'Forget the ideology. What are you doing to make

government work in a way that helps my family every day?'" In February 2003 Stabenow married Tom Athans, the co-founder of Democracy Radio, whose progressive format features hosts including Ed Schultz and Stephanie Miller. Stabenow has two grown children, Todd and Michelle, from her first marriage, which ended in divorce in 1990; from her marriage to Athans, she has a stepdaughter, Gina. Stabenow and Athans divide their time between their home in Lansing and Washington, D.C. Regarding her close connection with the city of Lansing, she told Schmitt: "It's where I bank and where my grocery store and dry cleaners are. I come home every weekend. I view this as a long-distance commute to work. That's not going to change."

—D.F.

Suggested Reading: Associated Press Sep. 20, 2000; *Detroit Free Press* B p1+ Nov. 29, 2004, p1+ Oct. 26, 2006; *New York Times* A p14 Nov. 13, 2000; *People* p105+ Nov. 5, 2001; *Washington Times* A p1+ Sep. 29, 2006; Duncan, Philip D. and Brian Nutting, eds. *Congressional Quarterly's Politics in America 2000: 106th Congress*, 1999; Hawkings, David and Brian Nutting, eds. *Congressional Quarterly's Politics in America 2004: 108th Congress*, 2003

Stein, Janice Gross

Apr. 16, 1943– Political scientist; educator; writer

Address: Munk Centre for International Studies, University of Toronto, 1 Devonshire Pl., Toronto, Ont., Canada M3P 3K7

Janice Gross Stein is a scholar who has devoted her professional life not only to research, writing, and teaching in the areas of international affairs, Middle Eastern politics, conflict resolution, and peacebuilding processes, but also to building bridges that connect specialists from the world of academia with people in government, nongovernmental organizations, and community groups and—of equal if not greater importance to her—members of the general public. A native of Canada, Stein is the founder and director of the Munk Centre for International Studies at the University of Toronto, in Ontario; she has taught at that school since 1981 and now holds the titles of university professor and Belzberg Professor of Conflict Management and Negotiation. In 2003 the Canada Council for the Arts, in recognizing her as "one of Canada's outstanding public intellectuals," awarded her its Molson Prize for her "outstanding lifetime contribution to the cultural and intellectual life of Canada." Stein, the council noted, "uses theory, not as an end in itself, but as a means of help-

Courtesy of the University of Toronto

Janice Gross Stein

ing people think intelligently about critical public policy and social problems." She has contributed to the forging of Canadian foreign and defense policies and even U.S. foreign policy, as a member of the Advisory Committee on International Peacekeeping of the Canadian minister for foreign affairs, vice chair of the Advisory Committee to the Canadian minister of defense, and member of the Committee on International Conflict Resolution of the U.S. National Academy of Sciences, to name only three of the many groups that she has served as an adviser. As an authority in her fields, she has regularly appeared on Canadian and U.S. television programs to comment on world and Canadian events. In 2000 Stein helped to launch the weekly Canadian television show *Going Global*, in which scholars, students, policy makers, and viewers (through telephone calls and E-mail messages) discuss current issues. Stein has written, co-written, or edited 20 books, among them *Rational Decision-Making: Israel's Security Choices, 1967*; *Psychology and Deterrence*; *Choosing to Co-operate: How States Avoid Loss*; *The Cult of Efficiency*; *Street Protests and Fantasy Parks: Globalization, Culture, and the State*; and *Networks of Knowledge: Collaborative Innovation in International Learning*. The subjects of the dozens of articles and book chapters she has written or co-written have ranged from psychology to U.S. foreign policy. Comparing Stein to the U.S. secretary of state during the second term of U.S. president Bill Clinton, Mark Pupo described her in *Toronto Life* (January 2002) as "Canada's answer to Madeleine Albright: a solemn academic with the tact of a diplomat."

Stein was born Janice Gross on April 16, 1943 in Montreal, Canada, to Clarence Gross, a lawyer, and Anne (Romoff) Gross, a homemaker and organization administrator. Her twin sister, Susan Gross Solomon, is a professor of Russian and East European studies at the Munk Centre. Stein's mother was among the first Canadian women to graduate from law school, completing her degree at McGill University in 1939; she never practiced law, however. After devoting herself to the care of her daughters when they were very young, she took high-level positions in philanthropic organizations, among them the National Women's League, the Canada-Israel Cultural Foundation, and the Canadian Zionist Federation. A person of great intellectual vigor, she awakened in her children social awareness and instilled in them a passion to make the world a better place. Stein became interested in national and international affairs during childhood. "One of my earliest memories was seeing the newspaper headlines about the war in Korea [1950–53] and before that, in 1948, in the Middle East," Stein told Paul Fraumeni for the University of Toronto publication *Edge* (Spring 2002). "I remember not understanding what was happening but also thinking, 'There must be a better way.' So as soon as I could, I began taking courses in high school in world history. I knew that was what I was going to do for life."

After her high-school graduation, Stein enrolled at McGill University, in Montreal, where she studied political science, security policy, and military history. After earning a B.A. degree, with first-class honors in history and political science, in 1964, she attended Yale University, in New Haven, Connecticut; she received an M.A. degree in international relations the following year as a Woodrow Wilson Fellow. Stein then returned to McGill, where, as a McConnell Fellow, she pursued a doctorate in political science. At the same time she began teaching political science at Carleton University, in Ottawa, Canada, with the rank of assistant professor. In 1968 she left Carleton to teach political science at McGill. She received a Ph.D. from McGill the next year and was promoted to associate professor in 1973. During the 1973–74 academic year, Stein briefly taught at the Hebrew University of Jerusalem as a visiting professor, gathering information related to conflict management in the Middle East.

In 1980 Stein wrote her first book, *Rational Decision Making: Israel's Security Choices, 1967*, in collaboration with the American political scientist Raymond Tanter. The book discusses Egypt's closing of the Straits of Tiran (which connect the Gulf of Aqaba with the Red Sea) to Israeli shipping, along with other events that led Israel to attack Egypt in 1967, launching what became known as the Six Day War. The war involved forces from Jordan, Iraq, and Syria as well as Israel and Egypt and ended with Israel in control of the Gaza Strip, the West Bank, the Sinai Peninsula, and the Golan Heights. Stein and Tanter examined Israel's decision to take preemptive military action as a case study in three contrasting models of decision making. The book attracted much attention among academics and earned Stein the Edgar Furniss Award of the Mershon Center of Ohio State University, given to an author "whose first book makes an exceptional contribution to the study of national and international security."

With her reputation as a scholar on the rise, in 1981 Stein landed a position as a professor of political science at the University of Toronto, one of the largest and most respected universities in Canada. She continued to produce books and articles in quick succession on such topics as negotiation theory, foreign-policy decision making, and international conflict management. While she focused largely on the political aspects of such topics, Stein offered a distinctive, multifaceted perspective on Middle Eastern and security issues by bringing other branches of knowledge to bear in her discussions. "One discipline can shed important light on another," she explained to Paul Fraumeni. "So I've also worked in history and psychology to bridge the insights, as well as sociology and organizational theory, with rudimentary work in economics and management. You ask a different set of questions that way, as opposed to working in only one discipline." In *Psychology and Deterrence* (1985), which she co-authored with two other leading political scientists, Robert Jervis and Richard Ned Lebow, Stein drew from psychology and conflict management to advance arguments that challenged accepted deterrence theory, which assumes that states act rationally. By considering psychological factors that might significantly influence the outcome of political deterrence strategies, Stein argued that governments that display their military might in order to intimidate others may instead provoke the types of actions that they seek to prevent. She built on that line of reasoning in *We All Lost the Cold War* (1994), co-authored with Richard Ned Lebow. In light of the ineffectuality of once-accepted deterrence strategies, Stein argued, states must clearly distinguish between the strategy of deterrence and reality. In the past, governments have taken the strategic approach, making misinformed assumptions and acting on them to produce counterproductive and extremely tense political situations. Stein maintained that if governments accurately assess the realities of both (or all) parties' interests and concerns, policy makers would be much more judicious about issuing threats or deploying military force. Among political scientists, Stein's arguments against the use of deterrence strategy in situations calling for conflict management and negotiation were praised as revolutionary and thought-provoking.

Among students at the University of Toronto, Stein is exceptionally popular, known for her ability to involve people of various majors in lively exchanges concerning political and social issues. She believes that discussion plays an important role in the learning process, not least because it alerts students to alternative viewpoints. Stein has also acted on her conviction that social scientists have obligations beyond the halls of academe. She envisioned the university's Munk Centre for International Relations, which she founded (it opened officially in 2000) and directs, as a venue for interdisciplinary research on global issues and open and thoughtful discourse linking researchers and teachers with the public. One of the center's divisions is called the Citizen Lab, which, according to its Web site, brings together social scientists, social activists, filmmakers, computer scientists, and artists and focuses on "advanced research and development at the intersection of digital media and world civic politics." In one past Citizen Lab project, Canadian and Mexican students lobbied government officials on North American water-policy issues; in another, three University of Toronto students with exceptional skills in computer hacking helped human-rights activists in Central America protect their privacy and freedom of speech through technology. On another front, in 2000 Stein co-created the weekly TV series *Going Global*, to stimulate discussions on world affairs in a call-in format. The series is filmed at the Munk Centre, with professors, policy experts, and students participating. "The philosophy in starting it was that we have many people in the university who think deeply about global issues and that we need to share that knowledge with the public," Stein told Paul Fraumeni. "People are genuinely interested in world affairs. They can get information easily enough, but the university can provide analysis that helps them understand the information. For example, we know what happened on Sept. 11. But why did it happen? That's what *Going Global* does. I think we've really struck a chord, and I'm thrilled about that." In its first season the show attracted 450,000 viewers—an impressive number in Canada, whose population is less than 33 million.

After the terrorist attacks of September 11, 2001, Stein found herself much in demand by the media for her expertise in Middle Eastern affairs and foreign policy, and she became a frequent commentator on Canadian and American television news programs. She has often appeared on *CBC News: The National*, a nightly news program produced for the Canadian Broadcasting Corp., and she is a regular panelist on the weekly TVOntario programs *Studio Two* and *Diplomatic Immunity*. Also in 2001 Stein delivered the Massey Lectures, a prestigious weeklong lecture series that is sponsored by the University of Toronto. (Past lecturers include John Kenneth Galbraith, Martin Luther King Jr., Carlos Fuentes, Doris Lessing, Jane Jacobs, and Noam Chomsky.) In a synopsis of the lectures for CBC-TV (on-line), Stein wrote that they were about "post-industrial society in the making. There is a growing emphasis on efficiency in this era of globalization, and the language of efficiency shapes the way citizens think about their most important shared values. But hidden in the polemics about efficiency are, I believe, much more important and enduring conversations about accountability and choice in post-industrial societies. . . . Surprisingly, I find that citizens want to see both less and more of the state. Although citizens in post-industrial society are less deferential, more distrustful of authority, and more confident of their capacity to make the important choices, the escape from the state is more apparent than real. Still another paradox lies deeper beneath the surface. Our conversation about efficiency has enabled not only a new discussion of accountability, but also about choice. Yet the way we think about choice hides many of the most intractable value conflicts in our society." The challenge, she concluded, is to "balanc[e] efficiency and accountability, rights and choice, to construct the public good." Stein expanded her Massey Lectures for her book *The Cult of Efficiency* (2001). Her book *Reflections on a Scholar's Journey into the World*, a collection of already-published and new essays, is slated to appear in 2008.

Stein has served as a member of the editorial boards of a dozen scholarly journals, among them *Études International, International Journal, Negotiation Journal, International Organization, Political Psychology,* the *European Journal of International Relations,* and the *American Political Science Review.* She is a fellow of the Royal Society of Canada and an honorary fellow of the American Academy of Arts and Sciences. She was a Trudeau Fellow for three years, beginning in 2003, and earned an honorary doctorate of laws from the University of Alberta in 2006.

"Imposing on TV, [Stein] is small and grandmotherly in person," Mark Pupo wrote. "She has the trained pundit's habit of nodding to the rhythm of her words." Stein is married to Michael B. Stein, a professor of political science at McMaster University, in Hamilton, Ontario. The couple live in Toronto and have two sons, Isaac and Gabriel.

—I.C.

Suggested Reading: *Time International* p121 Dec. 22, 2003; *Toronto Life* p6+ Jan. 2002; *Toronto Star* B p5 July 8, 2004; University of Toronto Web site; (University of Toronto) *Edge* (on-line) Spring 2002

Selected Books: *Rational Decision Making: Israel's Security Choices* (with Raymond Tanter), 1967; *Psychology and Deterrence* (with Robert Jervis and Richard Ned Lebow), 1985; *The Cult of Efficiency,* 2001; with Richard Ned Lebow— *When Does Deterrence Succeed and How Do We Know?,* 1990; *We All Lost the Cold War,* 1994; as editor—*Peacemaking in the Middle East: Problems and Prospects,* 1985; *Power Keg in the Gulf: Security in the Middle East,* 1995; *Street Protests and Fantasy Parks,* 2002

Stern, Jessica

Feb. 11, 1958– Expert on terrorism; writer; educator

Address: Kennedy School of Government, Rubenstein Bldg., Rm. 203, 79 John F. Kennedy St., Cambridge, MA 02138

When Jessica Stern entered the fledgling field of nuclear weaponry and terrorism, nearly two decades ago, few understood the significance of her work, through which she addresses the possibility that nuclear weapons will fall into the hands of terrorists and seeks ways to prevent such an occurrence. Many who knew Stern called her profession "bizarre." "I was used to people thinking I was very weird," she told Laura Shin for *Barnard Magazine* (Summer 2005). But after the terrorist attacks of September 11, 2001, terrorism and national security became ubiquitous topics for discussion, and news organizations have repeatedly published or broadcast statements obtained from terrorism experts. Few of those experts can boast of anything like the credentials, experiences, and accomplishments that have brought Stern renown. Having earned a bachelor's degree in chemistry, a master's degree in chemical engineering and technology policy, and a doctorate in public policy, she has worked in scientific laboratories, at the National Security Council (NSC), and, since 1999, as a lecturer at the Belfer Center for Science and International Affairs at Harvard University's John F. Kennedy School of Government. At the NSC she headed the Nuclear Smuggling Group, whose work inspired the film *The Peacemaker* (1997), which features a character based on Stern. Among her most unusual characteristics is her willingness, and even eagerness, to step beyond the safe boundaries of academia in conducting her research. For her critically acclaimed book *Terror in the Name of God: Why Religious Militants Kill* (2003), the diminutive Stern, who is of Jewish descent, interviewed some 75 terrorists around the world, many of them radical Muslims. While she has sought to understand the impulses that lead to hatred and violence, she hopes that her work will help to "make people feel better," as she told *Current Biography.* Her first book, *The Ultimate Terrorists,* was published in 1999.

Jessica Eve Stern was born on February 11, 1958 in New Rochelle, New York, to Ernest Stern, a solid-state physicist who had come to the U.S. as a refugee from Nazi Germany, and Shola Stern, a labor organizer. Her mother died three years after Jessica's birth. When Jessica Stern was about five, her father remarried and moved the family to Concord, Massachusetts, where Jessica was raised with her

Martha Stewart/Marthapix, courtesy of the Kennedy School of Government

Jessica Stern

sister, four stepsiblings, and two half-sisters. As a child Stern had a keen interest in an elementary form of chemistry. "I wanted to play around with stuff in the kitchen. I made my own [mixtures], what I decided was herbicide, but it really wasn't that at all," she told *Current Biography*. "I guess I was on the nerdy end of the spectrum." Nevertheless, she had no desire to attend college after her high-school graduation. Instead, for almost five years she worked in cafés, took dance classes, and read Russian novels. Then she enrolled at Barnard College (which is affiliated with Columbia University), in New York City. She considered herself the "arty" type and intended to focus on creative writing or Russian literature (she was fluent in the language), but she ended up majoring in chemistry, studying under the eminent organic chemist Jacqueline Barton. "Much to my surprise, it turned out that chemistry was the most fun for me and it turned out I was a bad writer. It was a lot easier on my ego to stick with science courses," she wrote for the Women of NASA Web site (1998).

For a time in the early 1980s, during her undergraduate years, Stern worked as an assistant to the commercial attaché (a specialist who worked for the U.S. State Department) in Moscow, in what was then the Soviet Union. She also took classes in technical Russian, went horseback riding in the Caucasus Mountains, studied ballet with a grand master, and attended performances at the Bolshoi Theater. The Cold War was raging then, and Stern was "very aware of what felt like the danger of war," as she told Lev Grossman for *Time* (December 17, 2001). "I became interested in national security living in Russia, and at that time, it was hard not to become interested in international security,"

she told *Current Biography*. "I still felt interested in chemistry, but I wanted to combine my interests, and so I was looking into nuclear weaponry to do that—something that people thought was a bizarre plan." Stern graduated from Barnard in 1985. At the suggestion of a friend, she abandoned her plan to pursue a Ph.D. in chemistry at Columbia and instead enrolled in an innovative master's-degree program in technology policy at the Massachusetts Institute of Technology (MIT), in Cambridge. "The program changed my life and allowed me to combine my interests in chemistry, Russia, and war," she wrote for Women of NASA. Stern gained expertise in such areas as science policy, engineering systems analysis, and economics. The subject of her master's thesis was chemical-weapons disarmament. She received an M.S. degree in chemical engineering and technology policy from MIT in 1988. She then entered the Kennedy School of Government, at Harvard University, also in Cambridge, to pursue a doctorate in public policy. For one year (1989–90) she was a Harvard MacArthur Fellow. Her dissertation was entitled "The Control of Chemical Weapons: A Strategic Analysis." She earned a Ph.D. from Harvard in 1992.

Stern next went to work as a postdoctoral fellow at Lawrence Livermore National Laboratory, in Livermore, California. She spent the next two years analyzing the potential for smuggling, or the unauthorized use of, nuclear weapons in Russia. In 1994 she was awarded an International Affairs Fellowship by the Council on Foreign Relations. That year, at the NSC, she helped to develop national policy aimed at preventing nuclear smuggling. "Normally [fellows] coming in for a year can't decide what they want to work on, and there are all these turf battles," Stern told Shin for *Barnard Magazine*. "But as it happened, nobody at the NSC was really working on the aspect of nuclear materials or weapons and the threat of nuclear terrorism." Thanks to her specialty, Stern was appointed the NSC's director of Russian, Ukrainian and Eurasian Affairs, in which her main task was the fashioning of national-security policy with regard to Russia and the former Soviet states. She also headed several other entities, among them the Nuclear Smuggling Group, which she had co-founded and which analyzed reports of nuclear theft and developed policies to reduce the threat of nuclear smuggling and terrorism. In addition, she helped oversee the final stages of Project Sapphire, a secret operation in which a large cache of highly enriched uranium was brought from Kazakhstan to a storage site in the U.S.

One day the NSC press office asked Stern to meet with the award-winning journalist Leslie Cockburn, who was known as something of a muckraker. A specialist in foreign affairs who had spent time in Russia, Cockburn knew that the smuggling of nuclear weapons was a real danger, and she asked Stern what the White House was doing to prevent it. Stern told Cockburn about the Nuclear Smuggling Group and the completed Project

Sapphire and, afterward, gave their conversation no more thought. But Cockburn used the information Stern had provided as the basis for her nonfiction book *One Point Safe* (1997), which discusses the efforts of the administration of President Bill Clinton to deal with the problem of unguarded nuclear weapons. Without Stern's knowledge, Cockburn adapted the book for a screenplay with Stern as the heroine and pitched the script to Dream-Works. Months later Stern received a telephone call from Michael Schiffer of DreamWorks and, at his request, met with him to discuss a filmscript about nuclear terrorism. To her surprise, she discovered that the reporter she had met earlier in the year for a seemingly routine interview had written the script. At the insistence of Stern, who served as a consultant for the movie, the studio renamed the character who was meant to be her and made that character less recognizable in other ways as well. "I thought [the movie] would be fun, but I also thought it could ruin my career," Stern told *Current Biography*. *The Peacemaker* centers on the frantic efforts of the main characters (played by Nicole Kidman and George Clooney) to prevent the detonation of a nuclear weapon in Manhattan; it drew mixed reviews and enjoyed moderate box-office success.

Stern left the NSC in 1995. In 1995–96 she held a fellowship at the Hoover Institution on War, Revolution and Peace, at Stanford University, in California. In 1998 and 1999 she worked at the Council on Foreign Relations, in Washington, D.C., as a so-called next-generation fellow; she was also known as a "superterrorism" fellow. Earlier, with the help of a MacArthur Foundation research and writing fellowship (1995–97), she had written *The Ultimate Terrorists*, which was published in 1999. The book offers a scholarly overview of the history of weapons of mass destruction, assesses the threat of chemical, biological, and nuclear terrorism (which, according to Stern, had been exaggerated in the media and by government spokesmen), and provides possible defenses against that threat. In a review of the book for *Salon* (March 23, 1999, online), Tim Cavanaugh wrote, "The ominous-sounding title . . . can't outweigh the balanced and blessedly concise arguments that Jessica Stern presents in the book itself." James T. Dunne wrote for *Security Management* (August 1, 2000), "*The Ultimate Terrorists* provides one of the better models of how such menaces might be approached, analyzed, and perhaps even countered. It's not the only book one should read on the topic, but it is one of the most incisive and refined."

For four years beginning in March 1998, while still working with the Council on Foreign Relations, Stern embarked on a project in which she ultimately interviewed 75 known terrorists of various religious affiliations, and family members of known terrorists, in the U.S. and widely scattered other parts of the world. She visited prisons and the homes of men who had killed ostensibly for reasons connected with their religious devotion.

Her decision to undertake the project, she admitted to *Current Biography*, was not particularly rational. "Usually, when you're in academia you do what you're trained to do, not what you're curious about. My whole career is on weapons of mass destruction and national security. I didn't get any training at all that would prepare me to talk to the perpetrators, but I was curious." Stern told a reporter for *BuzzFlash* (May 12, 2004, on-line), "It was only after Sept. 11 that I realized the nature of the real threat I had taken. For example, I did talk at length to the leader of a Pakistani jihadi group who is personal friends with bin Laden, and his group is very closely aligned with al-Qaeda. I knew that I didn't want to present myself to bin Laden. I thought that was not a very good idea, given my government experience. . . . But I didn't realize just how close I was getting. And of course, I did exactly what Daniel Pearl did"—a reference to a *Wall Street Journal* reporter who, after entering Pakistan in early 2002 in an attempt to meet and interview militants, was abducted and murdered. "I was scared on a number of occasions," Stern told Ron Hogan for *Publishers Weekly* (June 30, 2003), "but once I was in the presence of the militants, I didn't feel they were going to hurt me. My vulnerability as a woman alone also made me safer, ironically. I felt that I was entering a psychological compact: by making myself vulnerable to them, they would agree to take care of me and not kill me." But given the kidnappings and killings that have become everyday events in some areas, Stern told Buzzflash in 2004, "I would not, myself, repeat what I did in the post-Sept. 11 environment."

While growing up, as a member of a secular household, Stern had thought that "faith made people better—more generous, more capable of love," as she wrote in the introduction to *Terror in the Name of God: Why Religious Militants Kill* (2003), which is based on her 75 interviews. But after her first talk with Kerry Noble, the former second-in-command of Covenant, Sword and the Arm of the Lord (CSA), a violent apocalyptic cult active in the 1980s, she began asking herself, as she told Buzzflash.com, "How is it that people who profess strong moral values, who, in some cases, seem truly to be motivated by those values, can be brought to do evil things?" She tried to answer that question in the first part of *Terror in the Name of God*. In many cases, according to Stern, humiliation and fear of one thing or another lead people to join violent groups whose leaders persuade them that killing is a moral and religious duty and is not only looked on with favor by God, but commanded by Him. As is evident in the book, Stern questioned her subjects in a detached and nonjudgmental manner and seemed to empathize with them. "My colleagues have told me that they can't believe— they say they couldn't do it—that I am capable of sitting down and talking to someone whose views I reject completely, and, during the conversation, try to enter that person's head," she told Buzz-flash.com. "Try to really almost be that person for the period of the conversation, in terms of their thought process—to follow along with how they see the world. It's not just a matter of not expressing disapproval, but not allowing myself to think of disapproval." In the second part of her book, Stern described the structures of an array of terrorist organizations.

In one of the many enthusiastic reviews of the book, the neurologist and author Oliver Sacks wrote, as quoted on the book jacket, "Stern's extensive interviews with terrorists, and the empathetic (though never sympathetic) rapport she is able to establish, illuminates these states of mind which most of us can only regard with bewilderment and incomprehension. This is a psychological and moral achievement of a very rare order." In the *Boston Globe* (August 27, 2003), Scott Bernard Nelson wrote that *Terror in the Name of God* is "one of the most interesting books you'll ever read on terrorists and terrorism. . . . Stern opens an incredibly intriguing window into the minds of those who use God to justify violence against others." The London *Guardian* international-affairs columnist Isabel Hilton heralded Stern's work in the *New York Times Book Review* (November 16, 2003) as an "odyssey into the hearts and minds of religious terrorists. . . . On a subject that tends to be richer in rhetoric than in detail, a writer able and willing to get this close [to such extremists] is hard to find." Jonathan Schanzer, writing for the *Middle East Quarterly* (March 22, 2004), was similarly impressed: "Stern's work deserves praise. Most terror experts spend hours reading the tracts and communiqués of terrorists as a means to understand the radical mindset but never talk to terrorists directly.

Stern has taken that next step; her interviews bring the reader one step closer to getting inside the radical mind."

Stern currently lectures on public policy at Harvard. She is working on her next book, to be entitled "An Anatomy of Fear: An Inquiry into the Roots of Radicalism," which will examine how fear, especially of globalization and loss of identity, contributes to extremist behavior among individuals, and how fear "can also lead governments to react in a way that's even counterproductive and dangerous," as she told Shin for *Barnard Magazine*. Many op-ed pieces by Stern have been published in such major newspapers as the *New York Times*, the *Washington Post*, the *Boston Globe*, and *USA Today*. She has also written many articles for scholarly journals, among them *International Security*, the *Bulletin of Atomic Scientists*, the *Journal of the Centers for Disease Control and Prevention*, and the *Brookings Review*.

Stern lives in Cambridge, Massachusetts, with her son, Evan, who was five years old in 2006.

—I.C.

Suggested Reading: *Barnard Magazine* p17 Summer 2005; *BuzzFlash* (on-line) May 12, 2004; International Speakers Bureau Web site; ksgfaculty.harvard.edu; *Newsweek* p42 Oct. 1997; NPR.org; *Publishers Weekly* p71 June 2003; *Time* p62 Dec. 17, 2001; *Washington Post* B p1 Sep. 27, 1997; Women of NASA Web site, 1998

Selected Books: *The Ultimate Terrorists*, 1999; *Terror in the Name of God: Why Religious Militants Kill*, 2003

Stewart, Tony

May 20, 1971– Race-car driver

Address: c/o Joe Gibbs Racing, 5901 Orr Rd., Charlotte, NC 28213-6321

Decades ago, as Frank Deford noted in *Sports Illustrated* (November 28, 2005), Indy-car racing—involving sleek, open-wheel, single-seat cars with engines in the rear and open cockpits—"owned U.S. racing," while the National Association for Stock Car Auto Racing, or NASCAR, "was a regional sideshow, dismissed in sophisticated sports circles as a hillbilly carousel. Since then NASCAR has grown to be generally accepted as the fourth major American sport, after football, baseball and basketball." One driver who has succeeded in both Indy-car and NASCAR racing is Tony Stewart. As a boy, beginning when he was eight years old, Stewart won national titles in go-kart racing, and in 1995, in his mid-20s, he became the first driver ever to win the national midget, sprint-car, and sil-

ver-crown championships of the United States Auto Club (USAC). He then signed on as a NASCAR driver before joining the fledgling Indy Racing League (IRL); in 1997 he won the IRL championship. Since then, concentrating on NASCAR, Stewart has twice become the Nextel Cup (formerly Winston Cup) points champion, in 2002 and 2005.

Stewart's having bridged two worlds of auto racing might suggest that he is a conciliator of sorts; his behavior during competition, including sometimes violent clashes with racing officials, journalists, and other drivers, has proved otherwise. The former driver Benny Parsons said about Stewart, as reported by Hillary Wasch for ESPN.com, "You talk about a Jekyll and Hyde, that's Tony Stewart. Off the racetrack he's one of the most giving people that you've ever seen in your life. But on the racetrack, he has done some stupid things." The driver Jimmie Johnson explained to Mike Finney for the Wilmington, Delaware, *News Journal* (November 17, 2002) that Stewart is "a racer's racer. He might have done some things . . . that I'm sure he's not real happy with and that have left a negative mark

Chris Trotman/Getty Images

Tony Stewart

out there for him. But he loves the sport of racing and every racing fan respects that fact, that's he raced everything on the planet and won everything he's been in."

Anthony Wayne Stewart was born on May 20, 1971 in Rushville, Indiana, and was raised in Columbus, Indiana, less than one hour's drive from the Indianapolis Motor Speedway—a track that is often compared by racing enthusiasts, for its special place in the sport, to baseball's Yankee Stadium or Fenway Park. (The Indianapolis Moter Speedway is home to the annual Indianapolis 500, held on Memorial Day weekend.) Stewart's father, Nelson, worked in purchasing at the Indianapolis campus of Indiana University; his mother, the former Pam Boas, worked as a dental receptionist. His parents are now divorced. Stewart's sister, Natalie, and his mother help to run his official fan club.

When Stewart was six or seven years old, his father bought him a go-kart, and shortly afterward Stewart began entering races, under Nelson Stewart's tutelage. "He never let me settle for second," Stewart said about his father for his official Web site. "He didn't like it when we ran second, and he knew that I didn't like it when we ran second. . . . He never pressured me to be the best race car driver in the world, but he did pressure me to be the best race car driver that I could be. . . . That's probably why you see so much fire in me today." Beginning at an early age, Stewart looked up to the versatile, hot-tempered race-car driver A. J. Foyt, whom many consider to be one of the greatest American drivers of all time. (According to Bill Briggs, writing for the *Denver Post* [November 20, 2005], Stewart was named after Foyt, whose first name is Anthony.)

Stewart won his first national championship in 1980, at the Columbus Fairgrounds, in the four-cycle junior-class go-kart competition for rookie drivers aged eight to 12. In 1983, at 12, he won the championship in the Grand National division of the International Karting Federation, and he captured the World Karting Association national title in 1987. In 1989 Stewart jumped to competition in the higher-horsepower, open-wheel ranks of the United States Auto Club. Two years later he achieved USAC rookie-of-the-year honors as a sprint-car driver. (Sprint cars are smaller than standard-size race cars but larger than midget racers.) Stewart conceded to Bruce Lowitt for the *St. Petersburg (Florida) Times* (May 24, 1998) that with all the time he spent racing in his teen years, he had missed out on "normal teenage life, if there is such a thing."

In 1994 Stewart won his first USAC championship, with five victories in 22 midget starts, and finished sixth in the USAC silver-crown points championship. The following year he became the first driver to capture the USAC "triple crown," winning the 1995 national midget, sprint car, and silver-crown championships. His accomplishments led him to be compared to Jeff Gordon, who had enjoyed success in the USAC earlier in the decade before winning renown as a stock-car racer. "It's nice to be compared to him, but I don't want to be another Jeff Gordon," Stewart said to Al Pearce for the Newport News, Virginia, *Daily Press* (June 25, 1996). "I want to be Tony Stewart and do my best every time I get in a car."

While Stewart played down comparisons to Gordon, circumstances led him to turn his attention to NASCAR. As Bruce Lowitt reported, "By the time he was ready for some serious Indy-car racing," Stewart "discovered it was out of his league." Indeed, his parents had mortgaged their home just to pay the expenses of the go-kart races, and costs associated with the upper levels of Indy-car racing were beyond their means. "But the guys down south," Stewart told Lowitt, referring to NASCAR drivers, "they get hired to [drive] because of their talent, not what they have in their back pocket." Stewart signed a three-year contract with the Kentucky businessman and stock-car owner Harry Rainer to compete in the Busch series, a lower division of NASCAR.

Then, in January 1996, Stewart joined John Menard's Indy-racing team. That year the Championship Auto Racing Teams, a group of well-known, wealthy drivers and their teams, boycotted the Indianapolis 500, which provided unprecedented opportunities for lesser-known drivers—including Stewart, who competed in the upstart Indy Racing League. He had declined an offer to drive in the IRL for his boyhood idol, A. J. Foyt, who was by then a car owner; Foyt's condition was that Stewart not race in NASCAR, while Menard allowed him to maintain his affiliation with Rainer and drive in the NASCAR Busch series. Responding to critics who had misgivings about his split duties, Stewart said to Al Pearce, "Last year, people said I couldn't win three USAC championships in the same season. Now they're saying I can't run IndyCar and NASCAR in the same season. That makes me strive even harder to make it work."

In 1996 Stewart enjoyed a successful debut season in the Indy-racing ranks. Occupying the pole (or front) position in his first Indianapolis 500 start, as a result of the practice-round death of his teammate Scott Brayton, who had originally been assigned the position, Stewart led for many laps and was named the race's best rookie driver. For the season, Stewart finished in ninth place in the IRL's overall points standings and was tabbed the circuit's rookie of the year. That same year Stewart also started nine Busch series races for the Rainer racing team, affording him the opportunity to get used to the heavier NASCAR vehicles.

Stewart won the Indy Racing League title in 1997. (The championship is based on a points system, designed to reward consistency over a season.) He earned his first Indy-car victory that year in the circuit's inaugural event, at Pikes Peak, Colorado, and then coasted to the championship—aided by the slump that befell Davey Hamilton, the early points leader. Stewart also raced in a handful of NASCAR Busch-series events that year for Joe Gibbs, who had been head coach of the Washington Redskins football team (he returned to the Redskins in 2004). Like Menard, Gibbs was willing to let Stewart compete in various forms of racing, including occasional meets on dirt tracks. Stewart signed on with Gibbs to race in 22 Busch-series events in 1998. Many believed that those events would help prepare Stewart for NASCAR's more grueling Winston Cup competition. In 1998 he won two races from the pole position and achieved five top-five finishes. In Indy racing Stewart finished sixth in points in 1998, winning two races. In 1999 Gibbs promoted Stewart to the NASCAR Winston Cup division, whose demands effectively ended his IRL championship-racing career.

The sport of stock-car racing began as recreation among moonshiners in the South, who souped up their cars in order to evade government agents. NASCAR, founded in 1948, is currently the largest sanctioning body of motor sports in the United States. The three largest and most popular NASCAR series are the Busch series, which is akin to the triple-A leagues of professional baseball; the Craftsman Truck series; and the Nextel Cup series. The NASCAR Nextel Cup season, which was called the Winston Cup series from 1972 through 2003 and extends from February through November each year, consists of 26 regular-season point races, many of which are either 500 or 600 miles long. Each driver collects points based on his final position in a particular race; bonus points are awarded to the drivers who lead individual laps as well as to the driver who leads the most laps in one race. Since 2004, at the end of the regular season, NASCAR has held a 10-race play-off, the Chase for the Cup. Drivers who complete the regular season within the top 10 in points standings are eligible for the Chase, as is any driver within 400 points of the leader. As a spectator sport, stock-car racing has greatly increased in popularity in recent years; the Nextel series has split its television broadcast rights between the Fox and NBC networks.

Unlike other major U.S. sports, the NASCAR season begins with its crowning event, the Daytona 500 (also known as the "Great American Race"), which has been held every February since 1959 and is the highest-rated motor-sport event on television. Stewart made his Winston Cup debut at the 1999 Daytona 500, behind the wheel of an orange-and-black–trimmed, Home Depot–sponsored Pontiac Grand Prix; he began the race in the outside pole position, as the race's second-fastest qualifier. On September 11, 1999 Stewart won his first Winston Cup race, at the Richmond International Raceway, outside Richmond, Virginia. Overall, his first season was a resounding success, as he landed the highest points finish by a Winston Cup rookie (fourth) since 1972; achieved the most wins (three) by a rookie in Winston Cup history; and was awarded rookie-of-the-year honors after the season. On Memorial Day 1999 Stewart became one of only two drivers (the other was John Andretti) to race in both the Indianapolis 500 and the Coca-Cola 600, a Winston Cup race held that same evening in Charlotte, North Carolina. After finishing ninth in the first race, Stewart was transported by helicopter and then private jet to North Carolina, where he finished fourth in the Coca-Cola 600, despite suffering from lack of nourishment over the course of the event's final 100 laps. Stewart said after the race, according to Nancy Armour, writing for the Associated Press (May 31, 1999), "We were so concerned about keeping fluids in me we didn't think about getting food in." (Stewart completed that feat again in 2001, finishing sixth in the Indianapolis 500 and third in the Coca-Cola 600.)

During his second year of Winston Cup racing, in 2000, Stewart notched six victories, including two consecutive wins, but failed to improve on his rookie standing, and finished sixth in points. The following year, at the Daytona 500, Stewart's season began precariously, when he got into a crash and his vehicle tumbled several times. He recovered, however, to win three Cup races—at Richmond, Virginia; Sonoma, California, where Stewart and Joe Gibbs Racing each won a road-course race for the first time; and Bristol, Tennessee. Jeff Gordon finished several hundred points ahead of Stewart in 2001, capturing his fourth Winston Cup championship.

Rarely has Stewart completed a season of Winston/Nextel Cup racing without generating headlines for his aggressive behavior. In a Winston Cup race during his rookie season, following a crash with the driver Kenny Irwin Jr., Stewart exited his car and reached into Irwin's, attempting to land a punch. (A year later, in July 2000, Irwin was killed in a crash at New Hampshire International Speedway. Stewart won a racing trophy two days afterward and gave it to Irwin's family.) In July 2001 Stewart nearly came to blows with the Winston Cup series director, Gary Nelson, at the Pepsi 400 in Daytona, Florida, after receiving a black flag—used to summon drivers to the pits for disobeying rules. After the race Stewart smacked a tape recorder from a reporter's hand; NASCAR fined him $10,000 and placed him on probation for the remainder of the season for that act. Stewart is also known to have clashed with NASCAR officials over pre-race safety precautions. In addition, he has been outspoken about the steps taken by NASCAR at the behest of its corporate sponsors to punish drivers for aggressive behavior. Stewart told Ken Powers for the Massachusetts *Telegram & Gazette* (July 25, 2004), "I think NASCAR, in its effort to protect corporate America and their image, has taken a lot of the emotion out of racing. It's a manly sport, but NASCAR seems to be putting dresses on the drivers and crews." He added, "Drivers used to settle things themselves. Now, it's like we're in kindergarten. . . . I grew up in the Midwest driving midgets and sprints and silver crown cars, and guys would get in fistfights after the race and then they'd help each other load their cars and then stop for dinner together on the way home. It seemed problems settled themselves a lot quicker that way. I never saw a fistfight in the pits where someone had to be carried out on a stretcher. I've seen guys with bloody noses, bloody knuckles, but that was part of racing." That view notwithstanding, Stewart has consulted an anger-management specialist.

With six races remaining in the 2002 season, Stewart took the lead in points for the first time in his career, finishing second at a 500-mile race in Talladega, Alabama. Though he did not win any individual races in the remainder of the season, Stewart finished 38 points ahead of Mark Martin to win his first Winston Cup. Reflecting on the victory, Stewart was quoted as saying on his Web site, "If I had to retype my resume tomorrow, I'd put my NASCAR championship at No. 1. All of the championships I've been a part of were hard to acquire. None of them were easy. They had their unique set of circumstances, obstacles and challenges to overcome. But my heart tells me that this championship—right here in NASCAR—was my greatest accomplishment." The *Sporting News*, the National Motorsports Press Association, and the American Auto Racing Writers and Broadcasters Association later named him driver of the year.

Stewart failed to repeat as champion in 2003, finishing seventh in the points standings. He did, however, claim two victories, at Pocono, Pennsylvania, and Charlotte, North Carolina. In 2004 Stewart finished sixth in the overall points standings and again won two races, including his third road-course win, in Watkins Glen, New York. On November 20, 2005 Stewart won his second NASCAR Winston/Nextel championship, solidifying his status as one of the current generation's greatest race-car drivers. A string of races in the summer, in which Stewart won five times in seven starts, helped vault him into championship contention; over the final 22 races of the season, he notched an astonishing 19 top-10 finishes. He finished 35 points ahead of the drivers Greg Biffle and Carl Edwards in the season's final standings. "It's been a very special year," Stewart told Lars Anderson for *Sports Illustrated* (November 28, 2005). "This championship means ten times more than the one I won in 2002. I've had more fun this year than at any time in my life." In 2006 Stewart attempted to become the first Nextel/Winston Cup series driver to win consecutive championships since the 1997 and 1998 seasons, when Gordon did so. Stewart fell short, in a season that brought several accidents and injuries, including smash-ups in May that resulted in his being taken to the hospital two nights in a row. (On the second occasion he suffered a fractured right scapula.) In 11th place for the season, he was eliminated from the Chase for the Cup. Nonetheless, Stewart had three first-place finishes in 2006, at the DirecTV 500; the Pepsi 400; and the Banquet 400.

In 2003 Stewart founded the Tony Stewart Foundation, which supports "organizations that help care for critically ill children" and "families of race car drivers who have been injured in motorsports," according to a profile of Stewart on the Joe Gibbs Racing Web page. In addition, in 2003 Stewart made a $1 million contribution to the Victory Junction Gang Camp, an organization founded by the NASCAR driver Kyle Petty, which benefits children with chronic and life-threatening illnesses.

Tony Stewart, nicknamed "The Columbus Comet" and "Smoke," is five feet eight inches tall and weighs 185 pounds. He likes to shoot pool and bowl in his spare time. Stewart moved back to Indiana before the start of the 2005 Nextel Cup season. The move seemed to have a calming effect on the driver, who had divided his time between residences in Indiana and Charlotte, North Carolina. "I'm just so much more relaxed now," Stewart told Lars Anderson. His home, he said, "is the same house I grew up in. Every morning when I open the front door and let the dog out, it reminds me of when I was a kid. . . . Life isn't complicated for me here. . . . My neighbors think of me as the same punk kid who smacked baseballs into their aluminum siding. . . . Where I need to be, for my own peace of mind, is here."

—D.F.

Suggested Reading: *Denver Post* B p1 Nov. 20, 2005; ESPN.com; *Indianapolis Monthly* p100+ Aug. 2003; (Massachusetts) *Telegram & Gazette* D p1 July 25, 2004; (Newport News, Virginia) *Daily Press* D p1 June 25, 1996; *Sports Illustrated* p58+ Oct. 21, 2002, p78 Nov. 28, 2005; Tony Stewart Web site

Paul Hawthorne/Getty Images

Stringer, Howard

Feb. 19, 1942– Chairman and CEO of Sony Corp.

Address: 6-7-35 Kitashinagawa, Shinagawa-ku, Tokyo 141-0001, Japan

"That a foreigner is taking the helm of a proud Japanese firm like Sony is of great symbolic importance," an editorial in the *New York Times* declared on March 9, 2005. Days earlier Nobuyuki Idei, then the chairman and chief executive officer (CEO) of Sony, announced that in July 2005, Howard Stringer, a native of Wales (who was knighted by Queen Elizabeth II in 2000) and a naturalized American citizen, would succeed him as the company's chairman and CEO. "Symbolism has meaning," the editorial stated, "and by naming Sir Howard, Sony has shown that it means to change—a message that its domestic employees, shareholders and customers need to hear. Yet seen from a distance, the ascension of Sir Howard is neither surprising nor, in the end, especially relevant: in most ways the Sony Corporation is already an international company." Stringer arrived at Sony in 1997, to assume the position of president of Sony Corp. of America, with control over Sony's film, television, music, and consumer-electronics divisions in the U.S. During the next seven years or so, he acquired other titles (some concurrently): those of chairman of Sony Electronics, chairman and CEO of Sony Corp. of America, president of Sony Broadband Entertainment, director and then vice chairman of Sony Corp., and chief operating officer of the entertainment-business group. The first non-Japanese to serve as Sony's CEO, Stringer "must now integrate Tokyo's hardware-focused engineer-

ing culture with the media-driven sensibilities of New York and Los Angeles . . . ," according to the *New York Times* editorial, which went on to wonder, "After a breathtaking decades-long run, and despite its many strengths, can a company as large as Sony regain its agility by fusing the Japanese focus on the product with the American obsession with the customer?" Speaking of the company's Japanese employees (who make up only one-third of its entire payroll of more than 150,000 people worldwide), and alluding to Stringer's inability to speak Japanese, Idei said to Brent Schlender for *Fortune* (April 4, 2005), "It's funny, 100% of the people around here agree we need to change, but 90% of them don't really want to change themselves. So I finally concluded that we needed our top management to quite literally speak another language." Peter G. Peterson, a former Sony board member, a co-founder of the investment-banking firm the Blackstone Group, and the chairman of the Council on Foreign Relations, told Schlender, "Howard has a unique way of building affection, and he has demonstrated how he can get the trust and respect of people and get them to work together. . . . And he has demonstrated he can take on many of these problems that Sony is talking about and do something about them: cost cutting, integration, getting the right people in place." Regarding the challenges he faces as Sony's head, Stringer told Dominic Rushe for the London *Times* (March 13, 2005), "I'm prepared to throw myself in front of [a] truck to make this work. Perhaps that's why they chose me." More recently, he told Martin Fackler for the *New York Times* (May 29, 2006), "We need to rebuild the brand seriously, in terms of energy and perception around the world."

Stringer won nine individual Emmy Awards during the first three decades of his professional life, which he spent as a journalist, producer, and executive with CBS. In the late 1970s he served as the executive producer for *CBS Reports*, a highly respected series of award-winning documentaries. As the executive producer of the *CBS Evening News* in the early 1980s, he helped to restore the newscast to the number-one position in the ratings. As president of CBS News for several years later in the 1980s, he oversaw the development of the TV news magazine *48 Hours*, a prime-time hit. From 1988 to 1995 he occupied the post of president of the CBS Broadcast Group, with responsibility for the broadcasting of all of CBS's entertainment, sports, and news programs on both radio and television, and within a year CBS had risen from last place to first place in prime-time ratings. In 1993 Stringer played a key role in bringing the popular late-night talk-show host David Letterman to CBS from its rival NBC. For a few years in the mid-1990s, he was chairman and CEO of Tele-TV, a failed attempt by a trio of Bell companies to deliver television signals over phone lines. Stringer's many honors include the First Amendment Leadership Award of the Radio and TV News Directors Foundation (1996), the Public Service Award of

Phoenix House (2002), and the Britannia Award (2003) from BAFTA/LA (the Los Angeles arm of the British Academy of Film and Television Arts), for contributions to worldwide entertainment. In 2005 *Time* magazine listed him among the world's 100 most influential people.

The first of the two children of Harry Stringer and Marjorie Mary (Pook) Stringer, Howard Stringer was born on February 19, 1942 in Cardiff, Wales. His father was a squadron leader in the Royal Air Force and a talented recreational painter; his mother, according to the London *Evening Standard* (December 16, 1998), had a blue-collar job with a railroad before she became a schoolteacher. Stringer's brother, Rob, has worked in the music industry for many years; since mid-2004 he has served as chairman and CEO of Sony BMG Music Entertainment in the United Kingdom and Ireland. Until Howard Stringer was about four years old, his family lived on Barry Island (actually a peninsula), in the Vale of Glamorgan, Wales. After that the family frequently moved, because his father's air-force assignments often changed. The American soldiers whom young Howard saw on the bases where his father was stationed captivated Stringer in his youth, and he developed a strong attraction toward the United States; he also admired what he regarded as the competitiveness of Americans. The articles and stories he read in the popular weekly magazine the *Saturday Evening Post* also contributed to his positive ideas about the U.S. "To me, America was always bright with promise, and the aggressiveness that everybody else hated in Europe, I liked about it; a society where things could be done, where you didn't have to wait twenty years," he told a reporter for *Broadcasting* (December 12, 1988).

Stringer won a scholarship to attend Oundle School, a prestigious private school near Peterborough, England, about 80 miles north of London. Most of his classmates came from well-to-do families. "It was very much survival of the fittest," Stringer told Susan Schindehette for *People* (April 5, 1993). "My parents didn't own a car—and everyone else's had Rolls-Royces. I worked very hard to fit in. I became chameleon-like." At 19 Stringer received a full scholarship to Oxford University, also in England. At Oxford he was the president of the student body for a year and was chosen captain of the school's rugby team. His friendships with several Rhodes scholars from the U.S. further stimulated his interest in the United States. He graduated from Oxford in 1964 with both a bachelor's degree and a master's degree in modern history. He then worked as a long-distance truck driver, and within a year he had earned enough money to pay for a trip to the U.S. He sailed aboard the SS *United States* in 1965.

Soon after his arrival in New York, CBS-TV hired him as a desk assistant, a job that involved opening mail and performing other low-level tasks. Within only a few weeks, Stringer was drafted into the U.S. Army to serve in combat in the Vietnam War, despite his being a foreign national. (He did not become a U.S. citizen until 1985. He is still a British citizen as well.) "I was shocked," he recalled to *Broadcasting*. "I thought, maybe this was a mistake, maybe I can talk my way out of it. I wrote a letter to Senator Robert Kennedy and I sent a series of letters to the Army, but once in, I wasn't about to fly home on the first bad break, especially with a father who was in the Air Force." Stringer trained in South Carolina and Texas and then spent 10 months in Vietnam. He returned to the U.S. as a sergeant. For his meritorious service he received a U.S. Army Commendation Medal.

In 1968 CBS rehired Stringer and assigned him to the network's election-research unit. For eight months he visited three dozen states, analyzing voter-registration statistics in anticipation of the presidential election, in which the Republican Richard M. Nixon, who had served as vice president of the United States during the two terms of President Dwight D. Eisenhower, ran against Hubert H. Humphrey, the incumbent Democratic vice president. During this time Stringer also helped to come up with questions for a series of interviews with President Lyndon B. Johnson that the CBS producer John Sharnuk was preparing for the television show *CBS Reports*. According to some sources, during this period Stringer also worked as a news writer for WCBS Radio in New York City. In 1973 Perry Wolff, a producer of documentaries, recruited him for the staff of *CBS Reports*, and after that Stringer devoted himself exclusively to CBS television. He served at first as a researcher for the network's documentary unit, then quickly rose to the rank of director and, later, producer. He has credited both John Sharnuk and Burton Benjamin, who was then vice president of CBS News, with being "ideal teachers" who guided him as his responsibilities expanded. From 1974 to 1976 he earned nine individual Emmy Awards for his work as a writer, director, and producer. He was officially named executive producer of *CBS Reports* in 1975 and held that title until 1981. Among the notable documentary programs Stringer produced were "The Rockefellers," "The Palestinians," "A Tale of Two Irelands," "The Defense of the United States," "The Boat People," and "The Fire Next Door," the last of which spurred New York City officials to change related housing regulations. Between 1976 and 1981 his team earned 31 Emmy Awards and four Peabody Awards.

In 1981 Stringer was named executive producer of *CBS Evening News*. At that time the program was in transition, principally because of the recent retirement of its highly respected and popular anchorman Walter Cronkite, and its audience ratings trailed those of NBC's and ABC's evening newscasts. With the support of Dan Rather, Cronkite's successor, Stringer introduced relatively big changes to the newscast to attract viewers. The number of times live feeds from Washington interrupted the broadcast was decreased, for example, and the use of electronically generated graphics was increased. By 1982 *CBS Evening News with Dan Rather* had become the top-rated evening TV newscast.

In 1984 Stringer was named executive vice president of CBS News. The next year the Wall Street investor Laurence Tisch acquired a controlling interest in the CBS network. In October 1986 Stringer was promoted to the presidency of CBS's News Division, whose budget Tisch had cut by $30 million. Stringer oversaw the layoffs of approximately 200 employees and endured one of his most difficult times as an executive. Despite the stringent financial demands placed on CBS News during that time, Stringer guided the development of several new programs, including the award-winning TV news magazine *48 Hours*. *48 Hours* was heralded for its innovation: it presented a single news story as it unfolded over the span of two days, offering a novel spin on the sometimes stodgy feature news shows.

Both NBC and ABC were enjoying higher overall ratings than CBS when, in 1988, Stringer was appointed president of the CBS Broadcasting Group. The reason for CBS's poor showing, according to various observers, was that too many of CBS's programs (among them *60 Minutes* and *Murder, She Wrote*) appealed mostly to adults over the age of 35. With the idea of using that perceived disadvantage to the network's benefit, Stringer and CBS's programming chief, Jeffrey F. Stagansky, chose to aggressively target older audiences—for example, by adding to the CBS lineup such series as *Northern Exposure*, about the culture clashes that ensue after a neurotic young Jewish doctor from New York City opens a practice in a small, remote Alaskan town. "They went after the 35-to-54-year-old audience in earnest, even at the expense of the young viewers whom sponsors seem to crave," Mark Lander and Ronald Grover wrote for *Business Week* (October 19, 1992). By late 1992 CBS's ratings had improved significantly, resulting in a 14 percent rise in advertising revenues.

Especially noteworthy among Stringer's achievements as president of the CBS Broadcasting Group was his successful courting of the late-night talk-show host David Letterman. In 1993 Letterman left NBC for CBS, which reportedly had offered him $14 million a year (double his previous salary), along with the preferred 11:30 p.m. time slot and more creative control over his show than he had had at NBC. In its first two seasons at CBS, Letterman's show led the ratings among 11:30 p.m. programs. Stringer later told *Electronic Media* (September 2, 2002) that Letterman's being with CBS had served as a steadying influence for the network: "Even in the greatest days of the so-called Tiffany Network, when we were No. 1 in daytime, No. 1 in evening news, No. 1 in prime time, the bookends never worked. The morning news has had more anchors than the U.S. Navy, and [in the late-night slots] we were never able to dent Johnny Carson. So in retrospect, going after David Letterman was still the best thing I could have done. . . .

[Letterman's] guiding intelligence on that show is what gives the network its sheen and brands it, in a way connects it to the days of *M*A*S*H* and *Mary Tyler Moore*"—a reference to two immensely popular, long-running CBS series.

Stringer resigned the presidency of the CBS Broadcasting Group in February 1995, to become the chairman and CEO of Tele-TV, a media and technology company co-founded by Bell Atlantic, Nynex, and Pacific Telesis, three of the largest telephone companies in the U.S. at that time. An attempt by regional Bell carriers to deploy "wireless cable" technology and programming broadly, the venture did not succeed. The reasons, as Stringer told a Federal Communications Commission audience on October 17, 2002, as reported on Sony.com, were that "the infrastructure was not in place; business models were misconceived; and we lacked a common vision of the future." Stringer left the company in April 1997.

In the following month Stringer joined the Sony Corp. Headquartered in Tokyo, Japan, Sony is among the world's largest businesses; in particular, it is a leading manufacturer of consumer electronics products. It is perhaps best known as the producer, since 1979, of the portable cassette player known as the Walkman (a brand name that, in informal speech, has become generic). Founded in 1946 as the Tokyo Telecommunications Engineering Corp., with fewer than two dozen workers, the company offered as its first consumer product a rice cooker. In 1955 Sony (as it had been renamed) began selling transistor radios. Its second model of such radios could fit into a coat pocket; its third, introduced in 1957, could slip easily into a shirt pocket and became extremely popular—it had been made largely to satisfy the burgeoning craze for rock-and-roll music among American teenagers. The huge sales of Sony's transistor radios marked the beginning of the company's dominance of the consumer-electronics market. Among Sony's other widely known products are the reel-to-reel tape recorder (1950s); the Trinitron screen (late 1960s); the Betamax video recorder (1975–1998); and PlayStation, a video-game console (first model, 1994–2004; third model, 2006). In 1961 Sony became the first Japanese company to be listed on the New York Stock Exchange. The company grew significantly when it acquired CBS Records, the oldest and largest record company in the world (renamed Sony Music Entertainment), in 1988, and Columbia Pictures (Sony Pictures Entertainment), in 1989.

Stringer's first job with Sony was that of president of Sony Corp. of America, with control over the firm's film, television, music, and consumer-electronics divisions in the U.S. Among his first actions, he hired several new managers: Robert S. Wiesenthal, a banker, who became the company's chief financial officer; Andrew Lack, a former head of NBC, whom Stringer appointed to oversee Sony's music division; and Michael Lynton, a former president of Time Warner International, who was given the job of running Sony Pictures.

In 2001 Stringer sold 50 percent of Sony's holdings on the Game Show Network to the cable mogul John Malone of the Liberty Media Corp. He also sold Sony's stake in the Mexican television network Telemundo to NBC. In January 2003, as reported in the Japanese publication *Nikkei Weekly* (February 18, 2003), Sony and Royal Philips Electronics, the largest electronics firm in Europe, purchased InterTrust Technologies, "the owner of patents for most digital-rights-management technologies used to prevent piracy of movies and music," according to Brent Schlender. Also in the first half of the 2000s, Sony's movie studios released such hits as *Spider-Man*, which earned more than $403 million at U.S. box offices and was the highest-grossing American film of 2002; its much-anticipated sequel, *Spider-Man 2* (2004); and *Hitch* (2005), a romantic comedy, which grossed more than $177 million domestically. Stringer helped to arrange the merger, in 2004, of Sony's Music Entertainment unit with BMG, the music unit of the German media conglomerate Bertelsmann, as well as Sony's acquisition, in April 2005 (in partnership with the Comcast Corp. and two venture-capital banking firms), of Metro-Goldwyn-Mayer (MGM).

Despite those achievements, Sony's overall financial results for the quarter ending in December 2004 were dismal. During the previous 12 months, according to *Fortune* (April 4, 2005), its revenues had fallen 7.5 percent and its operating profits 13 percent. In March 2005, with Sony's projected revenues expected to drop to their lowest level in five years, the corporation's then–chairman and CEO, Nobuyuki Idei, announced that he planned to give up his titles in three months and bestow them on Stringer. Thus, in July 2005 Stringer became the first non-Japanese to lead Sony (or any other major Japanese electronics firm). "Forgive the awful pun, but he has kind of oriented himself to his Japanese colleagues," Peter G. Peterson told a *New York Times* (March 7, 2005, on-line) reporter. "It's a great achievement. They trust him. He's a harmonizer." "Howard is the ultimate diplomat," Victor Pacor, a former Sony executive who worked with Stringer for seven years, told the same reporter. "He is even-handed and will bring the kind of stability that the company needs."

Stringer's major challenge is to reverse the decline of Sony's position in the electronics market, which stems from the growing strength of its competitors, notably the South Korean company Samsung and the American firm Apple Computer. With that goal, he has been encouraging Sony's engineers to be more innovative and has attempted to remove longstanding obstacles, both bureaucratic and cultural, to the sharing of ideas. He has also taken steps to reduce expenses: on September 22, 2005 Sony announced that by the end of March 2008, among other measures, the company will have closed 11 plants and reduced its workforce by 10,000.

In April 2006 Sony announced that it had posted better-than-expected profits of $1.1 billion in the previous fiscal year—an accomplishment credited largely to Stringer's leadership. In an effort to improve Sony's brand name, Stringer has ended production of 600 of Sony's 3,000 electronic items. His agenda includes adding more marketable products to Sony's line and fostering better coordination between the company's electronics and entertainment divisions. Although the electronics division continued to struggle in the fiscal year ending in April 2006, sales of Sony's personal computers, digital camcorders, and flat-screen televisions grew. In another move designed to lead to an increase in Sony's profits, Stringer placed his brother, Rob, chairman and chief executive of Sony's British unit, in charge of the Sony Music Label Group.

In 1994 Stringer received the International Radio and Television Society's Foundation Award, which recognized him for his "uncommon vision" in the media industry. His many other honors include the 1996 First Amendment Leadership Award from the Radio and Television News Directors Foundation and the 1999 Steven J. Ross Humanitarian Award from UJA (United Jewish Appeal)-Federation of Jewish Philanthropies of New York. Stringer was inducted into the Broadcasting and Cable Hall of Fame in 1996 and into the Royal Television Society's Welsh Hall of Fame in 1999. The Literacy Partners, Teach for America, the New York Hall of Science, and the Center for Communication have also honored him. On December 31, 1999, in the New Year Honours list of Queen Elizabeth II, Stringer received the title of Knight Bachelor (Great Britain's oldest category of knight and one that ranks below all the others), which grants him the right to be addressed as "Sir Howard." In 2002 he received the Phoenix House Public Service Award. Stringer serves as the chairman of the American Film Institute board of trustees and sits on the boards of the Museum of Television, the InterContinental Hotels Group, the New York-Presbyterian Hospital, the American Theatre Wing, the American Friends of the British Museum, and the Corporate Leadership Committee of the Lincoln Center for the Performing Arts. He is a member of the Council on Foreign Relations.

The six-foot three-inch (four inches, according to some sources) Stringer is known for his dry wit; his firmness in making decisions that he knows will be unpopular; his capacity for remaining calm during crises; and his ability to nurture the talents of his employees. An avid sports fan, he follows rugby, tennis, and American football. He has amassed an impressive collection of autographed first-edition books, among them works by Graham Greene, Ian Fleming, and Thomas Hardy. Since 1978 he has been married to Jennifer A. K. Patterson, a dermatologist. The couple have two adopted children: a son, David, who is a young teenager, and a daughter, Harriet, who attends elementary school. By his own account, Stringer's desire to spend more time with his children led him to hesitate before he accepted Sony's top post. He maintains residences in New York City and Oxfordshire, England, and often commutes to Tokyo. According to *Who's Who in America*, he is a Presbyterian.

—D.F.

Suggested Reading: *Broadcasting* p95 Dec. 12, 1988; *Business Week* p114 Oct. 19, 1992; *Fortune* Apr. 4, 2005; (London) *Times* p6 Mar. 13, 2005; *New York Times* A p1+ Mar. 7, 2005, C p1+ May 29, 2006; *People* p61 Apr. 5, 1993; Sony Corp. Web site

Matthew Peyton/Getty Images

Talese, Nan

Dec. 19, 1933– Editor; publisher

Address: c/o Nan A. Talese/Doubleday, 1745 Broadway, 22d Fl., New York, NY 10019

As president, publisher, and editorial director of the Nan A. Talese imprint of Doubleday Books, Nan Talese oversees the publication of roughly 10 to 15 fiction and nonfiction titles a year, including works by such critically acclaimed authors as Margaret Atwood, Thomas Cahill, Pat Conroy, Thomas Keneally, Ian McEwan, and Barry Unsworth. Talese began her publishing career in the late 1950s at Random House, later serving as an editor at Simon & Schuster and Houghton Mifflin before joining Doubleday, now a division of Random House, in 1988. She is known for inspiring the loyalty of her authors, many of whom have followed her from one publishing house to another. Talese, in turn, rallies support for them among independent booksellers and critics. "I really am fierce about my authors getting the attention they deserve, whether it's in the publishing house or in bookstores," she told John Blades for the *Chicago Tribune* (October 26, 1990). "If it's really something I believe in, I don't take 'no' very easily." In addition to the works of celebrated novelists, Talese has published books by such figures as the former U.S. senator and Republican presidential nominee Bob Dole, the actress Mia Farrow, and, more recently, James Frey, a former alcoholic and drug addict, whose 2003 memoir, *A Million Little Pieces*, caused a national controversy when it was revealed that he had fabricated much of the material in the book.

According to Sybil Steinberg, writing for *Publishers Weekly* (April 15, 2002), Talese "displays the sort of ladylike calm and aplomb one expects of a social doyenne rather than a woman who manages renowned writers, a staff and a significant budget." Doubleday's president and publisher, Stephen Rubin, told Blades, "Nan is the quintessential lady, but she wears brass knuckles beneath those white gloves. She's a very determined publisher, who's tough as nails when it comes to getting what she wants for her books and her authors." Talese has shown particular faith and foresight in promoting the work of talented authors whose debut efforts sell modestly. McEwan and Atwood, for example, each saw sales of only about 7,000 copies in the United States when Talese first published their work; both have since gone on to achieve much greater sales and win some of the literary world's most prestigious awards. "It's so satisfying because you put your faith in a writer's excellence, and then readers catch up," Talese told Steinberg. In a talk with Laurel Touby for the Web site mediabistro.org (April 18, 2001), Talese said, "One often hears about MBAs who come newly into the world of publishing, who look at the best-sellers and say, Why don't you only do best-sellers? They suggest we mustn't contract for books that we're going to publish fewer than 15,000 copies of. But the fact is, many of those best-sellers come from those low numbers. If anyone could predict what it is that makes a book a best-seller, we'd have fewer publishers." Talese's stellar track record also reflects her deep passion for the written word. Outside the office she willingly edits the work of her husband, Gay Talese, a critically acclaimed author and a pioneer, with Tom Wolfe and others, of New Journalism, which combines fiction-like narrative elements with straightforward reporting. Nan Talese told Blades that being married to a writer "helps enormously, because I have seven days a week of understanding authors' needs, their insecurities, the kind of attention they require. On the other hand, if I didn't love books it would be very trying."

Talese was born Nan Ahearn on December 19, 1933 in New York City to James Ahearn, a banker, and Suzanne Sherman (Russel) Ahearn. She attended Manhattanville College of the Sacred Heart, in New York, where she studied philosophy. After graduating, in 1955, she studied foreign exchange at the First National City Bank in both London and Paris before working as an editorial assistant at the National Eugenics Society, in New York City, from 1957 to 1958. Talese then worked at *Vogue* magazine as an editorial assistant in the fashion department. After deciding that *Vogue* was "not the right place for me," as she told Michelle Lin during an interview for *New York Brain Terrain* (July 6, 2006, on-line), she took the advice of her fiancé, Gay Talese, and met with a book editor at Random House. At the time that company "was very different than we know it today," she said to Lin. "The offices were in the beautiful Villard mansion on Madison Avenue and 50th Street and publishing companies were separate entities. This was before the conglomerates blossomed." In 1959 (the year she married Gay Talese), she began working at Random House, starting out by proofreading mystery novels and doing some copyediting, mainly of books on philosophy. After what she described to Lin as "quite an apprenticeship," she began to work directly with authors. In one of her first collaborations with an author, Robert Penn Warren allowed Talese to edit the manuscript of his 1964 novel, *Flood*. Talese told Blades, "After 10 days of talking to him about words and phrases and the motivations of his characters, I thought I should have paid him a tuition fee, because he gave me such an insight into the writer's mind." Talese was promoted to associate editor in 1964 and senior editor in 1967. During her time at Random House, she worked with such famed writers as Neil Simon, Philip Roth, and Lorraine Hansberry.

In 1974 Talese left Random House for a senior-editor position at Simon & Schuster, also in New York. It was there that she began a series of long-term editorial relationships with such authors as Thomas Keneally, Ian McEwan, and Barry Unsworth. One of the first writers whose works Talese edited at Simon & Schuster was Margaret Atwood, who would go on to win the Booker Prize in 2000 for *The Blind Assassin*, published by Talese's imprint at Doubleday. Talese told Larry Weissman for the Random House on-line publication *Bold Type* (May 1997) that she is drawn to Atwood's writing because it reveals "her razor sharp mind, her sense of humor, her ability to cut straight through to the truth and to reveal it in story." She began editing Atwood's work in 1975, when the novelist "delivered an early draft (very unusual for her) of *Lady Oracle*," Talese told Weissman. "When I read it I was amazed at how she captured the dilemma of the many separate lives women were forced to lead at that time [1975]; how totally mad yet true the plot and picture she had divined; and how daring the story was. . . . Several senior editors had read it in the house, but somehow she seemed to like my

response to it, so I became her editor." Another writer Talese met at Simon & Schuster was Tom Keneally, whose book *Schindler's List* (about the real-life German industrialist Oskar Schindler, who saved more than 1,000 Polish Jews during the Holocaust) Talese published in the early 1980s. Keneally had conceived of the book (whose original title was *Schindler's Ark*) after having an encounter in a Beverly Hills, California, luggage store with a Holocaust survivor, and sold the story to Talese for $60,000. "I thought the story was extraordinary and needed to be told, but I had no idea of the market," she admitted to Steinberg. *Schindler's List* was made into an acclaimed film directed by Steven Spielberg. Before the release of the film, the book sold one million copies; afterward, sales rose by at least two million.

In 1981 Talese joined Houghton Mifflin as executive editor and vice president. She was hired as part of an effort to create a stronger New York presence for the Boston-based publisher. One of her first assignments was editing the 1,400-page manuscript of Pat Conroy's 1986 novel, *The Prince of Tides*. After "circling each other like fighters," as Talese said to John Blades (and engaging in "minor battles" which "Nan always won," as Conroy added), Talese and Conroy worked together for a week with the pages of the manuscript spread across her office floor, and Talese eventually slimmed the work down significantly. "She did a ton of work, cutting 500 pages," Conroy told Blades, "but she did it so sweetly that I barely knew the blood was pouring out of my wrists." After the tremendous success of that collaboration (*The Prince of Tides* sold five million copies and was made into a film starring Nick Nolte and Barbra Streisand), Conroy, along with several other authors, chose to follow Talese from Houghton Mifflin to Doubleday, where she became a senior vice president in 1988.

Two years after joining Doubleday, Talese formed her own imprint, Nan A. Talese Books, as a way to ensure that her writers would be unaffected by upper-level shakeups that were occurring in the company—such as the firing of the company's president, Nancy Evans, in 1990. Blades observed that having her own imprint put Talese in a "select circle" of editors whose names appear on the covers of books. The first book to carry the logo "A Nan Talese Book" was Brian Moore's novel *Lies of Silence*, published in September 1990. Talese has said that being in charge of an imprint has helped her sell works to bookstores, telling Steinberg, "If you've been publishing a certain author for a long time, bookstores have a sense of your standards, especially with new writers. They're more willing to take a chance on an unknown voice." (Readers, she admitted, tend to pay more attention to authors' names than to imprints.)

Talese's knack for recognizing and developing talent—which often involves forfeiting sales, at least initially—is well documented. To keep her imprint afloat financially, Talese practices "guerrilla marketing," personally and aggressively promoting her titles to booksellers and on-line audiences. Talese described her marketing practices to Touby: "For one of the books I published . . . *How the Irish Saved Civilization* [1995], by Thomas Cahill—it was thought that we shouldn't publish more than 6,000 copies of this book. But by getting some of our sales reps to read it we built enthusiasm for the book and printed 15,000 copies. The book has now sold over a million copies . . . and as the author pointed out to me, 'There are 40 million Irish Americans out there.' We haven't gotten to all of them yet." Furthermore, Talese told Steinberg, "I've always been aware that if you're publishing too many prospectively low-sales literary books, you have to balance them with something that's going to take care of the overhead"— that is, a best-seller.

An example of the latter was *A Million Little Pieces* (2003), an ostensible memoir by James Frey, a former screenwriter who had struggled with drug and alcohol addiction. The book, published by Talese, sold 3.5 million copies, largely because the talk-show host Oprah Winfrey made it an Oprah's Book Club selection for October 2005. Then, later in the year, the Web site The Smoking Gun exposed much of Frey's account of his addiction and recovery as fiction. When the allegations first surfaced, Winfrey remained supportive of Frey, calling in to defend the author during his appearance on the talk show *Larry King Live*. But as David Carr wrote for the *New York Times* (January 30, 2006), Winfrey changed her stance once "it was clear that it was not just [Frey's] reputation that was taking a pounding." In January 2006 Frey and Talese appeared on a much-discussed installment of *Oprah*, on which the host expressed disappointment in Frey and questioned Talese's judgment in allowing the book to be published as a memoir. Talese said on the program, as quoted by Edward Wyatt for the *New York Times* (January 27, 2006, on-line), "An author brings his book in and says that it is true, it is accurate, it is his own. I thought, as a publisher, this is James's memory of the hell he went through and I believed it." Many critics thought that Talese came across as unapologetic and blamed her and the publishing industry as a whole for failing to fact-check nonfiction books. Throughout the ordeal, Talese maintained that she had never known, or thought to ask, about the fictionalized sections of the book. "When the manuscript of *A Million Little Pieces* was received by us at Doubleday, it was received as nonfiction, as a memoir," she told Sheelah Kolhatkar for the *New York Observer* (January 23, 2006). "Throughout the whole process of publication, it had always been a memoir, and for the first year and a half it was on sale, it was always a memoir with no disputation." Frey, meanwhile, claimed that he had originally shopped the book as a work of fiction and that, once it was accepted for publication, he discussed with representatives at Doubleday whether to publish it as a memoir or a novel—a version of events that Talese has called inaccurate. The controversy only improved sales of the book. "We will continue to print the book as long as there is public demand for it," Talese said in an interview, as quoted by Jeffrey A. Trachtenberg in the *Wall Street Journal* (January 30, 2006).

Asked by Larry Weissman what satisfies her the most about being an editor, Talese cited "the chance to work with writers and to bring to the public's attention their works, which have the ability to move readers by their insight, wit and sheer story-telling ability, and who write about matters that are, to me, significant." Books recently published by the Nan A. Talese imprint include novels by Peter Ackroyd, Marti Leimbach, and Yasmina Khadra as well as Barry Werth's nonfiction work *31 Days*, about events during the first month after the resignation of President Richard Nixon. Nan and Gay Talese have two grown daughters: Pamela, a painter, and Catherine, a photographer.

—M.B.

Suggested Reading: *Chicago Tribune* Tempo p1 Oct. 26, 1990; *New York Observer* p1 Jan. 23, 2006; *Publishers Weekly* p36 Apr. 15, 2002

Frederick M. Brown/Getty Images

Tarver, Antonio

Nov. 21, 1968– Boxer

Address: c/o Star Boxing, 991 Morris Park Ave., Bronx, NY 10462

In an inspiring example of an individual's triumph over adversity, the boxer Antonio Tarver surmounted the difficulties of a fatherless childhood, the frustrations of menial jobs, the humiliations of poverty, and the desperation of drug addiction to become an Olympic medalist in 1996 and a light-heavyweight champion seven years later. The six-foot two-inch Tarver, a southpaw whose reach extends 75 inches, debuted as a professional in early 1997. In his efforts to rise to the top ranks of boxing, a prevailing motivation has been his determination to defeat Roy Jones Jr., who won a contest against him when both were 13 and who is considered one of the finest contemporary practitioners of the sport. "I'm training for Roy Jones. Every damn thing I do is for Roy Jones," Tarver told a reporter in 1999, as quoted by John C. Cotey in the *St. Petersburg (Florida) Times* (September 28, 2005, on-line). In 2004, after his second professional match against Jones and the first in which he prevailed over him, Tarver said, as quoted in *Jet* (June 7, 2004), "It takes a great fighter to beat a great fighter, and I am a great fighter." In their third meeting, in 2005, Tarver retained his light-heavyweight title with a unanimous 12-round decision over Jones. In June 2006 Tarver lost his title to Bernard Hopkins, bringing his win–loss record to 24–4, with 18 knockouts.

Antonio Deon Tarver was born on November 21, 1968 in Orlando, Florida. He and his three sisters were raised by their mother, Gwendolyn, in a single-parent home, their father having abandoned them when they were very young. At the age of 10, Tarver began boxing at the local Boys Club facility. The trappings of boxing captivated him, particularly "the uniforms, the pretty robes they had. And all those trophies," he recalled, as quoted by Richard Hoffer in *Sports Illustrated* (April 29, 1996). Tarver earned a score of trophies as a youngster and enjoyed presenting each one to his mother. A willful child, he often tried—unsuccessfully—to avoid doing his chores. Occasionally, his mother would haul him home from the Boys Club quarters and force him to complete the tasks she had assigned him. "I'd break my trophies for spite," he told Hoffer, "bury them in the yard in pieces. I knew it would hurt my mom. I knew how she cherished those trophies. I don't know how many more I gave to friends, all because I didn't get my way." At the 1982 Sunshine State Games, one of Tarver's opponents was his age-mate Roy Jones Jr., who won the fight. When he was about 14, Tarver gave up boxing, after his mother, eager to flee the rampant crime that beset their neighborhood, moved the family two-dozen miles across town, making the Boys Club facility inaccessible to him.

At Conway Middle School Tarver took up other sports, notably football, track, and basketball. By the time he entered Boone High School, also in Orlando, he had begun to focus on football and basketball, believing that he would be able to win an athletic scholarship for college. No scholarships came his way, though. Moreover, during his senior year he fathered a son. With the hope of helping to support his child, he took various part-time jobs. "The environment itself—it's hard out there when you can't get a job," Tarver told Mark McDonald for *Inside Sports* (May 1996). "And when you do get hired, you're washing dishes. All that takes a toll. My situation, my struggles with my son through high school, added a lot of pressures. I didn't have boxing to turn to at the time. I didn't feel I could turn anywhere, so I turned to the streets."

About a year after he graduated from high school, Tarver began experimenting with drugs. According to some reports, he developed a cocaine habit of such severity that he began stealing from his mother in order to support it. In 1990 he was arrested for drug possession. As part of a plea-bargain deal, he agreed to enter a six-month residential rehabilitation program, Phoenix South in Orlando; if he completed the program, he was promised, his arrest would be expunged from the criminal record. While at Phoenix South he gained an understanding of why he had responded to his disappointments, frustrations, and other problems as he had. A turning point came when he met the former heavyweight boxing champion—and recovering drug addict—Pinklon Thomas, who had become an inspirational speaker and came to Phoenix South in that role. After Tarver told Thomas that he wanted to resume boxing, the older man invited Tarver to call on him after he completed his rehabilitation.

In late 1990, after his six-month stay at Phoenix South ended, Tarver began a training regimen devised by Thomas. Almost immediately Tarver won the Florida light-heavyweight championship. Afterward, Thomas wanted Tarver to turn professional, but he balked at the suggestion. As a student of boxing history, he knew how many young fighters had entered the ranks of professionals prematurely and soon disappeared from view. In addition, he had another goal in mind—winning an Olympic gold medal. He had watched on television as Roy Jones Jr. competed as a member of the 1988 U.S. Olympic boxing team, and he longed to join the 1992 team, not least as a way to make up to his mother for all the awards he had destroyed or given away. After amiably parting ways with Thomas, he turned to the boxing coach Lou Harris, who worked with him at the Frontline Outreach Boxing Club in West Orlando, founded as a place where troubled youths could work out their anger. Although at first Harris did not consider Tarver Olympic material, he recognized Tarver's intense determination, as evidenced by his training harder and for more hours than anyone else at the club.

Under Harris's wing Tarver progressed quickly and seemed a likely contender for the 1992 Olympics, but a loss to the fighter Richard Bonds at the Eastern Olympic Trials ended his chance of competing in that year's Games. Despite that blow, he heeded Harris's urgings to persevere. In order to support himself and his son while training, he worked as a waiter and in the garden shop of Home Depot, the latter of which became an Olympic sponsor. In 1993 Tarver won a national championship, which helped him to recover some of his confidence. A temporary setback came in 1994, when he lost the national championship to Anthony Stewart. Later that year he beat Stewart in three additional bouts. In 1996 he became the only amateur boxer to win not only the U.S. National Championships but also the Pam-Am Games and the world championship in a single year. Along the way, in one bout, he beat Vassiliy Jirov (whose given name appears with various spellings in English-language sources) of Kazakhstan, a future cruiserweight champion. Going into the 1996 Olympics, held in Atlanta, Georgia, Tarver had not lost to anyone since 1994 and was regarded as an odds-on favorite to win a medal. In the first round he beat Dmitri Vybornov of Russia; in the second, David Kowah of Sierra Leone; and in the quarterfinals, Enrique Flores of Puerto Rico. In the semifinals Jirov bested him, 15–9. Tarver came home with the bronze medal and the belief that he had been cheated. "I dominated the second round of the fight I lost [to Jirov] and came out two points down," he said, as quoted on Starboxing.com. "I've always had great defense and when I look back at the fight now, I don't see how he was scoring any blows." Tarver told a reporter for the *Orlando (Florida) Sentinel* (on-line), "One fight doesn't make me, regardless of what medal I've got around my neck. It can't tell my story."

After the Olympics Tarver turned professional. He rehired as his trainer Jimmy Williams, who had worked with him during his years as an amateur. In his debut as a pro, on February 18, 1997 at the Blue Horizon, a famous boxing venue in Philadelphia, Pennsylvania, he scored a technical knockout (TKO) against Joaquin Garcia in the second round. Tarver won his next 15 fights. Then he fought a 12-round bout with Eric Harding, on June 23, 2000 in the Grand Casino in Biloxi, Mississippi. He dominated the match until the ninth round, when Harding broke his jaw and two ribs. Despite his injuries he knocked Harding down (but not out) in the 11th round, but the judges awarded the fight to Harding. "That broken jaw was a blessing," Tarver told Franz Lidz for *boxingtalk.com* (November 18, 2004). "A light clicked on in my head. I realized I had to reinvent myself." With that goal in mind, he recruited James "Buddy" McGirt, a former world welterweight champion, as his trainer and Dudley Pierce as his strength and conditioning coach. (Within a few years he was working with three strength and conditioning coaches simultaneously.) He also signed a deal with a promoter, Joe DeGuardia of Star Boxing. After his jaw and ribs healed, Tarver intensified his training. He returned to the ring on February 24, 2001 at the Ice Palace in Tampa, Florida, where he beat the previously undefeated Lincoln Carter by TKO in the fifth round. Tarver then faced another formidable opponent, Chris Johnson, on August 3, 2001, at the Yakama Legends Casino in Toopenish, Washington; he knocked Johnson out in the 10th round. After beating Reggie Johnson on January 25, 2002, at the Ramada Plaza in Rosemont, Illinois, Tarver found himself with a guaranteed opportunity to try

for the International Boxing Federation (IBF) light-heavyweight title. Instead, he chose to challenge Eric Harding again. At that match, held on July 20, 2002 at the Conseco Fieldhouse in Indianapolis, Indiana, Tarver pummeled Harding, beating him by TKO in five rounds.

Tarver's first attempt to win the IBF and World Boxing Council (WBC) world light-heavyweight titles came on April 26, 2003 at the Foxwoods Resort in Mashantucket, Connecticut, in a contest with Montell Griffin, a former world champion. Both organizations' light-heavyweight titles had been vacant since Roy Jones Jr. had given them up several months before, so that he could compete at the heavyweight level. Although Tarver knocked Griffin down in rounds one and two, Griffin remained in the ring for all 12 rounds. The judges unanimously awarded the fight—and the light-heavyweight championships—to Tarver.

In his first title defense, on November 8, 2003 at the Mandalay Bay Events Center in Las Vegas, Nevada, Tarver faced Roy Jones Jr., who had won the heavyweight title but had relinquished it to regain his light-heavyweight status. Until that match, for which Jones lost 20 pounds, the press had considered Jones to be almost unbeatable, but during the fight, according to Michael Katz, writing for the *New York Times* (November 9, 2003, on-line), Jones "appeared weak throughout" and "miss[ed] more than anyone could remember." Katz also wrote, "When it appeared as if Jones was finally in control, Tarver turned the tide with a vengeance, hammering away to the body again." After the final bell sounded, Katz reported, the crowd chanted, "Tar-ver, Tarver." Nevertheless, two of the three judges declared Jones the winner—an announcement greeted by many spectators' strenuous boos. In response to widespread demands for a rematch, Tarver and Jones met again, on May 15, 2004 at the Mandalay Bay Center. This time Tarver knocked out Jones in the second round with a single left hook. Jones dropped to the canvas immediately and attempted without success to get up. The victory not only returned the light-heavyweight championships to Tarver but also earned him $2 million. (Eight days before the fight, he had filed for bankruptcy, being nearly $900,000 in debt to the Internal Revenue Service, Star Boxing, and 17 other creditors.)

In his next contest, held on December 18, 2004 at the Staples Center in Los Angeles, California, Tarver took on Glen Johnson, who had recently become the second fighter to knock out Jones. After 12 rounds Tarver lost his championships to Johnson in a split decision. Feeling that he had been robbed of a victory, Tarver immediately asked for and was granted a rematch, held at the FedEx Forum in Memphis, Tennessee, on June 18, 2005. He won that 12-round fight with a unanimous decision. As the title holder once again, he faced Roy Jones Jr. for a third time, at the St. Pete Times Forum, in Tampa, Florida, on October 1, 2005. In most of the early rounds of that match, Tarver landed more blows and earned more points with the judges; then, as John Eligon reported for the *New York Times* (October 2, 2005, on-line), in the middle of the contest, "Jones came to life . . . and appeared to be in control for a couple of rounds. But Tarver kept plugging away, moving in for swift combinations, then stepping out." In the 11th round, with a right hook to the jaw, Tarver made Jones stagger, his knees buckling, and two more punches drove Jones back against the ropes, where Tarver continued to pound him. Jones recovered enough to tag Tarver several times in the 12th round. The judges unanimously awarded the fight to Tarver, who, like Jones, earned $5 million for his work. On June 11, 2006 Tarver lost his title to Bernard Hopkins in a stunning upset. After that fight Tarver announced that he would not appear in the ring for the rest of the year.

In an interview with Lisa Scott for *Fightnews.com* (June 2, 2004), Tarver said of his descent into drug abuse, "I guess it was one of those things I had to go through. That's life. If I had to do it all over again, I wouldn't change a thing. Because it was during those times, during my recovery, that I was able to build character. I *knew* there was nothing in this world that I could not achieve or

anything that I could not overcome. . . . It has made me a better person. I can be a role model and speak on things if need be and my advice is to believe in yourself and follow your dreams because they will come true. Life is hard. We all just have to endure. Right now, I feel that I am complete. I have everything together." Tarver will appear as the fictional heavyweight champion Mason "The Line" Dixon in the sixth installment of the *Rocky* film series, *Rocky Balboa*, scheduled for release at the end of December 2006. Never married, he lives in Tampa and has two sons, Antonio Tarver Jr. and Taylor Deon Tarver.

—C.M.

Suggested Reading: Antonio Tarver Web site; *Boxing News* (on-line) Oct. 1, 2005; *Boxing Talk* (on-line) Nov. 18, 2004; BoxRec.com; *Entertainment Weekly* p48 July 19, 1996; EPSN.com May 16, 2004; *fightnews.com* June 2, 20004; HBOPPV.com; *Inside Sports* p66+ May 1996; *Jet* p50 Dec. 1, 2003, p49+ June 7, 2004; *Sports Illustrated* p76+ Apr. 29, 1996, p99 Nov. 17, 2003, p82 May 24, 2004, p103 Oct. 10, 2005; Star Boxing (on-line)

Taylor, Herman A.

1954(?)– Cardiologist; educator

Address: Jackson Heart Study, 350 W. Woodrow Wilson Dr., Suite 701, Jackson, MS 39213

"If you have conversations with African-Americans from the South, they already suspect that a lot of things they love are no good for them," the University of Mississippi cardiologist Herman A. Taylor told Claudia Dreifus for the *New York Times* (February 7, 2006, on-line). As the lead investigator in the Jackson (Mississippi) Heart Study, the most widely conducted examination ever of the connections between race and cardiovascular disease, Taylor tries to uncover which "things" in particular have led to disproportionately high levels of the disease among southern blacks, and to determine whether the problem is genetic as well as environmental. African-Americans in Mississippi (the "fattest state in the union," according to Taylor) account for the greatest number of deaths from heart disease of any group in the United States. (Nationally, young and middle-aged blacks die of heart disease twice as frequently as whites.) Explanations for the particularly high rate of the disease in Mississippi include the high incidence of common factors: obesity, smoking, and high blood pressure are all prevalent in Mississippi, and inactivity and isolation are not unusual among many of the state's rural blacks. Other possible causes include an intolerance for salt common in

Courtesy of Heart to Heart International

African-Americans (salt intolerance being linked to hypertension) as well as the unhealthy cholesterol levels in southern "soul food." Also, studies of access to health care show a clear disparity between blacks and whites: in early 2002, 26 percent of blacks in Mississippi were without health insurance, while only 15 percent of whites were uninsured. While such figures are revealing, Taylor told Michael Kranish for the *Boston Globe* (March 10, 2002) that the cause of the high death rates may not lie in socioeconomic or environmental considerations alone: "I think genetics will wind up being an important issue," he said, adding that his statement is "potentially inflammatory."

The U.S. government selected Taylor to lead the Jackson Heart Study in the hope that the presence of an African-American director would lessen anxiety over a program that resembles in certain ways the disastrous Tuskegee Experiment. In that U.S. government study of the spread of syphilis, conducted from the 1940s to the 1970s in Alabama, researchers allowed black male participants (who did not know that they had the disease) to go untreated, even after penicillin was found to be an effective cure; dozens of the men died as a direct result. Michael Kranish wrote that Taylor's "job is no less than to heal racial wounds, to persuade black Mississippians to disclose the most personal information to the federal government and trust that it will be kept confidential, and even to change a state's diet and lifestyle." Nicknamed "heart man" among Jackson locals, Taylor has become a celebrated figure in the area. "Impeccably dressed and fittingly lean," Kranish wrote, "Taylor sports a politician's charisma."

Herman A. Taylor was born in about 1954 and grew up in Birmingham, Alabama. His father was a steelworker, his mother a teacher. Taylor told Dreifus, "During my childhood, I think there were two big influences, beyond my family: the incredibly heroic acts you saw from individuals like [the civil rights leader] Martin Luther King, and the space program. I wanted to grow up and help my people. I also dreamed about science. For me personally, the wonderful thing about working on [the Jackson Heart Study] is that it's a way for me to do both." Taylor was motivated to practice heart medicine after his two grandmothers died of strokes brought on by hypertension. He attended Princeton University, in New Jersey, graduating in 1976, then entered Harvard Medical School, in Cambridge, Massachusetts, where he learned about the Framingham Heart Study. That study, generally considered to be the most successful public-health survey ever conducted, would later provide the operational blueprint for Taylor's work in Jackson. Begun in 1948, the Framingham study tracked residents of Framingham, Massachusetts, over multiple generations, with researchers noting the effects of different activities on subjects' hearts. The study produced a great deal of the current knowledge about heart disease, revealing, for example, that smoking, high blood pressure, and obesity all contribute to the risk of cardiovascular failure.

At the time and place that the Framingham Study was conducted, white males were the main group known to suffer from heart disease, whose causes were once shrouded in mystery. Taylor told Dreifus, "You can probably count the number of blacks in the original study on one hand. Well,

maybe two," he explained. "It's no one's fault. When that study was first begun in 1948, the town of Framingham was mostly populated by second-generation immigrants and Yankees. That's just what it was." By the time Taylor learned about the study, though, there was an alarming growth in the number of blacks known to be afflicted with heart ailments, and a lack of medical research into possible causes. Taylor recognized the need for a study conducted in the black community.

Following his graduation from medical school, Taylor served as a senior assistant surgeon in the Commissioned Corps of the U.S. Public Health Care Service, an arm of the U.S. Department of Health and Human Services. The Commissioned Corps is the largest public-health program in the world, employing physicians, nurses, pharmacists, and researchers working in areas such as disaster relief, disease prevention, and food and drug regulation. Taylor earned a specialty certification in internal medicine in 1986 and in cardiovascular disease in 1989. He was an associate professor of medicine at the University of Alabama at Birmingham prior to taking a teaching post at the University of Mississippi.

The National Institutes of Health (NIH) shared Taylor's concern about the disproportionately high rate of heart disease–related deaths in black populations. "We must do something," Kranish quoted Taylor as saying. "We can't tolerate these huge differences within the boundaries of one country. It is like you are comparing two vastly different nations." With a budget of $54 million provided by the NIH's National Heart, Lung, and Blood Institute (NHLBI) and the National Center on Minority Health and Health Disparities (NCMHD), the Jackson Heart Study was launched in 1998, with initial examinations of patients starting in 2000; it is the largest investigation ever into the causes of cardiovascular disease among African-Americans. The study will follow 5,302 people aged 35–84, picked from three neighboring counties, until 2014. Taylor, who leads a team of 65 researchers, told Dreifus, "When you do a study like this, you want to figure out what's killing people. You enroll a large number and follow them. Over the years, some people will get sick; others won't. So the job is to try to determine the difference between those who got sick and those who didn't."

Roughly 2,500 of the subjects were guaranteed involvement in the Jackson study because of their participation in an earlier survey in the area, the Atherosclerosis Risk in Communities (ARIC) study. The rest were picked randomly from a computer-generated list of names, in order to ensure a representative sampling. The aim was to avoid choosing subjects according to their "willingness to participate or whatever," as Taylor told Nikki Burns for the *Mississippi Link* (August 1, 2001). "Sometimes only the healthiest people will participate in a study because they are knowledgeable and healthy. Sometimes people who already have a problem that they are worried about are the ones who will participate. . . . We want every day people, representing all facets of life in the African-American community." People who volunteered without being solicited, Taylor told Burns, were not turned away. "We don't tell people who call and want to participate, 'no.' We record those names and as a list is developed, we try to match those names with people on the list." The Jackson study seeks to differentiate itself from the Tuskegee survey by sharing, not withholding, information about patients' conditions. "If you don't share helpful information because you don't want to interfere with the natural history of their disease, then you're on a slippery slope. That was the rationale behind keeping information from the sick in the Tuskegee study . . . ," Taylor told Dreifus. "Also, when one of our medical exams shows something of clinical importance in a participant, we contact their physician. If they don't have one, we have a group of local doctors who've volunteered to take them on." In spite of such measures, after recruiting for 18 months, the Jackson Heart Study had signed up only about half of its desired number of subjects, suggesting a continued mistrust of the government.

Participants in the study are given blood-pressure tests using armbands; the tests last 24 hours and are administered at three-year intervals for the remainder of the subjects' lives. A one-time shopping center, converted into a clinic and nicknamed the "Medical Mall," serves as the study's headquarters. Data is coordinated at Jackson State University, and Tougaloo College and the University of Mississippi Medical Center have also granted the program use of their facilities. Participants are questioned on topics ranging from their diets to their methods of coping with racial discrimination. "One of the things we're looking at is, What kind of access do you have to a healthy lifestyle?" Taylor told Dreifus. "Can you get out . . . to walk, do exercise—or is the level of violence in your immediate surroundings so high that this would be a risky proposition? We look at how many grocery stores are in a certain area. Do you have to rely on the corner market with its jars of pickled eggs and pigs' feet on the counter?" Additionally, those of the subjects' family members who are in their 20s and older are studied. Taylor told Burns that that segment of the study is conducted to see "how disease runs in families, what part [of heart disease] is genetics versus what part is behavioral and environmental." The researchers' hope is that in finding causes of the elevated heart risks among black subjects, doctors will be able to help those subjects as well as introduce far-reaching health innovations for all Americans. That hope is grounded in part in research on the human genome, which revealed that there is more genetic diversity among blacks than there are differences between blacks and whites. Thus, should the Jackson Study reveal a genetic cause for heart disease, its findings would theoretically be useful for studying cardiovascular disease in all Americans.

The first sets of data gathered revealed high levels of obesity, diabetes, and hypertension. ("African-American women lead the way in obesity nationally, and our numbers here are significantly higher than that," Taylor told Dreifus.) Taylor attributes such figures less to diet than to inactivity. He told Dreifus that in a 1960s study taken in Georgia, blacks had a low heart-disease rate in spite of their regular consumption of soul food. He attributed that finding to the type of work the subjects did: "They were share croppers, people who did physical work. They didn't have nearly the access to bad things all day long that people have now." He added, "The problem today for people living under stressful conditions is that harmful stuff is sometimes a cheap way to take a load off their lives and feel less stressed. I think that drives a lot of eating and smoking."

In addition to leading the Jackson Heart Study, in 1989 Taylor founded the Heart to Heart Foundation, a nonprofit organization committed to providing health care and education to children in developing countries, including Bangladesh, Belize, Kenya, Pakistan, and Peru. Taylor is married and has two children. He lives in Jackson.

—M.B.

Suggested Reading: *Birmingham (Alabama) News* E p2 Feb. 16, 2002; *Boston Globe* A p1 Mar. 10, 2002; *Mississippi Link* p2 Aug. 1, 2001; *New York Times* (on-line) Feb. 7, 2006

Taylor, Jermain

Aug. 11, 1978– Boxer

Address: c/o DiBella Entertainment, 350 Seventh Ave., Suite 800, New York, NY 10001

"I've been boxing for 14 years, and if I got mad at all my opponents, I'd be the meanest person in the world," the middleweight boxing champion Jermain Taylor said to Don Steinberg for the *Philadelphia Inquirer* (July 16, 2005). "I mean, this is a sport. Whether I like [my opponent] or I don't like him, when we get in the ring, I'm going to take care of business. I'm a boxer, that's what I do. As far as outside the ring, it doesn't make a difference. I'd take him out to eat or whatever." Such graciousness and equanimity does little to explain Taylor's being known in the boxing world as "Bad Intentions." That nickname comes, instead, from his brutal efficiency in the ring. On July 16, 2005 the 156-pound Taylor defeated the veteran Bernard Hopkins in Las Vegas, Nevada, in a controversial split decision, claiming the middleweight titles of all four of boxing's major sanctioning bodies: the World Boxing Council (WBC), World Boxing Association (WBA), World Boxing Organization (WBO), and International Boxing Federation (IBF). In the

Jermain Taylor (right) in the ring with Bernard Hopkins at the world middleweight championship fight in Las Vegas on December 3, 2005

rematch with Hopkins in Las Vegas on December 3, Taylor won a unanimous decision, confirming his status as one of the best middleweight boxers of his generation. (Taylor relinquished his IBF title by choosing to fight Hopkins a second time.) On June 17, 2006 a match between Taylor and the boxer Ronald "Winky" Wright ended in a draw, leaving Taylor's middleweight championship intact. As of late October 2006 Taylor's record was 25–0–1, with 17 knockouts. His next bout, against the Ugandan pugilist Kassim Ouma, was scheduled for December 2006.

Remarking on the boxer's powerful overhand right, which he "throws like a baseball pitcher, ducking in under the arc of his arm to avoid counter shots," Steinberg also observed, "In the ring he moves gracefully and purposefully, firing long left jabs and hard rights whose power seems to emanate from the small of his wide, pivoting back and gather force while rippling up." Outside the ring, the Olympic bronze medalist is "polite, respectful to a fault," as Chris Givens put it in the *Arkansas Democrat-Gazette* (November 27, 2005); boxing observers as well as fellow fighters have praised Taylor for setting a good example for other boxers—and for young people—through his discipline and demeanor. "I'm hoping that I can be a role model for the kids," Taylor told a reporter for HBOPPV.com. "Not the earrings, the long hair, the sagging pants and big clothes. I think kids need a new role model."

The oldest of four children, Jermain Taylor was born in Little Rock, Arkansas, on August 11, 1978 and grew up in one of the city's poorer sections. Around the time that he was five years old, his fa-

ther, Lee Taylor, walked out on his mother, Carlois Reynolds, leaving her to raise her four small children alone. A nurse's assistant, Jermain's mother sometimes worked extra hours to make ends meet, and as the oldest child, Jermain assumed a great deal of responsibility for the family, helping bring up his three sisters—Tamicka, Tamara, and Gussie. Many biographical sketches of Taylor have remarked that the responsibility he accepted at an early age helped him mature into the disciplined fighter he is today. "We got by, though I don't know how," Taylor told Steve Springer for the *Los Angeles Times* (July 15, 2005). Taylor stuttered as a boy, and the shyness brought on by his speech impediment, coupled with his responsibilities at home, kept Taylor apart from children his age for a time. He attended McClellan High School in Little Rock but left without graduating; he later earned a General Educational Development (GED) diploma.

During Taylor's boyhood his mother, wanting him to escape the rough life of their neighborhood, tried to impress upon him the importance of pursuing a college education. Taylor, instead of concentrating on his studies, grew enamored of boxing. He became interested in the sport when a male cousin began training with Ozell Nelson at a local gymnasium. (Nelson and Pat Burns currently serve as Taylor's ringside trainers.) Taylor, who lost badly the first time he stepped into the ring, nonetheless recalled to Chris Givens, "I probably starting writing 'champ' at age 13. I had no idea what a champion really was, but I wrote it. If you start writing it at that age, it starts clicking in. . . . If you keep telling yourself you're No. 1, and work at it, eventually you're going to be No. 1." At first Taylor's mother opposed his desire to box, citing the dangers associated with the sport. Later, when she realized that Taylor was trying to join a local gang, she changed her mind. "I recognized the fact that if he didn't do something he wanted, he'd be doing something he had no business doing," she told Chris Givens. Taylor began training with Nelson in the gym regularly, keeping to a rigorous schedule and steadily improving as a boxer. (The benefits of his dedication to boxing became evident when a group of the then-teenager's friends were arrested after having robbed a gas station at gunpoint.)

Over time Nelson observed that Taylor relied too much on his right arm, to the point of enabling smaller opponents to gain an advantage over him. To remedy the problem, when Taylor was 16 Nelson began tying his protégé's right hand to the side of his head, forcing him to throw punches with his left hand and, in particular, to develop his left jab. "He started whipping everybody," Nelson told Richard Sandomir for the New *York Times* (July 14, 2005). Taylor later began traveling outside Little Rock to fight in tournaments.

The first notable event of Taylor's amateur career was his victory at the 1996 under-19 national championship. Later, Taylor won two Police Athletic League championships and several National Golden Gloves titles. In 1997 and 1998 he finished in second and third places, respectively, at the U.S. Boxing Championships. Also in 1998 Taylor won a bronze medal at the Goodwill Games held in New York City. The celebration of his Goodwill Games performance ended, however, when Taylor learned of the murder of his grandmother, Gussie Robertson, by her son—who subsequently committed suicide. At his grandmother's funeral, Taylor placed his medal from the Goodwill Games in the coffin. "Every time I get into the ring, she's the first person that pops into my head," Taylor told HBOPPV.com. "Before a fight, I go to a neutral corner, kneel down and say a prayer to God and my grandmother."

As a teenager Taylor watched television coverage of the boxing competition at the 1996 Olympics, and he made it a personal goal to represent the U.S. at the Games in the future. In 1998 Taylor entered the prestigious USA Boxing Camp in Marquette, Michigan, which helped him to secure a berth on the U.S. team competing in the 2000 Olympic Games, held in Sydney, Australia. (He thus became the first boxer from Arkansas to compete in the Olympics.) Boxing in the light-middleweight division at 156 pounds, Taylor defeated his first opponent, Dimitriy Usagin of Bulgaria, with a first-round punch that prompted the referee to stop the fight. Taylor went on to defeat Scott McIntosh of Canada by a 23–9 decision, with Evander Holyfield, then the WBA heavyweight boxing champion, watching from the crowd. By defeating McIntosh Taylor became a contender for the gold medal in his weight class, and with his next victory, a 19–14 decision over Adnan Catic, a former national champion in his native Germany,

Taylor guaranteed himself at least a bronze medal. In the next round of competition, Yermakhan Ibraimov of Kazakhstan beat Taylor in a match that was stopped early in the fourth round in observance of the 15-point "mercy" rule (Ibraimov was ahead by 29 to 14). Taylor was awarded a bronze medal and left the Olympics regarded as a major professional boxing prospect.

Taylor chose the promoter Lou DiBella to oversee the scheduling of his fights, signing a contract with DiBella Entertainment. He began his professional career in the 160-pound (or middleweight) class, taking on Chris Walsh on January 27, 2001 at New York's Madison Square Garden, as part of DiBella's "Night of the Olympians," broadcast on the cable network Home Box Office (HBO). Taylor scored a technical knockout (TKO) in the fourth round against the more experienced Walsh. (A TKO occurs when a referee pronounces a fighter unable to continue.) "I got in there without the headgear and I didn't know what to expect, but it felt great. I love this sport," Taylor told a reporter for the *Arkansas Democrat-Gazette (January* 28, 2001). He also noted, "In the fourth round, I was able to show him my right hand a little bit, and I caught him. I wanted to establish my jab. Everybody says, 'Jermain only has a right hand and no left hand,' so I used my jab to set up the right." Taylor dispatched each of his next six opponents, compiling a record of seven wins and no losses by the end of 2001. The following year he extended his winning streak to 13, including a first-round knockout of Keith Sims in Tulsa, Oklahoma.

The match that raised Taylor's profile significantly was that against Marcos Primera, on March 31, 2003, in Taylor's hometown of Little Rock. "Suddenly," the reporter for HBOPPV.com wrote, "the boxing world embraced Taylor, and was unable to ignore his jackhammer jab, concussive left hook, and veteran's poise between the ropes." Taylor rounded out 2003 with a fourth-round TKO against Nicholas Cervera on May 17, a victory by unanimous decision against Alfredo Cuevas on August 8, and a seventh-round TKO of Rogelio Martinez in Las Vegas on November 8. By defeating Cuevas, Taylor earned the vacant World Boxing Council Continental Americas middleweight title. Taylor was named *Ring* magazine's "Most Improved Fighter" of 2003, and at year's end his record stood at 18–0.

In his next fight, on January 9, 2004, Taylor dispatched Alex Rios with a first-round TKO. He earned a record of 20–0 when he scored a TKO against Alex Bunema in seven rounds on March 27, 2004. With that victory, Taylor had won eight of his previous nine fights by knockout or technical knockout. On June 19, 2004, at the Home Depot Center in Los Angeles, California, Taylor defeated the evasive veteran Raul Marquez when, between the ninth and 10th rounds, Marquez's corner decided to stop the fight. Having successfully defended his WBC title, Taylor was thought by Lou DiBella to be advancing toward a match against Bernard

Hopkins, who had been the undisputed middle-weight champion since his defeat of Felix Trinidad in 2001. "This was a great learning fight for [Taylor]," DiBella told Robert Turbeville for the *Arkansas Democrat-Gazette* (June 20, 2004). "It was exactly the kind of fight he needed. . . . Bernard Hopkins is an expert in knowing how to hold, release and hit. This Raul Marquez fight could be exactly what the doctor ordered." Appearing on HBO, on December 4, 2004, Taylor defeated the three-time former world middleweight champion William Joppy by unanimous decision after 12 rounds, again retaining his WBC Continental Americas crown.

Taylor faced the previously undefeated Daniel Edouard on February 19, 2005, in Los Angeles, winning a third-round TKO and clearing the way for a showdown with Hopkins. On July 16, 2005 in Las Vegas, in a controversial split decision, Taylor recorded a 12-round victory against Hopkins, thereby becoming the undisputed middleweight champion, as recognized by the WBC, WBA, WBO, and IBF. John Gregg, writing for the *Boxing Times* (December 3, 2005, on-line), noted that Taylor's "quicker reflexes" and his "ability to pull the trigger early and more often was the difference" for Taylor in securing the decision. The rematch between the two men, which took place in Las Vegas on December 3, 2005, was less controversial: all three judges scored the fight at 115–113 in favor of Taylor. "In a bout that featured intermittent action at best—no knockdowns, not even a big punch—it was clear that Taylor, who outjabbed Hopkins throughout and this time finished strong, was the better man," Richard Hoffer wrote for *Sports Illustrated* (December 12, 2005). "Not by much, but just enough." "The difference in this fight," Taylor told John Gregg, "was that I think he respected me more. I was determined to win the fight, but I take nothing away from Hopkins. He is a great fighter, a very clever fighter. You have to pull out every trick in the book to even hit him." Taylor's victory immediately generated talk of a match with the highly regarded middleweight boxer Ronald "Winky" Wright, whose record is 50–3 with 25 knockouts. Following a month of negotiations, the two agreed to meet in the ring on June 17, 2006. In that contest Taylor and Wright engaged in a punishing battle that ended after 12 rounds in a draw. The final scorecards from the ring's three judges—two were marked 115–113 in favor of Taylor, and the third read 114–114—reflected the closeness of the bout. Thus, Taylor retained his middleweight crown while his record changed to 25–0–1. Emanuel Steward, the legendary trainer from the Kronk Gym, in Detroit, Michigan, who prepared Taylor for the fight, told Clifton Brown for the *New York Times* (June 19, 2006), "Jermain did so many things wrong, but he still ended up keeping his championship, which really impressed me. He punches with so much power, even when Winky had his hands up, he moved his entire body. That's what a lot of judges are impressed by, power punches."

Don Steinberg remarked that Jermain Taylor is "magazine-model handsome, literally," noting that the boxer had been featured in a 15-page photo spread in the March 2005 issue of *Vogue*. In the summer of 2003, Taylor married the former Louisiana Tech basketball player Erica Smith, currently a member of the Washington Mystics of the Women's National Basketball Association (WNBA). The couple recently purchased a home in Little Rock, where they live with their daughter, Nia Jay, who was born in 2004. The boxer told Chris Givens for the *Arkansas Democrat-Gazette* (July 23, 2005) that he enjoys living in Arkansas because the people of that area "treat me so good, I can't say enough about them. I'll never leave Arkansas. I may have to move to a new house, but I won't leave. No one can represent Arkansas like I represent Arkansas; I love where I'm from." Taylor trains for his fights in Miami, Florida. "I think that in order to train a person needs to be away from his surroundings to take his mind off everything," Taylor explained to the reporter for HBOPPV.com. Regarding his future in boxing, Taylor said to Givens in November 2005, "I'm going to hold these belts as long as I can, and them I'm going to get out of boxing, when I'm ready. I'm not going to keep boxing because I need money. I want to get out of boxing early, I mean 32, 33. I want to take care of my family. If I'm still champ when I quit, don't be mad at me. I'm going to retire happy, on my terms, and live my life."

—D.F.

Suggested Reading: *Arkansas Democrat-Gazette* Nov. 27, 2005, Dec. 28, 2005; HBOPPV.com; *Los Angeles Times* D p9 July 15, 2005; *New York Times* D p1 July 14, 2005, D p8 June 19, 2006; *Philadelphia Inquirer* E p1 July 16, 2005

Thomas, William H.

Oct. 13, 1959– Geriatrician; writer

Address: The Eden Alternative, 742 Turnpike Rd., Sherburne, NY 13460

"I never wanted the words 'nursing home doctor' attached to my name in any way," William H. Thomas told Lou Waters on CNN's *Early Prime* (October 7, 1996). That sentiment notwithstanding, over the last 15 years, Thomas has become one of the most innovative nursing-home doctors in the world. With the two related programs that he has set up—the Eden Alternative and the Greenhouse Project—he has established an approach to nursing-home care that concerns itself more with the emotional well-being of residents than with their bodies. He has also written several books to explain and promote his philosophy and strategies, among them *The Eden Alternative: Nature, Hope,*

Courtesy of VanderWyk & Burnham

William H. Thomas

and Nursing Homes (1994), *Life Worth Living: How Someone You Love Can Still Enjoy Life in a Nursing Home: The Eden Alternative in Action* (1996), *Learning from Hannah: Secrets for a Life Worth Living* (1999), *What Are Old People For? How Elders Will Save the World* (2004), and *In the Arms of Elders: A Parable of Wise Leadership and Community Building* (2006). In comparing him to Benjamin Spock, a pediatrician who revolutionized child-rearing practices in the 1950s, and Fernand Lamaze, an obstetrician who revolutionized childbirth processes in the 1960s, observers claim that Thomas is helping to usher in what will likely be the last revolution of the baby boomers (generally defined as people born between 1946 and 1964). That group, Thomas believes, will insist that his innovations become standard. "The boomers have this rebellious streak in them, and at least some forward-thinking part of the boomer generation is going to say, 'Wait a minute, what is this? I'm not going to be afraid.' They're going to wake up and start telling everybody else that old age is cool," Thomas has said, as quoted by Jane Glen Haas in the *Orange County (California) Register* (November 11, 2004). According to Thomas, the baby boomers will then create what he has dubbed "eldertopia," a society in which the elderly are not segregated, all generations interact, and the oldest people are recognized as the most valuable members of the populace.

William H. Thomas was born on October 13, 1959 and raised in a rural community in upstate New York. After completing high school he entered the State University of New York (SUNY) at Cortland, where he studied biology to prepare himself for admission to medical school. While in college he became interested in politics; he was elect-

ed president of the student association and ran unsuccessfully for mayor of Cortland. He graduated from SUNY-Cortland summa cum laude in 1982. He then entered Harvard Medical School, in Cambridge, Massachusetts, from which he earned an M.D. degree in 1986. That year he began a three-year residency in family medicine at the University of Rochester, in New York State. After he completed his residency, he secured a job as an emergency-room doctor, concurrently planning to establish a rural family practice. (Other sources assert that he intended to make his career in emergency-room medicine.) In any event, in the early 1990s he was persuaded to take a job as the medical director of Chase Memorial Nursing Home, in New Berlin, New York, an 80-bed facility in which he served as the only in-house physician. "For the first time in my career," Thomas told Bruce Taylor Seeman for the *Miami (Florida) Herald* (December 26, 1996), "I was searching for the answer to the question: What does it mean to take care of another person?" He took to his new responsibilities with enthusiasm, recalling years later that he thought he had one of the best jobs on Earth.

Then, one day, Thomas told a conference audience in Australia, as Margaret Wenham reported for the Queensland, Australia, *Courier Mail* (December 9, 2000), "I was called to see a woman who had a rash on her arm. She reached up and took hold of my hand, pulled me over the bed and said: 'I'm so lonely.' In that moment all of my bravado, all my good cheer and professionalism escaped me. She was lonely. She was dying of loneliness." The episode transformed Thomas's perspective, making him understand that the people living in the nursing home were not simply patients who required physical care but also men and women who depended on the nursing-home staff to provide an emotionally satisfying world for them. He concluded that in that light, Chase Memorial, despite its reputation as one of the best nursing homes in the United States, was a distressingly bad failure. Those whom he had been hired to care for were suffering from acute loneliness, boredom, and feelings of helplessness—what Thomas has called the three plagues of the nursing-home environment. The roots of those plagues, he later wrote in his book *The Eden Alternative*, as quoted by Catherine Kozak in the *Virginian Pilot* (December 31, 1995), "cannot be traced neatly back to an imbalance of the metabolism or psyche. These three problems receive such little attention because they do not fit well with the medical model of care." That epiphany led to his conception of the Eden Alternative, whose name refers to the garden in the Bible's Book of Genesis; it has since become a registered trademark of Thomas's organization (which was founded in 1991 and has the same name).

The "Edenizing" of Chase Memorial began in 1991 with the assistance of a $200,000 grant from the federal and New York State governments. As a first step in the process, Thomas had pets, plants, and children brought into the facility. Introducing living things into a nursing home was not a new idea, but Thomas did so in a significantly different way. Rather than having children and animals at the home during regimented therapeutic activities, he integrated them into the daily lives of the residents. Dogs and cats were allowed to roam freely throughout the facility, and residents who wanted birds were allowed to care for them in their rooms. The presence of children, too, became usual at Chase, as the home established programs with local kindergartens so that the same children visited the home Monday through Friday. Residents could thus build relationships with individual children. Similarly, plants were placed not only in the lobby, as in other nursing homes, but throughout the home, and some residents welcomed the opportunity to take care of them. Thomas also introduced his charges to the pleasures of vegetable gardening and the rewards of eating what one has grown. The Edenizing process, however, is not only a matter of introducing animals, children, and plants into the nursing-home environment; it also requires changing the atmosphere so that the facility seems less like a hospital and more like an actual home.

Instituting those changes was not easy. Thomas had not anticipated some of the problems that arose, and his staff resisted taking on some new responsibilities, such as cleaning up after dogs. "We stumbled and fell at times," he told Laura Bruck for *Nursing Homes* (January 1997), "but we kept pushing. In the end, resistance became tolerance and, finally, acceptance as the vision began to materialize." Within three years of its start, Thomas's experiment had proven to be a success. Not only had the lives and emotional well-being of the home's residents improved, but in addition Chase's expenses had dropped, as demonstrated by a study conducted by the New York State Health Department. According to the *Orange County (California) Register* (October 12, 1998), there was "a 50 percent decrease in infections, a 71 percent drop in daily drug costs per resident and a 26 percent decrease in nurse's aide turnover"—the last-named problem a common one in nursing homes and one that raises costs because of the need to train new staff. The decline in expenses surpassed start-up costs at other homes where the program was adopted (often as much as $20,000) and the costs of caring for the animals and other elements of the program (approximately $21,000 per year). Chase's program was so successful that New York State introduced it to three other institutions, and Thomas established a nonprofit organization for the purpose of teaching workers at other nursing homes how to Edenize their facilities.

Drawing upon his experiences at Chase, Thomas formulated 10 basic Eden Alternative principles. Two principles concern the easy access of residents to plants, animals, and children. The other eight focus on the attitudes of nursing-home administrators and staff. They must recognize that loneliness, boredom, and helplessness are the primary causes of suffering among nursing-home resi-

dents; be willing to abandon the hierarchical model of authority found in most institutions by giving those working directly with residents more decision-making powers and giving residents opportunities for making choices as well; make it possible for residents to help maintain their surroundings; and minimize, to the extent possible, the use of prescription drugs and dependence on programmed activities, so as to encourage spontaneity.

As his name gained recognition within the nursing-home industry, Thomas began to introduce his ideas to a wider audience, through nationwide lectures and books. His goal had become, as he told Bruce Taylor Seeman, "to change every last nursing home in America. We are going to look back on the old nursing home with dismay." In some places his ideas were not welcomed. One administrator, he told an audience in North Carolina, said that his facility had gotten a dog but the staff could not care for the animal. "I'm thinking," Thomas told Ann Doss Helms for the *Charlotte (North Carolina) Observer* (March 27, 1997), "he wants to charge me $35,000 a year to take care of my mother, and they can't take care of a dog?" As he has often pointed out, the "top-down" model of authority in nursing homes is not consistent with the Eden Alternative, but making the necessary changes requires strong leadership. By the end of 1996, more than 100 nursing homes nationwide had adopted the Eden Alternative, and Thomas's organization had abandoned its nonprofit status. Earlier, he had published his first book, *The Eden Alternative: Nature, Hope, and Nursing Homes* (1994). He expanded and revised some of his ideas in his second book, *Life Worth Living: How Someone You Love Can Still Enjoy Life in a Nursing Home: The Eden Alternative in Action*, which contains a chapter on how the Eden Alternative can be adapted for use in private homes.

In 1997 the America's Award Foundation, established by the influential minister and writer Norman Vincent Peale, presented to Thomas its eponymous award, sometimes called "the Nobel Prize for Goodness," which "honors unsung heroes who personify the American character and spirit," according to various sources. By the end of 1998, the first Canadian nursing home to adopt his program was preparing to open. Thomas was optimistic about the prospects for his ideas in Canada, telling Monte Stewart for the *Calgary (Alberta, Canada) Herald* (October 27, 1998), "It's probably going to be more successful in Canada than the U.S." He added, as paraphrased by Stewart, "Canadian society is more community-minded while U.S. elder care is more profit-oriented." The year 1999 saw the publication of Thomas's book *Learning from Hannah: Secrets for a Life Worth Living,* a fictionalized account of the creation of the Eden Alternative in which he and his wife are shipwrecked on an island; during their yearlong stay they absorb the lessons of a society whose oldest members (among them a woman named Hannah) are valued for their wisdom and experience. After Thomas and his wife return home, they develop the Eden Alternative. To promote the book Thomas embarked on his Eden Across America Tour, during which, in addition to book-signing events and lectures, he presented a two-act, one-man show based on *Learning from Hannah*. According to Chuck Salter in *Fast Company* (February 2002), the show was an excellent medium for Thomas, whom he described as "alternately funny, exuberant, and sincere, offering glimpses of a natural theatricality."

In 1999 Thomas traveled to Australia to spread his message there. Then, the next year, he announced his idea for a radical alternative to the Edenization of large nursing homes: the Green House Project, through which ordinary houses would become homes to elderly people in need of nursing care. Each house would have 10 residents and round-the-clock staff. "The time has come to reinvent the long-term care environment in America for the 21st century," Thomas told the U.S. Newswire (September 25, 2000). "We believe that the Green House can become a high quality, safe, cost-effective alternative to institutionalization for the frail and disabled." "I want to create an environment where Eden-like ideas can flourish more readily than in a 200-bed nursing facility," Thomas explained to Julia Malone for the Cox News Service (September 26, 2000). "My heart breaks when I see how many people try hard to make it work and are knocked down by an institutional structure that is more powerful than they are." In the *Chicago Tribune* (July 24, 2005), Jane Adler reported that "Thomas has a map of the United States in his office with three pins showing the locations of existing Green Houses. He hopes his map will someday have 16,000 pins in it, representing the new Green Houses that have replaced all the nation's old nursing homes."

Moving as many as 150 nursing-home residents, some with serious illnesses, into 10 or 12 separate houses while still following state regulations was an arduous task, and initially the Green House Project was met with skepticism from senior-services companies. However, through diligent efforts at persuasion and the evidence provided by the positive results from his earliest Green Houses, Thomas's organization has gained momentum recently. In 2006 the Green House Project received a $10 million grant from the Robert Wood Johnson Foundation, to be used to replace more than 100 nursing homes (at least one in each of the 50 states) with clusters of small, comfortable homes. In Baltimore and New York City, apartment-style, vertical Green Houses will be built, so as to offer prospective residents the option of living in an urban area, according to Caroline Hsu in *U.S. News & World Report* (June 19, 2006).

Earlier, in 2004, Thomas published his fourth book, *What Are Old People For? How Elders Will Save the World*, in which he argued that people in the U.S. must "end the American tendency of equating being old with being sick. Seeing old age

solely in terms of disease and disability and condoning ageism damage all of society, especially the elderly. Instead, old age should be seen as a natural, developmental stage of life, rather than a difficult decline," as Korky Vann wrote for the *Orlando Sentinel* (November 1, 2004). To begin effecting that change in attitude, Thomas attempted to recreate people's understanding of the so-called ages of man. Instead of Shakespeare's seven ages, Erik Erikson's eight, or Sigmund Freud's five, Thomas focused on three: childhood, adulthood, and what he called "elderhood." Childhood, he explained, is a time of being, when humans simply experience the world and use their imaginations. Adulthood is a time of doing; in American society, as G. Allen Power wrote for the *Rochester Democrat and Chronicle* (April 2, 2004), "We value people for what they do, not who they are." During elderhood, humans once again seem to be rather than do. However, in Thomas's view, the elderly do not simply reenter a state of being and experience a second childhood. Rather, they become our greatest teachers: in his words, according to Power, "Elders . . . teach us how to make a community. When we come together to meet their needs, we learn how to live as human beings. They instruct us in the art of caring."

Thomas, his wife, Judy, and their five children live on a 258-acre working farm powered by solar and wind energy in Sherburne, a rural community in upstate New York. Thomas is developing his next project, a multigenerational "intentional community" called Eldershire, which he plans to create on his property. He writes daily and schedules 35 to 40 speaking engagements a year.

—A.R.

Suggested Reading: *Asheville (North Carolina) Citizen-Times* A p7 Apr. 28, 1999; *Chicago Tribune* C p4 July 24, 2005; *Detroit Free Press* A p1 Oct. 17, 1997; *Fast Company* p78+ Feb. 2002; *Orange County (California) Register* Nov 11, 2004; *Orlando (Florida) Sentinel* E p2 Nov. 1, 2004; *Ventura County (California) Star* E p1 Oct. 28, 2001

Selected Books: *The Eden Alternative: Nature, Hope, and Nursing Homes*, 1994; *Life Worth Living: How Someone You Love Can Still Enjoy Life in a Nursing Home: The Eden Alternative in Action*, 1996; *Learning from Hannah: Secrets for a Life Worth Living*, 1999); *What Are Old People For? How Elders Will Save the World*, 2004; *In the Arms of Elders: A Parable of Wise Leadership and Community Building*, 2006

Denise Applewhite/Courtesy of the Office of
Communications, Princeton University

Tilghman, Shirley M.

(TILL-man)

Sep. 17, 1946– Molecular biologist; educator

*Address: One Nassau Hall, Princeton University,
Princeton, NJ 08544*

On June 15, 2001, after serving for 15 years on the
faculty of Princeton University, Shirley Tilghman
became the school's 19th president and the first female to attain the post. Also a world-renowned
leader in the field of molecular biology, Tilghman
performed groundbreaking work in the area of genomic imprinting, or the "silencing" of certain
genes, and was one of the architects of the Human
Genome Project, a massive effort by the U.S. Department of Energy and the National Institutes of
Health (NIH) to map human DNA. In addition,
Tilghman has used her prominence to try to increase the numbers of women in faculty positions
in the sciences. "It has been my experience that the
problems that intrigue women about the natural
world are not always exactly the same as those that
attract men," she said during a speech at the
launch of the Earth Institute ADVANCE Program at
Columbia University, held on March 24, 2005. "By
encouraging women to embrace science, we likely
increase the range of problems under study, and
this will broaden and strengthen the entire enterprise."

The second of four daughters, Tilghman was
born Shirley Marie Caldwell on September 17,
1946 in Toronto, Ontario, Canada, to Shirley (Car-
re) Caldwell and Henry Wimmett Caldwell. Her father worked for the Bank of Nova Scotia. At an ear-

ly age Tilghman demonstrated a drive that brought
her success at school—and led to consternation
among her family members. "As a little girl, I never
knew anyone so impatient in my life," Shirley
Caldwell told Kathryn Federici Greenwood for the
Princeton Alumni Weekly (September 12, 2001,
on-line). "And how she ever took up science I don't
know because it must be the most demanding thing
to do. She was impatient with me and her sisters.
She wanted to get things done. She wanted to do
things her way." While she was growing up, math
was the subject that most fascinated Tilghman,
who frequently played arithmetic games with her
father. The two also played golf and practiced the
piano together. When Tilghman was in second
grade, she and her family relocated to the city of
Lethbridge, in Alberta, Canada, before heading
southwest to the city of London, Ontario. Two
years later they settled in Winnipeg, where Tilghman attended junior high and high school.

As a student at Kelbin High School, Tilghman
thrived socially as well as academically. In addition to being student council treasurer and yearbook editor, she was a member of the basketball,
volleyball, and track teams; she also skied and rode
horses. Although Tilghman was considered one of
the top students in her school, her 10th-grade history teacher, Leon Orlikow, told her parents that
she lacked "aggression about learning," which
served to increase her interest in her studies. Her
determination to succeed in her endeavors was further fueled by a high-school guidance counselor,
who said, based on the results of an aptitude test
Tilghman had taken, that she was most suited to
become an executive secretary. Tilghman has credited her father with helping her to set her sights
high. "I got my feminism from my father. He fought
for me every time there was an attempt to pigeonhole me as a woman," she said to Greenwood.
Tilghman decided to pursue a career in science
when she won a scholarship to attend the prestigious Queen's University in Kingston, Ontario. She
majored in chemistry and biochemistry and minored in math, receiving a bachelor's degree in
1968.

After graduation Tilghman taught chemistry to
high-school students in Sierra Leone, in western
Africa, as a volunteer with the Canadian University Service Overseas (CUSO), a volunteer organization. During that time she met Joseph Tilghman, a
Philadelphia, Pennsylvania, native and member of
the Peace Corps. The two were married in 1970,
following their return from Africa. While her husband attended law school, Tilghman enrolled at
Temple University, in Philadelphia, where she
studied biochemistry and earned her Ph.D. degree
in 1975. She was awarded the Fogarty International Fellowship at the NIH in Bethesda, Maryland,
and participated in cloning the mouse beta-globin
gene, the first mammalian gene to be cloned. Tilghman helped to clone the gene by isolating a single
gene from the entire genome of the organism. She
became one of the first to study the effects of intro-

ducing replicated genes into mice. In addition, she demonstrated that the coding sequences in the mouse genome were noncontiguous (not adjoining) and were interrupted by introns, or the sections of DNA that are not translated into protein. That finding was significant because the mouse genome and human genome share virtually the same set of genes and are similar in size; knowledge of the DNA sequence of the mouse genome is thus helpful in identifying and studying the function of human genes. Tilghman also identified the structure of the H19 gene in mice, later demonstrating that the gene was responsible for initiating and maintaining parental imprinting (that is, the tendency of gene expression to be determined by whether the gene is inherited from the male or the female parent). After completing her fellowship at the NIH, Tilghman returned to Temple University, where she worked for one year as an assistant professor at Fels Research Institute. She accepted a position as an independent investigator at the Institute for Cancer Research of Fox Chase Cancer Center, in Philadelphia, while also serving as an adjunct associate professor of human genetics, biochemistry, and biophysics at the University of Pennsylvania. She continued to study the structure and mechanism of expression of genes in the livers of mice during the development of embryos.

In 1986 Tilghman joined the faculty of Princeton University, in Princeton, New Jersey, as the Howard Prior Professor of Life Sciences in the Department of Molecular Biology. She continued to analyze a particular gene in mice and found that the gene's expression was not the same when it came from the mother as when it came from the father. During the process of genomic imprinting, which takes place inside the developing embryo, it is determined whether the copy of a given gene came from the mother or the father (most genes come in pairs, one from each parent); only one copy of the gene from one parent is expressed while the gene inherited from the other parent remains "silent," or is suppressed, usually the result of DNA chemicals known as the methyl groups. The results of Tilghman's study provided an understanding of why mammals' genes are expressed in a parent-specific manner during the maturation period; Tilghman also proposed the first model to explain the mechanism of parent-specific silencing of genes. Her additional research, into genes that affect embryo development, was made possible in 1988, when she became an investigator with the Howard Hughes Medical Institute, in Chevy Chase, Maryland. She also served during that time as an adjunct professor in the Biochemistry Department at the Robert Wood Johnson Medical School, in Piscataway, New Jersey.

In June 1991 Tilghman was appointed as one of 12 charter members of the National Advisory Council for Human Genome Research (NACHGR), who served as advisers on programs of the Human Genome Project. The goal of the project included identifying all of the genes in human DNA, finding out the sequences of the three billion chemical base pairs that make up human DNA, and storing the information in databases. Additional research involved studying the genes of nonhuman organisms, including the fruit fly and the laboratory mouse. In June 2000 the initial survey of the entire human genome was completed. In February 2001 the first draft of the study was published in *Nature*, mapping out the bulk of the human genome; the maps showed that there are only about 30,000 genes—many fewer than the 100,000 expected. The entire analysis of the human genome was completed and published in April 2003.

In 1993 Tilghman was appointed chairperson of Princeton University's Council on Science and Technology, which is concerned with the teaching of science and technology to students outside the science field. For her efforts Tilghman received the President's Award for Distinguished Teaching from the university in 1996. Two years later she received national attention for her report "Trends in the Early Careers of Life Scientists," published by the National Research Council, which she served as a committee chairman. Also in 1998 she was named the founding director of Princeton's Lewis-Sigler Institute for Integrative Genomics.

In May 2001, after 15 years of teaching at Princeton, Tilghman was selected to succeed Harold Shapiro as the university's president. She also became the first president in more than a century who has not received a degree from Princeton. Tilghman began her tenure by creating a task force on the status of female teachers in science and engineering and focusing on recruiting and retaining women professors in those fields. According to the task force's findings, released in a 2003 report, between 1992 and 2002 Princeton saw an overall increase in the percentage of women in the natural sciences and engineering, from 8.4 percent to 13.9 percent. While four departments at the university failed to report an increase in the proportion of female faculty members, the Department of Molecular Biology reported that the percentage of women in its department declined sharply, from 30 percent to 19 percent. It was found that while almost half of those who receive Ph.D. degrees in the field of molecular biology are women, only a quarter of the women apply for junior faculty positions at top universities. Among the task force's recommendations was the appointment of a special assistant to the dean of the faculty, who would focus on issues of gender equality. The university followed the recommendation. Tilghman also champions early exposure of students to the more current and exciting aspects of modern science. "Scientists love to teach the canon—Mendel's peas and Newton's first law—that's dry and not very inspiring," she told Donald Macleod for the London *Guardian Weekly* (January 27, 2006). She has also established the Princeton Postdoctoral Teaching Fellowship program, which provides postdoctoral students with yearlong opportunities to gain research and teaching experience at Princeton.

Tilghman's contributions to science and teaching have garnered her several prestigious awards, including Princeton University's Distinguished Teaching Award, the L'Oreal UNESCO Award for Women in Science, the Lifetime Achievement Award from the Society of Development Biology, and the Radcliffe Institute Medal. Tilghman helped to establish the blueprint for the Human Genome Project and was one of the founders of the National Advisory Council of the Human Genome Project Initiative at NIH. She is a member of the American Philosophical Society, the National Academy of Sciences, the Institute of Medicine, and the Royal Society of London. In 2005 Tilghman, who continues to teach at Princeton, was named to the board of directors at Google Inc. She is divorced and has two children, Rebecca and Alexander.

—B.M.

Suggested Reading: *New York Times* C p1 June 11, 1996; princeton.edu; *St. Louis Post-Dispatch* A p7 Oct. 22, 1992; *Washington Post* A p4 May 6, 2001

Tillerson, Rex

Mar. 23, 1952– Chairman and CEO of ExxonMobil Corp.

Address: ExxonMobil Corporate Headquarters, 5959 Las Colinas Blvd., Irving, TX 75039-2298

With revenues exceeding $360 billion and profits eclipsing $36 billion in 2005 alone—and with $29.3 billion in profits in 2006, as of November—ExxonMobil currently ranks as the United States' most profitable company and the world's largest publicly traded oil and gas producer. Rex W. Tillerson, the company's chairman and chief executive officer (CEO), has headed the petroleum giant since January 2006, when he replaced Lee Raymond, who served in those capacities from 1999 through 2005. Tillerson has worked for Exxon since 1975, when he was hired as a production engineer soon after graduating from the University of Texas at Austin with a degree in civil engineering. The many issues Tillerson faces as head of ExxonMobil include global warming and the growing concern among lawmakers and consumers about soaring gas prices; the retail price of one gallon of gasoline in the U.S. climbed to more than $3.00 on average late in the summer of 2005. (By the fall of 2006, the average had fallen to about $2.20 per gallon.) Upon his promotion, observers predicted that Tillerson would project a more approachable public image than that of his often impatient predecessor. Fadel Gheit, an oil-industry analyst, said to Thomas Catan for the *Financial Times* (April 23, 2006, on-line) that Tillerson "is very firm but with

a friendly manner. He can carry the same message [as his forerunners] but in a kinder, gentler manner. It will, I think, serve the company very well." Tillerson has a reputation as a shrewd deal broker and is known among the business press and his colleagues for his adeptness at negotiating with sometimes contentious heads of state, foreign ministers, and heads of oil companies in other countries, most notably those in the Middle East and Russia. "He is a businessman but also a diplomat . . . ," Gheit said to Catan. "This is probably one of his greatest attributes."

Americans consume an average of nearly 20 million barrels of oil per day, according to a Department of Energy study cited on the Web site of the Natural Resources Defense Council. ExxonMobil produces approximately 1.5 billion barrels of oil each year, or four million daily. Part of Tillerson's challenge as ExxonMobil's chief will be to negotiate an agreement for the company to extract oil from new sources, so that it can fulfill its promise of increasing its daily output to five million barrels by 2010. Tillerson told Susie Gharib for the PBS program *Nightly Business Report* (March 8, 2006) that he disagreed with the widespread notion that "the days of easy oil"—or of being able to supply oil with little effort—are over. "I've been in this business for more than 30 years now," he said. "I don't ever remember any easy days for oil and that's because we've always been on the edge of technology advances, finding the way to access the next new resource opportunity, deeper water, arctic conditions, harsher environments, new cultures, whatever the challenge may be. There's never been anything easy about it, and that's not any different than we find ourselves today."

Rex W. Tillerson was born on March 23, 1952 in Wichita Falls, Texas, near the border of Oklahoma. During the summers when he was a young man, he worked in construction. He attended the University of Texas at Austin, receiving his bachelor's degree in civil engineering, in about 1975. When he was a senior in college, a recruiter for the Exxon Co. USA persuaded him to visit the company's headquarters, in Katy, Texas, located just outside Houston. The recruiter explained to him that Exxon offered civil engineers a variety of positions with potential for growth. The visit convinced Tillerson that if he joined Exxon, he "would indeed have a say in selecting the job that would be right for me," as he said to Mike Long for ExxonMobil's employee publication, the *Lamp*. Tillerson further explained that in the Katy office he encountered young engineers who seemed genuinely pleased with their jobs, another factor in his decision to join the company. Soon afterward Exxon hired him as a production engineer, and he was assigned to its Katy office, which, "although it had Exxon USA's smallest production district engineering staff . . . ," Tillerman told Long, "offered just about anything you could want—major gas production, one of the company's largest gas processing plants, an expanding drilling program that re-

Chip Somodevilla/Getty Images

Rex W. Tillerson

quired leading-edge . . . techniques. It was a terrific experience that grounded me well for other assignments."

Initially, Tillerson changed positions roughly every 18 months, in keeping with the company's deep-rooted practice of diversifying new employees' portfolios. At the age of 29, he was assigned to the company's district office in Kingsville, Texas, which was larger than the Katy branch, and became the engineering manager. In that capacity he supervised a staff of 100 engineers and oversaw an annual budget of approximately $300 million. "That was a huge amount of money for someone my age," he explained to Long, "but that assignment is where I began to understand my own views about managing large organizations." In 1987 Tillerson accepted even greater responsibility, when he assumed the post of business-development manager for the company's Natural Gas Department; among his chief responsibilities were developing and implementing long-term plans for the commercialization of gas obtained from Alaska and the Beaufort Sea. Continuing his climb up Exxon's corporate ladder, in 1989 Tillerson was named the general manager of its Central Production Division, a sector responsible for oil and gas production operations throughout much of Texas, Oklahoma, Arkansas, and Kansas. He later served as a production adviser, relocating to Dallas, Texas, where he consulted on the company's merger of its South Texas Division and Central Division. That experience taught him "that when employees understand what the business needs to be successful, they always find a way to get it done," as he said to Long. He also said, "When you put two organizations together, you have to ensure that em-

ployees' pride in past accomplishments is preserved and that they don't feel they have lost their identity with the company. You want everybody working together." From 1992 to 1995 he served as the coordinator of Affiliate Gas Sales, in the company's international division, based in Florham Park, New Jersey.

In the latter half of the 1990s, Tillerson earned a reputation as a builder of relationships with foreign governments. Assigned to various positions overseas, he assumed the duties of, successively, president of Exxon Yemen Inc. and Esso Exploration and Production Khorat Inc. (Exxon is known in Europe as "Esso"); vice president of Exxon Ventures Inc.; and president of Exxon Neftegas Ltd. In the two latter roles, he oversaw the company's holdings in Russia and the Caspian Sea, including its dealings with the Commonwealth of Independent States (CIS), which comprises several former republics of the Soviet Union. Tillerson devoted most of his energy at that time to so-called "upstream" endeavors—or those involving energy exploration and production. (The term "downstream" applies to the refining and selling of petroleum products.) As the head of Exxon Neftegas, a multinational affiliate of Exxon, he negotiated a $15 billion production-sharing agreement (PSA), signed in June 1995, among the governments of the Russian Federation and Sakhalin, an island located off the coast of Russia, north of Japan, and four multinational oil companies, Exxon, Rosneft-Sakhalin, Sakhalinmorneftegas-Shelf, and the Sakhalin Oil Development Cooperation Co. Ltd. (SODECO), a Japanese company. The PSA, referred to as Sakhalin I, established the development of oil and gas reserves in three fields off the coast of Sakhalin and began pumping oil for export in late August 2006. (That area is expected to produce 250,000 barrels of oil per day by the end of 2006.) Also during that period, according to the *Lamp*, Tillerson negotiated a contract in Thailand for gas sales. Tillerson explained to Long that his experiences in the 1990s taught him "to maintain an enormous amount of patience and persistence. You cannot get discouraged." Regarding Tillerson's overseas successes, a person identified as his former boss said to Nelson D. Schwartz for *Fortune* (September 15, 2003), "He was extraordinary in Russia. He built relationships very quickly with the Russians, which wasn't easy to do." Eugene Lawson, president of the U.S. government's Russian Business Council (of which Tillerson is a board member), said to Schwartz for the April 17, 2006 issue of *Fortune*, "Russia was Rex's show. He's got a lot of gravitas, he's physically strong, he's a rancher—and the Russians just eat that stuff up. He's the best negotiator I've ever seen."

In late 1998 Lee R. Raymond, who had become Exxon's chief executive and chairman in 1993, announced the purchase of the Mobil Oil Co. for $77 billion. The merger created ExxonMobil, reuniting two of the biggest pieces of Standard Oil, the company that was founded by John D. Rockefeller in the latter half of the 19th century, grew into a monopoly, and was disbanded into 34 smaller companies in 1911. In December 1999 Tillerson was named vice president of ExxonMobil and relocated to Houston, Texas, where he was put in charge of the development and production of new oil and gas reserves. Then, in 2001, in a move watched closely by industry analysts, ExxonMobil reshuffled its corporate governance, elevating Tillerson and Ed Galante, the company's downstream expert, to senior vice president. Also in 2001 the company's board of directors asked Raymond, who according to reports was scheduled to retire in August 2003, to remain with the company for an indefinite period, during which he would groom a successor. In early March 2004 the company's board of directors promoted Tillerson to president, a position that had been vacant since 1996, and also named him to its board of directors. In August 2005 ExxonMobil announced that Raymond would step down at the end of the calendar year and that Tillerson would replace him as its chief executive officer and chairman.

Since he succeeded Raymond, Tillerson has worked to change Exxon's public position on climate change. For example, he acknowledged in an interview with Jad Mouawad for the *New York Times* (March 30, 2006) that fossil-fuel consumption contributes to higher global temperatures, a finding with which Raymond, as CEO, famously refused to agree. "We recognize that climate change is a serious issue," Tillerson said. "We recognize that greenhouse gas emissions are one of the factors affecting climate change." Tillerson has noted in interviews that Exxon has spent some $1 billion at its plants on co-generation, the process by which an industrial facility converts waste into heat or electricity and thereby reduces carbon-dioxide emissions. He has also pointed to the company's $100 million donation to Stanford University's Climate Energy Project, which is devoted to the development of a global energy system with low greenhouse-gas emissions. (Schwartz reported in 2006 that ExxonMobil has also given millions of dollars to such groups as the Competitive Enterprise Institute, a think tank that calls itself, according to Schwartz, "a leader in the fight against the global-warming scare.") Discussing the issue of global climate change with Schwartz for the 2006 *Fortune* article, Tillerson said, "What we support is continued efforts to understand the problem better." He added, "We need to work harder on articulating our views, and we're going to try to do better at that in the future." Despite that assertion, Tillerson has said that ExxonMobil will not invest in developing alternative energy sources, such as wind and solar power, which he believes have little potential for replacing oil and natural gas as the world's primary source of energy. "It's the same old wine in a new bottle," the analyst Fadel Gheit said to Mouawad, in discussing how ExxonMobil under Tillerson might alter its policies. "You can't expect a company this size to change on a dime,

but you might see changes in how it projects its image to the public, to its clients."

When asked by Susie Gharib to address President George W. Bush's declaration that the U.S. is "addicted" to oil and that it is vital for the country to end its dependence on that foreign energy source, Tillerson responded by saying: "We've said for some time that energy independence is not only unrealistic and unachievable, I guess I would add I'm not sure it's even desirable. From the standpoint of we live in a global community, our economies are interdependent and since energy is such a part of the economic growth, it's only natural that some of the energy supply demand is going to be interdependent as well." Tillerson said to Schwartz that the phrase "addicted to oil" represented "an unfortunate choice of words, quite frankly. Oil and natural gas have been the enablers of economic growth in this country. And to say that you're addicted to oil and natural gas seems to me to say you're addicted to economic prosperity." Tillerson also assured Gharib that ExxonMobil is not involved in "price gouging," a concern that many Americans shared: "Obviously we're not gouging the consumer. Our response to that is to do the things that we know how to do well and that's to continue to look for new sources of energy around the world, take the risk, huge amounts of capital required to develop new sources of energy, continue to develop technology that's going to open new resources that can become available to meet that energy demand."

On March 15, 2006, appearing as a witness before the U.S. Senate Judiciary Committee hearing investigating, among other issues, whether or not mergers and acquisitions in the oil industry have contributed to higher prices at U.S. gasoline stations, Tillerson defiantly stated that ExxonMobil would remain committed to its bottom line. As quoted by Schwartz, he said that the company's profits "accrue to the more than two million individual Americans who own our shares." Asked why ExxonMobil had not spent more money on finding renewable sources of energy, he said, "We are investing heavily in conventional oil and natural gas, which is the business we are in."

Overseas governments have been making it more difficult for multinational oil companies such as ExxonMobil to gain access to their oil deposits. In Venezuela, for example, President Hugo Chavez's Socialist government has proposed increasing royalties and other taxes on foreign investors, and in its recent agreements with other international petroleum companies, among them Chevron, BP, and Shell, Venezuela has dictated the terms of business agreements. ExxonMobil has publicly balked at some of the new conditions, refusing to sign an agreement with Venezuela that would essentially hand over control of the company's fields in that country. Russia has also recently taken steps to curtail foreign investment. As CEO Tillerson has enjoyed success in relations with other countries, however, personally negotiating agreements with the leaders of Indonesia and the United Arab Emirates that will enable the company to access those nations' previously untapped oil reserves. The company is believed to be preparing to increase its capital spending to $20 billion annually by 2010, and ExxonMobil hopes to increase its production to five million barrels per day by that year. According to the *New York Times* (March 30, 2006) ExxonMobil is investigating the viability of resource-extraction projects that could lead over the next three years to agreements with Angola, Malaysia, and Norway, among other nations.

In August 2006 ExxonMobil launched two ambitious projects relating to natural gas. The first was the building of a natural-gas pipeline from Alaska's North Slope to the lower 48 U.S. states; according to Barbara Shook, writing for *Natural Gas Week* (August 21, 2006), it is the "most expensive private construction venture ever envisioned." The second venture, a collaborative effort with Qatar Petroleum (QP), involves the construction of plants that will produce liquefied natural gas for the U.S. and European markets.

Ralph Nader, a noted American political activist and consumer advocate and a presidential candidate in 1996, 2000, and 2004, published an open letter to Tillerson on March 31, 2006. In the letter, which appears on the activist's Web site, Nader chided the ExxonMobil chief for what Nader saw as the company's continued abuse of power and wealth, which undermine the interests of the majority of Americans. He wrote, "Rarely has there been such a demonstration of corporate greed and insensitivity by a company that has received huge government welfare subsidies, de-regulation and tax expenditures over the years at the expense of the smaller taxpayers of America." Nader cited, in particular, ExxonMobil's refusal to "contribute some significant [tax] deductible money to charities which help impoverished American families pay the exorbitant prices for heating oil this past winter," as well as its "stubborn refusal to pay the modest $5 billion punitive damage award" that followed the 1989 *Exxon Valdez* oil spill, which "put so many small businesses out of business."

In the fall of 2006, Tillerson announced that ExxonMobil will undertake a series of philanthropic initiatives aimed at improving math and science education in U.S. schools. In one, ExxonMobil pledged to expand the Houston, Texas–based Bernard Harris Summer Science Camp (named in honor of the first African-American astronaut to walk in space), a science, technology, and engineering camp for middle-school students, to more than 20 other sites. In another, ExxonMobil will help to extend to educators nationwide an interdisciplinary math and science program for secondary-school teachers known as UTeach, which is based at the University of Texas at Austin.

Tillerson is married to the former Renda St. Clair. Loren Steffy, writing for the *Houston Chronicle* (May 7, 2006), described Tillerson as being "as avuncular as his predecessor [Raymond] was acerbic." The business press has described him as being deferential, unassuming, and matter-of-fact in person; he is also said to possess a sharp memory. The ExxonMobil chief is what has been called a "weekend rancher" and enjoys riding horses. Discussing Tillerson's work habits, a former colleague said to Schwartz in 2003, "If you send him an e-mail, you'll hear back within an hour. He doesn't leave it to his secretary." Tillerson is said to prepare meticulously for meetings with foreign heads of state by brushing up on those nations' history and culture. Since 1992, according to the Web site Newsmeat.com, which tracks the contributions made by prominent Americans to political parties and special-interest groups, Tillerson has donated $25,600 to the Republican Party or its candidates.

Regarding the company's potential for future growth, Tillerson said to Long: "This is a business about long time frames, very large investment commitments and huge risks. However, with patience and persistence and all of the things that we can bring to bear—the quality of our people, our technology, our management approach and our integrity—there is no doubt that we will be more successful than others. That was the case 100 years ago, and that's the case today."

—D.F.

Suggested Reading: *Financial Times* (on-line) Apr. 23, 2006; *Fortune* p116+ Sep. 15, 2003, p77+ Apr. 17, 2006; *New York Times* C p1 Mar. 30, 2006

Tomlinson, LaDainian

June 23, 1979– Football player

Address: San Diego Chargers, P.O. Box 609609, San Diego, CA 92160-9609

"My era goes back to [the legendary running back] Jim Brown and maybe a little bit before. I've seen them all," Marty Schottenheimer, the head coach of the San Diego Chargers of the National Football League (NFL), said to Bucky Gleason for the *Buffalo (New York) News* (November 19, 2005). Referring to the Chargers' running back LaDainian Tomlinson, Schottenheimer added, "It's hard to say, 'This guy is better than that guy,' but at the end of the day, if he stays healthy, I think he's going to stand as the best [running back] that's ever played." As a receiver at Texas Christian University, and in his first several seasons with the Chargers, beginning in 2001, Tomlinson saw his record-setting play overshadowed by the lackluster overall performance of his team. But every team Tomlinson has played for since his high-school days has improved on the strength of his consistently dazzling rushing efforts, and with the Chargers' recent resurgence, the compact five-foot 10-inch,

Getty Images

LaDainian Tomlinson

221-pound running back has begun to get the kind of attention many feel he has long merited. Tomlinson "strikes fear into the hearts of defenders every time he touches the ball," Michael Silver wrote for *Sports Illustrated* (September 6, 2004). His fearsome play on the field is balanced by a dedication to charity work and a rare humility away from it, qualities that have led him to be praised as a mature and generous person as well as a gifted athlete.

The second of the three children of Oliver Tomlinson and Loreane Chappell, LaDainian Tomlinson was born on June 23, 1979 in Marlin, Texas, outside Waco. LaDainian's father, a builder and truck driver, was 15 years older than his wife and had previously fathered five other children. The couple divorced in 1986, after Oliver Tomlinson suffered a disabling work-related injury that put a strain on the marriage. Loreane Chappell raised LaDainian and his younger brother, LaVar, and sister, Londria, on her own, working as a nurse's assistant and hospital-records clerk to keep the family afloat. Oliver remained in touch with his children initially but grew more distant from them as they got older. (As an adult LaDainian has reestablished contact with his father.) From an early age LaDainian followed football and was a particular fan of the Dallas Cowboys, whom he watched on television every week with his father. LaDainian first played organized football along with LaVar in a local Pop Warner League; their mother attended all of the games. LaDainian's favorite football player was the Cowboys' running back Emmitt Smith, whom he had followed since the latter's years as a college player.

Tomlinson entered University High School in Waco and hoped to get a scholarship to one of Texas's premier football colleges, such as the University of Texas or Texas A&M. During his first three high-school seasons, he was used in linebacker positions, in which he blocked for other runners instead of running the ball himself. By all accounts Tomlinson dutifully accepted those positions, though he believed that his talents could be put to better use. In his senior year Tomlinson was finally able to play tailback, and he immediately excelled at the position. By mid-season he had become a sensation in the local media, having rushed for over 1,000 yards. He totaled 2,554 yards and 39 touchdowns for the year and was named his school district's most valuable player. Nevertheless, he did not receive much attention from the colleges he had hoped would notice him, due to his short time in the tailback position and to his relatively small size (at that time he weighed roughly 195 pounds). Tomlinson was recruited by a handful of smaller schools, including North Texas, Texas Christian, and Kansas State Universities. He chose to attend Texas Christian (TCU), after favorable meetings with the head coach, Pat Sullivan, and because TCU's Fort Worth campus was close to Dallas, where his mother then lived and worked in real estate. (His mother, who moved to Dallas near the start of his senior year, agreed to let her son live with a friend's family in Waco so that he could finish his career at University High.)

In his freshman season Tomlinson gave a solid performance, with 538 yards rushing on 126 attempts. The team, however, finished the year with a dismal 1–10 record. For the next season TCU hired a new head coach, Dennis Franchione, who made more frequent use of Tomlinson and helped him to improve his strength through weight training. Tomlinson began his sophomore season at fullback, blocking for the running back Basil Mitchell, an upperclassman, but found more success when he was allowed to run the ball, rushing for 99 yards in a midseason upset of the Air Force Academy team. The TCU Horned Frogs made an impressive turnaround from the previous season, finishing with a 7–5 record, and upset the University of Southern California (USC) in the 1998 Sun Bowl. Tomlinson had 717 yards and eight touchdowns for the year and was voted Second Team All WAC (Western Atlantic Conference). In the off-season he concentrated on weight training as well as his classwork.

In July 1999 Tomlinson and the TCU basketball star Lee Nailon were arrested on suspicion of marijuana possession and trying to evade arrest, and Tomlinson spent 24 hours in jail. He told Franchione that he was innocent of the drug charge and had merely been in the wrong place at the wrong time, and he insisted on taking a drug test. The test results were negative, but the experience served as a lesson for him. "It really sunk in how fast trouble can get to you," he told Jennifer Floyd for the Fort Worth, Texas, *Star-Telegram* (August 15, 1999).

"Everybody had spent all summer telling me the sky is the limit for me, and I saw that it could've all been gone. I learned a lot that night, and it changed me in some ways." Tomlinson "was adamant that he wanted to prove that he wasn't involved," Franchione recalled, as quoted by Jim Trotter in the *San Diego Union-Tribune* (September 12, 2004). "I always thought he was a really good person, but that was just kind of a verification of what I thought, that he is what he seemed to me." While he was publicly absolved of wrongdoing, that development received far less media attention than the original charge.

NFL scouts began noticing Tomlinson's on-field performance early in the 1999 season, when he rushed for 269 yards against Arkansas State and 300 against San Jose State. In November of that year, he ran for 406 yards against the University of Texas–El Paso, setting a National Collegiate Athletic Association (NCAA) Division 1-A single-game record and becoming Texas Christian's all-time single-season rushing leader. TCU finished the season with a record of 8–4, its best in 40 years, and beat East Carolina in the 1999 Mobile Alabama Bowl, another upset. Tomlinson led the nation in rushing yards, finishing with 1,850. In a typically unselfish gesture, he gave his rushing-title trophy to the members of his offensive line. Following that season he considered entering the NFL draft but decided against it, as it was unlikely that he would be picked in the first round. His mother's desire for him to earn a degree also compelled him to stay in college. (Tomlinson recently completed all his coursework and earned a degree from TCU, fulfilling a promise to his mother. According to Tomlinson's Web site, he earned a degree in general studies with minors in psychology, sociology, and radio/TV/film.)

In the spring of 2000, LaDainian was the front-runner among running backs—though a longshot overall— for the Heisman Trophy, the award for the best college football player in any position, decided annually by a panel of voters around the country. Most of the other candidates for the trophy played for larger, more famous schools, so the TCU coaching staff launched a media campaign to widen Tomlinson's exposure. The school administration got involved, and the campaign came to focus not only on promoting Tomlinson but on attracting attention to the university itself. Tomlinson ended up as a finalist for the Heisman Trophy, which was awarded to the quarterback Chris Weinke of Florida State University. Also during that time, Tomlinson developed a reputation as a role model by appearing in a five-minute videotape, entitled "Teachers Are the Real Heroes," which was distributed to more than 300 schools around the Dallas/Fort Worth area, and making personal appearances at schools, to the delight of elementary and middle-school students. In preparation for the football season, he also continued to spend long hours in weight training.

In TCU's opening game that season, against Northwestern, Tomlinson rushed for 243 yards. In another victory, over the University of Hawaii, he rushed for 294 yards and had four touchdowns. At the height of their run, the TCU Horned Frogs, propelled by Tomlinson as well as other offensive players and a stellar defensive line, were ranked ninth in the nation and had the country's longest winning streak, with 12 straight victories dating back to the previous year. Although they lost some momentum toward the close of the season, Tomlinson finished with the fourth-highest single-season total of rushing yards in NCAA history, with 2,158, and the sixth-highest total of career rushing yards in NCAA Division 1-A history, with 5,263—despite his having run for only 1,255 yards in his first two seasons combined. He was also only the second player in NCAA history to rush for over 2,000 yards in a season and 5,000 yards in a career.

In 2001 the San Diego Chargers got first pick in the NFL draft because they had had the worst record in the NFL the previous season, finishing at 1–15. San Diego traded the first pick to Atlanta, in exchange for the fifth pick and the receiver Tim Dwight, and Tomlinson was drafted fifth by the Chargers. After lengthy negotiations Tomlinson was given a contract for $38 million over six years, with bonuses—a salary that earned him the nickname "Big Money" among his teammates. He bought new homes in Dallas, Texas, for his mother and sister and also purchased vacant buildings for their businesses. He bought himself an SUV (sport utility vehicle), with a license plate that read "Mr. LT," and rented a condominium in San Diego. As a pro-football player Tomlinson made rapid progress. In the Chargers' 2001 opening game, in which they beat the Washington Redskins, 30–3, Tomlinson rushed for 113 yards. Soon afterward he outplayed his boyhood hero Emmitt Smith, rushing for 90 yards in a 32–21 victory over the Dallas Cowboys. Although the Chargers finished the season at 5–11, Tomlinson became the first Charger ever to gain more than 1,600 yards from scrimmage in a season, with 1,603 (including 1,236 rushing yards and passes caught for 367) and was the runner-up for the NFL's Offensive Rookie of the Year honor.

The 2002 season began with another series of strong performances by San Diego, and especially Tomlinson, under a new head coach, Marty Schottenheimer. In the opening game Tomlinson ran for 116 yards in a defeat of the Cincinnati Bengals. A few weeks later, in a victory over the New England Patriots that brought San Diego to 4–0, LaDainian rushed for 217 yards, tying a team record. The team began to falter midway through the season, however, and lost seven of its last nine games. Tomlinson, meanwhile, was named the team's most valuable player and was also selected for the American Football Conference (AFC) Pro Bowl team. His most productive game of the year was against Denver, in which he gained 220 yards and made three touchdowns. During the season Tomlinson tied team records for yardage on the ground (1,683) and for receptions by a running back (79). He also became the 11th player in NFL history with total touchdowns in the double digits for consecutive seasons.

The following season was another disappointing one for the Chargers. While Schottenheimer had made significant lineup changes in attempts to improve the team's performance—such as trading the linebacker Junior Seau and acquiring the receiver David Boston—San Diego finished the 2003 campaign with a record of 4–12. Once again, Tomlinson had an extraordinary year despite his team's poor showing, rushing for 200 yards in a victory over Cleveland, and 243 yards—a team record—in a season-ending win against Oakland. His yardage from scrimmage totaled 2,370, the second most in NFL history, and he became the first player ever to rush for at least 1,000 yards and catch at least 100 passes in a single season. The Chargers rewarded him with a new, $60 million contract, the largest for a running back in the league's history.

With consistently impressive performances from the quarterback Drew Brees, the rookie tight end Antonio Gates, and the defense as a whole, as well as continued excellence from Tomlinson, the Chargers made a significant turnaround in 2004. After defeating Tampa Bay and Cleveland late in the year, they were guaranteed a spot in the playoffs. In their first postseason appearance, however, they lost in overtime to the New York Jets. Tomlinson finished the 2004 season with the most rushing touchdowns (17) and the fifth-most yards from scrimmage (1,776) in the NFL. He also set the single-season record for touchdowns rushed in consecutive games (12). In 2005 he scored a rushing touchdown in each of 14 consecutive games, surpassing the previous NFL record. That year he also broke the Chargers' record for touchdowns scored in a season, with 20, and career yards from scrimmage, with 9,753, as the Chargers finished with another winning record, 9–7. That season Tomlinson became one of only three players to rush for 1,200 or more yards in each of his first five seasons. (The others are Eddie George and Eric Dickerson.) In their September 11, 2006 season opener, the Chargers beat the Oakland Raiders, 27–0, with Tomlinson leading his team with 31 carries. As of early November of that year, Tomlinson led the NFL in touchdowns, having scored 11 in the season's first seven games.

Although he now receives the kind of recognition many feel he has long deserved, Tomlinson, in spite of what he has already achieved, continues to strive to outdo himself. The Philadelphia Eagles' coach, Andy Reid, was quoted by Charean Williams in the *Fort Worth Star-Telegram* (September 7, 2006) as saying, "He is good at everything. He is good at running the football, receiving the football, and obviously, if they need him to throw the ball, he's good at that, too." In the same article Schottenheimer was quoted as saying, "I think he's the best I've ever seen."

Tomlinson lives in Poway, California, in a 10,000-square-foot home, with his wife, LaTorsha. The couple met while they were both attending Texas Christian University. LaTorsha told Jim Trotter that at the beginning of her relationship with her husband, "I kept waiting for him to do something stupid so I could say, 'Oh, you're just like the rest of them.' But that big blunder I was waiting for never happened. He was always honest with me. . . . He just makes you believe in him. He seems so sincere and then you come to realize that it's because he is sincere." In his spare time Tomlinson enjoys attending Los Angeles Lakers basketball games and restoring classic cars. He is involved in a variety of charitable activities, including LT's 21 Club, which provides children from San Diego youth groups with tickets to Chargers home games. He also hosts an annual celebrity golf tournament, whose proceeds go to the LT School Is Cool Scholarship Fund and to victims of wildfires in San Diego. In addition, Tomlinson runs a yearly football camp in Waco, Texas, with a coach from his former high school. In her conversation with Jim Trotter, LaTorsha Tomlinson discussed her husband's modesty: "He has memorabilia of other stuff from other players, but he almost feels like it's being conceited to have people come to his house and there's stuff of himself everywhere. I have a friend who did a hand drawing of him running with the ball and I surprised him and had it framed, and he really didn't want to hang it on the wall because he didn't feel right about it. He always says football is not who I am, it's what I do."

—M.B.

Suggested Reading: (Fort Worth, Texas) *Star-Telegram* Sports Sep. 14, 2005; *San Diego Union-Tribune* C p1 Sep. 12, 2004; *Sporting News* p14 Aug. 12, 2005; *Sports Illustrated* p54 Nov. 6, 2000

Truss, Lynne

May 31, 1955– Writer

Address: Gotham Publicity, 375 Hudson St., New York, NY 10014

"With everything that's going on in the world, it is rather odd that people should be concerning themselves with semi-colons," the author Lynne Truss told Robert McCrum for the London *Observer* (June 13, 2004). "There must be a real comfort in looking at something with sets of rules, and which you can also have fun with when there are so many awful things going on." Perhaps that is part of the explanation for the success of Truss's 2003 book, *Eats, Shoots & Leaves*, which a writer for the London *Independent* (October 23, 2005) described as "the most unlikely publishing sensation of the past cou-

Lynne Truss

ple of years." Prior to writing that best-selling, humorous book on the use and abuse of punctuation, Truss had worked in her native Britain as an editor, columnist, sports journalist, writer of radio scripts, and radio host, and had earned some praise—and modest sales—for her fiction and nonfiction books, *With One Lousy Free Packet of Seed* (1994), *Making the Cat Laugh: One Woman's Journal of Single Life on the Margins* (1995), *Tennyson's Gift* (1996), *Going Loco: A Comedy of Terrors* (1999), and *Tennyson and His Circle* (1999). The reception of those books did not prepare her for the immediate, widespread success of her volume on punctuation. Truss turned her stickler's gaze on another subject—manners—for her newest work, *Talk to the Hand: The Utter Bloody Rudeness of the World Today, or Six Good Reasons to Stay Home and Bolt the Door* (2005). Her adaptation of *Eats, Shoots and Leaves* for children, which bears the subtitle *Why, Commas Really Do Make a Difference!* and has illustrations by Bonnie Timmons, was published in 2006.

Lynne Truss was born on May 31, 1955 and raised in Petersham, in the county of Surrey, England, in a council estate (the British equivalent of a housing project). Her father, a self-taught accountant and former member of Britain's Territorial Army, worked for the company that made Sellotape, while her mother was a telephone operator. Truss had an older sister, Kay, with whom she had a close but very competitive relationship while growing up. Though Truss has described her family life as rather unhappy, she has expressed gratitude for the love of reading that her parents instilled in her. "My parents were interested in books. They were readers. They had a lot of respect for reading and writing," she explained to Jo Ind for the *Birmingham (England) Post* (July 10, 2004). "My dad used to say, 'When I write a book . . .' which is quite an unusual thing for a working class man." Truss attended Tiffin Girls' Grammar School, in Kingston upon Thames, before enrolling at the University College London. While in school, she was painfully shy, as she recalled to Jane Wheatley for the London *Times* (October 15, 2005): "Everyone seemed cleverer than me and knew how to behave. I was so shy I didn't go to a dinner party until I was 35; I went out with the same boy from 18 till 30 but he was as bad as me and we just reinforced each other's inferiority complexes."

After graduating with honors, in 1977, Truss served as a sub-editor at the *Radio Times*, then moved to the *Times Higher Education Supplement*, where she worked as a books sub-editor. At the time she enjoyed editing other writers' work but seldom wrote herself. "I didn't begin writing properly until I was in my mid-thirties," she told Robert McCrum. "I had to overcome a big barrier. I thought that people were born with the right sort of certificate that said, 'This person is allowed to write' and I didn't have it." "I suppose I was ashamed of my background . . . ," she told Jo Ind. "I had a very high level of self-consciousness." Only after attending behavioral therapy did Truss resolve her self-esteem issues and begin writing. She also dealt with longstanding problems relating to her rivalry with her sister, Kay. "She had a lot of advantages," Truss told Jo Ind. "She was better looking than me; she had children; she did get divorced but she made good choices in her life, and she was very well liked." (Meanwhile, despite what Truss characterized as her sister's advantages, Kay often felt jealous of Lynne's academic and professional accomplishments. "If I was successful it was as though it took away from her," Lynne Truss told Jo Ind.) Truss was ultimately able to work out such issues during her therapy sessions and gained the confidence to begin writing; she also established a better, less competitive relationship with her sister.

In the late 1980s Truss spent several years as the literary editor of the now-defunct BBC publication the *Listener*, for which she wrote humorous columns. She also wrote dramatic plays that were performed on BBC Radio. Her first novel, *With One Lousy Free Packet of Seed*, was published in 1994, and she compiled some of her *Listener* columns into a book about single life, entitled *Making the Cat Laugh*, which was published in 1995. The following year she wrote *Tennyson's Gift*, a novel about a fictional conference among such Victorian figures as the poet Alfred, Lord Tennyson, the author Lewis Carroll, and the photographer Julia Margaret Cameron. Writing for the Glasgow *Herald* (August 3, 1996), Deirdre Chapman praised the novel as "a comedy of manners with the feel of summer rep, all grand entrances and exits, misunderstandings and monologues, interspersed with much stylish wit and wisdom." In 1999 Truss published her most recent novel, *Going Loco,* and the nonfiction work *Tennyson and His Circle,* the latter as part of the National Portrait Gallery's Character Sketches series.

Also during the 1990s Truss spent six years as a television critic for the London *Times.* After she declared in one column that few women want to read about sports, the *Times* offered her a job as a sportswriter. In that position she traveled to boxing and soccer matches across Europe, writing about them in a comedic, willfully clueless fashion. She was not happy in the job. "I felt actually if anything I wasn't really helping the cause of women's sports writing because I wasn't doing it from a proper sports writing perspective," she explained to Alan Taylor for the *Sunday Herald* (June 20, 2004) of Scotland. "So in a way I was confirming people's idea that women don't know a lot about sport because I was doing it from the point of view of someone who didn't know a lot about it." In 2000 Truss was slated to cover the Summer Olympic Games, in Sydney, Australia. After she discovered that her sister had been diagnosed with lung cancer, her superiors at the *Times* allowed her to write about the television coverage of the Games instead while she remained at home to lend her support to Kay. A short time later, Kay died, and Truss was devastated. "I was very proud of the relationship I had with my sister when she died," she told Jo Ind. "I was there with her and I was for her and we had a lot of fun and we didn't talk about any [sibling rivalry], we just got on with her." Following Kay's death, Truss could no longer handle the stress of the constant travel necessary for sportswriting, and she quit after four years on the job.

In 2002 Truss began hosting *Cutting a Dash,* a humorous series on BBC Radio 4 about punctuation. Later that year she encountered Andrew Franklin, the publisher of Profile Books (which had published Truss's first novel), at a Christmas party. When he asked her if she might be able to turn some of her material from *Cutting a Dash* into a book, Truss promptly rejected the idea. Soon, however, she began considering the suggestion more carefully and realized that there might be sufficient material for a book after all. She accepted a £15,000 advance (an amount equal to a little more than $25,000 at that time)—a relatively modest figure that was based on the sales of her previous books—and, in six months, produced a book entitled *Eats, Shoots & Leaves: The Zero Tolerance Approach to Punctuation,* which was published in Britain in 2003 and in the U.S. the following year. (The title refers to a joke in which a giant panda walks into a restaurant, eats a meal, takes out a gun, and fires a shot. When the waiter asks the animal why he did such an odd thing, the panda replies, "I'm a panda," and hands the waiter a poorly punctuated wildlife guide. In the guide, under the description of the panda's behavior, the text reads, "Eats, shoots and leaves," instead of the correct "Eats shoots and leaves.")

Initially, Truss was sure that her book would be a financial flop, of interest to very few people. "I just had this terrible sense of dread that I'd done something that would ruin the rest of my life," she told Alan Taylor. "I keep thinking back to what it was like to write it and in some ways it was like suicide. It was really public suicide." But Truss's book became a huge success, spending six months on the best-seller lists in England and 45 weeks on the *New York Times* best-seller list; the paperback edition, published in 2006, appeared on the *Times* paperback best-seller list for 16 weeks. As of late 2005 the book had sold more than three million hardcover copies worldwide. Moreover, *Eats, Shoots & Leaves* won the national British Book Award for book of the year and was selected as one of the best books of 2004 by *USA Today.* Truss's version of the book for children went on sale in the United States in the spring of 2006; it, too, became a best-seller. Truss was stunned by the reception of her book. "As an idea, it was a nonseller," she told Judith Long for *Newsday* (May 9, 2004), "something you'd do only out of the love of it. I really wrote it for myself." That comment notwithstanding, many readers and reviewers, particularly those in Britain, seized upon the book with enthusiasm. "Truss brings a droll sensibility to that driest of topics, the proper deployment of commas and dashes," Jan Freeman wrote for the *Boston Globe* (March 21, 2004). "Still, Truss doesn't overstate the gravity of her subject; she's a reformer with the soul of a stand-up comedian."

Not all reviewers, however, were pleased with Truss's book. The critique that drew the most attention, an article by the Pulitzer Prize–winning literary critic Louis Menand that was published in the *New Yorker* (June 28, 2004), was described by Dwight Garner, writing for the *New York Times* (February 6, 2005), as "one of the most withering reviews in recent memory." "The first punctuation mistake in *Eats, Shoots & Leaves* . . . appears in the dedication, where a nonrestrictive clause is not preceded by a comma," Menand wrote at the start of his indictment. "It is a wild ride downhill from there." He went on to catalog numerous errors in Truss's book, some of which, he acknowledged, were the result of the American publisher's failure to reedit the book for the U.S. market, where the rules of usage are different. "An Englishwoman lecturing Americans on semicolons is a little like an American lecturing the French on sauces," Menand wrote. "Some of Truss's departures from punctuation norms are just British laxness. In a book that pretends to be all about firmness, though, this is not a good excuse. The main rule in grammatical form is to stick to whatever rules you start out with, and the most objectionable thing about Truss's writing is its inconsistency. Either Truss needed a copy editor or her copy editor needed a copy editor. . . . 'I am not a grammarian,' Truss says. No quarrel there." Menand wondered why "a person who is not just vague about the rules but disinclined to follow them [would] bother to produce a guide to punctuation," and concluded that Truss was "set a-blaze" by the common misuse of apostrophes in advertisements and the lack of punctuation and capitalization in E-mail messages. "Are these portents of the night, soon coming, in which no man can read? Truss warns us that they are . . . but it's hard to know how seriously to take her, because her prose is so caffeinated that you can't always separate the sense from the sensibility. And that, undoubtedly, is the point, for it is the sensibility, the 'I'm mad as hell' act, that has got her her readers."

Many of Truss's compatriots writing for the British press bristled at Menand's article, particularly the assertion that they were more lax than Americans in their application of the rules of punctuation. Andrew Franklin, who described Menand as "a tosser"—a British epithet—with "no sense of humor," told John Mullan for the London *Guardian* (July 2, 2004) that the American critic's attack was "deeply xenophobic" and motivated by jealousy over Truss's tremendous book sales. Truss commented on language such as Franklin's in her next book, *Talk to the Hand*, which was published in late 2005. In the book, which focuses on the absence of manners and common politeness in society, Truss lamented that "abuse is becoming accepted as the quickest and smartest way of dealing with criticism in all areas of life." Noting the coarse tone that Franklin had used when defending her book against Menand's critique, she wrote: "Now, I loved my publisher for doing this, of course. He was defending my honour. . . . And although I have never read the article, I have heard enough about it to suspect that the chosen epithet actually had some merit in this case. But good grief, how embarrassing. Meanwhile, ripostes of this sort made by public figures are reported in the news, and quoted as if they were witty or thoughtful."

In her interview with Jane Wheatley, Truss explained her motivations for writing *Talk to the Hand*: "Once, a person might modify his behaviour for fear of disapproval but there is no longer the same peer pressure to conform to certain standards, to act in the common good. As a result, I don't feel the same sense of security, of being able to rely on others to react to objectionable behaviour in the same way as me." As with her previous effort, *Talk to the Hand* is a comedic lament in which Truss cast herself as an archetypical scold, wagging her finger at transgressions. "The scold is an innately comic figure," Deborah Solomon wrote for the *New York Times Magazine* (November 20, 2005), "and Truss's achievement has been to elevate it into classically unfunny and fussy realms, namely that of punctuation and manners." On the other hand, in the *New York Times* (November 7, 2005), Janet Maslin described the book as "a promising-looking volume that turns out to be a thin and crabby diatribe" and suggested that the "author may have been good for only one book-length conniption." Most assessments of *Talk to the Hand* were mixed, with reviewers acknowledging some flaws but praising Truss's witty and humorous approach to her subject. "Beyond her comic ranting and frenetic fuming, Truss makes a sincere and well-researched attempt to shed light on the dismal decorum of this darkest age," Bob Morris wrote for the *New York Times Book Review* (December 11, 2005). "If she fails at the task, she does so winningly."

In the wake of the success of *Eats, Shoots & Leaves*, four of Truss's earlier books, *With One Lousy Free Packet of Seed*, *Making the Cat Laugh*, *Tennyson's Gift*, and *Going Loco*, were reissued in 2004 by Profile Books and compiled in *The Lynne Truss Treasury* (published by the Gotham Books division of the Penguin Group) in 2005. Truss is currently writing more radio plays. Meanwhile, she has been enjoying the financial security that has accompanied her success. She paid off the mortgage on her home in Brighton, had some renovations done, rented an apartment in the Bloomsbury section of London, and bought herself a convertible Volkswagen Beetle. Additionally, she has paid off her mother's mortgage. "Maybe you're supposed to go and buy a helicopter. But if I had one I know I wouldn't use it," she told a reporter for the London *Independent* (October 23, 2005). "And if I started hanging around in clubs in London doing coke, I wouldn't know any of the people, so that would be a bit daft. Does this show a terrible lack of imagination?" Truss has remarked that she is glad that her great success arrived only after the death of her sister. "One of the awful, tragic things about her dying is that she would have hated this [success]," Truss told Robert McCrum. "She would have been very unhappy about [the book] doing so well, because she always hated it when nice things happened."

—K.J.E.

Suggested Reading: *Birmingham (England) Post* p45 July 10, 2004; (Glasgow, Scotland) *Sunday Herald* p3 June 20, 2004; (London) *Observer* p3 June 13, 2004; (London) *Times* Books p4 Oct. 15, 2005; Lynne Truss's Web site; *New York Times Magazine* p59+ Nov. 20, 2005

Selected Books: *With One Lousy Free Packet of Seed*, 1994; *Making the Cat Laugh: One Woman's Journal of Single Life on the Margins*, 1995; *Tennyson's Gift*, 1996; *Going Loco: A Comedy of Terrors*, 1999; *Tennyson and His Circle*, 1999; *Eats, Shoots & Leaves: The Zero Tolerance Approach to Punctuation*, 2003; *The Lynne Truss Treasury: Columns and Three Comic Novels*, 2005; *Talk to the Hand: The Utter Bloody Rudeness of the World Today, or Six Good Reasons to Stay Home and Bolt the Door*, 2005; for children—*Eats, Shoots and Leaves: Why, Commas Really* Do *Make a Difference*, 2006

Stephen J. Boitano/Getty Images

Valdes-Rodriguez, Alisa

Feb. 28, 1969– Writer

Address: c/o St. Martin's Press, 175 Fifth Ave., New York, NY 10010

With the publication of her first novel, *The Dirty Girls Social Club* (2003), Alisa Valdes-Rodriguez was heralded by the media as the "Latina Terry McMillan" for tapping into the large but often ignored market for books in the Hispanic community, in much the way that McMillan's 1992 novel, *Waiting to Exhale*, found many readers among African-Americans. With her book, Valdes-Rodriguez hoped to challenge the ethnic generalizations that she had faced in her work as a journalist for the *Boston Globe* and the *Los Angeles Times* and in society as a whole. The six major female characters are professional, middle-class women of Latina origin and of diverse ethnicities and races: Lauren, a half-Cuban newspaper columnist; Sara, a blue-eyed Cuban Jewish homemaker; Amber, an aspiring rock musician with Mexican roots; Elizabeth, a black Colombian television news anchor; Rebecca, the founder of a women's magazine who is of European and American-Indian origin; and Usnavys, a Puerto Rican nonprofit worker and social climber. As Valdes-Rodriguez told James H. Burnett III for the *Milwaukee Journal Sentinel* (June 7, 2004), "In writing my book, I didn't feel like I'd found any literature that had reflected a large diversity of Latina experiences. I tried to show sort of a more diverse group, religiously diverse, nationally diverse, skin tone diversity. Those things are probably what I've heard most about from people who have read the book, that

they hadn't seen that sort of diversity among Hispanics described elsewhere, either." After the success of the *Dirty Girls Social Club*, which has sold more than 350,000 copies, *Time* magazine honored Valdes-Rodriguez in 2005 as one of the 25 most influential Hispanics in America, referring to her as the "Godmother of Chica Lit" and praising her for writing a "hip, fast-paced novel" with "smart, funny" characters. Valdes-Rodriguez's next novel, *Playing with Boys*, appeared in 2004. Two novels by the writer were published in 2006: *Make Him Look Good* and *Haters*.

The younger of two children, Alisa Valdes-Rodriguez was born on February 28, 1969 in Albuquerque, New Mexico. Her father, Nelson Valdes, was a native of Havana, Cuba; her mother, Maxine Conant, an Irish-American, was born in rural New Mexico. When she was three years old, Valdes-Rodriguez moved with her parents and her brother, Ricardo, to the town of Bosque, New Mexico, where her maternal grandfather operated the trading post. In search of jobs, the family moved again, first to Glasgow, Scotland, when Valdes-Rodriguez was four years old, and then to New Orleans, Louisiana, when she was five. She was eight when she and her family returned to Albuquerque, after her father accepted a position as a janitor at the University of New Mexico. Valdes-Rodriguez has credited her mother with inspiring her passion for the written word. "I started writing stories at nine. My mom played word games with my brother and me. Walking to the hot car in the parking lot, she'd say, 'Get ready to bake like a potato and fry like a chicken.' I learned words were fun and reading was great," she told Nora Villagran for the *San Jose Mercury News* (May 19, 2003). When she was nine she began playing the saxophone, after hearing the instrument featured in a commercial during an episode of the television Western *Bonanza*.

When Valdes-Rodriguez was 11, her mother left the family and became a prostitute. Her father took on sole parental duties after his divorce from his wife, when Valdes-Rodriguez was 12. While working as a janitor, Nelson Valdes was encouraged by a fellow janitor, who was also of Cuban descent, to apply for a college scholarship. After taking that advice, Nelson Valdes attended the University of New Mexico, where he earned a bachelor's degree in Latin American studies (he had minored in Portuguese) and a doctorate in sociology. (He discovered years later, after attending the other janitor's funeral, that his dead friend had secretly funded the scholarship.) He now teaches at the University of New Mexico. "Seeing my father succeed in arts and letters taught me I could succeed," Valdes-Rodriguez told Carolyne Zinko for the *San Francisco Chronicle* (October 19, 2003). Valdes-Rodriguez attended high school in Albuquerque and during her freshman year served as class president until, as she told Patrick T. Reardon for the *Chicago Tribune* (August 22, 2002), she "got impeached. Well, actually, they asked me to step down," she explained. "For our prom, I suggested having an anti-nuclear sit-in at the mall." (As Reardon reported, many of her classmates' parents had jobs connected with the military.)

At that time, Valdes-Rodriguez told Wendy Pedrero for *Latino Leaders* (August 1, 2005, on-line), "I knew I loved writing, [but] I felt the writing was too easy and not challenging and it wouldn't be a valid career, so I went into music because it was a little harder for me." Following her high-school graduation, Valdes-Rodriguez attended the Berklee College of Music, in Boston, Massachusetts, where she studied saxophone performance, and supported herself financially by working as an aerobics instructor. During her college years she encountered what she perceived to be sexism, an example of which was her classical-music professor's failure to mention any famous female composers; Valdes-Rodriguez began leaving note cards with information about female classical composers in her professor's mailbox. She sent an article detailing those events to the *Boston Globe*, which published the piece two weeks before her graduation. Following the story's appearance, the school introduced new policies, including mandatory sensitivity training for its employees, and offered courses on the history of women in music. "Years later I got a letter from the college," Valdes-Rodriguez told Justino Águila for the *Orange County Register* (August 18, 2005, on-line). "They thanked me for making the school a better place. It inspired me to study journalism." Another subject that drew her interest was the Spanish language, which she learned when she was in her mid-20s.

Valdes-Rodriguez enrolled at Columbia University's Graduate School of Journalism, in New York City, earning her master's degree in 1994. Afterward the *Boston Globe* extended Valdes-Rodriguez an offer for a position as a staff writer. As a reporter she was critical of the newspaper's coverage of minorities, particularly its decision to run a front-page story about a woman missing from the wealthy suburb of Newton, Massachusetts, while one of her own articles, regarding the murder of a Dominican store owner in front of his daughter, was relegated to the newspaper's inside pages. As she recalled to Smith, "I started to talk about it. I was labeled a troublemaker." Valdes-Rodriguez was even more outspoken regarding the *Boston Globe*'s treatment of fellow reporters at the paper—one black (Patricia Smith) and one white (Mike Barnicle)—who both admitted to fabricating characters and quotes. While Smith was forced to resign in June 1998, Barnicle was suspended without pay for two months, prompting Valdes-Rodriguez to label the paper a "racist institution." (Barnicle resigned in August 1998 amid charges that he had fabricated characters for a 1995 column.) Valdes-Rodriguez also recalled being subjected to racial stereotyping in the newsroom. She told Warren that on one occasion a colleague asked her where to purchase Mexican jumping beans, and that another co-worker once said to her, "We're so glad you're here, representing your people." In 1998, af-

ter four years at the *Globe*, Valdes-Rodriguez moved to the *Los Angeles Times*, where she covered the Latin music industry, interviewing pop-music artists including Gloria Estefan and Christina Aguilera. She also taught journalism at the University of California at Los Angeles.

For a December 1998 feature story that appeared in the *Boston Globe* after she left, Valdes-Rodriguez provided a frank depiction of her family, writing: "My brother and his wife are crack addicts and high school dropouts. My mother, when money was tight, worked as a prostitute. She was held hostage once by her crazy, ex-convict boyfriend, who dunked her head in a toilet, at knifepoint. My cousin is in prison for stealing cars and checks from my aunt and grandmother. Her two teenage sons are in jail for murder. My grandmother lives in a trailer park. I am the only one of my American cousins to go to college. Now, let me tell you why I support the idea of looking at diversity—and disadvantage—in terms of economics, rather than race or ethnicity: All of the above-mentioned relatives are white. . . . My mother is Irish and English, with red hair and blue eyes, from a family that is lovingly described by her as 'white trash.' . . . The folks with bad grammar in my family tree are white. The ones on welfare, white. The ones in trouble with the law, white." Valdes-Rodriguez has since patched up her relationship with her mother.

In 1999 Valdes-Rodriguez married Patrick Jason Rodriguez, a screenwriter. The following year, while on medical leave due to a pregnancy-related illness, she resigned from her job at the *Los Angeles Times*. Her departure followed the controversial, 3,400-word letter she sent by E-mail to the paper, accusing the management of racism and sexism. She wrote, in part, as quoted by the *Floridian* (on-line): "In the process of covering so-called 'Latino' issues, I have stumbled upon a simple and disturbing fact: There is no such thing as a Latino. I have also seen this newspaper—and most others—butcher history and fact in an attempt to create this ethnic group. . . . After extensive study of history, I believe 'Latino'—as used in the *Los Angeles Times*—is the most recent attempt at genocide perpetrated against the native people of the Americas. I posit this new genocide is far more dangerous than the old fashioned murder and relocation efforts. Now, we simply rob people of their heritage, and force a new one upon them. They are no longer Indians, with a 30,000 year claim to these lands; they are now immigrants and 'Latinos.'" In the letter Valdes-Rodriguez also criticized the paper's treatment of the issue of race. "To me, it is telling that the *Times* rarely, if ever, writes of those people categorized as 'white' while identifying them by 'race' for the heck of it. While we endlessly profile 'Asian' authors and 'Black' celebrities, we never classify the 'white' people we write about as 'white' unless they have committed a hate crime, or are being compared in a poll or study to 'others.'" After the E-mail letter was made public over the Internet, Valdes-Rodriguez's reputation in the journalism field was tarnished. A year later, while she was still out of work, Valdes-Rodriguez addressed a follow-up E-mail letter to Jim Romenesko's Web site, medianews.org, as quoted on Luke Ford's Web site. "I was 10 days without food at the time I wrote the letter, frenzied, sweaty and crazy-eyed, wearing the same moldy nightgown for a week, smelly and sad and psycho in the loft of my condo, paranoid, the world spinning. . . . I never wanted to talk about this, especially in front of all of you, because in our industry if there is anything worse than being an arrogant little snot who writes a stupid resignation letter at one of the top newspapers on earth it is being a whiny little woman who blames hormones for her behavior and derails her career to have a baby. But it's true, and I want to be judged fairly, if possible, in the future, if I have one in this business—and I hope I do."

Following the birth of her son, Alexander, in 2000, Valdes-Rodriguez returned to Albuquerque, with the intention of pursuing a writing career. "I'm a writer who became a journalist—not a journalist who became a writer," she told Villagran. Struggling financially, Valdes-Rodriguez moved with her husband and their son into her father's home, located near the University of New Mexico, and received assistance from Medicaid. She remained unemployed until March 2002, when she was offered a job at a newspaper in Reno, Nevada. A few weeks later she left that paper to accept a position as the features editor of the *Albuquerque Tribune*. While working as an editor, Valdes-Rodriguez started writing again and mailed 65 query letters to literary agents. After receiving three responses, she signed with Leslie Daniels, an agent with the New York–based Joy Harris Literary Agency, who shopped her proposal for a nonfiction book based on the female Latin pop singers of the post-Selena generation. (The Mexican-American singer Selena Quintanilla Perez, who died in 1995, was considered one of the biggest stars of Tejano music.) Although publishers expressed little interest in her manuscript, they found her writing style very entertaining and asked Daniels if Valdes-Rodriguez had written a work of fiction. Unbeknownst to Daniels, Valdes-Rodriguez had written drafts of novels since high school; now she used them as raw material to conceive a story outline and a list of characters. In explaining the process of writing her first novel, Valdes-Rodriguez told Reardon, "After I wrote out the list of characters, then I went through my life, trying to think like each of them. . . . I tried to live the character before I sat down to write." Needing a quiet place to write, Valdes-Rodriguez left her son with her husband while spending 15 hours every day for two weeks at the local Starbucks coffee shop, writing on her laptop.

Those efforts resulted in the *Dirty Girls Social Club*, which chronicles the lives of six Latina professionals in their late 20s who met as Boston University freshmen and reunite twice a year during the decade after their graduation. The book's title is the English translation of the name Buena Sucia Social Club, which the women call themselves collectively. Each chapter of the novel is narrated in first-person by one of the characters.

Although several sources have reported that she wrote her debut novel in only six days, the novelist told Lydia Martin for the *Miami Herald* (June 10, 2003), "I had about 100 pages and then an agent asked me to finish it. So it was more like two weeks from the time she [Daniels] asked me to write it to the time I had a first draft 300 pages long." Following another four months of suggestions from her agent, the novel was ready to be submitted. The response from the publishing companies was overwhelmingly positive. In 2002 *The Dirty Girls Social Club* triggered a three-day bidding war among five major publishing houses; it was ultimately won by St. Martin's Press, which purchased the rights to her book for an advance of $475,000, a very high figure for a first-time novelist. A month and a half later, Valdes-Rodriguez resigned from her position at the *Albuquerque Tribune*. St. Martin's ordered a first printing of 125,000 copies in English and 10,000 copies in Spanish, making *Dirty Girls* the company's first novel to be published simultaneously in English and Spanish.

A week after its publication, in 2003, the book landed on the *New York Times* best-seller list for hardcover fiction, where it spent three months, peaking at number 20. Despite its commercial success, the book met with mixed reviews. Vicky Uland wrote for the *Rocky Mountain News* (May 16, 2003): "Valdes-Rodriguez's writing style is raunchy yet refined, with a variable cadence that echoes six different voices. But in the end, it's the complex, finely drawn characters who make the book work. . . . Weeks after finishing the book, I still find myself wondering how Rebecca's new romance is faring and whether or not Sara will make it in the career world." In contrast, Emiliana Sandoval wrote for the *Detroit Free Press* (May 4, 2003, on-line), "While it's high time there was a Latina Terry McMillan, as Valdes-Rodriguez is being hyped, she's not quite there yet. The novel feels a bit too much like a chip she needed to get off her shoulder. Now that she's established that Latinas aren't all one-sombrero-fits-all, she needs to develop some more believable story lines and characters, people who exist unto themselves, not just as servants to a message."

In September 2004 St. Martin's published Valdes-Rodriguez's second novel, *Playing with Boys*. The book explores the lives of a group of Latinas struggling to succeed in the entertainment industry. Valdes-Rodriguez's second novel had its share of detractors, some of whom found her guilty of the racial stereotyping about which she has complained. For the *San Jose Mercury News* (October 31, 2004), Nerissa Pacio wrote: "Throughout the novel, Valdes-Rodriguez peppers her characters' thoughts with biting commentary on the racist Hollywood institution that pigeonholes Latinos as criminals, housekeepers and sex objects. But she undercuts her efforts by painting unsympathetic caricatures of Latinas who are insecure, bitter and often one-dimensional." Aideen McCormick was far more complimentary, declaring in the *Calgary Herald* (October 23, 2004): "As the plot gains momentum, the reader becomes totally immersed in the rapidly escalating drama of Alexis, Marcella and Olivia's lives and loves." To date, the book has sold about 130,000 hardcover copies.

In 2005 Valdes-Rodriguez signed a development deal with Lifetime Television to create, write, and produce a series based on the *The Dirty Girls Social Club*, which is expected to air in the spring of 2006. She and Patrick Rodriguez founded the television and production company Dirty Girls Productions, for which her mother works as Valdes-Rodriguez's assistant. The writer is currently working with Nely Galan of Galan Entertainment, the creator and producer of the reality makeover show *The Swan*, to develop *The Dirty Girls Social Club* as a TV series. However, Valdes-Rodriguez has been increasingly unhappy with the direction of the project. As she told *Current Biography*, "I've asked for the rights back because I don't believe the new management at the network understand the project. I'm not willing to compromise on it. . . . As I like to joke, if anyone is going to screw up my book, I'd like it to be me." Valdes-Rodriguez is also writing a sequel to her book *Dirty Girls Social Club*.

In April 2006 Valdes-Rodriguez published two novels. *Make Him Look Good* explores the lives of six Miami women who are connected through their relationship with one man, a successful Latin pop singer. Valdes-Rodriguez targeted a youthful audience with her next book, *Haters*, about teenagers living in Orange County, California.

After noting the lack of Hispanic representation on Air America Radio, her favorite radio network, Valdes-Rodriguez was offered the chance to host a nationally syndicated political and cultural talk show entitled *Our America* with her father, Nelson Valdes. The first demo show was recorded on December 3, 2005 at KABQ, the Air America affiliate radio station in Albuquerque, and the second show was to be broadcast on December 10. In late 2006 the writer told *Current Biography* that she had abandoned her plan to host the program, because she had "lost interest" in it.

In 2002 *Hispanic Business Magazine* included Valdes-Rodriguez on its list of the 100 most influential Hispanics, and she was named one *of Latina Magazine*'s Women of the Year in 2003. She has twice married and twice divorced Patrick Rodriguez. Her ex-husband continues to work as a publicist at Dirty Girls Productions Inc. He and Valdes-Rodriguez live in Albuquerque, where they are raising their son, Alexander.

—B.M.

Suggested Reading: *Albuquerque Tribune* A p1 June 29, 2002; Alisa Valdes-Rodriguez's Web site; *New York Times* E p1 Apr. 24, 2003; *Orange County (California) Register* (on-line) Aug. 18, 2005; *San Diego Union-Tribune* F p1 Oct. 17, 2004

Selected Books: *The Dirty Girls Social Club*, 2003; *Playing with Boys*, 2004; *Haters*, 2006; *Make Him Look Good*, 2006

Van Zandt, Steven

Nov. 22, 1950– Musician; producer; actor; radio host

Address: c/o The Endeavor Agency, 10th Fl., 9601 Wilshire Boulevard, Beverly Hills, CA 90212

Nineteen ninety-nine was a banner year for the multifaceted performer Steven Van Zandt: he released his fifth solo album, *Born Again Savage*; he made his debut as an actor, appearing as Silvio Dante, a top adviser, or *consigliere,* to the ruthless mafia boss Tony Soprano, in HBO's runaway-hit series *The Sopranos*; and he reunited with Bruce Springsteen and the E Street Band on an extended world tour. As the E Street Band's eccentric, bandana-clad guitarist and raspy-voiced backup vocalist, from 1975 to 1984, "Van Zandt emerged—along with saxman Clarence Clemons—as one of the focal points of the band," Lynn Van Matre wrote for the *Chicago Tribune* (January 30, 1983), "whose contributions . . . played an integral part in shaping the E-Street sound." A savvy, streetwise studio hand, "Miami Steve" (as he became known to his fans) served as the band's part-time producer during that period of exceptional critical and commercial success, arranging the music to several of Springsteen's brooding tales of working-class angst. In 1982 Van Zandt changed his on-stage name to "Little Steven" and embarked on a solo career, teaming up with the Disciples of Soul to release several overtly political albums between 1982 and 1999. "Miami Steve was a sharpie sporting an everpresent fedora or beret and the aura of a small-time slick operator; Little Steven, with his bright headkerchief, black leather and multitude of scarves, has the look of an Italian Gypsy," Van Matre wrote, noting that Van Zandt had called his Little Steven persona "the real me."

Van Zandt is known for his political awareness, having organized Artists United Against Apartheid, which included such icons as Bob Dylan, Miles Davis, and Run-D.M.C. His music is recognized as containing elements of rhythm and blues, doo-wop, soul, and rock. Despite having a reedy

Evan Agostini/Getty Images

Steven Van Zandt

singing voice and no training as an actor, he was dubbed "the coolest guy in the entire state of New Jersey" by Jeffrey Goldberg, writing for the *New York Times* (December 26, 1999). Among his many achievements in the music industry, Van Zandt "helped create the archetypal Jersey bar-band sound," according to Jay Lustig, writing for *Newhouse News Service* (October 18, 1999). Since 2002 Van Zandt has been the host of the highly successful syndicated radio program *Little Steven's Underground Garage*, heard on more than 200 stations nationwide. Since 2004 Van Zandt has also produced for the subscriber-supported Sirius Satellite Radio two channels—*Underground Garage* and *Outlaw Country*—and one program, *The Wiseguy Show.*

Van Zandt was born Steven Lento on November 22, 1950 in Winthrop, Massachusetts, which is part of the greater Boston area. His father's family came from the Calabria region of southern Italy. When Van Zandt was an infant, his father died; not long afterward his mother remarried, and her new husband adopted young Steven. That explains "how somebody from an Italian family ends up with a Dutch name," Van Zandt told Lynn Van Matre. Van Zandt's younger brother, Billy, has written for such television comedies as *Newhart, Martin,* and *Yes, Dear,* among others. His sister, Kathi, is an executive at Victoria's Secret, a retail marketer of lingerie and women's beauty products.

Before Van Zandt entered middle school, his family moved from Massachusetts to Middletown, New Jersey, in Monmouth County, near the Jersey Shore. He spent the bulk of his childhood and adolescence a stone's throw from the state's beaches and pinball-arcade-lined boardwalks. Raised as a

Baptist, Van Zandt described his early religious awakening in an essay that accompanied the release of *Born Again Savage*, which is also posted on his official Web site: "I got very religious as a kid around the age of 10, 11, or 12. . . . I remember looking forward to the Easter Sunrise service every year. Waking up when it was still night and gathering at the mountain top was a rare mystical experience that seemed to connect to some dark, mysterious, long-past ritual in my subconscious." That development was soon followed by another epiphany, which occurred as he was listening to the song "Pretty Little Angel Eyes," by Curtis Lee. "A feeling of pure bliss flooded my body," Van Zandt wrote for his Web site. "It was my second epiphany in as many years and this one was even stronger than the first. It wouldn't become my life until two or three years later when the Beatles and the Rolling Stones would reveal my future, but from that moment on what would dominate the emotional part of my spiritual consciousness would be rock and roll. In other words, at that moment, rock and roll became my religion." He then purchased as many singles as he could afford, including "Tears on my Pillow" by Little Anthony and the Imperials, "Duke of Earl" by Gene Chandler, "Twist and Shout" by the Isley Brothers, "Sherry" by the Four Seasons, and "Pretty Little Angel Eyes."

By the time he was 16 years old, Van Zandt had formed his own band, named the Source, for which he played lead guitar and sang lead vocals. He also arranged the Source's music. "We were one of the first bands to break the mold," he explained to Terry Gross, host of the National Public Radio program *Fresh Air* (June 27, 2002). "In those days you had to play the top 40, and my band was one of the first to play FM radio rock type of album cuts. . . . I was playing songs by The Who and Buffalo Springfield and Youngbloods, people like that, which was a bit strange back then. There wasn't too many of us—there wasn't too many bands back then, actually. It was a very different world. It was not a viable way to make a living yet, so you were considered really one step above a criminal, you know, being in a rock 'n' roll band." Such earlier acts as the Drifters, Little Richard, and Gary "U.S" Bonds also influenced Van Zandt.

As a teenager, Van Zandt met and befriended Bruce Springsteen, a native of Freehold, New Jersey, who would become one of the most popular musicians of his generation. "We just had a thing right from the start," Van Zandt explained to Robert Hilburn for the *Los Angeles Times* (December 19, 1999). "I was one of the two guys in my high school of 3,000 with long hair. He was the only one in his high school with long hair. That meant you didn't really fit in. . . . This was before everyone wanted to be in a band. But we found something in the music that we believed in—even though no one else was supportive and there was no way of realistically thinking you were going to make a living at it." After they had both graduated from high school, Van Zandt and Springsteen performed together in various groups in clubs near and around the ocean town of Asbury Park, which is located south of Middletown and east of Freehold. Dr. Zoom and the Sonic Boom, the Bruce Springsteen Band, and the more popular Steel Mill were among the many bands for which the two musicians played. Van Zandt also performed with such rockers as Johnny Lyon and, much later, Jon Bon Jovi on that circuit.

While he loved performing, Van Zandt became disillusioned with the music industry and quit briefly to become a construction worker. He returned to his playing music around 1973, touring as a member of a backup band for the Dovells, a Philadelphia-based R&B and dance-music group who had recorded such hits as "Bristol Stomp" and "You Can't Sit Down" in the early 1960s. "The audience was just perfect for being creative because they didn't care if we lived or died," Van Zandt explained to Lynn Van Matre. "So we would do obscure Marvin Gaye things, whatever I felt like. That was where my personal musical identity really came together." Traveling around the country with the Dovells, Van Zandt played at such prominent venues as Madison Square Garden, in New York City, and he also performed with one of the men he had idolized in his youth, a doo-wop sensation named Dion DiMucci (better known to his fans as Dion), who had recorded such hits as "Runaround Sue" and "The Wanderer."

Afterward, in 1974, Van Zandt returned to New Jersey and collaborated with the musician and songwriter Johnny Lyon; together they cofounded Southside Johnny and the Kid. Later, the group changed its name to Southside Johnny & the Asbury Jukes, due in part to its growing membership and increasing popularity on the Jersey Shore's club circuit. Boasting a "horn-heavy, R&B-drenched sound," according to Jay Lustig, the Jukes' original lineup included such musicians as guitarist Billy Rush, keyboardist Kevin Kavanaugh, drummer Kenny Pentifallo, trumpeters Tony Palligrossi and Ricky Gazda, and trombonist Richie "La Bamba" Rosenberg. Van Zandt gained more experience as a songwriter and producer with the group, and he also worked inside a studio for the first time. "I just kept on doing what I had been doing all along," Van Zandt told Lynn Van Matre, "which was taking obscure R&B things and arranging them in more of a rock and roll way." He later served as the Jukes' manager, helping the band sign a contract with Epic Records in 1976, the year they released I Don't Want to Go Home. Kit Keifer, writing for the All Music Guide Web site, hailed that song as an "R&B Revivalist's delight."

Meanwhile, Van Zandt's friend Springsteen had successfully launched his own career, releasing Greetings from Asbury Park, N.J. (1973) and The Wild, the Innocent & the E Street Shuffle (1973). Prior to the recording of and release of Springsteen's third album for the Columbia label, Born to Run (1975), Van Zandt joined the E Street Band, assisting Springsteen in the studio with horn ar-

rangements for the album's tracks, playing some guitar, and singing backup vocals. He also promised Springsteen that he would perform live with the band for a short period on a promotional tour to promote the album's release. Born to Run, which has sold more than six million copies to date, was released on August 25, 1975, after Springsteen had "spent everything he had—patience, energy, studio time, the physical endurance of his E Street Band—to ensure that his third album was a masterpiece," according to a reviewer for Rolling Stone (November 1, 2003, on-line). Born to Run rose to number three on Billboard's pop charts, and both Time and Newsweek magazines put Springsteen on their covers on the same day, October 27, 1975. The album was considered by most reviewers to be Springsteen's best effort thus far.

Van Zandt's enduring and lucrative association with Springsteen was just beginning. Debuting their songs live rather than on the radio, at the suggestion of their agent, Frank Barsalona, Bruce Springsteen and the E Street Band secured a devoted following, playing to packed houses. During that time, Van Zandt became a fixture in the E Street Band, emerging on-stage as the band's effervescent, bandana-clad guitarist, "Miami Steve." Springsteen and the E Street Band followed up Born to Run with a string of successful albums, including Darkness on the Edge of Town (1978), the double-disc set The River (1980)—which Van Zandt co-produced—and Born in the U.S.A. (1984), which yielded seven hit singles in the U.S. and reached number one on the Billboard charts. By the summer of 1984, Bruce Springsteen and the E Street Band had become one of the most commercially successful and critically adored acts of all time.

Van Zandt, working with Springsteen, co-produced most of the tracks on Gary "U.S." Bonds's comeback albums Dedication (1981) and On the Line (1982). Van Zandt also produced Bonds's Standing in the Line of Fire (1984). But Van Zandt also wanted to become a successful solo artist in his own right. While touring and working tirelessly in the studio for Springsteen and others, he formed a 12-piece band called the Disciples of Soul, which included horn players from the Asbury Jukes and other musicians with whom he had developed close ties over the course of his career. In 1982 Little Steven and the Disciples of Soul released Men Without Women, which "in many ways . . . is the finest album the Asbury Jukes never made," Mark Deming wrote for the All Music Guide Web site. The name of the album, which appeared on the Razor & Tie label, came from a 1927 collection of short stories by the American writer Ernest Hemingway. Men Without Women was the first of six solo efforts released by Van Zandt between 1982 and 1999, and it is considered by most reviewers to be his best. "Van Zandt's guitar (and Jean Beauvior's bass) speak with the sound and fury of a true roots rock rebel. . . . On Men Without Women, Little Steven & the Disciples merged the brassy swing of a classic Motown side with the sweaty blare of an amped-up garage band," Deming wrote.

The album was also the first to express Van Zandt's emerging left-leaning political beliefs, which he began to expound with great fervor in his music and in the media. Having traveled overseas in the early 1980s, Van Zandt witnessed South Africa's brutal, government-sanctioned system of racial segregation, known as apartheid. What he saw had a profound impact on his life; his subsequent musical efforts addressed pressing political and social issues. Respectively, *Voices of America* (1984), *Freedom—No Compromise* (1987), *Revolution* (1989), and *Born Again Savage* (1999) explored issues of the family, the state, the economy, and religion. None of those albums brought Van Zandt the sort of mainstream success Springsteen had enjoyed as a solo artist. They sold more copies in Europe than in the U.S.; in Sweden two of the albums reached the Top 10. For the Artists United Against Apartheid record, released in 1985, Van Zandt wrote and produced the title song, "Sun City" (1985). The album was described as "certainly the most political of all the charity rock albums of the 1980s," by Stephen Thomas Erlewine, writing for *All Music Guide* Web site. Such acclaimed artists as Miles Davis, U2's Bono, Jackson Browne, Bobby Womack, Lou Reed, Bonnie Raitt, George Clinton, Bob Dylan, and Springsteen joined Van Zandt on the record.

In May 1997 Van Zandt served as the presenter for the induction ceremony of the Rascals—a popular blue-eyed soul group of the 1960s and 1970s— into the Rock and Roll Hall of Fame, in Cleveland, Ohio. Van Zandt's speech caught the attention of David Chase, a television producer and writer, who, at the time, was in the process of creating a weekly series for HBO. Chase later recalled thinking, according to the Montreal *Gazette* (April 15, 2003), that Van Zandt "was the face of New Jersey," which was to be the location of Chase's Mafia-family drama, *The Sopranos*. Though Van Zandt had no professional experience or training as an actor, Chase offered him a part on the show. The musician was initially reluctant to accept; he did not want to take work away from a more capable actor. He accepted the offer, though, when Chase told him he was creating a new character specifically for him. "David and I agreed the character was going to be the . . . throwback to the past, philosophically . . . that he should also reflect that physically," Van Zandt explained to Terry Gross. "We wanted to make sort of a '50s-looking guy, you know, a guy who never really left the 50s. . . . he's not particularly concerned with being fashionable or taking part in the modern world at all."

On *The Sopranos*, which has aired since 1999, Van Zandt plays Silvio Dante, a loyal adviser, or *consigliere*, to the New Jersey mob boss Tony Soprano. Silvio is also the proprietor of Bada Bing, a gentlemen's club where the show's sundry characters can often be found. *The Sopranos* has enjoyed unusual success, gaining widespread popularity and enthusiastic critical acclaim for its realism in depicting the lives of a contemporary Mafia family. Van Zandt told Robert Hilburn for the *Los Angeles Times* (December 19, 1999), "What I think makes the show connect with so many people is that the problems they have, generally speaking, are the problems that everybody has. Everybody has two families. Everybody has their family at home and their family at work. Everybody has those kind of complicated human relations. That's what a lot of the show is about. It's not just about gangster stuff. Take Silvio for instance . . . . When it comes to life-threatening situations, he's a very, very cool professional. But he'll completely lose his temper at his daughter's soccer game." *The Sopranos*'s sixth season began in March 2006. The following July Van Zandt signed another contract with HBO, according to which he reportedly was to earn $187,000 for each of the final eight episodes of that season.

Earlier, in 1999, Van Zandt joined Springsteen and the E-Street Band on an extremely successful reunion tour that lasted for over a year. Van Zandt performed with the E-Street Band on a long and fruitful tour for the band's studio release entitled *The Rising* (which represented Springsteen's first collaboration with the E-Street Band since the mid-1980s). The album, recorded in the wake of the September 11, 2001 terrorist attacks in New York City and Washington, D.C., was "one of the very best examples in recent history of how popular art can evoke a time period and all of its confusing and often contradictory notions, feelings, and impulses," according to Thom Jurek, writing for the *All Music Guide* Web site.

Around the same time, Van Zandt began hosting a Sunday-evening syndicated radio program, *Little Steven's Underground Garage*. The immensely popular show debuted from Los Angeles, California, on April 7, 2002, and now airs on more than 200 radio stations nationwide. *Little Steven's Underground Garage* features music spanning several decades of rock and roll and includes popular songs from such "garage rock" genres as rockabilly, British invasion, punk, and psychedelia, to name a few. "I miss those days when the deejay would turn you on to new things and you could develop a relationship with that deejay and a relationship with that station," Van Zandt told Terry Gross. "And that's what I'm trying to do. . . . Quite a bit of what I do is turning people on to, hopefully, new things." He told Valerie Block for *Crain's New York Business* (February 23–29, 2004): "I am a supporting player with *The Sopranos*, and I love it. I am a supporting player in Bruce Springsteen's life, which I am honored to be. This [*Little Steven's Underground Garage*] is my thing. It's become my artistic expression." According to Mark Brown, writing for the Denver *Rocky Mountain News* (April 29, 2006), *Little Steven's Underground Garage* "attract[s] more than 1 million listeners nationwide on 146 stations." Van Zandt also produces two channels for Sirius Satellite Radio: *Underground Garage*, a spin-off from Van Zandt's regular radio show, in which a series of rotating disc jockeys air an eclectic selection of little-known music, and *Outlaw Country*, which showcases edgier offerings from the country-music scene. He also produces *The Wiseguy Show*, hosted by the former *Sopranos* cast member Vincent Pastore and described in an Associated Press article (October 8, 2004) as a celebration of "life, the arts and meatballs."

Jeffrey Goldberg described Van Zandt as "the original white boy funk soul brother," who attends a lunch meeting "pretty much the same way he always dresses, which is to say he looks like some kind of purple-paisley snakeskin hippie gypsy pirate." The musician and actor is married to the actress Maureen Van Zandt, who joined the cast of *The Sopranos* as Silvio Dante's wife, Gabriella, during its second season. A classically trained dancer, Maureen Van Zandt was also raised in New Jersey. In 2001 she co-founded the With Out Papers Theatre Company, which has produced such plays as *Golden Boy, Simpatico, Kingdom of Earth,* and *Burn This.* Van Zandt and his wife live in Manhattan.

—D.F.

Suggested Reading: All Music Guide Web site; *Chicago Tribune* VI p17+ Jan. 30, 1983; Little Steven On-line; *New York Times* XIV p12 Nov. 7, 1999, VI p14 Dec. 26, 1999; *Newhouse News Service* Oct. 18, 1999

Selected Recordings: with Bruce Springsteen and the E Street Band—*Born to Run*, 1975; *Darkness on the Edge of Town*, 1978; *The River*, 1980; *Born in the U.S.A.*, 1984; with Little Steven & the Disciples of Soul—*Men Without Women*, 1982; *Voice of America*, 1984; *Freedom—No Compromise*, 1987; *Revolution*, 1989; *Born Again Savage*, 1999; with Southside Johnny and the Asbury Jukes—*I Don't Want to Go Home*, 1976; *This Time It's for Real*, 1977; *Hearts of Stone*, 1978; *Better Days*, 1991

Selected Television Shows: *The Sopranos*, 1999–

Selected Radio Shows: as producer—*Underground Garage*, 2004– ; *Outlaw Country*, 2004– ; *The Wiseguy Show*, 2004– ; as producer and host—*Little Steven's Underground Garage*, 2002–

Vargas, Elizabeth

Sep. 6, 1962– Broadcast journalist

Address: ABC News, 7 W. 66th St., New York, NY 10023

When she became a co-anchor of ABC's *World News Tonight*, in January 2006, Elizabeth Vargas also became the first Hispanic individual—and only the third woman—to anchor a nationally broadcast nightly news program. A 20-year veteran of television broadcasting, Vargas "exudes a smart, thoughtful and authoritative air—the kind of reassuring steadiness viewers crave in an increasingly chaotic world," as Liz Llorente wrote for *Hispanic* (June 2004, on-line). Over the last decade she has made a name for herself as a correspondent on news magazines such as *Dateline* and *20/20*, conducting interviews in a "penetrating and persistent, but always polite" manner, in Llorente's words. Still, Vargas, who began her career as a news anchor, never truly abandoned the role, having served in that capacity for the news segment of NBC's *Today Show* as well as for ABC's *World News Tonight Saturday* and *World News Tonight Sunday,* even as she pursued other opportunities.

The first of three children, Elizabeth Vargas was born in Paterson, New Jersey, on September 6, 1962 to Ralf Vargas, a Puerto Rican career army officer who retired with the rank of colonel, and his wife, Anne, an Irish-American. She spent much of her childhood overseas on army bases, first in Ja-

Peter Kramer/Getty Images

pan, when she was a toddler, and in Germany and Belgium during her adolescence. As a high-school student, she became interested in pursuing a career as a journalist but never expected to go into television. "I grew up without TV," she told Michael A. Lipton and Anne Longley for *People* (September 9, 1996). "My strength was writing"—indeed, she was editor in chief of her high-school newspaper. Her aspirations changed while she was attending the prestigious journalism program at the University of Missouri, in Columbia: she managed to secure a position as reporter-anchor on KOMU-TV, an NBC affiliate connected with the university. "We were No. 1 in the ratings, and I was being paid $3.35 an hour!" she told Lipton and Longley. "I had to waitress to make ends meet. [Customers] would say, 'Aren't you that newscaster?' and I'd say, 'Yes, I am, would you like rice pilaf or a baked potato with your entree?'"

After completing her degree, in 1984, Vargas moved to Reno, Nevada, to become a reporter-anchor with the CBS affiliate KTVN-TV. In 1986 she won the lead-reporter spot at the ABC affiliate KTVK-TV in Phoenix, Arizona. While she was working in Phoenix, Ken Lindner, a television agent who represents such on-air personalities as Matt Lauer of NBC, discovered her. "I was visiting a client in Phoenix and saw Elizabeth hanging from a helicopter doing a live shot," Lindner told Arissa S. Wang for *Electronic Media* (January 15, 2001). "I never saw anybody with more ownership of her material, or more compelling." In 1989, with the help of Lindner, Vargas landed a position in Chicago, a major news market, as a reporter and weekend-news co-anchor with the CBS affiliate WBBM-TV. In 1992 a shakeup at the station led to the removal of Vargas's co-anchor, Mike Parker, from the broadcast. Shortly thereafter, the station announced that Vargas would also be removed from her anchoring position after her contract ran out and "be used strictly in a 'prominent reporting role,'" as Robert Feder reported for the *Chicago Sun-Times* (July 27, 1992).

Again with Lindner's help, Vargas began looking for better opportunities. In 1993 she took a position with NBC in New York, working as a correspondent on *Now with Tom Brokaw and Katie Couric*, a TV news magazine, and as one of the anchors on the news segment of the *Today Show*. The following year *Now* was absorbed by NBC's *Dateline*, and Vargas became a regular presence on that program. She also continued working on *Today*, and in 1995 her role on the show was expanded to include substituting for Katie Couric as needed. The variety of her roles at NBC demonstrated her versatility, a quality that was in evidence on *Dateline*, for which she covered stories on breast-cancer research, a notorious drunk-driving case in New Mexico, and the mysterious life and death of the North Carolina tobacco heiress Doris Duke. Vargas thus caught the attention of television executives at other stations, and in 1996, the year her contract with NBC was set to expire, other networks began expressing interest in her. Vargas, meanwhile, was still vying for a more prominent position at NBC, seeking assurances that she would succeed the popular Couric as co-anchor of the *Today Show*. While the network's executives could not promise her that job, since Couric was expected to remain in her position, they reportedly offered her the an-

chor spot on *Today's* weekend edition and a continuing role as a correspondent on *Dateline*. Vargas was apparently not satisfied with the offer, and NBC broke off its contract negotiations with her, giving her the freedom to pursue offers from ABC and CBS.

In June 1996 Vargas debuted in the anchor position for the news segment of ABC's *Good Morning America*. By the end of the month, she was already taking on the role of a substitute co-host, sharing duties with Joan Lunden when Charles Gibson took a week off. The ABC News chief, Roone Arledge, publicly revealed that Vargas was Lunden's likely heir. Vargas herself reportedly began telling her new colleagues that she had been hired to replace Lunden, which created problems for her on the show. (Vargas and Lunden denied rumors that they were feuding.) In the fall of 1996, Vargas began taking on other roles at ABC, debuting as a correspondent on *Turning Point* with a story on gay marriage. The following year she moved from her position on *Good Morning America* and became a correspondent on ABC's prime-time news magazines, *20/20* and *PrimeTime Live*. She also became an anchor on ABC's *World News Tonight Saturday* and was given the opportunity to develop one-hour news specials. The first, *Diana: Legacy of a Princess* (1997), aired on September 6, 1997, the day of Princess Diana's funeral. Other specials included *Miracles* (1998), which investigated how the Catholic Church verifies miracles and determines whether a person will be granted sainthood, and *Secrets of the World of Fashion and Beauty* (1998), which dealt in part with the issue of drug use among models. In the summer of 1998, Vargas served as the host of ABC's weekly series *News Summer Thursday*, which aired reports on consumer and self-help issues.

Rumors that Vargas would land the co-anchor job on a struggling *Good Morning America* became widespread in early 1999, and later in the year, when her contract with ABC was set to expire, there was also talk that she might co-anchor *CBS This Morning*. Vargas, however, signed a three-year deal with ABC. She continued anchoring *World News Tonight Saturday*, began hosting a six-part series called *Vanished* about people who had disappeared, and became one of the hosts of *20/20 Downtown*, a refashioned version of *20/20's* Thursday edition that broadcast each week from different out-of-studio sites rather than the anchor's desk. That show featured hosts younger than those on the other editions of *20/20*, as part of a move by ABC executives to attract younger viewers. Vargas also continued serving as a correspondent on other editions of *20/20*. For the Wednesday edition, for example, she interviewed Cary Stayner, a man accused and later convicted of killing four women in Yosemite National Park. *20/20 Downtown* was taken off the air at the beginning of 2000, and Vargas turned her attention to making six new installments of the series *Vanished*, continued anchoring the weekend news, and substituted for Peter Jennings, then the host of *World News Tonight*, as needed during the week.

In 2002 *Downtown* was revived and was scheduled this time to air on Wednesdays. Vargas returned to her position on the program, while continuing to carry out her other duties with ABC. The following year she hosted a much-discussed special edition of *PrimeTime* that focused on Laci Peterson, a woman who had gone missing and was later found to have been murdered by her husband, Scott Peterson. That edition of *PrimeTime* openly questioned the integrity of the media, which had lavished attention on Laci Peterson while ignoring the cases of many other women who had been murdered or were missing, particularly minority women, some of whose circumstances were similar to Laci Peterson's. Vargas also hosted a news special called *Jesus, Mary, and DaVinci*. Inspired by the idea at the center of Dan Brown's best-selling novel *The DaVinci Code* (2003), the special considered the possibility that Mary Magdalene was married to Jesus and gave birth to his child. "For me, it's made religion more real and, ironically, much more interesting," Vargas told the Associated Press (October 30, 2003), "which is what we're hoping to do for our viewers." (Vargas's parents, who raised her in the Roman Catholic faith, said to her, "Oh, my goodness, what are you doing?" when they found out about the special, according to the Associated Press.)

In November 2003 Vargas's profile at ABC rose. In addition to working on news magazines and substituting occasionally for Jennings on *World News Tonight*, she was given the anchor position on *World News Tonight Sunday,* a prestigious job at the network. A year later she took over for Barbara Walters as a co-anchor of *20/20*. "I love doing all kinds of stories . . . I love breaking news and features and I don't mind doing the occasional celebrity profile," Vargas told Michael Starr for the *New York Post* (May 19, 2004). "We really have the entire world as options for stories [on *20/20*]." She said about Barbara Walters, "She's been a wonderful mentor and role model and has been exceedingly generous in a business that's not always that way." In her new post Vargas wasted little time in attempting to reinvigorate the show, airing, for example, a much-praised and risky installment arguing that the 1998 murder of Matthew Shepard in Laramie, Wyoming, which had been portrayed in the press as an anti-gay hate crime, was motivated by a drug-induced rage rather than homophobia. "None of this, as Ms. Vargas points out, changes the horror of the murder. . . . But getting the truth—in ABC's revisionist investigation, which seeks to overturn the powerful and canonical version of the facts and meaning of this crime—is worthwhile, as it thickens the description and adds to the mystery of what happened that night in Laramie," Virginia Heffernan wrote for the *New York Times* (November 26, 2004). Heffernan predicted that Vargas's work could help revive magazine shows, which had been declining in popularity.

In April 2005 Peter Jennings announced that he had been diagnosed with lung cancer, and shortly afterward he resigned his anchor's post on *World News Tonight*. (He died in August.) Vargas, along with Charles Gibson, began substituting for Jennings, while ABC looked for a long-term replacement. In December the network announced that Vargas and Bob Woodruff would share permanent anchor duty on *World News Tonight*. Vargas viewed that decision as a significant one for herself and others, saying, as the *Washington Post* (December 6, 2005) reported, "I'm a woman, I'm a working mother, I'm a minority. Being a mom is the biggest, most important role in my entire life. . . . Especially as a woman, I really, really want to do this well. It's important to have a woman be successful in this role." With two anchors, ABC was differentiating its world-news broadcast from those on the other major networks, which featured sole anchors. *World News Tonight* would introduce other differences as well, broadcasting live in three time zones, rather than broadcasting a live show in the East and re-airing it in other time zones, as is generally done; having the anchors broadcast daily Webcasts as well as contribute to a blog called the *World Newser*; and allowing each anchor to report regularly from locations, national and international, where news stories were developing. Vargas and Woodruff officially took their places on *World News Tonight* on January 3, 2006. Assessing their performances, Alessandra Stanley wrote for the *New York Times* (January 9, 2006), "Both Mr. Woodruff and Ms. Vargas are fine in the job: good-looking, highly polished and competent."

Before January came to a close, just as everyone involved in the show was getting comfortable with its new arrangement, ABC's dual-anchor format was placed in jeopardy. On January 29, while Woodruff and Doug Vogt, an ABC cameraman, were pursuing a story in Iraq, they were seriously injured by a roadside bomb that exploded near the vehicle in which they were traveling. ABC briefly considered making Vargas the program's sole anchor, but David Westin, the president of ABC News, was convinced that two anchors illustrated that "leading *World News* on camera had become too big for just one person," as Jacque Steinberg and Bill Carter wrote for the *New York Times* (February 1, 2006). Instead, Westin chose to have Diane Sawyer and Charles Gibson, the co-hosts of *Good Morning America,* work on an alternating basis with Vargas. Vargas, whom Westin praised for doing "a terrific job at being very solid and stable throughout this," as Matea Gold reported for the *Los Angeles Times* (February 6, 2006), expressed her determination to move forward in Woodruff's absence, preparing the way for his return. "We had all sorts of great plans," she remarked, according to Gold. "We're trying to figure out now how to persevere and to continue to put on the very best show we can, not only because we all want to, [but] because we all know that's what Bob would want. Selfishly, I want Bob to return to a strong show that we can all be proud of and that is competitive."

In May 2006 Vargas began a maternity leave of absence from ABC. Her departure, combined with Woodruff's absence and still undetermined return date, left the network in a tenuous position. (As of mid-October 2006, Woodruff was undergoing outpatient rehabilitation therapy.) Pressured by ABC executives to come up with a long-term replacement for Vargas on *World News Tonight*, Westin—despite his previous assertion that she would return as co-anchor when her maternity leave ended—eliminated Vargas's role on *World News* and hired Charles Gibson as the solo lead anchor. Joe Hagan reported for *New York* (June 19, 2006) that people close to Vargas told him that Westin's decision took her by surprise. According to Jacques Steinberg, writing for the *New York Times* (May 24, 2006), she said that she felt "an enormous amount of sadness" about losing the job. "In an interview . . . ,," Steinberg wrote, "Mr. Westin said he had also conveyed to Ms. Vargas that he did not see her as matching up with Mr. Gibson as well as she had with Mr. Woodruff, a conversation that Ms. Vargas recalled similarly." ABC has maintained that Vargas will be considered a candidate to succeed Gibson if he retires when his current contract ends, in 2009. Meanwhile, she is slated to co-anchor *20/20*, beginning in November 2006.

Vargas won an Associated Press Award for Outstanding Journalism and an Emmy Award in 2000 for her story on the six-year-old Cuban refugee Elian Gonzales. She is married to Marc Cohn, a songwriter best known for writing "Walking in Memphis." The couple have two sons: Zachary Rafael, born in early 2003, and Samuel Wyatt, born in mid-2006. Cohn also has two children from a previous marriage. Vargas has said that the birth of her first child changed the way she approaches her professional and private lives. "I don't know any parent who hasn't gone through a cataclysmic change," she told Llorente. "Having children changes your life irrevocably. It takes the whole paradigm and turns it upside down in the most wonderful way. Until you have a child, you've never been certain you'd give your life for someone, you've never been so proud, you've never felt so tired."

—A.R.

Suggested Reading: Associated Press Oct. 30, 2003; *Electronic Media* p78 Jan. 15, 2001; *Hispanic* p24 June 30, 2002, p18 June 30, 2004; *New York Times* IX p9 July 28, 2002, E p1 Jan. 9, 2006, A p1+ May 24, 2006; *People* p113 Sep. 9, 1996; *Washington Post* B p6 Feb 12, 1996, C p1 Dec. 6, 2005

Selected Television Shows: *Now with Tom Brokaw and Katie Couric,* 1993–94; *The Today Show,* 1993–96; *Dateline,* 1994–96; *Good Morning America,* 1996–97; *20/20,* 1997–2005; *World News Tonight Saturday,* 1997–2003; *World News Today Sunday,* 2003–05; *World News Tonight,* 2006; *20/20,* 2006–

Gareth Cattermole/Getty Images

Vaughn, Vince

Mar. 28, 1970– Actor

Address: c/o Mailmann, 15030 Ventura Blvd., #710, Sherman Oaks, CA 91403

The characters that Vince Vaughn has portrayed over the course of his career have frustrated some in their attempts to pigeonhole the handsome, six-foot five-inch actor. Another actor, Jon Favreau, one of Vaughn's closest friends and his occasional collaborator, told Susan Wloszczyna for *USA Today* (May 26, 2006), "When you look like [Vaughn], you are either the lead or the enemy of the lead who is trying to take his girl away. But what people don't realize is he is really a character actor at heart. That is why I lump him with Walter Matthau and Jack Nicholson." In 2006 Vaughn wrote, produced, and starred in *The Break-Up* and is now considered one of the top box-office draws in film comedy, a position that the actor reached rather circuitously: he has played serial killers and rakish cowboys, lotharios and clownish hit men, all to critical success. His breakthrough performance came in the 1996 independent film *Swingers*, which was written by Favreau and featured Vaughn as the charismatic, smooth-talking Trent—whose catchphrases (such as "You're so money!") can be heard across crowded clubs even today. After starring in an array of offbeat, under-watched thrillers, Vaughn entered the mainstream-studio comedy scene in 2003 with his featured role in *Old School*. The success of the hit comedy *Wedding Crashers* (2005), in which he starred opposite Owen Wilson, made Vaughn one of the most recognizable and sought-after comic actors in Hollywood.

Vincent Anthony Vaughn was born on March 28, 1970 and spent his early childhood in the small town of Buffalo Grove, Illinois. His father, Vernon, an Ohio native, had given up professional gambling to work in sales for a toy manufacturer; his mother, Sharon, who had emigrated from Ontario, Canada, was a real-estate agent and later worked as a stockbroker. Vaughn grew up with two older sisters, Victoria and Valerie, and three dogs, Viking, Vero, and Vladimir. When Vaughn was seven years old, the family moved out of their blue-collar neighborhood and relocated to Lake Forest, Illinois, an affluent suburb of Chicago. Because Vaughn initially had trouble adjusting to his new environment, his mother enrolled him in acting classes to help him connect with others. "My mom was always a big fan of theater," Vaughn told Fred Schruers for *Rolling Stone* (June, 12 1997, on-line), "and there was a local community theater that would put on musicals—a bunch of kids 10 and under doing the *King and I.* I'd be there morning till night—almost like day care. I really loved it."

During his years as a student at Lake Forest High School, Vaughn did not excel academically. For a time he dropped theater for such pursuits as football and wrestling. He was also the class clown. "I was a kid who didn't get very good grades, cut school, ran around with my friends, drank, always had a good time," Vaughn explained to Schruers. "I wasn't a mean kid; I was warm-spirited, but the teachers really had a problem with me." Vaughn was well liked by his peers, however, and popular enough to be elected class president in his senior year. A bad back, the result of an injury he sustained as a passenger in a car accident, forced Vaughn to give up sports. Searching for a new outlet for his energy, Vaughn tried out for the school play and won one of the lead roles. Soon he regained his interest in acting, which grew to be serious. Vaughn started traveling to Chicago on weekends to polish his natural improvisational skills under the direction of Del Close at Second City, an established improvisational-comedy troupe, many of whose performers had gone on to prominent television and film careers. After hiring a local agent, he landed a role in an educational film about sex and appeared in commercials, one of which, part of the automaker Chevrolet's "Heartbeat of America" campaign, ran during the Super Bowl.

In 1988, with the money—and confidence—he had gained by appearing in a nationwide commercial, Vaughn moved to Los Angeles, California, to pursue acting full-time. He was able to sign with a small agency but was surprised by the difficulty he had in landing roles. (In some cases he was rejected because of his height.) Eventually he earned parts in television after-school specials, and in the late 1980s and early 1990s, he appeared in brief roles on prime-time television shows such as *China Beach*, *21 Jump Street*, and *Doogie Howser, M.D.* He auditioned unsuccessfully for the feature films *School Ties* and *Dazed and Confused* but earned small roles in *For the Boys* (1991) and *Rudy* (1993),

a tearjerker about the Notre Dame University football team. While filming *Rudy* in Indiana, Vaughn met Jon Favreau, a fellow Chicagoan who had a larger role in the film. The two became friends, bonding over their shared Hollywood experiences as midwestern transplants without enough work. After his work in *Rudy*, Vaughn again struggled to find acting gigs and resorted to working as a lifeguard at the YMCA to help pay the rent on his studio apartment. "There was some discouragement during that period," Vaughn told Barry Koltnow for the *Orange County (California) Register* (October 6, 1997). "One day you wake up and you're not filled with that kind of naivete that can make this business so exciting. Suddenly, you realize that the odds are really stacked against you." Frustrated with the lack of fulfilling roles, Vaughn and Favreau decided to create some work for themselves. Favreau wrote a script titled *Swingers*, about out-of-work actors cruising the Los Angeles party scene, and the two tried to pitch it—and themselves, in the lead roles—to movie studios. With the major studios showing little interest, Favreau and Vaughn found a director for their film in the little-known Doug Liman, who also agreed to finance much of the production. Vaughn told Glen Schaefer for the *Vancouver Province* (October 31, 2001), "I always give the same advice, that if you're frustrated you really can't sit around and wait for someone else to give you an opportunity."

In the comedy *Swingers* (1996), a buddy movie set amid the singles-club scene in Los Angeles, Vaughn starred as Trent, a fast-talking ladies' man who tries to get his recently jilted friend Mike, played by Favreau, back into the world of dating. The film, made for the relatively low sum of $250,000 and with similarly modest expectations, became an overnight sensation. After a bidding war, Miramax bought the film for $5 million. The film picked up a great deal of momentum on the festival circuit, and critics began to view Vaughn as an up-and-coming star; he was offered follow-up roles before his breakout film even went into mainstream distribution. As Bruce Westbrook wrote for the *Houston Chronicle* (November 29, 1996), "In effect, based solely on the buzz from his first roles, [Vaughn] was a big star in Hollywood before the public had even seen him." Vaughn, stunned by the critical success of the film, later explained to Jim Slotek for the *Toronto Sun* (October 24, 2001), "The most we hoped to get from [*Swingers*] was some [audition] tape. The reception was so flattering and unbelievable." Bill Thompson wrote for the Charleston, South Carolina, *Post and Courier* (December 12, 1996), "As good as Favreau is, and he strikes all the right notes, it's Vaughn who steals the movie as the flamboyant Trent. . . . Trent makes it on audacity and bluff—and sets the tone for the entire picture."

While *Swingers* was still in production, Liman requested permission to use the theme music from the Oscar-winning director Steven Spielberg's 1975 film *Jaws* for a scene in which Vaughn's character attempts to pick up a woman. As a result Spielberg saw *Swingers* and was so impressed with Vaughn's talents that he encouraged the actor to audition for *The Lost World: Jurassic Park* (1997). Vaughn won the role of Nick Van Owen, an environmentalist photographer, in that blockbuster film. (The toy company Hasbro even modeled an action figure after his character.) "My objective is not fame," Vaughn said at the time to Bob Strauss for the *Port St. Lucie (Florida) News* (December 6, 1996). "For me, it's very important to do a good job. If Spielberg includes me in his film, that's a big honor for me and I want to make sure I do well for him." Also in 1997 Vaughn starred with Kate Capshaw, Spielberg's wife, in *The Locusts*. For that thriller Vaughn played Clay Hewitt, a handsome drifter who enters a small town looking for work; Capshaw played Delilah Potts, an older woman who hires him in an attempt to seduce him. *The Locusts*, set in 1960s Kansas, never found a substantial audience, but many were impressed with Vaughn's ability to carry a feature film. Bob Ivry wrote in a review for the Bergen County, New Jersey, *Record* (October 4, 1997), "Tall, lanky, impossibly good-looking in a James-Dean-meets-boy-next-door kind of way, Vaughn continues to display star power."

The year 1998 was a busy one for Vaughn: he starred in the romance *A Cool, Dry Place* and three darker-themed films, *Return to Paradise*, *Clay Pigeons*, and Gus Van Sant's remake of Alfred Hitchcock's classic 1960 thriller *Psycho*. Critics viewed Vaughn's roles in those films as risky ones for an actor who had just begun to make his reputation with a hit comedy and a high-profile Spielberg movie. "I wasn't sure [comedy] was the most interesting path for me to take," he told Ian Spelling for the Canadian publication the *Record* (June 17, 2004), "so I went in a different direction and did darker stuff." In *Return to Paradise*, based loosely on the 1989 French film *Force Majeure*, Vaughn played Sheriff, a New York City limousine driver who has just returned to the United States after five weeks of drugs, sex, and fun in Malaysia. Sheriff learns through a lawyer (played by Anne Heche) that a friend he has left behind in Malaysia has been arrested for possession of drugs and is in danger of execution. Vaughn's character is faced with the prospect of returning to share responsibility for the charges and reducing his friend's sentence to a few years in prison. Joseph Ruben, the director of *Return to Paradise*, said to Amy Longsdorf for the Allentown, Pennsylvania, *Morning Call* (August 8, 1998) that Vaughn "reminds me of an old-time movie star. Like Clark Gable, Vince has this remarkable presence." Heche was similarly impressed with her co-star, recommending him to Van Sant for *Psycho*. Vaughn reprised the role of Norman Bates (originally played by Anthony Perkins) for the new version of *Psycho*, which was well-publicized but universally panned.

Vaughn's streak of unconventional films and menacing roles continued with the thriller *The Cell* (2000), which co-starred Jennifer Lopez, and Harold Becker's *Domestic Disturbances* (2001). In the latter, Vaughn played Rick Barnes, a too-good-to-be-true businessman who enters the lives of a divorced woman and her son. John Travolta played the ex-husband who confronts Barnes after the son witnesses a murder. When asked about his taste for nefarious characters, Vaughn told Jamie Portman for the *Calgary Herald* (November 1, 2001), "There's fun in getting out of yourself and who you are and playing someone else. A lot of times, the characters who are more extreme socially are more interesting to play." Vaughn was never concerned that the psychotic characters he portrayed might limit his ability to appeal to a mass audience. He explained to Peter Howell, "I never really worried about [my characters] being liked in movies, as much as I worried about being truthful or being real."

In 2001, as part of his continued effort never to "establish one sort of thing," as he told Stephen Schaefer for the *Boston Herald* (June 18, 2004), Vaughn rejoined forces with Favreau to create, produce, and co-star in *Made*, a comedy about two would-be gangsters. "It's my responsibility, any time I'm getting locked into one thing or another, to either generate my own material, . . . or to find a filmmaker who sees me in a different light," he explained to Spelling. In *Made*, playing the dimmer of the two aspiring mobsters, Vaughn carried the film. Dennis Hunt wrote for the *San Diego Union-Tribune* (July 26, 2001), "[*Made*] is basically character-driven, without a sturdy plot, with Ricky [Vaughn] and Bobby [Favreau] careening through a series of misadventures." Vaughn, he wrote, "thoroughly dominates, acting everybody off the screen." The film did not develop the same cult following that *Swingers* engendered—which did not particularly bother Vaughn, who was more concerned with the process of creating the movie than with the critical or commercial response to it. "[It's] just so much more rewarding to work this way because you can share your point of view rather than just your interpretation of a role," he told Marc Horton for the *Edmonton Journal* (July 31, 2001).

After a brief appearance in Ben Stiller's *Zoolander* (2001), Vaughn moved successfully into mainstream-studio comedy with his role in Todd Phillips's *Old School* (2003), about a group of friends, well beyond their college years, who set up a frat house near a university campus. The low-brow humor of *Old School* apparently struck a chord with theatergoers and reviewers alike, prompting Andrew O'Hehir to write for *Salon.com* (February 21, 2003), "It's blissfully, pants-wettingly funny from beginning to end." Vaughn parlayed the success of *Old School* into featured roles in a string of successful comedies, including *Starsky & Hutch* (2004), *Dodgeball: A True Underdog Story* (2004), *Anchorman* (2004), and *Wedding*

Crashers (2005). Those films, with their themes of arrested adolescence and shifting casts of "A"-list comic actors, among them Vaughn, Will Ferrell, Ben Stiller, and Luke and Owen Wilson, have led some critics to refer to Vaughn and the others as the "Frat Pack." (The name is an allusion to the Rat Pack, the group of entertainers—led by Frank Sinatra—who appeared together in a string of film comedies in the 1960s.) Tom Maurstad wrote for the Dallas Morning News (July 16, 2005), "The defining trait of the Frat Pack comedies is a sophisticated sensibility that manages to be simultaneously ironic and sincere. The only difference between the good guys and the bad guys is that the bad guys are dumber or meaner than the good guys. But the good guys are just as selfish, unscrupulous and manipulative."

Wedding Crashers proved to be the biggest hit to date in the genre and, as the highest-grossing comedy of 2005, took Vaughn's reputation as a comic actor to a new level. Opposite Owen Wilson, Vaughn played Jeremy, a divorce negotiator who routinely crashes weddings to meet women—unwillingly falling in love with one of them. Bob Strauss wrote for the Los Angeles Daily News (July 10, 2005), "Vaughn's dirty-minded verbal dexterity astonishes," and the film's director, David Dobkin, said to Louis B. Hobson for the Calgary Sun (July 25, 2005) that Vaughn "is definitely the fireworks in the film." Vaughn, Dobkin, and Wilson reworked many of the scenes in Wedding Crashers to take advantage of the actors' improvisational skills.

In a departure from the Frat Pack comedies, Vaughn wrote, produced, and acted in The Break-Up (2006), which co-starred Jennifer Aniston. The main characters in The Break-Up are Gary (played by Vaughn) and Brooke (Aniston), a couple who break up but cannot figure out what to do with the condo they co-own. They decide to continue living together until a solution materializes, butting heads to comedic effect in the meantime. Vaughn wrote the script as a response to what he perceived as the cliché-ridden plots of many romantic comedies. "They always have this really ridiculous subplot to them . . . ," Vaughn groused to Susan Wloszczyna. "If you marry the girl, you will get the inheritance and run the company. And, if you don't, I'm going to give it to this mean guy who works for me. I'm more a fan of comedy that has some reality to it." Vaughn has described The Break-Up as an "anti-romantic" comedy and hopes that the project will begin a new phase of his career, which will involve more writing and producing.

Vaughn is romantically involved with his Break-Up co-star, Jennifer Aniston. He lives in Chicago, where he recently purchased a $12 million penthouse in the Palmolive Building.

—N.W.M.

Suggested Reading: Cosmopolitan p206 Oct. 1997; Dallas Morning News E p14 July 16, 2005; Details p203 Sep. 1997; Houston Chronicle p1 Nov. 29, 1996; Interview p34 June 1997; Rolling Stone (on-line) June, 12 1997; Salon (on-line) Feb. 21, 2003; USA Today D p4 June 16, 2004

Selected Films: Rudy, 1993; Swingers, 1996; The Lost World: Jurassic Park, 1997; The Locusts, 1997; A Cool, Dry Place, 1998; Return to Paradise, 1998; Clay Pigeons, 1998; Psycho, 1998; Made, 2001; Zoolander, 2001; Old School, 2003; Starsky & Hutch, 2004; Dodgeball: A True Underdog Story, 2004; Anchorman: The Legend of Ron Burgundy, 2004; Be Cool, 2005; Mr. & Mrs. Smith, 2005; Wedding Crashers, 2005; The Break-Up, 2006

Frazer Harrison/Getty Images

Wade, Dwyane

(dwayne)

Jan. 17, 1982– Basketball player

Address: Miami Heat, American Airlines Arena, 601 Biscayne Blvd., Miami, FL 33132

By nearly all accounts Dwyane Wade of the Miami Heat is among the most talented guards in the National Basketball Association (NBA). In three years with the NBA, he has emerged as one of the sport's most recognizable stars, capable of gravity-defying jumps that call to mind such luminaries of past decades as Dominique Wilkins of the Atlanta Hawks and Michael Jordan of the Chicago Bulls. In the 2005–06 season Wade cemented his status among the NBA's elite, leading the Heat to the NBA championship—the first in the franchise's 18-year-history—over the champion Dallas Mavericks in a hard-fought six-game series. Wade garnered the NBA Finals Most Valuable Player Award for a string of dazzling performances marked by prolific scoring (an average of 34.7 points per game for the series), clutch defense, and an apparently fierce will to win. According to Jack McCallum, writing for *Sports Illustrated* (July 5, 2006), the NBA finals marked "the coronation of Dwyane Wade as the second coming of Michael Jordan."

The multitalented Wade scores from the perimeter of the court, with a precise and reliable jump shot used to great effect at critical moments; he also moves with blazing speed and handles the basketball deftly with either hand. "There's an awe about Dwyane, not only in his game but in his whole approach to life. His sincerity, his humility," Pat Riley, the Heat's general manager, told Jill Lieber for *USA Today* (February 18, 2005). "All of those things are strengths when it comes to greatness." Wade first received national attention in 2003, as a junior at Marquette University, when he led the school's basketball team to its first appearance in over two decades in the National Collegiate Athletic Association (NCAA) Basketball Tournament Final Four. He was selected fifth overall by the Miami Heat in the 2003 NBA draft and has played in two NBA All-Star Games. Wade was a member of the U.S. Olympic basketball team that won a bronze medal in Athens, Greece, in 2004. Playing for the Heat, he and his teammate Shaquille O'Neal comprise one of the NBA's most formidable guard–forward duos. Known for displaying uncommon modesty both on and off the court, Wade donates 10 percent of his salary to a Chicago church. "He doesn't buy into the NBA superstar hype because he's a special kid," Damon Jones, then one of Wade's teammates, told Lieber. "He's all about the team. He wants to win at all costs, and he understands he's a very integral piece of what we're doing around here. I can't even count the number of game-saving plays he has made, and never once does he boast or brag." "He has a gift of honesty," Tom Crean, who coached Wade at Marquette, told Lieber. "He can be honest with himself and his teammates. What you see is what you get. In this day and age, so many people flash their agenda. His agenda is about winning, being a good teammate, being a good husband and a good father."

Dwyane Tyrone Wade Jr. was born in Chicago, Illinois, on January 17, 1982 to Jolinda and Dwyane Wade Sr. His parents split up when he was still an infant but maintained civil relations. He spent his early years on Chicago's rough South Side with his mother and her new husband; his older sister, Tragil, who is a schoolteacher; and his mother's two daughters, Deana and Keisha, from an earlier relationship. He has said that Tragil (who is five years his senior) played a big role in his upbringing. One day when he was about eight, she took him by bus to their father's house, telling him that she would come back for him in a few hours. Unbeknownst to him, his parents and Tragil had decid-

ed that they should shield him from the South Side's gangs and other potential dangers; he would fare better, they thought, in the home that his father (who worked for a printing plant) shared with his new wife and her three sons. Wade lived primarily with his father's family, in the Chicago suburb of Robbins, until his senior year of high school, when strife between his father and stepmother led him to move to the home of his girlfriend's mother.

Dwyane was a well-behaved boy; as he told Amy Shipley for the *Washington Post* (May 10, 2005), "I always wanted to keep my parents happy, let them know they were raising a good child." He liked playing sports with his stepbrothers, particularly basketball and football. He also enjoyed being with his father at a local recreational center where the elder Wade coached teenage basketball players. He and his father often competed with each other, too, shooting baskets in the family's backyard for many hours at a stretch. "He taught me the game," Wade told Shipley, "what I needed to know to win games." "My toughness on the court came from him knocking me down and not picking me up," he added. He and others have attributed his physical durability and mental focus largely to his years of training under his father's guidance.

Like his stepbrother Demetrius, Wade attended H. L. Richards High School, in Oak Lawn, a Chicago suburb. Demetrius was an important member of the school's fledgling basketball program, which was coached by Jack Fitzgerald. Unimpressed by Wade's performance on the court, Fitzgerald did not recruit him for the school's varsity basketball team. Instead, Wade played cornerback and wide receiver for Richards's football team. During the summer following his sophomore year, he prepared himself for the upcoming basketball season by working tirelessly to improve his ball-handling and shooting (both left- and right-handed), part of the time with one of Richards's coaches. Having grown several inches, to slightly over six feet, and having developed more muscle as well as improved skills, Wade joined the varsity team (known as the Bulldogs) as a junior and became its de facto leader. Excellent at both offense and defense, in his senior year Wade led the Bulldogs to a 24–5 record and to the Class AA sectional finals. He averaged more than 25 points and 10 rebounds per game. Meanwhile, before he entered his senior year, Wade (along with the future NBA player Darius Miles) had begun playing basketball with the Illinois Warriors, a team in the Amateur Athletic Union (AAU). During that period Wade grew adept at passing the ball to greatest effect late in games.

Because of Wade's low scores on the American College Testing (ACT) college-entrance exam, representatives of many of the major college-basketball programs lost interest in him. Among the few outstanding college programs willing to take a chance on him was that at Marquette University, in Milwaukee, Wisconsin, where Tom Crean was the head coach. During the previous two years, with Crean newly at the helm, Marquette (a member of Conference USA Division I) had secured winning records. Wade joined the team as a partial qualifier (the first in Marquette's history) due to his low test scores. He was not permitted to play in any games during the 2000–01 season or travel with the team but was allowed to practice with his teammates and sit next to the coaching staff during home games. Crean, Wade told Jill Lieber, "was harder on me than anybody else. When we lost, he'd come in the locker room and blame me, say it was my fault because I hadn't practiced hard enough. He wanted me to be a leader so he forced me to tell the guys how I felt about their performances. I wanted to call home and say, 'I can't do this.' It made me stronger, made me really want it more." Crean told Lieber, "We never treated him as a guy who sat out. We kept him at the front of the bench, either taking stats or notes. We never let him say, 'Woe is me.'"

In his first season (2001–02) with Marquette, Wade led the team in scoring, rebounding, assists, steals, and blocked shots. Following the team's opening-round, 71–69 loss to Tulsa in the 2002 NCAA Tournament, Wade made the All-Conference USA first team and received an honorable mention for All-America honors. In his second season he led Marquette to the Final Four. (The team's appearance in that contest was its first since 1977, the year the legendary college coach Al McGuire led the school to its first and only national championship in basketball.) In the Midwest Regional Finals of the NCAA Tournament (which precedes the Final Four), in which Marquette faced the number-one-seeded University of Kentucky, Wade recorded a triple-double—that is, in three important statistical categories, he posted double-digit figures: 29 points, 11 rebounds, and 11 assists, in an 83–69 victory. He was named a consensus First Team All-America player by the Associated Press (becoming the first Marquette player to earn that honor in over two and a half decades) and was voted Defensive Player of the Year and the Conference Player of the Year by Conference USA coaches and officials. Marquette was defeated by the University of Kansas in the national semifinals by a score of 94–61, thus ending their season.

Despite the loss, Wade became a bona fide star on the college level and recognized as one of the most talented young basketball players in the country. Those and other circumstances (he had become a father and married) led him, at the end of his junior year, to declare himself eligible early for the NBA draft. On June 26, 2003 the Miami Heat chose Wade in the fifth selection overall; the team and Wade later negotiated a rookie contract valued at slightly more than $7 million over three years. (Two of the players selected ahead of Wade were LeBron James, a high-school basketball sensation hailing from Akron, Ohio, taken first overall by the Cleveland Cavaliers, and Carmelo Anthony, a one-year college player who months earlier had led Syracuse University to a national championship, taken in the third pick by the Denver Nuggets.) The

Heat had floundered in recent years; in 2003 they ranked second to last in the NBA in points scored per game (85.6, on average). Their roster of young and unproven players was led by Pat Riley, the celebrated former head coach of both the Los Angeles Lakers and the New York Knicks. Before the season started Riley stepped down as coach to concentrate on his duties as the team's general manager. He was succeeded by his assistant Stan van Gundy.

During the early part of his debut season as a pro, Wade suffered an injury to his right wrist. He returned to the lineup in time for the team's advancement toward the play-offs. Posting solid numbers for a rookie, Wade finished the season averaging 16.2 points and slightly more than four assists and rebounds over 61 games. The Heat finished the regular season with a 42–40 record, placing second in the Atlantic Division of the Eastern Conference behind the New Jersey Nets. In the play-offs Wade demonstrated his reliability. Facing the New Orleans Hornets in the first round, Wade made critical jump shots toward the end of games one and five to lead his team to victory. The series between the two teams reached a decisive seventh game, which the Heat won, 85–77. In the second round, against the defensively robust, physical Indiana Pacers, Wade continued his steady performance. Although the Pacers defeated the Heat in six games, Wade again demonstrated his mettle as a leader: he led the Heat in scoring and assists, a feat accomplished by only three other NBA players during rookie seasons (Stephon Marbury, Michael Jordan, and Billy Ray Bates). After the season the Heat acquired the seven-foot center Shaquille O'Neal from the Los Angeles Lakers in exchange for three young players and a first-round draft pick.

Following the 2003–04 season Wade joined the men's basketball team that had been hurriedly assembled to compete in the 2004 Olympic Games. The squad included other young, inexperienced players like himself, among them the 2003 NBA draftees LeBron James and Carmelo Anthony. Their head coach, Larry Brown, was notoriously harsh on such athletes, and many observers expressed doubts about the U.S. team's prospects in the Games—presciently, as it turned out. The U.S. team endured its first two losses in Olympic basketball competition since 1992 (the first year that NBA stars played in the Games). Later, the U.S. team rebounded and defeated Lithuania, 104–96, to win the bronze medal. Wade averaged over 17 minutes per game but seemed unusually tentative in shooting the ball, and posted a field-goal percentage of only 38 percent.

In the 2004–05 season Wade emerged as one of the NBA's best players. With O'Neal providing a fresh source of rebounding and scoring assistance, Wade helped lead the Heat to the Eastern Conference's best record—59–23. He raised his average number of points per game to 24.1; he also averaged over one steal and one blocked shot per game. In February 2005 he was named a reserve on the

NBA's All-Star team. In rounds one and two of the play-offs, the Heat had eight consecutive victories, against the New Jersey Nets and Washington Wizards. They advanced as far as the Eastern Conference's championship round, in which they faced the Detroit Pistons. The Pistons and the Heat engaged in a hard-fought seven-game series, at the end of which the Pistons retained their title as Eastern Conference champions. Earlier, Wade joined the NBA Hall of Fame members Bob Cousy, Oscar Robinson, Wilt Chamberlain, Larry Bird, Magic Johnson, and Michael Jordan as one of the only players to have shot an average of better than 50 percent from the field in addition to averaging at least 25 points, eight assists, and six rebounds a game over the length of a play-off series.

Prior to the start of the 2005–06 season, the Heat added Antoine Walker and Jason Williams to their already talented roster. On December 12, 2005, after the team had gotten off to a mediocre 11–10 start, Riley took over as head coach, replacing Van Gundy, who retired for personal reasons. Under Riley's leadership, the Heat steamrolled through the next several months of the season, netting 30 additional victories and only 11 losses. They finished the regular season with a record of 52–30, the second best in the Eastern Conference. Wade, too, thrived under Riley's hard-nosed yet inspirational coaching, capping the season by posting career-high averages in points (27.2), rebounds (5.7), and assists (6.7) per game. In February 2006 Wade was selected to start in the NBA All-Star Game, in Houston, Texas.

Beginning in April 2006, during the NBA play-offs, Wade steered the Heat to successive victories over the Chicago Bulls, the New Jersey Nets, and the Detroit Pistons; with an impressive array of offensive weaponry, he averaged 28.4 points per game. Also noteworthy was Wade's performance in the NBA Finals, against the Heat's Western Conference rivals the Dallas Mavericks. After dropping the first two games of the series, the Heat returned to their home arena for Game Three. In that contest Wade scored 42 points (15 in the final quarter) to lead his team to victory. Wade almost single-handedly befuddled the Mavericks' defensive schemes over the next three games, which the Heat also won, thus capturing the championship. During the series Wade averaged 34.7 points per game, the third-highest average ever achieved by a player making his NBA Finals debut. Moreover, in Game Five Wade made a Finals series record with 21 free throws, prompting a Mavericks player, Darrell Armstrong, to complain to Jack McCallum for *Sports Illustrated* (July 5, 2006), "The kid spins, fades away, we don't touch him, and he goes to the [free throw] line? What does the NBA want? Ratings?" Wade was named the 2006 NBA Finals Most Valuable Player.

In the summer of 2006, Wade joined his NBA superstar contemporaries LeBron James and Carmelo Anthony as members of Team USA in that year's FIBA Men's World Championships, held in Japan.

Team USA beat Argentina 96–81 behind Wade's impressive 32-point effort to take home the bronze medal; they lost the chance to compete for the gold medal after suffering a loss to Greece in the semifinal round.

Wade is six feet four inches tall and weighs approximately 212 pounds. In the May 9, 2005 issue of *People*, he was named on the editors' list of the world's 50 most beautiful people. Recently he signed a lucrative contract with Converse sneakers. He donates 10 percent of his gross salary to what is identified in articles about him as the Blood, Water, and Spirit Ministry, a Baptist church in Chicago. Wade studied broadcasting in college and has said that he will consider a career in sports broadcasting when his playing days are over. Since childhood he has been a fan of the Chicago Bears football team. He lives in Doral, Florida, with his wife, Siohvaughn Funchess, whom he has known since the age of nine and married in 2002. The couple have one son, Zaire. In December 2004 Tom Crean established the Dwyane Wade Legacy of Leadership Award at Marquette.

—D.F.

Suggested Reading: dwyanewade.com; (Fort Lauderdale, Florida) *Sun Sentinel* (on-line) May 28, 2005; Jockbio.com; *Miami (Florida) Herald* D p1+ Sep. 28, 2003; *Oakland (Michigan) Press* (on-line) May 23, 2005; *USA Today* C p8 Feb. 18, 2005; *Washington Post* D p1+ May 10, 2005

Wales, Jimmy

1966– Founder and chairman of the Wikimedia Foundation

Address: Wikimedia Foundation Inc., 200 Second Ave. S. #358, St. Petersburg, FL 33701-4313

Jimmy Wales, a former futures and options trader, is the founder of Wikipedia, the Web-based encyclopedia that "anyone can edit," and the founder and chairman of the Wikimedia Foundation, a nonprofit corporation that operates a variety of open-source "wiki" projects. Since its launch, on January 15, 2001, Wikipedia has become one of the most popular destinations on the World Wide Web: as of late October 2006, the site boasted a library of more than 5.3 million articles in 250 languages. While 16 of those languages are represented by more than 50,000 articles each, the lion's share are English-language entries, of which there are more than 1.4 million—approximately 10 times the number of entries in the *Encyclopedia Britannica*. Those statistics notwithstanding, critics have expressed concerns about the accuracy of the site's content. Wikipedia uses wiki software, which encourages collaborative writing, enabling any visi-

Mario Tama/Getty Images

Jimmy Wales

tor to the site—be that person a reliable source or a vandal—to edit content quickly and easily. Vesting the anonymous masses with such authority is at the heart of what Wikipedia's critics, among them academics and librarians, in particular, call into question. "However closely a Wikipedia article may at some point in its life attain to reliability, it is forever open to the uninformed or semiliterate meddler," Robert McHenry, the former editor in chief of *Encyclopedia Britannica*, wrote in an oft-referenced article entitled "The Faith-Based Encyclopedia," which is posted on the TCS Daily Web site (November 15, 2004).

Wales and the thousands of volunteer editors who monitor Wikipedia's entries daily for vandalism, substandard reporting, and poor grammar argue that collaboration is what distinguishes Wikipedia from more formal reference sources. Discussing the future of the creation of information sources, he told Rhys Blakely for the London *Times* (December 30, 2005, on-line), "What we will see is a set of hybrid models with an increasing amount of citizen participation in the gathering of news and in feedback and in reporting and analysing the news." He added, "And at the same time, we'll have professional organisations managing the process—basically being the core framework."

One thing remains certain: Wikipedia "is unlike any other encyclopedic source in existence," as Danny P. Wallace and Connie Van Fleet wrote for *Reference & User Services Quarterly* (Winter 2005). "There is no centralized editorial control," Wallace and Van Fleet continued. "Instead content is influenced by individual contributors working collaboratively to achieve consensus and, when that fails, calling for a vote among interested contribu-

tors. The result can be thought of as a sort of democratized reference resource by, of, and for the people." James J. O'Donnell, the provost of Georgetown University and the author of *Avatars of the Word: From Papyrus to Cyberspace* (1998), told Peter Meyers for the *New York Times* (September 20, 2001), "A community that finds a way to talk in this way is creating education and online discourse at a higher level." Assessing the authoritativeness of his own site, Wales told Rhys Blakely, "If what you're after is 'who won the World Cup in 1986', it's going to be fine—no problem. If you want to know something a little more esoteric, or something that's going to be controversial, you should probably use a second reference—at least."

The oldest of four children, Jimmy "Jimbo" Donal Wales was born in 1966 in Huntsville, Alabama. Growing up, Wales was a devoted reader of his family's *World Book* encyclopedia, which his mother, a teacher, and his father, a grocery-store manager, had purchased from a door-to-door salesman. When he was three (some sources say four), his mother and grandmother, also a teacher, opened a private grammar school, dubbed the House of Learning. Located in a historic building in Huntsville, the school had a very small enrollment by today's standards; Wales was usually one of only four students in his class. The school was influenced by the Montessori method, which emphasizes individuality by giving students the freedom to choose their own curricula. Wales attended the House of Learning until the eighth grade, when he enrolled at the Randolph School.

After graduating from Randolph, at the age of 16, Wales attended Auburn University, in Alabama, receiving his bachelor's degree in finance. He later earned his master's degree in the same subject from the University of Alabama, in Tuscaloosa. While in college Wales "met all these great people online," as he told Chris Taylor and Coco Masters for *Time* (June 6, 2005), "and we were all discussing things on mailing lists no one ever looks at. I thought, Why not use the smarts of my friends and build something more long lasting, more fun?" As he continued his education, pursuing his doctorate and lecturing at Indiana University, in Bloomington, the entrepreneurial spirit reflected in that quote briefly lacked an outlet. Wales completed all of his doctoral course work but fell short of receiving his Ph.D., because he never wrote a dissertation.

In 1994 Wales entered the managed futures and options trading industry in Chicago. While working in finance he met Christine, his future wife, who was a steel trader for Mitsubishi Motors. In 1996 Wales founded Bomis, an Internet company that makes most of its money by selling advertising space for its search portal. The company also creates and hosts Web rings (groups of related Web pages). Although Wales is no longer actively involved in Bomis, sources indicate that he retained his stock-holding privileges for a while after selling the company.

While still running Bomis, Wales developed a keen interest in the open-source movement, in which a group of programmers argued that software should be distributed free of charge and designed so that anyone could modify it. According to the Web site for the nonprofit group Open Source Initiative (OSI), "The basic idea behind open source is very simple: When programmers can read, redistribute, and modify the source code for a piece of software, the software evolves. People improve it, people adapt it, people fix bugs. And this can happen at a speed that, if one is used to the slow pace of conventional software development, seems astonishing." The OSI Web site goes on to say, "This rapid evolutionary process produces better software than the traditional closed model, in which only a very few programmers can see the source and everybody else must blindly use an opaque block of bits." That approach to software development dovetailed with the philosophy expounded by Friedrich Hayek's 1945 article "The Use of Knowledge in Society," which Wales had read as an undergraduate. Hayek argued that an individual's knowledge of any subject is only partial, and thus the truth can be known only when a group of people pool their information.

In 2000 Wales founded Nupedia, a Web-based encyclopedia funded by Bomis. The decision to offer the encyclopedia for free was inspired by Wales's desire to quash ignorance, which he considers the cause of poverty, war, and terrorism. He hired Larry Sanger, a doctoral student in philosophy at the time, as the peer-reviewed site's editor in chief. Nupedia originally operated with a typical, top-down work flow: contributors were asked to write comprehensive, neutral articles, which were then vetted by the Nupedia Advisory Board, a team of reviewers and editors (mostly college professors and other experts). Only after an article passed through a seven-stage editorial review was it deemed suitable for publication.

After almost a year Nupedia had published only 21 articles—well short of what Wales and Sanger had envisioned—with another 150 drafts in various stages of approval. Jeremy Rosenfeld, a Bomis employee, proposed that a "wiki" be set up for Nupedia to speed the publication process. Earlier, a friend had directed Sanger to the programmer Ward Cunningham's innovative site WikiWiki-Web, which, when it was launched in 1994, was the first wiki, a type of Web site that allows visitors to add to and edit its content. The initial idea behind the Nupedia wiki was that visitors, using the wiki technology, could submit content for articles, which would then be inspected by the encyclopedia's editorial board. However, when a majority of the Nupedia Advisory Board rejected the plan, citing concern for the reliability and accuracy of visitor-authored entries, a separate Web site, operating under the domain name Wikipedia.com, was launched, on January 15, 2001. (According to some sources, Wales has claimed that converting to a wiki format was his idea. Sanger resigned from Nupedia and Wikipedia on March 1, 2002.)

By the end of its first month in operation, approximately 16 articles had appeared on Wikipedia, and after a year, 18,000 articles had been submitted. (Wikipedia added a .org domain name in 2002.) In a two-part memoir that appeared on the Slashdot Web site, Sanger outlined the early history of Wikipedia, citing the factors that enabled the encyclopedia to expand so quickly: "I think it was essential that we began the project with a core group of intelligent good writers who understood what an encyclopedia should look like, and who were basically decent human beings." Wales has also emphasized that the conscientious volunteers who were in place to help with Nupedia contributed greatly to Wikipedia's growth.

When the Wikipedia site first went on-line, anyone could create a new article or edit an existing one (a policy that later changed). Edits appear instantly, and an edit "history," which is also available for public scrutiny, keeps a chronological log of the changes made. Disagreements over the content—which sometimes become protracted debates, or "edit wars"—are commonly settled via a consensus and occasionally by a vote. Even entries that have been granted "featured article" status, meaning that reviewers have checked them for accuracy, reliability, neutrality, and style, are subject to visitors' edits. As a result, the content of the site is in constant flux.

While Wikipedia may be one of the most popular sites on the World Wide Web—as of October 2006 it ranked 15th on Alexa's list of the most-visited sites—the tolerant nature of its editorial process has sparked a contentious debate about the quality of the site's content. Detractors call into question the reliability and accuracy of a reference source that allows all visitors to add and subtract from any article. "The user who visits Wikipedia to learn about some subject, to confirm some matter of fact, is rather in the position of a visitor to a public restroom," Robert McHenry wrote. "It may be obviously dirty, so that he knows to exercise great care, or it may seem fairly clean, so that he may be lulled into a false sense of security. What he certainly does not know is who has used the facilities before him." The potential for vandalism and mudslinging are also common criticisms of Wikipedia. On more than one occasion, employees at the House of Representatives—who all share the same Internet Protocol (IP) address, thus making it impossible to identify which employees have edited Wikipedia—have vandalized the biographical entries on various politicians, leading the site's administrators to temporarily ban the entire law-making body from editing articles.

Critics also charge that the anonymity of the site prevents injured parties from seeking damages for defamatory material. On November 29, 2005 John Seigenthaler Sr., the former editor of the *Tennessean* and a onetime assistant to the former U.S. attorney general Robert F. Kennedy, published an opinion piece in *USA Today* charging that a biography of him that had appeared on Wikipedia for 132 days—and longer on two of Wikipedia's mirror sites, Answers.com and Reference.com—contained "scurrilous" information linking him to the assassination of Robert Kennedy and his brother President John F. Kennedy. "I am interested in letting many people know that Wikipedia is a flawed and irresponsible research tool," Seigenthaler wrote. Wales then instituted a new set of rules that prevented anonymous users from creating their own pages but did not prevent them from editing existing material. As Wales told *Current Biography*, since its founding Wikipedia has had a system by which the reliability and neutrality of articles are judged; disputed articles are marked with a "Stop Hand," alerting readers of the dispute.

Later that same year the scientific journal *Nature* published, in its December 15, 2005, issue, a peer-reviewed investigation into the accuracy of Wikipedia versus that of *Encyclopedia Britannica*. According to the study's author, Jim Giles, entries on topics from a "broad range of scientific disciplines" were chosen from both sources and then sent to experts in relevant fields for fact-checking. "The exercise revealed numerous errors in both encyclopaedias," Giles wrote, "but among 42 entries tested, the difference in accuracy was not particularly great: the average science entry in Wikipedia contained around four inaccuracies; *Britannica*, about three." Wales told Daniel Terdiman, writing for the CNET Web site (December 16, 2005, online), that he was delighted with the study, which he thought served as "a great counterpoint to the press coverage we've gotten recently, because it puts the focus on the broader quality and not just one article." Wales added, "I have very great respect for *Britannica*. [But] I think there is a general view among a lot of people that it has no errors, like: 'I read it in *Britannica*, it must be true.' It's good that people see that there are a lot of errors everywhere."

The Wikimedia Foundation, Wikipedia's parent organization, is an international nonprofit organization based in St. Petersburg, Florida. Its aim is "to develop and maintain open content, wiki-based projects and to provide the full contents of those projects to the public free of charge," according to a profile on Wikipedia (September 8, 2006). The Wikimedia Foundation manages a variety of sites, including Wikitionary, a multilingual, open-source dictionary and thesaurus; Wikiquote, an encyclopedia of famous quotations; and Wikibooks, a collection of such e-book resources as textbooks and public-domain works. Despite the high-volume traffic on its flagship site (which receives up to 14,000 hits per second), Wikimedia has yet to capitalize on any of those resources by selling ad space; it relies on charitable donations to pay its $750,000 annual budget, most of which is raised through contributions of $20 or less. Wales, who draws no salary for the many hours that he spends working on the sites every week, told Blakely that if Wikipedia carried advertising, it could generate hundreds of millions of dollars in revenue annually and that "at some point questions are going to be raised over the amount of money we are turning down." Nonetheless, he suspects, as he told Michael Hinman for the *Tampa Bay Business Journal* (September 23, 2005, on-line), that Wikipedia would not have become the success that it is, and that people would have been less likely to contribute, if the site had included ads. "I joke a lot that [choosing to be a nonprofit] was either the best thing or the worst thing I've ever done," he told Hinman.

In 2004 Wales and the Internet entrepreneur Angela Beesley founded Wikia (formerly known as Wikicities), a for-profit wiki-hosting service, which, as of October 2006, supported more than 1,500 wiki communities in 55 languages. Some of the more popular wikis include Memory Alpha, a reference stop devoted to *Star Trek*; Wookieepedia, a *Star Wars* wiki; and Uncyclopedia, a parody of Wikipedia. In the fall of 2006, Wales launched a new wiki called Students Wikia, aimed at university communities in the U.S. and overseas. According to Tristan Harris, who initiated the wiki at Stanford University, in California, Students Wikia aims to help "students looking for current, under-the-radar tips and tricks that only other students would know. . . . The beauty of creating a wiki on your university is that anyone can check out information on your school, but only those students who've experienced the school programs and 'extracurricular' activities can edit the content," as he told W. David Gardner for *TechWeb* (September 26, 2006, on-line).

Wales was appointed a fellow of the Berkman Center for Internet and Society at the Harvard Law School, in Cambridge, Massachusetts, in 2005. That same year he joined the board of directors for Socialtext, a company that establishes wiki sites for businesses. Wales was a featured speaker at Infovision 2006, a global summit for the "knowledge industry" and "knowledge society," held in Banglore, India; his speech focused on the surge of interest in India in Wikipedia, which by then had become the country's 17th-most-popular Web site. Also in 2006 *Time* included Wales on its list of the 100 most influential people in the world. Wikipedia has won a handful of awards, including the 2004 Golden Nica Award for Digital Communities from Prix Arts Electronica, the 2004 Web Creation Award from the Japan Advertisers Association, and the 2004 Webby Award for best community from the International Academy of Digital Arts and Sciences.

Wales and his wife, Christine, have one daughter, Kira, and live in the St. Petersburg area. He is a supporter of objectivism, a philosophical system attributed to the Russian-American writer Ayn Rand.

—D.F.

Suggested Reading: *Birmingham (Alabama) News* A p1 Dec. 31, 2005; *Florida Trend* p62+ Sep. 1, 2005; *Information Today* p49+ Sep. 2005; (London) *Times* (on-line) Dec. 30, 2005; *New York Times* G p2 Sep. 20, 2001, E p1 Nov. 10, 2004, IV p1 Dec. 4, 2005, III p5 Mar. 12, 2006; *New Yorker* p36+ July 31, 2006; *Newsweek* p34 Nov. 1, 2004; *Reference & User Services Quarterly* p100+ Winter 2005; *St. Petersburg Times* E p1 Nov. 8, 2004; *Tampa Bay Business Journal* (on-line) Sep. 26, 2005; *Time* p40+ June 6, 2005; Wikipedia Web site; *Wired* p124+ Mar. 2005

Warner, Mark R.

Dec. 15, 1954– Former governor of Virginia (Democrat); philanthropist

Address: Collis/Warner Foundation, 201 N. Union St., Suite 300, Alexandria, VA 22314

On political maps since the year 2000, Virginia has been classified as a so-called red state, because its voters have chosen the Republican candidate in every presidential election since 1964, most of its congressional representatives are Republicans, and Republicans hold the majorities in both houses of the state legislature. Nevertheless, in 2001 Virginians elected Mark R. Warner, a centrist Democrat, as the state's governor, and when he left office four years later, his approval rating stood at 80 percent. (State law prohibited him from running for reelection: in Virginia a governor may serve more than one term, but not consecutively.) The 51-year-old Warner, who has lived in Virginia for the last two decades, had never held public office before he became governor; his political experience until then consisted of brief stints as an aide to politicians and about two years as head of the Virginia Democratic Party. A lawyer by training, he never practiced law; rather, for 25 years he made his career in business, becoming a multimillionaire as a venture capitalist, originally in the sphere of cell-phone communications. After the failure of his bid for a seat in the U.S. Senate, in 1996, he had also engaged in philanthropic activities, mostly with the goal of improving the lives of Virginians. His belief that governments, too, must try to better the lives of citizens and help them to "tap their full potential" and "live the American dream," as he has put it—for example, by ensuring that every public school offers a good education and enabling qualified young people to attend college by providing scholarships and loans—places him within the mainstream of the Democratic Party. His support of the death penalty, laws requiring parental notification when a teenager seeks an abortion, and the right of individuals to own guns, however, along with his opposition to same-sex marriage and his

ability to convince traditionally Republican, rural voters of his sincerity, set him apart from many of his fellow Democrats. As governor he turned the state's huge deficit into a budget surplus, leading *Governing* magazine to name him and Virginia state senator John H. Chichester "public officials of the year 2004." After he left the governorship, Warner considered a run for the presidency in 2006 and, toward that end, established a political action committee (PAC) called Forward Together. On October 12, 2006 he announced that, because of family obligations, he had decided against seeking the Democratic presidential nomination. But he promised to remain involved in politics and did not rule out a future attempt to win an elective office. As of late October Forward Together was still operating.

Mark Robert Warner was born on December 15, 1954 in Indianapolis, Indiana, to Robert and Marjorie Warner. His father served as a Marine in World War II and later worked as a safety evaluator for Aetna Life & Casualty; his mother was a homemaker. Both parents tended to vote Republican but had no strong political ties, and they were active in local parent-teacher associations. By Warner's own account, his family's lives were typical of those of American middle-class families in the 1950s and early 1960s. When not in school, young Mark attended Boy Scout meetings and played basketball, football, and baseball; his parents coached some of his teams and helped out with Boy Scout activities. He also enjoyed collecting coins, playing the board game Risk, and reading history, particularly accounts of the Civil War, and from a young age held part-time jobs. On the Web site of Forward Together, he recalled that his parents taught him, "If somebody gives you a chance, you seize it; and whenever you have the opportunity, be bold."

When Warner was in the eighth grade, the family, which included his younger sister, Lisa, moved to Peoria, Illinois, before settling soon afterward in Vernon, Connecticut. That year—1968—he became very conscious of national and international events, among them the escalating war in Vietnam, the assassinations of the Reverend Martin Luther King Jr. and Senator Robert F. Kennedy of New York, and the raucous anti-war demonstrations that accompanied the Democratic National Convention, in Chicago, Illinois, and led to violent clashes between protestors and police officers. During that tumultuous period, Warner has said, he began to think about becoming a public servant, inspired in part by an aunt, who was a local ward leader in Indianapolis, and his social-studies teacher, Jim Tyler. "I was old enough to be touched by idealism but not old enough to be made cynical," he told Garrett M. Graff for the *Washingtonian* (February 2006).

In Vernon Warner attended Rockville High School and was elected class president in his senior year. He spent one summer as an exchange student in Buenos Aires, Argentina, where he learned Spanish. Following his high-school graduation, he attended George Washington University,

Michael Springer/Getty Images

Mark R. Warner

began investing in a variety of businesses. His first investment, in a new type of oil-burning furnace, cost him his savings ($5,000) in six weeks. His second, in a real-estate venture, shriveled up within six months. By his own account, during that period he often lived in the apartments of friends, sleeping on their couches or floors, and all his possessions fit into the trunk of his 1965 Buick.

While in Atlanta, Georgia, in connection with his second failed investment, Warner met Charles Thomas "Tom" McMillen, a professional basketball player, DNC donor, and future congressman from Maryland, who suggested that he invest in cellular phones. According to John F. Harris, writing for the *Washington Post* (March 28, 1993), Warner soon found out that the federal government had set up lotteries as a way to award free licenses to would-be cell-phone businesses. He considered the introduction of such lotteries "a dubious public policy," Harris wrote, "but it was a gold mine for people like him who developed expertise in helping those who won the licenses set up their businesses." After learning how to apply for those licenses, Warner sold the licenses to others. (Later, in his campaign speeches and on his Web sites, he would joke that friends of his tried to dissuade him from getting involved with cell-phone ventures, by telling him, "Mark, you're crazy! You've failed twice in business. Why don't you go and practice law? Nobody's going to want a telephone in their car.") Warner also became skilled at obtaining start-up funds; once, in 1982, after Warner talked for 20 minutes about his "impassioned vision of wireless communications," as a reporter for *Eastern* (Winter 2005, on-line), the Eastern Connecticut State University magazine, put it, the Connecticut industrialist and philanthropist David T. Chase contributed $1 million to Warner's newly founded cell-phone licensing company. In 1987, in one of his most successful ventures, Warner invested in Morgan O'Brien's new company FleetCall, which became the telecommunications giant Nextel. He later co-founded the Columbia Capital Corp., a venture-capital fund that specializes in technology start-ups. As a partner of Columbia Capital, Warner saw his personal fortune rise to $50 million by 1993; as of the 2001 gubernatorial campaign, his net worth was in the realm of $200 million. "It was just obscene for a while," Warner said to John F. Harris. "During the 1980s, the telecommunications industry went wild, and there was always another opportunity."

Earlier, in 1986, Warner had moved to Virginia, and three years later he had gotten married. During his honeymoon, spent overseas, his appendix burst—a life-threatening condition. Back in the U.S., he spent the next two months in the hospital. After his recovery he became the campaign manager for Virginia's then–lieutenant governor, the Democrat L. Douglas Wilder, who was running for governor of the state. He worked without pay and even contributed $60,000 of his own money to Wilder's campaign. On Election Day Wilder defeated

which had attracted him because of its location—four blocks from the White House, in Washington, D.C. Student loans and his earnings from part-time jobs enabled him to pay his tuition. On campus he became well-known as an organizer of all sorts of events, ranging from basketball games to parties. As an undergraduate he worked on Capitol Hill in the offices of several Connecticut legislators: Senator Abraham Ribicoff and U.S. representatives Ella Grasso and Christopher Dodd. The valedictorian of his class as well as the first member of his family to graduate from college, he received a B.A. degree in political science in 1977. He next enrolled at Harvard Law School, in Cambridge, Massachusetts, where he organized study groups and coached the school's first women's intramural basketball team. He became adept at remembering people's names and the names of their hometowns. His classmate Helen Blohn, the basketball team's captain then, told Graff, "He would often be the one planning the party, getting the group together, or doing social things that made us seem more connected to each other." Warner earned a J.D. degree in 1980.

Neither of the law firms with whom Warner had interned during summers offered him a job, and he turned down the only offer that came his way, through a man with political connections in Connecticut. Instead, he took a position as a fund raiser with the Democratic National Committee (DNC). While working at the DNC, he often found himself thinking about a congressional candidate who had ended his campaign some $300,000 in debt and in danger of losing his home. Warner decided that he would enter politics only when he had enough money set aside to do so, and toward that end, he his Republican opponent by a margin of victory of less than one percentage point; a recount confirmed his win. (Wilder was the first, and as of 2006 is the only, African-American to serve as governor of a U.S. state.) Warner directed Wilder's transition team; after the governor's inauguration, in January 1990, Warner was named to the Commonwealth Transportation Board, a part-time position that he held until 1994. (The state is officially known as the Commonwealth of Virginia.) In 1992 Warner helped to found, and for several years chaired, the Virginia Health Care Foundation, which is funded by both the state and private sources and helps the hundreds of thousands of Virginians who have no health insurance and/or do not have access to adequate medical care. Warner reportedly briefly considered running for Congress in 1990 and 1992. In the latter year he helped raise funds for Wilder's short-lived presidential campaign.

From 1993 to mid-1995 Warner chaired the Democratic Party of Virginia. He relinquished the chairmanship after announcing his intention to try to unseat the incumbent U.S. senator John W. Warner (the two are not related), a Republican, who would be running for reelection for the third time in 1996. At the Democratic state convention in June 1995, in which the former U.S. representative Leslie Byrne was also in the running, Warner won the nomination. In his tougher campaign against Senator Warner, in which he spent $10 million of his own money, Mark Warner portrayed himself as a moderate who had business knowhow and would be able to bring technology-related jobs to the state. He criticized Senator Warner's votes to cut funding for student loans and Medicare and his acceptance of campaign contributions from political action committees (PACs). Senator Warner, for his part, accused his Democratic opponent of being disingenuous in depicting himself as an "outsider" untainted by the political establishment, since he had been active with the Democratic National Committee for years. In the November 1996 general election, Senator Warner emerged victorious, with 52.5 percent of the vote to Mark Warner's 47.4 percent. Some observers attributed the latter's defeat in part to the widespread perception among voters that he seemed more like a manager than a lawmaker. But in comparison with Senator Warner's opponents in the 1984 and 1990 elections, who had captured only 29.9 and 18.7 percent of the votes, respectively, he had made a good showing, especially since at the start of the campaign he had had little name recognition among voters.

Since 1989 Warner had held the title of managing director at Columbia Capital Corp., and after his defeat he divided his time between his business affairs and various philanthropic efforts. Among the latter, supported in part by the Collis-Warner Foundation, which he set up with his wife in 1997, he established four regional Virginia small-business investment funds and the Virginia High-Tech Partnership, to help students at the five his-

torically black colleges and universities in Virginia secure internships and permanent jobs at high-tech firms. He also launched TechRiders, which offers Virginians free training in the use of computers and the Internet in libraries, community centers, and houses of worship. After his mother was diagnosed with Alzheimer's disease, he started an organization called SeniorNavigator, which provides on-line information regarding health and health providers, financial and legal problems, support groups, and other matters of relevance to middle-aged and old people. In 2000 he co-founded Venture Philanthropy Partners, to strengthen existing organizations that are helping children. Through such activities Warner became known to increasing numbers of voters.

Warner had no Democratic opponents when he threw his hat in the ring for the governorship in 2000. In the 2001 general election he faced the state attorney general, Mark Earley, a Republican with 14 years of government service. During his campaign he emphasized pocketbook issues, among them job creation and the state's unhealthy financial situation. His declaration that he would not raise taxes and his opposition to same-sex marriage and approval of capital punishment appealed to conservatives, and he made a favorable impression on many rural voters (most of them registered Republicans), not by pretending to be one of them but by showing that he respected them and understood their predilections and needs. His campaign sponsored a NASCAR truck and set up a Sportsmen for Warner network, which appealed to members of the National Rifle Association. By mid-September he held a comfortable lead in polls. Warner's candidacy drew more than $15 million in donations from approximately 10,000 individuals, and to deflect attention from his personal wealth, he waited until nearly the end of the campaign to spend his own funds, about $4.6 million. On November 6, 2001 Warner captured 983,404 votes, or 52.2 percent of the total.

Soon after he was sworn into office, in January 2002, Warner discovered that the state's projected deficit, supposedly $700 million, was actually more than $3 billion. He devoted much of the next two years to budget cutting. With the consent of the legislature, he eliminated approximately 3,000 state jobs and 50 state boards and reduced spending in almost every state department. He also consolidated the handling of various functions, such as procurement of goods and services, in some cases by combining agencies. "To make lemonade out of lemons," he told Alan Greenblatt for *Governing* (November 2004), "this may be the time when you can really make some really significant changes in government operations to bring about a more business-like approach." Such actions were insufficient to bring the state's finances out of the red, and in 2002 Warner acknowledged the need to raise taxes. He believed that Virginians would recognize that he had no other options. As he explained to Greenblatt, "If you're going to go out and ask people for more revenues, you have to have rock-solid credentials. You've got to show the taxpayer that you're going to squeeze every dollar and efficiency before you ask for more." In the legislature, both houses of which were controlled by Republicans, Warner found an unlikely ally—the chairman of the Senate Finance Committee, John H. Chichester, a Republican, who had been seeking to set Virginia on a path of long-term economic stability for some time. Indeed, Chichester had been drawing up his own tax bill, one that called for far larger hikes than the governor's plan and thus made the latter's more palatable to the public. Warner made the case for the tax increases in speeches at dozens of town-hall meetings and other local gatherings and, as Greenblatt wrote, "played a central role in the legislative process, helping to persuade a rump group of Republican House members to break ranks with their leadership and pass a compromise bill." The legislation, passed in the summer of 2004, lowered income and food taxes while raising taxes on alcohol, tobacco, gasoline, and businesses—a package totaling $1.17 billion, the largest tax increase in Virginia in four decades. The tax-code changes "will help make Virginia fiscally solvent for years to come," according to *Governing*, which named Warner and Chichester "public officials of the year 2004." "Raising taxes by a sufficient amount to stabilize the state's fiscal condition wasn't a choice the legislature made easily, or even—for many members—willingly," according to the Government Performance Project Web site. "It required rancorous special sessions that lasted long beyond the General Assembly's normal adjournment time. But in the end, it was done. Other states in similar fiscal condition shirked their responsibilities."

In 2005 Virginia, along with Utah, earned a grade of A minus (higher than those of any other states) after a two-year study of state-government performance conducted by the Pew Center on the States, a division of the Pew Charitable Trust. The study, part of what is called the Government Performance Project, evaluated performance in four categories: money (budgeting, accounting, contracting, etc.); people (the hiring, retaining, and training and development of state employees); physical infrastructure; and information (with regard to the use of information and technology to assess the effectiveness of state services and other activities). "There is little that Virginia does not do well in government management," the authors of the study declared, as quoted on results.gpponline.org. The study attributed Virginia's success to "an ethos of good management that has genuinely been institutionalized" and noted that the state "seems able to find its way back to the path of good managerial sense," even if "a governor betrays that culture," as the authors wrote that Warner's predecessor, James S. "Jim" Gilmore III, had, by instituting a popular tax cut that resulted in a $1 billion budget shortfall. The study praised Warner for introducing performance contracts for more than 100 top officials and for evaluating each one personally.

In November 2005, in one of his last actions as governor, Warner commuted the death sentence of a convicted killer one day before the man's scheduled execution, on the grounds that DNA evidence that might have cleared him had been destroyed. During his term as governor, 11 inmates sentenced to death in Virginia were executed. His successor as governor is Timothy M. "Tim" Kaine, a Democrat, who served as lieutenant governor under Warner. Kaine emphasized his association with Warner during his campaign, and in 2005 election results that provided evidence of Warner's popularity as well as his own, he captured a majority of the votes in traditionally Republican exurbs, among them Virginia Beach and Prince William County.

Warner served as chairman of the Southern Governors Association for a year, in 2003 and 2004, and as chairman of the National Governors Association for a year, in 2004 and 2005. His wife, Lisa Collis, has retained her maiden name. In addition to its other work, the Collis-Warner Foundation supports programs to prevent child abuse, an area in which Collis has worked for years. The Warners have three daughters, Madison, Gillian, and Eliza, born between 1990 and 1994. They have homes in Alexandria and Fredericksburg, Virginia. Warner's recreational activities include playing basketball.

—C.M.

Suggested Reading: *American Spectator* p30+ May 2004; *Atlantic Monthly* p42+ May 2006; *Governing* p24+ Nov. 2004; *Governing Finance Review* p63+ Apr. 2005; *National Review* p22+ Mar. 22, 2004; *New Republic* p16+ Oct. 29, 2001; *Newsweek* p26 Sep. 3, 2001, p48+ Aug. 2, 2004, p80 Jan. 3, 2005, p70+ Dec. 26, 2005–Jan. 2, 2006, p33+ May 8, 2006, (on-line) Dec. 9, 2005; *Washington Post* B p7 Apr. 7, 1990, B p3 Mar. 28, 1993, C p6 May 11, 1994; *Washingtonian* p52+ Feb. 2006

Warren, Rick

Jan. 28, 1954– Minister; writer

Address: Saddleback Valley Community Church, 1 Saddleback Way, Lake Forest, CA 92630

Rick Warren is the head pastor of Saddleback Valley Community Church, in California, which, with nearly 100,000 registered members, boasts the largest congregation in the United States. He is better known as the author of the phenomenally successful 2002 book *The Purpose-Driven Life: What on Earth Am I Here For?*, which has sold nearly 26 million copies, brought Warren international fame, and led the *Economist* (June 30, 2005) to call him "arguably the most influential evangelical pas-

Rick Warren

tor in America." Written in simple language that mirrors Warren's own down-to-earth persona, *The Purpose-Driven Life* is solidly grounded in Christian principles but has been embraced by secular institutions ranging from manufacturers to sports teams, who see it as a model for motivational leadership. Like many highly influential religious figures, Warren has sparked controversy. His many critics include other religious leaders, who have accused him of sugar-coating Christian teachings in order to appeal to a mass audience, as well as social activists, who feel that he attempts to impose religion on those his ministry seeks to help—including AIDS victims. Undeterred, Warren has recently sought to use his considerable public influence to address poverty, disease, and illiteracy on a global scale through an international network of churches. He has been invited to speak at the United Nations, the World Economic Forum, the African Union, the Council on Foreign Relations, and *Time*'s Global Health Summit, and the almost 157,000 subscribers to his weekly newsletter include religious leaders around the world.

Richard Duane Warren was born on January 28, 1954 and grew up in the small community of Redwood Valley, in northern California's rural Mendocino County. His father, Jimmy Warren Sr., a third-generation evangelist, was a Baptist minister; his mother, Dot, was a high-school librarian. Warren has a brother, Jimmy Warren Jr., and a sister, Chaundel. Their father was a self-described "church-builder," lending his skills as both a minister and a carpenter to create dozens of churches around the world. The family traveled to scenes of natural disaster, where they pastored and cooked meals for displaced people. Strangers were often present at the family's meals, and Warren's father kept a large vegetable garden for the purpose of giving food away. Warren told William Lobdell for the *Los Angeles Times* (September 19, 2003) that his "life has been profoundly affected by my parents' model of generosity and service." His father's last words were reportedly, "Save one more for Jesus."

As a teen Warren showed both a rebellious nature and an inclination for politics, and he was class president for several years at Ukiah High School. During his sophomore year there, he earned a job as a page in the U.S. Senate. The summer before he was set to take his job in Washington, D.C., he worked as a lifeguard at a Christian camp, an experience that transformed his interests radically. Though he had resisted pastoring as a career path, partly because it was a family tradition, Warren "kind of veered in that direction" after his time at the camp, as he told Ted Parks for the *San Diego Union-Tribune* (August 14, 2003). He gave up his opportunity in Washington and started a prayer group at his high school. He also put together a student musical and published a school newspaper, both of which had Christian themes. Warren gained recognition within evangelical circles as a teenage prodigy, and before he had graduated from high school, he was invited to speak at churches around California. Warren has recalled that by the time he was 20, he had spoken at more than 150 churches and camps on the West Coast.

In 1971 Warren enrolled at California Baptist University, where he received a bachelor of arts degree. During that period he married his longtime girlfriend, Elizabeth (who goes by Kay, her middle name). He received his master of divinity degree from Southwestern Baptist University, in Fort Worth, Texas, where his desire to start his own church increased. Toward the end of his time there, Warren researched the states that had the fewest churches per capita and found his native California on the list. He discovered that Lake Forest, in Orange County, 50 miles south of Los Angeles, was one of the fastest-growing communities in the United States, and though he had never been to the area, he decided to move there with his wife and baby daughter, Amy, to found a Southern Baptist church. Warren and his family rented a one-bedroom apartment and recruited the attending real-estate agent to be the first member of the congregation, which initially met in Warren's living room. Warren spent his first three months in Lake Forest going door-to-door, talking with as many non-churchgoers as he could about why they did not attend services and how a new church might appeal to them; he has said that his intention was not to alter the Christian message to win over potential parishioners but, rather, to ascertain the best way to get that message across to people who loosely defined themselves as Christian. Through his talks with such people, Warren developed a composite potential congregant whom he called "Saddleback Sam" (a name inspired by a nearby mountain): a well-educated, middle-class, 35-year-old man who preferred the casual to the formal and was skeptical of organized religion—feeling, among other things, that most churches were overly concerned with money and not relevant to everyday life. Warren designed his services to attract Saddleback Sam, sprinkling sermons with references to present-day situations, using very little theological vocabulary, and asking congregants to call him Rick. The first official service of the Saddleback Valley Community Church, which took place on Easter Sunday in 1980 at the Laguna Hills High School gymnasium, attracted more than 200 people. Warren dressed in casual clothing during services and replaced traditional Christian music with contemporary music because he "could find no one who listened to organ music in the car," he said, as paraphrased by Malcolm Gladwell in the *New Yorker* (September 12, 2005). Warren's approach had plenty of critics among evangelical Christians, who viewed it as pandering if not flirting with heresy. Warren justified his actions by citing Scripture. "Today, in America, the church must learn the culture and language of the 1990s to communicate," Warren told Barbara Bradley for the *Los Angeles Times* (December 10, 1995). "Now that may be a marketing principle, but it's also just a biblical principle that says: Start where people are. Jesus started where people were, not where he wanted them to be. So when he's with fishermen, he talks about fish. When he's with farmers, he talks about sowing seed. He started where people were, and he moved them to where people needed to be."

During the next 15 years, Warren's congregation grew rapidly but never established a permanent meeting place. The services took place in nearly 80 different buildings, including schools, recreation centers, restaurants, and theaters. Warren had several reasons for postponing the construction of a permanent facility. "I wanted to prove to the world that you don't have to have a building to grow a church," he told William Lobdell. He also did not want to limit the size of the congregation, which, by the mid-1990s, had more than 10,000 members. Warren told Gus Santoyo for the *Orange County (California) Register* (December 31, 1991), "Most churches build too soon and too small. I have always said that the shoes must never tell the foot how big to be." Eventually overwhelmed by the duties of managing his huge congregation (he passed out during one service), Warren divided it into small groups—organized by neighborhood or common interests—that met weekly for Bible discussion. The groups helped to foster an intimacy and familial spirit difficult to achieve in the larger congregation. In 1992 Warren began the three-year process of constructing a permanent building for the church. Again focusing on the needs and desires of his flock, Warren designed a campus to look and function more like a community center than a typical Southern Baptist church. The compound, constructed at 1 Saddleback Way in Lake Forest, California, on 120 acres of land, consists of two worship spaces, which seat 4,800 and 2,800, respectively; two 32,000-square-foot educational buildings; three athletic fields; a gymnasium; and a cafeteria. Along with weekend services, Saddleback offers 79 weekly programs ranging from child care to intensive Bible-study groups. The campus also serves as the headquarters for the church's community-service ministries. Warren believes that such amenities as ample parking and clean restrooms are nearly as important as the services themselves in ensuring that first-time visitors will return and become a part of the church community. Worshippers have differed in their reactions to Saddleback services. One attendee told Bradley, "Every time I come, it's like [Warren] knows my problems and is talking to me in a room by myself." Another likened Saddleback's campus to a department store and complained to Bradley of feeling "lost in the crowd."

By the early 1990s Warren and Saddleback Valley Community Church had become icons of the "mega-church" phenomenon. Pastors traveled from around the country to visit Saddleback and learn from Warren strategies to increase the sizes of their own churches. Warren felt that the success of his message lay in its simplicity and in his focus on the specific needs of his congregation. He began a lecture tour throughout the United States, often drawing crowds of more than 4,000 people, ranging from seminary students to corporate managers. "Were it a business, Saddleback would be compared with Dell, Google or Starbucks," Rich Karlgaard wrote for *Forbes* (February 16, 2004). The reception of Warren's message by such varied groups, and the rapid pace at which his congregation grew throughout the 1980s and 1990s, have led some to suggest that his greatest assets are organizational rather than spiritual, and that his formative influences come from management circles rather than religious ones. Marc Gunther in *Fortune* (October 31, 2005) called Warren "a protégé of management thinker Peter Drucker." Warren routinely quotes Drucker during interviews and has read his books as well as those of other business scholars such as Alvin Toffler, Ken Blancard, Tom Peters, and Jim Collins. In 1995 Warren published a guide for building churches, called *The Purpose-Driven Church*, which he sold at lectures and through networks of ministers around the world. Warren's strategies were aimed at creating what he called "healthy" churches, where the congregation attends weekly services out of a sense of purpose rather than because "it's what you do." The book was well received both within and outside religious circles, earning Warren a reputation as an expert on leadership, organization—and marketing. Karlgaard wrote that *The Purpose-Driven Church* was "the best book on entrepreneurship, business and investment that I've read in some time." The book went on to sell more than one million copies, and Warren used the proceeds to pay back the $3.5 million debt that had accrued during the construction of Saddleback Church.

In 2002 Warren took a seven-month sabbatical from Saddleback Church to write a follow-up to *The Purpose-Driven Church*, which he titled *The Purpose-Driven Life: What on Earth Am I Here For?* Warren wrote for 12 hours a day, seven days a week, struggling with the isolation that the project necessitated. "I knew the only way to write it was to plow into it and it about killed me to do it," Warren told Christie Storm for the *Arkansas Democrat-Gazette* (October 15, 2005). Using the same approach he had applied to the founding of his church, Warren wrote *The Purpose-Driven Life* for the uninitiated rather than those already immersed in the Christian faith. The book describes, in 40 chapters meant to be read in 40 consecutive days, a way for the reader to establish a sense of purpose, according to what Warren called "God's plan," through five principles: worship, fellowship, discipleship, ministry, and evangelism. As with his services at Saddleback, Warren felt that he was not providing new interpretations of the Bible but, as it were, simply changing the packaging. "Honestly," Warren told Linton Weeks and Alan Cooperman for the *Washington Post* (February 22, 2004), "I don't think that there's anything new in the book, anything that classic Christian writers have not said. I'm a translator, and I worked very, very hard at making it simple."

Part of what makes Warren's message appealing to many is his view that God wants "to be your best friend." That idea irked many evangelicals, who viewed it as a departure from traditional teaching and a "dumbing down" of the Gospels to appeal to a mass audience. "His actual message does a subtle violence to the rigors of belief," Chris Lehmann wrote for *Slate* (March 17, 2003 on-line). "In demanding so much of growth-minded Christian ministries, he winds up demanding too little of his fervently recruited believers. . . . Warren's God 'wants to be your best friend,' and this means, in turn, that God's most daunting property, the exercise of eternal judgment, is strategically downsized. When Warren turns his utility-minded feel-speak upon the symbolic iconography of the faith, the results are offensively bathetic." To illustrate his point, Lehmann quoted a passage from *The Purpose-Driven Life*: "When Jesus stretched his arms wide on the cross, he was saying, 'I love you *this* much.'"

Despite the controversial nature of *The Purpose-Driven Life* in religious circles, it resonated with its intended readership. As Lobdell wrote, "Scholars agree that Warren has a knack for tapping into needy psyches, giving people a sense of purpose when life can seem materialistic and meaningless." "It's a universal theme, not a niche book," Warren told Storm. "At some point in life you put your head down on a pillow and ask: 'Why am I here and why am I doing all this?' That is so universal, in every culture." *The Purpose-Driven Life* has sold more than 26 million copies in English and was translated into more than 20 languages in the first three years after publication, making it the

best-selling hardback book in American history, according to *Publishers Weekly*. Warren hoped that his message would attract readers outside church organizations, and that hope has been realized: in addition to the tens of thousands of churches that have bought copies of the book for their congregations, corporations such as Wal-Mart and Coca-Cola and sports teams including the Oakland Raiders and Green Bay Packers football teams have purchased it for their employees.

Directly after the publication of *The Purpose-Driven Life*, Warren launched a program he called "40 Days of Purpose"—a campaign of small-group readings of *The Purpose-Driven Life* that included projects meant to reinforce the messages in the book. To promote "40 Days of Purpose" to other churches, Warren designed a package of materials, including sermons, video presentations, and copies of *The Purpose-Driven Life*, that could be purchased by pastors at a reduced price for use in their churches. The pilot program of "40 Days of Purpose" included more than 1,500 churches in 10 countries, and by 2005 more than 32,000 churches had participated in the program. Warren created other items based on the campaign that individuals could purchase through his Web site, among them Bible covers, daily scripture cards, and confessional journals. Warren has sold $5 million worth of items related to *The Purpose-Driven Life*, and though he donates nearly all of his proceeds to foundations through Saddleback Church, many critics see his activities as representing the commercialization of religion. Philip D. Kenneson, an associate professor of theology and philosophy at Milligan College, told Lobdell, "At its best, I suspect the purpose-driven church could be a hub for genuine discipleship and Christian formation. At its worst, I fear that it may simply offer the latest venue for American consumers to forge an identity, only here it comes through purchasing certain religious goods and services."

In 2005 Warren started "40 Days of Community," which he called the second phase of the "40 Days of Purpose" campaign; rather than addressing the question "What on Earth am I here for?," it sought to answer the question "What on Earth are we here for?" "You cannot fulfill the purposes in life by yourself. You need other people," Warren told Storm. A central component of "40 Days of Community" was outreach, and each small group was asked to perform a mission project. The new campaign reflected the shifting orientation of Warren's evangelical movement. Saddleback Church fed 42,000 homeless people in Orange County as part of "40 Days of Community," an effort that demanded 9,200 volunteers and two million pounds of food. Warren told Storm that his goal was "to move American Christianity from total preoccupation with self—my needs, my interests, my hurts, my stress, my family, what's in it for me—and move away from the consumerist mentality. . . . Everything I do in America is simply to mobilize the American church to care about those that are less fortunate." Warren's shift in focus resulted from a period of soul-searching that followed the financial success of *The Purpose-Driven Life*. He told Gladwell that he came out of that period with the idea, inspired by Psalm 72 of the Bible, that "the purpose of influence is to speak up for those who have no influence." In keeping with that idea, Warren gave away most of his fortune to organizations that combat what he calls the five "Global Goliaths"—spiritual emptiness, egocentric leadership, extreme poverty, pandemic disease, and illiteracy. Warren created organizations called the Global PEACE Plan ("PEACE" is an acronym for Plant churches, Equip servant leaders, Assist the poor, Care for the sick, and Educate the next generation) and the Purpose-Driven Network (which promotes the use of his materials worldwide). Warren's dream is to have all churches be a part of a global network for humanitarian aid.

Warren's humanitarian projects have focused recently on care for HIV and AIDS victims. Saddleback Church is the first major evangelical congregation to start a local HIV ministry, and Warren's influence (he is a confidant of President George W. Bush and signed copies of *The Purpose-Driven Life* for all nine U.S. Supreme Court justices) has lent force to his humanitarian endeavors. The AIDS issue has created a great deal of controversy within Warren's constituency. Some members of his congregation are uncomfortable with frank discussions about sex and condom use and are unwilling to work with people whom they see as having rejected Jesus through their actions. Some have even left Saddleback. In Orange County, where the population most affected by HIV and AIDS is made up of gay men and single women, HIV health-care professionals are skeptical of Saddleback's intentions, fearing that, as an evangelical organization, it would demonize homosexuals. Alan Witchey, executive director of the AIDS Services Foundation, in Orange County, told Joe Garofoli for the *San Francisco Chronicle* (May 8, 2006), "There are people concerned that Saddleback would want to try to convert them from gay to straight." That Warren offers a sex-addiction workshop at Saddleback geared toward helping people "recover" from homosexuality reinforces that fear in the minds of local activists.

Nonetheless, Warren's interest in HIV and AIDS has linked him with other American evangelicals who are beginning to embrace international causes. In 2005 Warren led a delegation of 50 Saddleback members to the poverty-plagued nation of Rwanda. Warren believes that along with HIV/AIDS care, he could instill the "purpose-driven" philosophy in the governmental structure of that country. Warren told David Van Biema for *Time* (August 22, 2005) that he had sought in Rwanda "a small country where we could actually work on a national model." He has met with the president of Rwanda and that nation's parliament to discuss the idea. While Saddleback could help provide health care in that country, many are criti-

cal of other elements of the project. Alan Wolfe, director of the Boisi Center for Religion and American Public Life at Boston College, told Gunther, "I do not believe that Rick Warren has a bad bone in his body. But I do believe that his remarkable enthusiasm is fueled by considerable naivete." Gunther wrote, "As with so many things that touch on religion, what you make of Warren and his crusades may depend on where you stand. . . . But there is no doubt that he has shown himself to be his generation's great religious entrepreneur."

Warren's books include *Dynamic Bible Study* (1981), *The Power to Change Your Life* (1990), *Celebrate Recovery*, with John Baker (1998), and *Daily Inspiration for the Purpose-Driven Life* (2003). He lives with his wife, Kay, in Lake Forest, California. The couple have three grown children. In his free time Warren enjoys watching the History Channel and gardening, telling Ken Garfield for the *Lexington (Kentucky) Herald Leader* (October 22, 2005), "I'm wired to watch things grow." For the Saddleback Church's 25th anniversary, in 2005, Warren rented out the stadium of the Los Angeles Angels of Anaheim baseball team and offered the 38,000 congregants hot dogs and popcorn along with a sermon.

—N.W.M.

Suggested Reading: *Economist* (on-line) June 30, 2005; *Forbes* p39 Feb. 16, 2004; *Los Angeles Times* A p1 Dec. 10, 1995; *New Yorker* p60+ Sep. 12, 2005; *Orange County (California) Register* Local Nov. 2, 2003

Selected Books: *Dynamic Bible Study*, 1981; *The Power to Change Your Life*, 1990; *The Purpose-Driven Church: Growth Without Compromising Your Message & Mission*, 1995; *Celebrate Recovery* (with John Baker), 1998; *The Purpose-Driven Life: What on Earth Am I Here For?*, 2002; *Daily Inspiration for the Purpose-Driven Life*, 2003

Weinstein, Allen

Sep. 1, 1937– Archivist; historian; educator; writer

Address: National Archives & Records Administration, 8601 Adelphi Rd., Rm. 4200, College Park, MD 20740

On March 7, 2005, when Allen Weinstein was sworn in (for the second time in two weeks) as the ninth national archivist of the United States, Supreme Court justice Ruth Bader Ginsburg told those attending the ceremony that Weinstein is "a scholar whose work I have long admired," as Linton Weeks reported for the *Washington Post* (March 31, 2005). In his article Weeks called atten-

Courtesy of the National Archives and Records
Administration

Allen Weinstein

tion to Weinstein's 22-year career as a history professor at three major universities and his authorship or co-authorship of such books as *Perjury: The Hiss-Chambers Case* and *The Haunted Wood: Soviet Espionage in America—The Stalin Era*; he has edited or co-edited several others as well, among them *The Story of America: Freedom and Crisis from Settlement to Superpower*. After he made a name for himself in academia, Weinstein began, in the early 1980s, to try to affect history himself, by getting involved with organizations that sought to spread democracy throughout the world. The most prominent of them was the Center for Democracy, which Weinstein himself founded in 1985 and which gained importance in the early 1990s, during the early days of Russia's transition to democracy. Weinstein became the national archivist in spite of a significant amount of controversy among his peers, some of whom questioned his commitment to the free exchange of information. In his current post he is responsible for keeping safe and making available to the public the papers of former U.S. presidents, congressional records, important records associated with federal agencies, census data from 1790 to 1930, federal-court records, and the so-called Charters of Freedom (the Declaration of Independence, the Constitution, and the Bill of Rights), among other materials.

The youngest of three children, Allen Weinstein was born on September 1, 1937 in New York City. His father, Samuel Weinstein, and mother, the former Sarah Popkoff, were Russian-Jewish immigrants who owned a deli in the New York City borough of the Bronx. "I come from that Depression-World War II generation," he told Lewis Beale for the *Los Angeles Times* (April 7, 1992). "I don't

want to romanticize it, but there was a sense, particularly after the war, of opportunity, of things opening up. Culturally, historically, I am predisposed toward optimism, a sense of change." After he completed high school, Weinstein entered the City College of New York (now part of the City University of New York), where he earned a B.A. degree. He then entered Yale University, in New Haven, Connecticut, from which he received both an M.A. degree and, in 1967, a Ph.D. degree, both in American studies. In 1966 he had started teaching history at Smith College, in Northampton, Massachusetts. In 1968 he published two collections of essays that he edited with Frank Otto Gatell: *American Themes: Essays in Historiography* and *American Negro Slavery: A Modern Reader*. His next book, another essay collection edited with Gatell, was *The Segregation Era 1863-1954* (1970).

Weinstein's first original, book-length historical study, *Prelude to Populism: Origins of The Silver Issue, 1867-1878* (1970), reexamines the campaign to restore silver as legal tender in 19th-century America. In a mixed critique, C. M. Destler wrote for the *American Historical Review* (February 1971) that Weinstein was "to be congratulated upon his adherence to critical historical realism. . . . It is regrettable that this was not accompanied by complete coverage of the subject." R. E. Noble, by contrast, wrote for the *Annals of the American Academy of Political and Social Science* (March 1971), "This careful, detailed study will necessitate some important revisions in our understanding of the emergence of silver as a political issue in post-Civil War America." Weinstein followed *Prelude to Populism* with *The Growth of American Politics* (1972), a two-volume selection of essays that he edited with Gatell and Paul Goodman; *Freedom and Crisis: An American History* (1974); *Between the Wars: American Foreign Policy from Versailles to Pearl Harbor* (1974); and *Perjury: The Hiss-Chambers Case* (1978), about Alger Hiss and Whittaker Chambers, which brought Weinstein prominence and a nomination for an American Book Award.

Regarded by some as a definitive study, *Perjury* also inspired controversy, as has been true of nearly everything written about Hiss and Chambers. Hiss, a U.S. State Department employee in the 1930s, was convicted of perjury in 1950 for swearing under oath that he had not passed confidential government documents to Chambers when the latter was a member of the American Communist Party. After leaving the party and becoming a writer for *Time* magazine, Chambers had accused Hiss of being a double agent, and had testified for the prosecution at Hiss's trial. Weinstein had intended to prove Hiss innocent, but while doing research for the book (in the course of which he filed a lawsuit under the Freedom of Information Act to obtain materials related to the case), he changed his mind. In *Perjury* he argued that those who claimed that Hiss had been unjustly condemned because of America's anti-Communist paranoia were perpetuating a myth, one that had turned Hiss into a sort of countercultural hero. George F. Will, who reviewed *Perjury* for *Newsweek* (March 20, 1978), believed that the book would put an end to the pro-Hiss movement and that its publication was itself "a historical event," as he put it. Others, though, remained convinced that Hiss was innocent, and they attacked Weinstein's accuracy. Victor Navasky, the editor of the liberal publication the *Nation,* for example, charged that Weinstein had misrepresented his sources. "Working from galleys of the new book," Davide Gelman reported for *Newsweek* (April 17, 1978), "Navasky wrote [to] seven of Weinstein's key sources to ask if the historian had quoted them accurately. Six of the seven answered that he had distorted part or all of their quotes, Navasky reported. . . . [H]e also charged that Weinstein had woven in some damning evidence without indicating that the source was a book by . . . Chambers. Weinstein is 'hopelessly mired in the perspective of one side,' wrote Navasky." Weinstein accused his critics of being unable to stomach truths that made them uncomfortable. He then promised to make available to critics the primary sources he had used, first inviting them to his home to listen to his taped interviews and then pledging to deposit the materials in the Truman Library in Independence, Missouri. He has never fulfilled that promise; rather, he retracted his invitation and has kept the materials in his possession. "Weinstein's continuing refusal to make the disputed materials available to other scholars violates the AHA [American Historical Association] 'Statement on Standards of Professional Conduct,' adopted in 1987, which states that historians should 'make available to others their sources, evidence, and data, including the documentation they develop through interviews,'" Jon Wiener complained in the *Nation* (May 17, 2004). "Weinstein is also not complying with the 1989 AHA 'Statement on Interviewing for Historical Documentation,' developed jointly with the Oral History Association, the Organization of American Historians and the Society of American Archivists; it declares that 'interviewers should arrange to deposit their interviews in an archival repository that is capable of . . . making them available for general research.'"

That controversy notwithstanding, in 1981 Weinstein secured a professorship at Georgetown University, in Washington, D.C. Between 1981 and 1983 he edited the *Washington Quarterly*, a publication of that school's Center for Strategic and International Studies. He also joined the editorial staff of the *Washington Post*. Earlier, in 1980, he had become involved with Soviet dissidents who were organizing committees to monitor the Soviet Union's compliance with the Helsinki Accords on Human Rights (nonbinding agreements signed in Helsinki in 1975 by 35 nations, including the Soviet Union and the U.S.). At the end of 1983 and the beginning of 1984, Weinstein served as the acting president of the National Endowment for Democracy, a bipartisan, nongovernmental foreign-policy group that sought to encourage the creation of democratic institutions worldwide through initiatives emanating from the private sector. Later in 1984 he took on the presidency of the Center for the Study of Democracy, a think tank affiliated with the University of Santa Barbara, in California. Working out of the center's newly opened Washington, D.C., office, Weinstein successfully led an effort to bring together government officials and guerrilla leaders in El Salvador, a Central American country in the throes of civil war. He found himself at odds with the center's directors, whose ideas were "more cerebral and phlegmatic than mine," as he told Lewis Beale for the *Los Angeles Times* (April 7, 1992), and resigned at the end of the year. In a differing account of his departure, William R. Greer reported in the *New York Times* (February 7, 1985) that representatives of the center contended that Weinstein's contract was not renewed because "he refused to curtail . . . 'costly' conferences and other programs until the center could raise more money."

Weinstein left Georgetown University in 1984. For four years beginning in 1985, he taught at Boston University, in Massachusetts. Also in 1985 he founded, and became the president of, the Center for Democracy, a nonprofit organization for promoting democracy throughout the world. The center held conferences and worked with teams monitoring elections in various countries overseas, among them the Philippines in 1986 and Nicaragua in 1989. In the early 1990s the center drew attention when it formed a working relationship with Boris Yeltsin, who was serving as Russia's president when the Soviet Union disintegrated. In August 1991, when a right-wing coup was attempted in Moscow, Yeltsin was trapped in the Russian government headquarters; his only means of communication with the outside world was a fax machine. He used it to fax messages to the office of the Center for Democracy; thus, Weinstein became the source of information about events in Moscow for the White House, the State Department, and the press. After the coup was suppressed, Weinstein traveled to Russia to work with the Russian government on environmental policies and legal reforms, among other matters. He also helped American farmers to become linked with food-distribution programs operating in Russia.

Thanks to his work in Russia, Weinstein established contacts in former Eastern-bloc nations, among them Bulgaria. In 1991 his center, along with the Bulgarian president, Zhelyu Zhelev, set up a commission to investigate the alleged Bulgarian involvement in the 1981 assassination attempt on Pope John Paul II. The Bulgarian government gave Weinstein access to its intelligence files, which contained more than 30,000 pages of documents about that event. In three years of study of the file, Weinstein failed to unearth any "startling revelations," as R. C. Longworth reported for the *Chicago Tribune* (May 6, 1994). During that period

Weinstein revised *Perjury*, bolstering his arguments with information in documents newly available from sources in the former Soviet Union. As far as is publicly known, the material in the new version, published in 1997, failed to sway anyone who had believed Hiss to be innocent.

Weinstein wrote *The Haunted Wood: Soviet Espionage in America—The Stalin Era* (1998) with Alexander Vassiliev, a retired KGB officer. Their sources included documents from the files of the KGB, the Soviet Union's secret-police and intelligence agency, that they had viewed (and Vassiliev had translated) thanks to payments made to a group of retired KGB agents by the book's publisher, Random House. The authors' privileges had not included photocopying any paperwork, however. The unavailability of the documents to other scholars was perhaps the most controversial aspect of the book. As Ellen Schrecker wrote for the *Nation* (May 24, 1999), "Besides the ethical questions that buying exclusive access to official archives raises, it will be impossible to replicate—and thus check up on—the authors' research. . . . In addition, because no photocopying was permitted, other scholars cannot verify how accurately the documents were transcribed and interpreted." Christopher Lehmann-Haupt, writing for the *New York Times* (January 18, 1999), complained, "The authors offer no overview or perspective on their sources. . . . One symptom of the book's somewhat limited perspective is the extensive recapitulation of the Hiss-Chamber case. This turns out to be based not on K.G.B. files but on Mr. Weinstein's earlier study." By contrast, Harvey Klehr praised the book in a review for the *New Leader* (December 14, 1998): "The two [authors] have produced a fascinating, detailed and revealing portrait of Soviet intelligence activities in the United States during the Stalin era."

Weinstein next edited a collection of essays, *The Story of America* (2002). The following year he was named the senior adviser for democratic institutions and director of the Center for Democratic Initiatives at the International Foundation for Election Systems, for which he worked until 2005. (The foundation is a nonpartisan, nonprofit, international organization that offers help to governments making the transition to democracy.) Meanwhile, in 2004, President George W. Bush had nominated Weinstein for the post of national archivist. The nomination both surprised and raised "concerns among archivists and historians," as Tom Brune reported for *Newsday* (April 17, 2004). Some historians worried that the White House had chosen Weinstein because of his perceived penchant for secrecy, and they suggested that his appointment was a political move on the part of Bush to keep out of the hands of critics his father's presidential papers, which were to be made available to researchers in January 2005, as well as papers pertaining to the September 11, 2001 terrorist attacks on the U.S. "His history of sharing his information is not all that great," Anna K. Nelson, a professor of history

at American University, told Sheryl Gay Stolberg and Felicia R. Lee for the *New York Times* (April 20, 2004). "We don't know how he would run the archives. We ought to find out. How would he balance the public's right to know versus the president's right to protect his papers?" Such concerns led a dozen organizations—the Association of Research Libraries, the Council of State Historical Records Coordinators, the Organization of American Historians, the Society of American Archivists, the American Association for State and Local History, the American Library Association, the Association of Documentary Editors, the Council of State Historical Records Coordinators, the Midwest Archives Conference, the New England Archivists, Northwest Archivists Inc., and the Organization of American Historians—to question Weinstein's suitability for the position. Some of Weinstein's supporters, on the other hand, called attention to his public statements advocating openness, as well as his success in persuading the Church of Christ, Scientist to release documents related to Mary Baker Eddy, its founder. Other supporters suggested that those attacking Weinstein were trying to punish him for his attempts to demonstrate Alger Hiss's guilt.

On July 24, 2004 the Senate held a public hearing on Weinstein's nomination. Although Weinstein had no difficulties in responding to his questioners, testimony at the hearing revealed that the Bush administration had asked John W. Carlin, the archivist at the time, to resign and had not, as it had initially claimed, accepted a voluntary resignation from Carlin, who had said earlier that he intended to serve until July 2005. The revelation added to speculation that Weinstein had been appointed for political reasons. The Senate nevertheless confirmed Weinstein, and he was sworn in as national archivist on February 16, 2005. Weinstein told those attending the swearing-in ceremony, as the *US Fed News* (February 16, 2005) reported, "Under National Archivists during both Republican and Democratic presidencies, the tradition of nonpolitical and highest professional attention to the work involved has been the norm. It will continue to be so on my watch, as will an effort to deepen the interaction with Congress and with other government agencies." Weinstein was sworn in again at a second ceremony, on March 7, 2005, this time by Supreme Court justice Ruth Bader Ginsburg. Since he assumed his position, Weinstein has devoted much of his time to the National Archives' presidential library system—in particular, helping to incorporate the Nixon library into it—and to the multimillion-dollar Electronic Records Archives project, the aim of which is to preserve millions of digital documents from past and future presidential administrations.

Weinstein's academic awards include two Senior Fulbright Lectureships, an American Council of Learned Societies Fellowship, the Commonwealth Fund Lectureship at the University of London, and a Woodrow Wilson International Center for Scholars Fellowship. He has also received awards for his promotion of democracy, among them the United Nations' Peace Medal (1986) and two Silver Medals from the Council of Europe (1991 and 1996).

Weinstein married Adrienne Dominguez, a lawyer and businesswoman, in 1995. From an earlier union, he has two sons: Andrew Weinstein, a vice president at AOL, and David Weinstein, a Web designer with Yahoo. He also has one stepson.

—A.R.

Suggested Reading: *Chicago Tribune* N p10 May 6, 1994; *Los Angeles Times* E p1 Apr. 7, 1992; *Nation* p17 May 17, 2004; *New Leader* p11 Dec.

14, 1998; *Newsweek* p92 Apr. 17, 1978; *New York Times* A p23 Feb. 7, 1985, E p9 Jan. 18, 1999, A p14 Apr. 20, 2004; *Washington Post* C p1 Mar. 31, 2005

Selected Books: *Prelude to Populism: Origins of The Silver Issue, 1867–1878*, 1970; *Freedom and Crisis: An American History*, 1974; *Between the Wars: American Foreign Policy from Versailles to Pearl Harbor*, 1974; *Perjury: The Hiss-Chambers Case*, 1978; *The Haunted Wood: Soviet Espionage in America—The Stalin Era*, 1998

Evan Agostini/Getty Images

West, Kanye

(KHAN-yay)

June 8, 1977– Hip-hop artist; record producer

Address: Roc-A-Fella Records, 825 Eighth Ave., 19th Fl., New York, NY 10019-7416

The hip-hop artist and producer Kanye West came before the public eye in February 2004, with his multiplatinum solo debut, *College Dropout*. Selling more than 400,000 copies in its first week of release and spawning several hit singles, including "Through the Wire," "Slow Jamz," and "Jesus Walks," *College Dropout* won three Grammy Awards and announced West's arrival as one of hip-hop's wittiest satirists and most flamboyant

stars. The album, a mix of edgy beats, soulful hooks, spiritual themes, and smart humor, showcased West's primary musical signature—his artful "sampling," or creative manipulating (and appropriating) of classic tunes for modern musical application. Commenting on West's sampling techniques for *L.A. Weekly* (December 2, 2005), Ernest Hardy wrote, "[West] listens to old music and hears raw data, potential samples waiting to be chiseled from the fat. Unlike many of his peers, however, [West] . . . has both a heartfelt appreciation for that music in and of itself, and an intuitive knowledge of how to wield it." West's follow-up album, *Late Registration* (2005), took his sampling artistry to new heights. With production contributions from the noted folk-rock producer Jon Brion, *Late Registration* highlighted West's trademark samples, this time couched within lush pop arrangements; the hit single "Gold Digger," for example, incorporated Ray Charles's classic "I've Got a Woman," while "Addiction" featured an old Ella Fitzgerald rendition of "My Funny Valentine." West's second album also reflected his growing maturity as a lyricist, boasting such tracks as "Diamonds from Sierra Leone" and "Crack Music," two searing social critiques on materialism and drugs in America's inner cities. By 2006 *Late Registration*, like its predecessor, had reached the three-million mark in total album sales, and it received a Grammy Award for best rap album.

With the success of West's two solo albums, the general public has caught on to what the hip-hop community has acknowledged for years—namely, West's role as a creative force behind the notable records of other artists. Some of West's more substantive production contributions include samples for Jermaine Dupri's *Life in 1472* (1998), Jay-Z's *The Blueprint* (2001), Talib Kweli's *Quality* (2002), and Alicia Keys's *The Diary of Alicia Keys* (2003). But it is West's storied, egotistical, sometimes self-contradictory persona, perhaps more than his work itself, that has drawn the most attention. The product of a middle-class upbringing outside Chicago, Illinois, West eschewed the glamorized "gangsta"-

rap image in favor of preppy chic, becoming the rare artist who has successfully bridged the gap between street culture and bourgeois taste. Equally comfortable in Polo T-shirts and overly baggy pants, West is famous, as an artist and a person, for his embodying—perhaps pioneering—of classic-modern, street-suburban, sarcastic-reflective sensibilities. He said to Neil McCormick for the London *Daily Telegraph* (February 18, 2006), "I'm a popular artist but I'm a Pop artist too. Usually Pop art samples things, Andy Warhol taking Marilyn [Monroe] or Kanye West taking Ray Charles and giving it a new form, a new shape and making it something the masses today will connect with."

Kanye Omari West was born on June 8, 1977, the only child of Ray West, a former member of the Black Panther Party and currently a professor of sociology at the College of Southern Maryland, and Donda West, a literature professor and the recently retired chairperson of the English Department at Chicago State University. The intellectual energy and political convictions of his parents (who divorced when he was three) and of other family members left an indelible mark on West's consciousness and, later, his rhymes. Donda West's literary pursuits, in particular, helped to foster Kanye's love for language and knack for wordplay, and he has often cited the influence of his grandfather Portwood Williams, who was a civil rights activist in 1950s Oklahoma. By all accounts Kanye West, whose given name means "the only one" in Swahili, possessed a rare self-assuredness even as a young child growing up in the South Shore suburb of Chicago. He "displayed his charisma even in day care," his father noted to Rob Tannenbaum for *Playboy* (March 1, 2006). During his formative years West took art and music lessons and came up with rhymed variations on such children's tales as Dr. Seuss's *Green Eggs and Ham*. As his fascination with hip-hop's subculture grew, so did his abilities; he continued to experiment with rhythms and beats and showed a good ear for syncopation. After graduating from high school, in 1995, he matriculated at a local Chicago art academy, then at Chicago State University, before dropping out altogether to pursue his musical ambitions. His mother was not pleased with that development. "My plan was that he would get at least one degree, if not several," she told Josh Tyrangiel for *Time* (August 29, 2005). But Donda West could not overcome her son's determination. She recalled to Tyrangiel, "He said, 'Mom, I can do this, and I don't need to go to college because I've had a professor in the house with me my whole life.' I'm thinking, This boy is at it again. He always could twirl a word."

West's ascent into hip-hop lore began locally, when he developed a reputation as a crafty beat-maker for several Chicago-area rappers. He recognized the importance of beats early on. "Themes are important to me, but beats are what catches someone's ear and makes a record a hit," he declared to Robert Hilburn for the *Los Angeles Times* (August 28, 2005). West made his first sale—a collection of samples for $8,000—to the Chicago rapper Gravity and also forged a friendship with the city's rap star Common, who told Greg Kot for the *Chicago Tribune* (August 28, 2005), "I loved [West's] confidence, and I always thought he was clever, but he needed to grow as far as his delivery." Craig Bauer, who owned Hinge Studio—where West often recorded in the late 1990s—told Kot about West, "There was always something about the guy, even then, that commanded respect. He knew what he wanted, and he was always striving to make his beats sound like no one else's. He would lift samples and manipulate them—twist them around, turn them up an octave—until he got something fresh out of something that was made 20 or 30 years ago. He never wanted to be like someone else."

In 1998 West turned a professional corner with his contributions to the Atlanta, Georgia–based recording artist Jermaine Dupri's *Life in 1472*, producing the album's introductory track, "Turn It Out." In the wake of the album's release, West journeyed to one of hip-hop's bastions of hitmaking—New York City—in search of one of its elder statesman, the rapper Jay-Z. West's next major breakthrough came when Jay-Z commissioned five tracks originally sampled and produced by West for the 2001 album *The Blueprint*, including the single "Izzo (H.O.V.A.)," which recalled 1970s soul with its innovative sampling of the Jackson 5 track "I Want You Back." With his work on *The Blueprint*, West became a star in the world of hip-hop production.

As a result of that exposure, West oversaw production for a roster of other East Coast hip-hop notables, including DMX, Beanie Siegel, Foxy Brown, and the R&B singer Alicia Keys. Eager for greater celebrity of his own, he sought to parlay his reputation as a producer into a role as MC. He tried to enlist the support of Jay-Z and Damon Dash, the co-founders of Roc-A-Fella Records, who responded to West's requests with incredulity. As Dash recalled for Tyrangiel, he and Jay-Z did not consider West "street"—or street-smart—enough to make good rap music: "We all grew up street guys who had to do whatever we had to do to get by. Then there's Kanye, who to my knowledge has never hustled a day in his life. I didn't see how it could work." Others in the industry reacted similarly. "It was a strike against me that I didn't wear [typical 'gangsta' attire] and that I never hustled, never sold drugs," West said to Tyrangiel. "But for me to have the opportunity to stand in front of a bunch of executives and present myself, I had to hustle in my own way. I can't tell you how frustrating it was that they didn't get that. No joke—I'd leave meetings crying all the time." In the end, West's determination prevailed. Jay-Z explained to Lola Ogunnaike for *Rolling Stone* (February 9, 2006) his and Dash's reasons for taking on West: "We figured if we kept him close, at the very least we'd still have some hot beats."

In late 2001 West began crafting his debut album, *College Dropout*, which coupled his layered beats with self-effacing lyrics, signature highlights of West's style. One day about a year later, following a lengthy recording session, he fell asleep while driving home and crashed his car into another vehicle. For three weeks after that near-fatal episode, West was immobile, his jaw wired shut. He managed to draw inspiration and even humor from his condition and composed "Through the Wire," which became the anchor track for *College Dropout*. Influenced by Lauryn Hill's 1998 Grammy Award–winning album, *The Miseducation of Lauryn Hill*, West framed *College Dropout* in similar thematic terms, setting zany, ironic takes on the subculture of the streets, and suggestions of spirituality, against the soulful background loops of classic 1970s R&B. *College Dropout*, which featured cameos by a roster of former West collaborators—among them Jay-Z, Talib Kweli, and Mos Def—reached record stores on February 10, 2004 to great fanfare and critical praise, selling 400,000 copies in less than a week and peaking at number two on the *Billboard* Top 200 album chart. Describing his album's themes, West said to Renee Graham for the *Boston Globe* (March 21, 2004), "I make my lyrics about stuff people go through every day in the streets. And when I say the streets, I don't mean specifically selling drugs. I mean anybody who has to get up in the morning, get on the bus, or . . . drive to work. I mean any- and everybody." Ken Micallef, writing for *Remix* (February 1, 2004), hailed *College Dropout* as "the most socially responsible hip-hop album since Public Enemy's heyday," while Chris Salmon, in *Time Out* (February 18, 2004), declared that West's tunes "build from soul foundations, fizzing with inventive flourishes and laden with hooks capable of hauling Pharrell [a rival hip-hop artist] off his perch."

In addition to "Through the Wire," *College Dropout* spawned the hit singles "All Falls Down" and "Slow Jamz," an ode to witty, seductive soul songs, which sampled Luther Vandross's "A House Is Not a Home." The album's crowning achievement was the radio hit "Jesus Walks," a gospel-imbued song with choral arrangements and lyrics that teetered on moral ambiguity: "The only thing that I pray is that my feet don't fail me now / (Jesus Walks) / And I don't think there is nothing I can do now to right my wrongs / (Jesus Walks with me) / I want to talk to God but I'm afraid because we ain't spoke in so long." *College Dropout* went on to sell nearly three million copies, garnered 10 Grammy Award nominations (winning three), and cemented West as rap's newest solo star. The album also represented West's seeming contradictions, both as an artist and a person. Hua Hsu addressed that issue, writing for *Slate* (September 8, 2005, online), "West's expansive empathy and pendulum-like swing between arrogance and insecurity have made him into something more than a rapper. He's become a pop star, in the fullest sense of that term: He's someone whom people use as a guiding light,

with whom they identify, and whose experiences and ambitions seem universal."

The success of *College Dropout* allowed West to pursue a number of activities. He started his own record label (Getting Out Our Dreams, or GOOD, Records), created a fashion line (Pastelle Clothing, set to debut in late 2006), and initiated a philanthropic venture (the Kanye West Foundation) that promotes music education in schools. Meanwhile, his first year in the spotlight also exposed his now-legendary egotism. At the November 2004 American Music Awards ceremony, West walked out after being passed over, in favor of Gretchen Wilson, for the favorite-breakthrough-artist award. According to Ed Bumgardner, writing for *JournalNow.com* (November 17, 2005), West declared in a backstage press room, "I was the best new artist this year, so get that other [expletive] out of here."

In 2005 West began work on his highly anticipated follow-up album, *Late Registration*, which saw him move into new territory—undergirding the rhythms of hip-hop with lush pop melodies. He collaborated on the record with the producer Jon Brion, who was best known for his work with the folk-rock artists Aimee Mann and Fiona Apple. Brion saw his teaming with West as odd but promising. "[West's] knowledge and understanding of records across the board is great. That's the reason why we got along: We don't see music as something that happens in one genre," he said to Gail Mitchell for *Billboard* (September 3, 2005). West continued to refine his beats and lyrics, while Brion experimented with orchestrations and percussion. Brion fondly recalled to Kot for the *Chicago Tribune* article, referring to the process of producing the record, "There was [a] kind of lunacy going on. And then there was me conducting an orchestra who had to play these precisely timed phrases. The look of delight—everything from laughter to these shy smiles on some of the more prim members of the string section—while playing along with Kanye's raps in their headphones for the first time is something I'll never forget."

During the buildup to the release of *Late Registration*, West appeared on a promotional spot, "All Eyes on Kanye West," that aired on MTV on August 22, 2005. During the program he addressed the homophobia he saw as prevalent in the black community and elsewhere, referring to his own family experiences—namely, the recent disclosure that a favorite cousin of his was gay. As reported in the *Commercial Appeal* (August 20, 2005), West said that hip-hop had always been about "speaking your mind and about breaking down barriers, but everyone in hip-hop discriminates against gay people. . . . Not just hip-hop, but America just discriminates. And I wanna just, to come on TV and just tell my rappers, just tell my friends, 'Yo, stop it.'"

Late Registration landed in music stores on August 30, 2005 and became an instant hit, selling nearly 900,000 copies in its first week—more than double the debut sales of *College Dropout*. Hilburn wrote for the *Los Angeles Times* that *Late Registration* "is a 71-minute tour de force that mixes everyman tales with sonic invention—a record that could change the musical framework of rap," while Hua Hsu, in *Slate*, described it as "an amazingly intimate album, at once funny and sad and self-obsessed." Sasha Frere-Jones, the pop-music critic for the *New Yorker* (August 22, 2005), was more measured in his praise, writing, "There are few pop stars as consistently discontent and as obstreperously proud as the rapper and producer Kanye West. . . . listening to his thrilling and frustrating new record, *Late Registration*, is a bit like being chauffeured around in the fanciest car you can imagine by a driver who won't stop complaining about the mileage or the radio reception. You're annoyed, but at the same time you don't want the ride to end."

The album's singles reflected more of West's political and personal views than had his preceding work. "Diamonds from Sierra Leone" deals with Western materialism, citing the illegal diamond trade in Africa, which has funded civil wars throughout the continent; "Crack Music," a song about drug addiction, is critical of the black community; and "Hey Mama" offers a heartfelt tribute to the rapper's mother for the love and support she has given him. The hit track "Gold Digger" showcased, once again, West's ability to integrate classic samples (it opens with the actor Jamie Foxx singing Ray Charles's "I've Got a Woman") with quirky, humorous lyrics to make lightly sardonic commentary—this time about gender differences. West said to Tannenbaum about the process of creating his songs, "I beg for criticism. I'll get 30 opinions on what's wrong with a song and fix all of those things. So when it comes out, you can't tell me [anything]. You can't learn anything from a compliment."

Adding to the already considerable press coverage of West were the controversial remarks he made on September 2, 2005, during NBC's live telecast of *A Concert for Hurricane Relief*, which benefited the victims of Hurricane Katrina and the flooding it caused in and around New Orleans, Louisiana. As quoted in Ogunnaike's *Rolling Stone* article, West deviated from the show's script to voice his opinions about the federal government's slow relief efforts in the largely African-American city and the media's portrayals of the victims: "I hate the way they portray us in the media. You see a black family, it says they're looting. If you see a white family, it says they're looking for food." He capped his remarks with his widely publicized indictment of the president of the United States: "George Bush doesn't care about black people." Concerning his remarks, West later told Bumgardner, "I said what was on my mind. I had sized up the state of black Americans today, I had watched what was going on in New Orleans, and that was the conclusion I came to. I had no plans to come out and say that. I just listened to my heart. You can't live in fear." On the subject of the wide and varied reaction to his criticism of the president, West said to Ogunnaike, "Does anybody remember the whole thirty seconds I spent talking about how I turned away from the television set [during coverage of the flood damage], how I went shopping? No, all anyone remembers is 'George Bush doesn't care about black people.'"

By early 2006 West's *Late Registration*, like *College Dropout* before it, had gone triple platinum (that is, sold three million copies). It garnered eight Grammy Award nominations and took home three awards, one for best rap album. Meanwhile, West continued to generate controversy. The cover of the February 9, 2006 issue of *Rolling Stone* featured a picture of West, wearing what appeared to be a crown of thorns—an image meant to evoke Jesus—under the headline, "The Passion of Kanye West." In response, Jonah Goldberg wrote for the *National Review Online* (February 3, 2006), "Kanye West . . . sells himself as a victim of a society that can't handle his truth. Four million records sold and saturation adulation in the media suggest that it can handle his truth just fine. The problem is, it ain't the truth. It's just a scam for kids too stupid to recognize they're being played—again."

West composed two songs for the soundtrack of the big-budget 2006 film *Mission: Impossible III*, making a fan of the film's star and producer, Tom Cruise. He also recorded *Late Orchestration: Live at Abbey Road Studios*, a collection of his hits performed with a 17-piece string orchestra at the London studios where the Beatles had worked. The album was released only in Europe, with an accompanying DVD. Later in the year West appeared as the opening act at the first three concerts of the Rolling Stones' autumn U.S. tour. He continues to oversee the GOOD record label and its slate of recording artists, including Common and the R&B artist John Legend, whose debut, *Get Lifted*, produced by West, won him the prize for best new artist at the 2006 Grammy Awards ceremony.

According to reports that were widely published in the summer of 2006, West was engaged to marry his girlfriend, Alexis, whom he had begun to date before his 2002 car crash but with whom he had not been romantically involved consistently since then. Her last name and occupation did not appear in media accounts.

—D.J.K.

Suggested Reading: *Chicago Tribune* C p1+ Aug. 28, 2005; *Entertainment Weekly* p22+ Feb. 3, 2006; *Los Angeles Times* E p1+ Aug. 28, 2005; *Playboy* p49+ Mar. 1, 2006; *Rolling Stone* p3846 Feb. 9, 2006; *Time* p54+ Aug. 29, 2005

Selected Recordings: *College Dropout*, 2004; *Late Registration*, 2005

Peter Kramer/Getty Images

White, Armond

1953– Film and cultural critic

Address: New York Press, 333 Seventh Ave.,
14th Fl., New York, NY 10001

Writing for the *Boston Globe* (March 26, 2006), Wesley Morris called the African-American film critic Armond White "the last iconoclast of American criticism, putting us all on the defensive with his unfashionably contrarian positions." White himself, in an interview with Matthew Ross for *Filmmaker* (Winter 2004), objected to the term "contrarian," insisting that his sometimes controversial writing on film is motivated by a deeper principle: "I believe what I believe, and I respond to movies the way I do, which is typically not the way most people respond. And it's not the way most people respond because I think I care, and most people don't. . . . A good movie can help you to understand your humanity better, and others' as well. And it's not a matter of being contrary. There's a lot of garbage out there! And it irks me when garbage is praised as something else, so I feel I have to say so." Lamenting the state of contemporary film criticism, White told a writer for *Cineaste* (December 22, 2000), "Film critics have become virtually useless. They no longer retain the culture, providing historical or esthetic contexts for new releases or, more importantly, for younger, uninformed audiences. To be a mainstream critic with popular influence, one is required to cooperate with the industry's manipulation of ignorant, gullible viewers for whom every chase film, every film noir, every sex comedy, every blockbuster disaster flick is a 'new,' astonishing experience. . . . As a result,

'hype' is now the definition of what 'criticism' means to most people."

White, a former chairman of the prestigious New York Film Critics Circle, began his career as a reviewer for the Brooklyn, New York–based *City Sun* in the mid-1980s, moving in the following decade to the *New York Press*, where he serves as the chief film critic. He is a founder of, and contributor to, the on-line quarterly review *First of the Month*. White infuses his savvy, sometimes idiosyncratic readings of contemporary films with references to past works—from those of the French New Wave auteurs François Truffaut and Jean-Luc Godard to the work of the Hollywood directors Steven Spielberg and Brian De Palma—and has inspired controversy as well as acclaim with the moral seriousness and political edge of his writing. In the 1990s, for example, White praised the hip-hop group Public Enemy, the alternative-rock singer Morrissey, and the film director Robert Altman in his essay collection *The Resistance: Ten Years of Pop Culture that Shook the World* (1995), which argued for the importance of social activism in the arts. On the other hand, White excoriated the high-profile African-American artists Spike Lee and Eddie Murphy for creating what White viewed as caricatures and stereotypes of the black experience. White's iconoclasm co-exists with—might, in fact, be said to spring from—his optimism about the redemptive potential of the cinema. In trying to define the role of the responsible film critic, during his conversation with Jeremiah Kipp for the Senses of Cinema Web site, White said, "A critic is one who concerns him or herself with the ideas and aesthetics in a work of art. . . . Part of that is trying to observe and be specific about the content of the film, the way it affects me, and the way it affects society."

Armond White was born in 1953 in Detroit, Michigan, directly across the Detroit River from Windsor, Ontario, the southernmost city in Canada. Growing up near the Canadian border offered White exposure to a wide range of English-dubbed foreign-language films regularly broadcast by Canadian television networks; as a child he watched Hollywood movies and foreign films in equal measure. Movies such as *La Dolce Vita* (1960), by the celebrated Italian director Federico Fellini, which explored issues of personal morality, left indelible impressions on White. In his interview with Jeremiah Kipp, he likened the experience of absorbing the sophisticated visions of Fellini films including *La Dolce Vita* and *8½* (1963) to an awakening: "I didn't really know what was going on in those films, but they were fascinating. They were intriguing to me in ways I fear kids don't get from those sorts of films anymore. . . . That was a wonderful thing for me, to be able to look at the adult world and want to be a part of it. . . . I wanted movies about sexual adults—or *glamorous* adults. I may not even have known what sex was, but that world was pretty, and glamorous, and appealing. That was an early response to cinema." During his formative years White tried his hand at making movies of his own, drawing storyboards akin to comic strips, before realizing that his passion lay elsewhere. "As a child I did want to be a filmmaker, but I simply didn't have the wherewithal," he admitted to Brett W. Leitner for the Web site devoted to the work of Brian De Palma. "But my family did have a typewriter, and I just began to write." As early as junior high school, White began to consider writing reviews. "That was a way to deal with movies, to work with them, and also to be creative," he said to Leitner.

In the mid-1970s White entered Wayne State University, in Detroit, where he studied journalism and hosted a community-affairs program on WDET Radio, a local affiliate of National Public Radio. After graduating, in 1979, he relocated to New York City and enrolled in Columbia University's master of fine arts program in film history, theory, and criticism. In his studies White focused on film as a visual art form; his instructors, including Stefan Sharff, a former apprentice to the influential Russian-born director Sergei Eisenstein (1898–1948), enhanced White's understanding of films by having the class "literally analyze [movies] frame by frame with a stop-projection projector," as White noted for Matthew Ross. "That class was a revelation," he added. "I guess it informed my beliefs, my certainty that film is above all a visual medium: the images need to be interesting, the images need to say something, or else it's not a film. It's television or something else, a play. But it's not cinema." White expressed to Kipp his disdain for what he sees as misguided attempts to promote cheaper video technologies over the richer images of celluloid: "I think that our culture has lost an appreciation for the big screen images, and in some ways [has] lost an appreciation of what movie art is. I mean it's inevitable with DVDs and home video that these movies will be seen on a box on television, but nothing beats the big screen."

As Sharff helped lay the philosophical groundwork for White's film aesthetic, the legendary film critics Andrew Sarris and Pauline Kael inspired White's commitment to the craft of film criticism. Sarris, a longtime critic for the *Village Voice* who taught at Columbia, impressed White with his passion for film and encyclopedic knowledge of film history. "I loved his love of movies, which was a sophisticated love of cinema. He has a huge knowledge of film seemingly at his fingertips, and it's not a buff's knowledge, a geek's knowledge, it's a sophisticated artistic appreciation," White remarked to Ross. In Pauline Kael, the longtime film critic for the *New Yorker*, White found his "first inspiration," as he told Ross. "With Pauline, it was her willingness to go against hype, even back in the '60s. . . . She was willing not to swallow it or follow it. And that impressed me."

In 1984, after receiving his M.F.A. degree, White joined the editorial staff of the *City Sun*, a weekly newspaper that served an African-American readership. During his 12 years as a film critic and, later, arts editor for the paper, White established himself as a vociferous opponent of formulaic, shallow Hollywood offerings while championing sophisticated, often obscure films. Richard Morrison observed in the London *Times* (September 24, 1994), for example, that White stood as the lone dissenter beside "no fewer than 32 New York film critics" who praised the actor-director Robert Redford's 1994 film *Quiz Show*, about a fixed television quiz program in the 1950s. White said to Morrison about *Quiz Show*, "It's terribly dishonest. It portrays the cheats as victims. It raises a moral issue and does not deal with it. And it only pretends to deal with class in American society. If you are going to confront the whole White Anglo-Saxon Protestant thing, you don't cast a British actor [Ralph Fiennes] as the WASP. That only evades the issue."

While White intensified his rhetoric against the white-controlled Hollywood establishment, he reserved his harshest criticism for African-American moviemakers who, in his view, perpetuated racial stereotypes. In a 1988 review in the *City Sun*, he panned the film *Coming to America*, starring the African-American comedian-actor Eddie Murphy, labeling Murphy a "traitor to every instance of politics, history, sex and ethnic culture Black people have ever known," as quoted by a writer for *USA Today* (August 11, 1988). (As *USA Today* went on to report, Murphy responded to White's criticism with an ad in the *City Sun* that read in part, "The fact that [*Coming to America*] has sold $81.2 million in tickets . . . indicates that I must have some understanding of the tastes, morals and values of the Black community.") Throughout the 1990s White frequently clashed with Spike Lee, the acclaimed African-American director of renowned independent films including *Do the Right Thing* (1989), which examined race relations in urban America. When interviewed by Erin J. Aubry for the *L.A. Weekly* (July 2, 1999), White said that Lee had become a "first-rate marketer—he knows what a young audience wants, and he supplies it. He's a mainstream Hollywood filmmaker who really doesn't think in terms of film, of story. . . . Spike picks hot topics—basketball, interracial dating—but that doesn't mean you break ground. . . . The pretense of seriousness doesn't mean you're serious." White has praised the work of the lesser-known African-American filmmaker Charles Burnett, the director of *Killer of Sheep* (1978) and *To Sleep with Anger* (1990), among other movies. White described Burnett to Cynthia Lucia for *Cineaste* (March 22, 2001) as being "obscure as he ever was twenty years ago despite having made better and more pertinent films than Lee ever has."

In the mid-1990s White turned his attention to the broader arena of popular culture, writing two books that expressed his sociopolitical views on popular film and music: *The Resistance: Ten Years of Pop Culture that Shook the World* (1995), an anthology of White's essays originally penned for the *City Sun* and the journal *Film Comment*, and *Rebel for the Hell of It: The Life of Tupac Shakur* (1997). Seeing intellectual gravity in what other critics perceived as frivolous popular entertainment, White's essays in *The Resistance* venerated a motley assemblage of artists, ranging from the hip-hop group Public Enemy to the avant-garde filmmaker Alex Cox, who "challenged the hegemony of mainstream American perspectives," as Mark V. Reynolds noted in his review of *The Resistance* for *QBR: The Black Book Review* (February 28, 1996). John Nangle wrote for *Films in Review* (May/June 1996) that White's work "gets us to reconsider foggy positions and calcified ideas we'd long accepted as truths. We may not end up agreeing with him, but we do appreciate the prodding." *Rebel for the Hell of It*, the first published biography of the slain hip-hop artist Tupac Shakur, traced Shakur's career and impact on the larger American culture. The biography attracted publicity for the conflict between White and his publisher, Thunder's Mouth Press, over editorial revisions of the book. As Matthew Flamm reported for *Entertainment Weekly* (November 14, 1997), White claimed that the publishers made unauthorized changes to the text and added an "editor's note," which "force[d] a connection between the deaths of Tupac Shakur and [New York rapper] Biggie Smalls—which I took pains not to do and which I think reinforces certain racist stereotypes." After the biography's publication, in the fall of 1997, White distanced himself from its promotion.

After the *City Sun* closed its doors, in 1997, White joined the *New York Press*, a free alternative weekly newspaper in New York City, as its primary film and cultural critic. He drew the praise and ire of his audience for his eclectic film tastes and cynical readings of the racial politics and cultural philistinism he saw as driving Hollywood production. "I think the problem is Hollywood hegemony, that people have had one hundred years of indoctrination in the Hollywood system, in the Hollywood way of looking at movies and understanding movies. They think that's all there is and all there ought to be—not knowing there's a whole other world of cinema. You know, it's kind of jingoistic, nationalistic. . . . It's limited, it's narrow, it's not allowing movies to be anything other than a studio product," White said to Brett W. Leitner. Ironically, White often came to the defense of the successful Hollywood director Brian De Palma, whom he considered to be a visionary artist trapped within the formulaic constraints of commercial filmmaking. For example, in his praise of De Palma's 2000 film *Mission to Mars*—which was savaged by critics for being slow and sentimental and dismissed by most moviegoers—White said to Leitner, "[Moviegoers] are committed to seeing movies the 'Hollywood way,' not the 'art way.' And the 'art way,' that self-conscious, self-reflexive way of looking at making movies, scares and maybe bores some people. Because De Palma has that Godardian side to him [a reference to Jean-Luc Godard], that's the trouble he faces too, even though he works in a popular American medium." White also told Leitner, "A lot of critics feel compelled to keep moving with the trends rather than stay rooted in investigating what art is. Critics—no maybe I should call them 'reviewers' instead of critics—are looking for the *latest* thing rather than looking for the *truest* thing."

In September 1998 White and the former *City Sun* journalists Stanley Aronowitz, Benj DeMott, and Charles O'Brien launched the quarterly publication *First of the Month*, "a newspaper of the radical imagination . . . committed to cultivating the power of the powerless," according to its Web site. Featuring a mix of cultural criticism and edgy political commentary, *First of the Month* found a niche as "the only leftist publication I could imagine being read at both Columbia University and Rikers [Island prison]," a reviewer for *Time Out New York* wrote, as quoted on the *First of the Month* Web site. *First of the Month* provides a forum for White to write pieces that integrate his thoughts on race, class, and culture. In his November 2001 column, entitled "Citizen Jay-Z," for instance, White offered a rigorous exegesis of the hip-hop artist Jay-Z's 2001 album *The Blueprint*, hailing it as a "true depiction of African American striving," while calling the rapper a "pop-satirical 'citizen' willing to fight for his . . . people, country, planet and species." Yet in a June 2005 article, entitled "Tales from Behind the Black Curtain," White accused hip-hop culture of erecting a "black curtain" that separates African-American youth from hopes of success, by encouraging the socially unacceptable behavior that is hip-hop's "source—the engine of its innovation and perpetuation and commerciality."

In 2003 White became embroiled in a controversy involving the decision by Jack Valenti, the CEO of the Motion Picture Association of America (MPAA), to ban film companies' distribution of promotional DVD "screeners" (preview copies of Academy Award–nominated films) to journalists voting for Oscar contenders. (In recent times DVD screeners had opened channels for video piracy, a trend that Valenti hoped to combat.) Valenti's decision sparked widespread protests from filmmakers, independent studios, film publicists, critics, and even a writer for the *New York Times* editorial page, who all expressed the view that the ban would place less widely distributed independent films at a further disadvantage during the Oscar balloting. Among the few who sided with Valenti was White, who wrote an attention-getting piece for the *New York Press* (October 28, 2003) lambasting his colleagues for their complicity in perpetuating the Hollywood hyping of mediocre films—which, in White's view, was the real purpose of the screeners. "Contemporary journalists are so naïve about their professional mandate and social responsibility that they feel obligated to stroke the industry, cowering before publicists who hold the right to admit them into screenings, parties and gift them with swag. As today's DVD revolution crests, screeners . . . are the choicest swag of all," White wrote. The wide circulation of screeners, according to White, only confirmed that "advertising and buzz are more powerful than the non-rigorous criticism we have today, more important than the movies themselves." White also took the New York Film Critics Circle to task for its condemnation of the ban. He explained to Ross, "My whole point was that the Critics Circle should not make a statement about screeners. They should simply stay out of it, and see movies the way they were meant to be seen. . . . We are obligated to see the movies the way the public has seen them. If not, then become a DVD reviewer, don't become a film critic."

White continues to showcase his individualistic takes on movies as the lead film critic for the *New York Press*, lauding little-known independents such as *George Washington* (2000), by David Gordon Green, while dismissing audience favorites including *Match Point* (2005), by Woody Allen. (In a July 26, 2006 article, White argued that "Allen's artistic stature owes less to skill or vision than to his cemented media [cachet].") Over the last two decades, White has also distinguished himself in the field of music criticism, receiving the Deems-Taylor ASCAP award for music criticism in 1992.

He currently serves as chief curator for an annual music-video program at the Film Society of Lincoln Center, in New York City. White holds memberships in the New York Film Critics Circle (for which he served as chairman for a time, beginning in 1994) and the National Society of Film Critics. He has taught courses on American independent film and the history of film noir at Columbia, Fordham, and Long Island Universities. White has contributed essays to *Alfred Hitchcock's Rear Window* (2000) and *Doomed Bourgeois in Love: Essays on the Films of Whit Stillman* (2001) and writes book reviews for the *Nation*. He lives in New York City.
—D.J.K.

Suggested Reading: Brian De Palma Web site; *Cineaste* p27 Vol. XXVI No. 1 2000; *Filmmaker Magazine* (on-line) Winter 2004; *Los Angeles Weekly* July 2, 1999; Senses of Cinema Web site

Selected Books: *The Resistance: Ten Years of Pop Culture that Shook the World*, 1995; *Rebel for the Hell of It: The Life of Tupac Shakur*, 1997

Williams, Tad

Mar. 14, 1957– Fantasy and science-fiction writer

Address: c/o DAW Books, 375 Hudson St., Third Fl., New York, NY 10014

"One thing you have to understand about writing fantasy is that the country is very well mapped," the fantasy and science-fiction writer Tad Williams told Jo-Ann Goodwin for the London *Independent* (July 25, 1993). "Everything has been tried: the challenge is to use existing conventions to say something more or something different." Judging by their popularity and critics' enthusiasm for them, Williams has met that challenge in his fantasy series, Memory, Sorrow, and Thorn, and his science-fiction cum fantasy tetralogy, Otherland. His single-volume novels, *Tailchaser's Song, Child of an Ancient City, Caliban's Hour,* and *War of the Flowers*, have also won him a huge number of enthusiastic readers in the U.S. and abroad, where translations of one or another of his books exist in some 20 languages. Before he began to devote himself to writing full-time, when he was in his early 30s, Williams held a wide variety of jobs. He is unusually well-read, not only in the genres of fantasy and science-fiction but in history, science, and what is known as literary fiction. Moreover, according to many book reviewers and others among his admirers, he is uncommonly knowledgeable about, and imaginative in his portrayals of, the sorts of everyday problems and philosophical questions that people have grappled with for thousands of years. His clever, gripping, and often

Joerg Koch/AFP/Getty Images

complex story lines, vividly described settings, fully rounded, believable characters, and rich, evocative language have all contributed to his success. Williams's *Shadowmarch*, the first book in another projected fantasy trilogy, was published in 2004; the second volume, *Shadowplay*, is scheduled to appear in 2007.

The writer was born Robert Paul Williams on March 14, 1957 and raised in suburban Palo Alto, California, with his brother, Arthur. He dedicated all of his Otherland books to his father, Joseph Hill Evans. By his own account, his parents always encouraged their children, especially with regard to their creative impulses. When Tad was young his mother read to him often, introducing him to such classics as *The Wind in the Willows* and *Alice's Adventures in Wonderland*. (In recent years he has become reacquainted with his childhood favorites, by reading to his young son and daughter.) Early on he developed a passion for reading and had a special interest in both fantasy and science fiction, both of which fall into the category of speculative fiction. In science fiction, according to wikipedia.org, "the story depends (at least in part) upon some change in the world as we know it that is explained by science or technology (as opposed to magic)," while in fantasy, "the story's setting differs from our own universe in a manner that is not the result of science or technology, but rather the result of magic or other anomalous phenomena." (The two often overlap.) A few of the many writers whom Williams considers to be his favorites and/or to have had strong influences on him are Ray Bradbury, Philip K. Dick, Charles Dickens, Ursula Le Guin, Fritz Leiber, George R. R. Martin, A. A. Milne, Michael Moorcock, Theodore Sturgeon, James Tiptree Jr., J. R. R. Tolkien, and Roger Zelazny. Williams read Tolkien's Lord of the Rings trilogy a dozen times before the age of 18; he and a girlfriend even corresponded in Elvish (the name Tolkien chose for his constructed languages), as he told an audience at a reading in Bonn, Germany (one of several countries in which Williams fan clubs flourish), as reported for serendipita.org (October 27, 2000). As an adult with wide-ranging interests, he often reads six to eight books every week.

"I had the same trouble writing a 5-page paper in school that anybody else did," Williams remarked to Victoria Strauss for sff.net in 1999, "and now five pages is basically just like exhaling." After graduating from high school, he decided against attending college. "I was more interested in living on my own and supporting myself," he explained on his Web site. During the next decade he held a series of jobs, working as a taco maker, tile stacker, shoe salesman, insurance salesman, loan collector, manager of an art-supply store, and graphic designer; in the last-named job, he worked on manuals for the U.S. Army. For a while he served as the lead singer in a band called Idiot, and for a number of years, according to some sources, he hosted a syndicated radio talk show. From 1987 to 1990 he was employed by Apple Computer, where he gained expertise in multimedia. Meanwhile, he had begun to think seriously about becoming a professional novelist. "It seemed obvious to choose speculative fiction, because I felt I knew the conventions of the genre and was familiar with the larger body of work," he told Victoria Strauss for sfsite.com (Au-

gust 1999). "As I kept doing it, I realized that the nice thing about the genre is that it's as capable of being literary as anything else. It's mostly a question of whether you can keep people turning pages."

During that period Williams was living with cats for the first time and "started playing with the idea of a cat-o-centric universe," as he recalled on his Web site. His first book, *Tailchaser's Song*, follows the young tomcat Fritti Tailchaser as he journeys to find his female friend Hushpad, one of the many acquaintances of his who have mysteriously vanished. The disappearances, he discovers, are the work of evil cat gods who dwell underground. Williams sent the manuscript to a well-known American publisher of fantasy and received a rejection note that read, "We don't do works with non-human protagonists." When he pressed the publisher for a more detailed explanation of the decision, the response was, "We don't do animal books. We'd make an exception if this were a potential best-seller, but it isn't." Williams then sent the manuscript to DAW Books—the first publishing company devoted exclusively to science fiction and fantasy, according to its Web site. DAW accepted his novel, and in January 1985 he signed a contract with the firm. Published later that year, *Tailchaser's Song* was met with mixed reviews, but it became a DAW best-seller, and it earned Williams a nomination for the 1986 John W. Campbell Award for best newcomer in science fiction and fantasy.

Williams's contract with DAW next called for him to write a trilogy, to be completed by 1988. Partly because of personal troubles, including the dissolution of his first marriage, he had not yet finished the second book when DAW's deadline passed. "I was a mess," he wrote for his Web site, "and just getting out of bed sometimes seemed beyond my strength." When he ended the tale, he felt as if he had taken "responsibility for a world and for a lot of people in it, and [given] those characters and their world respect, and paid attention to what happened to all of them, and allowed each one the room to have his or her own story." The Memory, Sorrow, and Thorn trilogy consists of *The Dragonbone Chair* (1988), *Stone of Farewell* (1990), and *To Green Angel Tower* (1993), the last of which spent five weeks on the *New York Times* best-seller list. Totaling more than 2,300 pages in hardcover and more than 3,100 in paperback (with the last book published in two paperback volumes of 816 pages apiece), the series reflects elements of such epic tales as *Beowulf*, the legend of King Arthur, Celtic and Norse mythology, and The Lord of the Rings; it also drew comparisons to Leo Tolstoy's *War and Peace*. The setting, which bears similarities to first-millennium Great Britain, is a continent called Osten Ard. Its residents include humans, among them peoples reminiscent of Vikings, Celts, and Anglo-Saxons—the last called Erkynlanders, the current rulers of Osten Ard—and non-human races, including trolls and the Sithi, an immortal elf-like race that is scheming to regain power. The trilogy's protagonist is Simon, a 14-year-old orphan who dreams of knighthood. As *The Dragonbone Chair* opens, Simon, a lowly, clumsy worker in the kitchens of King John, becomes apprenticed to a magician. After the elderly king dies, his successor, Prince Elias, turns against his own brother, Prince Josua, and forms an alliance with the Sithi Storm King, Ineluki. Forced by circumstances to leave the castle, and presented with an opportunity to prove his valor, Simon embarks on a perilous quest to locate three magical swords—named Memory, Sorrow, and Thorn—without which the Storm King and Prince Elias cannot be defeated. He finds one sword, and as *Stone of Farewell* begins, a second sword is in the possession of the Siths. A troll and a Sithi prince who befriend Simon become his companions on his treacherous journey, which takes him into the underground realm of the Sithi. In a ferocious battle at the Stone of Farewell, Simon is horrified to find himself in a fight to the death against Elias's Erkynlander troops, including men whom he had known personally during his scullion days. With Elias's army and his confederates the Norns gaining the upper hand, Osten Ard becomes gripped in the bitter cold of an unending winter. *To Green Angel Tower* carries the story to the culminating battle between the forces of Elias, on one side, and Simon and his collaborators on the other.

Most professional critics praised the series highly. In the "Fantasy Finder" portion of the Swedish Web site hoh.se, Karl Henriksson echoed many other opinions when he wrote, "Williams has got not only a great story to tell, but also an amazing way of telling it. What a richness of expressions, what a talent for making a fantasy world truly come alive! You can feel the cold and the rain, the ache of the untrained rider spending too much time in the saddle, but also the . . . pleasure of a safe haven, a decent meal and a warm bed, as well as the pride and horrors the heroes and villains are experiencing." Williams's creation, Henriksson continued, "is not a masterpiece of inventive imagination . . . but it's one of the most believable fantasy worlds I've discovered so far. The plot is, when structurally analyzed, quite close to the standard fantasy plot. But I've never seen it built with such skill, nor heard it told with such elegance and style. Many of the characters have their equivalents in other fantasy epics, but they have never been given such depth before."

Earlier, before he completed *To Green Angel Tower*, Williams—with the help of the writer Nina Kiriki Hoffman—had reworked an Arabian Nights–inspired short story of his, which had appeared in *Weird Tales* magazine. The new version, a novel titled *Child of an Ancient City*, was published in 1992. His next book was *Caliban's Hour* (1994), which follows characters from William Shakespeare's *The Tempest* and is set 20 years later. In it a vengeance-seeking Caliban, whose fate is not revealed in the Shakespeare play, confronts Miranda, Prospero's daughter, whom he had both desired and despised, with the intention of killing her after giving her his version of long-past events. In *Library Journal* (November 15, 1994), Jackie Cassada wrote that *Caliban's Hour* revealed Williams's "talent for exploring the hidden recesses of one all-too-human heart."

Williams made his debut in science fiction with the Otherland tetralogy: *City of Golden Shadow* (1996), *River of Blue Fire* (1998), *Mountain of Black Glass* (1999), and *Sea of Silver Light* (2001). Discussing in his interview with Victoria Strauss for sfsite.com the river that links Otherland's many domains, and referring to novels built around rivers (among them Mark Twain's *Huckleberry Finn*, Joseph Conrad's *Heart of Darkness*, and Philip José Farmer's Riverworld series), he said, "I was trying to come up with a different way of approaching the river as metaphor, . . . and I thought, 'What if the river wasn't just a metaphor, but was literally metaphorical? What would a metaphorical river be?' And once I figured out a solution, which . . . was to make the river a virtual river, I realized that anything anyone could conceive of could be built along the banks, and a set of travelers forced to make a journey on this river could be exposed to almost anything a writer could come up with." The events in the trilogy take place in real-world locations; environments described in such classic literary works as *The Odyssey*, *Through the Looking Glass*, and *The Wizard of Oz*; and settings imagined by Williams, at a time in the near future when, thanks to advances in technology, people can enter computer simulations. In an interview posted on his Web site, Williams said that his research for the Otherland books involved "mortifying amounts of reading on zillions of different subjects," among them the real-world places mentioned in the book and World War I and other real historical events that figured in the story. The series has several converging story lines. One, set in Durban, South Africa, follows Renie Sulaweyo, a virtual-reality educator whose young brother becomes comatose one day while using the Internet. Renie discovers a plot hatched by a secret international group of wealthy men called the Grail Brotherhood, who are transferring the minds of children to a virtual world called Otherland in a scheme to ensure their own immortality; with her student and friend !Xabbu, one of the few surviving South African bushmen, and a few others, Renie enters a strange, golden, virtual city in a desperate attempt to restore her brother to consciousness. Well-received by critics and laypeople alike, the series earned for Williams a prestigious German award, the Corine Prize, in 2004.

In Williams's *The War of the Flowers* (2003), a human enters a land called Faerie, where he uncovers secrets about his family and birth. "The gritty and even rather grim faerie world . . . is hardly a refuge from reality," Roland Green noted for *Booklist* (April 15, 2003). "The war of the title is one of numerous factions fighting among themselves, and with it, Williams darkly satirizes every sort and condition of politics, ideology, religion, and other human foibles, much as he did in the Otherland saga."

With the first volume of Williams's most recent fantasy series, *Shadowmarch* (2004), Williams "open[ed] another of the intricate, intriguing sagas that are his stock-in-trade," Frieda Murray wrote for *Booklist* (October 15, 2004). Charles C. Finley, who reviewed the book for the *Columbus (Ohio) Dispatch* (December 9, 2004), described *Shadowmarch* as "terrific entertainment." He added, "Williams knows what fantasy readers expect and has a talent for twisting the genre in satisfying ways."

In July 2006 Williams's comic book *The Next*, illustrated by Dietrich Smith and Walden Wong, the first of a projected six-issue limited series, was published by DC Comics. The Next are young superheroes from the future who arrive on Earth while fleeing an oppressive government. October 2006 saw the publication of Williams's first collection of short stories, *Rite: Short Work*, available in limited clothbound and leather-bound editions. Williams's DC Comics projects include a second comic-book series, tentative titled "The Factory"; an issue of the Helmet of Fate miniseries; and the

series *Aquaman: Sword of Atlantis*, for which he will serve as a contributing writer beginning in early 2007.

Williams is married to Deborah Beale, a British-born writer and editor. The couple maintain homes in London, England, and near Silicon Valley, in California. They have a son, Connor, and a daughter, Devon.

—I.C.

Suggested Reading: (London) *Independent* Sunday Review p32 July 25, 1993; serendipita.org Oct. 27, 2000; sff.com; sfsite.com; tadwilliams.co.uk; tadwilliams.com; *Toronto Star* D p4 Apr. 8, 1997; wotmania.com July 14, 2003

Selected Books: *Tailchaser's Song*, 1985; *The Dragonbone Chair*, 1988; *Stone of Farewell*, 1990; *Child of an Ancient City* (with Nina Kiriki Hoffman), 1992; *To Green Angel Tower*, 1993; *Caliban's Hour*, 1994; *City of Golden Shadow*, 1996; *River of Blue Fire*, 1998; *Mountain of Black Glass*, 1999; *Sea of Silver Light*, 2001; *The War of the Flowers*, 2003; *Shadowmarch*, 2004; *The Next*, 2006

Willis, Dontrelle

Jan. 12, 1982– Baseball player

Address: Florida Marlins, Dolphin Stadium, 2267 Dan Marino Blvd., Miami, FL 33056

Baseball fans have come to identify the Florida Marlins' starting pitcher Dontrelle Willis with his unorthodox pitching motion, in which he raises his right leg above his head, turns his back to the batter, and looks away from home plate before uncoiling himself to launch his fastball, slider, or changeup. (The southpaw developed his style as a youngster growing up in Alameda, California, beguiling his opponents in a variant of baseball, aptly named "strikeout," that was played with tennis balls and broom handles.) He told Mike Bernardino for *Sports Illustrated for Kids* (Fall 2003) that his high-kicking motion "keeps my timing in order. It's the same reason Barry Bonds or Gary Sheffield flick their bats [before they hit]. It's all about timing. If my timing's off, it's harder for me to execute pitches." In 2003, his first season as a big-leaguer, Willis employed his whirling motion to great effect, keeping hitters off-balance to post a 14–6 record and a 3.30 ERA (earned-run average) and win National League Rookie of the Year honors; he was also named to the All-Star Game. That year he helped the Marlins win their second World Series championship since the franchise's inception, in 1993. In 2005 he enjoyed his best statistical season thus far: he achieved a major-league-best 22 wins (against 10 losses) and led or co-led the Na-

tional League in both shutouts and complete games.

Willis, who completed his fourth big-league season with the Marlins in 2006, is known as an ebullient personality, mixing his determination to achieve individual and team distinction with an air of enthusiasm, on and off the field. Gwen Knapp, writing for the *San Francisco Chronicle* (July 22, 2005), observed that Willis "projects a youthful exuberance and zeal that define him almost as much as his talent does." An all-around talent, Willis is also an accomplished hitter and above average in many other facets of the game. "Why he wins is because he is so good at so many things," Jack McKeon, Willis's manager from 2003 until 2005, said to Jeff Berlinicke for *Baseball Digest* (January 2006). "He fields his position. He bunts. He hits. He has a good pickoff move. He knows how to help himself. He always makes a good pitch when he has to, and that's the mark of a good pitcher."

Dontrelle Wayne Willis was born on January 12, 1982 in Oakland, California, and was raised by his mother, Joyce Harris, in neighboring Alameda, in the San Francisco Bay Area. His mother gave birth to a second child, Walter, in 1998. Dontrelle's father, Harold Willis, did not contribute to his son's upbringing, but the two maintain civil relations. Frank Guy, Dontrelle Willis's uncle, served as a role model for him during his youth. Willis lived with his grandmother Naomi for several years, during one particularly difficult period of his upbringing, when his mother was not working steadily; he has indicated that his grandmother was a strict dis-

Dontrelle Willis

Jed Jacobsohn/Getty Images

ciplinarian. Around 1991 his mother joined Local 378, an ironworkers' union, and over the next decade and a half, she rose through the union's ranks to become a foreman by the time Dontrelle was in the big leagues. Her often dangerous job took her to the tops of some of the area's most recognizable edifices, including the Golden Gate and San Francisco-Oakland Bay Bridges. She currently works for the Alameda County Building Trades Council; in that capacity she speaks to youth groups and other organizations about the benefits of a career in construction.

Willis's mother was an accomplished softball player (reportedly a slugging catcher) for more than 25 years in the Bay Area and elsewhere. According to numerous reports, she continued to play softball until she was seven months pregnant with Dontrelle. She played the sport well into Dontrelle's childhood as well. "I remember going out there to watch her play," Willis recalled to Chris Ballard for *Sports Illustrated* (June 30, 2003). "It was basically a bunch of mothers going out there and bashing." Joyce Harris taught Willis the finer points of playing baseball. Willis and many observers have attributed his maturity at such a young age, on and off the field, to the influence of his mother, with whom he has a very close-knit relationship. "We're almost too tight, almost like brother and sister instead of mother and son," Willis said to Robert Andrew Powell for the *New York Times* (May 11, 2005). "Those things a mother might normally shield from her son she didn't keep from me, so we went through the struggles together."

Growing up, Willis was an avid fan of the Oakland Athletics baseball team; in particular he idolized Dave Stewart, an African-American starting pitcher who helped the Athletics win the World Series in 1989. Precociously gifted on the baseball diamond and especially on the mound, Willis is said to have thrown a curve ball during a Little League game at age nine. (Such ability is uncommon for most until their teenage years. Experts generally recommend that youngsters not throw breaking pitches, or pitches with unusual motion, until their teen years, because doing so continually can damage one's arm.) Even when he attended Encinal High School, no one tampered with Willis's wild pitching windup and delivery; he used it to great effect as a pitcher for the varsity baseball team, beginning in his freshman year. That year he helped the team reach California's North Coast Section championship game, played at the Oakland-Alameda County Coliseum (currently McAfee Coliseum), the home of the Athletics. He threw for several innings as a reliever, after two of his teammates, both older than Willis, asked not to be placed in that high-pressure situation. (Encinal lost the game.) As a junior Willis joined an elite traveling team called the Area Codes. By that time professional scouts had grown interested in him and were often spotted at the games in which he pitched. In his senior year at Encinal, Willis attained a sparkling 12–1 record with a 0.82 ERA and 111 strikeouts in 70 innings pitched; he was named California's high-school player of the year for medium-size schools. He also proved to be a capable slugger, compiling a high batting average while also generating a high number of runs.

In early June 2000 the Chicago Cubs selected Willis in the eighth round of that year's amateur draft. He was then assigned to the Cubs' rookie team in Mesa, Arizona, where he pitched to a 3–1 record as a middle reliever. In the fall of 2001, Willis was promoted to the Cubs' Northwest League affiliate, the Hawks, in Boise, Idaho. Willis proved capable of handling the step up in competition, achieving eight wins and a 2.98 ERA as a starting pitcher and helping the Hawks post the league's best record. Meanwhile, he was named to the Northwest League All-Star team. On March 27, 2002 the Cubs traded Willis, along with then–minor-leaguers Jose Cueto and Ryan Jorgensen and the more established pitcher Julian Tavarez, to the Florida Marlins for the relief pitcher Antonio Alfonseca and the starting pitcher Matt Clement.

When he arrived at the Marlins' spring-training facility, in Melbourne, Florida, Willis performed so poorly in his first throwing session that Wayne Rosenthal, then the Marlins' pitching coordinator, questioned whether the southpaw would make it to the big leagues. Rosenthal also wondered if Willis's violent pitching motion ought to be subdued. "He threw a breaking ball about 6 feet in front of the plate. Changeups hit the back fence. It was nothing but arms, legs and balls," Rosenthal said to Joe Capozzi for the Florida *Palm Beach Post* (June 16, 2003). With his pitching motion unchanged, Willis, at 20, began the season playing single-A ball for the Kane County, Illinois, Cougars. Recovering control of his pitches, he became a Midwest League All-Star, posting a 10–2 record with a 1.83 ERA in 19 games. His performance triggered his promotion, in late July, to Jupiter, Florida, where in five starting appearances he went 2–0 with a 1.80 ERA. Willis was named the *Sports Weekly* minor-league pitcher of the year; meanwhile, the Marlins also selected him as their pitcher of the year.

In February 2003, while driving on a highway in Palo Alto, California, Willis lost control of his car, after one of its rear tires went flat. Though his car crashed into a guardrail and flipped over several times, no one was injured. Willis, who was wearing a seat belt, which he credits with shielding him from harm, has said that recalling the incident enables him to put bad performances on the mound into perspective. "Something like that really keeps you grounded about life in general," Willis said to Mark Emmons for the San Jose (California) News (August 22, 2003). "Nothing is as bad as it seems. Even if I give up eight runs, I realize I'm doing it in a major league game and I'm lucky."

Less than two weeks after the accident, Willis arrived at the Marlins' spring-training facility. The Marlins' staff was so impressed with Willis's ability to throw strikes with three different pitches—his repertoire by then included a slider, a recently honed changeup, and several variations on his fastball—that they promoted him to double-A ball to start the 2003 season. In six starts for the Carolina Mudcats (who play in Zebulon, North Carolina), Willis posted a 4–0 record with a 1.49 ERA. On May 9, 2003, at a point when the Marlins were low in the National League East divisional standings, Willis was called up to the majors as a replacement

for the right-handed pitcher A. J. Burnett, who had been sidelined due to surgery on his right elbow. Making his debut on the Marlins' home field, against the Colorado Rockies, he pitched six innings, allowing three runs and striking out seven batters, and received a no-decision. Just two days after Willis's major-league debut, Jeffrey Loria, the team's owner, feeling unhappy with the club's 16–22 start that season, hired Jack McKeon to replace Jeff Torborg as the team's manager. McKeon's advice to his players to relax and enjoy themselves paid off: after losing seven of the first 10 games for which McKeon was the manager, the Marlins went on to hold the best record in baseball from May 23 until the end of the season, finishing the year with a win–loss record of 91–71, second-best in the National League East.

Willis contributed significantly to the Marlins' turnaround. At the All-Star break, his record stood at 9–1 with a 2.08 ERA, and in July he was tapped for the National League All-Star Team when a replacement was needed for the injured Dodgers pitcher Kevin Brown. (At age 21 he became the youngest All-Star pitcher since Dwight Gooden, in 1985.) Willis became a major attraction in Miami and one of baseball's most-talked-about players. According to *Sports Illustrated*, the ratings generated by Willis's June 11 start against the Milwaukee Brewers were the highest for a local telecast of a Marlins game since 1998. Sportswriters and fans were awed by the rookie's precocity and whirling-dervish pitching mechanics, and many lauded Willis as being "good for baseball," because he exhibited an enthusiasm uncommon for players of the current generation. He was often compared to such pitchers as Gooden, Fernando Valenzuela, Mark Fidrych, Vida Blue, and Jim Palmer, each of whom, at a very early stage of his career, had befuddled major-league hitters. The Marlins won 19 of the 27 games Willis started. At the season's conclusion he was named the National League Rookie of the Year and also won the Larry Doby Award as the National League's best rookie, as voted on by the Negro League Baseball Museum. He finished the season with a 14–6 record and a 3.30 ERA, faltering some as the season progressed. (His 14 wins set a Marlins single-season record for a rookie.)

Having secured the National League wild-card berth, the Marlins entered the play-offs as underdogs against the San Francisco Giants. After losing the first game, 2–0, the Marlins won the next three in the best-of-five series, stunning the many sportswriters who had predicted that the "overmatched" Marlins would be knocked off in the first round. Willis appeared as a reliever in the eighth inning of Game Two, played in San Francisco. Tapped by McKeon as the starting pitcher for Game Four, he pitched well through the first four innings, allowing only one run, but tired in the fifth inning, in which he allowed four runs. At the plate Willis collected a run scored and three hits, including a triple—further evidence, sportswriters felt, of his all-around talent. In the National League Championship Series (NLCS), the Marlins faced the Chicago Cubs—the sentimental favorites of many fans and sportswriters to become the National League champions, as the franchise had not won a pennant since 1945 or a World Series since 1908. (The Marlins had won the 1997 World Series.) The Marlins defeated the Cubs in seven games, rallying from a three-games-to-one deficit to take the best-of-seven series. In the NLCS Willis's pitching was uncharacteristically poor: he surrendered six runs and recorded only seven outs as the starter in Game Four, a game the Cubs won by a score of 8–3. In Game Six, in Chicago's Wrigley Field, which the Marlins won, 8–3, Willis made a relief appearance, allowing a run on a wild pitch in one inning of work.

The 2003 World Series pitted the Marlins, whose payroll totaled about $50 million, against the New York Yankees, whose payroll topped $180 million—and who had won four world championships in the previous seven years. The Marlins entered Game Six of the best-of-seven series leading three games to one, prompting McKeon to make the unusual decision to start the 23-year-old pitcher Josh Beckett, who had had only three days to rest his arm since Game Three. Beckett pitched well, shutting out the Yankees and recording a complete game. The Marlins' 2–0 victory in Game Six marked the first time since 1981 that any team had beaten the Yankees in the World Series in Yankee Stadium. Willis, for his part, made relief appearances in Games One, Three, and Five, holding the Bronx Bombers to just four hits and no runs in over three innings pitched.

The year 2004 was a relatively unsuccessful one for Willis. He finished the season with a 4.02 ERA and a 10–11 record; many guessed that hitters had solved the puzzle presented by his unorthodox pitching motion. The Marlins finished in third place in the Eastern Division race with a record of 83–79 in 2004, repeating those statistics exactly in the following year. In the months leading up to the 2005 season, Willis kept to a rigorous conditioning program with the outfielder Juan Pierre, his then-teammate and close friend, and by early May he had put to rest the notion that he would be a "one-year wonder." He began the season with a 5–0 record and a minuscule 1.29 ERA. Willis and others within the organization credited his success in part to a slight adjustment to his pitching motion, which was suggested by Mark Wiley, then the Marlins' pitching coach. The alteration, through which Willis avoided turning his hip as far toward third base as he had before, allowed him to feel "more under control," as he explained to Albert Chen for Sports Illustrated (May 9, 2005). Willis added, "[The change] allows me to stay balanced and go toward home plate with a smooth effort." He finished the season with a career-best 2.63 ERA, shaving close to a run and a half from the important statistic. For the season he set a franchise record with 22 wins, the highest total in the majors that season, and also led the majors in shutouts, pitching five. In addition, he tossed seven complete games,

which tied him for the most in the National League. He finished second behind the St. Louis Cardinals' Chris Carpenter in the voting for the 2005 National League Cy Young Award, and he was named to his second All-Star team. Baseball Digest, meanwhile, named him its pitcher of the year. During the 2005 season Willis continued to perform well as a batter, too, leading major-league pitchers with 24 hits and 14 runs scored. On occasion, McKeon positioned Willis seventh in the team's batting order (pitchers traditionally bat ninth) and used him as a pinch hitter in critical run-scoring situations.

Before the start of the 2006 season, the Marlins reduced their payroll from $60 million to $15 million, trading away, or allowing to be signed elsewhere, such star players as the pitchers Beckett and Burnett, the infielders Carlos Delgado and Mike Lowell, and the outfielder Pierre. (McKeon retired as the team's manager after the 2005 season.) In the early part of the 2006 season, the team relied on young and unproven players to win games, a feat that had proven difficult for the Marlins' rookie manager, Joe Girardi. Although in late May the team's record had fallen to 17 games below .500, the second-lowest winning percentage in the National League, the Marlins gradually improved; in early July their record stood at 35–45. Despite a growing rift between Girardi and Jeffrey Loria, the team's owner, over managerial philosophy and decision-making, the players rallied, and the Marlins remained in play-off contention throughout August and September, ending the season with a 78–84 record. In October 2006 Loria fired Girardi and replaced him with Fredi Gonzales, the Atlanta Braves' third-base coach. Willis, meanwhile, after an uneven start, recaptured to some extent the poise he had shown in 2005, posting a 5–7 record and a 3.96 ERA during the first half of the season. In his final 10 starts, Willis finished strong, going 6–3 with a 2.76 ERA and ending the season with a 12–12 record and an ERA of 3.87. Many teams have expressed an interest in acquiring Willis via an in-season trade; in the offseason, to avoid salary arbitration, the pitcher signed a one-year contract valued at $4.35 million.

Willis stands six feet four inches tall and weighs 240 pounds. In his first two big-league seasons, he was known to have scrawled the word "Joyce" under the bill of his cap in honor of his mother. He is unmarried but told Ben Reiter for Sports Illustrated (May 15, 2006) that he is "not on the market" and that he has a serious girlfriend. He lives in Alameda in the off-season, according to the Florida Marlins' Web site. Willis enjoys listening to rap music prior to the start of games and relaxes by watching movies.

Discussing his views on baseball, Willis said to Jill Leiber for Baseball Digest (August 2005), "Home or away, when I see the fans out there, whether it's 15,000 or 50,000 people, that's a rush. When I see my name on the scoreboard, that's a rush. It's a beautiful thing to step onto the field, whether you're playing well or you're struggling." He also said to Leiber, "Baseball is not as complex as people make it, at least not for me. I try to break things down as simple as I can, as far as going about my work every day. I go out there, I throw the ball, I have a good time and I leave everything on the field. That's all that you can ask from a ball player, bottom line."

—D.F.

Suggested Reading: *Baseball Digest* (on-line) Aug 2005 Jan. 2006; Baseball Reference Web site; Florida Marlins Web site; jockbio.com; *New York Times* D p1+ May 11, 2005; *San Jose (California) Mercury News* D p1 Aug. 22, 2003; *Sports Illustrated* p40+ June 30, 2003

Wilson, Heather

Dec. 30, 1960– U.S. representative from New Mexico (Republican)

Address: 318 Cannon House Office Bldg., Washington, DC 20515

Heather Wilson, a Republican U.S. representative from New Mexico, is perhaps best known nationally for calling in early 2006 for a congressional inquiry into the National Security Agency's practice of domestic wiretapping—a practice revealed to the public late in the previous year. Her action, which represented a direct challenge to the Republican administration of President George W. Bush, was not the first instance of Wilson's disagreement with her party's leaders. While supporting such traditional GOP causes as fiscal conservatism and the banning of legalized abortion, Wilson has broken with the Republican ranks on issues related to homosexual rights and adoption. Wilson, a former Rhodes Scholar with a doctorate in international relations and a former U.S. Air Force officer (she is often identified as the only female armed-forces veteran in Congress), began her government career with the National Security Council under President George H. W. Bush. She served in the Cabinet of New Mexico governor Gary Johnson before winning the seat representing the state's First Congressional District in 1998. Since then she has been active in the areas of national security and intelligence; she has also championed drug benefits for senior citizens, worked to set stiff penalties for E-mail fraud, and served as an advocate for the energy industry (a force in her home state, which hosts three air-force bases and the Los Alamos and Sandia National Laboratories). Carter Pilcher, who attended the Air Force Academy with Wilson, told Gilbert Gallegos for the *Albuquerque (New Mexico) Tribune* (October 30, 2000), "One of her incredible attributes is she just doesn't do something unless it's clear and right. . . . Her conscience is huge."

In seeking reelection in 2006, Wilson found herself in a vigorously fought race against the Democratic challenger, the state's current attorney general, Patricia A. Madrid. A victory in that election would reinforce Wilson's position as a possible successor to her fellow Republican, U.S. senator Pete Domenici. Two days following the November 6, 2007 election, the race remained too close to call.

The second (and only girl) of three children, Heather Ann Wilson was born on December 30, 1960 in Keene, New Hampshire. Her grandfather, Scott Wilson, a native of Aberdeen, Scotland, joined the Royal Flying Corps during World War I and later moved across the Atlantic in search of work, settling with his wife in Keene during the Great Depression. Heather's father, George Douglas Wilson, joined the U.S. Air Force after high school, working as a crew chief at Walker Airfield in Roswell, New Mexico, before returning to New Hampshire to marry. When Heather was six years old, her father died in an automobile crash, leaving her mother, Martha Wilson-Kernozicky, to raise her three small children alone. Her mother's second marriage, to a feckless alcoholic, further complicated matters at home, and as a result Heather Wilson became independent at an early age. She focused on her studies as a refuge from the circumstances of her youth. Many years later, addressing a group of young female juvenile offenders in her role as the head of New Mexico's Children, Youth, and Families Department, she said about her own youth, as quoted by Susie Gran in the *Albuquerque (New Mexico) Tribune* (July 5, 1997), "I didn't dwell on weaknesses and didn't let them hold me back."

Wilson attended Keene High School, where she joined the band and the debate team and was voted by her classmates as most likely to succeed. During high school she considered pursuing a career in medicine or forestry. She eventually set her sights on becoming a pilot, in part to follow in the footsteps of her father and grandfather. On October 7, 1975 President Gerald R. Ford had signed into law legislation permitting women to enter the United States armed-services academies; on a full scholarship Wilson entered the Air Force Academy, in Colorado Springs, Colorado. As part of her training to become a fighter pilot, she parachuted from airplanes on several occasions. "I will never do that again . . . ," she said to Jackie Jadrnak for the *Albuquerque Journal* (May 5, 1996), adding, "falling is fine. Landing is terrible. It's like jumping off a two-story building." At the time, she said, "I was foolish and 18 and would do anything people dared me to do." She graduated with distinction in 1982, receiving a B.S. degree in international politics; her class was the third in the history of the Air Force Academy to include women. Upon earning her degree she was commissioned as a second lieutenant.

Wilson next attended Oxford University, in England, as a Rhodes Scholar, earning a master's degree in philosophy in 1984. The following year she

Luke Frazza/AFP/Getty Images

Heather Wilson

received her doctorate in international relations from the school. Her thesis was published by Oxford University Press under the title *International Law and the Use of Force by National Liberation Movements*; it earned the 1988 Paul Reuter Prize from the International Committee of the Red Cross. During that period, as an officer in the U.S. Air Force, she served for a time with the British Royal Air Force at the base in Mildenhall, England, and was also stationed in Brussels, Belgium, and Vienna, Austria, among other locations. In Brussels she worked with the U.S. mission to NATO for two years beginning in 1987. During her seven years in Europe, she attained the rank of captain. She returned to the U.S. in 1989.

While Wilson was giving thought to entering law school, a friend persuaded her to look into job opportunities in Washington, D.C. There, she landed a position with the National Security Council in the administration of President George H. W. Bush. As director for European Defense Policy and Arms Control, she advised the president during such important moments in history as the collapse of the Soviet Union and the reunification of what were then East and West Germany. Also while working in Washington, Wilson became reacquainted with Jay Hone, an attorney and law instructor from New Mexico who earlier had taught Wilson in the Air Force. The two were married in 1991 and moved to Albuquerque. There, in the same year, Wilson founded a consulting business, Keystone International, "to work with senior executives in large American defense and scientific corporations" on "business development and program planning work in the United States and Russia," according to her official Web site.

In 1994 Wilson competed with four other candidates for the post of Albuquerque school superintendent. Although another office seeker won the position, Wilson's campaign raised her profile among politicians in New Mexico. Later that year Gary Johnson, the state's newly elected Republican governor, offered her a Cabinet-level position in his administration. Early in 1995 she began her tenure as the head of the state's Children, Youth and Families Department. In that role Wilson demonstrated her decisiveness, at times engaging in disputes with community advocates who felt that her policies alienated the state's many poor families. For example, in her second year on the job, Wilson called for lowering the department's budget by 20 percent to eliminate what she considered needless government spending. Her critics charged that the proposed cuts would gut vital social programs meant to curtail the spread of juvenile delinquency. In her efforts to relieve the overcrowding of the state's juvenile-detention facilities, she oversaw the building of additional housing for detainees and opened New Mexico's first work camp for juveniles in the system. "[Those programs] had been ignored for some time," Nancy Jo Archer, then the executive director of a residential program for troubled juveniles in Albuquerque, said to Jackie Jadrnak. "She really put the debate into the public eye, stimulated a lot of discussion and debate. That's extremely healthy." Wilson also led efforts to implement stiffer penalties for juvenile offenders. "I don't brook much nonsense from a management perspective," Wilson said to Karen Peterson for the *Santa Fe New Mexican* (November 19, 1995), commenting on her leadership style. Explaining that she was "dispassionate about the department and compassionate toward the children it serves," she added, "It's hard to run this agency and not be moved by a lot of the circumstances children face today. Sometimes you go home on the weekend and just cry."

Wilson resigned her post in February 1998 and announced that she would seek a seat in the U.S. Congress, representing New Mexico's First Congressional District. The seat was then held by the Republican Steven H. Schiff, who in late January had announced that he would not seek reelection due to his fight with skin cancer. Surprising some, both Schiff and New Mexico's influential Republican U.S. senator Pete Domenici, who had had a longstanding policy against supporting those seeking nominations for federal posts, endorsed Wilson's candidacy. When Schiff died, on March 25, a special election was called for June 23, 1998, to fill the House seat for the remainder of his term in the 105th Congress. Since its creation, in 1968, Republicans have controlled New Mexico's First District, which includes the state's most populous city, Albuquerque; the district is also home to Los Alamos National Laboratory and Cannon Air Force Base. Representatives from the district have generally advocated fiscal conservatism and a strong military. Wilson ran on a platform that stressed simplifying the federal tax code, fighting crime, and making improvements to the educational system. Meanwhile, her chief opponent, the wealthy Democratic businessman Phil Maloof, tried to portray Wilson as a carpetbagger. In the special election, following a campaign that featured negative advertisements from both major candidates, Wilson emerged victorious, receiving 45 percent of the vote, with 40 percent going to Maloof. Some observers pointed to the presence of the Green Party nominee, Robert L. Anderson, who received some 15 percent of the vote, as helpful in securing Wilson's victory. Wilson became the first woman to represent New Mexico in Congress since Georgia Lusk, who held a House seat from 1946 to 1948. Wilson, Maloof, and Anderson squared off again in the fall of 1998, with similar results. Though Maloof outspent Wilson over the course of the year by four to one, Wilson captured a seven-point margin of victory over Maloof in the general election, to secure her first full term in Congress.

When Wilson arrived in Congress in June 1998 to serve the remainder of Schiff's term, Republicans assigned her to the Commerce Committee, a move some saw as being designed to attract campaign support from business interests for Wilson's impending general-election fight. In the 105th Congress Wilson embraced traditional Republican stances on many issues—supporting fiscal conservatism, opposing campaign-finance legislation, and voting to impeach President Bill Clinton, who was accused of obstruction of justice with regard to his extramarital affair with a former White House intern, Monica Lewinsky. On social issues, however, Wilson occasionally broke with her party. She backed Clinton's order to ban discrimination against homosexuals in the federal workplace and voted in favor of requiring insurance companies to cover birth control for federal workers. In August 1998 Wilson joined 29 other Republicans in voting with the minority against a law to prevent couples who are neither married nor related from adopting children in the District of Columbia. Her vote on that issue angered the Republican House Speaker, Newt Gingrich, according to *Politics in America 2000*.

In 1999 Wilson earned a seat on the House Permanent Select Committee on Intelligence. The committee, whose meetings are not open to the public, oversees and decides on the budgets of intelligence organizations, including the CIA. Wilson was also named to the Republican Policy Committee. In April of that year, she cautioned against sending U.S. ground troops to halt bloodshed in the Serbian province of Kosovo, in the former Yugoslavia; she called NATO's handling of the peace process, in the first major military operation of its 50-year history, "flawed." Republican strategists later tapped Wilson to represent the GOP position on the issue in talks with President Clinton and others. In the summer of 1999, Wilson was named to the House's Working Group on Juvenile Violence, a 10-member, bipartisan group charged with

forming a consensus on legislation intended to reduce youth violence. In July she was one of eight House members who voted against cutting the Energy Department's 2000 budget by $1.5 billion. Also in 1999, motivated in part by concerns that her own children might come across inappropriate advertisements for products and services, Wilson emerged as a leading supporter of legislation against "spam"—or mass, unsolicited E-mail messages. Wilson sponsored a bill that would have, among other provisions, enabled computer users to screen such messages. The measure passed in the House in July 2000 but was ignored by the Senate. Undeterred, in June 2003 she co-sponsored legislation with Representative Gene Green of Texas, the Wilson-Green Anti-Spam Act, that defined spam and required those sending it to give consumers the option of refusing the messages. The bill also set penalties for E-mail fraud. "The Internet has changed the way we communicate," Wilson said in a press release, as quoted by Andrew Webb in *New Mexico Business Weekly* (June 19, 2003, on-line). "Now, grandparents routinely get the latest grandkid news through quick e-mails, and commerce is conducted at light speed. As consumers, we should have the power to stop getting junk e-mail on our computers or on computers used by children." In November 2003 the Senate approved the legislation, which became law in 2004.

In 2000 Wilson endured a tough reelection battle against the Democratic nominee, John Kelly, a former U.S. attorney. Kelly had attracted national attention as the prosecutor in the case of the Taiwanese-born computer scientist Wen Ho Lee, an American citizen who worked at Los Alamos National Laboratory and was accused of supplying mainland China with nuclear secrets. (In September 2000 Lee gained his freedom after pleading guilty to one count of improperly downloading restricted data into his personal computer.) In his attempts to characterize Wilson as a puppet of the House Republican leadership, Kelly criticized Wilson for supporting a GOP-sponsored bill, passed by a small margin in late June 2000, that made the private sector responsible for developing medical-benefit policies for senior citizens. On Election Day Wilson won by slightly more than 15,000 votes (or seven percentage points) of the more than 200,000 cast; the Green Party candidate, Daniel Kerlinsky, won 6.5 percent of the vote. Wilson won reelection in 2002 and 2004 in similarly close contests, defeating the Democratic challenger Richard Romero both times. Following her Election Day victory in 2002, Wilson said, as quoted by Kate Nash in the *Albuquerque Tribune* (November 6, 2002), "Now it's time to go back to work for our families to make sure there is a great public school in every neighborhood for every kid to want to [attend]. We want to make sure we've got great jobs for our kids to take when they graduate from school so they don't have to leave New Mexico in order to get a good wage. We're going to keep taxes low. We're going to have fair regulation." She added, referring to the GOP plan to have Medicare cover both generic and brand-name drugs, "We're going to add that prescription drug benefit to Medicare."

In March 2001 House Republican leaders named Wilson the chairperson of the Subcommittee on National Security and Foreign Affairs. In that position she helped to shape the Republican Party's message on issues of defense and national security in the wake of the September 11, 2001 terrorist attacks against New York and Washington, D.C. Under Wilson's leadership, in February 2003 the subcommittee released a report that, according to *Politics in America 2004*, "challenged the government to do a better job of sustaining its nuclear weapons complex, investing more in research and development, and refining anti-proliferation programs." In her position, while helping to make the George W. Bush administration's case for military action in Afghanistan and Iraq, she also criticized the White House for the lack of sufficient U.S. troop strength in Iraq. In May 2005 Wilson was named the chair of the Republican Policy Subcommittee on Homeland and National Security.

In late September 2005, in the wake of Hurricane Katrina, which battered New Orleans in late August 2005—its 160-mile-per-hour winds uprooting trees, knocking down power lines, and strewing roadways with debris, leaving entire neighborhoods submerged under eight to 15 feet of water and New Orleans awash in floodwater, sewage, and corpses—Wilson called on House Speaker Dennis Hastert to create an oversight body and appoint an inspector general to ensure that the rebuilding effort was protected against fraud and mismanagement. "There must be no delay in getting this aid quickly and directly to those who need it most, and it is our duty to make certain these resources are not wasted," she wrote in a letter to Hastert, as quoted by *US Fed News* (September 23, 2005).

Breaking ranks with the Bush administration, Wilson generated headlines in February 2006, when she called for a full congressional inquiry into the secret domestic-wiretapping program of the National Security Agency (NSA). (She is the chairwoman of the House Intelligence Committee's Subcommittee on Technical and Tactical Intelligence, which oversees the NSA.) A front-page *New York Times* article had first publicized the program in early December 2005, revealing that the NSA, beginning in the months after September 11, 2001, had been—without warrants—wiretapping the international communications of people in the U.S. who were suspected of having ties to terrorists. "I think the argument that somehow, in passing the use-of-force resolution [through which Congress authorized the president to engage in war], that that was authorizing the president and the administration free rein to do whatever they wanted to do, so long as they tied it to the war on terror, was a bit of a stretch. And I don't think that's what most members of Congress felt they were doing," Wilson said to Sheryl Gay Stolberg for the *New York Times* (February 11, 2006). Wilson's criticism of the Bush administration seemed to encourage an outcry from lawmakers on both sides of the aisle. Wilson argued that under the Federal Intelligence Surveillance Act (FISA), the administration should explain its actions to the intelligence oversight committees of both houses of Congress, which it had failed to do previously. On February 8, 2006 Attorney General Alberto R. Gonzalez and Air Force general Michael V. Hayden, at the time the deputy director of national intelligence and a former NSA director, briefed the House Intelligence Committee, explaining the operations of the domestic-wiretapping program in testimony that Wilson described to Maura Reynolds for the *New York Times* as "very forthcoming and very helpful." Speaking at a press conference after the briefing, Wilson told reporters, as quoted by Reynolds: "The checks and balances in our system of government are very important, and it's those checks and balances that are going on and being executed now." She also said, "The president is the commander in chief of the military. He executes the laws and he administers the programs. In the Congress, we authorize programs, we set up agencies, we appropriate funds and we oversee the execution of programs. Those are very different roles under our Constitution, but that constitutional structure has kept us safe and free and the strongest country in the world for a very long time."

In the spring of 2006, with gasoline prices reaching $3 per gallon, Wilson proposed a federal gasoline price-gouging law, which called for the enforcement of "price-gouging penalties at any time, not just during times of crisis," as Michael Coleman reported in the *Albuquerque Journal* (May 2, 2006). (Wilson pushed a similar bill in late 2005, in the aftermath of the Hurricane Katrina crisis.) The bill passed overwhelmingly in Congress, by a vote of 389 to 34. "I hope the real impact of this bill is its deterrent effect—that knowing the federal government will come in and investigate will discourage people from playing games," Wilson told Michael Coleman for the *Albuquerque Journal* (May 4, 2006). Later, in September, Wilson, who had been critical of the NSA's secret domestic-wiretapping program earlier in the year, gave a boost to President Bush's controversial anti-terrorism initiatives, devising a bill that permitted warrantless wiretapping in the event of an imminent threat of a terrorist attack. The viability of the bill in the House and the Senate will be determined after both chambers reconvene for a lame-duck session after the November 2006 general elections.

In the fall of 2006, in one of the most closely watched of that year's congressional races, Wilson's bid to retain her seat became a struggle for her. Taking advantage of shrinking popular support for the U.S. war in Iraq, her Democratic challenger, New Mexico's attorney general, Patricia A. Madrid, has tried to link Wilson with what many have labeled as serious errors in the foreign policy of the Bush administration. Some of Madrid's television advertisements, for example, carry the written message "Lying for George Bush—Leaving America less safe," as reported by Andy Lenderman in the *Santa Fe New Mexican* (October 22, 2006). Wilson, in turn, has responded by painting herself as "a hardworking, highly disciplined moderate," in the words of Michael Coleman in the *Albuquerque Journal* (October 22, 2006), and as a woman with strong family values. "My responsibility to my kids doesn't end at the front step or the back porch. To me in some ways this [career choice] has always been about them and what kind of country do we want to leave for our kids," she told Coleman. In polls conducted in late October 2006, 44 percent of those questioned favored Wilson, while another 44 percent stated their intention to vote for Madrid. Wilson has vowed that if she is reelected, she will make national-intelligence reform her primary focus. As of November 9, 2006, the race between Wilson and Madrid remained too close to call.

"With short-cropped hair and her back ramrod straight," Heather Wilson "looks like she still would be at home in the Air Force blues she wore until 1989," according to John J. Lumpkin, writing for the *Albuquerque Journal* (October 8, 2000). Wilson divides her time between her home in Albuquerque and Washington, D.C. From her marriage to Jay Hone, she has three children: Scott (who is adopted), Joshua, and Caitlin Ann.

—D.F.

Suggested Reading: *Albuquerque Journal* A p1+ May 5, 1996, D p1+ May 2, 2006, A p1+ Oct. 22, 2006; *Los Angeles Times* A p1 Feb. 9, 2006; (Manchester, New Hampshire) *Union Leader* A p1 Mar. 15, 2003; *Politics in America 2000: 106th Congress*, 1999; *Politics in America 2004: 108th Congress*, 2003; *Santa Fe New Mexican* A p1+ Oct. 22, 2006

Scott Eells/Getty Images

Winchester, Simon

Sep. 28, 1944– Writer; journalist

Address: c/o Author mail, Seventh Fl., HarperCollins Publishers, 10 E. 53d St., New York, NY 10022

When the British journalist and nonfiction writer Simon Winchester graduated from the University of Oxford, in 1966, he intended to pursue a career in geology. He worked briefly on oil rigs in the North Sea and as a prospector in Africa before discovering that he was "an extremely bad, incompetent geologist," as he told Michael J. Ybarra for the *Los Angeles Times* (April 24, 2004). While still in Africa, Winchester retreated to his tent one night to read James Morris's *Coronation Everest*, a book that chronicled Edmund Hillary and Tenzing Norgay's historic climb up the highest peak in the world. "I read this book, and instantly I knew this is what I wanted to do," Winchester told Yvonne Nolan for *Publishers Weekly* (August 27, 2001). "It was about going on adventures and then telling people back home about those adventures. I wrote to . . . Morris and said I've just read *Coronation Everest* and basically my question is, 'Can I be you?'" Morris replied, and following his advice, Winchester returned to England to work as a reporter, later establishing a name for himself by covering the conflicts between Protestant and Catholic militants in Northern Ireland. Over the next three decades, he reported on such historic events as the formation of Bangladesh, the Jonestown massacre, and the assassination of the Egyptian president Anwar Sadat. He also published such highly praised travelogues as *The Sun Never Sets: Travels to the Remaining Outposts of the British Empire*, *Korea: A Walk Through the Land of Miracles*, and *The River at the Center of the World: A Journey Up the Yangtze and Back in Chinese Time*. Pico Iyer, writing for the *New York Times Book Review* (April 28, 1991), described Winchester as an "exceptionally engaging guide, an intrepid English traveler of the old school, at home everywhere, ready for anything, full of gusto and a seemingly omnivorous curiosity."

Midway through his career Winchester began to worry that publishers would soon stop financing his far-flung travels, particularly since the sales for his books were generally disappointing. He thus began writing historical nonfiction. He pored over locked-away files and letters at Broadmoor, an English asylum for the criminally insane, and learned the intricacies of lexicography for *The Professor and the Madman: A Tale of Murder, Insanity, and the Making of the* Oxford English Dictionary, which, in 1998, catapulted Winchester to bestseller lists for the first time. He applied the same approach, the illumination of scientific history through biography, in *The Map That Changed the World: William Smith and the Birth of Modern Geology* and later revisited the topic that made him famous with *The Meaning of Everything: The Story of the* Oxford English Dictionary. In a review of the latter book for the *Wilson Quarterly* (Autumn 2003), Clive Davis declared that in the overcrowded field of historical nonfiction, "Winchester's unobtrusive erudition and droll turn of phrase set him apart from the rest of the journalistic pack." Winchester's most recent books—*Krakatoa: The Day the World Exploded, August 27, 1883* and *A Crack in the Edge of the World: America and the Great California Earthquake of 1906*—examine important geological events.

When Simon Winchester was born, on September 28, 1944 in London, England, to Bernard Winchester and the former Andrée de Wael, his father, a British soldier who had been captured on D-day, was languishing in a German prison camp. "I've often thought it must have been quite a strain for my father," Winchester told Nolan. "He'd had a miserable time in Braunschweig POW Camp. He presumably wanted to come back to a woman who would look after him and be nice and tender. Instead, there was this seven-month-old strapping baby. I was sent off to boarding school in Dorset at the age of five, and I often think that was just my father saying, 'Look, I want to just be with your mother, thank you. And you've already intruded too much into my life. So go away!'" When Winchester was 14, his father disappointed him by accepting a job in the U.S. and then backing out. Young Winchester was so determined to see America, however, that shortly after graduating from boarding school, he hitchhiked his way across North America, traveling as far north as Montreal, Canada, and as far south as Mexico City—spending only $18 in the process. "People were so kind," he told Ybarra. "I just adore this country. I love the geology of America." Later, in 1976, Winchester published the travelogue *American Heartbeat: Some Notes from a Midwestern Journey*.

When Winchester returned to England, he tried to join the British Royal Navy but was rejected due to his color blindness. He then enrolled at St. Catherine's College, at the University of Oxford. After earning an M.A. degree in geology, in 1966, he accepted a job prospecting for copper in the Ruwenzori Mountains in western Uganda. Following the advice of James Morris (who published books under the name Jan Morris after undergoing a sex-change operation, in 1972), Winchester returned to England and in 1967 took a job as a correspondent for the *Journal*, a small newspaper in Newcastle upon Tyne. In 1970 he was hired by the Manchester *Guardian* and sent to Northern Ireland to cover the increasingly frequent clashes between Protestant and Catholic militants. "Before Northern Ireland, I was no-one," Winchester told a reporter for *Sunday Life* (September 19, 2004). "And then I came and covered the beginnings of the story, and managed to survive it. For me it was a formative time as a journalist. It was an amazing story to cut my teeth on." His experiences there also served as the basis for his first book, *In Holy Terror: Reporting the Ulster Troubles*, which came out in England in 1974 and was published in the U.S. the following year as *Northern Ireland in Crisis: Reporting the Ulster Troubles*.

From 1972 to 1976 Winchester served as the *Guardian*'s correspondent in Washington, D.C., covering, among other things, the Watergate affair and the resignation of President Richard Nixon. After a stint reporting from New Delhi, India, from 1977 to 1979, he returned to Washington as the chief U.S. correspondent for the London *Daily Mail*. In 1980 the firm Faber and Faber was set to publish Winchester's second book, *Their Noble Lordships: The Hereditary Peerage Today*, an unflattering portrait of the upper ranks of British society, when writs filed by five noblemen—who claimed that the book contained factual errors—forced the publisher to recall and pulp the first edition. The revised edition, published in 1981, was largely praised by critics, especially for the humorous anecdotes Winchester had collected through his extensive interviews.

By the time the U.S. edition—which was published as *Their Noble Lordships: Class and Power in Modern Britain*—reached bookstores, in 1982, Winchester was serving time in an Argentinian prison. While covering the Falkland Islands War for the London *Sunday Times* (for which he had begun working as a feature writer the year before), he had been mistaken for a British spy. He was released after three months and detailed that experience in the book *Prison Diary, Argentina* (1983), which failed to impress most reviewers; Malcolm Deas, writing for the *Times Literary Supplement* (February 10, 1984), called it "an ephemeral, sentimental and frustrated book." In 1983 Winchester also published *Stones of Empire: The Buildings of the Raj*, a survey of British architecture in India and Pakistan, for which he supplied the photographs and captions and his mentor, Morris, wrote the text.

In the mid-1980s Winchester moved to Hong Kong, where he reported on the Pacific region for the London *Guardian*, among other publications, and conducted some of the research for his next book, *The Sun Never Sets* (1985; published as *Outposts* in Britain), a travelogue of his journeys to the remaining British colonies, including Bermuda, Gibraltar, and St. Helena. It took Winchester three years to visit nearly all of the populated lands still under British rule, and reviewers were delighted with his observations. Andrew Harvey, writing for the New York Times Book Review (June 1, 1986), termed The Sun Never Sets a "warm, superbly written book," which serves not only as "a vivid account of far-flung islands" but also as "a meditation, by turns funny, melancholic and mocking, on the decline of modern Britain."

In 1987 Winchester began writing books and freelance articles full-time, and the following year he published Korea. To research that account of the people and history of the Republic of Korea, he traversed the country from the southern tip of the peninsula to the North Korean border. In a review for the London Guardian (July 15, 1988), Ruth Grayson described the book as "immensely readable" and praised Winchester for his thorough research.

In Pacific Rising: The Emergence of a New World Culture (1991), Winchester argued that the primacy of the nations with coastlines along the Atlantic Ocean would soon fall to the increasing influence of those of the Pacific Rim. The peoples of the Pacific were beginning to experience "an inchoate, undefined sense of oneness, of coterminous identity," he wrote, according to a reviewer for the Economist (February 23, 1991). Noting that the author "goes to elegant, erudite and amusing lengths" to convey that sense of identity as well, the Economist reviewer nonetheless remained unconvinced: "The quarter or more of the world's population who live around the rim of the Pacific are too diverse to be cutely grouped as the 'Pacific man' in the 'Pacific century,' so readily defined by fund managers and futurologists." Pico Iyer, on the other hand, found that "the singular charm of the book" is that Winchester "has no time for dull geopolitical surveys or dutiful claims of cultural unity; instead, he simply assembles a colorful encyclopedia of facts, adventures and perspectives based on his travels," presented with "a storyteller's fluency and panache."

In 1992 Winchester published Pacific Nightmare: How Japan Starts World War III, A Future History, a speculative work in which a catastrophic war is sparked by the British handover of Hong Kong to the Chinese in 1997. Malcolm Bosse wrote for the New York Times Book Review (October 18 1992) that Pacific Nightmare "illustrates both the strengths and the weaknesses" of the future-history genre: "The author's reach for authenticity often leads to so much detail that the reader must wade through it. . . . And the book has no emotional focus, since no single character, either fictional or historical, takes center stage, not even for a few pages. But each event is closely reasoned, precisely delineated. The writing and thinking are never shoddy. Wonderfully odd bits of information dot the pages."

In 1994 Winchester—traveling by boat, car, train, plane, bus, and on foot—followed the course of the Yangtze River (also called the Changjiang), which originates in the highlands of Tibet and snakes across China, emptying into the Pacific Ocean. He chronicled his experiences in The River at the Center of the World (1996), examining what he described as the "delicious strangeness of China," as quoted by a reviewer for Publishers Weekly (September 16, 1996). "Wryly humorous, gently skeptical, immensely knowledgeable as he wends his way along the 3900 miles of the great river, Winchester provides an irresistible feast of detail about the character of the river itself, the landscape, the cities, villages and people along its banks . . . ," the reviewer wrote. "Winchester is comfortable with the country's long, complex history and politics, and he writes about them with an easy grace that defies the usual picture of China as an enigma wrapped in a conundrum."

Not long after Winchester had struck out on his own as a freelance writer, he began to fear that he might "slide into a middle age of extreme penury," as he told Ybarra. Though many of his books received positive reviews, their sales were dismal; one of his books reportedly sold only 11 copies. Then, as he told Dave Weich for the Powell's Books Web site, while reading Jonathon Green's Chasing the Sun: Dictionary-Makers and the Dictionaries They Made (1996), Winchester noticed an intriguing footnote: "Readers will of course be familiar with the story of W. C. Minor, the convicted, deranged, American lunatic murderer, contributor to the OED." No one before Winchester had thought to write a book about the relationship between James Murray, editor of the Oxford English Dictionary, and William C. Minor, an American expatriate and Civil War veteran who had contributed thousands of entries to the first edition of the dictionary while confined to an English asylum for the criminally insane.

Though Winchester's publisher at the time passed on the project and advised him to drop it, HarperCollins agreed to publish The Professor and the Madman (1998)—which proved to be his breakthrough. The book was a best-seller in both Britain and the U.S. and thus far has sold more than a million copies worldwide. The Professor and the Madman (which was published as The Surgeon of Crowthorne in Britain) also received many critical accolades. "This book is representative of a type seen frequently of late . . . ," Benjamin Griffith wrote for the Sewanee Review (Summer 1999). "Winchester's superb account of Murray's first visit to Broadmoor and the growing friendship between the two scholars is a high point." David Walton, writing for the New York Times Book Review (August 30, 1998), called it an "imaginative retelling of these two 'inextricably and most curiously entwined' lives." Winchester wrote about a greater number of people involved in the creation of the Oxford English Dictionary in The Meaning of Everything (2003), which was short-listed for a British Book Award for history book of the year. In reviewing it for the Los Angeles Times (October 19, 2003), Robert McCrum wrote that its subject was "perfectly suited to Winchester's magpie mind. Winchester's account is an affectionate and frankly partisan study of the making of a great dictionary. It is also an offbeat portrait of an extraordinary society."

Interviewing Winchester shortly after Mel Gibson's production company bought the film rights to *The Professor and the Madman*, Mel Gussow reported for the *New York Times* (September 7, 1998) that the author sounded like a "newly retired explorer." Winchester told Gussow, "I think the idea of settling down and writing books about strange episodes in history, which somehow illuminate something rather greater, would be a nice way to spend a life, if I can wean myself from travel." He seemed unable, however, to completely abandon his peripatetic ways, visiting the Kosovar refugee camps in Macedonia for his next book, *The Fracture Zone: A Return to the Balkans* (1999). Having traveled through the region decades earlier on a road trip from Vienna, Austria, to Istanbul, Turkey, he was shocked by the "Bruegel-scene of mass misery" he discovered in a once-peaceful country that was being torn apart by conflicts between the ethnic Macedonians and the Albanian minority, as quoted by a reviewer for *Publishers Weekly* (September 27, 1999). "Taking a fatalistic attitude," the reviewer continued, Winchester "views the region's problems as little more than the fruit of 'classic Balkan hatreds, ancient and modern.' Still, Winchester's extensive interviews make his book notable. Almost every page contains the reflections of ordinary citizens, who reveal to Winchester their hatreds, their troubles and their hopes, lending richness and authenticity to his account. His unsentimental descriptions of the area's destroyed mosques, burned houses and virulent graffiti serve as a poignant reminder that the effects of war last long after the planes are gone."

Winchester's next book, *The Map That Changed the World* (2001), tells the story of William Smith, a British canal digger who labored for 22 years to create the first geological map, which was published in 1815. Though Smith is now known as the father of modern geology, he lived in poverty and obscurity, receiving little recognition for his work, until 1831, when he received the Geological Society of London's highest award and a lifetime pension from the king. "Winchester's such a fine historian, journalist and stylist that he manages to make this whole genre (popular science history refracted through partial biography) seem absolutely new," Kathryn Hughes wrote for the *New Statesman* (July 2, 2001). Hughes also praised the author for pointing out that Smith's discoveries—which contradicted the biblical tale of creation—paved the way for the crisis of faith in the Victorian age.

In *Krakatoa* (2003), Winchester described the 1883 eruption of the eponymous volcano—which was so powerful that the force of the explosion altered the configuration of the Sunda Strait, and the flow of lava and shower of rock and ash resulted in the formation of new islands in the Indian Ocean. "*Krakatoa* is a trove of wonderfully arcane information," Janet Maslin wrote for the *New York Times* (April 25, 2003). "The author has been able to attach so many tentacles to a single event . . . that there seems to be nowhere he can't go. . . . This manner of amplifying science or history with odd, figurative footnotes has become extremely popular; just read a full-length book about salt, for example. But since *The Professor and the Madman* . . . Winchester has emerged as the leading practitioner of the method. He incorporates research that ranges far and wide, serving up both real and cocktail-party science. And all the while, in scattering these trails of bread crumbs, he keeps track of his story's central path."

While packing the research materials for *Krakatoa*, Winchester noticed that the event was often lumped together with such other great natural disasters as the 1906 earthquake that devastated San Francisco, California. Realizing that the centennial of that event was fast approaching, he set to work on *A Crack in the Edge of the World* (2005). As Bryan Burrough noted for the *New York Times Book Review* (October 9, 2005), Winchester's book "is not a straightforward account of the earthquake and subsequent fire but a first-person melange of geology textbook and travelogue grafted onto a recounting of the events that destroyed San Francisco 100 years ago," and though the text is accompanied by charts, maps, and a glossary, "they adorn sections mined with passages as impenetrable as bedrock."

Winchester continues to contribute articles to U.S. and British publications, among them *Harper's*, *Smithsonian*, *National Geographic*, the *Spectator*, *Granta*, the *New York Times*, and the *Atlantic Monthly*. He has also written for and hosted television documentaries and has frequently contributed to the BBC radio show *From Our Own Correspondent*. In 2006 Winchester was made an Officer of the Order of the British Empire (OBE) by the queen of England in a ceremony at Buckingham Palace.

Winchester, who has been married twice, has three children (four, according to some sources) from his first marriage. He owns an apartment in New York City, a cottage on the Scottish island of Luing, and a small farm in the Berkshires, in Massachusetts.

—S.Y.

Suggested Reading: *Boston Globe* D p8 Apr. 20, 2003; *Economist* p93 Feb. 23, 1991, p119 May 16, 1992; *New Statesman* p47 July 3, 1998; *New York Times* E p1 Sep. 7, 1998, E p9 Sep. 16, 1998, E p43 Apr. 25, 2003; *New York Times Book Review* p10 Apr. 28, 1991, p12 Aug. 30, 1998, p24 Dec. 5, 1999, p18 Oct. 9, 2005; *Newsday* B p9 Aug. 12, 2001; *Publishers Weekly* p44 Aug. 27, 2001; *Sewanee Review* p lxxiv Summer 1999; *Smithsonian* p156+ Apr. 1987; *Washington Post Book World* p6 Jan. 16, 2000

Selected Books: *Northern Ireland in Crisis: Reporting the Ulster Troubles*, 1975; *American Heartbeat: Some Notes from a Midwestern Journey*, 1976; *Their Noble Lordships: Class and Power in Modern Britain*, 1982; *Stones of Empire: The Buildings of the Raj* (with Jan Morris), 1983; *Prison Diary, Argentina*, 1983; *The Sun Never Sets: Travels to the Remaining Outposts of the British Empire*, 1985; *Korea: A Walk Through the Land of Miracles*, 1988; *Pacific Rising: The Emergence of a New World Culture*, 1991; *Small World* (with Martin Parr), 1995; *The River at the Center of the World: A Journey Up the Yangtze and Back in Chinese Time*, 1996; *The Professor and the Madman: A Tale of Murder, Insanity, and the Making of the Oxford English Dictionary*, 1998; *The Fracture Zone: A Return to the Balkans*, 1999; *The Map That Changed the World: William Smith and the Birth of Modern Geology*, 2001; *Krakatoa: The Day the World Exploded, August 27, 1883*, 2003; *The Meaning of Everything: The Story of the Oxford English Dictionary*, 2003; *A Crack in the Edge of the World: America and the Great California Earthquake of 1906*, 2005; fiction— *Pacific Nightmare: How Japan Starts World War III, A Future History*, 1992

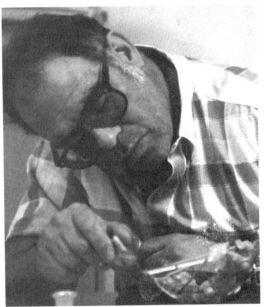

Courtesy of the University of Michigan

Wolpoff, Milford

Oct. 28, 1942– Paleoanthropologist

Address: 231 West Hall, University of Michigan, Ann Arbor, MI 48109

"The human population is best seen as a single, constantly evolving, interlinked species—like a moving stream linked by flows both in and out, of both genes and cultures," the paleoanthropologist Milford Wolpoff told Alison Shaw for the London *Independent* (September 9, 1997). Wolpoff, a professor of anthropology at the University of Michigan in Ann Arbor and an adjunct associate research scientist with the school's Museum of Anthropology, is best known as one of the architects of the Multiregional evolution theory of human development, which holds that human beings evolved as a single species throughout the globe and can count among their ancestors such hominids as *Homo erectus* and Neanderthals. According to *Race and Human Evolution: A Fatal Attraction* (1997), which he co-wrote with his second wife and colleague, Rachel Caspari, Wolpoff, "like most biological anthropologists of his generation, was steeped in the postwar credo that human races were arbitrary divisions of humanity." And after many years spent examining virtually the entire human and prehuman fossil record available in museums around the world, he became convinced that separate human populations could not have evolved in isolation—that distance and different environmental conditions account for variations among races and ethnicities.

Wolpoff's beliefs contrast greatly with those of the "Out of Africa" or "Eve" theorists, who trace humans back to one group of Africans, a new species that migrated outward 100,000 years ago, completely replacing *H. erectus*, Neanderthals, and other archaic humans. Both sides in the debate agree that early hominids—the family (*Hominidae*) of erect, bipedal primate mammals comprising recent humans together with extinct ancestral and related forms—appeared in Africa around five million years ago, and that there was an initial dispersal outward as early as two million years ago. The two sides, however, disagree as to whether human evolution occurred within one species, the one that spread throughout the world, or took place as one species replaced another. The question remains, as Wolpoff and Caspari put it, "Was the advent of humanity a single incident, like hominid origins when we parted from our last common ancestor with chimpanzees, or was it the culmination of many small changes that happened at different times and in different places? The Multiregional evolution hypothesis argues modernity was approached over a long time period as successful new features and behaviors appeared in different places and spread across the human range as people migrated or exchanged genes." Though recent analysis of mitochondrial DNA seems to bolster the Eve hypothesis, Wolpoff and his supporters still maintain, as Wolpoff and Caspari wrote, that "there was no singular event of modernization, no Rubicon to be crossed by widespread populations. Instead, [hominids'] continued contacts through migrations and mate exchanges created a network of genetic interchanges that linked even the most far-flung peoples."

Despite the current popularity of the Out of Africa theory, Wolpoff has said that future generations of scientists will understand why genetic and fossil data show it to be incorrect. Wolpoff and Caspari suggest that resistance to the Multiregional evolution theory is the result of the politics surrounding the concept of race. "If you ask the average person off the street, they'll tell you Out of Africa because it's easier to understand," Wolpoff told David Bricker for the *Michigan Daily* (November 4, 1997, on-line). "It's about 90 percent politics, and popular opinion is always behind the research."

Milford Howell Wolpoff was born on October 28, 1942 in Chicago, Illinois, to Ben Wolpoff and Ruth (Silver) Wolpoff. When he began his studies at the University of Illinois at Urbana-Champaign, he was a physics major; he later switched to anthropology, earning a B.A. degree in that field, with a minor in mathematics, in 1964. The following year, while pursuing his graduate studies at the same institution, he served as a research assistant to the noted anthropologist Eugene Giles (his graduate mentor and adviser) on a genetic analysis project in Ticul, Yucatán. During that time Wolpoff became fascinated with hominids known as australopithecines, who lived in southern and eastern Africa from six million years ago until roughly 1.5 million years ago. Although they possessed many ape-like features and relatively small brains, australopithecines walked upright and had near-human dentition. Wolpoff spent the final year of his graduate studies at the University of Wisconsin at Madison, studying australopithecines under the famous South African paleontologist John Robinson. According to Wolpoff and Caspari, "Robinson focused on the whole organism and believed there was much more to be learned from a few complete individuals than from piles of small fragments. . . . [Wolpoff] was more focused on the population and its attributes, which made him a reductionist (this also reflected his genetics training and the statistics forced on him as an undergraduate physics major), interested in the variation of features in samples that include few whole specimens. . . . He believed individuals could be best understood in this population context."

Wolpoff earned his doctorate in anthropology, with a double minor in archaeology and zoology, in 1969, submitting a dissertation entitled "Metric Trends in Hominid Dental Evolution." From 1968 to 1971 he was an assistant professor of anthropology at Case Western Reserve University, in Cleveland, Ohio. During that period he served as an associate curator at the Hamann-Todd Collection at the Cleveland Museum of Natural History. He began teaching in the Anthropology Department at the University of Michigan in 1971 and has remained there since.

From the late 1960s to the mid-1970s, Wolpoff supported a "single species hypothesis" of early human development, which ran counter to widely held theories at the time regarding early humans in southern Africa. Most scientists believed that there existed, in the period between three million and one million years ago, at least two species of early humans in southern Africa: *Australopithecus africanus* and *Paranthropus robustus*, whose fossils indicated that those two species co-existed in one place for a considerable length of time. Wolpoff believed that rather than representing two species, the differing fossils merely revealed normal population variation, relative differences due to size, and the sexual dimorphism—the differences in size and other characteristics between males and females of the same species—within a single species. (Over time he earned the nickname "the great American lumper," for his reluctance to designate recently discovered fossil finds as the remains of new species. "You see more variations in our own species on any street corner than you can see in some of these fossils," he told John Noble Wilford for an October 30, 1984 article for the *New York Times*.) Wolpoff argued that the *A. africanus* and *P. robustus* fossils could not represent two different species, because the fossil history of early humans had always shown that two ecologically similar species could not co-exist without entering into a struggle for existence in which one species became extinct. Nevertheless, the single species hypothesis was disproved in 1975, when *Homo ergaster* remains were found in the same layer of sediment as australopithecine remains, indicating that they were contemporaries.

Early in his career Wolpoff also studied sexual dimorphism as it had changed as humans evolved, noting that physiological differences between men and women not related to primary sex functions had decreased in human populations during recent millennia, perhaps following the invention of sophisticated weapons. In early hunter-gatherer societies, it was theorized, men's bigger muscles and quicker reactions better equipped them to hunt prey and respond to threats. Since the advent of advanced weapons, which made hunting less strenuous, it is believed, there has been a trend toward the feminization of males in the population, because, as Wolpoff told David Gelman for *Newsweek* (May 18, 1981), "the physical requirements of the male and female roles have become more similar."

In 1977, the same year he became a full professor at the University of Michigan, Wolpoff met Alan Thorne, an Australian paleoanthropologist, at the Eighth Pan-African Congress of Prehistory and Quaternary Studies, in Nairobi, Kenya. Thorne presented a paper, entitled "Center and Edge," which laid much of the foundation for what would later become Multiregionalism. When the conference ended, Wolpoff and Thorne stayed behind to examine the hominid remains in the National Museum of Kenya. The noted paleoanthropologist Richard Leakey also allowed them to examine the specimens—mostly australopithecine remains—that he and his colleagues had uncovered. The pair discovered that their interests—Wolpoff had focused on Neanderthal fossils, which have been found only in Europe, and Thorne on the origin of Australian Aborigines—complemented each other, particularly for the purpose of developing a broad theory of human origins, and they have continued to collaborate.

In early 1983 a debate broke out during a symposium held by the Institute of Human Origins, on hominid locomotion as it related to the relative limb lengths of Lucy, a famous *Australopithecus afarensis* fossil that is one of the most complete australopithecine skeletons ever found. William Jungers had suggested in "Lucy's Limbs: Skeletal Allometry and Locomotion in *Australopithecus afarensis*," an article published in the December 23, 1982 issue of *Nature*, that Lucy's relative limb lengths, when compared with those of modern humans and apes, indicate that while *A. afarensis* walked upright like human beings, their movements were less efficient. Wolpoff responded with "Lucy's Little Legs," a 1983 article published in the *Journal of Human Evolution*, in which he argued that though the legs of *Homo sapiens* were much longer than those of *A. afarensis*, the difference was proportional to the general increase in body size and therefore revealed nothing about the ancient species' efficiency in locomotion.

In 1984 Wolpoff and Thorne, along with a Chinese colleague, Wu Xinzhi, published their first detailed discussion of Multiregional evolution, in the anthology *Origins of Modern Humans*, which was edited by Fred Smith and Frank Spencer. By that time Wolpoff had established a reputation for making "frequent global expeditions [that had] brought him into contact with more original fossils secured in their home institutions than any other paleoanthropologist can boast," according to Roger Lewin in *Science* (May 4, 1984). That same year a judge in the Australian state of Victoria ordered the University of Melbourne to turn over its substantial collection of human remains—which contained fossils dating from as far back as 45,000 years, perhaps even 60,000 years ago—to Australian Aborigines, who felt that it was an affront to have the bodies of their ancestors held in laboratories and museums and wanted the remains returned for reburial. "If this decision goes through," Wolpoff told John Noble Wilford for the *New York Times* (July 24, 1984), "it will be an unmitigated tragedy. We're just beginning to recognize that Australia was the scene of an awful lot of evolutionary changes that affected east Asia and the islands of the region. If they bury all the evidence, we'll have nothing." While Wolpoff acknowledged that in the past anthropologists had engaged in such illicit practices as grave robbing to collect specimens, he emphasized the importance of re-

taining the fossils and, along with Thorne, rallied the support of other scientists to help the university retain its most crucial specimens. Ultimately all of the specimens were returned, but many have become available for continued scientific research under the control of their owners instead of museums and research laboratories.

The fossils at the University of Melbourne were of particular interest to Thorne and Wolpoff, who had collaborated in studies of a 30,000-year-old *H. erectus* fossil from China that, they noted, bore striking resemblances to Aboriginal fossils. While Thorne believed that the interbreeding of two different populations of early humans from Indonesia and China had led to the emergence of the modern Aborigines, Wolpoff took a more skeptical stance and considered past and present native Australian variation to be normal for a widespread population divided into small groups. However, he said that he believed that Thorne's assertion might be proven correct, and if so, "it will give us the first confirmed case of mixture between peoples coming from two different geographic origins," Wolpoff told Wilford for the July 24, 1984 *New York Times* article. "It will give us a model that we can apply to other places where we think that migration might have been important in evolution." Such a revelation, Wolpoff hoped, would reopen the argument about whether Neanderthals had interbred, as he told Wilford: "Arguments about what happened to the Neanderthals are just unending. One reason is that nobody really knows what would happen to a population in an area if there were persistent migrations coming from [someplace] else."

Wolpoff's confidence in Thorne's assertion grew to the point that, in a 1988 press interview, he used his colleague's conclusions about the origins of Aborigines as an example to refute the biochemist Allan C. Wilson's recently developed Mitochondrial Eve hypothesis. In 1987 a team from the University of California at Berkeley had analyzed genetic variations in the mitochondrial DNA of 147 women from populations in Africa, Asia, Europe, and elsewhere. Mitochondrial DNA, or mtDNA, is passed only through the maternal line and changes more quickly than nuclear DNA. The study found little variation in the DNA of the different groups, which supported the idea of a single recent origin for all modern humans. The DNA evidence seemed to indicate the existence of a "Mitochondrial Eve" from whom all modern humans descended—one woman who lived in Africa 140,000 to 280,000 years ago. "If the molecular evidence is correct, then the fossils become inexplicable," Wolpoff told Roger Lewin for *Science* (September 11, 1987). "But I believe the fossil evidence shows that the molecular biology is being wrongly interpreted. . . . They have calibrated the mutation rate incorrectly. With a much slower rate they would get a time of origin of 850,000 years ago, which I believe is correct." As Wolpoff told *Current Biography*, scientists later realized that because mitochondria play such an important role in metabolism, the development of those organelles (specialized components of cells) has been heavily influenced by natural selection, and therefore it is not possible to determine reliably, by examining mitochondrial DNA, when species diverged from one another.

In March 1988 the noted paleontologist and evolutionary biologist Stephen Jay Gould wrote an article for his regular column in *Natural History* titled "Honorable Men and Women," which ran with the subtitle, "Human unity is no idle political slogan or tenet of mushy romanticism." Commenting on a recent excavation in Israel, Gould accepted evidence, extracted from that site, that modern humans and Neanderthals lived in close proximity—but, he wrote, as quoted by Wolpoff and Caspari, the species "maintained their integrity without interbreeding." Wolpoff and his colleagues not only felt that the evidence did not support Gould's assertion but also saw the essay as an attack in which the Multiregional theory was "implicitly placed on the politically incorrect side of the stands." "Gould's essays invariably have a not-so-hidden agenda; it is one of the things that makes him such an interesting writer," Wolpoff and Caspari wrote. "The agenda here was not about Neanderthals, or even about punctuated equilibrium [a theory of Gould's], but about the moral implications of the Eve theory. . . . Gould was addressing the issue of human unity." It became evident to Wolpoff and Caspari, after the publication of that article, that some nonscientists saw the pair's stance as one that served a racist agenda by somehow indicating that the different races actually consisted of separate species. Wolpoff has stressed that "regional lineages were not like different species," as he told Shaw, because "there were also genetic and cultural exchanges between them." Thus no "race" (the term itself implies a more homogenous group than would exist under Wolpoff's model) could be more or less evolved than another. "Gould, in his assertions, had incorrectly assumed that Multiregional evolution was about *independent* evolution, when it was really about continued contacts between all human populations," Wolpoff told *Current Biography*. "We wondered what model of human evolution could better show human unity than the one based on constant human mixture, whenever people met or maintained relations."

Wolpoff and Caspari examined the history of the divisive debate over the origins of race in their book *Race and Human Evolution*, which was published in 1997. In it, they discussed past biological and anthropological schools of thought that shared some of Multiregionalism's tenets. Along with defending Multiregionalism and attacking the interpretations of the mitochondrial DNA evidence that bolstered the Eve hypothesis, the book offered lighthearted accounts of Wolpoff and Caspari's trips to Africa and Eurasia to study fossils. "Despite its intermittent forays into the lighter side of paleoanthropology, this is a book that needs to be taken seriously and read with care," Marvin Harris wrote in a review for the *Washington Post* (December 29, 1996). For *Race and Human Evolution*, Wolpoff and Caspari were awarded the W. W. Howells Book Prize in Biological Anthropology, presented by the Biological Anthropology Section of the American Anthropological Association.

On the strength of a 2000 study using anthropological, archaeological, and genetic evidence, Wolpoff and the anthropologist John Hawks reported that the first modern humans had indeed appeared two million years ago when a group of australopithecines manifested changes in behavior as well as brain and body size. Behavioral changes were revealed by archaeological evidence suggesting new patterns of hunting and gathering. Viewing the evidence as being consistent with their Multiregionalist stance, the authors argued that it represented the original appearance of *Homo sapiens*—direct ancestors of modern humans. They found no genetic or anthropological data to contradict the notion that the migrations of two million years ago were made by early humans. "It was the act of becoming humans that made these colonizations possible," Hawks was quoted as saying in an unsigned article for Ascribe Newswire (January 10, 2000).

As Multiregionalism's most vocal defender, Wolpoff has been quoted or cited in the *New York Times*, *Newsweek*, *New Scientist*, and *Discover*, among other publications. He is the author of the definitive textbook *Paleoanthropology*, which was published in 1980 and in revised form in 1999, and he has appeared regularly on television programs on PBS and the Discovery Channel. From 1973 to 1982 he served on the editorial board of the *Journal of Human Evolution*, and since 2002 he has served on the editorial board of *PaleoAnthropology*. He has received grants for his overseas research from the National Science Foundation, the National Academy of Sciences, and the Committee on Scholarly Communication with the People's Republic of China.

Wolpoff and Caspari have two children.

—M.B.

Suggested Reading: Ascribe Newswire (on-line) Jan. 10, 2000; (London) *Independent* N p8, Sep. 9, 1997; *Michigan Daily* (on-line) Nov. 4, 1997; *New Scientist* p2626 Apr. 14, 2001; *New York Times* C p1+ July 24, 1984, C p1+ Oct. 30, 1984, C p1+ Feb. 4, 1992; *Newsweek* p72 May 18, 1981; *Science* p477+ May 4, 1984, p1295 Sep. 11, 1987; *Washington Post* X p1+ Dec. 29, 1996

Selected Books: *Race and Human Evolution: A Fatal Attraction* (with Rachel Caspari), 1997

Courtesy of Kimberley S. Young

Young, Kimberly S.

1966(?)– Psychologist; writer; educator

Address: Center for Online Addiction, P.O. Box 72, Bradford, PA 16701

In 1994 Kimberly S. Young got a phone call from a friend who wanted to discuss a problem. The friend felt that her husband was spending too much time in chat rooms and was having on-line affairs that were threatening their marriage. Additionally, he was paying $350 a month in subscription fees to on-line services. Young, who was then a postdoctoral fellow at the Strong Memorial Hospital in Rochester, New York, began to wonder if it were possible to become addicted to the Internet in the same manner that some people are addicted to drugs, alcohol, sex, or gambling. She promptly launched a three-year study of the topic and compiled the results in a best-selling book entitled *Caught in the Net: How to Recognize the Signs of Internet Addiction—and a Winning Strategy for Recovery* (1998). Young also founded the Internet-based Center for Online Addiction (COLA), in 1995, and has since published another book, *Tangled in the Web: Understanding Cybersex from Fantasy to Addiction* (2001). As one of the most prominent researchers and authors in the relatively new field of Internet addiction, Young remains a controversial figure, alternately heralded as a pioneer and condemned as an alarmist.

Young was born in about 1966 and grew up near Buffalo, New York. She initially planned to pursue a career in business; she received her bachelor's degree in business administration, with concentrations in finance and management information sys-

tems, from the School of Management at the State University of New York (SUNY) at Buffalo in 1988. After graduation, she became a systems analyst for the Consortium of Precision Industries on Long Island, New York. While she held that position (from 1988 to 1990), Young also worked as a psychological associate for SUNY's Marital Therapy Clinic in Stony Brook, New York. In 1991 she obtained her master's degree in clinical psychology at Indiana University of Pennsylvania, in Indiana, Pennsylvania, and in 1994 she received her doctorate in behavioral medicine. During that period she worked as an outpatient therapist at the Western Psychiatric Institute and Clinic at the University of Pittsburgh School of Medicine, in Pennsylvania (in 1991), at the Center for Applied Psychology at the Indiana University of Pennsylvania (from 1990 to 1992), and at the Pain Evaluation and Treatment Institute at the University of Pittsburgh School of Medicine (1992). Young also worked as a psychological associate at the Harmarville Rehabilitation Center in Pittsburgh (from 1992 to 1993), at the same time that she served as an adjunct professor in the Psychology Department at the Indiana University of Pennsylvania. She then moved to Cleveland, Ohio, where she interned at both the Cleveland Clinic Foundation and the Cleveland Department of Veterans Affairs Medical Center. Upon receiving her doctorate in psychology, Young reportedly wanted to relocate to be closer to her ailing father in Buffalo, so in 1994 she joined the staff of Strong Memorial Hospital in Rochester as a postdoctoral fellow and taught at the University of Rochester School of Medicine.

When approached about her friend's aforementioned marital woes, Young decided to survey other computer users to determine if it were possible to become addicted to the Internet. She advertised on-line and posted fliers on college campuses, asking respondents to complete on-line surveys, which she conducted from 1994 to 1996. Of the 496 survey responses she received, Young eventually concluded that 396 were from addicts whose average weekly Internet usage was 38 hours. The consequences of such an addiction, she alleged, could include damaged relationships, depression, debt, anxiety, secretive behavior, and child neglect or endangerment. "Impairment to real life relationships appears to be the number one problem caused by Internet Addiction," she told S. J. Ross for the *Toronto Star* (May 21, 1998). "Marriages, dating relationships, parent-child relationships, and close friendships are . . . disrupted by excessive use of the Internet." She found on-line role-playing games and chat-room discussions to be particular sources of trouble, as such anonymous interactions with numerous faceless individuals allow Internet users to engage in on-line affairs and adopt different personas, sometimes at the expense of their real lives and relationships. "The fantasy component is fine in limited quantity, but when you start living the fantasy, prefer the fantasy, that's when the problems start," Young told Linton Weeks for the *Washington Post* (July 10, 1997).

In response to her findings, Young launched the Center for Online Addiction (COLA), in 1995. Through the organization's Web site, she offered surveys that people could take to determine whether or not they were addicts, information about Internet addiction, support groups, and, for a fee, counseling sessions. (In 1995 a 60-minute phone or on-line consultation with Young cost $30; by 2005 the fee had risen to $95.) After presenting her survey findings at the annual American Psychological Association conference in Toronto, Canada, in 1996, Young returned home to find nearly 100 messages from journalists on her desk. "A lot of people said 'you're juxtaposing a term like the Internet, which is so positive in our culture, with addiction, which was so negative,'" she told Tracey Drury for *Buffalo Business First* (February 16, 2004). "I didn't realize the magnitude of what I was doing."

In 1998 the publisher John Wiley & Sons brought out Young's *Caught in the Net*. Among mental-health professionals, reactions to the book varied greatly. "Kimberly S. Young is either a fearless pioneer or the Chicken Little of cyberspace," Vincent Kiernan wrote for the *Chronicle of Higher Education* (May 29, 1998). "It depends on whom you ask—and on what they think about the Internet." Many psychiatrists, including Ivan Goldberg, who had coined the term Internet addiction—as a joke—considered the very idea that someone could develop an addiction to the Internet invalid and unproven. Arlette Lefebvre, a staff psychiatrist at the Toronto, Canada, Hospital for Sick Children, told S. J. Ross, "Lots and lots of people have trouble moderating and controlling different aspects of their daily behavior, but we don't necessarily jump the gun and label this persistent habit as an addiction. . . . It's really tempting to dismiss as addictions the passions which we do not share or understand." Lefebvre and other critics objected to Young's methodology, citing the fact that participants in her study were volunteers. "Any scientific paper or study which relies exclusively upon voluntary responses to newspaper and Web advertisements for feedback has got to be a bit sloppy in design," Lefebvre told Ross. Malcolm R. Parks, an associate professor of speech communication at the University of Washington, questioned the accuracy of Young's survey, telling Kiernan that it counted "things as addiction that cannot be counted as addiction." Young replied that the criteria in her test had been modeled after the symptoms used by mental-health professionals to identify alcoholics and compulsive gamblers. Some critics complained that few of Young's articles had been published in peer-reviewed scholarly journals.

Regardless of the criticism Young has received, *Caught in the Net* became a best-seller and was translated into six languages. With the success of her book, Young has frequently served as an expert on the topic of Internet addiction in the print and broadcast media; she has appeared on ABC's *World News Tonight* and *Good Morning America* and

CNBC's *MarketWatch*, among other programs. She has published numerous articles about on-line abuse, has served as an expert witness in several state and federal cases, and is a frequent lecturer and consultant. Young serves on the editorial board of the publication *CyberPsychology & Behavior* and is the editor of *CyberHealth Newsletter*. Her second book, *Tangled in the Web: Understanding Cybersex from Fantasy to Addiction* (2001), offers a seven-step plan for dealing with Internet addictions.

Young earned a certificate in Web development from the University of Pittsburgh in 2000 and has since interwoven her interests in psychology, teaching, and business. She left the staff of the University of Pittsburgh in 2000 and, in 2002, assumed her present position as an associate professor in the department of management sciences at St. Bonaventure University School of Business, in St. Bonaventure, New York. She is a member of the American Psychological Association, Eastern Psychological Association, Pennsylvania Psychological Association, Employee Assistance Professionals Association, and National Council for Sexual Addiction and Compulsivity and a founding member of the International Society for Mental Health Online. In 2000 she received the Alumni Ambassador Award from the Indiana University of Pennsylvania, and in 2001 and 2004 she received the Psychology in the Media Award from the Pennsylvania Psychological Association. Young has been married since 1997 to James E. O'Mara. The couple have no children.

—K.J.E.

Suggested Reading: Center for Online Addiction Web site; *Chronicle of Higher Education* A p25 May 29, 1998; *Pittsburgh Post-Gazette* B p1 May 7, 1998; *Toronto Star* J p1 May 21, 1998, with photo

Selected Books: *Caught in the Net: How to Recognize the Signs of Internet Addiction—and a Winning Strategy for Recovery*, 1998; *Tangled in the Web: Understanding Cybersex from Fantasy to Addiction*, 2001

Zittel, Andrea

1965– Artist

Address: Andrea Rosen Gallery, 525 W. 24th St., New York, NY 10011

"My urge to simplify and pare things down is about creating a psychological state," the artist Andrea Zittel told Ariella Budick for *Newsday* (January 22, 2006). "We're encouraged to correct our lives by consuming instead of removing. . . . The best product you can buy is a black plastic trash bag.

Courtesy Andrea Rosen Gallery, New York

Andrea Zittel

Put everything in it and get rid of it." Zittel has won accolades for such ultra-functional creations as her uniforms for daily living, rock-shaped furniture, and portable living spaces, reflections of her continuing effort to simplify her own life and surroundings. Though some critics have suggested that her work—which is often compared to that which emerged from the early-20th-century Bauhaus school of architecture and applied arts—would be better classified as industrial design, others feel that Zittel creates designs made not to fit most lifestyles but to encourage an alternative way of living. "I have been using the arena of my life and day-to-day activities as a site for exploration and experimentation . . . ," Zittel has said, according to the Smithsonian American Art Collection Web site. "I often use my own experiences to try to construct an understanding of the world at large. . . . I am interested in how qualities which we feel are totally concrete and rational are really subjective, arbitrary or invented. Since I think that 'Art' is often seen as an area of expertise, a field requiring a vast body of knowledge in order to understand, I hope that my work ultimately bridges the most basic human concerns with those of contemporary artistic concerns." Zittel's distinctive, multipurpose creations have been showcased in more than 100 group exhibitions (including the prestigious Whitney Biennial in 1995 and 2004) and many solo shows, including two mid-career retrospectives in 2006—Andrea Zittel: Small Liberties at the Whitney Museum of American Art at Altria, in New York City, and Andrea Zittel: Critical Spaces, which toured nationally.

Andrea Zittel was born in Escondido, California, in 1965 to Miriam and Gordon Zittel, who were both schoolteachers. When she was young her family lived on a street that had only one other house, but by the time she reached high school, the Zittels' home was surrounded by tract housing. "Growing up in a community that's growing so rapidly really instilled a fear of growth," she told Scott Timberg for the *Los Angeles Times* (December 14, 2002). "You have no control over it at all. I think I wanted a place small enough that I could have some control over the way the entire community developed." She learned to appreciate solitude early on, as her parents often left her at home alone to take extended trips on their houseboat. After graduating from high school, she enrolled as a business major at San Diego State University, where the environment—which Timberg described as "one long frat party . . . which she had no interest in attending"—added to her sense of alienation. She also found her business classes devoid of intellectual stimulation. She changed her major to painting and sculpture after a college field trip to the Temporary Contemporary galleries (now called Geffen Contemporary), a division of the Museum of Contemporary Art in Los Angeles, where she first saw Al Ruppersberg's photographs depicting everyday life. After graduating with a B.F.A. degree, in 1988, Zittel attended the Rhode Island School of Design, in Providence, earning an M.F.A. degree in 1990.

Zittel then moved to the New York City borough of Brooklyn. Noticing the debris left out on the street curb for garbage collectors, she began taking home such broken and discarded objects as crockery and statuettes and fixing them, as part of her project Repair Work (1991). She found a job at the Pat Hearn Gallery; the pay was only $17,000 a year, and Zittel, who was required to dress professionally, felt at a loss to obtain appropriate attire. "Just getting dressed became so complicated—what you wear and what that means," Zittel wrote in the catalog for Andrea Zittel: Critical Space, as quoted by Molly Glentzer in the *Houston Chronicle* (December 21, 2005). "I started thinking of how complicated it was to have different outfits every day." Instead, she thought, having a uniform of sorts, a simple dress that she could wear daily and easily accessorize for various occasions, "would be much more liberating." Her first outfit, A–Z Six-Month Personal Uniform (1991), was a mid-length black wool jumper, which she wore every day for half a year. She later created a line of other, similarly austere black jumpers and also skirts. As an artist interested in function as much as form, Zittel regarded her daily wear of such uniforms as an active exhibition of her art. "The uniform is a reaction against a consumer capitalist culture that brainwashes people to think that constant variety is a form of freedom," she told Ariella Budick. "Coming up with the uniform was a conceptual exercise, but it was also a gift to myself." Over time she expanded her range of uniforms to include a greater assortment of colors and forms, comprising a collection she called A–Z Personal Panel Uniforms (1995–98). After 1998 she further simplified her line with the A–Z Single Strand Uniforms, which she crocheted rather than sewed, because, as she told Glentzer, "it required the least number of implements possible, a single crochet hook." Zittel did away with the hook when she learned how to crochet using just her fingers. With time she eliminated even the yarn; her latest creations are seamless felt made from organic, unprocessed woolen fibers.

Zittel experimented with other forms of expressions that challenged the traditional concept of art, breeding animals, for example, in her cramped, 200-square-foot apartment (actually a storefront) in the Williamsburg section of Brooklyn. "I was trying to design my own breed of chickens . . . ," she told Timberg. "I jokingly referred to it as the designer pet of the '90s—like pot-bellied pigs in the '80s or miniature horses in the '70s." She bred other animals as well, including quails, and in order to squeeze her expanding menagerie into her tiny apartment, she designed what she called Management and Maintenance Units, which held everything she needed to care for each animal.

Though Zittel's breeding experiments ended when the local board of health intervened, the Management and Maintenance Units inspired the creation of what later became her signature work. "Because my space was so tiny, and there was so much going on in it, it was always a real mess. One day I decided to make a unit for myself to simplify and consolidate my own life," she explained to Dave Freak for the Birmingham (England) Evening Mail (November 23, 2001). The unit, a box-like room with built-in amenities (a desk, a bench, a bed, etc.), became, Zittel told Dave Freak, "my first Living Unit, which I used to refer to as 'a little nucleus of perfection' which could be transported to comfort and protect me no matter what sort of larger environment I might live in." Using her apartment as a testing ground, she created other collapsible, transportable, multifunctional units; one of those early pieces, A–Z Management and Maintenance Unit, Model 003 (1992), consisted of a sink, cooking and dining area, and sleeping loft tucked into a roughly seven-by-eight-by-six-foot space. She exhibited some of the Living Units in her first solo exhibit, at the Jack Hanley Gallery in San Francisco in 1993.

As Zittel designed, developed, and utilized ever more units and functional accessories in her Brooklyn home, she christened her entire apartment A–Z (since renamed A–Z East). The name was born of necessity, as she recalled to Jori Finkel for the New York Times (September 25, 2005): When she called manufacturers to buy supplies for her projects, Zittel's "Southern California mall-girl twang" presented a problem, as salespeople "wanted to know who I was calling for. I would say 'me' and they'd basically hang up." She began attributing her requests to "A–Z Administrative Services"

instead and instantly commanded respect. Zittel expanded her range to include what she called Carpet Furniture (carpets woven with patterns that look like floor plans) and a line of household furniture and accessories, which were displayed in a 1993 solo show, titled A–Z Carpet Furniture, at the Christopher Grimes Gallery, in Santa Monica, California. Later that year the Andrea Rosen Gallery presented Purity, Zittel's first solo show in New York City; it featured 10 of her Living Units. Reviewing the exhibition for Art in America (June 1994), Jerry Saltz wrote, "Everything Zittel makes seems nearly sanitary yet not quite disinfected, which is nice. Her materials . . . feel modest and somehow egalitarian. The finished products are a little rickety and not quite perfect—not produced. They evoke the do-it-yourself experimentalism of modern design of the teens or the '20s." While acknowledging that he was "really attracted to Zittel's monkish, pared-down esthetic," Saltz admitted that he was disappointed with the show: "The problem is that . . . her work suggests a premodern condition without plumbing, toilets, zippers or buttons. Zittel questions everything, so you start to, too, which is good; she can really make you think about how you live your life. However she's not only provocative but controlling: she seems to say, 'This is the way you should live your life.' She also leaves you puzzling over whether her objects are as functional as she claims they are. Zittel is definitely a force to be reckoned with, but here her zealotry got in the way of her wonderfully quirky, immaculate poetry."

In 1998 Zittel used a grant from the Danish government to create A–Z Pocket Property, a 54-ton concrete island that floated off the coast of Denmark. "The A-Z Pocket Property combines your three most important possessions, your plot of land, your home and your vehicle into a hybrid prototype product," according to Zittel's Web site. "It is designed as a place with a unique potential for security, autonomy and independence." When the project was completed, in the summer of 2000, Zittel and some of her friends briefly inhabited the hollow interior of the island. "It's a fantastic idea—Huck Finn's raft meets a Robinson Crusoe RV," Kelly Klaasmeyer wrote for the Houston Press (October 20, 2005). The filmmaker Joachim Hamou, collaborating with Zittel, recorded the experiences of the island's inhabitants and produced the documentary Gollywobler (2000).

About two years earlier, Zittel had moved back to California—though she still retained ownership of A–Z East—and the confusion and disorder created by her move inspired her to create A–Z Raugh Furniture (1998). The two gray, rock-like formations that dominated the exhibit space at the Andrea Rosen Gallery were designed to comfortably accommodate people in sitting or reclining poses. Zittel told Patricia Leigh Brown for the New York Times (August 29, 2002) that she had initially developed the idea for the Raugh (pronounced "raw") furniture line while dating a slovenly man: "He was large and messy and broke all the furniture." Unable to "A-Z [her] boyfriend," Zittel began working on designs that would camouflage dirt and continue to look beautiful as they deteriorated. Though Gregory Volk, writing for *Art in America* (December 1998), called the Raugh furniture that was on display at Rosen's gallery "startlingly comfortable," Ken Johnson, writing for the *New York Times* (June 19, 1998), deemed it "an interesting but disappointing change" from Zittel's usual work: "This sprawling environment of simulated rock made of gray foam rubber, with old books, magazines and newspapers all around, is like a grungy zoo space for humans (or literate apes)."

The following year, 1999, Zittel exhibited her first public projects in the U.S., A–Z Point of Interest and A–Z Deserted Islands, both of which were commissioned by New York City's Public Art Fund. Located at Doris C. Freedman Plaza, which serves as an entrance to Central Park, the former of the two works was composed of two giant, faux rocks that mimicked outcroppings found within the park. A–Z Deserted Islands, originally designed for the 1997 Münster Sculpture Project, in Germany, featured a number of small, white, fiberglass islands, each equipped with a single padded seat, that floated in the pond adjacent to Freedman Plaza. Also in 1999 Zittel produced Free Running Rhythms and Patterns, a work inspired by a 168-hour period during which she isolated herself from "external" time by blocking out all natural sunlight and removing the television, radio, and all clocks from her residence. "Working from a video recording of the activities that filled this weeklong experiment," Stephanie Cash wrote for *Art in America* (April 1, 2006), "still images from which are interspersed on [27 mixed-media] panels, she used differently colored horizontal bars to indicate the amount of time she spent working, sleeping, cooking, cleaning, walking, brushing her teeth, etc. As the days pass, the breakdown in circadian time and her daily routine becomes apparent. For example, her sleeping pattern becomes erratic, with spurts of activity at 5 a.m. or mid-afternoon naps. . . . Interestingly, instead of feeling liberated by the lack of structured time, Zittel says she felt the pressure to constantly work . . . because, unable to track her progress, she was afraid that she was running out of time. Which illustrates another example of something she knows for sure: 'Things that we think are liberating can ultimately become restrictive, and things that we initially think are controlling can sometimes give us a sense of comfort and security.'"

In 2000 Zittel moved into a 700-square-foot, 1930s-era homesteader's cabin in the desert near Joshua Tree National Park, in California. She has traced her affinity for the desert to her frequent childhood visits to her grandparents' home in a nearby valley and moved to that locale largely for the space it offered. She immediately fashioned her new home into an artwork-in-progress and has dubbed it A–Z West. She has also opened her home

(and the 80 acres of desert on which it sits) to a steady stream of artists, and along with the artist Lisa Anne Auerbach, the collector Andy Stillpass, the art dealer Shaun Regen, and the curator John Connelly, she began an annual art "happening" called High Desert Test Sites, in which established and emerging artists create large, experimental artworks located in random spots in the desert. Julia Chaplin noted in the *New York Times* (April 21, 2006) that Zittel thus helped to begin a migration of architects, artists, musicians, screenwriters, and other creative types to the area, which now boasts a "full-fledged" art scene "hidden among the cactus, creosote and tract housing."

Inspired by the hundreds of tiny, abandoned shacks that dot the desert landscape—the result of a government policy from the early 20th century that granted free land to anyone who could "improve" it by constructing a homestead structure—Zittel produced the A–Z 2001 Homestead Unit. At less than 120 square feet, the unit, which is portable, is technically designated a temporary structure, and therefore does not require any building permits. During the same period Zittel also developed A–Z Wagon Stations, single-occupant shelters inspired by station wagons and covered wagons, and A–Z Cellular Compartment Units (2001), which she described on her Web site as "a cross between a modern apartment building and an elegant cabinet system."

In 2002 Zittel published *Diary #01*, the debut volume of Tema Celeste Editions, a series published by the multimedia group Gabrius, "in which contemporary artists use the model of a personal diary to interweave tales and conversation about their artistic practice," according to the e-flux Web site. The book details the development of Zittel's philosophy and contains photographs of her floating-island project in Denmark and her experimental habitat in the California desert.

Zittel applies the same organization to her daily life that she prizes in her work, sometimes dividing her days into two-hour chunks dedicated to such activities as exercise, work, reading, and correspondence. Since her boyfriend, David, moved into E–Z West, and their son, Emmett, was born, in 2004, she has not completely adapted her customarily super-organized lifestyle to the new arrangements.

Zittel is currently serving as an assistant professor at the Roski School of Fine Arts at the University of Southern California, in Los Angeles. She has also taught at Columbia University, in New York City, and Yale University, in New Haven, Connecticut. She has received many awards, including a 1995 fellowship from the German Academic Exchange Service (DAAD) and the 2005 Lucelia Artist Award, a $25,000 grant given annually by the Smithsonian American Art Museum to a leading American artist under the age of 50.

—K.J.E.

Suggested Reading: Andrea Zittel's A–Z Web Site; *Art in America* p124+ Apr. 1, 2006; *Los Angeles Times* V p1 Dec. 14, 2002; *New York Times* F p1 Aug. 29, 2002, II p36 Sep. 25, 2005; *Newsday* C p19 Jan. 22, 2006

Selected Works: Repair Work, 1991; A-Z Six-Month Personal Uniform, 1991; A-Z Management and Maintenance Unit, Model 003, 1992; A-Z Body Processing Unit, 1993; A-Z Personal Panel Uniforms, 1995–98; A-Z Escape Vehicles, 1996; A-Z Deserted Islands, 1997; A-Z Raugh Furniture, 1998; A-Z Point of Interest, 1999; Free Running Rhythms and Patterns, 1999; A-Z Pocket Property, 2000; A-Z 2001 Homestead Unit, 2001; A-Z Cellular Compartment Units, 2001

Selected Books: *Andrea Zittel: Personal Programs* (with Jan Avgikos and Zdenek Felix), 2001; *Diary #01*, 2002

Obituaries

Written by Kieran Dugan

ALLYSON, JUNE Oct. 7, 1917–July 8, 2006 Actress. Allyson is best remembered as a sweet-faced, husky-voiced movie star of the 1940s and 1950s who projected a sunny persona, especially in roles as the perfect girlfriend or wife. Of German and Dutch descent, Allyson was born Ella Geisman in the Bronx, New York City. When she was eight years old she suffered a bicycle accident that crippled her to the extent that physicians thought she might never walk again. A major contributing factor in her recovery was her aspiration to become a dancer/actress in emulation of Ginger Rogers. She made her first professional appearances in Broadway musicals, at first as a chorus girl, dancing in *Sing Out the News* in 1938 and *Very Warm for May* and *Higher and Higher* during the following two years. In the musical *Panama Hattie*, which opened in October 1940, she understudied Betty Hutton as Florrie, substituted for an ill Hutton in five performances, and was subsequently given a specialty dance in the show. In *Best Foot Forward* (1941–42) she had a featured speaking/dancing/singing ingenue role, which she reprised in the 1943 Metro-Goldwyn-Mayer screen adaptation. Under contract to MGM she was a specialty singer in several motion pictures before winning the lead role of Patsy Deyo in the musical *Two Girls and a Sailor* (1944). She achieved star billing in her first dramatic screen role, that of Barbara Ainsworth in *Music for Millions* (1944), and she went on to other starring or co-starring film roles, including that of Martha Canford Chandler, the demure younger sister in the period musical *Two Sisters from Boston* (1946), Penny Adams, the father-fixated adolescent in the psychological drama *The Secret Heart* (1946), Martha Teryton, the prim and proper New England schoolteacher in the comedy *The Bride Goes Wild* (1948), and Jo March in *Little Women* (1949). For her performance as Cynthia Potter in *Too Young to Kiss* (1951), she won a Golden Globe Award. She was cast as the steadfast wife opposite James Stewart in *The Stratton Story* (1949), *The Glenn Miller Story* (1953), and *Strategic Air Command* (1955), William Holden in *Executive Suite* (1954), and Alan Ladd in *The McConnell Story* (1955). Against type, she played Ann Downs, the malevolent wife of the José Ferrer character, in *The Shrike* (1955). She made a total of some 40 movies, including *Her Highness and The Bellboy* (1945), *The Sailor Takes a Wife* (1945), *High Barabaree* (1947), *The Reformer and the Redhead* (1950), *The Girl in White* (1950), *Remains to Be Seen* (1953), *The Opposite Sex* (1956), *A Stranger in My Arms* (1959), and *They Only Kill Their Masters* (1972). Her radio credits included roles in dramas on *Hallmark Playhouse* and *Lux Radio Theatre*. On the CBS television network, she hosted and occasionally starred in episodes of the half-hour dramatic anthology *The June Allyson Show*, also known as *The Dupont Show Starring June Allyson*, from 1959 to 1961. That show was produced by Four Star Films, co-founded by Dick Powell, her first husband. Her other television credits included appearances in some of the dramas in the half-hour series *The Dick Powell Show* (NBC, 1961–63) and in episodes of *The Love Boat* and *Murder, She Wrote*. In a return to the Broadway stage, she was top-billed in *Forty Carats* in 1970, and she starred on tour in a revival of *No, No Nanette* in 1971. Following the death of Dick Powell, in 1963, she was romantically involved with the writer/director Dick Summers and was married to and divorced from Alfred Glenn Maxwell, who had been Dick Powell's barber. She had two children, Pamela Allyson Powell (adopted) and Richard Powell Jr. Her survivors included her third husband, the dentist/actor David Ashrow. She died at her home in Ojai, California. See *Current Biography* (1952).

Obituary *New York Times* B p8 July 11, 2006

ANDERSON, JACK Oct. 19, 1922–Dec. 17, 2005 Journalist. Among the last of the purebred muckrakers, Anderson was the investigative reporter most feared in American halls of power, chiefly those in Washington, D.C., his home base, and the most popular political columnist of his time. During his heyday his exposés of corruption in high places were carried via his syndicated "Washington Merry-Go-Round" column (inherited from Drew Pearson) to some 45 million readers of more than 700 newspapers across the United States. He was especially dedicated to throwing light on what he described as "the incestuous relationship between government and big business [that] thrives in the dark." His modus operandi involved approaching for information not top officials but disgruntled career employees, and by all accounts his ability to extract the information was uncanny. Anderson grew up in a Mormon family in Cottonwood, a small town outside Salt Lake City, Utah. As a teenager he wrote for local newspapers, and between the ages of 19 and 21 he fulfilled his duty as a Mormon missionary. He then served in the U. S. Merchant Marine, briefly, and as China correspondent for the *Deseret News*, a Mormon-owned newspaper, also briefly. During part of his service as a draftee in the U.S. Army (1945–47), he worked for the *Stars and Stripes* newspaper. In 1947 Drew Pearson hired him as his assistant on "Washington Merry-Go-Round," a D.C.-insider gossip column that Pearson had launched with Robert S. Allen in 1932. (Allen left in 1942.) Anderson was Pearson's chief uncredited legman until 1965, when Pearson granted him an equal byline; the column became Anderson's when Pearson died, in 1969. Anderson was credited with the disclosures of financial malfeasance that led to the downfalls of U.S. Representative J. Parnell Thomas, chairman of the House Un-American Activities Committee, in 1948, and Sherman Adams, President Dwight D. Eisenhower's chief of staff, in 1958, and the censure of Senator Thomas J. Dodd, in 1967. Other early scandals he uncovered included, during the administration of President Harry S. Truman, the "Five Percenters," Representative Adam Clayton Powell's flouting of behavioral standards, and the CIA/Mafia conspiracy to assassinate Fidel Castro. In January 1972 he published secret papers prepared by employees of the White House during the presidency of Richard Nixon showing that Nixon wanted to "tilt" in favor of Pakistan in the India-Pakistan war, a contradiction of public professions of neutrality made by Henry Kissinger, President Nixon's adviser for national security affairs. That scoop made headlines around the world and brought Anderson the Pulitzer Prize for national reporting. He subsequently published a number of stories further enraging the Nixon administration, some concerning government involvement with the International Telephone and Telegraph Corp. and collusion of the CIA in plots against President Salvador Allende of Chile. In addition, he published the secret transcripts of the Watergate grand jury. Nixon operatives waged campaigns to discredit or even silence him. J. Edgar Hoover, the director of the FBI from 1924 to 1972, was a longer-term enemy, originally stirred to anger in the 1950s by Anderson's stories about the strength of organized crime, a national problem not taken seriously by Hoover (according to many observers in addition to Anderson) for questionable reasons. Also in the early 1970s, Anderson published—and retracted—drunk-driving allegations against Democratic U.S. senator Thomas Eagleton, who had just been nominated as his party's vice-presidential candidate, and he delivered details about the strange final days in the life of the reclusive but influential Las Vegas billionaire Howard Hughes. In the early 1980s Anderson found the Bulgarian connection in the attempted assassination of Pope John Paul II and the Iranian connection in the bombing of the American Embassy in Beirut, Lebanon. Just as he had been ambivalent in contributing to attacks on his former friend Joseph R. McCarthy, he was hesitant in the latter half of the 1980s in publishing his findings regarding the Iran-Contra scheme, developed by officials working in the administration of President Ronald Reagan. Later in the same decade, he exposed the "Keating Five," U.S. senators who had taken bribes from the savings-and-loan swindler Charles H. Keating Jr. In the years following his diagnosis with Parkinson's disease in 1986, his output and the syndication of his column progressively declined. Over the years he had depended on the help of many interns, including Les Whitten and Douglas Cohn. Cohn and Eleanor Clift took over the column when Anderson moved to the background in 2001. The United Features Syndicate stopped distributing "Washington Merry-Go-Round" in July 2004. With J. Peter Grace, Anderson co-founded Citizens Against Government Waste in 1984, and he succeeded Grace as chairman of that organization following Grace's death, in 1995. Anderson wrote or co-wrote more than a dozen books, including *The Anderson Papers* (with George Clifford, 1973), *Confessions of a Muckraker* (with James Boyd, 1979), and *Peace, War, and Politics: An Eyewitness Account* (with Daryl Gibson, 1999). "I have tried to break down the walls of secrecy in Washington," he once said. "But today the walls are thicker than ever." He died at his home in Bethesda, Maryland. His survivors included his wife, Olivia, five sons, four daughters, 41 grandchildren, and seven great-grandchildren. See *Current Biography* (1972).

Obituary *New York Times* p58 Dec. 18, 2005

APPEL, KAREL Apr. 25, 1921–May 3, 2006 Expatriate Dutch artist. Christiaan Karel Appel was an intentionally "barbaric" expressionist who attacked his canvases with the primal spontaneity and visceral vigor of an "action" painter but included surreal, often grotesque and violent figural elements that gave Jungian meaning to his quasi-abstract works, thick impastos typified by slashing lines and bold bright colors. Artistically, he was influenced by the work of Vincent Van Gogh, Henri Matisse, Pablo Picasso, Alberto Giacometti, Jean Dubuffet, and the German expressionists and by naïf art, including that of "primitive" people, mental patients, and, especially, children. Some critics have credited a Marxist influence, both intellectually and politically, as a partial explanation for his non-preachy occupation with such universal themes as world poverty, hunger, and injustice. While he viewed his work as an artist basically as "a constant struggle" to express himself intuitively, he described his execution of that work as "play"; as a child might, he sometimes squeezed paint directly from the tube or applied it with his fingers rather than a brush. After completing his studies at the Royal Academy of Fine Arts in Amsterdam, he held his first solo show in Groningen, the Netherlands, in 1946. In July 1948, unhappy with the geometric rigidity and austerity of the abstract style of the previous generation of such Dutch modernists as Mondrian and de Stijl, he and several other progressive young Dutch artists and writers—including the Nieuwenhuys brothers, Constant and Jan, and Cornelis van Beverley (a k a Corneille)—founded the Netherlands Experimental Group, also known as Reflex. Four months later the members of Reflex joined with others from Belgium and Denmark—including the painters Asger Jorn and Pierre Alechinsky and the poet Christian Dotremont—to form the international group Cobra (an acronym derived from Copenhagen, Brussels, and Amsterdam, the names of the native cities of its founders), a short-lived forerunner of the countercultural radicalism of the late 1960s. Dating from that period is one of Appel's best known paintings, *Hiep, Hiep, Hoera!* (*Hip, Hip, Hoorah!*), a 1949 canvas conveying a spirit of joyful artistic freedom through the depiction of hybrid human/bird creatures. After leaving the Netherlands in 1950, Appel lived in France for many years, first in Paris and subsequently in an old chateau he purchased in Molesmes, near Auxerre. He also lived on and off near Florence, Italy, and in New York City, and he traveled in Mexico, among other countries, before finally settling in Zurich, Switzerland. In New York he collaborated with the Beat poet Allen Ginsberg on a series of visual poems and painted portraits of the jazz musicians Count Basie, Miles Davis, Dizzy Gillespie, and Sarah Vaughan. Over the years he returned to his homeland for brief periods, chiefly when commissioned to paint murals on buildings in Amsterdam, Rotterdam, and the Hague. The first, actually commissioned just before he became an expatriate, was *Vragende Kinderen* (translatable as either *Children Begging* or *Children Questioning*), a fresco decorating a wall in the cafeteria of Amsterdam's city hall. The pathetic condition of the depicted juvenile figures, perhaps stirring memories of wartime suffering, offended municipal civil servants and initially provoked so much controversy that it was covered with wallpaper for a number of years. In 1960 Appel won first prize in the Guggenheim International Exhibition with his painting titled (in English translation) *Woman with Ostrich*. Turning to three dimensions, he sometimes incorporated relief into his canvases and murals, and he constructed and painted collages of found objects. Eventually he turned to large-scale stand-alone sculptures in painted wood, plastics, ceramics, and metal. On the occasion of the unveiling of his bronze sculpture titled (in translation) *Frog with Umbrella in the Hague* in 2001, Queen Beatrix of the Netherlands awarded him the Order of the Lion, the Dutch equivalent of a knighthood. In the United States his work, including prints, may be viewed in such public collections as those in the Museum of Modern Art and the Guggenheim Museum in Manhattan. Appel was married to the former Dutch fashion model Machteld. He died in Zurich, Switzerland. See *Current Biography* (1961).

Obituary *New York Times* B p7 May 9, 2006

AZCONA HOYO, JOSÉ Jan. 26, 1927–Oct. 24, 2005 President of Honduras (1986–90). Azcona was born in Ceiba, Honduras, to parents who had emigrated from Spain. According to some accounts, he lived with his maternal grandparents in Cantabria, Spain, from 1935 to 1949. He began his university studies in Honduras and completed them at the University of Monterrey in Mexico, where he earned a degree in civil engineering. Before entering government, he worked in supervisory positions in the design of infrastructure, urban development, and cooperative housing in Honduras. Meanwhile, he was active in politics, becoming a leader of the Action Front faction of the Pardido Liberal de Honduras (PLH, Liberal Party of Honduras). He was a PLH candidate for the Honduran National Congress in October 1963, when the election was cancelled by Colonel Oswaldo Lopez Arellano, who seized the presidency in a coup. He became a member of the PHL's central committee in 1977, secretary general of the party in 1981, and a member of the Honduran constituent assembly formed in 1981 after two decades of military rule. Pursuant to the election of October 1981, he took his seat in the National Congress early in 1982 and at that time became minister of communications, public works, and transport in the government of President Roberto Suazo Cordova. In succeeding Suazo in the presidency in 1986, he took part in the first peaceful transfer of power from one civilian president to another in more than 30 years. As president, he gave safe haven in Honduras to U.S.-backed Contra rebels fighting to overthrow the leftist Sandinista government in neighboring Nicaragua. When Sandinista forces invaded Honduras in pursuit of Contras, U.S. troops were sent to Honduras at his request. During his final months as president, after the Sandinistas lost power (through the electoral process) to a party led by Violetta Chamorro in Nicaragua, he began dismantling the Contra bases in Honduras. After leaving the presidency, he gave his full attention to his construction business. He died at his home in Tegucigalpa, Honduras. He was survived by his wife, Miriam, and three children. See *Current Biography* (1988).

Obituary *New York Times* C p19 Oct. 25, 2005

BARZEL, RAINER June 20, 1924–Aug. 26, 2006 German politician; lawyer. Rainer Candidus Barzel was a leader of the Christian Democratic Union (CDU) during the early decades of the existence of that right-center party, which was founded in West Germany (the Federal Republic of Germany) following World War II and continued to be a dominant political force after West Germany and Communist East Germany (the German Democratic Republic) reunified, under the banner of the Federal Republic of Germany, in 1990. Barzel ended his leadership of West Germany's Parliament, the Bundestag, in 1984 and retired from politics in 1987, under the cloud of a financial scandal. A Roman Catholic, he received his secondary education at a Jesuit school. During World War II he was a pilot in the air branch of the German navy. After the war he earned a law degree at the University of Cologne. In 1949, following the establishment of the Federal Republic of Germany, he entered the civil service of the state of North Rhine-Westphalia, where he soon became a speechwriter for the state's minister president, Karl Arnold (a left-leaning anomaly in the CDU), and an official in the state's ministry of foreign affairs. In 1957 he was elected to the Bundestag, where he became a protégé of the staunch anti-Communist Heinrich von Brentano. In 1961 Brentano became chairman of the CDU parliamentary group, with Barzel as his deputy. (On the federal level the CDU actually operated as one entity with its Bavarian alter ego, the Christian Social Union.) At that time Barzel drew criticism from some quarters for publishing a document exposing the Communist affiliations of more than 400 persons in West German public life. In 1962–63 Barzel was minister for all-German affairs in the CDU federal government of Chancellor Konrad Adenauer, a position in which he served as a liaison of sorts with East Germany and made regular broadcasts beamed to that Soviet-controlled country. After von Brentano fell ill in late 1963, Barzel served as acting chairman of the CDU Bundestag group; he succeeded to the chairmanship following Brentano's death, in 1964. As CDU parliamentary chairman, Barzel acted as the chief representative in the Bundestag of Chancellor Ludwig Erhard until 1966 and then of Chancellor Kurt Georg Kiesinger. From 1971 to 1973 he was national chairman of the CDU. Meanwhile, in 1969 Willy Brandt of the left-of-center Social Democratic Party, in coalition with the Free Democratic Party, had become chancellor, putting the CDU for the first time in opposition, a status in which it would remain for 13 years. Barzel came closest to becoming chancellor in 1972, when he called for a vote of no confidence against Chancellor Brandt in the Bundestag. (At issue was the nature of Brandt's policy of Ostpolitik—reconciliation with the Soviet bloc—which Barzel, a champion of reunification, viewed as overly conciliatory and likely to render permanent the division of Germany.) In that parliamentary contest, Barzel's motion lost by two votes. Subsequently, it was revealed that the East German espionage director Markus Wolf had bribed one or two conservative members of the Bundestag to vote against Barzel's motion. Brandt was pressured to resign when, in 1974, it came to light that Gunther Guilaume, the manager of his political office, was a spy working for East Germany. Brandt was succeeded by another Social Democratic chancellor, Helmut Schmidt, who governed in coalition with the Free Democrats until 1982, when the Social Democrats withdrew from the coalition and the CDU returned to power under Helmut Kohl. Barzel served as minister of inter-German affairs (1982–83) in Kohl's cabinet. In 1983 he became president of the Bundestag, the equivalent of Speaker in the U.S. House of Representatives. The following year he resigned that position under the cloud of the so-called Flick affair. That scandal broke when West German federal investigators found evidence of bribery and political influence peddling (including tax breaks) in the files of the giant Flick Industrial Holdings Co. The documents reportedly revealed that a number of members of all of the West German political parties in positions of power, with the exception of the Greens, had received undeclared financial gifts totaling 25 million deutschmarks from the Flick corporation. Barzel had allegedly received the equivalent of $556,000. He denied the charge, and a committee of inquiry subsequently supported his denial. He retired from politics in 1987. Barzel wrote several books on German politics. He died in Munich, Germany. He was survived by his third wife, Ute Cremer, and predeceased by his first wife, Kriemhild Schumacher, his second wife, Hilda Henselder, and a daughter by his first wife. See *Current Biography* (1967).

Obituary *New York Times* A p21 Aug. 30, 2006

BEDFORD, SYBILLE Mar. 16, 1911–Feb. 17, 2006
German-born British writer. As an expatriate writing in English, Bedford (neé Sybille von Schoenebeck) was a cosmopolite in a distinguished line of authors—including Joseph Conrad, Isak Dinesen, and Vladimir Nabokov—who chose to realize their full literary powers in a language that was not their native tongue. Growing up in an upper-class, multilingual German family, she had become fluent in four languages. Her family's history, along with tales she remembered her father telling, went into the creation of her masterpiece, *A Legacy*, a grand historical novel set in pre–World War I Germany. Her other novels, accounts of a vanishing milieu of European social elites where high privilege was combined with less high, often sybaritic morality, are sometimes barely distinguishable from memoirs. As a novelist, she wrote in a nuanced and somewhat oblique style that was greeted as mannered and snobbish by some critics but was marked by an elegance and wit—which sometimes erupted into farce—that was noticed by a select coterie of faithful admirers, including such luminaries as Evelyn Waugh, Nancy Mitford, V. S. Pritchett, and Aldous Huxley (her mentor and close friend). Parallel to her career as a novelist/memoirist, she was a widely esteemed trial and true-crime reporter, travel writer, and food and wine connoisseur. She was born in Charlottenburg (now part of western Berlin), Germany, to an elderly and eccentric Catholic baron (then already in his 60s) and a much younger Jewish mother of mixed (partly English) nationality whose friends or acquaintances included such literary and artistic figures as Thomas Mann, Bertolt Brecht, and Man Ray. After her parents separated, when she was about seven, she lived in Germany with her father until his death, when she was nine or 10. She subsequently lived in Italy with her mother and her Italian stepfather and was sent by her mother to study in England (where, in her words, she lived "with bohemian friends") before she settled with her mother and stepfather in the fishing port of Sanary-sur-Mer on France's Mediterranean coast. That town, a magnet for cosmopolitan literati, was her base for more than a decade. It was there that she met Aldous Huxley, her favorite author, and Huxley's wife, Maria, in 1928. To gain British citizenship, in the mid-1930s she entered into a quick marriage of convenience (arranged by the Huxleys) with the openly homosexual Walter Bedford, which enabled her to flee to England when the German Nazis occupied France in 1940. From England, she followed the Huxleys to California, and she remained in the United States for six years. Before returning to England after World War II, she traveled widely in Mexico. She had been writing since her mid-teens, producing three unpublished manuscripts for novels (all in imitation of Aldous Huxley) before she wove her Mexican notes into her first published book, the partly fictionalized travelogue *The Sudden View: A Mexican Journey* (1953; reissued as *A Visit to Don Otavio: A Traveller's Tale from Mexico* in 1960). In *A Legacy: A Novel* (1956), she evoked the glitter and corruption of Germany's Wilhelmine era and explored the development of tensions between the Catholic nobility of southern Germany, Berlin's Jewish mercantile class, and the Prussian officer class. In the climax of that novel, brutality and anti-Semitism in the military cadet schools contribute to the incubation of a scandal that threatens to bring down a government. Her quasi-autobiographical novels *A Favourite of the Gods* (1963), *A Compass Error* (1968), and *Jigsaw* (1989) were followed by *Quicksands: A Memoir* (2005), in which she recapitulated in open terms the previously veiled story of her life, with special emphasis on her childhood and her mother's later years. Meanwhile, she had for decades also been displaying her literary skill in court reportage for various magazines and in other writings on the law, often in conjunction with her travels. Those writings included the books *The Best We Can Do: An Account of the Trial of John Bodkin Adams* (1958), *The Faces of Justice: A Traveller's Report* (1961), and *As It Was: Pleasures, Landscapes and Justice* (1990). Among her other books were the two volumes comprising *Aldous Huxley: A Biography* (1973–74). In 1981 she was named to the Order of the British Empire. Later she became vice president of English PEN. She died in London. The American novelist Eda Lord, her longtime companion, predeceased her. See *Current Biography* (1990).

Obituary *New York Times* B p6 Feb. 27, 2006

BENCHLEY, PETER May 8, 1940–Feb. 12, 2006 American novelist. Peter Benchley's fictional entertainments, commonly described as "thrilling," were imaginatively spun out of experiences or subjects he knew well, one of which was the sea. The best known of his novels is *Jaws* (1974), a story about, in his words, "a great white shark that marauds an Eastern coastal town and provokes a moral crisis in the community." That book was on the *New York Times* best-seller list for almost a year and sold more than 20 million copies. The 1975 screen adaptation, directed by Steven Spielberg and co-scripted by Benchley (with Carl Gottlieb), is one of the most commercially successful motion pictures of all time, ranked by the American Film Institute second only to *Psycho* among the most frightening movies in Hollywood history. In the same "devil in the deep" vein, Benchley wrote the novels *The Deep* (1976), *The Island* (1978), *Beast* (1978), and *White Shark* (1994). (Both *The Deep* and *The Island* were made into feature films, released in 1977 and 1980, respectively.) *The Girl of the Sea of Cortez* (1982) was not written in quite the same vein, although it is a sea story and reiterates a theme common in the other novels, that human depredations disturb the balance of nature. Benchley drew on his two-year experience on President Lyndon B. Johnson's speechwriting staff for the political comedy in *Q Clearance* (1986). His *Rummies* (1989) is also a comic novel, about a patient in a substance-abuse rehabilitation center. Among his books of nonfiction are *Time and a Ticket* (1964), a memoir of a tour of the world he made just after he graduated from Harvard University with a degree in English, and two of his last books, *Shark Trouble* (2002) and *Shark Life* (2005). Benchley was a grandson of the humorist Robert Benchley and a son of the novelist Nathaniel Benchley. He was a journalist with the *Washington Post* in 1963 and 1964 and with *Newsweek* magazine from 1964 to 1967 and a freelance contributor to such magazines as *Life* and the *New Yorker*. Among the causes to which he contributed time and energy were the Environmental Defense Fund and Wild Aid. He died at his home in Princeton, New Jersey. His survivors included his wife, Wendy, a daughter, two sons, and five grandchildren. See *Current Biography* (1976).

Obituary *New York Times* A p21 Feb. 13, 2006

BENTSEN, LLOYD Feb. 11, 1921–May 23, 2006 American political leader; government official; lawyer; businessman. A giant in Texas Democratic politics, Lloyd Millard Bentsen Jr. served in the U.S. House of Representatives from 1949 to 1955 and in the U.S. Senate from 1971 to 1993; he was the nominee for vice president in the unsuccessful Democratic presidential campaign of 1988, and he was President Bill Clinton's first secretary of the treasury. As chairman of the Senate Finance Committee from 1987 to 1993, Bentsen championed international trade as well as such Texas interests as its oil and gas industries. As secretary of the treasury, from January 1993 to December 1995, he played a crucial role in winning congressional approval of the North American Free Trade Agreement (NAFTA), an historic expansion of the General Agreement of Tariffs and Trade (GATT), and a controversial budget package aimed at reducing the national deficit in part by raising taxes. Bentsen was one of two sons of a Lower Rio Grande Valley land and grocery tycoon. After earning a law degree, he served as a U.S. Army Air Force commander in World War II and later ran a successful insurance business in Houston, Texas. He subsequently founded Lincoln Consolidated, a financial holding company. Following his resignation as secretary of the treasury, he joined the Houston branch of the powerful Washington, D.C.–based law firm of Verner, Liipfert, Bernhard, McPherson & Hand. Bentsen died at his home in Houston. He was survived by his wife, Beryl Ann, two sons, a daughter, and seven grandchildren. See *Current Biography* (1993).

Obituary *New York Times* C p13 May 24, 2006

BREWER, ROY M. Aug. 9, 1909–Sep. 16, 2006 Labor-union official. As the Hollywood representative of the International Alliance of Theatrical Stage Employees (IATSE) from 1945 to 1953, Roy Brewer strenuously fought what he perceived to be Communist influence in the motion-picture industry. IATSE, which dates from 1886 and was chartered by the American Federation of Labor in 1893, now operates under the banner of the AFL-CIO. The range of its involvement in the entertainment industry is reflected in its current full name, adopted in 1995: the International Alliance of Theatrical Stage Employees, Moving Picture Technicians, Artists and Allied Crafts of the United States, Its Territories, and Canada. In his anti-Communist activity in Hollywood, Brewer worked in close association with the actor Ronald Reagan, the future U.S. president, when Reagan headed the Screen Actors Guild. Brewer had joined Local 586 of IATSE when he was a teenage silent-film projectionist at the Capitol Theater in Grand Island, Nebraska, in 1927, and he subsequently served as president of the local for 15 years. He also served three terms as president of the Nebraska State Federation of Labor. In 1940 he became secretary of an IATSE district covering nine states. During World War II he was chief of a division of the federal government's Office of Labor Production in Washington, D.C. When he became the representative of IATSE in Hollywood in March 1945, his immediate priority was a jurisdictional dispute between IATSE and a coalition of stagehand locals called the Conference of Studio Unions (CSU) over which of them should represent movie set designers and decorators. On the very day he arrived in the motion-picture capital, on May 12, the Screen Set Designers, Decorators, and Illustrators, a component of the CSU, went on strike. "Within a month we knew the Commies were behind the strike," he later said. "And we realized it was either them or us." When the strikers failed to obey a return-to-work order by the National War Labor Board, the studios fired 3,600 striking workers and gave their jobs to members of IATSE. The entire CSU union, 7,000 strong, then went out on a strike that lasted 18 months. The strike grew increasingly bloody and wreaked havoc in production at the movie studios; at Warner Brothers alone the violence resulted in the hospitalization of an estimated 150 employees. Brewer's home was placed under armed guard, and his eight-year-old daughter was escorted to and from school by a body-guard. In 1946 Brewer began a long-term association and friendship with Ronald Reagan. In 1950 he succeeded Reagan in the presidency of the Motion Picture Industry Council, for a one-year term. Brewer's anti-Communism was two-pronged, concerned with control of the content of motion pictures as well as the economic leverage inherent in control of Hollywood's craft labor. Testifying before the U.S. House of Representatives Un-American Activities Committee in Washington, D.C., he named 13 directors, actors, and writers whom he viewed as subversive. "I don't think you can stop anybody from singing the praises of Russia, if they believe it is a good country," he said in his testimony. "I think it is a part of our fundamental law that a man has got a right to say what he believes. But when he participates in American institutions and deliberately tries to subvert those institutions to become an instrument of a foreign power, that is something that is fundamentally wrong and has to be stopped." Writing jointly, the journalists Murray Kempton and Victor Riesel described Brewer as "the man the Comrades have tried to smear," whom they hate "more than they would a combination of Trotsky, Truman, and Tito." Following his tenure in Hollywood, Brewer worked as a labor-relations executive and consultant. In 1983 President Reagan appointed him to the Federal Service Impasses Panel, the final arbiter in disputes between federal unions and government employers. He became chairman of that panel in 1984. In the same year, Governor George Deukmejian of California named him to that state's Occupational Safety and Health Standards Board. Brewer died in the Los Angeles suburb of West Hills, California. He was predeceased by his wife, Alyce Auhl Brewer, and survived by a son, a daughter, 10 grandchildren, and 20 great-grandchildren. See *Current Biography* (1953).

Obituary *New York Times* C p10 Sep. 23, 2006

BUJONES, FERNANDO Mar. 9, 1955–Nov. 10, 2005 Ballet dancer, teacher, and director. Bujones, who as a dancer was chiefly associated with the American Ballet Theater, was one of the first American-born male ballet performers to achieve international stardom. He was a slim, handsome man of medium torso and long legs that tapered down to balletically perfect feet. While most acclaimed as a meticulous virtuoso classicist, he also included in his repertoire spirited performances of contemporary works. Whatever the vintage of the choreography, he electrified audiences with his high elevation, spectacular midair turns, and clean beats. Toward the end of his career, he worked increasingly as a director, and during the last five years of his life, he was the artistic director of the Orlando (Florida) Ballet (formerly the Southern Ballet Theater). Bujones was born in Miami, Florida, to Cuban parents who were divorced a few months after his birth. His mother, Maria Calleiro, took him with her back to Havana, where he began the study of ballet when he was six or seven. After his mother returned with him to the United States, when he was nine or 10, he continued to study ballet, partly under the tutorship of his cousin Zeida Cecilia Mendez, an alumna of the Ballet de Cuba. On the recommendation of New York City Bal-

let premier danseur Jacques d'Amboise (with whom his mother had arranged an audition when d'Amboise was performing in Miami with the touring troupe Ballet Spectacular), he obtained a scholarship to the School of American Ballet in Manhattan, New York City, beginning in 1967. While studying at that school (chiefly under Stanley Williams and André Eglevsky), he completed his academic schooling on a Ford Foundation grant at the Professional Children's School, also in Manhattan. Upon his graduation from the School of American Ballet, in 1972, he joined the corps of the American Ballet Theater, where he was promoted to soloist in 1973 and principal dancer in 1974. In July of the latter year he became the first American to win the gold medal in the senior division of the International Dance Competition in Varna, Bulgaria, the ballet world's equivalent of the Olympiad. For the better part of two decades, his association with the American Ballet Theater was congenial and mutually strengthening; he went from strength to strength in his performance not only of such 19th- and early 20th-century roles as Albrecht in *Giselle*, James in *La Sylphide*, and Solar in *La Bayadère* but also in works by such contemporary choreographers as George Balanchine, Anthony Tudor, Frederick Ashton, Jerome Robbins, Anton Dolin, and Harold Landers. In 1980 Mikhail Baryshnikov, Bujones's arch-rival at the American Ballet Theater, became the company's artistic director, succeeding Lucia Chase and Oliver Smith. Bujones became increasingly unhappy under Baryshnikov's administration, in part because of a paucity of new roles, and Baryshnikov dismissed him in 1985 for refusing to dance in the company's New York season. Meanwhile, Bujones had begun guesting with major opera companies in other countries, performing with the National Ballet of Canada and at the Edinburgh Festival in 1977 and the Paris Opera Ballet in 1981, for example. Soon after leaving the American Ballet Theater, in 1985, he briefly served as artistic director of the Rio de Janeiro Opera Ballet and danced with the Royal Ballet in London. He later performed with the Bolshoi Opera Ballet, the Stuttgart Ballet, the Vienna State Opera Ballet, and La Scala in Milan and guest-directed companies in Spain, Mexico, and Brazil. In the United States he danced with numerous regional companies, was a permanent guest artist with the Boston Ballet, and for a time was director of the Ballet Mississippi in Jackson. He returned to the American Ballet Theater during the 1989–90 season, after Baryshnikov was replaced in the directorship by Oliver Smith and Jane Hermann, and he remained with the company until 1995. In 1996 he was appointed choreographer-in-residence of the Dance Department at Texas Christian University. As artistic director of the Orlando Ballet beginning in 2000, he expanded that company's repertoire and improved its standards, elevating it from regional to national status. By his first marriage, to Marcia Kubitschek, he had a daughter, Alexandra. After that marriage ended, in divorce, he married Maria Arnillas. He maintained two homes in Florida, one in Hallandale, the other in Orlando. He died in Miami. See *Current Biography* (1976).

Obituary *New York Times* C p16 Nov. 11, 2005

BUTCHER, SUSAN Dec. 26, 1954–Aug. 5, 2006 Champion dog-sled racer. Susan Howlet Butcher, a trailblazer in the rearing and training of dogs, especially Siberian huskies, was a four-time winner of the annual Iditarod Trail Sled Dog Race, a 1,000-plus trek through blizzard conditions across the wilderness between Anchorage and Nome, Alaska. Butcher, who was born in Boston, Massachusetts, and raised in nearby Cambridge, "loved animals [especially dogs] and the outdoors," as she said, from early childhood. As a teenager she went to live with her grandmother in Maine, an environment more hospitable to the two huskies she owned. In 1972 she moved to Boulder, Colorado, where she worked as a veterinarian's assistant. Three years later she went to Fairbanks, Alaska, having been hired by the University of Alaska to work on a project to save endangered muskoxen and with the intention of practicing dog mushing. In 1977 the muskoxen project moved to Unalakleet, Alaska, where she met Joe Redington Sr., an organizer of the Iditarod Trail Sled Dog Race. Redington helped Butcher to find a sponsor, and in March 1978 she entered her first Iditarod race, finishing 19th. She placed ninth in the 1979 Iditarod, and following that race she and Redington led the only sled-dog team ever to reach the summit of North America's highest peak, Mount McKinley. In the Iditarod race she finished fifth in both 1980 and 1981, second in 1982, ninth in 1983, and second in 1984. She withdrew from the 1985 race when two of her dogs and 13 others were injured in an attack by a moose. She won the 1986 Iditarod in 11 days, 15 hours, and six minutes, a record time for the race's northern route, and the 1987 race in 11 days, two hours, and five minutes, a record for the shorter, southern route. In 1988 she covered the northern route in a new record time of 11 days, 11 hours, and 41 minutes. In 1989 she was runner-up to Joe Runyan. In 1990 she won the Iditarod in 11 days, one hour, and 43 minutes, a new mark for the northern route. With her husband, David Monson, Butcher operated Trail Breaker Kennels in Eureka, Alaska. Suffering from acute myelogenous leukemia, she underwent extreme chemo- and radiation therapy and a stem-cell transplant at the University of Washington Medical Center in Seattle, where she died. She was survived by her husband, David, and two daughters. See *Current Biography* (1991).

Obituary *New York Times* B p8 Aug. 7, 2006

BUTTONS, RED Feb. 5, 1919–July 13, 2006 Comedian; stage, screen, and television actor. The peaks in Buttons's career included the network television program *The Red Buttons Show* (1952–55)—a platform for the one-line zinging wit he had developed in burlesque, vaudeville, and nightclubs—and his winning the Academy Award for best supporting actor for his touching portrayal of Sergeant Joe Kelly in the motion picture *Sayonara* (1957). In the latter role—that of an American airman in occupied Japan in love with a young Japanese woman in contravention of military Occupation rules—he drew upon a dramatic skill he had honed on Broadway. A later generation of television viewers will perhaps remember the puckish Buttons in such performances as that of a witty regular on *The Dean Martin Celebri-*

ty Roast in the mid-1970s. Buttons holds place number 71 in Comedy Central's list of the 100 greatest standup comics of all time. Red Buttons was the stage name of Aaron Chwatt, who was born to Jewish immigrants from Poland on Manhattan's Lower East Side and grew up there and in the Bronx, New York City. Following an apprenticeship as an entertainer in the Borscht Belt of hotels in New York's Catskill Mountains, he toured as a comic on the burlesque circuit. He made his Broadway debut in the supporting role of Private Carter in the farce *Vickie* in 1942. Also on Broadway in the same year, he replaced one of the comedians in the vaudeville-style revue *Wine, Women and Song*. Inducted into the U.S. Army in 1943, he was assigned to an entertainment unit and cast as Whitey in a star-studded U.S. Army Air Forces theatrical production, the morale-boosting war drama *Winged Victory*, which ran on Broadway from November 1943 to May 1944 and subsequently toured. He reprised the role of Whitey in the screen adaptation of *Winged Victory* (1944). With another army unit he entertained troops in Europe in 1945. Back on Broadway after the war, he played Shyster Fiscal in the musical *Barefoot Boy with Cheek* (1947). At the National Theatre in Lower Manhattan in 1948, he was cast as Dinky Bennett in the musical *Hold It*. Moving into television, he scored impressively in October 1951 in the CBS anthology series *Suspense*, playing the lead in a half-hour drama about Joe E. Lewis, the nightclub singer who turned comedian after his vocal chords were damaged by Mafia hit men. In October 1952 the CBS television network launched *The Red Buttons Show*, a half-hour weekly comedy/variety program on which Buttons delivered monologues and performed in skits. On the show he developed several comic characters, including Rocky Buttons, a punch-drunk prizefighter, and introduced his nonsense theme song, cupping his ears and dancing about the stage while singing "Ho ho! He He! Ha Ha! Strange things are happening." During the 1953–54 season the show developed into a situation comedy, and it remained such when it moved to the NBC network in October 1954. It ran on NBC until May 1955. On the ABC network from January to September 1966, Buttons starred as a meek accountant hired to work as a counterspy by an American intelligence agency in *The Double Life of Henry Phyfe*. He later had recurring roles in the long-running prime-time television serial dramas *ER* and *Knots Landing* and made guest acting appearances on such shows as *Fantasy Island*, *The Cosby Show*, *It's Garry Shandling's Show*, and *Roseannne*. Buttons made a total of some 30 motion pictures. His feature-film credits subsequent to *Sayonara* included Corporal Chan Derby in *Imitation General* (1958), Private John Steele in *The Longest Day* (1962), Pockets in *Hatari!* (1962), Flight Officer Simon Shelley in *A Ticklish Affair* (1963), the sailor in *They Shoot Horses, Don't They?* (1969), James Martin in *The Poseidon Adventure* (1972), Ivan Cooper in *Gable and Lombard* (1976), Hoagy in *Pete's Dragon* (1977), and Walter Zakuto in *It Could Happen to You* (1994). Buttons returned to Broadway in a one-man autobiographical production, *Buttons on Broadway*, in 1995. Among the one-liners in that show were jokes about Abraham ("who said to God about a circumcision, 'Why not? It's no skin off my nose'"), King Solomon ("who looks at all of his wives and says, 'Okay, who doesn't have a headache tonight?'"), and Abe Lincoln ("who said, 'A House divided is a condominium'"). After his divorces from Roxanne Arlen and Helayne McNorton, Buttons married Alicia Pratt, who died in 2001. He was survived by a son and a daughter. Buttons died of vascular disease at his home in the Century City section of Los Angeles. See *Current Biography* (1958).

Obituary *New York Times* D p1 July 14, 2006

CALDWELL, SARAH Mar. 6, 1924–Mar. 23, 2006 American opera impresario; conductor. One of the most adventurous opera producers of her time, Caldwell was closely identified with the Opera Company of Boston. She founded that company (at first called the Opera Group of Boston) in 1958 and headed it throughout the more than three decades of its existence. Serving as its music and stage director as well as its administrator, she was responsible for the full gamut of functions, from fund-raising and talent hunting to the staging and conducting of some 100 operas, including new versions of old standards and the U.S. premieres of works by such composers as Paul Hindemith, Luigi Nono, Arnold Schoenberg, and Jean Philippe Rameau. One of her greatest achievements was the staging in 1972 of Berlioz's *Les Troyens*, in French and uncut. Among her other outstanding productions were Prokofiev's *War and Peace* (1974), Robert Sessions's *Montezuma* (1972), Mikhail Glinka's *Ruslan and Ludmila* (1977), Bernd Alois Zimmermann's *Die Soldaten* (1982), Peter Maxwell Davies's *Tavener* (1986), and Robert DiDomenica's *The Balcony* (1990). A trained violinist, she turned down several opportunities to play violin with symphony orchestras in order to assist Boris Goldovsky in directing the New England Opera Theater for a decade beginning in the late 1940s. Concurrently, she headed the opera department at Boston University for eight years (1952–60). Outside Boston, she staged productions for the New York City Opera, among other companies, and she made guest appearances on the podiums of many orchestras, including the New York Philharmonic, and opera companies, including the Metropolitan Opera, where she became the first woman to conduct (a performance of *La Traviata*) in 1976. She often conducted at such music festivals as Tanglewood, Wolf Trap, and Ravinia. Financial problems forced the Opera Company of Boston to close in 1991. She died in Portland, Maine. See *Current Biography* (1973).

Obituary *New York Times* A p13 Mar. 25, 2006

CARY, FRANK T. Dec. 14, 1920–Jan. 1, 2006 Corporate executive. Cary was chief executive officer of the International Business Machines Corp. from January 1973 through January 1981 and chairman of the board of IBM from January 1973 through February 1983. After earning a B.S. degree at the University of California at Los Angeles and an M.B.A. at Stanford, he joined IBM as a marketing representative in Los Angeles in 1948. He became president of IBM's data-processing division in 1964, a senior vice president in 1967, a member of the board of directors in 1968, and president in 1971. Under his watch as CEO, IBM set the course of the personal-computer industry

with its development of a PC more popular than those offered by Commodore or Apple. In buying software from the fledgling Microsoft, IBM set Microsoft's founder, Bill Gates, on the road to riches, and in marketing its PC it inspired many "IBM clones." IBM increased its revenues and earnings and remained among the world's top 10 corporations at a time when U.S. firms were declining in the international marketplace and corporations such as IBM were strongly challenged by Japanese imports. Cary defended IBM in a 13-year (1969–82) antitrust lawsuit brought by the federal government. He was a leader in rallying U.S. companies to support racial affirmative action at home and oppose apartheid in South Africa. When he retired from IBM, in 1981, the company was still generating profits, but the reputation of its stock was in decline. From 1986 to 1990 Cary chaired the Celgene Corp., a biopharmaceutical firm. He was also a director of Lexmark International and Vion Pharmaceuticals. He died at his home in Darien, Connecticut, leaving his wife, Anne, three children, and 12 grandchildren. See *Current Biography* (1980).

Obituary *New York Times* B p7 Jan. 6, 2006

CASSINI, OLEG Apr. 11, 1913–Mar. 17, 2006 French-born American couturier. Cassini, a dashing cosmopolite, was as celebrated for his public persona as he was for his eye for beauty in women and the fashions he designed for them. Those clothes ranged from figure-hugging, often risqué dresses to the elegant but simple garments that he designed for Jacqueline Kennedy when she was the First Lady of the United States and the movie actress Grace Kelly, a girlfriend of his before she married Prince Rainier of Monaco. "My philosophy," he once stated, "is this: do not tamper with the anatomy of a woman's body, do not camouflage it." Cassini was born to aristocratic Russian parents in Paris, France, and was raised in Denmark, Switzerland, and Italy. After working as a designer in Florence and Rome, he immigrated in 1936 to the U.S., where he designed for several New York fashion houses before opening his own studio. In 1940 he moved to Hollywood, where—with time out for military service during World War II—he spent two decades, designing costumes for 36 motion pictures produced by Paramount Pictures, Twentieth Century-Fox, and Eagle-Lion Studios (and establishing his reputation as a playboy). In Hollywood, he later recalled, he learned how to design "so as to trick the camera, which adds ten pounds to a woman's weight." In 1950 he returned to Manhattan and set up his Seventh Avenue wholesale fashion house, which became known for sheath dresses, knitted suits, and, as one observed noted, "modest little jackets over immodest little cocktail dresses." In addition to his ready-to-wear collections, he custom-designed fashions for an elite clientele, the most famous of whom was Jacqueline Kennedy. In 1960 Mrs. Kennedy, the wife of President-elect John F. Kennedy, chose him to be her personal couturier, and he proceeded, in her words, to "dress [her] for the part" of First Lady. Between 1960 and 1963 he created 300 outfits for Mrs. Kennedy, beginning with the white satin evening gown she wore at the preinaugural gala and the beige wool coat with small sable collar and muff and the pill-box hat that she wore at the presidential inauguration. The "Jackie look" that he helped create was an international fashion coup, setting a trend among women of all ages. Taking advantage of the concomitant growth of his name recognition, he, in his words, "created the concept of the designer franchise," licensing the use of his name on a number of products, from luggage to eyeglasses. In addition to his creations for women, he designed for men a "Johnny Carson" line of suits and colorful shirts and underwear, and he helped to popularize the Nehru jacket. In the 1990s he went into partnership with the David's Bridal firm. He published the autobiography *In My Own Fashion* in 1987 and the coffee-table book *A Thousand Days of Magic: Dressing Jacqueline Kennedy for the White House* in 1995. After his divorce from his first wife, Merry Fahney, he was married to and divorced from the movie actress Gene Tierney. Cassini died at North Shore University Hospital on Long Island, New York. His survivors included his third wife, Marianne Nestor Cassini (the president of Oleg Cassini Inc.), two daughters from his second marriage, and four grandchildren. See *Current Biography* (1961).

Obituary *New York Times* I p34 Mar. 19, 2006

CHAMBERLAIN, OWEN July 10, 1920–Feb. 28, 2006 Nuclear physicist; emeritus professor and member of the radiation laboratory at the University of California, Berkeley. With his Berkeley colleague Emilio Segrè, Chamberlain shared the 1959 Nobel Prize in Physics for history's second antimatter discovery, the recognition in 1955 of the antiproton, the mirror image of the proton, one of the chief components of the atomic nucleus. Chamberlain began his graduate studies in physics at Berkeley and earned his Ph.D. degree at the University of Chicago. During World War II he was among the Manhattan Project physicists who contributed to the development of the first atomic bomb at Los Alamos. He joined the Berkeley faculty in 1948 and became a full professor in 1958. His later work was on the interactions of antiprotons with deuterium and hydrogen, the production of antineutrons, and the emission of pions. He retired in 1989. His first two wives predeceased him. His survivors included his third wife, Sarah, three daughters, a son, and two stepdaughters. He died at his home in Berkeley, California. See *Current Biography* (1960).

Obituary *New York Times* B p8 Mar. 2, 2006

CHANDLER, OTIS Nov. 23, 1927–Feb. 27, 2006 Newspaper publisher. Chandler was the scion of the California dynasty that owned the Times Mirror Co., the third-largest publishing empire in the United States, until it was sold in 2000 to the Tribune Co., publisher of the *Chicago Tribune*. He was for 20 years the famously effective publisher of the *Los Angeles Times*, the hub of his family's journalistic domain. After earning a B.A. degree at Stanford University and serving on the ground with the U.S. Air Force during the Korean War, Chandler underwent a seven-year apprenticeship in the Times Mirror Co., rising from pressman and reporter to general manager of the *Los Angeles Mirror News*, an afternoon tab-

loid. He became publisher of the *Los Angeles Times* in 1960, when the newspaper was already the richest daily west of the Mississippi but still had a provincial reputation. He proceeded to double its circulation and advertising and move it into the front rank of nationally influential newspapers, establishing news bureaus throughout the world. In the process, he angered his traditionally Republican family by changing the *Times*'s editorial orientation from conservative to centrist-liberal. He resigned as publisher in 1980 and as chairman of the board in 1985. After his divorce from his first wife, Marilyn Brant, Chandler married Bettina Whitaker, in 1981. He died at his home in Ojai, California. His survivors included his wife Bettina, four children from his first marriage, and 15 grandchildren. See *Current Biography* (1968).

Obituary *New York Times* A p17 Feb. 28, 2006

CHARLES, EUGENIA May 15, 1919–Sep. 6, 2005 West Indian lawyer and stateswoman who was known as "Iron Lady of the Caribbean." A member of the "coloured bourgeoisie" in the class-stratified island nation of Dominica, Charles began her practice as her country's first female lawyer in 1949 (when Dominica was still a British crown colony) and became the Caribbean's first female head of state 31 years later. As a conservative prime minister of Dominica (and chairwoman of the Organization of Eastern Caribbean States as well), she drew international attention with her response to events in Grenada in 1983, when a power struggle in that neighboring island country culminated in the assassination of its moderate prime minister, Maurice Bishop. Sharing with President Ronald Reagan of the U.S. the interpretation of those events as an attempt at Cuban Communist expansion in the region, she provided Reagan with the request for intervention that lent a legal halo to his dispatch of U.S. Marines into Grenada. Charles's involvement in politics began in the 1950s in the form of letters she regularly wrote to the editor of a newspaper in Roseau, Dominica, as a concerned citizen criticizing whatever government was in power. In the 1960s she became increasingly angered at the corruption and abuses of power of the Dominica Labour Party government headed by Prime Minister E. O. Le Blanc. The last straw was the passage in 1968 of a Seditious and Undesirable Publications Act aimed at stifling the expression of dissent. In protest, she joined with others to form a broad-based group called the Freedom Fighters. Within weeks that group was organized into the right-of-center Dominica Freedom Party, with Charles at its head. Although she was not among the five Dominica Freedom Party MPs elected to Dominica's House of Assembly in 1970, she succeeded in obtaining one of the appointive legislative seats provided for in Dominica's constitution. Five years later she was elected an MP and became the leader of the opposition in the House of Assembly. Although the Dominica Freedom Party at first opposed independence from Britain on the ground that the country's status as a crown colony was more beneficial for the time being, Charles was a delegate to the talks in London that resulted in Dominica's becoming an independent republic, in 1978. During the following two years, she led the opposition first to the Dominica Labour government of Prime Minister Patrick John, which alienated even its organized-labor constituency with its repressive policies and mismanagement, and then to the more moderate Democratic Labour government of James Oliver Seraphine. In addition to the expected turnout of its relatively affluent urban base, Charles's Dominica Freedom Party received substantial support even among poorer rural voters when it was swept into power in the election of 1980. As prime minister, Charles brought not only integrity to the government of Dominica but also stability and efficiency. In the wake of the devastation wrought by Hurricane David in 1979, she oversaw the rebuilding of the country's infrastructure, notably its roads (reputed to be the best in the English-speaking Caribbean) and electric power, and the revival of its banana-dependent economy with international aid and favorable trade terms, which she was very effective in securing. She also protected and advanced Dominica's attractiveness as an unspoiled ecotourist destination, lush with flora and fauna and free of casinos, nightclubs, duty-free shops, and reckless development. Following her reelection in 1985, she assumed the portfolios of finance, foreign affairs, and trade and industry in addition to the prime ministership. In 1995, after serving three terms and surviving two coup attempts, she retired. "We've made our people more self-reliant," she said in retrospect. "If they want to achieve, they know they can achieve." Chief among the honors Charles garnered was a DBE (Dame of the British Empire), bestowed on her by Queen Elizabeth II in 1991. Never married, she lived with her father until his death, at age 107. She died in Fort de France on the French Caribbean island of Martinique, where she had been hospitalized with a broken hip. See *Current Biography* (1986).

Obituary *New York Times* C p15 Sep. 9, 2005

COFFIN, WILLIAM SLOANE June 1, 1924–Apr. 12, 2006 Progressive American Protestant clergyman; a leading activist in peace and social-justice causes, including civil rights. In the early 1960s, shortly after he became chaplain at Yale University, his alma mater, Coffin took part in interracial "freedom rides" challenging segregationist bus and restaurant laws in the South, and he subsequently gained national attention promoting civil disobedience, especially draft resistance, against the Vietnam War. Later, as senior minister at Riverside Church in New York City, he offered sanctuary to refugees from civil wars in Central America. He was also a leader in campaigns for nuclear nonproliferation and disarmament and against world hunger, and as an advocate for homosexual rights, he contributed to the development of the "open and affirming" movement within the United Church of Christ. Born into a prosperous blue-blood Manhattan family with ties to Union Theological Seminary and the Yale Corp., Coffin was raised in WASPish privilege and formatively imbued with a sense of noblesse oblige. He studied music in Paris, France, attended Deerfield Academy, and graduated from Phillips Andover Academy before earning a B.A. degree in government at Yale University. At Yale, a fellow student, George H. W.

Bush, a future president of the United States (1989–93), who had also been a classmate of his at Phillips Andover, sponsored his initiation into the secret society Skull and Bones. As a U.S. Army officer during World War II, Coffin—who was skilled in languages—was assigned to liaison work with the French and Soviet armies. The Russian-speaking assignment lasted for two years after the war, and he subsequently spent three years (1950–53) as a CIA agent in Germany, training anti-Stalinist Russians for subversive operations within the Soviet Union. After studying under Reinhold Niebuhr at Union Theological Seminary, he completed his preparation for the ministry at Yale Divinity School, where he received his bachelor of divinity degree in 1956. Shortly afterward, he was ordained a Presbyterian minister. In 1958, after serving as chaplain at Phillips Andover Academy and Williams College, successively, he became chaplain at Yale University, a position in which he remained for nearly 18 years, using his Battell Chapel pulpit as a platform for civil rights and antiwar activities. As an activist challenging southern Jim Crow laws, he was arrested in Montgomery, Alabama, in 1961, Baltimore, Maryland, in 1963, and St. Augustine, Florida, in 1964. In the antiwar movement, he co-founded the interfaith coalition Clergy and Laity Concerned About Vietnam in 1965, and two years later he embarked on a course of civil disobedience, publicly declaring his support for and complicity in "the Resistance," the antidraft movement among young men objecting to conscription for military service in Vietnam. On October 2, 1967 he chaired a press conference announcing the release of "A Call to Resist Illegitimate Authority," a manifesto signed by 320 eminent intellectuals. On October 16, 1967 he was one of the organizers of a rally in Boston at which 214 young men turned in their draft cards. Four days later he and others delivered to the Department of Justice in Washington, D.C., a total of more than 900 turned-in draft cards. In 1968 he and three others were convicted of "conspiracy to counsel, aid, and abet" disobedience of the Selective Service Act. The convictions were overturned on appeal two years later. Coffin was one of the members of the Committee of Liaison with Families of Servicemen Detained in North Vietnam, which went to Hanoi, North Vietnam, in 1972 to accompany three released prisoners of war on their return to the United States. In 1976 he resigned his chaplaincy at Yale, and the following year he became senior minister at Riverside Church in Manhattan. At the invitation of Iran's ruling Revolutionary Council, he and three other Christian churchmen visited American hostages held by militant Muslim students in Tehran at Christmastime in 1979. After resigning his ministry at Riverside Church, in 1987, he served for several years as president of SANE/Freeze (now called Peace Action), a merger of the Committee for a Sane Nuclear Policy and the Nuclear Weapons Freeze Campaign. He was selective in his peacemaking; while opposing the first Gulf War in 1991 and the U.S.-led invasion of Iraq in 2003, for example, he approved of the U.S.'s leading role in NATO's massive aerial bombardment of Kosovo in 1999. Coffin was eloquent in print as well as in the pulpit. In addition to his memoir, *Once to Every Man* (1977), he published his views on Christian theology and its social and political applications in *The Courage to Love* (1982), *Living the Truth in a World of Illusions* (1985), *A Passion for the Possible* (1993), *The Heart Is a Little to the Left* (1999), *Credo* (2004), and *Letter to a Young Doubter* (2005), and he co-wrote two books on civil disobedience. Coffin was the inspiration for the character Rev. Scot Sloan in the syndicated comic strip *Doonesbury*, created by Garry Trudeau. Coffin's first two marriages, to Eva Rubinstein and Harriet Gibney, ended in divorce. His survivors included his third wife, the former Virginia Randall Wilson, a son and a daughter from his first marriage, two step-children, three grandchildren, and four step-grandchildren. He was predeceased by another son from his first marriage. Coffin died at his home in rural Strafford, Vermont. See *Current Biography* (1980).

Obituary *New York Times* A p21 Apr. 13, 2006

CROSSFIELD, A. SCOTT Oct. 2, 1921–Apr. 19, 2006 Aviator; aeronautical engineer. Among the pioneers who led the exploration of the frontiers of space in rocket-powered experimental airplanes, the name of the civilian test pilot Scott Crossfield stands out, alongside that of the U.S. Air Force aviator Chuck Yeager. Yeager was the pilot who broke the sound barrier, reaching Mach 1 in a Bell X-1 rocket plane in 1948. Crossfield raised the record to Mach 2, or twice the speed of sound, piloting a Douglas D-558-II Skyrocket at 1,320 mph in 1953. Five years later, at the controls of an X-15 rocket plane, Crossfield became the first to nudge Mach 3, or thrice the speed of sound, and survive. (Mel Apt previously succeeded in reaching Mach 3 but had died in the doing.) With his many X-15 missions, Crossfield paved the way for the National Aeronautics and Space Administration's space shuttle and its Constellation exploration program. In a eulogy, NASA administrator Michael Griffin remembered Scott "not only as one of the greatest pilots who ever flew, but as an expert aeronautical engineer, aerodynamicist, and designer who made significant contributions to the design and development of the X-15 research aircraft and to systems tests, reliability engineering, and quality assurance for the Apollo command and service modules and Saturn V second stage." Crossfield learned to fly when he was a teenager. After serving as a pilot instructor in the U.S. Navy during World War II, he earned B.S. and M.S. degrees in aeronautical engineering at the University of Washington in Seattle. During five years (1950–55) with the National Advisory Committee for Aeronautics (NACA, the predecessor of NASA), he test-piloted such experimental aircraft as the F-100 and F-102 supersonic fighters, the X-1, X-4, and X-5 rocket planes, and the Douglas 558-II Skyrocket. He flew more than 130 supersonic air-launched rocket missions at heights up to 80,000 feet. In addition to flying, he participated in the planning and supervision of projects at NACA, including the prototype of the pressurized suit that would be worn by the Mercury, Gemini, and Apollo astronauts. He played a role in the conception and design of aircraft, including the X-15, the most advanced of the experimental rocket planes. Built to far exceed Mach 3 and to reach an altitude of 50 miles, the X-15 was conceived as the research tool for solv-

ing potential engineering problems that would be encountered in manned space flight. When the contract for constructing and testing the X-15 was awarded to North American Aviation Inc. in 1955, Crossfield left NACA and joined North American as design specialist and test pilot for the project. He piloted the X-15 in its first powered flight, in 1959, and the following year he flew it at Mach 2.97 to an elevation of 81,000 feet. In 1961 he was transferred to North American's space and information division, where he spent five years directing systems testing and quality assurance for such projects as the Hound Dog air-to-ground missile, the Apollo command and service module and launch and escape system, the Paraglider Gemini recovery system, and the Saturn S-11 booster. He was technical director of engineering systems development at North American from early 1966 to July 1967, when he joined Eastern Airlines (now defunct) as a director of flight research and development. He was a division vice president at Eastern from 1968 to 1973. As a senior vice president of Hawker Siddeley Aviation for a few months (1974–75), he set up that company's U.S. subsidiary for the design and marketing of the HS-146 transport plane in North America. From 1977 to 1993 he was a technical consultant on civil aviation with the House Committee on Science and Technology in the U.S. Congress. His numerous honors included induction into the National Aviation Hall of Fame, in 1983. With Clay Blair Jr., he wrote the autobiography *Always Another Dawn: The Story of a Rocket Test Pilot* (1960). Crossfield died when the small single-engine plane he was piloting, a Cessna 210A, crashed in a thunderstorm in a remote mountainous area of Gordon County, Georgia. His survivors included his wife, Alice, four sons, two daughters, and three grandchildren. See *Current Biography* (1969).

Obituary *New York Times* B p8 Apr. 21, 2006

DALY, MAUREEN Mar. 15, 1921–Sep. 25, 2006 Author. Literary historians commonly trace the genesis of the modern young-adult genre in American fiction to *Seventeenth Summer*, the first and most famous of Maureen Daly's books. When that coming-of-age novel—grounded, in large measure, as was all of her work, in her own experience—was published by Dodd, Mead and Co. in 1942, it anticipated by a quarter of a century the full flowering of fiction written about young people for young people by the likes of S. E. Hinton and Paul Zindel. *Seventeenth Summer* was reprinted repeatedly over a period of 50 years, most recently under the Simon Pulse imprint at Simon & Schuster in 2002. It has sold more than a million copies internationally. Maureen Daly was born in County Tyrone, Ulster, Ireland. Soon after her birth her father immigrated to the United States. When she was two years old, she, along with her mother and her two older sisters, Maggie and Kay, joined their father in Fond du Lac, Wisconsin. Her younger sister, Sheila, was the only Daly child born in the United States. In Fond du Lac Maureen attended the public elementary school and St. Mary's Springs Academy. As a socially withdrawn teenager, she found an outlet for her feelings, including the painful ones, in writing short stories that were essentially autobiographical. With "Fifteen," written when she was 15, she won fourth place in *Scholastic* magazine's short-story contest for high-school students. The following year she won first place in the annual *Scholastic* magazine competition with "Sixteen," which was reprinted in the *O. Henry Memorial Award Prize Stories of 1938*. It was while she was earning her B.A. degree in English and Latin at Rosary College in River Forest, Illinois, in the early 1940s that she completed the writing of *Seventeenth Summer* on a Dodd Mead literary fellowship. In that novel she remembered, as she said, "all the funny quirks and sadnesses and happiness you go through in adolescence." The central experience of the protagonist of the novel, Angie Morrow (a thinly veiled Maureen Daly), is her falling in love for the first time during the summer following her graduation from high school. Also in the early 1940s, Daly was employed by the *Chicago Tribune* as a police reporter and the writer of an advice column for teenagers. The column was syndicated to more than a dozen newspapers, and a number of the pieces were collected in *Smoother and Smoother* (1944). Daly was subsequently an associate editor of *Ladies' Home Journal* for several years. In 1946 she married the mystery writer William P. McGivern. With him and their two children, she traveled abroad for many years and had homes in France, Italy, Ireland, England, and Spain. In 1957 she published *Twelve Around the World*, comprising true accounts of the lives of a dozen teenagers in as many countries. She wrote several travel books, and with her husband she wrote *Mention My Name in Mombasa: The Unscheduled Adventures of an American Family Abroad* (1958). In 1959 she published *Patrick Visits the Farm*, the first of several books she wrote for young children. *The Ginger Horse* was published in 1965. Her short stories were collected in *Sixteen, and Other Stories* (1961). After the death of her husband, in 1982, she completed the writing of his last mystery novel, *Matter of Honor* (1984). Her book *Acts of Love* (1986) was inspired by her memory of the 17th summer of her daughter, Megan, who had died of cancer in 1983. Her last novel for young adults, *First a Dream*, was published in 1990. During the last decades of her life, Maureen Daly McGivern, as she was known in private life, lived in Palm Desert, California, where she wrote a restaurant-review column for the *Desert Sun* newspaper. She died (of non-Hodgkins lymphoma) at her home in Daly City. Her survivors included her son, Patrick, a sister, and two grandchildren. See *Current Biography* (1946).

Obituary *New York Times* C p12 Sep. 29, 2006

DELORIA, VINE JR. Mar. 26, 1933–Nov. 13, 2005 Native American scholar. Deloria was the preeminent intellectual and spiritual luminary of the modern American Indian renaissance, best known to the general public for his book *Custer Died for Your Sins*. Initially as a political activist but most famously as a prolific author armed with an elegant style and sardonic wit (typified by his reference to the Battle of the Little Big Horn as "a sensitivity-training session"), Deloria broke stereotypes and raised consciousness regarding the histories and cultures of North American indigenous peoples and the long trail of treachery and exploitation they suffered in their relationships with white settlers and the United States government (not to mention their depiction as savages by Hollywood), and he helped move Indian affairs increasingly out of the hands of bureaucrats in Washington—as well as white anthropologists, missionaries, and dilettantes—and into the control of Indians themselves. On a deeper level, he believed that pre-reservation Indians "had a very sophisticated idea of the human personality" that "can be very useful to us today," and he professed that his "overall goal" as a writer was to translate and transpose tribes' "complex ideas" into "principles of practical relationships" that "we can recognize and understand." His most important influence was on Indians themselves, especially young Indians. Wilma Mankiller, the former principal chief of the Cherokee Nation of Oklahoma, has observed that "no writer has more clearly articulated the unspoken emotions, dreams, and lifeways of contemporary Native people" than Deloria, and Norbert Hill, a member of the Oneida tribe, has testified that Deloria "helped us wake up from a great nap of oppression, and . . . made us think about who we were as Indian people, that we could become educated, be part of the mainstream without giving up being Indians." A Standing Rock Sioux from South Dakota, Deloria served in the U.S. Marines before earning a B.S. degree at Iowa State University and then, following in the footsteps of his father (an Episcopal minister), a master's degree at the Lutheran School of Theology in Chicago. From 1964 to 1967 he worked in Washington, D.C., as executive director of the National Congress of American Indians, an organization that had been in decline and that he revived. His lobbying and testifying on Capitol Hill and dealings with the U.S. Bureau of Indian Affairs motivated him to work for a law degree, which he received at the University of Colorado in 1970. He made his spectacular debut as an author with the runaway best-seller *Custer Died for Your Sins: An Indian Manifesto* (1969), which was both a scathing account of the treatment of the aboriginal inhabitants of the continent by white settlers and the United States government and a demand for a "cultural leave-us-alone agreement" that would allow for continuance of the framework of the system administered by the U.S. Department of the Interior, but with more of the authority subcontracted to tribal chiefs and councils. In *Custer Died for Your Sins*, Deloria made vivid such subjects as aboriginal rights (a civil rights claim that Indians alone among minority groups in the U.S. can make), broken treaties, genocide, and a positive presentation of neo-tribalism as a valid form of nationalism. He elaborated upon the last point in his second book, *We Talk, You Listen: New Tribes, New Turf* (1970), an argument for a return to Native American tribal standards as an escape route from the destructive climate of technology-oriented corporate America. In *God Is Red: A Native View of Religion* (1973), Deloria contrasted ecology-oriented Native cosmology with a Western Christian worldview supportive of an imperialistic exploitation not only of people but of the land itself. He subsequently published *Behind the Trail of Broken Treaties: An Indian Declaration of Independence* (1974), *Indians of the Pacific Northwest: From the Coming of the White Man to the Present Day* (1977), and *The Metaphysics of Modern Ex-*

istence (1979). In his autobiographical submission to *World Authors 1975–1980* he explained that with *Custer Died for Your Sins* he had played "the pre-assigned role for an Indian writer" and that *The Metaphysics of Modern Existence* was "infinitely deeper and took considerably more thought" and "was an effort to join the larger intellectual community." With Clifford Lytle, Deloria co-wrote *American Indians, American Justice* (1983) and *The Nations Within: The Past and Future of American Indian Sovereignty* (1984). In *Red Earth, White Lies: Native Americans and The Myth of Scientific Fact* (1995), he challenged, partly on the strength of Indian oral legends, prevailing scientific theories about the prehistory of Earth, the reliability of carbon dating in supporting those hypotheses, and in particular the Bering Strait "hoax," the assertion that Indians were not indigenous to America but had migrated from Asia. His essay collections *Spirit and Reason* and *For This Land: Writings on Religion in America* were published in 1999, as was his book *Singing for the Spirit: A Portrait of the Dakota Sioux* (1999). The sequel to *Red Earth, White Lies* was *Evolution, Creationism, and Other Modern Myths* (2002), in which he carried the argument of the earlier book into the religious arena, rejecting both the prevailing evolutionary and creationist theories and offering an alternative neocreationist "catastrophic" theory reflecting Indian folklore. In addition to his own writings, he edited or co-edited a number of books, including *Aggressions of Civilization: Federal Indian Policy Since the 1880s* (1984) and *American Indian Policy in the Twentieth Century* (1985), and he wrote the introduction to a new edition of *Speaking of Indians* (1998). The last mentioned was written by his aunt Ella Deloria, a social scientist, and was originally published in 1944. It includes detailed descriptions of the social and ceremonial life among pre-reservation Dakotas and the rapid social change that occurred with the dawn of the reservation era. Vine Deloria Jr. was a professor of political science at the University of Arizona from 1978 until 1990, when he joined the faculty of the University of Colorado, where he taught until 2000. Throughout his career he pressed the U.S. government to live up to its treaty obligations while allowing Indian people autonomy in their development. He died in Golden, Colorado. Among his survivors were his wife, Barbara, two sons, a daughter, and seven grandchildren. See *Current Biography* (1974).

Obituary *New York Times* A p25 Nov. 15, 2005

DIEBOLD, JOHN June 8, 1926–Dec. 26, 2005 Management consultant; founder of the Diebold Group and the Diebold Institute for Public Policy Studies. Diebold was a visionary pioneer in the modern revolution in communications technology and the adviser to myriad industrial, business, and other clients worldwide in the automating of their procedures. While his firm has no connection with Diebold Inc., the maker of ATMs, he was apprising banks of the benefits of a national system of electronic funds transfer years before interstate ATM networks became a reality. Serving in the U.S. Merchant Marine in the waning years of World War II, he kept thinking, as he later recalled, "If we can build tools and

. . . have automatic firing control [in anti-aircraft systems], why can't we have an automatic factory?" He pursued that line of inquiry—the application of electronic computers to factory mechanisms—in earning his M.B.A. degree (1951) at Harvard University and then carried that application on to wider usage. In his book *Automation: The Advent of the Automatic Factory* (1952), he tried, as he said, "to tell people, particularly managers, that something so significant was brewing that it would change everything, that technologies such as computers and automation would transform the way we do business." Following a stint as a junior consultant with a Chicago management-consultant firm, he launched the Diebold Group (originally called John Diebold & Associates Inc.) in 1954. From an office in the Diebold family home in Weehawken, New Jersey, the consulting firm expanded nationally over the following several years and internationally beginning in 1958. By the end of the following decade, Diebold was directing the activities of offices in 13 cities on five continents, persuading corporations, governments, banks, hospitals, and other entities to automate their data processing and other procedures, store their records electronically, and install interoffice computer networks, and he offered them help in doing so. In the United States alone his clients included scores of major corporations, such as Boeing, Xerox, IBM, and AT&T, as well as numerous smaller entities and the municipal governments of New York City and Chicago. Diebold published some dozen books, including *Man and the Computer: Technology as an Agent of Social Change* (1969) and *Making the Future Work: Unleashing Our Powers of Innovation for the Decades Ahead* (1984). After his divorce from his first wife, he married Vanessa Vonderporten. She survived him, as did their daughter, Emma, and son, John. Diebold died at his home in Bedford Hills, New York. See *Current Biography* (1967).

Obituary *New York Times* C p8 Dec. 27, 2005

DRUCKER, PETER F. Nov. 19, 1909–Nov. 11, 2005 Austrian-born American political economist, teacher, author, and consultant. Drucker, a bold thinker in the conservative tradition, is generally recognized as the founding father of the modern discipline of management studies. He acknowledged a debt to the pioneering contribution of Frederick J. Taylor (1866–1915) to the improvement of industrial efficiency, but that contribution had been restricted to scientific work studies, whereas Drucker prominently included considerations of common sense, human relations, and culture as well as a futuristic perspective in his approach to challenges and possibilities in industrial society. With his concepts of "management by objectives" and "core competencies" and other insights and his antipathy to bureaucracies and emphasis on risk-taking—and the pith and wit with which he articulated his ideas—he exerted a pervasive influence on the corporate and public-policy-making worlds. In his obituary in *Time* (November 21, 2005), Daniel Kadlec succinctly summed up Drucker's career: "[He] foresaw inflation in the 1970s, the rise of Japan Inc. in the 1980s, and the decline of unions in the 1990s, but his most far-reaching theories were on management and labor. He argued that if workers were allowed to participate in decisions, they would not only become happier and more productive but also provide valuable insights. . . . He was a free-market champion and staunch defender of profits. But he showed how those things need not be at odds with a dignified, productive work force." Before immigrating to the United States, in 1937, Drucker earned a law degree in Germany and worked as a journalist there and as an economist with an international banking house in the United Kingdom. In the United States he taught at a succession of schools, including New York University and Claremont Graduate University, where he was a professor of social science and management since 1971. He wrote more than 30 books, including *The End of Economic Man: A Study of the New Totalitarianism* (1939), *The Future of Industrial Man* (1942), *The Concept of the Corporation* (1946), *The Practice of Management* (1955), *Landmarks of Tomorrow* (1959; with a new introduction, 1996), *The Age of Discontinuity: Guidelines to Our Changing Society* (1969), *Management: Tasks, Responsibilities, Practices* (1973), *Managing for the Future* (1992), and *Managing in a Time of Great Change* (1995). In addition to his books of nonfiction, he published the novel *The Last of All Possible Worlds* (1982). His autobiography, A*dventures of a Bystander*, was published in 1979. The sparkling collection of bon mots *The Daily Drucker: 366 Days of Insight and Motivation for Getting the Right Things Done* (2004) was assembled with the assistance of Joseph A. Maciariello. In addition to his books, which were translated into more than 30 languages and sold in the millions, he contributed numerous articles to the *Harvard Business Review* and other publications and wrote a monthly column for the *Wall Street Journal* (1975–95). He died at his home in Claremont, California. His survivors included his wife, Doris, four daughters, a son, and six grandchildren. See *Current Biography* (1964).

Obituary *New York Times* A p13 Nov. 12, 2005

DUNHAM, KATHERINE June 22, 1909–May 21, 2006 American concert dancer; choreographer; teacher; dance anthropologist; social activist. Katherine Dunham revolutionized concert dance with her so-called Dunham technique. In developing that technique she borrowed movements and rhythms from dance, music, and ritual found in the sub-Saharan African diaspora in the Caribbean, South America, and the United States and integrated them into a regimen derived from classical European-derived ballet and modern dance, thus creating a new free-form American concert dance style. The epithet "matriarch of black dance" is commonly applied to her, but she rejected the racial exclusivity therein implied. "I am so tired of being considered a leader of black dance," she declared in 2003. "I am just a person who happens to be what in this country is called 'black.' I will insist on being called, one, a person, and, two, a human being." Dunham, who began her career in Chicago, projected a glamorous persona during her performing years. In 1938 she moved her dance company to New York City, where its performances of her revues on Broadway and in top nightclubs and other venues were great success-

es. In the early 1940s the Katherine Dunham Dance Company began touring North America and Mexico, and between that time and the late 1950s, it toured a total of 57 countries. Sometimes with her troupe, she also compiled a substantial filmography. In Manhattan in 1944 Dunham opened the Dunham School of Dance and Theater, also known as the Dunham School of Arts and Research. In addition to the Dunham technique in dance, the curricula of the school included an eclectic variety of classes in arts and humanities. The alumni of the school included a wide range of dancers and other entertainers, among them Alvin Ailey, Talley Beatty, Julie Belafonte, Peter Gennaro, Eartha Kitt, Janet Collins, Vanoye Aikens, Shelley Winters, James Dean, and Marlon Brando. The school remained in operation until 1957. Dunham also founded schools elsewhere, most importantly at Southern Illinois University, in East St. Louis, Illinois, and in Haiti. Dunham was born in Chicago, into a family that lived in nearby Glen Ellyn, Illinois. Her father, a tailor and dry cleaner, was African-American; her mother, a schoolteacher, was of mixed French-Canadian and North American Indian descent. After the death of her mother, when Katherine was three, she and her brother, Albert, were raised in Chicago and, later, Joliet, Illinois, where she attended high school. "I started dancing on my own," she recalled in an interview with Deardra Shuler for the *New York Beacon* (June 14, 2000). "After school [in Joliet] there was a teacher who exposed students to some ballet and a free-form dance style." She subsequently studied dance under Ludmilla Speranzeva and Mark Turbyfill in Chicago. In a storefront in Chicago in the early 1930s, with the help of her brother as well as that of Mark Turbyfill and Earl Delamarter, she started her first dance school and organized her first dance company, the Ballet Nègre. Meanwhile she was studying social anthropology at the University of Chicago, where she received a Ph.B. (bachelor of philosophy) degree in 1936. She subsequently wrote a master's thesis. On a Julius Rosenwald Foundation grant in the mid-1930s, she made the first of her many visits to the Caribbean, studying sub-Saharan-African–derived rituals and dances, especially in Haiti, where she would eventually establish a residence and become a mambo, or priestess, in the Voodoo religion. "Going to the West Indies gave me a sense of the body, and the use of the body, the so-called primitive techniques . . . ," she once told Carolyn P. Smith for the *Belleville (Illinois) News-Democrat*. "I always had classical training, but it was the idea of the body as instrument that appealed to me. My real effort was to free the body from restriction." Dunham also did anthropological fieldwork in Brazil. Her first full-length ballet, *L'Ag'Ya*, based on a Martinican fable, was initially staged as a WPA (Works Progress Administration) Federal Theater project in Chicago in 1938. Combining her ballet *Tropics* (1938) with supplemental material, Dunham, with her company, made her Broadway debut with *Tropics and Le Jazz Hot: From Haiti to Harlem* (February–May, 1940). Included was choreography based on early African-American social dances. In the same year Dunham contributed to the International Ladies' Garment Workers' Union (ILGWU) revue *Pins and Needles*. She assisted George Balanchine in creating the choreography for the hit Broadway musical *Cabin in the Sky* (1940–41), in which she starred as Georgia Brown and which featured her dancers. Subsequently on Broadway she directed two editions of her *Tropical Revue* (1943; 1944–45), choreographed *Blue Holiday* (1945–46) and *Carib Song* (1945), produced and performed in her *Bal Nègre* (1946), and directed, choreographed, and danced in successive productions of *Katherine Dunham and Her Company* (1950, 1955). Her joyous ballet *Choros* dated from 1944. Her ballet *Southland* (1951), inspired by the murder of Emmett Till, was an impassioned indictment of lynching. Her other ballets included *Rites du Passage* and *Bambouche*, produced on Broadway in 1962. In her Hollywood debut she originated the production of *Carnival of Rhythm* (1941), choreographed the dances in that short musical film, and danced the female lead. She designed and staged the dances in the motion picture *Pardon My Sarong* (1942), danced a solo in the feature musical *Star Spangled Rhythm* (1942), was one of the galaxy of musical stars in the screen classic *Stormy Weather* (1943), and choreographed and performed with her company in the dance scenes in *Casbah* (1948). She and her dancers also appeared in the Italian film *Botta e riposta* (1949) and the Mexican-made *Música en la noche* (1958). In the role of the dance teacher in *Mambo*, a Paramount picture made in Italy in 1954 and released in the U.S. in 1955, she is seen instructing the heroine (Silvana Mangano) and other students in the Dunham technique. Later she choreographed the movies *Green Mansions* (1959) and *The Bible* (1964). In 1967 Dunham became artist-in-residence at Southern Illinois University in Edwardsville, Illinois. She helped to create a dance anthropology program and a performing-arts center at the university, where Dunham Hall and Dunham Hall Theater are named in her honor. Under the aegis of the university, she founded in the nearby African-American ghetto of East St. Louis, Illinois, the East St. Louis Center for the Performing Arts and a related Dunham Museum, children's school, and community center offering multiple social services, especially for young people. For many years she lived in East St. Louis except for the winter months, which she spent in Haiti. Her social activism ranged from civil rights protests, including her refusal to perform before segregated audiences, to fasting in solidarity with the Haitian boat people. She wrote the books *Journey to Accompong* (1946), about the Marrons, a mountain people in Jamaica; *Dances of Haiti* (1983), her 1947 master's thesis; *A Touch of Innocence: Memoirs of Childhood* (1959); *Island Possessed* (1969), about Haitian culture; and *Kasamance: A Fantasy* (1974), a story for young people, set in Senegal. Following her divorce from her first husband, Jordis McCoo, in the late 1930s, Dunham married John Pratt, a white Canadian artist who had joined her company as the designer of its lavish sets and costumes. Pratt remained Dunham's husband and close artistic collaborator for more than four decades, until his death, in 1986. They had one child, a daughter. Katherine Dunham died in New York City. See *Current Biography* (1941).

Obituary *New York Times* B p7 May 22, 2006

EDWARDS, RALPH June 13, 1913–Nov. 16, 2005 American broadcaster. Edwards was an extraordinarily successful radio and television innovator, best known as the creator, producer, and host of two of the most popular shows in the history of the two electronic media. In 1940 he created the first of those durable hits, *Truth or Consequences*, a game show in which contestants who failed to answer trick questions correctly were required to perform wildly ridiculous stunts. He emceed that weekly program on network radio until 1950 and then on network television until 1956, when he turned over the hosting to Bob Barker. In a successful publicity ploy in 1950, he persuaded the town of Hot Springs, New Mexico, to rename itself Truth or Consequences in exchange for the show's being broadcast from there—a name change that has never been rescinded. On network radio in 1948, he introduced his second great popular creation, *This Is Your Life*, a weekly presentation of the "complete life story of a living American." Most of the biographees were celebrities; a few were ordinary folk. In each instance Edwards, with the collusion of the subject's colleagues and others, took the chosen person by surprise and reunited him or her on camera with people associated with events in his or her life. Remaining as host, in 1952 he took that show to network television, where it remained until 1961. It was later syndicated, beginning in 1970, and franchises were licensed to the BBC and ITV networks in the United Kingdom. Other shows Edwards produced (a total of some 20) included *Place the Face* and *Name That Tune*. In collaboration with Stu Billett, he produced *The People's Court*, a syndicated half-hour reality series (1981–93) in which a retired California Supreme Court judge heard real-life small-claims cases. (The parties in the suits agreed to accept the judge's rulings.) Edwards's innovations included his franchising of shows, his introduction of the multi-camera, live-on-film format that became standard in television situation comedies, and his incorporation of "cause marketing" into his programs. He was credited with selling $500 million in war bonds during World War II, and throughout his career he promoted numerous charities, including the Jimmy Fund, the American Heart Association, and the March of Dimes. Edwards began writing scripts for radio station KROW in Oakland, California, when he was a junior in high school. After earning a B.A. degree in English at the University of California at Berkeley, in 1936, he sought his fortune in New York City. He was hired as a staff announcer by the Columbia Broadcasting System in 1938. With CBS, he announced 45 radio shows a week, including those of Fred Allen, Phil Baker, and Major Bowes. While working at CBS, Edwards conceived *Truth or Consequences*, and he sold the concept to the National Broadcasting Co. The first television version of the show was broadcast by NBC briefly in New York beginning on July 1, 1941, five months before Pearl Harbor interrupted the development of the television industry in the United States. The network television broadcasts of the show began on CBS (1950–51) and continued to be telecast "live on film" on NBC from 1952 to 1965; reruns were syndicated from 1966 to 1974. Edwards licensed a British franchise of *Truth or Consequences* that ran in the United Kingdom for a number of years beginning in 1955. *This Is Your Life* was televised on NBC from 1952 to 1961; in a new syndicated version launched in 1983, reruns from the original series were combined with some new programs. The British versions of *This Is Your Life* ran longer than the American prototypes, until 2003. The American Academy of Television Arts and Sciences awarded Grammys to *Truth or Consequences* in 1950 and *This Is Your Life* in 1953 and 1954. Edwards himself received an Emmy Award for lifetime achievement in 2001, six years after he was inducted into the Radio Hall of Fame. On the periphery of his early career, he gathered several Hollywood acting credits, including a starring role in *The Bamboo Blonde* (1946). Edwards died at his home in West Hollywood, California. He was predeceased by his wife, Barbara Jean, and survived by a son, two daughters, six grandchildren, and two great-grandchildren. See *Current Biography* (1943).

Obituary *New York Times* A p28 Nov. 17, 2005

FERGUSON, MAYNARD May 4, 1928–Aug. 23, 2006 Canadian-born jazz musician; bandleader. Walter "Maynard" Ferguson was a bravura player of several wind instruments, most famously the trumpet, on which he routinely soared two octaves above high C. While some jazz purists took a dim view of his "screaming" style, his "strident exhibitionism," his crossovers into pop and rock, and his experiments with electronic instruments, Ferguson "stretched the range of the trumpet upwards beyond our wildest dreams, relished every note he ever played, brought on a multitude of young musicians within his bands, and wrapped every audience before whom he appeared in the wild elixir of his music," as Steve Voce wrote in an obituary of Ferguson for the London *Independent* (August 26, 2006). Over the span of half a century, in addition to his regular gigs in such venues as Manhattan's Birdland and Blue Note jazz nightclubs, Ferguson toured North America and nations overseas with his succession of bands, which ranged from sextets to big bands with upwards of 12 pieces. His discography, comprising more than 60 albums and CDs, documents his journey from big-band swing, cool jazz, and bebop into fusion with classical, operatic, Latin, disco, sonorities he learned in India, and other, more popular sources. The recording *M.F. Horn* (1970) spawned the hit pop single "MacArthur Park," and *Conquistador* (1977) was the first jazz album in 20 years to make the Top 40 on the charts. The latter album included his Grammy Award–nominated version of "Gonna Fly Now," the theme from the film *Rocky*. Among other audience favorites in his repertoire are "Ole," "Gospel John," which he co-wrote with Jeff Steinberg, his cover of "Maria," and a number of collaborations with the composer/arranger Jay Chattaway, including "Pagliacci" and "Superbone Meets the Bad Man." In addition to the trumpet, he played the flugelhorn, the valve trombone, and the saxophone, among other instruments. He invented several mouthpieces and instruments, including a valve trumpet played with the left hand rather than the right and two unique trombones, the Firebird and the Superbone. Born into a musical family in Verdun, a suburb of Montreal, Quebec, Canada, Ferguson grew up, as he said,

"with a cellar full of brass." In childhood he learned to play the piano and the violin as well as the trumpet and other wind instruments. While still a child he began formal training at the French Conservatory of Music in Montreal. After dropping out of high school, he began playing professionally in nightclubs in Montreal when he was 15. He made his U.S. debut with Boyd Raeburn's band in 1948, and within the same year he joined Jimmy Dorsey's orchestra. The following year he began an on-and-off relationship with Charlie Barnet's big band. As headline trumpeter with Stan Kenton's orchestra, he took first place in *Down Beat* magazine's popularity polls in 1950, 1951, and 1952. After leaving the Kenton organization, he spent three years in Hollywood as first-call studio trumpeter at Paramount Pictures, immortalized on the soundtracks of such motion pictures as *The Ten Commandments* (1956). In 1956 he formed his own band, a 13-musician group known first as Maynard Ferguson and the Dream Band of Birdland and subsequently as Maynard Ferguson's Dream Band. With its effulgent brass section, the band created a sensation when it made its first appearance at the Newport Jazz Festival, in 1958, and it placed second, behind Count Basie, in *Down Beat* magazine's 1959 poll. In the late 1960s Ferguson experimented with consciousness-altering drugs at Timothy Leary's commune in Millbrook, New York, and spent a year studying meditation and lecturing on music in India. (In later years he made annual trips to India to study at the guru Sai Baba's temple in Bangalore.) In 1968 he moved with his family to England, where he organized a new big band and established a business promoting and selling his customized musical instruments. In the early 1970s he returned with his family and his band to the United States, where American musicians gradually replaced the British members. In 1976 Ferguson was seen by millions of television viewers around the world when he performed at the closing ceremonies of the 1976 Olympic Games in Montreal, Canada, performing on the trumpet his electrifying version of "Pagliacci." After experimenting with synthesizers and other electronic devices during the 1980s, he returned to acoustics with his blues-influenced Big Bop Nouveau Band (which varied between fourteen and seventeen members) in the early 1990s. Interested in introducing the young to music, he spent much of his time in his later years visiting schools across the United States. His final gig was an engagement at the Blue Note in Manhattan in July 2006. Following his marriage to and divorce from the singer Kay Brown, Ferguson married his second wife, Floralou, who died in 2005. He was also predeceased by a son. He was survived by three daughters, a stepdaughter, and two grandchildren. Ferguson, who lived in Ojai, California, died at Community Memorial Hospital in Ventura, California. See *Current Biography* (1980) and WilsonWeb (1998).

Obituary *New York Times* C p10 Aug. 25, 2006

FOLON, JEAN-MICHEL Mar. 1, 1934–Oct. 20, 2005 Belgian artist. Folon's antic and gently surreal hand ranged into varied applications of several media, including sculpture, murals, tapestries, and stage décor, but he was at root a graphic designer, obsessed with drawing from early childhood, trained in draftsmanship as a young man, and originally best known for his whimsical and distinctively stylized pen-and-ink pictures, watercolors, engravings, aquatints, and other prints, especially those reproduced as posters or magazine, newspaper, and book illustrations. His graphic works are fanciful, bordering on the naïve, and compact and simple, in keeping with his motto, "Less is more." His signature motif is the Folon Everyman, a cartoonish figure with the torso of a giant pear (concealed by a tent-like raincoat) topped by a tiny head wearing a fedora, a lonely urban character boxed in by the technoculture and dreamily taking flight from it. Consistent with the leitmotif running through his art is his next-most-common recurring character, an avian/human with multicolored wings, expressing his sentiment that "when one flies, one is free." In reviewing a retrospective of his watercolors and prints at the Metropolitan Museum of Art in 1990, Edward M. Gomez wrote for *Time* magazine: "Folon's career can be seen, the artist proposes ironically, as a testament to the nurturing power of boredom. The son of a Brussels paper wholesaler, Folon quickly came to regard Belgium as 'a mental prison, the most boring place on earth.' Art became his means of escape from stifling surroundings, as it was, he suggests, for such other Belgian-born painters as James Ensor and René Magritte. Like them, Folon took a strong turn for the fantastic. . . . But Folon's pictures . . . have always owed more to the purposefully childlike simplicity of Paul Klee than to hallucinatory or dualistic styles." Reluctantly, out of deference to the wishes of his father, Folon studied architecture in Brussels for four years. When he was in his early 20s, he moved to Bougival on the outskirts of Paris, France, where he worked as an architectural draftsman while seeking recognition as a graphic artist. That recognition came very slowly and, in France, only after his drawings had found favor in the U.S. and Italy. A breakthrough came with "New York, Site Unseen," a set of line drawings published in the summer 1965 issue of the American magazine *Horizon*. As the title suggests, those drawings are imagined views of a metropolis he had not yet visited. They picture New Yorkers as anonymous herds of humans living and moving in the oppressive shadow of skyscrapers and television antennae. Such drawings were in part, he explained, his "revenge on what I had been taught in architecture school." After actually seeing Manhattan, he depicted it in a cover for the *New Yorker* (December 3, 1966) as a scene of intense clutter in which, amidst a sepia fog, the directional arrows in traffic signs point (not helpfully) in all directions (a basic Folon metaphor) and, in the foreground, human figures argue in imitation of the signs. "Arrows are the symbols of confusion of an entire era," he explained. "What would happen if, one night, someone were to remove all the traffic signs from the face of the earth?" The omnipresent arrows are included in "Laughter in the Labyrinth," a portfolio of seven drawings published in *Fortune* magazine in February 1966. Those drawings picture Folon's bewildered Everyman enmeshed in an urban maze consisting of walls of stairs leading nowhere and jumbles of streets in a canyon of skyscrapers. Folon also contributed drawings to *Esquire*, the At-

lantic Monthly, and the op-ed page of the *New York Times*, and he made four covers for *Time* magazine. His 1970 design "The Cry," executed with brush, pen, and colored inks, consists of 24 arrows sprouting from one central point but in helter-skelter fashion. In a visit to Italy during the late 1960s, Folon met and began a long-term professional relationship with Giorgio Soavi, the writer and publicity director of the Olivetti Corp., who commissioned him to design Olivetti ads as well as illustrations for books the company published as promotional gifts, among other projects. On commission from Olivetti in 1975 Folon created the mural *Paysage* (Landscape), which adorns a wall in the London Underground's Waterloo Station. Also in the mid-1970s, he designed a mural for the Metro in Brussels, and later he created murals for sites in Rome and Milan, Italy. At the same time he continued to turn out watercolors and other small-scale graphic designs, such as the quasi-surreal nature studies *The Look* (1975) and *One Morning* (1975) as well as *The Crowd* (1979), a reiteration of the theme of human alienation in a high-tech age. His most witnessed work was an animated cartoon he designed for state-run French television channel Antenne 2 (now defunct), in which his Everyman, dressed in blue, was seen floating skyward into the sunset. That sequence, accompanied by tranquilizing music, was the channel's nightly sign-off credit from 1975 into the 1980s. In addition to the numerous works by others that he illustrated, ranging from the tales of Jean de La Fontaine to the complete works of Jacques Prévert, he published a number of volumes devoted expressly to his art, including the books of watercolors *The Death of a Tree* (1976) and *The Eyewitness* (1980). The book *Posters by Folon* (1978) includes reproductions of posters he designed for three of his favorite causes— Greenpeace, Amnesty International, and the United Nations Children's Fund. An interchange between Folon and his friend the American graphic artist Milton Glaser is recorded in the slim volume *The Conversation* (1983). In 1985 Folon moved to Monaco, where he established space alongside other artists in a large communal workshop. There, he began sculpting, first in wood and later in clay, plaster, bronze, and marble. Some of his large sculptures can be seen at sites in Lisbon, Portugal, Brussels, Belgium, and Pietrasanta, Italy, among other cities. In 1989 he created the official logo for the celebration of the bicentennial of the French Revolution. Also in 1989, one of his tapestries was hung in the Palais des Congrès in Monaco, and stained-glass windows he designed were installed in the Chapelle de Pise in Pisa, Italy. His most acclaimed creations in stage décor were the sets and costumes he designed for a new production of La Bohème at the Puccini Festival in Torre del Lago near Pietrasanta, Italy, in the summer of 2003. In the year 2000 Folon established at the Chateau de La Hulpe near Brussels the Folon Foundation, including a museum where several hundred of his works are on display. Profits from the foundation are said to be dedicated to helping the disabled. Folon's art is represented in major museums internationally as well as numerous galleries, including his home galleries, the Galerie Guy Peters in Saint-Paul-de-Vence, France and the Nuages Gallery in Milan, Italy. His first marriage, to the writer and illustrator Colette Portal, ended in divorce. His survivors included his second wife, Paolina, and his son from his first marriage, François. He died in Monaco. See *Current Biography* (1981).

Obituary *New York Times* C p14 Oct. 22, 2005

FOWLES, JOHN Mar. 31, 1926–Nov. 5, 2005 British novelist. Fowles was an early postmodernist and a complex myth-making fabulist. His uncommon literary range and sensibility and his experimental metafictional devices—including open, ambiguous, or alternative endings—were combined with riveting storytelling (along with generous servings of sex), all of which enabled him to realize a mass popularity rare among authors so demanding of their readers. His intricately constructed, multilayered fiction was imbued with Heraclitan and existentialist philosophy, along with an anti-egalitarianism dividing society into the conformist herd, the "Many," and an elite "Few" capable of choosing their "authentic" destiny in a chaotic universe. The brute force of the Many too often overwhelms the Few, as in Fowles's sensational first published novel, *The Collector* (1963), a chilling tale of deadly, psychopathic sexual obsession. Fowles advanced his literary reputation with *The Magus* (1966), a complicated novel in which the protagonist finds himself in a labyrinthine "metatheater" controlled by an Aegean sorcerer, and he cemented it with the mystery-laden historical romance *The French Lieutenant's Woman* (1979), an intellectual tour de force that was his most successful work, both critically and commercially. He went on to publish three more novels and a collection of shorter fiction, *The Ebony Tower* (1974). He also published books of nonfiction, including *The Aristos* (1964), a volume of philosophical aphorisms, *The Tree* (1979), a book of reflections on nature and its relation to the creative arts, especially his own fiction, and *The Enigma of Stonehenge* (1980). *Wormholes*, a collection of his essays and occasional writings, was published in 1998. The first volume of his *Journals* was published in 2003; the second was slated to be published posthumously, in 2006. Fowles was a misanthropic rebel who traced his emphasis on individual free will and his "intense and continuing dislike of mankind en masse" to his scorn for the middle-class "pursuit of respectability" that surrounded him when he was growing up in Leigh-on-Sea in Essex, England, within commuting distance of London. When evacuated to the countryside of Devon as a teenager during World War II, he found in nature "the mystery and beauty that the human environment lacked." After boarding school and military service, he read French (or modern languages, according to one source) at Oxford University, where be became influenced by European traditions in literature, especially existentialism. Following his graduation, he lectured in English at the University of Poitiers in France (1950–51) and taught English as a second language at the Anargyrios and Korgialenios School, a boarding school for boys on the Greek island of Spetsai (1951–53), which provided the setting for *The Magus*. While teaching at Spetsai he found his muse in Elizabeth Christy, whom he wooed away from her husband, a fellow teacher. When he and Elizabeth married, in England in 1954,

she reluctantly left her daughter, a toddler, behind, in the custody of the child's father. After a stint at a finishing school in Herefordshire, Fowles taught English—ultimately serving as head of the department—at St. Godric's College in north London, until the success of *The Collector*, an instant best-seller, enabled him in 1963 to quit teaching and concentrate on writing. *The Collector* is an archetypal good-and-evil story in which the villain is Frederick Clegg, a poorly educated and sexually impotent clerk and amateur butterfly collector who turns his skills as a hunter and curator in the direction of human prey. The existential heroine of the story is the beautiful and talented Miranda Grey, an art student after whom Clegg has long lusted from afar and whom he "collects" and keeps imprisoned in his basement until she dies of pneumonia for want of medical attention. The most disturbing note in the suspenseful tale is struck at the end, when Clegg begins stalking a new victim, Marian, opening the prospect of serialism. *The Collector* was translated into more than a dozen languages and was made into a popular movie (1965). Fowles said he intended the book not as a crime novel but as "a parable . . . to show that our world is sick"; some critics blamed it for possibly inspiring or abetting the sickness of some real-life serial sexual predators. Nicholas Urfe, the protagonist of Fowles's second novel, *The Magus*, is, like the author, a British schoolteacher and, also like the author, a confessed cad with women. Visiting a remote Greek island, Urfe becomes the pawn in a "God-game" conjured up by trickery or magic by the title character, the rich Anglo-Greek cult leader Maurice Conchis. Fowles (essentially an atheist whose only god was an imagined deus abscondus, a diety who has vanished from his creation) described *The Magus* as "a fable" in which "the house of Conchis" is "a model of the universe," a literally godforsaken, "unpredictable" place in which "one has to decide how to act" in order to "impose an order on it" and "a meaningful pattern on [one's own] existence." Although he himself wrote the screenplay, he regarded the film adaptation of *The Magus* (1968) as "a disaster." His third and best-known novel, *The French Lieutenant's Woman*, set on the Dorset coast in 1867, is a triangular romance parodying the Victorian melodramatic style, with editorial asides by the omniscient 20th-century narrator. The triangle's members are Charles Smithson, an amateur geologist (like Fowles), his fiancée, Ernestina Freeman, and the mysterious anti-heroine of the title, Sarah Woodruff. The novel's many innovations include backward and forward shifts in time and multiple-choice endings. The enormous success of the novel was crowned by the great success of the screen adaptation (1972), written by Harold Pinter. Fowles's experience in Hollywood—including his assisting on the script for *The Collector*—provided much of the grist for his fourth novel, *Daniel Martin* (1977), in which a middle-aged British playwright and screenwriter looks back over his life with a critical eye. The surreal and ironic comic short novel *Mantissa* (1982) takes place entirely in the imagination of its protagonist, Mike Green, a novelist who awakes in a hospital with amnesia and proceeds to reconsider the process of novel writing and the relationship of the novelist to his muse. In that book Fowles wildly parodies his postmodernism and makes fun of the pervasive eroticism in his earlier novels and the importance he placed on sexual conquests in his personal life. He moved beyond existentialism in his sixth and last published novel, *A Maggot* (1985). That book begins ostensibly as an 18th-century historical novel but soon turns into a pastiche of several genres, including mystery and science fiction. The pastiche serves as a vehicle for the transmission of historical information and an examination of the nature of history and historiography. "There are two writers in John Fowles," Robert Nye wrote in his review of *The Maggot* for the London *Guardian*. "One of them is haunted by indelible images and fashions a powerful story when he follows those images to their logical conclusions. . . . This is the poet Fowles, who trusts the unconscious and has something of a genuine mythological imagination at work in him. The other Fowles, alas, is didactic, a preacher/teacher [given to] authorial interventions." Following a stroke he suffered in 1988, Fowles did little writing outside of his journals and occasional pieces. After the death of his first wife, in 1970, he had relationships with several younger women. In 1998 he married Sarah Smith, a longtime family friend. He died at his home overlooking the English Channel in Lyme Regis, Dorset, the subject of his book *A Short History of Lyme Regis* (1983). See *Current Biography* (1977).

Obituary *New York Times* A p25 Nov. 8, 2005

FRANCIOSA, ANTHONY Oct. 25, 1928–Jan. 19, 2006 Actor. Franciosa was a "method" actor whose natural intensity energized his performances on stage, screen, and television but sometimes affected his life and career deleteriously. Born into a broken Italian-American home in Manhattan, Franciosa grew up tough in an East Harlem slum. He ventured into acting by serendipity, when he accompanied a friend to an audition at the Lexington Avenue YMCA and found himself reading for a role that was not being filled. Immediately stage-struck, he embarked on a course of participation in works mounted by a series of small acting groups, culminating in the Actors Studio, the elite Manhattan theater workshop then directed by Lee Strasberg and devoted to training professional actors in the Stanislavski method of character development, from within one's self. On Broadway, he made his debut as Cadet Starkson in the military-academy drama *End as a Man* (1953–54) and he was subsequently cast as Ralph in *Wedding Breakfast* (1954–55). His breakthrough came with his performance as Polo Pope, the well-meaning brother and enabler of the drug addict Johnny Pope (Ben Gazzara) and the brother-in-law in love with Celia Pope (Shelley Winters) in *A Hatful of Rain*, which began a Broadway run of 389 performances in November 1955. That portrayal drew a Tony Award nomination and led to the burgeoning of his employment in such television dramatic showcases as *Studio One* and the *Kraft Television Theatre*. It also brought him the offer—which he accepted—of a major motion-picture supporting role, that of Joey De-Palma, the manipulative personal manager/promoter of the Andy Griffith character in the director Elia Kazan's *A Face in the Crowd* (1957). He then reprised—and drew an Oscar nomination

with—his portrayal of Polo Pope in the screen version of *A Hatful of Rain* (1957). In the romantic screen comedy *This Could Be the Night* (1957), he co-starred—opposite Jean Simmons—as the gangster/nightclub owner Tony Armotti. In his fourth feature film, the Western *Wild Is the Wind* (1957), starring Anthony Quinn and Anna Magnani, he was cast in the major supporting role of Bene, the lusty ranch hand and rival male love interest. He had the featured part of Jody Varner in the distinguished cast of *The Long, Hot Summer*, but by the time that film was released, in 1958, his Hollywood decline had begun. Growing insider gossip about alleged displays of irascible temperament during movie productions, from dressing-room sulking to volatile outbursts with directors and his fellow actors, was compounded by the public notoriety ensuing from reports of his being jailed for assaulting a press photographer in 1957 and for marijuana possession in 1959. While he did not disappear from the silver screen—he had roles as Goya in *The Naked Maja* (1958), Victor Santini in *The Story on Page One* (1959), Sam Lawson in *Career* (1959), Nick Stratton in *Go Naked in the World* (1961), Ralph Blitz in *Period of Adjustment* (1962), and Juan Luis Rodriguez in *Rio Conchos* (1964)—film offers diminished, and more of them came from foreign producers. Beginning in 1960, Franciosa returned increasingly to roles in television drama showcases, situation comedies, and adventure series. His own first network TV series was *Valentine's Day* (September 1964–September 1965), an ABC sitcom in which he played Valentine Farrow, a swinging Manhattan publishing executive. In November 1966 he co-starred with Susan Saint James in the pilot for the NBC crime show *The Name of the Game* (September 1968–September 1971). In the latter, playing Jeff Dillon, an investigative reporter for *Crime* magazine, he shared star billing for some time alternately with Gene Barry and Robert Stack before he was dropped from the cast for what Shelley Winters described as "erratic behavior." His acting credits, in feature films as well as on television, continued into the 1990s. After his marriage to and divorce from Beatrice Bakalyar (1952–57), Shelley Winters (1957–60), and Judy Balaban Kanter (1961–67), Franciosa married Rita Thiel, in 1970. He had a daughter from his third marriage and two sons from his fourth. He died in Los Angeles. See *Current Biography* (1961).

Obituary *New York Times* C p14 Jan. 21, 2006

FRANK, REUVEN Dec. 7, 1920–Feb. 5, 2006 Canadian-born American broadcast journalist. As a producer and top executive with the NBC network's news division, Frank was a founding father of TV journalism, one of the pioneers "who made up the rule book of television news as they went along," as Bill Carter once observed in the *New York Times*. In the view of the NBC News producer Steve Friedman, Frank "really invented the evening news." Frank received a B.S. degree in social science at the City College of New York before serving with the U.S. Army in World War II; after the war he earned an M.Sc. degree from the Graduate School of Journalism at Columbia University. From 1947 to 1950 he worked as a print journalist with the *Newark (New Jersey) Eve-*

ning News. He joined NBC News as a writer in 1950, and the following year he became news editor and chief writer for NBC's first evening news telecast, the *Camel News Caravan.* For several years beginning in 1954, he supervised such experiments in half-hour news discussion programs as *Outlook, Background,* and *Chet Huntley Reporting,* and he was the executive producer who developed the multitiered system of communication control that became standard in the coverage of political conventions by all three television networks. He created the celebrated newsanchor partnership of Chet Huntley and David Brinkley, and he later guided the rise of Tom Brokaw, Linda Ellerbee, and Andrea Mitchell. Huntley and Brinkley made their debut as a duo covering the national Democratic and Republican conventions in the summer of 1956, and they went on to replace the *Camel News Caravan* as the anchors of the *Huntley-Brinkley Report* the following October. The Huntley-Brinkley program almost immediately shot to first place in the Nielsen ratings for networktelevision evening newscasts, and it remained there for most of its 14-year run. During a sabbatical from supervision of the *Huntley-Brinkley Report,* Frank produced five documentaries, among them *The Tunnel,* an account of how 59 East Berliners dug their way under the Berlin Wall to West Berlin, which received the Emmy Award for best program of the 1962–63 television season. For other productions he won Peabody, George Polk, and DuPont-Columbia Awards. He was promoted to the executive vice presidency of NBC News in 1967 and to the presidency the following year. In 1973 he resigned as president and returned to the production of programs, including newsmagazines and documentaries. He again served as president from 1982 until he left NBC in 1984. His memoir, *Out of Thin Air: The Brief Wonderful Life of Nightly News,* was published in 1991. Frank died in Englewood, New Jersey. His survivors included his wife, Bernice, two sons, and a grandson and granddaughter. See *Current Biography* (1973).

Obituary *New York Times* A p18 Feb. 7, 2006

FREED, JAMES INGO June 23, 1930–Dec. 15, 2005 German-born American architect. Freed was a longtime professional partner of I. M. Pei and a reconstructed protégé of the master European modernist Ludwig Mies van der Rohe. For the better part of two decades early in his career, Freed's architectural designs were heavily influenced by modernism's spare and streamlined geometric style, stressing function and eschewing ornamentation, until he decided that "Mies's theories led to buildings that were too abstracted." Thereafter he sought to design buildings that would "appeal to all the senses" and invite human interaction. One of his major latter-day eclectic creations was the Jacob K. Javits Convention Center, his cavernous "crystal palace" on the west side of Midtown Manhattan, which opened in 1986. His greatest postmodernist legacy, completed in 1993, is the grimly expressionist United States Holocaust Memorial Museum in Washington, D.C., dedicated to the memory of the millions of Jews and others who suffered and died in Hitler's 12-year genocidal reign of terror. In designing that 265,000-square-foot complex of two auditoriums, several halls and galleries,

and other venues, he intended not simply to provide the housing for a library and research center, lecture space, and various multimedia exhibits relating to the Holocaust, incorporating films, recorded oral histories, and photographs as well as such artifacts as a boxcar, suitcases, shoes, and eyeglasses; he meant primarily to offer those entering therein an environment for "an awful experience," one of "mystery, fear, a sense of unbelieving." The effect is generally claustrophobic, with a notable exception in the atrium, called the Hall of Remembrance, which has a skewed three-story-high glass roof. As quoted by Blair Kamin in his obituary of Freed for the *Chicago Tribune,* Freed spoke about the last-named feature in these words: "Light is the only thing I know that heals. People at the [Nazi concentration] camps said the sky was the only way out." Freed, who was born into a nonreligious Jewish family in Essen, fled Nazi Germany and the continent of Europe in 1939, when he was nine and World War II was beginning. With his older sister, he immigrated to the United States and settled with relatives in Chicago, where the siblings were joined by their parents two years later. He became a student of Mies van der Rohe (himself a refugee from Germany) when he matriculated at the Armour Institute of Technology (later renamed the Illinois Institute of Technology), where Mies then headed the school of architecture. After receiving his bachelor of architecture degree in 1953, Freed spent two years with the U.S. Army Corps of Engineers, fulfilling his military service requirement, and then worked for a few months for Mies van der Rohe on the Seagram Building in New York City, the skyscraper widely regarded as Mies's masterpiece. With I. M. Pei's firm (then I. M. Pei & Partners), beginning in 1956, he contributed to the modernist designs for a large-scale urban-renewal project in Washington, D.C., and a variety of projects in New York City, including University Plaza, the Kips Bay Plaza high-rise residential complex, New York University Towers, consisting of three 30-story apartment buildings, and a 30-story office tower at 88 Pine Street in Manhattan's financial district. The last mentioned, completed in 1973, was, as he said, his "last overtly modernist building." His first design in a new direction was the National Bank of Commerce in Lincoln, Nebraska. Before the completion of that project (in 1976) he returned to the Illinois Institute of Technology, where he served as dean of the school of architecture for three years (1975–78). In 1978 he rejoined the Pei firm, which was renamed Pei Cobb Freed & Partners in 1980. He was the principal designer of One West Loop Plaza in Houston, Texas (1980), Gem City Savings Bank in Dayton, Ohio (1981), the Potomac Tower office building in Rosslyn, Virginia (1989), the First Bank Place office tower in Minneapolis, Minnesota (1992), and the expansion of the Los Angeles Convention Center (1993), in California. He later designed, among other buildings, the San Francisco Public Library's new main building and the Ronald Reagan Building, the Federal Triangle, and the International Trade Center in Washington, D.C. The execution of his design for the U.S. Air Force Memorial in Arlington, Virginia, was nearing completion at the time of his death. He died at his home in Manhattan. His survivors included his daughter, Dara Freed, and a grandson. His wife, the artist Hermine Freed, died in 1998. See *Current Biography* (1994).

Obituary *New York Times* B p8 Dec. 17, 2005

FRIEDAN, BETTY Feb. 4, 1921–Feb. 4, 2006 Writer; social activist. Friedan (née Bettye Goldstein) was a pioneering, catalytic polemicist in the women's-liberation movement, the so-called Second Wave of the feminist revolution that began with the women's suffrage struggle of the late 1800s and early 1900s. She was not without ideological adversaries in some feminist factions, but none can gainsay her role in setting the Second Wave in motion with her first book, *The Feminine Mystique* (1963). That now-classic best-seller raised the consciousness of millions of women and empowered homemakers to find "work and meaning outside of raising their children and feeding their husbands," as Anna Quindlen wrote in her introduction to the 1997 edition of the book. "Out of Friedan's argument that women had been coaxed into selling out their intellect and their ambitions for the paltry price of a new washing machine . . . came a great wave of change in which women demanded equality and parity under the law and in the workplace." Friedan began expounding leftist views on political and social issues as the editor of a campus weekly when she was majoring in psychology at Smith College. While at Smith she attended a summer course at the Highlander Folk School (now the Highlander Research and Education Center), in Tennessee, a center for leadership training in such progressive causes as labor and civil rights. After graduating summa cum laude from Smith (1942) and doing graduate work at the University of California, Berkeley (1942–43), she worked as a feature writer at Federated Press (1943–46), which provided news and features to union publications, and a staff reporter with the more radical *UE News* (1946–52), the newsletter of the United Electrical, Radio and Machine Workers of America. She married in 1947. With her second pregnancy, she was denied maternity leave and was fired by *UE News*. "My own conscious feminism," she later wrote, "began in later outrage at that mistaken either/or choice." During the mid-1950s, while she was writing noncontroversial freelance articles for women's magazines, the genesis of her first book was beginning, as she put it, as a "question mark in my own life." The microscopic question mark became macrocosmic in 1957, when she conducted a survey for a Smith College magazine revealing that her restiveness as a homemaker was shared by a large number of her sister alumnae. After several years of research and interviews with women nationwide, she published *The Feminine Mystique*, in which she debunked the myth of "happy female domesticity" (Marilyn French's paraphrase), an illusion fostered in large measure by advertising hype in the post–World War II years. Within four decades of its initial run, the book had sold more than three million copies worldwide. Her later books on the women's movement included *It Changed My Life* (1976), *The Second Stage* (1981), and *Rethinking Feminist Concerns* (1994). She explored aging and ageism in *The Fountain of Age* (1993). Her memoir *Life So Far* was published in 2000. Friedan was among the founders of the National Organization for Women, and she served as the first president of NOW (1966–70). She was also one of the founders of Naral Pro-Choice America (originally named the National Association for the Repeal of Abortion Laws) and the National Women's Political Caucus. She divorced in 1969. She died at her home, in Washington, D.C. Her survivors included her three children and nine grandchildren. See *Current Biography* (1989).

Obituary *New York Times* A p20 Feb. 5, 2006

GERBNER, GEORGE Aug. 1919–Dec. 24, 2005 Hungarian-born social scientist and educator. Gerbner was a leader in the field of communications research, specializing in the study of "mass-media message systems and the public images and assumptions that they cultivate." He pioneered the development of what is called cultivation theory, which links the content of television programs, especially situation comedies, dramas, and other story-telling shows, with the way viewers of them perceive the world. "If you can write a nation's stories," he once explained, "you needn't worry about who makes the laws." He told Michael Toms in a *New Dimensions* radio broadcast (program 2703): "A child today, for the first time in human history, is born into a home in which . . . it is no longer the parent who tells the stories, or the school, or the church, or the community. And in many cases around the world it's not even programming from the native country but essentially a handful of global conglomerates that basically have nothing to tell but a great deal to sell. That is the great human transformation of the past hundred years." After earning a B.A. degree in journalism at the University of California at Los Angeles, Gerbner worked briefly as a journalist in San Francisco before serving with the Office of Strategic Services behind enemy lines in World War II. While doing graduate work in communications at the University of Southern California between 1947 and 1955, he worked in a succession of positions in schools and school systems in Southern California. He earned a doctoral degree in 1955. He was research assistant professor in the Institute of Communications Research at the University of Illinois from 1956 to 1964, when he became dean of the Annenberg School of Communications at the University of Pennsylvania. At the request of the federal government and with federal grants, beginning in the late 1960s, he and his team of researchers studied violent content in network television programs and, through demographically wide surveys, measured the effect on viewers' perceptions of reality. One of his major conclusions was that heavy television viewing tends to result in a "mean world syndrome," in which the fearfulness of the state of society is exaggerated, making viewers more open to accepting political or social repression to relieve their insecurities. Those studies became the basis of his long-term and ongoing Cultural Indicators Project, a vast database of videotapes of prime-time network television shows amassed over the decades, along with a bibliography of hundreds of studies related to trends in the programming. The concerns of the studies span a wide range, including the manner of portrayal of sex roles, minorities, aging, ecological attitudes, occupations, and religion. Gerbner remained dean of the Annenberg School of Communications at the University of Pennsylvania until 1989, when he became professor of telecommunications at Temple University. He subsequently founded the Cultural Environment Movement, which, in his words, strived to "reassert democratic influence on the media." Articles he contributed to the quarterly *Journal of Communication* (of which he was executive editor) and the *International Journal of Communications* (of which he was chairman of the board) and other essays by him were collected in his book *Against the Mainstream* (2002). He co-wrote or co-edited books on such subjects as "the media's war" in the Persian Gulf, trends in television drama, the representation of women and minorities in the mass media, and how computers and other new communications technologies affect the social distribution of power. Several videorecordings made by him are available in libraries, including *The Electronic Storyteller* (1997) and *The Crisis of the Cultural Environment* (1997). Gerbner died at his home in Philadelphia. His wife, Ilona, predeceased him by 16 days. His survivors included two sons and five grandchildren. See *Current Biography* (1983).

Obituary *New York Times* B p7 Jan. 3, 2006

GOWDY, CURT July 31, 1919–Feb. 20, 2006 Broadcaster. As cited in the Peabody Awards presentations of 1969, Gowdy was network television's "most versatile sportscaster" in the pre-cable era. "Over the years," the Peabody citation read, "Mr. Gowdy has achieved top stature with a winning blend of reportorial accuracy, a vast fund of knowledge in many areas, intelligence, good humor, and an infectiously honest enthusiasm for his subject." Gowdy worked at radio stations in Cheyenne, Wyoming, and Oklahoma City, Oklahoma, before he gained fame, at first chiefly for his play-by-play reportage of major-league baseball. From the beginning of the 1949 baseball season through 1950, he backed up Mel Allen in calling the games of the New York Yankees on radio station WINS in New York City. As the lead announcer doing play-by-play reportage of Boston Red Sox baseball games from 1951 through 1965, he was heard on Boston radio station WHDH and, successively, on three Boston television stations. Beginning in 1961, when he was still broadcasting Red Sox games during the summers, he teamed up autumns with Paul Christman to report American Football League games—as well as some college football games—on network television, first on ABC (1961–65) and subsequently on NBC. After the AFL merged into the National Football League in 1970, he called NFL games for NBC. Under his long-term contract with NBC, his other assignments included *Game of the Week*, a Saturday afternoon play-by-play report of an outstanding major-league baseball game, from 1966 to 1975, and 10 consecutive World Series during the same period. After leaving NBC he did play-by-play baseball coverage on CBS radio. On the ABC television network from 1965 to 1984, he hosted *The American Sportsman*, a field-and-stream show featuring films of athletes and other celebrities on hunting and fishing trips. For three seasons (1974–77) on the Public Broadcasting Service, he hosted *The Way*

It Was, a sports nostalgia show on which he and guest athletes commented on film footage of great sports events. Record keepers disagree slightly on some of the figures, but the consensus is that Gowdy did network television coverage of at least 16 All-Star Games, 12 Rose Bowls, seven Olympic Games, 24 NCAA Final Four basketball championships, and eight Super Bowls. He was inducted into the broadcast wing of the Baseball Hall of Fame in 1984. Among his other honors was the naming of Curt Gowdy State Park in Wyoming in 1971. Outside of baseball, Gowdy became wealthy as the owner of a total of five radio stations in Lawrence, Massachusetts, and Laramie, Wyoming. He died at his home in Palm Beach, Florida. His survivors included his wife, Jerre, two sons, a daughter, and five grandchildren. See *Current Biography* (1967).

Obituary *New York Times* C p11 Feb. 21, 2006

HAMMOND, CALEB D. JR. June 24, 1915–June 5, 2006 Publisher and cartographer. As president (1948–74) and chairman (1974–98) of C. S. Hammond & Co., C. D. Hammond reinforced the family firm's status in cartography, second only to that of Rand McNally among American publishers of maps and atlases. He did so with the help of his chief cartographer, Herbert Pierce, his son, C. Dean Hammond, who succeeded him as chief executive officer, and the 100-plus draftspeople, artists, and researchers who were in his employ before they were replaced by computer technology. C. S. Hammond & Co. was founded in New York City by C. D.'s paternal grandfather in 1900. C. D. joined the company as a production manager in 1939, after earning a degree in mechanical engineering. He became a vice president upon the death of his father, in 1942. After World War II service with the U.S. Coast Guard, he returned to the company as vice president in charge of sales and management; he succeeded to the presidency upon the death of his uncle, Robert S. Hammond. In 1974 he was succeeded in the presidency by his son, and in 1998 he retired as chairman. C. S. Hammond & Co. was based for many decades in a plant in Maplewood, New Jersey. Sold to the Langenscheidt Group in 1999, the company is now known as the Hammond World Atlas Corp. and is located in Springfield, New Jersey. C. D. Hammond lived in Maplewood and died in Summit, New Jersey. He was survived by his wife, Patricia, his son, two daughters, eight grandchildren, and six great-grandchildren. See *Current Biography* (1956).

Obituary *New York Times* C p11 June 9, 2006

HARRER, HEINRICH July 6, 1912–Jan. 7, 2005 Austrian mountaineer and explorer; author. To those unfamiliar with the annals of mountain climbing and exploration, Harrer is perhaps best known by way of Brad Pitt's portrayal of him in the motion picture *Seven Years in Tibet* (1997), based on Harrer's best-selling memoir *Sieben Jahre in Tibet* (1952; *Seven Years in Tibet*, 1953). Born in Hüttenberg, Austria, Harrer spent much of his childhood and youth in the nearby Alps, mountain climbing during the summers and skiing during the winters. While working toward a degree in geography and physical training at Graz University, he won a place on the Austrian

Olympic ski team in 1936. Two years later, with three companions, he successfully undertook his first hazardous mountain-climbing project, the ascent of the formidable Mordwand, the north face of Mount Eiger, a 13,040-foot peak in the Bernese Alps, Europe's greatest mountaineering challenge, one that has lured a number of climbers to their deaths. To his expressed later regret, when Germany occupied Austria in 1938 he joined the Nazi Party and the SS, the party's police wing. He would later try to explain that he made the "stupid mistake" because of the perquisites, chiefly access to a sports-coaching job and participation in a government-financed Himalayan expedition. The goal of that expedition was the unconquered, sheer Diamir flank of Nanga Parbat in Kashmir, the ninth-highest peak in the world. The expedition was cut short in its preparatory stage, when World War II broke out, in 1939. Harrer was arrested by British troops and interned in a prisoner-of-war camp near Dehra Dun, India. He attempted to escape twice, unsuccessfully in 1943 and successfully in 1944. Making his way to Tibet, he met the Dalai Lama Tenzin Gyatso, who was then about nine years old, and a few years later became the boy's tutor. He remained in the young Buddhist spiritual leader's employ until Communist Chinese troops occupied Tibet. He fled to India via Sikkim in March 1951, shortly before the Dalai Lama himself was forced to flee. (The Dalai Lama remained his lifelong friend and supporter, having received Harrer's assurance that his conscience was clear regarding his Nazi past.) Before leaving the Himalayas and returning to Austria, Harrer joined a mountaineer from New Zealand named Thomas in scaling a previously unconquered peak in the Panch Chuli massif. He subsequently climbed mountains or explored remote areas in Indonesia, Suriname, the Andes, Alaska, and the Ruwenzori Mountains in Africa, among other places. He recounted his adventures in some dozen books, including those translated as *The White Spider: The Story of the North Face of the Eiger* (1959), *Return to Tibet* (1964), *I Come from the Stone Age* (1965), and *Ladakh: Gods and Mortals behind the Himalayas* (1980). *Lost Lhasa: Heinrich Harrer's Tibet* (1992) is a collection of photographs with text. His autobiography, *Mein Leben*, was published in 2002. Harrer also made many documentary films, and he founded a Tibetan museum in Austria. After he grew too old for mountain climbing and skiing, he became successful at golf. He was married three times and divorced twice. His survivors included his third wife, Katharina, and his son from his first marriage, Peter. He died in Friesach, Austria. See *Current Biography* (1954).

Obituary *New York Times* C p17 Jan. 10, 2006

HASHIMOTO, RYUTARO July 29, 1937–July 1, 2006 Japanese politician and statesman. Hashimoto, a leader of the conservative, pro-business Liberal Democratic Party (LDP), was prime minister of Japan from 1996 to 1998. He became prime minister at a time when Japan was in economic crisis; in the opinion of many, his supply-side approach to the demand-hungry Japanese economy was a factor in the worsening of the crisis. As an administrative reformer Hashimoto was more successful, laying the groundwork for the streamlining of the government's structure. On the diplomatic front he also scored high marks, in negotiating, for example, the return of a large part of the American military installation on the island of Okinawa to Japanese jurisdiction. Following his father into politics, Hashimoto in 1963 was elected to the first of his 12 terms in the House of Representatives, the lower house of the Japanese Diet, more powerful than the upper House of Councillors. In his first cabinet post, he was minister of health and welfare (1978–79). As minister of transport (1986–91), he helped to privatize the Japanese National Railways. In trade negotiations with the U.S. when he was minister of international trade and industry (beginning in June 1994), he stoutly and successfully refused to bow to the demand that a certain quota of American-made cars and auto parts be sold annually in Japan. In October 1994, when he was still minister of international trade and industry, he was named deputy prime minister in the coalition government of Prime Minister Murayama Tomiichi. He became prime minister when Tomiichi resigned in January 1996. Following a national election in October 1996, he assembled a new cabinet composed entirely of LDP members. Hashimoto resigned as prime minister when the LDP lost the upper-house national election in 1998. In the cabinet of Prime Minister Yoshiro Mori, he served as state minister in charge of administrative reform (2000–01). He remained leader of his LDP faction (officially known as the Heisei Study Group) until 2004, when he resigned under the cloud of a bribery scandal. In the magazine *Japan Inc.* (June 1, 2003) Gregory Clark tried to explain how "Tokyo's 'best and brightest' . . . managed to throw a basically strong economy into the dangerous deflationary spiral we see today." Clark wrote: "The rot really began in 1997 with the fiscal restraint policies introduced by . . . Ryutaro Hashimoto. Those policies quickly threw the economy into a swoon. . . . Hashimoto himself cannot be blamed too much, as he never pretended to be an economist. Much guiltier was the LDP Secretary General Koichi Kato. . . . Kato did most of the legwork to promote the foolish (and later withdrawn) legislation forcing the government to reduce deficit borrowing to zero within a fixed time limit. He also supervised the Darwinian policies that allowed the brutal bankruptcies of Yamaichi Securities and Takushoku Bank." By his wife, Kumiko, Hashimoto had two sons, three daughters, and two grandchildren. He died in Tokyo. See *Current Biography* (1998).

Obituary *New York Times* I p30 July 2, 2006

HAUGHEY, CHARLES Sep. 16, 1925–June 13, 2006 Irish politician and statesman. Although Charles J. Haughey was a notorious "fixer" and "self-aggrandizer," there was no gainsaying his energy and effectiveness as a long-term leader of the Fianna Fail Party (1979–92) and three-term taoiseach (prime minister) of the Republic of Ireland (1979–81; 1982; 1987–92). Born in County Mayo, Haughey was the son of Catholic parents who had fled Northern Ireland after Protestant Unionist raiders set fire to their family farm in County Derry. After studying accounting and law at University College, Dublin, and passing the bar (in 1949) he entered politics under the mentorship of his father-in-law, Sean F. Lemass, who was taoiseach from 1955 to 1966. Haughey was elected to the Dail, Ireland's legislature, in 1957, and between 1961 and 1970 he served in Fianna Fail governments as minister for, successively, justice, agriculture, and finance. In 1970 he was charged with complicity in gunrunning for the Provisional Irish Republican Army. Although acquitted of all charges, he spent three years in political limbo before winning reelection to the Dail in 1973. He served as minister for health and social services from 1977 until his election to leadership of the Fiana Fail Party and his first term as taoiseach, in 1979. During that first term, he and Margaret Thatcher, who was beginning her first term as prime minister of the United Kingdom, began to cooperate in their policies regarding the crisis in Northern Ireland; thus was initiated the slow London-Dublin rapprochement that would develop into the Anglo-Irish Agreement (1985), championed by Haughey during his third term as taoiseach. During his last two governments, he also "redirected a lethargic state-dominated [Irish] economy into a sustained export-led boom that halted decades of mass emigration," as Alan Murdoch observed in the London *Independent* (June 14, 2006). Beginning in 1982 there were allegations that Haughey authorized the wiretapping of unfriendly journalists. Following a revival of those allegations, party colleagues pressured him to resign the prime ministership in February 1992. During his years in office Haughey's critics had questioned his ability to maintain the lifestyle of a multimillionaire—including ownership of a yacht, helicopters, and a private island—on a lawful income equivalent to $150,000 a year. Their assumption of massive financial corruption was confirmed after his retirement, beginning in 1996 with the disclosure by Ben Dunne, the former chairman of the Dunnes Stores retail chain, that he had paid a total of £1.3 million ($2 million) into secret offshore accounts held in Haughey's name. Found guilty of having lied in court, Haughey was threatened with two years' imprisonment, but his lawyers reached an agreement with Irish authorities limiting his liability to the equivalent to several million dollars in legal fees and tax liabilities. He died at his estate in Kinsealy, north of Dublin. His survivors included his wife, Maureen, three sons, and one daughter. See *Current Biography* (1981).

Obituary *New York Times* B p8 June 14, 2006

HAYDEN, MELISSA Apr. 25, 1923–Aug. 9, 2006 Ballet dancer. Melissa Hayden, a prima ballerina with George Balanchine's New York City Ballet for more than 20 years, thrilled audiences with the combination of superb technical control and full-force emotion and energy she brought to her roles, including those by Balanchine, a large number of which were created expressly for her. The daughter of Russian immigrants, Hayden was born Mildred Herman in Toronto, Canada, where she began her ballet training under the Russian-born Boris Volkoff when she was 12. While in her teens, she moved to New York City, where she danced in the corps de ballet at Radio City Music Hall while continuing her training at

the School of American Ballet, where her teachers included Anatole Vilzak and Ludmilla Shollar. She changed her name (on the advice of the choreographer Antony Tudor) while dancing with the Ballet Theatre (now the American Ballet Theatre) for two and a half years. In 1948 she joined the New York City Ballet, founded two years earlier by Balanchine and the impresario Lincoln Kirstein. With her "formidable strength and attack," as Kirstein later wrote, she soon became the company's "strongest dramatic ballerina." With the exception of one year (1953–54), when she returned to the Ballet Theatre, she danced with the New York City Ballet until 1973. In addition to roles in ballets by Balanchine—including the *Second Pas de Trois*, *Agon*, *Firebird* (co-written by Jerome Robbins), *Stars and Stripes*, *Donizetti Variations*, *Ivesiana*, *Swan Lake*, *Brahms-Schoenberg Quartet*, *Orpheus*, *Allegro Brillante*, and *A Midsummer Night's Dream*—her repertory included roles in William Dollar's *The Duel*, Frederick Ashton's *Illuminations*, Jerome Robbins's *The Cage*, and Bergit Cullberg's *Medea*. Her entire repertory comprised some 60 roles. On the occasion of her retirement, George Balanchine created for her the ballet *Cortège Hongrois*. On the motion-picture screen, she danced as Claire Bloom's double in *Limelight* (1952). On television she was seen in the documentary *Dancing for Mr. B: Six Balanchine Ballerinas* (1989). After her retirement as a dancer, she headed the dance program at Skidmore College, in Saratoga Springs, New York, directed the School of Pacific Northwest Ballet in Seattle, was a guest teacher at the Royal Ballet School, and opened her own school in New York City. From 1983 until shortly before her death, she taught at the North Carolina School of the Arts in Winston-Salem, where she staged a score of ballets. She wrote several books, including *Melissa Hayden, Off Stage and On* (1963), *Ballet Dances for Figure, Grace & Beauty* (1969), *Dancer to Dancer: Advice for Today's Dancer* (1981), and *The Nutcracker Ballet* (1992), a retelling of the classic story, illustrated by Stephen T. Johnson. She died at her home in Winston-Salem, North Carolina. Her survivors included her husband, Donald Hugh Coleman Jr., a son, a daughter, and five grandchildren. See *Current Biography* (1955).

Obituary *New York Times* C p15 Aug. 10, 2006

HENDERSON, SKITCH Jan. 27, 1918–Nov. 1, 2005 Pianist and orchestra leader. The Grammy Award–winning Henderson, founder of the New York Pops Orchestra and a guest conductor of many symphony orchestras, was (with his Vandyke beard and genial manner) better known to millions of viewers as the first bandleader on the *Tonight Show Starring Johnny Carson* in the 1960s. Henderson changed his original first name, Lyle, to Skitch, a variation of "Sketch," early in his career, when he was working in motion pictures and radio. "I was called the Sketch Kid because of the way I would quickly sketch out a new score," he once explained. "Bing [Crosby] said, 'If you're going to compete, get your name straightened out. People always forget Christian names, but they never forget nicknames.'" Sources vary in relating the details of Henderson's birth and early childhood, but most agree that he was born to parents of Scandinavian descent in Birmingham, England, and grew up there and in the U.S., in Minnesota, Kansas, Oklahoma, and Illinois. He played the piano from approximately the age of six and began his professional career when he was a teenager. "I ran away," he once recalled, "and joined a rinky-dink band." In 1937 or 1938 he was playing at a hotel in the American Midwest, probably in Minnesota or Montana, when he met Judy Garland, who was with Mickey Rooney on a tour promoting their Andy Hardy movies. When the duo's piano accompanist fell ill, Henderson replaced him on the tour, and he accompanied Garland and Rooney back to Hollywood and gained employment in the music department at Metro-Goldwyn-Mayer studios. While on the West Coast in the late 1930s, he worked with the singer Dolores Reed and her husband, the comedian Bob Hope, on their radio program the *Pepsodent Show*. It was Hope who introduced him to Bing Crosby. As with the details of his earliest years, his military service in World War II is described differently in various sources, some of which credit him with service with either the British Royal Air Force or the Canadian Air Force early in World War II and most of which say that he was a bomber pilot with the U.S. Army Air Corps later in the war. After the war he formed and toured with his first dance band and was a pianist on the NBC network radio shows of Bing Crosby and Frank Sinatra (with whom he had done some recording sessions). In the early 1950s he entertained morning drive-time listeners as the disc jockey on the *Skitch Henderson Show*, the first of several radio programs he hosted on WNBC in New York City. Meanwhile, he pursued an interest in serious music, studying conducting with Albert Coates and Fritz Reiner and harmony with Arnold Schoenberg. He also secured some classical training under Ernst Toch and Arturo Toscanini. He first conducted the New York Pops Orchestra, then a tentative organization, in a series of concerts in Carnegie Hall in 1953. (The orchestra would not be formally organized until 1983.) Soon he was much in demand as a guest conductor of symphony orchestras, including the NBC Symphony, on whose podium he often substituted for Arturo Toscanini. He gained his first regular TV experience working on NBC's *The Bob Hope Show* in 1953–54. The next he joined Steve Allen's *Tonight!*, the prototype of the *Tonight* shows. After Allen moved to Los Angeles, Henderson remained in New York as the NBC network's musical director and the conductor of the RCA Orchestra while José Melis conducted the band on the *Jack Paar Tonight Show* (1957–62). When Johnny Carson succeeded Paar as host of *Tonight*, in 1962, Henderson assumed the podium, and he remained musical director of the *Tonight Show Starring Johnny Carson* until 1966. As pianist and conductor, Henderson made hundreds of recordings. In 1963 he received a Grammy Award for an album of selections from *Porgy and Bess* that he conducted. Following his divorce from his first wife, the actress Faye Emerson, Henderson married Ruch Einseidel Michaels in 1958. His second wife helped him to solidify the New York Pops organization (and became its president) and with him settled on their Hunt Hill Farm in New Milford, Connecticut. In New Milford they founded the Silo Inc., a combination art gallery,

cooking school, and country store, in 1972, and the Hunt Hill Farm Trust, in 2003. The trust has the double purpose of preserving the Henderson farm's land and buildings as well as celebrating Americana in music, art, and literature in collaboration with the Smithsonian Institution. Henderson died at his home in New Milford. He was survived by his wife, a son, a daughter, and four grandchildren. See *Current Biography* (1966).

Obituary *New York Times* C p19 Nov. 3, 2005

HERTZBERG, ARTHUR June 9, 1921–Apr. 17, 2006 Polish-born rabbi; scholar of Judaica; social activist; rabbi emeritus of the Conservative congregation Temple Emanu-El in Englewood, New Jersey; Bronfman Visiting Professor of the Humanities at New York University; president of the American Jewish Congress from 1972 to 1978; vice president of the World Jewish Congress from 1975 to 1991; president of the American Jewish Policy Foundation from 1976 until his death. Hertzberg, a prominent liberal rabbi of contrarian bent, was a provocative and sometimes controversial voice of Conservative Judaism, a form of the religion whose beliefs and practices lie between the rigid traditionalism of Orthodoxy and the more liberal individualism of Reform Judaism. The son of an Orthodox rabbi, Hertzberg broke away from the fundamentalism in which he was reared, but, as he said, he "never used my 'heresy' as the excuse to prefer the majority culture to my own." On the other hand, he eschewed parochialism and was engaged in the great issues and movements of his time, in civil rights, interfaith dialogue, war and peace, and world justice. As a Zionist, he had close ties to Israel dating back to its establishment in the late 1940s; he later became a strong advocate for Peace Now and for the two-state solution—that is, the return of the Arab lands occupied by Israel since the 1967 war—as the only route to peace in the Middle East. His numerous publications included the books *The Zionist Idea* (1959), *The French Enlightenment and the Jews: The Origins of Modern Anti-Semitism* (1968), *Being Jewish in America* (1979), *The Lessons of Emancipation* (1986), *The Jews in America: Four Centuries of an Uneasy Encounter* (1989), *Jewish Fundamentalism* (1992), *Jewish Polemics* (1992), *Jews: The Essence and Character of a People* (1998), *A Jew in America: My Life and a People's Struggle for Identity* (2002), and *The Fate of Zionism: A Secular Future for Israel and Palestine* (2003). Among his numerous lectures and published articles were "Who Is a Jew?" (1999) and "The Vatican's Sin of Omission" (2005). After earning a B.A. degree in history and Oriental languages at Johns Hopkins University and a master's degree in Hebrew literature at the Jewish Theological Seminary in New York City, he received rabbinic ordination in 1943. He later earned a Ph.D. degree in history at Columbia University. Before his appointment as rabbi at Temple Emanu-El in Englewood, in 1956, he had served as a Hillel director, a U.S. Air Force chaplain, and a pulpit rabbi in Philadelphia and Nashville. Before joining the faculty of New York University, in 1991, he had taught religion at Dartmouth College and history at Columbia University. After retiring into emeritus status at Temple Emanu-El, in 1985, he remained involved with that congregation as a teacher. He lived in Englewood, New Jersey, and died of heart failure en route from there to Pascack Hospital in Westwood, New Jersey. His survivors included his wife, Phyllis, two daughters, and four grandchildren. See *Current Biography* (1975).

Obituary *New York Times* A p25 Apr. 18, 2006

HILLER, STANLEY Nov. 15, 1924–Apr. 20, 2006 Inventor and entrepreneur; helicopter pioneer. Stanley Hiller Jr. was one of the four principal developers of vertical-flight aircraft beyond the autogiro stage. Igor Sikorsky came first in that hierarchy, introducing the first helicopter in 1941. Hiller came second, beginning his career in helicopter design when he was still a teenager, during World War II. (The other two helicopter pioneers, Frank Piasecki and Arthur Young, followed soon after with their designs.) While Hiller also created for the civilian market, most of his designs originated as military commissions. His helicopters were used by the French in their Indochinese war and by the U.S. military in Korea and Vietnam. Hiller's father was a professional airplane pilot, an engineer, and an inventor who held 40 patents, including one for a plane in which he taught his son, then a boy, to fly. When Stanley Jr. was about 12, he began die-casting and selling gas-propelled toy racing cars, an enterprise that, with his father's help, soon evolved into Hiller Industries, a manufacturer of other aluminum products as well, including parts for fighter planes sold after World War II broke out. Meanwhile, Stanley Jr. was becoming increasingly interested in helicopter design. In the early 1940s he dropped out of the University of California, sold Hiller Industries at a profit, and began to concentrate on helicopters. In 1944 he perfected his XH-44 (popularly known as the Hiller-Copter), the first all-metal rigid coaxial helicopter, with contra-rotating rotors eliminating the need for a tail rotor to control main rotor torque. Under a World War II U.S. military contract, he directed production of that helicopter as part of Kaiser Cargoes Inc. until the end of the war, when he founded his own company, United Helicopters Inc., later renamed the Hiller Aircraft Corp. Immediately after the war he produced the Commuter, a civilian contra-rotator, before turning to more conventional single-rotor-plus-tail-rotor designs for both civilian and military use. In his Hiller 360 he made the first helicopter flight across the United States, in 1949. He introduced his Hornet, an ultra-light two-seater powered by rotor-tip-mounted ramjet engines, in 1953 and his Flying Platform in 1955. Originally for the U.S. Navy, between 1954 and 1956 he created his Rotorcycle, a one-person foldable vehicle powered by rotor-tip jets. In its military application, that small helicopter could be parachuted behind enemy lines in a pod and assembled in nine minutes without tools. In the late 1950s Hiller proved the feasibility of a tilt-wing engine approach to high-speed heavy-weight vertical flight by developing the 17-ton X-18 troop transport. In 1960 the consortium of Hiller, Chance-Vought, and Ryan began production of an evaluation fleet of XC-142 transports, based on the X-18 design, for the U.S. Air Force. When Hiller Aircraft was acquired by the Fairchild Stratos Corp., in

1964, Hiller became an executive vice president of Fairchild Stratos, in charge of the merger's Hiller-Fairchild division. Pursuant to the merger, most of Hiller's military business was lost to the Hughes Corp. Disgusted, Hiller quit his position with Hiller-Fairchild in 1965 and began a second career in venture capitalism as a self-described "corporate paramedic." In 1966 he created the Hiller Group, devoted to turning around failing companies in diverse fields. Among those companies were G. W. Murphy Industries, a Houston oil producer, Bristol Compressors, the Bekins Co.mpany, the Reed Tool Co., and the York International Corp. Hiller died at his home in Atherton, California. His survivors included his wife, Carolyn, two sons, and seven grandchildren. See *Current Biography* (1974).

Obituary *New York Times* B p9 May 3, 2006

HRAWI, ELIAS Sep. 4, 1926–July 7, 2006 President of Lebanon (1989–98). Hrawi, a Maronite Christian who believed that national unity should take precedence over sectarian interests, was a reconciling figure in a nation torn by Christian-Islamic factionalism and caught in the middle of the Israel-Palestine dispute. Lebanon traditionally laid claim to being the only Christian country in the Arab world; it has 11 Christian denominations, the largest of which by far is the Maronite. The country, an offspring of the old Turkish Empire, came into existence as a French mandate, along with its Islamic neighbor Syria, in 1920, and it became an independent republic, as did Syria, in the early 1940s. Christians, who were then in the majority, assumed dominance in the country's power structure in keeping with the National Convention of 1943, which stipulated that public positions were to divided among persons from different confessional communities in accordance with the size of those communities. By the 1970s Muslims were outnumbering Christians and demanding a greater governmental and economic status, and Islamic militias were beginning to clash with Christian militias. In 1975 the clashes escalated into a full-blown civil war that would rage for 15 years; it ended under Hrawi's watch in 1990. That war was complicated and exacerbated by the presence of a Syrian army that occupied Lebanon for 29 years beginning in 1976, a pro-Israel Christian Lebanese Army that opposed the Syrian army as well as strongholds of the Palestine Liberation Organization, and Israeli military forces that invaded Lebanon in 1982. (After driving the PLO out of Lebanon, the Israeli forces retreated to a narrow "security zone" paralleling Lebanon's border with Israel in 1985, and they withdrew completely from Lebanon in 2000. Syria's troops withdrew in March and April 2005, following widespread allegations that Syria had been responsible for the assassination of former prime minister Rafik Hariri, in February 2005.) Because of his religious background, Elias Hrawi's primary sympathies lay with the Maronites, but because he came from Lebanon's heavily Islamic Becaa Valley, close to Syria, he was also in tune with the Muslims in his constituency. Hrawi began his career as an agricultural and food-processing and exporting/importing tycoon. He was elected to the National Assembly in 1972 and served as minister of public works under President

Elias Sarkis and Prime Minister Shafik Wazzan from 1980 to 1982. He achieved prominence as a champion of Christian-Muslim coexistence in 1981, when he was instrumental in defusing an imminent major battle between the Syrian forces and the Christian Lebanese Army at Zahlé, in the Becaa Valley. Following the assassination of President René Maowad, who was also a Maronite Christian dedicated to Muslim-Christian coexistence, the National Assembly elected Hrawi to a six-year term as president in November 1989. (In 1995 it voted to add three years to his term.) He was elected with a mandate to implement the Ta'if Accord, an Arab League–sponsored peace plan, and he was decisive in doing so, acting against the feuding militias and ending the civil war. In September 1990 he signed into law amendments to the constitution giving a greater measure of power and influence to Lebanese Muslims. In October 1990, with support from the Syrian army, he overcame a military challenge to his administration led by General Michel Aoun. In May 1991 he signed a Treaty of Fraternity, Coordination, and Cooperation with Syria. While he disarmed all Christian and most Muslim militias, he failed to disarm the Hezbollah, a powerful Shi'a Muslim fundamentalist militia. That failure opened the way for a second Israel-Lebanon conflict, known in Israel as the Second Lebanese War (July–August 2006), a conflict in which an estimated 1,200 Lebanese civilians were killed, 3,600 were wounded, and 256,000 were internally displaced. By his marriage to the former Mona Jammal, a Palestinian, Hrawi had two daughters. By a previous marriage, he had two sons and a daughter. He died in Beirut, Lebanon. See *Current Biography* (1992).

Obituary *New York Times* B p6 July 8, 2006

HUGHES, BARNARD July 16, 1915–July 11, 2006 Actor. Barnard Hughes was in the fourth decade of his career as a skilled and dependable character actor, with several hundred stage credits and dozens of television roles behind him, when he began to receive recognition. With his robust portrayal of the Brooklyn priest Father Stanislaus Coyne in *Hogan's Goat*, a hit of the 1965–66 Off-Broadway season, he made "Catholic morality a force and a benediction," as one critic observed. Subsequently, in one of the first of his then rare motion-picture roles, he was cast against type as the pathetic aging homosexual Towney, the last customer of hustler Joe Buck (Jon Voight), who beats and robs him in one of the most memorable scenes in *Midnight Cowboy* (1969). In the early 1970s he won acclaim for a number of roles in Joseph Papp's New York Shakespeare Festival, including Polonius in *Hamlet* (1972) and Dogberry in a production of *Much Ado About Nothing* (1972) that moved to Broadway in November 1972 and was filmed for presentation on the CBS television network in 1973. He starred as the avuncular physician of the title in the TV situation comedy *Doc* (CBS, September 1975–October 1976), and he won an Emmy Award for his guest appearance as the entertainingly senile Judge Felix Ruthman in an episode of the drama *Lou Grant* (CBS) during the 1977–78 television season. He reached the high point of his career on Broadway in his humorous and touch-

ing performance as the curmudgeonly title character in the Irish comedy *Da*, which brought him the Tony Award for best actor in the 1977–78 season. On television he starred in the sitcom *Mr. Merlin* (CBS, October 1981–September 1982) as Max Merlin, King Arthur's wizard, now living in San Francisco. Hughes was the son of immigrants from Ireland. He began his acting career in 1934 with a New York–based traveling repertory company called the Shakespeare Fellowship. On Broadway he made his debut in a bit part in *The Cat and the Canary* in 1937 and was cast as Joe Garibaldi in *Please, Mrs. Garibaldi* in 1939. After service with the U.S. Army during World War II, he toured military hospitals in a show called *Laugh That Off*. Back on Broadway, he played Martin in *The Ivy Green* in 1949 and Clancy in *Dinosaur Wharf* in 1951. Between 1949 and 1954 he was cast in many roles with the Tenthouse Theatre in Highland Park, Illinois. In the mid-1950s his credits included Captain McLean in a touring-company production of *Teahouse of the August Moon*. On Broadway between 1959 and 1964, he was seen as Inspector Norcross in *A Majority of One*, Senator Tom August in *Advise and Consent*, Bert Howell in *Nobody Loves an Albatross*, and Father Frank Feeley in *I Was Dancing*. His Broadway roles over the following two decades included Senator McFetridge in *How Now, Dow Jones*, Judge Belknap in *The Wrong Way Light Bulb*, General Fitzhugh in *Sheep on the Runway*, Fulbert in *Abelard and Eloise*, Father William Doherty in *Angels Fall*, and Philip Stone in *End of the World*. His last Broadway performances were as the Old Man in *Prelude to a Kiss* (1990) and Osgood Meeker in *Waiting in the Wings* (1999–2000). His television credits were many and varied, beginning with roles in teleplays presented on such showcases as Kraft Television Theatre during the golden age of live TV drama and ranging from his portrayals of the detective Father Brown in *Sanctuary of Fear* (1979) and Francis "Pop" Cavanaugh in the series *The Cavanaughs* (1986) to guest appearances on such sitcoms as *All in the Family* and recurring roles in such soap operas as *As the World Turns*. His motion-picture credits, which increased in frequency as he aged, included, in addition to his 1988 reprise of his role as *Da*, his portrayal of Tim McCullen in *Best Friends* (1982), Bishop Campbell in *Maxie* (1985), Jonathan Knowles in *Where Are the Children?* (1986), Grandpa in *The Lost Boys* (1987), Dr. Aurelius Hogue in *Doc Hollywood* (1991), and Henry Albertson in *The Fantasticks* (2000). Hughes died in New York Presbyterian Hospital in Manhattan. He was survived by his wife of 56 years, Helen Stenborg, his son, Doug, and his daughter, Laura. See *Current Biography* (1981).

Obituary *New York Times* C p11 July 12, 2006

HUNT LIEBERSON, LORRAINE Mar. 1, 1954–July 3, 2006 Opera and concert singer. In the contemporary revival of Baroque operas and oratorios, "the most luminous presence" was that of Lorraine Hunt Lieberson, as Charles Michener observed in a major profile for the *New Yorker* (January 5, 2004). Hunt Lieberson—known as Lorraine Hunt before her marriage to the composer Perter Lieberson in 1999—was a mezzo-soprano whose vocal power, mastery of melodic line, and deep and intense immersion in her roles drew comparisons to Maria Callas. In addition to excelling in the music of Monteverdi, Bach, Handel, and Mozart, she championed new works by such contemporary composers as John Adams, John Harbison, and her husband, and she included in her repertoire music by such 19th-century composers as Bizet, Berlioz, and Mahler. She had an unconventional career, in which she was for many years primarily a freelance violist before she began to concentrate on singing at age 30. In addition, as a singer she performed not as a member of any opera company but as a roving guest operatic performer, an independent recitalist, and a collaborator with intimate ensembles, including period-instrument and other chamber groups, as well as with major orchestras. Born in San Francisco to musical parents, she learned to play the piano and the violin in early childhood; she turned to the viola when she was 12. She studied both viola and voice at San Jose University, and she later studied voice at the Boston Conservatory. Partly in association with a boyfriend who was a jazz musician, she led a somewhat adventurous bohemian life when she was in her 20s. In the late 1970s she was the principal violist with the Berkeley (California) Free Orchestra. The turning point in her career came in 1984, when she sang the role of Tamiri in Mozart's *Il re pastore* in a concert performance with Emmanuel Music, a church-based Boston ensemble directed by Craig Smith. Immediately thereafter she successfully auditioned for the innovative and sometimes controversial theater and opera director Peter Sellars, who noted the "sheer concentrated energy" of her singing. The audition was for the role of Sesto in Sellars's updated production of Handel's *Julius Caesar*, presented at the Pepsico Summerfare Festival in Purchase, New York, in 1985. At the same festival two years later, Hunt Lieberson appeared as Donna Elvira in Sellars's over-the-top staging of Mozart's *Don Giovanni*. Her later collaborations with Sellars included the role of Irene in his production of Handel's *Theodora* at the Glyndebourne Festival in England in 1996 and a program of Bach cantatas, conceived and directed by him, which she performed in New York and London in 2001. In Paris in 1993 she sang the title role in Charpentier's *Médée* with the Les Arts Florissants ensemble under William Christie's direction. With the Boston Lyric Opera the following year, she sang the title role in Bizet's *Carmen*, and in the 1996–97 season, she sang Charlotte in Massenet's *Werther* at the Opéra de Lyon in Lyon, France. In other performances in the 1990s, she sang songs by Purcell and Offenbach and several Mozart roles, including Mozart's variation on the Sesto character in his opera *La clemenza di Tito*. With the Santa Fe Opera in 1997, she sang the role of Triraksha in the premiere of Peter Lieberson's opera *Asoka's Dream*. John Harbison wrote for her the role of Myrtle Wilson in his *The Great Gatsby*, which she sang in her first appearance with the Metropolitan Opera in New York City, in 1999. At the Met in February 2003, she gave a triumphant performance of her signature role as Dido in Berlioz's *Les Troyens*. With the Boston Symphony Orchestra in the fall of 2003, she sang Mélisande in Debussy's *Pélleas et Mélisande*. Her concert appearances included performances of Bach's *Magnificat* with the San Francisco Sympho-

ny, Berg's *Seven Early Songs* with the Berlin Philharmonia, Handel arias at Tanglewood with the Handel and Haydn Society, and a program of Mozart and Brahms with the Chamber Music Society at Lincoln Center. In recitals with the pianist Peter Serkin in Boston and New York in 2003, she sang a program that included songs by Mozart, Brahms, and Debussy and excerpts from Handel's *La Lucrezia*, delivered with an emotional combination of pathos and rage. After her marriage to Peter Lieberson, she added to her repertoire songs composed by him to poems by Pablo Neruda and Rainer Maria Rilke. Recordings of many of her performances are preserved in recordings on the Harmonia Mundi label. Hunt Lieberson died in Sant Fe, New Mexico. She was survived by her husband. See *Current Biography* (2004).

Obituary *New York Times* A p15 July 5, 2006

JACOBS, JANE May 4, 1916–Apr. 25, 2006 Civic activist and author. Jacobs (née Butzner), a community-spirited writer unlettered in city planning, was the most vocal and arguably the most effective North American critic of the destruction of dense and vibrant urban "ecosystems" (as she viewed them) in the name of slum clearance and big-scale urban renewal. In 1961—when she was an editor of *Architectural Forum* and a longtime resident of Greenwich Village, a Manhattan enclave epitomizing the kind of bustling, diverse-use downtown neighborhood she treasured—Jacobs published her seminal book, *The Death and Life of Great American Cities*, which she bluntly described as an "attack on current city planning." "I didn't have any ideology . . . ," she recalled in an interview with Jim Kuntsler for *Metropolis Magazine* (March 2001). "What was in my mind [was] we didn't care how our cities worked anymore." She subsequently examined the ideas presented in her first book from other perspectives, ranging from economic and scientific to sociological, philosophical, and moral, in a succession of books: *The Economy of Cities* (1969), *Cities and the Wealth of Nations: Principles of Economic Life* (1984), *Systems of Survival: A Dialogue on the Moral Foundations of Commerce and Politics* (1992), *The Question of Separatism* (1980), *The Nature of Economies* (2000), and *Dark Age Ahead* (2004). In an interview with Bill Steigerwald for *Reason* (June 2001), she said that the most important contribution for which she deserved to be remembered was her "discussion of what makes economic expansion happen" and how "expansion and development are two different things." After graduating from high school in Scranton, Pennsylvania, Jane Butzner worked briefly as a reporter with the *Scranton Tribune* newspaper. In New York City she at first earned a living as a temporary stenographer while beginning to write freelance articles about the city's neighborhoods. She became an associate editor with *Architectural Forum* in 1952. As a community activist during the 1960s, she led several successful protests against projects proposed by Robert Moses, New York's "master builder," including one to construct an expressway through Washington Square Park, the heart of Greenwich Village. Robert Caro, the author of *The Power Broker*, a biography of Moses, regards Jacobs as "one of the heroines of New York history," standing for "independent thought, smaller is better, that streetscapes have to be carefully crafted, that the car can't be allowed to dominate the city." With her husband, the architect Robert Hyde Jacobs Jr., and their children, she moved to Toronto, Canada, in 1969, and she became a Canadian citizen in 1974. (According to some sources, the move to Canada was motivated at least in part by her opposition to the war in Vietnam and her sons' being of draft age.) In her foreword to the Modern Library edition of *The Death and Life of Great American Cities* (1992), Jacobs wrote: "When I began work on this book in 1958, I expected merely to describe the civilizing and enjoyable services that good city street life casually provides— and to deplore planning fads and architectural fashions that were expunging these necessities and charms instead of helping to strengthen them. . . . That's all I intended. . . . But learning and thinking about city streets and the trickiness of city parks launched me into an unexpected treasure hunt. . . . One discovery led to another [and] at some point along the trail I realized I was engaged in studying the ecology of cities . . . [in which] diversity develops organically over time, and the varied components are interdependent in complex ways." In addition to making the analogy with natural ecosystems, she differentiated between "foot people" and "car people" and pointed out that the book "was instantly understood by foot people, both actual and wishful." "Experts of the time did not respect what foot people knew and valued," she wrote. "They were deemed old-fashioned and selfish—troublesome sand in the wheels of progress. It is not easy for uncredentialed people to stand up to the credentialed, even when the so-called expertise is grounded in ignorance and folly. This book turned out to be helpful ammunition against such experts. But it is less accurate to call this effect 'influence' than to see it as corroboration and collaboration [with foot people]. Conversely, the book neither collaborated with car people nor had an influence on them. It still does not, as far as I can see. . . . At the time of the book's publication, no matter whether the students [of city planning and architecture] were foot people or car people by experience and temperament, they were being rigorously trained as anticity and antistreet designers and planners. . . . The whole [city-planning] establishment . . . acted as gatekeepers protecting forms and visions inimical to city life. . . . Although the numbers of arrogant old gatekeepers have dwindled . . . anticity planning remains amazingly sturdy in American cities." Among Jacobs's concerns were monopolies being protected by zoning, collusion between urban developers and city governments, and the abuse of eminent domain, whereby property is expropriated from its owners and turned over to other private parties more favored by the local governments. Her most recent book, *Dark Age Ahead*, serves as "a grave warning to a society losing its memory" and offers "lessons to avoid decline," according to the jury that awarded her the 2005 Shaughnessy Cohen Prize for Political Writing. Jacobs died in Toronto, Canada. She was predeceased by her husband and survived by her daughter and two sons. See *Current Biography* (1977).

Obituary *New York Times* A p1+ Apr. 26, 2006

KING, CORETTA SCOTT Apr. 27, 1927–Jan. 30, 2006 The first lady of the U.S. civil rights movement. As the wife of the Reverend Dr. Martin Luther King Jr., Coretta Scott King kept a relatively low profile, at her husband's request, while he was engaged in his epochal campaigns for racial harmony, economic justice, and world peace and in preaching nonviolent disobedience to unjust segregationist laws. As the widow of the slain Dr. King, she emerged with dignity and grace as well as strength as an activist in her own right, a guardian of his "dream that one day this nation will rise up and live out the true meaning of its creed." Mrs. King had grown up as Coretta Scott in Heiberger, Alabama, where her parents ran a small truck farm and country store. After graduating from racially segregated schools in Heiberger and nearby Marion, Alabama, she studied education and music on a scholarship at Antioch College, in Ohio, where her older sister, Edythe, had earlier been the first black student. When she graduated from Antioch, in 1951, her aspiration was to be a classical singer. She moved to Boston, Massachusetts, to study at the New England Conservatory of Music on a small fellowship, augmented by her earnings from part-time work. In Boston she met Martin Luther King Jr., a Baptist minister from Atlanta, Georgia, who was working toward a Ph.D. degree in systematic theology at Boston University. Her wedding to Martin at her parents' home in Alabama in 1953 was a gala event, attended by approximately 350 guests. The couple spent the first months of their marriage in Atlanta, where Martin was preaching at Ebenezer Baptist Church, where his father was pastor. They moved to Montgomery, Alabama, when Martin accepted the post of pastor of the Dexter Avenue Baptist Church there in 1954, and back to Atlanta in 1960, when he became co-pastor with his father of the Ebenezer Baptist Church. It was in Montgomery that Dr. King began to earn his iconic reputation, with the first of his nonviolent campaigns, the designated leadership of the year-long boycott of city buses sparked by the arrest of Rosa Parks for her refusal to surrender her seat to a white passenger in December 1955. (During the boycott white supremacists lobbed a bomb onto the porch of the King home.) The success of the Memphis boycott set in motion a train of events that eventually brought down the Jim Crow system of racial segregation in the South and changed the course of race relations nationally. Dr. King went on to lead civil rights demonstrations in Birmingham and Selma, Alabama, as well as the massive March on Washington in 1963. During the 1960s he broadened his activism to include economic justice, international peace, and peace in Vietnam in particular. Mrs. King sometimes joined her husband in the demonstrations, and she accompanied him on his trip to Oslo, Norway, to receive the Nobel Peace Prize in 1964. On her own, she participated prominently in the Women's Strike for Peace movement, and she performed more than 30 "Freedom Concerts" in which she lectured, read poetry, and sang songs illustrating the history of the civil rights movement. The proceeds from the concerts were contributed to the Southern Christian Leadership Conference, co-founded by Dr. King. On April 4, 1968 Dr. King was felled by an assassin's bullet in Memphis, Tennessee, where he had been lending his leadership to a strike by sanitation workers. Four days later, even before he was buried, Mrs. King marched in his place at the head of a demonstration by the strikers. The following June she again stood in what would have been his place at the Poor People's Campaign at the Lincoln Memorial, in Washington, D.C., calling on American women to unite in the struggle against "the three great evils of racism, poverty, and war." In 1974 she co-founded another broad coalition, the Full Employment Council. She spent 12 years planning, raising the funds for, and creating the Martin Luther King Jr. Center for Nonviolent Social Change, a three-block memorial museum and civil rights library and archives built around Dr. King's tomb in Atlanta. The center, which opened in 1981, is part of a 23-acre national historic site that includes Dr. King's birthplace and the Ebenezer Baptist Church. After lobbying for a decade for a federal holiday honoring her late husband, Mrs. King realized success in 1983, when Congress enacted legislation authorizing the annual celebration of Martin Luther King Day on the third Monday in January. The legislation went into effect three years later. Marking the 20th anniversary of the historic 1963 March on Washington, Mrs. King in 1983 headed an even larger demonstration in the nation's capital by the Coalition of Conscience, comprising 200 human rights organizations. Until her health began to fail, she pursued a busy speaking and good-will itinerary, internationally as well as nationally. She published the autobiography *My Life with Martin Luther King Jr.* (1969; revised, 1993) and two collections of selections from Dr. King's speeches and writings. From the beginning, there were reports of a sibling-like rivalry, especially regarding fund-raising, between the Southern Christian Leadership Conference and the Martin Luther King Center. In the late 1990s, according to various reports, a real sibling rivalry began brewing between Mrs. King's two sons for control of the center, and that rivalry became more overt after she was incapacitated by a stroke and a heart attack in August 2005. Also diagnosed with advanced ovarian cancer, she was admitted to the Santa Monica Health Institute, an alternative-medicine facility in Rosarito Beach, Mexico, on January 26, 2006. She died of respiratory failure there. Among the dignitaries who spoke at the memorial service for her at the New Birth Missionary Baptist Church in Lithonia, Georgia, were President George W. Bush and his predecessor in the White House, Bill Clinton. Her survivors included her daughters, Yolanda and Bernice, and her sons, Martin Luther 3d and Dexter. See *Current Biography* (1969).

Obituary *New York Times* A p1+ Feb. 1, 2006

KUNITZ, STANLEY July 29, 1905–May 14, 2006 Poet; editor; teacher; consultant in poetry to the Library of Congress (1974–76); United States poet laureate (2000–01); New York State poet laureate (1987–89). Stanley Jasspon Kunitz was an unmistakably recognizable voice in 20th-century American verse. A poem came to him, as he said, "in the form of a blessing, like rapture breaking on the mind," but he crafted it to perfection with lapidarian patience and care for subtleties, without losing the original inspiration and passion. An essential focus of his was, in

his words, on the theme "that we are all living and dying at once," one he embraced with a sense that he was "grasping everything in this life that makes it beautiful, enjoyable, stimulating, and funny sometimes." In a eulogistic interview with Melissa Block on National Public Radio, Marie Howe, one of the many poets he had mentored and a longtime friend of his, observed that he "wrote always about transformation and change . . . at the intersection of time and eternity." She cited in particular his poem "The Layers," about surviving loss and grief and, in her words, "going on as a transformed being." Over the years Kunitz moved from an intellectual style, partly in the metaphysical tradition and marked by formal adherence to traditional rhyme and meter, to a leaner and more openly autobiographical style, with natural speech rhythms. "His later work is so transparent," Howe observed, "so seemingly simple on the surface, that all you hear is the sound of a soul speaking out." Kunitz, an agnostic, was born to Jewish parents who owned a dress-manufacturing business in Worcester, Massachusetts. Apparently depressed by marital as well as business problems, his father committed suicide (by drinking carbolic acid in a public park) a few weeks before Stanley's birth, and his mother (a seamstress who had emigrated from Lithuania) deleted every vestige of her late husband's memory from her speech and from the household. Along with a reiterated awareness of "the wild braid of nature," Kunitz's verse would be haunted by the mystery of his absent father, a subject explicitly addressed in such poems as "The Portrait" and "Father and Son." Among the many other influences on his verse-making were the sprung-rhythm poems of Gerard Manley Hopkins and, apparently, Jungian psychology. When he received a master's degree in English at Harvard University in 1927, an anti-Semitic university bureaucrat blocked his effort to remain at Harvard as a teaching assistant, and he left the school in what he later described as "a rage." After a stint as a reporter and feature writer with the *Worcester Telegram* newspaper, he moved to New York City. "By the time I came to New York," he would recall, "I was already a poet, a freethinker, and a rebel." In New York he joined the staff of the H. W. Wilson Co., a leading publisher of book and periodical indexes, among other reference books and databases. He edited the *Wilson Library Bulletin* from 1927 to 1943, when his employment at the Wilson Co. was interrupted by his induction into the U.S. Army for service in World War II (despite his conscientious objection to bearing arms). During his long association with the Wilson Co. he edited or co-edited (first with Howard Haycraft and later with Vineta Colby) nine volumes in the company's series of biographical/bibliographical dictionaries of literature, beginning with *Living Authors* (1931) and including *Twentieth Century Authors* (1942), *British Authors Before 1800* (1952), and *European Authors, 1000-1900* (1967). All the while he was writing poetry, slowly and scrupulously. His first book of verse, *Intellectual Things*, was published in 1930, and his second, *Passport to the War*, appeared 14 years later. He won the Pulitzer Prize with *Selected Poems, 1928–1958* (1958). That volume was followed by *The Testing Tree* (1971), *The Terrible Threshold* (1974), *The Coat Without a Seam* (1974), and *The Lincoln*

Relics (1978). *The Poems of Stanley Kunitz, 1928–1978* (1978) won the Lenore Marshall Poetry Prize, and *Passing Through: The Later Poems, New and Selected* (1995) won the National Book Award. *Next-to-Last Things: New Poems and Essays* was published in 1985 and *The Collected Poems of Stanley Kunitz* in 2000. Kunitz edited the Yale Series of Younger Poets (1966–77) and editions of the poetry of William Butler Yeats and John Keats, and he was a co-translator of several Russian poets. As an adjunct professor he taught in a graduate writing program at Columbia University from 1967 to 1985. He had previously taught at Bennington College and directed poetry workshops at several other schools. In Manhattan, where he lived, he co-founded Poets House, a literary meeting place for poets and the general public that contains the largest poetry archive in the U.S. In Provincetown, Massachusetts, where he maintained a summer home and cultivated a celebrated garden, he co-founded the Fine Arts Work Center, which each year provides residencies and stipends to 16 promising neophytes in the literary and visual arts. His talks with Genine Lentine, his literary assistant, were central in the creation of the essays accompanying the poems and photographs in *The Wild Braid: A Poet Reflects on a Century in the Garden* (2005). His honors included a Guggenheim Fellowship, a Bollingen Prize, and the National Medal of the Arts. His third wife, the painter Elise Asher, predeceased him. He had earlier been married to and divorced from Helen Pearce and Eleanor Evans. His survivors included a daughter (from his second marriage), a stepdaughter, five grandchildren, and three great-grandchildren. He died at his home in Manhattan. See *Current Biography* (1959).

Obituary *New York Times* A p22 May 16, 2006

LAKER, FREDDIE Aug. 6, 1922–Feb. 9, 2006 British airline entrepreneur. As the chairman and managing director of Laker Airways Ltd. (1966–82) and more specifically as the creator of that airline's transatlantic Skytrain service (1978–82), Laker—who was knighted in 1978—introduced low-cost, no-frills service to international air travel. He thus paved the way for Virgin Atlantic and Sky-Bus International, among other budget-conscious airlines. After leaving school, at 16, Laker learned the fundamentals of aviation engineering as an apprentice at Shorts Brothers, a British aircraft manufacturer. During World War II he was an engineer and pilot with the British Air Transport Auxiliary. In 1948, largely with borrowed money, he bought his first fleet of planes, 12 used Halton bomber-style aircraft. With that fleet he formed Aviation Traders, a major carrier of supplies during the Berlin airlift of 1948–49, and Air Charter, the chief independent airline carrying refugees on the Berlin run in the early 1950s. He himself piloted many of those flights. He later added Britannias and DC4s to his fleet and ventured into air-ferry services across the English Channel and down the west coast of Africa. In 1958 he sold his fleet to what became British United Airways, with himself as managing director. Under his management BUA prospered, gaining more than a dozen routes across Europe and to South America. Disagreements with BUA's chairman, Sir Myles Wyatt, led to his leaving BUA, in

1965. He then acquired another fleet and launched Laker Airways Ltd. in 1966. He ran the airline at first as a charter operation for package holidays to Mediterranean destinations. In 1969 he obtained "affinity charter" licenses allowing him to offer transatlantic fares far lower than those on scheduled airlines to "affinity groups," clubs and other organizations formed for purposes other than travel. That project was thwarted when, in the early 1970s, British and U.S. authorities found that many of the groups were not bona fide. Looking for another cheap-travel alternative for budget-minded travelers who could not plan ahead far enough to take advantage of charter flights, Laker came up with the idea of "something simple, like a train," a walk-on scheduled flight service not requiring reservations—that is, Skytrain, a daily transatlantic shuttle service that became a reality in 1978, after six years of legal battles. It was very successful until the largest scheduled airlines operating between Britain and the United States—including British Airways, Pan American World Airways, and Trans World Airlines—colluded in a war of "predatory pricing" (offering fares below cost) that drove Laker into bankruptcy in 1982. Laker's liquidator sued the colluding airlines, who settled out of court, paying several million dollars to Laker and his creditors in the mid-1980s. Laker took up residence in the Bahamas, where he and a partner ran a hotel and casino on Grand Bahama Island. In 1992 he established Laker Airways/Bahamas, offering flights between Grand Bahama Island and Florida; and three years later he returned to transatlantic service, founding (in partnership with Oscar S. Wyatt) Laker Airways Inc., offering scheduled and charter flights between Florida and London. He died at Memorial Regional Hospital in Hollywood, Florida. His survivors included his fourth wife, Jacqueline, and a son and daughter. Two of his sons predeceased him. See *Current Biography* (1978).

Obituary *New York Times* C p14 Feb. 11, 2006

LEM, STANISLAW Sep. 12, 1921–Mar. 27, 2006 Polish novelist, short-story writer, and philosopher of science. Lem became the titan of Eastern European speculative fiction with the stories that he imaginatively spun out of his knowledge of science and technology, including cybernetics and artificial intelligence, and their relationship to moral and cognitive issues and, more obliquely, political ones. He did so in a most unfavorable place and time, behind the Iron Curtain from the mid-1940s until Poland was freed of the grip of totalitarian Communism in 1990. He objected to being identified with writers of "pure fantasy" because, as he pointed out, he was writing "about the real world, . . . about what is happening, only in my own way, in my own terms." That way and those terms were fables. Lem "learn[ed] how to 'operate' the abstract, seemingly unreal worlds and concerns of science fiction, and to say exactly what he wished to say, in a code only dolts (that is, Party officials) would not be able to decipher immediately," John Clute wrote in his obituary of Lem for the London *Independent*. "This Aesopian language—the couching of hard subversive truths in sheep's clothing—Lem found extremely congenial, and his decision to stop writing fiction in 1989 may, at least in part, have come from a sense that . . . he no longer needed to tell fables." Lem explored the limitations of human understanding—a common theme with him—and took an oblique slap at Marxism's replacement of religion with a pseudoreligious science of human history in his most famous work, the 1961 novel *Solaris* (available in English only in an inferior 1970 translation via the French), in which cognitive scientists from Earth who are stumped and bamboozled in their efforts to communicate with an alien intelligence (an ocean of living plasma surrounding the planet Solaris) glorify their failed science by calling it Solaristics. *Solaris* was adapted for the silver screen twice, in Russian in 1972 and in English in 2002. The best translations of Lem's books into English have been those of Michael Kandel, beginning in 1973 with *Memoirs Found in a Bathtub* (co-translated by Christine Rose), a labyrinthine spy story set in Pentagon III, a vast underground espionage center in the Rocky Mountains run by a computer self-emancipated from its human creators. The narrator is a secret agent whose Kafkaesque assignment, dictated by the computer, is so confidential he does not know what it is. In 1974 Kandel published his translations of Lem's *The Cyberiad: Fables for the Cybernetic Age* as well as *The Futurological Congress*, Lem's novella about an overpopulated future world in which the ruling "chemocrats" suppress revolt and maintain order with "benignimizing" drugs. Later in the 1970s Kandel published his translations of Lem's *The Star Diaries* and *Mortal Engines* and in 1984 he published *His Master's Voice*, a Lem novel similar to *Solaris* in its treatment of the cognitive problem in human communication with alien entities. Kandel later translated *A Perfect Vacuum* (1999), Lem's "collection" of make-believe reviews of 16 nonexistent books, including one by Lem himself. "Did Lem really think," Lem wrote of himself, "he would not be seen through?" Kandel also edited *The Cosmic Carnival of Stanislaw Lem: An Anthology of Entertaining Stories by the Modern Master of Science Fiction* (1981). Lem was born into a nonobservant Jewish family in the Polish city of Lwow (also spelled Lvov and Lwiw), which is now in Ukraine. During World War II the city was occupied by Soviet troops, in 1939, then by German troops, in 1941, and by the Soviets again, in 1944. Intending to specialize in theoretical biology, Lem began the study of medicine at Lwow University in 1939. His studies, interrupted by the Nazi occupation during World War II, were completed at Jagiellonian University in Krakow between 1944 and 1950. He failed to obtain a medical degree, at least in part, according to some accounts, because of his refusal to accept the quack biological theories of Trofim Denisovich Lysenko, which had been made Stalinist doctrine. Lem began publishing his fiction in 1946 and achieved wide popularity in Europe with *Astronauci* ("The Astronauts," 1951; not yet translated into English). Censors held up for varying periods of time the printing of a number of his books, including *Czas nieutracony: Szpital przemienienia* (1955; *Hospital of the Transfiguration*, 1988), a non–sci-fi novella about a physician working in an insane asylum, the publication of which was delayed for eight years. Among his other novels were *Eden* (1959; translated into English in 1987) and a number that borrowed

from the mystery-story genre, including *Sledztwo* (1959; translated as *The Investigation*, 1974) and *Katar* (1976; translated as *The Chain of Chance*, 1978). Among his books of nonfiction are the autobiographical volume *Wysoki zamek* (1975; translated as *Highcastle*) and such philosophical works as *Dialogi* (1957; translated as *Dialogs*) and the untranslated tome *Summa Technologiae* (1964), in which he discussed human evolution and new scientific and technological advances and was prescient in his speculations on such topics as biological engineering and virtual reality. Lem died in Krakow, Poland. He was survived by his wife, Barbara Lesniak, a radiologist, and his son, Tomasz Lem, who runs the official Lem Web site. See *Current Biography* (1986).

Obituary *New York Times* B p7 Mar. 28, 2006

LOPEZ, AL Aug. 20, 1908–Oct. 30, 2005 Professional baseball player and manager. As a catcher in 18 National League seasons (1928, 1930–46) and one American League season (1947), Lopez played 1,918 games (1,950 according to some accounts), a career record for a major-league catcher at the time. As an American League manager, he guided the Cleveland Indians to first place in the league in 1954 and the Chicago White Sox to the same finish in 1959, thus interrupting the New York Yankees' otherwise unbroken pennant-winning streak between 1949 and 1964. His teams finished second to the Yankees nine times. Lopez, the son of immigrants from Spain, dropped out of high school in Tampa, Florida, to join the Tampa Smokers of the Florida State League in 1925. Two years later he advanced to Jacksonville, then in the Southeastern League. At the end of the 1927 season, Jacksonville sold him up to the National League's Brooklyn Dodgers. His first major-league games were three (in which he made three putouts and went hitless) with Brooklyn in 1928. In 1930, following a season with Atlanta in the Southern Association, he played the first of his six full seasons with Brooklyn. In 1934 he was named to the National League's All-Star team. He played with the Boston Bees (an interim National League franchise in Boston, preceded and followed by the Boston Braves) from 1936 until the middle of the 1940 season, when he was traded to the Pittsburgh Pirates. He was again a National League All-Star in 1941. After six and a half seasons with the Pirates and a total of 18 years in the National League, he finished his playing career with the Cleveland Indians in the American League in 1947. His career totals as a player included 6,454 putouts and a fielding percentage of .984 behind the plate and in seven games in the infield. At the plate, he had averages of .261 in batting and .337 in slugging. Lopez began his career as a manager with Indianapolis in the minor leagues' American Association, which he guided to an association pennant in 1948 and to second-place finishes in 1949 and 1950. As a major-league manager, he had a record of 570 wins and 354 losses with the Cleveland Indians (1951–56) and a 840–650 record with the Chicago White Sox (1957–69). His managerial tenure in Chicago was interrupted from the beginning of the 1966 season to July 1968, when Eddie Stanky managed and Lopez was an adviser. He was inducted into the Baseball Hall of Fame in 1977. Lopez died in Tampa, Florida. He was predeceased by his wife, Connie, and survived by his son, Al Lopez Jr., three grandchildren, and nine great-grandchildren. See *Current Biography* (1960).

Obituary *New York Times* B p7 Oct. 31, 2005

MACMITCHELL, LESLIE Sep. 26, 1920–Mar. 21, 2006 Track athlete. MacMitchell was a champion runner whose first major victories were the national interscholastic 1,000-yard and cross-country titles, earned when he was a student at George Washington High School in Manhattan in the mid-1930s. In 1937 he won the mile event at the Stuyvesant High School track meet. In 1941, when he was an undergraduate at New York University, he won the mile run in all five Madison Square Garden meets. In winning the Baxter Mile he equaled the world indoor record of 4 minutes 7.4 seconds, which had been set by Glenn Cunningham and Chuck Fenske. Outdoors that year he won the National Collegiate Athletic Association mile and the Amateur Athletic Union 1,500-meter championships. In the balloting by 600 sports authorities in March 1942, he was awarded the James E. Sullivan Trophy as the amateur athlete who during 1941 had "done the most to advance the cause of sportsmanship." In 1942 he won 19 consecutive mile competitions, including the Metropolitan, the AAU, the Wanamaker, the Hunter, and the Intercollegiate Association of Amateur Athletes of America mile events. Following his graduation from NYU, with a degree in physical education, in 1942, he saw World War II action as a U.S. Navy officer in the Atlantic and Pacific theaters. After the war he returned to running, but he never regained his earlier speed, and he quit competing when he failed to qualify for the U.S. Olympic team in 1948. Meanwhile, he had become an administrator at NYU. Following his divorce from his first wife, the former Mary Lee, he married Jill Kudlich, who survived him. His other survivors included two sons, two daughters, and three grandchildren. MacMitchell died in San Jose, California. See *Current Biography* (1946).

Obituary *New York Times* A p20 Mar. 28, 2006

MARKS, LEONARD H. Mar. 5, 1916–Aug. 11, 2006 Communications lawyer; director of the United States Information Agency in the administration of President Lyndon B. Johnson. Leonard Howard Marks earned a place in Johnson's inner circle in the late 1940s and early 1950s, when the future president was, successively, a U.S. congressman and a U.S. senator from Texas. At that time Marks helped Johnson's wife, Lady Bird Johnson, parlay a small radio station she owned into a rich cluster of media holdings under the banner of the Texas Broadcasting Corp. After earning his LL.B. degree at the University of Pennsylvania in 1938, Marks taught there for four years before joining President Franklin Delano Roosevelt's administration in Washington, D.C. during World War II as an attorney with the Office of Price Administration. He soon transferred to the Federal Communications Commission, where he became assistant counsel to the director. While with the FCC he began teaching in the law school of National University (which later merged with George Washington University). In 1946 he left the FCC and co-founded

the Washington-based law firm of Cohn & Marks, devoted to representing people interested in applying to the FCC for licenses for radio and television stations. The firm quickly grew into one of the largest in the field of communications, including radio, broadcast television, newspapers, cable television, satellites, and outdoor advertising. One of Marks's first clients was Lady Bird Johnson, the owner of KTBC, a radio station in Austin, Texas, that was licensed by the FCC to operate only from sunrise to sunset. Marks succeeded in obtaining for the station a license to broadcast full-time at a higher frequency. Later, when the FCC announced the allocation of a new television frequency in Austin in 1952, Lady Bird Johnson followed his advice and applied, successfully, for that station. "And that," as Marks said in an interview for *Bar Report* (June/July 2000), "was the beginning of the LBJ family fortune." In President Johnson's successful run for the presidency in 1964, Marks was treasurer of the Johnson for President Committee. In 1965 President Johnson named him director of the United States Information Agency, a position in which he served for three years. On a budget of $178 million, he oversaw at USIA such international operations as the Voice of America's radio broadcasts, the publication of magazines in dozens of languages, and the global distribution of hundreds of documentaries and other films. One of his proudest achievements at USIA was a cross-cultural exchange program with Egypt. After Johnson left office, Marks continued to work as his attorney. Much of Marks's time and energy in his later career was devoted to an effort to eliminate laws in 92 countries making it a crime for journalists to insult the political leaders of those countries. An advocate of public diplomacy, Marks served on such international communications panels as the World Press Freedom Committee and Radio Free Europe/Radio Liberty Fund Inc. He was on the board of the International Rescue Committee and was president of that committee from 1973 to 1979. He also served terms as chairman of the Foreign Policy Association and the executive committee of the American Academy of Diplomacy. In 2004 he published the memoir *The President Is Calling*. Marks was predeceased by his wife, Dorothy, and survived by two sons and five grandchildren. He died in Washington, D.C. See *Current Biography* (1966).

Obituary *New York Times* C p12 Aug. 16, 2006

McCARTHY, EUGENE J. Mar. 29, 1916–Dec. 10, 2005 Five-term Democratic U.S. representative (1949–59) and two-term Democratic U.S. senator (1959–71) from Minnesota. At root, McCarthy was a Catholic intellectual of sardonic and contrarian bent. In politics he was originally identified as a liberal; in the long run, he proved to be "committed to social justice but a skeptic about reform, about do-gooders, about the power of the state and the competence of government, and about the liberal reliance upon material cures for social problems," as Keith C. Burris, the editor of McCarthy's book *No-Fault Politics* (1998), has observed. In the defining moment of his career, he dared, in the words of President Bill Clinton, "to stand alone and turn the tide of history" by challenging President Lyndon B. Johnson on the issue of the Vietnam War in the 1968 Democratic electoral primaries. After earning degrees at St. John's University in Collegeville, Minnesota, and the University of Minnesota in Minneapolis, McCarthy taught in public schools and was a professor of economics at St. John's University and acting chairman of the Department of Sociology at the College of St. Thomas in St. Paul, Minnesota. He became a county chairman in the Democratic Farmer-Labor Party, Minnesota's version of the Democratic Party, in June 1948, and he was elected to Congress the following November. In the U.S. House of Representatives, he had a roll-call record that was consistently liberal in the New Deal tradition, and for the most part, he continued on that course after moving up to the U.S. Senate. He initially supported President Lyndon B. Johnson's Great Society social programs and was especially proud of his own promotion of civil rights legislation, but he became disillusioned when the Great Society programs were, in his view, pushed too far, beyond buoying working people, to providing "more welfare . . . an admission that the New Deal had failed or fallen." That perceived "failure" occurred simultaneously with Johnson's escalation of the war in Vietnam. In a speech at the Conference of Concerned Democrats in 1967, McCarthy said: "We have in politics today a new vocabulary in which the critical word is 'war'; war on poverty, war on ignorance, war on crime, war on pollution. None of these problems can be solved by war but only by persistent, dedicated, and thoughtful attention. But we do have a war which is properly called a war—a war in Vietnam . . . which is not defensible even in military terms . . . a war which is morally wrong." In 1967 the thought of a Democratic politician challenging the renomination of a sitting president was beyond the pale. McCarthy went beyond the pale in November 1967, announcing that he would be a war-protest candidate for the 1968 Democratic presidential nomination. In the first of the 1968 Democratic presidential primary elections, in New Hampshire on March 12, President Johnson received 49 percent of the vote and McCarthy finished second with 42 percent. The unexpected narrowness of the incumbent president's margin of victory shook Johnson to the core, and it emboldened a senator better known than McCarthy, Robert F. Kennedy of New York, to join the fray. Following Johnson's announcement of his withdrawal from pursuit of a second full term in office, on March 31, McCarthy and Kennedy went nip and tuck in the primaries until Kennedy was assassinated, on June 4. Later in June, when the Democratic presidential nomination went to Vice President Hubert H. Humphrey, President Johnson's hand-picked choice, anger among McCarthy's legion of young supporters contributed to the historic tumult at the Democratic National Convention in Chicago. Humphrey went on to lose to Republican Richard M. Nixon in the general election in November 1968. After leaving the Senate in 1971, McCarthy worked as a senior editor at the publishing firm of Harcourt, Brace, Jovanovich and at his own writing of poetry, essays (some in the form of syndicated newspaper columns), and books. In his writings, as in his public speaking, he often revealed a wry wit. In 1972 he again sought the Democratic presidential nomination, with less success than in 1968. Having

come to believe that there was no important difference between the Democrats and Republicans, he left the Democratic Party and ran for president as an independent in 1976. Four years later, out of antipathy to the administration of President Jimmy Carter, he first supported Libertarian presidential candidate Ed Clark and finally gave his endorsement to Republican candidate Ronald Reagan, who won the election. Running for president himself in 1988, he was identified differently on ballots in different states— as the Minnesota Progressive Party candidate in Minnesota, for example, and as the Consumer Party candidate in Pennsylvania. Returning to the Democratic Party, at least nominally, he entered the New Hampshire presidential primary a final time in 1992. On that occasion, excluded by party officials from most of the debates among the candidates, he had limited public exposure and garnered only 1 percent of the vote. He published a score of books, including the memoirs *Gene McCarthy's Minnesota* (1982) and *Up 'Til Now* (1987), such collections as *Required Reading: A Decade of Political Wit and Wisdom* (1988), and many books on American government, politics, and national and international affairs. His last book, *Parting Shots from My Brittle Brow: Reflections on American Politics and Life*, was published in 2005. He died in Washington, D.C. He was predeceased by his estranged wife, Abigail, and his daughter Mary. His survivors included his son, Michael, his daughters Ellen and Margaret, and six grandchildren. See *Current Biography* (1955).

Obituary *New York Times* A p25 Dec. 11, 2005

MCLEAN, JACKIE May 17, 1931–Mar. 31, 2006 Jazz musician; educator; one of the leading alto saxophonists of his time. McLean's work represented a transition from the rhythmically intense hard bop of the 1950s to free (also called progressive) jazz in the 1960s. "I've grown out of being just a bebop saxophone player, or being a free saxophone player," he told Jon Pareles for the *New York Times* in 1983. "I don't know where I am now. I guess I'm somewhere mixed up between all the saxophonists who ever played." The jazz critic Ira Gitler, who knew McLean and his work well, observed that he had "his own sound . . . a cry in his playing, and a lot of fire." Similarly, in his book *Hard Bop*, David H. Rosenthal described McLean's tone as "a true cry from the heart, piercing and ragged." One of McLean's great achievements as an educator was his creation of a degree program in jazz studies at the University of Hartford, where he founded the Jackie McLean Institute of Jazz. McLean was born into a musical family in the Sugar Hill section of Harlem, in New York City, in 1931. (Most reliable sources no longer accept 1932 as his year of birth.) The most important formative influences on his style included the bebop musicians Charlie Parker and Bud Powell. The latter, a Harlem neighbor, became his mentor when McLean was 16. Another influence was that of rhythm and blues, which McLean played with Danny Richmond and T. J. Anderson in gigs during a sojourn in Greensboro, North Carolina, in the early 1950s. The first recording in which he participated was an R&B piece called "Camel Walkin'" with Charlie Singleton's band. Soon afterward he joined Miles Davis in recording *Dig!*, widely regarded as the first hard-bop album. During the 1950s he played with Charles Mingus and Art Blakey, among others. His first recording as a bandleader in his own right was the album *The Jackie McLean Quintet* (1955). He subsequently recorded the albums *Lights Out!* (1956), *Jackie's Bag* (1959), *Vertigo* (1959), and *New Soil* (1959), which included his composition "Minor Apprehension." Among his other compositions were "Melody for Melonae," "Appointment in Ghana," "Dr. Jackie," and "Minor March." In 1959 he was cast as the saxophonist in *The Connection*, Jack Gelber's play about heroin addiction (a real-life problem of McLean's at that time), produced Off-Broadway by the Living Theater troupe. He subsequently toured with the production, and he reprised his stage role in the 1961 screen adaptation. McLean signaled the beginning of his transition from hard bop to free jazz with his album *Let Freedom Ring* (1962). He continued in that vein with such albums as *One Step Beyond* (1963) and *Demon's Dance* (1967). On his recording *New and Old Gospel* (1967), his featured guest sideman was Ornette Coleman, whose improvised departures from strict chord progression had made him the father of the new trend in jazz. During the 1960s McLean spent more and more of his time in community and educational service, counseling drug addicts and working with college students. In 1968 he began commuting from New York City to Hartford, Connecticut, to teach a saxophone course and serve as a drug counselor at the Hartt School of Music at the University of Hartford. In 1970 he joined the faculty of the Hartt School as a music instructor, and 10 years later he became the founding director of the school's African-American music department, renamed the Jackie McLean Institute of Jazz in 2000. In addition to his work at the university, he co-founded, with his wife, Dollie, in the city of Hartford the Artists Collective, a center devoted to teaching music, drama, dance, and the visual arts to inner-city youth. Meanwhile, with his revived quintet (which included his son René on tenor saxophone), he had made the comeback album *Dynasty* (1988), and during the 1990s he recorded five albums, including *Rites of Passage* and *Fire and Love*. His CD *Nature Boy* was released in 2000. He performed his last live gigs during a tour of Europe and the Middle East in 2004. McLean died at his home in Hartford. In addition to his wife, Dollie, and his son René, his survivors included another son, Vernone, a daughter, Melonae, five grandchildren, and five great-grandchildren. See *Current Biography* (2001).

Obituary *New York Times* B p6 Apr. 3, 2006

MERRIFIELD, R. BRUCE July 15, 1921–May 14, 2006. American biochemist; professor emeritus, Rockefeller University; Nobel laureate. Merrifield revolutionized polypeptide chemistry with his development of a solid-phase technique for automating the synthesis of the protein fragments called peptides. That technique opened vast new horizons in basic biochemical research and its applications in such fields as medicine, pharmacology, and genetic engineering. Previously, peptide synthesis had been done in liquid solutions with meager, painfully slow

results. In 1959 Merrifield began his search for "a rapid, quantitative, automatic method for the synthesis of long-chain peptides." The method that he hit upon was one in which the amino acids in each peptide chain were strung rapidly one upon the other in a solid plastic matrix. In 1962 he announced his success in swiftly producing large synthetic yields with that method. His next task was to design and construct a machine for the automating of his method. With his associates at Rockefeller University, he completed the first working model of an automated solid-phase synthesizer in 1965. Four years later he and Bernard Gutte accomplished the first successful synthesis of a naturally occurring enzyme, ribonuclease. Merrifield and his colleagues meanwhile were using his machine to synthesize bradykinin, peptide hormones, and, finally, a protein—insulin. Neither Merrifield nor Rockefeller University ever patented the solid-phase synthesis technique, allowing other institutions and commercial laboratories to freely use it in the preparation of peptide hormones, neuropeptides, toxins, protein growth factors, antibiotics, nucleotides, and nucleic acids. In recognition of the value of his development of a solid-matrix methodology for peptide synthesis, Merrifield was awarded the Nobel Prize in Chemistry in 1984. Merrifield had joined the faculty of Rockefeller University (then called the Rockefeller Institute for Medical Research) as an assistant biochemist in 1949, just after receiving his Ph.D. degree from the University of California at Los Angeles. He became an assistant professor at Rockefeller University in 1957, an associate professor in 1958, and a full professor in 1966. He was named John D. Rockefeller Jr. Professor in 1983. After retiring and assuming emeritus status, in 1992, he continued doing his laboratory work at Rockefeller University. His autobiography, *Life During a Golden Age of Peptide Chemistry*, was published in 1993. He died at his home in Cresskill, New Jersey. His survivors included his wife, Elizabeth, a son, and five daughters. See *Current Biography* (1985).

Obituary *New York Times* D p8 May 20, 2006

MILOSEVIC, SLOBODAN Aug. 20, 1941–Mar. 11, 2006 Serbian/Yugoslav politician and statesman. Milosevic was an erstwhile Yugoslav Communist turned militant Serbian nationalist. As two-term president of Serbia (1989–97), he pursued an aggressive "Greater Serbia" policy that ignited three Balkan wars and hastened the breakup of the Socialist Federal Republic of Yugoslavia, which comprised the area of the present-day independent states of Serbia, Montenegro, Slovenia, Croatia, Macedonia, and Bosnia (including Herzegovina). Constitutionally barred from seeking a third term as president of Serbia, Milosevic in 1997 was named by the federal assembly (dominated by his party) to the previously ceremonial and then appointive post of president of the Federal Republic of Yugoslavia, which by that time consisted of only Serbia and Montenegro. (Montenegro would declare its independence in the spring of 2006.) From that new seat of power, Milosevic escalated an already-in-progress civil war against ethnic Albanian insurgents in the Serbian province of Kosovo, which he lost when NATO intervened militarily in support of the ethnic Albanians in 1999. He died in his prison cell in The Hague, where he was on trial before the International Criminal Tribunal for the Former Yugoslavia on charges of war crimes and genocide. After studying law at Belgrade University, Milosovic worked as a banker and economic adviser to the mayor of Belgrade while rising through the ranks of the Yugoslav League of Communists to become chairman of the presidium of the party in Serbia in the mid-1980s. Following his election to the presidency of Serbia in 1989, he led the League of Communists of Serbia into a merger with the Socialist Alliance of Working People of Serbia, resulting in the formation of the arch-nationalistic Socialist Party of Serbia, with himself at its head. His effort as president of Serbia to rally ethnic Serbs in other Yugoslav republics into a "Greater Serbia" inflamed ethnic tensions and hastened the dissolution of theYugoslav federation. The first republic to leave was Slovenia (where ethnic Serbs were a tiny minority), in 1991. Milosevic used military force against Slovenia at that time, but only briefly. When, in May of the same year, Croatia (with a 12 percent ethnic Serb population) declared its independence, he sent in a strong force of Serbian-led Yugoslav army troops, Serbian police, and other paramilitaries who, in combination with local ethnic Serb militia, overran a third of Croatia within eight months, displacing tens of thousands of people and killing more than 10,000. After Bosnia (with a 31 percent ethnic Serb population) declared its independence in the spring of 1992, it suffered an even more intense attack by Milosevic's forces, who killed at least 100,000 and displaced hundreds of thousands, chiefly Muslims. At the same time, the Croatian army counterattacked, driving several hundred thousand ethnic Serbs out of Bosnia. There were ceasefires, but the wars in Croatia and Bosnia definitively ended only after the American-led NATO aerial bombardment of Serb positions in Bosnia in August and September 1995. By that time, 250,000 people had been killed, and there were 2.7 million refugees. Milosevic and representatives of Croatia and Bosnia signed the Dayton Peace Accords in November 1995. Meanwhile, trouble was brewing in Serbia's southern province of Kosovo, bordering Albania. While that province was sacred in the history of Christian Serbia, its population had become dominated by Muslim ethnic Albanians, also known as Kosovars. During the 1990s a small guerrilla band of ethnic Albanian separatists grew into the Kosovo Liberation Army (KLA). When the KLA declared open war against Serb Yugoslav authority in February 1998, Milosovic quickly responded with military might. Over the next several months, hundreds were killed and some 100,000 Kosovars were driven from their homes. American authorities at first condemned the KLA as "terrorist," but as Milosovic's crackdown became increasingly brutal, they tilted in favor of the Kosovars. On March 24, 1999 an American-led NATO air force began a bombardment of Serb targets—from military installations to bridges, oil refineries, and communications centers—that lasted 73 days and left Serbia's infrastructure and its economy in shambles. During the two stages of the Kosovo war that began in February 1998 and ended with the retreat of the Serbian military forces from the province in June 1999, several thousand people had been killed and half of the ethnic Albanian population had fled. In the aftermath of the war, most of Kosovo's Serb and Roma (Gypsy) populations fled into Serbia proper to escape Kosovar vengeance. After massive demonstrations against him following a disputed Yugoslav presidential election (the first to occur directly in the popular sector),Milosevic conceded victory by an opposition candidate and resigned the presidency. In March 2001 Yugoslav authories arrested him on charges of corruption and abuse of power. Three months later he was transferred to U.N. custody, whence he was turned over to the International Criminal Tribunal for the Former Yugoslavia in The Hague. His trial began in February 2002. When he died in his cell of a heart attack, some of his adversaries speculated that he may have failed to take his medicine for high blood pressure in the hope of impeding the trial on medical grounds; some of his sympathizers suspected either negligence or foul play on the part of his captors. He was survived by his wife, Mira, and a son and daughter. See *Current Biography* (1990).

Obituary *New York Times* I p34 Mar. 12, 2006

MOTLEY, CONSTANCE BAKER Sep. 14, 1921–Sep. 28, 2005 African-American jurist. Following her two decades of epochal work as a civil rights lawyer with the Legal Defense and Educational Fund of the National Association for the Advancement of Colored People (NAACP), Mrs. Motley became, in succession, the first black woman to be elected to the New York State Senate, the first woman of any race to serve as president of one of New York City's five boroughs (Manhattan, in her case), and the first black woman to be named a federal judge. She was born in New Haven, Connecticut, to parents who had immigrated to the U.S. from the British West Indies. Her father worked as a chef for various Yale University organizations, including the secret society Skull and Bones. Clarence W. Blakeslee, a white New Haven philanthropist impressed with her intelligence and oratorical ability, undertook the financing of her higher education. After a year and a half at Fisk University, she earned a B.A. degree in economics at New York University (1943) and an LL.B. degree at Columbia University Law School (1946) and was admitted to the New York State bar (1948). While studying law she interned in the New York office of the NAACP's Legal Defense and Educational Fund. She became a full-time clerk there in 1946, an assistant counsel in 1948, and an associate counsel in 1961. Between the late 1940s and the early 1960s, she played a role in the preparation of scores of NAACP legal briefs, including the draft complaint that became the basis for the litigation in the landmark U.S. Supreme Court desegregation case *Brown v. Board of Education of Topeka, Kansas* (1954). In particular, she was the NAACP team's chief point person in the South, acting as the principal trial attorney in numerous successful desegregation suits there, including those that broke down the racial barriers at colleges and universities in Alabama, South Carolina, Georgia, and Mississippi. In the best-known of those cases, she successfully argued before the Court of Appeals in the Fifth Circuit for the admission of James Meredith to the University of Mississippi in 1962. She also handled some elementary- and secondary-school cases, and she represented African-American plaintiffs in many desegregation suits involving restaurants and lunch counters, transportation, public accommodations, and recreational facilities and in defense of the plaintiffs' right to demonstrate. In the area of housing, she fought racial restrictions in cities in the North as well as the South. She was a close legal adviser to the Reverend Martin Luther King Jr. and a defender of his right to lead protest marches in Birmingham, Alabama, and Albany, Georgia. Of the 10 cases she argued before the U.S. Supreme Court, she won nine. Her entrance into politics came about when, early in 1964, she replaced on the ballot a Democratic New York State Senate candidate from Manhattan's Upper West Side who had been disqualified on an election-law technicality. Elected in February 1964 and reelected the following November, she remained in the Senate until February 1965, when the Manhattan members of the New York City Council elected her to fill a one-year vacancy in the office of president of the borough of Manhattan. She was elected to a full four-year term in the borough presidency in November 1965, but her work as borough president—including her initiation of a program for the revitalization of Harlem and East Harlem—was cut short when, in 1966, she accepted President Lyndon B. Johnson's appointment of her to a judgeship on the U.S. District Court for the Southern District of New York. She was the chief judge of the Southern District from 1982 until 1986, when she became senior judge, a status of virtual retirement that allowed her to resume work as a trial attorney. In 1993 Mrs. Motley was inducted into the National Women's Hall of Fame, and in 2001 she received the Presidential Citizens Medal. Her autobiography, *Equal Justice Under the Law*, was published in 1998. She died at New York University Downtown Hospital in Manhattan. Her survivors included her husband, Joel Wilson Motley Jr., her son, Joel III, and three grandchildren. See *Current Biography* (1964).

Obituary *New York Times* B p10 Sep. 29, 2005

MURPHY, THOMAS Dec. 10, 1915–Jan. 18, 2006 Corporate executive. Murphy was chairman and chief executive officer of the General Motors Corp. from December 1, 1974 to January 1, 1981. When he took the helm, GM was the world's leading automaker, but it was in crisis, because the Arab oil embargo that had begun just months before made more real the challenge presented to Detroit's gas-guzzlers by compact imports, chiefly Japanese. Under Murphy, GM made the transition to smaller, more fuel-efficient vehicles, including many models with front-wheel-drive power trains. In 1978 GM sold 9.55 million cars and trucks, 7.1 million of them in the United States alone, which stands as the best sales record in its history. Murphy held a degree in accounting from the University of Illinois. During Word War II he served in the U.S. Navy. Soon after joining GM as a clerk in the comptroller's office, he was transferred to the financial staff, where he worked his way up from accountant and statistician to, successively, director of financial analysis, comp-

troller, and treasurer. He served as vice president in charge of the car and truck division and vice chairman of the board before becoming chairman and CEO. According to Rick Wagoner, the corporation's current chairman and CEO, Murphy "personally set a tone of the highest morals and ethics . . . that has defined the culture in GM for decades since." Murphy died at his home in Boynton Beach, Florida. He was survived by his wife, Catherine Rita, two daughters, a son, eight grandchildren, and 10 great-grandchildren. See *Current Biography* (1979).

Obituary *New York Times* A p21 Jan. 19, 2006

NEWMAN, ARNOLD Mar. 3, 1918–June 6, 2006 Photographer. As the father of "environmental portraiture," Arnold Newman, in his own words, "took the portrait out of the studio and started getting into real life." Based in New York, Newman traveled widely with his camera, photographing the world's movers and shakers on location. Over a span of six decades, he compiled an immense gallery of prominent figures captured in settings related to their work. They included, in the fields of government and politics, Ariel Sharon, Yasir Arafat, and every president of the United States from Truman to Clinton; in science, J. Robert Oppenheimer and Jonas Salk; in literature or dramaturgy, Eugene O'Neill (photographed in his library), Henry Miller, Truman Capote, Isaac Asimov, and Lillian Hellman; in publishing, Henry Luce, Rupert Murdoch, and Arthur Sulzberger; in theater or film, Marlene Dietrich, Gypsy Rose Lee, Zero Mostel, Martin Scorsese, Vittorio de Sica, and a deglamorized Marilyn Monroe; in music, Leonard Bernstein, George Harrison, and Philip Glass; and in architecture, I. M. Pei and Philip Johnson. He photographed a number of fellow photographers, from Ansel Adams to Gordon Parks, and a legion of artists, including Georges Braque, Jean Miro, Pablo Picasso, Piet Mondrian, Marcel Duchamp, Edward Hopper, Salvador Dali, Max Ernst, Georgia O'Keeffe, Frank Stella, Claes Oldenburg, and Andy Warhol. His favorites were his portraits of Igor Stravinsky (seated at and dwarfed by his grand piano) and of the Nazi industrialist Alfried Krupp (an unflattering photograph, regarded by Newman as his "statement about the Holocaust"). In his camera work Newman was influenced not only by such photographers as Walker Evans and other Depression-era documentarians in the federal Farm Security Administration but also by such artists as the Cubists and the Flemish painters. A painter manqué himself, he did not so much pose his subjects as compose pictures that evoked the spirit of each sitter's personality in relation to his or her claim to fame. As Arthur Goldsmith once observed in the magazine *Popular Photography*, a Newman portrait is "an organization of visual elements which expresses . . . his interpretation of the personality portrayed." Colin Ford of Great Britain's National Portrait Gallery (which commissioned Newman to photograph 76 eminent British citizens) observed that a Newman portrait was "executed with all the thoroughness and depth of an oil painting." Conversations with his subjects were part of Newman's working routine. Newman studied art at the University of Miami from 1936 to 1938, when economic straits forced him to leave the university. Through a family friend he found a job as an assistant photographer with a commercial chain of portrait studios. After working in studios in Philadelphia and Allentown, Pennsylvania, and Baltimore, Maryland, he became manager of a studio in West Palm Beach, Florida, in 1939, and he opened his own business in Miami Beach in 1942. Meanwhile, he had begun exhibiting his work at the A–D Gallery in New York City, and he relocated to that city (where he had been born) in 1946. In that year he began contributing photographs to *Harper's Bazaar* and *Life*, and he subsequently became a contributor to other mass-circulation magazines, including *Look*, *Holiday*, *New York Times Magazine*, *Times Magazine* of London, *Travel and Leisure*, *Vanity Fair*, and *Paris Match*. In addition to his portraits, Newman did abstract and still-life photography. He is represented in the permanent collections of the Metropolitan Museum of Art and the Museum of Modern Art in New York City, the Corcoran Gallery in Washington, D.C., and many other major museums and galleries worldwide. His exhibition One World, One People, comprising 53 portraits, was held at the Jewish Museum of Florida in 2003 and subsequently toured the United States. He published 14 books of photographs, including *One Mind's Eye* (1974), *The Great British* (1979), *Faces USA* (1978), *Arnold Newman: Five Decades* (1986), *Arnold Newman's Americans* (1992), *Arnold Newman* (1999), and *Arnold Newman Breaking Ground* (2000). A definitive updated edition of *Arnold Newman*, Philip Brookman's illustrated biography of the photographer, was published in 2006. Newman died in Manhattan. He was survived by his wife, Augusta, two sons, and four grandchildren. See *Current Biography* (1980).

Obituary *New York Times* C p11 June 7, 2006

NILSSON, BIRGIT May 17, 1918–Dec. 25, 2005 Swedish soprano. Nilsson dazzled audiences in leading opera houses around the world with her great vocal purity, power (especially thrilling in the high notes), projection, and stamina. She was her generation's foremost interpreter of Wagnerian soprano roles, including Senta in *Der Fliegende Holländer*, both Elisabeth and Venus in *Tannhäuser*, and the very demanding roles of Isolde in *Tristan und Isolde* and Brünnhilde in the Ring cycle. Her repertoire also prominently included the title roles in Richard Strauss's *Elektra* and *Salome*, the Dyer's wife in Strauss's *Frau Ohne Schatten*, the title roles in Puccini's *Turandot* and *Tosca*, and the soprano leads in Mozart's *Idomeneo* and *Don Giovanni* and Verdi's *Macbeth*, *Un Ballo in Maschera*, and *Aida*, among other roles. She made her debut at the Royal Opera in Stockholm in 1946, and she joined that company's permanent roster the following year. She began performing in other European countries in 1951. Her first operatic performance in the Western Hemisphere was in Buenos Aires, Argentina, in 1955. In August 1956 she made her first appearance in the United States, as a guest artist with the Los Angeles Philharmonic, and the following October she made her American operatic debut with the San Francisco Opera Company. Following a three-year stint with the Chicago Lyric Opera, she made her de-

but with New York's Metropolitan Opera in 1959. Returning to the Met regularly over the following 24 years (except during an hiatus of five years when she was resolving a dispute with the U.S. Internal Revenue Service), she performed a total of more than 200 times there. A number of her performances are preserved in audio and video recordings. Her autobiography, *Mina minnesbilder* (1977), was translated into English in the United States as *My Memoirs in Pictures* (1981). After retiring as a performer, in 1983, she taught master classes, first at the Manhattan School of Music, in New York City, and subsequently in England, before returning to Sweden and settling in Vastra Karup, her natal village, with her husband, Bertil Niklasson. The couple had no children. She died in Vastra Karup. See *Current Biography* (1960).

Obituary *New York Times* A p1+ Jan. 12, 2006

NOFZIGER, LYN June 8, 1924–Mar. 27, 2006 Political consultant and communicator; former journalist. Nofziger was a shrewd conservative Republican strategist and spokesman who plied his craft in the disarming guise of a rumpled cutup who "wore Mickey Mouse ties, made awful puns, sported a goatee, and dressed like a refugee who had been outfitted by a charity that didn't know his size," as Lou Cannon, a biographer of Ronald Reagan, observed in his obituary of Nofziger for the *National Review*. Despite the clash of his personality with that of Nancy Reagan, Nofziger was best known for his long-term contribution to the political success of Ronald Reagan, the 33d governor of California (1966–74) and 40th president of the United States (1981–89). After serving in the U.S. Army during World War II and earning a degree in journalism at San Jose (California) State College, Nofziger worked as a newspaperman for 18 years, including eight (1958–66) as a Washington, D.C, correspondent for James S. Copley's chain of California and Illinois newspapers. Through Copley, the political supporters of Ronald Reagan persuaded him to serve as press secretary in the former movie actor's successful 1966 gubernatorial campaign. During the first 23 months (beginning in November 1966) of Governor Reagan's first four-year term in Sacramento, he remained at Reagan's side as his communications director, helping to maintain Reagan's high standing in the polls by preserving his image as an amateur rather than a professional politician. Among those close to Governor Reagan, Nofziger, along with Tom Reed, was the first to recognize his presidential potential. He continued to advise Reagan on a part-time basis after he left the gubernatorial team, in October 1968. After moving back to Washington, he served as President Richard M. Nixon's deputy assistant for congressional relations from July 1969 to February 1971, when he left the White House to become deputy chairman for communications of the Republican National Committee. In 1972 he directed the California sector of President Nixon's successful bid for reelection. When Ronald Reagan sought the Republican presidential nomination unsuccessfully in 1976, he was the Reagan campaign team's press secretary and national convention director. He founded the political action committee Citizens for the Republic, which kept the Reagan team together and made possible Reagan's nomination for the presidency at the Republican National Convention in the summer of 1980 and his election to the presidency the following November. During the general election campaign of 1980, Nofziger was Reagan's press secretary (and, briefly, communications director as well). During Reagan's first year in the White House, he was assistant to the president for political affairs (and simultaneously, for a brief period, press secretary). After he complained that too many Cabinet and sub-Cabinet positions were being filled by non-Reaganite moderates, he was given veto power over sub-Cabinet appointments. Upon leaving the White House in 1982, he opened a consulting, public relations, and lobbying firm in Washington in collaboration with Mark Bragg. Informally, he continued to advise Ronald Reagan throughout his two presidential terms. In 1988 he left that partnership and formed Nofziger Communications. Also in 1988 he was tried and found guilty of violating the Ethics in Government Act by lobbying illegally in the White House within months of leaving his government job; the conviction was overturned on appeal the following year. In addition to his political memoir, *Nofziger* (1992), he published four Western novels, including the trilogy comprising the volume *Tackett* (1998), and, under a pseudonym, a collection of limericks and other doggerel titled *Unbridled Joy: The Verse of Joy Skilmer* (2000). Nofziger died at his home in Falls Church, Virginia. His survivors included his wife, Bonnie, his daughter Glenda, and two grandchildren. His daughter Susan predeceased him. See *Current Biography* (1983).

Obituary *New York Times* B p7 Mar. 28, 2006

OBOTE, MILTON Dec. 28, 1924–Oct. 10, 2005 Ugandan politician and statesman. Obote, a dedicated Pan-Africanist and socialist in his youth, was driven to repressive authoritarianism when in power. He was the first prime minister (1962–66) and a two-time president (1966–71, 1980–85) of the Republic of Uganda, a country that had taken shape as a British protectorate beginning in the late 19th century. Without regard for local geography or natural and traditional demographics, the British cobbled together a colonial entity consisting of a score of disparate peoples, including several kingdoms south of Lake Kyoga, the largest and richest of which, Buganda, was designated as the seat of government. Relegated to second-class participation in that colonial arrangement were the Lango people living north of Lake Kyoga. Obote was a Lango, born into the family of a minor tribal chief in the village of Akokoro. He was educated at a local Protestant mission school, at colleges in Mwiri and Kampala, and through correspondence courses. In 1950 he migrated to neighboring Kenya, where, while working at various jobs, he was active in Jomo Kenyatta's Kenya National Union, Argwings Kodhek's African District Congress, and Tom Mboya's People's Convention Party. After returning to Uganda, in 1955, he was elected to the Legco, the colonial legislative council, in 1957, and proceeded to lead the Uganda National Congress into a merger with the Uganda People's Union, in 1960. The product of that merger was the Uganda People's Congress (UPC), a pro-independence party of which he became president-general. Through shrewd negotiation, by promising them federal autonomy, he succeeded in enlisting the hereditary rulers of the traditional tribal kingdoms, including Buganda, in the cause of national independence, which was achieved in 1962. The coalition of his UPC with the newly established Kabaka Yekka ("King Only") Party of Buganda enabled him to emerge from the national election of April 1962 with a backing of 67 seats in the 91-member National Assembly, a solid majority that gave him the prime ministership. In 1963, implementing his appeasement of the Kabaka Yekka Party, he orchestrated a largely rigged election that installed King Edward Mutesa II of Buganda in the office of president of Uganda. That office was to be ceremonial, Obote thought, but Mutesa turned out to be a restive figurehead, arguing with Obote over government policy, especially regarding disputed territory under Buganda's control. In 1966, in response to a more general governmental crisis—precipitated by charges of misappropriation of funds—Obote suspended the 1962 Ugandan constitution and installed himself as the all-powerful executive president under a new "republican" constitution. He outlawed the traditional Ugandan kingships—a draconian ban enforced by an army commanded by Idi Amin—and drove King Mutesa II into exile in London. To maintain power, he resorted to arbitrary detentions and other violations of justice, and, beset by scandals, became more and more dependent on the protection of Idi Amin's army. An assassination attempt in 1969, apparently instigated by a member of the Bugandan royal family, left him with facial wounds. In 1970 some 30,000 Kenyan workers were expelled from Uganda—again by force of Idi Amin's military—precipitating an economic crisis in Uganda. While Obote was attending a British Commonwealth conference in Singapore in 1971, Amin led a successful military coup and replaced Obote as Uganda's president. Obote lived in exile in nearby Tanzania until the collapse of Idi Amin's monstrous regime in 1979. He reassumed the presidency of Uganda when the UPC claimed victory in a disputed, apparently corrupt election in 1980. His second term as president was a bloody one, marked by civil war and gross violations of human rights, as well as by agricultural decline and economic scarcity. His army, led by General Tito Okello, had difficulty countering the bush maneuvers of guerrilla forces led by Yoweri Museveni and based largely in Buganda. Mass executions of hundreds of thousands of innocent civilians were reported as Obote's government strove to drive rural populations into cities. In 1985 General Okello turned against Obote and overthrew his government in a coup. Yoweri Museveni in turn overthrew Okello and moved into the presidency the following year. Meanwhile, Obote fled into exile, first in Kenya, finally in Zambia. Obote had three sons from as many marriages. He died in a hospital in Johannesburg, South Africa. See *Current Biography* (1981).

Obituary *New York Times* B p9 Oct. 11, 2005

PAIK, NAM JUNE July 20, 1932–Jan. 29, 2006 Korean-born avant-garde composer and intermedia performance artist. Paik was an amiably mischievous experimental musical artist, a "cultural terrorist," as the critic Alan Kaprow dubbed him. His kitschy, "happenings"-style "action concerts" could loosely be classified within the anti-art tradition of the Dadaists. More directly, he was influenced by the anti-harmonic "accidental" musical compositions of John Cage, although he took Cage's ideas "into areas where [Cage] would never have gone," as Cage himself observed. Most famously, he took them into the area of electronics, where he was the first to transform video into an artistic medium. Reviewing The Worlds of Nam June Paik, a retrospective that filled the Guggenheim Museum, in New York City, in 2000, David Joselit wrote for *Art in America*, "[Paik's] single-channel videotapes shatter narrative coherence by jumping rapidly between discontinuous images and by transforming the video signal into patterns that can be both psychedelic and grotesque. When combined in multi-monitor installations, [the effect is] a dynamic field of patterns that is alternately overwhelming and mesmerizing. . . . In Paik's hands, video distraction is reframed as a kind of media performance." Joselit wrote that entering the Guggenheim on that occasion was "exhilarating, as though one had entered a disco or a club where any stable opposition between 'viewers' and 'performers' necessarily disappears." After earning a degree in aesthetics at Tokyo University in 1956, with a thesis on the serial method of the composer Arnold Schoenberg, Paik moved to Germany, where he spent the next half-dozen years studying piano technique and music history, composition, and theory at the Freiburg Conservatory and the universities of Munich and Cologne and working with Karlheinz Stockhausen and others in Radio Cologne's Studio for Electronic Music. At the Internationale Ferienkurse für Neue Musik in Darmstadt, Germany, in the summer of 1958, he met and began to absorb the ideas of the American composer John Cage. Cage's basic ideas were that "everything we do is music" and that "there is no noise, only sound"; he found indeterminate musical sound in anything and everything—randomly and by chance, as with the haphazard tuning of radios, or with playful deliberation, as with his "prepared piano" stuffed with impedimenta for varied percussive effects. At his most perverse, Cage pretended to present musical performances with no sound at all. At the same summer school in new music in Darmstadt, Paik met George Maciunas, the founder of Fluxus, a group of musical "happening" performers (among them Yoko Ono) who were also influenced by Cage. With Fluxus in 1962, Paik performed his *One for Violin Solo*, consisting of two movements: (1) holding the instrument above his head and (2) crashing it to the floor. In some other performances he played the piano, badly. His first solo exhibition, in Wuppertal, Germany, in 1963, was the world's first show of video art; in it, he used sound waves to make images leap on 13 black-and-white television monitors. In Japan later in 1963, using color TVs, he staged the first "video painting." While in Japan he built his six-foot-tall robot K456 with the help of the electronics engineer Shuya Abe. He became known to Manhattan audiences through

his Off-Off-Broadway collaborations with the young classical cellist Charlotte Moorman, which continued for several years beginning in 1964. The pair created a succès de scandale with their stunts, in the most notorious of which Moorman performed fully or partially naked. In February 1967 they were briefly arrested for obscenity and indecent exposure following Moorman's bare-breasted performance of Paik's *Opéra Sextronique*. Paik responded to the arrests wittily, by creating "TV Bra for a Living Sculpture"—two minuscule televisions that covered Moorman's breasts. In 1967–68 Paik was artist-in-residence at the State University of New York at Stony Brook. On the Boston public television station WGBH in 1969, he contributed his *Electronic Opera No. 1* to *The Medium Is the Medium*, the first video-art broadcast ever. Subsidized by WGBH, he (again with Shuya Abe) invented an analog video synthesizer that enabled him to convert varied audio and video input into a limitless variety of fragmented patterns and colors, which could be fully appreciated only on multiple monitors. He made public use of the synthesizer for the first time in a four-hour audience-participation program on the station in August 1970. He began spending much of his time at the synthesizer's console, making footage he would then edit into videotapes, which became a principal source of his income. One of his best-known videotapes, made while he was artist-in-residence at television station WNET in New York City, was Global Groove (1973), a satirical work partly intended to make electronic technology itself look ridiculous. Among other videotapes of his with social or political messages were *Guadalcanal Requiem* (1977), which combined World War II footage with that of Solomon Islanders seeking independence from the United States and of Charlotte Moorman playing the cello, and *You Can't Lick Stamps in China* (1979). He became best known for his installations of multiple television sets, such as *The More the Better*, a work consisting of more than 1,000 monitors he created for the Seoul Olympics in 1988. In the 1990s he created a number of closed-circuit video sculptures, including *Piano Piece, 1993*, in which a mountain of monitors rested atop a "prepared" piano. He was also concentrating more and more on his "post video" treatments of energy and light with lasers, such as *Pyramid II* (1997) and *Modulation in Sync* (2000). Paik maintained two homes, one in Manhattan and another in Miami Beach, Florida. He died at his home in Miami Beach. See *Current Biography* (1983).

Obituary *New York Times* B p8 Jan. 31, 2006

PARKS, GORDON Nov. 30, 1912–Mar. 7, 2006 Photographer; filmmaker; writer; composer. Parks was an extraordinarily multitalented and prolific trailblazer in the arts, choosing the camera as his primary "weapon against poverty and racism" and also finding expression in the writing of fiction, nonfiction, poetry, and music. The youngest of 15 children, Parks was born into a poor but self-sustaining African-American farm family in Fort Scott, Kansas. As a boy he took to heart his mother's admonition that he never "give [his] color as a cause for failing" and the advice of a brother that "if you're going to fight [the world], use your brain." He learned, as he later said, that he had "a right to be bitter," but he "would not let bitterness destroy" him. Growing up in Fort Scott, and coming of age in St. Paul, Minnesota, he taught himself to play the piano and the trumpet and began composing songs. After dropping out of high school, he saw "how the rich lived" while he was a busboy at an exclusive club and later, during the 1930s, in his travels as a composer and vocalist with a white band and as a dining-car waiter on the North Coast railroad. In a pawnshop in 1937, he bought his first camera. Many of his earliest photos, including fashion shots, were published in African-American newspapers in St. Paul and Minneapolis, Minnesota. His fashion images caught the attention of Joe Louis's wife, who persuaded him to move to Chicago, where he set up a darkroom in the South Side Community Art Center. While earning a living shooting portraits of society women, he spent his spare time photographing scenes of poverty in Chicago's South Side ghetto, the first of the images of people in need for which he would become famous. Supported by a Julius Rosenwald Fellowship, he moved to Washington, D.C., where in 1942 he joined Roy Stryker's illustrious team of photographers (which included Walker Evans and Dorothea Lange) in the U.S. Farm Security Administration's information division, a bureau charged with documenting the human face of the Great Depression. After the FSA was disbanded, later in 1942, Parks moved with the rest of Stryker's team to the Office of War Information. In 1943 Stryker left the OWI to set up and head a major photodocumentary project in the private sector, under the aegis of the Standard Oil Co. of New Jersey. In 1944 Parks moved to the New York City area and joined Stryker's team at Standard Oil, remaining with it for four years. Concurrently, he became a freelance fashion photographer for *Glamour* and *Vogue* magazines. In 1948 *Life* magazine hired him as a staff photographer; he was posted in its Paris bureau until 1952. He remained with *Life* for more than two decades (until it changed from a weekly to a semiannual publication), completing 300 assignments, including coverage of Broadway, politics, crime, life in Harlem, racial segregation in the South, the civil rights movement, the Nation of Islam, the Black Panthers, and other black leaders, among them the Rev. Martin Luther King Jr. and Malcolm X. He also photographed many celebrities, from his socialite friend Gloria Vanderbilt to the musician Duke Ellington. His first books were the instruction manuals *Flash Photography* (1947) and *Camera Portraits* (1948). His books also include five collections of his photos accompanied by verse, including *Gordon Parks: A Poet and His Camera* (1968) and *Eyes with Winged Thoughts* (2005). *Born Black* (1971) is a collection of his biographical essays, with photographs. One of his photo essays for *Life* led to his book *Flavio* (1978), about a poor, gravely ill Brazilian boy for whom he was instrumental in obtaining lifesaving medical treatment. Parks wrote three novels: *The Learning Tree* (1963), a best-seller based on his childhood in Kansas, the historical novel *Shannon* (1981), about Irish immigrants in the early 1900s, and *The Sun Stalker* (1981), a fictionalization of the life of the British painter J. M. W. Turner. He published the memoirs *A Choice of Weapons* (1966), *To*

Smile in Autumn (1979), *Voices in the Mirror* (1990), and *A Hungry Heart* (2005) and the quasi-memoir *Half Past Autumn* (1997), published in conjunction with a touring exhibition of his photos. Parks became the first African-American to write, produce, and direct a feature film for a major Hollywood studio when he made the screen version of *The Learning Tree* (1969). In Hollywood he later directed the hit blaxploitation action-thriller *Shaft* (1971) and its sequel *Shaft's Big Score!* (1972), the action-comedy *The Super Cops* (1974), and the film *Leadbelly* (1976), about the folk singer/guitarist Huddie Ledbetter. On TV he directed several hour-long documentaries, including *The World of Piri Thomas* (1968) and the Emmy Award–winning *Diary of a Harlem Family* (1968), as well as the made-for-TV movie *Solomon Northrup's Odyssey* (1985), about a northern-born black man kidnapped into slavery in the 1840s. He himself was the subject of the TV documentary *Half Past Autumn: The Life and Works of Gordon Parks* (2000). In 1970 he helped to found the monthly magazine *Essence*. His musical compositions include the song "Don't Misunderstand," from the score for *Shaft's Big Score!*, concertos, sonatas, and the music for the ballet *Martin* (1989), dedicated to Martin Luther King Jr. (for which he also wrote the libretto). Parks's three marriages ended in divorce. The film director Gordon Parks Jr., his son from his first marriage, died in a plane crash in 1979. Gordon Parks was survived by a daughter from his first marriage and another from his second marriage, five grandchildren, and five great-grandchildren. He died at his home in Manhattan. See *Current Biography* (1992).

Obituary *New York Times* A p1+ Mar. 8, 2006

PARKS, ROSA Feb. 4, 1913–Oct. 24, 2005 African-American rights activist; a seamstress who, almost unwittingly, it would seem, became an internationally revered pioneer in the struggle for racial equality, described in the motto on the Congressional Gold Medal awarded her in 1999 as "the mother of the modern-day civil rights movement." Parks's claim to that title dated back to her arrest 44 years earlier, when she was traveling home from work on a city bus in downtown Montgomery, Alabama, and decided not to obey the white bus driver's command that she surrender her seat to a white passenger. With that simple, quiet act of civil disobedience, she sparked the train of events that brought down Jim Crow (the system of legalized racial segregation that had prevailed since the Reconstruction era) in the South and changed the course of race relations in the U.S. as a whole. Parks was born Rosa Louise ("Lee") McCauley in Tuskegee, Alabama, to a carpenter father and a teacher mother. From the ages of two to 11, she was raised by her mother and her maternal grandparents on their farm in Pine Level, Alabama. Her lifelong membership in the African Methodist Episcopal Church, in which she would become a deaconess, began in childhood. She dropped out of high school to help care for her ailing grandmother. In 1932 she married Raymond Parks, a barber by trade, who introduced her to the work of the National Association for the Advancement of Colored People (NAACP), especially in black voter registration.

She was secretary of the Montgomery branch of the NAACP for 14 years beginning in 1943. In the summer of 1955, she enrolled in a workshop at the Highlander Folk School in Monteagle, Tennessee. (The school, a center for training organizers and educating others in labor, civil rights, environmentalism, and other populist and progressive causes, is now the Highlander Research and Education Center, located in New Market, Tennessee.) Under Jim Crow in Montgomery, the buses operated (ostensibly "privately") by Montgomery City Lines Inc. were driven by white drivers primarily for the benefit of white passengers, although black passengers paid their fares with the same 10-cent tokens. White passengers not only had exclusive right to the first four rows but a preemptive right to seats as far back in the bus as occasion demanded. If any of the reserved front seats were occupied, black persons paying their fare at the front of the bus were not allowed even to proceed directly down the aisle to a seat in the rear. Instead, they had to get off and reenter the bus through the rear door. They could then seat themselves anywhere behind the "Colored" sign. But the location of the sign was not fixed. To accommodate the influx of white passengers, the driver could move it rearward, or even remove it altogether. This was the setting when, on December 1, 1955, Mrs. Parks boarded the Cleveland Avenue bus at approximately 6:00 p.m. She sat in the right-aisle seat in the fifth row, which consisted of four seats, two on either side of the aisle, immediately behind the whites-only section. The latter section became full at the bus's next stop. Then, at the third stop, the Empire Theater stop, a white male passenger entered the bus. The bus driver repositioned the "Colored" sign rearward, to row six, and demanded that Parks and the three other black passengers occupying row five vacate their seats to accommodate the lone white man. The other three reluctantly obeyed, but Parks remained in the row, sliding over to the now vacated window seat beside her. Soon afterward she was arrested. The blacks in Montgomery (who comprised three-quarters of the bus system's ridership) and their few white allies rallied to the cause. The Montgomery Improvement Association was formed, with the Rev. Martin Luther King Jr. as its president. The association managed the logistics of a mass boycott of the city bus system that began on December 5, 1955, the day of Parks's trial. In February 1956 Parks was among the 89 people indicted for their participation in the boycott, which lasted 381 days, until December 21, 1956, when Montgomery city buses were integrated for the first time. In 1957 Parks left Montgomery. She later moved to Detroit, where she worked as a seamstress until U.S. representative John Conyers hired her as a secretary and receptionist in his Detroit office, in 1965. She quit that job in 1988 in order to give more attention to the Rosa and Raymond Parks Institute for Self Development. With Elaine Eason Steele, she had founded the institute in 1987 in part to honor the memory of her husband, who had died in 1977. In 1992 Mrs. Parks published *Rosa Parks: My Story*, an autobiography written with Jim Haskins primarily for young readers. She subsequently published *Quiet Strength: The Faith, the Hope, and the Heart of a Woman Who Changed a Nation* (1994), a book of spiritual reflections written with Gregory J. Reed, and the collection of letters *Dear Mrs. Parks: A Dialogue with Today's Youth* (1996). Among the many honors she received during her life was the Presidential Medal of Freedom, bestowed by President Bill Clinton in 1996. In November 2005, after her death, Congress enacted legislation authorizing the placement of a life-size statue of her in Statuary Hall in the U.S. Capitol. Parks died in her apartment in a nursing home in Detroit. After lying in repose at St. Paul A.M.E. Church in Montgomery, her body was transported to Washington, D.C., where, by exceptional authorization of the U.S. Congress, it lay in state in the U.S. Capitol Rotunda on Sunday evening, October 30, 2005, and Monday morning, October 31. See *Current Biography* (1989).

Obituary *New York Times* A p1+ Oct. 25, 2005

PELIKAN, JAROSLAV Dec. 17, 1923–May 13, 2006
Author; professor emeritus of history and religious studies at Yale University. Pelikan, a Lutheran convert to Eastern Orthodoxy, was widely regarded as the foremost American scholar of Christianity of his time. Not counting those he wrote with others or edited, Pelikan published some 40 books, including the five volumes comprising *The Christian Tradition: A History of the Development of Doctrine*, which appeared between 1971 and 1989. Those five are *The Emergence of the Catholic Tradition (100–600)*, *The Spirit of Eastern Christendom (600–1700)*, *The Growth of Medieval Theology (600–1300)*, *Reformation of Church and Dogma (1300–1700)*, and *Christian Doctrine and Modern Culture (Since 1700)*. In his research for that monumental work, he consulted more than 4,000 sources in a dozen languages. Among the books he edited were a score of the volumes of Luther's *Works* issued by Concordia Publishing House between 1955 and 1970. The son of a Lutheran pastor from Slovakia and the grandson of the first bishop of the Slovak Lutheran Synod of North America, Pelikan was a prodigy, teaching himself to read when he was two, becoming multilingual when he was growing up in the polyglot immigrant neighborhoods of Pittsburgh, and matriculating in high school when he was nine. He went on to earn, simultaneously, in 1946, a bachelor's degree in divinity at Concordia Seminary in St. Louis (a school of the Lutheran Church's Missouri Synod) and a doctorate at the University of Chicago. Before joining the Yale faculty, he taught at Valparaiso (Indiana) University, Concordia Seminary, and the University of Chicago. At Yale he was Titus Street Professor of Ecclesiastical History from 1962 until 1972, when he was appointed Sterling Professor of History. He was acting dean of the Yale Graduate School in 1973–74 and dean of the school from 1975 to 1978. After his retirement from teaching, in 1996, he continued to write, publishing such books as the three volumes comprising *Credo: Historical and Theological Guide to Creeds and Confessions in the Christian Tradition* (2003) and the book *Whose Bible Is It? A History of the Scriptures through the Ages* (2005). With his wife, Sylvia, he was received into the Eastern Orthodox Church in a ceremony in the chapel at St. Vladimir's Orthodox Theological Seminary, in Crestwood, New York, in 1998. Succumbing to lung cancer, he died at his home in Hamden, Connecticut.

His survivors included his wife, two sons, a daughter, and three grandchildren. See *Current Biography* (1987).

Obituary *New York Times* A p23 May 16, 2006

PETERSON, MARTHA June 22, 1916–July 14, 2006 Educator. In a career spanning more than four decades, Peterson was best known for her presidency of Barnard College (1967–75), where she maintained relative calm when antiwar protests were disrupting other campuses, including that of Columbia University, Barnard's educational sibling and neighbor in Manhattan's Morningside Heights neighborhood. (Barnard is now officially a division of Columbia.) After earning a B.A. degree at the University of Kansas, in 1937, she taught Latin, German, and physical education in Kansas public schools until 1942, when she returned to the University of Kansas as a graduate student. The university awarded her an M.A. degree in 1943 and a Ph.D. degree in educational psychology and counseling in 1959. On the faculty of the University of Kansas, she was a teacher of mathematics (1943–46), assistant dean of women (1946–52), and dean of women (1952–57). At the University of Wisconsin at Madison, she was dean of women (1957–63) and special assistant to the president and dean for student affairs (1963–67). As president of Barnard for eight years beginning in 1967, Peterson also served as a dean of Columbia. She was not formally installed in the dual position until April 1968, when classes were interrupted at Columbia because of student riots there. Among those taking part in those actions were approximately 110 Barnard students who were arrested on April 30, 1968. Dorothy Urman Denburg, currently a dean at Barnard, was a Barnard student-government officer at the time. Denis Hevisi quoted her in the *New York Times* (July 20, 2006) as saying, "The campus came to a grinding halt. [Peterson] convened the entire community—faculty and students—in one of the largest rooms on campus to talk about what the college's response should be. The outcome was a series of compromises giving students options for completing their academic work." In 1975 Peterson left Barnard College to assume the presidency of Beloit College, in Beloit, Wisconsin, which was in fiscal disarray then. Through personnel cuts and other measures, she restored the college to solvency. She retired as president of Beloit College in 1981. Peterson died in Madison, Wisconsin. She was survived by Maxine Bennett, her longtime companion. See *Current Biography* (1969).

Obituary *New York Times* B p7 July 20, 2006

PIFER, ALAN J. May 4, 1921–Oct. 31, 2005 Philanthropy executive. Throughout his career in nonprofit educational work, Pifer's focus was on institutional accountability and high ethical standards as well as social justice, including gender-related and racial outreach. At the height of his career, he was president of the Carnegie Foundation for the Advancement of Teaching (1965–79), an institution devoted to strengthening schooling in the U.S., now located in Stanford, California. Concurrently, he was president of the related Carnegie Corp. of New York (1965–82), an organization with a capital fund of approximately $42 billion and grant-making expenditures of more than $80 million (in 2005). In addition to promoting literacy, urban-school reform, teacher-education reform, and greater participatory democracy in the U.S., the corporation contributes to the upgrading of higher education and libraries in British Commonwealth countries, especially Commonwealth (and former Commonwealth) countries in sub-Saharan Africa, one of Pifer's favorite areas of philanthropy. The corporation also funds programs to promote international peace and security and U.S.-Russian relations. Coming out of a privileged background, Pifer attended the Groton School and Harvard University before his education was interrupted by military service in World War II. For heroic conduct as an army captain in the Battle of the Bulge, he was awarded the Bronze Star. Resuming his education after the war, he received a B.A. degree in English at Harvard and, on a fellowship, completed a year of graduate work at Cambridge University, in England. As executive secretary of the U.S. Educational Commission in the United Kingdom from 1948 to 1953, he administered the Fulbright program of educational exchange and fellowships between the U.S. and Great Britain and the British Commonwealth. It was at that time that he became especially interested in raising the quality of education in the Commonwealth countries in Africa. During his first 10 years with the Carnegie Corp., as an executive assistant (1953–57) and executive associate (1957–63), he was instrumental in greatly increasing the corporation's funding of African programs. After his appointment to the vice presidencies of both the Carnegie Corp. and the Carnegie Foundation for the Advancement of Teaching in 1963, programs within the U.S. demanded more of his attention but he continued to make himself available as a consultant on African programs. He was acting president of both the Carnegie Corp. and the Carnegie Foundation for the Advancement of Teaching from August 1965 until April 1967, when he formally succeeded John W. Gardner in the presidencies. Carnegie's priorities during his presidential tenure ranged from projects in early-childhood learning, including participation in the launching of the Children's Television Workshop (now the Sesame Workshop) to projects in the improvement of postsecondary education, with special attention to helping traditionally disadvantaged groups, including women. Under his direction Carnegie laid the groundwork for the Pell Grants, and, jointly with the Rockefeller and Ford Foundations, it supported education-related lawsuits by civil rights organizations and the training of black lawyers in the South in public-interest law. After retiring from the Carnegie Corp., in 1982, he headed the Aging Society Project and co-edited the books *Our Aging Society* (1986) and *Women on the Front Lines: Meeting the Challenge of an Aging America* (1993). Pifer died in Shelburne, Vermont. He was predeceased by his wife, Erica, and survived by two sons and seven grandchildren. See *Current Biography* (1969).

Obituary *New York Times* A p15 Nov. 5, 2005

PROFUMO, JOHN Jan. 30, 1915–Mar. 9, 2006 British politician. Profumo is primarily remembered not for his life dedicated to public service but for a brief fall from grace, the interlude known as the "Profumo affair" of the early 1960s, a sexual indiscretion compounded by a lie that developed into one of the most sensational political scandals of the 20th century. Profumo—who inherited the title Fifth Baron Profumo but chose not to use it—was elected to the House of Commons in 1940 and reelected after heroic military service in World War II. By the late 1950s he was one of the Conservative Party's brightest rising stars. After Prime Minister Harold Macmillan formed his Conservative government in 1957, Profumo served as parliamentary undersecretary of state for the colonies (1957–58), parliamentary undersecretary of state for foreign affairs, and minister of state (1959–60). In 1960 he was promoted to the portfolio of secretary of state for war in the Macmillan cabinet. On July 8, 1961, when Profumo's 44-year marriage to the motion-picture actress Valerie Hobson was in its seventh year, Stephen Ward, a London osteopath notorious for arranging sex parties involving members of the British elite (and regarded by American as well as British intelligence agencies as a Cold War security risk), introduced Profumo to Christine Keeler, a "goodtime girl" 28 years his junior. Profumo was immediately smitten, and Keeler responded to his advances, chiefly because of his aura of power, as she later explained, and not with the passion she had for another of her lovers, Yevgeny Ivanov, a Soviet intelligence agent and assistant naval attaché at the Soviet embassy in London. Profumo's romantic liaison with Keeler lasted for several weeks. On August 9, 1961 the government's cabinet secretary, Norman Brook, relaying a message from MI5, Great Britain's security intelligence agency, warned Profumo to be careful in his involvement in the love triangle that included Keeler and Ivanov and in his conversations with Ward. Profumo terminated his relationship with Keeler soon afterward, but gossip about the affair lingered, and it exploded into international front-page news early in 1963. Summoned before the House of Commons in March 1963, Profumo swore that "there was no impropriety whatsoever in my acquaintanceship with Miss Keeler." Three months later, on June 3, 1963, admitting that his statement before the Commons had been a lie, he resigned as a minister of the crown, a member of Parliament, and a privy councilor. The scandal contributed to the resignation of Prime Minister Macmillan in November 1963 and the Conservative Party's loss to Labour in the elections of 1964. Seeking to atone, Profumo in April 1964 began doing soup-kitchen and other menial chores at Toynbee Hall, a then underfunded mission serving the poor, the alcohol and drug addicted, and other socially marginalized people in London's East End. He remained an unpaid volunteer at that charity for the rest of his life, contributing to the strengthening and expansion of its services as a prodigious fund-raiser and as its chairman (1982–85) and president (1985–2006). In recognition of that work, Queen Elizabeth appointed him a Commander of the Order of the British Empire in 1975. Profumo was predeceased by his wife and survived by his son, David, and three grandchildren. See *Current Biography* (1959).

Obituary *New York Times* C p14 Mar. 11, 2006

PROXMIRE, WILLIAM Nov. 11, 1915–Dec. 15, 2005 U.S. senator from Wisconsin (1957–89). Proxmire was an independent-minded Democrat, a maverick progressive. Unbeholden to party leaders or special interests and seemingly incorruptible, he was a tenacious fiscal watchdog, the nemesis of military-industrial-complex lobbyists, government boondogglers and pork-barrelers, the wealthy seeking tax loopholes, and businesses seeking "corporate welfare" (a term he coined). The American public knew him best for his monthly Golden Fleece Award for "the biggest or most ridiculous or most ironic example" of wasteful government spending. Winners of his mock prize included the $600 toilet seat purchased by the military, the Army Corps of Engineers for "the worst record of cost overruns in the entire federal government," and federal grants for the study of such subjects as the relationship between alcoholic intake and aggressiveness in fish and why inmates want to escape from prison. A native of Illinois, Proxmire moved to Wisconsin to run for political office, because that state's traditionally weak Democratic Party offered the best prospects for a neophyte candidate. He did so after serving in U.S. Army intelligence during World War II and earning degrees in English (at Yale University) and business administration and public administration (both at Harvard University). In Wisconsin he worked as a journalist, served one term (1951–52) in the Illinois State Assembly, and ran unsuccessfully for governor three times (in 1952, 1954, and 1956). In 1957 he won a special election to fill the U.S. Senate seat left vacant by the death of Republican senator Joseph R. McCarthy, and the following year he was elected to the first of his full six-year Senate terms, which would number five in all, a record for a senator from Wisconsin. In the Senate he was a daring loner, refusing to bow even to the dictates of Senator Lyndon B. Johnson of Texas, the swaggering Democratic leader; but he was influenced by at least one older senator—Paul H. Douglas of Illinois, who stressed the fiscal accountability of public officials and whose motto, "A liberal need not be a wastrel," became Proxmire's own. Proxmire's power in the Senate grew apace with his seniority on the Senate Committee on Banking, Housing, and Urban Affairs (which he would ultimately chair during two periods when the Democrats were in the majority), his alternating chairmanship of the joint House-Senate Economic Committee, and his chairmanship of that joint committee's Subcommittee on Priorities and Economy in Government. His major legislative accomplishments included sponsorship of the Consumer Credit Protection Act of 1968, popularly known as the Truth in Lending Act, and the Fair Credit Reporting Act of 1970, his subcommittee's disclosure in 1969 of a $2 billion cost overrun in the production of the U.S. Air Force's C-5A jumbo cargo plane, and the defeat in 1971 of funding for the civil supersonic transport plane known as the SST. In 1970 he failed in his effort to prevent the government's $271 million bailout of the Lockheed Corp., and in September 1981 he filibustered to no avail for 16 hours and 12 minutes against raising the ceiling on the national debt. During the 1980s he was highly critical of the contribution of the administration of President Ronald Reagan to the acceleration in the growth of the federal deficit. In his greatest display of tenacity, over a period of 19 years and some months beginning in 1967, he gave daily speeches on the Senate floor—3,211 in all—urging ratification of the U.N. Convention on Genocide. He realized what he regarded as his proudest achievement when the Senate finally ratified the convention, by a vote of 83–11, in 1986. (President Reagan signed legislation implementing the treaty in 1988.) Dairy price supports aside, he brought little or no federal "pork" back to his constituency, believing that Wisconsin was "best served when the federal government operates in prudent and careful ways and spends as little as possible." In his electoral campaigns Proxmire relied more on shoe leather and marathon hand-shaking than expensive television spots. In the two final campaigns, in 1976 and 1982, he won by landslides while refusing to accept any financial contributions; he spent less than $200 out of his own pocket, and most of that was for the cost of mailing money back to contributors. With an unrivaled attendance record at roll calls during his tenure, he cast 10,252 votes in the Senate, a mark dwarfing the career record of 2,941 previously held by Senator Margaret Chase Smith of Maine. He chose not to run for reelection in 1988. Proxmire wrote the books *Can Small Business Survive?* (1964), *Report from the Wasteland: America's Military-Industrial Complex* (1970), *Uncle Sam: The Last of the Bigtime Spenders* (1972), *The Fleecing of America* (1980), and two volumes on health and fitness. His first marriage, to the former Elise Rockefeller, ended in divorce. He was survived by his second wife, the former Ellen Hodges Sawall, two sons, a daughter, two stepdaughters, and nine grandchildren. He died in Sykesville, Maryland. See *Current Biography* (1978).

Obituary *New York Times* B p13 Dec. 16, 2005

PRYOR, RICHARD Dec. 1, 1940–Dec. 10, 2005 Comedian; monologist; actor. In its list of the 100 greatest standup comics of all time, the cable-television station Comedy Central in 2004 ranked the groundbreaking African-American humorist Richard Pryor number one. In his antic and edgy monologues, Pryor did not tell jokes; streetwise and gifted in verbal and physical mimicry, he told stories that transcended the expletives used in the telling, chiefly through the gallery of characters he created, among them junkies, poolroom hustlers, and, especially, the wino/philosopher Mudbone, his virtual alter ego. With his ribald but profound performance art, vibrant with a leitmotif rooted in the experience of social injustice, Pryor revolutionized American comedy, and he was especially effective in inspiring and opening the way for a host of younger irreverent black comics, from Eddie Murphy, Chris Rock, and the Wayans brothers to David Chapelle, Cedric the Entertainer, and Wanda Sykes. As one of them, David Lawrence, put it, Pryor made it "OK to tell it like it is." Pryor transmuted the profanity of mean ghetto streets and his own inner demons into a comedy of emancipation that "gave black people permission to laugh in front of white America the way we laughed among ourselves," as Eugene Robinson wrote in his obituary of Pryor for the *Washington Post*. Not all African-Americans were amused. "Pryor made explic-

itly public the dark, funky, bittersweet, and beautiful realities of black life behind the color line," as Mark Anthony Neal has noted, "and [thus] offended a great many black folk who wanted those realities to remain out-of-sight from the white gaze." For their part, many whites, shocked and/or scared, were unable to appreciate the social commentary or discern the underlying genius in Pryor's unfiltered, race-specific riffs. Pryor began gathering the grist for his routines while he was growing up, in a red-light district in Peoria, Illinois, and "saw things no child should see," as the comedian and comedy writer Paul Mooney, his close associate and confidant for 32 years, has said. Following service in the U.S. Army, Pryor performed on the so-called chitlin circuit until 1963, when he ventured into integrated clubs in Greenwich Village, in New York City. Within three years he had gained national exposure through appearances on the network television shows of Merv Griffin, Ed Sullivan, and Johnny Carson, among others. At that time he was working in the middle-brow mode of a generation of older black comedians (preeminently exemplified by Bill Cosby) who, with their "eyes on the prize" of civil rights, felt obliged to put "the best face of the race" on their humor and stress their commonalities with white audiences. Feeling that he was "turning into plastic," he soon began to rebel against what he called the "white bread" humor expected of him. He reached a decisive point in the late 1960s, when he had either a nervous breakdown or what he called an "epiphany" and cut short an engagement at the Aladdin Hotel in Las Vegas, Nevada, with onstage obscenity. While beginning his film career during a subsequent three-year retreat in Hollywood, he honed his more authentic standup act, described as a "new type of realistic theater" by David Felton in *Rolling Stone* magazine. At first he performed that act chiefly in black clubs; later, he appeared before packed audiences in mainstream venues from coast to coast. On network television in the early 1970s, he wrote for the *Sanford and Son* situation comedy, for Flip Wilson's show, and for Lily Tomlin's comedy/variety special *Lily*, for which he shared a best-writing Emmy Award in 1974. His success in hosting the seventh broadcast of the NBC sketch-comedy show *Saturday Night Live* in December 1976 led to a contract for *The Richard Pryor Show* (1977), but that program, hobbled by disputes with NBC censors, ended after only five broadcasts, one of them a repeat. He later hosted several NBC specials and *Pryor's Place* (1984–85), a CBS Saturday morning show for children. On the silver screen he scored dramatically in the supporting role of the drug-addicted piano player in *Lady Sings the Blues* (1972), as the Negro League baseball player trying to pass into the white major leagues in *The Bingo Long Traveling All-Stars and Motor Kings* (1976), and as one of the three factory-union activists in *Blue Collar* (1978). Among the best of his comic portrayals on film were those of Daddy Rich, the rascal preacher in *Car Wash* (1976), and Harry Monroe, who teaches the Gene Wilder character in *Stir Crazy* (1980) how to strut with a ghetto-blaster while saying "We bad, we bad." He had earlier co-starred with Wilder in *Silver Streak* (1976) and played the title role in *The Wiz* (1978), and he later wrote the screenplay for and directed himself in the semiautobiographical movie *Jo Jo Dancer, Your Life Is Calling* (1986). He co-scripted but did not act in *Blazing Saddles* (1974). As an actor he had more than 30 screen credits, including co-starring roles in *California Suite* (1978), *Harlem Nights* (1989), and *See No Evil, Hear No Evil* (1989). In addition to his feature pictures, his filmography includes *Richard Pryor: Live on the Sunset Strip* (1982) and a number of other concert documentaries. A nine-CD boxed collection of his complete Warner Bros. recordings (including his breakthrough 1974 album *That Nigger's Crazy*) was released with the title *. . . And It's Deep Too!* (2000). He won five Grammy Awards and was the first recipient of the Kennedy Center's Mark Twain Prize for American Humor. With Todd Gold, he wrote the autobiography *Pryor Convictions and Other Life Sentences* (1995). His public persona included vulnerability as well as volatility and manic boldness, and his private life was marked with a self-destructiveness that increased with his commercial success. His long history of substance abuse reached its nadir one day in 1980, when, in a state of drug-induced psychosis while he was freebasing cocaine, he soaked himself in high-proof alcohol and set himself afire. Suffering third-degree burns over half his body, he underwent several skin-graft operations. He subsequently underwent heart bypass surgery as well. Diagnosed with multiple sclerosis in the mid-1980s, he spent his last years in a wheelchair. Pryor was married seven times to five women, twice to two of them, one of whom, Jennifer Lee Pryor (his fourth wife), cared for him until his death. He died of cardiac arrest in Encino, Los Angeles County, California. In addition to Jennifer Lee Pryor, his survivors included four daughters and three sons. See *Current Biography* (1976).

Obituary *New York Times* p61 Dec. 11, 2005

QUINN, WILLIAM F. July 13, 1919–Aug. 28, 2006 Hawaiian political pioneer. William Francis Quinn, a Republican, was the last appointed governor and the first elected governor of Hawaii. Quinn was born in Rochester, New York. After serving as a U.S. Navy intelligence officer in Hawaii during World War II and earning an LL.B. degree at the Harvard University Law School, he joined the law firm of Robertson, Castle & Anthony in Honolulu, Hawaii, in 1947. He became a partner in the firm in 1950. He was appointed to the Honolulu Charter Commission in 1956 and to the Hawaii Statehood Commission in the following year. He ran unsuccessfully for the Hawaii Territorial Senate in 1956. President Dwight D. Eisenhower named him to the governorship of the Territory of Hawaii in July 1957, and he was sworn in as governor the following September. Two years later he was elected governor, taking office on August 21, 1959, the day that Hawaii became a state. In November 1962 he lost his bid for reelection to John A. Burns, who succeeded him as governor the following month. After leaving the governor's mansion, he resumed his private practice of law. In 1964 he joined the Dole Co. The following year he became president of that company, a position he held until 1972, when he returned to his law practice. Quinn died in an assisted-living facility on the island of Oahu, Hawaii. He was survived by his wife, Nancy,

two daughters, five sons, eight grandchildren, and one great-grandchild. See *Current Biography* (1958).

Obituary *Honolulu Star-Bulletin* (on-line) Aug. 30, 2006, *New York Times* A p22 Aug. 31, 2006

RAU, JOHANNES Jan. 16, 1931–Jan. 27, 2006 German politician and statesman. As a moderate Social Democratic Party leader and president of the Federal Republic of Germany (1999–2004), Rau sought to "reconcile, not divide." He was born into a devoutly religious family in the western city of Wuppertal in what is now the state of North Rhine-Westphalia. His father was a pastor in a Protestant denomination called the Confessing Church, and he himself was an activist in that church for many years. He dropped out of school to join the church-owned Protestant Youth Publishing House, and he remained with that firm for 18 years, working successively as traveling representative, business manager, and managing director. Meanwhile, he entered politics as a protégé of Gustav Heinemann. In 1952, three years after the founding of the Federal Republic in what was then West Germany, Heinemann formed the All-German People's Party, chiefly to promote reunification with East Germany (which would be realized in 1990) and to oppose German rearmament. After the All-German People's Party was dissolved (for want of membership) in 1957, Rau followed Heinemann into the Social Democratic Party. Heinemann subsequently served in Federal Republic governments as minister of justice (1966–69) and president (1969–74). Rau was elected to the North Rhine-Westphalia state legislature in 1958, to the mayoralty of Wuppertal in 1969, to the chairmanship of the Social Democratic Party in Rhine-Westphalia in 1977, and to the premiership of North Rhine-Westphalia in 1978. He remained both chairman and premier until 1998. In May 1999 he was named to a five-year term as president of the Federal Republic by the majority vote in a convention of 1,338 electors representing both the federal Parliament and Germany's 18 regional legislatures. He was ideally suited for the largely ceremonial post, a bully pulpit for moral arbitration, conciliation, and reconciliation. In his inaugural speech he said that he wanted "to be the president of all Germans and an interlocutor for all those who live and work here without a German passport." As president, he often traveled abroad in the hope of helping "to make the image of Germany as a peaceful and democratic country better known." The first German spoken in the Knesset, the Israeli parliament, came from his lips in 2000, when, addressing its members, he said: "With the people of Israel watching, I bow in humility before those murdered, before those who don't have graves where I could ask them for forgiveness. I am asking for forgiveness for what Germans have done, for myself and my generation, for the sake of our children and grandchildren, whose future I would like to see alongside the children of Israel." Rau died in Berlin. He was survived by his wife, Christina (a granddaughter of Gustav Heinemann, 26 years his junior) and their three children. See *Current Biography* (1987).

Obituary *New York Times* A p15 Jan. 28, 2006

RAWLS, LOU Dec. 1, 1933(?)–Jan. 6, 2006 Singer. Rawls had one of the most distinctive baritone voices in American popular music, described by Edward J. Hall in the New York *Daily News* as "sweet as sugar, soft as velvet, strong as steel, smooth as butter." Growing up, Rawls was a choir boy in a black Baptist church on Chicago's South Side. After serving in the U.S. Army, he toured the Bible belt with Sam Cooke and the Pilgrim Travelers and then proceeded, as he said, through "the full spectrum, from gospel to blues to jazz to soul to pop." A car accident on the road in Tennessee in 1958 took the life of one of the Pilgrim Travelers and left Rawls with a near-fatal brain injury. After a year-long recuperation, he made the transition from gospel halls to solo gigs in coffeehouses and small nightclubs by concentrating at first on such songs in his repertoire as "Every Day I Have the Blues," with which he felt comfortable in either milieu. Through appearances on network television, especially Steve Allen's late-night variety show, he gained national exposure, leading to a contract with Capitol Records in 1961. (He later switched, successively, to the MGM, Philadelphia International, Epic, and Blue Note labels.) He crossed over into the mainstream pop market with the gold album *Lou Rawls Live* in 1966. The single "Love Is a Hurtin' Thing" became his biggest hit to that date; another single, "Dead End Street," was in the Top 40 charts in 1966 and brought him his first Grammy Award, in 1967. He won his second Grammy with the single "A Natural Man," in 1972. His greatest commercial success came after his decision to go middle-of-the-road (called MOR in the music business), under the guidance of the producers/songwriters Kenny Gamble and Leon Huff in 1975. "You'll Never Find (Another Love Like Mine)" (1976) was his first gold single and biggest hit ever, and it became his signature song. In 1977, for the first time, one of his albums went platinum—*All Things in Time*—and he won his third Grammy (for best R&B vocal performance) with *Unmistakably Lou* (1977). Meanwhile, he had become a familiar guest on all the major TV variety programs, including Johnny Carson's *Tonight Show*, and his concert and club engagements were drawing sell-out audiences. In his performances, the songs were set within a monologue of friendly patter. In 1977 he starred briefly in the musical showcase *Lou Rawls on Broadway*. Later that year he toured Australia, and still later he put together and headed a USO show that entertained American troops on bases in Japan, South Korea, and the Philippines. On television, in 1977 he launched *The Lou Rawls Parade of Stars*, his annual celebrity-studded telethon for the United Negro College Fund, and in 1982 he hosted the CBS-TV special *Rhythm & Rawls*. He had a number of TV dramatic credits, and in children's programming he was the voice of the eponymous animated cat in the *Garfield* specials, Harvey the Milkman in Nickelodeon's *Hey Arnold* series, and the grandfather in Bill Cosby's animated *Fatherhood* series. For many years he was the commercial spokesman for the Anheuser-Busch brewing company. He appeared in 18 feature films, including *Angel, Angel, Down We Go* (1969), *Leaving Las Vegas* (1995), and *Blues Brothers 2000* (1998). On his own record label, Rawls & Brokaw, he released two volumes of *The Best of Lou Rawls* on

CD in the late 1990s. He released the gospel CD *I'm Blessed* on the Malaco label in 2001 and the CD *Rawls Sings Sinatra* on Savoy in 2003. Rawls died, of lung cancer, in Los Angeles. He was survived by his third wife, Nina, two sons, two daughters, and four grandchildren. See *Current Biography* (1984).

Obituary *New York Times* C p14 Jan. 7, 2006

REVEL, JEAN FRANCOIS Jan. 19, 1924–Apr. 30, 2006 French political philosopher and polemicist; prominent journalist. Revel (the pseudonym of Jean-François Ricard) was a maverick moderate socialist who antagonized his more orthodox cohorts on the European left with his "heretical" views, especially his championing of liberal democracy and American values. His "persistent intellectual thrust was as a philosopher of freedom in the tradition of Raymond Aron," as Douglas Martin observed in the *New York Times* obituary of him. Revel directed a formidable arsenal of humor and irony against his targets, including anti-globalists, the French "anti-Americanism obsession," the glorification of Charles de Gaulle, the philosophy of Martin Heidegger, the psychoanalytical theory of Jacques Lacan, the philosophical jargon dominant in French universities, inflated tourist-seducing Italian cultural claims and the purported virility of Italian men and the beauty of Italian women, and Marxist and Existentialist interpretations of the work of Marcel Proust. The most popular and provocative of his best-selling books was *Ni Marx Ni Jesus* (1970; *Without Marx or Jesus: The New American Revolution Has Begun*, 1971). In that book he ridiculed the hope that most European progressives were placing in Soviet Communism, Chinese Maoism, and the Third World. Those models represented "a revolutionary failure," in his view, because they stifled freedom of expression and participation of the individual in the exercise of power. He contended that the only revolution in modern history that had, albeit with failings, translated its ideals into reality was that which began in England in the 17th century and in the United States and France in the last part of the 18th century, and that is best carried forward in the U.S., partly because of that country's economic growth and technological competence, "without which no revolutionary project can proceed." "The revolution of the twentieth century will take place in the United States," he asserted. "It is only there that it can happen. And it has already begun." In the wake of the terrorist attacks on the United States mainland on September 11, 2001, Revel wrote the book entitled, in translation, *Anti-Americanism* (2002), in which he responded to those Europeans who blamed American foreign policy for provoking the attacks. In that book he wrote: "Obsessed by their hatred and floundering in illogicality, these dupes forget that the United States, acting in her own self-interest, is also acting in the interest of us Europeans and in the interests of many other countries threatened or already subverted and ruined by terrorism." Revel published some 30 books, including works on Proust, Descartes, the history of food, French culture, "the totalitarian temptation," and the vulnerability of the democratic impulse; a collection of French poetry; a book of memoirs; three volumes on the history of

Western philosophy; and *Le Moine et le Philosophe* (1997). The last mentioned was a dialogue with his son Matthieu Ricard, a Buddhist monk. Lettered in philosophy, Revel taught successively at schools in Algeria, Mexico, Italy, and France from 1947 through the 1950s, a period during which he made several visits to the United States. He was the chief literary editor of *France Observateur* from 1960 to 1963, became literary consultant to the publisher Editions Robert Laffont in 1965, and began writing a column for the weekly news magazine *L'Express* in 1966. He was a speechwriter for François Mitterrand, who was elected to two terms as president of France in the 1980s, a member of the Académie Française, and a radio commenatator. After his divorce from Yahne le Toumelin, he married Claude Sarraute, the daughter of the novelist Nathalie Sarraute. His survivors included his second wife, two sons, and a daughter. He died at the Kremlin-Bicetyre Hospital in suburban Paris, France. See *Current Biography* (1975).

Obituary *New York Times* B p7 May 2, 2006

RINFRET, PIERRE A. Feb. 1, 1924–June 29, 2006 Canadian-born American economist and investment counselor. Pierre Rinfret was a conservative economist eminent as a consultant in both the private and public sectors. As an adviser to President John F. Kennedy and President Lyndon B. Johnson, he participated in the formulation of the 1964 legislation authorizing tax cuts that resulted in a stimulation of American business and industry needed at that time. Later, he chided President Johnson for not raising taxes to halt undue expansionist tendencies in the economy. He was an adviser to Richard Nixon during Nixon's 1968 presidential campaign and the economic spokesman for President Nixon during his 1972 presidential campaign. Following service in combat with the U.S. Army during World War II, Rinfret earned an M.B.A. degree at New York University. He later received a doctorate in political economics at the University of Dijon, France. After joining Lionel D. Edie & Co. as a staff economist in 1951, he worked his way up the executive ladder of that investment management house to become chairman of the board in 1963. Leaving Lionel D. Edie & Co., he co-founded Rinfret-Boston Associates in 1967. As president of that consulting firm and manager of the Rinfret Mutual Fund, he provided economic reports and forecasts to industrial and financial firms and individual clients. A registered political Independent, he was persuaded to become the Republican candidate for governor of New York in 1990. Garnering only 21 percent of the vote, he lost to the Democratic incumbent, Mario Cuomo. Rinfret died on the island of Nantucket, Massachusetts. He was survived by his wife, Ida, a daughter, a son, and three grandchildren. See *Current Biography* (1972).

Obituary *New York Times* B p7 July 6, 2006

ROSENTHAL, A. M. May 2, 1922–May 10, 2006 Canadian-born American journalist. In his more than half a century with the *New York Times*, Abe Rosenthal became a Pulitzer Prize–winning correspondent and, subsequently, a demanding chief editor of relatively conservative social and political bent who, rather ironically, was credited with modernizing

and brightening American journalism's old "Gray Lady." With the backing of the *Times's* publisher Arthur Ochs ("Punch") Sulzberger, Rosenthal made extensive changes in the newspaper that resulted in the reversal of a decline in readership and a great increase in advertising and profits. He introduced new production technology, enlarged the newspaper's staff, expanded its domestic and global news operations, launched a national edition, and inaugurated numerous new feature sections. During his tenure the *Times* won several Pulitzer Prizes, most notably the one in 1972 for the paper's daring publication of the "Pentagon Papers," the classified government documents exposing Washington's step-by-step descent, during successive administrations, into the quagmire of the Vietnam War. Rosenthal's parents were natives of Byelorussia who immigrated to the Bronx, in New York City, via Ontario, Canada. He began his career with the *New York Times* as a campus stringer when he was an undergraduate majoring in the social sciences at the City College of New York in 1943. After becoming a staff reporter with the newspaper, in 1944, he completed his college courses at night, receiving a bachelor's degree in 1948. The *Times* assigned him to the United Nations from 1946 to 1954, when he was sent to New Delhi as India/Pakistan correspondent. He was the newspaper's Eastern European correspondent, based in Warsaw, from June 1958 to November 1959, when Poland's Communist government expelled him for "exposing too deeply the internal situation in Poland." His reporting from Warsaw (which prominently included a classic meditative piece written after his visit to the Nazi death camp at Auschwitz-Birkenau in southern Poland) was honored with the Pulitzer Prize for international reporting in 1960; it also brought him Overseas Press Club and Page One awards and the first of his two George Polk Memorial Awards. (The second award came in 1965.) Following his departure from Warsaw and a brief assignment in Geneva, Switzerland, he was based in Japan for two years. His career as a foreign correspondent ended in 1963, when he returned to Manhattan as metropolitan editor of the *Times*. He advanced to assistant managing editor in 1966, associate managing editor in 1968, managing editor in 1969, and executive editor in 1977. After resigning as executive editor, in 1986, he began writing the op-ed column "On My Mind," which ran in the *Times* twice a week for 13 years. When his views (described in an editorial in the *Times* itself as "strong, individualistic") fell from grace at the *Times*, in 1999, he took the column to the New York *Daily News*. President George W. Bush awarded Rosenthal the Presidential Medal of Freedom in 2002. Rosenthal's first marriage, to Ann Marie Burke, ended in divorce in 1986. He died in Manhattan. His survivors included his first wife, Ann, his second wife, Shirley (née Lord), three sons from his first marriage, and four grandchildren. See *Current Biography* (1960).

Obituary *New York Times* A p1+ May 11, 2006

ROTBLAT, JOSEPH Nov. 4, 1908–Aug. 31, 2005 Polish-born British physicist; Nobel Peace Prize laureate; a claimant to the title of "conscience of science in the nuclear age." Rotblat was born into a Jewish family in Warsaw, Poland, and earned a doctorate in physics at the University of Warsaw. During the 1930s he was a research fellow in radiology at the Scientific Society of Warsaw and assistant director of atomic physics at the Free University of Poland. In March 1939 an Oliver Lodge fellowship enabled him to leave Poland to join James Chadwick in his work in nuclear fission at the University of Liverpool, in England. His wife of two years, Tola Gryn, did not accompany him, because his fellowship stipend was too small to support both of them. His decision to remain working with Chadwick in England was sealed when Warsaw surrendered to the occupation forces of Nazi Germany in September 1939. Rotblat tried strenuously but without success to arrange for his wife's escape from Poland, and he lost track of her whereabouts in 1940. It is presumed that she died in the Holocaust. When, in 1943, James Chadwick was chosen to lead a team of British scientists assigned to the Manhattan Project, the secret U.S. effort to develop the first atomic bomb, Rotblat did not qualify for the team because he did not yet have British citizenship, a condition demanded by the American authorities. Chadwick finally persuaded the Americans to waive that condition, and Rotblat joined the Chadwick team at the Los Alamos National Laboratory, in New Mexico, in March 1944. From the beginning he was ambivalent about contributing to the creation of a weapon of awesome mass destruction, except for the purpose of beating the German dictator Hitler to the nuclear punch and thus deterring Nazi Germany from using such a weapon. His moral doubts grew when, in the months following his arrival in Los Alamos, it became clear that the prospect of the Nazis' developing an atomic bomb no longer existed and especially when, according to his account, he overheard General Leslie Groves state that the remaining, overriding purpose for the bomb was not to defeat Germany or even Japan but to intimidate the Soviet Union, a wartime ally perceived to be a potential postwar rival. In addition, Rotblat's conversations with the Danish physicist Niels Bohr at Los Alamos persuaded him of the danger of a future nuclear-arms race. When he ended his nine-month tenure at Los Alamos, his reasons of conscience were obscured by the cloud of an official accusation that he was a Communist sympathizer and a security risk. That accusation rose out of his friendship with a young Englishwoman, referred to as Ms. Elspeth, visiting Santa Fe, New Mexico. He later insisted that his conversations with Ms. Elspeth were never about the atom-bomb project and had been misunderstood or distorted by the informant who had overheard them. That person, he believed, was a Hispanic gardener with very limited facility in English. After returning to England in December 1944, Rotblat resumed his research and lecturing at the University of Liverpool, where, during the next five years, he became interested in the medical applications of nuclear physics. In 1949 he moved to London, to join the faculty of the University of London as a professor of physics at St. Bartholomew's Hospital Medical College and chief physicist at St. Bartholomew's Hospital. At St. Bartholomew's, he conducted research on the effects of radiation on living organisms in collaboration with the physiologist Patricia Lindop. He remained on the faculty of St. Bar-

tholomew's/University of London until 1976. Meanwhile, he had co-founded the Atomic Scientists Association (1946), the Pugwash Conferences on Science and World Affairs (of which he was secretary general from 1957 to 1973), and the U.K. Campaign for Nuclear Disarmament (1958). He was one of the 11 signatories of the Russell-Einstein Manifesto (1955), the document in which Albert Einstein and Bertrand Russell invited world scientists to unite in a campaign against any future use of nuclear weapons. In 1995 the Nobel Peace Prize was awarded jointly to Rotblat and the Pugwash Conferences "for their efforts to diminish the part played by nuclear arms in international politics and, in the longer run, to eliminate such arms." Rotblat's publications included a score of articles for the *Bulletin of the Atomic Scientists* and the many collections of Pugwash annals that he edited. He died in London. See *Current Biography* (1997).

Obituary *New York Times* B p7 Sep. 2, 2005

RUKEYSER, LOUIS Jan. 30, 1933–May 2, 2006 Journalist; broadcaster; financial and economic analyst. With his witty and commonsense approach, Louis Richard Rukeyser made accessible to millions of lay Americans the otherwise gray and complex worlds of finance and economics. The elegant but plainspoken Rukeyser was one of electronic journalism's pioneers, the creator and host of the first, highest-rated, and most durable of the television programs focused on business and the stock market, *Wall Street Week with Louis Rukeyser*, originally called *Wall Street Week*. On that half-hour show, broadcast on Friday nights on U.S. public television for 32 years, Rukeyser, with the help of a panel of experts, kept his mass audience apprised of events and trends in or related to the stock market and answered investment questions submitted by viewers. The program, produced by Maryland Public Television (MPT), was launched on the Eastern Educational Network in 1970 and was picked up by the Public Broadcasting Service (PBS) for national distribution two years later. It became PBS's most popular public-affairs show, attracting a peak audience of several million in the 1980s and keeping that audience above the million mark into the year 2002. In March 2002, anticipating the renegotiation of his contract in June, MPT announced that Rukeyser would be demoted to "senior correspondent" in a new format to be hosted by younger journalists from *Fortune* magazine and the Fox News Channel. Rukeyser objected, and he voiced his objections angrily on air on the Friday following the announcement. MPT immediately fired him, and he quickly went to the cable network CNBC, with which he signed a deal to host *Louis Rukeyser's Wall Street*. That show debuted on CNBC on April 19, 2002 at 8:30 p.m. EST, the same time slot in which *Wall Street Week with Fortune* was running on PBS. It quickly became CNBC's top-rated show, which Rukeyser hosted for 18 months, until he was incapacitated by multiple myeloma, the bone-marrow cancer that caused his death. He made his last appearance on *Louis Rukeyser's Wall Street* on October 3l, 2003, and the show itself went off the air two months later, at his request. (MPT terminated *Wall Street Week with Fortune* in June 2005.)

Rukeyser was one of four sons of the financial journalist Merryle Stanley Rukeyser. After graduating from the Woodrow Wilson School of Public and International Affairs at Princeton University, he served as editor of the European edition of *Stars and Stripes*, the U.S. Army newspaper, during a tour of military duty. During the following decade he was a reporter and foreign correspondent with the *Baltimore Sun* newspaper. In 1966 he joined the ABC television network as Paris correspondent for ABC News, and in 1967 he moved to London to head ABC's bureau there. From 1968 to 1973 he was with ABC News in New York City, writing and hosting documentaries, preparing special reports, and delivering thrice-weekly commentaries on economic issues on the *ABC Evening News*. In addition to his work on television, he lectured, broadcast two syndicated radio shows, published two newsletters, and wrote *How to Make Money in Wall Street* (1974) and *What's Ahead for the Economy* (1983), among other books. He died at his home in Greenwich, Connecticut. His survivors included his wife, Alexandra, and three daughters. See *Current Biography* (1983).

Obituary *New York Times* B p8 May 3, 2006

SABAH, JABER AL-AHMAD AL-JABER AL-, SHEIK June 29, 1926–Jan. 15, 2006 Kuwaiti sheik. In the royal line of the al-Sabah dynasty, Sheik Jaber served as the 13th emir of Kuwait, from 1977 until his death. He was the third emir since Kuwait's independence from Britain, in 1961. That independence was preserved in large measure because of Jaber's wise husbanding of Kuwait's rich oil revenues and his decision to align with the United States against the advice of some of those around him. When Kuwait was attacked and occupied by Saddam Hussein's Iraqi forces in August 1990, Jaber fled to Saudi Arabia, where he established a government in exile, financed by withdrawals from a contingency fund of approximately $120 billion. After seven months in exile, he returned to Kuwait after an American-led military coalition drove out the Iraqi occupiers early in 1991; he then began rebuilding his devastated country. In an earlier defining moment in his tenure as emir, in 1985, he survived an assassination attempt by Shiite Muslim militants, who drove a bomb-rigged car into his procession. Jaber had a distinguished record of public service dating back to 1949. He served as minister of finance and economy in 1962–63 and as minister of finance, industry, and commerce from 1963 to 1965. It was as minister of finance under Emir Abdullah al-Salem al-Sabah (his maternal uncle) that he established the framework for the Kuwaiti government's contingency fund, formally called the Future Generations Fund. He also implemented a policy of income redistribution through the application of oil revenues to public expenditures (including social-welfare programs) and through a land compensation plan. He was prime minister from 1965 until he succeeded his cousin Sheik Sabah al-Salim al-Sabah as emir in 1977. Jaber balanced his pro-Western policies (including donations to British charities) with generous financial aid to poorer Arab countries and to Arab nationalist causes, with trade missions to Communist countries, and with involvement in the creation of the Gulf Co-operation Council. Estimates of Jaber's marriages range into the dozens, but as a practicing Muslim, he never exceeded the canonical limit of four wives at one time. There has been no official enumeration of his offspring. See *Current Biography* (1988).

Obituary *New York Times* B p7 Jan. 16, 2006

SÁNDOR, GYÖRGY Sep. 21, 1912–Dec. 9, 2005 Hungarian-born American pianist. Sándor was a protégé of Béla Bartók, with whom he studied piano at the Liszt Academy in Budapest and to whom he remained close until Bartok's death in New York City, in 1945. Sándor championed Bartók's works, premiered some of them, and performed and made definitive recordings of all of them. He did so with technical brilliance, navigating the percussive cluster chords and other notoriously difficult passages with grace and legato finesse and stressing the folk-dance rhythms and lyricism that relieved the harshness. He once described his technique as "not in the fingers" but "in the muscles of the body." The piano compositions of Zoltán Kodály—with whom he studied composition in Budapest—and Sergei Prokofiev were also prominent in Sándor's performing and recording repertoire. Sándor made his debut as a concert pianist in Budapest in 1931 and subsequently toured Europe, including England, making his London debut in 1937. He immigrated to the United States late in 1938 and made his American debut at Carnegie Hall in February 1939. During World War II he served first with the U.S. Army Signal Corps and subsequently in the Intelligence and Special Services, until 1944. Following his military discharge, he toured South America, and he went on to perform internationally for more than half a century, with an itinerary that ranged from Australia, South Korea, and Singapore to Egypt. He included works by Liszt, Chopin, Brahms, Schumann, Bach, Rachmaninoff, Shostakovich, and Dukas, among others, in his concerts. In addition to his recitals, he performed major orchestras. His last concert was in Turkey in April 2005, when he was 92 years old. He maintained his busy touring schedule concurrently with his teaching at Southern Methodist University (1956–61), the University of Michigan (1961–81), and the Juilliard School of Music (1982–2005). In 1981 he published his book *On Piano Playing: Motion, Sound, and Expression*. Shortly before his death he completed the manuscript of a book on Bartók and his works. Sándor, who had been married to and divorced from Princess Christina of Habsburg, was survived by one son and three stepdaughters and predeceased by his pianist cousin, Arpád Sándor. He died at his home in Manhattan. See *Current Biography* (1947).

Obituary *New York Times* C p17 Dec. 14, 2005

SCHEUER, JAMES Feb. 6, 1920–Aug. 30, 2005 U.S. Democratic congressman from New York; lawyer; an unreconstructed liberal. During 13 terms in Congress (1965–73, 1975–93), Scheuer represented, because of redistricting, a succession of congressional districts covering parts of the Bronx, Queens, Brooklyn, and Nassau County. In the U.S. House of Representatives, he was fierce in his pursuit of environmental, consumer, and automotive protection, of fair housing, and of such educational programs as Head Start. On the Science, Space, and Technology Committee, he headed the subcommittee on natural resources and agricultural research. He also led the consumer-protection subcommittee of the Energy and Commerce Committee. Before entering politics he had made a fortune in real-estate development. As president of the Renewal and Development Corp., he oversaw the building of residential projects on cleared urban slum sites in eight American cities. The best-known of the projects was Capital Park, a 50-acre, 1,739-unit middle-income apartment and townhouse complex in southwest Washington, D.C. Beginning in 1955, he chaired the Housing Advisory Council of the New York State Commission Against Discrimination. In the early 1960s he became a charter member and executive committeeman of the New York Committee for Democratic Voters, a group of insurgent Democrats dedicated to reforming the Democratic Party in New York State in general and to toppling in particular Tammany Hall, the entrenched Democratic political machine in New York City, which included the fiefdom of Charles A. Buckley, at that time the Democratic boss in the city's borough of the Bronx. One of Buckley's chief lieutenants was U.S. congressman James C. Healey, representing the Bronx's Twenty-first Congressional District. Scheuer challenged Healey in the Democratic primary election in the Twenty-first C.D. in 1962 and lost, then challenged him again in 1964 and won, and he went on to defeat the Republican candidate, Henry Rose, in the general election in November 1964. He was reelected from the Twenty-first C.D. in 1964, 1966, and 1968. Adapting to redistricting, he ran successfully from the Twenty-second C.D. in 1970. Defeated in the election of 1972, he returned to Congress in the election of 1974, from the Eleventh C.D. He remained the representative of the Eleventh C.D. through the elections of 1974, 1976, 1978, and 1980. During his last five terms in Congress, from January 1983 through January 1993, he represented New York's Eighth C.D. In 1969 he published the book *To Walk the Streets Safely: The Role of Modern Science and Technology in Our Criminal Justice System.* He was heavily involved in projects in Israel, including the development of the new campus for the Hebrew Union College in Jerusalem. With his family, he maintained a residence in Jerusalem as well as a home in Washington, D.C. He died in Washington. He was survived by his wife, Emily, two daughters, two sons, and 10 grandchildren. See *Current Biography* (1968).

Obituary *New York Times* A p17 Aug. 31, 2005

SCHROEDER, FREDERICK R. July 20, 1921–May 26, 2006 Tennis player. Frederick Rudolph Schroeder was number one in world amateur tennis rankings in 1942 and number two from 1946 through 1949; in doubles play throughout the 1940s, he was known for his great partnership with his friend Jake Kramer. In 1939, while Schroeder was earning his B.A. degree in economics at Stanford University, he won the national juniors singles title. The following year he competed for the first time in what would later be known (beginning in 1968) as the U.S. Open, the final event in tennis's annual Grand Slam, occur-

ring just after Wimbledon. On that occasion he and Kramer won the men's national doubles championship. In 1941 they successfully defended that championship and in addition won the national clay-court doubles crown. In 1942 Schroeder won his second and third U.S. Open titles, the national men's singles championship and the mixed doubles (with Louise Brough), and in the same year, he won the intercollegiate singles and doubles (with Larry Dee). From 1942 to 1945 he served in the wartime U.S. Navy on destroyers and as a fighter pilot. After the war Schroeder and Kramer won the men's national doubles championship for the third time, in 1947. They were the dominant members of the American teams that took the Davis Cup from the Australians in 1946 and kept the prize in the U.S. in 1947, 1948, and 1949. Australia regained the Davis Cup in 1950, when Schroeder was beaten by Frank Sedgman and Ken McGregor. At Wimbledon in 1949 Schroeder won the singles title and was a finalist in the doubles. In the U.S. Open in the same year, he was a singles finalist. Concurrently with his career in tennis, he worked as a sales engineer for the Kold Hold Pacific Sales Co., dealers in commercial refrigeration equipment. After being promoted to vice president of Kold Hold in 1949, he decided against following Kramer into professional tennis. He retired from tennis playing in 1951. He was inducted into the International Tennis Hall of Fame in 1966. Schroeder died at his home in La Jolla, California. He was predeceased by his wife, Ann, and survived by his three sons. See *Current Biography* (1949).

Obituary *New York Times* A p14 May 27, 2006

SCHWARZKOPF, ELISABETH Dec. 9, 1915–Aug. 3, 2006 Opera and concert singer and recitalist. A lyric coloratura soprano and versatile performer, Elisabeth Schwarzkopf ranked alongside Maria Callas as a "diva assoluta" (absolute star) of her time. A German-born citizen of Great Britain, she was best known for her scrupulously studied and sensitive interpretations of soprano operatic roles composed by Richard Strauss (Zerbinetta, the Marschallin, and Countess Madeline) and Mozart (Donna Elvira, Countess Almaviva, Susanna, Constanze, and Fiordiligi) and for her promotion of German lieder, especially the art songs of Hugo Wolf. On the operatic stage and in her concerts and recitals, she made a stunning presence with her combination of Nordic beauty, poise, grace, and radiant and agile voice, with beautiful legato and sure ascent to the precise registering of the highest notes. A minority of critics faulted her for being a mannered "Prussian perfectionist," but as J. B. Steane pointed out in his book *The Great Tradition,* the "marvelously exact" calculation in her art manifested "a high degree of awareness—of colors and styles and of the existence of choices." As a student at the Hochschule für Musik in Berlin, Schwarskopf was mistakenly pegged as a contralto, a low-register soprano. Eventually, under the tutelage of Maria Ivogun and her husband, the accompanist Michael Raucheisen, she found her true voice, moving up through mezzo to lyric coloratura soprano. Aside from an earlier paid performance as a member of the chorus in a 1937 recording of Mozart's *The Magic Flute* under the baton of Sir Thomas

Beecham, she made her professional debut as a junior singer with the Deutsche Oper in suburban Berlin in 1938. During several years with that company, she sang many roles, including Adele in *Die Fledermaus*, Musetta in *La Bohème*, and, most impressively, Zerbinetta in *Ariadne auf Naxos*. At that time she became a member of the Nazi Party. Years later she explained that she did so for her career's sake, on the advice of her father, who had lost his position as a high-school principal because of his refusal to join the party. As a prima donna with the Vienna State Opera at the Theater an der Wein in Vienna from 1946 to 1948, Schwarzkopf sang a wide variety of roles, including Constanze in *Die Entführung aus dem Serail* (*The Abduction from the Seraglio*), Susanna in *La Nozze di Figaro*, Mimi in *La Bohème*, and Violetta in *La Traviata*. On tour with the Vienna State Opera, she sang the Marschallin in *Der Rosenkavalier* at La Scala in Milan and Donna Elvira in *Don Giovanni* at Covent Garden in London. After leaving the Vienna company, she returned to La Scala, where, with the resident troupe, she sang Beethoven's *Missa Solemnis* and such roles as Marguerite in *Faust*. In Venice in 1951 she created Anne Trulove in the world premiere of Igor Stravinsky's *The Rake's Progress*. With the Covent Garden Opera Company (as the Royal Opera Company was then known) in the late 1940s and early 1950s, she sang, among other roles, Violetta, Mimi, Pamina in *The Magic Flute*, Gilda in *Rigoletto*, the title role in Massenet's *Manon*, and Sophie in *Der Rosenkavalier*. Outside of her German repertory, all of that singing was in English. Schwarzkopf became a naturalized British citizen in 1953. In October of the same year, she married Walter Legge, the artistic director of EMI Records and the founder of the Philharmonia Orchestra, who became her manager. She first performed in the United States in 1953, touring as a recitalist. Two years later she made her American operatic debut, singing the Marschallin in San Francisco. Again as the Marschallin, she made her debut at the Metropolitan Opera in New York City in 1964. She performed at the Met in 1966 as Donna Elvira. During the remaining years of her operatic career, she concentrated on five roles: the Marschallin, Donna Elvira, Fiordiligi in *Così Fan Tutti*, Countess Madeleine in *Capriccio*, and Countess Almaviva in *La Nozze di Figaro*. She also impressed audiences with her interpretation of Alice Ford in *Falstaff*. During her operatic career she performed a total of 74 roles in 53 operas. After retiring from the operatic stage, in 1971, she continued giving recitals and performing in concerts until 1979. Foremost among her collaborators in her live performances and her recordings were the pianists Edwin Fischer and Walter Gieseking and the orchestra conductors Wolfgang Sawallisch and Herbert von Karajan. Her concert and recital repertory included Bach cantatas and oratorios and songs by Strauss, Schubert, Brahms, and Mahler as well as Hugo Wolf. In her retirement she conducted master classes at the Juilliard School in New York City and other venues in the United States and the United Kingdom, often in collaboration with her husband. On New Year's Day 1992, Queen Elizabeth II named her a Dame Commander of the British Empire. After living for many years in Zurich, Switzerland, Schwarzkopf settled in the town of Scruns,

Austria, where she died. She was predeceased by her husband, Walter Legge. There were no immediate survivors. Her legacy was her wealth of recordings of operatic roles and renditions of oratorios, cantatas, and leider. See *Current Biography* (1955).

Obituary *New York Times* B p7 Aug. 4, 2006

SCOTT, ROBERT L. JR. Apr. 12, 1908–Feb. 27, 2006 U.S. Air Force brigadier general, retired; author. Scott is best known for his best-selling World War II memoir *God Is My Co-Pilot* (1943), his account of his exploits as a highly decorated pilot in the China-Burma-India theater of operations. That book was made into a feature film starring Dennis Morgan, released in 1945. After graduating from West Point, in 1932, and earning his wings in the U.S. Army Air Corps (as it was then known), in 1933, Scott flew airmail, commanded a pursuit squadron in Panama, and instructed other pilots at bases in Texas and California. Early in 1942, following the U.S.'s entry into World War II, he was sent to India to prepare to take part in Task Force Aquila, a top-secret B-17 bomber raid on Tokyo, Japan. When that raid was cancelled, he remained in the Far East as a pilot in the Assam-Burma-China Ferry Command, which flew food and supplies from India over the Himalayas ("the Hump") to China. In China, he met Claire L. Chennault, who had formed the American Volunteer Group, also known as the China Air Task Force and better known as the Flying Tigers, to fight the Japanese under contract to the Nationalist Chinese government of Generalissimo Chiang Kai-Shek. In June 1942, after Chennault's group was incorporated into the U.S. Army Air Corps (where it was given the designation 14th Air Force), Scott became a flight commander with the group, directing the strafing of Japanese truck columns on the so-called Burma Road and the bombing of bridges along the Salween River. Piloting his Curtis P-40 fighter plane, he downed at least 13 enemy planes. In 1943 he was recalled to the United States to make a morale-boosting tour of war production plants and to help train other pilots. In 1944 he returned to the Far East to participate in air strikes using experimental rockets against Japanese supply trains in China and similar targets, chiefly ships, on and around Okinawa. During the 12 years following World War II, he had a variety of major assignments stateside and abroad in the U.S. Air Force (as the Army Air Corps became known when it was spun off into a separate branch of military service), including command of the 36th Fighter Bomber Wing in Fürstenfeldbruck, Germany, and Luke Air Force Base, in Arizona. After retiring from the air force, he worked as a life-insurance executive, walked much of the Great Wall of China, went on safaris in Kenya, and continued to fly and to write. He published some dozen books, including *Between the Elephant's Eyes!* (1955), *Flying Tiger: Chennault of China* (1959), and his autobiography, *The Day I Owned the Sky* (1988). He died in Warner Robins, Georgia. His wife, Kitty, predeceased him. His survivors included a daughter, Robin, and numerous grandchildren, great-grandchildren, and great-great-grandchildren. See *Current Biography* (1943).

Obituary *New York Times* A p16 Feb. 28, 2006

SETTLE, MARY LEE July 29, 1918–Sep. 27, 2005 Author. Settle, a native of West Virginia, spent many years living in foreign countries, including Turkey, where her experience as an expatriate provided the grist for *Blood Tie* (1977). That novel brought her a National Book Award, but her reputation rests even more firmly on her richly researched Beulah Land novels, in which she covered three centuries of history in telling the stories, beginning in England, of three fictional West Virginia (Beulah Land) families. Those works comprise a quintet beginning with *O Beulah Land* (1956) and including *Know Nothing* (1960), *Prisons* (1973), *The Scapegoat* (1980), and *The Killing Ground* (1982). The last named includes much of what had been cut from *Fight Night on a Sweet Saturday* (1964) by her editor. In the late 1930s Settle dropped out of Sweet Briar College, in Virginia, and joined a theatrical troupe in Abingdon, Virginia, an experience that was reflected in her first published novel, *Love Eaters* (1954). Her second published novel was *The Kiss of Kin* (1955). Following a stint as a fashion model in New York City, she went to England and served with the Women's Auxiliary Air Force, a branch of the Royal Air Force, during World War II. She recounted that wartime experience in the memoir *All the Brave Promises* (1966). Back in the United States in the postwar years, she worked successively on the staffs of *Harper's Bazaar* and *Flair* magazines and wrote a column for *Woman's Day* magazine. She taught at Bard College from 1965 to 1976 and later at the University of Virginia. In 1971 she published the novel *The Clam Shell*, which was a thinly veiled autobiography. Later she published the novels *Celebration* (1986) and *Charles Bland* (1989). Among her books of nonfiction were *Addie: A Memoir* (1998), about her grandmother Addie, and *Spanish Recognitions* (2004), a travel/history guide to Spain and its culture. She also wrote some short stories and juvenilia and several plays. She was the founder of the PEN/Faulkner fiction-award program, which carries annually a first prize of $15,000 and four runners-up prizes of $5,000 each, awarded by votes of authors, and which arranges for well-known writers of fiction to speak in schools. Settle, who was married three times, was divorced from her first two husbands and predeceased by her third, William L. Tazewell. Her survivors included a son, a grandson, a granddaughter, and four great-grandchildren. She died at her home in Charlottesville, Virginia. See *Current Biography* (1959).

Obituary *New York Times* B p9 Sep. 29, 2005

SHEARER, MOIRA Jan. 17, 1926–Jan 31, 2006 British ballerina and actress. Moira Shearer had barely begun her luminous tenure as a leading dancer with the Sadler's Wells Ballet (now the Royal Ballet) when she agreed to play Victoria Page, the tragic protagonist in *The Red Shoes* (1948), a landmark feature film set in the world of ballet. She did so reluctantly, and she later regretted taking on that role, because, while her exquisite performance as the beautiful young dancer torn between love and career made her the most famous ballerina in the world, it had a negative effect on her career. "Perhaps she had always had an instinct that *The Red Shoes* was a pact with the devil: it made her famous, yet it probably marked her down for vulgarity in the chilly world that controlled ballet," David Thompson observed in the London *Independent*. "So she danced, and she acted—and there was no doubt that among first-rank dancers she was a very fine actress—but in a strange way her career never moved farther ahead." Born in Scotland, Shearer, a strikingly elegant redhead, entered the Sadler's Wells School in 1940, joined the Sadler's Wells Ballet company in 1942, and soon began moving from the corps de ballet into major roles in the classical repertoire—including Odette in *Swan Lake* and the title part in *Giselle*—as well as new ballets by contemporary choreographers. Between 1943 and 1953 she danced (and in many instances created) principal roles choreographed by Ninette de Valois (the company's founder and director), Léonide Massine, Mikhail Fokine, André Howard, and, most notably, Frederick Ashton and Robert Helpmann. American and Canadian balletomanes had the opportunity to witness her impeccable technique and brilliant, graceful style in person when she toured cities in North America with the Sadler's Wells troupe in 1949. Michael Powell, the director of *The Red Shoes*, again recruited her for the roles of Stella and Olympia in his film *The Tales of Hoffmann* (1951). Subsequently, she starred opposite James Mason in the segment titled "The Jealous Lover" in the trifurcated film *The Story of Three Loves* (1953), and she played all four redheads in the comedy *The Man Who Loved Redheads* (1955). Meanwhile, she resigned from the Sadler's Wells roster in 1953 without having achieved her ambition to succeed Margot Fonteyn as prima ballerina. In the years immediately following, she occasionally made guest appearances with the Covent Garden–based company (which changed its name to the Royal Ballet in 1956) and other troupes. During a stint with Roland Petit's Les Ballets de Champs Élysées in Paris, her performance opposite Petit in *Cyrano de Bergerac* (choreographed by Petit to music by Marius Constant) was filmed, and it became one of the four balletic gems making up the motion picture *Les Coulant Noirs* (a k a *Un Deux, Trois, Quatre*, 1959), the English-language version of which is titled *Black Tights*. She was cast as the dancer Vivian in Michael Powell's controversial, disturbing psychological thriller *Peeping Tom* (a k a *Face of Fear*, 1960), about a psychopathic serial killer who photographs the faces of his dying female victims. She is among the many dancers represented in the MGM picture *That's Dancin'!* (1960), a compilation of selections from the golden age of the movie musical. As a stage actress, she played Titania in an Old Vic production of *A Midsummer's Night's Dream* at the Edinburgh Festival in 1954 and subsequently toured cities in the United States and Canada in the production. Back in Britain in the mid-1950s, she toured as Sally Bowles in *I Am a Camera* and played the title role in *Major Barbara* at the Old Vic. She returned to Covent Garden briefly as a guest dancer in 1967. Twenty years later she emerged from retirement to participate in a Northern Theatre Ballet production titled *A Simple Man*, a tribute to the painter L. S. Lowry on the 100th anniversary of his birth. The production was filmed for broadcast on BBC television and is available on DVD. In it, Shearer co-stars as the mother of Lowry, danced by Christopher Gable. During the 1970s she lectured widely on the history of ballet, and she gave readings of Scottish love poems with her husband, the author and broadcaster Sir Ludovic Kennedy. In 1973 she worked briefly as an announcer on BBC Radio 3. In her later years she reviewed books on ballet and theater for the London *Daily Mail* and wrote biographies of the actress Ellen Terry and the choreographer George Balanchine, who had been a great admirer of hers. She died in Oxford, England. In addition to her husband, her survivors included a son, three daughters, and seven grandchildren. At the time of her death, Sir Ludovic was working on a biography of her. See *Current Biography* (1950).

Obituary *New York Times* A p21 Feb. 2, 2006

SHUMWAY, NORMAN E. Feb. 9, 1923–Feb. 10, 2006 Cardiothoracic surgeon. The famously self-effacing Norman Shumway was the surgeon/scientist most responsible for developing the methodology that has made heart transplantation a fairly standard procedure, one that extends the lives of more than 4,000 patients annually around the world. As a U.S. Army draftee during World War II, Shumway was trained as a medic in an accelerated premedical course at Baylor University. After obtaining his M.D. degree at Vanderbilt University, in 1949, he interned at the University of Minnesota's medical center (1949–51), served in the U.S. Air Force's medical corps during the Korean War (1951–53), and returned to the University of Minnesota to earn a doctorate in cardiovascular surgery under the mentorship of the open-heart-surgery pioneers Owen H. Wangensteen and John Lewis. During those years at the University of Minnesota, he began to hone his expertise in the use of selective hypothermia on myocardial preservation, the artificial lowering of body temperature for the purpose of slowing metabolic processes, a sine qua non in heart transplantation. In San Francisco in 1958, he joined the faculty of Stanford University's School of Medicine as an instructor in surgery. Soon thereafter the school moved to Stanford University's new, expanded campus in Palo Alto, California, where it became part of the Stanford University Medical Center (along with an adult hospital and clinics and a children's hospital), and he became a full professor and chief of the school's division of cardiovascular surgery. In 1959, with the assistance of his first resident, Richard Lower, he performed his first heart transplant, from one dog to another. The dog receiving the heart lived for only eight days, because of blood clotting, a problem he proceeded to solve. Performing more than 300 dog heart transplants over the following eight years, he further perfected his technique, achieving a fairly good survival rate. On November 20, 1967 he announced that he was ready to attempt the first human heart transplant and was awaiting a suitable donor. When the announcement reached the ears of the more self-assertive South African heart surgeon Christiaan N. Barnard (who had studied alongside Shumway at the University of Minnesota), Barnard decided to "take a chance" and on December 3, 1967 transplanted a heart from one human to another, thus performing a transplant before Shumway, even though his own laboratory experi-

mentation with dog heart transplantation had been relatively brief and not very successful; the recipient died 18 days later. Shumway carried out the first adult human-heart transplant in the United States on January 6, 1968; the recipient died 15 days later. Meanwhile, a team of surgeons in New York had transplanted a heart into an infant (who lived for only six hours) and Barnard had performed his second transplant of a human heart, into a man who survived for 19 and a half months. During the following few months, 170 human heart transplants were carried out around the world. By 1971, 146 of the recipients had died either from rejection of their new hearts or from infection. Although Barnard went on briefly to achieve some more impressive results, the enthusiasm among heart surgeons for the heart-transplant operations, or even for further research and experimentation, dwindled to virtually naught. The only major American surgeon to persevere was Shumway, and he did so in spite of some formidable obstacles, such as the legal disputes over the definition of brain death among potential donors and the removal of the heart without an autopsy (an autopsy would have rendered the heart useless). With Lower and others in his laboratory team at Stanford, he returned to another decade of experimentation with dog heart transplantation to try to solve the twin problems of tissue rejection and infection. In an early breakthrough, he and his team devised a way to detect the occasions when rejection was beginning or about to occur and to limit increases in the dangerous immunosuppressive drug azathiaprine to those occasions. Later, they pioneered the use of a drug safer and more efficient than azathiaprine. That drug was cyclosporin, whose superior immunosuppressive properties control organ rejection without obliterating all resistance to infection. In addition to heart transplants, Shumway worked in lung transplantation, and in 1981 he and Bruce Reitz carried out the world's first successful combined heart-lung transplant. The recipient was Mary Gohike, who lived five more years and wrote a book about the experience. Shumway also transplanted hearts into infants, and he contributed to the advancement of the repair of congenital heart malformations in children. He did other kinds of open-heart surgery, including valve transplants, and he invented better methods of keeping donated hearts fresh. Since 1982, more than 75,000 human heart transplants have been performed worldwide, 60,000 of them in the United States, 1,240 at Stanford, and 800 by Shumway or under his supervision. On average, 85 percent of the recipients enjoy an extended life of at least one year and 70 percent go on to lead normal lives for more than five years, as many as 27 years to date. Shumway supervised the creation of the Department of Cardiothoracic Surgery at the Stanford University Medical Center in 1974 and chaired that department until his retirement, in 1993. He died at his home in Palo Alto. His survivors included his former wife, Mary Lou, a son, three daughters (including Sara J. Shumway, a professor of cardiovascular and thoracic surgery at the University of Minnesota who collaborated with him on a textbook on transplantation), and two grandchildren. See *Current Biography* (1971).

Obituary *New York Times* C p14 Feb. 11, 2006

SLAUGHTER, FRANK Feb. 25, 1908–May 17, 2001 Novelist and physician. In writing his best-selling novels, Frank Gill Slaughter drew on his biblical knowledge and his interest in history as well as his medical experiences. He began writing while he was a surgeon at Riverside Hospital in Jacksonville, Florida, from 1934 to 1943 and continued doing so while serving in the U.S. Army Medical Corps during World War II. After the war he devoted himself entirely to his writing. Among his scores of novels are *That None Should Die* (1941), *Air Surgeon* (1943), *Battle Surgeon* (1944), *Fort Everglades* (1951), *The Road to Bithynia* (1951), *The Galileans* (1953), *Sword and Scalpel* (1957), *The Crown and the Cross* (1959), *The Curse of Jezebel* (1961), *Upon This Rock* (1964), *The Sins of Herod* (1968), *Plague Ship* (1976), *Gospel Fever* (1980), *No Greater Love* (1985), and *Transplant* (1987). His novels *Sangaree* (1948) and *Doctors' Wives* (1967) were made into feature films with the same titles, released in 1953 and 1971, respectively. *The Song of Ruth* (1954) was adapted to the screen as *The Story of Ruth*; *The Warrior* (1956) was adapted as *Seminole* (1957). *Women in White* (1974) became the basis for the made-for-TV movie *Nurse* (1980) and for the television dramatic series *Nurse*, which aired on the CBS network from April 1981 until May 1982. Slaughter died at his home in Jacksonville, Florida. Two sons were among his survivors. See *Current Biography* (1942).

Obituary *New York Times* C p19 May 23, 2001

SPELLING, AARON Apr. 22, 1923–June 23, 2006 Television and motion-picture producer. Far and away, Aaron Spelling deserved the title of TV's "overachiever," as *Broadcasting & Cable* magazine once dubbed him. The sheer volume of Spelling's credits as a producer and executive producer is staggering. He earned his place in the *Guinness Book of World Records* by producing more than 3,800 hours of programming, including an unparalleled string of shows that became global hits. Spelling regarded his glittering productions as "mind candy." His greatest success was *Dynasty* (ABC, 1981–89), a lavish prime-time soap opera about love and villainy in an oil-rich Colorado family. A runner-up in popularity was his sexy "jiggle TV" coup *Charlie's Angels* (ABC, 1976–81), an hourlong weekly series about the adventures of three nubile crime fighters, glamorously clothed and groomed. Among his other hits were *Burke's Law* (ABC, 1963–65), *Daniel Boone* (NBC, 1964–70), *Honey West* (ABC, 1965–66), *The Mod Squad* (ABC, 1968–73), *Starsky and Hutch* (ABC, 1975–79), *Family* (ABC, 1976–80), *The Love Boat* (ABC, 1977–86), *Fantasy Island* (ABC, 1978–84), *Hart to Hart* (ABC, 1979–84), *T. J. Hooker* (ABC/CBS, 1982–87), *Hotel* (ABC, 1983–88), *Beverly Hills* 90210 (Fox, 1990–2000), and *Melrose Place* (Fox, 1992–99). Among the last of the series he produced were *Charmed*, which ran on the WB network from 1998 to 2006, and *7th Heaven*, which began its run on WB in 1996 and moved to the new CW network in 2006. Among the scores of movies he produced for TV were the Emmy Award winners *Day One* (1989) and *And the Band Played On* (1993). He also produced 13 feature films. Spelling was born to immigrant Orthodox Jewish parents in Dallas, Texas.

Following service with the U.S. Army Air Force in World War II, he began writing and directing plays as an undergraduate at Southern Methodist University, where he received a B.A. degree in 1950. While directing plays regionally in the Dallas and Los Angeles areas in the early 1950s, he found work as an actor in small roles on television and in motion pictures, from which he moved into scenario writing. He wrote, among other scenarios, 10 of the scripts for the Western anthology series *Dick Powell's Zane Grey Theatre* (CBS) during the 1956–57 television season. He continued to contribute scripts to that series during its five-year run, and he became producer of the series in 1960. The first of Spelling's three marriages, to Janice Carruth, was a brief union that ended in divorce. Spelling was then married to the actress Carolyn Jones for 11 years, until their divorce in 1964. Four years later he married Carole "Candy" Marer, by whom he had a son, Randy, and a daughter, the actress Tori Spelling. Aaron Spelling died in his home in Los Angeles. He was survived by his third wife and his son and daughter. See *Current Biography* (1986).

Obituary *New York Times* I p31 June 24, 2006

SPENCER, JOHN Dec. 20, 1946–Dec. 16, 2005 Actor. John Spencer capped his long career as a yeoman character actor on stage, film, and television with his Emmy Award–winning portrayal of Leo McGarry, the tough White House chief of staff on the TV show *The West Wing*. Spencer was a charter member of the cast of that weekly NBC serial drama, which began its run in 1999. For his role as top aide to President Josiah Bartlet (Martin Sheen), he was nominated for the Emmy Award for best supporting actor five times, and he won the award in 2002. (In the show's final, 2005–06 season, his McGarry character was a vice-presidential candidate.) Previously, Spencer was best known for his performance in the major supporting role of Detective Dan Lipranzer in the motion picture *Presumed Innocent* (1990) and for his membership in the ensemble cast of the television show *L.A. Law*. In the latter NBC dramatic series, about a fictional Los Angeles law firm, he played the fiery lawyer Tommy Mullaney from 1990 until 1994. Spencer's original surname was Speshock. He changed his name while attending the Professional Children's School in Manhattan. His first television role was in *The Patty Duke Show* (ABC, 1963–66), a situation comedy in which Patty Duke played the dual roles of Patty Lane, an outgoing Brooklyn teenager, and Cathy Lane, her visiting identical cousin, a prim British girl. Spencer was cast as Henry Anderson, Cathy's boyfriend. Over the following decade and a half, the actor worked in relative obscurity on the stage, mostly as an understudy and in minor roles in regional theater. A breakthrough came in 1981, when he received an Obie Award, Off-Broadway's highest honor, for his performance as Mark in Emily Mann's drama *Still Life*. In 1986 he won a Drama League award for his role in *Execution of Justice*, and in 1988 he was nominated for a Drama Desk award for his performance in the Manhattan Theatre Club's production of *The Day Room*. He made his motion-picture debut in the minor supporting role of Captain Jerry Lawson in *War Games*

(1983). His later screen credits included roles in *Forget Paris* (1995), *The Rock* (1996), *Cop Land* (1997), and *The Negotiator* (1998). In 1997 he returned to the New York stage as Dennis, the embittered civil-rights lawyer in the Manhattan Class Company's production of *Good as New*. Following a marriage and divorce in the 1970s, he lived for many years with the actress and choreographer Patti Mariano. He died in Los Angeles, following a heart attack. See *Current Biography* (2001).

Obituary *New York Times* B p8 Dec. 17, 2005

SPILLANE, MICKEY Mar. 9, 1918–July 17, 2006 Best-selling writer of crime novels. The literary establishment's protestations of his bad taste notwithstanding, the Brooklyn-born Frank Morrison Spillane was one of the most popular American authors of all time. Spillane was a workmanlike master of the hard-boiled detective genre, to which he brought a new level of lurid sex and sadistic violence. He personally cultivated a gritty public image in tune with that of his noir antihero, Mike Hammer, a brutal ultra-macho private investigator, tough-talking, womanizing, and remorselessly quick on the trigger. According to Spillane, "the first and only style of writing that ever influenced" him was that of Carroll John Daly (1889–1958), in such pulp magazines as *Black Mask* in the 1920s, *Dime Detective* in the 1930s, and *Thrilling Detective* in the 1940s and such fast-paced novels as *The Hidden Hand* (1929) and *Murder Can't Wait* (1933). Spillane's Mike Hammer was modeled after Daly's Race Williams, a New York shamus who was a one-man court of law, enforcing his personal code of vigilante justice on evildoers in quick-thinking action and escaping from dire situations with fists swinging or gun blazing. Spillane's first stories were scripts for *Captain Marvel*, *The Human Torch*, and other comic strips published by Funnies Inc. in the early 1940s. After stateside service with the U.S. Army Air Force in World War II, he returned to writing for comic books, on a freelance basis. He began writing novels in 1946 in order to raise the money he needed to buy property in Newburgh, New York, at the beginning of his first marriage. In his first novel, *I, the Jury* (1947), he introduced Mike Hammer, an alcohol-swigging, chain-smoking private eye who administers justice with a speed and efficiency beyond the capacities of the law. In the course of pursuing his target—which in that first book was a narcotics ring that killed his army buddy—he enjoys the sexual favors of a succession of well-endowed nubile women who find his raw masculinity irresistible. In the climax of *I, the Jury* the mob's ringleader is revealed to be a woman, the beautiful psychiatrist Charlotte Manning, whom Hammer shoots to death (in the belly) after she has stripped before him. *I, the Jury* fixed the mold for all of his books, which Max Allen Collins described in volume two of *Mystery and Suspense Writers* (1998), edited by Robin W. Winks: "Spillane writes with speed, and the rough-hewn poetry of his narrator creates a fantasy city, a New York of myth and dream, populated by the same character types as those found in the work of Daly, [Dashiell] Hammett, and [Raymond] Chandler—good girls, black widows, thugs, frustrated cops, gang lords, corrupt society

leaders—but delivered with unique fever-dream fervor." The second and third novels in the Mike Hammer series were *My Gun Is Quick* (1950) and *Vengeance Is Mine* (1950). In the latter Hammer's prey is a murderess who turns out to be a doppelgänger for Charlotte Manning. Hammer feels remorse for having killed the original Charlotte until he realizes her lookalike is a transvestite. The first three Hammer novels were brought together in volume one of *The Mike Hammer Collection* (2001). The next three—*One Lonely Night* (1951), *The Big Kill* (1951), and *Kiss Me Deadly* (1952)—make up volume two of the collection. Spillane became a Jehovah's Witness missionary in 1952, in a religious conversion that marked the beginning of a decade-long hiatus in his novel writing. Between 1962 and 1996 seven new (and somewhat tamer) Hammer books were published, bringing the series to a total of 13. In addition to that series, Spillane published *The Long Wait*, in 1951, *The Deep*, in 1961, and subsequently eight more non-Hammer crime novels and two children's books. With screenplays by Spillane, *I, the Jury*, *The Long Wait*, *Kiss Me Deadly*, and *My Gun Is Quick* were made into feature films in the 1950s, and the non-Hammer novel *The Delta Factor* was adapted for the screen in 1970. Spillane himself played Hammer in his screen adaptation of *The Girl Hunters* (1963). On television, Darren McGavin played Hammer in 78 syndicated episodes of *Mike Hammer* beginning in 1958 and Stacy Keach starred in the made-for-TV movie *Mickey Spillane's Mike Hammer* (CBS, 1983) and in the CBS series *Mike Hammer* (1984–87). Spillane's political perspective was well to the right of center. Among his fans was Ayn Rand, with whom he engaged in a lengthy correspondence. After his marriages to Mary Ann Parce and Sherri Malinou ended in divorce, Spillane married Jane Rodgers Johnson. According to his third wife, a number of his manuscripts remained unpublished at the time of his death. He died at his home in Murrells Inlet, South Carolina, where he had lived since 1954. In addition to his third wife, his survivors included two stepchildren (from his third marriage) and two daughters and two sons by his first wife. See *Current Biography* (1981).

Obituary *New York Times* B p7 July 18, 2006

STAPLETON, MAUREEN June 21, 1925–Mar. 13, 2006 Actress. Stapleton was an earthy and blowsy "method" actress, deeply grounded in theater but also esteemed for her work in motion pictures and on television. Although she was regularly top-billed early in her career and occasionally thereafter, she became most closely identified, especially as she grew more matronly in appearance, with her roles as homely characters, often mentally or emotionally vulnerable women. Once, when commenting on the glamorous typecasting that kept her friend Marilyn Monroe, the Hollywood sex icon, from full realization of her acting potential, Stapleton pointed out that she herself "never had that problem," that "people looked at me on stage and said, 'Jesus, that broad better be able to act.'" Among Stapleton's many Broadway successes were her Tony Award–winning creations of Serafina delle Rose, the fiery and love-hungry Sicilian-American widow in Tennessee Williams's drama *The Rose Tattoo* (1951), and Evelyn Meara, the alcoholic nightclub singer with a slumping career and an abusive lover in Neil Simon's tragicomedy *The Gingerbread Lady* (1970–71). In Hollywood she was nominated for the Academy Award for best supporting actress three times—for her portrayals of Fay Doyle (a k a Miss Lonelyhearts) in *Lonelyhearts* (1958), of Inez Guerrero in *Airport* (1970), and of Pearl in *Interiors* (1978)—before she won the Oscar with her performance as the anarchist revolutionary Emma Goldman in the film *Reds* (1981). Her many television credits included her Emmy Award–winning portrayal of Mary O'Meaghan, the lonely spinster who goes widower-hunting in a cemetery, in *Among the Paths to Eden* (1967), adapted from a story by Truman Capote. That TV film was combined with adaptations of two other Capote stories in the theatrical motion picture *Trilogy* (1969). Stapleton was born into an Irish-American Catholic family in Troy, New York, where she began acting in school plays at Catholic Central High School. When she was 18 she moved to New York City, where she studied acting under Robert Duff and Herbert Berghof and became a charter member of the Actors Studio, the Manhattan workshop devoted to training professional actors in the Stanislavski method of developing character psychologically, from within one's self. She made her Broadway debut as Sara Tensey in *The Playboy of the Western World* (1946–47) and was subsequently cast on Broadway as the serving maid Iras in *Antony and Cleopatra* (1947–48), Emily Williams in *The Bird Cage* (1950), Bella in *The Emperor's Clothes* (1953), and Elizabeth Proctor in *The Crucible* (1953). She created the roles of Ida in *The Cold Wind and the Warm*, in 1958, and Carrie in *Toys in the Attic*, in 1960. Her Broadway credits in plays by Tennessee Williams included her creations of Flora in *27 Wagons Full of Cotton* (1955) and Lady Torrance in *Orpheus Descending* (1956), her performances as Amanda Wingfield in two revivals of *The Glass Menagerie* (1965 and 1975–76), and her return to the role of Serafina delle Rose in a revival of *The Rose Tattoo* (1966). She created all three female protagonists—Karen Nash, Muriel Tate, and Norma Hubley—in the original cast of Neil Simon's three-playlet comedy *Plaza Suite* (1968–70). In revivals, she played Georgia Elgin in *The Country Girl* (1972) and Birdie Hubbard in *The Little Foxes* (1981). In *The Fugitive Kind* (1959), the screen version of *Orpheus Descending*, she was cast in the role of Vee Talbot. She had more than a score of other feature-film credits. During the golden age of live teleplays, beginning in the early 1950s, she had numerous roles in productions on such drama showcases as *Studio One* and *Playhouse 90*. Her later dramatic credits on television included Mrs. Hamilton in the situation comedy *The Thorns* (1988), appearances in episodes of several other series, and roles in made-for-TV movies, including Big Mama in *Cat on a Hot Tin Roof* (1976). In her autobiography, *A Hell of a Life* (1995), written with Jane Scovell, she wrote about such subjects as her alcoholism and her phobias, which included fear of elevators, flying, traveling on trains, and the possibility of being shot on stage by some deranged theatergoer. She was married to and divorced from Max Allentuck (1949–59) and David Rayfiel (1963–66). She died in Lenox,

Massachusetts. Her survivors included a son and daughter from her first marriage and two grandchildren. See *Current Biography* (1959).

Obituary *New York Times* B p9 Mar. 14, 2006

STRATTON, DOROTHY Mar. 24, 1899–Sep. 17, 2006 Educator; military officer. Dorothy Constance Stratton was Purdue University's first full-time dean of women and the U.S. Coast Guard's first female commissioned officer. She was the founding commandant of the SPARs, the Coast Guard women's auxiliary during World II. Later she was director of personnel with the International Monetary Fund (1947–50) and national executive director of the Girl Scouts of the U.S.A. (1950–60). After receiving a B.A. degree at Ottawa University in Ottawa, Kansas, in 1920, Stratton went on to earn a master's degree in psychology at the University of Chicago and a doctorate in student personnel administration at Columbia University. Early in her career she worked as a junior-high-school and high-school vice principal and principal. In 1933 she joined the faculty of Purdue University as dean of women and associate professor of psychology. She became a full professor in 1940. After the United States entered World War II, she served on the selection board for the WAACs (Women's Army Auxiliary Corps) Fifth Corps Area. After leaving Purdue, in 1942, she was commissioned a lieutenant in the U.S. Navy's women's reserve, the WAVES (Women Accepted for Volunteer Emergency Service, which later became Women in the Naval Services). She was later promoted to captain. When the U.S. Coast Guard Women's Reserve was established, in November 1942, she was sworn in as its first commandant. It was she who came up with the reserve's nickname, SPARs, an acronym derived from the Coast Guard's motto, "Semper Paratus," and its English translation, "Always Ready." The uniforms of the SPARs were the same as those of the WAVES, with the exception of the Coast Guard and Navy shields on the sleeves. As commandant, Stratton led 11,000 women, including 1,000 commissioned officers, in Coast Guard support-structure service. (Later, women would be admitted to the Coast Guard Academy and be eligible for all enlisted ratings and officer career fields.) For her wartime service, she was awarded the Legion of Merit. Her term of service ended with the demobilization of the SPARs in June 1946. Stratton's doctoral thesis was published as *Problems of Students in a Graduate School of Education* (1933; reprinted in 1972). With the late Helen B. Schleman, she co-wrote the book of etiquette *Your Best Foot Forward: Social Usage for Young Moderns* (1940; 1955). After living for many years in Newtown, Connecticut, Stratton moved in 1985 to West Lafayette, Indiana, to share a home there with Helen B. Schleman. She died in West Lafayette. See *Current Biography* (1943).

Obituary *New York Times* (on-line) Sep. 25, 2006

THOMSON, KENNETH R. Sep. 1, 1923–June 12, 2006 Canadian businessman and art collector; the former chairman and the controlling shareholder of the Thomson Corp. The only son of the self-made trans-Atlantic media mogul Roy Thomson, Kenneth

Thompson became the richest person in Canada and the ninth-richest in the world by guiding the multifaceted family business in new directions, most notably toward specialized electronic publishing. From his father he inherited the title of Second Baron Thomson of Fleet, but he avoided using the title in North America and never took his seat in the British House of Lords. After serving with the Royal Canadian Air Force in England during World War II, he earned a law degree at Cambridge University. Back in Canada after the war, he worked his way up in Thomson Newspapers Ltd. from cub reporter for the Timmins, Ontario, *Daily Press* in 1947 to general manager of the Galt, Ontario, *Evening Reporter* in 1950. In the early 1950s Roy Thomson bought the Edinburgh *Scotsman* and moved to the United Kingdom to oversee the operations of that newspaper, leaving Kenneth in Toronto as president and chairman of Thomson Newspapers, which at that time owned 24 dailies and eight weekly newspapers in Canada and 22 dailies and six weeklies in the United States. Roy Thomson subsequently bought the London *Times* and *Sunday Times*, among other newspapers, and he diversified widely, acquiring, for example, such interests as Britannia Airways, Thomson Travel (a British tour operator), Dominion-Consolidated Truck Lines, North Sea oil, and book and telephone-directory publishing. In the early 1960s Roy Thomson returned to Canada and sent Kenneth to London as chairman of the *Times* newspapers. With his wife and children, Kenneth lived in London for three years, beginning in late 1967. He returned to Toronto as chairman of Thomson Newspapers and co-chairman of the International Thomson Organization Ltd. in 1971, and upon the death of his father, five years later, he assumed control of the family conglomerate. Over the following years he progressively tightened and streamlined its operations, merging Thomson Newspapers and the International Thomson Organization Ltd. into the Thomson Organization (now the Thomson Corp.). He divested it of most of its travel, energy, and retail holdings, including the Hudson's Bay Company, Canada's largest department store chain, which he himself had acquired. At the same time, anticipating a decline in the profitability of print journalism, he sold off the London *Times* newspapers, the *Jerusalem Post*, most of the Thomson newspapers in Canada, and many of those in the United States. During the last decade of his life, he built the Thomson Corp. into a giant in the field of electronic information: a leading provider of on-line information and data for professionals and students in such fields as health and medicine, finance, law, science, and education. He retained a formidable foothold in print media through a 40 percent stake in Bell Globemedia, which owns the *Globe and Mail* newspaper, Canada's second-largest in circulation, as well as the CTV television network. The Thomson family holdings, which had been valued at approximately $500 million in 1976, appreciated to an estimated $29 billion by the end of 2005, when the revenues of the Thomson Corp. were almost $9 billion; profits in early 2006 were averaging more than $40 million a month. In 2002 Thomson turned the chairmanship of the Thomson Corp.—which includes the Westlaw (legal research) and First Call (financial data) companies—over to David, the elder of his two sons. He remained chairman of the Woodbridge Co. Ltd., the family's private holding company, which owns 70 percent of the Thompson Corp. stock. His personal fortune was estimated at $20 billion. After his retirement he donated the bulk of his art collection, comprising 3,000 paintings and sculptures worth $300 million, to the Art Gallery of Ontario. Thomson died in his office in Toronto, apparently of a heart attack. He was survived by his wife, Nora Marilyn Thomson, his sons, David and Peter, and his daughter, Lynne, also known as Taylor. See *Current Biography* (1989).

Obituary *New York Times* C p12 June 13, 2006

TROWBRIDGE, ALEXANDER B. Dec. 12, 1929–Apr. 27, 2006 Corporate executive; organization official; U.S. government official. Alexander Buel Trowbridge, an international oil executive and business lobbyist in the private sector, served as U.S. secretary of commerce (1967–68) in the administration of President Lyndon B. Johnson. Trowbridge majored in public and international affairs at Princeton University, where he received a B.A. degree in 1951. After serving as a Marine Corps officer in Korea, he joined the California Texas Oil Co. in 1954. Following a year in that firm's New York office, he worked for three years (1955–58) as marketing assistant for petroleum products with Caltex, a California Texas subsidiary in the Philippines. He left Caltex to join the Standard Oil Co. of New Jersey, which assigned him in 1959 to manage operations and marketing with its Esso Standard Oil subsidiary in the Caribbean and Central America. He was serving as president of Esso Standard Oil in Puerto Rico when the Johnson administration asked him to come to Washington. In Washington, he was assistant secretary of commerce for domestic and international business (1965–67) before his appointment as secretary of commerce. After leaving government he was president of the American Management Association until 1970, when he began a six-year tenure as president of the National Industrial Conference Board, a business research organization later renamed the Conference Board. As vice chairman of Allied Chemical from 1976 to 1980, he was instrumental in settling a massive pollution lawsuit against that corporation. As president of the National Association of Manufacturers (NAM) from 1980 to 1990, he was highly effective as that organization's chief spokesman and lobbyist in Washington. After leaving the NAM he headed the Washington consulting firm of Trowbridge Partners for more than a decade. He died at his home in Washington, D.C. His survivors included his wife, Eleanor Hutzler Trowbridge, two sons and a daughter from his earlier marriage to Nancey Horst (which ended in divorce), a stepdaughter, a stepson, and nine grandchildren. See *Current Biography* (1968).

Obituary *New York Times* B p8 Apr. 28, 2006

VIERECK, PETER Aug. 5, 1916–May 13, 2006 Political philosopher; poet; professor emeritus of European and Russian history, Mount Holyoke College. Peter Viereck, a seminal figure in the establishment of modern American conservatism as a mainstream movement, later became a dissenter from the course that movement took. A major essay on Viereck by Tom Reiss was published in the *New Yorker* (October 17, 2005) under the title "The First Conservative" and the subtitle "How Peter Viereck Inspired—and Lost—a Movement." Viereck was the son of the German-born American poet and journalist George Sylvester Viereck, from whose notorious fascist sympathies he forcefully distanced himself. The elder Viereck, a pro-German propagandist during World Wars I and II, was indicted for violation of the Foreign Agents Registration Act during World War II and served four years in a federal penitentiary, beginning in 1942. Peter Viereck, who received his Ph.D. degree in history at Harvard University that same year, remained estranged from his father for the next 16 years. Partly in reaction to his father's politics, he had issued the manifesto "But I'm a Conservative" in the *Atlantic Monthly* (April 1940). At that time, as Tom Reiss noted, "the word 'conservative' was associated primarily with fringe groups—anti-industrial Southern agrarians and the anti-New Deal tycoons who led the Liberty League." Viereck called for a "new conservatism" that would be opposed not only to the foreign "storm of totalitarianism" but also to domestic leftist "moral relativism and soulless materialism," including that represented by the Marxism that he claimed was a dominant influence at Harvard. While he recognized that domestic liberalism was morally benign in comparison, he argued that at base it shared with Nazism and Communism a utopianism that he regarded as naïve and mistaken. He later explained: "The liberal sees outer, removable institutions as the ultimate source of evil; sees man's social task as creating a world in which evil will disappear. His tools for this task are progress and enlightenment. The conservative sees the inner unremovable nature of man as the ultimate source of evil; sees man's social task as coming to terms with a world in which evil is perpetual and in which justice and compassion will both be perpetually necessary. His tools for this task are the maintenance of ethical restraints inside the individual and the maintenance of unbroken, continuous social patterns inside the given culture as a whole." Viereck refined and expanded the message of his 1940 essay in *Conservatism Revisited: The Revolt Against Revolt* (1949; revised as *Conservatism Revisited: The Revolt Against Ideology*, 2005). In that book he affirmed his approval of the moderate social programs and economic planning introduced by the New Deal and his commitment to the struggle against segregation and for racial justice in the United States, not by revolution but through gradual social evolution, as recommended by Edmund Burke (1729–97), a major influence on Viereck's thought. In the early 1950s Viereck supported the Democratic candidate, Adlai E. Stevenson, for president, and he tried to rally fellow conservatives against Senator Joseph R. McCarthy's anti-Communist witch hunt, which he regarded as a dishonest, anarchistic publicity stunt "subverting precisely those institutions that are the most conservative and organic." The latter effort contributed to his alienation from the very movement he was widely credited with having founded. Russell Kirk, for one, charged him with waging "McCarthyism against McCarthy." Years later, in January 2005, Viereck told Tom Reiss: "I think McCarthy was a menace not because of the risk that he would take over—that was never real—but because he corrupted the ethics of American conservatives, and that corruption led to the situation we have now. It gave the conservatives the habit of appeasing the forces of the hysterical right." Those forces include, in Reiss's paraphrase, "religious fundamentalists, paranoid patriotic groups, and big-business leaders, united in their loathing for the cosmopolitan elites on the nation's coasts." In his first book, *Metropolitics: From Wagner and the Romantics to Hitler* (1940; revised and enlarged in several successive editions), Viereck traced the intellectual roots of the Nazi mindset. His later books included *Shame and Glory of the Intellectuals: Babbit Jr. Versus the Rediscovery of Values* (1953), *The Unadjusted Man: A New Hero for Americans* (1956), *Conservatism: From John Adams to Churchill* (1956), and *Conservatism from Burke and John Adams Till 1982* (1982). In 1949 Viereck won the Pulitzer Prize for poetry for his first collection of verse, *Terror and Decorum* (1948). His later books of verse included *New and Selected Poems, 1932–1967* (1967) and *The Archer in the Marrow* (1987). Reviewing his last collection, *Tide and Continuities: Last and First Poems, 1995–1938* (1995) in the *New Leader*, Phoebe Pettingell noted the "wit" and "shrewd cultural judgments" to be found in Viereck's "spirited formal verse": "Viereck . . . knew how effective doggerel can be. . . . Doggerel's effects are often comic, but they also allow for philosophical musings, mockery, and even a species of folksy pathos. . . . Viereck and Garrison Keillor may be the only well-known writers who still love doggerel, and probably no one has put it through more paces than Viereck. In doing so, he proves once again its flexibility and emotional resonance." Viereck served as a U.S. Army intelligence analyst during World War II. He was the recipient of Guggenheim Fellowships in both history and poetry. After teaching briefly at Harvard University and Smith College, he joined the faculty of Mount Holyoke College, in South Hadley, Massachusetts, as an associate professor in 1948. He was a full professor at Mount Holyoke from 1955 to 1987. After retiring, with the status of professor emeritus, in 1987, he continued to teach a course in Russian history at the college until 1997. Viereck was twice married to and divorced from the late Anya de Markov before marrying Betty Martin Falkenberg in 1972. He was survived by his second wife, a son and a daughter by his first wife, three grandchildren, and one great-grandchild. Viereck died at his home in South Hadley, Massachusetts. See *Current Biography* (1943).

Obituary *New York Times* A p23 May 19, 2006

WARD, PAUL L. Feb. 4, 1911–Nov. 13, 2005 American educator and historian. Ward, a former Episcopal missionary/teacher in China, was a professor of history and the chairman of the History Department at the Carnegie Institute of Technology (now Carnegie Mellon University), in Pittsburgh, Pennsylvania (1953–60), president of Sarah Lawrence College, in Bronxville, New York (1960–65), and executive secretary of the American Historical Association, in Washington, D.C. (1965–74). He wrote the books *A Style of History for Beginners* (1959), *Elements of*

Historical Thinking (1971), and *Studying History: An Introduction to Methods and Structure* (1985), published many articles on British legal and constitutional history, and co-edited the books *Archeion* (1957) and *Confrontation and Learned Societies* (1970). Ward was born in Diyarbakir, Turkey, to American parents who were Congregational medical missionaries. In earning his doctorate at Harvard University, he specialized in the study of medieval and Elizabethan history, with special focus on the development of the British coronation ritual. In Washington, D.C., during World War II, he was an assistant section chief with the Office of Strategic Services, the precursor of the Central Intelligence Agency. After the war he taught Western history at Huachung University in Wuchang, China, under Protestant Episcopal Church auspices until his expulsion in 1950 by the then newly installed Communist regime in Beijing. Before joining the faculty of the Carnegie Institute of Technology, he taught history at Colby College, in Waterville, Maine, for two years (1951–53). While heading the American Historical Association, he served on the vestry of St. Augustine's Episcopal Church in Washington and was active in the Episcopal Peace Fellowship. He participated in the fellowship's demonstrations against the Vietnam War and helped to develop and teach a course on issues of war and peace at the Army War College, in Washington. In 1990 he moved from Alexandria, Virginia, to Gwynedd, Pennsylvania, where he died. He was survived by his wife, Catharine, a daughter, three sons, and grandchildren and great-grandchildren. See *Current Biography* (1962).

Obituary *New York Times* B p11 Nov. 18, 2005

WASSERSTEIN, WENDY Oct. 18, 1950–Jan. 30, 2006 Playwright. Among American women of her generation, Wendy Wasserstein was the preeminent translator of personal existential crises and career-related confusion into plays addressing issues raised by the modern feminist movement. André Bishop, the artistic director most closely associated with the Off-Broadway staging of her works (first at Playwrights Horizons and later at the Mitzi E. Newhouse Theater, at Lincoln Center), once observed that she wrote "plays of ideas that happen to be written as comedies." Peter Marks, a *Washington Post* theater critic, pointed out that she managed to locate feminism's elusive funny bone not by mocking feminism "but by making the intoxicating, bewildering choices it presented to women a natural ingredient of the human comedy." Wasserstein drew much attention in 1977 with the Off-Broadway success of *Uncommon Women and Other Choices*, her play about five close classmates at Mount Holyoke College (her alma mater) as they struggle, in their several ways, to become "uncommon" in a world of rapidly changing social and sexual mores without totally rejecting traditional roles, including motherhood. In what was a virtual sequel, she had even more success Off-Broadway in the early and mid-1980s with the long-running production *Isn't It Romantic*, in which two close college graduates—the somewhat pudgy, Jewish Janie (the author's counterpart) and the svelte WASP Harriet—discuss their different perspectives on love and success and struggle to maintain their friendship. Wasserstein's greatest success was *The Heidi Chronicles* (1988), which moved from Off-Broadway to a Broadway run of 622 performances beginning in 1989 and won both the Tony Award for the year's best play and the Pulitzer Prize for drama. In interrelated scenes, that play chronicles the life and career of Heidi Holland, an art historian, from her coming of age in the 1960s into the 1980s, when she begins to wonder if she has made the right choices in life. Wasserstein was born in Brooklyn, New York, to affluent Jewish immigrant parents. When she was growing up in Brooklyn and then on Manhattan's Upper East Side, her mother, Lola Wasserstein, introduced her to New York City's world of theater and dance and in particular to June Taylor of television's famous June Taylor Dancers, under whom she studied dance. After receiving a B.A. degree in history at Mount Holyoke College and an M.A. at the City College of New York (where she studied creative writing), she matriculated at Yale University's School of Drama, where she earned a master's degree in fine arts. Meanwhile, she began her connection to Off-Broadway theater through Louise Roberts, the former administrator of the June Taylor Dancers, who had become director of the Clark Center for the Performing Arts at Manhattan's West Side YWCA, the early home of Playwrights Horizons, a nonprofit theatrical company with a reputation for nurturing young talent. Louise Roberts brought a one-act play by Wasserstein, *Any Woman Can't*, to Robert Moss, the artistic director of Playwrights Horizons. Moss produced that play in 1973, and three years later he staged Wasserstein's short comedies *Happy Birthday* and *Montpelier Pa-zazz*. *Isn't It Romantic* flopped when it was first produced Off-Broadway, during the 1980–81 season. Under the guidance of Bishop, who had succeeded Moss at Playwrights Horizons, Wasserstein spent a year revising the play, and the new version became a box-office and critical hit first at Playwrights Horizons (1983–84) and then for 733 performances at the Lucille Lortel Theater, a larger venue. During the 1980s Wasserstein traveled widely in Europe, including Poland (where she looked in vain for traces of her Jewish roots). That cosmopolitan experience is reflected in her play *The Sisters Rosensweig*, about the reunion in London of three American sisters, Sara, Gorgeous, and Pfeni, on the occasion of the birthday of Sara, a fast-track international banker. First staged at Lincoln Center, that play moved to Broadway for a run of 556 performances beginning in March 1993. In her most overtly political play, *An American Daughter* (1992), Wasserstein told of the confirmation ordeal of a woman nominated for a White House Cabinet post. First produced at Lincoln Center, that play ran on Broadway in 1997. Wasserstein's *Old Money*, in which three characters travel in time between the early 1900s and the beginning of the new millennium, was produced at Lincoln Center in 2000–01. Among the one-act plays written by Wasserstein were *Welcome to My Rash, Tender Offer*, and *Third*. An expanded version of *Third*, about a feminist professor in her 50s taking stock of her life, was produced at Lincoln Center in 2005. Wasserstein wrote the screenplays for the feature film *The Object of My Affection* (1998) and the made-for-TV film *Kiss-Kiss, Dahlings!* (1992). Among the books published by Wasserstein were the self-help parody *Sloth* (2005), the children's book *Pamela's First Musical* (1996), and two volumes of essays, *Bachelor Girls* (1991) and *Shiksa Goddess: Or, How I Spent My Forties* (2001). Shortly before her death she completed her only novel, *Elements of Style*, which was published in 2006. She died in Manhattan. Her survivors included her six-year-old daughter, Lucy Jane, whom she had by artificial insemination and whose father's identity she never disclosed publicly. Lucy Jane is being raised by Wasserstein's brother Bruce, the chairman and CEO of the investment banking firm Lazard Frères and the owner of *New York* magazine. See *Current Biography* (1989).

Obituary *New York Times* A p1+ Jan. 31, 2006

WEAVER, DENNIS June 4, 1925–Feb. 24, 2006 Actor. The tall and lanky Weaver, who worked in relative obscurity on stage and screen at the beginning of his career, gained fame after he moved to television in the mid-1950s. Following service in the U.S. Navy, he earned a degree in theater arts at the University of Oklahoma. A fellow drama graduate, Lonny Chapman, who was going to New York to seek his fortune on the stage, persuaded Weaver to accompany him. Weaver understudied Chapman in the role of Turk Fisher in *Come Back, Little Sheba* on Broadway in 1950, and he took over the role of Turk in a national tour of the production. Shelley Winters, a fellow student at the Actors Studio, subsequently starred with him in a Los Angeles stage production of *A Streetcar Named Desire*, and she was instrumental in his finding work in Hollywood, where he had roles in numerous Westerns beginning in 1952. His later feature-film credits included the roles of John Brown Jr. in *Seven Angry Men* (1955), Sheriff Clyde Gibbons in *Ten Wanted Men* (1955), the Mirador Motel manager in *Touch of Evil* (1958), and Lieutenant Commander Andy Lowe in *The Gallant Hours* (1960). He first drew wide public attention as Chester Goode, the gimpy sidekick of Marshal Matt Dillon (James Arness) in the Western series *Gunsmoke* on the CBS television network beginning in 1955. For that portrayal he received an Emmy Award for best supporting actor in 1959. He left the cast of *Gunsmoke* in 1964 to accept the title role of the widowed veterinarian in the NBC comedy-drama series *Kentucky Jones* (1964–65), and he was next cast on CBS as Tom Wedloe, a Florida Everglades game warden whose son adopts a 600-pound bear as a pet, in *Gentle Ben* (1967–69). He reached the height of his popularity as Sam McCloud, a deputy marshal from Taos, New Mexico, on assignment with the police in New York City, in NBC's crime series *McCloud* (1970–77). During the 1980s he was cast successively as Detective Sergeant Daniel Stone in the series *Stone*, as Rear Admiral Thomas Mallory in the series *Emerald Point N.A.S.*, and as the no-nonsense title character, a surgeon, in the series *Buck James*. In 2005 he gave his last series performance, as Henry Ritter, the patriarch of a family running a thoroughbred farm, in *Wildfire* on the ABC Family cable channel. His made-for-TV film credits included the driver menaced by a tractor-trailer in Steven Spielberg's road-rage thriller *Duel* (1971), the title role in *The Ordeal of Doctor Mudd* (1980), the cocaine addict in

Cocaine: One Man's Addiction (1983), and the man hiding his illiteracy in *Bluffing It* (1987). His last feature-film roles were Grandpa Flint in *Escape from Wildcat Canyon* (1998) and Buck Stevens in *Submerged* (2000). Outside of show business, Weaver was a student of yoga, a passionate advocate of vegetarianism, and a champion of alternatives to fossil-fuel consumption and other environmental issues. With his wife, Gerry, he founded the Institute of Ecolonomics, an educational organization dedicated to promoting a sustainable future through the creation of a healthy ecological/economic synergy. Also with her, he built "Earthship," their solar-powered home in Ridgway, Colorado, constructed primarily of recycled tires and aluminum cans. With her and others, he founded LIFE (Love Is Feeding Everyone), a soup kitchen in Los Angeles. His autobiography, *All the World's a Stage*, was published in 2001. He died at his home in Ridgway, Colorado. His survivors included his wife, three sons, and three grandchildren. See *Current Biography* (1977).

Obituary *New York Times* A p16 Feb. 28, 2006

WEINBERG, ALVIN M. Apr. 20, 1915–Oct. 18, 2006 Nuclear physicist. Alvin Martin Weinberg was one of the theoretical physicists who contributed to the development of the first atomic bombs during World War II, and he subsequently directed research into peacetime applications of nuclear power at the Oak Ridge National Laboratory. After receiving his doctorate in physics at the University of Chicago, in 1939, Weinberg remained at the university as a research assistant in mathematical biophysics. In 1942 he joined the staff of the Metallurgical Laboratory, the code name for the University of Chicago's involvement in the Manhattan Engineering District (MED), informally known as the Manhattan Project, the top-secret wartime atomic-bomb development program conducted under the aegis of the U.S. Army Corps of Engineers. At the Metallurgical Laboratory he assisted Eugene P. Wigner in successfully applying the mathematical theory of diffusion to the production of plutonium-239, the synthetic element at the core of the implosion-style "Fat Man" type of atomic bomb tested (under the name "the gadget") at Trinity Site near Alamogordo, New Mexico, on July 16, 1945 and exploded over Nagasaki, Japan, on August 9, 1945. (The bomb exploded over Hiroshima, Japan, on August 6, 1945 was "Little Boy," a gun-type uranium-235 weapon.) In 1945 Weinberg joined the staff of the Oak Ridge National Laboratory (originally called the Clinton Engineer Works), which had been founded by the Corps of Engineers two years before as a "secret city" on remote farmland in the mountains of eastern Tennessee. At Oak Ridge he became director of the physics division in 1947 (when MED was formally replaced by the U.S. Atomic Energy Commission), research director in 1948, and overall director in 1955. He directed, among other research projects, those that produced the pressurized-water reactor system that became standard in the U.S. Navy's nuclear fleet and the isotopes now useful in medical diagnosis and therapy. Above all, he championed the commercial use of nuclear energy as a replacement for fossil fuels. In doing so, he concentrated chiefly at first on safety at nuclear-power plants. It was only much later, some of his critics pointed out, that he began to give serious attention to the problem of nuclear waste. After resigning as director at Oak Ridge, in 1973, he was associated with the consortium known as Oak Ridge Associated Universities (ORAU). Within ORAU he was instrumental in founding the Institute for Energy Analysis, which he directed from 1975 to 1985. Among the projects he directed at the institute were pioneering studies of the greenhouse effect in global warming, of various alternate energy sources, and of the comparative cost effectiveness of those sources. He was also concerned with public-policy issues related to energy and technology, including world peace. In May 1996 he was a principal figure in a Symposium on Non-Use of Nuclear Weapons. He was credited with coining the special usages within his field of such phrases as "big science," "Faustian bargain," and "technological fix." He published some dozen books, including *Nuclear Reactions: Science and Trans-Science* (1992), the memoirs *Reflections on Big Science* (1967) and *The First Nuclear Era: The Life and Times of a Technological Fixer* (1994), and several collections of essays. With Eugene P. Wigner he co-wrote *The Physical Theory of Nuclear Chain Reactors* (1958), which became a standard textbook. After the death of his first wife, Margaret Despres, Weinberg married Genevieve DePersio, who died in 2004. His survivors included a son and three grandchildren. He died at his home in Oak Ridge, Tennessee. See *Current Biography* (1966).

Obituary *New York Times* B p7 Oct. 21, 2006

WEINBERGER, CASPAR W. Aug. 18, 1917–Mar. 28, 2006 U.S. government official; Republican politician. "Cap" Weinberger served in the Cabinets of Presidents Richard M. Nixon and Gerald R. Ford and, more famously, as President Ronald Reagan's right-hand man in the strategy of outwitting the Soviets in the Cold War by outspending them militarily. He had begun his association with Reagan as his finance director when Reagan was governor of California in the late 1960s. While he held moderate to liberal views on social issues, he was, like Reagan, a fiscal conservative save in the cause of "peace through strength" internationally. As secretary of defense under President Reagan from 1981 to 1987, he presided over the most massive military buildup in U.S. peacetime history, one that included revival of the B-1 bomber program, development of the MX missile, and plans for the space-based missile-defense system popularly known as Star Wars. The implementation of that strategy at a cost of $2 trillion forced the USSR into unsustainable competition and hastened the implosion of the Soviet system. "I did not arm to attack . . . ," Weinberger explained in his memoir *In the Arena* (2001), written with Gretchen Roberts. "We armed so that we could negotiate from strength, defend freedom, and make war less likely." Weinberger, who was of Jewish descent paternally, was raised in his mother's Episcopal faith, which became, he said, "an enormous influence and comfort all my life." After earning a B.A. degree (1938) and a law degree (1941) at Harvard University, he served as a U.S. Army officer in the Pacific during World War II. After the war he worked as a law clerk in the

U.S. Ninth Circuit Court of Appeals (1945–47) and joined a San Francisco law firm (1947), in which he became a partner. He was elected to the California State Assembly in 1952 and reelected in 1954 and 1956. In the early 1960s he was, successively, vice chairman and chairman of the California Republican Central Committee. Following Ronald Reagan's election as governor of California in 1966, he served as chairman of the Commission on California State Government Organization and Economy (1967–68) and as state director of finance (1968–69). In January 1970 he went to Washington, D.C., to join the Nixon administration as chairman of the Federal Trade Commission. In July 1970 he moved to the Office of Management and Budget, where he served as deputy director until President Nixon promoted him to director in May 1972. The following November he became Nixon's secretary of health, education, and welfare, and in January 1973 he was in addition named counselor on human resources in Nixon's "super Cabinet." After Nixon resigned the presidency, in 1974, Weinberger continued to serve as secretary of HEW (1974–75) under President Ford. During a five-year hiatus from government (1975–80), he was vice president and general counsel of the Bechtel Group, a California-based engineering conglomerate. As President Reagan's secretary of defense, he did not escape being touched by the Iran-Contra affair, which began to surface in the mid-1980s. That affair was a political scandal in which several members of the Reagan administration were accused of secretly selling arms to Iran for the dual purpose of obtaining the release of Americans held hostage by pro-Iranian terrorists in Lebanon and then using the profits to fund covert support of the anti-Communist Contra guerrillas in Nicaragua. Weinberger was not one of the central figures in the affair—which he claimed he had opposed—but he was indicted on felony charges of perjury and obstruction of justice in the case (which was cut short when President George H. W. Bush pardoned all of the accused, in December 1992). In 1990 he published *Fighting for Peace*, an account of his tenure in the Pentagon. With Peter Schweizer, he wrote *The Next War* (1996), a book about defense strategy that included criticism of President Bill Clinton's cuts in military spending, and the novel *Chain of Command* (2005), a political thriller. His honors included the Presidential Medal of Freedom and a British knighthood. In 1989 he joined Forbes Inc. as publisher of *Forbes* magazine. In 1993 he became chairman of Forbes Inc., a position he held until his death. He died in Bangor, Maine. His survivors included his wife, Jane, a son, a daughter, three grandchildren, and four great-grandchildren. See *Current Biography* (1973).

Obituary *New York Times* A p21 Mar. 29, 2006

WHITE, GILBERT F. Nov. 26, 1911–Oct. 5, 2006 Geographer; professor emeritus of geography, University of Colorado. Gilbert Fowler White was an innovative geographer who exerted immense international influence with his ecologically and socially sensitive work in human interaction with nature. In addressing the problems of natural hazards and resource management and development, he stressed the importance of human accommodation with the environment and proposed a balanced range of tools rather than reliance on dams and other brute engineering projects alone—an approach once considered radical but now widely accepted by land-use planners and policy-makers. His best-known accomplishments were in flood control and water conservation, beginning with his contributions to floodplain management as a U.S. government employee (not his long-term modus operandi of choice) in the New Deal era and including his later participation in cooperative efforts to improve the sustainable water supply in developing countries. One of his out-of-the-box insights was the observation that levees and other engineering projects in risky areas (such as those below sea level) can actually increase risks by encouraging development. In his thinking as a geographer—and in his work in international relief and his attempt to be "an instrument of social change toward peace and justice" in the world—he drew inspiration from his religious faith as a member of the Society of Friends, better known as Quakers. Looking back over six decades of activity as a geographer and educator, he noted in "Autobiographical Essay," published in 2002, that he had "made some contributions to structures of thought in a few fields [and] several efforts to alter relevant public policy" and that he had done so "in a spirit of trying to be helpful to fellow humans by cooperative, nonviolent methods." White received a B.S. degree at the University of Chicago in 1932, and he went on to earn graduate degrees there. "Floods are acts of God," he wrote in his doctoral dissertation, published with the title "Human Adjustment to Floods" in 1942 (and, with the same title, as a book in 1945), "but flood losses are largely acts of man." In between his years of graduate study, he worked with the National Resources Board under the aegis of the federal Public Works Administration (1934–40), conducting and directing studies of recurrent floods in the Mississippi River Valley and other such land and water problems. At that time he wrote several government pamphlets on drought and flood control, and he lectured in the graduate school at American University (1938–40). In 1941 he was employed by the U.S. Bureau of the Budget as a legislative analyst assigned to reviewing a docket of reports relating to proposed land use and water conservation. Following the entry of the U.S. into World War II, in December 1941, White, a conscientious objector to military service, did alternative service with the American Friends Service Committee. As a delegate of that committee, he went to Vichy, the zone in southern France that remained unoccupied (although collaborationist) after France's surrender to Nazi Germany in 1940. There, he did relief work with refugees who, having fled war-torn places to the north and east, were trying to make their way to Spain and Portugal. After the Germans took over Vichy from the French government of Marechal Henri Philippe Pétain, in November 1942, White was interned in Germany for over a year, until he was released in an exchange of prisoners of war in 1944. While observing the German occupation of France, he became convinced that "man can no more conquer or preserve a civilization by war than he can conquer nature solely by engineering force [rather than] friendly adjustment." Upon his return to the United States, he was appointed an

assistant professor of geography at the University of Chicago. In 1945 he became assistant executive secretary of the American Friends Service Committee, and in that capacity he went to India to administer the American relief program there. Early in 1946 he helped to set up relief services in Germany, and later in the same year he became president of Quaker-founded Haverford College, in Pennsylvania, a position he held until 1955. During that period, in 1949, he was one of a group of prominent Quakers who held talks with American and Soviet diplomats in an effort to reduce Cold War tensions. He was professor of geography at the University of Chicago from 1956 to 1969 and visiting professor at Oxford University in 1962–63. From 1963 to 1969 he chaired the American Friends Service Committee. During the same period he headed the task force that laid the groundwork for the Federal Emergency Management Agency's National Flood Insurance Program, created by Congress in 1968. From 1970 to 1978 he was professor of geography and director of the Institute of Behavioral Science at the University of Colorado. At that university he founded the Natural Hazards Research and Applications Center, which he directed from 1976 to 1984 and from 1992 to 1994. Between 1996 and 1999 he took part in talks with Jordanian, Palestinian, and Israeli scientists and officials aimed at the improvement of water use in the Middle East. He had earlier been engaged in efforts at international cooperation on water systems in Southeast Asia and in Africa. He chaired or was a member of more than a score of Quaker, U.S. government, United Nations, and other panels on environmental and natural-resource matters, including the spread of deserts, losses due to earthquakes, emissions of greenhouse gases and other factors in global climate change, the real possibility of a "nuclear winter" in the event of a nuclear war, and geography education in high schools. He wrote several books, among them *Science and the Future of Arid Lands* (1960) and *Strategies of American Water Management* (1969), and numerous pamphlets and papers. Selections from his writings and lectures were brought together in the volume *Themes from the Work of Gilbert F. White* (1986). White was predeceased by his first wife, Anne Elizabeth Underwood White, and survived by his second wife, Claire Sheridan, and by a son, two daughters, two stepchildren, and four grandchildren. He died at his home in Boulder, Colorado. See *Current Biography* (1953).

Obituary *New York Times* C p10 Oct. 7, 2006

WILSON, AUGUST Apr. 27, 1945–Oct. 2, 2005 Playwright. Between the years 1980 and 2005, Wilson realized a singular theatrical achievement: his completion of an epic 10-play cycle chronicling African-American experience in each decade of the 20th century, chiefly as lived by his fictional families in Pittsburgh's Hill district, where he himself came of age. During Wilson's lifetime eight of his plays reached Broadway, six of them under the direction of Lloyd Richards (who had become Broadway's first black director with *Raisin in the Sun* in 1959): *Ma Rainey's Black Bottom* (1984–85), which earned Wilson the first of his four New York Drama Critics Circle Awards; *Fences* (1987–88), which won the Pulitzer

Prize for drama and the Tony Award for best play and brought James Earl Jones the best-actor Tony; *Joe Turner's Come and Gone* (1988), a Tony nominee; *The Piano Lesson* (1990–91), which garnered for Wilson his second Tony and second Pulitzer; *Two Trains Running* (1992), another Tony nominee; and *Seven Guitars* (1996). The fourth of sixth children, Wilson was born Frederick August Kittel in Pittsburgh, Pennsylvania. (He changed his surname to Wilson when he was 20.) His father was Frederick Kittel, a white baker who had emigrated in childhood from Germany; his mother was Daisy Wilson, a black cleaning woman from North Carolina. He seldom saw his father, who was for the most part an absentee from the household, a two-room cold-water flat in Pittsburgh's Hill district, a poor neighborhood, largely black, with an admixture of Jews and Italian-Americans. Shortly after Wilson graduated from elementary school, his mother divorced Kittel and married David Bedford, a black man who was embittered because of the racism that had cost him a college scholarship in football and whose anger contributed to some trouble with the law. Unlike Fredrick Kittel, Bedford was a good provider and a faithful presence in the family, but he was also a stepfather to whom Wilson could not relate. (Bedford was the inspiration for Troy Maxson, the father in *Fences*, an illiterate garbage collector and former baseball player whose bitterness at the white-controlled system that denied him athletic stardom creates obstacles in his relationships to those close to him.) The Bedfords moved to Hazelwood, a predominantly white working-class Pittsburgh neighborhood, where they experienced incidents of white racism, including a brick thrown through a window of their home. As a freshman at Central Catholic High School in Hazelwood, where he was the only black student, Wilson regularly found anonymous "Go home, nigger" notes on his desk. He transferred in quick succession to the Connelley Vocational School and then to Gladstone High School. He dropped out of Gladstone in the 10th grade, after an apparently racially biased teacher accused him of plagiarizing a paper he had written on Napoleon. From that point on he was self-taught, through omnivorous reading in the local public library and through life on "the street." "I grew up without a father," he once said, in an interview with Jim Davidson for the *Pittsburgh Gazette* (July 19, 1982). "When I was twenty I went down onto Center Avenue [in the Hill district] to learn from the community how to be a man. My education comes from the years I spent there. Mostly I'd listen to the older guys." Among other influences on his development as a black "cultural nationalist" (as he considered himself) were the poetry and plays of Amiri Baraka, the paintings of Romare Bearden, and, above all, the music known as the blues, in which he educated himself by collecting old vinyl recordings of Bessie Smith and other such singers and musicians that he found in thrift shops. "It's like our culture is in the music," he told Sandra G. Shannon in an interview for the *African American Review*. "And the musicians are way ahead of the writers I see. So I'm trying to close the gap." Following an abortive enlistment in the U.S. Army (1962–63), Wilson worked at various jobs, from gardener to short-order cook. In 1965 he bought

his first typewriter, a second-hand Royal. His early writings were poems—some of which were eventually published in two black-oriented little magazines at the University of Pennsylvania—and unpublished short stories in which he began to develop the mastery of authentic vernacular dialogue he would bring, slowly, over a period of many years, to his playwriting. In 1968, to "politicize the community and raise consciousness," he joined with the playwright and teacher Rob Penny in founding Black Horizons on the Hill, a combined art gallery and theatrical troupe in the Hill district. At Black Horizons, while continuing to support himself at menial jobs, he began trying his hand at directing, without ever having seen a professional play. That occurred in 1976, when he saw a production of Athol Fugard's *Sizwe Bansi Is Dead* at the Pittsburgh Public Theater. During that same year his tentative stage piece *The Homecoming* was produced at the Kuntu Repertory Theatre at the University of Pittsburgh. Another early short dramatic effort, *Fullerton Street*, was subsequently produced at the Allegheny Repertory Theater in Pittsburgh. In 1978 Wilson moved to St. Paul, Minnesota, where his friend Claude Purdy had become director of Penumbra, a black theatre troupe. With Purdy's encouragement, he progressed in his dramatic craftsmanship while supporting himself by cooking for a Catholic group called the Little Brothers of the Poor and writing educational scripts for children at the Science Museum of Minnesota. In 1980 he obtained a $200-a-month fellowship at the Minneapolis Playwrights Center. Additional financial support was provided by his second wife, Judy Oliver, a social worker whom he married in 1981. At Penumbra, Claude Purdy directed a production called *Black Bart and the Sacred Hills*, adapted from some of Wilson's poems. Wilson began to find his true theatrical voice in his revisions of *Jitney*, his first full-length play, on which he worked on and off for years. That two-act work, set in a Pittsburgh gypsy-cab station, was first produced by the Allegheny Repertory Theater in 1982. Its perfected version had its professional premiere at the Pittsburgh Public Theater 14 years later. Another long-nurtured project was the two-act *Ma Rainey's Black Bottom*. An exception to Wilson's usual Hill district settings, that play takes place in 1927 in a Chicago recording studio where the legendary blues singer Ma Rainey and her band are recording her version of the Black Bottom, a popular dance number of the time, under the exploitive control of a white producer and white agent. The play was submitted to the National Playwrights Conference, which gave it a staged reading at the Eugene O'Neill Center in Waterford, Connecticut, in 1982. Lloyd Richards, the artistic director of the conference as well as the dean of the Yale University School of Drama, coached Wilson in refining the play, staged its premiere at the Yale Repertory Theater in New Haven in April 1984, and took it to the Cort Theater in Manhattan the following October, initiating Wilson's string of Broadway productions. Wilson completed his 10-play cycle with *King Hedley II* (directed on Broadway by Marion McClinton in 2001), *Gem of the Ocean* (directed on Broadway by Kenny Leon in 2004–05), and *Radio Golf* (directed at Yale by Timothy Douglas in 2005). There was a long feud between Wilson and the white theatrical director and critic Robert Brustein, who believes that "theater works best as a unifying rather than a segregating medium." Wilson vehemently countered that assimilationist view with the declaration that African-American theater, like African-American experience, is a unique, discrete, and autonomous territory and that "we cannot allow others to have authority over our cultural and spiritual products." To him, the idea of an all-black cast playing *Death of a Salesman* was as much "an insult to our intelligence" as that of an all-white production of *Raisin in the Sun*. "We reject any attempt to blot us out, to reinvent our history, to ignore our presence. . . . We do not need colorblind casting; we need some theaters to develop our playwrights." Wilson was married three times and divorced twice. He was survived by this third wife, the theatrical costume designer Constanza Romero, and their daughter, Azula Carmen, and by another daughter, Sakina Ansari, from his first marriage, to Brenda Burton. He died in Seattle, Washington, where he had been living since 1990. See *Current Biography* (1987).

Obituary *New York Times* A p1+ Oct. 3, 2005

WINTERS, SHELLEY Aug. 18, 1922–Jan 14, 2006 Actress. One of the most durable of the movie stars who began their careers during the golden age of the old studio system, Shelley Winters amassed more than 100 feature-film credits over the span of half a century. The daughter of an immigrant tailor's cutter and an amateur operatic soprano, she was born Shirley Schrift in East St. Louis, Illinois. She lived there until she was 11, when her father, gravitating to Manhattan's garment district, took the family east. After some promising experiences in theater, including playing minor roles on Broadway, she moved in 1943 to Hollywood, where she shared an apartment with another starlet, Marilyn Monroe. Surviving what she described as the grade-B "dumb blond bombshell" typecasting that studios tried to force on her, she began establishing early on the reputation for impressive character portrayals that buoyed her career as she aged. She first attracted serious attention in the Desdemona-like role of Pat Kroll, the flirtatious young woman murdered by her mad Shakespearean actor lover (Ronald Colman) in *A Double Life* (1947), and she drew the first of four Academy Award nominations with her portrayal of another homicide victim, Alice Tripp, in *A Place in the Sun* (1951). Similarly, she was the murdered mother, Willa Harper, in *The Night of the Hunter* (1955) and the exploited starlet, Dixie Evans, who also met death, in *The Big Knife* (1955). For her supporting role as Mrs. Petronella Van Daan, one of the eight Dutch Jews hiding from Nazis in *The Diary of Anne Frank* (1959), she won the first of her two Oscars. The second was for her supporting performance as Rose-Ann D'Arcy, the abusive mother of a blind daughter in *A Patch of Blue* (1965). As Charlotte Haze Humbert, she was the tragically deceived mother of the nymphet in *Lolita* (1962). Her last Oscar nomination was for her role as Belle Rosen, the heroic former swimming champion in the ocean-liner disaster movie *The Poseidon Adventure* (1972). Among her other memorable screen roles were those

of the vulnerable Myrtle Wilson in *The Great Gatsby* (1949), the sexy title role in *Frenchie* (1950), Lola Manners in *Winchester '73* (1950), Ruby, the sexually insatiable girlfriend of the title character in *Alfie* (1966), Ma Barker in *Bloody Mama* (1970), Fay Lapinsky, a Jewish mother, in *Next Stop Greenwich Village* (1976), Queen Rachel in *King of the Gypsies* (1978), the powerful Hollywood agent Eva Brown in *S.O.B.*, and Mrs. Touchett, the selfish aunt in *The Portrait of a Lady* (1996). In addition to her feature-film roles, she had numerous dramatic credits on television, including the part of the grandmother in the situation comedy *Roseanne*. On Broadway, she created the role of Celia Pope in *A Hatful of Rain* in 1955 and that of Minnie in *Minnie's Boys* in 1970. Several one-act plays written by her were produced Off-Broadway in 1970 under the title *One Night Stands of a Noisy Passenger*. She wrote two autobiographies, *Shelley, Also Known as Shirley* (1960) and *Shirley II: The Middle of My Century* (1989). She was married to and divorced from three husbands: Paul Mayer, Vittorio Gassman, and Anthony Franciosa. On her deathbed she married Gerry DeFord, who had been her companion for 19 years. She died in Beverly Hills, California. In addition to DeFord, her survivors included her daughter, Victoria-Gina Gassman, and two grandchildren. See *Current Biography* (1952).

Obituary *New York Times* I p30 Jan. 15, 2006

WISE, ROBERT Sep. 10, 1914–Sep. 14, 2005 Filmmaker. Wise was a Hollywood cutting-room journeyman who matured into a masterly director and producer of outstanding motion pictures in a wide range of genres, from horror and the Western to caper, melodrama, and the musical. His *The Day the Earth Stood Still* (1951) is a classic in the science-fiction genre, as *The Haunting* (1963) is in the gothic genre. An early personal favorite of his among his works was *The Set-Up* (1949), a gritty, touching drama about the career denouement of an aging prize fighter. Another of his favorites was *I Want to Live!* (1955), a harrowing psychological rendering of the last days in the life of Virginia Graham, executed in San Quentin's gas chamber in 1955, a movie for which he was nominated for the Academy Award for best director. He first received that award for *Somebody Up There Likes Me* (1956), one of his biggest hits, a biographical picture based on the autobiography of the middleweight boxing champion Rocky Graziano (played by Paul Newman). His screen adaptation of the musical *West Side Story* (1961), a huge box-office success, brought him his second Oscar as director (shared with the choreographer Jerome Robbins) as well as his first as producer (that is, for best picture); it also earned several other Academy Awards. His ability to handle a bittersweet love story was confirmed with his direction of *Two for the Seesaw* (1962). He again won the best-director and best-picture Oscars with the musical *The Sound of Music* (1965), and he was nominated for best picture for *The Sand Pebbles* (1966), an action/romance movie starring Steve McQueen as a U.S. gunboat sailor on the Yangtze River in 1926. Wise began his career in 1933 as an editing-room messenger at RKO Pictures, where he became an apprentice to the seasoned editor T. K. Wood and worked his way up through sound editing to become a film editor in 1939. He was nominated for an Oscar for his editing of Orson Welles's *Citizen Kane* (1940), and he was Welles's surrogate in supervising the editing of *The Magnificent Ambersons* (1942). His first credit behind the camera was as co-director of the horror picture *The Curse of the Cat People* (1944), and his first as sole director was *Mademoiselle Fifi* (1944). Following a string of B pictures, he graduated to the A category with his direction of the adult Western *Blood on the Moon* (1948). After leaving RKO, in 1949, he directed variously under the aegis of Warner Brothers, Twentieth-Century-Fox, Metro-Goldwyn-Mayer, and several independent production companies, including his own. The first film that he produced was *Return to Paradise* (1953). The first that he produced/directed was *Odds Against Tomorrow* (1959), a taut, suspenseful heist movie with a documentary-like texture and an anti-racism message. He later produced/directed *The Andromeda Strain* (1971), *Two People* (1973), and *The Hindenburg* (1975). In 1967 he received the Irving G. Thalberg Memorial Award for his career work as a producer. As director alone he made some 30 movies, including *The Body Snatcher* (1945), *So Big* (1953), *Executive Suite* (1954), *Tribute to a Bad Man* (1956), *Run Silent, Run Deep* (1958), *Audrey Rose* (1977), *Star!* (1968), and *Star Trek: The Motion Picture* (1979). After nine years without credits, he directed the musical *Rooftops* (1989), his last theatrical film, and 12 years later he directed *A Storm in Summer* (2000) for television. He was married to Patricia Doyle from 1942 until her death, in 1975, and to Millicent Franklin from 1977 until his death. In addition to his widow, he was survived by a son from his first marriage, a stepdaughter, and a granddaughter. He died in Los Angeles. See *Current Biography* (1989).

Obituary *New York Times* B p8 Sep. 16, 2005

WYATT, JANE Aug. 12, 1911–Oct. 20, 2006 Actress. After establishing her versatility in comedy and drama on Broadway and in motion pictures in the 1930s and 1940s, Jane Wyatt turned to television, where she won regular roles during that medium's golden age of live drama, beginning in 1951, and later accrued myriad dramatic credits in filmed TV productions. She became best known as Margaret Anderson, the near-perfect pre-feminist suburban housewife and mother in the long-running situation comedy *Father Knows Best* (1954–62), a role for which she won three Emmy Awards. Jane Waddington Wyatt was born into a distinguished Catholic family in Campgaw, New Jersey, and raised in New York City, where she attended the exclusive Chapin School before matriculating at Barnard College. She was dropped from the New York Social Register soon after she left college to pursue a career as a professional actress. (She was later reinstated.) Between 1930 and 1933 she alternated between minor ingénue roles in summer stock and on Broadway. During 1933 she appeared on Broadway as, successively, Pauline Lacey in *Evensong*, Eva Locke in *Conquest*, and Lois Ardsley in *For Services Rendered*. Within the same year she replaced Margaret Sullavan as Paula Jordan in *Dinner at Eight*, and she remained in

that role on a national tour. Her subsequent Broadway credits included Theresa Farley Battle in the comedy *The Joyous Season* (1934), Janet Evans in Harry Segall's fantasy *Lost Horizons* (1934; not to be confused with the book and film *Lost Horizon*), Hester Grantham in *The Bishop Misbehaves* (1935), Princess Claudine in the comedy *Save Me the Waltz* (1938), Fay Tucker in the drama *Night Music* (1940), the female leads in *Quiet Please!* (1940) and *Hope for the Best* (1945), and Nina Denery in *The Autumn Garden* (1951). Between 1934 and 1950 she had predominantly beguiling or at least sympathetic roles in at least 27 motion pictures, ranging from Westerns and wartime military morale boosters to comedies and crime dramas. Among those portrayals were Sondra Bizet, the love interest of the Ronald Colman character in *Lost Horizon* (Frank Capra's 1937 screen adaptation of James Hilton's novel about Shangri-La), the supporting roles of Jane in *Gentleman's Agreement* (1947) and Lois Macauley in *Our Very Own* (1950), the featured roles of Aggie Hunter in *None But the Lonely Heart* (1944), Sue Forbes in *Pitfall* (1948), Miss Darlington in *No Minor Vices* (1948), and Janet Pringle in *My Blue Heaven* (1950), and the top-billed female roles of Madge Harvey in *Boomerang!* (1947), Dr. Edith Cabot in *Canadian Pacific* (1949), Mary Morgan in *Task Force* (1949), and Marjorie Byrne in *House by the River* (1950). Her final movie credit in that early phase of her career was her starring portrayal, against type, of Lois Frazer, the adulteress who kills her husband in the film noir *The Man Who Cheated Himself* (1950). She could not understand why her employability in the movie studios suddenly came to a halt in 1950 until a friend explained to her that she had been blacklisted and thus had become a victim of Hollywood's cooperation at that time with the congressional House Un-American Activities Committee's Cold War hunt for perceived political subversives. While Wyatt had never been a Communist, she was apparently stigmatized for having been, as she said, at the very worst, "prematurely anti-fascist." Moving into television, during the 1950s she was cast in many live productions in such dramatic showcases as *Robert Montgomery Presents*, *The Motorola Television Hour*, and *Studio One*. On the sitcom *Father Knows Best*, she played the understanding wife of Jim Anderson (Robert Young), an insurance salesman, and mother of their three children. The filmed weekly show began on the CBS network (1954–55), moved to NBC (1955–58), and finished its run back on CBS (1958–62). Tom Shales of the *Washington Post* has pointed out that while the Andersons were in many ways typical of the 1950s "vanilla-pudding" version of the American family, "the show operated on a higher plane than similar sitcoms" of the time. Shales recalled that, as Margaret Anderson, Wyatt "was pretty in a radiantly wholesome way," was a "heavenly mom who . . . had her little human failings," was "not so sweet as to be unbelievable," and "beautifully and memorably made believers of us all." Among Wyatt's later television credits were scores of roles in dramas and episodes of various dramatic series and situation comedies and a number of made-for-TV movies, including two *Father Knows Best* spin-offs. In *Journey to Babel* (1967), an episode of *Star Trek*, she played Amanda, the human mother of

Mr. Spock (Leonard Nimoy), Spock being the member of the spaceship *Enterprise* crew whose father was a native of the hypothetical planet Vulcan. She returned to that role in the feature film *Star Trek IV: The Voyage Home* (1986). Wyatt died at her home in Bel Air, California. She was predeceased by her husband, Edgar Bethune Ward, and survived by two sons, three grandchildren, and at least five—some sources say seven—great-grandchildren. See *Current Biography* (1957).

Obituary *New York Times* B p8 Oct. 23, 2006

YARD, MOLLY July 6, 1912–Sep. 21, 2005 Social activist; an indefatigable lifelong agitator in progressive causes who gained public recognition when she was elected president of the National Organization for Women (NOW), in 1987. After decades of work in the student, labor, and civil rights movements, Yard had joined the Pittsburgh chapter of NOW in 1974. Three years later she moved to NOW's headquarters in Washington, D.C., to head the organization's lobbying of Congress for an extension of the deadline for ratification of the Equal Rights Amendment (ERA) that had been passed by Congress in 1972. After the deadline was extended to 1982, she participated in lobbying state legislatures, but that effort fell short of obtaining the approval of the three-quarters necessary for ratification. Later, as a senior staff member of NOW's Political Action Committee and as NOW's political director (1985–87), she concentrated on the effort to elect more women to state legislatures. Under her presidency (1987–91), NOW organized the March for Women's Equality/Women's Lives that drew to Washington 600,000 marchers in support of abortion rights and the ERA and helped to bring about the rejection of the nomination of Judge Robert H. Bork for the U.S. Supreme Court, the passage of the Civil Rights Restoration Act of 1988, and the inclusion of women's rights in the Civil Rights Act of 1991. The fierce bellicosity that Yard brought to the feminist cause had its incubation in China, where she spent the first dozen years of her life. When she was born, to American Methodist missionary parents in Shanghai, her father's Chinese friends gave him a "consolation gift" for his not having been blessed with a son. "I grew up with that whole devaluation of myself because I was female," she said in retrospect. "It's outrageous, and it stays with you all your life." While at Swarthmore College, where she earned a degree in political science in the early 1930s, she led a successful effort to ban sororities and fraternities from the campus after a Jewish student was denied admission to the Kappa Alpha Theta sorority. After college she served successively as national organization secretary and chairperson of the American Student Union, positions that brought her into close acquaintance with Eleanor Roosevelt. She became a board member of Americans for Democratic Action, founded by Eleanor Roosevelt and others in 1947, and she was involved in Democratic Party politics locally and nationally, from reforming Philadelphia's city government and supporting Helen Gahagan Douglas in her unsuccessful U.S. Senate race against Richard M. Nixon in California to working regionally in the presidential campaigns of John F. Kennedy and George S. McGovern. Both locally and nationally, she was involved early on in the cause of racial equality, especially in housing, employment, and education, and her activism grew apace with the momentum of the civil rights movement in the 1950s and 1960s. In Pittsburgh, Pennsylvania, she chaired the YWCA's Civil Rights Committee; nationally, she worked with the Leadership Conference on Civil Rights and was heavily involved in the campaigns for the passage of civil rights legislation; in western Pennsylvania, she was the regional organizer for the 1963 March on Washington. After stepping down as president of NOW, Yard worked until the late 1990s at the Feminist Majority Foundation. She died at the Fair Oaks Nursing Home in Pittsburgh. She was predeceased by her husband, Sylvester Garrett, and a daughter and survived by two sons and five grandchildren. See *Current Biography* (1988).

Obituary *New York Times* C p19 Sep. 22, 2005

CLASSIFICATION BY PROFESSION—2006

ANTHROPOLOGY
Dawdy, Shannon Lee
Labov, William
Marcus, George E.
Reichs, Kathy
Wolpoff, Milford

ARCHAEOLOGY
Davis-Kimball, Jeannine
Dawdy, Shannon Lee

ARCHITECTURE
Duany, Andrés and Plater-
    Zyberk, Elizabeth
McDonough, William
Oppenheim, Chad

ART
Auth, Tony
Carone, Nicolas
Elgin, Suzette Haden
Hammons, David
Hancock, Trenton Doyle
Pennington, Ty
Prada, Miuccia
Zittel, Andrea

ASTRONOMY
Squyres, Steven

BUSINESS
Abrams, Jonathan
Barnes, Brenda
Barton, Jacqueline K.
Belcher, Angela
Bell, James A.
Buckingham, Marcus
Corzine, Jon
Dobbs, Lou
Fu, Ping
Hastings, Reed
Hunt, Swanee
Ive, Jonathan
Jones, Scott
Karpinski, Janis
Krawcheck, Sallie
Laimbeer, Bill
Lawal, Kase L.

Lee, Debra L.
Magliozzi, Tom and Ray
Musk, Elon
Nagin, C. Ray
Nooyi, Indra K.
Pennington, Ty
Posen, Zac
Prada, Miuccia
Rojas, Rudy
Romney, Mitt
Scott, H. Lee
Semel, Terry
Stringer, Howard
Tillerson, Rex
Wales, Jimmy
Warner, Mark R.
West, Kanye

COMPUTERS
Fu, Ping
Hastings, Reed

CONSERVATION
Beehler, Bruce
Benyus, Janine M.
McDonough, William

DANCE
Chase, Alison Becker

ECONOMICS
Bartlett, Bruce
Bernanke, Ben S.
Galbraith, James K.

EDUCATION
Alito, Samuel
Barton, Jacqueline K.
Behe, Michael J.
Belcher, Angela
Benyus, Janine M.
Bernanke, Ben S.
Bosselaar, Laure-Anne
Clarke, Richard
Dawdy, Shannon Lee
Elgin, Suzette Haden
Fagles, Robert
Fu, Ping

Gaines, Donna
Galbraith, James K.
Grossman, Edith
Gupta, Sanjay
Hastings, Reed
Hersch, Fred
Hollander, Robert B.
Hunt, Swanee
Jarecki, Eugene
Kavafian, Ani
Kim, Jim Yong
Klinkenborg, Verlyn
Knoll, Andrew H.
Koh, Jennifer
Labov, William
Leo, John
Lewis, Dorothy Otnow
Marcus, George E.
McDonough, William
Meier, Deborah
Murray, Donald M.
Olopade, Olufunmilayo
Palmer, Violet
Randall, Lisa
Reichs, Kathy
Spelke, Elizabeth
Squyres, Steven
Stabenow, Debbie
Stein, Janice Gross
Stern, Jessica
Taylor, Herman A.
Tilghman, Shirley M.
Valdes-Rodriguez, Alisa
Weinstein, Allen
Young, Kimberly S.

FASHION
Duff, Hilary
Posen, Zac
Prada, Miuccia

FILM
Burrows, James
Colbert, Stephen
Corbijn, Anton
Duff, Hilary
Falco, Edie

Flagg, Fannie
Haggis, Paul
Hastings, Reed
Haysbert, Dennis
Jarecki, Eugene
Ledger, Heath
Martin, Jesse L.
Meat Loaf
Parker, Mary-Louise
Pennington, Ty
Reeves, Dianne
Roberts, Tony
Semel, Terry
Silverman, Sarah
Smits, Jimmy
Vaughn, Vince
White, Armond

FINANCE
Lawal, Kase L.

GASTRONOMY
Bourdain, Anthony

GOVERNMENT AND
    POLITICS
Alito, Samuel
Bartlett, Bruce
Bernanke, Ben S.
Boehner, John
Bolten, Joshua
Bolton, John R.
Brazile, Donna
Clarke, Richard
Corzine, Jon
Durbin, Richard J.
Fitzgerald, Patrick J.
Hadley, Stephen
Hayden, Michael V.
Hunt, Swanee
Khalilzad, Zalmay
McCain, John S.
Nagin, C. Ray
Pace, Peter
Roberts, John G.
Romney, Mitt
Rounds, Michael
Rubin, Edward M.
Snow, Tony
Stabenow, Debbie
Stein, Janice Gross
Stern, Jessica
Warner, Mark R.
Weinstein, Allen

Wilson, Heather

JOURNALISM
Auth, Tony
Brooks, Geraldine
Cooper, Anderson
Dionne, E. J. Jr.
Dobbs, Lou
Guillen, Ozzie
Gupta, Sanjay
King, Florence
Klinkenborg, Verlyn
Kristof, Nicholas D.
Leo, John
Logan, Lara
Miller, Judith
Murray, Donald M.
Schieffer, Bob
Snow, Tony
Truss, Lynne
Valdes-Rodriguez, Alisa
Vargas, Elizabeth
White, Armond
Winchester, Simon

LAW
Alito, Samuel
Bolten, Joshua
Bolton, John R.
Durbin, Richard J.
Fitzgerald, Patrick J.
Hadley, Stephen
Hayes, Edward
Roberts, John G.

LITERATURE
Bosselaar, Laure-Anne
Bourdain, Anthony
Brooks, Geraldine
Carson, Anne
Clarke, Richard
Colbert, Stephen
Elgin, Suzette Haden
Fagles, Robert
Flagg, Fannie
Grossman, Edith
Hancock, Trenton Doyle
Hollander, Robert B.
King, Florence
Klinkenborg, Verlyn
Lethem, Jonathan
Murray, Donald M.
Pevear, Richard and
    Volokhonsky, Larissa

Reichs, Kathy
Smith, Ali
Truss, Lynne
Valdes-Rodriguez, Alisa
Williams, Tad
Winchester, Simon

MEDICINE
Gupta, Sanjay
Kim, Jim Yong
Olopade, Olufunmilayo
Rubin, Edward M.
Taylor, Herman A.
Thomas, William H.

MILITARY
Casey, George W. Jr.
Hayden, Michael V.
Karpinski, Janis
McCain, John S.
Pace, Peter
Wilson, Heather

MUSIC
Apple, Fiona
Black Eyed Peas
Clarkson, Kelly
Douglas, Dave
Duff, Hilary
Hersch, Fred
Kavafian, Ani
Koh, Jennifer
Meat Loaf
Miller, Marcus
Reeves, Dianne
Scelsa, Vin
Semel, Terry
Van Zandt, Steven
West, Kanye

NONFICTION
Auth, Tony
Bartlett, Bruce
Beehler, Bruce
Behe, Michael J.
Benyus, Janine M.
Bernanke, Ben S.
Bourdain, Anthony
Brooks, Geraldine
Buckingham, Marcus
Clarke, Richard
Davis-Kimball, Jeannine
de Waal, Frans
Dionne, E. J. Jr.

Dobbs, Lou
Elgin, Suzette Haden
Flowers, Vonetta
Gaines, Donna
Galbraith, James K.
Hayes, Edward
Holdsclaw, Chamique
Hollander, Robert B.
Hunt, Swanee
Karpinski, Janis
Kim, Jim Yong
King, Florence
Klinkenborg, Verlyn
Knoll, Andrew H.
Kristof, Nicholas D.
Labov, William
Leo, John
Lethem, Jonathan
Lewis, Dorothy Otnow
Magliozzi, Tom and Ray
Marcus, George E.
McCain, John S.
McDonough, William
Meier, Deborah
Miller, Judith
Murray, Donald M.
Osteen, Joel
Pennington, Ty
Schieffer, Bob
Squyres, Steven
Stein, Janice Gross
Stern, Jessica
Thomas, William H.
Truss, Lynne
Warren, Rick
Weinstein, Allen
White, Armond
Winchester, Simon
Wolpoff, Milford
Young, Kimberly S.

ORGANIZATIONS
Beehler, Bruce
Benyus, Janine M.
Elgin, Suzette Haden
Hunt, Swanee
Kim, Jim Yong

PALEONTOLOGY
Knoll, Andrew H.

PHILANTHROPY
Hastings, Reed
Hunt, Swanee

Warner, Mark R.

PHOTOGRAPHY
Corbijn, Anton
Friedlander, Lee
Hunt, Swanee
Winchester, Simon

PSYCHIATRY
Lewis, Dorothy Otnow

PSYCHOLOGY
de Waal, Frans
Spelke, Elizabeth
Young, Kimberly S.

PUBLISHING
Lee, Debra L.
Talese, Nan
Wales, Jimmy

RADIO
Brazile, Donna
Dobbs, Lou
Logan, Lara
Magliozzi, Tom and Ray
Scelsa, Vin
Schieffer, Bob
Truss, Lynne
Van Zandt, Steven

RELIGION
Behe, Michael J.
Hunt, Swanee
Jefferts Schori, Katharine
Osteen, Joel
Warren, Rick

SCIENCE
Barton, Jacqueline K.
Beehler, Bruce
Behe, Michael J.
Belcher, Angela
de Waal, Frans
Jefferts Schori, Katharine
Nachtigall, Paul E.
Olopade, Olufunmilayo
Randall, Lisa
Rubin, Edward M.
Stern, Jessica
Tilghman, Shirley M.
Winchester, Simon
Wolpoff, Milford

SOCIAL ACTIVISM
Kim, Jim Yong
Meier, Deborah
Tilghman, Shirley M.
Warren, Rick

SOCIAL SCIENCES
Gaines, Donna
Labov, William
Marcus, George E.

SPORTS
Bettis, Jerome
Blake, James
Cohen, Sasha
Cowher, Bill
Davis, Shani
Donovan, Landon
Duke, Annie
Flowers, Vonetta
Franco, Julio
Glavine, Tom
Guerrero, Vladimir
Guillen, Ozzie
Holdsclaw, Chamique
Laimbeer, Bill
Moss, Randy
Ohno, Apolo Anton
Palmer, Violet
Santana, Johan
Smith, Steve
Stewart, Tony
Tarver, Antonio
Taylor, Jermain
Tomlinson, LaDainian
Wade, Dwyane
Willis, Dontrelle

TECHNOLOGY
Abrams, Jonathan
Belcher, Angela
Ive, Jonathan
Jones, Scott
Musk, Elon
Semel, Terry
Stringer, Howard
Wales, Jimmy

TELEVISION
Bettis, Jerome
Bourdain, Anthony
Brazile, Donna
Burrows, James
Clarke, Richard

Colbert, Stephen
Cooper, Anderson
Dobbs, Lou
Duff, Hilary
Duke, Annie
Falco, Edie
Flagg, Fannie
Guillen, Ozzie
Gupta, Sanjay
Haggis, Paul
Hammer, Bonnie
Haysbert, Dennis
Lee, Debra L.
Logan, Lara
Martin, Jesse L.

Miller, Marcus
Osteen, Joel
Parker, Mary-Louise
Pennington, Ty
Reichs, Kathy
Roberts, Tony
Schieffer, Bob
Semel, Terry
Silverman, Sarah
Smits, Jimmy
Stein, Janice Gross
Stringer, Howard
Van Zandt, Steven
Vargas, Elizabeth

THEATER
  Burrows, James
  Colbert, Stephen
  Falco, Edie
  Flagg, Fannie
  Martin, Jesse L.
  Meat Loaf
  Parker, Mary-Louise
  Roberts, Tony
  Silverman, Sarah
  Smits, Jimmy

CUMULATED INDEX 2001–2006

This is the index to the January 2001–November 2006 issues. It also lists obituaries that appear only in this yearbook. For the index to the 1940–2005 biographies, see Current Biography: Cumulated Index 1940–2005.

Bedford, Sybille obit Yrbk
2006
Beehler, Bruce Aug 2006
Beene, Geoffrey obit Mar
2005
Beers, Rand Oct 2004
Behar, Ruth May 2005
Behe, Michael J. Feb 2006
Bel Geddes, Barbara obit Yrbk
2005
Belaúnde Terry, Fernando
obit Yrbk 2002
Belcher, Angela Jul 2006
Belichick, Bill Sep 2002
Bell, James A. Jul 2006
Bellow, Saul obit Aug 2005
Benchley, Peter obit Jun 2006
Benedict XVI Sep 2005
Bennett, Lerone Jr. Jan 2001
Bennington, Chester see
Linkin Park
Bentsen, Lloyd obit Oct 2006
Benyus, Janine M. Mar 2006
Benzer, Seymour May 2001
Berio, Luciano obit Yrbk 2003
Berle, Milton obit Yrbk 2002
Berlin, Steve see Los Lobos
Berlitz, Charles obit Yrbk
2004
Berman, Lazar obit Yrbk 2005
Bernanke, Ben S. Mar 2006
Bernhard Leopold, consort of
Juliana, Queen of the
Netherlands obit Mar 2005
Bernstein, Elmer Jun 2003
Berrigan, Philip obit Mar
2003
Berryman, Guy see Coldplay
Berton, Pierre obit Yrbk 2005
Bertozzi, Carolyn R. Jul 2003
Bethe, Hans obit Aug 2005
Bethune, Gordon M. Jun 2001
Bettis, Jerome Aug 2006
Bible, Geoffrey C. Feb 2002
Big Boi see OutKast
Bilandic, Michael A. obit Apr
2002
Biller, Moe obit Yrbk 2004
Birendra Bir Bikram Shah
Dev, King of Nepal obit Sep
2001
Bishop, Eric see Foxx, Jamie
Bittman, Mark Feb 2005
Björk Jul 2001
Black Eyed Peas Oct 2006
Black, Jack Feb 2002
Blackburn, Elizabeth H. Jul
2001
Blades, Joan see Blades, Joan
and Boyd, Wes
Blades, Joan and Boyd, Wes
Aug 2004
Blaine, David Apr 2001

Blake, James Mar 2006
Blakemore, Michael May
2001
Blanco, Kathleen Jun 2004
Blass, Bill obit Nov 2002
Blind Boys of Alabama Oct
2001
blink-182 Aug 2002
Block, Herbert L. obit Jan
2002
Bloomberg, Michael R. Mar
2002
Blount, Winton Malcolm obit
Jan 2003
Blur Nov 2003
Blythe, Stephanie Aug 2004
Bocelli, Andrea Jan 2002
Boehner, John Apr 2006
Boland, Edward P. obit Feb
2002
Bolten, Joshua Jul 2006
Bolton, John R. Feb 2006
Bond, Julian Jul 2001
Bontecou, Lee Mar 2004
Boorstin, Daniel J. obit Yrbk
2004
Borge, Victor obit Mar 2001
Borodina, Olga Feb 2002
Borst, Lyle B. obit Yrbk 2002
Bosch, Juan obit Feb 2002
Bosselaar, Laure-Anne Sep
2006
Boudreau, Lou obit Oct 2001
Boulud, Daniel Jan 2005
Bourdain, Anthony Jan 2006
Bourdon, Rob see Linkin Park
Bowden, Mark Jan 2002
Boyd, John W. Feb 2001
Boyd, Wes see Blades, Joan
and Boyd, Wes
Bracken, Eddie obit Feb 2003
Brady, Tom Aug 2004
Bragg, Rick Apr 2002
Branch, Michelle May 2005
Brando, Marlon obit Yrbk
2004
Bravo, Rose Marie Jun 2004
Brazile, Donna Mar 2006
Breathitt, Edward T. obit Sep
2004
Breen, Edward D. Jul 2004
Brenly, Bob Apr 2002
Brewer, Roy M. obit Yrbk
2006
Brier, Bob Sep 2002
Brier, Robert see Brier, Bob
Brin, Sergey and Page, Larry
Oct 2001
Brinkley, David obit Sep 2003
Brodeur, Martin Nov 2002
Brody, Adrien Jul 2003
Broeg, Bob May 2002
Brokaw, Tom Nov 2002

Bronson, Charles obit Mar
2004
Brooks & Dunn Sep 2004
Brooks, David Apr 2004
Brooks, Donald obit Yrbk
2005
Brooks, Geraldine Aug 2006
Brooks, Gwendolyn obit Feb
2001
Brooks, Kix see Brooks &
Dunn
Brooks, Vincent Jun 2003
Brower, David obit Feb 2001
Brown, Aaron Mar 2003
Brown, Charles L. obit Sep
2004
Brown, Claude obit Apr 2002
Brown, Dan May 2004
Brown, Dee obit Mar 2003
Brown, J. Carter obit Yrbk
2002
Brown, Jesse obit Yrbk 2002
Brown, Junior Nov 2004
Brown, Kwame Feb 2002
Brown, Lee P. Sep 2002
Brown, Robert McAfee obit
Nov 2001
Brown, Ronald K. May 2002
Browning, John obit Jun 2003
Brueggemann, Ingar Nov 2001
Brumel, Valery obit Jun 2003
Bryant, C. Farris obit Yrbk
2002
Brynner, Rock Mar 2005
Bryson, David see Counting
Crows
Buchanan, Laura see King,
Florence
Buchholz, Horst obit Aug
2003
Buckingham, Marcus Aug
2006
Buckland, Jon see Coldplay
Buckley, Priscilla L. Apr 2002
Budge, Hamer H. obit Yrbk
2003
Bujones, Fernando obit Yrbk
2006
Bundy, William P. obit Feb
2001
Bunim, Mary-Ellis obit Yrbk
2004 see Bunim, Mary-
Ellis, and Murray, Jonathan
Bunim, Mary-Ellis, and
Murray, Jonathan May 2002
Burford, Anne Gorsuch see
Gorsuch, Anne
Burgess, Carter L. obit Yrbk
2002
Burnett, Mark May 2001
Burroughs, Augusten Apr
2004
Burrows, James Oct 2006

Burrows, Stephen Nov 2003
Burstyn, Mike May 2005
Burtt, Ben May 2003
Bush, George W. Aug 2001
Bush, Laura Jun 2001
Bushnell, Candace Nov 2003
Busiek, Kurt Sep 2005
Butcher, Susan obit Yrbk 2006
Butler, R. Paul see Marcy, Geoffrey W., and Butler, R. Paul
Buttons, Red obit Yrbk 2006

Caballero, Linda see La India
Cactus Jack see Foley, Mick
Calderón, Sila M. Nov 2001
Caldwell, Sarah obit Yrbk 2006
Callaghan, James obit Yrbk 2005
Calle, Sophie May 2001
Camp, John see Sandford, John
Campbell, Viv see Def Leppard
Canada, Geoffrey Feb 2005
Canin, Ethan Aug 2001
Cannon, Howard W. obit Yrbk 2002
Cantwell, Maria Feb 2005
Canty, Brendan see Fugazi
Capa, Cornell Jul 2005
Capriati, Jennifer Nov 2001
Caras, Roger A. obit Jul 2001
Card, Andrew H. Jr. Nov 2003
Carlson, Margaret Nov 2003
Carmines, Al obit Yrbk 2005
Carmona, Richard Jan 2003
Carney, Art obit Yrbk 2004
Carone, Nicholas see Carone, Nicolas
Carone, Nicolas Jul 2006
Carroll-Abbing, J. Patrick obit Nov 2001
Carroll, Vinnette obit Feb 2003
Carson, Anne May 2006
Carson, Johnny obit Jul 2005
Carter, Benny obit Oct 2003
Carter, Jimmy see Blind Boys of Alabama
Carter, Regina Oct 2003
Carter, Shawn see Jay-Z
Carter, Vince Apr 2002
Cartier-Bresson, Henri obit Yrbk 2004
Cary, Frank T. obit May 2006
Casey, George W. Jr. Mar 2006
Cash, Johnny obit Jan 2004
Cassini, Oleg obit Yrbk 2006

Castle, Barbara obit Yrbk 2002
Castro, Fidel Jun 2001
Cattrall, Kim Jan 2003
Cavanagh, Tom Jun 2003
Cavanna, Betty obit Oct 2001
Cave, Nick Jun 2005
Cedric the Entertainer Feb 2004
Cela, Camilo José obit Apr 2002
Celmins, Vija Jan 2005
Chaban-Delmas, Jacques obit Feb 2001
Chafee, Lincoln Jan 2004
Chaikin, Joseph obit Yrbk 2003
Chamberlain, Owen obit Jul 2006
Champion, Will see Coldplay
Chandler, Otis obit Yrbk 2006
Chandrasekhar, Sripati obit Sep 2001
Chao, Elaine L. May 2001
Chapman, Duane Mar 2005
Chapman, Steven Curtis Oct 2004
Chappelle, Dave Jun 2004
Charles, Eugenia obit Yrbk 2006
Charles, Michael Ray Oct 2005
Charles, Ray obit Yrbk 2004
Chase, Alison Becker Nov 2006
Chase, David Mar 2001
Chauncey, Henry obit Mar 2003
Cheeks, Maurice Feb 2004
Cheney, Richard B. Jan 2002
Chertoff, Michael Oct 2005
Chesney, Kenny May 2004
Chiang Kai-shek, Mme. see Chiang Mei-Ling
Chiang Mei-Ling obit Mar 2004
Chieftains Mar 2004
Child, Julia obit Nov 2004
Chillida, Eduardo obit Yrbk 2002
Chisholm, Shirley obit Apr 2005
Churchland, Patricia S. May 2003
Claremont, Chris Sep 2003
Clark, Kenneth B. obit Sep 2005
Clarke, Richard May 2006
Clarkson, Kelly Sep 2006
Clarkson, Patricia Aug 2005
Clemens, Roger Aug 2003

Click and Clack, the Tappet Brothers see Magliozzi, Tom and Ray
Clinton, Hillary Rodham Jan 2002
Clooney, Rosemary obit Nov 2002
Clowes, Daniel Jan 2002
Clyburn, James E. Oct 2001
Coburn, James obit Feb 2003
Coca, Imogene obit Sep 2001
Cochran, Johnnie L. Jr. obit Oct 2005
Cochran, Thad Apr 2002
Coddington, Grace Apr 2005
Coffin, William Sloane obit Yrbk 2006
Cohen, Rob Nov 2002
Cohen, Sasha Feb 2006
Cohn, Linda Aug 2002
Colbert, Edwin H. obit Feb 2002
Colbert, Gregory Sep 2005
Colbert, Stephen Nov 2006
Coldplay May 2004
Coleman, Cy obit Feb 2005
Coleman, Norman Sep 2004
Coleman, Steve Jul 2004
Collen, Phil see Def Leppard
Collier, Sophia Jul 2002
Collins, Jim Aug 2003
Collins, Patricia Hill Mar 2003
Columbus, Chris Nov 2001
Cometbus, Aaron Mar 2005
Como, Perry obit Jul 2001
Conable, Barber B. obit Sep 2004
Conneff, Kevin see Chieftains
Connelly, Jennifer Jun 2002
Conner, Nadine obit Aug 2003
Connor, John T. obit Feb 2001
Conway, Gerry see Fairport Convention
Conway, John Horton Sep 2003
Cook, Richard W. Jul 2003
Cooke, Alistair obit Oct 2004
Coontz, Stephanie Jul 2003
Cooper, Anderson Jun 2006
Cooper, Chris Jul 2004
Coppola, Sofia Nov 2003
Corbijn, Anton Jun 2006
Corelli, Franco obit Mar 2004
Corzine, Jon Aug 2006
Coulter, Ann Sep 2003
Counsell, Craig Sep 2002
Counting Crows Mar 2003
Cowher, Bill Nov 2006
Cox, Archibald obit Yrbk 2004
Cox, Lynne Sep 2004

Coyne, Wayne *see* Flaming
Lips
Crain, Jeanne obit Sep 2004
Cranston, Alan obit Mar 2001
Creed May 2002
Creeley, Robert obit Yrbk
2005
Crick, Francis obit Yrbk 2004
Crittenden, Danielle Jul 2003
Cromwell, James Aug 2005
Cronyn, Hume obit Yrbk 2003
Croom, Sylvester Jr. Aug 2004
Crosby, John obit Yrbk 2003
Crossfield, A. Scott obit Yrbk
2006
Cruz, Celia obit Nov 2003
Cruz, Penelope Jul 2001
Cuban, Mark Mar 2001
Cummings, Elijah E. Feb 2004
Cunhal, Álvaro obit Yrbk
2005
Currie, Nancy June 2002
Curry, Ann Jun 2004

Dacre of Glanton, Baron *see*
Trevor-Roper, H. R.
Daddy G *see* Massive Attack
Daft, Douglas N. May 2001
Daly, Maureen obit Yrbk 2006
Dancer, Stanley obit Yrbk
2005
D'Angelo May 2001
Dangerfield, Rodney obit Feb
2005
Darling, Sharon May 2003
Davidson, Gordon Apr 2005
Davidson, Richard J. Aug
2004
Davis, Benjamin O. Jr. obit
Yrbk 2002
Davis, Glenn obit Yrbk 2005
Davis-Kimball, Jeannine Feb
2006
Davis, Nathanael V. obit Yrbk
2005
Davis, Ossie obit Yrbk 2005
Davis, Shani May 2006
Davis, Wade Jan 2003
Dawdy, Shannon Lee Apr
2006
de Branges, Louis Nov 2005
de Hartog, Jan obit Jan 2003
De Jong, Dola obit Sep 2004
de la Rúa, Fernando Apr 2001
de Meuron, Pierre *see* Herzog,
Jacques, and de Meuron,
Pierre
De Sapio, Carmine obit Yrbk
2004
De Valois, Ninette obit Aug
2001
de Varona, Donna Aug 2003
de Waal, Frans Mar 2006

Deakins, Roger May 2001
Dean, Howard Oct 2002
DeBusschere, Dave obit Yrbk
2003
DeCarlo, Dan Aug 2001 obit
Mar 2002
Deep Throat *see* Felt, W.
Mark
Def Leppard Jan 2003
Del Toro, Benicio Sep 2001
Delilah Apr 2005
Dellinger, David obit Yrbk
2004
DeLonge, Tom *see* blink-182
DeLorean, John Z. obit Yrbk
2005
Deloria, Vine Jr. obit Yrbk
2006
Delson, Brad *see* Linkin Park
DeMarcus, Jay *see* Rascal
Flatts
DeMille, Nelson Oct 2002
Densen-Gerber, Judianne obit
Jul 2003
Derrida, Jacques obit Mar
2005
Destiny's Child Aug 2001
Diamond, David obit Yrbk
2005
Diaz, Cameron Apr 2005
Dickerson, Debra Apr 2004
Dickinson, Amy Apr 2004
Diebold, John obit Yrbk 2006
Dillon, C. Douglas obit May
2003
Dimon, James Jun 2004
Dionne, E. J. Jr. May 2006
Dirnt, Mike *see* Green Day
Djerassi, Carl Oct 2001
Djukanovic, Milo Aug 2001
DMX Aug 2003
Dobbs, Lou Nov 2006
Domini, Amy Nov 2005
Donald, Arnold W. Nov 2005
Donaldson, William Jun 2003
D'Onofrio, Vincent May 2004
Donovan, Carrie obit Feb
2002
Donovan, Landon Jun 2006
Doubilet, David Mar 2003
Doudna, Jennifer Feb 2005
Douglas, Ashanti *see* Ashanti
Douglas, Dave Mar 2006
Douglas, Jerry Aug 2004
Douglas, John E. Jul 2001
Drake, James Jul 2005
Drozd, Steven *see* Flaming
Lips
Drucker, Eugene *see* Emerson
String Quartet
Drucker, Peter F. obit Apr
2006

Duany, Andrés *see* Duany,
Andrés and Plater-Zyberk,
Elizabeth
Duany, Andrés and Plater-
Zyberk, Elizabeth Jan 2006
Dude Love *see* Foley, Mick
Duesberg, Peter H. Jun 2004
Duff, Hilary Feb 2006
Dugan, Alan obit Oct 2004
Duke, Annie Aug 2006
Dunham, Katherine obit Yrbk
2006
Dunlop, John T. obit Sep
2004
Dunn, Ronnie *see* Brooks &
Dunn
Dunne, John Gregory obit
Yrbk 2004
Dunst, Kirsten Oct 2001
Durbin, Richard J. Aug 2006
Duritz, Adam *see* Counting
Crows
Dutton, Lawrence *see*
Emerson String Quartet
Dworkin, Andrea obit Yrbk
2005

Eban, Abba obit Mar 2003
Eberhart, Richard obit Yrbk
2005
Ebsen, Buddy obit Yrbk 2003
Eckert, Robert A. Mar 2003
Eddins, William Feb 2002
Edwards, Bob Sep 2001
Edwards, John R. Oct 2004
Edwards, Ralph obit Yrbk
2006
Egan, Edward M. Jul 2001
Egan, Jennifer Mar 2002
Eggleston, William Feb 2002
Ehlers, Vernon J. Jan 2005
Eiko *see* Eiko and Koma
Eiko and Koma May 2003
Eisner, Will obit May 2005
Elgin, Suzette Haden Aug
2006
Elizabeth, Queen Mother of
Great Britain obit Jun 2002
Elling, Kurt Jan 2005
Elliott, Joe *see* Def Leppard
Elliott, Sean Apr 2001
Emerson String Quartet Jul
2002
Eminem Jan 2001
Engibous, Thomas J. Oct 2003
Ensler, Eve Aug 2002
Epstein, Samuel S. Aug 2001
Epstein, Theo May 2004
Ericsson-Jackson, Aprille J.
Mar 2001
Estenssoro, Victor Paz *see* Paz
Estenssoro, Victor

Etherington, Edwin D. obit
Apr 2001
Eugenides, Jeffrey Oct 2003
Eustis, Oskar Oct 2002
Eustis, Paul Jefferson *see*
Eustis, Oskar
Evanovich, Janet Apr 2001
Evans, Dale obit Apr 2001
Evans, Donald L. Nov 2001
Eve Jul 2003
Everett, Percival L. Sep 2004
Everett, Rupert Jan 2005
Exon, J. James obit Yrbk 2005
Eyadéma, Etienne Gnassingbé
Apr 2002 obit Yrbk 2005
Eyre, Chris May 2003
Eytan, Walter obit Oct 2001

Faber, Sandra Apr 2002
Fadiman, Anne Aug 2005
Fagles, Robert Apr 2006
Fahd, King of Saudi Arabia
obit Yrbk 2005
Fahd, Prince of Saudi Arabia
see Fahd, King of Saudi
Arabia
Fairclough, Ellen obit Yrbk
2005
Fairport Convention Sep 2005
Falco, Edie Mar 2006
Fallon, Jimmy Jul 2002
Falls, Robert Jan 2004
Fangmeier, Stefen Aug 2004
Farhi, Nicole Nov 2001
Farmer, Paul Feb 2004
Farmer-Paellmann, Deadria
Mar 2004
Farrell, Dave *see* Linkin Park
Farrell, Eileen obit Jun 2002
Farrelly, Bobby *see* Farrelly,
Peter and Bobby
Farrelly, Peter and Bobby Sep
2001
Fast, Howard obit Jul 2003
Fattah, Chaka Sep 2003
Faulk, Marshall Jan 2003
Fausto-Sterling, Anne Sep
2005
Fawcett, Joy May 2004
Fay, J. Michael Sep 2001
Fay, Martin *see* Chieftains
Feifel, Herman obit Yrbk
2005
Felt, W. Mark Sep 2005
Fergie *see* Black Eyed Peas
Ferguson, Maynard obit Yrbk
2006
Ferguson, Stacy *see* Black
Eyed Peas
Ferré, Luis A. obit Mar 2004
Ferrell, Will Feb 2003
Ferrer, Rafael Jul 2001
Ferris, Timothy Jan 2001

Fey, Tina Apr 2002
Fiedler, Leslie A. obit Yrbk
2003
Fields, Mark Apr 2005
Finch, Caleb E. Sep 2004
Finch, Jennie Oct 2004
Finckel, David *see* Emerson
String Quartet
Firth, Colin Mar 2004
Fishman, Jon *see* Phish
Fitzgerald, Geraldine obit
Yrbk 2005
Fitzgerald, Patrick J. Jan 2006
Flagg, Fannie Nov 2006
Flaming Lips Oct 2002
Flanagan, Tommy obit Mar
2002
Fletcher, Arthur obit Yrbk
2005
Flowers, Vonetta May 2006
Foer, Jonathan Safran Sep
2002
Foley, Mick Sep 2001
Folon, Jean-Michel obit Yrbk
2006
Foner, Eric Aug 2004
Fong, Hiram L. obit Yrbk
2004
Fong-Torres, Ben Aug 2001
Foote, Shelby obit Yrbk 2005
Forrest, Vernon Jul 2002
Forsberg, Peter Nov 2005
Forsee, Gary D. Oct 2005
Forsythe, William Feb 2003
Fortey, Richard Sep 2005
Foss, Joseph Jacob obit Yrbk
2003
Fossett, J. Stephen *see*
Fossett, Steve
Fossett, Steve Apr 2005
Fountain, Clarence *see* Blind
Boys of Alabama
Fowles, John obit Apr 2006
Fox Quesada, Vicente May
2001
Foxx, Jamie May 2005
Franciosa, Anthony obit Yrbk
2006
Franciosa, Tony *see*
Franciosa, Anthony
Francis, Arlene obit Sep 2001
Francisco, Don Feb 2001
Franco, Julio Sep 2006
Frank, Reuven obit Yrbk 2006
Frankenheimer, John obit Oct
2002
Franklin, Shirley C. Aug 2002
Franks, Tommy R. Jan 2002
Franzen, Jonathan Sep 2003
Fraser, Brendan Feb 2001
Fredericks, Henry St. Clair
see Mahal, Taj

Freed, James Ingo obit Yrbk
2006
Freeman, Lucy obit Yrbk
2005
Freeman, Orville L. obit Yrbk
2003
Freston, Tom Aug 2003
Friedan, Betty obit May 2006
Friedlander, Lee May 2006
Friedman, Jane Mar 2001
Frist, Bill Nov 2002
Froese, Edgar *see* Tangerine
Dream
Froese, Jerome *see* Tangerine
Dream
Frum, David Jun 2004
Fry, Christopher obit Yrbk
2005
Fu, Ping Oct 2006
Fugazi Mar 2002
Fukuyama, Francis Jun 2001

Gades, Antonio obit Yrbk
2004
Gagne, Eric Jun 2004
Gaines, Donna Jun 2006
Galbraith, James K. Feb 2006
Galinsky, Ellen Oct 2003
Galloway, Joseph L. Sep 2003
Galtieri, Leopoldo obit Yrbk
2003
Gandy, Kim Oct 2001
Garcia, Sergio Mar 2001
Gardner, John W. obit May
2002
Gardner, Rulon Nov 2004
Garfield, Henry *see* Rollins,
Henry
Garofalo, Janeane Mar 2005
Garrels, Anne Mar 2004
Garrison, Deborah Jan 2001
Gary, Willie E. Apr 2001
Garza, Ed Jun 2002
Garzón, Baltasar Mar 2001
Gaskin, Ina May May 2001
Gates, Melinda Feb 2004
Gaubatz, Lynn Feb 2001
Gawande, Atul Mar 2005
Gayle, Helene Jan 2002
Gebel-Williams, Gunther obit
Oct 2001
Geis, Bernard obit Mar 2001
Gelb, Leslie H. Jan 2003
Gennaro, Peter obit Feb 2001
Gerberding, Julie Louise Sep
2004
Gerbner, George obit Yrbk
2006
Germond, Jack W. Jul 2005
Gerson, Michael Feb 2002
Giamatti, Paul Sep 2005
Giannulli, Mossimo Feb 2003
Gibson, Althea obit Feb 2004

Gibson, Charles Sep 2002
Gibson, Mel Aug 2003
Gierek, Edward obit Oct 2001
Gilbreth, Frank B. Jr. obit Jul 2001
Gillingham, Charles see Counting Crows
Gillis, John see White Stripes
Gilmore, James S. III Jun 2001
Ginzberg, Eli obit Yrbk 2003
Giroud, Françoise obit Jul 2003
Giulini, Carlo Maria obit Yrbk 2005
Gladwell, Malcolm Jun 2005
Glass, H. Bentley obit Yrbk 2005
Glavine, Tom Oct 2006
Goff, M. Lee Jun 2001
Gold, Thomas obit Yrbk 2004
Goldberg, Bill Apr 2001
Golden, Thelma Sep 2001
Goldman-Rakic, Patricia Feb 2003
Goldovsky, Boris obit Aug 2001
Goldsman, Akiva Sep 2004
Goldsmith, Jerry May 2001 obit Nov 2004
Goldstine, Herman Heine obit Yrbk 2004
Golub, Leon obit Yrbk 2004
Gomez, Jaime see Black Eyed Peas
Gonzales, Alberto R. Apr 2002
Gonzalez, Henry obit Feb 2001
Good, Mary L. Sep 2001
Good, Robert A. obit Yrbk 2003
Goodpaster, Andrew J. obit Yrbk 2005
Googoosh May 2001
Gopnik, Adam Apr 2005
Gordon, Bruce S. Oct 2005
Gordon, Cyrus H. obit Aug 2001
Gordon, Ed Jul 2005
Gordon, Edmund W. Jun 2003
Gordon, Mike see Phish
Gorman, R. C. Jan 2001
Gorsuch, Anne obit Yrbk 2004
Gorton, John Grey obit Yrbk 2002
Gottlieb, Melvin B. obit Mar 2001
Gould, Stephen Jay obit Aug 2002
Gourdji, Françoise see Giroud, Françoise
Gowdy, Curt obit Yrbk 2006

Gowers, Timothy Jan 2001
Gowers, William Timothy see Gowers, Timothy
Graham, Franklin May 2002
Graham, Katharine obit Oct 2001
Graham, Susan Oct 2005
Graham, Winston obit Yrbk 2003
Granholm, Jennifer M. Oct 2003
Grasso, Richard Oct 2002
Graves, Florence George May 2005
Graves, Morris obit Sep 2001
Gray, L. Patrick obit Yrbk 2005
Gray, Spalding obit Yrbk 2004
Greco, José obit Mar 2001
Green, Adolph obit Mar 2003
Green, Darrell Jan 2001
Green Day Aug 2005
Green, Tom Oct 2003
Greenberg, Jack M. Nov 2001
Greene, Wallace M. obit Aug 2003
Greenstein, Jesse L. obit Yrbk 2003
Greenwood, Colin see Radiohead
Greenwood, Jonny see Radiohead
Gregory, Frederick D. Oct 2005
Gregory, Wilton D. Mar 2002
Griffin, Michael Aug 2005
Griffiths, Martha W. obit Yrbk 2003
Grigg, John obit Apr 2002
Grohl, Dave May 2002
Groopman, Jerome E. Oct 2004
Grossman, Edith Mar 2006
Gruber, Ruth Jun 2001
Gruber, Samuel H. Aug 2004
Grubin, David Aug 2002
Gudmundsdottir, Björk see Björk
Guerard, Albert J. obit Mar 2001
Guerrero, Vladimir Jun 2006
Guillen, Ozzie May 2006
Guillermoprieto, Alma Sep 2004
Guinier, Lani Jan 2004
Gunn, Thom obit Yrbk 2004
Gupta, Sanjay Aug 2006
Gursky, Andreas Jul 2001

Haas, Jonathan Jun 2003
Hacker see Hackett, Buddy
Hackett, Buddy obit Oct 2003

Hadley, Stephen Nov 2006
Hagel, Chuck Aug 2004
Hagen, Uta obit Yrbk 2004
Haggis, Paul Aug 2006
Hahn, Hilary Sep 2002
Hahn, Joseph see Linkin Park
Hailey, Arthur obit Yrbk 2005
Hailsham of St. Marylebone, Quintin Hogg obit Feb 2002
Hair, Jay D. obit Jan 2003
Halaby, Najeeb E. obit Yrbk 2003
Halasz, Laszlo obit Feb 2002
Hall, Conrad L. obit May 2003
Hall, Deidre Nov 2002
Hall, Gus obit Jan 2001
Hall, Richard Melville see Moby
Hall, Steffie see Evanovich, Janet
Hall, Tex G. May 2005
Hallaren, Mary A. obit Yrbk 2005
Hallström, Lasse Feb 2005
Hamilton, Laird Aug 2005
Hamilton, Tom see Aerosmith
Hamm, Morgan see Hamm, Paul and Morgan
Hamm, Paul see Hamm, Paul and Morgan
Hamm, Paul and Morgan Nov 2004
Hammer, Bonnie Apr 2006
Hammon, Becky Jan 2003
Hammond, Caleb D. Jr. obit Yrbk 2006
Hammons, David May 2006
Hampton, Lionel obit Yrbk 2002
Hancock, Graham Feb 2005
Hancock, Trenton Doyle Apr 2006
Hanna, William obit Sep 2001
Hannity, Sean Apr 2005
Hansen, Liane May 2003
Harcourt, Nic Oct 2005
Harden, Marcia Gay Sep 2001
Hardin, Garrett obit Apr 2004
Hargis, Billy James obit Yrbk 2005
Hargrove, Marion obit Yrbk 2004
Harjo, Joy Aug 2001
Harper, Ben Jan 2004
Harrer, Heinrich obit Yrbk 2006
Harris, Eva Mar 2004
Harris, Richard obit Yrbk 2003
Harrison, George obit Mar 2002

Harrison, Marvin Aug 2001
Harrison, William B. Jr. Mar 2002
Hartke, Vance obit Yrbk 2003
Hartmann, Heidi I. Apr 2003
Hashimoto, Ryutaro obit Yrbk 2006
Haskins, Caryl P. obit Feb 2002
Hass, Robert Feb 2001
Hassenfeld, Alan G. Jul 2003
Hastings, Reed Mar 2006
Hauerwas, Stanley Jun 2003
Haughey, Charles obit Yrbk 2006
Hawkinson, Tim Aug 2005
Hax, Carolyn Nov 2002
Hayden, Melissa obit Yrbk 2006
Hayden, Michael V. Nov 2006
Hayes, Bob obit Jan 2003
Hayes, Edward May 2006
Haynes, Cornell Jr. see Nelly
Haynes, Todd Jul 2003
Haysbert, Dennis Nov 2006
Headley, Elizabeth see Cavanna, Betty
Heath, Edward obit Yrbk 2005
Heath, James R. Oct 2003
Hecht, Anthony obit Yrbk 2005
Heckart, Eileen obit Mar 2002
Heilbroner, Robert L. obit Yrbk 2005
Heilbrun, Carolyn G. obit Feb 2004
Heiskell, Andrew obit Yrbk 2003
Held, Al obit Yrbk 2005
Helms, Richard obit Yrbk 2003
Henderson, Donald A. Mar 2002
Henderson, Hazel Nov 2003
Henderson, Joe obit Oct 2001
Henderson, Skitch obit Apr 2006
Hendrickson, Sue Oct 2001
Henry, Brad Jan 2005
Henry, John W. May 2005
Hepburn, Katharine obit Nov 2003
Herblock see Block, Herbert L.
Herndon, J. Marvin Nov 2003
Herring, Pendleton obit Yrbk 2004
Hersch, Fred Apr 2006
Hertzberg, Arthur obit Yrbk 2006

Herzog, Jacques see Herzog, Jacques, and de Meuron, Pierre
Herzog, Jacques, and de Meuron, Pierre Jun 2002
Hewitt, Lleyton Oct 2002
Hewlett, Sylvia Ann Sep 2002
Heyerdahl, Thor obit Yrbk 2002
Heym, Stefan obit Mar 2002
Heymann, David L. Jul 2004
Hicks, Louise Day obit Jun 2004
Hidalgo, David see Los Lobos
Higgins, Chester Jr. Jun 2002
Hildegarde obit Yrbk 2005
Hill, Andrew Apr 2004
Hill, Dulé Jul 2003
Hill, Faith Mar 2001
Hill, George Roy obit Jun 2003
Hill, Grant Jan 2002
Hill, Herbert obit Yrbk 2004
Hillenburg, Stephen Apr 2003
Hiller, Stanley obit Yrbk 2006
Hiller, Wendy obit Yrbk 2003
Hines, Gregory obit Yrbk 2003
Hines, Jerome obit Jun 2003
Hinojosa, Maria Feb 2001
Hirschfeld, Al obit Jul 2003
Hobson, Mellody Aug 2005
Hobson Pilot, Ann May 2003
Hoffman, Philip Seymour May 2001
Hogg, Quintin see Hailsham of St. Marylebone, Quintin Hogg
Holden, Betsy Jul 2003
Holdsclaw, Chamique Feb 2006
Holl, Steven Jul 2004
Holland, Dave Mar 2003
Hollander, Robert B. Sep 2006
Holm, Ian Mar 2002
Hondros, Chris Nov 2004
Hong, Hei-Kyung Nov 2003
Hooker, John Lee obit Sep 2001
Hope, Bob obit Yrbk 2003
Hopkins, Bernard Apr 2002
Hopkins, Nancy May 2002
Hoppus, Mark see blink-182
Horwich, Frances obit Oct 2001
Hounsfield, Godfrey obit Yrbk 2004
Hounsou, Djimon Aug 2004
Houston, Allan Nov 2003
Houston, James A. obit Yrbk 2005
Howard, Tim Sep 2005

Howe, Harold II obit Yrbk 2003
Hoyer, Steny H. Mar 2004
Hoyle, Fred obit Jan 2002
Hrawi, Elias obit Yrbk 2006
Huckabee, Mike Nov 2005
Hughes, Barnard obit Yrbk 2006
Hughes, Karen Oct 2001
Hugo, Chad see Neptunes
Hull, Jane Dee Feb 2002
Hunt Lieberson, Lorraine Jul 2004 obit Yrbk 2006
Hunt, Swanee Mar 2006
Hunter, Evan obit Yrbk 2005
Hunter, Kermit obit Sep 2001
Hunter, Kim obit Yrbk 2002

Iakovos, Archbishop obit Yrbk 2005
Ifill, Gwen Sep 2005
Ilitch, Michael Feb 2005
Illich, Ivan obit Yrbk 2003
Immelt, Jeffrey R. Feb 2004
India.Arie Feb 2002
Inkster, Juli Sep 2002
Isbin, Sharon Aug 2003
Istomin, Eugene obit Feb 2004
Ive, Jonathan Oct 2006
Ivins, Michael see Flaming Lips
Izetbegovic, Alija obit Jun 2004

Ja Rule Jul 2002
Jackman, Hugh Oct 2003
Jackson, Alan Apr 2004
Jackson, Hal Oct 2002
Jackson, Lauren Jun 2003
Jackson, Maynard H. Jr. obit Yrbk 2003
Jackson, Michael Aug 2005
Jackson, Peter Jan 2002
Jackson, Thomas Penfield Jun 2001
Jacobs, Jane obit Yrbk 2006
Jagger, Janine Apr 2004
Jakes, T.D. Jun 2001
James, Alex see Blur
James, Bill Jun 2004
James, Edgerrin Jan 2002
James, LeBron Nov 2005
Janeway, Elizabeth obit Yrbk 2005
Jarecki, Eugene May 2006
Jarring, Gunnar obit Yrbk 2002
Jarvis, Erich D. May 2003
Jay-Z Aug 2002
Jeffers, Eve Jihan see Eve

Jefferts Schori, Katharine Sep 2006
Jeffery, Vonetta see Flowers, Vonetta
Jeffords, James Sep 2001
Jenkins, Jerry B. see LaHaye, Tim and Jenkins, Jerry B.
Jenkins, Roy obit Yrbk 2003
Jennings, Peter obit Sep 2005
Jennings, Waylon obit Apr 2002
Jensen, Oliver O obit Yrbk 2005
Jet see Urquidez, Benny
Jimenez, Marcos Perez see Pérez Jiménez, Marcos
Jin, Deborah Apr 2004
Jobert, Michel obit Yrbk 2002
Johannesen, Grant obit Yrbk 2005
Johansson, Scarlett Mar 2005
John Paul II obit Jun 2005
Johnson, Brian see AC/DC
Johnson, Eddie Bernice Jul 2001
Johnson, Elizabeth A. Nov 2002
Johnson, John H. obit Yrbk 2005
Johnson, Philip obit Sep 2005
Jones, Bobby Jun 2002
Jones, Chipper May 2001
Jones, Chuck obit May 2002
Jones, Edward P. Mar 2004
Jones, Elaine Jun 2004
Jones, Larry Wayne Jr. see Jones, Chipper
Jones, Norah May 2003
Jones, Sarah Jul 2005
Jones, Scott Jan 2006
Jonze, Spike Apr 2003
Joyner, Tom Sep 2002
Judd, Jackie Sep 2002
Judd, Jacqueline Dee see Judd, Jackie
Judson, Olivia Jan 2004
Juliana Queen of the Netherlands obit Yrbk 2004

Kabila, Joseph Sep 2001
Kael, Pauline obit Nov 2001
Kainen, Jacob obit Aug 2001
Kamen, Dean Nov 2002
Kane, Joseph Nathan obit Nov 2002
Kani, John Jun 2001
Kann, Peter R. Mar 2003
Kaptur, Marcy Jan 2003
Karbo, Karen May 2001
Karle, Isabella Jan 2003
Karon, Jan Mar 2003
Karpinski, Janis Apr 2006
Karsh, Yousuf obit Nov 2002

Karzai, Hamid May 2002
Kase, Toshikazu obit Yrbk 2004
Kass, Leon R. Aug 2002
Katsav, Moshe Feb 2001
Katz, Jackson Jul 2004
Kaufman, Charlie Jul 2005
Kavafian, Ani Oct 2006
Kazan, Elia obit Yrbk 2004
Kcho Aug 2001
Keane, Sean see Chieftains
Keegan, Robert Jan 2004
Keener, Catherine Oct 2002
Keeshan, Bob obit Yrbk 2004
Keith, Toby Oct 2004
Kelleher, Herb Jan 2001
Keller, Bill Oct 2003
Keller, Marthe Jul 2004
Keller, Thomas Jun 2004
Kelman, Charles obit Yrbk 2004
Kennan, George F. obit Yrbk 2005
Kennedy, Randall Aug 2002
Kennedy, Robert F. Jr. May 2004
Kent, Jeff May 2003
Kentridge, William Oct 2001
Kenyon, Cynthia Jan 2005
Kepes, György obit Mar 2002
Kerr, Clark obit May 2004
Kerr, Jean obit May 2003
Kerr, Mrs. Walter F see Kerr, Jean
Kerry, John Sep 2004
Kesey, Ken obit Feb 2002
Ketcham, Hank obit Sep 2001
Keys, Ancel obit Yrbk 2005
Keys, Charlene see Tweet
Khalilzad, Zalmay Aug 2006
Kid Rock Oct 2001
Kidd, Chip Jul 2005
Kidd, Jason May 2002
Kiessling, Laura Aug 2003
Kilbourne, Jean May 2004
Kilpatrick, Kwame M. Apr 2004
Kim, Jim Yong Nov 2006
King, Alan obit Yrbk 2004
King, Coretta Scott obit Apr 2006
King, Florence Apr 2006
Kittikachorn, Thanom obit Yrbk 2004
Klaus, Josef obit Oct 2001
Kleiber, Carlos obit Yrbk 2004
Klein, Naomi Aug 2003
Klein, William Mar 2004
Klinkenborg, Verlyn Jul 2006
Knievel, Robbie Mar 2005
Knipfel, Jim Mar 2005
Knoll, Andrew H. Apr 2006

Knowles, Beyoncé see Destiny's Child
Koch, Kenneth obit Yrbk 2002
Koff, Clea Nov 2004
Koh, Jennifer Sep 2006
Koizumi, Junichiro Jan 2002
Kolar, Jiri obit Yrbk 2002
Koma see Eiko and Koma
Konaré, Alpha Oumar Oct 2001
Koner, Pauline obit Apr 2001
Kopp, Wendy Mar 2003
Kostunica, Vojislav Jan 2001
Kott, Jan obit Mar 2002
Kournikova, Anna Jan 2002
Kramer, Joey see Aerosmith
Kramer, Stanley obit May 2001
Krause, David W. Feb 2002
Krawcheck, Sallie Mar 2006
Kreutzberger, Mario see Francisco, Don
Kripke, Saul Oct 2004
Kristof, Nicholas D. Feb 2006
Krugman, Paul Aug 2001
Kübler-Ross, Elisabeth obit Yrbk 2004
Kunitz, Stanley obit Aug 2006
Kushner, Tony Jul 2002
Kusturica, Emir Nov 2005
Kyprianou, Spyros obit May 2002

La India May 2002
La Montagne, Margaret see Spellings, Margaret
La Russa, Tony Jul 2003
Labov, William Mar 2006
Lacy, Dan obit Nov 2001
LaDuke, Winona Jan 2003
LaFontaine, Don Sep 2004
Lagardère, Jean-Luc obit Aug 2003
LaHaye, Tim see LaHaye, Tim and Jenkins, Jerry B.
LaHaye, Tim and Jenkins, Jerry B. Jun 2003
Laimbeer, Bill Jan 2006
Laker, Freddie obit Yrbk 2006
Lally, Joe see Fugazi
Lampert, Edward S. Sep 2005
Landers, Ann obit Nov 2002
Lange, David obit Yrbk 2005
Langevin, Jim Aug 2005
Lapidus, Morris obit Apr 2001
Lapp, Ralph E. obit Feb 2005
Lara, Brian Feb 2001
Lardner, Ring Jr. obit Feb 2001
Laredo, Ruth obit Yrbk 2005
Lassaw, Ibram obit Yrbk 2004

Lauder, Estée obit Yrbk 2004
Lavigne, Avril Apr 2003
Law, Ty Oct 2002
Lawal, Kase L. Nov 2006
Lax, Peter D. Oct 2005
Le Clercq, Tanaquil obit Mar 2001
Leakey, Meave Jun 2002
Lederer, Esther Pauline see Landers, Ann
Ledger, Heath Jun 2006
Lee, Andrea Sep 2003
Lee, Barbara Jun 2004
Lee, Debra L. Jun 2006
Lee, Geddy see Rush
Lee, Jeanette Oct 2002
Lee, Mrs. John G. see Lee, Percy Maxim
Lee, Peggy obit May 2002
Lee, Percy Maxim obit Jan 2003
Lee, Richard C. obit Jun 2003
LeFrak, Samuel J. obit Yrbk 2003
Lehane, Dennis Oct 2005
Leiter, Al Aug 2002
Lelyveld, Joseph Nov 2005
Lem, Stanislaw obit Yrbk 2006
Lemmon, Jack obit Oct 2001
Leo, John Sep 2006
Leon, Kenny Nov 2005
Leonard see Hackett, Buddy
Leone, Giovanni obit Feb 2002
Leslie, Chris see Fairport Convention
LeSueur, Larry obit Jun 2003
Lethem, Jonathan Mar 2006
Letterman, David Oct 2002
Levert, Gerald Oct 2003
Levin, Carl May 2004
Levine, Mel Nov 2005
LeVox, Gary see Rascal Flatts
Levy, Eugene Jan 2002
Lewis, Ananda Jun 2005
Lewis, David Levering May 2001
Lewis, David S. Jr. obit Yrbk 2004
Lewis, Dorothy Otnow May 2006
Lewis, Flora obit Yrbk 2002
Lewis, John obit Jun 2001
Lewis, Kenneth Apr 2004
Lewis, Marvin Nov 2004
Li, Jet Jun 2001
Li Lian Jie see Li, Jet
Libeskind, Daniel Jun 2003
Lifeson, Alex see Rush
Lilly, John C. obit Feb 2002
Lilly, Kristine Apr 2004

Lima do Amor, Sisleide see Sissi
Lincoln, Abbey Sep 2002
Lincoln, Blanche Lambert Mar 2002
Lindbergh, Anne Morrow obit Apr 2001
Lindgren, Astrid obit Apr 2002
Lindo, Delroy Mar 2001
Lindsay, John V. obit Mar 2001
Ling, James J. obit Yrbk 2005
Lingle, Linda Jun 2003
Link, O. Winston obit Apr 2001
Linkin Park Mar 2002
Linowitz, Sol M. obit Yrbk 2005
Lipinski, Anne Marie Jul 2004
Lippold, Richard obit Yrbk 2002
Little Steven see Van Zandt, Steven
Liu, Lucy Oct 2003
Lloyd, Charles Apr 2002
Locke, Gary Apr 2003
Logan, Lara Jul 2006
Lohan, Lindsay Nov 2005
Lomax, Alan obit Oct 2002
London, Julie obit Feb 2001
Long, Russell B. obit Yrbk 2003
Long, William Ivey Mar 2004
Lopez, Al obit Yrbk 2006
López Portillo, José obit Yrbk 2004
Lord, Walter obit Yrbk 2002
Los Lobos Oct 2005
Loudon, Dorothy obit Yrbk 2004
Love, John A. obit Apr 2002
Lowell, Mike Sep 2003
Lozano, Conrad see Los Lobos
Lucas, George May 2002
Luckovich, Mike Jan 2005
Ludacris Jun 2004
Ludlum, Robert obit Jul 2001
Ludwig, Ken May 2004
Luke, Delilah Rene see Delilah
Lumet, Sidney Jun 2005
Luns, Joseph M. A. H. obit Yrbk 2002
Lupica, Mike Mar 2001
Lyng, Richard E. obit Jun 2003
Lynne, Shelby Jul 2001

Mac, Bernie Jun 2002
Machado, Alexis Leyva see Kcho

MacKaye, Ian see Fugazi
MacKenzie, Gisele obit Jul 2004
MacMitchell, Leslie obit Yrbk 2006
Maddox, Lester obit Yrbk 2003
Madsen, Michael Apr 2004
Magliozzi, Ray see Magliozzi, Tom and Ray
Magliozzi, Tom see Magliozzi, Tom and Ray
Magliozzi, Tom and Ray Jun 2006
Magloire, Paul E. obit Nov 2001
Maguire, Tobey Sep 2002
Mahal, Taj Nov 2001
Maki, Fumihiko Jul 2001
Malina, Joshua Apr 2004
Malley, Matt see Counting Crows
Maloney, Carolyn B. Apr 2001
Manchester, William obit Yrbk 2004
Mankind see Foley, Mick
Mankoff, Robert May 2005
Mann, Emily Jun 2002
Mansfield, Michael J. see Mansfield, Mike
Mansfield, Mike obit Jan 2002
Marcinko, Richard Mar 2001
Marcus, George E. Mar 2006
Marcus, Stanley obit Apr 2002
Marcy, Geoffrey W. see Marcy, Geoffrey W., and Butler, R. Paul
Marcy, Geoffrey W., and Butler, R. Paul Nov 2002
Margaret, Princess of Great Britain obit May 2002
Markova, Alicia obit Yrbk 2005
Marks, Leonard H. obit Yrbk 2006
Marlette, Doug Jul 2002
Marshall, Burke obit Yrbk 2003
Marshall, Rob Jun 2003
Martin, A. J. P. see Martin, Archer
Martin, Agnes obit Apr 2005
Martin, Archer obit Yrbk 2002
Martin, Chris see Coldplay
Martin, George R. R. Jan 2004
Martin, James S. Jr. obit Yrbk 2002
Martin, Jesse L. Jul 2006
Martin, Kenyon Jan 2005
Martin, Kevin J. Aug 2005

Martin, Mark Mar 2001
Martinez, Pedro Jun 2001
Martinez, Rueben Jun 2005
Martinez, Vilma Jul 2004
Martz, Judy Mar 2005
Mary Kay see Ash, Mary Kay
Massive Attack Jun 2004
Masters, William H. obit May 2001
Mathers, Marshall see Eminem
Matsui, Connie L. Aug 2002
Matsui, Robert T. obit Apr 2005
Matta obit Yrbk 2003
Mauch, Gene obit Yrbk 2005
Mauldin, Bill obit Jul 2003
Mauldin, William Henry see Mauldin, Bill
Mayne, Thom Oct 2005
Mayr, Ernst obit May 2005
Mays, L. Lowry Aug 2003
Mayweather, Floyd Oct 2004
McBride, Martina Mar 2004
McCain, John S. Mar 2006
McCambridge, Mercedes obit Yrbk 2004
McCann, Renetta May 2005
McCarthy, Eugene J. obit Mar 2006
McCaw, Craig Sep 2001
McCloskey, Robert obit Yrbk 2003
McConnell, Page see Phish
McCracken, Craig Feb 2004
McCrary, Tex obit Yrbk 2003
McCurry, Steve Nov 2005
McDonald, Gabrielle Kirk Oct 2001
McDonough, William Jul 2006
McGhee, George Crews obit Yrbk 2005
McGrady, Tracy Feb 2003
McGrath, Judy Feb 2005
McGraw, Eloise Jarvis obit Mar 2001
McGraw, Phillip Jun 2002
McGraw, Tim Sep 2002
McGreal, Elizabeth see Yates, Elizabeth
McGruder, Aaron Sep 2001
McGuire, Dorothy obit Nov 2001
McIntire, Carl obit Jun 2002
McIntosh, Millicent Carey obit Mar 2001
McKeon, Jack Apr 2004
McKinney, Robert obit Yrbk 2001
McLaughlin, John Feb 2004
McLean, Jackie Mar 2001 obit Nov 2006

McLean, John Lenwood see McLean, Jackie
McLurkin, James Sep 2005
McMath, Sid obit Jan 2004
McNabb, Donovan Jan 2004
McNair, Steve Jan 2005
McNally, Andrew 3d obit Feb 2002
McQueen, Alexander Feb 2002
McWhirter, Norris D. obit Yrbk 2004
McWhorter, John H. Feb 2003
Meat Loaf Nov 2006
Mechem, Edwin L. obit Yrbk 2003
Meier, Deborah May 2006
Meiselas, Susan Feb 2005
Mendes, Sam Oct 2002
Menken, Alan Jan 2001
Merchant, Ismail obit Yrbk 2005
Merchant, Natalie Jan 2003
Meron, Theodor Mar 2005
Merrifield, R. Bruce obit Yrbk 2006
Merrill, Robert obit Feb 2005
Merton, Robert K. obit Yrbk 2003
Messick, Dale obit Yrbk 2005
Messier, Jean-Marie May 2002
Messing, Debra Aug 2002
Meta, Ilir Feb 2002
Meyer, Cord Jr. obit Aug 2001
Meyer, Edgar Jun 2002
Meyers, Nancy Feb 2002
Michel, Sia Sep 2003
Mickelson, Phil Mar 2002
Middelhoff, Thomas Feb 2001
Miller, Ann obit Yrbk 2004
Miller, Arthur obit Jul 2005
Miller, J. Irwin obit Yrbk 2004
Miller, Jason obit Yrbk 2001
Miller, John Aug 2003
Miller, Judith Jan 2006
Miller, Marcus Feb 2006
Miller, Neal obit Jun 2002
Millionaire, Tony Jul 2005
Millman, Dan Aug 2002
Mills, John obit Yrbk 2005
Milosevic, Slobodan obit Yrbk 2006
Milosz, Czeslaw obit Yrbk 2004
Mink, Patsy T. obit Jan 2003
Minner, Ruth Ann Aug 2001
Mirabal, Robert Aug 2002
Mitchell, Dean Aug 2002
Mitchell, Pat Aug 2005
Mitha, Tehreema May 2004
Miyazaki, Hayao Apr 2001
Moby Apr 2001

Mohammed, W. Deen Jan 2004
Moiseiwitsch, Tanya obit Jul 2003
Molina, Alfred Feb 2004
Molloy, Matt see Chieftains
Moloney, Paddy see Chieftains
Monk, T. S. Feb 2002
Monseu, Stephanie see Nelson, Keith and Monseu, Stephanie
Montresor, Beni obit Feb 2002
Moore, Ann Aug 2003
Moore, Dudley obit Yrbk 2002
Moore, Elisabeth Luce obit Yrbk 2002
Moore, Gordon E. Apr 2002
Moore, Paul Jr. obit Yrbk 2003
Moorer, Thomas H. obit Yrbk 2004
Morella, Constance A. Feb 2001
Morial, Marc Jan 2002
Morris, Butch Jul 2005
Morris, Errol Feb 2001
Morris, James T. Mar 2005
Morris, Lawrence see Morris, Butch
Morrison, Philip obit Aug 2005
Mortensen, Viggo Jun 2004
Mos Def Apr 2005
Moseka, Aminata see Lincoln, Abbey
Moses, Bob see Moses, Robert P.
Moses, Robert P. Apr 2002
Mosley, Sugar Shane Jan 2001
Mosley, Timothy see Timbaland
Moss, Adam Mar 2004
Moss, Frank E. obit Jun 2003
Moss, Randy Jan 2006
Moten, Etta see Barnett, Etta Moten
Motley, Constance Baker obit Feb 2006
Moynihan, Daniel Patrick obit Yrbk 2003
Muhammad, Warith Deen see Mohammed, W. Deen
Mulcahy, Anne M. Nov 2002
Murkowski, Frank H. Jul 2003
Murphy, Mark Sep 2004
Murphy, Thomas obit Yrbk 2006
Murray, Bill Sep 2004
Murray, Donald M. Jul 2006

Murray, Jonathan *see* Bunim, Mary-Ellis, and Murray, Jonathan

Murray, Jonathan *see* Bunim, Mary-Ellis, and Murray, Jonathan

Murray, Ty May 2002

Musharraf, Pervaiz *see* Musharraf, Pervez

Musharraf, Pervez Mar 2001

Musk, Elon Oct 2006

Mydans, Carl M. obit Yrbk 2004

Mydans, Shelley Smith obit Aug 2002

Myers, Joel N. Apr 2005

Myers, Richard B. Apr 2002

Nabrit, Samuel M. obit Yrbk 2004

Nachtigall, Paul E. Jan 2006

Nagin, C. Ray Jan 2006

Najimy, Kathy Oct 2002

Napolitano, Janet Oct 2004

Narayan, R. K. obit Jul 2001

Nash, Steve Mar 2003

Nason, John W. obit Feb 2002

Nasser, Jacques Apr 2001

Nathan, Robert R. obit Nov 2001

Navratilova, Martina Feb 2004

Ne Win obit Yrbk 2003

Neals, Otto Feb 2003

Neeleman, David Sep 2003

Negroponte, John Apr 2003

Nehru, B. K. obit Feb 2002

Nelly Oct 2002

Nelson, Gaylord obit Yrbk 2005

Nelson, Keith *see* Nelson, Keith and Monseu, Stephanie

Nelson, Keith and Monseu, Stephanie Jun 2005

Nelson, Marilyn Carlson Oct 2004

Nelson, Stanley May 2005

Neptunes May 2004

Neustadt, Richard E. obit Yrbk 2004

Newman, Arnold obit Yrbk 2006

Newman, J. Wilson obit Yrbk 2003

Newmark, Craig Jun 2005

Newsom, Lee Ann Oct 2004

Newton, Helmut obit Yrbk 2004

Nguyen Van Thieu *see* Thieu, Nguyen Van

Nicol, Simon *see* Fairport Convention

Nikolayev, Andrian obit Yrbk 2004

Nilsson, Birgit obit Sep 2006

Nitze, Paul H. obit Mar 2005

Nixon, Agnes Apr 2001

Nofziger, Lyn obit Yrbk 2006

Nooyi, Indra K. Nov 2006

Norton, Andre obit Yrbk 2005

Norton, Gale A. Jun 2001

Nottage, Lynn Nov 2004

Novacek, Michael J. Sep 2002

Nowitzki, Dirk Jun 2002

Nozick, Robert obit Apr 2002

Nugent, Ted Apr 2005

Obama, Barack Jul 2005

Obote, Milton obit Yrbk 2006

O'Brien, Ed *see* Radiohead

O'Connor, Carroll obit Sep 2001

O'Connor, Donald obit Apr 2004

O'Hair, Madalyn Murray obit Jun 2001

Ohno, Apolo Anton Feb 2006

O'Keefe, Sean Jan 2003

Okrent, Daniel Nov 2004

Olin, Lena Jun 2003

Ollila, Jorma Aug 2002

Olopade, Olufunmilayo Sep 2006

Olopade, Olufunmilayo Sep 2006

O'Malley, Sean Patrick Jan 2004

O'Neal, Jermaine Jun 2004

O'Neal, Stanley May 2003

O'Neill, Paul H. Jul 2001

Oppenheim, Chad Sep 2006

Orbach, Jerry obit Apr 2005

O'Reilly, Bill Oct 2003

Orlean, Susan Jun 2003

Orman, Suze May 2003

Ortiz, David Aug 2005

Ortner, Sherry B. Nov 2002

Osawa, Sandra Sunrising Jan 2001

Osborne, Barrie M. Feb 2005

Osbourne, Sharon Jan 2001

Osteen, Joel Jan 2006

Oudolf, Piet Apr 2003

OutKast Apr 2004

Oz, Mehmet C. Apr 2003

Paar, Jack obit Yrbk 2004

Pace, Peter Jun 2006

Page, Clarence Jan 2003

Page, Larry *see* Brin, Sergey, and Page, Larry

Paige, Roderick R. Jul 2001

Paik, Nam June obit Yrbk 2006

Palmeiro, Rafael Aug 2001

Palmer, Violet Nov 2006

Paltrow, Gwyneth Jan 2005

Park, Linda Sue Jun 2002

Park, Rosemary obit Yrbk 2004

Parker, Mary-Louise Apr 2006

Parker, Robert M. May 2005

Parks, Gordon obit Jun 2006

Parks, Rosa obit Jan 2006

Parsons, Richard D. Apr 2003

Pascal, Amy Mar 2002

Patchett, Ann Apr 2003

Patrick, Danica Oct 2005

Patty, Sandi Feb 2004

Pau, Peter Feb 2002

Paulson, Henry M. Jr. Sep 2002

Payne, Alexander Feb 2003

Paz Estenssoro, Victor obit Sep 2001

Peart, Neil *see* Rush

Peck, Gregory obit Sep 2003

Peck, M. Scott obit Yrbk 2005

Pegg, Dave *see* Fairport Convention

Pekar, Harvey Jan 2004

Pelikan, Jaroslav obit Yrbk 2006

Pelosi, Nancy Feb 2003

Pelzer, Dave Mar 2002

Pennington, Ty Feb 2006

Perdue, Frank obit Oct 2005

Pérez Jiménez, Marcos obit Feb 2002

Pérez, Louie *see* Los Lobos

Perkins, Charles obit Feb 2001

Perle, Richard Jul 2003

Perry, Joe *see* Aerosmith

Perry, Tyler Jun 2005

Person, Houston Jun 2003

Perutz, Max obit Apr 2002

Petersen, Wolfgang Jul 2001

Peterson, Martha obit Yrbk 2006

Pettibon, Raymond Apr 2005

Pevear, Richard *see* Pevear, Richard and Volokhonsky, Larissa

Pevear, Richard and Volokhonsky, Larissa Jun 2006

Peyroux, Madeleine Nov 2005

Phelps, Michael Aug 2004

Phillips, Sam Apr 2001

Phillips, Scott *see* Creed

Phillips, William obit Yrbk 2002

Phish Jul 2003

Phoenix *see* Linkin Park

Piano, Renzo Apr 2001

Picciotto, Guy *see* Fugazi

Pickering, William H. obit Yrbk 2004
Piel, Gerard obit Feb 2005
Pierce, David Hyde Apr 2001
Pierce, John Robinson obit Jun 2002
Pierce, Paul Nov 2002
Pierce, Samuel R. Jr. obit Feb 2001
Pifer, Alan J. obit Yrbk 2006
Pincay, Laffit Sep 2001
Pineda Lindo, Allan see Black Eyed Peas
Pingree, Chellie Jan 2005
Pitt, Harvey Nov 2002
Pitts, Leonard J. Oct 2004
Plater-Zyberk, Elizabeth see Duany, Andrés and Plater-Zyberk, Elizabeth
Plimpton, George obit Jan 2004
Plimpton, Martha Apr 2002
Poletti, Charles obit Yrbk 2002
Pollitt, Katha Oct 2002
Pomeroy, Wardell B. obit Yrbk 2001
Popeil, Ron Mar 2001
Posen, Zac Jul 2006
Posey, Parker Mar 2003
Potok, Chaim obit Yrbk 2002
Potter, Myrtle S. Aug 2004
Poujade, Pierre obit Yrbk 2004
Powell, Colin L. Nov 2001
Powell, Kevin Jan 2004
Powell, Michael K. May 2003
Prada, Miuccia Feb 2006
Prigogine, Ilya obit Yrbk 2003
Prince-Hughes, Dawn Apr 2005
Prinze, Freddie Jr. Jan 2003
Profumo, John obit Jun 2006
Prosper, Pierre-Richard Aug 2005
Proxmire, William obit Mar 2006
Pryor, Richard obit Apr 2006
Pujols, Albert Sep 2004
Pusey, Nathan M. obit Feb 2002

Queloz, Didier Feb 2002
Quine, W. V. obit Mar 2001
Quine, Willard Van Orman see Quine, W. V.
Quinn, Aidan Apr 2005
Quinn, Anthony obit Sep 2001
Quinn, William F. obit Yrbk 2006

Rabassa, Gregory Jan 2005
Racette, Patricia Feb 2003
Radiohead Jun 2001
Raimi, Sam Jul 2002
Rainier III, Prince of Monaco obit Yrbk 2005
Rakic, Patricia Goldman see Goldman-Rakic, Patricia
Rall, Ted May 2002
Ralston, Joseph W. Jan 2001
Ramirez, Manny Jun 2002
Ramirez, Tina Nov 2004
Ramos, Jorge Mar 2004
Rampling, Charlotte Jun 2002
Rampone, Christie Oct 2004
Randall, Lisa May 2006
Randall, Tony obit Yrbk 2004
Randolph, Willie Sep 2005
Rania Feb 2001
Rao, P. V. Narasimha obit Yrbk 2005
Rascal Flatts Aug 2003
Ratzinger, Joseph see Benedict XVI
Rau, Johannes obit Yrbk 2006
Rawl, Lawrence obit Yrbk 2005
Rawls, Lou obit Oct 2006
Ray, Rachael Aug 2005
Reagan, Ronald obit Sep 2004
Redd, Michael Mar 2005
Redgrave, Vanessa Sep 2003
Reeve, Christopher obit Jan 2005
Reeves, Dan Oct 2001
Reeves, Dianne Jul 2006
Regan, Donald T. obit Yrbk 2003
Rehnquist, William H. Nov 2003 obit Yrbk 2005
Reich, Walter Aug 2005
Reichs, Kathy Oct 2006
Reid, Antonio see Reid, L. A.
Reid, Harry Mar 2003
Reid, L. A. Aug 2001
Reilly, John C. Oct 2004
Reilly, Rick Feb 2005
Reinhardt, Uwe E. Mar 2004
Reinking, Ann Jun 2004
Reitman, Ivan Mar 2001
Rell, M. Jodi Sep 2005
Ressler, Robert K. Feb 2002
Reuss, Henry S. obit Mar 2002
Reuther, Victor obit Yrbk 2004
Revel, Jean Francois obit Yrbk 2006
Reynolds, John W. Jr. obit Mar 2002
Reynoso, Cruz Mar 2002
Rhodes, James A. obit Jul 2001

Rhodes, John J. obit Yrbk 2004
Rhodes, Randi Feb 2005
Rhyne, Charles S. obit Yrbk 2003
Rice, Condoleezza Apr 2001
Richler, Mordecai obit Oct 2001
Richter, Gerhard Jun 2002
Rickey, George W. obit Yrbk 2002
Ridge, Tom Feb 2001
Riefenstahl, Leni obit Yrbk 2004
Riesman, David obit Yrbk 2002
Riley, Terry Apr 2002
Rimm, Sylvia B. Feb 2002
Rimsza, Skip Jul 2002
Rines, Robert H. Jan 2003
Rinfret, Pierre A. obit Yrbk 2006
Riopelle, Jean-Paul obit Yrbk 2002
Ripley, Alexandra obit Yrbk 2004
Ripley, S. Dillon obit Aug 2001
Ritchie, Robert James see Kid Rock
Ritter, John obit Yrbk 2004
Rivers, Larry obit Nov 2002
Robards, Jason Jr. obit Mar 2001
Robb, J. D. see Roberts, Nora
Robbins, Anthony see Robbins, Tony
Robbins, Frederick C. obit Yrbk 2003
Robbins, Tony Jul 2001
Roberts, John G. Feb 2006
Roberts, John G. Jr. see Roberts, John G.
Roberts, Nora Sep 2001
Roberts, Tony Oct 2006
Robinson, Arthur H. obit Yrbk 2005
Robinson, Janet L. Mar 2003
Robinson, Marilynne Oct 2005
Rochberg, George obit Yrbk 2005
Roche, James M. obit Yrbk 2004
Rockefeller, Laurance S. obit Yrbk 2004
Roddick, Andy Jan 2004
Rodino, Peter W. obit Yrbk 2005
Rodriguez, Alex Apr 2003
Rodriguez, Arturo Mar 2001
Rogers, Fred obit Jul 2003

Rogers, William P. obit Mar
2001
Rojas, Rudy Jan 2006
Rollins, Edward J. Mar 2001
Rollins, Henry Sep 2001
Romenesko, Jim Feb 2004
Romer, John Jul 2003
Romero, Anthony Jul 2002
Romney, Mitt Sep 2006
Rooney, Joe Don *see* Rascal
Flatts
Rosas, Cesar *see* Los Lobos
Rose, Jalen Mar 2004
Rose, Jim Mar 2003
Rosenthal, A. M. obit Sep
2006
Ross, Gary May 2004
Ross, Herbert obit Feb 2002
Ross, Robert Oct 2002
Rostow, Eugene V. obit Yrbk
2003
Rostow, Walt W. obit Jul 2003
Rotblat, Joseph obit Feb 2006
Rote, Kyle obit Yrbk 2002
Roth, William V. Jr. obit Yrbk
2004
Rothschild, Miriam obit Yrbk
2005
Rounds, Michael Jun 2006
Rowan, Carl T. obit Jan 2001
Rowland, Kelly *see* Destiny's
Child
Rowley, Janet D. Mar 2001
Rowntree, David *see* Blur
Rubenstein, Atoosa Oct 2004
Rubin, Edward M. Jan 2006
Rudd, Phil *see* AC/DC
Rukeyser, Louis obit Nov
2006
Rule, Ja *see* Ja Rule
Rumsfeld, Donald H. Mar
2002
Rus, Daniela Feb 2004
Rusesabagina, Paul May 2005
Rush Feb 2001
Russell, Harold obit Apr 2002
Russell, Kurt Nov 2004
Rutan, Burt Jun 2005
Ryan, George H. Sep 2001
Ryder, Jonathan *see* Ludlum,
Robert
Ryer, Jonathan *see* Ludlum,
Robert

Saab, Elie Aug 2004
Sabah, Jaber Al-Ahmad Al-
Jaber Al-, Sheik obit Yrbk
2006
Safina, Carl Apr 2005
Sagan, Francoise obit Feb
2005
Said, Edward W. obit Feb
2004

Salinger, Pierre obit Feb 2005
Sánchez, David Nov 2001
Sanders, Ric *see* Fairport
Convention
Sandford, John Mar 2002
Sándor, György obit Yrbk
2006
Sanger, Stephen Mar 2004
Santana, Johan Jul 2006
Santos, José Nov 2003
Sapolsky, Robert Jan 2004
Sapp, Warren Sep 2003
Saramago, José Jun 2002
Savage, Rick *see* Def Leppard
Savimbi, Jonas obit Jun 2002
Sayles Belton, Sharon Jan
2001
Scammon, Richard M. obit
Sep 2001
Scaturro, Pasquale V. Oct
2005
Scavullo, Francesco obit Yrbk
2004
Scdoris, Rachael Jul 2005
Scelsa, Vin May 2006
Scelsa, Vincent *see* Scelsa,
Vin
Schaap, Phil Sep 2001
Schakowsky, Jan Jul 2004
Schell, Maria obit Yrbk 2005
Scheuer, James obit Apr 2006
Schieffer, Bob Aug 2006
Schilling, Curt Oct 2001
Schindler, Alexander M. obit
Feb 2001
Schjeldahl, Peter Oct 2005
Schlein, Miriam obit Yrbk
2005
Schlesinger, John obit Yrbk
2003
Schoenberg, Loren Feb 2005
Scholder, Fritz obit Yrbk
2005
Schott, Marge obit Yrbk 2004
Schriever, Bernard obit Yrbk
2005
Schroeder, Frederick R. obit
Yrbk 2006
Schroeder, Ted *see*
Schroeder, Frederick R.
Schultes, Richard Evans obit
Sep 2001
Schultz, Ed Aug 2005
Schwarzenegger, Arnold Aug
2004
Schwarzkopf, Elisabeth obit
Yrbk 2006
Scott, George obit Yrbk 2005
see Blind Boys of Alabama
Scott, H. Lee Oct 2006
Scott, Jill Jan 2002
Scott, Robert L. Jr. obit Yrbk
2006

Scott, Tony Nov 2004
Scottoline, Lisa Jul 2001
Scully, Vin Oct 2001
Sears, Martha *see* Sears,
William and Martha
Sears, William and Martha
Aug 2001
Seau, Junior Sep 2001
Sebelius, Kathleen Nov 2004
Sedaris, Amy Apr 2002
Selway, Phil *see* Radiohead
Semel, Terry Jul 2006
Senghor, Léopold Sédar obit
Mar 2002
Serrano Súñer, Ramón obit
Yrbk 2004
Settle, Mary Lee obit Yrbk
2006
Setzer, Philip *see* Emerson
String Quartet
Seymour, Lesley Jane Nov
2001
Seymour, Stephanie Oct 2002
Shahade, Jennifer Sep 2005
Shaheen, Jeanne Jan 2001
Shalhoub, Tony Nov 2002
Shapiro, Irving S. obit Nov
2001
Shapiro, Neal May 2003
Shaw, Artie obit Apr 2005
Shawcross, Hartley obit Yrbk
2003
Shearer, Harry Jun 2001
Shearer, Moira obit Yrbk 2006
Shepherd, Michael *see*
Ludlum, Robert
Shields, Mark May 2005
Shinoda, Mike *see* Linkin
Park
Shoemaker, Willie obit Apr
2004
Short, Bobby obit Nov 2005
Shriver, Lionel Sep 2005
Shumway, Norman E. obit
Yrbk 2006
Shyamalan, M. Night Mar
2003
Siddons, Anne Rivers Jan
2005
Silver, Joel Nov 2003
Silverman, Sarah Jul 2006
Simmons, Earl *see* DMX
Simon, Claude obit Yrbk 2005
Simon, Herbert A. obit May
2001
Simon, Paul obit Yrbk 2004
Simone, Nina obit Yrbk 2003
Simpson, Lorna Nov 2004
Sin, Jaime obit Yrbk 2005
Singer, Bryan Apr 2005
Sinopoli, Giuseppe obit Sep
2001
Sisco, Joseph obit Yrbk 2005

Sissi Jun 2001
Slater, Kelly Jul 2001
Slaughter, Frank obit Yrbk 2006
Slavenska, Mia obit Apr 2003
Smiley, Tavis Apr 2003
Smith, Ali Jun 2006
Smith, Amy Jun 2005
Smith, Chesterfield H. obit Yrbk 2003
Smith, Dante Terrell see Mos Def
Smith, Elinor Mar 2001
Smith, Howard K. obit Aug 2002
Smith, Jeff obit Yrbk 2004
Smith, Kiki Mar 2005
Smith, Maggie Jul 2002
Smith, Orin C. Nov 2003
Smith, Steve Sep 2006
Smits, Jimmy May 2006
Smylie, Robert E. obit Yrbk 2004
Snead, Sam obit Yrbk 2002
Snow, John Aug 2003
Snow, Tony Sep 2006
Soffer, Olga Jul 2002
Solomon, Susan Jul 2005
Sontag, Susan obit May 2005
Sothern, Ann obit Aug 2001
Souzay, Gérard obit Yrbk 2004
Spahn, Warren obit Yrbk 2004
Sparks, Nicholas Feb 2001
Spelke, Elizabeth Apr 2006
Spelling, Aaron obit Yrbk 2006
Spellings, Margaret Jun 2005
Spence, Hartzell obit Yrbk 2001
Spencer, John Jan 2001 obit Yrbk 2006
Spencer, Scott Jul 2003
Spergel, David Jan 2005
Spillane, Mickey obit Nov 2006
Spiropulu, Maria May 2004
Spitzer, Eliot Mar 2003
Sprewell, Latrell Feb 2001
Squyres, Steven Nov 2006
St. John, Robert obit Yrbk 2003
Stabenow, Debbie Feb 2006
Stackhouse, Jerry Nov 2001
Staley, Dawn Apr 2005
Stanfield, Robert Lorne obit Yrbk 2004
Stanley, Kim obit Jan 2002
Stanton, Andrew Feb 2004
Stanton, Bill May 2001
Stapleton, Maureen obit Nov 2006

Stapp, Scott see Creed
Stargell, Willie obit Sep 2001
Stassen, Harold E. obit May 2001
Steele, Claude M. Feb 2001
Steele, Michael S. Jul 2004
Steig, William obit Apr 2004
Steiger, Rod obit Yrbk 2002
Stein, Benjamin J. Sep 2001
Stein, Janice Gross Aug 2006
Steingraber, Sandra Sep 2003
Stern, Isaac obit Jan 2002
Stern, Jessica May 2006
Stevens, Ted Oct 2001
Steward, David L. Nov 2004
Stewart, Alice obit Yrbk 2002
Stewart, James "Bubba" Feb 2005
Stewart, Jon Jul 2004
Stewart, Tony Nov 2006
Stiefel, Ethan Apr 2004
Stoltenberg, Gerhard obit Mar 2002
Stone, W. Clement obit Yrbk 2002
Storr, Anthony obit Sep 2001
Stott, John May 2005
Straight, Michael obit Yrbk 2004
Stratton, Dorothy obit Yrbk 2006
Stratton, William G. obit Aug 2001
Straus, Roger W. Jr. obit Yrbk 2004
Streb, Elizabeth Apr 2003
Stringer, Howard Jan 2006
Stroman, Susan Jul 2002
Struzan, Drew Mar 2005
Stutz, Geraldine obit Yrbk 2005
Subandrio obit Apr 2005
Sucksdorff, Arne obit Sep 2001
Sugar, Bert Randolph Nov 2002
Sullivan, Daniel Feb 2003
Sullivan, Leon H. obit Sep 2001
Summers, Lawrence H. Jul 2002
Summitt, Pat Jun 2005
Sun Wen Apr 2001
Sutherland, Kiefer Mar 2002
Suzuki, Ichiro Jul 2002
Suzuki, Zenko obit Yrbk 2004
Sweeney, Anne Jun 2003
Swinton, Tilda Nov 2001
Syal, Meera Feb 2001

Taboo Nawasha see Black Eyed Peas
Taintor, Anne Jun 2005

Tajiri, Satoshi Nov 2001
Talese, Nan Sep 2006
Talley, André Leon Jul 2003
Talmadge, Herman E. obit Jun 2002
Tange, Kenzo obit Yrbk 2005
Tangerine Dream Jan 2005
Tarter, Jill Cornell Feb 2001
Tartt, Donna Feb 2003
Tarver, Antonio Jun 2006
Tauscher, Ellen O. Mar 2001
Taylor, Herman A. Jun 2006
Taylor, Jermain Apr 2006
Taylor, John W. obit Apr 2002
Taylor, Koko Jul 2002
Taylor, Lili Jul 2005
Taylor, Theodore obit Feb 2005
Tebaldi, Renata obit Apr 2005
Tebbel, John obit Mar 2005
Tejada, Miguel Jun 2003
Teller, Edward obit Sep 2004
Thain, John A. May 2004
Thaler, William J. obit Yrbk 2005
Theron, Charlize Nov 2004
Thieu, Nguyen Van obit Jan 2002
Thomas, Dave see Thomas, R. David
Thomas, R. David obit Apr 2002
Thomas, William H. Jan 2006
Thompson, Hunter S. obit Yrbk 2005
Thompson, John W. Mar 2005
Thompson, Lonnie Jan 2004
Thomson, James A. Nov 2001
Thomson, Kenneth R. obit Yrbk 2006
Thomson, Meldrim Jr. obit Sep 2001
Thurmond, Strom obit Nov 2003
Thyssen-Bornemisza de Kaszan, Baron Hans Heinrich obit Yrbk 2002
Tice, George A. Nov 2003
Tierney, John Aug 2005
Tigerman, Stanley Feb 2001
Tilghman, Shirley M. Jun 2006
Tillerson, Rex Sep 2006
Timbaland Mar 2003
Tisch, Laurence A. obit Yrbk 2004
Titov, Gherman obit Jan 2001
Tobin, James obit May 2002
Toledo, Alejandro Nov 2001
Toles, Thomas G. see Toles, Tom
Toles, Tom Nov 2002

Tolle, Eckhart Feb 2005
Tomlinson, LaDainian Oct 2006
Tre Cool *see* Green Day
Tremonti, Mark *see* Creed
Trenet, Charles obit Sep 2001
Trenkler, Freddie obit Yrbk 2001
Trevor-Roper, H. R. obit Jul 2003
Tridish, Pete Apr 2004
Trigère, Pauline obit Jul 2002
Tritt, Travis Feb 2004
Trotter, Lloyd Jul 2005
Trout Powell, Eve May 2004
Trout, Robert obit Jan 2001
Trowbridge, Alexander B. obit Yrbk 2006
Trudeau, Pierre Elliott obit Jan 2001
Truman, David B. obit Yrbk 2004
Truss, Lynne Jul 2006
Tsui Hark Oct 2001
Tull, Tanya Nov 2004
Tureck, Rosalyn obit Yrbk 2003
Turner, Mark Nov 2002
Turre, Steve Apr 2001
Tweet Nov 2002
Tyler, Steven *see* Aerosmith
Tyson, John H. Aug 2001

Unitas, Johnny obit Yrbk 2002
Uris, Leon obit Yrbk 2003
Urquidez, Benny Nov 2001
Urrea, Luis Alberto Nov 2005
Ustinov, Peter obit Aug 2004

Valdes-Rodriguez, Alisa Jan 2006
Valentine, Bobby Jul 2001
Van den Haag, Ernest obit Jul 2002
Van Duyn, Mona obit Nov 2005
Van Exel, Nick Mar 2002
Van Gundy, Jeff May 2001
Van Zandt, Steven Feb 2006
Vance, Cyrus R. obit Apr 2002
Vandiver, S. Ernest obit Yrbk 2005
Vandross, Luther obit Yrbk 2005
Vane, John R. obit Yrbk 2005
Vargas, Elizabeth Apr 2006
Varnedoe, Kirk obit Yrbk 2003
Vaughn, Vince Sep 2006
Verdon, Gwen obit Jan 2001

Vick, Michael Nov 2003
Vickrey, Dan *see* Counting Crows
Vieira, Meredith Apr 2002
Viereck, Peter obit Yrbk 2006
Vinatieri, Adam Sep 2004
Virilio, Paul Jul 2005
Viscardi, Henry Jr. obit Yrbk 2004
Vitale, Dick Jan 2005
Volokhonsky, Larissa *see* Pevear, Richard and Volokhonsky, Larissa
Voulkos, Peter obit Aug 2002

Wachowski, Andy *see* Wachowski, Andy and Larry
Wachowski, Andy and Larry Sep 2003
Wachowski, Larry *see* Wachowski, Andy and Larry
Wade, Dwyane Apr 2006
Wales, Jimmy Oct 2006
Walker, Mort Feb 2002
Walker, Olene S. Apr 2005
Wall, Art obit Feb 2002
Wallace, Ben Apr 2004
Wallis, Jim Jul 2005
Walsh, John Jul 2001
Walters, Barbara Feb 2003
Walters, Vernon A. obit Jul 2002
Walworth, Arthur C. obit Yrbk 2005
Ward, Benjamin obit Yrbk 2002
Ward, Paul L. obit Yrbk 2006
Ward, William E. Nov 2005
Ware, David S. Sep 2003
Warner, Mark R. Oct 2006
Warnke, Paul C. obit Feb 2002
Warren, Rick Oct 2006
Washington, Walter E. obit Yrbk 2004
Wasserman, Lew R. obit Yrbk 2002
Wasserstein, Wendy obit Yrbk 2006
Waters, Alice Jan 2004
Watkins, Donald Jan 2003
Watkins, Levi Jr. Mar 2003
Watson, Arthel Lane *see* Watson, Doc
Watson, Doc Feb 2003
Waugh, Auberon obit May 2001
Wayans, Marlon *see* Wayans, Shawn and Marlon
Wayans, Shawn and Marlon May 2001

Weaver, Dennis obit Yrbk 2006
Weaver, Pat obit Yrbk 2002
Weaver, Sylvester *see* Weaver, Pat
Webb, Karrie Aug 2001
Webber, Chris May 2003
Weber, Dick obit Yrbk 2005
Weinberg, Alvin M. obit Yrbk 2006
Weinberger, Caspar W. obit Jul 2006
Weinrig, Gary Lee *see* Rush
Weinstein, Allen Jun 2006
Weiss, Paul obit Yrbk 2002
Weisskopf, Victor F. obit Yrbk 2002
Weitz, John obit Apr 2003
Weizman, Ezer obit Aug 2005
Wek, Alek Jun 2001
Wells, David May 2004
Wellstone, Paul D. obit Yrbk 2003
Welty, Eudora obit Nov 2001
Wesley, Valerie Wilson Jun 2002
West, Kanye Aug 2006
Westmoreland, William C. obit Nov 2005
Wexler, Jerry Jan 2001
Weyrich, Paul Feb 2005
Wheeldon, Christopher Mar 2004
Whipple, Fred L. obit Yrbk 2005
Whitaker, Mark Aug 2003
White, Armond Oct 2006
White, Byron Raymond obit Jul 2002
White, Gilbert F. obit Yrbk 2006
White, Jack *see* White Stripes
White, John F. obit Yrbk 2005
White, Meg *see* White Stripes
White, Reggie obit Yrbk 2005
White Stripes Sep 2003
Whitehead, Colson Nov 2001
Whitford, Brad *see* Aerosmith
Whitford, Bradley Apr 2003
Whitson, Peggy Sep 2003
Wiesenthal, Simon obit Yrbk 2005
Wiggins, James Russell obit Mar 2001
Wilder, Ken Apr 2002
Wilder, Billy obit Yrbk 2002
Wilhelm, Hoyt obit Yrbk 2002
Wilkins, Maurice H. F. obit Yrbk 2005
Wilkins, Robert W. obit Yrbk 2003
will.i.am *see* Black Eyed Peas

Williams, Armstrong May 2004

Williams, Cliff *see* AC/DC

Williams, Harrison A. Jr. obit Mar 2002

Williams, Michelle *see* Destiny's Child

Williams, Pharrell *see* Neptunes

Williams, Serena *see* Williams, Venus and Williams, Serena

Williams, Tad Sep 2006

Williams, Ted obit Oct 2002

Williams, Venus *see* Williams, Venus and Williams, Serena

Williams, Venus and Williams, Serena Feb 2003

Willingham, Tyrone Nov 2002

Willis, Deborah Sep 2004

Willis, Dontrelle Aug 2006

Wilson, August obit Feb 2006

Wilson, Heather Jul 2006

Wilson, James Q. Aug 2002

Wilson, Kemmons obit Yrbk 2003

Wilson, Luke Feb 2005

Wilson, Marie C. Sep 2004

Wilson, Owen Feb 2003

Wilson, Sloan obit Yrbk 2003

Winchester, Simon Oct 2006

Winsor, Kathleen obit Yrbk 2003

Winston, Stan Jul 2002

Winters, Shelley obit Apr 2006

Wise, Robert obit Apr 2006

Witherspoon, Reese Jan 2004

Woese, Carl R. Jun 2003

Wojciechowska, Maia obit Yrbk 2002

Wolfe, Art Jun 2005

Wolfe, Julia Oct 2003

Wolff, Maritta M. obit Yrbk 2002

Wolfowitz, Paul Feb 2003

Wolfram, Stephen Feb 2005

Wolpoff, Milford Jul 2006

Wong-Staal, Flossie Apr 2001

Wood, Elijah Aug 2002

Wood, Kerry May 2005

Woodcock, Leonard obit Apr 2001

Woods, Donald obit Nov 2001

Woodson, Rod Oct 2004

Woodward, Robert F. obit Yrbk 2001

Wooldridge, Anna Marie *see* Lincoln, Abbey

Worth, Irene obit Aug 2002

Wright, Jeffrey May 2002

Wright, Steven May 2003

Wright, Teresa obit Yrbk 2005

Wright, Will Feb 2004

Wright, Winky Jul 2004

Wriston, Walter B. obit Aug 2005

Wrynn, Dylan *see* Tridish, Pete

Wyatt, Jane obit Yrbk 2006

Wylde, Zakk Oct 2004

Wyman, Thomas obit Yrbk 2003

Xenakis, Iannis obit Jul 2001

Yagudin, Alexei Feb 2004

Yard, Molly obit Apr 2006

Yashin, Aleksei *see* Yashin, Alexei

Yashin, Alexei Jan 2003

Yassin, Ahmed obit Yrbk 2004

Yates, Elizabeth obit Nov 2001

Yates, Sidney R. obit Jan 2001

Yokich, Stephen P. obit Yrbk 2002

Yorke, Thom *see* Radiohead

Young, Angus *see* AC/DC

Young, Kimberly S. Jan 2006

Young, Malcolm *see* AC/DC

Zahn, Paula Feb 2002

Zaillian, Steven Oct 2001

Zambello, Francesca May 2003

Zatopek, Emil obit Feb 2001

Zellweger, Renee Feb 2004

Zerhouni, Elias Oct 2003

Zeta-Jones, Catherine Apr 2003

Zhao Ziyang obit Yrbk 2005

Zhu Rongji Jul 2001

Ziegler, Ronald L. obit Jul 2003

Zimmer, Hans Mar 2002

Zinni, Anthony C. May 2002

Zito, Barry Jul 2004

Zittel, Andrea Aug 2006

Zivojinovich, Alex *see* Rush

Zollar, Jawole Willa Jo Jul 2003

Zorina, Vera obit Yrbk 2003

Zucker, Jeff Jan 2002

Zukerman, Eugenia Jan 2004